W9-AEH-628

HANDBOOK OF CHILD PSYCHOLOGY

HANDBOOK OF CHILD PSYCHOLOGY

Formerly CARMICHAEL'S MANUAL OF CHILD PSYCHOLOGY

PAUL H. MUSSEN EDITOR

FOURTH EDITION

Volume II

INFANCY AND DEVELOPMENTAL PSYCHOBIOLOGY

Marshall M. Haith and Joseph J. Campos
VOLUME EDITORS

JOHN WILEY & SONS
NEW YORK CHICHESTER BRISBANE TORONTO SINGAPORE

Library of Congress Cataloging in Publication Data:

Main entry under title:
Infancy and developmental psychobiology.

(Handbook of child psychology; v. 2)
Includes index.
1. Infant psychology. 2. Developmental psychobiology. I. Haith, Marshall M., II. Campos, Joseph J. 1937- . III. Series.

BF721.H242 1983 vol. 2 [BF719] 155.4s [155.4'22] 83-5073
ISBN 0-471-09055-7

Printed in the United States of America

10 9 8 7 6 5 4 3 2 1

PREFACE TO THE FOURTH EDITION

The *Handbook of Child Psychology* is a direct descendant of three editions of the *Manual of Child Psychology*. The first and second editions, edited by Leonard Carmichael, were published in 1946 and 1954, the third, called *Carmichael's Manual of Child Psychology,* which I edited, was published in 1970. Each of these editions attempted to provide a definitive account of the state of knowledge of child psychology at the time of its publication.

In the 13 years since the publication of the third edition of *Carmichael's Manual,* child psychology has been an extraordinarily lively and productive discipline, expanding in many directions and at a rapid rate. Only a few of the most important of the countless changes will be reviewed here. The volume of the research activity and the annual output of research articles and books have accelerated enormously. As more information accumulates, new questions are generated, new research approaches are invented and older ones are applied in new versions, established theories are challenged and revised, novel theories are proposed, concepts are redefined, and specialized fields of interest and investigation evolve. These changes are closely intertwined and constantly have an impact on one another. Investigation of a new issue (or a revised version of an older one) often requires novel research techniques and approaches. New research findings may evoke questions about the conclusions derived from earlier studies and about underlying theories, and these questions, in turn, lead to further research. These cycles of events are repeated, progress in the field is continuous, and the amount of accumulated data snowballs. Consequently, even an authoritative 1970 publication cannot give an adequate picture of the field in the 1980s. A brand new source book is needed and the present volumes are intended to satisfy this need.

This *Handbook* attempts to reflect the changes in child psychology that have occurred since 1970 and to present as comprehensive, balanced, and accurate a survey of the contemporary field as possible. It is twice the size of the earlier two-volume work and differs from it in many ways. The coverage is broader and more topics are included, discussed in greater depth, and organized according to different principles. Discussions of topics of enduring interest that were presented in chapters in the last edition of *Carmichael's Manual*—for example, Piaget's theory, learning, language, thinking, aggression, sex-typing, socialization in the family and peer group—are reconceptualized and brought up to date in chapters in this *Handbook.*

The reader may get a clearer understanding of the structure and contents of the *Handbook* by noting some of the most significant contrasts between it and the last edition of *Carmichael's Manual.* The *Handbook* includes more chapters on theories and fundamental approaches to research in child psychology (Volume I). The chapter by Piaget on his own theory has been retained. In addition, there are chapters on information processing and systems theories—previously applied to issues in perception, learning, cognition, and social organization—which have proven useful in integrating a substantial body of the data of developmental psychology and in stimulating research. Cross-cultural and field studies have become very fruitful in the last 20 years and these too are discussed in separate chapters, as are the latest advances in general research methodology and assessment. And, as the discipline has matured, there is heightened (or renewed) interest in its philosophical and historical antecedents, so two chapters of Volume I are centered on these issues.

Developmental psychologists have always been interested in the *origins* of behavior, and the factors involved in very early development have become more prominent foci of research attention in the last 10 or 15 years. The psychological study of infants has burgeoned, while advances in research methodology in physiology, ethology, genetics, and neurology have made possible more refined and penetrating explorations of the biological bases of behavior. These research emphases are examined in Volume II of this *Handbook*.

The content area of greatest activity since 1970 has been cognitive development and the results of this activity are apparent in Volume III. For example, the third edition of *Carmichael's Manual* contained one chapter on language development, and it dealt almost exclusively with the acquisition of grammar. In contrast, the *Handbook* has separate chapters on grammar, meaning, and communication. Much of the recent research in cognitive development confirms and extends Piaget's conclusions, but the results of other studies challenge aspects of Piagetian theory. Both kinds of findings are included in chapters in Volume III.

Several research areas that were new in 1970 have become well established, vigorous, and fruitful. Among these are social cognitive development, moral reasoning, and prosocial behavior; each of these is the topic of a chapter in this *Handbook*. In addition a number of traditional issues that had been somewhat neglected until recently have become more prominent in the literature of developmental psychology. For example, this *Handbook* contains chapters on representation, on logical thinking, play, the self, and on the school as an agent of socialization. None of these topics was discussed in the 1970 edition of *Carmichael's Manual*.

In response to social needs, developmental psychologists in increasing numbers conduct research on practical problems and attempt to apply their research findings to the solution of urgent problems, spelling out the implications of basic data for such areas as educational practice and social policy (see particularly the chapters on intervention and on risk factors in development in Volume II, on learning, memory, and comprehension in Volume III, and on treatment of children with emotional problems in Volume IV). The results of these activities are highly salutary for advancing the field of child psychology, for they extend the definitions of concepts investigated, test the findings of laboratory research in real-life settings, and illuminate the limitations of available data and theory.

The volume editors (William Kessen of Yale University, Marshall Haith and Joseph Campos of the University of Denver, John Flavell and Ellen Markman of Stanford, and E. Mavis Hetherington of the University of Virginia) and I met to plan and organize this *Handbook* over five years ago. Our objective was clear and straightforward: to prepare a source book that would present as complete, accurate, balanced, and up-to-date view of the field as possible.

Although there is no entirely satisfactory way of subdividing and organizing all of the vast body of theory, methods, and data in a field as large, varied, and ever-changing as developmental psychology, we constructed a table of contents that in our opinion included all the key topics—that is, all the topics that are currently receiving substantial amounts of research and theoretical attention. It soon became obvious that 4 volumes would be required, and we decided to arrange the material in accordance with the four predominant divisions of the field—theory and methods, biological bases of behavior and infancy, cognitive development, and social and personality development.

Comprehensive coverage was not our only aim; integrative summaries were to be accompanied by new perspectives and insights, critical analyses, and explications of deficiencies in existing data and theoretical orientations. We hoped to produce more than an encyclopedic review of accumulated knowledge; our goal was a source book that would encourage sophisticated thinking about fundamental issues, formulation of questions and hypotheses, and, ultimately, more good research.

We selected and invited a group of distinguished authorities in developmental psychology and related fields who were highly qualified to contribute chapters that would accomplish these goals. Almost all of our invitations were accepted and the assignments were carried out with extraordinary diligence, care, and thoughtfulness. Each working outline, preliminary draft, and final manuscript was reviewed by the volume editor, the general editor, and another authority on the subject, and suggestions for revision were communicated to the author. Although three of the chapters included in the original plan are missing, all the key chapters are included. We are therefore convinced that the *Handbook* provides the most comprehensive picture of contemporary child psychology that exists in one place.

If the objectives of the *Handbook* have been achieved, it is due primarily to the painstaking work, dedication, and creativity of the contributors and the volume editors. The lion's share of the basic work—preparation of scholarly, integrative, and critical chapters—was done by the authors. The contribution of the volume editors was indispensable; in their difficult roles of critic, advisor and guardian of high standards, they were infinitely wise, patient, and persistent. My debts to all these individuals are incalculable.

PAUL H. MUSSEN

PREFACE TO VOLUME II

The publication of the *Handbook of Child Psychology,* 4th Edition, as four separate thematically organized volumes reflects in microcosm the new maturity of developmental psychology. During the past two decades, developmental psychology has evolved from a sometimes esoteric or minor subdiscipline of psychology to a field that is of central relevance to most, if not all, areas of behavioral science. This recently acquired status arose from many sources, among them the decline of environmentalism, the influx of Piagetian theory, the concern by society about the long-term effects of events in early childhood, the discovery of the power of genetic influences on behavioral characteristics, and the emergence of new social and economic forces that have changed the fabric of family life and childrearing in the United States and abroad. The impact of general systems theory and ecological concerns, which began to be felt in the 1960s, created within psychology a sense of the critical importance of understanding the context of adult behavior, including the historical context of the origins of behavior in early childhood, the physiological context that constrains behavior, and the contemporary context of crucial life events.

Major methodological developments have also made it possible for the study of developmental processes to be as rigorous as the study of laboratory animals or college students. No longer is developmental psychology associated with global rating scales, psychometric assessments, and uncontrolled observations. Thus, both theory and methodology have combined to make developmental research interesting and exacting.

Volume II specifically documents the new importance that two areas of developmental research—human infancy and developmental psychobiology—have assumed in recent years. The importance of these two areas was recognized to some extent in the previous edition of the *Handbook,* which devoted a separate chapter to human infancy, covering well over 2,000 references, and treated developmental psychobiology in 3 separate chapters as well as in parts of others. This volume, by contrast, contains 7 chapters devoted to infancy, 6 to developmental psychobiology, and all 13 chapters interdigitate psychobiology and early behavior.

It was difficult to anticipate in the late 1960s—when the previous edition of the *Handbook* was planned—the sheer volume of research that would be generated in the two areas of human infancy and developmental psychobiology in the ensuing 12 to 15 years. It was also difficult to anticipate the significant advances that occurred in our conception of both the human infant and the physiological processes that underlie developmental changes. In the late 1960s, the study of infant development was largely the study of the newborn, and the discovery of new and unsuspected capacities was often the key agenda. The search for specific capacities often yielded single-study ventures rather than programs of research. On those relatively rare occasions when developmental changes were investigated, the age selection was typically arbitrary. There was little interest in, or theorizing about, the processes accounting for developmental changes.

In the area of physiology, much of the study of the human infant centered either on autonomic functions or on states of sleep and wakefulness measured by electroencephalographic parameters. There were preciously few studies of information processing by the brain in waking and intact infants. As in the study of infant behavior, there was little interest in the investigation of central nervous system processes that governed an infant's development.

All of these trends have changed and are reflected in both the selection of chapters for inclusion in this volume and in the coverage given to various topics by the contributors. The interest in processes that account for developmental change pervades all the chapters in the *Handbook.* No longer is the study of the human infant synonymous with the study of the newborn, nor is the study of development equated with changes merely in age. Moreover, new methodologies—for example single-cell research, anatomical marking techniques, recombinant DNA work, identification of the functions served by various strands of chromosomes—have caused an explosion of research in developmental biology, with significant impact on our understanding of psychological development. These and many other developments in the field are well documented in the chapters that follow.

In planning the present volume, we decided to request perspectives from the contributors rather than encyclopedic reviews of each domain of literature. Although the latter was once appropriate for a handbook of this type, the information explosion of the 1960s and 1970s has rendered this approach to research compendia obsolete. It is now the function of professional journals, such as the *Psychological Bulletin, Child Development,* and *Developmental Psychology,* to compile periodically what is known in discrete research domains. The frequency of such publications permits in-depth reviews of literature that are no longer possible for volumes that appear every 10 to 15 years. Accordingly, a volume such as the present one must deal with historical and theoretical perspectives on the broad domains of infancy and developmental psychobiology.

The chapters by Gottlieb and Hinde particularly demonstrate the value of broad, yet succinct, theoretical overviews. Although both chapters touch on a considerable volume of research, their main objective is to use research citations to document major theoretical and methodological points and especially to clarify widespread misconceptions about both developmental psychobiology and ethology.

A related strategy is taken by Goldman-Rakic and her coauthors. Although they chose to describe what is known about the developmental plasticity of the frontal lobes of infrahuman primates, the lessons to be learned have clear implications for the investigation of any other area of brain function as well.

The chapter by Parmelee and Sigman nicely dovetails with the chapter by Goldman-Rakic and her coauthors, inasmuch as both describe frontiers in developmental neurobiology. Thus, the relevance of this work to our understanding of human infant behavior is expanded. But perspectivistic caveats are also offered concerning the level of explanation toward which these new techniques are taking us.

Scarr and Kidd describe specific issues in behavior genetics to illustrate major points about gene-behavior interrelationships. Kopp also adopts this strategy: she illustrates—from what is known about the effects of prematurity and Down's syndrome—several general principles that apply to many risk factors in development.

Other authors have brought new theoretical perspectives into areas of research that have long and well-established traditions. This is particularly true of Olson and Sherman's chapter on attention, learning, and habituation. Although research on early learning traces its origins to the time of John Watson and before, this important line of work has languished since the 1960s. Olson and Sherman infuse a new vitality into this area by describing the applicability of contemporary information processing principles to the study of conditioning, memory, and attention in the human infant. Similarly, Banks and Salapatek in their chapter on visual development trace the outline of a theory of pattern perception that promises to integrate the hitherto separate areas of sensory psychophysics and form perception. The chapter by Campos and his colleagues on socioemotional development bridges two related but independent research literatures—that on early emotional development and that on adult emotionality. The authors employ the notions of goals and strivings in their conceptual sketch to enhance our understanding of emotions, their socialization, and their development. The chapter by Harris on cognition in infancy attempts to suggest an alternative perspective to Piaget's on some of the most important aspects of sensorimotor intelligence—a perspective closely related to Gibson's theory of space and form perception and ecological optics.

There are four chapters in the volume that not only provide a broad perspective but also present extremely thorough reviews of the literature. Interestingly, they are all chapters that deal with rather new areas of research. Kinsbourne and Hiscock's chapter on the development of hemispheric specialization—a chapter that provides an excellent critical survey of both the methods and theories in this controversial line of research. Aslin, Pisoni and Jusczyk's chapter nicely integrates a burgeoning field of research in the areas of early learning in speech perception. Clarke-Stewart and Fein's chapter on day care and social policy, reviews the major findings on the consequences of daycare for child attachment, personality development, and social interaction. Finally, Kopp's chapter presents a valuable integration of the work on risk factors in pregnancy, in early postnatal development with important methodological caveats.

Not all of the content areas relevant to infancy and developmental psychobiology are covered in this volume. Some chapters in each of the other three volumes are centrally related to the topics covered in Volume II, and the interested reader is referred to the other volumes for coverage of specific methodological and conceptual issues. The division of content areas into separate volumes is thus only partly appropriate.

It is customary to acknowledge the multiple contributions made by others to the preparation of volumes such as this one. We are particularly grateful to our contributors, who entered this venture with only a dim sense of the sheer volume of work and difficulty that faced them as they tried to make sense out of sometimes incoherent research areas. In a very real sense, this is their volume. In addition, we would like to express our deep appreciation to Betty Richardson, Denise Hall, and Charlotte Henderson for their assistance in various phases of the production of this volume. And last, we want to express our appreciation to our respective families who encouraged us to make this volume as strong as possible and who suffered frequently from benign neglect.

The planning and implementation of this volume transpired over a period of nearly five years, and we are grateful for several sources of support that facilitated our work during that time. Joseph J. Campos was supported, in part, by grant MH-23556 from the National Institute of Mental Health as well as a grant from the Spencer Foundation. Marshall M. Haith was supported by a John Simon Guggenheim Award, research grant MH-23412 from the National Institute of Mental Health, and by a Research Scientist Award, also from the National Institute of Mental Health.

JOSEPH J. CAMPOS
MARSHALL M. HAITH

CONTENTS

THE PSYCHOBIOLOGICAL APPROACH TO DEVELOPMENTAL ISSUES*

1

GILBERT GOTTLIEB, *University of North Carolina, Greensboro*

CHAPTER CONTENTS

INTRODUCTORY CONSIDERATIONS

A psychobiological approach signifies the study of the development of behavior from a broadly biological perspective. A broad biological point of view includes not only some interest in the physiological, biochemical, and anatomical correlates of behavior, but also embraces ecological and evolutionary considerations as well. More particularly, a biological perspective emphasizes the study of species-typical behavior observed in an organism's usual habitat or natural setting—that is the proper starting point for experimental analysis in the laboratory. Thus the chief investigative questions revolve around discovering, by experimental means, the developmental background to an organism's adaptation (or failure to adapt) in its species-typical ecology.

In the present context the term *developmental* is also of great importance. Getting across the "developmental point of view" is the object of this chapter.

*This chapter was prepared in connection with research activities supported by the North Carolina Division of Mental Health and by Grant HD-00878 (now HD-0-2-110-218-6XXXX-2001) from the National Institute of Child Health and Human Development.

There are essentially two phases of developmental study: (1) naturalistic or normative description and (2) experimental analysis. In the first phase we describe how an organism gets assembled and begins functioning, going, for example, from genes to nervous system to behavior, or, more often, from early behavior to later behavior. In the second, more sophisticated stage we ask about linkages and dependencies between earlier and later stages of development. The second phase is the real heart of developmental study; it attempts to show the causal factors in the development of behavior by experimental methods. Animal models are particularly useful in the second, analytic phase of developmental study. Such studies can shed light on similar developmental processes in humans as well as in the animals themselves.

Experimental manipulations of viable developing human fetuses and infants merely for the sake of providing scientific information are morally unacceptable and are not to be countenanced. However, there are societal and cross-cultural differences in rearing infants and children (e.g., Fishbein, 1976; Gollin, 1981; Reynolds, 1976; Sahlins, 1976), and accidents of nature also occur in humans. These occasions offer the possibility for us to learn about mechanisms or features of normal and abnormal human development without direct experimental intervention. Studies of infants suffering from phenylketonuria (PKU), for example, have greatly informed our view of the gene-behavior pathway, especially inveighing against the old and widespread idea that certain genetic deficiencies invariably lead to mental deficiency. When it was discovered that the PKU-infants lacked the genetic material to produce the enzyme system that metabolizes the amino acid phenylalanine, steps were taken to drastically reduce or entirely prevent food substances containing phenylalanine from entering the diet of these infants. This prevented a buildup of phenylalanine (or byproducts thereof) in the infant's nervous system, a course of events that otherwise seriously interferes with the normal growth and function of the brain and thereby causes mental deficiency (e.g., Koch, Graliker, Fishler, & Ragsdale, 1963). Thus, here we have a case where an environmental factor (diet) can interact with the genes to channel cerebral and intellectual development into the normal range in one environmental context (early dietary intervention) or into the deficient range in another environmental context (late or no dietary intervention). The fallacy of describing either outcome as exclusively environmentally or genetically determined is obvious. (It was once common to call the PKU syndrome the "genetic determination of mental deficiency.") Genes are of enormous importance but they in themselves cannot cause mental deficiency any more than they can cause mental superiority. The various ascending levels in the gene-behavior pathway must be analyzed during the course of development to indicate "what is really happening." In some cases the external environment may be important; in others some feature of the internal environment may be critical; in most instances both will be important. Developmental study always involves such "interactions" regardless of the level of analysis.

Thus, the PKU studies and many other experiments, particularly animal experiments, have helped to shape our present view of the gene-behavior pathway. An individual's genotype (i.e., genetic composition) is best viewed developmentally as setting limits to, or circumscribing, behavioral variation rather than establishing a blueprint from which behavioral expression invariably and inexorably flows. The most direct action of genes seems to be in the regulation of the biochemical aspects of metabolism, and even here there is suggestive evidence of a circular loop extending into the developing organism's external environment. For example, a preliminary finding by Uphouse and Bonner (1975) suggests the possibility of an increased transcription of DNA from RNA in the brains of rats reared in an "enriched" external environment. The increase was apparently specific to the brain; other organs (liver, for example) did not show the increase in DNA. (This preliminary demonstration has since been elegantly confirmed and extended by the work of Grouse and associates [Grouse, Schrier, Bennett, Rosenzweig, & Nelson, 1978; Grouse, Schrier, & Nelson, 1979].)

While the topic of the relationship of genes to behavioral development will be taken up in detail below and in several succeeding chapters, the point is that the gene-behavior pathway extends through neuroembryology and is only realized through the process of prenatal and postnatal development. In order to understand the brain and behavior, therefore, we must study early development. Not only do many behavioral scientists realize the necessity for a developmental point of view, many biological scientists working strictly at the level of cells, tissues, and organs also use the developmental method of study: It is the single most powerful method for coming to an analytic understanding of any phenotype, whether sociological, psychological, behavioral, anatomical, or physiological.

Practical Significance of a Developmental Psychobiological Point of View

Insistence on the importance of a developmental point of view is not merely academic—it has practical applications to pressing and controversial issues. For example, in recent years much controversy has appeared in the scientific and popular press about sociobiology, particularly involving the notions of social determinism versus genetic determinism. One aspect of the controversy, as it applies to human society, revolves around the extent to which traditional sex roles are partially or wholly constrained or encouraged by strictly biological (i.e., genetic) differences between the sexes. This question, as well as others in the sociobiology controversy, is one of the extent of behavioral plasticity or malleability. Although this is an investigative question (i.e., a question to be solved by empirical study), it is not always appreciated that it is an empirical question, and one that must be examined strictly in a developmental context. The point is that to hazard guesses about the proportion of social behavior that is genetically "fixed," as at least one sociobiologist has done (10% was his figure), has no meaning at the level of the individual or in a developmental context. Constraints on neural and behavioral development certainly exist, but it will take considerable patient observation, many naturally occurring developmental accidents, and much systematic cross-cultural developmental study to determine these limitations in relation to various "gene-environment" interactions.

Precisely the same reasoning applies to the controversial topic of racial differences in IQ. Black people in general score lower on IQ tests than white people. If this observed difference in the IQ of black and white populations is to be attributed to genetic differences in neurobehavioral development underlying intellectual functions, then a complete swap of rearing environments would have to be arranged, including the intrauterine environment, in order to appropriately test the hypothesis of "genetic inferiority" of blacks put forth by several scientists.

The closest behavioral geneticists can get to the impossible ideal "experimental" design above is to do studies of transracial adoption. This involves measuring the IQs of black children who have been adopted by white families and comparing the IQs of these children to those of the biological children in these white families and to black children reared by black families. It will be immediately obvious that this is far from a perfect experimental design. These kinds of studies, although very important and the best that can be done under the circumstances, are fraught with unresolved methodological difficulties which always cloud the interpretation, especially when differences between black and white IQ persist. Take, for example, a recent transracial adoption study by Scarr and Weinberg (1976). In that study the black children adopted by middle-class white families had an IQ of about 106, which is significantly higher than the mean of the general black population (85 to 90) but still significantly lower than the mean of their white cohorts (biological children of the adopting parents), who scored about 116. The interpretation of the results is clouded because, among other problems, age at adoption plays a role in IQ attainment, with earlier adopted children scoring higher than later adopted ones. The white children were obviously in the white families from birth, whereas the Black children were close to 3 years old on the average when they were adopted. Also, the prenatal factor (environment) cannot be shrugged off because antenatal care in blacks is by and large poorer than it is in whites and the brain, particularly the cortex, is undergoing its more formative period of growth during the prenatal period. (There is also a second growth spurt of the brain during the first 30 months after birth, when many of the black adoptees were not in the white family environment.)

Without discussing other possible psychological and sociological complications that make the comparison of intellectual function in black and white children in a predominantly white society difficult, it seems once again clear that this controversial issue in behavioral genetics can only be resolved satisfactorily (if at all) by a developmental approach to the problem.

Aims and Assumptions

One of the major aims of the study of the development of behavior is to gain an understanding of how fetal, infant, juvenile, adolescent, and adult behavior realizes itself. This aim carries with it the assumption that certain, if not all, aspects of behavior are determined or influenced by events that occur earlier in ontogenesis (i.e., history of the individual). According to the ontogenetic viewpoint, early experiences or events explain many important aspects of later behavior. The familiar saying, "The child is the psychological father of the man," is a succinct statement, even if an overstatement, of this point of view.

Sigmund Freud's (1953) psychoanalytic theory of personality development is a particularly striking example of the supposed *continuity* of early and later behavior: experiences of unusual gratification or excessive frustration during the early oral, anal, or genital periods of infancy and childhood are said to lead to the manifestation of particular kinds of neuroses in adulthood, as well as influencing adult character structure in nonneurotic individuals. While this aspect of Freudian theory is no longer as completely accepted as it once was, it does serve as a dramatic example of the view that continuity is an important aspect of the development of behavior. Whereas continuity in human personality development is usually inferred from observing the adult behavior of human beings and then reconstructing their past history through personal interviews, as we will see later, there is some very clear proof for the continuity point of view in the development of behavior in animals, where direct and highly controlled experimentation is both possible and practical, as well as ethical. (Stability is not the same as continuity, as the latter concept is being used here. Continuity implies a dependence of later behavior on an earlier event; the later behavior could be a change in phenotypic expression, not necessarily always a continued expression of a previous phenotype [stability].)

Most developmental theorists and investigators realize that the development of behavior involves the emergence of new functions or abilities that are not necessarily derived from previous stages. Therefore, the other major aim in the study of the development of behavior has to do with the understanding and analysis of transitions where *discontinuity* is a much more prominent and important feature than is continuity. As a matter of experimental strategy, the search for continuities in development has been emphasized somewhat at the expense of discontinuities. The reason for this is that it is much easier, and much more direct, to demonstrate experimentally that a current behavior has been derived or influenced by previous events in the history of the animal than it is to obtain convincing evidence that a current behavior is entirely free of influence from past ontogenetic events. Since the experimental study of behavioral development is itself in its infancy, it is much more practical and useful at this point in time to attempt to establish firm continuities than it is to prove the "null hypothesis," that is, that functions arise entirely *de novo,* without any direct dependence on any of the previous activities in the life of the organism.

Thus, at the present time in the short history of experimental behavioral science, the "child is the psychological father of the man" theory of behavioral development (strict developmental continuity) is more heavily emphasized than are the developmental discontinuities. Fortunately, discontinuity theory is not without its supporters, and they will be heard from later in this chapter (and elsewhere in this Handbook). A complete understanding of behavioral development will almost certainly include discontinuities and continuities in its wake, but we are nowhere near that goal now, nor will we be so in the forseeable future.

Outmoded Conceptions of Development

The most serious of the outmoded conceptions concerning the development of behavior have to do with the influence of phylogeny on ontogeny and the related problem of the role of genes in behavior development. While most readers will readily recognize these flawed ways of thinking in the raw form presented here, it is well to realize that some of these very same concepts occasionally resurface in today's literature, albeit in new guises.

"Ontogeny Recapitulates Phylogeny"

This generalization, sometimes called the biogenetic law, means that the succession of stages through which an individual passes in ontogenetic development repeats the sequence of *adult* stages through which one's remote ancestors passed in their evolutionary development. E. Haeckel (1891) originally invoked the law to *explain* the particular sequence in which certain structures make their appearance during embryonic or larval development (e.g., "gills" in human embryos) and the law has sometimes also been used to explain human behavioral development as well (e.g., by G. Stanley Hall, 1916).

That individuals of a given species usually pass through a number of behavioral stages in a regular succession or order is not to be doubted; that these regularities are to be explained by phylogeny is a misconception. These regularities can only be understood by a direct experimental analysis of the conditions under which they occur: that is, by an analysis of ontogenesis itself. The idea that phylogeny explains ontogeny proved a great stumbling block to the introduction of the causal-analytic (experimental) method of study in embryology in the late nineteenth century (de Beer, 1958; Oppenheimer, 1967), so we can benefit from that historical example. The older point of view was that, if phylogeny explains ontogeny, an experimental analysis of ontogenesis is superfluous. We now know that this idea was mistaken: It is only through experimental analysis that we can come to understand and fully appreciate the phenomena of development. Phylogeny does not illuminate the *mechanics* of behavioral development at all.

Haeckel's law implies that the major evolutionary mechanism is that of terminal addition (i.e., that evolutionary novelties first appear in the adult). This view of evolution necessarily implies that the order of events in early ontogenesis is very stable. On the contrary, there are many significant instances of ontogenetic instability during the course of evolution. For example, teeth were evolved before tongues, but in mammals today tongues develop before teeth (de Beer, 1958). As the embryologists Garstang (1922) and de Beer (1958) have persuasively argued, terminal addition is probably the least used mode of evolutionary change. Rather, deceleration of ontogenetic development, with ancestral characters "dropping off" the end, may be among the more prominent modes. (de Beer describes at least seven other modes of ontogenetic change that underlie evolution. For those interested in developmental psychology, it is of great interest to learn that developmental changes bring about evolution or, to put it differently, that phylogeny is based on ontogeny.) In the evolution of the human species, for example, it is believed that there has been a developmental delay ("fetalization" or neoteny) of our entire lifespan such that we retain the youthful characteristic of *plasticity* (a formidable capacity to adapt or change) well into adulthood. A specific and very important example of a deceleration in human development is the delay in closing of the cranial sutures until long after birth, thus allowing the brain to grow to its unusually large size (de Beer, 1958). The size of our brain compared to the size of our body exceeds that of all other vertebrate species, and our big brain is no doubt largely responsible for what we take to be our advanced psychological development compared to other primates, other mammals, and other vertebrates (Jerison, 1973).

In summary, Haeckel's recapitulation hypothesis is no longer endorsed in embryology or in evolutionary circles. It is sad to relate that it was largely unaccepted by biologists at the time G. Stanley Hall published his two volumes on *Adolescence* (1916), since the recapitulation idea served as his primary theoretical underpinning. [Gould (1977) has published a highly readable account of the pervasive influence of the recapitulation idea in various fields during the 1800s.] There is of course always some repetition of ancestral features in descendants—there would otherwise not be any basis to infer the occurrence of evolution. However, such repetitions are more usually of embryonic, fetal, neonatal, or juvenile characteristics rather than adult characteristics. That is why the study of development is so important for our understanding of evolution and phylogeny. Similar patterns of development signify close phyletic relationships, whereas disparities in development can shed light on evolutionary trends.

Nature Versus Nurture, or Instinct Versus Learning

This outmoded conception assumes that the developmental process is controlled by two completely different and independent factors, one phylogenetically derived (genes) and the other ontogenetically derived (environment).

It is common to hear or to read that some behaviors are genetically determined whereas some other behaviors are environmentally conditioned during the lifetime of the individual. The misconception is that the latter can be no less genetically determined than the former. There can be no behavior without an organism and there can be no organism without genes. No one knows of any organism, part of which was constructed by genes and the other part of which was constructed by the environment. The ability to respond to environmental factors or be affected by experience is as genetically determined as the maturation process: no more, no less.

A much more subtle misconception implied by the idea of the genetic determination of behavioral development is the rather horribly oversimplified view it imparts of the so-called gene-behavior pathway. When one uses the phrase "genetically determined" it is as if there were a direct or close relationship between the expression of the genes and the emission of behavior during development. Quite to the contrary, it is an absolutely humbling experience when one merely considers all the different levels of analysis (molecule → tissues → organ → organ system → organism) that must be traversed to get from the genes (DNA) to the overt behavior of an organism. Add to this the temporal dimension of change that is of such importance in developmental study and one becomes dubious about the precise meaning of the phrase "genetically determined."

At the present stage of science we do know (1) the genetic complement must set (currently unknown) limits (constraints) on behavioral development and (2) the species-specific genetic complement substantially increases the likelihood that the capability for certain forms of behavior will occur later in development. We simply do not yet know the developmental mechanisms whereby (1) and (2) are realized—these are as yet unanswered, even though highly active, investigative questions in the domain of developmental genetics (e.g., see the theoretical reviews by Davidson & Britten, 1973, and by Zuckerkandl, 1976). Thus, we must respect the "distance" between the genome and behavior and also try to avoid thinking of part of an organism's behavioral development as stemming from genetic determination and some other part from environmental determination. The capacity for the organism to react to the environment is as genetically determined as its *inability* to react to certain features of the environment. It does not seem that the genes could be any more responsible for one than the other.

Maturation Versus Experience

This fallacious dichotomy is related to the previous one on nature versus nurture. The misconception in the present case is that genes control anatomical maturation while the environment controls experience. Since there is evidence (to be mentioned later) that experience affects the maturation of the brain and other structures during development, the proper way to visualize the relationship in developmental terms is maturation *and* experience, rather than maturation versus experience. As Zing-Yang Kuo (1967), T. C. Schneirla (1956), and Daniel S. Lehrman (1953) have tried to make clear, maturation always takes place in some "experiential" context, where experience is defined broadly to include the various stimulative aspects to which organisms are subject during prenatal and postnatal life. One of the chief aims of developmental analysis is the specification of how early conditions or stimulative events interact with organic maturation to exert particular effects on later behavior. Unfortunately, the concepts of associative learning (conditioning), long the preoccupation of experimental psychologists, are not very useful in describing the contributions of experience to the species-typical development of behavior, so it has become necessary to devise a new vocabulary and new concepts in order to appropriately specify the variety of these maturation-experience interactions (Aslin, 1981; Gottlieb, 1976a, b, 1981a). These new concepts are described in a later section.

General Principles

The study of infancy has always had a close connection with biology. In fact, virtually all the principles of early behavioral and psychological development have been adapted from the field of embryology. Descriptive principles of development are apt to be the same whether one is abstractly describing the course of development of an organ or an organism; the difference comes in the formulation of concrete *explanations* of development at the level of organs or organisms. For example, as we will see below, a descriptive hallmark of all developing systems, whether organ or organism, is that they differentiate, which means that they progress from a relatively homogenous to a relatively heterogeneous state. The explanation for differentiation at the organ level involves the movements and interactions among cells and tissues, whereas the explanation at the level of the organism involves neural and other bodily maturation, self-produced activity, interactions with other organisms, and interactions with the physical environment. One of the chief aims of developmental analysis (in contrast to developmental description) is to show how these various interactions contribute to the final product or endpoint that one has chosen for study. The reason for going into a critical examination of general principles of development early in this chapter is so we won't confuse description with explanation, as has sometimes happened in the past and is likely to recur.

There are several exceptionally well-founded principles of development. Chief among these are the following.

Forward Reference

The behavioral capabilities of newborn animals are typically so very well adapted to their usual life circumstances that they have a *preadapted* quality. Indeed, investigations of embryonic and fetal development show that the behavioral capabilities of the neonate do arise during the prenatal phase. In fact, many of the behaviors that newborns must manifest in order to survive actually become functional (or capable of function) well before the time of birth or hatching (e.g., the suckling reflex in mammals).

The continuity of mammalian fetal experience and neonatal behavior is well illustrated by the finding that amniotic fluid applied to the teats induces nipple attachment in newborn rats. The fetus swallows amniotic fluid during gestation (Bradley & Mistretta, 1975), and the mother licks the newborns and licks herself, thus applying the necessary stimulus for nipple attachment during the usual course of perinatal events (Teicher & Blass, 1977). In a conceptually related experiment, Hall and Bryan (1980) found that hungry 3-day-old rats deprived of nutritive suckling were capable of adult-like independent ingestion (licking and lapping) long before the normal time of weaning (three weeks). In a rather different experiment, Vince, Reader, and Tolhurst (1976) were able to precociously elicit the coordinated movements associated with hatching several days early by prematurely exposing chick embryos to "clicking" sounds that ordinarily occur during the later hatching period when the embryos begin to breathe through their lungs.

The phenomenon of precocious functional maturation is so general that a number of embryological writers (Anokhin, 1964; Barcroft, 1938; Carmichael, 1963; Coghill, 1929) have broached the idea that many prenatal and early postnatal phenomena are "preparatory" or "anticipatory," that is, that early neurosensory and neuromuscular maturation has a forward reference. While this descriptive principle is certainly valid as far as it goes, it does not have any explanatory value, of course. That is, it is still necessary to undertake an experimental examination of early development (as was done to some extent in the examples above) in order to determine which factors affect or control the development of any behavior, regardless of how adaptive it may be. The principle of forward reference incorporates the well-known view that early neural and behavioral development affects later behavior, specifically that the adaptive behavior of the neonate emerges from a background of prenatal development (Gottlieb, 1973b; Hooker, 1952; Preyer, 1888, 1889).

Differentiation and Hierarchical Organization

These two descriptive principles also emerged from the study of embryology (von Baer, 1828, 1837). They are so pervasive at all levels of development that Heinz Werner (1948) was able to frame a rather comprehensive comparative account of psychological development in humans and animals based entirely on the notions of differentiation and hierarchical integration.

Generally speaking, as individual development proceeds, virtually every organism's behavior becomes more versatile or more highly differentiated. This simply means that as the repertoire of behavior increases with age so does the capacity for the elaboration of fine details in the perceptual sphere, the performance of finer muscular movements in the motor sphere, greater achievements in the cognitive sphere, and more "individuation" or style in personality. Later neural and behavioral differentiation builds on earlier differentiation within neural and behavioral systems, so that identifiable integrated hierarchies form. The evidence for hierarchical integration comes from neurology as well as psychology. During the embryonic and fetal period, the brain develops from a central core outward so the last layers to appear are the outermost cortical ones. The human brain continues to grow after birth, perhaps until we reach age 20 years or so. When the cortical layers of the brain are destroyed by disease in old age (senile dementia), the earliest fetal and neonatal reflexes reappear: sucking, rooting, grasping, and so on (Paulson & Gottlieb, 1968). In the fetus we know that oxygen deprivation (anoxia or asphyxia) causes the more recently developed secondary reflexes to disappear, leading to the reappearance of earlier developed primary reflexes (Humphrey, 1953). In this case, the later developing higher motor centers are knocked out first, reducing fetal behavior to an earlier stage of competence when only the earlier developed lower motor neurons are functional. In an experimental study on behavioral differentiation and hierarchical integration, Teitelbaum, Cheng, and Rozin (1969) surgically damaged a selected brain area (lateral hypothalamus) relevant to feeding in adult rats and observed that the sequence of recovery was an exact parallel of the sequential stages of the development of feeding in the newborn rat—a "reencephalization" as it were.

The pervasiveness of differentiation and hierarchical integration sometimes blinds us to the need for developmental analysis. Thus, we need to remind ourselves that the means or mechanisms whereby developmental changes in differentiation and hierarchical integration come about are among the most significant questions in the field (see, e.g., Gollin's critical review [1981] of the problem).

Optimum Stages

There are prenatal and postnatal periods or stages in development when the organism is dependent on certain forms of stimulation for subsequent normal (typical) development. Other ways of viewing these stages are that they are ones in which the organism is maximally susceptible to certain kinds of stimulation, or when ease of mastering certain behavioral tasks is much higher than at other times in the life cycle. These stages are sometimes referred to as critical periods of development. It is not correct to think of these behavioral stages as occurring at a highly fixed time in the life of each member of the species, nor as being of an invariant length. The best example of the various features of an optimum stage is the learning of spoken language(s) by children. Although this occurs most readily and with the greatest facility when the child is very young, the capacity continues into adulthood, albeit with diminished ease. (The biological and ontogenetic behavioral variables that control optimum stages of development is another investigative question of the first order.) On its weakest interpretation, the concept of an optimum or critical stage implies that the development of particular abilities or endpoints is not equipotential over the lifespan; on its strongest interpretation, the critical period concept means that certain experiences must occur during a delimited period early in development if subsequent development is to be normal (species-typical). It is likely that both interpretations are correct and apply to the development of different behavioral or psychological phenomena. (See Bateson, 1979, for a recent review.)

If examples of the weak interpretation of an optimum or critical period for skills other than language do not immediately come to mind, it may be that they are few in number or they have not yet been determined by the relatively little research oriented to that particular aspect of the question. Certainly, there are numerous well-researched examples in the early development of vision that seem to show that almost any deprivation, however little, always creates some deficit, however small, in later visual function (reviewed by Aslin, 1981). Developmental research on vision has tended to focus on the strong interpretation of sensitive periods and there is thus considerable evidence for such periods in the sphere of visual physiological and anatomical development. On the other hand, frank damage to the brainstem during early development can result in no later measurable cognitive deficits, depending on the rearing environment of the youngster (Broman, Nichols, & Kennedy, 1975).

The point of the matter is that the concept of critical periods originated in experimental embryology, so one should not expect the same rigidity to apply when the term is used with reference to the phenomena of developmental psychology. Some psychological phenomena eventually may be shown to warrant the strong version; others may not. While it is much too soon to take a position on the matter, it is most important just to be alert to such possibilities.

Individual Differences

There are large and significant individual differences in all quantitative aspects of behavioral development. In many instances, these differences become even more marked as development proceeds. Individual variation is what natural selection works on, so variation is an important psychobiological datum. Unfortunately, it is usually treated as a terrible nuisance in experimental work.

Lest we think that individual differences in psychological development reflect largely, or solely, genetic or biological factors, it has been documented that environmental (social, physical, geographical, etc.) factors also contribute to individuality, beginning not only in the neonatal period but in the fetal period (e.g., Cravioto, Birch, DeLicardie, Rosales, & Vega, 1969).

Sequence of Behavioral Stages

Despite significant individual differences in the quantitative aspects of development, the *sequence* in which behavioral stages follow each other in any given species is remarkably constant when typical developmental conditions prevail. (Again, this is a descriptive principle, so the systematic experimental alteration of species-typical developmental conditions is required to shed light on the various factors that participate in the sequencing of behavioral stages.) An example of a pervasive sequence that must have strong consequences on perceptual and cognitive development is the systematic order in which the sensory systems become functional during the ontogenetic development of vertebrates including humans. As shown in Figure 5, the somesthetic sense (touch) is the first to develop, followed by the vestibular (balance), auditory, and visual senses. An example of a higher order sequence is that proposed by Piaget (1970) for the development of thinking in humans, which he divides into three principal periods: the sensorimotor period (occurring during the first 18 or 24 months of postnatal life); succeeded by a period of "representative intelligence," involving concrete and, later, functional groupings of objects (11 to 13 years of age); and, finally, the period during which the capability appears for propositional or formal logic.

Any psychobiological theory of development will necessarily involve stages or epochs because the facts of neurosensory and neuromotor maturation, among other biological changes, necessarily mean that significant changes occur during ontogenesis. Key theoretical issues (largely unsettled ones) concern the relation of the stages to their predecessors and successors—that is, the issue of continuity and discontinuity discussed earlier.

Function

The role of function (use, exercise, practice, stimulation, experience) has always been a key question in the development of early behavior, especially where species-specific, instinctive, or innate behavior is involved. Some theorists have held that function is necessary merely to *maintain* innate behavior once it has developed fully, whereas others have held that function also *facilitates* or even channels (*induces*) behavior *during* the developmental process itself (see review by Gottlieb, 1976b). It is very likely that function is necessary for maintenance. The extent to which it also plays a role in the maturation process itself is, however, still an active investigative question. Several recent experiments (reviewed below) now suggest that function may play a constructive (facilitative and inductive) as well as a maintenance role in the complete species-typical (normal) differentiation of behavior (i.e., during the late stages of the neural maturation process itself).

There has been a great deal of a priori taking of sides concerning the role, if any, of function during embryonic neural and behavioral development. On the one hand, we find extreme statements to the effect "that the possibility is open for any sense-organ to acquire functional connection with any muscle" (Holt, 1931, p. 33). Holt was very much under the sway of the successes of Pavlovian conditioning when he wrote that remark—it is no doubt erroneous and one that the great physiologist Pavlov himself probably would have cringed at. On the other side of the fence, one can find statements to the effect that "the bulk of the nervous system must be patterned without the aid of functional adjustment" (Sperry, 1951, p. 271). Or, "Development in many instances . . . is remarkably independent of function, even in . . . [the] . . . sense . . . [of] function as a general condition necessary to healthy growth" (Sperry, 1951, p. 271). More recently, Sperry (1971) has written: "In general outline at least, one could now see how it would be entirely possible for behavioral nerve circuits of extreme intricacy and precision to be inherited and organized prefunctionally solely by the mechanisms of embryonic growth and differentiation" (p. 32).

In the wake of significant research at the neurophysiological and neuroanatomical level during early development in the last decade, Sperry (Meyer & Sperry, 1976) and those on the other side of the theoretical fence have come to see the possibility of function and maturation operating in a variety of interdependent ways, so this important theoretical matter has been completely reopened for empirical study.

Canalization

This principle has several different meanings. As originally put forward in the psychological literature by Holt (1931), it meant that as development proceeds the relative diffuseness or randomness of early (prenatal and postnatal) motor activity becomes more focused or highly specific as a consequence of spatial and temporal contiguity learning (conditioning, to be exact). Later, Kuo (1967) used the concept in the more accepted sense that as development proceeds the original great range of behavioral potentials or plasticity narrows, signifying that the range of possibilities of behavioral development always exceeds the range of behavior that is actualized during the course of individual development. The channeling of behavior, and the correlated decrease of plasticity, over the course of ontogenesis is to be explained by the individual's particular developmental history, which, for Kuo, included biochemistry, physiology, and anatomy, as well as experience. This is a much broader (if vaguer) explanatory idea than Holt's reliance on contiguity conditioning, and thus is probably much more appropriate to the complexity of life as it is actually lived by developing organisms.

The final sense in which canalization has been used is quite different from the above. It is the developmental geneticist Waddington's (1942) notion that early normal or species-typical physiological and anatomical development can withstand great assaults or perturbations and still return to (or remain on) its usual developmental pathway, thus producing the normal phenotype. Waddington's concept of canalization is one that says that usual developmental pathways are buffered and thus normal (typical) development can be only temporarily derailed. Waddington (1968) later used the term "chreod" to express this idea more succinctly: A chreod means a "fated" or predetermined path. For Waddington, embryonic anatomical and physiological development consists of a number of highly buffered (i.e., virtually fixed) pathways. Surely, this view would seem to have very narrow, if any, applicability to even the earliest development of perception, cognition, and motor competence of the infant. While one does not want to lose sight of the important property of "resiliency" that developing organisms exhibit, the concept of buffering seems to point more to a phenomenon that needs to be explained rather than offering an explanation for the phenomenon.

Since Waddington's concept of canalization now is being widely adopted in various developmental psychological models (Fishbein, 1976; Lumsden & Wilson, 1980; Parker & Gibson, 1979; Scarr-Salapatek, 1976), it becomes important to scrutinize critically the appropriateness of this adoption. While I have previously emphasized the general significance of embryological concepts for developmental psychobiology, in no previous instance has an embryological concept been incorporated so literally into our field. All the writers cited above use Waddington's concept of canalization to refer to the process that somehow produces species-typical constancies or regularities in psychobiological development. (Waddington originally used the concept to call attention to specific environmental features against which the system was buffered.) Since, in any case, the "epigenetic landscape" in which Waddington's (1957) channels are embedded is merely figurative or metaphorical, the concept is absolutely devoid of any empirical content and thus supplies us with no concrete understanding or hypotheses concerning the developmental process that is involved.

Since Waddington's concept of canalization does not really inform us of the developmental mechanisms underlying species-typical behavior or capacities, it would be much clearer and more to the point if the term were omitted, lest we deceive ourselves into thinking it does refer to some definite process. Most writers who use the term seem to mean simply that the capacity or behavior in question has a strong innate predisposition. Thus, to invoke Waddington's concept of canalization to refer to the process behind the phenotypic expression of regularities in species typical development gains us nothing by way of understanding—it only becomes a new word for "innate" with all the problems that term has historically created (Lehrman, 1970). (See Gollin, 1981, for yet another critique of Waddington's ideas as they might apply to developmental psychology.)

To put the problem in its most concrete terms, Waddington (1953) performed a very important transgenerational selection experiment in which it was shown that a feature of the organism (crossveinless wing) that was originally induced by heat shock (the "environment") during development would, in the course of a dozen or so generations, come to be produced endogenously (i.e., "innately") if the organisms that responded to the heat shock were selectively mated in each generation. Waddington termed this outcome the "genetic assimilation of an acquired character" and used the concept of canalization to explain the results of the experiment. Genetic assimilation signifies development that is presumed free from external influence and canalization was Waddington's attempt to describe figuratively what happened in ontogenetic terms. Thus, Waddington's concept of canalization should only be used (if at all) with reference to characteristics that have been genetically assimilated. When the term is used to refer to the development of behavior, it would be clearer (even if not necessarily accurate) to use the term innate or instinctive. Some current writers are incorrectly using Waddington's concept of canalization to refer to behavior which is a consequence of exposure to stable features of the species rearing environment (e.g., Fishbein, 1976; Lumsden & Wilson, 1980; Parker & Gibson, 1979; Scarr-Salapatek, 1976).

Historical Basis of Current Theoretical Concepts

Thought about the problem of development originated in antiquity. Certainly, it was one of the many important conceptual problems identified by the philosopher Aristotle, who more or less accurately described the abstract feature of *epigenesis,* or what we now take to be the correct conception of development, as one of individual phenotypic *transformation* over the course of time, whether behavioral or psychological. What this means for developmental psychology is that all patterns of activity and sensitivity are not immediately evident in the initial stages of embryonic or early postnatal development, and that the various capabilities of the organism become manifest only during the course of development under the influence of a variety of factors. All modern theories of development are thus epigenetic, contrary to what sometimes seems implied in the theoretical psychological literature (e.g., Moltz, 1965), or in some textbooks (Dewsbury, 1978). Disagreement exists about the fundamental character of the epigenesis of behavior, not about whether development is epigenetic or not. (For authoritative intellectual histories of the concept of epigenesis, see Adelmann, 1966, and Needham, 1959.) To understand this occasional misunderstanding, it will be useful to review briefly the earliest formulation of the nature-nurture controversy.

Preformation and Epigenesis

To Aristotle and all subsequent writers on the topic of development, it was evident that there are only two possible general explanations of development: (1) either all the organism's features are present, however indistinctly, at conception (preformation), or, (2) all the organism's features do not preexist but come into existence in a serial progression over the course of development (epigenesis). To most of those who took the trouble to actually observe the embryonic development of, say, a chick, it was fairly clear that development is epigenetic. But preformationists had a logical question for the epigeneticists. How could something come from nothing? Must not some aspect of the later developing "somethings" be present early on, so that something can come from something rather than from nothing?

To those familiar with the history of philosophy, especially the theories of Rationalism and Empiricism as approaches to knowledge, it will be clear that preformation was a rationalist necessity (forced by pure logic) as epigenesis was an empiricist necessity (forced by observation). This is somewhat of an oversimplification, of course, but somewhere it is written that the doctrine of preformation represented a triumph of the understanding over the senses. Needham castigated such a view by calling it rather "one of the most striking victories of the imagination over the understanding" (1959, p. 238). As Needham points out, the preformationists decided epigenesis was inconceivable, and only accepted observations that accorded with their view. Unfortunately, such a conviction eventually made an examination of the developing embryo superfluous, because the preformationists were convinced that structure and organization would be present, whether they could see it or not. In essence, the preformationists believed development consisted only of the growth of preexisting parts, whereas the epigeneticists believed that differentiation as well as growth characterized the developmental process.

Contemporary Epigenetic Conceptions

We now know that the "somethings" that had to be there in order to give rise to something are regulatory and structural genes (DNA). But feet, arms, and brains are not in the DNA; they emerge during the course of epigenetic development, given a species-typical genome and usual (species-typical) developmental conditions. The analytic task of developmental psychobiology is to specify these intervening events in as much detail as possible, at least as they pertain to interesting aspects of infant behavior and psychology.

There are two dominant views of the epigenetic process of behavioral development. They need not be exclusionary but sometimes it seems that they are. I will try to synthesize these views here in a way that I have presented them elsewhere (Gottlieb, 1973a).

While there is unanimous agreement on the epigenetic character of embryonic neural and behavioral development, there is disagreement on the character of neurobehavioral epigenesis itself. Some theories assume that the epigenesis of the nervous system and/or behavior is *predetermined,* while others hold that it is *probabilistic*.

Predetermined Epigenesis

To put it in the clearest possible way, the concept of predetermined epigenesis, as it applies to behavior, means that the development of behavior in larvae, embryos, fetuses, and neonates can be explained entirely in terms of neuromotor and neurosensory maturation (i.e., in terms of the proliferation, migration, differentiation, and growth of neurons and their axonal and dendritic processes). In this view, factors such as the use or exercise of muscles, sensory stimulation, mechanical agitation, environmental heat, gravity, and so on, play only a passive role in the development of the nervous system. Thus, according to predetermined epigenesis, the nervous system matures in an encapsulated fashion so that a sufficiently comprehensive account of the maturation of the nervous system will suffice for an explanation of embryonic and neonatal behavior, the key idea being that structural maturation determines function, and not vice versa. The notion that function is required to maintain the integrity of fully mature systems is fairly well documented. The possibly inductive or facilitative role of function prior to complete structural maturation has not been widely appreciated, however; so, until very recently, few experiments have been designed in such a way that these possibilities could even be evaluated. This state of affairs should be borne in mind when we hear or read critical remarks to the effect that we have little or no evidence for the role of function on the structural maturation process itself.

Perhaps the most dramatic and explicit statement of the predeterminist point of view concerning the nonparticipation of behavior or neural function in the maturation of the nervous system is the following:

> The architecture of the nervous system, and the concomitant behavior patterns result from self-generating growth and maturation processes that are determined entirely by inherited, intrinsic factors, to the exclusion of functional adjustment, exercise, or anything else akin to learning. (Hamburger, 1964, p. 21)

(In the ensuing period, Hamburger [1973] has modified his position, so the above quotation no longer reflects his point of view.)

Rather extreme statements have been made on both sides of the theoretical fence, and the above statement may be a necessary "corrective" for the outmoded point of view expressed by an influential psychologist some 40 years ago: "John Locke's doctrine of the *tabula rasa* rests on solid embryological as well as psychological ground" (Holt, 1931, p. 35). Or, as cited earlier, "It [the nervous system] allows afferent impulses to diffuse or spread so widely that the possibility is open for any sense-organ to acquire functional connection with any muscle" (Holt, 1931, p. 33).

Statements such as the above, coming as they do from leading practitioners in their respective fields, are apt to be taken as empirically justified by young students inside each field, and that can only lead to the persistence of long-standing antithetical attitudes which are not in fact justified by evidence.

While the concept of predetermined epigenesis may be correct for the very earliest stages of embryonic and larval development, when, in fact, there is no embryonic behavior or motility as such, or when the nervous system is not yet functioning, it seems unduly conservative to apply this conception to later stages when the embryo is capable of motility or behavior, or when neurons have become capable of function (spontaneous or evoked). Whereas the view of predetermined epigenesis rightly focuses on the enormous self-differentiating prowess of the nervous system and embryonic organismic development in general, it tends to become unduly narrow in conception when, in advance of supporting evidence, even a facilitative role is denied to functional factors.

Probabilistic Epigenesis

While the adherents to predetermined epigenesis cast a dubious if not downright jaundiced eye on the possible effects of stimulation, musculoskeletal use, and neural function on the development of embryonic and neonatal behavior, some theorists of the probabilistic persuasion seem almost overexuberant or utterly naive in their assumptions of the immediate and subsequent effects of such factors. While, by definition, the predeterministic conception is loathe to grant even a facilitating role to functional factors in the progressive expansion and development of the nervous system and behavior, the probabilistic conception holds that function not only facilitates neural maturation and behavioral development but that it is also capable of exerting an inductive influence as well. Further, an analysis (Gottlieb, 1970) of the assumptions underlying the main probabilistic theories of prenatal behavior development (Holt, 1931; Kuo, 1967) reveals that these theories seem to demand (implicitly) that functional factors be operative during the actual maturation of the various sensory and motor systems of the embryo and fetus—that is, functional and environmental factors are assumed to contribute in both a facilitative and an inductive way to neural maturation and not merely to maintain and/or channel behavior only after neural maturation is completed.

Thus, in summary, whereas the key assumption of predetermined epigenesis holds that there is a unidirectional relationship between structure and function whereby structural maturation determines function (structural maturation → function) but not the reverse, probabilistic epigenesis assumes a bidirectional or reciprocal relationship between structural maturation and function, whereby structural maturation determines function and function alters structural maturation (structural maturation ↔ function).

Before we turn to the specific theoretical issues of early behavioral development, it is perhaps important to mention briefly two other more or less subsidiary features that distinguish predetermined and probabilistic conceptions of behavioral development, both of which are implicit in the bidirectional structure ↔ function concept. Namely, probabilistic theories (e.g., Holt, 1931; Kuo, 1967; Schneirla, 1965) hold that (1) behavioral development is a gradual and continuous process, wherein (2) certain features of late embryonic, fetal, or early neonatal behavior can be traced to, and are in some sense dependent on, earlier behaviors or stimulative events for their maintenance, facilitation, or induction. Certain other viewpoints, on the other hand, are explicit in their emphasis of discontinuities in embryonic behavior such that, for example, later movements are envisaged as arising *de novo,* in which case these movements could bear nothing other than a permissive relationship to earlier movements (Hamburger, 1973).

Another distinction between predetermined and probabilistic conceptions—one that must at the moment be considered tentative because it only infrequently and inconsistently comes to the fore—concerns the question of variability in neural and behavioral *outcomes* and neural and behavioral *processes*. Probabilistic perspectives sometimes tend to emphasize (or suggest) variable means to variable and reversible end states, whereas predeterministic viewpoints sometimes emphasize (or imply) invariant means to invariable and irreversible terminal events. An example of these aspects of the probabilistic perspective on development can be seen in Fischer's (1980) structural theory of cognitive development, in which (1) different individuals develop different skill profiles (i.e., we are all better at doing certain things than other things), and, most significantly, (2) we may arrive at the same skills via different developmental pathways. This seems to be a very different conception of a structural theory of cognitive development than that of Piaget (1970), for example, in which sequences are portrayed as invariant and, one assumes, inexorable as long as some unspecified range of typical sociocultural developmental conditions prevail. Perhaps the apparent conflict can be resolved by seeing Piaget's theory as charting *macrodevelopmental* changes (the overall picture) and Fischer's theory as dealing with *microdevelopmental* transformations within the larger cognitive categories. Since Fischer accepts that cognitive development proceeds from sensorimotor actions to representations and then to abstractions, which is Piaget's scheme, that resolution seems appropriate. That macrodevelopment is more predetermined than microdevelopment, and vice versa, does not seem unreasonable. As a further example, that the macrodevelopmental sequence of sensory-system development (Figure 5) is predetermined, whereas lower order change in these systems (precise time of onset, duration of development, fineness of tuning, etc.) is probabilistic also does not seem unreasonable.

In summary, with regard to behavioral development, the predetermined conception stresses the unidirectionality of the structure-function relationship and the discontinuities between earlier and later stages. The probabilistic conception emphasizes the bidirectionality of the structure-function relationship (whether the function is regarded as spontaneous or whether it is evoked by stimulation), the maintaining, facilitative, and inductive nature of precursors, and thus the continuities between earlier and later behavior. While adherents to either approach recognize and appreciate the stability of behavioral development which is manifested within (and sometimes even between) species, they of course differ in their conceptualization of the events responsible for these highly predictable and recurrent regularities. The specific ways in which these conceptualizations differ on particular topics are presented below.

Gene Action During Development

Since it is so important for the student of ontogenesis to have a clear and correct idea of the role of genetic activity during individual development, I think it will be helpful to realize that the two views of epigenesis do not differ on the importance of genetics to neurobehavioral development but only on the extent of modulating influences on gene action during development:

Predetermined Epigenesis: Unidirectional Structure-Function Relationship
Gene Action → Structural Maturation → Function

Probabilistic Epigenesis: Bidirectional Structure-Function Relationship
Gene Action ⇆ Structural Maturation ⇆ Function

In the unidirectional view gene action gives rise to neural maturation processes that form a structure, which, when fully mature, begins to function in an essentially nonreciprocal way. In the bidirectional view, gene action gives rise to structural maturation processes that are susceptible to (in some cases, possibly dependent on) the influence of function before complete maturity is attained. At the anatomical level, the term *maturation* refers to the early phase of development during which neural cells are proliferating and migrating, and to the later phase in which the nerve cells' axonal and dendritic processes grow and differentiate. It is particularly with respect to the latter that the effects of function are most readily observed. In the bidirectional view, function would be considered a normal part of the late phases of neural maturation. In the past, it has not been usual to consider neural activity, sensory stimulation, feedback from motor movement, and so on, as normal features of neuroembryological development. The incorporation of function as a factor in the late stages of neuroembryological development does not disregard or underrate the powerful nonfunctional contributions to neural maturation (e.g., sprouting, neurotrophic factors); it only widens the traditional purview. The elegant tissue culture studies of Crain, Bornstein, and associates have shown the remarkable degrees to which fetal rodent cerebral cortex can differentiate anatomically and electrophysiologically even when electrical activity has been deliberately suppressed by a blocking agent (Crain, Bornstein, & Peterson, 1968; Model, Bornstein, Crain, & Pappas, 1971). This is reminiscent of Carmichael's (1926) classical study showing that amphibians become capable of swimming even when prior muscular movement has been prevented. I have elsewhere noted (Gottlieb, 1971, pp. 109–110) that we might expect imperfections in the final functional development of explanted neural cells deprived of normal activity and input. That expectation has recently been supported by Leiman, Seil, and Kelly (1975), who found incomplete electrophysiological development in such preparations. Whether the failure of explanted cortical cells to achieve complete electrophysiological or anatomical differentiation is a consequence of functional deprivation or other factors has not yet been clarified. In a groundbreaking series of experiments, Oppenheim and his colleagues (Pittman & Oppenheim, 1979; and unpublished experiments) have demonstrated a complex relationship between overt motor activity in the chick embryo and the death of motor neurons in the spinal cord. (Cell death is a normal feature of embryonic neural maturation.) They found that suppression of the overt motility of the chick embryo with neuromuscular blocking agents such as curare prevents the normal loss of thousands of motor neurons by natural cell death. These counterintuitive findings imply that early functional interactions play an important role in some of the initial stages in neurogenesis.

To return to the diagram above, it is probable that during development, genes are activated and deactivated by chemical events associated with neural maturation processes. Thus, in the diagram, there is an arrow going back to gene action from structural maturation to depict the probable bidirectionality of that relationship as well as of the structure-function relationship. Although the switching on and off of the activity of specific genes by hormones during development has not yet been demonstrated in the nervous system per se, it has been shown in other systems (e.g., O'Malley & Means, 1974). Therefore, it does not seem unreasonable to expect the same sort of mechanism to hold for neural maturation as well. Such a mechanism is clearly implied in the notion that thyroid hormone regulates the timing of some features of neural maturation (Hamburgh, 1969). For example, excess thyroxine accelerates the rate of development of synapses in the cerebellum in young rats, and it also is associated with a premature termination of the cellular proliferation phase in that region, resulting in a reduction in the number of synapses in the mature cerebellum (Nicholson & Altman, 1972). Interestingly, either reduced or excessive thyroxine in the neonatal period in rats is associated with behavioral deficiencies in adulthood (Eayrs, 1968). This poorer performance reflects not only endocrine disturbance as such, but an important disruption of timing in the early maturation of certain systems of the brain (e.g., Stone & Greenough, 1975). Normal development is brought about by the meshing of a number of separate though interrelated time schedules. This schedule is disrupted because excess or reduced thyroxine does not affect the activity of all systems but only some of them. The same sorts of deleterious upsets in the timing of neural development are caused by certain drugs (Slotkin, Smith, Lau, & Bareis, 1980). Thus, the probable bidirectionality between the activity of genes and neural structures and functions can be highly significant for behavior well beyond the early period of development in which the formative reciprocal interactions took place.

Thirty years ago, the developmental psychologist McGraw (1946) recognized that the structure-function relationship could very well be bidirectional in her study of the early motor development of the human infant. She stated:

> It seems fairly evident that certain structural changes take place prior to the onset of overt function; it seems equally evident that cessation of neurostructural development does not coincide with the onset of function. There is every reason to believe that when conditions are favorable function makes some contribution to further advancement in structural development of the nervous system. An influential factor in determining the structural development of one component may be the functioning of other structures which are interrelated. (McGraw, 1946, p. 363)

As Crowell (1967) has pointed out, although McGraw did not work out a systematic theoretical position, her notions did moderate the more extreme interpretation of Gesell's (1946) "maturational hypothesis" and thus were a step toward an appropriate resolution of the nature-nurture problem.

Various Roles of Experience

So far it has been possible to discriminate three main ways in which experience contributes to the development of species-typical behavior: maintenance, facilitation, and induction (Aslin, 1981; Gottlieb, 1976a, 1976b, 1981a). It may be helpful to study Figure 1 in conjunction with the discussion that follows.

Maintenance

The lowest level or weakest effect of function (experience) on the development of behavior or the maturation of the nervous system concerns the necessity of function merely to preserve an already developed state or endpoint regardless of how the state or endpoint itself was achieved.

A blatant example of maintenance can be seen in extreme instances of sensory deprivation that cause adult humans to behave inefficiently and perhaps even to undergo psychotic experience of hallucinations or delusions when their usual sensory input is so drastically reduced (e.g., Bexton, Heron, & Scott, 1954). Here the ordinary, everyday effects of activity or function seem to be necessary to maintain routine behavioral efficiency and, in some individuals at least, to preserve nonpsychotic perceptual and thought content.

At a developmental level, long-term sensory deprivation during early neonatal development can lead to atrophy and disintegration of neural tissue in the sensory system deprived of stimulation, as the earliest studies in this area amply demonstrated (e.g., Chow, Riesen, & Newell, 1957). On the motor side, however, it appears that very little, if any, normal embryonic motility is necessary for the maintenance of early neural and behavioral integrity in the chick (Oppenheim et al., 1978; Pittman & Oppenheim, 1979). On the sensory side, very little (but some) normal embryonic auditory experience is absolutely necessary to maintain normal postnatal responsiveness to the maternal call (Gottlieb, 1981b). Also, it would appear that if young domestic chicks are deprived of hearing the maternal call of their species for several days after hatching, they become relatively unresponsive to it (Graves, 1973; Spalding, 1873). In a similar vein, Dawkins (1968) attributes the persistence and ultimate specificity of the young chick's preference for pecking at solid hemispheres to the dual effects of rewarding experiences that maintain that preference and nonrewarding experiences which extinguish the proclivity to peck at flat objects. These results would seem to be prime examples of *functional validation* at the behavioral level (Jacobson, 1974).

In the so-called higher realms of learned behavior (fear conditioning in this case), Campbell and Jaynes' (1966) notion of *reinstatement* as an important developmental phenomenon is strictly of a maintenance character, involving as it does the periodic partial repetition of an earlier experience that is effective when the animal has had a specific earlier experience but relatively ineffective (i.e., does not induce learning) in the absence of the early experience. Campbell and Jaynes posit reinstatement as the means whereby the effects of certain earlier experiences persist into adulthood; in the absence of reinstatement, they contend that the early experiences would not influence adult behavior.

As an aside, it bears mention that much of the operant conditioning literature is concerned with the effectiveness of different reinforcement schedules on the maintenance of behavior, although there is unfortunately relatively little research emphasis on how the behaviors in question developed initially.

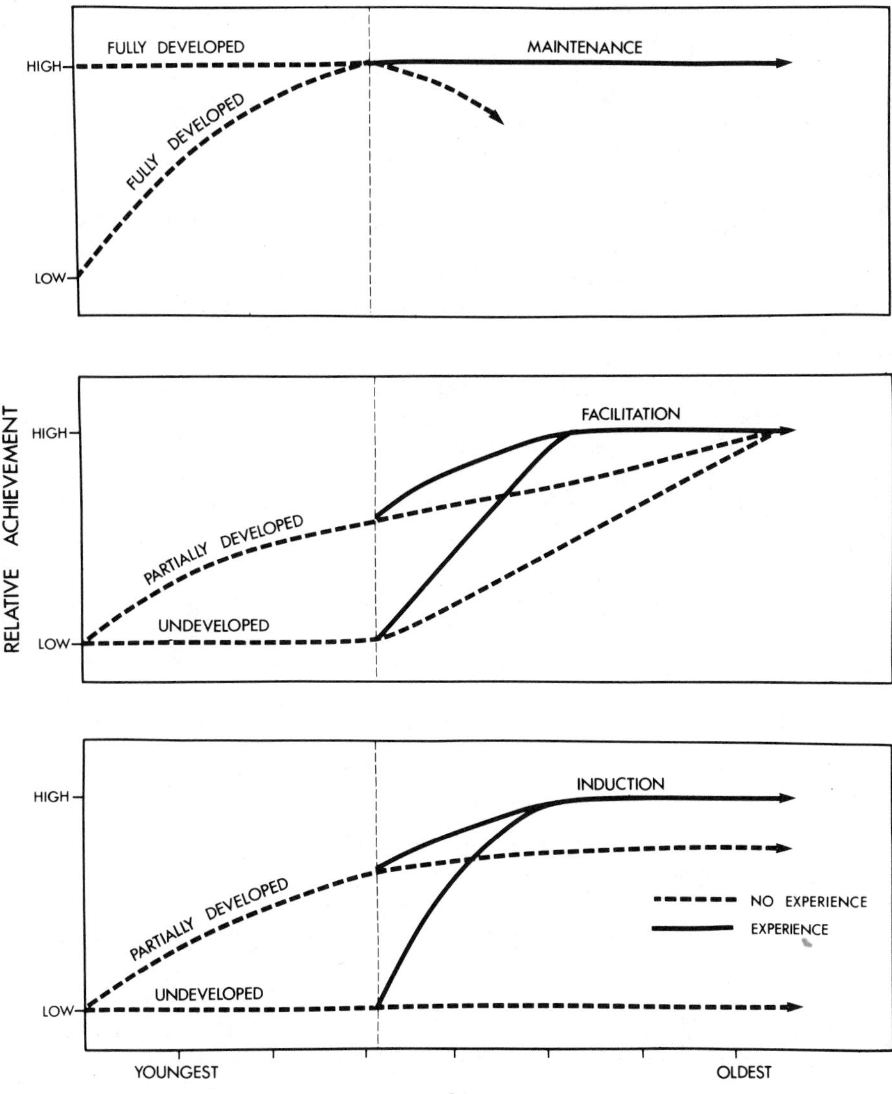

Figure 1. Three ways in which experience can contribute to species-typical development. *Maintenance* preserves already developed achievements. *Facilitation* acts as a temporal regulator of achievements which will nonetheless eventually be reached even if the organism is deprived of the normally occurring experience. *Induction* represents experience that is essential if the species-typical endpoint is to be fully achieved. (The current definitions of facilitation and induction are different from those given earlier [Gottlieb, 1976a, b] for reasons of logical consistency elaborated in Gottlieb, 1981. Figure 2 further illustrates these differences.) Vertical dashed line indicates when experience first occurs. "Fully developed," "partially developed," and "undeveloped" refer to stages of maturation of the system prior to experience.

The possibility of maintaining certain kinds of vocal behavior in young infants via operant social reinforcement has been demonstrated by Rheingold, Gewirtz, and Ross (1959), for example. An operant framework is currently being applied to the development of species-specific song in birds by Stevenson (1969). From her early results, it is virtually certain that maintenance is involved (in certain species, at least) in the "shaping" of the final song. (Auditory experience may also have facilitating and even inductive effects on the achievement of song [Marler & Mundinger, 1971].)

In sum, much behavior and neural circuitry which is considered innate, in the sense that it appears to develop and perfect itself in the absence of experience, could be nonetheless dependent on experience for its maintenance. This important distinction, that is, whether experience plays a contributory role in the maturation of the nervous system and in the development of the behavior or merely in their maintenance, is all too often not observed in discussions bearing on the nature-nurture problem and the neural specificity literature, even though it is an experimentally resolvable issue depending only on the use of appropriate developmental research strategies as, for example, outlined by Solomon and Lessac (1968). The research strategies that allow one to distinguish the precise role of experience in the normal development of behavior and the nervous system are rather demanding and not always immediately obvious, so perhaps that is why so few studies lend themselves to clear interpretation on this point.

Facilitation

This represents a temporal regulative effect of experience on the development of behavior (or the nervous system). An important difference between the maintenance and facilitative effects of experience is that the latter temporally assist (i.e., acceler-

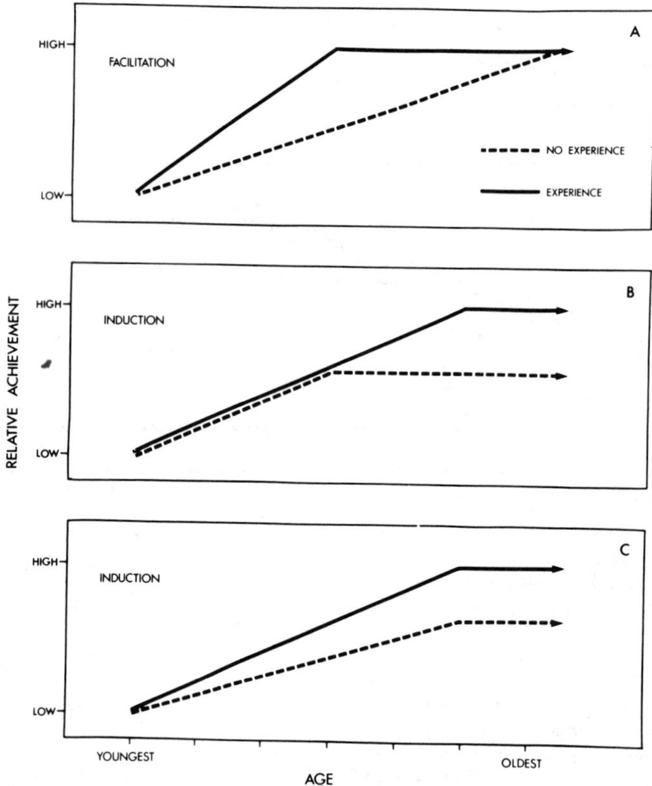

Figure 2. Difference between facilitation and induction. Facilitative experiences regulate the usual time of appearance of an achievement that will appear later even in the absence of experience. Inductive experiences are those that are essential if the usual level of terminal achievement is to be reached. In B the effect of experience becomes manifest later than in C. (Revised from Gottlieb, 1976b, Figure 2.)

ate) the developmental achievement of certain states or endpoints, whereas the former operate to preserve already achieved states or endpoints. The difference between facilitative and *inductive* effects of experience, on the other hand, is that the former refer to instances where development of the behavior (or neural structure and function) will eventually occur even in the absence of the experience, whereas in the absence of inductive experience the particular behavior (or neural connectivity or activity) would not develop. Facilitative experiences thus regulate maturation and behavioral development, whereas inductive experiences determine whether or not a given behavioral or neural aspect is present or not. Inductive (or determinative) experiences thus exert the strongest possible effect on development, maintenance the weakest, with facilitation intermediate and probably the most ubiquitous of the three. (See Figure 2 for a graphic representation of differences between facilitation and induction.)

An example of the facilitative effect of motor exercise comes from Zelazo, Zelazo, and Kolb (1972), who observed that deliberate and explicit prolongation of reflexive stepping in the human neonate between birth and 8 weeks of age resulted in an earlier onset of independent walking around 1 year of age. (''Early'' may not always be synonymous with good or better or even normal, as was made clear in the previously described experiments with thyroxine and certain drugs.)

Instances of the rather fundamental facilitative influences of sensory function would include the following. In the visual system, for example, the presence of appropriate sensory stimulation accelerates sensory functional (EEG) maturation (Paulson, 1965; Peters, Vonderahe, & Powers, 1956), and its absence decelerates functional (ERG) maturation (Zetterström, 1956).

A paradigmatic study of the roles of maintenance, facilitation, and induction in the development of depth perception is that by Tees (1974). In Tees' study, as summarized in Figure 3, neonatal rats were either allowed visual experience (light-reared) or denied visual experience (dark-reared) for various times after birth and then tested for the fineness of their depth discrimination in a visual cliff apparatus. Each group was tested at one age only in a design that allowed the discrimination of the various roles of experience. Tees' results indicate that depth perception in rats develops *and improves* in the absence of visual experience; the rate at which it improves is slower than in light-reared rats, however, and, most important, the ability of visually deprived rats to make fine discriminations never reaches the level of the visually experienced rats, thereby implicating the visual experience as inductive as well

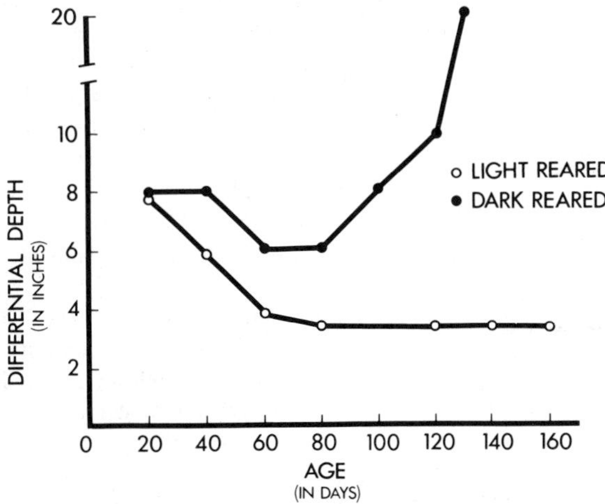

Figure 3. Experimental results which demonstrate the operation of facilitation, induction, and maintenance in the development of depth perception in rats. The fineness of depth perception develops earlier (facilitation) in rats reared in the light, although there is some improvement even when the animals are kept in the dark (compare points at 40 and 60 days). Rats reared in the dark do not develop the usual degree of fineness of depth perception of light-reared animals (induction). The achievement of some degree of depth perception is lost if the animals are deprived of visual experience beyond 80 days (maintenance). (Data from Tees, 1974.)

as facilitative (compare Figure 1 and Figure 3). In addition, after an even longer period of deprivation, rather than showing further improvement in their depth perception, the performance of light-deprived rats eventually begins to deteriorate in the continued absence of visual experience, thereby showing the maintenance aspect of visual stimulation.

In sum, Tees' excellent study makes clear the methodological necessity of recurrently sampling from the experience-deprived control group at various ages in order to be able to distinguish the facilitative effects of experience that result merely in acceleration from the effects that result in a persistent difference in ultimate level of attainment. These important distinctions are so often overlooked in the developmental literature that we have very few conclusive examples of the persistence of early advantages (or disadvantages) relative to numerous instances of acceleration (or deceleration) as such.

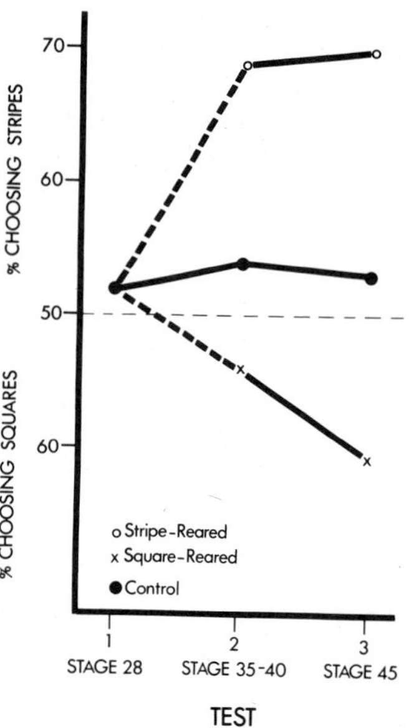

Figure 4. Red-legged frogs' choice of substrate ("habitat") pattern as a function of their larval rearing environment. The larvae were raised in a "featureless" white pan (control condition) until they had passed Stage 28, at which time some of them were placed in a striped pan or one with squares on its floor and walls. Subsequently, they were given choice tests premetamorphically (Stages 35 to 40) and postmetamorphically (Stage 45) to determine if the rearing environment determined their substrate preference. The stripe-reared larvae developed a significant preference for their substrate pattern but the square-reared larvae did not. The control group never exhibited a preference. (Data from Wiens, 1970.)

Induction

This is the most dramatic effect of experience, one that students of development find most significant and interesting: instances in which the presence or the absence of a particular experience (or set or sequence of experiences) completely determines whether or not a given species-typical neural feature or behavioral activity, whether sensory-perceptual or motor-behavioral, will manifest itself later on in development. While such "canalizing" effects are well known in embryology and developmental endocrinology where, for example, the presence or absence of certain gonadal hormones in the prenatal period determines whether the genitalia will be of the male or female type upon maturity (e.g., Goy, Bridgson, & Young, 1964; Willier, Gallagher, & Koch, 1937), there are very few clear-cut examples of the inductive experiential effects in the neural and behavioral literature when one seeks for them in the context of supplying the normal developmental underpinning for species-typical behavior or neural structure or function. While the determinative effects of induction clearly involve the notion of "plasticity," many experiments committed in the name of plasticity have unfortunately little to contribute to our understanding of experiential mechanisms underlying normal—that is, species-typical—development. (See Johnston, 1981, for a similar critique of the extensive literature on animal learning.) Imprinting would represent an inductive phenomenon par excellence in those instances where the early experience brings about a normal (usually occurring) later state of affairs, one that would not occur but for the early experience. Defined in this restrictive way, however, there are actually few examples of imprinting. One has the impression that there may be many such examples in normal or species-typical development, but they occur within such a complex web of biopsychological *constraints* that we have not yet been able to clearly grasp and appreciate them—imprinting does not really represent a "blank slate" model of development, although that model may be the one that most readily comes to mind in thinking about inductive influences in development.

A paradigmatic study of the inductive effects of experience in the normal development of behavior is that by Wiens (1970), involving an analysis of substrate preferences in red-legged frogs (*Rana aurora*). The usual habitat of these creatures is a shallow pond or overflow area, characterized by slender, emergent willow branches, cattails, submerged weed stems and grasses—all essentially linear structures that would cast more or less linear shadows on the muddy substrate. In the laboratory, Wiens reared red-legged larvae in one of three "habitats" and tested them pre- and postmetamorphically for their "habitat" preference. He reared one group in a white pan with parallel black stripes on its floor and walls, a second group in a white pan with black squares on its floor and walls, and a third group in a "featureless" white pan. The larvae were tested for their substrate ("habitat") preference by placing them in a chamber, half of which was covered by the striped pattern and half by the black squares. Each tadpole's preference was recorded by the amount of time it spent in each half of the test chamber during a three-minute test period. When tested premetamorphically (Stages 35 to 40 in Figure 4), the stripe-reared larvae showed a statistically significant preference for the striped side of the test compartment, whereas the square-reared group showed a slight but insignificant preference for the side with the square pattern. When tested postmetamorphically, the stripe-reared group continued to show a strong preference for the striped side and the square-reared group showed a slight increase in their bias toward the side with squares, but this was still a statistically nonsignificant preference. Most important, as shown in Figure 4, the group reared in the featureless pan continued not to show a preference for either of the two substrate patterns at any of the ages, thus allowing an unequivocal diagnosis of the experiential effect as an inductive one. Thus, the rearing environment of red-legged frog tadpoles determines their later choice of substrate pattern, and this determinative influence operates within perceptual constraints so a preference for certain types of patterns is more readily induced than others.

Since we are inclined to think of instances of induction as indicating the height of behavioral plasticity during development and perhaps as being relegated to vertebrate species, it is noteworthy that such plasticity occurs even in invertebrate species. For example, as shown by the behavioral experiments of Jaisson (1975), if young worker ants are removed from the colony on the day of hatching, they will care for the cocoons of many different species that are offered to them. If they are exposed to cocoons of a given species during the 15 days immediately after hatching, however, they will tend only that species and treat other species of cocoons (including their own) as food. In the normal course of development, these worker ants would ordinarily be exposed to cocoons of their own species and thus tend these and devour cocoons of other species. Jaisson's experiments show that this apparently rigid, stereotyped, species-specific behavioral outcome is a consequence of a highly plastic developmental process involving induction of a positive preference for tending that species of cocoon to which the developing worker ant has been exposed during a formative period of development. Thus, developmental plasticity is not restricted to birds and mammals, or even vertebrates, but extends at least to insects. It may be that the retention of embryonic or neonatal plasticity into later stages of ontogeny is what distinguishes the behavioral development of higher from lower forms (cf. Cairns, 1976; Mason, 1968).

T. C. Schneirla's Approach/Withdrawal Theory of Neonatal Behavior

Following the early lead of Z.-Y. Kuo (summarized in Kuo, 1967), Schneirla (1965) worked out the only extensive theory of how early embryonic or prenatal experience might affect behavior (perception) after birth. His theory holds that stimulative events occurring *in embryo* cause the neonate to approach (or prefer) certain stimulative configurations and withdraw from others after birth.

Schneirla's theory rests importantly on a most interesting and as yet untested assumption, namely, that *quantitative* features of tactile and proprioceptive stimulation (rhythms of activity, and so on) to which the young bird is recurrently exposed as an embryo affects its response to previously unencountered auditory and visual stimuli after hatching. This intermodality generalization mechanism, for which there is no direct developmental evidence at present, is akin to Klüver's (1933) principle of stimulus equivalence derived from perceptual experiments with adult monkeys. The essence of Klüver's principle is that if an animal gives the same response to physically dissimilar stimuli, these stimuli are psychologically (perceptually) equivalent to the animal. In his theory, Schneirla applies Klüver's principle to the development of perception, particularly the very early behavior of avian neonates, in order to account for the responses young animals address to previously unencountered forms of stimulation (such as auditory or visual patterns). Based on certain evidence that young birds tend to approach gradually changing, regular, low, or low-medium intensity forms of auditory and visual stimulation and tend to withdraw from abruptly changing, irregular, high-intensity forms of auditory and visual stimulation, Schneirla links the former (approach tendency) to the kinds of tactile and proprioceptive stimulation

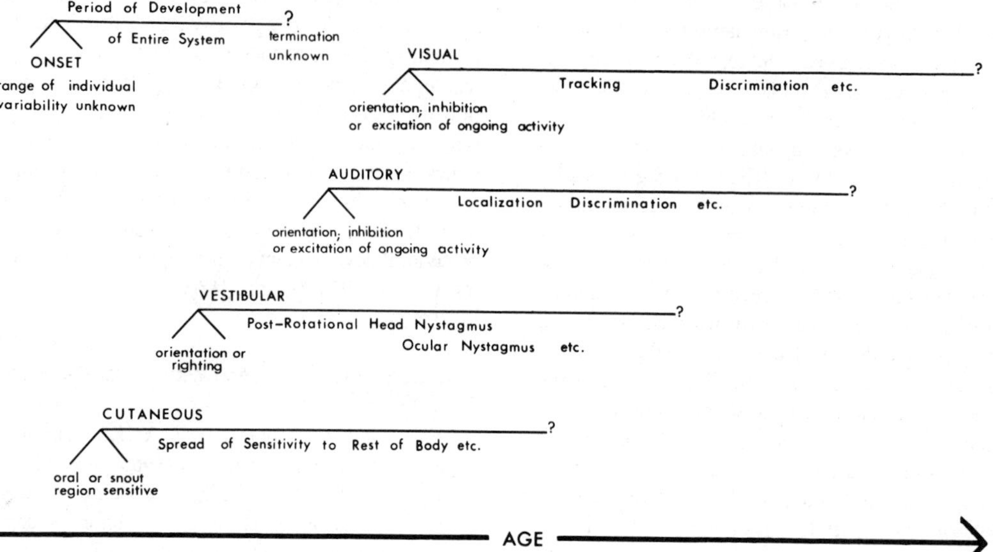

Figure 5. The ontogenetic sequence of development of four sensory systems derived from anatomical, physiological, and behavioral research on birds and mammals, including humans. In precocial species such as chicks, ducklings, guinea pigs, sheep, and the like, in which the newborn can locomote and is otherwise highly developed, these sensory systems become functional before hatching or birth. In altricial species, on the other hand, the auditory and visual systems usually become capable of function only after birth or hatching. Humans differ from other altricial species in that all of these sensory systems mature and become capable of functioning during the prenatal period (Gottlieb, 1971).

presumably encountered by the embryo and the latter (withdrawal tendency) to the presumed absence of such stimulation during embryonic development.

Thus, Schneirla's theory represents an effort to account for postnatal species-typical perceptual preferences on the basis of embryonic experience. It not only assumes (1) the *inductive* role of embryonic sensory stimulation on the development of perception, but it also assumes (2) that the quantitative aspects of experience in one sensory modality can influence the features to which the embryo or neonate will respond in other (later developing) sensory modalities. This second assumption is potentially very significant for our understanding of the development of species-typical perception, so it warrants careful experimental examination. Such cross-modal competence has been demonstrated in adult monkeys (Weiskrantz & Cowey, 1975), and there is clear evidence of it in 6- to 8-month-old (Allen, Walker, Symonds, & Marcell, 1977) and 1-year-old human infants (Gottfried, Rose, & Bridger, 1977). At younger ages the relevant dimensions may be different (Lewkowicz & Turkewitz, 1980), so such studies of cross-modal equivalence could be of the highest developmental significance, leading as they would to a delineation of change in central mediation with age and experience. Since we now have evidence of the relatively early onset of tactile sensitivity, and the relatively late onset of auditory and visual sensitivity in a variety of birds and mammals (including humans), the actual inter-modal direction and ease of establishment of these equivalences is predictable from a developmental point of view (Bradley & Mistretta, 1975; Gottlieb, 1971). Specifically, I think the tactile to auditory or visual route would be easier for the human neonate than the other way around, based on what is known about the sequential development of these systems (summarized in Figure 5). While this hypothesis may be construed as an "empiricist" approach to the development of perception, it is actually counter to what the great empiricist philosopher John Locke (1690/1961, p.

114) predicted about the relation of touch to sight. His theory held that a congenitally "blind man, at first sight, would not be able with certainty to say which was the globe, which was the cube, whilst he only saw them, though he could unerringly name them by his touch."

The hypothesized developmental perceptual relationship between touch and vision is borne out strikingly in a study of intersensory equivalence in children by Abravanel (1968). He found that the relation between haptic (active touch) exploration and visual matching was substantially better at virtually all ages (3 to 13 years) when the active touch preceded the visual matching, as opposed to the later haptic matching of an item that was first visually observed.

A thoughtful review of acoustic-optical correspondences and auditory-visual coordination in infancy has been published by Mendelson (1979). A similar set of correspondences between the tactile and the auditory and visual systems would help to guide research with young infants and neonates, leading to the delineation of changes in relevant dimensions with age and experience.

Z.-Y. Kuo's Program

In contrast to the relative specificity of Schneirla's theoretical proposals, Zing-Yang Kuo (1967) has put forth a general program to recognize the essentially multidisciplinary nature of the comparative study of behavioral development.

According to Kuo, we must actively consider anatomical and physiological factors because these set limits to behavior potentials, thus influencing the actual range and varieties of behavior patterns for a given species. Although the plasticity of a species' behavioral repertoire is often studied for its own sake, Kuo put forth a rationale for creating what he called *behavioral neophenotypes*. Namely, by severely altering typical developmental conditions, one can determine the actual immediate potential for the future evolution of behavior in a species. Although it is not often made explicit in accounts of the evolution of behavior, reconstructions of the prior evolution of a species' behavior is highly speculative and is necessarily limited to such matters as form of locomotion, sensory specializations, and possible modes of eating (see Hopson & Radinsky, 1980, for a sophisticated review). So, the experimental creation of new behavioral phenotypes has the great advantage of being an empirical enterprise that would exhibit the limits of plasticity and thus show the possible directions of behavioral evolution for the immediate future of the species. (This proposal is also apt for other epigenetic approaches to evolution that explicitly strive to go beyond conventional neo-Darwinian assumptions; see, e.g., Ho & Saunders, 1979.)

For Kuo, the proper starting point for developmental study is of course the embryo. In his view, many of the important movement patterns evident in the neonate represent a repetition and extension of the various components of embryonic motor activity, now *reorganized* and incorporated into a new motor pattern in response to the changed environmental context (birth or hatching introducing the new context), as well as changes in physiology and morphology. The central idea here is that the emergent neonatal motor behavior pattern is in some sense dependent on certain of its various components having been active during the embryonic state, although these components may not have entered into the same relationship prior to birth or hatching.

Kuo's theory assumes that throughout embryonic and neonatal development, new patterns of movement manifest themselves (due to changes in morphology, embryonic position, and so on), and that these almost always include some components that were active earlier in development. The extent to which the onset, threshold, rate of development, and/or coordination of the later movement patterns are dependent on the prior activity or exercise of certain of their components has not been tested in an experimental fashion, so the validity of Kuo's viewpoint on this issue has not been tested. In conceptual agreement with Kuo, Tryphena Humphrey's (1969, 1971) view on the ontogeny of patterned movement in human infants assumes that sequences of certain movements that occur in late embryonic or fetal life (or in early neonatal or perinatal behavior) are rather straightforward repetitions of the sequences of previous embryonic or fetal motor activity. She stresses (Humphrey, 1971, p. 35) that it is the repetition of fetal motor *sequences*, not of identical movements, which occurs when, for example, the neonate makes a certain train of oral and facial movements. While it is virtually certain that the central "control" mechanisms change during development, Humphrey (1969, p. 80) points out that the motor neurons involved are most likely the same in each case, so, in this sense, the earlier activity is the precursor to the later one.

Kuo has often been written off as a crass or extreme environmentalist, and certainly his early anti-instinct writings of 60 years ago lend themselves to that interpretation. In his 1967 book, however, published near the end of his life (he died in 1970), Kuo says (pp. 198–199) that he chose to call his point of view an epigenetic one so as to recognize genetic influences as well as environmental factors in the development of the individual behavioral repertoire. And that is certainly in keeping with the contemporary developmental point of view that has been sketched in the present chapter.

In closing, it remains to add that a principal forerunner of modern geneticists, August Weismann (1894), maintained an overriding interest in the process of ontogenetic development and, more particularly, of the role of external influences on individual development. If the brilliant author of the germ plasm theory placed so much emphasis on the importance of external influences on development, perhaps we may be countenanced in continuing this mode of inquiry at the level of brain, behavior, and psychology, just as long as we retain as our ultimate goal the illumination of species-typical development in its usual setting. To do otherwise, of course, runs the risk of continuing the utterly banal practice of demonstrating plasticity for its own sake.

REFERENCES

Abravanel, E. The development of intersensory patterning with regard to selected spatial dimensions. *Monographs of the Society for Research in Child Development*, 1968, *33*(2), 1–52.

Adelmann, H. B. *Macello Malpighi and the evolution of embryology*. Ithaca, N.Y.: Cornell University Press, 1966.

Allen, T. W., Walker, K., Symonds, L., & Marcell, M. Intrasensory and intersensory perception of temporal sequences during infancy. *Developmental Psychology*, 1977, *13*, 225–229.

Anokhin, P. K. Systemogenesis as a general regulator of brain development. In W. A. Himwich & H. E. Himwich (Eds.), *The developing brain*. New York: American Elsevier, 1964.

Aslin, R. N. Experiential influences and sensitive periods in development: A unified model. In R. N. Aslin, J. R. Alberts, & M. R. Petersen (Eds.), *Development of perception* (Vol. 2). New York: Academic Press, 1981.

von Baer, K. E. *Ueber Entwicklungsgeschichte der thiere*. Königsberg: Gebruder Bornträger, 1828, 1837.

Barcroft, J. *The brain and its environment*. New Haven: Yale University Press, 1938.

Bateson, P. How do sensitive periods arise and what are they for? *Animal Behaviour*, 1979, *27*, 470–486.

de Beer, G. *Embryos and ancestors* (3rd ed.). London: Oxford University Press, 1958.

Bexton, W. H., Heron, W., & Scott, T. H. Effects of decreased variation in the environment. *Canadian Journal of Psychology*, 1954, *8*, 70–76.

Bradley, R. M., & Mistretta, C. M. Fetal sensory receptors. *Physiological Reviews*, 1975, *55*, 352–382.

Broman, S. H., Nichols, P. L., & Kennedy, W. *Preschool IQ: Prenatal and early developmental correlates*. Hillsdale, N.J.: Erlbaum, 1975.

Cairns, R. B. Ontogeny and phylogeny of social interactions. In M. E. Hahn & E. C. Simmel (Eds.), *Communicative behavior and evolution*. New York: Academic Press, 1976.

Campbell, B. A., & Jaynes, J. Reinstatement. *Psychological Review*, 1966, *73*, 478–480.

Carmichael, L. The development of behavior in vertebrates experimentally removed from the influence of external stimulation. *Psychological Review*, 1926, *33*, 51–58.

Carmichael, L. The onset and early development of behavior. In L. Carmichael (Ed.), *Manual of child psychology*. New York: Wiley, 1963.

Chow, K. L., Riesen, A. H., & Newell, F. W. Degeneration of retinal ganglion cells in infant chimpanzees reared in darkness. *Journal of Comparative Neurology*, 1957, *107*, 27–42.

Coghill, G. E. *Anatomy and the problem of behaviour*. Cambridge, Eng.: At the University Press, 1929. (Reprinted 1964 by Hafner, New York.)

Crain, S. M., Bornstein, M. B., & Peterson, E. R. Maturation of cultured embryonic CNS tissues during chronic exposure to agents which prevent bioelectric activity. *Brain Research*, 1968, *8*, 363–372.

Cravioto, J., Birch, H. G., De Licardie, E., Rosales, L., & Vega, L. The ecology of growth and development in a Mexican preindustrial community. *Monographs of the Society for Research in Child Development*, 1969, *34* (5), 1–76.

Crowell, D. H. Infant motor development. In Y. Brackbill (Ed.), *Infancy and early childhood*. New York: Free Press, 1967.

Davidson, E. H., & Britten, R. J. Organization, transcription, and regulation in the animal genome. *Quarterly Review of Biology*, 1973, *48*, 565–613.

Dawkins, R. The ontogeny of a pecking preference in domestic chicks. *Behaviour*, 1968, *25*, 170–186.

Dewsbury, D. A. *Comparative animal behavior*.

New York: McGraw-Hill, 1978.

Eayrs, J. T. Developmental relationships between brain and thyroid. In R. P. Michael (Ed.), *Endocrinology and human behaviour*. London: Oxford University Press, 1968.

Fischer, K. W. A theory of cognitive development: The control and construction of hierarchies of skills. *Psychological Review*, 1980, *87*, 477–531.

Fishbein, H. D. *Evolution, development, and children's learning*. Pacific Palisades, Calif.: Goodyear, 1976.

Freud, S. *A general introduction to psychoanalysis*. New York: Permabooks, 1953.

Garstang, W. The theory of recapitulation. A critical restatement of the biogenetic law. *Journal of the Linnaean Society of London* (Zoology), 1922, *35*, 81–101.

Gesell, A. The ontogenesis of infant behavior. In L. Carmichael (Ed.), *Manual of child psychology*. New York: Wiley, 1946.

Gollin, E. S. Development and plasticity. In E. S. Gollin (Ed.), *Developmental plasticity*. New York: Academic Press, 1981.

Gottfried, A. W., Rose, S. A., & Bridger, W. H. Cross-modal transfer in human infants. *Child Development*, 1977, *48*, 118–123.

Gottlieb, G. Conceptions of prenatal behavior. In L. R. Aronson, E. Tobach, D. S. Lehrman, & J. S. Rosenblatt (Eds.), *Development and evolution of behavior*. San Francisco: Freeman, 1970.

Gottlieb, G. Ontogenesis of sensory function in birds and mammals. In E. Tobach, L. R. Aronson, & E. Shaw (Eds.), *The biopsychology of development*. New York: Academic Press, 1971.

Gottlieb, G. Introduction to Behavioral embryology. In G. Gottlieb (Ed.), *Behavioral embryology*. New York: Academic Press, 1973. (a)

Gottlieb, G. (Ed.). *Behavioral embryology*. New York: Academic Press, 1973. (b)

Gottlieb, G. Conceptions of prenatal development: Behavioral embryology. *Psychological Review*, 1976, *83*, 215–234. (a)

Gottlieb, G. The roles of experience in the development of behavior and the nervous system. In G. Gottlieb (Ed.), *Neural and behavioral specificity*. New York: Academic Press, 1976. (b)

Gottlieb, G. Roles of early experience in species-specific perceptual development. In R. N. Aslin, J. R. Alberts, & M. R. Petersen (Eds.), *Development of perception* (Vol. 1). New York: Academic Press, 1981. (a)

Gottlieb, G. Development of species identification in ducklings: VIII. Embryonic vs. postnatal critical period for the maintenance of species-specific perception. *Journal of Comparative and Physiological Psychology*, 1981, *95*, 540–547. (b)

Gould, S. J. *Ontogeny and phylogeny*. Cambridge, Mass.: Belknap Press of Harvard University Press, 1977.

Goy, R. W., Bridgson, W. E., & Young, W. C. Period of maximal susceptibility of the prenatal female guinea pig to masculinizing actions of testosterone propionate. *Journal of Comparative and Physiological Psychology*, 1964, *57*, 166–174.

Graves, H. B. Early social responses in *Gallus:* A functional analysis. *Science*, 1973, *132*, 937–938.

Grouse, L. D., Schrier, B. K., Bennett, E. L., Rosenzweig, M. R., & Nelson, P. G. Sequence diversity studies of rat brain RNA: Effects of environmental complexity on rat brain RNA diversity. *Journal of Neurochemistry*, 1978, *30*, 191–203.

Grouse, L. D., Schrier, B. K., & Nelson, P. G. Effect of visual experience on gene expression during the development of stimulus specificity in cat brain. *Experimental neurology*, 1979, *64*, 354–364.

Haeckel, E. *Anthropogenie oder Entwicklungsgeschichte des Menschen* (4th Rev. and Enl. ed.). Leipzig: Wilhelm Engelmann, 1891.

Hall, G. S. *Adolescence*. (2 vols.) New York: Appleton, 1916.

Hall, W. G., & Bryan, T. E. The ontogeny of feeding in rats: II. Independent ingestive behavior. *Journal of Comparative and Physiological Psychology*, 1980, *94*, 746–756.

Hamburger, V. Ontogeny of behaviour and its structural basis. In D. Richter (Ed.), *Comparative Neurochemistry*. Oxford: Pergamon, 1964.

Hamburger, V. Anatomical and physiological basis of embryonic motility in birds and mammals. In G. Gottlieb (Ed.), *Behavioral embryology*. New York: Academic Press, 1973.

Hamburgh, M. The role of thyroid and growth hormone in neurogenesis. In A. Moscona & A. Monroy (Eds.), *Current topics in developmental biology* (Vol. 4). New York: Academic Press, 1969.

Ho, M. W., & Saunders, P. T. Beyond neo-Darwinism—an epigenetic approach to evolution. *Journal of Theoretical Biology*, 1979, *78*, 573–591.

Holt, E. B. *Animal drive and the learning process* (Vol. 1). New York: Holt, 1931.

Hooker, D. *The prenatal origin of behavior*. Lawrence, Kansas: University of Kansas Press, 1952.

Hopson, J. A., & Radinsky, L. B. Vertebrate paleontology: New approaches and new insights. *Paleobiology,* 1980, *6,* 250–270.

Humphrey, T. The relation of oxygen deprivation to fetal reflex arcs and the development of behavior. *Journal of Psychology,* 1953, *35,* 3–43.

Humphrey, T. Postnatal repetition of human prenatal activity sequences with some suggestions of their neuroanatomical basis. In R. J. Robinson (Ed.), *Brain and early behaviour: Development in the fetus and infant.* New York: Academic Press, 1969.

Humphrey, T. Human prenatal activity sequences in the facial region and their relationship to postnatal development. *American Speech and Hearing Association* (ASHA) *Report,* 1971, No. 6, 19–37.

Jacobson, M. A plenitude of neurons. In G. Gottlieb (Ed.), *Aspects of neurogenesis.* New York: Academic Press, 1974.

Jaisson, P. L'impregnation dans l'ontogenese de comportements de soins aux cocons chez la jeune formi rousse (*Formica polyctena Forst*). *Behaviour,* 1975, *52,* 1–37.

Jerison, H. J. *Evolution of the brain and intelligence.* New York: Academic Press, 1973.

Johnston, T. D. Contrasting approaches to a theory of learning. *Behavioral and Brain Sciences,* 1981, *4,* 125–173.

Klüver, H. *Behavior mechanisms in monkeys.* Chicago: University of Chicago Press, 1933.

Koch, R., Graliker, B., Fishler, K., & Ragsdale, N. Clinical aspects of phenylketonuria. In *First inter-American conference on congenital defects.* Philadelphia: Lippincott, 1963.

Kuo, Z.-Y. *The dynamics of behavior development.* New York: Random House, 1967. (Reprinted in 1976 by Plenum Press.)

Lehrman, D. S. A critique of Konrad Lorenz's theory of instinctive behavior. *Quarterly Review of Biology,* 1953, *28,* 337–363.

Lehrman, D. S. Semantic and conceptual issues in the nature–nurture problem. In L. R. Aronson, E. Tobach, D. S. Lehrman, & J. S. Rosenblatt (Eds.), *Development and evolution of behavior.* San Francisco: Freeman, 1970.

Leiman, A. L., Seil, F. J., & Kelly, J. M. Maturation of electrical activity of cerebral neocortex in tissue culture. *Experimental Neurology,* 1975, *48,* 275–291.

Lewkowicz, D. J., & Turkewitz, G. Cross-modal equivalence in early infancy: Auditory-visual intensity matching. *Developmental Psychology,* 1980, *16,* 597–607.

Locke, John. *An essay concerning human understanding* (2nd ed.). London: Dent, 1961. (Originally published in 1690.)

Lumsden, C. J., & Wilson, E. O. Translation of epigenetic rules of individual behavior into ethnographic patterns. *Proceedings of the National Academy of Science USA,* 1980, *77,* 4382–4386.

Marler, P., & Mundinger, P. Vocal learning in birds. In H. Moltz (Ed.), *The ontogeny of vertebrate behavior.* New York: Academic Press, 1971.

Mason, W. A. Scope and potential of primate research. In J. H. Masserman (Ed.), *Science and psychoanalysis* (Vol. 12, *Animal and Human*). New York: Grune & Stratton, 1968.

McGraw, M. B. Maturation of behavior. In L. Carmichael (Ed.), *Manual of child psychology.* New York: Wiley, 1946.

Mendelson, M. J. Acoustic-optical correspondences and auditory-visual coordination in infancy. *Canadian Journal of Psychology,* 1979, *33,* 334–346.

Meyer, R. L., & Sperry, R. W. Retinotectal specificity: Chemoaffinity theory. In G. Gottlieb (Ed.), *Neural and behavioral specificity.* New York: Academic Press, 1976.

Model, P. G., Bornstein, M. B., Crain, S. M., & Pappas, G. D. An electron microscopic study of the development of synapses in cultured fetal mouse cerebrum continuously exposed to Xylocaine. *Journal of Cell Biology,* 1971, *49,* 362–371.

Moltz, H. Contemporary instinct theory and the fixed action pattern. *Psychological Review,* 1965, *72,* 27–47.

Needham, J. *A history of embryology.* New York: Abelard-Schuman, 1959.

Nicholson, J. L., & Altman, J. Synaptogenesis in the rat cerebellum: Effects of hypo- and hyperthyroidism. *Science,* 1972, *176,* 530–531.

O'Malley, B. W., & Means, A. R. Female steroid hormones and target cell nuclei. *Science,* 1974, *183,* 610–620.

Oppenheim, R. W., Pittman, R., Gray, M., & Maderdrut, J. L. Embryonic behavior, hatching and neuromuscular development in the chick following a transient reduction of spontaneous motility and sensory input by neuromuscular blocking agents. *Journal of Comparative Neurology,* 1978, *179,* 619–640.

Oppenheimer, J. M. *Essays in the history of embryology and biology*. Cambridge, Mass.: MIT Press, 1967.

Parker, S. T., & Gibson, K. R. A developmental model for the evolution of language and intelligence in early hominids. *Behavioral and Brain Sciences,* 1979, *2,* 367–408.

Paulson, G. W. Maturation of evoked responses in the duckling. *Experimental Neurology,* 1965, *11,* 324–333.

Paulson, G., & Gottlieb, G. Developmental reflexes: The reappearance of foetal and neonatal reflexes in aged patients. *Brain,* 1968, *91,* 37–52.

Peters, J. J., Vonderahe, A. R., & Powers, T. H. The functional chronology in developing chick nervous system. *Journal of Experimental Zoology,* 1956, *133,* 505–518.

Piaget, J. Piaget's theory. In P. H. Mussen (Ed.), *Carmichael's manual of child psychology* (Vol. 1, 3rd ed.). New York: Wiley, 1970.

Pittman, R., & Oppenheim, R. W. Cell death of motoneurons in the chick embryo spinal cord. IV. Evidence that a functional neuromuscular interaction is involved in the regulation of naturally occurring cell death and the stabilization of synapses. *Journal of Comparative Neurology,* 1979, *187,* 425–446.

Preyer, W. *The mind of the child.* Part 1. *The senses and the will.* New York: Appleton, 1888.

Preyer, W. *The mind of the child.* Part 2. *The development of the intellect.* New York: Appleton, 1889.

Reynolds, V. *The biology of human action.* San Francisco: Freeman, 1976.

Rheingold, H. L., Gewirtz, J. L., & Ross, H. W. Social conditioning of vocalizations in the infant. *Journal of Comparative and Physiological Psychology,* 1959, *52,* 68–73.

Sahlins, M. *The use and abuse of biology.* Ann Arbor: University of Michigan Press, 1976.

Scarr, S., & Weinberg, R. A. IQ test performance of Black children adopted by White families. *American Psychologist,* 1976, *31,* 726–736.

Scarr-Salapatek, S. Genetic determinants of infant development: An overstated case. In L. Lipsitt (Ed.), *Developmental psychobiology: The significance of infancy.* Hillsdale, N.J.: Erlbaum, 1976.

Schneirla, T. C. Interrelationships of the "innate" and the "acquired" in instinctive behavior. In P.-P. Grassé (Ed.), *L'Instinct dans le comportement des animaux et de l'homme.* Paris: Masson, 1956.

Schneirla, T. C. Aspects of stimulation and organization in approach/withdrawal processes underlying vertebrate behavioral development. In D. S. Lehrman, R. A. Hinde, & E. Shaw (Eds.), *Advances in the study of behavior* (Vol. 1). New York: Academic Press, 1965.

Slotkin, T. A., Smith, P. G., Lau, C., & Bareis, D. L. Functional aspects of development of catecholamine biosynthesis and release in the sympathetic nervous system. In H. Parvez and S. Parvez (Eds.), *Biogenic amines in development.* Amsterdam: Elsevier, 1980.

Solomon, R. L., & Lessac, M. S. A control group design for experimental studies of developmental processes. *Psychological Bulletin,* 1968, *70,* 145–150.

Spalding, D. A. Instinct: With original observations on young animals. *MacMillan's Magazine,* 1873, *27,* 282–293.

Sperry, R. W. Mechanisms of neural maturation. In S. S. Stevens (Ed.), *Handbook of experimental psychology.* New York: Wiley, 1951.

Sperry, R. W. How a developing brain gets itself properly wired for adaptive function. In E. Tobach, L. R. Aronson, & E. Shaw (Eds.), *The biopsychology of development.* New York: Academic Press, 1971.

Stevenson, J. G. Song as a reinforcer. In R. A. Hinde (Ed.), *Bird vocalizations.* Cambridge, Eng.: At the University Press, 1969.

Stone, J. M., & Greenough, W. T. Excess neonatal thyroxine: Effects on learning in infants and adolescent rats. *Developmental Psychobiology,* 1975, *8,* 479–488.

Tees, R. C. Effect of visual deprivation on development of depth perception in the rat. *Journal of Comparative and Physiological Psychology,* 1974, *86,* 300–308.

Teicher, M. H., & Blass, E. M. First suckling response of the newborn albino rat: The roles of olfaction and amniotic fluid. *Science,* 1977, *198,* 635–636.

Teitelbaum, P., Cheng, M.-F., & Rozin, P. Development of feeding parallels its recovery after hypothalamic damage. *Journal of Comparative and Physiological Psychology,* 1969, *67,* 430–441.

Uphouse, L. L., & Bonner, J. Preliminary evidence for the effects of environmental complexity on hybridization of rat brain RNA to rat unique DNA. *Developmental Psychobiology,* 1975, *8,* 171–178.

Vince, M., Reader, M., & Tolhurst, B. Effects of stimulation on embryonic activity in the chick.

Journal of Comparative and Physiological Psychology, 1976, *90,* 221–230.

Waddington, C. H. Canalization of development and the inheritance of acquired characters. *Nature,* 1942, *150,* 563–564.

Waddington, C. H. Genetic assimilation of an acquired character. *Evolution,* 1953, *7,* 118–126.

Waddington, C. H. *The strategy of the genes*. London: Allen and Unwin, 1957.

Waddington, C. H. The basic ideas of biology. In C. H. Waddington (Ed.), *Towards a theoretical biology*. 1. *Prolegomena*. Chicago: Aldine, 1968.

Weiskrantz, L., & Cowey, A. Cross-modal matching in the rhesus monkey using a single pair of stimuli. *Neuropsychologia,* 1975, *13,* 257–261.

Weismann, A. *The effect of external influences upon development*. London: Henry Frowde, 1894.

Werner, H. *Comparative psychology of mental development* (Rev. ed.). New York: International University Press, 1948.

Wiens, J. A. Effects of early experience on substrate pattern selection in *Rana aurora* tadpoles. *Copeia,* 1970, No. 3, 543–548.

Willier, B. H., Gallagher, T. F., & Koch, F. C. The modification of sex development in the chick embryo by male and female sex hormones. *Physiological Zoology,* 1937, *10,* 101–122.

Zelazo, P. R., Zelazo, N. A., & Kolb, S. "Walking" in the newborn. *Science,* 1972, *176,* 314–315.

Zetterström, B. The effect of light on the appearance and development of the electroretinogram in newborn kittens. *Acta Physiologia Scandanavica,* 1956, *35,* 272–279.

Zuckerkandl, E. Programs of gene action and progressive evolution. In M. Goodman, R. F. Tashian, & J. H. Tashian (Eds.), *Molecular anthropology*. New York: Plenum Press, 1976.

ETHOLOGY AND CHILD DEVELOPMENT* 2

ROBERT A. HINDE, *MRC Unit on the Development and Integration of Behaviour, Cambridge University*

CHAPTER CONTENTS

SOME PRINCIPLES OF ETHOLOGY RELEVANT TO CHILD PSYCHOLOGY

Introduction

This chapter is concerned with the contribution of ethologists and of ethological ways of thinking to the study of child development. From the start, however, I would emphasize that the distinction between ethology and developmental psychology is to be seen primarily in historical terms. In the past, when ethologists and developmental psychologists pursued their separate ways, a surprising number of conceptual, methodological, or empirical advances were made more or less simultaneously by members of both groups. With the currently increasing interpenetration of ideas which are fertile for both groups, it is to be hoped that the waste of endeavor which occurred in the past is being reduced. My aim is to facilitate that trend: if boundaries are necessary in science, they should be dictated as far as possible by the problems, not by -ologies. Of course, I am not

*This chapter was in part written while I held the Hitchcock Professorship at the University of California, Berkeley, and I would like to thank Drs. Steven Glickman and Paul Licht for their hospitality there. At other times, my work was supported by the Royal Society, Medical Research Council and Grant Foundation. A number of colleagues gave me valuable comments on earlier drafts, and I would like to thank especially Pat Bateson, Judy Dunn, Nick Humphrey, Harriet Oster, Michael J. A. Simpson, and Joan Stevenson-Hinde as well as the editors Joseph J. Campos and Marshall Haith.

claiming that the ethological tradition, hitherto concerned primarily with animal behavior, is likely to have much to say about such issues as the immediate bases of moral development or cultural differences. Ethology and developmental psychology are not coextensive. But there are many issues that can better, and perhaps only, be tackled when distinctions between the two disciplines cease to matter.

In focusing on the contribution of ethologists to developmental psychology, I have had to forgo any attempt to convey to child developmentalists the excitement of much empirical ethological work and the humility in the face of the diversity of nature that it engenders (e.g., see Tinbergen, 1958). I have not even attempted to review all ethological work on animals that might be relevant to studies of child development nor all studies of child development that might be called ethological. Instead, in the discussion on *Selected Issues,* I have focused on orientational and conceptual issues of common interest. My aim is not to propagate an ethology of child development but rather to persuade child developmentalists, where appropriate, to think ethologically. I have confined more detailed data reviews to some selected issues.[1]

The Nature of Ethology

It is necessary first to indicate what is meant by ethology. That, however, is not easy: Ethology has too often been defined as concerning phenomena or involving concepts, theories, or techniques which many who call themselves ethologists would regard as only part of the whole or even disown altogether. Perhaps a brief historical view will help.

Although the origins of ethology have been traced to the nineteenth century naturalists (Thorpe, 1979), the bases of modern ethology were laid in the 1930s by Konrad Lorenz in Germany and by Niko Tinbergen in Holland. Both were keen observers, fascinated by the diversity of nature and by the intricacy of the adaptations shown by animals to their environment. In his early work, Lorenz, much influenced by Heinroth (e.g., 1911), opened up the study of imprinting (Lorenz, 1935) and showed how stereotyped and species-characteristic movements (fixed action patterns) could be used as taxonomic characters (Lorenz, 1941). He also provided theories on the relations between instinct and learning and on the nature of motivation based on an astonishing knowledge of diverse species (Lorenz, 1937, 1939). Tinbergen's early work included a number of field studies (e.g., 1939), some of which included experimental work on orientation in insects and on camouflage in a wide range of species (Tinbergen, 1935, 1958). His laboratory studies of the courtship behavior of the three-spined stickleback (Tinbergen, 1951) exemplified the combination of observation and experiment which was to characterize so much subsequent ethological work, and his field study of the herring gull initiated a program of research which is still in progress (Tinbergen, 1959).

Lorenz and Tinbergen worked together briefly before World War II (e.g., Lorenz & Tinbergen, 1939), and summaries of their ideas were published in English during the 1940s (Thorpe, 1948; Tinbergen, 1942, 1948). However, it was Tinbergen's *The Study of Instinct* (1951) that produced the first real impact in the English-speaking world. This work included material relevant to the four questions which he has since (e.g., Tinbergen, 1963) emphasized as crucial for the full understanding of behavior: What causes this behavior? / How did it develop? / What is its biological function? / How did it evolve? (see *The Four Whys*).

Given the gross approximations necessary in a brief historical survey of this sort, it is fair to say that during the 1950s ethologists in Germany and Scandinavia were influenced primarily by Lorenz, those in the Low Countries and in the U.K. (where Tinbergen settled in 1949) by Tinbergen, and those in the United States rather more by Lorenz than by Tinbergen. This is important because during the 1950s and 1960s, ethologists, although united on the main issues, came to differ in emphasis on others. Again summarizing a complex situation, it is true to say that most of those influenced by Lorenz continued to distinguish between innate and learned behavior, to use (overtly or covertly) energy models of motivation, and to suggest that natural selection operated for the benefit of the group, whereas those influenced by Tinbergen adopted an interactionist approach to development, an intervening variable (in the sense of MacCorquodale & Meehl, 1948) type of approach to problems of motivation, and a concept of natural selection as acting on individuals.

The difficulties that beset attempts to define ethology may now be apparent. Ethology can not be delimited as the study of innate behavior. It is not merely descriptive, and it does not involve any particular theory of development or motivation. So, a rather discursive definition may be repeated (Hinde, 1970):

> The term ethology is applied particularly to the work of students who, although differing widely in the problems they tackle, the level of analysis at which they work, the methods they use and the

theoretical interpretations (if any) they adopt, share certain orienting attitudes which are, perhaps, more important as unifying factors than any particular theoretical scheme. Many of these attitudes are a consequence of the zoological training of the early ethologists. They felt, for instance, that the description and classification of behaviour is a necessary preliminary to its analysis; that the behaviour of an animal cannot be properly studied without some knowledge of the environment to which its species has become adapted in evolution; and that questions about the evolution and biological function of behaviour are, in principle, as valid and important as those about its immediate causation [and, it may be added, development]. (p. vii)

To some, a crucial aspect of ethology has been its interfertility with other disciplines. Contact has been made with a variety of physiological and biological sciences with various branches of psychology, and with several of the social sciences (Hinde, 1982a, 1983). Relations with two branches of psychology require comment in the present context. Some comparative psychologists, such as F. A. Beach, entered into discussion with ethologists before World War II, but others, such as T. C. Schneirla, were bitterly opposed to the new discipline. There were two main bones of contention. First, Schneirla was much concerned with differences between the capacities of animals at different phyletic levels and felt that the ethologist's generalized concepts often concealed differences in mechanism. On their side, ethologists (used to making precise comparisons between closely related species in evolutionary studies) felt that gross comparisons between different phyla were too crude to be useful. They defended their concepts on the grounds that they were functional, not causal in nature: Just as anatomists use the term legs for locomotory appendages in insects and vertebrates without implication of evolutionary homology or similarity in structure or mechanism, so did ethologists use the term social releasers for movements or structures specialized for signaling in any species. Second, Schneirla emphasized the role of experience in development, regarding the ethologists' emphasis on innateness as an evasion of important developmental problems, whereas ethologists felt the comparative psychologists neglected the importance of genetic factors. It could also be said that up to the early 1950s ethologists were not sophisticated about psychology, although they saw themselves as more hard-headed than the European subjectivists (e.g., Bierens de Haan, 1947) and less constrained by laboratory techniques than the American behaviorists.

Perhaps in part because of his obscure prose style, Schneirla's criticisms of ethology were relatively ineffective. However, a hard-hitting attack on ethology by his pupil Lehrman (1953) led, surprisingly, to a permanent rapprochement between the two disciplines. This was due largely to the compatible personalities of the protagonists. Lehrman, Lorenz, Tinbergen, and other ethologists were all at heart naturalists, more interested in the bird outside the window than in theoretical differences. They recognized that common problems provided important ties which overrode theoretical divergence. On the comparative issue, the differences in approach were recognized and accepted, whereas on ontogeny both sides (with some individual exceptions) withdrew from their somewhat extreme positions. Although some differences in emphasis remained, ethologists and comparative psychologists became largely indistinguishable.

Although Lorenz early on (e.g., 1939) speculated about the applicability of ethological concepts to the human species, ethology did not start to have an impact on developmental psychology until later. Two sources of influence, one conceptual and the other methodological, deserve mention. One was a series of papers, and later books, by John Bowlby (1969, 1973, 1980), a London psychoanalyst. Bowlby had earlier noted that young delinquents had often had a history of separation from their families, and he set out to conceptualize how infant-mother attachment develops and how the bond affects subsequent development. During the 1950s and 1960s a group used to meet regularly at the Tavistock Clinic—a group including Freudian and Kleinian analysts, Hullian and Skinnerian learning theorists, a Piagetian, psychiatric social workers, an ethologist, and sometimes an antipsychiatrist—theoretically heterogeneous but united by an interest in parent-child relationships. Bowlby, with scientific eclecticism especially remarkable in a psychoanalyst, assimilated what he felt to be useful; his subsequent theory of attachment included a major ethological contribution.

The second important event was the publication of a book, edited by Blurton Jones (1972c), a pupil of Tinbergen. Besides a number of empirical studies, mostly of nursery school children, this contained a masterly summary by Blurton Jones of a fairly extreme ethological position. Emphasis was laid particularly on the need for objective description in terms of behavioral elements, with more global concepts, such as aggression, attachment, and anxiety, being eschewed. Blurton Jones's introduction provided powerful arguments for the use of an ethological approach. As the dust has settled, it has, I believe, become apparent that he overstated his case on some issues. For example, in criticizing rating scales, he neglected the contexts in which they are useful; in arguing against the use of interviews as a means of finding out about child behavior, he overlooked the fact that what a mother feels about her child may be, for some purposes, as important as what she can be seen to do with it; and in arguing against the attachment concept, he appears to have misunderstood the concept and overrated the power of factor analysis (see *The Current Status of Attachment Concepts*). These issues are mentioned here only because Blurton Jones's work was so clearly of pioneering importance in this field. His views are of interest because they, as well as the comparable overstatements by the more traditional child developmentalists, exemplify the frictions that often first arise when representatives of different backgrounds meet over a common problem but which can then pave the way for fruitful cooperation.

Interestingly, entirely independently of the growth of ethology, a number of studies appeared that ethologists would have been happy to claim. Although Darwin's observational studies (e.g., 1872) were long neglected, some of the classic studies of child development, notably those of Piaget, depended on careful observation and description. During the 1930s, a number of excellent observational studies of child behavior were carried out (e.g., M. Smith, 1933; Swan, 1938; Washburn, 1932). Such studies subsequently fell into disrepute, in part because some used rather unreliable methods and in part because the better ones provided material for more analytical studies. As other early examples, Ahrens (1954) carried out a pioneering study of the stimuli eliciting smiling in infants and Gunther (1955), a London pediatrician investigating difficulties in the establishment of breast feeding, carried out an ethological analysis of the sucking sequence (with considerable clinical implications). Prechtl, formerly a student of Lorenz, became interested in the same problem (1958) and subsequently developed a method for the neurological examination of the newborn that has widespread application (Prechtl & Beintema, 1964). In recent years, advances in our understanding of several aspects of child development (perhaps most notably developmental psycholinguistics) have come from close attention to what actually happens in natural situations, and it is becoming apparent that a similar approach is essential both for posing the right questions and in seeking for answers elsewhere (e.g., the study of nonverbal communication, empathy and cooperation, and friendship). An integration of ethological and developmental psychological approaches is clearly timely.

In their contacts with other disciplines, ethologists have been able to make substantial contributions, not by annexing a group of phenomena as their own but rather by marrying their approach to that of those already in the field. Partly for that reason, the recent tendency to segregate a science of human ethology seems retrogressive. But there are also other reasons. An important characteristic of much ethological work lies in its comparative nature. The peculiarities of the behavior of one species are seen, explicitly or implicitly, against a background of the behavior of others, and in many cases comparisons are used as a specific source of data (see *The Comparative Method*). Human ethology implies an ethology cut off from its comparative roots. Another issue is that, whereas ethology has traditionally been concerned with behavior, a full understanding of much human action requires us also to come to terms with the meanings ascribed to actions and with what individuals think they do, hope to do, or feel they should do (Dunn, 1979; Harré & Secord, 1972). Thus, although human ethology may be a useful label for some courses, textbooks, and the like, if isolated it could become largely limited to superficial interpretations of rather trivial phenomena. In the present context, however, this means only that ethologists tackling problems traditionally in the province of developmental psychology must do so with humility. As I hope to show, ethologists have made and are continuing to make important contributions.

Because of the difficulties in defining ethology, because many studies that might conceptually or methodologically be called ethological were carried out by people who did not call themselves ethologists, and above all because attempts to erect boundaries between areas of scientific endeavor are nearly always counterproductive, the approach here is catholic. I shall discuss some of the topics to which an ethological approach has made a substantial contribution, whether or not the primary training of the workers concerned was ethological.

Special Issues in the Integration of Ethology and Developmental Psychology

Although many of the orienting attitudes of ethologists are entirely compatible with those of developmental psychologists, three issues require special explication.

The Comparative Method

Many attempts to draw from animal data lessons applicable to the human case involve, explicitly or implicitly, the use of an animal model. A particular nonhuman species, resembling humans in certain respects, is presumed also to resemble them in others. Whereas this may work well enough in some cases, no nonhuman species is very like humans, and the dangers of false conclusions are considerable (Hinde, 1976b; Lehrman, 1974; Seay & Gottfried, 1975). Animal species differ not only from the human species but also among themselves in complexity of organization as well as in detail, and apparently similar behavioral effects may depend on different processes in different species (Schneirla, 1949).

Nevertheless, the comparative method can facilitate understanding of the human case. For one thing, processes contributing to complex phenomena can often be studied more readily in simpler organisms: examples are provided in the study of attachment (see *Ethological Studies . . .* and *The Current Status of Attachment Concepts*). Another approach is to compare a range of species, abstract principles from the comparisons and, then, to assess the applicability of those principles to the human species. Such a comparative approach means to the ethologist much more than comparing a particular animal species with the human species. One example has implications for the frequency with which newborns should be suckled. Comparative studies of a wide range of mammals show that frequency of suckling is inversely related to the protein content of the milk. Although some species nurse their young almost continuously, others, producing milk with a high protein content, nurse them only once a day or even less. Human milk has a low protein content, suggesting that newborn infants are adapted to be suckled more frequently than the four hourly feeds that have been standard in many maternity hospitals (Blurton Jones, 1972b). This is in harmony with the findings that breast-fed babies cry more over the first 10 days and more after feedings than do bottle-fed babies because bottled milk has a higher protein concentration (Bernal, 1972).

Other examples of the value of a comparative approach will appear later in this chapter. However, one caution is necessary. Where there is variability between human cultures, it must not be assumed that procedures closer to the nonhuman primate condition, let alone to some particular nonhuman species, are necessarily to be preferred. Consider, for instance, the issue of contact comfort.

All monkeys and apes—and we may exclude here the more primitive prosimians—spend the greater part of their early life in physical contact with another individual. Young infants usually cling to their mothers in a ventro-ventral position, which gives them ready access to the nipple when the mother is seated and enables them to use the nipple as a fifth point of support when the mother is walking or climbing. Later, they often ride dorsally, clinging to their mother's back or neck. Figure 1 illustrates that frequent physical contact of an infant with the mother lasts for a considerable part of its developmental period for a species which develops fairly rapidly and that an infant is carried by other family members as well as the mother (Ingram, 1977). Furthermore, it has been established experimentally that contact with the mother or mother surrogate can be comforting in anxiety-provoking situations (Candland & Mason, 1968; Harlow & Zimmerman, 1959; Mason & Berkson, 1975). But the ubiquity of physical contact between mother and infant in other primate species does not, of course, mean that human babies *must* have near-continuous physical contact with an adult. In many cultures, they do; but equally in many cultures they do not. In each society, a whole com-

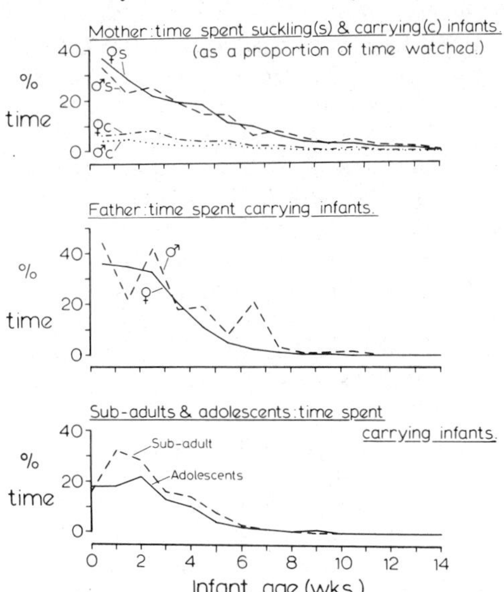

Figure 1. Proportion of observation time that infant marmosets spent on various social companions. Data for mother show suckling times and carrying but not suckling times separately. Data for mother and father show male and female infants separately. Animals lived in family groups and were observed during the morning hours. (Ingram, 1977, p. 814.)

plex of practices has, through the joint action of biological and cultural forces, become more or less standardized. In comparing cultures or species, one must compare those complexes of practices in the contexts in which they occur, not independent aspects of child care. But the ubiquity of bodily contact between infant and caregiver in nonhuman primates does give a certain perspective to some facts about babies—for instance, that swaddling and rocking can soothe, how readily children become attached to blankets or soft toys with which they have contact in bed (see also Hong & Townes, 1976; Passman, 1977; Passman & Weisberg, 1975), and the efficacy of the dummy (or pacifier). Such data indicate that the use of substitute contact objects is inversely related to the availability of the mother (Hong & Townes, 1976). Furthermore, observations in a culture where babies are carried in bodily contact with their mothers indicate that many infant reflexes function (or functioned) to readjust position on the mother or to grasp the mother as she gets up or moves off (Blurton Jones, 1974; Konner, 1972). Even such trite universals as contact comfort in nonhuman primates are worth studying if they indicate features of the environment to which infants are biologically adapted and if they integrate a number of facets of infant development.

The Four Whys

As indicated earlier, ethologists regard full understanding of any one item of behavior as entailing answers to four questions. It is worthwhile to consider these in a little more detail.

The causal analysis of behavior is concerned with the question, What made the organism behave in this way? Normally, an essential preliminary to causal analysis is description and classification of the behavioral events. An attempt is then made to specify relations between the behavioral events and to relate them to antecedent conditions. For instance, if an ethologist finds that a particular avian display is frequently associated with certain other patterns of behavior, such as striking a rival, she may classify them together, perhaps giving them the label aggressive behavior. If the display can be elicited by a mirror, visual stimuli must be important. If the display occurs more at certain seasons than at others, internal (motivational) factors are likely to be important. If the display is less likely to be elicited by familiar individuals than by strangers, experience plays a role—and so on. Of course, such a preliminary analysis depends heavily on the use of correlations between events, but if we bear in mind that temporal correlations may arise in more than one way and that they are in any case only a guide for further analyses or experimentation, that will not matter. Experiments designed with knowledge of the natural situation may follow. The behavioral level of analysis may in itself lead us to explanatory concepts which will suffice for prediction and control of the behavior, at any rate within a specified range of conditions. Complete understanding of causation is likely to require study at finer analytical levels, involving physiological and physicochemical techniques, but that is unnecessary for many issues.

A second group of problems is also primarily concerned with causation but involves delving further into the past. As an organism develops, its behavior changes: the course of ontogeny demands analysis and understanding. Here, again, we must start with description: How does the behavior change? From a descriptive base, we can, then, pose such causal questions as: To what extent do the changes observed depend on environmental influences? and How do such influences produce their effects? In practice, the distinction between problems of immediate causation and problems of ontogeny is often blurred. For example, delinquent behavior in adolescents may depend on propensities acquired in childhood, be made more probable by the effects of continuing recent frustration (e.g., a long hot summer in a ghetto area), and be precipitated by example from peers (see Fig. 2).

Processes studied in the course of ontogenetic analysis have as consequences processes studied in the analysis of immediate causation. But these latter processes also have their consequences, and they, in turn, pose a third set of problems. Some of these problems constitute the situation toward which the behavior was directed (goals), and these or other consequences may affect the probability that the behavior is repeated (reinforcers). Thus, searching may lead to food (goal) and the food or further consequences of eating increase the probability that the animal will search in the same place again. Some consequences may affect the individual animal's chances, or its relative's chances, of survival or reproduction. Thus, some variations in consequences are of long-term evolutionary importance (functions strict sense [ss]), whereas other consequences, although beneficial, are by-products of natural selection, being fully achieved in all individuals. Yet other consequences may be neutral with respect to all these issues or even harmful (see Fig. 2). These categories only partially overlap. For instance, aggression directed toward a peer may be reinforced by parental attention or a sexual conquest may have

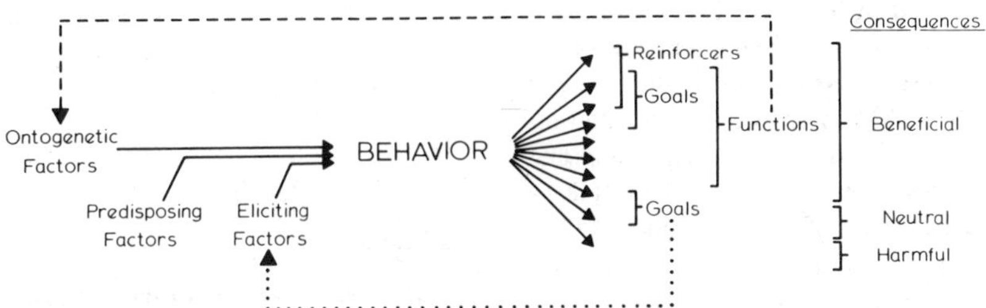

Figure 2. Relations between ontogenetic and causal factors and consequences. The distinctions between ontogenetic and predisposing factors and between predisposing and eliciting factors are often somewhat arbitrary. Among the consequences, the categories of reinforcers, goals, and functions only partially overlap. Although a goal is normally achieved as a consequence of behavior, an internal representation (anticipation) may contribute to causation (dotted line). Consequences may be beneficial, yet not provide material for the action of natural selection (i.e., not be functions in a strict sense). Exceptionally, harmful consequences can be goals. The discontinuous line indicates evolutionary consequences on the next generation. (Hinde, 1982a, p. 81.)

reproductive consequences quite separate from the goal of peer adulation which led to it. But it will be apparent that the analysis of cause and consequence may merge. Because the interval of time over which a causal analysis is made is limited, the consequences of earlier events in the sequence of behavior may affect later ones: for example, reinforcers become causes of subsequent actions.

A fourth question concerns the evolutionary origins of the behavior in question. Often, comparisons between closely related species enable us to erect hypotheses about the course of evolution of particular aspects of behavior. We shall see some examples later (see *Sign Stimuli, Social Releasers . . .* and *The Current Status of Attachment Concepts*).

Functional and evolutionary questions might seem irrelevant to students of child development if only because the environments in which nearly all children now live are so different from the "environment of evolutionary adaptedness," to use Bowlby's (1969) phrase. However, this is not necessarily the case because we gain perspective if we see apparently functionless behavior as part of a repertoire that was formerly adaptive. For example, the distress of a child confronted by a stranger or left alone in a room of toys seems functionless in a secure civilized society, but it may be crucially important in other societies and must have been so at an earlier stage in our evolution. Bowlby's theory of attachment (see *Ethological Studies . . .* and *The Current Status of Attachment Concepts*) was, in fact, built up on this basis—a young primate depends on its mother for protection as well as for food and other necessities and is, therefore, equipped with a repertoire of behavior patterns for maintaining proximity with her (see also *The Comparative Method*).

More recently Trivers (1974) has attempted to account for the course of the mother-infant relationship in terms of the difference in the biological benefits and costs to mother and offspring of the latter's independence. In brief, if benefits and costs are measured in terms of future reproductive potential, continued dependence on the mother produces obvious benefits and entails little cost for the infant. However, it involves considerable costs on the mother because of its effects on the probability of her conceiving and successfully rearing further offspring. The mother also benefits in evolutionary terms less than the infant because, although most genes are identical in mother, infant, and father, the infant carries on average only half of the maternal genes that are not shared with the father. It is, thus, to be expected that the mother should encourage the infant's independence—an expectation supported by data on nonhuman species (see *The Current Status of Attachment Concepts* and *The Dynamics of the Parent-Child Relationship*). Such considerations may help us maintain a balanced perspective when considering the course of human mother-infant interaction.

Sometimes functional considerations can help us to understand apparently abnormal behavior. Attachment behavior, normally functional, can become pathologieal clinging; observational data suggest that fear leading to avoidance of social encounters is crucial in some conditions labeled as childhood autism (Hutt & Ounstead, 1966; Richer,

1976; Tinbergen & Tinbergen, 1972). Although functional considerations can be illuminating for ontogenetic or causal analyses, speculations about function are not always worthwhile—they can involve crude comparisons between humankind and its hypothetical ancestors, outdated biological theory, and even a naive view of function (Hinde, 1975).

In studies of child development, considerations of biological function—which is measurable only in terms of inclusive fitness (Hamilton, 1964) or gene survival—often merge with studies of more immediate consequence. It is, therefore, especially important to maintain the distinction between causal and functional questions. When we say a baby's crying is "really" just attention getting, do we mean that the behavior is one evolved to promote proximity to parent (functional explanation), that it merely produces parental proximity (beneficial consequence), or that it is goal directed by the infant toward that end (causal explanation)? If we say smiling enhances the mother-infant bond, we imply a functional explanation, but if we say the child's smile elicits maternal tenderness, we are talking in causal terms.

In this chapter, we shall be concerned primarily with questions of ontogeny, causation, and immediate (as opposed to long-term evolutionary) consequence. However, it will be apparent that the questions of biological function and evolutionary history are not irrelevant in studies of child development.

The Study of Processes Versus Behavioral Categories

A third issue concerns a traditional difference in orientation between ethologists and psychologists. The former, although they have long discarded classical instinct theory, still like to classify types of behavior into groups on causal or functional grounds, for instance, into sexual, aggressive, or feeding behavior. Insofar as the relations between these categories or between their constituent members are discussed, the emphasis is on their mutually inhibitory or facilitatory influences. Psychologists, by contrast, have been concerned with characteristics of processes, such as perception, motivation, or learning, which transcend the ethologists' categories. The ethologists' bias may lead to shortcomings in their approach to development, where such categories can be misleading, and in studies of the behavior of higher organisms, where cognitive functions may link causal or functional categories of behavior (see *The Current Status of Attachment Concepts*). The psychologists' bias retarded their recognition of the importance of response or situation-specific constraints on learning (see *Principles of Development*). Integration between these approaches is clearly essential.

SELECTED ISSUES

Methodology

Observational and Descriptive Studies

With their emphasis on the importance of description as a basis for analysis, ethologists have paid considerable attention to techniques for describing behavior. Their work has gone on in parallel with, but regretably largely in isolation from, that of developmental psychologists: each group could have learned much from the other. Because methodological issues are discussed in Volume I of the Handbook, discussion here is limited to some basic issues. It is, of course, important to stress that a purely behavioral approach is unlikely to be adequate for many investigations and that, to elucidate meaning, other techniques are often necessary in addition to, or instead of, behavioral ones.

Initial Conceptual Issues. The importance of description has often been neglected, especially by those scientists who modeled their approach on that of classical physics. Classical physics dealt mainly with everyday events—floating boats, falling apples, and the like, which were already familiar. But less mundane phenomena, such as the movements of the planets or the colors produced by a prism, required careful descriptive work before they could be understood. The course of child development is indeed an everyday matter, but experience shows that we are not always adept at noticing that which later turns out to be important; for many projects, careful description is a wise first step. Of course, this does not mean that every investigation must start with a descriptive phase, but many have gone astray by not doing so.

Observation of behavior inevitably involves abstraction. This is necessary because of our inability to deal with unique events: it is a reasonable assumption that each instance of behavior differs from all others, and it is necessary for us to group instances into classes by abstracting properties that, to a degree of precision appropriate to the problem being tackled, recur in more than one instance.

Observation, thus, involves selection. Indeed while observing one aspect of behavior, we must neglect others which are going on simultaneously: if we are interested in a child's eye movements, for instance, we may disregard his respiration or the way he curls his toes. In addition, we must confine our observations to a limited span of time. Behavior involves a continuous stream of events, yet we must neglect many of those that precede the instances on which we have focused as well as many of their consequences. Sometimes we will regret our omissions, but the practical necessities of observation and data handling force us to be selective. Unfortunately, selection is likely to be influenced by cultural or theoretical predilections: we must be constantly on our guard against the resultant bias.

Having selected what we would describe, there are basically two methods of description available. The first involves reference ultimately to the strength, degree, and patterning of muscular contractions (or change in some other physiological property). In practice, such a complete description is often both impracticable and unnecessarily cumbersome, and description is limited to patterns of limb or body movement, such as raised eyebrows or Moro's reflex or walk. Sometimes, however, as in the study of facial expression, description in terms of patterns of muscular contraction can provide a firmer base (e.g., Ekman & Friesen, 1975; Oster, 1978; Oster & Ekman, 1978).

In classifying together instances on the basis of such descriptions, we group instances by similarity in selected aspects of the spatiotemporal patterns of muscular contraction. Which characteristics are chosen must, of course, be specified objectively, but we must recognize that variation of motor pattern is not necessarily paralleled by a similar variability in basic mechanism: depending on the nature of the surface, what is being carried, and so on, the precise movement patterns used in walking are extremely variable, yet the distinctions from crawling or running are usually clear.

The second method for describing behavior may be called description by consequence. Lever pressing, picking up the toy, or approaching mother—such phases do not refer to particular patterns of muscular contraction but cover all patterns that lead, or could lead, to the result specified. Here, a brief description can cover a multitude of motor patterns—approaching may involve crawling, walking, or running—and, thus, provide an essential shorthand.

Description by consequence often calls attention to essential features of the behavior that would not appear in physical descriptions, such as orientation with respect to some object or person (approaching *mother*) or responsiveness to external stimuli (searching for *mother*). Classification of instances in terms of consequence is often more free from errors of observation than classification in terms of movement patterns—whether or not the child picked up a toy or moved her head sufficiently to operate a microswitch are matters which brook no argument.

However, there are disadvantages in description by consequence. Sometimes it may bias theorizing: Was the child approaching its mother or fleeing from a stranger, or both? And such descriptions can be taken to imply reciprocal relations between behavior classes specified in terms of muscular contraction such that a decrease in frequency of one would be followed by a compensatory increase in another (MacCorquodale & Meehl, 1954). That may or may not be so. A child who could not walk to his mother might crawl, but a baby who could not operate a microswitch even with a simple response, such as a head movement, would not necessarily be able to do so with a more complex action, such as bringing his hand to it.

Whichever type of description is used (and often a combination is desirable), there will be rejection of some of the data and a selection of features to be studied. If we do not select, we shall wallow in a mass of detail and our attention will be diverted from the essentials of the problem. Yet, it is essential always to be aware of the dangers of rejecting important information, of using units too large or too small, or of using information that is irrelevant for the task at hand.

Having described behavior in a manner which enables us to group instances together as examples of the same type of behavior, it is usually then convenient to categorize the types of behavior that we recognize. Four types of category may be recognized. First, types of behavior may be classified together on the view that they share causal factors, for instance, we might classify together all the types of behavior a baby shows when it has not been fed for a long time or when a pin is sticking into her. Second, we may classify behavior in terms of consequence—all the behavior that increases the probability that the mother will approach or all behavior that leads to destruction of property or is disruptive of our social system. Or we may group items of behavior according to their evolutionary origin, for instance, the human smile and the monkey fear grin may have a common evolutionary origin (see *Sign Stimuli, Social Releasers* . . .). Finally, we may group items together because they were acquired in the same way, for instance, patterns of behavior that were learned or learned from models.

These systems of classification are distinct and

must not be confused. Causal and consequential categories often overlap, but we must be clear whether we mean common causation or common consequence when we use terms like sexual behavior or aggressive behavior.

Choice of Approach. The methods available for obtaining data on a child's behavior or interactions fall roughly into four groups (determined in part by the amount and nature of the data selection that occurs at the time of observation):

1. Direct permanent recording. A near complete and permanent record is obtained on film, videotape, or audiotape. Data selection occurs subsequently and can depend on criteria determined after the data are collected.
2. Direct observation. Here, the observer records preselected aspects of behavior, by spoken commentary onto tape, by use of a checksheet, or by a keyboard operating either a pen recorder or a computer-compatible magnetic tape.
3. Indirect reports. Data are obtained from individuals who spend much time with the child. Included here are such methods as maternal interviews, diaries, teachers' questionnaires, and so on. The data ultimately involve the reporter's perception of the child's behavior and that perception may be the focus of interest. However, it is essential to be able to distinguish between reports of feelings about events and the events themselves. For the latter, detailed but flexible and skilled interviewing may be necessary (Rutter & Brown, 1966). However, observers' judgments can be of special value in conveying a synthesis of the overall quality or style of behavior (Block, 1977).
4. Self-reports. It is possible to ask older children what they do, feel, or think. Once again, reported events may not correspond to actual ones. However, what a child thinks or feels or what he says he thinks or feels may be crucial.

Although the main distinction emphasized here is the degree of preselection of the aspects of behavior to be recorded, this is often, but not necessarily, paralleled by differences in the fineness of detail. Very fine details of behavior can be obtained only from a direct and permanent record, whereas indirect records often concern rather global properties of behavior, although this is not necessarily the case.

Developmental psychologists have been concerned with the relative values of different methods for some years (e.g., Hutt & Hutt, 1970; Lytton, 1971) and some have made direct comparisons between methods. For example, Willems and Willems (1965) assessed the relative validity of coded interviews, a card-sorting technique, and a checklist completed by adolescent subjects, all of these methods being concerned with why the subjects participated in certain group activities. The results were validated against the number of activities in which the subjects actually participated. The interview data proved to have the highest validity but was the most costly in terms of time and effort; the checklist was least costly but also least valid. Lytton (1974) compared behavioral counts based on naturalistic home observations; overall ratings based on observation, interview, and a 24-hr. diary; and measures obtained in an experimental playroom situation. When construct validity was assessed in terms of the extent of the network of correlations with theoretically predicted variables that the data sources generated, the experimental approach came off worst. Measures obtained from behavioral observations entailed the greatest costs. Of course, the generality of comparisons between particular methods applied in particular ways to particular problems can always be called in question, but it is clear that ease of data collection is not always related to high validity.

Most ethological work has involved or at least started from direct observation. Ethologists were, however, early to recognize the value of a permanent record (e.g., Thorpe, 1961), and they have exploited novel methods for the analysis of film and video recordings (e.g., Golani, 1976, and Weisler, 1978, have used a dance notation for describing movement).

Enthusiastic over the power of direct observational techniques, some ethologists have been critical of interview methods and of observer ratings, especially of such global aspects of behavior as negativism or aggressiveness (Blurton Jones, 1972a). However, direct comparisons of observational measurements with observers' ratings (Lytton, 1974), teachers' questionnaire ratings (Roper & Hinde, 1979), and maternal interview material (Dunn & Kendrick, 1980b) involving behaviorally defined items have shown that indirect methods can be reliable. These methods are now being used in studies of children by ethologists. In fact, their use has been extended to animal studies. Stevenson-Hinde, Stillwell-Barnes, and Zunz (1980) have shown that observers' ratings of items (defined in behavioral terms) about the individual characteristics of rhesus monkeys show high interobserver agreement and high validity where they can be compared with observational measures. Ratings of maternal characteristics permitted prediction of infant characteristics at 1 year to an extent greater than has yet been possible using behavioral items (see *Relation Between Characteristics of the Mother or Mother-Infant Relationship and Those of the Offspring*).

However, the need for caution in interpreting measures of the validity of observer ratings is emphasized by a recent study of nursery school children. By a multiple-scan sampling technique (see *Sampling Methods*), aspects of the behavior of children in turn were recorded. These included assessments of the degree of social participation as self, parallel, group, and interactive play—based on the categories used by Parten (1932). A principal-components analysis of the data subsequently suggested that these categories do not form a scale—how much a child played on her own (self-play) loading heavily on a dimension orthogonal to that concerned with how interactively she played when alongside other children (parallel, group, and interactive play). A teacher's questionnaire was completed by teachers and observers before the results of the principal-components analysis were known. From the observational data, 10 measures were relevant to 15 items in the questionnaire and showed good agreement. But a principal-components analysis of the questionnaire data yielded a first factor loaded positively with such items as socially appropriate behavior, talkative, confident, and so on, and loaded negatively with alone. Thus, the analysis of the questionnaire data, unlike that of the observational data, suggested that items relevant to interactive or group play or to self-play lay on a continuum. Apparently the respondents to the questionnaire, including the present writer, were influenced by an implicit personality theory (Bruner & Tagiuri, 1954) that self-play is inversely related to interactive play but not influenced sufficiently to disrupt the correlations on individual items. Thus, validity at the data level does not necessarily imply similarity of structure.

In an extension of this work, teacher ratings were compared with observational data for children who were 42 months old (mostly in their second term in preschool) and 50 months old. Agreement was better at the former age. In many cases, the reduction in agreement at 50 months could be accounted for on the hypotheses that the teachers were more observant of the children while they were still settling into the school and that they tended to assess the children in terms of their own behavior to them rather than in terms of their behavior to each other (Hinde, Easton, & Meller, in press).

Sampling Methods. Whether a permanent record or direct observation is to be used, it is necessary to decide how to sample the stream of behavior to obtain data on the items of interest. The issues that arise here, present even if only one individual or dyad is being studied, become even more acute if a group of individuals (e.g., in a classroom or playgroup) are under observation. Decisions about sampling methods must be taken with an eye on the specific questions that are to be asked. Altmann (1974) has classified the sampling methods available and the classification used here departs only slightly from hers.

1. *Ad libitum sampling*. In ad libitum sampling, the observer records as much as he can or whatever is most easily observed or most interesting to him. This is the method most used in preliminary studies and in natural history observations. It can produce definitive data of exceptionally conspicuous events, but it must usually be superceded by more precise methods as the investigation proceeds.

2. *Sociometric matrix completion*. Ad libitum sampling may be supplemented by obtaining additional data on particular individuals or pairs of individuals. For instance, if relative dominance within dyads is under study and ad libitum observations provide adequate data for some dyads but not for others, attention may be focused on the latter. But no meaning can be attached to the row and column totals in any matrix drawn up from such data, and use of the method greatly restricts the sorts of questions that can be answered.

3. *Focal individual sampling*. An individual (or group of individuals) is selected and all occurrences of specified types of behavior are recorded throughout the duration of a specified sampling period. Thus, the observer may focus on the baby rather than on the mother or sibling or she may focus on one child in a group. (It may be necessary in playground situations to record separately the durations of intervals for which the target individual is out of sight.) Under some conditions, it is possible to obtain a record not only of the focal individual's actions but also a record of responses directed to him by others or of responses to his actions by others.

4. *Sampling all occurrences of some behavior types*. In some circumstances, it is possible to record all occurrences of certain types of behavior in a group of individuals. The events must be attention catching and never too frequent for recording. For instance, such a method might be suitable for recording questions to the teacher or fights in a classroom.

5. *Sequence sampling*. The focus of attention in sequence sampling is an interaction sequence, not a particular individual. Recording starts when one out of a specified number of types of interaction starts—

for example, a baby starts to cry or a child asks a teacher a question—and is continued until that sequence is concluded in one of a number of specified ways.

6. *One-zero sampling*. The occurrence or nonoccurrence of particular items of behavior in successive time periods is recorded. Thus, a focal individual may be selected and records made of whether that individual was in certain states (e.g., asleep) or performed certain actions in successive periods (often 10 sec. or 30 sec.). What is recorded is not the frequency of each type of behavior but the frequency of intervals that include any amount of time spent in that behavior. This is not necessarily closely related to actual frequency or duration. Altmann (1974), therefore, argued strongly against the use of this technique (see also Dunbar, 1976; Kraemer, 1979; Simpson & Simpson, 1977). Hinde (1973) also recognized its possible inaccuracies but considered that it could have certain advantages for durational activities in spite of the loss in accuracy. Hinde also pointed out that it could capture rare but important events which might be lost by instantaneous sampling. Tyler (1979) found one-zero sampling to be generally less satisfactory than others he examined but points out that every convention can give accurate or inaccurate estimates depending on the parameters of the behavior studied.

7. *Instantaneous sampling*. In instantaneous sampling, the observer records the current activity at preselected moments in time (e.g., every minute on the minute). This samples behavioral states rather than events. The data may concern a preselected focal individual or group of individuals; in the latter case, individual records would have to be taken at different points in time (near-instantaneous scans). This method is perhaps the ideal one for estimating the percentage of time individuals spend in different (reasonably common) activities: extended records may be necessary for estimates of the frequencies of rare events.

8. *Multiple-scan sampling*. Multiple-scan sampling combines focal individual sampling with near-instantaneous scans. Each individual is watched for a specified time; then, the observer focuses on another individual and continues the process up to a specified number (e.g., the complete class). Then, the sequence is repeated. This is useful where instantaneous sampling is inadequate to interpret the behavior being shown and where a number of individuals must be studied in the same time period (e.g., Roper & Hinde, 1978).

It will be apparent that some combinations of these methods are possible. For instance, instantaneous sampling may be used for states of a focal child, but all interactions may be recorded as they occur. Whatever method is used, decisions as to when sampling sessions should be started and finished must be made: it is usually essential that such decisions should be independent of the behavior observed. According to the problem under study, it will be necessary to decide how to allocate observation time between individuals, whether one individual or many should be studied, and how the subjects should be selected and the observations scheduled.

Experimental Approaches

Having achieved an adequate description, most ethologists adopt an experimental approach. Although their contribution to techniques of experimentation has not been great, one issue deserves mention. Tinbergen's early work depended heavily on field experiments, that is, his experiments did not involve placing the animal in a rigidly controlled (thus, unnatural) situation but rather involved experimental control of one or more factors in the natural environment. In studies of child development, the techniques used must of course be suited to the problem, but for some purposes such semistructured situations can have more validity than artificial test procedures. Developmental psychologists have, of course, reached similar conclusions independently. In practice, the techniques vary from manipulation of the "natural" situation, as when space or number of toys available in a nursery school are varied, through procedures in which a "natural" event is contrived in a laboratory situation (e.g., the Ainsworth strange-situation technique—see *The Current Status of Attachment Concepts*) to more rigidly controlled laboratory procedures.

Principles of Development

Ethologists have devoted much research effort to problems of development. The aim here is not to review this work but rather to focus on some theoretical issues of current mutual interest to ethologists and child developmentalists.

Functional Considerations

First, one issue of perspective must be stressed. Child development is usually studied by adults, who perceive the course of development as culminating in adulthood. But, looked at from a functional viewpoint, natural selection has shaped the immature stages of organisms not as miniature adults but so that they will succeed in their developmental task (Tinbergen, 1963). Caterpillars are superb leaf eaters, but they do not pretend to be butterflies. The very word development too often diverts us from considering each stage in its own right.

Of course, this does not mean that it is necessarily the case that everything an infant does is directly functional. For instance, Thelen (1979), in a longitudinal study of 20 normal infants over their first year, described 47 movement patterns showing constancy of form and development. Groups of stereotyped movements involving particular parts of the body or body postures had characteristic ages of onset, peak performance, and decline. Thelen suggests that rhythmic stereotypes are a consequence of incomplete cortical control of endogenous patterning in maturing neuromuscular pathways.

Dichotomies in Development

It is now virtually universally accepted that a dichotomy between innate and learned behavior is neither accurate nor heuristically valuable. In the first place, such a dichotomy implies that the factors influencing behavior are of two types only: genetic and those associated with learning—in practice nutrition, stress and many other factors are known to affect behavioral development in ways that would not come within any generally accepted definition of learning. Second, the dichotomy implies that it is possible to classify items of behavior into those that are influenced only by genetic determinants and those on which innate factors have no influence: in reality both genetic and environmental factors influence all aspects of behavior. It is, however, sometimes useful to recognize that aspects of behavior are distributed along a continuum from those that are environmentally stable (i.e., unmodifiable by any environmental conditions within the viable limits) to those that are environmentally labile (i.e., varying greatly with environmental influences). Thus, the form of the smile at 1 year of age is stable, but the situations eliciting it have considerable lability. Such an approach encompasses the basic postulate that the development of all behavior involves both genetic and environmental influences and can recognize that behavior may be stable over one stage of its development and labile at another (Hinde, 1959).

Turning from behavior to the processes involved in its development, it is sometimes convenient to distinguish consequences of maturation from those of experience (e.g., Schneirla, 1966), although here the dichotomy is only a convenient abstraction which depends on the universe of discourse. When applied to tissue growth and differentiation, maturation is applied to processes that are unaffected by environmental factors because they occur within an environment whose characteristics are maintained within limits by regulatory mechanisms. When applied to behavioral development, maturation usually refers to environmentally stable (see above) characters which appear to be unaffected by differences in the social or physical environment during development. That stability may, however, be due either to self-regulatory properties in the individual or, as we shall see later, perhaps more usually to self-regulatory properties in the parent-child relationship.

A third type of dichotomy, and one with more heuristic value, concerns the sources of differences in behavior. If we rear organisms known to differ genetically in similar environments, any difference in behavior can be safely ascribed to genetic factors. For example, different species of finch reared in closely similar environments grow up to have different seed preferences. A role of genetic differences between the species in determining seed preferences thus seems highly likely. However, this does not imply that learning is of no importance. In practice, the seed preferences develop in part because species have different-sized beaks and learn to select those seeds that they can open most efficiently with the beaks they possess (Kear, 1962).

Alternatively, if organisms of (actually or statistically) similar genetic constitution are reared in different environments, differences in behavior can be ascribed to environmental factors. Again, this does not mean that genetic factors are unimportant. With a slight change in genetic constitution, development might occur similarly in the two environments because genes determine responsiveness to the environment. Such a dichotomy between the causes of differences in behavior poses further questions: How do the genetic factors influence behavior? / What environmental factors operate? / How do environmental factors produce their effects? (See *Scarr & Kidd, vol. II, chap. 6.*)

An important issue here concerns the extent to which organisms are predisposed to learn some things and constrained from learning others. The earlier view that it would be possible to find laws of learning valid for all species in all situations and that what acts as an effective reinforcement in one situation will also do so in another is now seen to have been overoptimistic. Comparative evidence shows that what an individual will learn and the situations in which an individual will learn vary between species (Hinde & Stevenson-Hinde, 1973; Seligman & Hager, 1972). To give but one example, song development in many birds depends on imitative learning, but the song repertoire that each individual acquires is more or less limited to those characteristic of the species. Furthermore, this limitation is achieved in different ways in different species, for example, the chaffinch will learn only songs with a note structure similar to that of normal chaffinch song, whereas the bullfinch is predisposed to imitate its father or foster father (Thorpe, 1961). It seems certain that much human learning is to be seen in a similar light. For a variety of reasons, ranging from trivial to highly complex, at each stage in our lives, we are more likely to learn some things than others (e.g., Hutt, 1973). In the human case, constraints on what is learned and predispositions to learn some things more than others may differ markedly between cultures.

Beyond that, in considering how inherited and environmental factors affect behavior, further classificatory categories may prove valuable. For instance, factors of either sort may have either specific effects on a rather narrow aspect of behavior or more general consequences on much or all of the behavioral repertoire (Bateson, 1976b; Hinde, 1970; Lehrman, 1970; Schneirla, 1956). Again these factors may act to initiate, facilitate, or maintain processes involved in behavioral development (e.g., Bateson, 1978b; Gottlieb, 1976). Thus, developmental determinants may be inherited or environmental, they may initiate, facilitate, or maintain consequences which are relevant to limited or to more general aspects of behavior. Furthermore, the effects of any one determinant may vary with the others present. For instance, a given factor may act in one way or be more or less general in its effects, depending on the other factors present.

Such a classification of the determinants of behavior is, of course, only an aid toward understanding the processes involved. And at every stage, there are dangers in overgeneralization from experimental data. Although an investigator is unlikely to conclude from the finding that one genetic or environmental factor is important, that others are not also relevant, it is possible to be misled into concluding, from the finding that a number of factors tested one by one are without effect, that they never have any effect. Interactions between independent variables are virtually ubiquitous, the effectiveness of any one in influencing the behavior in question is always likely to depend on the presence of other variables (e.g., Denenberg, 1970, 1979).

Organism-Environment Interaction

Turning more specifically to the question of process, development involves a continuing interaction between a changing organism and (usually) a changing environment (transaction, as Sameroff, 1975, likes to call it although the term seems to embody no new concept). To take first a concrete example, female canaries are brought into reproductive condition by a change in day length and other external stimuli. These result in a change in endocrine state, which results in the display of nest-building behavior. Such behavior leads to the construction of a nest; stimuli from that nest cause further changes in behavior, both directly and through endocrine intermediaries. Thus, the bird changes its environment and the environmental change induces further changes in the bird and, thus, in behavior (Hinde, 1970). Usually (perhaps) the change lies not in the actual environment, but in the perceived or effective environment. The environmental factors that matter to a 1-month-old baby differ from those that matter at 1 year; the nest a canary builds is not only a new source of stimulation but induces hormonal changes which make the canary increasingly sensitive to that nest and cause changes in her building behavior.

Such cases can be described in more general terms: the responses of an organism to environmental events produce changes in the organism so that its response either to similar or to quite other environmental events differs from that shown earlier. In the cases cited, the effects were such that progressive changes in behavior were facilitated—for example, through response to environmental factors, the canary's hormonal state changes in such a way that it becomes more sensitive to certain stimuli—and as a result development to a new reproductive stage proceeds. We shall see shortly that the same form of words covers also changes that tend to preserve the status quo, or at least the current developmental track.

Sensitive Periods

By definition, the individual changes throughout development. It is, thus, to be expected that susceptibility to environmental influences will change as development proceeds. The more obvious examples concern the dependence of late-developing skills on abilities acquired earlier. More interesting (and more controversial) are cases in which individual characteristics can be influenced by particular environmental events more strongly at one stage than either earlier or later.

It is important here to distinguish the strong concept of critical periods in development from the more useful concept of sensitive periods. The former derived its popularity in the behavioral literature largely from experiments on imprinting in birds: the young of many bird species will learn to respond to a moving object as they would normally respond to a parent, provided that the object is presented to them within a period starting a few hours after birth and finishing a few hours or days later (Lorenz, 1935). Lorenz regarded this period as immutable and the process of imprinting as irreversible: thus the term critical period became current in the literature (e.g., Hess, 1959; Scott & Marston, 1950).

However, it soon became apparent that the limits of the period were not irrevocably fixed by inherent developmental processes (e.g., Guiton, 1961; Moltz & Stettner, 1961) and that imprinting was not irreversible (e.g., Fabricius & Boyd, 1954; Hinde, Thorpe, & Vince, 1956; Moltz, 1960). The term sensitive period, thus, became more popular. Its implication is simply that a given event produces a stronger effect on development or that a given effect can be produced more readily during a certain period than earlier or later. It does not imply that the period is necessarily closely tied to chronological age nor that equivalent effects cannot be obtained (although perhaps with more difficulty) later (Clarke & Clarke, 1976).

Seen in this way, sensitive period provides a useful label, for example, for the suggestions that events in the immediately postnatal period are of special importance in the establishment of the mother-infant relationship (e.g., Kennell, Trause, & Klaus, 1975) or that a period of separation between mother and child may have more marked effects at some ages than others (e.g., Bowlby, 1951). Similarly, data on the effects of various rearing conditions on the development of social behavior in rhesus monkeys show that particular treatments are more effective at some ages than at others and that each response system is more susceptible to modification by aspects of the social environment over some age ranges than others (Suomi & Harlow, 1978a, 1978b). The processes involved in the changes in sensitivity are, of course, likely to differ from case to case (e.g., Bateson, 1979). The question of subsequent compensation for early deficiencies is considered later.

Continuity and Discontinuity

Given a continuing interaction between a changing organism and a changing physical and social environment, the question arises as to whether development should be seen as proceeding smoothly and gradually or as punctuated by periods of marked changes in organization. Over periods within the first few years of life, at least, individual differences in some aspects of behavior show significant consistency (e.g., Thomas, Chess, Birch, Hartzig, & Karn, 1963). And early experience can have long-term consequences—to cite but one example, studies of children reared in institutions with multiple caretakers revealed continuities between clinging and diffuse attachments in infancy, attention seeking and indiscriminate friendliness later, and impaired social relationships somewhat later still (Tizard, 1977; Tizard & Hodges, 1978). Nevertheless, longitudinal studies, although providing evidence for consistency over some age spans, indicate rather marked discontinuities at others. For instance, Kagan (1971) assessed a number of dependent variables at 4, 8, 13, and 27 months and found moderate stability between 8 and 13 months and between 13 and 27 months, but not from 4 to later months. McCall, Eichorn, & Hogarty in 1976 (cited in Kagan, 1978) analyzed data in which the Bayley scale was administered at frequent intervals over the first 5 years and found discontinuities in the principal components' scores at 3, 8, 13, and 20 months. Mainly on the basis of these studies, Kagan (1978) postulated major psychological changes around 8 months and again after the first birthday.

Such major discontinuities have also been identified in the more controlled conditions possible in the animal laboratory. For example, an impressive body of evidence indicates that rats progress from a stage at which learning, extinction, and other responses to change in reinforcement occur without cognitive intermediaries to a stage in which goal anticipation plays a crucial role (Amsel & Stanton, 1980). The transition occurs between 10 and 20 days of age. Before this period, the course of learning can be accounted for on the assumption that the incremental effects of reinforcement and the decremental effects of nonreinforcement are governed by the same mechanism, as in many classical accounts (e.g., Bush & Mosteller, 1955; Rescorla & Wagner, 1972). Later, certain paradoxical effects appear, for instance, intermittent reinforcement yields a lower density of rewards during acquisition than continuous reinforcement but there is greater resistance to extinction and large magnitudes of reward in acquisition lead to faster extinction than small magnitudes. Amsel and Stanton (1980) suggest that this ontogenetic change is comparable to the phylogenetic difference in capacity between the fish-reptile and bird-mammal phylogenetic levels, cognitive intermediaries becoming important in the learning process. A change in the nature of the learning processes in infant rats between 10 and 20 days is suggested also by an apparent change in the mechanisms responsible for maintaining mother-infant interaction. In the early period, suckling (even in the absence of milk reinforcement) and contact with the mother are very persistent. After about 14 days, the incentive properties of suckling become more deprivation related and learned persistence is determined by the magnitudes and schedule of the reinforcement received.

As another example, Barrett and Bateson (1978) found a marked developmental discontinuity in the development of play in cats between 7 and 8 weeks after birth. Not only were there major changes in the frequencies of some patterns but also individual differences were not predictable from 4 to 7 weeks to the 8 to 12 week period.

It can be assumed that extreme views over the issue of continuity versus discontinuity are likely to be wrong. On the one hand, as indicated above, development lacks total continuity. On the other hand, even apparent discontinuity may conceal threads of continuity. To take an animal example, the consequences of larval learning may persist even through the almost total reorganization involved in insect and amphibian metamorphosis. Thus, the ichneumonid wasp *Nemeritis canescens* normally lays its eggs on the larva of the moth *Ephestia kuhniella*. Thorpe and Jones (1937) showed that if *Nemeritis* are raised artificially on the larva of a strange species (*Meliphora grisella*), they become positively attracted to its odor in adulthood. Again, if larval newts *Triturus cristatus* are taught a simple discrimination task for food reward, the preference is retained by the adult newts after metamorphosis (Hershkowitz & Samuel, 1973). And in the human case, McCall, Hogarty, and Hurlbert (1972) have suggested on the basis of IQ data that early behavior in infancy might form the basis from which later childhood skills emerge, without itself directly predicting them.

There are, in any case, great practical and conceptual difficulties both in assessing the nature of apparent continuity and in locating discontinuity (Dunn, 1976, 1977, 1979). For example, Dunn (1977) found a significant correlation between babies' sucking rates during the first 10 days of life and measures of verbal demands at 14 months. But she points out the difficulties involved in interpreting this. Even the sucking measure, although carried out as early as day 8, may not be independent of the previous course of interaction between mother and baby. And the correlation over the 14-month period could be due to continuity in the mother's behavior, the baby's behavior, or the relationship between them. Ainsworth's (e.g., 1979) finding that so-called maternal behaviors show more stability over the first year than do infant behaviors would be in keeping with the first of these possibilities.

Several types of evidence can lead to the identification of discontinuities (Bateson, 1978a, 1978b). One is the occurrence of a marked alteration in the rate of development, such as the growth spurt before puberty. Another, and perhaps the most commonly used, depends on repeated measures of a given aspect of behavior in a group of subjects: if the individuals show a consistent rank ordering for a time, evidence for discontinuity would be provided by a sudden fall in correlations in the rank ordering of individuals between age periods. Some examples were cited above. Yet, another type of evidence, and one perhaps more reliably indicative of a change in behavioral organization, is a change in the pattern of correlations between behavioral measures. Such a change was found in the several measures of cat play in the study by Barrett and Bateson (1978). Another example, immediately concerned with discontinuity in a relationship rather than an individual, is shown in Figure 3. Here it can be seen that the pattern of correlations between various aspects of the mother-firstborn relationship changes dramatically with the arrival of a new sibling (Dunn & Kendrick, in press-a).

The types of discontinuity implied by these several sorts of evidence are themselves quite different, and discontinuity of one type does not necessarily imply discontinuity of another. Discontinuity is, thus, itself a heterogeneous category. And within any one type there is always the difficulty of knowing that a given item of behavior assessed at one age is "really" the same as an apparently similar item

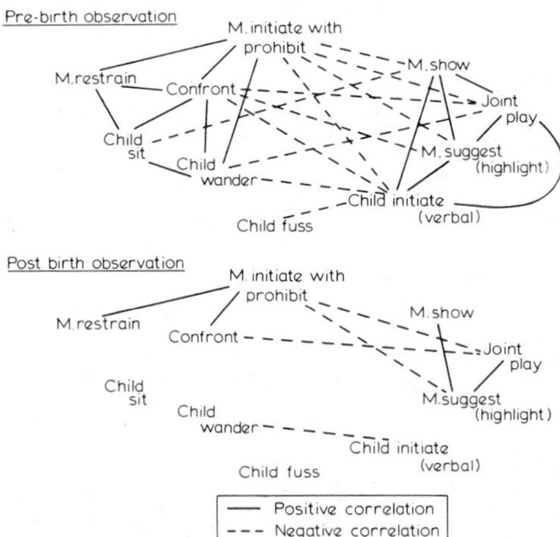

Figure 3. Correlations between measures of mother and child behavior before and after the birth of a sibling. The lines indicate significant correlations. (Dunn & Kendrick, 1980a.)

measured later. Furthermore, Bateson (1978a, 1978b) points out that apparent discontinuities may appear for quite trivial reasons, such as a reduction in variability (floor or ceiling effect), individual differences in rate of development that have only temporary effects, or temporary perturbations with subsequent recovery. To these may be added environmental changes, for example, the major psychological changes which Kagan (1978) postulated at 8 and at 12+ months could, for instance, be due to a change in mothering style or even to a lack of change because it has yet to be shown that mothers who promote optimum development at one age also do so at another. Distinguishing these diverse possibilities from intrinsic discontinuities, if such exist, is clearly no easy task.

Yet another issue arises from the finding that the consistency to be found in successive assessments of adult subjects varies with the data source. Observer ratings or evaluations and self-ratings indicate that personality characteristics show considerable consistency and continuity, whereas data derived from objective tests in laboratory situations do so much less often (Block, 1977). Many of the data for discontinuities in infancy and childhood are of the latter type. We shall see later, in considering the concept of attachment (see *Attachment*), that there may be continuities in organization of behavior even when there appear to be no continuities in individual measures.

Such considerations indicate a need for caution: evidence for discontinuity does not imply the occurrence of unanalyzable reorganization, it merely specifies the next problem to be tackled. Debate on the general issue of the relative importance of continuity versus discontinuity is likely to fade into insignificance as understanding of developmental processes increases. However, time may well prove that Kagan's (1978) attack on the Zeitgeist of continuity will increase that understanding. In fact he acknowledged both that continuity is evident where the environment promotes or maintains the infant's particular qualities and that there is a tendency to grow toward health. If his position is adequately summed up in the words, "there *need* not be *closely* dependent relations between *all* the structures of successive stages" (Kagan, 1978, p. 72; emphasis added), his position is in fact a moderate one.

Self-regulatory Mechanisms

A crucial question, from both a practical and a theoretical point of view, is whether everything that happens to a young organism necessarily matters in the long run. Do all environmental factors that produce marked changes (or differences) in behavior at one stage necessarily produce long-term effects? Over the last decade, studies of rhesus monkeys have provided considerable evidence that apparently gross abnormalities produced by temporary separation from the mother (Hinde & Spencer-Booth, 1971a) or by early social deprivation are susceptible to rehabilitation, at least in some degree (reviewed Suomi & Harlow, 1978a, 1978b; see *Studies of the Effects of Early Rearing Conditions . . .*). Bell (1974), Clarke and Clarke (1976), Dunn (1976), and Bateson (1976a) have emphasized that behavioral development often has a knack of returning toward its original track, even though it has suffered deviations along the way. Dunn (1976) cites a number of studies in which aspects of behavioral development, for instance, IQ, language, or social development, seemed to catch up after a period of retardation. Acknowledging the importance of recent work on the subtlety of early mother-infant interaction, she nevertheless warns, "Because psychologists demonstrate that something happens between a mother and baby it does not necessarily follow that it is important in the long run" (p. 486). In a similar vein, Clarke and Clarke (1976) have collected a body of data indicating that, as a consequence of either continued plasticity or regulation, the effects of early adversity are not necessarily irreversible (see also Bakeman & Brown, 1980; Tizard & Rees, 1975).

Recovery of the original developmental track after divergence through unfavorable circumstances is usually ascribed to self-correcting features or internal control of development, and the achievement of a particular end state by diverse routes is labeled equifinality (e.g., Bertalanffy, 1968). Although, for practical and conceptual reasons, equifinality is hard to prove, the occurrence of self-correcting tendencies cannot be doubted. But such labels, at least at first sight, have an almost mystical air, and the systems theory with which they are often linked, although sometimes fertile in suggesting avenues of research (e.g., Bateson, 1978a), can carry a veneer of sophistication hardly suited to the crude behavioral data as yet available to us.

In practice, some examples of regulation in development may depend on very simple mechanisms. Given that only some aspects of the environment matter to the developing organism (see *Sign Stimuli, Social Release . . .*), there may be mechanisms for keeping the environment more or less constant. If the mother leaves, a child may follow and thereby maintain proximity; if she disappears, attachment to another individual may be sought.

In any case, rather than setting interaction theorists and control theorists in opposition to each other, there is more heuristic value in integrating their views (Bateson, 1976a). One route to this end is to see regulation as a particular sort of interaction. Whereas progressive developmental change can depend on a response to environmental events producing change in the organism so that its responsiveness alters (see *Organism-Environment Interaction*), so also can maintenance of the developmental track. The simplest case is perhaps that of habituation: stimuli initially producing a response that potentially diverts development produce a change in the organism whereby these stimuli eventually cease to elicit a response.

In practice, virtually all development must involve changing responsiveness to environmental events, but the mechanisms may be quite simple. For example, the size of prey objects and the amount of food eaten changes as a fish increases in size. Whatever mechanisms regulate feeding behavior at one stage, they must be subject to readjustment as the fish develops. The mechanism could involve nothing more than growth-linked changes in the reward/cost ratios of seeking different-sized prey items (Hinde, 1959). A number of other cases are described by Bateson (1976a) as involving rules for changing rules. For example, aspects of the behavior of young chicks can be described as involving a rule to approach a wide range of conspicuous objects and a further rule for limiting the stimuli that elicit approach to those objects that are familiar. Bateson (1978a) has shown that in this case phrasing the phenomena in systems-theory terms can lead to computer modeling useful for elaborating hypotheses about development.

In child development, many self-correcting mechanisms may lie in the child's relationships with others rather than in the child himself. That dyadic relationships and families have powers for self-regulation has been emphasized for many years by clinicians (e.g., Jackson, 1959; Watzlawick, Beavin, & Jackson, 1967; Wertheim, 1975). Although stability within a defined range is ensured, limited change in particular directions may yet be possible. An example from rhesus monkeys is shown in Figure 4. After a short separation experience, rhesus monkey infants are often very demanding on their mothers and spend much less time off the mother than before the separation. In most cases, however, the relationship reverts to its original track. This occurs apparently because the mother at first accedes to the infant's demands. We can picture this as a deviance in one partner producing behavior in the other that removes the deviance in the former. However dyadic self-regulation does not always occur, as shown by one dyad in Figure 4—the regulatory mechanism is effective only within limits. The marked oscillations in measures of the relationship in the days and weeks after reunion resemble those of a poorly damped homeostat and reveal the processes involved in the gradual reestablishment of the relationship (see Hinde, 1974; Hinde & McGinnis, 1977).

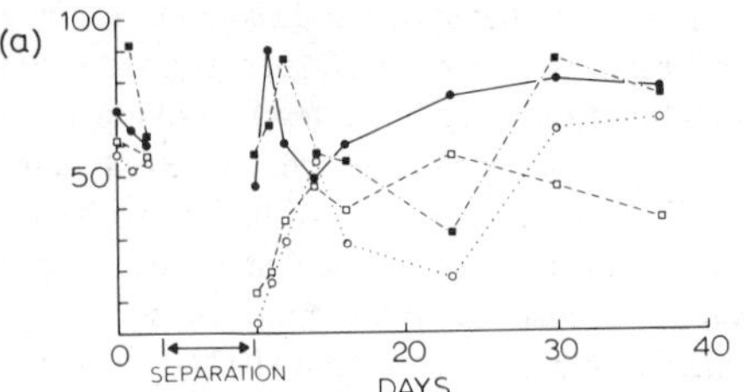

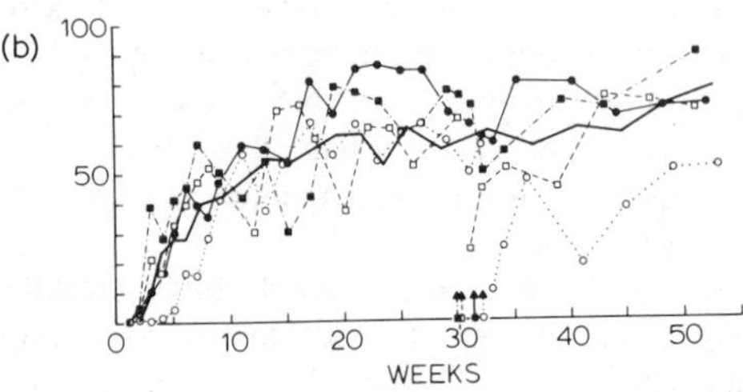

Figure 4. Effects of a 6-day removal of the mother from the social group on the time that infants later spent off the mother: (a) Short-term effects for four mother-infant dyads; each line refers to a different dyad. (b) Longer term effects. Data for the same four infants over the first year of life. Dates of separation experience indicated on the ordinate. The thick line shows the median for nonseparated infants. (Spencer-Booth & Hinde, 1967.)

Many cases of apparent self-regulation in the behavioral development of children will probably turn out in fact to involve dyadic regulation. Indeed, the special importance for development of relationships with particular others, as opposed to an anonymous social environment, may lie in the potential for regulation that a relationship with a known other provides.

These examples indicate that regulation in behavioral development can involve quite simple mechanisms either within the individual or, perhaps more usually, within the dyad. Even the latter do not involve any new issues of principle. The characteristics of both mother and child (say) are such that each responds to certain changes in the other with behavior likely to restore the status quo (Hinde, 1974).

However, any regulatory system is effective only

within limits. After a temporary separation, the rhesus monkey mother-infant relationship returns to its original course only under certain conditions (Hinde, 1974; Hinde & McGinnis, 1977). In the human species, Sameroff (Sameroff, 1975; Sameroff & Chandler, 1975) has reviewed data showing that perinatal trauma produces significant long-term effects only in socially disadvantaged families, and Quinton & Rutter (1976) showed the same to be true of early separation experiences (see *Attachment*). Sameroff and Chandler proposed a continuum of caretaking effectiveness. At one end, supportive, compensatory, and normalizing environments appear to be able virtually to eliminate the effects of early problems, whereas at the other end, caretaking by deprived stressed, or poorly educated parents tends to exacerbate early difficulties. An unusual developmental course is, thus, likely to be a consequence either of an earlier above-threshold deviation or of a continuing malfunction in the mechanisms of homeostasis. The latter could be due to the former or to continuing environmental pressures.

Relationships and Personality

It is implicit in what has been said that a child's relationships with others form the most important aspects of her environment. If development is to be understood, therefore, the properties and dynamics of relationships must also be understood. Just as an interaction between two individuals can have properties that are simply not relevant to the behavior of individuals in isolation (e.g., synchrony, behavioral meshing, competitiveness), so can relationships have properties that are emergent from the relative frequency and patterning of interactions over time. For instance, a mother-infant relationship is described as rejecting, controlling, or permissive not on the basis of one interaction or even one type of interaction, but on the frequencies and relative frequencies of several types of interaction over a period of time (Hinde & Simpson, 1975). Thus, a first requirement is a means for describing the properties of relationships.

Beyond that, if we are to understand the development of personality, we must understand both the ways in which the dynamics of relationships depend on the personalities of the participants and how relationships affect the participants. Although the influence of individual nature on relationships is clear throughout life, the influence of relationships on personality is perhaps more important in the early years. Thus, developmental psychologists must come to terms with a continuing dialectic between relationships and personality. We shall see later how this problem is critical, for instance, in understanding the categorization resulting from the Ainsworth strange-situation technique (see *Attachment*).

The dynamics of relationships are influenced not only by the personalities of the participants but also by the social situations in which they are embedded. A relationship is influenced by the other relationships of the participants and by the social norms that regulate their behavior. Conventions about how mothers should behave differ dramatically between cultures. But the social situation is composed of, and, thus, affected by, its constituent dyadic (and higher order) relationships, and social norms are transmitted and transmuted through relationships. There is, therefore, a need also to come to terms with a dialectic between relationships and society. It seems clear not only that a study of social relationships could facilitate integration between diverse branches of psychology (including the study of personality and social psychology) and sociology but also that developmental psychology must play a crucial role (Hinde, 1979).

Sign Stimuli, Social Releasers, Fixed Action Patterns, and the Development of Communication

Three concepts basic in the development of ethology have contributed to analyses of the early development of social behavior. The first is that of the sign stimulus.

At any moment, we respond to some of the physical changes that impinge on our sense organs and disregard others. Perception is, thus, always selective—a fact exploited by the caricaturist, who exaggerates those features on which recognition usually depends. When a particular set of stimuli elicits a specific response, group of responses, or propensity to respond, those stimuli are referred to as sign stimuli. For example, many species of small birds show a mobbing response to owls. Elicitation of this response depends on a number of features of owls, the eyes (cf. Coss, 1979) and the general color or patterning being of major importance (see Fig. 5).

Owls behave as if they disliked being mobbed and often fly off, so it is unlikely that the characteristics of their eyes and plumage were evolved to increase their effectiveness in eliciting mobbing. In some cases of selective responsiveness, however, there is strong evidence that the stimulus characters in question evolved in relation to their effectiveness in eliciting a particular response. For example, Tinbergen (e.g., 1948) showed that quite crude models

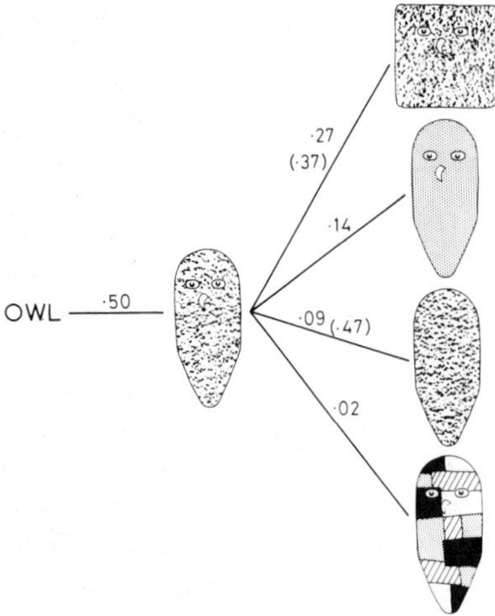

Figure 5. Stimulus characteristics of owls effective in eliciting the mobbing call from chaffinches. Each pair of models was tested in eight counterbalanced presentations with at least four wild-caught chaffinches. The numbers represent the median ratio between the number of calls elicited by the second model and the number elicited by the first. Numbers in parentheses are for tests with four or more hand-reared chaffinches who had never seen owls. (Hinde, 1982a, p. 36.)

of a three-spined stickleback were effective in eliciting agonistic behavior from a territory-owning male stickleback, provided that they had a red belly. Models lacking that character, although otherwise closely resembling sticklebacks, were relatively ineffective (see Fig. 6). The red belly is, in fact, displayed in a threat posture made to rival males. This and other comparative evidence strongly suggest that the red belly was evolved in relation to its signal function. Such sign stimuli are known as social releasers. The concept of sign stimulus implies selective responsiveness by the respondent, and, as used by ethologists, it has usually implied selectivity common to all individuals of the species. Social releaser implies the evolution not only of selective responsiveness in the respondent but also of especially effective stimulus features, often enhanced by accompanying movements, in the signaler. The evolution of social releasers is referred to as ritualization: often elaboration of structural characters and accompanying movements have proceeded simultaneously (Blest, 1961; Tinbergen, 1948, 1959).

Sign stimuli are often displayed in the course of, or elicit, relatively stereotyped movements which are also characteristic of the species. These are usually referred to as fixed action patterns (e.g., Lorenz & Tinbergen, 1939; Tinbergen, 1942) or modal action patterns (Barlow, 1968). Fixed action pattern is a useful general concept even though authors disagree as to how it should be defined (Dewsbury, 1978), and the extent to which the movement is fixed or stereotyped is a matter of degree (Barlow, 1968). Lorenz and Tinbergen (1939) distinguished between the invariant *Erbkoordination* and the orientation component whereby it is directed with respect to the environment, because orientation may be determined by aspects of the stimulus situation different from those that elicit the *Erbkoordination*. Thus, a goose will retrieve an egg that has rolled out of its nest by putting the beak beyond it and then moving its beak toward its breast. The wobbling movements of the egg are compensated by side to side movements of the bill. The *Erbkoordination* is elicited by visual and tactile stimuli from the egg and, once elicited, continues to completion. The side-to-side orientation movements depend on stimuli on the side of the beak and disappear as soon as the egg is removed. However, two components are not always separable in this way.

The terms sign stimulus, social releaser, and fixed action pattern have been applied by ethologists primarily to environmentally stable, species-characteristic features. However, the principle of selectivity in responsiveness and the use of stereotyped signal movements do not imply that experience played no role in shaping the characteristics in question. In the cases of the caricatur and of many idiosyncratic signals, experience is primary. In practice, because of the existence of species-characteristic constraints on learning in some directions and predispositions to learn in others, the distinction is not always so important as it once seemed (see *Dichotomies in Development*).

Species-characteristic responsiveness does in fact play an important role in early infant-mother attachment. For example, the rooting response of the newborn is part of a sequence of responses which facilitates attachment to the nipple. While moving its head from side to side, the neonate is selectively responsive to tactile stimulation in a certain area of the lips and cheek: If stimulated appropriately, the head is turned so that the mouth moves toward the point stimulated. Mouth opening occurs simultaneously; grasping of the nipple and sucking are elicited by subsequent links in a chain of stimuli to which the infant is selectively responsive (Gunther, 1955; Prechtl, 1958). An understanding of this sequence enabled Gunther to assist mothers with early nursing difficulties.

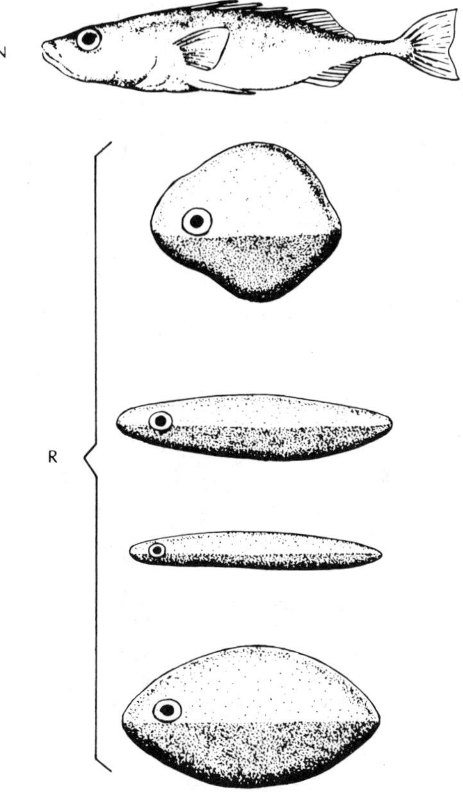

Figure 6. Models used for eliciting aggressive behavior from territory-owning three-spined sticklebacks. N = Normal off-season coloration; R = with red belly. (Hinde, 1974, after Tinbergen, 1951.)

Nor is the operation of sign stimuli limited to the baby's side of the interaction. Lorenz's (1950) suggestion that mothers respond selectively to certain features characteristic of babies, such as their bulging foreheads and uncoordinated gait—features that have been exploited by cartoonists—has received some experimental support (Gardner & Wallach, 1965; Sternglanz, Gray, & Murakami, 1977; see also Hess, 1970). There is also evidence that responsiveness to these stimulus features increases in girls around the age of puberty and in boys a year or two later (Fullard & Reiling, 1976). As Fullard and Reiling point out, such evidence does not indicate the relative importance of social versus biological factors in the development of responsiveness. But there seems little doubt that the baby's smile and cry qualify as social releasers—their special effectiveness must surely be the consequence of selection for signaling effectiveness by elaboration of the movement pattern (e.g., Freedman, 1964).

In the case of the smile, some interesting suggestions concerning its probable phyletic origin have been made. Studies of animal signals have shown that some, such as the display postures used in threat and courtship, depend on two incompatible behavioral tendencies. For instance, many threat postures depend on simultaneous tendencies to attack or approach and to flee or withdraw from the rival (e.g., Baerends, 1975). Changes in the absolute or relative levels of these tendencies may be associated with changes in the nature of the display posture. On the basis of evidence drawn from a wide variety of sources, van Hooff (1972) has suggested that smiling and laughter similarly vary along at least two dimensions, in this case those of friendliness and playfulness. A full smile denotes the former, a full

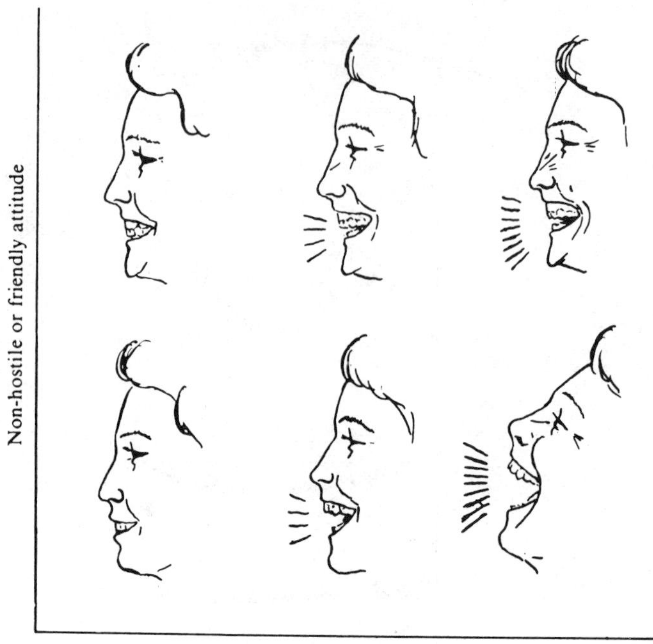

Figure 7. Two dimensions of variation of the smile-laugh continuum. With increased friendliness, there is increased baring of the teeth. Increasing playfulness is accompanied by mouth opening and vocalization. (After van Hooff, 1972.)

laugh the latter (Fig. 7). He suggests that this continuum may be derived from two distinct facial expressions in nonhuman primates. First, many species have a play face, often accompanied by vocalizations, that seems to signify "What I do is only in play, and not serious." Second, many species have a fear grin, or silent, bared-teeth display, sometimes accompanied by vocalizations, which is usually given by a frightened animal to a superior and seems to signify "I am harmless, and you need not attack me." But in some cases, this display is also used by superiors to inferiors, when it seems to mean "Don't be afraid, I will not attack you." In the chimpanzee, the latter display exists in three fairly distinct types, one being primarily friendly, one submissive, and one soothing in function. A possible course of evolution, illustrated by modern forms, is shown in Figure 8. In man, the grin of terror remains as a rather separate entity. Van Hooff's suggestion has come in for some criticism, chiefly on the grounds that it does not account for all instances of smiling, especially not for nonsocial smiles (e.g., Vine, 1973). However, van Hooff specifically stated that the dimensions in Figure 7 were unlikely to be the only ones involved. Furthermore, a hypothesis about the evolution of the movement patterns of smiling and laughter would not be expected to produce explanations for all the contexts in which they appear in humans. Van Hooff's hypothesis is compatible with the complexities in development and in contextual factors reviewed by later writers (e.g., Sroufe & Waters, 1976), and it does introduce a note of caution concerning unitary explanations, such as that in terms of tension release postulated by Sroufe & Waters.

Detailed comparisons of other aspects of nonverbal communication between nonhuman primates and humans seem so far to be lacking. The obvious resemblances between, for instance, infant tantrums and those shown by young monkeys (Chance & Jones, 1974; Hinde, Rowell, & Spencer-Booth, 1964; Jay, 1962) or between adult threat behavior and that of chimpanzees (van Lawick-Goodall, 1968) suggest that a rich field awaits the investigator (e.g., see Redican, 1975).

We have seen that the essential issue in the sign stimulus and social-releaser concepts is that of selective responsiveness. Some aspects of the total situation are much more important than others in eliciting the response in question. This applies no matter how

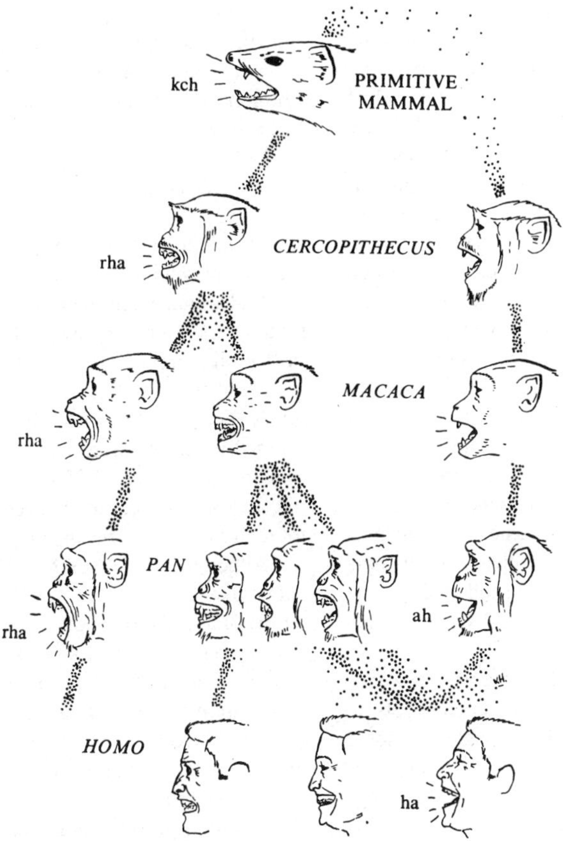

Figure 8. The phylogenetic development of laughter and smiling as suggested by homologues in existing members of the phyletic lines leading to *Homo*. On the left is the silent, bared-teeth display and the bared-teeth scream. The former, initially submissive, later becomes also a friendly response and converges with the relaxed open-mouth or play face (on the right). (After van Hooff, 1972.)

extensively experience is involved in shaping either the signal or the response to it. However, in the past, an overemphasis on the role of experience led to a rather sharp division of opinion between ethological studies of nonverbal communication and those (e.g., Birdwhistell, 1963, 1967; La Barre, 1947) studying human facial expression and gesture within other traditions. For instance, Eibl Eibesfeldt (1972), a pupil of Lorenz, studied cross-culturally movement patterns, such as smiling and crying, as well as more complex entities, such as the patterns used in greeting and flirting. Impressed by the similarities, he argued that most human expressive gestures were characteristic of the species and developed with minimal cultural influence, although he conceded that many had acquired different meanings, were accentuated to different extents, or were used in different ways in different cultures. On the other hand, some social psychologists and anthropologists, impressed by the complexity of human nonverbal communication and by its cultural diversity, held that concepts derived from the study of animal behavior could contribute nothing to the understanding of human communication (e.g., Birdwhistell, 1963; La Barre, 1947; Leach, 1972).

Fortunately, a more balanced view now prevails. On the one hand, certain movement patterns (e.g., smiling and crying) and syndromes of behavior (e.g., anger, flirting) are similar among cultures. In most cases, not only the motor patterns themselves but also the motivational bases of the movements and their interpretations by the reactor are pancultural. However, motivational bases and the interpretations are more labile than the movement patterns. Similarities among cultures occur especially with signals that concern personal or emotional characteristics. At the other extreme, some nonverbal signals, especially those closely dependent on verbal language, are specific to particular cultures. Much of the progress in this previously confused field is due to the conceptually sophisticated cross-cultural studies of Ekman & Friesen (1969), who carefully classified the various types of nonverbal signals, describing the extent to which each is pancultural and the nature of such cultural differences as occur. Those that have a pancultural basis are mostly affect displays. These involve the primary affects (happiness, surprise, fear, sadness, anger, disgust, and interest) and combinations between them. Although the movement patterns show considerable constancy across cultures, their motivational and situational antecedents, the extent to which they are amplified or suppressed, and their consequences on others show cultural variability. Other categories of signal movement, such as the emblems that can substitute for words and signals that illustrate and regulate verbal interchanges, are usually culturally specific and individually learned.

There are some ways in which the very power of the sign-stimulus and social-releaser concepts in lower vertebrates has resulted in a neglect of some aspects of the communicatory process among ethologists. For instance, studies of the dramatic signals used in threat and courtship displays led to neglect of the trivial and often idiosyncratic movements which are often also important in communication. Slight nuances of posture and seemingly trivial movements of hands or eyes may yet be powerful regulators of social intercourse (e.g., Simpson, 1973). Whereas infant research first focused on the smile and cry, many other aspects of infant behavior affect the mother (e.g., Stern, 1977).

Again, social releasers were often identified or assessed by the immediate response, often a fixed action pattern, of the reacting individual. This tended to obscure the fact that the effects of some social releasers are cumulative: for instance, a male bird's courtship may produce a gradual change in the endocrine state of the female.

The social-releaser approach also led to an underestimation of the communicatory significance of contextual factors. In their earlier writings, Lorenz and Tinbergen spoke of social releasers as more or less automatically eliciting particular responses, as a key opens a lock. But more recently, W. J. Smith (e.g., 1965; 1977) has pointed out that the effect of a particular signal varies with the context. He refers to the common factor in all the states of the communicator in the situations in which the signal is given together with any identificatory information it may carry as the message. Its meaning depends also on the context and can be deduced from the response of the recipient, thus:

$$\text{Message plus Context} \rightarrow \text{Meaning}$$

For example, a bird may give the same call in a variety of situations in which it hesitates to take flight. Coming from an intruder, the call would elicit attack from a territory owner, but the same call from a fledgling would evoke feeding from a parent. A similar distinction had in fact been made by the linguist Bloomfield in the 1930s, but had been quite missed by ethologists. The importance of this distinction in studies of, for instance, the ability of mothers to differentiate between the different cries of their babies will be apparent.

Although W. J. Smith (1965) emphasized the situational context, Beer (1976) has argued that the effect of a signal on another individual may depend on the context of other signals accompanying it. In this view, the full understanding of nonverbal communication may require a grammar.

A final issue to be mentioned in connection with the social-releaser approach concerns the extent to which signals actually convey information about the state of the signaler. Somewhat simplifying the situation, behavioral evidence shows that many signal movements are associated with conflicting tendencies, for instance, to attack or flee from the rival, to approach, or to stay put (Baerends, 1975). Part of this evidence comes from studies of the behavior that follows a display movement. For instance, a given threat display may be followed sometimes by an attack on the rival, sometimes by a flight away, and sometimes by neither. In species with several distinct threat postures, it has been shown that each posture is associated with different relative probabilities of attacking, fleeing, and staying put (e.g., Moynihan, 1955; Stokes, 1962). Furthermore, comparative evidence shows how the evolutionary processes of ritualization have enhanced the effectiveness of signal movements. But this does not mean that such display movements indicate exactly what the displaying individual will do next. In some circumstances, it would clearly be against his interests to convey such information: in a competitive situation, for instance, an individual that was certainly going to attack or to flee would do best to do so immediately, without signaling his intention beforehand. It seems, in fact, that some signals are given in situations of uncertainty, perhaps when what the signaler will do next depends on the response of the other individual (Hinde, 1974), and the signal conveys only a range of possible subsequent actions. Indeed, some current evolutionary theorists emphasize that natural selection favors individuals who successfully manipulate the behavior of others, whether or not this is to the advantage of the latter (Dawkins & Krebs, 1978). Although this argument has most force in the analysis of threat behavior, it is relevant to work in child development. Thus, we should see natural selection as producing not babies who tell their mothers how hungry they are, but babies who spend energy in crying when the urgency of their needs and the probability of those needs being met make it worth their doing so.

Recent work on nonverbal communication in children is reviewed in more detail by Paul Harris (*vol. II, chap. 9*). From an ethological viewpoint, the studies fall into several more or less distinct categories. Description and classification is an essential first step—although a great deal has been achieved with both infants (Oster, 1978; Oster & Ekman, 1978; Young & Décarie, 1977) and older individuals (e.g., Blurton Jones, 1972b; Brannigan & Humphries, 1972; Ekman & Friesen, 1975; Grant, 1969; McGrew, 1972; Smith, Chase, & Katz, 1974), much remains to be done, especially on a cross-cultural basis (e.g., Ekman, 1973).

Categorization of the movements as described must be made with respect to criteria relevant to the task in hand—ontogenetic, causal, functional, or evolutionary. Causal and functional categories often overlap, but there have been relatively few studies specifically investigating the effectiveness of particular signal movements. Among the recent exceptions are Camras's (1977) study of the use of an aggressive face in defence of an object and the study of Ginsburg, Pollman, and Wauson (1977) investigating the effect of a diminution in stature on the aggression of a rival.

As a solid descriptive base is laid, attention can be focused on age changes in the form or variety of signal movements and in the contexts in which they are used (e.g., Jancovic, Devoe, & Wiener, 1975), although much of the evidence on the role of experience in producing such age changes must come from experiments with animals (e.g., Kenny, Mason, & Hill, 1979). Special interest lies in studies of the increasing sophistication with which children use and interpret signal movements. For example, Cheyne (1976) has attempted to build on the earlier suggestion of Brannigan and Humphries (1972) that most smiles can be subsumed into three categories—a simple smile, appearing in solitary play; an upper smile, used in social situations and often combined with eye-to-eye contact; and a broad smile, often used in play, especially rough-and-tumble play. (It must be noted, however, that Brannigan & Humphries, 1972, did not show how far these differences were genuinely situational ones, and how much differences in intensity.) Cheyne (1976) showed that smiling at peers increases between the ages of 2 and 5 but that this is true only of the upper smile, which also comes to be used with increasing selectivity. Unfortunately, it is not clear whether the increase can be attributed to a general increase in social activity.

As another example, Zivin (1977) has described a facial expression used in encounters between children which strongly predicts that the child making the face will win. Her data indicate that its use becomes increasingly sophisticated so that top-ranking 7- to 10-year-olds do not use it much during obviously agonistic episodes but more in subtle challenges. Age changes occur also in the ability to interpret facial expressions (e.g., Abramovitch & Daly, 1978). The finding that preschool children could assess, from a videotape of their mother's head and torso, whether she was interacting with a stranger or familiar person, but that they were unsuccessful with similar videotapes of strange mothers, although the mothers were successful with the videotapes of strangers, suggests that children first learn to interpret the subtleties of expressive movements from those familiar to them and then generalize to a larger group (Abramovitch, 1977).

Special interest attaches to the study of nonverbal communication in infancy. Sophisticated recording techniques are now providing new insights into the nature of facial expression in early infancy (e.g., Oster, 1978). But beyond that, its importance both to research workers in interpreting the behavior of nonlinguistic infants and as a determinant of the behavior of the infants themselves is now being recognized. Dunn and Kendrick (1982) described social capacities in young infants which surpass what might be expected from current views of their cognitive development and emphasize their sophisticated use of nonverbal clues. Interaction of infants of less than 18 months with their older siblings is primarily nonverbal but shows surprising insights into the emotional state of the other child. From a functional point of view, it is hardly surprising that infants of this age should be equipped to interpret nonverbal cues. Campos and Sternberg (1981) have argued that the conventional learning paradigms are too narrow to be useful in understanding early emotional development, and they especially emphasize the importance of social referencing.

It is perhaps appropriate to end this discussion by referring to a dispute which has caused some difficulties in the past, that is, the meaning of the term communication. At one time, ethologists (including the present writer) tended to limit the term to species-characteristic signals for which there was reasonable evidence that ritualization had occurred. Those interested in communication systems, however, argued that the term was improperly applied unless there was evidence of intent to communicate (MacKay, 1972)—an issue very difficult to investigate with young children. But if the nature of social development is under study, it is surely necessary to include all means by which individuals affect each other, whether or not the signals are intended and whether they are characteristic of the species or are idiosyncratic (e.g., Lock, 1976).

Ethological Studies of the Early Parent-Offspring Relationship

Introduction

Inspired initially by Lorenz's (e.g., 1935) work on imprinting and Tinbergen's (e.g., 1948) work on sign stimuli, studies of the development of social behavior and of the parent-offspring relationship have provided a special focus of interest for ethologists. Some of the earlier work in this area was used by Bowlby (e.g., 1958, 1969) in his treatment of the mother-infant relationship. Attachment theory, as Bowlby's approach has come to be known, incorporated also elements from elsewhere,—especially Piagetian theory, information processing approaches to cognition, and systems theory. Here we are concerned primarily with animal data on the formation of early parent-offspring relationships and their application by attachment theorists and others to the human case. Some concepts used in the study of attachment and their ethological origins are considered in the discussion on *The Current Status of Attachment Concepts*.

Some Processes Involved in the Early Establishment of the Relationship

Consider first a very simple case. Moorhens reared by hand can learn to go to an infrared heater for warmth, to take food from forceps, and to follow practically any moving object with which they are presented repeatedly as they would have followed their parents. Thus, three responses that in nature would all have been directed toward aspects of the parent are under artificial conditions directed toward quite different objects. And the fact that the feeding response, for instance, can be elicited in naive chicks by stimuli as different as a pair of forceps and a parent's head indicates that these responses can initially be elicited by a wide range of stimuli. But once the responses have become directed to an artificial object, they cannot easily be elicited by a real moorhen nor vice versa. Thus, learning occurs that narrows the range of effective stimuli to those objects that have actually elicited the response.

In a similar way, the young monkey or human baby is equipped with a repertoire of responses. In monkeys, although to a lesser extent in humans, clinging can be induced by certain textural stimuli, and monkeys can be reared on inanimate mother surrogates (Harlow & Zimmermann, 1959). In both monkey and humans, suckling is the culmination of a sequence of responses appearing when the baby is hungry, most of the responses being elicited by particular stimuli from the breast or nipple. It can be elicited also by artificial stimuli, such as those provided by a bottle, but once a baby has been fed from a bottle for a while, it is far from easy to get it to feed from the breast. Similarly, at 1 to 2 months, smiling can be elicited by a wide range of stimuli, but a few weeks later smiling comes to be elicited preferentially (at least for a while) by stimuli from the mother's face.

The learning processes associated with sucking, smiling, and so on, have been studied in considerable detail (the complexities revealed are discussed in *vol. II, chap. 8*). Here the emphasis is on how that learning contributes to the formation of the relationship between infant and mother. In this context, work on the manner in which young nidifugous birds (e.g., chicks and ducks) come to direct their following behavior preferentially to one particular model is of some relevance.

The following response can be studied by using a moving model which, suspended from a rotating arm, is carried round a runway. Chicks follow such a moving object fairly readily, especially if it also emits intermittent sounds. However, very young chicks cannot follow, and the tendency for newly hatched naive chicks to follow at first increases, then decreases again—in other words, there is a sensitive period (see *Sensitive Periods*; review Bateson, 1979).

The beginning of the sensitive period is apparently set in part by maturation of the neuromuscular apparatus. Gottlieb (1961) and Landsburg (1976) have shown that it is affected both by the developmental age of the chick (i.e., the time since incubation started) and by the age since hatching. However, an increase in the functional effectiveness of the visual system probably also plays a role (Paulson, 1965).

The end of the sensitive period coincides with the appearance of persistent fleeing responses from strange objects. If a chick is first exposed to the model soon after hatching, it will gradually start to follow. A chick first shown a model a day or so later initially avoids it, but may change over to following if the test is prolonged. If the first test occurs later still, fleeing is sustained. But if a chick is shown a model on successive occasions starting reasonably early in this period, persistent following comes to predominate (see Fig. 9). Apparently following depends on the object acquiring a degree of familiarity, a view substantiated by the finding that previous experience of some aspects of the model facilitates following (Bateson, 1964b; Hoffman & Ratner, 1973; Hoffman, Ratner, & Eiserer, 1972). The sensitive period is, thus, a time during which the chick learns the characteristics of the familiar environment, although, of course, further learning may continue after it is over. Once the chick has acquired a background of the familiar, stimulus situations that are strange elicit avoidance. But there can be no response to what is strange until the organism has acquired a background of the familiar.

At any point in this period, some objects are more effective in eliciting following than others. In many species, objects emitting a noise resembling the mother's call are especially effective. If effective objects are not present, the sensitive period may be extended. For example, chicks reared in isolation can be imprinted on an experimental object at an older age than can chicks reared in a group (Guiton, 1959; Smith & Nott, 1970).

In the early days of studying the attachment of the following response to the mother, it was supposed that the learning involved was special, and it was called imprinting. It was thought to have characteristics that differed from learning as studied in laboratory situations (Lorenz, 1935). This view has turned out to be incorrect. Of the laboratory paradigms most used in studies of learning, all three can, in fact, be applied to the imprinting situation:

1. Exposure learning. Chicks reared in pens painted with horizontal or vertical stripes subse-

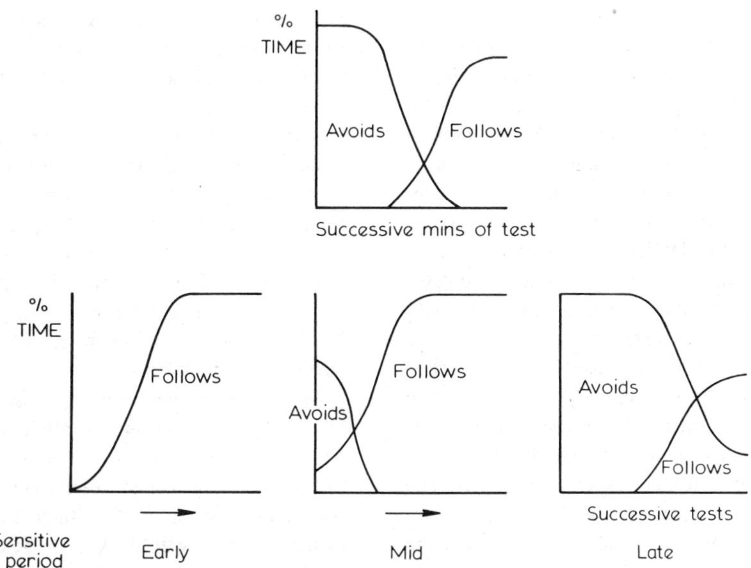

Figure 9. Idealized data showing the acquisition of the following response by chicks. The top diagram shows the changing incidence of avoiding and following over one test in a chick first tested in the middle of the sensitive period. The bottom diagrams show the incidence in successive tests for chicks tested in the early, in the middle, and in the late phase of the sensitive period.

quently follow models painted similarly to their rearing pen more readily than models painted differently (Bateson, 1964b). They will also learn a discrimination that involves such patterns more readily than one that involves unfamiliar patterns (Bateson, 1964a). This study is comparable to one of the classic studies of exposure learning (Gibson, Walk, Pick, & Tighe, 1958). Thus, the same early training that facilitated learning in an imprinting situation also facilitated exposure in discrimination learning (see also Salzen, 1967).

2. Classical conditioning. Once a chick has been imprinted to a stimulus, emission of distress calls is suppressed by its presence. A second initially ineffective stimulus can acquire the capacity to suppress distress calls if it is appropriately (i.e., according to the classical conditioning paradigm) paired with an imprinted stimulus. By this means, the behavioral control that characterizes an imprinted stimulus can be extended to other features of the imprinted object or of the environment (Hoffman & De Paulo, 1977; Hoffman & Ratner, 1973).

3. Operant conditioning. A flashing light, just like a moving box, elicits approach from a chick. If chicks are given the opportunity to perform a response (e.g., stepping on a pedal) that switches on a flashing light, they will show that response with increasing frequency (Bateson & Reese, 1969).

Thus, the learning which occurs in the imprinting situation is by no means simple. The chick learns about its mother by exposure learning and at the same time learns responses that bring it into her presence through operant conditioning. Additional properties of the mother or the situation may become associated with stimuli that initially elicited the approach response by classical conditioning.

Although studies of the processes involved in the establishment of parent-young attachment in chicks have been concerned with the following response, it is highly likely that other responses become attached to the mother in the same way. Because the mother elicits a number of different responses, characteristics of the mother may come by conditioning to be relevant to more than one response (Fig. 10). The chick learns about the mother and to direct his responses to the mother at the same time. And as the mother becomes familiar, strange objects come to elicit avoidance so that responsiveness becomes limited to her.

Two other issues which augment the chicks' attachment to its mother must be mentioned. First, although marked novelty evokes fear responses, chicks are attracted toward objects that look slightly

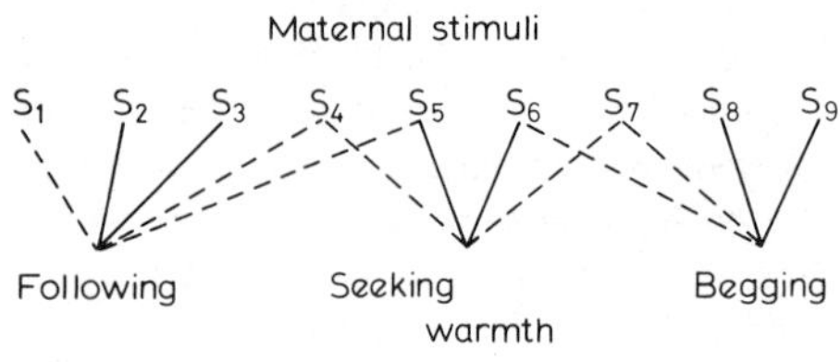

Figure 10. Proposed process contributing to the transformation of the parent as a collection of eliciting stimuli to the parent as an individual. Continuous lines indicate initially effective stimuli, discontinuous lines those that become so by conditioning.

different from how they usually look (Bateson & Jaeckel, 1976). The same is true for human infants (Hopkins, Zelazo, Jacobson, & Kagan, 1976). In the chick, at least, the degree of discrepancy from the familiar standard that is preferred decreases as a result of experience with the standard. It will be apparent that increased attentiveness to the mother when seen in a novel posture, in a novel light, and from a novel angle would be likely to augment learning of her characteristics by an organism as yet lacking adult powers of object constancy and could, indeed, facilitate the acquisition of object constancy (Bateson, 1976a; Hinde, 1961).

Another issue is that chicks (and also monkeys) exposed to two stimuli a few seconds apart find a discrimination involving those two stimuli more difficult than do animals exposed to novel stimuli. This is not so with stimuli to which the chick has been exposed at different times. Apparently, seeing two stimulus objects in rapid succession leads to the chick classifying them together. Such a process might be important in building up a concept of the mother. When the chick attends to a slightly unfamiliar view of the mother and then has a familiar view, the unfamiliar pattern would be classified with the familiar one (Bateson & Chantrey, 1972; Chantrey, 1972, 1976).

We have seen that as some objects become familiar, strange objects come to elicit fear responses. Whether this is the whole story is not quite clear because infants are capable of discriminating strange from familiar stimuli before they show fear to the former (see Kenny et al., 1979). Be that as it may, another matter over which there is something in common between chick, monkey, and humans, at least at a descriptive level, concerns the mother's role as a secure base. As the young individual becomes able to locomote, to explore his environment, even perhaps to feed, he starts to leave his mother for brief trips into the wider world and then to return to her. He uses her as a secure base. If danger threatens, he returns to her and his fears are allayed. If suddenly placed in a strange situation, a young monkey may be terrified and quite unable to cope. But if his mother is present, he is able by degrees to leave her and explore.

At this point it may be helpful to list the processes that have been identified in young-parent attachment in at least some nonhuman vertebrates:

1. The young organism's responses are each elicited by a stimulus situation which is rather ill defined so that each response can, under artificial conditions, be elicited by stimuli other than those provided naturally by the mother.
2. The range of stimuli effective for each response becomes narrowed from those initially effective to those that have actually elicited it.
3. Characteristics of the mother may be learned through simple exposure learning.
4. Conditioning of each response to features of the mother not initially relevant to the response can lead to an overlap between the stimuli effective for each response.
5. Responses that produce stimulus situations that are attractive become strengthened by operant conditioning.
6. Slight discrepancy produces a positive response.
7. Stimuli seen in rapid succession tend to be classified together.
8. Unfamiliar stimuli elicit fear responses.
9. The attachment object acquires anxiety-allaying properties.

Here it is appropriate to underline the eclecticism of the ethological approach. Most other workers (although see, e.g., Chalmers, 1978; Hoffman, 1978) have attempted to explain the phenomena of attachment in terms of one or at most two laboratory paradigms: operant conditioning (Gewirtz, 1961, 1976); classical conditioning (Hoffman & De Paulo, 1977; Hoffman & Ratner, 1973); contiguity conditioning (Cairns, 1966, 1979); or opponent processes (Hoffman & Solomon, 1974). Ethologists by contrast have long stressed the need to interpret learning as it occurs under natural circumstances in terms of interdigitated learning paradigms (Thorpe, 1963); in studying attachment, they seek to integrate this with the concept of behavioral systems (see *Attachment Behavioral System*). Their approach is not in opposition to learning theories in general, as some writers (e.g., Rajecki, Lamb, & Obmascher, 1978) would have it, but only to attempts to interpret the phenomena of attachment in terms of only one paradigm.

It seems not unreasonable to suppose that processes comparable to those listed above may be important also in the early attachment of human infants to mothers, although, of course, there is no implication that they are the only processes involved. There is no suggestion here that the early development of the infant-parent relationship in any particular species of bird or mammal is the same as in humans—ethologists are aware that bird and mammal have undergone separate evolutionary differentiation since Permian times. Nor is there any implication that similarity in behavioral processes necessarily implies similarity in mechanism, but only that, insofar as studies of nonhuman species are easier than that of man, they may give us indications of the sorts of processes that may contribute to attachment in humans.

The Range of Infant Responses and Maternal Sensitivity

In humans, the diversity of responses involved in mother-infant interaction is, of course, much greater than in other animals. Bowlby (e.g., 1958, 1969) and Ainsworth (1969, 1972) laid primary emphasis on responses whereby the infant gained or maintained proximity and contact, such as grasping and clinging, and on those whereby the infant caused adults to approach or remain nearby, such as crying and smiling. Just as with imprinting in birds, the range of stimuli effective for these fixed action patterns becomes narrowed to those that have actually elicited them. Fear responses, including both a wariness of the unfamiliar and, later, learned aversions (Bronson, 1978), play a role. Further patterns, such as crawling and walking, come to be elicited by these familiar stimuli.

In part as a reaction to emphases on feeding by psychoanalysts and on primary drive reduction by learning theorists, Bowlby (1969) played down the importance of nutritive responses in the attachment of infant to mother. However, as we shall see (*The Current Status of Attachment Concepts*), attachment refers to only certain aspects, albeit perhaps the most important aspects, of the infant-mother relationship, namely, those concerned with the acquisition by the infant of felt security from the mother's presence or proximity. Although there is abundant evidence that nursing is not essential for infant-mother attachment in animals or humans, it may well play a role in the infant-mother relationship as a whole. Not only feeding but also many other types of behavior, including games (e.g., Brazelton, Tronick, Adamson,

Als, & Weise, 1975; Fogel, 1977; Stern, 1977), may play a role in other aspects of the relationship. These types of behavior may also contribute to the mother's effectiveness as a security figure, especially in older children. Although maternal availability and sensitivity to distress signals may well be crucial early on, her behavior in a wide range of contexts may be important later (Ainsworth, Blehar, Waters, & Wall, 1978; also see Bretherton, in press).

So far, we have discussed the mother as a more or less passive provider, but there is considerable evidence that her responsiveness to the infant's signals are important. Infants signal their needs for care, food, stimulation, and rest, and the sensitive mother responds appropriately (Ainsworth et al., 1978; Brazelton et al., 1975; Stern, 1977). Observational data indicate that a complex of properties that may be described as maternal sensitivity is an important determinant of the nature of the infant-mother relationship in both humans (Ainsworth et al., 1978; Schaffer & Emerson, 1964) and monkeys (Hinde & Spencer-Booth, 1971a). Some experimental data are also compatible with this view. Although monkeys can become attached to inanimate mother surrogates, mobile objects are better (Anderson, Kenney, & Mason, 1977; Mason & Berkson, 1975; Wood, Mason, & Kenney, 1979) and dogs, who are presumably responsive to infants, are probably better still (Mason & Kenney, 1974).

Experimental data on human babies in harmony with the view that maternal responsiveness might be an important determinant of the nature of the mother-infant relationship have been provided by Watson (1972). Not only will the frequency of an infant's response increase if that response operates a mobile, but the baby will often smile and direct other social responses to a mobile whose movement is contingent upon her behavior. Of special interest in this context are the peekaboo and other games that mother and infant play, games that seem to be based on a reinforcing effect of making something happen, the learning process being perhaps comparable with that of the chick turning on a flashing light. Conceivably, the reinforcing effectiveness and pleasure-giving properties of a wide (although not unlimited) range of response-contingent events, such as the movement of a mobile, could be regarded as a by-product of a mechanism primarily functional in making mother come.

A somewhat sterile controversy is now developing (see Lamb, 1976a; Rajecki et al., 1978) over whether parental proximity or parental sensitive responsiveness is the more important in influencing the course of the relationship. It seems self-evident that a certain minimum (possibly quite a large minimum) of time together is essential, but given adequate time together, maternal sensitivity may be crucial.

But in studies of both animals and humans, the maternal side of the bond has been rather neglected. Bowlby postulated a maternal behavior system which complemented that of the infant, and we have already seen that special sign stimuli may be involved. But the mother's diffuse responsiveness to her baby's needs lends itself less readily to ethological analysis than the infant's more circumscribed behavior. Although ethologists did show that the first few minutes or hours after birth were crucial for some ungulate mothers to become attached to their infants (Blauvelt, 1956; Klopfer & Klopfer, 1968; this may also involve labeling her infant with her own odors, see Gubernick, Corbeau Jones, & Klopfer, 1979), the maternal side of the relationship was long neglected. It is now becoming possible that this early period may be important also in humans (e.g., Hales, Lozoff, Sosa, & Kennell, 1977; but see Svejda, Campos, & Emde, 1980); Kennell et al., 1975), although the reasons may be quite different. Of course, the finding that the early postnatal period may be of special importance for the mother's feelings about her baby must not blind us to the multiplicity of other factors—experiential and immediately environmental, physiological and psychological, familial and social—that are also important. It is clear that many important research problems await to be tackled in this area.

Temporal Variations in Proximity: The Set Goal

The amount of proximity to the caregiver demanded by the infant varies with time. To describe this, Bowlby used the concept of set goal (see Miller, Galanter, & Pribram, 1960). The degree of proximity required was seen as varying with factors internal (e.g., fatigue) and external (e.g., danger) to the infant.

This use of control-theory concepts was directed in the first instance to the behavior of young children and has aided attempts at formalization which may yet yield fruit (e.g., Bischof, 1975). Although Bowlby repeatedly emphasized the importance of affective/cognitive intermediaries in older children (Bowlby, 1969, 1973; see also Ainsworth, 1972), his use of mechanical-sounding control-theory concepts led to his being misunderstood by workers from other backgrounds. In fact, the implications of cognitive development are under active consideration by attachment theorists. Bischof (1975) and Sroufe and Waters (1977)—the latter concerned primarily with 12- to 18-month-old children—have argued for regarding the set goal in terms of felt security and for treating adaptive behavior as mediated by affect. Proximity seeking would, thus, depend on the infant's evaluation of internal and external state in terms of his subjective experience of security/insecurity. Such an emphasis clearly becomes more necessary the older the infant under consideration. That this affective-bond approach to attachment becomes more difficult to operationalize (Bernal, 1974; Cairns, 1972; Gewirtz, 1972; Weinraub, Brooks, & Lewis, 1977) is a matter that, in the opinion of Sroufe & Waters (1977), must be accepted.

In the same mode, Bretherton (in press) has argued that the meshing between the behavior of infant and mother which appears gradually toward the end of the first year must depend on expectancies that each has about the behavior of the other. Bretherton postulates that infants first construct nonsymbolic or sensorimotor models which cannot be used for long-term predictions or in the partners' absence but only during actual interactions with the caregiver. (This concept, Bretherton suggests, is comparable to, but more complex than, the Piagetian schema.) These non-symbolic models give way to symbolic representation as the infant grows up.

The Current Status of Attachment Concepts

In elaborating his theory of how the child becomes attached to her mother, Bowlby (1969) labeled the several responses whereby contact and proximity between mother and infant are maintained "attachment behavior." He spoke of them as constituting the "attachment behaviour system," and as leading to "attachment." He regarded attachment behavior as biologically functional in an "environment of evolutionary adaptedness." These concepts have been further discussed by Ainsworth et al. (1978) and Ainsworth (1979). We may consider them in turn.

Attachment Behavior

Attachment behavior is simply a category label for the various types of behavior whereby a child maintains or increases proximity to, or contact with a mother figure or causes the mother figure to come to it. As such, this label lies clearly within the data language (MacCorquodale & Meehl, 1954) of the system Bowlby and Ainsworth have built.

The Attachment Behavioral System

The Concept of Behavioral System. This requires a digression, because behavioral system has been used in a rather special sense by ethologists to refer to systems postulated as controlling a group of behavior patterns that together serve to achieve a given biological end. The concept of a behavioral system is, in fact, related to one meaning of the term instinct (McDougall, 1923) and has been used, for instance, in relation to the nest-provisioning behavior of the wasp *Ammophila campestris* (Baerends, 1941), the reproductive behavior of the three-spined stickleback (*Gasterosteus aculeatus*) (Tinbergen, 1942), and the reproductive behavior of both the great tit (*Parus major*) (Hinde, 1953) and the herring gull (*Larus argentatus*) (Baerends, 1976). In each case, observations of a number of related types of behavior led to the postulation of interacting systems which could explain the occurrence of the several types of behavior and the interrelations between them. These interrelations were of diverse types: some patterns might be appetitive to others and some might be alternatives to others; some might share positive causal factors and others might share negative (consummatory) factors; some might be mutually facilitatory and others might be mutually inhibitory. In some cases, the precise nature or relative frequency of the responses might change with time, that is, with ontogenetic or reproductive development. Although the behavioral systems were postulated to explain the observed behavior, there was no necessary implication of isomorphous mechanisms in the brain. The explanation is a software one, comparable to a computer program which performs a particular job irrespective of the details of the hardware of the computer into which it is fed (Baerends, 1976; Dawkins, 1976).

Each behavioral system is seen as interacting with other behavioral systems. The behavior shown at any one instant is, thus, a consequence of interactions between behavioral systems. Indeed, recent ethological theorizing has emphasized that the boundaries between behavioral systems are often hard to define—the systems overlap, influence each other, and so on. Furthermore, the extent to which a behavioral system depends on factors external to it or is self-activating and self-integrating varies with time and with its current state (Fentress, 1976).

Attachment behavioral system refers to the system controlling the several types of attachment behavior. Among those who apply the concept of an attachment behavioral system to human infant-mother interaction there are some differences in exactly what is implied. For instance, Bowlby (1969) took the view that the system was either switched on, with the resultant display of attachment behavior, or switched off when the set goal was achieved. Bretherton (in press), however, prefers to ascribe also a monitoring function to the system, a function that operates continuously even when the behavior is switched off. Be that as it may, the concept of attachment behavioral system is concerned with the control of and relations between the several types of attachment behavior. It thus lies in the theory language. As attachment behavior serves one or more particular interpersonal relationships, the attachment behavior system must incorporate sensitivity to, and expectations about, the other—what Bowlby (1969) called a working model of the other. The attachment behavior system, thus, becomes differentiated with each new relationship—a theory-language way of saying that new relationships are affected by the nature of earlier ones.

The Development of the Attachment Behavior System. In this case the concept's ethological origins have not stimulated an adequately analytical approach. Studies of the development of behavior in a wide variety of species show that animals may show movement patterns in near-perfect form before they have had opportunity to practice them, and that they may have predispositions to respond to some stimulus characters rather than others. These studies also show that initially independent movement patterns may become integrated into functional sequences in circumstances in which specific learning seems extremely improbable. For example, nest building in canaries involves picking up material, carrying it to a nest site, and performing there a number of different building movements. Individuals kept without material may show isolated and functionless fragments of this sequence but, when given material, functional nest-building behavior may occur within seconds (Hinde, 1958). That learning plays some role in the full development of nest-building behavior is not the issue here. Instead, the point is that the whole complex of responses becomes integrated without trial and error leading to the normal functional end point. Even though the data do not rule out a role of learning, the rapidity with which integration is achieved implies that individuals are predisposed to learn in a species-characteristic manner (see *Dichotomies in Development*).

Ethologists, thus, tend to assume that a young organism's behavior has a structure which is not solely a consequence of earlier environmental contingencies. Instead, a young organism's capacities, limitations, and predispositions as well as its experience are seen as contributing to the building up of a number of interacting behavioral systems, some of which concern relations with the mother. However, although the principle is clear enough, the detailed developmental processes in the ontogeny of a behavioral system have been tackled in very few cases (e.g., Kortlandt, 1955; Kruijt, 1964).

Here lies both a strength and a weakness in the ethologists' bias. On the one hand, in studying the integrated attachment behavior of a 14-month-old child, ethologists have not so far felt it necessary to account for every aspect of that integration in terms, for instance, of known learning paradigms—they can say, "This is the way our species develops." This facilitates a focus on the forest rather than the trees. And for many purposes the forest may be more important. But, in the longer term, it could lead to the assumption that aspects of development that progress normally under most circumstances will progress similarly under all.

To be more specific, we have described how in Bowlby's (1969) theorizing the early attachment behavior of the infant is seen as comprising a group of fixed action patterns (crying, smiling, etc.), each elicited under appropriate circumstances but with little inherent organization. At about the middle of the first year, he suggested, these patterns become organized and integrated in a manner which can best be described as involving a hierarchically organized goal-correcting system, which incorporates a working model of the parent. The processes involved in the development of this organization, however, have not so far been studied in any depth. Although ethologists can properly claim that it was necessary to see the forest first, it is now necessary to examine the trees. Detailed cognitive developmental analysis will clearly be necessary. Although much relevant research has been carried out (e.g., Schaffer, 1971), much of it has been concerned primarily with language or general intellectual development, not with the development of social attachments. Integration of work on cognitive development and work on attachment is only just beginning (e.g., Trevarthen, 1977, 1978).

A particular example may be mentioned. Young rhesus monkeys that have been reared by natural mothers or on cloth-covered surrogates are comforted by the presence of their attachment object in anxiety-provoking situations. Young monkeys fed from wire-mesh mother surrogates are not comforted in this way (Harlow & Zimmermann, 1959). It thus seems that a surrogate that merely reduces hunger does not allay anxiety in fear-provoking situations, whereas one that provides contact comfort does. If these data are correct, they clearly raise the important ontogenetic question: How does this situation come about? Why should clingability experienced at least mostly in nonanxiety-provoking situations reduce anxiety when suckability by itself does not? This is the sort of issue that ethologists and attachment theorists could merely accept as a given.

Ainsworth (Ainsworth, 1967; Ainsworth et al., 1978), however, has shown some concern with the development of the attachment behavior system. Although infants *can* gain or maintain proximity or contact with their attachment figures by a variety of behavior patterns, some of these patterns come to figure prominently in the relationship, whereas others become splintered off. This view was prompted by the observation that infants given free access to the breast were more disturbed by weaning than those given the breast only on maternal initiative. In the former case, Ainsworth suggests that sucking had become integrated into the system of behaviors mediating attachment, whereas in the latter case, by contrast, sucking did not contribute in an important way to attachment nor did weaning constitute rejection by the attachment figure.

Attachment

Ainsworth et al. (1978) refer to attachment as "the affectional bond or tie that an infant forms between himself and his mother figure" (p. 302), which is inferred "from a stable propensity over time to seek proximity and contact with a specific figure" (p. 303). Attachment is, thus, an aspect—and for most purposes the most important aspect—of a child's relationship with the parent figure. As we have seen (*Relationships and Personality*), relationships both include the properties of their constituent interactions and possess properties that are consequent upon the absolute and relative frequency and patterning of these interactions over time. Attachment refers to a subset of such properties. Although attachment, thus, lies primarily in the data language, it is sometimes used also in an explanatory sense. Thus, Ainsworth et al. (1978) refer to attachment as "an inner organization of behavioral systems" (p. 303). However, most ethologists, conscious of the spectre of the old instinct theories, will be cautious of such isomorphisms between behavior and postulated underlying mechanism. Indeed, the very existence of properties of attachment emergent from the patterning of interactions over time (Hinde, 1979) would make any equation between data and postulated mechanism suspect. Thus, it seems preferable to use the term attachment in a primarily descriptive sense. Where attachment enters into an explanatory scheme or where the nature of attachment is said to be prognostic of an aspect of future development, a correlation between an aspect of the attachment relationship and the measured characteristic is implied, but attachment does not of itself imply mechanism. Attachment (abstracted from data language) is to be explained by the state or activity of a behavioral system (theory language).

One aspect of attachment requires emphasis. Bowlby and Ainsworth regard it as exclusively directed toward one particular caregiver or, at most, to a very few caregivers. Bowlby (1969) proposed the term monotropy to refer to this. It is important to note that he was concerned primarily with the child's tendency to seek security from one particular figure and did not imply that relationships with other individuals might not be important in other ways. A child who is ill or under stress may single out its mother, yet prefer to play with its father when well (Lamb 1977). Nor does monotropy imply that, in the absence of the primary attachment figure, distress cannot be alleviated by the presence of a secondary figure, at least in some degree; the data show that it can (Robertson & Robertson, 1971).

Work on attachment has come in for criticism by those who have mistakenly regarded attachment as an intervening variable, with measures of attachment behavior as dependent variables. If attachment were to be useful in that way, such measures should show reasonable correlation with each other (Miller, 1959). In addition, attachment was seen as an enduring trait, with the implication that individual differences in the several indices of attachment should be stable over time. Evidence that correlations between measures were low and that the measures did not show temporal stability (Coates, Anderson, & Hartup, 1972; Maccoby & Feldman, 1972) was taken as evidence that attachment was not a useful concept (Cairns, 1972; Gewirtz, 1972; Masters & Wellman, 1974; Weintraub, Brooks, & Lewis, 1977). Such criticisms have come from inside as well as from outside ethology, although with inside criticism (Blurton Jones & Leach, 1972) there was some acknowledgment that attachment might be useful to refer to a complex causal system.

But the criticisms are irrelevant if attachment is seen not as an intervening variable or trait but as embracing aspects of behavior that may be alternative to each other and change with age. In this view, attachment cannot be assessed by counting the frequencies or durations of any one type of behavior. Indeed, it is unlikely that the outputs of any behavior system could be assessed along a simple dimension.

Sroufe and Waters (1977) (see also Ainsworth et

al., 1978) emphasize that attachment is best assessed by reference to the organization of attachment behavior with respect to the caregiver with due regard to context. Specific aspects of behavior are not useful in isolation because different types of behavior can serve the same function.

> Babies who vocalize and show a toy in one reunion episode may smile in another: both are positive greetings. Similarly, babies who seek proximity on reunion at one age may smile and vocalize when they are older: both are ways of reestablishing contact. (Sroufe & Waters, 1977, p. 1188)

See also Lamb (1976a, 1976b) and Rosenthal (1973).

In this view, the amount of contact behavior is not a measure of strength of attachment. A securely attached baby may need less contact with the caregiver than a less securely attached one. Instead, an attempt is made to evaluate attachment in terms of qualitative differences in the way the various types of attachment behavior are organized. This requires a brief description of the strange-situation, the technique which has been most used by attachment theorists for 1- to 2-year-old children (Ainsworth et al., 1978). The procedure involves eight episodes staged in a standard way in a laboratory playroom (see Table 1). Because parents are instructed to behave in a particular way, classification is based on the infants' behavior, with special reference to the two reunion episodes (Table 2). Infants classified as *secure* actively seek proximity and contact following

Table 1. **Summary of Strange-Situation Procedure**

Episode	Persons Present[a]	Time	Events and Procedures
1	M, B	Variable (approx. 1 min.)	M and B are introduced into S/S room by E. If necessary, M interests B in toys before being seated. M does not initiate interaction but is responsive to bids from B.
2	M, B	3 min.	M remains seated and is responsive to bids for interaction but does not initiate.
3	M, B, S	3 min.	S enters and is seated, sits silently for 1 min., talks to M for 1 min., engages B in interaction or toy play for 1 min.
4	B, S	3 min. (less if B extremely distressed)	M leaves room, S allows B to play alone but remains responsive to interactive bids. If B is crying, S offers contact and tries to comfort. If B refuses or resists, S does not persist. Terminate episode after 1 min. hard crying or on M's request.
5	M, B	3 min.	M calls B from outside door and steps inside, pausing at doorway to greet B and to reach and offer contact. If necessary, B is held and comforted and then reinterested in toys; otherwise, M is seated and remains responsive to bids from B but does not initiate.
6	B	3 min. (less if B extremely distressed)	M leaves room; B remains alone. Terminate episode if 1 min. hard crying ensues or on M's request.
7	B, S	3 min. (less if B extremely distressed)	S returns and is seated. If B is crying or begins to cry without pause, S offers contact and tries to comfort. If B cannot be comforted and crying continues (or on M's request), terminate episode.
8	M, B	3 min.	M calls B from outside door and steps inside, pausing at doorway to greet B and to reach and offer contact. If necessary, B is held and comforted and then reinterested in toys; otherwise, M is seated and remains responsive to bids from B but does not initiate if B is content in toy play.

[a]*Note:* M = mother; B = baby; S = stranger.
(After Waters, 1978)

separation and are readily comforted by this. Insecurely attached infants are not readily comforted and fall into two main groups. Upon a parent's return, an *avoidant* infant actively avoids and ignores the parent, showing no distress or anger. An *ambivalent* infant both seeks and resists proximity. The classification is normally done from videotape according to a system developed by Ainsworth and her colleagues (Ainsworth et al., 1978), and agreement between trained judges is very high. Distribution of children within the three main categories varies little for the white middle-class samples seen throughout the United States: one half to two thirds are judged *secure*; one fifth to one third are judged *avoidant*; and a small minority are judged *ambivalent* (see also Main & Weston, 1982).

It will be apparent that a much greater range of patterns of response could occur in the strange-situation than are described by the eight subcategories in Table 2. The categories are based on specific predictions about the behavior that will appear; in practice, the majority of cases do fit one or other category. Sroufe and Waters (Sroufe & Waters, 1977; see Waters, 1978), for example, found no infants who avoided the mother on reunion and were wary of the stranger or cried when left with the stranger, although in the absence of a theory such a pattern would be quite conceivable. However, recent work indicates that the infants who do not fit the Ainsworth categories constitute a sufficiently large proportion not to be neglected (Main & Weston, 1982).

A number of studies testify that the strange-situation categorization taps enduring aspects of the parent-child relationship. First, in middle-class families, the assessments show remarkable stability, at least over the 12- to 18-month-age range. This stability resides, it must be emphasized, not in the particular behavior shown but in the categories, for example, infants who avoided contact by turning away at one age might ignore their mothers or show gaze aversion six months later (Ainsworth et al., 1978; Sroufe & Waters, 1977; Waters, 1978).

Further studies of mother-infant interaction in the home before or after the strange situation categorization at 1 year of age indicate clear differences between the A, B, and C categories. The so-called B babies (Table 2) tended to cry little and gave frequent positive greetings to their mothers, frequently tended to initiate and show positive reactions to close bodily contact, and yet tended to show positive responses to cessation of contact. They communicated better with their mothers and were more compliant. In all those respects, they differed from the A and C babies.

A number of studies, reviewed by Ainsworth et al. (1978), show that strange-situation behavior is related to a variety of antecedent variables that could affect the mother-infant relationship. Of special interest is the fact that mothers of infants subsequently placed in category B (securely attached) are more sensitive and responsive to their babies, and even in the first few months of life hold them more carefully than do mothers in A and C dyads (Ainsworth, 1979;

Table 2. **Summary of Main Categories Used in Strange-Situation Procedure**[a]

Classification[b]	Descriptor	Proximity Seeking	Contact Maintaining	Proximity Avoiding	Contact Resisting	Crying
A (2 subcategories)	Avoidant	Low	Low	High	Low	Low (preseparation), high or low (separation), low (reunion)
B (4 subcategories)	Secure	High	High (if distressed)	Low	Low	Low (preseparation), high or low (separation), low (reunion)
C (2 subcategories)	Ambivalent	High	High (often preseparation)	Low	High	Occasionally (preseparation), high (separation), moderate to high (reunion)

Notes:
[a]Classification criteria (from reunion episodes 5 and 8).
[b]Typical of the group as a whole; subcategories differ in nonreunion episodes and to some extent in reunion behavior. See Ainsworth et al. (1978) for detailed classification instructions. (After Waters, 1978)

Ainsworth, Bell, & Stayton, 1971). Mothers in A dyads differed from those of C dyads in showing more rejection, aversion to bodily contact, controlled anger, and a generally compulsive kind of adjustment (Main, 1977; Main et al., 1979). There is also evidence that babies in dyads subsequently categorized as C differ from others on the Brazelton (Brazelton & Freedman, 1971) neonatal assessment (Waters, Vaughn, & Egeland, 1980).

Other research reviewed by Ainsworth et al. (1978) validate the strange-situation technique by relating its categorization to other antecedent variables (e.g., twins vs. singletons) and to contemporaneous or subsequent assessments of cognitive functioning, other aspects of the mother-infant relationship, and responses to strangers and peers.

Although the attachment construct is, thus, clearly valuable as an integrating construct and is supported by a considerable body of data, there are still some difficulties over exactly what is being measured in the strange situation.

One issue is that behavior in the strange situation involves the infant's attempts to achieve and maintain proximity and contact and also to avoid or resist it, to explore her environment, play with toys, and so on. Thus, as Ainsworth et al. (1978) emphasize, to assess attachment behavior in the strange situation it is necessary to trace through "the interplay among attachment behavior, wary/fearful behavior, exploratory behavior and, in some episodes, social (or affiliative) behavior directed towards the stranger" (p. 15). This is a formidable task. One problem is that a given type of behavior may subserve more than one behavioral system (*Werkzeugreaktionen* in the older ethological terminology, e.g., in Tinbergen, 1942). Another is that the behavioral outcome of any one behavioral system is affected by the degree of activation of others (Fentress, 1976). Although relevance of behavior to attachment can be partially ensured by taking context into account (Waters, 1978), interactions between behavioral systems are inevitably involved (see, e.g., Ainsworth et al., 1978).

A second issue arises from the fact that the parent is asked to behave in a constant way, whereas the infant's behavior is free to vary and forms the basis for later categorizing; this can lead to the mistaken view that it is inherent characteristics of the infants that are being measured. Given the dialectic between personality and relationship (see *Relationships and Personality*), it seems more accurate to regard the strange situation as intruding on a relationship at a particular point in time and of assessing an aspect of that relationship from the infant's point of view. Indeed, such a view is necessary to accommodate the finding that an infant may be classified in one category with his mother but in another quite different category with his father (Grossmann & Grossmann, 1982; Main & Weston, 1981). It is also in keeping with the finding that although categorization in middle-class samples is stable over the 12- to 18-month period, in less privileged families it can change in parallel with changes in the stability of the mother's environment (Vaughn, Egeland, Sroufe, & Waters, 1979).

Environment of Evolutionary Adaptedness

Why should a child be distressed in the mother's absence? What is the child afraid of? Why do children show attachment behavior? Bowlby (1969, 1973, 1980) argued that the answers to such questions provided by current theoretical approaches were unsatisfactory and that much light would be thrown on them by consideration of humankind's evolutionary history. In the environment of evolutionary adaptedness of the human species, safety for the child lay in her proximity to the mother, and both child and mother must have been adapted to maintain it. In support of this view, Bowlby drew on extensive evidence from nonhuman primates, evidence which need not be repeated here. Although proximity-seeking behavior is no longer so obviously necessary under modern conditions, it persists. The nature of the child is still such that healthy development is promoted by the continuing proximity or availability of a mother figure. The attachment behavior system is adapted to this end.

But whereas such biological considerations provided an essential background to Bowlby's theorizing, some caution is now necessary. In part because we now know more about the selective forces acting on parent-infant relationships than was the case 20 years ago and in part because interest has shifted from general considerations about the mother-infant relationship to considerations of interdyadic differences, two points may be made. First, the view that maternal behavior has been adapted to mesh with infant behavior easily leads to the view that natural selection has operated to promote an idyllic partnership between mother and infant. In practice, mothers of probably all species actively promote their infants' independence before the infants are ready for it (Hinde, 1969), and it is in the mothers' biological interest to do so (Trivers, 1974). Infants are presumably adapted to cope with mothers who reject them. Thus, although Bowlby was right that natural selection would favor protective mothers, it is also the case that it favors mothers who promote their infants' independence. In turn, infants must be adapted to emerge from such relationships adjusted to the society in which they live.

The second reservation concerns the view that natural selection will promote a particular style of sensitive mothering. Evidence from samples in the United States shows that it is better to be securely attached as assessed in the strange situation, in the sense that such dyads have the more harmonious mother-infant relationships, do better subsequently on developmental tests, and so on. Noting that such dyads are the most frequent in U.S. samples, Ainsworth (e.g., 1979) also argues that such babies have "developed normally, i.e. along species-characteristic lines." And because intermother differences are more important than interinfant ones in determining the nature of the relationship, she regards infants as preadapted to mothers who are responsive, intervene promptly when they cry, and so on. It is not with the view that securely attached dyads are likely to do better that difficulties arise, but with the use of a biological argument.

In general, the styles of mothering that are most biologically advantageous will vary with circumstances. Consider first a relatively simple monkey example. Altmann (1980) points out that restrictive baboon mothers are likely to have infants which survive better in the early months but are less likely to survive if orphaned. Because infants of dominant individuals are less susceptible to dangers in their early months than infants of subordinate mothers, Altmann suggests that selection may tend to favor a more laissez faire style with more dominant mothers. Thus, natural selection is likely to favor alternative strategies (If dominant be laissez faire in case you die; if subordinate, be restrictive to maximize infant survival), with decision rules for choosing between them. The concept of an environment of evolutionary adaptedness, although useful for an early stage in our thinking, is only a crude approximation even for monkey societies. An argument that one particular mothering style is best based on biological considerations inevitably runs into difficulties.

This issue is even more pertinent in human societies, which are both more complex and more varied than those of any monkey species: (1) within any one society, the mothering technique that will produce the "best" infants (as judged in terms either of biological inclusive fitness or by cultural standards) will vary according to whether the child is male or female, its ordinal position in the family, and with many aspects of the social and material situation; and (2) cultural differences will affect mothering strategies, their outcomes and desiderata for the offspring. Thus, an argument from natural selection theory that any one mothering style is best is on dangerous ground. Interestingly, it now appears that securely attached dyads are not the most common everywhere—a sample (yet to be replicated) in Bielefeld, West Germany, had a preponderance in the avoidant category (Grossmann & Grossmann, 1982).

In conclusion, it must be emphasized that the argument here concerns not whether or not babies from securely attached dyads do better, but, instead, the use of evolutionary arguments (see Blurton Jones, 1976; Hinde, 1982b) to support a view about what is best.

General

The use of attachment concepts does not constitute a tight set of propositions in the learning theory tradition. Instead, as Ainsworth et al. (1978) have emphasized, it is an open-ended system "intended both to help us to understand research findings to date and to provide guidelines for future research." She further argues that her approach "is clearly open to extension, modification, and refinement in the light of research findings" (p. 436). As such, its heuristic value is to be found not only in studies of child development but also in work on the later consequences of the lack or loss of adequate attachment figures (e.g., Bowlby, 1980; Rutter, 1972), on adult anxiety (e.g., Bowlby, 1973), and on bereavement (e.g., Bowlby, 1980; Parkes, 1972). However such open endedness also carries some dangers—dangers, for instance, of unverifiability and of circularity. One way to minimize these dangers has been suggested—the maintenance of a clear distinction between description and explanation, with avoidance of the reification of descriptive concepts into explanatory ones (see also Chalmers, 1978; Kovach, 1978). Other interrelated needs would seem to be: (1) a deeper understanding of the development of the human attachment behavior system, including further understanding of the implications of cognitive development for this and other systems; and (2) an advance from the ethological tradition of discrete behavior systems to an understanding of how such systems interact at the behavioral level (see *Attachment Behavior*) and are transcended at the cognitive level (see *The Study of Processes Versus Behavioral Categories*). Only by pursuing such aims will we be able to specify the place of attachment behavior (i.e., behavior promoting proximity/contact to a security figure) in the infant-mother relationship; how much, if at all, other types of behavior contribute to attachment; how far the concept of monotropy is applicable to attachment or to the infant-mother relationship as a whole—or neither; how both attachment in particular and the infant-mother relationship in general contribute to relationships in adulthood, and so on. Some more recent work is presented in Parkes and Stevenson-Hinde (1982).

The Dynamics of the Parent-Child Relationship

In preceding discussions, it has been assumed that the parent-child relationship, like any other interpersonal relationship, involves mutual influences of each partner on the other. Such a view is relatively recent in the study of child development. Not long ago, most developmental psychologists assumed that control rested firmly in the hands of the mother. From a practical point of view, this was natural enough—pediatricians could tell a mother what to do, but not a baby. However, Yarrow (1963) argued that the same caregiver behaved differently to different infants, and R. Q. Bell (1968) pointed out that many aspects of ongoing interactions are controlled by the infant. This has led to numerous studies on the "effects of the infant on his caregiver" (Lewis & Rosenblum, 1974). By contrast, ethologists, interested both in parental stimuli that elicit filial behavior and in stimuli from the infant that elicit parental behavior, usually regarded the relationship in terms of mutual influence (Harper, 1970). However, impressed by changes correlated with the rapid physical development of the young, ethologists sometimes assumed that the temporal course of the relationship was largely determined by the physical development of the young—a view which, as we shall see shortly, is equally misleading.

The issues here are complex and require discussion in depth.

A long-term relationship involves successive interactions between the participants. Analyses of behavioral sequences can, thus, throw considerable light on the dynamics of relationships (e.g., Patterson, 1975), although the complexities involved in the analysis of sequential data are considerable. However, within a long-term relationship, each interaction is liable to be affected by preceding interactions and by expectations of interactions in the future, so that the states of the participants may change from one interaction to the next. Analysis in stimulus-response terms, although invaluable in some contexts, is liable to be cumbersome and, however hard nosed it may be, to founder in others. We are, in fact, confronted with continuing mutual influences of the natures of the participants on the relationship and of the relationship on the natures of the participants (see *Relationships and Personality*): no measure of behavior that we take in the dyadic situation can be regarded as a measure of the behavior or characteristics of either individual in isolation from the other. But recent studies of the mother-infant relationship in nonhuman primates have shown that examination of correlations between measures can lead to some progress. The approach depends on framing the questions being asked very precisely.

To illustrate this by example from the mother-infant relationship it is necessary to introduce three measures used in studies of rhesus monkeys:

Time off. This is a measure of the time the infant spends off its mother, expressed as a percentage of observation time (Fig 11a).

Frequency of rejections. The frequency with which the mother rejects the infant's attempts to make contact with the mother per unit time observed (Fig 11b).

The infant's role in the maintenance of contact (Fig 11c). This can be assessed in terms of an index calculated from the proportion of contact makes that were due to movement by the infant and the proportion of contact breaks that were due to movement by the infant:

$$\left(\frac{Mk_I \times 100}{Mk_I + Mk_M} - \frac{Bk_I \times 100}{Bk_I + Bk_M} \right)$$

If the infant is responsible for a higher proportion of makes than of breaks and is, thus, primarily responsible for contact, the index will be positive. In the opposite case, where the infant is responsible for a higher proportion of breaks than makes, it will be negative, indicating that the mother is primarily responsible for contact (see Hinde, 1979; Hinde & White, 1974).

The argument which follows involves correlations between the first of the above measures and the other two, but it could be applied to any two measures of a relationship, provided one could be said to affect the other. We may now consider three questions concerning the mother-infant relationship.

1. *Is the mother or infant primarily responsible for determining the length of contacts during each age period?* As noted above, the answer to this question is indicated directly by the index % Mk_I − % Bk_I. Figure 11(c) shows that in the early weeks the mother is primarily responsible, whereas later, the infant becomes so.

2. *Are the age changes in the amount of ventro-ventral contact due more immediately to changes in*

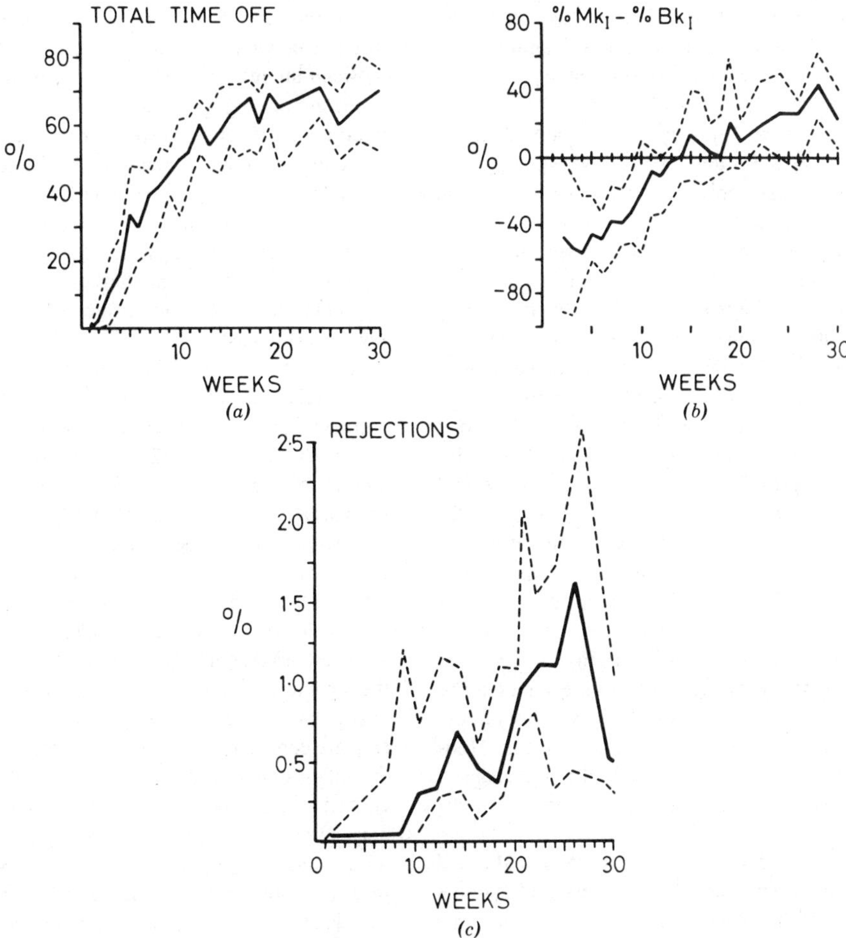

Figure 11. Three measures of the rhesus monkey mother-infant relationship; (a) time infant spends off mother, as percentage of the time observed; (b) frequency with which mother rejects infant's attempts to gain contact; (c) infant's role in the maintenance of contact. In each case the median and interquartile range is shown.

the mother or to changes in the infant? If the time off mother increased owing to a change in the behavior of the infant, we should expect the frequency of rejections and the index of the infant's role in contact to decrease; but if the time off increased owing to a change in the mother, we should expect both to increase. Figure 11 (a and b) shows the latter to be the case, and thus it seems that it is changes in the mother that immediately determine the increase in independence of the infant.

Three assumptions in this argument must be mentioned. First, it is assumed that the individuals have characteristics which, although subject to influence from the mother, the mother-infant relationship, or elsewhere, have some duration in time. Second, a degree of stationarity is implied, that is, it is assumed that the infant responds more or less similarly to the mother's signals at successive age points. Third, it is assumed that the dyad has limited flexibility: for instance, if the infant seeks proximity to the mother more, the mother will reject the infant more but, nevertheless, accede a little to the infant's demands. Each of these assumptions seems reasonable.

Because the increase in independence is correlated with the infant's physical growth, increasing locomotor activity, and the tendency to explore the physical and social environment, the conclusion that it is changes in the mother that immediately govern the rate of increase in the infant's independence is at first sight surprising. Nevertheless, it is in harmony with the finding that infants reared on inanimate surrogate mothers or without mothers but in pairs maintain a considerable amount of contact to a greater age than do infants reared on natural mothers (Hansen, 1966; Harlow & Harlow, 1965). The explanation in both cases presumably lies in the absence of the rejecting behavior of the natural mother.

There is no implication that the changes in the mother that promote the infant's independence arise endogenously. They may be initiated by the infant's increase in size, demands for milk, or more vigorous locomotor play. But these, in turn, depend on maternal care, which, in turn, depends on communication with the infant, and so on. Furthermore, the rate at which the infant gains independence will be influenced also by many other factors, such as the social situation (Berman, 1978; Hinde & Spencer-Booth, 1967; Suomi, 1976). Indeed, although this argument is concerned primarily with changes in the relationship that arise from changes in the partners, it is not always easy to specify whether a given change is endogenous or exogenous in origin, for instance, whether or not the mother becomes pregnant may be influenced by the infant as well as by factors in the external social situation (Simpson, Simpson, Hooley, & Zunz, 1981). This is only the first stage in teazing apart the ongoing interaction between mother and infant.

Study of individual curves reveals additional complexity and permits further understanding of the dynamics of the relationship. For instance, in some individuals, the rise in time off may precede the rise in rejections and coincide with a decrease in maternal restrictiveness. Here, the change is again due primarily to a change in the mother, but the mechanism is different from that implied above. In other individuals, the rise in time off may again precede the rise in rejections but coincide with an increase in social play and an increase in maternal restrictiveness. Here, the short-term change must be ascribed primarily to a change in the infant (M. J. A. Simpson, 1980). Although study of individual curves reveals many complexities, the overall trend over the first 20 to 30 weeks in all individuals is in conformity with that implied by the group means.

3. *At any one age, are the differences in the amount of contact between mother-infant dyads due primarily to differences between mothers or to differences between infants*? Here again correlations between measures are helpful. If, at any one age, those infants who spend most time off their mothers are the ones who play the greatest role in contact and are rejected the most, the differences in amount of contact would be primarily due to differences between mothers. If the reverse were the case, the differences would be due primarily to differences between infants. In practice, the correlation coefficients are not high, indicating that intermother and interinfant differences are both important. However, the correlation coefficients show interesting and consistent age changes, being consistently positive (sometimes significantly so) in the early weeks and negative (sometimes significantly so) later. Thus with young infants intermother differences are more important than interinfant differences, but later the reverse is the case.

It will be noted that the three questions posed so far are all of the general type "Is this partner or that partner responsible?" Yet the answers are very different. During the first 12 weeks or so, it is mothers who are primarily responsible for contact, but it is changes in mothers that are primarily responsible for the increases in independence of the infant. And at later ages, although the latter still applies, it is differences between infants that are primarily responsible for differences between dyads.

These arguments can be generalized in terms of the scheme shown in Table 3. Four possible types of change or difference in the mother-infant relationship are considered—the mother seeks contact with the infant either more or less and the infant seeks contact with the mother more or less. The measures considered so far are shown in columns 1 to 3. Columns 4 and 5 represent predictions for two further measures—the proportion of time off that the infant spends at a distance from its mother (out of arm's reach or > 60 cm) and an index of the infant's role in the maintenance of proximity based on the difference between the proportion of approaches and leavings over the 60-cm boundary for which the infant was responsible. The symbols indicate the predicted direction of change in each measure, given a change in the relationship of the type shown on the left. It will be apparent that columns 1 and 2, 1 and 3, and 4 and 5 change in the same direction if the change or difference is primarily maternal, but they change in different directions if it is due to the infant.

The changes indicated on the left of Table 3 suggest that time off the mother and the proportion of that time spent at a distance from the mother are positively correlated with each other. This is usually so, although sometimes it is not (Hinde, 1974). Lack of correlation is an indicator of greater complexity than the model indicates and might, for instance, be anticipated in human babies who both avoided and sought contact with their mothers (see Main & Weston, 1982; see also Table 2, group C, and *Attachment*).

Of course, the questions discussed so far repre-

Table 3. **Predicted Direction of Changes (or Differences) in Five Measures of the Mother-Infant Relationship, Given the Four Types of Change (or Difference) Shown on the Left**

	Contact			Proximity	
	(1) Time Infant Off Mother	(2) Infant's Relative Role in Contact	(3) Mother Rejects Infant's Attempt at Contact	(4) Proportion of Time Off Infant Away from Mother	(5) Infant's Relative Role in Proximity
M − I →	−	−	−	−	−
M − I ←	+	+	+	+	+
M − I ←	−	+	+	−	+
M − I →	+	−	−	+	−

sent only the first stages in understanding the dynamic influences of the individuals on the relationship and vice versa. Further progress depends on asking further questions which will help unravel the dialectic between the changing relationship and the changing characteristics of the partners. One such step, shown in Figure 12, depends on combining questions about the overall change in the relationship with questions about individual differences. In a new set of data Simpson (1980) has shown that (1) rank ordering of dyads in terms of frequency of maternal rejections and in terms of time off are consistent in data collected every other week; (2) the frequency of rejections in week 2 is positively related to the change in time off between weeks 2 and 4; and that (3) during weeks 2 and 4, rejections are positively correlated with time off.

The last point is consistent with the view that differences between mothers are primarily responsible for differences in time off in these early weeks, but not (or to a lesser extent) later. Item (2) suggests that individual differences in frequency of maternal

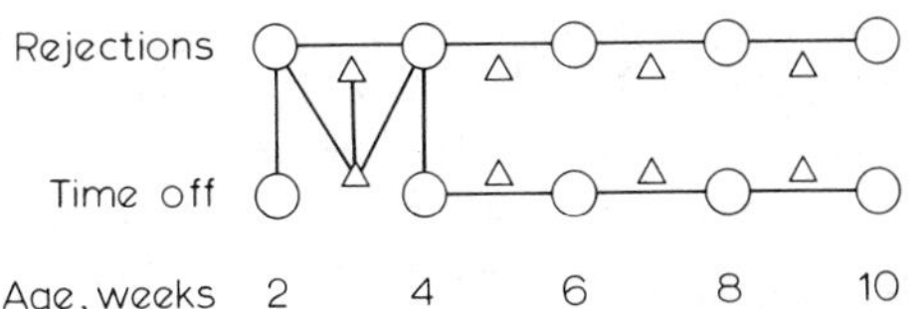

Figure 12. Rank order correlations between frequency of maternal rejections and time spent off mother by infant rhesus monkeys (circles) and changes in those measures (triangles). Lines joining symbols indicate a rank order correlation with $p < .05$. (Simpson, 1980.)

rejections determined the changes in time off from weeks 2 to 4. Subsequently, both the individual differences in time off and in the changes in time off were presumably due to differences between both mothers and infants, although item (1) indicates that the differences established in one period tended to persist to the next. However, because median time off and median frequency of rejections both increased with age, this age change in the median was primarily due to changes in the mothers.

Although most of the data discussed above were pooled within 6-hr. observation periods—so that the changes in, or differences between, relationships discussed have referred to mean measures over such periods—the method is, in principle, applicable to any periods for which adequate data could be obtained. It would, for instance, be possible to compare the relationship in the 10 min. before a rest period (Simpson, 1979) with the 10 min. after and to ask whether the differences in the relationship between those periods were due to differences between infant or mother. Furthermore, the model described may be applied not only in the context of the questions listed above but also to differences between two (groups of) dyads living under different conditions, to differences between measures before and after treatment, to differences between the relationships of one individual with two others (Hinde, 1969, 1977), and so on.

The scheme is also applicable to many aspects of human relationships. For example, mothers and infants engage in play sequences involving bouts of mutual eye contact and social interaction interspersed with looking away (Stern, 1977). The interactions are complex, apparently involving both simple responses to stimuli and in some sense preprogrammed sequences on the part of both infant and mother. The questions of how far differences in the frequency or duration of such sequences between mother-infant dyads are due to differences between mothers or infants and how far age changes are due to changes in one or the other could easily be answered from data on who initiated or terminated the sequences. On a longer time scale, it seems intuitively likely that the progression of the human child toward independence—the changes from milk to solid food, from crib to bed, and from home to school—are paced by changes in the mother.

Although the methods principally discussed in this chapter have not yet been applied to human development, they would seem to have a certain potential. At the very least, the clear lesson that questions asked about the development of a relationship must be framed precisely should carry over (see Ainsworth, 1979).

It is appropriate here to refer briefly to the method of cross-lagged analysis already used by developmental psychologists (e.g., Clarke-Stewart, 1973). This concerns a somewhat different question, that is, the influence of one aspect of the relationship during one time period on a different aspect in a later period. Although it is usual to assume that the measures inserted into the analysis are measures of parent behavior or child behavior, this is not necessary to the analysis. An assumption of stationarity is, however, inherent to the method. Some of the precautions that must be observed are discussed by Eron, Huesmann, Lefkowitz, and Walder (1972) and Kenny (1975).

The Child, the Dyad, and the Group

So far we have been concerned either with the child or with the mother-child relationship. But the nature of the mother-child relationship is itself affected in a number of ways by the total social situation: even infants soon have relationships with individuals other than the mother. Studies of nonhuman primates have, indeed, consistently demonstrated that every relationship is embedded in a nexus of other relationships and cannot be considered in isolation. Three studies relevant to early development may be cited.

The first concerns the influence of group companions on the mother-infant relationship. It has been observed that the rhesus monkey mother-infant relationship differs between dyads living in small social groups and dyads living in similar cages but alone. The segregated infants spend more time off their mothers and go to a distance from their mothers more often. In agreement with the argument in the discussion of *The Dynamics of the Parent-Child Relationship,* the difference lies mainly in the mothers, who are more rejecting or permissive in the absence of group companions. Although the infants go to a distance from their mothers more often, they spend fewer long bouts there, presumably because they have no peers to play with (Hinde & Spencer-Booth, 1967; see also Howe & Simpson, personal communication.)

Even when the caging conditions are identical, small groups of monkeys may differ markedly in social structure and interaction patterns. In a comparison of six groups of rhesus monkeys of similar composition, Howe and Simpson (1982) showed that the infants in each group, although born of different mothers at different times, resembled each other more than infants in other groups. For instance, there were significant intergroup differences in the frequencies with which infants made contact with their mothers and the duration of ventro-ventral contact at 8 weeks as well as in the frequency of maternal rejections and of contact calls by the infants at 16 weeks.

The third example concerns not the effect of others on the mother-infant relationship, but the influence of the infant on the mother's relationship with her peers. Seyfarth (1976), studying a troop of baboons in South Africa, found that the amount of grooming a mother received tended to increase after the birth of her infant. The effect was present, however, only in low-ranking individuals, more dominant females receiving much grooming both before and after the birth (Fig. 13).

Such findings (see also Vaitl, 1978) suggest that the first-order zone of an infant macaque or baboon can be represented as in Figure 14. The continuous bars represent relationships, their thickness roughly proportional to their importance, and the discontinuous lines represent the effects of relationships on relationships. For example, in the group in question, the adolescent female coveted the infant, playing with it or cuddling it if she had the opportunity. The mother could seldom challenge the adolescent directly because the male came to the adolescent's assistance. The mother thus became more restrictive. Thus, the male-adolescent, mother-adolescent, adolescent-infant, and mother-infant relationships formed a system of mutual influences. The various effects of relationships on relationships pictured in Figure 14 were all supported by quantitative or reasonably hard qualitative data.

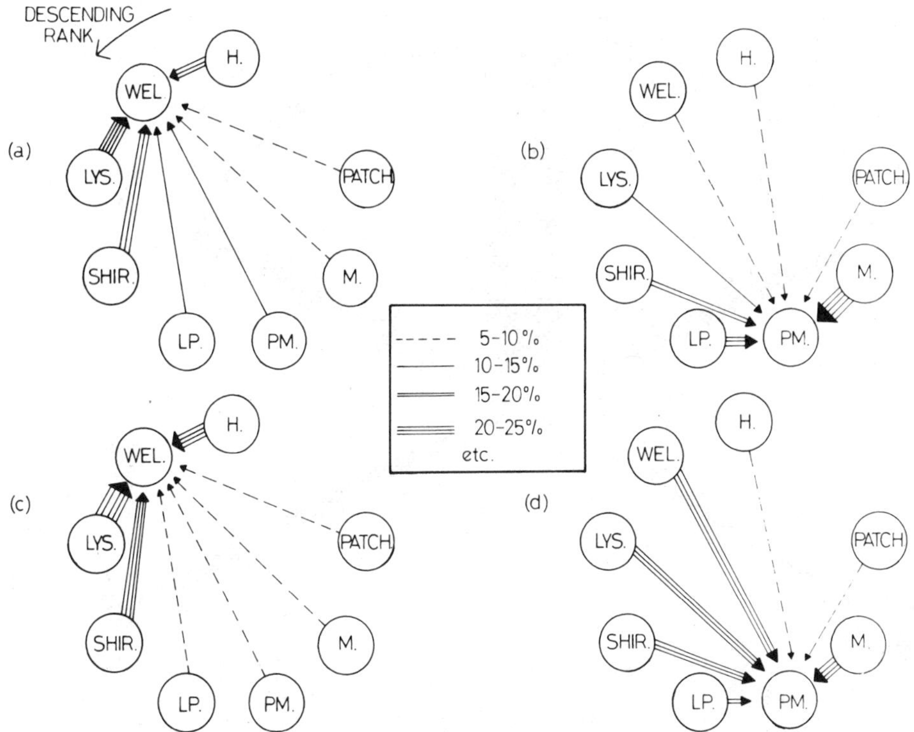

Figure 13. Changes in the distribution of grooming received by two baboon females during the first 10 weeks of lactation: (a) and (b) illustrate the distribution of grooming received by females named Wellesley (ranked second) and PM (ranked sixth) throughout the 15-month study; (c) and (d) illustrate the distribution of grooming received by each female during the first 10 weeks of lactation. Based on instantaneous sampling. (Seyfarth, 1976.)

The influences of relationships on relationships have of course frequently been acknowledged by developmental psychologists and have sometimes been the specific focus of study. In a human family the birth of a second child may produce marked changes in the mother-first born relationship (Dunn & Kendrick, 1980; see *Continuity and Discontinuity*).

Such intrafamily influences have recently been categorized by Parke, Power, and Gottman (1979). Although their scheme will be most congenial to ethologists, it will also force them to recognize that the issues involved extend far beyond the realm of comparative studies. The effect, for instance, on a mother's feelings for her husband when she sees her husband caressing the baby she loves may be susceptible to description in balance theory terms, but it has no known parallels in lower species. And the extent to which family members are influenced by socially accepted norms is a peculiarly human matter (Hinde, 1979).

Aggression and Dominance

A review of the literature on aggression and dominance would require a chapter in itself. My aim here is to mention three issues concerned with classificatory or conceptual issues which have arisen in recent ethological work.

The Heterogeneity of Aggressive Behavior

Aggressive behavior has been given many definitions, but there is common agreement that behavior directed toward causing physical harm to another individual is properly labeled as aggressive. Whether predatory behavior, verbal abuse, or intergroup strife are to be placed in the same category as interindividual aggression are issues that need not detain us here. We are concerned with the central core, namely, behavior directed toward causing physical harm. But aggressive behavior in this sense often results in the settling of status, precedence, or access to some object or space. Whether this is true

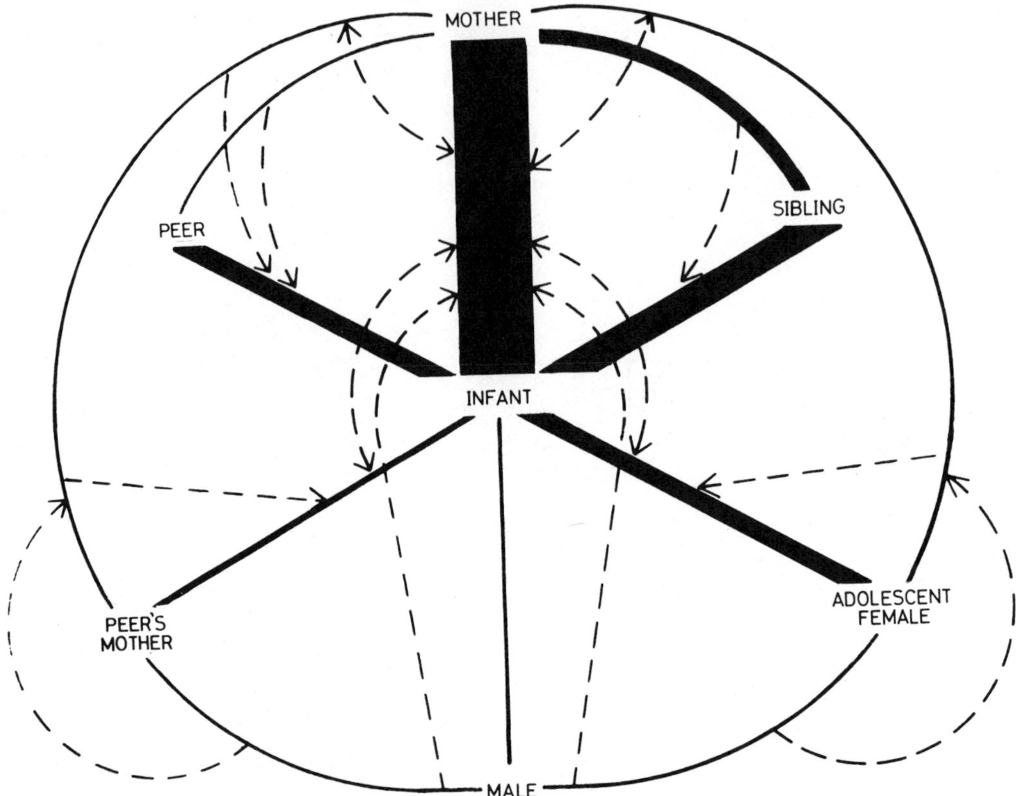

Figure 14. First order zone for an infant rhesus monkey in a small captive group. Continuous lines indicate relationships between individuals, with the thickness of the line indicating roughly the importance of the relationship. Discontinuous lines indicate effects of relationships on relationships.

of all aggressive behavior is largely a matter of definition. Insofar as an individual who causes physical injury is subsequently avoided, his aggressive behavior has determined access to space around him. But the complementary question of whether all behavior directed toward settling status, precedence, or access should properly be labeled as aggressive is at the basis of much disagreement in discussions about aggression. The popular use of the term aggressive as equivalent to go-getting in such phases as an aggressive salesperson has led to unjustified assumptions about the motivational bases of go-getting behavior (Hinde, 1974).

Furthermore, both ethologists and comparative psychologists have often warned that behavior falling within even a narrow definition of aggressive behavior may have diverse causal bases. Moyer (1968), for instance, distinguishes six types of aggression: intermale, fear induced, irritable, territorial, maternal, and instrumental. Whether or not these categories have any generality, they call attention to the need for caution. Similar distinctions have appeared in the child development literature: for instance, Feshbach (1964, 1970) distinguished instrumental from hostile aggression. Here, three studies of nursery school children that have taken the matter a little further may be mentioned.

As discussed earlier, Blurton Jones (1972a) warned against the dangers inherent in the uncritical use of global categories of behavior. In his own studies of nursery school children, he recorded at a much finer level of analysis and subsequently assessed the relations between items by factor analysis. One result was a clear distinction of laugh-play face, run, jumps, hit at, and wrestle from other aggressive items, such as fixate, frown, hit, push, and take-tug-grab. The former represent rough-and-tumble play, the latter aggression in the strict sense. Blurton

Jones's data strongly suggest that, at the nursery school age, the two groups have distinct motivational bases.

The second study, although more in the nature of a pilot investigation, is of interest because it focuses not on different types of aggression per se, but on categories of children distinguished by the type (rather than frequency) of hostility the children displayed (Manning, Heron, & Marshall, 1978). An act was defined as hostile if it usually evoked a reaction implying physical damage, insult, intimidation, or interference. Three categories of hostility were recognized:

1. Specific hostility. Specific hostility occurs in a specific situation which annoys or frustrates the aggressor, for instance, in the context of property disputes, social exclusion, ordering about, precedence, or judgment for transgressions.
2. Harassment. Unprovoked aggression, often directed at the same person repeatedly, for instance, physical harassment, teasing, or threats.
3. Games hostility. Socially unacceptable roughness in rough-and-tumble play, bullying, or imprisonment against the victim's will in imaginative games, and so on.

Manning et al. used these categories of hostility to classify 3- to 5-year-old children according to their predominant style of hostility. The 14 to 17 children in the study were ranked in order of the ratio of specific to specific-plus-harassment hostility. This rank order was then arbitrarily divided into groups in ascending order of the ratio. Group 1 showed hostility mainly in the games situation, where they tended to lose control. Elsewhere they tended to be timid. Group 2, the teasers, were among the most hostile and violent children present. Group 3 tended to be bossy as well as teasing, not especially violent, and showed hostility mainly outside the games situation. Group 4 showed little hostility, but when they did, it was mostly of the specific type.

Although the grouping of the children seems a little arbitrary, the interest of the study lies in its apparent validation in follow-up work. Differences between the groups remained at ages 7 to 8. Although Group 4 showed no signs of behavioral disturbance, all other groups did so. Furthermore, the latter children came from families with difficulties which could have formed part of the etiology.

The third study to be mentioned is even more ambitious. Szegal (Szegal, 1979; Szegal & Benis, 1979) has produced a detailed scheme for the study of aggressive behavior in young children. This comprises 14 dimensions, such as moral evaluation (e.g., antisocial, asocial), organization (e.g., temper tantrums, directed attack), mode (action vs. reaction), and form of execution (verbal, instrumental). This scheme has been applied to a study of 228 children in foundling homes or day nurseries in Budapest. The relation of frequency of aggressive acts and their characteristics along the 14 dimensions to a considerable number of independent variables, including aspects of the personality of some of the parents and nurses, were assessed. For instance, in a subsample of children, aggression was found to correlate positively with the aggressiveness of the fathers (as assessed by an inventory) and negatively with the anxiety of the mothers (as assessed by a projective test). Unfortunately, the data of this interesting study are available in English only in summary form.

Dominance Relationships and Dominance Hierarchies

The concept of dominance—whose use in biology and psychology stems largely from the work of Schjelderup-Ebbe (1922) on chickens—has had a checkered history. Recent ethological work has emphasized that dominance as applied to dyadic relationships may have a heuristic value different from the concept of dominance hierarchy as applied to a group. In the former case, dominance acts as an intervening variable whose value depends on the extent of the correlations between the aspects of behavior it is held to explain. As applied to a social group, its value depends on the extent to which the individuals can be arranged in a linear dominance order without triangular relationships of the type *A* bosses *B*, *B* bosses *C*, but *C* bosses *A* (Hinde, 1978).

Although dominance has, indeed, proved a useful principle for understanding some aspects of group organization in children ranging from preschoolers to early teenagers, the studies are difficult to compare because of the wide range of measures of dominance used. These include disputes over objects, avoidance, glances at superiors, and teachers' assessments (e.g., Anderson & Willis, 1976; Hold, 1976; McGrew, 1972; Omark & Edelman, 1976; Savin-Williams, 1976; Sluckin & Smith, 1977; Strayer & Strayer, 1976).

Furthermore, it is essential to remember that dominance is only one of a number of principles relevant to group structure (e.g., Gartlan, 1968). For example, the structure of monkey groups is much more complex than had previously been supposed. In macaques, the permanent organization depends on the females who are arranged in matrifocal families, with the daughters in inverse age order of dominance; the families are arranged in a dominance order within genealogies of families with related mothers; and the genealogies within a troop are subordinated to each other (e.g., Dolhinow, McKenna, & Laws, 1979; Kawai, 1958; Kawamura, 1958; Sade, 1972). The males have relationships both with each other and with the females, the nature of those relationships varying with age. Such complex structures demand a number of principles for their understanding (Hinde, 1976a). It is clear that groups of children have even greater complexity. Indeed, friendships, coalitions, and subgroups have been shown to be crucial for understanding the distribution of social behavior in a number of studies (e.g., Clark, Wyon, & Richards, 1969). In a detailed study of one group, Guttstein (1975) and Strayer (1980) showed that, although the distribution of some types of interaction could be explained in terms of a dominance hierarchy, the formation of subgroups was also an important aspect of the dynamics of the group.

Studies of Temporary Social Separations

In the postwar years, both Bowlby (1951) and Spitz (1946, 1950) suggested that a period of separation between mother and infant could have long-term effects on the psychological development of the infant (see also Ainsworth, 1962). In part because of the impossibility of testing this hypothesis experimentally with human subjects, a number of investigators undertook to assess the effects of a separation experience in nonhuman primates. This work has been reviewed a number of times recently (e.g., Hinde & McGinnis, 1977; Mineka & Suomi, 1978); a brief indication of the findings is included here because of their implications not only for hospital practice but also for understanding the dynamics of relationships.

The subjects have been of diverse ages from infancy to adulthood and the separations involved mothers or peers (the studies discussed here involved mother-infant separation unless stated otherwise). Before separation, the mother-infant dyad may have been confined alone or living in a social group. The techniques have involved removal of subject from mother or surrogate, or vice versa. The separation may have lasted from a few minutes to several weeks and may or may not have been repeated.

A consistent finding is that infants respond to separation first by active protest (distress calling [the analogue of crying] and searching) followed by depression, with a decrease in locomotor activity, play, and so on, and the frequent assumption of a hunched, depressed posture (e.g., Hinde, Spencer-Booth, & Bruce, 1966; Jensen & Tolman, 1962; Kaufman & Rosenblum, 1969; Seay, Hansen, & Harlow, 1962). These symptoms are similar to those shown by children, although avoidance of the mother on reunion, frequently observed in children (e.g., Bowlby, 1973; Spitz, 1946), is rarely observed in nonhuman primates.

After reunion, the mother-infant relationship is usually somewhat disturbed, with the infant demanding much close contact with the mother. Readjustment gradually occurs and the relationship usually returns to something near its original course. However, some effects have been found to persist for many months after reunion (Hinde, Leighton-Shapiro, & McGinnis, 1978; Hinde & Spencer-Booth, 1971a; Mitchell, Harlow, Griffin, & Møller, 1967). There is also some evidence that early mother-infant and peer-peer separations may lower the threshold of response to separations later in life (Mineka & Suomi, 1978; Young, Suomi, Harlow, & McKinney, 1973).

There is considerable variation both between and even within species in the response to a separation experience (e.g., Lewis & McKinney, 1976), and the bases of this variation are far from understood. However, the short and medium-term responses have been found to depend upon a number of factors:

1. Separation per se. Infants separated from their mothers exhibit more distress than infants merely removed from the social group with their mothers. The distress is greater the more complete the separation (Suomi, Collins, Harlow, & Ruppenthal, 1976). However, there are considerable species differences in the response to separation (e.g., Dolhinow, 1978; Jones & Clark, 1973; Kaufman & Rosenblum, 1969; Preston, Baker, & Seay, 1970; Schlottman & Seay, 1972). These may be, in part, a consequence of species differences in maternal or social behavior.

2,3. Preseparation and postseparation mother-infant relationship. Rhesus infants separated for 1 week at 20 to 32 weeks show more distress after reunion the higher the frequency of maternal rejections and the greater the role of the infant relative to that of the mother in staying near the mother when off her (cf. Fig. 11). Distress immediately after reunion is more closely related to these measures of tension before separation, whereas a few days later it is more closely related to contemporaneous measures. Distress is not related to the absolute amount of time the infant spent on or close to its mother (Hinde & Spencer-Booth, 1971a).

4,5. Preseparation and postseparation maternal social relationships. The mother-infant relationship is affected by the mother's relationships with others, which affect the outcome of a separation experience indirectly (Hinde & McGinnis, 1977; McGinnis, 1979). It can be assumed that the outcome is also affected by the many other factors that influence the mother-infant relationship (Brandt, Baysinger, & Mitchell, 1972; Castell & Wilson, 1971; Kaplan, 1972; Rosenblum, 1974; White & Hinde, 1975).

6. Preseparation infant social relationships. Bonnet macaque infants have less exclusive relationships with their mothers and relate to others more readily in their mother's absence than do pigtail macaque infants (Kaufman & Rosenblum, 1969). This affects the outcome of a separation experience (see item 10 below).

7. Postseparation infant social relationships. Infants separated by removal from their social group on reunion spend considerable time in interactions with their peers; this affects their relationship with their mothers, although the long-term effects are not known (Hinde & McGinnis, 1977). Infants temporarily removed from a peer group settle back less easily on reunion if the group contains infants who are themselves disturbed by separation experiences (Chappell & Meier, 1975; Suomi & Harlow, 1975).

8. Nature of the separation experience. Rhesus infants left in the home pen after their mother has been removed go through the phase of protest into depression more rapidly than do infants removed alone to a strange pen for a similar period. In the former case, depressive symptoms persist longer after reunion, perhaps as a result of conditioning to the environment (Gewirtz, 1961). The former (mother-removed) infants are more severely affected by the separation experience than are the infant-removed infants. Two factors seem to be important. First, the persisting depression of the mother-removed infants makes them less effective in gaining their mother's attention. Second, mothers who have been removed must, on their return, reestablish their relationship with their own social companions: apparently, as a consequence of this, they show less interest in their infants. By contrast, mothers of infant-removed infants, having been at home all the time, focus on their infants (Hinde & McGinnis, 1977).

9. Duration of separation. In rhesus monkeys, one 13-day separation produces greater effects than two 6-day separations and these, in turn, produce greater effects than one 6-day separation (Hinde & Spencer-Booth, 1971a).

10. Alternative sources of mothering during the separation period. In species in which adult females are attracted to young infants, their alternative mothering can ameliorate the effects of a separation experience (Kaufman & Rosenblum, 1969). This is especially the case in langur monkeys, where the effect seems to depend more on the availability than the adequacy of substitute care. Adoptive mothers are sometimes retained even if the mother is returned (Dolhinow, 1978).

In species where the available adult females are unfamiliar or are not attracted to infants, this effect is much less marked (Kaufman & Stynes, 1978; Schlottman & Seay, 1972; Suomi & Harlow, 1977). The presence of peers can also ameliorate distress (Suomi, Collins, & Harlow, 1973).

11. Sex of infant. There is some evidence that males are more disturbed than females (Hinde & Spencer-Booth, 1971a).

12. Age of infant. This is certainly an important variable, although the only systematic studies have covered too narrow an age range to demonstrate a dramatic effect (Hinde & Spencer-Booth, 1971a; but see Suomi et al., 1973). Near-independent young squirrel monkeys show little disturbance at separation (Kaplan, 1970).

13. Other characteristics of the infant. That infants differ in their resilience is not to be doubted, but this has not been studied in nonhuman species.

14. Direct effects of separation on the mother. It is possible that cessation of suckling may have physiological effects on the mother, making her less ready to initiate contact with the infant after reunion.

15. Infant's previous experience. Repetitive separations between mother and infant seem not to produce dramatically different effects (Chappell & Meier, 1975; Hinde & Spencer-Booth, 1971a). However, repetitive separations between infants brought up in a peer-peer situation do (Suomi, Harlow, & Domak, 1970; Young et al., 1973)—the cumulative effect seems to have been particularly noticeable in an unpublished study cited by Mineka and Suomi (1978). Monkeys lacking in social sophistication as a result of preceding social deprivation find readjustment during reunion more difficult (Suomi, 1976).

These data indicate that the consequences of temporary separation from the mother depend on diverse factors that interact in a complex way. Studies of separation of infants from an inanimate mother surrogate or from peers (Erwin, Maple, Mitchell, & Willott, 1971; Singh, 1977; Suomi et al., 1970; Suomi & Harlow, 1975; Suomi, Seaman, Lewis, De Lizio, & McKinney, 1978) and separation between older individuals (e.g., McKinney, Kliese, Suomi, & Moran, 1973; Suomi, Eisele, Grady, & Harlow, 1975) are reviewed by Mineka and Suomi (1978) and will not be discussed here. In general, the young subjects showed responses comparable to those seen in mother-infant separation, whereas the older subjects showed minimal effects unless separation from a peer group was followed by social isolation. Studies of separation from individuals other than the mother, in general, provide further evidence for the independent variables listed above but (except as already mentioned) do not substantially add to, or contradict, it.

In general, studies of the effects of separation experiences are of interest from several points of view:

First, they have been used to study the physiological concomitants of protest and depression (e.g., Kraemer & McKinney, 1979; Lewis & McKinney, 1976; Reite, Kaufman, Pauley, & Stynes, 1974; Reite, Short, & Seiler, 1978; Short & Reite, 1977; Suomi & Harlow, 1977).

Second, they have implications about the effects of mother-child separation in our own species. First, if the response of human infants to separation is similar to that of monkey infants, which are nonverbal and presumably operate at a relatively simple level of cognitive functioning, this places limits on the complexity of explanation needed in the human case. Second, the empirical findings may also be applicable to humans. Of course, the relative importance of the various independent variables differs even between nonhuman primate species (Kaplan, 1970; Preston et al., 1970; Rosenblum & Kaufman, 1968; Schlottman & Seay, 1972), let alone between monkeys and humans (e.g., Hinde, 1976b; Lehrman, 1974). Although the response of human children to reunion after separation often includes a period of detachment (Bowlby, 1973) and even hostility (Robertson & Robertson, 1971), which is seldom seen in monkeys, most of the 15 independent variables mentioned above as important in monkeys seem also to be so in man (e.g., [2]: Bowlby, 1973. [3]: Heinicke & Westheimer, 1966; Vernon, Foley, Sipowicz, & Schulmans, 1965; Robertson & Robertson, 1971. [4,5]: Robertson, 1965, 1970; Rutter, 1971. [6]: Mead, 1962. [9]: Rutter, 1972. [10]: Bowlby, 1973; Robertson & Robertson, 1971. [11]: Bowlby, 1973; Rutter, 1972. [12]: Bowlby, 1973. [13]: Robertson & Robertson, 1971).

With human infants, the stress of separation is likely to be greater if the infant is moved to strange surroundings than if it remains at home (Douglas & Bloomfield, 1958; Rutter, 1972); this, at first sight, contradicts the monkey data (item 7 above). However, the important issue in the monkey data is that the effect on the infant is greater in the circumstances in which the mother-infant relationship is most affected. In monkeys, removal of the mother affects the mother-infant relationship more than removal of the infant, but this may not be so in humans.

Third, these experiments have provided material for diverse theories relevant to the mechanisms by which separation produces its effects and, thus, to the nature of attachment in the first place. The main ones are:

1. The ethologically based view of Bowlby (1969) and Ainsworth (e.g., 1979) that attachment behavior is a product of natural selection and is conducive to infant survival. Attachment includes the use of the mother as a secure base from which to explore: protest and despair result from its disappearance.

2. The suggestion of Kaufman (Kaufman, 1973; Kaufman & Rosenblum, 1967) that the protest-despair sequence to separation is but one example of a fight-flight reaction followed by conservation and withdrawal that is seen in many stressful situations (Engel, 1962).

3. Approaches that emphasize the role of learning in the formation of attachment, either on the operant conditioning (e.g., Gewirtz, 1961, 1972), classical conditioning (e.g., Hoffman & Ratner, 1973), or contiguity (e.g., Cairns, 1966) paradigm or that invoke the concept of learned helplessness (Seligman, e.g., 1975). In the latter case, the despair phase is explicable in terms of learned helplessness, but the initial protest must be regarded as a response to loss of freedom and control (Brehm, 1976).

4. The opponent process theory (Hoffman & Solomon, 1974).

These theoretical approaches are discussed by Mineka and Suomi (1976) and Rajecki et al. (1978), and they are not in total conflict—the urgent need would seem to be not to try to specify which is right and which wrong but to attempt to integrate them.

All these theoretical approaches focus on the infant. However, many (perhaps all) of the factors listed above as affecting the consequences of temporary separation can be seen as operating through the mother-infant relationship. The importance of the continuing dialectic between the infant's characteristics and its relationships with others, especially its mother (see *Relationships and Personality; The Current Status of Attachment Concepts;* and *The Child, the Dyad, and the Group*), has already been stressed. We have also seen that the mother-infant relationship has powers of regulation which can permanently ameliorate a degree of infant distress (see *Self-regulatory Mechanisms*). Thus, whatever the mechanisms underlying the infant's immediate response to separation, understanding of the long-term consequences of such an experience must include understanding of the infant's relationships. This is in harmony with the finding that maternal separation in man is much more likely to have long-term effects if the children come from disadvantaged or stressed homes (Douglas, 1975; Quinton & Rutter, 1976).

Effects of Early Experience

Many ethological studies have involved manipulation of early experience and assessment of the effects on subsequent behavioral development. Some of those involving separation of infant primates from mother or peer were reviewed in the discussion of *Studies of Temporary Social Separations*. Many of the others were directed toward assessing the importance of particular types of early experience or of social experience in general for subsequent behavioral development. Comprehensive review is impossible here, but five groups of studies concerned with differences in early experience or their sequelae have been selected for special mention.

Sexual Imprinting in Birds

The filial imprinting discussed earlier (*Ethological Studies . . .*) influences the elicitation of responses normally given by a newly hatched bird to its parents. In a number of species, experience in the early weeks also influences subsequent choice of a sexual partner (Bateson, 1978a, 1978c; Immelmann, 1969; Klinghammer, 1967; Schutz, 1965). The sexual imprinting, as the learning processes involved are often termed, may occur rather later than filial imprinting.

There is evidence that the mate eventually chosen by male Japanese quail resembles, but differs to some extent from, the birds with which he was reared. Bateson (1978a) suggests that this is a mechanism conducive to optimal outbreeding—the bird mates with a member of its own species but not with a close relative. In harmony with this view, the period of maximal sensitivity for sexual imprinting comes just after the age at which the young gain their adult plumage but before the family disperses, that is, an age at which learning of the siblings' individual characters could be adequate to prevent mating with them in adulthood. Such findings are reminiscent of studies indicating that close familiarity in childhood mitigates against stable pair bonds in humans (e.g., Demarest, 1977; Shepher, 1971; Wolf, 1970) and raises the possibility that in some cultures where brother-sister marriages are or were frequent, the individuals concerned may yet be reared apart (see also Weinberg, 1976).

Studies of the Effects of Early Rearing Conditions on Behavioral Development in Monkeys

Monkeys of several species have been reared in total social isolation with various types of mother surrogate and with various combinations of mothers, other adults, adolescents, and peers. Their subsequent behavioral development has been compared with each others' and with that of wild-born individuals. The data have recently been reviewed by Sackett and Ruppenthal (1973) and Suomi & Harlow (1978a).

Not surprisingly, monkeys reared in social isolation show many subsequent abnormalities, including rocking and other stereotyped behavior, self-directed aggression, abnormally low levels of exploration, and excessive fear of novel objects. They also show abnormal and/or deficient self-grooming and social behavior, including play, and abnormal adult aggressive, sexual, and maternal behavior (e.g., Chamove, 1966; Harlow & Harlow, 1969; Mason & Berkson, 1975; Mitchell, Raymond, Ruppenthal, & Harlow, 1966; Suomi & Harlow, 1972). They may also give abnormal responses to painful stimuli and have abnormal metabolism (reviewed by Sackett & Ruppenthal, 1973). The effects are more marked in rhesus than in pigtail macaques (Sackett, Holm, & Ruppenthal, 1976). Although responsiveness to some expressive movements appears to be independent of experience (Sackett, 1966), there is also evidence that isolation produces deficiencies in social communication (Miller, Caul, & Mirsky, 1967).

Comparable deficiencies are found in rhesus monkeys reared under conditions of partial social isolation, that is, in bare wire cages and able to see and hear but not interact with other monkeys. Non-nutritional orality and externally and self-directed threat are especially affected. Such symptoms may persist into adulthood (Cross & Harlow, 1963; Griffin & Harlow, 1966) together with abnormalities in aggressive, sexual, and maternal behavior (e.g., Ruppenthal, Arling, Harlow, Sackett, & Suomi, 1976).

Such social deprivation at any point during infancy is likely to produce behavioral abnormalities later, but there is some evidence that the period of 3 to 9 months is of special importance—animals isolated for 3 months but then exposed to social situations, develop fairly normally (Griffin & Harlow, 1966; Mitchell et al., 1966), whereas 6 months' isolation produces more severe long-term consequences (Harlow & Harlow, 1969). However, rhesus monkeys reared by their mothers for their first 16 to 120 days of life and then separated permanently from them also showed many abnormalities in behavior; these were ameliorated in individuals kept with a peer after separation from the mother (Suomi et al., 1973).

Macaques reared by their mothers but without other social companions develop qualitatively normally (Alexander & Harlow, 1965; Jensen, Bobbitt, & Gordon, 1973; Meier, 1965; Spencer-Booth, 1969). However, such animals are usually hyperaggressive when subsequently exposed to peers and may show some abnormalities in social behavior throughout life. Aggressive behavior usually develops after infants have had a good deal of social experience in peer-peer play: in its absence, aggressive behavior develops abnormally.

In one study, the effects of giving mother-reared animals 2 hr. of daily contact with age mates was studied. Three groups were given such treatment from 15 days or 4 months of age and after separation from their mothers at 9 months. Both delayed groups were more aggressive toward peers than the 15-day group and, at 9 months, they were more aggressive to a neonate (Alexander, 1966). Impairment of social behavior persisted into adulthood (Ruppenthal et al., 1976), indicating that the mother alone does not provide a fully adequate social environment (see also Spencer-Booth, 1969).

Such a finding could be due to the fact that mothers behave differently to their infants when peers are not present than when they are. As reported earlier (*The Child, the Dyad, and the Group*), mothers of infants without peers tend to be more rejecting than if peers are present, although the effect of this on time on mother probably depends on cage conditions (see Alexander, 1966; Jensen & Bobbitt, 1967).

Infant rhesus monkeys reared without mothers but with peers show rather different abnormalities (Chamove, Rosenblum, & Harlow, 1973; Suomi & Harlow, 1975). Having no mother, they clasp each other and develop high levels of self-orality. Both clinging and sucking persist for longer than in mother-reared infants. Peers apparently provide a less adequate secure base than a mother, and such monkeys tend also to be unusually timid. But play, although appearing rather late, and aggression develop normally, and such animals show fairly normal social behavior in adulthood. The males, however, show some abnormalities in sexual behavior (Goy & Goldfoot, 1973) and the females are inadequate mothers (Ruppenthal et al., 1976).

The effects of inconsistent mothering have been studied by rotating infants between mothers every fortnight so that they had a new "mother" every two weeks. Such multiple-mothered infants showed more fear during infancy than controls, but they otherwise differed little (Griffin, 1966). However, later they were more violent and dominant.

An important recent finding from the University of Wisconsin (Madison) laboratory concerns the rehabilitation of socially deprived monkeys. Although isolation-reared monkeys when placed with socially reared age mates were overwhelmed by their playfulness and aggressiveness (Mitchell et al., 1966), Suomi and Harlow (1972) suggested that rehabilitation might come through exposure to younger socially reared animals who sought contact with the isolates in a nonthreatening manner. Such proved to be the case: 6-month-old isolates were paired with 3-month-old socially reared "therapists" for 10 hr. a week for 6 months. The isolates gradually lost their aberrant behavior patterns and subsequently developed near-normal social behavior. In a later study, Novak and Harlow (1975), using a similar procedure, achieved almost complete rehabilitation of 12-month-old isolates (see also Chamove, 1978; Erwin et al., 1974). These principles have been applied with success to the rehabilitation of socially withdrawn children (Furman, Rahe, & Hartup, 1979).

Finally, as an example of the subtleties of social behavior that may be influenced by early experience, Anderson and Mason's (1974) comparison of rhesus monkeys reared under conditions of social deprivation with monkeys reared by mothers and with age mates may be cited. The socially experienced animals interacted more often as trios and in larger subgroups, the response structure of the triadic subgroups was more complex, and the functional organization of triadic interactions suggested that each individual recognized the status relations of the other two.

Interdyad Differences in the Mother-Infant Relationship

Much of the work discussed so far has been concerned with rather gross differences in early relationships. If these produce long-term consequences, more subtle differences in quality of relationships may also be important. Of eight categories of dimensions considered likely to be useful in describing human interpersonal relationships (Hinde, 1979), five are clearly relevant to the monkey mother-infant relationship and four of these show clear interdyad differences:

1, 2. Content and diversity of interactions within the relationship. Most types of maternal-filial interaction are, of course, common to all dyads. However, some mother-infant dyads play a game involving the mother walking a little way from the infant and then waiting for it to come to her. Other dyads do not (Hinde & Simpson, 1975). Of course, dyads differ also in the frequency of some types of interaction, such as mother-infant grooming.

3. Quality of interactions. Quality, of course, is not easy to measure, but dyads with 8-week-old infants, for instance, show consistent differences in the frequency with which the mother accepts the infant's attempts to gain close contact by either putting her arm round it or by initiating such contact herself (Hinde & Spencer-Booth, 1971b; Simpson & Howe, 1980). Special interest attaches to measures of coordination or behavioral meshing between mother and infant. Although the mother-infant relationship grows more distant as the infant gets older, it also becomes better meshed (Hinde & White, 1974), and at any one age dyads show marked individual differences in meshing (Hinde & Simpson, 1975).

4. Relative frequency and patterning of interactions. Some properties of relationships depend not on one type of interaction but on the relations between interactions of several types. For instance, one would not assess a dyad as high on maternal warmth solely on the grounds that the mother often groomed her infant, but if she often also picked it up, was quick to put her arm round it when it came to her, and so on, one is more prone to do so.

In some cases properties depend on the direction and degree of correlations between measures of different sorts. For example, in rhesus monkeys, measures of maternal restrictiveness can vary independently of measures of maternal rejection (Simpson & Howe, 1980). Dyads high on both might be regarded as high on maternal control, and dyads low on both as high on maternal permissiveness (Hinde & Simpson, 1975). Dyads do, in fact, differ in this dimension reliably (Simpson & Hooley, 1980).

A final point is that not only absolute frequencies of interactions but also relative frequencies may be important. For example, the number of times a mother rejected her infant relative to the number of times the infant attempted to make contact might be more revealing of tension than the absolute number of rejections (Hinde & Hermann, 1977).

5. The final dimension concerns the reciprocity versus the complementarity of the interactions. A reciprocal interaction is one in which the two participants do the same thing, either simultaneously or in alternation, as when one child chases another and then the latter chases the erstwhile chaser. In a complementary interaction, each participant behaves in a way different from, but complementary to, the other. In mother-infant relationships virtually all interactions are complementary along nurturant/succorant or dominant/subordinate dimensions.

Bases of Interdyad Differences in the Mother-Infant Relationship

First, there is some evidence that the relationships of individual mothers with successive infants show some consistency. Howe and Simpson (personal communication) found that certain measures of the relative roles of mother and infant in the maintenance of proximity were more similar between successive infants of the same mother than between all the infants born in the same group.

Second, the mother's own rearing conditions are known to be important. Females reared without mothers or peers (motherless mothers) were themselves inadequate mothers, generally failing to nurse their infants and being either indifferent or actively abusive to them (Arling & Harlow, 1967). The maternal behavior of such females was improved by the presence of peers during rearing and by even brief exposure to their own first born. Thus, they often showed much improved maternal behavior with their second and later babies (Harlow, Harlow, Dodsworth, & Arling, 1966). Part of this improvement may have been due to opportunities to observe other females with their infants. Dienske, van Vreeswijk, and Koning (1980) have evidence that opportunity to observe another female with an infant is important in the development of adequate maternal behavior. Although early reports suggested that the infants of inadequate motherless mothers did surprisingly well (Seay, Alexander, & Harlow, 1964), later reports indicate long-term social defects, such as hyperaggressiveness (Arling & Harlow, 1967).

The two variables considered so far are fairly gross, and it is hardly surprising that they affect the mother-infant relationship. Data on more subtle influences are complex and indicate important interactional effects between the independent variables. For example, White and Hinde (1975) examined the influence of six independent variables on group-living rhesus mother-infant relationships: maternal parity, source of mother (born in or imported into the colony), number of infants previously borne in the colony, dominance status, sex of infant, and presence of peers for the infant. All variables appeared to affect the relationship except (surprisingly) maternal parity. However, none of the effective variables produced differences independent of the other variables operating or consistent over age of the infant. As an example of the complexities that arise, in another study the aggression received by the mother from other individuals (itself inversely correlated with the time she spent with the male) was positively correlated with maternal restraining of 8-week-old female infants and with maternal rejection of 8-week-old male infants (Howe & Simpson, personal communication). Maternal dominance status was negatively correlated with maternal restrictiveness in captive groups but positively in a free-living troop (Berman, 1978).

There are, as might be expected, differences between mother-infant relationships, depending on the sex of the infant, but these again are complex and vary with age. For example, White and Hinde (1975) found that male infants in the first few months were off their mothers less than female infants, but after about 8 months they were off more. Of special interest is an apparent effect of the sex of the infant on the interbirth interval. Colony-living rhesus mothers with sons are more likely to conceive within a year of their sons' birth than mothers who have borne daughters. This may be related to the greater activity of male infants because among mothers with daughters, those with the more active daughters were more likely to conceive early (Simpson et al., in preparation). In this context, it is interesting to note that in bonnet macaques, young females are attacked more by females from other lineages than are young males (Silk, Rodman, & Samuels, 1981).

Relation Between Characteristics of the Mother or Mother-Infant Relationship and Those of the Offspring

Data on the relation between characteristics of the mother or mother-infant relationship and those of the offspring are extremely scarce. However, some data are available from a study using observer ratings of individual characteristics on behaviorally defined items. Principal component analyses yielded three main dimensions: *confident* to *fearful, excitable* to *slow,* and *sociable* to *solitary*. These showed remarkable stability from year to year in adult females. *Confident* mothers tended to have *confident* 1-year-old daughters, *sociable* mothers had *sociable* daughters, and *excitable* mothers tended to have *excitable* daughters. The significant correlations for sons were rather different. Whereas *sociable* mothers tended to have *sociable* 1-year-old sons, *excitable* mothers tended to have sons who were *not confident* (Stevenson-Hinde et al., 1980).

Mother-infant interactions over the first year of life indicated how these mother-daughter and mother-son correlations might have developed. Confident mothers were relatively accepting of daughters at the age of weaning. Nonexcitable mothers spent much time in contact with very young sons, with little restricting and little coming and going at the age of weaning. The outcome, confident mothers producing confident daughters and excitable mothers producing not-confident sons, has parallels with the development of secure attachment in human infants (Stevenson-Hinde & Simpson, 1981).

In another study, infant vervet monkeys receiving the least amount of maternal care in the first 3 months were found to be more socially competent with their peers at 6 months (Johnson, Gilbert, & Herdt, 1979). Although the generality of any one finding must always be questioned, further work on the long-term consequences of interdyad differences in the mother-infant relationship should clearly have high priority.

Conclusion

To integrate the diverse themes touched on in this chapter is hardly a feasible goal. However, it will I hope be apparent that ethological methods, concepts, ways of analysis, and data have much to contribute to the study of child development. If one issue stands out, it is perhaps that a child's development cannot be understood without reference to the relationships in which the child is involved, both within and outside the family. There is nothing new in this, yet it seems to require emphasis. Although psychology has focused on the nature and development of behavior in the individual on the one hand and on the nature and dynamics of groups on the other, there seems to be no integrated body of knowledge about dyadic relationships. Two possible reasons for this lie in the absence of a descriptive base on which a science of interpersonal relationships could be based and in the multiplicity of explanatory concepts used in studies of interpersonal relationships (referring often to diverse levels of analysis), with a dearth of attempts to integrate them. A search for a descriptive base was hinted at earlier (*Relationships and Personality*). In the meanwhile, study of many aspects of child behavior could surely be facilitated were they seen in the naturalistic context of the nexus of interpersonal relationships in which the child is embedded.

NOTE

1. Because the full understanding of psychopathology requires understanding of the processes of development, some ethological contributions to child development are also of interest to psychiatry. The contents of this chapter overlap with those of the chapter, *Ethology and Psychiatry*, written simultaneously (Hinde, 1983).

REFERENCES

Abramovitch, R. Children's recognition of situational aspects of facial expression. *Child Development*, 1977, *48*, 459–463.

Abramovitch, R., & Daly, E. M. Children's use of head orientation and eye contact in making attributions of affiliation. *Child Development*, 1978, *49*, 519–522.

Ahrens, R. Beitrage zur Entwicklung des Physiognomie und Mimikerkennes. *Zeitschrift für experimentelle und angewandte Psychologie*, 1954, *2*, 402–454, 599–633.

Ainsworth, M. D. S. The effects of maternal deprivation: A review of findings and controversy in the context of research strategy. In *Deprivation of maternal care*. Geneva: World Health Organization, 1962.

Ainsworth, M. D. S. *Infancy in Uganda: Infant care and the growth of attachment*. Baltimore: The Johns Hopkins University Press, 1967.

Ainsworth, M. D. S. Object relations, dependency and attachment: A theoretical review of the infant-mother relationship. *Child Development*, 1969, *40*, 969–1025.

Ainsworth, M. D. S. Attachment and dependency: A comparison. In J. L. Gewirtz (Ed.), *Attachment and dependency*. Washington, D.C.: Wiley, 1972.

Ainsworth, M. D. S. Attachment as related to mother-infant interaction. *Advances in the Study of Behavior*, 1979, *9*, 2–52.

Ainsworth, M. D. S., Bell, S. M., & Stayton, D. J. Individual differences in strange situation behavior of one-year-olds. In H. R. Schaffer (Ed.), *The origins of human social relations*. New York: Academic Press, 1971.

Ainsworth, M. D. S., Blehar, M. C., Waters, E., & Wall, S. *Patterns of attachment*. Hillsdale, N.J.: Erlbaum, 1978.

Alexander, B. K. *The effects of early peer deprivation on juvenile behavior of rhesus monkeys*. Unpublished doctoral dissertation, University of Wisconsin, Madison, 1966.

Alexander, B. K., & Harlow, H. F. Social behavior of juvenile rhesus monkeys subjected to different rearing conditions during the first 6 months of life. *Zoologisches Jahrbuch Abteilung 3, Allgemeine Zoologie und Physiologie*, 1965, *71*, 489–508.

Altmann, J. Observational study of behavior: Sampling methods. *Behaviour*, 1974, *9*, 227–267.

Altmann, J. *Baboon mothers and infants*. Cambridge: Harvard University Press, 1980.

Amsel, A., & Stanton, M. The ontogeny and phylogeny of the paradoxical reward effects. *Advances in the Study of Behavior*, 1980, *11*, 227–275.

Anderson, C. O., Kenney, A., & Mason, W. A. Effects of maternal mobility, partner and endocrine state on adolescent rhesus monkeys. *Developmental Psychobiology*, 1977, *10*, 421–434.

Anderson, C. O., & Mason, W. A. Early experience and complexity of social organization in groups of young rhesus monkeys (*Macaca mulatta*). *Journal of Comparative Physiology and Psychology*, 1974, *87*, 681–690.

Anderson, F. J., & Willis, F. N. Glancing at others in preschool children in relation to dominance. *Psychological Record*, 1976, *26*, 467–472.

Arling, G. L., & Harlow, H. F. Effects of social deprivation on maternal behavior of rhesus monkeys. *Journal of Comparative Physiology and Psychology*, 1967, *64*, 371–377.

Baerends, G. P. Fortpflanzungsverhalten und Orientierung der Grabwespe (*Ammophila campestris*). *Jur. Tijdschr Ent.*, 1941, *84*, 68–275.

Baerends, G. P. An evaluation of the conflict hypothesis as an explanatory principle for the evolution of displays. In G. P. Baerends, C. Beer, & A. Manning (Eds.), *Function and evolution in behaviour*. Oxford: Clarendon, 1975.

Baerends, G. P. The functional organization of behaviour. *Animal Behaviour*, 1976, *24*, 726–738.

Bakeman, R., & Brown, J. V. Early interaction: Consequences for social and mental development at three years. *Child Development*, 1980, *51*, 437–447.

Barlow, G. W. Ethological units of behavior. In D. Ingle (Ed.), *Central nervous system and fish behavior*. Chicago: University of Chicago Press, 1968.

Barrett, P., & Bateson, P. P. G. The development of play in cats. *Behaviour,* 1978, *66,* 106–120.

Bateson, P. P. G. An effect of imprinting on the perceptual development of domestic chicks. *Nature,* 1964, *202,* 421–422. (a)

Bateson, P. P. G. Effect of similarity between rearing and testing conditions on chicks' following and avoidance responses. *Journal of Comparative Physiology and Psychology,* 1964, *57,* 100–103. (b)

Bateson, P. P. G. Rules and reciprocity in behavioural development. In P. P. G. Bateson & R. A. Hinde (Eds.), *Growing points in ethology*. Cambridge: At the University Press, 1976. (a)

Bateson, P. P. G. Specificity and the origins of behavior. *Advances in the Study of Behavior,* 1976, *6,* 1–20. (b)

Bateson, P. P. G. Early experience and sexual preferences. In J. B. Hutchison (Ed.), *Biological determinants of sexual behavior*. London: Wiley, 1978. (a)

Bateson, P. P. G. How does behavior develop? In P. P. G. Bateson & P. H. Klopfer (Eds.), *Perspectives in ethology*. New York: Plenum, 1978. (b)

Bateson, P. P. G. Sexual imprinting and optimal outbreeding. *Nature,* 1978, *273,* 659. (c)

Bateson, P. P. G. How do sensitive periods arise and what are they for? *Animal Behaviour,* 1979, *27,* 470–486.

Bateson, P. P. G., & Chantrey, D. F. Retardation of discrimination learning in monkeys and chicks previously exposed to both stimuli. *Nature,* 1972, *237,* 173–174.

Bateson, P. P. G., & Jaeckel, J. B. Chicks' preferences for familiar and novel conspicuous objects after different periods of exposure. *Animal Behaviour,* 1976, *24,* 386–390.

Bateson, P. P. G., & Reese, E. P. The reinforcing properties of conspicuous stimuli in the imprinting situation. *Animal Behaviour,* 1969, *17,* 692–699.

Beer, C. Some complexities in the communication behavior of gulls. *Annals of the New York Academy of Science,* 1976, *280,* 413–432.

Bell, R. Q. A reinterpretation of the direction of effects in studies of socialization. *Psychological Review,* 1968, *75,* 81–85.

Bell, R. Q. Contributions of human infants to caregiving and social interaction. In M. Lewis & L. A. Rosenblum (Eds.), *The effects of the infant on its caregiver*. New York: Wiley, 1974.

Berman, C. M. *Social relationships among free-ranging infant rhesus monkeys*. Unpublished doctoral dissertation, Cambridge University, 1978.

Bernal, J. Crying during the first 10 days of life, and maternal responses. *Developmental Medicine and Child Neurology,* 1972, *14,* 362–372.

Bernal, J. Attachment: Some problems and possibilities. In M. P. M. Richards (Ed.), *The integration of the child into the social world*. Cambridge: At the University Press, 1974.

Bertalanffy, L. von. *General systems theory*. New York: George Braziller, 1968.

Bierens de Haan, J. A. Animal psychology and the science of animal behaviour. *Behaviour,* 1947, *1,* 71–80.

Birdwhistell, R. L. The kinesis level in the investigation of the emotions. In P. H. Knapp (Ed.), *Expressions of the emotions in man*. New York: International Universities Press, 1963.

Birdwhistell, R. L. Communication without words. In P. Alexandre (Ed.), *L'aventure humaine*. Paris: Société d'Etudes Litteraires et Art, 1967.

Bischof, N. A systems approach towards the functional connections of attachment and fear. *Child Development,* 1975, *46,* 801–817.

Blauvelt, H. Neonate-mother relationship in goat and man. In B. Schaffner (Ed.), *Group processes. Transactions of the 2nd Conference*. New York: Josiah Macy, Jr., 1956.

Blest, A. D. The concept of ritualization. In W. H. Thorpe & O. L. Zangwill (Eds.), *Current problems in animal behaviour*. Cambridge: At the University Press, 1961.

Block, J. Advancing the psychology of personality: Paradigmatic shift or improving the quality of research. In D. Magnusson & N. S. Endler (Eds.), *Personality at the crossroads*. New York: Wiley, 1977.

Bloomfield, L. *Language*. New York: Holt, Rinehart & Winston, 1933.

Blurton Jones, N. G. Characteristics of ethological studies of human behaviour. In N. G. Blurton Jones (Ed.), *Ethological studies of child behaviour*. Cambridge: At the University Press, 1972. (a)

Blurton Jones, N. G. Comparative aspects of mother-child contact. In N. G. Blurton Jones (Ed.). *Ethological studies of child behaviour*. Cambridge: At the University Press, 1972. (b)

Blurton Jones, N. G. (Ed.) *Ethological studies of child behaviour*. Cambridge: At the University Press, 1972. (c)

Blurton Jones, N. G. Ethology and early socialization. In M. P. M. Richards (Ed.), *The integration of a child into a social world*. Cambridge: At the University Press, 1974.

Blurton Jones, N. G. Growing points in human ethology: Another link between ethology and the social sciences? In P. P. G. Bateson & R. A. Hinde (Eds.), *Growing points in ethology*. Cambridge: At the University Press, 1976.

Blurton Jones, N. G., & Leach, G. M. Behaviour of children and their mothers at separation and greeting. In N. G. Blurton Jones (Ed.), *Ethological studies of child behaviour*. Cambridge: At the University Press, 1972.

Bowlby, J. *Maternal care and mental health*. London: HMSO, 1951.

Bowlby, J. The nature of the child's tie to his mother. *International Journal of Psycho-Analysis*, 1958, *39*, 350–373.

Bowlby, J. *Attachment and loss*, vol. 1, *Attachment*. London: Hogarth Press, 1969.

Bowlby, J. *Attachment and loss*, vol. 2, *Separation*. London: Hogarth Press, 1973.

Bowlby, J. *Attachment and loss*, vol. 3, *Loss*. London: Hogarth Press, 1980.

Brandt, E. M., Baysinger, C., & Mitchell, G. D. Separation from rearing environment in mother-reared and isolation-reared rhesus monkeys. *International Journal of Psychobiology*, 1972, *2*, 193–204.

Brannigan, C. R., & Humphries, D. A. Human nonverbal behaviour, a means of communication. In N. G. Blurton Jones (Ed.), *Ethological studies of child behaviour*. Cambridge: At the University Press, 1972.

Brazelton, T. B., & Freedman, D. G. The Cambridge neonatal scales. In J. J. van der Werff ten Bosch (Ed.), *Normal and abnormal development of brain and behavior*. Leiden: Leiden University Press, 1971.

Brazelton, T. B., Tronick, E., Adamson, L., Als, H., & Weise, S. Early mother-infant reciprocity. In *Parent-infant interaction* (CiBa Foundation Symposium No. 33). Amsterdam: Elsevier, 1975.

Brehm, J. W. Responses to loss of freedom: A theory of psychological reactance. In J. W. Thibaut, J. T. Spence, & R. C. Carson (Eds.), *Contemporary topics in social psychology*. Morristown, N.J.: General Learning Press, 1976.

Bretherton, I. Young children in stressful situations. In G. V. Coehlo & P. Ahmed (Eds.), *Uprooting*. New York: Plenum, 1980.

Bronson, G. Aversive reactions to strangers: A dual process interpretation. *Child Development*, 1978, *49*, 495–499.

Bruner, J. S., & Tagiuri, R. The perception of people. In G. Lindzey (Ed.), *Handbook of social psychology*. Cambridge, Mass.: Addison-Wesley, 1954.

Bush, R. R., & Mosteller, F. *Stochastic models for learning*. New York: Wiley, 1955.

Cairns, R. B. Attachment behavior of mammals. *Psychological Review*, 1966, *73*, 409–426.

Cairns, R. B. Attachment and dependency: A psycho-biological and social-learning synthesis. In J. L. Gewirtz (Ed.), *Attachment and dependency*. New York: Winston, 1972.

Cairns, R. B. *Social development: The origins and plasticity of interchanges*. San Francisco: W. H. Freeman, 1979.

Campos, J. J., & Sternberg, C. R. Perception, appraisal and emotion. In M. E. Lamb & L. Sherrod (Eds.), *Infant social cognition*. Hillsdale, N.J.: Erlbaum, 1981.

Camras, L. A. Facial expressions used by children in a conflict situation. *Child Development*, 1977, *48*, 1431–1435.

Candland, D. K., & Mason, W. A. Infant monkey heartrate: Habituation and effects of social substitutes. *Developmental Psychobiology*, 1968, *1*, 254–256.

Castell, R., & Wilson, C. Influence of environment on development of mother-infant interaction in pigtail monkeys. *Proceedings 3rd International Congress of Primatology*, 1971, *3*, 121–124.

Chalmers, N. Comments on Rajecki, Lamb, & Obmascher. *Behavioral and Brain Sciences*, 1978, *3*, 441–442.

Chamove, A. S. *The effects of varying peer experience on social behavior in the rhesus monkey*. Unpublished doctoral dissertation, University of Wisconsin, Madison, 1966.

Chamove, A. S. Therapy of isolate rhesus: Different partners and social behavior. *Child Development*, 1978, *49*, 43–50.

Chamove, A. S., Rosenblum, L. A., & Harlow, H. F. Monkeys (*Macaca mulatta*) raised only with peers. A pilot study. *Animal Behaviour*, 1973, *21*, 316–325.

Chance, M. R. A., & Jones, E. A protracted startle response to maternal rejection in infants of *Macaca fascicularis*. *Folia Primatologica*, 1974, *22*, 218–236.

Chantrey, D. F. Enhancement and retardation of discrimination learning in chicks after exposure to the discriminanda. *Journal of Comparative Physiology and Psychology*, 1972, *81*, 256–261.

Chantrey, D. F. The behaviour of domestic chicks during exposure to two stimuli. *Animal Behaviour,* 1976, *24,* 780–785.

Chappell, P. F., & Meier, G. W. Modification of the response to separation in the infant. *Biological Psychiatry,* 1975, *10,* 643–657.

Cheyne, J. A. Development of forms and functions of smiling in preschoolers. *Child Development,* 1976, *47,* 820–823.

Clark, A. H., Wyon, S. M., & Richards, M. P. M. Free play in nursery school children. *Journal of Child Psychology and Psychiatry,* 1969, *10,* 205–216.

Clarke, A. M., & Clarke, A. D. B. *Early experience: Myth and evidence.* London: Open Books, 1976.

Clarke-Stewart, K. A. Interactions between mothers and their young children: Characteristics and consequences. *Monographs of the Society for Research in Child Development,* 1973, *38*(6–7, Serial No. 153).

Coates, B., Anderson, E., & Hartup, W. W. The stability of attachment behaviors of human infants. *Developmental Psychology,* 1972, *6,* 218–230.

Coss, R. G. Perceptual determinants of gaze aversion by normal and psychotic children: The role of two facing eyes. *Behaviour,* 1979, *69,* 228–254.

Cross, H. A., & Harlow, H. F. Prolonged and progressive effects of partial isolation on the behavior of macaque monkeys. *Journal of Experimental Research on Personality,* 1963, *1,* 39–49.

Darwin, C. *The expression of the emotions in man and the animals.* London: John Murray, 1872.

Dawkins, R. Hierarchical organization: A candidate principle for ethology. In P. P. G. Bateson & R. A. Hinde (Eds.), *Growing points in ethology.* Cambridge: At the University Press, 1976.

Dawkins, R., & Krebs, J. R. Animal signals: Information or manipulation. In J. R. Krebs, & N. B. Davies (Eds.), *Behavioural ecology.* Oxford: Blackwell, 1978.

Demarest, W. J. Incest avoidance among human and non-human primates. In S. Chevalier-Skolnikoff & F. E. Priorier (Eds.), *Primate biosocial development.* New York: Garland, 1977.

Denenberg, V. H. Experimental programming of life histories and the creation of individual differences. In M. R. Jones (Ed.), *Effects of early experience.* Coral Gables, Fla.: University of Miami Press, 1970.

Denenberg, V. H. Paradigms and paradoxes in the study of behavioral development. In E. B. Thoman (Ed.), *Origins of the infant's social responsiveness.* Hillsdale, N.J.: Erlbaum, 1979.

Dewsbury, D. A. What is (was?) the "fixed action pattern?" *Animal Behaviour,* 1978, *26,* 310–311.

Dienske, H., Vreeswijk, W. van, & Koning, H. Adequate mothering by partially isolated rhesus monkeys after observation of maternal care. *Journal of Abnormal Psychology,* 1980, *89,* 489–492.

Dolhinow, J. Comments on Rajecki, Lamb, & Obmascher, 1978. *Behavioral and Brain Sciences,* 1978, *3,* 442–443.

Dolhinow, P., McKenna, J. J., & Laws, J. V. H. Rank and reproduction among female langur monkeys. *Aggressive Behaviour,* 1979, *5,* 19–30.

Douglas, J. W. B. Early hospital admissions and later disturbances of behaviour and learning. *Developmental Medicine and Child Neurology,* 1975, *17,* 456–480.

Douglas, J. W. B., & Bloomfield, J. M. *Children under five.* London: Allen & Unwin, 1958.

Dunbar, R. I. M. Some aspects of research design and their implications in the observational study of behaviour. *Behaviour,* 1976, *58,* 78–98.

Dunn, J. How far do early differences in mother-child relations affect later development? In P. P. G. Bateson & R. A. Hinde (Eds.), *Growing points in ethology.* Cambridge: At the University Press, 1976.

Dunn, J. Patterns of early interaction: Continuities and consequences. In H. R. Schaffer (Ed.), *Studies in mother-infant interaction.* London: Academic Press, 1977.

Dunn, J. Understanding human development: Limitations and possibilities in an ethological approach. In M. von Cranach, K. Foppa, W. Lepenies, & D. Ploog (Eds.), *Human ethology: Claims and limits of a new discipline.* Cambridge: At the University Press, 1979.

Dunn, J., & Kendrick, C. The arrival of a sibling: Changes in patterns of interaction between mother and first born child. *Journal of Child Psychology and Psychiatry,* 1980, *21,* 119–132. (a)

Dunn, J., & Kendrick, C. Studying temperament and parent-child interaction: Comparison of interview and direct observation. *Developmental Medicine and Child Neurology,* 1980, *22,* 484–496. (b)

Dunn, J., & Kendrick, C. *Siblings: Love, envy and understanding.* Cambridge: Harvard University Press, 1982.

Eibl Eibesfeldt, I. Similarities and differences between cultures in expressive movements. In R. A. Hinde (Ed.), *Non-verbal communication*. Cambridge: At the University Press, 1972.

Ekman, P. Cross-cultural studies of facial expression. In P. Ekman (Ed.), *Darwin and facial expression*. New York: Academic Press, 1973.

Ekman, P., & Friesen, W. V. The repertoire of nonverbal behavior: Categories, origins, usage and coding. *Semiotica*, 1969, *1*, 49–98.

Ekman, P., & Friesen, W. V. *Unmasking the face*. Englewood Cliffs, N.J.: Prentice-Hall, 1975.

Engel, G. L. Anxiety and depression-withdrawal: The primary affects of unpleasure. *International Journal of Psychoanalysis*, 1962, *43*, 89.

Eron, L. D., Huesmann, L. R., Lefkowitz, M. M., & Walder, L. O. Does television violence cause aggression? *American Psychologist*, 1972, *27*, 253–263.

Erwin, J., Maple, T., Mitchell, G., & Willott, J. Follow-up study of isolation-reared and mother-reared rhesus monkeys paired with preadolescent conspecifices in late infancy: Cross-sex pairings. *Developmental Psychology*, 1974, *10*, 808–814.

Fabricius, E., & Boyd, M. Experiments on the following reactions of ducklings. *Wildfowl Trust Annual Report*, 1954, *1952–1953*, 84–89.

Fentress, J. Dynamic boundaries of patterned behavior: Interaction and self-organization. In P. P. G. Bateson & R. A. Hinde (Eds.), *Growing points in ethology*. Cambridge: At the University Press, 1976.

Feshbach, S. The function of aggression and the regulation of aggressive drive. *Psychological Review*, 1964, *71*, 257–272.

Feshbach, S. Aggression. In P. H. Mussen (Ed.), *Carmichael's manual of child psychology* (Vol. 2). New York: Wiley, 1970.

Fogel, A. Temporal organization in mother-infant face-to-face interaction. In H. R. Schaffer (Ed.), *Studies in mother-infant interaction*. London: Academic Press, 1977.

Freedman, D. G. Smiling in blind infants and the issue of innate vs. acquired. *Journal of Child Psychology and Psychiatry*, 1964, *5*, 171–184.

Fullard, W., & Reiling, A. M. An investigation of Lorenz's "babyishness." *Child Development*, 1976, *7*, 1191–1193.

Furman, W., Rahe, D. F., & Hartup, W. W. Rehabilitation of socially withdrawn preschool children through mixed-age and same-age socialization. *Child Development*, 1979, *50*, 915–922.

Gardner, B. T., & Wallach, L. Shapes of figures identified as a baby's head. *Perceptual and Motor Skills*, 1965, *20*, 135–142.

Gartlan, J. S. Structure and function in primate society. *Folia Primatologica*, 1968, *8*, 89–120.

Gewirtz, J. L. A learning analysis of the effects of normal stimulation, privation and deprivation on the acquisition of social motivation and attachment. In B. M. Foss (Ed.), *Determinants of infant behaviour* (Vol. 1). London: Methuen, 1961.

Gewirtz, J. L. Attachment, dependence, and a distinction in terms of stimulus control. In J. L. Gewirtz (Ed.), *Attachment and dependency*. Washington, D.C.: V. H. Winston, 1972.

Gewirtz, J. L. The attachment acquisition process as evidenced in the maternal conditioning of cued infant responding (particularly crying). *Human Development*, 1976, *19*, 143–155.

Gibson, E. J., Walk, R. D., Pick, H. L., & Tighe, T. J. The effect of prolonged exposure to visual patterns on learning to discriminate similar and different patterns. *Journal of Comparative Physiology and Psychology*, 1958, *51*, 584–587.

Ginsburg, H. J., Pollman, V. A., & Wauson, M. S. An ethological analysis of non-verbal inhibitors of aggressive behavior in male elementary school children. *Developmental Psychology*, 1977, *13*, 417–418.

Golani, I. Homeostatic motor processes in mammalian interactions: A choreography of display. In P. P. G. Bateson & P. H. Klopfer (Eds.), *Perspectives in ethology* (Vol. 2). New York: Plenum, 1976.

Gottlieb, G. Developmental age as a baseline for determination of the critical period in imprinting. *Journal of Comparative Physiology and Psychology*, 1961, *54*, 422–427.

Gottlieb, G. The roles of experience in the development of behavior and the nervous system. In G. Gottlieb (Ed.), *Studies on the development of behavior and the nervous system* (Vol. 3). New York: Academic Press, 1976.

Goy, R. W., & Goldfoot, D. A. Experiential and hormonal factors influencing development of sexual behavior in the male rhesus monkey. In F. O. Schmitt & F. G. Worden (Eds.), *The neurosciences: Third study program*. Cambridge: MIT Press, 1973.

Grant, E. C. Human facial expression. *Man*, 1969, *4*, 525–536.

Griffin, G. A. *The effects of multiple mothering on the infant-mother and infant-infant affectional systems*. Unpublished doctoral dissertation, University of Wisconsin, Madison, 1966.

Griffin, G. A., & Harlow, H. F. Effects of three months of total social deprivation on social adjustment and learning in the rhesus monkey. *Child Development,* 1966, *37,* 534–547.

Grossman, K., & Grossmann, K. Parent-infant attachment relationships in Bielefeld: A research note. In G. W. Barlow, K. Immelmann, M. Main, & L. Petrinovich (Eds.), *Behavioural ontogeny*. Cambridge: At the University Press, 1982.

Gubernick, D. J., Corbeau Jones, K., & Klopfer, P. H. Maternal "imprinting" in goats? *Animal Behaviour,* 1979, *27,* 314–315.

Guiton, P. Socialization and imprinting in brown leghorn chicks. *Animal Behaviour,* 1959, *7,* 26–34.

Guiton, P. The influence of imprinting on the agonistic and courtship responses of the brown leghorn cock. *Animal Behaviour,* 1961, *9,* 167–177.

Gunther, M. Instinct and the nursing couple. *Lancet,* 1955, 575–578.

Guttstein, J. *An ethological study of social interactions among children*. Unpublished master's thesis, University of Wisconsin, Madison, 1975.

Hales, D. J., Lozoff, B., Sosa, R., & Kennel, J. H. Defining the limits of the maternal sensitive period. *Developmental Medicine and Child Neurology,* 1977, *19,* 454–461.

Hamilton, W. D. The genetical theory of social behaviour. *Journal of Theoretical Biology,* 1964, *7,* 1–52.

Hansen, E. W. The development of maternal and infant behavior in the rhesus monkey. *Behaviour,* 1966, *27,* 107–149.

Harlow, H. F., & Harlow, M. K. The affectional systems. In A. M. Schrier, H. F. Harlow, & F. Stollnitz (Eds.), *Behavior of non-human primates*. New York: Academic Press, 1965.

Harlow, H. F., & Harlow, M. K. Effects of various mother-infant relationships on rhesus monkey behaviors. In B. M. Foss (Ed.), *Determinants of infant behaviour* (Vol. 4). London: Methuen, 1969.

Harlow, H. F., Harlow, M. K., Dodsworth, R. O., & Arling, G. L. Maternal behavior or rhesus monkeys deprived of mothering and peer associations in infancy. *Proceedings of the American Philosophical Society,* 1966, *110,* 58–66.

Harlow, H. F., & Zimmermann, R. R. Affectional responses in the infant monkey. *Science,* 1959, *130,* 421–432.

Harper, L. V. Ontogenetic and phylogenetic functions of the parent-offspring relationship in mammals. *Advances in the Study of Behavior,* 1970, *3,* 75–119.

Harré, R., Secord, P. F. *The explanation of social behaviour*. Oxford: Oxford University Press, 1972.

Heinicke, C., & Westheimer, I. *Brief separations*. London: Longman's Green, 1966.

Heinroth, O. Beiträge zur Biologie, namentlich Ethologie und Psychologie der Anatiden. *5th International Ornithologiches Kongress,* 1911, 589–702.

Hershkowitz, M., & Samuel, D. The retention of learning during metamorphosis of the crested newt (*Triturus cristatus*). *Animal Behaviour,* 1973, *21,* 83–85.

Hess, E. H. Imprinting. *Science,* 1959, *130,* 133–141.

Hess, E. H. Ethology and developmental psychology. In P. H. Mussen (Ed.), *Carmichael's manual of child psychology* (vol. 1). New York: Wiley, 1970.

Hinde, R. A. Appetitive behaviour, consummatory act, and the hierarchical organization of behaviour—with special reference to the great tit (*Parus major*). *Behaviour,* 1953, *5,* 189–224.

Hinde, R. A. The nest-building behaviour of domesticated canaries. *Proceedings of the Zoological Society of London,* 1958, *131,* 1–48.

Hinde, R. A. Behaviour and speciation in birds and lower vertebrates. *Biological Review,* 1959, *34,* 85–128.

Hinde, R. A. The establishment of the parent-offspring relation in birds, with some mammalian analogies. In W. H. Thorpe & O. L. Zangwill (Eds.), *Current problems in animal behaviour*. Cambridge: At the University Press, 1961.

Hinde, R. A. Analyzing the roles of the partners in a behavioral interaction—mother-infant relations in rhesus macaques. *Annals of the New York Academy of Science,* 1969, *159,* 651–667.

Hinde, R. A. *Animal behavior: A synthesis of ethology and comparative psychology*. New York: McGraw-Hill, 1970.

Hinde, R. A. On the design of check-sheets. *Primates,* 1973, *14,* 393–406.

Hinde, R. A. *The biological bases of human social behavior*. New York: McGraw-Hill, 1974.

Hinde, R. A. The concept of function. In G. P. Baerends, C. Beer, & A. Manning (Eds.), *Function and evolution in behaviour*. Oxford: Clarendon, 1975.

Hinde, R. A. Interactions, relationships and social structure. *Man,* 1976, *11,* 1–17. (a)

Hinde, R. A. The uses of differences and similarities in comparative psychopathology. In G. Serban & A. Kling (Eds.), *Animal models in human psy-*

chopathology. New York: Plenum, 1976. (b)

Hinde, R. A. Assessing the bases of partner preferences. *Behaviour,* 1977, *62,* 1–9.

Hinde, R. A. Dominance and role-two concepts with dual meanings. *Journal of Social and Biological Structures,* 1978, *1,* 27–38.

Hinde, R. A. *Towards understanding relationships*. London: Academic Press, 1979.

Hinde, R. A. *Ethology*. London: Fontana; New York: Oxford University Press, 1982. (a)

Hinde, R. A. Attachment: Some conceptual and biological issues. In C. Parkes & J. Stevenson-Hinde (Eds.), *The place of attachment in human behavior*. New York: Basic Books, 1982. (b)

Hinde, R. A. Ethology and psychiatry. In M. Shepherd (Ed.), *The scientific foundations of psychiatry*. Cambridge: At the University Press, 1983.

Hinde, R. A., Easton, D. F., & Meller, R. E. Teacher questionnaire compared with observational data on effects of sex and sibling status on preschool behaviour. *Journal of Child Psychology and Psychiatry,* in press.

Hinde, R. A., & Herrmann, J. Frequencies, durations, derived measures and their correlations in studying dyadic and triadic relationships. In H. R. Schaffer (Ed.), *Studies in mother-infant interaction*. London: Academic Press, 1977.

Hinde, R. A., Leighton-Shapiro, M., & McGinnis, L. Effects of various types of separation experiences on rhesus monkeys 5 months later. *Journal of Child Psychology and Psychiatry,* 1978, *19,* 199–211.

Hinde, R. A., & McGinnis, L. Some factors influencing the effects of temporary mother-infant separation—some experiments with rhesus monkeys. *Psychological Medicine,* 1977, *7,* 197–212.

Hinde, R. A., Rowell, T. E., & Spencer-Booth, Y. Behaviour of socially living rhesus monkeys in their first six months. *Proceedings of the Zoological Society of London,* 1964, *143,* 609–649.

Hinde, R. A., & Simpson, M. J. A. Qualities of mother-infant relationships in monkeys. In *Parent-infant interaction*. (CiBa Foundation Symposium No. 33). Amsterdam: Elsevier, 1975.

Hinde, R. A., & Spencer-Booth, Y. The effect of social companions on mother-infant relations in rhesus monkeys. In D. Morris (Ed.), *Primate ethology*. London: Weidenfeld and Nicolson, 1967.

Hinde, R. A., & Spencer-Booth, Y. Effects of brief separation from mother on rhesus monkeys. *Science,* 1971, *173,* 111–118. (a)

Hinde, R. A., & Spencer-Booth, Y. Towards understanding individual differences in rhesus mother-infant interaction. *Animal Behaviour,* 1971, *173,* 165–173. (b)

Hinde, R. A., Spencer-Booth, Y., & Bruce, M. Effects of 6-day maternal deprivation on rhesus monkey infants. *Nature,* 1966, *210,* 1021–1023.

Hinde, R. A., & Stevenson-Hinde, J. *Constraints on learning: Limitations and predispositions*. London: Academic Press, 1973.

Hinde, R. A., Thorpe, W. H., & Vince, M. A. The following response of young coots and moorhens. *Behaviour,* 1956, *9,* 214–242.

Hinde, R. A., & White, L. The dynamics of a relationship—rhesus monkey ventro-ventral contact. *Journal of Comparative Physiology and Psychology,* 1974, *86,* 8–23.

Hoffman, H. S. Comments on Rajecki, Lamb, & Obmascher. *Behavioral and Brain Sciences,* 1978, *3,* 441–442.

Hoffman, H. S., & De Paulo, P. Behavioral control by an imprinting stimulus. *American Scientist,* 1977, *65,* 58–66.

Hoffman, H. S., & Ratner, A. M. A reinforcement model of imprinting: Implications for socialization in monkeys and men. *Psychological Review,* 1973, *80,* 527–544.

Hoffman, H. S., Ratner, A. M., & Eiserer, L. A. Role of visual imprinting in the emergence of specific filial attachments in ducklings. *Journal of Comparative Physiology and Psychology,* 1972, *3,* 399–409.

Hoffman, H. S., & Solomon, R. L. An opponent process theory of motivation: III. Some affective dynamics in imprinting. *Learning and Motivation,* 1974, *5,* 149–164.

Hold, B. Attention structures and rank-specific behavior in pre-school children. In M. R. A. Chance & R. Larsen (Eds.), *The social structure of attention*. New York: Wiley, 1976.

Hong, K. M., & Townes, B. D. Infants' attachment to inanimate objects: A cross-cultural study. *Journal of the American Academy of Child Psychiatry,* 1976, *15,* 49–61.

van Hooff, J. A. R. A. M. A comparative approach to the phylogeny of laughter and smiling. In R. A. Hinde (Ed.), *Non-verbal communication*. Cambridge: At the University Press, 1972.

Hopkins, J. R., Zelazo, P. R., Jacobson, S. W., & Kagan, J. Infant reactivity to stimulus schema discrepancy. *Genetic Psychology Monographs,* 1976, *93,* 27–62.

Howe, S., & Simpson, M. J. A. Personal communication, 1982.

Hutt, C., & Ounstead, C. The biological significance of gaze aversion with particular references to the syndrome of childhood autism. *Behavioral Science,* 1966, *11,* 346–356.

Hutt, S. J. Constraints upon learning: Some developmental considerations. In R. A. Hinde & J. Stevenson-Hinde (Eds.), *Constraints on learning.* London: Academic Press, 1973.

Hutt, S. J., & Hutt, C. *Direct observation and measurement of behavior.* Springfield, Ill.: Charles C. Thomas, 1970.

Immelmann, K. Song development in the zebra finch and other estrildid finches. In R. A. Hinde (Ed.), *Bird vocalizations.* Cambridge: At the University Press, 1969.

Ingram, J. C. Interactions between parents and infants, and the development of independence in the common marmoset (*Callithrax jacchus*). *Animal Behaviour,* 1977, *25,* 811–827.

Jackson, D. D. Family interaction, family homeostasis and some implications for conjoint family psychotherapy. In J. H. Masserman (Ed.), *Individual and familial dynamics.* New York: Grune & Stratton, 1959.

Jancovic, M., Devoe, S., & Wiener, M. Age-related changes in hand and arm movements as nonverbal communication: Some conceptualizations and an empirical explanation. *Child Development,* 1975, *46,* 922–928.

Jay, P. C. Aspects of maternal behavior among langurs. *Annals of the New York Academy of Science,* 1962, *102,* 468–476.

Jensen, G. D., & Bobbitt, R. A. Implications of primate research for understanding infant development. In J. Hellmuth (Ed.), *The exceptional infant* (Vol. 1). Seattle: Special Child Publications, 1967.

Jensen, G. D., Bobbitt, R. A., & Gordon, B. N. Mothers' and infants' roles in the development of independence of *Macaca nemestrina. Primates,* 1973, *14,* 79–88.

Jensen, G. D., & Tolman, C. W. Mother-infant relationship in the monkey *Macaca nemestrina:* The effect of brief separation and mother-infant specificity. *Journal of Comparative Physiology and Psychology,* 1962, *55,* 131–136.

Johnson, C. K., Gilbert, M. D., & Herdt, G. H. Implications for adult roles from differential styles of mother-infant bonding. *Journal of Nervous and Mental Disease,* 1979, *167,* 29–37.

Jones, B. C., & Clark, D. L. Mother-infant separation in squirrel monkeys living in a group. *Developmental Psychobiology,* 1973, *6,* 259–269.

Kagan, J. *Change and continuity in infancy.* New York: Wiley, 1971.

Kagan, J. Continuity and stage in human development. In P. P. G. Bateson & P. H. Klopfer (Eds.), *Perspectives in ethology* (Vol. 3). New York: Plenum, 1978.

Kaplan, J. The effects of separation and reunion on the behavior of mother and infant squirrel monkeys. *Developmental Psychobiology,* 1970, *3,* 43–52.

Kaplan, J. Differences in the mother-infant relations of squirrel monkeys housed in social and restricted environments. *Developmental Psychobiology,* 1972, *5,* 43–52.

Kaufman, I. C. Mother-infant separation in monkeys: An experimental model. In J. P. Scott & E. Senay (Eds.), *Separation and depression: Clinical and research aspects* (Reference No. 94). Washington, D.C.: American Association for the Advancement of Science, 1973.

Kaufman, I. C., & Rosenblum, L. A. The reaction to separation in infant monkeys: Anaclitic depression and conservation-withdrawal. *Psychosomatic Medicine,* 1967, *29,* 648–675.

Kaufman, I. C., & Rosenblum, L. A. Effects of separation from mother on the emotional behavior of infant monkeys. *Annals of the New York Academy of Science,* 1969, *159,* 681–695.

Kaufman, I. C., & Stynes, A. J. Depression can be induced in a bonnet macaque infant. *Psychosomatic Medicine,* 1978, *40,* 71–75.

Kawai, M. On the system of social ranks in a neutral group of Japanese monkeys. *Primates,* 1958, *1,* 111–148.

Kawamura, S. Matriarchal social ranks in the Minoo-B troop: A study of the rank system of Japanese monkeys. *Primates,* 1958, *2,* 181–252.

Kear, J. Food selection in finches with special reference to interspecific differences. *Proceedings of the Zoological Society of London,* 1962, *138,* 163–204.

Kennell, J. H., Trause, M. A., & Klaus, M. Does human maternal behaviour after delivery show a characteristic pattern? In *Parent infant interaction* (CiBa Foundation Symposium No. 33). Amsterdam: Elsevier, 1975.

Kenny, D. A. Cross-lagged panel correlation: a test for spuriousness. *Psychological Bulletin,* 1975, *82,* 887–903.

Kenney, M. D., Mason, W. A., & Hill, S. D. Effects of age, objects and visual experience on affective responses of rhesus monkeys to strangers. *Developmental Psychology,* 1979, *15,* 176–184.

Klinghammer, E., Factors influencing choice of

mate in altricial birds. In H. W. Stevenson, E. H. Hess, & H. L. Rheingold (Eds.), *Early behavior*. New York: Wiley, 1967.

Klopfer, P. H., & Klopfer, M. S. Maternal "imprinting" in goats: Fostering of alien young. *Zeitschrift für Tierpsychologie*, 1968, *25*, 862–866.

Konner, M. J. Aspects of the developmental ethology of a foraging people. In N. G. Blurton Jones (Ed.), *Ethological studies of child behaviour*. Cambridge: At the University Press, 1972.

Kortlandt, A. Aspects and prospects of the concept of instinct. *Archives Neérlandisches Zoologie*, 1955, *11*, 155–284.

Kovach, J. K. Comments on Rajecki, Lamb, Obmascher. *Behavioral and Brain Sciences*, 1978, *3*, 451–452.

Kraemer, G. W., & McKinney, W. T. Interactions of pharmacological agents which alter biogenic amine metabolism and depression. *Journal of Affective Disorders*, 1979, *1*, 33–54.

Kraemer, H. C. One-zero sampling in the study of primate behavior. *Primates*, 1979, *20*, 237–244.

Kruijt, J. P. Ontogeny of social behaviour in Burmese red junglefowl (*Gallus gallus spadiceus* Bonnaterre). *Behaviour Suppl. No. 12.*, 1964.

La Barre, W. The cultural basis of emotions and gestures. *Journal of Personality*, 1947, *16*, 49–68.

Lamb, M. E. Proximity seeking attachment behaviors: A critical review of the literature. *Genetic Psychology Monographs*, 1976, *93*, 63–89. (a)

Lamb, M. E. The role of the father: An overview. In M. E. Lamb (Ed.), *The role of the father in child development*. New York: Wiley, 1976. (b)

Lamb, M. E. Father-infant and mother-infant interaction in the first year of life. *Child Development*, 1977, *48*, 167–181.

Landsberg, J. W. Posthatch age and developmental age as a baseline for determination of the sensitive period for imprinting. *Journal of Comparative Physiology and Psychology*, 1976, *90*, 47–52.

Lawick-Goodall, J. van. Behaviour of free-living chimpanzees of the Gombe Stream area. *Animal Behaviour Monographs*, 1968, *3*.

Leach, E. The influence of cultural context on non-verbal communication in man. In R. A. Hinde (Ed.), *Non-verbal communication*. Cambridge: At the University Press, 1972.

Lehrman, D. S. A critique of Konrad Lorenz's theory of instinctive behavior. *Quarterly Review of Biology*, 1953, *28*, 337–363.

Lehrman, D. S. Semantic and conceptual issues in the nature-nurture problem. In E. R. Aronson, E. Tobach, D. S. Lehrman, & J. S. Rosenblatt (Eds.), *Development and evolution of behavior*. San Francisco: W. H. Freeman, 1970.

Lehrman, D. S. Can psychiatrists use ethology? In N. F. White (Ed.), *Ethology and psychiatry*. Toronto: University of Toronto Press, 1974.

Lewis, J. K., & McKinney, W. T. Mother-infant separation in rhesus monkeys as a model of human depression. *Archives of General Psychiatry*, 1976, *33*, 699–705.

Lewis, M., & Rosenblum, L. A. (Eds.). *The effect of the infant on its caregiver*. New York: Wiley, 1974.

Lock, A. Acts instead of sentences. In W. von Raffler-Engle & Y. Lebrum (Eds.), *Neurolinguistics*, vol. 5, *Baby talk and infant speech*. Amsterdam: Swets & Zeitlinger, 1976.

Lorenz, K. Der Kumpan in der Umwelt des Vogels. *Journal für Ornithologie*, 1935, *83*, 137–213, 289–413.

Lorenz, K. Über die Bildung des Instinktbegriffes. *Naturwissenschaften*, 1937, *25*, 289–300, 307–318, 324–331.

Lorenz, K. Vergleichende Verhaltensforschung. *Zoo. Anz. Suppl. Bd.*, 1939, *12*, 69–102.

Lorenz, K. Vergleichende Bewegungsstudien an Anatinen. *Supplement Journal für Ornithologie*, 1941, *89*, 194–294.

Lorenz, K. Ganzheit und Teil in der tierischen und menschlichen Gemeinschaft. *Studium Generale*, 1950, *3/9*.

Lorenz, K., & Tinbergen, N. Taxis und Instinkthandlung in der Eirollbewegung der Graugans: I. *Zeitschrift für Tierpsychologie*, 1939, *2*, 1–29.

Lytton, H. Observational studies of parent-child interaction: A methodological review. *Child Development*, 1971, *42*, 651–684.

Lytton, H. Comparative yield of three data sources in the study of parent-child interaction. *Merrill-Palmer Quarterly*, 1974, *20*, 53–64.

Maccoby, E., & Feldman, S. Mother-attachment and stranger reactions in the third year of life. *Monographs of the Society for Research in Child Development*, 1972, *37*(Serial No. 146).

MacCorquodale, K., & Meehl, P. E. On a distinction between hypothetical constructs and intervening variables. *Psychological Review*, 1948, *55*, 95–107.

MacCorquodale, K., & Meehl, P. E. Edward C. Tolman. In W. K. Estes, S. Koch, K. MacCorquodale, P. E. Meehl, C. G. Mueller, Jr., W. N. Schoenfeld, & W. S. Verplank (Eds.), *Modern learning theory*. New York: Appleton-Century-Crofts, 1954.

MacKay, D. M. Formal analysis of communicative processes. In R. A. Hinde (Ed.), *Non-verbal communication*. Cambridge: At the University Press, 1972.

Main, M. Analysis of a peculiar form of reunion behavior seen in some daycare children: Its history and sequelae in children who are home-reared. In R. Webb (Ed.), *Social development in daycare*. Baltimore: The Johns Hopkins University Press, 1977.

Main, M. Avoidance in the service of proximity. In K. Immelmann, G. W. Barlow, M. Main, & L. Petrinovitch (Eds.), *Behavioral development: The Bielefeld interdisciplinary project*. New York: Cambridge University Press, 1982.

Main, M., Tomasini, L., & Tolan, W. Differences among mothers of infants judged to differ in security. *Developmental Psychology,* 1979, *15,* 472–473.

Main, M., & Weston, D. R. The quality of the toddler's relationship to mother and to father: Related to conflict behavior and the readiness to establish new relationships. *Child Development,* 1981, *52,* 932–940.

Main, M., & Weston, D. R. Avoidance of the attachment figure in infancy: Descriptions and interpretations. In C. M. Parkes & J. Stevenson-Hinde (Eds.), *The place of attachment in human behavior*. New York: Basic Books, 1982.

Manning, M., Heron, J., & Marshall, T. Styles of hostility and social interactions at nursery, at school and at home. An extended study of children. In L. A. Hersov, M. Berger, & D. Shaffer (Eds.), *Aggression and anti-social behaviour in childhood and adolescence*. Oxford: Pergamon, 1978.

Mason, W. A., & Berkson, G. Effects of maternal mobility on the development of rocking and other behaviors in rhesus monkeys: A study with artificial mothers. *Developmental Psychobiology,* 1975, *8,* 197–211.

Mason, W. A., & Kenney, W. D. Redirection of filial attachments in rhesus monkeys: Dogs as mother surrogates. *Science,* 1974, *183,* 1209–1211.

Masters, J., & Wellman, H. Human infant attachment: A procedural critique. *Psychological Bulletin,* 1974, *81,* 218–237.

McCall, R. B., Hogarty, P. S., & Hurlbert, N. Transitions in infant sensori-motor development and the prediction of childhood I.Q. *American Psychologist,* 1972, *27,* 728–748.

McDougall, W. *An outline of psychology*. London: Methuen, 1923.

McGinnis, L. Maternal separation vs. removal from group companions in rhesus monkeys. *Journal of Child Psychology and Psychiatry,* 1979, *20,* 15–28.

McGrew, W. C. *An ethological study of children's behavior*. New York: Academic Press, 1972.

McKinney, W. T., Kliese, K. A., Suomi, S. J., & Moran, E. C. Can psychopathology be reinduced in rhesus monkeys? An experimental investigation of behavioral sensitization. *Archives of General Psychiatry,* 1973, *29,* 630–634.

Meier, G. W. Other data on the effects of social isolation during rearing upon adult reproductive behaviour in the rhesus monkey. *Animal Behaviour,* 1965, *13,* 228–231.

Miller, G. A., Galanter, E., & Pribram, K. H. *Plans and the structure of behavior*. New York: Holt, 1960.

Miller, N. E. Liberalization of basic S-R concepts. In S. Koch (Ed.), *Psychology, a study of a science: Study I* (Vols. 1, 2). New York: McGraw-Hill, 1959.

Miller, R. E., Caul, W. F., & Mirsky, I. A. Communication of affects between feral and socially isolated monkeys. *Journal of Personality and Social Psychology,* 1967, *7,* 231–239.

Mineka, S., & Suomi, S. J. Social separation in monkeys. *Psychological Bulletin,* 1978, *85,* 1376–1400.

Mitchell, G. D., Harlow, H. F., Griffin, G. A., & Møller, G. W. Repeated maternal separation in the monkey. *Psychonomic Science,* 1967, *8,* 197–198.

Mitchell, G. D., Raymond, E. J., Ruppenthal, G. C., & Harlow, H. F. Long-term effects of total social isolation upon behavior of rhesus monkeys. *Psychological Reports,* 1966, *18,* 567–580.

Moltz, H. Imprinting: Empirical basis and theoretical significance. *Psychological Bulletin,* 1960, *57,* 291–314.

Moltz, H., & Stettner, L. J. The influence of patterned-light deprivation on the critical period for imprinting. *Journal of Comparative Physiology and Psychology,* 1961, *54,* 279–283.

Moyer, K. W. Kinds of aggression and their physiological basis. *Communications in Behavioral Biology,* 1968, *2,* 65–87.

Moynihan, M. Some aspects of reproductive behavior in the black-headed gull (*Larus ridibundus* L.) and related species. *Behaviour,* 1955, *4* (Supplement)

Novak, M. A., & Harlow, H. F. Social recovery of monkeys isolated for the first year of life. I: Rehabilitation and therapy. *Developmental Psychology,* 1975, *11,* 453–465.

Omark, D. M., & Edelman, M. S. The development of attention structures in young children. In M. R. A. Chance & R. Larsen (Eds.), *The social structure of attention.* New York: Wiley, 1976.

Oster, H. Facial expression and affect development. In M. Lewis & L. A. Rosenblum (Eds.), *The development of affect.* New York: Plenum, 1978.

Oster, H., & Ekman, P. Facial expression in child development. In A. Collins (Ed.), *Minnesota Symposia on Child Psychology* (Vol. 11). 1978.

Parke, R. D., Power, T. G., & Gottman, J. Conceptualizing and quantifying influence patterns in the family triad. In M. E. Lamb, S. J. Suomi, & G. R. Stephenson (Eds.), *The study of social interaction: Methodological issues.* Madison: University of Wisconsin Press, 1979.

Parkes, C. M. *Bereavement studies in adult life.* London: Tavistock, 1972.

Parten, M. B. Social participation among preschool children. *Journal of Abnormal Social Psychology,* 1932, *27,* 243–269.

Passman, R. H. Providing attachment objects to faciliate learning and reduce distress: Effects of mothers and security blankets. *Developmental Psychology,* 1977, *13,* 25–28.

Passman, R. H., & Weisberg, P. Mothers and blankets as agents for promoting play and exploration by young children in a novel environment: The effects of social and non-social attachment objects. *Developmental Psychology,* 1975, *11,* 170–177.

Patterson, G. R. A three-stage functional analysis for children's coercive behaviors. In B. C. Etzel, J. M. LeBlanc, & D. M. Baer (Eds.), *New developments in behavioral research: Theory, methods, and applications. In honor of Sidney W. Bijou.* Hillsdale, N.J.: Erlbaum, 1975.

Paulson, G. W. Maturation of evoked responses in the duckling. *Experimental Neurology,* 1965, *11,* 324–333.

Prechtl, H. F. R. The directed head turning response and allied movements of the human baby. *Behaviour,* 1958, *13,* 212–242.

Prechtl, H. F. R., & Beintema, D. J. *The neurological examination of the full term newborn infant.* London: Heinemann, 1964.

Preston, D. G., Baker, R. P., & Seay, B. M. Mother-infant separation in the patas monkey. *Developmental Psychology,* 1970, *3,* 298–306.

Quinton, D., & Rutter, M. Early hospital admissions and later disturbances of behaviour: An attempted replication of Douglas's findings. *Developmental Medicine and Child Neurology,* 1976, *18,* 447–459.

Rajecki, D. W., Lamb, M. E., & Obmascher, P. Toward a general theory of infantile attachment: A comparative review of aspects of the social bond. *Behavioral and Brain Sciences,* 1978, *3,* 417–464.

Redican, W. K. Facial expressions in non-human primates. In L. A. Rosenblum (Ed.), *Primate behavior* (Vol. 4). New York: Academic Press, 1975.

Reite, M., Kaufman, I. C., Pauley, J. D., & Stynes, A. J. Depression in infant monkeys: Physiological correlates. *Psychosomatic Medicine,* 1974, *36,* 363–367.

Reite, M., Short, R., & Seiler, C. Physiological correlates of maternal separation in surrogate-reared infants: A study in altered attachment bonds. *Developmental Psychobiology,* 1978, *11,* 427–435.

Rescorla, R. A., & Wagner, A. R. A theory of Pavlovian conditioning. In A. H. Black & W. F. Prokasy (Eds.), *Classical conditioning* (Vol. 2). New York: Appleton-Century-Crofts, 1972.

Richer, J. The social-avoidance behaviour of autistic children. *Animal Behaviour,* 1976, *24,* 898–906.

Robertson, J. Mother-infant interaction from birth to twelve months: Two case studies. In B. M. Foss (Ed.), *Determinants of infant behaviour* (Vol. 3). London: Methuen, 1965.

Robertson, J. *Young children in hospital* (2nd ed.). London: Tavistock, 1970.

Robertson, J., & Robertson, J. Young children in brief separation: A fresh look. *Psychoanalytic Study of the Child,* 1971, *26,* 264–315.

Roper, R., & Hinde, R. A. Social behavior in a play group: Consistency and complexity. *Child Development,* 1978, *49,* 570–579.

Roper, R., & Hinde, R. A. A teacher's questionnaire for individual differences in social behaviour. *Journal of Child Psychology and Psychiatry,* 1979, *20,* 287–298.

Rosenblum, L. A. Sex differences, environmental complexity, and mother-infant relations. *Archives of Sexual Behavior,* 1974, *3,* 117–128.

Rosenblum, L. A., & Kaufman, I. C. Variations in infant development and response to maternal loss in monkeys. *American Journal of Orthopsychiatry,* 1968, *38,* 418–426.

Rosenthal, M. Attachment and mother-infant interaction: Some research impasses and a suggested change in orientation. *Journal of Child Psychology and Psychiatry,* 1973, *14,* 201–207.

Ruppenthal, G. C., Arling, G. L., Harlow, H. F., Sackett, G. P., & Suomi, S. J. A 10-year perspective of mother-less mother monkey behavior. *Journal of Abnormal Psychology,* 1976, *85,* 341–349.

Rutter, M. Parent-child separation: Psychological effects on the children. *Journal of Child Psychology and Psychiatry,* 1971, *12,* 233–260.

Rutter, M. *Maternal deprivation reassessed.* Harmondsworth, Eng.: Penguin, 1972.

Rutter, M., & Brown, G. W. The reliability and validity of measure of family life and relationships in families containing a psychiatric patient. *Social Psychiatry,* 1966, *1,* 38–53.

Sackett, G. P. Monkeys reared in isolation with pictures as visual input: Evidence for an innate releasing mechanism. *Science,* 1966, *154,* 1468.

Sackett, G. P., Holm, R. A., & Ruppenthal, G. C. Social isolation rearing: Species differences in behavior of macaque monkeys. *Developmental Psychology,* 1976, *12,* 283–288.

Sackett, G. P., & Ruppenthal, G. C. Development of monkeys after varied experiences during infancy. In S. A. Barnett (Ed.), *Ethology and development.* Philadelphia: Lippincott, 1973.

Sade, D. S. A longitudinal study of social behavior of rhesus monkeys. In R. Tuttle (Ed.), *The functional and evolutionary biology of primates.* Chicago: Aldine-Atherton, 1972.

Salzen, E. A. Imprinting in birds and primates. *Behaviour,* 1967, *28,* 232–254.

Sameroff, A. J. Early influences on development: Fact or fancy? Merrill-Palmer Quarterly, 1975, *21,* 276–294.

Sameroff, A. J., & Chandler, M. J. Reproductive risk and the continuum of caretaking causality. In F. D. Horowitz, M. Hetherington, S. Scarr-Salapatek, & G. Sregel (Eds.), *Review of child development research* (Vol. 4). Chicago: University of Chicago Press, 1975.

Savin-Williams, R. C. An ethological study of dominance formation and maintenance in a group of human adolescents. *Child Development,* 1976, *47,* 972–979.

Schaffer, H. R. *The growth of sociability.* Harmondsworth, Eng.: Penguin, 1971.

Schaffer, H. R., & Emerson, P. E. The development of social attachments in infancy. *Monographs of the Society for Research in Child Development,* 1964, *29*(Serial No. 3).

Schjelderup-Ebbe, T. Beiträge zur Sozialpsychologie des Haushuhns. *Zeitschrift für Psychologie,* 1922, *88,* 225–252.

Schlottman, R. S., & Seay, B. M. Mother-infant separation in the Java macaque. *Journal of Comparative Physiology and Psychology,* 1972, *79,* 334–340.

Schneirla, T. C. Levels in the psychological capacities of animals. In R. W. Sellers, V. J. McGill, & M. Farber (Eds.), *Philosophy for the future.* New York: Macmillan, 1949.

Schneirla, T. C. Interrelationships of the ''innate'' and the ''acquired'' in instinctive behavior. In *L'instinct dans le comportement des animaux et de l'homme.* Paris: Fondation Singer Polignac, 1956.

Schneirla, T. C. Behavioural development and comparative psychology. *Quarterly Review of Biology,* 1966, *41,* 283–302.

Schutz, F. Sexuelle Prägung bei Anatiden. *Zeitschrift für Tierpsychologie,* 1965, *22,* 50–103.

Scott, J. P., & Marston, M. V. Critical periods affecting the development of normal and maladjustive social behavior of puppies. *Journal of Genetic Psychology,* 1950, *77,* 25–60.

Seay, B. M., Alexander, B. K., & Harlow, H. F. Maternal behavior of socially deprived rhesus monkeys. *Journal of Abnormal Social Psychology,* 1964, *69,* 345–354.

Seay, B. M., & Gottfried, N. W. A phylogenetic perspective for social behavior in primates. *Journal of Genetic Psychology,* 1975, *92,* 5–17.

Seay, B. M., Hansen, E. W., & Harlow, H. F. Mother-infant separation in monkeys. *Journal of Child Psychology and Psychiatry,* 1962, *3,* 123–132.

Seligman, M. E. P. *Helplessness.* San Francisco: W. H. Freeman, 1975.

Seligman, M. E. P., & Hager, J. L. *Biological boundaries of learning.* New York: Appleton-Century-Crofts, 1972.

Seyfarth, R. M. Social relationships among adult female baboons. *Animal Behaviour,* 1976, *24,* 917–938.

Shepher, J. Mate selection among second generation kibbutz adolescents and adults: Incest avoidance and negative imprinting. *Archives of Sexual Behavior,* 1971, *1,* 293–307.

Short, R., & Reite, M. Alpha activity in the infant *Macaca nemestrina* following maternal separation. *Abstracts of the American Society of Primatology,* 1977, *1,* 22–23.

Silk, J. B., Clark-Wheatley, C. B., Rodman, P. S., & Samuels, A. Differential reproductive success and facultative adjustment of sex ratios among female bonnet macaques (*Macaca radiata*). *Animal Behaviour,* 1981, *29,* 1106–1120.

Simpson, M. J. A. The social grooming of male

chimpanzees. In J. H. Crook & R. P. Michael (Eds.), *The comparative ecology and behaviour of primates*. London and New York: Academic Press, 1973.

Simpson, M. J. A. Daytime rest and activity in socially living rhesus monkey infants. *Animal Behaviour*, 1979, *27*, 602–612.

Simpson, M. J. A. Personal communication, 1980.

Simpson, M. J. A., & Hooley, J. Personal communication, 1980.

Simpson, M. J. A., & Howe, S. The interpretation of individual differences in rhesus monkey infants. *Behaviour*, 1980, *72*, 127–155.

Simpson, M. J. A., & Simpson, A. E. One-zero and scan methods for sampling behaviour. *Animal Behaviour*, 1977, *25*, 726–731.

Simpson, M. J. A., & Simpson, A. E. Birth sex ratios and social rank in rhesus monkey mothers. *Nature*, in press.

Simpson, M. J. A., Simpson, A. E., Hooley, J., & Zunz, M. Infant-related influences on birth intervals in rhesus monkeys. *Nature*, 1981, *290*, 49–51.

Singh, S. D. Effects of infant-infant separation of young monkeys in a free-ranging natural environment. *Primates*, 1977, *18*, 205–214.

Sluckin, A. M., & Smith, P. K. Two approaches to the concept of dominance in preschool children. *Child Development*, 1977, *48*, 917–923.

Smith, F. V., & Nott, K. H. The "critical period" in relation to the strength of the stimulus. *Zeitschrift für Tierpsychologie*, 1970, *27*, 108–115.

Smith, M. A method of analyzing the interaction of children. *Journal of Juvenile Research*, 1933, *17*, 78–88.

Smith, W. J. Message, meaning and context in ethology. *American Naturalist*, 1965, *99*, 405–409.

Smith, W. J. *The behavior of communicating*. Cambridge: Harvard University Press, 1977.

Smith, W. J., Chase, J., & Katz, A. Tongue showing: A facial display of humans and other primate species. *Semiotica*, 1974, *11*, 201–246.

Spencer-Booth, Y. The effects of rearing rhesus monkey infants in isolation with their mothers on their subsequent behaviour in a group situation. *Mammalia*, 1969, *33*, 80–86.

Spencer-Booth, Y., & Hinde, R. A. The effects of separating rhesus monkey infants from their mothers for six days. *Journal of Child Psychology and Psychiatry*, 1967, *7*, 179–197.

Spitz, R. A. Anaclitic depression. *Psychoanalytic Study of the Child*, 1946, *2*, 313–342.

Spitz, R. A. Anxiety in infancy: A study of its manifestations in the first year of life. *International Journal of Psychoanalysis*, 1950, *31*, 138–143.

Sroufe, L. A., & Waters, E. The ontogenesis of smiling and laughter: A perspective on the organization of development in infancy. *Psychological Review*, 1976, *83*, 173–189.

Sroufe, L. A., & Waters, E. Attachment as an organizational construct. *Child Development*, 1977, *48*, 1184–1199.

Stern, D. *The first relationship: Infant and mother*. London: Fontana/Open Books, 1977.

Sternglanz, S. H., Gray, J. L., & Murakami, M. Adult preferences for infantile facial features: An ethological approach. *Animal Behaviour*, 1977, *25*, 108–115.

Stevenson-Hinde, J., & Simpson, M. J. A. Mothers' characteristics, interactions, and infants' characteristics. *Child Development*, 1981, *52*, 1246–1254.

Stevenson-Hinde, J., Stillwell-Barnes, R., & Zunz, M. Subjective assessment of rhesus monkeys over four successive years. *Primates*, 1980, *21*, 66–82.

Stokes, A. W. Agonistic behaviour among blue tits at a winter feeding station. *Behaviour*, 1962, *19*, 118–138.

Strayer, F. F. Social ecology of the preschool peer group. In W. A. Collins (Ed.), *Development of cognition, affect, and social relations*. Hillsdale, N.J.: Erlbaum.

Strayer, F. F., & Strayer, J. An ethological analysis of social agonism and dominance relations among preschool children. *Child Development*, 1976, *47*, 980–989.

Suomi, S. J. Factors affecting responses to social separation in rhesus monkeys. In G. Serban & A. Kling (Eds.), *Animal models in human psychopathology*. New York: Plenum, 1976.

Suomi, S. J. Differential development of various social relationships by rhesus monkeys. In M. Lewis & L. A. Rosenblum (Eds.), *The social network of the developing infant*. New York: Plenum, 1978.

Suomi, S. J., Collins, M. L., & Harlow, H. F. Effects of permanent separation from mother on infant monkeys. *Developmental Psychology*, 1973, *9*, 376–384.

Suomi, S. J., Collins, M. L., Harlow, H. F., & Ruppenthal, G. C. Effects of maternal and peer separations on young monkeys. *Journal of Child Psychology and Psychiatry*, 1976, *17*, 101–112.

Suomi, S. J., Eisele, C. J., Grady, S. A., & Harlow, H. F. Depression in adult monkeys following separation from nuclear family environment. *Journal of Abnormal Psychology*, 1975, *84*, 576–578.

Suomi, S. J., & Harlow, H. F. Social rehabilitation of isolate-reared monkeys. *Developmental Psychobiology,* 1972, *6,* 487–496.

Suomi, S. J., & Harlow, H. F. Effects of differential removal from group on social development of rhesus monkeys. *Journal of Child Psychology and Psychiatry,* 1975, *16,* 149–164.

Suomi, S. J., & Harlow, H. F. Production and alleviation of depressive behaviors in monkeys. In J. Maser & M. E. P. Seligman (Eds.), *Psychopathology: Experimental models.* San Francisco: W. H. Freeman, 1977.

Suomi, S. J., & Harlow, H. F. Early experience and social development in rhesus monkeys. In M. E. Lamb (Ed.), *Social and personality development.* New York: Holt, Rinehart & Winston, 1978. (a)

Suomi, S. J., & Harlow, H. F. Early separation and behavioral maturation. In A. Oliviero (Ed.), *Genetics, environment and intelligence.* Amsterdam: Elsevier, 1978. (b)

Suomi, S. J., Harlow, H. F., & Domak, C. J. Effect of repetitive infant-infant separation of young monkeys. *Journal of Abnormal Psychology,* 1970, *76,* 161–172.

Suomi, S. J., Seaman, S. F., Lewis, J. K., De Lizio, R., & McKinney, W. T. Antidepressant effects of imipramine treatment on separation-induced social disorders in rhesus monkeys. *Archives of General Psychiatry,* 1978, *35,* 321–325.

Svejda, M., Campos, J. J., & Emde, R. N. Mother-infant bonding: Failure to generalize. *Child Development,* 1980, *51,* 775–779.

Swan, C. Individual differences in the facial expressive behavior of pre-school children: A study by the time-sampling method. *Genetic Psychology Monographs,* 1938, *20,* 557–650.

Szegal, B. A. *Continuity and discontinuity in the development of aggression in early childhood.* Paper presented at the Institute for the Study of Behavior Development, Lund, Sweden, 1979.

Szegal, B. A., & Benis, M. *The trends of the development of aggression in early childhood.* Paper presented at the International Congress of Child Psychology, Paris, July 1979.

Thelen, E. Rhythmical stereotypes in normal human infants. *Animal Behaviour,* 1979, *27,* 699–715.

Thomas, A., Chess, S., Birch, H. G., Hartzig, M. E., & Karn, S. *Behavioral individuality in early childhood.* New York: New York University Press, 1963.

Thorpe, W. H. The modern concept of instinctive behaviour. *Bulletin of Animal Behaviour,* 1948, *7,* 2–12.

Thorpe, W. H. *Bird song.* Cambridge: At the University Press, 1961.

Thorpe, W. H. *Learning and instinct in animals* (1st ed.). London: Methuen, 1963.

Thorpe, W. H. *The origins and rise of ethology.* London: Heinemann, 1979.

Thorpe, W. H., & Jones, F. G. W. Olfactory conditioning and its relation to the problem of host selection. *Proceedings of the Royal Society (Series B),* 1937, *124,* 56–81.

Tinbergen, E. A., & Tinbergen, N. Early childhood autism—an ethological approach. *Advances in Ethology,* 1972, *10,* 1–53.

Tinbergen, N. Über die Orientierung des Bienenwolfes (*Philanthus triangulum* Fabr.). *Zeitschrift für vergleichende Physiologie,* 1935, *21,* 699–716.

Tinbergen, N. *The behavior of the snow bunting in spring. Transactions of the Linnaeus Society* (New York). No. 5, 1939.

Tinbergen, N. An objectivistic study of the innate behaviour of animals. *Bibliotheca Biotheoretica,* 1942, *1,* 39–98.

Tinbergen, N. Social releasers and the experimental method required for their study. *Wilson Bulletin,* 1948, *60,* 6–51.

Tinbergen, N. *The study of instinct.* Oxford: Oxford University Press, 1951.

Tinbergen, N. *Curious naturalists.* London: Country Life, 1958.

Tinbergen, N. Comparative studies of the behaviour of gulls (Laridae): A progress report. *Behaviour,* 1959, *15,* 1–70.

Tinbergen, N. On aims and methods of ethology. *Zeitschrift für Tierpsychologie,* 1963, *20,* 410–433.

Tizard, B. *Adoption: A second chance.* London: Open Books, 1977.

Tizard, B., & Hodges, J. The effect of early institutional rearing on the development of eight year old children. *Journal of Child Psychology and Psychiatry,* 1978, *19,* 99–118.

Tizard, B., & Rees, J. The effect of early institutional rearing on the behaviour problems and affectional relationships of 4 year old children. *Journal of Child Psychology and Psychiatry,* 1975, *16,* 61–74.

Trevarthen, C. Descriptive analyses of infant communicative behaviour. In H. R. Schaffer (Ed.), *Studies in mother-infant interaction.* London: Academic Press, 1977.

Trevarthen, C. Communication and cooperation in early infancy. In M. Bullowa (Ed.), *Before speech: The beginnings of human communica-*

tion. Cambridge: At the University Press, 1978.

Trivers, R. L. Parent-offspring conflict. *American Zoologist,* 1974, *14,* 249–264.

Tyler, S. Time-sampling: A matter of convention. *Animal Behaviour,* 1979, *27,* 801–810.

Vaitl, E. Nature and implications of the complexly organized social system in non-human primates. In D. J. Chivers & J. Herbert (Eds.), *Recent advances in primatology*. London: Academic Press, 1978.

Vaughn, B., Egeland, B., Sroufe, L. A., & Waters, E. Individual differences in infant-mother attachment at twelve and eighteen months: Stability and change in families under stress. *Child Development,* 1979, *50,* 971–975.

Vernon, D. T. A., Foley, J. M., Sipowicz, R. R., & Schulmans, J. L. *The psychological responses of children to hospitalization and illness*. Springfield, Ill.: Charles C. Thomas, 1965.

Vine, I. The role of facial visual signalling in early social development. In M. von Cranach & I. Vine (Eds.), *Social communication and movement: Studies of men and chimpanzees*. London: Academic Press, 1973.

Washburn, R. W. A scheme for grading the reactions of children in a new social situation. *Journal of Genetic Psychology,* 1932, *40,* 84–99.

Waters, E. The reliability and stability of individual differences in infant-mother attachment. *Child Development,* 1978, *49,* 483–494.

Waters, E., Vaughn, B. E., & Egeland, B. R. Individual differences in infant-mother attachment behaviors at age one. *Child Development,* 1980, *51,* 208–216.

Watson, J. S. Smiling, cooing and "the game." *Merrill-Palmer Quarterly,* 1972, *18,* 323–339.

Watzlawick, P., Beavin, J. H., & Jackson, D. D. *Pragmatics of human communication*. New York: W. W. Norton, 1967.

Weinberg, P. *Incest behavior*. Secaucus, N.J.: Citadel Press, 1976.

Weintraub, M., Brooks, J., & Lewis, M. The social network: A reconsideration of the concept of attachment. *Human Development,* 1977, *20,* 31–47.

Weisler, A. *Temporal patterns of rhesus mother-infant interactions*. Unpublished doctoral dissertation, Cambridge University, 1978.

Wertheim, E. S. The science and typology of family systems: II. Further theoretical and practical considerations. *Family Process,* 1975, *14,* 285–309.

White, L., & Hinde, R. A. Some factors affecting mother-infant relations in rhesus monkeys. *Animal Behaviour,* 1975, *23,* 527–542.

Willems, E., & Willems, G. Comparative validity of data yielded by three methods. *Merrill-Palmer Quarterly,* 1965, *11,* 65–71.

Wolf, A. P. Childhood association and sexual attraction: A further test of the Westermarck hypothesis. *American Anthropologist,* 1970, *72,* 503–515.

Wood, B. S., Mason, W. A., & Kenney, M. D. Contrasts in visual responsiveness and emotional arousal between rhesus monkeys raised with living and those raised with inanimate substitute mothers. *Journal of Comparative Physiology and Psychology,* 1979, *93,* 368–377.

Yarrow, L. J. Research in dimensions of early maternal care. *Merrill-Palmer Quarterly,* 1963, *9,* 101–114.

Young, G., & Gouin Décarie, T. An ethology-based catalogue of facial/vocal behaviour in infancy. *Animal Behaviour,* 1977, *25,* 95–107.

Young, L. D., Suomi, S. J., Harlow, H. F., & McKinney, W. T. Early stress and later response to separation. *American Journal of Psychiatry,* 1973, *130,* 400–405.

Zivin, G. On becoming subtle: Age and social rank changes in the case of a facial gesture. *Child Development,* 1977, *48,* 1314–1321.

PERINATAL BRAIN DEVELOPMENT AND BEHAVIOR | 3

ARTHUR H. PARMELEE, JR., *University of California, Los Angeles*
MARIAN D. SIGMAN, *University of California, Los Angeles*

CHAPTER CONTENTS

INTRODUCTION

The purpose of this chapter is to provide a bridge between the chapters on anatomic and physiological development and those on behavioral development. The relation of brain maturation to behavioral development is such a complex topic that no attempt will be made to provide a fully comprehensive review. Instead, we will present what we consider to be some of the major issues and will give examples of brain and behavioral research that addresses these issues.

Our principal aim is to illustrate that, despite the remarkable advances in developmental neuroanatomy and neurophysiology and in the descriptions of behavioral development, there are still many problems in relating brain and behavior causally (Davidson & Davidson, 1980; Puccetti & Dykes, 1978; Thompson, Hicks, & Shuyrkov, 1980; Wolstenholme & O'Connor, 1979). Knowledge of brain maturation and understanding of behavioral development have developed largely along parallel tracks. We have had to be satisfied in many instances with inferences of causality through temporal coincidence of changes in brain morphology or physiology and the appearance of new behaviors. Some current research is focused on ways of determining precisely the relation between the development of specific brain morphology, neurophysiology, and neurochemistry and the appearance of very limited but well specified behaviors (Kandel, 1977, 1979; Lynch, Gall, & Dunwiddie, 1978; Spinelli & Jensen, 1979).

In the 1946 version of this book, chapters by Carmichael, Gesell, and McGraw were concerned with the problem of maturation and learning. These authors stressed the importance of the immaturity of the nervous system in the fetus and young infant in restricting learning in the early stages of development. By acknowledging the possibility of environmental influences, these reviewers attempted to lay the nature-nurture problem to rest. In the 1940s maturation referred in large measure to growth change in the nervous system, although all aspects of physical maturation were included. The details of the morphological and neurophysiological changes in the brain were referred to only grossly. Much was still unknown about brain function in general and even less about ontogenetic changes in brain structure. A major thrust of the research of Tilney and McGraw in the 1930s was on comparative studies of brain development and behavioral change in infant animals and humans but the investigators were greatly hampered by the limited research techniques available. As McGraw states,

> The studies reported in *Neuromuscular maturation of the human infant* were initiated in 1930 for the expressed purpose of determining the relationship between behavior development and the maturation of neural tissues, particularly those of the brain. That goal was never experimentally achieved, but an interpretation of developing motor activities common to the human infant was presented in the light of available literature on the cellular structures of the nervous system. Perhaps the original purpose could never have been achieved even if we had been able to carry through to completion the histological studies as originally planned. Early in the program we became aware that histological studies of dead tissues could not disclose the whole story of a function and the neural counterparts that mediated the behavior. But histological and reconstructive techniques were the established neurological methods of investigation at that time. (McGraw, 1963, p. xi)

There was little discussion of the effect of environmental stimulation on the development of specific forms of brain morphology, nerve cell metabolism, or synaptic transmission. They were, however, concerned in a general way with how much the unfolding of the nervous system was genetically predetermined and for how long (McGraw, 1946, 1963; Tilney, 1933; Tilney & Kubie, 1931).

We are still left with the problem of determining how long and the extent to which genetically predetermined brain development leads to new behaviors thereby permitting more complex interaction with the environment and when and the degree to which environmental stimulation, by inducing new behaviors, generates developmental changes in the brain. Presumably, the relation of environmental stimulation and brain development varies at different stages of maturation. Our viewpoint is that prior to about a month before term, 40 weeks gestation, the human fetus or preterm infant may be relatively unaffected by sensory input due to limitations of the nervous system, particularly in sensory receptors and in the limited transmission from these receptors to the cortex. Following this period, the nervous system develops to the point that environmental factors become prepotent in determining behavioral and cognitive development. In fact, the environment becomes so crucial that cognitive operations can develop even in the presence of neurological damage, whether or not there are behavioral limitations. An example is the development of many children with cerebral palsy whose overall cognitive functioning is normal although motorically their development may be limited. Another example is the preterm infant who recovers from medical trauma and neurological insult so that environmental factors become a major determinant of development (Sigman & Parmelee, 1979).

This chapter will examine brain maturation and sensory development primarily in human infants and kittens. Study of the human fetus born preterm but still viable is necessary to explore the issue of genetic unfolding and environmental stimulation on brain maturation and development in humans. We are also interested in the development of preterm infants because so many now survive and we need to understand the potential effects of the artificial world we create for them. For comparative animal research, we will refer to studies done with kittens. In the following paragraphs, we will review the advantages of particular animal models for the study of preterm and full-term infants.

CHOICE OF APPROPRIATE ANIMAL MODELS

There will always be many neuroanatomical, neurochemical, and neurophysiological studies that will not be possible with human fetal and infant brains for practical and ethical reasons. For example, for some forms of neuronal staining or fixation for anatomical studies or for extraction of chemicals, particularly enzymes, the brain material must be obtained immediately after death. Neurophysiological studies requiring electrode placement in brain tissue and brain lesion studies are primarily limited to animals. Naturally occurring or acquired brain lesions in the human fetus and infant generally provide limited information because of the poor definition of their structure and extent and the inaccuracy in timing their onset.

The selection of the appropriate animals for useful comparative studies with infants depends on the maturity of their nervous system at birth. The guinea pig, for example, is not very useful because the brain development is so advanced when the animal is born. While it might be possible to deliver guinea pig fetuses prematurely for study, the difficulty of keeping them alive has made this impractical. Mice and rats have very immature nervous systems at birth and for this reason could be good models for comparison with human preterm as well as full-term infants. Their brain maturation is, however, very rapid making it difficult to identify concurrent changes in neuroanatomy, neurophysiology, and behavior, particularly when environmental manipulations are superimposed. Furthermore, since neonatal and early infant rats and mice are so small few neurophysiological studies have been done with them and behavioral studies until recently have been limited. On the other hand, neurochemical investigations have largely been carried out with mice and rats. Monkeys of various breeds are particularly suitable for neurophysiological and behavioral studies for comparison with human infant studies. Their expense in purchase and daily care has however limited the extent of these studies. The number of monkeys that would need to be sacrificed at each age level for combined ontogenetic studies of all aspects of nervous system maturation and behavior have made such studies infrequent. The excellent studies that have been done have been confined to a few laboratories.

The kitten is one of the most useful and practical animals for comparative study. At birth the kitten is like the human infant of 24 to 26 weeks gestation, about 15 weeks before the expected term gestational age of 40 weeks, in the cytoarchitecture of the nervous system, the metabolic maturity of the neurons, time of peak rate of neuronal mitoses, neuronal dendritic and axonal growth, type and maturity of synapses, visual and auditory evoked potentials, spontaneous EEG, and sleep state organization. The kitten's nervous system matures at an approximate rate of 1 to 5 compared to the human infant. Therefore at 3 weeks of age the kitten has matured to the level of an infant born at term and by 6 weeks to that of an infant 15 weeks past term (Kitten: Hoppenbrouwers & Sterman, 1975; Marty, 1967; Noback & Purpura, 1961; Rose, 1981; Rose & Ellingson, 1970; Scheibel & Scheibel, 1963; Shipley, Buchwald, Norman, & Guthrie, 1980; Verley, 1974; Voeller, Pappas, & Purpura, 1963; Infant: Conel, 1939; Dobbing & Sands, 1973; Gruner, 1970; Molliver, Kostovic, & Van Der Loos, 1973; Parmelee & Stern, 1972; Poliakov, 1967; Purpura, 1975; Rabinowicz, 1964; Starr, Amlie, Martin, & Sanders, 1977; Takashima, Chan, Becker, & Armstrong, 1980; Umezaki & Morrell, 1970; Weitzman & Graziani, 1968). It is necessary to remember that only approximate maturational comparisons can be made and these will only be valid for certain kitten functions. Basically, the kitten is born with a nervous system that is quite immature and matures slowly enough for careful behavioral and neurophysiological studies to be done over an extended period. Furthermore, a great deal is known about the neuroanatomy and neurophysiology of kittens and cats. Less is known about their neurochemistry but this is currently under exploration. Behavioral studies of kittens are also expanding rapidly, thus, providing data for the development of a complete animal model.

HISTORICAL REVIEW

Before we discuss more general issues, we will present a brief historical review of some of the many approaches that have been used to study brain maturation and its relation to behavior. The purpose of this historical review is to provide some awareness of the way in which simple notions of brain development and function have become increasingly complex. As we have learned more about smaller and smaller units of the nervous system, earlier concepts of the relation of brain maturation and behavioral development seem untenable. New techniques have led to an increasing reductionism so that it is often difficult to conceptualize the relation between behavioral development and anatomical change.

Anatomic Studies

Various anatomic structures and substances have been studied as possible indices of physical maturation and functional development. These indices include: (1) the appearance of myelin, (2) the structure of axons and dendrites, (3) the amount of Nissl substance, and (4) the formation of synapses and the nature of neurotransmitters. While each index has proved roughly useful as a measure of physical maturation, most investigators have come to recognize that the anatomy described could not specify the level of functioning.

Myelin

Significant impetus to ontogenetic studies of brain development was provided by Fleschig (1876; Clark & O'Malley, 1968) who observed, in neuroanatomical studies of fetuses, newborn, and young infants, that myelin appeared in areas of the brain and spinal cord tracts at different ages and matured at different rates (Figure 1). Myelin is an easily stained, fat-containing substance that surrounds nerve axons and aids nerve conduction. We now know that the presence of myelin in axonal

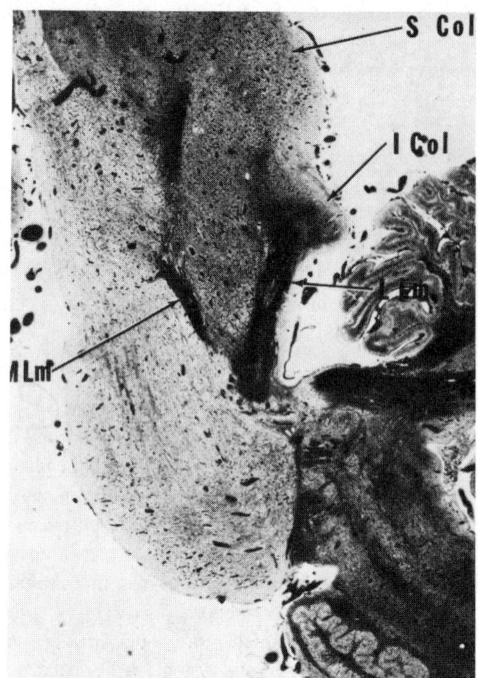

Figure 1. Myelin stained axonal fiber tracts in a longitudinal section through the brain stem of a 35-week fetal infant. Included are the superior and inferior colliculi and upper end of the medulla. The myelinated fiber tracts are stained black and can be seen as black streaks extending from the inferior colliculus (I Col), the auditory system in the lateral lemniscus (LLM) but not from the superior colliculus (S Col), that is, visual system. A few myelinated fibers are beginning to appear in the medial lemniscus, MLM, the pathway to the thalamus for some auditory fibers. (From Yakovlev & Lecours, 1967.)

tracts correlates only roughly with the development of function. Fleschig's myelogenic studies of brain development allowed him to identify a large number of brain areas and tracts that were related to each other by the appearance and rate of development of myelin. Since these brain areas were known to be functional systems such as the visual, auditory, and motor systems, he concluded that myelin might signal the onset of function, a conclusion that has had to be modified by subsequent research. Myelogenic studies of the nervous system and the correlation of these with function became popular. Tilney and Casamajor (1924) studied the development of myelin and the motor activities of kittens and determined that there was a close correlation between myelin development and onset of motor functions. Langworthy (1929, 1933) repeated these myelin and behavioral studies in the kitten and extended them to the human infant. While a general coincidence of the myelinization of fiber tracts and certain behavioral functions was observed, Langworthy (1933, p. 50) states,

> Both the physiological and morphological data concerning the human fetus and infant are far from complete, but certain conclusions can be arrived at from the material that has accumulated. From the study of the pouch-young opossum and of the human fetus, it is quite clear that reflex activity may be observed a considerable period before any pathways are myelinated in the nervous system. This activity consists of movements involving large portions of the body, slow, of small amplitude and often tremulous. The sensory zone is very large and the motor response diffuse.

In subsequent studies Humphrey (1964, p. 113) states,

> At the age when the first reflex follows perioral stimulation there is no evidence for myelination of any cranial or spinal nerve fibers, peripherally or centrally. . . . Evidently the beginning of myelin formation is not necessary for the functioning of the reflex arcs which first appear. Since myelin has appeared in late developing tracts such as the cortical spinal long before there is any evidence of function, it is of particular interest that the fibres utilized by these early appearing reflexes do not myelinate until some time after they have begun functioning.

The study of myelinization does, however, provide a useful general index of nervous system maturation that can be applied to large brain segments (Figure 1, Yakovlev & Lecours, 1967).

Dendrites and Axons

The description of a silver stain (Clark & O'Malley, 1968; Golgi, 1866) which made it possible to identify the dendrites and axons of individual neurons permitted the study of the network of nerve cells, (Figure 2). Using this staining technique Ramon y Cajal (1891, Clark & O'Malley 1968) established neurons as units anatomically independent from each other. Subsequent studies by Conel (1939), Rabinowicz (1964), Purpura, Shofer, Housepian, and Noback (1964), Adinolfi (1971), Purpura (1975), and others using Golgi's staining techniques have traced the development of neuronal dendrites and axons in the brains of animal and human fetuses and infants. The arborization of neuronal dendrites and the development of synaptic spines along these are found to parallel the develop-

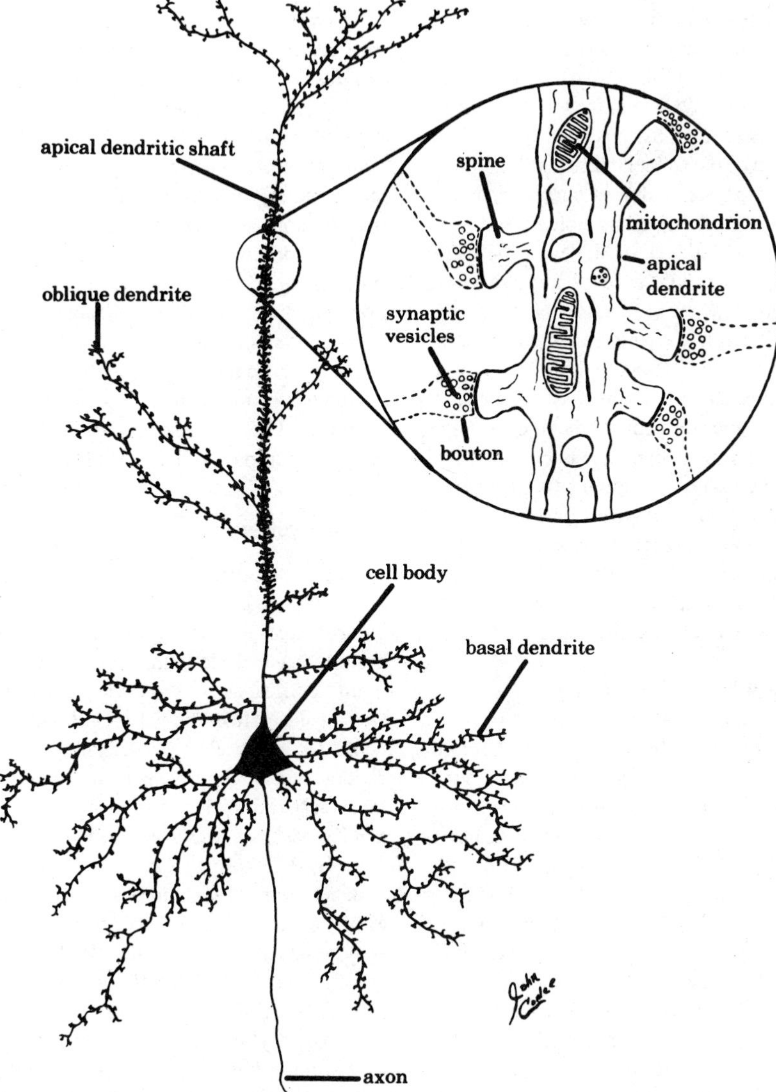

Figure 2. A typical Golgi-stained pyramidal neuron whose cell body is in Layer 5 of the cortex. The dendrites (apical, oblique, basal) receive synaptic input from other nerve cells. The axon conducts the neuron's output to other nerve cells. The enlargement on the right side of the figure presents a segment of the apical shaft as it might appear in the electron microscope. At high magnification (30,000 to 40,000 power) the dark projections from the dendrite appear as protoplasmic extensions called spines. These spines form synapses with the vesicle-filled axon terminals, or boutons, from other neurons. Synapses on the cell body do not utilize spines and hence cannot be visualized with Golgi-staining techniques. (From Greenough, 1975.)

ment of behavioral changes in the fetus and infant as will be discussed in the next section. The difficulty with this technique as with all microscopic studies is that only very small segments of the brain can be studied at one time.

Nissl Substance

Maturational changes in the ultrastructure and metabolism of individual neurons were also recognized as important in determining the relation of brain maturation to behavioral function. Special staining techniques were developed that permitted observation of particular characteristics of neurons under the microscope. Nissl (1894) introduced a stain that made it possible to identify structures within the cell bodies of neurons. Nissl was guarded in the interpretation of the stained particles. Later they were determined to be related to the chemistry of cell functioning and were accepted as indicators of neuronal functioning (Clarke & O'Malley, 1968). For example, Humphrey (1965) used the appearance of Nissl granules as evidence of functioning of the neurons in the vestibular nuclei and related this to some behavioral observations. However, we now know that the appearance and amount of Nissl substance is not sufficient evidence to specify either the presence or degree of functioning. Many other cell stains and chemical procedures were subsequently developed for the study of neuronal ultrastructure and metabolism. Many developed in recent years remain to be tried in maturational studies (Pearse, 1967). The development of electron microscopy has also permitted more extensive study of cellular morphology.

Synapses and Neurotransmitters

Ontogenetic studies of the formation of synapses, their location, and the nature of the structure on either side of the separating space have been made possible by the electron microscope. The number of synaptic vesicles increases with maturation suggesting changes in synaptic transmission with age (Adinolfi, 1971; Gruner, 1970). Bodian's (1966, 1968) studies with the electron microscope of the neuronal and synaptic development of the spinal cord of the fetal monkey and the coincidental development of motor behavior illustrates an early ontogenetic application of this technique. Unfortunately, electron microscope studies deal with even smaller segments of the nervous system than light microscopy, thus limiting even further the interpretations that can be made between anatomy and complex behaviors.

In addition to studies of neuron cell structure and metabolism, there are important recent investigations of the chemistry of transmitter substances at synapses. These studies have also been advanced by the development of special staining techniques (Broderson, Westrum, & Sutton, 1974; Falck, Hillarp, Thieme, & Torp, 1962; Fuxe, Hökfelt, Jonsson, & Ungerstedt, 1970) Neurotransmitters have been found to change with maturation and the nature of these changes may be very important to our understanding of behavioral development. This is one of the most active and important areas of brain research today.

As we have indicated, from the last part of the nineteenth century to the present there has been a progressive refinement of techniques for the morphological and biochemical study of the development of the nervous system. There has also been a constant effort to correlate changes in nervous system structure with behavioral development. Most investigators, however, have recognized that the anatomy described could not specify the level of functioning. Furthermore, the microscopic descriptions pertained to only small samples of the entire nervous system. The observed behavioral changes might be related to some area of the nervous system not under anatomic study and independent of the anatomic changes in the area studied. The need for parallel neurophysiological studies was evident.

Neurophysiological Studies

EEG Activity

Berger (1929, 1930, 1932) was the first investigator to study the ongoing electrical activity of the brain extensively in humans. His attempt to record brain electrical activity in the newborn human infant was unsuccessful. The youngest infant in whom he could record an electroencephalogram (EEG) was 35 days. With improvement in amplifying equipment and experimentation with electrode placement, EEG recordings were obtained from newborn infants by J. R. Smith (1938). At the time he was collaborating with Tilney and McGraw in their efforts to find relations between brain development and behavior. J. R. Smith (1938) and Lindsley (1939) began describing the development of EEG activity in infants and young children. There was still difficulty, however, in determining which neurons were involved in generating the EEG activity and the EEG's relation to behavioral development. Again the problem was that one could only specify by coincidence in time, the appearance of a specific brain morphology, the first appearance of an EEG pattern, and a specific behavioral development.

Evoked Potentials

The evoked potential is the response within the spontaneous EEG that is time locked to the sensory stimulus. The parameters studied are latency, form, and amplitude of the cortical responses. Although brain cortical evoked potentials to visual stimulation were sought and identified by Caton in 1875 (Brazier, 1958), his finding of continuous brain electrical activity, was applied first by Berger and others since this was more readily recorded than brain evoked potentials with the existing equipment. The evoked potentials were of small amplitude and difficult to identify in the ongoing EEG activity. Much later the improvement in amplifiers and the development of special purpose computers for identification of evoked potentials led to a rapid development of such studies, essentially from 1950 to the present (Dawson, 1951; Donchin, 1977).

The study of visual, auditory, and somesthetic cortical evoked potentials provided the opportunity to investigate the development of sensory systems neurophysiologically and this will be discussed more fully in the next sections. Initially, cortical evoked potentials to peripheral sensory stimulation indicated that a signal was progressing from the receptor to the brain but said nothing about sensory information processing. Cortical evoked potentials were useful to identify areas of the brain participating in the reception of sensory inputs through various systems. Recent studies of cortical evoked potentials using sophisticated computer analyses have associated specific types of responses with anticipation and selected cognitive activities (Donchin, 1977; Duffy, Burchfiel, & Lombroso, 1979; Sutton, Braren, Zubin, & John, 1965). Developmental studies in infants are currently an area of great interest.

When sensory evoked cortical potentials and spontaneous brain electrical activity were first identified their anatomic origin was unknown. Whether this electrical activity was generated in the cerebral cortex or in subcortical areas could not be determined. The development of single unit neuronal recording helped resolve this problem (Figure 3 and Figure 4). These recordings were either extracellular but adjacent to a single neuron or intracellular for study of the dynamics of neuronal electrical activity. Such recordings, as well as transcortical recordings have determined that the mid- and long latency evoked potentials as well as electroenceph-

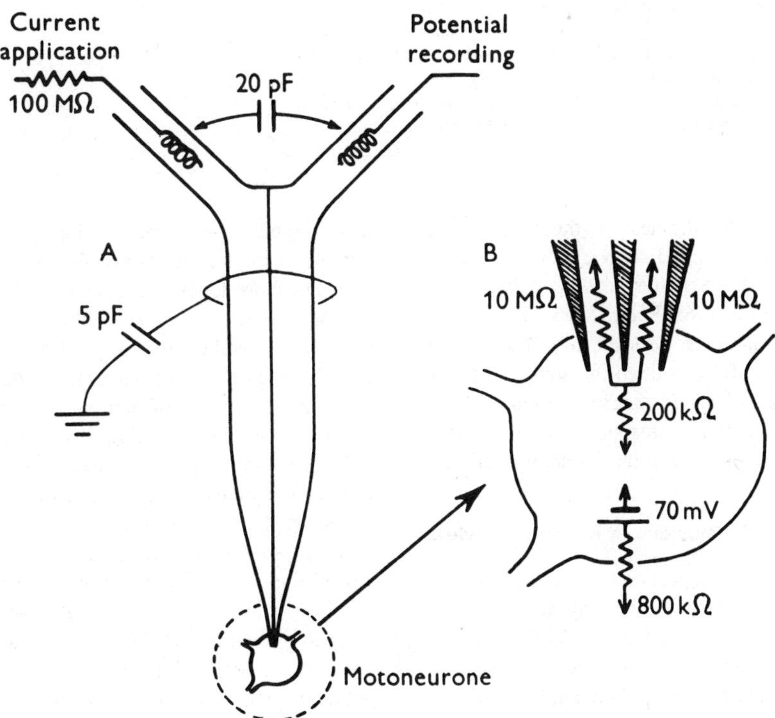

Figure 3. Double-barreled microelectrode and its immediate connections are shown in A. Typical values are given for the several electrical characteristics which are significant in the use of the electrode. B is an enlarged view of the microelectrode tip in the motoneurone. The motoneurone properties represented are the potential and resistance (ignoring the reactance) between the inside and outside of the inactive cell. For diagrammatic purposes the microelectrode tip is shown greatly magnified relative to the motoneurone. (Coombs, Eccles, & Fatt, 1955a, from Eccles, 1957.)

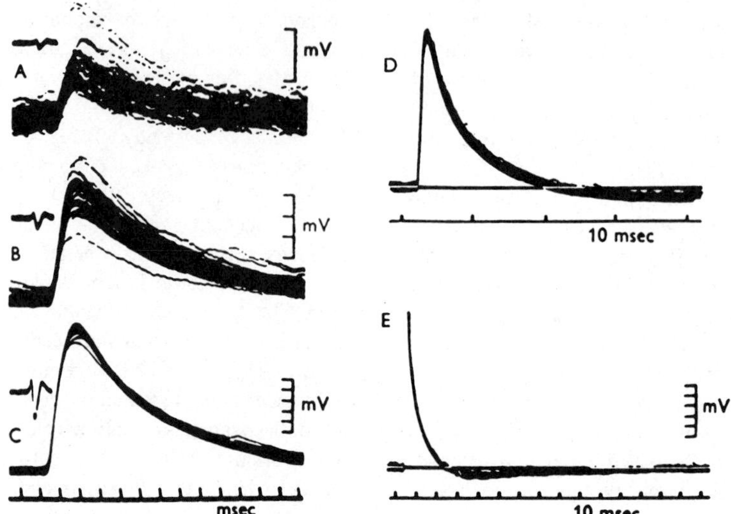

Figure 4. Microelectrode intracellular recording in a spinal motor neurone of excitatory postsynaptic potentials (EPSPs). All records are formed by the superposition of about 40 faint tracings with positive upward. Each response to synaptic input follows the same time course. In A through C on the left the amplification is decreased as the responses increase. In D and E are the same EPSPs at slower time scales and with a base line drawn through the initial level of potential. (Coombs et al., 1955b, from Eccles, 1957.)

alographic activity originate in the cortical neurons and their dendrites (Bishop & Clare, 1952; Calvet, Calvet, & Scherrer, 1964; Creutzfeldt, Watanabe, & Lux, 1966; Eccles, 1957; Freygang & Frank, 1959; Garma & Verley 1965). These single unit recordings also permitted the study of the ontogeny of spontaneous neuronal activity, the strength and duration of responses to stimulation, rate of responsiveness, and the refractory periods.

Summary and Conclusions of Historical Review

In this brief historical review, we have described some changes in our understanding of the nervous system in the last hundred years. With each new development, there has been a tendency to overestimate the amount of behavioral change that could be accounted for by a temporal coincidence in brain development. The difficulty is that studies of brain maturation have not been designed in terms of their relevance for the development of behavioral functions but have been determined by the availability of special techniques. These have ranged from tissue staining techniques to electron microscopy for anatomic studies and electronic transducers, amplifiers, and computers for neurophysiological studies. With our increasing technical expertise, we have learned more and more about smaller and smaller units of the nervous system. The size of the units chosen for study has limited the relevance of the new information for behavioral development. On the other hand, these refined studies of neuronal functioning have improved our understanding of larger nervous network functioning as represented by sensory cortical evoked potentials, EEG, reflex motor responses, and sleep state organization.

In the succeeding sections, we will review current studies of brain maturation selected primarily for their relevance to behavioral development. In order to present a more integrated view of the relation between brain and behavior, we will discuss the ontogeny of form and function in the visual and auditory systems. These systems will be used as models to illustrate how we can study brain development and behavior, avoid oversimplification, and identify important areas for future study. Furthermore, our review will be used to exemplify our viewpoint that plasticity in behavior is rather limited in the preterm infant because of neurological and neurophysiological limitations particularly in sensory reception and that behavioral development becomes increasingly influenced by environmental stimuli during infancy.

STUDIES OF BRAIN MATURATION

The functioning of the brain depends at any stage of development on several factors:

1. Number and location of neurons in the brain.
2. Maturity of structure and metabolism of these neurons.
3. Their ability to generate action potentials spontaneously or when stimulated.
4. Number of connections between axons and dendrites.
5. Development of synapses.
6. Neurochemical transmitters.
7. Organization of the total network for sensory reception, information processing, and action response.

We will focus on these developmental processes in the order given. The section dealing with nervous system networks will be subdivided into sections on the development of the EEG, evoked potential, and sleep states.

The Number and Location of Neurons; Nervous System Cytoarchitecture

Cytoarchitecture refers to the structure of the nervous system as defined by the location and arrangement of cells of various types in relation to each other. For example, neurons of particular types are organized in nuclear clusters such as the caudate nucleus, the thalamic nuclei, the lateral geniculate nucleus, and so forth. The brain cortex is organized in six layers identified by the size and other characteristics of the neurons which predominate in each layer. Furthermore, these layers in adult animals and humans can be further subdivided into areas such as the visual, auditory, motor, and association cortex, and then even into further subsections.

At one time, it was hoped that by determining when these various structures and regions of the cortex were formed one might account for behaviors appearing coincidentally in time. However, as we have indicated in the introduction, it has gradually become clear that many other factors also are essential to behavioral development.

Studies of the ontogeny of brain development are increasingly concerned with how and when undifferentiated neurons migrate from a central germinal matrix, develop into specialized types of neurons, and arrive at their ultimate location. Such information potentially can help us understand abnormal brain development and alterations induced in brain development genetically and biochemically. While most of our knowledge comes from animal studies, the migration of neurons and the development of the ultimate cytoarchitecture seems to be quite similar in all mammals including humans. Of course, the ages at which each level of development is achieved varies with each species (Berry, 1974; Cowan, 1979; Larroche, 1962; Marin-Padilla, 1970; Noback & Purpura, 1961; Poliakov, 1967; Rabinowicz, 1964; Rodier, 1980; Sidman & Rakic, 1973; Takashima, Chan, Becker, & Armstrong, 1980).

Our knowledge of the mechanisms of development in the human fetus is still limited, but several principles seem to be established. The first is that the oldest neurons form the lower layers of the cortex. This means that the cortex forms from the inside out and that succeeding layers are formed by cells migrating through layers of neurons already in position (Figure 5). The second principle is that cells migrate in columns of related cells (Sidman, 1970; Sidman & Rakic, 1973). The cortex, then, ultimately consists of horizontal layers of particular types of neurons and vertical columns extended across the layers made up of many types of cells. The purpose of this type of organization is currently being researched. There is increasing interest in the columns representing unit modules that are similar from one area of the cortex to the next. Their different functions seem to depend not on the form of the columns, which are very much alike, but on the distribution of specific inputs to the various areas of the cortex (Hubel, Wiesel, & LeVay, 1977; Mountcastle, 1979). These are exciting new concepts for understanding brain function that are now being explored further.

We have some understanding of human fetal brain development. Most of the general cytoarchitecture of the brain including the six cortical layers is recognizable by the seventh month of fetal life, but there is great variability in the rate of development of cortical regions. From the seventh month on, the definition of the cytoarchitecture becomes clear in all areas. The development of the cytoarchitecture of the cerebellum is unique and is much delayed relative to the rest of the brain, with most of its development in the first year postnatally in the infant. The cerebellum therefore is particularly sensitive to toxins late in pregnancy or early postnatally (Conel, 1939, 1941, 1947; Larroche, 1962; Marin-Padilla,

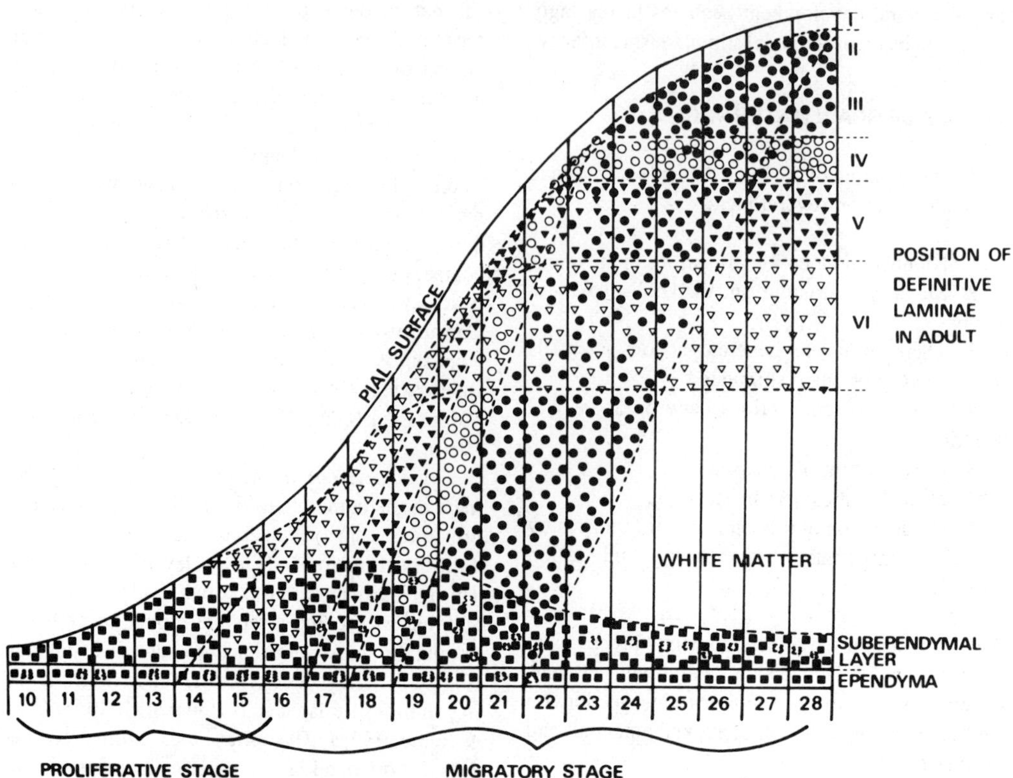

Figure 5. A schematic representation of the pattern of migration of neuroblasts (developing neurons) in the fetal rat with age expressed in days from conception along the base. The final layers of the neocortex are indicated in Roman numerals vertically on the right. Cells formed along the ventricular margins, ependyma, ■, in the first 16 days migrate to Layer VI, ▽. Those cells formed about day 17 migrate to Layer V, ▼, and those on day 18 to Layer IV, ○. The cells formed on days 19, 20, and 21 migrate through all these to Layers III and II, ●. Thus neocortical layers form from inside out. Cells undergoing mitosis, ⌇⌇, persist in the subependymal layer throughout. (From Berry, 1974.)

1970; Mountcastle, 1979; Poliakov, 1967; Rabinowicz, 1964, 1976; Rodier, 1980; Sidman & Rakic, 1973; Takashima et al., 1980).

At present, we do not understand the significance of the number of neurons in the brain at any particular stage of development. When new neurons are developing rapidly, they are more sensitive to toxins or malnutrition. The technique of measuring the chromosomal substance DNA made it possible to determine the rate of development of new brain cells since only new cell division creates more DNA. This technique, however, does not differentiate between neurons and glial cells. Microscopic brain studies demonstrate that the early increases in cell number are primarily neuronal and that this is followed by glial development. For the human infant, most neuronal mitoses have been completed one to two months before term with glial development continuing for several months after birth. The significance of glial cells for brain function is not understood. Behavioral functioning is disturbed by malnutrition and fetal illnesses associated with small head size and diminished number of neurons. However, malnutrition and early infant illness are usually also associated with other disturbances in brain growth besides the number of brain cells, such as dendritic branchings, numbers of synapses, and neurotransmitter development. Any poor behavioral functioning therefore may be as highly related to the latter as to reduced neuronal numbers (Dobbing, 1976; Dobbing & Sands, 1973; McConnell, 1980; Winick, 1971, 1980; Winick & Rosso, 1969).

Currently there is interest in the observation that an excess of neurons are formed initially and the final structure of the brain and spinal cord is achieved by the elimination of some neurons in the shaping processes. It suggests that the absolute number of neurons in early development is not so important as the number ultimately selected to survive. Whether some of this shaping is a function of sensory interaction with the environment is not clear, particularly since much of this seems to occur very early in brain development (Jacobson, 1974). Nevertheless, this presents another important area for further exploration of the brain growth and functional development.

Neuronal Structure and Metabolism

In addition to the multiplication and migration of the neurons to form the ultimate architecture of the nervous system, the development of the internal structure or ultrastructure of the neuron also needs to be considered. This ultrastructure helps determine the metabolism of the neuron for its chemical and electrical responsiveness to stimuli and for its continuous lifelong renewal of structure. This ultrastructure includes the cell nucleus and the surrounding cytoplasm containing the organelles such as the endoplasmic reticulum and ribosomes, Nissl substance, Golgi apparatus, and mitochondria (Figure 6). As previously mentioned, Nissl substance was identified by a special stain in 1894, and was soon found to be composed of protein, iron, and phosphorous. It was considered an important marker of neuronal cell development because it frequently appeared coincidental with the appearance of some evidence of function (Figure 6). We now know that Nissl substance includes portions of the endoplasmic reticulum and attached ribosomes. The latter contain ribonucleic acid, RNA, and produce proteins important for nerve cell activity and survival. This organelle system along with Golgi bodies appears generally after neurons have reached their final point of migration and the dendritic and axonal networks are beginning to grow. These and other organelles in the cytoplasm develop gradually over time, as we now know from electron microscopic studies (Jacobson, 1978; LaVelle & LaVelle, 1970; Palay & Palade, 1955; Tennyson, 1970). No precise relationships between the level of development of these systems in a neuron and the complexity of its functional capacity have been determined, though some correlation clearly exists.

From the anatomic studies of the maturational changes in the ultrastructure of neurons one infers

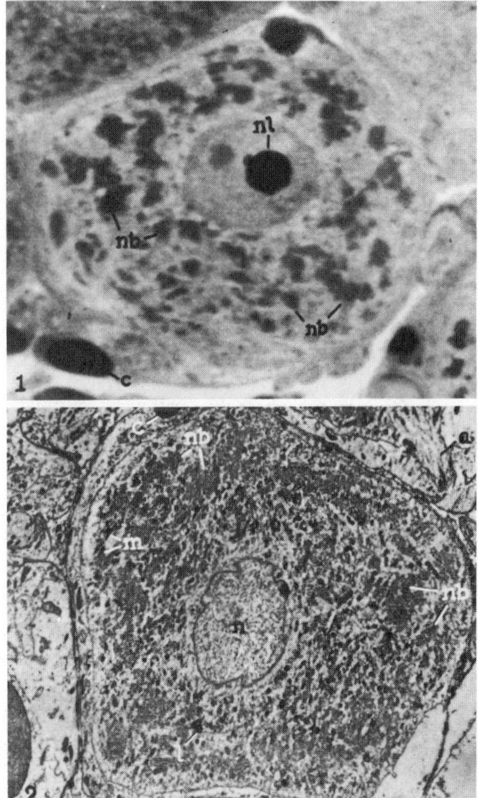

Figure 6. Nerve cell structure *Top*. A photomicrograph through a dorsal root ganglion cell, showing irregularly shaped Nissl bodies (nb), a nucleus with a dense nucleolus (nl), and capsule cells (c) surrounding the perikaryon. *Bottom*. An electron micrograph from the same tissue as the picture above showing irregular Nissl bodies (nb), mitochondria (m), a nucleus (n), and lipid droplets (1). (From Palay & Palade, 1955. Reproduced from the *The Journal of Cell Biology*, 1955, vol. 1, p. 89 by copyright permission of The Rockefeller University Press.)

parallel changes in their metabolic processes considered important to neuronal action potentials necessary for transmission of signals. Studies of maturational changes in the chemical contents of the brain, including enzymes in both animal and human fetuses and infants, help identify what these metabolic changes may be. The enzymes most frequently sought are those related to glucose metabolism, the primary source of energy in the brain. There are two main pathways for their metabolism: one aerobic requiring oxygen and the other anerobic, requiring no oxygen (Eiduson, Geller, Yuwiler, & Eiduson, 1964; Guroff, 1980; Pearse, 1967; Swaiman, 1970). Specification of areas with different rates and types of metabolism have been obtained from analyses of separate portions of the brain. This is part of the continuing search for evidence that certain parts of the brain may become functional before others or have specific functions early. Special stains for these important metabolic processes were developed to stain specific enzymes in the neurons making them visible on microscopic study. The location of the cells stained permits tracing the ontogeny of certain enzymic distributions in all areas of the brain and the density of the stain reflects the amount of enzyme present. Such studies have been carried out in human fetuses and children's brains by Farkas-Bargeton, 1978. She stained enzymes in the glucose metabolic cycle, two in the aerobic cycle, succinate dehydrogenase (SCH) (Figure 7) and malate dehydrogenase (MDH), two in the anaerobic pathway, pyruvate kinase (PK) and lactate dehydrogenase (LDH) and one enzyme in glucose and in lipid metabolism, glycerophosphate dehydrogenase (GPDH). Little or no LDH was visible in the human fetus of 22 weeks gestation, but it was easily identified in the deeper layers of all areas of the cortex of 36 to 38 weeks

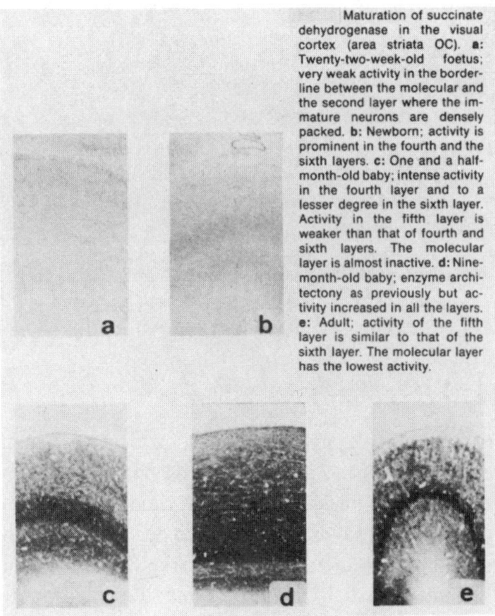

Maturation of succinate dehydrogenase in the visual cortex (area striata OC). **a:** Twenty-two-week-old foetus; very weak activity in the borderline between the molecular and the second layer where the immature neurons are densely packed. **b:** Newborn; activity is prominent in the fourth and the sixth layers. **c:** One and a half-month-old baby; intense activity in the fourth layer and to a lesser degree in the sixth layer. Activity in the fifth layer is weaker than that of fourth and sixth layers. The molecular layer is almost inactive. **d:** Nine-month-old baby; enzyme architectony as previously but activity increased in all the layers. **e:** Adult; activity of the fifth layer is similar to that of the sixth layer. The molecular layer has the lowest activity.

Figure 7. Metabolic enzyme development in fetal, newborn, and adult occipital calcarine (OC) cortex. Maturation of succinate dehydrogenase in the visual cortex (area striata OC). A. Twenty-two-week-old fetus; very weak activity in the borderline between the molecular and the second layer where the immature neurons are densely packed. B. Newborn; activity is prominent in the fourth and the sixth layers. C. One and a half-month-old baby; intense activity in the fourth layer and to a lesser degree in the sixth layer. Activity in the fifth layer is weaker than that of fourth and sixth layers. The molecular layer is almost inactive. D. Nine-month-old baby; enzyme architectony as previously but activity increased in all the layers. E. Adult; activity of the fifth layer is similar to that of the sixth layer. The molecular layer has the lowest activity. (From Farkas-Bargeton & Diebler, 1978.)

gestation becoming progressively more dense in all laminae by 4½ months past term and continuing to increase in density to 11 years. There is a similar increase with age with enzymes MDH, PK, and LDH. GPDH is diffusely present and stains densely in the fetus with diminution in density in infants and young children, except in specific deeper laminae of the cortex. There are some cortical regional differences in these changes but these are small compared to general changes described. These findings are paralleled by brain extraction studies of lactate dehydrogenase and malate dehydrogenase by Chabás, Briones, and Sabater (1979a,b, 1980). What these maturational metabolic changes mean to neuronal functioning has not yet been fully explored.

A new and exciting technique has been developed to measure the rate of glucose metabolism in the brain in live humans and animals during specific activities. It is given the general name Positron-Emission Tomograph (PET). With this technique one can determine areas of increased glucose uptake during and immediately after a specific activity (Kennedy, Sakwada, Shinohara, Jehle, & Sokoloff, 1978; Reivich, Kuhl, Wolf, Greenberg, Phelps, Ida, Casella, Fowler, Hofman, Alavi, Som, & Sokoloff, 1979; Sokoloff, Reivich, Kennedy, Des Rosiers, Potlak, Pettigrew, Sakwada, & Shinohara, 1977). This is done with radioactive labeled glucose that can be observed accumulating in any area of the brain by computer tomography during and immediately after the specific activity. For example, Phelps, Kuhl, and Mazziotta (1981) demonstrated that adult human subjects had a rapid accumulation of 2-^{18}F fluro-2-deoxy-D-glucose (FDG) in the brain cells of area 17 of the visual cortex while looking at a flashing light. There was little spread to occipital association cortex areas 18 and 19 until these subjects looked at a complex image (Figure 8). These studies demonstrate that metabolic processes in neurons are significantly increased during sensory stimulation and in the expected areas such as the visual cortex in the case of visual stimulation. In animals other sensory modalities have been studied with corresponding involvements of expected areas of the brain. With time studies of this type will undoubtedly be extended to look for involvement of unexpected areas particularly during the processing of complex stimuli. So far there are no reported ontogenetic studies. These studies are a major step forward in understanding areal variations in brain metabolism in real time during the conduct of a task, but do not as yet tell us which neurons are involved in the areas studied or how the information is processed and stored.

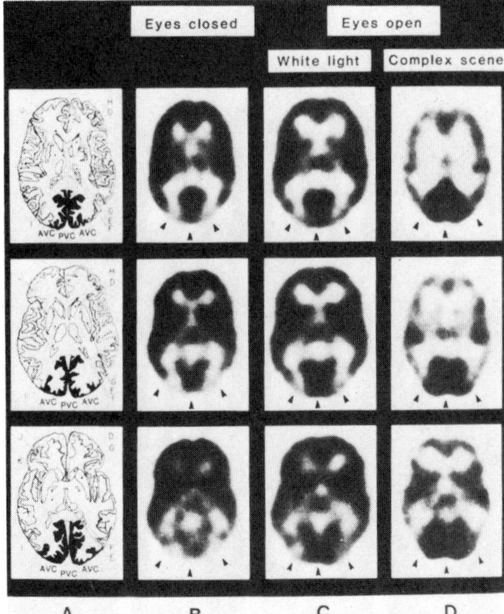

Figure 8. Brain metabolism of radioactive glucose in occipital areas in an adult subject; with eyes closed (B), when looking at a white light (C), and a complex picture (D), using positron emission tomography (PET) at three horizontal levels. Sketches of brain sections (A) corresponding to the tomography pictures show in black the primary visual cortex (PVC) and associative visual cortex (AVC); the black arrows in the tomography pictures point to these same areas. In the tomography pictures there is less glucose metabolism in the visual cortex when the subject's eyes are closed (B) than when the eyes are open (C and D). With the subject only looking at a light the glucose metabolism is greatest in the primary visual cortex (C) while when the subject is looking at a complex scene the associative visual cortex is also included (D). (From Phelps, Kuhl, & Mazziotta, 1981. Courtesy of Michael E. Phelps, UCLA School of Medicine. Copyright 1981 by the American Association for the Advancement of Science.

Neuron Action Potentials

Neuron action potentials are the source of the signals that are transmitted from one neuron to another and are therefore fundamental for the reception of sensory information and transmission of these signals through the brain for processing and for the ultimate response behaviors. These action potentials are dependent on the ultrastructure of the neuron and its energy metabolism, which has just been discussed, and the number and quality of the synaptic inputs.

Nothing is known of single neuron impulses or action potentials in the spinal cord or brain of the human fetus or infant in whom intracellular and extracellular recordings of nervous activity are not possible. However numerous studies in kittens have determined that the structure and metabolism of neurons in various locations in the nervous system of newborn kittens are mature enough to sustain a large membrane potential across the cell membrane and to produce an action potential or nerve impulse when these neurons are stimulated. From intracellular and extracellular unit recording in the kitten it has been determined that spontaneous action potentials of single neurons are infrequent and the responses to stimulation are limited in the first two weeks after birth, with major increases in frequency of firing between two and four weeks, and then more gradual increases to adult levels after that (Figure 9). These changes vary somewhat depending on where the recordings are made, but the trend from infrequent spontaneous firing of action potentials in the first week to more frequent firing by three to four weeks seems consistent in all areas. A second characteristic of the immature neurons is refractoriness to repeated rapid stimulation, (Figure 10). This clearly puts a limit on the rate at which incoming stimuli can be processed and the possible information content which can be carried (Adrien & Roffwarg, 1974; Bowe-Anders, Adrien, & Roffwarg 1974; Huttenlocher, 1967; Huttenlocher, & Rawson, 1968; Levine, Cherubini, Novack, Hull, & Buchwald, 1979; Lidsky, Buchwald, Hull, & Levine, 1976; Morris, Levine, Cherubini, Buchwald, & Hull, 1979; Purpura & Shofer, 1972; Purpura et al., 1964; Scheibel & Scheibel, 1978).

It is not clear to what extent the infrequency of spontaneous impulse activity of the neurons and their refractoriness to repeated stimulation is a function of their immature metabolic system, their reduced number of synaptic contacts, or the limits on neurotransmission at the synapses. Purpura and Shofer (1972) using intracellular recordings of neurons in the cortex and hippocampus have described a stronger postsynaptic inhibitory potential than excitatory potential in newborn kittens. They think this phenomenon may account for some of the infrequency of spontaneous impulses and the refractoriness to repeated stimulation. That this is not true of all brain neurons in newborn kittens has been demonstrated by Morris et al. (1979) in caudate neurons where excitatory postsynaptic potentials dominate. Despite this domination by excitatory postsynaptic potentials, caudate neurons also have infrequent spontaneous activity and are refractory to repeated stimulation. Both studies show a sharp shift toward more mature type responses in the kitten between the second and fourth week after birth.

The observations concerning neuronal ultrastructure, metabolism, and action potential development in the kitten are associated with coincidental changes in behavior. In the period from 2 to 4 weeks after birth of the kitten, when the rapid increase in spon-

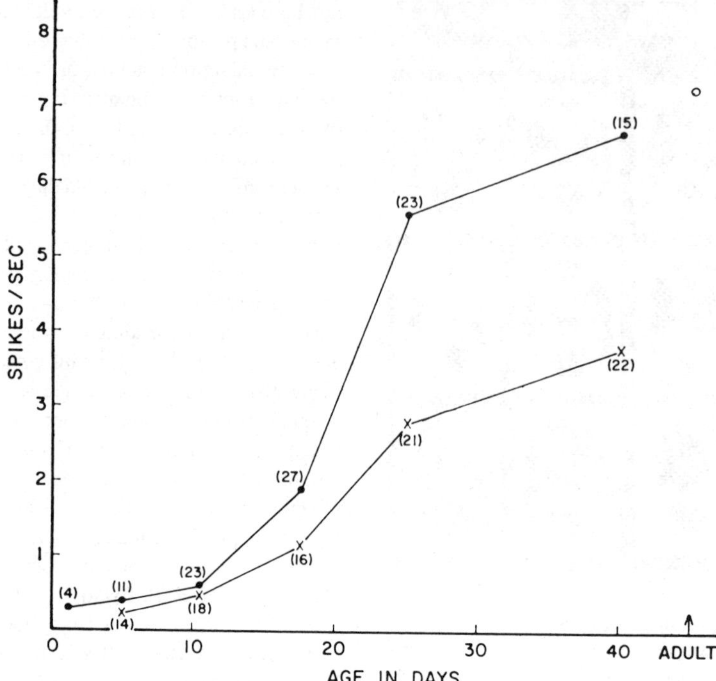

Figure 9. Spontaneous neuronal activity in the kitten. The mean spontaneous activity in 192 single-cell units recorded in sensorimotor (•) and visual (X) cortex of kittens between 1 day and 6 weeks. Numbers in parentheses indicate number of units recorded for each plot point. (From Huttenlocher & Rawson, 1968.)

taneous neuronal activity and responsiveness to repeated stimuli occurs, the first evidence of behavioral responsiveness to visual and auditory stimuli is manifest and increasing stimulus sensitivity is shown in the next period from 4 to 9 weeks (Blakemore, 1974; Bowe-Anders et al., 1974; Carlier, Abonnenc, & Pujol, 1974; Hubel & Wiesel, 1963; Levine et al., 1980; Pujol, 1976). The coincidence of anatomical, neurophysiological, and behavioral development in the kitten will be reviewed further in the next section.

Dendrites and Axons

The individual neurons that make up the nervous system communicate with each other through their dendritic and axonal processes. In general the dendrites form the input system and the axons the output system for each neuron. These structures begin to develop rapidly after the neurons stop migrating. The dendrites and axons provide the complex neural networks of the brain with elaborate feedback loop systems that ultimately control sensory processing and behavior. It is difficult, however, to relate the development of specific behaviors directly to the changes in such networks since generally only small samples from a limited number of areas are studied because of the complexity of the process of staining and microscopic analysis.

The development of neuronal axons and dendrites have been extensively studied both in animals and humans, largely by Golgi silver staining of nervous tissue. The sequences of development is very similar in animals and humans. We will discuss the general sequence of development as it has been described for the human fetus, newborns and young infants and for kittens. Type I or *pyramidal neurons* develop apical dendrites and axons first and later basilar dendrites (Figure 11). These neurons have a triangular shape, hence their name pyramidal; the apical dendrites grow out of the upward point and basilar dendrites from the corners of the base. The axon grows down from the middle of the base. The exact timing of the developmental changes varies in different areas of the nervous system, but the sequence generally remains the same. Type II or *stellate neurons or microneurons* develop later. They are small and star shaped and have no apex or base

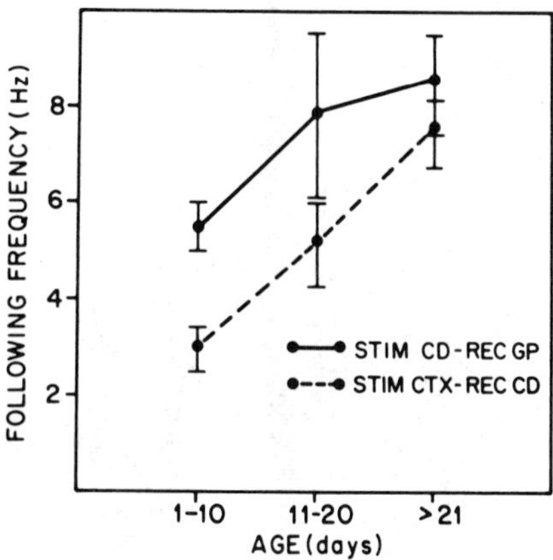

Figure 10. Age related changes in the ability of neurons to respond to repetitive stimulation. The following frequency is limited from 1 to 10 days of age but improves rapidly at 21 days and later with the continuing change most prominent in the caudate nucleus (CD) neuronal responses to cortical (CTX) stimulation. Each point represents average following frequency and range markers represent ± 1 S.E. Following frequencies were determined by assessing the ability of each unit to respond to trains of three pulses at each frequency.

•——• Stimulation in the caudate nucleus and recording in the globus palidus (GP).

•– – –• Stimulation in the cortex and recording in the caudate nucleus.

(From Levine, Cherubini, Novack, Hull, & Buchwald, 1979.)

but more radially symmetric dendritic branching and short axons (Figure 11).

In the just viable preterm infant of 25 to 30 weeks gestation, 2½ to 3 months before term, the cortical Type I (pyramidal) neurons have mainly apical dendrites with limited branching, few basilar dendrites, and short axons (Figure 12). The same is true of similar neurons in the newborn kittens, (Figure 11). In the preterm infant, the apical dendrites soon begin to branch and between 34 and 36 weeks gestation, (Figure 13), 1½ to 1 month before term, basilar dendrites are present in significant numbers and size and Type II (stellate) neurons are evident with expanded dendritic branching. The 2-week kittens' cortical neurons appear similar in development. In the last month before term, the preterm infants' cortical neurons are similar to those of full-term infants but the dendritic branching is less dense. From term birth through infancy and childhood the major changes are in the increased length and branching of the dendrites of the neurons and lengthening of the axons. The kitten of 3 weeks has cortical neurons like those in the term infants and these develop in the next weeks as those in the infants in the first months of life (Infants: Conel, 1939, 1941, 1947; Marin-Padilla, 1970; Poliakov, 1967; Purpura, 1975; Rabinowicz, 1964; Takashima et al., 1980); (Kittens: Adinolfi, 1971; Noback & Purpura, 1961; Purpura et al., 1964; Scheibel & Scheibel, 1963; 1971, 1978).

Exact age comparions of the ontogeny of dendritic and axonal growth between fetuses or infants of the same age or kittens of the same age or between kittens and infants is difficult because of the variation among individuals in degree of development at each age level. Kittens from the same litter can vary in these characteristics at birth (Scheibel, personal communication). This becomes particularly significant in evaluating the studies of human fetuses, preterm, newborn and young infants. Usually only one to five infants are studied at a given age level, not enough to be secure about the range of variability at any age. A statement, therefore, about the degree of advancement or delay in development of the dendritic growth of a given infant is tenuous.

Takashima, Becker, and Chan (1982) report that the neuronal dendritic growth in six preterm infants who had lived several weeks after birth was similar to that of a control group of preterm infants who died soon after birth at the same conceptional age as those who had lived for several weeks. In four additional cases the dendritic growth was delayed. Purpura (1975) found both accelerated and delayed cortical neuronal dendritic growth in preterm infants who survived several weeks. Purpura (1975, 1976) in some very elegant studies has related the development of the characteristics of visual evoked potentials in preterm infants to the ontogenetic characteristics of the apical and basilar dendrites of pyramidal cells in the visual cortex. This will be discussed in more detail later. With this technique he has been able to demonstrate deviant development of visual evoked potential when there is abnormal development of the dendrites of visual cortical neurons. This certainly supports the importance of this type of anatomic study but the results may only pertain when the deviations are extreme.

There is evidence that environmental stimulation can increase dendritic growth (Greenough & Juraska, 1979). Spinelli, Jensen, and Viana Di Prisco (1980) trained kittens from ages 4 to 6 weeks to withdraw one forepaw to avoid a mild shock. Samples of tissue from the somatosensory cortex from the trained and untrained sides were analyzed for the amount of apical and basilar dendritic branching. Increased apical and basilar branching was found only on the trained side. The training experience clearly generated an anatomic change in the direction of more rapid dendritic growth. It is important to note, however, that the training period was not begun until the kittens were 4 weeks old and the brain

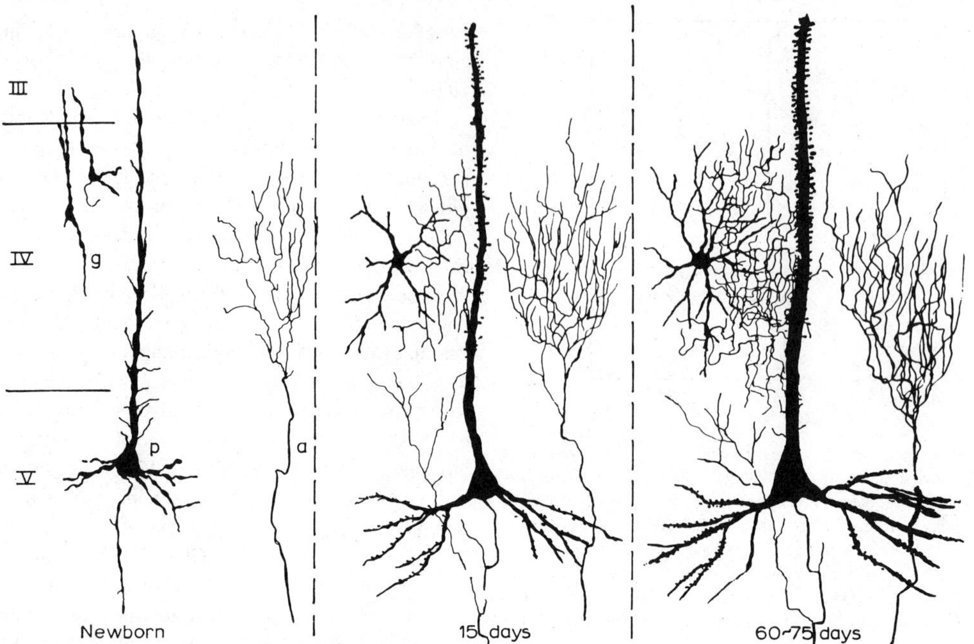

Figure 11. Golgi-stained cortical neurons in kittens, ages 1, 15, and from 60 to 75 days. In the newborn kitten the pyramidal neuron (p) has a long apical dendrite with little branching extending from Layer V to III, a few short basilar dendrites, and a thin axon extending downward from the base. There is an axon (a) of a thalamic neuron extending upward into the cortex. The short axon neuron in Layer IV (g) is a stellate neuron, Golgi II. It starts as a primitive bipolar neuron in the newborn kitten and then generates increasingly dense dendritic and axonal plexuses which seem to reach maturity between 60 and 90 days. The pyramidal neurons with maturation develop more dendritic branches, particularly in the basal area, and numerous dendritic spines. The axonal afferents, extending into the cortex, also develop more branching. (From Scheibel & Scheibel, 1964.)

and sensory system had a sufficient degree of maturity to respond adequately. Whether such training given earlier would have had the same effect is still to be tested. These findings are consistent with those of Greenough and Volkmar (1973) who compared infant rats raised in complex environments with others raised in standard cages and found increases in dendritic growth. These animals were also in these environments for extended age periods when their brains were relatively mature. The question is then, not whether environmental circumstances can alter dendritic growth, but how early in life this can occur. These are questions that undoubtedly will be explored as extensions of present studies.

Synapses

The ultimate point of transmission between neurons is through synaptic contacts, usually between axons and dendrites, but also between axons and neuron cell bodies and between dendrites. The development of synapses in animals and in human fetuses, newborns, infants, and children have been well studied both by light microscopy and electronmicroscopy. In the study of developing dendrites, multiple small projections or spines were observed in Golgi-stained preparations under light microscopy. Eventually, with electronmicroscopy, it was confirmed that the spines on the dendrites represented synapses (Figure 2). In the brain the development of synapses follows the same sequence described for dendritic branching. Initially, most of the synapses are between axons and apical dendrites and only later appear on basilar dendrites and cell somas and between dendrites (Infants: Purpura, 1975; Rabinowicz, 1964; Takashima et al., 1980); (Kittens: Adinolfi, 1971; Noback & Purpura, 1961; Purpura et al., 1964; Scheibel & Scheibel, 1963, 1971, 1978).

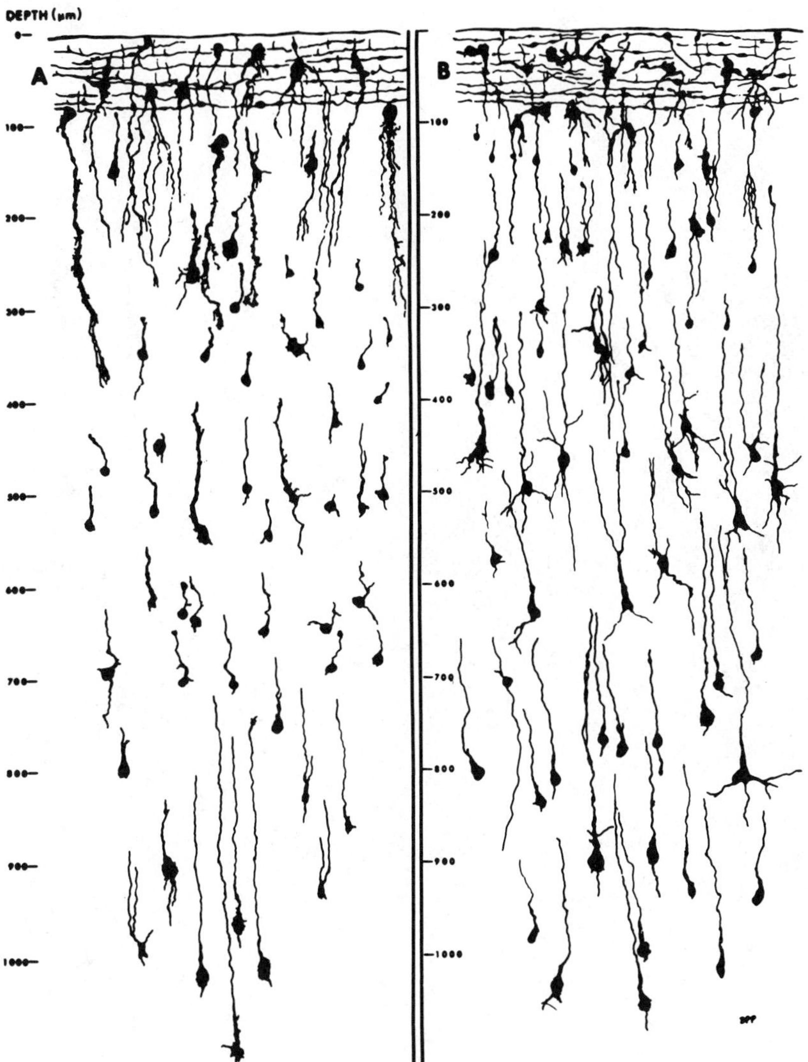

Figure 12. The visual cortex of preterm infants of 26 and 27 weeks conceptional age. This is a camera lucida composite drawing of neurons in calcarine (visual) cortex, from (A) a 26 to 27 week and (B) a 27-week preterm infant. Both infants show limited dendritic branching on pyramidal cells, particularly in the basilar area. There are scattered bipolar stellate cells. The basilar dendritic branching of the pyramidal cells in infant B is greater than in infant A and indicates more maturity of nervous system development in this infant. The stellate cells in infant B also show more dendritic branching. Dendritic spines are not present in either infant. (From Purpura, 1975.)

When the dendrites are sparse, so are the spines on them and as the dendrites develop so do the spines. The latter, however, go through a period of excessive development and some are ultimately lost. For some structures spines develop some time after dendritic growth and show a differential gain on distal portions of the dendrites and a loss on proximal regions. Many investigators believe that this is the way synaptic specificity develops and brain function is shaped. As yet, we do not know the developmental stage at which the arrangement of synapses becomes more a function of input stimulation rather

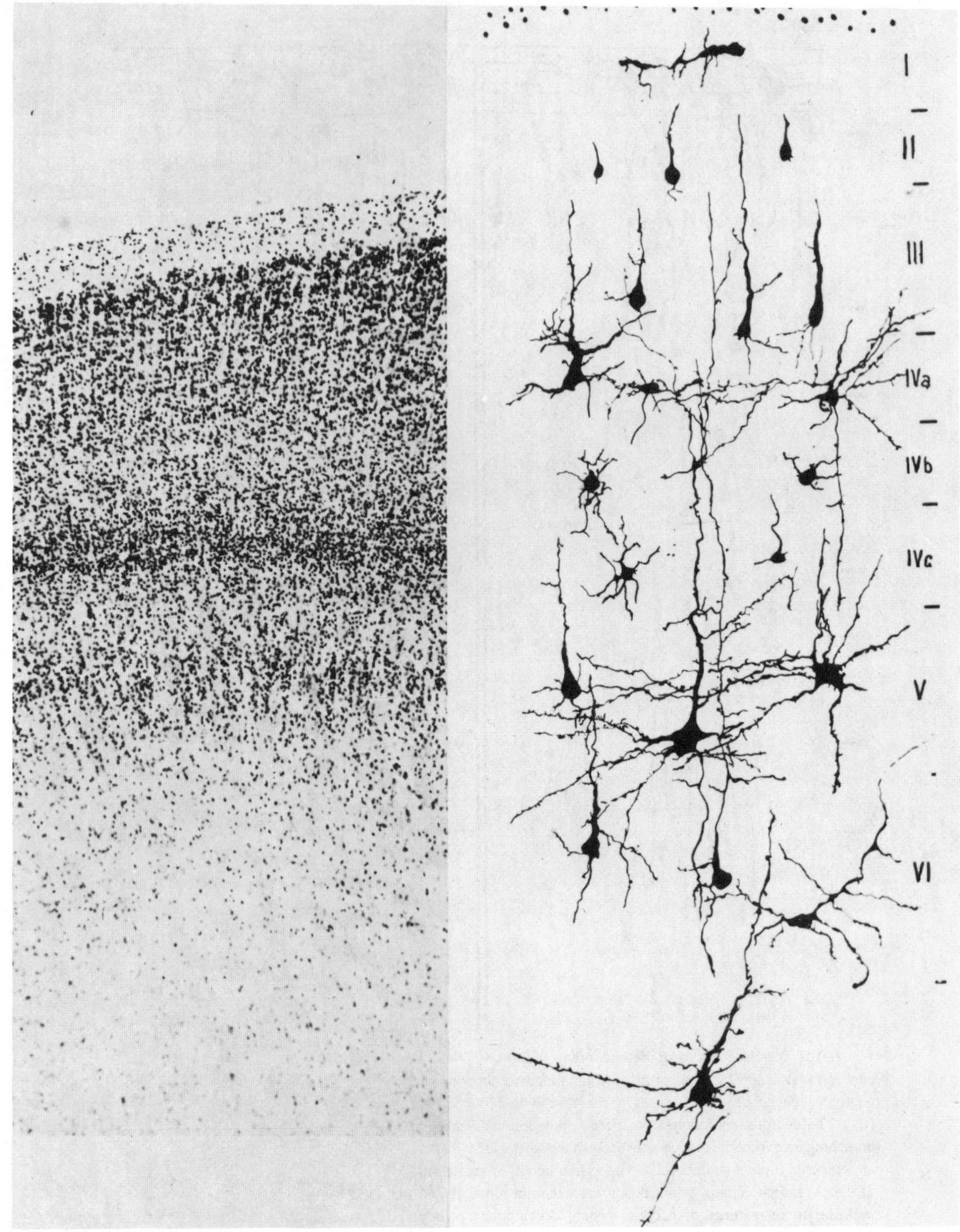

Figure 13. Visual calcarine fissure cortex of a preterm infant of 8 months gestation. On the left is a section stained with Cresyl violet to show all of the cells and their easily recognizable layering; the cortex surface is at the top. On the right are drawings from a Golgi-Cox stain of the same area. This technique stains individual neurons and their dendrites and axons. Small stellate, Golgi II, are clearly seen in Layer IVa, b, c and large pyramidal cells, Golgi I, in Layers IV, V, and VI with the largest in V. Basilar dendritic branching in the pyramidal cells is at this age more extensive than in younger preterm infants (see Figure 12). (From Rabinowicz, 1964.)

than the result of a predetermined genetically coded growth pattern (Berry, Bradley, & Borges, 1978; Changeux & Donchin, 1976; Cowan, 1979; Hull, McAllister, Levine, & Adinolfi, 1981; Purves & Lichtman, 1980).

Dendritic synapses can be seen in preterm infants as early as 15 weeks gestation, six months before term, but are rare and their form is immature. More synapses are seen by 25 weeks that are predominantly axodendritic, and by 32 weeks gestation there are many such synapses that are also more mature in appearance. Mature synapses are present by 35 weeks, one month before term, and axosomatic synapses are present (Gruner, 1970; Molliver et al., 1973; Purpura, 1975).

In kittens at birth, most synapses are axodendritic and on apical dendrites as in the 25 to 30 week gestation infant. In the 2-week old kitten, axosomatic synapses are more frequent and are more mature as in the 35-week gestation infant (Adinolfi, 1971; Voeller et al., 1963).

How well immature synapses function is still undetermined. As previously mentioned, the form of neuron action potentials and their refractoriness to rapid stimulation may be largely determined by the number and functional capacity of these synapses.

Neurotransmitters

Most synaptic stimulus transmission is now thought to be chemical by substances labeled neurotransmitters. Approximately 30 neurotransmitters have been identified to date. The location of the synapses and the biochemical composition of the neurotransmitter determines whether the stimulus transmitted is excitatory or inhibitory. The duration of the action of the neurotransmitter is dependent on the presence of other agents and enzymes that terminate their chemical activity to permit multiple stimuli to be transmitted per second (Figure 14). The types of neurotransmitters present and the strength of their deactivators changes with maturation. Normal behavioral development is undoubtedly dependent on the progressive maturation of this biochemistry of synaptic transmission (Axelrod, 1974;

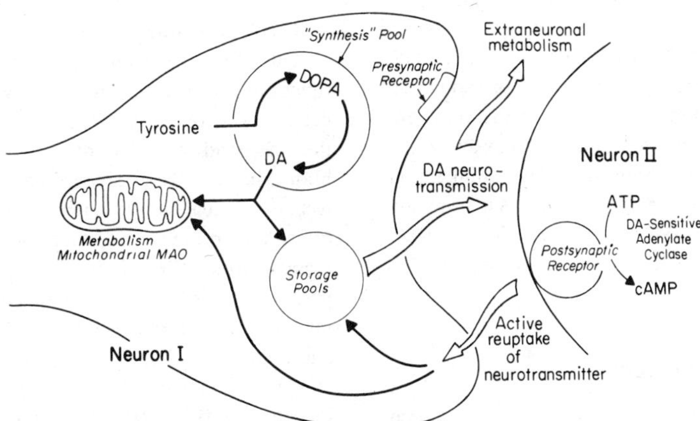

Figure 14. Neurotransmitters at synapses. An idealized model of a dopaminergic synapse. Dopamine (DA) is synthesized in two steps from the amino acid tyrosine and then stored in synaptic vesicles. An action potential depolarizes the presynaptic membrane, resulting in the release of dopamine into the synaptic cleft, which it diffuses across to interact with specific postsynaptic receptors. Interaction of dopamine with its receptors initiates a series of complex events including changes in membrane permeability to ions and formation of cyclic adenosine monophosphate (ATP), which, in turn, activates other intracellular reactions. There also is some evidence for presynaptic receptors which may help to regulate dopamine synthesis as a function of synaptic activity. The signal is terminated as dopamine is removed from the synaptic cleft, primarily by an active mechanism that takes dopamine back up into the presynaptic terminal, where it is metabolized by monamine oxidase (MAO) or restored for future use. (From Barchas, Abil, Elliott, Holman, & Watson, 1978.)

Ellison, 1979; Iverson, 1979; McGeer, Eccles, & McGeer, 1978).

We know a little about neurotransmitters and their ontogeny in the human fetus and infant (Graybiel & Ragsdale, 1980; Kaplay, 1977; Krmpotić-Nemanić, Kostović, Kelović, & Nemanić, 1980), but we are dependent on studies in animals for the details (Kristl, 1979). Even in animals it is difficult to isolate the minute amounts of these chemicals present and know from which synapses they were obtained. Special fluorescent staining techniques available for some neurotransmitters have demonstrated that they are not randomly distributed in the brain so that functionally related systems have common neurotransmitters (Axelrod, 1974; Falck et al., 1962; Iverson, 1979).

Although our understanding of the ontogeny of neurotransmitters or even the number that may exist is limited, it is clear that this is an important area of research. Many drugs and neurotoxins alter behavior in adult animals and humans in predictable and dramatic ways through blocking or enhancing the effect of specific neurotransmitters, either transiently or for prolonged periods. Studies of these drug effects have provided valuable information about the behavioral significance of specific neurotransmitters. What has been surprising have been the unexpected reversals of the effects of some drugs affecting neurotransmitters on the behavior of newborn and infant animals as compared with adult animals. We therefore still have a great deal to learn about organization of neurotransmitter systems in the developing organisms and the action of neurotransmitters in immature synapses (Adrien, 1979; Cohen & Young, 1977; Mueller, Mailman, & Breese, 1980; Shimizu & Himwich, 1969).

Nervous System Networks

We have reviewed the development of the neuron, the basic unit of the nervous system. As we have indicated, there are many factors in the development of the neuron that influence its effectiveness in the total nervous system such as its own metabolic processes, growth of the axon and of the dendritic branches, and the growth in the numbers and types of synapses. The neurons, of course, work together in complex networks whose functioning is dependent on the independent neuron, and may be more influenced by some neurons in the system than others. We have emphasized the importance of the development of the sensory receptors and their pathways in any conceptualization of the influence of external stimuli on the development of the central nervous system. We have pointed out, and will elaborate more fully, that a transient reaction of an organism to a stimulus does not tell us much about the amount, form, or duration of the stimulus transmitted to the central nervous system. The information we have suggests that the early reactions to stimuli are only to selected components of a stimulus, such as the onset of the stimulus. This is due to the refractory nature of the first level neurons in the transmission chain from the peripheral to the central nervous system, as well as in the fine tuning of the receptor organs. This will be discussed in more detail relative to vision and audition in the next section.

There are many ways to study the neuronal network neurophysiologically and behaviorally. We will discuss three approaches: (1) the electroencephalogram (EEG), (2) sensory evoked potentials, and (3) state organization. Although they are interrelated in many ways, all three approaches also are used independently of each other. We will present state organization last to emphasize it as an integration of neurophysiological and behavioral measures. While the EEG, for example, may be one of the neurophysiological parameters of sleep state studies, it is not an essential part, particularly in infants.

Electroencephalogram

One of the first techniques used for studying the functioning of neuronal networks was the electroencephalogram (EEG) recorded in human infants from the scalp and in infant animals generally from the brain surface. These recordings reflect the neurophysiological activity within the cortex of the brain and represent the summations of the activity of many neurons. Changes in the EEG activity during a period of recording are presumed to be responses to inputs from subcortical centers such as the thalamus and brain stem. The source of these inputs may be changes in sensory stimulation from the environment or shifts in state organization such as from wake to sleep or within sleep from active, rapid eye movement (REM) sleep to quiet (non-REM) sleep.

Berger (1929) first described the dominant EEG activity during wakefulness as alpha rhythm, usually with a frequency of 10 Hz and this continued to be the predominant rhythm studied for many years. Berger in 1930 in his second report commented, "I had been struck by the fact that in many experiments subjects' opening of the eyes . . . caused an immediate change in the EEG and that during mental tasks, e.g., when solving a problem of arithmetic, the mere task caused the same change of the EEG" (Gloor, 1969, p. 83). This observation has been repeatedly confirmed so that the alpha rhythm is considered a measure of attention. The alpha rhythm disappears or is greatly suppressed when the subject attends to a task. This rhythm is most pronounced in the occipital or visual area when the subject is awake and quiet with eyes closed. Opening the eyes and looking at a light suppresses the alpha rhythm, but it returns unless the subject attends to an object or task. The attending can be visual or a mental activity (Brazier, 1960). Measurements of alpha rhythm changes during performance of tasks are still used as criteria of brain function but have been refined by computer analyses (Duffy, Denckla, Bartels, Sandini, & Kiessling 1980; Walter, Rhodes, Brown, & Adey, 1966). Unfortunately, this or a similar rhythm that blocks with eye opening and focus of attention has not been found in newborn or very young infants. In part, this may be because they quickly drift off to sleep when they close their eyes obscuring any eyes closed awake rhythm. It is also difficult to record the EEG of awake infants without many movement artifacts. Lindsley (1939) found a slower rhythm of 4 to 6 Hz in waking infants of 4 months and older that was suppressed with eye opening or by shining a light in their eyes. He suggested that this was the early form of the adult alpha rhythm of 10 Hz. Others (Bernhard & Skoglund, 1939, 1942; Smith, 1938) supported this in older infants and described a linear relation through childhood between this alpha rhythm frequency and age. At 1 year the mean alpha frequency is 8 Hz and by 16 years the mean is 10 Hz. Alpha frequency has become a measure of brain maturation. Used in this way it has been found that the alpha frequency is more rapid at each age level up to adolescence in females as compared to males, but from adolescence on, there are no longer any sex differences (Eeg-Olofsson, 1971; Petersén & Eeg-Olofsson, 1970/1971). It has also been found that the alpha frequency is more similar in monozygotic than dizygotic twins suggesting a strong genetic component to individual differences in the frequency of this rhythm (Dumermuth, 1968).

We have discussed the awake alpha rhythm even though it has not been important so far in infant studies because it was the central focus of EEG studies in children and adults from the beginning. There has always been great disappointment that the alpha rhythm studies, so fruitful in older children, could not be carried out in young infants. With greater knowledge of state organization and computer analyses, these studies may still be possible.

In the early studies of infant EEG, only brief recordings of 15 to 20 min. were made. This was the usual practice in recording older children and adults and was sufficient for the study of the waking EEG. As previously stated, it was difficult to get waking tracings free of movement artifact in newborn and young infants. Those who persevered did get some recordings and observed that throughout the first year and later, there was a gradual shift from a general dominance of slower rhythms to more rapid rhythms as a function of brain maturation (Brandt & Brandt, 1955; Corbin & Bickford, 1955; Gibbs & Gibbs, 1951; Henry, 1944; Lindsley, 1936, 1938; Petersén & Eeg-Olofsson, 1970/71).

In some of the early studies of sleep in newborn infants the statement was made that there were no EEG changes between wake and sleep. This was probably because the infants went directly from wake into unrecognized rapid eye movement (REM) sleep in which the EEG activity is very similar to that of the awake infant. Since the recordings were of short duration, samples of quiet (non-REM) sleep EEG were not often observed. A few investigators, even with short recordings, did eventually observe major EEG changes when the sleeping newborn infant was very quiet and breathing regularly (Dreyfus-Brisac, Samson, Blanc, & Monod, 1958; Ellingson, 1958). About this time the concept of REM and non-REM sleep was being developed from adult sleep studies using all night sleep recordings (Dement & Kleitman, 1957). Shortly, extended recording of newborn infants began with the recognition of REM, active sleep and, non-REM, quiet sleep in them. These were then combined with polygraphic recordings of eye and body movements, respiration, and heart rate to define these sleep states by non-EEG parameters (Delange, Castan, Cadilhac, & Passouant, 1961; Dreyfus-Brisac, 1964; Parmelee, Wenner, Akiyama, Stern, & Flescher, 1967; Prechtl, Akiyama, Zinkin, & Grant, 1968; Roffwarg, Dement, & Fisher, 1964).

In the healthy adult there is a very high correlation between particular patterns of EEG activity and sleep states so that one can determine sleep states fairly accurately from the EEG alone. This is not so true of newborn infants. While certain EEG patterns of activity are more frequent in each sleep state, the consistency is less than in adults so that it is difficult to predict behaviorally and polygraphically determined sleep states from the EEG alone. In addition, the EEG patterns in each state change rapidly with maturation while non-EEG behavioral and polygraphic criteria of state remain fairly similar at each age.

We can now describe the EEG patterns expected in sleep and waking states in infants at all ages and in preterm infants from 26 weeks gestation to term (Figure 15). These patterns can be recognized visu-

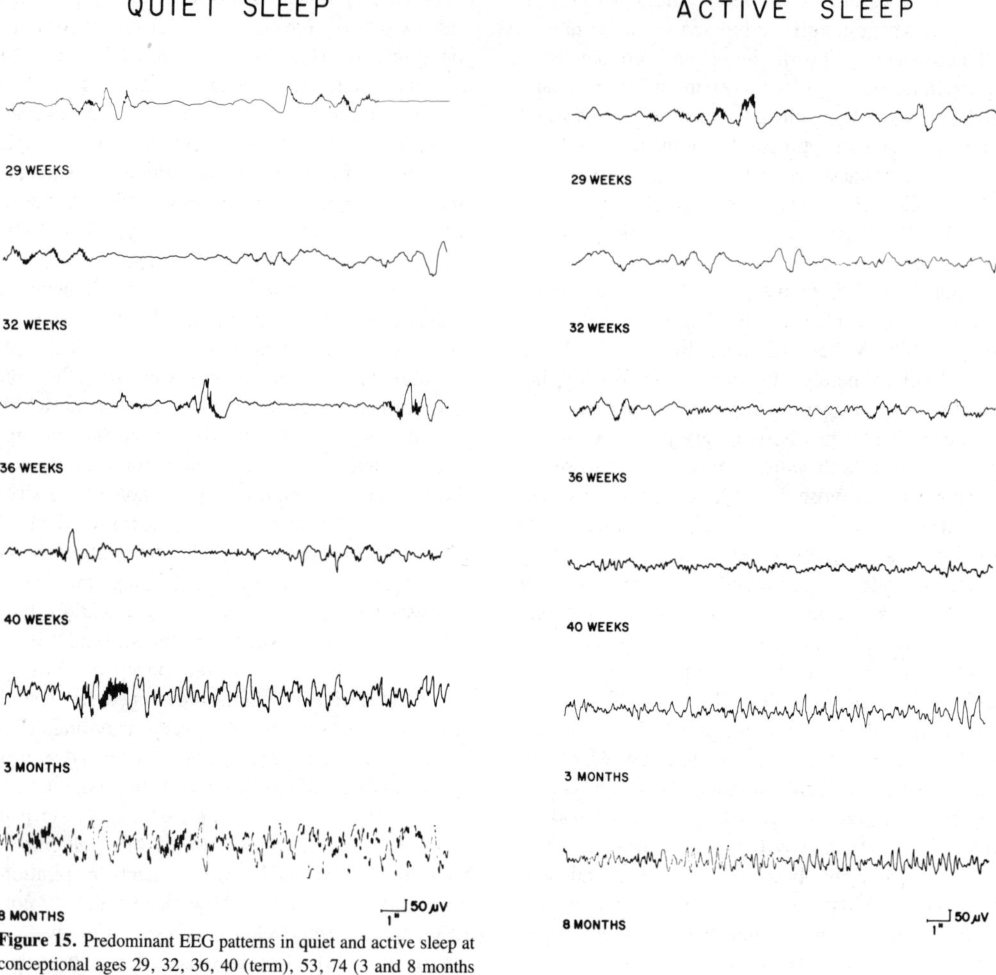

Figure 15. Predominant EEG patterns in quiet and active sleep at conceptional ages 29, 32, 36, 40 (term), 53, 74 (3 and 8 months past term) weeks. Sleep states were determined by the non-EEG parameters of eye movements, respiratory patterns, and body movements. At 28 weeks the EEG patterns tend to be similar in all states. With maturation, differences in EEG patterns in sleep states gradually develop and are quite distinct by 40 (term) weeks. In late preterm and newborn infants certain EEG patterns become more characteristic of specific sleep states but also occur so frequently in indeterminate states that they cannot be used for state classification. At 3 and 8 months past term EEG patterns become more tightly linked to specific sleep states as in adults but even at these ages this is found primarily for normal infants and adults.

ally on paper writeouts and by computer analyses of magnetic tape recorded EEG. With this information, the ontogenetic coincidences of changes in neuroanatomy, in EEG pattern and in behavioral state of the infant can be identified (Dreyfus-Brisac, 1979; Dreyfus-Brisac et al., 1958; Ellingson & Peters, 1980a,b; Haas & Prechtl, 1977; Havlicek, Childaeva, & Chernick, 1977; Parmelee, 1974; Parmelee et al., 1967; Parmelee, Akiyama, Schultz, Wenner, & Schulte, 1969; Parmelee, Akiyama, Schultz, Wenner, Schulte, & Stern, 1968; Parmelee, Schulte, Akiyama, Wenner, Schultz, & Stern, 1968; Prechtl, 1974; Prechtl et al., 1968; Sterman, Harper, Havens, Hoppenbrouwers, McGinty, & Hodgman, 1977; Watanabe, Iwase, & Hara, 1974).

The development of the spontaneous EEG in the preterm infant as in the kitten reflects the maturation of the cerebral cortex: the number of synapses, their depth from the surface, and number of interneurons, and recurrent collateral intracortical connections. Initially the EEG consists of bursts of high-voltage slow-wave activity, alternating with periods of very low-voltage attenuated activity with little or no variation in this pattern. A second pattern of continuous slow-wave activity appears between 28 and 30 weeks conceptional age. At 33 to 36 weeks a third pattern of continuous slow waves and irregular activity of lower voltage appears. Then at 40 weeks conceptional age an even lower voltage and more irregular activity with more rapid rhythms emerges. Preterm infants of like conceptional ages, though of different gestational and postnatal ages, have similar EEG patterns. At 40 weeks conceptional age the predominant patterns of preterm and full-term newborn infants are visually similar. The EEG patterns continue to develop in parallel fashion after term in preterm and term infants of like conceptional ages. Both develop readily identifiable sigma spindles (11 to 15 Hz) between 4 and 8 weeks past term, and at 3 months the EEG patterns associated with sleep states are approaching adult forms for both (Dreyfus-Brisac, 1964; Parmelee, 1974; Parmelee, Akiyama et al., 1968; Parmelee, Schulte et al., 1968).

Although the similarities predominate, there are some differences in the development of the EEG patterns of preterm and full-term infants at equivalent conceptional ages. At term the preterm infants have a scattered residual of immature EEG patterns that are not found in full-term infants (Dreyfus-Brisac, 1964; Parmelee, Schulte et al., 1968). Metcalf (1969) also demonstrated that preterm infants develop recognizable sleep sigma spindles about 2 to 4 weeks earlier than do full-term infants. More recently Ellingson and Peters (1980b) have confirmed this observation and added the finding that the alternating tracing (TA) found during quiet sleep in newborns disappears between 3 and 4 weeks past term in preterm infants and not until 5 to 6 weeks in full-term infants. This, like the earlier development of sleep spindles, suggests a more rapid development of these EEG parameters in preterm infants in the early months past term. With further studies, more differences will undoubtedly be found in the future. This does not change the significance of the predominant and surprising similarities in EEG development of infants of the same conceptional age.

The EEG of the kitten progresses from a nonvarying slow-wave pattern in all states to more rapid low-amplitude activity during wakefulness and rapid eye movement sleep and to high-voltage slow waves during sleep without eye movements at about 2 to 3 weeks of age. These changes parallel the changes seen in preterm infants (Hoppenbrouwers & Sterman, 1975; McGinty, Stevenson, Hoppenbrouwers, Harper, Sterman, & Hodgman, 1977; Valtax, Jouvet, & Jouvet, 1964).

The EEG is a very useful measure of pathological brain activity, particularly seizure activity, even in the newborn infant (Figure 16). It can also be used for identification of localized brain problems such as tumors and hemorrhages at all ages (Gibbs & Gibbs, 1951). It has been less useful in identifying differences in behavioral development, temperament, and intelligence. There are, however, significant correlations between EEG activity and age.

The brain cortical activity, as represented by the EEG, does undergo clear maturational changes in all states of sleep and wake beginning in fetal life and continuing through adult life. In normal children the process appears to be relatively independent of environmental circumstance (Ellingson, 1958; Gibbs & Gibbs, 1951; Petersén & Eeg-Olofsson, 1971; Petersén, Selldén, & Bosaeus, 1976), although this maturational progression can be altered by trauma, illness, and metabolic and genetic problems.

Sensory Evoked Potentials

Cortical evoked potentials are measured from the scalp in infants and the cortical surface in animals in the same manner as the electroencephalogram. The evoked potential is the recorded response within the spontaneous EEG activity that is time-locked to the presentation of a sensory stimulus. The stimulus may be visual, auditory, or somesthetic. The response to a single stimulus often can be seen in the ongoing spontaneous EEG activity but also may be missed by visual inspection. After multiple stimuli are presented sequentially, the 500 to 1000 msec of EEG following each stimulus can be summed by a computer, and the evoked EEG response that is time-locked to the stimulus is enhanced and stands out while the spontaneous non-time-locked EEG is diminished. In this manner, the shape, amplitude, and latencies of the recorded responses to the stimuli can be abstracted from the EEG. Mature evoked responses usually have multiple positive and negative waves or peaks with latencies from 25 to 500 msec. In the immature nervous system, the cortical evoked potential responses have long latencies and only surface negative peaks. The long latencies are due to the long transmission time across immature synapses and over immature unmyelinated axons even though the actual distances from sensory receptors to cortex are shorter than in adult animals or humans. The maturation of synaptic neurotransmitters helps speed conduction across synapses and the

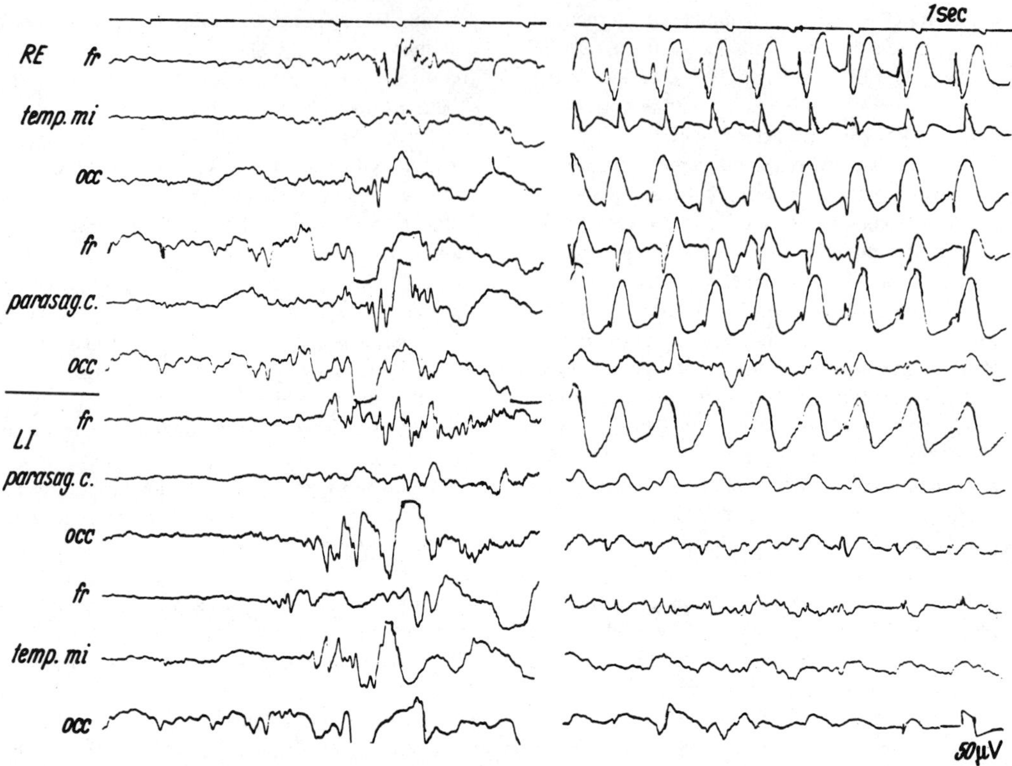

Figure 16. An abnormal EEG pattern in a 4-day-old infant with seizures due to congenital toxoplasmosis infection. The EEG on the left side of the illustration demonstrates bursts of polymorphic waves and on the right side regular repeated monomorphic waves occurring in paroxysms. The high amplitude regular waves are in all EEG leads in the right (RE) hemisphere and only in the left (LI) frontal (fr) region. Right hemisphere, RE; left hemisphere, LI; EEG leads: frontal, fr; mid-temporal, temp mi; occipital, occ; central parasaggital, parasag c. (From Joppich & Schulte, 1968.)

development of myelin helps speed conduction time along axons.

The maturational changes in the latencies and wave form of the evoked potential have been well described for infants and children for auditory, visual and somato sensory evoked potentials (Barnet, Friedman, Weiss, Ohlrich, Shanks, & Lodge, 1980; Barnet, Ohlrich, Weiss, & Shanks, 1975; Desmedt, Brunko, & Debecker, 1976; Ellingson, 1960; Engel & Benson, 1968; Weitzman & Graziani, 1968). This will be discussed in more detail when we review the development of the visual and auditory systems in subsequent sections of this chapter.

Changes in the first component of the sensory evoked potential from a negative to a positive wave form follow closely the anatomic development of the cortex (Desmedt et al., 1976; Marty, 1967; Purpura, 1975; Rose & Lindsley, 1968; Umezaki & Morrell, 1970). We now know from recordings in animals from single neurons that the negative sensory evoked potentials are generated in the cortex by activity at the axodendritic synapses (Creutzfeld, Watanabe, & Lux, 1966; Purpura et al., 1964). As we have previously described, in the immature nervous systems of preterm infants of 25 to 30 weeks gestation and in newborn kittens the axons from thalamic nuclei transmitting sensory stimuli synapse only on apical dendrites that are near the brain surface (Adinolfi, 1971; Purpura et al., 1964). The theoretical result of the neuronal activity being initiated so close to the surface should be a surface negative field of electric activity relative to the deeper levels where the neuron cell bodies are. In fact, the first component of sensory evoked potentials in preterm infants and newborn kittens is negative. With maturation of the cortical neurons, as we have described, basilar dendrites develop deeper in the cortex and the axons now initiate the neuronal activity at these syn-

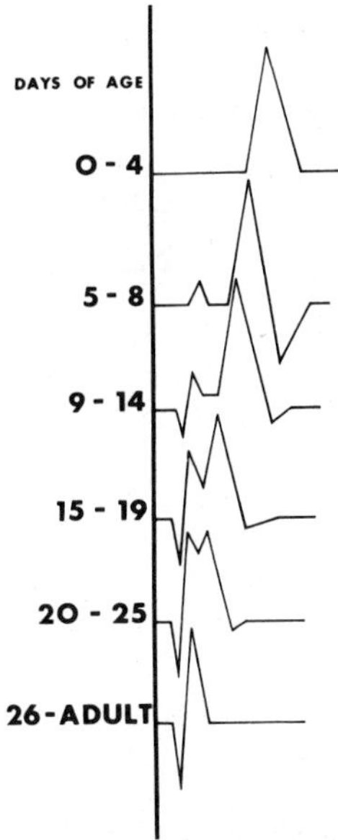

Figure 17. Visual cortical evoked responses from kittens and adult cats schematically represented with a deflection upward designated as a negative wave and downward as positive. From 0 to 4 days of age only a long latency negative wave is present; at 5 to 8 days an additional shorter latency negative wave appears; next at 9 to 14 days positive wave precedes both negative waves; then all latencies shorten and the two negative waves fuse into a single short latency wave. These schemas are from studies of evoked potentials in anesthetized (pentobarbital) kittens. (From Rose, Gruenau, & Spencer, 1972.)

apses. This results in the negative electrical field developing away from the cortical surface which remains relatively positive for the first wave. As expected at this developmental stage, in older preterm and full-term infants and older kittens the first component of sensory evoked potentials is positive.

The shift of the initial evoked potential wave from negative to positive is not only a function of the anatomic development of basilar dendrites on pyramidal neurons but also the total number of synaptic contacts for each neuron. The latter change the nature of the action potential of neurons generated by stimulation. In the neurons of the more immature cortex, the postsynaptic action potential has a large and prolonged inhibitory component that would add to the surface negative response. With maturation the postsynaptic potential develops a larger initial positive component adding to the development of surface positive waves (Hull & Fuller, 1975). Thus, sensory evoked potentials follow closely in form the anatomic development of the cortex, and provide a dynamic understanding of this part of the nervous system network (Desmedt et al., 1976; Marty, 1967; Purpura, 1975; Rose & Lindsley, 1968; Umezaki & Morrell, 1970)—see Figures 17 and 18.

Brainstem evoked potentials can be recorded to auditory stimuli reflecting the activity at a series of brainstem nuclei as the auditory signal ascends from the cochlea to the inferior colliculus. In the recording a series of five peaks are seen. The first peak, about 1 msec after the stimulus, is thought to reflect activity in the cochlear nerve and each succeeding wave a msec later another transmission point in the mature nervous system. Since these evoked potentials are of such short latency and are recorded from the vertex of the head they could not be transmitted to the cortex via neuronal pathways, as the transmission time would be too long. Instead the brain above the brainstem is considered to act as a volume conductor. It is for this reason these evoked potential are called far field potentials. The brainstem auditory evoked potentials, particularly the first peak, can be used to determine whether or not the cochlea is functioning and can diagnose deafness at this level. They also give us a window on brainstem functioning. Increased latencies and lower amplitude of the five peaks have been found in patients with a variety of neurological disorders and medical problems including neonatal hypoxic episodes. The significance of these in predicting later behavior is not yet clear. At present we have information on the ontogeny of brainstem evoked potentials in preterm infants and infants and children in the first months and years of life. The more immature the brain, for example, in the preterm infant, the longer the latencies of all peaks, the more irregular their form, and the louder the auditory stimulus must be to elicit them—see Figures 19 and 20—(Barden & Peltzman, 1980; Despland & Galambos, 1980; Goldstein, Krumholz, Felix, Shannon, & Carr, 1979; Kileny, Connelly, & Robertson, 1980; Salamy, Mendelson, Tooley, & Chaplin, 1980; Starr et al., 1977).

Studies of the ontogeny of auditory brainstem evoked potentials in the kitten are in progress. Animal studies permit experimental lesions and single-unit recordings in order to determine the sites of origin of each evoked peak and the changes in the latencies and amplitudes of evoked potentials at different age levels (Shipley et al., 1980).

Sensory evoked potentials indicate that the sensory receptor can respond to a stimulus, that the pathways to the cortex are functioning, and that the cortical neurons can respond. Sensory evoked responses as traditionally recorded do not delineate how much of the signal is involved nor the degree to which it is being processed by either the peripheral receptors, the more central nuclei, or the cortex. A normal visual or auditory evoked response in an infant, for example, demonstrates that the basic system is operating but not whether there is visual or auditory perception.

The use of more complex stimuli rather than the traditional light flash or click in producing evoked potentials has made it possible to obtain information about the portions of the stimuli being processed even in very young infants as well as preschool children. For visual stimuli, complex checkerboard targets have been used with brief intermittent flashing illumination or sinusoidal rapid checkerboard reversal. With these techniques both the visual acuity and attention to complexity can be evaluated (Karmel & Maisel, 1975; Sokol, 1978). More complex auditory stimuli, such as human speech sounds, have been used in the study of auditory evoked potentials in infants. These studies have been particularly useful in studying hemispheric differences in types of speech discrimination (Molfese, 1980; Molfese & Hess, 1976). Such studies will undoubtedly continue to extend our understanding of sensory information processing particularly in early infancy.

Some recent evoked potential studies have attempted to address the issue of brain information processing and memory. These techniques require presentations of stimuli that allow anticipation and estimation of the probability of another stimulus. The evoked potential responses are called *event related potentials* (ERP). One is the *contingent negative variation* (CNV). The CNV is a negative shift in brain potential during the period between a warning stimulus and a later imperative stimulus requiring a mental or motor response. It is interpreted as a response related to expectation and preparation for the command stimulus and an index of memory activity (Desmedt, 1981; Walter, Cooper, Aldridge, McCallum, & Winter, 1964). This procedure has been used mostly with older children and adults but may ultimately be extended to infants.

Another event-related potential is the late positive wave with latencies of 300 to 900 msecs, $\overline{\text{P300}}$. The $\overline{\text{P300}}$ wave measures attention and decision making regarding task relevant stimuli. Active attention toward target signals of a serial cognitive task (with or without a motor response) are necessary to enhance the $\overline{\text{P300}}$ wave. To ignore identical stimuli designated as task irrelevant on a later run will reduce the $\overline{\text{P300}}$ wave in the same subject. Use of this technique appears to be very fruitful in the study of cognitive processes in adults and older children (Courchesne, 1978; Desmedt, 1981; Donchin, 1977; Donchin, Tueting, Ritter, Kutor, & Heffley, 1975; Squires, Squires, & Hillyard, 1975; Sutton et al., 1965). In children 6 to 8 years old the $\overline{\text{P300}}$ wave may have a latency as great as 900 msec. Cour-

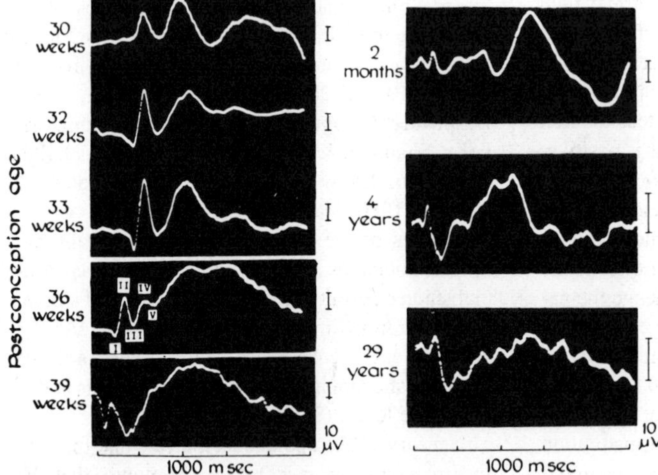

Figure 18. Visual cortical evoked potentials in preterm infants of 30, 32, 33, 36, and 39 weeks conceptional age, 2 months past term, 4 years, and 29 years. An upward deflection is a negative wave and a downward deflection is positive. At 30 weeks conceptional age there are two negative waves with long latencies, and by 33 weeks there is a clear positive wave before the two negative waves and the latencies are shorter. This is reminiscent of the responses in kittens of 5 to 8 days and 9 to 14 days respectively (see Figure 17). (From Umezaki & Morrell, 1970.)

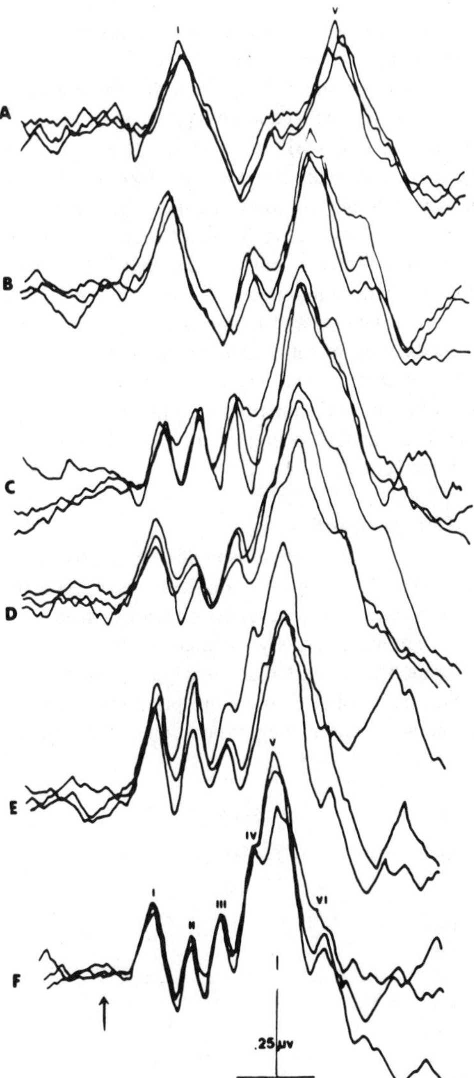

Figure 19. Maturational changes in brainstem auditory evoked potentials in humans (A, newborn; B, 6 weeks old; C, 3 months old; D, 6 months old; E, 1 year old; F, adults). Each trace represents an average of 2400 brainstem evoked potentials from a different subject. There is a progressive decrease in latency and definition of wave form. In F waves I through VI are designated. Note the very short time scale for these evoked potentials. All occur within 6 to 8 msec in contrast to cortical evoked potentials that have latencies of 25 to 1000 msec. In this illustration positivity is indicated by an upward deflection. (From Salamy & McKean, 1976.)

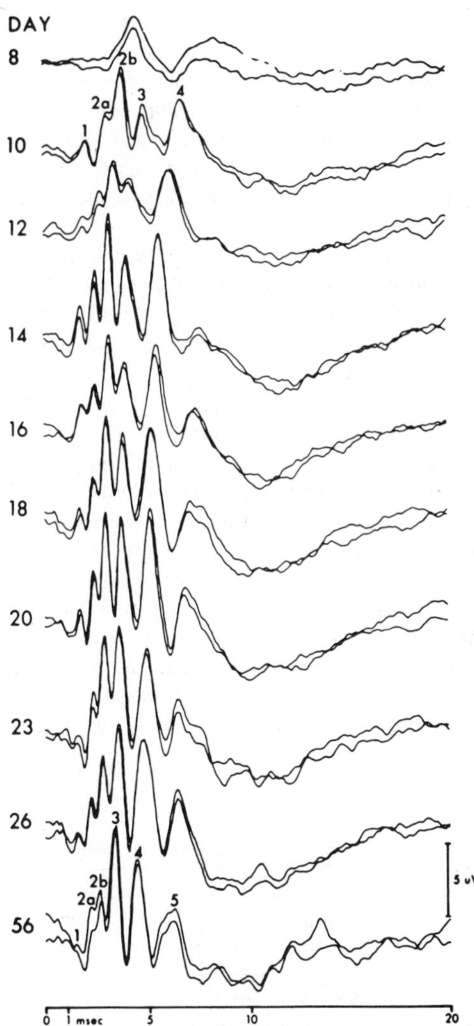

Figure 20. The development sequence of brainstem auditory evoked potentials from one kitten from 8 to 56 days of life. Note the decreasing latency and greater definition of the wave forms with age. The waves are numbered 1 to 5 at 10 and 56 days of age. The stimulus (45 db HL, 10/sec clicks) occurs at the trace onset. (From Shipley et al., 1980.)

chesne (1978) has suggested that this difference in latency in children corresponds to a different mode of processing used to evaluate the content of events rather than differences in sensory processing.

Extension of $\overline{\text{P300}}$ studies to younger children and infants is feasible and is being explored. Such studies should provide valuable information about memory and decision making in infants (Courchesne, Ganz, & Norcia, 1981; Hoffman, Salapatek, & Kuskowski, 1981; Karmel, Kay, & John, 1978).

Unfortunately at present nothing is known about the neurophysiological origin and mechanisms of the $\overline{\text{P300}}$ wave. Such studies necessarily require animal experiments with depth electrode recording from the brain and placement of focal lesions, and so on. Recently Wilder, Farley, and Starr (1981) reported obtaining $\overline{\text{P300}}$ waves in cats similar to those in humans. If these results are confirmed, the way for the necessary animal experiments will be open.

As we have already indicated in our discussion of the EEG, there are current efforts to do combined

EEG and evoked potential analyses. These studies include the presentation of complex stimuli and various tasks to elicit the event related potentials and simultaneous recording from multiple areas of the brain. The amount of information obtained in such studies is overwhelming. To deal with these data, promising complex computer analysis techniques have been devised. Two of these techniques are neurometrics (John, Karmel, Corning, Easton, Brown, Ahn, John, Harmony, Prichep, Toro Gerson, Bartlett, Thatcher, Kaye, Valdes, & Schwartz, 1977; Karmel et al., 1978) and brain electrical activity mapping (BEAM).

The BEAM techniques provide a color-coded display of the changes in the brain electrical activity in each brain area as represented on a grid corresponding to the brain surface. The color coding can represent actual brain electrical activity in each area, differences between areas, or differences from an expected response. The display can take place in real time during the coding or later from tape (Duffy & Als, 1982; Duffy et al., 1979; Duffy et al., 1980; Duffy, Denkla, Bartels, Sandini, & Kiessling, 1980). These techniques already have been used successfully to identify children with learning disorders but have not been used with infants except for limited explorations of the possibilities.

As we gain more skill at coordinating information processing with neurophysiological measures of the neuronal network, we tend to move away from the immediate brain responses to response displays derived through complex mathematical analyses. These are, however, inclusive of more stimuli and brain areas. Thus we move farther and farther away from an understanding of the contribution of any individual neuron and its synapses but gain more understanding of total neuronal network functioning. It will take many years of study of brain unit structure, network functioning, and behavior to approach an understanding of their interdependence and interaction.

Ontogeny of States

Studies of the development of sleep, sleep states, and waking bring together simultaneous observation and recording of spontaneous behavior such as body and eye movements, physiological functions such as respiration and heart rate, and brain activity, the EEG. Studies of sleep in infants permit the study of the ontogeny of the integration of these separate pa-

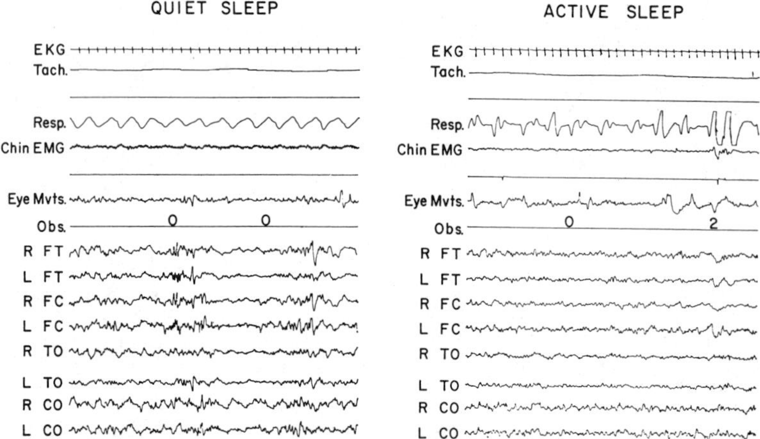

Figure 21. A polygraphic recording of a full term newborn infant illustrating the characteristics of quiet and active sleep. Recorded are heart rate as EKG and on a tachometer (Tach), respirations (Resp), chin muscle electromyogram (EMG), eye movements as corneal-retinal potentials (Eye Mvts), movements by observation code (Obs), and eight bipolar channels of EEG. Quiet sleep is characterized by a regular heart rate with slow steady undulations of rate, regular respirations, chin EMG activity present, no eye movements, no body movements as indicated under Obs by the zeros, and an EEG pattern of alternating bursts of activity, trace alternant. Active sleep is characterized by an irregular heart rate (not well illustrated here), irregular respirations, no chin EMG activity, eye movements present, small body movements present as indicated under Obs by the number 2, and an EEG pattern of continuous low voltage rapid activity. (From Parmelee, Akiyama et al., 1968.)

rameters into organized complex units of behavior signaling the development of the more global brain networks. Within the described organized states one can pursue the development of both behavioral and brain evoked responses to stimulation in order to further define brain network ontogeny.

Sleep states and waking are fairly well organized at birth in full-term infants. Sleep is usually defined behaviorally as any period when the infant's eyes are closed. Sleep can be further subdivided into active (rapid eye movement or REM) sleep and quiet (no rapid eye movement or non-REM) sleep by both behavioral observation and recording of eye movements that are clearly visible beneath the closed eyelids. Active sleep is further characterized by frequent brief muscle jerks both in the face and in the extremities but absent tonic muscle tone. In the face these twitches often resemble smiles and frowns. Respiration and heart rate are also irregular in this state. Quiet sleep is characterized by an absence of eye movements and body movements except for occasional total body jerking, the presence of tonic muscle tone, and regular respirations and heart rate (Figure 21). As discussed previously, the EEG in these two sleep states in newborn and young infants, while demonstrating some patterns of activity most characteristic of each state, does not have the close correlation of specific patterns with states seen in adults. It is not, therefore, easy to predict sleep state in the infant from EEG patterns alone before about 3 to 4 months past term.

Cycles of active and quiet sleep alternate rhythmically in infants as in adults (Figure 22). Newborn infants generally go from waking through a short transition period into active sleep which lasts for 15 to 20 min. and then through a short transition into quiet sleep for 15 to 20 min. and back into active sleep, alternating in this fashion for 3 to 4 hr. until the infant awakens. Infants usually awaken from active sleep. As infants mature the active sleep periods become shorter and the quiet sleep periods longer, but the total cycle length remains the same, 50 to 60 min. Older infants are more likely to enter sleep in the quiet sleep state but continue to waken from active sleep (Anders, 1978; Anders, Emde, & Parmelee, 1971; Aserinsky & Kleitman, 1955; Bernstein, Emde, & Campos, 1973; Dreyfus-Brisac, 1968, 1970, 1979; Emde & Walker, 1976; Parmelee, 1974; Parmelee, Akiyama et al., 1968; Parmelee, Schulte et al., 1968; Parmelee & Stern, 1972; Parmelee, Wenner, Akiyama, Schultz, & Stern, 1967; Petre-Quadens, 1967; Prechtl et al., 1968; Roffwarg, Muzio, & Dement, 1966; Stern, Parmelee, Akiyama, Schultz, & Wenner, 1969).

The waking state is usually defined behaviorally by the observation of open eyes and apparent visual alertness; additional observations of quietness or movement are used to further subdivide this state. Crying is usually included in the awake state as well. While one can define the waking state in the young infant by multiple parameters such as open eyes, eye movements present, respirations irregular, muscle tone present, and a low-voltage-fast-activity EEG pattern, the other subdivisions used do not necessarily define different state levels within waking. Brief periods of higher levels of arousal or alertness usually are so variable and context dependent that they do not fit the classic definition of a state (Ashton, 1973; Prechtl, 1974). We need a different terminology for varying levels of arousal and attentiveness within the waking state.

In adults, visual, auditory, and somesthetic

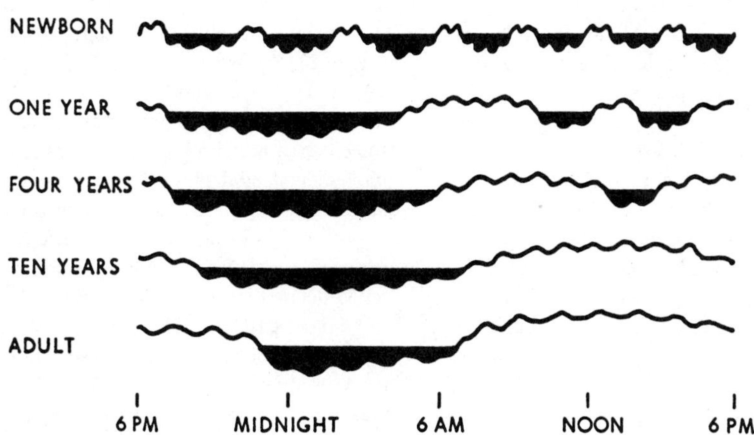

Figure 22. Schematic representation of the basic rest-activity cycle superimposed on the sleep-wake cycles. Black areas represent sleep. (From Kleitman, 1963.)

evoked potentials have different characteristics when obtained during wakefulness, non-REM sleep or REM sleep. Generally, the lowest amplitudes are obtained in REM sleep and the clearest definitions of each peak in Non-REM sleep. These state differences in evoked responses are not present in full-term or preterm newborn infants or even in infants 3 months past term. When differences in amplitude are found in late peaks in preterm infants, these appear to be due to background EEG amplitude (Akiyama, Schulte, Schultz, & Parmelee, 1969; Desmedt & Debecker, 1972; Ellingson, 1970, 1973; Watanabe, Iwase, & Hara, 1973). The early short latency components of sensory evoked potentials are independent of state even in adults as are brainstem auditory evoked potentials (Ellingson, 1973; Salamy & McKean, 1976). It must be remembered that these are responses to light flashes, clicks, or electrical skin stimulation. Response latencies and wave forms to more salient stimuli in these states is now being explored.

The behavioral responses of infants are dependent on state, and judging state of arousal at the time of sensory stimulation is an important part of the behavioral evaluation of newborn full-term and preterm infants as well as young infants. For example, in the quiet awake state they may turn away from strong visual or auditory stimuli and turn toward more gentle and salient voices or visual images (Als, Lester, & Brazelton, 1979; Brazelton, 1973). Prechtl was one of the first investigators of newborn behavior and neurology to recognize the degree to which neurological and behavioral responses of the newborn are altered by state changes. He and his colleagues have systematically investigated these in a series of elegant studies of reflexes, postural responses, and responses to tactual, visual, and auditory stimuli (von Bernuth & Prechtl, 1969; Casaer, 1979; Lenard, von Bernuth, & Prechtl, 1968; Prechtl, 1972, 1974; Prechtl & Beintema, 1968; Prechtl, Vlach, Lenard, & Kerr Grant, 1967; Vlach, von Bernuth, & Prechtl, 1969). Some of Prechtl's results are listed in Table 1.

In his classification State 1 is non-REM or quiet sleep, State 2 is REM or active sleep, and State 3 is quiet awake. The proprioceptive reflexes such as the knee jerk and biceps jerks (muscle stretch reflexes) and Moro reflex (neck articulation and vestibular stimulation) are all increased in State 1, quiet sleep, and essentially absent in State 2, active REM sleep. This is consistent with the marked reduction of muscle tone during REM sleep presumably due to supraspinal influences that inhibit the alpha motor neurons and the general loss of postural control in this state. Exteroceptive skin reflexes and auditory orienting, on the other hand, persist in REM sleep indicating a continuing receptiveness in this state but responses are absent in quiet sleep. Some reflexes that are nociceptive appear to be independent of state. Differences in responses in each state between infants and adults are probably due to immaturity of state organization in the infant. Studies of kittens have shown opposite responses in the jaw closing and opening reflex as a function of state when compared with adult cats (Chase, 1972). By 4 weeks the kitten reflex patterns vary with state like those of the adult cat. In preterm infants some reflexes such as the Babkin and Palmomental reflexes (skin pressure reflexes) are not state dependent but become state dependent by term (Lenard et al., 1968; Parmelee, 1963 a,b; Prechtl, 1972).

Even within the defined sleep states we have difficulty knowing whether these states are truly similar across all ages. There is some agreement that this may be so from 3 to 4 months past term on and perhaps even in the newborn period. The definition of sleep states in preterm infants becomes more difficult and we are more inclined to define them by partial criteria. For example, some investigators have described increasing amounts of REM sleep the more immature the preterm infant such that the just viable infant of 25 weeks gestation has only REM sleep (Roffwarg et al., 1966). This is based on their frequent movement, irregular respiration, and sporadic occurence of eye movements during all sleep. Muscle tone and EEG criteria at this age are not useful. On closer inspection, the eye movements, while present, are not frequent and sometimes are widely scattered. Other investigators have preferred to describe this sleep as indeterminate or transitional since it may not be analogous to later REM sleep. More clearly definable active or REM sleep appears between 34 to 36 weeks gestation, a month before term when quiet, non-REM sleep also emerges—see Figure 23 (Parmelee & Stern, 1972; Parmelee et al., 1967a; Petre-Quadens, 1967). From then on eye movements become more frequent and more confined to periods with irregular respiration and phasic movements and depressed tonic muscle tone. Even at this stage of clearer definition of active or REM sleep it may still not be entirely comparable to the active or REM sleep of older infants or adults. The REM sleep of infants 3 to 4 months past term seems to be most analogous to adult REM sleep. Perhaps some other terminology for these states should be used for infants younger than 3 months. It is for this reason that Prechtl, for example, prefers to use numerical designations such as States I and II in newborn infants.

Researchers of sleep in newborn animals have

Table 1. **Responses to Stimulation in Different States***

	State 1	State 2	State 3
Proprioceptive reflexes			
Knee jerk	+++	±	++
Biceps jerk	+++	±	++
Lip jerk	+++	±	++
Ankle clonus	+++	–	–
Moro tap	+++	–	++
Moro head drop	+++	–	++
Exteroceptive skin reflexes			
Tactile			
Rooting	–	–	++
Palmar grasp	–	+	++
Plantar grasp	–	++	++
Lip protrusion	–	+++	++
Finger reflex	–	+	++
Toe reflex	–	++	++
Tibial reflex	±	++	++
Fibular reflex	±	++	++
Axillary reflex	±	++	++
Pressure			
Babkin	–	+	++
Palmomental	–	++	++
Nociceptive			
Babinski reflex	++	+++	+++
Abdominal reflex	++	+++	+++
Thigh	++	+++	+++
Pubic	++	+++	+++
Inguinal	+++	+++	+++
Auditory orienting	±	++	+++
Visual pursuit	–	–	++
Vestibulo-ocular	–	++	+++

State I = Eyes closed, regular respiration, no movements.
State II = Eyes closed, irregular respiration, no gross movements.
State III = Eyes open, no gross movements.

***From Prechtl, 1974.**

been faced with the same problem. Newborn kittens and rat pups have only one state of constant twitching and irregular respiration; eyes are closed with eye movements variable. There is no tonic muscle tone and the EEG is invariant. In the kitten identifiable sleep states begin to appear between 10 to 14 days after birth (Jouvet-Mounier, Astic, & Lacote, 1970), comparable with the appearance of organized sleep states in premature infants at 34 to 36 weeks gestation.

The following are neurophysiological and neurochemical studies that provide further evidence of developmental differences in sleep state organization between infants and adults. Ponto-geniculate-occipital neuronal activity is associated with the phasic somatic phenomena of active or rapid eye movement (REM) sleep in adult cats, particularly with the eye movement bursts. These have been considered to be manifestations of the fundamental triggering mechanism of REM sleep in the adult cat (Benoit & Adrien, 1975). Although kittens have a form of active sleep with jerking body movements and some eye movements from birth, ponto-geniculate-occipital spikes could not be recorded in the lateral geniculate nuclei until after 2 weeks of age. Rapid bursts of ponto-geniculate-occipital spikes did not begin to appear until the third week but were mature in character by 4 weeks (Figure 24). Before 3 weeks postnatally there was no clear association of ponto-geniculate-occipital spikes to sleep states, but by 4 weeks they were almost exclusively confined to REM sleep, as in adult cats—see (Figure 25) (Benoit & Adrien, 1975; Bowe-Anders et al., 1974).

Studies of the development of neuronal unit activity in the lateral geniculate nuclei of kittens along the visual pathway to the cortex demonstrated that

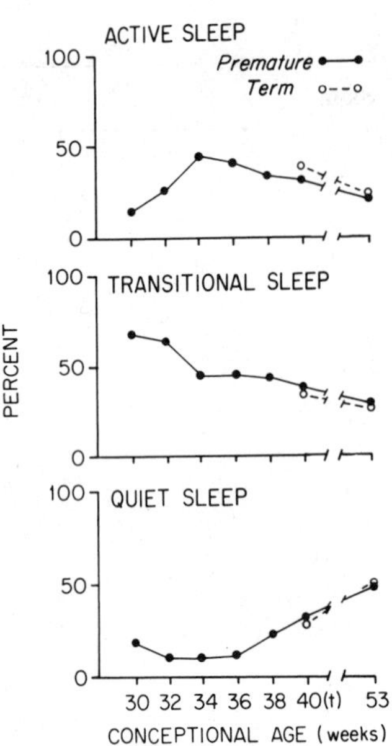

Figure 23. Development of distribution of sleep states in preterm and term infants in three-hour interfeeding polygraphic recordings. Criteria for quiet sleep (QS) were no body or eye movements and regular respiration; and for active sleep (AS) presence of eye movement and irregular respiration. Sleep that did not meet the criteria for QS or AS was classified transitional. Before 34 weeks most sleep is unclassifiable. Then AS can be identified in insignificant amounts as a separate state, but there is little QS. The latter develops after 36 weeks and rapidly increases in amount to 3 months past term 53 weeks' conceptional age. At term and 3 months the distribution of sleep states is the same for preterm and full-term infants. (From Parmelee & Stern, 1972.)

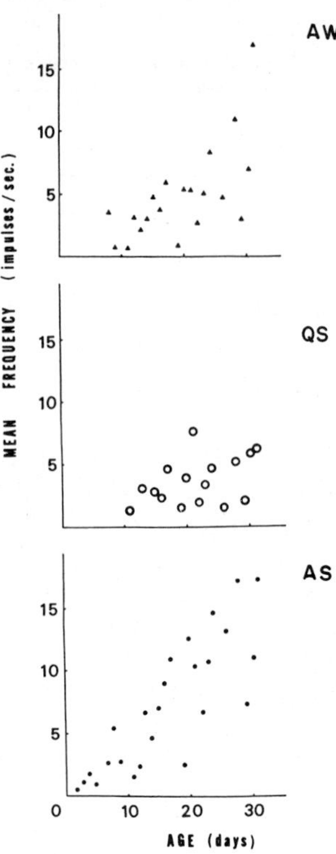

Figure 25. Unit activity in the lateral geniculate nucleus, LGN, demonstrating the evolution of the mean frequency of unit discharge in three states during the first month of life: awake state (AW), quiet sleep (QS), and active sleep (AS). There is little activity in any state before 10 to 20 days of age and no clear association with state. After 20 days there is increased unit activity during AS and AW with a suppression of activity in QS. (From Adrien & Roffwarg, 1974.)

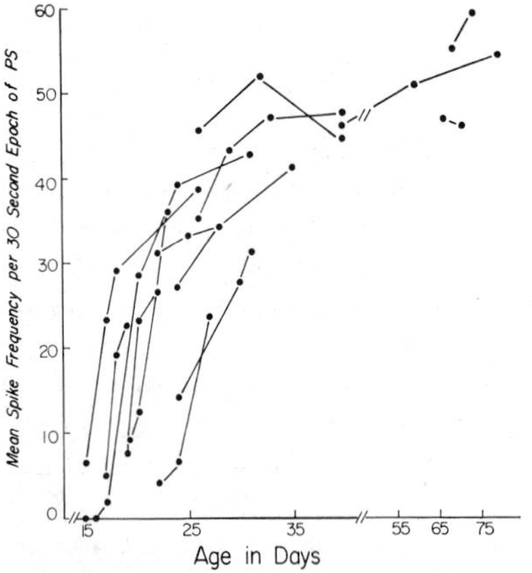

Figure 24. Evolution of lateral-geniculate nucleus (LGN) activity as part of the ponto-geniculate-occipital, PGO, activity in 14 kittens. There is very little activity around 15 days of age with a rapid increase in frequency of spikes to 25 days, when PGO waves are initially observed, with a leveling off after 35 days. Each dot represents the mean of all frequencies recorded in active or paradoxical sleep (PS). (From Bowe-Anders et al., 1974.)

spontaneous discharges were infrequent regardless of state (fewer than 5 impulses per sec) in the first 2 weeks. At 3 weeks there was a sharp increase in the discharge rate to more than 10 per sec during rapid eye movement (REM) sleep and more than 5 per sec during wakefulness. The rate of spontaneous discharges did not increase during quiet sleep until after 2 weeks, suggesting a state-dependent depression of these after this time (Adrien & Roffwarg, 1974).

In adult cats the serotonin neurotransmitter system associated with the posterior median raphe in the brain stem is associated with the control of quiet or non-REM sleep, and the norepinephrine neurotransmitter system associated with the locus coeruleus of the brain stem is important in controlling REM sleep (Figure 26). Destruction of either of these systems in the adult can profoundly alter the state organization of the system involved. Adrien (1978) found that destruction of one or the other of these systems in newborn kittens did not immediate-

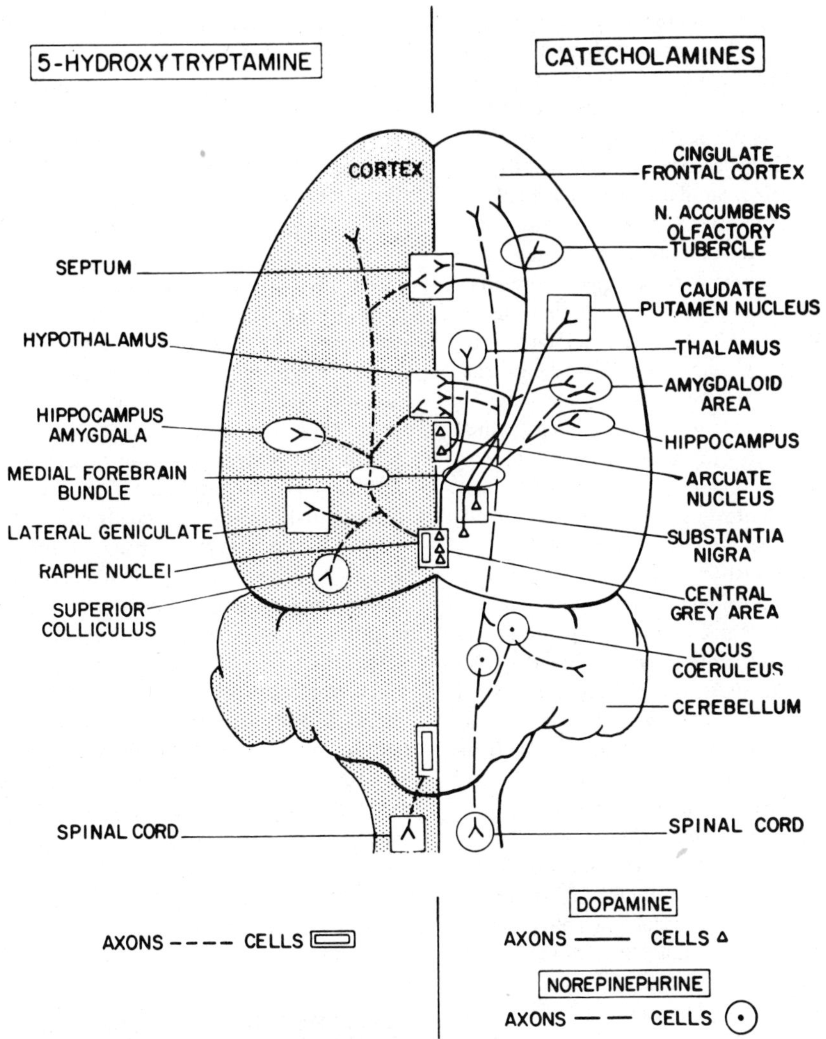

Figure 26. Neurotransmitter pathways for three important neuroregulators of behavioral states. The dopaminergic and noradrenergic (catecholamine) pathways and the serotonergic (5-Hydroxy-tryptomine) pathway in the rat brain are shown in a simplified horizontal cross section of brain. (From Barchas, Abil, Elliott, Holman, & Watson, 1978.)

ly alter their sleep states or the development of their sleep states in the next weeks, whereas similar lesioning in 3-week-old kittens did alter sleep state organization. This also suggests that what we perceive as state organization in immature organisms has to some degree a different underlying mechanism. Disturbances in states at this developmental level may have different neurophysiological and possibly behavioral meaning than similar disturbances in states observed at later ages.

There are, nevertheless, definite signs of progressive organization of states associated with maturation of the brain. This is manifest by the increasing evidence of control in each parameter used to identify states. For example, as preterm infants mature there are more and longer periods of regular respiration and of regular heart rate with each requiring increasingly elaborate mechanisms for monitoring rate and regularity and feedback controlling mechanisms (Harper, Hoppenbrouwers, Sterman, McGinty, & Hodgman, 1976; Parmelee & Stern, 1972; Parmelee, Stern, & Harris, 1972). In very small and immature preterm infants muscle tone is constantly shifting and there are frequent phasic movements.

With neurological maturation there are more frequent and longer periods without movement alternating with longer periods of phasic movement. These are associated with long periods of steady muscle tone and suppressed and phasic muscle tone respectively (Eliet-Flescher & Dreyfus-Brisac, 1966; Schulte, 1974). Similarly, eye movements are scattered in preterm infants with varying intervals between each movement. With maturation, eye movements become more densely packed in bursts of more equal intervals between eye movements (Becker & Thoman, 1982; Dittrichova, Paul, & Pavlikova, 1972; Petre-Quadens, 1972; Petre-Quadens, DeLee, & Remy, 1971; Prechtl & Lenard, 1967). Each of these parameters, as well as their gradual concordant appearance for sustained periods to form identifiable states, provide evidence for the increasing development of nervous system controlling feedback mechanisms (Parmelee & Stern, 1974).

These maturational changes in sleep state organization can be used to identify maturation age and disturbance in development of sleep organization in infants who have suffered neonatal problems or who are offsprings of mothers who are heroin or alcohol addicted. Fortunately most of these changes are transient (Havlicek et al., 1977; Monod, Dreyfus-Brisac, Eliet-Flescher, Pajot, & Plassart, 1963; Parmelee & Stern, 1972; Schulman, 1969; Theorell, Prechtl & Vos, 1974; Thoman, Dennenberg, Sievel, Zeidner, & Becker, 1980). The individual parameters of sleep states within the context of state organization can also be used to identify neurophysiological disorganization. For example, increased episodes of apnea have been found in sleep recording of infants who later suffered from sudden infant death syndrome (SIDS) (Guilleminault, Ariagno, Forno, Nagle, Baldwin, & Owen, 1979; Thoman, Miano, & Freese, 1977); increased eye movement "storms" at 6 months in REM sleep show a relationship to poor performance on behavioral assessment at one year (Becker & Thoman, 1981); and reduced eye movement frequency in REM sleep is associated with mental retardation in infants and children (Petre-Quadens, 1972).

The development of sleep state organization and the parameters within each state provide another global view of the maturation of the total nervous system network. In addition, we have more anatomical, neurophysiological, and biochemical information from animal studies related to state organization than to any other general cluster of behavioral organization. While most of these studies have been done in the adult cat—and hence the findings are not always applicable to the kitten—these investigations usefully guide research in the kitten. We still need increasingly detailed studies of kitten behavioral development to relate to the detailed studies of infant behavior.

At present it seems reasonable to postulate that evidence of identifiable sleep state organization neurophysiologically and behaviorally in the kitten at 2 to 3 weeks and in the human preterm infant at 34 to 36 weeks conceptional, one month before term, signals a level of maturational development that permits the nervous system to be more interactive with the environment. Prior to this time the limited capacity of the nervous system to interact with the environment diminishes the degree to which the environment can influence brain development.

Throughout this section we have focused on the development of the nervous system during the transition period from the genetically encoded development of the embryo to the period of developmental sensitivity to sensory inputs found in early infancy. In the human this transition period is best exemplified by the preterm infant from 25 to 35 weeks gestation, 1 to 3 months before term, and in the kitten from birth to 3 weeks after birth. We have chosen to emphasize this transition period not only because it is the least understood of all stages of nervous system development as related to behavior but also because it has practical significance in the management of preterm and newborn infants.

The next section will detail the relation of nervous system and behavioral development during this transition period for two sensory systems, auditory and visual.

DEVELOPMENT OF VISUAL AND AUDITORY SENSITIVITY AND BEHAVIOR

The question of when sensory stimulation can begin to affect brain development is of both theoretical and practical importance. The clinical issue concerns the effects of early stimulation on the development of preterm infants. Some infants are born as much as 10 to 15 weeks before their expected date of birth, term, and survive to adulthood. During this preterm period before expected birth, they are exposed to auditory and visual stimuli from which they would normally be shielded. Those who care for these infants in special intensive-care nurseries are greatly concerned that the preterm infant may be grossly overstimulated in some ways and possibly understimulated in others. We will review what is known about the development of the auditory and visual system in preterm infants. We will present evidence that the extreme immaturity of the nervous system before 35 to 37 weeks of gestation or one month before term, may provide a form of protection by its limited capacity to process stimuli despite the ability to respond behaviorally in limited ways. Animal and human studies related to audition and vision which support this hypothesis will be presented.

Development of Auditory Sensitivity in Infants

Preterm infants probably are exposed to more and different sounds than in utero. Among these are noises within incubators—for example, air circulation motors—that may be at a 70 to 80 db level in the frequency range of 63 to 250 Hz with the peak at 125 Hz. This is continuous noise without patterning. Additional and more varied increases in sound level come from the clatter of doors, handling of equipment and nursery staff conversation (Bess, Peck, & Chapman, 1979; Blennow, Svenningsen, & Almquist, 1974; Committee, Academy of Pediatrics, 1974; Lawson, Daum, & Turkewitz, 1977; Seleny & Streczyn, 1969).

The effects of this noise on the later auditory perception of preterm infants have been difficult to determine. Other factors that can cause hearing losses confound the results of follow-up studies. These include hypoxia, infections, drugs, and hyperbilirubinemia, all potentially harmful to the auditory system, and frequent complications for preterm infants.

Schulte and Stennart (1978) in a follow-up study of preterm infants found 12.4% with some neurosensory loss compared with a generally reported .5% incidence for all children. There was no correlation of the neurosensory hearing loss in the preterm infants with gestational age or length of stay in the incubator. There was, however, a correlation with a perinatal nonoptimal risk score. Similar findings have been reported by Abramovich, Gregory, Slemick and Stewart (1979). This suggests that the hearing losses are related more to illnesses during pregnancy, and delivery and immediate postnatal problems than to nursery noise pollution. As will be discussed later, longitudinal studies show that auditory evoked potentials in the neonatal period are also not altered in their development by the nursery environment.

Preterm infants have been reported to have language difficulties in childhood with somewhat greater frequency than full-term infants (DeHirsch, Jansky, & Langford, 1964; Neligan, Kolvin, Scott, & Garside, 1976). Variables other than preterm birth have been difficult to control in such studies. For example, we are increasingly aware of the considerable importance of demographic and social variables such as the nature of parent-infant interactions in language development. Cohen, Beckwith, and Parmelee (1978) found specific influences of parental caregiving on the receptive language competence of 2-year-old preterm infants as measured by an assessment of receptive language capacity (Beckwith & Thompson, 1976). Neligan et al. (1976) also found a strong environmental influence on language competence of preterm infants at 5 and 7 years of age.

O'Connor (1980) studied 50 preterm and full-term infants at 4 months of age using a variable trials habituation-dishabituation procedure in an auditory discrimination task with heart rate as a response measure. The preterm and full-term infants were indistinguishable on the habituation parameters. Included in the preterm group were many infants who were in incubators for prolonged periods since the mean gestational age for the group was 32 weeks with a range of 26 to 37 weeks. Nevertheless, there was no correlation between the gestational age of the preterm infants and their performance. Thus, while the potential for auditory and language difficulties in preterm infants seems to be present, it is still unclear that the unusual auditory environment of the preterm has a significant persisting impact on the immature but rapidly developing auditory system or language development.

There is limited information and some confusion about the early responses of the human fetus and preterm infant to auditory stimulation (Parmelee, 1981). Mothers have reported fetuses responding to music or loud noises in the environment with movement as early as 6 months and fetal heart rate response to extrauterine auditory stimulation has been reported in one infant at 30 weeks gestation (Murphy & Smyth, 1962). In systematic studies of larger numbers of subjects, however, these observations have not been confirmed (Bench & Vass, 1970; Fleischer, 1955) and consistent responses of the fetus to environmental sounds are found only after 34 weeks of gestation. The responses of younger fetuses may be secondary to the effect of the sound stimulus on the mother (Sontag, Steele, & Lewis, 1969).

There are a few studies of the responses of preterm infants to auditory stimulation. Such responses have been observed as early as 28 to 32 weeks gestation but are brief and inconsistent and disappear with repeated stimulation. Furthermore, loud stimuli are necessary to elicit a response. The older preterm infants of 34 weeks gestational or conceptional age demonstrate more varied and selective responses

(Als et al., 1979; Bench & Parker, 1971; Gesell & Amatruda, 1945; Monod & Garma, 1971).

Cortical and brainstem auditory evoked potentials can be obtained from the youngest viable preterm infants of 25 to 28 weeks gestation. These early evoked potentials require very loud stimuli and have very long latencies and the form of the evoked waves is different than in term infants. As discussed previously, the initial cortical evoked potential wave is negative in polarity in the young preterm infant with a positive wave appearing first, near term. In general the cortical and brainstem auditory evoked potentials of preterm infants at their expected date of term birth and full-term newborns at birth have similar latencies and wave forms. When differences are found these can be attributed to the medical complications of the preterm infant (Akiyama et al., 1969; Hecox & Galambos, 1974; Salamy et al., 1980; Schulman-Galambos & Galambos, 1975, 1979; Starr et al., 1977; Weitzman & Graziani, 1968).

By contrast, infants after term, 40 weeks conceptional age, have rapidly growing auditory competence that is far greater than that of the fetus in utero or of preterm infants. Infants in the first weeks past term respond to sound more consistently and with a greater variety of behavioral responses. They show some selectivity for the frequency range and patterning of human speech sounds. They also show marked maturational changes in electroencephalographic characteristics of auditory evoked potentials and heart rate responses to auditory stimuli (Berg & Berg, 1979; Butterfield & Cairns, 1976; Eisenberg, 1976; Morse, 1979; Schneider, Trehub, & Bull, 1979; Trehub, Schneider, & Endman, 1980).

Development of Auditory Sensitivity in Kittens

A review of some of the anatomical, neurophysiological, and behavioral studies of kittens gives some support for the concept of period of limited environmental influence. As previously stated, the kitten at birth is in several ways anatomically and neurophysiologically similar to human infants of about 25 weeks gestation or 15 weeks before full term, 40 weeks. The kitten's nervous system matures at a rate of about 1 week to 5 for the human infant and therefore the kitten of 3 weeks is like the full-term newborn infant. A description of the development of the auditory system in the kitten may help us understand the prenatal development of the auditory system in the human infant.

At birth the kitten's external auditory canals are closed and open gradually with increasing depth of the canals during the first two weeks. Nevertheless responses can be seen to sound stimuli as early as 2 to 5 days, and to the mother cat vocalizations with consistent discrete responses by 10 to 15 days (Olmstead & Villablanca, 1980). Brainstem auditory evoked responses can also be obtained in free-field stimulation as early as 4 days to loud stimuli (Olmstead & Villablanca, 1980; Shipley et al., 1980).

In the kitten the cochlea becomes responsive to auditory stimulation through surgically opened auditory canals only 2 to 3 days following birth; yet primitive cortical auditory evoked responses can be obtained at birth by stimulation of the auditory nerve. Thus, the central nervous system is responsive to stimulation before the transducer, the cochlea, is responsive. Neurophysiological recordings from the auditory nerve demonstrate that the first responses from the cochlea to auditory stimulation have long latencies and do not follow the stimulus duration or frequency characteristics. High-intensity stimulation is required to get responses. Within the first 2 weeks these characteristics improve rapidly coincident with maturational changes in the fine structure of the cochlea. Single-unit recording in the cochlear nucleus of kittens reveals limited spontaneous activity until 2 to 3 weeks. Auditory stimulation induces spike activity in these neurons in kittens less than one week of age but the stimulus must be intense, and the response has a long latency and is limited only to the onset of the auditory stimulus and is refractory to repeated stimuli (Figure 27). Thus at the first level of transmission along the auditory pathway there are limitations placed on the amount of response and the quality and nature of information transmitted from an auditory signal at this age.

Similar limitations in neuronal unit spontaneous and stimulated activity can be found along the auditory pathway at the inferior colliculus and the auditory cortex. With maturation the amount of spontaneous neuronal activity increases, the responses to stimuli begin to correspond to the duration of the stimulus, at first intermittently and then continuously and the refractoriness to higher frequency stimulation rates of stimulation also decreases (Figure 27). Some of these early limitations of response to the stimulus characteristics is in the cochlea as determined by recordings from the auditory nerve but not all, especially in kittens 2 weeks of age and older. There continue to be significant changes in the neurophysiological response patterns well after 3

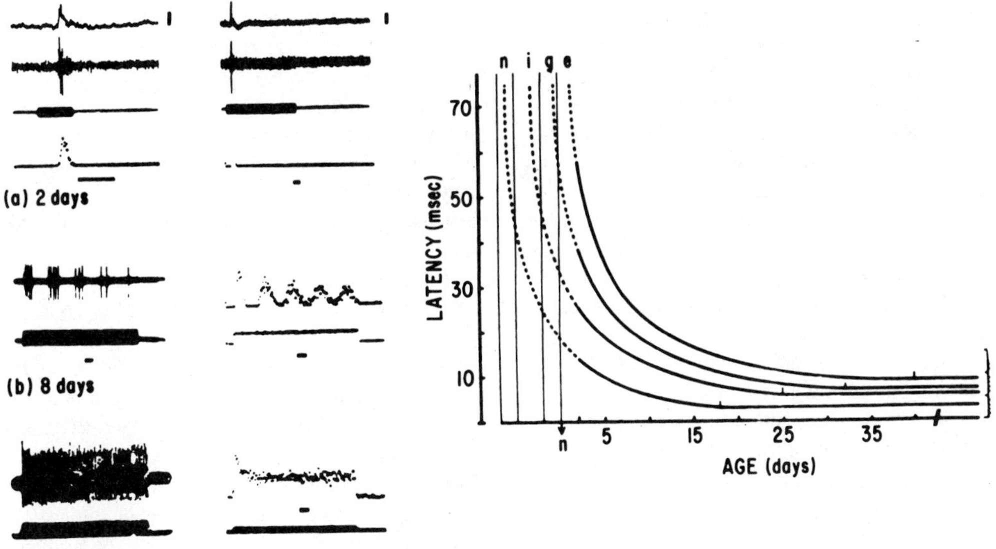

Figure 27. Two physiological criteria for evaluation of the maturation of the auditory system in the kitten. Left: Maturation of unit responses in the cochlear nerve. The response to a sound of long duration is (A) only an "on" response at 2 days with wide distribution of spikes, (B) an intermittent rhythmic response at 8 days, (C) continuous response at 21 days. Sound duration in A is 500 msec and in B and C, 800 msec. Right: Decrease in latencies to auditory evoked potentials in different places in the auditory path in the kitten, Cochlear Nucleus (n), Inferior Colliculus (i), Medial Geniculate (G), Cerebral Cortex (c). (From Pujol, 1976.)

weeks in the kitten (Aitkin & Moore, 1975; Brugge, Javel, & Kitzer, 1978; Carlier et al., 1974; Carlier, Lenoir, & Pujol, 1979; Carlier & Pujol, 1978; Javel, 1980; Konig, Pujol, & Marty, 1972; Pujol, 1976; Romand & Marty, 1975).

These studies indicate that long after there is an initial demonstrable response in the kitten to an auditory stimulus this response is to only a limited part of the stimulus. Moreover, the short duration of the response limits the potential impact of auditory stimulation on individual neurons in the auditory pathway. The major change in these limitations in the kitten comes between 2 and 3 weeks of age.

One cannot make ready judgments about the onset, level, or complexity of function in the auditory system or other neurological functional systems from anatomical studies alone. In many ways, the kitten's auditory system is very mature anatomically and more auditory response might be expected. For example, the otic capsule of the kitten is adult size at birth, although only the first coil of the lamina spiralis is ossified; histologically most of the components of the adult cochlear organ can be identified in an immature state; and the neural components of the cochlea have a myelin sheath. Recent studies of the development of the fine structures of the cochlea and the neurons and nuclei along the auditory pathway have provided some clues to the neurophysiological limitations found in the kitten's auditory system (Pujol, Carlier, & Devigne, 1978; Pujol & Hilding, 1975; Pujol & Marty, 1970; Rubel, 1978; Sans & Chat, 1976).

We have emphasized the difficulty of determining the onset, level, or degree of function of the auditory system in the kitten from anatomic studies because in the past many reports on human auditory development have made such assumptions. The inner and middle ear and the general contour of the cochlea develop rapidly in human fetal life to near adult proportions as in the kitten and some myelination of auditory pathways occurs as early as the fifth month of gestation (Bast & Anson, 1949; Yakovlev & Lecours, 1967). These two observations in the past have stimulated considerable speculation concerning early onset and rather complete functioning of the auditory system. On the other hand, similar to the kitten, the cochlea is slow to develop microscopic structures considered important to auditory function and myelination of spiral ganglion neurons is very late (Arnold, Wang, & Linnenkohl, 1980; Kimuro, Otu, & Takahashi, 1979). Unfortunately, we have very limited information on the fine structural development of the human cochlea (Bredberg, 1967; Parmelee, 1981; Selnes & Whitaker, 1976; Tuchman-Duplessis, David, & Haegel, 1972). In addition we have no unit recording of neuronal responses along the auditory pathway from the cochlea to the auditory cortex. For this kind of information we will always be dependent on animal studies such as those in kittens.

To the extent that the development of auditory functioning in the kitten from birth to 3 weeks old may parallel the development of auditory functioning in the preterm infant from 25 weeks gestation to term, we can understand that there are major restrictions placed on the impact of any auditory stimulus on the central nervous system until 2 to 3 weeks of age in the kitten or 35 to 40 weeks gestational or conceptional age in the preterm infant.

Development of Visual Sensitivity in Infants

The visual system has been investigated more extensively than the auditory system in preterm and full-term newborns and young infants. It is clear that preterm infants are capable of responding to visual stimuli well before term date. Several investigators have described a progressive increase in the quality of attention from 32 weeks so that active attention is commonly noted by 34 to 36 weeks conceptional age (Dubowitz, Dubowitz, Marante, & Verghote, 1980; Hack, Miranda, & Fantz, 1975; Hack, Mostow, & Miranda, 1976; Hack, Muszynski, & Miranda, 1981). Furthermore, visual recognition memory, in some rudimentary form, is evidenced by conditioned sucking in preterm infants of 35 weeks gestational age (Werner & Siqueland, 1978).

While some investigators have found no differences in the visual preferences of preterm and full-term infants tested at matched conceptional ages (Dubowitz et al., 1980; Fantz & Fagan, 1975; Fantz, Fagan, & Miranda, 1975; Miranda, 1976), some differences have been reported by others particularly in the early months of life. Clinical observers (Gesell & Amatruda, 1945; Saint-Anne Dargassies, 1966) noted differences in visual behaviors between preterm and full-term infants at 40 weeks conceptional age and interpreted these as indicating a greater visual competence in the preterm infant. However, recent observations in controlled situations suggest that the preterm infant may be slower to process visual information. At 40 weeks conceptional age, preterm infants take more time to reach a response decrement criterion (Friedman, Jacobs, & Werthmann, 1981) and decrease their visual responsiveness more slowly (Kopp, Sigman, Parmelee, & Jeffrey, 1975; Sigman, Kopp, Littman, & Parmelee, 1977) than full-term infants of the same conceptional age. These differences are independent of postnatal age and seem to reflect either an inability to inhibit visual responsiveness or a slower rate of information intake.

The differences reported at 40 weeks conceptional age are also identified later in the first year. Caron and Caron (1981) report a reduced ability to abstract invariant relational information in preterm infants. This was evident as early as 12 weeks of age postterm and was manifested at this age by lack of discrimination of face versus nonface stimuli following habituation. In another series of studies (S. A. Rose, 1980, 1981; Rose, Gottfried, & Bridger, 1978), preterm infants at several ages were less able to use information than full-term infants. At 6 months old, full-term infants showed visual differentiation between novel and familiar stimuli when familiarized to a constant visual stimulus, while preterm infants of the same conceptional age did not differentiate between novel and familiar stimuli. Furthermore, full-term infants at 12 months of age were able to overcome interfering tactual exposure to stimuli whereas preterm infants were not. At 12 months preterm infants were able to show the type of visual differentiation that was absent at 6 months. S. A. Rose (1980, 1981) attributes the differences to a deficit in the speed of encoding visual information among preterm infants. When longer familiarization times were provided, preterm infants were better able to differentiate between novel and familiar stimuli.

Our own research findings (Sigman, 1976; Sigman & Parmelee, 1974) support those reported by S. A. Rose and her colleagues. At 4 months, a group of full-term infants showed significant preferences for novel stimuli that were not shown by preterm infants of the same conceptional age (Sigman & Parmelee, 1974). Furthermore, preterm infants were slower to turn away from familiar objects explored manually and visually at 8 months old. Visual preferences were also related to risk factors in our studies and those by Siqueland and his collaborators (Siqueland, 1981; Werner & Siqueland, 1978). In our study of a large sample of infants, those infants who showed a discrimination between novel and familiar stimuli had suffered fewer birth complications (Parmelee & Sigman, 1976).

An environmental association with deficits in visual responses has been suggested by several research findings. Among preterm infants, slow visual processing of the unchanging patterns at term date was most pronounced among infants experiencing the least social interaction at home (Sigman & Beckwith, 1980). Furthermore, the degree of preference for novel stimuli in female preterm infants at 4 months corrected age was related to social stimulation in the home measured at one month (Sigman, Cohen, & Forsythe, 1981). S. A. Rose (1980) has shown that neonatal intervention centered on tactual and vestibular modalities enhanced visual recognition memory 6 months later.

While environmental factors in the nursery and home seem to affect subsequent processing of visual information, so far the evidence exists only for infants of 35 weeks conceptional age and older. Our observations were made at 40 weeks conceptional age (term) and most of our subjects had returned home at about 35 to 36 weeks conceptional age. Intervention in the studies by S. A. Rose and her collaborators (1980) was begun about 35 weeks conceptional age. Thus, the effects of neonatal stimulation have been demonstrated at about 35 weeks conceptional age, the age when most preterm infants return home. The evidence for earlier effects of environmental stimulation are lacking. Younger infants may not be neurologically mature enough to process visual information even if these infants show some of the appropriate behavioral responses reviewed above.

Just as visual responsiveness increased with maturation, visual evoked potentials in infants also show a very interesting sequence of development. This sequence parallels that found in the kitten, as will be pointed out in the following section. In the preterm infant of 28 to 30 weeks gestation, only long latency negative waves, single or double, are seen. As discussed in the section on sensory evoked potentials, these long latency negative waves suggest that there is a predominance of apical dendritic synapses near the cortical surface. After 32 to 34 weeks gestation, the positive-negative complex is present coincidental with the development of some axosomatic and axodendritic basilar synapses.

At term, a prominent positive-negative (P_2, N_2) complex is almost always present, occasionally preceded by a low amplitude very short latency positive-negative complex (P_1, N_1). Between the first and second month a third positive-negative complex (P_3, N_3) of greater amplitude than the other two develops. All three positive-negative complexes are well formed by 3 months, and the form of the visually evoked potential becomes stable and like that of the adult (Ferriss, Davis, Dorsen, & Hackett, 1967).

There is a gradual decrease in the latencies of all components of the visually evoked potential in preterm infants to term (Ellingson, 1960; Engel, 1965; Engel & Benson, 1968; Hrbeck, Karlberg, & Olsson, 1973; Umezaki & Morrell, 1970; Watanabe, Iwase, & Hara, 1972). Umezaki and Morrell (1970) found no significant correlation between this decrease in latency and postnatal age, but they did find a significant correlation with conceptional age.

Ellingson (1974) and Engel (1965) reported the latencies of preterm infants at term to be significantly slower than those of full-term infants. However, Ellingson (1974) states that by 6 months past term there are no longer any differences in latencies. All authors describe a significant amount of interindividual variability. Of great interest is the sharp drop in latency of the visually evoked potential between 1 and 2 months past term. This was first described by Ellingson (1960) and subsequently confirmed by others. After 3 months past term the latencies decrease very gradually reaching adult levels by 2 to 4 years (Ellingson, 1960).

The change in form of the visually evoked potential identifies the maturational changes in the cortical neurpil and may be useful as a general marker of maturity. The change in the form of the evoked potential may reflect an increase in the complexity of the visual material that can be processed. On the other hand, the change in latency with maturation may have some bearing on the speed and attentional aspect of visual information processing. Certainly the rapid decrease in latency of the visually evoked potential between 1 and 2 months parallels dramatic changes in the visual behavior of infants. These concepts are elaborated in additional studies by Karmel and Maisel (1975) who presented evidence for different visual processing mechanisms before and after about 6 weeks of age.

Another important aspect as indicated earlier is that of visual decoding by the retina. Little is known about the neuroanatomical development of the human retina. Much of the discussion has centered around the development of rod and cone cells, particularly cone cells in the foveal area. Some older anatomic studies suggested the cones in the fovea are poorly developed in the full-term newborn infant. More recent study indicates the presence of cones in the foveal area even in preterm infants. A current study demonstrates the presence of cones in the fovea of full-term infants but states that they are poorly formed (Abramov, Gordon, Hendrickson, Hainline, Dobson, & La Bossiere, 1982; Haith, 1978, 1980; Horsten & Winkleman, 1962; Mann, 1964;

Maurer, 1975). Recordings of electrical potential responses of the retina to light flashes, the electroretinogram (ERG), have demonstrated a photopic response, attributed to cones, as well as a scotopic response, attributed to rods, present even in preterm infants of 34 to 36 weeks conceptional age and certainly in full-term infants (Barnet, Lodge, & Armington, 1965; Horsten & Winkelman, 1962; Samson-Dollfus, 1968).

The strong interest in the development of cone cells in the fovea stems from the importance of cone cells for acute central vision. We know that newborn infants will follow a moving target visually and prefer targets with large configurations to plain targets. These visual tasks could be accomplished without much central foveal vision. One study of full-term newborn infants found more central fixation to a single vertical black line than to a blank field and concluded that this was evidence that central vision was more sensitive than peripheral vision (Lewis, Maurer, & Kay, 1978). Another study used cortical evoked potential latencies to various sized checkerboard stimuli as a measure of central and peripheral vision. The investigators concluded that since recordable signals could not be obtained to the small checks, seen by adults with central vision, until the infants were 12 to 16 weeks of age, peripheral vision dominated until then (Sokol & Jones, 1979). This issue is unresolved by the determination of the presence of cones in the fovea since their level of function is not known. We need to keep in mind that retinal functioning also depends on other neuronal components, such as the amacrine and the ganglion cells.

In the human infant we have neither the neuroanatomic picture of the newborn or young infant's retina nor the necessary neurophysiological studies to have a level of understanding that approximates our knowledge of kitten retinal functioning, limited as that is. We do know that newborn infants make some visual discriminations and follow objects. We also know that their visual acuity at birth and for several months thereafter is very low compared to adults (Dobson & Teller, 1978). The sensory receptive limitations of the retina only add further to the limitations of visual sensory transmission and cortical reception already discussed relative to the rest of the visual pathway in preterm infants and that we will discuss in kittens in the following section.

Development of Visual Sensitivity in Kittens

The identification of the innate specificity of some neurons in the newborn kitten's visual cortex has stimulated much fruitful research (Hubel & Wiesel, 1963). These investigators demonstrated that some neurons in the visual cortex of the newborn kitten responded specifically to horizontal or vertical movements across the visual field. In addition, some cells responded to stimulation in both eyes, and other cells responded to stimulation of only one eye. Obliteration of the vision of one eye in a kitten from birth to 6 weeks of age caused a loss in the number of neurons responding to that eye as well as many of the binocularly responsive neurons and an exaggeration of the number responding to the normal eye. This demonstrated the need for continuing visual input after birth to sustain the specificity of the neurons. In addition, it was demonstrated that the neurons were particularly sensitive to the loss of visual input between 3 and 6 weeks postnatally (Hubel & Wiesel, 1970).

Barlow and Pettigrew (1971) and Pettigrew (1974) found that the number of cells with innate specificity may not be as great as Hubel and Wiesel suggested. Instead, in addition to the innately specific neurons, the newborn kitten may also have many nonspecific neurons in its visual cortex. The latter may be stimulated by visual experience to respond specifically. Pettigrew (1974), though demonstrating that visual input is necessary for significant development of neuronal specificity, finds this sensitivity to visual input only after 4 weeks of age. Blakemore and Mitchell (1973) also describe the sensitive period as starting after 3 weeks. These findings are consistent with a concept of a relatively insensitive period in the first weeks. The nature of the sensitive period from 3 to 9 weeks has been extensively studied by a large number of investigators, along with the mechanisms and neuroanatomy involved and how and under what circumstance recovery of normal function can occur (Blakemore, 1974; Freeman & Bonds, 1979; Hirsch & Leventhal, 1978; Leventhal & Hirsch, 1980; Pettigrew, 1978; Spinelli & Jensen, 1979; Tumosa, Tieman, & Hirsch, 1980; Wilkinson, 1980). Recent studies have demonstrated that some of the cortical responsiveness induced by monocular deprivation in kittens in the sensitive period can be blocked or reversed neurochemically adding to the factors that may contribute to brain plasticity in this period (Duffy, Snodgrass, Burchfiel, & Conway, 1976; Kasamatsu & Pettigrew, 1979; Kasamatsu, Pettigrew, & Ary, 1979). The issues of this complex subject are well reviewed by Pettigrew (1978).

Some of the delay in visual sensitivity of kittens to stimulation may in part be a function of the immaturity of their eyes. Kittens do not open their eyes until 8 to 10 days after birth and the media is cloudy until 15 to 30 days (Villablanca & Olmstead, 1979). This does not seem to be the major limiting factor. The immaturity of the retina in the first three weeks may be more significant, particularly in limiting the complexity and frequency of neuronal signals transmitted centrally (Cragg, 1975; Hamasaki & Flynn, 1977; Johns, Rusoff & Dubin, 1979; Rusoff & Dubin, 1978).

Rose and Lindsley (1968) studied the development in the kitten of the cortical evoked potential to visual stimuli and found the first characteristics of a mature response at 3 weeks and fully developed mature responses at 4 to 6 weeks postnatally. Rose and Collins (1975) used the mature, visual-cortical evoked potential as a marker of maturity of the visual processing system of the kitten for the study of visual behavior. They correlated 11 visual behavioral responses with this marker without intending to imply a causal relation. Only eyeblink to light and optokinetic nystagmus appear before 2.5 weeks, and visual home orienting and tracking appear between 2 and 3 weeks. The remaining seven behaviors appear after 3 weeks with the four most complex after 4 weeks postnatal age when the cortical evoked potential has adult configuration (Figure 28). Based on these observations they trained two groups of kittens on a light-dark discrimination learning task. Group A (younger) began their discrimination trials at 21 to 23 days of age and Group B (older) at 35 to 37 days. The more immature Group A kittens reached criterion after 90 trials at 48 days postnatally, and the more mature Group B kittens reached criterion after 60 trials and at 46 days. This demonstrated again that there must be a definite level of neurological organization before kittens can process visual information. Further extensions of these studies in kittens and other animals and their importance to developmental psychobiology have been reviewed by G. H. Rose (1981).

With these observations of the relative lack of plasticity of visual cortex neurons and the delay in visual learning in the first 3 weeks of the kitten's life in mind, we will review some of the concomitant neuroanatomical and neurophysiological phenomena previously discussed more generally under various subheadings. We will review primarily changes that may relate to visual evoked potentials and visual signal processing. We are making this limitation in order to make comparisons with infant data. We recognize that neuroanatomic and physiological maturational changes are taking place at all levels in the visual pathway.

As we have previously indicated, Purpura et al. (1964) described the sequences of neuronal development in the cerebral cortex of kittens. First, the apical dendrites branch and develop spinous processes; then the basilar dendrites branch and myelination of the axons also begins to develop. The greatest changes in basilar dendritic branching and axonal growth are between the second and fourth weeks postnatally. Scheibel and Scheibel (1963, 1964, 1971) made similar observations and also described the appearance of thalamocortical axons with axodendritic synapses appearing at approximately 2 weeks. In addition, cortical Golgi type II short axon interneurons and axonal recurrent branching to cortical neurons appear between 2 and 4 weeks. These greatly enhance the number of synaptic contacts between cortical neurons. Adinolfi (1971) in detailed studies of synapses in the kitten cortex confirmed the appearance of axodendritic synapses before axosomatic synapses. At approximately 3 weeks the axodendritic synapses in the molecular layer become predominantly axospinuous when axodendritic branchlets and axosomatic contacts and axodendritic synapses in the basilar area are developing. The ultrastructure of the synapses of Layers I and II appears to be mature by 4 weeks postnatally.

These neuroanatomical studies can be used to illustrate the paucity and immaturity of cortical synapses in the newborn kitten. The cortical synapses increase in number and maturity particularly between 2 and 4 weeks and are almost mature by 6 weeks. This development is at least coincidental with the sensitive period of corcial neurons at 3 to 6 weeks as described by Blakemore and Mitchell (1973) and Pettigrew (1974) and of discrimination learning at 4 to 7 weeks, demonstrated by Rose and Collins (1975).

In addition to the neuroanatomical structural changes in this time period, as we have previously indicated, there are significant neurophysiological changes. These are best illustrated by the spontaneous rate of discharge recorded in neurons along the visual pathway. Huttenlocher (1967) and Huttenlocher and Rawson (1968) studied the spontaneous discharge rate of kitten visual cortical neurons and found these to be very sparse in the first 2 weeks postnatally; there was a sharp increase in the discharge rate between 3 and 4 weeks which almost reached adult levels by 6 weeks (Figure 9). Adrien and Roffwarg (1974) have described a similar development of neuronal activity in the lateral geniculate nucleus in the visual pathway from the retina to the cortex (Figure 25). This lower rate of activity of neurons in the cortex and along sensory pathways and lower rate of responsiveness to stimulation has already been described for the auditory system. It

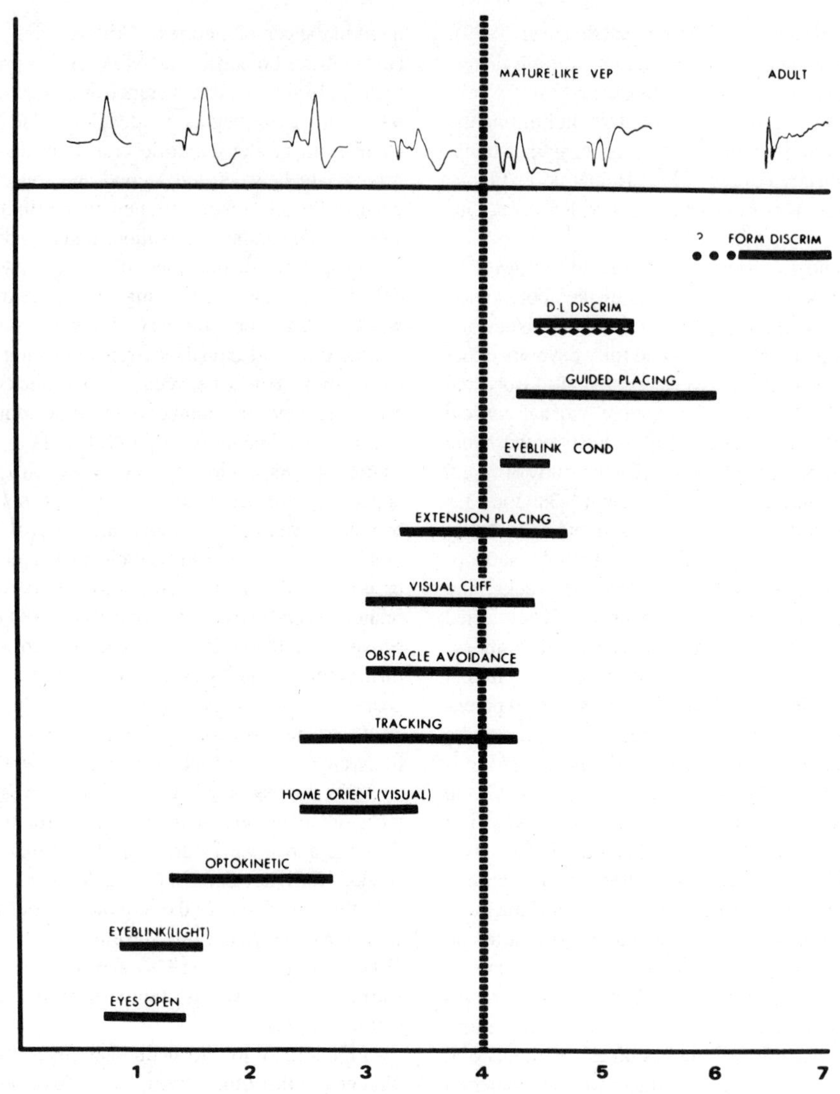

Figure 28. Visual behavior and electrocortical maturation in kittens. The visually evoked potential (VEP) illustrated at the top is used as an electrophysiological marker. At 4 weeks of age the VEP is designated as mature, as indicated by the broken line. Kitten behaviors are indicated by the labeled dark bars. (From Rose & Collins, 1975.)

tends to be a general phenomenon in many neural pathways and systems in the immature kitten. It is true, for example, of the basal ganglia which are very important in the regulations of response and cognitive sets (Buchwald, Hull, Levine, & Villablanca, 1975; Morris et al., 1979).

The ontogeny of visually evoked cortical potential in kittens shows a parallel postnatal evolution reflecting the neuroanatomical and neurophysiological maturation of the brain previously discussed. In the kitten there is at first only one long latency negative wave and later two. A little later a positive shorter latency wave preceding a shorter latency negative wave appears. Gradually between 3 and 5 weeks the two negative waves coalesce. From then on the visually evoked potential is similar in form and in latencies to that of the adult cat (Figure 17) (G. H. Rose, 1981; Rose, Gruenau, & Spencer, 1972; Rose & Lindsley, 1968).

As mentioned earlier in this chapter, the way in which the visually evoked potential develops in the kitten is of special interest because it is compatible with the sequences of neuroanatomic development of the kitten cortex and the neurophysiological concepts of the origins of cortical electrical activity.

Developmental studies of the kitten retina demonstrate that neurological functioning cannot be assumed simply given the presence of neuronal structures. Johns et al. (1979) report that all the ganglion cells in the kitten retina are present at birth and all the other neurons are present in the central retina with some later development of neurons in periphery. Hamasaki and Flynn (1977) recorded the responses from single optic tract fibers in 3-week-old kittens to varying sizes of circular light stimuli and established that the recorded activity was from ganglion cells in the retina. They found very low level spontaneous activity in the kitten ganglion cells compared to adult cats. The firing rate was lower in the kitten than in cats for all intensities of stimulation. The response rate to intermittent stimulation was less in the kitten and there was a greater latency of the responses (Figure 29). The ganglion cells did show an adultlike pattern of a center-surround organization of the receptive fields. Once again it is clear that the anatomic presence of various neuronal structures does not define the degree of neurophysiological functioning.

CONCLUSIONS

In this review we have discussed the many facets of brain development that are occurring simultaneously in order to emphasize the complexity of the brain and the difficulty of relating isolated behaviors to specific areas or forms of brain development. Historically, behavioral development has been attributed to the appearance of isolated anatomic findings such as myelin, Nissl substance, and neuronal distribution in cortical areas, concepts now known to be overly simplistic. Knowledge was limited to the available staining, microscopic, and neurophysiological techniques, as we have indicated. Each new decade has brought advances in many areas of our understanding of brain development and function through the steady development of new procedures and techniques. These range from new anatomic stains, radioactive labeling of cells during migration, and cell metabolic processes, to fluorescent labeling of neurotransmitters; from improved light microscopic procedures, to electron microscopy; and from complex computer analyses of single neuron action potential recordings, to similar analyses of recordings of large neuronal networks during a variety of complex stimulation procedures. We have every reason to expect even greater advances in the coming years. Many procedures will of necessity be limited to animal studies so we will need many more comparative studies across various species of animals and humans, particularly in the

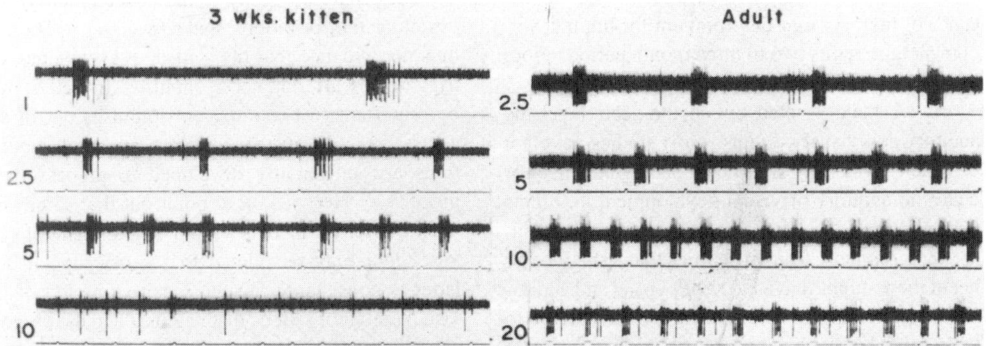

Figure 29. Retinal ganglion cell responses to different rates of visual stimulation in a 3-week-old kitten and an adult cat as recorded from single optic tract fibers. The retinal ganglion cells of the 3-week-old kitten can follow frequencies up to 5 Hz but not 10 Hz whereas those of the adult cat readily follows visual stimulation frequencies of 10 and 20 Hz. Note the increase in recording strip speed in the adult recordings at 20 Hz. The stimulus intensity was $3.4 \times 10^2 cd/m^2$ for the kitten and $1.1 \times 10^2 cd/m^2$ for the adult. Background luminance was .5 cd/m^2. (From Hamasaki & Flynn, 1977.)

behavioral area. For those interested in infants and children, it is important that such studies are extended to the ontogeny of brain development and behavior both in animals and humans. Fortunately, there is currently considerable momentum in this direction.

An important issue in the ontogeny of brain development is the length of time and degree to which the growth and organization of the brain is largely genetically predetermined. We do know that at some point environmental sensory inputs play an increasingly important role in brain organization, or at least in maintenance of the organization already developed. We do not know for sure when the environmental sensory influences begin to have a greater impact. The transition may be gradual over a period of time and at different times for different systems, or the transition may be in significant steps. In either case, the development of the various sensory systems appears to be coordinated to converge at a particular stage of advancement (Scherrer, 1974). Certain animals such as cats, rabbits, and rats have very immature nervous systems at birth and in them environmental sensory influences are deferred a few days or weeks after birth, where as the guinea pig, for example, has a very mature nervous system at birth and is more immediately influenced by environmental sensory stimulation.

The problem might not be of such great significance for human infants, who have quite well-developed brains at full-term birth, except for the fact that a number of infants are born 8 to 12 weeks preterm and survive. These infants have immature brains at birth. This poses the practical issue of the significance of their sensory environment for brain development during this two to three month period before their expected date of birth.

As we have pointed out in the section on the auditory and visual systems, most studies have not been able to identify significant lasting advances or delays in auditory or visual development in infants born preterm that is directly attributable to their sensory environment. The difficulties that a small number of these infants have later with visual and auditory perception appear to be primarily attributable to their frequent medical problems in the neonatal period.

In order to gain some insight into neuroanatomical and neurophysiological explanations for these observations, we have reviewed some comparative animal studies, particularly in kittens. As we have pointed out, there are many neuroanatomic and neurophysiologic parallels in the ontogeny of the kitten brain from birth to 3 or 4 weeks, and that of the preterm infant from 25 weeks gestation to term, 40 weeks conceptional age.

A general principle that appears to emerge from our observations and the studies reviewed is that the brain and central sensory pathways develop functionally somewhat ahead of the peripheral receptors. In the kitten, for example, at birth, direct electrical stimulation of the auditory or optic nerve elicits a cortical evoked potential when external auditory and visual stimuli do not. These early responses from direct nerve stimulation are, nevertheless, very immature with long latencies and resistant to repeated stimulation. From the first relay nuclei on to the cortex in both auditory and visual systems, there are neurophysiological obstructions to the transmission of the complete signals in terms of their duration and frequency. Thus, even central to the peripheral receptors, there is some "protection" of cortical neurons from stimulation.

Gradually, as the kitten matures, cortical responses can be obtained from external auditory and visual stimuli and the central pathways become more responsive. In the early weeks, however, there continues to be a lag between the development of the central pathways and the peripheral receptors, the retina, and the organ of Corti. The sensory receptors are slower to develop and provide a significant limitation to the complexity or amount of information in the signal transmitted centrally.

It has been postulated that it is important for the cortex and central brain pathways to be somewhat protected by the limitations of the receptors during this early phase of development. Cragg (1975), in his neuroanatomic study of the development of the visual system in kittens states (p. 164), "There is thus no evidence that the start of synaptogenesis is triggered by afferent nerve impulses. Indeed, it may be important to keep afferent impulses out of the central nervous system until the synaptic connections are sufficiently developed to process them properly." He goes on to point out that somewhat later after birth, there is a rapid development of synapses that may be related to sensory inputs. The latter is consistent with the sensitive period of the visual cortex of kittens that begins when the kitten is about 3 weeks old.

After a certain level of central and peripheral nervous system maturity is reached, external sensory stimuli become very important. This importance is illustrated most clearly by the defects that occur when there is insufficient stimulation. The brain appears to be particularly vulnerable at this time, a vulnerability that does not seem very advantageous to a developing organism. Pettigrew (1978) addresses this paradox and states (p. 311), "I believe that the critical period for primary visual cortex is not merely a potential handicap for the developing organism. Rather, it may be a time when neural activity brings about the fine tuning of a cortical organization which is not complete prior to the animal's first experience." We would only modify this statement by suggesting that this fine tuning may not start with the animal's very first experiences after birth depending on the brain maturity of the particular animal at birth. When it starts, however, it plays an important part in brain development. We have suggested that in human infants this period probably does start at full-term birth or perhaps even a month earlier in preterm infants.

Of course, the fact that the sensory systems of the young preterm infant cannot be affected by the environment does not mean that environmental influences do not matter at all. It may be that visual, auditory, and tactile inputs influence the infant's capacity to modulate state and motor responses. In this way, the nature of early stimulation may affect the underpinning of later sensory responsiveness. It is difficult to imagine that throughout development there is not a continuous environment-organism interaction which the organism seeks and needs in order to arrive at the next step of differentiation (Als, personal communication).

We do not know how long the sensitive period for fine tuning lasts in normal infants but we would presume it lasts at least for the first several months of life. In kittens the sensitive period is usually described as extending from 3 to 12 weeks after birth. This does not imply that modifications of the central nervous system due to environmental stimuli is limited to this period. We are only discussing a presumed peak period of sensitivity.

In infants, this period is quickly followed by, or overlaps with, a period of rapid cognitive growth. Some aspects of cognitive growth may not be dependent on much identifiable structural change within the brain in terms of synaptic or dendritic growth, since concept generalizations can be integrations of previous sensory perceptions.

Most animal studies do not effectively address this aspect of cognitive plasticity which in some measure may be uniquely human (Sigman, 1982). Animal studies do include what is referred to as behavioral plasticity, but this is generally very task specific and follows specific task training. Even when nonspecific enriched environments are provided animals, the outcome measures are likely to be task specific. Any specific structural brain changes found in these animals could be related to very specific sensory experiences or tasks in the environment and not to their integration. We are left, therefore, without adequate animal models for brain studies of concept formations and abstract generalizations. We come quickly to the ever present mind-body problem which remains unanswered by current knowledge of brain structure and function, however much we may believe in the unitary relation of mind and body. In this chapter we have, therefore, deferred from discussing the relationship between brain and cognitive development in later infancy and childhood because the questions raised become increasingly complex and involve a new set of theoretical and empirical issues.

REFERENCES

Abramov, I., Gordon, J., Hendrickson, A., Hainline, L., Dobson, V., & LaBossiere, E. The retina of the newborn human infant. *Science,* 1982, *217,* 265–267.

Abramovich, S. J., Gregory, S., Slemick, M., & Stewart, A. Hearing loss in very low birthweight infants treated with neonatal intensive care. *Archives of Diseases in Childhood,* 1979, *54,* 421–426.

Adinolfi, A. M. The postnatal development of synaptic contacts in the cerebral cortex. In M. B. Sterman, D. J. McGinty, & A. M. Adinolfi (Eds.), *Brain development and behavior.* New York: Academic Press, 1971.

Adrien, J. Ontogenesis of some sleep regulations: Early postnatal impairment of the monamineegic systems. In M. B. Corner, R. E. Baker, N. E. van de Poll, & D. F. Swabb (Eds.), *Maturation of the nervous system. Progress in brain research* (Vol. 48). Amsterdam: Elsevier, 1978.

Adrien, J., & Roffwarg, H. P. The development of unit activity in the lateral geniculate nucleus of the kitten. *Experimental Neurology,* 1974, *43,* 261–275.

Aitkin, L. M., & Moore, D. R. Inferior colliculus. II: Development of tuning characteristics and tonotopic organization in central nucleus of the neonatal cat. *Journal of Neurophysiology,* 1975, *38,* 1208–1216.

Akiyama, Y., Schulte, F. J., Schultz, M. A., & Parmelee, A. H., Jr. Accoustically evoked responses in premature and full-term newborn infants. *Electroencephalography and Clinical Neurophysiology,* 1969, *26,* 371–380.

Als, H., & Duffy, F. H. Assessing infant individuality. In T. B. Brazelton, & B. M. Lester (Eds.), *Infants at risk: Toward plasticity and in-*

tervention. New York: Elsevier, 1982.

Als, H., Lester, B. M., & Brazelton, T. B. Dynamics of the behavioral organization of the premature infant: A theoretical perspective. In T. Field, S. Goldberg, A. Sostek, & H. H. Shuman (Eds.), *The high risk newborn*. New York: Spectrum, 1979.

Anders, T. Home recorded sleep in two- and nine-month-old infants. *Journal of the American Academy of Child Psychiatry*, 1978, *17*, 421–432.

Anders, T., Emde, R., & Parmelee, A. H. (Eds.). *A manual of standardized terminology, techniques and criteria for scoring of states of sleep and wakefulness in newborn infants*. Los Angeles: UCLA Brain Information Service/BRI Publications Office, 1971.

Arnold, W., Wang, J. B., & Linnenkohl, S. Neue Aspekte zur Anatomie des menschlichen Spiralganglions. *Archives of Oto-rhino-laryngology*, 1980, *228*, 69–84.

Aserinsky, E., & Kleitman, N. A motility cycle in sleeping infants as manifested by ocular and gross bodily activity. *Journal of Applied Physiology*, 1955, *8*, 11–18.

Ashton, R. The state variable in neonatal research. *Merrill-Palmer Quarterly of Behavior Development*, 1973, *19*, 3–20.

Axelrod, J. Neurotransmitters. *Scientific American*, 1974, June, *230*, 59–71.

Barchas, J. D., Abil, H., Elliott, G. R., Holman, R. B., & Watson, S. J. Behavioral neurochemistry: Neuroregulators and behavioral states. *Science*, 1978, *200*, 964–981.

Barden, T. P., & Peltzman, P. Newborn brain stem auditory evoked responses and perinatal clinical events. *American Journal of Obstetrics and Gynecology*, 1980, *136*, 912–919.

Barlow, H. B., & Pettigrew, J. D. Lack of specificity of neurones in the visual cortex of young kittens. *Proceedings of the Physiological Society*, 1971, *218*, 98–100.

Barnet, A. B., Friedman, S. L., Weiss, I. P., Ohlrich, E. S., Shanks, B., & Lodge, A. VEP development in infancy and early childhood. A longitudinal study. *Electroencephalography and Clinical Neurophysiology*, 1980, *49*, 476–489.

Barnet, A. B., Lodge, A., & Armington, J. C. Electroretinogram in newborn human infants. *Science*, 1965, *148*, 651–654.

Barnet, A. B., Ohlrich, E. S., Weiss, I. P., & Shanks, B. Auditory evoked potentials during sleep in normal children from ten days to three years of age. *Electroencephalography and Clinical Neurophysiology*, 1975, *39*, 29–41.

Bast, C. H., & Anson, B. J. *The temporal bone and the ear*. Springfield, Ill.: Charles C. Thomas, 1949.

Becker, P. T., & Thoman, E. B. Rapid eye movement storms in infants: Rate of occurrence at 6 months predicts mental development at one year. *Science*, 1981, *212*, 1415–1416.

Becker, P. T., & Thoman, E. B. REM storms in infants indicate neurobehavioral instability. *Developmental Psychobiology*, 1982, *15*, 203–210.

Beckwith, L., Cohen, S. E., Kopp, C. B., Parmelee, A. H., & Marcy, T. G. Caregiver-infant interaction and early cognitive development in preterm infants. *Child Development*, 1976, *47*, 579.

Beckwith, L., Sigman, M., Cohen, S. E., & Parmelee, A. H. Vocal output in pre-term infants. *Developmental Psychobiology*, 1977, 10, 543–554.

Beckwith, L., & Thompson, S. K. Recognition of verbal labels of pictured objects and events by 17- to 30-month-old infants. *Journal of Speech and Hearing Research*, 1976, *19*, 690–699.

Bench, R. J., & Parker, A. Hyper-responsivity to sounds in the short-gestation baby. *Developmental Medicine and Child Neurology*, 1971, *13*, 15–19.

Bench, R. J., & Vass, A. Fetal audiometry. *Lancet*, 1970, *1*, 91–92.

Benoit, O., & Adrien, J. PGO activity as a criterion of paradoxical sleep. A critical review. In G. C. Lairy, & P. Salzarulo (Eds.), *Experimental study of human sleep: Methodological problems*. Amsterdam: Elsevier, 1975.

Berg, W. K., & Berg, K. M. Psychophysiological development in infancy: State, sensory function and attention. In J. Osofsky (Ed.), *Handbook of infant development*. New York: John Wiley & Sons, 1979.

Berger, H. Über das Elektrenkephalogramm des Menschen. *Archiv für Psychiatrie und Nervenkrankheiten*, 1929, *87*, 527–570.

Berger, H. Über das Electrenkephalogramm des Menschen, II. *Journal für Psychologie and Neurologie*, 1930, *40*, 160–179.

Berger, H. Über das Elektrenkephalogramm des Menschen, fünfte Mitteilung. *Archiv für Psychiatrie und Nervenkrankheiten*, 1932, *99*, 213–254.

Berkson, G., Wasserman, G. A., & Behrman, R. Heart rate response to an auditory stimulus in premature infants. *Developmental Psychobiol-*

ogy, 1974, *11*, 244–246.

Bernhard, C. G., & Meyerson, B. A. Early ontogenesis of electrocortical activity. In P. Kellaway & I. Petersén (Eds.), *Clinical Electroencephalography of Children*. Stockholm: Almquist & Wiksell, 1968.

Bernhard, C. G., & Skoglund, C. R. On the alpha frequency of human brain potential as a function of age. *Skandinavischer Archiv für Physiologie*, 1939, *81*, 178–184.

Bernhard, C. G., & Skoglund, C. R. On the blocking time of the cortical alpha rhythm in children. *Acta Psychiatrica et Neurologica*, 1942, *17*, 159–170.

Bernstein, P., Emde, R., & Campos, J. REM sleep in four-month infants under home and laboratory conditions. *Psychosomatic Medicine*, 1973, *35*, 322–329.

Bernuth, H. von, & Prechtl, H. F. R. Vestibulo-ocular response and its state dependency in newborn infants. *Neuropeodiatrie*, 1969, *1*, 11–24.

Berry, M. Development of the cerebral neocortex of the rat. In G. Gottlieb (Ed.), *Studies on the development of behavior and nervous system. Aspects of Neurogenesis* (Vol. 2). New York: Academic Press, 1974.

Berry, M., Bradley, P., & Borges, S. Environmental and genetic determinants of connectivity in the central nervous system—An approach through dendritic field analysis. In M. B. Corner, R. E. Baker, N. E. Van de Poll, & D. F. Swabb (Eds.), *Maturation of the nervous system. Progress in brain research* (Vol. 48). Amsterdam: Elsevier, 1978.

Bess, F. H., Peck, B. F., & Chapman, J. J. Further observations on noise level in infant incubators. *Pediatrics*, 1979, *63*, 100–106.

Birch, H. Introduction. In D. Purpura & G. P. Reaser (Eds.), *Methodological approaches to the study of brain maturation and its abnormalities*. Baltimore: University Park Press, 1965.

Bishop, G. H., & Clare, M. H. Sites of origin of electric potentials in striate cortex. *Journal of Neurophysiology*, 1952, *15*, 202–219.

Blakemore, C. Effects of visual experience on the developing brain. In S. R. Berenberg, M. Caniaris, & N. P. Masse (Eds.), *Pre- and postnatal development of the human brain* (Vol. 13). Basel: S. Karger, 1974.

Blakemore, C., & Cooper, G. F. Development of the brain depends on the visual environment. *Nature*, 1970, *228*, 447–478.

Blakemore, C., & Mitchell, D. E. Environmental modification of the visual cortex and the neural basis of learning and memory. *Nature*, 1973, *241*, 467–468.

Blennow, G., Svenningsen, N. W., & Almquist, B. Noise levels in infant incubators (Adverse effects?). *Pediatrics*, 1974, *53*, 39–42.

Bodian, D. Development of fine structure of spinal cord in monkey fetuses. I: The motoneuron neuropil at the time of onset of reflex activity. *Bulletin of Johns Hopkins Hospital*, 1966, *119*, 129–149.

Bodian, D. Development of the fine structure of spinal cord in monkey fetuses. II. Pre-reflex period to period of long intersegmental reflexes. *Journal of Comparative Neurology*, 1968, *133*, 113–166.

Bosher, S. Morphological and functional changes in the cochlea associated in the inception of hearing. In J. P. Bench, A. Pye, & J. D. Pye (Eds.), Sound reception in mammals. *Symposia of the Zoological Society of London*, No. 37. Oxford: Academic Press, 1975.

Bowe-Anders, C., Adrien, J., & Roffwarg, H. P. Ontogenesis of ponto-geniculo-occipital activity in the lateral geniculate nucleus of the kitten. *Experimental Neurology*, 1974, *43*, 242–260.

Brandt, S., & Brandt, H. The electroencephalographic patterns in young healthy children from zero to five years of age. *Acta Psychiatrica Scandinavica*, 1955, *30*, 77–89.

Brazelton, T. B. *Neonatal behavioral assessment scale*. Philadelphia: Lippincott, 1973.

Brazier, M. A. B. The development of concepts relating to the electrical activity of the brain. *Journal of Nervous and Mental Diseases*, 1958, *126*, 303–321.

Brazier, M. A. B. *The electrical activity of the nervous system*. New York: Macmillan, 1960.

Bredberg, G. The human cochlea during development and aging. *Journal of Laryngology and Otology*, 1967, *81*, 739–758.

Broderson, S. H., Westrum, L. E., & Sutton, A. E. Studies of the direct coloring thiocholine method for localizing cholinesterase activity. *Histochemistry*, 1974, *40*, 13–23.

Brugge, J. F., Javel, E., & Kitzer, L. M. Signs of functional maturation of peripheral auditory system in discharge patterns of neurons in anteroventral cochlear nucleus of kitten. *Journal of Neurophysiology*, 1978, *41*, 1557–1579.

Buchwald, N. A., Hull, C. D., Levine, M. S., & Villablanca, J. The basal ganglia and the regulation of response and cognitive sets. In M. A. B. Brazier (Ed.), *Growth and development of the brain*. New York: Rover Press, 1975.

Butterfield, E. C., & Cairns, G. G. The infant's auditory environment. In T. D. Tjossem (Ed.), *Intervention strategies for high risk infants and young children*. Baltimore: University Park Press, 1976.

Calvet, J., Calvet, M. C., & Scherrer, Jr. Etude stratographique corticale de l'activité EEG spontanee. *Electroencephalography and Clinical Neurophysiology*, 1964, *17*, 109–125.

Carlier, E., Abonnenc, M., & Pujol, R. Maturation des responses unitaires à la stimulation tonale dans le nerf cochleare du chaton. *Journal de Physiologie*, 1974, *70*, 129–138.

Carlier, E., Lenoir, M., & Pujol, R. Development of cochlear frequency selectivity tested by compound action potential tuning curves. *Hearing Research*, 1979, *1*, 197–201.

Carlier, E., & Pujol, R. Role of inner and outer hair cells in coding sound intensity: An otogenetic approach. *Brain Research*, 1978, *147*, 174–176.

Caron, A. J., & Caron, R. F. Processing of relational information as an index of infant risk. In. S. L. Friedman & M. Sigman (Eds.), *Preterm and psychological development*. New York: Academic Press, 1981.

Casaer, P. *Postural behavior in newborn infants*. Philadelphia: Lippincott, 1979.

Caton, R. The electric currents of the brain. *British Medical Journal*, 1875, *2*, 278.

Chabás, A., Briones, P., & Sabater, J. Prenatal development of isocitrate- and glucose-6-phosphate dehydrogenase in the human brain. *Brain Research*, 1979, *176*, 180–184. (a)

Chabás, A., Briones, P., & Sabater, J. Prenatal human brain development, I. Catalytic and electrophoretic studies on lactate dehydrogenase. *Developmental Neuroscience*, 1979, *2*, 65–73. (b)

Chabás, A., Briones, P., & Sabater, J. Prenatal human brain development. II. Studies on malate dehydrogenase. *Developmental Neuroscience*, 1980, *3*, 19–27.

Changeux, J. P., & Donchin, A. Selective stabilization of developing synapses as a mechanism for the specification of neuronal networks. *Nature*, 1976, *264*, 705–712.

Chase, M. H. Patterns of reflex excitability during ontogenesis of sleep and wakefulness. In C. D. Clemente, D. P. Purpura, & F. E. Mayer (Eds.), *Sleep and the maturing nervous system*. New York: Academic Press, 1972.

Clarke, E., & O'Malley, C. D. *The human brain and spinal cord*. Los Angeles: University of California Press, 1968.

Cohen, D. J., & Young, J. G. Neurochemistry and child psychiatry. *Journal of Child Psychiatry*, 1977, *48*, 152–157.

Cohen, S. E., Beckwith, L., & Parmelee, A. H., Jr. Receptive development in pre-term infants as related to caregiver-child interaction. *Pediatrics*, 1978, *61*, 1620.

Committee on Environmental Hazards of the American Academy of Pediatrics, Noise pollution: Neonatal aspects. *Pediatrics*, 1974, *54*, 476–479.

Conel, J. L. *The cortex of the newborn. The postnatal development of the human cerebral cortex* (Vol. 1). Cambridge: Harvard University Press, 1939.

Conel, J. L. *The cortex of the one-month infant. The postnatal development of the human cerebral cortex* (Vol. 2). Cambridge: Harvard University Press, 1941.

Conel, J. L. *The cortex of the three-month infant. The postnatal development of the human cerebral cortex* (Vol. 3) Cambridge: Harvard University Press, 1947.

Coombs, J. S., Eccles, J. C., & Fatt, P. The electrical properties of the motoneurone membrane. *Journal of Physiology*, 1955, *130*, 291–325. (a)

Coombs, J. S., Eccles, J. C., & Fatt, P. Excitatory synoptic action in motoneurones. *Journal of Physiology*, 1955, *130*, 374–395. (b)

Corbin, H. P. F., & Bickford, R. G. Studies of the electroencephalogram of normal children: Comparison of visual and automatic frequency analyses. *Electroencephalography and Clinical Neurophysiology*, 1955, *7*, 15–28.

Courchesne, E. Neurophysiological correlates of cognitive development: Changes in long latency event-related potentials from childhood to adulthood. *Electroencephalography and Clinical Neurophysiology*, 1978, *45*, 468–482.

Courchesne, E., Ganz, L., & Norcia, A. M. Event-related brain potential to human faces in infants. *Child Development*, 1981, *52*, 804–811.

Cowan, W. M. Selection and control of neuogenesis. In F. O. Schmitt, & F. Worden (Eds.), *The Neuroscience Fourth Study Program*. Cambridge, Mass.: MIT Press, 1979.

Cragg, B. G. The development of synapses in the visual system of the cat. *Journal of Comparative Neurology*, 1975, *160*, 147–166.

Creutzfeldt, O. D., Watanabe, S., & Lux, H. D. Relations between EEG phenomena and potentials of single cortical cells. I. Evoked responses after thalamic and epicortical stimulation. *Electroencephalography and Clinical Neurophysiol-*

ogy, 1966, *20*, 1–18.

Crowell, D. H., & Kapuniai, L. E. Autoregressive spectral estimates of newborn brain maturational level: Classification and validation. *Psychophysiology*, 1977, *15*, 204–208.

Davidson, J. M., & Davidson, R. J. (Eds.). *The psychobiology of consciousness*. New York: Plenum Press, 1980.

Dawson, G. D. A summation technique for detecting small signals in a large irregular background. *Journal of Physiology*, 1951, *115*, 2–3.

DeHirsch, K., Jansky, J. J., & Langford, W. S. The oral language performance of prematurely born children and controls. *Journal of Speech and Hearing Disorders*, 1964, *29*, 60–69.

Delange, M., Castan, P., Cadilhac, J., & Passouant, P. Etude E. E. G. des divers stades du sommeil de nuit chez l'enfant. Consideration sur le stode IV ou d'activite onirique. *Revue Neurologique*, 1961, *105*, 176–181.

Dement, W., & Kleitman, N. Cyclic variations in EEG during sleep and their relation to eye movements, body mobility, and dreaming. *Electroencephalography and Clinical Neurophysiology*, 1957, *9*, 673–690.

Desmedt, J. E. Scalp-recorded cerebral event-related potentials in man as point of entry into the analysis of cognitive processing. In F. O. Schmitt, F. G. Worden, G. Adelman, & S. G. Dennis (Eds.), *The organization of the cerebral cortex*. Cambridge: MIT Press, 1981.

Desmedt, J. E., Brunko, E., & Debecker, J. Maturation of the somatosensory evoked potentials in normal infants and children, with special reference to the early N_1 component. *Electroencephalography and Clinical Neurophysiology*, 1976, *40*, 43–58.

Desmedt, J. E., & Debecker, J. The somatosensory cerebral evoked potentials of the sleeping human newborn. In C. D. Clemente, D. P. Purpura, & F. E. Mayer (Eds.), *Sleep and the maturing nervous system*. New York: Academic Press, 1972.

Despland, P., & Galambos, R. The auditory brain stem response (ABR) is a useful diagnostic tool in the intensive care nursery. *Pediatric Research*, 1980, *14*, 154–158.

Dittrichova, J., Paul, K., & Pavlikova, E. Rapid eye movements in paradoxical sleep in infants. *Neuropeodiatrie*, 1972, *3*, 248–257.

Dobbing, J. Vulnerable periods in brain growth and somatic growth. In D. F. Roberts & A. M. Thomson (Eds.), *The biology of human fetal growth*. London: Taylor & Francis, 1976.

Dobbing, J., & Sands, J. Quantitative growth and development of human brain. *Archives of Diseases of Childhood*, 1973, *48*, 757–767.

Dobson, V., & Teller, D. Y. Assessment of visual activity in infants. In J. Armington, J. Krauskopf, & B. Wooton (Eds.), *Visual psychophysics and physiology*. New York: Academic Press, 1978.

Donchin, E. Event-related brain potentials: A tool in the study of human information processing. In H. Begleiter (Ed.), *Brain potentials and behavior*. New York: Plenum Press, 1977.

Donchin, E., Tueting, P., Ritter, W., Kutor, M., & Heffley, E. On the independence of the CNV and the $\overline{\text{P300}}$ components of the human averaged evoked potential. *Electroencephalography and Clinical Neurophysiology*, 1975, *38*, 449–461.

Dreyfus-Brisac, C. The electroencephalogram of the premature infant and full-term newborn: Normal and abnormal waking and sleeping patterns. In P. Kellaway & I. Petersen, (Eds.). *Neurological and electroencephalographic correlative studies in infancy*. New York: Grune & Stratton, 1964.

Dreyfus-Brisac, C. Sleep ontogenesis in early human prematurity from 24 to 27 weeks of conceptional age. *Developmental Psychobiology*, 1968, *1*, 162–169.

Dreyfus-Brisac, C. Ontogenesis of sleep in human prematures after 32 weeks conceptional age. *Developmental Psychobiology*, 1970, *3*, 91–121.

Dreyfus-Brisac, C. Neurophysiological studies in human premature and full-term newborns. *Biological Psychiatry*, 1975, *10*, 485–496.

Dreyfus-Brisac, C. Ontogenesis of brain bioelectrical activity and sleep organization in neonates and infants. In F. Falkner & J. Tanner (Eds.), *Human growth* (Vol. 3). New York: Plenum Press, 1979.

Dreyfus-Brisac, C., Samson, D., Blanc, C., & Monod, N. Electroencephologramme: de l'enfant, normal de moins de 3 ans. *Etude Neonatalé*, 1958, *7*, 143–175.

Dubowitz, L. M. S., Dubowitz, V., Morante, A., & Verghote, M. Visual function in the preterm and full term newborn infants. *Developmental Medicine and Child Neurology*, 1980, *22*, 465–475.

Duffy, F. H., & Als, H. Neurophysiological assessment of the newborn. In T. B. Brazelton & B. M. Lester (Eds.), *Infants at risk: Toward plasticity and intervention*. New York: Elsevier, 1982.

Duffy, F. H., Burchfiel, J. L., & Lombroso, C. T. Brain electrical activity mapping (BEAM): A method for extending the clinical utility of EEG and evoked potentials data. *Annals of Neurology*,

1979, *5*, 309–321.

Duffy, F. H., Denckla, M. B., Bartels, P. H., & Sandini, G. Dyslexia: Regional differences in brain electrical activity by topographic mapping. *Annals of Neurology*, 1980, *7*, 412–420.

Duffy, F. H., Denckla, M. B., Bartels, P. H., Sandini, G., & Kiessling, L. S. Dyslexia: Automated diagnosis by computerized classification of brain electrical activity. *Annals of Neurology*, 1980, *7*, 421–428.

Duffy, F. H., Snodgrass, S. R., Burchfiel, J. R., & Conway, J. L. Bicuculline reversal of deprivation amblyopia in the cat. *Nature*, 1976, *260*, 256–257.

Dumermuth, G. Variance spectra of electroencepholograms in twins. In P. Kellaway, & I. Petersen (Eds.), *Clinical electroencephalography of children*. Stockholm: Almquist & Wiksell, 1968.

Eccles, J. C. *The physiology of nerve cells*. Baltimore: Johns Hopkins Press, 1957.

Eeg-Olofsson, O. The development of the electroencephalogram in normal adolescents from the age 16 through 21 years. *Neuropeodiatrie*, 1971, *2*, 117–151.

Eeg-Olofsson, O. Longitudinal development course of electrical activity of brain. *Brain and Development*, 1980, *2*, 33–44.

Eiduson, S., Geller, E., Yuwiler, A., & Eiduson, B. T. *Biochemistry and behavior*. Princeton: D. Van Nostrand, 1964.

Eisenberg, R. B. *Auditory competency in early life: The roots of communicative behavior*. Baltimore: University Park Press, 1976.

Eliet-Flescher, J., & Dreyfus-Brisac, C. Le sommeil du nouveau-né et du prematuré, II. Relations entre l'électromyogramme mentonnier au cours de la maturation. *Biology of the Neonate*, 1966, *10*, 316–339.

Ellingson, R. J. Electroencephalograms of normal full-term newborns immediately after birth with observations on arousal and visual evoked responses. *Electroencephalography and Clinical Neurophysiology*, 1958, *10*, 31–49.

Ellingson, R. J. Cortical electrical responses to visual stimulation in the human infant. *Electroencephalography and Clinical Neurophysiology*, 1960, *12*, 663–667.

Ellingson, R. J. Variability of visual evoked responses in the human newborn. *Electroencephalography and Clinical Neurophysiology*, 1970, *29*, 10–19.

Ellingson, R. J. Variability of visual evoked potentials in human infants and adults. *Electroencephalography and Clinical Neurophysiology*, 1973, *34*, 113–124.

Ellingson, R. J., Danahy, T., Nelson, B., & Lathrop, G. H. Variability of auditory evoked potentials in human newborns. *Electroencephalography and Clinical Neurophysiology*, 1974, *36*, 155–162.

Ellingson, R. J., & Peters, J. F. Development of EEG and daytime sleep patterns in normal full-term infants during the first three months of life: Longitudinal observations. *Electroencephalography and Clinical Neurophysiology*, 1980, *49*, 112–124. (a)

Ellingson, R. J., & Peters, J. F. Development of EEG and daytime sleep patterns in low risk premature infants during the first year of life: Longitudinal observations. *Electroencephalography and Clinical Neurophysiology*, 1980, *50*, 165–171. (b)

Ellingson, R. J., & Wilcott, R. C. Development of evoked responses in the visual and auditory cortices of kittens. *Journal of Neurophysiology*, 1960, *23*, 363–375.

Ellison, G. D. Chemical systems of the brain and evolution. In D. A. Oakley & H. G. Plotkin (Eds.), *Brain behaviour and evolution*. London: Methuen, 1979.

Emde, R. N., & Koenig, K. L. Neonatal smiling, frowning and rapid eye movement states. *Journal of the American Academy of Child Psychiatry*, 1968, *8*, 57–67.

Emde, R. N., & Walker, S. Longitudinal study of infant sleep: Results of 14 subjects studied at monthly intervals. *Psychophysiology*, 1976, *13*, 456–461.

Engel, R. Maturational changes and abnormalities in the newborn electroencephalogram. *Developmental Medicine and Child Neurology*, 1965, *7*, 498–506.

Engel, R., & Benson, R. C. Estimate of conceptional age by evoked response activity. *Biology of the Neonate*, 1968, *12*, 201–213.

Falck, B., Hillarp, N. A., Thieme, G., & Torp, H. Fluorescence of catecholamine and related compounds condensed by formaldehyde. *Journal of Histochemistry and Cytochemistry*, 1962, *10*, 348–354.

Famiglietti, E. V., Jr., & Kolb, H. Structural basis for on- and off-center responses in retinal ganglion cells. *Science*, 1976, *194*, 193–195.

Fantz, R. L., & Fagan, J. F., III. Visual attention to size and number of pattern details by term and pre-term infants during the first six months. *Child Development*, 1975, *46*, 3–18.

Fantz, R. L., Fagan, J. F., III, & Miranda, S. B. Early visual selectivity as a function of pattern variables, previous exposure, age from birth and conception, and expected cognitive deficit. In L. B. Cohen & P. Salapatek (Eds.), *Infant perception: From sensation to cognition* (Vol. 1). New York: Academic Press, 1975.

Farkas-Bargeton, E., & Diebler, M. F. A topographical study of enzyme maturation in human cerebral neocortex: A histochemical and biochemical study. In M. A. B. Brazier & H. Petsche (Eds.), *Architectonics of the cerebral cortex*. New York: Raven Press, 1978.

Fleischer, J. Untersuchungen zur Entwiklung der innenohr Funktion. Intrauterine Kindesbewegungen nach Schallreizen. *Zeitschrift für Laryngologie, Rhinologie, Otologie und Ihre Grenzgebiete,* 1955, *34,* 733–740.

Fleschig, P. *Die Leitungsbahnen in Gehirn und Ruckenmark des Menschen auf grand entwickelungs geschichtlicher untersuchungen.* Leipzig: W. Engleman, 1876.

Freeman, R. D., & Bonds, A. B. Cortical plasticity in monocularly deprived immobilized kittens depends on eye movements. *Science,* 1979, *206,* 1093–1095.

Freygang, W. J., Jr., & Frank, K. Extracellular potentials from single motoneurons, *Journal of General Physiology,* 1959, *42,* 749–760.

Friedman, S. L., Jacobs, B. S., & Wertmann, M. W., Jr. Sensory processing in pre- and full-term infants in the neonatal period. In S. L. Friedman & M. Sigman (Eds.), *Preterm birth and psychological development.* New York: Academic Press, 1981.

Fuxe, K., Hökfelt, T., Jonsson, G., & Ungerstedt, U. Fluorescence microscopy in neuroanatomy. In W. J. H. Nauta & S. O. E. Ebbesson (Eds.), *Contemporary research methods in neuroanatomy,* New York: Springer-Verlag, 1970.

Garma, L., & Verley, R. Generateurs corticaux etudier par electrodes implantees chez de lapin nouveau-ne. *Journal de Physiologie,* 1965, *57,* 811–818.

Gesell, A., & Amatruda, C. S. *The embryology of behavior*. New York: Harper, 1945.

Gibbs, F. A., & Gibbs, E. L. *Atlas of electroencephalography* (Vol. 1). Reading, Mass.: Addison-Wesley, 1951.

Gloor, P. (Ed. and trans.). Hans Berger on the electroencephalogram of man. *Electroencephalography and Clinical Neurophysiology,* 1969. (Supplement 28)

Goldman, P. S., & Galkin, T. W. Prenatal removal of frontal association cortex in the fetal rhesus monkey: Anatomical and functional consequences in postnatal life. *Brain Research,* 1978, *152,* 451–485.

Goldstein, P. J., Krumholz, A., Felix, J. K., Shannon, D., & Carr, R. F. Brain stem-evoked response in neonates. *American Journal of Obstetrics and Gynecology,* 1979, *135,* 622–628.

Golgi, C. Sur l'anatomie microscopique des organes centraux du systeme nerveux. *Archives Italiennes de Biologie,* 1886, *7,* 15–47.

Graybiel, A. M., & Ragsdale, Jr., C. W. Clumping of acetylcholinesterase activity in the developing striatum of the human fetus and young infant. *Proceedings National Academy of Science,* 1980, *77,* 1214–1218.

Greenough, W. T. Experiential modification of the developing brain. *American Scientist,* 1975, *63,* 37–46.

Greenough, W. T., & Juraska, J. M. Experience-induced change in brain fine structure: Their behavioral implications. In M. E. Hahn, C. Jensen, & B. C. Dudek (Eds.), *Development and evolution of brain size: Behavioral implications.* New York: Academic Press, 1979.

Greenough, W. T., & Volkmar, F. R. Pattern of dendritic branching in occipital cortex of rats reared in complex environments. *Experimental Neurology,* 1973, *40,* 490–504.

Gruner, J. E. The maturation of human cerebral cortex in electron microscopy study of post-mortem punctures in premature infants. *Biology of the Neonate,* 1970, *16,* 243–255.

Guilleminault, C., Ariagno, R. L., Forno, L. S., Nagle, L., Baldwin, R., & Owen, M. Obstructive sleep apnea and near miss for SIDS: Report of an infant with sudden death. *Pediatrics,* 1979, *63,* 837–843.

Guroff, G. *Molecular neurobiology.* New York: Marcel Dekker, 1980.

Haas, G. H., & Prechtl, H. F. R. Normal and abnormal EEG maturation in newborn infants. *Early Human Development,* 1977, *1,* 69–90.

Hack, M., Miranda, S., & Fantz, R. Early pattern fixation in preterm infants. *Pediatric Research,* 1975, *9,* 383.

Hack, M., Mostow, A., & Miranda, S. Development of attention in preterm infants. *Pediatrics,* 1976, *58,* 669–674.

Hack, M., Muszynski, B. A., & Miranda, S. State of awakeness during visual fixation in preterm infants. *Pediatrics,* 1981 *68,* 87–92.

Hagne, I. Development of the waking EEG in normal infants during the first year of life. In P. Kellaay & I. Petersen (Eds.), *Clinical electroencephalography of children.* Stockholm: Almquist & Wiksell, 1968.

Haith, M. M. Visual competence in early infancy. In R. Held, H. W. Leibowitz, & H. L. Tauber (Eds.), *Handbook of sensory physiology. Perception* (Vol. 4). New York: Springer-Verlag, 1978.

Haith, M. M. *Rules that babies look by.* New Jersey: Lawrence Erlbaum Assoc., 1980.

Hamasaki, D. I., & Flynn, J. T. Physiological properties of retinal ganglian cells of 3-week-old kittens. *Vision Research,* 1977, *17,* 275–284.

Harper, R. M., Hoppenbrouwers, T., Sterman, M. B., McGinty, D. J., & Hodgman, J. Polygraphic studies of normal infants during the first six months of life. I. Heart rate and variability as a function of state. *Pediatric Research,* 1976, *10,* 945–951.

Havlicek, V., Childaeva, R., & Chernick, V. EEG frequency spectrum characteristics of sleep states in full-term and pre-term infants. *Neuropeodiatrie,* 1975, *6,* 24–40.

Havlicek, V., Childaeva, R., & Chernick, V. EEG frequency spectrum characteristics of sleep states in infants of alcoholic mothers. *Neuropaediatrie,* 1977, *8,* 360–373.

Hecox, K. Electrophysiological correlates of human auditory development. In L. B. Cohen & P. Salapatek (Eds.), *Infant perception: From sensation to cognition. Perception of space, speech, and sound.* (Vol. 11). New York: Academic Press, 1975.

Hecox, K., & Galambos, R. Brain stem auditory evoked responses in human infants and adults. *Archives of Orolaryngology,* 1974, *99,* 30–33.

Henry, C. E. Electroencephalograms of normal children. *Monographs of the Society for Research in Child Development,* 1944, *9* (3, Serial No. 39), 1–71.

Hirsch, H. V. B., & Leventhal, A. G. Functional modification of the developing visual system. In M. Jacobson (Ed.), *Handbook of sensory physiology: Development of the sensory system.* Berlin: Springer-Verlag, 1978.

Hirsch, H. V. B., & Spinelli, D. N. Modification of the distribution of receptive field orientation in cats by selective visual exposure during development. *Experimental Brain Research,* 1971, *13,* 509–527.

Hoffman, M. J., Salapatek, P., & Kuskowski, M. Evidence for visual memory in the averaged and single evoked potentials of human infants. *Infant Behavior and Development,* 1981, *4,* 185–205.

Hoppenbrouwers, T., & Sterman, M. B. Development of sleep patterns in the kitten. *Experimental Neurology,* 1975, *49,* 822–838.

Horsten, G., & Winkelman, J. Electrical activity of the retina in relation to histological differentiation in infants born prematurely and at full term. *Vision Research,* 1962, *2,* 269–276.

Hrbek, A., Karlberg, P., & Olsson, T. Development of visual and somatosensory evoked responses in pre-term and newborn infants. *Electroencephalography and Clinical Neurophysiology,* 1973, *34,* 225–232.

Hubel, D. H., & Wiesel, T. N. Receptive fields of cells in striate cortex of very young, visually inexperienced kittens. *Journal of Neurophysiology,* 1963, *26,* 994–1002.

Hubel, D. H., & Wiesel, T. N. The period of susceptibility to the physiological effects of unilateral eye closure in kittens. *Journal of Physiology,* 1970, *206,* 419–436.

Hubel, D. H., Wiesel, T. N., & LeVay, S. Plasticity of ocular dominance columns in monkey striate cortex. *Philosophical Transactions of the Royal Society of London. Series B: Biological Sciences,* 1977, *278,* 377–409.

Hull, C. D., & Fuller, D. R. G. Discussion: Development of postsynaptic potentials recorded from immature neurons in kitten visual cortex. In M. A. B. Brazier (Ed.), *Brain mechanisms in mental retardation.* New York: Academic Press, 1975.

Hull, C. D., McAllister, J. P., Levine, M. S., & Adinolfi, A. M. Quantitative developmental studies of feline neostriatal spinz neurons. *Developmental Brain Research,* 1981, *1,* 309–332.

Humphrey, T. Some correlations between the appearance of human fetal reflexes and the development of the nervous system. In D. P. Purpura & J. P. Schade (Eds.), *Growth and maturation of the brain: Progess in brain research* (Vol. 4). Amsterdam: Elsevier, 1964.

Humphrey, T. The embryologic differentiation of the vestibular nuclei in man correlated with functional development. *International Symposium on Vestibular and Oculomotor Problems.* Extraordinary Meeting of the Japan Society of Vestibular Research, University of Tokyo, 1965, 51–56.

Huttenlocher, P. R. Development of cortical neuronal activity in the neonatal cat. *Experimental Neurology,* 1967, *17,* 247–262.

Huttenlocher, P. R., & Rawson, M. D. Neuronal activity and adenosine triphosphatase in immature cerebral cortex. *Experimental Neurology,* 1968, *22,* 118–129.

Iverson, L. L. The chemistry of the brain. *Scientific American*, 1979, *241*, 134–149.

Jacobson, M. A plentitude of neurons in studies on the development of behavior and the nervous system. In G. Gottlieb (Ed.), *Studies on development of behavior and nervous system. Aspects of neurogenesis* (Vol. 2). New York: Academic Press, 1974.

Jacobson, M. *Developmental neurobiology* (2nd ed.) New York: Plenum Press, 1978.

Javel, E. Neurophysiological correlates of auditory maturation. *Annals of Otology, Rhinology and Laryngology*, 1980, *74*, 103–113. (Supplement)

Johansson, B., Wedenbert, E., & Westin, B. Measurement of tone response by the human fetus. *Acta Oto-laryngologica*, 1964, *57*, 188–192.

John, E. R., Karmel, B. Z., Corning, W. C., Easton, P., Brown, D., Ahn, H., John, M., Harmony, T., Prichep, L., Toro, A., Gerson, I., Bartlett, F., Thatcher, R., Kaye, H., Valdes, P., & Schwartz, E. Neurometrics. Numerical toxonomy identifies different profiles of brain functions within groups of behaviorally similar people. *Science*, 1977, *196*, 1393–1410.

Johns, P. R., Rusoff, A. C., & Dubin, M. W. Postnatal neurogenesis in the kitten retina. *Journal of Comparative Neurology*, 1979, *187*, 545–556.

Joppich, G., & Schulte, F. J. *Neurologie der neugeborenen*. Berlin: Springer-Verlag, 1968.

Jouvet-Mounier, D., Astic, L., & Lacote, D. Ontogenesis of the states of sleep in rat, cat, and guinea pig during the first postnatal month. *Developmental Psychobiology*, 1970, *2*, 216–239.

Kandel, E. R. Neuronal plasticity and the modification of behavior. In *Handbook of physiology*. Bethesda, Md.: American Physiological Society, 1977.

Kandel, E. R. Psychotherapy and the single synapse: The impact of psychiatric thought on neurobiological research. *New England Journal of Medicine*, 1979, *301*, 1028–1037.

Kaplay, S. S. Cholinesterase activity of developing human brain. *Indian Journal of Biochemistry and Biophysics*, 1977, *14*, 389–391.

Karmel, B. Z., Kay, H., & John, E. R. Developmental neurometrics: The use of quantitative analysis of brain electrical activity to probe mental function throughout the life span. In W. A. Collins (Ed.), *Minnesota Symposia on Child Psychology*, (Vol. 11). Hillsdale, N.J.: Lawrence Erlbaum Associates, 1978.

Karmel, B. Z., & Maisel, E. B. A neuronal activity model for infant visual attention. In L. B. Cohen & P. Salapatek (Eds.), *Infant perception: From sensation to cognition* (Vol. 1). New York: Academic Press, 1975.

Kasamatsu, T., & Pettigrew, J. D. Preservation of binocularity after monocular deprivation in the striate cortex of kittens treated with G-hydroxydopamine. *Journal of Comparative Neurology*, 1979, *185*, 139–162.

Kasamatsu, T., Pettigrew, J. D., & Ary, M. Restoration of visual cortical plasticity by local microprofusion of norepinephrine. *Journal of Comparative Neurology*, 1979, *185*, 163–182.

Kennedy, C., Sakwada, O., Shinohara, M., Jehle, J., & Sokoloff, L. Local cerebral glucose utilization in the normal conscious macaque monkey. *Annals of Neurology*, 1978, *4*, 293–301.

Kileny, P., Connelly, C., & Robertson, C. Auditory brain stem responses in perinatal asphyxia. *International Journal of Pediatric Otorhinolaryngology*, 1980, *2*, 147, 159.

Kimura, R. S., Ota, C. Y., & Takahashi, T. Nerve fiber synapses on spiral ganglion cells in the human cochlea. *Annals of Otology, Rhinology, and Laryngology*, 1979, *88*, 1–17. (Supplement)

Kleitman, N. *Sleep and wakefulness*. Chicago: University of Chicago Press, 1963.

Konig, N., Pujol, R., & Marty, R. A laminar study of evoked potentials in the auditory cortex of the postnatal cat. *Brain Research*, 1972, *37*, 469–473.

Kopp, C. B., Sigman, M., Parmelee, A. H., & Jeffrey, W. E. Neurological organization and visual fixation in infants at 40 weeks conceptional age. *Developmental Psychobiology*, 1975, *8*, 165–170.

Kristl, D. A. Development of neocortical circuitry: Quantitative ultrastructural analysis of putative monoaminergic synapses. *Brain Research*, 1979, *178*, 69–88.

Krmpotić-Nemanić, J., Kostović, I., Kelović, Z., & Nemanić, D. Development of acetylcholinesterase (AChE) staining in human fetal auditory cortex. *Acta Otolaryngdica*, 1980, *89*, 388–392.

Langworthy, O. R. Correlated study of the development of reflex activity in fetal and young kittens and myelinization of trac in the nervous system. *Contribution to Embryology* (No. 114), Carnegie Institute of Washington (Publication No. 394), 1929, *20*, 127–170.

Langworthy, O. R. Development of behavior patterns and myelinization of the nervous system in the human fetus and infant. *Contribution to Embryology* (No. 139), Carnegie Institute of Washington (Publication No. 139), 1933, *24*, 1–57.

Larroche, J. C. Quelques aspect anatomique du developpement cerebral. *Biology of the Neonate,* 1962, *4,* 126–153.

LaVelle, A. Nucleolar and Nissl substance development in nerve cells. *Journal of Comparative Neurology,* 1956, *104,* 175–205.

LaVelle, A., & LaVelle, F. W. Cyto differentiation in neurons. In W. A. Himwich (Ed.), *Developmental Neurobiology.* Springfield, Ill.: Charles C. Thomas, 1970.

Lawson, K., Daum, C., & Turkewitz, G. Environmental characteristics of a neonatal intensive care unit. *Child Development,* 1977, *48,* 1633–1639.

Lenard, H. G., Bernuth, H. von, & Prechtl, H. F. R. Reflexes and their relationship to behavioral state in the newborn. *Acta Paediatrica Scandinavica,* 1968, *3,* 177–185.

Lenard, H. G., Schulte, F. J., Eichorn, W., Meyer, S., & Busse, C. Die Entwicklung sensorischer Funktionen bei Frühgeborenen in den ersten lebens Wochen. *Monatsschrift für Kinderheilkunde,* 1977, *125,* 383–385.

Leventhal, A. G., & Hirsch, H. V. B. Receptive-field properties of different classes of neurons in visual cortex of normal and dark reared cats. *Journal of Neurophysiology,* 1980, *43,* 1111–1132.

Levine, M. S., Cherubini, E., Novack, G. D., Hull, C. D., & Buchwald, N. A. Development of responses of globus pallidus and entopeduncular nucleus neurons to stimulation of the caudate nucleus and precruciate cortex. *Experimental Neurology,* 1979, *66,* 479–492.

Levine, M. S., Hull, C. D., & Buchwald, N. A. Development of motor activity in kittens. *Developmental Psychobiology,* 1980, *13,* 357–371.

Lewis, M. Infants' responses to facial stimuli during the first year of life. *Developmental Psychology,* 1969, *1,* 75–86.

Lewis, T. L., Maurer, D., & Kay, D. Newborns' central vision: Whole or hole? *Journal of Experimental Child Psychology,* 1978, *26,* 193–203.

Lidsky, T. I., Buchwald, N. A., Hull, C. D., & Levine, M. S. A neurophysiological analysis of the development of cortico-caudate connections in the cat. *Experimental Neurology,* 1976, *50,* 283–292.

Lindsley, D. B. Brain potentials in children and adults. *Science,* 1936, *84,* 354.

Lindsley, D. B. Electrical potentials of the brain in children and adults. *Journal of General Psychology,* 1938, *19,* 285–306.

Lindsley, D. B. A longitudinal study of the occipital alpha rhythm in normal children: Frequency and amplitude standards. *Journal of Genetic Psychology,* 1939, *55,* 197–213.

Lynch, B., Gall, C., & Dunwiddie, T. V. Neuroplasticity in the hippocampal formation. In M. A. Corner, R. E. Baker, N. E. van de Poll, & D. F. Swabb (Eds.), *Maturation of the nervous system: Progress in brain research* (Vol. 48). New York: Elsevier, 1978.

Maffei, L., & Fiorentini, A. Electroretinographic responses to alternating gratings before and after section of the optic nerve. *Science,* 1981, *211,* 953–955.

Mann, I. *The development of the human eye.* London: British Medical Association, 1964.

Marin-Padilla, M. Prenatal and early postnatal ontogenesis of the human motor cortex: A Golgi study. I. The sequential development of the cortical layers. *Brain Research,* 1970, *23,* 167–183.

Marty, R. Maturation post-natale du système auditif. In A. Minkowski (Ed.), *Regional development of the brain in early life.* Oxford: Blackwell, 1967.

Maurer, D. Infant visual perception: Methods of study. In L. B. Cohen & P. Salapatek (Eds.), *Infant perception: From sensation to cognition.* New York: Academic Press, 1975.

McConnell, P. Nutritional effects on non-mitotic aspects of central nervous system development. In P. S. McConnell, G. J. Boer, H. J. Romijm, N. E. van de Poll, & M. A. Corner (Eds.), *Adaptive capabilities of the nervous system. Progress in brain research* (Vol. 53). New York: Elsevier, 1980.

McGeer, P. L., Eccles, J. C., & McGeer, E. G. *Molecular neurobiology of the mammalian brain.* New York: Plenum Press, 1978.

McGinty, D. J., Stevenson, M., Hoppenbrouwers, T., Harper, R. M., Sterman, M. B., & Hodgman, J. Polygraphic studies of kitten development: Sleep state patterns. *Developmental Psychobiology,* 1977, *10,* 455–469.

McGraw, M. B. Maturation of behavior. In L. Carmichael (Ed.), *Manual of child psychology.* New York: John Wiley & Sons, 1946.

McGraw, M. B. *The neuro-muscular maturation of the human infant.* New York: Hafner Publishing, 1963.

Metcalf, D. R. The effect of extrauterine experience on the ontogenesis of EEG sleep spindles. *Psychosomatic Medicine,* 1969, *31,* 393–399.

Metcalf, D. R. The ontogenes of sleep-wake states from birth to 3 months. *Electroencephalography and Clinical Neurophysiology,* 1970, *28,* 421.

Miranda, S. B. Visual attention in defective and high risk infants. *Merrill-Palmer Quarterly,* 1976, *22,* 201–228.

Molfese, D. L. Hemispheric specialization for temporal information: Implications for the perception of voicing cues during speech perception. *Brain and Language,* 1980, *11,* 285–299.

Molfese, D. L., & Hess, T. M. Hemispheric specialization for VOT perception in preschool children. *Journal of Experimental Child Psychology,* 1976, *26,* 71–84.

Molliver, M. E., Kostovic, I., & Van Der Loos, H. The development of synapses in cerebral cortex of the human fetus. *Brain Research,* 1973, *50,* 403–407.

Monod, N., Dreyfus-Brisac, C., Eliet-Flescher, J., Pajot, N., & Plassart, E. Les troubles de l'organization du sommeil chez le nouveau-né pathologique. *Revue Neurologique,* 1963, *115,* 469–474.

Monod, N., & Garma, L. Auditory responsivity in the human premature. *Biology of the Neonate,* 1971, *17,* 292–316.

Morris, R., Levine, M. S., Cherubini E., Buchwald, N. A., & Hull, C. D. Intracellular analysis of the development of responses of caudate neurons to stimulation of cortex, thalamus and substantia nigra in the kitten. *Brain Research,* 1979, *173,* 471–487.

Morse, P. A. The infancy of infant perception: The first decade of research. *Brain, Behavior and Evolution,* 1979, *16,* 351–373.

Mountcastle, V. B. An organizing principle for cerebral function: The unit module and the distributed system. In F. O. Schmitt & F. G. Worden, *The Neurosciences Fourth Study Program.* Cambridge, Mass.: MIT Press, 1979.

Mueller, R. A., Mailman, R. B., & Breese, G. R. Behavioral and monoaminergic consequences of exposure to neurotoxins during development. In H. Parnes & S. Parvey (Eds.), *Biogenic amines in development.* Amsterdam: Elsevier, 1980.

Murphy, K. P., & Smyth, C. N. Response of foetus to auditory stimulation. *Lancet,* 1962, *2,* 972–973.

Nakai, Y. An electron microscopic study of the human fetus cochlea. *Practica Oto-rhino-laryngologica,* 1970, *32,* 257–267.

Neligan, G. A., Kolvin, I., Scott, D. M., & Garside, R. F. *Born too soon or born too small.* Philadelphia: J. B. Lippincott, 1976.

Nissl, F. Uber die sogenannten Granula der Nervenzellen. *Neurologisches, Zentralblatt,* 1894, *13,* 676–685, 781–789, 810–814.

Noback, C. R., & Purpura, D. P. Postnatal ontogenesis of neurons in cat neocortex. *Journal of Comparative Neurology,* 1961, *117,* 291–308.

O'Connor, M. J. A comparison of preterm and full-term infants on parameters of habituation at 4 months and performance on the Bayley Scales of Infant Development at 18 months. *Child Development,* 1980, *51,* 81–88.

Olmstead, C. E., & Villablanca, J. R. Development of behavioral audition in the kitten. *Physiology and Behavior,* 1980, *24,* 705–712.

Palay, S. L., & Palade, G. E. The fine structure of neurons. *Journal of Biophysical and Biochemical Cytology,* 1955, *1,* 69–87.

Parmelee, A. H., Jr. The hand-mouth reflex of Babkin in premature infants. *Pediatrics,* 1963, *31,* 734–740. (a)

Parmelee, A. H., Jr. The palmomental reflex in premature infants. *Developmental Medicine and Child Neurology,* 1963, *5,* 381–387. (b)

Parmelee, A. H., Jr. Ontogeny of sleep patterns and associated periodicities in infants. In S. R. Berenberg, M. Caniaris, & N. P. Masse (Eds.), *Pre- and postnatal development of the human brain* (Vol. 13). Basel: S. Karger, 1974.

Parmelee, A. H., Jr. Neurophysiological and behavioral organization of premature infants in the first months of life. *Biological Psychiatry,* 1975, *10,* 501–512.

Parmelee, A. H., Jr. Auditory function and neurological maturation in preterm infants. In S. L. Friedman & M. Sigman (Eds.), *Preterm birth and psychological development.* New York: Academic Press, 1981.

Parmelee, A. H., Jr., Akiyama, M. A., Schultz, M. A., Wenner, W. H., & Schulte, F. J. Analysis of the electroencephalogram of sleeping infants. *Activitas Nervosa Superior,* 1969, *11,* 111–115.

Parmelee, A. H., Jr., Akiyama, Y., Schultz, M. A., Wenner, W. H., Schulte, F. J., & Stern, E. The electroencephalogram in active and quiet sleep in infants. In P. Kellaway & I. Petersen (Eds.), *Clinical electroencephalography of children.* New York: Grune & Stratton, 1968.

Parmelee, A. H., Jr., Kopp, C. B., & Sigman, M. Selection of developmental assessment techniques for infants at risk. *Merrill-Palmer Quarterly,* 1976, *22,* 177–199.

Parmelee, A. H., Jr., Schulte, F. J., Akiyama, Y., Wenner, W. H., Schultz, M. A., & Stern, E. Maturation of EEG activity during sleep in premature infants. *Electroencephalography and Clinical Neurophysiology,* 1968, *24,* 319–329.

Parmelee, A. H., Jr., & Sigman, M. Development

of visual behavior and neurological organization in pre-term and full-term infants. In A. D. Pick (Ed.), *Minnesota Symposia on Child Psychology* (Vol. 10). Minneapolis: University of Minnesota Press, 1976.

Parmelee, A. H., Jr., & Stern, E. Development of states in infants. In C. Clemente, D. Purpura, & F. Meyer (Eds.), *Sleep and the maturing nervous system.* New York: Academic Press, 1972, 199–228.

Parmelee, A. H., Jr., Stern, E., & Harris, M. A. Maturation of respiration in prematures and young infants. *Neuropeodiatrie,* 1972, *3,* 294–304.

Parmelee, A. H., Jr., Wenner, W. H., Akiyama, Y., Schultz, M., & Stern, E. Sleep states in premature infants. *Developmental Medicine and Child Neurology,* 1967, *9,* 70–77. (a)

Parmelee, A. H., Jr., Wenner, W. H., Akiyama, Y., Stern, E., & Flescher, J. Electroencephalography and brain maturation. In A. Minkowski (Ed.), *Regional brain development in early life.* Oxford: Blackwell, 1967. (b)

Pearse, A. G. E. Fundamentals of functional neurochemistry. *Brain Research,* 1967, *4,* 125–134.

Peterseń, I., & Eeg-Olofsson, O. The development of the electroencephalogram in normal children from the age of 1 through 15 years. *Neuropeodiatrie,* 1970/71, *2* and *3,* 1–151.

Peterseń, I., Selldén, U., & Bosaeus, E. The relationship between IQ, social class and EEG by child-psychiatric methods. *Scandinavian Journal of Psychology,* 1976, *17,* 189–197.

Petre-Quadens, O. Ontogenesis of paradoxical sleep in the human newborn. *Journal of the Neurological Sciences,* 1967, *4,* 153–157.

Petre-Quadens, O. Sleep in mental retardation. In C. D. Clemente, D. P. Purpura & F. E. Mayer (Eds.), *Sleep and the maturing nervous system.* New York: Academic Press, 1972.

Petre-Quadens, O., DeLee, C., & Remy, M. Eye movement density during sleep and brain maturation. *Brain Research,* 1971, *26,* 49–56.

Pettigrew, J. D. The effect of visual experience on the development of stimulus specificity by kitten cortical neurones. *Journal of Physiology,* 1974, *237,* 49–74.

Pettigrew, J. D. The paradox of the critical period for striate. In C. W. Cotman (Ed.), *Neuronal plasticity.* New York: Raven Press, 1978.

Phelps, M. E., Kuhl, D. E., & Mazziotta, J. C. Metabolic mapping of the brain's response to visual stimulation in humans. *Science,* 1981, *211,* 1445–1448.

Poliakov, G. I. Embryonal and post embryonal development of neurons of the human cerebral cortex. In R. Hassler & H. Stephens (Eds.), *Evolution of the forebrain, phylogenesis and ontogenesis of the forebrain.* New York: Plenum Press, 1967.

Prechtl, H. F. R. Patterns of reflex behavior related to sleep in the human infant. In C. D. Clemente, D. P. Purpura, & F. E. Mayer, Eds., *Sleep and the maturing nervous system.* New York: Academic Press, 1972.

Prechtl, H. F. R. The behavioral states of the newborn infant (a review). *Brain Research,* 1974, *76,* 185–212.

Prechtl, H. F. R., Akiyama, Y., Zinkin, P., & Grant, D. K. Polygraphic studies of the full-term newborn: I. Technical aspects and qualitative analysis. In R. MacKeith & M. Bax (Eds.), *Studies in infancy* (Clinics in Developmental Medicine No. 27). Lavenham, Eng.: Spastics International Medical Publications in Association with William Heinemann Medical Books, Ltd., 1968.

Prechtl, H. F. R., & Beintema, D. J. *The neurological examination of the full-term newborn infant.* (Clinics in Developmental Medicine No. 12). London: Heinemann, 1968.

Prechtl, H. F. R., & Lenard, A. G. A study of eye movements in sleeping newborn infants. *Brain Research,* 1967, *5,* 477–493.

Prechtl, H. F. R., Theorell, K., & Blair, A. W. Behavioral state cycles in abnormal infants. *Developmental Medicine and Child Neurology,* 1973, *15,* 606–615.

Prechtl, H. F. R., Vlach, V., Lenard, H. G., & Kerr Grant, D. Exteroceptive and tendon reflexes in various behavioral states in the newborn infant. *Biology of the Neonate,* 1967, *11,* 159–175.

Prechtl, H. F. R., & Vos, J. E. Verlaufsmuster der Frequenzspektren und Koharenzen bei schlafenden normalen und neuologisch abnormalen Neugeborenen. In G. K. Schenck (Ed.), *Beitrage Zum Symposium: Die Quantifizierunge des Elektroencephalogramms.* Konstanz: AEG-Telefunken, 1973.

Puccetti, R., & Dykes, R. W. Sensory cortex and the mind-brain problem. *The Behaviorial and Brain Sciences,* 1978, *3,* 337–395.

Pujol, R. Maturation du système auditif. *Revue de Laryngologie,* 1976, *97,* 551–562. (Supplement)

Pujol, R., Carlier, E., & Devigne, C. Different patterns of cochlear innervation during development of the kitten. *Journal of Comparative Neurology,* 1978, *177,* 529–535.

Pujol, R., & Hilding, D. A. Anatomy and physiology of the onset of auditory function. *Acta Otolaryngolica* (Stockholm), 1975, *76*, 1–12.

Pujol, R., & Marty, R. Postnatal maturation in the cochlea of the cat. *Journal of Comparative Neurology*, 1970, *139*, 115–126.

Purpura, D. P. Morphogenesis of the visual cortex in preterm infants. In M. A. B. Brazier (Ed.), *Growth and brain development*. New York: Raven Press, 1975.

Purpura, D. P. Structure-dysfunction relations in the visual cortex of preterm infants in brain dysfunction. In M. A. B. Brazier, & F. Coceani (Eds.), *Infantile febrile convulsions*. New York: Raven Press, 1976.

Purpura, D. P., & Shofer, R. J. Principle of synoptogenesis and their application to ontogenetic studies of mammalian cerebral cortex. In C. D. Clemente, D. P. Purpura, & F. E. Mayers (Eds.), *Sleep and the maturing nervous system*. New York: Academic Press, 1972.

Purpura, D. P., Shofer, R. J., Housepian, E. M., & Noback, C. R. Comparative ontogenesis of structure-function relations in cerebral and cerebellar cortex. In D. P. Purpura & J. P. Schade (Eds.), *Growth and maturation of the brain, progress in brain research* (Vol. 4). New York: Elsevier, 1964.

Purves, D., & Lichtman, J. W. Elimination of synapses in the developing nervous system. *Science*, 1980, *210*, 153–157.

Rabinowicz, T. The cerebral cortex of the premature infant of the 8th month. In D. P. Purpura & J. P. Schade (Eds.), *Growth and maturation of the brain. Progress in brain research* (Vol. 4). New York: Elsevier, 1964.

Rabinowicz, T. Morphological features of the developing brain. In M. A. B. Brazier & F. Coceani (Eds.), *Brain dysfunction in infantile febrile convulsions*. New York: Raven Press, 1976.

Rakic, P., & Sidman, R. L. Histogenesis of cortical layers in human cerebellum, particularly the lamina dissecans. *Journal of Comparative Neurology*, 1970, *139*, 473–500.

Ramon y Cajal, S. Sur la structure de l'ecorce cerebrale de quelques mammiferes. *Cellule*, 1891, *7*, 123–176.

Reivich, M., Kuhl, D., Wolf, A., Greenberg, J., Phelps, M., Ida, T., Casella, V., Fowler, J., Hoffman, E., Alavi, A., Som, P., & Sokoloff, L. The [18F] fluorodeoxyglucose method for the measurement of local cerebral glucose utilization in man. *Circulation Research*, 1979, *44*, 127–137.

Rodier, P. M. Chronology of neuron development: Animal studies and their clinical implications. *Developmental Medicine and Child Neurology*, 1980, *22*, 525–545.

Roffwarg, H. P., Dement, W. C., & Fisher, C. Preliminary observations of the sleep-dream patterns in neonates, children and adults. In E. Harms (Ed.), *Problems of sleep and dreams in children. International Series of Monographs on Child Psychiatry* (Vol. 2). New York: Macmillan, 1964.

Roffwarg, H. P., Muzio, J. N., & Dement, W. C. Ontogenetic development of the human sleep-dream cycle. *Science*, 1966, *152*, 604–619.

Romand, R., & Marty, R. Postnatal maturation of the cochlear nuclei in the cat: A neurophysiological study. *Brain Research*, 1975, *83*, 225–233.

Rose, G. H. Animal studies in developmental psychobiology: Commentary on method theory and human implications. In S. L. Friedman & M. Sigman (Eds.), *Preterm birth and psychological development*. New York: Academic Press, 1981.

Rose, G. H., & Collins, J. P. Light-dark discrimination and reversal learning in early postnatal kittens. *Developmental Psychobiology*, 1975, *8*, 511–518.

Rose, G. H., & Ellingson, R. J. Ontogenesis of evoked potentials. In W. A. Himwich (Ed.), *Developmental neurobiology*. Springfield, Ill.: Charles C. Thomas, 1970.

Rose, G. H., & Gruenau, S. P., & Spencer, J. W. Maturation of visual electrocortical responses in unanesthetized kittens: Effects of barbiturate anesthesia. *Electroencephalography and Clinical Neurophysiology*, 1972, *33*, 141–158.

Rose, G. H., & Lindsley, D. B. Development of visually evoked potentials in kittens: Specific and nonspecific responses. *Journal of Neurophysiology*, 1968, *31*, 607–623.

Rose, S. A. Enhancing visual recognition memory in preterm infants. *Developmental Psychology*, 1980, *16*, 85–92.

Rose, S. A. Lags in the cognitive competence of prematurely born infants. In S. L. Friedman & M. Sigman (Eds.), *Preterm birth and psychological development*. New York: Academic Press, 1981.

Rose, S. A., Gottfried, A. W., & Bridger, W. H. Cross-modal transfer in infants: Relationship to prematurity and socioeconomic background. *Developmental Psychology*, 1978, *14*, 643–652.

Rubel, E. W. Ontogeny of structure and function in the vertebrate auditory system. In M. Jacobsen (Ed.), *Handbook of sensory physiology. Development of sensory systems* (Vol. 9). Berlin: Springer-Verlag, 1978.

Rusoff, A. C., & Dubin, M. W. Kitten ganglion

cells: Dendritic field size at 3 weeks of age and correlation with receptive field size. *Investigative Ophthalmology and Visual Science,* 1978, *17,* 819–821.

Saint-Anne Dargassies, S. Neurological maturation of the premature infant of 28 to 41 weeks gestational age. In F. Falkner (Ed.), *Human development.* Philadelphia and London: W. B. Saunders, 1966.

Salamy, A., & McKean, C. M. Postnatal development of human brainstem potentials during the first year of life. *Electroencephalography and Clinical Neurophysiology,* 1976, *40,* 418–426.

Salamy, A., Mendelson, T., Tooley, W. H., & Chaplin, E. R. Contrasts in brainstem function between normal and high-risk infants in early postnatal life. *Early Human Development,* 1980, *4,* 179–185.

Samson-Dollfus, D. Developpement normal de l'eletroretinogramme depuis l'age faetal de sept mois et demi jusqu'a l'age de quatre mois apres la naissance a terme. *Bulletin des Societes d'Ophtolmologie de France,* 1968, *4,* 1–9.

Sans, S., & Chat, M. Maturation postnatale des noyaux vestibulaires chez le chat: Etude histologique par la methode de Golgi-Cox. *Brain Research,* 1976, *111,* 13–30.

Scheibel, M. E., & Scheibel, A. B. Some structural and functional substrates of development in young cats. In W. A. Himwich & H. E. Himwich (Eds.), *The developing brain. Progress in brain research* (Vol. 9). New York: Elsevier, 1964.

Scheibel, M. E., & Scheibel, A. B. Some structural and functional substrates of development in young cats. In W. A. Himwich & H. E. Himwich (Eds.), *Progress in brain research* (Vol. 9). New York: Elsevier, 1964.

Scheibel, M. E., & Scheibel, A. B. Selected structural-functional correlations in postnatal brain. In M. B. Sterman, D. J. McGinty, & A. M. Adinolfi (Eds.), *Brain development and behavior.* New York: Academic Press, 1971.

Scheibel, M. E., & Scheibel, A. B. The development of somotosensory thalamus in mammals. In M. Jacobsen (Ed.), *Handbook of sensory physiology. Development of sensory systems* (Vol. 9). Berlin: Springer-Verlag, 1978.

Scherrer, J. Electrophysiologie et ontogenèse du système nerveux. In S. R. Berenberg, M. Coniaris, & N. P. Masse (Eds.), *Pre- and postnatal development of the human brain.* Basel: Karger, 1974.

Schneider, B. A., Trehub, S. E., & Bull, D. The development of basic auditory process in infants. *Canadian Journal of Psychology,* 1979, *33,* 306–319.

Schulman, C. Effects of auditory stimulation on heart rate in premature infants as a function of level of arousal, probability of CNS damage, and conceptional age. *Developmental Psychobiology,* 1969, *2,* 172–183.

Schulman-Galambos, C., & Galambos, R. Brain stem auditory evoked responses in premature infants. *Journal of Speech and Hearing Research,* 1975, *18,* 456–465.

Schulman-Galambos, C., & Galambos, R. Brain stem evoked response audiometry in newborn hearing screening. *Archives of Otolaryngology,* 1979, *105,* 86–90.

Schulte, F. J. The neurological development of the neonate. In J. A. Davis & J. Dobbing (Eds.), *Scientific Foundations of Pediatrics.* London: Heinemann, 1974.

Schulte, F. J., & Stennart, E. Hearing defects in preterm infants. *Archives of Disease in Childhood,* 1978, *53,* 269–270.

Schulte, F. J., Stennert, E., Wulbrand, H., Eichorn, W., & Lenard, H. G. The ontogeny of sensory perception in pre-term infants. *European Journal of Pediatrics,* 1977, *126,* 211, 224.

Seleny, F. L., & Streczyn, M. Noise characteristics in the baby compartment of incubators. *American Journal of Diseases in Children,* 1969, *117,* 445–450.

Selnes, O. A., & Whitaker, H. A. Morphological and functional development of the auditory system. In R. W. Rieber (Ed.), *The neurophysiology of language, essays in honor of Eric Lennenberg.* New York: Plenum Press, 1976.

Shimizu, A., & Himwich, H. E. Effects of psychotropic drugs on the sleep-wakefulness cycle of the developing kitten. *Developmental Psychobiology,* 1969, *2,* 161–167.

Shipley, C., Buchwald, J. S., Norman, R., & Guthrie, D. Brain stem auditory evoked response development in the kitten. *Brain Research,* 1980, *182,* 313–326.

Sidman, R. L. Autoradiographic methods and principles for study of the nervous system with Thymidine-H^3. In W. J. H. Nauta & S. O. E. Ebbesson (Eds.), *Contemporary research methods in neuroanatomy.* New York: Springer-Verlag, 1970.

Sidman, R. L., & Rakic, P. Neuronal migration, with special reference to developing human brain: A review. *Brain Research,* 1973, *62,* 1–35.

Sigman, M. Early cognitive development of preterm and full-term infants: Exploratory behavior in eight-month-old infants. *Child Development,* 1976, *37,* 606–612.

Sigman, M. Plasticity in development: Implications for intervention. In L. Bond & J. M. Joffee (Eds.), *Facilitating infant and early childhood development.* Hanover, N.H.: University Press of New England, 1982.

Sigman, M., & Beckwith, L. Infant visual attentiveness in relation to caregiver-infant interaction and developmental outcome. *Infant Behavior and Development,* 1980, *3,* 141–154.

Sigman, M., Cohen, S. E., Forsythe, G. B. The relation of early infant measures to later development. In S. L. Friedman & M. Sigman (Eds.), *Preterm birth and psychological development.* New York: Academic Press, 1981.

Sigman, M., Kopp, C. B., Littman, B., & Parmelee, A. H., Jr. Infant visual attentiveness as a function of birth condition. *Developmental Psychology,* 1977, *13,* 431–437.

Sigman, M., & Parmelee, A. H., Jr. Visual preferences of four-month-old premature and full-term infants. *Child Development,* 1974, *45,* 959–965.

Sigman, M., & Parmelee, A. H., Jr. Longitudinal follow-up of premature infants. In T. M. Field, A. M. Sostek, S, Goldberg, & H. H. Shuman (Eds.), *Infants born at risk.* New York: Spectrum, 1979.

Siqueland, E. R. Studies of visual recognition memory in preterm infants: Differences in development as a function of perinatal morbidity factors. In S. L. Friedman & M. Sigman (Eds.), *Preterm birth and psychological development.* New York: Academic Press, 1981.

Smith, J. R. The electroencephalogram during normal infancy and childhood: I. Rhythmic activities present in the neonate and their subsequent development. *Journal of Genetic Psychology,* 1938, *53,* 431.

Smith, J. R. The electroencephalogram during normal infancy and childhood: II. The nature of the growth of the alpha waves. *Journal of Genetic Psychology,* 1938, *53,* 455.

Sokol, S. Measurement of infant visual acuity from pattern reversal evoked potentials. *Vision Research,* 1978, *18,* 33–39.

Sokol, S., & Jones, K. Implicit time of pattern evoked potentials in infants: An index of maturation of spatial vision. *Vision Research,* 1979, *19,* 747–755.

Sokoloff, L., Reivich, M., Kennedy, C., Des Rosiers, M. H., Potlak, C. S., Pettigrew, K. D., Sakwada, O., & Shinohara, M. The [14C] deoxy glucose method for the measurement of local cerebral glucose utilization: Theory, procedure and normal values in the conscious and anesthetized albino rat. *Journal of Neurochemistry,* 1977, *28,* 897–916.

Sontag, L. W., Steele, W. G., & Lewis, M. The fetal and maternal cardiac response to environmental stress. *Human Development,* 1969, *12,* 1–9.

Spinelli, D. N., & Jensen, F. E. Plasticity: The mirror of experience. *Science,* 1979, *203,* 75–78.

Spinelli, D. N., Jensen, F. E., & Viana Di Prisco, G. Early experience effect on dendritic branching in normally reared kittens. *Experimental Neurology,* 1980, *68,* 1–11.

Squires, N. K., Squires, K. C., & Hillyard, S. A. Two varieties of long-latency positive waves evoked by unpredictable auditory stimuli in man. *Electroencephalography and Clinical Neurophysiology,* 1975, *38,* 387–401.

St. James-Roberts, I. Neurology plasticity, recovery from brain insult, and child development. In H. W. Reese & L. P. Lipsitt (Eds.), *Advances in Child Development and Behavior* (Vol. 14), New York: Academic Press, 1979.

Starr, A., Amlie, R. M., Martin, W. H., & Sanders, S. Development of auditory function in newborn infants revealed by auditory brain stem potentials. *Pediatrics,* 1977, *60,* 831–839.

Sterman, M. B., Harper, R. M., Havens, B., Hoppenbrouwers, T., McGinty, D. J., & Hodgman, J. E. Quantitative analysis of infant EEG development during quiet sleep. *Electroencephalography and Clinical Neurophysiology,* 1977, *43,* 371–385.

Stern, E., Parmelee, A. H., Jr., Akiyama, Y., Shultz, M. A., & Wenner, W. H. Sleep cycle characteristics in infants. *Pediatrics,* 1969, *43,* 65–70.

Sutton, S., Braren, M., Zubin, J., & John, E. R. Evoked-potential correlates of stimulus uncertainty. *Science,* 1965, *150,* 1187–1188.

Swaiman, K. F. Energy and electrolyte. Development changes during maturation. In W. A. Hemwich (Ed.), *Developmental neurobiology.* Springfield, Ill.: Charles C. Thomas, 1970.

Takashima, S., Becker, L. E., & Chan, F. Retardation of neuronal maturation in premature infants compared with term infants of the same postconceptional age. *Pediatrics,* 1982, *69,* 33–39.

Takashima, S., Chan, F., Becker, L. E., & Armstrong, D. L. Morphology of the developing visual cortex of the human infant. *Journal of Neuropathology and Experimental Neurology,*

1980, 39, 487–501.

Tennyson, V. The fine structure of the developing nervous system. In W. A. Himwich (Ed.), *Developmental neurobiology*. Springfield, Ill.: Charles C. Thomas, 1970.

Theorell, K., Prechtl, H. F. R., & Vos, J. E. A polygraphic study of normal and abnormal newborn infants. *Neuropaediatrie,* 1974, *5,* 279–317.

Thoman, E. B., Denenberg, V. H., Sievel, J., Zeidner, L., & Becker, P. Behavioral state profiles in infancy are predictive of later medical or behavioral dysfunction. *Neuropaediatrie,* 1980, *12,* 45–54.

Thoman, E. B., Miano, V. N., & Freese, M. P. The role of respiratory instability in the sudden infant death syndrome. *Developmental Medicine and Child Neurology,* 1977, *19,* 729–738.

Thompson, R. F., Hicks, L. H., & Shuyrkov, V. B. (Eds.). *Neural mechanisms of goal-directed behavior and learning*. New York: Academic Press, 1980.

Tilney, F. Behavior in its relation to the development of the brain: II. Correlation between the development of the brain and behavior in the albino rat from embryonic states to maturity. *Bulletin of the Neurologic Institute of New York,* 1933, *3,* 252–358.

Tilney, F., & Casamajor, L. Myelinogeny as applied to the study of behavior. *Archives of Neurology and Psychiatry,* 1924, *12,* 1–66.

Tilney, F., & Kubie, L. S. Behavior in its relation to the development of the brain. *Bulletin of the Neurologic Institute of New York,* 1931, *1,* 229–313.

Trehub, S. E., Schneider, B. A., & Endman, M. Developmental changes in infants' sensitivity to octave-band noises. *Journal of Experimental Child Psychology,* 1980, *29,* 282–293.

Tuchman-Duplessis, H., David, G., & Haegel, P. *Illustrated human embryology. Nervous system and endocrine glands* (Vol. 3). New York: Springer-Verlag, 1972.

Tumosa, N., Tieman, B., & Hirsch, H. V. B. Unequal alternating monocular deprivation causes asymmetric fields in cats. *Science,* 1980, *208,* 421–423.

Umezaki, H., & Morrell, F. Developmental study of photic evoked responses in premature infants. *Electroencephalography and Clinical Neurophysiology,* 1970, *28,* 55–63.

Valtax, J. L., Jouvet, D., & Jouvet, M. Evolution electroencephalographique des differents etats de sommeil chez le chaton. *Electroencephalography and Clinical Neurophysiology,* 1964, *17,* 218–233.

Verley, R. Essai sur les critères électrophysiologiques qui permettraient de comparer entre elles les évolutions de diverses espèces, en particulier de l'homme. In S. R. Berenberg, M. Caniaris, & N. P. Masse (Eds.), *Pre- and postnatal development of the human brain* (Vol. 13). Basel: Karger, 1974.

Villablanca, J. R., & Olmstead, C. E. Neurological development of kittens. *Developmental Psychobiology,* 1979, *12,* 101–127.

Vlach, V., Bernuth, H. von, & Prechtl, H. F. R. State dependency of exterceptive skin reflexes in newborn infants. *Developmental Medicine and Child Neurology,* 1969, *11,* 353–362.

Voeller, K., Pappas, G. D., & Purpura, D. P. Electron microscope study of development of cat superficial neocortex. *Experimental Neurology,* 1963, *7,* 103–130.

Walter, D. O., Rhodes, J. M., Brown, D., & Adey, W. R. Comprehensive spectral analysis of human EEG generators in posterior cerebral regions. *Electroencephalography and Clinical Neurophysiology,* 1966, *20,* 224–237.

Walter, W. C., Cooper, R., Aldridge, V. J., McCallum, W. C., & Winter, A. L. Contingent negative variation: An electric sign of sensorimotor association and expectancy in the human brain. *Nature,* 1964, *203,* 380–384.

Watanabe, K., Iwase, K., & Hara, K. Maturation of visual evoked responses in low-birthweight infants. *Developmental Medicine and Child Neurology,* 1972, *14,* 425–435.

Watanabe, K., Iwase, K., & Hara, K. Visual evoked responses during sleep and wakefulness in pre-term infants. *Electroencephalography and Clinical Neurophysiology,* 1973, *34,* 571–577.

Watanabe, K., Iwase, K., & Hara, K. Development of slow-wave sleep in low-birthweight infants. *Developmental Medicine and Child Neurology,* 1974, *16,* 23–31.

Weitzman, E. D., & Graziani, L. J. Maturation and topography of the auditory evoked response of the prematurely born infant. *Developmental Psychobiology,* 1968, *1,* 79–89.

Werner, J. S., & Siqueland, E. R. Visual recognition memory in the preterm infant. *Infant Behavior and Development,* 1978, *1,* 79–94.

Wilder, M. B., Farley, G. R., & Starr, A. Endogenous late positive component of the evoked potential in cats corresponding to $\overline{\text{P300}}$ in humans. *Science,* 1981, *211,* 605–607.

Wilkinson, F. E. Reversal of the behavioral effects of monocular deprivation as a function of age in the kitten. *Behavioral Brain Research,* 1980, *1,* 101–123.

Windle, N. F. Development of neural elements in human embryos of four to seven weeks gestation. *Experimental Neurology,* 1970, *5,* 44–83. (Supplement)

Winick, M. Cellular growth during early malnutrition. *Pediatrics,* 1971, *47,* 969–978.

Winick, M. Nutrition and central nervous system development. In P. S. McConnell, G. J. Boer, J. J. Romijm, N. E. Van de Poll, & M. A. Corner. *Progress in brain research. Adaptive capabilities of the nervous system* (Vol. 53). New York: Elsevier, 1980.

Winick, M., & Rosso, P. Head circumference and cellular growth of the brain in normal and marasmic children. *Journal of Pediatrics,* 1969, *74,* 774–778.

Wolff, P. H. Organization of behavior in the first three months of life. In J. I. Nurnberger (Ed.), *Biological and environmental determinants of early development.* Baltimore: Williams & Wilkins, 1973.

Wolstenholme, G., & O'Connor, M. (Eds.). Brain and Mind. *Ciba Foundation Symposium* (No. 69). Amsterdam: Ecerpta Medica, 1979.

Yakovlev, P., & Lecours, A. The myelogenetic cycles of regional maturation of the brain. In A. Minkowski (Ed.), *Regional development of the brain in early life.* Oxford: Blackwell, 1967.

THE NORMAL AND DEVIANT DEVELOPMENT OF FUNCTIONAL LATERALIZATION OF THE BRAIN* | 4

MARCEL KINSBOURNE, *The Eunice Kennedy Shriver Center, Waltham, Massachusetts, and Harvard Medical School*
MERRILL HISCOCK, *University of Saskatchewan, Saskatoon, Saskatchewan, Canada*

CHAPTER CONTENTS

The first author's work was supported by a grant from the National Institute for Child Health and Development. The second author's work was supported by a grant from the Medical Research Council of Canada.

INTRODUCTION: THE MAJOR ISSUES

The human nervous system can be mapped with reference to the three Cartesian co-ordinates. John Hughlings Jackson proposed a useful and influential conceptual scheme based on the vertical dimension, or the *y*-axis (Taylor, 1932). Progression upward along the neuraxis, from spinal cord to neocortex, corresponds to increasing complexity in behavior, increasing voluntary control over behavior, and less predetermined organization. The highest levels—those of greatest interest to psychologists—are the most complex, the most voluntary, and the least organized at the time of birth. This Jacksonian view of the nervous system provides a heuristic for understanding phylogenetic and ontogenetic change. Differences between species in the quality or extent of the behavioral repertoire as well as developmental changes in behavior, may be related to the "encephalization" of function (Miller, Goldman, & Rosvold, 1973; Sarnat & Netsky, 1974). We refer to this issue later (see Ontogeny of Lateralization: Theoretical Considerations). But the thrust of our discussion is toward a different coordinate, as it relates to the organization of the highest level of the vertical co-ordinate, the forebrain.

Whereas the *y*-axis of the nervous system remains the principal axis along which brain development and associated behavioral changes may be plotted, the lateral, or *x*-axis, has preoccupied neuropsychologists during the past two decades. As a result of a proliferation of studies dealing with brain-behavior correlations at the highest level of the neuraxis, the level of cerebral cortex, it now is feasible to consider neuropsychological development with respect to the lateral dimension of the forebrain.

Why favor the lateral dimension? Clinical experience shows that the location of a cerebral lesion along the anterior-posterior dimension, the *z*-axis, is at least as relevant as its lateral position to the nature of the resulting behavioral deficit. Insofar as the frontal region of the cerebral cortex matures after the central and posterior regions (Crelin, 1973; Luria, 1966; Rabinowicz, 1974), the anterior-posterior dimension is relevant to the study of brain and behavioral development. We emphasize the lateral dimension only because it provides a useful organizing principle for summarizing much of the contemporary research in developmental neuropsychology. Research concerning left versus right differences in brain function is sufficiently cohesive to allow treatment in a single chapter. At the same time, it has implications for the more general question of how higher mental functions are represented in the developing brain. An analysis of the literature on hemispheric specialization will serve to illustrate many fundamental issues in developmental neuropsychology.

There is another reason for organizing this chapter around the topic of left-right differences. The study of hemispheric specialization has become so popular that people in many disciplines and many settings have been made aware of various findings and claims regarding functional differences between the left and right hemispheres. Since the time of Samuel T. Orton (1937), claims have been made about anomalous cerebral dominance as a causal factor in some cases of learning disability and educators continue to read about unusual hemispheric specialization in learning-disabled children (e.g., see Witelson, 1977a) or about right-brained children in left-brained schools (e.g., see Hunter, 1976). Hemispheric specialization has been related to schizophrenic vulnerability in children (Blau, 1977), schizophrenic and manic-depressive syndromes in adults (Flor-Henry, 1976), and other phenomena of interest to psychiatrists (Galin, 1974; Parsons, 1977). Sex differences in certain cognitive abilities have been attributed to differences in the cerebral lateralization of these skills (Waber, 1977; Witelson, 1976b). It has been suggested that individual differences in attributes such as ego strength (Palmer, 1964), creativity (Bogen & Bogen, 1969), cognitive style (Pizzamiglio, 1974), hypnotic susceptibility (Bakan, 1969), and personal values (Weiten & Etaugh, 1973) are somehow related to the degree or nature of hemispheric specialization, the relative prepotency of the two hemispheres, or the degree of communication between them. Because notions such as these are so prevalent, it is likely that readers who are familiar with no other aspect of neuropsychology will be familiar with, and interested in, research concerning differences between the cerebral hemispheres.

If this is the era of laterality in neuropsychology, there must be a reason. As often is the case in science, the reason is technological. During the past thirty years, several new clinical and experimental techniques have become available for the study of functional differences between the left and right cerebral hemispheres. Of the clinical techniques, the most dramatic and best known takes advantage of the commissurotomy procedure, or the surgical splitting of the brain (Myers & Sperry, 1953; Sperry, 1964). A few patients with disconnected left and right hemispheres provided researchers an unprecedented opportunity to study the hemispheres in relative isolation, and the fascinating results of those studies were reported to a wide audience (Bogen, 1969a, 1969b; Bogen & Bogen, 1969; Gazzaniga, 1970; Kinsbourne & Smith, 1974; Levy-Agresti & Sperry, 1968; Ornstein, 1972). At nearly the same time, Kimura (1961a, 1961b) discovered that right-ear superiority for perception of competing (dichotic) messages is related to the lateralization of language-processing capacity to the left cerebral hemisphere. Thus, a noninvasive and relatively simple technique became available for studying the lateralization of various perceptual processes in normal adults and children. This dichotic-listening technique constituted an important link between neurology and experimental psychology and attracted many psychologists and linguists to the study of functional specialization of the cerebral hemispheres. While these two new methodologies were being exploited and publicized, other important techniques were being developed. It was found that the speech-dominant hemisphere in prospective neurosurgical patients could be identified unequivocally by injecting a fast-acting soluble barbiturate into the carotid artery supplying one or the other cerebral hemispheres with blood (Wada & Rasmussen, 1960). With most of one hemisphere briefly incapacitated by the barbiturate, one could determine some behavioral capacities and limitations of the opposite hemisphere (Rasmussen & Milner, 1975). As a result of advances in computer technology and nuclear medicine, it is possible to observe changes in blood flow within the left and right hemispheres as patients perform different physical and mental activities (Lassen & Ingvar, 1963). Computerized axial tomography (CAT scanning) greatly facilitates clinical studies of left- and right-hemispheric function insofar as it is now possible to localize quite precisely the structural abnormality associated with a particular behavioral deficit. Positron emission tomography and nuclear magnetic resonance (NMR) imaging promise even further insight. Positron emission tomography affords a direct measure of the metabolic rate of parts of the brain (although its resolving power over time is inferior to that of the regional blood-flow techniques). With further development of NMR techniques, clinical investigators probably will acquire the capability to measure localized metabolic activity with high temporal as well as spatial precision. Noninvasive behavioral techniques other than dichotic listening also have been developed and refined. Visual (taistoscopic) asymmetries frequently are used as a basis for inferences about hemispheric specialization but the methodological problems are enormous (Swanson, Ledlow, & Kinsbourne, 1978; White, 1969b, 1972). Tactile tasks have been adapted for the study of hemispheric specialization (Hawn & Harris, 1979; Rudel, Denckla, & Hirsch, 1977; Rudel, Denckla, & Spalten, 1974; Witelson, 1974). The dual-task paradigm of human factors research has been applied to questions of resource limitations within a cerebral hemisphere (Kinsbourne & Cook, 1971). The development of computer technology has facilitated the study of electrical activity in the left and right halves of the brain during various tasks. Powerful laboratory computers permit the use of sophisticated techniques, such as averaging of cortical evoked potentials and power spectral analysis of spontaneous electrical activity (Donchin, Kutas, &

McCarthy, 1977) as well as the topographical mapping of changes in such variables over time, that is, brain electrical activity mapping—BEAM (Duffy, Burchfield, & Lombroso, 1979).

Each of these techniques has contributed some information to our fund of knowledge about similarities and differences between the left and right sides of the human cerebrum. Without them, a chapter written today about the lateralization of the brain would differ little from a chapter that might have been written 30 years ago. Nevertheless, most of the major questions in this area of research remain unanswered, not primarily because the technology is deficient but because our conceptual sophistication fails to match the sophistication of our technology. In the next several paragraphs, we will outline what we regard as the major issues in the study of brain development from a left-right perspective; and in so doing, we will provide an overview of the organization of this chapter.

Phylogenetic Antecedents of Cerebral Asymmetry

An obvious starting point is the issue of phylogeny. Any biological characteristic of a species has a natural history. Did the characteristic arise from continuous natural selection or from natural selection during some phase of the species' evolution? Alternatively, can the characteristic be attributed to the absence of selective pressure favoring an opposite or incompatible characteristic? In the case of asymmetry between the cerebral hemispheres, we may ask whether the forces of natural selection have favored asymmetry for some reason or whether asymmetry exists because the forces favoring symmetry have been relaxed?

Theories about the natural history of cerebral asymmetries vary in scope with respect to (1) evolutionary perspective and (2) the range of phenotypic characteristics under consideration. One may narrow one's focus of attention to laterality differences between humans and other mammalian species or among different human cultures (Frost, 1980; Hewes, 1973, 1979). Alternatively, one might consider asymmetric and bisymmetric aspects of organisms across the entire animal kingdom, from one-celled animals to humans (Kinsbourne, 1974a). One may emphasize only the possible adaptive advantage associated with a particular phenotypic characteristic, such as hand preference (Levy, 1972), or one may consider the adaptive significance of the full range of neuromuscular and behavioral symmetries and asymmetries. It is our contention that the phylogenetic antecedents and adaptive value of a particular pattern of cerebral organization can be understood only in the context of the full evolutionary spectrum and only when cerebral dominance is considered as part of an integrated system containing asymmetric and bisymmetric components. Therefore, we will present an account for the evolution of cerebral asymmetries that begins with simple one-celled organisms and we will describe the evolution of neural asymmetry within a broad biological context. From this perspective, it can be appreciated that the lateral dimension is as fundamental a dimension of brain organization as is the vertical.

Human Asymmetries: The Adult Base State in Summary

The description of change is limited by knowledge of its end points. Biological and behavioral changes that take place between conception and maturity cannot be understood in the absence of knowledge about the initial state of the organism and about the nature of the mature organism. We know far more about cerebral lateralization of higher mental functions in adults than in children. Consequently, we preface our discussion of the ontogeny of cerebral dominance with a summary of current knowledge about hemispheric asymmetry in the adult. What is the evidence for anatomical asymmetries in the brain? What are the implications with respect to function? What do findings from clinical studies reveal about the nature of hemispheric specialization in adults and its significance in terms of higher mental functions? To what extent are the clinical findings supported by studies of laterality in normal adults? How useful are neuropsychological concepts in explaining psychopathology? Clarification of these issues will facilitate our interpretation of the evidence concerning cerebral lateralization and its significance in infancy and childhood.

Indices of Cerebral Lateralization: Measurement Issues

Many of the ambiguities and inconsistent findings in the research literature concerning adult laterality can be ascribed to methodological and interpretative problems. Insofar as the same problems beset studies of laterality in children, we will discuss these problems of measurement and inference at some length. We will begin with a critique of the traditional method of neuropsychology, namely, investigation of the cognitive consequences of focal lesions. Lesion studies have yielded much information about the lateralization of higher mental functions; nevertheless, this source of information must be scrutinized closely. How precisely can lesions be defined? How adequate is the measurement of behavioral deficits? What are the consequences of unrepresentative sampling? What are some of the factors that may alter the relationship between lesion lateralization and behavioral consequences? Can the extrapolation of findings to the normal brain be justified? Some of these considerations are particularly important in clinical studies of children.

Without attempting a definitive analysis of the highly specialized topic of electrophysiological asymmetries, we will describe the fundamental principles underlying EEG techniques; the major technical, procedural, and analytic problems; and some of the findings most relevant to questions of brain lateralization. We will discuss some methodological variables that must be considered when doing EEG laterality research and when interpreting the findings. We will also offer an explanation for stimulus-dependent electrophysiological asymmetries that are seen very early in life.

Much of the section on measurement will be devoted to techniques for measuring behavioral asymmetries, namely, dichotic listening, lateral presentation of visual stimuli using a tachistoscope, tactile recognition techniques, hemisphere priming, the dual-task technique, and observation of lateral eye movements. Although these methods have yielded a substantial body of interesting and potentially useful findings, we ask whether the findings really have answered any major questions about the way in which higher mental processes are organized in the brain. Do behavioral asymmetries faithfully reflect the functional specialization of the cerebral hemispheres or are they influenced to a large degree by other factors? If behavioral asymmetries are multiply determined, what are the factors other than hemispheric specialization that influence such asymmetries? Can these extraneous factors be controlled? Are they really extraneous or are they an integral part of human laterality? Consideration of anomalies and extraneous factors in laterality leads us to the question of the mechanism or mechanisms underlying behavioral asymmetries. Some of the findings are anomalous and unexpected only in the context of a particular theoretical viewpoint. Auditory and visual asymmetries were initially assumed to conform to a structural model (Kimura, 1961a, 1961b, 1967) that attributed them to the combined effects of hemispheric specialization and the conduction properties of afferent pathways. Many findings, however, are more readily explained in terms of an attentional model (Kinsbourne, 1970a, 1973b, 1974c, 1975), in which asymmetries are thought to index the balance of activation between the hemispheres. For instance, crosscoupling between an asymmetric information processor and an orientational control system tends to orient the organism in a direction opposite to the side of the more highly activated cerebral hemisphere. Or, the more activated hemisphere (subserving a lateralized mental set) is the more efficient processor (unless overloaded, in which case its efficiency is diminished). All these complexities, and more, must be considered if we are to make sense of the developmental data.

Ontogeny of Lateralization: Theoretical Considerations

There are two contrasting possibilities regarding the ontogeny of hemispheric specialization. Specialization for a particular function may change during the lifespan or it may remain invariant throughout development. If the cerebral lateralization of a function changes during development, it may either become more pronounced or less pronounced with increasing age. The hypothesis of progressive language lateralization is ingrained in the neurological and psychological literature (e.g., see Lenneberg, 1967), but there is little consideration of the possibility that the degree of lateralization may decrease during development (Kocel, 1980). What are the implications of regressive and progressive lateralization in terms of underlying assumptions about brain-behavior relationships and what kind of evidence might be used to support each hypothesis? What are the implications of developmental invariance in degree of cerebral lateralization (Kinsbourne & Hiscock, 1977)?

A difficult issue in ontogeny is how to differentiate developmental changes in cerebral lateralization of a skill from changes in the lateralized development of that skill. May a hemisphere be specialized for a function before that function has developed? How does one determine stability or change in the brain substrate for behaviors that undergo marked quantitative and qualitative changes during development? Do apparent changes in the lateralization of a function reflect a developmental shifting of localization or only changes in the manner in which the function is performed?

The plasticity of the nervous system must also be considered if we are to understand the various findings relevant to ontogeny. Is recovery of function after unilateral injury to the brain attributable to replication of functions in the opposite hemisphere or to neuroplasticity (the ability of the immature brain to reorganize itself in such a way as to compensate for the damage)? If the speed or completeness of recovery decreases with increasing age—and this seems to be the case—is that developmental change attributable to decreasing neuroplasticity or to departure from an initial bilaterality in cerebral organization?

Ontogeny of Lateralization: Findings and Implications

Insofar as the higher mental functions develop during childhood, it is not possible to assess the lateralization of those functions in infancy. However, we may look for precursors of cerebral lateralization in the infant. Certain neuroanatomical asymmetries exist at birth and even prior to birth (Wada, Clarke, & Hamm, 1975; Witelson & Pallie, 1973). These recent findings of morphological asymmetry in the infant brain are ironic for, in an earlier era, it was the supposed lack of such asymmetry that first led physicians to believe that the cerebral hemispheres are not specialized at birth (Dennis & Whitaker, 1977). Of clearer relevance to cerebral lateralization, however, is evidence of functional differences between the right and left sides of the infant brain. The infant is asymmetric in posture and orienting behavior, in reaching and grasping, and in perception of environmental sounds. Some of these asymmetries appear to be tonic, whereas others are phasic (i.e., stimulus dependent). It has been found repeatedly that speech sounds elicit higher amplitude evoked responses from the left side of the brain than from the right side and that this difference in amplitude is reversed for music and other nonspeech sounds (e.g., see Molfese, 1977; but see Shucard, Shucard, Cummins, & Campos, 1981, for a failure to replicate). Is there a common principle uniting these various manifestations of asymmetry in the infant? Does a lateralized, stimulus-dependent activation system exist long before the brain is sufficiently developed to process the stimuli fully? Do infant asymmetries predict laterality later in life?

For many decades, knowledge about the development of cerebral dominance for language was based solely on clinical studies of childhood aphasia. We will examine that data base as well as more recent research dealing with behavioral asymmetries in normal children of different ages. Although the two different sources appear at first to lead to contradictory conclusions, a closer look at the clinical data suggests that earlier interpretations were incorrect. Methodological deficiencies and inferential problems made it possible to draw erroneous conclusions from the childhood aphasic data. Moreover, the more recent studies of childhood aphasia contradict the earlier studies (Woods & Teuber, 1978a). Results from these more recent clinical studies are compatible with the majority of findings from studies of behavioral asymmetries in normal children. Nevertheless, the existence of developmental changes in the lateralization of functions other than language remains a disputed issue.

Some interesting issues related to ontogeny will be discussed, namely, the influence of gender, social class, and maturational rate upon degree of cerebral lateralization for different functions; the relevance of hemispheric specialization to gender differences in spatial ability; and the lateralization of the second language of bilinguals. It has been claimed (1) that boys and girls are differentially lateralized for certain kinds of spatial functions (Witelson, 1976b) or, alternatively, that spatial ability is related to its degree of lateralization and (2) that gender differences are secondary to differences in maturation rate (Waber, 1977). Other investigators have claimed that the degree of hemispheric specialization for speech perception is related to children's socioeconomic class (Geffner & Hochberg, 1971) and that the respective languages of bilinguals are represented in opposite hemispheres (e.g., see Albert & Obler, 1978). These well-publicized claims will be analyzed in light of the methodological and conceptual considerations discussed elsewhere in the chapter. In addition, we will discuss hypotheses that cerebral lateralization undergoes changes across the entire life span.

Deviant Lateralization in Behavioral Deficit

If a given cerebral organization for higher mental functioning is the norm for the human species, what are the consequences of deviations from that norm? Because linguistic functions usually are represented in the left cerebral hemisphere, is there some advantage associated with left-lateralized language? Is there some disadvantage associated with right-lateralized language or bilaterally represented language? Specifically, is anomalous lateralization associated with cognitive deficit?

We will attempt to answer these questions in two ways. First, we will summarize findings concerning cognitive abilities in left-handers. Because anomalous lateralization of language is known to be relatively common among left-handers, we might expect to observe some degree of cognitive deficiency in these people as a group if deviations from the predominant pattern of cerebral organization have any functional significance. However, meaningful answers can be obtained from investigations of left-handers only if one distinguishes between those people who are left-handed because of early insult to the brain (pathological left-handers) and those who are left-handed from nonpathological (presumably genetic) causes. Our second approach is to look for associations between hemispheric specialization and behavioral deficit in a variety of disorders. We will begin with a discussion of the implications of dysfunction of the corpus callosum and then evaluate claims of abnormal hemispheric specialization in several clinical entities: instances of reading disabilities and speech problems, deafness, stuttering, and infantile autism. Finally, we will comment on the claim that extreme environmental deprivation leads to anomalous cerebral organization of higher mental functions.

SOME CONCEPTS, DEFINITIONS, AND DISTINCTIONS

Lateralization of Brain Functions

The central concept we deal with here is the cerebral lateralization of higher mental functions. The higher mental functions are characteristically human—although not uniquely human—skills involving perception, attention, memory, motor performance, and logical reasoning. Speaking a language, remembering a face, and playing a musical instrument are examples. Luria (1971) estimated that at least 75% of the human cortex is dedicated to functions that are (1) social in origin, (2) highly complex, (3) not localized in a single brain center, (4) represented in various brain structures, and (5) goal directed and self-regulated. These higher mental functions may be contrasted with elementary sensory and motor functions, such as light perception and limb flexion, whose representation in the cerebral cortex can be mapped quite precisely. With respect to higher mental functions, the concept of cerebral lateralization is constrained by the complexity of the functions and by the complexity of their representation in the brain. For instance, the question of whether arithmetic is lateralized is not a satisfactory question. Arithmetic comprises a large set of component skills, each of which itself is complex and may or may not be represented in the brain in the same fashion as another component skill. A particular arithmetic task entails some combination of reading or aural comprehension, memory, spatial manipulation, arithmetic reasoning, computation, writing or speaking, and so on. Unless all the components are similarly lateralized, one may discover that no generalization about the lateralization of arithmetic is universally valid. Different tasks will yield different indications of lateralization, depending on which component it is whose efficiency limits the efficiency of the performance as a whole. One must, therefore, decompose cognitive tasks into component processes before attempting to reach conclusions about lateralization. Even in the case of language, which usually is assumed to be left lateralized in all aspects, there appears to be a major difference between receptive functions and expressive functions in the degree to which the nondominant hemisphere is potentially involved (Searleman, 1977).

The concept of cerebral lateralization of activities involving higher mental processes is further constrained by the complex distribution of the representation of the component processes in the brain. One cannot designate a region of the cerebral cortex and state that a given activity or skill is represented there. Activities involving higher mental functions defy such straightforward localization. Whether one accepts Luria's (1974) hierarchical model of sequential analysis of information or Brown's (1977) notion of simultaneous microgenesis, it is clear from clinical studies that the higher mental functions and even some of their elementary component processes involve various brain structures. Localization of function is a specialization of brain regions so that different regions contribute different component processes to the programming and execution of a particular function. Cerebral lateralization is a special case of lateralization in which the crucial component processes of an activity (i.e., those that are performance limiting) are all localized in one hemisphere. If either hemisphere can program and execute a task, the manner in which the task is performed should differ between hemispheres. For example, if a problem can be solved by use of either a verbal or a visuospatial strategy, the verbal strategy might be left lateralized and the visuospatial strategy right lateralized.

This viewpoint regards hemispheric specialization as absolute. The hemisphere specialized for a function performs it, even if the input to be processed is initially projected to the other hemisphere. Both Kimura's (1966, 1967) structural model and Kinsbourne's (1970, 1973b, 1974, 1975) attentional model assume absolute lateralization, and they do so based on a century of supporting evidence derived from the study of unilateral cerebral lesion effects on human behavior. More recently a contrasting assumption has crept into the literature, more by implication than by assertion. This is that the hemisphere of entry processes the input, well or less well, depending on whether it is or is not specialized for that processing. This appears to be true for many tasks given split-brain subjects (Zaidel, 1978b). But when applied to intact people, this view gives license to the overliteral interpretation of behavioral asymmetry findings that we criticize later. Specifically, scores for material presented to each ear or each visual half field (VHF) are assumed to index the best efforts of the respective contralateral hemisphere. There is no supporting evidence for the notion that one can so simply tap the isolated capabilities of the two highly connected halves of the cerebrum.

One cannot measure cerebral lateralization directly but must rely on indirect evidence. Traditionally, observations of cerebral symptomatology have led to conclusions about the lateralization of higher mental functions. Localization of function is inferred from the dissimilar behavioral results of approximately equivalent lesions in different cerebral regions. Ideally, this takes the form of double dissociation. Damage in one area impairs performance *A* more than *B;* damage in the other area impairs performance *B* more than *A*. Similarly, lateralization of function is inferred from observations that left- and right-hemispheric lesions of approximately corresponding locus and extent have dissimilar behavioral results. The evidence is indirect. The clinical investigator sees deficits and infers the functions. Lesion studies show lateralization of deficits, not lateralization of functions. Evidence from other sources is more obviously inferential. For example, electrophysiological data consist of voltages recorded on the scalp that relate, in unknown ways, to actual brain functioning. Although techniques, such as dichotic listening and VHF studies, measure functions (i.e., behaviors), it is a conjecture that asymmetries in those measurable behaviors faithfully reflect underlying brain asymmetries. Factors in addition to cerebral lateralization influence observed asymmetries.

Speculative Claims Regarding Cerebral Lateralization

Popular formulations of hemisphere contributions to mental function cluster around a distinction between a linear and sequential, as compared to a parallel and holistic, logic as well as the creative and intuitive powers that characterize certain individuals (e.g., see Kane & Kane, 1979; Willems, 1979). These formulations are groundless (Corballis, 1980; Hardyck & Haapanen, 1979). Beyond its verbal role, the involvement of the left hemisphere in serial recognition (Kinsbourne & Warrington, 1962b), temporal differentiation (Efron, 1963), and sequential movement (Kimura & Archibald, 1974) is well known. In contrast, the left hemisphere has never been identified by inference, either from clinical deficit or laterality findings, as a purveyor of a dispassionate, materialist logic. The right hemisphere's control of the processing of relationships in visual and haptic space (DeRenzi, 1982) is certain. Its idealization into a holistic humanism seems to be based on nothing more persuasive than the view that what is nonverbal is presumably ineffable. Both hemispheres are specialized for functions properly described as analytic. The left specifies items in perception and action; the right specifies their relationships in space. Insofar as these functions can be abstracted (e.g., into algebra and geometry), they are properly described as higher than the representation of sensorimotor function and of ambient extrapersonal space, which appear to be bilateral (Trevarthen, 1978). But reasoning and logic have never been shown to be represented in one hemisphere, nor, indeed, has creative thinking. It appears that those mental operations that are exempt from bilateral representation cannot properly be described as programming intuition or logic. Instead, these mental operations are instruments of behavioral control that are used by different individuals with varying degrees of intuitive weight or logical incisiveness. The extent to which they are so used more probably depends on the specificity of selective neuronal activation than on the existence of lateralized centers for intuition or reason. Functions that are lateralized may be abstract, such as certain verbal semantic or visual imaginal processes, or they may be concrete, such as the ability to perform a gesture or recognize a face. Either hemisphere may program abstract or concrete mental processes, depending on the process in question.

Complementary hemispheric specialization could be adaptive (Kinsbourne, 1978a; Levy, 1969, 1972; Semmes, 1968). But some mental operations may be asymmetrically represented simply because they do not refer to locations in ambient space and, therefore, need not be deployed from both hemispheres (Kinsbourne, 1974a).

This brief discussion should caution us to resist assertions about, for instance, the right hemispheric nature of primary process (Galin, 1974) or the left hemispheric mentality of Western adults (Ornstein, 1972). It is no more true that undifferentiated perception is right hemispheric than that verbal expression reflects the contribution of the left hemisphere only (the formulation of words may be left lateralized but that of the thoughts they express is not so constrained).

In summarizing the vast literature on hemispheric specialization, we will not have space to address speculative issues, such as hemisphericity, or individual tendencies to use a mode or style of thinking that suggests the preeminence of one hemisphere or the other (e.g., see Bakan, 1969; Bogen,

1969a, 1969b; Bogen & Bogen, 1969; Ornstein, 1972) or the philosophical question of whether consciousness is unitary or dual (Bogen, 1977; Jaynes, 1976; Kinsbourne, 1982; Popper & Eccles, 1977; Puccetti, 1973; Sperry, 1968).

Three terms related to cerebral lateralization require clarification: cerebral dominance, double dominance, and laterality.

Cerebral Dominance

The term cerebral dominance has two meanings (Zangwill, 1962). One is synonymous with cerebral lateralization. It means that one hemisphere is specialized or preeminent for a particular function, such as speech or manipulation. Thus, the left hemisphere (of right-handers) is dominant for speech. Cerebral dominance can also imply an executive function that is not implied in the term cerebral lateralization: the notion of a master hemisphere—a hemisphere that exerts control over its counterpart or generally is prepotent in controlling behavior (Orton, 1937). The master-hemisphere concept is a vestige of an earlier era in which the special functions of the right hemisphere were unknown; the right hemisphere was thought to be a largely redundant appendage to the dominant hemisphere (Dimond, 1972; Zangwill, 1962). Now that the right hemisphere is known to be more specialized than the left for certain functions and equally competent for others, continued use of the master-hemisphere concept implies at least one of three assumptions about the brain and brain functions. The first is that language is an exalted faculty, uniquely human and qualitatively different from other skills. The special significance of language implies an inequality between the hemispheres. It may be argued that nonlinguistic capabilities are represented in the right hemisphere by default because the left hemisphere is reserved for language (Corballis & Morgan, 1978). A second assumption is that whereas either hemisphere may organize mental processes, the left hemisphere, with its highly developed linguistic and motor capacity, controls implementation of the decisions. It acts as an output buffer not only for processing that occurs within the left hemisphere but also for processing within the right hemisphere. Verbal and manual programming in the left hemisphere mediate most or all responses from brain to environment. A third and weaker assumption is that the left hemisphere is the executive hemisphere only because people function within a predominantly verbal environment.

Double Dominance

One way of updating the concept of cerebral dominance without abandoning the executive-control concept is to postulate that dominance may shift from one situation to another (Dimond, 1972). The left hemisphere may assume dominance for the performance of some tasks and the right hemisphere may assume dominance for the performance of others. The difficulty with this double-dominance concept lies in specifying how executive control is relinquished by one hemisphere so that it can be assumed by its counterpart. It is more parsimonious to dismiss the unverified concept of unilateral executive control (except in patients whose hemispheres have been separated by callosal section, see Kinsbourne, 1974b; Levy & Trevarthen, 1976; Trevarthen, 1974) and to postulate simply that processing capacity for different tasks is distributed asymmetrically in the cerebrum. Double dominance, without the implication of lateralized control, is best described by such terms as cerebral lateralization, hemispheric specialization, bilateral asymmetry (Levy, 1974), or dual-functional asymmetry (Kimura, 1966).

Laterality

Unlike dominance and lateralization, which refer to hypothetical patterns of cerebral organization, laterality refers to observable asymmetries of perceptual and motor functioning. Differences between the ears in the perception of dichotic speech or between the hands in performance of a motor task are examples of laterality. An estimate of degree of laterality may be based on a single measurement of a dimension, such as hand preference; it may be based on multiple measures of a single dimension; or it may be based on measures of various dimensions, such as hand preference, manual dexterity, auditory perception, or eye dominance. Even though measures of laterality sometimes are combined to yield a composite index of sidedness (e.g., see Orton, 1937), the meaningfulness of any global measure of laterality is questionable. Different dimensions of laterality are, at best, only loosely correlated (Hines & Satz, 1974; Porac & Coren, 1978; Shankweiler & Studdert-Kennedy, 1975); and even correlations among what are supposed to be different measures of the same dimension are modest (Hiscock & Caplan, 1979; Shankweiler & Studdert-Kennedy, 1975). Consequently, we will refer to laterality with respect to a particular measure and not assume that a person's laterally biased behavior can be characterized by a single laterality index.

Bilaterality

The word bilaterality can be used to denote behavioral symmetry. A person who performs equally with the left and right hands on a unimanual task, for example, may be described as ambilateral, meaning bilaterally symmetric. Bilaterality, however, has a second, more specific meaning. Vertebrate nervous systems are known to be bisymmetrically organized, in that the fundamental sensory and motor functions are represented in corresponding, or homologous, regions of the left and right neuraxis. In humans, each cerebral hemisphere receives sensory input primarily from one side of the body or from one side of space and each controls motor output primarily to one side of the body or one side of space. Except for the uncrossed olfactory function, each hemisphere is responsible primarily for the contralateral side of the body and of space. The functional relationships between either hemisphere and the body is asymmetric or lateralized; however, because the functional organization of the second hemisphere at least approximately mirrors that of the first, the system as a whole is bisymmetrically, or bilaterally, organized with respect to simple sensory and motor functions. In other words, bilaterality (also bilateral symmetry or bisymmetry) refers to a situation in which the functions of one hemisphere are duplicated in the other hemisphere. This duplication is not to be construed as redundancy. Each hemisphere has a complete sensorimotor repertoire, but it deploys this capability with respect to half only of the body and of extrapersonal space. Bilaterality is the general rule in vertebrate nervous system organization, although numerous exceptions to this rule have been discovered (Denenberg, 1981). The asymmetric representation of higher mental functions in the human cerebrum is one of those exceptions.

Summary

In this section, we ask, "What is lateralized in the human brain?" and "What is the nature of the lateralization?" with reference to higher mental functions. Each of these functions comprises a complex set of component skills and even the component skills may engage various brain structures. Nevertheless, if all critical components of a function are represented within the same hemisphere, it may be said that the function is lateralized. We argue that lateralization is absolute. If one hemisphere is specialized for a particular function, then that hemisphere always performs the function. Popular claims regarding fundamental differences between the hemispheres—abstract versus concrete, linear versus parallel, logical versus intuition, and so on—are without empirical basis. Both hemispheres perform analytic functions, although the nature of the analysis differs between them. In addition, the meanings and implications of the terms cerebral dominance, double dominance, laterality, and bilaterality are discussed.

PHYLOGENETIC ANTECEDENTS OF CEREBRAL LATERALIZATION

What Does Asymmetry Imply?

Implicit but pervasive in neuropsychological thought is the unwarranted assumption that bisymmetry of form and function is the primitive base state. Against this backdrop, asymmetry may appear as a refinement whose probability of occurrence varies with (1) the species' position on an evolutionary scale for degree of behavioral control, (2) the organism's maturational status, and (3) the degree to which the relevant behavior is abstract. Such a hierarchical formulation neatly accommodates the popular stereotype that of all species, the human becomes most lateralized as he matures, especially with respect to his higher mental functions. Animals are less lateralized than humans, children than adults, and sensorimotor function than abstraction (into verbal, spatial, and other modes). In this chapter we will subject these beliefs to an overdue critical appraisal. We will consider in the most detail the ontogenetic issue. By what developmental process are those functions established for which one or the other hemisphere is specialized? But first we will wonder, does the appearance of asymmetry in the evolution of species always index an advance (i.e., some additional sophistication in body organization)? Is asymmetry truly most characteristic of the behaviorally most elaborated species? Is asymmetry necessarily most marked with respect to those forms of behavioral control that are the most abstract?

Evolutionary Status of Asymmetries

Various forms of symmetry and myriad departures from them abound among invertebrates (Ludwig, 1932). Bilateral symmetry evolved, not in deference to some ideal, but because it is adaptive to mobility. By virtue of streamlining, an elongated body progressing along its longest axis has advantage in movement. Mobility entails need for more effective distance receptors, corresponding to the enlargement of the individual's effective action space. Being elaborate, distance receptors are concentrated at the leading end. To deploy them in all directions, the organism must be able to turn quickly to either side. This involves bilaterally symmetrical musculature and, therefore, calls for bilaterally symmetrical central neural control. The relationship between mobility and bisymmetry is easily demonstrable. Many species evolved into regressive sessile forms; others metamorphose from motile larvae to sessile mature form within a lifespan. In both cases, the sessile form commonly exhibits gross departures from bisymmetry. Nor is bisymmetry applicable to all body parts. Parts not involved in locomotion, such as the viscera, are single and eccentric or, if paired, depart from mirror-image form and may not lie at the same segmental level. We learn that bisymmetry serves an adaptive need. If the adaptive need relaxes, symmetry relations become variable. Departures from bisymmetry may be for negative reasons—no need for it—or for positive reasons—adaptive advantage for asymmetry. Neither can be taken for granted. In every instance, a specific determination must be made.

By and large, motile organisms remain approximately bisymmetrical but minor departures abound. Among fish, the locomotive musculature is symmetrical but the fins are not. Right-finnedness prevails in the majority of species (Hubbs & Hubbs, 1944). Flatfish are grossly asymmetrical. Most of the over 500 species have both their eyes on the same side of the head. Equal numbers show asymmetry in favor of right and of left (Policansky, 1982). Among humans, minor asymmetries are the rule. Right-handers have heavier bones and muscles on the right (excepting a certain few) and their skull bulges rightward frontally (and to the left posteriorly). The non-right-handed minority more nearly approximates bisymmetry (Hicks & Kinsbourne, 1978).

Within the nervous system, asymmetries exist. The human brain bulges to the right in front, to the left in the rear, in conformity with the shape of the skull (the cause-effect relation between the two being unknown). Asymmetries between sections of the temporal lobes have been discussed (e.g., see Geschwind & Levitsky, 1968; Rubens, 1977). A mysterious asymmetry in amphibians is the larger size of the left of the paired habenular nuclei, whose functional role is not known. We will see later that even when function is asymmetrical, morphology may be similar on both sides (e.g., song control of the chaffinch).

The many instances of asymmetry suggest that this phenomenon is not to be subsumed under any single organizing principle. Sometimes it does develop as a refinement of bisymmetry; at other times it is the base state upon which bisymmetry is superimposed. It may exist because of selection pressures or because of the relaxation of selection processes. There is no justification for reasoning, in the human case, that the more primitive, less mature organism and the less abstract form of behavioral control are necessarily represented with greater bisymmetry. Nor does the mere existence of an anatomical asymmetry imply a corresponding specialization. Nor can we assume that developmental failures are, or even can be, due to a failure of asymmetry to emerge from bisymmetry during ontogeny. As such an assumption has often been made, it is worth noting that in every case substantiating evidence is lacking.

Phylogeny

The phylogenesis of lateralization would be directly relevant to its ontogeny only if it were indeed true that, as annunciated by Ernst Haeckel (1908), "ontogeny recapitulates phylogeny." But this maxim is more often breached than observed. Therefore, we will briefly review proven as well as suggestive instances of brain lateralization in birds and nonhuman mammals primarily for the ontogenic information contained in these reports and to establish the basic point that brain lateralization is not confined to humans. For any formulation about the specialized function of either hemispheres to have generality, it should be conceptualized within a biological framework.

Birds

Songbirds (the chaffinch, canary, white-crowned sparrow) are largely left lateralized for control of song (Nottebohm, 1970, 1971, 1972). The same applies to the white-throated sparrow (Lemon, 1973). This lateralized control is demonstrable from the very beginning of song, that is, this instance of lateralization is developmentally invariant. There is no hint of any early tendency to bilaterality or of progressively asymmetrically shrinking brain base for song control. Instead, the left hypostriatum ventrale, pars caudale, is in control from the beginning (Nottebohm, Stokes, & Leonard, 1976). Note, however, that its right-sided counterpart, with little or no such role, is histologically similar and not smaller in volume. Yet, in the females of these species, who do not sing, both hypostrata are much less developed. So, contrary to the emphasis of Geschwind and Levitsky (1968) and others, a search for gross histological differentiation may not be a particularly fruitful way of studying brain lateralization. A further parallel with the human situation is with respect to plasticity. Left hypoglossal lesion (disconnecting the left brain from the syringeal mechanism that affects vocalization) instantly abolishes established bird song. But, if left section is performed before any song has developed, the right side takes over and the bird does sing, although somewhat imperfectly (Nottebohm, 1979).

Lest we overreach ourselves in generalizing from these findings—for instance, by considering sequential output (which is common to song and speech) as the sufficient cause of the evolution of lateralized neural control—we should note that the parrot's vocalizations are bilaterally controlled (Nottebohm, 1976). Lateralization of voice control does not apply to all vocal birds, only to those birds who learn their song.

Lateralization in birds is not limited to song. Young chicks have been shown to be left lateralized for visual discrimination and for shifting attention from target to target (Rogers & Anson, 1979). In contrast, the right brain is more in control of attack and copulation (Rogers, 1980), although the left brain exerts some inhibitory control on the right brain's propensity to generate these behaviors. Andrew, Mench, and Rainey (in press) found young chicks to discriminate visually faster with left eye occluded (thus evoking the right-eye/left-brain system), whereas escape behavior was more readily triggered by enlisting the left-eye/right-brain system.

Rats

Rat populations have been reported to be systematically biased with respect to turning and body positioning. The bias originates before birth and is especially marked in females (Denenberg, Rosen, Hofman, Gale, Stockler, & Yutzey, 1981, for a review). Denenberg and his colleagues have also investigated the effects of early handling and of enriching the environment on behavioral and brain asymmetries. The results defy simple exposition. Handling potentiates the emergence of asymmetrical hemisphere lesion effects on activity. In a laboratory-case environment, the left hemisphere is more in control of activity; in an enriched environment, the right hemisphere is more in control (Denenberg, Garbanati, Sherman, Yutzey, & Kaplan, 1978). But with respect to turning behavior, even unhandled animals show asymmetry, that is, when left lesioned, their left-turning bias is greater than is their right-turning bias when right lesioned (Sherman, Garbanati, Rosen, Yutzey, & Denenberg, 1980). So, we must conclude that the right hemisphere generates a more powerful contralateral turning bias than the left hemisphere but that, presumably by cross-inhibition, this is held in check in the intact animals. Note that a similar imbalance, but in the opposite direction, is revealed by lateral brain lesions in adult humans and is even overtly apparent in human neonates (see Ontogeny of Lateralization: Findings and Implications).

R. G. Robinson (1979) has found that right-hemisphere lesions made rats hyperactive, whereas left-brain lesions did not. Subsequent chemical analysis found catecholamine depletion of intact hemisphere and brain stem in right-lesioned rats but not in left-lesioned rats. It would appear that the right hemisphere has some superordinate remote control of catecholamine levels and that this asymmetry could be involved in the mechanism of lateralization of emotional control. Possibly related is the finding that rats exhibit asymmetry in their bilateral dopaminergic nigrostriatal systems and exhibit corresponding turning biases (Glick & Jerussi, 1974; Glick, Jerussi, & Zimmerberg, 1977). Paw preference in animals generally seems to be a poor indicator of the orienting biases that exist. The obvious reason would be that, whereas turning is clearly a survival-related behavior, such actions as lever pressing by rats or grasping by rhesus monkeys in a laboratory situation (Deuel & Dunlop, 1980) lack ecological validity and do not appear to be behaviors that have been subjected to longstanding selection pressures.

Nonhuman Primates

Early reports of hemispheric dominance in split-brain monkeys given visual-discrimination tasks (Gazzaniga, 1963; Hamilton & Lund, 1970; Hamilton, Tieman, & Farrell, 1974) have been disconfirmed (Hamilton, 1977). But in the auditory modality, Dewson (1979) found a deficit apparently associated with left temporal cortical damage, but not right. Petersen, Beecher, Loloth, Moddy, & Stebbins (1978) report ear asymmetries for discriminating natural Japanese macaque coo sounds, which suggested to them a left-hemisphere superiority in that processing (although as yet tested on rather few animals).

Summary

As investigators focus increasingly on ecologically valid performance, brain asymmetries in function will probably emerge as a common finding in many species. It is too early to ask, what is the ontogeny of such animal asymmetries? But it is clear that brain asymmetry is neither unique to humans nor confined to the representation of high-level cognitive processes. A single organizing principle for the miscellany of animal findings may or may not emerge. But, given asymmetries in so many species, we should not be surprised to find them strikingly present in human infants well before they develop evidence of higher mental function.

HUMAN ASYMMETRIES: THE ADULT BASE STATE IN SUMMARY

Neuroanatomic Asymmetries

There are well-documented structural differences between the left and right cerebral hemispheres of the right-handed adult human. It has been found repeatedly that the planum temporale, the auditory association area on the superior surface of the temporal lobe, is on the average larger on the left side than on the right side (Geschwind & Levitsky, 1968; Teszner, Tzavaras, Gruner, & Hécaen, 1972; Wada et al., 1975; Witelson & Pallie, 1973). Although a similar asymmetry was found in the chimpanzee brain, the gross morphology of the temporale surface was symmetric in monkeys (Pfeiffer, 1936; von Economo & Horn, 1930; Yeni-Komshian & Benson, 1976). But insofar as claims regarding anatomical asymmetries in the human brain have been based largely on measurements of surface distance and areas rather than on volumetric measures, they are inconclusive. A detailed study of the auditory cytoarchitectonic areas in one adult brain did reveal that the temporoparietal cortex was more than seven times as large on the left side as on the right side (Galaburda, LeMay, Kemper, & Geschwind, 1978).

What do these anatomical asymmetries imply about hemispheric function? Some investigators (e.g., Galaburda et al., 1978; Geschwind & Levitsky, 1968) have expressed confidence that structural differences between the hemispheres ultimately can be related to functional differences. At least, there are several conceptual and practical difficulties to be surmounted in relating gross structure to differentiated function. First, measurement of regional anatomical asymmetries is an imprecise and arbitrary enterprise (Rubens, 1977). Marked individual differences in the location and shape of cortical gyri and sulci often preclude unambiguous delineation of a region. A narrow gyrus between deep sulci may present as much cortical surface areas as a wide gyrus between shallow sulci. The small size of one region may be offset by unusually large adjacent regions that perform the same or similar functions. Second, even if different cortical regions could be defined more meaningfully and measured more accurately, it seems unlikely that any simple relationship between a region's size and its function would be found (unless the size differential is related to pathology—see Ratcliffe, Dila, Taylor, & Milner, 1980). Consider, for example, the Geschwind and Levitsky (1968) finding that the left planum temporale is larger than that on the right. Of 100 adult brains, only 65% showed the effect; the right planum temporale was larger than the left in 11% of the cases, and 24% showed no measurable asymmetry. If we assume that at least 95% of the general population has speech represented primarily in the left hemisphere (Rasmussen & Milner, 1975; Zangwill, 1960), then it is clear that the 65% incidence rate for left-sided superiority in size is much too low. The reports of temporal lobe asymmetries must be interpreted in the context of various other structural asymmetries found in the human brain, some of which favor the right hemisphere. For example, the right carotid artery provides a more direct blood supply route from heart to brain than does the left carotid artery. Perhaps for this reason, perfusion of the right hemisphere appears to be greater than that of the left (Carmon & Gambos, 1970; Carmon, Harishanu, Lowinger, & Lavy, 1972). Wada et al. (1975) reported that the frontal operculum of the right hemisphere is larger than that of the left. On the basis of CAT scan data, LeMay (1976) reported that right-handed adults tend to have both wider right frontal lobes than left frontal lobes and wider left occipital lobes than right occipital lobes. These differences are reported to be quite striking; however, there are no obvious functional concomitants. A convincing argument against anatomico-behavioral correlation is presented by Rubens (1977). He cites evidence that two different language areas of the left hemisphere—the frontal operculum and the angular gyrus—are smaller than the homologous regions in the right hemisphere. The left frontal operculum is associated with speech production and the left angular gyrus is associated with reading.

A model that postulates a general dominance of the left hemisphere fails because some regions of the left hemisphere are smaller than homologous regions of the right hemisphere. A double-dominance model that predicts superior size of language areas in the left hemisphere and superior size of certain other areas in the right hemisphere also fails insofar as some presumed language areas in the left hemisphere appear to be smaller than corresponding areas in the right hemisphere.

Corballis (1980) asserts, "It would indeed be magical if functional differences could not be attributed ultimately to structural ones" (p. 286). Actually, metabolic differences have potent influence on function, holding structure constant. Nor need relevant anatomy include the particular morphological differences between hemispheres that have been reported to date. It may prove necessary to examine brain structure at a cellular level, with methods more adequate than those at present available, before an anatomical analysis of the neural basis of cognition can be accomplished.

Functional Asymmetries

The facts of differential specialization of the cerebral hemispheres are under continual review (e.g., see DeRenzi, 1982; Dimond, 1972; Hécaen & Albert, 1978; Kinsbourne, 1978a; Milner, 1973; Zangwill, 1960). They arise from observed differences in the symptomatology of right- as compared to left-hemispheric disorders and from behavioral and psychophysiological asymmetries in intact people.

Asymmetries in Cerebral Hemispheric Damage

The left and right cerebral hemispheres differ most strikingly in their capacity for language processing. Since the clinical observations of Dax and Broca in the 19th century (Boring, 1950; Critchley, 1979), neurologists have recognized that aphasia, the acquired disruption of language, frequently is associated with insult to the left but not the right hemisphere. The 19th-century neurologists, however, did not have our present understanding of either the relationship between language lateralization and handedness nor the specialization of the right hemisphere. Clinical studies continue to provide information about the manner in which various higher mental functions break down as a consequence of unilateral cerebral damage. From these studies, we can make some inferences about which functions are lateralized and, in particular, about the representation of linguistic functions in the brains of left- and right-handed people.

Case studies of adult aphasics (e.g., see Annett, 1975; Gloning, Gloning, Haub, & Quatember, 1969; Hécaen & Sauget, 1971; Luria, 1970; Roberts, 1969; Zangwill, 1967) imply that more than 95% of the right-handed population has speech represented in the left hemisphere. Contrary to early beliefs, most left-handers also have left-hemispheric speech representation, but the proportion of left-handers with deviant speech representation is about 30% to 40%. These figures have been confirmed by testing performed on patients while one hemisphere is incapacitated by a barbiturate (Rasmussen & Milner, 1975; Rossi & Rosadini, 1967). Injection on separate occasions of sodium amobarbital into the arterial system supplying each hemisphere incapacitates most of the hemisphere for a few minutes. The patient, with only one hemisphere functional, remains conscious, thus permitting various functions to be assessed. Of right-handed patients, more than 95% become mute when the left hemisphere is disabled (Rasmussen & Milner, 1975). About 70% of the left-handed and ambidextrous patients who have been tested also seem to depend solely on the left hemisphere for their speech. The remaining non-right-handed patients appear to have speech represented primarily in the right hemisphere or to have substantial speech representation in both hemispheres.

These estimates of the incidence of left-hemispheric speech facilitate the interpretation of cognitive differences between right- and left-handers, when they occur. Left-handers are expected to have anomalous speech representation more often than an equal number of right-handers. This heterogeneity can be exploited to determine the behavioral costs, if any, of anomalous cerebral organization. Also, the incidence figures provide a basis for estimating the validity of noninvasive measures of cerebral lateralization. If at least 95% of right-handers have left-sided language, then a valid and reliable measure of language lateralization should classify approximately the same proportion of people as left lateralized (Satz, 1977). Both points will be elaborated later.

Many of the deficits associated with damage to the right cerebral hemisphere are less obvious than the speech defects that may result from damage to the left cerebral hemisphere; nevertheless, numerous clinical reports substantiate the generalization that various nonverbal skills are impaired as a result of lesions in the right hemisphere (DeRenzi, 1982). Spatial and constructional deficits, in particular, characteristically follow lesions in the temporal and occipitoparietal regions of the right hemisphere (e.g., see Hebb, 1939; McFie, Piercy, & Zangwill, 1950; Paterson & Zangwill, 1944; Piercy & Smyth, 1962). In addition, right-hemisphere lesions are associated with neglect of the left side of space (Brain, 1941; Weinstein & Friedland, 1977) and with defects in musical ability (Bogen, 1969b; Luria, 1963; Milner, 1962), recognition of faces (Benton, 1980; DeRenzi & Spinnler, 1966; Hécaen & Angelergues, 1962; Warrington & James, 1967), perception of line orientation (Benton, Hannay, & Varney, 1975; Benton, Varney, & Hamsher, 1978), and visual memory (Kimura, 1963; Milner, 1968). There are some notable exceptions. Finger agnosia (an inability to recognize finger identity based on finger position) (Kinsbourne & Warrington, 1962b), difficulty in figure-ground discrimination (Russo & Vignolo, 1967), and deficits in identifying countries from their maps (Luria, 1966) tend to be associated with left-hemispheric lesions, even though these defects are not mediated by language disturbance (Kinsbourne & Warrington, 1962b; Luria, 1966). Rhythms are processed by the left hemisphere, whether they involve speech or not (Robinson & Solomon, 1974); even face recognition has components that are left lateralized (Benton, 1980; Sergent & Bindra, 1981). Similarly, different components of musical skills are lateralized to different sides (Henninger, 1981; Milner, 1962). Further, largely supportive evidence for a high degree of discrete specialization of left hemisphere for diverse verbal functions (Ojemann & Whitaker, 1978) and right hemisphere for visuospatial function (Fried, Mateer, Ojemann, Wohns, & Fedio, 1982) derives from results of direct electrical stimulation of cortex in the conscious patient undergoing neurosurgery.

The picture of hemispheric specialization that emerges from the commissurotomy data generally confirms that already established through the study of unilateral cerebral lesion effects. Any contradictions between conclusions from the two respective sources pertain largely to the question of hemispheric specialization for language. No evidence from commissurotomy contradicts the conclusion that, in general, nonverbal processes are heterogeneously lateralized and each hemisphere is specialized for particular nonverbal tasks (DeRenzi, 1982).

Gazzaniga (1970), summarizing findings from the early commissurotomy studies, claimed:

> The left hemisphere is of course capable of speech, whereas the adult right hemisphere is predictably incapable. Information presented to the left hemisphere is normally handled, but identical stimulation of the right yields no response. (p. 129)

Among the first group of commissurotomy patients, some appeared to be able to comprehend certain nouns and, to a lesser degree, adjectives, but they never understood verbs with the isolated right hemisphere (Gazzaniga, 1970). However, technically more sophisticated commissurotomy studies (Zaidel, 1978a) suggest that the linguistic competence of the right hemisphere much exceeds that demonstrated in the early commissurotomy patients (Nebes, 1978; Searleman, 1977).

Two distinctions help clarify the right hemisphere's linguistic competence: (1) the distinction between speech comprehension and speech production and (2) the distinction between the linguistic potential of the right hemisphere under extraordinary circumstances (i.e., the functions for which the right hemisphere can compensate) and its usual linguistic functions (i.e., functions the right hemisphere actually performs in the intact brain). Patients whose left hemispheres have been removed or severely damaged during adulthood can provide information about the upper limits of right-hemispheric linguistic capability in the adult; commissurotomized patients can provide information about linguistic functions of the right hemisphere in people whose left hemisphere remains functional.

The right hemisphere possesses substantial receptive language competence. When the left hemisphere is anesthetized with sodium amobarbital, patients still comprehend verbal instructions (Rasmussen & Milner, 1975; Wada et al., 1975). Zaidel (1978a), after extensive testing of two commissurotomy patients and one patient whose left hemisphere had been removed after pubescence, concluded that the right hemisphere under these circumstances "can have substantial auditory language comprehension" (p. 269). It can form semantic concepts, store concepts in an abstract form, and use those concepts as a basis for matching pictures of physically different but semantically related objects. It has a "surprisingly rich" vocabulary on the Peabody Picture Vocabulary Test (PPVT). Contrary to the claims of Gazzaniga (1970), Zaidel (1978a) reported that the right hemisphere comprehends verbs about as well as it comprehends nouns; this has been confirmed by H. W. Gordon (1980). Nevertheless, Zaidel's (1978a) studies led him to conclude that the right hemisphere is deficient in phonetic discrimination and that patients who depend on their right hemisphere for linguistic functions show an assortment of aphasic characteristics. The presence of comprehension deficits in aphasia does not really conflict with reports of right-hemispheric linguistic competence in the disconnected or isolated right hemisphere; in both cases, there clearly are limits to the ability of the right hemisphere to comprehend speech. If aphasic comprehension is sometimes more limited than that of commissurotomy or hemispherectomy patients, one possible explanation is that the damaged left hemisphere suppresses the functions of the right hemisphere or perhaps adds "noise" to the system (Kinsbourne, 1974b).

In 1874, John Hughlings Jackson (Taylor, 1932) stated his conviction that the sparse and flawed speech output of global aphasics emanates from the right hemisphere. Outside the context of aphasia, there is considerable evidence that the right hemisphere is almost totally mute. Right-handers almost invariably cease speaking when sodium amobarbital is introduced into the left carotid artery (Rasmussen & Milner, 1975). Commissurotomy patients are unable to generate speech with the right hemisphere (Gazzaniga, 1970). In the case of expressive speech, the distinction between the typical and maximal capacity of the right hemisphere is important. When the left hemisphere is functional or has recently been so—as in many of the patients undergoing sodium amobarbital testing as well as commissurotomized patients—the right hemisphere cannot control speech production. In contrast, an adult's right hemisphere can gradually assume control over expressive speech when the left hemisphere is damaged or excised. This was demonstrated through sodium amobarbital testing of aphasics (Kinsbourne, 1971). In the three cases reported, it was right-sided, not left-sided, injections that caused the flawed aphasic speech to cease. Subsequent amobarbital work, on a much larger number of aphasic patients, has indicated that aphasic language usually originates in the intact right hemisphere rather than in the damaged left hemisphere (Czopf, 1972).

The neuropsychological (clinical) evidence regarding hemispheric specialization in adults can be summarized as follows:

1. Speech control is lateralized to the left cerebral hemisphere in more than 95% of right-handers. At least 30% of all left-handers have deviant speech representation, that is, right-hemispheric or bilateral speech.
2. Although right-hemispheric specialization for nonverbal functions is not as clearcut as is left-hemispheric specialization for speech, certain functions, such as tonal perception, visual memory, and perception of line orientation, seem to be lateralized to the right hemisphere.
3. The right hemisphere possesses substantial capacity for verbal comprehension, even when the left hemisphere's linguistic functions are unimpaired or minimally impaired. The ability of the right hemisphere to control speech production, although as a rule less complete than its ability to comprehend speech, seems to depend on the status of the left hemisphere. In the absence of a functional left hemisphere, the right hemisphere can control the emission of speech, albeit an imperfect variety of speech. Under normal circumstances—when linked to a linguistically competent left hemisphere—the right hemisphere appears to be mute and remain so, even when the left hemisphere is temporarily incapacitated by a barbiturate.

Asymmetries in Neurologically Intact Adults

For more than 100 years, knowledge about hemispheric specialization in the adult brain was based almost entirely on clinical evidence. Then, in 1961, Kimura (1961a, 1961b) adapted a noninvasive and relatively simple behavioral measure for ascertaining cerebral dominance for speech perception. She administered Broadbent's (1954) dichotic-digits task to patients whose cerebral dominance for speech was verified independently. The patient reported as many digit names as possible, given three pairs of names in such a way that one member of each pair was presented to the left ear at the same time that the other member was presented to the right ear. Patients with left-hemispheric speech representation showed a right-ear advantage (REA) when reporting these stimuli, whereas patients with right-hemispheric speech representation showed a left-ear advantage (LEA). Normal, right-handed control subjects also showed a REA, which presumably reflected their left-hemispheric speech representation. Subsequently, several investigators adapted visual-perception tasks (e.g., see Bryden & Rainey, 1963) and, less frequently, tactile tasks (L. J. Harris, 1980b) for the study of laterality in neurologically intact people. More recently, studies of interference between concurrent tasks have been used for the same purpose (Kinsbourne & Hiscock, 1983).

These techniques have been widely applied and have yielded supportive but few definitive results. Tachistoscopic studies of visual laterality in particular have been controversial (McKeever & Huling, 1971b; White, 1969b, 1972, 1973a). Findings from all of the three perceptual modalities studied often have been disparate and the laterality effects typically are weak and unstable. Different paradigms applied to the same subject sample often give results that are at variance with each other with respect to the construct that is presumably being studied. Nevertheless, certain aspects of the various findings do confirm the inferences about cerebral asymmetry that are based on clinical case studies. Most notable of these is the consistent finding of a dichotic-listening REA when stimuli are verbal sounds, such as words, digit names, and consonant-vowel (CV) nonsense syllables (Berlin & McNeil, 1976; Studdert-Kennedy & Shankweiler, 1970). Nonverbal stimuli, such as music or environmental sounds, usually yield either a LEA or no significant asymmetry (Curry, 1967; Kimura, 1964; Milner, 1962; Spellacy & Blumstein, 1970). Tactile studies tend to yield a left-hand advantage for identification of objects and patterns, a finding that is consistent with the notion that the right cerebral hemisphere is specialized for activity of that nature (L. J. Harris, 1980b; Witelson,

1974). Although tachistoscopic studies usually yield a right visual half-field (VHF) advantage for words, it is not clear whether that asymmetry is attributable to left-hemispheric specialization for verbal processing (McKeever & Huling, 1971b) or to poststimulus scanning effects associated with reading habits (Mishkin & Forgays, 1952; Terrace, 1959). In the tachistoscopic laterality paradigm, nonverbal stimuli have yielded a variety of asymmetrical effects ranging from strong right VHF superiority (e.g., see Bryden & Rainey, 1963; Wyke & Ettlinger, 1961) to strong left VHF superiority (e.g., see Geffen, Bradshaw, & Wallace, 1971; Kimura, 1966), but probably the most common finding with nonverbal stimuli is an absence of VHF differences (e.g., see Bryden, 1960, 1973; Heron, 1957; Kimura & Durnford, 1974; Terrace, 1959).

The dual-task laterality paradigm assumes that two concurrently performed activities will interfere with each other to a greater or lesser extent, depending on the functional distance between their respective areas of representation in the cerebrum (Kinsbourne & Hicks, 1978a, 1978b). Thus, if speech is represented in the left hemisphere, speaking should interfere with concurrent manual activity being controlled by the left hemisphere to a greater degree than it interferes with the same manual activity being controlled by the right hemisphere. Because control of the movements of each hand resides primarily in the contralateral cerebral hemisphere (Brinkman & Kuypers, 1972, 1973), speaking should disrupt concurrent right-hand activity more than concurrent left-hand activity. Several studies have shown that, in fact, speaking does interfere selectively with the right hand's performance of a skilled manual task, such as dowel-rod balancing (Hicks, 1975; Kinsbourne & Cook, 1971) or sequential finger movement (Hicks, Provenzano, & Rybstein, 1975). Other verbal activities also have a right-lateralized effect on manual performance, whereas nonverbal activities usually affect both hands equally or the left more than the right (Kinsbourne & Hiscock, 1983).

The limited amount of definitive information about hemispheric specialization that derives from various noninvasive tasks documents the difficulty of investigating normal brain organization by means of behavioral techniques. It is encouraging, however, that certain consistent outcomes lend converging validation to conclusions drawn from clinical evidence. The value of corroborative data from studies of normal people is sufficient to justify continuing interest in laterality tasks. Data from normal subjects can be accrued much more quickly than can clinical data from neurological patients. Moreover, data obtained from normal subjects are not biased by the difficult sampling problems that plague the clinical investigator.

To a limited degree, psychophysiological asymmetries also corroborate clinically based inferences about hemisphere specialization in the adult. Although the extant collection of EEG and evoked-potential studies fails to provide a simple pattern of results, there are numerous instances of task-dependent asymmetries in electrical activity measured from the scalp. (These findings are summarized in our discussion of the *Indices of Cerebral Lateralization: Measurement Issues*.) In the majority of instances, the pattern of left-right differences conforms to that expected on the basis of concepts about left- and right-hemispheric specialization that have been derived from the clinical evidence. Stronger and more detailed conclusions are not possible as many discrepant outcomes must be explained; even the expected differences between the left and right sides of the head often are small in magnitude and variable across subjects (Donchin et al., 1977; Friedman, Simson, Ritter, & Rapin, 1975; Marsh, 1978). The complexity of these techniques is such that laterality investigators are still discovering the phenomena to look for and the best means of identifying and measuring them. At present, the cumulative findings from electrophysiological studies provide only the most general confirmation of the results from clinical and noninvasive studies of hemispheric specialization in adults but, in the future, electrophysiological evidence is likely to constitute an important link between studies of deficits in brain-injured patients and studies of behavioral asymmetry in normal people.

Asymmetries in Psychopathology

Patients with left-hemisphere damage tend to exhibit a sad mood and even catastrophically to decompensate, whereas patients with right-hemisphere lesions exhibit a bland indifference or even euphoria to their disabilities (Denny-Brown, Meyer, & Horenstein, 1952; Dobrokhotova & Braghina, 1974; Gainotti, 1972; Hécaen, 1962). Some studies of intracarotid sodium amobarbital inactivation of one cerebral hemisphere at a time have elicited from normal volunteers a depressive reaction after inactivation of the left hemisphere and a euphoric or even maniacal mood after inactivation of the right hemisphere (Perria, Rosadini, & Rossi, 1961; Rossi & Rosadini, 1967; Terzian, 1964). Conversely, irritative lesions that presumably enhance the excitation of the lesioned hemisphere relative to the other one seem to generate auras and interictal phenomena consistent with the preceding formulation. Thus, right focal seizures may be ushered in by paroxysmal weeping (dacrystic epilepsy), whereas left lesions more commonly trigger paroxysmal laughter (gelastic epilepsy). During a seizure, right-hemispheric epileptics showed more negative affect than those with left foci (Sackheim, Greenberg, Weiman, Gur, Hungertaken, & Geschwind, 1982). Interictally this pattern is reversed; left-hemispheric seizures brought on negative feelings (Bear & Fedio, 1977; Deglin & Nikolaenko, 1975). Evidence on this point is not completely consistent. For instance, in polyarteritis nodosa right-hemispheric involvement results in a depressive illness, whereas left-hemispheric involvement does not (Kulesha, Moldofsky, Urowitz, & Zeaman, 1981). Also, the amobarbital studies have the peculiar aspect that emotional reactions are released not during the inactivation of the anesthetized hemisphere but in the course of its recovery from anesthetization. Electroencephalographic desynchronization, more marked on the right than on the left, occurred during a manipulation leading subjects to indulge in sad thoughts (Tucker, 1981). Consistent with the findings previously summarized, this suggests that an excitation-inhibition balance in favor of the right hemisphere accompanies negative affect. A study of lateral gaze has shown relatively more left gaze in response to certain questions with negative emotional connotation than in response to questions of positive valence (Ahern & Schwartz, 1979).

Mental illness has only recently been credited with its own neuropsychology. In line with the current popularity of a cognitive and even neurological approach to psychopathology, the hunt for lateralized and localized signs in psychiatric patients is now on. Neuropsychological tests were designed to detect focal structural brain damage; but failing evidence of such damage in psychiatric populations, these tests are allegedly sensitive to correspondingly localized cerebral dysfunctions. An approximate summary of conclusions so far is that the left hemisphere is dysfunctional and overaroused in schizophrenia and perhaps in obsessive-compulsive neurosis, the right hemisphere in depression and perhaps in hysteria, and the frontal lobes are supposedly dysfunctional and overaroused in anxiety states but dysfunctional and underaroused in psychopathy (Abrams & Taylor, 1979; Flor-Henry & Yeudall, 1979; Gruzelier & Hammond, 1977; Klonoff, Fibiger, & Hutton, 1970; Smokler & Shevrin, 1979).

Before inquiring whether these changes are causes or only products of these psychiatric diseases, we must satisfy ourselves that the findings really justify this kind of conclusion. We will separately consider neuropsychological tests and laterality tests.

After focal cerebral damage, the patient develops specific symptomatology, finds that certain activities have become disproportionately difficult, and does very poorly on a specific subset of mental tests. Psychiatric patients, in whom evidence of brain damage is wanting or nonspecific, lack the neurological symptoms and signs but may also score relatively poorly on clusters of tests that roughly correspond to ones indicative of particular cerebral lesions. Can parallel inferences be drawn from test performances of people who are not known to have focal brain lesions? Only if confounding variables are scrupulously eliminated. It is possible to fail any test for more than one reason and there is no guarantee that a mentally disturbed person fails a particular test for the same reason that a brain-damaged person fails it. The factorial structure of tests is not necessarily the same in these two populations.

Language tests are hard for aphasics, but they are also hard for illiterates, the deaf, and those who use their verbal abilities in unusual ways. When schizophrenics lose points on verbal tests, is this because they cannot perform or because they differently construe the nature of the task? On the basis of total test scores only, members of these groups could often easily be confused. But, clinically, the differences in history, manner of presentation, and patterns of erroneous performance are apparent. A relatively lower score on the Wechsler Adult Intelligence Scale (WAIS) verbal than performance tests does not qualify schizophrenics as aphasics. Clinically, they behave like no subtype of aphasia ever described. If schizophrenics' poor verbal performance is not due to aphasia, possibly it arises from some dysfunction specific to the psychosis that disturbs the verbal functioning of the left hemisphere in its own idiosyncratic manner. But, for such a strong inference, positive evidence is needed. Pending such evidence, we can only reaffirm that schizophrenics, having unusual thoughts, say strange things. Nonverbal tests of left-hemispheric function do exist, and these could be used to deconfound left-hemispheric integrity and things schizophrenics say.

Both unipolar and bipolar depressives may do worse on the performance than the verbal subscale of the WAIS (or WAIS-R). The tests are novel, call for on-the-spot problem solving, and are mostly time limited. A patient with psychomotor retardation would be unlikely to make the mental effort to live up to his cognitive potential for succeeding on such testing. (The same applies to senile people; they, too, have been accused of disproportionate right-hemispheric deterioration.) Right-hemispheric tests exist that are neither arduous nor call for performance under time pressure (e.g., see Benton & Van Allen, 1968; Benton et al., 1978). They could be used to deconfound right-hemispheric function and a sad and sluggish attitude.

Frontal-lobe deficits may lead to impulsive behavior; impulsive behavior may lead to prison. That does not render an impulsive approach to certain tests diagnostic of frontal-lobe dysfunction in people in whom there is no other converging evidence of such dysfunction. As has been made clear in the course of the notorious controversy on nature versus nurture in IQ testing, one rushes from test scores to the brain at one's peril and at the risk of stigmatizing as permanently brain damaged people who are, in fact, subject to transitory situational pressures. One may at times use some parts of one's brain more effectively than others on account of habit, modeling, cognitive style, or motivation. In short, the analogy between test profiles in cerebral and psychiatric symptomatology remains an analogy for further study.

Laterality findings in psychopathology abound and are suggestive but conflicting in their outcomes (see the review by Gruzelier, 1981). Certainly, if the direction of an asymmetry is simplistically interpreted as indicating the side of lateralization of the processes tested, then lateralization in the psychopathologies is not only bewildering and deviant but also subject to inexplicable variation from time to time and under the influence of situational circumstances. In fact, this segment of laterality science can only be organized with a semblance of coherence if laterality relationships are admitted to index the relative activation of the hemispheres, which, in turn, is determined not only by their specialization but also with the way they are in fact used—a way that in mentally disturbed people may seem capricious and certainly is often deviant. Variables, such as set, strategy, motivation, and affective coloring, all of which can bias laterality outcomes in normal people, are particularly apt to do so in the mentally disturbed.

Up to now, this work has been virtually limited to adults and adolescents, probably for no more profound reason than that they are relatively amenable to the test procedures used. But as the medical model of psychopathology implicit in the influential *Diagnostic and Statistical Manual* (*DSM-III*) issued by the American Psychiatric Association increasingly displaces the currently more popular dynamic-developmental approaches, we will find an increase of studies in children analogous to those in adults. In developing and evaluating such studies, the above-cited methodological considerations are not only relevant but also compounded by the interaction of the mental disease with developmental status. Structural models of brain abnormality should be explanations of last resort, applicable only when it has been proven (1) that the many cognitive and affective variables that determine which parts of the brain are used for what purpose have all been brought under experimental control and (2) that those variables, neither singly nor in combination, can account for the neuropsychological findings.

Summary

This discussion outlines current knowledge about structural and functional asymmetries in the adult brain. Although various anatomical differences between the left and right hemispheres have been discovered, it is unclear whether they are related to functional specialization of the hemispheres. Attempts to link structural and functional asymmetries have been limited by the crude nature of the anatomical measurements and by the failure of the evidence, thus far, to support any plausible model of anatomico-behavioral correlation.

Information about functional asymmetries in the adult brain is derived both from the study of patients with hemisphere damage or disconnection and from noninvasive experiments with neurologically intact people. The clinical evidence indicates that speech control is left hemispheric in more than 95% of right-handers and in as many as 70% of left-handers. Certain nonverbal functions are lateralized to the right hemisphere, others are impaired by damage to either hemisphere. The right hemisphere has substantial capacity for linguistic comprehension and limited capacity for control of expressive speech. Both the receptive and expressive competencies of the right hemisphere seem to depend on the functional status of the left hemisphere with which it is paired. Behavioral and psychophysiological asymmetries in normal adults corroborate and extend clinically based inferences about the general nature of left- and right-hemispheric specialization. The methodological considerations that render these findings less than definitive are briefly previewed. Evidence from psychopathology raises the possibility that different affective perceptions and responses also differentially engage the hemispheres.

INDICES OF CEREBRAL LATERALIZATION: MEASUREMENT ISSUES

Effects of Lateralized Lesions

The data base for human neuropsychology consists primarily of evidence about behavioral deficits associated with injury to the brain. Investigators rely on experiments of nature to gather data that for ethical reasons cannot be provided from controlled experimentation. Nature's experiments are imperfectly controlled; consequently, methodological and interpretative problems associated with clinical studies are numerous and often intractable. We will begin with a general description of these problems. The problems that most directly affect our ability to draw inferences about the developmental course of language lateralization are examined further in our discussion on *Ontogeny of Lateralization: Findings and Implications*.

Evidence from people with localized brain lesions consists of information about structural and physiological characteristics of the damaged brain on the one hand and about associated behavioral deficits on the other hand. To the degree that information about the lesion and about the deficits is complete and accurate, it is possible to make inferences about brain-behavior relationships. Thus, we begin by discussing identification of the lesion and measurement of behavioral deficits. A third methodological factor is choice of person, that is, the degree to which the sample of patients under study represents the general population of children or adults. Fourth, there is a long list of variables that affect the nature and severity of the deficits being measured.

Identifying the Lesion

In the past, although some information about the lesion could be deduced from neurological examination, definitive information was not available until autopsy. But often, no autopsy is performed or the pathologist's report is unavailable. If the patient's brain lesions are static and the patient dies of unrelated causes, lesion at autopsy should approximate its state at the time of behavioral assessment. But the child with a static deficit will usually outlive the investigator. If the neurological disease is progressive, especially if it is fatal, changes in brain tissue occurring subsequent to the time of testing obfuscate the relationship between lesion and resultant behavioral deficits (Reitan & Davison, 1974).

Technological advances have lessened the need to rely on autopsy. Angiography and CAT scanning are powerful methods of revealing structural lesions of various kinds in the living brain, although they do provide less direct anatomic information than does autopsy (Benson, 1967). Small lesions of functional importance may be missed and the extent of lesions misinterpreted on CAT scan. NMR yields superior resolution of lesion sites but has not as yet been widely used for neuropsychological studies. Positron emission tomography and regional cerebral blood-flow studies give functional information.

Irrespective of how the lesion is to be detected and defined, the investigator cannot avoid the possibility that the damaged area responsible for the behavioral deficit has been missed. One may know that a lesion exists in a particular brain region but not be sure that damage does not also exist elsewhere in the brain. As an example, this false negative problem was invoked by Woods and Teuber (1978a) when they speculated that cases of childhood aphasia reported in the older literature resulted from undetected dysfunction of the left hemisphere rather than from more obvious dysfunction of the right hemisphere (see *Ontogeny of Lateralization: Findings and Implications*).

Measuring the Deficits

If the functional significance of cerebral lesions is to be understood, the appropriate mental functions must be tapped, the test must be sufficiently selective to permit proper interpretation, and the test results must be integrated in such a fashion as to lead to reasonable conclusion about the precise nature of the deficits (Lezak, 1976).

A neuropsychological test may be described in terms of its selectivity and its sensitivity. Some tests, such as the Symbol-Digit Modalities Test (A. Smith, 1968) and the Trail Making Test (Reitan, 1958), are useful for screening because they are very sensitive to the effects of brain dysfunction irrespective of etiology or lesion site. Broadband tests high in sensitivity are low in selectivity. They would probably fail to reveal differences associated with lesion site, even where such differences exist. Any differences between patient groups probably would reflect general differences in level of functioning rather than differences in a single, circumscribed skill. Other tests—for example, tests of line-orientation judgment (Benton et al., 1978) and face recognition (Benton & Van Allen, 1968)—are sensitive and selective. Tests such as these are well suited for studies of patients with relevant focal lesions.

Many widely used psychological tests are neither sensitive nor selective with respect to neurologically based deficits. For example, IQ tests tap many complex cognitive functions often resistant to the effects of focal brain injury (Lezak, 1976; Matarazzo, 1972). Especially when composite scores, such as verbal IQ, performance IQ, and full-scale IQ, are used in lieu of subtest scores to measure patients' performance, IQ tests are mediocre neuropsychological instruments (Dennis & Whitaker, 1977). Perhaps for this reason, attempts to relate side of lesion and verbal IQ/performance IQ discrepancy have yielded inconsistent results for children (Hammill & Irwin, 1966; McFie, 1961; Reed & Reitan, 1969) as well as adults (Matthews & Reitan, 1964; Reitan, 1955; A. Smith, 1966; Todd, Coolidge, & Satz, 1977).

Clinical studies fall into three categories. Some findings are based on clinical impressions. Investigators may judge the patient to be impaired on the basis of either negative evidence (e.g., failure to talk or failure to repeat a series of digits) or positive evidence (e.g., paraphasic speech errors or order reversals in digit repetition). Especially with children, positive findings are more convincing than negative findings. But the results of clinical observation are subject to various observer biases. The second category uses general-purpose psychometric instruments, such as the xechsler IQ tests. Although these tests are comprehensive and can be used objectively they may be insensitive to lesser degrees of impairment. The third category of deficit-measurement procedures consists of sensitive and selective special-purpose tests for measuring functions known to be altered by injury to a particular brain region. In many cases, specialized neuropsychological tests will reveal clear-cut deficits that are not detected by clinical examinations or by psychometry.

Controversy lingers between those who believe in specific localization of function and those who favor Flourens's (1960) principle of *action commune*, or homogeneity of function within each of the major structures of the brain. To a large extent, this fundamental issue revolves about deficit measurement, namely, the selectivity and sensitivity of behavioral measures. If only a few selective tests are used, deficits other than those expected will not be found. One will not find that which is not sought. If many selective tests or a few sensitive, nonselective tests are used, behavioral impairment is likely to appear to be more extensive.

Sampling from Clinical Populations

Sampling problems are especially severe in clinical research. If the study of brain-injured people is to clarify brain-behavior relationships in normal children and adults, the brain-injured population must be representative of the general population with respect to brain organization. In many instances, brain-injured people are not representative because preexisting neurologic disease or malformation has altered the structure or physiology of the brain. A major cerebrovascular accident or stroke, for example, may have been preceded by vascular disease and undetected small strokes that damaged various regions of the brain and resulted in compensatory reorganization. The behavioral effects of a subsequent major stroke may be altered as a consequence of preexisting damage so that a relationship between a behavioral deficit and the region damaged by the major stroke may characterize that particular patient but not others. Abrupt neurologic insult—particularly head trauma and some tumors—might alleviate the problem were it not that tumors and closed head injuries seldom produce circumscribed and well-defined regions of damage. It is for such reasons that previously healthy young soldiers who sustain penetrating missile wounds in the head during warfare have constituted so valuable a source of neuropsychological data.

Another sampling problem that especially affects left- versus right-hemispheric comparisons is selective reporting of clinical cases. Unexpected and extraordinary findings are more likely to be overrepresented in the published literature. The overrepresentation of exceptions may cause a serious distortion of aggregate incidence figures. One should regard with skepticism box score tabulations that fail to consider sampling biases as well as other aspects of methodological merit in the studies. Each report should include a detailed description of sampling procedures so that the likelihood of sampling error may be estimated.

Controlling Extraneous Variables

Brain lesions may be specified and matched with varying degrees of precision. It is not instructive to contrast left- and right-lesioned patients unless the respective lesions are equivalent in terms of their location within the hemisphere, as patients with left-sided damage may differ behaviorally from those with right-sided damage—not because of the lateralization of the lesion but because of differences in location on the anterior versus posterior, superior versus inferior, and cortical versus subcortical dimensions. In practice, precise specification and matching are but starting points if meaningful comparisons among patients are to be made. The mapping of relationships between brain lesions and behavioral deficits would be a much simpler matter if the lesion site were the only factor of consequence. In fact, the location of the lesion is but one of several variables that affect the quality and degree of behavioral deficit (Lezak, 1976; Reitan & Davison, 1974; A. Smith, 1975). Unless these variables can be controlled, comparison of left versus right lesions, anterior versus posterior lesions, and so on, leads to ambiguous findings.

An obvious potential confound is the extent of the lesion or, to be more precise, the extent of the region whose functioning is disrupted by the lesion. Greater behavioral deficits tend to be associated with greater destruction of neural tissue. Nevertheless, it has been reported that a focal lesion within a temporal lobe causes greater impairment than the removal of the entire lobe (Nielsen & Raney, 1939) and that a lesion within a cerebral hemisphere causes impairments not found after removal of the entire hemisphere (Kinsbourne, 1976). Beyond some critical lesion size, the damaged portion of the brain appears to contribute so much "noise" to the overall functioning of the brain that complete silencing of that portion constitutes an improvement. In any event, between-group comparison of deficits are interpretable only if lesion size is comparable.

Etiology of lesion is important. Two reasons have already been mentioned, that is, strokes may represent the culmination of an undetected but chronic disease process that has altered brain organization and tumors and blows on the head tend to cause damage that cannot be delineated precisely. There are further reasons for matching patients according to etiology of damage. Because damage that is due to tumor often progresses, whereas that which is due to stroke recedes, initially matched tumor and stroke patients become increasingly different over time. Some lesions tend to alter cerebral blood flow more dramatically than do others, some are associated with edema sufficient to disrupt functioning over a wide expanse of cortical territory, and some are epileptogenic. Both seizures and subclinical seizure activity themselves may impair functioning. Medical treatment, which varies according to etiology of lesion, may confound measurement of deficits. The fact that a particular kind of damage affects one side of the brain more frequently than the other constitutes a statistical artifact that must be dealt with when attempting to estimate the incidence of left- and right-hemispheric representation of a particular function in the general population (Satz, 1979). In all respects mentioned, lesion types in children differ from those in adults. For instance, in midchildhood, the relative incidence of extracerebral trauma as a cause for brain damage is greater than either in infancy or adulthood, and this carries a better prognosis regardless of age (Van Dougen & Loonen, 1977).

The time interval between neurologic insult and behavioral testing must be controlled whenever possible as many patients show either progressive impairment or recovery of function over time. Moreover, within the same patient, one mental function may recover while another remains indefinitely impaired. But one can match for interval only when the onset of the pathological process can be specified. In cases of neoplasm, dementia, and some infectious diseases, it is unclear when the significant damage began. The element of time is paramount in studies of children in whom deficits may diminish or disappear in a few days. In contrast, the course over which the disease develops may be lengthy. This is true even of cases of spastic hemiplegia, which provide much of the evidence about language lateralization in children (Byers & McLean, 1962).

Ideally, brain-damage effects can be differentiated from deficits associated with the affective state of the patient and medication. In practice, this may not be the case. Higher mental functions represent a complex and continually changing interaction among endogenous and exogenous variables. Results from even the most valid and selective neuropsychological instruments can be biased by factors, such as depression, preoccupation, suboptimal arousal, fatigue, fear, malingering, and intentional uncooperativeness. Altered affective states may stem directly from brain pathology or be a consequence of unfamiliar, threatening, and (perhaps) painful circumstances. Adults and older children may be obsessed with concerns about their impaired functioning and their uncertain future; younger children may be fearful and uncooperative. Drug symptoms include drowsiness, behavioral slowing, difficulty in focusing attention, emotional lability, and difficulties of limb control. In clinical studies of brain-behavior relationships, there is risk of finding deficits that are associated indirectly, or not at all, with the damaged region of the brain.

Children's capacity to perform many tasks irrespective of acquired impairment will vary with age, and tests and criteria for evaluating results must be adjusted accordingly. Deficit assessment in adults is relatively straightforward, given a stable background of higher mental functioning. In children, however, the deficit may be obscured by maturation and new learning or it may be accentuated if the child's acquired handicaps preclude the learning of new material. Scores on many neuropsychological tests decline as a consequence of "normal" aging processes. Decreasing neuroplasticity across the lifespan (see *Ontogeny of Lateralization: Theoretical Considerations*) has implications for deficit measurement in people of different ages.

Age affects neurological as well as behavioral aspects of clinical studies. The size and weight of various regions change. There are developmental changes in number of neurons (Huttenlocher, 1979), myelination, arborization of dendrites, and levels of neurotransmitters. At different stages of development, regions of the brain are differentially susceptible to different kinds of insult, such as that from toxic substances and anoxia. For instance, the newborn's brain is relatively resistant to anoxia. The incidence of various diseases and structural defects changes markedly as a function of age. For all these reasons, it is difficult to make meaningful comparisons of neurologic status among people of different ages.

Aphasia studies and sodium amobarbital investigations (described in our discussion of *Human Asymmetries: The Adult Base State in Summary*) indicate that the probability of left-hemispheric representation of expressive speech differs between right- and left-handed adults, even though the majority, irrespective of handedness, has left-sided speech. Effects of unilateral electroconvulsive therapy (ECT) also suggest an elevated incidence of right-sided language among left-handers (e.g., see Fleminger, de Horne, & Nott, 1970; Pratt & Warrington, 1972; Pratt, Warrington, & Halliday, 1971; Warrington & Pratt, 1973). For language, left-handers appear less lateralized and more variable from person to person than right-handers simply because there are proportionately far more left-handers with right-sided speech. In addition, it appears that, in the individual left-hander, hemispheric specialization is often less focal than in the individual right-hander (Hécaen & Piercy, 1956; Hécaen & Sauget, 1971; Luria, 1970; Marcie, 1972; Roberts, 1969; Subirana, 1958). Clearly, the cerebral organization of left-handers is different from that of right-handers, and the differences exist in children as well as in adults (Herron, 1980). Even when the emphasis is on some aspect of brain-behavior correspondence other than hemispheric specialization, left-handers may differ sufficiently from right-handers in cerebral organization so that including their data with data from right-handers will distort the findings.

Premorbid cognitive strengths and weaknesses are usually unknown. In a neurologic patient, a deficit may be unrelated to the brain pathology and may instead reflect a lifelong characteristic. Some deficits violate specieswide expectations, (Lezak, (1976)). For example, adult humans in all cultures can speak and understand at least one language. Loss of such abilities can be attributed unambiguously to neurologic disease, unless it preexisted the lesion. When the deficit is more subtle or involves a skill for which there are no universal expectations (e.g., interpretation of proverbs, memory for lists of words, making designs with blocks), the poor performance may reflect an extreme instance of natural variability rather than a consequence of brain injury. Single-case reports are particularly vulnerable to misinterpretations of this kind.

Significant individual differences exist in the structure of the brain and its vascular system. The configuration of the cerebral vasculature deviates from the norm in some normal people. Occlusion of the same cerebral artery at identical sites may have severe consequences for one patient and few, if any, consequences for another because collateral blood supply in the second patient is sufficient to maintain functioning in the region that was infarcted in the first patient. Similarly, topographical landmarks on the cortical surface vary considerably among people and between the two hemispheres of the same person (Rubens, 1977). The high degree of anatomical and physiological variability from person to person and from hemisphere to hemisphere complicates the correspondence between brain lesions and cognitive deficits.

Another complication is von Monakow's (1914) diaschisis. Diaschisis (see also *Ontogeny of Lateralization: Theoretical Considerations*) refers to the observation that damage to a circumscribed area of the cortex disrupts the functioning not only of that area but also temporarily that of other areas that normally receive stimulation from the damaged region. Diaschisis is separable in concept from tissue damage but the behavioral effects are not separable until such time as diaschisis effects have disappeared. Consequently, the deficits associated with a focal lesion may be overestimated if behavioral testing following the injury takes place early (Smith, 1966).

Conclusions

It is rarely possible to overcome all the problems and avoid all the pitfalls that we have described. Awareness of the problems and pitfalls, however, is a prerequisite for designing clinical studies that are as sound as possible. The researcher and the reader who are aware of the methodological problems inherent in clinical research can avoid overinterpretation and overgeneralization of the findings. Moreover, the limitations of clinical neuropsychological research define the need for experimental studies of normal people that—although they entail serious methodological problems of their own—promise to provide information about hemispheric specialization that will complement the information obtained from clinical studies. But the single most important precaution is to rely only on findings that are large in scale. Conventional levels of significance (e.g., 5% level) may be grossly misleading and prove unreplicable.

Irrespective of the methodological adequacy of clinical studies, one must be cautious in using the results to draw conclusions about normal brain organization. It may appear to be a short logical step to infer functional lateralization from lateralized deficits but such inferences may be specious. Ablation of brain tissue provides information about functions the brain can perform in the absence of that tissue rather than about functions that the ablated tissue normally performs. In more concrete terms, the fact that function *A* is spared by a lesion in region *X* does not prove that function *A* normally is independent of region *X*. Function *A* may depend on region *X* in the intact brain, but there may be compensatory mechanisms that allow function *A* to persist after destruction of region *X*. Conversely, the fact that function *B* is disrupted by a lesion in region *Y* does not prove that function *B* is represented in region *Y*. The lesion may have destroyed pathways that are necessary for the expression of function *B*. In applying this caveat to lateralization of function, we reiterate the distinction between deficits and functions. In showing lateralization of deficits, lesion studies provide a basis for inferring lateralization of function. Such evidence does not constitute proof that functions are lateralized in the undamaged brain. Corroboration from the study of neurologically intact people is required.

Psychophysiological Asymmetries

Since Berger (1929) discovered that rhythmic patterns of electric potential differences can be measured between sites on the human scalp, it has been accepted that such patterns (EEG) reflect electrical activity of the brain. The scalp EEG has been used in clinical neurology to detect and localize seizure foci, tumors, destructive lesions, and so on (Case & Bucy, 1938; Gibbs, Lennox, & Gibbs, 1936; Walter, 1936). Given that electrical activity on the scalp is sensitive to localized dysfunction of the underlying brain, it might likewise reflect localized events in the normal brain. Comparing activity on the left and right sides of the head thus becomes a strategy for investigating lateralization of function.

Electroencephalogram: Characteristics and Methods

The EEG offers some advantages for the study of brain lateralization. One is the presumed directness with which EEG taps brain functioning. The EEG albeit is a very complex phenomenon that presumably reflects additive and interactive contributions from various brain regions (Lindsley, 1969) and that is subject to contamination by noncerebral generators (e.g., see Anderson, 1976). Nevertheless, unlike most among noninvasive event-related measures, it measures neural activity and not some behavioral characteristic that is an end product of neural events. In contrast to CAT scans and angiography, EEG provides information about function. Thus, EEG provides a more direct view of the brain function than do measures of either behavior or brain structure. With computer analysis, the resolution of EEG data with respect to time has become unsurpassed. Certain brainstem evoked potential waveforms can be measured so accurately that lesions in the auditory pathways can be pinpointed at each of several levels (Starr & Achor, 1975; Stockard & Rossiter, 1977). Although EEG does not provide excellent spatial resolution with respect to the cerebral cortex, that is, cerebral localization, it is sensitive to changes in several regions at one time. Thus, it is well suited for the current state of the art in lateralization research, in which it may be more realistic to predict overall right versus left differences than differences between more circumscribed regions within each hemisphere and in which the investigator may wish to determine empirically the regions that show the clearest left versus right differences. In some applications, when complex "naturalistic" tasks are to be performed, the ability of EEG to document electrical activity over a long period of time may be counted as an advantage. Electrophysiological measures are of particular value in working with infants and severely impaired people because useful data can be obtained without the necessity for overt behavioral responses.

The directness of electrophysiological methods leads to high expectations for consistent, compelling, and clear-cut findings. In general, with respect to the lateralization of higher mental processes, such expectations have not been met (Butler & Glass, 1974; Donchin et al., 1977; Friedman et al., 1975; Galambos, Benson, Smith, Shulman-Galambos, & Osier, 1975; Hillyard & Woods, 1979; Marsh, 1978; Mayes & Beaumont, 1977; Shelburne, 1972, 1973). Even questions concerning lateral differences for simple sensory processes cannot be answered definitively (cf. Andreassi, De Simone, Friend, & Grota, 1975; Butler, Keidel, & Spreng, 1969; Calmes & Cracco, 1971; Harmony, Ricardo, Fernandez, & Valdes, 1973; Peronnet, Michel, Echallier, & Girod, 1974; Peters & Mendel, 1974; Rhodes,

Obitz, & Creel, 1975; Ruhm, 1971; Vaughan & Ritter, 1970). We will summarize what conclusions may or may not be drawn from the extant data and some of the methodological problems and shortcomings of electrophysiological research into hemispheric specialization. More detailed reviews are available (Donchin et al., 1977; Friedman et al., 1975; Marsh, 1978).

The basic phenomenon of interest is a minute, constantly changing potential difference between two sites on the scalp. From this common ground, studies diverge. Some entail the recording of ongoing or "spontaneous" EEG, others the computer averaging of event-related EEG. These categories—spontaneous EEG versus averaged event-related EEG—correspond to the frequency domain and the time domain respectively (Donchin et al., 1977). Some of the other characteristics that differentiate various EEG studies are relevant mainly to one category of study or the other; some are common to both.

Recording of spontaneous EEG requires the continuous acquisition of potential-difference data over a period that usually lasts from several minutes to several hours. Customarily, analogue tracings are obtained and interpreted subjectively or by applying specified scoring criteria. Some typical tracings are shown in Figure 1. Such EEG procedures as these are used in clinical neurology (e.g., see Kooi, 1971) and in the psychophysiological study of sleep (Rechtschaffen & Kales, 1968). Most recent investigations of hemispheric differences have attempted to detect shifts in the left versus right balance of EEG power as a function of the task being performed. The EEG amplitude is integrated over time to obtain power estimates (e.g., see Galin & Ornstein, 1972; Morgan, McDonald, & MacDonald, 1971) or else spectrum analyses are performed (e.g., see Doyle, Ornstein, & Galin, 1974; Gardiner & Walter, 1977). Because mental effort is associated with desynchronization of the EEG, especially in the alpha band of 8 to 12 Hz (Adrian & Matthews, 1934), a decrease in power from one side of the scalp relative to the opposite side indicates that the balance of cerebral activation has shifted in favor of the side showing decreased power.

The recording of event-related EEG, or average evoked potentials (AEPs), requires that the recording be time locked to a stimulus. Typically, recording begins with the onset of a brief stimulus, such as a light flash, and continues for a period ranging from a few to several hundred milliseconds. The resultant waveform is digitized and stored in computer memory. The entire sequence is repeated several times, and each amplitude value is added to previous values

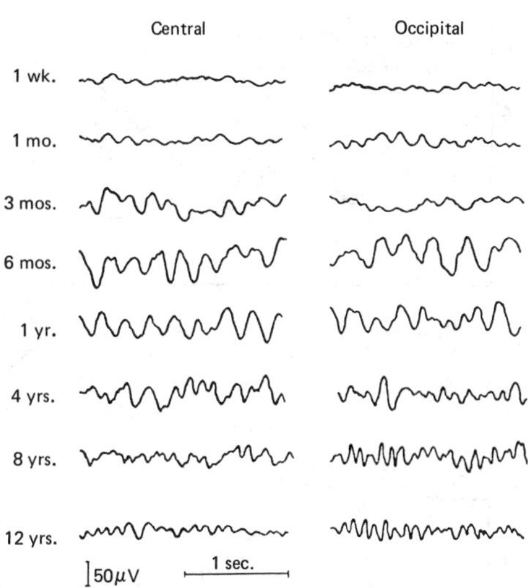

Figure 1. Normal waking patterns of spontaneous EEG at various ages. Samples were selected to show typical age-related variations of frequency and amplitude. (Reproduced from Kooi, 1971. Copyright, Harper & Row, Publishers; reprinted by permission.)

for that particular point in time relative to the stimulus. Changes in electrical potential that are temporally related to the stimulus will enhance as data from successive trials are summed, but potential changes that are independent of the stimulus will diminish over trials. The resultant waveform, when averaged over trials, often resembles those depicted in Figure 2. To the extent that extraneous electrical activity is random with respect to the stimulus, its algebraic sum over a large number of trials will approach zero. The signal-to-noise ratio varies as a function of the square root of the number of trials; consequently, the sensitivity of the technique increases as the number of trials is increased. There is no single, consensual method of measuring evoked potentials. Depending on the stimulus, the task, and the interval over which potentials are recorded, there may be several positive and negative peaks. These are usually labeled according to their approximate latency, for example, the P300 wave occurs about 300 msec following stimulus onset. In many instances, the investigator simply makes judgments as to similarities and differences in waveforms on the basis of visual inspection (e.g., see Goff, Matsumiya, Allison, & Goff, 1969). Alternatively, the investigator may measure the latency and amplitude of a particular deflection in the averaged waveform. Although gross characteristics of the averaged waveform may provide satisfactory data under some

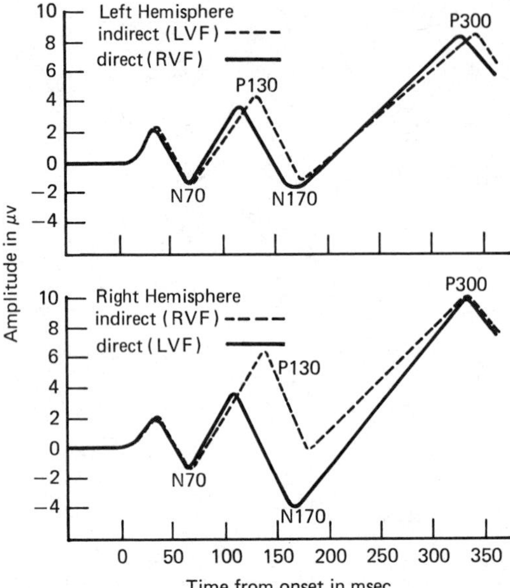

Figure 2. Composite averaged visual evoked potentials from eight normal right-handed adult males. Stimuli consisted of single letters and pairs of letters presented for 40 msec in either the left or right visual half-field (LVF or RVF). (Reproduced from Ledlow, Swanson, & Kinsbourne, 1978. Copyright, American Psychological Association, Inc.; reprinted by permission.)

circumstances, it is desirable in other situations to be able to perform multivariate analyses upon the digital data derived from each trial (Donchin, 1969).

Donchin et al. (1977) divide AEPs into three categories. Exogenous components of the waveform, that is, those occurring within about 150 msec of stimulus onset, are determined largely by stimulus parameters. Endogenous components, that is, those with latencies in excess of 150 msec, are more dependent on task parameters than on stimulus characteristics. Endogenous components may be subclassified into those that occur after the stimulus and those that appear prior to the stimulus and presumably represent anticipation of the stimulus (Walter, Cooper, Aldridge, McCallum, & Winter, 1964). Most studies of lateral differences in the evoked potential have focused on poststimulus endogenous components. It is also possible to distinguish among evoked-potential studies according to the association between the eliciting stimulus and the task being performed by the subject. In most cases, the stimulus is an integral part of the task, as when the stimulus is a letter to be read or a sound to be identified. In other cases, however, the stimulus that triggers the averaging computer is irrelevant to the task (Galin & Ellis, 1975). The stimulus serves as a probe to sample asymmetries that presumably result from the performance of some ongoing activity. A flash of light may occur randomly or periodically as the subject is engaged in different tasks. Because the light flash remains constant across conditions, any differences in the evoked potential can be attributed to alteration in the state of the brain owing to the task rather than the light flashes.

Electroencephalographic studies, irrespective of whether spontaneous or event-related activity is measured, differ in several ways. The independent variable usually is a task manipulation of some kind, although it may be a selected (individual-difference) variable, such as handedness or age. Numerous tasks have been used in EEG studies. In some studies, different active tasks have been compared; in others, certain tasks were contrasted with a base-line condition. Potential confounding factors, such as eye movements, oral responses, and manual responses, have been dealt with in various ways or not at all. Electrode sites have been chosen on the basis of different placement systems, and different choices have been made from within standard systems. The EEG signal may contain all components capable of being amplified by the amplifier or filters may be used to pass only certain frequencies. When filtering is used, the width of the passband varies, as does the center frequency to be passed. The time period over which EEG is sampled may vary from study to study. As we will see, the wide assortment of choices has contributed substantially to the difficulty of interpreting divergent outcomes. Before outlining the common methodological problems, however, we will briefly summarize the findings with respect to cerebral lateralization.

A Summary of EEG findings

Spontaneous EEG recorded from homologous sites over the left and right hemispheres of normal people is similar (Adrian & Matthews, 1934) but not identical (Hoovey, Heinemann, & Creutzfeldt, 1972; Remond, Lesevre, Joseph, Rieger, & Lairy, 1969). There is some evidence that interhemispheric differences in amplitude and phase can be predicted on the basis of the person's handedness or other laterality characteristics (Cornil & Gastaut, 1947; Giannitrapani, Darrow, & Sorkin, 1964; Raney, 1939). However, amplitude differences between dominant and nondominant hemispheres are not found consistently (see Aird & Gastaut, 1959; Glanville & Antonitis, 1955; Lindsley, 1940; Provins & Cunliffe, 1972) and phase differences seem to depend on some combination of subject and task variables that is not well understood (Donchin et al., 1977).

It is not clear why electrical activity over the dominant hemisphere should differ from that over the nondominant hemisphere when the subject is relaxed during a base-line condition (Butler & Glass, 1974). But a stronger case can be made for predicting that EEG power will decrease over the hemisphere that is utilized primarily in performing a task or that the right-left power ratio will change as a function of the degree to which the task requires processing by the left and right hemispheres. One need not hypothesize that normal human beings alternate between left- and right-hemispheric modes of thinking (Galin & Ornstein, 1972); even continuous collaboration between the hemispheres would result in EEG imbalances if it is assumed that one hemisphere is more highly activated than the other at any instant. Since 1970, several groups of investigators have reported task-related shifts in EEG power between the left and right sides of the scalp (Butler & Glass, 1974; Doyle et al., 1974; Dumas & Morgan, 1975; Galin & Ornstein, 1972; Harmon & Ray, 1977; McKee, Humphrey, & McAdam, 1973; Morgan, MacDonald, & Hilgard, 1974; Morgan et al., 1971; Osborne & Gale, 1976; Warren, Peltz, & Haueter, 1976). These studies are heterogeneous with respect to the putative left- and right-hemispheric tasks used, electrode placement, EEG frequencies being amplified, adequacy of the experimental design, and method of analyzing the data. Nevertheless, most of the studies do succeed in showing that tasks selected as left- or right-hemispheric tasks on a priori grounds may produce a lateral shift in relative EEG power that is in the direction predicted. Interpretation of these results is limited by the diversity of the studies; one can conclude only that right-left power ratios and laterality indices do vary as a function of task and that the direction of change is usually in accord with that predicted from a differential hemispheric utilization model. As Donchin et al. (1977) point out, however, the data do not substantiate the conclusion that EEG is selectively suppressed in the hemisphere that is dominant for a particular task. The use of right-left ratios and difference ratios obscures the picture: "It is not possible to tell if a ratio has been modified by changing the numerator, the denominator, or both when only the ratio figure is presented" (Donchin et al., 1977, p. 345).

Certain subject variables, such as age, sex, occupation, and experience with a particular category of stimulus, seem to influence task-related EEG asymmetries (e.g., see Davidson & Schwartz, 1977; Doktor & Bloom, 1977; Dumas & Morgan, 1975; McLeod & Peacock, 1977; Morgan et al., 1971, 1974; Tucker, 1976). At least, it is clear that task effects vary considerably among subjects and that group averages do not reflect the data of all subjects within the group. Moreover, it appears that some measures of individual differences in task-related EEG asymmetry are stable over time (Amochaev & Salamy, 1979; Ehrlichman & Wiener, 1979). From these findings, we learn that it is often impossible to predict an individual subject's pattern of task-related asymmetry on the basis of the tasks themselves.

In a study of EEG asymmetries in infants (Gardiner & Walter, 1977), four 6-month-old infants heard several brief presentations of speech and music respectively; EEG recordings were chosen from times when the infants appeared to be attending to the auditory stimulus. Data analysis yielded laterality indices for different placement sites (primarily parietal and posterior temporal) and different frequency bands. Although the findings differed across sites and frequency bands, the most striking and consistent findings showed relatively low power on the left side during speech epochs and relatively low power on the right side during music epochs. Gardiner and Walter suggested that the task-related EEG shifts in their infants were equivalent to those reported in adults. The differences reported by Gardiner and Walter are clearest in the frequency band centered at 4 Hz and not at adult alpha frequency. The authors suggested that these shifts at 4 Hz are homologous to alpha-band shifts in adults, and this is plausible but remains to be proven.

Davidson & Fox (1982) measured EEG desynchronization (indicating activation of underlying brain) in 10-month-old infants while they viewed an actress looking either happy or sad. They found more left- than right-frontal desynchronization with the happy face and more left-frontal desynchronization with the happy than the sad face. These findings support the claim that the left and right sides of the brain are differentially specialized early in life for positive and negative affect respectively.

Evoked-Potential Studies

In turning from spontaneous EEG to evoked potentials, we will begin by noting that numerous investigations of early components—those that Donchin et al. (1977) label as exogenous—fail to reach a consensus with respect to lateralization. The most frequent finding, irrespective of stimulus modality, is that left-sided stimulation and right-sided stimulation do produce different distributions of evoked potentials. Often, as would be expected, stimulation of one side of the body elicits responses of greater amplitude or shorter latency on the opposite side of the scalp (e.g., see Butler et al., 1969; Calmes & Cracco, 1971). However, even these early components are subject to modulation by attentional or cognitive factors (Ledlow, Swanson, & Kinsbourne, 1978a, 1978b). Perhaps for this reason, the findings are not consistent across studies and become less consistent when left- versus right-hemispheric differences as well as when ipsilateral versus contralateral effects are considered (cf. Harmony et al., 1973; Peronnet et al., 1974; Peters & Mendel, 1974; Rhodes et al., 1975; Vaughan & Ritter, 1970). It is one matter to state that contralateral responses are larger or faster than ipsilateral responses irrespective of hemisphere but quite a different matter to state that left-hemispheric responses are different from right-hemispheric responses. For instance, higher amplitude left-hemispheric responses result from auditory stimulation at the right ear than at the left ear and vice versa (Andreassi et al., 1975; Butler et al., 1969; Peronnet et al., 1974; Vaughan & Ritter, 1970), but it is difficult to specify whether right- or left-ear stimulation elicits the more asymmetric scalp responses (cf. Peronnet et al., 1974; Peters & Mendel, 1974; Ruhm, 1971; Vaughan & Ritter, 1970). The laterality of exogenous evoked potentials may vary as a function of individual-difference factors, such as handedness, eye preference, and sex (Culver, Tanley, & Eason, 1970), but it is unlikely that the role of such factors can be specified until stimulus factors affecting the early components of the evoked potential are better understood.

Perhaps the primary implication of the early-components data, with their inconsistencies and contradictions, pertains to studies of perceptual asymmetry, a topic to be discussed later in this section. From a structural perspective, in which perceptual asymmetries are attributed to the fixed conduction properties of specific pathways from receptor organ to cortex, it is disturbing that the early components of the evoked potential exhibit so much variability and inconsistency from one study to the next and perhaps from one person to the next.

Following Donchin et al. (1977), the later components of the evoked potential—the endogenous components—may be divided into those that precede the stimulus and those that follow the stimulus. Prestimulus potentials related to voluntary limb movement serve to validate the evoked-potential methodology as an index of localized brain activity. For example, it has been shown that the slow negative shift preceding movement of the hand and arm is greater in amplitude on the side of the scalp contralateral to the responding limb (Gilden, Vaughan, & Costa, 1966; Kutas & Donchin, 1974; Vaughan, Costa, & Ritter, 1968). The contingent negative variation, or expectancy wave (Walter et al., 1964), occurs when a first, or conditional, signal is followed by a second, or imperative, signal, which typically requires a manual response, such as a button press (J. Cohen, 1969). The slow negative shift seen between signals usually has greatest amplitude when recorded from the midline (vertex), and it initially was thought that the response was symmetrical along the transverse axis of the head (J. Cohen, 1969; Low, Borda, Frost, & Kellaway, 1966). Subsequently, slight asymmetries favoring the side contralateral to the responding hand have been reported (Otto & Leifer, 1973; Syndulko, 1969, 1972). It seems plausible to conclude that the contingent negative variation reflects an asymmetric component associated with the manual response in addition to a symmetric component associated with the cognitive aspect of the task (Donchin, Kutas, & McCarthy, 1974; Gazzaniga & Hillyard, 1973).

Even if the cognitive components of manual-response anticipation are not lateralized, the neural activity associated with speech preparation may be greater over the left side than over the right side. McAdam and Whitaker (1971) reported a negative potential shift over the left but not the right frontal region as normal subjects were about to speak. Nonverbal oral movements were not preceded by this asymmetric shift. Similarly, Low, Wada, and Fox (1976) found greater amplitude of contingent negative variation over the left hemisphere than over the right hemisphere prior to speech in patients in whom this electrophysiological asymmetry was correlated with speech dominance as ascertained by sodium amobarbital testing. Although these data provide encouragement for investigators who seek to find an orderly relationship between event-related electrophysiological asymmetry and other measures of hemispheric specialization, the evidence is far from conclusive. Of particular concern is the contamination of evoked potentials by eye-movement artifacts (cf. Anderson, 1977; Grözinger, Kornhuber, & Kriebel, 1975; Morrell & Huntington, 1971).

Considerable attention has been devoted to the potentials that follow presentation of linguistic and nonlinguistic stimuli in both the visual and the auditory modality, that is, to potentials associated with perception. Data from studies of auditory perception are particularly interesting insofar as the technique can be applied to infants as well as to older children and adults (e.g., see Molfese, Freeman, & Palermo, 1975). Different stimuli and tasks sometimes have unequal effects on auditory evoked responses from the left and right sides of the scalp in adults, and many of the findings imply that language is processed primarily in the left hemisphere. As seems to be the case with all varieties of electrophysiological laterality studies, however, the auditory studies considered collectively are not sufficiently systematic to permit stronger inferences about hemispheric specialization. In the literature dealing with auditory stimulation, the stimuli include clicks (e.g., Cohn, 1971; Neville, 1974), nonsense words (e.g., Morrell & Salamy, 1971), real words (e.g., Matsumiya, Tagliasco, Lombroso, & Goodglass, 1972), a musical chord (Molfese et al., 1975), and noise (Molfese et al., 1975). Stimuli usually are presented binaurally, but they may be presented in dichotic competition (Neville, 1974). Moreover, there is variability in the responses being recorded, which range from waves with latency of only a few milliseconds to P300, which occurs about 300 msec after stimulus presentation (Friedman et al., 1975). In all likelihood, different waves reflect different combinations of acoustic, phonetic, phonemic, semantic, and perhaps nonlinguistic cognitive processes. Additionally, under some circumstances, the later components may be confounded by motor processes (Wood, Goff, & Day, 1971).

Despite the heterogeneity of variables represented in investigations of auditory evoked potentials, two conclusions may be drawn. One is that linguistic and nonlinguistic stimuli often elicit responses that differ in predictable ways. Thus, verbal stimuli but not nonverbal stimuli may produce lateral differences in the evoked response (Hillyard & Woods, 1979; Neville, 1974), or verbal stimuli may produce asymmetries favoring one side and nonverbal stimuli may produce asymmetries favoring the opposite side (Cohn, 1971; Molfese et al., 1975). Other investigators, however, have reported little or no difference with respect to laterality between responses elicited by verbal stimuli and those elicited by nonverbal stimuli (Friedman et al., 1975; Galambos et al., 1975; Roth, Kopell, & Bertozzi, 1970). When differential effects are seen, one cannot be sure that they are attributable to the verbal versus nonverbal distinction or to some associated difference between categories of stimuli (Matsumiya et al., 1972). The second and more compelling claim is that a given stimulus may elicit different lateral distributions of scalp potentials depending on the way in which the stimulus is processed. Wood et al. (1971) reported that the amplitude of a medium latency wave (100 to 200 msec) over the left hemisphere depended on whether the subject was required to discriminate among the consonant stimuli on a linguistic or an acoustic basis. Teyler, Harrison, Roemer, and Thompson (1973) and Brown, Marsh, and Smith (1973) both showed that left-hemispheric evoked potentials varied as the meaning of the stimuli was changed by manipulating the context in which the stimuli was heard.

Studies of relatively late potentials evoked by visual stimulation have generated a smaller but equally diverse set of findings. Buchsbaum and Fedio (1969) reported that three-letter words elicited responses that could be differentiated from responses to both random dot patterns and designs composed from dots. Although the authors claimed that the waveforms for verbal and nonverbal stimuli differed more on the left side than on the right side, this finding was not consistent either across time or across classes of stimuli. In addition, responses to words were more similar between hemispheres than those elicited by the nonverbal stimuli. A subsequent investigation (Buchsbaum & Fedio, 1970), in which stimuli were presented to the left or right visual half field, yielded similar findings. Shelburne (1972) failed to find any consistent differences in amplitude or latency of waveforms associated with three-letter words and nonsense syllables that were presented in a sequential, letter-by-letter fashion. Galin and Ellis (1975) averaged the potentials elicited by flashing lights as subjects performed either a writing task or a block-construction task. They found that the left versus right distribution of evoked-potential power and amplitude varied with cognitive task. A shift toward one hemisphere in evoked-potential power and amplitude corresponded to a similar shift in alpha power (although high evoked-potential amplitude and low alpha power are usually taken to be concomitant indicators of attention or effort). In any event Mayes and Beaumont (1977) could not duplicate these findings.

Molfese and his colleagues have reported striking stimulus-dependent asymmetries in the auditory evoked potentials of infants as well as in older children and adults. In their early studies (Molfese, 1973; Molfese et al., 1975), adults, children, and infants ranging in age from 1 month to 10 months heard three kinds of sounds, namely, CV syllables, words, and mechanical sounds (a piano chord and a noise burst). Amplitude was measured from the largest negative component to the following positive peak. Although the latencies of these landmarks varied markedly as a function of age group, the asymmetries were similar across the three groups. The evoked response to speech stimuli was larger over the left temporal region than over the right, and the evoked response to mechanically produced stimuli was larger over the right temporal region than over the left. For the CV syllables and mechanical stimuli, the degree of asymmetry decreased with increasing age. It subsequently was found that amplitude differences between hemispheres in response to synthesized speech stimuli depend on an acoustic factor (band width) but not on any of several properties usually considered to be phonetic, namely, presence or absence of the initial transition that distinguishes CV syllables from steady-state vowel sounds, changes in voicing within phoneme categories, changes in voicing across phoneme categories, and change in place of articulation with voicing held constant. An initial application of multivariate analytic techniques failed to show any laterality effects for either acoustic or phonetic cues (Molfese, Nunez, Seibert, & Ramanaiah, 1976), but more recent work of this nature (Molfese & Molfese, 1979, 1980) has shown that one or more orthogonal factors in the evoked-response patterns of neonates and even preterm infants are strongly lateralized. The findings suggest the presence of a uniquely left-hemispheric process that discriminates between different phonetic transitions in stimuli with the formant structure of speech but not in stimuli with sine-wave formant structure. This work suggests early hemispheric specialization for analysis of speech-specific acoustic cues, although the mechanism in infants does not appear to be identical to that in adults (Molfese, 1978).

The disparity between the infant and adult data with respect to factors that influence auditory evoked potential asymmetry is but one of several reasons for using caution in interpreting the infant findings. Molfese et al. (1976) describe a study in which cats showed asymmetrical responses over the insular temporal cortex but not over the primary auditory or visual cortex after presentation of both broad- and narrow-band acoustic signals. Thus, the presence of asymmetric components in the auditory evoked response need not be a precursor of linguistic competency. In humans, asymmetric responses to simple repetitive visual stimuli (the right hemisphere being more responsive than the left hemisphere) seem to reflect nervous system immaturity (Crowell, Jones, Kapuniai, & Nakagawa, 1973; Crowell, Kapuniai, & Garbanati, 1977). At least, these asymmetries are known to decrease with increasing age to the point that bilaterality is the most common finding with adults. This asymmetry of the infant evoked response has been attributed not to early specialization of the right hemisphere but to late functional development of the interhemispheric commissures (Crowell et al., 1973). Interpretation of infant asymmetries in terms of hemispheric specialization for linguistic and nonlinguistic processes is further complicated by the experiments of Davis and Wada (1977, 1978). In infants as well as normal adults, Davis and Wada found greater left- than right-sided evoked responses to clicks and greater right- than left-sided responses to brief flashes of light. The differential response patterns were ascribed to differences between stimuli in degree of structure, that is, the clicks provide highly structured auditory information but the flashes provide unstructured information. On the basis of their own data and other evidence, Davis and Wada (Davis & Wada, 1977, 1978; Wada, 1977; Wada & Davis, 1977) speculate that the left hemisphere is specialized for processing stimuli that can be identified easily or related readily to past experience. Such identification or referential processing is claimed to be independent of language and may develop prior to language. The right hemisphere, according to this argument, processes stimuli that are not readily referable to past experience.

Thus, there is reason to suspect that the very early electrophysiological asymmetries elicited by linguistic stimuli are independent of language processing per se. We would even argue that these asymmetries do not reflect information processing of any kind. Instead we suggest that the neonatal brain is preprogrammed so that one side becomes more activated than the other in response to stimuli with certain physical properties (Kinsbourne & Hiscock, 1977). According to this explanation, the brainstem generates a material-specific activation pattern long before the neuronal equipment of the association areas is sufficiently mature to process the incoming information. If sounds with certain acoustic characteristics elicit responses from the left brain that are not found over the right brain, (e.g., see Molfese & Molfese, 1979), that fact need not imply that the newborn infant's left brain already is processing such sounds differently from the right brain or that the left brain is attuned to acoustic cues that are overlooked by the right brain. The asymmetric component or components of the evoked potential may indicate only that the left half of the brain is being activated by the brainstem in a manner qualitatively or quantitatively different from the way in which the right half of the brain is being activated. The left brain is receiving electrical stimulation that has no functional significance at the time but will have great importance when cortically based linguistic skills begin to develop. Then, the material-specific activation pattern will ensure that the cerebral hemisphere specialized for processing a particular variety of stimulus material will be activated when that material is being presented. We will return to this topic when discussing the ontogeny of hemispheric specialization because it appears that material-specific asymmetries of activation are the precursors of the information processing asymmetries that characterize the brain at a subsequent stage of development.

Methodological and Interpretive Problems

In summarizing the EEG and evoked-potential literature, we have emphasized problems associated with the unsystematic diversity among studies. These problems can be resolved only with additional studies to fill present gaps in our knowledge and especially to vary stimulus and task factors parametrically. Additional studies will clarify issues, however, only if they are well designed and only if they avoid certain methodological pitfalls described below.

As Donchin et al. (1977) point out, differences between left- and right-side scalp potentials tend to be subtle. Moreover, there is a great deal of variability from one person to the next. These two characteristics—differences of small magnitude and large intersubject variability—impose constraints on the design of electrophysiological laterality studies. Between-group comparisons are insensitive to true task-dependent effects if there is a high level of variability within groups. Consequently, repeated-measure (within-subject) designs are preferable, although such designs often require careful counterbalancing to avoid contamination of results from habituation, practice effects, and carry-over of strategy from one task to the next.

When effects are weak, statistical power (J. Cohen, 1977) must be relatively great if true effects are to be detected with any regularity. Statistical power is increased by increasing the sample size, but the nature of electrophysiological research is such that the number of subjects who can be tested is limited. Negative findings are uninterpretable if the statistical power of the F test is so low that the probability of detecting a weak effect is markedly less than unity. On the other hand, experiments with small sample sizes are susceptible to spurious findings owing to sampling error. If a substantial minority of the population shows a stable but deviant pattern of task-dependent scalp activity (Amochaev & Salamy, 1979; Ehrlichman & Wiener, 1979), a fortuitous overrepresentation of that minority in a small sample will lead to irreproducible results.

Developmental studies are especially difficult to design and interpret because scalp potential patterns change substantially between infancy and adulthood. In the realm that Donchin et al. (1977) term the frequency domain, it is EEG frequency that changes (Gardiner & Walter, 1977); in the time domain, it is primarily the latency of the waveforms that changes (Molfese et al., 1975). In both cases, the differences between infancy and adulthood are dramatic. Insofar as these differences are age dependent and not individual differences, replacing cross-sectional designs with longitudinal designs will not solve the problem. Comparability between EEG measures in subjects from different age groups cannot be assured until the neurophysiological basis of various electrocortical phenomena is known. Without such knowledge, we must consider any statements about laterality changes (or constancy) across age classification to be tentative rather than definitive.

Irrespective of whether spontaneous EEG or AEPs are being recorded, the laterality experiment usually investigates task-dependent differences between the left and right sides. Given asymmetric patterns for a linguistic task for instance (e.g., see Morrell & Salamy, 1971), little can be learned in the absence of a control condition, especially because very simple, meaningless stimuli also elicit asymmetric scalp potentials (Thatcher, 1977). The use of a base-line condition, a time-honored practice in electrophysiological research, is of dubious value in the study of phenomena related to higher mental activity because no one knows what cognitive activity subjects are using to entertain themselves during this so-called base-line condition. A similar criticism can be directed at tasks that entail no observable behavior. A more satisfactory alternative involves choosing tasks on which subjects make overt, scorable responses and then analyzing performance as well as the electrophysiological data. Two studies by Ledlow, Swanson, & Kinsbourne (1978, 1981) illustrate the successful use of reaction time and evoked-potential measures concurrently within the same laterality experiment. Even when experiments avoid the common pitfalls of task selection, they may nevertheless be unsatisfactory because the respective tasks or stimuli are too dissimilar. A good example of this problem, as cited by Friedman et al. (1975), is the Cohn (1971) experiment in which auditory potentials to clicks and words were contrasted. The differential laterality effects in this experiment are difficult to interpret because the stimuli are so different in their physical characteristics. The lateralized early component might be attributable to differences between kinds of stimuli in any of several acoustic properties. The information gained from comparing stimuli increases as the differences between stimuli decrease. Molfese's recent work (e.g., see Molfese & Molfese, 1979) illustrates that laterality effects in the evoked potential may vary as a specific acoustic cue is altered while other physical parameters are held constant. Another powerful technique entails manipulation of a signal's significance or meaning to the subject, perhaps through contextual changes, while the physical properties of the signal are held constant (e.g., see Brown et al., 1973; Teyler et al., 1973; Wood et al., 1971).

Failure to consider two additional stimulus and task factors may lead to spurious negative results (Donchin et al., 1977). First, the task must in fact require differential processing by the two cerebral hemispheres. It must either engage one hemisphere to a greater degree than the other or it must require a different kind of processing in one hemisphere than in the other. When stimuli or tasks are chosen merely on their face validity as left-hemisphere or right-hemisphere stimuli or tasks, the significance of a failure to find the expected electrophysiological asymmetry is unclear. If lateralized processing cannot be validated by concurrent behavioral measurement (e.g., see Ledlow et al., 1978, 1981), then investigators should at least strive to use tasks known to yield stable behavioral asymmetries or tasks whose lateralization is well documented in the clinical literature. A less obvious task factor is the level at which the independent variable is applied (Donchin et al., 1977). As in behavioral studies, a stimulus or task manipulation may exert influence at one range of values but not at others; thus, asymmetries may fail to materialize if the task is outside that range, for example, if the stimulus is too bright or too dim or if the task is too easy or too difficult. Kutas and Donchin (1974) have shown that forceful motor responses generate a lateralized motor potential, even though movements with much less muscular involvement do not (Donchin, Kutas, & Johnson, 1974). Donchin et al. (1977) report asymmetry of the contingent negative variation for only a relatively difficult cognitive task, although the design did not permit the effects of difficulty to be isolated from the effects of concomitant factors.

Much of the variability in the results of EEG and evoked-potential studies can be attributed to subject variables of two kinds. Group differences, especially differences between right- and left-handers, account for some of the variability, even though it is impossible to specify on an a priori basis the importance of these differences in any given experiment. Other subject variables are true individual differences, which cannot be attributed to the traditional group classifications or perhaps to any group variable (Amochaev & Salamy, 1979; Ehrlichman & Wiener, 1979). Insofar as scalp potentials provide a relatively direct measure of underlying brain activity, seemingly anomalous but consistent patterns in certain people deserve close inspection.

Switching from independent to dependent variables, we first note that the recording montage itself may be a source of ambiguity, even when electrode placement conforms to usual standards (Jasper, 1958). Friedman et al. (1975) point out two evoked-potential studies in which bipolar recordings were made from pairs of electrode sites on the left and on the right sides of the scalp. In this case, a larger response on one side indicates a greater potential difference between the two points on that side relative to the corresponding two points on the opposite side, but it fails to provide definitive information about potential differences on either side relative to midline. Other suboptimal recording configurations are commonplace in studies of EEG and evoked-potential asymmetries (Donchin et al., 1977).

Both spontaneous EEG and evoked potentials are rich sources of data that require selection of manageable subsets for analysis or other means of simplifying the data set. Under these circumstances, false positives and false negatives are both likely. True asymmetries may be overlooked because attention is focused on the wrong components or spurious asymmetries may be found as a consequence of making a large number of comparisons (Friedman et al., 1975). These problems are most evident when multiple univariate tests are used. The univariate approach is conceptually straightforward and findings often lend themselves to fairly straightforward interpretation. However, univariate analyses may not be sufficiently comprehensive or systematic to ensure that subtle features of the data are discovered. Thus, univariate analyses are most appropriate under circumstances in which critical features of the waveform have been established through previous research, that is, when the investigator knows what to look for and where to find it. Multivariate techniques, such as principal-components analysis, provide a means of overcoming many of the problems inherent in analysis of complex data sets (Chapman, 1973; Donchin, 1969). In principal-components analysis, the complex matrix of values in the waveform is decomposed into the relatively small number of orthogonal dimensions that most economically account for the maximal amount of variance. Factor scores may then be computed for each subject, and univariate analyses of variance may then be performed on the factor scores to evaluate the effect on each factor of the independent variables, such as left versus right hemisphere (e.g., see Molfese & Molfese, 1979). Even though the arguments in favor of multivariate analysis of evoked-potential data are persuasive, this approach is not without its difficulties. First, there are numerous possible analytic techniques, and different techniques may very well lead to disparate results. When the latency of evoked-potential components is shifted by an independent variable, additional factors that provide no information about the morphology of the waveform are needed to account for the latency shift (Donchin, 1969). Similar studies may yield discrepant factor structures (cf. Molfese & Molfese, 1979, 1980), which makes it difficult to compare the results. Perhaps the fundamental problem with multivariate techniques is that they replace biological phenomena with abstract, mathematical entities called factors or dimensions. Consequently, the unique directness of EEG techniques is compromised and the results may become difficult to interpret with reference to brain activity. Donchin's (1969) comment about a particular technique—discriminant analysis—would seem to apply to multivariate techniques in general: "While the analysis can provide more information, it cannot assure that any deeper insights will be obtained from the data" (p. 216).

Conclusions

The promise and the problems of electrophysiological methods for studying cerebral lateralization are equally impressive. The state of the art is expressed well in two sentences by Thatcher (1977): "The fact that left-right AEP asymmetries have been observed is indisputable. However, their functional significance is currently poorly understood" (p. 429). These conclusions could be applied to spontaneous EEG as well as to evoked potentials. A recurrent theme in our discussion of EEG and evoked-potential research is that more experiments are needed and that the studies must be more carefully designed than most of those published in the past. It is especially important that stimulus and task factors be controlled to the point that asymmetries in the scalp potential can be attributed unambiguously to a specific, circumscribed difference between two stimuli or two tasks.

A few tentative conclusions may be based on the currently available data. With respect to evoked potentials, it appears that asymmetries in the medium and late components, which are associated with cognitive processing, are more reliable across studies than asymmetries in the early components. Several findings—from studies of spontaneous EEG as well as from those using evoked potentials—suggest that the more verbal or linguistic of two tasks or stimuli activates the left hemisphere more than the right hemisphere. The findings are especially impressive in a small number of experiments in which the nature of the task is manipulated without concomitant changes in the stimuli or responses. Individual variation in electrophysiological laterality is surprisingly great, and some of the variation seems to represent fairly robust and stable patterns. Although there are pronounced developmental changes in spontaneous EEG and evoked potentials alike, asymmetries resembling those obtained or expected in adults have been observed repeatedly in infants and children. We speculate that the asymmetries in infants reflect an innately programmed brainstem activation mechanism that responds differentially according to the physical properties of the stimulus.

Behavioral Asymmetries

Although certain perceptual asymmetries were described three decades earlier (Crosland, 1931; Glanville & Dallenbach, 1929), it was not until 1961 that perceptual asymmetries in normal adults were linked to cerebral lateralization (Kimura, 1961a, 1961b). Kimura administered Broadbent's (1954) dichotic-listening task to adults with known left- or right-hemispheric speech representation and found that more digits were reported from the ear contralateral to the hemisphere dominant for speech than from the ipsilateral ear. Cerebral dominance had been considered—and rejected (Mishkin & Forgays, 1952)—as an explanation for asymmetries in visual perception. However, subsequent to Kimura's (1961a, 1961b) demonstration of the relationship between listening asymmetry and speech lateralization, asymmetries in the visual modality commonly have been attributed to hemispheric specialization (Kimura, 1966). Most perceptual asymmetry studies have focused on the auditory and visual modalities, although tactile asymmetries also have been ascribed to cerebral lateralization (e.g., see Rudel et al., 1974; Wagner & Harris, 1979; Witelson, 1974). A recent trend is increased attention to hemispheric priming, the alteration of perceptual asymmetries through manipulation of a prior or concurrent task (e.g., see Hellige & Cox, 1976; Kinsbourne, 1970a, 1973b). Also recently developed are competition tasks that may be used to study the laterality of speech production as well as that of speech reception and cognitive activity (e.g., see Kinsbourne & Cook, 1971; Kinsbourne & McMurray, 1975). The subject performs an activity, such as oral recitation, at the same time as an attention-demanding unimanual task. In right-handers, speech interferes disproportionately with right-hand performance, presumably because the functional distance between the cerebral regions for speech and right-hand control is less than that between the regions for speech and left-hand control (Kinsbourne & Hicks, 1978a, 1978b). Still another putative index of cerebral lateralization is lateral eye movement (Bakan, 1969; Day, 1964). It has been claimed that lateral gaze shifts during deliberation reflect asymmetric activation of the left and right hemispheres. Presumably, the asymmetric activation associated with lateralized cognitive processing overflows into the homolateral frontal eye field thus eliciting an aversive deviation of gaze (Kinsbourne, 1972, 1974b).

The availability of noninvasive measures of cerebral lateralization engendered many studies during the 1960s and 1970s. It seemed likely that information derived from normal children and adults would complement the clinical data accumulated over a period of several decades. However, payoff from the new noninvasive techniques has yet to fulfill early expectations. After two decades of intensive research into perceptual asymmetries, it seems that no major issue concerning hemispheric specialization has been resolved as a result of laterality studies (Kinsbourne, 1978b; Kinsbourne & Hiscock, 1978; Satz, 1976; Studdert-Kennedy, 1975; White, 1969b, 1972). Instead, these studies are revealing the complex and multifaceted nature of behavioral asymmetries. Consider, for example, dichotic listening, the most widely studied of the perceptual techniques. Even though most normal adults and children do show a right-ear superiority for dichotically presented linguistic stimuli, the incidence of right-ear superiority usually fails to approximate the incidence of left-lateralized speech as inferred from clinical evidence (Berlin & Cullen, 1977; Kinsbourne & Hiscock, 1977; Satz, 1977). The retest reliability of the ear-difference score is lower than one would expect of an index of some fixed property of the nervous system (Berlin & Cullen, 1977; Blumstein, Goodglass, & Tartter, 1975). Ear asymmetry is susceptible to influence from several nonphysiological factors, for example, the context in which the stimuli are heard (Spellacy & Blumstein, 1970), the person's previous experience with the stimulus material (Bever & Chiarello, 1974; Johnson, 1977; Papcun, Krashen, Terbeek, Remington, & Harshman, 1974; Van Lancker & Fromkin, 1977), and diverse attentional and strategic factors (Bryden, 1978b; Goldstein & Lackner, 1974; Hiscock, Hampson, Wong, & Kinsbourne, 1981; Hiscock & Kinsbourne, 1980a; Hiscock, Kinsbourne, Caplan, & Swanson, 1979; Milberg, Whitman, Rourke, & Glaros, 1981). The concept of ear asymmetry may itself be misleading insofar as the asymmetry is related to the spatial location of the sound source rather than the ear of entry (Morais & Bertelson, 1975).

In this section, we describe techniques for eliciting perceptual asymmetries in the auditory, visual, and tactile modalities as well as methods for studying hemispheric priming, dual-task interference, and lateral eye movements. We specify the variables that account for discrepancies from study to study. The shortcomings of laterality techniques may be explained in different ways, but it seems parsimonious to conclude that each of these techniques is influenced by factors other than functional specialization of the cerebral hemispheres. Except in regard to the visual modality, researchers have devoted relatively little attention to factors other than hemispheric asymmetry that might contribute to behavioral asymmetries. Consequently, these factors are not well understood and discrepant results that might be attributed to these extraneous factors remain unexplained.

Consideration of anomalies and extraneous factors in perceptual laterality can lead to one of two outcomes, both of which are desirable. One possibility is that various nonstructural factors will be identified and understood sufficiently well so that they may be controlled. With these factors neutralized, perceptual asymmetries should constitute a valid index of cerebral lateralization. Alternatively, the nonstructural factors themselves may turn out to be due to hemispheric specialization (Kinsbourne, 1970a, 1973b, 1974b, 1975). Attentional biases, response sets, expectancies, and context may alter perceptual asymmetry to the extent that they influence the relative activation of the left and right halves of the brain. If this is true, then further investigation of these factors should lead to a more adequate understanding of cerebral functioning in general and hemispheric specialization in particular.

Auditory Asymmetries

In dichotic listening, competing messages are delivered to the respective ears by means of stereophonic headphones. Typically, the subject reports the messages irrespective of ear of entry. A right-ear superiority for linguistic stimuli, such as strings of digit names, usually is assumed to reflect (1) functional prepotency of the contralateral ear-to-cortex pathway relative to the ipsilateral pathway (Kimura, 1967) and, therefore, (2) left-hemispheric specialization for the perception of linguistic material. Kimura (1967) suggested that, at some point of overlap, the contralateral pathways occlude impulses from the ipsilateral pathways. However, ear asymmetry can be obtained with monaural stimulation (e.g., see Bakker, 1967, 1968, 1969, 1970; Bever, 1971; Haydon & Spellacy, 1974; Morais & Bertelson, 1973; Morais & Darwin, 1974; Provins & Jeeves, 1975; Simon, 1967). Therefore, occlusion is not necessary to elicit listening asymmetry. Possibly, the contralateral pathways are more efficient than the ipsilateral pathways, perhaps because of a slight difference in the number of fibers (Rosenzweig, 1951). Individual variation in degree of ear asymmetry could then be ascribed to variation in the relative efficiency of the input channels (Teng, 1981). Alternatively, ear asymmetry may be independent of any difference in the conduction properties of crossed and uncrossed pathways (or any other structural asymmetry). Studies of perceptual asymmetries in callosally sectioned subjects suggest that at any time one hemisphere may be in control, its influence being mediated to the other side by brainstem centers (H. W. Gordon, 1980; Kinsbourne, 1974c; Levy & Trevarthen, 1976; Trevarthen, 1974). Listening asymmetry in intact people may be a specific manifestation of a more general tendency to shift attention to the side of space opposite to the more highly activated cerebral hemisphere (Kinsbourne, 1970a, 1973b, 1974b, 1975). An expectancy for verbal material, for instance, may be associated with activation of the left hemisphere and the asymmetry of activation may shift attention toward the right side of space. The orientational model of listening asymmetry relates ear differences to the spatial location of the sound source rather than to the ear at which the sound is heard (as validated by Morais & Bertelson, 1975).

For whatever reason, dichotic presentation of verbal material yields an overall REA in samples of normal adults; nonverbal material, such as music and environmental sounds usually (although less constantly), yields a LEA (e.g., see Blumstein et al., 1975; Curry, 1967; Kimura, 1964; Spellacy & Blumstein, 1970). However, the incidence of right-ear superiority falls well short of that expected on the basis of aphasia and sodium amobarbital studies (Rasmussen & Milner, 1975; Zangwill, 1967). The discrepancy in incidence is sufficient to invalidate dichotic listening as a noninvasive means of assessing speech lateralization in normal children and adults. If 95% of the general population has speech represented in the left hemisphere and if 70% of people sampled from that population show a REA, then a Bayesian analysis can be used to evaluate the likelihood that different conclusions about individuals' speech lateralization will be correct. Satz (1977) calculated that, given the specified conditions, there is a .97 probability that subjects who show a REA will have left-lateralized speech. However, the probability of left-lateralized speech is .90 even for those people who show a LEA. If we infer anomalous speech representation on the basis of a LEA, we will be wrong 9 times out of 10.

Beyond its shortcomings in determining language representation in an individual, in any between-group comparison the low predictive power of dichotic listening is likely to result in erroneous and inconsistent findings. When dichotic techniques are used to compare normal and learning-disabled children, outcomes are diverse (Satz, 1976). If only learning-disabled children's asymmetry varied from study to study, we might suspect sampling error as the source of the variability. However, normal subjects as well show significant group right-ear superiority in some studies but not in others, and considerable individual variability (Bakker, Vander Vlugt, & Claushuis, 1978; Berlin, 1977; Blumstein, Goodglass, & Tartter, 1975; Pizzamiglio, De Pascalis, & Vignait, 1976; Ryan & McNeil, 1974; Schulman-Galambos, 1977; Shankweiler & Studdert-Kennedy, 1975; Teng, 1981). Consequently, methodological differences must account for the heterogeneous results. Methodological factors might also explain inconsistent age trends in listening asymmetry (e.g., see Porter & Berlin, 1975; Satz, Bakker, Teunissen, Goebel, & Van der Vlugt, 1975). Some potentially important methodological variables will be discussed later.

Fundamental to dichotic listening are the physical (i.e., acoustic) properties of frequency, intensity, and time (Berlin & Lowe, 1972). These basic properties of sound determine the specifications of dichotic stimuli in terms of such variables as intensity level, band width, signal-to-noise ratio, and degree of asynchrony between competing signals. Acoustic differences between the left and right channels can enhance or diminish the REA for linguistic material (Berlin & Cullen, 1977; Berlin & McNeil, 1976), and the magnitude of ear asymmetry changes as the perceptual difficulty of the material is varied on both channels (Godfrey, 1974). Even the robust REA for CV nonsense syllables can be nullified (Berlin, Lowe-Bell, Cullen, Thompson, & Loovis, 1973) or reversed (Studdert-Kennedy, Shankweiler, & Schulman, 1970) if left-ear signals are made to lag behind right-ear signals by 20 or 30 msec.

Phonetic variables similarly can influence listening asymmetry (Studdert-Kennedy & Shankweiler,

1970). For example, unvoiced stop consonants (/p/, /k/, /t/) tend to override the corresponding voiced stop consonants (/b/, /g/, /d/) in dichotic competition (Berlin, Lowe-Bell, Cullen, Thompson, & Loovis, 1973; Gerber & Goldman, 1971; Lowe, Cullen, Berlin, Thompson, & Willett, 1970).

Acoustic and phonetic variables are especially critical when the objective is to understand central auditory deficits or to explore the mechanisms of speech perception. In these cases, the investigator must be able to manipulate certain aspects of the signal while controlling others. When the aim of research is the comparison of ear asymmetry among groups, less rigorous control over physical and phonetic factors may be acceptable, provided that there are no differences between left- and right-ear stimuli. A major advantage of dichotic listening, relative to techniques for studying visual laterality, is that the channels can be equated by simply reversing the headphones. Thus, even if the entire realm of physical and phonetic variables cannot be measured and controlled, it is possible to preclude any inherent differences between channels from biasing the ear-difference score. Nevertheless, even when the two channels are properly counterbalanced between ears, acoustic and phonetic factors may produce differences among subjects (if the counterbalancing is between subjects) and among different studies. For instance, if a dichotic task is made too difficult by degrading the signal-to-noise ratio or by precise matching of competing stimuli, a floor effect may obscure any ear asymmetry.

Insofar as ear asymmetry depends on the kind of stimulus material being heard, differences among studies may be attributable to stimulus type. One should not expect comparable degrees of asymmetry between two different studies simply because verbal stimuli are used in both. For example, CV nonsense syllables generate larger REAs than do either vowel sounds (Shankweiler & Studdert-Kennedy, 1967; Studdert-Kennedy & Shankweiler, 1970) or consonant-vowel-consonant (CVC) nonsense words (Caplan & Kinsbourne, 1981), and CV nonsense syllables and strings of digit names have produced conflicting results in young children (Porter & Berlin, 1975). With dichotic digit names, the limiting factor seems to be one's ability to organize and report the stimuli before they are lost from memory; in contrast, dichotic CV stimuli challenge one's perceptual ability. In other words, different kinds of stimulus material seem to tap different stages of speech perception (Porter & Berlin, 1975; Studdert-Kennedy, Shankweiler, & Pisoni, 1972).

Procedural variables also influence ear asymmetry. In most dichotic-listening studies, investigators have used a free-report procedure in which the subject is instructed to report as many stimuli as possible in any order. The free-report procedure confounds perceptual asymmetry with order-of-report factors (Bryden, 1967; Bryden & Allard, 1978; Inglis & Sykes, 1967). In most cases, order of report alone cannot account for ear differences (Bryden, 1967). Moreover, order-of-report biases may stem from perceptual asymmetries (Bryden, 1963, 1967). Nevertheless, the influence of response factors may under some circumstances be sufficient to impair the task as a measure of perceptual asymmetry (Freides, 1977). The response-bias problem is particularly important because the confounding of perceptual asymmetry and asymmetrical order of report appears to enhance the ear difference under some circumstances and to attenuate it under others. When the number of digit names presented during each trial approaches or exceeds the subject's memory span, adults tend to show an exaggerated REA (Hines & Satz, 1974). Adults presumably respond to the overload by reporting signals from the favored ear first, thus failing to retrieve many signals from the opposite ear. Young children, in contrast, seem to show a less consistent asymmetry under free-report instruction than when instructed to report signals selectively from one ear on each trial (Hiscock & Kinsbourne, 1980a; Hiscock et al., 1979; Satz et al., 1975). To complicate matters further, report strategies change as the presentation rate of stimuli is varied (Bryden, 1964, 1972; Witelson & Rabinovitch, 1971). Adults and children above the age of 9 years report dichotic stimuli in a channel-by-channel fashion if the presentation rate exceeds one pair per second; at slower rates, they switch to a pair-by-pair order of report. Consequently, the degree of bias introduced by a tendency to report signals from one ear first depends on the rate at which the signals are presented.

There are several alternative procedures for administering dichotic-listening tasks that avoid the ambiguities of the free-report methodology. In one study with 3-year-old children (Kinsbourne & Hiscock, 1977), a signal-detection paradigm was used to obtain a significant REA for digit names. Children simply indicated the presence or absence of a target digit on each trial. A REA for verbal material also can be obtained with instructions to report signals from one ear prior to those from the opposite ear (e.g., see Bryden, 1963; Satz, Achenbach, Pattishall, & Fennell, 1965) and with instructions to report signals from only one ear on each trial (e.g., see Geffen, 1978; Hiscock & Kinsbourne, 1977,

1980a). As mentioned previously, ear asymmetries can be shown under certain circumstances with monaural stimulation (Henry, 1979). This can be accomplished using a reaction-time paradigm (e.g., see Morais & Darwin, 1974; Provins & Jeeves, 1975; Simon, 1967) or by presenting long strings of stimuli (e.g., see Bakker, 1967, 1968).

In recent years, a selective-listening (or focused-attention) procedure has been used successfully with children (Geffen, 1978; Geffen & Wale, 1979; Hiscock & Kinsbourne, 1977, 1980a; Kinsbourne & Hiscock, 1977). Children monitor one ear on any given trial and report only signals arriving at that ear. This procedure seems to minimize volitional shifting of attention from one ear to the other; perhaps for that reason it yields consistent and unambiguous right-ear superiority for dichotic digit names in young children (Hiscock & Kinsbourne, 1977, 1980a; Kinsbourne & Hiscock, 1977). Ironically, this procedure—which appears to reduce the "noise" in dichotic listening—generates a potent order effect that limits the validity of the REA as an index of an individual child's speech representation. The order effect is generated simply by asking a child to monitor one ear for a number of consecutive trials (as few as 12), then asking the child to switch attention to the opposite ear. If the right ear is monitored first, there will be an exaggerated REA. If the left ear is monitored first, the usual REA will be reduced to statistical nonsignificance (Hiscock & Kinsbourne, 1980a) and right-ear performance may even be slightly inferior to left-ear performance (Hiscock et al., 1979). We will describe this order effect more thoroughly in our discussion of asymmetric priming.

Visual Asymmetries

Asymmetries of visual perception are demonstrated by using a tachistoscope or cathode ray tube to flash stimuli to the left or right of fixation. If it disappears before a fixating eye movement can be made, a stimulus to the right of fixation will impinge on the left half of each retina and a stimulus to the left will impinge on the right half of each retina. The architecture of the visual system is such that the right VHF stimulus will be conducted to the left visual cortex and the left VHF stimulus will be conducted to the right visual cortex. Presumably, signals originating from one side of space will reach the cerebral hemisphere on the same side only by an indirect route that involves recrossing the midline at the corpus callosum. Kimura (1966) suggested that the preferential recognition of stimuli from one side of space or the other can be attributed to a more direct pathway from that side of space to the cerebral hemisphere that is specialized for processing that particular kind of material. Thus, verbal material is more readily recognized in the right VHF than in the left VHF because right VHF stimuli are more directly transmitted to the parieto-occipital region of the left hemisphere, which is thought to play a major role in the process of reading. Visual asymmetries are less consistent across studies than are dichotic-listening asymmetries (White, 1969b, 1972, 1973a), and they are particularly sensitive to nonstructural factors, such as orientational bias (Kinsbourne, 1970a, 1973b) and lateral scanning of the iconic memory trace (Heron, 1957; Terrace, 1959).

In early studies, English letters were presented briefly in rows that extended across the subject's visual field (Crosland, 1931; Glanville & Dallenbach, 1929). Letters on the left were more likely to be reported than letters on the right, but no inferences about cerebral dominance were drawn. Mishkin and Forgays (1952) subsequently obtained a significant right VHF advantage for English words and a nonsignificant left VHF advantage for Yiddish words in bilingual adults (cf. Orbach, 1953). Mishkin and Forgays (1952) reasoned that neither cerebral dominance nor any other unilateral factor could account for the dissociation between the results for English words and for Yiddish words. Subsequent findings also seemed to be inconsistent with a cerebral dominance explanation. Heron (1957) reported that English letters and letter groups were more likely to be recognized in the left than in the right VHF when stimuli appeared simultaneously in both half fields. Only unilateral presentation of letters yielded a consistent right VHF advantage (Bryden, 1960; Harcum & Jones, 1962; Heron, 1957; Terrace, 1959). Thus, prior to the early 1970s, the belief that visual asymmetries reflect cerebral dominance was tempered by early findings that seemed incompatible with a cerebral lateralization explanation. Reviews by White (1969b, 1972, 1973a), which described some of the numerous variables that may influence visual laterality, provided additional reasons to use caution in ascribing laterality effects to cerebral dominance.

Despite White's (1969b) conclusion that "laterality differences in perception would appear to be a composite function of many factors" (p. 402), researchers have continued to interpret their findings largely in terms of cerebral dominance. This confidence in cerebral dominance explanations perhaps can be traced to demonstrations by McKeever and Huling (McKeever, 1971; McKeever & Huling, 1971a, 1971b) of right VHF superiority for bilaterally presented verbal material. McKeever and Huling (1971b) attributed earlier findings of left VHF superiority for the recognition of linguistic material to certain methodological deficiencies: (1) use of random-letter series rather than words, which are more meaningful, (2) presentation of stimuli across the entire visual field rather than only in the lateral half fields, (3) excessive exposure times, and (4) lack of positive control over subjects' fixation. With the rectification of these presumed methodological flaws, a strong right VHF superiority for bilaterally presented verbal material usually is found (Hines, 1972, 1975; Kershner & Jeng, 1972; McKeever, 1971; McKeever & Huling, 1971a, 1971b; Moore & Weidner, 1974; Pirozzolo & Rayner, 1977; Walters & Zatorre, 1978). Thus, one may obtain a right VHF superiority for verbal material irrespective of whether stimuli are presented in one VHF at a time or in both VHFs simultaneously. This conclusion, coupled with the expected absence of right VHF advantage with nonverbal stimuli (Bryden, 1960, 1973; Bryden & Rainey, 1963; Geffen et al., 1971; Heron, 1957; Kimura, 1966; Kimura & Durnford, 1974; Terrace, 1959) can be used to argue that a right VHF advantage for verbal material reflects left-hemispheric specialization for linguistic processes. Nevertheless, there are contradictory findings and alternative explanations (White, 1973a). The fixation control procedure recommended by McKeever and Huling (1970b), which entails reporting a centrally presented fixation stimulus prior to the lateral stimuli, may not eliminate trace scanning artifacts so much as bias the direction of the scan to favor the report of stimuli from the right VHF. Also, the verbal nature of the fixation stimulus (e.g., a digit) may induce left-hemispheric priming and thereby bias attention to the right (cf. Carter & Kinsbourne, 1979, discussed later; Kershner, Thomae, & Callaway, 1977).

The relatively simple tachistoscopic paradigm described in the early literature has become complicated with "a multiplicity of stimulus materials, stimulus arrangements, attentional-set controls, stimulus intensities, viewing conditions, and report instructions" (White, 1969b, p. 388). Unless these diverse stimulus and experimental variables can be specified, it is difficult to predict the outcome of any visual laterality study and even more so to attribute it to cerebral lateralization alone. Variation among studies arises from: (1) stimulus properties, (2) procedures used to present stimuli, and (3) response factors.

Stimulus Properties. Stimulus category or some associated property often determines whether asymmetries will be found. Usually stimuli are dichotomized into verbal and nonverbal categories (e.g., see Kimura & Durnford, 1974). Stimuli considered to be verbal include single letters, letter groups, words, single digits, and groups of digits. Verbal stimuli may be taken from different languages, and they may vary in physical and semantic characteristics as well as in statistical properties, such as frequency of occurrence in the language from which they are drawn. Stimuli considered to be nonverbal are even more diverse because they include outline drawings, nonsense forms, geometric forms, dots, line segments, and photographs of faces. With random unilateral presentation, verbal stimuli usually produce an asymmetry favoring the right VHF, and at least some kinds of presumably nonverbal stimuli may yield a left VHF advantage. Laterality effects associated with nonverbal stimuli tend to be variable, perhaps because many putatively nonverbal stimuli may, in fact, be processed with the aid of linguistic coding (White, 1969b, 1972). Different verbal stimuli probably are not uniform in the extent to which they call for verbal processing and different nonverbal stimuli are even less likely to be equally nonverbal.

Stimulus category alone does not necessarily determine laterality effects. For instance, dot stimuli may yield a right VHF advantage, a left VHF advantage, or no asymmetry, depending in part on whether accuracy of localization or of detection is being measured and on whether the dots appear within a frame (Allard & Bryden, 1979; Bryden, 1973, 1976; Kimura, 1969; Kimura & Durnford, 1974; Pohl, Butters, & Goodglass, 1972). Similarly, letters may or may not yield a right VHF advantage, depending on the kind of script in which they appear (Bryden & Allard, 1976). Even the right VHF advantage for words may be abolished by presenting the words in vertical orientation (Ethier, 1980). Patterns of asymmetry thought to be associated with stimulus category may, in fact, be attributable to related characteristics, such as orientation, size, shape, directionality, or response factors, rather than to the visual or verbal nature of the stimulus per se. This kind of confound is avoided only if the stimulus is held constant (Geffen, Bradshaw, & Nettleton, 1972) or words differing only in semantic properties are compared (Ellis & Shepherd, 1974; Hines, 1977; Seamon & Gazzaniga, 1973).

Several stimulus properties other than general category influence the degree or direction of visual-laterality effects. Directionality is one (Harcum & Finkel, 1963). Whenever words are presented in their usual orientation, scanning habits are likely to influence their perception (cf. Barton, Goodglass, & Shai, 1965; Ethier, 1980; Goodglass & Barton, 1963; Harcum & Finkel, 1963). On the other hand, if verbal material is presented vertically or in some other unusual orientation, the stimuli then become unnatural and unrepresentative of verbal material in general. Another important variable is the number of elements in the display. When multiple-element displays, such as words or letter groups, are presented at the relatively long exposure times necessary for adequate performance, postexposural scanning of the memory trace largely accounts for any laterality effects obtained (White, 1969b). When multiple-element displays are used, recognition of elements in different portions of the visual field varies with the spacing between elements (Bryden, 1966; Bryden, Dick, & Mewhort, 1968; Crovitz & Schiffman, 1965; Dick & Mewhort, 1967; Harcum, 1964; Mewhort, 1966). Letter spacing interacts with scanning tendencies to enhance, attenuate, or even reverse the asymmetries generated by directional scanning.

Another stimulus property of importance is exposure duration. It varies across laterality studies from a few milliseconds (e.g., see Bryden, 1973; Mewhort, 1974) to several hundred milliseconds (e.g., see Ayres & Harcum, 1962; Fitzgerald & Marshall, 1967). A primary concern is that the stimulus should have disappeared before a saccadic eye movement can be made. If the subject has time to fixate the stimulus, then it will impinge on the fovea centralis of the retina, and the stimulus information will be transmitted simultaneously to the visual cortex of both hemispheres. Insofar as the latency of human saccades is about 200 msec (Gay, Newman, Keltner, & Stroud, 1974; D. A. Robinson, 1968), the exposure duration in most studies is sufficiently brief to preclude fixation on the stimulus. Nevertheless, variations in exposure time may affect the scanning of the memory trace. Bryden (1966) reported that the starting point for left-to-right scanning shifted farther to the left as the exposure duration of bilaterally presented letters was lengthened. He also suggested that exposure time interacts with letter spacing; the spacing between letters is of little consequence if the exposure duration is sufficient for the subject to scan the peripheral elements of the stimulus array. If postexposural scanning varies as a function of exposure time, then studies that differ substantially in exposure duration may not be comparable even if they yield similar results; different mechanisms may underlie the similar results.

Sometimes, when the experiment is designed to compare VHF differences across different kinds of stimuli, different exposure durations for the respective material are used to counteract the disparity in overall performance that would result if exposure durations were equal (e.g., see Levy & Reid, 1978). A similar situation arises when the object of an experiment is to compare groups. If the groups are likely to differ in overall performance, as when children of different ages are compared, exposure duration can be adjusted to equalize performance. Even when there is no need to equate performance levels across stimuli or groups, the exposure time for each subject can be "titrated" so that performance is relatively constant across individuals. In each of these circumstances, we are confronted with a virtually insoluble dilemma. Whereas it may be impossible to compare asymmetry scores in a meaningful way when performance levels are disparate (Richardson, 1976), equalizing performance by adjusting exposure duration introduces a potential confound. Asymmetry differences among individuals or groups or differences associated with the stimulus type may, in fact, be attributable to differential scanning patterns or other factors that are related not to hemispheric specialization but to exposure duration.

Other stimulus variables that may influence the outcome of visual-laterality experiments include the displacement of stimuli from midline, size, complexity, luminance, contrast between stimulus and background, and the rise and decay characteristics of the tachistoscopic lamps or cathode ray tubes. The precise manner in which these factors influence visual laterality is uncertain.

Procedures. There are nearly as many procedures used to present visual stimuli as there are stimulus parameters. Stimuli may be presented in both VHFs simultaneously or in one VHF per trial; viewing may be either binocular or monocular; the subject's fixation may be uncontrolled or controlled through various techniques; poststimulus masking patterns may or may not be used; and presentations of a particular kind of stimulus material may be massed into a block of trials or interspersed with presentations of dissimilar material.

Of these various procedural variables, none is more important than presentation format, that is, whether stimuli are presented simultaneously in both VHFs or sequentially in one VHF per trial. One can no longer conclude that verbal material will yield a left VHF advantage when presented bilaterally and a right VHF advantage when presented unilaterally; nevertheless, it is difficult to specify the conditions under which a right VHF advantage will be observed with bilateral presentation. McKeever and Huling (1971b) attributed the left VHF superiority for verbal material in earlier studies (Crosland, 1931; Heron, 1957) to lengthy exposure times and lack of fixation control as well as to certain stimulus variables, but subsequent experiments have yielded right VHF superiority despite exposure times of 100 msec or more (Kershner & Jeng, 1972; Moore & Weidner, 1974) and in the absence of a fixation-control task (Kershner & Jeng, 1972; MacKavey, Curcio, & Rosen, 1975). White (1973a) pointed out that some investigators have found left VHF superiority for bilaterally presented verbal material and right VHF superiority for unilaterally presented material when both kinds of presentation were mixed within blocks of trials (Crovitz, Schiffman, Lipscomb, Posnick, Rees, Schaub, & Tripp, 1966; Heron, 1957; Mathewson, Miller, & Crovitz, 1968; White, 1969a, 1969c, 1969d, 1970, 1973b). This outcome cannot be dismissed as an artifact associated with poor fixation control. Instead, the most likely explanation for the disparate results with bilateral presentation of verbal stimuli seems to involve the stimuli themselves. It appears that, to obtain a right VHF advantage with simultaneous bilateral presentation, one must use as stimuli either words or letters that are grouped in each VHF with a gap in the center (Hirata & Bryden, 1976). Until the dissimilarities between bilateral and unilateral procedures are better understood, it cannot be assumed that the same factors underlie perceptual asymmetries observed in the two respective situations.

Viewing condition merits consideration. Typically, subjects view the stimulus material with both eyes. The homolateral halves of the two retinas project to the same cerebral hemisphere. Thus, a stimulus presented to the right of fixation is transmitted to the left hemisphere through the temporal hemiretina of the left eye and the nasal hemiretina of the right eye. The fact that the signal is transmitted through both crossed and uncrossed pathways does not undermine the logic of binocular tachistoscopic experiments. In the case of monocular viewing, however, any VHF asymmetry for either eye is confounded with differences between crossed (nasal retina) and uncrossed (temporal retina) pathways. It appears that the crossed pathways are superior to the uncrossed in some experimental situations (Bower & Haley, 1974; Crovitz & Lipscomb, 1963; Harcum & Dyer, 1962; Maddess, 1975; Poffenberger, 1912; Sampson, 1969; Sampson & Spong, 1961) but inferior in others (Markowitz & Weitzman, 1969; McKeever & Huling, 1970b; Neill, Sampson, & Gribben, 1971). These apparent differences between crossed and uncrossed optic pathways imply that monocular laterality effects may differ between left and right eyes (e.g., see McKeever & Huling, 1970b; Overton & Wiener, 1966). As a rule, one can expect to obtain similar results with binocular and monocular viewing if other task parameters remain constant. However, if monocular data are based on the performance of only one eye (e.g., see Walters & Zatorre, 1978), the possibility of differences between crossed and uncrossed pathways obscures the meaning of the results.

Fixation control is another important procedural variable. In early tachistoscopic studies (e.g., see Heron, 1957), the subject typically was instructed to look at a central fixation dot when a ready signal was given and to maintain central fixation until the stimulus or stimuli were flashed. Fixation instructions may be reinforced by informing the subject that central fixation will maximize performance, but the subject's actual fixation point is indeterminate unless there is some other means of insuring that the eyes are centrally positioned at stimulus onset. One approach to fixation control entails monitoring eye position so that the experimenter can await proper fixation before exposing the stimulus (e.g., see Moore & Weidner, 1974) or exclude data from trials on which a deviation from midline fixation occurs (e.g., see Maddess, 1975). Another approach compels central fixation without direct observation of the eyes. Commonly, a central stimulus must be reported prior to the lateral display (Sperry, 1968). The experimenter invalidates trials on which the fixation stimulus is not reported correctly (e.g., see McKeever & Huling, 1971b). Both methods of fixation control can be effective, but, as suggested by White (1973a), use of a fixation stimulus may introduce a confound into an already-complicated situation. The fixation task may not so much prevent as alter scanning. Subjects may begin their left-to-right scan with the fixation stimulus rather than with the stimulus in the left VHF. This tendency would favor detection of stimuli in the right VHF. In addition, a fixation stimulus may generate leftward or rightward biases, depending on its categorical nature (Carter & Kinsbourne, 1979; Kershner, Thomae, & Callaway, 1977). The evidence will be described when we discuss asymmetrical priming effects.

The effect of backward (poststimulus) masking (Kinsbourne & Warrington, 1962a) on VHF differences has not been systematically investigated. If the fixation dot is present in the postexposure field—a situation that cannot be avoided with two-channel tachistoscopes—then it constitutes a masking stimulus for the fixation-control stimulus or any other stimulus presented on midline. In contrast, the preexposure- and postexposure-masking pattern used by McKeever and Huling (1971b) apparently masked the lateral stimuli but not the fixation-control digits. This pattern consisted of six lines radiating in the manner of the spokes of a wheel from an open space in the center of the card. Klein, Moscovitch, and Vigna (1976) employed a similar masking pattern with a dot in the center of the pattern instead of an open space. Levy and Reid (1978) used a postexposure-masking field of visual "noise." The effects of these different masking patterns on VHF asymmetry are unknown.

Response Factors. As in dichotic listening, perceptual asymmetries in the visual modality may be exaggerated, nullified, or even reversed by response factors that in many cases are overlooked in the design of the experiment. For example, Neill et al. (1971) attempted to investigate the asymmetry of letter recognition while requiring subjects always to report stimuli from left to right. In studies that compare laterality for verbal and nonverbal material (e.g., see Hellige, 1978; Klein et al., 1976), subjects often respond vocally to verbal stimuli and manually to nonverbal stimuli. This cascading of stimulus and response factors precludes unambiguous interpretation of the results; VHF differences between verbal and nonverbal material may be attributable less to the nature of the stimuli than to the nature of the response.

With multielement displays, there is an association between the order in which an item is reported and the likelihood that it will be reported correctly (Bryden, 1960; Glanville & Dallenbach, 1929; Mewhort, 1966). This association raises several questions. Are certain elements reported first because they are perceived more clearly than others or are they perceived more clearly because they are processed first? Will left or right VHF superiority disappear if order of report is modified? Will performance deteriorate if order of report is altered? Finally, does hemispheric specialization influence the order in which items are reported? In other words, is order of report an extrinsic factor that modifies and perhaps obfuscates the effects of cerebral lateralization or is order of report itself a manifestation of cerebral lateralization? Even though no general answers have been found for these questions, a substantial amount of information has been accumulated about the ways in which reporting order influences performance and the circumstances under which order effects exert the greatest influence (Harcum, 1978). Changing the order of report alters left versus right differences, but the degree to which asymmetry can be changed depends on the kind of stimulus material and other factors. When left-to-right processing is most strongly established, as with letters (Anderson & Crosland, 1933; Bryden, 1960; Dick & Mewhort, 1967; White, 1969c) and words (McKeever, 1971), a right-to-left reporting order will impair overall performance but have minimal effect on laterality; when directional processing is less constrained, as with nonverbal forms (Bryden, 1960), an imposed reporting order is likely to influence laterality markedly while having little or no effect on overall performance. Moreover, the order in which elements are processed is likely to affect laterality depending on the memory demands of the task (White, 1969b) as well as exposure duration (Kimura, 1959), symmetry of the material (Harcum, 1964), and the spacing between elements (Bryden, 1966).

In most studies of visual laterality, recognition accuracy is the dependent variable. In others, reaction time (RT), or response latency, is the dependent measure of primary interest. One approach of RT studies is similar to recognition studies in most respects. Typically, a complex stimulus, such as a face or a word, is presented in the left or right VHF; the subject is required to indicate manually or vocally whether the stimulus is the same as, or different from, a previously presented item. As in recognition studies, the object is to show VHF differences as a function of stimulus category. Geffen et al. (1971), for example, found that manual responses in a face-matching task were faster when faces appeared in the left VHF than when they appeared in the right VHF, but identification of digits was faster when the digit appeared in the right VHF than in the left VHF. Reaction-time studies of this variety are subject to many of the same methodological problems that we summarized in connection with recognition studies, and the results usually are interpreted in the same ways.

The second kind of RT study seeks information that is not obtainable from recognition studies, namely, an estimate of interhemispheric transfer time (IHTT). The IHTT paradigm (Poffenberger, 1912) is based upon Helmholtz's subtraction method of RT analysis, which originally was developed to measure the velocity of nerve conduction (Swanson et al., 1978). The time required for information to cross from one hemisphere to the other is estimated by comparing RTs obtained under two circumstances: (1) when the response is initiated by the hemisphere to which the stimulus is projected and (2) when the response is initiated by the opposite hemisphere. Direct reaction (right-hand response to right VHF stimulation or left-hand response to left VHF stimulation) should be faster than indirect reaction (right-hand response to left VHF stimulation or left-hand response to right VHF stimulation) by a constant number of milliseconds that reflects the time required for information to cross the corpus callosum.

Results from these RT studies have failed to yield an unqualified measure of IHTT. Estimates of IHTT range from 3 msec (Berlucchi, Heron, Hyman, Rizzolati, & Umilta, 1971) to 100 msec (Jeeves, 1965), and attempts to account for the variability among estimates in terms of stimulus factors have not been convincing (cf., Berlucchi et al., 1971; McKeever & Gill, 1972; Poffenberger, 1912; Swanson & Kinsbourne, 1976 [also described in Swanson et al., 1978]). It appears that the subject's expectancy with respect to stimulus position accounts for some of the variability. When stimuli are presented in blocked left and right VHF trials, the resultant IHTT estimate tends to be on the order of a few milliseconds; but when the location of stimuli is randomized across trials, the IHTT estimate is substantially greater (cf. Berlucchi et al., 1971; Bradshaw & Perriment, 1970; Filbey & Gazzaniga, 1969, Moscovitch & Catlin, 1970; Poffenberger, 1912; Swanson & Kinsbourne, 1976 [also described in Swanson et al., 1978]). This expectancy effect suggests that much of the variance in these RT studies is attributable to factors other than nerve conduction time. One such factor is stimulus-response (S-R) compatibility. An anatomically direct S-R combination, for example, right VHF and right hand, implies a response in the direction of the stimulus; an indirect combination, for example, right VHF and left hand, implies a response to the side opposite the stimulus. Anatomical pathway and S-R compatibility can be deconfounded by requiring the subject to respond with arms crossed (Simon, Hinrichs, & Croft, 1970). If differences between direct and indirect reactions reflect conduction properties of the nervious system, then IHTT estimates from the arms-crossed condition should not differ from estimates obtained with the arms uncrossed. If, however, S-R compatibility influences RT, IHTT estimates will vary depending on whether the arms are crossed or not. In a between-subjects comparison of arms-crossed and arms-uncrossed responding, Wallace (1971) reported an IHTT value of 50 msec for the uncrossed condition and −52 msec for the crossed condition. With subjects' arms crossed, the anatomically direct reaction required more time than the indirect reaction. Similar results were obtained in an experiment in which arm configuration was varied as a within-subject variable (Swanson & Kinsbourne, 1976 [also described in Swanson et al., 1978]). The IHTT estimate for the arms-crossed condition exceeded 20 msec, but the estimate for the uncrossed condition was −40 msec. Swanson and his colleagues (1978) conclude that the S-R compatibility effect "is large enough to completely overshadow the IHTT effect" (p. 288). Reviewing this literature, Bashore (1981) accepts the minimal estimate of Berlucchi et al. (1971) of 3 msec as a valid measure of IHTT, based on the view that their paradigm was free of the above confounds. But a further confound cannot readily be overcome. When the stimulated hemisphere programs response, it has the benefit of activation by the stimulus, which could accelerate its response programming (cf. Ledlow et al., 1981). Thus, the 3-msec advantage for homolateral response could be wholly, or in part, a stimulation effect rather than a measure of IHTT.

Of the various behavioral techniques discussed here, the tachistoscopic method seems to be the most difficult to use effectively with young children. Many methodological complexities and interpretive ambiguities in studies of visual asymmetry in adults are exacerbated with children. The tachistoscopic method has been applied to the question of the relationship between laterality and reading ability (Marcel, Katz, & Smith, 1974; Marcel & Rajan, 1975; McKeever & Huling, 1970a; Witelson, 1976a; Yeni-Komshian, Isenberg, & Goldberg, 1975) as well as that of developmental change in normal children (Forgays, 1953; Miller & Turner, 1973; Olson, 1973; Reitsma, 1975; Tomlinson-Keasey, Kelly & Burton, 1978), but neither line of research has yielded consistent results.

Tactile Asymmetries

Several clinical studies suggest that the right hemisphere is more proficient than the left hemisphere in the perception of number, pattern, direction, and shape through the tactile modality (Carmon & Benton, 1969; Fontenot & Benton, 1971; Milner & Taylor, 1972; Nebes, 1971). Consequently, one expects a general left-hand superiority among normal people who are performing a tactile-recognition task. If the stimuli are linguistic or if there are linguistic aspects to the task, one might expect the left-hand advantage to be diminished or reversed.

Early studies of blind adults (Critchley, 1953; J. M. Smith, 1929) showed a left-hand superiority for Braille reading, despite the fact that the task contains linguistic as well as spatial components. Hermelin and O'Connor (1971) confirmed this finding in children as well as adults and found that the left-hand superiority is greater when subjects read with the unpracticed middle finger instead of the practiced index finger. Nevertheless, because blind people often read with their left hand, studies of Braille reading in the blind are confounded by differential practice. Rudel et al. (1974) found a significant left-hand advantage for reading Braille symbols in sighted 13- and 14-year-old children, thus demonstrating that hand differences need not depend on differential practice or experience. Because the Braille characters were learned and read in a left-to-right direction, irrespective of hand, the left-hand superiority could reflect an advantage for adductive over abductive movements in tactile perception. In addition, the hand differences in the Rudel et al. (1974) experiment interacted with age, sex, and the order in which the hands performed. Overall, boys performed significantly better with the left hand and girls performed significantly better with the right hand. When data from boys and girls were combined, there was a significant right-hand superiority among 7- and 8-year-olds. Left-hand performance benefited from the right-hand's prior experience with the task, but right-hand performance did not differ significantly as a function of order. A more recent study of sighted children's ability to read Braillelike characters (Wagner & Harris, 1979) revealed a significant left-hand superiority for 9- and 11-year-old girls but not for boys of the same age. Again, left-hand performance was enhanced if tested after the right hand, but right-hand performance did not benefit from the previous experience of the left hand.

Braille patterns were presented in a nonlinguistic context by Rudel, Denckla, & Hirsch (1977), who required sighted children and adults to make same/different judgments without having learned the name of each pattern. Although there was an overall left-hand superiority, it was found only among subjects above the age of 10 years; it was further qualified by a three-way interaction among age, sex, and hand. Apart from the nonmonotonic developmental trends and the irregular deviations between hand differences for females and males, the Rudel et al. (1977) results are interesting because they resemble results from the earlier (Rudel et al., 1974) study of Braille letter learning. It does not seem to matter whether the dot patterns constitute a linguistic symbol to be associated with an English letter or a spatial pattern to be matched to another spatial pattern.

Another procedure for investigating asymmetries of tactile perception is Witelson's (1974) "dichhaptic" task, which entails the simultaneous palpation of unseen stimuli by the second and third fingers of each hand. In her 1974 study, two different kinds of stimulus material were used. One kind consisted of pairs of Styrofoam nonsense shapes, which were presented for 10 sec. per trial. The subject responded by pointing to two stimuli from a visual display of six. The other kinds of stimulus material consisted of pairs of rubber upper case letters. On each trial, two consecutive pairs of letters were presented for 2 sec. each and the subject responded by naming the four letters he had felt. There was no significant difference between left- and right-hand performance on the letter-naming task. The nonsense shape-identification task yielded a pronounced left-hand advantage, but only when it was administered first. When the shape task followed the letter task, the left-hand superiority failed to materialize. In a subsequent administration of the dichhaptic nonsense shapes to 200 normal children aged 6 to 13 years, Witelson (1976b) reported a significant left-hand advantage for boys of all ages but no asymmetry for girls. She suggested that by 6 years of age, the right hemisphere of boys is specialized for spatial processing but that girls have spatial functions represented bilaterally at least until adolescence. Elsewhere, Witelson (1976a, 1977b) has speculated that differences in tactile laterality between normal and reading-disabled boys reflect bilateral representation of spatial functions in the reading-disabled group.

Data from tactile studies are too sparse to permit a comprehensive assessment of tactile methods for measuring laterality, but they do point to certain problems. Stimulus variables probably are as important in tactile as in auditory and visual laterality studies, but they are more difficult to specify and control in tactile studies in which the subject is free to palpate the stimuli in an idiosyncratic fashion. In the dichhaptic task with nonsense shapes (Witelson, 1974), the subject has 10 sec. in which to explore the two objects. A left-hand superiority in perception could be due to more extensive or more efficient exploratory activity on the part of the left hand or to a tendency to attend to the left-hand stimulus before processing the right-hand stimulus. The technique used by Rudel et al. (1974) for perception of Braille letters constrains the direction of the tactile sweep with each hand as well as the order in which the hands are attended to, but there may be systematic differences between the hands in the speed or firmness of touch that generate differences in recognition accuracy. As suggested previously, there may be an advantage in adduction over abduction. Even if overall left-hand superiority cannot be attributed to such differences, these differences may account for some of the age, sex, and order effects.

Procedural variables, for the most part, remain to be explored. The unimanual tactile task differs in several respects from the dichhaptic procedure, and it is not known whether the two procedures would yield similar results if the same stimulus material were used. When they required normal adults to match nonsense shapes by touch, Webster and Thurber (1978) found that response latency was less with the left hand than the right hand when the shapes were presented dichhaptically but not when they were presented to one hand at a time; however, neither the dichhaptic nor unimanual conditions yielded any significant asymmetry in accuracy. The fact that Braille studies (e.g., Rudel et al., 1974) and dichhaptic studies (e.g., see Witelson, 1976b) have shown different patterns of asymmetry in girls and boys of different ages may reflect stimulus differences rather than unimanual versus bimanual differences. In tactile studies, as in tachistoscopic studies, there is risk of obfuscating stimulus effects by covarying response factors along with stimulus factors. The results of Witelson's (1974) dichhaptic study are difficult to interpret because subjects named the letters but pointed to the nonsense shapes that they had felt. On the other hand, Rudel et al. (1976, 1977) concluded that the results of Braille studies are similar irrespective of whether subjects associate each dot pattern with an English letter or merely match dot patterns without learning any linguistic association. However, asymmetries in Braille learning are altered if subjects are familiarized with visual representations of the Braille characters prior to performing the tactile task (Rudel & Denckla, 1979).

The small body of literature on tactile asymmetry suggests two factors that act to decrease the validity of manual asymmetry as an index of hemispheric specialization. The first of these phenomena is strategy. The minimal constraints on the subject's exploration of the stimulus, particularly in the dichhaptic situation, allows several individualized approaches. As suggested previously, subjects may tend to concentrate on one hand longer than, or before, the other. Also, subjects may work in either an analytical, sequential, feature-detecting manner or in a holistic or gestalt fashion. When adult subjects were instructed to approach a dichhaptic shape-matching task with a sequential, feature-detection strategy, the ratio of right-hand to left-hand response time did not differ significantly from unity; when other subjects were instructed to use a strategy that involved construction of holistic visual images, however, left-hand response time was faster and the right-to-left ratio was significantly greater than that for the first group (Webster & Thurber, 1978). The second phenomenon is susceptibility to order effects. The magnitude and sometimes even the very existence of tactile asymmetries seem to depend on the order in which the hands are tested (Rudel et al., 1974; Wagner & Harris, 1979) or on the order in which different kinds of tasks are performed (Witelson, 1974). These effects are discussed next.

Asymmetric Priming

We proposed earlier that anomalies and extraneous factors in perceptual laterality should be investigated further for two reasons: (1) so that the so-called extraneous factors may be better controlled for the purpose of yielding purer measures of hemispheric specialization and (2) so that at least some of these factors may be appreciated not as nuisance variables but as variables that can tell us something about the fundamental nature of cerebral organization. Insofar as most attempts to account for nonstructural factors affecting perceptual asymmetry have been guided by an attentional, or orientational, model (Kinsbourne, 1970a, 1973b, 1974a, 1975), we will begin with a brief overview of that model and its implications for priming effects.

The orientational model is based on the tendency for each cerebral hemisphere to direct orientation toward the contralateral side of space. Differential activation of the two hemispheres produces an overt or covert shift of attention away from the side of the more highly activated hemisphere. This phenomenon can be traced back to infancy; when linguistic or other structured auditory stimuli impinge on the neonate, subcortical arousal mechanisms activate the left side of the brain to a greater degree than the right (Gardiner & Walter, 1977; Molfese, 1977; Molfese, et al., 1975). Other kinds of stimulation—either auditory (Molfese, 1977; Molfese & Molfese, 1979, 1980) or visual (Davis & Wada, 1977)—produce different distributions of activation (but see Shucard et al., 1981, for a failure to replicate). Accordingly, infants are more likely to respond to novel linguistic stimuli from their right side than from their left side and to novel nonlinguistic stimuli from their left side than from their right side (Entus, 1977; Glanville, Best, & Levenson, 1977). Similarly, in older children and adults, listening to speech as well as speaking or even thinking verbally tends to bias attention toward the right side of space; performance of visuospatial or other nonverbal tasks tends to bias attention toward the left side (e.g., see Kinsbourne, 1972, 1974b; Kocel, Galin, Ornstein, & Merrin, 1972). Attentional biases may be relatively automatic and inflexible in the neonate but become increasingly modulated by cortical influence. Situational and experiential factors then become important determinants of orientation in space. Cognitive variables, such as mental set, expectancy, and previous experience, influence the manner in which stimuli are perceived, interpreted, and processed. For instance, ambiguous auditory stimuli might be interpreted as linguistic or nonlinguistic, depending on the context in which they are heard, and one or the other hemisphere would be activated accordingly (Spellacy & Blumstein, 1970). Listening to music might result in activation of either the right or left hemisphere, depending on the listener's strategy, which, in turn, may depend on familiarity with music (Bever & Chiarello, 1974; Johnson, 1977) or on strategies deployed (Henninger, 1981). As the nervous system matures, attention can be allocated in a more flexible manner. The older child or adult more readily overcomes inbuilt biases, such as that which links lateralized cerebral activation to laterally biased orientation. This ability to override the innate "wiring" of the nervous system contributes to the lack of perfect correlation between the direction or degree of asymmetry and the presumed lateralization of language in a given individual.

The orientation model not only allows us to understand laterality findings that would be uninterpretable from a structural viewpoint but also leads to predictions concerning the way in which perceptual asymmetries may be biased by antecedent conditions and concurrent activities.

Let us first consider antecedent conditions. It is clear from the perceptual laterality literature that auditory, visual, and tactile procedures for assessing laterality share a susceptibility to bias from prior experience of many kinds. Whether this influence is called a priming effect, a preexposural set, an order effect, or something else, it represents a category of related phenomena, each involving the influence of some previous activity upon subsequent perceptual asymmetry. In some instances, the bias stems from a person's long-term familiarity with a particular kind of stimulus material (Bever & Chiarello, 1974; Johnson, 1977; Papcun et al., 1974; Van Lancker & Fromkin, 1977). In other cases, the bias can be attributed to an activity that immediately preceded the laterality task (Hiscock & Kinsbourne, 1980a; Hiscock et al., 1979; Kimura & Durnford, 1974; Klein et al., 1976; Rudel & Denckla, 1979; Rudel et al., 1974).

Reading habits affect visual laterality. Mishkin and Forgays (1952) found among English-Yiddish bilinguals right VHF superiority for English words but not for Yiddish words. Orbach (1953) reported similar results, although a left VHF advantage for Yiddish words was found only among those subjects who had learned Yiddish before learning English. In an attempt to minimize horizontal scanning, Barton et al. (1965) presented English and Hebrew words in a vertical orientation; they reported a significant right VHF superiority irrespective of language. So, asymmetries in word recognition may vary depending on whether the words are read from left to right or right to left. Moreover, Orbach's (1953) findings suggest that people who have learned to read a left-to-right and a right-to-left language may show differential laterality patterns, depending on which language was learned first. Developmental changes in asymmetry for tachistoscopically presented verbal material also may be interpreted as effects of experience. In studies showing an age-related increase in degree of asymmetry (e.g., see Forgays, 1953; Miller & Turner, 1973; Reitsma, 1975; Tomlinson-Keasey et al., 1978), the increase could be attributable to the greater experience of the older children in left-to-right reading rather than a greater degree of cerebral lateralization.

In certain auditory studies, degree of familiarity with the stimulus material is a determinant of laterality pattern. Bever and Chiarello (1974) found that musicians showed a REA for the detection of monaurally presented tonal melodies, even though nonmusicians showed the expected left-ear superiority. Bever and Chiarello suggested that the musicians applied an analytic strategy to the task, whereas naive listeners perceived the tones in a gestalt fashion. But perhaps the greater musical knowledge of the musicians allowed them to label various aspects of the music, thus rendering it a linguistic task. In any event, the Bever and Chiarello (1974) findings were supported by Johnson (1977), who found a similar difference between musicians and nonmusicians who listened to dichotically presented violin melodies. At this level of analysis, analytic and labeling strategies are confounded. Henninger (1981) performed a finer grained study and was able to refer the left hemisphere's role in musicians to the trained performance of tonal analysis. Van Lancker and Fromkin (1977) found that Thai speakers show a REA for intoned Thai words but that English speakers do not. Presumably, these intoned words have linguistic value only to people who understand them. A similar explanation can be applied to a finding by Papcun et al. (1974), namely, that trained Morse code users show a significant REA for Morse code letters but that naive subjects show a significant LEA. However, the familiar intelligible stimuli might well attract more analytic attention so that, in those cases, linguistic and analytic factors remain confounded.

Although this evidence from auditory tasks does not reveal what differences between groups cause them to show different laterality effects for the same material, the results can be explained parsimoniously in terms of strategy differences and orientational biases. If the group in each experiment that is more familiar with the stimulus material uses a verbal strategy, this would tend to shift attention toward the right side of space (Kinsbourne, 1970a, 1973b, 1974b, 1975). In the cases cited, the people who can be presumed to use a verbal-strategy show a REA.

Perceptual biases also arise from activities within the experimental setting that immediately precede the laterality task. Biases of this kind include carry-over effects of one task upon a subsequent task of a different nature as well as effects of attention to one side of space or one side of the body upon subsequent performance on the same task when attention is switched to the opposite side of space or the body. An early example of a carry-over effect from one task to another can be found in Kimura and Durnford's (1974) description of a tachistoscopic experiment that comprised both a letter-identification task and a geometric-form-identification task. One group of subjects attempted the letter-identification task immediately prior to the form-identification task; another group of subjects accomplished the two tasks in reverse order. There was a right VHF superiority for letters irrespective of the order in which the tasks were administered. However, laterality effects for the geometric forms were not so robust; there was a nonsignificant tendency toward a left VHF superiority if the forms preceded the letters but a significant right VHF superiority if the forms followed the letters. Even though it is not made clear how priming phenomena fit into Kimura's (1966) structural model of visual asymmetries, Kimura and Durnford (1974) attribute the order effect for form laterality to verbal priming of one hemisphere and perhaps a "resultant scanning tendency" (p. 40). Kimura and Durnford cited a similar order effect in a study that involved perception of pictures and letters (Paivio & Ernest, 1971). There was a right VHF advantage for pictures only when they were preceded by the series of letter-identification trials. More recently, priming effects in the visual modality have been reported by Klein et al., (1976). In Experiment I of this study, adult subjects were presented 40 trials of bilaterally presented faces either before or after presentation of 40 trials of bilaterally presented words. Subjects who accomplished the face-recognition task first recognized more items (both faces and words) in the left VHF and fewer in the right VHF than did subjects who accomplished the word-recognition task first. However, when the procedure was modified in Experiment II so that subjects pointed to correct words rather than naming them, there was no longer any trace of a priming effect. The inconsistency between Experiments I and II illustrates the fragile nature of priming effects, that is, their dependency on various experimental and extraexperimental factors.

Witelson's (1974) tactile-identification study, which we summarized earlier, revealed a carry-over effect similar to those described above in connection with tachistoscopic experiments. One group of boys accomplished a block of 10 shape-identification trials prior to a block of 10 letter-identification trials; another group accomplished the letter-identification task first. The expected left-hand superiority for recognition of shapes was found only when the shape-identification task was accomplished first. There was no significant asymmetry in shape perception if the task was preceded by the letter-recognition task. Letter-recognition performance was symmetric irrespective of the order in which the tasks were administered. It should be noted that there was a 2- to 3-week interval between the two tasks.

Because it is not usually feasible to present blocked trials of left VHF or right VHF stimuli, tachistoscopic tasks do not yield information about the effects of prior attention to one side of space or the other. Auditory and tactual tasks, however, have provided some striking evidence of order effects that occur when a subject's attention is directed to one side of space or of the body and subsequently is switched to the opposite side.

Previously, we referred to an order effect that arises consistently from dichotic-listening experiments with children in which attention is focused on one ear or the other for a series of trials and then switched to the opposite ear. The children show marked difficulty in listening to the previously unattended ear, and their performance while listening to the second ear is characterized by numerous intrusion errors from the previously attended ear (Hiscock & Kinsbourne, 1980a; Hiscock et al., 1979). This phenomenon seems to represent a priming effect, that is, practice in attending to one side of space apparently establishes an expectancy or sensitization for signals from that side. This is difficult to overcome when the child subsequently is asked to attend to the opposite side. The phenomenon resembles what Schneider and Shiffrin (Schneider & Shiffrin, 1977; Shiffrin & Schneider, 1977) have termed automatic-attention responses. After practice in the identification of signals from one side of space, subsequent signals from the same side gain the ability to direct attention automatically to that side. The effect is not merely the result of fatigue or a transitory attention-switching effect. It persists unabated over an interval as long as 1 week between the monitoring of one ear and the monitoring of the other, and it does not seem to dissipate with practice in monitoring the previously unattended ear (Hiscock & Bergstrom, 1981; Hiscock & Kinsbourne, 1980a; Hiscock et al., 1979). This priming effect influences subsequent free-report performance as well as selective-listening performance, and it can be observed in adults as well as in children (Hiscock & Stewart, 1979). Thus far, auditory priming effects have been demonstrated with digit strings as stimulus material but not with CV nonsense syllables (Hiscock & Stewart, 1979) or with digit names presented to young children in single pairs (Parlow, 1978). This pattern of results suggests that auditory priming effects depend on localization of signals in space. Unless signals can be identified readily as originating from the right or from the left, an expectancy for sounds from that side of space cannot be established.

A somewhat similar order effect is found in tactile laterality when each hand is tested separately (Rudel & Denckla, 1979; Rudel et al., 1974; Wagner & Harris, 1979). Right-hand performance remains about constant, irrespective of testing order, but left-hand performance is enhanced quite dramatically by the previous experience of the right hand. It seems that left-hand superiority for Braille learning actually is attributable to asymmetric transfer of training and that no asymmetry would be found using a between-subjects design in which half of the children are tested only with the left hand and the other half are tested only with the right hand. Only after hands are switched does the left emerge as the superior hand.

These various reports of carry-over effects show that subjects may begin a laterality task with a preexisting lateral bias stemming from familiarity with the stimulus material, performance of a previous task, or prior attention to one side of space or of the body. In addition, certain aspects of the laterality task itself may generate lateral biases. Investigators have long recognized the possibility that the subject's expectancy, or preexposural set, on any trial might influence laterality effects for that trial (Heron, 1957; Terrace, 1959). Heron (1957) reported that, when letter groups appeared about 3° and 4° from fixation in a tachistoscopic recognition task, advance knowledge of the VHF in which they would appear was associated with improved left VHF recognition. Most subsequent investigations of visual laterality have attempted to preclude the possibility of preexposural sets favoring either VHF by randomizing presentations between VHFs. To prevent the formation of a preexposural set for type of material, Terrace (1959) randomized the presentation of words and forms as well as the VHF in which they appeared. He found a right VHF advantage for words and no significant VHF difference for forms, and he, consequently, concluded that right versus left differences in word recognition can be attributed to postexposural processes and not to preexposural sets. Nevertheless, in the same report, Terrace referred to a pilot study in which it was found that subjects tend to deflect their eyes to the right if they know that only letters will be presented. Subsequent experiments have shown that there are several different circumstances under which laterality biasing expectancies, or priming effects, may arise from the experimental task itself.

The issue raised by Terrace (1959), that is, preexposural sets in tachistoscopic experiments involving homogeneous sets of stimuli, still has not been resolved. Dee and Hannay (1973) randomly mixed random shapes with three-letter nonsense words and found a significant left VHF superiority for the shapes but no significant asymmetry for the nonsense words. They claimed that their results failed to support the preexposural set hypothesis, but their experiment is inconclusive for the same reasons that Terrace's (1959) was inconclusive, namely, there is no way of ascertaining what results their stimuli and procedures would have yielded under circumstances conducive to the formation of preexposural sets. It is necessary to compare results from mixed presentation with those obtained from presentation of "pure" sets of verbal or nonverbal stimuli. In the one such study, Hellige (1978) found that asymmetry in the recognition of random shapes did shift from the "pure-list" to the mixed-list condition. Although four-letter nouns yielded a significant right VHF advantage irrespective of whether they were presented in a homogeneous set or mixed randomly with the shapes, the shapes yielded a left VHF advantage when presented in a homogeneous set and a right VHF advantage when mixed with the nouns. Hellige's findings show that preexposural sets are indeed a contributing factor in tachistoscopic laterality experiments.

One report in the dichotic-listening literature (Spellacy & Blumstein, 1970) strongly suggests that the subject's mental set can influence auditory laterality. This dichotic-listening study was analogous to Hellige's (1978) tachistoscopic study insofar as different kinds of stimuli were mixed randomly to influence the subject's expectancy. Subjects who heard dichotic CVC nonsense words mixed with real English words showed a significant REA for vowel-varied pairs of nonsense words, but subjects who heard the same CVC nonsense words mixed with nonlinguistic sounds showed a significant LEA.

Another potential source of lateral bias is the fixation stimulus. A verbal-fixation stimulus might favor right VHF recognition either because the fixation stimulus itself is read from left to right (thus generating a left-to-right scan that continues into the right VHF) or because it activates the left hemisphere and, thus, biases orientation toward the right side of space (Kinsbourne, 1970a, 1973b, 1974b, 1975). Either mechanism could account for the consistent right VHF superiority obtained in studies using McKeever and Huling's (1971b) procedure. Only the orientational mechanism, however, would clearly predict a left VHF superiority in instances when a nonverbal-fixation stimulus is used. In two studies involving children (Carter & Kinsbourne, 1979; Kershner et al., 1977), the nature of the fixation stimulus did, in fact, alter VHF differences in the perception of laterally presented digits. In both studies, either a digit or a geometric shape was presented centrally at the same time that digits were presented bilaterally and the children were instructed to report the fixation digit or shape prior to reporting the stimuli in the lateral fields. Both studies yielded very similar results, namely, a right VHF advantage when digits served as fixation stimuli and a left VHF advantage when geometric forms served as fixation stimuli. These studies show that, at least under some circumstances, the fixation stimulus may have a major effect on visual laterality. Under other circumstances, in adults, consistent asymmetries have been obtained irrespective of alterations in the fixation task (Ethier, 1980; Hines, 1978).

Most of the biases discussed up to this point occur spontaneously in laterality experiments. Other experimental situations have been contrived for the specific purpose of demonstrating lateral biases. Most of these situations entail concurrent performance of two tasks, one of which is intended to generate a lateral bias that affects the asymmetry of performance on the other. The fixation-control procedure discussed earlier may be thought of as a secondary task, but we described it separately because it usually is used to ensure midline fixation rather than to create a lateral bias.

Kinsbourne (1970a) first showed that a secondary task can modify perceptual asymmetry. Normal adults were asked to determine whether briefly presented squares were complete or broken by a single gap. On half of the trials, they held six words in mind while performing the perceptual task. In the absence of a concurrent memory load, the likelihood of failing to detect gaps to the left of fixation and to the right of fixation did not differ significantly. When concurrent verbal storage was required, however, performance was significantly better for right-sided gaps than for left-sided gaps. Similar results were obtained in subsequent gap-detection experiments (Earl & Kinsbourne described in Kinsbourne, 1973b; Kinsbourne, 1973b). Moreover, Bruce & Kinsbourne (described in Kinsbourne, 1973b) found that a concurrent verbal-memory task biased laterality for the perception of nonsense shapes; there was a significant asymmetry (favoring the right VHF) only when subjects were attempting to hold six words in memory. Other studies suggested that concurrent musical activity can bias attention to the left (Bruce & Kinsbourne, described in Kinsbourne, 1973b; Gardner, Eagan, & Branski, 1973; Goodglass, Shai, Rosen, & Berman, 1971). There have been subsequent failures to find biases of the kind predicted by the orientational model (Allard & Bryden, 1979; Boles, 1979; Gardner & Branski, 1976; Schwartz, 1980), but these negative results are equivocal owing to inappropriate choices with respect to either the tasks themselves or to task parameters, such as degree of difficulty. The methodological and conceptual complexities of concurrent-task experiments are illustrated in the work of Hellige and his colleagues (Hellige, 1978; Hellige & Cox, 1976; Hellige, Cox, & Litvac, 1979). For instance, either a concurrent verbal task or random mixing of words and nonsense forms can alter laterality for form recognition, but the combined effect of both variables is not greater than the effect of either variable in isolation (Hellige, 1978; Hellige & Cox, 1976). As the concurrent memory load increases from zero to six nouns, its biasing influence on form recognition changes in a nonmonotonic fashion, that is, the effect appears as memory-set size increases from zero to two nouns, remains substantial at four nouns, but dissipates completely at a set size of six (Byrd & Kinsbourne, 1983; Hellige & Cox, 1976). It is clear from these results that an experiment may fail either because the secondary task is too easy or too difficult. Biasing effects also appear to differ between VHFs and as a function of whether the stimuli to be recognized are verbal or not (Hellige & Cox, 1976; Hellige et al., 1979).

In some instances, laterality may be influenced by direct manipulation of attention to one side or the other. The REA in dichotic listening may be overcome simply by instructing children to listen to the left ear, although the ability to monitor verbal material at the left ear is less than the ability to monitor the same material at the right ear (Geffen, 1978; Geffen

& Wale, 1979; Hiscock & Kinsbourne, 1977, 1980a). Other studies suggest that lateral shifts of visual attention can alter listening asymmetry. Goldstein and Lackner (1974) reported that ear differences for the perception of CV nonsense words varied as subjects' visual fields were displaced laterally by prisms. The usual REA was enhanced with rightward visual displacement and diminished with leftward displacement. Watching an optokinetic nystagmus (OKN) drum has similar effects on the laterality of CV nonsense-word perception. When the OKN contours move from the subject's left to right, the REA is significantly greater than when the contours move from right to left (Hiscock et al., 1981). In the same study, it was found that laterality for dichotic-musical stimuli is influenced by saccadic eye movements that are synchronous with the onset of the auditory stimuli. A left-ear superiority for identification and localization of the musical stimuli was obtained only when eye movements were to the left; upward and rightward eye movements were associated with a REA.

Asymmetries of Interference Between Concurrent Tasks

Thus far, performance of concurrent tasks has been discussed only in connection with perception, that is, in terms of altered perceptual laterality as a consequence of concurrent cognitive activity. However, the laterality of motor performance also may be altered by requiring subjects to perform a concurrent task.

The literature on asymmetries of dual-task performance deals mainly with interference and, in particular, with the interfering effects of a concurrent task upon left- and right-hand performance. Initially, the focus on interference may seem contrary to the concurrent-task studies of perceptual laterality insofar as the concurrent task in the perceptual studies often seems to have a facilitative effect. Activation of a cerebral hemisphere for one task appears to enhance that hemisphere's role in perception, as when a concurrent verbal task generates a right VHF advantage (e.g., see Kinsbourne, 1970a). Other studies, however, provide evidence of interference between tasks (Byrd & Kinsbourne, 1983; Hellige & Cox, 1976; Hellige et al., 1979). Depending on (1) the nature of the respective tasks and (2) task difficulty, a lateralized concurrent task may have a facilitative, interfering, or negligible effect on perception of stimuli in either VHF. All three contingencies—facilitation, interference, and the absence of an effect—no doubt can be demonstrated as well in situations requiring concurrent performance of two motor tasks or of a cognitive and a motor task; but as a rule division of attention between tasks yields a decrement in the performance of one or both tasks, even if the tasks are relatively nondemanding (Kahneman, 1973; Kinsbourne, 1981b; Welford, 1968).

The tendency of a concurrent activity to affect the performance of limbs on one side of the body more than on the other may be accounted for in terms of a functional-distance principle of cerebral organization (Kinsbourne, 1981b; Kinsbourne & Hicks, 1978a, 1978b): the functional distance between cerebral regions decreases as the interaction between them, in the performance of concurrent tasks, increases. In the highly interconnected mammalian brain, some pairs of centers or regions are more highly linked than others. Homologous (mirror-image) sites in the two halves of the brain are especially closely connected (Kinsbourne, 1974a). Differences in degree of linkage, according to the functional-distance principle, are reflected in differential overflow or crosstalk between regions. Depending on the nature of the responses being controlled by two regions, cross talk may be facilitative or disruptive. Facilitation occurs when one task generates positive transfer for the other task (Hicks, Frank, & Kinsbourne, 1982), helps optimize arousal for the other task (Posner & Boies, 1971), or when one task selectively activates the hemisphere required for performing the other task and shifts attention toward the appropriate side of space (Kinsbourne, 1970a, 1973b). Under other circumstances, cross talk is disruptive. Different pairings of the four limbs yield different degrees of interference in a two-limb tracking task (Briggs & Kinsbourne, 1975), and the rank ordering of limb pairs in terms of interference matches the rank ordering of limb pairs on the basis of electromyographic cross talk (Davis, 1942a, 1942b) and transfer of training (Cook, 1933a, 1933b, 1934). The evidence, in each instance, suggests that functional distance is least between centers that control homologous limbs, intermediate for loci controlling ipsilateral limbs, and greatest for loci controlling diagonally paired limbs (Kinsbourne & Hicks, 1978a).

Excepting the special case of homologous callosally connected areas, it is reasonable to assume that the functional distance between two cortical regions is less (other factors remaining constant) if both regions lie within the same hemisphere than if the two regions are located in opposite hemispheres. The expressive speech area in the left frontal lobe, for example, should be closer in functional (as well as anatomical) distance to the hand-control region of the left hemisphere than to the hand-control region of the right hemisphere. This assumption is supported by data of McAdam and Whitaker (1971), who found greater electrical activity over the left motor cortex than the right motor cortex as subjects spoke. This presumed difference between within-hemisphere and between-hemisphere functional distance serves as a basis for studying how various activities interfere with concurrent manual performance. If speech output, for example, is lateralized in the left hemisphere, then speech should interfere to a greater degree with skilled manual performance by the right hand than with performance by the left hand (given that each hand is controlled at the cortical level primarily by the contralateral hemisphere [Brinkman & Kuypers, 1972, 1973]).

Numerous findings confirm that verbal activity interferes more with right- than left-hand performance. Kinsbourne and Cook (1971) showed that, in normal, right-handed adults, concurrent speech has an unequal effect on the duration of dowel-rod balancing with the left and right hands. Speaking (repeating a sentence) continuously disrupted balancing with the right hand but not with the left hand. This result was confirmed by Hicks (1975), who also reported that speech was equally disruptive of left- and right-hand performance in left-handed adults (or disrupted left performance more if their sinistrality was familial). In several subsequent studies of normal, right-handed adults, similar asymmetries of interference between speech and manual performance have been reported (Bowers, Heilman, Satz, & Altman, 1978; Dalby, 1980; Hellige & Longstreth, 1981; Hicks et al., 1975; Hicks, Bradshaw, Kinsbourne, & Feigin, 1978; Lomas, 1980; Lomas & Kimura, 1976; Thornton & Peters, 1982). Total failure to find the effect has been infrequent (Majeres, 1975), although it has failed to materialize under certain conditions, for example, when the manual task is too difficult or too easy (Lomas & Kimura, 1976) or when the measure of manual performance is timing accuracy rather than speed or duration (Wolff & Cohen, 1980). The verbal activity need not be overt to interfere asymmetrically with concurrent manual activity. The effect has been found when subjects listened to stories (Bowers et al., 1978), read silently (Hellige & Longstreth, 1981), and rehearsed letter strings silently (Hicks et al., 1975; Summers & Sharp, 1979) as well as when subjects engaged in verbal tasks requiring only minimal vocalization (McFarland & Ashton, 1978b, 1978c). Conversely, nonverbal cognitive activity tends either to disrupt the performance of both hands equally or to affect the left more than the right (Bowers et al., 1978; Dalby, 1980; Hellige & Longstreth, 1981; McFarland & Ashton, 1975b; 1978a, 1978b, 1978c).

The dual-task procedure has been applied to children, primarily to investigate the ontogeny of cerebral dominance for speech, and (as with adults) the results have been quite consistent. Those results will be described later (see *Ontogeny of Lateralization: Theoretical Considerations* and *Ontogeny of Lateralization: Findings and Implications*). For present purposes, it is sufficient to state that concurrent speech interferes more with right- than with left-hand performance in children of age 3 and older (Hiscock & Kinsbourne, 1978, 1980b; Kinsbourne & McMurray, 1975; Piazza, 1977; White & Kinsbourne, 1980).

The dual-task technique, thus, is a useful means of obtaining information about speech lateralization in normal children and adults. Careful analysis of the literature, however, reveals some potential problems and limitations (Kinsbourne & Hiscock, 1983).

1. A variety of cognitive activities may be incorporated into dual-task experiments. While engaging in a manual activity, people may talk aloud, "talk" subvocally, listen to speech, read, encode nonverbal material for later recall, and so on. The diversity of possible cognitive activities represents a major asset of the dual-task method but, in the absence of corroborative evidence regarding the lateralization of the components of these activities in normal brains, it often is difficult to interpret differences in laterality from one task to another. Failures to find consistently lateralized interference with humming (e.g., see Hicks, 1975; Johnson & Kozma, 1977; Lomas & Kimura, 1976; Piazza, 1977) may reflect opposing influences of left-hemispheric specialization for vocalization and right-hemispheric specialization for music processing or they may reflect bilateral representation of music. But most likely, it depends on the characteristics of what is hummed. Repeated failures to show the expected lateralized interference with visuospatial tasks (Bowers et al., 1978; McFarland & Ashton, 1978a; Summers & Sharp, 1979; White & Kinsbourne, 1980) may be attributed to a verbal-response artifact in some instances or perhaps to the absence of motor components of the tasks (Hellige & Longstreth, 1981), although in other studies, nonverbal tasks without major motor components did generate interference that was greater on the left side than on the right side (Dalby, 1980; McFarland & Ashton, 1978b, 1978c). Of course, it is possible that most nonverbal tasks elicit bilateral processing. In the absence of independent information about what task components are represented in each hemisphere, dif-

ferences among interference effects for various visuospatial tasks—as well as differences between verbal and visuospatial tasks—are difficult to interpret because tasks vary in so many ways.

2. Measuring performance on the nonmanual task is necessary if dual-task experiments are to be interpreted without ambiguity. Otherwise, one might attribute interference asymmetries to an asymmetric tradeoff between tasks. If the right hand is more affected by the concurrent task, it is possible that the person is giving priority to the manual task while performing with the left hand and to the nonmanual task while performing with the right hand. But some tasks, such as humming, are not readily quantified and scored. Even if the concurrent task does lend itself to quantitative assessment, different aspects of performance may yield different results. For instance, concurrent tapping actually enhanced the rate of children's speech production, although it increased the error rate even more dramatically (Hiscock, 1982).

3. Many dual-task studies cannot be interpreted correctly until the relationship between laterality and task difficulty is understood. It has been claimed that the differential outcomes associated with different manual tasks have important theoretical bases, but it seems likely that some of those differences reflect disparate difficulty levels. For example, Lomas and Kimura (1976) concluded that speech interferes asymmetrically with sequential hand movements but not with repetitive movements. Lomas (1980) further claimed that lateralizes interference occurs only when the manual task required nonvisual control (cf. Thornton & Peters, 1982). However, in experiments that failed to show a lateralized effect, the overall reduction in tapping rate relative to control conditions was as little as 3.6% (Lomas, 1980) and 4% (Lomas & Kimura, 1976). Even if so little interference is statistically significant, it is not optimal for showing a lateralized effect. Under some circumstances, there may be no interference at all. Lomas and Kimura (1976) found that speaking interferes asymmetrically with the dowel-rod balancing performance of males but not of females. Males balanced the rod for an average of 48.2 sec. in the control conditions; their mean balancing time dropped by 17% in the speaking conditions. Females, however, balanced for only 19.2 sec. in the control conditions; their mean time actually increased by 11% in the speaking conditions. Clearly, there can be no asymmetry of interference if there is no interference (Johnson & Kozma, 1977).

The relationship between task difficulty and laterality is not straightforward. As the results of Lomas (1980) and Lomas and Kimura (1976) illustrate, the dual-task method may yield no useful information about laterality if one of the tasks is so easy—or so difficult—that there is little or no measurable interference between tasks. Hicks (1975) found that, in adults, the asymmetry of interference increased as the phonetic difficulty of the speaking task increased. Similarly, Hiscock, Antoniuk, and Prisciak (1982a) found that the effect of reading on concurrent finger tapping was more asymmetric in poor readers (for whom the reading task was relatively difficult) than in good readers. Hicks and his colleagues (Hicks, Bradshaw, Kinsbourne, & Feigin, 1978) also reported that interference becomes increasingly asymmetric as the difficulty of the manual task increases. On the other hand, there is evidence that disruption of manual activity remains constantly asymmetric as the difficulty of the concurrent task increases (Hellige & Longstreth, 1981; Hicks, Provenzano, & Rybstein, 1975; Hiscock, Kinsbourne, Samuels, & Krause, 1983) as well as evidence that the laterality of interference decreases as either the manual task (Summers & Sharp, 1979) or the concurrent task (McFarland & Ashton, 1978b) increases in difficulty. Even in a commissurotomized (split-brain) patient, a difficult cognitive task disrupted finger tapping bilaterally, whereas easier tasks had only unilateral effects (Kreuter, Kinsbourne, & Trevarthen, 1972). Because different tasks differ in respects other than difficulty and because different groups may differ in respects other than ability to perform the tasks, definitive conclusions about the relation between laterality and difficulty cannot be stated. Parametric studies of task difficulty and of performance tradeoffs between tasks are needed (see Kinsbourne & Hiscock, 1983; Navon & Gopher, 1979; Norman & Bobrow, 1975).

4. From the functional distance hypothesis (Kinsbourne, 1981b; Kinsbourne & Hicks, 1978a, 1978b), it follows that interference between concurrent tasks, if lateralized at all, should be mutually lateralized. If verbal activity interferes more with right- than left-hand motor performance, then the right-hand activity should interfere more with verbal performance than does left-hand activity (Botkin, Schmaltz, & Lamb, 1977; Dalby, 1980; McFarland & Ashton, 1978b, 1978c). In most cases, however, performance of speaking or other nonmanual tasks is affected equally by concurrent activity of the left and right hands (Bowers et al., 1978; Dalby & Gibson, 1981; Hellige & Longstreth, 1981; Hicks et al., 1975; Hiscock, 1982; Hiscock & Kinsbourne, 1978, 1980b; Majeres, 1975). When the expected asym-

metry is found, it frequently is inconsistent from one experiment to another within the same study (e.g., see Hicks, 1975; Summers & Sharp, 1979; White & Kinsbourne, 1980). The most obvious reason for the absence of a lateralized effect of manual activity upon the nonmanual task is that there is little overall interference in that direction, that is, neither hand seems to interfere substantially with performance of the nonmanual task. Speaking appears to be particularly insusceptible to interference from concurrent manual activity. In a study of normal children, we found that recitation of a nursery rhyme decreased finger-tapping speed by about 19% relative to the base-line speed, but tapping decreased verbal production by only 4% relative to a control speaking condition (Hiscock & Kinsbourne, 1980b). Consequently, it was assumed that children's tendency to "protect" their speaking performance (Kahneman, 1973) accounts for the minimal amount of interference and, thus, for the lack of asymmetrical interference. This explanation is not satisfactory insofar as an emphasis on the manual task and deemphasis of the speaking task produced a dramatic rise in error rate but no asymmetry (Hiscock, 1982). In the absence of further data, we can only conclude that mutual asymmetry of interference between manual and nonmanual tasks is observed quite infrequently and that it is most likely to occur when the nonmanual task consists of an activity other than speaking (e.g., see Botkin et al., 1977; Kinsbourne, LaCasse, & Hicks cited in Kinsbourne & Hicks, 1978a; McFarland & Ashton, 1978c).

The problem and limitations of the dual-task paradigm discussed above are specific to that method. The method also shares at least some of the problematic attributes of other noninvasive techniques for investigating hemispheric specialization. The retest reliability of children's asymmetry scores over an interval of a year is low (Hiscock & Kinsbourne, 1980b). The proportion of children inferred to be left-hemisphere dominant for speech is comparable to that derived from dichotic studies (approximately 70%), although it rose to 85.5% when the number of trials in each condition was increased (Hiscock, 1982). The number of correct classifications may be limited only by the reliability of measurement. The dual-task method offers the greatest flexibility of any noninvasive technique for exploring functional differences between the two hemispheres. The technique has yielded remarkedly consistent results in several studies of children (Dalby & Gibson, 1981; Hiscock, 1982; Hiscock & Kinsbourne, 1978, 1980b; Hiscock et al., 1983; Kinsbourne & McMurray, 1975; McFarland & Ashton, 1975a; Obrzut, Hynd, Obrzut, & Leitgeb, 1980; Piazza, 1977; White & Kinsbourne, 1980). Nevertheless, it is clear that like all behavioral asymmetry paradigms, the method currently cannot determine organization within an individual child or adult.

Asymmetry of Lateral Gaze

The obvious function of saccadic eye movements is to position the eyes rapidly so that information can be acquired from a selected portion of the visual field (D. A. Robinson, 1968). Consequently, saccades usually have been studied in connection with visual information processing, such as reading and scanning pictures (Rayner, 1978). Nevertheless, saccades occur when there is little or no visual information to be processed (C. S. Moore, 1903; Teitelbaum, 1954). The laterality of these stimulus-independent eye movements was observed by Day (1964, 1967a, 1967b; 1968), who contended that people look consistently to one side when asked a question requiring some reflection. Day dichotomized people as left-movers and right-movers. He claimed that the two groups differ primarily in the way in which they experience anxiety, that is, the anxiety of left-movers has an internal locus, whereas that of right-movers has an external locus. Subsequently, Bakan (1969) suggested that asymmetries in lateral eye movement stem from the functional asymmetry of the brain. A tendency to look to one side was thought to be "symptomatic of easier triggering of activities in the hemisphere contralateral to the direction of eye movement" (Bakan, 1969, p. 930). Bakan further speculated that differences in the ease with which the left and right hemispheres are triggered might be associated with individual differences in cognitive, personality, and physiological characteristics. As an alternative to the trait (or typologic) concept of gaze laterality proposed by Bakan, others have viewed the lateral eye movement as a response to the information processing demands of a particular task. In 1972, independent reports by Kinsbourne and by Kocel and her colleagues showed that, within subjects, the direction of eye moving was influenced by the nature of the task. Kinsbourne (1972) found that verbal questions elicited more rightward eye (and head) turning in right-handers than did spatial or numerical problems. In a second experiment, subjects turned rightward more often while preparing to repeat a sentence than while visualizing its meaning. Kocel et al. (1972) found that verbal and arithmetic questions elicited more rightward eye movements than did spatial or musical questions.

The empirical association between lateral eye movements and lateralized cognitive processing has a straightforward theoretical explanation (Kinsbourne, 1974a). Unilateral electrical stimulation of several cortical areas in primates and other mammals evokes a contralateral movement of the head and eyes (e.g., see Ferrier, 1876; Mott & Shafer, 1890). Moreover, unilateral cerebral ablation alters eye, head, and body turning in such a way as to confirm that each hemisphere subserves orientation toward the opposite side of space (e.g., see Goltz, 1876; Kennard & Ectors, 1938). Electrical stimulation (Penfield & Roberts, 1959) and unilateral cerebral disease (Kinsbourne, 1970a) in humans lead to the same conclusion (see review by Gowne, 1983). When stimulated by the cortex (through one of at least two parallel cortex-to-brainstem pathways—Schiller, True, & Conway, 1979), the brainstem generates a saccade that is a weighted mixture of opposing signals from the left and right hemispheres (D. A. Robinson, 1968). If both hemispheres are activated simultaneously, the resultant saccade will be to the side opposite the more highly activated hemisphere. From these neurophysiological facts, one may infer that an imbalance in hemispheric activation associated with lateralized cognitive processing might overflow into those cortical areas involved in shifting orientation (Kinsbourne, 1970b, 1972, 1973b, 1974a, 1975). Thus, thinking verbally should be associated with rightward eye (and head) turning and spatial information processing should be associated with leftward turning.

Despite the plausible link between gaze laterality and hemispheric specialization and despite the encouraging findings from early studies (Bakan, 1969; Kinsbourne, 1972; Kocel et al., 1972), the lateral eye movement has not been validated as a useful indicator of cerebral lateralization. Experimental outcomes have been diverse; even the most basic findings—for example, predominantly rightward movements with verbal questions and predominantly leftward movements with visuospatial questions—have been obtained usually, but not consistently (Ehrlichman & Weinberger, 1978; Ehrlichman, Weiner, & Baker, 1974).

Because we have exempted the topic of hemisphericity from the purview of this chapter, we will not summarize the literature that has evolved from Bakan's (1969) paper (i.e., studies that attempt to find associations between left or right lateral-eye-movement tendencies and a host of personality, cognitive, and cognitive-style attributes) except to comment that the findings have been contradictory and that some of the most frequently mentioned correlates of left- or right-moving, such as hypnotic susceptibility, have not been validated independently as characteristics of either hemisphere. The shortcomings of the hemisphericity literature are much less damaging to the validity of the lateral eye movement as a laterality measure than are the mixed outcomes of studies in which the task is varied. Although the basic findings of Kinsbourne (1972) and Kocel et al. (1972) have been replicated several times (e.g., see Galin & Ornstein, 1974, Experiment 2; Gur, Gur, & Harris, 1975; Hiscock & Bergstrom, 1981, Experiment 1; Schwartz, Davidson, & Maer, 1975; Weiten & Etaugh, 1974), there have been many failures to replicate (e.g., see Ahern & Schwartz, 1979; Berg & Harris, 1980; Ehrlichman, Weiner, & Baker, 1974; Galin & Ornstein, 1974, Experiment 1; Hiscock & Bergstrom, 1981, Experiments 2 & 3; Rodin & Singer, 1976; Säring & von Cramon, 1980). Even when similar procedures are used by the same experimenters, the results may be contradictory from one experiment to the next (Galin & Ornstein, 1974; Hiscock & Bergstrom, 1981). Extensions of the paradigm beyond the basic verbal versus visuospatial task manipulation also have failed to yield consistent findings. For instance, the claim of Gur et al. (1975) regarding the critical importance of experimenter location in lateral-eye-movement research was confirmed only in part by Hiscock (1977) and not at all by Berg & Harris (1980). Investigations of the effect of affective state upon lateral-eye-movement direction have not yielded totally consistent results, although it is possible that lateral eye movement will prove to be a more satisfactory index of affective states than of cognitive processes. Schwartz et al. (1975) found that emotionally loaded questions elicited a preponderance of leftward gaze shifts, thus suggesting an enhancement of right hemispheric activation. Although this finding was duplicated by Tucker, Roth, Arneson, & Buckingham (1977), subsequent findings suggest that affect is related to lateral-eye-movement direction in a complex fashion (Ahern & Schwartz, 1979). A claimed association between experimentally manipulated stress and leftward eye movements (Tucker et al., 1977) received no support from other studies (Berg & Harris, 1980; Hiscock, 1977).

Little is known about lateral eye movements in children. Day (1967b) had failed to detect the LEM phenomenon in any of 50 children below the age of 4 years. Reynolds and Kaufman (1980) did find a statistically significant number of LEMs in most children below 4, although eye shifts were much more frequent in children above the age of 3½ than in younger children. In the Reynolds and Kaufman

(1980) study, the direction of children's LEMs was not influenced by the nature of the task (verbal and numerical questions versus visuospatial questions).

It seems fair to characterize the association between LEM direction and cognitive task as a real but fragile phenomenon. Obtaining the expected verbal versus visuospatial task effect depends either on some critical factor as yet unidentified or on some combination of factors. Ehrlichman and Weinberger (1978) discussed several potentially important factors under the categories of (1) question characteristics, (2) scoring factors, and (3) characteristics of the physical and social situations. Questions differ in complexity, difficulty, or the amount of reflection required; in the specific kind of processing required; and in the nature of the required response. They also differ in structural properties, such as syntax and number of words. The initial phase of some questions may elicit processing, whereas other questions may not be meaningful until the final word is pronounced. In general, questions have been categorized as verbal or visuospatial without independent validation as to either the kind of processing actually required or the hemisphere actually activated during that processing. The methods and criteria for scoring eye movements also vary from study to study. Movements have been scored using direct observation, video recording, and electro-oculography. Criteria for scoring a deflection as a LEM—size, timing, presence or absence of a vertical component, necessity for initial fixation on midline—also vary. Different statistical treatments of the scores may lead to divergent conclusions. The physical and social factors of possible relevance are numerous. The experimenter may be positioned in front of the subject, behind the subject, or even out of the room. If the experimenter faces the subject, the distance between the two may influence gaze behavior quite dramatically. The experimenter's own gaze tendencies may influence those of the subject. If the experimenter is absent or behind the subject, the subject may sit in symmetrical and homogeneous surroundings or in an environment replete with incidental points of fixation. The subject often faces the lens of a video camera and may have a microphone to look at as well. The experimenter may attempt to disguise (with various degrees of success) the fact that eye movements are being observed; the setting or instructions may induce an unpredictable amount of stress, anxiety, or self-consciousness.

The LEM is enigmatic. One could offer numerous procedural explanations for any failure to obtain predicted results but, as Ehrlichman and Weinberger (1978) suggest, one investigator usually will have obtained the desired outcome despite commission of the presumed procedural error yet another investigator probably has failed even though the error was expunged. Perhaps the answer lies in the phenomenon itself, that is, in arbitrary selection of one event—the first lateral eye shift following a question—as the event of exclusive interest. Especially when the subject is not facing an examiner, the LEM is not an isolated event but part of a complex pattern of gaze shifts (Hiscock, 1977). We know too little about the larger pattern of oculomotor events: stares, vertical movements, head movements, rate of ocular motility, duration of gaze deviation, changes over time, and so on. There has been relatively little attention to the consistent finding that visuospatial questions tend to elicit either stares or vertical eye movements (Ehrlichman & Weinberger, 1978; Kinsbourne, 1972). In fact, following visuospatial questions, ocular motility in the horizontal plane is sharply reduced relative to motility following verbal questions (Hiscock & Bergstrom, 1981; Weiner & Ehrlichman, 1976). This robust finding may reflect bilateral activation of the cerebrum during visuospatial thinking, although other explanations must be considered as well (Hiscock & Bergstrom, 1981).

Laterality Indices

In our introduction we allude to the assumption that performance associated with an ear, visual half field, or hand reflects the processing capability of the contralateral hemisphere. That assumption implies a direct relationship between degree of behavioral asymmetry and degree of cerebral lateralization for the processing being performed. We question the validity of the assumption on grounds that (1) when a function is lateralized, the difference between hemispheres, from clinical evidence, appears to be qualitative rather than quantitative and (2) numerous factors influence behavioral laterality. Irrespective of the validity of the assumption, it is legitimate to ask whether one person or group is more asymmetric than another in performing a particular task. If there are differences of degree, for example, between the laterality of younger and older children, those differences might be attributable to a number of factors other than cerebral lateralization, but the behavioral finding itself is a starting point. Conversely, if the groups do not differ in degree of behavioral asymmetry, then there is no basis for claiming that one group has a greater or lesser degree of cerebral lateralization than the other. Thus, it is helpful to be able to compare people with respect to degree of behavioral laterality.

Such comparisons present no special difficulty when overall performance (i.e., right plus left) is similar. In practice, however, equivalent performance is the exception rather than the rule. When different tasks are compared, average difficulty usually varies from one to another. When groups are compared, there usually are differences in competence to perform the task, as when younger children are compared with older children and when learning-disabled children are compared with control subjects. If overall performance varies among groups, apparent differences in laterality may be spurious. The most extreme case is that in which ceiling or floor effects are present. If performance is near 100%, there can be little difference between left and right scores. The same is true if overall performance is near zero or the level expected by chance alone. However, even when there is no ceiling or floor effect in a strict sense, the possible range of asymmetry may be constrained by the level of overall performance. For this reason, numerous statistical treatments, often referred to as laterality indices, have been proposed (Bryden & Sprott, 1981; Harshman & Krashen, 1972; Hawles, 1969; Kuhn, 1973; Marshall, Caplan, & Holmes, 1975; Repp, 1977; Studdert-Kennedy & Shankweiler, 1970).

We will illustrate the problem of comparing degrees of laterality with a simple hypothetical example in which older and younger children obtain left- and right-ear scores from a dichotic-listening test. There are 60 trials consisting of one left-ear and one right-ear stimulus each. The younger children obtain an average score of 20 from the left ear and 25 from the right ear. The older children score 40 from the left ear and 50 from the right. Because the absolute REA of the older children is twice that of the younger children, an analysis of variance for raw scores from each ear or for difference scores (right minus left [RA − AL]) would quite likely indicate that [R − L] older children show greater asymmetry than younger children. In contrast, two proportional laterality indices—right-ear score divided by total score and R − L score divided by total score—would indicate that the degree of asymmetry is identical for both groups. Another index, Kuhn's (1973) phi coefficient, would indicate that the older children are about 2.25 times as strongly lateralized as the younger children, whereas Harshman and Krashen's (1972) percent-of-error score would indicate that the groups differ in degree of lateralization by a factor of 1.25. Although these figures in actuality would be somewhat different (because our computations are based on group averages rather than scores of individual children), they illustrate the dilemma of trying to compare degrees of laterality when overall performance is disparate. In Figure 3, four different indices are plotted as a function of overall performance for each of three possibilities: (1) positive correlation between R − L scores and overall performance (R + L), (2) no correlation between R − L and R + L, (3) negative correlation between R − L and R + L. It is clear that the indices in some instances have strikingly dissimilar effects and that the effect of any index depends on the correlation between overall performance and the absolute amount of asymmetry.

Recently, laterality indices have received considerable attention in neuropsychology literature (Birkett, 1977; Colbourn, 1978; Hellige, Zatkin, & Wong, 1981; Richardson, 1976; Stone, 1980). Although some of the indices now available are more sophisticated than those used in the past (Bryden & Sprott, 1981), the basic assumptions underlying all attempts to quantify laterality have come under attack (Colbourn, 1978; Richardson, 1976). Traditionally, emphasis has been placed on finding the best laterality index, that is, one that is independent of total performance. Now, there is doubt concerning the desirability of that criterion. Until there is some theoretical basis for specifying the relationship between laterality and overall performance, the criterion of orthogonality is an arbitrary one (Richardson, 1976).

If the criterion itself is suspect, it is impossible to know which laterality index is best. Some authors have suggested the substitution of nonparametric methods for the usual analyses of laterality scores (Colbourn, 1978; Richardson, 1976). Alternatively, it seems that the laterality indices might be retained if investigators ascertain how various indices will bias their data and then select indices with opposing effects. If the comparison among tasks or among groups leads to the same conclusion, irrespective of the index used, then the finding may be accepted as valid and robust. If not, the nonparametric statistical techniques may be used or the answer to the research question may be considered indeterminante.

Conclusions

Several paradigms have been applied to the study of behavioral asymmetry during the past 20 years. Some have corroborated clinically derived inferences about functional lateralization of the cerebrum and others have given rise to new speculations about the organization of the brain. Even when research has failed to uncover the desired information about left- and right-hemispheric specialization, the experiments often have provided useful by-products

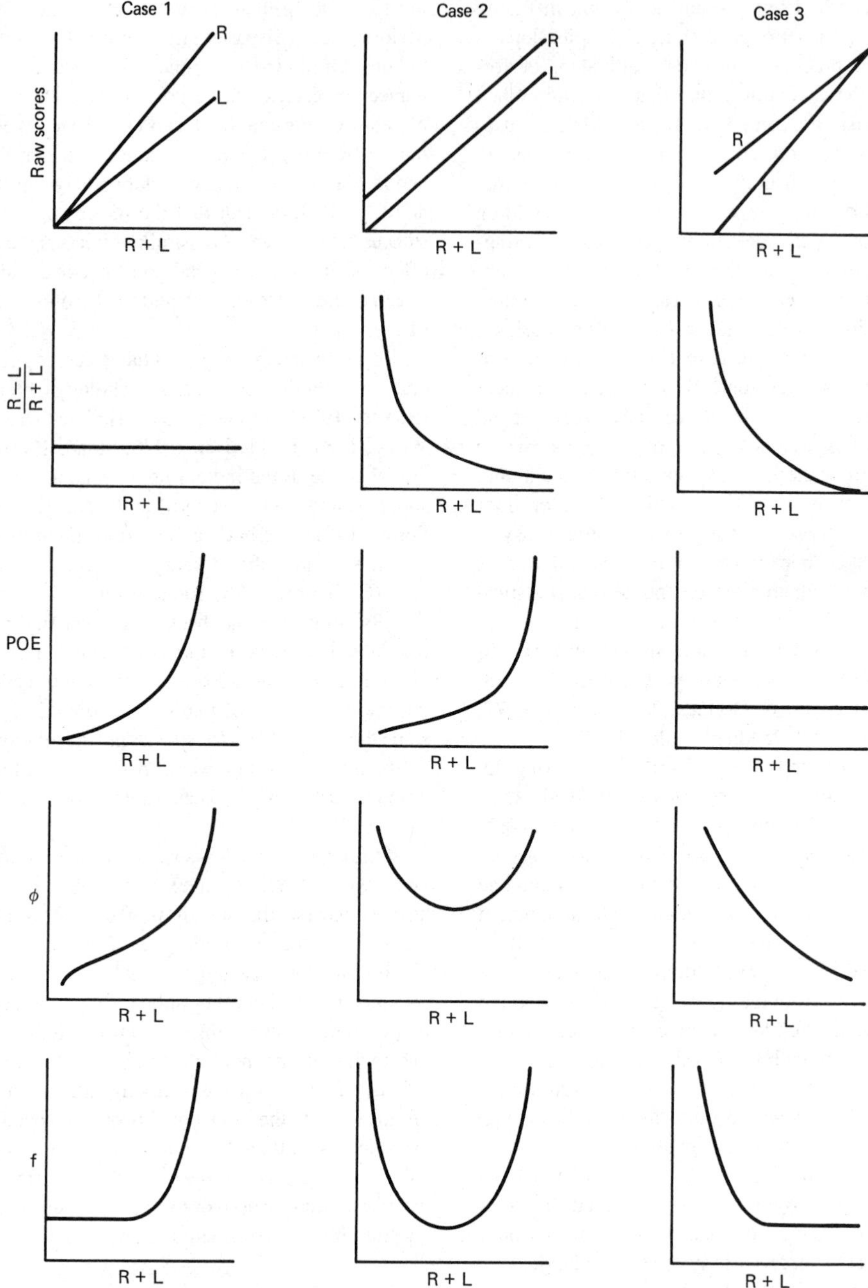

Figure 3. An illustration of the manner in which each of four popular laterality indices varies as a function of total performance (R + L). Considered separately are Case 1, in which the difference between right (R) and left (L) raw scores increases with increasing total performance; Case 2, in which the difference between R and L remains constant as total performance increases; and Case 3, in which the difference between R and L decreases as total performance increases. The laterality indices depicted are: (R − L)/(R + L) (e.g., Studdert-Kennedy & Shankweiler, 1970); Percent of Error (POE) (Harshman & Krashen, 1972); the phi coefficient (Kuhn, 1973); and *f*, which is (R − L)/(R + L) for (R + L) < 50% and (R − L)/(T − (R + L)) for (R + L) > 50%, where *T* represents the maximum possible number of correct responses (Marshall, Caplan, & Holmes, 1975). Curves were generated with the following constraints: 60 trials, 2 responses per trial, mean R − L difference of 10. From Hiscock, Mackay, & Kinsbourne, in preparation.

in the form of information about human perception, attention, memory, language, and motor skill.

Of the techniques, dichotic listening has been the most successful. The REA for linguistic stimuli is a phenomenon that stands alone in laterality research for its robustness. Yet, even this phenomenon leaves much to be desired as a measure of hemispheric specialization. Cerebral lateralization and trace-scanning tendencies are so intricately confounded in visual perception as to make the study of visual laterality exceedingly difficult. Despite a great volume of facts from tachistoscopic experiments, the basic mechanisms of visual asymmetry remain to be determined. Relatively few studies of tactile laterality have been published, but it appears that the left hand shows a general superiority for tactile recognition. Perceptual laterality, irrespective of modality, often is influenced by attentional and cognitive factors, such as past experience with the stimulus material, previous attention to one side of space, the context in which stimuli are perceived, and the subject's strategy. Incidental findings as well as findings from experiments into which biasing factors were deliberately incorporated document the existence of powerful priming effects. Two less developed methods—the study of dual-task interference and of lateral gaze shifts—provide capability for investigating the lateralization of many cognitive processes whose lateralization cannot be studied using perceptual methods. The dual-task method, in particular, has yielded results that are consistent with other evidence about cerebral lateralization, and this technique promises to be a useful new tool for the laterality researcher.

Although relatively little attention has been paid to the psychometric properties of laterality measures, it is now clear that certain psychometric issues must be dealt with. There is doubt concerning not only the adequacy of various laterality indices but also the meaningfulness of quantifying laterality in the absence of a theory specifying the relationship between laterality and overall performance.

Summary

Because our knowledge of the functional lateralization of the brain is inferential, it is imperative that we consider carefully the kinds of evidence on which inferences are based. We have presented a critical appraisal of clinical, physiological, and behavioral methods for studying cerebral lateralization because only through appreciation of the severe limitations inherent in each of these approaches can one properly evaluate the evidence and reach correct conclusions.

Evidence from unilateral brain lesions is paradoxical, in that it is the strongest and yet potentially the most misleading evidence available. Examining brain function through clinical studies alone is not unlike examining a complex organism through a microscope. It is possible to obtain much information about a sample that may be unrepresentative of the entity from which it was taken. Generalizing from the abnormal to the normal brain must be done with great care. The inferential problems inherent in clinical research provide incentive to develop and refine alternatives. There are EEG and behavioral alternatives available, although thus far the results obtained from these techniques have not been definitive, mainly because both EEG and behavioral asymmetries are influenced by a number of factors in addition to hemispheric specialization. Nevertheless, in some instances, the results have corroborated clinical evidence; in other instances, the results have provided a basis for new models of cerebral organization.

Lesion studies and noninvasive methods have complementary strengths and weaknesses. The clinical method is direct but the results may not be generalizable to the normal brain; noninvasive methods may be applied to normal subjects but they are indirect. Future advances in our understanding of cerebral lateralization will depend on the convergence of evidence from these different sources.

ONTOGENY OF LATERALIZATION: THEORETICAL CONSIDERATIONS

The principles of hemispheric equipotentiality and progressive lateralization of language have been established as neurological doctrine since the 19th century (Dennis & Whitaker, 1977; Woods & Teuber, 1978a). Equipotentiality implies that different areas of the brain are equally capable of becoming specialized for a particular function. Pierre Marie (1922), an influential proponent of the equipotentiality argument, dismissed the possibility that a lateralized speech center already exists in the infant brain on the grounds that the known perceptual and motor centers were invariably bilateral and symmetric. The apparent anatomical symmetry of the cerebral hemispheres served to reinforce belief in the equipotentiality hypothesis, as did instances of language development in children with atrophy of the left hemisphere. Moreover, the idea that cerebral lateralization develops during childhood appeals to common sense. Because language in the adult develops from a nonlinguistic neonatal state, it seems reasonable to conclude that the language substrate undergoes a corresponding developmental change between infancy and adulthood. If it is in addition assumed that bisymmetry is a simpler or less evolved pattern of neural organization than asymmetry, it follows that the lateralized adult brain develops from a functionally symmetrical neonatal brain.

Evidence for and against equipotentiality and progressive lateralization will be discussed later. Before reviewing that evidence, we will consider some implications of the progressive lateralization hypothesis as well as alternative models. Then we will point out some conceptual problems encountered in attempting to study the cerebral lateralization of functions as they are emerging. Finally, we will discuss the concept of neuroplasticity as it relates to hemispheric specialization.

Progressive Lateralization

Although equipotentiality and progressive lateralization usually are linked together (e.g., see Lenneberg, 1967), the two concepts may be dissociated. Operationally, equipotentiality only manifests when the area of brain that normally subserves a function becomes inactivated. The notion that this is a property of the brain at some specified stage of development, usually the time of birth, is common, but not integral to the concept. Perhaps equipotentiality of the hemispheres ends when a skill begins to develop in one hemisphere. One could argue, for example, that there is equipotentiality for language until language begins to develop; when language development begins, however, it does so within the left hemisphere only. This incorporates equipotentiality but not progressive lateralization. Conversely, one could speculate that complete lateralization of language will be achieved only after years of maturation, but that damage to the left hemisphere at any age would limit the ultimate level of language development. This model incorporates progressive lateralization but not equipotentiality.

Progressive lateralization implies a brain basis for a particular function that shrinks with development. The function initially is bilaterally represented, but it ultimately is represented only in one hemisphere (Lenneberg, 1967). Although this principle of a shrinking brain basis for a behavior is not necessarily incorrect, it is a novel concept, lacking precedent in neurobiology. That the degree of recovery from aphasia diminishes with increasing age (Lenneberg, 1967) is more parsimoniously attributed to the established principle of decreasing neuroplasticity than to the novel and unconfirmed principle of a shrinking brain basis for behavior. The fact that the immature right hemisphere can assume linguistic functions after damage to the left hemisphere does not prove that the right hemisphere subserved those functions prior to the damage.

In criticizing the shrinking-substrate principle, we should point out the distinction between that principle and two confusable concepts. The first is that of a shifting brain base for a specific behavior, from lower to higher levels of organization, which is known as encephalization of function (Miller et al., 1973; Sarnat & Netsky, 1974). Increasing functional sophistication may be associated with increasing cortical control, but this is quite different from stating that the brain base decreases in size. The other confusable principle is automatization of behavior. There is reason to believe that as a function becomes well practiced its execution depends on less cortical territory than when it is being learned or when its execution demands a high level of attention (Kinsbourne, 1976; Whitaker, 1980). In cybernetic terms, automatized performance involves an open loop rather than a closed loop. Insofar as open-loop control tends to evolve with learning and maturation (Kinsbourne, 1976), the cortical territory required for the execution of certain functions may decrease during development. In other words, more functions become automatized as the child grows older, and because automatized functions require less cerebral territory than nonautomatized functions, it is likely that certain functions can be performed with less cortical involvement in the adult than in the young child. When circumstances require attention, however, performance in both the adult and the child should require equivalent amounts of cerebral territory. The concept of automatization, thus, concerns the degree to which available brain resources are deployed in the performance of certain tasks. The concept of a shrinking-brain basis for behavior, in contrast, pertains to developmental changes in the hard wiring of the brain.

Regressive Lateralization

If degree of cerebral lateralization does undergo change during maturation, it may decrease rather than increase. Despite occasional suggestions that electrophysiological and behavioral asymmetries are more prominent in infants (Entus, 1977; Molfese, 1977) and young children (Kinsbourne & Hiscock, 1977) than in older children and adults, writers have consistently ignored the possibility that the degree of cerebral lateralization decreases during ontogeny. A regressive-lateralization hypothesis implies that the brain basis for various functions becomes more extensive with increasing maturation. The concept of an expanding substrate is consistent with a Jacksonian view of the nervous system, although developmental expansion in Jackson's scheme was due to cortical representation being added to preexisting subcortical representation. In contrast, according to a regressive-lateralization notion, behaviors already under cortical control in one hemisphere would fall to an increasing degree under the control of the opposite hemisphere as well.

The concept of regressive lateralization can be supported by contrasting the presumed nature of functional asymmetries in infants to those in older children and adults. The electrophysiological asymmetries found in neonates (Davis & Wada, 1977, 1978; Molfese, 1977) presumably reflect the innate activity of brainstem arousal mechanisms. Certain acoustic properties of linguistic stimuli and other highly structured auditory stimuli seem to cause selective activation of the left side of the brain. This asymmetry, which tends to be marked, most likely is independent of experiential and cognitive influences that play a role only after the cerebral cortex has reached a more advanced state of maturation. It can be argued that, after language develops in the cortex, it never is as clearly lateralized as the activating mechanism that is being tapped in the infant studies (Searleman, 1977). For example, certain quasi-linguistic processes, such as the use of visual imagery and metaphors, may depend on the right hemisphere (Ellis & Shepherd, 1974; Seamon & Gazzaniga, 1973).

To recapitulate, the argument for regressive lateralization rests upon the assumption that different levels of neural organization are being tapped at different stages of development. Early asymmetries reflect subcortical mechanisms; later asymmetries reflect a greater degree of cortical influence. Insofar as the right hemisphere contributes to language performance in the adult (Searleman, 1977), language in the adult might be considered to be more bilateral than its precursors in the infant.

Unchanging Lateralization

The remaining possibility is that the degree of lateralization neither increases nor decreases during development but, rather, that it remains constant across the lifespan. The mechanisms that underlie measured asymmetries may shift from predominantly subcortical to predominantly cortical substrate as the brain matures, but the degree of lateralization remains invariant. The developmental-invariance hypothesis (Kinsbourne, 1975b; Kinsbourne & Hiscock, 1977) carries with it some important implications for understanding the brain basis of cognitive deficiency. If the brain is lateralized from the time of birth, it makes no sense to invoke the concept of delayed lateralization to explain cognitive deficits or to claim that a particular stage of cognitive development is associated with an optimal degree of lateralization. There would be no justification for attempting to accelerate the course of lateralization by special training. There would be only two conclusions that one could reach regarding cerebral lateralization in a group of abnormal children. Either the brains of these children are lateralized in the usual manner or, if not, the children having anomalous lateralization will reach maturity without ever acquiring lateralization in its common form.

The concept of developmental invariance need not imply that the cerebral organization of a particular complex skill remains fixed across the lifespan. It is quite likely that, as a new skill develops, its brain basis changes in some way. For instance, the automatization of certain components of the skill may be associated with alterations in the brain substrate for that skill. What presumably remains constant is the left hemisphere's specialization for some basic functions and the right hemisphere's specialization for others. The degree to which the respective functions of each hemisphere are utilized in performing a newly acquired skill may change as the skill develops, but these are changes in strategy rather than changes in the basic organization of the brain. Consider, for instance, a hypothetical skill that may be performed with or without the aid of linguistic mediation. When the skill first develops, children may rely heavily on nonverbal processes, perhaps because their linguistic mediation skills are not sufficiently developed. With further practice in performing the hypothetical skill as well as further language development, it may become increasingly adaptive and feasible to use a linguistic strategy to perform the skill. In one sense, the neural basis of the skill has evolved from right hemispheric or bilateral representation to left hemispheric representation; however, there is no reason to believe that there has been any change in the lateralization of the verbal and nonverbal underpinnings of the skill.

Interpreting Developmental Change

Clinical Evidence

Until recently, clinical studies of childhood aphasia constituted the sole source of information about the ontogeny of cerebral dominance for speech. Other sources of information are now available but the clinical data remain influential. Consequently, it is important to note the risks of using clinical evidence to draw conclusions about the developmental course of hemispheric specialization in normal children.

Let us first consider the conclusions that may be drawn about speech lateralization from cases of right-hemispheric damage. What can we infer from the claim that young children frequently become aphasic as a consequence of damage to the right hemisphere? This observation, if correct, still fails to confirm Lenneberg's (1967) hypothesis that early language is bilaterally represented. Aphasia after right-hemispheric insult merely shows that language was represented in the right hemisphere; establishing bilaterality on the basis of aphasia evidence is much more difficult. One must first define what is meant by bilaterality. If bilaterality is construed to entail redundancy of language in the two hemispheres, then it would require bilateral damage to produce aphasia. Another possible construction of bilaterality is that both hemispheres are necessary for language and neither hemisphere by itself is sufficient. In that case, insult to either side would be likely to impair language. One would assume *a priori* that aphasia would be equally probable following left- or right-sided damage. A third possibility is that one cerebral hemisphere performs some language functions and the opposite hemisphere performs others. Damage to either hemisphere again would be likely to disrupt language, but the nature of the aphasia would vary as a function of the hemisphere involved. Unless the respective functions of the two hemispheres proved to be invariant across individuals, it would be impossible to confirm this kind of bilaterality on the basis of aphasia resulting from unilateral damage. Even if the principle were correct, a given aspect of language might be represented in the left hemisphere of some children and in the right hemisphere of others. Moreover, damage to either hemisphere probably would result in diverse aphasic manifestations, depending on such factors as size and locus of the lesion.

It is clear that inferences about the bilaterality of language representation cannot be made without studying both hemispheres of an individual. The sodium amobarbital procedure (Wada test) represents one approach, but there is rarely medical necessity for performing the test on young children. Observations of language deficits after unilateral insult can provide definitive evidence of bilaterality only if there should happen to be two successive injuries, one to one hemisphere and the other to the opposite hemisphere. Bilaterality of the third variety (some linguistic functions in the left hemisphere, others in the right hemisphere) would be confirmed if the initial injury results in a partial aphasia and if subsequent damage to the opposite hemisphere terminated the remaining linguistic skills.

For the purpose of demonstrating the right hemisphere's putative role in children's language processing, the incidence of aphasia following right- and left-hemispheric damage has been of primary interest. Childhood aphasia studies have provided an additional kind of information, namely, data regarding recovery of language function after unilateral damage. It is assumed that rapid and virtually complete restitution of function after left-hemispheric damage reflects incompleteness of lateralization, that is, language in the right as well as the left hemisphere. It follows that if the degree of language lateralization increases with increasing age, then recovery of language after left-hemispheric injury should be slower and less complete in older children than in younger children. The first difficulty in applying this logic is a practical one: it is virtually impossible to ascertain the comparability of lesions in the brains of children of diverse ages. However, even in the ideal case—in which the lesions are assumed to be exactly comparable—age differences in speed or degree of recovery cannot be unequivocally attributed to increasing degrees of lateralization. In making such an inference, one must disregard the likelihood that neuroplasticity decreases with increasing age (Isaacson, 1968; Stein, Rosen, & Butters, 1974). Any reported changes in recovery of function following unilateral damage may be attributed more parsimoniously to the well-established principle of diminishing plasticity than to the unproven principle of a shrinking cerebral substrate for language (Kinsbourne & Hiscock, 1977).

Anatomical Correlates of Behavioral Development

The cognitive skills that become available by virtue of hemispheric specialization are presumably enabled by maturation of the neural substrate. It is, therefore, natural that attempts have been made to link the emergence of individual mental operations with observable change in some index of neural maturation. This effort has, to date, been of no avail because no concensus exists about what constitutes the relevant index for the change at the neural level.

Brain cells cease to form in the second year of life (Dobbin & Sands, 1973), whereas brain weight increases subsequently by a further third. By far the most attention has been paid to myelination—no doubt because it is easily demonstrable histologically—and especially to myelination in the corpus callosum, both because the callosum is morphologically distinct and because of the popular appeal of split-brain studies. However, myelination may not be a useful index. First, neurons do conduct impulses, even before they are myelinated. The functional implication of this is unknown. Also, there is no guarantee that once a neural system is myelinated, it springs into action forthwith (Goldman, 1974). Second, myelination serves those neurons that communicate at a distance. There is no reason to assume that it is the ability to communicate the proceeds of processing from neural system to neural system that is rate limiting for cognitive development. The development of the dendritic network (neuropil) and specifically of inhibitory connections (e.g., those mediated by gamma-aminobutyric acid) may be much more closely linked to mental function. But we cannot readily measure this at present. Nor is it clear what role the *loss* in synaptic density with increasing age in childhood (reported by Huttenlocher, 1979) has to do with function. Does it support behavioral differentiation by rendering neurons more differentially connected with each other? (See also Brockes, 1976.) It seems likely that the needed index of neural maturation will be related to synaptic organization rather than to as gross a feature as the insulation of nerve cables.

Even if myelination were relevant, its emergence is so staggered over time as to render it virtually useless as an explanatory principle. For instance, the corpus callosum myelinates gradually from age 2 to 8 (Yakovlev & LeCours, 1967). This slow process could potentially explain any cognitive advance during this lengthy stage of the lifespan; it, therefore, explains none. How much myelination is enough for function (i.e., for which function)? Until we can perform event-related measures of callosal activity in humans, we should treat the use of the myelinating callosum as an explanatory principle with reserve.

Two studies illustrate the attempt to invoke interhemispheric transmission as explanatory of mental development. Galin, Johnstone, Nakell, & Herron (1979) have shown that young children can perform successive haptic matches better within a hand than between hands; Davidson et al. (1982) made similar observations with a limited group of poor readers (as compared to controls) who showed no difference between the uncrossed and crossed conditions. This work is, of course, suggestive. But we should keep in mind that the change in hand used for the successive matches interpolates an additional event into the memory task. This could cause interference regardless of the crossing attribute of the maneuver. The studies lack the control of a similarly distracting maneuver that does not entail shifting control from one hemisphere to another. When one controls for this factor, one no longer finds evidence for relatively limited interhemispheric information transmission in either young children or dyslexics (Kinsbourne, da Silva, & Kershner, 1983).

Statements that young children are "split-brain" (Gazzaniga, 1970) go beyond our present knowledge. They imply that higher mental systems mature in each hemisphere before their interconnections mature. No such knowledge exists about any human cognitive system. Not only the corpus callosum but also the hemisphere is slow to mature, particularly in the association areas. No one knows specifically whether a given processing center becomes functional before, at the same time, or after its interhemispheric connection becomes functional.

Developmental Change in Laterality

Later in our discussion, we will cite laterality evidence suggesting that basic functions, such as speech perception and speech production, remain lateralized in the same manner and to the same degree across childhood. Certain other tasks yield asymmetries that appear later in development or change in some way during development. Although these latter findings frequently are interpreted in terms of shifting patterns of cerebral lateralization (e.g., see Tomlinson-Keasey & Clarkson-Smith, 1980; Witelson, 1976b), they may reflect developmental changes in strategy superimposed upon a constantly lateralized substrate (Carey & Diamond, 1977; Carey, Diamond, & Woods, 1980; Leehey, Carey, Diamond, & Cahn, 1978; Webster & Thurber, 1978).

If cerebral lateralization is alleged to increase or decrease during development or to wax and wane in some nonmonotonic manner, it is difficult to isolate changes in the way that a function is performed (i.e., strategy changes) from putative changes in the degree to which the hemispheres are specialized (i.e., lateralization changes). A developmental trend from functional symmetry to asymmetry may reflect a developmental change in the way a skill is being performed (with lateralization of the neural substrate remaining constant) or it may reflect a shift in lateralization of the skill (with the functional organization of the skill remaining constant). In the absence of evidence favoring one interpretation or the other, it should be kept in mind that the two alternative interpretations represent different levels of inference. If children of different ages differ in degree of asymmetry on a perceptual task, for example, the inference that their brains are differentially lateralized is a stronger, less conservative conclusion than is the inference that they are approaching the task with different strategies. Consequently, the differential-strategy explanation should be ruled out before one concludes that different degrees of asymmetry reflect different degrees of hemispheric specialization.

Lateralization of cognitive function cannot be studied before that function's neural substrate has matured to a point sufficient for the child to be able to exercise the function to some measurable extent. In other words, one cannot study a function before its developmental sequence has begun. Clear in principle, this point is nevertheless difficult to operationalize. Type-one and type-two errors are at risk: one may assume the sequence has begun either before it has or after it has. A type-one error may occur if one equates a function with a performance. The recognition of faces may be an instance. Even very young children are known to respond differentially to faces (e.g., Fantz, 1966). Yet, a left visual-field advantage for face recognition sometimes is not found below the age of 9 years (Leehey, 1976). If face recognition corresponds one-to one to a particular process, it could reasonably be inferred that that process begins in bilateral representation and lateralizes subsequently. However, not only laterality changes over time but also skill in the performance increases. A neurologizing interpretation would be that the same process is able to function more efficiently because it is concentrated in one hemisphere rather than spread thinly across the cortex and is less subject, therefore, to interference or to failures of cross-callosal synchronization, and so on. However, the assumption that the task, face recognition, elicits the same strategies on the part of the observer at different ages may not be justified. Perhaps the onset of the laterality effect indexes the recruitment to the task of an additional strategy—a more subtle use of relational information that the right hemisphere has now become mature enough to implement. If so, the emerging laterality could index the inclusion into the repertoire of face-recognizing operations an additional developmental sequence, previously not available, but that itself might well have been lateralized from the start. Our strategy-based explanation is supported by the fact that changes in stimuli and procedures seem to alter the age at which asymmetries emerge (Broman, 1978; Leehey, 1976; Marcel & Rajan, 1975; Young & Ellis, 1976).

Similar considerations apply at the motor level. It is often argued that handedness is not fully established until the 2nd or even the 5th year of life. Operationalized as reliable preference for use of one hand in a set of prescribed situations, this may well be true (Coren, Porac, & Duncan, 1981). But again, it may not be justifiable to rush to the brain for an explanation. It is possible that the hand preference was established physiologically much earlier. However, other variables may have been more capable of interfering with the phenotypic expression of a handedness genotype in the younger child. An instance is the variable of crossing the midline. Infants tend not to reach across the midline. Given the difficulty of keeping an infant in a stable centered condition, one can readily see how a study of reaching might fail to find a lateral preference because the preference is overridden by the tendency to reach with the arm ipsilateral to the stimulus. In this example of a type-one error, one has been observing, in the infant, a different determinant of behavior than one discovers in the older child, although the task is held constant. Add to this the presumed effects of practice and habit formation as well as the possible effect of self-definition ("I am a left-hander") in further polarizing differential hand choice, and one can readily see how a trend toward increased handedness over time may be independent of any change in the neural basis of the hand preference itself.

A type-two error may be made through too strict definition of the behavior being examined. One may regard language-output behavior as originating in the first differential vocal response to different referents toward the end of the 1st year. But differential vocalizing starts earlier, as babbling, although lacking the stable reference; selective attention to different referents, although without the accompaniment of intelligible utterances, begins earlier still. Recognizing that behaviors commonly evolve first outside the adaptive context to which they later will be applied, we may suspect babbling as being part of a developmental sequence leading to referential utterance. Recognizing that early utterance has a cognitive base (Bloom, 1970, 1973), namely, selective attention to salient percepts (Lempert & Kinsbourne, in press), the evolving ability to orient selectively may be another developmental precursor of utterance. With respect to babbling, laterality considerations appear not to have been studied. But selective orientation has a partially mapped-out laterality history, and this is potentially pertinent to the development of speech and its lateralization.

Thus, even though it may not be possible to detect lateralization of a function before that function has developed to a measurable extent, one may look for lateralized precursors. As a general principle of child development, typical patterns of an activity are seen before the child is capable of performing the activity adaptively. Toddlers, for instance, toddle from one place to another for no apparent reason. Infants place objects into containers and remove objects from containers, again without demonstrable reason. They emit a wide variety of speech sounds before being able to use them to communicate. In all these instances, considerable patterning of behavior precedes the adaptive application of the behavior. Given these observations, it seems plausible that certain asymmetries related to language lateralization might be observed before any highly organized, goal-directed language capacity develops. Asymmetric turning tendencies, in particular, may reflect unequal activation of the two halves of the brain (Liederman & Kinsbourne, 1980a, 1980b). Perhaps the electrophysiological (Davis & Wada, 1977, 1978; Gardiner & Walter, 1977; Molfese et al., 1975; Molfese & Molfese, 1979, 1980) and perceptual (Best, Hoffman, & Glanville, 1982; Entus, 1977; Glanville, et al., 1977; Segalowitz & Chapman, 1980) asymmetries found in infants are related to these general turning tendencies. They suggest that there is an innately programmed mechanism, presumably located in the brainstem, that activates one side of the brain more than the other in response to particular categories of stimulation. The side of the brain that later will process language, thus, shows its material-specific activation pattern long before its neuronal equipment is sufficiently mature to mediate observable, goal-directed language.

Lateralization and Neuroplasticity

The term neuroplasticity refers to the ability of the nervous system to compensate for loss of functional tissue. Compensatory recovery of function occurs in the mature brain following focal injury, but the plasticity of the young brain is thought to be much greater. Even in the neonate, however, recovery cannot be attributed to physiological repair of damaged nerve cells because neurons in the human brain do not regenerate after the axon is severed (Cajal, 1928). There may be some growth in the damaged region of the axon along with the establishment of compensatory synaptic junctions by other neurons (Kerr, 1975; LeVere, 1975), but the damaged neurons themselves do not regain their functions.

To understand neuroplasticity in neonates and children, we begin by considering possible mechanisms underlying recovery of function in the adult. If brain functions are not localized, then explaining compensatory recovery of function is a trivial matter. Loss of any part of the cerebrum might diminish overall cerebral efficiency but there would be no selective loss of function because there is no specialization. Clearly, this is contrary to the preponderance of clinical evidence, which suggests that functions are localized. The first question, then, is how to explain recovery of function in a specialized brain. If the entire cerebrum is dedicated to various specialized functions, how do we account for recovery after a function is lost? Rosner (1974) summarized four classical explanations:

1. Hierarchical organization (Jackson, reprinted in Taylor, 1932). A given function is represented at various levels of the neuraxis; damage at a higher level allows lower levels to assume control over the behavior in question.
2. Diaschisis (von Monakow, 1914). When intact regions of the cerebrum are deprived of stimulation from the damaged area, a widespread, but temporary, disturbance occurs. Restitution of function is merely the dissipation of diaschisis.
3. Substitution (Munk, 1881). Cerebral regions not otherwise committed assume control of functions lost through focal injury.
4. Dynamic reorganization (e.g., Luria, Naydin, Isvetkova, & Vinarskaya, 1969). Recovery of function is attributable to the reorganization of intact brain regions. Lost functions are performed in new ways.

The latter two mechanisms assume a degree of plasticity that may not be present in the mature brain. LeVere (1975) has argued that the mature nervous system resembles other biological systems in possessing a fairly high level of stability. He asserted that behavioral capacities following brain damage reflect sparing of the relevant neural mechanisms and not reorganization of other neural tissue. Recovery can be attributed to mechanisms such as regaining access to the spared system (Meyer, 1972), correcting adverse changes in the inhibitory-facilitory balance between components of the damaged system (Sprague, 1966), and counteracting a tendency for behavioral control to shift from damaged to undamaged systems (Lashley, 1932).

The next question concerns the developing brain. Why might plasticity be greater in the young than in the mature brain? Does one or more of the mechanisms listed above operate to a greater extent in the young brain? Or is the plasticity of the immature brain attributable to mechanisms not present in the mature brain?

As noted by Goldman (1974), there are two predominant hypotheses for explaining the relatively great compensatory ability of the young brain. One invokes anatomical restructuring. Early lesions in the rodent brain (e.g., see Hicks & D'Amato, 1970; Schneider, 1970; Schneider & Jhaveri, 1974) frequently are followed by the development of anomalous axonal connections. Although some abnormal axonal growth may occur after lesions are sustained in adulthood (Lynch, Stanfield, & Cotman, 1973), the restructuring appears to be much more extensive if damage occurs during a period early in the animal's life. Little is known about compensatory axonal changes in humans and, even in rodents, the relationship between anomalous connections and behavioral sparing is not always clear. Schneider and Jhaveri (1974) observe that "having more anomalous connections may even be maladaptive" (p. 71).

The other hypothesis is that the young animal (or child) develops alternative strategies that allow the expression of a behavior without reliance on the damaged brain regions that normally subserve the behavior. It resembles Luria's concept of dynamic reorganization. The use of compensatory strategies is difficult to confirm. In humans, especially, it is difficult to differentiate compensatory strategies from the variety of individual differences in strategy that exist for nonpathologic reasons. Also, one might expect that adult animals—humans in particular—might have a fairly wide choice of alternative strategies to use after brain damage. Consequently, unless the availability of strategies in different stages of life can be specified, the strategy explanation for functional sparing does not explain why plasticity might change during development.

Goldman (1974) has proposed an alternative to the respective hypotheses of new axonal connections and new strategies. Her work with lesioned monkeys suggests that functional sparing in the young animal cannot be understood without considering the maturational state of different brain regions at the time of damage and at the time of testing. A function will appear to be preserved despite an early lesion if testing is performed prior to full development of the neural substrate for that function. For example, monkeys with early lesions in the dorsolateral frontal lobes failed to show significant deficits on a delayed-response task when tested at the age of 1 year, but deficits were seen subsequently at the age of 2 years. Presumably, delayed-response performance at 1 year of age is mediated primarily by structures other than the dorsolateral cortex. Thus, the ability to perform the task at that age does not reflect compensation but, instead, it suggests that the function had not been lost. Similarly, an early lesion may or may not produce a behavioral deficit, depending on the maturational status of intact structures that are available to serve as an alternative substrate. In monkeys with early lesions to the dorsolateral cortex, adequate delayed-response performance at the age of 1 year apparently depends on other structures (viz., orbital cortex, caudate nucleus, and dorsomedial nucleus of the thalamus) that have reached functional maturity by the age of 1 year. Although Goldman's work does not rule out the development of new connections nor reliance on new strategies as mechanisms of functional sparing, it does suggest that neither of these mechanisms need be invoked to explain some of the sparing observed in early-lesioned monkeys. What appears to be plasticity may be attributable to differential maturation and a shifting brain basis for certain behaviors. Goldman's reasoning does presuppose that the performance (delayed response) is controlled by the same variables in young and older animals. It may not be. The older animal may deploy additional strategies (e.g., to fend off distractors) that the young animal does not use or even need (and those may rely on functioning frontal lobes). This possibility appears not to have been investigated.

Having considered some possible brain-based reasons why recovery from brain damage is more complete if the damage occurs early, we should admit that this proposition has itself been challenged. There are many differences between the usual scope and circumstances of early and of later damage, and existing studies fail to hold these factors constant (James-Roberts, 1979). Long-term sequelae of early damage depend not only on its time of occurrence but also on its extent and etiology (Towbin, 1978); on the child's gender, maturational state, and early experience; and on characteristics of the child's environment following the injury (Chelune & Edwards, 1981; Rudel, 1978). Insofar as learning ability is affected by the damage, the younger brain-injured child is disadvantaged by having previously learned little of what there is to be learned. Moreover, one's impression of the child's recovery may be overly favorable if it depends largely on clinical examination or on IQ tests; substantial deficits may exist long after more obvious signs of abnormality have disappeared (Rudel, 1978). To quite an extent the greater recovery potential of the immature brain may prove to have been exaggerated.

Language is relatively resistant to early damage

(Rudel, 1978). For clinical purposes, it is useful to know that early damage, if restricted to either cerebral hemisphere, does not preclude normal or near-normal development of language. It is of theoretical importance, however, to be able to specify precisely the degree to which a single left or right hemisphere can serve as substrate for linguistic and other cognitive abilities. Most clearcut is the evidence of linguistic competency following damage in childhood to the left cerebral hemisphere. We will subsequently outline the evidence that the left brain is specialized for language from at least the time of birth. Nevertheless, linguistic competency can be demonstrated after extensive damage to the language areas of the left hemisphere and even after removal of the entire hemisphere—striking testimony of the degree to which functions may recover.

Lenneberg (1967) summarized the clinical evidence regarding recovery of linguistic function after unilateral cerebral damage in children of different ages. If damage occurs during the first 2 years of life, before a substantial degree of language has been acquired, the consequences with respect to language development will be minimal. According to Lenneberg, language will develop either normally or with only a few months' delay. If a damaged 3- or 4-year-old loses language, recovery will involve traversing the stages of language acquisition but ultimately will be complete (at least as judged from the absence of clinically obvious aphasia). Damage to children between the ages of 4 years and pubescence also will be reversed in most cases to the point that there is no obvious residual aphasia, although if recovery is not complete by pubescence, there will be little additional recovery after that time. After puberty is reached, recovery is like that in adults, that is, more limited, with persisting manifestations of aphasia.

A strong version of equipotentiality regards both cerebral hemispheres as equally good substrates for any cognitive function. In contrast, if the left and right halves of the brain show signs of differential specialization at the time of birth or shortly thereafter (e.g., see Entus, 1977; Molfese, 1977), one might expect that the upper limits of a hemisphere's capacity to subserve a particular function would depend on whether it normally subserves that function. Although the right hemisphere may be capable of subserving linguistic functions after early damage to the left hemisphere, the isolated right hemisphere might never develop a level of linguistic competency equivalent to that which would have developed in the isolated left hemisphere.

Many lesion studies have addressed the issue of equipotentiality between the hemispheres, but there are too many confounding factors in these studies to allow definite conclusions about whether the two hemispheres differ in their ability to subserve various linguistic and nonlinguistic functions. The best evidence comes from a few carefully studied patients who have had one cerebral hemisphere (or at least the cortex of one hemisphere) removed surgically. A. Smith (1972) described a young man whose left cerebral hemisphere was removed in childhood because of epileptogenic structural damage that probably occurred very early in life. Even though this man had no left hemisphere, his verbal IQ from the WAIS was 130; he performed so well on the Peabody Picture Vocabulary Test that no ceiling could be established. A. Smith's patient has since graduated from university and apparently is performing successfully as a highway traffic engineer. More than any other known case in the neurological literature, A. Smith's patient demonstrates the impressive capacity of an isolated right hemisphere to subserve those functions for which the left hemisphere normally is specialized. Nevertheless, remarkable as it is, this example falls short of proving equipotentiality between the left and right hemispheres as substrates for language development. Had the boy's right hemisphere been damaged instead of his left, Smith's patient might, for all we know, have shown even more impressive verbal skill. Moreover, we cannot be sure that he is free of psycholinguistic deficits because measures such as verbal intelligence tests fail to tap important components of language competency, such as ability to comprehend and generate certain difficult syntactic constructions.

Dennis and her collaborators (Dennis, 1980a, 1980b; Dennis & Kohn, 1975; Dennis & Whitaker, 1976, 1977; Kohn & Dennis, 1974) seek to uncover subtle linguistic deficits in hemidecorticate patients whose only cerebral cortex is that of the right hemisphere. The first three children reported by Dennis were born with Sturge-Weber-Dimitri syndrome, a condition characterized by seizures and progressive mental backwardness. The entire cerebral cortex of one hemisphere was excised in the 1st year of life to bring the seizures under control and facilitate mental development. There was little opportunity for language to develop in the hemisphere that was excised so early in life. At the age of 9 years, the children's intellectual abilities were about average and there was neither clinically obvious aphasia nor deficient verbal IQ in the two children without a left cerebral cortex. However, more specialized linguistic testing revealed that the two children with only a right hemisphere intact were deficient in their ability to understand certain syntatic information, such as that conveyed by the words when, after, and before. In contrast, the child with only a left cerebral cortex performed above age norms on various psycholinguistic tests, but he showed marked deficits on the visual association and visual closure subtests of the Illinois Test of Psycholinguistic Abilities (Kirk, McCarthy, & Kirk, 1968). Dennis and her colleagues conclude that, when a single cerebral hemisphere develops in isolation, its capacity for certain kinds of cognitive performance depends on whether it is a left or a right hemisphere. An isolated right hemisphere cannot attain the degree of proficiency in auditory language processing that is possible with an isolated left hemisphere. An isolated left hemisphere is likely to be deficient in certain visuospatial skills.

Such a conclusion is obviously premature, considering the tiny sample size and the host of uncontrolled variables, notably the extent of the hemidecortication (Jacobs, 1977). Yet when Dennis (1980a) added three more right- and four more left-operated cases, the situation was not eased because these were widely diverse in age at operation and testing and no assurance was given that some of them were not bilaterally involved. Bishop (in press) presents a detailed critique of this series of studies, pointing out sampling biases and flaws in statistical analysis that render the conclusions unacceptable. One impressive finding does emerge. Some of the left-operated patients did as well on the psycholinguistic measures as the right-operated cases. So, it is possible for the right hemisphere, under some circumstances, to sustain language development equal to that supported by the left. Hemispheric equipotentiality is supported by this result.

What can we conclude about neuroplasticity and its relationship to hemispheric specialization in the child? Although the plasticity of the young brain may be attributable, in part, to sprouting of new axonal connections, it seems likely that much apparent sparing or recovery of function reflects differential maturation rates for different brain structures and a shifting neural substrate for certain functions (Goldman, 1974). Some deficits may resolve over time, but only because the more mature expression of a function depends on an intact brain region rather than on the damaged region. Conversely, when a behavior is spared after cerebral damage, deficits may appear subsequently as the damaged region assumes responsibility for the more mature form of the behavior. Goldman's demonstrations of delayed deficits support the neurodevelopmental-lag model of cognitive deficiency (Kinsbourne, 1973a), which postulates that early brain damage may have no observable behavioral consequences until such time as the skills subserved by the damaged region normally would emerge as a result of maturation. Implicit in these conclusions is an assumed inability of any healthy brain region to duplicate exactly the functions previously provided by another region that subsequently sustains damage. Yet, the existing data from hemispherectomy and hemidecortication patients show that the cerebrum of the human infant possesses a substantial degree of plasticity. An isolated right hemisphere may subserve average or above-average linguistic abilities, such as those measured by verbal IQ tests, although careful testing could still reveal deficits in some aspects of language. Similarly, it remains to be ascertained whether the isolated left hemisphere is capable of performing certain visuospatial functions at a level commensurate with its other capabilities. There is preliminary evidence that compensation for the right-hemispheric role in visuospatial functioning is less impressive than the compensation for left-hemispheric loss (Woods, 1980). In short, it remains to be determined whether there are selective limitations to plasticity. That there are cannot simply be inferred from the fact that the sides of the brain show signs of differentiated functioning very early in life (e.g., see Segalowitz & Gruber, 1977). Indeed, it is by no means clear that the early differential functioning should be ascribed to the infant's hemispheres (which are probably not even functional at the time—cf. Conel, 1939–1967). The lateral specialization may be at the brainstem in structures that implement task-specific hemispheric activation (Kinsbourne, 1980b). The view that each hemisphere is wired in a way that fosters its predestined specialized mode of functioning (Semmes, 1968) remains unsupported by evidence. Alternatively, brainstem selectors determine which hemisphere will be active during which task (and do so even in infants before the task can be attempted). If this were true, then the limits on contralateral compensation might be set, not by incompatible wiring characteristics, but by the extent to which the brainstem control centers are able to activate the intact hemisphere for purposes of the compensatory functioning.

Summary

This section has set the stage for a review and interpretation of the evidence dealing with the ontogenesis of cerebral lateralization. We have pointed out some implications of progression, regression, and invariance models of hemispheric specialization. We have discussed the difficulties encountered when using lesion data to study cerebral lateralization in children, when relating cerebral lateralization to anatomical maturation, and when attempting to assess change in the lateralization of functions while the functions are emerging. We have emphasized the distinction between developmental changes in brain organization and changes in the way in which a complex function is performed, and we have recommended that strategy changes be ruled out before concluding that the substrate has become more or less lateralized. We have also presented a rationale for seeking lateralized precursors of functions that have not yet developed. Finally, in discussing neuroplasticity, we have argued that the remarkable capacity of the immature brain to recover functions after injury is not inconsistent with the principle of early specialization of the cerebral hemispheres.

ONTOGENY OF LATERALIZATION: FINDINGS AND IMPLICATIONS

Early Anatomical Asymmetries

As noted previously in this chapter, certain anatomical asymmetries are known to exist in the adult cerebrum (Geschwind & Levitsky, 1968; Teszner et al., 1972; Wada et al., 1975; Witelson & Pallie, 1973; Yeni-Komshian & Benson, 1976). Similar asymmetries have been found in the neonatal cerebrum (Wada et al., 1975; Witelson & Pallie, 1973). Of particular interest is the finding that the temporal speech region (planum temporale) usually is larger on the left side than on the right side in the infant as well as in the adult brain. As with the adult brain, the functional implications of topographic asymmetries in the immature brain are unknown. It could be argued that left-hemispheric dominance for handedness and language stems from structural asymmetries; or it could be argued that the structural asymmetries have no obvious implications for the development of functional asymmetries. Wada et al. (1975) reported that the degree of asymmetry in the planum temporale of adults is more marked than in children. Although this apparent developmental change toward greater asymmetry may be a valid observation, the functional significance of such a change remains to be determined. The same applies to the apparent phylogenetic progression in cerebral asymmetry noted by Yeni-Komshian and Benson (1976). They found the left sylvian fissure to be equally as long as the right in rhesus monkeys, somewhat longer in chimpanzees, and relatively longer still in humans. We can at least conclude that there is a rough parallel, with respect to phylogeny as well as ontogeny, between morphological asymmetry in the sylvian region and the organism's capacity for symbolic communication. Nevertheless, anatomical asymmetries in infancy are notable mainly because they refute one of the basic observations underlying the equipotentiality hypothesis, namely, that the two cerebral hemispheres in the neonate are physically identical.

Infant Precursors of Cerebral Lateralization

The beginning of a developmental sequence is not always easily identified. The first use of intelligible words might reasonably be regarded as initiating the development of expressive language. However, psycholinguists might argue that language in the strict sense unique to humans is not properly represented by nominalizing, which is what infants mostly do when they first speak. Conversely, one might see in babbling a precursor to speaking. Here a distinction should be made between emotive babbling, which is perhaps more closely related to archaic limbic circuitry and emotive animal cries (Jergens & Ploog, 1981), and the babbling that accompanies cognitive behavior. What cognitive behavior is accompanied by babbling and particularly by early verbalizations? If we can establish this, then we can enquire whether that cognitive behavior is itself asymmetrical or whether the asymmetry emerges only when speech control is initiated.

A wealth of evidence indicates that early utterances generally refer to perceptually salient things or activities and that they accompany an orienting response to the stimulus (Lempert & Kinsbourne, in press). The orienting response, in addition to its general component, has a selective component, which may consist in hand and gaze deviation, directional hand movement, or even full-fledged pointing. It is in selective orienting rather than in specific dyadic communicative routines, such as "joint regard" (Bruner, 1975), that speech sounds emerge. It is to emerging orienting behavior that we, therefore, look first for any evidence of asymmetry.

Posture and Orientation

Infants display asymmetries of posture. The tonic-neck reflex, which involves the head and all four limbs, is an inherently asymmetric posture in which the majority of infants, even premature infants, orient to the right (Gesell, 1938; Gesell & Ames, 1950). Head and eyes are turned to the right and the right hand is extended. Asymmetry in intrauterine position is associated with, but does not account for, the neonatal head-orientation bias (Michel & Goodwin, 1979). Instead, this asymmetric posture suggests an early prepotency of the left side of the brain, existing as early as at 34 weeks of postconceptual age (Fox & Lewis, 1982). A possible explanation is that not only in the mature brain but also perhaps to an even greater degree in the immature brain, lateral brain activation overflows into contralateral turning tendency (Kinsbourne, 1972). Although this has so far been studied in adults as a phasic phenomenon, it could also have a tonic component in early development (perhaps associated with asymmetric maturational spurts). This is one explanation for the observation that in the period of 16 to 22 months following birth, children show increasing right-turning bias corresponding to an acceleration in their verbal development (Kagan, 1982). It has also been established that neonates turn their heads spontaneously to the right much more often than to the left (Siqueland & Lipsitt, 1966; Turkewitz, Gordon, & Birch, 1965a, 1965b) and that they show a rightward bias when stimulated (Liederman & Kinsbourne, 1980a; Turkewitz, Moreau, Birch, & Crystal, 1967). Siqueland and Lipsitt (1966) found it difficult to condition right turning in infants because they tend to turn to the right spontaneously. Moreover, the rightward bias appears to be a motor bias rather than a result of differential sensitivity to the left and right sides of the body (Liederman & Kinsbourne, 1980a, 1980c). Each of these asymmetries can be taken as evidence that (1) the left side of the brain is dominant early in life and (2) the putative connection between turning asymmetries and laterality is bolstered by the finding that rightward-biased turning is characteristic of children with two right-handed parents but not of children with one nonright-handed parent (Liederman & Kinsbourne, 1980b).

Reaching and Grasping

Even though it is commonly believed that consistent hand preference emerges long after infancy (e.g., see Cernacek & Podivinsky, 1971; Gesell & Ames, 1947; Giesecke, 1936), a statistically significant right-hand preference has been demonstrated in infants only 3 months of age (Caplan & Kinsbourne, 1976). In this study, infants retained an object significantly longer in the right hand than in the left hand. This finding recently has been duplicated with infants as young as 17 days (Petrie & Peters, 1980) and a tendency for the stepping reflex to lead off with the right leg has also been found at that age (Peters & Petrie, 1979). It is likely that previous failures to find very early hand preference can be attributed to inappropriate choice of response measures. Insofar as infants tend to reach with both hands at once and usually fail to reach across the midline (Provine & Westerman, 1979), reaching tasks are not well suited for demonstrating early handedness unless special precautions are taken, in which case the predominance of right-handedness becomes manifest (Hawn & Harris, 1979). Directional bias in neonatal head turning predicts hand preference in reaching at 16 and 22 weeks (Michel, 1981). Neonatal head-orientation preference predicts side of longer lasting grasp in the 2-month-old child (Hawn & Harris, 1979) as well as reaching at 3 months (Michel & Goodwin, 1979) and at 5 months (Hawn & Harris, 1979). It also correlates significantly with lateral preference at age 7 years (Viviani, Turkewitz, & Karp, 1978). It does seem clear that there is in most people an inherent rightward-turning bias, which is manifested in neonatal head orienting (Liederman & Kinsbourne, 1980a), related to right-handedness in their parents (Liederman & Kinsbourne, 1980b), expressed in both right-sided grasp superiority (Caplan & Kinsbourne, 1976) and reaching preference (Hawn & Harris, 1979; Michel & Goodwin, 1979), and associated with rapid diminution of a primitive reflex on the right side (Liederman & Coryell, in press). But phases appear to exist during which this right-turning bias is temporarily neutralized or overridden. Franco, Muir, and Dodwell (1978) observed reaching more often with the left arm as early as 2 months of age; Halverson (1931) claimed the same for children at 1 month; and Gesell and Ames (1947) and Seth (1973) inferred left preference for several subsequent months, although (as Young 1977, has shown) on no convincing data base. Ramsay (1980) found 7- but not 5-month-old infants to reach for toys with the right hand more often than the left hand. Lewkowitz and Turkewitz (1982) found no reaching preference in 6-month-old infants, but A. I. Cohen (1966) did at age 8 months. By the time infants reach the age of 10 months, an overall right-hand advantage for tapping performance as well as a right-hand preference can be observed (Ramsay, 1979).

Perceptual Asymmetries

Because infants are able to discriminate among speech sounds (Eimas, Siqueland, Jusczyk, & Vigorito, 1971; Moffitt, 1971; Trehub & Rabinovitch, 1972), it is feasible to look for asymmetries in the perception of speech sounds as well as other environmental stimuli. It has been shown that, when pairs of CV nonsense syllables are presented in dichotic competition, infants between the ages of 22 and 140 days show a REA for the detection of transitions from one syllable to another (Entus, 1977). The right-ear superiority is evident from the infants' differential nonnutritive sucking patterns in response to transitions at the left and right ear; infants were more likely to detect transitions at the right ear (i.e., to recover from habituation of sucking) than at the left ear. However, the opposite ear advantage was seen when infants heard dichotically presented musical stimuli. All together, 34 of 48 infants (71%) showed a REA for the CV nonsense syllables and 38 of 48 infants (79%) showed a LEA for the musical stimuli. Although these findings were not confirmed in a subsequent study (with some methodological adjustments) of 2-month-olds (Vargha-Khadem & Corballis, 1979), Glanville et al., (1977) confirmed the major conclusions of the Entus (1977) study. Recovery from cardiac instead of sucking habituation was the measure of auditory perception in 12 infants of average age of 15 weeks. Despite this departure from the procedure used by Entus (1977), the results were very similar, that is, greater response recovery followed transition from one CV syllable to another at the right ear than at the left ear, and the reverse held for transition from one musical stimulus to another. These independent demonstrations of early perceptual asymmetries were supported by evidence of differential reduction in limb tremor after speech and music in premature infants (Segalowitz & Chapman, 1980). After repeated exposure to either speech or music, infants only 36 gestational weeks old were fitted with accelerometers to record limb tremors. The group exposed to speech showed a disproportionate reduction of right-hand movements relative to the group exposed to music and to a no-treatment control group. Although this finding does not demonstrate perceptual asymmetry per se, it does serve to substantiate other findings of early left-brain prepotency in response to speech.

Recently, Best et al. (1982) repeated the Glanville et al. (1977) cardiac habituation procedure with a larger sample of infants. When results for all forty-eight of the 2-, 3-, and 4-month-olds were considered together, they duplicated the previous findings, that is, right-ear superiority for phonetic discrimination and left-ear superiority for discrimination of musical timbre. However, separate analysis of the performance of each age group revealed that 2-month-old infants not only failed to show a significant REA for speech stimuli but also apparently failed to discriminate changes in speech sounds irrespective of the ear into which the sounds were presented. In contrast, these 2-month-olds were able to detect changes in timbre if the musical notes were heard at the left ear. As Best et al. (1982) point out, their failure to find a REA for phonetic discrimination in the youngest children reflects a "floor effect in phonetic memory ability" (p. 80) and, as such, cannot be attributed to an absence of brain lateralization. Of the nine 2-month-old infants who did respond to phonetic contrasts, six showed a REA.

Electrophysiological Asymmetries

Electrophysiological asymmetries are evident early in infancy (Crowell, et al., 1973; Davis & Wada, 1977; Gardiner & Walter, 1977; Molfese & Molfese, 1979, 1980; Molfese et al., 1975, 1976). Such asymmetries have been found during the first day of life (Molfese & Molfese, 1979) and in preterm infants whose average conceptional age was only 36 weeks (Molfese & Molfese, 1980). Although most of this research has involved the recording and computer averaging of AEPs, stimulus-related asymmetries in the spontaneous EEG also have been reported (Gardiner & Walter, 1977).

Molfese and his colleagues (Molfese & Molfese, 1979, 1980; Molfese et al., 1975, 1976) repeatedly have found (1) that speech stimuli, such as CV nonsense syllables and CVC words, elicit higher amplitude responses over the left hemisphere than over the right hemisphere and (2) that nonspeech sounds, such as a piano chord and a burst of noise in the speech-frequency range, elicit higher amplitude responses over the right hemisphere than over the left hemisphere. These asymmetries are generally consistent with those found by Gardiner and Walter (1977), who recorded spontaneous EEG from the left and right sides of the heads of 6-month-old infants as they heard continuous speech or music. Gardiner and Walter found that the left-to-right power ratio in the 3- to 5-Hz band shifted in response to stimulus type and that the direction of the shift was identical to that found in the alpha (8- to 12 Hz) activity of adults. In other words, the power shifts seemed to reflect predominant left-brain activation in response to speech sounds and predominant right-brain activation in response to music.

The more recent studies (e.g., see Molfese & Molfese, 1979, 1980) have focused on specific stimulus characteristics that might account for the differential responding of the left and right hemispheres to speech and nonspeech material. There are some inconsistencies between studies of infants (cf. Molfese

& Molfese, 1979, 1980) and between the infant findings and findings from a study of AEP in adults (Molfese, 1978), but the results tentatively point to some speech-specific acoustic variables to which only the left hemisphere seems to respond. Even if these preliminary conclusions are valid, however, the variables under study by Molfese do not appear capable of accounting for all of the electrophysiological asymmetries found in infants. Specifically, they do not explain why clicks and light flashes also yield asymmetric evoked responses (Davis & Wada, 1977). The asymmetries of temporo-occipital coherence and power found by Davis and Wada suggest an early prepotency of the left hemisphere for processing nonverbal auditory information. This implies that the neonatal brain is lateralized with respect to functions more rudimentary than language processing. Regardless of whether Davis and Wada are correct in attributing differential left- and right-sided electrophysiological activity to differences in stimulus familiarity, it is clear from their findings that the language versus nonlanguage dichotomy is not a completely satisfactory basis for explaining the asymmetries that have been found.

Irrespective of the underlying mechanism, the speech versus nonspeech asymmetries of cephalic electrical activity at least superficially resemble those found in adults. The degree of asymmetry is reported greater in infants than in adults (Molfese, 1977). In addition, there is preliminary EEG evidence that the expected pattern of hemispheric specialization for affect, namely, greater left-brain than right-brain activation when viewing a happy face, is present prior to the end of the 1st year of life (Davidson & Fox, 1982).

An Interpretation of Infant Asymmetries

Do the various signs of early asymmetry represent different manifestations of the same mechanisms or independent phenomena? Do they reflect lateralized processing or a more primitive asymmetry of orientation? If they reflect a single underlying mechanism, how is that mechanism related to hemispheric specialization in the more mature human? What is the relationship between tonic and phasic asymmetries?

These questions alert us to the possibility that phasic changes in the balance of activation between the hemispheres of adults, as they adopt verbal or spatial mental sets, may be superimposed, at least in right-handers, on a base state of activation that is itself asymmetrical between the hemispheres. The various asymmetries found in infancy may represent some early manifestations of phasic- as well as tonic-turning tendencies that persist throughout the lifespan. In fact, we speculate that the perceptual asymmetries found in adults reflect the vestigial effects of those primitive turning tendencies.

After lateral brain damage, the tendency to orient differentially to the side of space opposite the *intact* hemisphere is most marked when it is the left hemisphere that has remained intact (Kinsbourne, 1977). Possibly, the left hemisphere exerts a tonic right-turning influence, which in the intact brain is kept in check by cross-inhibition from the right hemisphere. When the relevant parts of the right hemisphere are rendered inactive by disease, that inherent bias is disinhibited and manifests as neglect of left space (Kinsbourne, 1977). For supportive observations in promising animal models see Denenberg (1981).

With respect to the origins of speech, we summarize by pointing out that right head-turning bias and more frequent or prolonged right-hand use in grasping, reaching, and (although this has not yet been studied) pointing could be precursors of the referential aspect of naming (Kinsbourne & Lempert, 1978).

The electrophysiological evidence that has been offered for lateralization of speech-receptive mechanisms in infants could constitute an artifact of differential head turning. As described previously, Molfese et al. (1975, 1976) reported converse asymmetries in infants for scalp potentials evoked by speech and nonspeech stimuli. However, Molfese et al. (1975) used 10 infants across the wide age range of 1 week to 10 months. The evoked-potential peak latencies were very late as compared to available normative data (Barnet, Uhlrich, Weiss, & Shanks, 1975; Ellingson, Danahy, Nelson, & Lathrop, 1974). In addition to the ambiguities in interpreting that result, a potentially significant biasing variable appears not to have been held constant—that is, infant state. Because increased arousal enhances asymmetrical head-turning tendencies (Liederman & Kinsbourne, 1980a), it could be that state happened to vary between speech and nonspeech conditions. Also, if speech happened to be more arousing for the infants, it could lead to a right-turning bias and evoked potential asymmetry for nonspecific rather than categorical reasons. Shucard et al. (1981) did control state and found no evoked-potential asymmetries relative to the categorical nature of stimulation. They did, however, find an intriguing double dissociation—males exhibited higher amplitude evoked potentials over the right convexity of the skull, females over the left convexity of the skull (raising the possibility of sex-differential early hemispheric maturation). But, holding stimulation constant, males are known to be more readily aroused than females. To what extent this effect contributes to the findings remains to be determined. In older infants, EEG evidence has been offered for differential hemispheric activation relative to emotional state (Davidson, et al., 1982). Working with 6- and 8-month-old children, Lewkowitz and Turkewitz (1982) showed that the categorical nature of input (speech versus music) interacts with ear of presentation in determining latency of reaching. Here there were complex interactions with sex. Whether the sex effects are direct or mediated by systematic state differences is unclear. With respect to the findings of more dishabituation in infants for dichotic speech on the right side and for nonspeech on the left (Best et al., 1982; Entus, 1977; Glanville et al., 1977), gross changes in head position were not ruled out as mediators of differential effects. The same applies to Davis and Wada's (1977) finding of differential evoked-potential asymmetries to flashes and clicks in infants aged 2 to 10 weeks.

Thus, studies reporting categorical dissociations in infants have to rule out potential biases based on variations in state. Such effects as survive could be due to differential brainstem activation and need not indicate cerebral processing per se. These strictures do not, however, diminish the importance of a dramatic recent finding (Mac Kain, Studdert-Kennedy, Spieker, & Stern, 1983). In this study, 5- to 6-month-old infants maintained gaze longer on a speaker displayed on video if the concurrent sound track presented speech that corresponded to the speaker's visible articulatory movements. Of interest to laterality theory is the finding that the infants showed this effect only while looking rightward. It has been shown in adults that rightward orienting facilitates verbal processing (Kinsbourne, 1973b; Lempert & Kinsbourne, 1982). The demonstration of such an effect in preverbal infants suggests that left-sided brain mechanisms are predisposed to process intermodal speech correspondence as opposed to other aspects of a display (or, conversely, that when the infant adopts the mental set to process verbally, brainstem selector systems differentially generate left-sided activation (Kinsbourne, 1980b).

Cerebral Lateralization During Childhood

The absence of initial bisymmetry does not preclude the possibility that the degree of hemispheric specialization increases in some manner during childhood. We will summarize the relevant evidence from clinical case studies and from studies of laterality in normal children.

Clinical Evidence

For more than 100 years, the doctrines of equipotentiality and progressive lateralization derived empirical support almost exclusively from clinical studies of childhood aphasia (e.g., see Woods & Teuber, 1978a). They were recently forcefully articulated by Lenneberg (1967), who based his argument largely on two conclusions from the clinical data of Basser (1962). The first is that aphasia in children when caused by unilateral brain damage is less severe and more transitory than aphasia produced by comparable damage in the adult. Lenneberg (1967) attributed this developmental change to a decreasing role of the right hemisphere with respect to language. However, as we pointed out in the previous section, such observations can be explained more parsimoniously in terms of decreasing plasticity than in terms of a shrinking brain base for language.

Lenneberg's second observation was that, in children under the age of 10 years, damage to either cerebral hemisphere has similar consequences with respect to language. It was claimed that, if injury occurs prior to speech onset, the course of subsequent language acquisition is the same irrespective of the hemisphere involved and that, if injury occurs in children between the ages of 2 and 10 years, damage to either hemisphere is likely to produce aphasia. Therefore, claimed Lenneberg, the younger the child, the greater the degree to which both hemispheres are involved in language processing. Logical pitfalls in this line of reasoning were noted in the previous section. In addition, much of the evidence itself is questionable. Krashen (1973), after reviewing Basser's (1962) report, pointed out that it includes no evidence for aphasia following a right-hemispheric lesion after the age of 5 years. Consequently, Krashen concluded that the lateralization of language is complete by 5 years of age.

Whereas Krashen's (1973) critique of Lenneberg's (1967) hypothesis led him to modify the time frame for lateralization without abandoning the concept of progressive lateralization, Woods and Teuber (1978a) directly challenged the doctrines of equipotentiality and progressive lateralization. Among 65 children with acquired hemiparesis, Woods and Teuber found that left-hemispheric damage resulted in aphasic impairment of language in 74% of the cases; right-hemispheric damage produced language impairment in only 13% of the cases, and half of those children were left-handed premorbidly. Thus, the incidence of aphasia following right-hemispheric injury in right-handed children was only about 7%, which is very close to the incidence of crossed aphasia in right-handed adults (e.g., see Conrad, 1949; Newcombe & Ratcliff, 1973; Russell & Espir, 1961). Moreover, among those children in the Woods and Teuber study who had acquired aphasia as a result of their lesion, there was no simple relationship between age when the lesion occurred and the time required for recovery.

Because their findings contradict established teaching about childhood aphasia, Woods and Teuber (1978a) undertook an extensive review of the clinical literature. They concluded that the findings changed dramatically about 1940. Prior to the 1930s, about one third of all aphasia cases were attributed to right-hemispheric damage; after 1940, less than 10% of the aphasias were attributed to right-hemispheric lesions and the incidence dropped to 5% if known left-handers were excluded. Woods and Teuber speculated that the abrupt decrease in the incidence of crossed aphasia in children corresponds to the introduction of antibiotics and mass immunization. It is argued that the older series of cases contained children with systemic infections capable of producing focal cortical lesions in addition to diffuse encephalopathy. The focal signs would lead investigators to classify the lesion as unilateral when, in fact, the encephalopathy might involve both hemispheres. Woods and Teuber note that, in the most recent studies, lesions tend to be of a vascular nature and there is less likelihood of diffuse encephalopathy. Although Basser's (1962) influential data seem to run contrary to their argument, Woods and Teuber (1978a) point out that many of Basser's patients acquired their lesions in the late 1930s or early 1940s and thus may not have received antibiotics or other modern medical treatment.

Regardless of whether Woods and Teuber (1978a) are correct about why the older and the more recent clinical data differ, their literature review as well as their own case studies must be considered damaging to the progressive lateralization hypothesis. From the time that speech is acquired, damage to the right hemisphere appears to disrupt language only rarely in right-handed children. After applying methods for estimating speech organization distributions to the relatively recent studies, Carter, Hohenegger, and Satz (1982) concluded that the association between side-of-lesion and incidence of aphasia is the same in children as in adults. For complete certainty, each report, if not each clinical case, must be evaluated according to its adequacy with respect to four criteria (Kinsbourne & Hiscock, 1977).

First, there is the problem of representative sampling. Basser (1962), for example, compiled many of his cases from sporadic reports in the literature. This procedure is almost certain to result in overrepresentation of the more exceptional cases. For instance, cases of aphasia after right-hemispheric damage probably are more likely to be reported than cases of aphasia after left-hemispheric damage simply because aphasia after right-hemispheric damage is considered less common.

Second, the children themselves may not be representative of the general childhood population. This is a subtle but ubiquitous problem when clinical samples are used as a basis for inferences about normal functioning or normal development. Many causes of aphasia, such as cerebrovascular accidents, are potentially recurrent and, thus, more likely to occur in children who already have suffered some previous undiagnosed brain damage. If right-hemispheric damage causes language impairment in a particular child, this outcome might be attributable to previous damage to the left hemisphere that caused the right hemisphere to become dominant for language.

Third, although it is relatively easy for the neurologist to determine that a particular region of the brain is involved, it is logically and practically impossible to be equally sure that another region is not involved. Even with modern techniques, such as CAT scan, one cannot rule out impaired functioning at some site distant to the known lesion. Woods and Teuber's (1978a) argument about diffuse encephalopathy is one example of how bilateral involvement might be misinterpreted as unilateral involvement. Another example occurs in a report by Hécaen (1976), who observed aphasic symptoms in 15 of 17 children with cerebral damage classified as left-hemispheric and in 2 of 6 children with damage classified as right-hemispheric. Even though the incidence of aphasia after right-sided damage is reported as 33%, 1 of the 2 children with right-sided aphasia was left-handed and the other had incurred cranial trauma. Hécaen concedes that he is unable to rule out bilateral involvement in the trauma cases. In a box score tabulation, Hécaen's study, with its 33% incidence rate for right-sided aphasia, probably would be grouped with others that favor the hypothesis of progressive lateralization. However, if stringent criteria for lesion localization are applied (and if only right-handed children are considered), the incidence of right-sided aphasia is 0%.

The fourth criterion concerns the definition of aphasia. Without strict and consistent criteria for defining aphasia, the comparability of various studies is questionable. When reviewing the records of children at the Hospital for Sick Children in Toronto who reportedly suffered aphasia as the result of early brain damage (Kinsbourne & Hiscock, 1977), we found cases in which the only evidence for aphasia consisted of a note in the chart that the children would not talk to the doctor. When these cases were included in the series, 4 cases of aphasia out of 30 that occurred before the age of 6 years were attributed to right-hemispheric damage. When strict criteria for aphasia were invoked, there was no instance of right-hemispheric damage among 8 cases of aphasia in children below the age of 6 years.

The clinical data that traditionally have been used to support the doctrines of equipotentiality and progressive lateralization no longer can be accepted uncritically. Apart from logical concerns about making inferences with respect to normal development on the basis of lesion studies, there now are concerns about the reproducibility of classical findings. Many modern studies of childhood aphasia suggest that the incidence of aphasia following left- and right-hemispheric damage respectively does not differ substantially from comparable statistics in the adult literature (Carter, Hohenegger, & Satz, 1982; Satz & Bullard-Bates, 1981). Ambiguities among studies will be resolved only with the publication of new studies in which stringent criteria for sampling of cases, definition of the lesion, and definition of aphasia are employed.

Laterality in Normal Children

In the 15 years since the publication of Lenneberg's (1967) influential book, the controversy concerning the development of cerebral lateralization has centered less around childhood aphasia data than around developmental patterns of behavioral asymmetry. As noted previously, the absence of initial bisymmetry does not preclude the possibility that the degree of hemispheric specialization increases in some manner during childhood. Some investigators, on the basis of developmental changes in perceptual asymmetry, have suggested that the degree of cerebral lateralization does increase during the childhood years (Bryden & Allard, 1978; Satz et al., 1975). We suggested previously that developmental changes in degree of asymmetry may reflect changes in strategy that are superimposed on a constantly lateralized neural substrate. With respect at least to some laterality paradigms, proper interpretation of developmental changes in degree of asymmetry is an academic question because most studies reveal no developmental change.

Dichotic Listening. Several dichotic-listening studies have shown a right-ear superiority for perception of verbal material in preschool children (Bever, 1971; Geffner & Dorman, 1976; Gilbert & Climan, 1974; Hiscock & Kinsbourne, 1977; Ingram, 1975; Kinsbourne & Hiscock, 1977; Piazza, 1977). The asymmetry has been found in the youngest children tested, that is, children as young as 2½ years of age, and its magnitude does not appear to increase between that age and the age of 5 years (Hiscock & Kinsbourne, 1977). One particular study of selective listening in 3-year-olds, using dichotically presented digit names as stimuli, yielded a REA substantially larger than that typically found with older children and adults (Kinsbourne & Hiscock, 1977). Studies encompassing a wider age range also fail to show any consistent developmental change in degree of asymmetry (Berlin, Hughes, Lowe-Bell, & Berlin, 1973; Chasty, 1979; Geffen, 1978; Goodglass, 1973; Hiscock & Kinsbourne, 1980a; Hynd & Obrzut, 1977; Kimura, 1963, 1967; Kinsbourne & Hiscock, 1977; Knox & Kimura, 1970; Kraft, 1982; Satz et al., 1975; Schulman-Galambos, 1977). With the exception of two studies (Bryden & Allard, 1978; Satz et al., 1975), there is no indication that the magnitude of the right-ear superiority for verbal material increases with increasing age (Bryden & Allard, 1981, failed to replicate their earlier result). As an attempt to reconcile the discrepant findings, Porter and Berlin (1975) suggested that some dichotic-listening tasks tap auditory or phonetic processes but other tasks require higher level semantic and mnemonic processes. According to the Porter and Berlin argument, auditory and phonetic processes mature early in the left hemisphere but higher level linguistic processes continue to undergo significant change after the age of 4 years. Consequently, it is argued that stimuli that demand higher level processing—for example, strings of digit names—are more likely to yield a developmental increase in ear asymmetry than are stimuli that require mainly phonetic discrimination. Although the levels-of-processing explanation seems plausible, a recent study using strings of digit names produced results contrary to those predicted on that basis, that is, there was no developmental increase in the magnitude of the REA for perception of those complex stimuli (Hiscock & Kinsbourne, 1980a). Although the findings cited above all rely on a cross-sectional design, the one longitudinal study in the literature (Bakker, Hoefkins, & Van der

Vlugt, 1979) also failed to detect any developmental change in the magnitude of the REA for dichotic-digit names.

Dual-Task Performance. The unchanging degree of asymmetry seen in most studies of dichotic listening in children is also seen in developmental studies of verbal-manual output competition. First to apply the dual-task paradigm to children was a study by Kinsbourne and McMurray (1975) in which kindergarten students were asked to tap as rapidly as possible with their left or right index finger while performing a concurrent vocalization task. Even though right-hand tapping was significantly faster than left-hand tapping in the control conditions (i.e., with no concurrent vocalization), left- and right-hand tapping rates were equivalent in the concurrent-task conditions. In other words, concurrent speech disrupted right-hand performance more than it disrupted left-hand performance. This outcome is analogous to that of dual-task studies with adults (e.g., see Hicks, 1975; Kinsbourne & Cook, 1971; McFarland & Ashton, 1978a), and it suggests that speech control is lateralized to the left hemisphere by the age of 5 years. Piazza (1977) subsequently reported similar findings with 3-, 4-, and 5-year-old children. Application of the dual-task paradigm to larger samples of normal, right-handed children (Hiscock & Kinsbourne, 1978, 1980b; White & Kinsbourne, 1980; Hiscock, Kinsbourne, Samuels & Krause, 1983) showed that the degree to which verbal-manual interferences is asymmetric remains constant across the age range of 3 to 12 years (even though time-sharing capacity increases greatly). Thus, findings from dual-task studies mirror findings from dichotic-listening studies insofar as both paradigms show asymmetries that are suggestive of early left lateralization of language and do not change in magnitude with increasing age.

Visual and Tactile Perception. In contrast to remarkably consistent dichotic-listening and dual-task findings, various developmental courses have been reported for the laterality of tachistoscopic word recognition (Butler & Miller, 1979; Forgays, 1953; Lewandowski, 1982; Marcel & Rajan, 1975; Marcel et al., 1974; Miller & Turner, 1973; Olson, 1973; Reitsma, 1975; Tomlinson-Keasey et al., 1978), face recognition (Broman, 1978; Leehey, 1976; Marcel & Rajan, 1975; Young & Ellis, 1976), Braille reading (Rudel et al., 1974, 1977; Wagner & Harris, 1979), and recognition of shapes in a dichhaptic task (Etaugh & Levy, 1981; Witelson, 1976b). In many instances, no significant degree of asymmetry is found in young children. With increasing age, asymmetries appear and then level off. In some cases, significant asymmetries are found in the youngest children tested (e.g., see Butler & Miller, 1979; Young & Ellis, 1976). In still other instances, there are striking gender differences in the pattern of laterality (e.g., Rudel et al., 1974; Witelson, 1976b; Jones & Anunza, 1982). The developmental pattern of perceptual asymmetries in the visual modality is particularly unclear. Some tachistoscopic studies have shown right VHF superiority for words in children as young as 7 years (Butler & Miller, 1979; Lewandowski, 1982; Marcel & Rajan, 1975; Marcel et al., 1974; Olson, 1973), or even 3 years (Jones & Anunza, 1982). Others have failed to show a right VHF superiority in children younger than 10 to 12 years (Forgays, 1953; Miller & Turner, 1973; Reitsma, 1975; Tomlinson-Keasey et al., 1978). Left VHF superiority for dot enumeration was noted in children as young as 5 years and did not increase with increasing age (Young & Bion, 1979). However, the age at which a left VHF superiority for face recognition is first observed ranges from 5 years (Young & Ellis, 1976) to 9 or 10 years (Leehey, 1976).

Although developmental changes in asymmetry of visual perception have been attributed to an emerging hemispheric specialization for certain functions, it is curious that a brain that is lateralized from birth for the processing of speech sounds should become lateralized for other functions only after the passing of several years.

We suggested in the previous section of this chapter that developmental changes in degree of asymmetry probably reflect developmental changes in the behavioral organization of the skill rather than a shifting neural base for a constantly organized set of component skills. As a skill develops in the maturing brain, additional lateralized components may be recruited to the performance of the skill and asymmetries observed for the first time. When performance of the younger child is symmetric, this need not imply that the lateralized components have not yet become lateralized; instead, the lateralized components may not yet be functional or integrated into the organization of the skill. In support of this explanation, we can point to evidence (previously described) that perceptual tasks are susceptible to influence from nonstructural variables, such as strategy, expectancy, and previous experience with the stimulus material. For example, a right VHF advantage for recognition of digits depends on whether a digit or geometric shape is presented at midline as a fixation control measure (Carter & Kinsbourne, 1979; Kershner et al., 1977) and a right VHF advantage for geometric forms may be obtained if letters are presented prior to the forms (Kimura & Durnford, 1974). Webster and Thurber (1978) altered subjects' asymmetry in performing Witelson's (1974) dichhaptic-recognition task by instructing them to use different problem-solving strategies. Hand differences in Braille-recognition studies as well as dichhaptic studies depend on the order in which the two hands are tested (Rudel & Denckla, 1979; Wagner & Harris, 1979; Witelson, 1974). Perceptual tasks are not merely measures of some structural property of the brain. It seems plausible that age-related changes in degree of asymmetry reflect different approaches to the task rather than different degrees of cerebral lateralization.

Time-Limited Changes in Degree of Asymmetry

With respect to a variety of independent variables, investigators have pointed out different degrees of perceptual asymmetry at different life stages. For example, Bakker (1973) has addressed differences in dichotic ear advantage between beginning and more accomplished readers; Waber (1977) has postulated different degrees of lateralization for early and late physical and sexual maturers of a given peripubertal age; and Leehey (1976) has demonstrated a reversal in the emergence of perceptual asymmetry for preadolescents in a presumptively right-hemispheric-related task (Carey, Diamond, & Woods, 1980). In such cases, it is tempting to resort to a structural rationale and posit spurts and lags in lateralization to correspond to the data points. But, given the formidable set of variables potentially biasing perceptual asymmetry, it is necessary to rule these out as differentiating between groups or within groups at different life stages before fitting the organization of the brain to every nook and cranny of the laterality data. Quite possibly, once event-related psychophysiological variables become more generally applicable and more easily interpretable, it will become possible to test the more ambitious brain-based explanations for laterality findings.

Meanwhile, we can evaluate these claims on a logical basis. If we reject the concept of progressive lateralization during childhood, then we must reject or at least modify these derived notions. It no longer makes sense to attribute cognitive deficits to delayed lateralization if, in fact, lateralization is not an emergent phenomenon; neither does it make sense to talk about developmental stages of lateralization and their relationship to skills, such as reading (e.g., see Bakker, 1973; Bakker & Reitsma, 1973; Sparrow & Satz, 1970), nor to design interventions for the purpose of accelerating the course of functional lateralization. These implications are of special importance in the realm of learning disabilities (Hiscock & Kinsbourne, 1980c). With respect to putative sex differences in cerebral lateralization, an absence of developmental change is not inconsistent with claims of sex differences in children (Buffery, 1976) or adults (e.g., see Lake & Bryden, 1976; McGlone & Davidson, 1973; McGlone & Kertesz, 1973), but it is inconsistent with claims that there are sex differences in lateralization at some ages and not at others (e.g., see Witelson, 1976b). Of particular relevance is Waber's (1977) suggestion that sex differences in cognitive abilities are related to individual differences—within as well as between the sexes—in rate of somatosexual maturation. Waber argued that early maturation confers an advantage in verbal development and that late maturation confers an advantage in spatial development and that because males, on the average, mature later than females, differential maturation rate can account for the tendency for females to perform better than males on certain verbal tasks and for males to outperform females on certain visuospatial tasks (Maccoby & Jacklin, 1974). Waber (1977) took her argument one step further in claiming that the rate of somatosexual development is related to the rate at which asymmetry evolves, as measured by a standard dichotic-listening test. Waber did find, among the older group only (13-year-old girls and 15-year-old boys), that the absolute value of the ear advantage, irrespective of its direction, was significantly greater for the later maturers than for the early maturers. However, the evidence necessary to support the differential lateralization argument more convincingly—evidence of faster developing and ultimately more extreme asymmetry for one kind of task in one sex and for the other kind of task in the opposite sex—has yet to be obtained.

One other viewpoint that is linked to the progressive lateralization hypothesis is the claim that children from low socioeconomic backgrounds are slow to show signs of cerebral dominance for language. Kimura (1967) reported that she twice failed to find a REA for perception of dichotic-digit names in 5-year-old boys from a low-to-middle-class background, even though she did find a REA in 5-year-old girls from the same kind of background and in 5-year-olds of both sexes from higher socioeconomic-status families. Other investigators (Geffner & Hochberg, 1971) reported the absence of a significant REA in 4-, 5-, and 6-year-old children from low socioeconomic backgrounds. Subsequent research, however, has failed to duplicate these class differences (Dorman & Geffner, 1974; Geffner & Dorman, 1976). It appears that when socioeconomic-status effects are found, they are attributable to the inability or unwillingness of children from lower status backgrounds to perform as well as children of higher socioeconomic status on a challenging task. Failures to respond, perseverative responses, and so on, will minimize the differences between ear scores (Geffner & Dorman, 1976; Kinsbourne, 1975b). When less difficult, age-appropriate tasks are used and when other measures are taken to prevent floor effects (Dorman & Geffner, 1974; Geffner & Dorman, 1976), there appears to be little or no difference between the listening asymmetry of children from disparate socioeconomic backgrounds. Consequently, the research dealing with socioeconomic-status effects on degree of laterality does not lead to conclusions that are incompatible with the hypothesis of developmental invariance for the cerebral lateralization of language.

Development of Sex Differences in Spatial Laterality

Although Maccoby and Jacklin (1974) concluded that sex differences in spatial ability are absent until adolescence, there is plentiful evidence (summarized by Newcombe, Bandura, & Taylor, in press) that they do exist in children. Even the claim that these differences are small in young children and increase with age (Droege, 1967; Flanagan et al., 1964; Wilson, DeFries, McClearn, Vandenberg, Johnson, & Rashad, 1975) is not upheld in some studies (Porteus, 1965; Vandenberg & Kuse, 1978; Witkin, Goodenough, & Karp, 1967). As for the cause of these differences, studies to date have not succeeded in deconfounding genetic, hormonal, and experiential explanations. This is the reason why some have studied the laterality aspect of the differential performance. If, corresponding to performance differences, laterality differences can be demonstrated, this would bolster biological explanations of the sex differences.

A logical way of proceeding would then be:

1. To identify patterns of cerebral representation that engender inefficient performance.
2. To identify the specific factors of intellect with respect to which performance is different between the sexes.
3. To demonstrate that, more frequently in one sex than the other, the factors in question but not other factors are represented in the manner known to make for inefficient performance.

Not one of these steps has even approximately been completed.

A suitable population for studying the relationship between laterality and performance is the subgroup of left-handers, which accounts for about 10% of the general population. It is known that many left-handers have anomalous laterality patterns (e.g., reversed [i.e., verbal right, spatial left] or bisymmetric [i.e., both verbal and spatial functions bilaterally represented], see Goodglass & Quadfasel, 1954; Hécaen, De Agostini, & Monzon-Montes, 1981; Rasmussen & Milner, 1975). Early claims notwithstanding (Levy, 1969; Miller, 1971), studies that have used adequate sample size have found no selective differences in intellectual profile between right- and left-handed people in the general population (e.g., see Briggs, Nebes, & Kinsbourne, 1976; Hardyck, Petrinovich, & Goldman, 1976; Newcombe & Ratcliff, 1973). Subsets of left-handers have also been studied with respect to degree of left-handedness, presence of familial sinistrality, and the use of an "inverted" hand posture while writing. Although significant differences in test scores (after interacting with gender) have been reported, they are complex, contradictory, and not readily understood (e.g., see Bradshaw, Nettleton, & Taylor, 1981; Gregory, Alley, & Morris, 1980; Gregory & Paul, 1980; Healey, 1980; Johnson & Harley, 1980; Kocel, 1977). A further complication is the possibility that the relationship between handedness and cognitive skills interacts with age. Swanson, Kinsbourne, and Horn (1980) followed right-handed, left-handed, and mixed-handed children longitudinally, testing them on the Primary Mental Abilities Tests in fourth grade and again in seventh grade. The left-handed group in fourth grade scored higher and the mixed-handed lower than the right-handed group. More interestingly, both left-handed and mixed-handed groups subsequently decreased in performance relative to the right-handed group, particularly on spatial and numerical tests. If this result on a small sample replicates, it could indicate that cerebral organization in the left-handed and the mixed-handed is less adapted to the more complex levels of spatial and numerical tasks than to simpler ones. However, other explanations are also possible. At the present time, whether any particular pattern of cerebral representation of function is less suited to efficient performance than the rest is simply not known.

Attempts to specify the spatial process on which gender differences in performance are based have had similarly equivocal outcomes. The right hemisphere has been loosely credited with dominance for spatial functions of all kinds, based on extrapolation from a rather limited and variable set of clinical and behavioral laterality findings. Females have been alleged to be deficient in a similar spread of factorially complex tasks. But closer analysis leads to no clear resolution. There is also the well-known distinction between factors called spatial orientation and spatial visualization (Guilford, 1967—but see Carroll & Maxwell, 1979). If one accepts this distinction, one learns from Richmond (1980) that only the former is subject to sex difference, whereas tests loaded on the latter factor have repeatedly been reported by others to be better performed by males (e.g., see Keogh & Ryan, 1971; Witkin, et al., 1967). When spatial performance is subdivided into face-valid components of spatial memory and spatial manipulation, then some studies find females to be less efficient in spatial memory (Kail & Siegel, 1977; Samuels, Hiscock, & Kinsbourne, 1978), whereas others incriminate spatial manipulation (Guilford, 1967; Kail, Pellegrino, & Carter, 1980). Yet another source of information suggests that males make better use of cues in pattern copying (Keogh & Ryan, 1971; Vasta, Regan, & Kerley, 1980). Further complicating the issue are findings that females outperform males on some spatial tasks (Bahrick, Bahrick, & Wittlinger, 1975). We conclude that at this time no precise statement can be made as to which spatial-component process females find relatively difficult. It is not even clear whether a specific subset of intellectual activity is involved or whether these difficulties are more varied and scattered, as one would expect if they were largely based on differential experience. Given this uncertainty, the attempt to identify the inefficient pattern of lateralization of those spatial skills in females is premature. Nevertheless, it has been made.

Are there lateralization differences between males and females? McGlone (1980) inferred a more diffuse representation of function in females from her finding that aphasia in females is milder than in males after allegedly comparable brain damage. This conclusion is unacceptable in view of methodological and logical flaws (Kinsbourne, 1980c). Bryden (1978) concluded that evidence for sex differences in lateralization was most conspicuous by its absence and that what evidence did exist could more conservatively be interpreted as reflecting sex differences in strategic approach to tasks, involving different patterns of hemispheric usage in individuals whose pattern of hemispheric specialization could be identical.

Hemispheric usage can be monitored by physiological recording of hemispheric activation. Thus, Furst (1976) and Gur and Reivich (1980), using EEG and blood-flow methodology respectively, found performance in spatial tasks to correlate significantly with evidence of right-hemispheric activation in the brain in their male subjects. Ray, Newcombe, Semon, and Cole (1981) corroborated this finding for high ability males, found the reverse for low ability males, and found no relationship at all between activation pattern and performance for females. Such findings lend themselves more readily to explanation in terms of different strategies than different laterality.

Perceptual asymmetries have been treated as indices of lateralization (although we have noted that they may reflect hemispheric activation directly, lateralization only indirectly). In any case, relationships between dichotic (Fennell, Bowers, & Satz, 1978; Herbst, 1980; McGlone & Davidson, 1973; Waber, 1977), VHF (Birkett, 1977; Fennell et al., 1977), and dichhaptic (Newcombe & Bandura, 1983) asymmetries and spatial performance are weak or absent. Nor can it be assumed that if there were a relationship between laterality and performance, the more lateralized subjects would be the ones to perform better. Reviewing the dichotic-listening literature, Witelson (1977b) showed that girls, who are credited with better verbal development (Gaddes & Crockett, 1975; Garai & Scheinfeld, 1968; T. Moore, 1967), if anything are less lateralized for verbal processing. Hiscock and Kinsbourne (1978, 1980b) have constantly failed to find sex differences in degree of lateralized verbal-manual interference in both cross-sectional and longitudinal studies. This paradigm does not appear to permit much strategic or attentional variation, and perhaps this is why sex differences do not obtrude.

An imaginative attempt to explicate sex differences in verbal and spatial ability was made by Waber (1977), who, it will be recalled, proposed that early maturation favors verbal and later maturation favors spatial development. She did not find a selective advantage for verbal tasks among early maturers, nor have others. With the spatial component of the hypothesis, the situation is more complex. Waber (1977) herself did find the relationship, as did Carey and Diamond (1980), Herbst (1980), and, rather weakly, Newcombe and Bandura (1983). Others have failed to find the relationship (Herbst & Peterson, 1979; Peterson, 1976). In a subsequent study, Waber, Bauermeister, Cohen, Ferber, and Wolff (1981) found it to hold only for a middle class subset of the total sample. This would suggest an effect of differential experience rather than the envisaged biological phenomenon. In any case, Strauss and Kinsbourne (1981) found no relationship between age at menarche and either verbal- or spatial-test performance in young adult females. So the phenomenon, if it exists, is perhaps transitory (Waber, 1977).

The evidence for lateralization differences relative to maturity is still less convincing. Waber (1977) reported greater dichotic asymmetries for verbal stimuli in early maturers (although they did not differ in verbal ability) and that only among the older subjects (although the sex differences in spatial performance existed among her younger subjects). If there are systematic differences in laterality relative to maturity, they appear to be unrelated to the differences in intellectual profile that they were supposed to explain.

Regardless of any relationship to performance, do males and females develop laterality in different ways? Molfese and Molfese (1979, 1980) have found sex to interact with stimulus material in averaged evoked-potential studies in infants. Shucard et al. (1981) failed to replicate the Molfeses' findings of double dissociation between verbal and musical conditions. They found double dissociation by sex instead, with males sharing greater right-sided and females greater left-sided amplitude for both stimulus categories. In school-age children, findings are quite contradictory for asymmetries in hemifield (Leehey, 1976; Young & Bion, 1979) and dichhaptic (Cranney & Ashton, 1980; Flanery & Balling, 1979; Newcombe & Bandura, 1983; Witelson, 1976) experiments.

We conclude that (1) sex differences in behavioral asymmetries do exist, but that they index sex differences in lateralization has not been established and (2) maturational differences in behavioral asymmetries may exist, but have not been related to other variables. In neither case is there any systematic relationship between laterality findings and ability to perform tasks categorically related to the test used for laterality purposes.

Laterality in Bilingualism

The question has often been asked, is a second language lateralized within the same territory as the first or elsewhere? Rationales have been adduced for expecting either early bilinguals or late bilinguals to have deviant lateralization for their second language; the second language is often suggested as either occupying both hemispheres or being centered on the right side. Studies of this issue have been performed on adults rather than children, but insofar as they relate to the end point of a developmental process, they can be scrutinized for any light they might cast on this issue. Information about the laterality of second-language representation derives from two main and one subsidiary source: the effect of lateralized brain lesions, laterality testing in intact people, and, potentially, electrophysiological studies (Kinsbourne, 1981a).

A few striking case reports have suggested a dissociation in hemispheric representation of first and second languages (Albert & Obler, 1978; Silverberg & Gordon, 1979). However, the divergent clinical syndromes of aphasia reported for the two languages could have been the result of quantitative differences in the degree to which patients are fluent in the two languages (being more vulnerable to the more severe syndrome in the less practiced language). Larger scale series have failed to show substantial dissociations (Charlton, 1964; Watamori & Sasanuma, 1978). In general, use of both languages is impaired to a comparable degree.

Laterality studies similarly vary in reported outcome, but the most extensive and controlled investigations lead to congruent conclusions, that is, both tachistoscopic and dichotic-listening studies converge on the conclusion that bilinguals are lateralized like monolinguals for both their languages (Gordon & Zatorre, 1981; Soares, in press; Soares & Grosjean, 1981). Admittedly, the restrictions that these paradigms impose on the level of complexity of linguistic material that can be used makes them an imperfect index of language behavior. More ecological validity can be achieved by use of the dual-task interference paradigm, which permits natural speech to occur as part of the experimental arrangement. Two studies have taken advantage of this opportunity. Sussman, Franklin, & Simon (1982) compared monolinguals with late bilinguals and reported bilateral interference of speech in the second language. They inferred a bilateral organization for the second language. However, they arrived at this conclusion by using an idiosyncratic group-laterality index. If the data are reanalyzed more conventionally, such as by a direct-difference measure, then the apparent difference between the first and second languages of bilinguals disappears. Soares (in press) has listed other methodological deficiencies of the Sussman et al. (1982) study, which he overcame in his own more stringent design. Soares's study used among other conditions, one of a spontaneous conversation between the experimenter and the subject in both the first and the second languages (the experimenter also being bilingual). Soares's study confirms the previously gained impression, that is, that interference was equally lateralized for monolinguals and for bilinguals in both first and second languages.

The convergence of evidence is clear. First-language territory also becomes second-language territory regardless of whether the second language is acquired early or late. Any laterality outcome differences depend on different strategies used, and therefore different neural areas enlisted, rather than the use of different areas for the same process (see Galloway, 1982 for a comprehensive review). Here as elsewhere in neuropsychology, simplistic theories of crowding out of one function by another from a specific cerebral space remain unsupported. Instead, the finding illustrates a point that appears to be basic in hemispheric-specialization theory (Kinsbourne, 1982). Where different performances represent alternative choices for the subject (such as whether to speak in one or the other language), then the same or neighboring cerebral territories can represent those performances. It is when disparate performances have to be integrated into a final product that separate and even distant representation is encountered.

Lifespan Trends in Laterality

Three proposals have been made for laterality changes beyond the first decade of life:

1. Lateral specialization progressively increases (Brown & Jaffe, 1975).
2. Lateral specialization decreases (Kocel, 1980).
3. Right-hemispheric specialization decreases relative to left-hemispheric specialization (Kleisz, 1978).

Late progressive lateralization was conceived as a continuation of the supposed progressive lateralization in childhood; the concept is based on the finding that the peak incidence of Broca's (expressive) aphasia occurs a few years earlier than that of Wernicke's (receptive) aphasia (e.g., see Obler, Albert, Goodglass, & Benson, 1978). Confirming this, Brown and Grober (in press) found in a stroke population that "motor aphasia tended to dominate through the fourth decade; mixed and total aphasia, the fifth decade; and sensory aphasia, the sixth." Although Brown and Jaffe (1975) attributed this age difference to continued specialization of the right hemisphere, rendering it less able in older people to compensate for receptive loss owing to left-hemispheric lesion, it could be that stroke tends toward a more posterior impact with advancing age (so, having a higher probability of temporal lobe—Wernicke's area—involvement). However, trauma cases (Brown & Grober, in press) and tumor cases (Miceli, Caltagirone, Gianotti, Masullo, Silveri, & Villa, 1981) show a similar pattern of greater mean age for sensory than motor aphasia. Also, sensory aphasia is uncommon, although by no means unknown, in children; at times, it even occurs when the lesion is posteriorly located (i.e., in the territory that in the adult is thought to be committed to speech decoding, Hécaen, 1976).

Brown and Grober (in press) interpret these phenomena as indicating "a progressive differentiation or regional specification within the dominant hemisphere language zone." They envelop this claim in the more general view (for which we already have given grounds to reject) that "language representation gradually develops from a diffuse, bilateral organization to a unilateral and focal one," although the former proposition does not depend on the latter more global view because it is based on a microgenetic perspective on ontogenesis, which Brown (1972, 1977) defends elsewhere. Broad issues apart, the empirical facts hardly justify such sweeping interpretation. We can summarize these facts as follows: the older the patient, the more severe the aphasia and the more likely to include a sensory deficit. Both findings could be sufficiently accounted for by a decline with age of compensatory potential of the right hemisphere simply because of increasing probability that it, too (although perhaps less dramatically), is subject to disease—neuronal fallout, microinfarcts, and so on. At any age, the right hemisphere seems better able to compensate for lost left-hemispheric input- than for output-processing capability (Searleman, 1977); with increasing age even this compensatory potential becomes, on the average, more limited.

Kocel (1980) suggests that communication between the hemispheres increases with advancing age, implying (for her) decreased lateralization. This claim is based on complex interactions between age and left-handedness in a psychometric study. Laterality, as such, was not measured, and the suggestion has too little empirical basis to be useful at this time.

It has repeatedly been suggested that the right hemisphere deteriorates differentially with advancing age (e.g., Kleisz, 1978). Certainly, cerebral neuropathology in aging does not reveal any predominance of abnormality in either hemisphere (Roth, 1980). If the right hemisphere ages faster than the left hemisphere, it does so by some as-yet unidentifiable mechanism. The most comprehensive study of this issue, based on the Halstead-Reitan test battery (Goldstein & Shelly, 1981) found evidence neither of a predominance of right- over left-hemispheric focal deficit nor of any more generally greater deterioration of the specialized functions of the right hemisphere. The pattern of loss on the two sides was not comparable, but until replication convinces us that the disparities were other than fortuitous, theorizing about these differences is premature. In intact people, premature aging of the right hemisphere should result in increased right biases for verbal tasks and decreased left biases for spatial tasks. Watson, Elias, and Pentz (1975) for letter matching, Elias, Winn & Wright, (1979) for word and shape matching, and Stern (1980) for simple RT found no age laterality interactions. In dichotic listening, Clark and Knowles (1973) and Johnson (1977) found greater REA in the elderly. But they used multiple pairs of stimuli per trial, setting the scene for a confounding effect of task difficulty. Given the usual strategy of reporting first from one ear, overall lower performance would disproportionately prejudice report from the second ear. Borod and Goodglass (1980) found age-related effects neither for digit names (REA) nor for melodies (LEA).

At least with respect to interpreting psychometric findings, the notion of prior right-hemispheric decline is probably an artifact of a confounding variable. This is the extent to which the subtests measure fluid intelligence (age sensitive) versus crystalized intelligence (age insensitive) (Cattell, 1963; Horn & Cattell, 1967). Verbal tests tend to incorporate more crystalized content. When Elias and Kinsbourne (1974) held everything constant in a RT test other than the mode of stimulus presentation (verbal versus spatial), they found no differential age effects between modes.

We conclude that no acceptable evidence exists of any physiological changes in laterality in the adult years.

Summary

Traditional assumptions regarding absence of asymmetry (functional as well as morphological) in the infant brain have been disproven. Much recent evidence establishes that the left and right halves of the human brain are differentially specialized from the time of birth if not before. We have argued that behavioral and electrophysiological asymmetries in infancy are manifestations of tonic turning tendencies upon which stimulus-dependent phasic turning tendencies may be superimposed. These turning tendencies are thought to be precursors of hemispheric specialization in later life. Even though the literature on childhood aphasia has served for several decades as a basis for claims that language lateralization increases in degree during childhood, neither this clinical evidence nor the results from laterality studies of normal children provide compelling evidence that cerebral lateralization in young children is any different from that in older children or adults. Similarly, empirical support is lacking for other popular assertions, namely, that there are certain time-limited changes in cerebral lateralization, that sex differences in spatial ability are related to differences in the cerebral representation of spatial functions, that different languages are represented differentially in the brains of bilinguals, and that cerebral lateralization undergoes developmental change during the adult years.

DEVIANT LATERALIZATION IN BEHAVIORAL DEFICIT

Two issues lie at the heart of attempts to link anomalous lateralization of higher mental functions with various kinds of behavioral abnormality. One is empirical, namely, whether there is a statistical assocation between signs of deviant lateralization and a particular kind of behavioral pathology. Is there a high incidence of bilaterality among the mentally retarded, the learning disabled, children who stutter, and so on? This question, or questions like it, would not be of much interest unless there were some suspicion as to why such an association might be found. That is the second issue, namely, cause. Does anomalous cerebral organization per se cause cognitive deficit or some other form of behavioral abnormality? Is anomalous lateralization of functions per se maladaptive? Would the child's brain function properly if the existing processing circuitry could be rearranged so that its topography matches that of the majority of brains?

There is a dilemma inherent in attempting to determine if deviant arrangement of cerebral circuitry contributes to deficiency of any kind. We must study people with no evidence of brain pathology because deficiency in brain-injured people could be attributed to the loss of processing capacity rather than anomalous spatial distribution of the capacity. However, people without known or suspected brain damage cannot ethically be subjected to invasive procedures for determining the hemisphere in which different functions are localized, and there are no proven noninvasive procedures that are capable of classifying individuals as left or right lateralized with the necessary degree of accuracy. Without further technological advance, this dilemma remains intractable. Consequently, we must be content to look for empirical associations and only speculate as to cause and effect if such associations are found. Nevertheless, there is one circumstance under which we can acquire some limited information about the effect of anomalous cerebral lateralization upon cognitive ability. We can examine the implications of left-handedness.

Left-handedness and Cognitive Deficit

Left-handedness in the General Population

If practically all right-handers but fewer than two thirds of left-handers have left-sided speech (Rasmussen & Milner, 1975; Zangwill, 1967), then there is a substantially greater proportion of left-handers than of right-handers with deviant language lateralization, that is, with either bilateral or right-sided speech (Milner, Branch, & Rasmussen, 1966). If anomalous lateralization of speech per se contributes to cognitive deficiency, left-handed groups without known or suspected brain damage should (1) score lower than right-handers on tests of cognitive ability and (2) show more variability than right-handers on those tests.

Research has failed to reveal consistent differences between left- and right-handers in cognitive ability (Hicks & Kinsbourne, 1978). Two studies did report significantly lower nonverbal ability in left-handers and mixed-handers than in right-handers (Levy, 1969; Miller, 1971); a third study (Nebes, 1971) reported a relative deficiency in part-whole matching among left-handers. Levy (1969) argued that bilaterally represented language in left-handers disrupts the nonverbal processing that presumably takes place in the nondominant hemisphere. Although the findings and Levy's interpretation are intriguing, the findings are based on small samples and Levy's sample, in particular, consisted of very bright graduate students who are not at all representative of the general population. Other studies, many of which are based on larger and more representative samples of subjects, have failed to find any substantial deficiency among left-handers in either overall intelligence or in nonverbal ability (Briggs et al., 1976; Fagan-Dubin, 1974; Hardyck et al., 1976; Keller, Croake, & Riesenman, 1973; Newcombe & Ratcliff, 1973; Orme, 1970; Roberts & Engle, 1974; Wilson & Dolan, 1931). Newcombe and Ratcliff (1973), for instance, failed to find differences in verbal or performance IQ among 26 pure left-handers, 139 mixed-handers, and 658 right-handers. Pure left-handers differed from other people only in that their variability was very low, a finding that runs counter to the hypothesis that anomalous lateralization of higher mental functions is maladaptive. In an exhaustive study that was described in a U.S. Government National Health Survey Report (Roberts & Engel, 1974), Wechsler vocabulary and block-design tests were administered to more than 7,000 children between the ages of 6 and 11 years. Despite the great statistical power of tests for group differences (a consequence of the sample size), scores for the 762 left-handed children in the sample did not differ significantly from scores for the right-handers. Similarly, Hardyck et al. (1976) administered a battery of ability and achievement tests to 6,947 right-handed and 741 left-handed children but failed to find a single significant difference between the two groups. Possibly a late-developing decline in the ability of left-handed children can be detected if longitudinal designs are used (Swanson et al., 1980), but evidence to that effect is as yet inconclusive.

The several negative findings, especially those that derive from studies in which large and representative samples were used, suggest that left-handers in the general population are as intelligent as their right-handed counterparts. When deviant lateralization of language occurs in the absence of brain pathology, there seems to be no unfavorable consequence with respect to cognitive ability. It remains possible that behavioral tendencies other than cognitive skill are affected adversely by anomalous lateralization and that maladaptive anomalies of cerebral organization exist that are no more frequent among left-handers than among right-handers. Nevertheless, to the degree that cognitive ability in normal left-handers is a valid indicator of the cost of anomalous lateralization of higher mental processes, we find no proof of any cost associated with anomalous lateralization per se.

Pathological Left-handedness

The high incidence of left-handedness in epilepsy (Bingley, 1958; Bolin, 1953), mental retardation (Bakwin, 1950; Burt, 1950; Doll, 1933; M. Gordon, 1921; Hicks & Barton, 1975; McAnulty, Hicks, & Kinsbourne, 1983; Porac, Coren, & Duncan, 1980; Wilson & Dolan, 1931; Zangwill, 1960), and probably in other types of developmental psychopathology (L. J. Harris, 1980a) has occasioned two major hypotheses. One is the pathological left-handedness concept (M. Gordon, 1921; Redlich, 1908; Satz, 1972, 1973). This proposes that the excess of left-handers in pathological groups, as compared to the general population, is attributable to a subset of genotypic dextrals who assumed a sinistral phenotype (i.e., shifted hand preference) on account of left-hemispheric damage (presumably invading the left motor strip) sufficient to render the right hand unsuitable for its genetically programmed leading role. The presumptive cause is usually loosely labeled birth stress, leaving a wide range of adverse prenatal, perinatal, and postnatal events as candidates. The converse view is that a prevalence of left-handedness indexes families subject to an elevated risk of birth damage (Bakan, 1971). According to this latter view, all left-handedness is of pathological origin.

Acceptable evidence supports the application of the construct of pathological left-handedness to epilepsy. Yanowitz, Willmore, and Rice (1982) used EEG to study epileptics with focal lesions. They found the locus of the raised incidence of left-handedness among those patients who had sustained left focal lesions before 2 years of age. This group showed a corroborating feature—the right foot was more than ½ cm shorter than the left foot. This is taken to represent a trophic shortfall owing to presumed left-brain damage. This finding does not rule out the notion of familial left-handedness as a risk factor. In the case of mental retardation, this notion is supported. McAnulty et al. (1983) present a detailed documentation of the increased incidence of left-handedness among individuals with IQs below 50. As expected in any theory, the more retarded the person, the higher the probability of left-handedness. The hand preference of the retarded probands did not correlate significantly with that of their parents. But, the more severely affected retardates, as a group, had parents with a higher incidence of sinistrality. Familial sinistrality is, therefore, a risk factor for mental retardation and perhaps for pathological left-handedness also. This finding supports the pathological left-handedness notion.

According to the notion of a "continuum of reproductive casualty" (Pasamanick & Knobloch, 1960), adverse consequences of birth stress are a matter of degree; many apparently normally developing individuals do have a history of birth stress. Does birth stress substantially (Corballis & Beale, 1976; Zangwill, 1955) or even—as Bakan (1971) has claimed—totally account for left-handedness in the general population? Some retrospective data of Bakan, Dibb, and Reed (1973) pointed in that direction, but a formidable number of retrospective studies that have failed to confirm this relationship are now on record (Annett & Ockwell, 1980; Duseck & Hicks, 1980; Hicks, Elliot, Garbesi, & Martin, 1979; Hicks, Evans, & Pelligrini, 1978; Hubbard, 1971; Schwartz, 1977). A massive study including 17,733 cases failed to show any excess of left-hand use by those who scored highest on a weighted measure of birth stress (Spiegler & Yeni-Komshian, 1982). A much more comprehensively analyzed sample of 8,285 children studied prospectively also failed to reveal any relation between adverse prenatal, perinatal, and postnatal events and the incidence of left-handedness (McManus, 1980). However, Searleman, Porac, and Coren (1982) did find a higher incidence of history of birth stress in the subset of lefthanders that use inverted hand posture for writing (Levy & Reid, 1978; Parlow & Kinsbourne, 1981).

Whereas pathological left-handedness has implicitly been related to early damage induced by discrete events with observable concomitants, it does not logically follow that in the absence of evidence of such events, left-handedness must have been genotypic. It is quite possible that adverse influences on left-hemispheric development could occur during fetal life without currently observable concomitants and result in deviation to a sinistral phenotype (and perhaps, at times, also to other deficiencies in left-hemispheric function). Operationally, this alternative would be supported if evidence for delayed left-hemispheric development were found in left-handers who had neither the expected family background of sinistrality nor a history of prenatal or perinatal adversity.

The situation with respect to other conditions associated with excess of left-handedness is not fully clarified. The most numerous population is that classified as dyslexic. The necessary large-scale family study has not been done. Pending this work, it remains unclear whether pathological left-handedness is an appreciable factor among these children, whether the anomalous laterality relationships found in some left-handers predispose to difficulties in learning to read, and whether certain families are subject to a risk factor that variably expresses itself in nonright-handedness, dyslexia, or a combination of the two (perhaps even in association with autoimmune disease, as suggested by Geschwind & Behan, 1982, and supported by Kinsbourne & Bemporad, 1983).

In fact, it appears that reproductive casualty is not a continuum. Instead, minor degrees of birth stress lead to consequences that are self correcting (except when the child develops in an adverse environment [Sameroff & Chandler, 1975]). Only relatively infrequent, very severe adversity in pregnancy and delivery leads to definite subsequent neurological abnormality and mental retardation (and increased prevalence of left-handedness [Hicks, in preparation]).

Dysfunction of the Corpus Callosum

Effects of deficient callosal function could be inferred on the basis of two quite different mechanisms: (1) deficient interhemispheric information transfer or (2) insufficient inhibition of bilateral cerebral representation of sensorimotor functions.

Split-brain symptomatology is usually explained in terms of deficient interhemispheric information flow (e.g., see Bogen, 1969a, 1969b; Bogen & Bogen, 1969; Gazzaniga, 1970), although an explanation in terms of excitation-inhibition imbalances between hemispheres is equally viable (Guiard, 1980; Kinsbourne, 1974a). Similar claims have been made for young children (Galin, 1977; Gazzaniga, 1970; Kletzkin, 1980; Kraft, 1981). It is conceivable that failure of contact between the products of right-hemispheric pattern perception and left-hemispheric verbal codes could complicate learning to read (Vellutino, Bentley, & Phillips, 1978). But in the absence of a detailed and consensual model of the cognitive interactions in beginning reading, this is nothing but guesswork. It would be supported (and light cast on dyslexia) if a dyslexia subtype could be identified in which interhemispheric information transfer is demonstrably deficient.

Evidence for an inhibitory function of the corpus callosum was reviewed by Kinsbourne (1974a). At the sensorimotor levels, callosal agenesis studies (Dennis, 1977) suggest that the corpus callosum inhibits hemispheric control of the ipsilateral side of the body, leaving each hemisphere in undisputed control of most of the contralateral side. In its absence (in agenesis) or pending its maturation (in young children), contralateral associative movements are frequent (Dennis, 1977; Woods & Teuber, 1978b; Chiarello, 1980) and, according to Dennis (1977), the specificity of sensorimotor function within each hand is itself imperfect. Mirror movements persisting unduly are listed among manifestations of minimal brain dysfunction, and impaired finger localization is a component of the developmental Gerstmann variant of dyslexia (Kinsbourne & Warrington, 1963b) and was the most effective predictor of reading problems in a longitudinally studied sample of school boys (Satz, Taylor, Friel, & Fletcher, 1979). At the cognitive level, lack of callosal inhibition could, as has been suggested in agenesis (Saul & Gott, 1976), leave both hemispheres specialized for both pattern perception and verbal coding. According to the information-transfer model, this actually could be helpful for beginning reading, in that access of these representations to each other is preserved; however, several models of brain organization predict interference between these diversely specialized functions if housed in the same hemisphere (Kinsbourne & Hicks, 1978; Levy, 1969, 1972; Witelson, 1976a, 1977a). If a subtype of dyslexia could be identified in which tests demonstrate deficient callosal inhibition, this approach would receive support.

Poffenberger's (1912) method for measuring IHTT was adopted for children and applied to callosal agenesis by Jeeves (1965), who inferred greatly prolonged IHTT from his data. This, however, Kinsbourne and Fisher (1971) could not confirm. As discussed previously, recent assessments of this paradigm (Ledlow et al., 1978, 1981) have shown it to be too confounded with cognitive variables to be interpretable in the manner originally intended. We, therefore, resort to the more recently described methods of Galin and his colleagues (Galin, 1977; Galin et al., 1979), that is, the finger localization and the texture-matching tests. Both compare errors made in successive comparisons within and between hands.

In the test of finger localization, the child indicates the finger touched by the experimenter (uncrossed) or the homologous finger of the hand opposite to that touched by the experimenter (crossed). Galin (1977) found an excess of crossed over uncrossed errors among normal children aged 4.9 to 10.1 years; the disparity was more marked in the younger children. He attributed the interaction with age to less complete callosal maturation and, therefore, less interhemispheric information transfer in the younger children. However, the outcomes are confounded by the requirement to identify a homologous digit and touch it in the crossed condition. This act itself is not necessarily effortless for the young child and could account for some, or all, of the excess difficulty of the crossed condition without need to invoke interhemispheric transmission as an explanatory principle.

Similar methodological difficulties beset Galin's other callosal test (Galin et al., 1979). The palmar surface of the children's fingers is touched with fabrics varying in texture. In succession, the fingers are touched either by the same texture twice or by two different textures. Again, crossed errors in same/different judgments predominate—particularly, the younger children found it more difficult to make correct judgments when the two stimulated surfaces are on opposite hands as compared to when they are on the same hand. But in the uncrossed condition, the same surface is stimulated twice; in the crossed condition, different surfaces are touched. Lingering sensation from the first of the two rapidly successive touches could have accounted for the fact that the uncrossed matching was easier, in that it became partly a simultaneous rather than a successive matching task. It is possible that such an effect will be more marked in younger children. Kinsbourne et al (1983) introduced a control condition in which successive ipsilateral matches were performed by different pairs of fingers of the same hand. Even in the younger children, this condition proved no easier than the one presumably involving callosal transmission. Kletzkin (1980) studied children aged 9 to 11 who are either good or poor readers. In both groups she found an excess of crossed errors on the finger-localization test. Uncrossed-error incidence did not differ significantly between groups, whereas the poor readers made a significantly greater number of crossed errors. However, this appears to be due to a ceiling effect for uncrossed localization, as the error rate for both groups was only about half that in the crossed condition. More recently, Strausbaugh, Kinsbourne, and Languis (1983) found no uncrossed/crossed performance difference in a sample of dyslexic children. The question of callosal maturity as studied by this test in learning-disabled children remains unresolved.

Callosal function may also be studied using tasks involving transfer of training. When one limb is practiced in a skill, something is learned by the other side also, as judged by savings in the number of trials it takes for the other limb subsequently to achieve the same performance criteria (e.g., see Hicks, Frank, & Kinsbourne, 1982). It appears that the central representations of the movements of the hand not being trained are implicitly modified at the time of the initial training. Two possible mechanisms come to mind, that is, information about the relevant motor program is transferred to the other hemisphere transcallosally, and ipsilateral as well as contralateral connections mediate the training. If the former is the case, then training should transfer to an increasing degree as the child and his corpus callosum mature. If the latter is the case and the callosum actually inhibits ipsilateral influence, as claimed by Dennis (1977), the the opposite should hold, that is, transfer should decrease with increase in age.

Transfer may be positive or negative. In positive transfer, the skill that is taught the first limb is then taught the second (Hicks, Frank, & Kinsbourne, 1982). Negative transfer is elicited when the second limb is taught a movement sequence contradictory to, or incompatible with, that acquired by the first. So, the individual who experiences greater positive transfer (i.e., savings) when the skill to be taught is held constant should experience greater negative transfer (i.e., interference) and do less well in second hand training in the negative transfer paradigm. If younger children show less savings, is that simply one more instance of the fact that younger children generally perform less well than older ones? If so, they would show fewer savings in positive transfer, yet more interference in negative transfer (contradicting the callosally related models).

Callosal inhibition may be inferred from the absence of left-right associated movements. If mirror movements were callosally transmitted, they would be expected to increase with the increasing callosal maturation and age of the child. In fact, they are well known to decrease with increasing age (Connally & Stratton, 1968). If this decrease is due to overflow of innervation into ipsilateral motor pathways (Green, 1967) and this, in turn, is a consequence of callosal underdevelopment (Dennis, 1977; Woods & Teuber, 1978b), then the incidence of mirror movements would relate to scores on the other callosal tests.

The absence of a fully functional corpus callosum may have diverse behavioral manifestations, depending on several factors. Most important are the age at which the callosum became dysfunctional and coexisting neurological abnormality. Children with agenesis of the corpus callosum do not show the marked degree of behavioral laterality that is characteristic of patients whose callosum was surgically sectioned during adult life (Saul & Sperry, 1968). It has been suggested (Ferriss & Dorsen, 1975) that functions usually lateralized in the normal brain are duplicated in both hemispheres of agenesis patients. Agenesis patients should then show less than the usual degree of asymmetry; some dichotic-listening studies, but not others, have supported that prediction (Bryden & Zurif, 1970; Ettlinger, Blakemore, Milner, & Wilson, 1972, 1974; Netley, 1977). It is unlikely that agenesis cases will provide much information about the role of the corpus callosum, as the number of available cases is small, the completeness of the agenesis is variable, and the disorder often entails additional neurological abnormality of severity sufficient to obfuscate the significance of the defective corpus callosum.

Laterality in Children with Reading and Speech Problems

It has long and often been asserted that children with dyslexia have incomplete cerebral dominance. The particular hemispheric mechanism proposed by

Orton (1928, 1937), who emphasized mirror-image reversals as a cardinal manifestation, need no longer be entertained, but the suspicion that many retarded readers are ill-lateralized for language persists (Hiscock & Kinsbourne, 1982).

Using handedness as an approximate index of lateralization, investigators have compared children with contrasting hand preference on measures of reading achievement. The expected inferiority among the nonright-handed sample was found by some (Dearborn, 1931, 1933; A. J. Harris, 1957; Zangwill, 1960) but not by others (Bennett, 1938; Coleman & Deutsch, 1964; Gates & Bond, 1936; Rutter, 1969; Sparrow, 1969; Witty & Kopel, 1936). Nevertheless, the view persists that nonright-handedness indexes incomplete lateralization, which, in turn, impairs reading acquisition, (Critchley, 1970; Sadick & Ginsburg, 1978; Zangwill, 1960). An analogous relationship between anomalous cerebral asymmetry and a subset of dyslexics has been suggested (Hier, LeMay, Rosenberger, & Perlo, 1978) but not confirmed (Haslam, Dalby, Johns, & Rademaker, 1981).

Laterality-based theories of reading disability undoubtedly gained fuel from the postulate of progressive cerebral dominance because a developmental lag model of dyslexia (Satz, Fletcher, Clark, & Morris, 1981) would simply regard dyslexics as having made little or no progress in lateralizing, at least language, to their left hemisphere. It is an easy logical step to institute procedures that purport to hasten this hypothesized lagging process, and this step has often been taken (Ayres, 1968, 1979; Delacato, 1959; Tomatis, 1978). Empirical validation of these approaches is lacking. Now that the notion of progressive cerebral lateralization is itself suspect, the time is opportune to question the theoretical basis for these methodologies.

What is incomplete cerebral dominance? Taking the left hemisphere and language as cases in point, these possibilities are most salient:

Model 1. Language function is spread across both hemispheres rather than lateralized. The pathological mechanism would presumably be some interference between language and other functions localized in the same cerebral space.

Model 2. Some language functions are left lateralized, others are right lateralized. Perhaps there is, then, a communication problem.

Model 3. The left hemisphere incompletely dominates (e.g., incompletely inhibits) the right during verbal activity. Then, interference between hemispheres might contaminate language performance.

Model 4. A possibility exists for this model, but it is a conceptual error to classify it with the rest. It is the possibility that the specialization for language of the left hemisphere simply does not occur or lags (Witelson, 1977a,b). That would certainly be a problem in hemispheric maturation but not in lateralization per se. In other words, lateralization-deficit hypotheses posit that the language function is abnormally represented in the brain. In the case of lagging specialization, the lateralization would be in the normal place, but it does not unfold normally (Hiscock & Kinsbourne, 1980c). Thus, reading problems may derive from maldevelopment within the classic language area of the left hemisphere (although the striking single case report to this effect by Galaburda and Kemper, 1979, leaves one uncertain whether this is a likely hypothesis for such frequently encountered problems). Even where this is so, diminished or reversed asymmetries of verbal perception need not necessarily result.

Model 5. Even if specialization has properly occurred, this is no guarantee that the hemisphere will be deployed at the proper time. If adopting a verbal mental set involves activation of left-hemispheric language areas, then this process itself, as distinct from the specialization, might be subject to failure (Kinsbourne, 1980b; Oexle & Zenhausern, 1981).

What would be the consequences of these models for laterality testing? If the processes tapped were, in fact, right lateralized in reading-disabled children, a reversed asymmetry would result; but this is rarely claimed and not found. But all models could accommodate an asymmetry that is less than the usual. In the cases of Models 1, 2, and 3 for structural reasons of brain organization; in Model 4 for reason of processing deficit; and in Model 5 for reason of selection deficit. Only one of the models, however, could accommodate the findings of no differences in asymmetry. This is Model 4. Suppose the selection mechanism for the left hemisphere during verbal mental set is normally active. It activates an incompetent hemisphere but, nevertheless, sets up the activation gradient between hemispheres that can generate a perceptual asymmetry. The point in principle is: a normal perceptual asymmetry—and, by implication, normal hemispheric activation—is no guarantee of normal hemispheric functioning. Holding task difficulty constant, Models 1 through 4 do call for stable laterality findings with the dyslexic sample across different laterality tasks; Model 5 does not. When there is a selective-activation impairment, the precise conditions of testing could have a major influence (to the extent that they do or do not facilitate left-hemispheric activation for the task).

In investigating backward readers, dichotic listening (e.g., see Bryden, 1970; Caplan & Kinsbourne, 1981) and hemifield viewing have most often been applied. The former method is indirect, in that it examines spoken-language lateralization in children whose problem is in reading (although a less dramatic oral-language deficit frequently coexists (Kinsbourne & Warrington, 1963a; Pirozzolo, 1979; Vellutino, 1979). The latter has the drawback of its advantage. It investigates reading directly (if in a simplistic manner) but is limited to single words too briefly exposed to decode by word attack. However, by studying a performance that is by definition defective in the experimental group and normal in the control group, it sets up a comparison that is clearly illegitimate.

Many studies find a right half-field advantage for retarded readers, many do not (Satz, 1976). The diversity of samples could account for this, but even if samples of backward readers were uniform (and dyslexia were a unitary condition), the degree of reading difficulty could still differ among children and this would affect two variables that profoundly influence perceptual asymmetry: coding strategy and effort.

At different levels of reading expertise, different strategies are used for decoding words. These are not fully understood, but obvious extreme examples would be spelling-to-sound conversion and reading as word association to a visual pattern. The former method might draw more exclusively on left-hemispheric skills (Young & Ellis, 1981). Level of difficulty has a less well-understood, but possibly even greater, effect. The fluent reader might adopt an efficient verbal set and the left-hemispheric activation involved would generate a substantial right VHF advantage. Poor readers might (1) do this also and show equal asymmetry, (2) not attempt this because they expect to fail, (3) not be able to do this on account of physiological abnormality, or (4) not bother to do this because they are undermotivated. The diminished or absent asymmetry cannot be translated into diminished or absent language lateralization unless these potential biases are held constant. They have not been.

Some preliminary evidence does suggest a somewhat deviant cognitive style among backward readers, tending toward the nonverbal (Caplan & Kinsbourne, 1982), that lines older poor readers up with younger normal children and shows no qualitative difference (see also Oexle & Zenhausern, 1981). It remains to be determined whether cognitive style is cause or effect of the reading problem.

If one matches retarded readers with younger normal readers at the same achievement level, then one might overcome the differential coding problem—but only if the maturational-lag hypothesis of selective reading disability is correct (Satz & Van Nostrand, 1973). Only if the dyslexic attempts to read as would a normal child and the deficit is quantitative are similar strategies to be expected. But if the dyslexic reading is qualitatively different, then such groups are still unmatched. This is probably aggravated by the remedial instruction that such children often receive. Intense emphasis on a particular teaching method (e.g., phonics) could induce the child to use special strategies and make mistakes uncharacteristic of readers taught in conventional group situations. Worse still, there is evidence for diverse subtypes of reading disability (Boder, 1970; Doehring & Hoshko, 1977; Fisk & Rourke, 1979; Kinsbourne & Warrington, 1963a; Lyon, Stewart, & Freedman, 1983; Mattis, 1978; Myklebust, 1975; Petrauskas & Rourke, 1979; Pirozzolo, 1979; Rourke, 1982) though for methodological reasons they cannot as yet be precisely specified (Satz & Morris, 1981), and it is quite possible that whereas one subtype represents a general lag of reading-related processes, others represent imbalances in these processes that would compel the beginning reader to resort to unusual approaches.

An instance of the possible impact of subtyping of dyslexia on laterality considerations is offered by Pirozzolo (1979). Following Kinsbourne and Warrington (1963a), he classified dyslexias into an auditory-linguistic and a visual-spatial form, both attributable to left-hemispheric dysfunction or immaturity, but in different brain areas. The auditory-linguistic cases who give evidence of language difficulties beyond the written word showed no right half-field advantage. Possibly, they were unable to implement verbal mental set via selective left-hemispheric activation (Model 5). The visual-spatial cases had the usual asymmetry favoring the right.

Dalby and Gibson (1981) classified their backward readers into dysphonetic (particularly limited in word attack), dyseidetic (limited in vocabulary), and nonspecific. They used tactile directional orientation and verbal-manual interference to establish laterality for spatial and verbal processing. They found no asymmetries for dysphonetics, only spatial (right) lateralization for dyseidetics, and only verbal (left) lateralization for nonspecifics. Insofar as the classifications used by them and Pirozzolo (1979) can be assumed to overlap, we have congruence with respect to lack of the normal laterality in verbal tasks for the auditory-linguistic subtype. But further comparisons cannot be made. Cermak, Cermak, Drake, and Kenney (1978) classified dyslexic children into two contrasting subgroups in terms of at least 15-point discrepancy between WISC verbal and performance IQ. Neither group showed the expected right-ear dichotic advantage, but for the verbally deficient group, it was reinstated when children concurrently finger tapped, although only when using the left hand. Bakker (1979); Bakker, Teunissen, and Bosch (1976); and Bakker, Licht, Kok, and Bouma (1980) have sought to relate laterality (side of dichotic ear advantage for verbal stimuli) to pattern of reading difficulty. They interpret their findings as indicating two dyslexic subtypes, characterized by overinvolvement of the right and left hemisphere respectively in the reading process. This group further claims to have improved reading performance by delivering stimulation to the underinvolved hemisphere in each type (Bakker, Moerland, & Groekoop-Hoetkens, 1981). Conclusions drawn must be tentative, but findings such as these make it clear that wholesale studies in laterality in poor readers of indeterminate subtype will give unintelligible results.

Children with overt delays in developing spoken language have been less often studied with respect to their laterality, presumably because they are fewer in number than children with reading difficulty and also because the more severely affected children are hard to test by the usual methods. Some such studies show diminished or absent right-sided advantage in perceptual asymmetry paradigms that use verbal material (Petitt & Helms, 1974; Rosenblum & Dorman, 1978; Starkey, 1974). Others do not (Sommers & Taylor, 1972; Springer & Eisenson, 1977; Tobey, Cullen, & Rampp, 1976). Absent right-sided advantage would be consistent with Models 4 or 5 (or the two in combination). To make a case for the more ambitious Models 1 through 3, one would have to show by event-related variables not only diminished language activity on the left but also increased language activity on the right. As no such evidence has been offered, we concede that the conservative postulate of left-hemispheric immaturity or underactivation remains the most plausible at present.

In summary, failure of verbal processes to lateralize to the left hemisphere cannot be considered an acceptable explanation for reading or language difficulties in children. Delayed or deviant left-hemispheric maturation could be involved but for reasons proper to that hemisphere rather than on account of failure of a hypothetical shift of verbal representation from a bisymmetrical to an asymmetrical pattern. Attempts to shift language representation toward the left hemisphere by peripheral manipulations are irrational.

Deafness

Unable to use the auditory modality, the congenitally deaf presumably attempt many tasks with strategies far different from those hearing children and adults normally deploy. Therefore, they would use different brain areas for such purposes, and this difference in brain use would emerge in the results of event-related measurements, among which are the various behavioral asymmetry paradigms. When the deaf show deviant laterality patterns, the conservative conclusion is that they are setting about the task differently. Only if they can be proven to be using the same strategy as controls can laterality differences be credibly referred to different patterns of functional cerebral specialization in the deaf. A prediction of the conservative position is that the more the experimenter successfully constrains the deaf subject's strategy, the closer to the norm will be the laterality findings.

Different studies of perceptual laterality in the deaf have found atypical patterns of laterality (Gibson & Bryden, 1982; Kelly & Tomlinson-Keasey, 1981; LaBreche, Manning, Gobel, & Markman, 1977), a reduced degree of laterality (McKeever, Hoemann, Florian, & Van Deventer, 1976; Scholes & Fischler, 1979), and laterality resembling that of subjects with normal hearing (Cranney & Ashton, 1980; Poizner, Battison, & Lane, 1979). Some investigators have voiced different expectations for the laterality pattern of oral and signing deaf subjects. Phippard (1977) reported that oral subjects showed left VHF advantage for verbal as well as nonverbal stimuli, whereas signing subjects showed no asymmetry for either. Neville (1977) reported the exact opposite findings. Scholes and Fischler (1979) found no perceptual asymmetry for verbal material in their deaf subjects, but Scholes and Fischler (in press) found the expected differential right-manual-performance decrement in a verbal-manual interference paradigm, as did Ashton and Beasley (1982).

These findings conform to expectations, based

on differential strategy, in that the output paradigms—over which the experimenter has the most control—give findings close to the norm. The input paradigms give findings that conflict not only with the norm but also with each other.

Stuttering

Among the disorders that Orton (1928) identified as involving deviant lateralization was stuttering, and this claim has often been made since (Brady, Sommers & Moore, 1973; Jones, 1966; Travis, 1931). Although the idea that rivalry between competing speech control centers could cause a person to stutter is not without appeal, the natural history of the disorder makes it unlikely that stuttering is attributable to fixed structural abnormalities of any kind.

Stuttering begins not when children first speak, but at age 4 to 6 years. Most children who stutter during this period subsequently cease to do so without therapy. Some continue to stutter. But before the appearance of speech disorder, their speech development was normal. Moreover, all stutterers, however severe their disorder, are capable of normal utterance at times. It, therefore, seems likely that speech and language have developed normally but that functions go awry under certain circumstances.

Recent attempts to investigate language lateralization by using dichotic-listening and related paradigms have proved inconclusive or negative for the deviant-lateralization hypothesis (Brady & Berson, 1975; Curry & Gregory, 1969; Dorman & Porter, 1975; Gruber & Powell, 1974; Quinn, 1972; Rosenfield & Goodglass, 1980; Slorach & Noehr, 1973; Sommers, Brady, & Moore, 1975; Sussman & MacNeilage, 1975), but these were on tests on speech-input processing. Only if language lateralization were necessarily all of a piece would one expect the lateralization of speech-decoding mechanisms to index lateralization of speech-output control. There is no logical basis for supposing this, and we know that some language functions can be left lateralized and others right lateralized in the same person, at least in certain left-handers who were studied with intracarotid sodium amobarbital (Rasmussen & Milner, 1975). An adequate laterality test for stutterers would address the output function directly, for instance, by using vocal-manual interference (Kinsbourne & Hicks, 1978) as a lateralizing paradigm. Using this technique, Sussman (1982) found laterally symmetrical interference for stutterers (like lefthanders). He also used nonsupportive interference and found the surprising outcome of right hand (left hemisphere) selective interference. Neurophysiological correlates of vocalisation by stutterers and controls have been compared, with inconclusive results (Pinsky & McAdam, 1980; Zimmerman & Knott, 1979).

Still more directly, each hemisphere may selectively be inactivated by intracarotid amobarbital injection and the consequences for stutterers' speech noted. Jones (1966) found evidence of bilaterality speech control in 4 stutterers with structural brain lesions. Of 10 developmental stutterers who have been so studied, 4 had bilateral speech representation (Andrews, Quinn, & Sorby, 1972; Luessenhop, Boggs, LaBorwit, & Walle, 1973), so it may be that bilateral speech control is a sufficient, but not a necessary, condition for stuttering to develop.

Infantile Autism

Some investigators of this perplexing syndrome have incriminated hemispheric brain mechanisms (see reviews by McCann, 1981, and by Prior, 1979). Acquired generalized brain damage has been reported to have induced autism in a previously normal 10-year-old child (Weir & Salisbury, 1980). It is currently fashionable to emphasize the language deficit as opposed to the behavioral deviance of autistic children (Baker, Cantwell, Rutter, & Bartak, 1976; Rutter & Bartak, 1971). By implication, the left hemisphere (at least of genotypic dextrals) is suspected of malfunction or even structural anomaly and the search for pathological left-handedness and right-hemispheric cognitive style has begun.

Hauser, DeLong and Rosman (1975) reported pneumoencephalographic findings for 18 autistic children. The left lateral ventricle was enlarged in 15 of them, raising the possibility of left-hemispheric atrophy owing to early structural damage. Hier, LeMay, & Rosenberger (1979) used CAT to search for hemispheric asymmetries. Whereas the majority of control (retarded and neurologically impaired) children exhibited a left parieto-occipital region that was wider than the right, 9 of 16 autistic children showed the reverse asymmetry. Subject to the reservation that these hospital-based samples might include a relatively high proportion of autistic children with gross brain lesions, these findings do, albeit weakly, support the idea of a disordered left hemisphere in at least some autists. However, serious methodological problems render these results inconclusive (Tsai, Jacoby, Stewart, & Beisler, 1982). Dawson, Warrenburg, and Fuller (1982) recently reported that a sample of 10 male autists differed from control subjects to the laterality of EEG alpha activity recorded from over the parietal region. The right-to-left alpha ratios suggested a preponderance of right-hemispheric activation among the autistic subjects, relative to the controls, during the performance of spatial tasks, but the EEG index did not differentiate the two groups while they performed either of two verbal tasks. Because the autists were markedly deficient in verbal ability (but not visuospatial ability), it is likely that factors such as subjective difficulty and strategy would have greater effects during performance of the verbal tasks than performance of the spatial tasks.

Further circumstantial evidence derives from the higher incidence of nonright-handedness among autistic children than in the general population (Barry & James, 1978; Colby & Parkinson, 1977) or as compared to their parents (Boucher, 1977). This is similar to the phenomenon that exists among mentally retarded children, with the prevalence of nonright-handedness increasing with the degree of retardation (Hicks & Barton, 1975). In the case of both disordered populations, the following explanation may apply: whereas sinistrality in the general population appears to be genetically determined (Hicks & Kinsbourne, 1976), its excess incidence in autists (and the retarded) is contributed by pathological left-handers (Satz, 1972). Brain damage that involves the hemispheres unequally can shift handedness away from the genotypically selected side. As genotypic dextrality is by far the most frequent, such pathological hand preference will favor the left hand, raising the incidence of left-handedness from the usual 10% to anything up to near 50%. If it were true that autistic children have left cortical damage, then this would plausibly explain the handedness findings. It would also explain the adoption of a right-hemispheric orienting strategy documented by Blackstock (1978). He found that autistic children listened to a sound source more often with the left ear in contrast to controls. The left turning could index right-hemispheric predominance. Perhaps for the same reason, Prior and Bradshaw (1979) found absence of a dichotic REA overall for an autistic sample, in contrast to controls. However, this study leaves room for ambiguity, in that it is unclear with what categorical mental set the language-deficient autistic children were approaching the linguistic dichotic task.

If dominance relationships are anomalous in some or many autistic children, (Dawson, Warrenburg, & Fuller, 1982), this could be for one or both of two reasons: (1) early lateralized cerebral malfunction or frank damage and (2) genetic sinistrality with its expected heterogeneous dominance concomitants. However, in the absence of hard neurological signs, the evidence for left-hemispheric damage is weak. Also, the hypothesis is illogical in view of the compelling evidence for right-hemispheric language compensation even after the most severe left-hemispheric destruction in children. At the very least, the left-hemisphere hypothesis must additionally assume an influence that precludes the right hemisphere from realizing its compensatory potential for language development. One could, at this point, invoke cross-inhibition, but this takes us so far beyond the data that it is not at this time worth considering. It is at least as possible that the disorder involves the brainstem (Fein, Skoff, & Mirsky, 1981) in such a way as to distort selection mechanisms for regional cerebral activation. Theorizing apart, any suggestion that the autistic language deficit represents a failure to lateralize language lacks empirical support (Kinsbourne, 1979).

Language Deprivation

Although we offered an alternative explanation for the frequent failure of deaf children to show normal patterns of perceptual laterality, some investigators (e.g., see Kelly & Tomlinson-Keasey, 1981) have inferred from this evidence that deprivation of auditory-verbal stimulation leads to anomalous cerebral organization. Because of their heterogeneity with respect to degree and kind of hearing loss as well as the nature and proficiency of their communicative skills, deaf children probably will not provide definitive evidence of the effects of linguistic deprivation. But what if a child with normal sensory acuity were deprived of linguistic stimulation throughout the period in which children normally acquire language? If language subsequently is acquired by that individual, what would be the nature of its cerebral representation?

An extraordinary case of physical and social deprivation was described by Curtiss (1977). From the age of 20 months to 13½ years, a girl referred to by Curtiss as Genie was confined to a small room in which she received very little auditory and almost no linguistic stimulation. Although Genie apparently had begun to acquire language at the time her confinement began, she became mute shortly thereafter and exhibited no expressive language when she emerged from isolation nearly 12 years later. Even her ability to comprehend speech at that time was suspect. During subsequent years of intensive training, as her linguistic and other cognitive skills developed, Genie was administered several linguistic and psychological tests, including tests of dichotic listening and of tachistoscopic perception. Cortical evoked potentials from the left and right sides of the scalp also were measured.

The results from all laterality measures deviated from the norm and suggested that Genie's language was lateralized to the right hemisphere. She is right-handed. The laterality test results as well as Genie's pattern of strengths and weaknesses on various psychometric instruments led Curtiss (1977) to characterize Genie as a "right-hemisphere thinker." Curtiss concluded that Genie's case illustrates the inability of the left hemisphere to acquire language outside Lenneberg's (1967) critical period of 2 years to puberty.

The case of Genie is interesting for many reasons, but it tells us little about the effects of extreme isolation on brain organization. First, the evidence suggesting right-hemispheric lateralization of her language is weak. Genie's atypical asymmetries are more plausibly attributed to idiosyncratic strategy than to deviant brain organization. As we have pointed out previously, a substantial minority of normal children and adults shows laterality patterns that deviate from the norm. It is hardly surprising, in light of her lack of opportunity to learn language, that Genie is more proficient at nonverbal than verbal skills. Even if the right-hemispheric locus of Genie's language could be confirmed, it would be impossible to know whether it is attributable to auditory-linguistic deprivation or to any number of other factors, including the possibility that she is one of those sporadic right-handers with right-hemispheric language or that early head trauma, malnutrition, or disease (at least one instance of serious febrile illness is reported by Curtiss) produced neurological damage sufficient to alter cerebral organization.

Summary

The study of deviant hand preference (i.e., left-handedness) suggests two conclusions: (1) anomalous cerebral organization when unaccompanied by brain pathology has no deleterious consequences for cognitive development and (2) the empirical association between left-handedness and behavioral deficit in clinical populations can be ascribed to a familial vulnerability to early brain pathology that leads to both behavioral deficits and (pathological) left-handedness. Claims regarding the developmental and clinical significance of callosal functioning are not substantiated by the extant evidence. Nor is there adequate empirical basis for one of the oldest and most widespread assertions about hemispheric specialization, namely, that children's reading and speech problems are attributable to deviant cerebral lateralization. Analysis of various hypothetical models of deviance shows that absence of left lateralization of language cannot explain these disorders, although abnormal development of the left hemisphere (apart from any abnormality of lateralization) might. Bilateral speech control in some stutterers may contribute, but it cannot account for all or even most instances of stuttering. Although samples of deaf and autistic children sometimes show deviant patterns of behavioral and electrophysiological asymmetry, it is likely that such patterns reflect the use of deviant strategies rather than anomalous cerebral lateralization. A case of delayed language development following prolonged extreme isolation provides no conclusive evidence of the putative inability of the left hemisphere to acquire language after the so-called critical period.

CONCLUDING REMARKS

The answers of the 1960s reverted into questions in the 1970s, and so remain. That humans are unique in, and because of, the lateralization of their higher mental functions; that maturity of mental development is a triumph of progressive lateralization; that failed lateralization explains diverse failures in mental development; that from beast to man, infant to adult, even female to male, poor to rich, a continuum of lateralization underlies a continuum of behavioral refinement. These simple, sweeping formulations are now thoroughly undermined, and no alternative certitudes replace them. The fantasy of the 1970s, that is, that the right hemisphere is purveyor of an alternative life style, is over. The conceptual core itself of yesterday's neuropsychology, the switchboard model of brain as a communication network (disconnected in its parts by disease) has outlived its heuristic value. It is not that the ideas were devoid of merit or that we are no further than 20 years ago. On the contrary, while the disinformation summarized was developed, much else was learned. As science progresses, questions may receive different answers. But more significantly, they are replaced by different (and more searching) questions. The vagaries of experimental outcome compel a more rigorous methodology and the error variance turns out to be a source of basic insights. A new composite begins to form, that is, the brain as a cybernetic device, connected yet exquisitely differentiated and its maturation the refinement of checks and balances—complicated in detail but, in principle, conforming to a blueprint already apparent in the infant.

The questions themselves, now stripped of answers, represent an adversary (either/or) approach to scientific inquiry, which is at best a point of departure in the search for a more sophisticated dialectic. The reductionism of assertion and refutation, claim and counterclaim, attractive as it may be to bewildered editors of scientific journals, leads to impasse. Alternative hypotheses may represent equally valid perspectives on a complex whole, and converging operations perhaps should converge, not on the "right" explanation but on the correct account of the boundary conditions within which a given explanation has simplifying value. If the 1980s are a decade of doubt, current retreat from certainty may be an opportune basis for the next step forward by developmental neuroscience.

REFERENCES

Abrams, R., & Taylor, M. A. Laboratory studies in the validation of psychiatric diagnoses. In J. H. Gruzelier & P. Flor-Henry (Eds.), *Hemisphere asymmetries of function in psychopathology.* Amsterdam: Elsevier North-Holland, 1979.

Adrian, E. D., & Matthews, B. H. C. The Berger rhythm: Potential changes from the occipital lobes in man. *Brain,* 1934, *57,* 355–385.

Ahern, G. L., & Schwartz, G. E. Differential lateralization for positive versus negative emotion. *Neuropsychologia,* 1979, *17,* 693–698.

Aird, R. B., & Gastaut, Y. Occipital and posterior electroencephalographic rhythms. *Electroencephalography and Clinical Neurophysiology,* 1959, *11,* 637–656.

Albert, M. L., & Obler, L. K. *The bilingual brain: Neuropsychological and neurolinguistic aspects of bilingualism.* New York: Academic Press, 1978.

Allard, F. A., & Bryden, M. P. The effect of concurrent activity on hemispheric asymmetries. *Cortex,* 1979, *15,* 5–17.

Amochaev, A., & Salamy, A. Stability of EEG laterality effects. *Psychophysiology,* 1979, *16,* 242–246.

Anderson, I., & Crosland, H. R. A method of measuring the effect of primacy of report in the range of attention experiment. *American Journal of Psychology,* 1933, *45,* 701–713.

Anderson, S. W. Language-related asymmetries of eye-movement and evoked potentials. In S. Harnad, R. W. Doty, L. Goldstein, J. Jaynes, & G. Krauthamer (Eds.), *Lateralization in the nervous system.* New York: Academic Press, 1977.

Andreassi, J. L., De Simone, J. J., Friend, M. A., & Grota, P. A. Hemispheric amplitude asymmetries in the auditory evoked potential with monaural and binaural stimulation. *Physiological Psychology,* 1975, *3,* 169–171.

Andrew, R. J., Mench, J., & Rainey, C. Right-left asymmetry of response to visual stimuli in the domestic chick. In D. J. Ingle, R. J. W. Mansfield, & M. A. Goodale (Eds.), *Advances in the analysis of visual behavior.* Cambridge: MIT Press, 1980.

Andrews, G., Quinn, P. T., & Sorky, W. A. Stuttering: An investigation into cerebral dominance for speech. *Journal of Neurology, Neurosurgery and Psychiatry,* 1972, *35,* 414–418.

Annett, M. Handedness in families. *Annals of Human Genetics,* 1973, *37,* 93–105.

Annett, M., & Ockwell, A. Birth order, birth stress and handedness. *Cortex,* 1980, *16,* 181–188.

Ashton, R., & Beasley, M. Cerebral laterality in deaf and hearing impaired children. *Developmental Psychology,* 1982, *18,* 294–300.

Ayres, A. J. Sensory interpretative processes and neuropsychological learning disabilities. In J. Hellmuth (Ed.), *Learning disorders* (Vol. 3). Seattle: Special Child Publications, 1968.

Ayres, A. J. *Sensory integration and the child.* Los Angeles: Western Psychological Services, 1979.

Ayres, J. J., & Harcum, E. R. Directional response-bias in reproducing brief visual patterns. *Perceptual and Motor Skills,* 1962, *14,* 155–165.

Bahrick, H. P., Bahrick, P. O., & Wittlinger, R. P. Fifty years of memory for names and faces: A cross-sectional approach. *Journal of Experimental Psychology: General,* 1975, *104,* 54–75.

Bakan, P. Hypnotizability, laterality of eye-movements and functional brain asymmetry. *Perceptual and Motor Skills,* 1969, *28,* 927–932.

Bakan, P. Handedness and birth order. *Nature,* 1971, *229,* 195.

Bakan, P., Dibb, G., & Reed, P. Handedness and birth stress. *Neuropsychologia,* 1973, *11,* 363–366.

Baker, L., Cantwell, D. P., Rutter, M., & Bartak, L. Language and autism. In E. R. Ritvo, B. J. Freeman, E. M. Ornitz, & P. E. Tanguay (Eds.), *Autism: Diagnosis, current research and management.* New York: Spectrum, 1976.

Bakker, D. J. Left-right differences in auditory perception of verbal and nonverbal material by children. *Quarterly Journal of Experimental Psychology,* 1967, *19,* 334–336.

Bakker, D. J. Ear-asymmetry with monaural stimulation. *Psychonomic Science,* 1968, *12,* 62.

Bakker, D. J. Ear-asymmetry with monaural stimulation: Task influences. *Cortex,* 1969, *5,* 36–42.

Bakker, D. J. Ear-asymmetry with monaural stimulation: Relations to lateral dominance and lateral awareness. *Neuropsychologia,* 1970, *8,* 103–114.

Bakker, D. J. Hemispheric specialization and states in the learning-to-read process. *Bulletin of the Orton Society,* 1973, *23,* 15–27.

Bakker, D. J. Hemispheric differences and reading strategies: Two dyslexias? *Bulletin of the Orton Society,* 1979, *29,* 84–100.

Bakker, D. J., Hoefkens, M., & Van der Vlugt, H. Hemispheric specialization in children as reflected in the longitudinal development of ear asymmetry. *Cortex,* 1979, *15,* 619–625.

Bakker, D. J., Licht, R., Kok, A., & Bouma, A. Cortical responses to word reading by right- and left-eared normal and reading disturbed children. *Journal of Clinical Neuropsychology,* 1980, *2,* 1–12.

Bakker, D. J., Moerland, R., Groekoop-Hoetkens, M. Effects of hemisphere-specific stimulation on the reading performance of dyslexic boys: A pilot study. *Journal of Clinical Neuropsychology,* 1981, *3,* 155–159.

Bakker, D. J., & Reitsma, P. Ear dominance and reading ability. *Cortex,* 1973, *9,* 301–312.

Bakker, D. J., Teunissen, J., & Bosch, J. Development of laterality-reading patterns. In R. M. Knights & D. J. Bakker (Eds.), *The neuropsychology of learning disorders.* Baltimore: University Park Press, 1976.

Bakker, D. J., Van der Vlugt, H., & Claushuis, M. The reliability of dichotic ear asymmetry in normal children. *Neuropsychologia,* 1978, *16,* 753–757.

Bakwin, H. Psychiatric aspects of pediatrics: Lateral dominance right- and left-handedness. *Journal of Pediatrics,* 1950, *36,* 385–391.

Barnet, A. B., Ohlrich, E. S., Weiss, I. P., & Shanks, B. Auditory evoked potentials during sleep in normal children from ten days to three years of age. *Electroencephalography and Clinical Neurophysiology,* 1975, *39,* 29–41.

Barry, R. J., & James, A. L. Handedness in autistics, retardates, and normals of a wide range. *Journal of Autism and Childhood Schizophrenia,* 1978, *8,* 315–323.

Barton, M. I., Goodglass, H., & Shai, A. Differential recognition of tachistoscopically presented English and Hebrew words in right and left visual fields. *Perceptual and Motor Skills,* 1965, *21,* 431–437.

Bashore, T. R. Vocal and manual reaction time estimates of interhemispheric transmission time. *Psychological Bulletin,* 1981, *89,* 352–368.

Basser, L. S. Hemiplegia of early onset and the faculty of speech with special reference to the effects of hemispherectomy. *Brain,* 1962, *85,* 427–460.

Bear, D., & Fedio, P. Quantitative analysis of interictal behavior in temporal lobe epilepsy. *Archives of Neurology,* 1977, *34,* 454–467.

Bennett, C. C. *An inquiry into the genesis of poor reading.* New York: Bureau of Publications, Teachers College, Columbia University, 1938.

Benson, D. F. Fluency in aphasia: correlation with radioactive scan localization. *Cortex,* 1967, *3,* 373–394.

Benton, A. L. The neuropsychology of facial recognition. *American Psychologist,* 1980, *35,* 176–186.

Benton, A. L., Hannay, H. J., & Varney, N. R. Visual perception of line direction in patients with unilateral brain disease. *Neurology,* 1975, *25,* 907–910.

Benton, A. L., & Van Allen, M. W. Impairment in facial recognition in patients with cerebral disease. *Cortex,* 1968, *4,* 344–358.

Benton, A. L., Varney, N. R., & Hamsher, K., de S. Visuospatial judgement. *Archives of Neurology,* 1978, *35,* 364–367.

Berg, M. R., & Harris, L. J. The effect of experimenter location and subject anxiety on cerebral activation as measured by lateral eye movements. *Neuropsychologia,* 1980, *18,* 89–93.

Berger, H. Über das Elektrenkephalogramm des Menschen. *Archiv für Psychiatrie und Nervenkrankheiten* 1929, *87,* 527–570.

Berlin, C. I. Hemispheric asymmetry in auditory tasks. In S. Harnad, R. W. Doty, L. Goldstein, J. Jaynes, & G. Krauthamer (Eds.), *Lateralization in the nervous system.* New York: Academic Press, 1977.

Berlin, C. I., & Cullen, J. K. Acoustic problems in dichotic listening tasks. In S. J. Segalowitz & F. A. Gruber (Eds.), *Language development and neurological theory.* New York: Academic Press, 1977.

Berlin, C. I., Hughes, L. F., Lowe-Bell, S. S., & Berlin, H. L. Dichotic right ear advantages in children 5–13. *Cortex,* 1973, *9,* 394–402.

Berlin, C. I., & Lowe, S. S. Temporal and dichotic factors in central auditory testing. In J. Katz (Ed.), *Handbook of clinical audiology.* Baltimore: Williams & Wilkens, 1972.

Berlin, C. I., Lowe-Bell, S. S., Cullen, J. K., Jr., Thompson, C. L., & Loovis, C. F. Dichotic speech perception: An interpretation of right-ear advantage and temporal offset effects. *Journal of the Acoustical Society of America,* 1973, *53,* 699–709.

Berlin, C. I., & McNeil, M. R. Dichotic listening. In N. J. Lass (Ed.), *Contemporary issues in experimental phonetics.* Springfield, Ill.: Charles C. Thomas, 1976.

Berlucchi, G., Heron, W., Hyman, R., Rizzolati, G., & Umilta, C. Simple reaction times of ipsilateral and contralateral hand to lateralized visual stimuli. *Brain,* 1971, *94,* 419–430.

Best, C. T., Hoffman, H., & Glanville, B. B. Development of infant ear asymmetries for speech and music. *Perception & Psychophysics,* 1982, *31,* 75–85.

Bever, T. G. The nature of cerebral dominance in speech behavior of the child and adult. In R. Huxley & E. Ingram (Eds.), *Language acquisition: Models and methods.* London: Academic Press, 1971.

Bever, T. G., & Chiarello, R. J. Cerebral dominance in musicians and non-musicians. *Science,* 1974, *185,* 537–539.

Bingley, T. Mental symptoms in temporal lobe epilepsy and temporal lobe gliomas with special reference to laterality of lesion and the relationship between handedness and brainedness. *Acta Psychiatrica et Neurologica,* 1958, *33* (Suppl. No. 120).

Birkett, P. Measures of laterality and theories of hemispheric process. *Neuropsychologia,* 1977, *15,* 693–696.

Bishop, D. V. M. Linguistic impairment after left hemidecortication for infantile hemiplegia? A reappraisal. *Quarterly Journal of Experimental Psychology,* in press.

Blackstock, E. G. Cerebral asymmetry and the development of early infantile autism. *Journal of Autism and Childhood Schizophrenia,* 1978, *8,* 339–353.

Blau, T. H. Torque and schizophrenic vulnerability. *American Psychologist,* 1977, *32,* 997–1005.

Bloom, L. *Language development: Form and function in emerging grammars.* Cambridge: MIT Press, 1970.

Bloom, L. *One word at a time: The use of single-word utterance before syntax.* The Hague: Mouton, 1973.

Blumstein, S., Goodglass, H., & Tartter, V. The reliability of ear advantage in dichotic listening. *Brain and Language,* 1975, *2,* 226–236.

Boder, E. Developmental dyslexia: A new diagnostic approach based on the identification of three subtypes. *Journal of School Health,* 1970, *40,* 289–290.

Bogen, J. E. The other side of the brain I: Dysgraphia and dyscopia following cerebral commissurotomy. *Bulletin of the Los Angeles Neurological Societies,* 1969, *34,* 73–105. (a)

Bogen, J. E. The other side of the brain II: An appositional mind. *Bulletin of the Los Angeles Neurological Societies,* 1969, *34,* 135–162. (b)

Bogen, J. E. Further discussion on split-brains and hemispheric capabilities. *Brit. J. Phil. Sci.,* 1977, *28,* 281–286.

Bogen, J. E., & Bogen, G. M. The other side of the brain III: The corpus callosum and creativity. *Bulletin of the Los Angeles Neurological Societies,* 1969, *34,* 191–220.

Boles, D. B., Laterally biased attention with concurrent verbal load: Multiple failures to replicate. *Neuropsychologia,* 1979, *17,* 353–361.

Bolin, B. J. Left handedness and stuttering as signs diagnostic of epileptics. *Journal of Mental Science,* 1953, *99,* 483–488.

Boring, E. G. *A History of Experimental Psychology.* New York: Appleton-Century-Crofts, 1950.

Borod, J. C., & Goodglass, H. Lateralization of linguistic and melodic processing with age. *Neuropsychologia,* 1980, *18,* 79–83.

Botkin, A. L., Schmaltz, L. W., & Lamb, D. H. "Overloading" the left hemisphere in right-handed subjects with verbal and motor tasks. *Neuropsychologia,* 1977, *15,* 591–596.

Boucher, J. Hand preference in autistic children and their parents. *Journal of Autism and Childhood Schizophrenia,* 1977, *7,* 177–187.

Bower, T. G. R., & Haley, L. J. Temporal effects in binocular vision. *Psychonomic Science,* 1974, *1,* 409–410.

Bowers, D., Heilman, K. M., Satz, P., & Altman, A. Simultaneous performance on verbal, nonverbal and motor tasks by right-handed adults. *Cortex,* 1978, *14,* 540–556.

Bradshaw, J. L., Nettleton, N. C., & Taylor, M. J. Right hemisphere language and cognitive deficit in sinistrals? *Neuropsychologia,* 1981, *19,* 113–132.

Bradshaw, J. L., & Perriment, A. D. Laterality effects and choice reaction time in a unimanual two-finger task. *Perception & Psychophysics,* 1970, *7,* 185–188.

Brady, J. P., & Berson, J. Stuttering, dichotic listening and cerebral dominance. *Archives of General Psychiatry,* 1975, *32,* 1449–1452.

Brady, J. P., Sommers, R. K., & Moore, W. H. *Central speech processing in stuttering children and adults.* Paper presented at the meeting of the

American Speech and Hearing Association, Detroit, 1973.

Brain, W. R. Visual disorientation with special references to lesions of the right cerebral hemisphere. *Brain,* 1941, *64,* 244–272.

Briggs, G. G., & Kinsbourne, M. *Cerebral organization as revealed by multilimb tracking performance.* Unpublished manuscript, Duke University Medical Center, 1975.

Briggs, G. G., Nebes, R. D., & Kinsbourne, M. Intellectual differences in relation to personal and family handedness. *Quarterly Journal of Experimental Psychology,* 1976, *28,* 591–602.

Brinkman, J., & Kuypers, H. G. J. M. Split-brain monkeys: Cerebral control of ipsilateral and contralateral arm, hand and finger movements. *Science,* 1972, *176,* 536–539.

Brinkman, J., & Kuypers, H. G. J. M. Cerebral control of contralateral and ipsilateral arm, hand and finger movements in the split-brain rhesus monkey. *Brain,* 1973, *96,* 653–674.

Broadbent, D. E. The role of auditory localization in attention and memory span. *Journal of Experimental Psychology,* 1954, *47,* 191–196.

Brockes, J. Suppression of foreign synapses. *Nature,* 1976, *260,* 281.

Broman, M. Reaction-time differences between the left and right hemispheres for face and letter discrimination in children and adults. *Cortex,* 1978, *14,* 578–591.

Brown, J. W. *Aphasia, apraxia, and agnosia.* Springfield, Ill.: Charles C. Thomas, 1972.

Brown, J. W. *Mind, brain, and consciousness.* New York: Academic Press, 1977.

Brown, J. W., & Grober, E. Age, sex and aphasia type: Evidence for a regional cerebral growth process underlying lateralization. In I. Alter (Ed.), *Limits of functional localization.* New York: Raven Press, in press.

Brown, J. W., & Jaffe, J. Hypothesis on cerebral dominance. *Neuropsychologia,* 1975, *13,* 107–110.

Brown, W. S., Marsh, J. T., & Smith, J. C. Contextual meaning effects on speech evoked potentials. *Behavioral Biology,* 1973, *9,* 755–761.

Bruner, J. S. The ontogeny of speech acts. *Journal of Child Language,* 1975, *2,* 1–19.

Bryden, M. P. Tachistoscopic recognition of nonalphabetic material. *Canadian Journal of Psychology,* 1960, *14,* 78–86.

Bryden, M. P. Ear preference in auditory perception. *Journal of Experimental Psychology,* 1963, *65,* 103–105.

Bryden, M. P. The manipulation of strategies of report in dichotic listening. *Canadian Journal of Psychology,* 1964, *18,* 126–138.

Bryden, M. P. Accuracy and order of report in tachistoscopic recognition. *Canadian Journal of Psychology,* 1966, *20,* 262–272.

Bryden, M. P. An evaluation of some models of laterality effects in dichotic listening. *Acta Otolaryngologica* (Stockholm), 1967, *63,* 595–604.

Bryden, M. P. Laterality effects in dichotic listening: Relations with handedness and reading ability in children. *Neuropsychologia,* 1970, *8,* 443–450.

Bryden, M. P. *Perceptual strategies, attention, and memory in dichotic listening* (Res. Rep. No. 43). Waterloo, Canada: University of Waterloo, 1972.

Bryden, M. P. Perceptual asymmetry in vision: Relation to handedness, eyedness, and speech lateralization. *Cortex,* 1973, *9,* 418–432.

Bryden, M. P. Response bias and hemispheric differences in dot localization. *Perception & Psychophysics,* 1976, *19,* 23–28.

Bryden, M. P. Evidence for sex differences in cerebral organization. In M. A. Wittig & A. C. Peterson (Eds.), *Sex-related differences in cognitive functioning: Developmental issues.* New York: Academic Press, 1978. (a)

Bryden, M. P. Strategy effects in the assessment of hemispheric asymmetry. In G. Underwood (Ed.), *Strategies of information processing.* London: Academic Press, 1978. (b)

Bryden, M. P., & Allard, F. A. Visual hemifield differences depend on typeface. *Brain and Language,* 1976, *3,* 191–200.

Bryden, M. P., & Allard, F. A. Dichotic listening and the development of linguistic processes. In M. Kinsbourne (Ed.), *Asymmetrical function of the brain.* New York: Cambridge University Press, 1978.

Bryden, M. P., & Allard, F. A. Do auditory perceptual asymmetries develop? *Cortex,* 1981, *17,* 313–318.

Bryden, M. P., Dick, A. O., & Mewhort, D. J. K. Tachistoscopic recognition of number sequences. *Canadian Journal of Psychology,* 1968, *22,* 52–59.

Bryden, M. P., & Rainey, C. A. Left-right differences in tachistoscopic recognition. *Journal of Experimental Psychology,* 1963, *66,* 568–571.

Bryden, M. P., & Sprott, D. A. Statistical determination of degree of laterality. *Neuropsychologia,* 1981, *19,* 571–581.

Bryden, M. P., & Zurif, E. B. Dichotic listening

performance in a case of agenesis of the corpus callosum. *Neuropsychologia,* 1970, *8,* 371–377.

Buchsbaum, M., & Fedio, P. Visual information and evoked responses from the left and right hemispheres. *Electroencephalography and Clinical Neurophysiology,* 1969, *26,* 266–272.

Buchsbaum, M., & Fedio, P. Hemispheric differences in evoked potentials to verbal and nonverbal stimuli in the left and right visual fields. *Physiology and Behavior,* 1970, *5,* 207–210.

Buffery, A. W. H. Sex differences in the neuropsychological development of verbal and spatial skills. In R. M. Knights & D. J. Bakker (Eds.), *The neuropsychology of learning disorders.* Baltimore: University Park Press, 1976.

Burt, C. *The backward child.* London: University of London Press, 1950.

Butler, R. A., Keidel, W. D., & Spreng, M. An investigation of the human cortical evoked potential under conditions of monaural and binaural stimulation. *Acta Oto-laryngologica* (Stockholm), 1969, *68,* 317–326.

Butler, S. R., & Glass, A. Asymmetries in the electroencephalogram associated with cerebral dominance. *Electroencephalography and Clinical Neurophysiology,* 1974, *36,* 481–491.

Butler, D. C. & Miller, L. K. Role of order of approximation to English and letter array length in the development of normal laterality. *Developmental Psychology* 1979, *15,* 522–529.

Byers, R. K., & McLean, W. T. Etiology and course of certain hemiplegias with aphasia in childhood. *Pediatrics,* 1962, *29,* 376–383.

Byrd, M., & Kinsbourne, M. *Hemispheric priming and interference by a concurrent lateralized task.* Manuscript submitted for publication, 1983.

Cajal, S. R. *Degeneration and regeneration of the nervous system.* London: Oxford University Press, 1928.

Calmes, R. L., & Cracco, R. Q. Comparison of somatosensory and somatomotor evoked responses to median nerve and digital nerve stimulation. *Electroencephalography and Clinical Neurophysiology,* 1971, *31,* 547–562.

Caplan, B., & Kinsbourne, M. Cerebral lateralization, preferred cognitive mode, and reading ability in normal children. *Brain and Language,* 1981, *14,* 349–370.

Caplan, B., & Kinsbourne, M. Cognitive style and dichotic asymmetries of disabled readers. *Cortex,* 1982, *18,* 357–366.

Caplan, P. J., & Kinsbourne, M. Baby drops the rattle: Asymmetry of duration of grasp by infants. *Child Development,* 1976, *47,* 532–534.

Carey, S., & Diamond, R. From piecemeal to configurational representation of faces. *Science,* 1977, *195,* 312–314.

Carey, S., & Diamond, R. Maturational determination of the developmental course of face encoding. In D. Caplan (Ed.), *Biological studies of mental processes.* Cambridge: MIT Press, 1980.

Carey, S., Diamond, R., & Woods, B. T. Development of face recognition—a maturational component? *Developmental Psychology,* 1980, *16,* 257–269.

Carmon, A., & Benton, A. L. Tactile perception of direction and number in patients with unilateral cerebral disease. *Neurology,* 1969, *19,* 525–532.

Carmon, A., & Gambos, G. H. A physiological vascular correlate of hand-preferences: Possible implications with respect to hemispheric cerebral dominance. *Neuropsychologia,* 1970, *8,* 119–128.

Carmon, A. Harishanu, Y., Lowinger, E., & Lavy, S. Asymmetries in hemispheric blood volume and cerebral dominance. *Behavioral Biology,* 1972, *7,* 853–859.

Carroll, J. B., & Maxwell, S. E. Individual differences in cognitive abilities. *Annual Review of Psychology,* 1979, *30,* 603–640.

Carter, R. L., Hohenegger, M. K., & Satz, P. Aphasia and speech organization in children. *Science,* 1982, *218,* 797–799.

Carter, G. L., & Kinsbourne, M. The ontogeny of right cerebral lateralization of spatial mental set. *Developmental Psychology,* 1979, *15,* 241–245.

Case, T. J., & Bucy, P. C. Localization of cerebral lesions by electroencephalography. *Journal of Neurophysiology,* 1938, *1,* 245–261.

Cattell, R. B. Theory of fluid and crystallized intelligence: A critical experiment. *Journal of Educational Psychology,* 1963, *54,* 1–22.

Cermak, S. A., Cermak, L. S., Drake, C., & Kenney, R. The effect of concurrent manual activity on the dichotic listening performance of boys with learning disabilities. *American Journal of Occupational Therapy,* 1978, *32,* 493–499.

Cernacek, J., & Podivinsky, R. Ontogenesis of handedness and somatosensory cortical response. *Neuropsychologia,* 1971, *9,* 219–232.

Chapman, R. M. Evoked potentials of the brain related to thinking. In F. J. McGuigan & R. A. Schoonover (Eds.), *The psychophysiology of thinking: Studies of covert processes.* New York: Academic Press, 1973.

Charlton, M. H. Aphasia in bilingual and polyglot patients—a neurological and psychological study. *Journal of Speech and Hearing Disorders,* 1964, *29,* 307–311.

Chelune, G. J. & Edwards, P. Early brain lesions: Ontogenetic-environmental considerations. *Journal of Consulting and Clinical Psychology,* 1981, *49,* 777–790.

Chasty, H. T. Functional asymmetry of the brain in normal children and dyslexics. *Dyslexia Review,* 1979, *2,* 9–12.

Chiarello, C. A house divided? Cognitive functioning with callosal ogenosis. *Brain and Language,* 1980, *11,* 128–158.

Clark, L. E., & Knowles, J. B. Age differences in dichotic listening performance. *Journal of Gerontology,* 1973, *28,* 173–178.

Cohen, A. I. Hand preference and developmental status of infants. *Journal of Genetic Psychology,* 1966, *108,* 337–345.

Cohen, J. Very slow brain potentials relating to expectancy: The CNV. In E. Donchin & D. B. Lindsley (Eds.), *Average evoked potentials, methods, results, and evaluations* (NASA–191). Washington, D.C.: U.S. Government Printing Office, 1969.

Cohen, J. *Statistical power analysis for the behavioral Sciences.* New York: Academic Press, 1977.

Cohn, R. Differential cerebral processing of noise and verbal stimuli. *Science,* 1971, *172,* 599–601.

Colbourn, C. J. Can laterality be measured? *Neuropsychologia,* 1978, *16,* 283–289.

Colby, K. M., & Parkinson, C. Handedness in autistic children. *Journal of Autism and Childhood Schizophrenia,* 1977, *7,* 3–9.

Coleman, R. I., & Deutsch, C. P. Lateral dominance and right-left discrimination: A comparison of normal and retarded readers. *Perceptual and Motor Skills,* 1964, *19,* 43–50.

Conel, J. L. *The postnatal development of the human cerebral cortex* (8 vols.). Cambridge: Harvard University Press, 1939–1967.

Connally, K., & Stratton, P. Developmental changes in associated movements. *Developmental Medicine and Child Neurology,* 1968, *10,* 49–56.

Conrad, K. Über aphasische Sprachstörungen bei hirnverletzten Linkshändern. *Nervenartz,* 1949, *20,* 148–154.

Cook, T. W. Studies in cross education. 1. Mirror tracing the star-shaped maze. *Journal of Experimental Psychology,* 1933, *16,* 144–160. (a)

Cook, T. W. Studies in cross education. 2. Further experiments in mirror tracing the star-shaped maze. *Journal of Experimental Psychology,* 1933, *16,* 679–700. (b)

Cook, T. W. Studies in cross education. 3. Kinesthetic learning of an irregular pattern. *Journal of Experimental Psychology,* 1934, *17,* 749–762.

Corballis, M. C. Laterality and myth. *American Psychologist,* 1980, *35,* 284–295.

Corballis, M. C., & Beale, I. L. *The psychology of left and right.* Hillsdale, N.J.: Erlbaum, 1976.

Corballis, M. C., & Morgan, M. J. On the biological basis of human laterality: I Evidence for a maturational left-right gradient. *Behavioral and Brain Sciences,* 1978, *2,* 261–336.

Coren, S., Porac, C., & Duncan, P. Lateral preference behaviors in preschool children and young adults. *Child Development,* 1981, *52,* 443.

Cornil, L., & Gastaut, H. Etude électroencephalographique de la dominance sensorielle d'un hémisphère cérébral. *La Presse Medicale,* 1947, *37,* 421–422.

Cranney, J., & Ashton, R. Witelson's dichhaptic task as a measure of hemispheric asymmetry in deaf and hearing populations. *Neuropsychologia,* 1980.

Crelin, E. S. *Functional anatomy of the newborn.* New Haven, Conn.: Yale University Press, 1973.

Critchley, M. *The parietal lobes.* New York: Hafner, 1953.

Critchley, M. *The dyslexic child.* London: Heinemann, 1970.

Critchley, M. *The divine banquet of the brain.* New York: Raven Press, 1979.

Crosland, H. R. Letter position effects, in the range of attention experiment, as affected by the number of letters in each exposure. *Journal of Experimental Psychology,* 1931, *14,* 477–507.

Crovitz, H. F., & Lipscomb, D. B. Dominance of the temporal visual field at a short duration of stimulation. *American Journal of Psychology,* 1963, *76,* 631–637.

Crovitz, H. F., & Schiffman, H. R. Visual field and the letter span. *Journal of Experimental Psychology,* 1965, *70,* 218–223.

Crovitz, H. F., Schiffman, H. R., Lipscomb, D. B., Posnick, G., Rees, J., Schaub, R., & Tripp, R. Identification and localization in the letter span. *Canadian Journal of Psychology,* 1966, *20,* 455–461.

Crowell, D. H., Jones, R. H., Kapuniai, L. E., & Nakagawa, J. K. Unilateral cortical activity in newborn humans: An early index of cerebral dominance. *Science,* 1973, *180,* 205–208.

Crowell, D. H., Kapuniai, L. E., & Garbanati, J. A.

Hemispheric differences in human infant rhythmic responses to photic stimulation. In J. E. Desmedt (Ed.), *Cerebral motor control in man: Cerebral event-related potentials*, vol. 4, *Progress in clinical neurophysiology*. White Plains, N.Y.: S. Karger, 1977.

Crowne, D. P. The frontal eye field and attention. *Psychological Bulletin*, 1983, *93*, 232–260.

Culver, M., Tanley, J. C., & Eason, R. G. Evoked cortical potentials: Relation to hand dominance and eye dominance. *Perceptual and Motor Skills*, 1970, *30*, 407–414.

Curry, F. K. W. A comparison of left-handed and right-handed subjects on verbal and non-verbal dichotic listening tasks. *Cortex*, 1967, *3*, 343–352.

Curry, F. K. W., & Gregory, H. H. The performance of stutterers on dichotic listening tasks thought to reflect cerebral dominance. *Journal of Speech and Hearing Research*, 1969, *12*, 73–82.

Curtiss, S. *Genie. A psycholinguistic study of a modern-day "wild child"*. New York: Academic Press, 1977.

Czopf, J. Über die Rolle der nicht dominanten Hemisphäre in der Restitution der Sprache der Aphasischen. *Archiv für Psychiatrie und Nervenkrankheiten*, 1972, *216*, 162–171.

Dalby, J. T. Hemispheric timesharing: Verbal and spatial loading with concurrent unimanual activity. *Cortex*, 1980, *16*, 567–573.

Dalby, J. T., & Gibson, D. Functional cerebral lateralization in subtypes of disabled readers. *Brain and Language*, 1981, *14*, 34–48.

Davidson, R. J., & Fox, N. Asymmetrical brain activity discriminates between positive versus negative affective stimuli in ten month old infants. *Science*, 1982, *218*, 1235–1236.

Davidson, R. J., Nirenberg, E. & Saron, C. Intermodal and interhemispheric transfer in reading disabled and normal children. Paper to the international Neuropsychological Society, Pittsburgh, February, 1982.

Davidson, R. J., & Schwartz, G. E. The influence of musical training on patterns of EEG asymmetry during musical and nonmusical self-generation tasks. *Psychophysiology*, 1977, *14*, 58–63.

Davis, A. E., & Wada, J. A. Hemispheric asymmetries in human infants: Spectral analysis of flash and click evoked potentials. *Brain and Language*, 1977, *4*, 23–31.

Davis, A. E., & Wada, J. A. Speech dominance and handedness in the normal human. *Brain and Language*, 1978, *5*, 42–55.

Davis, R. C. The pattern of muscular action in simple voluntary movements. *Journal of Experimental Psychology*, 1942, *31*, 347–366. (a)

Davis, R. C. The pattern of response in a tendon reflex. *Journal of Experimental Psychology*, 1942, *30*, 452–463. (b)

Dawson, G., Warrenburg, S., & Fuller, P. Cerebral lateralization in individuals diagnosed as autistic in early childhood. *Brain and Language*, 1982, *15*, 353–368.

Day, M. E. An eye-movement phenomenon relating to attention, thought, and anxiety. *Perceptual and Motor Skills*, 1964, *19*, 443–446.

Day, M. E. An eye-movement indicator of individual differences in the physiological organization of attentional processes. *Journal of Psychology*, 1967, *42*, 51–62. (a)

Day, M. E. An eye-movement indicator of type and level of anxiety: Some clinical observations. *Journal of Clinical Psychology*, 1967, *23*, 438–441. (b)

Day, M. E. Attention, anxiety and psychotherapy. *Psychotherapy: Theory, Research and Practice*, 1968, *5*, 146–149.

Dearborn, W. F. Ocular and manual dominance in dyslexia. *Psychological Bulletin*, 1931, *28*, 704.

Dearborn, W. F. Structural factors which condition special disability in reading. *Proceedings and addresses of the 57th annual session of the American Association on Mental Deficiency*. 1933.

Dee, H. L., & Hannay, H. J. Asymmetry in perception: Attention versus other determinants. *Acta Psychologica*, 1973, *37*, 241–247.

Deglin, V. L., & Nikolaenko, N. N. Role of the dominant hemisphere in the regulation of emotional states. *Human Physiology*, 1975, *1*, 394.

Delacato, C. H. *The treatment and prevention of reading problems*. Springfield, Ill.: Charles C. Thomas, 1959.

Denenberg, V. H. Hemispheric laterality in animals and the effects of early experience. *Behavioral and Brain Sciences*, 1981, *4*, 1–49.

Denenberg, V. H., Garbanati, J. A., Sherman, G. F., Yutzey, D. A., & Kaplan, R. Infantile stimulation induces brain lateralization in rats. *Science*, 1978, *201*, 1150–1152.

Denenberg, V. H., Rosen, G. D., Hofman, M., Gall, J., Stockler, J., & Yutzey, D. A. Neonatal postural asymmetry and sex differences in the rat. *Developmental Brain Research*, in press.

Dennis, M. Imparied sensory and motor differentiation with corpus callosum agenesis: A lack of callosal inhibition during ontogeny? *Neuropsychologia*, 1977, *14*, 455–459.

Dennis, M. Capacity and strategy for syntactic comprehension after left and right hemidecortication. *Brain and Language*, 1980, *10*, 287–317. (a)

Dennis, M. Language acquisition in a single hemisphere: Semantic organization. In D. Caplan (Ed.), *Biological studies of mental processes.* Cambridge: MIT Press, 1980. (b)

Dennis, M., & Kohn, B. Comprehension of syntax in infantile hemiplegics after cerebral hemidecortication: Left hemisphere superiority. *Brain and Language,* 1975, *2,* 475–486.

Dennis, M., & Whitaker, H. A. Language acquisition following hemidecortication: Linguistic superiority of the left over the right hemisphere. *Brain and Language,* 1976, *3,* 404–433.

Dennis, M., & Whitaker, H. A. Hemisphere equipotentiality and language acquisition. In S. J. Segalowitz & F. A. Gruber (Eds.), *Language development and neurological theory.* New York: Academic Press, 1977.

Denny-Brown, D., Meyer, J. S., & Horenstein, S. The significance of perceptual rivalry resulting from parietal lesion. *Brain,* 1952, *75,* 433–471.

DeRenzi, E., & Spinnler, H. Facial recognition in brain-damaged patients. *Neurology,* 1966, *16,* 145–152.

DeRenzi, E. *Disorders of space exploration and cognition.* New York: Wiley, 1982.

Deuel, R. V., & Dunlop, N. L. Hand preference in the rhesus monkey. *Archives of Neurology,* 1980, *37,* 217–221.

Dewson, J. H., III. Toward an animal model of auditory cognitive function. In C. L. Ludlow & M. E. Doran-Quine (Eds.), *The neurological bases of language disorders in children: Methods and directions for research* (NINCDS Monograph No. 22). Washington, D.C.: U.S. Government Printing Office, 1979.

Dick, A. O., & Mewhort, D. J. K. Order of report and processing in tachistoscopic recognition. *Perception & Psychophysics,* 1967, *3,* 573–576.

Dimond, S. *The double brain.* London: Churchill Livingstone, 1972.

Dobbin, J., & Sands, J. Quantitative growth and development of human brain. *Archives of Diseases in Childhood,* 1973, *48,* 757–767.

Dobrokhotova, T. A., & Braghina, N. N. Functional asymmetry of the cerebral hemispheres in psychopathological cases due to brain lesions. *Voprosy Psikhologii,* 1974, *2,* 95–103.

Doehring, D. G., & Hoshko, I. M. Classification of reading problems by the Q-technique of factor analysis. *Cortex,* 1977, *13,* 281–294.

Doktor, R., & Bloom, D. M. Selective lateralization of cognitive style related to occupation as determined by EEG alpha asymmetry. *Psychophysiology,* 1977, *14,* 385–387.

Doll, E. A. Psychological significance of cerebral birth lesions. *American Journal of Psychology,* 1933, *45,* 444–452.

Donchin, E. Data analysis techniques in evoked potential research. In E. Donchin & D. B. Lindsley (Eds.), *Average evoked potentials, methods, results, and evaluations* (NASA–191). Washington, D.C.: U.S. Government Printing Office, 1969.

Donchin, E., Kutas, M., & Johnson, R., Jr. The CNV does not behave like a "motor" potential. *Electroencephalography and Clinical Neurophysiology,* 1974, *37,* 434.

Donchin, E., Kutas, M., & McCarthy, G. *Comparison of the hemispheric asymmetries of the readiness potential and CNV.* Paper presented at the meeting of the Psychonomic Society, Boston, November 1974.

Donchin, E., Kutas, M., & McCarthy, G. Electrocortical indices of hemispheric utilization. In S. Harnad, R. W. Doty, L. Goldstein, J. Jaynes, & G. Krauthamer (Eds.), *Lateralization in the nervous system.* New York: Academic Press, 1977.

Dorman, M. F., & Geffner, D. S. Hemispheric specialization for speech perception in six-year-old black and white children from low and middle socioeconomic classes. *Cortex,* 1974, *10,* 171–176.

Dorman, M. F., & Porter, R. J. Hemispheric lateralization for speech perception in stutterers. *Cortex,* 1975, *11,* 181–185.

Doyle, J. C., Ornstein, R. E., & Galin, D. Lateral specialization of cognitive mode: II. EEG frequency analysis. *Psychophysiology,* 1974, *11,* 567–578.

Droege, R. C. Sex differences in aptitude maturation during high school. *Journal of Counseling Psychology,* 1967, *14,* 407–411.

D.S.M. III. Diagnostic and statistical manual of mental disorders. (Third Edition). Washington, D.C.: American Psychiatric Association, 1980.

Duffy, F. M., Burchfield, J. L., & Lombroso, C. T. Brain electrical activity mapping (BEAM): A method for extending the clinical utility of EEG and evoked potential data. *Annals of Neurology,* 1979, *5,* 309–321.

Dumas, R., & Morgan, A. H. EEG asymmetry as a function of occupation, task, and task difficulty. *Neuropsychologia,* 1975, *13,* 219–228.

Duseck, C. M., & Hicks, R. A. Multiple birth risk factors and handedness in elementary school children. *Cortex,* 1980, *16.*

Efron, R. The effect of handedness on the perception

of simultaneity and temporal order. *Brain,* 1963, *86,* 261–284.

Ehrlichman, H., & Weinberger, A. Lateral eye movements and hemispheric asymmetry: A critical review. *Psychological Bulletin,* 1978, *85,* 1080–1101.

Ehrlichman, H., Weiner, S. L., & Baker, A. H. Effects of verbal and spatial questions on initial gaze shifts. *Neuropsychologia,* 1974, *12,* 265–277.

Ehrlichman, H., & Wiener, M. S. Consistency of task-related EEG asymmetries. *Psychophysiology,* 1979, *16,* 247–252.

Eimas, P. D., Siqueland, E. R., Jusczyk, P., & Vigorito, J. Speech perception in infants. *Science,* 1971, *171,* 303–306.

Elias, J. W., Winn, F. J., & Wright, L. L. Age, sex and hemisphere asymmetry difference induced by a concurrent memory processing task. *Experimental Aging Research,* 1979, *5,* 217–237.

Elias, M. F., & Kinsbourne, M. Age and sex differences in the processing of vérbal and non-verbal stimuli. *Journal of Gerontology,* 1974, *29,* 162–171.

Ellingson, R. J., Danahy, T., Nelson, B., & Lathrop, G. H. Variability of auditory evoked potentials in human newborns. *Electroencephalography and Clinical Neurophysiology,* 1974, *36,* 155–162.

Ellis, H. D., & Shepherd, J. W. Recognition of abstract and concrete words presented in left and right visual fields. *Journal of Experimental Psychology,* 1974, *103,* 1035–1036.

Entus, A. K. Hemispheric Asymmetry in processing of dichotically presented speech and nonspeech stimuli by infants. In S. J. Segalowitz & F. A. Gruber (Eds.), *Language development and neurological theory.* New York: Academic Press, 1977.

Etaugh, C. F., & Levy, R. Hemispheric specialization for tactile-spatial processing in preschool children. *Perceptual and Motor Skills,* 1981, *53,* 621–622.

Ethier, L. *Effects of imagery value and response factors upon word recognition in left and right visual half-fields.* Unpublished master's thesis, University of Saskatchewan, 1980.

Ettlinger, E. G., Blakemore, C. B., Milner, A. D., & Wilson, J. R. Agenesis of the corpus callosum: A behavioural investigation. *Brain,* 1972, *95,* 327–346.

Ettlinger, E. G., Blakemore, C. B., Milner, A. D., & Wilson, J. R. Agenesis of corpus callosum: A further behavioural investigation. *Brain,* 1974, *97,* 225–234.

Fagan-Dubin, L. Lateral dominance and development of cerebral specialization. *Cortex,* 1974, *10,* 69–74.

Fantz, R. L. Pattern discrimination and selective attention as determinants of perceptual development from birth. In A. H. Kidd & J. L. Rivoire (Eds.). *Perceptual development in children.* New York: International Universities Press, 1966.

Fein, D., Skoff, B., & Mirsky, A. F. Clinical correlates of brainstem dysfunction in autistic children. *J. Autism. Dev. Disord.,* 1981, *11,* 303–315.

Fennell, E. B., Bowers, D., & Satz, P. Within-modal and cross-modal reliabilities of two laterality tests. *Brain and Language,* 1977, *4,* 63–69.

Ferrier, D. *The function of the brain.* London: 1876.

Ferriss, G. S., & Dorsen, M. M. Agenesis of the corpus callosum. I. Neuropsychological studies. *Cortex,* 1975, *11,* 95–122.

Filbey, R. A., & Gazzaniga, M. S. Splitting the normal brain with reaction time. *Psychonomic Science,* 1969, *17,* 335–336.

Fisk, J. L., & Rourke, B. P. Identification of subtypes of learning-disabled children at three age levels: A neuropsychological multivariate approach. *Journal of Clinical Neuropsychology,* 1979, *1,* 289–310.

Fitzgerald, R. E., & Marshall, A. J. Left-right field differences with partial report of letters. *American Journal of Psychology,* 1967, *80,* 370–376.

Flanagan, J. C., David, F. B., Darley, J. T., Shaycroft, M. F., Orr, D. B., Goldberg, I., & Neyman, C. A. *Project Talent:* The identification, development and utilization of human talent. Pittsburgh, Project Talent Office, University of Pittsburgh, 1964.

Flanery, R. C., & Balling, J. D. Developmental change in hemispheric specialization for tactile spatial ability. *Developmental Psychology,* 1979, *15,* 364–372.

Fleminger, J. J., de Horne, D. J., & Nott, P. Unilateral electroconvulsive therapy and cerebral dominance: Effect of right- and left-sided electrode placement on verbal memory. *Journal of Neurology, Neurosurgery and Psychiatry,* 1970, *33,* 408–411.

Flor-Henry, P. Lateralized temporal-limbic dysfunction and psychopathology. In S. R. Harnad, H. D. Steklis, & J. Lancaster (Eds.), "Origins and evolution of language and speech." *Annals of the New York Academy of Sciences,* 1976, *280,* 777–795.

Flor-Henry, P., & Yeudall, L. T. Neuropsychological investigation of schizophrenia and manic-depressive psychoses. In J. H. Gruzelier & P. Flor-Henry (Eds.), *Hemisphere asymmetries of function in psychopathology,* Amsterdam: Elsevier North-Holland, 1979.

Flourens, P. Investigations of the properties and the functions of the various parts which compose the cerebral mass. In G. von Bonin (Ed.), *The cerebral cortex,* Springfield, Ill.: Charles C. Thomas, 1960.

Fontenot, D. J., & Benton, A. L. Tactile perception of direction in relation to hemispheric locus of lesion. *Neuropsychologia,* 1971, *9,* 83–88.

Forgays, D. G. The development of differential word recognition. *Journal of Experimental Psychology,* 1953, *45,* 165–168.

Fox, N., & Lewis, M. Motor asymmetries in preterm infants: Effects of prematurity and illness. *Developmental Psychology,* 1982, *15,* 19–23.

Franco, D., Muir, D. W., & Dodwell, P. C. "Reaching in very young infants." *Perception,* 1978, *7,* 385–392.

Freides, D. Do dichotic listening procedures measure lateralization of information processing or retrieval strategy? *Perception and Psychophysics,* 1977, *21,* 259–263.

Fried, I., Mateer, C., Ojemann, G., Wohms, R., & Fedio, P. Organisation of visuospatial functions in human cortex. Evidence from electrical stimulation. *Brain,* 1982, *105,* 349–371.

Friedman, D., Simson, R., Ritter, W., & Rapin, I. Cortical evoked potentials elicited by real speech words and human sounds. *Electroencephalography and Clinical Neurophysiology,* 1975, *38,* 13–19.

Frost, E. T. Tool behavior and the origins of laterality. *Journal of Human Evolution,* 1980, *9,* 447–460.

Furst, C. J. EEG asymmetry and visuospatial performance. *Nature* (London), 1976, *260,* 254–255.

Gaddes, W. H. A., & Crockett, D. J. The Spreen-Benton aphasia tests; Normative data on a measure of normal language development. *Brain and Language,* 1975, *2,* 257–280.

Gainotti, G. Emotional behavior and hemispheric side of the lesion. *Cortex,* 1972, *8,* 41–55.

Galaburda, A. M., & Kemper, T. L. Cytoarchitectonic abnormalities in developmental dyslexia: A casy study. *Annals of Neurology,* 1979, *6,* 94–100.

Galaburda, A. M., LeMay, M., Kemper, T. L., & Geschwind, N. Right-left asymmetries in the brain. *Science,* 1978, *199,* 852–856.

Galambos, R., Benson, P., Smith, T. S., Shulman-Galambos, C., & Osier, H. On hemispheric differences in evoked potentials to speech stimuli. *Electroencephalography and Clinical Neurophysiology,* 1975, *39,* 279–283.

Galin, D. Implications for psychiatry of left and right cerebral specialization. *Archives of General Psychiatry,* 1974, *31,* 572–583.

Galin, D. Lateral specialization and psychiatric issues: Speculations on development and the evolution of consciousness. *Annals of the New York Academy of Sciences,* 1977, *299,* 397–411.

Galin, D., Diamond, R., & Herron, J. Development of crossed and uncrossed tactile localisation on the fingers. *Brain and Language,* 1977, *4,* 588–590.

Galin, D., & Ellis, R. R. Asymmetry in evoked potentials as an index of lateralized cognitive processes: Relation to EEG alpha asymmetry. *Psychophysiology,* 1975, *13,* 45–50.

Galin, D., Johnstone, J., Nakell, L., & Herron, J. Development of the capacity for tactile information transfer between hemispheres in normal children. *Science,* 1979, *204,* 1330–1332.

Galin, D., & Ornstein, R. E. Lateral specialization of cognitive mode: An EEG study. *Psychophysiology,* 1972, *9,* 412–418.

Galin, D., & Ornstein, R. E. Individual differences in cognitive style. I. Reflective eye movements. *Neuropsychologia,* 1974, *12,* 367–376.

Galloway, L. M. Bilingualism: Neuropsychological considerations. In G. Hynd (Ed.), *Neuropsychological perspectives in education.* Special issue of the *Journal of Research and Development in Education,* 1982, 12–28.

Garai, J. E., & Scheinfeld, A. Sex differences in mental and behavioral traits. *Genetic Psychology Monographs,* 1968, *77,* 169–299.

Gardiner, M. F., & Walter, D. O. Evidence of hemispheric specialization from infant EEG. In S. Harnad, R. W. Doty, L. Goldstein, J. Jaynes, & G. Krauthamer (Eds.), *Lateralization in the nervous system.* New York: Academic Press, 1977.

Gardner, E. B., & Branski, D. M. Unilateral cerebral activation and perception of gaps: A signal detection analysis. *Neuropsychologia,* 1976, *14,* 43–53.

Gardner, E. B., Eagan, M. J., & Branski, D. M. Attentional bias in gap-detection: An investigation of "the Kinsbourne effect." Paper presented at the meeting of the American Psychological Association, Montreal, August 1973.

Gates, A. L., & Bond, G. L. Relation of handedness, eyesighting, and acuity dominance to reading. *Journal of Educational Psychology,* 1936, *27,* 450–456.

Gay, A. J., Newman, N. M., Keltner, J. L., & Stroud, M. H. *Eye movement disorders.* St. Louis: C. V. Mosby, 1974.

Gazzaniga, M. S. Effects of commissurotomy on a preoperatively learned visual discrimination. *Experimental Neurology,* 1963, *8,* 14–19.

Gazzaniga, M. S. *The bisected brain.* New York: Appleton-Century-Crofts, 1970.

Gazzaniga, M. S., & Hillyard, S. A. Attention mechanisms following brain bisection. In S. Kornblum (Ed.), *Attention and performance* (Vol. 4). New York: Academic Press, 1973.

Geffen, G. The development of the right ear advantage in dichotic listening with focused attention. *Cortex,* 1978, *14,* 11–17.

Geffen, G., Bradshaw, J. L., & Nettleton, N. C. Hemispheric asymmetry: Verbal and spatial encoding of visual stimuli. *Journal of Experimental Psychology,* 1972, *95,* 25–31.

Geffen, G., Bradshaw, J. L., & Wallace, G. Interhemispheric effects on reaction time to verbal and nonverbal visual stimuli. *Journal of Experimental Psychology,* 1971, *87,* 415–422.

Geffen, G., & Wale, J. Development of selective listening and hemispheric asymmetry. *Developmental Psychology,* 1979, *15,* 138–146.

Geffner, D. S., & Dorman, M. F. Hemispheric specialization for speech perception in four-year-old children from low and middle socioeconomic classes. *Cortex,* 1976, *12,* 71–73.

Geffner, D. S., & Hochberg, I. Ear laterality performance of children from low and middle socioeconomic levels on a verbal dichotic listening task. *Cortex,* 1971, *8,* 193–203.

Gerber, S. E., & Goldman, P. S. Ear preference for dichotically presented verbal stimuli as a function of report strategies. *Journal of the Acoustical Society of America,* 1971, *49,* 1163–1168.

Geschwind, N., & Behan, P. Left-handedness: Association with immune disease, migraine, and developmental learning disorder. *Proc. Natl. Acad. Sci., U.S.A.,* 1982, *79,* 5097–5100.

Geschwind, N., & Levitsky, W. Human brain: Left-right asymmetries in temporal speech region. *Science,* 1968, *161,* 186–187.

Gesell, A. The tonic neck reflex in the human infant. *Journal of Pediatrics,* 1938, *13,* 455–464.

Gesell, A., & Ames, L. B. The development of handedness. *Journal of General Psychology,* 1947, *70,* 155–175.

Gesell, A., & Ames, L. B. Tonic-neck reflex and symmetro-tonic behavior. *Journal of Pediatrics,* 1950, *36,* 165–178.

Giannitrapani, D., Darrow, C. W., & Sorkin, A. Asleep and awake interhemispheric EEG phase relationships in left- and right-handed subjects. *American Psychologist,* 1964, *19,* 480–481.

Gibbs, F. A., Lennox, W. G., & Gibbs, E. L. The electroencephalogram in diagnosis and in localization of epileptic seizures. *Archives of Neurology and Psychiatry,* 1936, *36,* 1225–1235.

Gibson, C., & Bryden, M. P. Cerebral lateralization in deaf children using a dichhaptic task. Paper presented at the meeting of the International Neuropsychological Society, Pittsburgh, February 1982.

Giesecke, M. The genesis of hand preference. *Monographs of the Society for Research in Child Development,* 1936, *1*(5, Serial No. 5).

Gilbert, J. H. V., & Climan, I. Dichotic studies in two and three year olds: A preliminary report. In *Speech Communication Seminar, Stockholm* (Vol. 2). Upsala: Almqvist & Wiksell, 1974.

Gilden, L., Vaughan, H. G., & Costa, L. D. Summated human EEG potentials associated with voluntary movement. *Electroencephalography and Clinical Neurophysiology,* 1966, *20,* 433–438.

Glanville, A. D., & Antonitis, J. J. The relationship between occipital alpha activity and laterality. *Journal of Experimental Psychology,* 1955, *49,* 294–299.

Glanville, A. D., & Dallenbach, K. M. The range of attention. *American Journal of Psychology,* 1929, *41,* 207–236.

Glanville, B. B., Best, C. T., & Levenson, R. A cardiac measure of cerebral asymmetries in infant auditory perception. *Developmental Psychology,* 1977, *13,* 55–59.

Glick, S. D., & Jerussi, T. P. Spatial and paw preferences in rats: Their relationship to rate-dependent effects of d-amphetamine. *Journal of Pharmacology and Experimental Therapeutics,* 1974, *188,* 714–725.

Glick, S. D., Jerussi, T. P., & Zimmerberg, B. Behavioral and neuropharmacological correlates of nigrostriatal asymmetry in rats. In S. Harnad, R. W. Doty, L. Goldstein, J. Jaynes, & G. Krauthamer (Eds.), *Lateralization in the nervous system.* New York: Academic Press, 1977.

Gloning, I., Gloning, K., Haub, G., & Quatember, R. Comparison of verbal behavior in right handed and non-right handed patients with anatomically verified lesions of one hemisphere. *Cortex,* 1969, *5,* 41–52.

Godfrey, J. J. Perceptual difficulty and the right ear

advantage for vowels. *Brain and Language*, 1974, *1*, 323–335.

Goff, W. R., Matsumiya, Y., Allison, T., & Goff, G. D. Cross-modality comparisons of averaged evoked potentials. In E. Donchin & D. B. Lindsley (Eds.), *Average evoked potentials, methods, results, and evaluations* (NASA–191). Washington D.C.: U.S. Government Printing Office, 1969.

Goldman, P. S. An alternative to developmental plasticity: Heterology of CNS structures in infants and adults. In D. G. Stein, J. J. Rosen, & N. Butters, *Plasticity and recovery of function in the nervous system*. New York: Academic Press, 1974.

Goldstein, G., & Shelly, C. Does the right hemisphere age more rapidly than the left? *Journal of Clinical Neuropsychology*, 1981, *3*, 65–78.

Goldstein, L., & Lackner, J. R. Sideways look at dichotic listening. *Journal of the Acoustical Society of America*, 1974, *55*. (Suppl. S10[A].)

Goltz, F. Über die Vernichtungen des Grosshirnes. *Pflügers Archiv für die Gesamte Physiologie des Menschen und der Tiere*, 1876, *13*, 1–44.

Goodglass, H. Developmental comparison of vowels and consonants in dichotic listening. *Journal of Speech and Hearing Research*, 1973, *16*, 744–752.

Goodglass, H., & Barton, M. I. Handedness and differential perception of verbal stimuli in left and right visual fields. *Perceptual and Motor Skills*, 1963, *17*, 851–854.

Goodglass, H., & Quadfasel, F. A. Language laterality in left-handed aphasics. *Brain*, 1954, *77*, 521–548.

Goodglass, H., Shai, A., Rosen, W., & Berman, M. *New observations on right-left differences in tachistoscopic recognition of verbal and nonverbal stimuli*. Paper presented at the meeting of the International Neuropsychological Society, Washington, D.C., February 1971.

Gordon, D. P., & Zatorre, R. J. A right-ear advantage for dichotic listening in bilingual children. *Brain and Language*, 1981, *13*, 389–396.

Gordon, H. W. Right hemisphere comprehension of verbs in patients with complete forebrain commissurotomy: Use of the dichotic method and manual performance. *Brain and Language*, 1980, *11*, 76–86.

Gordon, M. Left-handedness and mirror-writing, especially among defective children. *Brain*, 1921, *43*, 313–368.

Green, J. B. An electromyographic study of mirror movements. *Neurology* (Minneapolis), 1967, *17*, 91–94.

Gregory, R. J., Alley, P., & Morris, L. Left-handedness and spatial reasoning abilities. The deficit hypothesis revisited. *Intelligence*, 1980, *4*, 151–159.

Gregory, R. J., & Paul, J. The effects of handedness and writing posture on neuropsychological test results. *Neuropsychologia*, 1980, *18*, 231–235.

Grözinger, B., Kornhuber, H. H., & Kriebel, J. Methodological problems in the investigation of cerebral potentials preceding speech. *Neuropsychologia*, 1975, *13*, 263–270.

Gruber, L., & Powell, R. L. Responses of stuttering and nonstuttering children to a dichotic listening task. *Perceptual and Motor Skills*, 1974, *38*, 263–264.

Gruzelier, J. H. Cerebral laterality and psychopathology: Fact and fiction. *Psychological Medicine*, 1981, *11*, 219–227.

Gruzelier, J. H., & Hammond, N. V. The effect of chlorpromazine upon bilateral asymmetries of bioelectric skin reactivity in schizophrenia. *Studia Psychologia*, 1977, *19*, 40–50.

Guiard, Y. Cerebral hemispheres and selective attention. *Acta Psychologica*, 1980, *46*, 41–61.

Guilford, J. P. The nature of human intelligence. New York: McGraw-Hill, 1967.

Gur, R. C., & Reivich, M. Cognitive task effects on hemispheric blood flow in humans: Evidence for individual differences in hemispheric activation. *Brain and Language*, 1980, *9*, 78–92.

Gur, R. E., Gur, R. C., & Harris, L. J. Cerebral activation, as measured by subjects' lateral eye movements, is influenced by experimenter location. *Neuropsychologia*, 1975, *13*, 35–44.

Haeckel, E. *The evolution of man: A popular exposition of the principal points of human ontogeny and phylogeny* (Vol. 1). New York: Appleton, 1908.

Halverson, H. H. An experimental study of prehension in infants by means of systematic cinema records. *Genetic Psychology Monographs*, 1931, *10*, 107–286.

Hamilton, C. R. Investigations of perceptual and mnemonic lateralization in monkeys. In S. Harnad, R. W. Doty, L. Goldstein, J. Jaynes, & G. Krauthamer (Eds.), *Lateralization in the nervous system*. New York: Academic Press, 1977.

Hamilton, C. R., & Lund, J. S. Visual discrimination of movement: Midbrain or forebrain? *Science*, 1970, *170*, 1428–1430.

Hamilton, C. R., Tieman, S. B., & Farrell, W. S. Cerebral dominance in monkeys. *Neuropsychologia*, 1974, *12*, 193–197.

Hammill, D., & Irwin, O. C. I.Q. differences of right and left spastic hemiplegic children. *Per-*

ceptual and Motor Skills, 1966, *22,* 193–194.

Harcum, E. R. Effects of symmetry on the perception of tachistoscopic patterns. *American Journal of Psychology,* 1964, *77,* 600–606.

Harcum, E. R. Lateral dominance as a determinant of temporal order of responding. In M. Kinsbourne (Ed.), *Asymmetrical function of the brain.* New York: Cambridge University Press, 1978.

Harcum, E. R., & Dyer, D. W. Monocular and binocular reproduction of binary stimuli appearing right and left of fixation. *American Journal of Psychology,* 1962, *75,* 56–65.

Harcum, E. R., & Finkel, M. E. Explanation of Mishkin and Forgay's result as a directional-reading conflict. *Canadian Journal of Psychology,* 1963, *17,* 224–234.

Harcum, E. R., & Jones, M. L. Letter recognition within words flashed left and right of fixation. *Science,* 1962, *138,* 444–445.

Hardyck, C., & Haapanen, R. Educating both halves of the brain: Educational breakthrough or neuromythology? *Journal of School Psychology,* 1979, *17,* 219–230.

Hardyck, C., Petrinovich, L., & Goldman, R. Left-handedness and cognitive deficit. *Cortex,* 1976, *12,* 266–279.

Harmon, D. W., & Ray, W. J. Hemispheric activity during affective verbal stimuli: An EEG study. *Neuropsychologia,* 1977, *15,* 457–460.

Harmony, J., Ricardo, G. O., Fernandez, S., & Valdes, P. Symmetry of the visual evoked potential in normal subjects. *Electroencephalography and Clinical Neuropsychology,* 1973, *35,* 237–240.

Harris, A. J. Lateral dominance, directional confusion, and reading disability. *Journal of Psychology,* 1957, *44,* 283–294.

Harris, L. J. Left-handedness: Early theories, facts, and fancies. In J. Herron (Ed.), *Neuropsychology of left-handedness.* New York: Academic Press, 1980. (a)

Harris, L. J. Which hand is the "eye" of the blind?—A new look at an old question. In J. Herron (Ed.), *Neuropsychology of left-handedness.* New York: Academic Press, 1980. (b)

Harshman, R., & Krashen, S. An "unbiased" procedure for comparing degree of lateralization of dichotically presented stimuli. *UCLA Working Papers in Phonetics,* 1972, *23,* 3–12.

Haslam, R. H. A., Dalby, J. T., Johns, R. D., & Rademaker, A. W. Cerebral asymmetry in developmental dyslexia. *Archives of Neurology,* 1981, *38,* 679–682.

Hauser, S. L., DeLong, G. R., & Rosman, N. P. Pneumographic findings in the infantile autism syndrome. *Brain,* 1975, *98,* 667–688.

Hawles, T. G. Effects of dichotic fusion on the perception of speech. *Supplement to Status Reports on Speech Research.* New Haven, Conn.: Haskins Laboratories, 1969.

Hawn, P. R., & Harris, L. J. *Hand asymmetries in grasp duration and reaching in two and five month old human infants.* Paper presented at the meeting of the International Neuropsychological Society, New York, February 1979.

Haydon, S. P., & Spellacy, F. J. Monaural reaction time asymmetries for speech and non-speech sounds. *Cortex,* 1974, *9,* 288–294.

Healey, J. Individual differences in the pattern and degree of cerebral lateralization of cognition. Unpublished doctoral dissertation, City University of New York, 1980.

Hebb, D. O. Intelligence in man after large removals of cerebral tissue: Defects following right temporal lobectomy. *Journal of General Psychology,* 1939, *21,* 437–446.

Hécaen, H. Clinical symptomatology in right and left hemispheric lesions. In V. B. Mountcastle (Ed.), *Interhemispheric relations and cerebral dominance.* Baltimore: The Johns Hopkins University Press, 1962.

Hécaen, H. Acquired aphasia in children and the ontogenesis of hemispheric functional specialization. *Brain and Language,* 1976, *3,* 114–134.

Hécaen, H., & Albert, M. L. *Human neuropsychology.* New York: Wiley-Interscience, 1978.

Hécaen, H., & Angelergues, R. Agnosia for faces (prosopagnosis). *Archives of Neurology,* 1962, *7,* 92–100.

Hécaen, H., De Agostini, M., & Monzon-Montes, A. Cerebral organization in left-handers. *Brain and Language,* 1981, *12,* 261–284.

Hécaen, H., & Piercy, M. F. Paroxysmal dysphasia and the problem of cerebral dominance. *Journal of Neurology, Neurosurgery and Psychiatry,* 1956, *19,* 194–201.

Hécaen, H., & Sauget, J. Cerebral dominance in left-handed subjects. *Cortex,* 1971, *7,* 19–48.

Hellige, J. B. Visual laterality patterns for pure-versus mixed-list presentation. *Journal of Experimental Psychology: Human Perception and Performance,* 1978, *4,* 121–131.

Hellige, J. B., & Cox, P. J. Effects of concurrent verbal memory on recognition of stimuli from the left and right visual fields. *Journal of Experimental Psychology: Human Perception and Performance,* 1976, *2,* 210–221.

Hellige, J. B., Cox, P. J., & Litvac, L. Information processing in the cerebral hemispheres: Selective hemispheric activation and capacity limitations. *Journal of Experimental Psychology: General,* 1979, *108,* 251–279.

Hellige, J. B., & Longstreth, L. E. Effects of concurrent hemisphere-specific activity on unimanual tapping rate. *Neuropsychologia,* 1981, *19,* 395–406.

Hellige, J. B., Zatkin, J. L., & Wong, T. M. Intercorrelation of laterality indices. *Cortex,* 1981, *17,* 129–133.

Henninger, P. *Problem-solving strategies of musically trained and untrained subjects and hemisphere activation.* Doctoral dissertation, University of Toronto, 1981.

Henry, R. G. J. Monaural studies eliciting an hemisphere asymmetry: A bibliography. *Perceptual and Motor Skills,* 1979, *48,* 335–338.

Herbst, L. Timing of maturation, brain lateralisation and cognitive performance. Paper to the American Psychological Association, Montreal, September 1980.

Herbst, L., & Peterson, A. C. Timing of maturation, brain lateralisation and cognitive performance in adolescent females. Paper to the 5th Annual Conference on Research on women and education. Cleveland, Ohio, November 1979.

Hermelin, B., & O'Connor, N. Functional asymmetry in the reading of Braille. *Neuropsychologia,* 1971, *9,* 431–435.

Heron, W. Perception as a function of retinal locus and attention. *American Journal of Psychology,* 1957, *70,* 38–48.

Herron, J. (Ed.) *Neuropsychology of left-handedness.* New York: Academic Press, 1980.

Hewes, G. W. Primate communication and the gestural origin of language. *Current Anthropology,* 1973, *14,* 5–32.

Hewes, G. W. Lateral dominance, culture, and writing systems. *Human Biology,* 1979, *21,* 233–245.

Hicks, R. A., Elliot, D., Garbesi, L., & Martin, S. Multiple birth risk factors and the distribution of handedness. *Cortex,* 1979, *15,* 135–137.

Hicks, R. A., Evans, E. A., & Pelligrini, R. J. Correlation between handedness and birth order: Compilation of five studies. *Perceptual and Motor Skills,* 1978, *46,* 53–54.

Hicks, R. E. Intrahemispheric response competition between vocal and unimanual performance in normal adult human males. *Journal of Comparative and Physiological Psychology,* 1975, *89,* 50–60.

Hicks, R. E. The association between mental retardation, left handedness and indices of early brain damage. In preparation.

Hicks, R. E., & Barton, A. K. A note on left-handedness and severity of mental retardation. *Journal of Genetic Psychology,* 1975, *127,* 323–324.

Hicks, R. E., Bradshaw, G. J., Kinsbourne, M., & Feigin, D. S. Vocal-manual tradeoffs in hemispheric sharing of human performance control. *Journal of Motor Behavior,* 1978, *10,* 1–6.

Hicks, R. E., Frank, J. M., & Kinsbourne, M. The locus of bimanual skill transfer. *Journal of General Psychology,* 1982, *107,* 277–281.

Hicks, R. E., & Kinsbourne, M. On the genesis of human handedness: A review. *Journal of Motor Behavior,* 1976, *8,* 257–266.

Hicks, R. E., & Kinsbourne, M. Handedness differences: Human handedness. In M. Kinsbourne (Ed.), *Asymmetrical function of the brain.* New York: Cambridge University Press, 1978.

Hicks, R. E., Provenzano, F. J., & Rybstein, E. D. Generalized and lateralized effects of concurrent verbal rehearsal upon performance of sequential movements of the fingers by the left and right hands. *Acta Psychologica,* 1975, *39,* 119–130.

Hicks, S. P., & D'Amato, C. J. Motor-sensory and visual behavior after hemispherectomy in newborn and mature rats. *Experimental Neurology,* 1970, *29,* 416–438.

Hier, D. B., LeMay, M., & Rosenberger, P. B. Autism and unfavorable left-right asymmetries of the brain. *Journal of Autism and Developmental Disorders,* 1979, *9,* 153–159.

Hier, D. B., LeMay, M., Rosenberger, P. B., & Perlo, V. P. Developmental dyslexia: Evidence for a subgroup with reversal of cerebral asymmetry. *Archives of Neurology,* 1978, *35,* 90–92.

Hillyard, S. A., & Woods, D. L. Electrophysiological analysis of human brain function. In M. S. Gazzaniga (Ed.) *Handbook of behavioral neurobiology* (Vol. 2). New York: Plenum, 1979.

Hines, D. Bilateral tachistoscopic recognitions of verbal and nonverbal stimuli. *Cortex,* 1972, *8,* 315–322.

Hines, D. Independent functioning of the two cerebral hemispheres for recognizing bilaterally presented tachistoscopic visual-half field stimuli. *Cortex,* 1975, *11,* 132–143.

Hines, D. Differences in tachistoscopic recognition between abstract and concrete words as a function of visual half-field and frequency. *Cortex,* 1977, *13,* 66–73.

Hines, D. *Verbal versus nonverbal fixation control in bilateral tachistoscopic recognition.* Paper presented at the meeting of the International Neuropsychological Society, Minneapolis, Minn., February 1978.

Hines, D., & Satz, P. Cross-modal asymmetries in

perception related to asymmetry in cerebral function. *Neuropsychologia,* 1974, *12,* 239–247.

Hirata, K., & Bryden, M. P. Right visual field superiority for letter recognition with partial report. *Canadian Journal of Psychology,* 1976, *30,* 134–139.

Hiscock, M. Effects of examiner's location and subject's anxiety on gaze laterality. *Neuropsychologia,* 1977, *15,* 409–416.

Hiscock, M. Verbal-manual time sharing in children as a function of task priority. *Brain and Cognition,* 1982, *1,* 119–131.

Hiscock, M., Antoniuk, D., & Prisciak, K. Dual-task performance as a function of children's age and academic skill level. In preparation, 1983.

Hiscock, M., & Bergstrom, K. J. Ocular motility as an indicator of verbal and visuospatial processing. *Memory & Cognition,* 1981, *9,* 332–338.

Hiscock, M., & Bergstrom, K. J. The lengthy persistence of priming effects in dichotic listening. *Neuropsychologia,* 1982, *20,* 43–53.

Hiscock, M., & Caplan, B. Developmental studies of listening asymmetry. In M. Hiscock (Chair), *Symposium on the ontogeny of language lateralization: Current perspectives on the Lenneberg hypothesis.* San Diego, Calif.: Academy of Aphasia, 1979.

Hiscock, M., Hampson, B., Wong, S. C. P., & Kinsbourne, M. *Effects of eye movements on the recognition and localization of dichotic stimuli.* Paper presented at the meeting of the International Neuropsychological Society, Atlanta, Ga., February 1981.

Hiscock, M., & Kinsbourne, M. Selective listening asymmetry in preschool children. *Developmental Psychology,* 1977, *13,* 217–224.

Hiscock, M., & Kinsbourne, M. Ontogeny of cerebral dominance: Evidence from time-sharing asymmetry in children. *Developmental Psychology,* 1978, *14,* 321–329.

Hiscock, M., & Kinsbourne, M. Asymmetries of selective listening and attention switching in children. *Developmental Psychology,* 1980, *16,* 70–82. (a)

Hiscock, M., & Kinsbourne, M. Asymmetry of verbal-manual time sharing in children: A follow-up study. *Neuropsychologia,* 1980, *18,* 151–162. (b)

Hiscock, M., & Kinsbourne, M. Individual differences in cerebral lateralization: Are they relevant to learning disability? In W. M. Cruickshank (Ed.), *Approaches to learning: The best of ACLD, 1978–79* (Vol. 1). Syracuse, N.Y.: Syracuse University Press, 1980. (c)

Hiscock, M., & Kinsbourne, M. Laterality and dyslexia: A critical view. *Annals of Dyslexia,* 1982, *32,* 177–228.

Hiscock, M., Kinsbourne, M., Caplan, B. J., & Swanson, J. M. Auditory attention in hyperactive children: Effects of stimulant medication on dichotic listening performance. *Journal of Abnormal Psychology,* 1979, *88,* 27–32.

Hiscock, M., Kinsbourne, M., Samuels, M., & Krause, A. E. *The development of dual-task performance: I. Effects of speaking upon children's finger tapping.* Article in preparation.

Hiscock, M., Kinsbourne, M., Samuels, M., & Krause, A. E. The development of dual-task performance: Effects of speaking and memory-encoding upon the rate and variability of children's finger tapping. In press, 1983.

Hiscock, M., Mackay, M., & Kinsbourne, M. On choosing a laterality index. Article in prep, 1983.

Hiscock, M., & Stewart, C. *Altering the right-ear advantage in dichotic listening: Effects of unequal experience in attending to the right and left ears.* Paper presented at the meeting of the Canadian Psychological Association, Quebec City, Canada, June 1979.

Hoovey, Z. B., Heinemann, U., & Creutzfeldt, O. D. Interhemispheric "synchrony" of alpha waves. *Electroencephalography and Clinical Neurophysiology,* 1972, *32,* 337–347.

Horn, J. L., & Cattell, R. B. Age differences in fluid and crystallized intelligence. *Acta Psychologica,* 1967, *26,* 701–719.

Hubbard, J. I. Handedness is not a function of birth order. *Nature,* 1971, *232,* 276–277.

Hubbs, C. L., & Hubbs, L. C. Bilateral asymmetry and bilateral variation in fishes. *Papers of the Michigan Academy of Sciences,* 1944, *30,* 229–311.

Hunter, M. Right-brained kids in left-brained schools. *Today's Education,* 1976, November–December, 45–49.

Huttenlocher, P. Synaptic density in human frontal cortex: Developmental changes and effects of aging. *Brain Research,* 1979, *163,* 195–205.

Hynd, G. W., & Obrzut, J. E. Effects of grade level and sex on the magnitude of the dichotic ear advantage. *Neuropsychologia,* 1977, *15,* 689–692.

Inglis, J., & Sykes, D. H. Some sources of variation in dichotic listening performance in children. *Journal of Experimental Child Psychology,* 1967, *5,* 480–488.

Ingram, D. Cerebral speech lateralization in young children. *Neuropsychologia,* 1975, *13,* 103–105.

Isaacson, R. (Ed.), *The neuropsychology of development.* New York: Wiley, 1968.

Jacobs, J. An external view of neuropsychology and its working milieu. In S. J. Segalowitz & F. A. Gruber (Eds.), *Language development and neurological theory*. New York: Academic Press, 1977.

Jaffe, J. Coupling between a symmetric and an asymmetric neural system. *Mount Sinai Journal of Medicine*, 1974, *41*, 153–155.

James-Roberts, I. Neurological plasticity, recovery from brain insult, and child development. *Advances in Development and Behavior*, 1979, *14*, 253–319.

Jasper, H. H. The ten-twenty electrode system of the international federation of societies for electroencephalography: Appendix to report of the committee on methods of clinical examination in electroencephalography. *Electroencephalography and Clinical Neurophysiology*, 1958, *10*, 371.

Jaynes, J. *The origin of consciousness in the breakdown of the bicameral mind*. Boston: Houghton Mifflin, 1976.

Jeeves, M. A. Psychological studies of three cases of congenital agenesis of the corpus callosum. In E. G. Ettlinger (Ed.), *Functions of the corpus callosum*. London: Churchill, 1965.

Johnson, O., & Harley, C. Handedness and sex differences in cognitive tests of brain laterality. *Cortex*, 1980, *16*, 73–82.

Johnson, O., & Kozma, A. Effects of concurrent verbal and musical tasks on a unimanual skill. *Cortex*, 1977, *13*, 11–16.

Johnson, P. R. Dichotically stimulated ear differences in musicians and nonmusicians. *Cortex*, 1977, *13*, 385–389.

Jones, R. K. Observations on stammering after localized cerebral injury. *Journal of Neurology, Neurosurgery and Psychiatry*, 1966, *29*, 192–195.

Jones, B., & Anunza, T. Sex differences in cerebral lateralization in 3- and 4-year old children. *Neuropsychologia*, 1982, *20*, 347–350.

Jurgen, V., & Ploog, D. On the neural control of mammalian vocalisation. *Trends in Neuroscience* 1981, *4*, 135–137.

Kagan, J. Unpublished manuscript, 1982.

Kahneman, D. *Attention and effort*. Englewood Cliffs, N.J.: Prentice-Hall, 1973.

Kail, R. V., Pellegrino, J., & Carter, P. Developmental changes in mental rotation. *Journal of Experimental Child Psychology*, 1980, *29*, 102–116.

Kail, R. V., & Siegel, A. W. Sex differences in retention of verbal and spatial characteristics of stimuli. *Journal of Experimental Child Psychology*, 1977, *23*, 341–347.

Kane, N., & Kane, M. Comparison of right and left hemisphere functions. *Gifted Child Quarterly*, 1979, *23*, 157–167.

Keller, J. F., Croake, J. W., & Riesenman, C. Relationships among handedness, intelligence, sex, and reading achievement of school age children. *Perceptual and Motor Skills*, 1973, *37*, 159–162.

Kelly, R. R., & Tomlinson-Keasey, C. The effect of auditory input on cerebral laterality. *Brain and Language*, 1981, *13*, 67–77.

Kennard, M. A., & Ectors, L. Forced circling in monkeys following lesions of the frontal lobe. *Journal of Neurophysiology*, 1938, *1*, 45–54.

Keogh, B. K. Preschool children's performance on measures of spatial organization, lateral preference, and lateral usage. *Perceptual and Motor Skills*, 1972, *34*, 299–302.

Keogh, B. K., & Ryan, S. R. Use of three measures of field organization with young children. *Perceptual and Motor Skills*, 1971, *33*, 466.

Kerr, F. W. L. Structural and functional evidence of plasticity in the central nervous system. *Experimental Neurology*, 1975, *48*, 16–31.

Kershner, J. R., & Jeng, A. G. R. Dual functional hemispheric asymmetry in visual perception: Effects of ocular dominance and post exposural processes. *Neuropsychologia*, 1972, *10*, 437–445.

Kershner, J. R., Thomae, R., & Callaway, R. Nonverbal fixation control in young children induces a left-field advantage in digit recall. *Neuropsychologia*, 1977, *15*, 569–576.

Kimura, D. The effect of letter position on recognition. *Canadian Journal of Psychology*, 1959, *13*, 1–10.

Kimura, D. Cerebral dominance and the perception of verbal stimuli. *Canadian Journal of Psychology*, 1961, *15*, 166–171, (a).

Kimura, D. Some effects of temporal-lobe damage on auditory perception. *Canadian Journal of Psychology*, 1961, *15*, 156–165, (b).

Kimura, D. Speech lateralization in young children as determined by an auditory test. *Journal of Comparative and Physiological Psychology*, 1963, *56*, 899–902.

Kimura, D. Left-right differences in the perception of melodies. *Quarterly Journal of Experimental Psychology*, 1964, *16*, 355–358.

Kimura, D. Functional asymmetry of the brain in visual perception. *Neuropsychologia*, 1966, *4*, 275–285.

Kimura, D. Functional asymmetry of the brain in dichotic listening. *Cortex,* 1967, *3,* 163–175.

Kimura, D. The neural basis of language qua gesture. In H. Avakian-Whitaker & H. A. Whitaker (Eds.), *Current trends in neurolinguistics.* New York: Academic Press, 1977.

Kimura, D., & Archibald, Y. Motor functions of the left hemisphere. *Brain,* 1974, *97,* 337–350.

Kimura, D., & Durnford, M. Normal studies on the function of the right hemisphere in vision. In S. J. Dimond & J. G. Beaumont (Eds.), *Hemisphere function in the human brain.* New York: Halsted Press, 1974.

Kinsbourne, M. The cerebral basis of lateral asymmetries in attention. In A. F. Sanders (Ed.), *Attention and performance* (Vol. 3). Amsterdam: North-Holland, 1970. (a)

Kinsbourne, M. A model for the mechanism of unilateral neglect of space. *Transactions of the American Neurological Association,* 1970, *95,* 143–145. (b)

Kinsbourne, M. The minor cerebral hemisphere as a source of aphasic speech. *Archives of Neurology,* 1971, *25,* 302–306.

Kinsbourne, M. Eye and head turning indicates cerebral lateralization. *Science,* 1972, *176,* 539–541.

Kinsbourne, M. Minimal brain dysfunction as a neurodevelopmental lag. *Annals of the New York Academy of Sciences,* 1973, *205,* 263–273, (a).

Kinsbourne, M. The control of attention by interaction between the cerebral hemispheres. In S. Kornblum (Ed.), *Attention and performance* (Vol. 4). New York: Academic Press, 1973. (b)

Kinsbourne, M. Direction of gaze and distribution of cerebral thought processes. *Neuropsychologia,* 1974, *12,* 279–281. (a)

Kinsbourne, M. Lateral interactions in the brain. In M. Kinsbourne & W. L. Smith (Eds.), *Hemispheric disconnection and cerebral function.* Springfield, Ill.: Charles C. Thomas, 1974. (b)

Kinsbourne, M. Mechanisms of hemispheric interaction in man. In M. Kinsbourne & W. L. Smith (Eds.), *Hemispheric disconnection and cerebral function.* Springfield, Ill.: Charles C. Thomas, 1974. (c)

Kinsbourne, M. The mechanism of hemispheric control of the lateral gradient of attention. In P. M. A. Rabbitt & S. Dornic (Eds.), *Attention and performance* (Vol. 5). London: Academic Press, 1975. (a)

Kinsbourne, M. The ontogeny of cerebral dominance. In D. R. Aaronson & R. W. Rieber (Eds.), Developmental psycholinguistics and communication disorders. New York: New York Academy of Sciences, 1975. (b)

Kinsbourne, M. The neuropsychological analysis of cognitive deficit. In R. G. Grenell & S. Grabay (Eds.), *Biological foundations of psychiatry.* New York: Raven Press, 1976.

Kinsbourne, M. Hemi-neglect and hemispheric rivalry. In E. A. Weinstein & R. P. Friedland (Eds.), *Advances in neurology,* (Vol. 18), *Hemi-inattention and hemispheric specialization.* New York: Raven Press, 1977.

Kinsbourne, M. (Ed.). *Asymmetrical function of the brain,* New York: Cambridge University Press, 1978. (a)

Kinsbourne, M. Asymmetry and the brain. *Science,* 1978, *200,* 651–652. (b)

Kinsbourne, M. The neuropsychology of infantile autism. In L. A. Lockman, K. F. Swaiman, J. S. Druge, K. B. Nelson & H. M. Marsden. Neurological Basis of Autism. NINCDS Monograph No. 23, Bethesda, Md., U.S. Dept. of HEW, 1979.

Kinsbourne, M. Language lateralization and developmental disabilities. *Advances in Behavioral Pediatrics,* 1980, *1,* 69–95. (a)

Kinsbourne, M. A model for the ontogeny of cerebral organization in nonrighthanders. In J. Herron (Ed.), *Neuropsychology of left-handedness.* New York: Academic Press, 1980. (b)

Kinsbourne, M. If sex differences in brain lateralization exist, they have yet to be discovered. *Brain and Behavioral Sciences,* 1980, *3,* 241–242. (c)

Kinsbourne, M. Neuropsychological aspects of Bilingualism. *Annals of the New York Academy of Sciences,* 1981, *379,* 50–58. (a)

Kinsbourne, M. Single channel theory. In D. H. Holding (Ed.), *Human skills.* Chichester, England: Wiley, 1981. (b)

Kinsbourne, M. Hemispheric specialization and the growth of human understanding. *American Psychologist,* 1982, *37,* 411–420.

Kinsbourne, M., & Bemporad, B. Syndrome of dyslexia, familial sinistrality and familial vulnerability to auto-immune disease. In preparation, 1983.

Kinsbourne, M., & Cook, J. Generalized and lateralized effects of concurrent verbalization on a unimanual skill. *Quarterly Journal of Experimental Psychology,* 1971, *23,* 341–345.

Kinsbourne, M., da Silva, M., & Kershner, J. Cross manual tactile matching and the corpus callosum: A methodological note. In preparation, 1983.

Kinsbourne, M., & Fisher, M. Latency of uncrossed and of crossed reaction in callosal agenesis. *Neu-*

ropsychologia, 1971, *9,* 471–472.

Kinsbourne, M., & Hicks, R. E. Functional cerebral space: A model for overflow, transfer and interference effects in human performance. In J. Requin (Ed.), *Attention and performance* (Vol. 7). Hillsdale, N.J.: Erlbaum, 1978. (a)

Kinsbourne, M., & Hicks, R. E. Mapping cerebral functional space: Competition and collaboration in human performance. In M. Kinsbourne (Ed.), *Asymmetrical function of the brain.* New York: Cambridge University Press, 1978. (b)

Kinsbourne, M., & Hiscock, M. Does cerebral dominance develop? In S. J. Segalowitz & F. A. Gruber (Eds.), *Language, development and neurological theory.* New York: Academic Press, 1977.

Kinsbourne, M., & Hiscock, M. Cerebral lateralization and cognitive development. In J. S. Chall & A. F. Mirsky, (Eds.), *Education and the brain* (Yearbook of the National Society for Study of Education). Chicago, Ill.: University of Chicago Press, 1978.

Kinsbourne, M., & Hiscock, M. Asymmetries of dual-task performance. In J. B. Hellige (Ed.), *Cerebral functional asymmetry: Theory, measurement, and application.* New York: Praeger, 1983.

Kinsbourne, M., & Lempert, H. Does left brain lateralization of speech arise from right-biased orienting to salient percepts? *Human Development,* 1978, *22,* 270–275.

Kinsbourne, M., & McMurray, J. The effect of cerebral dominance on time sharing between speaking and tapping by preschool children. *Child Development,* 1975, *46,* 240–242.

Kinsbourne, M., & Smith, W. L. (Eds.) *Hemispheric disconnection and cerebral function.* Springfield, Ill.: Charles C. Thomas, 1974.

Kinsbourne, M., & Warrington, E. K. The effect of an after-coming random pattern on the perception of brief visual stimuli. *Quarterly Journal of Experimental Psychology,* 1962, *14,* 223–235. (a)

Kinsbourne, M., & Warrington, E. K. A study of finger agnosia. *Brain,* 1962, *85,* 47–66. (b)

Kinsbourne, M., & Warrington, E. K. Developmental factors in reading and writing backwardness. *British Journal of Psychology,* 1963, *54,* 145–156. (a)

Kinsbourne, M., & Warrington, E. K. The developmental Gerstmann syndrome. *Archives of Neurology,* 1963, *8,* 490–501. (b)

Kirk, S. A., McCarthy, J. J., & Kirk, W. D. *Examiner's manual: Illinois test of psycholinguistic abilities.* Urbana: University of Illinois Press, 1968.

Klein, D., Moscovitch, M., & Vigna, C. Attentional mechanisms and perceptual asymmetries in tachistoscopic recognition of words and faces. *Neuropsychologia,* 1976, *14,* 55–66.

Kleisz, D. Neuropsychological evaluation in older persons. In M. M. Storandt, I. C. Siegles, & M. F. Elias (Eds.), *The clinical psychology of aging.* New York: Plenum, 1978.

Kletzkin, D. *Electroencephalographic, neurological and psychometric correlates of right and left cerebral hemisphere functions in on grade and below grade elementary school boys.* Unpublished doctoral dissertation, Rutgers University, 1980.

Klonoff, H., Fibiger, C. G., & Hutton, G. H. Neuropsychological problems in chronic schizophrenia. *Journal of Nervous and Mental Disease,* 1970, *150,* 291–300.

Knox, C., & Kimura, D. Cerebral processing of nonverbal sounds in boys and girls. *Neuropsychologia,* 1970, *8,* 227–237.

Kocel, K. M. Cognitive abilities: Handedness, familial sinistrality and sex. Annals of The New York Academy of Sciences, 1977, 299, 233–243.

Kocel, K. M. Age-related changes in cognition abilities and hemispheric specialization. In J. Herron (Ed.), *Neuropsychology of left-handedness.* New York: Academic Press, 1980.

Kocel, K. M., Galin, D., Ornstein, R. E., & Merrin, E. L. Lateral eye movement and cognitive mode. *Psychonomic Science,* 1972, *27,* 223–224.

Kohn, B., & Dennis, M. Selective impairments of visuo-spatial abilities in infantile hemiplegics after right cerebral hemidecortication. *Neuropsychologia,* 1974, *12,* 505–512.

Kooi, K. A. Fundamentals of electroencephalography. New York, Harper & Row, 1971.

Kraft, R. H. Asymmetric brain specialization: Proposed relationship between its development and cognitive development. In V. Rentel (Ed.), *Psychobiological aspects of reading.* Oxford: Pergamon, 1981.

Kraft, R. H. Relationship of ear specialization to degree of task difficulty, sex and lateral preference. *Perceptual and Motor Skills,* 1982, *54,* 703–714.

Krashen, S. D. Lateralization, language learning, and the critical period: Some new evidence. *Language Learning,* 1973, *23,* 63–74.

Kreuter, C., Kinsbourne, M., & Trevarthen, C. Are

deconnected cerebral hemispheres independent channels? A preliminary study of the effect of unilateral loading on bilateral finger tapping. *Neuropsychologia,* 1972, *10,* 453–461.

Kuhn, G. M. The phi coefficient as an index of ear differences in dichotic listening. *Cortex,* 1973, *9,* 450–456.

Kulesha, D., Moldofsky, H., Urowitz, M., & Zeaman, R. Brain scan lateralization and psychiatric symptoms in systemic lupus erythematous. *Biological Psychiatry,* 1981, *16,* 407–412.

Kutas, M., & Donchin, E. Studies of squeezing: Handedness, responding hand, response force, and asymmetry of readiness potential. *Science,* 1974, *186,* 545–548.

La Breche, T. M., Manning, A. A., Gobel, W., & Markman, R. Hemispheric specialization for linguistic and non-linguistic tactual perception in a congenitally deaf population. *Cortex,* 1977, *13,* 184–194.

Lake, D. A., & Bryden, M. P. Handedness and sex differences in hemispheric asymmetry. *Brain and Language,* 1976, *3,* 266–282.

Lashley, K. S. Studies of cerebral function in learning. VII. A reanalysis of data on mass action in the visual cortex. Journal of Comparative Neurology, 1932, *54,* 77–84.

Lassen, N. A., & Ingvar, D. H. Regional cerebral blood flow measurement in man. *Archives of Neurology and Psychiatry,* 1963, *9,* 615–622.

Ledlow, A., Swanson, J. M., & Kinsbourne, M. Reaction times and evoked potentials as indication of hemispheric differences for laterally presented name and physical matches. *Journal of Experimental Psychology: Human Perception and Performance,* 1978, *4,* 440–454. (a)

Ledlow, A., Swanson, J. M., & Kinsbourne, M. A comparison of RT and AEP differences as a function of direct and indirect neural pathways. *Annals of Neurology,* 1978, *3,* 525–530. (b)

Leehey, S. *Face recognition in children: Evidence for the development of right hemisphere specialization.* Unpublished doctoral dissertation, Massachusetts Institute of Technology, 1976.

Leehey, S., Carey, S., Diamond, R., & Cahn, A. Upright and inverted faces: The right hemisphere knows the difference. *Cortex,* 1978, *14,* 411–419.

LeMay, M. Morphological cerebral asymmetries of modern man, fossil man and nonhuman primate. In S. R. Harnad, H. D. Steklis, & J. Lancaster (Eds.), "Origins and evolution of language and speech." *Annals of the New York Academy of Sciences,* 1976, *280,* 349–366.

Lemon, R. E. Nervous control of the syrinx in white-throated sparrows. (*Zonotrichia albicollis*). *Journal of Zoology* (London), 1973, *171,* 131–140.

Lempert, H., & Kinsbourne, M. Effect of laterality of orientation on verbal memory. *Neuropsychologia,* 1982, *20,* 211–214.

Lempert, H., & Kinsbourne, M. Perceptual constraints on the acquisition and use of language by young children. In K. Nelson (Ed.), *Children's language.* New York: Gardner Press, in press.

Lenneberg, E. H. *Biological foundations of language.* New York: Wiley, 1967.

LeVere, T. E. Neural stability, sparing, and behavioral recovery following brain damage. *Psychological Review,* 1975, *82,* 344–358.

Levy, J. Possible basis for the evolution of lateral specialization of the human brain. *Nature,* 1969, *224,* 614–615.

Levy, J. Lateral specialization of the brain: Behavioral manifestations and possible evolutionary basis. In J. A. Kiger, Jr. (Ed.), *Proceedings of the 32nd annual biology colloquium on the biology of behaviors.* Corvallis: Oregon State University Press, 1972.

Levy, J. Psychobiological implications of bilateral asymmetry. In S. J. Dimond & J. G. Beaumont (Eds.), *Hemisphere function of the human brain.* London: Paul Elek, 1974.

Levy, J., & Reid, M. Variations in cerebral organization as a function of handedness, hand posture in writing, and sex. *Journal of Experimental Psychology: General,* 1978, *107,* 119–144.

Levy, J., & Trevarthen, C. Metacontrol of hemispheric function in human split-brain subjects. *Journal of Experimental Psychology: Human Perception and Performance,* 1976, *2,* 299–312.

Levy-Agresti, J., & Sperry, R. W. Differential, perceptual capacities in major and minor hemispheres. *Proceedings of the National Academy of Science,* 1968, *61,* 1151.

Lewandowski, L. Hemispheric asymmetries in children. *Perceptual and Motor Skills,* 1982, *54,* 1011–1019.

Lewkowicz, D. J., & Turkewitz, G. Influence of hemispheric specialization in sensory processing on reaching in infants: Age and gender related effects. *Developmental Psychology,* 1982, *18,* 301–308.

Lezak, M. D. *Neurological assessment.* New York: Oxford University Press, 1976.

Liederman, J., & Coryell, J. Movements are less reflex-bound during right rather than left-hand rotation in human infants. *Developmental Psychobiology,* in press.

Liederman, J., & Kinsbourne, M. The mechanism of neonatal rightward turning bias: A sensory or motor asymmetry? *Infant Behavior and Development,* 1980, *3,* 223–238. (a)

Liederman, J., & Kinsbourne, M. Rightward motor bias in newborns depends upon parental right-handedness. *Neuropsychologia,* 1980, *18,* 579–584. (b)

Liederman, J., & Kinsbourne, M. Rightward turning biases in neonates reflect a single neural asymmetry in motor programming. *Infant Behavior and Development,* 1980, *3,* 245–251. (c)

Lindsley, D. B. Bilateral differences in brain potentials from the two cerebral hemispheres in relation to laterality and stuttering. *Journal of Experimental Psychology,* 1940, *26,* 211–225.

Lindsley, D. B. Average evoked potentials—achievements, failures and prospects. In E. Donchin & D. B. Lindsley (Eds.), *Average evoked potentials, methods, results, and evaluations* (NASA–191). Washington, D.C.: U.S. Government Printing Office, 1969.

Lomas, J. Competition within the left hemisphere between speaking and unimanual tasks performed without visual guidance. *Neuropsychologia,* 1980, *18,* 141–150.

Lomas, J., & Kimura, D. Intrahemispheric interaction between speaking and sequential manual activity. *Neuropsychologia,* 1976, *14,* 23–33.

Low, M. D., Borda, R. P., Frost, J. D., Jr., & Kellaway, P. Surface-negative slow-potential shift associated with conditioning in man. *Neurology,* 1966, *16,* 771–782.

Low, M. D., Wada, J. A., & Fox, M. Electroencephalographic localization of the conative aspects of language production in the human brain. In W. C. McCallum & J. R. Knott (Eds.), *The responsive brain.* Bristol: John Wright, 1976.

Lowe, S. S., Cullen, J. K., Jr., Berlin, C. I., Thompson, C. L., & Willett, M. E. Perception of simultaneous dichotic and monotic monosyllables. *Journal of Speech and Hearing Research,* 1970, *13,* 812–822.

Ludwig, W. *Das Rechts-Links-Problem im Tierreich und beim Menschen.* Berlin: Springer-Verlag, 1932.

Luessenhop, A. J., Boggs, J. S., LaBorwit, L. J., & Walle, E. L. Cerebral dominance in stutterers determined by Wada testing. *Neurology,* 1973, *23,* 1190–1192.

Luria, A. R. *Restoration of function after brain injury.* Oxford: Pergamon, 1963.

Luria, A. R. *Higher cortical functions in man.* New York: Basic Books, 1966.

Luria, A. R. *Traumatic aphasia. Its syndromes, psychology and treatment* (D. Bowden, trans.). Paris: Mouton, 1970.

Luria, A. R. The functional organization of the brain. *Scientific American,* March 1970. Reprinted in Richard C. Atkinson (Ed.), *Contemporary psychology.* San Francisco: W. H. Freeman, 1971.

Luria, A. R. *The working brain* (B. Haigh, trans.). New York: Basic Books, 1974.

Luria, A. R., Naydin, V. L., Isvetkova, L. S., & Vinarskaya, E. N. Restoration of higher cortical function following local brain damage. In P. J. Vinken & G. W. Bruyn (Eds.), *Handbook of clinical neurology* (Vol. 3). Amsterdam: North-Holland, 1969.

Lynch, G., Stanfield, B., & Cotman, C. W. Developmental differences in post-lesion axonal growth in the hippocampus. *Brain Research,* 1973, *59,* 155–168.

Lyon, R., Stewart, N., & Freedman, D. Neuropsychological characteristics of empirically derived subgroups of learning disabled readers. *Journal of Clinical Neuropsychology,* 1983, *4,* 343–365.

Maccoby, E. E., & Jacklin, C. N. *The psychology of sex differences.* Stanford, Calif.: Stanford University Press, 1974.

MacKavey, W., Curcio, F., & Rosen, J. Tachistoscopic word recognition performance under conditions of simultaneous bilateral presentation. *Neuropsychologia,* 1975, *13,* 27–33.

Maddess, R. J. Reaction time to hemiretinal stimulation. *Neuropsychologia,* 1975, *13,* 213–218.

Majeres, R. L. The effect of unimanual performance on speed of verbalization. *Journal of Motor Behavior,* 1975, *7,* 57–58.

Manning, A. A., Gobel, W., Markman, R., & La Breche, T. M. Lateral cerebral differences in the deaf in response to linguistic and nonlinguistic stimuli. *Brain and Language,* 1977, *4,* 309–321.

Marcel, T., Katz, L., & Smith, J. M. Laterality and reading proficiency. *Neuropsychologia,* 1974, *12,* 131–139.

Marcel, T., & Rajan, P. Lateral specialization for recognition of words and faces in good and poor readers. *Neuropsychologia,* 1975, *13,* 489–497.

Marcie, P. Writing disorders in 47 left-handed patients with unilateral cerebral lesions. *International Journal of Mental Health,* 1972, *3,* 30–37.

Marie, P. Existe-t-il, dans le cerveau humain des

centres innés ou préformés de langage? *La Presse Medicale,* 1922, *17,* 117–181.

Markowitz, H., & Weitzman, D. O. Monocular recognition of letters and Landolt Cs in left and right visual hemifields. *Journal of Experimental Psychology,* 1969, *79,* 187–189.

Marsh, G. R. Asymmetry of electrophysiological phenomena and its relation to behavior in humans. In M. Kinsbourne (Ed.), *Asymmetrical function of the brain.* New York: Cambridge University Press, 1978.

Marshall, J. C., Caplan, D., & Holmes, J. M. The measure of laterality. *Neuropsychologia,* 1975, *13,* 315-321.

Matarazzo, J. D. *Wechsler's measurement and appraisal of adult intelligence* (5th ed.). Baltimore: Williams & Wilkens, 1972.

Mathewson, J. W., Jr., Miller, J. C., Jr., & Crovitz, H. F. The letter span in space and time. *Psychonomic Science,* 1968, *11,* 69–70.

Matsumiya, Y., Tagliasco, V. L., Lombroso, C. T., & Goodglass, H. Auditory evoked response: Meaningfulness of stimuli and interhemispheric asymmetry. *Science,* 1972, *175,* 790–792.

Matthews, C. G., & Reitan, R. M. Correlations of Wechsler-Bellevue rank orders of subtest means in lateralized and non-lateralized brain-damaged groups. *Perceptual and Motor Skills,* 1964, *19,* 391–399.

Mattis, S. Dyslexia syndromes: A working hypothesis that works. In A. L. Benton & D. Pearl (Eds.), *Dyslexia: An appraisal of current knowledge.* New York: Oxford University Press, 1978.

Mayes, A., & Beaumont, G. Does visual evoked potential asymmetry index cognitive activity? *Neuropsychologia,* 1977, *15,* 249–256.

McAdam, D. W., & Whitaker, H. A. Language production: Electroencephalographic location in the normal human brain. *Science,* 1971, *172,* 499–502.

McAnulty, G., Hicks, R. E., & Kinsbourne, M. Left handedness in mental retardation: Familial or pathological? Manuscript submitted for publication, 1983.

McCann, B. S. Hemispheric asymmetries and early infantile autism. *Journal of Autism and Developmental Disorders,* 1981, *11,* 401–411.

McFarland, K. A., & Ashton, R. A developmental study of the influence of cognitive activity on an ongoing manual task. *Acta Psychologica,* 1975, *39,* 447–456. (a)

McFarland, K. A., & Ashton, R. The lateralized effects of concurrent cognitive activity on a unimanual skill. *Cortex,* 1975, *11,* 283–290. (b)

McFarland, K. A., & Ashton, R. The influence of brain lateralization of function on a manual skill. *Cortex,* 1978, *14,* 102–111. (a)

McFarland, K. A., & Ashton, R. The influence of concurrent task difficulty on manual performance. *Neuropsychologia,* 1978, *16,* 735–741. (b)

McFarland, K. A., & Ashton, R. The lateralized effects of concurrent cognitive and motor performance. *Perception & Psychophysics,* 1978, *23,* 344–349. (c)

McFie, J. The effects of hemispherectomy on intellectual functioning in cases of infantile hemiplegia. *Journal of Neurology, Neurosurgery and Psychiatry,* 1961, *24,* 240–249.

McFie, J., Piercy, M. F., & Zangwill, O. L. Visual spatial agnosia associated with lesions of the right cerebral hemisphere. *Brain,* 1950, *73,* 167–190.

McGlone, J. Sex differences in human brain asymmetry: A critical survey. *Behavioral and Brain Sciences,* 1980, *3,* 215–264.

McGlone, J., & Davidson, W. The relation between cerebral speech laterality and spatial ability with special reference to sex and hand preference. *Neuropsychologia,* 1973, *11,* 105–113.

McGlone, J., & Kertesz, A. Sex differences in cerebral processing of visuospatial tasks. *Cortex,* 1973, *9,* 313–320.

McKain, K., Studdert-Kennedy, M., Spieker, S. & Stern, D. Infant intermodal speech perception is a left hemisphere function. *Science,* 1983, *219,* 1347–1349.

McKee, G., Humphrey, B., & McAdam, D. W. Scaled lateralization of alpha activity during linguistic and musical tasks. *Psychophysiology,* 1973, *10,* 441–443.

McKeever, W. F. Lateral word recognition: Effects of unilateral and bilateral presentation, asynchrony of bilateral presentation, and forced order of report. *Quarterly Journal of Experimental Psychology,* 1971, *23,* 410–416.

McKeever, W. F., & Gill, K. M. Interhemispheric transfer time for visual stimulus information varies as a function of the retinal locus of stimulation. *Psychonomic Science,* 1972, *26,* 308–310.

McKeever, W. F., Hoemann, H. W., Florian, V. A., & Van Deventer, A. D. Evidence of minimal cerebral asymmetries in the congenitally deaf. *Neuropsychologia,* 1976, *14,* 413–423.

McKeever, W. F., & Huling, M. D. Lateral dominance in tachistoscopic word recognition of children at two levels of ability. *Quarterly Journal of Experimental Psychology,* 1970, *22,* 600–

604. (a)

McKeever, W. F., & Huling, M. D. Left-cerebral hemisphere superiority in tachistoscopic word-recognition performance. *Perceptual and Motor Skills,* 1970, *30,* 763–766. (b)

McKeever, W. F., & Huling, M. D. Bilateral tachistoscopic word recognition as a function of hemispheric stimulated and interhemispheric transfer time. *Neuropsychologia,* 1971, *9,* 281–288. (a)

McKeever, W. F., & Huling, M. D. Lateral dominance in tachistoscopic word recognition performances obtained with simultaneous bilateral input. *Neuropsychologia,* 1971, *9,* 15–20. (b)

McLeod, S. S., & Peacock, L. J. Task-related EEG asymmetry: Effects of age and ability. *Psychophysiology,* 1977, *14,* 308–311.

McManus, I. C. Handedness and birth stress. *Neuropsychologia,* 1980, *18,* 347–355.

Mewhort, D. J. K. Sequential redundancy and letter spacing as determinants of tachistoscopic recognition. *Canadian Journal of Psychology,* 1966, *20,* 435–444.

Mewhort, D. J. K. Accuracy and order of report in tachistoscopic identification. *Canadian Journal of Psychology,* 1974, *28,* 383–398.

Meyer, D. R. Access to ENGRANS American Psychologists, 1972, *27,* 124–133.

Miceli, G., Caltagirone, C., Gianotti, G., Masullo, C., Silveri, C., & Villa, G. Influence of age, sex, literacy, and pathologic lesion on incidence, severity and type of aphasia. *Acta Neurologica Scandinavica,* 1981, *64,* 370–382.

Michel, G. F. Right handedness: A consequence of infant supine head orientation preference? *Science,* 1981, *212,* 385–387.

Michel, G. F., & Goodwin, R. Intrauterine birth position predicts newborn supine head position preferences. *Infant Behavior and Development,* 1979, *2,* 29–38.

Milberg, W. P., Whitman, R. D., Rourke, D., & Glaros, A. G. Role of subvocal motor activity in dichotic speech perception and selective attention. *Journal of Experimental Psychology: Human Perception and Performance,* 1981, *7,* 231–239.

Miller, E. A. Handedness and the pattern of human ability. *British Journal of Psychology,* 1971, *62,* 111–112.

Miller, E. A., Goldman, P. S., & Rosvold, H. E. Delayed recovery of function following orbital prefrontal lesion in infant monkeys. *Science,* 1973, *182,* 304–306.

Miller, L. K., & Turner, S. Development of hemified differences in word recognition. *Journal of Educational Psychology,* 1973, *65,* 172–176.

Milner, B. Laterality effects in audition. In V. B. Mountcastle (Ed.), *Interhemispheric relations and cerebral dominance.* Baltimore: The Johns Hopkins University Press, 1962.

Milner, B. Visual recognition and recall after right temporal-lobe excision in man. *Neuropsychologia,* 1968, *6,* 191–210.

Milner, B. Hemispheric specialization: Scope and limits. In F. O. Schmitt & F. G. Worden (Eds.), *The neurosciences: Third study program.* Boston: MIT Press, 1973.

Milner, B., Branch, C., & Rasmussen, T. Evidence for bilateral speech representation in some non-right handers. *Transactions of the American Neurological Association,* 1966, *91,* 306–308.

Milner, B., & Taylor, L. B. Right hemisphere superiority in tactile pattern recognition after cerebral commissurotomy: Evidence for nonverbal memory. *Neuropsychologia,* 1972, *10,* 1–16.

Mishkin, M., & Forgays, D. G. Word recognition as a function of retinal locus. *Journal of Experimental Psychology,* 1952, *43,* 43–48.

Moffitt, A. R. Consonant cue perception by twenty to twenty-four week old infants. *Child Development,* 1971, *42,* 717–731.

Molfese, D. L. Central asymmetry in infants, children and adults: Auditory evoked responses to speech and music. *Journal of the Acoustical Society of America,* 1973, *53,* 363–373.

Molfese, D. L. Infant cerebral asymmetry. In S. J. Segalowitz & F. A. Gruber (Eds.), *Language development and neurological theory.* New York: Academic Press, 1977.

Molfese, D. L. Left and right hemisphere involvement in speech perception: Electrophysiological correlates. *Perception & Psychophysics,* 1978, *23,* 237–243.

Molfese, D. L., Freeman, R. B., & Palermo, D. The ontogeny of brain lateralization for speech and non-speech stimuli. *Brain and Language,* 1975, *2,* 356–368.

Molfese, D. L., & Molfese, V. J. Hemisphere and stimulus differences as reflected in the cortical responses of newborn infants to speech stimuli. *Developmental Psychology,* 1979, *15,* 505–511.

Molfese, D. L., & Molfese, V. J. Cortical responses of preterm infants to phonetic and nonphonetic speech stimuli. *Developmental Psychology,* 1980, *16,* 574–581.

Molfese, D. L., Nunez, V., Seibert, S. M., & Ramanaiah, N. V. Cerebral asymmetry: Changes in factors affecting its development. In "Origins and evolution of language and speech." *Annals of the New York Academy of*

Sciences, 1976, *280,* 821–833.

Moore, C. S. Control of the memory image. *Psychological Review Monograph Supplement,* 1903, *4*(1, Whole No. 17).

Moore, T. Language and intelligence: A longitudinal study of the first eight years. Part I: Patterns of development in boys and girls. *Human Development,* 1967, *10,* 88–106.

Moore, W. H., & Weidner, W. E. Bilateral tachistoscopic word perception in aphasic and normal subjects. *Perceptual and Motor Skills,* 1974, *39,* 1003–1011.

Morais, J., & Bertelson, P. Laterality effects in dichotic listening. *Perception,* 1973, *2,* 107–111.

Morais, J., & Bertelson, P. Spatial position versus ear of entry as determinant of the auditory laterality effects: A stereophonic test. *Journal of Experimental Psychology: Human Perception and Performance,* 1975, *1,* 253–262.

Morais, J., & Darwin, C. J. Ear differences for same-different reaction times to monaurally presented speech. *Brain and Language,* 1974, *1,* 383–390.

Morgan, A. H., MacDonald, H., & Hilgard, E. R. EEG alpha: Lateral asymmetry related to task and hypnotizability. *Psychophysiology,* 1974, *11,* 275–282.

Morgan, A. H., McDonald, P. J., & MacDonald, H. Differences in bilateral alpha activity as a function of experimental task with a note on lateral eye movements and hypnotizability. *Neuropsychologia,* 1971, *9,* 459–469.

Morrell, L. K., & Huntington, D. A. Electrocortical cortical localization of language production. *Science,* 1971, *174,* 1359–1360.

Morrell, L. K., & Salamy, J. G. Hemispheric asymmetry of electrocortical response to speech stimuli. *Science,* 1971, *174,* 164–166.

Moscovitch, M., & Catlin, J. Interhemispheric transmission of information: Measurement in normal man. *Psychonomic Science,* 1970, *18,* 211–213.

Mott, F. W., & Shafer, E. A. On associated eye movements produced by cortical faradization of the monkey's brain. *Brain,* 1890, *13,* 165–173.

Munk, H. *Über die Funktionen der Grosshirnrinde.* Gesammelte Mitteilungen aus den Jahren 1877–1880. Berlin: August Hirshwald, 1881.

Myers, R. E., & Sperry, R. W. Interocular transfer of a visual form discrimination habit in cats after section of the optic chiasm and corpus callosum. *Anatomical Record,* 1953, *175,* 351–352.

Myklebust, H. Learning disabilities and minimal brain dysfunction in children. In D. B. Tower (Ed.), *The nervous system* (Vol. 3): *Human communication and its disorders.* New York: Raven, 1975.

Navon, D., & Gopher, D. On the economy of the human information processing system: A model of multiple capacity. *Psychological Review,* 1979, *86,* 214–225.

Nebes, R. D. Handedness and the perception of part-whole relationships. *Cortex,* 1971, *7,* 350–356.

Nebes, R. D. Direct examination of cognitive function in the right and left hemisphere. In M. Kinsbourne (Ed.), *Asymmetrical function of the brain.* New York: University of Cambridge Press, 1978.

Neill, D. O., Sampson, H., & Gribben, J. A. Hemiretinal effects in tachistoscopic letter recognition. *Journal of Experimental Psychology,* 1971, *91,* 129–135.

Netley, C. Dichotic listening of callosal agenesis and Turner's syndrome patients. In S. J. Segalowitz & F. A. Gruber (Eds.), *Language development and neurological theory.* New York: Academic Press, 1977.

Neville, H. J. Electrographic correlates of lateral asymmetry in the processing of verbal and nonverbal auditory stimuli. *Journal of Psycholinguistic Research,* 1974, *3,* 151–163.

Neville, H. J. Electroencephalographic testing of cerebral specialization in normal and congenitally deaf children: A preliminary report. In S. J. Segalowitz & F. A. Gruber (Eds.), *Language development and neurological theory.* New York: Academic Press, 1977.

Newcombe, F., & Ratcliff, G. Handedness, speech lateralization and ability. *Neuropsychologia,* 1973, *11,* 399–407.

Newcombe, N. & Bandura, M. M. Effect of age at puberty on spatial ability in girls: a question of mechanism. *Developmental Psychology,* 1983, *19,* 215–224.

Newcombe, N., Bandura, M. M., & Taylor, D. G. Sex differences in spatial ability and spatial activities. *Sex roles,* in press.

Nielsen, J. M., & Raney, R. B. Recovery from aphasia studied in cases of lobectomy. *Archives of Neurology and Psychiatry,* 1939, *42,* 189.

Norman, D. A., & Bobrow, D. G. On data-limited and resource-limited processes. *Cognitive Psychology,* 1975, *7,* 44–64.

Nottebohm, F. Ontogeny of bird song. *Science,* 1970, *167,* 950–956.

Nottebohm, F. Neural lateralization of vocal control in a passerine bird. I. Song. *Journal of Experimental Zoology,* 1971, *177,* 229–262.

Nottebohm, F. Neural lateralization of vocal control in a passerine bird. II. Subsong, calls and a theory of vocal learning. *Journal of Experimental Zoology,* 1972, *179,* 35–50.

Nottebohm, F. Phonation in the orange-winged Amazon parrot, *Amazona amazonica. Journal of Comparative Physiology,* 1976, *108,* 156–170.

Nottebohm, F. Origins and mechanisms in the establishment of cerebral dominance. In M. S. Gazzaniga (Ed.), *Handbook of behavioral neurobiology* (Vol. 2). New York: Plenum, 1979.

Nottebohm, F., Stokes, T. M., & Leonard, C. M. Central control of song in the canary, *Serinus canarius. Journal of Comparative Neurology,* 1976, *165,* 457–486.

Obler, L. K., Albert, M. L., Goodglass, H., & Benson, D. F. Aphasia type and aging. *Brain and Language,* 1978, *6,* 318–322.

Obrzut, J. E., Hynd, G. W., Obrzut, A., & Leitgeb, J. L. Time sharing and dichotic listening asymmetry in normal and learning-disabled children. *Brain and Language,* 1980, *11,* 181–194.

Oexle, J. E., & Zenhausern, R. *International Journal of Neuroscience,* 1981, *15,* 31–36.

Ojemann, G., & Whitaker, H. Language localisation and variability. *Brain and Language,* 1978, *6,* 239–260.

Olson, M. E. Laterality differences in tachistoscopic word recognition in normal and delayed readers in elementary school. *Neuropsychologia,* 1973, *11,* 343–350.

Orbach, J. Retinal locus as a factor in the recognition of visually perceived words. *American Journal of Psychology,* 1953, *65,* 555–562.

Orme, J. E. Left-handedness, ability and emotional instability. *British Journal of Social and Clinical Psychology,* 1970, *9,* 87–88.

Ornstein, R. E. *The psychology of consciousness.* San Francisco: W. H. Freeman, 1972.

Orton, S. T. A physiological theory of reading disability and stuttering in children. *New England Journal of Medicine,* 1928, *199,* 1045–1052.

Orton, S. T. *Reading, writing and speech problems in children.* New York: W. W. Norton, 1937.

Osborne, K., & Gale, A. Bilateral alpha differentiation of stimuli. *Biological Psychology,* 1976, *4,* 185–196.

Otto, D. A., & Leifer, L. J. The effect of modifying response and performance on the CNV in humans. In W. C. McCallum & J. R. Knott (Eds.), *Event-related slow potentials of the brain.* New York: Elsevier, 1973.

Overton, W., & Wiener, M. Visual field position and word-recognition threshold. *Journal of Experimental Psychology,* 1966, *71,* 249–253.

Paivio, A., & Ernest, C. Imagery ability and visual perception of verbal and nonverbal stimuli. *Perception & Psychophysics,* 1971, *10,* 429–432.

Palmer, R. D. Development of a differentiated handedness. *Psychological Bulletin,* 1964, *62,* 257–272.

Papcun, G., Krashen, S. D., Terbeek, D., Remington, R., & Harshman, R. Is the left hemisphere specialized for speech, language and/or something else? *Journal of the Acoustical Society of America,* 1974, *55,* 319–327.

Parlow, S. E. *Does left-hemispheric "attention" interfere with subsequent perception of language by the right hemisphere in a selective listening task?* Unpublished master's thesis, University of Toronto, 1978.

Parlow, S. E., & Kinsbourne, M. Handwriting posture and manual motor asymmetry in sinistrals. *Neuropsychologia,* 1981, *19,* 687–696.

Parsons, O. A. Human neuropsychology: The new phrenology. *Journal of Operational Psychiatry,* 1977, *8,* 47–56.

Pasamanick, B., & Knobloch, H. Brain damage and reproductive casualty. *American Journal of Orthopsychiatry,* 1960, *30,* 298–305.

Paterson, A., & Zangwill, O. L. Disorders of visual space perception associated with lesions of the right cerebral hemisphere. *Brain,* 1944, *67,* 331–358.

Penfield, W., & Roberts, L. *Speech and brain mechanisms.* Princeton, N.J.: Princeton University Press, 1959.

Peronnet, F., Michel, F., Echallier, J. F., & Girod, J. Coronal topography of human auditory evoked responses. *Electroencephalography and Clinical Neurophysiology,* 1974, *37,* 225–230.

Perria, L., Rosadini, G., & Rossi, G. F. Determination of side of cerebral dominance with amobarbital. *Archives of Neurology,* 1961, *4,* 173–181.

Peters, J. F., & Mendel, M. I. Early components of the averaged electroencephalic response to monaural and binaural stimulation. *Audiology,* 1974, *13,* 195–204.

Peters, M., & Petrie, B. N. Functional asymmetries in the stepping reflex of human neonates. *Canadian Journal of Psychology,* 1979, *33,* 198–200.

Petersen, M. R., Beecher, M. D., Loloth, S. R., Moddy, D. B., & Stebbins, W. C. Neural lateralization of species-specific vocalizations by Japanese macaques (*Macaca fuscata*). *Science,* 1978, *202,* 324–327.

Peterson, A. C. Physical androgyny and cognitive functioning in adolescence. *Developmental Psychology,* 1976, *12,* 524–533.

Petitt, J. M., & Holms, S. B. Hemisphere language

dominance of language-disordered, articulation-disordered, and normal children. *Journal of Learning Disabilities,* 1974, *12,* 12–17.

Petrauskas, R-J., & Rourke, B. P. Identification of subtypes of retarded readers: A neuropsychological multivariate approach. *Journal of Clinical Neuropsychology,* 1979, *1,* 17–38.

Petrie, B. N., & Peters, M. Handedness: Left/right differences in intensity of grasp response and duration of rattle holding in infants. *Infant Behavior and Development,* 1980, *3,* 215–221.

Pfeiffer, R. A. Pathologie des Hoerstrahlung und der Corticalen Hoersphaere. In O. Bumke & O. Foerster (Eds.), *Handbuch der Neurologie* (Vol. 6). Berlin: Springer-Verlag, 1936.

Phippard, D. Hemifield differences in visual perception in deaf and hearing subjects. *Neuropsychologia,* 1977, *15,* 555–561.

Piazza, D. M. Cerebral lateralization in young children as measured by dichotic listening and finger-tapping tasks. *Neuropsychologia,* 1977, *15,* 417–425.

Piercy, M. F., & Smyth, V. Right hemisphere dominance for certain nonverbal intellectual skills. *British Journal of Psychiatry,* 1962, *83,* 775–790.

Pinsky, S. D., & McAdam, D. W. Electroencephalographic and dichotic indices of cerebral laterality in stutterers. *Brain and Language* 1980, *11,* 374–397.

Pirozzolo, F. J. *The neuropsychology of developmental reading disorders.* New York: Praeger, 1979.

Pirozzolo, F. J., & Rayner, K. Hemispheric specialization in reading and word recognition. *Brain and Language,* 1977, *4,* 248–261.

Pizzamiglio, L. Handedness, ear-preference, and field-dependence. *Perceptual and Motor Skills,* 1974, *38,* 700–702.

Pizzamiglio, L., De Pascalis, C., & Vignati, A., Stability of dichotic listening test. *Cortex,* 1974, *10,* 203–205.

Poffenberger, A. T. Reaction time to retinal stimulation with special reference to the time lost in conduction through nerve centers. *Archives of Psychology,* 1912, *23,* 1–73.

Pohl, W., Butters, N., & Goodglass, H. Spatial discrimination systems and cerebral lateralization. *Cortex,* 1972, *8,* 305–314.

Poizner, H., Battison, R., & Lane, H. Cerebral asymmetry for American sign language: The effects of moving stimuli. *Brain and Language,* 1979, *7,* 351–362.

Policansky, D. Flatfishes and the inheritance of asymmetries. *Behavioral and Brain Sciences,* 1982, *5,* 262–266.

Porac, C., & Coren, S. Relationship between lateral preference behaviors in humans. *The Behavioral and Brain Sciences,* 1978, *2,* 311–312.

Porac, C., Coren, S., & Duncan, P. Life-span age trends in laterality. *Journal of Gerontology,* 1980, *35,* 715–721.

Porter, R. J., & Berlin, C. I. On interpreting developmental changes in the dichotic right ear advantage. *Brain and Language,* 1975, *2,* 186–200.

Porteus, S. D. *Porteus maze test: Fifty years' application.* Palo Alto, Calif.: Pacific Books, 1965.

Posner, M. I., & Boies, S. J. Components of attention. *Psychological Review,* 1971, *78,* 391–408.

Pratt, R. T. C., & Warrington, E. K. The assessment of cerebral dominance with unilateral E.C.T. *British Journal of Psychiatry,* 1972, *121,* 327–328.

Pratt, R. T. C., Warrington, E. K., & Halliday, A. M. Unilateral E.C.T. as a test for cerebral dominance, with a strategy for treating left-handers. *British Journal of Psychiatry,* 1971, *119,* 78–83.

Prior, M. R. Cognitive abilities and disabilities in infantile autism: A review. *Journal of Abnormal Child Psychology,* 1979, *7,* 357–380.

Prior, M. R., & Bradshaw, J. L. Hemisphere functioning in autistic children. *Cortex,* 1979, *15,* 73–81.

Provine, R. R., & Westerman, J. A. Crossing the midline: Limits of early eye-hand behavior. *Child Development,* 1979, *50,* 437–441.

Provins, K. A., & Cunliffe, P. The reliability of some motor performance tests of handedness. *Neuropsychologia,* 1972, *10,* 199–206.

Provins, K. A., & Jeeves, M. A. Hemisphere differences in response time to simple auditory stimuli. *Neuropsychologia,* 1975, *13,* 207–211.

Puccetti, R. Brain section and personal identity. *British Journal of the Philosophy of Science,* 1973, *24,* 339–355.

Quinn, P. T. Stuttering—cerebral dominance and dichotic word test. *Medical Journal of Australia,* 1972, *2,* 639–642.

Rabinowicz, T. Some aspects of the maturation of the human cerebral cortex. In S. R. Berenberg, M. Caniaris, & N. P. Masse (Eds.), *Pre- and postnatal development of the human brain.* Basel: S. Karger, 1974.

Ramsay, D. S. Manual preference for tapping in infants. *Developmental Psychology,* 1979, *15,* 437–442.

Ramsay, D. S. Onset of unimanual handedness in

infants. *Infant Behavior and Development,* 1980, *3,* 377–385.

Raney, E. T. Brain potentials and lateral dominance in identical twins. *Journal of Experimental Psychology,* 1939, *24,* 21–39.

Rasmussen, T., & Milner, B. Clinical and surgical studies of the cerebral speech areas in man. In K. J. Zulch, O. Creutzfeldt, & G. Galbraith (Eds.), *Otfrid Foerster symposium on cerebral localization.* Heidelberg: Springer-Verlag, 1975.

Ratcliffe, G., Dila, C., Taylor, L., & Milner, B. The morphological asymmetry of the hemispheres and cerebral dominance for speech: A possible relationship. *Brain and Language,* 1980, *11,* 87–98.

Ray, W. J., Newcombe, N., Semon, J., & Cole, P. M. Spatial abilities, sex differences and EEG functioning. *Neuropsychologia,* 1981, *19,* 719–722.

Rayner, K. Eye movements in reading and information processing. *Psychological Bulletin,* 1978, *85,* 618–660.

Rechtschaffen, A., & Kales, A. (Eds.), *A manual of standardized terminology, technique and scoring system for sleep stages of human subjects.* Bethesda, Md.: HEW Neurological Information Network, 1968.

Redlich, E. Epilepsie und Linkshändlichkeit. *Archiv Psychiat,* 1908, *44,* 59–83.

Reed, J. C., & Reitan, R. M. Verbal and performance differences among brain-injured children with lateralized motor deficits. *Perceptual and Motor Skills,* 1969, *29,* 747–752.

Reitan, R. M. Certain differential effects of left and right cerebral lesions in human adults. *Journal of Comparative and Physiological Psychology,* 1955, *48,* 474–477.

Reitan, R. M. Validity of the trail making test as an indicator of organic brain damage. *Perceptual and Motor Skills,* 1958, *8,* 271–276.

Reitan, R. M., & Davison, L. A. *Clinical neuropsychology: Current status and applications.* New York: Winston/Wiley, 1974.

Reitsma, P. Visual asymmetry in children. In Boerhaave Committee for Postgraduate Education (Ed.). *Lateralization of brain functions.* Leiden, the Netherlands: University of Leiden Press, 1975.

Remond, A., Lesevre, N., Joseph, J. P., Rieger, H., & Lairy, G. C. The alpha average. I. Methodology and description. *Electroencephalography and Clinical Neurophysiology,* 1969, *26,* 245–265.

Repp, B. H. Measuring laterality effects in dichotic listening. *Journal of the Acoustical Society of America,* 1977, *62,* 720–737.

Reynolds, C. R., & Kaufman, A. S. Lateral eye movement behavior in children. *Perceptual and Motor Skills,* 1980, *50,* 1023–1037.

Rhodes, L. E., Obitz, F. W., & Creel, D. Effect of alcohol and task on hemispheric asymmetry of visually evoked potentials in man. *Electroencephalography and Clinical Neurophysiology,* 1975, *38,* 561–568.

Richardson, J. T. E. How to measure laterality. *Neuropsychologia,* 1976, *14,* 135–136.

Richmond, P. G. A. A limited sex difference in spatial test scores with a preadolscent sample. *Child Development,* 1980, *51,* 601–602.

Roberts, J., & Engle, A. *Family background, early development, and intelligence of children 6–11 years.* In National Center for Health Statistics, Data from the National Health Survey, Series II, No. 142, DHEW No. (HRA) 75–1624. Washington, D.C.: U.S. Government Printing Office, 1974.

Roberts, L. Aphasia, apraxia and agnosia in abnormal states of cerebral dominance. In P. J. Vinken & G. W. Bruyn (Eds.), *Handbook of clinical neurology* (Vol. 4). Amsterdam: North-Holland, 1969.

Robinson, D. A. Eye movement control in primates. *Science,* 1968, *161,* 1219–1224.

Robinson, R. G. Differential behavioral and biochemical effects of right and left hemispheric cerebral infarction in the rat. *Science,* 1979, *205,* 707–710.

Robinson, G. M. & Solomon, D. J. Rhythm is processed by the speech hemisphere. *Journal of Experimental Psychology,* 1974, *102,* 508–511.

Rodin, J., & Singer, J. L. Eye-shift, thought, and obesity. *Journal of Personality,* 1976, *44,* 594–610.

Rogers, L. J. Functional lateralization in the forebrain revealed by cycloheximide treatment. *Proceedings of the 17th International Ornithological Congress, West Berlin, 1980.*

Rogers, L. J., & Anson, J. M. Lateralization of function in the chicken fore-brain, 1979, *19,* 679–686.

Rosenberger, P. B., & Hier, D. B. Cerebral asymmetry and verbal intellectual deficits. *Annals of Neurology,* 1980, *8,* 300–304.

Rosenblum, D. R., & Dorman, M. F. Hemispheric specialization for speech perception in language deficient kindergarten children. *Brain and Language,* 1978, *6,* 378–389.

Rosenfield, D. B., & Goodglass, H. Dichotic testing of cerebral dominance in stutterers. *Brain and Language,* 1980, *11,* 170–180.

Rosenzweig, M. R. Representations of the two ears at the auditory cortex. *American Journal of Physiology,* 1951, *167,* 147.

Rosner, B. G. Recovery of function and localization of function in historical perspective. In D. G. Stein, J. J. Rosen, & N. Butters, *Plasticity and recovery of function in the nervous system.* New York: Academic Press, 1974.

Rossi, G. F., & Rosadini, G. Experimental analysis of cerebral dominance in man. In C. F. Millikan & F. L. Darley (Eds.), *Brain mechanisms underlying speech and language.* New York: Grune & Stratton, 1967.

Roth, M. Senile dementia and its borderlands. In J. O. Cole & J. E. Parrett (Eds.), *Psychopathology and the aged.* New York: Raven Press, 1980.

Roth, W. T., Kopell, B. S., & Bertozzi, P. E. The effect of attention on the average evoked response to speech sounds. *Electroencephalography and Clinical Neurophysiology,* 1970, *29,* 38–46.

Rourke, B. P. Central processing deficiencies in children: Toward a developmental neuropsychological model. *Journal of Clinical Neuropsychology,* 1982, *4,* 1–18.

Rubens, A. B. Anatomical asymmetries of human cerebral cortex. In S. Harnad, R. W. Doty, L. Goldstein, J. Jaynes, & G. Krauthamer (Eds.), *Lateralization in the nervous system.* New York: Academic Press, 1977.

Rudel, R. G. Neuroplasticity: Implications for development and education. In J. S. Chall & A. F. Mirsky (Eds.), *Education and the brain* (Yearbook of the National Society for the Study of Education). Chicago, Ill.: University of Chicago Press, 1978.

Rudel, R. G., & Denckla, M. B. Feeling our way toward a theory of hemispheric asymmetry: Braille studies continued. In M. Hiscock (Chair), *Hemispheric specialization in the developing brain.* Symposium presented at the meeting of the International Neuropsychological Society, New York, 1979.

Rudel, R. G., Denckla, M. B., & Hirsch, S. The development of left-hand superiority for discriminating Braille configurations. *Neurology,* 1977, *27,* 160–164.

Rudel, R. G., Denckla, M. B., & Spalten, E. The functional asymmetry of Braille letter learning in normal-sighted children. *Neurology,* 1976, *24,* 733–738.

Ruhm, H. B. Lateral specificity of acoustically evoked EEG responses. I. Non-verbal, non-meaningful stimuli. *Journal of Auditory Research,* 1971, *11,* 1–8.

Russell, W. R., & Espir, M. L. E. *Traumatic aphasia. A study of aphasia in war wounds of the brain.* London: Oxford University Press, 1961.

Russo, M., & Vignolo, V. A. Visual figure-ground discrimination in patients with unilateral cerebral disease. *Cortex,* 1967, *3,* 113–127.

Rutter, M. The concept of dyslexia. *Clinical Developmental Medicine,* 1969, *33,* 129–139.

Rutter, M., & Bartak, L. Causes of infantile autism: Some considerations from recent research. *Journal of Autism and Childhood Schizophrenia,* 1971, *1,* 20–32.

Ryan, W. J., & McNeil, M. Listener reliability for a dichotic task. *Journal of Acoustical Society of America,* 1974, *56,* 1922–1923.

Sackheim, H., Greenberg, M. S., Weiman, A. L., Gur, R. C., Hungerbaken, J. P., & Geschwind, N. Hemispheric asymmetry in the expression of positive and negative emotions. *Archives of Neurology,* 1982, *39,* 210–218.

Sadick, T., & Ginsburg, B. The development of lateral functions and reading ability. *Cortex,* 1978, *14,* 3–11.

Sameroff, A. J., & Chandler, M. J. Reproduction risk and the continuum of caretaking casualty. In F. D. Horowitz, E. M. Hetherington, S. Scarr-Salapatek, & G. M. Siegel (Eds.), *Review of child development research* (Vol. 4). Chicago: University of Chicago Press, 1975.

Sampson, H. Recall of digits projected to temporal and nasal hemiretinas. *Quarterly Journal of Experimental Psychology,* 1969, *21,* 39–42.

Sampson, H., & Spong, P. Handedness, eye-dominance, and immediate memory. *Quarterly Journal of Experimental Psychology,* 1961, *13,* 173–180.

Samuels, M., Hiscock, M., & Kinsbourne, M. Development of strategies for recalling letter sequences. *Journal of Experimental Child Psychology,* 1978, *25,* 298–314.

Säring, W., & von Cramon, D. Is there an interaction between cognitive activity and lateral eye movements? *Neuropsychologia,* 1980, *18,* 591–596.

Sarnat, H., & Netsky, M. G. *Evolution of the nervous system.* New York: Oxford University Press, 1974.

Satz, P. Pathological left-handedness: An explanatory model. *Cortex,* 1972, *8,* 121–135.

Satz, P. Left-handedness and early brain insult: An explanation. *Neuropsychologia,* 1973, *11,*

115–117.

Satz, P. Cerebral dominance and reading disability: An old problem revisited. In R. M. Knights & D. J. Bakker (Eds.), *The neuropsychology of learning disorders*. Baltimore: University Park Press, 1976.

Satz, P. Laterality tests: An inferential problem. *Cortex,* 1977, *13,* 208–212.

Satz, P. A test of some models of hemispheric speech organization in the left- and right-handed. *Science,* 1979, *203,* 1131–1133.

Satz, P., Achenbach, K., Pattishall, E., & Fennell, E. Order of report, ear asymmetry and handedness in dichotic listening. *Cortex,* 1965, *1,* 377–396.

Satz, P., Bakker, D. J., Teunisson, J., Goebel, R., & Van der Vlugt, H. Developmental parameters of the ear asymmetry: A multivariate approach. *Brain and Language,* 1975, *2,* 171–185.

Satz, P., & Bullard-Bates, C. Acquired aphasia in children. In M. T. Sarno (Ed.), *Acquired Aphasia*. New York: Academic Press, 1981.

Satz, P., Fletcher, J. M., Clark, W., & Morris, R. Lag, deficit, delay, and rate constructs in learning disability: A re-examination. In A. Ansara, N. Geschwind, A. M. Galaburda, M. L. Albert, & N. Gartrell (Eds.), *Sex differences in dyslexia.* New York: Orton Dyslexia Society, 1981.

Satz, P., & Morris, R. Learning disability subtypes: A review. In F. J. Pirozzolo & M. C. Wittrock (Eds.), *Neuropsychological and cognitive processes in reading*. New York: Academic Press, 1981.

Satz, P., Taylor, H. G., Friel, J., & Fletcher, J. M. Some developmental and predictive precursors of reading disabilities: A six-year follow-up. In D. Pearl & A. Benton (Eds.), *Dyslexia: A critical appraisal of current theory*. New York: Oxford University Press, 1978.

Satz, P., & Van Nostrand, G. K. Developmental dyslexia: An evaluation of a theory. In P. Satz & J. Ross (Eds.), *The disabled learner: Early detection and intervention*. Rotterdam: Rotterdam University Press, 1973.

Saul, R. E., & Gott, P. S. Language and speech lateralization by amytal and dichotic listening tests in agenesis of the corpus callosum. In D. O. Walter, L. Rogers, & J. M. Finzi-Fried (Eds.), *Conference* on *human brain function*. Los Angeles: Brain Information Service, UCLA, 1976.

Saul, R. E., & Sperry, R. W. Absence of commissurotomy symptoms with agenesis of the corpus callosum. *Neurology,* 1968, *18,* 307.

Schiller, P. H., True, S. D., & Conway, J. L. Effects of frontal eye field and superior colliculus ablations on eye movements. *Science,* 1979, *206,* 590–592.

Schneider, G. E. Mechanisms of functional recovery following lesions of visual cortex or superior colliculus in neonate and adult hamsters. *Brain, Behavior and Evolution,* 1970, *3,* 295–323.

Schneider, G. E., & Jhaveri, S. R. Neuroanatomical correlates of spared or altered function after brain lesions in the newborn hamster. In D. G. Stein, J. J. Rosen, & N. Butters, *Plasticity and recovery of function in the nervous system.* New York: Academic Press, 1974.

Schneider, W., & Shiffrin, R. M. Controlled and automatic human information processing: I. Detection, search, and attention. *Psychological Review,* 1977, *84,* 1–88.

Scholes, R. J., & Fischler, I. Hemispheric function and linguistic skills in the deaf. *Brain and Language,* 1979, *7,* 336–350.

Schulman-Galambos, C. Dichotic listening performance in elementary and college students. *Neuropsychologia,* 1977, *15,* 577–584.

Schwartz, G. E., Davidson, R. J., & Maer, F. Right hemisphere lateralization for emotion in the human brain: Interactions with cognition. *Science,* 1975, *190,* 286–288.

Schwartz, M. Left-handedness and high risk pregnancy. *Neuropsychologia,* 1977, *15,* 341–344.

Schwartz, M. Inconsistencies and problems with visual asymmetries. In M. Schwartz & M. Hiscock (Chair), *Progress and problems of the study of human laterality.* Symposium presented at the Canadian Psychological Association, Calgary, Canada, 1980.

Seamon, J. G., & Gazzaniga, M. S. Coding strategies and cerebral laterality effects. *Cognitive Psychology,* 1973, *5,* 249–256.

Searleman, A. A review of right hemisphere linguistic capabilities. *Psychological Bulletin,* 1977, *84,* 503–528.

Searleman, A., Porac, C., & Coren, S. The relationship between birth stress and writing hand posture. *Brain and Cognition,* 1982, *1,* 158–164.

Segalowitz, S. J., & Chapman, J. S. Cerebral asymmetry for speech in neonates: A behavioral measure. *Brain and Language,* 1980, *9,* 281–288.

Segalowitz, S. J., & Gruber, F. A. (Eds.), *Language development and neurological theory.* New York: Academic Press, 1977.

Semmes, J. Hemispheric specialization: A possible cue to mechanism. *Neuropsychologia,* 1968, *6,* 11–26.

Sergent, J., & Bindra, D. Differential hemispheric processing of faces: Methodological considerations and reinterpretation. *Psychological Bul-*

letin, 1981, *89,* 541–554.

Seth, G. Eye-hand co-ordination and "handedness": A developmental study of visuomotor behavior in infancy. *British Journal of Educational Psychology,* 1973, *43,* 35–49.

Shankweiler, D. P., & Studdert-Kennedy, M. Identification of consonants and vowels presented to left and right ears. *Quarterly Journal of Psychology,* 1967, *19,* 59–63.

Shankweiler, D. P., & Studdert-Kennedy, M. A continuum of lateralization for speech perception? *Brain and Language,* 1975, *2,* 212–225.

Shelburne, S. A., Jr., Visual evoked responses to word and nonsense syllable stimuli. *Electroencephalography and Clinical Neurophysiology,* 1972, *32,* 17–25.

Shelburne, S. A., Jr., Visual evoked responses to language stimuli in normal children. *Electroencephalography and Clinical Neurophysiology,* 1973, *34,* 135–143.

Sherman, G. F., Garbanati, J. A., Rosen, G. D., Yutzey, D. A., & Denenberg, V. H. Brain and behavioral asymmetries for spatial preference in rats. *Brain Research,* 1980, *192,* 61–67.

Shiffrin, R. M., & Schneider, W. Controlled and automatic information processing II. Perceptual learning, automatic attending, and a general theory. *Psychological Review,* 1977, *84,* 127–190.

Shucard, J. L., Shucard, D. W., Cummins, K. R., & Campos, J. J. Auditory evoked potentials and sex related differences in brain development. *Brain and Language,* 1981, *13,* 91–102.

Silverberg, R., & Gordon, H. W. Differential aphasia in two bilingual individuals. *Neurology,* 1979, *29,* 51–55.

Simon, J. R. Ear preference in a simple reaction-time task. *Journal of Experimental Psychology,* 1967, *75,* 49–55.

Simon, J. R., Hinrichs, J. V., & Croft, J. L. Auditory S-R compatibility: Reaction time as a function of ear-hand correspondence and ear-response-location correspondence. *Journal of Experimental Psychology,* 1970, *86,* 97–102.

Siqueland, E. R., & Lipsitt, L. P. Conditioned head turning in human newborns. *Journal of Experimental Child Psychology,* 1966, *4,* 356–357.

Slorach, N., & Noehr, B. Dichotic listening in stuttering and dyslalic children. *Cortex,* 1973, *9,* 293–300.

Smith, A. Certain hypothesized hemispheric differences in language and visual functions in human adults. *Cortex,* 1966, *2,* 109–126.

Smith, A. The symbol-digit modalities test: A neuropsychologic test of learning and other cerebral disorders. In J. Helmuth (Ed.), *Learning disorders* (Vol. 3). Seattle: Special Child Publications, 1968.

Smith, A. Dominant and nondominant hemispherectomy. In W. S. Smith (Ed.), *Drugs, development and cerebral function.* Springfield, Ill.: Charles C. Thomas, 1974.

Smith, A. Neuropsychological testing in neurological disorders. In W. J. Friedlander (Ed.), *Advances in neurology* (Vol. 7). New York: Raven Press, 1975.

Smith, J. M. Which hand is the eye of the blind? *Genetic Psychology Monographs,* 1929, *5,* 209–252.

Smokler, I. A., & Shevrin, H. Central lateralization and personality style. *Archives of General Psychiatry,* 1979, *36,* 949–954.

Soares, C. Converging evidence for left hemisphere language lateralization in bilinguals: use of the concurrent activities paradigm. Manuscript in preparation.

Soares, C., & Grosjean, G. Left hemisphere language lateralization in bilinguals and monolinguals. *Perception & Psychophysics,* 1981, *29,* 599–604.

Sommers, R. K., Brady, W. A., & Moore, W. H. Dichotic ear preferences of stuttering children and adults. *Perceptual and Motor Skills,* 1975, *41,* 931–938.

Sommers, R., & Taylor, L. Cerebral speech dominance in language-disordered and normal children. *Cortex,* 1972, *8,* 224–232.

Sparrow, S. S. Reading disability and laterality. *Proceedings of the 77th Convention of American Psychological Association* (Vol. 4). 1969.

Sparrow, S. S., & Satz, P. Dyslexia, laterality and neuropsychological development. In D. J. Bakker & P. Satz (Eds.), *Specific reading disability: Advances in theory and method.* Rotterdam: Rotterdam University Press, 1970.

Spellacy, F. J., & Blumstein, S. The influence of language set on ear preference in phoneme recognition. *Cortex,* 1970, *6,* 430–439.

Sperry, R. W. The great cerebral commissure. *Scientific American,* 1964, *210,* 42.

Sperry, R. W. Hemispheric disconnection and unity in conscious awareness. *American Psychologist,* 1968, *23,* 723–733.

Spiegler, B., & Yeni-Komshian, G. H. Birth trauma and left-handedness: Test of a theory. Paper presented at the meeting of the International Neuropsychological Society, Pittsburgh, February 1982.

Sprague, J. M. Interaction of cortex and superior colliculus in mediation of visually guided behavior in the cat. *Science,* 1966, *153,* 1544–1547.

Springer, S. P., & Eisenson, J. Hemispheric specialization for speech in language disordered children. *Neuropsychologia,* 1977, *15,* 287–293.

Starkey, K. A dichotic test for subjects having limited functional speech and writing abilities. Paper to the American Speech and Hearning Association, Las Vegas, 1974.

Starr, A., & Achor, L. J. Auditory brainstem responses in neurological disease. *Archives of Neurology,* 1975, *32,* 761–768.

Stein, D. G., Rosen, J. J., & Butters, N. *Plasticity and recovery of function in the nervous system.* New York: Academic Press, 1974.

Stockard, J. J., & Rossiter, V. S. Clinical and pathological correlates of brainstem auditory response abnormalities. *Neurology,* 1977, *27,* 316–325.

Stone, M. A. Measures of laterality and spurious correlation. *Neuropsychologia,* 1980, *18,* 339–345.

Strausbaugh, L., Kinsbourne, M., & Languis, M. Do dyslexics have deficient interhemispheric communication? In preparation, 1983.

Strauss, E., & Kinsbourne, M. Does age of menarche affect the ultimate level of verbal and spatial skills? *Cortex,* 1981, *17,* 323–325.

Studdert-Kennedy, M. Dichotic studies II: Two questions. *Brain and Language,* 1975, *2,* 123–130.

Studdert-Kennedy, M., & Shankweiler, D. P. Hemispheric specialization for speech perception. *Journal of the Acoustical Society of America,* 1970, *48,* 579–594.

Studdert-Kennedy, M., Shankweiler, D. P., & Pisoni, D. Auditory and phonetic processes in speech perception: Evidence from a dichotic study. *Cognitive Psychology,* 1972, *3,* 455–466.

Studdert-Kennedy, M., Shankweiler, D. P., & Schulman, S. Opposed effects of a delayed channel on perception of dichotically and monotically presented CV syllables. *Journal of the Acoustical Society of America,* 1970, *48,* 599–602.

Subirana, A. The prognosis of aphasia in relation to cerebral dominance and handedness. *Brain,* 1958, *81,* 415–425.

Summers, J. J., & Sharp, C. A. Bilateral effects of concurrent verbal and spatial rehearsal on complex motor sequencing. *Neuropsychologia,* 1979, *17,* 331–343.

Sussman, H. M. Contrastive patterns of intrahemispheric interference to verbal and spatial concurrent tasks in right-handed, left-handed and stuttering populations. *Neuropsychologia,* 1982, *20,* 675–684.

Sussman, H., Franklin, P., & Simon, T. Bilingual speech, bilateral control. *Brain and Language,* 1982, *15,* 125–142.

Sussman, H. M., & MacNeilage, P. F. Hemispheric specialization for speech production and perception in stutterers. *Neuropsychologia,* 1975, *13,* 19–37.

Swanson, J. M., & Kinsbourne, M. *S-R compatibility and interhemispheric transfer time.* Paper presented at the meeting of the American Psychological Association, Washington, D.C., August 1976.

Swanson, J. M., Kinsbourne, M., & Horn, J. M. Cognitive deficit and left-handedness: A cautionary note. In J. Herron (Ed.), *Neuropsychology of left-handedness.* New York: Academic Press, 1980.

Swanson, J. M., Ledlow, A., & Kinsbourne, M. Lateral asymmetries revealed by simple reaction time. In M. Kinsbourne (Ed.), *Asymmetrical function of the brain.* New York: Cambridge University Press, 1978.

Syndulko, K. Relationships between motor potentials and CNV. *Electroencephalography and Clinical Neurophysiology,* 1969, *27,* 706.

Syndulko, K. *Cortical slow potential shifts in humans during sensory and motor tasks.* Unpublished doctoral dissertation, University of California, Los Angeles, 1972.

Taylor, J. (Ed.). *Selected writings of John Hughlings Jackson* (Vol. 2). London: Hodder & Stoughton, 1932.

Teitelbaum, H. A. Spontaneous rhythmic ocular movements. Their possible relation to mental activity. *Neurology,* 1954, *4,* 350–354.

Teng, E. L. Dichotic ear difference is a poor index for the functional asymmetry between the cerebral hemispheres. *Neuropsychologia,* 1981, *19,* 235–240.

Terrace, H. S. The effects of retinal locus and attention on the perception of words. *Journal of Experimental Psychology,* 1959, *58,* 382–385.

Terzian, H. Behavioral and EEG effects of intracarotid sodium amytal injection. *Acta Neurochirurgica,* 1964, *12,* 230–239.

Teszner, D., Tzavaras, A., Gruner, J., & Hécaen, H. L'asymétrie droite-gauche du planum temporale. A propos de l'étude anatomique de 100 cerveaux. *Revue Neurologique,* 1972, *126,* 444–449.

Teyler, T., Harrison, T., Roemer, R., & Thompson, R. Human scalp recorded evoked potential correlates of linguistic stimuli. *Journal of the Psychonomic Society Bulletin,* 1973, *1,*

333–334.

Thatcher, R. W. Evoked-potential correlates of hemispheric lateralization during semantic information-processing. In Harnad, S., Doty, R. W., Goldstein, L., Jaynes, J., & Krauthamer, G. (Eds.), *Lateralization in the nervous system.* New York: Academic Press, 1977.

Thornton, C. D., & Peters, M. Interference between concurrent speaking and sequential finger tapping: Both hands show a performance decrement under both visual and nonvisual guidance. *Neuropsychologia,* 1982, *20,* 163–169.

Tobey, E. A., Cullen, J. P., Jr., & Rampp, D. L. Performance of children with auditory-processing disorders on a dichotic, stop-vowel identification task. Paper presented at the meeting of the International Neuropsychological Society, Toronto, February 1976.

Todd, J., Coolidge, F., & Satz, P. The Wechsler adult intelligence scale discrepancy index: A neuropsychological evaluation. *Journal of Consulting and Clinical Psychology,* 1977, *45,* 450–454.

Tomatis, A. A. *Education et dyslexie.* Paris: Editions E.S.F., 1972. (Translated as *Education and dyslexia*) Montreal: France-Quebec Editions, 1978.)

Tomlinson-Keasey, C., & Clarkson-Smith, L. *What develops in hemispheric specialization?* Paper presented at the meeting of the International Neuropsychological Society, San Francisco, February 1980.

Tomlinson-Keasey, C., Kelly, R. R., & Burton, J. K. Hemispheric changes in information processing during development. *Developmental Psychology,* 1978, *14,* 214–223.

Towbin, A. Cerebral dysfunctions related to perinatal organic damage: Clinical-neuropathologic correlations. *Journal of Abnormal Psychology,* 1978, *87,* 617–635.

Travis, L. E. *Speech pathology.* New York: Appleton-Century, 1931.

Trehub, S. E., & Rabinovitch, M. S. Auditory-linguistic sensitivity in early infancy. *Developmental Psychology,* 1972, *6,* 74–77.

Trevarthen, C. Functional relations of disconnected hemispheres with the brain stem and with each other: Monkey and man. In M. Kinsbourne & W. L. Smith (Eds.), *Hemispheric disconnection and cerebral function.* Springfield, Ill.: Charles C. Thomas, 1974.

Trevarthen, C. Manipulative strategies of baboons and origins of cerebral asymmetry. In M. Kinsbourne (Ed.), *Asymmetrical function of the brain.* New York: Cambridge University Press, 1978.

Tsai, L., Jacoby, C. G., Stewart, M. A., & Beisler, J. M. Unfavorable left-right asymmetries of the brain and autism: A question of methodology. *British Journal of Psychiatry,* 1982, *140,* 312–319.

Tucker, D. M. Sex differences in hemispheric specialization for synthetic visuospatial functions. *Neuropsychologia,* 1976, *14,* 447–454.

Tucker, D. M. Lateral brain function, emotion, and conceptualization. *Psychological Bulletin,* 1981, *89,* 19–46.

Tucker, D. M., Roth, R. S., Arneson, B. A., & Buckingham, V. Hemisphere activation during stress. *Neuropsychologia,* 1977, *15,* 697–700.

Turkewitz, G., Gordon, E. W., & Birch, H. G. Head turning in the human neonate: Effect of prandial condition and lateral preference. *Journal of Comparative and Physiological Psychology,* 1965, *59,* 189–192. (a)

Turkewitz, G., Gordon, E. W., & Birch, H. G. Head turning in the human neonate. Spontaneous patterns. *Journal of Genetic Psychology,* 1965, *107,* 143–148. (b)

Turkewitz, G., Moreau, T., Birch, H. G., & Crystal, D. Relationship between prior head position and lateral differences in responsiveness to somesthetic stimulation in the human neonate. *Journal of Experimental Child Psychology,* 1967, *5,* 548–561.

Vandenberg, S. G., & Kuse, A. R. Mental rotations, a group test of three-dimensional spatial visualization. *Perceptual and Motor Skills,* 1978, *47,* 599–604.

Van Dongen, H. R., & Loonen, M. C. Factors related to prognosis of acquired aphasia in children. *Cortex,* 1977, *13,* 131–136.

Van Lancker, D., & Fromkin, V. A. Hemispheric specialization of pitch and "tone." Evidence from Thai. *Journal of Phonetics,* 1977, *1,* 101–109.

Vargha-Khadem, F., & Corballis, M. C. Cerebral asymmetry in infants. *Brain and Language,* 1979, *8,* 1–9.

Vasta, R., Regan, K. G., & Kerley, J. Sex differences in pattern copying: spatial cues or motor skills. *Child Development,* 1980, *51,* 932–934.

Vaughan, H. G., Costa, L. D., & Ritter, W. Topography of the human motor potential. *Electroencephalography and Clinical Neurophysiology,* 1968, *25,* 1–10.

Vaughan, H. G., & Ritter, W. The sources of auditory evoked responses recorded from the human scalp. *Electroencephalography and Clinical Neurophysiology*, 1970, *28*, 360–367.

Vellutino, F. R. Toward an understanding of dyslexia: Psychological factors in specific reading disability. In A. L. Benton & D. Pearl (Eds.), *Dyslexia: An appraisal of current knowledge*. New York: Oxford University Press, 1978.

Vellutino, F. R. *Dyslexia, theory and research*. Cambridge: MIT Press, 1979.

Vellutino, F. R., Bentley, W., & Phillips, F. Inter-versus intra-hemispheric learning in dyslexic and normal readers. *Developmental Medicine and Child Neurology*, 1978, *20*, 71–80.

Viviani, J., Turkewitz, G., & Karp, E. A relationship between laterality of functioning at 2 days and at 7 years of age. *Psychonomic Science*, 1978, *12*, 189–192.

von Economo, C., & Horn, J. L. Über Windingsrelief, Masse und Rindenarchitektonik der Supratemporalfläche, ihre Individuellen und ihre Seitenunterschiede. *Zentralblatt für die Gesamte Neurologie und Psychiatrie*, 1930, *130*, 687–757.

von Monakow, C. *Die Lokalisation im Grosshirrinde und der Abbau der Funktion durch korticale Herde*. Wiesbaden, W. Germany: J. F. Bergmann, 1914.

Waber, D. P. Sex differences in mental abilities, hemispheric lateralization and rate of physical growth at adolescence. *Developmental Psychology*, 1977, *13*, 29–38.

Waber, D. P., Bauermeister, M., Cohen, C., Ferber, R., & Wolff, P. H. Behavioral correlates of physical and neuromotor maturity in adolescents from different environments. *Developmental Psychobiology*, 1981, *14*, 513–522.

Wada, J. A. Pre-language and fundamental asymmetry of the infant brain. *Annals of the New York Academy of Sciences*, 1977, *299*, 370–379.

Wada, J. A., Clarke, R., & Hamm, A. Cerebral hemispheric symmetry in humans. *Archives of Neurology*, 1975, *32*, 239–246.

Wada, J. A., & Davis, A. E. Fundamental nature of human infants' brain asymmetry. *Canadian Journal of Neurological Sciences*, 1977, *4*, 203–207.

Wada, J. A., & Rasmussen, T. Intracarotid injection of sodium amytal for the lateralization of cerebral speech dominance. *Journal of Neurosurgery*, 1960, *17*, 266–282.

Wagner, N. M., & Harris, L. J. *Hand asymmetries in braille letter learning in sighted nine- and eleven-year-olds: A cautionary note on sex differences*. Paper presented at the meeting of the International Neuropsychological Society, New York, February 1979.

Wallace, R. J. S-R compatibility and the idea of a response code. *Journal of Experimental Psychology*, 1971, *88*, 354–360.

Walter, W. G. The localization of cerebral tumors by electroencephalography. *Lancet*, 1936, *2*, 305–312.

Walter, W. G., Cooper, R., Aldridge, V. J., McCallum, W. C., & Winter, A. L. Contingent negative variation: An electric sign of sensorimotor association and expectancy in the human brain. *Nature*, 1964, *203*, 380–384.

Walters, J., & Zatorre, R. J. Laterality differences for word identification in bilinguals. *Brain and Language*, 1978, *6*, 158–167.

Warren, I. R., Peltz, L., & Haueter, E. S. Patterns of EEG alpha during word processing and relations to recall. *Brain and Language*, 1976, *3*, 283–291.

Warrington, E. K., & James, M. An experimental investigation of facial recognition in patients with cerebral lesions. *Cortex*, 1967, *3*, 317–326.

Warrington, E. K., & Pratt, R. T. C. Language laterality in left-handers assessed by unilateral E.C.T. *Neuropsychologia*, 1973, *11*, 423–428.

Watamori, T. S., & Sasanuma, S. The recovery processes of two English-Japanese bilingual aphasics. *Brain and Language*, 1978, *6*, 127–140.

Watson, W. E., Elias, M. F., & Pentz, C. A. Hemisphere-hand interactions for the matching of letters. *Experimental Aging Research*, 1975, *1*, 293–305.

Webster, W. G., & Thurber, A. D. Problem-solving strategies and manifest brain asymmetry. *Cortex*, 1978, *14*, 474–484.

Weiner, S. L., & Ehrlichman, H. Ocular motility and cognitive process. *Cognition*, 1976, *4*, 31–43.

Weinstein, E. A., & Friedland, R. P. (Eds.), *Advances in Neurology*, vol. 18, *Hemi-inattention and hemispheric specialization*. New York: Raven Press, 1977.

Weir, K., & Salisbury, D. M. Acute onset of autistic features following their change in a ten-year-old child. *Journal of Autism and Developmental Disorders*, 1980, *10*, 185–191.

Weiten, W., & Etaugh, C. F. Lateral eye movement as related to verbal and perceptual-motor skills and values. *Perceptual and Motor Skills*, 1973, *36*, 423–428.

Weiten, W., & Etaugh, C. F. Lateral eye movement as a function of cognitive mode, question sequence, and sex of subject. *Perceptual and Motor Skills,* 1974, *38,* 439–444.

Welford, A. T. *Fundamentals of skill.* London: Methuen, 1968.

Whitaker, H. A. *Current problems in neurolinguistics.* Augusta, Ga.: North Atlantic Treaty Organization Advanced Study Institute, 1980.

White, M. J. Identification and localization within digit and letter spans. *Psychonomic Science,* 1969, *14,* 279–280. (a)

White, M. J. Laterality differences in perception: A review. *Psychological Bulletin,* 1969, *72,* 387–405. (b)

White, M. J. Order of report and letter structure in tachistoscopic recognition. *Psychonomic Science,* 1969, *17,* 364–365. (c)

White, M. J. Visual field differences and the recognition of alphanumeric material. *Australian Journal of Psychology,* 1969, *21,* 311–317. (d)

White, M. J. Retinal locus and the letter span error function. *Perception & Psychophysics,* 1970, *8,* 107–109.

White, M. J. Hemispheric asymmetries in tachistoscopic information-processing. *British Journal of Psychology,* 1972, *63,* 497–508.

White, M. J. Does cerebral dominance offer a sufficient explanation for laterality differences in tachistoscopic recognition? *Perceptual and Motor Skills,* 1973, *36,* 479–485. (a)

White, M. J. Vocal and manual response latencies to bilateral and unilateral tachistoscopic letter displays. *Quarterly Journal of Experimental Psychology,* 1973, *25,* 41–47. (b)

White, N., & Kinsbourne, M. Does speech output control lateralization over time? Evidence from verbal-manual time-sharing tasks. *Brain and Language,* 1980, *10,* 215–223.

Willems, A. L. Beginning reading: Are we doing only half the job? *Kappa Delta Pi Record,* April 1979, 124–126.

Wilson, J. R., DeFries, J. C., McClearn, G. E., Vandenberg, S. G., Johnson, R. C., & Rashad, M. N. Cognitive abilities: Use of family data as a control to assess sex and age differences in two ethnic groups. *International Journal of Aging and Development,* 1975, *6,* 261–276.

Wilson, M. O., & Dolan, L. B. Handedness and ability. *American Journal of Psychology,* 1931, *43,* 261–268.

Witelson, S. F. Hemispheric specialization for linguistic and nonlinguistic tactual perception using a dichotomous stimulation technique. *Cortex,* 1974, *10,* 3–17.

Witelson, S. F. Abnormal right hemisphere specialization in developmental dyslexia. In R. M. Knights & D. J. Bakker (Eds.), *The neuropsychology of learning disorders.* Baltimore: University Park Press, 1976. (a)

Witelson, S. F. Sex and the single hemisphere: Right hemisphere specialization for spatial processing. *Science,* 1976, *193,* 425–427. (b)

Witelson, S. F. Developmental dyslexia: Two right hemispheres and none left. *Science,* 1977, *195,* 309–311. (a)

Witelson, S. F. Neural and cognitive correlates of developmental dyslexia: Age and sex differences. In C. Shagass, S. Gershon, & A. J. Friedhoff (Eds.), *Psychopathology and brain dysfunction.* New York: Raven Press, 1977. (b)

Witelson, S. F., & Pallie, W. Left hemisphere specialization for language in the newborn: Neuroanatomical evidence of asymmetry. *Brain,* 1973, *96,* 641–646.

Witelson, S. F., & Rabinovitch, M. S. Children's recall strategies in dichotic listening. *Journal of Experimental Child Psychology,* 1971, *12,* 106–113.

Witkin, H. A., Goodenough, D. R., & Karp, S. A. Stability of cognitive style from childhood to young adulthood. *Journal of Personality and Social Psychology,* 1967, *7,* 291–300.

Witty, P. A., & Kopel, D. Sinistral and mixed manual-ocular behavior in reading disability. *Journal of Educational Psychology,* 1936, *27,* 119–134.

Wolff, P. H., & Cohen, C. Dual task performance during bimanual co-ordination. *Cortex,* 1980, *16,* 119–133.

Wood, C. C., Goff W. R., & Day, R. S. Auditory evoked potentials during speech perception. *Science,* 1971, *173,* 1248–1251.

Woods, B. T. The restricted effects of right-hemisphere lesions after age one: Wechsler test data. *Neuropsychologia,* 1980, *18,* 65–70.

Woods, B. T., & Teuber, H. L. Changing patterns of childhood aphasia. *Annals of Neurology,* 1978, *3,* 273–280. (a)

Woods, B. T., & Teuber, H. L. Mirror movements after childhood paresis. *Neurology,* 1978, *28,* 1152–1158. (b)

Wyke, M., & Ettlinger, G. Efficiency of recognition in left and right visual fields. *Archives of Neurology,* 1961, *5,* 95–101.

Yakovlev, P. I., & Lecours, A. R. The myelogenetic cycles of regional development of the brain. In A. Minkowski (Ed.), *Regional development of the brain in early life: Symposium.* Oxford: Blackwell, 1967.

Yanowitz, J. S., Willmore, L. J., & Rice, W. J.

Clinical correlates of early brain damage: Relationship between EEG and pedal asymmetry as indices of hemispheric laterality and pathological left-handedness. Paper presented at the meeting of the International Neuropsychological Society, Pittsburgh, February 1982.

Yeni-Komshian, G. H., & Benson, D. A. Anatomical study of cerebral asymmetry in the temporal lobe of humans, chimpanzees and Rhesus monkeys. *Science,* 1976, *192,* 387–389.

Yeni-Komshian, G. H., Isenberg, S., & Goldberg, H. Cerebral dominance and reading disability: Left visual field deficit in poor readers. *Neuropsychologia,* 1975, *13,* 83–94.

Young, A. W., & Bion, P. J. Hemispheric laterality effects in the enumeration of visually presented collections of dots by children. *Neuropsychologia,* 1979, *17,* 99–102.

Young, A. W., & Ellis, A. W. Asymmetry of cerebral hemispheric function in normal and poor readers. *Psychological Bulletin,* 1981, *89,* 183–190.

Young, A. W., & Ellis, H. D. An experimental investigation of developmental differences in ability to recognize faces presented to the left and right cerebral hemispheres. *Neuropsychologia,* 1976, *14,* 495–498.

Young, G. Manual specialization in infancy: Implications for lateralization of brain function. In S. J. Segalowitz & F. A. Gruber (Eds.), *Language development and neurological theory.* New York: Academic Press, 1977.

Zaidel, E. Auditory language comprehension in the right hemisphere following cerebral commissurotomy and hemispherectomy: A comparison with child language and aphasia. In A. Caramazza & E. B. Zurif (Eds.), *Language acquisition and language breakdown: Parallels and divergencies.* Baltimore: The Johns Hopkins University Press, 1978. (a)

Zaidel, E. Lexical organization in the right hemisphere. In P. Buser & A. Rougeul-Buser (Eds.), *Cerebral correlates of conscious experience.* Amsterdam: Elsevier, 1978. (b)

Zangwill, O. L. Discussion on parietal lobe syndromes. *Proceedings of the Royal Society of Medicine,* 1951, *44,* 343–346.

Zangwill, O. L. *Cerebral dominance and its relation to psychological function.* London: Oliver & Boyd, 1960.

Zangwill, O. L. Dyslexia in relation to cerebral dominance. In J. Money (Ed.), *Reading disability.* Baltimore: The Johns Hopkins University Press, 1962.

Zangwill, O. L. Speech and the minor hemisphere. *Acta Neurologica et Psychiatrica Belgica,* 1967, *67,* 1013–1020.

Zimmerman, G., & Knott, J. R. Slow potentials of the brain related to speech in normal speakers and stutterers. *Electroencephalography and Clinical Neurophysiology,* 1974, *37,* 599–607.

THE NEUROBIOLOGY OF COGNITIVE DEVELOPMENT* | 5

PATRICIA S. GOLDMAN-RAKIC, AMI ISSEROFF, MICHAEL L. SCHWARTZ, NELLIE M. BUGBEE, *Yale University School of Medicine*

CHAPTER CONTENTS

*Preparation of this chapter was supported by PHS Grants NS-16666 and MH-00298.

INTRODUCTION

Researchers in developmental psychology have accumulated a large store of behavioral information concerning the ontogeny of cognitive abilities in children. However, comparatively little is known about the neurological bases of these abilities or about the errors of biological development that can cause children to become autistic, schizophrenic, or mentally retarded. In the past few years, the prospects for relating biological structure to higher order functions have changed dramatically, and significant progress has been made in describing the anatomical, biochemical, and functional properties of systems that subserve cognition in experimental animals and in humans. The present chapter focuses on developments in understanding the role of prefrontal association cortex in the cognitive development of nonhuman primates. We have chosen this area for several reasons. First and foremost, the integrity of prefrontal association cortex is essential for organization and continuity of behavior toward the achievement of future goals (e.g., Brickner, 1936; Denny-Brown, 1951; Luria, 1966; Pribram & Luria, 1974). As such, no subject could be of greater interest for students of child development and human potential. Second, in humans, this phylogenetically significant area occupies a larger proportion of cerebral cortex than any other functional subdivision: for example, prefrontal cortex accounts for 25% of the cerebral cortex whereas primary visual cortex (Brodmann's area 17), for example, occupies only about 3% (Filimonov, 1949). Third, its involvement in complex cognitive operations appears relatively late in ontogeny as do the cognitive functions themselves (Goldman, 1976a). Fourth, in recent years a great deal of evidence has accumulated concerning the anatomical, biochemical, and functional development and plasticity of prefrontal cortex which is not reviewed in other literature on psychological or neurological development. Because of its distinctive qualities, comparisons of findings in frontal association cortex with the results of similar investigations of sensory or motor cortex can reveal which principles of development and plasticity are general to all cortical areas and which are specific to association cortex.

We believe that progress in understanding the biological bases of behavior requires a multidisciplinary approach, that is, one that involves diverse psychological, anatomical, and physiological techniques. Such an approach is reflected in the present chapter. Accordingly, methods will be discussed that will probably not be mentioned elsewhere in this volume. Some anatomical and biochemical terms will be introduced to most readers possibly for the first time. Every effort has been made to define terms and methods as clearly as possible in an attempt to convey to the interested reader the richness of conceptual and technical approaches that are now available to the biologically oriented student of cognitive development. Our philosophical premise is that the study of complex human behavior will be importantly informed by an understanding of the machinery which mediates that behavior, as has been true in the realm of sensory, motor, and reflex functions.

Although neuropsychological studies of prefrontal cortex have been conducted in a variety of species, this chapter emphasizes studies of the monkey, a nonhuman primate that is unparalleled as a model of human developmental phenomena. We will first review evidence implicating the prefrontal cortex in control of cognitive behavior in adult monkeys and data linking the functional maturation of those cortical areas with the ontogenetic development of cognitive behavior. The anatomy and neurochemistry of the prefrontal cortex is then discussed. The revolution in techniques for tracing anatomical circuitry, including the visualization and analysis of the exact position, inputs, and outputs of individual neurons has made it possible to obtain very detailed data on many systems, including the frontal association cortex. Similarly, newly developed neurochemical methods have allowed the identification of many classes of neurotransmitters in the brain and their localization within specific neuronal systems. Studies of the development of neurotransmitter function may provide important clues to the mechanisms underlying functional maturation of the prefrontal areas. Moreover, recent studies have shown that the frontal association is rich in the neurotransmitter, dopamine (Tassin, Bockaert, Blanc, Stinus, Thierry, Lavielle, Premont, & Glowinski, 1978). Deficiencies in the dopamine system may be responsible for a host of behavioral pathologies including those associated with stress (Thierry, Blanc, Sobel, Stinus, & Glowinski, 1973), aging (Bartus, Fleming, & Johnson, 1978) and cognition (Brozoski, Brown, Rosvold, & Goldman, 1979). In the concluding section we will discuss mechanisms of neural and behavioral plasticity occurring after cortical damage in developing primates. This subject may be of particular relevance to an understanding of the variety of cognitive deficits that appear in development as well as the wide degree of latitude in the achievements of brain-injured or environmentally deprived children. No less important is our understanding of the effects of experience on the maturational potential of normal individuals. The information to be presented in this chapter should help to bridge the disparate worlds of cognitive psychology and developmental neurobiology and to provide a basis for a more integrated science of cognition.

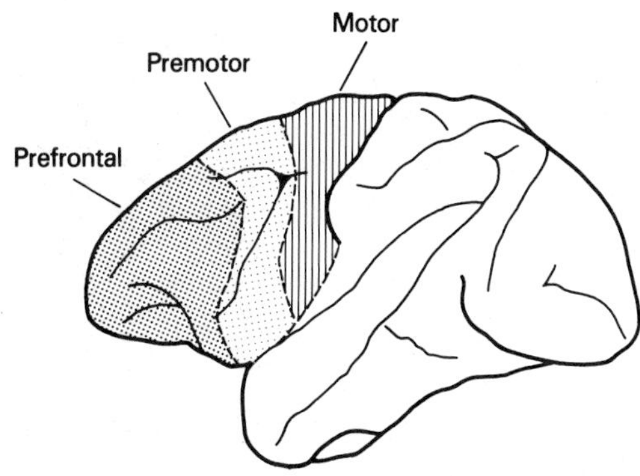

Figure 1. The three major subdivisions of neocortex in the frontal lobe of rhesus monkey based on cytoarchitectonic and hodological criteria. The prefrontal cortex (dense dots), which is highly developed in primates, extends onto the ventral surface of the frontal lobe, and a large proportion of it is buried within the banks and depths of sulci. (From Goldman-Rakic, 1981.)

FUNCTIONS OF PREFRONTAL CORTEX IN NONHUMAN PRIMATES

Behavioral Observations

The prefrontal cortex reaches its peak size and complexity in the human brain, in which it occupies more than a fourth of the cortical mantle (Filimonov, 1949). Since the frontal lobes are so prominent in humans, it is not surprising that appreciation of their function can best be gained from clinical studies of patients with various frontal lesions. The dominant features of such lesions were recognized over a century ago and have been subject to little disagreement among clinical observers. Damage to sizable portions of a human's frontal cortex—whether through accidental injury, brain disease, or neurosurgery—results in manifold symptoms including impairment in synthetic reasoning (Brickner, 1936; Goldstein, 1949; Milner, 1964), inability to utilize past experience and plan for the future (Denny-Brown, 1951), lack of initiative (Kleist, 1934), spatial disorientation (Semmes, Weinstein, Ghent, & Teuber, 1963), lack of behavioral restraint (Brickner, 1936; Elder & Miles, 1902), and inappropriate social affect and disintegrated personality (Brickner, 1936; Luria, 1966; Rylander, 1939). Primary sensory and motor processes generally remain intact.

The importance of the prefrontal cortex in human cognition and affect has stimulated extensive study of the anatomy and function of this region in animal subjects. As mentioned, nonhuman primates have been the subjects of choice for such research because of their well-developed prefrontal cortex, and phylogenetic proximity to humans. In primates, all cortex forward of the central sulcus is considered frontal cortex (Figure 1). This large cortical expanse can be divided into a posterior "motor" and an anterior "prefrontal" area separated by a transitional region, the premotor area including the frontal eye fields. Prefrontal cortex is further subdivided into various functional and structural regions. The most common partition is between (1) a dorsolateral prefrontal area and (2) an orbital prefrontal region (Fulton, 1951; Livingston, Fulton, Delgado, Sachs, Brendler, & Davis, 1948; Porrino, Crane, & Goldman-Rakic, 1981). The dorsolateral area is defined as all cortex on the dorsolateral convexity forward of the arcuate sulcus, including the banks and fundus of the principal sulcus (Figure 2). The orbital prefrontal cortex occupies the ventral surface of the frontal lobe (Figure 2). These two prefrontal subdivisions can also be distinguished on the basis of their relationship to the thalamus, a major subcortical integrative relay center deep within the brain. The dorsolateral prefrontal region receives projections from the laterally situated part of the mediodorsal thalamic nucleus whereas the more medial subdivision projects to the ventrally situated orbital cortex (Akert, 1964; Pribram, Chow, & Semmes, 1953; Walker, 1940).

Although not all features of the devastating frontal lobe syndrome manifested in humans are easily reproduced in laboratory animals, resections of frontal association cortex in primates and other animals produce clear and reliable cognitive (Harlow, Davis, Settlage, & Meyer, 1952; Jacobsen, 1936), motivational (Bianchi, 1922; Ferrier, 1886), and social (Myers, Swett, & Miller, 1973) impairments that are in some respects analogous to symptoms found in humans. Of the various classes of deficit that can be measured in laboratory animals with frontal lesions, cognitive disorders have been the most thoroughly investigated. For this reason, this chapter focuses on cognitive functions.

The Delayed-Response Tasks

Under proper conditions, nonhumans and humans are able to remember the location of an object following only a single presentation and retain such information for hours and even days (Hunter, 1913; Tinklepaugh, 1928). This ability can be measured in tests of delayed reaction originally devised by Hunt-

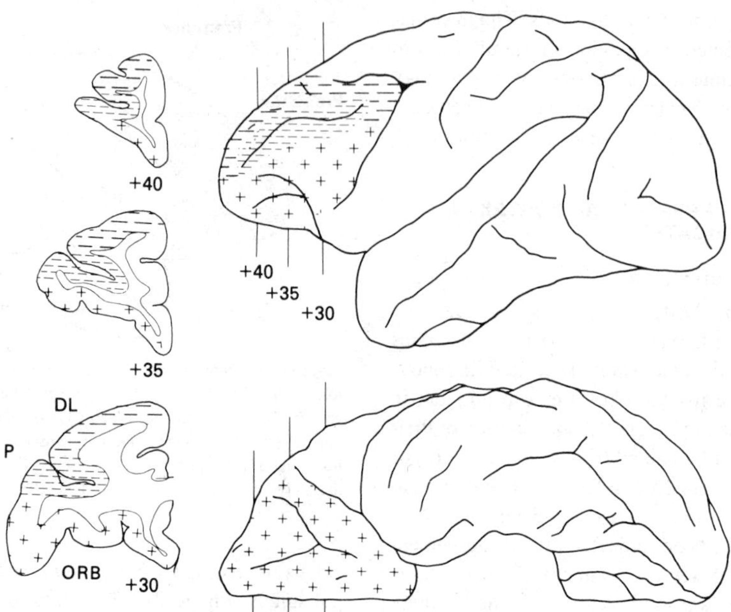

Figure 2. The regional subdivisions of the prefrontal association cortex. Dashed lines represent the dorsolateral prefrontal cortex; crosses represent the orbital prefrontal cortex. The principal sulcus (P), which is part of the dorsolateral (DL) cortex, is shown with more closely spaced lines. The subdivisions are based to a large extent on functional (Goldman, 1971; Goldman & Rosvold, 1970; Goldman et al., 1971) and anatomical (e.g., Goldman, 1979; Goldman & Nauta, 1976, 1977a,b; Johnson, Rosvold, & Mishkin, 1968) investigations.

er (1913) for comparative psychological studies. In the classical or widely used standard two-choice version of this test, the subject is shown the location of a food morsel which is then hidden from view by an opaque screen (Figure 3). Following a delay period, the subject is allowed to choose the correct location out of two or more choices. In a variation of this task, delayed alternation, the subject is required to alternate between left and right food wells on successive trials which are separated by delay periods. In the latter task, the subject's choice on any given trial is predicated on faithful memory of the preceding choice. Tests of spatial delayed reaction have been much maligned by psychologists perhaps because they may seem too simple; yet, they have proven to be useful experimental tools in the study of brain damage (Jacobsen, 1936), pharmacological treatment (Brozoski et al., 1979), aging (Bartus et al., 1978), and most significantly for present purposes, development (Harlow, Blomquist, Thompson, Schiltz, & Harlow, 1968). It should be pointed out that use of the delayed response task provided the first behavioral demonstration of deficits in memory function attributable to a localized region of the central nervous system—the prefrontal cortex in monkeys (Jacobsen, 1936). The dependence of delayed response function on prefrontal cortex remains one of the best and most solidly established structure-function relationships in neuropsychology. The elemental capacity to recognize that an object exists despite its temporary disappearance reflects an ability to behave in terms of anticipated or remembered outcomes. Such an ability has to be considered a building block, if not the very cornerstone of cognitive development. The delayed-response task certainly resembles the object-permanence task which has been used so extensively in children (Piaget, 1954). Spatial delay memory tasks are relatively quickly mastered by normal adult monkeys; adult lobectomized monkeys perform only at chance levels (e.g. Goldman, 1971; Goldman & Rosvold, 1970; Goldman, Rosvold, Vest, & Galkin, 1971; Jacobsen, 1936).

Functional Subdivisions

The type and severity of impairment that follows prefrontal lesions varies with the particular region of prefrontal cortex ablated. While behavioral tests indicate that both orbital and dorsolateral cortex are involved in spatial delay processing, these regions differ in the extent of their involvement. Lesions of either cortical region result in deficits on delayed

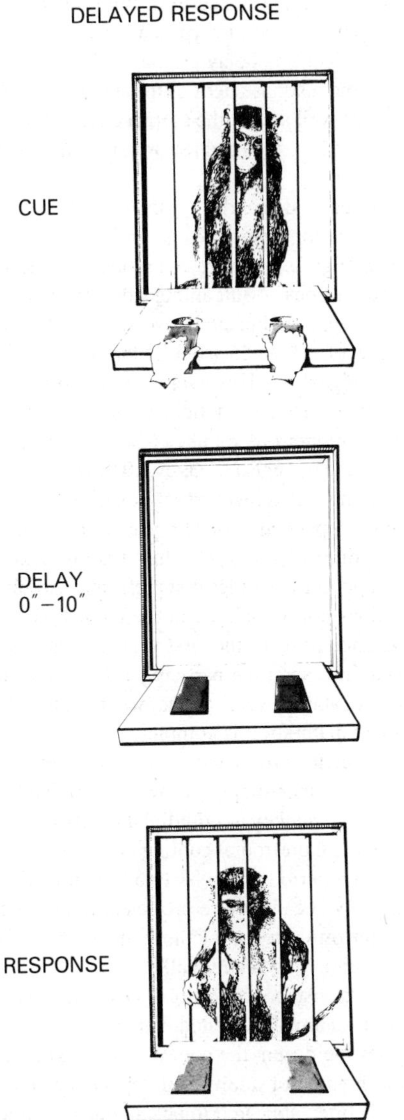

Figure 3. The three components of a delayed-response trial. In the cue period (top panel), the monkey watches an experimenter bait one of the wells with a food morsel and then both wells are covered with cardboard plaques. During the delay phase, an opaque screen is lowered for one or more seconds. In the response phase, the screen is raised and the monkey is allowed to select the correct well, that is, the one containing the reward.

alternation and delayed-response tasks (Goldman 1971; Goldman et al., 1971), but the deficits following orbital ablation are less severe than those consequent to dorsolateral removal. With sufficient retraining, animals with orbital lesions eventually attain criterion performance on these tasks (Goldman, 1971, 1976*b;* Miller, Goldman, & Rosvold, 1973). However, monkeys with orbital lesions are impaired on a wide range of other nonspatial tasks including object discrimination reversals (Goldman, 1971), learning set (Mishkin, 1964), and object matching or color matching problems (Mishkin & Manning, 1978).

In contrast, ablation of the dorsolateral cortex results in profound impairments only on spatial-mnemonic tasks, and these impairments persist even after prolonged postoperative training (Goldman & Rosvold, 1970; Goldman et al., 1971). It is important to note that the deficits which follow ablation of dorsolateral cortex are evident only in those tasks in which temporal delays and spatial information are combined (Goldman & Rosvold, 1970; Goldman et al., 1971). Operated subjects are able to perform simple color and pattern discriminations (Battig, Rosvold, & Mishkin, 1962; Goldman, 1971) indicating that they do not suffer from visual, motor, or motivational impairments. They perform within the range of normal monkeys on such complex tasks as learning set (Mishkin, 1964), object reversal (Goldman, 1971), object alternation (Mishkin & Manning, 1978), and crossmodal matching (Petrides & Iversen, 1976), showing that impairment is not merely a function of the degree of problem difficulty. Moreover, these monkeys can solve spatial problems not involving temporal delays (Goldman & Rosvold, 1970) as well as delay problems lacking a spatial component (Goldman et al., 1971; Passingham, 1975). Lesions confined to the principal sulcus of the dorsolateral cortex produce deficits as severe as those following complete dorsolateral removal (Butters, Pandya, Stein, & Rosen, 1972; Goldman et al., 1971; Gross & Weiskrantz, 1964; Mishkin, 1964) indicating that this circumscribed region serves as a focus for prefrontal control of spatial delay performance.

Development of Prefrontal Function

Early studies by Hunter (1913) in humans, and more systematic investigations by Harlow and his colleagues in monkeys (Harlow, 1959; Harlow, Harlow, Rueping, & Mason, 1960) established that the delayed-response capabilities mediated by the prefrontal cortex and associated structures mature at a relatively late point in ontogeny. This concept received support from studies in which young monkeys, whose prefrontal cortex had been ablated in early infancy, were tested on spatial delay tasks (Akert, Orth, Harlow, & Schiltz, 1960; Goldman, 1971; Tucker & Kling, 1967). In contrast to the devastating spatial impairment observed in adult monkeys, the immature animals showed no deficits in delayed-response performance when compared to age-matched unoperated controls (see *Developmental Plasticity of Primate Prefrontal Cortex* in this chapter). These results argue that the prefrontal cortex does not assume its mature role in spatial delay processing until relatively late in postnatal life.

However, the interpretation of studies in which lesions are used to study cerebral development is complicated by secondary tissue damage resulting from degeneration of injured neurons, as well as by the possibility of compensatory neural reorganization which could occur during the weeks or months intervening between surgery and behavioral assessment. To bypass the inherent limitations of the lesion approach, Goldman and Alexander (1977) studied the functional development of prefrontal cortex using the procedure of cryogenic depression, a method by which neuronal processes in a given brain area can be functionally inactivated through local hypothermia. The chief advantage of this method is that its effects are entirely reversible, so that each animal can serve as its own control. In addition, the relatively brief episodes of functional ablation produced by a cooling block are unlikely to allow time for compensatory neural reorganization to alter the basic anatomical and physiological properties of the system under investigation. Because hypothermia does not result in neuronal death, both primary lesions and secondary tissue degeneration can be avoided. Previous studies had already demonstrated that local cooling of the dorsolateral prefrontal cortex of adult rhesus monkeys produces spatial memory deficits quite similar to those that attend prefrontal lesions (Fuster & Alexander, 1970; Goldman & Alexander, 1977).

To achieve reversible cyrogenic depression of dorsolateral prefrontal cortex, cooling probes were implanted on the dura mater, the membrane casing of the brain, in the region overlying the principal sulcus. At the same time, thermistors were inserted beneath the dura directly on the cortical surface to monitor subdural temperature and to verify that cooling was confined to its intended target (Alexander & Goldman, 1978). Experimental testing began one week after surgery, and consisted of repeated sessions in which the subjects' performance was assessed before, during, and after cooling to 20°C.

The behavioral paradigm used to assess the effects of prefrontal cooling was the delayed-response (DR) task mentioned previously, the classical marker for the functional integrity of prefrontal association cortex. As indicated, the subject is allowed to observe an experimenter bait one of two recessed wells with food (the cue period). Both wells are then covered, and a screen interposed between the wells and the subject (the delay period). When the screen is raised (the response period) the subject is allowed to open one well and, if the correct choice is remembered, to retrieve the food reward or, if incorrect, to go unrewarded.

In 3-year-old nearly sexually mature rhesus monkeys, cooling block results in DR impairments similar though less severe than those produced by prefrontal lesions. Adult animals demonstrate a significant, reproducible and reversible performance decrement of 21% to 25% during the period of hypothermia (Figure 4). However, cooling to the same temperatures produces deficits of only 7% to 8% in 19- to 31-month-old monkeys, and no detectable deficits in the youngest monkeys, 9 to 16 months old (Fig. 4). Thus, as subjects reach sexual maturity, the degree of dependence of DR performance on prefrontal cortex increases. This finding provides strong support for the idea that prefrontal association cortex does not participate in the mediation of DR performance prior to the first year and one-half of postnatal life, and then participates to only a minor extent until about 3 years of age, when the process of functional maturation is complete.

Evidence for protracted maturation of prefrontal function is further supported by data obtained from studying one monkey longitudinally as its sensitivity to dorsolateral prefrontal cooling developed. Over a three month period (from 31 to 34 months of age), this monkey became more proficient in delayed-response performance during those times when its prefrontal cortex was functionally intact, i.e., during the pre- and postcool conditions. Over the same time period, this animal exhibited increasing decrements in DR testing during the cooling phase. The transition to maximal or adult level dependence on dorsolateral cortex appeared to be smooth and gradual, without disruptive effects on behavior. Thus, the neural mechanisms which underly DR performance early in life are apparently supplanted, but not entirely replaced, by maturation of the dorsolateral prefrontal cortex.

It is important to emphasize that these behavioral results cannot easily be attributed to any systematic variation in the topographic limits of the area functionally inactivated by cooling. Intracerebral temperature gradients measured during cooling revealed that the area cooled to 20°C was limited to the regions of dorsolateral cortex located directly beneath the cooling chambers and did not vary as a function of age (Alexander & Goldman, 1978). The demonstration that a portion of the cerebral cortex con-

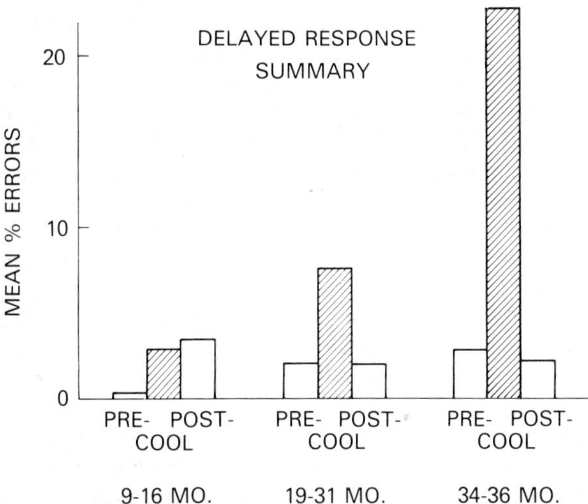

Figure 4. Delayed-response (DR) performance as a function of cryogenic depression of the dorsolateral prefrontal cortex (DLC). Mean percentage errors (%) on the DR trials presented before, during, and after DLC cooling for groups of monkeys in the age spans indicated: percentage of DR errors for each animal and condition were subjected to an arcsin transformation, and the transformed data (age groups and DLC cooling condition) underwent a 3 × 3 factorial analysis of variance with repeated measures on the last-named variable. The main effect for DLC cooling conditions was significant [F(2, 10) = 28 1, *P* .001], as was the age × DLC cooling condition interaction [F(4, 10) = 8.8, *P* .005]. Comparisons of mean DR errors in the different DLC conditions within groups were made using Tukey's *A* test with the critical level of *P* .01. Both groups II (ages 19–31 months, n = 3) and III (ages 34–36 months, n = 2) made significantly more errors during cooling than either before or after while their performance under the two latter conditions did not differ significantly. In contrast, for Group I (ages 9 to 16 months, *n* = 3), there were no significant differences in performance among any of the three conditions. (From Goldman & Alexander, 1977.)

cerned with selective cognitive processes does not become functionally mature until or after puberty may be relevant to neurological mechanisms involved in human cognitions, which likewise do not become fully functionally mature until or after puberty.

Neuronal Activity in Prefrontal Cortex

Electrophysiological methods have been used for some time to study neuronal processes and connections in the central nervous system; however, unit recording techniques have been extended to awake, behaving animals only in the last two decades (Bizzi, 1970; DeLong, 1971; Evarts, 1966, 1968). This type of study has proven to be most feasible in primates, animals which can be trained to perform difficult tasks over long periods under conditions of chair restraint.

Until recently, almost all investigations of neuronal activity in relation to ongoing behavior have been conducted in motor or sensory systems. Sensory systems are particularly amenable to electrophysiological analysis because precisely controlled external stimuli can be used to "trigger" neuronal firing. In studies of motor systems, the lack of such an external trigger has been overcome by timelocking recordings of neuronal activity to the subject's own response indicators (Evarts, 1966, 1968). Application of similar timelocking procedures to the well-defined components of the delayed response task—the cue, delay and response periods—has made it possible to extend electrophysiological analysis to an even more complex behavioral system, the temporospatial processing of prefrontal association cortex.

Studies in Adult Monkeys

To date, most electrophysiological studies of the frontal lobe have recorded the activity of neurons in the dorsolateral prefrontal cortex (including the banks and depths of the principal sulcus) in monkeys performing either spatial delayed alternation (Kubota & Niki, 1971; Niki, 1974a & b) or spatial delayed response (Alexander, Witt, & Goldman-Rakic, 1980; Fuster, 1973; Fuster & Alexander, 1971; Niki, Sakai, & Kubota, 1972; Niki, 1974c) tasks. The types of neurons identified in these investigations has depended to a large extent on the specific behavioral conditions employed. For example, Kubota and Niki (1971) described two types of unit responses: an "expectancy unit" that fires several hundred msec in advance of the response in a delayed alternation task, and a "delay unit" that fires preferentially during the delay interval of the same task. Using the delayed response paradigm, Fuster (1973) described six types of units, two of which were similar to those that are prominent in delayed alternation paradigms. By designing more explicit behavioral conditions, Niki (1974a,b,&c) and Niki and Watanabe (1976) were able to further characterize delay units into two types: one dependent on cue location and independent of the direction of the impending response and another related to the direction of the impending response and independent of the cue location (Niki, 1974a,b,&c; Niki & Watanabe, 1976). In studies in which the duration of the delay is varied, a subclass of neurons that fire only during the initial seconds of the delay has been discovered (Kojima & Goldman-Rakic, 1982). The last finding is in agreement with a number of studies that indicate that the early part of the delay period is particularly critical for spatial-temporal processing. Negative steady potential shifts in prefrontal cortex are maximal early in the delay period (Stamm & Rosen, 1969), and electrical stimulation of principal sulcal cortex (Stamm, 1969) or behavioral distraction (Kojima, 1980) is most disruptive to delayed-response performance when imposed during the first few seconds of the delay period. Such studies provide some indication that prefrontal lesions may produce deficits in registration rather than in retrieval or storage of memories.

The task-related unit activity in the studies described above is not an artifact of movements or uncontrolled sources of stimulation. Careful electromyographic recording of various muscle groups, including the extraocular musculature is not correlated with the activity of these prefrontal neurons (Fuster, 1973; Kubota & Niki, 1971). Units that show sustained elevation of firing during the delay phase of a delayed response trial do not fire in mock trials in which no reward is hidden (Fuster, 1973) or in trials in which the delay is bridged by an external cue (Niki, 1974a). Finally, although extensive cortical mapping has not been done, it is significant that units firing in definite relationship to delayed-response tasks have been found in the banks and depths of the principal sulcus and in areas anatomically connected with the principal sulcus including the parietal association cortex (Alexander, Witt, & Goldman-Rakic, 1980; in preparation), the anterior cingulate cortex (Fuster, 1973), the mediodorsal nucleus of the thalamus (Alexander, Witt, & Goldman, 1978; Fuster & Alexander, 1971), and caudate nucleus (Niki, Sakai, & Kubota, 1972).

These electrophysiological studies in behaving primates demonstrate that the activity of a large percentage of prefrontal neurons, as high as 50%, can be related to the parameters (cue, delay, and response) of delayed-response tasks. In terms of the neurophysiology of memory and cognition, the most interesting of these are the neurons that fire preferentially during the delay interval of a delayed response or delayed alternation trial. Furthermore, recording and stimulation studies demonstrate the importance of the early part of the delay period in the storage of spatial information. Although exhaustive surveys of neuronal activity in other regions of the brain have not yet been carried out, the finding of behaviorally relevant classes of neurons around the cortex of the principal sulcus, and in several anatomically connected structures, adds substantial support to the evidence from ablation studies that the dorsolateral prefrontal cortex of adult rhesus monkeys is highly specialized for processing and retention of spatiotemporal information.

Development of Neuronal Activity

For a number of reasons, studies of the development of neurophysiological activity in behaving animals have been rare. Young animals are difficult to train and to record electrophysiologically; moreover, it is often a problem to obtain comparable performance from younger and older subjects. Thus, most developmental studies of unit activity have been carried out in anesthetized preparations where the response of neurons in visual cortex to various parameters of stimulation usually is examined (Buisseret & Imbert, 1976; Hubel & Wiesel, 1963a; Imbert & Buisseret, 1975; Pettigrew, 1974).

To examine the neuronal activity associated with maturation of delayed-response performance, Alexander, Witt, and Goldman-Rakic (1980) recorded from individual neurons in the dorsolateral prefrontal cortex of immature (12 months old) and mature (36 months old) monkeys as they performed the DR task. Figure 5 shows the data collected from an adult subject and demonstrates the firing characteristics seen during a typical DR trial. During the control period the subject merely awaits the onset of the next trial, and the neuron being monitored shows a fairly constant base-line firing rate. At the onset of the "cue period" a visual stimulus appears on either the right or left side of the response panel signaling the location of the eventual food reward; this is followed by a 12-sec. delay during which the subject is no longer able to visualize the cue. Previous studies have demonstrated that a substantial proportion of neurons in dorsolateral prefrontal cortex show increased rates of discharge during the delay period,

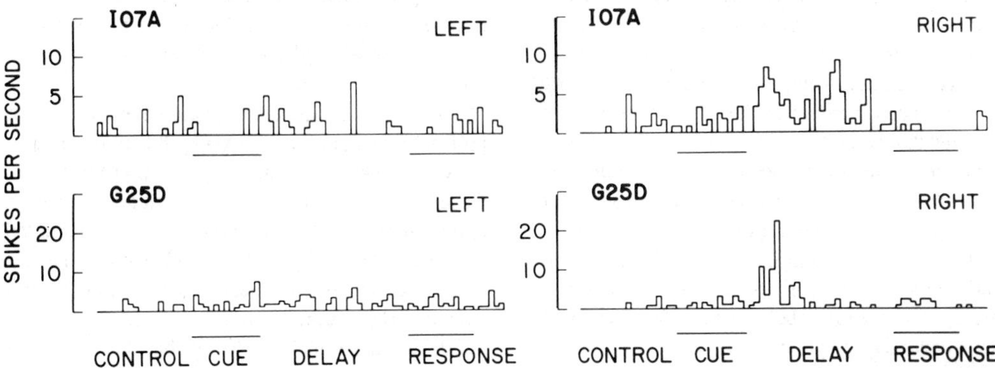

Figure 5. Two examples of prefrontal neurons that exhibit delay-related spatially discriminative activity while the monkey from which they were recorded was performing a delayed-response task. In this experiment, the cue and response periods lasted 5 sec; the duration of the delay was 12 sec. (From Alexander, Witt, & Goldman-Rakic, unpublished.)

regardless of whether the cue is presented on the right or left. In this developmental study, 38% of the neurons in prefrontal association cortex of adult rhesus monkeys could also be characterized as "delayed-activated" neurons (Figure 6). In contrast, in immature monkeys, only 20% of prefrontal units manifested increased rates of discharge during the delay period. The use of stringent control paradigms such as "mock delay" (in which no cue is presented) or "action withholding" (in which the animal is allowed to visualize the cue throughout the delay period) show that these delay-related increases in firing rate are task-specific and do not occur unless the animal is required to retain and eventually utilize the spatial information presented in the cue period. Other discharge parameters, such as the magnitude and spatial selectivity of unit responses, did not differ significantly between recordings from mature and immature monkeys; nor were there any age-related differences in the number of units showing activation during the cue and response periods.

Thus, the population of delay-activated neurons

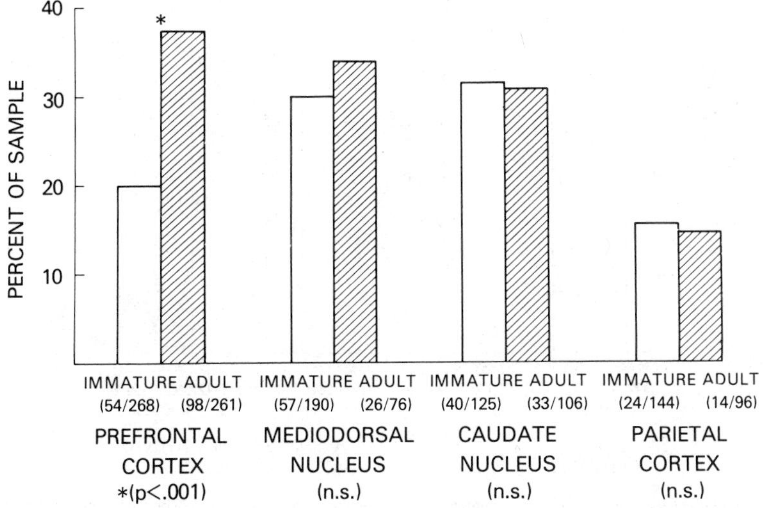

Figure 6. Percentage of delay-related neurons in the prefrontal cortex, the mediodorsal nucleus of the thalamus and caudate nucleus and in the parietal cortex of immature and adult monkeys. Note that there is a difference in incidence of such units in younger and older monkeys only in prefrontal cortex. (From Rakic & Goldman-Rakic, 1982.)

of prefrontal cortex expands by as much as twofold in the course of the first 3 years of postnatal life. Since in primates the number of cortical neurons remains essentially constant from birth to maturity, the age-related increase in delay-activated neurons indicates that some form of functional or structural recruitment must occur postnatally. In young animals, the proportion of uncommitted prefrontal neurons (i.e., those that do not respond to any phase of the DR-testing paradigm) is slightly, but significantly, greater than in adults. This subpopulation of unresponsive cells may be the source from which the later appearing delay-activated cells are recruited.

The quantitative changes in delay-activated neurons may provide a partial explanation for the monkeys' gradually increasing dependence on prefrontal cortex for the solution of spatial problems. In order to determine whether any qualitative factors of neuronal response also contribute to the postnatal maturation, a number of other characteristics of delay-activated neurons were analyzed. There were no age-related changes in the base-line firing rate of the cells, in the rate of increase during a delay, or in their response magnitudes. The spatial selectivity of these neurons was also examined in order to determine whether individual units responded preferentially to contralateral or to ipsilateral cue presentations. Interestingly, in both young and adult monkeys, one-third of the units responded to ipsilateral, one-third to contralateral, and one-third to cue presentations on either side.

In order to compare the functional maturation of prefrontal association cortex with that of other brain regions, analysis of unit activity during DR testing was also carried out in areas of parietal association cortex, in the head of the caudate nucleus and in the mediodorsal nucleus (MD) of the thalamus. In parietal cortex, which is connected anatomically to prefrontal cortex, some neurons were activated during the delay phase of the DR trial, but the number of such units was very small and did not differ between infants and adults (Figure 7). Cells of the caudate and MD nuclei were studied because these subcortical structures also have strong anatomical connections with prefrontal cortex (Akert, 1964; Goldman & Nauta, 1977b), and because lesions of these structures result in DR impairment in both infants and adults (Goldman & Rosvold, 1972; Isseroff, Galkin, Rosvold, & Goldman-Rakic, 1982). In these regions, a relatively large proportion of neurons showed activity changes associated with the events of DR testing. However, as in parietal regions, their relative number remained constant from infancy to adulthood. Thus, quantitative aspects of subcortical

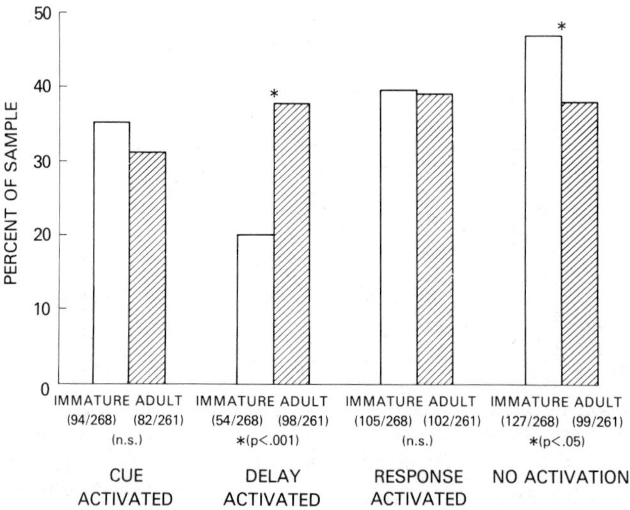

Figure 7. Developmental changes in specific classes of prefrontal neurons. Only the percentage of prefrontal cells that fire preferentially during the delay increases significantly between 1 and 3 years of age in rhesus monkeys. The percentage of unresponsive prefrontal neurons decreases significantly over the same age span. (From Alexander, Witt, & Goldman-Rakic, unpublished.)

and other cortical participation in delayed-response performance seem to mature within the first year of life whereas the functional contribution of prefrontal cortex continues to increase throughout the first 3 years of postnatal life. This cortical area's increasing participation in cognitive function appears to correspond to a gradual increase in the proportion of prefrontal neurons whose discharge characteristics are timelocked to mnemonic events of the delayed-response task. In addition to providing important contributions to our current understanding of functional development of cortex, these studies open the door for further analysis of the postnatal maturation of cortical neurons. For instance, Alexander, et al. (1980), have succeeded in combining the procedures of cryogenic depression of prefrontal cortex and single-unit recording in subcortical structures of the same animal. Simultaneous application of these two sophisticated techniques makes it possible to follow the activity of subcortical neurons before, during, and after cortical cooling and thus to determine how the prefrontal cortex affects the firing characteristics of caudate or thalamic neurons in awake, behaving animals at different developmental stages. Preliminary results from these studies indicate that even before prefrontal cortex is fully active in mediating spatial memory tasks, it is capable of modulating the neuronal activity of delay-related units in the caudate and MD nuclei (Alexander et al., 1980).

2-Deoxyglucose Metabolic Labeling

Methodological Background

In recent years, neurobiologists have developed powerful new tools for investigating the relationship between functional activity in specific brain regions and the ongoing behavior of an individual subject. These techniques are all based on the close coupling between neuronal activity on one hand, and cerebral oxygen consumption, blood flow, and glucose metabolism on the other. The most promising of these techniques is Sokoloff's (Sokoloff, Reivich, Kennedy, Des Rosiers, Patlak, Pettigrew, Sakurada, & Shinohara, 1977) 2-deoxyglucose method (2DG) for measuring brain glucose metabolism, a technique that permits simultaneous functional mapping of the entire brain of a behaving animal.

In primates, the brain is one of the most metabolically active structures of the body, accounting for 20% of resting oxygen consumption. Glucose, in turn, is the only measurably significant energy source for brain metabolism. Nearly all of brain oxygen uptake is attributable to glucose oxidation; moreover, energy sources other than glucose which supply other organs of the body fail to pass the blood-brain barrier. To an overwhelming degree, the energy-consuming activity of the brain is confined to neuronal electrical activity, either in the form of action potentials themselves, or in the form of the cellular maintenance necessary for the production of action potentials (Sokoloff et al., 1977). Thus, the brain is unlike other bodily tissue in two important ways: (1) it has but one activity of note, neuronal signaling, and (2) it has but one significant energy substrate, glucose. Consequently, measurement of glucose consumption provides a highly accurate picture of the functional activity of the brain, and detection of local variations in the rate of glucose consumption by the 2-deoxyglucose method affords a means of comparing the functioning of discrete structures in the brain.

The (^{14}C) dexoyglucose molecule is a radioactive isotope of glucose differing in that it lacks one oxygen atom and carries the (^{14}C) label. As a glucose analogue and glucose consumption indicator, it has three virtues: (1) it crosses the blood-brain barrier and cell membranes using the same carrier as does glucose; (2) it is phosphorylated by hexokinase, as is glucose; and (3) once in its phosphorylated form, (^{14}C) DG-6-P, it is metabolized no further and is sequestered effectively within the cell. If added to the blood of an experimental subject in a manner that assures its uniform diffusion through the plasma and if introduced in tracer amounts so as to avoid disrupting the normal uptake of glucose, (^{14}C) deoxyglucose uptake over time will be virtually identical to that of glucose. Unlike glucose, which is rapidly metabolized, however, the presence and quantity of the radioactive deoxyglucose can be systematically determined through autoradiography. Thus, an experimental subject can be injected with (^{14}C) deoxyglucose, allowed to engage in a particular behavior for approximately 45 min. to ensure that all deoxyglucose is taken up by brain tissue, and then sacrificed. The brain is quickly removed and frozen to prevent diffusion of the trapped (^{14}C)-6-P, and the frozen tissue is cut in 20μ sections. These sections are then placed in an X-ray cassette, and covered with medical X-ray film. After a period of from 5 to 7 days, the films are removed and developed, providing a radiographic picture of the brain section. Those regions of the brain which were most metabolically active during the testing session, and thus sequestered the largest amounts of the (^{14}C)-6-P, will be most densely labeled in the autoradiogram. Thus, the autoradiograms provide a map of the regional differences in neural activity which occur during specific behavioral tasks.

Studies in Juvenile or Adult Monkeys

In its earliest applications, the 2DG method was used to differentially mark functionally active motor and sensory brain structures. Sharp (in Plum, Gjedde, & Samson, 1976) applied the technique to monkeys trained to rapidly squeeze a rubber ball in order to obtain a juice reward. Autoradiograms of these animals revealed increased optical density (i.e., 2DG uptake) in the face and hand regions of the motor and sensory cortex. Metabolic mapping of the visual system (Kennedy, Des Rosiers, Sakurada, Shinohara, Reivich, Jehle, & Sokoloff, 1976) showed that in subjects exposed to bilateral retinal stimulation, glucose utilization in striate cortex is not homogeneous throughout the cytoarchitectural layers; greatest levels of activity are found in layer IV. Unilateral retinal stimulation with 2DG injection reveals the separate layers of the lateral geniculate body and produces a pattern of stripes in visual cortex which correspond to ocular dominance columns. In a more sensitive test of the method, Hubel, Weisel, & Stryker (1978) injected 2DG into monkeys exposed to a visual stimulus consisting of only vertical lines. Autoradiograms showed bands of label in the visual cortex which the authors believed to be the cortical orientation columns hypothesized on the basis of earlier electrophysiological findings.

The first quantitative determination of local cerebral glucose utilization (LCGU) in primates was carried out by Kennedy, Sakurada, Shinohara, Jehle, & Sokoloff (1978). Subjects were seven conscious young adult rhesus monkeys; while their exact ages were not known, estimations based on their weights indicate that they were between 2 and 3 years old. During the 45 minutes between 2DG administration and sacrifice, subjects were restrained in primate chairs and exposed to the auditory and visual stimulation of the laboratory.

Rates of glucose utilization fell into two major categories. In white matter (fibers) LCGU was low (ranging between 11 and 23 μmoles/100 g/min.) and was relatively uniform from one part of the brain to the other. In contrast, gray matter (cortex and nuclear groups) rates were quite heterogeneous and generally three to five times greater than those of white matter. In general, the highest rate of glucose utilization was found in the auditory system. In the inferior colliculus, a subcortical component of the auditory system, LCGU was 103 μmoles/100 g/min, an extremely high metabolic rate. Glucose utilization values in cortex ranged from a low of 44 μmoles/100 g/min in motor cortex to 79 μmoles/100 g/min in auditory cortex. Metabolic activity of the caudate and putamen were nearly identical at from 52 to 53 μmoles/100 g/min.

LCGU During Performance of Cognitive Tasks

The development of techniques for measuring cerebral blood flow and local cerebral glucose utilization have made it possible to explore central questions regarding brain-behavior relationships in adult animals which in turn set the stage for studies of development and plasticity. Because this is potentially a powerful approach for analysis of cognitive development, this section will describe in detail a recent 2-deoxyglucose analysis of metabolic activity in mature monkeys performing a cognitive task (Bugbee & Goldman-Rakic, 1981). In this study, six rhesus monkeys of various ages were trained on a delayed-response (DR) task, while four control (CON) animals were tested under identical circumstances with the same number of trials and reinforcements, except that no delay was interposed; these subjects were allowed to respond as soon as the target was presented. To ensure that motor activity and auditory input were similar for both groups, all subjects were restrained in primate chairs and exposed to amplified white noise. At the beginning of its final testing session, each monkey received an intravenous pulse of ^{14}C-2DG (100 uCi/kg) via a femoral catheter. Subjects worked steadily over the 45 minute period of 2DG administration, with DR animals performing at 90% correct.

Local cerebral glucose utilization (LCGU) quantified according to the procedures described by Sokoloff et al. (1977), was measured in eight cortical regions: prefrontal, motor, auditory, striate, extrastriate, entorhinal, and superior and inferior temporal gyrus. Statistical comparisons demonstrated that only LCGU values of the prefrontal cortex differed for the DR and CON groups ($p < .05$, t-test, two-tailed). None of the other cortical areas examined could be differentiated according to behavioral task (Table 1). To determine whether prefrontal metabolic activity was specific to spatial-mnemonic aspects of the delayed-response task or reflected instead the more general and nonspecific attentional demands of the task, 2-deoxyglucose analysis was also performed in a group of monkeys trained to perform a visual pattern discrimination task which, according to results of ablation studies, depends on the integrity of visual association cortex in the temporal lobe (Harlow et al, 1952). These animals were tested in the same apparatus as those performing delayed-response tasks but were rewarded for distinguishing visual pattern rather than for memorizing for spatial location as is required in DR tasks. The same cortical areas examined in monkeys performing DR were subjected to densitometric analysis in those performing the visual pattern task.

Table 1. **Outcome of Statistical Comparisons on Local Cerebral Glucose Utilization Ratios for Groups of Monkeys Performing Delayed Response (DR), Visual Discrimination (VD), and Control (CON) Tasks**

	Group Comparisons		
Cortical Areas	DR vs. CON	VD vs. CON	DR vs. VD
Prefrontal			
Dorsolateral	$p < .01$	NS	NS
Orbital	$p < .05$	NS	NS
Motor	NS	NS	NS
Parietal	NS	NS	NS
Cingulate	$p < .05$	$p < .05$	NS
Entorhinal	NS	NS	NS
Inferior temporal	NS	$p < .01$	NS
Superior temporal	NS	NS	NS
Auditory	NS	NS	NS
Visual	NS	NS	NS

Bugbee and Goldman-Rakic (in preparation) found that the prefrontal LCGU ratios of monkeys performing the visual discrimination task were intermediate between those found in monkeys performing the DR task and those in monkeys performing in the nonassociative control condition. In the inferior temporal cortex, on the other hand, although the LCGU ratios of both task groups were intermixed, only those performing the pattern task were significantly different from controls (Table 1). And in a third cortical region, the cingulate cortex, a limbic area thought to play a role in arousal and motivation, both delayed-response and visual discrimination groups differed statistically from the control monkeys (Table 1). Thus, the 2-deoxyglucose method not only bore out prior evidence and theories about cortical function, but at the same time revealed new dimensions of cortical involvement in various functions. For example, whereas monkeys with prefrontal lesions do not exhibit deficits in performance on visual pattern tasks, the 2DG method has revealed that prefrontal cortex, nevertheless, plays a role in this and perhaps other behaviors though its engagement is less than for delayed-response tasks. The 2-deoxyglucose method thus provides a way to analyze the simultaneous contribution of many areas to a given function and conversely to assess the role of a single area in multiple functions.

Studies of Metabolic Labeling and Blood Flow in Humans

Because the 2DG method is a noninvasive method performed in normal animals without lesions, it provides a valuable link to theoretically similar techniques that have been developed to study dynamic brain processes in humans, for example, computerized cerebral tomography in conjunction with administration of the glucose analogue, 2-fluoro-2-deoxyglucose (F-18), (Phelps, Huang, Hoffman, Selin, Sokoloff, & Kuhl, 1979; Reivich, Kuhl, Wolf, Greenberg, Phelps, Ido, Cosella, Fowler, Hoffman, Alavi, Sow, & Sokoloff, 1979). Due to the fact that blood flow is controlled to a large extent by the metabolism of neuronal tissue, studies of cerebral blood flow in humans are also valuable sources of comparative data between experimental animals and humans (Ingvar & Lassen, 1975; Lassen & Ingvar, 1972). Roland and Skinhoj (1981) recently analyzed blood flow in 254 different regions of the human cortex during the performance of various visual shape discrimination problems. Increases in blood flow were found in many visual cortical areas known to be involved in visual perception. However, increases in blood flow were also observed in several portions of the human frontal lobe, a finding reminiscent of the results obtained in the 2DG analysis of visual pattern discrimination by monkeys described above (Bugbee & Goldman-Rakic, in preparation). Perhaps the finding of greatest relevance to the topic of the present chapter, is that normal human subjects at rest exhibit ''hyperfrontality,'' that is, elevation of blood flow and presumably metabolic activity in frontal, as compared with posterior, regions of the cerebral cortex (Ingvar, 1979). States of increased awareness during cognitive demands to solve an intellectual problem induce more marked hyperfrontality than is observed at rest (Risberg & Ingvar, 1973) consistent with the LCGU results obtained in monkeys performing the delayed-response task (Bugbee & Goldman-Rakic, 1981). Thus, metabolic labeling studies in animals offer new possibilities for testable extrapolations to human behavior.

Ingvar has now studied blood flow in 40 patients diagnosed as chronic schizophrenics (Ingvar, 1980). The "hyperfrontal" pattern present in normal subjects at rest was found to be much less pronounced in chronic schizophrenics and in some patients the pattern was reversed such that temporal and parietal regions exhibited higher cerebral blood flow ratio than did frontal regions (Ingvar, 1980). Ingvar interprets these findings to indicate that the fundamental deficit in schizophrenia is the way the brain filters sensory information and programs behavior. By implication, prefrontal cortical functions break down in this mental disease.

Development of Metabolic Activity

Because the 2DG method is relatively new and expensive to employ in research, few studies have yet been carried out in developing primates. However, some efforts have begun in this area. Kennedy and coworkers recently measured LCGU in newborn rhesus monkeys (Kennedy, Sakurada, Shinohara, Mijaoka, & Sokoloff, 1982). These infants were separated from their mothers 12 to 28 hours after birth, were hand held during the 2DG procedure, and were exposed to auditory and visual stimuli comparable to that of the adults. Comparison of the LCGU values of neonatal and pubescent animals revealed a number of noteworthy differences. In white matter, LCGU values of neonates generally exceeded those of pubescents, perhaps reflecting metabolic activity of ongoing myelin formation. In gray matter, age-related differences in metabolic activity varied according to position along the neuraxis. In neonates, the LCGU of brainstem structures such as the vestibular nuclei, the superior colliculus, and relay nuclei of the auditory pathway was generally equal to or higher than that measured in pubescent animals. Metabolic activity of parts of the cerebellum (the flocculus and cerebellar vermis) in neonates also exceeded rates in the older monkeys. Conversely, in the more rostral forebrain regions of the neuraxis, metabolism was generally low in neonates as compared to pubescent animals. For example, although in auditory and somatosensory cortex LCGU values were approximately equal to those of the 2- to 3-year-olds, metabolic activity of frontal and parietal association areas was well below their more mature levels. The inferior temporal cortex, a visual association area, was particularly low, approaching the metabolic rate of white matter. Interestingly, the single cortical region where neonatal glucose utilization was above that of the older subjects was the medial orbital region of prefrontal association cortex. There was a correspondingly high LCGU in the magnocellular part of the mediodorsal thalamic nucleus which projects to medial orbital cortex. LCGU of the caudate (23 μmoles/100 g/min) and putamen (37 μmoles/100 g/min) were low, but unlike older subjects, activity in the putamen was consistently higher than that of the caudate. The significance of these differences is not well understood at present.

Data on the developmental progression and/or sequence of metabolic changes in different regions of the mammalian brain have also been sparse. Since maturation of the brain is characterized by profound morphological and functional reorganization and differentiation, alterations in energy metabolism may be expected in various regions of the central nervous system. Measurements in local blood flow have been carried out in Beagle dogs from birth through maturity (Kennedy, Grave, Jehle, & Sokoloff, 1972). Blood flow is regulated and adjusted to local metabolic demand and can be taken as indirect indication of metabolic activity in different structures (Kennedy et al., 1972). In all regions of the canine brain examined, values were generally low at birth and rose to maximal levels between 3 and 7 weeks of postnatal age; however, subsequently, blood flow values declined toward adult levels by 13 weeks of postnatal age. The peak levels at earlier ages may reflect a summation of changes in energy demands associated with biosynthetic processes essential for growth and development on the one hand, and with increasing functional demands on the other (Kennedy et al., 1972). In preliminary studies on developing rhesus monkeys the autoradiographic method of measuring of LCGU indicates that a similar pattern of development may characterize the development of cerebral metabolic activity in many areas of the primate brain as well (Bugbee, Kennedy, Sokoloff, & Goldman-Rakic, unpublished results). Future application of the 2DG method will be to examine metabolic activity in brains of monkeys while they perform various tasks at different developmental stages.

ANATOMICAL DEVELOPMENT OF PREFRONTAL CORTEX

The study of structure-function relations in the nervous system of developing and mature organisms has had an uneven history. Indeed, for some time the pervasive view was that structure had little to do with function. In the earlier 1940s this point was articulated by Lashley (1941) as follows:

> It may, indeed, be stated as a general principle of behavior that psychological functions are of such a character that they must be independent of the particular nerve cells excited and be determined by the patterns or relations between points of excitation.
>
> Much of my own work, based on operative destruction of parts of the brain combined with experimental studies of learning, has shown a similar independence of function from the structural details of the brain. (p. 464)

As our behavioral paradigms have become more sophisticated it is clear that certain functions may be localized to certain regions of the brain (see discussion in previous section with regard to spatial abilities and the prefrontal cortex), yet we still have relatively little detailed knowledge about specific structure-function relations within these regions. One approach to this problem has been to selectively eliminate portions of an area, or to alter certain constituent structures within an area and to assess the effects on behavior. These approaches are discussed in the previous section, as well as in the last section of this chapter. An alternative approach is to carefully examine the anatomy and connections of these regions and to chart their development, relative to the development of behavioral function. In this section we will focus on the anatomy, connectivity, and development of the prefrontal cortex as a basis for understanding the maturation of cognitive activity. It should be pointed out, however, that while cognitive activity is expressed postnatally, the neurological foundation for cognitive development cannot be fully understood without appreciation of the sequence of critical developmental events that begin long before birth. As such, it is important to examine prenatal anatomical development as well. This point is dramatically demonstrated in the section of this chapter dealing with plasticity, where the sparing of behavioral function which occurs following damage to the cerebral cortex *in utero* will be discussed.

Until recently, analysis of the anatomical organization of association cortical regions such as the prefrontal cortex has been hampered by the lack of sensitive and reliable methodologies. However, the recent introduction and refinement of techniques for tracing anatomical pathways and for visualizing entire neurons and their relationships with other cell populations at the light and electron microscopic (EM) levels have enhanced our understanding of the primate prefrontal cortex and associated structures. In addition to their use in studying structural organization in mature animals, most of these techniques are now being employed to examine and characterize development and plasticity (see *Developmental Plasticity of Primate Prefrontal Cortex*) in the central nervous system. In the present section we will examine some aspects of the mature prefrontal cortex and characterize the development of both local and long tract connections of this region. No attempt will be made to catalogue either all the connections of this area or all that is known about its development, but instead we will focus on selected aspects of each which may be particularly relevant to an understanding of structure-function relations of this area.

Prefrontal Cortex in Adults

Before proceeding, it will be helpful for the reader to be familiarized with some terminology that is essential for an understanding of the material to be presented. The recently devised methods for tracing neural connections have significantly advanced our knowledge of connectivity within the nervous system. These methods are generally classified as *retrograde* methods, those which allow axons to be traced from their synaptic terminations back to the cell body from which they arise, and *orthograde* methods, which trace connections starting from the cell body and proceeding toward areas of synaptic termination. By using these methods it is possible to identify the neurons projecting to a particular area of interest as well as the pattern of termination in the target structure. The principle orthograde tracing technique utilized today is the autoradiography of radioactively labeled amino acids. In this procedure, labeled amino acids are injected into an area of interest where they are *taken up by cell bodies* and incorporated into proteins. These proteins are then transported down the axon to the terminal or synaptic areas of that neuron. The animal is sacrificed; sections of the brain are mounted on glass slides and then coated with a film emulsion which becomes exposed by the radioactively labeled amino acid. By examining the emulsion (lying over the tissue) in serial sections through the area of interest, it is possible to identify terminal regions of the injected area. A number of retrograde tracing methodologies are currently popular, for example, HRP and fluorescent dyes, which have a common mode of action. After these substances are injected into the brain they are *taken up at synaptic or terminal areas* of a neuron and transported down the axon toward the cell body. After sectioning of the brain and various steps of chemical processing, the cell bodies giving rise to terminals in the injected area fluoresce a specific color (after fluorescent dye injections) or appear opaque (after HRP injections) relative to unlabeled cells.

When examining a section of cortical tissue which has been stained for the identification of cells by conventional cell stains, one is struck by fluctuations in both cellular density and variations in cell shape at different depths of the cortex (see Figure 8). Careful examination of this cytoarchitecture (cellular architecture) reveals a laminar arrangement which, in neocortex, may be divided into six primary lamina or layers. Although these laminae are seen in all cortical regions, the thickness and proportionate size of the laminae vary throughout the brain. On the basis of these variations in cytoarchitecture, the brain has been subdivided into a number of cytoarchitectonic areas (see Figure 9). For example, visual cortex (area 17) has a thick and sharply delineated layer IV (see Figure 8), which is in clear contrast to motor cortex (area 4), in which layer IV is so poorly represented that it is barely identifiable. Prefrontal cortex, with which we will be most concerned, lies anterior to the motor and premotor regions of the frontal lobes (see Figure 1) and is characterized by a thin, but well demarcated layer IV.

In addition to variations in cytoarchitecture, cortical areas may also be delineated on the basis of their connectivity with other regions of the brain. Therefore, as with variations in cytoarchitecture, the prefrontal cortex is distinguished from adjacent re-

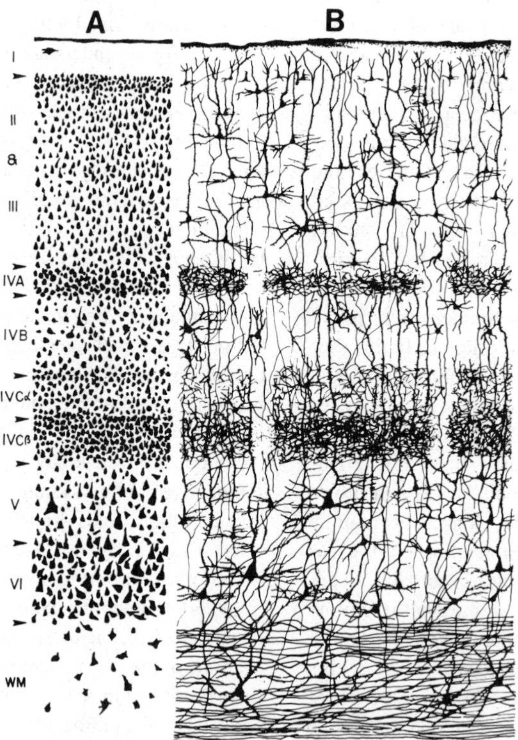

Figure 8. The laminar (layered) organization of neurons in the primary visual cortex of the rhesus monkey. On the left (A) the cytoarchitectonic appearance of visual cortex (Brodmann's area 17) in Nissl stain (cell stain) displays horizontal cell stratification. As with all neocortical areas six primary layers are designated according to cell type and density. In some cortical regions, some of these layers may be further subdivided, for example, in area 17 layer IV is frequently subdivided. On the right (B) is a composite drawing of neurons impregnated by the Golgi method and superimposed afferent axons in sublayers IVA and IVC. The Golgi method impregnates only a fraction of the neurons and allows one to visualize the dendritic arbor of a neuron as well as its axon. This technique provides the necessary information for neuronal classification which is unavailable in Nissl stained sections. (Adapted from Rakic, 1979a.)

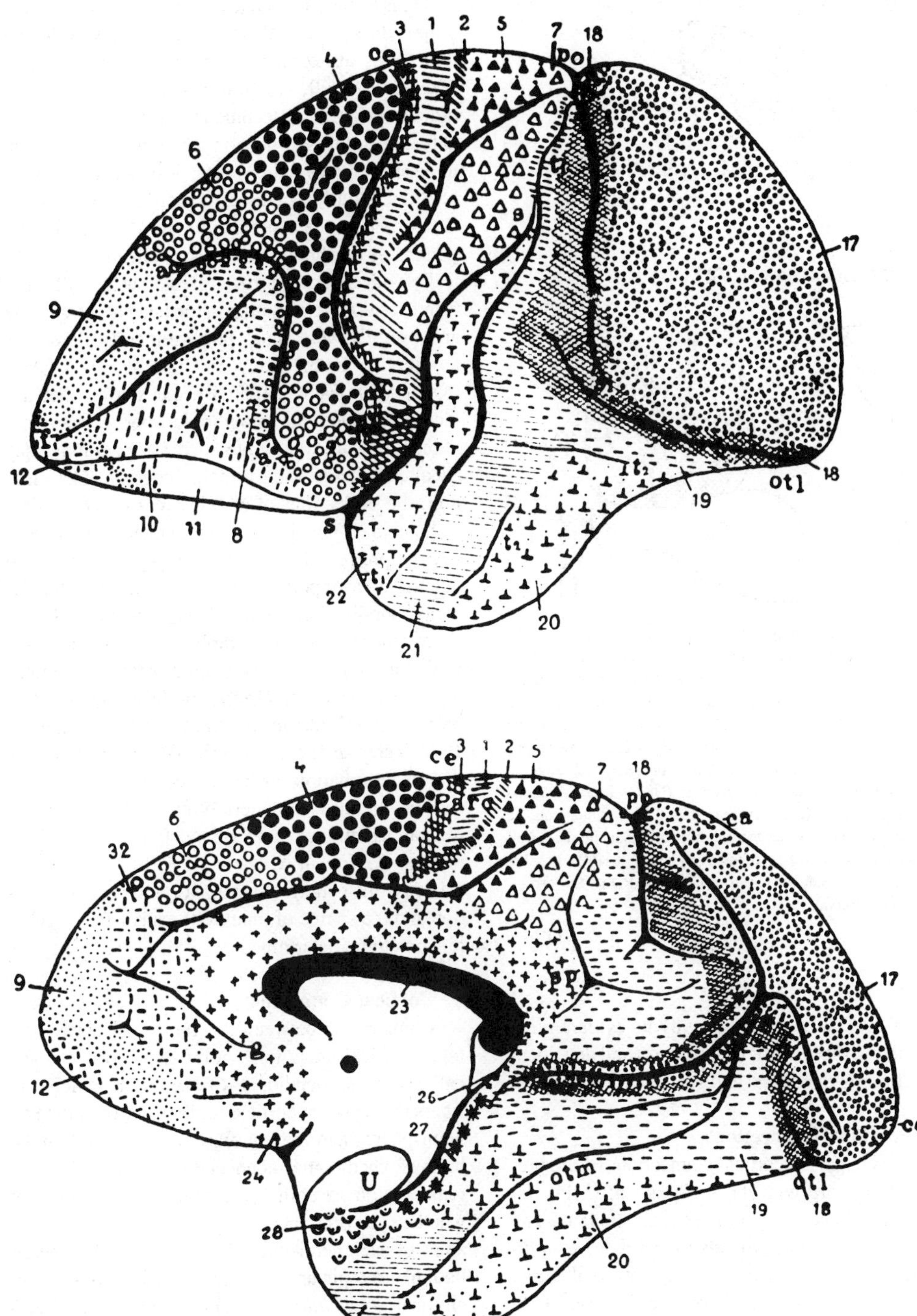

Figure 9. Brodmann's map of monkey cerebral cortex shown on lateral (top) and medial (bottom) views of the monkey brain. The divisions of cortex are assigned numerical values and are based on differences in the cellular composition (cytoarchitecture) between areas. A similar map of human cortex has been made by Brodmann. (Adapted from Von Bonin & Bailey, 1947.)

PREFRONTAL CORTEX

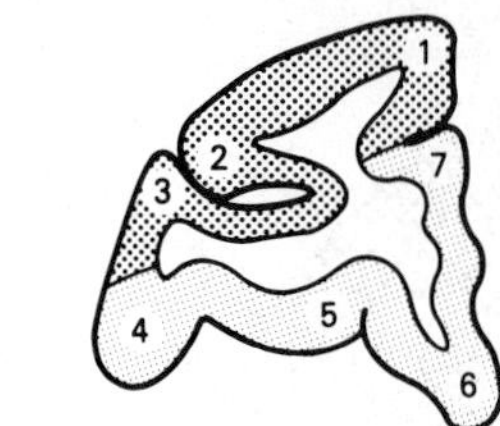

MEDIODORSAL NUCLEUS

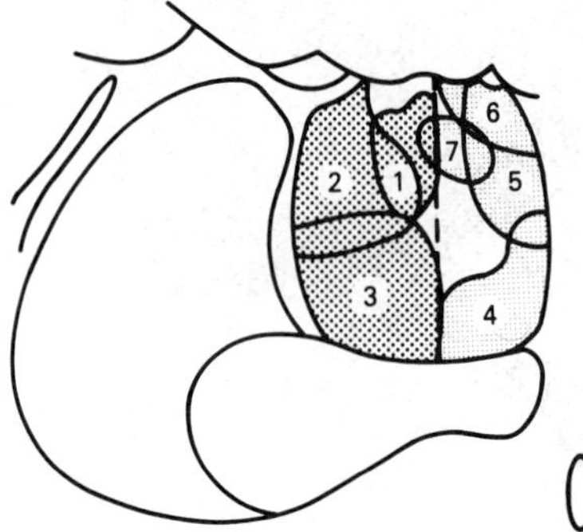

Figure 10. The topography of thalamocortical connections in the prefrontal cortex of the rhesus monkey. The detailed arrangement of thalamocortical cell groups was revealed by employing retrograde cell labeling with horseradish peroxidase (HRP) in seven cases arbitrarily numbered 1 to 7. With the arbitrary numbering system used, the register of MD neurons and their synaptic targets in the prefrontal cortex are shown. Areas numbered 1, 2, and 3 in the top figure represent dorsolateral cortex (DL) and areas 4, 5, and part of 6 represent orbital cortex (see Figure 2 for a comparison). In the bottom figure the border between parvocellular (on the left of the broken line) and magnocellular (on the right) MD is schematized by the broken line. (From Goldman-Rakic & Porrino, unpublished observations.)

gions of the cerebrum not only by its cytoarchitecture, but also on the basis of its pattern and density of connections with cortical and subcortical structures.

Subcortical Connections

The principal subcortical connections of the prefrontal cortex are with the mediodorsal (MD) nucleus of the thalamus and the caudate nucleus. The MD thalamic nucleus projects to and receives a direct projection from all areas of the prefrontal cortex (Akert, 1964; Jacobson, Butters, & Tovsky, 1978; Walker, 1940). These reciprocal connections are topographically organized such that the orbital and dorsolateral subdivisions of prefrontal cortex are associated with the medial magnocellular and lateral parvocellular subdivisions of the nucleus, respectively (Figure 10) (Akert, 1964; Tobias, 1975).

Unlike the MD nucleus, the caudate does not project directly onto the prefrontal cortex, although it receives an extensive projection from this area (Kemp & Powell, 1970). Recent studies using autoradiographic tracing techniques have revealed several features of this projection which were not evident in earlier studies using older, less sensitive methodologies. Earlier investigations had suggested that the cortico-caudate projection from this and other regions of cerebral cortex was arranged topographically with anterior cortical areas, such as the prefrontal region, terminating in the head of the caudate and progressively more posterior cortical regions terminating in the body and tail of this nucleus (Kemp & Powell, 1971). Recent studies that use more sensitive autoradiographic fiber tracing techniques indicate that while such a topography may adequately describe the principal regions of termination, the projections of certain areas to the caudate nucleus may have been underestimated. In particular, the prefrontal cortex now appears to innervate not just anterior portions of the nucleus, but all of its major subdivisions (Goldman & Nauta, 1977b). Furthermore, autoradiographic studies have revealed a previously unsuspected pattern of inhomogeneity in the terminal zones of the cortico-caudate projection (Goldman & Nauta, 1977b; Kunzle, 1975; Yeterian & Van Hoesen, 1978). The distribution of termination of the cortico-caudate pathway exhibits an intricate pattern of channels and islands of input which surround terminal-free areas (see Figure 11) (Goldman & Nauta, 1977b). The significance of this pattern of termination to caudate function and the source of input to the label-free regions remains to be determined.

Cortical Connections

Connections between the prefrontal cortex and other cortical areas fall within two broad classes, callosal and associational. *Callosal* connections are fibers that connect cortical regions between the two hemispheres and may be further subdivided on the basis of whether they connect the same cytoarchitectonic region in both hemispheres (homotopic) or whether they connect different cytoarchitectonic areas of each hemisphere (heterotopic). In general, both heterotopic and homotopic connections are reciprocal. *Associational* fibers are those which connect different cortical areas within the same hemisphere and, as with callosal projections, these also tend to be reciprocal. The dorsolateral prefrontal area of one hemisphere is connected across the callosum with the homotopic cortical region in the opposite hemisphere as well as with several heterotopic

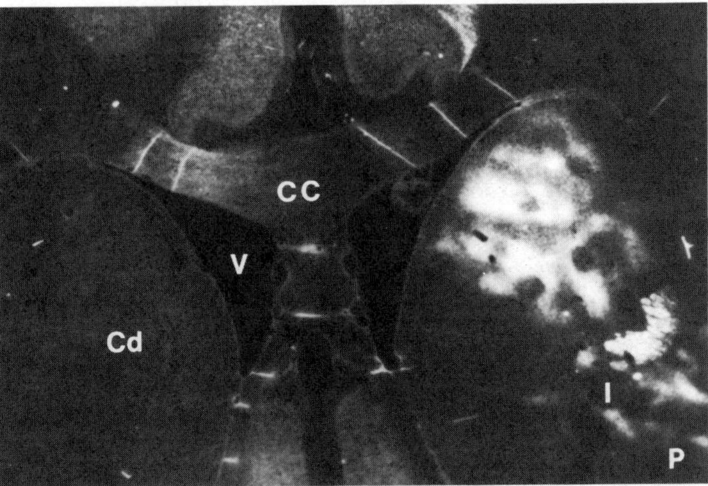

Figure 11. Photograph under dark-field illumination of the caudate nucleus in a normal rhesus monkey whose homolateral principal sulcus (right hemisphere) was injected with tritiated amino acids. The dark-field autoradiogram displays the intricate pattern of fiber clusters originating in prefrontal cortex. These fiber clusters often surround elliptically shaped territories devoid of prefrontal input. (From Goldman, 1978.)

areas (Goldman & Nauta, 1977; Jacobson & Trojanowski, 1977b). This area of prefrontal cortex also has extensive reciprocal associational connections in the same hemisphere, with the posterior parietal, cingulate, and temporal areas of cortex (Goldman & Nauta, 1977a; Jacobson & Trojanowski, 1977a). A more detailed and extensive discussion of the cortico-cortical connections of the prefrontal cortex can be found in several comprehensive papers and reviews (Jacobson & Trojanowski, 1977a,b; Nauta, 1972; Pandya & Vignola, 1971).

The analysis of cortico-cortical connections like that of the cortico-caudate projection, has also benefited from the autoradiographic methodology. Both the callosal and associational projections of the prefrontal cortex have been found to terminate in a disjunctive pattern of columns or patches (Figure 12) (Goldman & Nauta, 1977a), in many ways similar to the pattern of ocular dominance columns described in primary visual cortex of cats and monkeys (Figure 13) (Hubel & Freeman, 1977; Hubel & Wiesel, 1977; Shatz, Lindstrom, & Wiesel, 1977). Although both the thalamo-cortical terminations of the ocular dominance columns and the cortico-cortical termi-

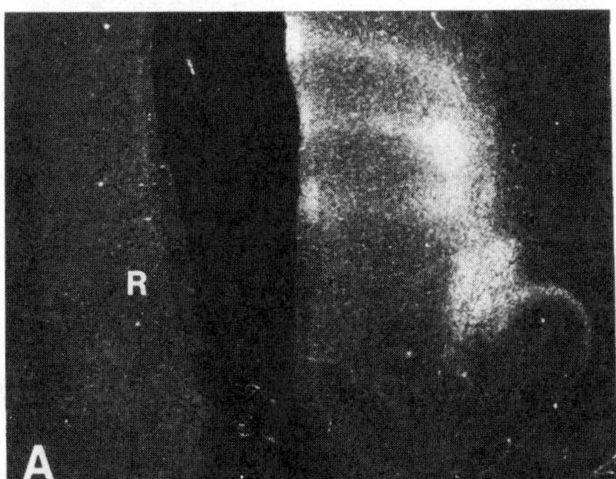

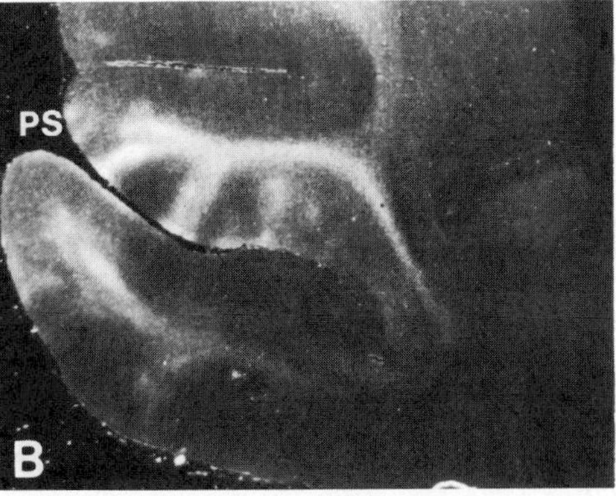

Figure 12. Dark-field autoradiogram illustrating columns in the ipsilateral retrosplenial (R) cortex following a single injection of ^{3}H-leucine and ^{3}H-proline into the cortex of the dorsal bank of the principal sulcus in a 4-day-old monkey (*A*) × 25. Dark-field autoradiogram of columns in the homotopical region of the principal sulcus (PS) in the contralateral hemisphere of the same 4-day-old monkey given a single injection in the dorsal bank of the principal sulcus of the opposite hemisphere (*B*) × 25. (Modified from Goldman & Nauta, 1977a.)

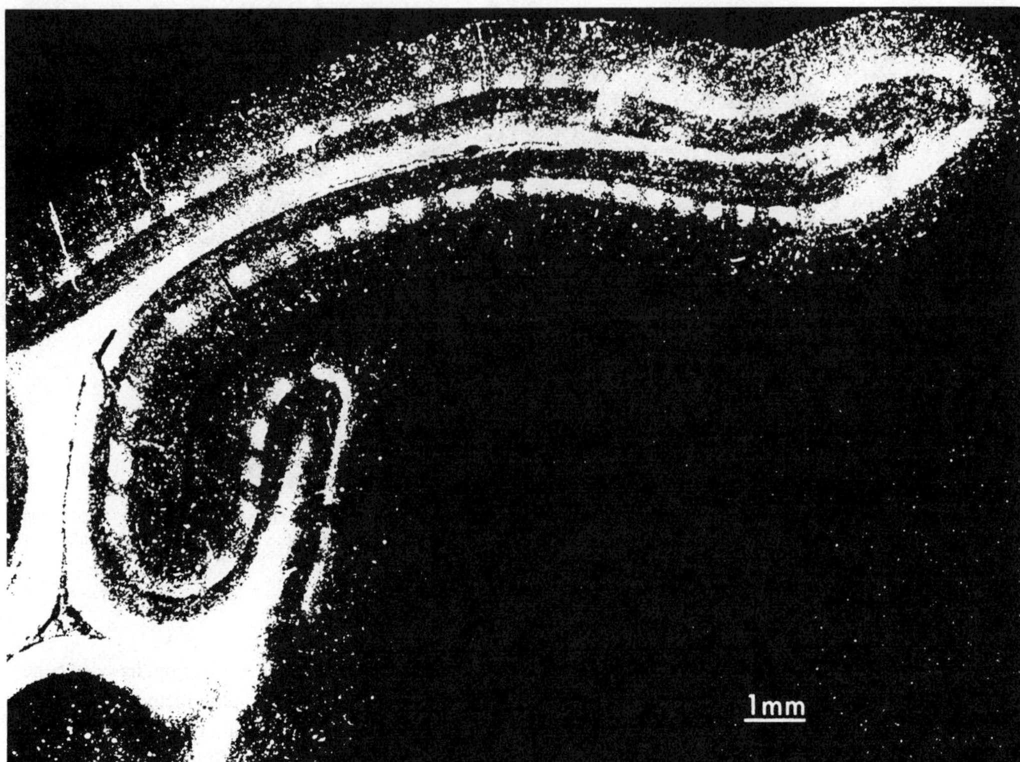

Figure 13. Dark-field autoradiogram of striate cortex in adult monkey following injection of tritiated proline-fucose in the ipsilateral eye. As can be seen, the thalamocortical terminal zones of each eye in the visual cortex are organized as alternating columns, and tend to be restricted to layer IV. (From Hubel & Wiesel, 1977.)

nations of the prefrontal cortex represent a vertical pattern of anatomical organization which is superimposed upon the laminar or horizontal structure of the cortex, they differ in fundamental aspects of their structure and functional organization. For example, the thalamo-cortical terminal zones of the visual system are restricted to layer IV of this area (Figure 13), while the callosal and associational columns of the prefrontal cortex span the entire cortical depth with principle terminations in layers I–V (see Figure 11).

This variation in the laminar termination zones may have important functional implications, as many neurons within layers III, V, and VI are output neurons that send axons to distant cortical and subcortical targets, while cells within layer IV tend to have axons that remain within the same cortical area. These factors may reflect the amount of local processing of information that the thalamic versus cortical message receives prior to the conveyance of this signal to other regions.

A second and more fundamental difference between the columnar organization of sensory and association cortex terminal zones is the nature of the input interposed between columns. In the primary visual cortex, adjacent ocular dominance columns are equivalent fiber systems representing the two eyes. In prefrontal cortex, callosal terminals interdigitate with associational terminals. As with left and right eye ocular dominance columns, the two sets of cortico-cortical afferents tend to occupy mutually exclusive columnar territories (Goldman-Rakic & Schwartz, 1982). The extent to which this relationship of ipsilateral and contralateral connections represent a general principle of organization remains to be determined. Further knowledge of the interrelationships among converging inputs to these zones will provide a significant step in our understanding of the mediation of functional activity by this cortical network.

Development of Prefrontal Cortex

In contrast to the numerous investigations of the intrinsic organization and extrinsic connections of prefrontal cortex in adult monkeys, until recently only a few studies have focused on the development of this area or its connections. In the following sections we will assess what is known about the neural development of prefrontal cortex, sùpplementing, where gaps exist, information obtained from the study of other cortical areas.

Time of Cell Origin

In all structures of the developing central nervous system (CNS), the generation of neural constituents and their migration to appropriate positions relative to other structures are critical developmental events. In the developing monkey and human brain these events occur prenatally and are completed well in advance of birth.

All neurons in the developing CNS are generated in germinal zones which are usually distant from the positions which their progeny will eventually occupy in the mature organism. These proliferative or germinal zones lie within the ventricular regions of the developing neural tube. Although it is beyond the scope of this section to go into detail about the embryonic development of the central nervous system, it is useful to point out that all divisions of the CNS arise from the embryonic neural tube. Additionally, as the neural tube undergoes conformational changes during development, it is possible to identify regions which in the fully formed organism will correspond with the divisions of the CNS ventricular system. It is at the surface of these ventricular regions that the germinal zones are found during development. The relations between the sites of neural generation and the ultimate destination of cells is rigidly specified. For example, cells destined for the neocortex are generated in the ventricular zone of the lateral ventricle (see Figure 14), with subregions of this proliferative area responsible for the generation of particular subdivisions within the cerebral cortex (Rakic, 1978). Constituent neurons of adult neo-

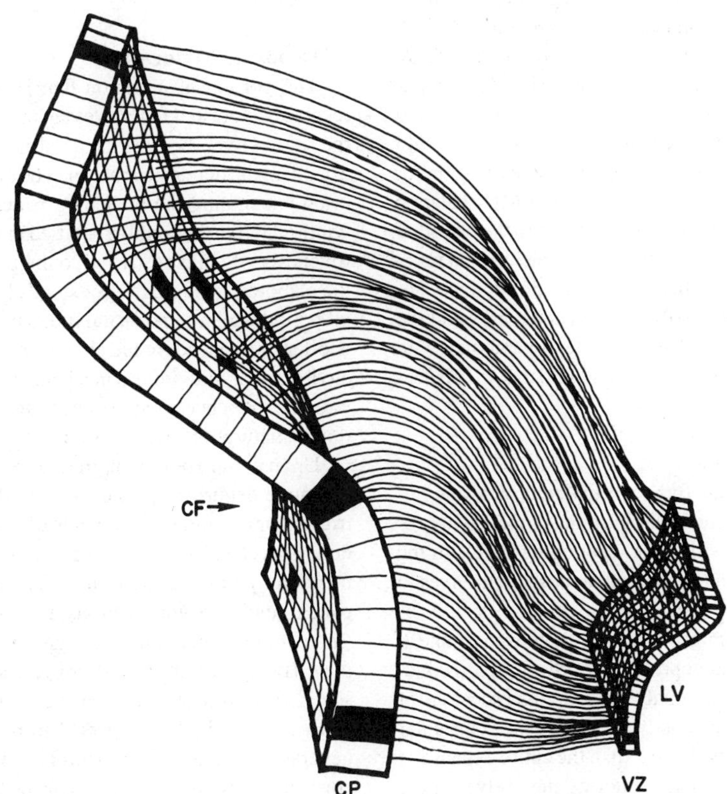

Figure 14. Schematic three-dimensional reconstruction of the portion of the medial cerebral wall of the occipito-parietal junction in an 80-day-old monkey fetus. The reconstruction is confined to the level of the incipient calcarine fissure (CF) to display the relationship between the parcellation of the ventricular zone (VZ) and that of the cortical plate (CP). The corresponding regions are connected by radial glial fibers which span the full thickness of the cerebral wall from the lateral ventricle (LV) to the pial surface. Rakic postulated that these elongated cords provide lateral constraints during cell migration and enable precise reproduction of the mosaicism of the ventricular zone on the enlarged and distorted cerebral surface. (From Rakic, 1978.)

cortex are generated only within this germinal zone and must then migrate from this area to their final resting position.

Using the technique of ^{3}H-thymidine autoradiography it is possible to determine the spatial and temporal origin and migration pattern of neurons destined for specified neocortical and subcortical structures. This procedure involves injecting ^{3}H-thymidine into pregnant females or newborn animals at known gestational or postnatal ages. The ^{3}H-thymidine is then incorporated into the DNA of actively dividing cells providing a radioactive tag or label in neurons "born" at the time of injection. These animals are subsequently sacrificed and sections of the brain are exposed to a photographic film emulsion sensitive to the emission energy of the ^{3}H-thymidine (Sidman, 1970). Examination of sections prepared in this way allows "labeled" cells to be identified and analyzed for number and position. Utilizing this methodology it has been determined that all cells that comprise the prefrontal cortex in the monkey are generated over a 50-day period beginning at embryonic day 40 (E40) and reaching completion by E90 of the 165-day gestational period (Wikmark & Rakic, unpublished observations). The MD nucleus of the thalamus is generated over a shorter period beginning at E30, reaching completion by E45 (Dekker & Rakic, 1980). The times of cell origin for the prefrontal cortex and the related MD thalamic nucleus show a remarkable similarity to the period of neuronal generation for other anatomically and functionally distinct cortical and thalamic regions. For example, neurons destined for visual cortex and the related thalamic nucleus, the lateral geniculate, are generated from E45 to E102 and E30 to E45, respectively (Rakic, 1974, 1977).

Cell Migration

Following their final cell division, neurons migrate from the ventricular germinal zones to appropriate positions within the developing brain. In the cortex, young neurons closely appose themselves to elongated radial glial fibers which they use as "guides" in the migration from the germinal zone to the surface of the appropriate cortical area (Rakic, 1978). These radial glial fibers are the processes of glial cells whose cell body remains in the ventricular zone, yet whose processes span the entire expanse of the developing cortex, anchoring themselves at the surface of the brain. It is possible, therefore, for a neuron to be generated in the ventricular zone and follow the path of a single radial glial fiber to its cortical destination (Rakic, 1972, 1978). Upon arrival in the developing cortical plate, successive waves of newly arriving neurons pass through earlier arriving neurons and assume progressively more superficial laminar positions. Although some mixing may occur, in general these neurons will retain these laminar positions throughout the life of the organism.

Using the ^{3}H-thymidine method to examine the rate of neural migration in the developing primate cortex, Rakic (1978) has determined that the period between a neuron's generation and its arrival in the cortical plate varies depending on the stage of cortical development. The results of this investigation revealed that early in development neurons may arrive in the cortical plate within three days of their last cell division, while in the final stages of this period migration may take up to three weeks. These migration rates and the data available on neurogenesis indicate that in primates, such as the rhesus monkey, all neural constituents of the cortex are generated and in position well before birth; thus these events appear to be largely under genetic control and may be relatively impervious to external environmental influences.

Dendritic Maturation

The portion of a neuron that is specialized for receiving input and for conveying this information to the soma or cell body is the dendrite. In the mature organism the dendritic arbor may be quite extensive, often resembling the branching pattern of a tree in winter. Unlike the rigidly specified program for neurogenesis which is restricted to the prenatal period, the elaboration of dendrites extends from the prenatal period well into postnatal life. This development is often influenced by the character of the postnatal environment, providing a mechanism by which individual experiences may be integrated into the functional maturation of developing neural structures.

Upon completion of migration, neurons begin to elaborate dendritic appendages. While the specific trigger for the initiation of dendritic growth is uncertain, it has been suggested that initial dendritic segments may arise as the result of an interaction between newly arriving neurons and monoaminergic (monoamine-containing) fiber groups in the cortical plate (Berry, 1982; Pinto Lord & Caviness, 1979; see also *Neurochemical Development of Cerebral Cortex*). As might be expected from the pattern of generation and migration, neurons within the deeper cortical layers initiate dendritic growth prior to cells within more superficial laminae (Jones, 1982; Juraska & Fifkova, 1979); however, despite differences in the time of onset, the dendritic arbors of cells in all cortical laminae seem to reach maturity at roughly equivalent times (Berry, 1982; Jones, 1982).

Cells of the same morphological class also share a precise and orderly sequence of dendritic elaboration even though they may be located in different laminae. For example, the pyramidal neuron is found in nearly all cortical laminae except layers I and IV and has three primary dendritic systems: (1) the *apical* or primary dendrite which is aligned perpendicular to the cortical surface, and issues from the apex of the cell body and crosses several laminar boundaries, (2) the *basilar* dendrites which arise from the base of the neuron and are generally restricted to a single cortical lamina, and (3) the *oblique* dendrites which branch off of the apical dendrite in various laminae. For this class of neuron the sequence of dendritic development is ordered such that the apical dendrite is the first to appear, followed shortly by the emergence of the basilar dendrites, and finally by the growth of the oblique branches (Juraska & Fifkova, 1979). This progression appears to be evident for neurons of this type in all layers and across species.

Although little information is available on the dendritic development of prefrontal cortical neurons in monkeys, a comprehensive study of the human frontal cortex by Schade and van Groenigen (1961) provides some interesting insights into the relationships between higher cognitive functions and neural maturation in this region. Their results indicate that this area is relatively immature at birth, with all dendritic systems of pyramidal neurons in layers 2, 3, and 5 appearing quite rudimentary and lacking extensive branching. In contrast, neurons of the relatively early maturing visual cortex have numerous basal and oblique branches and have apical dendrites, which though still relatively thin, nonetheless cross several laminar borders at birth (Takashima, Chan, Becker, & Armstrong, 1980). Neurons of the prefrontal cortex undergo an extensive elaboration of dendritic area after birth, with dendritic length increasing five- to tenfold within the first six months (Schade & Groenigam, 1961). This elaboration of dendritic area continues, although at a reduced rate, until well beyond 24 months of age in humans.

Synaptic Development

The synapse is the area of communication between neurons. It is at this specialized site between an axon and dendrite or cell body (or in some cases between an axon and another axon) that chemical messages are relayed (see *Neurochemical Development of Cerebral Cortex*). As with dendritic development, synaptogenesis in primate neocortex begins prenatally but does not reach completion until well into postnatal life. Although the time at which synaptogenesis begins has not been precisely specified in primate neocortex, studies of rodent cortex indicate that synaptic profiles can be identified soon after the emergence of initial dendritic segments (Juraska & Fifkova, 1979). Investigations of synaptic density beginning at birth in both humans and monkeys indicate that synaptic proliferation must be extensive during the postnatal period (Huttenlocher, 1979; Lund, Boothe, & Lund, 1977; Takashima et al., 1980). In spite of the considerable number of synapses present at birth, synaptic density in the frontal lobes continues to increase postnatally until maximal levels are attained between 1 and 2 years of age (Huttenlocher, 1979).

An interesting aspect of cortical synaptogenesis is that, at least for some regions, the initial proliferation of synapses may overshoot the number found in mature individuals. This phenomena has been quantified in human frontal cortex (Huttenlocher, 1979) as well as in monkey and rat visual cortices (Boothe & Lund, 1976; Lund et al., 1977; Parnavelas & Globus, 1976). This initial overproduction of synapses is followed by a period of consolidation during which synaptic density is gradually reduced until adult levels are reached. This developmental sequence is similar to the overproduction of neurons in some areas of the peripheral nervous system during ontogeny and the subsequent period of cell death during which the organism prunes the population to adult levels. Investigations in human frontal cortex indicate that this consolidation period may continue from the period at which maximal density of synapses is reached at 1 to 2 years of age, until 16 years of age (Huttenlocher, 1979). These observations have important implications for our understanding of the relation between synaptic density and behavior, since it has generally been assumed that a larger number or a greater density of synapses implies a higher functional capacity or increased potential for neuronal plasticity. In contrast, these results suggest that beyond a certain level, high synaptic density may also be maladaptive or reflect developmental arrest; indeed, unusually high numbers of synapses have been observed in some cases of human mental deficiency (Cragg, 1975).

Environmental and Aging Influences on Dendritic Development

Both the periods of dendritic growth and of maturation in synaptic density extend well into postnatal life providing ample opportunity for environmental factors to interact with the maturation and pattern of growth of both structures. As has been observed on many occasions (for review see Globus, 1975; Riesen, 1966; Rothblat & Schwartz, 1979b), numerous investigations have provided evidence that the character of the early postnatal environment may profoundly influence the dendritic and synaptic organization within a given cortical area. Three general principles have emerged from these investigations. First, limiting the level of environmental stimulation significantly reduces synaptic density as well as the length and branching of dendrites in affected cortical regions (Borges & Berry, 1978; Coleman & Riesen, 1968; Fifkova, 1970; Valverde, 1967), while enhancing the level of environmental stimulation has the opposite effect (Greenough & Volkmar, 1973; Parnavelas & Globus, 1976). Second, the effects of postnatal stimulation tend to be restricted to the sensory modality deprived or hyperstimulated. Third, the effects of stimulation or deprivation on morphological development tend to be most pronounced during a sensitive period in early postnatal life; this period may vary from one cortical area to the next depending on the level and rate of neural maturation (Fiala, Joyce, & Greenough, 1978; Rothblat & Schwartz, 1979a). The majority of these studies have utilized cats or rodents as experimental subjects and have focused on alterations of the sensory environment. Thus the extent to which primate cortical association areas may also be modified by alterations in, or interaction, with the postnatal environment remains undetermined. However, a recent study of primates reared under various environmental conditions has indicated that nonsensory areas such as the cerebellum respond morphologically to variations in the early environment (Floeter & Greenough, 1979).

Modifications of dendritic arborization and synaptic density tend to diminish with increasing age. Investigations of aging in a number of species including humans (Buell & Coleman, 1979; Huttenlocher, 1979; Scheibel, Lindsay, Tomisayu, & Scheibel, 1975, 1976) and infrahuman primates (Cupp & Uemura, 1980; Uemura, 1980) indicate that in extreme old age and senescence synaptic density may be reduced and that there is a progressive reduction of dendritic length and branching within a select population of cortical neurons. Interestingly, the sequence of dendritic loss in affected neurons mirrors the order of original elaboration (Scheibel, 1982). For example, pyramidal neurons show a reduction in dendritic surface that is first evident for the basilar and oblique branches, followed some time later by the diminution of the apical dendrite. This mirroring of development in the degradation of dendritic systems has intriguing functional implications. For example, one obvious possibility is that the pattern of loss of cognitive and intellectual skills in senescence or senile dementia may be the reverse of the general pattern of their development. Such issues remain to be evaluated. However, it is tempting to speculate that as the structural and functional consequences of aging become better understood, they may provide some insight into the structural basis of cognitive development.

Synaptic Density and Mental Capacity

The precise relationship between synaptic density and behavioral capacity remains unclear. Traditionally, the density of synaptic structures has been considered to be positively correlated with functional capacity. This reasoning has been reinforced by investigations of synaptic number in mentally retarded individuals or individuals with impaired mental abilities due to chromosomal aberrations such as Down's or Patau's syndromes (Marin-Padilla, 1972, 1974). In general, these individuals have abnormally low synaptic densities and show alterations in synaptic morphology. Conversely, conditions that are associated with improved learning capacity, such as environmental enrichment, frequently result in abnormally high synaptic levels (Globus, Rosenzweig, Bennett, & Diamond, 1973).

Although it is tempting to speculate that functional capacity and synaptic number may be monotonically or linearly related, several lines of evidence indicate that this may be an oversimplification. Thus, Cragg (1975) has observed that in some instances of mental deficiency, synaptic numbers may exceed those found in normal mature individuals. In addition, recent investigations of the rodent visual system indicate that some early environmental manipulations may produce behavioral impairments although synaptic density may be normal or supranormal (Anderson & O'Steen, 1972; Parnavelas & Globus, 1976; Schwartz & Rothblat, 1980).

These results argue against the exclusive use of morphological criteria of synaptic development as an index of behavioral and cognitive development and capacity. Indeed, anatomical maturity does not necessarily imply functional maturity. For example, Farkas-Bargeton and Diebler (1978) have provided evidence that the appearance of dendritic spines may not in itself be an accurate index of a functioning or mature synapse. They indicate that in normal development a morphologically mature spine may be present well in advance of the enzyme constituents which are necessary for the adult-like functioning of these synaptic specializations.

Development of Cortico-Cortical Connections

Unlike the proliferation of dendrites and synaptic structures, the development of cortico-cortical connections of the monkey prefrontal cortex occurs

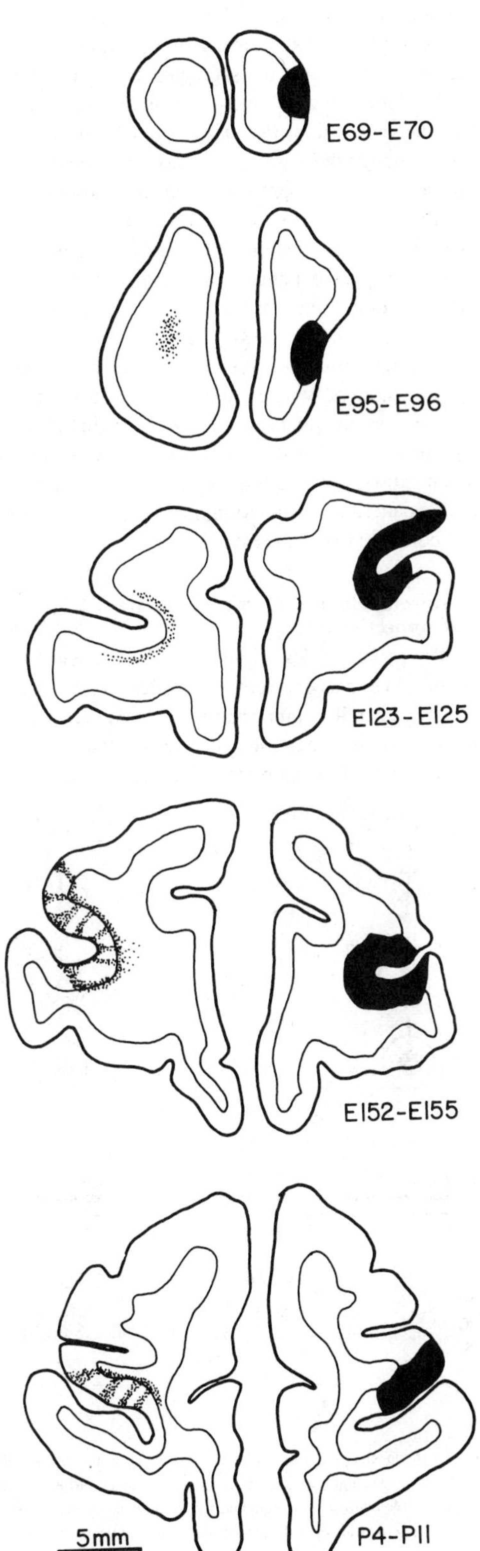

Figure 15. Callosal fibers at different embryonic (E) and postnatal (P) ages. The first number beneath each drawing indicates the age in days when the animal was injected and the second number refers to the age in days at which it was sacrificed. Callosal fibers do not reach the contralateral hemisphere until after E70 and do not enter the cortical plate before E123. Callosal axons invade the cortex between E125 and E152, and by the end of this period they are already segregated into the "modular" pattern characteristic of the neocortex in postnatal monkeys.

largely prior to birth (Goldman-Rakic, 1981). As so much of the development of these connections is completed prenatally, only recently with the introduction of reliable fiber tracing methodologies and advances in prenatal surgical techniques has it been possible to trace and characterize the development of these connections. Goldman-Rakic (1981) has utilized these methodologies to map the development of selected callosal and associational connections of the dorsolateral prefrontal cortex. Following injections of radioactively labeled amino acids into the presumptive prefrontal cortex of fetuses at embryonic day 69 (E69) Goldman-Rakic observed labeled fibers descending from the injection site to the subjacent intermediate zone (prospective white matter) and into the developing callosum (Figure 15). Fibers of ipsilateral associational connections were not evident at this age. Between the ages of E69 and E123, associational fibers began to emerge and the number of both callosal and associational fibers steadily increased as they approached their cortical targets. Ipsilateral associational fibers had arrived at and penetrated one of their targets, the retrosplenial cortex (a portion of cortex on the medial surface of the brain in the posterior one-third of the hemisphere) by E123; however, the callosal fibers were not as advanced and, although they had arrived at the homotopic contralateral prefrontal cortex, they had not yet penetrated the cortical plate. By E155, roughly 2 weeks before term, both the callosal and associational fibers had arrived at their respective targets, penetrated all cortical laminae, and displayed a pattern of columnar organization indistinguishable from that observed in mature monkeys.

The rapid prenatal development of cortico-cortical connections of the prefrontal cortex contrasts with the protracted postnatal maturation of the thalamo-cortical ocular dominance system in monkeys (Rakic, 1976; LeVay, Wiesel, & Hubel, 1980). These columnar systems differ not only in the time of maturation, but also in the sequence of segregation for terminal regions and in the reliance on environmental input for normal development. For example, the fibers of callosal and associational connections of prefrontal cortex are already segregated into columns before they enter their cortical targets. In contrast, the thalamic fibers representing the two eyes enter the visual cortex in an overlapping manner and only gradually segregate into alternating ocular dominance columns representing one, then the other eye (Rakic, 1979a&b) (Figure 16). In addition, although the segregation into a columnar organization occurs in prefrontal terminal zones prenatally in the absence of external input, the maturation and segregation of ocular dominance columns is highly dependent on, and responsive to, visual stimulation through both eyes (Rakic, 1979a&b; Swindale, 1981).

It is clear from the comparison of developmental features of these two columnar systems that while a columnar arrangement of afferent fiber distribution may be a general feature of central nervous system organization, the functional significance and impact of this pattern of termination may vary greatly from one cortical area to the next.

Development of Cortico-Caudate Connections

The principal development of the caudate fiber system, like that of the cortico-cortical connections, occurs prenatally. It may be recalled that the caudate nucleus is one of the subcortical centers that receives a major output from prefrontal cortex (cortico-caudate). This pathway is thought to be the principle route by which the prefrontal cortex ultimately influences voluntary motor behaviors. However, unlike the cortico-cortical connections which are already segregated when they invade their target areas, cortico-caudate fibers initially distribute with a uniform density throughout the caudate nucleus and only gradually develop the patchy pattern of termination that characterizes the adult organization (see Figure 17) (Goldman-Rakic, 1981). Utilizing methods identical to those used to trace the development of cortico-cortical connections, Goldman-Rakic (1981) has mapped the maturation of cortico-caudate fibers originating from the prefrontal area of cortex. Following injections of radioactively labeled amino acids into the prefrontal cortex of fetuses at E69 it is possible to detect labeled fibers that are evenly distributed throughout the head of the ipsilateral caudate nucleus (Figure 17). Although the density of fibers increases dramatically with increasing age, no detectable variation in the distribution is seen until around E105. At E105 the first evidence of segregation of terminal label is observed, although the boundaries of labeled and unlabeled regions are not crisp. By E152 the network of terminal clusters and label-free islands has become indistinguishable from that in mature animals.

As yet the mechanism(s) by which the cortico-

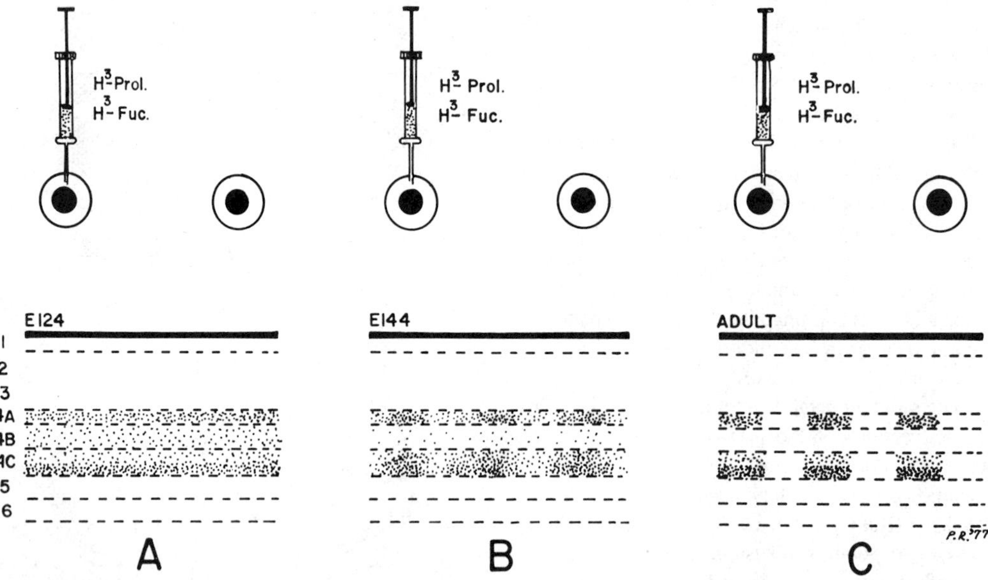

Figure 16. Development of ocular dominance columns in layer 4 of the primary visual cortex of the rhesus monkey at various ages (E124, E144, adult). This sequence was visualized in autoradiograms following transneuronal transport of radioactive tracers (^{3}H-fucose and ^{3}H-proline) injected into one eye 14 days before sacrifice. Cortical layers indicated by numerals 1 to 6 are delineated according to Brodmann's (1905) classification. (From Rakic, 1979a.)

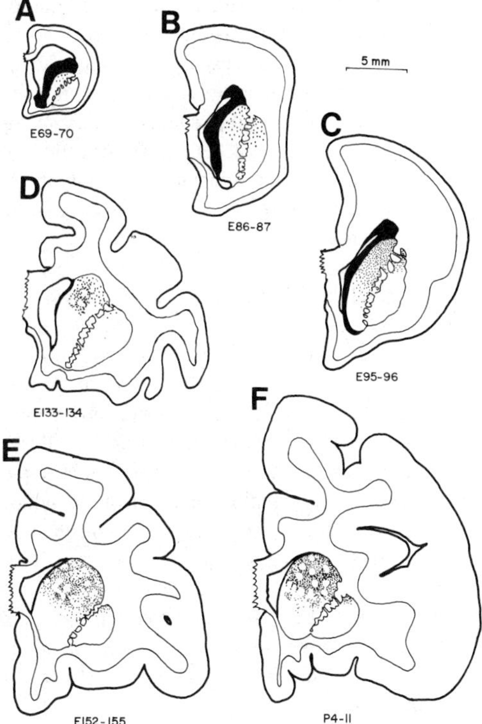

Figure 17. Time and mode of establishment of prefrontocaudate connections in the rhesus monkey. Prefrontal fibers enter the caudate nucleus as early as E69 but they are distributed uniformly at this and subsequent embryonic ages. Segregation of cortical terminals begins at or around E123 (not shown) and is well developed, if not virtually completed, by E152. (From Goldman-Rakic, 1981.)

caudate fibers shift from a homogeneous distribution during early development to a segregated and patchy pattern in the mature monkey are unclear and the functional consequences of such a shift are similarly obscure. One possibility is that the arrival of new afferents from other cortical or subcortical areas may differentially displace fibers of the prefrontal cortex through a competition for synaptic space. Alternatively, inhomogeneity may arise as the result of the development and organization of intrinsic neuronal networks within the nucleus. Indeed, recent observations in neonatal and adult monkeys indicate that the label-free cores within the caudate nucleus are occupied by rounded or elliptically shaped islands of densely packed small neurons (Goldman-Rakic, 1981). The relationship between the appearance of these cellular islands and the emergence of terminal segregation remains to be elucidated, but may provide some clue as to the mechanism of segregation for cortical terminations.

Functional Implications

The orderly distribution of connections within specific sensory systems has been recognized for some time. The orderly topography of retinal projections on the lateral geniculate body (Matthews, Cowan, & Powell, 1960; Minkowski, 1913; Polyak, 1957) and of the cochlear representation in auditory cortex (Ades, 1943; Merzenich & Brugge, 1973; Woolsey & Walzl, 1942) and the functional and anatomical columnar arrangements in the visual cortex (Hubel & Wiesel, 1963b, 1969) are examples of anatomical and cytoarchitectonic features that correlate with function in a relatively straightforward manner. In contrast, the organization of cognitive behaviors is not readily suggestive of any particular neuroanatomic arrangements, and the structural bases of such behaviors have long been thought to be rather diffuse. However, the discovery of columnar organization in the cortical projections of prefrontal cortex (Goldman & Nauta, 1977a) and the patterning in prefronto-caudate projections (Goldman & Nauta, 1977b) seem to indicate that the neuroanatomical substrates mediating complex cognitive activity may be as highly structured as the areas subserving sensory processing. The functional significance of these findings are as yet unclear, but some preliminary results (Bugbee & Goldman, unpublished data) indicate that prefrontal columns and prefronto-caudate patterning may have their counterparts in areas of differing local metabolic rates as measured by the 2-deoxyglucose method, which was discussed earlier.

The intricate structuring of functional relationships within the sensory system has provided the framework for our present understanding of the neural basis of sensory behavior. Similarly, we have every reason to expect that further elucidation of the anatomical organization of areas which may be involved in cognitive function, such as the prefrontal cortex, may shed light on the functional organization underlying cognition. Such data would in turn allow further advances in the study of the neuroanatomical basis of normal and pathological cognitive development.

NEUROCHEMICAL DEVELOPMENT OF CEREBRAL CORTEX

While anatomical pathways establish the structural framework of connectivity of the central nervous system, communication between cells is mediated via chemical messengers or transmitters. The neurochemical environment of the developing brain does not remain constant, but shows ontogenetic fluctuation and variation. Investigations of these neurochemical alterations—their causes, functions, and relationships to behavior—provide a perspective on the problems of development which is separate from but complementary to that of anatomy.

Presently, over 30 putative transmitters have been identified in the central nervous system. This discussion will focus on a particular subset of these, the monoamines, so named because their molecular structure is characterized by a single amine group. The particular monoamines to be discussed are serotonin (an indoleamine) and norepinephrine and dopamine (both catecholamines). Although dopamine is formed as an intermediate step in the manufacture of norepinephrine, considerable evidence indicates that it also acts as a transmitter in its own right.

The monoamines have been selected for discussion for a number of reasons. Because they were among the first transmitter substances to be identified, they have been the most thoroughly studied and are consequently among the best understood. In humans, clinical and pharmacological evidence has linked the monoamines to the expression of emotional and cognitive behaviors (Hornykiewicz, 1974) and in nonhuman primates, dopamine has been shown to play a particularly important part in functions subserved by prefrontal cortex (Brozoski, Brown, Rosvold and Goldman, 1979). Moreover, the potential role of the monoamine systems in cortical development is of great interest for a number of reasons. Studies of cell proliferation (Coyle & Molliver, 1977; Hanaway, McConnell, & Netsky, 1972; Lauder & Bloom, 1974; Levitt & Rakic, 1979; Loizou, 1976) and of transmitter levels and synthetic capacity (Coyle & Axelrod, 1972a,b; Levitt & Moore, 1979; Loizou & Salt, 1970) all indicate that catecholamine neurons arise early in development. The precocious maturation of these systems has led to the hypothesis that monoamines may exert an inductive or regulatory influence on the development of the cerebral cortex (Coyle & Axelrod, 1972a,b; Lauder & Bloom, 1974; Olson & Seiger, 1972).

The basic mechanisms of neurochemical communication in the central nervous system have been worked out for a number of years. Most neurons are composed of distinct receiving (dendrites and soma) and transmitting (axon) zones, and communication between cells generally occurs only at specialized junctions called synapses. A nerve impulse or action potential in the first (presynaptic) of two communicating neurons commences near the cell body and sweeps along the axon toward the axon terminal. Upon reaching the axon terminal, the impulse causes stored packets of neurotransmitter molecules to be released into the synaptic space. A small number of these molecules diffuse across the synapse and lock into special receptor complexes located in the membrane of the postsynaptic cell. The activation of these receptors alters the postsynaptic membrane in such a way as to trigger an action potential in the postsynaptic neuron.

While this traditional model of synaptic communication may hold for most neuronal systems, it has been recently established that many other kinds of synaptic interactions can occur (Shepherd, 1979). For instance, the dendrite of one neuron may synapse with the dendrite of another, and information between these two may flow bidirectionally. Moreover, morphological evidence suggests that some neurotransmitters, including members of the monoamine group, may be released from nonsynaptic sites for diffusion to targets more distant than those found in conventional synaptic transmission. Substances released from diffuse axonal projections could alter the responsiveness of vast domains of target cells, and thereby produce global effects on behavioral state.

The first step in neurochemical transmission is the manufacture of transmitter molecules. Transmitters are synthesized in the cell body of the neuron and are carried to the axon terminals by the process of anterograde axonal transport. In most cases, a neuron can synthesize only one kind of transmitter, which it releases from all the terminals of its axon. The transmitter molecules are not manufactured *de novo,* but are prepared by the modification of precursor molecules—usually amino acids—through a series of one or more enzyme-catalyzed reactions. The synthesis of catecholamines begins with the amino acid, tyrosine, which is taken up into the nerve terminal from the bloodstream. Tyrosine is first converted into the intermediate substance, L-dopa; a second enzyme converts L-dopa into dopamine, and a third enzyme converts dopamine into norepinephrine. The amino acid precursor for serotonin is tryptophan, which is enzymatically converted to 5-hydroxytryptophan and eventually to 5-hydroxytryptamine (5-HT) or serotonin.

At the synapse, only a small proportion of the transmitter molecules released from the presynaptic membrane actually reaches the postsynaptic receptors. The remainder may be taken back into the presynaptic membrane (re-uptake) or may be degraded by enzymes present in the synaptic space. Thus, the amount of a particular transmitter in a given volume of brain tissue reflects not only the rate at which that transmitter is being synthesized but also the rate of enzymatic degradation of the transmitter.

Monoamine Systems in Adults

Sources of Monoamines in the Brain

One of the most important advances in understanding the neurochemistry of brain function has been the development of methods for identification of neurons containing a particular transmitter. These techniques have been used to reveal the distribution of the cell bodies and axonal projections of monoamine-containing neurons. In the histofluorescence technique developed by Falck and his colleagues (Falck, Hillarp, Thieme, & Torp, 1962), the natural transmitter is converted into a derivative which fluoresces when exposed to ultraviolet radiation in the fluorescence microscope. When brain tissue is treated with formaldehyde vapors or glyoxylic acid, the neurons containing catecholamines fluoresce green and indoleamines fluoresce yellow. More recently, radioactively labeled transmitters (Parent, Descarries, & Beaudet, 1981) or antibodies specific to a particular transmitter or synthetic enzyme (Steinbusch, 1981; Swanson & Hartman, 1975) have been used to map neurochemical pathways.

The techniques described above have shown that monoamines are not randomly distributed throughout the brain, but are localized in discrete clusters of neurons whose axons project to specific brain regions. The remarkably extensive norepinephrine projection system originates in two major sites: cell groups within the lateral tegmentum and the nucleus locus coeruleus (see review by Moore & Bloom, 1978).

Cells of the locus coeruleus are notable for the extensive collateralization of their axons, such that a single neuron may project to widespread regions of the cortex and cerebellum (Olson & Fuxe, 1971; Ungerstedt, 1971). The diffuseness and lack of topographical organization of norepinephrine-containing fibers has been interpreted as suggestive of a nonspecific role of this monoamine system in modulating cortical activity.

In contrast to norepinephrine, the dopamine system has a precise and discrete topography and a more restricted terminal distribution. All of the dopamine of the telencephalon originates in two regions of the midbrain, the substantia nigra and the ventral tegmentum.

Fibers from the substantia nigra project primarily to the caudate and putamen of the neostriatum. As the dopamine axons enter these structures, they undergo extensive collateralization, and each collateral branch is studded by numerous swellings or varicosities. Because the degeneration of the nigrostriatal system gives rise to the muscular rigidity and tremors of Parkinson's disease, striatal dopamine has been hypothesized to play a critical role in the control of complex movements (Hornykiewicz, 1979).

The second dopamine system originates in a cell group of the brainstem generally described as the ventral tegmental area. Anatomical data from a number of species indicates that these tegmental cells project heavily to the prefrontal cortex (Divac, Bjorklund, Lindvall, & Passingham, 1978; Porrino & Goldman-Rakic, 1982). Thus, both the cortical and subcortical components of the prefrontal system are characterized by strong dopaminergic input, with the prefrontal cortex receiving dopamine from the ventral tegmental area and the caudate nucleus receiving dopamine from the substantia nigra.

The cells of origin of the serotonin system are clustered in the region of the brainstem known as the raphe nuclei. The neurons of the raphe project to the hypothalamus, the thalamus, and many other brain regions (Brodal, Taber, & Walberg, 1960).

Cortical Distribution of Monoamines

While clinical research has revealed the importance of monoamines in the cognitive and emotional behavior of humans, until recently most anatomical evidence concerning the distribution of cortical monoamines has been based on rodent studies. However, cortical fields which are topographically and functionally discrete in the primate are compressed into completely or partially overlapping territories in the rodent. In order to determine the levels and localization of monoamines in a species in which cortical differentiation and behavioral capabilities are more similar to those of man, a series of studies was undertaken to provide a quantitative analysis of the distribution and maturation of monoamines in selected cortical and subcortical structures of the monkey (Brown, Crane, & Goldman, 1979; Brown & Goldman, 1977, 1979; Goldman-Rakic & Brown, 1981a,b). Monoamine content (the amount of transmitter in a given brain region) and turnover (an index of the rate of *in vivo* synthesis) were first measured in 11 young adult monkeys of 2 to 3 years of age (Brown et al., 1979). Data from the young adults were then used as a reference point for studying the ontogenesis of monoamine systems in developing animals, and examining the effects of aging in these systems (Goldman-Rakic & Brown, 1981a,b).

In young adult rhesus monkeys (24 to 36 months of age), catecholamine levels vary across cortical regions. Dopamine concentration peaks in the prefrontal cortex, and then declines in an almost linear fashion along the anterior-posterior axis (Figure 18). Concentrations decrease along the premotor, precentral, postcentral, and parietal cortices, and reach a low within the visual cortex at the occipital pole.

Unlike its distribution in rodent species, the norepinephrine content of the rhesus monkey brain shows a distinct pattern of regional variation. As shown in Figure 18, norepinephrine exhibits a frontal-occipital distribution gradient similar to that described for dopamine; however, the norepinephrine distribution is more irregular. Peak concentrations of norepinephrine are observed in the postcentral somatosensory cortex where levels are nearly double those observed in the motor cortex of the precentral gyrus. The lowest norepinephrine concentrations are found in the occipital cortex.

Compared to the well-defined gradients observed for cortical catecholamines, the topographic distribution of serotonin in 24- to 36-month-old monkeys is more uniform (Figure 18). Slightly above average concentrations are found in somatosensory and occipital cortex; in remaining cortical areas, serotonin is evenly distributed in relatively low concentrations.

Functional Implications

In rodents, norepinephrine has been reported to be rather evenly distributed throughout all cortical areas (Kehr, Lindquist, & Carlsson, 1976; Levitt & Moore, 1978). This lack of regional variation has been used to argue that monoamines must play a rather nonspecific role in cortical function. However, Brown and Goldman's (1977) finding that in primates transmitter levels vary with cortical region suggests more specific functions for these substances than have been suspected previously. For instance, norepinephrine levels peak in somatosensory cortex, suggesting that this monoamine may play a role in somesthetic function. This suggestion is supported by a recent description of selective norepinephrine innervation of somatosensory cortex of the rat (Lidov, Rice, & Molliver, 1978) and by reports of high levels of norepinephrine in human thalamic nuclei which project to somatosensory cor-

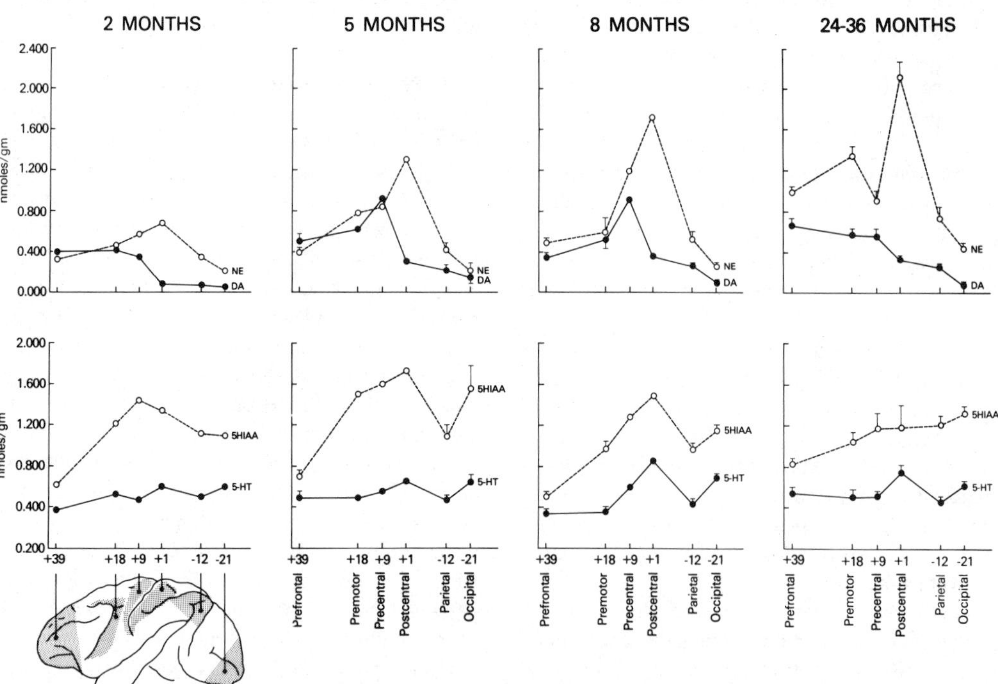

Figure 18. Topographical distribution in nmole/gm concentrations of norepinephrine (NE), dopamine (DA), serotonin (5-HT), and the serotonin metabolite, 5-HIAA, in six functionally distinct regions of dorsal neocortex. In order to emphasize topographical differences, the concentrations have been plotted along a horizontal axis representing Horsley-Clark coordinates of the anterior-posterior axis of the brain. (From Goldman-Rakic and Brown, 1982.)

tex (Oke, Keller, Medford, & Adams, 1978). Interestingly, toxic doses of drugs which potentiate the action of norepinephrine, such as cocaine and amphetamine, often produce tactile hallucinations and paresthesias (Ellenwood, 1969; Kramer, Fischman, & Littlefield, 1967). Similarly, the finding that serotonin levels are highest in visual cortex may relate to the observation that ingestion of LSD—a drug known to interact with the serotonergic system (Aghajanian, 1972)—produces profound visual hallucinations.

Of particular interest to the study of frontal lobe function is the finding of high dopamine levels in the prefrontal association cortex of the rhesus monkey, a finding that suggests that dopamine plays some role in the mnemonic and spatial capacities of this region. To test this hypothesis, Brozoski et al. (1979) examined the spatial memory capacities of monkeys in which the prefrontal cortex had been selectively depleted of dopamine. Before undergoing this treatment, monkeys were trained on a delayed alternation task to determine the span of time over which they could remember spatial information; at the same time, they were trained on a visual discrimination task that did not involve spatial memory. After behavioral base–lines were established, the subjects were pretreated with DMI, a substance that protects norepinephrine terminals, and injections of the neurotoxin 6-hydroxydopamine were placed directly into prefrontal cortex. This substance selectively and permanently destroys the axon terminals of catecholamine neurons, and, hence, when administered with DMI produces a preferential reduction of dopamine content in the injected region.

All subjects recovered rapidly and displayed normal appetitive behavior and motor activity in their home cages. However, when retested, the dopamine-depleted animals showed a profound deficit in delayed alternation performance, a deficit nearly as severe as that seen in animals with surgical lesions of the prefrontal cortex. This impairment did not represent a general deterioration of cognitive ability because these same subjects continued to perform the visual discrimination task at pretreatment levels. In control subjects in which either norepinephrine or serotonin was depleted, alternation performance was affected only slightly if at all.

Further evidence that the spatial memory impairment is directly related to dopamine is indicated by the demonstration that the effect could be selectively reversed. When the affected subjects received systemic injections of the dopamine precursor, L-dopa (a substance that can pass through the blood brain barrier and thus elevate levels of brain dopamine), their alternation performance returned to predeficit levels. Drugs that did not act on the dopaminergic system did not produce significant behavioral recovery. More recent studies in rodents have confirmed the finding that reduction of prefrontal dopamine content produces selective impairment on spatial alternation tasks (Simon, Scatton, & LeMoal, 1979, 1980). In these experiments the ventral tegmental area, which is the source of prefrontal dopamine, was destroyed either by surgical lesions or direct injections of 6-hydroxydopamine.

The findings of Brozoski et al. (1979) demonstrate that the high levels of dopamine found in prefrontal cortex are linked directly to the expression of cognitive behaviors. Moreover, they suggest that the cognitive impairments associated with certain forms of Parkinson's disease (Lieberman, Dziatolowski, Kupersmith, Serby, Goodgold, Korein, & Goldstein, 1978; Loranger, Goodell, Lee, & McDowell, 1972) or with advancing age may result from the lowering of cortical dopamine known to accompany these conditions. Evidence of age-related declines in cortical dopamine will be discussed in a later portion of this chapter.

Maturation of Cortical Monoamines

After determining the regional distribution of monoamines in adults, Brown and Goldman (1977) and Goldman-Rakic and Brown (1981b) investigated the postnatal maturation of these systems in monkeys ranging in age from newborns to young adults. In all age groups studied, catecholamines showed the characteristic distribution already described for young adults—highest concentrations were found in prefrontal regions and lowest in occipital cortex. However, the relative concentrations of norepinephrine and dopamine differed with age. Norepinephrine showed a progressive increase from birth through 2 to 3 years of age. The increase in prefrontal, postcentral, parietal and occipital cortex between the neonatal period (0 to 2 months) and young adulthood (2 to 3 years) ranged from 171% to 719%.

Developmental changes in dopamine levels were generally more complex and erratic than those exhibited by norepinephrine. In general, dopamine reached peak concentration earlier in ontogeny than corresponding norepinephrine values—typically by 5 months of age (Figure 18). In most cortical regions examined, dopamine concentration at 5 months of age was higher than that at 2 months, and differed very little from levels at 2 to 3 years of age. An exception to this general rule occurred in prefrontal cortex, where dopamine concentration peaked at birth and did not differ significantly from young adult values. However, the dopamine content of prefrontal cortex exhibited a characteristic decline over an 18-month period before increasing again at 2 to 3 years. This pattern of change contrasted with that in the motor cortex, in which dopamine exhibits a peak value at 5 months, followed by a marked decrease at subsequent ages. In visual cortex, dopamine remains at the same low levels from birth to maturity.

Among the three monoamines studied, serotonin showed the least drastic alterations and most rapid development from birth through 3 years of age. In posterior parietal and visual cortices, serotonin content reached adult levels by 2 months of age and changed very little thereafter. Serotonin content in the postcentral gyrus reached adult status by 5 months of age. In prefrontal and premotor cortex, serotonin development paralleled that of dopamine. Similar concentrations and developmental fluctuations are observed in the two transmitters from 2 months through 36 months of age in both regions.

Developmental Changes in Monoamine Gradients

To emphasize the topography of monoamine distributions, the cortical content of norepinephrine, dopamine, and serotonin are plotted along stereotaxic coordinates in Figure 18. This plot shows that at 2 months of age, norepinephrine is almost evenly distributed throughout cortex, but over a two to three year period it becomes concentrated in somatosensory cortex, to yield the well-differentiated pattern characteristic of young adults.

The same figure shows that dopamine is most highly concentrated in prefrontal cortex at all ages. In the cortex posterior to the central sulcus, the dopamine concentration is consistently lower than in prefrontal cortex. Between 2 months and 5 months, there is a slight increase in dopamine content which remains at a constant level thereafter. Throughout development, the topography of serotonin distribution is somewhat irregular but consistent over age, with highest concentrations occurring in postcentral somatosensory and occipital cortices.

Developmental Changes in Monoamine Synthesis

In addition to measuring endogenous levels of monoamines, the rate at which these substances are synthesized or manufactured by their brainstem cells of origin also was studied developmentally (Goldman-Rakic & Brown, 1981b). Again, striking regional differences were observed. In prefrontal cortex, catecholamine synthesis increased steadily from birth to 3 years of age, while in adjacent premotor regions, adult levels of synthetic capacity were attained by 8 months. In posterior parietal cortex, catecholamine synthesis was unchanged from birth through 15 to 18 months, but then increased rapidly. Catecholamine activity of visual cortex showed a gradual but modest increment over the course of postnatal maturation.

Development of biosynthetic capacity differed not only with respect to cortical region, but according to transmitter. In prefrontal cortex, where catecholamine synthesis increased steadily over the first 3 years of life, serotonin synthesis remained constant from birth through adulthood. In contrast the serotonin synthesis in visual cortex continued to increase between 8 and 24 months. As a general rule, in areas of cortex where synthesis of catecholamines is high, that of serotonin is low.

Instead of developing hand in hand, monoamine levels and biosynthetic capacity were found to be dissociated at different ages. For example, in prefrontal cortex, dopamine and serotonin levels showed developmental oscillations in spite of the fact that dopamine synthesis matured gradually and serotonin synthesis remained constant with age. In parietal and visual cortices, the biosynthetic capacity of serotonin did not reach mature levels until 15 to 18 months, long after serotonin levels had asymptoted. While the basis for these dissociations are not completely understood, they may reflect developmental processes such as the maturation of postsynaptic targets and mechanisms of uptake and storage (Coyle & Axelrod, 1971; Coyle & Molliver, 1977; Tissari & Suurhasko, 1971) and shifts in catabolic enzyme activity (Bourgoin, Artand, Adrien, Hery, Glowinski, & Hamon, 1977).

Mechanisms and Significance of Developmental Shifts

At present, neither the causes nor the functional significance of the developmental shifts in monoamine balance are apparent. A better understanding of these neurochemical alterations in primate neocortex might provide some clue to the basis of the differential response to some drugs, notably amphetamine, exhibited by children and adult humans. The developmental dynamics of cortical neurochemistry also may shed light on the age-dependency of functional deficits following brain damage at various stages of postnatal development.

It is possible that these changes are secondary to metabolic or morphological events in cortical maturation. In human neocortex, the age at which certain enzyme activity shifts from an oxygen-independent (anaerobic) to an oxygen-dependent mode varies across cortical regions, and even across different laminae within a cortical field (Farkas-Bargeton & Diebler, 1978). In rodents, monoamine and catabolic enzyme activity also show developmental variation (Bourgion et al., 1977). Such alterations in enzyme activity could account for the changes in monoamine levels that occur even when synthetic activity remains constant. Developmental changes in the neuron's capacity for uptake and storage of neurotransmitters probably also contribute to the dissociation between monoamine synthesis and levels seen in very young rhesus monkeys. In some neuronal systems, there may be a gap between the time at which a cell can produce a particular transmitter, and the time at which it is able to regulate that production in response to events in the neuronal milieu. Developmental studies in nonprimates indicate that the short-term regulation of the dopaminergic and serotonergic systems develops postnatally (Coyle & Axelrod, 1971), while the mechanisms for regulation of norepinephrine are well developed in the newborn (Kellogg & Wennerstrom, 1974). Such differences could explain the fluctuations seen in serotonin and dopamine levels, as opposed to the gradual and steady increase in norepinephrine content of the primate cortex.

Role of Catecholamines in Neuronal Plasticity

A particularly intriguing explanation of the age-related monoamine shifts is the suggestion that the function of these transmitters may change as development progresses. Because of the early development and wide ramifications of the locus coeruleus system, a number of investigators suggested that catecholamines may play a trophic role in brain development and plasticity (Lauder & Bloom, 1974; Lewis, Patel, Bendek, & Balazs, 1974; Seiger & Olson, 1971).

One of the few experimental tests of this hypothesis is the exploration of the impact of catecholamines on the plasticity of visual cortex in neonatal kittens (Kasamatsu & Pettigrew, 1976, 1979; Kasamatsu, Pettigrew, & Ary, 1979). Kittens which are monocularly deprived during a brief critical period in infancy lack the usual complement of binocularly activated neurons; instead, most of the cells in visual cortex are driven exclusively by the nondeprived eye. To determine the role of catecholamines on cortical modifiability, Kasamatsu and Pettigrew examined kittens in which the entire neocortical arborization of the catecholamine system was destroyed by interventricular injections of 6-hydroxydopamine. Subjects that had received this treatment, along with littermates that received control injections, were then subjected to a period of monocular deprivation. In the vehicle-injected group, and in another control group which received 6-hydroxydopamine *after* occlusion, cortical neurons demonstrated the usual effect of monocular deprivation—the vast majority of cells could be driven only by the eye which had been open. However, the catecholamine-depleted kittens were unaffected by the occlusion, suggesting that catecholamines facilitate the process by which visual deprivation brings about changes in ocular dominance.

To prove that the observed lack of cortical plasticity did not result from nonspecific neuronal changes, another group of kittens was fitted with skull-mounted osmotic minipumps capable of perfusing small areas of cortex with catecholamines. These kittens were subjected to the same experimental treatment as the earlier group. However, during the deprivation period, small regions of visual cortex received direct perfusion of norepinephrine via the pumps. Recording from these subjects showed that regions of cortex reached by the norepinephrine contained neurons dominated by the open eye whereas surrounding, catecholamine-depleted neurons were binocular. Surprisingly, local norepinephrine perfusion also restored some degree of cortical plasticity outside the accepted age limits of the critical period (Kasamatsu et al., 1979). The reorganization of neuronal connections which is presumed to underly these shifts in ocular dominance occurs only in the presence of both the amine and an abnormal pattern of input to visual cortex. In norepinephrine-perfused animals given normal binocular experience, no change in ocular dominance was observed. Thus, the role of norepinephrine appears to be modulatory or permissive, and does not itself cause the change in connectivity.

In terms of frontal lobe function, it is conceivable that the early postnatal decline in dopamine and later increase at 2 to 3 years reflect a change from trophic to transmitter function for this substance. This possibility is supported by primate behavioral studies which show that the ability to perform tasks mediated by prefrontal cortex shows a steady improvement over the course of postnatal development (Alexander & Goldman, 1978) rather than reflecting the fluctuations of dopamine levels. If there is a shift in the neural substrate of delay tasks, the transfer from subcortical to cortical mediation may not occur until prefrontal dopamine levels reattain adultlike levels.

Monoamine Systems in the Aging Brain

Endogenous concentrations and biosynthetic activity of dopamine, norepinephrine, and serotonin were also studied in the brains of aging rhesus monkeys (Goldman-Rakic & Brown, 1981). In this species, sexual maturity is reached around the third year of life, and in captivity, mean life span is estimated to range between 15 years and 20 years (Brizzee, Ordy, Hansche, & Kaack, 1976). The oldest recorded age of a rhesus monkey is 29 years (Altman & Dittmer, 1964).

The most striking finding within the frontal lobe of these aging animals was a marked drop in the concentration of dopamine in the prefrontal and premotor cortex (Figure 19). In prefrontal cortex, dopamine content did not change significantly between 2 to 3 and 5 years of age, but was reduced over 50% in monkeys 10 and 18 years of age. Dopamine concentration in other cortical areas also declined with age, but to a lesser extent than in prefrontal cortex. For example, between 2 years and 18+ years, dopamine in premotor cortex fell 34%, but in motor cortex it fell only 14%.

The age-dependent changes in prefrontal cortex are specific to dopamine. No comparable decline was observed in levels of norepinephrine or serotonin over the same age range. Serotonin in prefrontal cortex is as high at 10 years and 18 years as at 2 to 3 years, but in premotor and motor cortex it declines at 18+ years. Thus, advancing age results in a marked loss of dopamine in prefrontal and premotor cortex and a modest loss of serotonin in precentral cortex.

In the temporal lobe, age-related changes in dopamine concentration are smaller than those of the prefrontal cortex, ranging from a 15% to 39% drop. The norepinephrine content of the temporal lobe shows a moderate loss from 2 to 3 years to 18+ years. Serotonin content of the temporal lobe increases up to 10 years of age before falling to or below young adult values at 18 years of age.

In the parietal and occipital lobes, cortical levels of the catecholamines remain surprisingly steady from 2 to 18+ years of age. As in the temporal lobe, increases in serotonin concentrations are observed in some regions. In both the parietal and visual cortical areas, this monoamine increases significantly between the ages of 3 years and 5 years before falling off at older ages. Data obtained in neonates and animals ranging up to 2 to 3 years indicate that serotonin concentrations in various temporal cortical regions show a progressive increase through 5 years, suggesting that functional maturation of serotonergic mechanisms may continue until this age. If so, in the temporal lobe at least, the development of this monoamine would be considerably more protracted than that of the catecholamines in the same cortical regions.

Selective Depletion of Catecholamines

These results demonstrate the dramatic changes in monoamine systems that occur in the second half of the primate life span. Most striking is the finding that the aging process affects the catecholaminergic fiber systems, especially dopaminergic neurons, to a far greater extent than the serotonergic system. Moreover, the magnitude of catecholamine change varies markedly in different regions of the cerebral cortex, being most pronounced in prefrontal association areas.

While the mechanisms underlying the age-related dissociation of serotonin and catecholamines are not known, one contributing factor may be the differential sensitivity of these two systems to hypoxia. Catecholamine activity appears to be more severely compromised by acute hypoxic states than is serotonergic activity (Brown, Snyder, & Carlsson, 1974; Davis & Carlsson, 1973). Since in old age and dementia, the cerebral cortex (especially the frontal and temporal lobes) is subject to chronic states of reduced cerebral circulation (Gustafson, Hagberg, & Ingvar, 1978; Kety, 1956), decreased oxygen uptake may be a critical factor in the selective loss of catecholamine activity.

Depletion of cortical monoamines with age is probably at least partially due to degeneration of presynaptic neurons which supply these transmitters. Data from the substantia nigra of humans (McGeer & McGeer, 1977) and primates (Sladek & Sladek, 1978) and from the locus coeruleus of humans (Vijayashankar & Brody, 1979) indicate that these cell groups undergo a process of functional deterioration or loss through life. Another possibility is that the postsynaptic receptors for monoamines are lost with aging. In rabbits, increased age is associated with selective losses of dopamine receptor binding sites in frontal and limbic cortex, as well as in neostriatum (Lloyd & Hornykiewicz, 1972).

Functional Implications

Several investigators (Bartus & Dean, 1979; Bartus, Fleming and Johnson, 1978) have shown that the behavioral profile of aged monkeys is strikingly similar to that found in young adults following ablation (Jacobsen, 1936; Mishkin, 1964) or 6-OHDA injections (Brozoski et al., 1979) of prefrontal cortex. Thus, at least some of the cognitive impairments associated with extreme old age are likely to be related to prefrontal dopamine depletion. Other evidence for prefrontal dopamine deficiency in old age is the

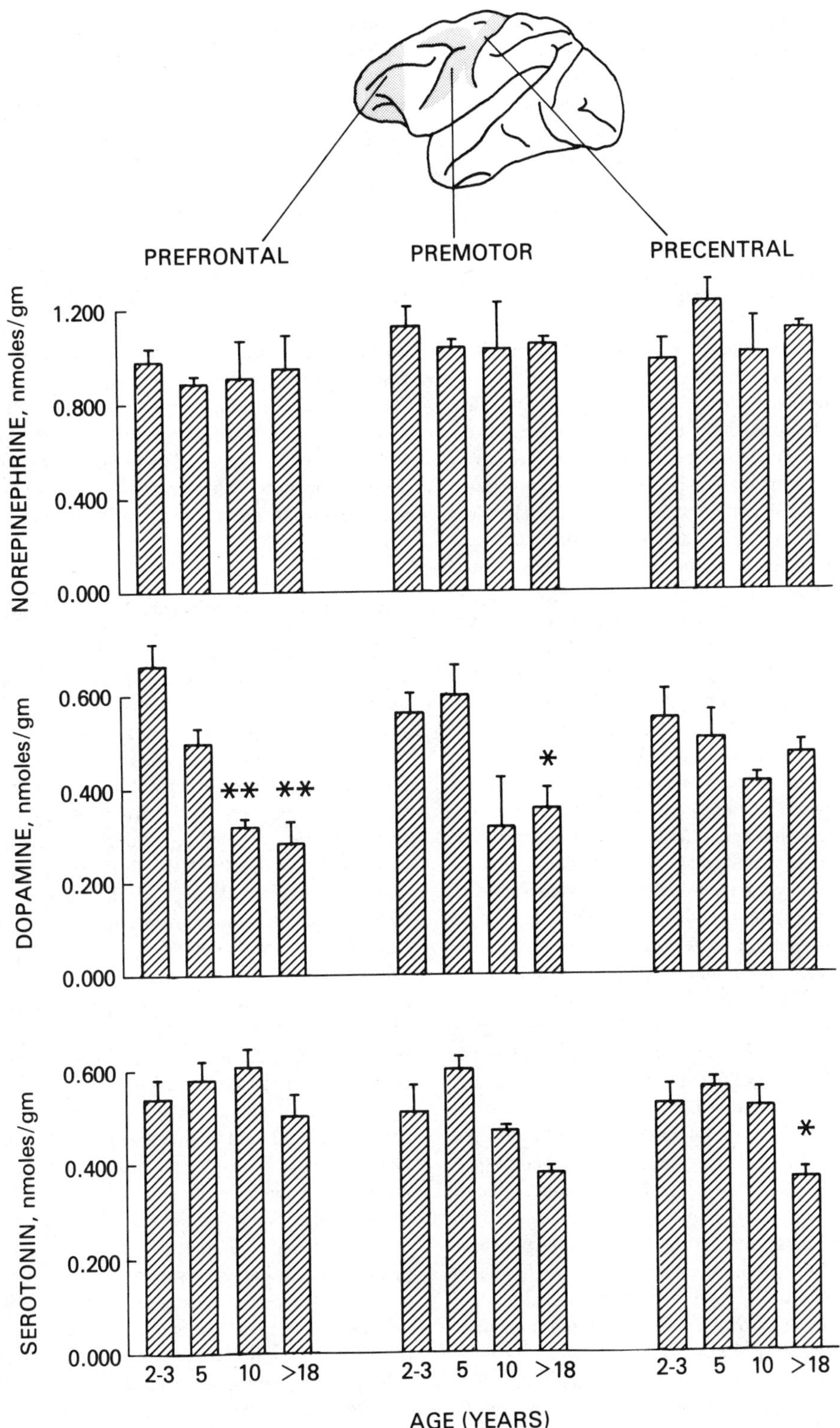

Figure 19. Concentration of norepinephrine, dopamine, and serotonin in three major cortical subdivisions of the frontal lobe. Concentration is in nmoles/gm with standard error of the mean (S.E.M.) indicated by the bars. For the 2- to 3-year-old monkeys, $n = 10$ for prefrontal cortex, $n = 8$ for premotor, and $n = 5$ for precentral. $N = 4$ for all 3 areas of 5-year-olds, $n = 2$ for these areas in 10-year-olds, and $n = 3$ for the same regions in 18-year-olds. Asterisks indicate significance of specific comparisons between the 2- to 3-year-old age group and each of the other age groups ($*p = .05$, $**p = .01$). (From Goldman-Rakic & Brown, 1981.)

observation that Parkinson's disease is frequently accompanied by cognitive disorders (Lieberman et al., 1978; Loranger et al., 1972) and L-dopa therapy is reported to improve memory in these patients as well as in patients suffering from other forms of dementia (Arbit, Boshes, & Blonsky, 1970; Gottfries, 1978).

DEVELOPMENTAL PLASTICITY OF PRIMATE PREFRONTAL CORTEX

This section will examine anatomical and behavioral development following destruction of prefrontal association cortex in infancy. Like the studies described in previous sections, one goal of this research is to understand the factors that govern development in normal animals. These studies are aimed also at understanding the differences in behavioral outcome following brain damage at different ages.

Development is a process of functional and anatomical differentiation. During this process, different groups of cells become committed to forming a given structure with a certain set of functional attributes. Damage to one portion of a developing system is one factor that might affect the functional and anatomical commitment of other cells in that system. Early observations indicated that brain damage in infancy may spare behaviors that are impaired following comparable lesions in adult animals. From these findings it has often been inferred, but rarely demonstrated, that damage to one portion of the brain may induce other still immature areas to alter their developmental commitment and take over the behavioral functions normally mediated by the destroyed tissue in adults (Kennard, 1938; Lenneberg, 1967; Soltmann, 1876). The studies to be described in this section indicate that behavioral sparing following early brain damage may in part be due to the reassignment of the control of these behaviors to undamaged neural systems. Some neural systems seem to be largely committed to a given mode of development rather early in life, even before they have attained complete functional maturity (Goldman, 1971, 1974). However, functional commitment can be altered during development by factors such as early environmental stimulation (Goldman & Mendelson, 1977), hormonal manipulation (Goldman & Brown, 1975), and brain damage (Goldman, 1971, 1974).

If changes in functional commitment do occur following brain damage in infancy, one might expect to find corresponding alterations in anatomical development. Recent studies have demonstrated altered anatomical connections and other structural anomalies following early lesions in the prefrontal cortex and other areas (e.g., Goldman, 1978; Goldman & Galkin, 1978; Hicks & D'Amato, 1970). However, as our discussion will show, it may prove difficult to understand the relationship between the behavioral effects of early damage and these anatomical anomalies.

The methods involved in assessing the behavioral and anatomical effects of brain damage are, in principle, straightforward. However, elucidation of the significance of these effects can be treacherously difficult. Not surprisingly, interpretations of such research have provoked a great deal of controversy (Isaacson, 1975; Lashley, 1938; Laurence & Stein, 1978; Levere, 1975; Sperry, 1958; Young, 1970). An extensive treatment of this topic is beyond the scope of the present chapter; however, we shall consider some of the main issues relevant to our discussion.

Inferences from Experimental Brain Damage

Pierre Flourens (1824) first used the lesion technique to study localization of function in the central nervous system. With the relatively crude methods available to him, Flourens was able to demonstrate that damage to different parts of the pigeon brain resulted in characteristic behavioral deficiencies. He was the first to show the involvement of the cerebellum in motor function, refuting the claims of phrenologists (Gall, 1822) that this area is concerned with sex behavior. Flourens' method was ridiculed by his opponents, who claimed that nothing could be learned about the behavior of normal animals by studying "mutilated" creatures (Young, 1970). Nonetheless, many of the inferences made by Flourens proved to be correct, and the lesion technique remained the mainstay of experimental neurology for well over a century.

Flourens also made some notable errors, which illustrate the pitfalls and limitations of the technique. He was unable to observe major behavioral impairments after damage to different parts of the forebrain and concluded that it functions as an undifferentiated mass. This error was partly due to his method of assessment, casual observation. Obviously, some behavioral capacities cannot be evaluated without the use of sophisticated and extensive behavioral tests. Even then, impairments may go unnoticed either because inappropriate paradigms are used to measure the deficit or because the impairments are difficult to observe and quantify.

Two problems raised by these limitations are particularly relevant to the present discussion. First, our understanding of the neural bases of different behaviors is directly related to the ease with which they can be detected and quantified. Thus, sensory and motor systems are better understood than are the mechanisms subserving cognition; relatively little is known about the neural bases of affective and social behaviors, which are difficult to study in laboratory animals. Second, in considering the results of injury in infancy, we should bear in mind that while these animals may do well in tests which are sensitive to similar injury in adults, they may suffer impairments which we have neglected to or cannot as yet measure.

Thus, failure to observe a behavioral impairment following damage to a given area does not necessarily mean that there is no impairment. On the other hand, an impairment that appears following destruction of a particular region is not always due to loss of functions mediated by that region. A lesion that is restricted to one structure may produce functional disturbances or cell death in other areas. For instance, injury in one area may cause inflammation, pressure, or disturbance in blood supply in adjacent areas of the brain which may or may not be functionally and anatomically related to the destroyed tissue. Another example of a disturbance that may disrupt the functions of distant but anatomically related areas is diaschisis, that is, transitory traumatic disturbances in intact portions of the brain (von Monakow, 1914). Diaschisis was supposed, by von Monakow, to be due to the propagation of functional depression along neural pathways leading from the site of the lesion, but only in recent years has there been any electrophysiological and neurochemical evidence of such a phenomenon (Glassman, 1971, 1973; Kempinsky, 1958; Meyer & Welch, 1972; Moore, 1970; for a review see Goldman & Lewis, 1978). It has also been known for a long time that neurons die if a significant portion of their terminals are lost (e.g., Gudden, 1870). Since lesions of a given structure destroy the afferent terminals distributed in that area, the cells of origin of these inputs often die as well. This phenomenon, retrograde degeneration, occurs with such regularity that it has been used for many years to trace the anatomic connections of different areas (e.g., Cajal, 1909). In addition, cells which lose some of their afferent innervation may exhibit abnormalities such as supersensitivity to other inputs (Cannon & Rosenblueth, 1949), and in some cases, they may undergo degeneration and die (Cowan, 1970). These phenomena result in a loss of tissue in areas other than the site of the original injury, and these effects probably have a profound influence on the behavioral changes noted after brain damage.

Mechanisms of Recovery of Function

Damage to a given area of the brain does not inevitably result in a fixed constellation of impairments. Even after brain damage in adulthood, some restitution of function usually occurs. Lesions that are inflicted in infancy often produce less behavioral impairment than those occuring in adults (Goldman, 1974; Isaacson, 1975; Kennard, 1938; Lashley, 1938; Lenneberg, 1967). Thus, the brain, like other bodily organs, has some recuperative powers. However, functional recovery following brain damage is difficult to explain, since the cells destroyed by a lesion never grow back.

Numerous explanations have been offered to account for functional restitution following brain damage. If a given impairment recovers following a lesion in adulthood, it is often assumed that the deficit was due to diaschisis (von Monakow, 1914; Prince, 1910). For example, destruction of prefrontal cortex may produce temporary motor impairments (Jacobsen, 1936). The motor impairments may be attributed to the action of diaschisis in adjacent premotor and motor cortex, and the recovery is attributed to return of function in these intact areas. The "residual" impairments in delayed response tasks are thought to reflect the loss of behavioral capacities normally mediated by the prefrontal cortex. In this instance, the inference is probably correct; however, it should be realized that recovery is not always associated with disappearance of diaschisis. Some permanent behavioral deficits may result such as long lasting depletion of neurotransmitter levels in intact areas of the brain (Moore, 1970). Conversely, behavioral recovery can occur for reasons other than dissipation of diaschisis.

Behavioral recovery can sometimes occur without any return of the functions that were lost following brain damage. In these cases, animals use their remaining functional capacities to overcome the limitations imposed by their disabilities. Such behavioral substitution may result in seemingly normal test scores or performance, which are achieved in anomalous ways. Sometimes the difference from normal behavior may be quite obvious. If rats that were taught to run down a maze are then deprived of their motor coordination by damage to the cerebellum, they will roll their bodies down the maze instead (Beach, Hebb, Torgan, & Nissen, 1960). In other cases, behavioral substitution can only be detected by detailed and painstaking analyses of the subtlest aspects of performance (e.g., Goldberger & Murray, 1978; Sperry, 1945, 1947).

Another explanation of recovery following brain damage posits that intact areas can actually assume the functions of destroyed tissue. The proposition that such reorganization can occur in adults has been especially controversial (for a historical review, see Teuber, Eidelberg & Stein, 1974). In its most radical form, reorganization theory proposes that reeducation can, in effect, create new functional entities in the brain (Luria, 1966). This proposition is difficult to reconcile with present knowledge of structure-function relationships. Another form of the reorganization hypothesis attributes behavioral recovery to anatomic and functional anomalies that occur to a limited extent following lesions in adult animals (Eidelberg & Stein, 1974; Goldberger & Murray, 1978). However, many investigators take the position that such anomalies must necessarily lead to anomalous behavior (Levere, 1975; Raisman, 1969; Sperry, 1958).

Developmental Aspects of Recovery from Brain Damage

The experimental study of brain damage in infant animals was pioneered by Soltmann (1876). He examined the effects of unilateral or bilateral damage to the motor cortex and adjacent areas in puppies and full-grown dogs. He found that whereas such lesions resulted in severe and permanent disruption of motor function in adult animals, they had no observable immediate or long-term effects in newborn puppies. The clumsy motor behavior of newborn puppies suggested that the motor cortex had not yet matured at this stage of development. Soltmann was able to support this hypothesis using the then newly discovered technique of electrical stimulation (Fritsch & Hitzig, 1870). He found that in adults, electrical stimulation of the motor cortex caused muscular contractions, whereas no such responses were evoked by stimulation of the cortex of puppies. Soltmann therefore concluded that the functional immaturity of the motor cortex in infancy was a key factor in explaining the absence of behavioral symptoms following early damage to that area.

A systematic study of recovery from lesions of the motor cortex in infant monkeys was undertaken by Kennard (1938, 1940, 1942; Kennard & McCulloch, 1943). These investigations confirmed that early damage allowed considerable escape of motor function. Moreover, Kennard's findings suggested that surrounding association cortex had assumed some of the functions of the tissue destroyed in infancy. In monkeys that had suffered motor cortex lesions as infants, lesions of the adjacent association areas produced motor disturbances. Such effects were not noted after similar lesions in animals with intact motor areas (Kennard, 1942). In addition, following lesions of the motor cortex in infancy, the threshold for evoking muscular contractions by electrical stimulation was considerably lower in surrounding association regions (Kennard & McCulloch, 1943). These results provided strong support for the proposition that recovery following early brain damage could be attributed to reorganization of function in intact portions of the immature nervous system.

In humans, the best known example of functional restitution following early brain damage is the recovery or sparing of language functions following injury to the left hemisphere in infancy (Lenneberg, 1967). Language behaviors are mediated by the cortex of the left hemisphere in 90% of the normal adult population. Destruction of this hemisphere in adulthood results in more or less permanent impairments in speech, writing, and other language related capacities. However, in a large sample of individuals who had suffered profound damage to the left hemisphere prior to age 5, it was found that language functions were essentially normal in adulthood. In the overwhelming majority of these cases, it was determined that the right hemisphere, rather than the left, was dominant for language behavior.

As we have noted, these results have been interpreted as evidence that immature areas of the brain can alter their functional commitment to compensate for capacities lost following early damage. While this may be true, the evidence for reorganization is not always as conclusive as it may seem. Extensive behavioral testing often reveals considerable impairment following early damage. Thus, in Kennard's studies (1938, 1940), monkeys that appeared to develop normally soon after early damage to their motor cortex later began to show disorders in fine coordination and dexterity, the same functions supposedly controlled by that tissue. When behavioral recovery does occur, it is not always possible to provide evidence that reorganization, rather than some other mechanism, was responsible. It may be particularly difficult to single out the structure that has taken over the functions of the destroyed tissue. Damage to intact areas may reinstate an impairment, as in Kennard's study (1942). However, it has also been found that destruction of many different areas may cause a recurrence of symptoms in animals that have recovered from brain damage (Butters, Rosen,

& Stein, 1974). This does not necessarily mean that all of these areas of the brain had taken on the functions of the damaged tissue.

The mechanism underlying reorganization is not clear at present. If it is solely a learning process, then it would be difficult to explain why similar learning cannot take place after damage in adulthood. If it is primarily due to anatomical changes, it is difficult to understand how it is ensured that such changes result in adaptive behavior. The proposition that one area can assume the functions of another is equally ambiguous. Do these new functional centers operate in exactly the same way as the damaged areas they have "replaced"? Or are the existing functional capacities of intact areas used to provide alternative means of performing behaviors which normally require the integrity of the damaged tissue (Luria, Naydin, Tsvetkova, & Vinarskaya, 1969)? In the latter instance, reorganization may be indistinguishable from behavioral substitution.

Other explanations of recovery following early brain damage are equally problematic. Some instances of sparing following lesions in infancy may be due to behavioral substitutions, whereas others might be due to dissipation of diaschisis (Isaacson, 1975). However, one would still have to explain why such processes do not occur following similar damage in adulthood.

The research we will discuss below illustrates the contention that behavioral development in normal and brain damaged individuals is influenced by a great many factors. It is probable that as the different mechanisms responsible for recovery following brain damage are elucidated, it will become apparent that some correspond to one or another of the classical explanations of recovery, whereas others may involve novel principles of development or neural organization which could not be anticipated.

Behavioral Consequences of Early Damage to Prefrontal Cortex

The effects of circumscribed lesions of the prefrontal cortex in infant monkeys were first studied by Akert et al. (1960). They reported that when infant-operated animals were tested in a delayed response task at 1 year of age, they showed no evidence of impairment. In contrast, monkeys that had been given similar lesions at an older age, and allowed postoperative recovery periods of the same length, were severely impaired in this task. Later studies with larger lesions of the dorsolateral portion of the prefrontal area essentially confirmed this basic result (Harlow et al., 1968; Tucker & Kling, 1967). However, when prefrontal lesions in infant monkeys induced damage to the orbital prefrontal cortex, the lesion produced a severe deficit in delayed alternation, and a moderate deficit in delayed response performance of delayed alternation; monkeys that had undergone orbital lesions in infancy performed as poorly on these tests as did animals operated as juveniles, and like the juveniles, were also impaired in object reversal. Some of these results are shown in Figure 20.

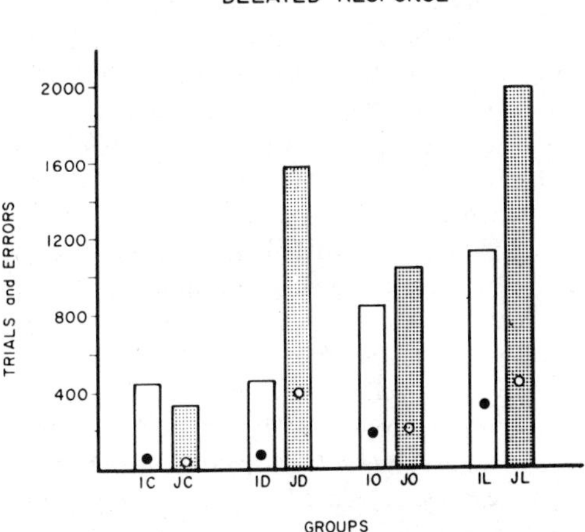

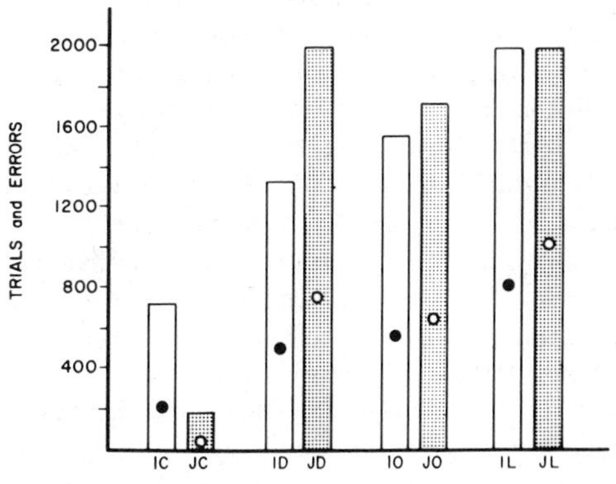

Figure 20. Effects of locus of damage upon sparing of spatial memory abilities—left, delayed-response performance; right, delayed-alternation performance. Bars indicate trials to criterion; circles errors to criterion. IC, infant unoperated control group; JC, juvenile unoperated controls; ID, group given dorsolateral lesions in infancy; JD, group given dorsolateral lesions in the juvenile period; IO, group given orbital lesions as infants; JO, group given orbital lesions as juveniles, IL group lobectomized as infants; JL, group lobectomized as juveniles. (From Goldman, 1971.)

The differences in the effects of infant orbitofrontal and dorsolateral damage which were apparent in animals tested at about 1 year of age suggested that the development of these two areas proceeds at a different rate. One possibility is that the dorsolateral cortex is less mature at age 50 days when the damage was inflicted. Another possibility is that the differences observed in these studies reflected the maturity of the two systems at the age at which the animals were tested. Accordingly, one might expect that different behavioral results would be observed if the animals were tested at other stages of development. Longitudinal studies of behavior after early brain damage were undertaken to test this hypothesis.

Longitudinal Studies: Consequences of Prefrontal Cortex Damage

In the studies of Goldman (Goldman, 1971; Goldman, Rosvold, & Mishkin, 1970b), monkeys that had suffered lesions of the dorsolateral frontal area were relatively proficient in delayed response behavior when tested at age 12 months, and delayed alternation behavior was at least partically spared as well. Common sense would seem to dictate that further testing would show improvements in the performance of these monkeys either because they had more opportunity to recover from the lesion or because they were able to transfer the training from previous testing or because the animals had matured and therefore had greater cognitive capacity. To examine these possibilities, the same animals originally tested at 1 year of age continued to be tested as they grew older. The most revealing results were the scores on delayed alternation tests, conducted when the infant-operated animals and their age-matched unoperated controls were approximately 30 months old. As expected, the intact animals showed considerable improvement in performance. However, the monkeys that had received dorsolateral lesions as infants exhibited a quite different pattern of development. When they were retested on delayed alternation they performed no better as a group than they had scored originally. Two monkeys improved their performance, but two others that had originally learned the task were now unable to reach criterion within the limits of testing. Although these observations were based on an admittedly small number of subjects, they suggested that neural systems which mediate delayed alternation learning and/or performance in the 15-month old monkeys may not be the same as those that were operating when the animals were retested at age 30 months.

One explanation for these results is that the dorsolateral prefrontal cortex had not yet become functionally committed to mediation of delayed response behaviors at 1 year of age and was consequently dispensable in 1-year old monkeys. Therefore, the effects of damage to this region of prefrontal cortex was not apparent in animals tested on delayed alternation at 1 year, but became evident at older ages, when the normal timetable of maturation called for participation of prefrontal cortex in delayed-response behaviors. This surmise was confirmed by the reversible lesion studies described in an earlier part of this chapter, showing that cooling of the dorsolateral area did not produce maximum deficits in delayed-response performance until monkeys were nearly 3 years old. These studies provide strong evidence that maturational status is a critical factor in the outcome of neural damage. On the other hand, it should be emphasized that monkeys operated on in infancy do retain some advantage over those undergoing surgery as juveniles or adults, which is probably attributable to mechanisms of neural reorganization. Although early-operated monkeys fail to advance, they still perform some delayed-response tasks that adult-operated animals cannot. Thus, it seems that lesions in specific regions of developing brain may have at least two consequences: (1) arrest the development of functions dependent on the resected tissue and (2) induce reorganization in related or other neural systems that remain.

Subcortical Involvement in Delayed-Response Function

The finding that the dorsolateral prefrontal cortex has a protracted development extending into the third year of life makes it difficult to explain the neural basis of delayed-response function prior to this age. After all, normal monkeys perform delayed-response tasks with varying degrees of proficiency even within the first year of life (Goldman, 1971; Harlow et al., 1960). The most logical candidates for this role are subcortical regions, such as the caudate nucleus or thalamic mediodorsal nucleus, which have close anatomical connections with the prefrontal cortex, and appear to have similar behavioral functions. Lesions of the caudate nucleus (Battig, Mishkin, & Rosvold, 1960) and the thalamic mediodorsal nucleus (Goldman, 1974; Isseroff et al., 1982; Schulman, 1964) produce deficits in delayed-response tasks in adult monkeys. These structures are apparently functional in infant monkeys, as indicated by electrophysiological and lesion studies (Alexander et al., 1980; Goldman & Rosvold, 1972). In fact, as shown in Figure 21, lesions of the caudate nucleus in infant monkeys produce as much

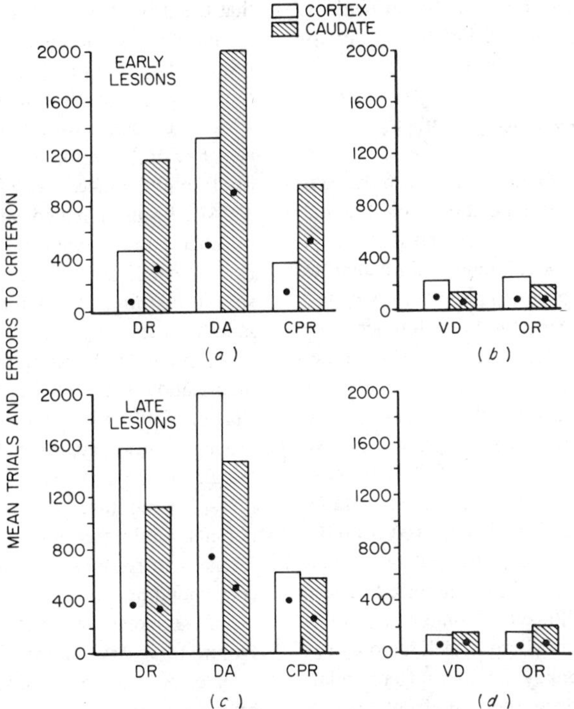

Figure 21. Contrasting effects of dorsolateral cortical and anterodorsal caudate lesions at different stages of development: (*a,b*) Performance on tests given after the age of 1 year but before 2 years, after lesions performed in infancy. (*c,d*) Performance on the same tests given at the same time intervals after surgery performed in young adults. Abbreviations: DR, delayed response; DA, delayed alternation; and CPR, conditioned position response—all spatial tests affected by dorsolateral lesions in adults; VD, visual pattern discrimination; OR, object discrimination reversal; control tests not dependent on the integrity of the dorsolateral cortex. (From Goldman, 1974.)

behavioral impairment in infants as in adults, whereas prefrontal cortical damage produces greater impairment in adults than it does in infants. These are precisely the results one would expect if the caudate nucleus mediated these tasks in infancy, while the prefrontal cortex became progressively more involved in delayed response function in later stages of development.

Given that structures other than the dorsolateral prefrontal cortex are able to mediate delayed-response capacities in infancy, it is difficult to understand why the same structures cannot compensate for the loss of dorsolateral cortex in adult monkeys. One possibility is that the functional organization of these areas in the infant nervous system represents an interim arrangement. Perhaps this arrangement evolved to allow the animal to learn and function while a large portion of the association system remains immature. The prolonged development of the prefrontal cortex and other phylogenetically advanced areas may be necessitated by their functional complexity. An alternative and not altogether unrelated possibility is that the *effective* cortical lesion is not the same in infants and adults. Perhaps cortical lesions in adults but less so in infants cause permanent disruption of the functions mediated by the subcortical structures which are deprived of their cortical input by the lesion (see Goldman, 1974, for elaboration). In any case, it appears that once these areas have matured, the functional organization of the nervous system changes so that the arrangement which operated in the infant brain is no longer functional.

This heterology in the functional organization of the infant and adult brain has profound implications for our understanding of normal cognitive maturation and of developmental pathologies in humans. Developmental shifts in neural organization may explain why children learn languages and mathematical concepts in different ways than do adults and why most early childhood memories are lost. Such shifts may also account for the fact that certain learning or affective disorders may be "outgrown" as children mature, while other disturbances may appear only in adolescence or adulthood.

Behavioral Effects of Prenatal Brain Damage

The studies discussed so far provide strong evidence that symptoms tend to be attenuated if neural damage occurs closer to birth rather than at maturity. Could the resilience of developing brain extend to circumscribed lesions sustained prenatally, when so many critical events of structural development take place and the brain is undergoing its most rapid development? Recent advances in the techniques of fetal surgery have made it possible to examine the effects of prenatal lesions on subsequent cognitive development (Goldman & Galkin, 1978). In these experiments, a pregnant rhesus monkey is operated on during gestation. The fetus is removed from the womb, a lesion is made in the prospective association cortex, and the fetus is then replaced. These pregnancies are then allowed to come close to full term (165 days) before the baby is delivered by cesarean section. One monkey that had suffered bilateral destruction of the dorsolateral prefrontal cortex at 119 embryonic days and was examined over a 2½-year postnatal period consistently exhibited performance in delayed-response alternation and various discrimination tasks that was as good or better than that of the normal controls (Goldman & Galkin, 1978). Preliminary results of studies of the effects of unilateral destruction of the dorsolateral prefrontal areas in more than a dozen monkeys operated as fetuses indicate that such lesions also allow considerable behavioral sparing relative to the same damage inflicted in adult animals (Goldman-Rakic, Schwartz, & Isseroff, unpublished observations).

Sex Differences in Development Following Orbital Prefrontal Lesions

In parallel with the research on the dorsolateral prefrontal area, a series of studies examined the behavioral development of animals suffering early orbitofrontal damage. The results of these experiments illustrate the diversity and complexity of factors involved in normal maturation, and in behavioral recovery following early brain damage. As discussed above, lesions of the orbitofrontal area at about 50 days of age, unlike those restricted to the dorsolateral cortex, produce severe impairments in delayed alternation when animals are first tested at 15 months (Goldman et al., 1970a, 1970b). On the basis of these findings, Goldman (1971) proposed that the orbitofrontal system undergoes a developmental shift in functional organization similar to that proposed for the dorsolateral one. She suggested that this shift may occur at an earlier age in the orbital system. Evidence for this view comes from a study of behavioral development in monkeys suffering orbitofrontal damage at age 50 days (Goldman et al., 1974). Brain-damaged animals and intact age-matched controls were tested in object discrimination reversal, delayed alternation, and delayed-response learning at different ages beginning at 2.5 months of age. A pattern of initial sparing, followed by eventual deterioration of behavior was observed in this study, similar to the development occurring at a later age following dorsolateral damage. Quite surprisingly, however, this pattern was evident only in female monkeys. Male infants were impaired as early as 2.5 months, whereas females did not show deficits until after their first year. The sex differences in response to early damage suggested a corresponding difference in normal maturation of orbital association cortex in males and females. Failure to observe an impairment in brain-damaged females prior to 15 months of age indicates that the orbital cortex of female monkeys does not mature until that age, whereas it matures at 2.5 months in males. In support of this inference, normal intact males perform the object reversal task better than intact females at 2.5 months, but not at 15 months of age, indicating that orbital cortical mechanisms mature earlier in males than in females.

Goldman and Brown (1975) examined the effect of hormonal manipulations on these differences. Pregnant female monkeys were subjected to high doses of the male hormone testosterone during a critical period of gestation. Androgenization caused the genetically female offspring to be born as pseudohermaphrodites, that is, females with male primary sex characteristics. Like normal males, the pseudohermaphrodites were superior to females in tests of orbital cortex function in early infancy. Moreover, the androgenized females exhibited the male reaction to early orbitofrontal damage, since such lesions produced deficits in these animals at 2.5 months of age, as they do in normal males.

At present one can only speculate as to the full significance of these sex differences. Certainly, they have interesting implications regarding the development of cognitive abilities in primates, including humans. Such differences might also affect the prognosis of developmental pathologies, of which some, such as dyslexia (Critchley, 1960), have a higher incidence in males than in females.

Effects of Experience on Recovery from Orbitofrontal Damage

Studies of behavioral development following infant orbitofrontal damage have shown that in both normal and brain-damaged animals, functional maturation of neural systems subserving cognition are strongly affected by sex differences. As will be discussed, these systems can also be quite powerfully affected by early experience.

To demonstrate the role of experience, capital was made of the finding that although monkeys with orbital prefrontal lesions typically are impaired on orbital functions at age 15 months, they are much improved when retested beginning at 24 months of age. Such change could of course result from normal maturational processes or it might be due to repair processes initiated following the lesion. It seemed possible that the recovery displayed by these animals was dependent on the repeated testing they received, since different types of postoperative experience facilitate postoperative recovery (Isseroff & Isseroff, 1978; Lashley, 1938; Luria et al., 1969; Will, Rosenzweig, & Bennett, 1976; Will, Rosenzweig, Bennett, Herbert, & Morimoto, 1977).

Goldman (1976) assessed the effects of postoperative experience upon recovery from orbitofrontal damage by testing normal and early operated monkeys for the first time when they were 2 years old and comparing the results to performance of monkeys with identical lesions tested initially at 1 year of age and then again at 2 years. The results of that experiment, shown in Figure 22, were that orbitofrontal lesions produced a severe impairment in delayed alternation in animals tested for the first time at 1 or 2 years of age. However, this impairment was markedly reduced in the animals that had been *retested* at this age, even though the same animals showed severe impairments in their earlier tests. As might be expected, intact controls showed considerable retention of their previous learning upon retesting. Furthermore, monkeys operated on as juveniles were unable to learn the task in 2000 trials of training in the original test and failed similarly when retested. Finally when operated monkeys tested initially at 2 years of age were retested upon reaching their third birthday, they showed improved performance (Figure 22). Thus, it became clear that postoperative experience was an important factor in recovery from the behavioral effects of orbitofrontal damage, but only when the injury was sustained in infancy.

These results gave no indication of why the delayed-alternation performance of early operated monkeys had been improved by experience. The effect might have been due to transfer of specific skills associated with the task, as has been shown in some studies (Isseroff & Isseroff, 1978; Lashley, 1929, 1938). Alternatively, the animals might have learned more general associations connected with the behavioral testing situation, such as familiarity with the apparatus (Lovejoy, 1966; Sutherland, 1959; Zeaman & House, 1963). Early experience might also have facilitated recovery by providing stimulation of a general nature, rather than through learning of specific associations (Harlow, 1939; Hughes, 1965; Will et al., 1976; Will et al., 1977).

A subsequent study indicated that early experience may operate in a very nonspecific manner; furthermore, it may affect cognitive development in intact animals in the same way as it influences that of brain-damaged monkeys (Goldman & Mendelson, 1977). In this investigation, a naive group of monkeys given lesions of the orbital cortex at 50 days of age and a group of unoperated subjects were trained as neonates in object reversal discrimination beginning at 75 days of age. These animals, together with groups of operated and intact monkeys that had no previous test experience, were tested on the same object discrimination reversal plus a delayed-alternation test starting at age 15 months. As shown in Figure 23, early experience with object discrimination facilitated the subsequent performance of operated subjects on delayed alternation, but paradoxically did not affect their impairment in object reversal learning at age 15 months. Since experience with one task selectively facilitated performance on the *other* test, the effect could hardly have been due to transfer of specific or more general learning, and must have resulted from nonspecific stimulation.

Early experience with object reversal learning also facilitated the subsequent delayed-alternation performance of unoperated monkeys. From these data, Goldman & Mendelson (1977) suggested that stimulation in infancy altered the functional development of an area that is normally involved in delayed-alternation behavior, but not in object reversal, probably the dorsolateral prefrontal cortex. Such experience would have a diminishing effect on developmental commitment as the affected system reached maturity. This explains why postoperative experience did not improve the performance of monkeys operated as juveniles, or alter performance on a task mediated by the early developing orbital cortex. Moreover, this hypothesis is supported by the finding that object reversal training was most effective in promoting recovery when it was admin-

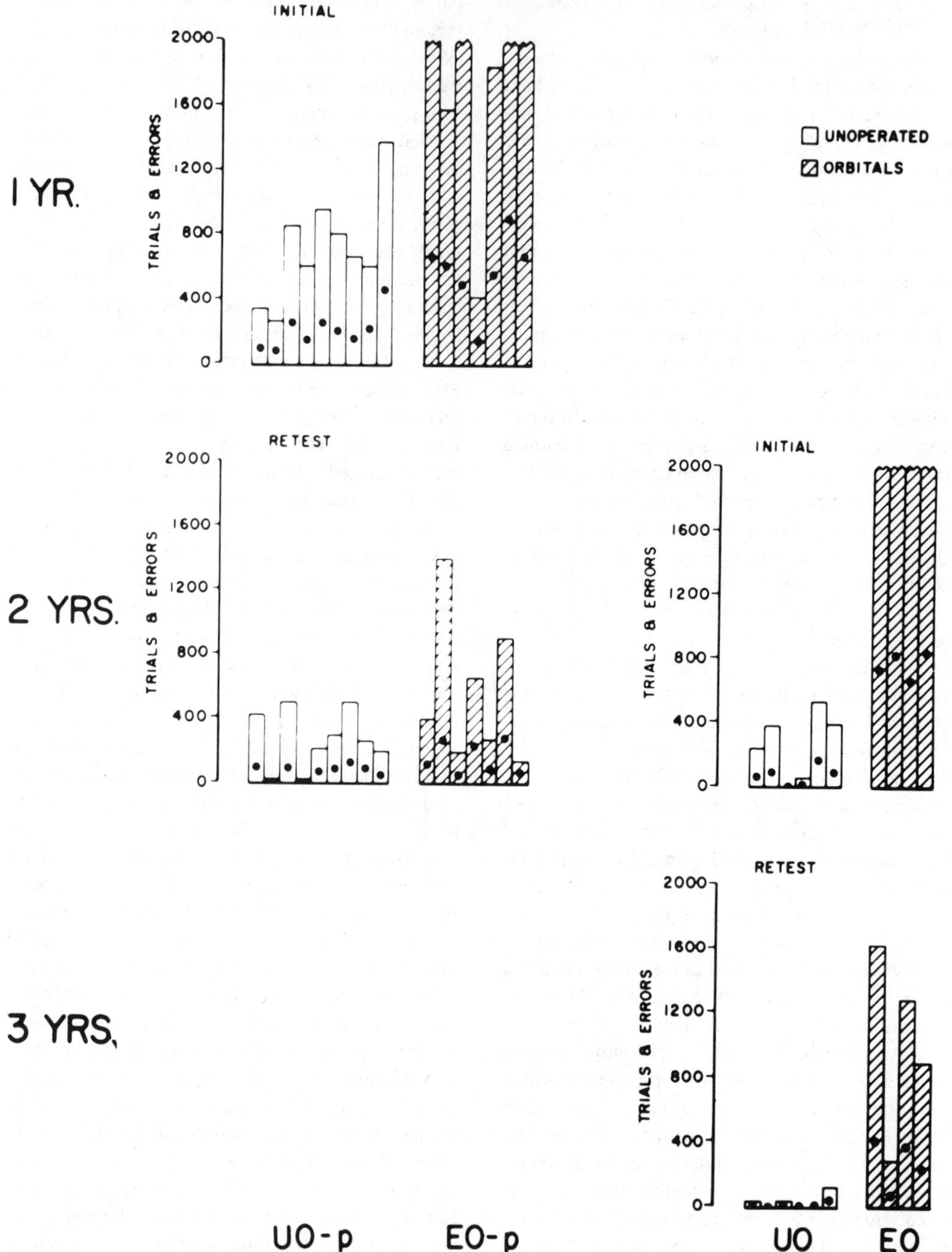

Figure 22. Effects of repeated testing upon performance following early orbitofrontal lesions. UO, unoperated; EO, early operated; -p indicates groups with early test experience. Note that monkeys with orbital lesions show impairments upon initial testing but recover when retested about a year later, independent of age. Test experience apparently can promote recovery even when performance is poor. (From Goldman, 1976.)

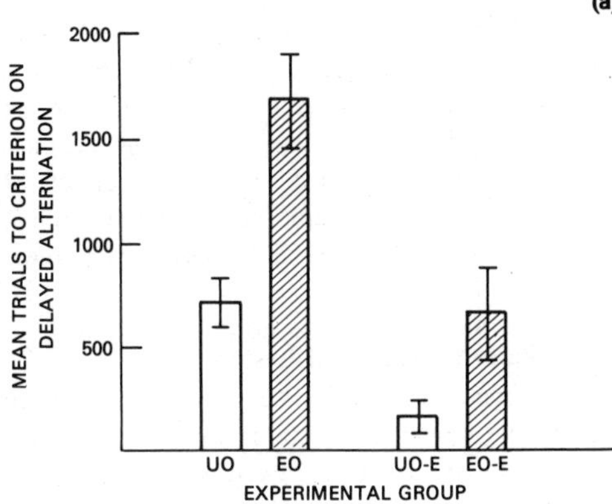

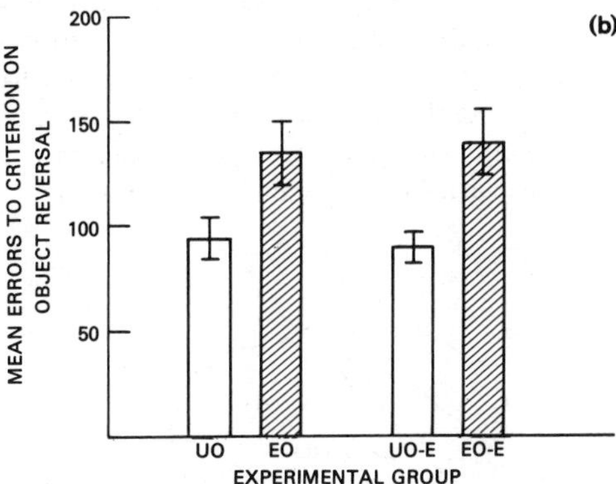

Figure 23. Effects of early experience with object reversal learning upon subsequent (15-month) performance on delayed-alternation (top) and object reversal (bottom) tasks following infant orbitofrontal lesions. Paradoxically early object reversal training improves delayed-alternation performance but not object reversal relearning. UO, unoperated; EO, early operated; UO-E, unoperated with experience; EO-E, early operated with experience. (From Goldman & Mendelson, 1977.)

istered at younger ages. Infant-operated animals that were given experience at age 2.5 months (Goldman & Mendelson, 1977) were superior to those given their first test experience when they were over 1 year old, and these monkeys were in turn, better able to perform delayed alternation than those that had received their first test experience at 2 years old (Goldman, 1976).

Summary: Factors Influencing Cognitive Development in Normal and Brain-damaged Monkeys

These studies illustrate a number of useful principles to help in understanding both normal cognitive development and the effects of early brain damage on behavior.

Longitudinal and cross-sectional investigations of behavioral development following lesions of the dorsolateral or orbital areas in infancy indicate that the effects of such damage are not static; they depend on the age at which animals are tested as well as upon the age at which the lesions are inflicted. The functional outcome of such injury may be influenced by various compensatory mechanisms; however, it is also determined by changes in functional organization that occur during the normal sequence of development.

The maturation of the infant brain does not proceed linearly from a nonfunctional to a functional state. At different stages of development, structure-function relationships are apparently arranged to make optimal use of the functional capacities available at that age. Such shifts in functional organization during development are suggested by the findings that behavioral capacities of animals suffering brain damage in early life may appear normal at first, but fail to develop at the same rate as those of intact animals (Goldman, 1971; Kennard, 1940; Lawrence & Hopkins, 1970). These developmental changes in neural function may also explain the qualitative differences between infant and adult humans in cognitive behavior and conceptual thinking (Piaget, 1954).

The systems we have been studying must become largely committed to a particular mode of functional organization rather early in life, though this organization may not become operational until much later in development. However, the plan of development is not entirely rigid. These studies have shown that it can be altered by such factors as early environmental stimulation and by hormonal manipulations. Injury to these systems in infancy may also produce some functional reorganization, thus allowing varying degrees of behavioral sparing relative to damage in mature animals.

Influence of Early Brain Injury on Anatomical Development

The study of behavioral effects of early brain damage began when there were few techniques for studying neural function and neuroanatomical circuitry. Consequently, explanations such as "reorganization" and "diaschisis" and concepts such as "commitment" were inferences about hypothetical properties of neural systems, based primarily on observations of behavioral changes. It was obvious, however, that the behavioral differences between animals suffering brain damage at different stages of development must have some counterpart in anatomical and physiological alterations occurring after injury to the infant nervous system. Early investigators attempted to provide corroborative electrophysiological evidence for the maturational and reorganization mechanisms they had inferred from behavioral data (Kennard & McCulloch, 1943; Soltmann, 1876). Only recently, however, have advances in neuroanatomical tracing methods made it possible to study some types of anatomical changes which occur following damage to the developing central nervous system. These phenomena may account for some of the behavioral differences between animals injured in infancy or as adults (Castro, 1975, 1977; Eidelberg & Stein, 1974; Hicks & D'Amato, 1970; Schneider, 1970).

Anatomical phenomena that occur following brain lesions may be divided into several classes. Damage to the prospective target neurons of a growing fiber pathway may cause the fibers to form altered but nonetheless functional patterns of synaptic contacts in still intact portions of the brain (Devor, 1975; Schneider, 1970). In mammals, such redirected growth of immature axons is largely limited to the infant central nervous system. A different type of alteration may occur in areas where neurons remain intact, but lose a portion of their synaptic input. These vacated synaptic spaces may be filled by collateral sprouting, that is, growth of collateral branches and terminals from nearby axons (Lynch, Deadwyler, & Cotman, 1973a; McCouch, Austin, Liu, & Liu, 1958; Raisman, 1969). Collateral sprouting has been observed in adults as well as infants, but appears to be more extensive following damage in infancy (Goldman & Galkin, 1978; Lynch, Stanfield, & Cotman, 1973b; Raisman & Field, 1973). Denervated neurons may also become innervated by axons that normally do not terminate in that region at all, resulting in the formation of aberrant fiber tracts (Castro, 1975, 1977; Hicks & D'Amato, 1970; Schneider, 1970). This type of change seems to occur only after damage to the immature nervous system.

Since the study of axonal growth phenomena in the mammalian brain is relatively recent, the behavioral effects of these alterations have not been fully explored. The vast majority of such experiments have been conducted in rodents, and in most instances there was little or no attempt to investigate the behavior of these animals. In some studies, however, strong links have been established between axonal growth phenomena and behavioral sparing or impairment (Devor, 1975; Schneider, 1970; Schneider & Jhaveri, 1974); in others, the results are at least suggestive of a relation between the observed anatomical and behavioral changes (Goldberger & Murray, 1978; Hicks & D'Amato, 1970).

Recent investigations (Goldman, 1978; Goldman & Galkin, 1978; Goldman-Rakic, 1981) have documented some of the anatomical alterations that may occur after damage to the prefrontal cortex in infant or fetal monkeys. A number of hitherto unsuspected differences in the anatomical effects of prefrontal damage at different stages of development were revealed, and these will be described below.

Anatomical Anomalies Following Early Unilateral Prefrontal Lesions

Two types of anomalous connections have been observed following unilateral lesions of the primate dorsolateral prefrontal cortex inflicted either prenatally or in monkeys up to 2 months old (Goldman & Galkin, 1978; Goldman-Rakic, 1981). In these studies, animals are given lesions of the prefrontal cortex of one hemisphere. After sufficient time has transpired for the anatomical changes to occur, the intact prefrontal area of the opposite hemisphere is injected with radioactive amino acids (see section on

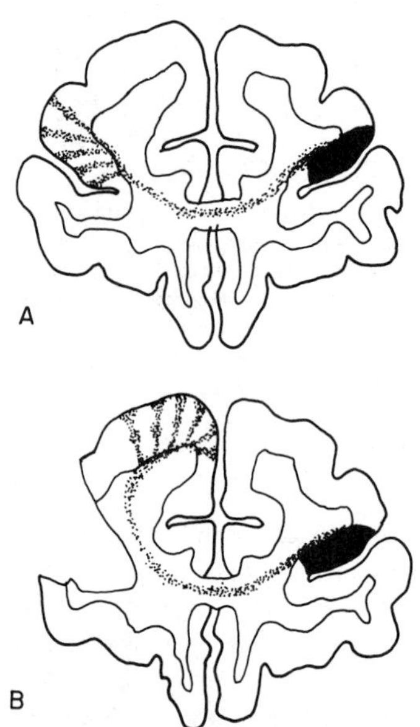

Figure 24. Efferent callosal projections from principal sulcus as revealed by autoradiography of transported radiolabeled amino acids. A normal monkey sacrificed 3 weeks after an injection of labeled tracer (A) and a monkey that had undergone unilateral excision of prefrontal cortex at 8 weeks of age, followed by injection of tracer in the contralateral principal sulcus at 4 months and sacrificed 3 weeks later (B). In the intact monkey (A) note the pattern of alternating columns in the projection to homotopic cortex. In the animal with early damage (B) the same pattern is evident in anomalous projections to dorsomedial cortex. Thus, a normally homotopic callosal connection has become heterotopic. (From Goldman-Rakic, 1981.)

anatomy). Following survival times sufficient to allow for transport of the amino acids from the neurons in the injection site to their terminations, the animals are sacrificed. Frozen sections are cut from their brains, mounted on slides, and then dipped in photographic emulsion. The sections are exposed for several weeks, developed, and counterstained. The resulting autoradiograms show the distribution of amino acids transported from the neurons of the prefrontal area to their terminations in various parts of the brain.

In intact monkeys, the prefrontal cortex of each hemisphere projects to the same area in the opposite hemisphere. The prefrontal cortex also sends ipsilateral projections to various cortical and subcortical areas. Following destruction of the dorsolateral prefrontal area of one hemisphere in infant or fetal monkeys, the intact dorsolateral prefrontal cortex issues an abnormal projection to the contralateral dorsomedial convexity (Goldman-Rakic, 1981). As shown in Figure 24, following removal of target cortex, normally homotopic callosal axons can become heterotopic.

A second anatomical anomaly is found in the subcortical projections of the intact dorsolateral prefrontal area following contralateral prefrontal lesions in early development. Normally, this area has a heavy ipsilateral projection to the head of the caudate nucleus, with a characteristic "fenestrated" mode of termination, as shown in Figure 11 (Goldman & Nauta, 1977b). Following perinatal damage, injections of tritiated amino acids into the principal sulcus of the intact hemisphere reveal both the normal ipsilateral termination, and a greatly enhanced projection field in the contralateral (denervated) caudate nucleus (Goldman 1978, Figure 25). The fenestrated pattern of termination of the anomalous projections is similar to that evident in the normal ipsilateral termination.

The origins of these anomalous cortical and subcortical projections are not yet completely understood. Possible mechanisms have been discussed elsewhere in detail (Goldman, 1978; Goldman-Rakic, 1981). These contralateral projections are not observed in normal fetuses at any stage of development (Goldman-Rakic, 1981). Thus, the anomalies do not represent retention of infantile "exuberant" terminations which are normally eliminated during the course of development. It is possible that denervation of the contralateral caudate nucleus and dorsomedial cortex stimulates the expansion of sparse contralateral projections that are normally present but difficult to detect; in fact, the normal contralateral projection to the head of the caudate may be somewhat more extensive than previously suspected (Fallon & Ziegler, 1979; Goldman, 1978; Leichnetz, 1981). A similar mechanism has been proposed to explain aberrant terminations formed by collateral sprouting in other parts of the central nervous system (Goldowitz, White, Steward, Lynch, & Cotman, 1975; Hicks & D'Amato, 1970). A second possibility is that the anomalous connections are due

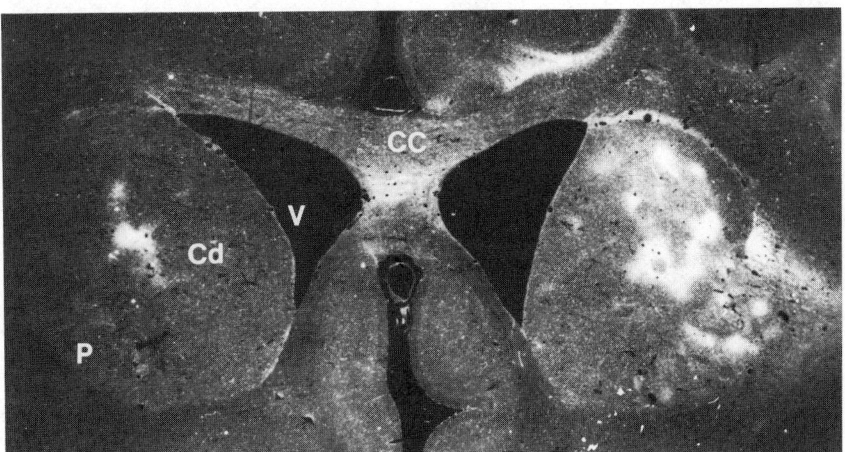

Figure 25. Photomicrograph of the head of the caudate nuclei in left and right hemispheres under dark-field illumination in a monkey whose prospective left dorsolateral prefrontal cortex was resected at embryonic day 119. The right principal sulcus was injected with tritiated amino acids when the animal was 5 days old, and the monkey was sacrificed 1 week later. Bright areas indicate labeled fibers from frontal cortex. Note the intricate pattern of label in the right (ipsilateral) caudate, and the anomalous projection to the left (contralateral) caudate. Compare with Figure 11. (From Goldman, 1978.)

to deflection of callosal fibers that would normally grow into the dorsolateral prefrontal area. Since the contralateral homotopic area is destroyed by the lesion, these fibers are deprived of their original target; they may then grow either dorsally into the dorsomedial cortex, or turn ventromedially into the head of the caudate nucleus.

Morphological Consequences Following Prenatal Bilateral Prefrontal Lesions

Another striking morphological change observed following prenatal lesions is a radical alteration in the surface topography of the cerebral mantle. This consists of anomalous sulci and gyri which appear following bilateral or unilateral damage prior to day 119 of gestation, about 45 days before birth (Goldman & Galkin, 1978). Some of these alterations are shown in Figure 26. They occur not only in prefrontal cortex adjacent to the damage area, but also in far removed temporal and occipital areas. Moreover, in unilaterally operated monkeys, the surface anomalies develop bilaterally, and thus cannot be attributed solely to gross mechanical disturbances provoked by the lesion. The locations of the abnormal sulci and gyri is highly selective, and may be related either to the schedule of anatomical maturation of these areas, or may be a function of anatomical connectivity with the prefrontal cortex (for discussion, see Goldman-Rakic, 1981).

The reasons for the formation of these extra sulci and gyri are not well understood. Since migration of cortical neurons into the dorsolateral area was not completed at the time the damage was inflicted, these neurons may have been spared, and may have then migrated to an adjacent areas; the resulting displacement would have produced a distortion of the cortical surface. This mechanism could not, however, account for abnormalities found in cortical areas quite distant from the site of the damage (Goldman & Galkin, 1978).

Abnormal fissuration has been reported in humans suffering from gross central nervous system pathology (Courville, 1971; Larroche, 1977; Yakovlev & Wadsworth, 1946) and has been associated with disasterous behavioral effects. Similar anomalies have been induced by prenatal anoxia

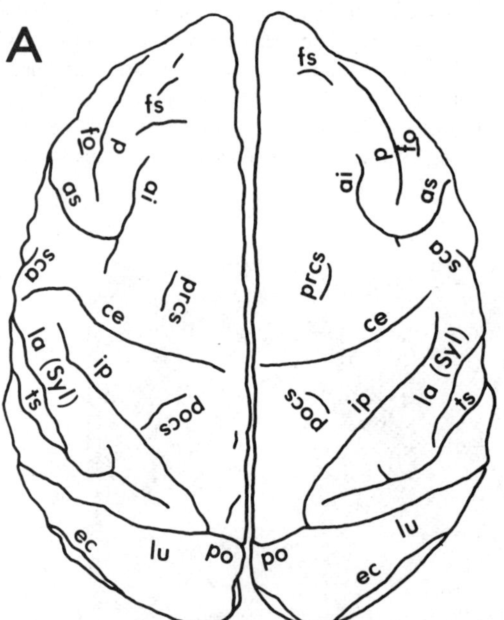

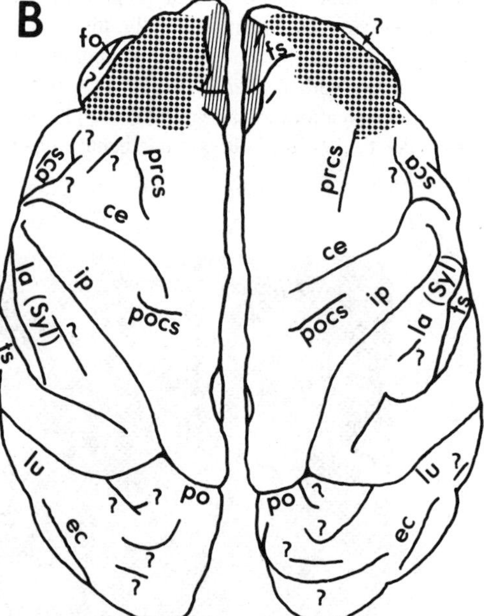

Figure 26. Dorsal view reconstruction of the brain of an unoperated 2½-year-old monkey (a). Dorsal view of the 2.5-year-old monkey operated at E106 illustrating size of the resection and location of the anomalous sulci indicated by question marks (b). Note the preponderance of ectopic sulci in the prefrontal, temporal, and occipital lobes and their relative absence in the central portion of the cortical surface. ai, inferior ramus of arcuate sulcus; as, superior ramus of arcuate sulcus; ce, central sulcus; ec, ectocalcarine sulcus; fo, orbital-frontal sulcus; fs, sulcus frontalis superior; ip, intraparietal sulcus; lu, lunate sulcus; la (Syl), lateral (Sylvian) fissure; po, parieto-occipital incisure; pocs, superior postcentral sulcus; prcs, superior precentral dimple; sca, anterior subcentral dimple, ts, superior temporal sulcus. (From Goldman & Galkin, 1978.)

(Meyers, 1969; Windle, Jacobson, deRamiriz, de Arellano, & Combs, 1967). One study reported alterations of the cortical surface immediately surrounding the lesion site in kittens operated on neonatally or as juveniles (Isaacson, Nonneman, & Schmaltz, 1968). The observations in monkeys suffering prefrontal damage are, however, the first indication that widespread anomalies of fissuration can be induced by focal cortical damage during development. It may be noted that unlike the findings in humans, the alterations in fissural patterns induced by discrete damage in monkeys could not be related to any obvious behavioral impediment.

A second morphological change observed following prenatal destruction of the dorsolateral prefrontal area is the preservation of thalamic neurons which normally project to that area (Goldman & Galkin, 1978). As discussed earlier, the parvocellular portion of the mediodorsal thalamic nucleus sends a massive projection to the dorsolateral prefrontal cortex. Cortical lesions in older animals destroy this projection, provoking a retrograde reaction that is transmitted back to the thalamic neurons and results in their death (Akert, 1964; Pribram et al., 1953; Walker, 1938). Lesions of the dorsolateral prefrontal area in fetal monkeys produces only slight degeneration in the parvocellular portion of the mediodorsal nucleus whereas in monkeys suffering lesions during infancy or as juveniles, complete degeneration occurs. This finding is all the more remarkable because such degeneration phenomena have usually been found to be greater following brain damage in developing animals (Bleir, 1969; Cowan, 1970; Gudden, 1870).

The reasons for retrograde degeneration following destruction of axons are only partially understood. However, since neuronal survival depends fundamentally upon the maintenance of a requisite minimum of connections (Clarke & Cowan, 1976; Hamburger, 1975; Kerr, 1975; Schneider & Jhaveri, 1974), it must be assumed that, following prenatal destruction of their cortical projection areas, thalamic neurons find new synaptic contacts elsewhere. One possibility is that destruction of thalamic terminals in the prefrontal areas may have induced the thalamic neurons to sprout collaterals in other portions of their terminal fields. Another alternative is that since a portion of the thalamic input may not yet have entered the cortex at the age the damage was inflicted, these thalamocortical fibers might escape injury and be redirected into adjacent cortical areas. This explanation might also account for some of the extra sulci and gyri observed following prenatal damage, since these may have formed to create more surface area for the anomalous projections.

Neuroanatomical Changes and Behavior

As has been pointed out, bilateral lesions of the dorsolateral area in infant monkeys and, to a greater extent, bilateral or unilateral lesions incurred prenatally spare some of the behavioral capacities which are normally lost following similar damage in mature animals. The finding that early injury to these areas results in anomalous anatomical development suggests a possible basis for the behavioral sparing. However, it is by no means a simple matter to conclusively link anatomical change with specific behavioral sparing. Although one source of evidence for linkage is that lesions often induce anatomical, physiological, and neurochemical changes, with the same time course, this clustering of effects also makes it difficult to isolate the factor or factors that are responsible for behavioral recovery. In a system that subserves cognitive and integrative functions, such as the prefrontal cortex, the problem is doubly difficult since the normal anatomical bases of these behaviors are not yet well understood, and cognitive functions are usually more difficult to evaluate than are motor or sensory abilities.

Evaluation of the behavioral significance of rearranged anatomical connections following brain damage is of great interest, because it may hold the key to the resolution of a major theoretical dilemma. As we have observed, it seems likely that the dramatic and enduring differences in learning capacities between adult- and infant-operated animals are due to equally dramatic differences in neural circuitry. However, the notion that altered circuitry could be responsible for normal, adaptive behavior has been greeted with skepticism, because it implies that there is no strict relation between neural organization and behavioral function (Dawson, 1973; Isaacson, 1975; Levere, 1975; Sperry, 1958). The dilemma is not resolved satisfactorily by explanations that invoke behavioral substitution or diaschisis; one would still have to account for the fact that younger animals are able to learn the alternate strategies postulated by behavioral substitution theories, or cope with the functional disturbances posited by diaschisis whereas older animals are not.

The solution to the dilemma posed by findings of behavioral sparing after early damage may lie in the gradually accumulating evidence which indicates that anomalous projections might result in adaptive behavior by preserving or enhancing the functions of intact tissue. The most straightforward example of such anatomical sparing is the prevention of retrograde degeneration by sprouting of collaterals in intact areas. This mechanism might, as we have noted, be responsible for the sparing of mediodorsal thalamic neurons after early prefrontal damage. While the new synaptic contacts may have little or no functional value, the preservation of parvocellular mediodorsal tissue may allow these cells to develop their normal connections with other subcortical regions. Destruction of the mediodorsal thalamic nucleus can impair spatial memory performance (Isseroff et al., 1982; Schulman, 1964); thus, sparing of such tissue following prefrontal damage in fetal monkeys should have some beneficial effect. However, it should be noted that only prenatally operated monkeys showed substantial sparing of mediodorsal neurons, whereas prenatal or early postnatal injury allowed some behavioral sparing.

There is also increasing evidence that altered or enhanced projections induced by brain damage can enhance the functions of intact areas. These changes may allow the intact tissue to substitute its own capacities for those of the damaged area. Thus, "behavioral substitution" may actually be an expression of anatomical reorganization rather than a strictly behavioral mechanism of recovery. In cats and kittens, lesions of the spinal dorsal roots of sensory nerves deprive the motor reflex arc of sensory feedback, and therefore result in severe disturbances of motor function. These animals exhibit partial behavioral recovery, but the recovered motor behavior is apparently guided by anomalous sensory cues (Goldberger & Murray, 1978). These lesions also produce several anatomical anomalies, including expansion of the terminal fields of descending projections. The time course of these changes parallels the improvement in behavioral functions. Damage to descending projections can abolish the recovered motor behavior in cats that had previously suffered lesions of the dorsal roots, though it has only mild behavioral effects in otherwise intact animals. Goldberger and Murray (1978) concluded that the enhanced projections enabled central motor areas to exert greater descending control over spinal reflexes, thus allowing them to mediate some of the behavioral capacities formerly controlled by the destroyed sensory input.

In some cases, continued growth of axons following early lesions may recreate a portion of the neural connections destroyed by a lesion. Schneider (1970, 1979; Schneider & Jhaveri, 1974) has been studying the behavioral and anatomic effects of early damage in the hamster visual system. Normal hamsters will immediately turn toward a sunflower seed or other relevant stimulus placed in their field of vision. Such behavior is abolished following lesions of the upper layers of the optic tectum (superior colliculus) in adult hamsters. Considerable sparing of function may be noted following similar damage in infancy. Anatomical studies reveal that in infant hamsters, the optic fibers deprived of their normal targets in the superior colliculus continue to grow and make contact instead with neurons in the deeper layers of the tectum—in other words, with neurons that do not normally receive such input. The orientation behavior of these animals shows sparing, although head-turning movements are not as accurate as they are in intact hamsters. For example, in some animals, visual stimuli elicit a turning response in the opposite than normal direction. In these cases, retinal fibers have been shown to innervate the "wrong" side of the tectum (Schneider, 1970; 1979).

Another way in which anatomical anomalies may result in adaptive behavior is indicated by findings that postlesion growth may create or expand pathways that are not normally very prominent in the species being studied but may be normal in other species. One such example comes from research into the effects of damage to the rat hippocampal formation. This is an area of the limbic system consisting of the hippocampus and a closely associated structure known as the dentate gyrus. These areas receive extensive projections from ipsilateral adjacent limbic cortical regions, including the entorhinal cortex. Lesions of the ipsilateral entorhinal cortex have been shown to induce expansion of a normally very sparse projection from the contralateral entorhinal cortex to the denervated dentate gyrus (Goldowitz et al., 1975; Lynch et al., 1973b). The expansion of this normally sparse terminal field allows the connection to become electrophysiologically functional (Steward, Cotman, & Lynch, 1974). This expanded contralateral projection, which is anomalous in the rat, is present normally in the rabbit (Hjorth-Simonsen & Zimmer, 1975). One might propose that there are a number of potentially functional arrangements of neural circuitry. In the course of normal development and differentiation, the optimal arrangement for a particular species may be singled out and other circuits may fail to develop or else be crowded out by competition. However, when the competitive inputs are removed following damage early in development, the normally less developed circuitry may expand and become functional, forming anomalous connections for that species but not necessarily maladaptive ones. The reasons for such differences between species are not clear. They may be dictated by functional differences related to species-specific behaviors; if so, emergence of projections typical of other species following a lesion might produce a corresponding alteration in behavior. One may speculate that some such phenomenon is responsible for "behavioral substitution" observed in monkeys suffering lesions of the prefrontal cortex. Orbach (1962) noted that following such lesions, Old World monkeys, including rhesus macaques, may solve the delayed-response problem by positioning their bodies in front of the correct food well. Such behavior is not common in unoperated monkeys. "Positional cueing" behavior has occasionally been observed in monkeys that have undergone prefrontal lesions in infancy; however, the basis of their solutions to delayed-reaction problems has not yet been analyzed systematically (Goldman-Rakic, unpublished observations).

We hasten to point out that the mechanisms discussed here are highly speculative. They are meant to illustrate how anatomical anomalies following early brain damage might mediate behavioral recovery without violating present conceptions of structure-function specificity in the central nervous system. It would appear that some such mechanisms must exist to explain the existence of permanent behavioral differences between early and late brain-damaged animals. However, it is equally cogent to argue that the widespread anatomic anomalies found after infant damage must result in some behavioral deficiency and that the sparing of cognitive abilities following early damage must have its "price" in terms of other functions not disturbed by lesions in older monkeys. Such anomalies have not been observed in prefrontal operates, but that may reflect the difficulty of examining more than a small fraction of the behavioral repertoire of these animals in controlled laboratory tests. We do not know, for example, how these lesions affect social and emotional behavior at different stages of development.

Conclusions

The study of cognitive and anatomical development following early damage to the prefrontal areas is admittedly far from complete. However, the data obtained so far seem to be instructive both about the nature of normal development and about the mechanisms that may underly differences following damage incurred in infancy or adulthood. The phenomenon of deterioration of function after early lesions may be a useful model for understanding the etiology of late appearing cognitive and affective pathologies. It is probable that the shift in functional organization proposed for the prefrontal system is not unique to those structures. Other areas may undergo similar reorganization during development; thus heterology of function in the developing nervous system may account for many qualitative changes in behavior during maturation. The permanent behavioral differences between animals suffering brain damage at different stages of development seem to have their counterpart in altered anatomical connections. Attempts to relate the anatomical and behavioral phenomena are important not only for the understanding of recovery mechanisms, but also for understanding the bases of normal functional organization.

Traditionally, there have been several separate approaches to the study of central nervous system development. Psychologists, physiologists, and anatomists each attempted to describe the phenomena they observed in terms of their own disciplines. It should be obvious, however, that these various disciplines are interdependent. It is not possible to explain phenomena such as recovery from early brain damage without invoking hypothetical intervening processes in the nervous system such as reorganization. It is equally difficult to explain the qualitative changes in personality and cognitive processes that occur in normal development without invoking some change in the neural mechanisms governing behavior. These explanations cannot be validated without a detailed understanding of the anatomical and functional bases of neural development. Without such validation, developmental psychology would remain largely a descriptive discipline. Conversely, descriptions of the myriad anatomical connections or electrophysiological events occurring in the nervous system make no sense unless they are directed toward understanding how these phenomena are related to the behavioral functions of the nervous system. Such multidisciplinary research has only become practical in recent years, thanks in part to vast improvements in anatomical, neurochemical, and electrophysiological techniques. The continued application of these techniques, in conjunction with sophisticated and innovative behavioral approaches, promises a corresponding revolution in our understanding of the biological bases of behavior and behavioral development.

REFERENCES

Ades, H. W. A secondary acoustic area in the cerebral cortex of the cat. *Journal of Neurophysiology*, 1943, *6*, 59–64.

Aghajanian, G. K. LSD and CNS transmission. *An-*

nual Review of Pharmacology, 1972, *12,* 157–168.

Akert, K. Comparative anatomy of the frontal cortex and thalamocortical connections. In J. M. Warren and K. Akert (Eds.), *The frontal granular cortex and behavior.* New York: McGraw-Hill, 1964.

Akert, K., Orth, O. S., Harlow, H. F., & Schiltz, K. A. Learned behavior of rhesus monkeys following neonatal bilateral prefrontal lobotomy. *Science,* 1960, *132,* 1944–1945.

Alexander, G. E., & Goldman, P. S. Functional development of the dorsolateral prefrontal cortex: An analysis utilizing reversible cryogenic depression. *Brain Research,* 1978, *143,* 233–249.

Alexander, G. E., Witt, E., & Goldman-Rakic, P. S. Neuronal activity in the prefrontal cortex, caudate nucleus and mediodorsal thalamic nucleus during delayed response performance of immature and adult rhesus monkeys. *Neuroscience Abstracts,* 1980, *6,* 86.

Altman, P. L., & Dittmer, D. S. (Eds.), *Biology data book.* Washington, D.C.: 1964.

Anderson, K. V., & O'Steen, W. K. Black-white and pattern discrimination in rats without photoreceptors. *Experimental Neurology,* 1972, *34,* 446–454.

Arbit, J., Boshes, B., & Blonsky, R. Behavior and mentation changes during therapy. In A. Barbeau & F. H. McDowell (Eds.), *L-DOPA and Parkinsonism.* Philadelphia: F. A. Davis Company, 1970.

Bartus, R. T., & Dean, R. L. Recent memory in aged non-human primates: Hypersensitivity to visual interference during retention. *Experimental Aging Research,* 1979, *5,* 385–400.

Bartus, R. T., Fleming, D., & Johnson, H. R. Aging in the rhesus monkey: Debilitating effects of short-term memory. *Journal of Gerontology,* 1978, *33,* 858–871.

Battig, K., Mishkin, M., and Rosvold, H. E. Comparison of the effects of frontal and caudate lesions on delayed response and alternation in monkeys. *Journal of Comparative and Physiological Psychology,* 1960, *53,* 400–404.

Battig, K., Rosvold, H. E., & Mishkin, M. Comparison of the effects of frontal and caudate lesions on discrimination learning in monkeys. *Journal of Comparative and Physiological Psychology,* 1962, *55,* 458–463.

Beach, F. A., Hebb, D. O., Torgan, C., & Nissen, H. W. (Eds.), *The Neuropsychology of Lashley.* New York: McGraw-Hill, 1960.

Berry, M. J. Cellular differentiation: Development of Dendritic arborization under normal and experimentally altered conditions. In P. Rakic & P. S. Goldman-Rakic (Eds.), *Development and modifiability of the cerebral cortex.* Boston: MIT Press, 1982.

Bianchi, L. *The mechanism of the brain and the function of the frontal lobes* (J. H. MacDonald, trans.). New York: W. Wood & Company, 1922.

Bizzi, E. Single unit activity in the frontal eye fields of unanesthetized monkeys during eye and head movement. *Experimental Brain Research,* 1970, *10,* 151–158.

Bleier, R. Retrograde transsynaptic cellular degeneration in mammillary and ventral tegmental nuclei following limbic decortication in rabbits of various ages. *Brain Research,* 1969, *15,* 365–393.

Blum, J. S., Chow, K. L., & Pribram, K. H. A behavioral analysis of the organization of the parieto-temporo-preoccipital cortex. *Journal of Comparative Neurology,* 1950, *92,* 53–100.

Boothe, R. G., & Lund, J. S. A quantitative study of pyramidal cell spine density in developing visual cortex of normal and dark-reared macaque monkeys. *Neuroscience Abstracts,* 1976, *2,* 1103. (Abstract)

Borges, S., & Berry, M. The effects of dark-rearing on the development of the visual cortex of the rat. *Journal of Comparative Neurology,* 1978, *180,* 277–300.

Bourgoin, S., Artaud, F., Adrien, J., Hery, F., Glowinski, J., & Hamon, M. 5-Hydroxytryptamine catabolism in the rat brain during ontogenesis. *Journal of Neurochemistry,* 1977, *28,* 415–422.

Brickner, R. M. The intellectual functions of the frontal lobes. New York: Macmillan, 1936.

Brizzee, K. R., Ordy, J. M., Hansche, J., & Kaack, B. Quantitative assessment of changes in neuron and glial cell packing density and lipofuscin accumulation with age in the cerebral cortex of a non-human primate (Macaca mulatta). In R. D. Terry & S. Gershon (Eds.), *Aging, Neurobiology of Aging* (Vol. 3). New York: Raven Press, 1976.

Brodal, A., Taber, E., & Walberg, F. The raphe nuclei of the brain stem in the cat. II. Efferent connections. *Journal of Comparative Neurology,* 1960, *114,* 239–259.

Brown, R. M., Crane, A. M., & Goldman, P. S. Regional distribution of monoamines in the cerebral cortex and subcortical structures of the rhesus monkey: Concentrations and in vivo synthesis rates. *Brain Research,* 1979, *168,* 133–150.

Brown, R. M., & Goldman, P. S. Catecholamines in neocortex of rhesus monkeys: Regional distribution and ontogenetic development. *Brain Research,* 1977, *124,* 576–580.

Brown, R. M., & Goldman, P. S. Developmental changes in catecholamine content and activity in circumscribed regions of the cerebral cortex in the rhesus monkey. In E. Usdin, I. J. Kopin, & J. Barchas (Eds.), *Catecholamines: Basic and clinical frontiers* (Vol. 1). New York: Pergamon Press, 1979.

Brown, R. M., Kehr, W., & Carlsson, A. Functional and biochemical aspects of catecholamine metabolism in brain under hypoxia. *Brain Research,* 1975, *85,* 491–509.

Brown, R. M., Snyder, S. R., & Carlsson, A. Changes in biogenic amine synthesis and turnover induced by hypoxia and/or foot shock stress. II. The central nervous system. *Journal of Neural Transmission,* 1974, *35,* 293–305.

Brozoski, T., Brown, R. M., Rosvold, H. E., & Goldman, P. S. Cognitive deficit caused by regional depletion of dopamine in prefrontal cortex of rhesus monkey. *Science,* 1979, *205,* 929–932.

Buell, S. J., & Coleman, P. D. Dendritic growth in the aged human brain and failure of growth in senile dementia. *Science,* 1979, *6,* 854–856.

Bugbee, N. M., & Goldman-Rakic, P. S. Compartmentalization of prefrontal projections: Comparisons of cortical columns and striatal islands in old and new world monkeys. *Neuroscience Abstracts,* 1980, *6,* 822.

Bugbee, N. M., & Goldman-Rakic, P. S. Functional 2-deoxyglucose mapping in association cortex: Prefrontal activation in monkeys performing a cognitive task. *Neuroscience Abstracts,* 1981, *7,* 416.

Buisseret, P., & Imbert, M. Visual cortical cells: Their developmental properties in normal and dark-reared kittens. *Journal of Physiology,* London, 1976, *255,* 511–525.

Butters, N., Pandya, D., Stein, D., & Rosen, J. A search for the spatial engram within the frontal lobes of monkeys. *Acta Neurobiologiae Experimentalis,* 1972, *32,* 305–329.

Butters, N., Rosen, J. J., & Stein, D. G. Recovery of behavioral functions after sequential ablation of the frontal lobes of monkeys. In D. G. Stein, J. J. Rosen, & N. Butters (Eds.), *Plasticity and recovery of function in the central nervous system.* New York: Academic Press, 1974.

Cajal, S. Ramon Y. *Histologie du sytème nerveux de l'homme et des vertèbres.* Paris: Maloine, 1909.

Cannon, W. B., & Rosenblueth, A. *The supersensitivity of denervated structures; A law of denervation.* New York: Macmillan, 1949.

Castro, A. J. Ipsilateral corticospinal projections after large lesions of the cerebral hemisphere in neonatal rats. *Experimental Neurology,* 1975, *46,* 108.

Castro, A. J. Limb preference after lesions of the cerebral hemisphere in adult and neonatal rats. *Physiology and Behavior,* 1977, *18,* 605–608.

Chow, K. L. Effects of ablation. In G. C. Quarton, T. Melnechuk, & F. O. Schmitt (Eds.), *The Neurosciences. A study program* (Vol. 1). New York: The Rockefeller University Press, 1967.

Clark, W. E. L., & Boggon, R. H. On the connections of the medial cell group of the thalamus. *Brain,* 1933, *56,* 83–98.

Clark, W. E. L., & Boggon, R. H. The thalamic connections of the parietal and frontal lobes of the brain in the monkey. *Philosophical Transactions of the Royal Society of London; B: Biological Sciences,* 1935, *224,* 313–359.

Clarke, P. G. H., & Cowan, W. M. The development of the isthmo-optic tract in the chick, with special reference to the occurrence and correction of developmental errors in the location and connections of isthmo-optic neurons. *Journal of Comparative Neurology,* 1976, *167,* 143–163.

Coleman, P. D., & Riesen, A. H. Environmental effects on cortical and dendritic fields. I. Rearing in the dark. *American Journal of Anatomy,* 1968, *102,* 363–374.

Courville, C. B. Birth and brain damage. An investigation into the problems of antenatal and paranatal anoxia and allied disorders and their relation to the many lesion-complexes residual thereto. Pasadena, Calif.: N. F. Courville, 1971.

Cowan, W. M. Anterograde and retrograde transneuronal degeneration in the central and peripheral nervous system. In W. J. H. Nauta & S. O. E. Ebbesson (Eds.), *Contemporary research methods in neuroanatomy.* New York: Springer-Verlag, 1970.

Coyle, J. T., & Axelrod, J. Development of the uptake and storage of L-[^{3}H]-norepinephrine in the rat brain. *Journal of Neurochemistry,* 1971, *18,* 2061–2075.

Coyle, J. T., & Axelrod, J. Dopamine-beta-hydroxylase in the rat brain: Developmental characteristics. *Journal of Neurochemistry,* 1972, *19,* 449–459. (a)

Coyle, J. T., & Axelrod, J. Tyrosine hydroxylase in

the rat brain: Developmental characteristics. *Journal of Neurochemistry,* 1972, *19,* 1117–1123. (b)

Coyle, J. T., & Molliver, M. E. Major innervation of newborn rat cortex by monoaminergic neurons. *Science,* 1977, *196,* 444–447.

Cragg, B. G. The density of synapses and neurons in normal, mentally defective and ageing human brains. *Brain,* 1975, *98,* 81–90.

Critchley, M. *The dyslexic child.* Springfield, Ill.: Charles C. Thomas, 1960.

Cupp, C. J., & Uemura, E. Age related changes in prefrontal cortex of Macaca mulatta: quantitative analysis of dendritic branching patterns. *Experimental Neurology,* 1980, *69,* 143–163.

Davis, J. N., & Carlsson, A. The effect of hypoxia on monoamine synthesis, levels and metabolism in rat brain. *Journal of Neurochemistry,* 1973, *21,* 783–790.

Dawson, R. G. Recovery of function: Implications for theories of brain function. *Behavioral Biology,* 1973, *8,* 439–460.

Dekker, J. J., & Rakic, P. R. Genesis of neurons in the motor cortex and VA-VL thalamic complex in rhesus monkey. *Neuroscience Abstract,* 1980, *6,* 205.

DeLong, M. R. Activity of pallidal neurons during movement. *Journal of Neurophysiology,* 1971, *34,* 414–427.

DeLong, M. R. Motor functions of the basal ganglia: Single unit activity during movement. In F. O. Schmitt & F. G. Worden (Eds.), *The neurosciences, third study program.* Cambridge, Mass.: MIT Press, 1974.

DeLong, M. R., & Strick, P. L. Relation of basal ganglia, cerebellum and motor cortex to ramp and ballistic limb movements. *Brain Research,* 1974, *71,* 327–335.

Denny-Brown, D. The frontal lobes and their function. In A. Feiling (Ed.), *Modern trends in neurology.* New York: Hoeber, Inc., 1951.

Devor, M. Neuroplasticity in the sparing or deterioration of function after early olfactory tract lesions. *Science,* 1975, *190,* 998–1000.

Divac, I., Bjorklund, A., Lindvall, O., & Passingham, R. Converging projections from the mediodorsal thalamic nucleus and mesencephalic dopaminergic neurons to the neocortex in three species. *Journal of Comparative Neurology,* 1978, *180,* 59–72.

Eidelberg, E., & Stein, D. G. (Eds.), Functional recovery after lesions of the nervous system. *Neurosciences Research Program Bulletin,* 1974, *12,* 191–303.

Elder, W., & Miles, A. A case of tumour of the left prefrontal lobe removed by operation. *Lancet,* 1902, *1,* 363.

Ellenwood, E. H., Jr. Amphetamine psychosis: A multi-dimensional process. *Seminars in Psychiatry,* 1969, *1,* 208–226.

Evarts, E. V. Pyramidal tract activity associated with a conditioned hand movement in the monkey. *Journal of Neurophysiology,* 1966, *29,* 1011–1027.

Evarts, E. V. Relation of pyramidal tract activity to force exerted during voluntary movement. *Journal of Neurophysiology,* 1968, *31,* 14–27.

Falck, B., Hillarp, N. A., Thieme, G., & Torp, A. Fluorescence of catecholamines and related compounds condensed with formaldehyde. *Journal of Histochemistry and Cytochemistry,* 1962, *10,* 348–354.

Fallon, J. H., & Ziegler, B. T. S. The crossed cortico-caudate projection in the rhesus monkey. *Neuroscience Letters,* 1979, *15,* 29–32.

Farkas-Bargeton, E., & Diebler, M. F. A topographical study of enzyme maturation in human cerebral neocortex: A histochemical and biochemical study. In M. A. B. Brazier & H. Petsche (Eds.), *Architectonics of the cerebral cortex.* New York: Raven Press, 1978.

Ferrier, D. *The functions of the brain* (2nd ed.). New York: G. P. Putnam's Sons; London: Smith, Elder, 1886.

Fiala, B. A., Joyce, J. N., & Greenough, W. T. Environmental complexity modulates growth of granule cell dendrites in developing but not adult hippocampus of rats. *Experimental Neurology,* 1978, *59,* 372–382.

Fifkova, E. The effect of monocular deprivation on the synaptic contacts of the visual cortex. *Journal of Neurobiology,* 1970, *1,* 285–294.

Filimonov, I. N. Cortical cytoarchitecture—general concepts. Classification of the architectonic formations. In S. A. Sarkisov, I. N. Filimonov, & N. S. Preobrazhenskaya (Eds.), *Cytoarchitecture of the cerebral cortex in man.* Moscow: Medgiz, 1949.

Floeter, M. K., & Greenough, W. T. Cerebellar plasticity: Modification of purkinje cell structure by differential rearing in monkeys. *Science,* 1979, *206,* 227–229.

Flourens, P. *Recherches experimentales sur les propriétés et les fonctions du système nerveux dans les animaux vertébrés,* Crevot, Paris, 1824.

Fritsch, G., & Hitzig, E. Uber die elektrische Erregbarkeit das Grosshirns. *Arch. Anat. Physiol. wiss. Med.,* 1870, *37:* 300–332.

Fulton, J. F. *Frontal lobotomy and affective behavior*. New York: W. W. Norton, 1951.

Fuster, J. M. Unit activity in prefrontal cortex during delayed-response performance: Neuronal correlates of transient memory. *Journal of Neurophysiology*, 1973, *36*, 61–78.

Fuster, J. M., & Alexander, G. E. Delayed response deficit by cryogenic depression of frontal cortex. *Brain Research*, 1970, *20*, 85–90.

Fuster, J. M., & Alexander, G. E. Neuron activity related to short-term memory. *Science*, 1971, *173*, 652–654.

Gall, F. J. *Sur les fonctions du cerveau er sur celles de chacune de ses parties*. Paris, 1822.

Glassman, R. B. Recovery following sensorimotor cortical damage: Evoked potentions, brain stimulation and motor control. *Experimental Neurology*, 1971, *33*, 16–29.

Glassman, R. B. Similar effects of infant and adult sensorimotor cortical lesions on cat's posture. *Brain Research*, 1973, *63*, 103–110.

Globus, A. Brain morphology as a function of presynaptic morphology and activity. In A. H. Riesen (Ed.), *The developmental neuropsychology of sensory deprivation*. New York: Academic Press, 1975.

Globus, A., Rosenzweig, M. R., Bennett, E. L., & Diamond, M. C. Effects of differential experience on dendritic spine counts in rat cerebral cortex. *Journal of Comparative Physiological Psychology*, 1973, *82*, 175–181.

Goldberger, M. E., & Murray, M. Recovery of movement and axon sprouting may obey some of the same laws. In C. W. Cotman (Ed.), *Neuronal Plasticity*. New York: Raven Press, 1978.

Goldman, P. S. Functional development of the prefrontal cortex in early life and the problem of neuronal plasticity. *Experimental Neurology*, 1971, *32*, 366–387.

Goldman, P. S. Developmental determinants of cortical plasticity. *Acta Neurobiologie Experimentalis*, 1972, *32*, 495–511.

Goldman, P. S. An alternative to developmental plasticity: Heterology of CNS structures in infants and adults. In D. G. Stein, J. J. Rosen, & N. Butters (Eds.), *Plasticity and recovery of function in the central nervous system*. New York: Academic Press, 1974.

Goldman, P. S. Maturation of the mammalian nervous system and the ontogeny of behavior. In J. S. Rosenblatt, R. A. Hinde, E. Shaw, & C. Beer (Eds.), *Advances in the study of behavior*. New York: Academic Press, 1976. (a)

Goldman, P. S. The role of experience in recovery of function following prefrontal lesions in infant monkeys. *Neuropsychologia*, 1976, *14*, 401–412. (b)

Goldman, P. S. Neuronal plasticity in primate telencephalon: Anomalous crossed cortico-caudate projections induced by prenatal removal of frontal association cortex. *Science*, 1978, *202*, 768–770.

Goldman, P. S. Contralateral projections to the dorsal thalamus from frontal association cortex in the rhesus monkey. *Brain Research*, 1979, *166*, 166–171.

Goldman, P. S., & Alexander, G. E. Maturation of prefrontal cortex in the monkey revealed by local reversible cryogenic depression. *Nature*, 1977, *267*, 613–615.

Goldman, P. S., & Brown, R. M. The influence of neonatal androgen on the development of cortical function in the rhesus monkey. *Neuroscience Abstracts*, 1975, *1*, 494.

Goldman, P. S., Crawford, H. T., Stokes, L. P., Galkin, T. W., & Rosvold, H. E. Sex-dependent behavioral effects of cerebral cortical lesions in the developing rhesus monkey. *Science*, 1974, *186*, 540–542.

Goldman, P. S., & Galkin, T. W. Prenatal removal of frontal association cortex in the fetal rhesus monkey: Anatomical and functional consequence in postnatal life. *Brain Research*, 1978, *152*, 451–485.

Goldman, P. S., & Lewis, M. E. Developmental biology of brain damage and experience. In C. Cotman (Ed.), *Neuronal plasticity*. New York: Raven Press, 1978.

Goldman, P. S., & Mendelson, M. J. Salutary effects of early experience on deficits caused by lesions of frontal association cortex in developing rhesus monkeys. *Experimental Neurology*, 1977, *57*, 588–602.

Goldman, P. S., & Nauta, W. J. H. Autoradiographic demonstration of a projection from prefrontal association cortex to the superior colliculus in the rhesus monkey. *Brain Research*, 1976, *116*, 145–149.

Goldman, P. S., & Nauta, W. J. H. Columnar distribution of cortico-cortical fibers in the frontal association, limbic, and motor cortex of the developing rhesus monkey. *Brain Research*, 1977, *122*, 393–413. (a)

Goldman, P. S., & Nauta, W. J. H. An intricately patterned prefronto-caudate projection in the rhesus monkey. *Journal of Comparative Neurology*, 1977, *171*, 369–386. (b)

Goldman, P. S., & Rosvold, H. E. Localization of

function within the dorso-lateral prefrontal cortex of the rhesus monkey. *Experimental Neurology*, 1970, *27*, 291–304.

Goldman, P. S., & Rosvold, H. E. The effects of selective caudate lesions in infant and juvenile rhesus monkeys. *Brain Research*, 1972, *43*, 53–66.

Goldman, P. S., Rosvold, H. E., & Mishkin, M. Evidence for behavioral impairment following prefrontal lobectomy in the infant monkey. *Journal of Comparative Physiological Psychology*, 1970, *70*, 454–463. (a)

Goldman, P. S., Rosvold, H. E., & Mishkin, M. Selective sparing of function following prefrontal lobectomy in infant monkeys. *Experimental Neurology*, 1970, *29*, 221–226. (b)

Goldman, P. S., Rosvold, H. E., Vest, B., & Galkin, T. W. Analysis of the delayed alternation deficit produced by dorsolateral prefrontal lesions in the rhesus monkey. *Journal of Comparative Physiological Psychology*, 1971, *77*, 212–220.

Goldman-Rakic, P. S. Development and plasticity of primate frontal cortex. In F. O. Schmitt, F. G. Worden, S. G. Dennis, & G. Adelman (Eds.), *The organization of cerebral cortex*. Cambridge, Mass.: MIT Press, 1981.

Goldman-Rakic, P. S., & Brown, R. M. Regional changes of monoamines in cerebral cortex and subcortical structures of aging rhesus monkeys. *Neuroscience*, 1981, *6*, 177–187.

Goldman-Rakic, P. S., & Brown, R. M. Postnatal development of monoamine content and synthesis in the cerebral cortex of rhesus monkeys. *Developmental Brain Research*, 1982, *4*, 339–349.

Goldman-Rakic, P. S., & Schwartz, M. L. Interdigitation of contralateral and ipsilateral columnar projections to frontal association cortex in primates. *Science*, 1982, *216*, 755–757.

Goldowitz, D., White, W. F., Steward, O., Lynch, G., & Cotman, C. Anatomical evidence for a projection from the entorhinal cortex to the contralateral dentate gyrus of the rat. *Experimental Neurology*, 1975, *47*, 433–441.

Goldstein, K. Frontal lobotomy and impairment of abstract attitude. *Journal of Nervous and Mental Disease*, 1949, *110*, 93–111.

Gottfries, C. G. Biochemical aspects of dementia. In H. M. Van Praag, M. H. Lader, O. J. Rafaelsen, & E. J. Sachar (Eds.), *Handbook of biological psychiatry. Part IV Brain mechanisms and abnormal behavior*. New York: Marcel Dekker, 1978.

Greenough, W. T., & Volkmar, F. R. Pattern of dendritic branching in occipital cortex of rats reared in complex environments. *Experimental Neurology*, 1973, *40*, 491–504.

Gross, C. G., & Weiskrantz, L. Some changes in behavior produced by lateral frontal lesions in the macaque. In J. M. Warren & K. Akert (Eds.), *The frontal granular cortex and behavior*. New York: McGraw-Hill, 1964.

Gudden, B. Experimentaluntersuchungen uber das peripherische und centrale nervensystem. *Archiv für Psychiatrie und Nervenkrankheiten*, 1870, *2*, 693–723.

Gustafson, L., Hagberg, B., & Ingvar, D. H. Speech disturbances in presenile dementia related to local cerebral blood flow abnormalities in the dominant hemisphere. *Brain and Language*, 1978, *5*, 103–118.

Hamburger, F. Cell death in the development of the lateral motor column of the chick embryo. *Journal of Comparative Neurology*, 1975, *160*, 535–546.

Hanaway, J., McConnell, J. A., & Netsky, M. G. Histogenesis of the substantia nigra, ventral tegmental area of tsai and interpeduncular nucleus: An autoradiographic study of the mesencephalon in the rat. *Journal of Comparative Neurology*, 1971, *142*, 59–74.

Harlow, H. F. Recovery of pattern discrimination in monkeys following unilateral occipital lobectomy. *Journal of Comparative Psychology*, 1939, *27*, 467–489.

Harlow, H. F. The development of learning in the rhesus monkey. *American Scientist*, 1959, *47*, 459–479.

Harlow, H. F., Blomquist, A. J., Thompson, C. I., Schiltz, K. A., & Harlow, M. K. Effects of induction age and size of prefrontal lobe lesions on learning rhesus monkeys. In R. Isaacson (Ed.), *The neuropsychology of development*. New York: Wiley, 1968.

Harlow, H. F., Davis, R. T., Settlage, P. H., & Meyer, D. R. Analysis of frontal and posterior association syndromes in brain-damaged monkeys. *Journal of Comparative Physiological Psychology*, 1952, *45*, 419–429.

Harlow, H. F., Harlow, M. K., Rueping, R. R., & Mason, W. A. Performance of infant rhesus monkeys on discrimination learning, delayed response, and discrimination learning set. *Journal of Comparative Physiological Psychology*, 1960, *53*, 113–121.

Hebb, D. O. *Organization of behavior*. New York: Wiley, 1949.

Hicks, S. P., & D'Amato, C. J. Motor-sensory and visual behavior after hemispherectomy in newborn and mature rats. *Experimental Neurology*, 1970, *29*, 416–438.

Hjorth-Simonsen, A., & Zimmer, J. Crossed pathways from the entorhinal area to the fascia dentata. I. Normal in rabbits. *Journal of Comparative Neurology*, 1975, *144*, 215–232.

Hornykiewicz, O. Some remarks concerning the possible role of brain monoamines (dopamine, noradrenaline, serotonin) in mental disorders. *Journal of Psychiatric Research*, 1974, *11*, 249–253.

Hornykiewicz, O. Brain dopamine in Parkinson's disease and other neurological disturbances. In A. S. Horn, J. Korf, & B. H. C. Westerink (Eds.), *The neurobiology of dopamine*. New York: Academic Press, 1979.

Hubel, D. H., & Freeman, D. C. Projection into the visual field of ocular dominance columns in macaque monkey. *Brain Research*, 1977, *122*, 336–343.

Hubel, D. H., & Wiesel, T. N. Receptive fields of cells in striate cortex of very young, visually inexperienced kittens. *Journal of Neurophysiology*, 1963, *26*, 994–1002. (a)

Hubel, D. H., & Wiesel, T. N. Shape and arrangement of columns in the cat striate cortex. *Journal of Physiology*, 1963, *165*, 559–568. (b)

Hubel, D. H., & Wiesel, T. N. Anatomic demonstration of columns in the monkey striate cortex. *Nature*, 1969, *221*, 747–750.

Hubel, D. H., & Wiesel, T. N. Functional architecture of macaque monkey visual cortex. *Proceedings of the Royal Society of London; B: Biological Sciences*, 1977, *193*, 1–59.

Hubel, D. H., Wiesel, T. N., & Stryker, M. P. Orientation columns in macaque monkey visual cortex demonstrated by the 2-deoxyglucose autoradiographic technique. *Nature*, 1978, *269*, 328–330.

Hughes, K. R. Dorsal and ventral hippocampus lesions and maze learning: influence of preoperative environment. *Canadian Journal of Psychology*, 1965, *19*, 325–332.

Hunter, W. S. The delayed reaction in animals and children. *Behavior Monographs*, 1913, *2* (Whole No. 1).

Huttenlocher, P. R. Synaptic density in human frontal cortex—developmental change and effects of aging. *Brain Research*, 1979, *163*, 195–205.

Imbert, M., & Buisseret, P. Receptive field characteristics and plastic properties of visual cortical cells in kittens reared with or without visual experiences. *Experimental Brain Research*, 1975, *22*, 25–36.

Ingvar, D. H. "Hyperfrontal" distribution of the cerebral gray matter flow in resting wakefullness; on the functional anatomy of the conscious state. *Acta Neurologica Scandinavica*, 1979, *60*, 12–25.

Ingvar, D. H. Abnormal distribution of cerebral activity in chronic schizophrenia: A neurophysiological interpretation. In C. Baxter & T. Melnechuk (Eds.), *Perspectives in schizophrenia*. New York: Raven Press, 1980.

Ingvar, D. H., & Lassen, N. A. (Eds.), *Brain work*. Copenhagen: Munkdsgaard, 1975.

Isaacson, R. L. The myth of recovery from early brain damage. In N. R. Ellis (Ed.), *Aberrant development in infancy*. Potomac, Md.: Lawrence Erlbaum Associates, 1975.

Isaacson, R. L., Nonneman, A. J., & Schmaltz, L. W. Behavioral and anatomical sequelae of damage to the infant limbic system. In R. L. Isaacson (Ed.), *The neuropsychology of development*. New York: Wiley, 1968.

Isseroff, A., Galkin, T., Rosvold, H. E., & Goldman-Rakic, P. S. Spatial memory impairments following damage to the mediodorsal nucleus of the thalamus in rhesus monkeys. *Brain Research*, 1982, *232*, 97–113.

Isseroff, A., & Isseroff, R. G. Experience aids recovery of spontaneous alteration following hippocampal damage. *Physiology and Behavior*, 1978, *21*, 469–472.

Jacobsen, C. F. Studies of cerebral function in primates. *Comparative Psychology Monographs*, 1936, *13*, 1–68.

Jacobson, S., Butters, N., & Tovsky, N. J. Afferent and efferent subcortical projections of behaviorally defined sectors of prefrontal granular cortex. *Brain Research*, 1978, *159*, 279–296.

Jacobson, S., & Trojanowski, J. Q. Prefrontal granular cortex of the rhesus monkey. I. Intrahemispheric cortical afferents. *Brain Research*, 1977, *132*, 209–233. (a)

Jacobson, S., & Trojanowski, J. Q. Prefrontal granular cortex of the rhesus monkey. II. Interhemispheric cortical afferents. *Brain Research*, 1977, *132*, 235–246. (b)

Johnson, T. N., Rosvold, H. E., & Mishkin, M. Projections from behaviorally defined sectors of the prefrontal cortex to the basal ganglia, septum, and diencephalon of the monkey. *Experimental Neurology*, 1968, *21*, 20–34.

Jones, D. G. Quantitative investigations of development of synaptic junctions in cortex. In P. Rakic & P. S. Goldman-Rakic (Eds.), *Development and modifiability of the cerebral cortex*. Boston: MIT Press, 1982.

Jones, E. G., Coulter, J. D., & Hendry, S. H. C. Intracortical connectivity of architectonic fields in the somatic sensory, motor and parietal cortex of monkeys. *Journal of Comparative Neurology*, 1978, *181*, 291–348.

Juraska, J. M., & Fifkova, E. A golgi study of the early postnatal development of the visual cortex of the hooded rats. *Journal of Comparative Neurology*, 1979, *183*, 247–256.

Kasamatsu, T., & Pettigrew, J. D. Depletion of brain catecholamines: Failure of ocular dominance shift after monocular occlusion in kittens. *Science*, 1976, *194*, 206–209.

Kasamatsu, T., & Pettigrew, J. D. Preservation of binocularity after monocular deprivation in the striate cortex of kittens treated with 6-hydroxydopamine. *Journal of Comparative Neurology*, 1979, *185*, 139–162.

Kasamatsu, T., Pettigrew, J. D., & Ary, M. Restoration of visual cortical plasticity by local microperfusion of norepinephrine. *Journal of Comparative Neurology*, *185*, 163–182.

Kehr, W., Lindqvist, M., & Carlsson, A. Distribution of dopamine in the rat cerebral cortex. *Journal of Neural Transmission*, 1976, *38*, 173–180.

Kellogg, C., & Wennerström, G. An ontogenetic study on the effect of catecholamine receptor-stimulating agents on the turnover of noradrenaline and dopamine in the brain. *Brain Research*, 1974, *79*, 451–464.

Kemp, J. M., & Powell, T. P. S. The cortico-striate projection in the monkey. *Brain*, 1970, *93*, 525–546.

Kemp, J. M., & Powell, T. P. S. The site of termination of afferent fibers in the caudate nucleus. *Philosophical Transactions of the Royal Society of London; B: Biological Sciences*, 1971, *262*, 413–427.

Kempinsky, W. H. Experimental study of distant effects of acute focal brain injury—a study of diaschisis. *Archives of Neurology and Psychiatry*, 1958, *79*, 376–389.

Kennard, M. A. Reorganization of motor function in the cerebral cortex of monkeys deprived of motor and premotor areas in infancy. *Journal of Neurophysiology*, 1938, *1*, 477–496.

Kennard, M. A. Relation of age to motor impairment in man and in subhuman primates. *Archives of Neurology and Psychiatry*, 1940, *44*, 377–397.

Kennard, M. A. Cortical reorganization of motor function: Studies on series of monkeys of various ages from infancy to maturity. *Archives of Neurology and Psychiatry*, 1942, *48*, 227–240.

Kennard, M. A., & McCulloch, W. S. Motor response to stimulation of cerebral cortex in the absence of areas 4 and 6 (Macaca Mulatta). *Journal of Neurophysiology*, 1943, *6*, 181–190.

Kennedy, C., Des Rosiers, M. H., Sakurada, O., Shinohara, M., Reivich, M., Jehle, J. W., & Sokoloff, L. Metabolic mapping of the primary visual system of the monkey by means of the autoradiographic (^{14}C) deoxyglucose technique. *Proceedings of the National Academy of Sciences*, 1976, *73*, 4230–4234.

Kennedy, C., Grave, G. D., Jehle, J. W., & Sokoloff, L. Changes in blood flow in the component structures of the dog brain during postnatal maturation. *Journal of Neurochemistry*, 1972, *19*, 2423–2433.

Kennedy, C., Sakurada, O., Shinohara, M., Jehle, J., & Sokoloff, L. Local cerebral glucose utilization in the normal conscious macaque monkey. *Annals of Neurology*, 1978, *4*, 293–301.

Kennedy, C., Sakurada, O., Shinohara, M., Mijaoka, M., & Sokoloff, L. Local cerebral glucose utilization in the newborn macaque monkey. *Annals of Neurology*, 1982, *12*, 333–340.

Kerr, F. W. L. Neuroplasticity of primary afferents in the neonatal cat and some results of early deafferentation of the trigeminal spinal nucleus. *Journal of Comparative Neurology*, 1974, *163*, 305–328.

Kety, S. S. Human cerebral blood flow and oxygen consumption as related to aging. *Research Publications of the Association for Research in Nervous and Mental Disease*, 1956, *35*, 31–45.

Kleist, K. *Gehirnpathologie*. Leipzig, Ger.: Barth, 1934.

Kojima, S. Short-term memory in the rhesus monkey: A behavioral analysis of delayed-response performance. *Journal of the Experimental Analysis of Behavior*, 1980, *33*, 359–368.

Kojima, S., & Goldman-Rakic, P. S. Delay-related activity of prefrontal cortical neurons in rhesus monkeys preforming delayed response. *Brain Research*, 1982, *248*, 43–49.

Kramer, J. C., Fischman, V. S., & Littlefield, D. C. Amphetamine abuse: Pattern and effects of high doses taken intravenously. *Journal of the American Medical Association*, 1967, *201*, 89–93.

Kubota, K., & Niki, H. Prefrontal cortical unit activity and delayed cortical unit activity and delayed alternation performance in monkeys. *Jour-*

nal of Neurophysiology, 1971, *34,* 337–347.

Künzle, H. Bilateral projections from precentral motor cortex to the putamen and other parts of the basal ganglia. *Brain Research,* 1975, *88,* 195–210.

Künzle, H. An autoradiographic analysis of the efferent connections from premotor and adjacent prefrontal regions (areas 6 and 9) in Macaca fascicularis. *Brain, Behavior and Evolution,* 1978, *15,* 185–234.

Larroche, J. C. *Developmental pathology of the neonate.* Amsterdam: Elsevier, 1977.

Lashley, K. S. *Brain mechanisms and intelligence: A quantitative study of injuries to the brain.* Chicago: University of Chicago Press, 1929.

Lashley, K. S. Factors limiting recovery after central nervous lesions. *Journal of Nervous and Mental Disease,* 1938, *88,* 733–755.

Lashley, K. S. Coalescence of neurology and psychology. *Proceedings of the American Philosophical Society,* 1941, *84,* 461–470.

Lassen, N. A., & Ingvar, D. H. Radio-isotopic assessment of regional cerebral blood flow. *Progress in Nuclear Medicine,* 1972, *1,* 376–409.

Lassen, N. A., Ingvar, D. H., & Skinhoj, E. Brain function and blood flow. *Scientific American,* 1978, *239,* 62–71.

Lauder, J. M., & Bloom, F. E. Ontogeny of monoamine neurons in the locus coeruleus, raphe nuclei and substantia nigra of the rat. I. Cell differentiation. *Journal of Comparative Neurology,* 1974, *155,* 469–482.

Laurence, S., & Stein, D. G. Recovery after brain damage and the concept of localization of function. In S. Finger (Ed.), *Recovery from brain damage.* New York: Plenum Press, 1978.

Lawrence, D. G., & Hopkins, D. A. Bilateral pyramidal lesions in infant rhesus monkeys. *Brain Research,* 1970, *24,* 543–544.

Leichnetz, G. R. The median subcallosal fasciculus in the monkey: A unique prefrontal corticostriate and cortico-cortical pathway revealed by anterogradely transported horseradish peroxidase. *Neuroscience Letters,* 1981, *21,* 137–142.

Lenneberg, E. H. *Biological Foundations of Language.* New York: Wiley, 1967.

LeVay, S., Wiesel, T. N., & Hubel, D. H. The development of ocular dominance columns in normal and visually deprived monkeys. *Journal of Comparative Neurology,* 1980, *191,* 1–51.

Levere, T. E. Neural stability, sparing, and behavioral recovery following brain damage. *Psychological Review,* 1975, *82*f, 344–358.

Levitt, P., & Moore, R. Y. Noradrenaline neuron innervation of the neocortex in the rat. *Brain Research,* 1978, *139,* 219–231.

Levitt, P., & Moore, R. Y. Development of the noradrenergic innervation of neocortex. *Brain Research,* 1979, *162,* 243–259.

Levitt, P., & Rakic, P. Genesis of central monoamine neurons (MA) in the rhesus monkey. *Neuroscience Abstracts,* 1979, *5,* 341.

Lewis, P. D., Patel, A. J., Béndek, G., & Balázs, R. Effect of reserpine on cell proliferation in the developing rat brain: A quantitative histological study. *Brain Research,* 1977, *129,* 299–308.

Lidov, H. G. W., Grzanna, R., & Molliver, M. E. The serotonin innervation of the cerebral cortex in the rat: An immunohistochemical analysis. *Neuroscience,* 1980, *5,* 207–227.

Lidov, H. G. W., Rice, F. L., & Molliver, M. E. The organization of the catecholamine innervation of somatosensory cortex: The barrel field of the mouse. *Brain Research,* 1978, *153,* 577–584.

Lieberman, A., Dziatolowski, M., Kupersmith, M., Serby, M., Goodgold, A., Korein, J., & Goldstein, M. Dementia in parkinson disease. In *Annals of Neurology* (Vol. 6, No. 4). Boston: Little, Brown, & Company, 1978.

Livingston, R. B., Fulton, J. F., Delgado, J. M. R., Sachs, E., Brendler, S. J., & Davis, G. D. Stimulation and regional ablation of orbital surface of frontal lobe. *Research Publications of the Association for Research in Nervous and Mental Disease,* 1948, *27,* 405.

Lloyd, K. G., & Hornykiewicz, O. Occurrence and distribution of aromatic L-amino acid (L-DOPA) decarboxylase in the human brain. *Journal of Neurochemistry,* 1972, *19,* 1549–1559.

Loizou, L. A. Postnatal ontogeny of monoamine-containing neurons in the CNS of the rat. *Brain Research,* 1976, *40,* 375–418.

Loizou, L. A., & Salt, P. Regional changes in monoamines of the rat brain during postnatal development. *Brain Research,* 1970, *20,* 467–470.

Loranger, A. W., Goodell, H., Lee, J. E., & McDowell, F. Levodopa treatment of parkinson's syndrome. *Archives of General Psychiatry,* 1972, *26,* 163–168.

Lovejoy, E. Analysis of the overlearning reversal effect. *Psychological Review,* 1966, *73,* 87–103.

Lund, J. S., Boothe, R. G., & Lund, R. D. Development of neurons in the visual cortex (area 17) of the monkey (Macaca nemestrena): A Golgi study from fetal day 12 to postnatal maturity. *Journal of Comparative Neurology,* 1977, *176,* 149–

188.

Luria, A. R. *Higher cortical functions in man.* New York: Basic Books, 1966.

Luria, A. R. *Human brain and psychological processes.* B. Haigh (trans.), Harper and Row, N.Y.: 1966. Freeman, W., & Watts, J. W. Retrograde degeneration of the thalamus following prefrontal lobotomy. *Journal of Comparative Neurology,* 1947, *86,* 65–93.

Luria, A. R., Naydin, V. L., Tsvetkova, L. S., & Vinarskaya, E. N. Restoration of higher cortical function following brain damage. In R. J. Vinken & G. W. Bruyn (Eds.), *Handbook of clinical neurology* (Vol. 3). Amsterdam: North Holland Publishers, 1969.

Lynch, G., Deadwyler, S., & Cotman, C. Postlesion axonal growth produces permanent functional connections. *Science,* 1973, *180,* 1364–1366. (a)

Lynch, G., Stanfield, B., & Cotman, C. W. Developmental differences in post-lesion axonal growth in the hippocampus. *Brain Research,* 1973, *59,* 155–168. (b)

Marin-Padilla, M. Structural abnormalities of the cerebral cortex in human chromosomal aberrations: A golgi study. *Brain Research,* 1972, *44,* 625–629.

Marin-Padilla, M. Structural organization of the cerebral cortex (motor area) in human chromosomal aberrations: A golgi study. I. D_1(13–15) trisomy, Patau syndrome. *Brain Research,* 1974, *66,* 375–391.

Matthews, M. R., Cowan, W. M., & Powell, T. P. S. Transneuronal cell degeneration in the lateral geniculate nucleus of the macaque monkey. *Journal of Anatomy,* 1960, *94,* 145–169.

McCouch, G. P., Austin, G. M., Liu, C. N., & Liu, C. Y. Sprouting as a cause of spasticity. *Journal of Neurophysiology,* 1958, *21,* 205–216.

McGeer, P. L., & McGeer, E. G. and Suzuki, J. S. Aging and extrapyramidal function. *Archives of Neurology,* 1977, *34,* 33–35.

Merzenich, M. M., & Brugge, J. F. Representation of the cochlear partition on the superior temporal plane of the macaque monkey. *Brain Research,* 1973, *50,* 275–296.

Mettler, F. A. Extracortical connections of the primate frontal cerebral cortex. II. Cortico-fugal connections. *Journal of Comparative Neurology,* 1947, *86,* 119–166.

Meyer, J. S., & Welch, K. M. A. Relationship of cerebral blood flow and metabolism to neurological symptoms. In J. S. Meyer & J. P. Schade (Eds.), *Progress in brain research: Cerebral blood flow* (Vol. 35). Amsterdam: Elsevier, 1972.

Meyers, R. E. Brain pathology following fetal vascular occlusion: An experimental study. *Investigative Ophthalmology,* 1969, *8,* 41–50.

Miller, E. A., Goldman, P. S., & Rosvold, H. E. Delayed recovery of function following orbital prefrontal lesions in infant monkeys. *Science,* 1973, *182,* 304–306.

Milner, B. Some effects of frontal lobectomy in man. In J. M. Warren & K. Akert (Eds.), *The frontal granular cortex and behavior.* New York: McGraw-Hill, 1964.

Minkowski, M. Experimentelle Untersuchungen uber die Beziehungen der Grosshirnrinde und der Netzhaut zuden Primaren Optischen Zentren, besonders zum Corpus genieu latum externum. *Abreiten Hirnanatomie Institute,* Zurich, 1913, *7,* 255–362.

Mishkin, M. Perseveration of central sets after frontal lesions in monkeys. In J. M. Warren & K. Akert (Eds.), *The frontal granular cortex and behavior.* New York: McGraw-Hill, 1964.

Mishkin, M., & Manning, F. J. Non-spatial memory after selective prefrontal lesions in monkeys. *Brain Research,* 1978, *143,* 313–323.

Monakow, C. von. *Die Lokalisation im Grosshirnrinde und der Abbau der Funktion dorch Corticale Herde.* Wiesbaden, Ger. : J. F. Bergmann, 1914.

Moore, R. Y. Brain lesions and amine metabolism. In C. C. Pfeiffer & R. Smythies (Eds.), *International Review of Neurobiology,* 1970, *13,* 67–92.

Moore, R. Y., & Bloom, F. E. Central catecholamine neuron systems: Anatomy and physiology of the dopamine systems. *Annual Review of Neurosciences,* 1978, *1,* 129–169.

Myers, R. E., Swett, C., & Miller, M. Loss of social group affinity following prefrontal lesions in free-ranging macaques. *Brain Research,* 1973, *64,* 257–269.

Nauta, W. J. H. Neural associations of the frontal cortex. In J. Konorski, H. -L. Teuber, & B. Zernicki (Eds.), *The frontal granular cortex and behavior. Acta Neurobiologicae Experimentalis,* 1972, *32,* 125–140.

Niki, H. Prefrontal unit activity during delayed alternation in the monkey. I. Relation to direction of response. *Brain Research,* 1974, *68,* 185–196. (a)

Niki, H. Prefrontal unit activity during delayed alternation in the monkey. II. Relation to absolute versus relative direction of response. *Brain Re-*

search, 1974, *68*, 197–204. (b)

Niki, H. Differential activity of prefrontal units during right and left delayed response trials. *Brain Research*, 1974, *70*, 346–349. (c)

Niki, H., Sakai, M., & Kubota, K. Delayed alternation performance and unit activity of the caudate head and medial orbitofrontal gyrus in the monkey. *Brain Research*, 1972, *38*, 342–353.

Niki, H., & Watanabe, M. Prefrontal unit activity and delayed response: Relation to cue location *versus* direction of response. *Brain Research*, 1976, *105*, 79–88.

Oke, A., Keller, R., Medford, R. I., & Adams, R. N. Lateralization of norepinephrine in human thalamus. *Science*. 1978, *200*, 1411–1413.

Olson, L., & Fuxe, K. On the projections from the locus coeruleus noradrenaline neurons: The cerebellar innervation. *Brain Research*, 1971, *28*, 165–171.

Olson, L., & Seiger, A. Early prenatal ontogeny of central monoamine neurons in the rat: Fluorescence histochemical observations. *Anatomy and Embryology*, 1972, *137*, 301–316.

Orbach, J. Proprioceptive and positional cues in solving delayed response problems. *Science*, 1962, *135*, 667–668.

Pandya, D. N., & Vignola, L. A. Intra- and interhemispheric projections of the precentral, premotor and arcuate areas in the rhesus monkey. *Brain Research*, 1971, *26*, 217–233.

Parent, A., Descarries, L., & Beaudet, A. Organization of ascending serotonin systems in the adult rat brain. A radioautographic study after intraventricular administration of (^{3}H) 5-hydroxytryptamine. *Neuroscience*, 1981, *6*, 115–138.

Parnavelas, J. G., & Globus, A. The effect of continuous illumination of the development of cortical neurons in the rat: A Golgi study. *Experimental Neurology*, 1976, *51*, 637–647.

Passingham, R. Delayed matching after selective prefrontal lesions in monkeys (Macaca mulatta). *Brain Research*, 1975, *92*, 89–102.

Petrides, M., & Iverson, S. D. Cross-model matching and the primate frontal cortex. *Science*, 1976, *192*, 1023–1024.

Pettigrew, J. D. The effect of visual experience on the development of stimulus specificity by kitten cortical neurons. *Journal of Physiology*, 1974, *237*, 49–74.

Phelps, M. E., Huang, S. C., Hoffman, E. J., Selin, C., Sokoloff, L., & Kuhl, D. E. Tomographic measurement of local cerebral glucose metabolic rate in humans with (F-18) 2-fluoro-2-deoxy-d-glucose: Validation of method. *Annals of Neurology*, 1979, *6*, 371–388.

Piaget, J. *The construction of reality in the child.* New York: Basic Books, 1954.

Pinto Lord, M. C., & Caviness, V. S. Determinants of cell shape and orientation: A comparative golgi analysis of cell-axon interrelationships in the developing neocortex of normal and reeler mice. *Journal of Comparative Neurology*, 1979, *187*(1), 49–70.

Plum, F., Gjedde, A., & Samson, F. E. Neuroanatomical functional mapping by the radioactive 2-deoxy-d-glucose method. *Neurosciences Research Program Bulletin*, 1976, *14*, 461–518.

Polyak, S. L. *The vertebrate visual system.* Chicago: University of Chicago Press, 1957.

Porrino, L. J., Crane, A. M., & Goldman-Rakic, P. S. Direct and indirect pathways from the amygdala to the frontal lobe in rhesus monkeys. *Journal of Comparative Neurology*, 1981, *198*, 121–136.

Porrino, L., & Goldman-Rakic, P. S. Brain stem innervation of prefrontal and anterior cingulate cortex in the rhesus monkey revealed by retrograde transport of HRP. *Journal of Comparative Neurology*, 1982, *205*, 63–76.

Pribram, K. H., Chow, K. L., & Semmes, J. Limit and organization of the cortical projection from the medial thalamic nucleus in monkey. *Journal of Comparative Neurology*, 1953, *98*, 433–448.

Pribram, K. H., & Luria, A. R. *Psychophysiology of the frontal lobes.* New York: Academic Press, 1973.

Prince, M. Cerebral localization from the point of view of function and symptoms—with special reference to von Monakow's theory of diaschisis. *Journal of Nervous and Mental Disease*, 1910, *37*, 337–354.

Raisman, G. Neuronal plasticity in the septal nuclei of the adult rat. *Brain Research*, 1969, *14*, 25–48.

Raisman, G., & Field, P. M. Sexual dimorphism in the neuropil of the preoptic area of the rat and its dependence on neonatal androgen. *Brain Research*, 1973, *54*, 1–29.

Rakic, P. Mode of cell migration to the superficial layers of fetal monkey neocortex. *Journal of Comparative Neurology*, 1972, *145*, 61–84.

Rakic, P. Neurons in rhesus monkey visual cortex: Systematic relation between time of origin and eventual disposition. *Science*, 1974, *183*, 425–427.

Rakic, P. Prenatal genesis of connections subserving ocular dominance in the rhesus monkey. *Nature*, 1976, *261*, 467–471.

Rakic, P. Genesis of the dorsal lateral geniculate nucleus in the rhesus monkey: Site and time of origin, kinetics of proliferation, routes of migration and patterns of distribution of neurons. *Journal of Comparative Neurology,* 1977, *176,* 23–52.

Rakic, P. Neuronal migration and contact guidance in the primate telencephalon. *Postgraduate Medical Journal,* 1978, *54,* 25–40.

Rakic, P. Genesis of visual connections in the rhesus monkey. In R. D. Freeman (Ed.), *Developmental neurobiology of vision.* New York: Plenum Press, 1979. (a)

Rakic, P. Genetic and epigenetic determinants of local neuronal circuits in the mammalian central nervous system. In F. O. Schmitt & F. G. Worden (Eds.), *The neurosciences fourth study program.* Cambridge, Mass.: MIT Press, 1979. (b)

Rakic, P., & Goldman-Rakic, P. S. Development and modifiability of the cerebral cortex. *Neuroscience Research Program Bulletin,* 1982, MIT Press.

Reivich, M., Kuhl, D., Wolf, A., Greenberg, J., Phelps, M., Ido, T., Cosella, V., Fowler, J., Hoffman, E., Alavi, A., Sow, P., & Sokoloff, L. The ^{18}F-fluorodeoxyglucose method for the measurement of local cerebral glucose utilization in man. *Circulation Research,* 1979, *44,* 127–137.

Riesen, A. H. Sensory deprivation. In E. Stellar, & J. Stellar (Eds.), *Progress in physiological psychology.* New York: Academic Press, 1966.

Risberg, J., & Ingvar, D. H. Patterns of activity in the gray matter of the dominant hemisphere during memorization and reasoning. *Brain,* 1973, *96,* 737–756.

Roland, P. E., & Skinhoj, E. Extrastriate cortical areas activated during visual discrimination in man. *Brain Research,* 1981, *122,* 166–171.

Rosvold, H. E., & Szwarcbart, M. Neural structures involved in delayed-response performance. In J. M. Warren & K. Akert (Eds.), *The frontal granular cortex and behavior.* New York: McGraw-Hill, 1964.

Rothblat, L. A., & Schwartz, M. L. The effect of monocular deprivation on dendritic spines in visual cortex of young and adult albino rats: evidence for a sensitive period. *Brain Research,* 1979, *161,* 156–161. (a)

Rothblat, L. A., & Schwartz, M. L. Altered early environment: Effects on the brain and visual behavior. In R. D. Walk & H. L. Pick (Eds.), *Perception and experience.* New York: Plenum Press, 1979. (b)

Rylander, G. *Personality changes after operations on the frontal lobes.* Copenhagen: E. Munksgaard, 1939.

Sanides, F. Structure and function of the human frontal lobe. *Neuropsychologia,* 1964, *2,* 209–219.

Schade, J. P., & van Groenigen, D. B. Structural organization of the human cerebral cortex. I. Maturation of the middle frontal gyrus. *Acta Anatomica,* 1961, *47,* 47–111.

Scheibel, A. B. Age related changes in the human forebrain. In P. Rakic & P. S. Goldman-Rakic (Eds.), *Development and modifiability of the cerebral cortex.* Cambridge, Mass.: MIT Press, 1982.

Scheibel, M. E., Lindsay, R. D., Tomisayu, U., & Scheibel, A. B. Progressive dendritic changes in aging human cortex. *Experimental Neurology,* 1975, *47,* 392–403.

Scheibel, M. E., Lindsay, R. D., Tomisayu, U., & Scheibel, A. B. Progressive dendritic changes in the aging human limbic system. *Experimental Neurology,* 1976, *53,* 420–430.

Schneider, G. E. Mechanisms of functional recovery following lesions of visual cortex or superior colliculus in neonate and adult hamsters. *Brain, Behavior and Evolution,* 1970, *3,* 295–323.

Schneider, G. E. Is it really better to have your brain lesion early? A revision of the *Kennard principle. Neuropsychologia,* 1979, *17,* 557–584.

Schneider, G., & Jhaveri, S. Neuroanatomical correlates of spared or altered function after brain lesions in the newborn hamster. In Stein, D. G., Rosen, J. J., & Butters, N. (Eds.), *Plasticity and recovery of function in the central nervous system.* New York: Academic Press, 1974.

Schulman, H. S. Impaired delayed response from thalamic lesions. *Archives of Neurology,* 1964, *11,* 477–499.

Schwartz, M. L., & Goldman-Rakic, P. S. Callosal and associational axon collaterals of prefrontal cortical neurons in the rhesus monkey demonstrated by retrograde fluorescent tracers. *Nature,* 1982, *299,* 154–156.

Schwartz, M. L., & Rothblat, L. A. Behavioral and dendritic spine deficits in monocularly deprived rats: The role of reduced photic stimulation. *Neuroscience Abstracts,* 1980, *6,* 635.

Seiger, A., & Olson, I. Late prenatal ontogeny of cnal monoamine neurons in the rat: Fluorescence histochemical observations. *Anatomy and Embryology,* 1971, *140,* 281–318.

Semmes, J., Weinstein, S., Ghent, L., & Teuber, H.-L. Correlates of impaired orientation or personal and extrapersonal space. *Brain,* 1963, *86,* 747–772.

Shatz, C. J., Lindstrom, S., & Wiesel, T. N. The distribution of afferents representing the right and left eyes in the cat's visual cortex. *Brain Research,* 1977, *131,* 103–116.

Shepherd, G. *The synaptic organization of the brain.* Oxford: Oxford University Press, 1979.

Sidman, R. L. Cell proliferation, migration, and the interaction in the developing mammalian central nervous system. In F. O. Schmitt (Ed.), *The neurosciences. Second study program.* New York: Rockefeller University Press, 1970.

Simon, H., Scatton, B., & LeMoal, M. Definitive disruption of spatial delayed alternation in rats after lesions in the ventral mesencephalic tegmentum. *Neuroscience Letters,* 1979, *15,* 319–324.

Simon, H., Scatton, B., & LeMoal, M. Dopaminergic A10 neurones are involved in cognitive functions. *Nature,* 1980, *286,* 150–151.

Sladek, J. R., & Sladek, C. D. Relative quantitation of monoamine histofluorescence in young and old non-human primates. In C. E. Finch, D. E. Potter, & A. D. Kenny, (Eds.), *Parkinson's Disease* (Vol. 2). New York: Plenum Press, 1978.

Sokoloff, L., Reivich, M., Kennedy, C., Des Rosiers, M. H., Patlak, C. S., Pettigrew, K. D., Sakurada, O., & Shinohara, M. The (^{14}C) deoxyglucose method for the measurement of local cerebral glucose utilization: Theory, procedure, and normal values in the conscious and anesthetized albino rat. *Journal of Neurochemistry,* 1977, *28,* 897–916.

Soltmann, O. Experimentelle studien über die functionen des grosshirns der neugeborenen. *Jahrbuch für Kinderhielkunde,* 1876, *9,* 106–148.

Sperry, R. W. The problem of central nervous reorganization after nerve regeneration and muscle transposition. *Quarterly Review of Biology,* 1945, *20,* 311–369.

Sperry, R. W. Effect of crossing nerves to antagonistic limb muscles in the monkey. *Archives für Neurologie und Psychiatrie,* 1947, *38,* 452–473.

Sperry, R. W. Physiological plasticity and brain circuit theory. In H. Harlow & C. Woolsey (Eds.), *Biology and biochemical bases of behavior.* Madison: University of Wisconsin Press, 1958.

Stamm, J. S. Electrical stimulation of monkey's prefrontal cortex during delayed-response performance. *Journal of Comparative and Physiological Psychology,* 1969, *67,* 535–546.

Stamm, J. S., & Rosen, S. C. Electrical stimulation and steady potential shifts in prefrontal cortex during delayed response performance by monkeys. *Acta Biologia Experimentalis,* 1969, *29,* 385–399.

Stein, D. G., Rosen, J. J., & Butters, N. (Eds.), *Plasticity and recovery of function in the central nervous system.* New York: Academic Press, 1974.

Steinbusch, H. W. M. Distribution of serotonin-immunoreactivity in the central nervous system of the rat-cell bodies and terminals. *Neuroscience,* 1981, *6,* 557–618.

Steward, O., Cotman, C. W., & Lynch, G. S. Growth of a new fiber projection in the brain of adult rats: Re-innervation of the dentate gyrus by the contralateral entorhinal cortex following ipsilateral entorhinal lesions. *Experimental Brain Research,* 1974, *20,* 45–66.

Sutherland, N. S. Stimulus analyzing mechanisms. In *Proceedings of a symposium on the mechanization of thought processes* (Vol. 2). London: H. M. Stationary Office, 1959.

Swanson, L. W., & Hartman, B. K. The central adrenergic system. An immunofluorescence study of the location of cell bodies and their efferent connections in the rat utilizing dopamine-B-hydroxylase as a marker. *Journal of Comparative Neurology,* 1975, *163,* 467–506.

Swindale, N. V. Absence of ocular dominance patches in dark-reared cats. *Nature,* 1981, *290,* 332–333.

Takashima, S., Chan, F., Becker, L. E., & Armstrong, D. L. Morphology of the developing visual cortex of the human infant. *Journal of Neuropathology and Experimental Neurology,* 1980, *39,* 487–501.

Tassin, J. P., Bockaert, J., Blanc, G., Stinus, L., Thierry, A. M., Lavielle, S., Premont, J., & Glowinski, J. Topographical distribution of dopaminergic receptors of the anterior cerebral cortex of the rat. *Brain Research,* 1978, *154,* 241–251.

Teuber, H. L. Recovery of function after brain injury in man. In *Outcome of severe damage to the central nervous system,* Ciba Foundation (Vol. 34). Amsterdam: Elsevier, 1975.

Thierry, A. M., Blanc, G., Sobel, A., Stinus, L., & Glowinski, J. Dopaminergic terminals in the rat cortex. *Science,* 1973, 182, 499–501.

Tilney, F. Preface. In R. M. Brickner (Ed.), *The intellectual functions of the frontal lobes.* New York: Macmillan, 1936.

Tinklepaugh, O. L. An experimental study of representational factors in monkeys. *Journal of Comparative Psychology,* 1928, *8,* 197–236.

Tissari, A. H., & Suurhasko, B. V. A. Transport of 5-HT in synaptosomes of developing rat brain. *Acta Pharmacologica et Toxicologica,* 1971, *29,* Supplement IV 59.

Tobias, T. J. Afferents to prefrontal cortex from the thalamic mediodorsal nucleus in the rhesus monkey. *Brain Research,* 1975, *83,* 191–212.

Tucker, T. J., & Kling, A. Differential effects of early and late lesions of frontal granular cortex in the monkey. *Brain Research,* 1967, *5,* 377–389.

Uemura, E. Age related changes in prefrontal cortex of Macaca mulatta: synaptic density. *Experimental Neurology,* 1980, *69,* 164–172.

Ungerstedt, U. Stereotaxic mapping of the monoamine pathways in the rat brain. *Acta Physiologica Scandinavica,* 1971, *367,* 1–48. (Suppl.)

Valverde, F. Apical dendritic spines of the visual cortex and light deprivation in the mouse. *Experimental Brain Research,* 1967, *3,* 337–352.

Vijayashankar, N., & Brody, H. A quantitative study of the pigmented neurons in the nuclei locus coeruleus and subcoeruleus in man as related to aging. *Journal of Neuropathology and Experimental Neurology,* 1979, *38,* 490–497.

Von Bonin, G., & Bailey, P. *The neocortex of macaca mulatta.* Urbana: University of Illinois Press, 1947.

Walker, A. E. *The primate thalamus.* Chicago: University of Chicago Press, 1938.

Walker, A. E. The medial thalamic nucleus: A comparative anatomical, physiological and clinical study of the nucleus medialis dorsalis thalami. *Journal of Comparative Neurology,* 1940, *73,* 87–115.

Will, B. E., Rosenzweig, M. R., & Bennett, E. L. Effects of differential environments on recovery from neonatal brain lesions, measured by problem solving scores. *Physiology and Behavior,* 1976, *16,* 603–611.

Will, B. E., Rosenzweig, M. R., Bennett, E. L., Herbert, M., & Morimoto, H. Relatively brief environmental enrichment aids recovery of learning capacity and alters brain measures after postweaning brain lesions in rats. *Journal of Comparative and Physiological Psychology,* 1977, *91,* 31–50.

Windle, W. F., Jacobson, H. N., deRamiriz, P., de Arellano, M. I., & Combs, C. M. Structural and functional sequelae of asphyxia neonatorum in monkeys (Macaca mulatta). *Research Publications of the Association for Research in Nervous and Mental Disease,* 1967, *39,* 169–182.

Woolsey, C. N., & Walzl, G. M. Topical projections of nerve fibers from local regions of the cochlea to the cerebral cortex of the cat. *Johns Hopkins Medical Journal,* 1942, *71,* 315–344.

Yakovlev, P. I., & Lecours, A. R. The myelogenetic cycles of regional maturation of the brain. In A. Minkowski (Ed.), *Regional development of the brain in early life.* Oxford: Blackwell Scientific Publications, 1967.

Yakovlev, P. I., & Wadsworth, R. C. Schizencephalies, a study of the congenital clefts in the cerebral mantle. II. Clefts with hydrocephalis and lips separated. *Journal of Neuropathology and Experimental Neurology,* 1946, *5,* 169–206.

Yeterian, E. H., & Van Hoesen, G. W. Cortico-striate projections in the rhesus monkey: The organization of certain cortico-caudate connections. *Brain Research,* 1978, *139,* 43–63.

Young, R. M. *Mind, brain and adaptation in the nineteenth century: Cerebral localization and its biological context from Gall to Ferrier.* Oxford: Clarendon Press, 1970.

Zeaman, D., & House, B. J. The role of attention in retardate discrimination learning. In N. R. Ellis (Ed.), *Handbook of mental deficiency.* New York: McGraw-Hill, 1963.

Zecevic, N. R., & Molliver, M. E. The origin of the monoaminergic innervation of immature rat neocortex: An ultrastructural analysis following lesions. *Brain Research,* 1978, *150,* 387–397.

DEVELOPMENTAL BEHAVIOR GENETICS 6

SANDRA SCARR, *Yale University*
KENNETH K. KIDD, *Yale University*

CHAPTER CONTENTS

INTRODUCTION TO DEVELOPMENTAL BEHAVIOR GENETICS

Development is the process by which the genotype becomes the phenotype. To understand the role of genetic programs in development requires at least three kinds of mind-sets. First, one needs an evolutionary perspective on the nature of human development and of human variation. Second, one needs an introduction to the complex ways in which genes, through functions such as determining enzyme structure within the cell, can affect all levels of human functioning, including brains and behaviors. And, third, one needs to think dynamically about the changing forms of adaptation that humans experience across the lifespan. As the individual develops and matures, the requirements for successful adaptation change because development brings people into contact with different experiences from infancy to adulthood.

Because we wish to consider behavior genetics in both developmental and evolutionary contexts we will review evolutionary theory as the context for behavior genetic studies of human development. Rather than review the phenomena of development, we will provide the evolutionary perspective and describe genetic aspects of development. We will review (1) basic genetic principles as the mechanisms by which genetic differences are translated into human behavioral variation and (2) research on human differences, particularly developmentally important phenotypes. We will discuss the development of human behavior from an epigenetic perspective that includes the coaction of genes and environments in the production of observable behaviors and other behaviorally relevant phenotypes.

Evolutionary Theory

The two central tenets of evolutionary theory are *variation* and *selection*. Within a breeding group individuals will usually differ from one another in a variety of ways. These apparent (or *phenotypic*) differences among individuals depend to some extent on genetic (*genotypic*) differences among them. Whenever individuals in one generation do not reproduce equally, there is a genetic change in the population from that generation to the next. Natural selection occurs when the differential rates of reproduction are caused by phenotypic differences; we say those different phenotypes have different fitnesses. Natural selection will change the frequencies of the genotypes from generation to generation if the different phenotypes are the result of different genotypes. A measure of the opportunity for natural selection is the amount of variation among individuals in their reproductive contribution to the succeeding generation. In the presence of such reproductive variation each succeeding generation tends to resemble, both phenotypically and genetically, those individuals in the preceding generation who were reproductively more successful or fit.

The idea of natural selection working through phenotypic variability to produce genetic change over time is such a simple idea that many have wondered why it was not thought of long before Darwin and Wallace. Despite the idea's simplicity, many biologists of the last century vigorously resisted the unifying concept that evolution applied to all living organisms. Similarly, behavioral scientists of this century have barely begun to grasp the implications of evolutionary theory for theories of human behavior (Ghiselin, 1969).

One reason for the resistance to evolutionary ideas comes from the insistence and beliefs of some religious groups that the human species should not be considered in the same terms as lesser organisms. This is not the source of resistance for most contemporary scientists. Rather, Plato and Aristotle did us a great disservice in popularizing typological thinking. For Plato, individual variation resulted from imperfect reproductions of the ideal form. Thus, species were types that individuals resemble more or less perfectly. Contemporary population thinking turns idealism on its head. Individual variation is the reality from which species-typical types are mere abstractions.

The Species and Populations

From a population and genetic view a species can be defined as a group of potentially interbreeding individuals that have most of their genetic, morphologic, and behavioral characteristics in common and that is reproductively isolated from all other such groups. This definition suffers an occasional difficulty in the face of complex biological reality, because individuals of one species may, in fact, be interfertile with members of another species. In such cases, reproductive barriers of some other sort, be it geographical isolation or behavioral incompatibilities, prevent or severely restrict gene flow between species.

The genetic variation present in any mammalian species is not uniformly distributed throughout that species. A species can usually be subdivided at several levels. For example, in humans there are clear differences between Scandinavians and Southern

Europeans at one level and between Europeans as a group and Eastern Asians at another level. The subdivisions often can be hierarchically organized and in some species the levels are given taxonomic status. Within a group at any level the individuals are generally, on average, more similar to each other than they are to individuals in another group at that level, but the differences between groups need not be qualitative. Phenotypic similarity is a reflection of genetic similarity. A group at any of these hierarchical levels can be termed a population, but it is more common to use *population* to refer to a smaller group with, preferably, nearly random mating within the group and little mating outside the group. The term *Mendelian population* (Dobzhansky, 1951) is often used with this meaning.

Even limited amounts of reproduction across group boundaries can serve to keep an entire species from fragmenting into two or more species. This *gene flow* need not occur every generation and need only involve exchange among closely related groups. For example, though one tends to think of human races as distinct, easily defined entities, there are populations intermediate between all races and globally no clear boundary exists between races. Thus, gene flow has kept and continues to keep *Homo sapiens* as one species. In spite of the obvious phenotypic and genotypic variation within the species, one human is more like any other human, both genetically and phenotypically, than either is to any other higher primate, including most of our extinct ancestral lineage.

To reiterate, populations within species and species themselves consist of individuals with different genotypes and phenotypes. A population is *not* an ideal genotype around which the less perfect forms are distributed. In fact, a well adapted population consists of diverse individuals, each of whom is adapted to some portion of the population's niche. The environmental demands of adaptation are not uniform across populations because there is always differentiation of function among individuals and some diversity in the environmental demands of different portions of the niche. The best adapted populations are genetically and phenotypically diverse.

If one can think in population terms, one can experience a revelation about the nature of human diversity. Because most people find and build their own niches within a human population, there cannot be one best-adapted genotype, whether one's concern is intelligence, sociability, or altruism. The expression, "It takes all kinds. . . ." is very true in a larger sense. Evolution need operate in a way that would cause uniformity to develop. Rather, a well-adapted population usually retains extensive genetic diversity that can serve as material for evolutionary responses to changing conditions (Mayr, 1970).

The Maintenance of Genetic Diversity in Populations

Genetic diversity in populations is maintained by the recombination of genes into new genotypes, by mutations, and by gene flow from other populations. The importance of particulate inheritance and the recombination of genes was not appreciated by Darwin and his contemporaries, who believed in blending inheritance. As Mayr (1970) notes, it was Mendel's spectacular insight to realize that the genetic factors that fathers and mothers contribute to new zygotes do not lose their identity but segregate and reassort in the next generation. Particulate inheritance guarantees that the gene pool retains much the same variability from generation to generation, in part because much of that variability is hidden in each generation and thus immune from selective pressure. In the absence of selective pressure, the particulate nature of inheritance assures that existing variation does not diminish (Cavalli-Sforza & Bodmer, 1971).

Genetic variability can be increased by mutations and in-migration and decreased by selection and accidents of sampling from generation to generation. Whatever the distribution of genotypes in the present generation, the population retains enormous genetic variability that is hidden until segregation, assortment, and recombination reveal another small portion in the next generation, and until one or more of the factors that increase or decrease variability act on the distribution of genes in the population.

Random changes in the genetic material, mutations, are the ultimate raw material for natural selection. Although nearly all mutations are reduced in frequency or eliminated by natural selection, the net effect of mutations is to produce new genetic variability. Genes also migrate into populations from other populations through the interbreeding of members of two or more groups, thereby increasing the variability in any one population. Of course, migration does not require the permanent relocation of peoples. Invading armies have always left their genes behind and contributed to gene flow over long distances, even if the invaders themselves eventually were driven out. For example, the Viking raids in the Mediterranean over a thousand years ago are believed responsible for the blue-eyed Sicilians today.

Differential reproductive success, through different rates of fertility and mortality, is the process of natural selection. The effect of most natural selection is to reduce the genetic variability of a population because the less fit genotypes become rarer. Another factor that also operates to reduce genetic variation is chance events accumulated over many generations. New mutations and gene flow to carry new genes to different populations counteract the loss of genetic variation and thereby maintain the raw material of evolution.

Selection acts on the whole phenotype. It is individuals who have varied reproductive and survival rates, not genes per se. For some purposes individuals can be seen as temporary receptacles for the gene pool. In the case of selection, all of the individual's genes share the same fate; the unit of selection is the whole person. The fact that selection acts on phenotypes, not genotypes, is exceedingly important. Where there is a simple relationship between genotype and phenotype, as in the blood groups, phenotypic selection is highly related to genetic selection. The more complex the relationship between genotype and phenotype, the less clear is the relationship of selection to genetic change.

In sum, there are changes in the frequencies of genes from one generation to another. Some changes are due to chance determining which egg and sperm actually get together. Other changes are more directed, with some forces increasing and some decreasing the genetic variability of the population. The models of selection against various genetic disorders are too complicated to detail here (see Cavalli-Sforza & Bodmer, 1971). But the general point is that a great deal of genetic variability is and always has been present in human populations in spite of obvious selection operating to eliminate it. There are also numerous mechanisms whereby natural selection favors greater variability, thus actively maintaining genetic variation. Though less often documented, such selection does exist in humans. For example, in the presence of endemic malaria, natural selection maintains Hb^S (the sickle cell gene) in spite of its causing severe anemia when it replaces both copies of the normal gene.

Microevolutionary Differences

Since even the very large evolutionary changes in animals arise, in most cases, by the accumulation of small changes, an understanding of the origin and fate of microevolutionary differences is required—particularly so in the case of human evolution where most questions are those of a microevolutionary nature because the evolutionary separation of humans from any nearest "relatives" is rather recent. Consequently, one important approach to the study of human evolution is the study of the variation that exists within the species and of the origin and histories of the many ethnic groups that embody this variation. Although these studies must be based on differences, the most immediately obvious character differences, such as skin color, hair color and form, physiognomy, and so on, are not ideal, partly because such character differences are subject to environmental variation, and partly because there may be convergent evolution and/or sexual selection. However, the main problem with such character differences is that their genetic basis is unknown or only very poorly understood. For instance, it is possible that the Australian aborigines and African natives may have a largely different genetic basis for superfically similar skin pigmentation. Physical anthropologists have attempted to overcome these difficulties by measuring many small aspects of body and/or skeletal form, and by removing the environmental variation with suitable statistical analyses.

In order to reconstruct evolutionary relationships of species or populations geneticists prefer to study human variation using data as closely related to the genes as possible. Direct measurement of such genetic differences seems much more suitable for studying evolutionary relationships than more complex (behavioral) phenotypes. Ideally, one would like to study differences in the DNA itself. At the microevolutionary level studying normal genetic variation, such as different blood groups, closely approximates the study of DNA, and fortunately gene frequencies for such normal variants have been studied in many human populations. Even though we often lack a precise understanding of the biochemical relationship of the genes to the phenotypes (as with many blood group antigens), these traits do nonetheless identify a particular DNA segment and its alternative forms that vary in frequency among populations. Data on gene frequency variation among populations provide a good basis for the study of human microevolution for three reasons. First, the relative amount of random variation is largest at the microevolutionary level and allows the construction of models and the development of statistical methods of analysis, as will be discussed later. Second, there are many independent genetic systems that can be studied, making the results largely independent of vagaries at any one locus. Third, there are extensive data available for use in such analyses, a pragmatic but important consideration.

With respect to these last two reasons, the tremendous genetic variation that exists among human populations has been well documented in many recent studies. Studies of primitive populations, such as the Melanesians on Bougainville (Friedlander, 1971) and the Yanomama in the Amazon valley (Neel, 1970), show a very great variation in gene frequencies over a small, apparently uniform area. Low migration between villages and the consequent high local inbreeding may be a major factor and may reflect the situation that existed through much of human evolution.

Restrictions on Phenotypic Variability

Despite the maintenance of great genetic variability in the population, there must be some restriction on the variability of phenotypes. Although humans are very flexible in learning about their environments, there must be some bounds on human variation. Species adaptation depends on a rather limited range of behavioral phenotypes. Some characteristically human patterns need to emerge in every individual. There are genetically determined regulatory mechanisms that limit the possible number of phenotypes that can develop. These mechanisms compensate for perturbations in the genome and the environment and help to keep the organism on a normal developmental course.

Canalization is the term used to describe a genetic predisposition for the development of a certain form of adaptation, guided along internally regulated lines. Environmental features are necessary for complete development or for the full expression of the adaptation, but the direction of the development is difficult to deflect. Environmental inputs that are necessary for canalized development to occur must be universally available to the species, or else this form of adaptation would not work.

Embryologists, particularly Waddington (1962), have long recognized the "self-righting" tendencies of many aspects of growth. The difficulty of deflecting an organism from its growth path (which Waddington calls a creod) is expressed in the idea of canalization. Canalization restricts phenotypic diversity to a limited species range while maintaining desirable genetic diversity. If all genetic diversity were phenotypically expressed, there would be such enormous behavioral differences among people that it is difficult to see how any population could reproduce and survive (Vale & Vale, 1969). There are obviously functional equivalences in many genotypes (they produce similar phenotypes) for the most basic human characteristics.

The total genome is a "physiological team." No genes are soloists; they must play harmoniously with others to achieve selective advantage, because selection works on the whole person and on whole coadapted gene complexes in the population. As Dobzhansky (1955) has said, evolution favors genes that are "good mixers," ones that make the most positive contributions to fitness against the greatest number of genetic backgrounds. Selection is always for coadapted gene complexes that fit a developmental pattern. The sheer number of gene differences between individuals or species is not a good measure of developmental and functional difference between the organisms. To express individual or population differences as differences in the number of nucleotide pairs of the DNA is like trying to express the difference between the *Holy Bible* and Dante's *Divine Comedy* in terms of the frequency of letters used in the two works (Mayr, 1970).

Every human characteristic is genetically based (because the entire organism is), but a useful distinction can be made between genetic differences and nongenetic differences. Nongenetic means simply that the differences between two phenotypes are not caused by genetic differences. The capacity of a single genotype to produce two or more phenotypes is itself genetically controlled, of course (Mayr, 1970; see also the section titled *Developmental Examples*). The notion of a genetic blueprint for ontogeny means that each genotype has its own canalized course of development, from which it is difficult to deflect.

The Evolution of Human Development

Every period of the human life span is the product of evolution. Selection has acted on the primate developmental program to produce the uniquely *human* features of human development, from the prenatal period to old age. (Occasionally, colleagues in psychology are surprised to think of puberty as a genetically programmed, developmental event!) The whole of development is governed by developmental genetic programs that act on the phenotype in concert with the surrounding environments from the cellular to social. Fitness, after all, depends not just on the birth of offspring but on their successful development to become reproductive adults themselves. Thus, natural selection has acted on all of the phenotypes and their changes from the prenatal period to the end of reproduction. It is possible to imagine means for selection to act on the postreproduction phenotype as well. Perhaps, healthier older adults with stronger ties to their families could enhance the survival rates of relatives, thereby indirectly creating selection pressures for individuals who grow old gracefully.

> Behavior is perhaps the strongest selection pressure operating in the animal kingdom. Hominid evolution is rich in behavioral shifts: Each of these shifts initiated new selection pressures; some facilitating and speeding up hominidization; some of the later ones reversing or at least halting previous trends. One of the most significant aspects of hominid behavior is parental care. (Mayr, 1970, pp. 387–388)

Parental care, greatly extended in the human species over that of any other species, is of particular interest in relation to the evolution of an extended infancy and childhood. While parents became more attentive to fewer and fewer offspring, the offspring evolved into more and more immature creatures who require more attentive and extended care. This prolonged period of infancy and childhood is what we now refer to as the period of socialization. Indeed, the very complex of child and parent behaviors that evolved make socialization both necessary and possible. Let us take a longer look at the evolution of infancy.

The Evolution of Infancy

Infancy is a mammalian theme. A period of suckling the dependent young evolved as an efficient way to increase the survival chances of fewer and fewer offspring. The evolutionary strategy of high investment in a small number of offspring reaches its most extreme development in humans. While extended care of the dependent young is a burden and a risk for parents, it is of great evolutionary importance because it increases fitness through improved survival of the offspring. The more an organism is protected from the vicissitudes of the environment, the greater the role of intraspecific competition. What one offspring requires of its parents are energy and resources not available to another offspring of those same parents. It became advantageous to have fewer and better equipped offspring rather than many offspring and to have long life spans. Both competition for females and demands for long parental care put a premium on long life span, and this again decreased the number of offspring still further (Mayr, 1970).

Primate infancy is an elaboration (exaggeration?) of the mammalian pattern—a single infant born not more than once a year and requiring years of parental care. Aside from being a strategy for improving fitness, what advantages can such a pattern confer? Highly developed parental care allows a fundamental change in the genetics of behavioral development. Primate infants have a more open program for learning than other mammals. Such an open program requires a far larger brain in the adults who provide the care and in the infants who must learn what information is needed. Primate intelligence is a coadapted product of evolutionary changes in the duration and the intensity of infant dependence and parental care. No one product could have evolved independently of the others.

The pattern of development for human infants in the sensorimotor period is basically the same as that in closely related primates. The distinct recent evolutionary histories of apes and humans have led to species differences in the degree of immaturity at birth, the degree of flexibility in learning, and the length of the socialization period. However, in infancy there are incredible similarities in the sensorimotor period, similarities that should be considered apart from the more obvious differences. Prolonged infancy evolved as a primate variation on the mammalian theme. Human infancy is a further evolution of the primate pattern.

Every period of human life span is a product of selection (Mayr, 1970). Multiple pressures, which we can only speculate about post hoc, must have played interacting roles in the evolution of prolonged infancy. LaBarre (1954) argued for an increasing specialization of human infants in brains and as infants (1973). One-seventh of the newborn's weight is brain. Conflicting selective forces, on the one hand, favor increased fetal brain development and, on the other hand, select against greatly increased size of the birth canal. One resolution of the conflict is to postpone much of the development to after birth. Infants being born less and less mature assures the safe passage of the big-brained fetus into the world.

Changes in adult behaviors must have accompanied the increasingly long dependence of a less mature infant. LaBarre's (1954) account of the evolution of human immaturity is highly speculative. It postulates coordinated changes in adult male, adult female, and infant adaptations and includes the structure of the family. Further, any of several adaptations—(1) the female pelvic size being increased, (2) pregnancy being shortened, or (3) more brain growth being postnatal—would permit further evolution of brain size. No increase in brain size has occurred in the last 30,000 years of human evolution, presumably because there is no longer a selective premium on it. Omenn and Motulsky (1972) noted that human newborns are delivered at a less advanced stage of development than newborn apes and monkeys, a fact that they attribute to two adaptational differences. First, the female pelvis narrowed with the adaptation to bipedal locomotion, and the restriction in the bony birth canal required earlier birth of fetuses. Second, the slow maturation of human infants is ideally adapted to the molding of species-specific behaviors by social input.

It is impossible at present to decide which set of factors in evolutionary history accounted for the correlated shifts in infant intelligence, immaturity, and parental behaviors. They are coadapted. The total phenotype is, after all, a compromise of all selection pressures, some of which are opposed to each other (Mayr, 1970). The evolution of neoteny and infant intelligence most likely represents a compromise solution among pressures on adults to provide increased infant care (a liability), pressures for increasing brain size and flexible learning ability (a benefit, we presume), reproductive economy, and other factors we can only guess.

Biology and Culture

It has been tempting for many to think that the evolution of human behavior has ceased, because (1) there has been no important change in human brain capacities over the past 30,000 to 100,000 years, (2) human cultures insulate us from further evolutionary pressures, and (3) evolution has little to do with human behavior, anyway. Although we will deal with each proposal in turn, the principal point is very simple: *As long as there is any differential rate of reproduction and mortality among individuals, there is evolutionary change.* Because individuals are genetically variable, and because there are differential rates of reproduction and mortality, the likelihood that all phenotypes are reproducing at the same rate is vanishingly small. Fitness, one must remember, is not defined by good looks, high intelligence, or any other socially valued traits. Fitness is merely a function of the number of surviving offspring in proportion to the offspring of others in the population. Those who place the most genes in the next generation will be defined as the most fit and will shape the genetic destiny of the next generation to a greater extent than those who reproduced less successfully.

First, it is true that no important changes in the human brain capacity have occurred in the last 30,000 to 100,000 years. It is speculation to try to account for why a very rapid increase in brain size should come to such an abrupt halt (Mayr, 1970). It must be that for many reasons there was no longer a premium on brain increase in the human population. Perhaps, once most members of the species were able to learn culture, communication, and social norms, evolutionary pressures on brain size per se were reduced. There are no data on the evolution of the structural and functional complexity of human brains.

Second, culture has probably reduced some selective pressures on the human species. As Dobzhansky said (1962), it has not been necessary for people to grow fur in order to keep warm in cold climates when they could don clothing. We do not have to grow wings to fly, or develop more rods in the retina to see at night. Many cultural inventions have reduced selective pressures for *specific* adaptations and permitted us to extend the species range to previously uninhabitable niches.

On the other hand, culture has posed new selective pressures on the species to be able and willing to learn the culture and to live in social groups. Thus, while the human brain volume may have been relatively constant over the last tens of thousands of years, it is not clear that evolution of the brain has stopped. Organization of the brain might still be changing. McClearn (1970), in the previous edition of the *Handbook*, emphasized the role that the development of culture played in the further selection of mankind. People who adapted better to new forms of communication and accumulation of material and formal culture were probably at a selective advantage over those who adapted less well. Specifically, culture shaped the further evolution of mankind by imposing requirements on individuals to meet the demands of group living, governed by norms and even formal laws.

Our gradual accumulation of culture has great relevance to our evolution. Culture provided new environments to which childhood and adult adaptations could occur. As McClearn (1970) said:

> First steps toward culture provided a new environment in which some individuals were more fit, in the Darwinian sense, than others; their offspring were better adapted to culture and capable of further innovations; and so on. The argument can be made that, far from removing mankind from the process of evolution, culture has provided the most salient natural selection pressure to which man has been subject in his recent evolutionary past. (p. 57)

The pressures of culture on the evolution of intelligence are self-evident. Far from being separate forces in the development of the species, biological and cultural forces go hand in hand in the evolution of the human species.

Third, the idea that evolution has little to do with human behavior is readily discounted. The remarkable fossil record of hominid evolution and the development of larger and larger brains (Jerison, 1973) should convince anyone that evolution has shaped contemporary human behaviors. Comparative studies of humans and the great apes show many commonalities but also important differences, especially in behaviors. Blood group and hemoglobin similarities among primates are far greater than morphological and behavioral resemblances. Our divergence from other species, indeed the divergence of any species, is most clearly seen in their behaviors and in the morphology that facilitates those behaviors. King and Wilson (1975) have discussed the "discrepancy" between the relatively large morphological differences between humans and their nearest relatives and their close similarity on the molecular levels that have been examined. They conclude that much of recent human evolution is at the regulatory level, not the level of production of new proteins.

As the complexity of mammalian brains has increased, there has been selection for generalized adaptability rather than prespecified responses. Adaptability for problem solving has been overlaid on reflex responses, as the neocortex has covered the older cortex and midbrain. The evolution of the human mind has been toward greater flexibility in learning, an adaptation that is compatible with the greater immaturity of the human child and the longer and more intense parenting required for successful rearing of the human child.

The fact that human children learn is of paramount importance to understanding the evolution of human development. All normal babies interact with their social and physical worlds, structure and interpret their experiences, and modify their subsequent interactions. As Piaget has described, human children set about learning in a graded sequence of intellectual stages that reflects their growing awareness of the effects of their actions and of the properties of the physical and social worlds around them. A critical feature of human learning is its flexibility. In infancy we see the major transitions from reflex organization to a flexible, experimental approach to the world. By 1 to 1½ years old babies have become impressive, practical experimenters. The rapid development of practical intelligence leaves the rest of the preadolescent period for mental adaptations. While formal operational thought may not develop in all normal species members, sensorimotor and concrete operational intelligences do.

In a brilliant and provocative paper Bruner (1972) outlined the nature and uses of immaturity for human development. He identified the "tutor-proneness" of the young, their readiness to learn through observation and instruction. Infants are ever ready to respond to novelties provided by the adult world. Further, they use play, according to Bruner, as an opportunity to work out their knowledge in safety, without the consequences that would befall adults who were in the initial stages of learning sensorimotor skills and how to be a responsible social animal. The distinctive pattern of immaturity lends itself to more flexible adaptation for the species. The usefulness of opportunities for learning depends on the behavioral flexibility of the infant to acquire by learning what has not been "built into" the genome.

Two facts of human evolutionary history are particularly salient for the evolution of immaturity: the necessity of the mother-child dyad and the consistent availability of a larger human group into which the dyad is integrated. No surviving child was without a social context throughout human history. The evolution of child development has occurred, therefore, in the context of normal human environments. This context has profound implications for the lack of developmental fixity (Lehrman, 1970) in human behavior. Foremost, it has been unnecessary for selection to build into the genotype those behaviors that all children would develop experientially in their human groups. All normal children have close contact with mothers and other conspecifics and with tools and material culture, thus giving them opportunities to learn object manipulation, social bonds, and a human language. What has evolved genotypically is a bias toward acquiring these forms of behavior, a bias that Dobzhansky (1967) calls human educability.

Cavalli-Sforza (1971) has drawn parallels between biological inheritance and evolution and the inheritance and evolution that can occur on a completely cultural level. The last 10,000 years since the beginning neolithic have seen a remarkable evolution of human culture based on the ability to transmit culture from parent to child. As we will see, attempts to understand the genetic factors in human behavioral variation cannot ignore the phenomenon of cultural inheritance.

REVIEW OF BASIC GENETIC PRINCIPLES

What Is a Gene?

Genetics is the science of heredity, the science of how traits are passed from generation to generation. As such, genetics is concerned with the nature of the genetic material, its organization, its transmission from cell to daughter cell and from parent to offspring, and the way in which the genetic material controls the development of traits during the life of an individual. The classical tool of genetics has been variation among individuals. Mendel studied such clear alternative traits as tall versus short peas and defined factors that control this alternative development of the plant. He inferred there was a unique pair of factors controlling each of the traits he studied. These discrete inherited elements that corresponded to the observed functional or developmental alternatives became known as genes. In the last decades biochemical methods have become as important to genetics as variation. As more and more knowledge has been accumulated on the biochemical and molecular nature of the genetic material, the complexity discovered has made it nearly impossible to define in molecular terms exactly what constitutes any particular gene.

The Molecular Nature of a Gene

The genetic material in general is quite well defined—it is a chemical called *deoxyribonucleic acid,* or *DNA*. Watson and Crick (1953) were the winners in a scientific race to understand how this chemical could encode all of the information needed for the life of a complex organism (see Judson, 1979; Watson, 1965). Nearly three decades of intensive research later, the structure of DNA is known to be essentially that proposed by Watson and Crick. Figure 1 is a schematic representation depicting the now classical double helix structure of DNA and its replication. Each strand is a linear sequence of nucleotide bases joined together along a backbone of alternating sugar (deoxyribose) and phosphate. The two strands pair with great precision; the sugar-phosphate chains are on the outside and the bases pair across the middle. Each base has only one possible complementary base with which it pairs—adenine (A) always pairs with thymine (T) and guanine (G) always pairs with cytosine (C). Thus the two strands in the double helix are exactly complementary and each can serve as a template for replication of the whole molecule.

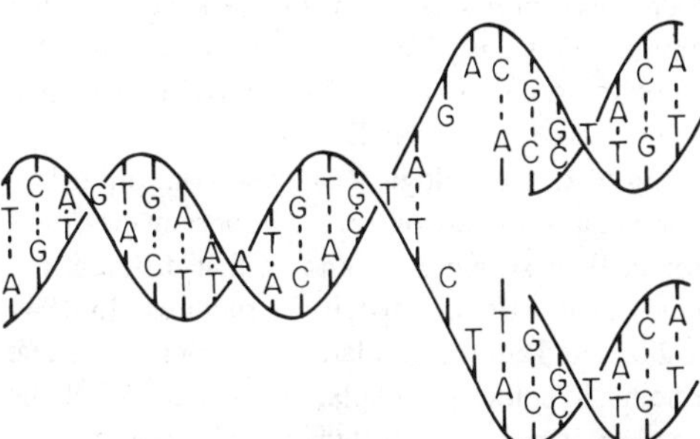

Figure 1. A highly stylized representation of DNA replication. The alternating sugar-phosphate backbone of DNA is simplified to a line in this drawing. In their sequence along the molecule the bases that carry the information are simplified to letters: A for adenine, C for cytosine, G for guanine, and T for thymine. The basis always pair to form a double helix with two exactly complementary strands: A always pairs with T and G always pairs with C. When DNA replicates, the strands separate and, as shown on the right, new strands are synthesized exactly complementing each original strand. The diagram omits the several enzymes that do all the work of fitting the new bases in and then joining them together to make a new continuous backbone.

The amount of DNA in a single human cell is about 6×10^{-12} gs. A human sperm or human egg contains only half that amount. This very small quantity, however, contains an extremely large amount of information. The information is contained in the sequence of the bases along the molecule. Though the molecule has a very precise chemical structure, the bases can occur in any sequence along the molecule; instead of an alphabet of 26 letters the information is ''written'' in an alphabet of the four letters A, T, G, and C. The information in the sequence serves many functions, not all of them yet understood. However, the most well understood and possibly most important function is the control of the synthesis of protein molecules.

Proteins are complex molecules that serve either as important structural proteins (hair, collagen, etc.) or as the enzymes controlling the biochemical machinery in the cells. Each kind of protein molecule is extremely complex and many are very large. Protein molecules are built from smaller units, the amino acids, which are linked together into a long linear sequence. The linear sequence of nucleotide bases in DNA determines the linear sequence of amino acids in protein molecules. The process through which DNA controls protein synthesis involves many individual steps that can be grouped into transcription of the information into a messenger and translation of the message into protein.

As schematically shown in Figure 2, the first step, transcription, is the copying of a given section of DNA. The copy is made out of similar bases but the chemical structure of the sugar in the sugar-phosphate backbone of the nucleic acid is ribose instead of deoxyribose, hence it is called *ribonucleic acid,* or *RNA*. Particular sequences of nucleotides, as yet largely unknown, apparently serve as starting signals and stopping signals for the production of RNA copies of a defined segment of DNA. The nucleotide sequences must be recognized by enzymes that control the synthesis of a copy. The RNA molecule is single stranded and is a transcript of only one of the two DNA strands. Once the copy has been made in

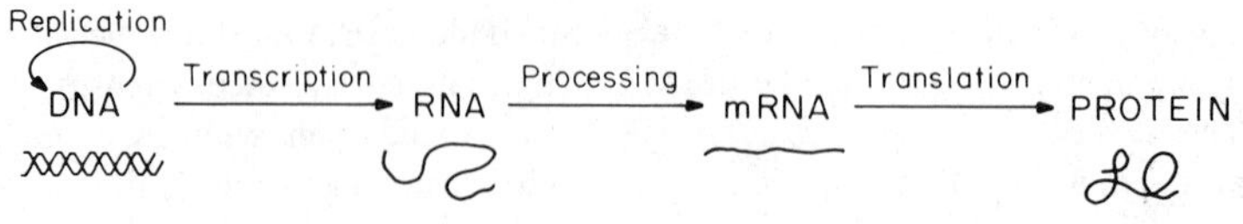

Replication

DNA → Transcription → RNA → Processing → mRNA → Translation → PROTEIN

Figure 2. The flow of information from DNA to protein molecules. As shown in Figure 1, the information in DNA replicates itself. The information contained in the base sequence in DNA is preserved when DNA is transcribed into single-stranded RNA molecules. These RNA molecules are then processed into mature mRNA, which is then translated in the process of protein synthesis into a sequence of the amino acids that make up a protein. The genetic code specifies how a series of three nucleotide bases (a triplet) determines a specific amino acid. The 64 possible triplets (or codons) are translated into one start codon, three stop codons, and 60 specifying the 20 amino acids.

the nucleus, the long molecule is usually processed by other enzymes and transported out of the nucleus into the cytoplasm. During processing, large segments in the middle of the sequence are removed and the pieces rejoined to each other. A special cap is put on the "front end" of the RNA strand and a tail of several consecutive adenosines (poly A) is added to the "back end." Once the processing is completed, the resulting mature *messenger RNA* (*mRNA*) molecule is ready to be translated into a protein molecule.

The complex translation process occurs in the cytoplasm, involves many individual components, and has its own regulation mechanisms. The logical process of translation is quite simple: the messenger RNA is read in groups of three sequential bases; each triplet codes for a specific amino acid. The coding triplet is called a *codon.* Since there are four different bases in the messenger RNA, just as in the DNA, and they can occur in any sequence, a total of 64 different codons can occur. One of the 64 is a start signal that indicates the point at which translation into a protein is to begin. Three of the codons are stop signals that indicate the position at which translation is to terminate. The remaining 61 codons specify amino acids. Because there are only 20 amino acids, the code is redundant with from 2 to 6 codons specifying a particular amino acid. There is no ambiguity, a specific codon codes for only one amino acid. The codons are nonoverlapping so any codon can, in theory, follow any other.

The biochemical process by which this simple, logical code is actually translated from messenger RNA (mRNA) into a protein molecule is quite complex. A large structure, called a *ribosome,* composed of several RNA molecules and several different proteins, attaches to the mRNA around the initiation or start codon. This molecule then, in effect, moves along the mRNA and causes the translation to take place. As the ribosome moves to each subsequent codon, it "finds" a small *transfer RNA (tRNA)* molecule that matches the specific codon. These small tRNA molecules exist in many different kinds, one for each of the codons that specifies an amino acid. Part of the tRNA molecule contains a sequence that is complementary to its particular codon; attached to the other end of the molecule is the amino acid that represents this codon. Thus, the tRNAs are the molecules that effect the translation. As the ribosome matches a tRNA molecule with the next codon on the messenger, the amino acid attached to that tRNA is joined to the amino acid of the preceding codon. As the ribosome moves along the messenger RNA, the chain of amino acids grows. The amino acids are cut loose from the tRNA after they have been joined to the growing chain of amino acids and the tRNA is released to be recycled elsewhere in the cell by having a new molecule of its specific amino acid attached to it. When the ribosome reaches a termination codon, the chain of amino acids (called a polypeptide because the amino acids are joined by peptide bonds) is released. This polypeptide may be a completed protein molecule or may subsequently be modified or combined with other polypeptides to form an even larger, more complex, molecule. The hemogoblin molecule, for example, is composed of four polypeptides, two each of two different kinds.

Enzymes, the biological catalysts controlling cellular metabolism, are one of the important classes of protein. It has long been known that different enzymes have different specific structures. In 1941 Beadle and Tatum formulated the "one gene, one protein" hypothesis to explain the way in which the genetic material controlled the functions of the cells and of the organism. Of course, since some enzymes are composed of more than one type of polypeptide chain, the concept actually was closer to the less euphonious "one gene, one polypeptide chain." With the understanding of how genes determined protein structure, it was possible to think of a gene in terms of the DNA. Though it has long been recognized that some sort of control mechanisms must exist at the DNA level, the gene has often been considered to be that section of the DNA that corresponds to the segment of messenger RNA that is translated into protein. That concept is, unfortunately, too simplistic.

In just the last few years we have learned that the DNA often has a structure, or informational content, that is much more complex than just the sequence of codons for a polypeptide. Some of this informational complexity and its role in protein synthesis are illustrated in Figure 3. In a very real sense our image of the gene was exploded in 1977 (Proudfoot, Shander, Manley, Gefter, & Maniatis, 1980). In that year it was first learned that additional segments of DNA normally intervene between the sequences that code for amino acids. These intervening sequences are removed as the RNA transcript is processed to form mRNA, in effect splicing the pieces of the "classical gene" back together again. It is clear now that the existence of these intervening sequences, and their specific DNA sequences, are important in the production of mRNA. These parts of the DNA that never become translated into protein are nonetheless vital to the synthesis of the specific protein molecule being coded for by the surrounding DNA. The parts of the DNA that signal points for initiation of transcription and termination of transcription must also be considered relevant to the synthesis of the particular protein. In fact, the sequences that code for the amino acid sequence of protein represent only a small part of the DNA. A large amount of DNA that never appears as mRNA and some of the information that exists in the messenger but that is not translated into protein—the sequences preceding the initiation codon and following the termination codon—may very likely be relevant to regulation, even though they are not relevant to the amino acid composition of proteins. When a protein is produced and how much product is produced are functions of these other parts of the DNA (see *Developmental Examples*). Such genetic regulatory functions play a crucial role in development; indeed, they are the basis for development. Because we cannot assay those functions easily, we have no clear estimates of their functions or of the normal genetic variation in these relevant parts of DNA. It is easiest to think of the gene as that whole segment of the DNA that is "responsible" for the production of one particular molecule.

Unfortunately, even this concept is not universally applicable. Recent discoveries in the virus SV-40 show that "genes" can overlap with the same segment of DNA coding for amino acid sequences in two or three *different* proteins. The RNA transcript can be processed in alternative ways. Depending on which of the start signals or splicing options is chosen, the sequence from one part of the DNA becomes part of the mRNA for different proteins.

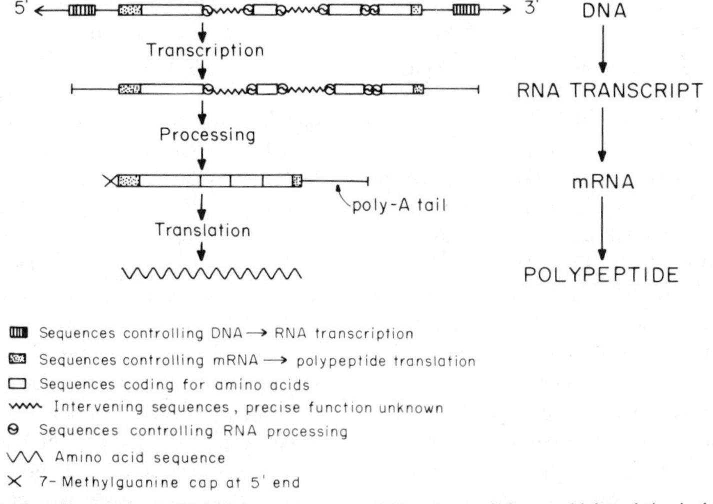

Figure 3. The organization of a typical gene in a higher organism, such as a human, from the DNA level to the final protein. At the DNA level there are coding sequences that are not completely contiguous. Intervening sequences as well as flanking sequences are all transcribed into RNA. Still additional sequences control the initiation of RNA transcription but are not themselves copied into RNA. During the processing step, specific ends are attached to the RNA to protect it from rapid degradation in the cell and the intervening sequences are spliced out at precisely determined positions. The mature mRNA thus represents only a fraction of the information content contained in the DNA. That message, however, is specific and sufficient for determining the amino acid sequence in a protein molecule. Many identical protein molecules can be synthesized, one after another, from the same mRNA template molecule.

But, though it is the same nucleotide sequence, the amino acid sequence produced is different because it is translated in a different reading frame—sequences of triplets shifted over one or two bases with respect to each other (see Reddy, Thimmuppaya, Dhar, Subramanian, Zain, Pan, Ghosh, Celma, & Weissman, 1978, for detailed review). Such a situation is not known for humans, but we have barely begun to explore human DNA. Even the existence of intervening sequences was unknown until 1977 but appears to be the norm, not the exception.

Transmission: The Classic Understanding of Inheritance

Whatever its precise extent in molecular terms, the gene is in some sense a segment of the DNA molecule and, hence, a piece of the chromosome. When Mendel hypothesized his factors, they had no known correspondence to real elements within the cell but nonetheless were shown to follow very strict rules of transmission from generation to generation. What Mendel postulated for peas is essentially what we know today to be true for humans as well, though we understand the mechanism for the rules of transmission—the behavior of chromosomes in ordinary cell division and in the special cell divisions that form the gametes, the sperm, and the egg.

A human is a diploid organism: all chromosomes occur in pairs. The chromosome cycle described in the following section—the preservation of diploidy in the adult organism, the reduction division in the production of gametes and the restoration of diploidy at fertilization—is responsible for the patterns of inheritance first clearly described by Mendel. Every individual has two copies of each gene and only one of each pair is included in a gamete. To any specific child a parent transmits only one copy of each pair of genes. Chance determines which copy—that inherited from the mother or that inherited from the father—will be included in a gamete and transmitted to an offspring. The restoration of the diploid state at fertilization also restores the paired nature of the genes. While this process occurs for every gene, its effects cannot be observed directly. The passage of a given copy of a gene down through successive generations of a family can only be detected if that copy is a variant form of the gene that determines a difference in the appearance in the individuals carrying it.

Because *gene* is an ambiguous word, specific terms distinguish between the general unit of heredity as a segment of the chromosome and the specific information contained in one particular copy of that unit. Since the genetic material is organized in a specific order along the chromosome and a given gene always occurs in the same place on the chromosome, *locus* is the general term geneticists use with reference to the function or characteristic affected by the genetic information in a particular place on a chromosome. *Allele* is used to refer to the information to be found at a particular locus on one chromosome. Thus, in humans there is a colorblindness locus with alleles for normal vision and alleles for colorblindness. In a group of several individuals more than two different alleles (forms) of a given locus may exist. For example, the ABO blood group system has I^A alleles determining production of the A antigen, I^B alleles controlling production of the B antigen, and *i* alleles which specify neither antigen. Because humans are diploid—the chromosomes occur in pairs—only two alleles (representatives) of a specific locus will exist in any one individual. When the allele on one chromosome is identical to the allele at the same locus on the homologous chromosome, the individual is said to be homozygous at that locus. When the two alleles at a locus are different the individual is said to be heterozygous at that locus. Because of their greater specificity and because of the ambiguity of the word *gene,* the terms *locus* and *allele* are preferable. The preceding sentences show that the word *allele* has two slightly different usages. It can refer either to specific copies or specific forms of the information at a locus. Thus, only two alleles (representatives) of any locus occur in the cells of any diploid individual—one on each chromosome of the pair—but those two may be different alleles (forms) from the two alleles (representatives) occurring in another individual.

The ordinary process of cell division involves exact replication of all parts of the genetic material and distribution into the two daughter cells of two exactly identical sets of genetic material. At the molecular level the DNA is replicated to form two identical copies. This is accomplished by the complementary strands of the double helix separating with each strand serving as a template for the synthesis of a new complementary strand. This ability for a molecule to serve as a copy for its own duplication is an important element of the genetic material. The chromosomes, the structures which contain the DNA, are then duplicated, one around each copy of the DNA. The complex part of cell division called *mitosis* involves the distribution of the duplicated chromosomes and assures that all of the genetic material is present in each of the daughter cells.

DNA replication occurs while the chromosomes are loosely intertwined in a seemingly amorphous mass throughout the cell nucleus. When the cell is ready to divide, the chromosomes begin to contract and gradually become highly condensed structures with tightly packed DNA. The DNA has been fully replicated but the duplicated chromosomes are still held together at one point, the centromere. The nuclear membrane breaks apart and the chromosomes gradually become obviously doubled structures, though still attached. These chromosomes align themselves into a plate across the center of the cell. Each chromosome becomes attached at the centromere to a complex structure of fibers running from this equatorial plate to points at opposite poles of the cell. The chromosomes synchronously divide at the last attachment, the centromere, and the two daughters are pulled apart by contraction of the fibers attaching them to opposite poles. When the chromosomes reach the opposite poles they begin to associate, become less condensed, and are enclosed in a new nuclear membrane. A new cell membrane forms along the equatorial plate and two cells exist where one existed before. Each of the daughter cells has an identical set of genetic information.

A different and more complicated sequence of divisions, called *meiosis,* is responsible for the production of gametes. A detailed description of meiosis (and mitosis) can be found in any biology or general genetics book. Here it is sufficient to note that the process assures that instead of one copy of each chromosome being included in each of the daughter cells, one copy of each pair of chromosomes is included in the final cell, a gamete. This reduction division is essential for the preservation of a constant chromosome number in the species while allowing both parents to have equal genetic contribution to the off spring. Since each gamete has only half the genetic information from the parent, when the two gametes unite, a full complement of genetic material is restored.

Human Chromosomes and Chromosomal Variations

Organization of Genome into Chromosomes

The human genome is organized into 23 pairs of chromosomes. One of these pairs is responsible for sex determination and its chromosomes—the *X* and the *Y*—are appropriately referred to as the sex chromosomes. The chromosomes of the other 22 pairs are referred to as autosomes. The autosomes occur in identical pairs and account for the bulk of the genetic material. The sex chromosomes, on the other hand, are not always present in identical pairs.

The genetic constitutions of the two types of sex chromosome differ: the *X* chromosome is relatively large and contains many loci of known function; the *Y* chromosome is relatively small and contains no loci that have yet been identified by precise function. Females have two *X* chromosomes and therefore all loci in females, those on the *X* as well as those on the autosomes, are present in duplicate. Males have only one *X* chromosome and, instead of a second *X* chromosome, have a *Y* chromosome. The loci on the *X* chromosome are present only in single copy in males and consequently show a different pattern of inheritance. In meiosis in a female, no special problems arise and all gametes contain one copy of each pair of chromosomes, one *X* and one each of the 22 autosomes. In contrast, meiosis in a male results in two kinds of gametes. The *X* and *Y* chromosome associate in meiosis so that they segregate into different gametes. Thus, every sperm contains one chromosome from each pair, but the sex chromosome pair is represented by either an *X* chromosome or a *Y* chromosome. The sex of the zygote is determined by whether an *X*-bearing sperm (producing a female) or a *Y*-bearing sperm (producing a male) fertilizes the egg.

Normal Human Chromosomes

Each of the 24 types of chromosomes (22 autosomes, *X* and *Y*) can now be individually identified under the microscope in material that has been appropriately prepared. The chromosomes can be classified and hence identified, by three characteristics. The first and most obvious is total length of the chromosome. The autosomes are numbered from 1 for the longest to 22 for the shortest. The relative position of the centromere provides another means of identification. It is useful for identification because the position of the centromere is constant and representative of each individual chromosome. Unambiguous identification of each chromosome has only come about since 1970 with the development of staining techniques that produce banding patterns on human chromosomes. Different staining techniques produce different banding patterns but each chromosome has a distinct and characteristic banding pattern. The banding pattern seen using one group of techniques is shown in the photomicrograph of a chromosome preparation (Figure 4). The different banding patterns of different pairs are obvious when the chromosomes in a photograph of a single cell are rearranged into a standardized format. Figure 5 shows such an arrangement of the chromosomes of a normal human male.

While the banding patterns are generally identical for each individual chromosome across individuals, small-scale variations, called heteromorphisms, have been identified. These heteromorphisms are apparently normal variations that are genetically stable characteristics of a particular chromosome. The banding techniques have also made it

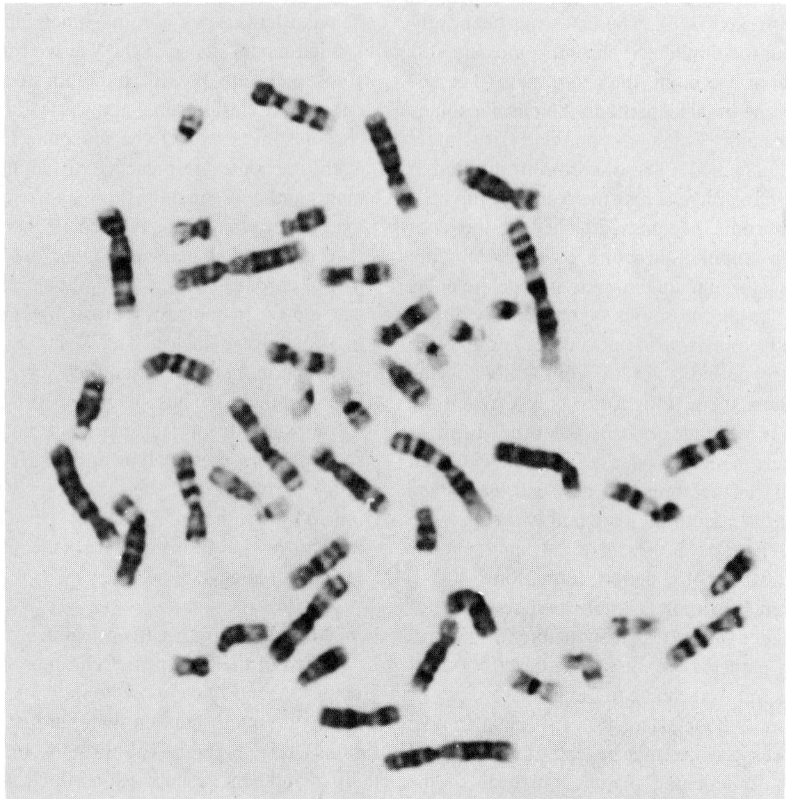

Figure 4. A photomicrograph of a human chromosome preparation. Cells were grown in culture medium in the laboratory and treated so that the chromosomes would be caught in the middle of the cell division process and would be spread, as seen, when the cells burst as they were dropped onto the microscope slide. The bands are the result of specific staining procedures. (This example showing the chromosomes of a normal male is courtesy of Dr. Roy Breg.)

possible to identify chromosomal aberrations with much more specificity than had been possible before. It is now known that Cri-du-chat syndrome, a syndrome of mild mental retardation and certain behavioral abnormalities including a cat-like cry in infancy (hence the name), is caused by a deletion of part of the short arm of chromosome 5. Such children have only one copy of the genetic material in this region and this genetic imbalance somehow causes the disorder. Using banding techniques to study possible associations of specific symptoms and their severity with the specific bands deleted, Wilkins and Brown (1980) found no clear relationship for physical abnormalities and chromosome segments. They did find that measured IQ was significantly negatively correlated ($r = -.69, p < .01$) with the size of the deletion.

Comparative Cytogenetics

The amount of genetic material represented by the complete set of 46 human chromosomes is approximately the same amount found in most other mammalian species (Ohno, 1967). However, that genetic material is arranged quite differently in different species. Different species frequently have different chromosome numbers—48 for the chimpanzee, 64 for the horse, 78 for the dog, 40 for the mouse, 27 for the toad (for example, see Strickberger, 1976). In addition, the individual chromosomes vary in length, position of the centromere, and banding pattern. These differences make it possible to identify all the specific chromosomes in the human-mouse hybrid cells that derive from the fusion in culture medium of a somatic cell of a mouse with a somatic cell of a human (Ruddle, 1973; Ruddle & Kucherlapati, 1974). Knowing which chromosomes are derived from the mouse parent and which chromosomes are derived from the human parent has contributed to major advances in understanding gene organization.

There is one remarkable exception to this shuffling of genetic material into different chromosomal

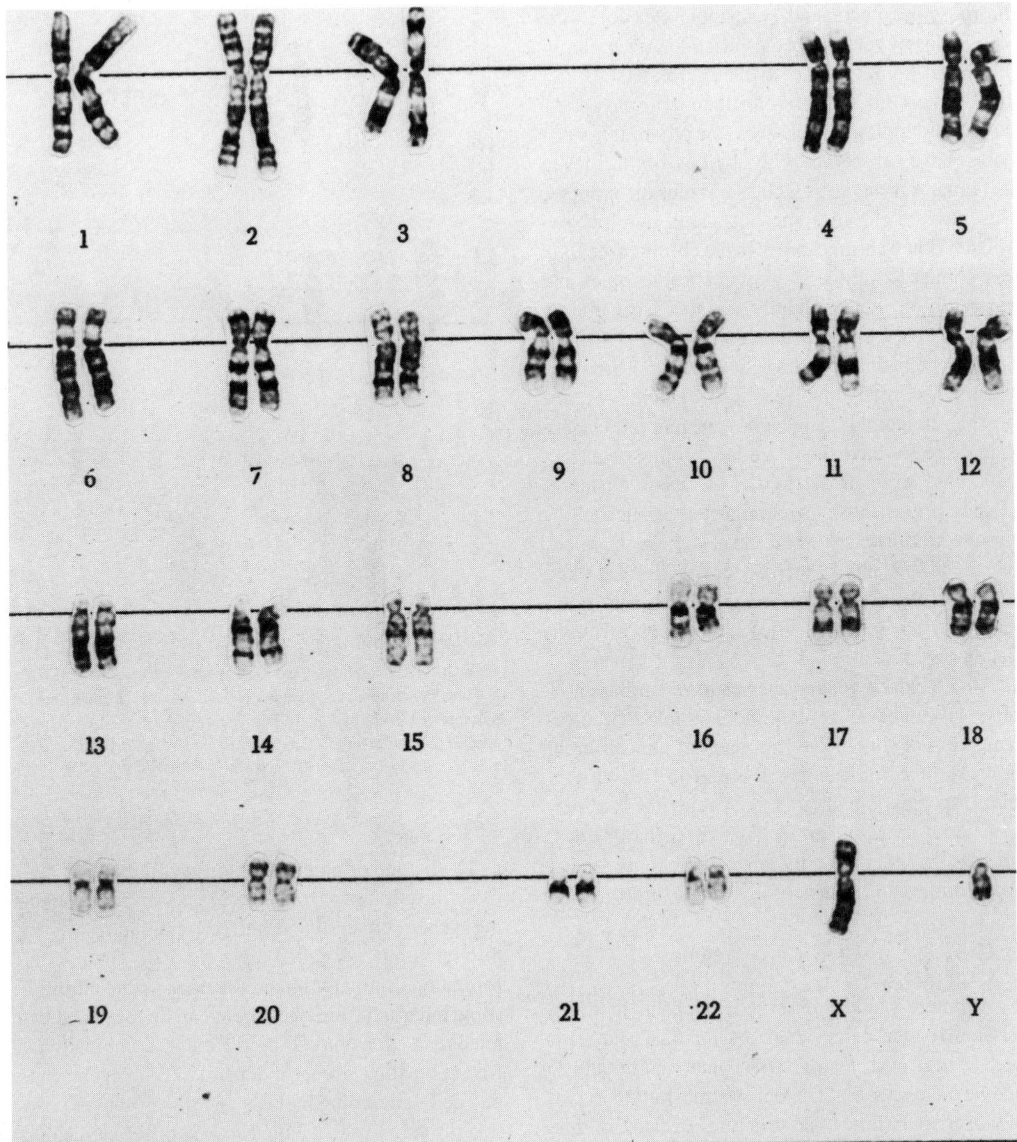

Figure 5. A human karyotype. Chromosomes seen under the microscope as in Figure 4 have been cut from a photograph and artificially arranged so that members of each pair are together. The pairs are arranged in order of decreasing size, and numbered according to convention from 1 for the largest pair of autosomes to 22 for the smallest pair. The X and Y chromosomes are so labeled. (This karyotype of a normal human male—not the same male as in Figure 4—is courtesy of Dr. Uta Francke.)

packets: the *X* chromosome is conserved throughout all mammalian species. Though there is variation in the order of the loci on the X chromosome in different species, the same set of genes, representing about 1/9 of the genetic information in a gametic set of chromosomes, is present on all mammalian X chromosomes (Ohno, 1967; Pearson, Roderick, Davisson, Garner, Tharburton, Lalley, & O'Brien, 1979). This conservation of the X chromosome has occurred because of the complications introduced by its being part of the sex-determining mechanism. For genes to be moved either from or to the X chromosome interferes with the genetic adaptation to the sex determination mechanism.

The rearrangement of loci occurs as part of evolution. Just as random gene mutations can occur and some small percentage of them become established in the species, so also can rearrangements of the chromosomes occur and occasionally become the norm. Closely related species often have very similar chromosomes while distantly related species show almost no similarity in their chromosomes. Our nearest biological relatives, the other higher primates, have karyotypes with obvious similarities to the human karyotype as well as obvious differences. Most have 48 chromosomes instead of our 46. Several individual chromosomes in the chimpanzee look very similar to individual human chromosomes and apparently do have virtually identical sets of loci (Pearson et al., 1979; Seuanez, 1979).

As schematically shown in Figure 6, the rearrangements usually involve whole segments of chromosome containing many genes. In general, closely related species have more similar chromosomes and they share larger intact blocks of DNA. Distantly related species show few similarities in their chromosomes. However, when gene loci are mapped, even such distantly related species as humans and mice still show small blocks of genes that have apparently been together since very early in mammalian evolution.

Not all closely related species have similar chromosome numbers. An extreme example of the organization of similar genetic material into different numbers of chromosomes is found in two closely related species of muntjac. One species has its genetic material arranged in 23 pairs of chromosomes, whereas the other has only three "pairs," two pairs of autosomes and unusual sex chromosomes.

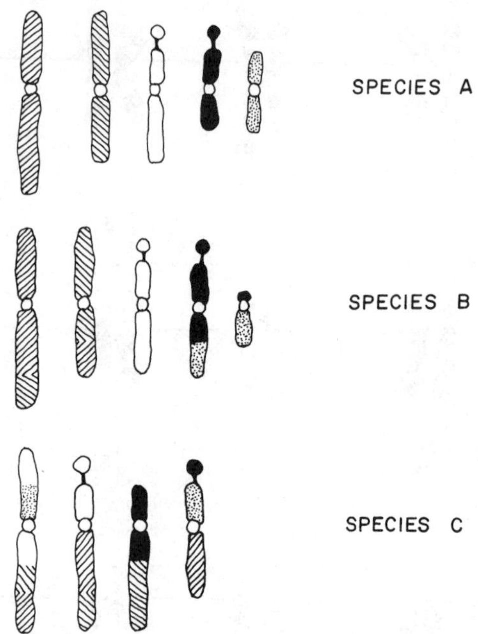

Figure 6. The evolutionary rearrangement of genetic material. The shading shows how genetic material found on one chromosome in one species (A) can be found slightly rearranged in a closely related species (B) and greatly rearranged in a more distantly related species (C).

Genetic Consequences of Genome Organization

Although Mendel observed independent transmission for the pairs of factors for different traits such as seed coat, flower color, plant height, and so on, we have seen that the loci are transmitted as part of the larger chromosome structure. Because of this, Mendel's law of independent assortment does not hold for loci close together on the same chromosome. When loci are located on the same chromosome they are said to be *syntenic,* from the Latin for "held together." In somatic-cell hybrids between species, this syntenic block of genes behaves as a single unit; all loci are present if the chromosome is present and all are absent if the chromosome is absent. In normal sexual reproduction, the tendency of syntenic genes to be transmitted together varies with the distance between them.

Genetic linkage is the nonrandom assortment in meiosis of alleles at different loci because the loci involved are located close together on the same chromosome. During meiosis the two chromosomes of a pair—the one of paternal origin and the one of maternal origin—can exchange blocks of corresponding genetic material. This recombination occurs through a process called crossing over. Genetic information originally linked together in one chromosome inherited from one parent can thereby be separated and transmitted in different combinations. Recombination occurs independently in each separate cell undergoing meiosis and the crossover position is randomly distributed among different meiotic events. The frequency of recombination between two different genetic sites or loci on the chromosome is a function of the actual physical distance between them. Alleles at loci close together will usually be inherited together, while alleles at loci at opposite ends of a long chromosome will be inherited independently. An evolutionarily important consequence of the recombination process is that mutations arising at different loci can eventually recombine even though they are on the same chromosome.

Genetic linkage is measured as the recombination frequency, which can be zero for loci immediately adjacent to each other or any value up to .5. The maximum frequency of 50% recombinant gametes occurs when the two loci segregate completely independently. Chromosome linkage maps are constructed with map units of 1% recombination, but accurate map distances can only be directly measured over small distances. For loci located further apart, multiple crossover events can occasionally occur between the loci, reducing the observed rate of recombination. The longer chromosomes in humans, such as numbers 1 and 2, are more than 300 map units long. Because random segregation shows an apparent recombination of 50%, this is the maximum that can actually be observed. Therefore, loci more than about 60 to 70 map units apart normally show no deviation from random or independent segregation in meiosis, even though they are on the same chromosome.

The loci for colorblindness and hemophilia, which are closely linked on the *X* chromosome, illustrate the tendency for closely linked loci to be transmitted together. If a woman inherits the allele for normal clotting and the allele for colorblindness on the *X* chromosome from her father and inherits the hemophilia allele and allele for normal color vision on the *X* chromosome from her mother, she will tend to have two kinds of sons depending on which one of her two *X* chromosomes is transmitted: those with colorblindness and normal clotting and those with hemophilia and normal vision. Among her daughters' children, those grandsons with colorblindness will generally not have hemophilia, and those with hemophilia will generally not have colorblindness. In such a family there would be a negative association between the two abnormal traits because the abnormal alleles happen to be on separate chromosomes. In other families there might be a positive association because the abnormal alleles happen to occur on the same chromosome. However, in the population at large there will be no association between the abnormal traits. Linkage is a tendency for whatever alleles occur at the linked loci to be transmitted together; in the total population there is no tendency for certain alleles at these loci to occur disproportionately together. Finding an association in a population, for example the reported association between the presence of myopia and higher average IQ scores (Karlsson, 1973, 1975), does not imply that linkage exists.

The Human Gene Map

From a combination of the somatic-cell techniques and classical linkage analyses of segregation patterns in families it has been possible to construct an early map of the human genome (Ruddle & McKusick, 1977). The state of this map in early 1980 is shown in Figure IIB 4. Additional and more precise assignments of loci continue. The introduction of the new recombinant DNA techniques promises to provide many more reference points on the human gene map (Botstein, White, Skolnick, & Davis, 1980; Wyman & White, 1980). In 15 years the human gene map has gone from nothing to this present state. In another 10 years it may be the best genetic map of any species.

Value of a Linkage Map for Behavioral Analyses

As explained in greater detail in subsequent sections, the relationship between genotype and the complex behaviors of interest is almost certainly not going to be a simple one. Polymorphic loci allow a researcher to follow the transmission of blocks of genetic material (the statistically defined segment from that marker locus to the nearest crossover on either side) without knowing what genes occur in that region. Use of linkage markers in families makes it possible to determine whether or not some gene near the marker may be affecting the behavior. For example, genetic linkage studies have been pursued in families with bipolar affective disorder—the classic manic-depressive illness. Though no results are yet definitive (Morton & Kidd, 1980), there are families in which susceptibility to the illness appears to be transmitted on the *X* chromosome and linked to the locus for colorblindness (Mendlewicz, Linkowski, Guroff, & Van Praag, 1979) as well as families which show no evidence of such linkage (Gershon, Targum, Matthysee, & Bunney, 1979). In other families susceptibility to the illness appears to show linkage to the HLA (Human Leukocyte Antigen) loci in the major histocompatibility complex on the short arm of chromosome 6 (Smeraldi, Negri, Melica, & Scorza-Smeraldi, 1978). The apparent conflict between these two results may simply be indicative of genetic heterogeneity—the existence of two or more genetic loci, any one of which alone has alleles that can cause manic-depressive disorder, that is, different genetic mechanisms giving rise to the same phenotype. Genetic linkage is an excellent means for identifying and resolving such heterogeneity.

In experimental organisms such as the fruit fly (*Drosophila melanogaster*) genetic linkage with known marker loci has also allowed researchers to identify major loci that affect a polygenic trait (Thoday, 1977) and a quantitative behavioral trait (Jayakar, Della Croce, Scacchi, & Guazzotti, 1977). This approach should allow, in the next few decades, the identification of the major individual loci

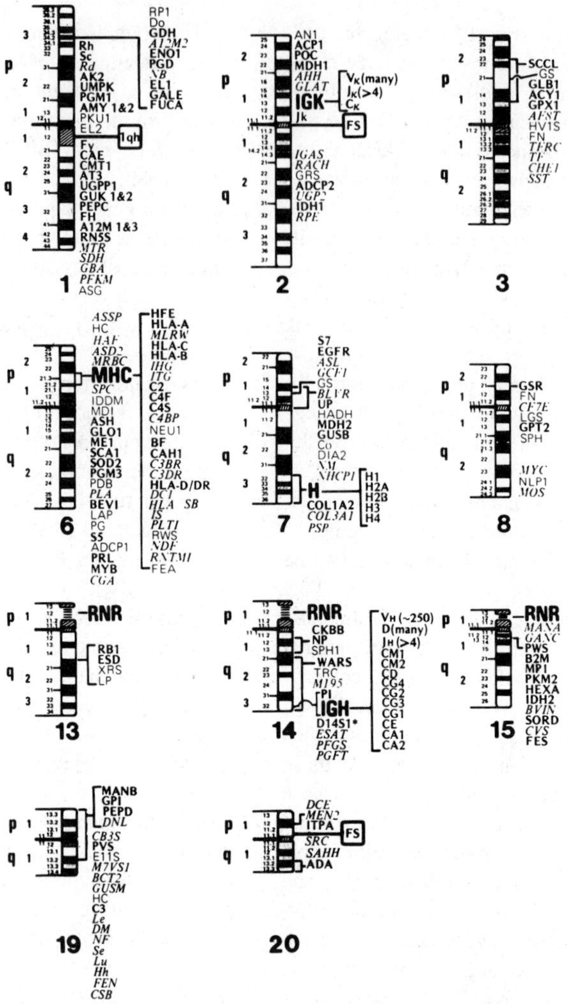

Figure 7. The human linkage map. Information is rapidly accumulating on the locations of the DNA sequences for specific functions in the human genome. This diagram shows the map as of December, 1982. The ABO blood group locus is on chromosome 9, the Rh blood group locus is on chromosome 1, the two common color blindness loci (CBD and CBP) are on the X chromosome. A full explanation of many of the remaining gene symbols can be found in Thompson & Thompson (1980, pp. 247–249). (Diagram courtesy of Dr. Victor McKusick.)

affecting polygenic traits in humans. Our understanding of the genetic control of normal human development will then take a quantum leap.

Human Genetic Variation

Normal Variation at Single Loci

It is obvious to everyone that humans differ greatly from one another. There are blondes and brunettes, blue-eyed people and brown-eyed people, tall people and short people. The variation one sees, however, is very superficial and may not be representative of total genetic variation among humans. At the level of genetic variation at a single locus there have been two schools of thought. One favored the concept of a normal allele and rare individual variants. The other favored a more dynamic concept of normal variation with many loci having two or more alleles, no one of which could be identified as the normal allele. Which of the two schools applied to humans was not clear until the late 1960s when the work of Harris (1975) and his colleagues showed clearly that there was no single normal allele at a large proportion of human loci. Harris studied several enzymes found in red blood cells and found that about 30% had variant alleles that were sufficiently common that the locus was polymorphic. (A locus is considered polymorphic if the most frequent allele

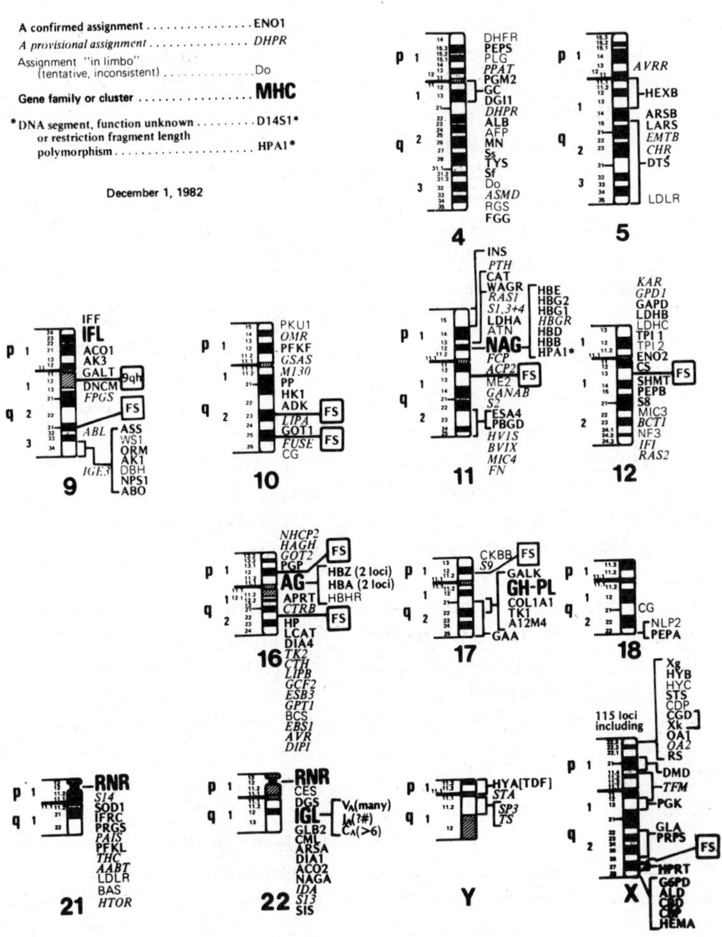

Figure 7—*continued*

occurs with a frequency of less than 99%; that is usually equivalent to more than one allele having a frequency greater than 1%.)

The polymorphic human loci that Harris and his colleagues identified are all polymorphic for normal alleles; the enzymes produced by these alleles perform the required enzymatic functions correctly but have minor structural differences that allow them to be identified. The amount of genetic variation uncovered was surprisingly large. Extrapolation from the unbiased sample of 30 or so enzymes studied suggests that as much as 30% of the loci coding for proteins might show significant normal genetic variation in a population and that any given individual might be heterozygous for different normal alleles at 10% of the loci.

Some newer methods have found little genetic variation but countering this finding are studies showing that the techniques that found 30% of the loci polymorphic probably are grossly underestimating the actual amount of variation among those loci that are polymorphic. Use of many different techniques for each single enzyme has shown in *Drosophila* that what originally was thought to be one allele often was several different alleles (Coyne, 1976; Coyne & Felton, 1977, Singh, Lewontin, & Felton, 1976). In the same sample of alleles from natural populations one enzyme in *Drosophila per-*

similis was found to have 23 alleles instead of 6 (Coyne, 1976) and the same enzyme, but in *D. pseudoobscura,* to have 27 instead of 8 alleles (Singh et al., 1976). Work with other loci is summarized by Coyne, Felton, and Lewontin (1978) who conclude that loci already known to be polymorphic may have much more variation than had previously been believed but that those loci with no known genetic variation still appear to be monomorphic with the newer techniques. The sharp distinction between monomorphic loci and highly polymorphic loci indicates differences in the action of natural selection.

Two concerns have arisen. First, is this sample of enzymes from the serum and red blood cells a representative sample of the genome? Second, are these variants that have been detected in any sense meaningful in terms of differential fitness and natural selection or are they completely neutral variants? The scientific debate over these two questions continues with some population geneticists favoring the neutrality of the existing alleles and others favoring the existence of functional differences. A direct test is very difficult because *in vitro* conditions certainly differ from those *in vivo.* It seems likely that loci of different functional classes also have different degrees of polymorphism in humans. Whatever the overall figure for polymorphism might be, it is clear that considerable normal variation exists in humans.

With the recent advances in the techniques of studying and analyzing DNA has come a whole new class of human genetic polymorphisms. They are called restriction fragment length polymorphisms and are variants in the DNA nucleotide sequence. The unique aspects of these variants is that they are detectable even if the altered DNA sequence occurs between loci or in the intervening sequences. Available evidence indicates that DNA-level polymorphisms are common. Several have been detected around the β-globin complex on chromosome 11 (e.g. Kan & Dozy, 1978, 1980). In one study of randomly picked segments of the genome, one of three such segments had a very high level of DNA polymorphism associated with it (Wyman & White, 1981).

Single Locus Genetic Abnormalities

A very large number of human genetic defects has been identified (McKusick, 1978). Virtually all of these exist with allele frequencies too small to qualify as polymorphisms. They also have deleterious effects in at least some genetic combinations, usually when homozygous. Though the sum total of deleterious genes is quite large—it has been estimated that each human is, on average, a carrier for the equivalent of four different abnormal genes any one of which would be lethal when homozygous—individually they are rare abnormal alleles. The carrier (heterozygote) frequency for some of these variants, however, can approach 1% of the population. Thus, if the carrier showed a slight effect of the abnormal allele, it could contribute to the normal variation in the population. Also, many of these genetic disorders have known behavioral consequences. (See Ehrman & Parsons 1981, Omenn & Motulsky, 1972.)

Normal Biochemical Variations

Might some of the normal genetic variation be relevant to behavioral differences among humans? While the intuitive answer is yes, there are virtually no data that clearly associate specific "normal" genetic variation with a behavioral difference. Of course, there are numerous examples of abnormal variations being associated with behavioral differences (PKU, Lesch-Nyhan, homocystinuria, etc.).

Classical Patterns of Inheritance. The normal relationship(s) between genotype and phenotype are complex. The exceptional cases in humans are the simple autosomal dominant and autosomal recessive (and their *X*-linked counterparts) modes of inheritance such as were described by Mendel. The simplicity of the relationship between phenotypic state and genotype is the reason that classical Mendelian traits are the exception in any higher organism. A classical autosomal dominant trait is one in which the dominant phenotype is associated with the heterozygote and one of the two homozygotes for a single locus with only two alleles. The recessive phenotype is the alternative trait which is expressed only by the other homozygote. The *X*-linked counterparts show the same pattern in females, but since males only have one *X*-chromosome and can be neither homozygous nor heterozygous (they are termed hemizygous), whatever allele is present is expressed. Figure 8 shows a tabular representation of these classical genotype-to-phenotype relationships. Also represented is the co-dominant relationship in which the heterozygote expresses both alleles, a form of inheritance common for human blood groups such as the MNS system.

The terms *dominant* and *recessive* are logical because the recessive trait recedes or is masked in the heterozygote, though there is still present a copy of the allele that, when homozygous, results in that trait. It is common to refer to that allele as the "recessive allele" and the alternative as the "dominant allele." Such terminology has always been shorthand, is technically incorrect, and is often a source

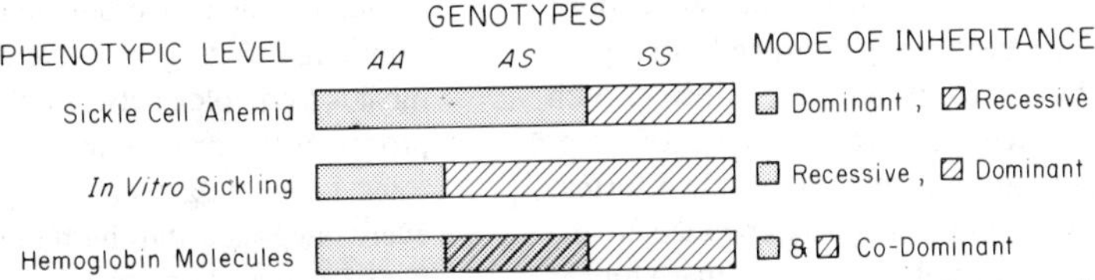

Figure 8. A diagram of genotype-phenotype relations. The classical modes of inheritance are diagrammed according to different definitions of phenotypes associated with the *HbA* and *HbS* alleles at the beta hemoglobin locus, as discussed in the text. The three shaded columns represent the three genotypes; in a given row similar shading in two columns indicates those two genotypes have the same phenotype, as defined on the left.

of tremendous confusion. A simple example illustrates both the errors in such shorthand and the importance of defining the level of the phenotype. Sickle-cell anemia is a well known disorder, most common among blacks; it is caused by homozygosity for an abnormal form of one of the polypeptide chains in the hemoglobin molecule. The medical disorder is clearly autosomal recessive—the heterozygote has no clinical problems under almost all of the broad range of normal experiences and environments. However, under extremely low oxygen concentrations, readily obtainable *in vitro,* the cells of a heterozygote also show sickling. Thus, though there are quantitative differences, the qualitative trait of red cell sickling under low oxygen concentrations shows autosomal dominant inheritance. That is a completely different phenotype from the clinical anemia, though the two are clearly related (we might consider it as drawing thresholds at two different levels of a continuum). With biochemical techniques it is possible to study the abnormal hemoglobin molecule itself (HbS) and distinguish it from the normal molecule (HbA). Using these techniques to define the phenotype at a molecular level, one defines a codominant trait because both HbA and HbS are expressed in the heterozygote. Thus, phenotypes relate to the three possible genotypes at this locus as codominant, autosomal dominant, or autosomal recessive, depending on the definition of the phenotype. Of course, the individual alleles are either present or absent.

Such simple models of inheritance are largely irrelevant to human behavioral genetics, because most behavioral traits show patterns that are called multifactorial inheritance; their transmission depends on more than one genetic or environmental factor. Usually, there is a clear familial concentration of affected persons, so that genetic transmission can be presumed to be involved, but there may also be environmental factors that operate differently in different individuals (genotype-environment interactions), environmental factors that are correlated with individual differences (genotype-environment correlations), or even familial transmission, called cultural inheritance (Cavalli-Sforza & Feldman, 1981). Multifactorial traits may depend on one gene locus or a few major loci, but be modified in the phenotype by other loci or genetic background that interacts with one or more of the major genes; this effect is called epistasis. Multifactorial traits may also result from many genes that combine in simple, additive fashion to produce the trait; this effect is called polygenic.

Many birth defects and developmental disorders show multifactoral inheritance: cleft lip and palate, pyloric stenosis, juvenile onset diabetes, ankylosing spondylitis, and multiple sclerosis. Some human behavioral disorders that show multifactorial patterns of inheritance, rather than simple Mendelian ratios, are language disorders of stuttering and cluttering, reading disorders, schizophrenia, affective disorders, and Tourette's syndrome, to be described later.

Many investigators have developed techniques for studying multifactorial inheritance, because so many major human disorders show this pattern. Pedigree analysis, the tracing of affected persons through a family of related persons, is used to demonstrate the familial concentration. At present, methods are being developed to include biochemical correlates of the trait, to use genetic markers that are linked with the trait, and to incorporate indices of environmental variables that are related to the development of the disorder in powerful statistical models that can help to clarify the mode of inheritance. These approaches will be discussed in the section on the problems of genetic inference.

Developmental Genetics: From the Gene to the Phenotype

The earlier discussion of protein synthesis indicates that the mechanism of gene expression is a very complex one. But the expression of a gene as a protein molecule is only the first step in determining the phenotype that an organism will have and in realizing the role of a particular gene in that phenotype.

Additional complexities of metabolic interactions and metabolic feedback are determined largely by the ways in which protein molecules interact with other protein molecules, with molecules of other types and with the environment. While the information allowing these interactions is encoded in the DNA, the DNA is not itself involved at these higher levels. It is clear, however, that the realization of the function specified by any segment of DNA (i.e. any gene) is dependent directly on the whole protein synthesis mechanism for the translation of the information into a protein and on the entire metabolism of the cell and the whole organism—a gene cannot express its function in a vacuum. Indeed, not only the biological environment but the physical and social environment required for the organism to develop are necessary for the expression of many phenotypes. There is no controversy over whether genes or environment are more important; both are essential. The development of an organism can only occur through the joint action of genetic information and the necessary environmental factors that allow that information to be expressed.

The relationship of genotype to phenotype in human development is an extremely complicated topic. No simple summary is possible, but we can make three points: (1) different genotypes can, and often do, produce different phenotypes; (2) different genotypes can, and often do, produce phenotypes that are indistinguishable, and (3) the same genotype is often capable of producing more than one phenotype, depending on environmental conditions. As Dobzhansky (1970) has emphasized, the relationship of genotype to phenotype is far more complex than can be learned from study of an isolated locus:

> The process of the development of an organism should not be misinterpreted as a gradual accumulation and superposition of individual contributions of its genes. Actually, the development is a complex network of processes. In these processes the genes play, of course, the leading roles; taken altogether these processes are, however, integrated into harmonious systems capable of being alive. In other words, the genetic material are aggregations of particulate or atomistic genes; the development is a unified network of interrelated events.

Epigenetic Forces

Waddington (1962) has proposed an epigenetic model to describe the development of a genotype into a phenotype. There are four "spaces" in his model, as shown in Figure 9. Each horizontal pathway represents the developmental course of one individual. On the far left is the genotypic space. Each dot represents a different genotype. The second space is the epigenetic or developmental process. The arrows in the center are genotypic pushes on the developing organism, altering the developmental trajectory. The larger, dashed arrows represent the environmental elements that also push and alter the course of the organism's development. In the epigenetic space, therefore, Waddington represents the course of development and the combined effects of genetic programs and environmental influences on the expression of the genotype.

In the third space, five phenotypes are presented as clusters of genotypes. Within each cluster, the different genotypes appear as equivalent phenotypes. Some individuals have been deflected in the epigenetic space to a phenotype different from what would have been expected for their genotype. What is not shown here is that the path through the epigenetic space can be largely independent for each individual. Thus, the same genotype can produce

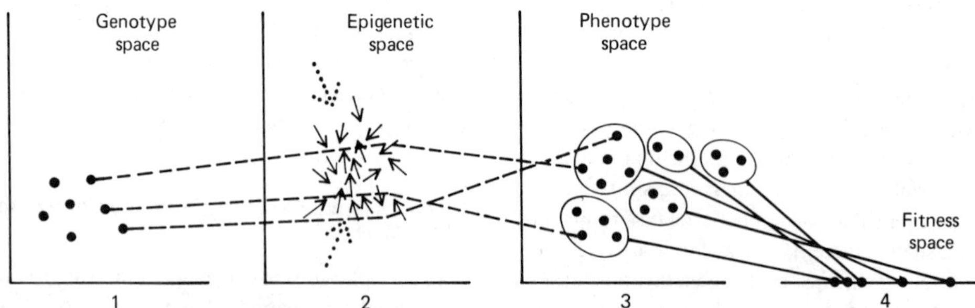

Figure 9. The development of genotypes into phenotypes takes place in an epigenetic space in which environmental forces, from the cellular to the social levels, affect the phenotypic outcomes. There is no one-to-one correspondence of genotypes and phenotypes because each genotype has many possible responses to environmental events. Fitness, or differential reproduction and survival, is a one-dimensional space in which only the number of viable offspring is relevant.

different phenotypes because of different experiences in the epigentic process.

The fourth space represents fitness. It is one-dimensional because fitness is measured only by the differential reproduction and survival of offspring, and the subsequent contribution of an individual to the gene pool of the next generation. Waddington's diagram makes clear the difficulty of predicting either from the genotype to fitness or from fitness to underlying genetic structure in populations. From the genotype to fitness there are indeterminancies in the epigenetic space and in the phenotypic space. It is impossible to know how fit a given genotype will be unless one knows what experiences it will undergo and to which phenotypic class it will belong. From the other direction, from fitness to genetic makeup, it is even more difficult to predict. As Waddington points out, the prediction from fitness to genotype is a one-to-many dimensional mapping. In addition, there is indeterminancy in the spaces that intervene between genotype and fitness, as before.

In sum, the relationship between genotype and phenotype is extremely complicated by the epigenetic process, which is in part internally regulated by the individual's genetic program for development and in part by environmental factors from the cellular to the social levels.

Reaction Range: A Developmental Model

The concept of reaction range refers to the quantitatively different phenotypes that can develop from the same genotype under varying environmental conditions (Gottesman, 1963; Lewontin, 1974). Ginsburg & Laughlin (1971) have used the term genomic repertoire to refer to the potential for development into any one of a number of phenotypes. A given genotype has a specific inherent repertoire or range of reaction. The actual phenotype that develops is achieved through genotypic expression in a set of environments over the entire span of development. It is not correct, however, to say that heredity sets the limits on development while environment determines the extent of development. Both are half-truths because they ignore the constant transaction between genotype and environment during development.

Ginsburg (1968) and his colleague (Ginsburgh & Laughlin, 1966, 1971) have summarized evidence on the genomic repertoires of a number of inbred strains of mice. Since each strain is essentially made up of identical genotypes, strain differences are analogous to individual human differences. The important developmental findings are (1) genotype-environment interactions are frequent, (2) environmental circumstances that will alter the behavioral development of one strain may have no effect on another and an opposite effect on a third, (3) the period during development at which a given effect can be most readily induced by a given environmental circumstance is genotype-specific.

An excellent example of genotype-environment interaction is provied by a study of three species of macaques (Sackett, Ruppenthal, Fahrenbruch, & Holm, 1981). Beginning soon after birth, infant rhesus (*Macaca mulatta*), pigtail (*M. nemistrina*), and crab-eating (*M. fascicularis*) monkeys were reared alone in completely enclosed, sound-attenuated chambers until they were from 6 to 7 months old. After the isolation period, they were tested daily for 1 month on social interaction in a playroom containing toys and normally reared peers. The normal and isolation-reared infants were rated on passive behaviors, nonsocial play, isolate syndrome behaviors, positive social interactions, and on socially elicited fear or withdrawal. The three species of macaques were reliably different in many aspects of behavior when reared in isolation. Rhesus exhibited the classic syndrome of self-destructive and stereotypic behavior, low exploration, and nonpositive social behavior. Pigtail macaques had low levels of isolate syndrome behavior, were highly exploratory, but also had little positive social behavior. Crab-eating macaques had a moderately high degree of isolate syndrome behavior, coupled with high exploration and positive social behavior.

All three species of macaques have similar social organization and close association between mothers and infants. But only the rhesus exhibited the devastating pattern so well described by Harlow and his colleagues, of low social interaction, low exploration, high fear, and isolate syndrome behavior. The high exploratory behavior of the pigtail was coupled with low social interaction, and the high isolate syndrome behavior of the crab-eaters was associated with nearly normal levels of social interaction.

> All this suggests that an adequate explanation of social deprivation rearing effects in primates must involve at least two relatively independent mechanisms. One mechanism must be compatible with genotypic differences in risk for developing self-directed and stereotyped behaviors during the rearing period. The other must be compatible with genotypic differences in the amount or quality of social and nonsocial experience during infancy that is necessary to maintain exploratory behaviors and to initiate and maintain species-typical social behavior during post-

rearing development. (Sackett et al., 1981, pp. 10–11)

The genotypic differences in this study are species differences among three closely related groups of monkeys. Within each species there are individual genotypic differences that can also affect the vulnerability of the organism to detrimental experiences, although Sackett et al. do not describe individual variability in this study. Ginsburg's work on inbred mouse strains, each of which represents a single genotype, illustrates the role of individual genetic variability, whereas Sackett's work describes the average effects of genotypic differences among species faced with the same social deprivation.

There are no general laws of reaction range that can predict *a priori* the development of individuals. Only for certain abnormal genotypes can the reaction range be roughly specified under existing environments. As Hirsch (1971, p. 94) has said,

> The more varied the conditions, the more diverse might be the phenotypes developed from any one genotype. Of course, different genotypes should not be expected to have the same norm of reaction; unfortunately psychology's attention was diverted from appreciating this basic fact of biology by half a century of misguided environmentalism. Just as we see that, except for monozygotes, no two human faces are alike, so we must expect norms of reaction to show genotypic uniqueness. . . . Extreme environmentalists were wrong to hope that one law or set of laws described universal features of modifiability. Extreme hereditarians were wrong to ignore the norm of reaction.

The hypothetical reaction ranges for IQ in Figure 10 are fairly simple. Much more complex reaction ranges can exist as reviewed by Lewontin (1974). Figure 11 shows another hypothetical example in which two different genotypes have opposite reactions to variation in the environment. That such examples can actually occur is illustrated by data of Dobzhansky and Spassky (1944) in which different genotypes in *Drosophila* showed different viabilities as a function of temperature. An important point to note is that, if the genotypes exist in a population in appropriate frequencies, opposite reaction norms will effectively cancel out and the mean of the population remains constant as the environment changes, as illustrated by the dashed lines in the figure. The amount of difference in phenotype caused by these genetic differences is a function of the mean and breadth of environments encountered. In Environment 1 the genotypes have little effect on phenotype while in Environment 2 the effect is quite striking (see Figure 11).

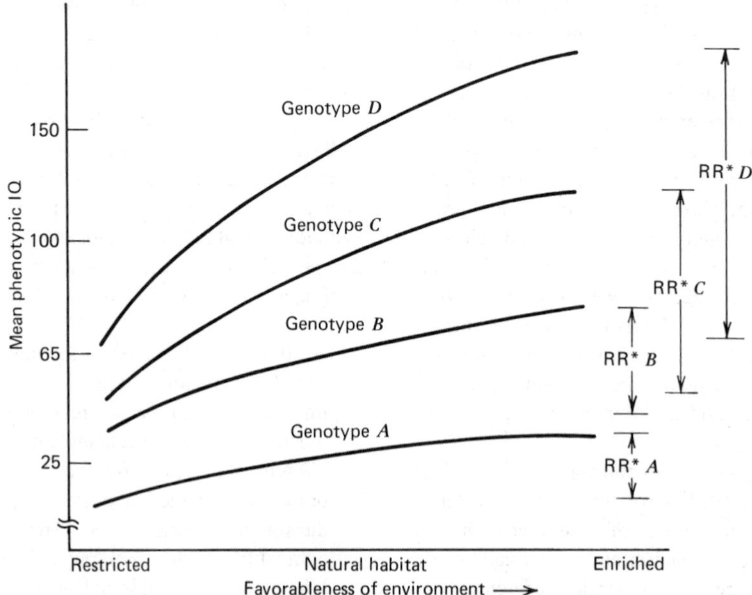

Figure 10. A hypothetical set of reaction ranges of intellectual development of several genotypes under environmental conditions that range from poor to good. Although each genotype responds favorably to improved environments, some are more responsive to environmental deprivation and enrichment than others. (From Gottesman, 1963.)

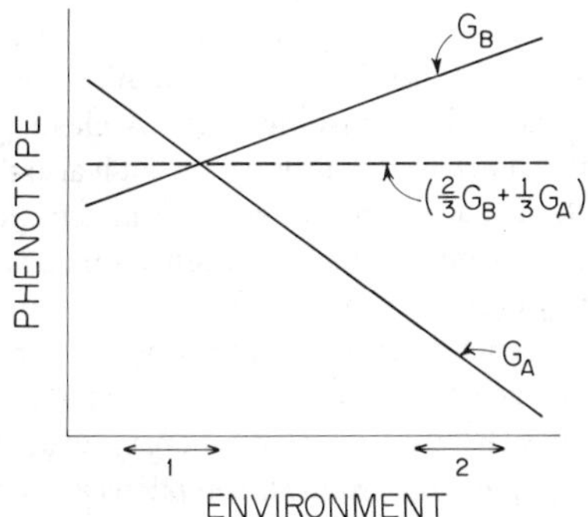

Figure 11. A hypothetical reaction range. The two different genotypes react in opposite directions to changes in the environment. The dashed line illustrates a population composed of a mixture of the two genotypes; it would show no change in the mean phenotype with a change in environmental mean. However, as the phenotypes of the two genotypes diverged, the population variance would increase dramatically.

Two human genetic diseases serve as clear examples of the dependence of the phenotype on both the genotype and the environment. Phenylketonuria (PKU) is a well-known genetic disease that, if untreated, results in irreversable mental retardation. This genetic disorder is the result of the complete absence of a particular enzyme, phenylalanine hydroxylase, that converts phenalanine, one of the amino acids in proteins, into tyrosine, thereby eliminating excesses of phenylalanine. In the absence of this enzyme excess phenylalanine from protein in the diet is not utilized and accumulates in the body. With the higher concentration, spillover into other degradative pathways results in an excess of phenylketones and other chemicals normally present only in minute quantities. These products are toxic to the development and growth of the central nervous system. Their high concentrations in children with untreated PKU result in reduced brain development and irreversable mental retardation.

The treatment for PKU is simple—almost completely eliminating the intake of phenylalanine. Dietary management of these patients is reasonably complex but the idea is simple and it works. With sufficiently reduced dietary intake there is no excess of phenylalanine, the toxic byproducts do not accumulate, and the brain appears to develop nearly normally. Thus, an alteration in the environment can cause a marked alteration in the phenotypic consequences of a genetic defect. PKU individuals still have the genetic defect and the primary abnormality, absent phenylalanine hydroxylase, but the most serious phenotypic consequence has been averted.

Interestingly, PKU also provides an example of environmental input mimicking a genetic defect. The treatment for PKU has existed long enough that there are now sexually mature individuals with PKU who are otherwise quite normal. Because the mature central nervous system appears quite resistant to the toxic effects resulting from high phenylalanine concentrations, these individuals do not need to follow the strict low phenylalanine diet. However, a fetus growing in the uterus of a PKU female may be born with severe mental retardation even though the fetus has normal phenylalanine hydroxlase inherited from the father. If the mother is not on a low phenylalanine diet, the high concentration of toxic substances swamps the circulation of the fetus and causes abnormal neurological development *in utero*. The child is born with mental retardation resulting from PKU even though the child does not have PKU.

Another example of environmental modification of symptoms is propionic acidemia caused by deficiency of the enzyme propionyl-CoA-carboxylase (PCC). This defect arises from the inability to break down other components of protein. The consequent accumulation of toxic products results in severe mental retardation, seizures, and often death in the first few months to years of life. Though no completely effective treatment is known for all cases, there are individuals who respond quite well to a low-protein diet. Since the average diet contains much more protein than is necessary for normal growth and development, much of the protein eaten is metabolized for energy and other uses. By reducing total protein intake to only the amount required for normal growth and development, the consequences of PCC deficiency are greatly diminished (Brandt, Hsia, Clement, & Provence, 1972).

Untreated autosomal recessive enzyme deficiencies, such as PCC deficiency, have been thought always to result in some degree of clinical abnormality, though the degree of impairment could differ. In one large family PCC deficiency showed a great variability in clinical expression prior to diagnosis and medical intervention (Kidd, Wolf, Hsia, & Kidd, 1980). A brother and sister with comparable enzyme deficiency exhibited markedly different clinical courses; the brother had classical features of severe propionic acidemia, with seizures and mental retardation, while his older sister remained asymptomatic. The sister had had three mild episodes of seizure in the first 13 months of life but had received no therapy. At three years of age she spontaneously restricted her protein intake and, fortunately, her dietary preferences were respected by her parents. When the enzyme deficiency was diagnosed at the age of 8, her growth was average and her verbal and performance scores were average. Four years later, she continued to be asymptomatic and on a medically unrestricted protein diet, because her food preferences result in a low normal protein intake.

From the foregoing discussion it should be clear that saying that genes are relevant to differences among individuals is not a linear determinism. As a final example, we note that genetic differences among individuals are very important in determining differences in susceptibility to various infectious diseases—for example, not everyone is equally susceptible to a given virus. Apart from whether or not an individual has had a prior virus infection and, hence, has the antibodies, genetic differences exist for susceptibility to infection. Nonetheless, viral infections are not called genetic diseases because, clearly, exposure to the virus is much more important than slight differences in susceptibility. In such a framework the genetics of a behavioral trait must be approached considering that both genetic and nongenetic factors are important. Their relative magnitudes and the ways in which they interact are then the object of study.

Distributions of Genes in Populations

Patterns of Genetic Similarity Among Human Ethnic Groups

Physical anthropologists have invested great efforts over the last decades describing variation in the human species. It is quite clear that there are major differences that are often concentrated in groups. Though extensive efforts have been made to define races in humans, no classification scheme has been completely satisfactory (Dobzhansky, 1962). The difficulty stems in part from the fact that the race concept does not fit the reality of human evolution. By any classification yet devised there are populations that are intermediate between groups or for some other reason difficult to classify. Thinking of human races or "ethnic groups" may be a useful way of conceptualizing the variation in the species but the groups do not exist as discrete entities. The human species shows nearly continuous variation across the two-dimensional surface of the earth. We can only consider the *relative* similarities and differences of groups sampled from this distribution.

Students of human evolution are interested in knowing how the existing variation in our species arose in time. Ideally, we want to know both the origin of the genetic relationships and the changes that have occurred through time. Unfortunately, history is all too often a poor indicator of genetic relationships (though in some cases it can be informative) and covers only a tiny fraction of time in a true evolutionary sense. Most of the variation within the species arose in prehistoric times. Archeology has provided much useful information but it also tells all too little about the genetic relationships of populations to each other. The best information on the evolutionary origins of human variation may well be the existing genetic variations among populations. The observed genetic relationships among ethnic groups can be used to postdict the evolutionary relationships among populations. Some assumptions are required to make these inferences and, of course, there are complications. Not only is there gene flow between adjacent populations, but major migrations have taken place and continue to take place. These long-scale migrations create new hybrid populations. Thus, it may be impossible to quantify genetic relationships among human groups in a purely two-dimensional space. The third dimension of time causes rearrangements and distortions of the space.

Still, the existing variation represents the net evolutionary divergence among human populations. Thus, we wish to study the genetic relationships among these groups. There are two ways of looking at the genotype and at differences among population genotypes. The genotypes can be assessed directly via known polymorphisms or indirectly by physical traits that are controlled by the genotype. Thus, comparisons among human ethnic groups can be based on overall phenotypic similarity—such as skin color, physical traits, and so on—or on genetic similarity measured as gene frequency similarities. The two types of data generally give similar answers for comparison among populations that belong to the same major ethnic group or large geographic area—Africa, Europe, or Eastern Asia, for example. However, when comparing populations from different major groups (or areas) the different types of data give results that differ in some fundamental relationships. (Cavalli-Sforza & Bodmer, 1971; Howells, 1973; Kidd, 1973).

In a gene frequency analysis, Caucasians are closer to Africans, and the Southwest Pacific populations are closer to American Indians. The basic dichotomy separates Western populations from Eastern populations. This contrasts with the results using craniometric or other anthropometric data; those analyses show Africans closest to the Southwest Pacific populations and Caucasians closest to American Indians, a separation of Northern populations from Southern populations (Kidd, 1973). Guglielmino-Matessi, Gluckman, and Cavalli-Sforza (1979) found that the anthropometric data were highly correlated with a composite index of climate while the gene frequency data were not. Their analysis shows that natural selection can affect the genome quite "selectively." Relationships inferred from gene frequency data are closer to the historical and net genetic relationships of the populations.

Some similarities among contemporary populations are due to one single outward radiation and some are due to a cline. A cline is a gradation in adaptation resulting from natural selection in different environmental niches. For example, skin color varies from light pigmentation in more northern climates to darker in more equatorial climates, where more pigment provides greater protection from ultraviolet radiation from the sun. There is a cline of skin color from north to near the equator. Body types also vary from more compact to more linear from colder to warmer climates. Adjacent populations are also more likely to interbreed, so that some of the gradation of a cline can be due to the amount of interbreeding in the series overlapping breeding groups. A cline is influenced by natural selection, by gene flow between adjacent populations, and by genetic drift.

Distributions of Genes Within a Population

The allele frequency is often used to describe the extensive variation that exists among individuals within a population. The allele frequency characterizes the total breeding population for the locus. In addition, the frequencies of the genotypes can, with simple assumptions, be determined directly from the allele frequency. When mating is at random, the frequency of individuals homozygous for any allele is simply the square of the allele frequency, that is, the probability that two genes pulled at random from the population to form a zygote are identical alleles. So long as mating is random among individuals and loci are unlinked, this simple probability can be extended to genotypes of any sort of any number of loci. Thus, allele frequencies are a simple summary that can give a good general indication of the genotypes present in the population and their frequencies.

Allele frequency changes can also be used as a simple summary of evolution. Selection operates on individuals but in the presence of random mating the most immediate effect is that the allele frequencies are altered in the next generation. Changes in allele frequencies indicate changes in genotype frequencies.

Many different types of selection can exist and their effects on the genotypes in subsequent generations can be predicted mathematically. Many simple models have been studied in considerable detail. Books about population genetics, such as Bodmer and Cavalli-Sforza (1976), Cavalli-Sforza and Bodmer (1971), Hartl (1978), and Spiess (1977), give the mathematical derivations and cite examples for simple selection affecting genotypes determined by one locus. In humans, one of the best known examples at a locus that is polymorphic is the hemoglobin S (HbS) polymorphism in which the *AS* heterozygote is more resistant to malaria than is the normal *AA* homozygote. Selection operates to increase the frequency of the gene for HbS up to between from 10% to 15% even though the homozygous *SS* individual has sickle-cell anemia and very low fitness. If the gene frequency were higher than this range, however, the proportionately greater frequency of homozygotes for HbS would result in selection against the *S* allele. Thus, in the presence of malaria the effect of natural selection is to maintain this polymorphism in a balanced state—both homozygotes are less fit than the heterozygote.

The mathematical formulations of population genetics also are helpful for indicating the speed with which natural selection can change the population. A simple example is the effect of natural selection on HbS in populations no longer subjected to malaria. In the U.S. black population the frequency of the *S* allele is about 5%. That predicts that about ¼ of 1% of the U.S. black population has sickle cell anemia ($.05 \times .05 = .0025$). Because selection only operates on those homozygotes, it is not very effective when there is such a low frequency of homozygotes; most of the HbS genes are present in heterozygotes. Nonetheless, unless there is a remarkable medical breakthrough in treatment of sickle cell anemia, selection will relentlessly eliminate HbS alleles and slowly decrease the frequency. The frequency will approach zero in an asymptotic fashion but it is easy to calculate how long it will take for the frequency to be reduced from 5% to 1% assuming only selection is operating. Using formulae found in most population genetics books, approximately 80 generations are required for this change in the worst case of sickle cell patients never having children. At roughly 25 years per generation in the U.S. population, this translates into 2000 years.

The finding of very large numbers of polymorphisms in most species, including humans, has spurred population geneticists to formulate theories explaining their presence. Two schools of thought have developed: one favors the maintenance of these polymorphisms by some form of natural selection; the other considers most of the variation that is observed to be in effect selectively neutral with no differential fitness among the various genotypes. As discussed by Lewontin (1974a, 1974b) the argument is very academic in the most pejorative sense of that word because both schools can adequately explain the existing data and virtually no information short of direct measurement of fitness of each genotype can allow clear discrimination between the two hypotheses.

As the phenotype becomes more distantly related to any single polymorphic locus, the effect of selection on the allele frequencies at that locus is diminished. Depending on the complexities of the determination of varying phenotype, it may be extremely difficult to predict the effects on the alleles of selection on the phenotype. This point was made earlier in the context of discussing the epigenetic space hypothesized by Waddington (1962).

The most common assumption in population genetics is that individuals mate at random with respect to their genetic differences. In considering behavioral phenotypes that is distinctly untrue. There is quite clear mating preference for similarity in height between spouses and there is strong evidence for assortative mating on the basis of intelligence (Johnson, Ahern, & Cole, 1980). Assortative mating is defined as a population parameter representing the degree to which choice of spouse in a population is nonrandom. It is still possible for a large proportion of the matings to be between individuals that are not particularly similar so long as more pairs are similar than would be expected by chance alone. The effect of assortative mating on a population is to increase the variance in the population for the particular trait. If the trait in question is a continuously distributed quantiative trait, such as height and IQ, the effect will be a slightly broader distribution with the amount of increased variance a function of the degree of assortative mating. Assortative mating is not related to fitness. Individuals with an average value for the trait prefer to mate with individuals with an average value while those below average prefer mates that are also below average. Thus, there is no overall tendency for the mean to shift under assortative mating.

Population genetics also makes predictions for quantitative traits that are determined by the effects of many genes as well as by environmental variation: the offspring of any given couple will tend to be, on average, closer to the mean of the population than are the parents. This regression toward the mean is a function of three main factors: (1) the degree to which environmental factors are important in varying the quantitative trait, (2) the degree to which genetic segregation produces new genetic combinations, and (3) the degree to which genotypes do not have strictly additive effects in determining the phenotype.

Developmental Examples

In this section we will summarize what is known about genetic control of development of the nervous system and of behavior, but we will not limit ourselves to these areas only. Developmental genetics is a broad area that is only beginning to be understood. Each system that has been studied has been complex and difficult to elucidate. Each system is unique and no general model has emerged yet to guide research. Part of the reason for the lack of an overall model is the complexity of reality. The actual biochemical and developmental pathways for genetic influences on human behavior are numerous and complex, and the following examples serve as models for their complexity.

Human Hemoglobin

Though not directly related to behavior, human hemoglobin is the archetypal example of human developmental genetics. Hemoglobin is not just one molecule, but a succession of different, though related, molecules produced at different times during development (Figure 12). Starting very early in prenatal development an embryonic hemoglobin is produced. At about 8 weeks of gestation and lasting until birth, two fetal hemoglobins are produced. These are nearly identical to each other and similar to the embryonic hemoglobin. Soon after the early fetus starts producing fetal hemoglobins, the embryonic hemoglobin stops being produced. A very clear developmental switch occurs in the production of hemoglobins. Shortly before birth a second switch occurs with initation of synthesis of adult hemoglobins and the "cessation" of production of fetal hemoglobins. By about the sixth month after birth two adult hemoglobins account for over 99% of the hemoglobins with small amounts (< 1%) of fetal hemoglobin often present. The two adult hemoglobins, A and A_2, normally exist in very unequal proportions, ~97% A and ~2% A_2. These two are not as similar to each other as are the two fetal hemoglobins but are more similar than either is to fetal hemoglobin. Normal human development thus involves five different hemoglobins that are produced at different ages.

The hemoglobin molecule is not the product of one single gene. Rather, it is a molecule that is composed of four polypeptide chains, two each of two

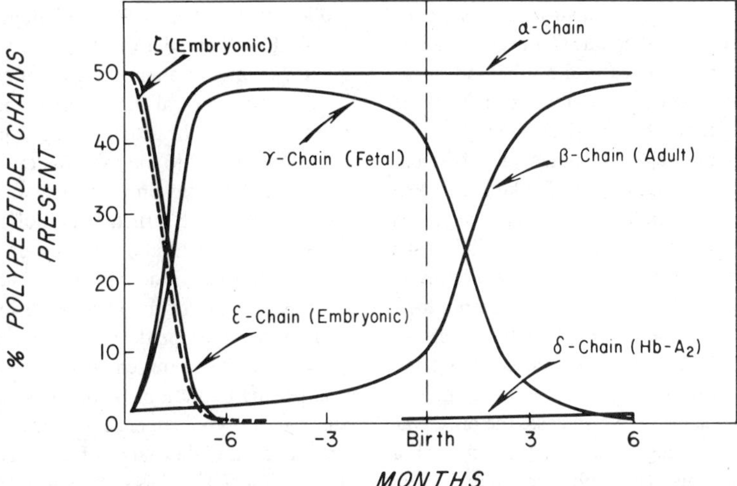

Figure 12. The developmental sequence of human hemoglobins. The left half of the diagram covers the period from conception to birth. The embryonic hemoglobins, zeta and epsilon, disappear by about the third month. Alpha and gamma chains are produced in equal quantities and combine to form fetal hemoglobin starting sometime before the second month. In the third trimester fewer gamma chains are synthesized and more beta chains are synthesized. The trend continues, essentially unaffected by birth itself, so that by six months after birth, only adult hemoglobin, which is made of equal numbers of alpha and beta chains, is the predominant hemoglobin. Tiny amounts of fetal hemoglobin continue to be synthesized throughout adult life. Delta chains, which combine with alpha chains to produce the minor adult hemoglobin a_2, are synthesized from late fetal life throughout adult life. (Reproduced with permission from Bunn, Forget, & Ranney, 1977.)

different types, called alpha (α) and beta (β). The α and β chains have much of their amino acid sequence in common, showing that they evolved from a duplication of an ancestral gene. The duplication is thought to have occurred roughly 500 million years ago, early in vertebrate evolution, since most vertebrates have two hemoglobin chains related to the human α and β (Dayhoff, 1972).

The developmental shifts observed in hemoglobin are the result of shifts in the production of types of chains. There are two different chains in the α-chain family—zeta (ζ) and α. There are five different chains in the β-chain family—epsilon (ϵ), two gamma chains, ($^A\gamma$, $^G\gamma$), delta (δ), and β itself. These would give rise to 10 different types of hemoglobin if both α-like chains could combine with all five β-like chains. Not all occur in the developmental sequence of hemoglobins as a result of the turning on and turning off of the genes sequentially. The ζ locus and the ϵ locus are turned on in the production of embryonic hemoglobin. The developmental shift from embryonic hemoglobin to fetal hemoglobins is caused by a shift from the production of ζ chains to α chains and from production of ϵ chains to γ chains. Thus, in normal development the combinations of ζ with the γ chains is not possible except during a very brief transition phase. The coordinated transition from functioning of the ζ and ϵ loci to functioning of the α and γ loci is an important developmental phenomenon and a model for developmental changes in general. The mechanism is not understood, but the shift shows a remarkable similarity in timing with the disappearance of the yolk sac (Vogel & Motulsky, 1979). Through the rest of life α chains continue to be produced. The second developmental shift involves only β-like loci; shortly before birth the hemoglobin production shifts from active synthesis of the two γ chains to synthesis of β and δ chains. Again two loci are inactivated and two loci are activated in a coordinate fashion.

Our understanding of the molecular structure and developmental genetics of the loci controlling human hemoglobins is more advanced than that any other genetic system. These genes have been objects of study for over 50 years because of the very large number of disorders of hemoglobin synthesis in humans (Bank, Mears, & Ramirez, 1980; Forget, 1979). The existence of numerous different deleterious mutants as well as variants with selective advantage in the presence of malaria has provided the raw material for extensive genetic studies. Since the mid 1970s these have exploited the newer recombinant DNA technologies. The convenient packaging of large quantities of globin mRNA in readily accessible corpuscles made these genes obvious and easy early candidates for gene cloning. Added incentive was provided by the many developmental and genetic questions that had been asked about these most important genes in the lifeblood of the species. Most of these questions remain unanswered at this early stage, but the surprises abound.

Each of the globin-chain loci thus far studied has two intervening sequences. In the β-like globin loci they occur in exactly the same places in the chains and are approximately the same length. The α-like globin loci also have the intervening sequences in places analogous to those of the β-like globin loci. The precise DNA sequences of the intervening sequences show much more divergence among the various loci than do the sequences in the regions coding for amino acids. Nevertheless, the preservation of these intervening sequences through such a long evolutionary history emphasizes their importance for normal gene functioning.

Though the α-chain family and the β-chain family of genes are not linked, the structural loci for the chains within each family are closely linked. The close clustering into two globin-chain domains reflects the more recent gene duplication but probably has functional significance in development as well (Proudfoot et al., 1980). Within each of the globin-gene clusters there is at least one pair of adjacent loci that apparently have recent, common origin and coordinate expression in development. In the α-chain cluster there are two α-chain loci, both of which function in normal individuals and produce the same amino acid sequence. The nucleotide sequences in their intervening and flanking regions are nearly identical. Also, in the α-chain cluster is a pair of two ζ-chain loci but it is not as clear that both function equally. In the β-like globin domain there are also two pairs of loci. The two γ loci are virtually identical to one another throughout their coding sequences, their intervening sequences, and their flanking sequences (Slightom, Blechl, & Smithies, 1980); the primary observable difference is one amino acid difference in the coding sequence. In contrast, the δ and β loci are highly homologous in their sequences coding for amino acids but have diverged considerably in their intervening and flanking sequences. In terms of function each of the human globin loci appears to be an individual transcription unit. With the exception of the δ-globin gene, the various loci are apparently transcribed with roughly equal efficiency when they are active.

Interesting developmental findings are the observations that the loci within each domain are expressed through development in the order in which they are arranged in the chromosome. Another important observation based on many of the hemoglobinopathies that are the result of gene deletions is the finding that control of the developmental sequence of globin-chain production can be affected by deletions several thousands of nucleotide base pairs away from the actual coding sequences. This is being interpreted to indicate that these domains are functional domains and that deletions within them alter chromosome structure and affect the normal pattern of differential expression of the loci. Such domains of related loci may be the normal state for the organization of the genome of higher animals.

In addition to the developmental implications in the study of the globin-chain domains there has been a surprising evolutionary finding—vestigial genes. Since the DNA sequence is largely known for a stretch of many thousands of base pairs, it has been possible to identify DNA sequences that correspond to globin-chain sequences but produce no product. In the current terminology these are being referred to as pseudogenes but *relic* and *vestigial* seem more appropriate qualifiers. Two relics have been identified in the β-chain region but have not yet been extensively characterized in man. Extensive characterization in rabbit and mouse of the analogus (homologus?) sequences shows that they are incapable of leading to a functional polypeptide sequence because of small deletions and other alterations (Leder, Hansen, Konkel, Leder, Nishioka, & Talkington, 1980). However, they maintain a sequence homology with the functioning loci of from 75% to 80%. These are probably the remnants of past gene duplication and subsequent mutational/evolutionary divergence. That may not be a sufficient explanation as witnessed by their frequent occurrence and the observance that all of the mammalian globin-gene clusters studied to date have at least one such sequence between the early (embryonic or fetal) functional loci and the loci for the adult chains. Thus, there may be a functional role as yet unidentified for these sequences.

It is interesting to note that theories on evolution by gene duplication with subsequent divergence of one copy outside the constraint of natural selection have been supported by the DNA sequence findings in mammalian globin-chain domains. Leder and his colleagues (1980) discussed the evolutionary implications of the findings in the mouse. They have also speculated on the significance of the pseudogenes, although to what degree the vestigial sequences could in the future become active genes for very different proteins is uncertain. We now know that specific coding sequences at the beginning and end of each of the intervening sequences are also essential to function, as are the intervening sequences themselves. Thus, more than just the coding sequence is necessary for a gene to function. However, the DNA sequence homology between these vestigial sequences and the nearby functional loci provides opportunity for unequal crossing over and insertion of part of the relic's divergent sequence into the corresponding coding sequence of a functional gene. Thus, a new globin gene could arise in a one-step event but show considerable amino acid sequence difference from the existing globin chains. While such a protein may serve no value as a globin chain, such events may be the raw material for rapid and extensive innovative evolutionary change in response to novel selective pressures.

The story of hemoglobins in evolution and development is more complete than for any behavioral phenotype so far described. To what degree hemoglobins can serve as a model for other loci, including those relevant to behavioral characteristics, remains to be seen. The developmental switches in the production of the various hemoglobins and the presence of various allelic forms are likely models for behavioral development. The presence of vestigial information in the DNA with no present product is a provocative idea that could link us to our primate past.

Genetic Control of Neurological Development

A major advance in mammalian developmental genetics was the development of techniques for combining cells of two different genotypes into a single mouse (Mintz, 1962, 1965; Tarkowski, 1961). Using such chimeric animals, it is often possible to examine whether the expression of a given genotype is inherent to the affected cell(s) or whether the original site of gene action is the differentiated cells distinct from those ultimately expressing the phenotype. These techniques are beginning to be applied to the study of development and differentiation of the central nervous system. The results from even the few initial studies are beginning to eliminate the diverse developmental mechanisms that occur between gene and behavior phenotype.

Production of chimeric animals is still quite a technical art, but the concept is simple. Briefly, embryos at about the 8-cell stage of development (two days after mating) are flushed from the oviduct of female animals. The extracellular envelopes are removed and two embryos from different females, usually of different strains, are placed in contact in culture medium and incubated. By the following day the cells have usually mixed together to form a double-sized morula and then blastocyst. These blastocysts are then surgically transplanted into uteruses of females that are pseudopregnant. Development then occurs normally and the chimeras are born as normal individuals, except that some fraction of their cells are derived from one set of parents and the rest are derived from a completely different set of parents. If those sets of parents differed in coat color, the chimeric individual will have patches of the two types of coat color. If the two early embryos differed for some biochemical variant that can be histologically detected, it is possible to identify individual cells as to their genetic origin.

The results of the first neurologic mutation to be investigated with mouse chimeras have been reviewed by LaVail and Mullen (1976). These studies by several different groups involve the retinal degeneration mutation that in mice leads to the death of the developing photoreceptor cells between 10 and 20 days after birth. In chimeras involving cells homozygous for retinal degeneration and cells that are homozygous normal, the neural retina contained patches of normal tissue and patches in which the photoreceptors had completely degenerated. These chimeras also differed at the albino locus so that the genotype of the pigment epithelium overlying the photoreceptors could be determined in sectioned material. In the normal eye the physiology of the photoreceptor is dependent on the pigment epithelium but in the chimeras the state of the photoreceptors, normal or degenerated, was unrelated to the genotype of those pigment epithelial cells. These experimental results indicate that the retinal degeneration genotype expresses itself in each individual photoreceptor cell and that the genotype of the adjacent pigment epithelial cell is not important in determining whether or not the photoreceptor cell degenerates.

The results for a phenotypically similar trait in rat, retinal dystrophy, are distinctly different from those in the mouse (Mullen & LaVail, 1976). In rat chimeras the degeneration of the photoreceptor cells was found only in those cells adjacent to mutant pigment epithelium. Both mutant and normal photoreceptor cells survived, depending on their position. Thus, this mutant in the rat apparently acts in the individual pigment epithelial cell and causes degeneration of the adjacent photoreceptor cells but not of the pigment epithelial cell itself. The contrast between these two mechanisms for the same ultimate phenotypic effect illustrates both the complexity of development and one way in which a quite specific disorder (in this case photoreceptor degeneration) can be genetically heterogeneous.

Chimeric mice have recently been used to examine in greater detail the development of the cerebellum. Herrup and Mullen (1979) studied chimeras for the mutant straggerer. Staggerer homozygotes have a greatly reduced cerebellum with abnormal Purkinje cells. In the chimeras, the Purkinje cells that were normal in size and position had the homozygous normal genotype at the staggerer locus. The abnormal Purkinje cells had the staggerer genotype. Thus, the several Purkinje cell defects in this mutant appear to be expressions intrinsic to the affected cell. Neither the existence of normal cells adjacent nor the overall physiology of a largely normal mouse had any effect on the expression of the mutant in the homozygous Purkinje cells. Very similar findings have been found for Purkinje cell degeneration, a different mutant in which virtually all Purkinje cells degenerate between 30 and 40 days after birth (see Mullen & Herrup, 1978, for review).

A quite different result was found for the mutant reeler in which cells do not degenerate but are abnormally placed. Mullen and Sidman (cited in Mullen and Herrup, 1979) produced several chimeras of homozygous reeler and homozygous normal cells. In the chimeras many genetically reeler Purkinje cells occur in normal position. Genetically normal cells also occurred in normal positions. The aberrantly positioned Purkinje cells (i.e., the reeler phenotype) were also a mixture of the two cell types. Thus, the cells appear to be positioned in the cerebellum by extrinsic instructions, though the precise nature of those and the specific cells involved are not yet understood. It does appear, however, that each cell is being positioned individually, depending on whether or not it receives normal or "reeler" instructions from some specific cell contracts.

Genetic Control of the Anatomic Structure and Number of Individual Neurons

For over 100 years it has been recognized that the nervous systems of lower organisms could show considerable variation among individuals (Lubbock, 1858). The number of neurons involved in any structure can vary as can the morphology of those neurons. Recent work in experimental organisms has convincingly demonstrated that this variation in neuron number and morphology is largely under genetic control. One of the best demonstrations is the work by Goodman (summarized in Goodman, 1979) on some neurons in grasshoppers that have a sufficiently specific location and morphology that they are easily recognizable. In addition to the finding that the differences among individual grasshoppers in the number and morphology of these particular cells is largely under genetic control, one of the intriguing surprises was the demonstration that the amount and specific type of nongenetic variation is also under genetic control.

The genetic "trick" used by Goodman is the creation of isogenic grasshopper lines. In this case *isogenic* means that all individuals within a line are, to the best of our knowledge, identically homozygous at all loci. Thus, the individual animals can be thought to represent a clone in which the genome is held constant among individuals. Such a grasshopper clone is analogous to a line of *highly* inbred mice except that in these grasshoppers a line of completely inbred animals can be obtained in only two generations. The particular means used is the exploitation of parthenogenetic reproduction for two consecutive generations—grasshoppers of the genus *Schistocerca* can be induced in the laboratory to reproduce from unfertilized eggs. Each individual produced parthenogenetically is homozygous at all loci. After only one generation of parthenogenesis, the siblings are not identical because they result from different meiotic events. However, a single female from parthenogenetic reproduction will be completely homozygous and will only be able to produce a single type of gamete. Therefore, a second generation of parthenogenetic reproduction from a single female produces offspring that are all genetically identical to each other and to their mother—each female will produce a clone identical to herself. These different clones can then be used to compare variation with clones and between clones. This procedure provides a method for studying questions of the role the genome plays in the variation observed in the natural population and the degree to which the system is developmentally controlled by the genome.

Goodman has collected data on variation in the number and morphology of identified neurons both within each of several isogenic groups and among isogenic groups. By definition the identified neurons show relatively little variation in number and morphology among individuals in the species, but some differences are seen. For example, the parental strain of grasshoppers showed both occasional absence of a particular neuron as well as occasional presence of that neuron in two copies. In general, the isogenic groups showed less variation than the parental strain, but each isogenic strain had its own pattern of variation. For example, in one experiment a particular neuron that occasionally occurred duplicated in the parental strain was rarely or never duplicated in some isogenic groups but frequently duplicated in one other isogenic group. Since all individuals in each isogenic group have the same genotype, those duplications occur or do not occur during development as a function of nongenetic variation. Since the rearing conditions were controlled within and among isogenic groups, the conclusion is that the genotype determines the degree to which nongenetic variation can occur. Several different series of isogenic groups support that general conclusion with data on other neurons and on other types of variation such as morphology and total absence of the neuron.

Extrapolation of these results would suggest that the developmental responsiveness of an organism to environmental variation is itself under genetic control.

Genetic Inference

The approaches to analyses of disorders as qualitative traits are often different from those for normal variation. For disorders the emphasis is on determining the mode of inheritance and identifying any gene-environment interactions. Psychiatric and behavioral disorders in man have many of the same problems for researchers as other complex disorders. Etiologies are either unknown or poorly understood; the specific pathogenesis for each disorder is largely unknown. In many cases no clear single-locus etiology is evidenced by either a specific biochemical defect or a Mendelian pattern in families. Attempts to understand these complex disorders require advancement on several fronts: nosologic, biochemical, and genetic, in particular. Advancement along genetic lines has recently involved the mathematical formulation of genetic models so that family data could be rigorously compared with the various genetic hypotheses.

Genetic models for complex traits serve as hypotheses that relate genes and genotypes, their frequencies in the population, and other relevant variables to the phenotypes and the distributions of phenotypes within the population and within individual families. These models aid in the design of data collection strategies that will optimize the amount of relevant information collected, not only for genetic but also for biochemical and nosologic studies. Thus, using a genetic model for analyzing specific traits can provide considerable insight into the biology of the disorder. However, use of the term *model* makes explicit that these are simplifications and approximations to the biological reality. In choosing a model for the analysis of data on any specific complex trait, one must be guided by existing knowledge of the biology of that trait.

Genetic models make several assumptions that are very likely to be violated by any biological system. Although the degree to which specific assumptions are violated and the effect on any outcome may be trivial, the effect may also be sufficient to invalidate an analysis. Researchers must always be aware of what assumptions are being made. The commonest assumption is that of a Gaussian distribution. Sufficient counterexamples exist to make this reasonable assumption one that ultimately needs confirmation. Most models that involve more than one factor also assume a simple additive effect of those factors at some level. The existence of a Gaussian distribution for the phenotype does not constitute proof that underlying factors combine in a simple additive fashion.

Another parameter for many genetic models is *penetrance*. In the models penetrance is the probability that a specified genotype will develop a specified phenotype. Penetrance values are estimated, within the context of the model, from the frequencies of the phenotypes among many individuals of each relevant genotype. Thus, penetrance includes such diverse elements as background genotype, environmental factors, and random aspects of development. The actual biological mechanism that determines whether or not a given individual with a susceptible genotype does or does not manifest a disorder may be unique to each individual—a peculiar environment in one case, a rare interaction among genes in another, and so on. That does not invalidate the concept of penetrance but limits its biological interpretation.

Two related considerations must always be held as caveats in analyses of behavioral disorders. The definition of the phenotype and genetic-etiologic heterogeneity. Genetic studies of psychiatric disorders—whether twin, family, linkage, or adoption studies—have until recently been hampered by the imprecision and variability in diagnostic criteria. In fact, most variation in results among different studies can be explained by the differences in diagnostic methods. The two major sources of unreliability in diagnosis are (1) the method of collecting information necessary for making diagnostic distinctions and (2) the rules for using the data to classify patients into diagnostic categories. New diagnostic methodologies that take into account these sources of variation and improve reliability have become available (Andreason, Endicott, Spitzer, & Winokur, 1977; Spitzer, Endicott, & Robins, 1978) and are now being applied to genetic studies. Similar problems have arisen in defining other behavioral disorders such as dyslexia; different investigators have defined this disorder differently. The improved definition of diagnostic categories and the greater accuracy with which individuals can be classified will undoubtedly improve future genetic studies. For many disorders greater diagnostic uniformity will be necessary to allow meaningful comparisons among studies.

Genetic models generally assume a single basic etiology with no allowance, other than as an error term, for completely separate genetic mechanisms leading to the same disorder. Pursuit of models with separate genetic systems that independently cause the disorder does not seem profitable. A better course is to strive for data sets in which the disorder is as homogeneous as possible. That can be achieved by (1) defining the phenotype as rigorously as possible, (2) controlling in the sample for possibly relevant nongenetic variables, and (3) collecting data from a population as genetically homogeneous as possible.

Genetic homogeneity is more likely to occur in a sample from the same ethnic group than in a random sample; it is even more likely to occur in an inbred isolate population. Genetic homogeneity is most like to be found in a single pedigree. Matthysse and Kidd (1976) showed that ascertainment through two affected children results in a more homogeneous set of pedigrees, and selection for additional affected individuals among remote relatives has the same effect. If homogeneity is achieved by collecting data from a population with a restricted gene pool (isolate or single pedigree), however, the results obtained may not generalize to the same phenotype in other populations, for which the genetic causes may differ.

One important factor in analyses using genetic models is parameterization. Some of the models may appear to have very few parameters only because some parameters are judged to be less important or to have known fixed values. When more parameters are estimated from a finite amount of data, all the parameter estimates will be less precise. A good strategy to reduce this problem is the use of preliminary analyses to eliminate some parameters from the final analysis, either by fixing their values or by eliminating them altogether.

The importance of hypothesis testing deserves emphasis for two reasons. First, general qualitative agreement of a data set with the predictions of a hypothesis does not constitute a statistical test of that hypothesis. As popularized by Popper (1959), scientific understanding advances primarily by excluding hypotheses. This latter is especially relevant in the case of genetic models since frequently two or more quite different genetic models achieve statistically acceptable fit to a given set of data. Apparently, most common types of family pattern can often be explained by quite divergent hypotheses. Reasonable hypotheses appear to differ primarily in their predictions for very uncommon family constellations, for example, the risk of two normal parents having four affected children (Kidd, 1979). Even very large data sets may be quite deficient in that information that discriminates best among hypotheses. Hence, finding a hypothesis with which the data are compatible cannot be considered as strong support for that hypothesis being true. However, the hypothesis can and should serve as a guide for further research designed to elucidate the genetic and environmental factors, and their interactions, that are relevant to the etiology of the disorder.

Genetic Models for Behavioral Disorders

Genetic studies of human behavioral disorders attempt to identify the specific genetic mechanism underlying the transmission of a disorder within a family. It is well recognized that genetic heterogeneity may exist, as was discussed earlier and that complex genetic mechanisms may be the basis for the disorder. However, it is specifically for disorders, behaviors that fall outside of the normal range, that there is the greatest likelihood that one or a very few loci may be primarily responsible. For most disorders that have been studied to date little, if any, information is available on the specific biochemical or developmental anomalies that underlie the observed symptomatology. The main approach to the genetics of such disorders has been attempting to fit the parameters of specific genetic models to the data. If one model should allow a quite acceptable fit of the population and family data while other models will not allow such a fit, the model that fits the data would be strongly supported as the mechanism underlying the disorder. Unfortunately, this approach has had limited success because for most disorders we do not yet have enough information to decide among alternative models. Examples of the problems will be given in the later section on specific disorders. Here it is sufficient to give a brief overview of some of the models.

Many of the problems and assumptions underlying parameterization of these models have been discussed earlier in this section. Several recent reviews of these models have been published (Elston & Rao, 1978; Kidd, 1981; Kidd & Gladstein, 1980; Pauls & Kidd, 1981). There are models based on one major locus with two alleles or one major locus with three alleles; there are models based on two loci; there are polygenic models in which each locus has an infinitesimal effect; there are models based on a major locus and a polygenic background. The important point is that these models can be formulated in precise mathematical terms so that the frequencies of different types of offspring can be predicted as functions of such underlying parameters as allele frequencies, penetrances, relative magnitude of environmental variation, and so on. Within the context of a specific model it is possible to estimate the proportion of the variance in the population due to genetic variation. For a qualitative trait—affected or unaffected—the total variance is a function of what proportion is affected and what proportion is not. But because the genetic variation differently in different models, the proportion attributable to genes is different for different models. Even when the various models explain the available data equally well, they often predict different heritabilities.

Genetics of Continuous Traits

Evolutionary and developmental principles suggest that variation within the normal range of behavior is very unlikely to be the result of genetic variation at one or even a few loci. Moreover, the near future will not likely see a greater understanding of the developmental phenomena that result in certain behaviors and of the ways in which variation in development gives rise to the normal range of variation in the population. Even more unlikely is an understanding of the development of the specific behavioral profile of a single individual. An attempt to understand biochemical or genetic mechanisms for a significant fraction of normal variation in human behavior seems beyond current capabilities. Of course, individual components of a behavior may be identified and their development specified; an attempt to understand variation in a simpler component seems more likely. Still, we are not optimistic in the near future.

Nonetheless, it is often of great interest and sometimes of importance to know whether variation in a given behavior is to some degree the result of genetic variation among individuals. Heritability can be a useful summary statistic conveying information on this point. It has often been abused and misinterpreted but its basic interpretation is quite clear, if limited.

Heritability

The concept of "heritability" has often been used to estimate the magnitude of the genetic contribution, but this term has semantic and mathematical ambiguities. Although the dictionary definition of heritable as "capable of being inherited" is unobjectionable, the geneticist uses a different and more precise definition. First, the total variation of a trait within a population (measured as the variance) is divided into genetic and environmental components and a component representing their interaction. The genetic component is then further divided into "additive" and "dominance" effects. The distinction between the latter components is best understood by recalling that each individual has two alleles (genes) at each locus, one from each parent. If one form of the gene is pathogenic and the other is not, an individual can be genetically normal at the locus, heterozygous (single dose of the pathogenic allele), or homozygous (double dose). If the effect of a single dose is exactly half that of a double dose, the allele is said to be additive. Otherwise there will be dominance variation as well as additive genetic variation. Thus, *narrow heritability* in the genetic definition is the proportion of a trait's variance in the population that is due to additive genetic variance among individuals. *Broad heritability* is that proportion of a trait's variance in the population that is due to the total of all genetic variances.

The ways in which narrow and broad heritability can be estimated for human traits are described in general texts such as Ehrman and Parsons (1981) and Plomin, DeFries, and McClearn (1980).

Limitations of the Concept of Heritability. In its precise form, the heritability concept has several limitations. First, the heritability of a trait depends on the range of relevant environmental variation in the population being studied. If the population is subjected to a wider range of relevant environments, heritability will decrease; conversely, if the relevant aspects of the environment are held constant, heritability will increase. Furthermore, it frequently happens that the range of environments in the sample studied is not representative of the general population, so the heritability estimate cannot be safely extended to the population as a whole. In fact, drug therapy and psychotherapy can be considered as novel environments so that, logically speaking, one would have to conclude that the heritability of schizophrenia changed when these modalities were introduced.

A second limitation is that heritability requires quantitative definition of a trait. When there are several different ways of defining a trait (as is always the case in psychiatry), there will be several different heritability estimates. Gottesman and Shields (1967) first applied the multifactorial model of Falconer (1965) to schizophrenia and obtained a heritability estimate of about 80%. The attribute to which this heritability applies is not actually a measured trait; it is a hypothetical underlying continuous and normally distributed variable called "liability." One can also calculate heritability for schizophrenia defined as an all-or-none trait (i.e., arbitrary discrete scores for normal and affected individuals). With this definition of the attribute, heritability would be placed at from 20% to 40% for a single-gene model. It is also possible to construct a single-locus model with an underlying continuous liability that is not normally distributed (Kidd 1975; Kidd & Cavalli-Sforza, 1973); heritability of the liability scores is in the range from 0% to 15%. Thus, three different definitions of the trait result in three different heritabilities.

The third problem is that in order to calculate heritability, it is necessary to assume that genetic and environmental components contribute additively to the trait, that they are not correlated with each other (Layzer, 1974; Moran, 1973), and that the rearing environment is not dependent on whether the parents have the trait. When there is "cultural transmission," as in learning a language, the last assumption certainly breaks down.

In summary, heritability does not provide information on etiology, is not able to predict response to novel environments, and often cannot be estimated unambiguously from data. Therefore, it is our conclusion that heritability is not a meaningful concept or statistic for schizophrenia, even though the disease has a clear genetic component. For discontinuous traits, it may be possible to test competing models of genetic transmission. For continuous traits, heritability may be a useful statistic about a defined population, but its limitations are severe.

EXAMPLES OF SPECIFIC BEHAVIORAL DISORDERS

After reviewing the basic principles of evolutionary theory, developmental genetics, and Mendelian genetics, it is appropriate to mention several developmental problems that have clear genetic bases. The goal of this section is to illustrate the many ways in which genes can shape the development of behavioral abnormalities. Some of the pathways are clear, others obscure; some of the biochemical abnormalities are known, others not. In any case, it seems that there are important genetic variants that underlie the disorders. Although the genotypes underlying each disorder are probably heterogeneous, there is reason to suspect that each is primarily a genetic disorder. This is not to say that environmental events have no effect; in fact, some are environmentally controllable. It is to say that the origin of the disorder is probably or certainly in a defective metabolic or developmental pathway.

Mental Retardation

There are more than 150 known gene defects that are associated with mental retardation (Anderson, 1972). There are many ways for development to go awry. At the minimum, we know that many genes must perform properly in the chorus for the performance of normal intelligence to go on stage. Genes that fail to code for enzymes required for normal metabolism (PKU, galactosemia, Lesch-Nyhan Syndrome, and so on) are inborn errors of metabolism, many of which have mental retardation as a feature. Other single gene disorders code for incorrect enzymes, fail to code for proper proteins, or produce indigestible products somewhere in the gene action pathway. The literature in genetics is replete with examples of rare and specific gene defects that lead to mental retardation. But what does this tell us about the development of normal intelligence? Models of gene action gone awry tell us very little about the role of genetic differences in intelligence per se. Perhaps, they serve to confirm the view that genetic variants are present in the human organism, that normal intellectual development is a complex feat of genetic programming, and that genetic variation "counts" in explaining normal variation in intelligence.

Apart from single gene models, one cannot fail to note the extensive literature on chromosomal abnormalities. Having too much or too little chromatin will affect intelligence, always for the worse. Is it surprising that having the species-typical amount of genetic material should make the development of intelligence in the normal range more likely or that having an abnormal amount of chromatin makes mental retardation more likely? Having too many or too few sex chromosomes is not as disastrous to intelligence as too many or too few *autosomes* (the last is evidently lethal as there are no living examples). Intellectual development is adversely affected by the wrong amount of genetic material, which evidently messes up the program for brain development.

Retardation: Nongenetic Causes

There are many environmental events that can intervene in the normal development of the human brain. Beginning in the first trimester of pregnancy, radiation, drugs, and diseases can all exert damaging effects on the fetal brain. When the damage occurs in a period of rapid brain development, the damage is generally extensive and more severe than if the same events occurred later or earlier in development. After birth, major infections of the brain, high fevers, and severe traumas to the head can all result in brain damage and mental retardation.

There is considerable interest in the 1980s in the long-term effects of alcohol consumption by the pregnant woman on the brain development of the fetus. Heavy alcohol consumption has been linked to elevated rates of mental retardation and language disorder in the offspring (Iosub, Fuchs, Bingol, & Gromisch, 1981). Even moderate, social drinking has been shown to result in higher rates of mild mental and language impairments.

Nonetheless, the largest group of mentally retarded persons in the United States is the so-called cultural-familial retarded. Children born to parents who either are retarded themselves or have retarded first-degree relatives are at much greater risk for retardation than children born to parents of normal IQ from families without retarded members. (See the next section.) Although there are clearly genetic reasons for the persistence of familial retardation, there are also differences in the rearing environments of children with retarded and normal IQ parents. The levels of intellectual stimulation and instruction provided by retarded parents can hardly match those provided by normal parents. Among the nearly 300 adopted children studied by Scarr and Weinberg (1976, 1978), no child reared from infancy in the adoptive homes had an IQ score of less than 75, even though several of their natural parents were known to be retarded. Surely, some of the persistence of retarded intellectual development in "cultural-familial" group arises from the poor environments for intellectual development provided by the families of these children.

Genetic Causes of Familial Retardation

It has not been possible to differentiate a major gene model from a polygenic one in the determination of familial mental retardation. The possibility of making such a discrimination depends on the rarity of the trait, and mental retardation is too common to make the choice among models possible (Anderson, 1974). Pauls (1972) studied nearly 6,000 individuals, none of whose parents was retarded, and calculated a heritability estimate for retardation of .62, very close to contemporary estimates for intelligence in general. There was no evidence from the analysis of the family data that major genes accounted for a major part of the retardation.

As Anderson indicated in his review (1974) several features of the literature on mental retardation are relevant to a quantitative genetic theory: (1) the frequency of retardation is higher among males, (2) retarded females are more likely to reproduce than retarded males, and (3) the risk of retardation is higher among the offspring of female than male retardates. In summary, the risk for retardation is highest among the sons of affected mothers and lowest among the daughters of affected fathers. As Anderson indicates, these results are congruent with an hypothesis that familial mental retardation results from multigenes with a sex-modified threshold, which predicts that, when a trait is more common among males, the least risk will be for the female relatives of retarded males. Because more severely affected females than males reproduce, the offspring of retarded mothers have a higher rate of retardation than the offspring of (less severely) retarded males. The females have, on the average, greater "genetic loading" for retardation, so that part of the maternal effect for retardation may be genetic. Another part may be the rearing environment, which is more related to the mother's mental status than the father's.

Familial Versus Clinical Retardation

Although there are overlapping or indistinct boundaries between categories, most workers in the field of retardation hold that there are two broad categories of retarded individuals: the lower grade mental defectives with major chromosome, genetic, or traumatic disabilities, and the higher grade, "familial" retardates, without histories of specific etiology or known defect—just much lower than average IQ and social competencies. Roberts (1952) found that the siblings of children with severe mental retardation are more likely to have normal IQ scores than the siblings of the higher grade mental retardates. If the causes of severe retardation were rare chromosomal anomalies, recessive single gene defects, and environmental events, then most sibs would be unaffected and those affected would have the same severe defect if the cause were genetic. If the higher grade mental retardates are the lower end of the normal curve of polygenic inheritance for intelligence, then their sibs would be likely to have lower IQs as well.

Kamin (1974) questioned the methods of the Roberts' study and ridiculed the results. To reexamine Roberts' hypotheses with new data, Johnson, Ahern, and Johnson (1976) looked at the siblings and parents of 289 retarded probands, reported by Reed and Reed (1965). Forty-seven of the probands had no IQ score or no sibling; data on the 242 remaining probands and their siblings are presented in Table 1.

It is clear from the table that higher grade retardates have more retarded siblings than lower grade retardates ($\chi^2 = 26.22, p < .001$). Of the siblings of retardates with IQs less than 40, 21.5% are retarded. Of the siblings of retardates with IQ scores above 40, 31% are retarded. Also in keeping with Roberts' results the siblings of the higher grade retardates were more likely to be of higher grade retardation themselves. If severely retarded probands had affected sibs, the sibs were likely to be severely retarded themselves.

The authors suggested that the groups, clinical and familial retardates, were not as clearly divisible as is sometimes suggested, for the severely retarded had some higher grade retarded sibs. But the parents of the retardates with IQ scores below 40 were far less likely to be described occupationally as indigent or unskilled than the parents of higher grade retardates, thus, supporting the notion of familial retardation. The percentage of parents who were themselves retarded also differed between the groups: of the severely retarded probands, 12.7% had both parents defective and 28.8 had one parent defective; of the probands with IQ scores > 40, 22.3% has both parents defective and 33.8 per cent had one parent defective. Interestingly, the defective parents of the severely retarded probands were equally divided between mothers and fathers, whereas the mothers of the higher grade retardates were more likely to be retarded than the fathers, in keeping with the polygenic theory developed by Anderson (1974), which posits a greater genetic loading for retarded women than men.

Selected Psychiatric Disorders

A vast literature exists on the genetics of psychiatric disorders but little is known definitively about any of the disorders except that most of the major disorders appear to have a significant, if unspecified, genetic component. A major problem has been a consistent objective diagnosis of the various disorders. American psychiatry has recently made a major advance toward more uniform and objective psychiatric diagnoses with the publication of the third edition of the *Diagnostic and Statistical Manual of Mental Disorders* (American Psychiatric Association, 1980), referred to commonly as DSM III. In addition to providing information on prognosis for each disorder, DSM III contains specific diagnostic criteria for each. These objective criteria take the form of minimal qualifications for making the diagnosis in terms of specific symptoms, their duration, and so on. There are also specific exclusion criteria that are particularly useful in differential diagnosis.

Data with less confusion of different disorders sbould be easier to interpret genetically. But, as the following three examples show, it is still difficult to determine the specific genetic component in any psychiatric disorder.

Schizophrenia

Genetic studies of schizophrenia have been numerous and the published conclusions and opinions range the limit from the disorder being purely genetic (biochemical) to its being purely environmental. Perhaps no other disorder has such a testy literature about its genetics. The debate continues and few definitive conclusions can be reached about the involvement of genes in determining the disorder, or about the specific mode of genetic transmission. Part of the uncertainty in the past may be attributable to ambiguities in the definition of schizophrenia and to variation in the diagnostic criteria applied by different investigators in their individual studies. Certainly, if the trait being studied is defined differently in different studies, it would not be surprising to find different results. Indeed, Kidd and Cavalli-Sforza (1973) showed that the reported frequencies of schizophrenia among relatives (as summarized in Rosenthal, 1970) were significantly heterogeneous.

One of the primary differences in diagnostic criteria has been the distinction between the European tradition of schizophrenia being a severe chronic disorder and the American tradition which encompassed milder, even transitory, illness if the appropriate symptoms were present. With the advent of the DSM III diagnostic criteria, the American definition has become stricter and more like the European one. Schizophrenia shows not only individual and geographic variation in definition, but also temporal variation. In spite of these uncertainties, it is not hopeless to look for a common pattern, since most researchers agree on the diagnosis in the more severe cases and since many studies do consider severe schizophrenia.

Evidence in favor of a genetic component to chronic schizophrenia comes from three sources—twin data, adoption data, and biochemical data. First, the probandwise concordance rates in monozygotic (MZ) twins range from 14% to 79% in 11 different studies reviewed by Rosenthal (1970), but is practically always higher than that in dizygotic (DZ) twins (ranging from 2% to 15%); both are higher than the population prevalence of chronic schizophrenia. A recent review of the literature using more

Table 1. Status of Full Siblings of Reed and Reed Probands by IQ Level of Probands

		Sibs							
IQ Level of Probands	Number of Probands[a]	Dead[b]	Retarded	Normal or of Unknown Ability[c]	Total Number of Sibs	Percentage Retarded of Retarded, Normal, and Unknown Sibs	Number of Probands with One or More Retarded Sibs	Percentage of Probands with Retarded Sibs	Mean IQ of retarded Sibs of Probands[d]
0–19	47	81	34	169	284	16.70	17	36.17	28.12 (N = 19)
20–29	32	57	41	104	202	28.28	14	43.75	34.21 (N = 19)
30–39	31	33	35	127	195	21.60	17	54.84	35.78 (N = 9)
40–49	54	65	77	195	337	28.31	35	64.85	47.56 (N = 18)
50–59	37	40	42	119	201	26.09	21	59.46	58.12 (N = 17)
60–79[e]	41	56	68	106	230	39.08	33	80.49	60.50 (N = 24)
Total	242	332	297	820	1449	26.59	137	56.61	45.32 (N = 106)

[a] Only probands with IQ scores and full siblings are included in this table.
[b] Includes recorded miscarriages, stillbirths, infant and neonatal deaths.
[c] Internal evidence (Reed and Reed, 1965, Table 27, p. 39) indicates that persons of unknown ability nearly always are of normal ability, despite the fact that too little is known about them to state that they are of normal ability.
[d] Only sibs with known IQ scores are included.
[e] Only one proband was above IQ 69. (From Johnson, Aherin & Johnson, 1976).

stringent criteria (O'Rourke, Gottesman, Suarez, Rice, & Reich, 1982) gives a range of from .35 to .68 for MZ and from .09 to .26 for DZ concordances; the general finding still holds. Second, adoption studies of the biological relatives of a schizophrenic proband (Heston, 1966; Kety, Rosenthal, Wender, & Schulsinger, 1968; Kety, Rosenthal, Wender, Schulsinger, & Jacobsen, 1975), and a small number of MZ twins brought up apart, show that cultural transmission or social correlations among relatives are inadequate to explain the elevated frequencies in biological relatives of schizophrenics—some genetic transmission must be involved (see Kessler, 1980, for a recent review). Third, the biochemical findings on platelet MAO in schizophrenics suggest that genetic variation for this enzyme affects susceptibility to schizophrenia as well as to other psychiatric disorders (Wyatt, Potkin, & Murphy, 1979).

The evidence speaks in favor of an important genetic contribution; on the other hand, the role of environmental differences is also important. Not all identical cotwins of schizophrenics are also schizophrenic, so identical genotypes do not always lead to the identical phenotype. Thus, nongenetic events must have some influence: some aspect of development is moderated by nongenetic factors. It is not known whether the relevant developmental events are pre- or postnatal, psychosocial or physical. The intrauterine environment, the nutritional status of the young child, and the number and severity of childhood diseases are all environmental factors that affect the growth and development of the individual and hence are theoretically relevant environmental factors in schizophrenia. For the sake of clarity it should be noted that the environmental factors being considered produce a lifetime liability or susceptibility to the disorder; they are not environmental factors that act to precipitate an episode of illness. Even the relative contribution of genetic and environmental factors has not been assessed because the nature of the genetic contribution is not known (Kidd, 1975; Matthysse & Kidd, 1976).

Part of the uncertainty over the role of genetics stems from the heterogeneity in specific results among the studies. Some sources of that heterogeneity—the variation in severity of the disease and that of the diagnostic criteria employed by different authors—are discussed by Rosenthal (1970) in some detail. In the tabulation of MZ and DZ twins, for instance, the outcome of studies is given by a low and a high figure, usually depending on the severity of the criteria employed, because concordance is apparently higher for more severe cases. Further uncertainties in interpreting the family data arise from the large and significant discrepancy between the frequency of schizophrenia in parents of schizophrenic offspring, ascertained through the offspring (.08% to 11.1%) and the frequency of the disorder in offspring of one schizophrenic parent (7.1% to 19.4%) (O'Rourke et al., 1981). Many reasonable explanations for the difference have been offered in the literature. The most likely is that since severe schizophrenics rarely reproduce (especially the males) it will be rare for any individual to have a schizophrenic parent. Therefore, the higher risk estimates for children of a schizophrenic who does reproduce may be closer to the expected risk.

Though there is uncertainty about the exact frequencies with which schizophrenia occurs in families of schizophrenics, several studies have been done to determine what the mode of inheritance might be. The more recent attempts to fit precise models of inheritance to specific family data or to some consensus figures include Slater's (1958) monogenic hypothesis and Gottesman and Shields' (1967) application of the multifactorial-polygenic model of Falconer (1965). In both cases the model being studied appeared to provide an adequate explanation of the data.

By the early 1970s almost everyone had decided that schizophrenia was a multifactorial-polygenic trait on the basis of the Gottesman and Shields (1967) analysis. Heston (1970) proposed simpler single locus inheritance if the milder schizoid disease were considered. Then, Elston and Campbell (1971) used family data on chronic schizophrenia and showed that a single-major-locus hypothesis could explain those data. They concluded that it was premature to reject the hypothesis that schizophrenia might have a major gene underlying it. Kidd and Cavalli-Sforza (1973) also concluded that a generalized single-major-locus hypothesis was tenable.

In an attempt to circumvent the problem of heterogeneity among different studies and do a more powerful test of genetic hypotheses, Elston, Namboodiri, Spence, & Rainer (1978) used multigenerational segregational analysis on many of the large pedigrees collected by Kallman, generally not previously published by him but used in his studies (e.g., Kallmann, 1946). They concluded with reservations about whether a single locus could be responsible for those data. Matthysse and Kidd (1976) adopted a different strategy and concluded that neither a multifactorial-polygenic or single-major-locus model could adequately account for all of the data. Stewart (1980) and Stewart, Debray, and Caillard (1980) have constructed genetic models for schizophrenia with one, two, and four loci and applied them to data on large pedigrees of 25 schizophrenic probands in Paris. All of the models fit but the exact parameters obtained led them to conclude that the etiology of schizophrenia is heterogeneous or even nongenetic. They decided that a simple one locus model is potentially the most useful working hypothesis.

Two recent analyses have used stricter criteria for selection of published data and more sophisticated statistical procedures to reexamine the simplest single locus and polygenic models. O'Rourke et al. (1981) have reviewed the data and various attempts to find a genetic model for schizophrenia, including some not mentioned in this brief review. They applied the method of Suarez, Rice, and Reich (1978) to the suitable data found in their review and concluded that no possible single-locus, two-allele model could explain the inheritance of schizophrenia considered as a homogeneous disorder. Rao, Morton, Gottesman, and Lew (1981) used path analysis rather than directly estimating variance components to analyze data summarized by Gottesman (1978). They elaborated the statistical approach to allow a transmitted environmental component as well as the genetic component. Although the estimates obtained from the analysis indicated a sizable environmental component that was transmitted—the cultural heritability was about 20% and the genetic heritability was nearly 80%—the model had to be rejected because the fit was so poor. The data for frequency of schizophrenia in three classes of relatives—first cousins, uncle and niece, and children—contributed 97% of the huge goodness of fit χ^2. The explanation was not obvious. Even the model without the cultural transmission had to be rejected.

Within the last 10 years our understanding of the genetics of schizophrenia has gone from having at least two statistically acceptable models to having no acceptable models. Yet, there are still modifications of the approaches that might make a model agree with the data more closely. For example, Morton, Kidd, Matthysse, and Richards (1979) have shown that it is theoretically possible to obtain more precise risk estimates if a spectrum of diagnostic certainty is incorporated into the different genetic models. However, in practice, it will be extremely difficult to use statistical analyses of the patterns of occurrences of schizophrenia in families. Additional information should also be obtained from incorporation of relevant biological data. For example, none of the genetic analyses has incorporated the recent findings of a clear, if small, association of platelet MAO activity and schizophrenia.

It is reasonable to conclude that both genetics and environment contribute in an important way to the manifestation of schizophrenia. However, heterogeneity among studies makes an accurate analysis very difficult. For this reason, the solution is unlikely to come from statistical techniques alone. Future advances in physiological, toxicological, and biochemical research are more likely to supply a firmer basis to the understanding of the genetic component of this disorder. Another conclusion about schizophrenia is that genetic heterogeneity almost certainly exists (Matthysse, 1978). In some affected individuals the disorder has a different etiology from that in others.

Genetic analyses cannot yet identify the precise nature of the genes involved in the transmission of schizophrenia. The fault lies in two areas: (1) genetic analyses incorporating environmental effects are not sophisticated relative to other types of genetic analyses, and (2) the common types of family data collected lack information that would enable one to discriminate among hypotheses. As more data become available, and as our methods of genetic analysis become more powerful, a much more definitive statement should become possible. However, these analyses are not useless at the current state; some make useful quantiative predictions that can guide future genetic research in schizophrenia.

Affective Disorders

Affective disorders today include many diagnoses that are related in symptomology but may not always be the result of the same etiology. The severe disorders are characterized either by episodic or chronic mood states of depression and/or mania that occur without other preexisting psychiatric illness. The main diagnoses are unipolar illness (UP) in which only depression occurs and bipolar illness (BP; also called manic-depressive illness, MDI) periods of mania are interspersed with periods of depression. The depressive symptoms in manic depressive illness (MDI) are the same as those in the unipolar form, but it is not clear to what degree unipolar represents a less complete expression of the same illness. Lithium carbonate, for example, has been a highly effective drug for MDI; it is reported effective in some cases of pure depression but several other drugs not effective in MDI are highly effective against depression.

Onset for both unipolar and bipolar affective disorder can occur at virtually any age. Age-of-onset distributions suggest a median onset age of about 40 for UP and about 26 for BP. Lifetime prevalence for affective disorders has been variously estimated at from 1% to over 20%. In one epidemiologic study using the DSM III diagnostic criteria, the lifetime prevalences were 16% for UP and 1.2% for BP. Females have been found to be 1.5 to 3.6 times more likely to develop an affective disorder than males. Sex ratios (females:males) for specific diagnoses are 1.6 for BP and 2.9 for UP (Weissman & Klerman, 1977). Both diagnoses are often treatable, but with different drugs.

The episodic nature of the symptoms is probably controlled by non-genetic factors but does not show that environmental factors are involved in the basic susceptibility. A significant genetic contribution to the affective disorders is suggested by four types of genetic data—family data, adoption data, twin data, and linkage data. The responsiveness of both UP and BP patients to drug therapy and a variety of biochemical findings in patients (see Gershon, Targum, Kessler, Mayure, & Bunney, 1977 for review) suggest a fundamental biochemical disorder and hence a genetic etiology.

The family data show a consistent pattern of patients' relatives having an increased frequency of affective illnesses (Table 2). Genetic analyses of the family data on affective disorder have considered either sex differences (Leckman & Gershon, 1977) or severity differences (Gershon, Baron, & Leckman, 1975) as defining thresholds in genetic models. Gershon, Buron, and Leckman (1975), using analyses in which severity differences (unipolar versus bipolar) define thresholds in single-major-locus (SML) and multifactorial-polygenic (MFP) models, found that both of these models gave acceptable fits to their data. Leckman and Gershon (1977), using analyses in which sex differences define separate thresholds in the SML and MF models, found that both models gave acceptable fits to some of the data sets analyzed (Gershon, Mark, Cohen, Belizon, Baron, & Knobe, 1975; Goetzl, Green, Whybrow, & Jackson, 1974; James & Chapman, 1975) while neither model provided an acceptable fit to other data sets (Mendelwicz & Rainer, 1974; Winokur & Clayton, 1967). Analyses in which the sexes were given equal thresholds in the SML and MFP models also showed that both models provided good fits to some of the data sets (Goetzl et al., 1974; Gershon et al., 1975b).

Table 2. **Affective Illness in First-Degree Relatives**

Bipolar Probands (BP)	Number at Risk	Morbid Risk (%) BP	UP
James and Chapman, 1975	239	6.4	13.2
Gershon et al., 1975b	341	3.8	6.8
Goetzl et al., 1974	212	2.8	13.7
Helzer and Winokur, 1974	151	4.6	10.6
Winokur and Clayton, 1967	167	10.2	20.4
Perris, 1966	627	10.2	0.5
Angst, 1966	161	4.3	3.0
Total	1898	6.8	8.3
Unipolar Probands (UP)			
Angst, 1966	811	0.3	5.1
Perris, 1966	684	0.3	6.4
Gershon et al., 1975b	96	2.1	11.5
Total	1591	0.4	6.0

(From Gershon et al., 1977).

Two adoption studies of affective disorders both report an increased frequency of affective diagnoses among biological relatives of patients over both adoptive relatives of the patients and the biological relatives of controls (Cadoret, 1976; Mendlewicz & Rainer, 1974). Unfortunately, the sample sizes are small and these data cannot be considered conclusive. Most twin data predate the current objective diagnostic classifications, but a summary by Gershon et al. (1977) reported MZ concordances of 69.2% ± 4.8% and DZ concordances of 13.3% ± 2.3% without distinguishing UP and BP forms.

The excess of females among patients and the low frequency of male to male transmission, especially for BP, led several investigators to consider *X*-linked inheritance as an explanation. The results have been conflicting and some studies have even indicated autosomal linkage. Kidd (1982) reviewed the linkage studies in BP families and concluded that the data suggest at least three genetic forms of BP affective disorder, but do not yet definitely demonstrate the existence of any one of them: an *X*-linked form, an autosomal form closely linked to the HLA region of chromosome 6, and at least one other form that is neither *X*-linked nor linked to HLA. Since a much greater number of genetic markers should be available in the next decade, additional genetic linkage studies of the affective disorders should further clarify the heterogeneity and the specific genetics of each type.

Gilles de la Tourette Syndrome

Gilles de la Tourette (1885) vividly described a neuropsychiatric syndrome with a unique constellation of clinical features, for example, multiple motor tics, phonic symptoms, compulsions, and other behavioral phenomena, such as the irresistable urge to echo or imitate. He observed its predominance in males, its childhood onset, and lifelong duration, and speculated that its cause might lie in neurological vulnerability perhaps on an inherited basis. Increasing attention has been given this disorder in the past 20 years and now hundreds of cases and series of patients have been described in the world literature, leaving little doubt that Tourette syndrome (TS) is a clinically recognizable disorder with a stable pattern of expression across cultures (Abuzzahab & Anderson, 1976; Shapiro, Shapiro, Brunn, & Sweet, 1978). Today, a diagnosis of TS is based on chronic multiple motor and vocal tics, a changing pattern of specific tics, and a waxing and waning course. Not all patients have all symptoms, but onset appears always to be in childhood (2 to 16 years old) with facial tics almost always the first to appear (Jagger, Prusoff, Cohen, Kidd, Carbonari, & John, 1982). Onset and progression of specific symptoms seems to follow a cephalo-caudal sequence (Mahler, Luke, & Daltroff, 1945). Since Tourette's first paper, studies have consistently reported many more male patients than female patients.

Tourette syndrome was once thought to be a rare clinical curiosity. However, since the discovery of the therapeutic value of haloperidol in the mid-1960s (Shapiro & Shapiro, 1968), there has been increasing recognition of the disorder and more frequent, earlier diagnosis (Shapiro et al., 1978). A modest literature now exists on the familial nature of TS and multiple tics. A high proportion of Tourette patients have a positive family history of either TS or multiple tics (Eldridge, Sweet, Lake, Ziegler, & Shapiro, 1977; Nee, Caine, Polinsky, Eldridge, & Ebert, 1980). Wilson, Garron, and Klawans (1978) presented a thorough review of the relevant literature through early 1978. They concluded that the studies of both Tourette syndrome and tics have found on average about 30% of patients to have a positive family history of tics. Shapiro et al. (1978) found a sex difference in the frequency of positive family history—47% of female patients (32% counting only first-degree relatives) had a positive family history of tics while only 28% of male patients (24% counting only first-degree relatives) had such a positive family history. Since the determination of "positive family history" considers several relatives simultaneously, it can only be related to the prevalence of tics if family sizes are specified. Since family sizes generally were not reported, 30% of families in the general population might be chance alone contain at least one present or former tiquer. Wilson et al. (1978) concluded that the positive family history findings in Tourette syndrome, *as reported,* cannot support the hypothesis that the condition has a significant genetic component. Conversely, the percentage of "positive family history" does not argue against a genetic hypothesis unless the percentage is extremely low.

Table 3. **Frequency of TS and/or MT Among 231 First-Degree Relatives**

Type of Relative	Sex of Proband: Male	Sex of Proband: Female
Fathers	**.229 ± .061**	**.333 ± .111**
Mothers	**.125 ± .048**	**.111 ± .074**
Brothers	**.162 ± .061**	**.462 ± .138**
Sisters	**.091 ± .050**	**.188 ± .098**
Total	**.157 ± .029**	**.262 ± .055**

(From Kidd et al., 1980).

More recently Kidd, Prusoff, and Cohen (1980) presented data on the frequencies of TS and/or multiple tics (MT) among parents and siblings in 66 families of TS patients (Table 3). Kidd et al. (1980b) concluded that (1) multiple tics appear to be a milder form of TS, (2) there is vertical transmission since the effect of an an affected parent is significant, (3) the sex difference in the prevalence of TS is real, and (4) this sex difference is related to the transmission of susceptibility for either multiple tics and/or TS. Hence, a sex-modified form of transmission was demonstrated without having to assume a specific etiologic model—either genetic or cultural. These results support previous findings but avoid the "positive family history" trap pointed out by Wilson et al. (1978). Genetic models seem adequately to fit the data, but other cultural/environmental models may fit as well. Although conclusive proof is lacking, recent biochemical findings (Cohen, Shaywitz, Young, Carbonari, Nathanson, Lieberman, Bowers, & Maas, 1979; Hanin, Merikangas, Merikangas, & Kopp, 1979) support the conclusion that TS is an inherited neurologic disorder.

Speech and Language Disorders

Speech and language disorders are among a large group of behavioral disorders that in the past were not usually thought to have a genetic component, but genetic influences are now recognized as important (Lenneberg, 1967; McClay & Osgood, 1959). Lenneberg (1967) stressed the involvement of both genes and environment in determining the course of language acquisition.

> It seems unlikely that genes actually transmit behavior as we observe it in the living animal because the course that an individual takes in its peregrinations through life must necessarily depend on environmental contingencies which could not have been "programmed and prepared for" in advance. Inheritance must confine itself to propensities, to dormant potentialities that await actualization by extra-organic stimuli, but it is possible that innate facilitatory or inhibitory factors are genetically transmitted which heighten the likelihood of one course of events over another. When put into these terms, it becomes quite clear that nature-nurture cannot be a *dichotomy* of factors but only an *interaction* of factors. To think of these terms as incompatible opposites only obscures the interesting aspects of the origin of behavior. (p. 22)

Language appears to be innate in humans; it is spontaneous, universal, and its acquisition follows a fixed sequence, correlated with physical development (Lenneberg, 1968). It is dependent on an extremely complex set of interactions including cortical maturation, neuromuscular development, and other morphologic requisities for the organization and operation of speech. Even the act of speaking is very complex since more than 100 muscles are involved. Movement from one speech sound to the next depends on differences in muscular adjustments; for each sound each muscle must contract, relax, or maintain its tonus. Different muscle groups are activated prior to, during, and after speech (Lenneberg, 1967). Approximately 140,000 neuromuscular events must be coordinated for each second of motor speech production (Bateman, 1977). Given the complexity of speech, it is not surprising that many recognized genetic disorders with neurologic and/or muscular effects also disturb fluent speech. There probably exist other genetic variants that primarily affect speech or language.

Some relevant variables in neural function, possibly under genetic control, include: (1) competence of the neural receptors, (2) strength of spontaneous rhythms in neuronal assemblies, (3) strength and speed of transmission of the neural patterns, (4) competence of synaptic potentials, and (5) efficiency of feedback controls. Any deficiency or alteration in these variables may result in a developmental lag in language and speech acquisition.

Assuming a genetic defect, a sex difference would be expected because of (1) the known differences in speech and language development between the sexes, (2) the generally high frequency of sex differences for medical-genetic disorders ([Kidd, Kidd, & Records, 1978; Kidd, Matthysse, Carmelli, Cavalli-Sforza, Elston, Lange, Motulsky, Rao, Reich, & Wyatt, 1978]), and (3) the increased frequency of speech disorders among males. The reported sex ratios (male:female) for various speech and language disorders are: delayed speech development, 2.1:1; general language disorders, 2.5:1; cluttering, 3.4:1; stuttering, 4:1 (Luchsinger & Arnold, 1965).

These and many other specific speech and language disorders are also known to be familial. General language disability is thought by some to represent a hereditary disorder (Luchsinger & Arnold, 1965), though its transmission pattern is not readily interpretable. Children with developmental aphasia—a childhood language disorder characterized by delayed, sometimes aberrant, development of speech, reading, and writing—often have a family history of similar difficulties and a dominant mode of inheritance has been suggested (Irwin & Marge, 1972). Four times more males are reported to be affected than females (Luchsinger & Arnold, 1965). Congenital dyspraxia, a psychomotor childhood disorder characterized by unusual bodily clumsiness and overall late motor maturation, might be related to the inherited delayed maturation of the motor nerves (Karlin, 1958). Two other familial speech disorders that deserve consideration in more detail are cluttering and stuttering.

Cluttering

Cluttering is characterized by speech disfluency plus a general language disability, including grammatical deficiency, impaired reading ability, bizarre handwriting, poor musical ability, and bodily incoordination (Perkins, 1977). The primary deficit in the clutterer appears to be an underlying language problem that results in stuttering-like speech, as well as articulation and phonation problems. Weiss (1964) defined cluttering as the verbal manifestation of a central language imbalance. In cluttering, the rate and rhythm of articulation are so disrupted that speech is slurred, rapid, confused, and irregular in tempo. The unclear speech has many sounds either omitted or imperfectly formed (Rousey, 1971). However, when the clutterer is forced to articulate slowly, the speech is perfect.

Luchsinger and Arnold (1965) summarized five characteristics of cluttered speech: (1) respiratory dysrhythmia resulting in a disrupted breathing pattern for speaking and oral reading, so that the clutterer jumps in irregular spurts from one group of words to the next; (2) faulty phonation, breaks on stressed vowels, and monotonous or inappropriate speech inflection; (3) increased rate of speech so that words virtually tumble over one another (Seeman [1966] considered acceleration the most typical symptom of cluttering); (4) irregular rhythm of speech—the clutterer's speech sputters and tumbles in disrupted spurts of half-swallowed words; (5) articulation that is hasty, slurred, inaccurate, with unstressed syllables skipped and major word particles replaced by the schwa (the sound "uh").

The striking disruption of the rhythm, rate, and timing in speech seems to reflect a basic disorganization of all musical elements. The clutterer cannot generally keep time with simple musical rhythms, even drum beats, and usually is tone deaf and melody mute. This has been variously attributed to a deficit in fine extrapyramidal coordination (Luchsinger & Arnold, 1965), to a defect in the inhibitor mechanism in feedback control exerted by the temporal lobe (Karlin, Karlin, & Gurren, 1965), or to a breakdown in the reticular control of voluntary motor activities (Berry, 1969). Research has consistently shown more neurologic disability (such as EEG abnormalities) and other language disabilities among clutterers than stutterers (Perkins, 1977).

One of the primary differences between the clutterer and stutterer is that the clutterer is unaware of the speech problem, and is unconcerned about carelessness in articulation. If asked to concentrate on speech or to speak up, the clutterer's speech will be greatly improved. Also, unlike the stutterer, the clutterer will speak better to superiors, in new situations, and when asked to repeat what has been said. Another difference is shown in the response to delayed auditory feedback. Delayed auditory feedback causes a speaker's voice to be fed back to his or her ears with a delay of 0.1-0.5 sec by means of a modified tape recorder device. While the speech of a fluent speaker and a clutterer will deteriorate under this delayed feedback, the stutterer's speech will improve (Langova & Moravek, 1964).

As in other complex behavioral disorders, it seems likely that the etiology of cluttering is heterogeneous. The variable nature of the symptoms of cluttering suggests clinical subclasses that may reflect genetic heterogeneity (Op't Hof & Uys, 1974). Differential diagnoses are needed to separate the various types of cluttering before a genetic study can be undertaken. Cluttering may prove to be a plethora of different specific inherited neurologic variants.

Stuttering

The analyses of data on stuttering illustrate many aspects of a systematic approach to the genetics of childhood disorders and its value. Though stuttering has frequently been labeled purely psychologic it may be largely the consequence of specific genetic variation. Kay (1964) who was the first to examine stuttering by using genetic models concluded: (1) stuttering is a heterogeneous disorder, (2) nonspecific environmental factors may trigger stuttering in individuals with a genetic predisposition, and (3) although the mode of inheritance is uncertain, genetic transmission could explain inheritance in some pedigrees.

The only other large genetic study of stuttering has been described by Kidd and Records (1979). Those data are the bases of several analyses. In one preliminary analysis several possible explanations of the excess of males among individuals who stutter were examined; only the gene-environment interaction hypothesis was consistent with the data (Kidd, Kidd, & Records, 1978). The large sex difference observed was also related to transmission of the trait, clearly indicating that the sex difference needs to be incorporated in any subsequent analysis aimed at understanding etiology of this trait. Biases introduced by the different modes of ascertainment were present. Families were ascertained in three ways: (1) child probands were obtained primarily through speech pathologists in schools and private clinics, (2) most adult probands were obtained through enrollment in an intensive therapy program, and (3) other adult probands were obtained through clinics and the Councils of Adult Stutterers in several large cities. The families of the children were significantly different from those of the adult groups. The families of the two adult groups were not different from each other. For child probands, parents more frequently had a history of stuttering than they had for adult probands. Analyses indicated that this was caused by a higher frequency of agreeing to participate in our study among families in which a parent of the proband had also stuttered. This apparent bias could shift analyses toward accepting the hypothesis that stuttering is transmitted. Therefore, only families of adult probands have so far been used for subsequent analyses.

Among the adult probands, there were three times as many males as females. The adult male probands were classified by whether any parent had ever stuttered. The data for siblings of these classes of male probands are given in Table 4. Analyses of these and comparable data from female stutterers showed that the frequencies of affected siblings are significantly increased if a parent had also ever stuttered. Although the statistical analysis incorporated no genetic hypotheses, this significant difference

Table 4. **Numbers of Relatives (Percent who ever Stuttered) by Parental Type[a] for Male Probands**

Parental type	N	F	M	B
Number of Families:	267 Families	65 Families	19 Families	5 Families
Brothers[b]				
S	58 (17.21)	24 (32.43)	6 (35.29)	2 (33.33)
NS	279	50	11	4
Total	337	74	17	6
Sisters[b]				
S	7 (2.56)	8 (10.39)	1 (5.56)	3 (37.5)
NS	266	69	17	5
Total	273	77	18	8

[a] Parental types: N—neither parent ever stuttered; F—only father ever stuttered; M—only mother ever stuttered; B—both parents stuttered.
[b] Classifications of siblings: S—ever stuttered; NS—never stuttered.
(From Kidd & Records, 1979).

provides strong support for the hypothesis that susceptibility to stuttering is vertically transmitted.

A more elaborate statistical analysis of the family data of 294 adult male probands and 103 adult female probands used a logistic model (Cox, 1970). The main factors found to increase the risk of stuttering in a sibling child of a stutterer were (1) starting with a female stutterer, (2) looking at a male relative, (3) having a parent who had ever stuttered, and (4) looking at a child rather than a sibling of the stutterer.

Another analysis used data on a subset of 184 adult stutterers and their families to examine whether any variables were predictors of severity of stuttering in the proband (Kidd, Oehlert, Heimbuch, Records, & Webster, 1980). None of the variables tested, including stuttering among first-degree relatives, was a predictor of severity of stuttering in the index stutterer. Apparently this measure of severity—frequency of disfluent syllables in reading a passage—is not related to the factors that predispose to stuttering.

Vertical transmission and sex-modified expression exist, but what is the nature of the transmission? It might be genetic. Stuttering does not follow a clear single-gene pattern, but it may very well be explained by a general single-major-locus model with two alleles and three genotypes; nongenetic variation or other gene loci (epistasis) could modify the risk of stuttering for each genotype. Heterozygotes could stutter if they have a sufficiently stressful environment, and homozygotes may not stutter if they have a sufficiently benign or ameliorating environment. The parameters that give the closest explanation to the data are given in Table 5. This solution explains the family data quite well with the transmission having a purely genetic basis. The gene frequency in the solution is 4%, not a rare gene, but not a very common one either. Most individuals in the total population lack the gene. About 8% of the population is heterozygous and less than 2 in a 1,000 are actually homozygous. The penetrances—the probability that an individual with a particular genotype will ever stutter, as a function of sex—are virtually zero for the normal genotype; they are one (or 100%) for homozygotes for the stuttering allele. A striking sex difference is found for heterozygotes; penetrance is about 38% for a heterozygous male but only 11% for a heterozygous female. These parameter values predict lifetime prevalences of about 4% of the population of males and about 1% of the population of females, roughly the observed values for the lifetime prevalence of ever stuttering at some time in childhood.

Table 5. **Best Fit of the Single Major Locus Model to the Family Incidence Data on Stuttering**

Stuttering allele (S) frequency = .040 ± .007
Predicted general incidences, .35 for males; .010 for females
Penetrances for each genotype and sex

	Genotypes		
	NN	NS	SS
Male	0.005 ± 0.003	0.378 ± 0.025	1.0
Female	0.0002 ± 0.0002	0.107 ± 0.019	1.0

The goodness of fit $\chi^2_3 = 4.65$, $p = .22$

(From Kidd & Records, 1979).

Finding an acceptable solution does not constitute proof that a single locus is responsible for stuttering, but it is highly suggestive. Especially noteworthy is that the model does not require that the interaction of genetic and nongenetic factors be confined to heterozygotes. Biological principles would suggest such interaction is most likely to be significant in heterozygotes. Arguing against a single-major-locus (SML) explanation is the finding that a multifactorial-polygenic model (MFP) can also explain the data (Kidd, 1977). In the MFP model genetic factors explain the transmission; the model also explains the sex differences observed.

In summary, the overall pattern of occurrences of stuttering within families is definitely nonrandom. Genetic analyses of the data reveal that this pattern of stuttering can be explained by genetic transmission of susceptibility and sex-modified interaction with environment. Although the mode of transmission is not yet clearly defined, two genetic models with sex-specific thresholds closely fit the data and may help to identify the genetic nature of susceptibility to stuttering.

However, nongenetic hypotheses must also be considered before any firm conclusion can be reached. Certain models of purely cultural inheritance can be excluded by the data. The simplest cultural model—imitating the speech of a family member who stutters—could not explain more than a small fraction of all stuttering in children (Kidd, Kidd, & Records, 1978). This finding is consistent with the high familial concentration of stuttering because most stutterers recover before adulthood. For example, in 20% of these families the father had at some time stuttered but in one-half of those cases he had recovered before the birth of the child who later stuttered. Some more complex cultural hypotheses have involved a general nervousness being culturally transmitted since, for example, anxiety is known to exacerbate symptoms in a stutterer. Such hypotheses predict that the severity of stuttering would be associated with the frequency of relatives who stutter. One reliable measure of the severity of stuttering is the frequency of words on which a stutterer has some difficulty. This measure of severity is *not* associated with the frequency or distribution of stuttering among relatives and, therefore, we conclude severity is not related to the transmitted factors that predispose to stuttering. Hence, hypotheses of general anxiety being the culturally transmitted cause of stuttering appear to be excluded by these data. At this time definite proof is elusive, yet all available evidence suggests that susceptibility to stuttering is genetically transmitted.

Dyslexia

Specific reading disability (RD, developmental dyslexia) has been defined by Critchley (1970) and others as a disorder characterized by difficulty in learning to read despite conventional instruction, normal intelligence, and adequate sociocultural opportunity. Much work has been done in an attempt to understand this disorder more completely (see Herschel, 1978 for a review). The diagnosis of RD is not uniform and it is not always clear that the results from various studies can easily be compared. In addition, the disorder is quite likely to be heterogeneous.

Attempts have recently been made to identify possible subtypes. Johnson and Myklebust (1967) and Boder (1971) observed that the spelling errors made by dyslexic persons could be categorized into dysphonetic and phonetic types. On that basis Boder (1971) suggested three subtypes of RD. Mattis, French and Rapin (1975) suggested a different set of three distinct subtypes of RD based on neuropsychological tests. Several other attempts have been made to classify subtypes (Bateman, 1968; Doehring & Hoshko, 1977; and Ingram, Mason, & Blackburn, 1970). In almost all cases the categories defined include an auditory type of dysfunction, a visual type of dysfunction, and a mixed type with characteristics of both the others. Unfortunately, all attempts use slightly different diagnostic schemes and none has been cross validated. Obviously work needs to be done in this area, so that if there are distinct subtypes they can be accurately defined and diagnosed. It may be that genetic methodologies may prove useful in helping to identify homogeneous subtypes (Omenn & Weber, 1978; Smith, Pennington, Kimberling, & Lubs, 1979).

Reading disability is familial. As early as 1905, Fisher published a report in which the proband's maternal uncle also had RD. Several other early reports (Stephenson, 1907; Thomas, 1905) described families with multiple cases of the disorder. Orton (1937), Marshall and Ferguson (1939), and Eustis (1947) also reported the familial nature of RD and in addition noted that affected individuals usually had normal intelligence. Hallgren (1950) published the results of one of the largest family studies of RD to date. There were 116 probands in the sample with 391 first degree relatives. Hallgren reported an excess of males among affected individuals. Of the 116 probands, 89 were male. The sex difference was also observed among the first-degree relatives. Of the fathers and brothers 47% were affected, whereas only 38% of mothers and 35% of sisters were affected. In total 160 of the 391 (40.9%) first-degree relatives were affected. Hallgren calculated segregation ratios based on several Mendelian models and suggested that dyslexia was an autosomal dominant trait with sex-modified expression. Other studies also showed the familial nature of RD but no specific genetic model was tested (DeFries, Singer, Foch, & Lewitter, 1978; Finucci, Guthrie, Childs, Abbey, & Childs, 1976; McGlannon, 1968; Owen, Adams, Forrest, Stolz, & Fisher, 1971; Walker & Cole, 1965). Each of these studies confirmed the observation that RD runs in families and that more males are affected than females.

Symmes and Rapaport (1972) and Zahalkova, Vrzal, and Kloboukova (1972) suggested two different hypotheses which would account for the observed sex difference. Symmes and Rapaport suggested sex-linked recessive inheritance after studying the families of 54 reading disabled children. Zahalkova et al. (1972) studied the families of 65 dyslexic children and calculated a segregation ratio of .42 ± .06. Based on that result, they suggest autosomal dominant inheritance with partial sex limitation.

Lewitter (1977, 1979) performed segregation analyses on families collected through 133 RD children to test the hypotheses proposed by previous investigators. She also analyzed three subsets of the total data: families of male probands, families of female probands, and families of severely affected probands. No one hypothesis was supported in all the analyses and she stated that the results suggested that RD was genetically heterogeneous. When she restricted her analysis to children only, she was unable to reject the hypothesis of a single major locus. The results for children only may be more meaningful than those from analyses in which parents were included.

Although the tendency to cluster in families suggest that RD is transmitted, it does not prove that the transmission is genetic. Additional evidence for a genetic contribution to the manifestation of the trait has come from at least two other sources.

The first source is twin studies. Zerbin-Rudin (1967) reviewed the literature and found that of 17 MZ pairs reported all were concordant for RD, whereas only 12 of 34 DZ pairs were concordant for the trait. Additional data on twins have been collected. In all reported studies except one, concordance has been 100% among MZ twin pairs. Bakwin (1973) examined 338 pairs of same-sexed twins and found 97 of the 676 twins to be affected with RD. Of the 31 MZ pairs in which at least one twin had RD, 26 of the cotwins were also affected; in contrast, only 9 of the 31 DZ twin pairs were concordant. The greater concordance rate among MZ twins suggests a genetic contribution, but the fact that the MZ concordance is less than 100% suggests some environmental factors to be important in the etiology of the trait.

A second source of evidence for a genetic contribution comes from linkage studies. The demonstration of linkage of a purported locus for a trait with a known genetic marker locus is strong evidence for a genetic component to the etiology of that trait. Smith et al. (1979) studied eight families with multiple affected individuals. They purposely selected families with several affected in order to minimize heterogeneity. Their results strongly suggest linkage of RD to a heteromorphic section of chromosome 15. Although additional work needs to be done, these results suggest that at least one type of dyslexia may be caused by some genotypes at a single locus.

A major problem for dyslexia research is the probable existence of heterogeneity. As noted above, several attempts have been made to identify different subtypes. Two studies (Omenn & Weber, 1978; Smith et al., 1979) have used the classification schemes of Boder (1971) to see if the subtypes defined would "breed true" within families. Omenn and Weber (1978) studied 21 families with multiple members with RD. Eleven probands were classified as visual-predominant, seven as auditory-predominant, and three as mixed. Most of the affected relatives who could be diagnosed had the same subtype as the proband, giving "support for the hypothesis that the phenotypic subtypes reflect independent familial predispositions." Smith et al. (1979) were unable to show any correlation between subtypes defined by the Mattis et al. (1975) and Boder (1971) classification schemes. In addition, the Mattis et al. (1975) scheme did not discriminate well between affected and unaffected relatives. Smith et al. (1979) did not indicate whether those affected with poor spelling tended to come from a few families or were randomly distributed over all of the families.

As noted above, the preponderance of individuals affected with RD are males. Several authors have suggested that RD may be a trait with a sex-modified threshold important for its expression (Childs & Finucci, 1979; Herschel, 1978). If the genetic mechanism for the trait is also related to its differential expression in the sexes, then the risk to relatives should differ depending on the sex of the proband. That is, since females are less frequently affected, the risk to the relatives of female probands should be greater than the risk to relatives of male probands. This is not the case for RD. Childs and Finucci (1979) state that the risk to the relatives of females is not significantly greater than the risk to the relatives of males. Omenn and Weber (1978) show that the risk is greater for relatives of females but not significantly so. When the data presented by Finucci et al. (1976) are separated by sex of proband, the risks are not different for the two classes of relatives. These results could mean one of two things; first, in each of these studies the sample size is too small to obtain significance or, second, the sex difference observed is not related to the transmission of the trait.

If the sex difference is not related to the transmission of RD, then it could be explained by one of several possibilities. The social-educational environment could be more favorable to girls, so that they would express the trait less often, even when they were genetically predisposed. If that were the case, one might expect a lower concordance rate for male than for female MZ twins. Bakwin (1973) reported concordance rates for male and female MZ twins to be 84% and 83%, respectively. Hence, it is unlikely that different educational environments account for the observed difference. Another explanation for the observed difference could be that the developmental processes of males and females interact differently with the genetic predisposition for RD and the interaction produces more severe effects in males than it does in females. If that is the case, one would also expect males to be more severely affected than females. This appears to be the case (Herschel, 1978).

In summary, it is clear that much work remains to be done to gain a better understanding of RD and its etiology. From the work already done, we know that RD is familial and we believe part of the reason for familial clustering is underlying genetic mechanisms. What is not known is what the genetic mechanisms are. Several models have been proposed; the most frequently mentioned is an autosomal dominant with reduced and sex-modified penetrance. Few, if any, of the alternative hypotheses have been rigorously excluded. Diagnostic uncertainty and a probable etiologic and phenotypic heterogeneity cloud the picture. More work is needed to establish useful criteria for all age ranges and to determine if in fact there are phenotypic differences that tend to cluster within families as suggested by Omenn and Weber (1978).

NORMAL HUMAN VARIATIONS

Genetic and Environmental Differences in Intelligence

The idea of genetic differences as a source of individual and group differences in intelligence is one of the most controversial issues in the history of psychology. Some experts advocate the view that no evidence to date should compel anyone to accept the idea that genetic differences have anything to do with individual or group differences in anything we measure as intelligence (Kamin, 1974, 1981; Schwartz & Schwartz, 1974; Taylor, 1980). Other experts claim that the evidence points to a very high degree of genetic determination of differences in intelligence (Eysenck, 1973, 1979; Jensen, 1973a,b,c, 1978a,b). Most investigators in behavior genetics conclude from the evidence that about half (± .1) of the current differences among individuals in U.S. and European white populations in measured intelligence result from genetic differences among them (Loehlin, Lindzey, & Spuhler, 1975; Nichols, 1978; Plomin & DeFries, 1980).

It is curious that so many experts examining the same evidence could reach such different conclusions. To understand the controversy and the differing views, one must examine some of the history of investigations of genetic differences in intelligence and take a new look at the major pieces of evidence. Further, one must understand the theoretical and methodological approaches in genetics to the study of human behavior, for they are profoundly different and often confused by behavioral scientists. We will review the older and the more recent evidence on genetic and environmental differences in general and specific abilities and propose a future course for research.

What We Used to Know

Nearly 40 years ago, the distinguished psychologist, R. S. Woodworth, was asked by the Social Science Research Council to review the research on *Heredity and Environment* (Woodworth, 1941) that had recently been obtained from several studies of twins and foster (adopted) children and studies of nursery schools. There was much dispute at the time between the Stanford (Terman, McNemar, & Burks), Minnesota (Leahy & Goodenough) and Iowa (Wellman, Skodak, & Skeels) groups over the interpretation of evidence favoring heredity or environment as the predominant source of intellectual variation. After a judicious review of the evidence from studies of twins reared together and apart, from studies of foster children, orphanage children, and those with and without nursery school experience, Woodworth wrote a conclusion that stands today as a fine summary of what we know about genetic and environmental differences in intelligence.

1. Both heredity and environment contribute to differences among and within families.

2. Intrafamily differences are subtle and undissected. Sibling differences depend in part on their

own genetic differences and in part on their environments, with which we now know birth order differences are correlated.

3. Interfamily environmental differences among U.S. whites are a very small part of the total individual variation in IQ, probably as Woodworth says, because of the uniformity of environments produced by public schooling and other public agencies.

4. It is still possible to raise the general level of intelligence by improving the environment, but that will not by any means annul individual differences due to heredity.

A Brief Political History of Genetic Differences in IQ

There is a remarkable ratio of cant to data in this field. Many people express opinions (and write polemics in reviews) and relatively few people do empirical research. Since the mid-1970s the ratio is improving as more investigators see the possibilities of important research questions and approaches, particularly through the study of adopted children (DeFries & Plomin 1978; Scarr-Salapatek 1975).

To understand the controversy over the very study of genetic variance in intelligence, one has to place oneself into a political frame of mind and, on the one hand, decide to suppress the evil consequences of such knowledge and its possible uses. On the other hand, one needs to consider oneself the appointed guardian of an awful truth—that genetic differences among human beings and among groups of people are so pervasive, so terrifyingly strong that the knowledge is essential to bring before the public for their consideration in social policy issues. Now, the stage is set for a confrontation, a noisy conflict that has persisted from the early twentieth century to the present (see Block & Dworkin, 1976 for a good collection of articles).

It seems that some scientists fear that knowledge of the current sources of intellectual differences in a population will foreclose attempts to search for ways to improve the intellectual states of distribution of resources of the population. If current differences in intelligence are attributable half to genetic differences, about 10% to differences among family environments, and the rest to differences among individuals within families, are we led to abandon a commitment to improve children's lives? We fail to see the connection.

As Anderson (1974, pp. 20–21) pointed out:

> Genetics as a discipline cuts across the four levels of biological study—molecular, cellular, organismal, and populational. At each level testable hypotheses can be stated and the results at one level may lead to questions which may be investigated at other levels. Genetic studies treat variability as the primary focus for investigation, not merely as noise to be eliminated or disregarded. This variation must be examined both within families and between families. If only one pair of genes is involved, the incidence among relatives will follow simple ratios, but with multigenic inheritance there is a more complex set of expectations.

Consider the following questions that one might ask about the role of genetic differences in intelligence.

1. How do genes affect intelligence? (Which pathways of gene-protein-enzyme activity to physiology and brain function cause differences in intelligence?)
2. What are the sources of individual (and group) differences in intelligence? (What are the sources of *variation* in a population at the present time?)
3. Why and in what ways does human intelligence differ from that of other primates? (What is the evolutionary history of primate species?)
4. Why is there a distribution of individual differences in intelligence within a population, and perhaps between populations? (What is the evolutionary history and structure of human populations?)

Confusion about the different nature of each of these questions has led many critics of the study of genetics and intelligence to commit amazing feats of illogic. Most common is the confusion of questions (1) and (2) in the psychological literature. It is asserted that one cannot study the sources of individual differences in a population because both genes and environments are required for individual development. Well, yes, we all assume that development requires both genes and environments that act together to program human development. But, as Woodworth said, that is not an answer to question (2), about sources of variation. Many species-typical developments depend on the same or functionally equivalent genotypes and environments for development within bounds that are normal for the species. Individual differences depend on functional differences in genotypes and/or environments that cause noticeable variations in phenotypes.

Variation in Infant Intelligence

In several studies of infant twins, monozygotic pairs were found to be as similar as the same individual tested twice. (Broman, Nichols, & Kennedy, 1975; Wilson, 1972a, 1972b, Wilson & Harpring, 1972). Wilson and his collaborators found that dizygotic twins are far more similar than their genetic resemblance would account for; that is, the DZ correlations are between .61 and .74, depending on the age at testing. Nichols and his collaborators found that the DZ correlations in the National Perinatal Study were consonant with a genetic correlation of about .50. All of these studies used the Bayley Scales of Mental Development.

Siblings who are not twins, on the other hand, are found to be much less similar than DZ twins, even when the sibs are tested at the same ages in infancy. In the Perinatal Study, the correlations at 8-month tests for 1684 pairs of siblings was only .20. Thus, the high degree of DZ twins resemblance in infant intelligence arises not just from genetic resemblance, but presumably from the shared prenatal and postnatal environments.

Unlike the studies of older DZ twins and siblings, who are generally found to have similar levels of correlation when tested in childhood, adolescence and adulthood, the effects of simultaneously shared infant environments seems to increase the intellectual resemblance of twins. Differences in early environments reduce the resemblance of biological siblings, whose IQ scores are more similar in later childhood and adulthood than in the first year of life.

There is little reason to believe that infant intelligence is the same phenotype (or genotype) as later, conceptual intelligence (Scarr-Salapatek, 1976), and the importance of *environmental* differences for infant mental scores stands in sharp contrast to the results of later IQ tests.

Twin Studies of Intelligence

Robert Nichols (1978) compiled 211 studies of intelligence and abilities that compare the resemblance of indentical (MZ) and fraternal (DZ) twins. His results for 1100 to 4500 pairs of MZ and a like number of DZs are given in Table 6.

For general intelligence, the mean correlation for MZ twins, taken from a variety of tests, is .82; for DZ twins, .59. Although the MZ correlation exceeds the DZ coefficient by .22 (using a *z* transformation to subtract correlation coefficients), it is clear that being genetically related and reared as twins in the same family are potent determinants of individual differences in measured intelligence. From the comparison of MZ and DZ correlations from the 30 studies, one can calculate an estimate of the broad heritability (see preceding section on heritability) of IQ in the white U.S. population of adolescents (who made up most of the studies' subjects) as somewhere between .3 and .7, with a most likely value in the .5 range given a correction for assortative mating of the parents and without correcting for the reliability of the tests. Nichols corrected for the reliability of measurement, and calculated a most likely estimate of genetic differences as accounting for about .60 to .70 of the IQ variation.

As anyone fond of sampling theory would have smilingly predicted, the studies summarized by Nichols (1978) form a distribution of results. The population of studies of general intelligence and other abilities have means and variances of their own. In Figure 13 Nichols indicates the results of each study with a circle and, by an arrow, the weighted mean correlation coefficient for MZ and DZ twin for each measure. As anyone who is knowledgeable about statistical distributions would expect, there are some outlying values and more studies clustered nearer to the middle of the distribution. In Nichols' sample, however, there are some unusually low correlation values, outlying by themselves, which raise suspicions about measurement, test administration, sampling restriction, and the like.

Critics of the twin study method have seized on the outliers in distributions of studies to raise questions about the overall pattern of results. Kamin (1974), in particular, has made much of equivocal findings from some twin and adoption studies (Kamin, 1981). McAskie and Clark (1976) used the variance of parent-child study results for the same purpose. A more sophisticated, statistical look at the twin results is persuasive evidence for the greater average similarity of MZ than DZ cotwins for measures of general and specific abilities. The greater similarity of MZ twins is usually interpreted as due to their greater genetic similarity, but that conclusion is based on the critically important assumption that the environments of MZ twins do not bias their behavioral similarities by their more similar treatment. The objection to the twin study method is that MZ twins are made more similar by the greater similarity of their treatment by others, based on their striking physical similarity.

Environmental Similarity of MZ and DZ Twins

There are three approaches to testing the effects of greater environmental similarity of MZ than DZ twins. First, Scarr (1968) and Scarr and Carter-Saltzman (1979) compared the actual intellectual, personality, and physical similarities of twins who were correctly and incorrectly classified as MZ and DZ by themselves, their parents, and others. There

Table 6. **Mean Intraclass Correlations from Twin Studies of Various Traits**

Trait	Number of Studies	Mean Intraclass Cor.		Difference $r_{MZ}-r_{DZ}$	
		r_{MZ}	r_{DZ}	Mean	Stand. Deviation
Ability					
General intelligence	30	.82	.59	.22	.10
Verbal comprehension	27	.78	.59	.19	.14
Number and mathematics	27	.78	.59	.19	.12
Spatial visualization	31	.65	.41	.23	.16
Memory	16	.52	.36	.16	.16
Reasoning	16	.74	.50	.24	.17
Clerical speed and accuracy	15	.70	.47	.22	.15
Verbal fluency	12	.67	.52	.15	.14
Divergent thinking	10	.61	.50	.11	.15
Language achievement	28	.81	.58	.23	.11
Social studies achievement	7	.85	.61	.24	.10
Natural science achievement	14	.79	.64	.15	.13
All abilities	211	.74	.54	.21	.14
Interests					
Practical interest	20	.50	.37	.13	.15
Science interest	15	.54	.29	.25	.11
Business interest	22	.45	.30	.15	.14
Clerical interest	10	.44	.26	.18	.09
Helping interest	18	.48	.30	.18	.14
Artistic interest	16	.50	.32	.18	.13
All interests	116	.48	.30	.18	.13
Personality					
Extraversion-introversion	30	.52	.25	.27	.14
Neuroticism	23	.51	.22	.29	.21
Socialization	6	.49	.23	.27	.17
Dominance	13	.53	.31	.23	.18
Masculinity-femininity	7	.43	.17	.27	.21
Hypochondriasis	9	.37	.19	.18	.28
Conformity	5	.41	.20	.22	.15
Flexibility	7	.46	.27	.19	.27
Impulsiveness	6	.48	.29	.19	.12
All personality	106	.48	.29	.19	.12

Note: Mean correlations are unweighted averages of the studies involved. Because most twin studies employ multiple measures, the same twin sample may be represented in several traits. (From Nichols, 1978).

appeared to be little bias from the belief in zygosity, as the incorrectly classified MZs and DZs were as similar on most measurements as the correctly classified pairs. On intellectual measures, belief in zygosity had no significant effect on actual similarity. On personality and physical measures, both actual zygosity and belief in zygosity were related to measured similarities. It is hard to imagine that twins grow taller or shorter, have greater or lesser skeletal maturity because someone believes them to be identical or fraternal twins. Thus, we concluded that for personality and physical measures, actual similarity is a basis for the judgment of zygosity, not likely the reverse.

Lytton (1977) has taken a second approach to the issue of environmental similarity between identical and fraternal twins. With extensive observations of the parental response and initiation of interactions with very young twins, Lytton showed that the parents of MZs treat their children more similarly than do the parents of DZs, because the identicals give the parents more similar stimuli to respond to. He observed no difference in parental treatment of MZs and DZs that would create additional similarities or differences to bias comparisons between the types of twins.

A third approach to the study of the role of more similar environment for identical than fraternal

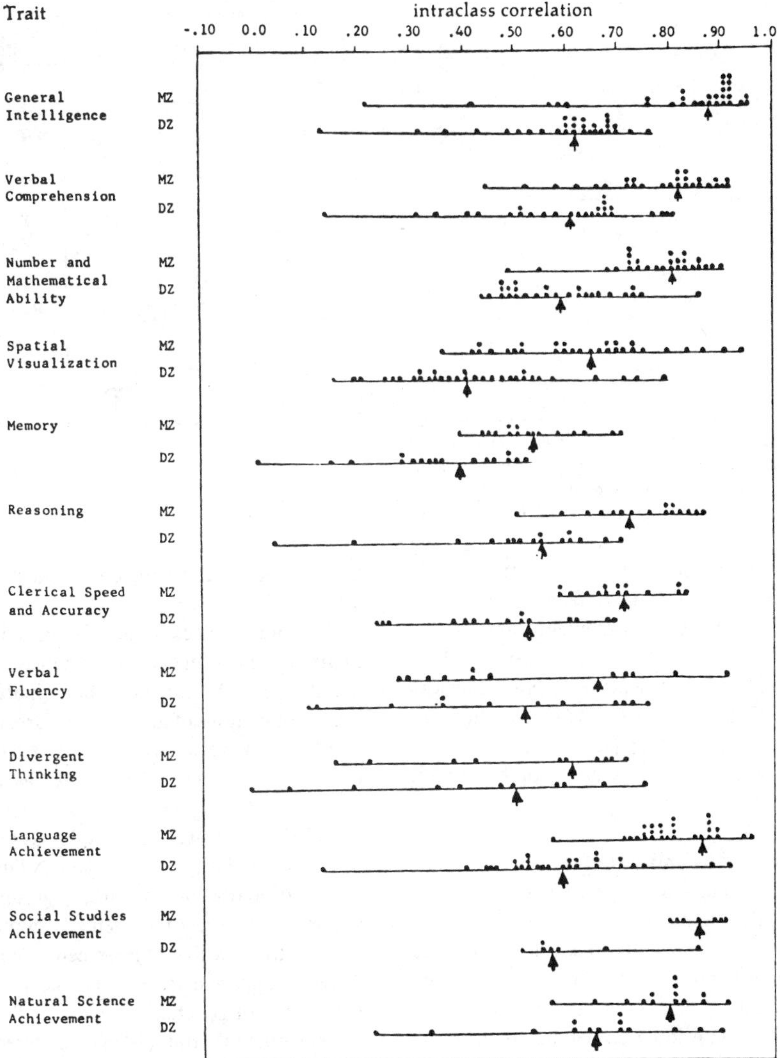

Figure 13. Twin studies of various abilities. The intraclass correlations obtained in each study for MZ (identical) and DZ (fraternal) twins are indicated by the dots along each horizontal line. The mean correlation, weighted by the number of cases in each study, is indicated by the arrow below each line. (Reproduced with permission from Nichols, 1978.)

twins was developed by Plomin, Willerman, and Loehlin (1976). Their reasoning was as follows: If identical twins are more similar *because* they are treated more similarly, then those identicals who experience more similar environments should be more similar than those identicals who experience less similar environments. Sharing the same room, friends, classrooms, and receiving similar parental treatment, for example, should increase the behavioral similarity of some MZs over that of others. In short, those environmental similarities that differ *between* identical and fraternal twins ought to affect the degree of similarity *among* identical twins as well.[1]

The result of Plomin et al.'s (1976) analysis of the effect of greater similarities on the environmental factors that differentiate between MZ and DZ twins was clear—greater environmental similarity in parental treatment and experience, as reported by the

[1]Fraternal twins were not used, because some pairs are genetically more similar than others, a confounding factor in any analysis of greater and lesser environmental similarity. To some extent, greater genetic similarity may lead some DZ pairs to select and receive more similar environments than others.

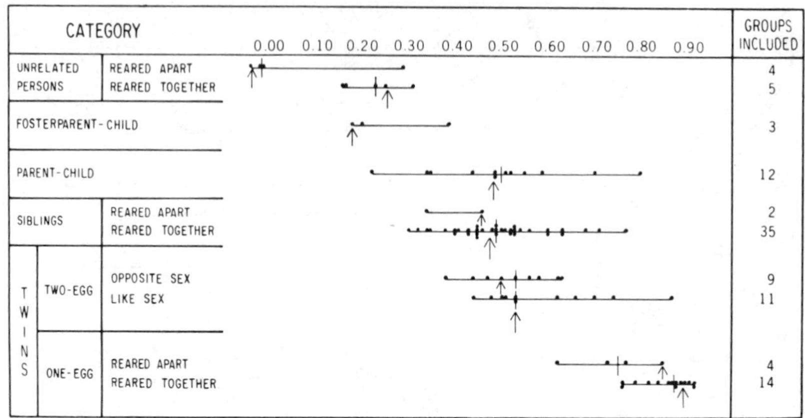

Figure 14. IQ correlations of twins, biological, and adopted relatives, reared together and apart, excluding the correlations reported by Burt. (From Rimland & Munsinger, 1977.)

twins, does not inflate actual similarities among identical twins on intellectual or personality dimensions. Rather, it seems likely that more similar genotypes develop greater behavioral similarity and select more similar environments more often than less similar (e.g., DZ) genotypes. The greater environmental similarity of MZ than DZ twins is, therefore, primarily a result and not a cause of behavioral similarity.

Studies of Twins and Families

Following on the summary by Nichols (1978) it seems appropriate to mention the famous review of the literature on genetic differences in intelligence by Erlenmeyer-Kimling and Jarvik (1963). They presented a chart of 52 studies, excluding some of the twin studies with low correlations included by Nichols and showing the median correlations for the various degrees of kinship and rearing closeness. Unfortunately, their chart included data from the "studies" of Sir Cyril Burt, now considered questionable at least, fraudulent at most (Hearnshaw, 1979).

The older, selected studies of genetic differences in measured intelligence supported a conclusion that about 70% of the variance among individuals in the white populations of the U.S. and Great Britain were due to genetic variation. The omission of Burt's data does little to change the picture, as Rimland and Munsinger (1977) showed in their annotated graph from Erlenmeyer-Kimling and Jarvik (1963) (Figure 14). The regularity of these data and the magnitude of the differences among kinship groups, with some variance due to rearing together, supported a strong genetic hypothesis. More recent data, as will be shown, support a more moderate position on the heritability of general intelligence.

Rowe and Plomin (1978) compared Burt's data to those surveyed by Jencks (1972), based entirely on U.S. samples. Their data, given in Table 7, again support more moderate estimates of heritability than Burt's data.

***Table 7.* A Comparison of Data from Burt's Studies and from Other Behavior Genetic Studies**

	Burt's studies		Other behavior genetic studies	
	Correlation	*N*/pairs	Correlation	*N*/pairs
MZ together	0.930	95	0.857	526
DZ together	0.537	127	0.534	517
MZ apart	0.841	53	0.741	69
Sibs together	0.525	264	0.545	1671
Unrelated together	0.267	136	0.376	259

(From Rowe & Plomin, 1978).

Table 8. **Regression and Correlation Analyses of Block Design Test Scores and Finger Print Ridge Counts**

	Block Design		Ridge Count	
	Coefficient	*N*	Coefficient	*N*
Regressions				
Son/daughter on father/mother	.28 ± .04	572	.42 ± .05	564
Nephew/niece on twin uncle/aunt	.23 ± .06	318	.37 ± .05	310
Nephew/niece on spouse uncle/aunt	−.01 ± .06	241	−.06 ± .07	247
Offspring on midparent	.54 ± .07	254	.82 ± .07	254
Correlations				
Monozygotic twins	.68 ± .06	65	.96 ± .03	60
Full siblings	.24 ± .08	297	.36 ± .08	296
Half-siblings	.10 ± .12	318	.17 ± .12	310
Father-mother	.06 ± .10	102	.05 ± .10	98

(From Rose, 1979).

Twin Family Studies. A particularly interesting design for the estimation of genetic and environmental effects on intelligence is the study of families of identical twins, who are themselves adults with offspring. Suppose that an identical twin pair of males marry two unrelated women and each have two children. The children of one are equally related genetically to the cotwin, with whom the children do not live, and not related at all to the spouse of the cotwin. Thus, these families provide examples of parent-child pairs together and in different households (albeit correlated environments). Furthermore, the children of the MZ twins are more than ordinary first cousins; they are half-siblings, having genetically the same father and a different mother. The design also provides for the study of ordinary full siblings, spouse correlations, and maternal versus paternal effects, depending on the gender of the MZ twin pair. Nance and Corey (1976) have proposed models for the analysis of such data, and Rose (1979) has reported initial data from 65 such family constellations for the Wechsler Block Design. The data for Block Design and fingerprint ridge count are given in Table 8.

One notable feature of the results is that the regression of genetic offspring on genetic parent (whether actual parent or twin uncle/aunt) is only slightly lower when they do not reside in the same household, whereas the regression of offspring on the genetically unrelated spouse of the twin is zero. The twin, sibling, and half-sibling data are all consistent with the parent-child results and heritability estimates in the .4 to .6 range. A comparison of the Block Design and fingerprint ridge count data show a very similar pattern of family resemblance, with the physical measure being more heritable (an estimated range of .68 to .84). The study of twin families seems to be a very appealing one and a design that will yield more defensible estimates of genetic variance than the study of twins alone.

Another study that incorporates both twins and siblings is the Louisville Twin Study (Wilson, 1977). At about 8 years old the twins and one of their siblings were tested with the WISC. The data are shown in Table 9 (combined results of Wilson's Tables 2 & 3).

The correlations for siblings are very close to those of DZ twins, with whom they are genetically related as sibs and who are genetically related to each other as ordinary sibs. (Twins were designated A and B according to the alphabetical order of their legal first names.) Identical (monozygotic) twins are far more similar in WISC scores than any of the sibling groups. Wilson concludes, and we agree,

> The concordance for full-scale IQ and verbal IQ showed no significant change from dizygotic twins to sibling pairs to twin-sibling sets, so the unique experiences of being born and raised as twins did not promote significantly greater similarity in IQ. Nor did the differential experiences of twin versus singleton lead to greater disparities in school age IQ among the twin-sibling sets. From this perspective, the concordance among age-matched zygotes from the same family was negligibly related to the experiences of being a twin or a singleton. The more potent determinants appeared to be the proportion of shared genes plus the common family environment. (p. 214)

Not only are the full-scale, verbal and performance scores per se heritable in a range of .5 to .8, but the *pattern* of verbal and performance scores also

Table 9. **Within-Pair Correlations on the Wechsler Scale for Different Sets of Siblings and Twins**

	Full Scale IQ	Verbal IQ	Performance IQ	Difference Between Verbal and Performance IQs	No. of Sets
Sibling-sibling pairs	.46	.42	.37	.21	56
Sibling and MZ twin A	.41	.46	.24	.24	65
Sibling and MZ twin B	.46	.48	.29	.26	65
Sibling and DZ twin A	.47	.35	.47	.17	53
Sibling and DZ twin B	.28	.39	.09	.24	53
Dizygotic twins (8 years)	.45	.41	.41	.27	71
Monozygotic twins (8 years)	.82	.79	.67	.49	86

In those families where two siblings were available, the sibling closest to age 8 was used. (From Wilson, 1977).

shows evidence of moderate heritability. The fourth column in the table gives the correlations of the difference between the two subscores for the related pairs. The first-degree relatives' patterns are correlated about .24, whereas the identical twins' patterns are correlated .49.

MZ Twins Reared "Apart." Like DeFries, Vandenberg and McClearn (1976), we believe that adoption studies offer the best evidence for genetic differences in intelligence. Although many people find the study of identical twins reared apart most compelling, there are reasons of nonrandom selection and nonrandom assignment to environments that render the study of MZs apart less useful than research on adopted children. If there were a study of identical twins reared in uncorrelated environments, genetic differences would be controlled, while both within-family and between-family environmental variables are free to vary. This would be an ideal study of genetic differences. Unfortunately for science, there are simply too few pairs of MZs reared apart, too peculiarly sampled, to make these subjects useful to social science. The most notable studies of MZ twins reared in separate households for at least most of their growing years (but not entirely separated and reared in uncorrelated environments) are those of Newman, Freeman, and Holzinger (1937) and Shields (1962). The average IQ correlation of MZs reared in correlated but not the same households is .76, considerably higher than DZ twins reared in the same household. Thus, these studies provide some evidence for the importance of genetic differences in intelligence.

Adoptive Families. Adopted children, on the other hand, provide data almost as useful as the rare identical twins reared apart, and they are far more available. Adopted children are not genetically descended from the family of rearing, so that environmental differences between families are not confounded with genetic differences in the children, if the adopted children are randomly placed by adoption agencies. Theoretically, regressions of adopted child outcomes on adoptive family characteristics will provide genetically unbiased estimates of true environmental effects in the population. Unfortunately, adoptive families are selected by agencies for being above average in many virtues, including socioeconomic status. Thus, they are always an unrepresentative sample of the population to which one would like to generalize. Although it is possible that the adoptive family coefficients on background are good estimates of the population values, it is difficult to know without modeling the way in which the families were selected. An easier corrective for the possible bias of selected adoptive families is to have a comparison sample of biological families that are similarly selected.

A complete adoption study design would include comparable information on the intelligence of the natural parents of the adopted children. No study to date has reported IQ data on both the natural mothers and fathers of "adopted-away" children, but the prospective adoption study being conducted by Robert Plomin and his colleagues at the University of Colorado will provide information on the IQs of both natural parents, as well as the adoptive parents and the adopted children. The studies of Skodak and Skeels (1949) and Horn, Loehlin, and Willerman (1979) reported IQ test scores on the natural mothers of the adopted children. Other studies have been forced to use educational level of the natural parents as indices of intelligence because there were no IQ tests given to most of the natural parents.

Bias in the Adoption Study Methods? Comparisons of adopted and biologically related relatives assume that the greater behavioral similarity usually found among biological relatives is due to their greater genetic similarity. Critics of behavior genetic methods assert, to the contrary, that important biases creep into comparisons of genetically related and unrelated families through parental and child expectations of greater similarity among biological than adoptive relatives. If biological parents see themselves in their offspring and expect them to develop greater similarity to the parents, then the children may develop more similarly in many ways. Adoptive parents, knowing that there is no genetic link between them and their children, may expect less similarity and thus not pressure their children to become like the parents. The greater expectation of similarity among biological than adoptive relatives could well bias the comparisons of genetically related and unrelated families, confounding genetic relatedness with environmental pressures toward similarity that run in the same direction.

To test the hypothesis that knowledge of biological or adoptive status influences actual similarity, Scarr, Scarf, and Weinberg (1980) correlated absolute differences in objective test scores with ratings of similarity by adolescents and their parents in adoptive and biological families. Although biological family members see themselves as more similar than adoptive family members, there are also important generational and gender differences in perceived similarity that cut across family type. There is moderate agreement among family members on the degree of perceived similarity in intelligence and temperament. However, family members are more accurate about shared social attitudes.

Knowledge of adoptive or biological relatedness is related to the degree of perceived similarity, but perceptions of similarity are not related to objective similarities and thus do not constitute a bias in comparisons of measured differences in intelligence and temperament in adoptive and biological families.

The Classic Adoption Studies. The adoption studies of the 1920s and 1930s were crucial to conclusions about the role of genetic and environmental differences in intelligence in the white, nonethnic population of the United States. Despite their detractors (Kamin, 1974) these are remarkable studies, which the contemporary psychologist is unlikely to appreciate without more intimate contact with them.

Barbara Burks (1928, 1938), Alice M. Leahy (1935), and Marie Skodak and Harold Skeels (Skeels, 1938; Skodak, 1938; Skodak & Skeels, 1949) contributed unique and valuable information to the nature-nurture debate. Their studies supported the following points: (1) the above-average intellectual level of adopted children reared in advantaged homes, and hence the malleability of IQ scores, and (2) the lesser resemblance of adopted than natural children to their adoptive parents, and hence the role of genetic resemblance in intellectual resemblance. The more recent Texas and Minnesota adoption studies support their principal conclusions.

Texas Adoption Project. The Texas Adoption Project was begun in 1973 soon after the discovery of an adoption agency that had routinely administered over 1000 IQ and personality tests to the unwed mothers in their care. The agency administered these tests in order to provide their clients with occupational and educational counseling. The final sample consisted of 300 adoptive families, who were administered IQ tests by 22 different licensed psychologists across the state. The average age of the adopted children was about 8 years old. The adoptive families were well above average socioeconomically and intellectually. In this study the biological mothers of the adopted children also came from advantaged families, because the private home for unwed mothers from which the sample was drawn asked that the families of the unwed mothers contribute ''significant amounts of money to offset the costs of caring for their daughters'' (Horn, Loehlin, & Willerman, 1979). The average IQ of the natural mothers of the adopted children in this sample was 108.7 on the Beta. The average IQ scores of the adoptive patents on the Beta was 113.8 and on the WAIS, 113.9. The IQ scores of the adopted and biological offspring of the adoptive families are similar and in the range of from 109 to 114. Unlike the Burks (1928) and the Minnesota Adoption Studies to be described, but consonant with Leahy's (1935) results, the Texas Adoption Project found no average difference between the IQ scores of the adopted and biological children of the same families.

Parent-Child Correlations. Table 10 gives the correlations for adoptive and biological parents with their children. Although the biological relatives tend to have higher correlations with their offspring than the adoptive relatives, all of the correlations are quite low. The magnitude of the IQ correlation of the biological mother with her adopted-away child is as high as the correlations of the adoptive parents with their own offspring. There is evidence for considerable selective placement in these families, as the IQ score of the biological mother of one adopted child in a family is correlated .19 with the IQ score of another (unrelated) adopted child being reared in the same family and .08 with the biological child of the family that is rearing her adopted-away child.

Sibling Correlations. The overall IQ correlation of biological offspring of the adoptive parents

Table 10. **Correlation of Parent's Beta IQ with Child's IQ Tests[a]**

	Child Test			
	Wechsler Performance IQ		Wechsler or Binet total IQ	
Correlational Pairing	*r*	*N*	*r*	*N*
Adoptive father and				
biological child	**.29**	**144**	**.28**	**163**
adopted child	**.12**	**405**	**.14**	**462**
Adoptive mother and				
biological child	**.21**	**143**	**.20**	**162**
adopted child	**.15**	**401**	**.17**	**459**
Unwed mother and				
her child	**.28**	**297**	**.31**	**345**
other adopted child in same family	**.15**	**202**	**.19**	**233**
biological child in same family	**.06**	**143**	**.08**	**161**

[a]*N*'s refer to the number of pairings (= the number of children)—the same parent may enter more than one pairing. In the case of twins, the second twin was excluded from the unwed mother–other child comparisons. (From Horn, Loehlin & Willerman, 1979).

reared together was .35. Genetically unrelated children reared together had IQ scores that correlated .26, a statistically lower coefficient, but quite high!

Environmental and Genetic Effects on Adoptees' IQ Scores. Willerman (1979) divided the Texas adoptees into two extreme groups by natural mothers' IQ scores. For the low IQ group he selected natural mothers with IQ scores below 95, and for the high IQ group mothers with IQ scores of 120 or above. Table 11 shows the average of the adoptive parents' IQ scores (the midparent IQ), the mean IQ scores of the offspring of the high and low IQ natural mothers, and the percentage of the adopted children with IQ scores below 95 or equal to or above 120.

Although there is some evidence of selective placement for the adopted children, because the adoptive parent groups differ by 4 points in IQ, the 13 point IQ difference between the offspring of high and low IQ mothers shows that individuals of different genetic backgrounds differ in their responsiveness to the generally good environments of adoptive homes. Although the offspring of the low IQ mothers score above the population mean, they are not as bright as the offspring of high IQ mothers in similar environments.

The Minnesota Adoption Studies. Two large adoption studies were launched in 1974 for two quite different purposes.

In Minnesota the Transracial Adoption Study in 1974 to 1976 tested the hypothesis that black and interracial children reared by white families (in the culture of the tests and of the schools) would perform on IQ tests as well as other adopted children (Scarr & Weinberg, 1976). Adopted children ranged in age from 4 to 16 years.

In the transracial families there were 143 biological children, 111 children adopted in the first year of

Table 11. **IQs of Adoptees as a Function of Biological Mother's IQ**

Biological Mother (Beta)	Adoptive Midparent (Beta)	Adoptee (WISC/Binet)	Adoptees ≥ 120 IQ	Adoptees ≤ 95 IQ
Low IQ				
(*N* = 27; *M* = 89.4)	**110.8**	**102.6**	**0%**	**15%**
High IQ				
(*N* = 34; *M* = 121.6)	**114.8**	**118.3**	**44%**	**0%**

Note: WISC—Wechsler Intelligence Scale for Children; Binet—Stanford-Binet Intelligence Scale. (From Horn, Loehlin & Willerman, 1979).

life (called the Early Adoptees), and 65 children adopted after 12 months of age—up to 10 years old at the time of adoption. Most of the later adoptees were in fact placed with adoptive families before 4 years old, but they were not the usually studied adopted children who have spent all of their lives past the first few months with one adoptive family. As described by Scarr & Weinberg (1976), the later adoptees have checkered preadoptive histories.

> The 101 participating families included 176 adopted children, of whom 130 were socially classified as Black (29 with two Black natural parents and 101 with one Black natural parent and one natural parent of other or unknown racial background), and 25 as white. The remaining 21 included Asian, North American Indian, and Latin American Indian children. All of the adopted children were unrelated to the adoptive parents. Adopted children reared in the same home were unrelated, with the exception of four sibling pairs and one triad adopted by the same families, who were excluded from the analyses of family similarity. (Scarr and Weinberg, 1976, p. 728.)

IQ Levels of Family Members. Both the parents and the natural children of the families were found to score in the bright average to superior range on age-appropriate IQ tests. The black and interracial adopted children were also found to score above the average of the white population, regardless of when they were adopted. The black children adopted in the first 12 months of life scored on the average at IQ 110 (Scarr & Weinberg, 1976). This remarkable result was interpreted to mean that adopted children were scoring at least 20 points above comparable children being reared in the Black community. We interpreted the dramatic change in the IQ scores and school performance of the black and interracial children to mean that (1) genetic racial differences do not account for a major portion of the IQ or academic test performance difference between racial groups, and (2) black and interracial children reared in the culture of the tests and the schools perform as well as white adopted children in similar families (Burks, 1928; Horn, Loehlin, & Willerman, 1979; Leahy, 1935; Scarr & Weinberg, 1978). The adopted children scored 6 points below the natural children of the same families, however, as Burks (1928) and our second adoption study also found.

Family Correlations of IQ Scores. Table 12 shows the correlations of the parents and children in the transracial adoption study. The adoptive families had adopted at least one black child, but there were also other adopted children and many biological offspring of these same parents. The children ranged in age from 4 to about 18 years old. Because of the age range, children from 4 to 7 years were given the Stanford-Binet, children from 8 to 16 the WISC, and older children and all parents the WAIS. The adopted children averaged age 7, and the natural children about 10.

Table 12 shows the parent-child IQ correlations for all of the adopted children in the transracial adoptive families, regardless of when they were adopted. The total sample of adopted children is just as similar to their adopted parents as the early adopted group! The midparent-child correlation for all adoptees, regardless of age at adoption, was .29, and for the early adoptees, .30. Mothers and all adopted children were equally similar, and fathers more similar

***Table 12*. Comparisons of Biological and Unrelated Parent–Child IQ Correlations in 101 Transracial Adoptive Families**

	N (pairs)	*r*
Parents–Biological Children		
Adoptive mother–biological child	**141**	**.34**
Natural mother–adopted child[a]	**135**	**.33**
Adoptive father–biological child	**142**	**.39**
Natural father–adopted child[a]	**46**	**.43**
Parents–Unrelated Children		
Adoptive mother–adopted child	**174**	**.21 (.23)**[b]
Natural mother–biological child of adoptive family[a]	**217**	**.15**
Adoptive father–adopted child	**170**	**.27 (.15)**[b]
Natural father–biological child of adoptive family[a]	**86**	**.19**

[a]**Early adopted only ($N = 111$).**
[b]**Educational level, not IQ scores.**
(From Scarr & Weinberg, 1976).

than they were to the early adopted children alone.

Table 12 also shows the correlations between all adopted children's IQ scores and their natural parent's educational levels. Because we did not have IQ assessments of the natural parents, education is used here as a proxy. Despite this limitation, the correlations of natural parents' education with their adopted-away offspring's IQ scores are as high as the IQ correlations of biological parent-child pairs and exceed those of the adopted parent-child IQ scores. The mid-natural parent-child correlation of .43 is significantly greater than the mid-adopted parent-child of .29.

Because the adoptive parents are quite bright, their scores had considerably restricted variance. In Table 12 the correlations between parents and their natural and adopted children are not corrected for restriction of range in the parents' IQ scores. When corrected, the correlations of biological offspring with their parents rise to .49 and .54, and the midparent-child correlation is .66. Adopted child-adoptive midparent IQ resemblance rises to .37 (Scarr & Weinberg, 1977).

The correlations between natural parents of adopted children and biological children of the same families is an estimate of the effects of selective placement. If agencies match educational and social class characteristics of the natural mothers with similar adoptive parents, then the resemblance between adoptive parents and children is enhanced by the genetic, intellectual resemblance of natural and adoptive parents. Selective placement also enhances the correlation between natural parents and their adopted-away offspring, because the adoptive parents carry out the genotype-environment correlation that would have characterized the natural parent-child pairs, had the children been retained by their natural parents. Thus, neither the adoptive parent-child correlations nor the natural parent-adopted child correlations deserve to be as high as they are. Scarr and Weinberg (1977) adopted the solution proposed by Willerman et al. (1977) to subtract half of the selective placement coefficient of .17 from both the natural parent-adopted child correlation. There are other corrections that could be justified by the data set, but we will leave the "ultimate" solution(s) to biometricians. The simple figuring of these data yield "heritabilities" of .4 to .7.

In Table 13 the sibling correlations reveal a strikingly different picture. Young siblings are quite similar to each other, whether genetically related or not! The IQ correlations of the adopted sibs, genetically unrelated to each other, are as high as those of the biological sibs reared together. Children, reared in the same family environments and who are still under the major influence of their parents, score at similar levels on IQ tests.

Table 13. **Sibling IQ Correlations Natural and All Adopted Children of Adoptive Families**

	N (Pairs)	*r*
Natural sibs	**107**	**.42**
Natural sibs-adopted sib	**230**	**.25**
Natural sib-early adopted sib	**34**	**.30**
All adopted sibs	**140**	**.44**
Early adopted sibs	**53**	**.39**

The major point is that the heritabilities calculated from young sibling data are drastically different from those calculated from the parent-child data. As Christopher Jencks (1972) pointed out, the correlations of unrelated young siblings reared together do not fit any biometrical model, because they are too high. This study only makes the picture worse.

The Adolescent Adoption Study. This study was conceived to assess the cumulative impact of differences in family environments on children's development at the end of the childrearing period (Scarr & Weinberg, 1978; Scarr & Yee, 1980). All of the adoptees were placed in their families in the first year of life, the median age being 2 months. We administered the short-form of the WAIS to both parents and to two adolescents in most of the 115 adoptive families. A comparison group of 120 biological families had children of the same ages. Both samples of families were of similar socioeconomic status, from working to upper-middle class, and of similar IQ levels, except that the adopted children scored about 6 points lower than the biological children of similar parents. Table 14 gives these results.

Parent-Child and Sibling Correlations. Table 15 gives the parent-child and sibling correlations for the WAIS IQ and the four subtests on which it is based. The parent-child IQ correlations in the biological families were what we were led to expect from our earlier study and others—around .4 when uncorrected for the restriction of range in the parent's scores. The correlations of the adolescent adoptees with their adoptive parents, however, were lower than those of the younger adopted children and their adoptive parents. And the IQ correlation of adolescent adopted children reared together was zero! Unlike the younger siblings (who, after all, are

Table 14. Means, Standard Deviations, and Correlations of Adoptive and Biological Family Characteristics

	Biological Children (N = 237)											Mean	Standard Deviation
	1	2	3	4	5	6	7	8	9	10	11		
1 Child's IQ		.26	.24	.10	.22	−.19	−.21	.39	.39			112.82	10.36
2 Father's education	.10		.51	.61	.44	.01	−.36	.56	.24			15.63	2.83
3 Mother's education	.10	.51		.36	.39	.02	−.36	.43	.46			14.68	2.24
4 Father's occupation	.12	.57	.25		.47	.01	−.30	.37	.13			62.47	24.73
5 Family income	.06	.50	.40	.46		.00	−.25	.38	.19			24,987.34	8,770.43
6 Birth rank	−.19	.05	.03	.06	.15		.08	−.00	.03			1.62	0.63
7 Family size	−.05	.04	.11	−.00	.21	.10		−.30	−.10			3.85	1.48
8 Father's IQ	.15	.53	.30	.40	.45	.08	.14		.20			118.02	11.66
9 Mother's IQ	.04	.29	.44	.19	.21	.07	.12	.30				113.41	10.46
10 Natural mother's age	−.10	.04	.03	.12	−.02	−.11	−.04	−.10	.03				
11 Natural mother's education	.21	.33	.24	.29	.43	.09	.14	.20	.10	.07			
12 Natural mother's occupation	.12	−.00	.13	.11	.06	−.06	.11	.11	.15	.28	.33		

	1	2	3	4	5	6	7	8	9	10	11	12
Mean	106.19	14.90	13.95	60.30	25935.00	1.43	2.87	116.53	112.43	22.46	11.97	30.44
Standard Deviation	8.95	3.03	2.06	24.14	10196.78	0.57	1.20	11.36	10.18	5.80	1.66	23.24

Adopted children (N = 150)

$r \geq .16$, $p < .05$

(From Scarr & Weinberg, 1978).

Table 15. Correlations Among Family Members in Adoptive and Biologically Related Families (Pearson Coefficients on Standardized Scores by Family Member and Family Type) for Intelligence Test Scales

			Family Correlations			
Child Score	Reliability[a]		Mother–Child	Father–Child	Siblings	Mid-Parent/Child
Total WAIS IQ	(.97)	Biological	.41[b]	.40[b]	.35[b]	.52[b]
		Adoptive	.09	.16	−.03	.14
Subtests						
Arithmetic	(.79)	Biological	.24[b]	.30[b]	.24[b]	.36[b]
		Adoptive	−.03	.07	−.03	−.01
Vocabulary	(.94)	Biological	.33	.39[b]	.22	.43[b]
		Adoptive	.23	.24	.11	.26
Block design	(.86)	Biological	.29[b]	.32[b]	.25[b]	.40[b]
		Adoptive	.13	.02	.09	.14
Picture arrangement	(.66)	Biological	.19[b]	.06	.16	.11[b]
		Adoptive	−.01	−.04	.04	−.03
N		Biological	270	270	168	268
		Adoptive	184	175	84	168

[a] Reliability reported in the WAIS manual for late adolescents.

[b] Biological family correlations exceed adoptive family correlations, $p < .05$.

also of different races), these white adolescents reared together from infancy do not resemble their genetically unrelated siblings at all.

The IQ heritabilities from the adolescent study vary from .38 to .61, much like the parent-child data in the study of younger adoptees, but very unlike that data on younger sibs.

The interpretation of these results (Scarr & Weinberg, 1978) is that older adolescents are largely liberated from their families' influences and have made choices and pursued courses that are in keeping with their own talents and interests. Thus, the unrelated sibs have grown less and less alike. This hypothesis cannot be tested fully without longitudinal data on adopted siblings; to date all of the other adoption studies sampled much younger children, at the average age of 7 or 8 years. We can think of no other explanation for the markedly low correlations between the adopted sibs at the end of the childrearing period, in contrast to the several studies of younger adopted sibs, who are far more similar.

Sibling Correlations. Further details of sibling resemblance are given in Table 16. As one can see, the effects of being reared in the same household, neighborhood, and schools are negligible unless one is genetically related to one's brother or sister. The correlations of the biological siblings are modest but statistically different from zero.

With the most simple version of the heritability coefficient and an assumption that parental assortative mating is the same for aptitude and achievement as for IQ, we multiply the difference between the biological and adopted siblings' correlations by 1.6. The heritability estimates vary from .22 to .61 with a median estimate of .37. Although these values are not .8, as some would claim, neither are they zero. There seems to be no consistent difference in heritability by the kind of test.

The negligible differences in heritability for IQ, aptitude and achievement scores in this study of late adolescents is congruent with Lloyd Humphreys' findings of equal heritabilities for all cognitive measures in the Project Talent data (Hymphreys, 1980) and the Texas Adoption Study result of equal sibling resemblances of IQ and school achievement measures in a sample of younger children (Willerman et al., 1977). In other words, there seems to be no greater sibling resemblance for one or another kind of intellectual achievement, when they are all "g" loaded. We agree with Humphreys, however, that some specific skills may have different heritabilities.

Racial Differences in Intelligence. Arthur Jensen proposed that racial differences in measured intelligence could have a genetic basis.

> In view of all the most relevant evidence which I have examined, the most tenable hypothesis, in my judgment, is that genetic, as well as environmental, differences are involved in the average disparity between American Negroes and whites in intelligence and educability, as here defined. All the major facts would seem to be comprehended quite well by the hypothesis that something between one-half and three-fourths of the average IQ difference between American Negroes and whites is attributable to genetic factors, and the remainder to environmental factors

***Table 16.* Sibling Correlations of IQ, Aptitude, and Achievement Test Scores of Adopted and Biologically Related Adolescents**

	Biological		Adopted		
	N (pairs)	r	N (pairs)	r	$h^2 = 1.6(r_{bio} - r_{adopt})$
WAIS Verbal	168	.23	84	.07	.26
Performance	168	.21	84	.07	.22
IQ	168	.35	84	−.03	.61
Aptitude					
Verbal	141	.29	68	.13	.26
Numerical	61	.32	49	.07	.40
Total	61	.32	49	.09	.37
Achievement					
Reading	106	.27	73	.11	.26
Math	104	.35	58	−.11	.53
Total	104	.33	58	−.03	.58

(From Scarr & Yee, 1980).

> and their interaction with the genetic differences. (Jensen, 1973a, p. 363)

The evidence to which Jensen refers is the (1) unbiased nature of cognitive tests (see also, Jensen, 1980), (2) the heritability of individual differences within each racial group studied, (3) the inability of environmental factors that account for individual variation within racial groups to account for racial differences between groups, and (4) the poor performance of U.S. black groups compared to Indians and Mexican Americans, whose social conditions are even worse than those of blacks. Jensen admits that none of these arguments addresses directly the issue of genetic racial differences between blacks and whites in the United States.

In 1975 Loehlin et al. published their SSRC-sponsored review of the literature on racial differences in intelligence. Their equivocal conclusion that genetic differences may or may not be involved in intellectual differences between the races led many social scientists to accept their view as the most respectable scientific stance of the day. Since that time, two investigations on the possible genetic origins of racial differences in performance on school and IQ test have rejected the hypothesis of genetic differences as the major source of intellectual differences between the races. First, transracial children reared by socioeconomically advantaged white families (Scarr & Weinberg, 1976) score very well on standard IQ tests and on school achievement tests. Being reared in the culture of the test and the school resulted in intellectual achievement levels for black children that were comparable to adopted white children in similar families. Therefore, it is highly unlikely that genetic differences between the races could account for the major portion of the usually observed differences in the performance levels of the two groups.

A second study on the relation of black ancestry to intellectual skills within the black population (Scarr, Pakstis, Katz, & Barker, 1977) showed that having more or less African ancestry was not related to how well one scored on cognitive tests. In other words, holding constant social identity and cultural background, socially classified blacks with more African ancestry scored as highly on the tests as blacks with less African ancestry. A strong genetic difference hypothesis cannot account for this result.

Briefly, blood groups were used to estimate the proportion of each person's African and European ancestry. This is roughly possible because the parent populations differ in the average frequencies of many alleles at many loci and differ substantially at a few loci. Therefore, a person with a particular allele was assigned a probability that the allele was from one of the two populations. Although there is undoubtedly a large error term in these estimates, they had several satisfactory characteristics, such as appropriately large sibling correlations and correlations with skin color. What is most important here is that the estimates of ancestry did not correlate with any measures of intellectual performance in the black sample. Thus, the conclusion that degree of white ancestry had little or no effect on individual levels of performance within the black group is insufficient. Other explanations must be sought.

Separate Cognitive Abilities. Discussions about the behavior genetics of separate cognitive abilities often focus on data from multivariate studies indicating that some abilities that correlate highly with one another are more heritable than other clusters of abilities. There is considerable dispute about the strength of such a claim and about its implications for a theory of intelligence. Many behavior geneticists continue to doubt that different kinds of intellectual functioning are differentially heritable (Loehlin & Nichols, 1976; Nichols, 1978). Despite the general finding of moderate to high correlations among tests of specific cognitive abilities, the existence of sharp discontinuities of intellectual performance has kept alive the hope that there may be discrete and uncorrelated components of information processing that contribute to what is loosely construed as intelligence. The existence of "idiot savants," individuals with subnormal psychometric IQ scores but who excel in specific areas such as music, art, or numerical abilities, has been cited as testimony for the separate abilities approach to intelligence (Anastasi & Levee, 1959; Minton & Schneider, 1980). Additional support for this position has come from evidence of differential rates of decline with age for verbal and spatial abilities (Botwinick, 1977; Wechsler, 1950).

There would be no good rationale for asking questions about genetic and environmental mechanisms for separate cognitive abilities if we believed that all cognitive abilities developed in the same way and responded identically to differences in genetic constitution, biological factors, and environmental circumstances. However, this is not the case. There is good evidence for differential cognitive development, not only from the factor analytic studies that are commonly cited, but from studies of cognitive dysfunction. We know, for example, that women with Turner's syndrome, a chromosomal anomaly involving the *X* chromosome, while normal or above normal in verbal functioning often show defects in spatial thinking (Garron, 1970). If this genetic anomaly had deleterious effects on intellectual functioning in general, there would be an overall decrement in cognitive skills. Similarly, if the physical consequences of Turner's syndrome (short stature, webbed neck, absence of secondary sexual characteristics, infertility, and others) led to treatment by parents, siblings, and teachers that would depress cognitive performance, it would be expected that the performance depression would not be restricted to spatial thinking.

Overall, attempts to specify and elaborate the routes from genes to behaviors have not met with great success when general level of intellectual functioning has been the object of study. It is possible, however, that the mechanistic approach will have greater utility with respect to specific cognitive abilities. There are certain clinical syndromes with known or suspected genetic etiologies (Turner's syndrome, autism, dyslexia) in which only certain kinds of cognitive functions are disrupted while others are quite intact. There are other conditions with known genetic antecedents in which the precise nature of the cognitive impairment has not been fully explored (PKU, Down's syndrome, Klinefelter's syndrome, and Huntington's chorea, for example). Although the prospect of carrying out detailed biochemical analyses on probands and their families may seem arduous and painstaking, it is only by doing such studies that we can hope to understand the biological substrates of abnormal cognitive development and develop effective treatments for affected individuals.

The bulk of recent behavior genetic research on IQ and general intellectual ability has focused on normal development rather than on clinical populations. The same has not been true in studies of specific cognitive abilities. Researchers seem here to fall into two camps—those who take a population approach and administer cognitive tests to large numbers of individuals who differ in the extent to which they share common genes and common rearing environments, and those who sample from populations with a specific deficit, and study either those individuals intensively or those individuals *and* their relatives, in an attempt to explore possible biological and sociocultural mechanisms underlying the condition. With the first approach, the goal is to determine what proportion of total variance can be attributed to genetic and nongenetic factors. While the second approach may also attempt to explain some variance in the population, the major focus seems to be one of developing explanatory, mechanistic models that might lead to effective interventions, at whatever level.

Multivariate Studies of Specific Cognitive Abilities. As mentioned earlier in this chapter, there is no convincing evidence that any one kind of cognitive ability is substantially more heritable than any other. Although some studies have reported greater familiarity for verbal abilities, others have found no significant differences.

The most comprehensive and largest twin studies to date have come up with mixed results, and have led us to conclude that the twin data cannot be used to support the notion that there are genetically mediated differences in the relative degree of familial resemblance across different cognitive abilities (Brunn, Markkanen, & Partanen, 1966; Loehlin & Nichols, 1976; Schoenfeldt, 1968). Although the heritability estimates for specific and general cognitive abilities from twin studies do not differ significantly (.42 for specific abilities; .48 for general IQ), an examination of the magnitudes of the MZ and DZ correlations suggests that within-family environmental influences may affect specific cognitive abilities more than general cognitive functioning (Plomin, DeFries, & McClearn, 1980).

Family studies have also come up with inconsistent findings. Williams (1975) reported that family resemblance was greater for Verbal than Performance subscales on Wechsler tests in a study of 55 boys (aged 10 years) and their parents. Verbal test correlations were not consistently higher than correlations for other tests, however, in a study of cognitive performance in 192 Israeli families with two children aged 13 or older (Loehlin, Sharan, & Jacoby, 1978).

Data from the largest family study to date, the Hawaii Family Study, have been combined with data from a study of 209 Korean families (Park, Johnson, DeFries, McClearn, Mi, Rashad, Vandenberg, & Wilson, 1978) in an attempt to present comparable information on three different ethnic groups. After age corrections had been made, midchild (the average of the children's) scores were regressed on midparent scores for individual cognitive tests and for factor scores. Both the Americans of European ancestry and the Americans of Japanese ancestry had somewhat higher familial similarity on Verbal and Spatial factors than on Perceptual Speed and Visual Memory (see Figure 15). This pattern is not evident for the Korean sample, however, in which, although the value for Visual Memory is the lowest of the four factors, all factors reflect substantial familiality.

Few adoption studies have looked at specific cognitive abilities, but those that have are consistent with the twin and family studies in that they report significantly higher correlations for biological relatives than for adoptive relatives, but do not present convincing evidence that any one kind of cognitive process is more heritable than another (Carter-Saltz-

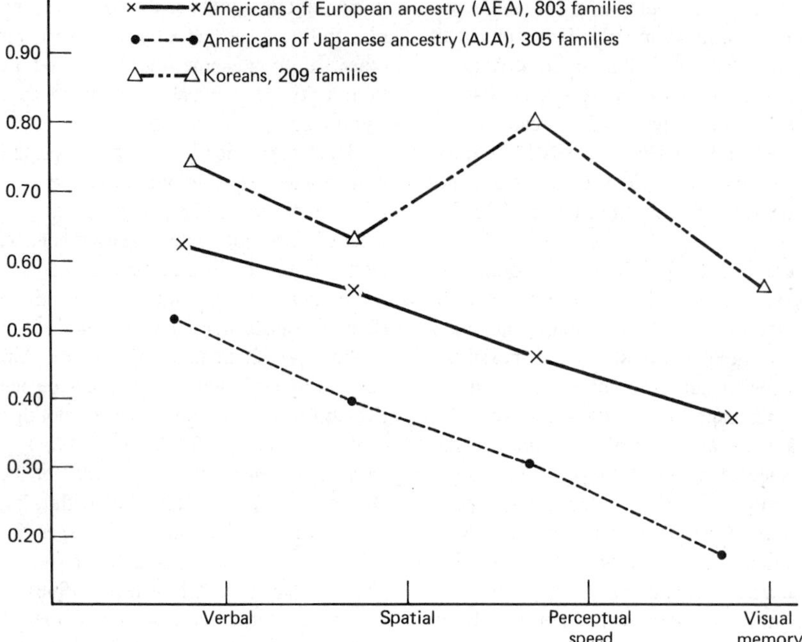

Figure 15. Regressions of mid-child on mid-parent for four different factor scores in three ethnic groups. (Drawn from data in DeFries et al., 1970, and Park et al., 1978).

man, 1978; Claeys, 1973; Scarr & Weinberg, 1978). A reexamination of Table 15 will indicate that although biological relatives are more similar than adoptive relatives on WAIS subtests, the patterns of correlations (especially when assortative mating coefficients are considered) do not lead us to make any strong statements about differential heritability of specific abilities.

Spatial Thinking. Spatial abilities have received more attention from behavior geneticists than any other kind of cognitive processes, and there are several reasons why. First, there are substantial individual and group differences in some kinds of spatial thinking. In particular, strong and consistent sex differences in "spatial visualization" have been replicated many times and have led to the formulation and testing of specific genetic models to account for the distributional and family correlational patterns obtained. Second, psychologists have somewhat more precisely defined spatial ability than other cognitive abilities, so the phenotype under consideration can be clearly differentiated from other cognitive phenotypes. Factor analytic studies have greatly facilitated this differentiation, and have even enabled us to distinguish among various kinds of spatial thinking (*not* all of which show the aforementioned sex differences). Finally, some clinical subgroups show striking patterns of deficits and advantages in spatial thinking. In Turner syndrome, a chromosomal disorder, there is a definite disturbance of spatial thinking. Knowledge that Turner syndrome women differ from other women by the absence of the second *X* chromosome has led investigators to focus attention on possible *X*-chromosome involvement in spatial thinking.

Sex Differences. Differences between the sexes favoring males have been found across a wide range of spatial tasks by many different investigators. The strongest and most consistent differences have been discerned on tasks that have a visualization component, and this difference is rarely detected before puberty. Although some early sex differences in spatial abilities have been reported (see Vandenberg & Kuse, 1979, for review) the most discriminating tests that tap visualization have proven too difficult for both young boys and girls. Differences emerge in adolescence, when males move well ahead of their female peers, most of whom never manage to catch up (Harris, 1977, 1979; Maccoby & Jacklin, 1974). Of course, not all females lack spatial visualization ability, although there are more males than females in whom this talent is expressed.

Questions about the nature of the mechanisms

underlying this sex difference still remain unresolved, despite considerable vigilance on the part of several investigators. Hypotheses about the effects of sociocultural, physiological, endocrinological, and genetic mechanisms have been tested. We will review the genetic models that have been proposed, and will assess the state of the field in the light of family studies that have been conducted to date. It is sometimes forgotten that behavior genetic methodologies allow us to test environmental models as well as genetic models. Some of the data obtained from family studies have been used to explore the power and specificity of environmental effects on the development of spatial thinking.

X-linkage Model of Inheritance. Results from twin studies and studies of biological and adoptive families have indicated that spatial abilities are as heritable as other kinds of cognitive abilities (Claeys, 1973; DeFries et al., 1976, 1978; Osborne & Gregor, 1968; Vandenberg, 1962, 1967; Williams, 1975).

Due to both the difficulties inherent in accurate assessment of the phenotype—there is, for instance, no absolute cut-off level on a particular test above which one can reliably diagnose the presence of spatial visualizing ability—and to correct designation of genotype, speculations about the genetic mechanisms influencing sex differences have been vague. Results from a number of early studies lent support to a hypothesis involving *X* linkage (Bock & Kolakowski, 1973; Corah, 1965; Guttman, 1974; Hartlage, 1970; Stafford, 1961). This hypothesis was most clearly articulated by Bock and Kolakowski (1973), who proposed that spatial visualization ability, although probably influenced by multiple autosomal alleles, was "enhanced" by a recessive gene located on the X chromosome. The frequency of this gene was calculated to be about .50 in North American white populations. As expected with a gene frequency of .50, about 50% of all males and about 25% of all females in these populations would express the trait, since males express whatever is on their single *X* chromosome whereas females require two of the recessive alleles for the trait to be expressed (Bock & Kolakowski, 1973). A large number of studies found support for the *X*-linkage hypothesis with the distribution of scores; only about one quarter of females scored above the median score for males on a variety of spatial tests (Bock & Kolakowski, 1973; Bouchard & McGee, 1977; Loehlin, Sharan, & Jacoby, 1978; O'Connor, 1943; Yen, 1975).

The patterns of family correlations from early studies also supported the *X*-linkage hypothesis. The expected pattern of correlations is as follows: equally high mother-son and father-daughter correlations would be expected since a son receives his only *X* chromosome from his mother, and a father passes on his only *X* chromosome to his daughter; the correlation between fathers and sons should be very close to zero because sons receive no *X* chromsomes from their fathers; and the correlation between mothers and daughters should be intermediate, as neither mothers nor daughters necessarily express what is coded on the single *X* chromosome they share. Therefore, the order of correlations for an *X*-linked trait should be as follows:

Mother-son = Father-Daughter > Mother-Daughter > Father-Son

For sibling correlations it is expected that sisters would be most similar, since they share the paternally derived *X*, and have a 50% chance of sharing an *X* chromosome from the mother; brothers would have a 50% chance of having the same maternal *X* chromosome; and brother-sister pairs would be the least similar, since their 50% chance of sharing the maternally-derived *X* chromosome is offset by the certainty that the sister will receive an *X* from the father and the brother will not. The expected order of sibling correlations, then is

Sister-Sister > Brother-Brother > Sister-Brother

Results from the early studies supported an *X*-linked hypothesis for spatial visualization, but later ones have not. For more detailed treatments of these investigations, the reader is referred to recent reviews by McGee (1979) and Vandenberg and Kuse (1979). The overwhelming conclusion from the more recent studies is that the *X*-linkage hypothesis cannot be supported by the rank order of intrafamilial correlations.

Turner's Syndrome and Spatial Performance. Studies of the cognitive performance patterns of women with Turner syndrome are of particular interest for several reasons. First, Turner syndrome has a known genetic antecedent involving the *X* chromosome. In the classic Turner syndrome, the entire second *X* chromosome is missing, leaving the patient with a total of only 45 chromosomes (45, *X*). Some women with Turner Syndrome are mosaics, with some of their cells showing the classic 45, X patterns, and others having the normal 46, *XX* chromosome complement. Still others show variations of the short arm of the second *X* chromosome: deletions, translocations, or complete absence of the arm (Serra, Pizzamiglio, Boari, & Spera, 1978; Stern, 1973). Because of the *X*-linkage hypothesis about the transmission of spatial abilities, there has been considerable interest in studying possible *X*-chromosome involvement in spatial thinking. If spatial visualization were *X*-linked one would expect the spatial performance of Turner syndrome women to resemble that of normal males, since any information coded on the *X*-chromosome should be expressed. In contrast to that expectation, women with Turner syndrome perform exceptionally poorly, on the average, on tests of spatial thinking. In addition, this deficit seems to be quite specific to spatial thinking; performance on tests of verbal ability is at or above normal levels.

Hormonal Models for Differences in Spatial Ability. Models linking spatial performance to hormonal events—prenatally, at puberty, and in adulthood—have made a respectable showing over the past fifteen years, and most are still viable today. These models have tried to account for cognitive differences as a function of maturation rate (Waber, 1976; 1977), physical androgyny (Klaiber, Broverman, & Kobayashi, 1967; Mackenberg, Broverman, Vogel, & Klaiber, 1974; Peterson, 1976), and hormonal fluctuations during the menstrual cycle (Englander-Golden, Willis, & Dienstibier, 1976; Klaiber, Broverman, Vogel & Kobayashi, 1974). Although research in this area is of great importance and will surely enhance our eventual understanding of the biological mechanisms underlying cognitive performance patterns, no studies to date have employed behavior genetic methods. For recent reviews and critiques of these models the reader is referred to Dan (1979), McGee (1979), Petersen (1979), and Waber (1979).

It has been suggested that the *Y* chromosome retards maturation rate, permitting fuller expression of the genome in males than females (Ounsted & Tayler, 1972). This would presumably be reflected in more complete penetrance in males (already proposed in some of the genetic models reviewed above), as well as in greater male variance for a wide array ofphenotypes. Wilson and Vandenberg (1978) have reported that in the Hawaii study variance was greater for males than females on 11 of 15 cognitive tests (the difference was significant for Mental Rotations, Subtraction and Multiplication, and Word Beginnings and Endings). Existing data sets can be examined for sex differences in variances, and the question can partially be addressed in that manner. In addition, it should be possible to look at the rates of physical maturation and cognitive development in individuals with *Y*-chromosome anomalies.

McGee (1979) has proposed that there may be an *X*-linked gene that controls the timing of androgen release at puberty, and has related his suggestion to the work of Petersen (1976) and Broverman, Klaiber, Kobayashi, and Vogel (1968), who found that high spatial performance was associated with late maturation and low androgenization (determined by physical characteristics) in males, and with highly androgenized body types in females. This notion is consistent with Waber's (1976, 1977, 1979) reports that for both males and females, late maturers performed at higher levels than early maturers on tests of spatial ability. These formulations would be strengthened considerably by data indicating a strong positive relationship between the timing of puberty and ratings of physical androgeny. One would also want to look at familial patterns in the timing of the onset of puberty to see if there was any evidence of *X*-linked inheritance. To our knowledge such studies have not yet been undertaken.

Studies of the relationship between cognitive performance profiles and hormonal status have not been numerous, but we do not know of a single one in which affected subjects showed higher spatial than verbal performance. Dawson (1972) has reported higher Verbal than Performance scores on Wechsler tests for four different groups of subjects with sex hormone anomalies: genetic males with testicular feminization (Masica, Money, & Ehrhardt, 1969); males with Klinefelter syndrome; females with Turner syndrome; and West African males with gynecomastia (breast-enlargement) due to Kwashiorkor (Dawson, 1967a; 1967b). It may be that an optimal balance of steroid hormones at one or more periods during development is a prerequisite for the development of high spatial ability. Levine (1971) has suggested that early hormones are crucial during some critical periods of neurological differentiation. He proposed that "the function of gonadal hormones in infancy is to organize the central nervous system with regard to neuroendocrine control of behavior" (p. 15), and suggested that the differential responsiveness of males and females to externally administered hormones might be dependent on hormonal events occurring in the prenatal and neonatal periods (Levine, 1971).

Genetic Factors in Visual Illusion and Perception. The existence of individual differences in visual perception is well established (Berry, 1971; Pick & Pick, 1970; Segal, Campbell, & Herskovits, 1966). Strangely enough, no one seems to have tried to relate those differences—for example, in visual acuity, lens pigmentation, illusion susceptibility, persistence of a visual image, brightness judgment, and many other basic aspects of visual processing—to performance on cognitive tests of visuospatial performance. Instead, the very limited literature on individual differences in vision has concentrated on linking such variation to differences in age (see Pick & Pick, 1970, for review), culture (Deregowski, 1973; Segal et al., 1966), or sex (McGuinness, 1976a, 1976b; McGuinness & Lewis, 1976).

Genetic factors have been found to contribute to susceptibility to both primary illusions (those that show a decrease in errors with age) and secondary illusions (those that show an increase in errors with age), and to an illusion that shows a quite complex relationship to age changes. Twin data supporting this general conclusion have been reported for the Mueller-Lyer illusion (Smith, 1949) and the double trapezium illusion (Matheny, 1973), both primary illusions, and for the Ponzo illusion (Matheny, 1971), a secondary illusion.

In a family study including 203 mother-father-offspring triads and 303 sibling pairs, Coren and Porac (1979) found evidence of significant family resemblance for the Muller-Lyer illusion and for the underestimated segment of the Ebbinghaus illusion. In their informative review of the possible cognitive and sensory processes underlying illusion susceptibility, the authors concluded that several heritable optical and neural mechanisms might be responsible for both the Muller-Lyer illusion and the underestimated part of the Ebbinghaus, but that no such mechanisms could be invoked to explain Ebbinghaus overestimation.

Although there has been relatively little work by behavior geneticists on visual perception, the data that exist suggest that both genetic and nongenetic factors are important in the development of perceptual processes, and that such processes are related to cognitive functioning. The field is wide open for a more programmatic approach to the problem.

Sex Differences. Because of the robust sex difference in spatial visualization, we were led to ask about sex differences in visual perception. Are there any? If so, do we know anything about how such differences develop? It will perhaps surprise some students of perception and cognition that there is considerable evidence for the existence of sex differences in visual perception (see McGuinness, 1976a, 1976b, for reviews). A few of the differences are: male superiority in both dynamic and static visual acuity (Burg, 1966; Roberts, 1964); longer persistence of visual sensation in males than females (McGuinness & Lewis, 1976); female superiority in some perceptual learning and visual discrimination tasks (Laughlin & McGlynn, 1967; Pishkin, Wolfgang, & Rasmussen, 1967; Stevenson, Hale, Klein, & Miller, 1968); greater amount of lens pigmentation for males (Porac, Coren, Girgus, & Verde, 1979).

Investigations of sex differences in susceptibility to visual illusions have indicated that although there are no sex differences for two-dimensional, static illusions (Fraisse & Vautrey, 1956; Pressey & Wilson, 1978; Porac et al., 1979), sex differences have been found for Necker cube reversals (Immergluck & Mearini, 1969), an illusion that involves reorganization of a three-dimensional array.

The finding of sex differences only for a three-dimensional illusion is inconsistent with results reported for spatial visualization tasks. Although sex differences are sometimes found for two-dimensional spatial tests, those findings are less robust and less consistent across studies. The only family studies on visual illusions to date have been limited to two-dimensional illusions.

Conclusions: Spatial Thinking. There are clearly large individual differences in spatial thinking. Because so much research effort has been spent on this area, we have chosen to devote considerable attention to it. The results of numerous behavior genetic studies have led to the conclusion that genetic factors do contribute to the observed differences, although it is difficult to estimate precisely the magnitude of that contribution.

Of all cognitive abilities that have been psychometrically assessed, none has shown greater sex differences, at least in North American Caucasian populations, than spatial visualization. To date, the mechanisms mediating those differences have not been specifically delineated, although several genetic models have been proposed and tested. Some of these models have involved differential penetrance in males and females, and have most recently been subjected to complex statistical analyses.

The most intriguing (and most widely-tested) hypothesis has been the one involving *X* linkage. The most recent family data do not favor the hypothesis that enhanced spatial visualization is an *X*-linked recessive trait, but distributional data and the results of recent linkage study still do not allow us to discard the idea. Although the pattern of cognitive abilities of women with Turner syndrome seem in direct opposition to the *X*-linkage hypothesis, it is possible that early (possibly prenatal) hormonal events may prime the subsequent pattern of spatial thinking. Turner syndrome women differ from both men and other women with a normal chromosome complement in such hormonal events.

Because there may be some relationship between hormonal status and spatial thinking, it is also possible that the timing of androgen release at puberty and the rate of sexual maturation may be related to level of spatial ability. The extent to which genetic factors are important to such a relationship has not yet been addressed with behavior genetic methods. It is only through a longitudinal behavior genetic study that one would be able to demonstrate a clear relationship among normal events, spatial performance (at a later point in time), and genetic constitution.

Personality Variations

The essence of personality is behavioral consistency across time and place. People are said to "have" certain personality characteristics when they are observed by others or themselves to behave in predictably similar ways over variable events and situations. The very notion of personality was challenged by Mischel (1968), who proposed that (1) consistencies are so low as to be trivial, and (2) whatever consistency exists is primarily in the eye of the beholder. He emphasized the situational inconsistency in people's behaviors. Throughout the history of personality study there have been arguments over the relative importance of situational determinants of behavior versus individual consistency in behavior. Advocates of the importance of situationalism necessarily favor environmental explanations of behavior; advocates of personal consistency have often proposed some genetic basis for individual differences in personality.

Despite the popularity of situationalism over the past 15 years, there is growing awareness that personal consistency does exist, at least for "some of the people some of the time" (Bem & Allen, 1974). And there is growing awareness that the claims of extreme situationalism are based in (large) part on unreliable measurements of behaviors, which necessarily result in low correlations across times and places (Moskovitz & Schwarz, 1982). At the other extreme, ideas of fixed traits have given way to more moderate views of person-situation interactions that shape personality development.

If personal consistency develops from combinations of genetic background and individual experiences, then biologically related persons should be more similar in personality than unrelated persons. People who live together should share more common experiences and therefore be more similar in their behaviors than others who do not live together. Thus, parents and their genetic offspring and biologically related siblings should score more similarly on personality measures than unrelated adoptive parents and their children or unrelated children reared as siblings. Unrelated persons who live together should be more similar than unrelated persons reared apart. Monozygotic twins should be more similar than first-degree relatives, including dizygotic twins.

Studies of Temperament

The term *temperament* is usually applied to behavioral dispositions of infants and young children and connotes a constitutional origin for personality differences. The principal model that attempts to describe the role of genetic differences in temperament proposes that individual differences, present in the first days of life, have genetic and prenatal environmental origins that interact with caretaking differences in infancy to produce differences in child and adult personality (Escalona 1968; Thomas & Chess, 1977). Thomas and Chess (1977) have described nine dimensions of temperament that have been assessed longitudinally through parental interviews and questionnaires (Carey & McDevitt, 1977). From the ages of 1 to 5 years old, only one dimension proved to be even modestly stable. At any one age, however, MZ twin resemblance tends to exceed that of DZ twins for most or all temperamental traits (Freedman, 1965; Matheny, Dolan, & Wilson, 1976; Torgeson & Kringlen, 1978).

In the Louisville Twin Study, Matheny et al. (1976) used the Bayley Infant Behavior Record to assess the temperamental and behavioral similarities of 1-year old twins. For the 23 behaviors rated by the Bayley examiners during the first year of life, the average MZ correlation was .57 and the average DZ correlation was .35.

In a longitudinal study of temperament in twins, Goldsmith and Gottesman (1981) showed that MZ twin correlations exceed those of DZs for a variety of temperamental characteristics at 8 months and at 4 and 7 years of age. From the Collaborative Perinatal Project, the Bayley Infant Behavior Record ratings by test examiners of the infant and childhood temperament were factored for more than 100 MZ and 200 DZ pairs at the three ages. The median correlation for temperamental traits, such as activity, attention, task persistence, and irritability were generally higher for MZ than DZ pairs. They found that the median correlations for both MZ and DZ pairs declined with age, falling from .46 to .33 for MZs and from .30 to .12 for DZs in the period of 8 months to 7 years. Many of the more "heritable" temperamental traits are know to be highly correlated with intellectual performance (McCartney, Scarr, Phillips, Grajek, & Schwarz, 1981; Scarr, 1981), so that these findings are not easily interpretable as temperamental, genetic variation per se.

Temperamental differences among twins have

been assessed in several studies by Plomin and his colleagues. With the cooperation of the National Mothers of Twins Clubs in several states, they obtained parents' ratings of themselves and their young twin children on the EASI scales (Buss & Plomin, 1975). Correlations of the parents' ratings on Emotionality, Activity, Sociability, and Impulsivity (EASI) averaged .55 for the MZ twins and −.07 for the DZ pairs! The twin data suggest very high heritability for the EASI temperamental traits; assuming no assortative mating, double the difference between the MZ and DZ coefficients gives an h^2 of .96. There is no evidence for any effect of common home environment, as the DZ twin correlation is actually slightly negative.

By contrast, the average mother-child and father-child personality correlations were only .17 and .10, respectively. Thus, the parent-child data yield an upper-limit heritability between .20 and .34, far below the estimate from the twin data. The fact that the children were between 2 and 6 years old and the parents averaged 30 years of age led the authors to suggest that the traits may have different meanings in the two age groups. As we shall see in the study of adopted and biologically related families with adolescents, however, the parent-child correlations in this study are similar to those obtained in a study of much older offspring (Scarr, Webber, Weinberg, & Wittig, 1981). The twin data are discrepant from both family studies.

The role of temperament in the development of infant-mother attachments was explored by Plomin in a study of 46 twin pairs who ranged in age from 13 to 37 months. Visitors to the home administered and rated the twins' attachment behaviors in a standard series of interactions with the mother and the experimenter, including approach by and play with stranger and mother, cuddling with stranger and mother, and separation from mother. Significant differences were found between the similarities of MZ and DZ twins for social behaviors directed toward the stranger but not for social behaviors directed toward the mother. Plomin concluded that, in infancy, genetic differences affect social responding to unfamiliar persons more than to familiar ones. Environmental effects were largely differences *within* families, rather than between them.

In the longitudinal, prospective adoption study in Colorado, DeFries, Plomin, Vandenberg, and Kuse (1981) reported no consistent pattern of resemblance between the temperament in adoptive or in the biologically related control families. Natural mothers' scores on personality tests were also unrelated to their adopted-away infants' temperament scores. Because the true correlations between biologically related pairs may be as low as .20, the sample size in this study to date may not be sufficient to detect such relationships.

Twin Studies of Personality

Studies of personality resemblance between adolescent and young adult cotwins are numerous and fairly consistent in finding moderate similarity among MZ twins and greater MZ than DZ twin resemblance. Nichols (1978) reviewed the published studies of personality resemblance of twins and reported a weighted mean correlation of .52 for identical twins and .25 for fraternal twins. There were no consistent differences among personality measures in the magnitude of their broad heritabilities. Dozens of personality scales administered to thousands of twin pairs in more than 30 studies yielded the result that all measured aspects of personality seem to be equally heritable. In a review of twin studies using the California Personality Inventory (Carey, Goldsmith, Tellegen, & Gottesman, 1978), the authors also reported no consistency in the heritabilities of the various scales across studies, but suggested that there was more stability for MZ than DZ coefficients. The authors favor the view, as did Scarr (1968), that social introversion-extraversion is more heritable than other traits, although the evidence is inconclusive.

In a remarkably large study of 12,898 pairs of twins from the Swedish twin registry, Floderus-Myrhed, Pederson, and Rasmuson (1980) administered by mail a shortened version of the Eysenck Personality Inventory (EPI). The same-sex twin pairs ranged in age from 16 to 48 years of age. The results are consonant with Nichols's (1978) summary: the MZ correlations for Psychosocial Instability (Neuroticism) and Extraversion were .48 and .50, respectively, and the DZ correlations were .23 and .21. From these twin coefficients, the authors calculated heritability coefficients of .54 and .58.

Twin correlations for personality measures are found to be consistently lower than those for measures of ability. Nichols' (1978) review of twin studies of abilities yielded a weighted mean correlation of .82 for MZ pairs and .59 for DZ pairs. For measures of general ability, identical twins are about as similar as the same person tested twice, which Plomin & DeFries (1980) estimated as .82, whereas MZ twin correlations for personality measures do not approach the reliability of contemporary personality measures, which range in the high .70s and .80s. The results of Nichols' tabulations are shown in Table 17.

Table 17. **Summary of Mid-Parent-Child Resemblance on Personality Measures of Introversion–Extraversion and Neuroticism–Anxiety**

	Biological r_{iB}	Adoptive r_{iA}	t
Introversion–extraversion	.19	−.00	1.78[a]
Social closeness	.28	−.00	2.93[b]
Social potency	.21	.10	1.10
Impulsivity	.14	−.02	1.53
Neuroticism	.25	.05	2.09[a]
Social anxiety	.03	.17	−1.43[a]
Physical anxiety	.21	.06	1.56
Total anxiety	.14	.11	.29
Defensiveness (lie)	.20	.06	1.53
Single parent–child median r_i	.20	.06	
Mid parent–child median r_i	.15	.04	

Single parent–child $h^2 = 2(r_{iB} - r_{iA}) = .22$
Midparent–child $h^2 = (r_{iB} - r_{iA}) = .14$

[a] $p < .05$
[b] $p < .01$

Curiously, however, the *differences* between the MZ and DZ correlations are about the same for measures of ability and personality. The implication of this result is that the heritabilities of ability and personality measures are the same! Loehlin and Nichols (1976) concluded:

> Identical twins correlate about .20 higher than fraternal twins, give or take some sampling fluctuation, and it doesn't matter much what you measure—whether the difference is between .75 and .55 on an ability measure, between .50 and .30 on a personality scale, or between .35 and .15 on a self-concept composite. (p. 35)

Loehlin, Horn, and Willerman (1981) and Loehlin and Nichols (1976) attribute the higher correlations of ability than personality measures, for both MZ and DZ twins, primarily to the effects of common home environment (or differences among homes) on the development of abilities, but not personality.

Family Studies of Personality

Many studies of parental childrearing practices suggest that the characteristic ways in which parents behave toward their children are correlated with the children's personality (e.g., Harrington, Block & Block, 1978). Many studies show also that the personality characteristics of parents are modestly related to those of their offspring. Crook (1937) reported an average biological parent-child correlation of .16 for personality measures, and an average sibling correlation of .18. Given that both parent-child and sibling pairs share about half of their genes, the coefficients are modest indeed. In addition, siblings share more similar rearing environments than parents and children, but sibling resemblance hardly exceeds that of parents and children. Given that siblings were more likely to have been given the same personality measures, because they are more nearly the same ages, whereas parents were often given an adult test, the slightly greater similarity of sibling than parent-child pairs may be nothing more than measurement similarity.

Studies of Young Adopted and Biologically Related Children. Two recent adoption studies have included children whose average ages were between 7 and 10 years. The Texas Adoption Project (Horn et al., 1979) reported personality correlations for about 200 families in which the children were old enough to complete a paper-and-pencil personality inventory. Although all of the families had adopted children, many also had biological offspring. Similarly, Scarr and Weinberg (1976, 1977) reported on 101 adoptive families, each of which had adopted at least one black or interracial child, also had many biological offspring, and, in some cases, adopted children of other races. In the Texas Adoption Project, the average age of the children was about 8 years; in the Minnesota Transracial Study the adopted children averaged age 7 and the biological offspring about age 10.

The striking finding in the Texas study is the lack of personality resemblance for people who live together, regardless of their genetic resemblance. Loehlin, Horn, & Willerman (1981) reported a median correlation of .05 for 24 pairs of biological siblings and .04 for 109 pairs of adopted siblings for 13 personality scales (from the *Cattell 16 PF*). Children who have lived together all of their lives and those who are genetically related by half might as well be strangers on such personality inventories. Parent-child correlations were equally discouraging. The Texas parents' personality scores correlated .09 with their biological offspring (N = 178) and .08 with their adopted children (N = 409). Loehlin's careful analysis of the patterns of resemblance for the various personality scales revealed no consistent pattern of results.

In the Minnesota study, the three scales of the *Junior Eysenck Personality Inventory* yielded a mean sibling correlation of .19 for 40 biologically related pairs, and .01 for unrelated children. Thus, in the Minnesota study of young children, there is evidence for genetic effects in the personality scales of the *Junior EPI*, but no support for the effects of environmental differences among families. The Minnesota parents' EPI scores correlated with their biological children's scores on the Junior version of the test .01 (N = 162) and with their adopted children .05 (N = 92). The parent-child data provide no evidence for sizable effects of genetic differences or effects of common family environment. The necessity of different tests for parents and children, however, renders the results ambiguous.

In attempting to reconcile these adoption study results with earlier twin studies, one might argue that the problem with assessing personality in children so young is that their personalities have not developed or differentiated to the extent of their adult parents and thus cannot be assessed as similar. Or, one might argue that the measurements of children's personalities are simply unreliable, although the evidence for the reliability of the Junior version of the Eysenck test is impressive (Eysenck, 1965). Compared to several thousand DZ twins (young adults), whose weighted mean correlation for personality measures was found to be .25, the weighted mean correlation for 64 biological pairs of siblings in the two adoption studies is only .14. Clearly, the personality resemblance of ordinary siblings is not as high as that of DZ twins, which implies that there is something special about the twin environment that increases the similarity of siblings who happen to be the same age and sex.

Adolescent-Parent Personality Resemblance. In another study, (Scarr et al., 1981), personality resemblance of adolescents, who were adopted in infancy, to their families, was compared to personality resemblance in biologically related families.

Parent-child and sibling correlations are given in Tables 17 and 18. The median mid-parent-child correlation for the personality measures was .20 for bi-

Table 18. **Correlations of Twins and Siblings for Personality Test Scores in Late Adolescence**

	Twins		Siblings	
	MZ	**DZ**	**Biological**	**Adopted**
Genetic Correlation	**1.00**	**.50**	**.50**	**.00**
Personality Measure				
Introversion–extraversion	**.52***	**.25**	**.06**	**.07**
Social closeness			**.10**	**.13**
Social potency			**.20**	**.07**
Impulsivity	**.48[a]**	**.29**	**.20**	**.05**
Neuroticism	**.52[a]**	**.22**	**.28[a]**	**.05**
Social anxiety			**.17**	**.36**
Physical anxiety			**.24**	**.04**
Total anxiety			**.32**	**.29**
Defensiveness (lie)			**.18**	**.26**
Median:	**.52[a]**	**.25[a]**	**.20[b]**	**.07[b]**

***MZ > DZ** $h^2 = 2\,(r_{iMZ} - r_{iDZ}) = .54$ $h^2 = 2(r_{iB} - r_{iA}) = .26$
Biological > Adopted
[a]27 CPI Scales (Nichols, 1978)
[b]16 listed measures (From Scarr, Webber, Weinberg, Wittag, 1981).

ologically related pairs and .06 for adoptive pairs as shown in Table 17. Single parent-child resemblance was .15 for biological pairs and .04 for adoptive pairs. These results are in accord with the older studies of parent-child resemblance and not congruent with the studies of DZ twins. The heritability that could be estimated from parent-child resemblance is .22, substantially less than the .52 estimated from studies of MZ and DZ twins.

Biologically related sibling resemblance in personality traits is more like that of DZ twins, with a median of .20 for the 10 measures in this study. The median correlation for unrelated siblings is .07, significantly lower than the coefficient for biologically related sibs. Table 18 shows the correlations of biological and adopted sibs, compared with the correlations of MZ and DZ twins. The most notable feature of the table is the far higher heritability estimate from twin than sibling studies. Whereas MZ twin correlations exceed those of DZs by .27 for the traits measured, the biological sib correlation exceeds the adopted sib coefficient by only .13, or half as much. Note that the degrees of resemblance are 1.00 versus .50 and .50 versus .00 in the two cases, equally disparate comparisons. Thus, one must conclude that the evidence from family studies is not congruent with the twin studies. The correlations of siblings and parents and children support the conclusion that only about 25% of the personality variance is due to genetic differences among individuals. What are we to make of this contradiction?

Most of the variance in personality measures is not accounted for by either genetic differences or by environmental differences *between* families. Most of the variance (not explained by errors of measurement) in personality must lie with individuals within families. That is, the experiences of siblings must be sufficiently different that personality development proceeds quite differently for even biologically related members of the same family. It is clear that we need much more complex models of how individual environments work to shape personality. Individuals within families are vastly different in the personality characteristics we measured, and psychology has no theory to explain the individuality.

It may be that individual genotypes evoke and select different responses from their environments, thereby creating genotype-environment correlations of great importance. Lytton's (1977) study of parental responses to the behaviors of MZ and DZ twins supports the notion that parents react to the individual differences of their offspring in ways that correlate with the genotypes of the children. Thus, it may be for individual children; their unique genotypes may determine much of the environment they experience and explain much of the variance we are unable to measure in studies of personality.

Interests and Attitudes

Twin research on patterns of interests gives results similar to those of twin studies on personality: the MZ correlations are in the area of .50 and the DZ correlations about half as high. Thus the conclusions from twin studies of interests is that there is indeed a genetic component to differences in interests and that the magnitude of the heritability is sufficient to explain all of the family resemblance in interests. There is no need to refer to common rearing environments.

In the only study of adopted and biologically related families that included measures of interests and attitudes, Grotevant, Scarr & Weinberg, (1977) reported the biological family members—parent-child and sibling pairs—resemble each other in interests with correlations in the .2 to .3 range, whereas adoptive family members are not at all similar on patterns of interests. The data look just like the personality results. Nichols (1978) summarized the literature on twin studies of interest patterns shown in Table 17. MZ twins have a median weighted correlation of .52 for interests, whereas DZ twin correlations were about .28—much like the twin results for personality inventories. There are not sufficient data on twin studies of attitudes to report a general result.

Grotevant (1978) assessed parent-child and sibling resemblance in patterns of interests with high and low parental agreement in interests. In those families where parents share similar interests, their children were more likely to resemble their parents in interests than in those families where the parents' interest patterns were quite different. Thus, there is some evidence for the effects of rearing environments on children's interests, if parental agreement is taken into account. The results applied to both adopted and biological offspring, even though there was a greater degree of family resemblance for biological parent-child pairs when parents shared similar interests.

Attitudes, on the other hand, may have a much larger cognitive component than interests or personality. Eysenck has studied conservatism and found a considerable heritability. Because of the high negative correlation of conservative and authoritarian attitudes with IQ, Scarr and Weinberg (reported in Scarr, 1981) found that both parent-child and sibling resemblance for attitudes was similar to that for general ability. Thus, the biological relatives tend to have correlations in the .4 to .5 range, whereas the adopted relatives' correlations are generally less than .2.

Conclusions: Personality

Unlike the studies of resemblances in abilities, where the twin and family results both support a moderate role for genetic differences in the development of individual differences, in measures of personality there are marked and consistent differences in the estimated role of genetic differences from twin and family studies. Twin studies support a moderate heritability of about half the variance being due to genetic differences in personality. The studies of parent-child and sibling resemblances in biologically related and adoptive families yield estimates of one-quarter or less of the personality variance being due to genetic differences. Because family relationships of the parent-child and sibling variety are more generalizable to the population as a whole, we favor the lower estimates of the importance of genetic variability in personality development.

Both the twin and family studies are in agreement on the lack of importance for differences between families on personality differences. Because adopted children hardly resemble each other at all, and because the estimates of heritability can fully account for the resemblances of biological relatives, there seems to be little role for the common experiences of rearing in the same family. Personality differences arise primarily from individual differences in experiences within the family and from individual genetic variability.

SUMMARY AND CONCLUSIONS

What Do We Know?

There are several clearly established facts in developmental behavior genetics. A brief list follows.

1. There are hundreds of genetic disorders that arise from miscodings at the DNA-RNA level and that have important ramifications for intellectual and other behaviors. Normal development is impeded by the presence of defective genes.

2. There are abnormalities of autosomal chromosome number that adversely affect, usually severely, not only the normal physical, but also intellectual and other behavioral development of affected individuals.

3. There are abnormalities of sex chromosome number that adversely affect at least some aspects of normal intellectual and other behavioral development. Too few *X* chromosomes, as in Turner's syndrome, have less severe behavioral consequences than too many X chromosomes, as in Klinefelter's syndrome. Having the wrong number of sex chromosomes is less deteterious to behavioral development than having the wrong number of autosomal chromosomes.

4. Single gene and chromosomal disorders have multiple consequences. There is no one-to-one relationship between genotype and phenotype, although there may be some characteristic kinds of disorder associated with particular gene or chromosome disorders, such as spatial or right hemisphere functioning in the absence of one of the *X* chromosomes or such as language disorders in Lesch-Nyhan Syndrome.

5. With respect to numerous behavioral disorders it is possible to show that there is a familial concentration, perhaps even vertical transmission, of the disorder. But most show familial patterns quite different from those expected for simple modes of inheritance. For many there is no clear biochemical abnormality. Thus, it is not possible to discriminate between genetic and cultural transmission. If one assumes, as seems likely for many disorders, that the transmission is genetic and not cultural, it is still usually impossible to specify the genetic mechanism.

6. In the normal range of variation, greater genetic resemblance is associated with greater behavioral resemblance, quite strongly in the intellectual domain and to a lesser extent in personality and interests. The effects of genetic differences on intellectual differences is evident in early childhood and persists into late adulthood.

7. Being reared in the same family accounts for some portion of intellectual differences among people in studied populations, but common rearing accounts for little of the variance among individuals in personality or interests. One reason for this discrepancy may be that families exert similar pressures on their offspring for intellectual development, where the desirable direction is clearly upward, whereas they do no push all of their children toward similar personality or interests, where neither extreme is especially desirable. There is no clear advantage to rearing children who are extreme in extraversion or introversion, high or low activity, mechanical or social interests. Although we often think that parents want "chips off the old block," in fact parents are probably quite respectful of individual differences in offspring.

What Do We Need to Know?

There are no arguments about the benefits of knowing the pathways by which genetic disorders affect development. The work of genetics has many success stories of previously incurable, severe developmental problems that have yielded to treatments, once the pathways are known from gene action to phenotypic development. One should be optimistic that many more specific disorders will be revealed, understood, and treated successfully. Although important to those afflicted with genetic disorders, such discoveries will not solve all of the problems of mental retardation or mental disorders as they are now defined.

Understanding variation in the normal range of development is a very much more complicated problem than discovering the genetic pathways implicated in a specific disorder. Familial or sociocultural mental retardation will not yield to single gene models. Nor is it likely that schizophrenia or affective disorders will. The likelihood is that these disorders will be better understood in evolutionary and population genetic terms—that is, of variation and selection and of multiple gene effects and genetic heterogeneity. Certainly, to understand the differences between siblings with IQs of 100 and 130 requires a polygenic perspective. Models of cultural and genetic inheritance, their interactions and correlations, will better describe variation in the normal range than more molecular models of gene action pathways, at least for the foreseeable future.

Developmental models of genetic differences across the life span are essential to our understanding of development. Too few psychologists think about the role of genetic variation in the development of behavioral phenotypes in infancy, childhood, adolescence, and adulthood. Although most of us recognize the species-typical patterns of development that Piaget and Erikson, for example, have described, few psychologists account for these human patterns in evolutionary, genetic terms. Psychologists look constantly for the immediate, proximal correlates of behavioral change and call these causes. At best, the proximal causes are a partial explanation of developmental phenomena. At worst, they are a distraction from the more important, evolved developmental causes that have emerged with the species, over millions of years. Puberty is not an environmentally caused accident of adolescent development; it is a programmed event of a sexually reproducing species. Aging is not merely "wearing out"; it is a developmentally programmed course of post-reproductive life. Both puberty and aging can be affected by good nutrition, healthy social interactions, and countless other environmental events, but the basic program is in the species and cannot be eliminated, nor should it be ignored.

As a species, we have a developmental program that directs, within some limits, all aspects of our development from the fertilized, single cell, to the end of the life span. This human program is the product of eons of evolution; it is conservative and it probably has some seldom-or never-used portions. It also has redundancy that helps to ensure development within a normal species range. And it has individual variability at the genetic level that reverberates in the development of individual differences at all phenotypic levels. Although human behavioral individuality *is* responsive to environmental variations, that very responsiveness is also part of the genetic program and shows its own individual variability.

In developmental psychology, an evolutionary perspective on the field can bring new questions to the forefront, direct attention to new levels of analysis, and provide more enduring facts on which to base improvements in human lives.

REFERENCES

Abuzzahab, F. S., & Anderson, F. O. (Eds.). *Gilles de la Tourette's syndrome.* St. Paul, Minn: Mason Publishing, 1976.

Anastasi, A., & Levee, R. F. Intellectual defect and musical talent. *American Journal of Mental Deficiency,* 1959, *64,* 695–703.

Anderson, V. E. Discussion. In L. Ehrman, G. S. Omenn, & E. Caspari (Eds.), *Genetics, environment, and behavior.* New York: Academic Press, 1972.

Anderson, V. E. Genetics and intelligence. In Joseph Wortis (Ed.), *Mental retardation (and developmental disabilities): an annual review* (Vol. VI). New York: Brunner/Maze, 1974.

Andreasen N. C., Endicott J., Spitzer R. L., & Winokur, G. The family history method using diagnostic criteria. *Archives of General Psychiatry,* 1977, *34,* 1229–1235.

Baker, S. W., & Ehrhardt, A. A. Prenatal androgen, intelligence and cognitive sex differences. In R. C. Friedman, R. N. Richard, & R. L. Vande Wiele (Eds.), *Sex differences in behavior.* New York: John Wiley, 1974.

Bakwin, H. Reading disability in twins. *Developmental Medicine and Child Neurology,* 1973, *15,* 184–187.

Bank, A., Mears, J. G., & Ramierez, F. Disorders of human hemoglobin. *Science,* 1980, *207,*

486–493.

Bateman, B. *Interpretation of the Illinois test of psycholinguistic abilities*. Seattle: Special Child Publication, 1968.

Bateman, H. E. *A clinical approach to speech anatomy and physiology*. Springfield, Ill.: Charles C. Thomas, 1977.

Beadle, G. W., & Tatum, E. L. Genetic control of biochemical reactions in neurospora. *Proceedings of the National Academy of Science*, 1941, *27*, 499–506.

Bem, D. J., & Allen, A. On predicting some of the people some of the time: The search for cross-situational consistencies in behavior. *Psychological Review*, 1974, *81* (6), 506–520.

Berry, J. W. Muller-Lyer susceptibility: Culture, ecology, race? *International Journal of Psychology*, 1971, *6*, 193–197.

Berry, M. F. *Language disorders in children: The bases and diagnosis*. New York: Appleton, 1969.

Block, N. J., & Dworkin, G. (Eds.). *The IQ controversy: Critical readings*. New York: Pantheon Books, 1976.

Bock, R. D., & Kolokowski, D. Further evidence of sex-linked major-gene influence on human spatial visualizing ability. *American Journal of Human Genetics*, 1973, *25*, 1–14.

Boder, E. Developmental dyslexia–prevailing diagnostic concepts and a new diagnostic approach. In R. H. Myklebust (Ed.), *Progress in learning disabilities*. New York: Grune and Stratton, 1971.

Bodmer, W. F., and Cavalli-Sforza, L. L. *Genetics, evolution, and man*, San Francisco: W. H. Freeman, 1976.

Borich, G. D., & Bauman, P. M. Convergent and discriminant validation of the French and Guilford-Zimmerman spatial orientation and spatial visualization factors. *Educational and Psychological Measurement*, 1972, *32*, 1029–1033.

Botstein, D., White, R. L., Skolnick, M., & Davis, R. W. Construction of a genetic linkage map in man using restriction fragment length polymorphisms. *American Journal of Human Genetics*, 1980, *32:* 314–331.

Botwinick, J. Intellectual abilities. In J. C. Birren & K. W. Schaie (Eds.), *Handbook of the psychology of aging*. New York: Van Nostrand Reinhold, 1977.

Bouchard, T. J., Jr., & McGee, M. G. Sex differences in human spatial ability: Not an X-linked recessive gene effect. *Social Biology*, 1977, *24*, 332–335.

Brandt, I. K., Hsia, Y. E., Clement, D. H., & Provence, S. A. Propionic acidemia (Ketotic hyperglycinemia): Dietary treatment resulting in normal growth and development. *American Journal of Human Genetics*, 1972, 24.

Breakefield, X. O., Edelstein, S. B., & Costa, M. R. C. Genetic analysis of neurotransmitter metabolism in cell culture: Studies on the Lesch-Nyhan syndrome. In X. O. Breakefield (Ed.), *Neurogenetics: Genetic approaches to the nervous system*. New York: Elsevier, 1979.

Breakefield, X. O., Pintar, J. E., Cawthon, R. M., Barbosa, J., Hawkins, M., Jr., Castiglione, C., Haseltine, F., & Francke, U. Biochemical and genetic studies of human monamine oxidase. *American Journal of Human Genetics* (Abstract), 1982, *34*, 111.

Broman, S., Nichols, P., & Kennedy, W. A. *Preschool IQ: Prenatal and early developmental correlates*. Hillsdale, N.J.: Lawrence Erlbaum Associates, 1975.

Broverman, D. M., Klaiber, E. L., Kobayashi, Y., & Vogel, W. Roles of activation in inhibition in sex differences in cognitive abilities. *Psychological Review*, 1968, *75*, 23–50.

Bruner, J. S. The nature and uses of immaturity. *American Psychologist*, 1972, *27*, 687.

Brunn, K., Markkanen, T., Partanen, J. Inheritance of drinking behavior, a study of adult twins. *Helsinki: The Finnish Foundation for Alcohol Research*, 1966.

Buchsbaum, M. S., & Rieder, R. O. Biologic heterogeneity and psychiatric research. *Archives General Psychiatry*, 1979, *36*, 1163–1169.

Bunn, F., H., Forget, B. G., & Ranney, H. M. *Human hemoglobins*. Philadelphia: Saunders, 1977.

Burg, A. Visual acuity as measured by dynamic and static tests: A comparative evaluation. *Journal of Applied Psychology*, 1966, *50*, 460–466.

Burks, B. S. The relative influence of nature and nurture upon mental development: A comparative study of foster parent-foster child resemblance and true parent-true child resemblance. *27th Yearbook, National Society for Studies in Experimental Education*, 1928, *27*(1), 219–316.

Burks, B. S. On the relative contributions of nature and nurture to average group differences in intelligence. *Proceedings of the National Academy of Sciences*, 1938, *24*, 276–282.

Buss, A. H., & Plomin, R. *A temperament theory of personality development*. New York: Wiley,

1975.

Cadoret, R. The genetics of affective disorders. In R. G. Grennell & S. Gabay (Eds.), *Biological foundations of psychiatry*. New York: Raven Press, 1976.

Carey, G., Goldsmith, H. H., Tellegen, A., & Gottesman, I. I. Genetics and personality inventories: The limits of replication with twin data. *Behavior Genetics,* 1978, *8,* 299–313.

Carey, W. B., & McDevitt, S. C. Revision of the infant temperament questionnaire. *Pediatrics,* 1977, *61,* 735–739.

Carter-Saltzman, L. Patterns of cognitive functioning in relation to handedness and sex-related differences. In M. A. Wittig & A. C. Petersen (Eds.), *Sex-Related differences in Cognitive Functioning: Developmental Issues.* New York: Academic Press, 1979.

Cavalli-Sforza, L. L., Similarities and dissimilarities of sociocultural and biological evolution. In F. R. Hodson, D. G. Kendall, & P. Tautu (Eds.), *Mathematics in the archeological and historical sciences.* Edinburgh: Edinburgh University Press, 1971, 535–541.

Cavalli-Sforza, L. L., & Bodmer, W. F. *The genetics of human populations.* San Francisco: W. H. Freeman, 1971.

Cavalli-Sforza, L. L. & Feldman, M. W. Cultural transmission and evolution: A quantitative approach. Princeton, N.J.: Princeton University Press, 1981.

Childs, B., & Finucci, J. M. The genetics of learning disabilities. CIBA Foundation Symposium, 1979, *66,* 359–376.

Claeys, W. Primary abilities and field-dependence of adopted children. *Behavior genetics,* 1973, *3* (4), 323–338.

Cohen, D. J., Shaywitz, B. A., Young, J. G., Carbonari, D. M., Nathanson, J. A., Lieberman, D., Bowers, M. B., & Maas, J. W. Central biogenic amine metabolism in children with the syndrome of chronic multiple tics of Gilles de la Tourette. *American Journal Child Psychiatry,* 1979, *180,* 320–341.

Corah, N. L. Differentiation of children and their parents. *Journal of Personality,* 1965, *33,* 300–308.

Coren, S., & Porac, C. A new analysis of life-span age trends in visual illusion. *Developmental Psychology,* 1978, *14* (2), 193–194.

Coren, S. & Porac, C. Heritability in visual-geometric illusions: A family study. *Perception,* 1979, *8,* 303–309.

Cox, D. R. *Analysis of binary data.* New York: Chapman and Hall, 1970.

Coyne, J. A. Lack of genetic similarity between two sibling species of Drosophila as revealed by varied techniques. *Genetics,* 1976, *84,* 593–607.

Coyne, J. A., & Felton, A. A. Genetic heterogeneity at two Adh loci in D. pseudoobscura and D. persimilis. *Genetics* 1977, *87,* 285.

Coyne, J. A., Felton, A. A., & Lewontin, R. C. Extent of genetic variation at a highly polymorphic esterase locus in Drosophila pseudoobscura, *Proceedings of the National Academy of Sciences,* United States, 1978, *75,* 5090.

Critchley, M. *The dyslexic child.* London: Heinemann, 1970.

Crook, J. Intra-family relationships in personality test performance. *Psychological Record,* 1937, *1,* 479–502.

Dan, A. J. The menstral cycle and sex-related differences in cognitive variability. In M. A. Wittig & A. C. Petersen (Eds.), *Sex-related differences in cognitive functioning.* New York: Academic Press, 1979.

Dawson, J. L. M. Cultural and psychological influences upon spatial-perceptual processes in West Africa: Part I. *International Journal of Psychology,* 1967, *2,* 115–128. (a)

Dawson, J. L. M. Cultural and psychological influences upon spatial-perceptual processes in West Africa: Part II. *International Journal of Psychology,* 1967, *2,* 171–185. (b)

Dawson, J. L. M. Effects of sex hormones in cognitive style in rats and man. *Behavior Genetics,* 1972, *2,* 21–42.

Dayhoff, M. O. *Atlas of protein sequence and structure,* National Biomedical Research Foundation, Washington, D.C., 1972.

DeFries, J. C., & Plomin, R. Behavioral genetics. *Annual Review of Psychology,* 1978, *29,* 473–515.

DeFries, J. C., Plomin, R., Vandenberg, S. G., & Kase, A. R. Parent-offspring resemblance in cognitive abilities in the Colorado adoption project: Biological, adoption, and control parents and one-year-old children. *Intelligence,* 1981, *5,* 245–277.

DeFries, J. C., Singer, S. M., Foch, T. T., & Lewitter, F. I. Familial nature of reading disability. *British Journal of Psychiatry,* 1978, *132,* 361–367.

DeFries, J. C., Vandenberg, S. G., & McClearn, G. E. Genetics of specific cognitive abilities. *Annual Review of Genetics,* 1976, *10,* 179–207.

de la Tourette, G. Étude sur une affection nerveuse, caracterisée par de l'incoordination motrice accompagnée de'écolalie et de coprolalie. *Arch Neurol* (Paris), 1885, *9,* 158.

Deregowski, J. B. Illusion and culture. In R. L. Gregory & G. M. Gombrich (Eds.), *Illusion in nature and art.* New York: Charles Scribner, 1973.

Dobzhansky, T. *Genetics and the origin of species.* New York: Columbia University Press, 1951.

Dobzhansky, T. A review of some fundamental concepts and problems of population genetics. *Cold Spring Harbor Symposium on Quantitative Biology,* 1955, *20,* 1–15.

Dobzhansky, T. *Mankind evolving: The evolution of the human species.* New Haven: Yale University Press, 1962.

Dobzhansky, T. On types, genotypes, and the genetic diversity in populations. In J. Spuhler (Ed.), *Genetic diversity and human behavior.* Chicago: Aldine, 1967.

Dobzhansky, T. *Genetics of the Evolutionary Process.* New York: Columbia University Press, 1970.

Dobzhansky, T., & Spassky, B. Genetics of natural populations. XI. Manifestation of genetic variants in Drosophila pseudoobscura in different environments. *Genetics,* 1944, *29,* 270–290.

Doehring, D. G., & Hoshko, I. M. Classification of reading problems by the Q-technique of factor analysis. *Cortex,* 1977, *13,* 281–294.

Ehrman, L., & Parsons, P. A. *The genetics of behavior.* Sunderland, Mass.: Sinauer Associates, 1981.

Eldridge, R., Sweet, R., Lake, C. R., Ziegler, M., & Shapiro, A. Gilles de la Tourette syndrome: Clinical, genetic, psychologic and biochemical aspects of 21 selected families. *Neurology,* 1977, *27,* 115–124.

Elston, R. C., & Campbell, M. A. Schizophrenia: Evidence for the major gene hypothesis. *Behavior Genetics,* 1970, *1,* 3–10.

Elston, R. C., Namboodiri, K. K., & Hames, C. G. Segregation and linkage analyses of dopamine-β-hydroxylase activity. *Human Heredity,* 1979, *29,* 284–292.

Elston, R. C., Namboodiri, K. K., Spence, M. A., & Rainer, J. D. A genetic study of schizophrenia pedigrees. II. One-locus hypotheses. *Neuropsychobiology,* 1978, *4,* 193–206.

Elston, R. C., & Rao, D. C. Statistical modeling and analysis in human genetics. *Annual Review of Biophysics and Bioengineering,* 1978, *7,* 253–286.

Englander-Golden, P., Willis, K. A., & Dienstibier, R. A. *Intellectual performance as a function of repression and menstrual cycle.* Paper presented to American Psychological Association Meetings, September, 1976.

Erlenmeyer-Kimling, L., & Jarvik, L. F. Genetics and intelligence: A review. *Science,* 1963, *142,* 1477–1479.

Escalona, S. K. *The roots of individuality.* Chicago: Aldine, 1968.

Eustis, R. S. Specific reading disability. *New England Journal of Medicine,* 1947, *237,* 243–249.

Eysenck, H. J. *The inequality of man.* London: Temple Smith, 1973.

Eysenck, H. J. *The structure and measurement of intelligence.* New York: Springer-Verlag, 1979.

Eysenck, S. B. G. *Junior Eysenck Personality Inventory.* San Diego: Educational and Industrial Testing Service, 1965.

Falconer, D. S. The inheritance of liability to certain diseases, estimated from incidence among relatives. *Annals of Human Genetics,* 1965, *29,* 51–71.

Fennema, E., & Sherman, J. Sex-related differences in mathematics achievement, and spatial visualization, and affective factors. *American Educational Research Journal,* 1977, *14,* 51–71.

Finucci, J. M., Guthrie, J. T., Childs, A. L., Abbey, H., & Childs, B. The genetics of specific reading disability. *Annals of Human Genetics,* 1976, *40,* 1–23.

Fisher, J. H. A case of congenital word-blindness (inability to learn to read). *Ophthalmic Review* 1905, *24,* 315–318.

Floderus-Myrhed, B., Pederson, N., & Rasmuson, I. Assessment of heritability for personality based on a short-form of the Eysenck Personality Inventory: A study of 12,898 twin pairs. *Behavior Genetics,* 1980, *10,* 153–162.

Forget, B. G. Molecular genetics of human hemoglobin synthesis. *Annals of Internal Medicine,* 1979, *91,* 605–616.

Fraisse, P., & Vautrey, P. The influence of age, sex, and specialized training on the vertical-horizontal illusion. *Quarterly Journal of Experimental Psychology,* 1956, *8,* 114–120.

Freedman, Daniel. An ethological approach to the genetic study of human behavior. In S. G. Vandenberg (Ed.), *Methods and goals in human behavior genetics.* New York: Academic Press: 1965.

Friedlaender, J. S. The population structure of South-Central Bougainville. *American Journal of Physical Anthropology,* 1971, *35,* 13–25

Friedlaender, J. S., Sgaramella-Zonta, L. A., Kidd, K. K., Lai, L. Y. C., Clark, P., & Walsh, R. J.

Biological divergences in South-Central Bougainville: An analysis of blood polymorphism gene frequencies and anthropometric measurements utilizing tree models, and a comparison of these variables with linguistic, geographical, and migrational "distances." *American Journal of Human Genetics,* 1971, *23,* 253–270.

Garron, D. C. Sex-linked, recessive inheritance of spatial and numerical abilities, and Turner's syndrome. *Psychological Review,* 1970, *77,* 147–152.

Gershon, E. S., Baron, M., & Leckman, J. R. Genetic models of the transmission of affective disorders. *Journal of Psychiatric Research,* 1975, *12,* 301–317.

Gershon, E. S., Mark, A., Cohen, N., Belizon, N., Baron, M., & Knobe, K. Transmitted factors in the morbid risk of affective disorders: A controlled study. *Journal of Psychiatric Research,* 1975, *12,* 283–299.

Gershon, E. S., Targum, S. D., Kessler, L. R., Mazure, C. M., & Bunney, W. E., Jr. Genetics studies and biologic strategies in affective disorders. *Progress in Medical Genetics,* 1977, (New Series, Vol. II) 103–164.

Gershon, E. S., Targum, S. D., Matthysse, S., & Bunney, W. E. Color blindness not closely linked to bipolar illness. *Archives General Psychology,* 1979, *36,* 1423–1430.

Ginsburg, B. E. Genotypic factors in the ontogeny of behavior. *Science and Psychoanalysis,* 1968, *12,* 12–17.

Ginsburg, B. E., & Laughlin, W. The multiple bases of human adaptability and achievement: A species point of view. *Eugenics Quarterly,* 1966, *13,* 240–257.

Ginsburg, B. E., & Laughlin, W. Race and intelligence, what do we really know? In R. Cancro (Ed.), *Intelligence: Genetic and environmental influences.* New York: Grune & Stratton, 1971.

Goetzl, U., Green, R., Whybrow, P., & Jackson, R. X-linkage revisited. *Archives of General Psychiatry,* 1974, *31,* 665–672.

Goldsmith, H. H., & Gottesman, I. I. Origins of variation in behavioral style: A longitudinal study of temperament in young twins. *Child Development,* 1981, *52,* 91–103.

Goodenough, D. R., Gandini, E., Okin, I., Pizzamiglio, L., Thayer, D., & Witkin, H. A. A study of X chromosome linkage with field dependence and spatial visualization. *Behavior Genetics,* 1977, *7,* 373–387.

Goodman, C. S. Isogenic grasshoppers: Genetic variability and development of identified neurons. In X. O. Breakefield (Ed.), *Neurogenetics: Genetic approaches to the nervous system.* New York: Elsevier-North Holland, 1979.

Gottesman, I. I. Genetic aspects of intelligent behavior. In N. Ellis (Ed.), *Handbook of Mental Deficiency.* New York: McGraw-Hill, 1963.

Gottesman, I. I. Schizophrenia and genetics: Where are we? Are you sure? In L. C. Wynne, R. L. Cromwell, and S. Matthysse (Eds.), *The nature of schizophrenia: New approaches to research and treatment.* New York: Wiley, 1978.

Gottesman, I. I., & Shields, J. A polygenic theory of schizophrenia. *Proceedings National Academy of Sciences, U.S.A.,* 1967, *58,* 199–205.

Grotevant, H. D. Sibling constellations and sex typing of interests in adolescence. *Child Development,* 1978, *49,* 540–542.

Grotevant, H., Scarr, S., & Weinberg, R. A. Intellectual development in family constellations with adopted and natural children: A test of the Zajonc and Markus model. *Child Development,* 1977, *48,* 1699–1703.

Guglielmino-Matessi, C. R., Gluckman, P., & Cavalli-Sforza, L. L. Climate and the evolution of skull metrics in man. *American Journal Physical Anthropology,* 1979, *50,* 549–564.

Guttman, R. Genetic analysis of analytical spatial ability: Raven's progressive matrices. *Behavior Genetics,* 1974, *4,* 273–284.

Hallgren, B. Specific dyslexia. *Acta Psychiatrica et Neurologica Suppl.,* 1950, *65,* 1–287.

Hanin, I., Merikangas, J. R., Merikangas, K. R., & Kopp, U. Red cell choline and Gilles de la Tourette syndrome. *New England Journal of Medicine,* 1979, *301,* 661–662.

Harrington, D. M., Block, J. H., & Block, J. Intolerance of ambiguity in preschool children: Psychometric considerations, behavioral manifestations, and parental correlates. *Developmental Psychology* 1978, *14,* 242–256.

Harris, H. *The principles of human biochemical genetics* (2nd ed.). New York: Elsevier, 1975.

Harris, L. J. Sex differences in spatial ability: Possible environmental, genetic and neurological factors. In M. Kinsbourne (Ed.), *Asymmetrical function of the brain.* Cambridge, England: Cambridge University Press, 1979.

Hartl, D. L. *Principles of population genetics.* Sunderland, Mass.: Sinauer Assocs., 1980.

Hartlage, L. C. Sex-linked inheritance of spatial ability. *Perceptual and Motor Skills,* 1970, *31,* 610.

Hearnshaw, L. *Cyril Burt, Psychologist.* Ithaca, N.Y.: Cornell University Press, 1979.

Herrup, K., & Mullen, R. J. Regional variation on absence of large neurons in the cerebellum of the staggerer mouse. *Brain Research,* 1979, *172,* 1–12.

Herschel, M. Dyslexia revisited. *Human Genetics,* 1978, *40,* 115–134.

Heston, L. L. Psychiatric disorders in foster home reared children of schizophrenic mothers. *British Journal of Psychiatry,* 1966, *112,* 819–825.

Heston, L. L. Genetics of schizophrenic and schizoid disease. *Science,* 1970, *167,* 249–256.

Hirsch, J. Behavior-genetic analysis and its biosocial consequences. In R. Cancro (Ed.), *Intelligence: Genetic and environmental influences.* New York: Grune & Stratton, 1971, 23–39.

Horn, J. M., Loehlin, J. C., & Willerman, L. Intellectual resemblance among adoptive and biological relatives: The Texas adoption project. *Behavior Genetics,* 1979, *9,* 177–207.

Howells, W. W. Cranial variation in man: A study by multivariate analysis of patterns of difference among recent human populations. *Peabody Museum Papers,* 1973, (Vol. 67). Harvard University, Cambridge.

Humphreys, L. The primary mental ability. In M. Friedman, J. P. Das, & N. O'Connor (Eds.), *Intelligence and Learning.* New York: Plenum, 1981.

Immergluck, L., & Mearini, M. C. Age and sex difference in response to embedded figures and reversible figures. *Journal of Experimental Child Psychology,* 1969, *8,* 210–221.

Ingram, T., Mason, A., & Blackburn, I. A retrospective study of 82 children with reading disability. *Developmental Medicine and Child Neurology,* 1970, *12,* 271–281.

Iosub, S., Fuchs, M., Bingol, N., & Gromisch, D. S. Fetal alcohol syndrome revisited. *Pediatrics,* 1981, *68,* 475–479.

Irwin, J. V., & Marge, M. *Principles of childhood language disabilities.* New York: Appleton, 1972.

Jagger, J., Prusoff, B. A., Cohen, D., Kidd, K., Carbonari, C., & John, K. The epidemiology of Tourette syndrome: A pilot study. *Schizophrenia Bulletin,* 1982, *8,* 267–278.

James, N. M., & Chapman, C. J. A genetic study of bipolar affective disorder. *British Journal of Psychiatry,* 1975, *126,* 449–456.

Jayakar, S. D., Della Croce, L., Scacchi, M., & Guazzotti, G. A genetic linkage study of a quantitative trait in D. melanogaster. In E. Pollak, O. Kempthorne, & T. B. Bailey, Jr. (Eds.), *Proceedings of the International Conference on Quantitative Genetics.* Ames: Iowa State University Press, 1977.

Jencks, C. *Inequality: A reassessment of the effect of family and schooling in America.* New York: Basic Books, 1972.

Jensen, A. R. *Educability and group differences.* New York: Harper & Row, 1973. (a)

Jensen, A. R. *Genetics and education.* New York: Harper & Row, 1973. (b)

Jensen, A. R. Let's understand Skodak and Skeels, finally. *Educational Psychologist,* 1973, *10,* 10–35. (c)

Jensen, A. R. The current status of the IQ controversy. *Australian Psychologist,* 1978, *13* (L), 7–27. (a)

Jensen, A. R. Genetic and behavioral effects of nonrandom mating. In R. T. Osborne, C. E. Noble, & N. Weyl (Eds.), *Human variation: Biopsychology of age, race and sex.* New York: Academic Press, 1978. (b)

Jensen, A. R. *Bias in mental testing.* New York: Basic Books, 1980.

Jerison, H. J. *Evolution of the brain and intelligence.* New York: Academic Press, 1973.

Johnson, C. A., Ahern, F. M., & Johnson, R. C. Level of functioning of siblings and parents of probands of varying degrees of retardation. *Behavior Genetics,* 1976, *6,* 473–477.

Johnson, D., & Myklebust, H. *Learning disabilities: Educational principles and practices.* New York: Grune & Stratton, 1967.

Johnson, R. C., Ahern, F. M., & Cole, R. E. Secular change in degree of assortative mating for ability? *Behavior Genetics,* 1980, *10,* 1–8.

Judson, H. G. *The eight day of creation.* New York: Simon & Schuster, 1979.

Kallman, F. J. The genetic theory of schizophrenia: An analysis of 691 twin index families. *American Journal of Psychiatry,* 1946, *103,* 309–322.

Kamin, L. J. *The science and politics of IQ.* Potomac, Md.: Erlbaum Associates, 1974.

Kamin, L. J. Commentary in S. Scarr, *IQ: Race, social class, and individual differences: New studies of old issues.* Hillsdale, N.J.: Lawrence Erlbaum Associates, 1981.

Kan, Y. W., & Dozy, A. M. Polymorphism of DNA sequence adjacent to human B-globin structural gene: Relationship to sickle mutation. *Proceedings of the National Academy of Sciences, U.S.A.,* 1978, *75,* 5631–5635.

Kan, Y. W., & Dozy, A. M. Evolution of the hemoglobin S and C genes in world populations. *Science,* 1980, *209,* 388–391.

Kaplan, E. B., & Elston, R. C. Program package for

general pedigree analysis (GENPED). University of North Carolina Institute of Statistics Mimeo Series.

Karlin, I. Speech and language-handicapped children. *Journal diseases of Children*. 1958, *95*, 370.

Karlin, I. W., Karlin, D. B., & Gurren, K. *Development and disorders of speech in childhood*. Springfield, Ill.: Charles C. Thomas, 1965.

Karlins, M., Schuerkoff, C., & Kaplan, M. Some factors related to architectural creativity in graduating architecture students. *Journal of General Psychology*, 1969, *81*, 203–215.

Karlsson, J. L. Influence of the myopia gene on brain development. *Clinical Genetics*, 1975, *8*, 314–318.

Karlsson, J. L. Genetic relationship between giftedness and myopia. *Hereditas*, 1979, *73*, 85–88.

Kay, D. W. The genetics of stuttering. In G. Andrews & M. Harris (Eds.), *The syndrome of stuttering*. London: William Heinemann, 1964.

Kessler, S. The genetics of schizophrenia: A review. *Schizophrenia Bulletin*, 1980, *6*, 404–416.

Kety, S. S., Rosenthal, D., Wender, P. H., & Schulsinger, F. The types and prevalence of mental illness in the biological and adoptive families of adopted schizophrenics. *Journal of Psychiatric Research*, 1968, *6*(s.1), 345–362.

Kety, S. S., Rosenthal, D., Wender, P. H., Schulsinger, F., & Jacobsen, B. Mental illness in the biological and adoptive families of adoptive individuals who have become schizophrenic: A preliminary report based on psychiatric interviews. In R. Fieve, D. Rosenthal, & H. Brill (Eds.), *Genetic Research in Psychiatry*. Baltimore: Johns Hopkins University Press, 1975.

Kety, S. S., Rosenthal, D., Wender, P. H., Schulsinger, F., & Jacobsen, B. The biologic and adoptive families of adopted individuals who became schizophrenic: Prevalence of mental illness and other characteristics. In L. C. Wynne, R. L. Cromwell, & S. Matthysse (Eds.), *The nature of schizophrenia: New approaches to research and treatment*. New York: Wiley, 1978.

Kidd, J. R., Wolf, B., Hsia, Y. E., & Kidd, K. K. Genetics of propionic acidemia in a Mennonite-Amish kindred. *American Journal of Human Genetics*, 1980, *32*, 236–245.

Kidd, K. K. Genetic approaches to human evolution. In Quaderno No. 182, *Atti del Colloqui Internazainale sul Tema: L'Origine Dell'Uomo*. Rome: Accadamie Nazionale dei Lincei, 1973. pp. 149–174.

Kidd, K. K. On the possible magnitudes of selective forces maintaining schizophrenia in the population. In R. R. Fieve, D. Rosenthal, & H. Brill (Eds.), *Genetic Research in Psychiatry*. Baltimore: Johns Hopkins University Press, 1975.

Kidd, K. K. A genetic perspective on stuttering. *Journal of Fluency Disorders*, 1977, *2*, 259–269.

Kidd, K. K. Empiric recurrence risks and models of inheritance: Part II. In C. J. Epstein, C. R. Curry, S. Packman, S. Sherman and B. D. Hall (Eds.), *Risk, communication, and decision making in genetic counseling*, Chapter 4. New York: Alan R. Liss, 1979.

Kidd, K. K. Genetic models for psychiatric disorders. In E. S. Gershon, S. Matthysse, X. O. Breakefield, and R. D. Ciarnello (Eds.), *Psychobiology and psychopathology:* (Vol. 1) *Genetic research strategies in psychobiology and psychiatry*. Pacific Grove, Cal.: The Boxwood Press, 1981.

Kidd, K. K. Genetic linkage markers in the study of psychiatric disorders. In E. Usdin & I. Hanin (Eds.), *Biological markers in psychiatry and neurology*. Oxford: Pergamon Press, 1982.

Kidd, K. K., & Cavalli-Sforza, L. L. An analysis of the genetics of schizophrenia. *Social Biology*, 1973, *20:* 254–265.

Kidd, K. K., & Gladstien, K. Alternative models for genetic analyses of complex human traits. In M. Melnick, D. Bixler and E. Shields (Eds.), *Progress in clinical and biological research: Etiology of cleft lip & cleft palate* (Vol. 46). New York: A. R. Liss, 1980.

Kidd, K. K., Kidd, J. R., & Records, M. A. The possible causes of the sex ratio in stuttering and its implications. *Journal of Fluency Disorders*, 1978, *3*, 13–23.

Kidd, K. K., & Matthysse, S., with Carmelli, D., Cavalli-Sforza, L. L., Elston, R., Lange, L., Motulsky, A., Rao, D. C., Reich, T., & Wyatt, R. Research design for the study of gene-environment interactions in psychiatric disorders: Report of an FFRP panel. *Archives of General Psychiatry*, 1978, 35, 925–932.

Kidd, K. K., Oehlert, G., Heimbuch, R. C., Records, M. A., & Webster, R. L. Familial stuttering patterns are not related to one measure of severity. *Journal of Speech and Hearing Research*, 1980, *23*, 539–545.

Kidd, K. K., Prusoff, B. A., & Cohen, D. J. The familial pattern of Tourette syndrome. *Archives of General Psychiatry*, 1980, *37*, 1336–1339.

Kidd, K. K., & Records, M. A. Genetic methodologies for the study of speech. In X. O.

Breakefield (Ed.), *Neurogenetics: Genetic approaches to the nervous system*. New York: Elsevier-North Holland, 1979.

King, M. C., & Wilson, A. C. Evolution at two levels in humans and chimpanzees. *Science*, 1975, *188*, 107–116.

Klaiber, E. L., Broverman, D. M., & Kobayashi, Y. The automatization cognitive style, androgens, and monoamine oxidase (MAO). *Psycholopharmacologia*, 1967, *11*, 320–336.

Klaiber, E. L., Broverman, D. M., Vogel, W., & Kobayasbi, Y. Rhythms in plasma MAO activity, EEG, and behavior during the menstrual cycle. In M. Ferin, F. Halberg, R. M. Richart, & R. L. Vande Wiele (Eds.), *Biorhythms and human reproduction*. New York: Wiley, 1974.

LaBarre, W. *The human animal*. Chicago: University Press, 1954.

LaBarre, W. The development of mind in man in primitive cultures. In F. Richardson (Ed.), *Brain and intelligence: The ecology of child development*. Hyattsville, Md.: National Educational Press, 1973.

Langova, J., & Moravek, M. Some results of experimental examinations among stutterers and clutterers. *Folia Phoniatr.*, 1964, (Basel) *16*, 290–296.

Laughlin, P. R., & McGlynn, R. P. Cooperative versus competitive concept attainment as a function of sex and stimulus display. *Journal of Personality and Social Psychology*, 1967, *7*, 398–402.

LaVail, M. M., & Mullen, R. J. Experimental chimeras: A new approach to the study of inherited retinal degeneration in laboratory animals. In M. B. Landers, M. L. Wolbarsht, J. E. Dowling, & A. M. Laties (Eds.), *Retinitis pigmentosa: Clinical implications of current research*. New York: Plenum, 1976.

Layzer, D. Heritability analyses of IQ scores: Science or numerology? *Science*, 1974, *183*, 1259–1266.

Leahy, A. M. Nature-nurture and intelligence. *Genetic Psychology Monographs*, 1935, *17*, 237–308.

Leckman, J. F., & Gershon, E. S. Autosomal models of sex effect in bipolar-related major affective illness. *Journal of Psychiatric Research*, 1977, *13*, 237–246.

Leder, P., Hansen, J. N., Konkel, D., Leder, A., Nishioka, Y., & Talkington, C. Mouse globin system: A functional and evolutionary analysis. *Science*, 1980, *209*, 1336–1342.

Lehrman, D. Semantic and conceptual issues in the nature-nurture problem. In L. R. Aronson, W. Tobach, & E. Shaw (Eds.), *Development and Evolution of Behavior*. San Francisco: Freeman, 1970.

Lenneberg, E. H. *Biological foundations of language*. New York: Wiley, 1967.

Lenneberg, E. H. A biological perspective of language. In R. C. Oldfield & J. C. Marshall (Eds.), *Language*. Baltimore: Penguin Education, 1968.

Levine, S. Sexual differentiation: The development of maleness and femaleness. *California Medicine*, 1971, *114*, 12–17.

Lewitter, F. I. *Genetic models of reading disability*. Unpublished doctoral dissertation, University of Colorado, 1977.

Lewitter, F. I. Investigation of genetic heterogeneity of reading disability. *Behavior Genetics*, 1979, *9*, 465.

Lewontin, R. C. The analysis of variance and the analysis of causes. *American Journal of Human Genetics*, 1974, *26*, 400–411. (a)

Lewontin, R. C. *The genetic basis of evolutionary change*. New York: Columbia University Press, 1974. (b)

Loehlin, J. C. Are personality traits differentially heritable? *Behavior Genetics*, 1982, *12*, 417–428.

Loehlin, J. C., Horn, J. M., & Willermen, L. Personality resemblances in adoptive families. *Behavior genetics*, 1981, *11*, 309–330.

Loehlin, J. C., Lindzey, G., & Spuhler, J. N. *Raw differences in intelligence*. San Francisco: Freeman, 1975.

Loehlin, J. C., & Nichols, R. *Heredity, environment, and personality: A study of 850 sets of twins*. Austin: University of Texas Press, 1976.

Loehlin, J. C., Sharan, S., & Jacoby, R. In pursuit of the "spatial gene": A family study. *Behavior Genetics*, 1978, *8*, 27–41.

Lubbock, J. On the digestive and nervous systems of *Coccus hesperidum. Proceedings Royal Society, London* (Biology), 1858, *9*, 480–486.

Luchsinger, R., & Arnold. G. E. *Voice-speech-language, clinical communicology: Its physiology and pathology*. Belmont, Cal.: Wadsworth, 1965.

Lytton, H. Do parents create, or respond to, differences in twins? *Developmental Psychology*, 1977, *13*, 456–459.

Maccoby, E. E., & Jacklin, C. N. *The psychology of sex differences*. Stanford, Cal.: Stanford University Press, 1974.

Mackenberg, E. J., Broverman, D. M., Vogel, W., & Klaiber, E. L. Morning-to-afternoon changes in cognitive performances and in the electroencephalogram. *Journal of Educational Psychology,* 1974, *66,* 238–246.

Mahler, M. S., Luke, J. A., & Daltroff, W. Clinical and follow-up study of the tic syndrome in children. *American Journal of Orthopsychiatry,* 1945, *15,* 631–647.

Marshall, W., & Ferguson, J. H. Heredity word-blindness as a defect of selective association. *Journal of Nervous and Mental Disease,* 1939, *39,* 164–173.

Masica, D. N., Money, J., & Ehrhardt, A. A. Fetal sex hormones and cognitive patterns: Studies in the testicular feminizing syndrome and androgen insensitivity. *Johns Hopkins Medical Journal,* 1969, *124,* 34–43.

Matheny, A. P. Genetic determinants of the Ponzo illusion. *Psychonomic Science,* 1971, *24,* 155–156.

Matheny, A. P. Hereditary components of the response to the double trapezium illusion. *Perceptual and Motor Skills,* 1973, *36,* 511–513.

Matheny, A. P., Dolan, R. S., & Wilson, R. S. Relation between twins' similarity: Testing an assumption. *Behavior Genetics,* 1976, *6,* 343–351.

Matthysse, S. W. Etiological diversity in the psychoses. In N. E. Morton & C. S. Chung, (Eds.), *Genetic Epidemiology.* New York: Academic Press, 1978.

Matthysse, S. W., & Kidd, K. K. Estimating the genetic contribution to schizophrenia. *American Journal of Psychiatry,* 1976, *133,* 185–191.

Mattis, S., French, J. H., & Rapin, I. Dyslexia in children and young adults: Three independent neuropsychological syndromes. *Developmental Medicine and Child Neurology,* 1975, *17,* 281–300.

Mayr, E., *Populations, species, and evolution.* Cambridge, Mass.: Harvard University Press, 1970.

McAskie, M., & Clark, A. M. Parent-offspring resemblances in intelligence: Theories and evidence. *British Journal of Psychology,* 1976, *67,* 243–273.

McCartney, K., Scarr, S., Phillips, D., Grajek, S., and Schwarz, J. C. Environmental differences among day care centers and their effects on children's levels of intellectual, language and social development. In E. Zigler & E. Garden (Eds.), *Day Care: Scientific and social policy issues.* Boston: Auburn House, 1981.

McClay, H., & Osgood, E. I. Hesitation phenomena in spontaneous English speech. *Word,* 1959, *15,* 19–44.

McClearn, G. E. Genetic influences on behavior and development. In P. Mussler (Ed.), *Carmichael's manual of child psychology,* vol. I. New York: Wiley, 1970.

McClearn, G. E. Genetic determination of behavior (animal). In L. Ehrman, G. S. Omenn, and E. Caspari (Eds.), *Genetics, environment, and behavior.* New York: Academic Press, 1972.

McGee, Mark G. Human spatial abilities: Psychometric studies and environmental, genetic, hormonal, and neurological influences. *Psychological Bulletin,* 1979, *86* (5), 889–918.

McGlannon, F. K. Familial characteristics of genetic dyslexia preliminary report from a pilot study. *Journal of Learning Disabilities,* 1968, *1,* 185–191.

McGuinness, D. Away from a unisex psychology: Individual differences in visual sensory and perceptual processes. *Perception,* 1976, *5,* 279–294. (a)

McGuinness, D. Sex differences in the organization of perception. In B. Lloyd & J. Archer (Eds.), *Exploration of sex differences.* London: Academic Press, 1976. (b)

McGuinness, D., & Lewis, I. Sex differences in visual persistence: Experiments on the Ganzfeld and afterimages. *Perception,* 1976, *5,* 295–301.

McKusick, V. A. *Mendelian inheritance in man: Catalogs of autosomal dominant, autosomal recessive, and X-linked phenotypes.* (5th ed.). Baltimore: Johns Hopkins University Press, 1978.

Mendlewicz, J., Linkowski, P., Guroff, J. J., & Van Praag, H. M. Color blindness linkage to bipolar manic-depressive illness. New evidence. *Archives of General Psychology,* 1979, *36,* 1442–1447.

Mendlewicz, J., & Rainer, J. D. Morbidity risk and genetic transmission in manic-depressive illness. *American Journal of Human Genetics,* 1974, *26,* 692–701.

Minton, H. L., & Schneider, F. W. *Differential psychology.* Monterey, Cal.: Brooks/Cole, 1980.

Mintz, B. Formation of genotypically mosaic mouse embryos. *American Zoologist,* 1962, *2,* 432.

Mintz, B. Genetic mosaicism in adult mice of quadriparental lineage. *Science,* 1965, *148,* 1232–1233.

Mischel, W. *Personality and assessment.* New York: Wiley, 1968.

Moran, P. A. P. A note on heritability and the correlation between relatives. *Annals of Human Genetics,* 1973, *37,* 217.

Morton, L. A., & Kidd, K. K. Likelihood analysis of high-density pedigrees of stuttering. *Behavior Genetics,* 1979, *9,* 470. (Abstract)

Morton, L. A., & Kidd, K. K. The effects of variable age-of-onset and diagnostic criteria on the estimates of linkage. An example using manic-depressive illness and color blindness. *Social Biology,* 1981, *27,* 1–10.

Morton, L. A., Kidd, K. K., Matthysse, S. W., & Richards, R. L. Recurrence risks in schizophrenia: Are they model dependent? *Behavior Genetics,* 1979, *9,* 389–406.

Moskovitz, D. S., & Schwarz, J. C. Validity comparisons of behavior counts and ratings by knowledgeable informants. *Journal of Personality and Social Psychology,* 1982, *42,* 518–528.

Mullen, R. J., Eicher, E. M., & Sidman, R. F. Purkinje cell degeneration, a new neurological mutation in the mouse. *Proceedings of the National Academy of Sciences, U.S.A.,* 1976, *73,* 208–212.

Mullen, R. J., & Herrup, K. Chimeric analysis of mouse cerebellar mutants. In X. O. Breakefield (Ed.), *Neurogenetics.* New York: Elsevier, 1979.

Mullen, R. J., & LaVail, M. M. Inherited retinal dystrophy: Primary defect in pigment epithelium determined with experimental rat chimeras. *Science,* 1976, *192,* 799–801.

Nance, W. E., & Corey, L. A. Genetic models for the analysis of data from families of identical twins. *Genetics,* 1976, *83,* 811–826.

Nee, L. E., Caine, E. D., Polinsky, R. J., Eldridge, R., & Ebert, M. H. Gilles de la Tourette syndrome—Clinical and family study of 50 cases. *Annals of Neurology,* 1980, *17,* 41–49.

Neel, J. V. Lessons from a "primitive" people. *Science,* 1970, *170,* 815–822.

Newman, H. G., Freeman, F. N., & Holzinger, K. J. *Twins: A study of heredity and environment.* Chicago: University of Chicago Press, 1937.

Nichols, R. C. Heredity and environment: Major findings from twin studies of ability, personality and interests. *Homo,* 1978, *29,* 158–173.

O'Connor, J. *Structural visualization.* Boston: Human Engineering Laboratory, 1943.

Ohno, S. *Sex chromosomes and sex-linked genes.* Berlin: Springer-Verlag, 1967.

Omenn, G. S., & Motulsky, A. G. Biochemical genetics and the evolution of human behavior. In L. Ehrman, G. S. Omenn, & E. Caspari (Eds.), *Genetics, environment, and behavior.* New York: Academic Press, 1972.

Omenn, G. S., & Weber, B. A. Dyslexia: search for phenotypic and genetic heterogeneity. *American Journal of Medical Genetics,* 1978, *1,* 333–342.

Op't Hof, J., & Uys, I. C. A clinical delineation of tachyphemia (cluttering): A case of dominant inheritance. *South African Journal of Medical Science,* 1974, *48,* 1624–1628.

O'Rourke, D. H., Gottesman, I. I., Suarez, B. K., Rice, J., & Reich, T. Refutation of the general single-locus model for the etiology of schizophrenia. *American Journal of Human Genetics,* 1982, *34,* 630–649.

Orton, S. T. *Reading, writing and speech problems in children.* New York: W. W. Norton, 1937.

Osborne, R. T., & Gregor, A. J. Racial differences in heritability estimates for tests of spatial abilities. *Perceptual and Motor Skills,* 1968, *27,* 735–739.

Ounsted, C., & Taylor, D. (Eds.). *Gender differences: Their ontogeny and significance.* London: Churchill Livingstone, 1972.

Owen, F. W., Adams, P. A., Forrest, T., Stolz, L. M., & Fisher, S. Learning disorders in children: Sibling studies. *Monographs of the Society for Research in Child Development,* 1971, *36,* 1–77.

Pandey, G. N., Dorus, E., Shaughnessy, R., & Davis, J. M. Genetic control of platelet monoamine oxidase activity: Studies on normal families. *Life Sciences,* 1979, *24,* 1173–1178.

Park, J., Johnson, R. C., DeFries, J. C., McClearn, G. E., Mi, M. P., Rashad, M. N., Vandenberg, S. G., & Wilson, J. R. Parent offspring resemblance for specific cognitive abilities in Korea. *Behavior Genetics,* 1978, *8* (1), 43–52.

Pauls, D. L. A genetic analysis of mental retardation and high intelligence. Doctoral dissertation, University of Minnesota, 1972.

Pauls, D. L., and Kidd, K. K. Genetics of childhood behavior disorders. In B. B. Lahey and A. E. Kazdin (Eds.) *Advances in clinical child psychology.* New York: Plenum, 1981.

Pearson, P. L., & Roderick, T. H., with Davisson, M. T., Garver, J. J., Warburton, D., Lalley, P. A., & O'Brien, S. J. Report of the committee on comparative mapping. *Human Gene Mapping 5,* Edinburgh Conference (1979). S. Karger AG: Basel.

Perkins, W. H. *Speech pathology: An Applied Behavioral Science.* St. Louis: Mosby, 1977.

Petersen, A. C. Physical androgyny and cognitive functioning in adolescence. *Developmental Psychology,* 1976, *12,* 524–533.

Petersen, A. C. Hormones and cognitive functioning in normal development. In M. A. Wittig & A. C. Petersen (Eds.), *Sex-related differences in cognitive functioning.* New York: Academic Press, 1979.

Pick, H. L., Jr., & Pick, A. D. Sensory and perceptual development. In P. H. Mussen (Ed.), *Car-*

michael's Manual of Child Psychology, (3rd ed.). New York: Wiley, 1970.

Pishkin, V., Wolfgang, A., & Rasmussen, E. Age, sex, amount and type of memory information in concept learning. *Journal of Experimental Psychology*, 1967, *73*, 121–124.

Plomin, R., & DeFries, J. C. Genetics and intelligence: Recent data. *Intelligence*, 1980, *4*, 15–24.

Plomin, R., DeFries, J. C., & McClearn, G. E. *Behavioral genetics: A primer*. San Francisco: Freeman, 1980.

Plomin, R., Willerman, L., & Loehlin, J. C. Resemblance in appearance and the equal environments assumption in twin studies of personality. *Behavior Genetics*, 1976, *6*, 43–52.

Pollack, R. H. Some implications of ontogenetic changes in perception. In W. J. Flavell & D. Ellcind (Eds.), *Studies in cognitive development; Essays in honor of Jean Piaget*. New York: Oxford University Press, 1969.

Popper, K. R. *The logic of scientific discovery*. London: Hutchinson, 1959.

Porac, C., Coren, S., Girgus, J. S., & Verde, M. Visual-geometric illusions: Unisex phenomena. *Perception*, 1979, *8*, 401–412.

Pressey, A. W., & Wilson, A. E. Another look at age changes in geometric illusion. *Bulletin of the Psychonomic Society*, 1978, *12*, 333–336.

Proudfoot, N. J., Shander, M. H. M., Manley, J. L., Gefter, M. L., & Maniatis, T. Structure and in vitro transcription of human globin genes. *Science*, 1980, *209*, 1329–1336.

Rao, D. C., Morton, N. E., Gottesman, I. I., & Lew, R. Path analysis of qualitative data on pairs of relatives: Application to schizophrenia. *Human Heredity*, 1981, *31*, 325–333.

Reddy, V. B., Thimmappaya, B., Dhar, R., Subramanian, K. N., Zain, B. S., Pan, J., Ghosh, P. K., Celma, M. L., & Weissman, S. M. The genome of simian virus 40. *Science*, 1978, *200*, 494–502.

Reed, E. W., & Reed, S. C. *Mental retardation: A family study*. Philadelphia: W. B. Saunders, 1965.

Reinisch, J. M., Gandelman, R., & Spiegel, F. S. Prenatal influences on cognitive abilities: Data from experimental animals and human endocrine syndromes. In M. A. Wittig & A. C. Petersen (Eds.), *Sex-related differences in cognitive functioning*. New York: Academic Press, 1979.

Rimland, B., & Munsinger, H. Burts IQ data. *Science*, 1977, *195*, 248.

Roberts, J. A. F. The genetics of mental deficiency. *Eugenics Review*, 1952, *44*, 71–83.

Roberts, J. *Binocular visual acuity of adults*. Washington: U.S. Department of Health, Education and Welfare, 1964.

Rose, R. J. Genetic variance in non-verbal intelligence: Data from the kinship of identical twins. *Science*, 1979, *205*, 1153–1155.

Rosenthal, D. *Genetic theory and abnormal behavior*. New York: McGraw-Hill, 1970.

Rousey, C. L. The psychopathology of articulation and voice deviations. In L. E. Travis (Ed.), *Handbook of speech pathology and audiology*. Englewood Cliffs, N.J.: Prentice-Hall, 1971.

Rowe, D. C., & Plomin, R. The Burt controversy: A comparison of Burt's data on IQ with data from other studies. *Behavior Genetics*, 1978, *8*, 81–84.

Ruddle, F. H. Linkage analysis in man by somatic cell genetics. *Nature*, 1973, *242*, 165–169.

Ruddle, F. H., & Kucherlapati, R. S. Hybrid cells and human genes. *Scientific American*, 1974, *231*, 36–44.

Ruddle, F. H., & McKusick, V. The status of the gene map of the human chromosomes. *Science*, 1977, *196*, 390–405.

Sackett, G. P., Ruppenthal, G. C., Fahrenbruch, C. E., & Holm, R. A. Social isolation rearing effects in monkeys vary with genotype. *Developmental Psychology*, 1981, *17*, 313–318.

Scarr, S. Environmental bias in twin studies. *Eugenics Quarterly*, 1968, *15*, 34–40.

Scarr, S. *Race, social class and individual differences, M IQ: New studies of old problems*. Hillsdale, N.J.: Lawrence Erlbaum Associates, 1981.

Scarr, S., & Barker, W. The effects of family background: A study of cognitive differences among black and white twins. In S. Scarr (Ed.), *IQ: Social class and individual differences*. Hillsdale, N.J.: Lawrence Erlbaum Associates, 1981.

Scarr, S., & Carter-Saltzman, L. Twin method: Defense of a critical assumption. *Behavior Genetics*, 1979, *9:* 527–542.

Scarr, S. & Carter-Saltzman, L. Genetics and intelligence. In R. Sternberg, (Ed.), *Handbook of intelligence*. New York: Cambridge University Press, 1982.

Scarr, S., Pakstis, A. J., Katz, S. H., & Barker, W. B. The absence of a relationship between degree of white ancestry and intellectual skills within a black population. *Human Genetics*, 1977, *39*, 69–86.

Scarr, S., Scarf, E., & Weinberg, R. A. Perceived and actual similarities in biological and adoptive families: Does perceived similarity bias genetic inferences? *Behavior Genetics*, 1980, *10*, 445–458.

Scarr, S., Webber, P. L., Weinberg, R. A., & Wittig, M. A. Personality resemblance among adolescents and their parents in biologically-related and adoptive families. *Journal of Personality and Social Psychology*, 1981, *40*, 885–898.

Scarr, S., & Weinberg, R. A. IQ test performance of black children adopted by white families. *American Psychologist*, 1976, *31*, 726–739.

Scarr, S., & Weinberg, R. A. Intellectual similarities within families of both adopted and biological children. *Intelligence*, 1977, *1*, 170–191.

Scarr, S., & Weinberg, R. A. The influence of "family background" on intellectual attainment. *American Sociological Review*, 1978, *43*, 674–692.

Scarr, S., & Yee, D. Heritability and educational policy: Genetic and environmental effects on IQ, aptitude, and achievement. *Educational Psychologist*, 1980, *15*, 1–22.

Scarr-Salapatek, S. Race, social class, and IQ. *Science*, 1971, *174*, 1285–1295.

Scarr-Salapatek, S. Genetics and intelligence. In F. D. Horowitz, *Review of child development research* (Vol. 4). Chicago: University of Chicago Press, 1975.

Scarr-Salapatek, S. An evolutionary perspective on infant intelligence. In M. Lewis (Ed.), *Origins of intelligence: Infancy and early childhood*. New York: Plenum, 1976, 165–197.

Schoenfeldt, L. F. The hereditary components of the Project TALENT two-day test battery. *Measurement and Evaluation in Guidance*, 1968, *1*, 130–140.

Schwartz, M., & Schwartz, J. Evidence against a genetical component to performance on IQ tests. *Nature*, 1974, *248* (5443), 84–85.

Seeman, M. Speech pathology in Czechoslovakia, In R. W. Rieber & R. S. Brubaker (Eds.), *Speech pathology*. Philadelphia: Lippincott, 1966, 439–457.

Segal, M. H., Campbell, D. T., & Herskovits, M. J. *The influence of culture on visual perception*. Indianapolis: Bobbs-Merrill, 1966.

Serra, A., Pizzamiglio, L., Boari, A., & Spera, S. A comparative study of cognitive traits in human sex chromosome aneuploids and sterile and fertile euploids. *Behavior Genetics*, 1978, *8*, 143–154.

Seuanez, H. N. *The phylogeny of human chromosome*. New York: Springer-Verlag, 1979.

Shapiro, A. K., & Shapiro, E. Treatment of Gilles de la Tourette syndrome with haloperidol. *British Journal of Psychiatry*, 1968, *114*, 345–350.

Shapiro, A., Shapiro, E., Brunn, R., & Sweet, R. *Gilles de la Tourette syndrome*. New York: Raven Press, 1978.

Shepard, R. N., & Metzler, J. Mental rotation of three-dimensional objects. *Science*, 1971, *171*, 701–703.

Shields, J. *Monozygotic twins brought up apart and brought up together*. London: Oxford University Press, 1962.

Silbert, A., Wolff, P. H., & Lilienthal, J. Spatial and temporal processing in patients with Turner's syndrome. *Behavior Genetics*, 1977, *7*, 11–21.

Singh, R. S., Lewontin, R. C., & Felton, A. A. Genetic heterogeneity with electrophoretic "alleles" of xanthine dehydrogenase in D. pseudoobscura. *Genetics*, 1976, *84*, 609–629.

Skeels, H. M. Mental development of children in foster homes. *Journal of Consulting Psychology*, 1938, *2*, 33–43.

Skodak, M. Children in foster homes. *University of Iowa Child Welfare*, 1938, *15* (4), 191.

Skodak, M., & Skeels, H. M. A final follow-up study of one-hundred adopted children. *Journal of Genetic Psychology*, 1949, *75*, 85–125.

Slater, E. The monogenic theory of schizophrenia. *Acta Genetica*, 1958, *8*, 50–56.

Slightom, J., Blechl, A., & Smithies, O. Human fetal Gγ- and Aγ-globin genes. Complete nucleotide sequences suggest that DNA can be exchanged between these duplicated genes. *Cell*, 1980, *21*, 627–638.

Smeraldi, E., Negri, F., Melica, A. M., & Scorza-Smeraldi, R. HLA system and affective disorders: A sibship genetic study. *Tissue Antigens*, 1978, *12*, 270–274.

Smith, G. *Psychological studies in twin differences*. Lund, Sweden: Gleerup, 1949.

Smith, S. D., Pennington, B. F., Kimberling, W. J., & Lubs, H. A. Investigation of subgroups within specific reading disability utilizing neuropsychological and linkage analyses. *American Journal of Human Genetics*, 1979, *31*, 83A. (Abstract)

Spiess, E. B. *Genes in populations*. New York: Wiley, 1977.

Spitzer, R. L., Endicott, J., & Robins, E. Research diagnostic criteria rationale and reliability. *Archives of General Psychiatry*, 1978, *35*, 773–782.

Stafford, R. E. Sex differences in spatial visualization as evidence of sex-linked inheritance. *Per-*

ceptual and Motor Skills, 1961, *13*, 428.

Stephenson, S. Six cases of congenital word-blindness affecting three generations of one family. *Ophthalmoscope*, 1907, *5*, 482–484.

Stern, C. *Principles of human genetics*. San Francisco: Freeman, 1973.

Stevenson, H. W., Hale, G. A., Klein, R. E., & Miller, L. K. Interrelations and correlates in children's learning and problem solving. *Monographs of the Society for Research in Child Development*, 1968, *33*.

Stewart, J. Schizophrenia: The systematic construction of genetic models. *American Journal of Human Genetics*, 1980, *32*, 47–54.

Stewart, J., Debray, Q., & Caillard, V. Schizophrenia: The testing of genetic models by pedigree analysis. *American Journal of Human Genetics*, 1980, *32*, 55–63.

Strickberger, M. W. *Genetics* (2nd ed.). New York: Macmillan, 1976.

Suarez, B. K., Rice, J., & Reich, T. The generalized sib pair IBD distribution: Its use in the detection of linkage. *Annals of Human Genetics*, 1978, *42*, 87.

Symmes, J. S., & Rapaport, J. L. Unexpected reading failure. *American Journal of Orthopsychiatry*, 1972, *42*, 82–91.

Tarkowski, A. K. Mouse chimeras developed from fused eggs. *Nature*, 1961, *190*, 857–860.

Taylor, H. J. *The IQ game: A methodological inquiry into the heredity-environment controversy*. New Brunswick: Rutgers University Press, 1980.

Thoday, J. M. Effects of specific genes. In E. Pollak, O. Kempthorne, & T. B. Bailey, Jr. (Eds.), *Proceedings of the International Conference on Quantitative Genetics*. Ames, Iowa: State University Press, 1977.

Thomas, A., & Chess, S. *Temperament and development*. New York: Brunner/Masel, 1977.

Thomas, C. J. Congenital "word blindness" and its treatment. *Ophthalmoscope*, 1905, *3*, 380–385.

Thompson, James, S., & Thompson, Margaret W. *Genetics in medicine*, 3rd Ed. Philaldelphia: Saunders, 1980.

Torgeson, A. M., & Kringlen, E. Genetic aspects of temperamental differences in infants: A study of same-sexed twins. *Journal of American Academy of Child Psychiatry*, 1978, *17*, 433– 444.

Vale, J. R., & Vale, C. A. Individual differences and general laws in psychology. *American Psychologist*, 1969, *24*, 1093.

Vandenberg, S. G. The hereditary abilities study: Hereditary components in a psychological test battery. *American Journal of Human Genetics*, 1962, *14*, 220–237.

Vandenberg, S. G. Hereditary factors in normal personality traits (as measured by inventories). *Recent advances in biological psychiatry* (Vol. 9). New York: Plenum Press, 1967.

Vandenberg, S. G., & Kuse, A. R. Mental rotations: A group test of three-dimensional spatial visualization. *Perceptual and Motor Skills*, 1978, *47*, 599–604.

Vandenberg, S. G., & Kuse, A. R. Spatial ability: A critical review of the sex-linked major-gene hypothesis. In M. A. Wittig & A. C. Petersen (Eds.), *Sex-related differences in cognitive functioning*. New York: Academic Press, 1979.

Vogel, F., & Motulsky, A. G. *Human genetics problems and approaches*. New York: Springer-Verlag, 1979.

Waber, D. P. Sex differences in cognition: A function of maturation rate. *Science*, 1976, *192*, 572–574.

Waber, D. P. Sex differences in mental abilities, hemispheric lateralization and rate of physical growth at adolescence. *Developmental Psychology*, 1977, *13*, 29–38.

Waber, D. P. Cognitive abilities and sex-related variations in the maturation of cerebral cortical functions. In M. A. Wittig & A. C. Petersen (Eds.), *Sex-related differences in cognitive functioning*. New York: Academic Press, 1979.

Waddington, C. H. *New patterns in genetics and development*. New York: Columbia University Press, 1962.

Walker, L., & Cole, E. M. Familial patterns of expression of specific reading disability in a population sample. *Bulletin of the Orton Society*, 1965, *15*, 12–24.

Watson, J. D. *Molecular biology of the gene*. New York: W. A. Benjamin, 1965.

Watson, J. D., & Crick, F. H. C. Molecular structure of nucleic acids. *Nature*, 1953, *171*, 737–738.

Wechsler, D. *The measurement of adult intelligence* (3rd ed.). Baltimore: Williams & Wilkins, 1950.

Weiss, D. *Cluttering*. Englewood Cliffs, N.J.: Prentice-Hall, 1964.

Weissman, M. M., & Klerman, G. L. Sex differences and the epidemiology of depression. *Archives of General Psychiatry*, 1977, *34*, 98–111.

Wilkins, L. E., & Brown, J. A. High resolution mapping of chromosome five in 18 cases of cri-du-chat syndrome. *American Journal of Human Genetics*, 1980, *32*, 93. (Abstract)

Willerman, L. Effects of families on intellectual development. *American Psychologist,* 1979, *34,* 923–929.

Willerman, L., Horn, J. M., & Loehlin, J. C. The aptitude-achievement test distinction: A study of unrelated children reared together. *Behavior Genetics,* 1977, *7,* 465–470.

Williams, T. Family resemblance in abilities: The Wechsler scales. *Behavior Genetics,* 1975, *5,* 405–409.

Wilson, J. R., & Vandenberg, S. G. Sex differences in cognition: Evidence from the Hawaii family study. In T. E. McGill, D. A. Dewsbury, & B. D. Sachs (Eds.), *Sex and behavior: Status and prospectus.* New York: Plenum, 1978.

Wilson, R. S., Twins: Early mental development. *Science,* 1972, *175,* 914–917. (a)

Wilson, R. S. Similarity in developmental profile among related pairs of human infants. *Science,* 1972, *178,* 1005. (b)

Wilson, R. S. Twins and siblings: Concordance for school-age mental development. *Child Development,* 1977, *48,* 211–216.

Wilson, R. S., Garron, D. C., & Kalwans, H. L. Significance of genetic factors in Gilles de la Tourette syndrome: A review. *Behavior Genetics,* 1978, *8,* 503–510.

Wilson, R. S., & Harpring, E. B. Mental and motor development in infant twins. *Developmental Psychology,* 1972, *7,* 277.

Winokur, G., & Clayton, P. Family history studies. I. Two types of affective disorders separated according to genetic and clinical factors. In J. Wortis (Ed.), *Recent advances in biological psychiatry* (Vol. 9). New York: Plenum, 1967.

Witkin, H. A. Individual differences in ease of perception of embedded figures. *Journal of Personality,* 1950, *19,* 1–15.

Woodworth, R. S. *Heredity and environment: A critical survey of recently published material on twins and foster children.* A report prepared for the Committee on Social Adjustment. New York: Social Science Research Council, 1941.

Wyatt, R. J., Potkin, S. G., & Murphy, D. L. Platelet monoamine oxidase activity in schizophrenia: A review of the data. *American Journal of Psychiatry,* 1979, *136,* 377–385.

Wyman, A. R., & White, P. A highly polymorphic locus in human DNA. *Proceedings of the National Academy of Science, U.S.A.,* 1980, *77,* 6754–6758.

Yen, W. M. Sex-linked major-gene influences on selected types of spatial performance. *Behavior Genetics,* 1975, *5,* 281–298.

Zahalkova, M., Vrzal, V., & Kloboukova, E. Genetical investigations in dyslexia, *Journal of Medical Genetics,* 1972, *9,* 48–52.

Zerbin-Rudin, E. Congenital word-blindness. *Bulletin of the Orton Society,* 1967, *17,* 47–54.

INFANT VISUAL PERCEPTION* | 7

MARTIN S. BANKS, *The University of Texas at Austin*
in collaboration with
PHILIP SALAPATEK, *University of Minnesota*

CHAPTER CONTENTS

*Preparation of this chapter was supported in part by NIMH Research Scientist Development Award MH00318 and NIH Research Grant HD12572 to M.S.B. and by NIH Program Project Grant HD01136 to the Institute of Child Development, and NSF Program Project Grant P2BI389 to the Center for Research in Human Learning at the University of Minnesota. We are indebted to a number of people who aided in the preparation of this chapter. Duane Albrecht, Dick Aslin, Randy Blake, Velma Dobson, Daphne Maurer, Sam Sokol, Ben Stephens, Davida Teller, and Al Yonas gave us very useful comments on various sections of an earlier draft. Marshall Haith provided thoughtful, detailed editorial comments on the entire manuscript. Joanne Bergman, Robin Ditto, and Anne Yemma assisted with the references, library searches, and typing. Finally, M.S.B. thanks Cristina Banks for her patience and support.

INTRODUCTION

Our understanding of the development of infant visual perception grew significantly in the last decade. Regrettably, Robert Fantz, the scientist whose work laid the foundation for this growth, passed away in 1981. We wish to dedicate this review to his memory.

Fantz brought scientific feasibility to the study of early visual perception by establishing various paradigms to document detection, discrimination, and recognition of visual stimuli. Between 1956 and 1961, he published a series of papers that used the visual preference paradigm. These papers documented the ability of young infants to discriminate visual stimuli on the basis of differences in form. In 1962, Fantz initiated psychophysical investigations of infant vision using optokinetic nystagmus and an adaptation of the visual preference paradigm. Later, he documented the ability of young infants to retain and recognize visual information using a precursor of the habituation paradigm. Fantz' empirical and theoretical work was clearly the foundation for the work reviewed here.

We had hoped initially to use broad theories of perceptual development to guide our review of infant visual perception. This proved to be impossible, however, because the span of work in this area has become much broader than the existing theories. For this reason, we have chosen instead to use three broad "themes" to guide the review. They will appear from time to time throughout the chapter.

1. One theme we will emphasize is the need for developmentalists to consider the purpose of vision in general and of various visual capabilities in particular. Without an understanding of the purposes of vision and visual capabilities, it is very difficult, if not impossible, to distinguish significant developmental changes from trivial ones. Barlow (1979) provides an example that illustrates this point well. If one believed that the heart's function was to warm the blood, then we might think that the heart is underdeveloped at birth because newborns do not thermoregulate well. Whereas, if one believed that the heart's main function was to circulate blood, we would conclude that the newborn's heart is reasonably mature. In the current context, the point is that one cannot determine how significant a difference is between the neonatal and adult status of one part of the visual system unless one knows what that difference means for normal visual functioning in everyday environments. With this point in mind, we have attempted in each section of this chapter to present a plausible account of the purpose of the visual capability in question before considering its development.

It would be useful here, however, to discuss the most general purpose(s) of vision before discussing specific capabilities. The visual system has evolved to convey information about the environment we inhabit. Gibson (1966) pointed out that this environment is restricted. Humans and most animals live on or close to the surface of the earth. As they move about, they need to guide their movement according to the location and identity of objects on the surface. Most of these objects are rigid or nearly so. They are also not self-luminous, but rather reflect light from other sources such as the sun. The objects are frequently in motion; indeed, the perceiver is often in motion, too. The visual system is designed to extract environmental information in the context of these and other constraints. But what information is it designed to extract? Marr (1982) has argued that the primary purposes of vision are to recognize and identify objects and to determine their spatial layout. These, of course, are not easy tasks. For one thing, the same object can produce vastly different retinal images as the source of illumination changes, as the object moves, or as the observer's station point changes. The key is to capitalize on invariant properties of objects wherever possible. These properties (e.g., reflectance and objective size) are more "valid" clues to an object's identity than are other properties that change with irrelevant variations in the environment (e.g., level of illumination, projective size, etc.). How the visual system accomplishes this is largely unknown, but, as we will see, some significant advances in our understanding have been achieved.

We advocate consideration of the purpose or function of different aspects of vision throughout this chapter. This general point of view is certainly not a new one (e.g., Gibson, 1966; Marr, 1982). But we have attempted to translate it specifically to the various areas of infant visual research. We hope these specific points of view can facilitate the field's ability to distinguish significant from trivial developmental changes and to focus on real-world phenomena rather than on specific laboratory tasks or paradigms.

2. We will emphasize an obvious trend that has emerged in the field of infant perception. Developmental researchers have adapted numerous hypotheses and methodologies that were originally developed in the adult literature. With suitable modifications, these have often been applied quite successfully to the study of infant perception. It has even become reasonably common to see both infant

and adult data in developmental publications. In our opinion, the use of techniques and models originally developed in adult work has been fruitful for three reasons. First, comparing infant and adult capabilities has helped to set the infants' capabilities in a lifespan perspective. Second, obtaining adult data using the stimuli and procedures to be used with infants has helped to determine if the stimuli and procedures have any flaws (e.g., if one were measuring infant spectral sensitivity, one should be able to obtain adult data that match previous reports in the literature). Third, studies of adult vision have a much longer and more extensive history than do studies of infant vision. Thus, several powerful models and techniques have gradually evolved in the adult literature. It makes sense for developmental researchers to benefit, where possible, from the decades of methodological and theoretical refinements in this literature. A case in which this strategy has been quite successful is recent work on infant color vision (e.g., Teller & Bornstein, in press). The value of many of the techniques used (e.g., the neutral-point test) is not superficially apparent; rather, the techniques evolved from decades of theoretical and empirical work with adults.

Use of techniques derived from adult studies requires an assumption, however. This assumption is that the structure and function of the immature version of a particular capability is qualitatively (not necessarily quantitatively) similar to that of the mature version. If this assumption were violated, researchers using techniques and models based on adult work might miss something important developmentally. A hypothetical example illustrates this. Use of adult models in the literature on infant color vision has often assumed that an early color deficiency would fall into one of the classes of color deficiency observed in adults. We might be misled, however, if early color vision were qualitatively different from later. If, for example, the immature color system had two cone pigments, just as some color-deficient adults do, but these pigments were sensitive to quite different spectral bands than the adults' pigments were, specific versions of most color deficiency tests would not detect the infant's deficiency.

Thus, developmental researchers should, we believe, be aware of methodological and theoretical advances in the adult literature. These advances might help one design a powerful line of developmental research. Developmental researchers should also be cautious, however, not to overextend adult models because, in so doing, they may miss something important developmentally. In keeping with this theme, we review basic findings in the adult literature concerning each of the visual capabilities reviewed below before considering their development.

3. The last theme we emphasize is a strictly developmental one. It is well recognized (e.g., Bower, 1974) that the relationship between proximal stimuli (e.g., binocular disparity in the retinal image) and their distal correlates (the relative distance of two objects) generally changes with age due to growth of the eye, head, and body. This changing relationship demands continual recalibrations to preserve the accuracy of visually guided behavior. We believe that this problem is actually more serious than most researchers realize. Every structure in the visual system undergoes substantial and complex changes postnatally. We briefly describe two examples here which are treated in greater detail later. First, the receptors in the retina seem to migrate toward the fovea during early infancy, so a given feature in the environment will actually stimulate different populations of receptors at different ages. Second, the number of interneuronal connections in the visual cortex grows astronomically after birth and probably does not stabilize during infancy. Thus, the cortical representation of any feature in the environment must change tremendously with age. In spite of these changes in the neural structures which subserve visual behavior, infants after a few months of experience seem capable of maintaining reasonably constant perceptions. For instance, their reaches maintain some accuracy after 4 to 5 months, and they recognize common objects perhaps even earlier. Using computer terminology, it appears that the "output" of visuomotor programs attains some sort of stability before the "hardware" of the system does. This is a fascinating aspect of visual development which may imply, using computer terminology again, that the system's "software" is continually evaluating outputs and, through software modifications, compensating for growth in the hardware. We point out several instances of such compensations in the following sections.

Finally, we should mention the topics we have chosen to review and some of those we have chosen not to review. The major sections of this chapter cover developmental anatomy/physiology, visuomotor mechanisms, pattern vision, color vision, temporal vision, and depth perception. These topics were chosen because they are all basic components of visual perception and because they are not covered elsewhere in this *Handbook*. We have devoted considerable space to developmental anatomy/physiology in particular because work in this field has advanced dramatically in the last decade and because it is beginning to have an important influence on the study of visual perception in human infants. Some major topics, such as pattern recognition and face perception, have been omitted because they are covered in other chapters.

DEVELOPMENTAL ANATOMY AND PHYSIOLOGY

Neural mechanisms in the retina and central visual system subserve visual perception. Consequently, anatomical and physiological work is an important component of the study of perceptual development.

Our knowledge of anatomical and physiological development has expanded astronomically over the last 15 years. Understandably, this work has had an obvious impact on the infant perception literature. In particular, several researchers have attempted to explain various aspects of perceptual development with anatomical/physiological findings concerning single neurons in the central visual system (Fantz, Fagan, & Miranda, 1975; Haith, 1980; Karmel & Maisel, 1975; Maurer & Lewis, 1979). We believe that such attempts are often useful, but that one should be quite cautious in these attempts. Marr (1982) has presented a very reasonable viewpoint concerning the relationship between anatomical/physiological observations and perceptual function. His viewpoint is best illustrated by the following passage.

> Almost never can a complex system of any kind be understood as a simple extrapolation from the properties of its elementary components. Consider, for example, some gas in a bottle. A description of thermodynamic effects—temperature, pressure, density, and the relationships among these factors—is not formulated by using a large set of equations, one for each of the particles involved. Such effects are described at their own level, that of the enormous collection of particles; the effort is to show that in principle the microscopic and macroscopic descriptions are consistent with one another. (p. 19)

In the current context the point is that the relationship between the "hardware" (neurons and synapses) and the functioning of the visual system as a whole is loose. A given function, say the localization of a spot of light, could be subserved by any of the wide variety of neurons and synapses that exist in the nervous system. Thus, one should be cautious in using a known anatomical/physiological change at the level of the neuron to explain the development of a particular visual behavior. The utility of such explanations depends on the particular aspect of visual perception in question. Some relatively low-level phenomena such as light adaptation (see our discussion *Light and Dark Adaptation* below) lend themselves to anatomical/physiological hypotheses because they involve fairly simple, uniform, and automatic processes that have been studied extensively with physiological and anatomical techniques. Visual scientists frequently look for consistency between anatomical/physiological and psychophysical data concerning light adaptation and use such information to advance their understanding of the phenomenon (e.g., Geisler, 1979, 1980). Other behavioral phenomena such as visual scanning, to which we devote an entire section below, involve more complex, high-level mechanisms (Tversky, 1974; Yarbus, 1967) and, consequently, do not lend themselves so readily to anatomical/physiological explanations. If, on the other hand, one's intent is to use anatomical/physiological data simply to guide one's thinking about a behavioral phenomenon of this sort rather than to explain the phenomenon, anatomical/physiological data can be quite useful.

Another cautionary note is worth mentioning. The interpretation of the developmental anatomy/physiology of a particular structure depends to a great extent on one's theory of the function of that structure. We discussed this point in the introduction and illustrated it with Barlow's (1979) example concerning the heart's maturity early in life. We do not mean that nothing useful can be said about development until the mature organism is fully understood; some worthwhile descriptions of growth have emerged without any knowledge of ultimate function. Yet it is much more likely that important developmental changes, and not epiphenomenal ones, will be emphasized in cases where the function of a structure is understood. The function of many structures in the adult visual system is understood at least in broad outline, but there is still room for considerable debate. For example, Barlow (1979) advanced three plausible theories of visual cortical function. The three theories are similar in that they posit cortical involvement in pattern discrimination and recognition but are dissimilar in the specific role they ascribe to the cortex. Without resolving this uncertainty about cortical function, it may be difficult to know how significant postnatal cortical development is.

With this general point in mind, we emphasize, where possible, what is known of the ultimate function of a particular structure before describing relevant developmental data. Unfortunately, we can provide only sketchy, somewhat uncertain descriptions of function for some structures because not enough is known of their function yet.

Our primary interest in this review is anatomical/physiological findings relevant to the development of visual perception in human infants. Consequently, we concentrate, wherever possible, on data from humans or infrahuman species such as the macaque monkey. Unfortunately, most developmental research has been conducted with cats, not primates. Accordingly, we also review some cat work. We hasten to point out, though, that the visual systems of cats and higher primates differ in a number of important ways. Thus, one should be cautious in extrapolating from cats to humans. As we will see, failures to appreciate inter-species differences have led some researchers to propose implausible theories of neural-behavioral linkages.

The Retina

The retina transduces distributions of light into neural signals and preliminarily processes these signals. In this section, we describe, in order, the structure and function of the mature human retina, the anatomical development of the retina in humans and related species, and, finally, the physiological development of the retina in humans and related species.

A schematic and a photograph of the mature human retina are shown in Figures 1 and 2, respectively. The retina is clearly layered. The outer nuclear layer is formed by the nuclei of the rods and cones. The inner nuclear layer is formed by the nuclei of the bipolar, horizontal, and amacrine cells. Finally, the ganglion cell layer is formed by the retinal ganglion cells. Synaptic contacts among these neurons occur in the inner and outer plexiform layers.

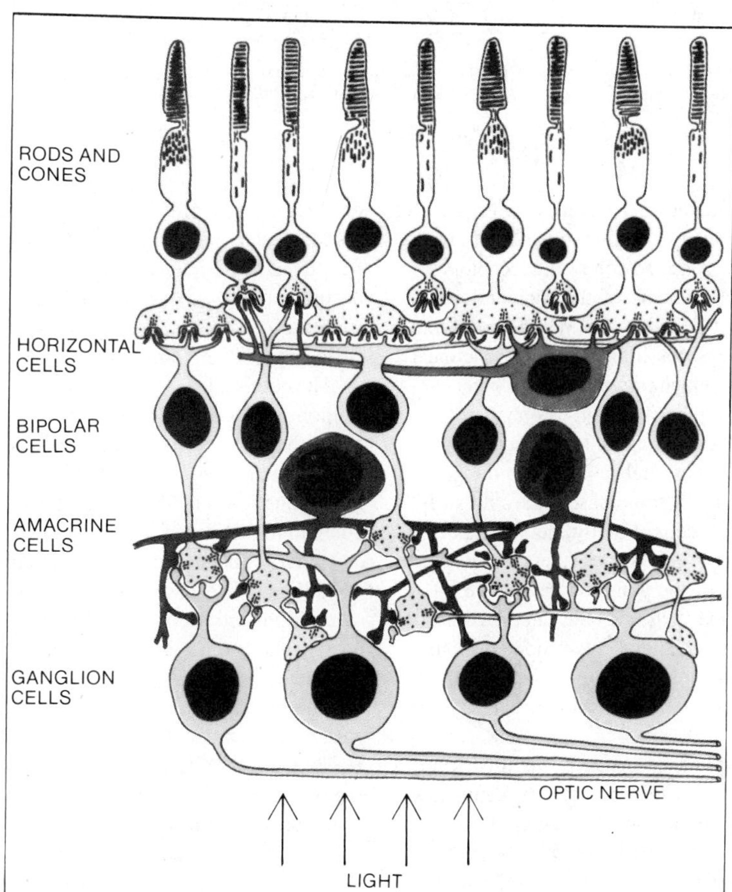

Figure 1. Schematic diagram of the retina. This diagram shows the primary neural elements and connections of the primate retina. The regions where cells are contiguous are synapses. (From Kuffler & Nicholls, 1976.)

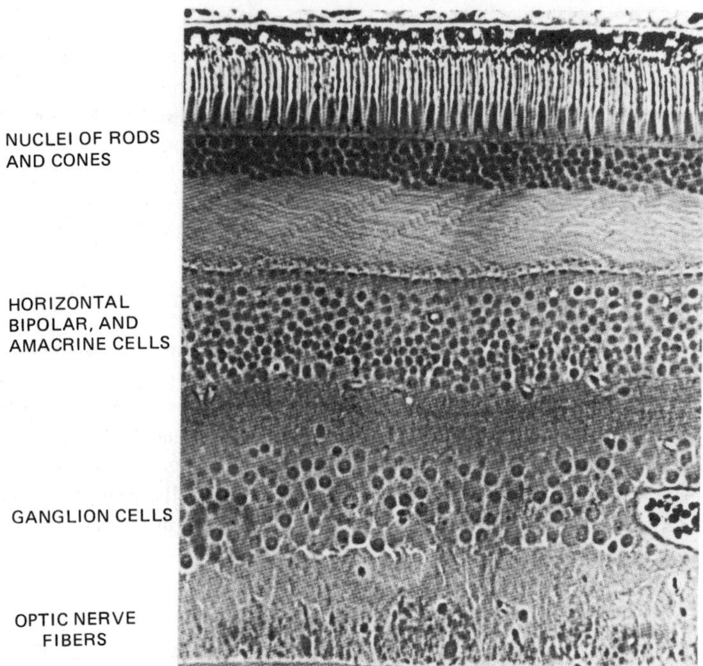

Figure 2. Photograph of the retina. This cross section shows the five types of neural elements arranged in layers. The orientation of the cross section is the same as that of Figure 1. (From Kuffler & Nicholls, 1976.)

Light reaches the retina from below in Figures 1 and 2 and hence traverses the various retinal layers before reaching the rods and cones, the receptors for vision. The outer segments of the rods and cones contain photosensitive pigments. When a molecule of photopigment absorbs light, an electrochemical signal is triggered, which travels from the outer segment to the base of the receptor. From there, the signal is passed across synapses to the bipolar cells. The bipolar cells pass signals, in turn, to the ganglion cells, although, in some cases, they do so by way of the amacrine cells. Finally, neural impulses leave the eye along optic nerve fibers, which are actually the axons of the ganglion cells. The horizontal and amacrine cells provide lateral connections in the retina—horizontal cells among receptors and amacrines among bipolars. As we will see, these lateral interactions serve an important visual function.

The gross morphology of the retina differs noticeably from one region to another. In the center lies the fovea, which contains no rods and whose cones are unusually long, slender, and densely packed. Moreover, other neural elements (bipolars, ganglion cells, etc.) are swept to the side to form the foveal pit and to allow light to fall directly on the photoreceptors. The fovea is small in human adults, occupying only about 2 deg of the visual field. Visual acuity is much greater in this part of the field than in the parafovea or periphery. Outside of the fovea, rods become mixed with cones and the inner nuclear and ganglion cell layers overlay the receptors. In the periphery, rods predominate.

The retina of each eye contains more than 100 million rods and 10 million cones. Yet there are fewer than 1 million ganglion cells. So information from many receptors must in general converge on a given ganglion cell. These proportions, however, do not hold for the fovea. The number of ganglion cells and other retinal neurons devoted to foveal vision is roughly equal to the number of foveal cones. The connections from cones to ganglion cells are thus nearly one-to-one in the fovea but not in the periphery.

The functioning of various types of retinal neurons can be characterized by their receptive fields. Receptive field refers to the area on the retinal surface (or, alternatively, in the visual field) that, when illuminated, influences a neuron's responses. The receptive fields of photoreceptors are quite simple. When the area immediately above a given receptor is illuminated, the receptor's response increases. Stimulation of a nearby region leads to a small response increase or none at all. The receptive fields of retinal

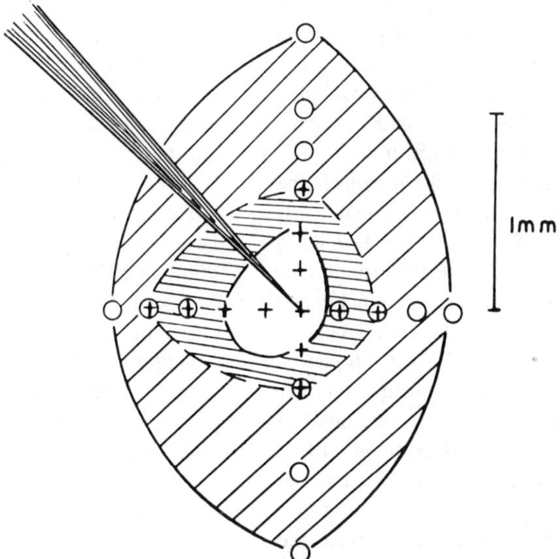

Figure 3. Receptive field of a retinal ganglion cell. The center region marked with plus signs (+) yields bursts of activity when stimulated with small spots. These are *on* responses. The outer region marked with circles (o) yields *off* responses. The intermediate region marked with pluses and circles gives *on–off* responses. A microelectrode in also shown. (From Kuffler, 1953.)

ganglion cells are more complicated because they reflect the processing that occurs among neurons between the receptors and ganglion cells. Figure 3 illustrates the receptive field of a typical "on-center" ganglion cell. A small spot of light shone on or near the center of the field evokes a burst of activity. The locations where this occurs are marked with plus signs in the figure (+). This region is called the on-center. Presenting a small spot further from the field's center does not evoke activity but, interestingly, turning the spot off does. This region is marked with circles. Thus, this region, which is called the "off-surround," responds in quite a different fashion from the on-center. There are two basic types of ganglion cells: those with an on-center and off-surround and those with an off-center and on-surround. In both types, the center and surround regions are antagonistic. So, for example, a spot of light in the surround of an on-center, off-surround cell actually inhibits any on-going activity due to stimulation of the center. For this reason, ganglion cells do not respond much at all to changes in uniform illumination. The center-surround arrangement of ganglion cell receptive fields is produced by lateral interactions mediated by horizontal and amacrine cells.

Enroth-Cugell and Robson (1966) described two functionally distinct classes of cat ganglion cells, both of which include on-center and off-center varieties. They called these X cells and Y cells. In cats, these cells differ in a number of ways (Lennie, 1980; Stone, Dreher, & Leventhal, 1980). X cells exhibit linear spatial summation,[1] but Y cells do not. X cells exhibit a reasonably sustained response to a long-duration stimulus, whereas Y cells typically respond transiently at stimulus onset and offset. Y cells respond to faster moving stimuli than X cells. Moreover, their response travels more rapidly up the optic nerve. X cells tend to have smaller receptive fields (and hence greater acuity). Finally, the relative proportions of X and Y cells vary across the retina. Y cells are generally fewer in number than X cells and are distributed fairly uniformly across the retina. X cells are concentrated in the central retina. The properties of monkey ganglion cells have been studied much less extensively, but separate populations of X and Y cells seem to exist with many of the properties observed in cats (de Monasterio, 1978). The X/Y distinction has attracted considerable interest in part because the two ganglion cell types seem to project to separate neuronal populations in the central visual system (Lennie, 1980; Stone et al., 1980). This observation, and some theoretical statements concerning it, is considered later in this section.

More recently, a third type of ganglion cell, the W cell, has been observed in cats (Stone & Fukuda, 1974). Since less is known about these cells, we do not consider them in detail.

One way to summarize the functions served by the retina in visual processing is to describe the way in which visual information is transformed from the retinal image itself to the "neural image" that is carried to the central visual system. The spatial distribution of stimulation is modified somewhat but is basically preserved; the "neural image" has retinotopic ordering (neighboring regions in the "neural image" correspond to neighboring regions in the visual stimulus), but the foveal region is magnified relative to the peripheral. Considerable information is also lost within the retina. Information about spatial detail is lost in two ways. First, the retinal image is digitized in a fashion because the photoreceptors sample the image at discrete points only. It can be shown mathematically that spatial information finer than the grain of the photoreceptor mosaic cannot be transmitted without distortion (Goodman, 1965; Snyder, 1979). Stated more precisely, the sampling frequency of the receptor mosaic (the density of receptors; specifically, the reciprocal of twice the average separation between receptors) sets a limit to the highest spatial frequency (the finest pattern of stripes) that can be accurately transmitted. It is interesting to note in this regard that the highest spatial frequency an adult human can resolve matches the sampling frequency of the receptor mosaic in the fovea (Green, 1970). Second, spatial information has been summated considerably by the time a signal reaches the ganglion cells, particularly in the peripheral retina, so additional spatial detail is lost, presumably in the interest of increased sensitivity. The spatial information in the retinal image is also transformed in another, more interesting fashion. Because of the lateral interactions evident in the center-surround antagonism of retinal ganglion cells, the output of the retina tends to signal sharp intensity gradients (e.g., contours) in the retinal image but not gradual ones (e.g., diffuse shadows). Because of this, the retina's output signals relative intensity between adjacent regions quite well, but signals absolute intensity rather poorly. Information about temporal variations in the retinal image is also lost in the course of retinal processing. Very high rates of intensity change are not signaled because even cones, the faster of the two photoreceptors, do not follow stimulus variations greater than about 60 cycles per second (Hz). Slow rates of intensity change are also conveyed poorly because inhibitory interactions in the inner nuclear layer tend to obscure them. The result is that sudden intensity changes are signaled better than slow ones.

Development

We now turn to the development of the retina. The anatomical development of the human retina has been investigated at two levels. The microstructural level concerns the fine structure of neurons and synaptic contacts. The macrostructural level concerns the gross morphology of the retina (its layering, distribution of neuron types, etc.). In this section, we consider postnatal retinal development at both levels.

The human retina is more mature at birth than that of many species, such as the cat (Donovan, 1966), dog (Shively, 1971), and rat (Weidman & Kuwabara, 1969), but less mature than the retina of some primates, such as the macaque (Hendrickson & Kupfer, 1976). In spite of these differences in maturity at birth, some authors have noted cross-species similarities in sequences of retinal development (Dunn, 1972; Kahn, 1974).

Our knowledge of the postnatal development of the human retina is limited. Only three detailed investigations have appeared in the literature: Bach and Seefelder (1914), Horsten and Winkelman (1962), and Abramov, Gordon, Hendrickson, Hainline, Dobson, and LaBossiere (1982). The oft-cited reviews by Mann (1964) and Duke-Elder and Cook (1963) are based on the Bach and Seefelder report.

Most retinal structures differentiate during the first trimester of fetal life. Differentiation first occurs near the posterior pole of the eye (which ultimately becomes the foveal region) and proceeds centrifugally to the extreme periphery (Mann, 1964). In spite of centrifugal growth during fetal development, the peripheral retina at birth is more mature in many respects than the central retina (Abramov et al., 1982; Bach & Seefelder, 1914).

It is important to make clear what is meant by "mature" here because there has been some confusion about this in the literature. We think that two meanings have been used. Bronson (1974) and others have used what we will call *relative maturity*, and Haith (1980) has used what we will call *absolute maturity*. Relative maturity refers to the status of a structure at a given age relative to its adult status. Absolute maturity refers to the status of a structure at a given age according to absolute criteria such as the number or density of cells, number of synapses, degree of arborization of processes, and so forth. In most cases the second term is not particularly useful because maturity can only be defined relative to the adult state. But, as we will see, the concept of absolute maturity is useful in evaluating differences in functional status between the peripheral and central retina.

In comparing the maturity of the peripheral and central retina, we first consider the status of the peripheral retina. Figure 4 illustrates the structure of

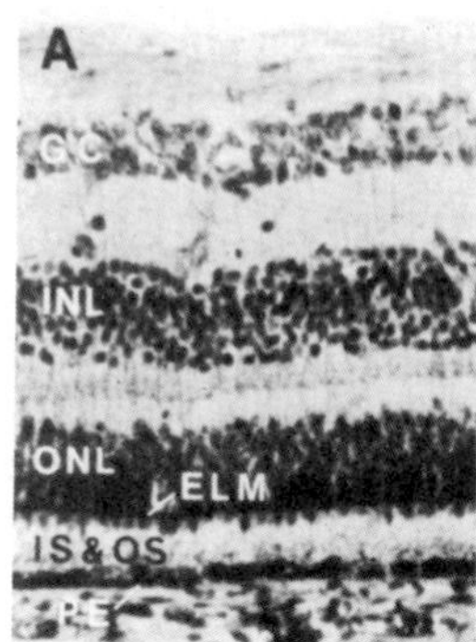

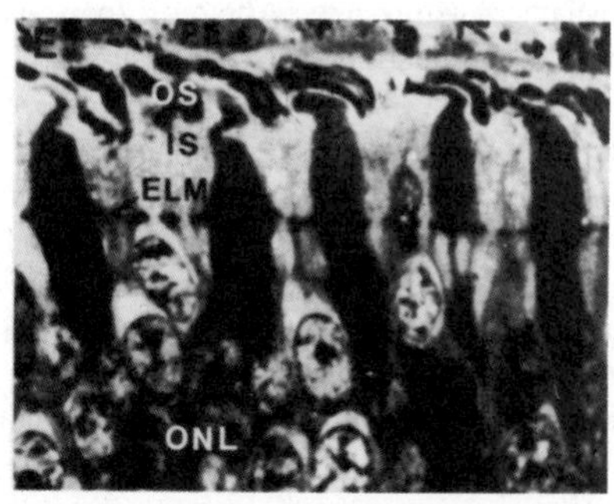

Figure 4. Peripheral retina of a full-term, 8-day-old human infant. (A) Retina section stained with modified Cason's stain. The photomicrograph is of peripheral retina between the fovea and optic nerve head. (E) Retina section stained with azure 11-methylene blue. Abbreviations: GC, ganglion cells; INL, inner nuclear layer; ONL, outer nuclear layer; ELM, external limiting membrane; IS and OS, inner and outer segments of receptors; PE, pigment epithelium. (From Abramov et al., 1982.)

the developing peripheral retina as reported by Abramov et al. Bach and Seefelder's observations, though less detailed, generally agree with those of Abramov and his colleagues. At a macrostructural level, all retinal layers in the periphery are distinct and adultlike at birth. Closer examination reveals that the dimensions of peripheral cones and rods are also nearly adultlike. Both inner and outer segments are well developed. Synaptic contacts appear to be well formed before birth (Spira & Hollenberg, 1973). The foveal region, in contrast, exhibits a number of immature properties at birth. Although the adult fovea can be seen clearly in fundus photographs, the newborn's fovea is not distinct in such photographs (Bulpitt & Baum, 1969). This suggests that the fovea is not clearly differentiated from the rest of the retina at this age. Closer examination shows that the lamination of the newborn fovea is quite different from that of the adult. Figure 5 illustrates the foveal retina's structure at birth as reported by Abramov et al. A depression in the retinal surface (the so-called foveal pit) is present but is not as distinct and deep as it is later on. The newborn's ganglion cell and inner nuclear layers, though thinner than in the periphery, have not yet separated to the extent they do in adults. The inner nuclear layer is actually two layers at this age. Such double layering appears throughout the retina during the second trimester of fetal development but apparently disappears in all but the fovea by birth. The cones in the

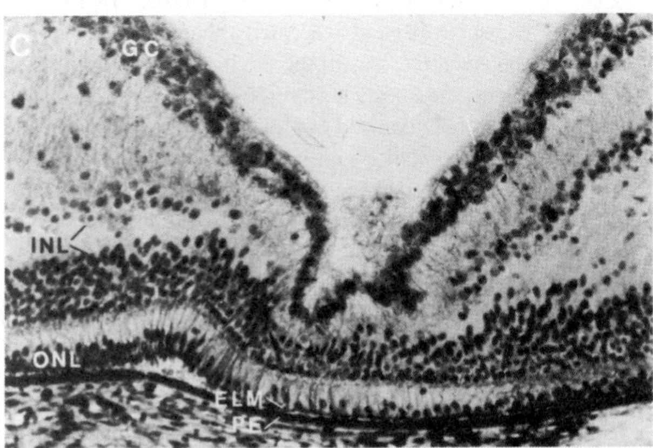

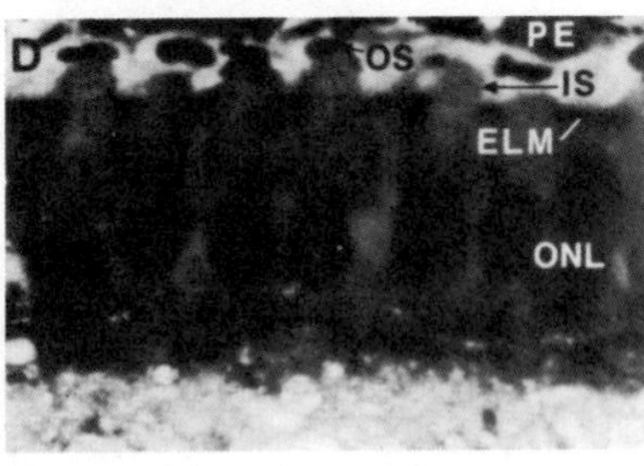

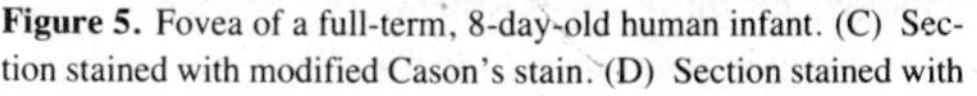
Figure 5. Fovea of a full-term, 8-day-old human infant. (C) Section stained with modified Cason's stain. (D) Section stained with azure 11-methylene blue. (From Abramov et al., 1982.)

foveal region are not densely packed in marked contrast to foveal cones in the adult retina. It even appears that foveal cones are packed less densely than parafoveal cones at this age, Abramov (personal communication), a situation which contrasts sharply with receptor distributions in the adult (Oesterberg, 1935). One reason for this may be that the neonate's foveal cones are quite short and thick relative to the adult's. Thus, the foveal, but not the peripheral, region of the retina appears quite immature at birth in many respects. Of course, one cannot conclude from this that the neonatal fovea is incapable of function, but some degree of functional immaturity seems likely. Abramov et al. estimated that the region of anatomical immaturity subtends roughly 5 deg of visual angle, so fixation accuracy may be affected.

The above account of foveal development disagrees somewhat with the observations of Horsten and Winkelman (1962). They reported few differences in maturity between the periphery and the "centre of retina" in a full-term infant. Abramov et al. note, however, that Horsten and Winkelman's photograph of the central retina did not exhibit any foveal depression. Thus, they hypothesize that this section was from the parafoveal rather than foveal region.

In summary, the Abramov et al. and Bach and Seefelder observations show clearly that, in the relative sense mentioned above, the foveal region of the retina is less mature anatomically than the peripheral region. The neonatal fovea is markedly different from the adult fovea, but the neonatal periphery is reasonably similar to the adult periphery. It is not as clear whether the fovea is less mature than the periphery in the absolute sense mentioned above. Some evidence suggests equivalent levels of absolute maturity; for example, both regions possess all major cell types and a significant number of synapses at birth. Other evidence suggests that the fovea is less mature absolutely than the periphery. For example, double layering of the inner nuclear layer is present in the fovea but not the periphery, and the number of photoreceptors in the fovea is actually less than in the near periphery.

The next question of interest is how the fovea develops postnatally. Bach and Seefelder traced foveal development from birth to 4 months of age. They reported that the ganglion cell and inner nuclear layers continue to separate during this period to form the foveal depression. By 4 months, the foveal cones are thinner and longer and are packed more densely than they were at birth but still not to the degree they are in adults. It is not known when the fovea first becomes adultlike, but Abramov et al. provide some preliminary evidence that it does so before 11 months.

The macaque retina is more mature at birth than the human retina, but postnatal changes are qualitatively similar in the two species (Hendrickson & Kupfer, 1976; Samorajski, Keefe, & Ordy, 1965). Again, the periphery appears more adultlike at birth, but the fovea is clearly marked by a separation of the ganglion cell and inner nuclear layers. This separation continues until at least 2 months and, consequently, the foveal depression deepens. Cones are packed more densely in the fovea than in the parafovea and periphery but not as densely as in the adult fovea (Hendrickson & Kupfer, 1976). The foveal cones are somewhat short and thick in the neonate macaque but not to the same extent as in humans.

Hendrickson and Kupfer note that no new cones and retinal neurons differentiate in the foveal region postnatally. Thus, the decreasing density of the ganglion cell and inner nuclear layers over the fovea and the increasing density of foveal cones imply that a complex migration occurs. Namely, ganglion cells and the constituents of the inner nuclear layer (bipolars, amacrines, and horizontals) must migrate centrifugally (radially away from the fovea) and foveal cones must migrate centripetally (i.e., radially toward the fovea). They also note that connections between cones and higher order retinal neurons do not appear to break and re-form during this migration. If in humans a similar migration occurs (which is implied by Abramov et al., 1982) and the connections between receptors and ganglion cells are not broken and re-formed, an interesting problem arises. A given set of ganglion cells will respond to different features in the environment at different ages. Thus, a set of ganglion cells that responds to the presentation of a straight line at one age might respond to a curved line at a different age. Such a change in the mapping between features in the environment and the set of retinal neurons whose response represents those features may demand continual recalibration. (It is interesting that a similar change occurs in auditory development. The mapping between the proximal stimulus, and the central representation of it, changes with age; Lippe & Rubel, 1983; Rubel & Ryals, 1983).

We now turn to the physiological development of the retina. Unfortunately, only photoreceptors and retinal ganglion cells have been examined and only in cats. This is unfortunate because the anatomy reviewed above suggests that important physiological changes might occur postnatally in primates.

Our understanding of the functional development

of photoreceptors is quite limited. To our knowledge, only one report has appeared. Tucker, Hamasaki, Labbie, and Muroff (1979) recorded the late receptor potential from the retinas of 9- to 26-day-old kittens and adult cats. The late receptor potential is a multiple-unit response that reflects activity in the inner and outer segments of receptors in a restricted patch of retina. Tucker et al. found that the shape and duration of the response did not change much with age. However, there were enormous changes in threshold (i.e., the stimulus intensity needed to elicit a criterion response amplitude). Nine- to 11-day thresholds were at least 5 log units (a factor of 100,000) higher than 15- to 16-day thresholds! Threshold decreased another ½ log unit by 23 to 26 days at which time adultlike values were obtained. Because the late receptor potential is a multiple-unit response, it is difficult to determine the characteristics of individual photoreceptors from these data. Nonetheless, the sheer magnitude of the age effects argues that the sensitivity of individual photoreceptors must increase significantly during the first month of life. By most anatomical measures, monkey and human photoreceptors are more mature than cat receptors at birth. Thus, it is not surprising that electroretinographic (ERG) recordings in humans suggest that both rods and cones are functional at birth (Barnet, Lodge, & Armington, 1965; Horsten & Winkelman, 1962; Lodge, Armington, Barnet, Shanks, & Newcomb, 1969). The ERG, however, is not a precise response measure, so intraretinal primate data are sorely needed to determine the potential significance of postnatal photoreceptor development to infant vision.

Kitten ganglion cells respond fairly briskly to visual stimuli by 3 weeks, the earliest age tested (Hamasaki & Flynn, 1977; Hamasaki & Sutija, 1979; Rusoff & Dubin, 1977). Nonetheless, the receptive fields of these cells differ from adults' in a number of ways. The center and surround mechanisms are larger (when expressed in visual degrees) and less sensitive than those seen in mature cats. The size and sensitivity of the center mechanism approach adult values by 6 weeks of age. (Part of the size change results from the growth of the eye, which decreases the visual angle subtended by a piece of retina; Rusoff & Dubin, 1978.) The antagonistic surround mechanism develops more slowly. It is often not detectable at 3 weeks and does not approach adultlike size or sensitivity until 8 or 9 weeks (Rusoff & Dubin, 1977). Thus, the contour-enhancing and gain control effects of lateral inhibition may not be present until about 2 months of age. According to one report, the proportion of Y cells relative to X cells is higher among kittens than cats (Hamasaki & Sutija, 1979). However, using somewhat different classification criteria, others did not observe such a developmental shift (Rusoff & Dubin, 1977).

Visual deprivation has no obvious impact on cat retinal ganglion cells and, by inference, on more peripheral retinal neurons. The ganglion cells of monocularly and binocularly deprived cats do not exhibit any unusual properties. The proportions of X, Y, and W cells appear to be the same as in normally reared cats (Sherman & Stone, 1973). The spatial and temporal resolution of X and Y cells also seem to be normal (Kratz, Mangel, Lehmkuhle, & Sherman, 1979). Consequently, the deprivation effects observed at higher levels of the visual pathway (the lateral geniculate and visual cortex) are probably not caused by changes in retinal mechanisms.

Summary

The function of the mature retina is to transduce distributions of light into neural signals and to process these signals preliminarily. Visual information is transformed in a number of ways during transduction and subsequent processing. Some spatial detail is lost because of discrete sampling by the receptor mosaic and because of spatial summation between receptors and ganglion cells. Visual information is transformed further by lateral inhibitory connections; sharp spatial and temporal intensity gradients are emphasized at the expense of gradual gradients. This facilitates the signaling of relative intensities rather than absolute intensities, the importance of which we describe in our discussion *Light and Dark Adaptation* below.

The retinas of cats, monkeys, and humans are clearly not adultlike anatomically at birth, cats being the least mature and monkeys the most. The retina of the human newborn is immature throughout, but the foveal region is most obviously different from its ultimate status. The foveal pit is not formed. The foveal cones are distinctly short and thick and are not packed nearly as densely as they will be later in life. These morphological immaturities lead one to expect that the spatial resolution capability of the central retina, which presumably corresponds to the line of sight, is poor in newborns. This implies, in turn, that fixation accuracy (see *Saccadic Eye Movements* and *Visual Scanning* below) and visual acuity (see section on *Visual Acuity* below) are poor early in life. The human retina matures fairly rapidly thereafter so, by 11 months (or perhaps earlier), the major structures are adultlike anatomically.

How well the various components of the retina

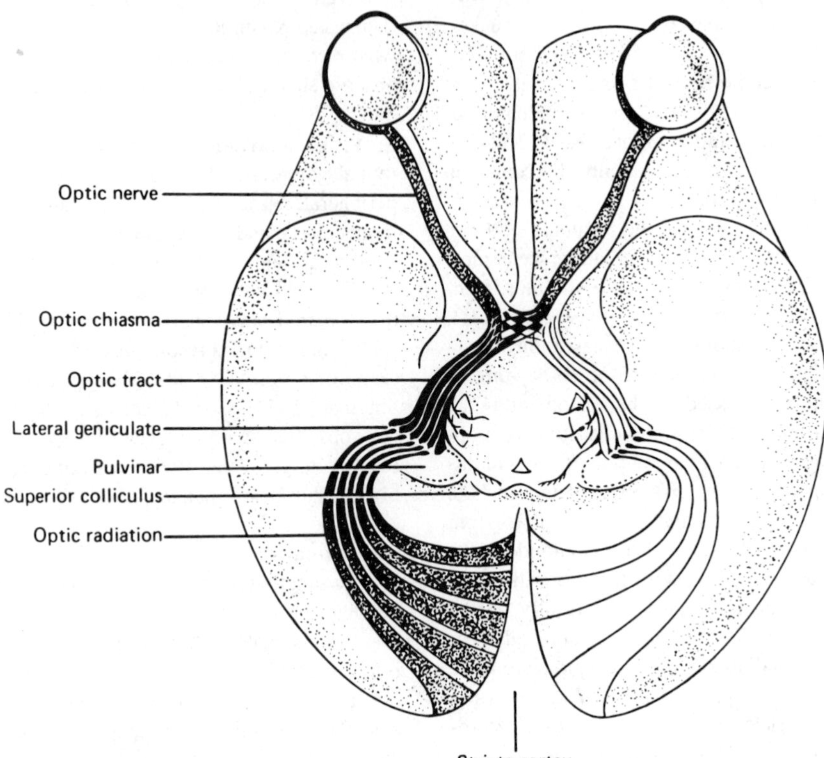

Figure 6. Major pathways from the eyes to the central nervous system. Fibers of the optic nerve from the temporal halves of each retina remain on the same side of the head; that is, they project to the ipsilateral hemisphere of the brain. Fibers originating from the nasal halves of each retina cross at the optic chiasma and then project to the contralateral hemisphere. The lateral geniculate nuclei are part of the thalamus. The superior colliculi are part of the mid-brain. The striate cortices are part of the cerebral cortex. (From Kaufman, 1974.)

function early in life is largely unknown. Rods and cones are functional at birth in humans, but little more is known. Detailed physiological studies have examined kittens only and, since their retinas are less mature anatomically at birth than human retinas, one cannot extrapolate from those data to humans. In kittens, the sensitivity of photoreceptors and ganglion cells improves dramatically during the first 2 to 3 weeks. Lateral inhibitory connections seem to develop even later. If similar trends occurred in humans, several visual capabilities would be affected including contrast sensitivity and light adaptation.

Lateral Geniculate Nucleus

The lateral geniculate nucleus (LGN) is the next major structure in the ascending visual pathway. In this section, we consider, in order, the structure and function of the mature LGN in humans, monkeys, and cats, the anatomical development of the LGN in humans, monkeys, and cats, and, finally, the physiological development of the LGN in monkeys and cats.

After leaving the eye, optic nerve fibers segregate and cross partially at the optic chiasm. These pathways and the decussation are schematized in Figure 6. Most of the optic nerve fibers then terminate on neurons of the left and right lateral geniculate nucleus (LGN), but some branch off to enter the superior colliculi.

The LGN is distinctively layered. In the cat, there are three well-defined layers, one of which has been further subdivided. The LGNs of monkeys and humans are remarkably similar (Hickey & Guillery, 1979). For example, both have six layers. Two contain relatively large neurons and hence are called magnocellular layers. The others contain smaller neurons and are called parvocellular layers. In cats, monkeys, and humans, fibers from both eyes project to both lateral geniculate nuclei, but each geniculate layer is supplied by fibers from one eye only. Those inputs are arranged in a highly ordered, retinotopic fashion. Neighboring regions of the retina make connections on neighboring regions of the LGN. This topographical arrangement is preserved across layers, so the receptive fields of cells in one layer, serving one eye, represent the same position in the visual field as the receptive fields of cells in a neighboring layer, serving the other eye, do. As one might expect from the distribution of cells in the retina, much of the cat, monkey, and, presumably, human LGN represents the central visual field; relatively few cells are devoted to the peripheral visual field. The heavy representation of the central visual field presumably facilitates detailed vision.

The LGN is generally considered a relay station because it does not transform visual information drastically. The receptive fields of LGN neurons are similar to those of retinal ganglion cells. Geniculate neurons and ganglion cells both exhibit center-surround antagonism, although it is stronger in the geniculate. Both on-center and off-center types exist. The spatial resolution or visual acuity of geniculate cells is not obviously different from that of ganglion cells. All geniculate cells respond well to sharp spatial contrast (e.g., contours) and to rapid temporal change (e.g., movement or flicker) but weakly, if at all, to diffuse spatial contrast or slow changes in uniform illumination. Thus, the "neural image" traveling upstream is not changed greatly between entering and exiting the geniculate. Perhaps the most significant change is further enhancement of sharp spatial and temporal contrast, a process that began in the retina.

X and Y cells are less easily dichotomized in the LGN than in the retina, but the distinction has still proven useful (Lennie, 1980). As in the retina, geniculate X cells exhibit linear spatial summation and Y cells do not, but the sustained-transient distinction is less clear in the geniculate. X cells exhibit somewhat better spatial resolution but poorer temporal resolution than Y cells (Derrington & Fuchs, 1979). It was thought that monkeys exhibit a greater degree of anatomical segregation of X and Y cells than cats in that Y cells appear predominantly in the magnocellular layers and X cells in the parvocellular layers (Dreher, Fukada, & Rodieck, 1976; Sherman, Wilson, Kaas, & Webb, 1976). Recently, however, Kaplan and Shapley (1982) have reexamined this issue using more rigorous classification criteria. They agree that the monkey's parvocellular layers contain only X cells but, in contrast to earlier reports, they find that the magnocellular layers contain more X cells than Y cells. They also report some important functional distinctions among these cells. The parvocellular X cells are generally color-opponent cells and have poor contrast sensitivity. The magnocellular X and Y cells, on the other hand, are generally not color-opponent and have high contrast sensitivity. Hubel and Wiesel (1972) observed that parvocellular and magnocellular cells project to distinct cortical layers in monkeys, which does not imply that X and Y cells do.

Development

We now turn to the development of the geniculate. The prenatal and postnatal development of the LGN is remarkably similar in monkeys and humans (Hitchcock & Hickey, 1980; Rakic, 1977). Thus, the monkey may provide a good model for geniculate development in humans. In contrast, the developing and mature geniculate in cats is different in some important ways from the human LGN, so caution is called for in extending research findings on cats to human development. We discuss this point in more detail later.

The LGN of the newborn human has many characteristics of the mature structure (Hickey, 1977). Six layers, two magnocellular and four parvocellular, are readily observed, but the cell bodies in each layer are smaller than in adults. Neurons in the parvocellular layers grow very rapidly from birth to 6 months and then more slowly until 12 months, when they are adultlike in size. Neurons in the magnocellular layers grow more slowly and hence do not reach adult size until 2 years after birth (Hickey, 1977). Development in the monkey geniculate is quite similar but occurs more rapidly (Rakic, 1977). Because periods of cell growth are correlated with sensitive periods in other species, Hickey (1977) has speculated that a visual sensitive period may exist from birth to 2 years in humans. This is not inconsistent with the sparse data that exist on sensitive periods in humans (Awaya, Miyake, Amaizumi, Shiose, Kanda, & Komuro, 1973; Banks, Aslin, & Letson, 1975; Hohmann & Creutzfeldt, 1975). These postnatal anatomical changes, however, do not necessarily imply functional change in the geniculate.

As mentioned above, the functional development of the LGN seems to differ in cats and monkeys; thus we discuss these two species separately. The response properties of kitten geniculate cells are quite immature at first. The retinotopic arrangement of receptive fields across the geniculate is adultlike, but individual cells are very slow to respond, fatigue quite easily, have abnormally large receptive fields, and exhibit weak surround inhibition, if any at all (Daniels, Pettigrew, & Norman, 1978; Norman, Pettigrew, & Daniels, 1977). Moreover, "silent" areas are encountered during physiological recording, suggesting that several cells are simply not responsive to visual stimulation. The X/Y distinction is much less marked in the kitten than in the adult cat. For example, kitten cells categorized as X or Y by spatial summation have widely overlapping conduction velocities (Daniels et al., 1978; Norman et al., 1977). Postnatal development proceeds fairly rapidly particularly among X cells. They attain adultlike receptive field size and center-surround antagonism by 4 to 5 weeks of age. Y cells require a few more weeks. It is interesting to note that this trend is the oppposite of that observed among retinal ganglion cells (Hamasaki & Sutija, 1979; but see Rusoff & Dubin, 1977). There is some evidence (Daniels et al., 1978) that the physiological immaturities observed in the LGN are more marked than among ganglion cells, so changes in the geniculate may not just reflect retinal development.

There is widespread agreement that monocular deprivation disrupts anatomical development in kitten geniculate more than binocular deprivation does. Specifically, monocular deprivation causes marked cell shrinkage in the deprived layers, whereas binocular deprivation does not (Guillery, 1973; Shapley & So, 1980; Sherman, Hoffmann, & Stone, 1972). This supports the notion that some sort of binocular competitive mechanism normally modulates cell growth in the geniculate (Guillery, 1972). (There is recent evidence that the cell shrinkage in the LGN is secondary to deprivation effects in the visual cortex; e.g., see Cynader & Mitchell, 1977.) The physiological consequences of deprivation are not so clear. Sherman et al. (1972) reported that monocular deprivation reduced the proportion of functional Y cells dramatically in the layers supplied by the deprived eye. Proportions of X and Y cells were normal in layers supplied by the nondeprived eye. The few Y cells that were encountered in deprived layers exhibited normal receptive fields, but the remaining X cells suffered a loss in visual acuity (Lehmkuhle, Kratz, Mangel, & Sherman, 1980; Mower & Christen, 1982). However, Shapley and So (1980), using somewhat different experimental techniques, did not observe any reduction in the relative number of Y cells. Derrington and Hawken (1981) also failed to observe Y cell loss as a result of deprivation and, in contrast to Lehmkuhle et al. and Mower and Christen, did not detect any change in X cell acuity. These disagreements are as yet unresolved, but one cause may be sampling bias resulting from the use of different types of microelectrodes. In fact, Shapley and So found that the relative proportions of X and Y cells observed differed for the two types of electrodes they used.

The physiological development of the monkey LGN is similar in some ways but dissimilar in others to that of the cat. Geniculate cells in very young monkeys respond quite sluggishly and fatigue easily (Blakemore & Vital-Durand, 1980). Figure 7 shows the visual acuities of geniculate cells supplied by

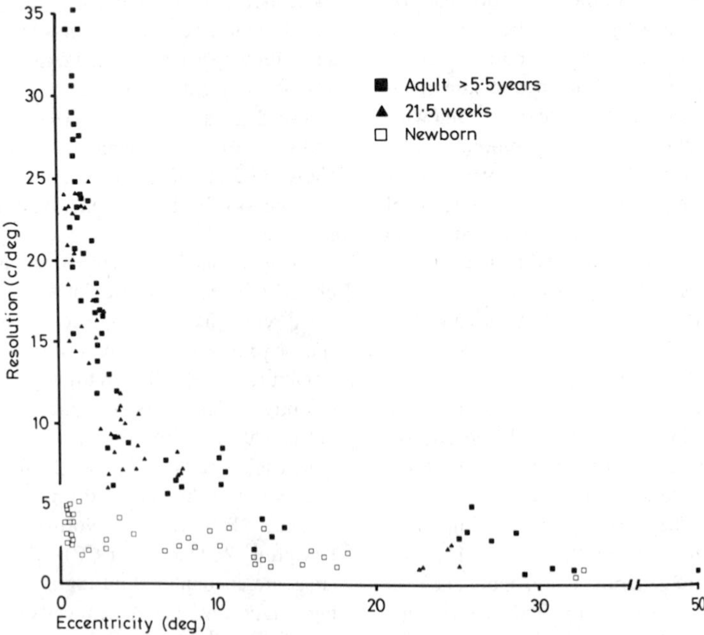

Figure 7. Visual acuity of X cells in the monkey lateral geniculate at three different ages. Resolution of X cells serving different retinal eccentricities are shown for newborns, 5-month-olds, and adults. (From Blakemore & Vital-Durand, 1980.)

different retinal regions at birth, 21 weeks, and adulthood. In newborn monkeys, the acuity of cells supplied by the fovea is slightly higher than that of cells supplied by the periphery. In absolute terms then, foveal geniculate cells are more advanced early in life than peripheral cells. Notice, however, that the visual acuity of foveal geniculate cells improves with age much more dramatically than the acuity of peripheral cells. Thus, in relative terms, foveal geniculate cells are less advanced early in life than peripheral cells. The foveal/peripheral discrepancy is probably caused in large part by differences in foveal and peripheral retinal development. This example illustrates the potential utility of the absolute/relative maturity distinction described earlier. Figure 7 also illustrates that geniculate development proceeds fairly slowly in monkeys. Specifically, the resolution of cells supplied by the central retina does not attain mature values until 7 months of age.

The X/Y distinction is readily observed in monkeys even shortly after birth using tests of spatial summation. It is not evident, however, using tests of response duration; X and Y cells both respond transiently to long-duration stimuli (Blakemore & Vital-Durand, 1980). Thus, the basic structure of receptive fields—the "Xness" or "Yness"—is probably present at birth though many properties, even those correlated with the X/Y distinction, develop postnatally.

There may be some important developmental differences between monkey and cat geniculate. For one thing, the kitten geniculate seems to be more susceptible to deprivation. The cell shrinkage accompanying monocular deprivation is more dramatic among kitten Y cells than among Y or X cells in monkeys (Vital-Durand, Garey, & Blakemore, 1978). Moreover, the physiological consequences may also be greater in kittens. There are, according to some reports (Lehmkuhle et al., 1980; Mower & Christen, 1982; Sherman et al., 1972), pronounced functional changes among kitten geniculate cells after monocular deprivation (but see Derrington & Hawken, 1981; Shapley & So, 1980). In contrast, there are apparently no observable changes among monkey cells even after prolonged deprivation (Blakemore & Vital-Durand, 1980).

Summary

The mature LGN is generally thought of as a relay station because it does not transform visual information dramatically. There are significant postnatal changes in the anatomy and physiology of cat and monkey LGN. The monkey, and not the cat, seems to provide a reasonably accurate model of human development. The most obvious postnatal functional changes in monkey LGN are an overall decrease in response sluggishness and fatigability and an increase in the visual acuity of cells serving the fovea. The latter finding reflects, in part, the postnatal growth of the fovea itself and is closely related to behavioral measures of acuity in developing monkeys (Teller, Allen, Regal, & Mayer, 1978).

Visual Cortex

Visual information is transformed dramatically in the visual cortex so it has been examined extensively in both mature and developing organisms. In this section, we consider, in order, the structure and function of the visual cortex in mature cats, monkeys, and humans, its structural development in the same species, and, finally, its functional development in cats and monkeys.

Axons from the lateral geniculate nucleus fan out in the optic radiation and then terminate in the visual cortex. The visual cortex in cats and higher primates lies posteriorly in the cerebrum (see Figure 6). Three different areas—17, 18, and 19—can be distinguished by several criteria. Incoming fibers from the LGN terminate primarily in area 17 in monkeys (also called the striate cortex). Areas 18 and 19 are adjacent to 17 and receive inputs from it. In cats, fibers from the LGN project to areas 18 and 19 as well as 17.

There is a wealth of neurons and connections of various sorts in these three areas, which suggests that a great deal of information processing is performed here. In light of this, it is fortunate for researchers that some segregation of function into different parts of the cortex exists. For one thing, cells in the mammalian cortex are arranged in layers. Figure 8, a cross section of area 17 in a mature monkey, shows this. The lamination is more apparent in monkeys and humans than in cats. The numbering scheme illustrated in Figure 8 is used to classify the laminae. Layer IV, which has been further subdivided into layers IVa, IVb, and IVc, is the primary receiving site for afferents from the LGN. Axons from the parvocellular and magnocellular layers of the geniculate terminate in different parts of layer IVc, the lower and upper halves, respectively. This suggests at least partial segregation of X and Y cell inputs to the cortex (but see Kaplan & Shapley, 1982). The deeper layers—V and VI—also receive some afferents from the LGN. The superficial cortical layers—I, II, and III—receive almost all of their input from the deeper layers; that is, they receive few

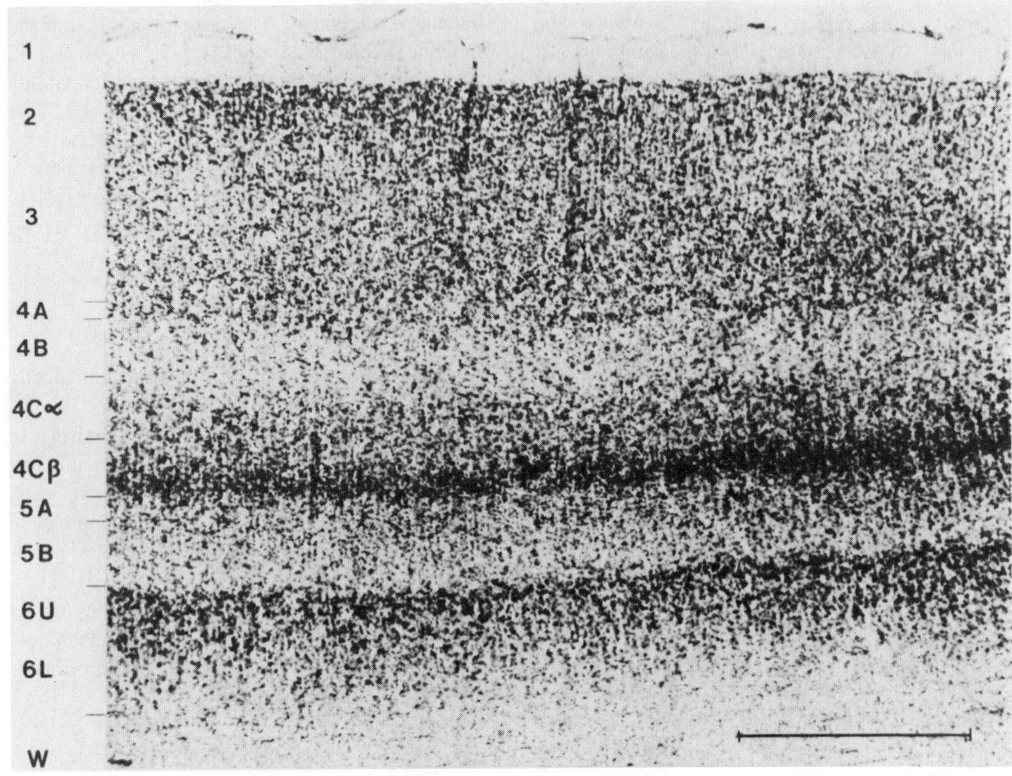

Figure 8. Cross section of monkey visual cortex. This Nissl-stained section shows the layering of the visual cortex. Labels on the left indicate the various layers. See text for further details. (From Lund, 1981.)

afferent fibers from other parts of the central nervous system. Layer II sends efferent fibers to area 18 in monkeys. The corticotectal tract, another significant pathway, originates from layer V. Other smaller projections from area 17 go to a number of higher and lower level structures including the LGN, inferior pulvinar, cortical area 19, and the visual association cortex. Most of these projections have not been investigated developmentally, so they are not considered here. The exception is the corticotectal pathway from the visual cortex to the superior colliculus, which we discuss in the next section.

The lamination of the visual cortex is correlated with functional specializations; that is, different types of receptive fields are observed among neurons residing in different layers. The receptive fields of cortical neurons are quite distinct from those of retinal and geniculate neurons, but they do share at least two properties with those lower level neurons: (1) the visual field is represented in a strictly topographical map and (2) cells respond little, if at all, to changes in overall illumination. The latter property is a further enhancement of the signaling of sharp spatial or temporal change at the expense of response to diffuse or gradual change. Of most importance, however, are the unique properties of cortical receptive fields. Virtually all visual cortical neurons respond best to elongated contours of a particular orientation. Different cells prefer different sorts of contours. Some respond best to light bars and some to dark bars, while others prefer a single light-dark contour (an edge). The selectivity for orientation is reasonably precise; typically, a change of $\pm$ 10–15 deg from the optimal orientation reduces the response by 50%. Unlike retinal and geniculate cells, cortical neurons are generally responsive to input from either eye and they generally prefer stimuli moving in a particular direction.

In work they recently received the Nobel Prize for, Hubel and Wiesel (1962, 1968) classified cortical neurons into three categories based on their receptive field characteristics: simple cells, complex cells, and hypercomplex cells. The defining characteristic of simple cells is that their receptive fields can be mapped with stationary flashing spots into separate on and off subregions. There is summation within each of these regions and antagonism between them. The optimal stimulus, a properly oriented edge or bar of a particular width, can be roughly predicted from the on and off subregions. As the edge or bar is moved across the receptive field, simple cells respond with one or two short bursts of activity. In other words, simple cells only respond when the stimulus is in a particular position. They are particularly common in layer IV and appear to receive a direct input from X cells in the geniculate (Hoffmann & Stone, 1971; Hubel & Wiesel, 1968).

Complex cells also respond to contours of a certain orientation but, unlike simple cells, their receptive fields cannot be mapped into separate on and off subregions. Complex cells do not require precise positioning of the contour in order to respond; they respond continuously as a properly oriented bar or edge drifts across their field. Therefore, the meaning of signals arising from complex cells and simple cells differs somewhat. Simple cells localize a bar (or edge) of a certain orientation and width to a particular position in the visual field. Complex cells signal the presence of a bar (or edge) with a particular orientation and width without strict reference to position.

Hubel and Wiesel (1962, 1968) originally described another cell type—the hypercomplex cell—but more recent work suggests that it is not a distinct category. Now most neurophysiologists distinguish two types of simple and complex cells, those with end inhibition and those without. This property, when present, makes these cells respond optimally to properly oriented bars (or edges) of a certain length as well as width.

Recently, the responses of cortical neurons to sine wave gratings of different spatial frequencies and orientations have been examined (e.g., Campbell, Cooper, & Enroth-Cugell, 1969b; DeValois, Albrecht, & Thorell, 1982). The motivation for using gratings as visual stimuli is beyond the scope of this section but is described below under *Contrast Sensitivity*. Suffice it to say that cortical neurons respond quite selectively to gratings; changing a grating's spatial frequency, for example, has a significant influence on response rate (Albrecht, DeValois, & Thorell, 1980).

The responsivity of cortical neurons is affected by several other properties of visual stimuli. Most are influenced by input from either eye, but from cell to cell the relative influence varies. Hubel and Wiesel (1968) used the so-called ocular dominance histogram to classify cells along this dimension. The histogram is composed of seven categories, ranging from cells influenced by the contralateral (opposite side of the head) eye only to cells influenced equally by both eyes to cells influenced by the ipsilateral (same side of the head) eye only. In mature monkeys, about 30% of the neurons in area 17 are monocular; that is, they are influenced by input to one eye only. The proportion of monocular cells in adult cats is somewhat lower. The majority of the remaining binocular neurons in cats and monkeys exhibit sensitivity to binocular disparity; that is, response rate varies as a binocular stimulus is moved from behind to in front of the plane of fixation. Some cells actually prefer positions behind the fixation plane while others prefer closer positions (Barlow, Blakemore, & Pettigrew, 1967; Hubel & Wiesel, 1970a). This is undoubtedly part of the neural substrate for stereoscopic depth perception, a topic we take up again in the last major section. Cortical neurons also respond selectively to different wavelengths and combinations of wavelengths. This presumably is part of the encoding process involved in color vision; we return to this topic later. They also respond differentially to stimuli moving in different directions and at different rates. This is probably part of the encoding used in the perception of motion, a topic we discuss below in the section on *Temporal Vision*.

Although the visual cortex is layered (see Figure 8), an important feature is its structural and functional organization into columns perpendicular to the layers. In close examinations of cross sections, it is apparent that most cortical axons and dendrites run vertically, that is, perpendicular to the cortical surface. Lateral connections are generally rather short in comparison. Hubel and Wiesel (1962, 1965b, 1968) observed in cats and monkeys that different columnar regions contained neurons with some functional property in common. They described columnar clusterings according to the neurons' preferred position in the visual field, ocular dominance, and orientation. Maffei and Fiorentini (1977) recently described functional "rows" in area 17 of the cat's cortex. These rows were perpendicular to the columns described above and contained neurons with the same preferred spatial frequency (or size). More recent evidence, however, contradicts this report. Tootell, Silverman, and DeValois (1981) found that preferred spatial frequencies were organized in columns rather than rows.

Hubel and Wiesel (1974a) noted an important regularity across orientation columns. As they moved their recording electrode from column to column, preferred orientation changed gradually and systematically. A total orientation shift of 180 deg took place over a distance of about 1 mm before another sequence of orientation shifts began. A similar regularity seemed to exist across ocular dominance columns; a complete shift from one eye to the other took place over a distance of about 1 mm. Hubel and Wiesel coined the term "hypercolumn" to designate the 1 × 1 mm block of cortex that contains one complete set of columns subserving all stimulus orientations and both eyes. Different hypercolumns subserve different positions in the visual field, so any one hypercolumn has the cortical machinery needed to "digest a region of visual field, examining it for light-dark contours in all orientations and with both eyes" (Hubel & Wiesel, 1977, p. 40).

Interestingly, these hypercolumns and the cells within them are very similar across area 17; that is, hypercolumns supplied by the fovea are remarkably similar to those supplied by the peripheral retina. Superficially, this observation seems difficult to reconcile with the obvious behavioral differences between foveal and peripheral vision (e.g., Aulhorn & Harms, 1972). Hubel and Wiesel (1974a) point out, however, that the differences probably lie in the inputs to the cortex, not in the cortical machinery itself. A section of monkey cortex devoted to the fovea generally serves a very small segment of the visual field, whereas a comparably sized section devoted to the retinal periphery may cover 30 to 40 times more (Cowey & Rolls, 1974; Hubel & Wiesel, 1974b). Stated another way, a given segment of the central visual field is represented by 30 to 40 times more cortex than a segment of equivalent area in the far periphery. This is the so-called cortical magnification factor, which has been shown to predict reasonably accurately the eccentricity-dependence of a number of visual capabilities. For example, the dramatic changes in visual resolution from the fovea to the far periphery are predictable from changes in the cortical magnification factor with eccentricity (Cowey & Rolls, 1974; Virsu & Rovamo, 1979; for discussions of other visual capabilities, see Koenderink, Bouman, Bueno de Mesquita, & Slappendel, 1978; McKee & Nakayama, 1982; and Virsu, Rovamo, Laurinen, & Näsänen, 1982). The apparent similarity of neural circuitry in different parts of the visual cortex may reflect an economic strategy for cortical development. Specifically, the genetic and experiential programs necessary to specify the structure of various cortical regions would be simplified if they only had to specify one basic structure and then duplicate it many times.

We can use the "neural image" characterization to summarize crudely how the visual cortex represents visual inputs. Consider what the cortex' neural image of a solid square might be. Since cortical cells do not respond well to the absolute level of uniform illumination, responses would be confined to the square's boundary. These responses could signal the position, orientation, length, and binocular disparity (stereoscopic depth) of the square's boundaries. The speed and direction of motion could also be signaled. Because of the cortical magnification factor, some of these stimulus attributes (position and binocular disparity) could be conveyed with greater precision if the square were in the central rather than the peripheral visual field.

It is important for the following discussion on cortical development to consider what functions the mature visual cortex serves for the organism. Without an understanding of this, it is difficult to know which aspects of cortical immaturity are important and which are not.

Experiments in which the visual cortices are removed demonstrate that a number of visual capabilities are at least partially dependent on cortical function. Unfortunately, the specific effects of cortical ablation vary somewhat from species to species (Stone & Freeman, 1973), so this literature cannot be summarized easily. In cats, ablation does not significantly affect the ability to detect and orient to objects (Spear & Braun, 1969; but see Sherman, 1977, for an interesting exception), nor does it affect optokinetic nystagmus (Spear & Braun, 1969; but see Wood, Spear, & Braun, 1973, for an interesting exception). On the other hand, these cats are unable to follow moving targets smoothly and reliably (Spear & Braun, 1969). They are also unable to perform complex pattern discriminations, except on the basis of simple flux (overall intensity) or size cues (Dodwell & Freedman, 1968; Spear & Braun, 1969). In monkeys, the consequences of cortical ablation are somewhat more severe. The ability to detect, localize, and follow moving objects is disrupted, but not eliminated (Humphrey & Weiskrantz, 1967) and even optokinetic nystagmus is affected to some degree (Pasik & Pasik, 1964). The most obvious deficits, however, involve pattern vision. Thresholds for detecting pattern are much worse than in normal monkeys (Miller, Pasik, & Pasik, 1980). Furthermore, the ability to discriminate complex patterns is noticeably affected (Humphrey & Weiskrantz, 1967; Klüver, 1941; Pasik, Pasik, & Schilder, 1969) and even those discriminations that can be made may be dependent on picking up local flux cues while moving the head. Monkeys also lose the capacity for hue discrimination following ablation (Klüver, 1942).

Thus, the visual cortex in cats and monkeys appears to play an important role for at least some types of visuomotor behavior, for pattern vision, and, in monkeys, for color vision. (One would expect that depth perception would also be affected, but this has not been investigated rigorously.) The question is: Exactly what are those roles? There are no firm answers to this question, just a number of hypotheses. One possibility is to extend the Lettvin, Maturana, Pitts, and McCulloch (1961) trigger feature hypothesis to the visual cortex. Such an extension would hold that individual visual cortical neurons encode a single attribute (say, the presence of a right angle) of the visual scene. Thus, a single cell, by responding vigorously, would signal the presence of its trigger feature. This hypothesis can be rejected. As we have shown, each cell in the visual cortex actually responds selectively to a number of stimulus attributes (e.g., orientation, position, width, direction of motion, etc.). Thus, a change in a cell's response is multiply ambiguous; it could imply an alteration in any of these attributes. Information about the individual features of a visual scene, therefore, requires some form of integration of responses among a population of neurons. Barlow (1979) and Marr (1982) have hypothesized that local regions of the visual cortex perform computations that, in effect, transform visual information into a language more suitable for recognizing objects in a visual scene. Barlow, for example, proposed that a patch of visual cortex performs a crude Fourier transform (see *Contrast Sensitivity* below) on a local region in the visual scene. The spatial frequency and orientation information that results is then distributed to other centers that look for similarities and dissimilarities between different parts of the scene.

In conclusion, the function of the mature cortex is understood only in broad outline. Thus, it is difficult at this time to know which aspects of cortical development are most significant. Accordingly, our review of the developmental literature is fairly broad and, where we have been selective, our choices were based on the belief that the cortex is particularly important for pattern vision.

Development

We now turn to the development of the visual cortex. The structural development of the cortex appears in broad outline to be similar in cats, monkeys, and humans. There are, however, cross-species differences in time course.

The differentiation of neurons and the subsequent migrations to their ultimate positions are best understood in monkeys, but indirect evidence suggests a similar developmental pattern in humans and cats. The full complement of prospective cortical neurons is produced well before birth in ventricular and subventricular zones below the monkey's cortex (Rakic, 1981). The same is true in humans (Rakic & Sidman, 1968). After differentiation, young neurons migrate a considerable distance in order to reach their final positions. The migration is an inside-out process in monkeys and other mammals (Jacobson, 1978). The first neurons to differentiate take up positions in deep cortical layers. Neurons that differentiate later migrate past the older neurons to adopt positions in progressively more superficial layers. In each case, the path of migration is radial, that is, perpendicular to the cortical surface. This radial pattern may facilitate the development of the orientation and ocular dominance columns observed in adult monkeys and cats. At birth, neurons in monkeys and humans reside in all cortical layers, so the lamination characteristic of adult cortex (see Figure 8) is apparent.

Individual neurons in monkey cortex undergo marked morphological changes after birth (Boothe, Greenough, Lund, & Wrege, 1979; Lund, Boothe, & Lund, 1977). All neurons in area 17 appear to go through a common developmental sequence at very similar times. Just before birth, axons and dendrites are easily recognized, but dendrites are short and poorly arborized. All neurons then grow a large number of dendritic spines, the greatest number occurring at about 2 months after birth. This may mean that a large number of synaptic contacts are being formed during this time, but there are no direct data on this point. Thereafter, the number of spines gradually diminishes until adult levels are reached several months later. Boothe et al. (1979) noted that neurons in the lower half of layer IVc start and complete this developmental sequence somewhat before neurons in the upper half of IVc, so perhaps cells receiving input from the parvocellular layers of the LGN develop more rapidly than those receiving inputs from the magnocellular layers. From Kaplan and Shapley's observations of lateral geniculate function, discussed earlier, this implies that cells that ultimately have low contrast sensitivity may develop before cells that ultimately have high contrast sensitivity.

Similar changes in neuronal morphology occur in humans. Conel (1939–1963) has examined the structural development of the human cortex from birth to 2 years. Figure 9 shows cross sections of area 17 at birth, 1 month, 3 months, and 6 months. As in the monkey, the number and amount of arborization of dendrites increase greatly postnatally. At each age, the neurons of layer IVc, the receiving site for fibers from the lateral geniculate, are more advanced than neurons in other layers. The general prolifera-

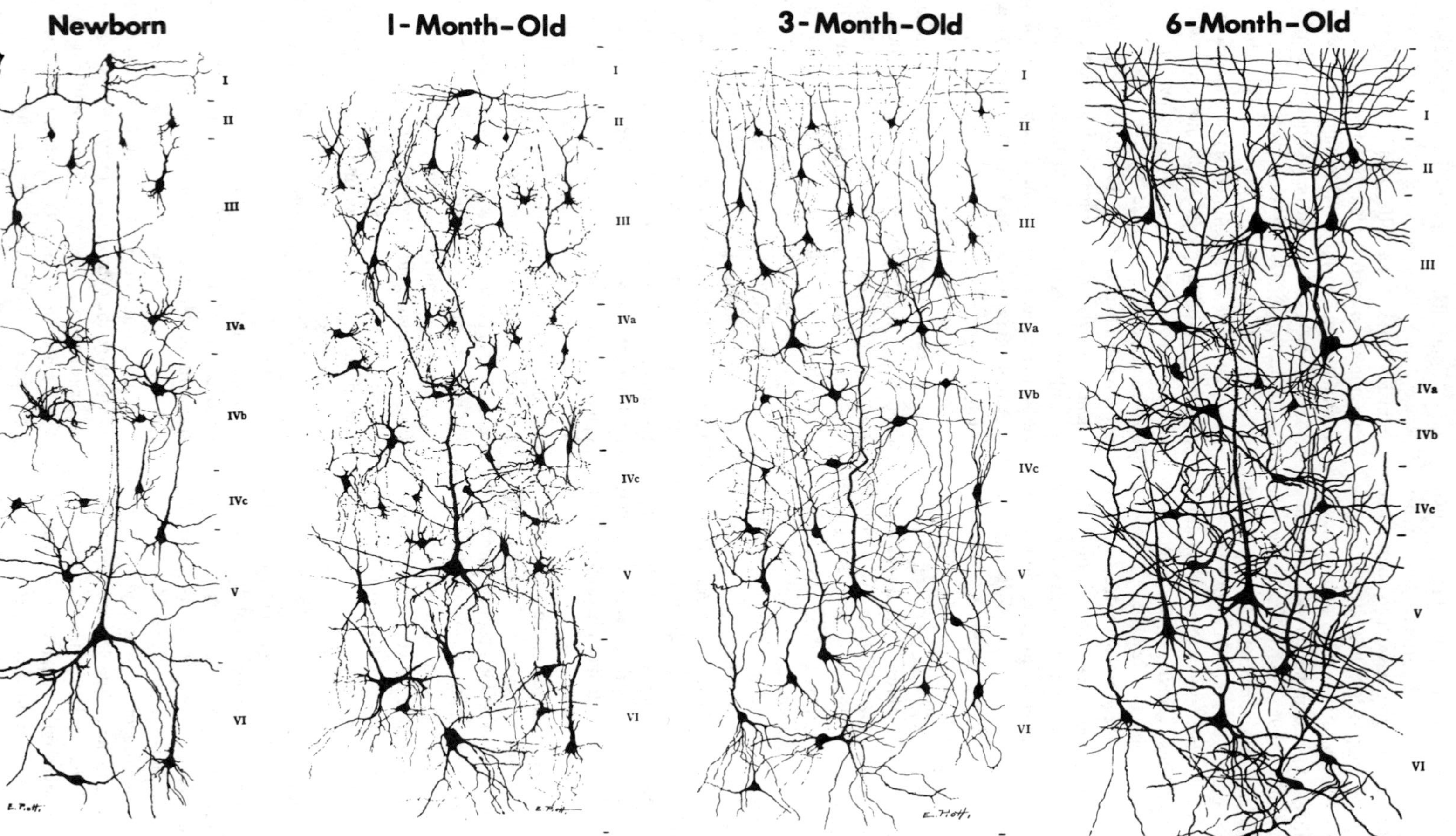

Figure 9. Drawings from cross sections of the visual cortex of human newborns, 1-month-olds, 3-month-olds, and 6-month-olds. The drawings are based on Golgi-Cox preparations. The Roman numerals refer to different cortical layers. See Figure 8 and the text for reference. (From Conel, 1939–1963.)

tion of dendrites takes place more gradually in humans than in monkeys, since it does not appear to peak until roughly 6 months. The vertical organization of dendritic trees, which presumably underlies columnar organization of function, is apparent from birth onward.

As neurons grow they form synaptic connections with other neurons. Unfortunately, little is known about the formation of synapses within the developing primate cortex. It is known that afferent fibers from the LGN reach cortical layer IV before birth, but it is not known when they form connections with cortical cells (Rakic, 1981). These afferent fibers are not initially segregated according to ocular dominance. Instead, a gradual segregation occurs until the adult pattern is achieved by about 1 month after birth (Hubel, Wiesel, & LeVay, 1977). A similar sequence occurs in kittens (LeVay, Stryker, & Shatz, 1978).

Cragg (1975a, 1975b) has examined the formation of synapses in the kitten cortex. Synaptogenesis begins before birth, but by the time the kitten's eyes open only a very small fraction of the normal adult complement of synapses is present. Between that age and 5 weeks, a burst of synaptogenesis occurs. This phase is at least partially dependent on visual input (Cragg, 1975a) and is followed by a partial loss of synapses until adult levels are reached at about 3 months. It is not exactly clear what the functional implications of these findings are because the linkage between number of synapses and neuronal function has not been specified. But surely the enormous postnatal growth in synaptic density has a significant impact. Unfortunately, there are no data on synaptogenesis in humans and monkeys comparable to Cragg's cat data, but the large proliferation of dendritic spines followed by partial loss observed in these two species suggests that a similar sequence of synapse formation may occur.

Finally, myelin, the sheath that insulates axons and dendrites, is still being formed in the visual pathways after birth. Yakovlev and LeCours (1967) state that myelination in humans proceeds from peripheral sites to the visual cortex. The optic nerve is fully myelinated by 3 months and the visual cortex somewhat later.

Clearly, the structure of the visual cortex changes postnatally at both macrostructural and microstructural levels. One expects then that cortical functioning changes as well. Electrophysiological studies of single cortical cells generally confirm this expectation. We review this work in the remainder of this section. Almost all of the work concerns the visual cortex of kittens, but we emphasize, where appropriate, work on young monkeys.

To understand the development of any structure, one certainly needs information about how it changes from birth to maturity in the context of a normal environment. But information about its development within aberrant settings is also extremely useful; such information reveals the extent to which development is under genetic versus environmental control. Accordingly, we consider cortical development under both normal and restricted rearing conditions. To date, the physiological work in this area has focused on the properties of single cells, but some recent advances in anatomical methodology (e.g., Sokoloff, Reivich, Kennedy, Des Rosiers, Patlak, Pettigrew, Sakurada, & Shinohara, 1977) have provided insights into the functions of large clusterings of cells (e.g., LeVay, Wiesel, & Hubel, 1980).

The first two questions we consider are: (1) What is the status of the visual cortex in the very young, visually inexperienced organism? (2) How does this status change with age? At birth, kittens' eyes are closed and, even when they do open at about 1½ weeks, the optics of their eyes are noticeably cloudy (Bonds & Freeman, 1978). Thus, the receptive field properties of cortical neurons are difficult to assess until about 3 weeks of age when the optics become less cloudy. Nonetheless, several researchers have measured the receptive field properties of area 17 neurons in very young kittens (Blakemore & Van Sluyters, 1975; Bonds, 1979; Buisseret & Imbert, 1976; Frégnac & Imbert, 1978; Hubel & Wiesel, 1963; Pettigrew, 1974). As one might expect, there are similarities and dissimilarities among these accounts. They all agree that these cells exhibit some reasonably mature properties at the youngest ages testable. These properties are retinotopicity (the topographic mapping of visual fields onto the cortex), direction selectivity, and, to some extent, binocularity. The reports also agree that these neurons respond quite sluggishly and fatigue easily. The major disagreements concern pattern variables such as orientation and bar width. Hubel and Wiesel (1963), for example, reported that all cells exhibited clear orientation preferences, although the specificity of such preferences was less precise than in adults. They also observed recognizable examples of simple and complex cells. Pettigrew (1974), on the other hand, found very few, if any, orientation-selective neurons and could not distinguish simple and complex receptive fields. The disagreement, Pettigrew argued, derived from differences in how orientation selectivity was assessed; Hubel and Wiesel did not attempt to isolate orientation preferences from direction preferences, while Pettigrew did. Subsequent reports indicate that the truth may lie somewhere between these two extremes. When an attempt is made to distinguish orientation from direction selectivity, most cells do not have a distinct orientation preference shortly after birth, but some cells do (Blakemore & Van Sluyters, 1975; Bonds, 1979; Buisseret & Imbert, 1976; Frégnac & Imbert, 1978). Figure 10 shows the proportion of orientation-selective and nonorientation-selective cells in 1-week-old kittens, the youngest age group testable. About 20% of the cells encountered are truly orientation selective. Those few cells tend to be monocular, to prefer vertical or horizontal orientations, and to reside in cortical layer IV. Figure 10 also shows how the proportion of orientation-selective cells changes with age. Adultlike proportions are reached by 5 to 6 weeks. Furthermore, by this age, the range of orientations a typical cell will respond to is adultlike (Bonds, 1979).

Different aspects of the spatial properties of cortical receptive fields can be measured using sine wave gratings (Campbell et al., 1969b; see *Contrast Sensitivity* below). For this reason, Derrington and Fuchs (1981) used gratings of various spatial frequencies to characterize the cortical cells of kittens from 2 to 12 weeks of age. Sensitivity and acuity were quite low at 2 weeks but improved rapidly up to

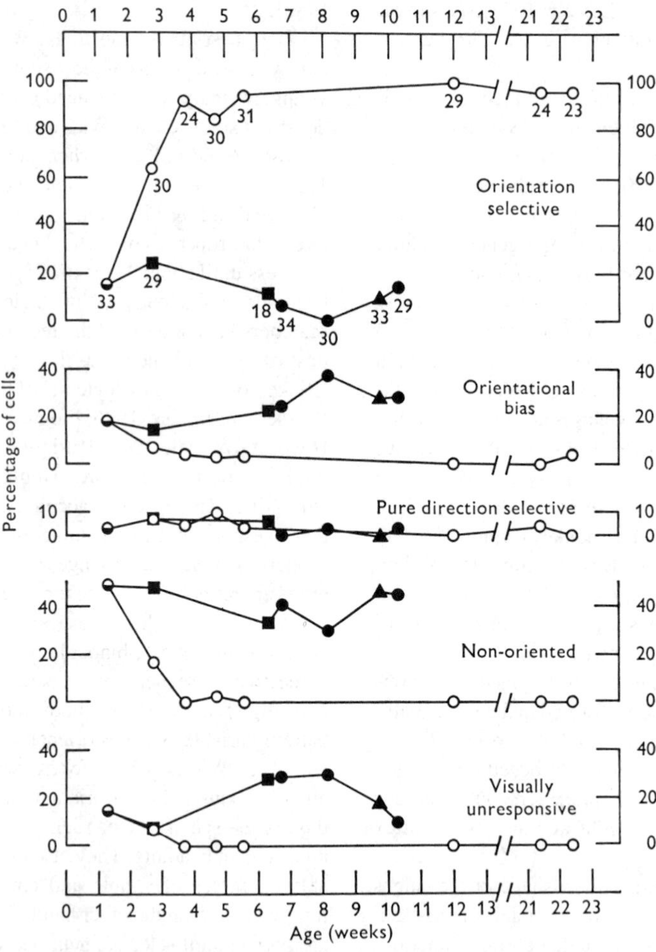

Figure 10. Proportions of orientation-selective and nonoriented cells in kittens of different ages. Cells are classified into five categories as shown. The open symbols represent proportions in normally reared kittens. The filled symbols represent proportions in visually deprived kittens; the squares are for dark-reared kittens, the circles for lid-sutured kittens, and the triangles for nictitating-membrane-sutured kittens. The numbers beneath the data points for the top pair of curves indicate the total number of cells represented in the point. (From Blakemore & Van Sluyters, 1975.)

adult values by 6 weeks. Furthermore, the range of frequencies these cells responded to (the cell bandwidth) decreased dramatically from 2 to 6 weeks. Thus, two means of analyzing receptive fields—mapping with bars and edges and mapping with sine wave gratings—evidence a marked increase in specificity to pattern variables from birth to 6 weeks of age.

Disparity selectivity is an important property of mature cortical neurons, but only Pettigrew (1974) has examined its development. He reported that disparity tuning was strikingly imprecise in very young kittens; the binocular disparity of an otherwise optimal stimulus could be varied by several degrees of visual angle without influencing response rate. Tuning improved rapidly thereafter, approaching adult values by 5 to 6 weeks.

We can use the "neural image" characterization to summarize these observations. Position in the visual field and direction of motion are probably represented reasonably faithfully in the newborn kitten's "cortical image." On the other hand, pattern information, such as contour, orientation, and bar width or spatial frequency content, is probably not conveyed very faithfully. Depth information, as specified by binocular disparity, is also not represented faithfully. These encoding deficits are short-lived, however, because each property is conveyed with adultlike precision by 5 to 6 weeks. It is perhaps not surprising then that the visual behavior of kittens is very immature during the first few weeks. They do not orient to and follow visual stimuli reliably, nor avoid obstacles (Norton, 1974). By 5 to 6 weeks, however, their vision is much improved; at this time they orient to and follow visual stimuli, avoid obstacles and drop-offs (Norton, 1974), and their visual acuity has improved substantially (Mitchell, Giffin, Wilkinson, Anderson, & Smith, 1976).

Unlike kittens, monkeys are born with their eyes open and with clear optics. The receptive field properties of cortical cells in young monkeys are probably more mature than those in young kittens, which is not too surprising since monkeys' visual behavior is more advanced at birth than kittens. Wiesel and Hubel (1974) were struck by the absence of unresponsive, sluggish, and nonoriented cells in newborn monkeys. Most cells responded briskly when stimulated visually, preferred a relatively narrow band of orientations, and exhibited either simple or complex receptive fields. Furthermore, ocular dominance and preferred orientation changed systematically as Wiesel and Hubel advanced their recording electrode, suggesting that columnar organization was present. It is difficult, however, to draw firm conclusions from this one report since these same authors concluded that the kitten cortex was more mature than other investigators did. Thus, others, using different techniques and criteria, might give somewhat less favorable accounts of the maturity of the neonatal monkey cortex.

The next questions we consider are (1) whether postnatal cortical development is under mostly genetic or environmental control, and (2) if environmental factors are indeed important, which factors are most significant and what roles do they play? Answers to these questions have been sought in experiments that manipulate the visual diet of kittens and monkeys during infancy.

The most obvious manipulation is to deprive a developing animal of visual input altogether. This condition has been produced experimentally by dark rearing and has been approximated by suturing the eye lids of both eyes closed. Although there is evidence that the impact of long-term dark rearing is more severe than that of binocular lid closure, both have pronounced effects. In cats deprived since birth, many cells are unresponsive to visual stimulation and those that are responsive are erratic and easily fatigable (Blakemore & Van Sluyters, 1975; Frégnac & Imbert, 1978; Leventhal & Hirsch, 1977; Wiesel & Hubel, 1965). Few cells exhibit orientation selectivity, but most are binocular and show direction selectivity. The abnormality of the binocularly deprived cortex relative to the normally reared cortex does not emerge until 4 to 5 weeks of age. Before 4 weeks, the cortical cells of normally reared and binocularly deprived kittens are essentially indistinguishable (Blakemore & Van Sluyters, 1975; Frégnac & Imbert, 1978). After 4 weeks, the cells in deprived animals become less and less responsive and selective in comparison to cells in normal animals. Indeed, if deprivation continues, the receptive field properties of single cells actually regress to neonatal status or worse. This later finding means that there is little, if any, passive maturation beyond 4 weeks of age.

Early binocular deprivation also severely disrupts the selectivity of cortical cells in monkeys (Crawford, Blake, Cool, & von Noorden, 1975). Indeed, the cortex of a deprived adult monkey is probably considerably less organized than that of a newborn monkey. Clearly, then, some sort of visual experience is required for the development or maintenance of normal cortical function in both cats and monkeys.

Thus, the next question is: What kind of experience is required? To answer this difficult question, researchers have looked at the unique properties of cortical cells. Recall that, unlike cells in the retina and LGN, cortical cells exhibit binocularity, disparity selectivity, orientation selectivity, and direction selectivity. Researchers have invented several environmental manipulations to examine the influence of visual experience on each of these properties.

Monocular deprivation, for example, has been used in part to study the development of binocularity. Although monocular deprivation is a less severe environmental manipulation than binocular deprivation, its physiological consequences are in many ways more profound. It causes a dramatic loss of responsiveness through the deprived eye in both cats and monkeys (Blakemore, Garey, & Vital-Durand, 1978; Blakemore & Van Sluyters, 1974; Crawford et al., 1975; Wiesel & Hubel, 1965). Thus, very few binocular cells are observed in monocularly deprived animals. As one would expect, this loss of influence by the deprived eye is accompanied by changes in the ocular dominance columns. In cats and monkeys, the columnar regions supplied by the nondeprived eye expand at the expense of regions that otherwise would have been supplied by the deprived eye (Hubel et al., 1977; Shatz & Stryker, 1978). The more severe consequences of monocular deprivation relative to binocular deprivation prompted Hubel and Wiesel (1965a) and others to propose that competitive interactions between inputs from the two eyes play an important role in cortical development. We can conclude from the work on monocular deprivation that one requirement for normal development is binocular visual experience.

One wonders then if any binocular experience will do or whether there are certain restrictions. This question has been examined in an elegant series of experiments by Blakemore (1976). He asked initially if the loss of binocularity due to monocular lid suture was caused by an imbalance in the overall intensity of the two retinal images or by an imbalance in the clarity of pattern information in the two images. To answer this question, he developed two rearing conditions that allowed him to manipulate independently interocular differences in illumination and pattern clarity. Kittens raised with a diffuser in front of one eye and a clear neutral density filter (chosen to match interocular illumination) in front of the other did not exhibit many binocular cells when tested. Thus, an imbalance in pattern clarity alone disrupted binocularity. In contrast, kittens raised with a clear neutral density filter (which reduced illumination tenfold) over one eye developed normal cortical binocularity. Therefore, an imbalance in retinal illumination did not disrupt binocularity. We can conclude that the presentation of similar pattern information to the two eyes is a necessary condition for the maintenance of binocularity.

The question then becomes: What aspects of pattern information must be similar? This question has been explored by raising kittens and monkeys with their visual axes artificially misaligned. This rearing condition does not allow the same features in the visual field to fall on corresponding retinal points and hence mimics the human clinical condition of strabismus ("crossed eyes" or "wall eyes"). Several researchers have found that months of artificial strabismus beginning near birth greatly reduce the proportion of binocular cells in cats and monkeys (Baker, Grigg, & von Noorden, 1974; Blakemore, 1976; Hubel & Wiesel, 1965a; Van Sluyters & Levitt, 1980). Obviously, the ability to encode binocular disparity is disrupted as well. Hubel and Wiesel hypothesized that the disruption of cortical binocularity was caused by the lack of registration between the two retinal images. Additional evidence for this idea comes from the fact that alternately depriving kittens' eyes day by day disrupts cortical binocularity (Blakemore, 1976; Hubel & Wiesel, 1965a). We can conclude from this work that another requirement for normal cortical development is that the binocular visual experience be concordant and synchronous. Since strabismus in humans seems to affect the development of binocularity adversely (Banks et al., 1975; Hohmann & Creutzfeldt, 1975), the experiential requirements may be similar for humans.

Binocular experience with nondisparate patterns is needed to maintain binocularity and, presumably, to develop disparity selectivity, but what sorts of visual inputs are needed for orientation selectivity to develop normally? Pettigrew and Freeman (1973) and Van Sluyters and Blakemore (1973) guessed that extended contours are required. To test this, they raised kittens in environments composed of small, randomly arrayed spots in order to eliminate extended contours from their visual experience. Most cells did not develop normal orientation selectivity. Indeed, they seemed to prefer spots rather than bars or edges, a preference that contrasts sharply with that of cells in normal cats.

Further evidence for the import of extended contours comes from experiments in which kittens were reared in environments with contours of only one or two orientations. Blakemore and Cooper (1970) raised kittens in cylindrical drums with either vertical or horizontal stripes painted on their walls. Hirsch and Spinelli (1970, 1971) outfitted kittens with goggles that presented vertical stripes to one eye and horizontal stripes to the other. Both groups of investigators discovered significant alterations in orientation preferences among these kittens' cortical cells. In Blakemore and Cooper's experiment, most cortical cells preferred orientations close to the one experienced during rearing. In Hirsch and Spinelli's experiments, cells responsive to the eye that had experienced vertical stripes preferred vertical or nearly vertical orientations. Similarly, cells responsive to the other eye preferred horizontal or nearly horizontal orientations. Hirsch and Spinelli also encountered many cells that were simply not orientation selective.[2] Thus, experience with contours of one orientation can change the distribution of orientation preferences among cortical cells.

Several researchers have asked whether stripe rearing actually induces orientation preferences among cells that would otherwise develop a different preference or whether it just maintains selectivity among a fraction of cells while allowing the others to atrophy. This question has not been answered clearly. Some researchers have found sizable numbers of nonoriented or unresponsive neurons in stripe-reared cats, a result consistent with the atrophy hypothesis (Hirsch & Spinelli, 1970, 1971; Leventhal & Hirsch, 1975; Stryker, Sherk, Leventhal, & Hirsch, 1978). Others have continued to report strong biases in the distributions of preferred orientations and small numbers of nonoriented or unresponsive cells, a result consistent with the induction view (Blakemore, 1976; Blakemore & Cooper, 1970).

A human analog of these stripe-rearing experiments has been reported (Mitchell, Freeman, Millodot, & Haegerstrom, 1973), so it seems likely that experience with extended contours influences human cortical development, too. This experiment is discussed in a later section.

Now that the need for binocular experience with extended contours has been established, one naturally wonders whether experience with motion is important. One obvious property to investigate is direction selectivity, another characteristic property of cortical cells in cats and monkeys. Recall that this property is present even in very young animals. Cynader and Chernenko (1976) reared kittens under stroboscopic illumination in order to deprive them of experience with moving stimuli. The proportion of direction-selective neurons was radically reduced, but other receptive field properties were unaffected. To establish the importance of motion in another way, Cynader, Berman, and Hein (1975) reared kittens in an environment with contours moving in one direction only. They found that the distribution of preferred directions changed toward the experienced direction. Thus, a visual diet of contours moving in different directions is required to maintain the direction selectivity of neonatal neurons.

Another important question concerning environmental modification of the cortex is: When is the appropriate visual experience required? The answer to this question varies somewhat from one environmental manipulation to another and from one cortical cell property to another (e.g., Cynader, Berman, & Hein, 1976; Daw, Berman, & Ariel, 1978). Nonetheless, the period of susceptibility to environmental manipulation generally appears to be limited in duration. In cats, the so-called sensitive period extends from roughly 2 to 14 weeks of age (e.g., Hubel & Wiesel, 1970a). In monkeys, the sensitive period is roughly similar in length (Crawford et al., 1975). It appears to be substantially longer in humans (Awaya et al., 1973; Banks et al., 1975; Hohmann & Creutzfeldt, 1975). These sensitive periods are correlated roughly with periods of dendritic growth and synaptogenesis (e.g., Boothe et al., 1979; Conel, 1939–1963; Cragg, 1975b).

In summary, studies of newborn animals indicate that at least a skeleton of mature organization of cortical receptive fields appears before visual experience. The skeleton may be better articulated in the newborn monkey than in the newborn kitten. Aberrant experience has been shown to affect all receptive field properties of cortical cells with the possible exception of retinotopicity (but see Shlaer, 1971). Therefore, rich visual experience with contours of various orientations moving in different directions and falling on corresponding retinal points is needed to maintain the existing organization and to facilitate further refinements.

Significant progress has obviously been achieved in understanding genetic and environmental influences on cortical development. Nonetheless, the purposes of environmental influences have not been elucidated fully. In the remainder of this subsection, we focus on hypotheses concerning the purposes of cortical plasticity. We also point out that, without a clear notion of the purposes of cortical plasticity, work in this area faces significant interpretative difficulties. (This point is, of course, consistent with the functional theme we introduced above.) We describe these interpretative difficulties first and then introduce some existing hypotheses to illuminate the difficulties.

The manipulations of visual experience employed in the experiments reviewed above have generally been quite gross. It is possible that some may have been too gross to elucidate the role of experience in normal development. Thus, we recommend that the conclusions drawn from these studies be treated cautiously until more is known about what function plasticity normally serves. Just as one needs some understanding of the function the mature cortex serves before one can state with confidence how mature the neonate's cortex is, one also needs some understanding of how and why visual experience shapes cortical development before one can assess with confidence the relevance of various environmental manipulations. The risk is that some environmental manipulations that researchers have used may depart too much from the range of environmental variability that the visual cortex has evolved to cope with. The results from such experiments might then mislead attempts to understand the normal function of cortical plasticity.

An example should clarify this point. One theory of the environment's role in shaping cortical development holds that the mechanisms of binocular integration and disparity encoding require modification and tuning (Blakemore, 1979; Pettigrew, 1978). Specifically, modifications based on visual experience may be required to ensure that binocular cells respond to precisely the same feature in the visual field through inputs from two eyes. Pettigrew and Blakemore describe several considerations that make this an attractive account of the teleology of cortical plasticity. We mention a few of these. First, experiential effects are demonstrable only in cortices of animals with binocular vision (e.g., Chow & Spear, 1974). Second, stereopsis, the perceptual consequence of disparity encoding, is fairly precise in cats but is astonishingly so in monkeys and humans. The human visual system, for example, is capable of detecting, in one retinal image compared to the other, a displacement much smaller than the diameter of a single photoreceptor (Berry, 1948). This implies that binocular mechanisms allow a very precise comparison of environmental features viewed through the two eyes. The attainment of such precision is particularly remarkable because postnatal eye growth (see *Optics* below) and photoreceptor migration (see *The Retina* above) cause continual modifications in the relationship between features in the visual field and their central representations. Consequently, Pettigrew and Blakemore argue that modifications based on visual experience may be needed to develop and maintain appropriate receptive field correlations. The third piece of evidence is the most interesting and supports our contention that gross environmental manipulations may obscure the normal role played by visual experience. Blakemore, Van Sluyters, Peck, and Hein (1975) and Shinkman and Bruce (1977) asked whether individual cells can modify their orientation preferences to compensate for rotating visual input in one eye with respect to the other. Blakemore et al. examined this by surgically rotating one eye of a young kitten 90 deg about its visual axis. This condition could be called a torsional strabismus. They observed a marked decrease in the number of binocular cells. Of most interest, however, were the orientation preferences of the few remaining binocular cells; the correlation between preferred orientations for one eye versus the other was strikingly lower than the correlation observed in normally reared cats. This experiment alone suggests then that compensation for visual field rotation cannot occur and casts doubt on Pettigrew's and Blakemore's theory of cortical plasticity. Shinkman and Bruce (1977) showed, however, that the cortex could compensate for a subtler manipulation. They raised kittens with prisms placed in front of both eyes. The prisms rotated the visual fields either 24, 16, or 0 deg with respect to one another. The 24 deg manipulation disrupted binocularity and was not compensated for by changes in preferred orientation, a finding consistent with Blakemore et al. (1975). The 16 deg manipulation, however, produced the opposite result: It did not disrupt binocularity and the rotation was compensated for by interocular changes in preferred orientation. Taken together, these observations illustrate that cortical plasticity is probably not capable of more than slight modifications of innate organization. When presented highly aberrant visual inputs, such as 24 or 90 deg rotations of one visual field with respect to the other, the normal mechanisms of plasticity break down and a highly abnormal cortex develops. Thus, future research in this area should consider carefully the roles visual experience might play in normal development. We hope a better understanding of these roles will help researchers to identify "ecological" environmental manipulations and to avoid being misled by the consequences of "nonecological" manipulations.

Summary

The visual cortex of kittens is quite immature at birth in a number of ways. Thus, the young kitten's ability to encode pattern information and binocular disparity must be fairly primitive. Most cortical properties attain adultlike status by 5 to 6 weeks, so deficits that result from cortical immaturities must be short-lived. The monkey's visual cortex is apparently more mature at birth than the kitten's. It too attains adultlike status fairly rapidly. The differences in maturity at birth and some differences between the visual cortices of adult cats and monkeys illustrate the need for caution in extrapolating from kitten data to the human case.

Studies of experiential and genetic factors in the development of the kitten's cortex have yielded a number of fascinating observations. Some cortical properties emerge early in life without the benefit of visual experience. In those cases, experience is often needed to maintain the property's integrity. Some cortical properties emerge later and their emergence is guided by visual experience. Unfortunately, most of our knowledge about the experiential requirements for the development of different cortical properties is based on cat data. A few studies have been conducted with monkeys and they generally yield results similar to those obtained with cats. But, again, our understanding of the neural substrate of human visual development would benefit greatly from additional observations of monkey cortical development.

Superior Colliculus

Another major visual area is the superior colliculus, a bilateral structure in the mid-brain (see Figure 6). In fish, amphibia, and birds its homologue—the optic tectum—is the primary central visual area, but in mammals the colliculus is less predominant because of the elaboration of the geniculocortical system. Thus, the superior colliculus is considered a phylogenetically older, perhaps more primitive, module of the mammalian visual system. In this section, we review the structure and function of the mature superior colliculus in cats and monkeys, and then the anatomical and physiological development of the superior colliculus.

The superior colliculus of cats and monkeys performs functions of sensorimotor integration. Accordingly, it receives inputs from and sends outputs to an overwhelming number of structures (Edwards, Ginsburgh, Henkel, & Stein, 1979; Goldman & Nauta, 1976). Among these, there are two primary visual inputs: a direct path from the retina and an indirect path through the visual cortex. The retinal path projects directly to the colliculus from the ipsilateral half of both retinas (i.e., the right superior colliculus receives fibers from the right half of both eyes). In the cat, the crossed path from the contralateral eye is larger than the uncrossed path from the ipsilateral eye (Sterling, 1973). The indirect path, which is called the *corticotectal tract*, projects from the ipsilateral visual cortex in both cats and monkeys. Since the cortex also receives fibers from the ipsilateral half retinas, the corticotectal tract represents the same half retinas as the direct retinal path to the colliculus. Thus, both paths represent the contralateral half of the visual field.

The superior colliculus is layered in both cats and monkeys, though not as distinctly as the lateral geniculate nucleus. Seven layers can be distinguished, but researchers generally divide them simply into superficial layers and deep layers. This dichotomous classification is based on a number of anatomical, physiological, and behavioral distinctions in several mammals (Harting, Hall, Diamond, & Martin, 1973; Mohler & Wurtz, 1976). Simply stated, the superficial layers exhibit fairly specific connections that are typical of sensory structures, while the deep layers exhibit more diffuse connections. The superficial layers seem primarily concerned with visual processing, whereas the deep layers seem more concerned with orienting movements of the eyes in response to visual, auditory, and tactile stimulation.

We first review the properties of the superficial layers. As in other visual areas of the brain, the majority of experimental observations concerns the single cell so, by necessity, most of our review will be at this level. Superficial cells are quite responsive to a variety of visual stimuli. As in the cortex and lateral geniculate, their receptive fields are retinotopically organized (Cynader & Berman, 1972; Sterling & Wickelgren, 1969). Hence, neighboring regions in the colliculus subserve neighboring regions in the visual field. The retinotopic map, as in the cortex and lateral geniculate, overrepresents the central visual field. This central magnification is more pronounced in monkeys than in cats; fully one-third of the monkey colliculus is devoted to the central 10 deg of the visual field (Cynader & Berman, 1972).

Beyond this, there are few similarities between the properties of superficial colliculus cells and cortical cells. Colliculus cells, for example, habituate much more easily than cortical cells. Consequently, they signal the first appearance of a target quite well but not subsequent presentations. Colliculus cells, unlike cortical cells, appear to be quite insensitive to variations in the size and shape of a stimulus so long as it is confined to the receptive field (Sterling & Wickelgren, 1969). The receptive fields are also quite large by cortical or geniculate standards: Fields as large as 20 to 30 deg are observed even near the fovea. As one might expect from such large fields, colliculus cells respond only to very low spatial frequencies (0.05 to 0.2 c/deg; Pinter & Harris, 1981).

Suppressive flanks exist around the receptive field proper, but they are too weak to eliminate response to changes in overall illumination. Also unlike cortical and geniculate cells, superficial colliculus cells are strikingly more responsive to moving than to flashed, stationary stimuli. Most cells in the cat have, in addition, a distinct preference for stimuli moving in one direction, generally from the fovea outward (Sterling & Wickelgren, 1969). This is not the case in monkeys, since only 5% of their cells are direction selective (Goldberg & Wurtz, 1972a). Superficial cells are generally binocular and exhibit crude disparity selectivity, which Berman, Blakemore, and Cynader (1975) have argued might be used to guide vergence eye movements.

One of the most unique and interesting properties of superficial colliculus cells has been called behavioral modulation. Many cells in alert monkeys respond more vigorously to the introduction of a visual stimulus if the animal is about to make a saccadic eye movement to the stimulus (Goldberg & Wurtz, 1972b). The response enhancement is not a general arousal effect because it is spatially specific; that is, the response is enhanced only when a saccade is about to be made into the cell's receptive field. Thus, the visual responses of many superficial cells are influenced by the behavioral significance of a stimulus within their receptive field.

The overall impression is that superficial cells sacrifice the ability to resolve and discriminate changes in pattern such as size, shape, and orientation. They are suited instead for detecting the introduction of a visual stimulus and signaling its location, velocity, direction of motion, and behavioral significance. It is not clear, however, whether superficial colliculus cells can signal these properties, with the exception of behavioral significance, more accurately than cortical cells can.

The superior colliculus as a whole exhibits some columnar organization of function. So as a researcher's electrode advances downward from the most superficial to intermediate and then deep layers, the cells encountered generally represent the same position in the visual field and, if they exhibit direction selectivity, share a common preferred direction. Cells in the deep layers are, nonetheless, quite distinct in a number of ways from those in superficial layers. We describe three of these distinctions. First, many deep cells are not responsive to visual stimuli and those that are have even larger receptive fields than superficial cells (Gordon, 1973). Second, the responses of many deep cells are intimately tied to the execution of saccadic eye movements. Many deep cells discharge just before a saccade is executed. Unlike superficial cells, these discharges are not dependent on visual stimulation because they occur in the dark as well as in conjunction with a visual stimulus (Schiller & Koerner, 1971). The response leads execution of the saccade by as little as 50 msec in some cells, so they may be the output neurons of the superior colliculus. Significantly, each cell discharges only before a saccade to a particular region of the visual field, the so-called movement field (Wurtz & Goldberg, 1972). These movement fields are arranged retinotopically in registration with the receptive fields of overlying superficial cells. So, for example, a cell in the deep layers with a movement field centered 20 deg above the fovea lies just below cells in the superficial layers whose receptive fields are centered roughly 20 deg above the fovea. This fascinating correspondence suggests an integration of sensory and motor maps, a point we return to shortly. It should be emphasized that the movement fields of deep cells and the receptive fields of superficial cells are organized by retinal coordinates. In other words, both sorts of fields are referenced to the point of fixation regardless of the position of the eyes.

The third major distinguishing characteristic of deep cells as compared to superficial cells is their multimodal input. Many deep cells in cats and monkeys are responsive to auditory and tactile as well as visual stimulation (Updyke, 1974; Wickelgren, 1971). Interestingly, the auditory receptive fields are in register with the above-mentioned movement fields (Stein, Magalhães-Castro, & Kruger, 1976; Wickelgren, 1971). The tactile receptive fields are also roughly in register (Stein et al., 1976). So a trimodal cell with an auditory receptive field and a visual movement field 20 deg to the right may have a tactile receptive field on the right side of the face. The registration of auditory receptive fields, tactile receptive fields, and visual movement fields in the deep layers and the visual receptive fields of the overlying superficial layers suggests that a local region in the superior colliculus can signal the position of an event in the environment independent of the particular sensory modality(s) stimulated. Notice, however, that the registration of these maps would be disrupted whenever the eyes are fixating laterally rather than straight ahead (Pöppel, 1973). In cats, this is not a serious problem because they have a strong bias to orient with a combination of an eye movement and a head movement in order to keep their eyes in central position (Blakemore & Donaghy, 1980). It remains a problem to be explained in monkeys (and presumably humans), however, because they often orient with eye movements alone; thus, frequently, their eyes are not positioned centrally.

Since two major visual pathways project to the superior colliculus—the direct retinal path and the corticotectal tract—an obvious question is: What roles do these pathways play in shaping the functional properties of colliculus cells? This question has been examined by observing the effects on single colliculus cells of eliminating influence due to the corticotectal tract. This manipulation has quite different effects in cats and monkeys, so we describe them separately. In cats, ablation or reversible cooling of the visual cortex changes the characteristics of superficial colliculus cells dramatically. They become monocular, less responsive to moving stimuli, and lose their direction selectivity (Rosenquist & Palmer, 1971). The cells of deep layers lose their ability to respond to visual stimuli altogether (Stein, 1978). A similar experimental manipulation in monkeys has no obvious effect on cells in the superficial layers (Schiller, Stryker, Cynader, & Berman, 1974). There is even no noticeable loss of responsiveness to foveal stimulation, despite anatomical observations that the fovea is not represented in the direct retinal path (Wilson & Toyne, 1970; but see Cowey & Perry, 1980). As in cats, however, cortical ablation or cooling causes cells in the deep layers to lose their ability to respond to visual stimuli completely (Schiller et al., 1974). Thus, the corticotectal tract influences the properties of superficial cells in the cat but not in the monkey and influences the properties of deep cells in both species.

One extremely important property of the deep layers of the superior colliculus is revealed by direct electrical stimulation. In alert monkeys, stimulation of a particular region leads to a conjugate saccadic eye movement into the movement fields of cells in that region (Schiller & Stryker, 1972). For example, stimulating a region whose movement fields lie 50 deg to the right of the point of fixation is followed by a large conjugate saccade to the right. Such saccades are often followed by head movements in unrestrained monkeys, but the colliculus does not appear to control those movements (Robinson & Jarvis, 1974). The phenomenon is somewhat different in cats. Stimulation of deep cells whose movement fields lie within 25 deg of the point of fixation is followed by corresponding saccadic eye movements and pinna movements (Harris, 1980; Stein & Clamann, 1981). Stimulation of cells with more eccentric movement fields, however, is followed by a coordinated eye and head movement as well as pinna movements. Thus, the colliculus is involved in the control of orienting head movements in cats, but not monkeys. Nonetheless, these stimulation experiments illustrate a unique feature of the superior colliculus in both species. Namely, the motor map, as revealed by observing the amplitude and direction of orienting movements when a collicular region is electrically stimulated, is in register with the sensory maps for visual, auditory, and tactile stimulation. Thus, the superior colliculus is well-suited for encoding the position of a sight or sound and initiating a saccadic eye movement to place the stimulus on the fovea.

Ablation studies confirm the view that the superior colliculus is important to the guidance of visual orienting and is not important to pattern perception. Monkeys with total collicular lesions eventually learn to make visually guided saccadic eye movements to peripheral targets, but the latency, precision, and form of eye movements are clearly abnormal (Mohler & Wurtz, 1977; Schiller, True, & Conway, 1980). Similar, but somewhat more significant, deficits are observed in cats with colliculus lesions (Sprague & Meikle, 1965). In contrast, ablation of the superior colliculus affects pattern discrimination little, if at all, in monkeys and cats (Anderson & Symmes, 1969; Myers, 1964; Rosvold, Mishkin, & Szwarcbart, 1958).

Development

We now turn to the development of the superior colliculus. As in the review of cortical development, we first consider how the colliculus normally changes from birth to maturity and then consider its development in the context of aberrant environments. Our review concerns only kittens because there are currently no developmental data on primates. This is particularly unfortunate because one would expect the development of primate and kitten colliculi to differ nontrivially given the obvious differences in the adult structures. Consequently, our ability to infer what the development of the human colliculus might be like is quite limited.

The two primary visual pathways—the direct retinal and corticotectal paths—have invaded the kitten's colliculus by birth (Stein & Edwards, 1979; Williams & Chalupa, 1982). The connections are not functional, however, because responses to visual stimuli cannot be elicited (Stein, Lábos, & Kruger, 1973b). Only cells in deep layers are responsive and then only to tactile stimulation. By 5 days of age, a few deep cells respond to auditory stimuli, but the first hint of visual responsiveness occurs among superficial cells at 7 days (Stein et al., 1973b). The first trimodal cells are observed a week later. The sequence of tactile, auditory, and visual responsivity among colliculus cells is the same as the developmental sequence of modality-specific orienting behaviors. For this reason, Stein (1978) suggested that colliculus development may determine in part the emergence of general orienting behaviors regardless of the modality of stimulation.

After 7 days of age, more and more visually responsive cells emerge, but they remain decidedly immature in a number of ways. They fatigue quite easily, even by colliculus standards. Unlike mature colliculus cells, most respond better to flashed, stationary stimuli than to moving stimuli. Virtually all are monocular, responding only to input to the contralateral eye. Receptive fields are quite large and ill-defined because suppressive surrounds are not yet present. By 10 to 14 days after birth, some superficial cells begin to exhibit binocularity, preference for moving stimuli, and direction selectivity (Norton, 1974; Stein, Lábos, & Kruger, 1973a, 1973b). The number of such cells increases to 5 to 7 weeks when the superficial layers of the colliculus are adultlike.

Norton (1974) has considered the relationship between the maturation of single cells in the superficial colliculus and the development of visuomotor behaviors. The status of some visuomotor behaviors (e.g., visual orienting and following) is coupled in time with the development of cell properties. However, several other visuomotor behaviors (e.g., visual placing and triggered placing) do not emerge until after colliculus development is complete. From this and some ablation work (Norton & Lindsley, 1971), Norton concluded that the development of visuomotor behaviors involving orientation of a stationary self to a moving stimulus (following and orienting) is dependent on colliculus development, whereas the development of behaviors involving response of a moving self to a stationary stimulus (placing) is not. This hypothesis concerns cats only because, as we mentioned above, nothing is known of the functional development of the monkey's superior colliculus.

One dogma of developmental neurobiology is that mid-brain structures develop more rapidly than cortical structures (Jacobson, 1978). The kitten's visual system, however, seems to violate this. At an age when the superior colliculus is not responsive to visual stimulation at all, the visual cortex is reasonably responsive and even exhibits some adultlike stimulus selectivity (e.g., Blakemore & Van Sluyters, 1975). Moreover, the two structures acquire adultlike status at similar ages. One cause of this apparent anomaly is the dependence of colliculus cell properties on the corticotectal tract; some properties of colliculus cells may have to await the maturation of cortical cells and their projections to the corticotectal tract. Stein and Gallagher (1981) tested this hypothesis by examining in young kittens the effects of reversible cooling of the visual cortex on the properties of colliculus cells. Up to 10 to 14 days after birth, no obvious effects were detected. Thereafter, as binocular and direction-selective cells began to appear in the superficial layers, cortical cooling affected an increasing number of cells. The only cells affected were, however, "mature" cells; those cells that exhibited binocularity and direction selectivity before cortical cooling became monocular and unselective after cooling. Thus, much of the development of visual cells in the kitten colliculus seems to be dependent on the maturation of the visual cortex. One strongly suspects that the same would not be true of monkeys since ablating the visual cortex in adult monkeys has no significant influence on superficial cells. However, this has not been examined experimentally.

The notion that the development of the cat superior colliculus depends heavily on cortical development is reinforced by the results of selective rearing experiments. For example, binocular deprivation produces an abnormal superior colliculus, but much of the abnormality is probably secondary to deprivation effects at the cortex. Binocular deprivation causes cells in the superficial layers of the colliculus to lose their binocularity and direction selectivity (Hoffmann & Sherman, 1975). In addition, the visual fields of these kittens, when tested monocularly, become quite restricted; only the nasal half retinas (and hence the temporal visual fields) appear to be responsive (Sherman, 1977). Two considerations suggest that this deficit is caused by changes in the visual cortex that are conferred on the superior colliculus through the corticotectal tract. First, binocular deprivation is known to affect the responsivity and specificity of cortical neurons significantly (Blakemore & Van Sluyters, 1975). Second, the consequences of binocular deprivation to the superior colliculus (loss of binocularity, direction selectivity, and nasal visual fields) are quite similar to the consequences of cortical ablation (Rosenquist & Palmer, 1971).

The effects of stimulus motion have also been explored by rearing kittens under stroboscopic illumination and in unidirectional environments. Stroboscopic rearing, which eliminates stimulus motion altogether, causes a notable drop in the number of direction-selective cells (Flandrin, Kennedy, & Amblard, 1976). Again, however, this effect is probably secondary to a change at the visual cortex—in this case, a change in the direction selectivity of cortical cells (Cynader & Chernenko, 1976). The effects of unidirectional rearing are less certain; Flandrin and Jeannerod (1975) observed a shift in the distribution of direction preferences toward the exposed direction, while Cynader et al. (1975) observed no change. In summary, the properties of cells in the superficial layers of the superior colliculus are somewhat dependent on visual experience for normal development. It seems, however, that the most significant experiential effects may be conferred on colliculus cells through the corticotectal tract. Again, nothing is known about how deprivation affects the development of the monkey superior colliculus.

Although the superior colliculus seems to be intimately involved in the initiation of orienting behaviors, developmental researchers have hardly considered its motor functions. Kittens' visuomotor behavior is extremely crude until at least 2 to 3 weeks of age (Norton, 1974). Orienting behaviors to tactile and auditory stimuli can, however, be elicited in younger animals. This suggests that sensory immaturities may be more responsible than motor immaturities for the early deficits in visuomotor behaviors. Stein, Clamann, and Goldberg (1980) explored this by stimulating the deep layers of the superior colliculus of very young kittens. Kittens as young as 2 days elicited saccadic eye movements when a region of the colliculus was electrically stimulated. The movements were immature in some ways—their length was shorter than is typical of adult cats and some obvious trial-to-trial variability existed—but Stein et al. were impressed with the quality of the responses. The eye movements were conjugate. Moreover, their length and direction were correlated with the locus of stimulation, so at least a rudimentary motor map was present. These results support the notion that development of the sensory components of the saccadic control system lags behind the development of the motor components. A similar suggestion has been made for the accommodative control system (see *Visual Accommodation* below).

Summary

The mature superior colliculus is important to sensorimotor behavior. In both cats and monkeys, it receives inputs from three sensory modalities and represents these inputs in complementary sensory maps. Stimulation of the colliculus leads to conjugate saccadic eye movements to different regions in the visual field. The motor map, which represents the amplitude and direction of such movements, is in register with the above-mentioned sensory maps. Thus, the superior colliculus appears to be designed to detect and locate sights and sounds and then initiate eye movements to direct the foveas to the source of such stimulation.

There are some obvious, and potentially important, differences between the colliculi of adult cats and monkeys. For example, the corticotectal tract seems to be much more important to the normal function of the cat's colliculus than it is to the monkey's. Our current understanding of collicular development is based almost entirely on kitten data and not at all on monkey data. This is quite unfortunate because, given the differences between the colliculi of adult cats and monkeys, one suspects that the developmental stories are different, too. Our ability to relate the anatomical/physiological development of the superior colliculus to human behavioral development is correspondingly limited.

The kitten data, nonetheless, show that their superior colliculus is quite immature early in life. This immaturity is more marked for sensory functions than for motor functions. Indeed, very few visually responsive cells are observed at first. This finding violates the dogma that subcortical structures are more mature early in life than cortical structures. Early deficits in kittens' visuomotor behaviors seem to be caused by these sensory deficits rather than by motor dysfunctions. Once visually responsive cells are observed, the superior colliculus develops fairly rapidly, attaining adultlike status by 5 to 6 weeks, and visuomotor behavior improves as well.

Neurally Based Theories of Infant Visual Perception

In the past decade, some reasonably comprehensive theories of early visual development have appeared. They are different versions of the two-visual-systems theory (Bronson, 1974; Karmel & Maisel, 1975; Maurer & Lewis, 1979; Salapatek, 1975) and the cortical firing rate theory (Haith, 1980). Since all five theories are based on neural mechanisms, they are introduced here. Each makes reasonably specific predictions concerning early visual perception and its subsequent growth, but the predictions concern a variety of perceptual phenomena, ranging from eye movements to pattern discrimination. Consequently, to present an evaluation of the various predictions, we have adopted the somewhat awkward strategy of distributing evaluative statements among the several sections below and, finally, reviewing the evaluations in the conclusion.

Bronson (1974) has hypothesized that early visual development can be characterized by differential rates of development among two parallel visual systems. Salapatek (1975) and Karmel and Maisel (1975) have presented similar models. One system—the so-called primary visual system—consists of the visual projection from the retina to the lateral geniculate and then to the visual cortex. This system is elaborated in higher mammals but not in lower mammals, birds, amphibia, and fishes. In phylogenetic terms, it is a young system. The other, so-called secondary, visual system consists of the visual projection to the superior colliculus. This system is phylogenetically older since it is the dominant visual system in all but higher mammals.

The claim that the visual system can be described as two parallel systems is not new. Several researchers have described two systems: the primary and secondary systems (Held, 1968; Schneider, 1969) and focal and ambient vision (Trevarthen, 1968). Bronson's developmental elaboration of this view emphasizes several structural and functional distinctions between the primary and secondary systems. Most of these have been described above, so here we simply emphasize the major distinctions Bronson elaborated. The components of the primary system greatly overrepresent the fovea, have excellent visual acuity, and respond quite selectively to changes in pattern variables (size, shape, orientation, etc.). As such, this system is supposedly devoted to fine pattern analysis and to the control of stable binocular fixation. The components of the secondary system, Bronson claims, do not overrepresent the fovea, have poor visual acuity, and are not particularly sensitive to changes in pattern variables; however, they are quite sensitive to stimulus location and to temporal parameters such as stimulus onset and motion. As such, the secondary system is supposedly devoted to the detection and localization of targets presented in the peripheral visual field and to the initiation and control of saccades to such targets. The secondary system is also involved in the control of visual tracking of large targets.

Bronson's developmental account is based on the assumption that the secondary system matures more rapidly than the primary system. In particular, the secondary system supposedly governs visual behavior before 1 month of age, after which the primary system begins to play a significant role. From this perspective, a neonate's visual behavior should correspond roughly to a decorticate adult's visual behavior.

We consider the specific predictions of the two-visual-systems model in subsequent sections. It is worthwhile, however, to consider the proposed anatomical and physiological mechanisms here. The general notion that the visual cortex and superior colliculus subserve different functions is clearly supported by anatomical and physiological findings as well as ablation studies. However, some of the anatomical/physiological details of Bronson's model may not be correct; we mention three here. First, Bronson's claim that the retinal periphery is overrepresented in the secondary system is false. The superior colliculus of both cats and monkeys actually underrepresents the periphery relative to the fovea. Even the direct retinal path seems to overrepresent the fovea in monkeys (Cowey & Perry, 1980; Schiller et al., 1974), despite earlier claims to the contrary (Wilson & Toyne, 1970). However, Bronson's argument that the fovea is poorly represented in the neonate's visual system may still be correct. As described above, the neonate's fovea is immature structurally compared to the parafovea (Abramov et al., 1982). Thus, Bronson's claim that the fovea is weakly represented shortly after birth may be correct, but the cause is retinally based rather than collicularly based. Second, the notion that the cortical and subcortical projections represent distinct, parallel systems is somewhat misleading because there are significant interactions between the two projections. Indeed, the properties of deep cells in the monkey's superior colliculus depend heavily on cortical influence, and Bronson himself proposes interaction between the systems at higher stages. Third, the development of the superior colliculus, in cats anyway, does not generally precede the development of the visual cortex. As described above, at least some cortical cells in kittens exhibit adultlike response properties before any colliculus cells respond to visual stimulation at all (Blakemore & Van Sluyters, 1975; Stein et al., 1973b). Unfortunately, there are no relevant data on primates.

Maurer and Lewis (1979) have proposed a related version of the two-visual-systems model. Their version emphasizes the differences between X and Y cells. Recall that X cells project solely to the visual cortex and exhibit linear summation, relatively high visual acuity, and low temporal resolution. Y cells, on the other hand, project to the visual cortex and superior colliculus, subserve different functions, and exhibit nonlinear summation, high temporal resolution, and low visual acuity. On these grounds, Maurer and Lewis argue, as others have, that X cells are designed for fine pattern analysis and Y cells for the detection and localization of visual events. Their model of visual development states that only the X pathway to the cortex and the Y pathway to the colliculus are functional at birth. The Y pathway to the cortex supposedly becomes functional between 1 and 2 months and, consequently, so does the Y pathway (the corticotectal tract) from the cortex to the colliculus. Unlike Bronson's model, Maurer and Lewis claim that both the visual cortex and superior colliculus are immature at birth and become functional by roughly 2 months, when the geniculocortical and corticotectal Y pathways become functional. They also argue that in some ways (X projection) the visual cortex is functional at birth.

The model makes a number of specific predictions concerning early visual development. We consider these in subsequent sections. It is worthwhile here, however, to consider the anatomical and physiological claims of this model. We believe that the Maurer and Lewis model should be questioned on two grounds. First, X and Y cells do not form two distinct categories of cells because only some properties of X and Y cells (spatial summation and conduction velocity) are really dichotomous. The other properties that supposedly distinguish the two cell types are distributed continuously rather than dichotomously (Lennie, 1980). Moreover, many cells of one type can be made to exhibit properties of the other type by manipulating the adaptation level of the cell (Lennie, 1980). The X/Y distinction is even less clear in young animals. For example, only tests of spatial summation segregate X and Y cells clearly in young kittens (Daniels et al., 1978). For these reasons, X and Y cells probably do not constitute two functionally dichotomous populations. Second, Maurer and Lewis base the developmental aspects of their model primarily on kitten data. As mentioned in the last three sections, there are very important differences in the anatomy and physiology of various structures in the cat and monkey (and thus probably between cats and humans). Until we know more about the function of the visual system, it will be unclear how important these differences are. They do, nonetheless, point to the need for caution in extrapolating from cat data. We describe three examples to illustrate this point. (1) The superficial layers of the cat's superior colliculus are strongly dependent on cortical influence, but those of the monkey are not. Thus, it is not surprising that the development of superficial layers in kittens is dependent on cortical development. There are no comparable developmental data in monkeys, but one suspects that cortical development would be less significant to the function of superficial colliculus cells. (2) The uncrossed direct retinal path to the cat's colliculus is weaker than the crossed path. Thus, elimination of cortical influence renders the cat's colliculus monocular (responsive to the contralateral eye only; Rosenquist & Palmer, 1971). The asymmetry between the two paths must be less pronounced in monkeys because elimination of cortical influence does not leave the colliculus monocular (Schiller et al., 1974). (3) The anatomical segregation of X and Y cells in the lateral geniculate appears to be different in cats and monkeys. Some have reported that X and Y cells reside in different laminae in the monkey but not in the cat (see Lennie, 1980). More recent evidence suggests that the anatomical segregation of monkey X and Y cells is not as distinct as previously thought (e.g., Kaplan & Shapley, 1982), but it still appears to be more distinct than in cats. Again, it is unclear how important these differences between cats and monkeys are to the predictions of the Maurer and Lewis model. The presence of these differences suggests, however, that an extrapolation from cats to humans should be treated cautiously.

Finally, Haith (1980) and Karmel and Maisel (1975) have proposed "cortical firing rate" models. These models state that the visuomotor behavior of young infants is guided by the magnitude of cortical firing. So, for example, a newborn scans stimuli in such a way to maximize some, as yet unspecified, measure of cortical firing. The model's specific predictions are considered in subsequent sections, but we examine the specific anatomical and physiological claims here. One important claim of the model is that the visual cortex controls visuomotor behavior in newborns. This claim cannot be evaluated yet, but it is important to note that many of the visuomotor behaviors Haith considers can be elicited in fairly refined form in decorticate animals (Spear & Braun, 1969). Another important claim is that the fovea is overrepresented in the cortical projection of newborns. (Otherwise, the cortical firing rate would not be maximized by foveating a contour.) In actuality, recent anatomical evidence suggests that the newborn's fovea is less mature than other retinal regions (Abramov et al., 1982). For example, receptor packing density is lower in the fovea than in the parafovea. Thus, it is quite unlikely that the newborn's foveal visual field is overrepresented in the cortical projection. It is probably only after postnatal receptor migration that the fovea becomes overrepresented.

We have described some reasonably comprehensive neural models of human visual development. All have some specific deficiencies, which we discuss below. Nonetheless, they have been quite useful in guiding both empirical and theoretical work in this field.

VISUOMOTOR MECHANISMS

Unlike mechanical devices such as cameras, the visual system does not have the same resolution capability throughout its field of view. The very center of the retina—the fovea—has much higher visual acuity than more peripheral regions. This spatial inhomogeneity allows quite precise processing, but only over a fraction of the visual field. Consequently, when the eyes are stationary, the "picture" received has sharp detail only in its center and progressively less detail with greater distance from the center. The majority of the "picture" is quite blurred.

Such an arrangement would be quite unacceptable if it were not for saccadic, smooth pursuit, vestibular-controlled, and optokinetic eye movements. Saccadic eye movements allow the effective visual field to be expanded by shifting the eyes from one position to another. Smooth pursuit eye movements allow the eyes to hold fixation on a moving object. Vestibular-controlled and optokinetic movements allow stable fixation while the observer is moving. Several investigators have argued that vestibular-controlled and optokinetic eye movements are controlled by different neural structures than those controlling saccadic and smooth pursuit movements (e.g., Leibowitz & Post, 1982). If these eye movements really are controlled by different mechanisms, one would expect them to develop at different rates. Accordingly, we consider the development of each of these types of eye movements in the next few sections.

Vergence, another type of eye movement which allows the eyes to maintain alignment on objects of different distances, is considered under *Depth Perception* below.

To capitalize on the resolution capability of the fovea, the visual system must focus images sharply on the retina. We consider the development of two mechanisms that are part of this process—optics and visual accommodation—in two sections below.

Visual information is also used to maintain postural stability. We consider the development of this capability in the last section of this part of the chapter.

Saccadic Eye Movements

A saccadic eye movement is a rapid change in fixation from one visual stimulus to another. The saccadic system is thus used to relocate targets in the peripheral visual field onto the fovea for fine pattern analysis. In the adult, saccadic eye movements are conjugate (both eyes move in unison), very rapid (up to 800 deg/sec), and accurate (only a 10% undershoot error in the first saccade to a target; Alpern, 1969, 1971). Adult saccades are also ballistic; that is, once a saccadic eye movement is initiated, it continues to its computed endpoint without significant further correction. It appears that the motor programs for saccades are actually set about 80 msec prior to the execution of the movement (Wheeless, Boynton, & Cohen, 1966). Head movements are often programmed in conjunction with saccades, particularly for targets 20 deg or more from the fovea.

Only a handful of studies have examined the development of the saccadic system. Tronick and Clanton (1971), Tronick (1972), Harris and MacFarlane (1974), and Aslin and Salapatek (1975) observed young infants' saccades to peripheral targets under a number of conditions. They found that the likelihood of an infant executing a saccade in the correct direction is quite high if the peripheral target is fairly close to the initial line of sight and is the only one present in the field. They also found that 2-month-olds are more likely to localize a distant target than newborns or 1-month-olds are.

With the exception of the Aslin and Salapatek experiment, the response measures used were too imprecise to tell us much about the magnitude and character of infant saccades. Aslin and Salapatek, however, obtained reasonably accurate records of saccadic eye movements using electrooculography or EOG (measurement of eye movements by recording electrical potentials produced by the eye; see Maurer, 1975, for details). Infant saccades differed from adults' in a number of ways. One- and 2-month-olds were much slower to initiate a saccade than adults were. The median latency to initiation of a saccade was greater than 1 sec in 1-month-olds and slightly less than 1 sec in 2-month-olds. These latencies were roughly 5 times greater than adult values. The most interesting difference between young infants and adults concerned the form of infant saccades. The first saccade to a peripheral target generally did not move the line of sight 90% of the distance required, as it would in an adult. Instead a series of saccades, roughly equal in amplitude, were executed until the target was reached. Examples of such multiple saccades are represented in Figure 11. It appeared that the distance of the peripheral target was taken into account before a multiple saccade was begun because the magnitude of the component movements increased with target distance. This un-

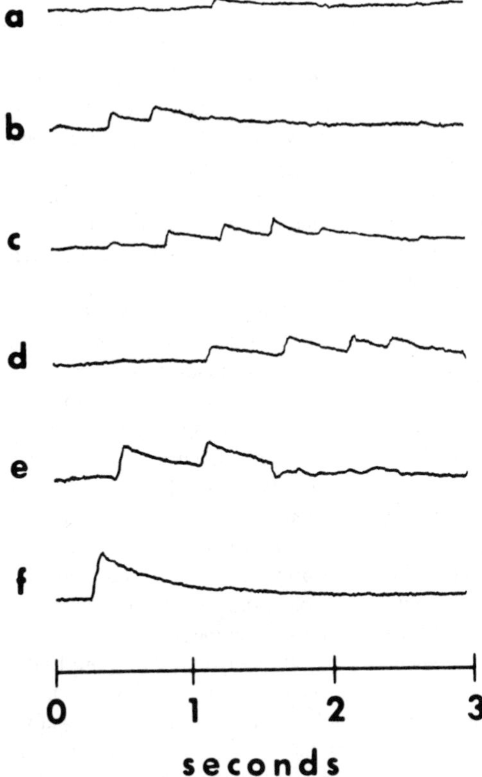

Figure 11. Electrooculographic (EOG) records of infant (a through e) and adult (f) saccades. (a) A single saccade to a target 10 deg in the periphery. (b) A double saccade to a target at 20 deg. (c) A triple saccade to a target at 30 deg. (d) A quadruple saccade to a target at 40 deg. (e) A double saccade to a target at 30 deg followed by a return movement. (f) A typical adult saccade to a target at 30 deg. Time marks represent seconds after target onset. (From Aslin & Salapatek, 1975.)

usual form of eye movement persists until at least 2 months of age, the oldest group tested.

Aslin and Salapatek (1975) speculated that the dramatic undershooting of the infant saccadic system might, in part, result from the programming of, but failure to execute, head movements in conjunction with saccades. This seemed quite possible because the infants' heads were restrained in this experiment. Regal and Salapatek (1982) tested this hypothesis recently by examining infants' saccades under restrained and unrestrained conditions. Although head movements appeared to play an important role in target localization, multiple saccades were equally prevalent in the two conditions. Thus, multiple saccades are not caused by an inability to execute head movements. Goodkin (1980) also examined the coordination of eye and head movements in young infants. When he presented a stationary peripheral target to 3-month-olds, they generally executed a saccade followed immediately by a head movement, much as adults do. Two-month-olds, on the other hand, did not execute a head movement soon after a saccadic eye movement. These results suggest that significant improvements in eye-head coordination occur during the second month of life.

Salapatek, Aslin, Simonson, and Pulos (1980) attempted to unravel the contents of infants' saccadic programs. Specifically, they asked whether the initial saccadic component in a multiple saccade series is simply reapplied without reprogramming of step size. They presented 1- and 2-month-olds a target 10, 20, or 30 deg from the initial line of sight. In one condition, the peripheral target remained on long enough for completion of a multiple saccade to it. In another, the peripheral target was extinguished the instant a saccade in the appropriate direction was detected electronically. Multiple saccades were observed in both conditions. Total eye rotation was greater on the interrupted (peripheral target extinguished) trials than on the continuous trials. This appeared to be the result of a slight increase in both the size and number of individual saccades in the interrupted trials relative to the continuous. These results suggest, though not convincingly, that a similar eye movement program was operating in both types of trials. The authors suggest that the program consists of the programming of a relatively fixed, grossly hypometric saccade that is continually reapplied until the target is foveated, motivation is lost, or the eyes can rotate no further.

Bechtold, Bushnell, and Salapatek (1979) examined young infants' saccades to both visual and auditory stimuli. They found that infants generally moved their eyes in the direction of the auditory stimulus, but that eye movement magnitude was uncorrelated with the eccentricity of the sound.

In summary, the saccadic eye movement system is functional at birth, allowing the neonate to localize stimuli of interest onto the central retina. The system is not adultlike, however, in several respects. The effective visual field for eliciting saccades grows postnatally. Whether this is a manifestation of motor development or sensory development (or both) is unknown. The latency to initiate a saccade is much longer in infants than in adults. Furthermore, the multiple saccades of infants are distinct from adult saccades. Thus, the existing data imply that the neonatal saccadic eye movement system is less proficient than the adult system at directing the fovea rapidly and accurately to peripheral targets. Experiments with older infants are needed to learn when and how the transition from infantile to adultlike movements occurs. More detailed studies of the velocity and acceleration of infant saccades, of the nature of corrective saccades, and of the coordination between saccades and head movements would also be helpful. An important question that still warrants thorough investigation is: How does the imprecise and slow saccadic eye movement system of young infants affect their acquisition of visual information? This question is considered below under *Visual Scanning*.

Smooth Pursuit Eye Movements

Saccadic eye movements occur when an observer shifts his or her fixation from one stationary target to another. When an observer attempts to hold fixation on a moving target, a different sort of eye movement occurs. These movements, which are called smooth pursuit eye movements, are more continuous and much slower in velocity than saccadic eye movements. Thus, they allow observers to hold fixation on moving targets over a fairly broad range of velocities.

When a target first starts to move, one or two saccades usually bring the line of sight close to the target before smooth pursuit actually begins. Thereafter, smooth pursuit movements keep the fovea on the target. In spite of their cooperation in such cases, there is considerable evidence that the smooth pursuit system in adults is reasonably independent of the saccadic system (Rashbass, 1961). For example, the saccadic system programs eye movements ballistically, while the smooth pursuit system continuously samples visual inputs and, thus, allows reprogramming during the course of a movement in response to a change in target velocity (Young, 1971).

The character of smooth pursuit eye movements is typically described in the adult literature by three properties. (1) Amplitude gain is the magnitude of an eye movement divided by the magnitude of a target excursion. For example, if an eye movement of 8 deg is elicited in response to a target movement of 10 deg, the amplitude gain would be 0.8. (2) Velocity gain is the velocity of a pursuit movement divided by the velocity of the target. (3) Phase lag is a representation of the delay of the eye relative to the target. Large phase lags mean the position of the eye is lagging behind the target.

Most early studies of the development of smooth pursuit eye movements claimed that newborns were unable to execute smooth pursuit movements and that horizontal pursuit was present at an earlier age than vertical (Barten, Birns, & Ronch, 1971; Beasley, 1933; Guernsey, 1929; Wolff, 1959). These studies used rather crude measurement techniques, however, so nothing more can be concluded from them.

Dayton and Jones (1964), Dayton, Jones, Steele, and Rose (1964b), and Kremenitzer, Vaughan, Kurtzberg, and Dowling (1979) used electrooculography (EOG) to measure smooth pursuit movements to relatively small targets in very young infants. They found that even newborns' eye movements were generally in the appropriate direction, but the movements consisted of a jerky series of saccadic refixations of the moving target. The jerkiness of these movements decreased during the first year of life, but smooth pursuit movements were common by 2 months (Dayton & Jones, 1964).

Aslin (1981) has examined the development of smooth pursuit in greater detail using a corneal photography recording system (see Maurer, 1975, for details). Infants from 3 to 17 weeks of age were presented a black bar that moved back and forth sinusoidally on a bright uniform background. The frequency of sinusoidal oscillation was varied from 0.33 to 1.0 Hz to estimate the accuracy of pursuit movements as a function of velocity. Figure 12 displays some typical data. Before 5 to 6 weeks, tracking was completely saccadic even for low target velocities. The first noteworthy pursuit was observed at 8 weeks, but only at low velocities. Even at those velocities, the velocity gain was considerably less than 1.0 at this age, so saccades were frequently needed to catch up to the target. By 10 to 12 weeks, smooth pursuit was quite common for a range of target velocities, and velocity gain was closer to 1.0.

Aslin also observed an increase in the accuracy of smooth pursuit over trials in some 10-week-olds. This suggests that these infants benefitted from repeated stimulus presentations and, consequently, may be indicative of predictive control of tracking.

It is interesting to note that smooth eye movements are present in optokinetic nystagmus (OKN) from birth onward (see section on *Optokinetic Nystagmus* below). Bronson (1974) has noted that the eliciting stimuli for typical smooth pursuit and for reflexive smooth movements in OKN differ. Smooth pursuit movements are elicited by a single, relatively small target, while smooth movements in OKN are elicited by motion of all, or a major portion, of the visual field. Bronson argued that the newborn's ability to perform smooth movements in OKN implies that the neural structures involved in processing whole-field motion develop earlier than structures that process movement of discrete targets on a stationary background. This notion is consistent with the current opinion in the adult literature that

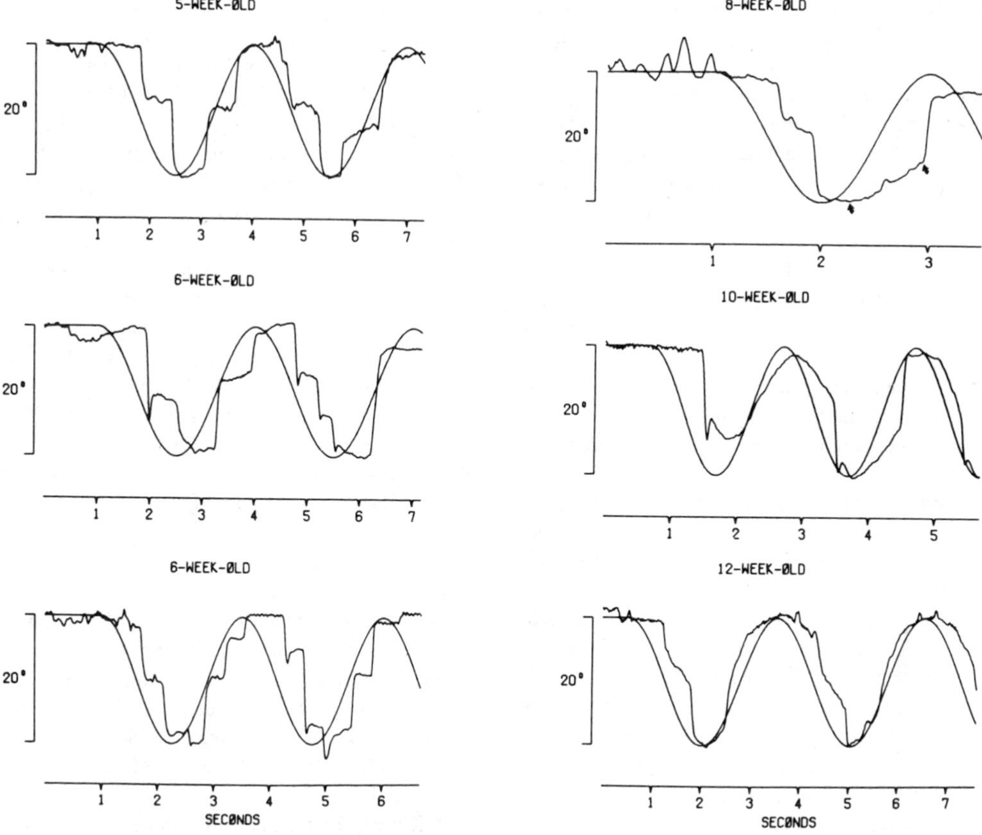

Figure 12. Records of tracking eye movements by infants of different ages. The infants were presented a target that moved sinusoidally. This target motion is represented by the smooth lines. The eye movements are represented by the other lines. (From Aslin, 1981.)

smooth pursuit and OKN are controlled by quite different neural structures (e.g., Leibowitz & Post, 1982).

Aslin (1981) noted that the absence of smooth pursuit early in life and its subsequent development may be caused by early deficits and subsequent improvements in a number of factors including attention, anatomical and neuromuscular structures, sensory mechanisms, and sensorimotor control mechanisms. We hope that the most significant factors will be revealed in the next decade.

Vestibular Control of Eye Movements

The eye movements we have considered thus far are generally elicited in a stationary observer. In everyday situations, however, the body and head are often in motion. Different sorts of eye movements are elicited in such situations. Two of these are static reflex movements and statokinetic reflex movements (Alpern, 1969) or, simply, vestibulo-ocular reflex movements (Dichgans & Brandt, 1978). These eye movements compensate for motion of the head and thereby help to maintain fixation on a constant point in space. They are induced by signals from the vestibular apparatus that accompany acceleration of the head. The static reflex consists of upward or downward eye movements when the head is tilted forward or backward and of counterrolling of the eyes when the head is tilted to the side. These movements occur with the eyes open or closed. Statokinetic reflex movements are typically elicted by angular rotations of the head or body. A series of smooth movements (opposite to the direction of rotation), followed by saccadic refixations (in the direction of motion), occurs when the rotation is large in magnitude and fairly rapid. These nystagmus movements also occur whether the eyes are open or not. Single compensatory smooth movements occur when the head/body rotation is smaller in magnitude. The smooth phase of the nystagmus movements and the single compensatory movements compensate more accurately for head movements when the eyes are open (i.e., when a visual target is present) than when the eyes are closed. These smooth portions of vestibular-controlled eye movements are also qualitatively different in adults from smooth pursuit movements to small moving targets (Robinson, 1968).

Vestibulo-ocular reflex eye movements are generally present at birth (Peiper, 1963). The prewired nature of these movements is illustrated by Peiper's observation of them in blind infants. Compensatory eye movements are in fact reliable enough in normal young infants that they have been used to calibrate eye movement recording systems (Tronick & Clanton, 1971).

Goodkin (1980) examined the development of vestibular-controlled eye movements using the EOG so he could determine their velocity gain. He rotated the bodies of infants 2 and 3 months of age under three conditions of visual stimulation. He found that statokinetic reflex movements in the dark (no visual target present) were similar in 2- and 3-month-olds and in adults. The velocity gain at each age was somewhat less than 1.0, suggesting that the eye movements were undercompensating (moving less rapidly than the head). When a stationary visual target was added, the velocity gain of 3-month-olds and adults increased to 1.0, suggesting that the eye movements were compensating quite accurately for head rotations. The gain for 2-month-olds, however, remained less than 1.0 (undercompensating). Finally, Goodkin found that when the visual target rotated in synchrony with the head, 3-month-olds and adults were able to suppress statokinetic movements and thereby maintain fixation on the target. Two-month-olds were not able to suppress the statokinetic movements; they continued to make movements compensating for head rotation and hence were unable to maintain fixation on the target.

In summary, vestibular-controlled eye movements are observed at birth. Yet even by 2 months of age, these movements are not well coordinated with other forms of eye movements. Consequently, vestibular-controlled eye movements alone do not enable accurate fixation of a target while the head is rotated until 3 months of age.

Optokinetic Nystagmus

A large moving visual pattern elicits a rhythmic series of smooth movements in the direction of the pattern's movements, followed by saccadic refixations in the opposite direction. These eye movements, which are called optokinetic nystagmus (OKN), can be elicited when the observer's head is stationary. However, Robinson (1976) has argued convincingly that this is an overly artificial situation that does not illuminate the true purpose of eye movements produced by the OKN system. Instead, the OKN system, he argues, is designed to produce compensatory eye movements to hold fixation on a consistent point in space while the observer is in motion. Thus, the OKN system probably serves a function similar to that of the vestibular eye movement systems, but, in this case, the signal is produced by uniform motion of the visual field rather than by vestibular excitation. This viewpoint is supported by the observation that OKN can also be elicited by moving an observer with constant velocity before a large, stationary visual stimulus (Alpern, 1969).

Schor and Narayan (1981) have recently examined the stimulus determinants of OKN in adults. They found that the ability to elicit OKN is dependent on target velocity, target size, and the spatial frequency of the target. These parameters will be discussed further in our discussion on *Visual Acuity*, but it is worth noting here that reliable OKN is elicited for only certain combinations of velocity, size, and spatial frequency.

OKN can be elicited in newborns by a moving field of vertical stripes (Dayton, Jones, Aiu, Rawson, Steele, & Rose, 1964a; Enoch & Rabinowicz, 1976; Fantz, Ordy, & Udelf, 1962; Gorman, Cogan, & Gellis, 1957, 1959). OKN thus appears to be mature before saccades and smooth pursuit, but roughly at the same time as the other motion-compensating movements (static reflexes and statokinetic reflexes). Bronson (1974) has argued that these differential rates of maturation reflect the fact that these eye movement systems are primarily subserved by different neural structures (see *Neurally Based Theories of Infant Visual Perception* above). This notion is consistent with hypotheses in the adult literature (e.g., Dichgans & Brandt, 1978; Leibowitz & Post, 1982).

Atkinson and Braddick (1979, 1981) examined OKN in infants from 1 to 3 months of age. When viewing the stimulus binocularly, infants of all ages elicited reliable OKN regardless of the direction of stimulus motion. A different result was obtained under monocular viewing conditions. Three-month-olds again elicited reliable OKN for both directions of stimulus motion, but 1-and 2-month-olds did so only for temporal to nasal movement of the stimulus field. Nasal to temporal movement of the stimulus field did not evoke reliable OKN at 1 and 2 months. Atkinson and Braddick labeled the behavior of the 1- and 2-month-olds under monocular conditions as *asymmetric OKN*, and the behavior of 3-month-olds as *symmetric OKN*. They repeated this experiment with infant monkeys and observed a similar phenomenon, but at different ages. Monkeys less than 1 month of age generally exhibited asymmetric OKN and older monkeys generally exhibited symmetric OKN. Atkinson and Braddick noted that asymmetric OKN is also observed in deprived and decorticate cats (Van Hof-van Duin, 1978; Wood et al., 1973) and in children and adults known to have abnormal binocularity (Atkinson & Braddick, 1979). From this, they argued that the development of symmetric OKN may depend on the development of binocular mechanisms in the visual cortex.

In summary, eye movement systems that compensate for motion of the observer (vestibular-controlled and OKN) are more mature early in life than systems that compensate for motion of the stimulus (saccades and smooth pursuit). This is somewhat curious since neonates move their heads and bodies less than older infants so, if anything, one would expect the demand for vestibular-controlled and OKN movements to be less than for saccadic and smooth pursuit movements. Perhaps the best view at this stage of our understanding is that the different rates of maturation simply reflect different rates of subcortical and cortical development (Bronson, 1974).

Optics

The mature visual system is capable of resolving quite small features in a visual stimulus. The optics of the eye, which are responsible for forming the retinal image, are obviously an essential component of this capability. For several reasons, the development of the eye's optics has become an important research topic. Much of the work is technical in nature, so we only attempt to highlight it here. For more detailed reviews, see Banks (1980a) and Howland (1982).

The major optical components of the eye are depicted in Figure 13. The cornea and lens are the components responsible for refracting light and thereby forming a retinal image. Thus, the dimensions of the cornea and lens (radius of curvature, thickness, index of refraction, etc.) are important to the quality of the eye's optical processing. Other ocular dimensions are important, too. These include the distance from the cornea to the lens, the distance from the lens to the retina, and the shape of the

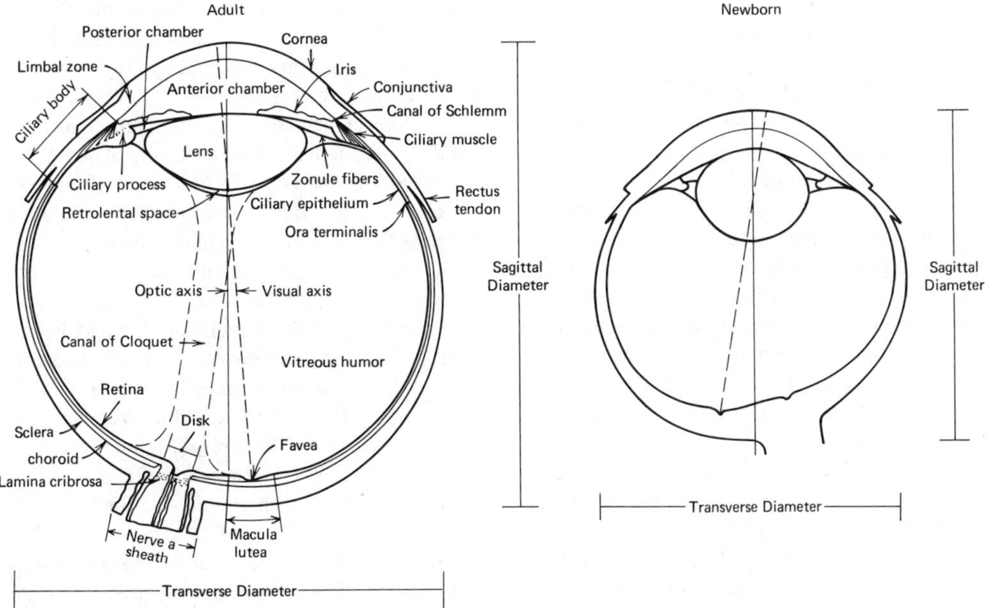

Figure 13. Cross-sectional drawings of the adult and newborn eye. The adult eye on the left is a horizontal section of the right eye. Important structures are labeled. The visual axis is represented by the broken line and the optic axis by the solid line. The newborn eye on the right is also a horizontal section of the right eye. It is drawn to scale to represent its size relative to the adult eye. (Adapted from Salapatek, 1975, and Wilmer & Scammon, 1950.)

retina. The optical quality of the adult eye is quite good, but with all of these components contributing, it is not surprising that the quality is imperfect. The retinal images formed are somewhat degraded versions of the information presented to the eye. Several factors can contribute to this degradation: cloudy optic media, spherical and chromatic aberration, diffraction resulting from the pupil, spherical refractive error, and cylindrical or astigmatic refractive error (Bennett & Francis, 1969). In this section, we discuss what is known about these errors in the growing eye and consider their impact on visual perception.

Spherical and chromatic aberration and diffraction resulting from the pupil have not been examined developmentally, but they are almost certainly trivial relative to the other errors (see Salapatek & Banks, 1978). The clarity of the optic media is also reasonably good; details of the retinal structure (e.g., blood vessels) can be seen readily in ophthalmoscopic observations of the newborn's eye (Cook & Glasscock, 1951). This contrasts with observations of the eyes of 1- to 3-week-old kittens in which retinal structures appear quite blurred (Bonds & Freeman, 1978).

Spherical refractive errors might present a more serious constraint. Such errors exist when the distance to which the eye is best focused differs from the distance to the visual stimulus. In other words, when spherical errors exist, the retinal image of the stimulus is brought to a focus either in front of or behind the retina and, consequently, it is blurred. The two primary types of spherical refractive error are myopia and hyperopia. Myopia exists when the retinal image is focused in front of the retina or, in other words, the eye is best focused to a distance closer than the stimulus under inspection. Hyperopia exists in the opposite situation; the retinal image is focused behind the retina, so the eye is best focused to a distance greater than the stimulus distance (Bennett & Francis, 1969). Cylindrical or astigmatic refractive errors exist when one stimulus orientation is focused in a different plane than the orthogonal orientation. Thus, astigmatism yields a retinal image in which lines of one orientation are focused more sharply than lines perpendicular to that orientation (Bennett & Francis, 1969).

Spherical and astigmatic refractive errors in infants have been assessed under two conditions: (1) a cycloplegic condition in which drugs are used to paralyze the muscles of accommodation temporarily, and (2) a noncycloplegic condition in which no drugs are used and, therefore, accommodation is allowed. Noncycloplegic measures of spherical error really concern the study of accommodation, so they are described in the next section.

The traditional view is that cycloplegia induces a refractive state that represents the eye "at rest." Thus, such measurements reveal whether an eye is myopic (near-sighted) or hyperopic (far-sighted) in its resting state. However, this view of the eye's resting state has been seriously questioned recently (Leibowitz & Owens, 1978). It now seems that the cycloplegic state is actually the least myopic (or most hyperopic) refractive state that the eye is mechanically capable of.

Several reports dating back to the nineteenth century have examined the spherical refractive errors of full-term newborns under cycloplegia (reviewed by Banks, 1980a). The measurement technique used in almost all of these reports was retinoscopy (described by Bennett & Francis, 1969). In spite of differences in subject populations and methodologies, there is substantial agreement that the spherical errors of newborn populations are normally distributed with a mean of about 2 diopters of hyperopia and a standard deviation of 2 diopters. Thus, the average newborn appears to be quite farsighted. However, this apparent hyperopia may result in part from a measurement error inherent to retinoscopy. Glickstein and Millodot (1970) demonstrated a measurement error in the hyperopic direction in small eyes such as those of newborns. Millodot (1972) and Howland (1982) have estimated the magnitude of this error in the newborn eye as .8 and .5 diopters, respectively. Thus, even if the contribution of a small eye measurement error is partialled out, the average newborn appears to be more than 1 diopter hyperopic under cycloplegia.

Cycloplegic studies of young adult populations yield mean spherical refractive errors of about 0 diopters with a standard deviation of 1 (Stromberg, 1936). Thus, a comparison of neonates and adults suggests that the developmental trend is from variable, generally hyperopic refractions to less variable, less hyperopic refractions. Unfortunately, few developmental data exist on infants beyond the neonatal period, but those data that do exist suggest a general decline in the average hyperopia observed (reviewed by Banks, 1980a). Moreover, the mean refractive error under cycloplegia among school-age children approaches 0 (Hirsch, 1963).

The tendency of children's and adults' cycloplegic refractive errors to remain small despite growth of the eye has been called *emmetropization* (van Alphen, 1961). The eye grows in a complicated fashion postnatally. Most ocular components increase in size, but different components grow at different rates as illustrated in Figure 13 (Larsen, 1971; Sorsby & Sheridan, 1961; Wilmer & Scammon, 1950). Therefore, the growth of the eye must be a coordinated process to maintain nearly emmetropic refractions across age. Two general hypotheses of the source of this coordination have been proposed. First, the coordination may be governed by a genetically prespecified maturational program that determines the appropriate relationships among optical components at various ages (Sorsby, Benjamin, & Sheridan, 1961). Since many ocular structures grow at dissimilar rates, the program would have to be quite complex. For this reason, a second hypothesis has been proposed. The coordinating program might be a negative feedback system in which the eye's habitual accommodative state influences the growth of particular optical components (van Alphen, 1961). In other words, this hypothesis holds that visual experience plays an important role in the development of the eye's refraction.

The negative feedback account of emmetropization is supported by experiments in which animals are reared in different visual environments. Monkeys reared in hoods and cats reared in small cages develop refractions 1 to 2 diopters more myopic than animals reared in less restricted spaces (Belkin, Yinon, Rose, & Reisert, 1977; Young, 1963). The restricted animals presumably habitually accommodated to near distances and, thus, according to the negative feedback hypothesis, a myopic refraction more suitable for near vision would develop.

Homologous effects have been observed in humans. For example, Bedrossian (1971) examined the development of refractive errors in 75 school-age children who had been reported to exhibit myopia. After the diagnosis of bilateral myopia, one eye of each child was treated daily for one year with a cycloplegic drug that paralyzed the refractive state of that eye to the far point of accommodation. The other eye was untreated and thus allowed to accommodate normally for one year. At the end of the year, the cycloplegic refractions of both eyes were measured. Bedrossian found that the treated eyes were on the average 1 diopter less myopic than the untreated eyes. Preventing normal accommodation appeared to reduce the tendency toward greater myopia. Thus, it is possible that the habitual accommodative state of the young human eye is in part responsible for the developmental process of emmetropization.

Other environmental effects are known to cause the development of myopia in animals and humans, but it is not clear whether these illuminate the normal process of emmetropization. For example, suturing the eyelid closed during infancy causes monkeys to develop myopia (Wiesel & Raviola, 1979; but see von Noorden & Crawford, 1978). Children born with ptosis (drooping eyelids) in one eye tend to develop myopia in that eye (O'Leary & Millodot, 1979). A similar tendency is apparent among children who had cataracts, macular dystrophy, and other ocular pathologies during infancy (Rabin, Van Sluyters, & Malach, 1981).

Another type of optical defect manifest in some adult eyes is a cylindrical refractive error also known as astigmatism. An astigmatism exists when the refraction for one orientation differs from that of another orientation. Significant astigmatism (two axes differing by 1 diopter or more) is very common in young infants (reviewed by Banks, 1980a) relative to the incidence among school-age children and adults (e.g., Woodruff, 1971). The high incidence of astigmatism in infants has been demonstrated using a variety of techniques including conventional retinoscopy under cycloplegia (Fulton, Dobson, Salem, Mar, Petersen, & Hansen, 1980; Santonastaso, 1930), near retinoscopy (Mohindra, Held, Gwiazda, & Brill, 1978), and photorefraction (Howland, Atkinson, Braddick, & French, 1978). The incidence appears to peak sometime during the first year and to decline thereafter (Atkinson, Braddick, & French, 1980; Fulton et al., 1980; Ingram & Barr, 1979). The process by which astigmatism declines after the first year is not clear, but Howland (1982) has shown that most infantile astigmatic errors are caused by asymmetries in the cornea.

An important question for both researchers and clinicians is: Do the large astigmatisms frequently present among young infants have perceptual consequences? The answer is an unambiguous yes. Atkinson and French (1979) and Held (1979) have demonstrated that uncorrected astigmatic refractive errors lead to predictable reductions in visual acuity for gratings of particular orientations.

It is also likely that early astigmatisms, if they persist, lead to uncorrectable acuity deficits for stimuli whose orientation matches that of the astigmatic error. Fortunately, most early astigmatisms either decline in magnitude or disappear altogether after the first year, so acuity deficits resulting from early astigmatism are relatively rare. The experimental work on this topic is discussed in the section on *Visual Acuity* below.

Summary

The optical quality of the young infant's eye is quite good. Indeed, we argue in a later section that the optics actually exceed the resolution capabilities of the rest of the neonate's visual system. Spherical refractive errors are common early in life, but usually diminish because of the intriguing, but as yet unexplained, process of emmetropization. Astigmatic errors are also surprisingly common and they, too, typically disappear during infancy.

Visual Accommodation

The eye can only be sharply focused for one viewing distance at a time. An object at another distance gives rise to a blurred retinal image. The mature eye, however, can shift its plane of best focus by changing the curvature of the lens. For near objects, curvature is increased, which increases refractive power and thereby moves the plane of best focus toward the eye. For distant objects, curvature is decreased, refractive power reduced, and the focal plane moves away from the eye. These adjustments of the plane of best focus are called visual accommodation.

Under normal circumstances, adults' accommodative responses are rapid and accurate. Hence we generally do not recognize the operation of the accommodation system. However, we become acutely aware of its operation under special conditions that impede accommodation (e.g., extended near vision, or the hardening of the lens with age), because inaccurate focus degrades the retinal image and causes a loss of visual resolution. To avoid such inaccuracies, the mature accommodation system uses information from a variety of sources to guide its responses. These sources include convergence (Fincham & Walton, 1957), blur or contrast (Alpern, 1958; Owens, 1980), chromatic information (Fincham, 1951), and a variety of depth cues such as size and linear perspective (Ittelson & Ames, 1950).

These complexities lead one to expect that adultlike accommodation should emerge rather late since, for example, the ability to detect contrast improves until at least 6 months of age (see *Contrast Sensitivity* below). Unfortunately, the study of accommodative development is still in its own infancy, so only a handful of rudimentary observations exist. Until 1965, very little work on the development of accommodation had appeared at all. It was known that the refractive state of a newborn's eye could vary under some conditions. For example, large changes occurred with the introduction of accommodation-paralyzing cycloplegic drugs (Santonastaso, 1930). It was not known, however, if the refractive state varied in correspondence with changes in stimulus distance.

Haynes, White, and Held (1965) were the first to study accommodation experimentally. Naturally, this experiment was conducted without cycloplegic drugs. A small target whose distance varied from 8 to 100 cm was presented to infants ranging from 6 days to 4 months. Haynes et al. measured the distance of the focal plane for each stimulus distance using dynamic retinoscopy. The results can be represented by plotting the distance of the focal plane for each stimulus distance. The slopes of functions plotted in this manner are the index of accommodation performance. A slope of 1 would indicate perfect accommodation; that is, the focal distance is adjusted appropriately to the target distance for all distances presented. A slope of 0 would indicate no accommodation; that is, focal distance is fixed at one value regardless of target distance. The slopes obtained by Haynes et al. are represented by the filled circles in Figure 14. Their results indicated that infants less than 1 month of age exhibited no accommodation; the median fixed focal distance was just under 20 cm. Considerable improvement in accommodation thus occurred from 1 to 4 months. Indeed, accommodative performance for 3- to 4-month-olds resembled adult performance.

The Haynes et al. experiment has been criticized on two grounds. First, young infants' poor visual acuity and contrast sensitivity may have rendered the visual stimulus used—a small patterned shield—a less than optimal stimulus for accommodation. Consequently, they may have underestimated the accommodative ability of the younger infants. To examine this possibility, Banks (1980b) and Brookman (1980) conducted extensive retinoscopic studies using targets designed to provide an optimal stimulus to accommodation.

Banks used a large, high-contrast checkerboard whose angular subtense was constant for all target distances. Target distance varied from 25 to 100 cm. He conducted two developmental studies in 1- to 3-month-olds using two different retinoscopic techniques. Banks' results are represented in Figure 14 by open squares and diamonds. Note that accommodative slope was higher, age for age, than that observed by Haynes et al. The difference was most apparent at 1 month. Thus, the use of a larger, higher contrast target appeared to enhance young infants' accommodative responding.

Brookman (1980) used a similar method to measure accommodation in infants from 2 to 20 weeks for target distances from 10 to 50 cm. His results are represented by the crosses in Figure 14. The accommodative slopes appeared to be lower than those observed by Haynes et al. (1965) and Banks (1980b). This resulted from the use of very short target distances; if accommodative slopes are computed for just the 25 and 50 cm distances, the slopes are very similar to those reported by Banks.

The second criticism of the Haynes et al. experiment was raised by Braddick, Atkinson, French, and Howland (1979). They pointed out that retinoscopy

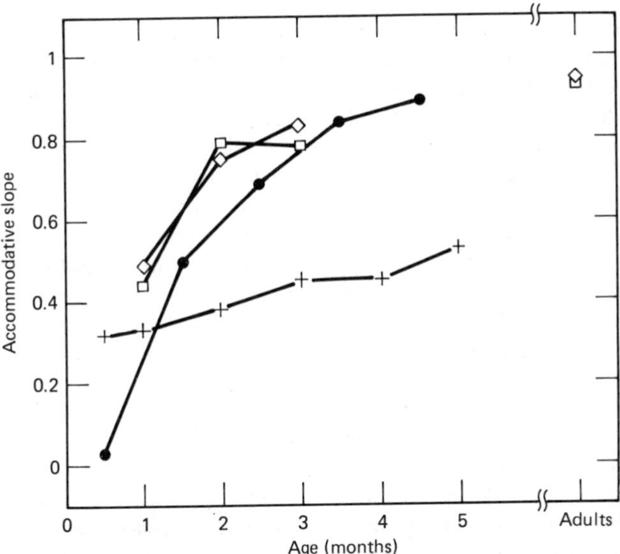

Figure 14. Accuracy of accommodation at different ages. The slope of accommodation functions is plotted as a function of age. A slope of 1 indicates perfect accommodation, while a slope of 0 indicates no accommodation (see text for further explanation). Filled circles: results from Haynes et al. (1965). Open squares and diamonds: results from Banks (1980). Crosses: results from Brookman (1980).

requires a certain amount of time to obtain one measurement of refractive state. Thus, that technique cannot yield information about accommodative variations more rapid than the measurement interval. Given infants' limited attention, such variations may be significant in infant experiments. Consequently, Braddick et al. argued that retinoscopic studies like those of Haynes et al. (1965), Banks (1980b), and Brookman (1980) could underestimate the accommodative capability of young infants.

To pursue this possibility, Braddick and his colleagues studied infant accommodation using a rapid photographic technique developed by Howland and Howland (1974). This technique, which is called *photorefraction,* allows one to assess the refractive state of the eye in a single photograph. The advantage for work with infants is that attention to the target is only required for the instant the photograph is taken. Braddick et al. tested infants ranging in age from 1 day to 12 months at two stimulus distances, 75 and 150 cm. The camera operator served as the visual target. Unfortunately, photorefraction does not always allow one to determine the sign of an accommodative error (myopic or hyperopic relative to the target distance) nor to separate the defocusing effects of accommodative error from those of other optical errors such as spherical aberration (see previous section). Consequently, Braddick et al. presented their findings as the percentage of infants exhibiting accommodative responses within a criterion range of the target distance. Infants were characterized as "consistent" or "inconsistent" focusers (or neither) depending on the number of criterion responses they exhibited. The younger infants, particularly those 1 to 9 days old, exhibited more accurate accommodation to the 75-cm target than to the 150-cm target. In contrast, nearly all of the older infants accommodated consistently to both target distances.

Although direct quantitative comparisons are difficult, these results seem to agree quite well with the results of Banks (1980b). In particular, they corroborate Banks' conclusion that Haynes et al. underestimated the accommodative ability of very young infants. Most of the 1-week-olds in the Braddick et al. study, for example, focused between 40 and 75 cm for the 75-cm target, whereas the 1-week-olds in the Haynes study exhibited focal distances between 12 and 25 cm for all target distances.

The results of infant accommodation studies indicate that considerable improvement occurs between birth and 3 months in the ability to focus to both distant and near targets. Newborns and 1-month-olds display significant focusing errors (overaccommodation for distant targets and underaccommodation for near targets), whereas 3-month-olds display small errors.

One might expect from these results that newborns and 1-month-olds see objects more clearly at some distances (ones to which they can accommodate accurately) than at others. More specifically, one might predict that acuity would vary with target distance. Surprisingly, this simple prediction is not supported by empirical data. Fantz, Ordy, and Udelf (1962), Salapatek, Bechtold, and Bushnell (1976), and Atkinson, Braddick, and Moar (1977b) have all found that 1-month acuity (measured using preferential looking) does not vary with target distance. Recently, this apparent paradox has been discussed in depth (Banks, 1980b; Braddick et al., 1979; Salapatek et al., 1976). Banks, for example, argued that depth of focus (the distance through which an object can be moved, in the absence of accommodative change, without a noticeable reduction in image sharpness) may be so large in young infants that substantial focusing errors would not cause noticeable increases in blur. Consequently, one should not expect visual acuity to vary with target distance.

Green, Powers, and Banks (1980) pursued this hypothesis quantitatively. They noted that the small pupil diameter and low acuity of young infants should result in large depth of focus. They calculated depth of focus for different ages and concluded that infants' focusing errors did not exceed the estimated depth of focus. Thus, very young infants, although not capable of accurate accommodation, may accommodate just well enough to maintain constant acuity across a range of distances. This analysis also suggests a related explanation of why early accommodation is poor and how it improves with age. If depth of focus is very large in young infants, in-focus and out-of-focus retinal images could not be discriminated and, consequently, there would be no cue for accommodation. As pupil size and visual acuity increase with age, depth of focus should decrease. Consequently, the discriminability of in-focus and out-of-focus images would improve, thereby providing a better cue for accommodation. In support of this idea, Banks (1980b) has shown that accommodative performance in 1-, 2-, and 3-month-olds can be predicted quite accurately from their respective depth of focus estimates. This account of accommodative development must be qualified in view of Brookman's (1980) finding that infants do not accommodate to very near targets until about 5 months of age. This suggests that some limitation (e.g., convergence, mechanical problems with the lens) other than large depth of focus must exist for very near targets.

Accommodation can be activated either by changing target distance or by placing ophthalmic lenses in front of the eyes. Recently, some developmental studies have employed the second technique to examine the development of accommodation and depth of focus. Three studies (Harter, Deaton, & Odom, 1977a; Powers & Dobson, 1982; Sokol, Moskowitz, & Paul, in press) involved placing lenses in front of both eyes to allow binocular viewing. One study (Boltz, Manny, & Katz, in press) tested the infants monocularly. All four studies found that positive (convex) lenses generally led to a reduction in visual acuity because the blur induced by positive lenses cannot be overcome by accommodation (except in subjects with large hyperopic refractive errors). The three binocular studies also found that acuity dropped when negative lenses were used, suggesting an inability to accommodate and thereby overcome the induced blur. If the effect of placing lenses in front of the eyes is really analogous to changing target distance, such a finding contradicts earlier reports that acuity does not vary with distance (Atkinson et al., 1977b; Fantz et al., 1962; Salapatek et al., 1976). Of course, another possibility is that the effect of placing lenses in front of the eyes is not analogous to changing target distance. In particular, placing lenses in front of the eyes changes the accommodative stimulus but not the convergence stimulus. Changing target distance, on the other hand, changes both the accommodative and convergence stimuli in a correlated manner. Accommodation and convergence appear to be linked in infants, though probably not as closely as they are in adults (Aslin & Jackson, 1979). The lenses may then cause conflict and, therefore, may not induce adequate accommodative changes. This hypothesis is supported by the results of the Boltz et al. experiment. Because their infants were tested monocularly, no convergence stimulus was present to contradict the accommodative stimulus. Interestingly, their subjects appeared to accommodate appropriately; they showed no change in acuity over a considerable range of negative lenses.

Visual experience appears to play at least an indirect role in the development of accommodation. Adults with abnormal early visual experience often develop reduced acuity in one eye (amblyopia). Wood and Tomlinson (1975) have shown that these people do not accommodate accurately with their amblyopic eye. Indeed, their accommodation resembles that of young infants. This and other relationships between adult and infant accommodation have led Banks (1980b) and Owens and Held (1978) to speculate that the basic mechanisms of accommodation are similar in infants and adults and that the age-related changes observed are the results of improvements in other visual functions such as visual acuity.

Summary

Visual accommodation improves notably during the first several months of life. It appears, however, that accommodation is accurate enough, even at 1 month, to maintain constant visual resolution across a wide range of distances. The growth of accommodative accuracy appears to depend more on improvements in visual processing than on improvements in motor capability.

Postural Control

Gibson (1966) noted that vision not only functions to provide information about external events (exteroception) but also to provide feedback about an observer's own movements (proprioception). The latter feedback comes from changes in visual stimulation caused by the observer's activity. For example, centrifugal textural flow can indicate that one is falling forward.

Lee and Aronson (1974) were the first to study infants' use of visual information to maintain postural stability. They constructed a large experimental room whose walls and ceiling could be moved. When the room was moved forward, away from an adult observer, subjects felt as though they were falling backward and, to compensate, made forward postural corrections. Infants 12 months of age or older, all of whom could stand unsupported, behaved in a similar fashion when tested in the experimental room; that is, they swayed or fell in the direction of the room's motion. Butterworth and Hicks (1977) observed similar behavior in younger infants who experienced the room's motion while seated. These experiments show quite convincingly that infants capable of upright posture, whether standing or sitting, use kinetic visual information to guide postural control.

Brandt, Wenzel, and Dichgans (1976) investigated visual control of posture more quantitatively from 12 months to adulthood. They found that visual information influenced posture to an increasing extent up to 2 years of age, after which visual influence declined to adult values.

This is an interesting area of research that warrants further investigation, since several questions remain unanswered. At what age does visual information first affect postural control? How good is postural control in locomoting infants when visual information is absent rather than misleading? The experience question: Is the use of visual information correlated with how long the infant has been able to sit or stand? We hope that these questions and others will be answered in the next decade.

PATTERN VISION

Thus far our discussion has centered on visual capabilities that are used primarily to localize objects in the environment. As described in the introduction, the ability to recognize and identify objects is equally important. Accordingly, we now turn our attention to the major visual capabilities involved in object recognition and identification: pattern vision and color vision (the discussion on *Color Vision* follows this one).

The ability to recognize, classify, and identify objects on the basis of pattern information is arguably the most complex and sophisticated of our visual capabilities. This point is illustrated by the difficulty computer scientists have had in producing general pattern recognition devices (e.g., Dodwell, 1970). For this reason, the study of the development of pattern vision has traditionally attracted more experimental and theoretical interest than any other topic in infant perception. The same has been true during the last decade.

Unfortunately, there is no consensus on what is meant by the term pattern nor by many related terms. We offer the following definitions, which are reasonably consistent with the most common usages.

Contour: Any localized and perceptible transition in brightness or hue.

Pattern: Any field in which one or more contours are present.

Figure: A contour(s) defining a figure-ground relationship.

Form or shape: The aspect of a pattern or object that remains constant despite changes in low-order variables such as brightness, contrast, size, position, context, and, to some extent, local features and orientation.

Object: A graspable physical entity that has a location in space.

Configuration: Any arrangement of contours, figures, forms, or objects.

Element: The component contours, figures, forms, or objects in a configuration.

Notice that pattern is defined most broadly, so we will use this term whenever no specific meaning is intended.

In an attempt to simplify our discussion of the vast literature on infant pattern vision, we have divided the topic into three reasonably natural categories: pattern detection, pattern discrimination, and pattern recognition. Pattern detection refers to the simplest of pattern vision capabilities: the ability to perceive that a stimulus is patterned rather than unpatterned or uniform. An infant's ability to detect a pattern has usually been assessed in one of two ways. First, many have used a preferential looking procedure to look for differential behavior toward a patterned relative to an unpatterned field (e.g., Atkinson et al., 1977b). Second, the visually evoked potential has been used to look for a significant response to a patterned stimulus relative to an unpatterned one (e.g., Marg, Freeman, Peltzman, & Goldstein, 1976). We review pattern detection work in the next three sections. Pattern discrimination refers to the somewhat more complex ability of distinguishing two (or more) detectable patterns from one another. Thus, pattern discrimination presupposes pattern detection. Infants' pattern discrimination abilities have usually been assessed in one of two ways. First, a vast number of studies have employed preferential looking procedures to reveal differential responses to two (or more), presumably detectable, patterns (e.g., Fantz, 1961). Second, some researchers have habituated infants to one presumably detectable pattern and then looked for differing responses to that pattern and one or more other detectable patterns (e.g., McGurk, 1970). Pattern recognition refers to the yet more complex ability of determining whether a pattern has been seen previously. This requires not only the ability to detect the familiar pattern and discriminate it from other nonfamiliar patterns, but also the ability to store a representation of the pattern in memory. We do not review work on pattern recognition explicitly, although many habituation studies address issues of discrimination and recognition (see *Vol. II, chap. 2* for a review of recognition work).

Within the framework presented here, the relationships among these aspects of pattern vision are asymmetrical; that is, experiments focusing on higher levels require some knowledge of lower level function. For example, to test the ability to discriminate two stimuli on the basis of pattern presupposes that the patterns in the two stimuli are detectable. Thus, some knowledge of detectability must precede experiments on discrimination.

Visual Acuity

As we argued above, a primary visual function is to represent pattern information in a manner that allows the recognition and identification of objects and their spatial layout. This function depends on the ability to detect differences in intensity or wavelength composition because such differences create the contours of patterns in the first place. However, it is not enough to just detect intensity or wavelength differences. Object recognition and identification depend further on the ability to encode the spatial distribution of such differences. The study of visual acuity addresses the question of how accurate this encoding of spatial distribution is. To be more precise, it concerns how finely the visual system can partition spatial distributions of intensity and wavelength. The term visual acuity thus refers to the threshold or maximum resolving capability of the visual system.

Measurements of visual acuity generally involve high-contrast, black-and-white test patterns. A subject's performance is assessed as the distance or separation is varied between two contours within the pattern. The separation for which the subject is just able to detect or resolve the pattern serves as the measure of visual acuity and is expressed in degrees of visual angle.

Several types of acuity tasks using different sorts of patterns exist. We discuss three: minimum visible acuity tasks, minimum separable acuity tasks, and vernier acuity tasks. As one might expect, the just-resolvable separation of contours varies among these tasks.

Minimum visible tasks involve a single black line on a white background (or a single white line on a dark background). Adults can, under optimal conditions, detect such a line when it is only ½ second of arc wide (Hecht & Mintz, 1939). Unfortunately, minimum visible acuity measurements cannot be logically separated from the intensity discrimination capacity of the eye (Riggs, 1965). Consequently, they probably should not be regarded as measures of acuity.

Minimum separable acuity tasks require the subject to respond to a separation between elements of a pattern. The most common pattern is a series of alternating black and white stripes of equal width (a square wave grating). The finest grating the subject can resolve is taken as the measure of acuity. It is generally expressed in terms of spatial frequency, the number of pattern repetitions per degree of visual angle. (Other units for expressing acuity are displayed in Figure 17.) Adult minimum separable acuity under optimal conditions is 45 to 60 cycles/degree (c/deg), which corresponds to a stripe width of ½ to ⅔ minutes of arc.

Vernier acuity tasks require the subject to discriminate displacements of one line with respect to another. Specifically, one must distinguish whether an upper vertical line is displaced to the left or right of a lower vertical line. The just-discriminable offset, under optimal conditions, is about 2 seconds of arc for adults (Berry, 1948). Clearly then different sorts of tasks yield quite discrepant estimates of visual acuity. Westheimer (1979, 1982) has argued, in fact, that minimum separable and vernier acuity tasks actually tap different visual mechanisms. This is an intriguing, but as yet unconfirmed, idea.

Parenthetically, we would like to point out an important implication of the fact that different sorts of acuity tasks yield widely different estimates of visual resolution. Because the resolution limit varies from one pattern to another, one cannot use an acuity estimate obtained with one sort of pattern to predict the limit of resolution for another sort of pattern. This has important implications for infant research. Several investigators have used estimates of minimum separable acuity (specifically, the angular subtense of one stripe when the grating is at threshold) to argue that the pattern elements in another stimulus (e.g., the individual features in a schematic face) are resolvable. This is, in general, inappropriate because, as we have described here, acuity estimates actually vary greatly from one pattern to another and hence cannot be used to predict one another in any simple way. The next section considers an approach that offers solutions to this problem.

One motivation for studying visual acuity (and, as we will see, for studying the growth of visual acuity) is the expectation that it will provide insight into optical, anatomical, and physiological influences on visual performance. In tests of visual acuity, the visual system's ability to encode the spatial distribution of stimulation is pushed to the limit. Accurate processing is required from many stages, beginning with the eye's optics and proceeding to central neural networks. Psychophysical estimates of acuity have actually helped uncover quantitative relationships between adults' visual performance on the one hand and optical and neural mechanisms on the other. A brief discussion of this work will help set the framework for much of the infant work on acuity development.

Two classical observations illustrate the influence of optical and neural factors on adult visual acuity. First, minimum visible, minimum separable, and vernier acuity, all depend heavily on the average luminance of the stimulus. Adult minimum separable acuity, for example, increases more than a hundredfold from dark scotopic to bright photopic conditions (Shlaer, 1937). Second, all three measures of acuity depend significantly on the retinal eccentricity of the target (retinal eccentricity refers to the angular distance from the fovea to the retinal region being tested). For example, adult minimum separable acuity is highest in the fovea and falls dramatically, but steadily, as the target is moved into the periphery (Mandelbaum & Sloan, 1947).

Both optical and neural factors contribute to the increase in acuity with higher luminance. Consider first the contribution of optical factors. As luminance is increased, the pupil constricts. This improves the sharpness of the retinal image (and thereby improves visual acuity) because restricting light to the center of the cornea and lens minimizes the defocusing effects of spherical and chromatic aberrations (see our discussion above on *Optics*). Neural factors, however, are more important because dramatic improvements in acuity with increasing luminance are still observed even when pupil diameter (and hence optical quality) is held constant. Two neural mechanisms seem to be involved. First, the shift from rod to cone activation (that accompanies an increase in light level) enhances resolution because cones are packed much more densely than rods in the central retina. Furthermore, the cones do not pool their responses at higher level neurons as much as rods do. Second, there is physiological evidence that the receptive fields of retinal neurons change with light level. Barlow et al. (1957) and Enroth-Cugell and Robson (1966) observed that the antagonistic surround of retinal ganglion cells disappeared at low light levels and, consequently, that the resolution of the cells dropped.

Neural factors also seem to be primarily involved in the change in visual resolution from the fovea to the far periphery. The optical quality of the eye is much worse for the retinal periphery than for the fovea, but Green (1970) has shown nonetheless that optical quality does not constrain acuity in the periphery. He measured adult minimum separable acuity at various eccentricities under two conditions: (1) using conventional gratings viewed under normal conditions and (2) using laser-generated gratings that were formed directly on the retina and hence were impervious to optical degradation. Peripheral acuity was identical for the two conditions suggesting that, despite their poor quality, optical factors do not constrain resolution in that part of the retina. Foveal acuity was somewhat higher for the laser gratings than for the conventional gratings. So in spite of the relatively good quality of foveal optics, it partially constrains acuity for that part of the retina. Since optical factors apparently do not cause the fall in acuity with retinal eccentricity, what neural mechanisms cause them? Green (1970) showed that, once optical factors were partialled out, acuity in the central 5 deg of the retina could be predicted precisely from the average separation of cones. As mentioned in our discussion above on *The Retina*, it can be shown mathematically that minimum separable acuity cannot exceed the density (or sampling frequency) of the receptor mosaic. But acuity could, of course, be worse than the limit set by the mosaic. The fact that it is not indicates that acuity in the fovea is constrained primarily by the density of cones in that region. Beyond 5 deg, Green found that acuity was actually somewhat worse than would be predicted from receptor density. The primary constraint then must be further upstream.

The optical and neural substrates of minimum visible and vernier acuity are less clear than those of minimum separable acuity. For one thing, resolution thresholds in these tasks can be as low as 1 second of arc, a distance which is 20 to 30 times smaller than the diameter of a single photoreceptor! Obviously then simple hypotheses based on the grain of the receptor mosaic cannot account for these thresholds in the same manner they did for minimum separable thresholds. Recently, a quantitative model of the optical and neural substrates of vernier acuity has appeared (Crick, Marr, & Poggio, 1981), but it is too involved to describe here.

Development

We now turn to the development of visual acuity. There have been two fundamental motivations for studying acuity growth. First is the expectation that such studies will provide insight into the relationship between visual performance and the optical, anatomical, and physiological development of the infant's visual system. This expectation is fostered by the success this approach has had in adult work. Second, infant researchers have measured acuity in an attempt to characterize the visual system's sensitivity to patterns at different ages. We argue in the next section that acuity measurements actually do not provide a general index of pattern sensitivity. Nonetheless, visual acuity has an important impact on pattern vision. Pattern elements that are smaller than the resolution limit cannot be detected. If such an element was the distinguishing feature of an object in a particular situation, the object could not be correctly identified. Hence the second motivation for studying acuity growth should be stated more narrowly: Acuity estimates may allow researchers to determine which pattern elements or features are too small to be detected at different ages.

Casual observation suggests that visual acuity is quite low early in life and that it improves dramatically during the first year. For example, neonates seem to attend only to large objects, whereas older infants notice quite small objects or features that even their parents have difficulty detecting.

These casual observations are confirmed by the now extensive literature on infant visual acuity. Unfortunately, all but one report in the literature has measured minimum separable acuity. Nevertheless, different response measures and different stimuli have been used, so one cannot summarize the literature by just stating acuity estimates for various ages because, as in adults, the estimates of acuity depend on the responses and stimuli used.

In order to keep our review of this work reasonably brief and to represent the dependence on response measure, we have chosen to describe only three representative studies in detail—each with a different response measure—and to present the findings of other studies only as supplements. Discussion of stimulus variables is sprinkled throughout this section and the next. The three response measures represented—optokinetic nystagmus (OKN), visually evoked potentials (VEP), and preferential looking—account for virtually all of the acuity studies to date (see Dobson & Teller, 1978; Maurer, 1975, for reviews).

Fantz et al. (1962) used OKN to estimate infant acuity. OKN is the rhythmic pattern of slow, pursuitlike movements followed by saccadic refixations that is elicited when a subject looks at a repetitive moving pattern (see our discussion above on *Optokinetic Nystagmus*). As in most OKN procedures, Fantz et al. used a moving square wave grating that covered most of the infant's visual field. The spatial frequency of the grating was varied from 0.75 to 6 c/deg. Fantz et al. tested 46 healthy infants, 4 days to 6 months of age. The presence or absence of OKN was judged on-line by an adult observer. Acuity estimates were based on the highest spatial frequency at which reliable OKN was observed. We have reanalyzed their results and plotted in Figure 15 the estimated spatial frequency at which 50% of the infants in each age group would yield reliable OKN. The acuity estimates increased reasonably monotonically from about 2 c/deg (20/300 Snellen) at ½ month to greater than 6 c/deg (20/100 Snellen) at 5½ months. These acuity values agree reasonably well with the OKN acuities observed by Enoch and Rabinowicz (1976) and Gorman et al. (1957, 1959). Dayton et al. (1964a) reported acuities of 4 c/deg for many newborns, a value higher than the others obtained. Banks and Salapatek (1981), however, have shown that their stimulus contained spatial frequencies lower than 4 c/deg. Thus, Dayton et al. probably overestimated OKN acuity.

Sokol (1978) used the steady-state visually evoked potential (VEP) to measure infant acuity. The stimuli were checkerboards that reversed in phase 12 times per second (6 Hz). Check size was

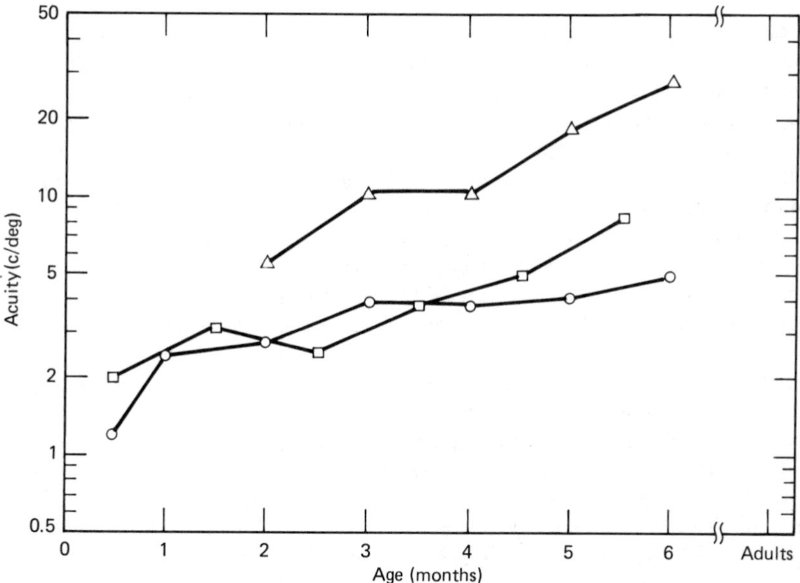

Figure 15. Visual acuity at different ages. The highest spatial frequency is plotted as a function of age. Open circles: acuity estimates from Allen's (1978) preferential looking experiment. Open squares: estimates from the Fantz et al. (1962) OKN experiment. Open triangles: estimates from Sokol's VEP experiment.

varied from 7.5 to 90 minutes of arc, and the amplitude of the VEP was noted for each size. Fifteen infants were tested, in most cases longitudinally, at monthly intervals from 2 to 6 months of age. Extrapolation to zero response amplitude on an amplitude versus check-size plot allowed Sokol to estimate the threshold check size for each infant. (Campbell & Maffei, 1970, and Regan & Richards, 1971, have shown that such an extrapolation predicts adult psychophysical acuity thresholds.) The results from this experiment are also plotted in Figure 15. This Figure shows the fundamental spatial frequency corresponding to threshold check size for each age. Estimated acuities increase monotonically from 5.7 c/deg at 2 months to 28 c/deg at 6 months. These results agree reasonably well with those of other steady-state VEP studies (Harris, Atkinson, & Braddick, 1976; Sokol & Dobson, 1976) and with those of one transient VEP study (Marg et al., 1976). Other transient VEP studies have yielded lower estimates of acuity (Harter, Deaton, & Odom, 1977a, 1977b; Harter & Suitt, 1970).

Allen (1978) used the forced-choice preferential looking technique (FPL) to measure acuity in infants from ½ to 6 months. Recently, the FPL technique has become popular. Since it may not be familiar to the reader, we use Allen's experiment to describe it (see Teller, 1979, for more information). The infants were shown two fields simultaneously of equal size, luminance, and hue. The fields differed only in that one was a stationary, high-contrast square wave grating while the other was unpatterned. An adult observer, who did not know which side the grating was on, tried to identify the grating's location based on the infant's behavior. The observer was given trial-by-trial feedback to allow him or her to recognize a particular infant's most reliable cues. Any aspect of the infant's behavior could be used, but typically an infant's inherent preference to look at a patterned rather than an unpatterned field produced more and longer fixations to the grating side. The spatial frequency of the grating was varied from 0.38 (wide stripes) to 12 (narrow stripes) c/deg. The observer's percent correct typically varied from about 50%, which is chance performance, for high spatial frequencies to about 100% for low spatial frequencies. Allen estimated the spatial frequency required to achieve 75% correct responding by interpolation, and this value was considered as the acuity estimate. These estimates are shown in Figure 15. The acuity estimates increased monotonically from 1.3 c/deg at ½ month to 5 c/deg at 6 months. Allen's data agree reasonably well with those of other preferential looking studies (Atkinson, Braddick, & Moar, 1977a, 1977b; Banks & Salapatek, 1978; Fantz et al., 1962; Gwiazda, Brill, Mohindra, & Held, 1978; Salapatek et al., 1976; Teller, Morse, Borton, & Regal, 1974).

These estimates of acuity should, of course, be regarded as lower bound estimates of infants' resolution capabilities since the failure of an infant to elicit a positive response is not strong evidence for an inability to detect. With this provision in mind, let us consider the general findings. Although there are obvious differences in the response measures used (and some in the stimuli used as well), these reports agree on two points. First, the finest grating or checkerboard to which a neonate responds reliably has a spatial frequency of about 1 c/deg. Thus, minimum separable acuity is about 20/600 in Snellen notation, roughly 30 times lower than normal adult acuity. Second, the highest detectable spatial frequency increases monotonically from birth to at least 6 months of age. The reports often disagree on one point: Many VEP studies obtained higher acuity estimates than preferential looking and OKN studies particularly after 3 months of age. This discrepancy suggests that response convergence (Yonas & Pick, 1975) may not obtain and raises the question of which technique yields the most meaningful estimates of visual acuity.

Dobson and Teller (1978) considered this discrepancy between VEP and OKN or preferential looking acuity estimates in some detail. They presented three possible explanations, two of which suggest that the differences are more apparent than real. First, the discrepancy might be the result of differences in the stimuli used in the three techniques. Specifically, the stimuli used in VEP studies, because they were modulated temporally, may yield higher acuity estimates, regardless of the response measure used, than the static gratings used in preferential looking studies. This hypothesis is weakened by the results of two studies that compared preferential looking acuities with both static and nonstatic stimuli. Dobson, Teller, and Belgum (1978) used FPL to measure visual acuity in 2-month-olds with two types of stimuli: (1) phase-alternating checkerboards similar to those used in many VEP studies and (2) static square wave gratings like those used in many preferential looking studies. Similar acuity estimates were obtained with the two patterns. Similarly, Atkinson et al. (1977a) measured FPL acuity in 1-, 2-, and 3-month-olds using static and drifting sine wave gratings. They, too, found no difference between stationary and moving gratings. It should be noted, however, that results from older infants would have been more relevant to the issue at hand because VEP and preferential looking (PL) acuities are generally not very different until after 3 months. Moreover, Atkinson et al. drifted the gratings in a fashion that made the drift velocity inversely proportional to spatial frequency. Consequently, the relatively high-frequency gratings used to measure acuity in the 2- and 3-month-olds may have been moving too slowly to elicit a preference for temporal modulation (see our discussion on *Temporal Vision* below).

Second, Dobson and Teller considered the possibility that the discrepancy between VEP and other estimates of acuity may be the result of the different scoring techniques used for different response measures. In preferential looking studies, acuity is usually estimated by somewhat strict criteria—for example, the spatial frequency required to elicit 75% correct responding. VEP acuity, on the other hand, is usually estimated with much more generous criteria—for example, the spatial frequency for which VEP amplitude will be zero or just above zero. Use of more generous scoring criteria in preferential looking studies (60% or 55%) would increase the acuity estimates by 1 to 1.5 octaves. Thus, much of the difference between acuities estimated by VEP and PL techniques may be attributable to differences in the scoring criteria used. It seems, however, that this cannot be the whole story since it does not explain why the discrepancy is so much more pronounced after 3 months than it is before.

Dobson and Teller considered a third possibility. Perhaps the three techniques yield different acuity estimates at some ages because they tap different visual mechanisms. This hypothesis is difficult to evaluate at this stage because not enough is known about preferential looking, VEP, and OKN in infants.

A simple way to determine if these response measures reflect the same mechanisms is to examine whether they are influenced similarly by changes in stimulus parameters. For example, if VEP and OKN acuity estimates are affected in quite different ways by changes in light level, they probably do not tap the same mechanisms. Adult work has in fact shown that VEP, OKN, and psychophysical acuity estimates are affected in different ways by changes in stimulus parameters; this implies that the three responses tap somewhat different mechanisms in adults. For example, Regan (1978) has argued that VEP and psychophysical measures are affected differently by changes in stimulus parameters. Specifically, he showed that pattern-reversal VEPs in adults exhibit two components: (1) a pattern component due to the phase-reversing changes in the pattern and (2) a local flicker component due to changes in luminance over time. To estimate acuity, researchers have held the rate of phase reversal constant and varied the size of pattern elements in the stimulus.

Unfortunately, the relative magnitude of the two VEP components varies significantly with both the size of the pattern elements and the rate of phase reversal. Thus, one's choice of temporal frequency influences the estimate of acuity. Interestingly, changes in temporal frequency also affect psychophysical estimates of acuity (Robson, 1966) but not in the same manner as VEP estimates are affected. In other words, spatial-temporal interactions in the VEP appear to be different than those observed in psychophysical tasks. This suggests that the two techniques may tap somewhat different mechanisms. One could argue that this problem can be avoided simply by choosing the temporal frequency so as to match VEP and psychophysical acuity estimates. Unfortunately, the appropriate frequency for infants is probably different from the one for adults. Moskowitz and Sokol (1980) have shown that significant spatial-temporal interactions exist in infant VEPs and that these interactions change with age. Thus, a choice of temporal frequency based on adult work could yield an inaccurate estimate of visual acuity for the particular age tested.

Very recently a report has appeared that offers a more optimistic view of the correlation between VEP and psychophysical estimates of pattern detection capabilities. Cannon (1983) reported a new VEP technique for measuring detection thresholds in adults. The details of the technique are beyond the scope of this chapter, but it might be fruitfully applied to infant work. A few of Cannon's observations in his adult studies are worth mentioning here. He measured VEP and psychophysical detection thresholds but, unlike other researchers, he presented precisely the same stimulus in both tasks. VEP thresholds were consistently higher than psychophysical thresholds, but they were nearly perfectly correlated. Specifically, as Cannon changed a subject's optical correction or changed the spatial frequency of the stimulus (as in contrast sensitivity measurements; see the next section), VEP and psychophysical thresholds varied in unison. These results contradict earlier studies that reported low correlations between VEP and psychophysical thresholds and suggest that at least one VEP technique may reveal the same mechanisms as psychophysical techniques do.

Little is known of the substrates of OKN acuity in infants, so we must turn again to adult work for clues. Several adult studies suggest that OKN acuity reflects different visual mechanisms than psychophysical acuity. For example, Pearson (1966) and Reinecke and Cogan (1958) have shown that adult OKN acuity estimates are not well correlated with psychophysical estimates. Furthermore, Schor and Narayan (1981) have shown that OKN and psychophysical acuity estimates are affected differently by changes in stimulus parameters. They examined the effects of a number of stimulus parameters in eliciting involuntary OKN in adults. As in the infant studies described above, the stimulus was a drifting grating. They found that the highest velocity at which OKN could be elicited was the same as the highest detectable velocity in a psychophysical task. They also found that the acuity cut-off for OKN was well below the psychophysical acuity for some conditions. Specifically, psychophysical acuity was unaffected by changes in stimulus field size whereas OKN acuity was considerably lower for large fields than for small fields. (OKN acuity appeared to match the psychophysical acuity for the most peripheral part of the retina stimulated by the drifting grating.) To summarize, the fact that OKN and psychophysical acuities in adults are affected differently by changes in stimulus parameters implies that the two types of acuity are mediated by different mechanisms.

We have seen that VEP, OKN, and psychophysical estimates of adult acuity are affected differently by variations in stimulus parameters such as rate of temporal modulation and field size. This means the three response measures probably tap somewhat different visual mechanisms in adults unless one is careful, like Cannon (1983), to choose parameters and procedures wisely. It is tempting to conclude that the same must be true of VEP, OKN, and preferential looking acuity estimates in infants. Unfortunately, such a conclusion is unwarranted until more is learned of how various stimulus parameters, such as those examined in the adult studies mentioned above, affect the techniques' estimates of infants' visual capability. It is worth restating in this context, however, that VEP, OKN, and preferential looking acuities do not appear to diverge until after about 3 months. This might mean that the three response measures reflect the same mechanism early in infancy and different mechanisms later on.

There is another important reason for examining the effects of different response measures and stimulus parameters on estimates of infant visual acuity. The literature clearly indicates that neonates' minimum separable acuity is quite poor in comparison to adults' acuity and that it improves significantly during the first half year. These observations motivate two fundamental questions: Why is early acuity so poor, and how does it improve so rapidly during the first half year? There are three types of mechanisms that might govern early acuity growth: optical, neural, and attentional mechanisms. As we will see, the use of different response measures and the effects of different stimulus parameters can aid the evaluation of these three alternatives.

First, consider optical mechanisms. Perhaps the optics of the young eye are the primary constraint on early acuity. The sharpness of the retinal image depends on the quality of the cornea, lens, and other optic media. Consequently, as optical quality and hence retinal image sharpness improves with age, so might visual acuity. This hypothesis, however, does not seem to account for the data adequately (Dobson & Teller, 1978; Salapatek & Banks, 1978). Several sorts of optical errors can affect adult acuity: spherical aberration, chromatic aberration, diffraction resulting from the pupil, and clarity of the optic media. All of these errors, however, appear to be far too small in young infants to account for their low acuity values (see section on *Optics* above for more details).

Another optical error—accommodative error—might be a more viable candidate since accommodation, like acuity, improves notably with age. If accommodative error were an important constraint, one would expect young infants' acuity to vary with target distance. On the contrary, several investigators have shown that infants' acuity does not vary with distance (Atkinson et al., 1977b; Fantz et al., 1962; Salapatek et al., 1976). Thus, accommodative error also does not appear to be a significant limitation to infant acuity.

These considerations imply that the quality of the retinal image exceeds the acuity observed in young infants and, therefore, that optical factors do not limit acuity significantly. Thus, neural mechanisms or attentional factors must be the primary limit on early resolution. Attentional factors cannot be ruled out with certainty, but two facts suggest that they are not a primary limiting factor, at least before 3 months of age. First, involuntary responses, like the VEP and OKN, are presumably relatively unaffected by attentional lapses. Yet they yield acuity estimates similar to those obtained with preferential looking before 3 months. Second, the addition of reinforcement in the preferential looking paradigm should reduce the impact of any motivational deficit; yet Mayer and Dobson (1982) have shown that the use of reinforcement does not yield higher acuity estimates in young infants. One interpretation of this result is that little, if any, motivational deficit exists in the traditional preferential looking technique, at least before 3 months of age.

The third type of mechanism that might account for the early acuity deficit and subsequent growth is a broad class of neural mechanisms. A number of the neural mechanisms known to influence adult acuity are potentially involved in early acuity development. One mechanism is the spacing of photoreceptors. Recall that the average angular separation between foveal cones predicts minimum separable acuity in adults; smaller separations (higher density) near the center of the fovea lead to higher acuity, and the larger separations (lower density) in the parafovea lead to somewhat lower acuity in that part of the retina (Green, 1970). Foveal cone separation is known to decrease postnatally in humans (Abramov et al., 1982; Mann, 1964) and monkeys (Hendrickson & Kupfer, 1976), so the factor probably contributes to age-related changes in infants' minimum separable acuity. Indeed, Abramov (personal communication) has observed that the average angular separation of foveal cones decreases by a factor of 10 to 20 from birth to adulthood. Hence this factor alone may account for most of the roughly thirtyfold increase in minimum separable acuity over the same age range. A problem arises, however, in trying to relate these numbers: No one is certain of the part of the retina infants use in acuity tasks. If they do not use the fovea, then one should not use anatomical data from the foveal region to assess the contribution of receptor spacing. Thus, measurements of minimum separable acuity as a function of retinal eccentricity are needed along with more quantitative estimates of receptor density for different eccentricities before one can evaluate the receptor spacing hypothesis in infants. Unfortunately, nothing is known of the relationship between infant minimum separable acuity and retinal eccentricity. Lewis, Maurer, and Kay (1978) found that newborns could detect a narrower light bar against a dark background when it was presented near the fixation point than when it was presented in the periphery. But their task measured minimum visible acuity, which is in general not predictable from the dimensions of the receptor mosaic.

A second type of neural mechanism may also influence early acuity development: the spatial tuning of neurons at different levels of the visual system. The size of a neuron's receptive field limits its spatial resolution, with larger fields exhibiting lower acuity (e.g., Enroth-Cugell & Robson, 1966). The size of retinal ganglion cell receptive fields decreases significantly postnatally in cats (Rusoff & Dubin, 1977), so one would expect a concomitant decrease in visual acuity. Mitchell et al. (1976) have shown that kittens' acuity improves considerably postnatally, but no quantitative links between the receptive fields of ganglion cells and behavioral acuity have been drawn. The spatial resolution of lateral geniculate and cortical neurons also improves postnatally in cats and monkeys (e.g., Blakemore & Vital-Durand, 1980; Derrington & Fuchs, 1981). This, too, should affect visual acuity. There are, of course, no physiological data on receptive field sizes in developing humans, but several lines of evidence suggest that receptive field development may be similar in human and macaque infants (Boothe, 1981).

Summary

One form of visual acuity—minimum separable acuity—is by all accounts quite poor early in life and grows steadily until at least 6 months of life. The acuity estimates at different ages can be used to calculate roughly what objects or features in the environment are too small to be resolved. Unfortunately, different response measures yield different estimates of acuity, particularly after 3 months. It is possible that the measures tap different visual mechanisms in infants, but more experimental and theoretical attention must be devoted to this issue before firm conclusions can be drawn.

Various neural factors such as the grain of the photoreceptor mosaic and the spatial tuning of retinal, geniculate, and cortical receptive fields may determine early visual resolution and its subsequent development. Not enough is known currently to pinpoint which of these are the major determinants. Nonetheless, it appears that the primary limitation to early acuity is not the quality of the retinal image but rather the nervous system's ability to process that image.

Clinical Implications

Another issue that has been important in the study of acuity development, for both theoretical and clinical reasons, has been the role of visual experience. In the last 10 years there has been a number of demonstrations that early visual experience can play an important role in visual development. Behavioral measures of visual functions in cats and monkeys indicate susceptibility to abnormal early experience during a specific period of development (Dews & Wiesel, 1970; Muir & Mitchell, 1973; von Noorden, Dowling, & Ferguson, 1970). Neurophysiological studies of these same animals have shown that several properties of neurons in the visual cortex are affected by abnormal experience during this sensitive or critical period (see our discussion on *Visual Cortex* above).

There is now evidence that abnormal visual experience during infancy and early childhood can result in relatively permanent deficits in human visual acuity. In particular, adults with a history of early astigmatism (Freeman, Mitchell, & Millodot, 1972; Mitchell et al., 1973) or myopia (Fiorentini & Maffei, 1976) exhibit lower acuity than normal adults even if the astigmatic or myopic refractive error was corrected during childhood or adulthood. The presence of cataracts or patching early in life has even more severe effects (Awaya et al., 1973; Gstalder & Green, 1971).

These demonstrations of experiential effects are all retrospective; that is, the evidence is from adults with particular developmental histories. Obviously such experiments provide little information on when and how the deficits developed in these individuals. Thus, there has been considerable interest in examining acuity development in infants with astigmatism, cataracts, or some other impediment to receiving normal visual experience.

The retrospective studies of the effects of early astigmatism show that adult astigmats exhibit an uncorrectable acuity deficit for gratings in the habitually blurred orientation but not in others (Mitchell et al., 1973). This orientation-specific acuity loss has been called *meridional amblyopia*. Held (1978) and Teller et al. (1978) have studied the development of acuity in astigmatic infants to ascertain the ages at which meridional amblyopia first appears and when the sensitive period for its development is. The experimental procedures involved the measuring of minimum separable acuity using gratings of different orientations with and without optical correction for the astigmatism. Held found that without optical correction infants from 3 to 12 months exhibited lower acuity for the blurred orientation. Teller et al. obtained the same result in an infant tested at 4 and 5 months. With proper optical correction, the infants in the Held and Teller studies no longer exhibited the orientation-specific deficit they had without correction. Thus, meridional amblyopia must develop after the first year of life.

Enoch and Rabinowicz (1976) published a case history that is relevant to our understanding of the role of visual experience. The history concerns a full-term, healthy infant born with a dense unilateral cataract. The infant's cataract was removed and partial visual correction initiated at 4 days of age. Visual acuity was then assessed using OKN over a period of 4½ months. The acuity of the good eye improved steadily over this period. The acuity of the aphakic eye, however, did not increase at all until a more accurate visual correction was provided at 25 days. From that age on, acuity improved at similar rates in both eyes such that the aphakic eye exhibited a consistent deficit relative to the good eye.

The role of experience in acuity development has also been examined by comparing the acuity development of infants born prematurely with that of full-term infants. Miranda (1970) and Dobson, Mayer, and Lee (1980) both found that the acuity of premature infants matched that of full-term infants when they were compared on gestational rather than postnatal age. These findings suggest that the amount of visual experience does not determine the rate of acuity development, at least up to 12 weeks of age, because the preterm infants often had had 4 weeks more experience than full-term infants of equivalent gestational age. Thus, early acuity growth in humans is somewhat independent of visual experience.

The fact that abnormal visual experience during infancy appears to cause functional deficits later in life points to the importance of establishing developmental acuity norms and efficient techniques for early screening. Dobson, Teller, Lee, and Wade (1978) and Mayer and Dobson (1982) have described preferential looking techniques that show some promise with children from birth to 5 years of age. Sokol (1980) has described VEP techniques that might also be useful clinically.

Contrast Sensitivity

Measurements of visual acuity index the visual system's ability to resolve the smallest objects at high contrast. This is, of course, an important aspect of the system's pattern detection capabilities, but the visual world actually consists of objects of many different sizes at varying contrast levels. Indeed, many visual functions do not require acute vision at all. For example, the use of visual information to regulate posture does not depend on fine pattern information (Leibowitz, Shupert-Rodemer, & Dichgans, 1979). Thus acuity measurements alone are a poor index of the visual system's general ability to detect pattern information in everyday environments. A better index is provided by the contrast sensitivity function (CSF). This function represents the visual system's sensitivity to everything from very coarse to very fine spatial patterns. Specifically, the CSF relates the contrast required to just detect a sine wave grating (a repeating series of stripes whose luminance varies sinusoidally) to the grating's spatial frequency (the number of stripes per degree of visual angle). Figure 16 provides examples of high-contrast sine wave gratings that differ in spatial frequency.

Figure 16. Two sine wave gratings differing in spatial frequency. Both gratings are high-contrast, but the grating on the left is lower in spatial frequency. If the figure is held at arm's length, the grating on the left has a spatial frequency of 2 c/deg and the one on the right has a frequency of 7 c/deg.

The CSF of a typical adult is shown in Figure 17. Contrast sensitivity (the reciprocal of the contrast required to detect the grating) is plotted as a function of spatial frequency. Notice the bandpass characteristic; sensitivity is higher to intermediate frequencies than to low or high spatial frequencies.

The CSF has been extremely useful in the study of adult pattern vision. There are two reasons for this. The primary reason derives from Fourier's theorem and linear systems analysis. Fourier's theorem implies that any two-dimensional pattern can be represented by its spatial frequency content (see Banks & Salapatek, 1981; Cornsweet, 1970; Gaskill, 1978). Thus, even a complex pattern such as the picture of a face can be exactly reproduced by combining a set of sine wave gratings of various spatial frequencies, contrasts, and orientations. Linear systems analysis utilizes this fact to allow, in principle, the prediction of sensitivity to any pattern once the CSF of a visual system is known. The validity of linear systems analysis depends, however, on certain assumptions about the system under study. The adult visual system does not satisfy these assumptions in detail but, with certain restrictions, the approach has been very successful in predicting sensitivity to a wide variety of patterns (Banks & Salapatek, 1981; Cornsweet, 1970). This generalization capability has allowed researchers to synthesize a wide variety of observations.

The second reason that CSFs have been useful is related to the first. CSFs reveal the properties of some important aspects of pattern vision. These include visual acuity, intensity discrimination, low-frequency attenuation, and multiple feature-selective channels. We describe each of these in a moment.

Many of the infant studies concerning CSFs have been designed to capitalize on the generalizability afforded by linear systems analysis and to reveal the properties of the above-mentioned aspects of pattern

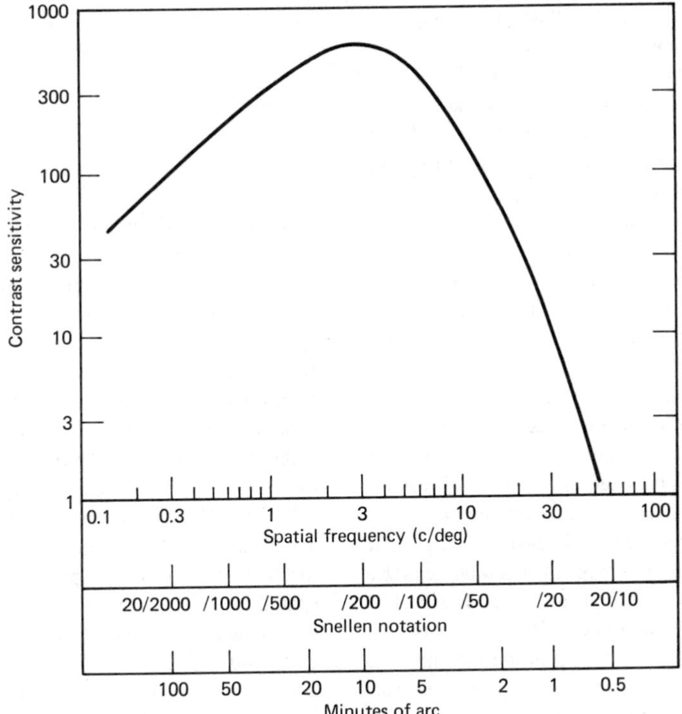

Figure 17. Typical adult contrast sensitivity function (CSF). Contrast sensitivity, the reciprocal of contrast at threshold, is plotted as a function of spatial frequency, the number of pattern repetitions per degree of visual angle. Scales relating spatial frequency to Snellen equivalents and stripe width in minutes of arc are shown for comparison. (From Banks & Salapatek, 1978.)

vision. In other words, the theoretical background for much of the infant work is based on rules and phenomena uncovered in previous adult work. We outline this background by presenting a few illustrative examples from the adult literature.

The CSF has proven a useful index of adult visual acuity. The point at which the high-frequency side of the CSF intersects the abscissa is called the high-frequency cutoff and is an estimate of visual acuity. Are such acuity estimates derived from the CSF more useful than other measures of acuity? Yes, because one can use the CSF to predict accurately the ability of adults to resolve various sorts of acuity targets. The converse is not true. An example can illustrate this. Adults exhibit remarkable resolution when the acuity target is a single black line on a white background (minimum visible acuity). Hecht and Mintz (1939) reported that adults can detect a single line when it is only a few seconds of arc wide. On the other hand, the widths of single stripes in the finest resolvable sine wave grating are about 1/2 minute of arc wide (Campbell & Green, 1965). In spite of this apparent contradiction, Campbell, Carpenter, and Levinson (1969a) showed that the narrowest detectable single line can actually be predicted from a straightforward application of the CSF and linear systems analysis.

Bodis-Wollner (1972) provided another striking example of the utility of the CSF. He reported case histories of patients with cortical lesions who were experiencing great difficulty reading and performing other pattern recognition tasks. The visual acuity of the patients was normal, and hence suggested no dysfunction. The patients' CSFs, however, revealed a large deficit for intermediate spatial frequencies. These deficits probably caused the reading disturbances because, subsequent to treatment, the mid-frequency deficit lessened and normal reading ability returned.

The CSF has also been a useful indicant of intensity discrimination in adults. Since intensity differences generally define patterns in the first place, the discrimination of intensities is obviously a fundamental aspect of pattern vision. Each point on the CSF represents the contrast necessary to just detect that an intensity difference is present. Is the CSF a better index of this capacity than other measures? Again a positive answer is justified. Adult psychophysical studies have revealed that no single value can characterize intensity discrimination capabilities. For example, discriminability depends critically on stimulus size and on illumination level (Vos, Lazet, & Bouman, 1956; see next section, *Light and Dark Adaptation*). Van Meeteren (1967) has shown, however, that CSFs measured at different illumination levels can be used to predict intensity discrimination thresholds for various background illumination levels and spots of various sizes.

Yet another important property revealed in CSF measurements is low-frequency attenuation. As previously described, lateral inhibitory connections are present in the early stages of visual processing. These connections serve to attenuate the visual system's response to gradual intensity changes. In CSFs, this attenuation is manifest as a relative insensitivity to low spatial frequencies (see Figure 17). Consider the function of lateral inhibition in pattern vision. To simplify processing of the astronomical amount of information entering the eye, the visual system must filter out certain types of information. Lateral inhibition is an integral part of this filtering. Lateral inhibitory networks tend to filter out gradual intensity changes (diffuse shadows, gradual changes in lighting, etc.). Hence the pattern information that passes through lateral inhibitory networks appears to be the most "valid" information, namely the position and shape of contours that define patterns in the first place. The argument that lateral inhibitory processing is reflected by the low-frequency falloff of the CSF is supported by several physiological and psychophysical studies. For example, it is known from physiological experiments that the magnitude of retinal lateral inhibition is less for low than for high luminances (Barlow, Fitzhugh, & Kuffler, 1957). Adult psychophysical experiments have shown that the slope of the low-frequency CSF falloff is also less for low than for high luminances (Van Nes & Bouman, 1967). In other words, at high luminances where lateral inhibition is strong, the low-frequency falloff of the adult CSF is pronounced. At low luminances where inhibition is weak, the low-frequency falloff is much less distinct.

To summarize, the CSF has been a very useful index of adult pattern sensitivity. Because of the generalization capability afforded by Fourier's theorem and linear systems analysis, the CSF has provided a reasonably general index from which sensitivity to a variety of patterns can be predicted. The CSF has also been a useful indicant of visual acuity, intensity discrimination, and contour enhancement provided by lateral inhibition.

Development

Because the CSF has been so useful to adult work, it has been measured in infants as well. Three laboratories have published reports of CSF development during early infancy (Atkinson et al., 1977b; Banks & Salapatek, 1978; Pirchio, Spinelli, Fiorentini, & Maffei, 1978). The methodologies of the three differ, so we describe each of them briefly.

Atkinson et al. (1977b) used the FPL technique (and a first fixation measure) to test 1-, 2-, and 3-month-olds. On each trial sine wave gratings appeared on one of two oscilloscopes; the other oscilloscope presented a uniform field of the same hue and average luminance. Each display was circular and subtended 15 deg. The gratings were either stationary or drifting. The results—the contrast necessary to elicit 70% correct responding as a function of spatial frequency—revealed a large increase in contrast sensitivity, primarily at high spatial frequencies, from 1 to 2 months and essentially no change from 2 to 3 months. The low-frequency falloff in sensitivity that is characteristic of adult CSFs was not observed consistently at 1 month, but was observed at 2 and 3 months.

Banks and Salapatek (1978) also used a preferential looking technique to measure CSFs in 1-, 2-, and 3-month-olds. The response measure used was first fixation. They used a projection system to present much larger stimuli (48 deg × 40 deg) than Atkinson et al. (1977b). The grating and uniform fields were again equal in hue and average luminance, but they were adjacent to one another. The observer always waited until the infant was fixating midline before presenting the stimuli. Consequently, the grating in the Banks and Salapatek study would, when first presented, have appeared close to the infant's fixation point. The sine wave gratings were always static. The results are shown in Figure 18. Again, there is an increase with age in contrast sensitivity, primarily at high spatial frequencies, but not as large an increase as observed by Atkinson et al. Again the low-frequency falloff was not observed consistently at 1 month but was at 2 and 3 months.

In summary, these two behavioral experiments agree substantially on the shape and height of the CSF at 2 and 3 months of age. They disagree concerning the overall sensitivity of 1-month-olds but agree on the shape of the CSF at that age. The disagreement at this age may be the result of differences in the field sizes employed. This argument is supported by recent findings that 1-month-olds do not

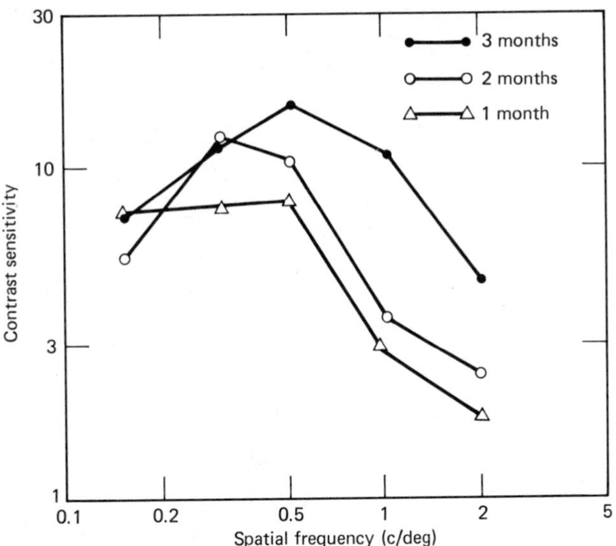

Figure 18. Contrast sensitivity functions (CSFs) for 1-, 2-, and 3-month-olds as reported by Banks and Salapatek. The average contrast sensitivity for each age group is plotted as a function of spatial frequency. (From Banks & Salapatek, 1978.)

appear to process pattern information presented within a frame (see *Internal-External Effects* below).

Comparing the adult CSF in Figure 17 to the infant functions in Figure 18 reveals distinct differences. Clearly, infant CSFs are shifted to a lower band of spatial frequencies. Moreover, infants appear to have a substantial deficit in overall contrast sensitivity relative to adults. Such comparisons motivate an important question: To what extent are these early deficits the result of nonvisual factors such as motivation?

Evoked potential measurements can answer this question to some extent because they presumably are not as subject to motivational factors as behavioral techniques might be. Pirchio et al. (1978) used steady-state VEPs to measure CSFs in one infant from 2½ to 6 months of age. They also measured two points on the CSF (the high-frequency cutoff and the peak) in a number of infants from 2 to 10 months. The sine wave gratings were presented in 7 to 25 deg fields depending on the infant's age. The gratings were flickered at a rate of 8 Hz. Threshold was estimated by plotting VEP amplitude versus contrast and extrapolating to find the contrast yielding zero amplitude. The results for the infant tested longitudinally are shown in Figure 19. Again, overall contrast sensitivity and the low-frequency falloff increased notably with age. The 2½-month data were quite similar to the 2- and 3-month results of the two behavioral studies. The results from the other infants (not shown in Figure 19) indicated that the high-frequency cutoff increased from 2 c/deg at 2 months to about 20 c/deg by 10 months and that peak contrast sensitivity improved from 4 to 40 over the same age range.

Harris et al. (1976) actually measured CSFs in one 6-month-old using both the VEP and preferential looking. In spite of differences in some of the stimulus parameters and the obvious differences in response measures, the two techniques yielded similar estimates of the CSF. It should be noted parenthetically that the 6-month-old's CSF still exhibited a twofold deficit in high-frequency sensitivity relative to adults. Thus, CSF development is not complete by 6 months.

The VEP results of Pirchio et al. (1978) and Harris et al. (1976) suggest that the contrast sensitivity differences between adults and young infants observed in the earlier behavioral studies result in large part from visual factors rather than from nonvisual, motivational factors. Thus, the pattern information to which infants are sensitive appears to be a small fraction of the information available to adults.

It is interesting to note that CSF development in macaque monkeys, a species whose mature visual system is very similar structurally and functionally to human adults (Boycott & Dowling, 1969; De-Valois, Morgan, & Snodderly, 1974), is similar to CSF development in humans except that it occurs

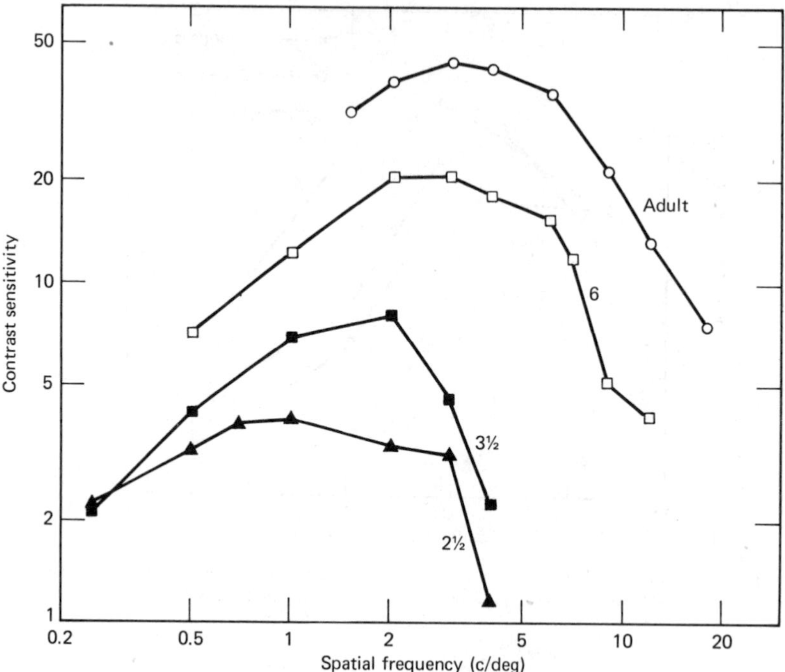

Figure 19. Contrast sensitivity function (CSFs) for one infant at different ages and one adult as reported by Pirchio et al. The infant's age in months is shown to the right of each of the infant functions. (From Banks, 1982.)

more rapidly in macaques (Boothe, Williams, Kiorpes, & Teller, 1980).

Another important question concerning CSF development is: To what extent are the age differences observed caused by differences in neural processing versus differences in optical quality? An explanation based on optical quality is somewhat attractive because deficits in young infants are most pronounced for high spatial frequencies, and high-frequency sensitivity suffers more from optical aberrations than does low-frequency sensitivity (Green et al., 1980). Nonetheless, it is very unlikely that optical aberrations contribute significantly to early contrast sensitivity deficits. The reasoning behind this conclusion is detailed in our section on *Visual Acuity*, where we consider whether optical aberrations constrain acuity to its low levels early in life.

To summarize the infant CSF work reviewed thus far, the evidence is reasonably persuasive that the young infant is sensitive to a much lower and perhaps more restricted range of spatial frequencies than the adult visual system is. Similarly, the range of contrasts to which infants are sensitive is quite restricted early on. The ranges of detectable frequencies and of detectable contrasts increase steadily during the first half year. Neural mechanisms appear to be more responsible than optical structures for the early deficits and subsequent growth. It appears then that the young visual system is sensitive initially to only a fraction of the information to which the adult system is sensitive and that this fraction increases steadily through at least the first half year of life.

Banks and Salapatek (1981) have referred to the fraction of pattern information to which young infants are sensitive as their "window." Evidently, the "window" is quite restricted early in life, but before concluding that young infants must be virtually blind, two points should be kept in mind. (1) Concerning the low overall contrast sensitivity of infants relative to adults, the contours of many common objects have contrasts greater than the threshold contrasts indicated in Figures 18 and 19. For example, faces often exhibit contrasts of 0.7 to 0.9 between the skin and hair, a value high enough to be detected by young infants. Thus, even though contrast sensitivity in infants is quite low relative to adults, it is sufficient for the detection of many typical intensity gradients in the environment. (2) Concerning the shift of sensitivity to low spatial frequencies in infants, the spatial frequencies of the sine wave components in an object change systematically with viewing distance. As the object is brought closer, its angular subtense increases and the major components are translated toward lower frequency values. The low-frequency "window" in infants is best suited for perceiving objects in the immediate rather than the distant visual environment. As the "window" grows with age, infants' ability to perceive distant objects (or small near objects) should increase correspondingly. Interestingly, Ginsburg (1978) has demonstrated that adult pattern recognition is not affected significantly when high spatial frequencies are deleted. His demonstrations emphasize the utility of low-frequency information in the recognition of all but very small objects (e.g., fine print).

As mentioned earlier, the CSF allows one, in principle, to predict sensitivity to a variety of patterns. It also reveals three important aspects of pattern vision: visual acuity, intensity discrimination, and low-frequency attenuation. We now discuss these points in the context of work on infants.

Recall that the CSF has been used in adult work to predict acuity thresholds for a variety of targets. Atkinson, Braddick, and Moar (1977c) and Banks and Salapatek (1981) demonstrated that similar predictions can be drawn from infant CSFs. Banks and Salapatek reanalyzed two experiments—Dayton et al. (1964a) and one described by Fantz, Fagan, and Miranda (1975)—that had used atypical patterns to estimate visual acuity. These experiments were of particular interest because both reported higher acuity values than others who used more conventional stimuli. The details of the reanalyses are beyond the scope of this chapter but, in both cases, application of linear systems analysis and the CSF for the appropriate age group revealed that higher acuity values were actually predictable given the patterns used in the experiments. Hence the results of Dayton et al. and Fantz et al. were actually consistent with other investigators' estimates.

Atkinson et al. (1977c) developed a unique measure of acuity using facial photographs. Two faces, one focused and one defocused to varying degrees, were presented to 1- to 3-month-olds in a discrimination task. When the one face was badly defocused, infants preferentially fixated the focused version. Atkinson and her colleagues varied the amount of defocus to find the point at which infants preferred the focused face on 70% of the trials. Once they obtained these thresholds, the experimenters used CSF measurements from another experiment (Atkinson et al., 1977b) in an attempt to predict the amount of just-detectable defocus. The predictions were quite accurate given the inherent variability of infant data. Thus, the CSF and a simple application of linear systems analysis allowed the prediction of a rather unique estimate of visual acuity. Parenthetically, the success of this experiment argues that the use of "nonecological" stimuli such as sine wave gratings has not badly misrepresented infants' visual sensitivity. If it had, "nonecological" measurements would presumably be unable to predict sensitivity obtained with more "ecological" stimuli like faces. So Banks and Salapatek (1981) and Atkinson et al. (1977c) have shown that infant CSFs provide a flexible, reasonably general index of the growth of visual resolution.

The second aspect of pattern vision revealed by the CSF concerns intensity discrimination or sensitivity to contrast. Each point on the function represents the intensity difference (or contrast) necessary for an infant to detect the presence of nonuniformity. Peeples and Teller (1978) measured intensity discrimination in 2-month-olds. They found that 2-month-old infants could discriminate stripes (square wave gratings) whose intensity differed by only 12% from the background intensity. This corresponds to a contrast sensitivity of 17.5. The predicted contrast sensitivity, based on Banks and Salapatek's (1978) 2-month CSF data, is 14.0, a reasonably close match considering the differences in procedures.

Clearly, however, describing the contrast sensitivity or intensity discrimination ability of the developing visual system with single values at different ages is inappropriate because those abilities are highly dependent on stimulus size and shape (and other factors such as luminance; see the next section). Following this reasoning, Banks and Stephens (1982) demonstrated how the CSF approach can be used to predict contrast sensitivity for different sorts of patterns. Specifically, they measured the contrast sensitivity of 10-week-olds for five types of rectangular wave gratings. The spatial frequency of the gratings was always 1 c/deg, but they differed in duty cycle (the relative widths of light and dark stripes). An adult was also tested but at a spatial frequency of 7 c/deg. The adult and infant results were very similar except for a large difference in contrast sensitivity. In both cases, sensitivity varied systematically with duty cycle. Banks and Stephens used linear systems theory to derive predicted contrast sensitivities as a function of duty cycle. The predicted functions fit the infant and adult data very well. The close match between the predicted and observed functions illustrates the utility of linear systems analysis and the CSF in predicting infants' sensitivity to different sorts of patterns.

The third aspect of pattern vision revealed in CSFs is low-frequency attenuation. Recall that this attenuation is a product of contour-enhancing, lateral inhibitory processing. Low-frequency attenuation seems to develop between 1 and 2 months of age. As is evident in Figure 18, a low-frequency falloff is observed in infants 2 months of age or older but not in 1-month-olds. Atkinson et al. (1977b) examined the development of low-frequency attenuation in detail. They tested a number of 1- to 3-month-olds at three low spatial frequencies. The results clearly showed that the low-frequency falloff is generally not present until 2 months of age. The implication is that lateral inhibition is not functional until that age. This hypothesis is supported by two observations. First, it is known from physiological studies that the magnitude of lateral inhibition in the retina is less for low than for high luminances (Barlow et al., 1957). Thus, if the low-frequency falloff in the CSF is caused by lateral inhibition, one would expect the falloff to become shallower at low luminances. Banks and Salapatek (1981) tested this in 2-month-olds. They measured CSFs at two luminances and found a lower falloff slope at the lower luminance. Second, physiological studies of kitten retinal ganglion cells have found that lateral inhibitory mechanisms are not adultlike until 8 to 9 weeks, which is considerably delayed relative to the development of excitatory mechanisms (Hamasaki & Sutija, 1979; Rusoff & Dubin, 1977). Thus, the contour-enhancing properties of early visual processing may not emerge until about 2 months after birth.

Another fundamental property of pattern vision that can be revealed in CSF experiments is the presence of multiple, feature-selective channels. All sensory systems possess many parallel pathways, each specialized to carry information about a particular type of stimulus. In the visual system, different sorts of pattern information from the same location in the visual field are signaled by different neurons. For example, different cells in the visual cortex are tuned to stimuli of different orientations (Hubel & Wiesel, 1962, 1968; and see our discussion above on *Visual Cortex*). Moreover, such cells respond to different sizes (or bands of spatial frequency), one cell responding to large pattern elements (low frequencies) and another to small pattern elements (high frequencies; Albrecht et al., 1980). A number of psychophysical experiments in adults have suggested that pattern information is processed in parallel by a number of different "channels" analogous to the cortical cells mentioned above. Different channels appear to be tuned to different orientations and spatial frequencies (reviewed by Braddick, Campbell, & Atkinson, 1978). The evidence for spatial-frequency tuning among these channels lies in the fact that spatial frequencies interact in experiments on detection, adaptation, and masking, but only if they lie within about one octave (a factor of 2) of each other. Significantly, these channels appear to be involved in the perception of size (Blakemore & Sutton, 1969).

In spite of the importance of these processes to pattern recognition (Ginsburg, 1978; Marr, 1982) and the electrophysiological evidence that channel specificity develops postnatally in kittens (Derrington & Fuchs, 1981), the development of spatial frequency and orientation channels in humans has received very little experimental attention. The only relevant experiment we are aware of is one recently conducted by Banks and Stephens (cited by Banks, 1982). Using a masking paradigm borrowed from auditory research, they measured the frequency bandwidth of channels in 1½-month-olds, 3-month-olds, and adults. They found in all age groups that a masker whose spatial frequency was similar to a test grating caused an increase in the threshold of the grating. However, when the masker and grating differed in frequency by 2 octaves (a factor of 4), the grating's threshold was unaffected by the masker in 3-month-olds and adults. This indicates that pattern information whose frequency content differs by 2 octaves is processed by separate channels. In 1½-month-olds, the masker affected the grating's threshold even when they differed by 2 octaves and, consequently, separate channels were not demonstrated over this range. Banks and Stephens used their data to estimate channel bandwidth as a function of age. The estimates were ± 1.2 octaves for 3-month-olds and adults. A bandwidth could not be estimated at 1½ months because no frequency-selective masking was observed. The results imply that the spatial-frequency tuning (or size tuning) of such channels becomes more precise with age. One might suspect from this that the ability to discriminate patterns according to size should improve correspondingly with age. Unfortunately, no data on the development of size discrimination per se exist, so this hypothesis cannot be evaluated.

Summary

The CSF and linear systems analysis have only recently been applied to the study of visual development. Already this approach has proven to be a useful general index of pattern detection capabilities. It has also illuminated several important aspects of pattern vision and how they change with age.

Several important questions remain to be explored. For one, how do spatial-temporal interactions influence infants' detection of pattern? This is an important question for future research because spatial-temporal interactions have significant effects in adults (Kelly, 1979). Moreover, Moskowitz and Sokol (1980) have already shown that spatial-temporal interactions influence infants' VEPs and that those interactions change with age. Atkinson et al. (1977a) have confirmed this in a preliminary behavioral CSF experiment. They found that the contrast sensitivity of infants 1 to 3 months of age was slightly higher for drifting than for static gratings.

Another important question for the future concerns the encoding of spatial relationships among detected contours. The potential importance of this is illustrated by an example from the adult literature. Researchers have noted that they often cannot predict adult amblyopes' acuity for letters (Snellen acuity) from their CSFs. (Amblyopia is a developmental anomaly in which visual acuity and some pattern discrimination capabilities are reduced.) The Snellen acuity is typically worse than predicted. Pass and Levi (1982) may have discovered why. They measured conventional CSFs in amblyopic adults and found a small but reliable high-frequency deficit relative to normal adults. They also measured thresholds for the identification of spatial relationships among detectable patterns. The amblyopes exhibited a large deficit in this task. This suggests that, in addition to a contrast sensitivity deficit, amblyopes also have a spatial-encoding deficit. Similar types of experiments in infants might reveal important properties of the developing visual system.

Finally, one wonders how well the rules and phenomena uncovered in CSF work might extend to the study of pattern discrimination. Recently, two laboratories (Banks & Ginsburg, in press; Banks & Salapatek, 1981; Gayl, Roberts, & Werner, 1983) have used the CSF and linear systems analysis to investigate suprathreshold pattern preferences. This work is reviewed in the section on *Pattern Preferences*.

Light and Dark Adaptation

Thus far we have discussed what is known of the development of pattern vision at fixed levels of illumination. Of course, the environment actually presents stimuli across a virtually infinite range of light levels. The visual system has evolved to maintain reasonably proficient pattern vision for a substantial portion of this range. For instance, Ripps and Weale (1969) have estimated that pattern vision is possible over a 10 log unit range of light levels. Thus, we can still discern patterns when the light is 10 billion times more intense than the smallest amount of light detectable in the dark. This remarkable feat is accomplished by adjusting the visual system's sensitivity according to the ambient level of illumination. Such adjustments are usually not obvious subjectively because they occur so efficiently. They are obvious only when light level changes suddenly and drastically. On those occasions, the visual system is temporarily "blinded" but readapts fairly rapidly so that pattern vision is once again possible. The processes of adapting to increases and decreases in illumination are called light and dark adaptation, respectively.

Before turning to the developmental research on adaptation, let us discuss the perceptual task of recognizing objects presented under different levels of illumination. An object is generally defined by differences in intensity (or hue; see *Color Vision* below) between the object and its background or between features within the object. The apparent brightness or luminance of an object or a feature within an object depends both on its reflectance (the percentage of incident light reflected) and the amount of light falling on it. Consequently, two adjacent parts of an object with different reflectances will always differ in luminance and form a contour, if they are bathed in the same light. If the amount of light falling on the object is changed, the *ratio* of the luminances does not change. So, the luminance ratio defining the contour would be the same under sunlight or moonlight. Fortunately, the mature visual system capitalizes on this invariance: Light and dark adaptation operate to ensure that the visual system responds to luminance ratios rather than absolute luminances. In this way, contours remain approximately equally visible for a large range of illumination levels. This property is illustrated by Weber's Law, which simply states that the smallest intensity increment needed for a target to be detected against an otherwise uniform background is a constant percentage of the background's intensity. Weber's Law is illustrated by increment threshold functions which plot the logarithm of the just-detectable increment intensity against the logarithm of the background intensity. Figure 20 shows a typical adult increment threshold function. Weber's Law holds where the slope of this function is 1.0; thus it appears to hold over a large range of intensities in adults.

The mechanisms mediating adaptation in adults are gradually yielding their secrets to visual physiologists and psychophysicists (see Barlow, 1972). Several mechanisms contribute to this process. First, pupillary changes modulate the amount of light falling on the retina in an appropriate, albeit insignificant, manner. The area of the adult pupil in bright light is about one-sixteenth its area in darkness. Therefore, pupillary changes aid adaptation but are really quite insignificant given the total dy-

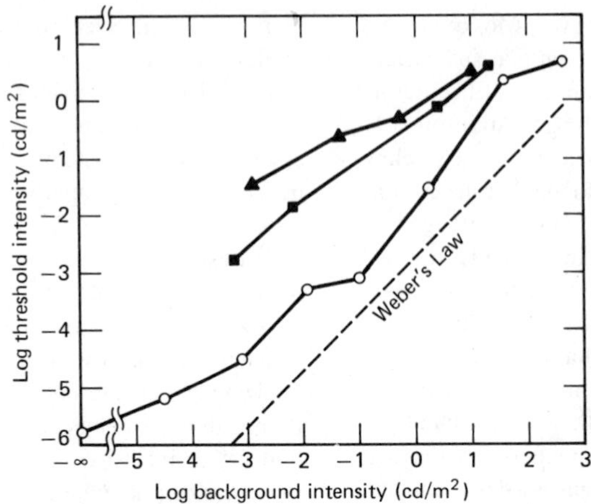

Figure 20. Increment threshold functions for 7-week-olds, 12-week-olds, and adults as reported by Dannemiller and Banks. The logarithm of the intensity increment needed to detect the target is plotted as a function of the logarithm of background intensity. Weber's Law is illustrated by the dashed line. Open circles: the average adult increment thresholds. Filled triangles: average 7-week increment thresholds. Filled squares: average 12-week increment thresholds. (Adapted from Dannemiller & Banks, 1983.)

namic range of the visual system. Second, the presence of two types of photoreceptors—rods and cones—aids adaptation by dividing the total dynamic range roughly in half. Rods are about 4 log units (10,000 times) more sensitive than cones, so they function over the range of dim light levels while cones operate at high levels. But even this staggering of sensitivity cannot fully account for light adaptation in adults. Additional photochemical and neural mechanisms must, therefore, contribute (Barlow, 1972).

Development

Developmentalists have only recently studied the effects of illumination changes on pattern vision. Consequently, the experimental questions to date have been elementary. Hansen and Fulton (1981) and Dannemiller and Banks (in press) measured increment threshold functions at a number of ages to examine the extent to which adaptation occurs to different levels of illumination. Hansen and Fulton measured increment thresholds in the scotopic range (low light levels at which rods operate) using the forced-choice preferential looking (FPL) procedure. Although only one infant was tested at each age, two developmental trends were evident. First, increment thresholds at all background intensities decreased with age. Second, thresholds decreased more at low background intensities than at high; so the slopes of the increment threshold functions increased steadily from about 0.62 at 2 weeks to an adultlike value of 0.90 at 12 weeks. Thus, adultlike adaptation (Weber's Law) did not appear to hold, at least for scotopic stimuli, until 12 weeks of age.

Dannemiller and Banks (in press) presented both scotopic and photopic (cone vision) levels to a much larger number of infants. They also used the FPL procedure. Their results are summarized in Figure 20. They observed the same two developmental trends. First, increment thresholds declined in general with age. Second, increment threshold function slopes increased with age; slopes of 0.56 and 0.79 were observed at 7 and 12 weeks, respectively. Adult slopes in the same apparatus over the same luminance range were 0.88 on the average, a close approximation to Weber's Law.

Hence, the two groups of investigators concur that adultlike changes in visual sensitivity do not occur with changes in background intensity until 3 to 4 months of age.

Dannemiller and Banks (in press) considered several explanations for the postnatal changes in increment threshold function slopes they and Hansen and Fulton observed. First, adaptation mechanisms per se may be immature at birth and improve up to 3 or 4 months. Second, adaptation mechanisms may be mature before 3 to 4 months, but other sensory or nonsensory factors that can affect increment threshold functions may change. The researchers favored the second class of explanations, but more work is needed to confirm this. Nonetheless, the results of these experiments suggest that, for whatever reason, detection thresholds (expressed relative to background intensity) are affected more by changes in background intensity during the perinatal period than afterward. At 1 month, the increment intensity required for detection is a much higher percentage of the background intensity at low light levels than it is at high levels. At 3 to 4 months, on the other hand, increment intensity at threshold is nearly a constant percentage of background intensity across a large range of light levels. Thus, by this age, the visual system appears to capitalize on the invariance of relative intensities in the environment by responding to luminance ratios.

Pattern Preferences

People generally prefer to fixate some patterns over others. Such pattern preferences have been examined extensively in infants but not in adults. Consequently, the pattern preference literature is uniquely developmental.

Until Fantz' refinement of the preference paradigm, very little was known about infants' pattern perception. Thus, the initial empirical question raised was quite basic: Can infants demonstrate any evidence of pattern perception? Fantz (1961, 1963) measured relative preferences in infants from birth to 6 months for six grossly different patterns: a schematic face, a bull's eye, newsprint, and three discs of different colors. Infants of all ages, including newborns, exhibited differential fixation times among most of these patterns. Other early work found differential preferences for yet other stimuli (Fantz, 1965; Fantz & Nevis, 1967). It was clear then that even young infants have at least primitive pattern discrimination capabilities.

Subsequent work turned to more refined questions. For example, (1) What features or properties of patterned stimuli allow infants of different ages to discriminate them? And a closely related question, (2) What features or properties are most preferred at different ages? The pursuit of answers to these questions has produced a massive literature. In spite of all of this work, we believe that the preference literature has not yielded very useful characterizations of the development of pattern perception. For this reason, we have chosen to review only portions of it: two lines of work, both of which began in the early 1960s and continued to the present. We chose these particular lines of inquiry because they have both provided clear empirical findings, generated a number of empirical investigations, and, unfortunately, led to theoretical quandries which we believe characterize the current state of the preference literature as a whole.

The first line of work stems from Fantz and Nevis' (1967) work with the bull's eye and grating, shown in the inset of Figure 21. They measured relative preferences for these patterns as a function of age. The patterns were useful because they were similar in overall size, brightness, contrast, element width, and amount of contour. Figure 21 summarizes the results. Before 1 month of age, the grating was slightly preferred over the bull's eye. By 2 months, a strong preference for the bull's eye emerged that persisted until 6 months, the oldest age tested. These findings demonstrated that even young

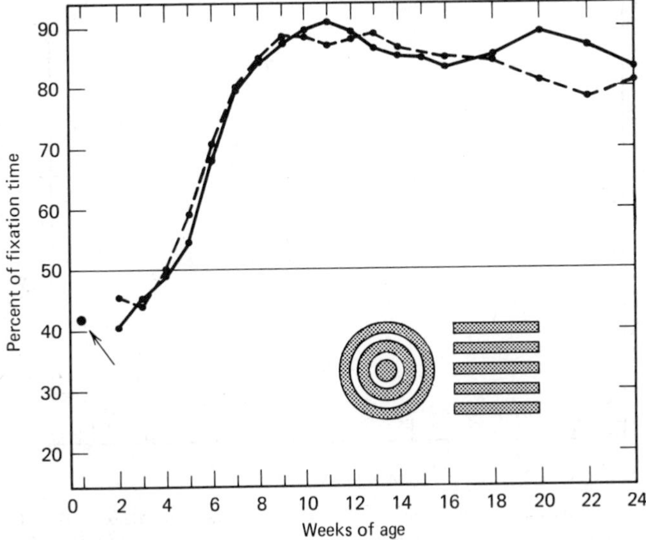

Figure 21. Relative preference for a bull's eye versus a grating at different ages. The inset displays the bull's eye and grating patterns used to collect these data. The abscissa of the graph represents age in weeks, while the ordinate represents the percentage of fixation time on the bull's eye rather than the grating. The solid lines are data from infants reared at home. The broken lines are data from infants reared in an institution. The arrow indicates data from a newborn population. (From Fantz & Nevis, 1967.)

infants can discriminate stimuli on the basis of seemingly subtle differences in pattern configuration.

Fantz and others asked what aspects of these patterns determined the discrimination. They realized that bull's eyes and gratings differ in a number of ways. Bull's eyes are concentric whereas gratings are not. Bull's eyes are composed of connected, curved lines; gratings of disconnected linear lines. Bull's eyes have many different orientations; gratings only one. Accordingly, Fantz and others set out to study the pattern variables that were responsible for the bull's eye versus grating discrimination (Fantz, Fagan, & Miranda, 1975; Fantz & Miranda, 1975; Fantz & Nevis, 1967; Karmel, 1969; Miranda, 1970; Ruff & Birch, 1974; Spears, 1964, 1966).

Fantz et al. (1975) partialled out the concentricity and connectedness dimensions in a series of experiments with 2- to 5-month-old infants. Even though there were wide variations in the types of patterns presented, a preference almost always emerged for the most curvilinear member of a pair. Fantz et al. concluded that infants 2 months of age and older can discriminate curved and straight contours and prefer curved contours. Hence, at least part of the bull's eye over grating preference probably involved curvilinearity. One cannot determine, however, from the Fantz et al. experiments whether curvilinearity is the only critical variable in the bull's eye versus grating preference. Consequently, Ruff and Birch (1974) explored three dimensions—concentricity, number of orientations, and curvilinearity—in 3-month-olds. They used 10 stimuli that allowed independent manipulation of the three dimensions. The results demonstrated fairly convincingly that differential preferences existed for stimuli varying along any of the three dimensions. Curvilinear patterns were preferred over linear when concentricity and number of orientations were equated. Similarly, concentric patterns were preferred over nonconcentric, and multiple orientation patterns were preferred over single orientation when the other dimensions were equated. Ruff and Birch concluded that all three dimensions were involved in 3-month-olds' strong preference for bull's eyes over gratings. Before evaluating the utility of this line of work concerning bull's eyes and gratings, we describe the second line of empirical work, since our evaluation of the bull's eye and grating work applies to the second line as well.

The second line of pattern preference work we review stems from Berlyne's (1958) research, which demonstrated that infants seemed to prefer the more

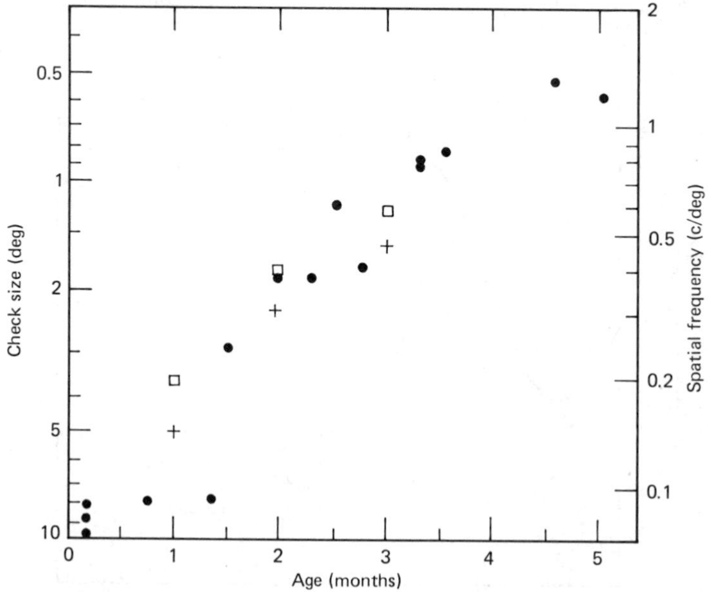

Figure 22. Preferences for checkerboards with different check sizes as a function of age. The most preferred check size is plotted on the left ordinate and the corresponding spatial frequency of the fundamental component on the right ordinate. The filled symbols represent the results of a number of different experiments as analyzed by Karmel and Maisel (1975). The open squares and the crosses represent the predictions of the linear systems model of Banks and Ginsburg; the squares are predictions based on the largest component rule and the crosses predictions based on the square root of sums rule. (From Banks & Ginsburg, 1983.)

complex of two stimuli. A great deal of subsequent research explored the effects of stimulus complexity on infants' preferences and discriminations. Brennan, Ames, and Moore (1966) defined complexity as the number of elements in a checkerboard. They presented infants of various ages checkerboards differing in the number of elements (2 × 2, 8 × 8, 24 × 24). One-month-olds fixated the 2 × 2 checkerboards longer than the other checkerboards. In contrast, 2-month-olds and 3½-month-olds preferred the 8 × 8 and 24 × 24 checkerboards, respectively. Thus, the most preferred number of elements increased with age. Since number of checks and check size were inversely related in these patterns, another way to state this is that the most preferred check size decreased with age. A number of subsequent investigations confirmed this observation. Figure 22 summarizes these findings. Each point represents the most preferred check size as a function of age. Although these points were drawn from different experiments using different procedures, a clear result emerges: The optimal check size decreases monotonically with age. This result has been interpreted as evidence that complexity is an important determinant of infant pattern preferences.

Defining complexity in other ways led to similar findings. Hershenson, Munsinger, and Kessen (1965) used random polygons that differed in number of angles. Neonates showed a reasonably clear preference for those with an intermediate number of angles. Munsinger and Weir (1967) showed that the optimal number of angles in such polygons was greater in older infants.

The checkerboard and polygon studies demonstrated that some variable(s) that is (are) at least correlated with the complexity of the stimulus influenced infants' preference and discrimination capabilities. Several researchers recognized that this did not necessarily imply that infants actually encode complexity per se and respond on the basis of it. Perhaps some other variable(s) related to complexity was (were) mediating the response.

Miranda and Fantz (1971) proposed that the size and number of pattern elements were the primary determinants. To explore this they varied the size and number of pattern elements using the set of stimuli shown in Figure 23. Relative preferences of neonates were measured by presenting all possible pairs of these stimuli. The lower number to the right of each pattern is the average looking time for that pattern. One can see that, when the number of elements was equated (e.g., 2-2 vs. 2-1 in Figure 23), the member with larger elements was preferred. When element size was equated (e.g., 2-1 vs. 8-1), the member with more elements was preferred. Fantz and Fagan (1975) extended these findings in a massive and carefully conducted experiment. The subjects were 5-, 10-, 15-, 20-, and 25-week-old full-term and preterm infants (age here refers to weeks past the due date). In addition, a 1-week group of preterm infants was tested. The stimulus set was expanded to include nine size and number combinations.[3] As Miranda and Fantz (1971) had found in newborns, infants of all ages preferred the member with larger elements among pairs equated for number of elements. Likewise, infants of all ages preferred the member with more elements among pairs equated for element size. There were, in addition, some interesting developmental trends. The size variable was a better predictor of preferences than the number variable at 5 weeks, while the reverse was true at older ages. Fantz and Fagan concluded that age-related changes in checkerboard preferences were better explained by changes in size and number preferences than by developmental changes in optimal complexity.

Karmel (1969) also questioned the usefulness of describing changes in checkerboard preferences according to complexity. He presented two types of checkerboards to 3- and 5-month-olds. For one type, the square pattern elements were arranged regularly to form a conventional checkerboard. For the other, the squares were arranged randomly to form a so-called random checkerboard. Four check sizes were used for each type of checkerboard. Karmel used naive adult complexity ratings as an index of the complexity of each stimulus. The results revealed

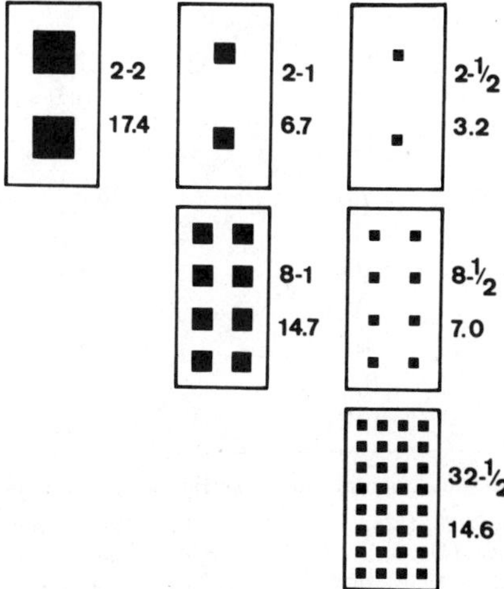

Figure 23. Stimuli used in the size and number experiment of Miranda and Fantz. The numbers to the right of each stimulus represent the number and size of pattern elements and the average fixation times. (From Miranda & Fantz, 1971.)

that looking times were influenced by both check size and checkerboard type. Interestingly, average looking times did not appear to be closely related to complexity; some patterns given similar complexity ratings yielded large differences in looking times and some patterns given dissimilar ratings were just about equally preferred. Karmel argued reasonably convincingly that infants' preferences for regular and random checkerboards were better predicted by contour density. We describe this hypothesis in more detail a bit later.

In our opinion, these two lines of preference research, and several others we have not reviewed, have not yielded very useful characterizations of early pattern perception. There are several reasons for this. To describe them, we again use the bull's eye versus grating line of research as an example.

An unambiguous picture of what determines the preference for bull's eyes over gratings never emerged. One reason was that it proved impossible to manipulate all of the potentially relevant dimensions independently of the others. For example, changing connectedness also changed contour density (Karmel & Maisel, 1975). This, however, is not the most significant problem.

More damaging problems become apparent when one asks: What has this approach told us about the development of pattern perception in general? Everyone who examined a particular preference, in this case bull's eyes versus gratings, seemed to note another, potentially relevant stimulus dimension. Unfortunately, empirical tests revealed that each new dimension affected preference at some age and, therefore, could not be ignored. Where this has led us is summarized in Table 1 (which has been adapted from Banks, in press). This table lists only stimulus dimensions that may distinguish bull's eyes and gratings and have been shown to influence infants' visual preferences. For each dimension, qualitative weightings are given at different ages. Remember that Table 1 was created with only the bull's eye versus grating preference in mind. It would be much longer if more types of stimuli were considered. This table illustrates a number of unsatisfying aspects of the current status of this research. First, the list seems to be expanding endlessly, which raises the possibility that it is part of an infinite regress. Second, without a theory of how the items are related to one another, one cannot use the list to predict preferences for a new stimulus that has not yet been stud-

Table 1. **Dimensions of Bull's Eye vs. Grating Preference as a Function of Age**

Age (months)	Curvilinearity	Concentricity	Number of Orientations	Number of Elements	Point Symmetry
0	0 (M1)		**0** (F1)	+ (M2)	**0** (F1)
	+ (F4)				
	0 (F1)				
1	0 (F1)		**0** (F1)	+ (F2)	**0** (F1)
	0 (G)				
2	+ (F3)	++ (F3)	**0** (F1)	++ (F2)	+ (F1)
	+ (F1)				
3	**+** (R)				
	+ (F1)				
	+ (F3)	**++** (R)	**+** (R)		
	++ (G)	++ (F3)	+ (F1)	++ (F2)	**0** (F1)
4	++ (F3)				
	+ (F1)	++ (F3)	**0** (F1)	++ (F2)	**0** (F1)
5	+ (F3)				
	+ (F1)	++ (F3)	**0** (F1)	++ (F2)	**0** (F1)

Note: **Boldface symbols indicate those experiments in which the indicated dimension was isolated reasonably well.**

R = Ruff & Birch, 1974. **F1 = Fantz & Nevis, 1967.**
M1 = Miranda, 1970. **F2 = Fantz & Fagan, 1975.**
M2 = Miranda & Fantz, 1971. **F3 = Fantz et al., 1975.**
G = Greenberg & O'Donnell, 1972. **F4 = Fantz & Miranda, 1975.**

0 = Preference for indicated dimension between 41% and 59% of total looking time.
+ = Preference for indicated dimension between 60% and 69% of total looking time.
++ = Preference for indicated dimension between 70% and 79% of total looking time.

ied. In other words, it is unclear how general statements can be extracted from what has been learned. Third, the implicit description of development is unsatisfying. Development is represented by changes in the weightings of different, unconnected items in a list. Curvedness, for example, becomes more heavily weighted with age, while concentricity does not. This developmental description is unsatisfying because one cannot use it to gain any feeling for how an infant's pattern perception changes with age. We cannot use the list to answer even simple questions. Do 3-month-olds have a greater pattern discrimination capacity than newborns? One could not tell from the information given.

An additional problem commonly encountered in pattern preference experiments is the interpretation of negative results. Specifically, if an infant does not exhibit a differential preference, can one infer an inability to discriminate? Obviously one cannot because, as McGurk (1970) demonstrated so clearly, infants often exhibit evidence for discrimination in habituation experiments for patterns for which they exhibit no differential preferences. The problem of interpreting negative results is present in all infant paradigms, but experiments like McGurk's suggest that it is more common in preference experiments than others.

We have argued that the conventional uses of the pattern preference paradigm have not produced useful developmental characterizations. Our argument was based on the manner in which stimuli have been characterized and chosen for study. Haith (1980) has criticized the preference paradigm on other grounds. He argued that the paradigm implies an overly restrictive view of the motivation for infants' visual behavior and a misleading view of how infants process stimuli.

Before discussing alternatives to the traditional preference paradigm, we review the current theories of infant preferences because therein lie some potentially useful hints for future directions.

In the remainder of this section we describe and evaluate models of infant pattern preferences. We intentionally avoid discussing pattern discrimination here (recall our definition above) because we believe it is useful to regard it as a separate theoretical problem. We consider four models: complexity, size and number, contour density, and linear systems analysis. We evaluate each model's ability to predict preferences among a wide set of meaningless, two-dimensional, achromatic patterns. Other important variables such as color and depth are considered in other sections. Our approach may be a bit unjustified because at least one of the models (size and number) may not have been intended as a general model. Thus, our evaluations should not be taken to imply that these models are not useful within limited domains.

Complexity

A number of researchers have argued that stimulus complexity is the major determinant of infants' pattern preferences (Berlyne, 1958; Dember & Earl, 1957; Greenberg & O'Donnell, 1972; among others). This hypothesis originates from the view that the infant's information-processing capacity grows with age and, consequently, that different levels of stimulus complexity provide optimal stimulation at different ages. The relationship between stimulus complexity and the optimal level for different infants has been thought of in two ways (Kessen, Haith, & Salapatek, 1970). First, there is a stimulus viewpoint, which claims that patterns with more elements, angles, or contours are more complex. Second, there is a cognitive viewpoint, which claims that complexity is defined by the interaction between the stimulus and the infant's previous experience with it or related stimuli. The stimulus viewpoint has generally been called *complexity theory;* the cognitive viewpoint is called *discrepancy theory*. We do not discuss discrepancy theory further since it falls to some extent outside the domain of this chapter and has been thoughtfully criticized in other places (Thomas, 1971; Welch, 1974).

The complexity model predicts that some level of complexity is most preferred at any given age and, furthermore, that this optimal level increases with age. Although the complexity model has intuitive appeal, it has not fared very well. One critical problem has been that of defining "complexity." Several definitions have been employed, but none has yet been agreed on. Some have used predictability as the index of complexity. This definition has been applied fruitfully in studies using sequentially blinking lights (Cohen, 1969; Haith, Kessen, & Collins, 1969) but has been more difficult to implement with patterns. Consequently, other definitions such as number of elements (Brennan et al., 1966; Greenberg & O'Donnell, 1972; Hershenson, 1964; among others) and number of angles (Hershenson et al., 1965; McCall & Kagan, 1967; Munsinger & Weir, 1967) have been used with patterns. These too have not proven very useful. As mentioned above, number of elements alone is not a good predictor of infant preferences (Fantz & Fagan, 1975; McCall & Melson, 1970; Miranda & Fantz, 1971). Number of angles is also not a good predictor of infant preferences among stimuli with the same number of elements (e.g., Greenberg & O'Donnell, 1972), and several have found no differential preferences among stimuli with different numbers of angles (e.g., Fantz & Nevis, 1967). The problem with definitions based on the number of elements or the number of angles is that they are not rich enough. Specifically, neither alone is sensitive to several pattern dimensions that seem intuitively to affect the complexity of a stimulus. For example, irregularly arranged patterns strike one as more complex than regularly arranged ones, yet definitions based on the number of elements or the number of angles are insensitive to the dimension of irregularity. Consequently, another approach has been to use naive adults' complexity ratings, without regard to the particular dimensions they might be attending to, as the index of stimulus complexity (Karmel, 1969; McCall & Melson, 1970; Thomas, 1965). This definition is appealing in some respects, but not in others. One unappealing feature is that different raters assign somewhat different complexity orderings to the same set of stimuli. This problem aside, adult complexity ratings also do not seem to be good predictors of infant pattern preferences. As mentioned above, both McCall and Melson (1970) and Karmel (1969) observed no differential preferences among stimuli that differed substantially in rated complexity, and Karmel (1969) observed significant differential preferences among stimuli that did not differ in rated complexity. In conclusion, it appears that complexity theory is not a viable general account of infant pattern preferences.

Size and Number

Fantz and Fagan (1975) proposed that the size and number of pattern elements are important determinants of preferences. Their model essentially consists of a post hoc analysis of preferences among the size and number stimuli Fantz and his colleagues have employed (see Figure 23). Recall that both the number of elements and the size of elements influenced looking time in their experiments and that the relative influence of number increased with age. Fantz and Fagan argued that a model that combined the effects of the size and number of pattern elements predicted infant preferences better than either complexity or contour density alone. In fact, size and number alone cannot account for preference behavior very well. Both size and number are insensitive to changes in the shape and arrangement of pattern elements, yet differential preferences are observed at a number of ages for curved over straight lines (Fantz & Nevis, 1967; Ruff & Birch, 1974) and for irregular over regular arrangements (Fantz & Fagan, 1975; Fantz et al., 1975). In addition, Pipp (1978) has reported that size and number were not good predictors of preference among the set of patterns she used. Thus, the size and number model does not appear to be useful as a general account of infant pattern preferences.

Contour Density

Karmel's contour density model has been quite influential in recent years. The model was developed in post hoc fashion from the results of Karmel's (1969) experiment with regular and random checkerboards. He defined contour density as the total length of contour in a stimulus divided by the total area of the stimulus. Karmel (1974) cautioned, however, that one should convert the dimensions of the stimulus into degrees of visual angle before computing contour density. This allows greater generality than linear units such as centimeters because it takes variations in viewing distance into account.

Karmel (1969) used a post hoc polynomial regression analysis to determine hypothetical functions that best described the relationship between contour density and preference at different ages. These functions are illustrated in Figure 24. The thick lines for infants 13 and 20 weeks old were computed from Karmel's data. The thin lines for newborns, 3-week-olds, and 8-week-olds were computed from the data of Hershenson (1964) and Brennan et al. (1966).[4] Note that a close fit was found between Karmel's data (the circles and Xs) and the hypothetical functions. This, of course, is not surprising since these functions were derived from the data. The same holds for the newborn, 3-week, and 8-week functions fit to the Hershenson and Brennan et al. data. Karmel and his colleagues realized this, so they examined how well their hypothetical functions predicted preferences for different sorts of patterns (Karmel, 1974; Maisel & Karmel, 1978). We describe these experiments in some detail in the next part of this section, but suffice it to say here that the contour density model generally predicted those preferences quite well.

There is some evidence, though, that contour density does not predict preferences well for some sets of stimuli. The contour density metric is insensitive to some dimensions of pattern that are known to affect infant visual behavior. For instance, the arrangement of unconnected pattern elements has no effect on contour density, yet infants often prefer the more irregular of two arrangements (Fantz & Fagan, 1975; Fantz et al., 1975; Fantz & Nevis, 1967). Contour density is also unaffected by at least two other variables known to influence infant visual be-

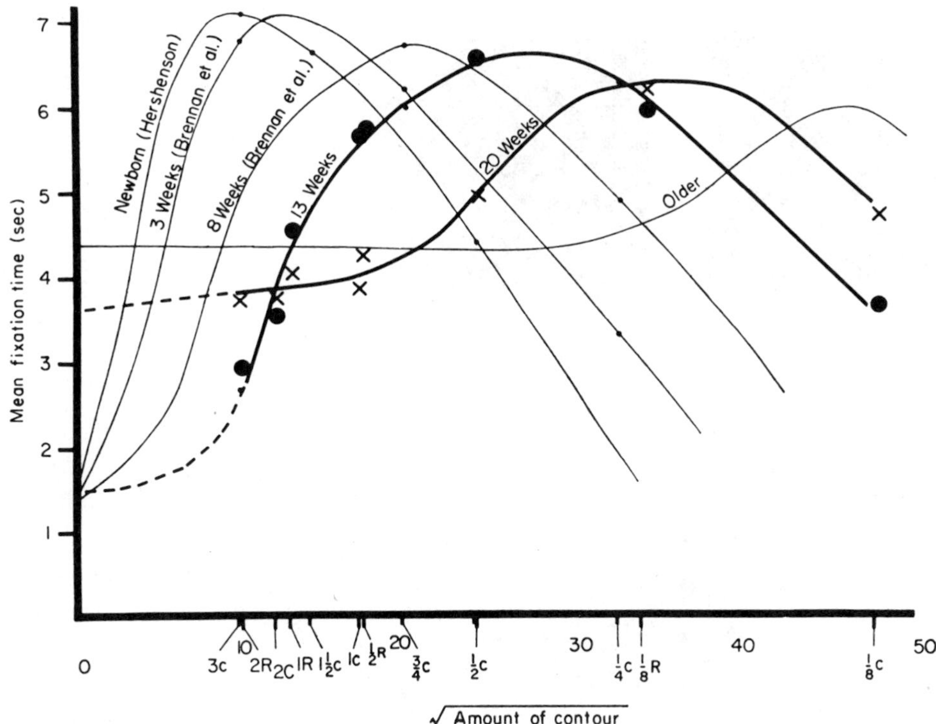

Figure 24. Hypothetical preference functions based on Karmel's contour density model. The abscissa represents contour density, while the ordinate represents predicted fixation times. The heavy solid curves were derived from Karmel's (1969) data for 13- and 20-week-olds. The light solid curves were derived from Hershenson's (1964) data for newborns and from Brennan et al. (1966) for 3- and 8-week-olds. The filled circles and crosses are Karmel's data for 13- and 20-week-olds, respectively. (From Karmel, 1969.)

havior: contrast (Banks & Salapatek, 1981) and overall size (Cohen, 1972).[5] As we point out below, however, the contour density model seems to provide reasonably good predictions for a number of pattern types.

Linear Systems Analysis

Recently, Banks and Salapatek (1981), Banks and Ginsburg (in press), and Gayl et al. (1983) have proposed preference models based on linear systems analysis and the contrast sensitivity function (CSF). The use of linear systems analysis and the CSF in visual science, in general, and infant research, in particular, was described earlier. In very simple terms, the approach allows one, in principle, to characterize a system's input-output relationships for an endless variety of stimuli.

A simple example of how the approach works is provided in Figure 25. Row 1 of the figure displays a 6 × 6 and a 16 × 16 checkerboard of equal overall size. Row 2 depicts the sine wave grating components of which these two patterns are composed. Each of these graphs shows the so-called amplitude spectrum of the patterns. Each dot represents a sine wave component. The component's spatial frequency is represented by the distance between the dot and the origin of the graph. The orientation of each component is depicted by the angle between the horizontal axis and the dot. Contrast, or amplitude, is represented by the area of the dot. Phase is not represented in this particular figure, but is nonetheless an important variable in linear systems analysis. Notice that the two amplitude spectra are identical except that the components of the 16 × 16 checkerboard are five times greater in spatial frequency than those of the 6 × 6 checkerboard. The step taken between rows 2 and 3 mimics what happens when a pattern is processed by a "visual system" with a low-frequency CSF. Row 3 shows the so-called output amplitude spectrum that results when the spectra of row 2 are filtered by a CSF, which passes information below 2 c/deg but blocks information above that spatial frequency. Notice that the higher frequency components of both patterns have been lost in the filtering

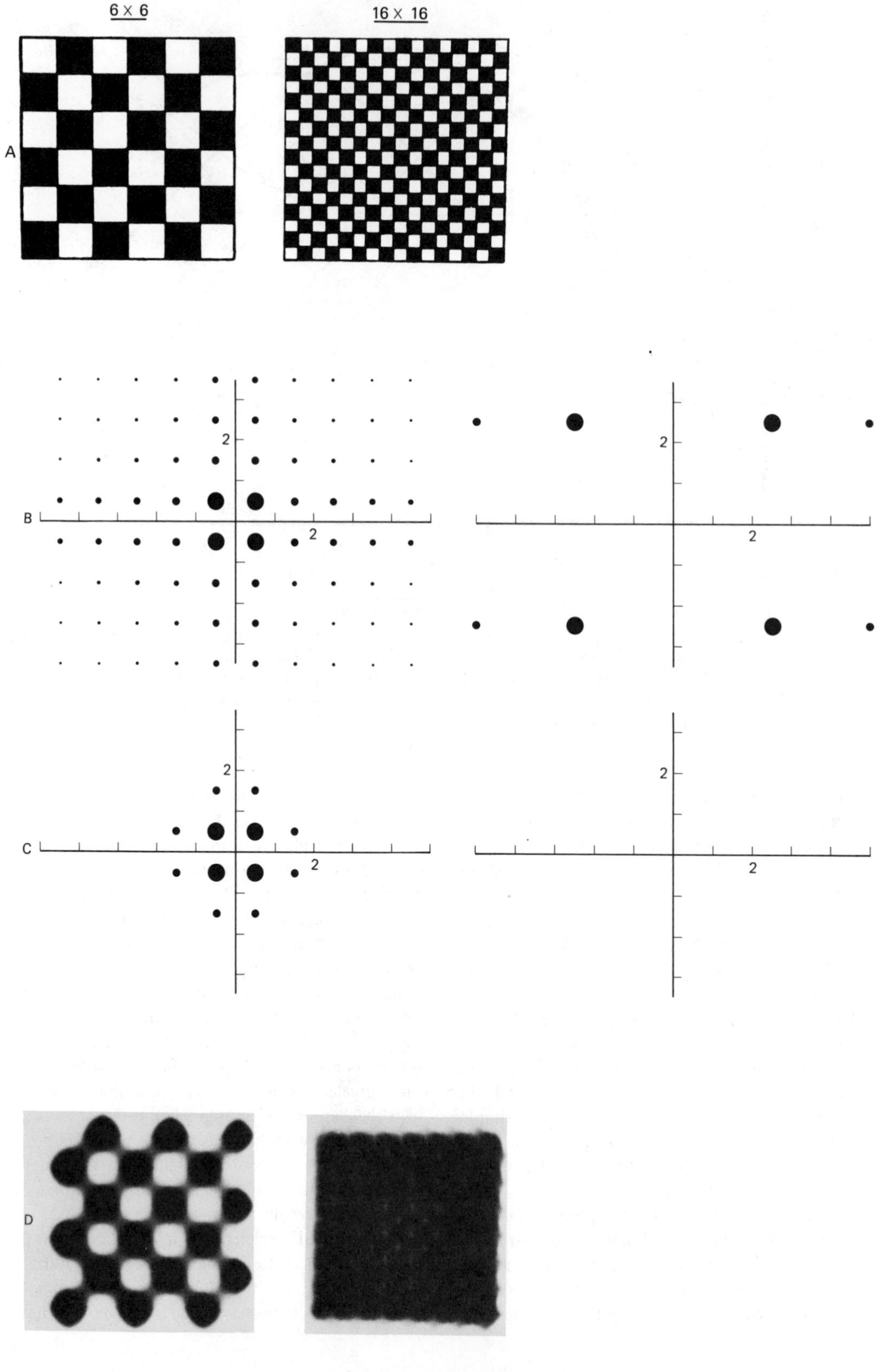

6 × 6 16 × 16

A

B

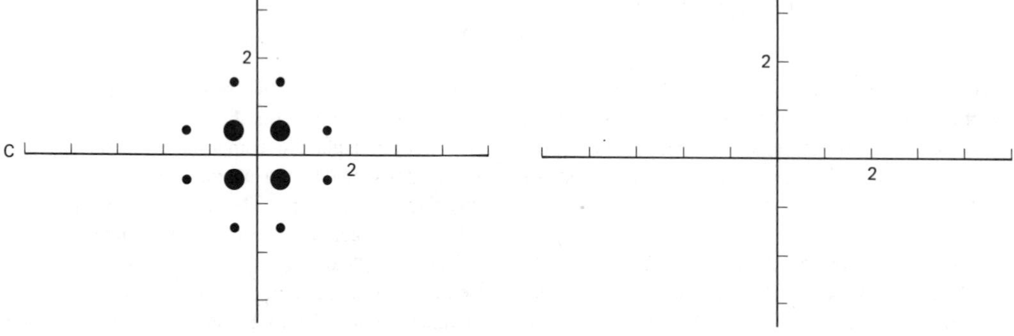

D

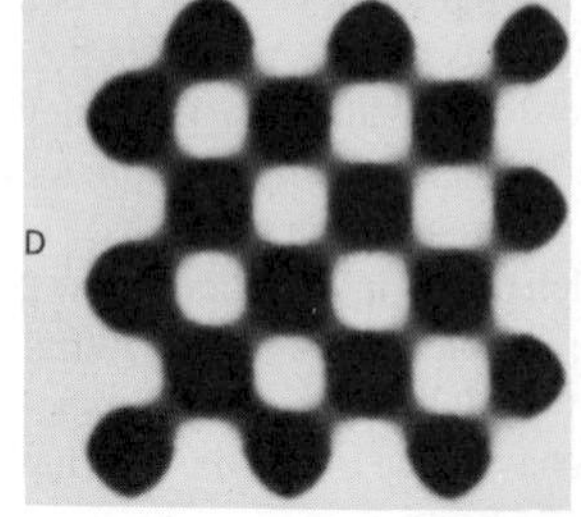

Figure 25. An example of the application of linear systems analysis. The left column depicts the technique for a 6 × 6 checkerboard. The right column depicts the technique for a 16 × 16 checkerboard. The rows depict in sequence, from top to bottom, how linear systems analysis can be used to predict the outputs for the two checkerboards when processed by a visual system similar to the infant's. (A) The 6 × 6 and 16 × 16 checkerboards. (B) The so-called amplitude spectra of the two checkerboards. These spectra show the spatial frequency, orientation, and amplitude of the checkerboards' sine wave components. Each dot represents one component. Spatial frequency is represented by the distance of the dot from the origin. Orientation is represented by the angle of a vector running from the origin to the dot. Contrast or amplitude is represented by the area of the dot. (C) The amplitude spectra of the two checkerboards, once filtered by a visual system sensitive to frequencies between 0 and 2 c/deg only. (D) The resultant appearance of the checkerboards themselves. Note that the patterning of the 16 × 16 checkerboard is lost but that of the 6 × 6 remains.

process. Finally, row 4 illustrates the checkerboards themselves after filtering by the low-frequency CSF. These patterns are simply the result of adding together all of the sine wave components shown in the output amplitude spectra.

This example illustrates roughly how linear systems analysis can be used to determine how well various patterns are passed through the visual system. Of course, the CSF used was much simpler than the CSFs of real visual systems, but the principles involved are the same.[6]

The linear systems analysis model assumes that infant pattern preferences are governed by the pattern information available to decision centers in the central nervous system. There are three facets of this assumption. First, the pattern information available to central decision centers is only a small fraction of the information impinging on the infant's eye; considerable information is lost in processing by the ocular media, retina, and visual pathways. This process of information loss can be thought of as filtering. Second, the model assumes that the CSF is a reasonably good description of the filtering characteristics of the infant's visual system. Third, the model assumes that infants tend to direct their visual attention (i.e., orient to or hold fixation on or near) toward the most "salient" pattern, once filtered by the CSF. "Salience" has been defined in different ways in these three papers, but the two definitions proposed by Banks and Ginsburg make some physiological and psychophysical sense and are reasonably easy to implement. These are the "largest component rule" and the "square root of sums rule." The interested reader should consult Banks and Ginsburg (in press) for a detailed description of these rules. Both rules can be used to compute a predicted preference value for any two-dimensional, time-invariant pattern.

Banks and Ginsburg tested the linear systems analysis model by reanalyzing several pattern preference experiments in the literature. Their approach was simply to compute predicted preference values for a variety of patterns that had been presented to 1- to 3-month-old infants and then to compare these predictions with observed preferences. The first pattern they considered was the checkerboard. Recall from our earlier discussion that the most preferred check size decreases with age. Figure 22 illustrates this relationship as revealed by a number of different experiments. Banks and Ginsburg used the average CSFs of 1-, 2-, and 3-month-olds, as reported by Banks and Salapatek (1981), to compute predictions of the most preferred check size at each of these ages. In Figure 22, the open squares represent the predictions of the largest component rule, and the crosses the predictions of the square root of sums rule. The agreement between the data and the predictions of both rules is quite good.

Banks and Ginsburg also reanalyzed the size and number experiment of Fantz and Fagan (1975). They used Banks and Salapatek's average CSFs for 1-month-olds and 3-month-olds to predict Fantz and Fagan's 5-week and 10-week data. The correlation between the predictions of the square root of sums rule and Fantz and Fagan's average looking times was .92 and .95 for 5-week-olds and 10-week-olds, respectively. The correlations were lower for the largest component rule. Banks and Ginsburg also computed contour density predictions based on Karmel's (1969) hypothetical functions. The correlations between predicted and observed looking times were .69 and .98 for 5-week-olds and 10-week-olds, respectively.

These applications of the linear systems model both involved linear, nonconcentric patterns, so Banks and Ginsburg next examined the model's ability to predict preferences for different sorts of patterns. They used Maisel and Karmel's (1978) data on preferences of 5- and 9-week-olds for bull's eyes varying in the size and number of concentric rings, concentric squares varying in the size and number of squares, and checkerboards varying in check size and number. (They did not analyze the fourth pattern Maisel and Karmel used for technical reasons.) They used the 1- and 2-month CSFs of Banks and Salapatek for the 5-week-olds and 9-week-olds, respectively. The linear systems predictions were again quite good. The correlation between the observed and predicted most preferred stimulus among each of the three pattern types was .96. Banks and Ginsburg also computed contour density predictions based on Karmel's hypothetical functions. The observed-predicted correlation in this case was .80.

Gayl et al. used an approach very similar to Banks and Salapatek's (1981) and Banks and Ginsburg's (in press) to reanalyze Karmel's (1969) experiment with regular and random checkerboards. They used the 3-month CSF of Banks and Salapatek to compute predictions for Karmel's 13-week-olds. Gayl et al. found that a rule, similar to Banks and Ginsburg's square root of sums rule, predicted looking times for Karmel's stimuli very well (r = .91). Unfortunately, their particular rule, unlike Banks and Ginsburg's, had a free parameter that they allowed to vary in order to maximize prediction accuracy. Thus, the high correlation between observed and predicted preferences was possibly artifactual. Gayl et al. noted that the contour density model also predicted these data quite well (r = .90), but this too is not very compelling because Karmel's hypothetical functions were derived in post hoc fashion from this set of data.

In summary, the linear systems analysis model has been very successful to date in predicting the preferences of 1- to 3-month-olds for various sorts of patterns. The contour density model of Karmel (1969) also predicted 1- to 3-month-old preferences for the same set of patterns, although not quite as accurately as the linear systems model. Thus, it appears that both models are reasonably useful accounts of early pattern preferences. This implies, in turn, that there is considerable overlap between the linear systems and contour density models, a point that was anticipated by Karmel and Maisel (1975). Banks and Ginsburg (in press) agree to a limited extent with this assessment, but point out that the linear systems model is sensitive to many of the pattern manipulations that the contour density model is not sensitive to. For example, the shape and arrangement of pattern elements influence a pattern's amplitude spectrum and, thus, the predictions of the linear systems model. These same variables often do not affect a pattern's contour density (e.g., the curved vs. linear lines of Fantz & Nevis, 1967, and the regular vs. irregular arrays of Fantz & Fagan, 1975) and consequently, cannot influence contour density predictions.

Overall Evaluation

Of the four preference models we considered, the linear systems model seems to be the most successful account of early preferences for a reasonably broad set of patterns. The contour density model has also been reasonably successful but is not rich enough to account for how preferences change with element shape and arrangement.

As mentioned earlier, two general classes of preference models have been proposed in the developmental literature: (1) models based on the infant's perceptual/cognitive state and (2) models based on the stimulus. For the purposes of evaluating preference models, we refer to the former as neural substrate models. The neural substrate models proposed that young infants' preferences are governed by the responses of neurons in the central visual system (Haith, 1980; Karmel & Maisel, 1975). Patterns that match the size and shape of these neurons' receptive fields evoke greater activity and thereby attract or hold fixation. Finer patterns become more preferred with age because the receptive fields of such neurons become smaller. We have not considered these models in detail in this section because they cannot be tested experimentally in their present form. To test them, one would need some independent assessment of receptive field size as a function of age. This, of course, is currently impossible with human infants, but physiological data from closely related species might eventually help.

The linear systems model might share important features with these neural substrate models. It holds, just as the neural models do, that the most preferred pattern is the one that best fits the infants' visual "window." The linear systems view uses the CSF as the description of this window. The neural substrate models use the size and shape of hypothetical receptive fields. Presumably, the size and shape of the CSF are dependent on receptive field size and shape at, as yet unspecified, locations in the visual system. Thus, the CSF "window" could conceivably be a manifestation of the visual cortical receptive fields proposed by Haith (1980) and Karmel and Maisel (1975).

The success of the linear systems model to predict infant pattern preferences leads to an intriguing question: Why should infants' visual behavior obey such a simple rule as proposed by the linear systems model? In other words: Why should infants look at the pattern whose filtered output is greatest? Banks and Ginsburg (in press) considered this question in some detail. They noted, much as Haith (1980) has, that exposure to pattern information aids the postnatal development of the visual cortex and perhaps other visual centers in the central nervous system. Blakemore (1976), for example, has shown that exposure to patterned stimuli, not just light, is required to maintain or facilitate normal development of the cat visual cortex. Banks and Ginsburg (in press) and Haith (1980) speculated that human infants' looking behavior may reflect a fixation strategy that tends to expose the central retina to salient patterns in order to provide the stimulation required for cortical development to proceed optimally.

It is also interesting to note, as Banks and Salapatek (1981) have, that the linear systems and contour density models, as they stand, are insensitive to the "significance" or "meaning" of a stimulus. These models were originally developed as accounts for preferences among abstract, nonrepresentational patterns, but consider their potential application with more meaningful stimuli. Both models would not predict a strong preference for a facelike over a similar, but nonfacelike, pattern except to the degree that the facelike pattern provided spatial frequency or contour information that fit the infant's filter better. This is an intriguing and potentially testable hypothesis. It is not clear to us at this time whether additional processes beyond these sensory-based models must be postulated before 3 months of age. After that age, it is probable as Banks and Salapatek (1981) have noted, that neither the linear systems nor contour density view can account adequately for preference behavior in general. Preference models in older infants would assuredly have to incorporate more sophisticated attention mechanisms and long-term memory to account for results like the differential preference between familiar and strange faces (Barrera & Maurer, 1981). This is not to say, though, that the linear systems model should not be part of such an account; even with older infants, the filtering of pattern information, as captured by the CSF, would be a useful component.

Summary

Even neonates exhibit differential preferences among stimuli differing in pattern. These preferences change with age. We can conclude then that some pattern discrimination capacity exists at birth and that it changes with age. Not much more than that can be concluded from the pattern preference literature, however, because no general guidelines for stimulus characterization have been used. Thus, we cannot generalize the current set of findings to as yet unstudied patterns. Moreover, one cannot glean from the preference literature any general characterization from which one could determine whether pattern discrimination capabilities improve with age and, if so, how they improve. Some new models of infant pattern preferences—the contour density model and, particularly, the linear systems analysis model—have proven to be successful predictors of preferences from birth to 3 months of age. These offer the possibility of synthesizing much of the existing literature and generalizing current findings to as yet unstudied stimuli. But neither of these models offers a theory of pattern discrimination per se, nor do they seem applicable, in isolation, to preference behavior in older infants.

Visual Scanning

While one looks at a complex visual scene, saccadic eye movements continually move the fovea from one feature in the scene to another. Research on infants, children, and adults has shown that some features are much more likely to be fixated than others (e.g., Salapatek & Kessen, 1966; Yarbus, 1967). Hence eye movements provide the researcher readily observable behavior that is, presumably, linked in some way to the processing of pattern information.

The visual scanning paradigm as employed in infant work grew out of interest in the relationship between eye movements and perceptual learning. Currently, it is a common research tool. It involves measurement of infants' fixations relative to pattern elements presented in the visual field. Fixation is generally measured using corneal photography, a technique that estimates eye position from the locations of reflections off the cornea relative to the pupil (see Maurer, 1975, for details). The visual scanning paradigm differs from the traditional visual preference paradigm in the precision of the response measure. In preference experiments, the loci of fixations are generally divided into three gross categories: left stimulus, right stimulus, and off target. In scanning experiments, much greater precision is possible. Furthermore, *how* the infant looks as well as *where* he or she looks can be assessed to some extent. For these reasons, Haith (1980) has argued that the scanning paradigm offers considerable advantages over the preference paradigm.

In our opinion, the advantage one of these two paradigms might have over the other depends on the experimental question being asked and on the relationship between visual scanning and visual processing. First, consider the issue of the experimental question being asked. For example, consider two patterns such as a face and a field of vertical stripes. If one simply wanted to know if those two patterns could be discriminated on any basis, the preference paradigm would be as useful as the scanning paradigm and much easier to implement. If, on the other hand, one wanted to know which particular feature of the two patterns allowed infants to discriminate them, the scanning paradigm would be more appropriate; if fixations clustered around one element on the face and were distributed evenly across the striped field, one might argue that discrimination was based primarily on a single feature on the face compared to multiple features in the striped field.

Now consider the issue of the relationship between visual scanning and visual processing. The form of this relationship has a significant bearing on the value of the scanning paradigm. Three possible relationships exist. (1) Scanning may play an essential role in the process of learning about objects in the environment and, furthermore, may be crucial to the subsequent recognition and identification of such objects. (2) Scanning may play an important, but nonessential, role in the process of learning and subsequent recognition and identification. (3) Scanning may not be important to these processes at all.

Several pieces of evidence make the first and third possible relationships unlikely. The champions of the first view proposed that motor involvement is crucial to perceptual learning. For example, Hebb (1949) and Zaporozhets and Zinchenko (1966) proposed that motor excitations are the basis for defining the shape of patterns. Indeed, Hebb maintained that infants initially generate sensorimotor representations of patterns with sequential scanning routines. It has been shown, however, that infant monkeys do not require eye movements to learn simple patterns and to recognize them subsequently (Ganz & Wilson, 1967). Given the well-documented similarities between the visual systems of adult monkeys and humans (e.g., DeValois et al., 1974) and recently reported similarities between their visual systems early in life (e.g., Boothe et al., 1980), it seems likely that eye movements are not required for the human infant's learning of simple patterns either. This, however, has not yet been tested directly.

Another observation that argues against the first possible relationship concerns the relationship between scanpaths and visual processing in adults. Despite claims to the contrary (e.g., Noton & Stark, 1971), there does not appear to be a close relationship between scanpaths and processing in adults. Adults exhibiting quite different scanpaths may extract the same information from a stimulus (Nodine, Carmody, & Kundel, 1978), or they may extract different information while exhibiting very similar scanpaths (Tversky, 1974). These findings do not imply, of course, that scanpaths are not closely linked to processing in infants. They should, however, serve as a reminder that such a linkage should not be assumed without an empirical demonstration of it.

Yet another argument against the first relationship is the fact that the point of fixation, in adults anyway, is not the only important locus of processing. The peripheral visual field provides considerable information that aids the reading process (Rayner, 1978), identification of patterns (Day, 1957), and other skills.

Some evidence argues against the third possible relationship (that scanning is not important to visual processing). It is reasonable to assume, in adults anyway, that the point of fixation corresponds to the region in which the most detailed processing can occur (e.g., Hochberg, 1970; Rayner, 1978) since the fovea has much higher acuity and a much greater cortical representation than the periphery. A similar line of reasoning supports this assumption in infants. However, recall that the young infant's fovea is less specialized than the adult's (see our discussion above on *The Retina*). Thus, one might expect a linkage between fixation and pattern processing in infants, but it is probably somewhat looser than it is in adults.

These considerations imply, but do not prove, that the second of the above relationships (that scanning is important, but not essential, to infants' visual processing) is the most plausible. Thus, research should turn to questions about the precise functions that eye movements actually serve in visual perception. Unfortunately, with few exceptions, infant scanning experiments have not dealt with effects on visual processing. Instead, most experiments have simply described how various stimulus variables affect eye movements.

Before describing the empirical work on infant scanning, a few words on methodology are appropriate. Scanning experiments generate astronomical amounts of data that must be reduced for ease of interpretation. Quite different approaches to this task have been used. Some involve few statistical computations, whereas others rely heavily on them. Some present individual subject data, whereas others present only group data. At one extreme, Salapatek and his colleagues generally have simply plotted, separately for each subject, fixation points relative to the pattern presented (Salapatek, 1975; Salapatek & Kessen, 1966, 1973). At the other extreme, Haith (1980) has presented mean positions, standard deviations, and other statistical indices for group data. There is no clear advantage of either of these techniques, but they are different enough to make comparisons between studies very difficult indeed. Some instances of this will be discussed later on.

Given the uncertain relationship between scanning and visual processing, few strong conclusions about visual perception can be drawn from the infant scanning literature. Consequently, we have adopted the neutral strategy of ordering our review simply on the basis of stimulus complexity. Stimulus complexity has varied from very simple stimuli such as uniform dark or bright fields to quite complex patterns such as faces.

Haith (1980) presented the simplest stimuli possible—unpatterned dark and bright fields—to newborns. He found that eye movements were more "controlled" for the dark field than for the bright; that is, there were fewer large movements and fewer "nystagmus-like" movements. Salapatek and Kessen (1966) also found that newborns scanned bright uniform fields broadly under binocular conditions. With monocular viewing, only the side of the field in front of the uncovered eye was scanned (Salapatek, 1968). Salapatek (1975) reported that older infants did not scan uniform fields for more than a few seconds. Instead, they fussed and looked off to the side.

The next question to consider is: What happens when a pattern is introduced? Kessen, Salapatek, and Haith (1972) presented newborns very simple patterns: either a vertical or horizontal contour. The vertical contour was offset to either the left or right of midline. The horizontal contour was offset up or down. Kessen et al. observed many more fixations near the contour when the vertical contours were presented than in the same regions when a uniform control field was presented. Surprisingly, they did not observe a significant increase in fixations near the contour when the horizontal contours were presented relative to the uniform control fields. In the case of the horizontal contour in the down position, the failure to demonstrate an increase in fixations may have been the result of a ceiling effect. Specifically, a large proportion of fixations occurred near the region of the horizontal-down contour when the uniform control field was present. Thus, it may have been difficult to increase fixations in that region by the introduction of any pattern.

Haith (1980) replicated these findings to some extent. He presented a vertical or horizontal contour to newborns. The vertical contour was offset horizontally and the horizontal contour vertically so that each lay at the mean fixation position during the unpatterned control trials. By placing the two contours in these positions, Haith hoped to ensure that differential looking to one contour relative to the other could not be explained by an endogenous bias to fixate one position over the other. He observed a significant increase in looking in the contour region for both the vertical and horizontal contours relative to the control stimuli. However, the increase was greater for the vertical contour. Haith also found that eye movements tended to cross the vertical contours rather than follow along them.

In summary, both Kessen et al. (1972) and Haith (1980) found a significant increase in fixations near the region of a contour when a vertical contour was introduced. Neither found as large an increase when a horizontal contour was presented, although this trend was small in Haith's study.

Three explanations for this vertical-horizontal asymmetry have been offered. The first explanation proposes that the newborn's visual acuity is higher for vertical than for horizontal contours, so a vertical edge is simply more visible. Since there are no data on newborn acuity thresholds as a function of stimulus orientation, it is somewhat difficult to evaluate this hypothesis. There are data on very young infants (ages 1 to 6 months), however, that reveal no differences in acuity between vertical and horizontal gratings (Gwiazda et al., 1978; Teller et al., 1974; but also see Leehey, Moskowitz-Cook, Brill, & Held, 1975). The second hypothesis proposes that the vertical eye movements needed to foveate a horizontal contour are more difficult to program and execute than the horizontal movements needed for a vertical contour. Haith (1980) pointed out that the motor actions for executing horizontal movements are in fact much simpler than those for vertical movements. A vertical movement involves the coordinated action of all six extraocular muscles. In contrast, horizontal movements involve only two extraocular muscles. Aslin and Salapatek's (1975) data on saccadic eye movements are consistent with this hypothesis. They found that 1- and 2-month-olds were more likely to make a saccadic eye movement toward a circular target that appeared left or right of the fixation point than they were to make a saccadic eye movement toward a target appearing above or below the fixation point. A third possibility is that newborns simply prefer vertical contours (perhaps because it is easier to program and execute eye movements to them). This explanation seems to be ruled out by Slater and Sykes' (1977) observation that horizontal gratings are preferred to vertical. This observation means that verticality per se is not preferred.

The next logical question to consider is: What happens when more complex patterns are presented? Salapatek and Kessen (1966) investigated this question in newborns. They presented three conditions, each for 100 sec: the standard uniform field control, an upright black equilateral triangle, and an inverted black equilateral triangle. The individual subject data for the control condition are illustrated in the left half of Figure 26. The triangle shown in each plot represents the positions of the marker lights; that is, the light positions have been connected by lines. The newborns, of course, did not see these lines. The figure shows that fixations generally did not cluster near the marker lights. The results for the triangle conditions are illustrated in the right half of Figure 26. The outer triangles represent the boundaries of the solid triangles that were presented to the newborns. Clearly, fixations were more likely to occur in the regions around the triangle vertices in these conditions than in the control conditions. Indeed, many subjects fixated a single vertex throughout a 100-sec stimulus presentation. This observation is consistent with earlier reports that very young infants are "captured" by limited parts of the stimulus field (Ames & Silfen, 1965). The single-feature scanning and stimulus "capture" observations are interesting because they imply that neonates only process a few parts, at most, of an extended figure. Why angles seem to be favored over linear contours is not yet clear, but Haith (1980) has pointed out that local contour density is greater for acute angles than for linear contours.

A more recent experiment suggests that Salapatek and Kessen (1966) may have somewhat overestimated the prevalence of single-feature scanning in newborns. Salapatek and Kessen (1973) examined the effects of repeated presentations of the triangles they used in their earlier experiment. They wanted to know if prolonged exposure to a triangle would increase scanning extensiveness. Most of the neonates did not scan the triangles for more than a few minutes, so only five subjects yielded sufficient data. Nonetheless, single-feature scanning and extensive scanning were observed both within and between subjects; single-feature scanning appeared to be more common but, given the small sample size, this could not be stated categorically. There were no obvious indications that one form of scanning preceded another.

Hainline and Lemerise (1982) have hypothesized that newborns' scanning extensiveness depends on stimulus size. Specifically, they suggested that more extensive scanning might be obtained with smaller stimuli. Salapatek (1966, 1968) explored this. Salapatek presented large, medium, and small circles and triangles. Before discussing his results, however, it is necessary to define *scanning extensiveness* more clearly. Two quite different implicit definitions have been used in the scanning literature. One, which is that intended by Salapatek and his colleagues, concerns the distribution of fixations relative to the stimulus pattern. An extensive scan by this definition is one that carries the fixation point to a number of different regions on the pattern. We refer to this definition as *relative* extensiveness. The other definition, which is implied in some of the analyses conducted by Hainline and Lemerise, concerns the absolute distribution of fixations without regard to their location relative to the stimulus figure. We refer to this definition as *absolute* extensiveness. Salapatek (1966, 1968) analyzed his data in terms of relative extensiveness to the degree that was possible and also in terms of absolute extensiveness. He found no significant difference in relative scanning extensiveness between the large and medium figures. Relative extensiveness was greater for the small figures, but this may not be a meaningful effect; the measurement errors inherent in infant scanning studies have much larger effects on the computation of relative extensiveness for small figures than for large figures (because such errors are largely constant errors). The contribution of such errors would, of course, inflate relative extensiveness scores. Thus, Salapatek's (1966, 1968) results are consistent with the hypothesis that the relative extensiveness of scanning is not influenced by stimulus size, at least for stimuli large enough to allow reasonably accurate computations of relative extensiveness. Salapatek also found that absolute extensiveness decreased for small figures.

Haith (1980) also investigated newborns' scanning of multiple contour stimuli. In one study he presented four versions of an outline right angle differing only in orientation, two versions to each subject. He also presented a bright unpatterned control field. To analyze the scanning data, he divided each right angle into three square subregions of equal size. One square was centered at the vertex of the angle and the others on the vertical and horizontal arms. The results demonstrated convincingly that introduction of the angle increased the number of fixations in the three square subregions. Haith concluded, however, that the subregion centered on the angle vertex was not any more attractive than the subregions centered on the arms. Close inspection of his data reveals that a ceiling effect around the center subregion may have operated against showing a large experimental effect for that subregion. Specifically, 69% of the fixations that fell on any of the three subregions during the control condition fell on the center subregion. Consequently, even though the number of fixations on the center subregion increased noticeably with the introduction of the right angle, the proportion of fixations falling on the center decreased. Thus, a ceiling effect may have

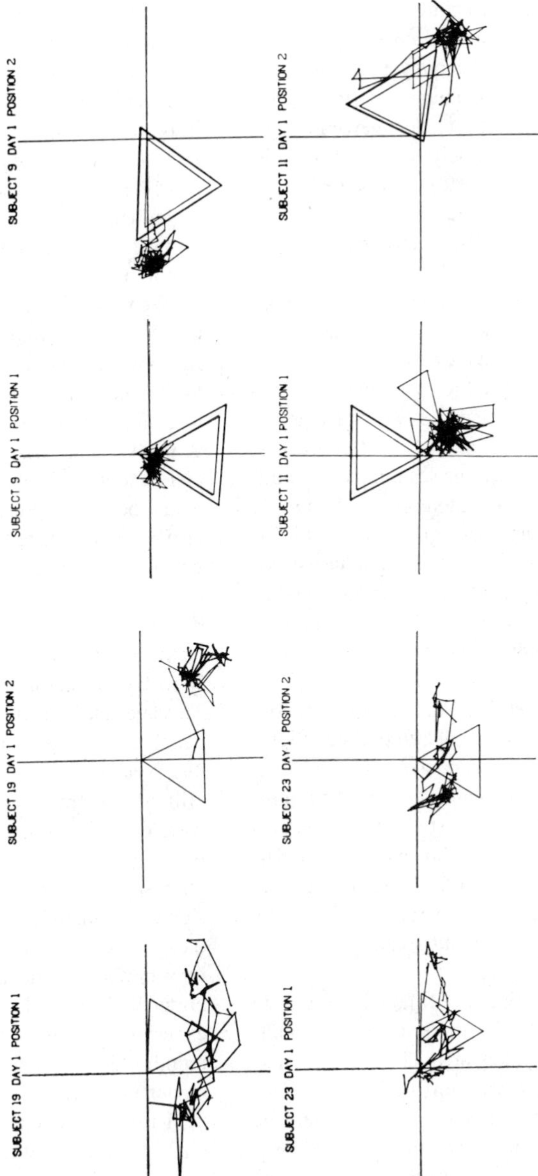

Figure 26. Scanning patterns of newborns. The left portion shows scanning patterns when newborns were presented a homogeneous field. Each dot represents eye position at one time sample. The lines connecting the dots simply connect eye positions at adjacent time samples. The vertices of the triangles represent infrared marker light positions. Thus, the triangles shown were actually not present during these trials. The right portion of this figure shows scanning patterns when newborns were presented a solid black triangle on an otherwise homogeneous field. The outer triangle on each record represents the triangle's contours. The vertices of the inner triangles represent the marker light positions. (From Salapatek & Kessen, 1966.)

caused this unusual result. This issue could be resolved by conducting a study similar to Haith's but with the position of the right angle varied.

Let us summarize the newborn scanning work briefly before considering older infants. Clearly, newborns can and do fixate contours introduced into the visual field. Some contours appear to be more attractive than others, but it is not yet clear what the cause of this is. The first scanning experiment (Salapatek & Kessen, 1966) reported that newborn scanning was not extensive; namely, the large majority of newborns appeared to fixate only one feature for long periods of time. Subsequent experiments revealed the occurrence of some extensive scanning in newborns.

One obvious question is whether older infants exhibit more extensive scanning than newborns. One might expect this to be the case since adult scan patterns are considerably more extensive than newborn patterns (Noton & Stark, 1971; Salapatek & Kessen, 1966). Salapatek and Miller (reported by Salapatek, 1975) examined the scanning of five different figures by 1- and 2-month-olds. Figure 27 illustrates the scanning plots for typical subjects. They have been adjusted by the optic axis/visual axis correction factor suggested by Slater and Findlay (1972). Figure 27 illustrates that 2-month-olds scanned the figures more extensively than 1-month-olds.

Leahy (1976) investigated the scanning of four types of figures—an open angle, an outline ellipse, an outline ellipse with a gap, and an outline triangle—in infants 1 and 3 months of age. The figures were presented in pairs, so this study shared features of both the scanning and two-choice preference paradigms. Although his method of evaluating scan breadth differed somewhat from Salapatek's, Leahy also concluded that older infants scan more extensively than 1-month-olds.

Hainline and Lemerise (1982) failed to replicate this result. They measured the scanning of small, medium, and large squares in 1-, 2-, and 3-month-olds. The discrepancy between their observations and Salapatek's and Leahy's may, however, be more apparent than real. For a number of reasons, Hainline and Lemerise were unable to assess the relative extensiveness of scanning.[7]

Thus, most experiments have found an increase in scanning breadth with age. This finding is consistent with the notion that development involves a change from processing only parts of stimuli to processing stimuli as wholes (Hebb, 1949; Jeffrey, 1968). The mechanism for this age-related change is not yet clear, but Jeffrey's serial habituation hypothesis provides a feasible explanation. His account of scanning holds that an infant fixates a particular feature until that feature becomes familiar. At that point, the infant shifts his or her fixation to a less familiar feature. If one adds the assumption that familiarization occurs more rapidly in older infants, one would predict shorter fixation durations (and hence more fixations per unit time) in older than in younger infants. Leahy (1976) tested this hypothesis in 1- and 3-month-olds. He found that the number of fixations of the most preferred feature decreased from the first to the second half of a stimulus presentation. However, the number of fixations of less preferred features also dropped, so the serial habituation hypothesis was not supported.

We now turn from the scanning of simple figures to that of compound figures. Salapatek and Moscovich (reported by Salapatek, 1975) presented the simple and compound stimuli shown in Figure 28 to 1- and 2-month-olds. The fixations of individual subjects are superimposed on the stimuli. Both 1- and 2-month-olds fixated the small square or squares when they were presented alone. Both age groups also generally fixated the contour of the large square when it was presented alone. The most interesting result, however, involves the compound stimuli. One-month-olds typically did not fixate the internal elements. In contrast, 2-month-olds were more likely to fixate internal rather than external elements. This age-related shift in the tendency to fixate internal elements might underlie the developmental shift observed by Milewski (1976) in the ability to discriminate internal elements. We discuss this topic in more detail in our discussion below on *Internal-External Effects*. Suffice it to say here that the most interesting result may not be the 1-month-olds' aversion to internal elements but, instead, the 2-month-olds' attraction to them. A simple argument that infants prefer to fixate large stimuli, an argument supported by Fantz and Fagan's (1975) size and number experiments, can account for the result with 1-month-olds. Explanation of the 2-month-olds' behavior may involve more complicated hypotheses.

Three experiments have investigated infant scanning of faces, a yet more complex stimulus (Hainline, 1978; Haith, Bergman, & Moore, 1977; Maurer & Salapatek, 1976). The findings are striking and in general agreement among themselves and with the Salapatek and Moscovich observations mentioned above. For example, Haith et al. (1977) observed that infants, before 2 months, mainly fixated regions of high contrast such as the border of the face. After 2 months, fixations were much more likely to cluster around internal features, particularly

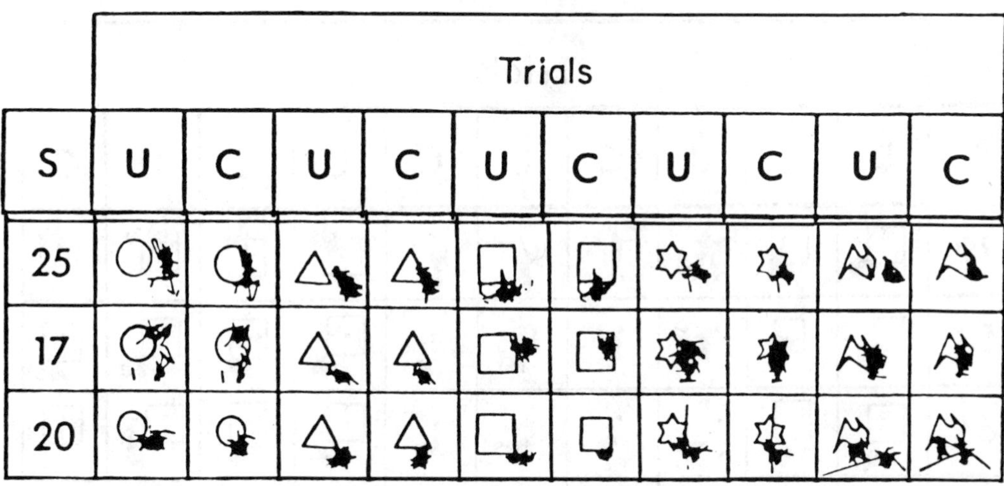

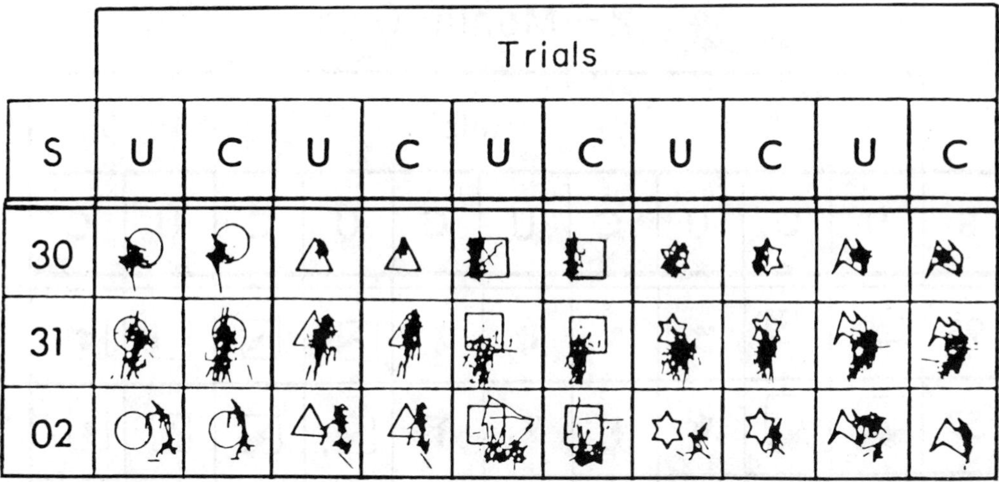

Figure 27. Scanning patterns of 1-month-olds and 2-month-olds when presented different stimuli. Five different outline shapes were presented to each subject. Scanning patterns are illustrated by connecting successive estimates of eye position. The first plot, labeled U, is based on uncorrected estimates of the line of sight. The second plot, labeled C, has been corrected for errors in the corneal photography technique (Slater & Findlay, 1972). (From Salapatek, 1975.)

the eyes. Thus, they found a shift from external to internal scanning similar to that Salapatek and Moscovich had observed with geometric patterns.

To date, a number of reasonably consistent findings have emerged from the infant scanning literature, but what can we tell from these results about visual perception? First, it is clear from this literature that even newborns can detect the presence of a contour and move their eyes to fixate it in the central visual field. By 1 month of age, the visuomotor programs involved must carry direction and distance information since initial movements, upon introduction of a contour, are not random (Aslin & Salapatek, 1975). Second, newborn scanning differs as a function of both contour orientation (Haith, 1980) and stimulus size (Salapatek, 1968), so the neonate's visual system must have information about pattern orientation and size. Surprisingly, no one has

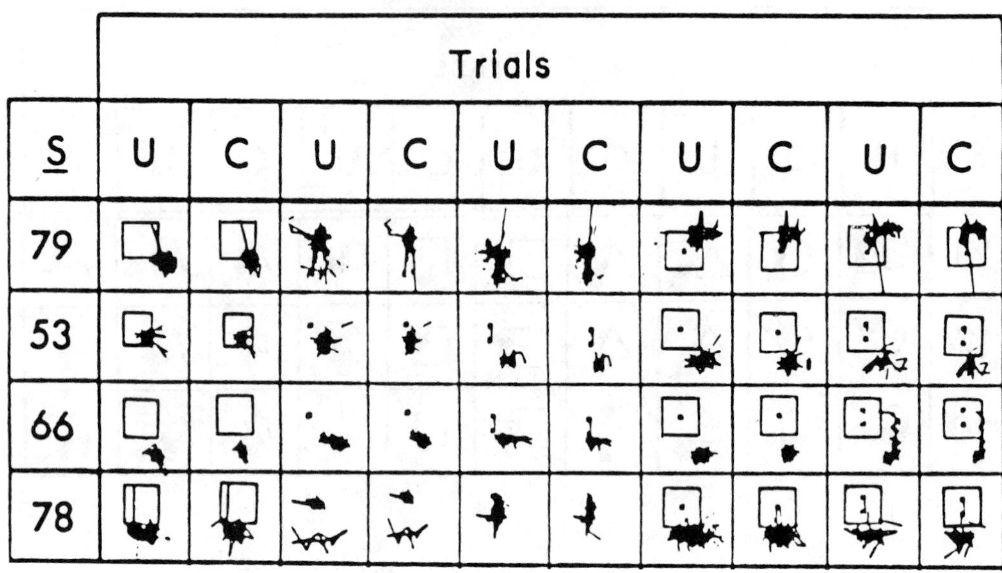

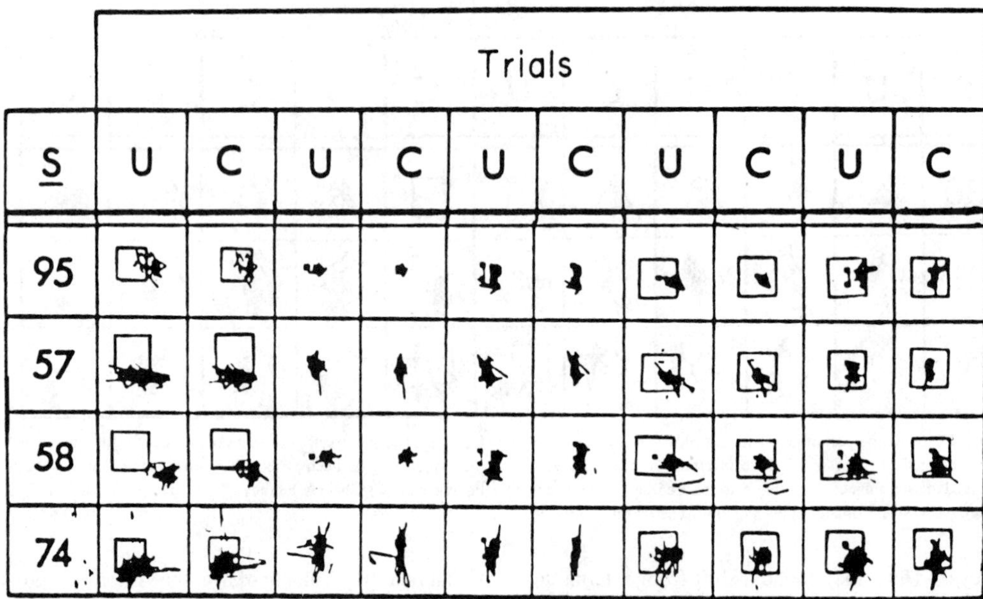

Figure 28. Scanning patterns of 1-month-olds and 2-month-olds when presented simple and compound stimuli. Details as in Figure 27. (From Salapatek, 1975.)

determined if and when scanning shape is dependent on the shape of the stimulus. Third, scanning seems to change with age; older infants exhibit broader scans (Leahy, 1976; Salapatek, 1975), which include the internal elements of compound stimuli (Haith et al., 1977; Salapatek, 1975). Whether this developmental shift involves sensory or motor maturation, or both, is as yet unclear. It seems then that the scanning literature has provided only rudimentary information about visual perception primarily because the experimental questions asked to date have been fairly primitive.

Bronson (1982) has broken somewhat with tradition and attempted to answer several questions that had not typically been addressed in the scanning literature. How large a region around the fixation point is normally processed? How does the region's size depend on the pattern information presented and the task at hand? What is the relationship between fixation duration and processing? What is the relationship between an infant's familiarization with different parts of a stimulus and scanning (see also Leahy, 1976)? To what extent is scanning recursive? How important is recursiveness to the acquisition and recognition of pattern information?

The experiments Bronson conducted do not answer all of these questions unambiguously. Nonetheless, his approach is innovative empirically and theoretically and should motivate future research concerning these issues. He tested a small number of infants between 2 and 5 months of age. The experiments are too complicated to describe here, so the interested reader should consult Bronson's monograph. The results showed that infants at each age tested were attracted to the location of a familiarized square when it was replaced by an ellipse of similar size, but only when this event occurred 5 deg rather than 15 deg from the fixation point. This suggests that pattern discrimination in the peripheral visual field may be poor early in life. Presumably, a more profound change in pattern would have been detected (Maurer & Lewis, 1979). Bronson also found, in contrast to the predictions of Jeffrey's (1968) serial habituation hypothesis, that individual infants' scanpaths were usually similar rather than dissimilar with repeated presentations of a complex stimulus. In support of Salapatek's (1975) summary, he observed that extensiveness of scanning increased with age. Bronson argued that this reflects an increased willingness among older infants to override stimulus salience.

Bronson's experiments could not answer many of the questions he posed because he did not have an independent means of assessing visual processing. Nonetheless, his monograph argues, as we have above, for the need to examine the relationship between scanning and processing. One plausible way to do this is to measure scanning during the course of a typical pattern discimination task (e.g., Haith, Goodman, Godwyn, & Montgomery, 1982). If instances of successful discrimination were associated with fixation of distinguishing features and instances of failure to discriminate were associated with fixation of nondistinguishing features, a linkage between scanning and pattern processing would be implied.

Principles of Organization

Everyday scenes are usually complex, like the one illustrated in Figure 29. This scene consists of an entangled network of contours and textures. Fortunately, we do not see it that way. Instead, we segregate the scene into two components: a plant and a fence behind it. This segregation process, which is generally called *perceptual organization,* is crucial to the perception of objects in everyday environments. Without it, visual scenes would be confusions of dissociated contours.

How the visual system accomplishes segregation is largely unknown.[8] The Gestaltists studied perceptual organization extensively with abstract, two-dimensional patterns (Koffka, 1935; Köhler, 1959; Wertheimer, 1923). They did not explain the general organization process convincingly, but they did discover several principles of organization that the visual system seems to use. Five of these principles are illustrated in Figure 30: (1) *Good continuation:* Elements that appear to follow in the same direction, such as along a straight line or smooth curve, tend to be grouped together (Figure 30A). (2) *Proximity:* Elements that are relatively close together tend to be grouped together (Figure 30B). (3) *Similarity:* Elements that are similar in shape, brightness, and hue tend to be grouped together (Figure 30C). (4) *Symmetry:* Elements that are mirror images of one another tend to be grouped together (Figure 30D). (5) *Common fate:* Elements that move in the same direction tend to be grouped together. Other Gestalt principles exist (Hochberg, 1971a), but we chose the five in Figure 30 because they have been used in developmental studies. The Gestaltists believed that all of the principles of organization reflected a tendency for organization to yield "good" or "simple" figures; patterns were supposedly organized in the manner that yielded the "simplest" perceptual outcome. Figure 30A illustrates this: The sine wave and straight line are perceived because they are "simpler" than other possible outcomes. Ginsburg (1978) has presented a series of demonstrations that suggest that most of the Gestalt principles are byproducts of filtering by low spatial frequency mechanisms (see our discussion above on *Contrast Sensitivity*).

It is important to note that the Gestalt principles of organization generally lead to a veridical perception of real scenes (for a more detailed discussion, see Rock, 1975). For example, grouping elements

Figure 29. Photograph illustrating the need to segregate components in everyday scenes. Local intensity differences alone do not allow complete segregation of the plant and the fence behind it. Higher-order clues, like good continuation and occlusion, must also be used. (From Marr, 1982.)

on the basis of good continuation usually leads to appropriate segregation; contours from one object rather than from different objects are grouped together. Thus, the diagonal straight lines in Figure 29 exhibit good continuation and are, appropriately, grouped together.

The importance of segregation in perception and the usefulness of the Gestalt principles in doing so have led several investigators to consider whether visually inexperienced organisms manifest these organizing principles. Some have argued that the principles are probably learned because they are manifest in everyday scenes (e.g., Brunswik, 1956). Others have argued that they must be innate because

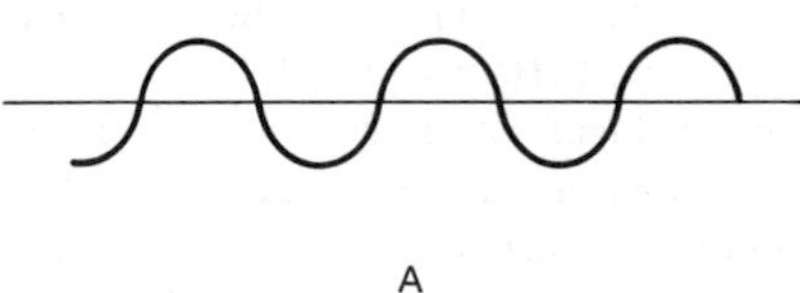

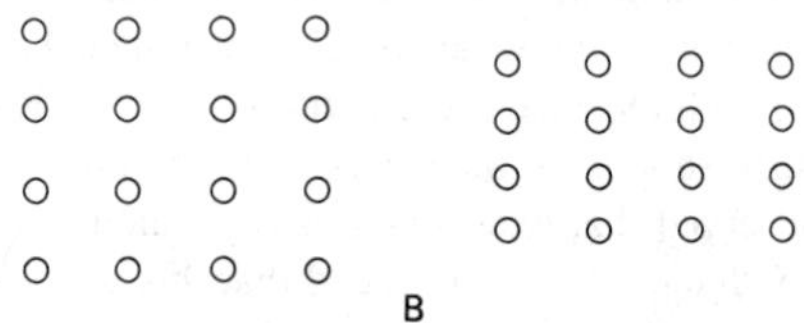

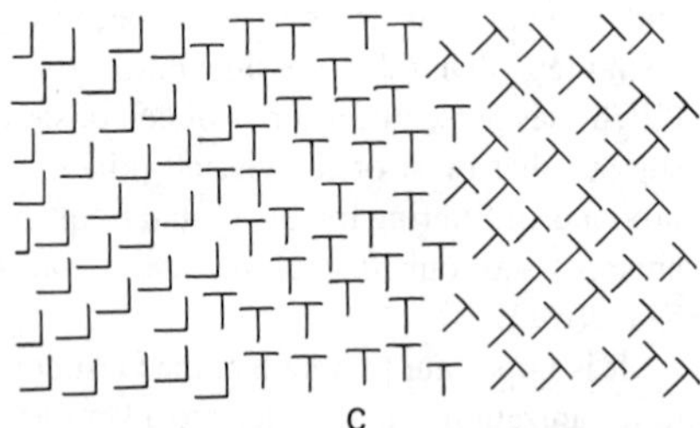

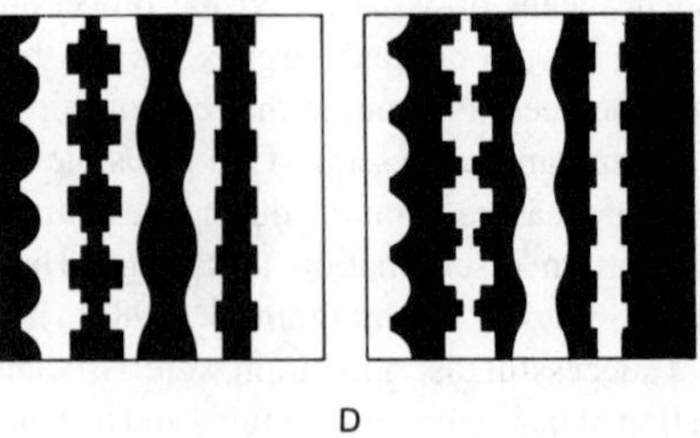

Figure 30. Examples of various Gestalt principles of organization. (A) Good continuation. (B) Proximity. (C) Similarity. (D) Symmetry. (Adapted from Hochberg, 1971a.)

without some ability to segregate contours properly, perceptual development could not commence (e.g., Köhler, 1959; Zuckerman & Rock, 1957). Unfortunately, only a handful of developmental studies has been conducted, so this controversy is still alive. We review the developmental literature below; the review is ordered according to organizing principle.

Bower (1965a) examined the principles of proximity, common fate, and good continuation in infants from 1 to 9 months of age. He presented stimulus transformations that were either consistent or inconsistent with each of those principles and measured sucking rate when each of the stimuli was presented. He reasoned that infants who possess a particular principle would exhibit surprise (i.e., a decrease in sucking) when a transformation inconsistent with that principle was presented. Infants of all ages exhibited a decrement in sucking to transformations inconsistent with common fate. Infants did not exhibit surprise to transformations inconsistent with good continuation nor proximity until 7 months. Bower concluded that the organizing principle of common fate is present at 1 month, but that good continuation and proximity are not present until 7 months. A subsequent study (Bower, 1967) confirmed the proximity result, but not the good continuation result. Specifically, 1-month-olds again did not exhibit surprise at a transformation inconsistent with proximity but did to one inconsistent with good continuation. These results suggest, then, that some Gestalt principles (common fate and good continuation) are present very early in life and at least one other (proximity) is not. Bower concluded from this that common fate and good continuation are not learned but innate. These results are intriguing, but should be replicated.

More recently, Kellman and Spelke (1981) confirmed the presence of common fate early in life, but did not see evidence for good continuation. They habituated 4-month-olds to a partially occluded object: a rod partially hidden behind a block. They then examined the infants' responses to the rod alone and to a broken rod. (The broken rod was composed of the two segments of the rod that could be seen above and below the block during habituation.) The infants did not fixate one of the test stimuli over the other, so the authors concluded that good continuation was not operating. When the rod was moved back and forth during habituation, however, infants subsequently fixated the complete over the broken rod. Thus, the authors reasoned that common fate was operating by 4 months.

Treiber and Wilcox (1980) and Bertenthal, Campos, and Haith (1980) investigated infants' perception of stimuli that to adults produce subjective contours. Since the subjective contour phenomenon involves the completion of co-linear, but unconnected contours, these studies can be thought of as investigations of good continuation. Treiber and Wilcox habituated 1- to 4-month-olds to a Kanizsa triangle. (The Kanizsa figure is composed of three angles but no sides.) Their infants dishabituated to a similar pattern in which the orientations of the corners were altered and to a dissimilar pattern. They failed, however, to dishabituate when presented a real triangle. Treiber and Wilcox concluded that infants as young as 1 month perceived the subjective triangle in the Kanizsa figure and hence exhibited the principle of good continuation. Unfortunately, their results were contaminated by a significant difference in inherent preferences for the three test patterns. The Bertenthal et al. experiment was better controlled. They too used a habituation-dishabituation paradigm and Kanizsa figures. Five- and 7-month-olds were habituated to either a subjective contour pattern (four corners of a square in proper arrangement) or a pattern that did not create such contours (two other arrangements of the four corners). Once habituated, infants were presented either the subjective contour pattern or one of the two nonillusion patterns. Seven-month-olds dishabituated to a change from the subjective contour to a nonillusion pattern, or vice versa. Five-month-olds, on the other hand, did not consistently dishabituate to such changes. They concluded that subjective contours are not perceived until about 7 months.

Finally, van Giffen and Haith (submitted) examined the sensitivity of 1- and 3-month-olds to good continuation using a visual scanning paradigm. The stimuli were 12 dashed line segments arranged in either a square or circular configuration. In some cases, all of the line segments were aligned according to the principle of good continuation. In others, one of the segments was rotated 90 deg or displaced radially to form a local region in which good continuation did not hold. Three-month-olds reliably fixated the discrepant region in the stimulus with the rotated segments, but 1-month-olds did not. Thus, this study evidences sensitivity to good continuation at 3 months, but not at 1 month.

We are left with a somewhat confusing picture of the development of good continuation. Bower (1967) and Treiber and Wilcox (1980) reported findings consistent with the presence of good continuation at 1 month of age. Bower (1965a), Kellman and Spelke (1981), van Giffen and Haith (submitted), and Bertenthal et al. (1980) did not. These discrepancies may be the result of experimental artifacts in some of the studies. On the other hand, they may not be contradictory at all; perhaps the early use of good continuation, or any other organizing principle, depends critically on the particular stimuli involved.

Salapatek (1975) developed a paradigm to investigate the principle of similarity. He used stimuli like those shown in Figure 31. A small matrix of one kind of element was embedded within a larger matrix of different elements. When adults and preschoolers viewed these stimuli, they tended to fixate the small matrix of discrepant elements. The cause of this, Salapatek reasoned, was the dissimilarity of the two types of elements. Because it was composed of discrepant elements, the small matrix was grouped together and segregated from the rest of the stimulus. Surprisingly, 2-month-olds did not fixate the discrepant region consistently. Instead, they seemed to fixate the region of highest contour density whether it was a discrepant region or not. One interpretation of this result is that the organizing principle of similarity is not present at 2 months. Another is that young infants may use similarity to detect the discrepancy but are not attracted to that region.

Another organizing principle—symmetry—has been investigated indirectly. Bornstein, Ferdinandsen, and Gross (1981) and Fisher, Ferdinandsen, and Bornstein (1981) examined the role of symmetry in the encoding and discrimination of simple patterns. A number of experiments were conducted with 4-month-olds. Overall, the results showed that infants habituated more rapidly to vertically symmetric than to horizontally symmetric or asymmetric patterns. Moreover, vertically symmetric patterns were discriminated more readily from asymmetric and horizontally symmetric patterns than horizontally symmetric patterns were from asymmetric. The infants failed to demonstrate discrimination of various asymmetric patterns from one another. The authors concluded that vertical symmetry promotes encoding and discrimination early in life. This may suggest that young infants use vertical symmetry to organize patterns, but more direct investigations of this are required.

Strauss and Curtis (1981) also examined the influence of symmetry on infant pattern discrimination. They used patterns that were either "good," "intermediate," or "poor" forms according to adult ratings. The "good" forms were vertically and horizontally symmetric; the "poor" forms were not. Two versions of each type of pattern were presented.

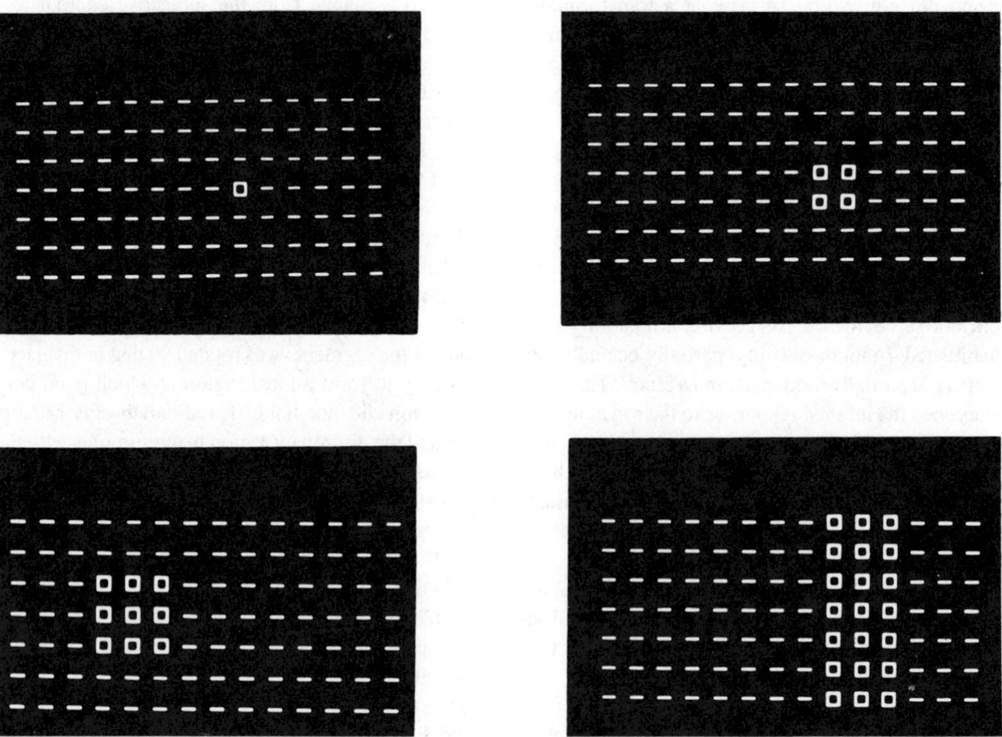

Figure 31. Examples of the matrix stimuli used by Salapatek. (From Salapatek, 1975.)

Three-, 5-, and 7-month-olds were habituated to one version and then tested with the other. Three-month-olds demonstrated discrimination among the "good" forms but not the others. Five-month-olds discriminated the "good" and "intermediate" forms, and 7-month-olds discriminated all three. These results indicate, as one would suspect, that pattern discrimination improves from 3 to 7 months. They may also show, Strauss and Curtis argue, that figural "goodness" (and symmetry) are important early determinants of discrimination. There is, however, one problem with this interpretation of the effect of figural "goodness." Only two stimuli were used to represent each category of "goodness." Since no independent measure of similarity was provided, it is possible that the particular "good" forms employed were more discriminable than the particular "poor" forms. A larger experiment with more stimuli and some index of similarity apart from figural "goodness' is required to clarify this issue.

Summary

Pattern segregation is an important but poorly understood process. The developmental literature on this topic is sparse and somewhat confusing, but there are indications that some Gestalt organizing principles are functional early in life. Several important issues have not been resolved. To what extent does the development of these principles depend on experience? Are the various principles yoked developmentally? If the principles are not innate, how can they be learned unless the infant has some independent means of separating a figure from ground or one figure from another? How does use of the principles depend on stimulus variables such as familiarity, complexity, size, and depth? We hope the next decade will yield answers to these intriguing but difficult questions.

Internal-External Effects

Figures or objects in everyday scenes are rarely simple. Generally, from the observer's standpoint, they are embedded within or overlap with other figures or objects. In this section we consider the situation in which one is embedded within, or is adjacent to, another. Several lines of work suggest an interesting developmental shift in the ability to process small figures placed either within or adjacent to a larger figure. This effect was originally called the *externality effect* but, as we will see, this is probably an inappropriate term.

Visual scanning experiments, for instance, found that 1-month-olds tend to fixate only the outer contour of a face or a compound geometric pattern. Two-month-olds and 3-month-olds, on the other hand, tend to scan both internal and external contours (Haith et al., 1977; Maurer & Salapatek, 1976; Salapatek, 1975).

This scanning bias in very young infants led researchers to ask whether 1-month-olds could discriminate changes in the internal element(s) of a compound pattern. Fantz and Miranda (1975) examined newborn pattern preferences for curved versus straight lines. When the lines were not bounded by an external contour, newborns looked longer at the curved lines. This shows that they could discriminate them. When an external contour was added, no consistent preferences were found; that is, the newborns failed to demonstrate an ability to discriminate curved from straight lines.

Milewski (1976, 1978) used compound patterns like those in Figure 32 to investigate the effects of external frames. He habituated 1- and 4-month-olds to a particular compound and then changed the shape of either the external figure, the internal figure, or both. Four-month-olds discriminated all three changes. One-month-olds, on the other hand, did not demonstrate that they could discriminate changes in the internal figure. Milewski called the 1-month-olds' discrimination failure the externality effect. Bushnell (1979) replicated this particular finding. Milewski also conducted a second experi-

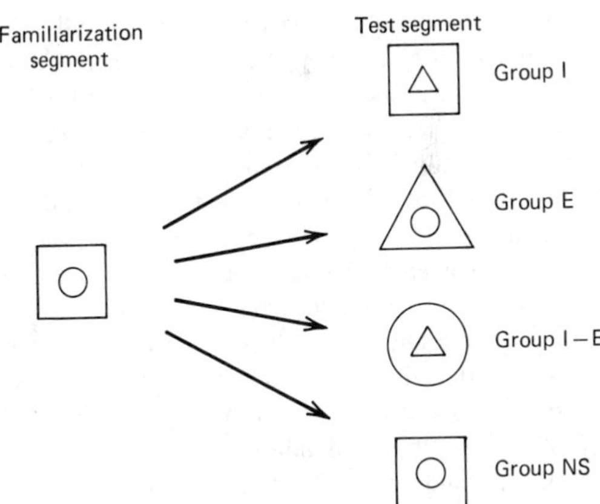

Figure 32. Representative stimuli used in the Milewski experiment. The compound figure on the left is one of the familiarization stimuli used. Infants were exposed to this for a number of trials and then tested with one of the four stimuli on the right. The stimulus for Group I had the same external figure but a different internal figure. The stimulus for Group E had the same internal figure but a different external figure. The stimulus for Groups I–E had different internal and external figures. The stimulus for Group NS was the same as the familiarization stimulus. (Adapted from Milewski, 1976.)

ment that showed that the 1-month-olds' inability was not due to the size of the internal figure alone; they discriminated changes in the "internal" figure when it was presented in isolation. He showed in subsequent experiments that the inability seemed to be due to the size of the smaller "internal" figure *relative* to the "external" figure; when a small figure was presented adjacent to rather than within a larger figure, 1-month-olds again failed to exhibit the ability to discriminate a change in the smaller figure's shape. Milewski (1978) concluded that, in very young infants, the inability to discriminate the internal element in a compound pattern resulted from a bias for processing the largest figure in the field rather than a bias for external contours.

More recent experiments have examined whether the "salience" of an internal figure embedded in an external figure influences 1-month-olds' ability to discriminate changes in figure shape. Bushnell (1979) showed that 1-month-olds discriminated changes in the shape of an internal figure when it was flickered or moved within an external figure but not when the internal and external figures were static or moved together. Girton (1979) obtained similar results with a schematic face whose eyes moved. These results suggest that relative motion increased the 1-month-olds' ability or willingness to process the internal figure. Bushnell also showed that motion of the internal figure did not eliminate the ability to discriminate changes in the external figure.

Ganon and Swartz (1980) also examined the influence of stimulus salience on 1-month-olds' discrimination of changes in internal elements. They placed either a bull's eye or a checkerboard, which are highly preferred patterns for young infants, inside an outline figure. Under these conditions, 1-month-olds readily distinguished a change in the internal figure (from a bull's eye to a checkerboard or the reverse) and a change in the external figure (from a square to a triangle or the reverse).

These findings as a whole suggest that the externality effect is misnamed. The effect is probably better thought of in terms of pattern salience. In infants less than 2 months of age, the relative size, motion, and configuration of a pattern all seem to influence whether the pattern is processed sufficiently for later recognition. Infants older than 2 months are not so limited. This age-related change in discrimination with these compound patterns may be caused by a change from scanning only limited, salient parts of the visual array to more extensive scanning (Salapatek, 1975), but scanning experiments with the stimuli used in the above-mentioned discrimination studies should be conducted to verify this. Why very young infants choose such a limited scanning strategy and older infants do not is, of course, the most important question. There is no firm answer as yet, but we discuss some possibilities in our discussion on *Visual Scanning* above.

Before leaving this topic, it is interesting to note that discrimination failures similar to those obtained with 1-month-olds have been observed in other contexts. An example is the so-called crowding phenomenon observed in human adults with amblyopia, a developmental anomaly which causes a reduction in visual acuity and pattern discrimination capabilities. The crowding phenomenon is demonstrated by comparing an observer's ability to identify a letter or Landolt C when presented in isolation compared to when it is surrounded by other letters or pattern elements. The performance of a normal eye is not affected significantly by the surrounding letters or elements, but the performance of an amblyopic eye is severely affected by the presence of surrounding contours (Flom, Weymouth, & Kahneman, 1963; Stuart & Burian, 1962). Interestingly, the crowding phenomenon is also observed in the peripheral visual field of normal adults (Andriessen & Bouma, 1976). Whether crowding effects also occur when a small target is placed adjacent to, rather than within, masking targets is unknown.

Humphrey (1970, 1974) observed an externality effect in a rhesus monkey whose visual cortex had been removed. The monkey learned to reach and grasp raisins under visual control. When the raisins were placed within a large frame, however, she did not exhibit any attempt to reach for them. Thus, it appears that one by-product of a normal visual cortex is the ability to detect and discriminate small figures embedded in larger ones. It will be important in developing theories of infant pattern discrimination to determine if the crowding effects observed in destriate monkeys are homologous with those observed in very young human infants. If so, one might argue that crowding effects are a reflection of cortical immaturity. It may also be theoretically fruitful to determine if the crowding effects seen in amblyopic adults and in the peripheral visual field of normal adults are homologous with the effect observed in young infants.

Form Discrimination and Generalization

The mature visual system is remarkably adept at recognizing an object even when it is presented in varying sizes, intensities, positions, contexts, and, to some extent, orientations. For example, a familiar face can be recognized despite gross variations in viewing distance, lighting, and background. This marvelous capability is essential to recognizing objects in the varying conditions of everyday scenes. We consider the development of this capability in the next two sections on form discrimination and size and shape constancy.

Recall our earlier definition of form. It is the aspect of a pattern that remains constant in spite of changes in low-order variables such as brightness, contrast, color, size, position, local features, context, and, to some extent, orientation. Thus, form refers to the configuration of a pattern. Because the ability to extract form information despite changes in low-order variables is requisite for object recognition, an important research question is: How does the ability to extract form information develop?

Unfortunately, it has proven very difficult to study form perception in nonverbal organisms such as human infants because so many low-order variables can contaminate an experiment. Some examples are provided in the animal literature on form discrimination. Most relevant in the current context are studies of discrimination capabilities in cats and monkeys who have either been visually deprived or have had their visual cortices removed. Ganz and Haffner (1974), for example, tested cats who had undergone various amounts of deprivation early in life. These cats were trained to discriminate the gratings shown on the left in Figure 33. All cats learned this discrimination. One might conclude from this that deprived cats could perceive and discriminate the orientations of these gratings, but subsequent tests did not support this. The cats were tested for generalization of the horizontal-vertical discrimination with the gratings shown in columns A, B, C, and D. The performance of nondeprived cats was unaffected by any of these transformations. In contrast, the performance of deprived cats was adversely affected by all of the transformations. Ganz and Haffner concluded that the deprived cats' original discrimination was based on local flux (amount of light) cues at the bottom of the gratings because altering this flux caused performance to fall. Similar phenomena have been observed in destriate cats and monkeys (Humphrey, 1974; Loop & Sherman, 1977). Thus, visual deprivation and visual cortical ablation affect an organism's ability to extract invariant form information much more severely than their ability to discriminate patterns on the basis of low-order pattern variables such as flux. In other words, deprived and destriate cats and monkeys exhibit deficits in form discrimination per se.

The animal work illustrates how important it is to define criteria clearly which, if demonstrated, would constitute evidence for form discrimination. We offer two criteria that are similar to Ruff's (1978). First, one must show that two stimuli that differ in form can be discriminated when all potential low-order variables are either equated or rendered irrelevant. Second, one must show generalization between two stimuli that are identical in form but whose low-order variables differ. Unfortunately, these two criteria have turned out to be rather difficult to demonstrate. To illustrate this difficulty, we have chosen two examples from the infant literature of experiments that have not met these criteria. Both

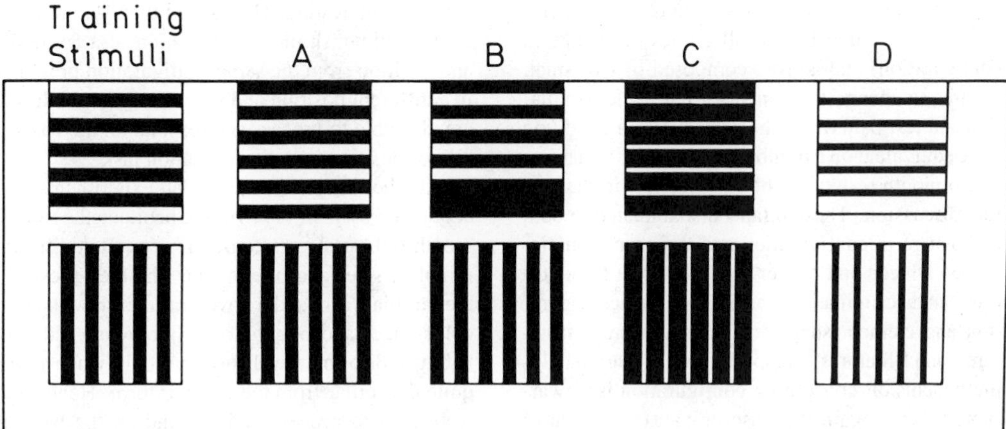

Figure 33. Training and test stimuli used by Ganz and Haffner. Cats were trained to make the horizontal grating versus vertical grating discrimination shown in the first column. They were then tested with the pairs of stimuli in columns A to D. (From Ganz, 1978.)

experiments tested infants' ability to discriminate changes in the configuration of patterns composed of identical elements.

Fantz and Nevis (1967) used a preference paradigm to test 1-week-olds to 4-month-olds. The stimuli were 25 identical square elements presented in four different configurations: a bull's eye, a checkerboard, a lattice, and an irregular lattice. Because they were constructed in this fashion, they were equal in brightness, contrast, overall size, and contour length. Fantz and Nevis did not find clear differential preferences among the four configurations until 2½ months of age when the bull's eye and checkerboard were preferred over the lattices. They concluded tentatively that infants 2½ months of age and older can discriminate on the basis of pattern configuration alone. This conclusion is not justified, however, because the stimuli could have been discriminated on the basis of low-order pattern variables. In particular, discrimination could have been mediated by the orientation of a single element or a small cluster of elements. In the lattice configurations, all of the elements were oriented vertically or nearly so. In the bull's eye and checkerboard configurations, diagonal orientations were available. Consequently, discrimination may have been based on the orientation of a few elements. The discrimination could also have been based on differences in local contour density. The bull's eye and checkerboard had regions of high contour density (where the corners of elements touched). The lattices did not.

Dineen and Meyer (1980) used a habituation-dishabituation paradigm to examine the ability of 3- and 6-month-olds to discriminate configurations. Each infant was first habituated to a pattern composed of five small circles arranged in a cross. They were presented two novel test patterns: an X composed of the same five small circles (a change in configuration) and a cross composed of five small squares (a change in elements). Thus, the habituation and test patterns in the configuration condition were equivalent on a number of low-order variables. The 6-month results are of most interest to the current discussion. These infants dishabituated to both the change in configuration and the change in elements. Dineen and Meyer concluded that 6-month-olds can discriminate on the basis of both configuration and element shape (their terms were "structure" and "features," respectively). Unfortunately, the conclusion concerning configuration is unwarranted. Once again, the discrimination could have been mediated by low-order variables. For example, the infants may have simply responded to the change in absolute position of one of the elements.

Other experiments in the infant literature have had similar shortcomings (Cornell, 1975; Fagan, 1977; Vurpillot, Ruel, & Castrec, 1977). Demonstration of form discrimination uncontaminated by low-order variables had become a vexing problem. Recently, however, three experiments by Milewski (1979), Ruff (1978), and Schwartz and Day (1979) have largely overcome these problems and shown reasonably convincingly that infants can discriminate on the basis of form by 3 months.

Milewski (1979) used a habituation-dishabituation paradigm to test 3-month-olds. The stimuli were two configurations of three dots on an otherwise uniform field. One configuration formed a vertical straight line; the other formed a triangle. The two configurations were identical in contrast and overall brightness. The dots were not connected in either stimulus, so the configurations could not be discriminated according to local features. Infants were habituated to one of these configurations and then tested with either the same or the other configuration. The configuration's size and position were varied randomly during habituation, so discrimination could not be based on size, position, or local density cues. Milewski found that infants dishabituated significantly when a novel configuration was introduced but not when the familiar configuration with a novel size and position was introduced. These elegant results appear to satisfy both criteria for demonstrating form discrimination and hence constitute convincing evidence that 3-month-olds can process and respond on the basis of form. The form discrimination demonstrated, however, may be a very simple one (e.g., linear vs. nonlinear configuration).

It is somewhat tangential to the current discussion, but one of Milewski's follow-up experiments was also interesting. He showed that 3-month-olds could distinguish one configuration of a fixed size and position from the same configuration presented in a different position and size. Thus, 3-month-olds are also able to process and respond on the basis of size or position in a discrimination task.

Another important series of experiments was conducted by Ruff (1978). She habituated 6- and 9-month-olds to objects constant in form but differing in color, size, and orientation. She then presented the familiar form and a novel form, both with novel color, size, and orientation. Nine-month-olds dishabituated to the novel form but only when it was quite dissimilar from the familiar form. Hence they were able to process and respond on the basis of form, at least for quite dissimilar forms. Six-month-olds did not demonstrate such an ability even for the more dissimilar forms. Her results, when compared to Milewski's, suggest that infants' ability to exhibit form discrimination depends on the particular forms used.

Schwartz and Day (1979) conducted an extensive series of habituation-dishabituation experiments with 3-month-olds. The stimuli presented in one of the most interesting experiments are shown in Figure 34. Infants were habituated to stimulus A and then tested with A, B, C, and D. A and B were the same form; they differed in orientation only. C and D were different forms. Note that all four stimuli were equivalent in several low-order variables such as brightness and contrast. The results were clear; infants dishabituated to D and C but not to A and B. Discrimination of C and D from A could have been based on differences in form or on differences in local cues, such as the orientation of the upper right line. However, infants failed to demonstrate discrimination of A and B, which suggests that discrimination was not based on the orientation of one line. Thus, 3-month-olds responded differentially to stimuli that differed in form but did not to stimuli that differed in orientation only. This and other experiments conducted by Schwartz and Day suggest that young infants can process form information and respond on its basis. Schwartz and Day noted that the ability to extract form independent of orientation depended to some extent on stimulus complexity. Infants responded differentially to orientation changes with simple forms, such as squares and open angles composed of two lines, but did not with more complex forms like rectangles and those shown in Figure 34.

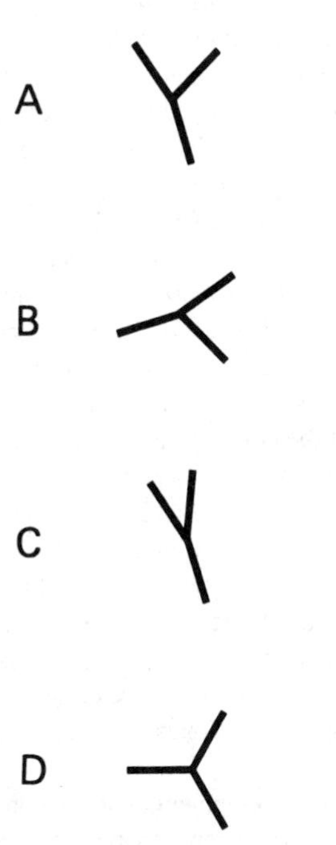

Figure 34. The stimuli used in one of Schwartz and Day's experiments. Infants were habituated to stimulus A and then tested with stimuli A through D. (From Schwartz & Day, 1979.)

Summary

Three recent studies, which controlled the contaminating effects of low-order variables fairly well, provide persuasive evidence that 3-month-olds can discriminate and generalize on the basis of form. They also revealed, as one might suspect, that this ability is dependent on the complexity of the stimuli. Younger infants have not yet been tested in a well-controlled experiment. Consequently, we do not yet know if neonates exhibit severe deficits like those observed in animals with poorly developed or ablated visual cortices.

Perceptual Constancies

As one moves about in the environment and views objects, the retinal image associated with those objects changes continually. This variation presents a difficulty for the task of recognizing and identifying objects. To recognize and identify objects unerringly, the visual system needs a stable representation that varies little, if at all, with one's viewpoint. Hence Marr (1982) and others have reasoned that at some point the object must be represented in an object-centered rather than viewer-centered fashion.

How the visual system might translate viewer-centered representations, such as the retinal image, into an object-centered language is poorly understood, but there is reasonably persuasive evidence that such a translation actually does occur. For example, consider the perceptual constancies. As you walk around and away from an object, the associated retinal image changes shape and shrinks. Yet the object's apparent shape and size do not change. The stability of apparent size, despite changes in projected retinal image size, is called *size constancy*. Similarly, the stability of apparent shape, despite changes in projected image shape, is called *shape constancy*. In this section, we consider research on the development of size and shape constancy.

Several other important constancies that also reveal object-centered descriptions have been identified but are not included in this section. The development of brightness, color, and egocentric constancy (Day & McKenzie, 1977; Hochberg,

1971b) has not been investigated directly, but related material appears in other sections of this chapter. Identity-existence constancy, or object permanence (Day & McKenzie, 1977), has been researched extensively and is discussed in this volume by Harris (Vol. II, Chap. 9).

The conventional explanation of size constancy is that the visual system judges size on the basis of both retinal image size and information concerning the object's distance. In other words, as an object draws farther away, the decrease in image size is somehow compensated for by the increase in perceived distance.

Several researchers have asked at what ages size constancy is present. This is, of course, an important research question since the onset of size constancy may mark the emergence of object-centered representations in the nervous system. Unfortunately, the literature is currently somewhat confusing. Consequently, here we simply present the data as they stand and draw conclusions that seem the most reasonable at this stage.

Cruikshank (1941) and Misumi (1951) were the first to investigate size constancy in infants. However, neither experiment yielded compelling results, so Bower's (1964, 1965b) conditioning experiments were the first well-controlled investigations. Bower (1964) conditioned infants 1½ to 3 months of age to turn their heads when presented with a 12-in. cube at a distance of 3 ft. He then assessed generalization to (1) the same stimulus, (2) a 12-in. cube at 9 ft, (3) a 36-in. cube at 3 ft, and (4) a 36-in. cube at 9 ft. The last cube had the same projected size as the conditioned stimulus. As one would expect, postconditioning response rate was greatest for condition 1. Of most interest though were the responses to conditions 2, 3, and 4. Response was less to condition 2 and 3 than to 1, but significantly greater than to condition 4. Thus, the infants appeared to respond more on the basis of the true size and distance of the object than the projected size. Bower concluded that shape constancy was present by 1½ to 3 months of age. He subsequently confirmed this result and suggested that motion parallax was the primary cue used to assess distance (Bower, 1965b).

McKenzie and Day (1972, 1976) and Day and McKenzie (1977) conducted four size constancy experiments in infants from 1½ to 5 months of age using habituation and conditioning paradigms. None of the experiments confirmed Bower's earlier findings. Indeed, it appeared that infants were responding on the basis of object distance rather than real or projected size.

In contrast, McKenzie, Day, and their colleagues recently obtained positive evidence for size constancy in 4- to 8-month-old infants. McKenzie, Tootell, and Day (1980) habituated 4-, 6-, and 8-month-olds to a large mannequin head at 60 cm. They then presented either (1) the same stimulus, (2) the large head at 30 cm, (3) a small head at 60 cm, or (4) a small head at 30 cm. Six- and 8-month-olds dishabituated significantly when presented with the stimuli that differed in real size from the habituation stimulus (3 and 4). They did not dishabituate to stimuli whose real size was identical to the habituation stimulus (1 and 2). The 4-month-olds exhibited a roughly similar pattern of results, but no statistically significant trends due to increased variability. Because these findings with 4-month-olds were ambiguous, Day and McKenzie (1981) re-examined this age group. Using a different habituation procedure and set of stimuli, they found clear evidence for size constancy in 4-month-olds. The discrepancy between the McKenzie et al. (1980) and Day and McKenzie (1981) results exemplifies a common problem in infant perception research—the uncertain relationship between competence and performance. Too often two experiments designed to index a particular skill yield discordant results. In this case, the same researchers testing the same age group with generally similar stimuli and procedures obtained different results. Such occurrences remind us of the need for replication in this area.

What can we conclude about the development of size constancy? All existing data are consistent with the conclusion that some form of size constancy is present by 6 months of age. The data, however, are unclear concerning younger age groups: Bower (1964, 1965b) and Day and McKenzie (1981) reported positive findings whereas McKenzie and Day (1972, 1976), McKenzie et al. (1980), and Day and McKenzie (1977) did not. Thus, we can only conclude that it is unclear whether size constancy operates before 6 months of age. This frustrates attempts to construct theories of the development of constancies. Nonetheless, it is worthwhile to point out that a number of skills emerge between 4 and 6 months of age that could be important determinants of the development of size constancy. These skills include visually guided reaching (White, Castle, & Held, 1964) and the appreciation of several new depth cues such as familiar size (Yonas, Pettersen, & Granrud, 1982) and linear perspective (Yonas, Cleaves, & Pettersen, 1978).

Next we consider the development of shape constancy, the stability of apparent shape despite changes in the shape of the projected image. Some researchers have argued that shape constancy is a special case of size constancy (e.g., Rock, 1975). Their reasoning is the following. Consider a rectangle slanted relative to the frontoparallel plane. If the distance of the farther side is taken into account by size constancy mechanisms, then the size of that side will be perceived veridically. The same reasoning applies to the nearer side. The two sides will then appear to be similar in size, which means the rectangle's shape should be perceived veridically. Developmental research could help determine if this view is correct. For example, if shape constancy emerges before size constancy, it cannot be dependent on size constancy.

Bower (1966) pioneered research on the development of shape constancy. He conditioned 2-month-olds to turn their heads when presented with a rectangle slanted 45 deg relative to the infants' line of sight. He then measured response generalization to (1) the same rectangle in its original orientation, (2) the same rectangle but presented perpendicular to the line of sight, (3) a trapezoidal object presented perpendicular to the line of sight so that its projective shape was the same as the conditioned stimulus, and (4) the same trapezoid slanted 45 deg. Infants responded about equally often to conditions 1 and 2 in which the stimulus had the same objective shape as the conditioned stimulus. They responded less frequently to condition 3 (same projective shape) and condition 4 (same slant). Bower concluded from this and two related studies that shape constancy is present by 2 months of age.

Day and McKenzie (1973) studied infants 1½ to 4 months old. They habituated infants across trials to either (1) a solid cube presented in one orientation, (2) the same cube presented in varying orientations, or (3) photographs of the cube in varying orientations. The authors reasoned that habituation should be more rapid in condition 1 than in conditions 2 or 3 if the infants did not possess shape constancy, because different instances of conditions 2 and 3 would be perceived as different stimuli. Infants actually habituated equally rapidly in conditions 1 and 2 (solid cubes) but did not habituate in condition 3 (photograph). The authors concluded, therefore, that shape constancy exists at this age. Cohen, DeLoache, and Strauss (1979) have questioned this interpretation. They pointed out that Day and McKenzie may have demonstrated only that infants habituate more rapidly to objects than to photographs.

Caron, Caron, and Carlson (1979) also looked for evidence of shape constancy in young infants. They habituated 3-month-olds to either a square or a trapezoid presented at a number of different slants. In this way they hoped to desensitize the infants to slant and make them attend to objective shape. The infants were then presented either a square or a trapezoid in the frontoparallel plane. Dishabituation was much greater when the test stimulus differed from that of the habituation stimulus than when it did not. Thus, these results suggest that shape constancy is present by 3 months.

What can we conclude about the development of shape constancy? The existing data are consistent with the statement that shape constancy operates by 3 months of age. This, in turn, suggests that some ability to represent objects in an object-centered rather than viewer-centered fashion exists early in life before locomotion and visually guided reaching are possible. It is too early to state with any confidence whether shape constancy actually emerges before size constancy, so this remains an interesting research question.

COLOR VISION

As described earlier in this chapter, pattern vision is critical for the recognition and identification of various objects. Many animals function well visually despite the absence of color vision because most objects are defined reasonably unambiguously by contours created by differences in luminance. Thus, the question is often asked: What advantage does color vision offer? We do not have a definitive answer to this question, but it should be noted that chromatic information probably aids object perception in a number of everyday situations. In cases in which an object and its background are equal in luminance, the object's shape can still be perceived based on chromatic cues. Chromatic information can also help distinguish one version of an object (a red apple) from another (a green apple) and can aid the figure segregation process (see our discussion above on *Principles of Organization*) in complex patterned environments (e.g., a red apple can be segregated from surrounding green foliage based on chromatic cues).

The study of color vision can be divided into two domains: sensory psychophysics and perception. The relationship between these two research areas is not symmetrical in the sense that a knowledge of sensory functions (e.g., spectral sensitivity) is required for the study of perceptual functions (e.g., preferences). Thus, we review work on infant color vision in the sequence implied by this asymmetry. Our review of this literature was aided by other recent reviews: Bornstein (1978), Werner and Wooten (1979), and, particularly, Teller and Bornstein (in press).

The Psychophysics of Color Vision

The psychophysical study of color vision has been particularly interesting to visual scientists. In the study of adult color vision, certain psychophysical observations have been strong indicators of what the underlying physiological mechanisms must be. Since this has been true for adults, Teller and Bornstein (in press) argue that it may prove to be true for the study of infant color vision as well. Many of the studies of infant color vision have been designed from this theoretical point of view. Consequently, the justification for some experiments may be obscure unless one knows some of the psychophysical-physiological relationships that have been determined historically. For this reason, we devote some time to describing basic features of adult color vision before reviewing the infant literature.

The term *color* refers to the component of visual experience characterized by the psychological attributes of brightness, hue, and saturation. Two of these—hue and saturation—are chromatic attributes. The other—brightness—is actually an achromatic attribute. These attributes are correlated with, but not isomorphic to, particular physical dimensions of stimulation. Hue and saturation are primarily correlated with the wavelength composition of the stimulus, and brightness with stimulus intensity. Thus, hue and saturation are the attributes most closely associated with our everyday notion of "color." To avoid confusion, we use the term *chromatic vision* instead of color vision to refer to the class of visual capabilities that involve the chromatic attributes, hue and saturation, and that do not involve the achromatic attribute, brightness.

The first stage of the visual process—the photoreceptors—is also the first important stage in color vision. The adult visual system has four types of photoreceptors, one type of rod and three types of cones, each of which is sensitive to a different, but overlapping, band of wavelengths. The rods function at low light levels and hence subserve night or scotopic vision. The three cone types function at higher light levels to subserve day or photopic vision. The three cone types are usually called short-wavelength-sensitive, middle-wavelength-sensitive, and long-wavelength-sensitive cones, but we use the less formal terms "blue," "green," and "red" cones, respectively. (Please note that the latter terms are not meant to imply that "blue" cones, for example, are solely responsible for the perceptual experience of blue. They cannot be solely responsible because the sensitivities of the three cone systems are widely overlapping.) Each type of photoreceptor responds in an untagged fashion; that is, the only aspect of their response that varies with changes in the incident light is quantity. The consequences of untagged responding are profound. The output of any single photoreceptor can be driven to a given level by virtually any wavelength of light simply by adjusting the light's intensity. Thus, wavelength information cannot be extracted from the output of a single photoreceptor. All rods share a common spectral sensitivity. So under scotopic viewing conditions (dim illumination), when only rods operate, wavelength information cannot be extracted from photoreceptor responses. Under photopic viewing conditions (bright illumination), three types of cones operate, each most sensitive to a different, but overlapping, band of wavelengths. Any one type cannot convey wavelength information by itself, but the relative activities of the three types can. It is this attribute—the relative activities of three kinds of cones—that signals wavelength information in the earliest stage of visual processing (Boynton, 1979; Teller & Bornstein, in press).

Obviously, photoreceptor characteristics cannot be the whole story because the subsequent stages of the visual process must preserve wavelength information to allow the conscious experience of color. Psychophysical evidence from adult humans and physiological evidence from adult monkeys indicate that the signals of the three cone types undergo a major transformation within the retina. Signals from two or three kinds of cones are combined additively to form achromatic channels (which code brightness primarily) and are combined subtractively to form two kinds of chromatic channels (which code hue primarily). The subtractive, chromatic channels have been called *opponent processes* because different wavelength bands evoke different directions of neural response. In one type of channel, for example, long wavelengths evoke a response increase and short wavelengths a response decrease.

As mentioned earlier, many of the characteristics of photoreceptors and subsequent neural stages outlined above were originally inferred from adult behavioral studies. Part of the interest in the behavioral studies of infants arises from the possibility that they will lead to similar insights concerning the development of the mechanisms of color vision.

Development

The most basic question to ask about the development of color vision is: When can infants discriminate stimuli on the basis of hue alone? In other words, when is chromatic vision present? Before 1975, a large number of studies had attempted to demonstrate chromatic vision in infants (reviewed by Bornstein, 1978; Kessen, Haith, & Salapatek, 1970). Unfortunately, each of these studies failed to eliminate the possibility that infants were basing their discriminations on brightness cues rather than hue (or saturation) cues. This is a serious shortcoming because infants' sensitivity to small intensity differences can be quite high.

To rule out brightness artifacts, we require some knowledge of the relationship between wavelength and brightness. This relationship is characterized by the spectral sensitivity function which plots the reciprocal of light intensity at threshold as a function of wavelength. Two examples of such functions are shown in Figure 35. One is the adult photopic spectral sensitivity curve representative of cone functioning. The other is the adult scotopic spectral sensitivity curve representative of rod functioning. Although only cones are responsible for chromatic vision, Figure 35 illustrates that both rods and cones are differentially sensitive to lights of different wavelengths.

Early efforts to measure spectral sensitivity in infants showed that the general shapes of photopic and scotopic functions were at least similar to those of adult functions (e.g., Peiper, 1927; Trincker & Trincker, 1955). They also suggested the existence of different functions under scotopic and photopic viewing conditions, indicating early functioning of both rods and cones. Unfortunately, each of these studies was flawed in one way or another. They have been summarized and criticized in a number of places (e.g., Bornstein, 1978; Dobson, 1976). Recently, more rigorous experiments have been conducted to measure both scotopic and photopic spectral sensitivity in young infants.

Scotopic spectral sensitivity has been assessed twice. Werner (1982) conducted a VEP study of nine subjects, two of whom were infants (4 and 5 months of age). Each subject was dark-adapted for 10 to 15 minutes and was then presented a series of lights of many different wavelengths. For each wavelength, light intensity was increased gradually and a running average of the VEP was recorded. A spectral sensitivity curve was derived for each subject by plotting the intensity required at each wavelength to evoke a criterion VEP amplitude. For much of the visible spectrum the infant curves were similar to the adult. Below 450 nm, however, one of the infants (and one of the toddlers) showed a systematic elevation in relative sensitivity compared to adults. A larger number of subjects was tested at only two wavelengths. The results from this sample also suggested an elevation in the average short-wavelength

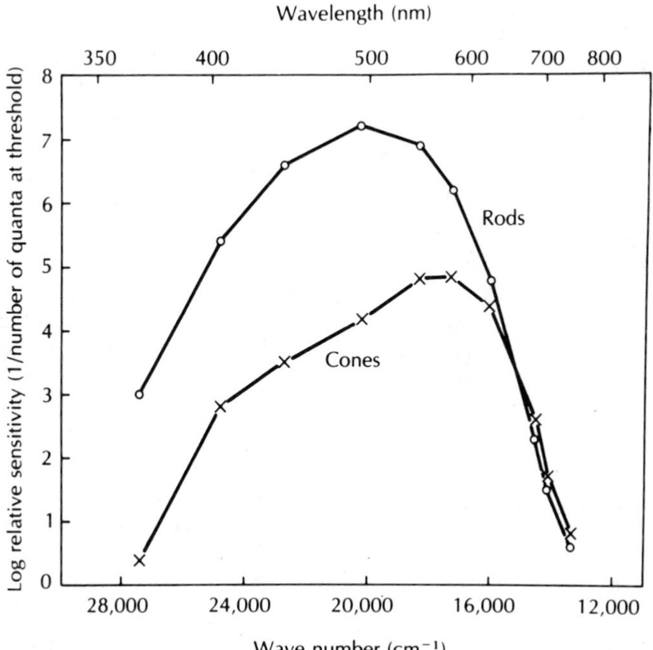

Figure 35. Adult photopic (cone) and scotopic (rod) spectral sensitivity curves. Sensitivity (the reciprocal of number of quanta at threshold) is plotted as a function of wavelength. Note that rods are generally more sensitive than cones and that the peak sensitivity of rods occurs at a lower wavelength. (From Cornsweet, 1970.)

sensitivity in infants and toddlers compared with adults. Werner (1982) hypothesized that enhanced short-wave sensitivity reflects less dense lens and macular pigmentation early in life (Boettner & Wolter, 1962), a proposal raised earlier by Dobson (1976).

Powers, Schneck, and Teller (1981) conducted a behavioral study of scotopic spectral sensitivity in 1- and 3-month-old infants. They used the FPL technique (see our discussion above on *Visual Acuity*) to measure dark-adapted thresholds for lights of various wavelengths. Figure 36 shows the average spectral sensitivity for each age group tested. Absolute sensitivity is plotted on the ordinate. Although the infants were somewhat less sensitive on the whole than the adults, the shapes of the curves were quite similar across age. The 1-month-olds exhibited a slight elevation in relative sensitivity at short wavelengths compared to adults. The 3-month-olds did not.

To summarize, the two modern studies reveal that infant scotopic spectral sensitivity is similar in shape to adult sensitivity. From this it appears that rods function early in life. The absolute sensitivity values observed by Powers et al. show that the rods are not just capable of functioning but in fact are quite sensitive.[9]

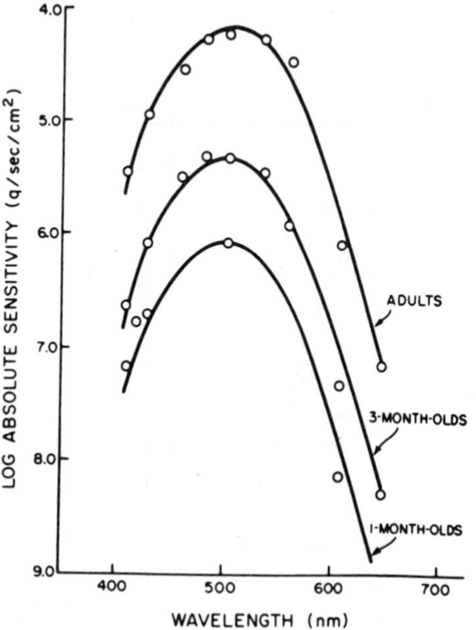

Figure 36. Average scotopic spectral sensitivity for 1-month-olds, 3-month-olds, and adults. The solid curves represent the CIE standard sensitivity function for scotopic vision in adults. They have been shifted vertically to fit the data points for each age group. The adult and 3-month data fit this function well. The 1-month data are slightly elevated at the shorter wavelengths. (From Powers et al., 1981.)

Photopic spectral sensitivity has also been assessed recently. Dobson (1976) used the VEP to examine sensitivity in adults and infants 1½ to 3 months old. The flashed stimuli were presented on a dark background. She varied the light intensity at each wavelength to find the value necessary to elicit a criterion response. Figure 37 summarizes Dobson's infant and adult findings. The average relative sensitivity for medium and long wavelengths appeared to be similar for infants and adults. At short wavelengths, the infants exhibited somewhat higher relative sensitivity. Moskowitz-Cook (1979) employed a similar VEP methodology to measure photopic spectral sensitivity at a number of ages. The flashed stimuli were presented on a dim white background. By 5 months, the infant sensitivity curves agreed closely with the adult curves. Younger infants, however, again exhibited higher relative sensitivity to short wavelengths. Moskowitz-Cook's data then confirm Dobson's findings for 2-month-olds and suggest that the short-wave elevation disappears by 5 months of age.

Peeples and Teller (1978) used the FPL technique to measure white-adapted, photopic spectral sensitivity in 2- to 3-month-olds. They varied the intensity of lights of various wavelengths presented on a white background to ascertain the intensity necessary for threshold responding. Their results are summarized in Figure 37. Overall, the spectral sensitivity curves of both infants and adults were quite flat, a typical finding with conditions of white adaptation. However, the shapes of the infant and adult curves were very similar. There was no evidence for an elevation of short-wavelength sensitivity in infants; this particular result is not necessarily in conflict with Dobson and Moskowitz-Cook because those studies either did not employ a white-adapting background or used a dim one.

To summarize, the three modern studies concur that infants' photopic spectral sensitivity is reasonably similar to adults' except that two of the studies indicate a tendency for infants less than 5 months of age to be more sensitive in relative terms to short wavelengths. This may be the result of less dense lens and macular pigmentation early in life (Boettner & Wolter, 1962; Hering, 1885).

The general similarities of infant and adult spectral sensitivity suggest the presence of normal cone functioning early in life, which in turn suggests the possibility of adultlike chromatic vision. Of course, this alone is not sufficient evidence; to demonstrate

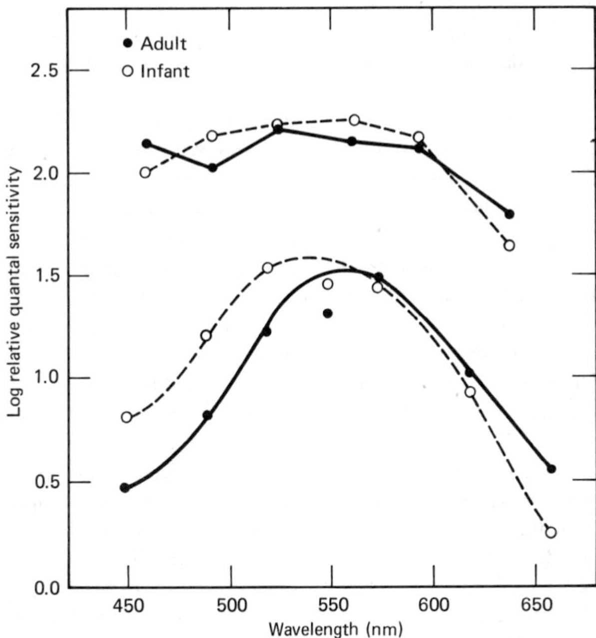

Figure 37. Average photopic spectral sensitivity for 2- to 3-month-olds and adults. The two upper curves are from Peeples and Teller. The infant curve has been shifted vertically to match the adult curve. The two lower curves are from Dobson (1976). Again, the infant curve has been shifted vertically to match the adult. See text for details. (From Werner & Wooten, 1979.)

chromatic vision, one must show that infants can discriminate on the basis of hue alone. The spectral sensitivity data have been useful in this endeavor because they have helped researchers eliminate brightness artifacts. Most modern infant studies have presented two chromatic stimuli and looked for systematic response to one as evidence for hue discrimination. They have eliminated brightness cues by one of two strategies. One strategy involves using the photopic spectral sensitivity data reviewed above to match the brightnesses of the two stimuli to a first approximation. Then, the luminances of the stimuli are varied unsystematically from trial to trial over a wide enough range to ensure that one is not always brighter than the other. Systematic responding by the infant to one of the two chromatic stimuli, across luminances, can therefore not be attributed to brightness discrimination. Schaller (1975) and Oster (1975) used this strategy, but different response measures, to demonstrate chromatic vision in 3-month-olds and 2-month-olds, respectively.

The second strategy for eliminating brightness cues was developed by Peeples and Teller (1975). They, too, used spectral sensitivity data to match approximately the brightnesses of their stimuli. They then varied luminance systematically around the estimate of the brightness match. Several luminances were presented, bridging a 0.8 log unit range in small steps. Consequently, at least one of the luminance pairings must have been equivalent in brightness for each of the infants. Peeples and Teller showed that 2-month-olds could discriminate red stripes from a white background for all luminance pairings. They concluded that 2-month-olds can discriminate on the basis of hue alone.

In summary, three 1975 reports from different laboratories using different techniques provided convincing demonstrations that 2- to 3-month-old infants can make at least some discriminations on the basis of hue alone. Thus, young infants must have at least rudimentary chromatic vision.

Adult studies have shown that an observer who has only two cone types can still make the discriminations 2- and 3-month-olds demonstrated in 1975 (Boynton, 1979). This kind of observer has dichromatic vision, the most common of color deficiencies. So the 1975 studies showed that quite young infants have at least two cone types and some neural machinery to encode wavelength information. The next question posed was: Do they have trichromatic vision and therefore possess all three cone types? Two approaches, borrowed from the adult literature, have been employed in pursuing this question.

One approach involves so-called *Rayleigh discriminations*. To explain the logic of this approach, we need to discuss adult color deficiencies. There are three types of dichromats: protanopes who seem to lack red cones, deuteranopes who seem to lack green cones, and tritanopes who seem to lack blue cones (Boynton, 1979). The first two types are much more common than the last one. Protanopes and deuteranopes, unlike color-normal trichromats, cannot distinguish one long-wavelength stimulus (550 nanometers or greater) from another if brightness cues are eliminated.

Bornstein (1976) used a version of the Rayleigh discrimination test coupled with a habituation-dishabituation procedure to examine 3-month-olds. He familiarized the infants to a 570 nanometer (nm) stimulus for 15 trials and then presented 560, 570, and 580 nm stimuli in random order. Infants exhibited the ability to differentiate the 560 nm light from the other two. Thus, they made a Rayleigh discrimination, showing that they were probably not deuteranopes nor protanopes. Bornstein actually concluded from his results that 3-month-olds have trichromatic vision but, as we explain below, this conclusion is unwarranted.

Hamer, Alexander, and Teller (1982) also explored Rayleigh discriminations in young infants. They used an FPL procedure to demonstrate that few 1-month-olds, most 2-month-olds, and virtually all 3-month-olds can make long-wavelength discriminations. This confirms Bornstein's finding and argues convincingly that most infants 2 months of age or older are not protanopes nor deuteranopes.

The second approach that has been used to determine if infants are trichromats involves the so-called *neutral-point test*. Color-deficient dichromats do not see all wavelengths of light as different from white; there is at least one point or zone in the visible spectrum that is seen as achromatic and indistinguishable from white. Trichromats, on the other hand, can distinguish all wavelengths from white. The subclasses of dichromacy can be diagnosed by noting the wavelength of their neutral point. It falls in the blue-green part of the spectrum, between roughly 490 and 500 nm, in adult protanopes and deuteranopes, the two most common kinds of dichromacy. It falls in the yellow part of the spectrum at about 570 nm for tritanopes (Boynton, 1979).

Bornstein (1976) used a habituation-dishabituation procedure and a shortened version of the neutral-point test. He familiarized 3-month-olds to various wavelengths in the 490 to 500 nm range, the range in which most adult dichromats (protanopes and deuteranopes) are unable to distinguish chromatic from achromatic stimuli. To rule out brightness artifacts, luminance was varied unsystematically during familiarization. Following the familiarization phase, infants exhibited recovery of looking (dishabituation) to a white light whose luminance was approximately equal to the average luminance of the monochromatic familiarization stimuli. In other words, they were able to discriminate the achromatic test stimulus from the chromatic familiarization stimuli. Since the infants did not exhibit a neutral point in the spectral region from 490 to 500 nm, Bornstein concluded that 3-month-olds probably possess trichromatic color vision.

This conclusion has been criticized. Salapatek and Banks (1978) and Werner and Wooten (1979) pointed out that Bornstein's results do not rule out the possibility that infants possess tritanopia, a form of dichromacy that is rare among adults but may not be among infants. Werner and Wooten argued further that Bornstein's data did not even rule out the other forms of dichromacy: protanopia and deuteranopia. They pointed out that the position of the neutral point in any dichromat is dependent on the relative sensitivities of the two remaining cone systems. Consequently, age-related differences in lens and macular pigmentation, photopigment concentrations, and neural weighting factors could shift the deuteranopic or protanopic neutral point outside the 490 to 500 nm range Bornstein tested. Werner and Wooten's argument regarding deuteranopia and protanopia loses force, however, given the above-mentioned Rayleigh discrimination results.

Teller, Peeples, and Sekel (1978) also used an adaptation of the neutral-point test to ascertain whether 2-month-olds are dichromats or trichromats. Their experiment was more exhaustive than Bornstein's in that they sampled a number of spectral regions. Infants readily discriminated red, orange, blue-green, blue, and some purple stimuli from white. They failed, however, to demonstrate a discrimination of yellow-greens and some purples from white. Consequently, Teller et al. could not conclude that 2-month-olds are trichromats. Adult tritanopes (who lack blue cones) exhibit a pattern of discrimination failures that is suggestively, but not conclusively, close to the pattern infants exhibited. Teller et al. pointed out, however, that their data alone do not warrant the conclusion that young infants are tritanopes because other reasonable interpretations of their findings exist.

Seeking more direct evidence for a blue-cone deficiency early in life, Teller's group turned to a chromatic adaptation paradigm (Pulos, Teller, & Buck, 1980). The FPL technique was used to assess spectral sensitivity under two conditions of chromatic adaptation. The shape of the spectral sensitivity curve generally changed below 560 nm for all ages tested. This means that at least two kinds of photoreceptors were functioning in the short-wave end of the spectrum. The 3-month and adult data evidenced the existence of blue cones. The 2-month data generally did not. The authors concluded that the blue cone system may be absent or relatively insensitive in most 2-month-olds and that it develops by 3 months. This result is consistent with the hypothesis that 2-month-olds are tritanopic dichromats.

In summary, infants by 2 months are at least dichromats and, consequently, must possess at least two cone systems. Most 2- and 3-month-olds can make wavelength discriminations that adult protanopes and deuteranopes cannot. Thus, they do not possess either of the two most common adult forms of color deficiency. This implies, in turn, that they possess at least green and red cone systems. Two-month-olds may be tritanopic dichromats; that is, they may have a dysfunctional or insensitive blue cone system. Three-month-olds appear less likely to have such a deficiency.

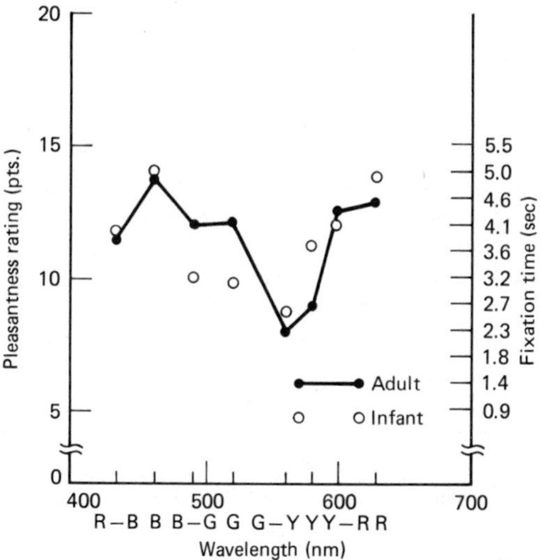

Figure 38. Adults' pleasantness ratings and infants' fixation times for lights of different wavelengths. The two ordinate scales have been adjusted to maximize agreement. The letters beneath the abscissa refer to red-blue, blue, blue-green, green, green-yellow, yellow, yellow-red, and red. (From Bornstein, 1975.)

Color Perception

With this background of current psychophysical knowledge, we now consider the development of color perception. The major question in this area has been: Do infants perceive colors in a manner analogous to adults? More specifically, two research questions have been asked: (1) Do infants' color preferences match adults' preferences? (2) Do infants perceive hues categorically and, if so, are their hue categories similar to adult categories?

One would expect color preferences to be quite variable across individuals. Yet reasonably consistent color preferences are observed in children and adults, even across cultures (Berlin & Kay, 1969; Bornstein, 1978). Given this, Bornstein (1975) wondered if infant preferences match those of adults. He showed 4-month-olds eight monochromatic stimuli spanning the visible spectrum. The stimuli were matched in brightness by adult standards which, as described above, should have yielded a reasonably close brightness match for infants. The stimuli were presented in pairs for some infants and singly for others. The average looking time for each wavelength is shown in Figure 38. Bornstein also asked adults to rate the pleasantness of the same stimuli. Their average pleasantness ratings are also shown in Figure 38. Note that the two ordinate scales (pleasantness rating and fixation time) have been adjusted to maximize agreement. The infant looking times corresponded reasonably well with adult ratings. The fact that preferences of young infants, who have had no instruction concerning colors, are similar to those of adults refutes the view that color preferences are determined culturally. Bornstein argues instead that color preferences emerge from the neural substrate of color vision.

Before describing work on hue categorization, a few definitions are needed. Hence, let us return for a moment to the dimensions of color described earlier. Hue is the closest psychological correlate of wavelength, a physical dimension of light. Thus, hue is the most salient aspect of our experience of colors. But the correspondence between hue and wavelength is imperfect. If the wavelength of a light is changed gradually and continuously, the perceived hue changes somewhat discontinuously. Generally, all of these hues can be described with four basic color names or hue categories: blue, green, yellow, and red (Boynton, 1979). The phenomenological centers of these categories are called *unique hues*. Unique hues are singular; that is, they yield a percept of only one hue. For instance, there is not blue, yellow, or red in unique green. Unique hues are in this sense central exemplars of hue categories. Hue-naming experiments with adults reveal that the relationship between hue names and wavelength is quite consistent. Different adults, even from different cultures, place category centers and boundaries at similar wavelengths (Berlin & Kay, 1969).

Bornstein (1978) argued that the cross-cultural consistency observed in hue-naming experiments implies that hue categories, like hue preferences, are not dependent on instruction. To test this hypothesis, Bornstein, Kessen, and Weiskopf (1976) examined hue categorization in 4-month-old infants using a habituation-dishabituation paradigm. Fourteen conditions were presented altogether. In each condition, a single wavelength was presented repeatedly during the habituation phase. Two types of test conditions were presented: (1) Boundary groups saw the original habituation stimulus, a second wavelength selected from the same adult hue category, and a third wavelength selected from an adjacent hue category; (2) category groups saw the original habituation stimulus and two other stimuli from the same hue category. For both types of groups, the novel wavelengths were equal physical distances (in nm) from the original habituation wavelength. Again, all stimuli were matched in brightness according to adult standards.

The results were quite complicated. In general, infants maintained habituation to the familiarized wavelength, and generalized habituation to wavelengths from the same adult hue category as the habituation stimulus, but dishabituated to wavelengths from an adjacent hue category. Overall, this implied that between-category changes are more salient than physically identical, within-category changes. Bornstein et al. (1976) drew two conclusions. First, 4-month-olds perceive hue categorically much as the voice-onset times of stop consonants in speech are perceived (see Vol. II, Chap. 8). Second, since the categories Bornstein et al. used were determined from adult experiments, 4-month-olds categorize wavelengths in much the same way as adults do.

Although both of these conclusions are interesting, they may be unjustified at this point (Werner & Wooten, 1979). Concerning the categorical perception of hue, the authors whose definition of "categorical perception" is most commonly employed explicitly discounted hue perception as an exemplar (Studdert-Kennedy, Liberman, Harris, & Cooper, 1970). Specifically, adult hue discrimination functions are not a mirror image of adult hue identification (naming) functions (Boynton, 1979), a property which is required, by definition, for categorical perception.[10] If hue perception in adults is not an exemplar of categorical perception, it is unwise to conclude that the Bornstein et al. (1976) results demonstrate adultlike categorical hue perception in infants.

Concerning the similarity of infant and adult results: Werner and Wooten (1979) argued that all of the Bornstein et al. conditions failed to eliminate the influence of hue preferences on posthabituation looking times. This is particularly evident in condition 6 where infants looked *less* at the novel stimulus from a novel category than they did to either the familiar stimulus or to the novel stimulus from the familiar category. Bornstein's (1981) counterargument that the original experimental design eliminated confounding due to hue preference is not compelling; the logical possibility remains that a low preference for particular wavelengths could have masked the presence of an ability to discriminate those wavelengths from the habituation stimulus. We believe this actually could have occurred. Low preference for the critical wavelength(s) actually exists (Bornstein, 1975) in 8 of 10 conditions in which low preference could have affected the interpretation of the results. (Bornstein's earlier preference study did not include the wavelengths necessary to assess three of the four remaining conditions. The other remaining condition was a control condition.) Consequently, the important issue of whether infant and adult hue categorization is similar must await further research.

Summary

Remarkable advances in our understanding of infant color vision have marked the last half decade. We now know that many fundamental aspects of chromatic vision are reasonably adultlike by 3 months of age or earlier. This is not to say, however, that chromatic vision is mature by that age. Many important aspects have simply not been examined in infants. In particular, we know little of the precision of early chromatic vision. We do not know, for example, what the smallest discriminable change in wavelength is early in life and how it changes with age. This and other indices of precision may reveal important developmental changes in chromatic vision beyond 3 months just as measures of acuity and contrast sensitivity have revealed such changes in pattern vision.

TEMPORAL VISION

Most research on infant visual perception has disregarded or at least minimized the time-varying or temporal aspects of vision. In reality, the infant picks up information in a series of eye movements, moving from one thing to another. Moreover, many objects of interest are not stationary themselves.

Consequently, from moment to moment, the eye may pick up entirely different distributions of light. To interpret these distributions accurately requires temporal processing. As we describe below, temporal information is probably used to make important perceptual inferences about the structure of the outside world. For these reasons, the temporal response properties of the infant visual system must be examined. We consider two aspects of temporal vision: the perception of flicker and the perception of motion. Both of these topics have been examined extensively in adults (see Kelly, 1972; Sekuler, 1975; for reviews).

Flicker

The most basic experimental question in flicker work is: What is the highest rate of flicker that can be perceived as varying with respect to time? This just-detectable flicker rate is known as the critical flicker frequency (CFF). CFF is an important index of temporal processing because it reflects the temporal summating properties of the system. Infants' CFFs have been examined in both electrophysiological and behavioral studies.

The most informative of the electrophysiological studies have used the electroretinogram (ERG), a measure of changes in electrical potential in the retina when it is exposed to light (see Armington, 1974; Maurer, 1975; for details). The ERG in adults exists at quite high flicker frequencies. Indeed, CFFs measured psychophysically and with the ERG correspond quite well so long as relatively intense stimuli are used (Dodt & Wadensten, 1954; Heck, 1957). In infants, the ERG has been used mostly to examine the response to single flashes, but a few studies have used flickering stimuli to measure the CFF. Heck and Zetterström (1958) measured CFFs in 1-day to 2-month-old infants. The stimulus field, which was large and unpatterned, was flashed on and off at various rates. Their results are shown in Figure 39. They found ERGs in response to a large flickering stimulus at all ages tested. CFF increased both with age and luminance. At the highest luminance, CFF improved from about 15 Hz at 1 day of age to 65 Hz, or nearly adultlike performance, by 2 months. CFF increased monotonically with luminance at all ages.

Horsten and Winkelman (1964) also used the ERG to investigate CFF at a number of ages. They, too, observed an increase of the CFF with increasing luminance for all ages tested. Surprisingly, however, no differences across age were reported. CFF at the highest luminance was about 70 Hz from birth to adulthood. The difference in these findings compared to those of Heck and Zetterström is most probably the result of differences in recording technique since the stimuli and subject populations appeared quite similar in the two experiments.

In summary, flicker ERG experiments disagree on the state of temporal resolution during the neonatal period but agree that adultlike resolution occurs by 2 months. Hence the retina is able to signal rapid

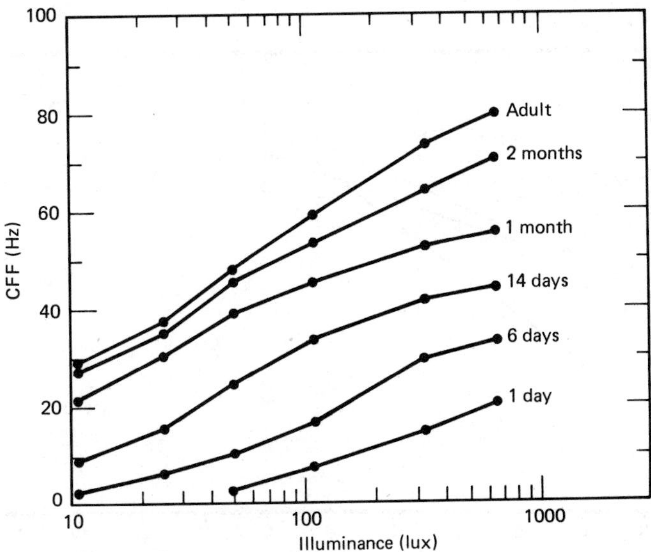

Figure 39. Critical flicker frequency (CFF) as a function of intensity as reported by Heck and Zetterström (1958). The highest flicker frequency to elicit a recordable electroretinogram (ERG) is plotted as a function of both flash illuminance and age. (From Banks, 1982.)

temporal changes with adultlike precision by 2 months of age. This does not tell us, however, what the young visual system as a whole is capable of resolving.

The VEP has been used to investigate the temporal resolution of stages beyond the infant's retina (Ellingson, 1960; Vitova & Hrbek, 1972). The VEP, unfortunately, may not be a good index of temporal resolution. Regan (1972) has noted that the range of temporal frequencies that elicits a strong VEP in adults is different from the range of frequencies that the same adults perceive as flickering. In particular, the highest flicker frequency that elicits a VEP does not generally correspond with an adult's psychophysical CFF. Consequently, we will not review VEP work concerned with the development of temporal resolution.

Recently, two behavioral studies of infant flicker perception have appeared. Nystrom, Hansson, and Marklund (1975) tested two age groups: 6-week-olds and 10-week-olds. They employed a preference paradigm. Two unpatterned, flickering stimuli were presented on every trial. In general, all possible pairings of 1, 5, 10, 20, and 100 Hz were presented to each infant. The 100-Hz stimulus was assumed to appear nonflickering because it was well above the adult CFF. Nystrom et al. observed that both groups of infants preferentially fixated the higher of the two frequencies presented, with one notable exception: When the 100-Hz stimulus was presented, the other frequency was preferentially fixated (the younger group also preferred 10 to 20 Hz). This one finding shows that infants as young as 6 weeks can demonstrate behaviorally the ability to detect flicker frequencies of at least 20 Hz. Unfortunately, frequencies between 20 and 100 Hz were not presented, so this study shows only that CFF is 20 Hz or higher at a young age.

Regal (1981) tested infants more systematically to estimate CFF as a function of age. He tested 1-, 2-, and 3-month-olds cross-sectionally and longitudinally using the FPL technique (described above under *Visual Acuity*). On each trial, two unpatterned, flickering stimuli were presented. One was always flickered at 75 Hz, a value higher than the adult CFF and, presumably, higher than the infant CFF, too. The observer judged the location of the lower frequency stimulus on each trial. The results are summarized in Figure 40. Correct responding rates of 75% were achieved on the average at 41 Hz for 1-month-olds, 50 Hz for 2-month-olds, 51 Hz for 3-month-olds, and about 53 Hz for adults. Consequently, Regal concluded that CFF is essentially adultlike by 2 months of age. This astonishing result suggests that temporal resolution unlike its spatial analogue—visual acuity—develops to adult levels very early in life.

To date, no infant work has examined sensitivity to flicker rates well below the CFF. This could be accomplished by measuring the temporal analogue of the spatial contrast sensitivity function. This function—the temporal contrast sensitivity function—represents an observer's sensitivity to unpatterned, sinusoidally flickering stimuli as a function of flicker

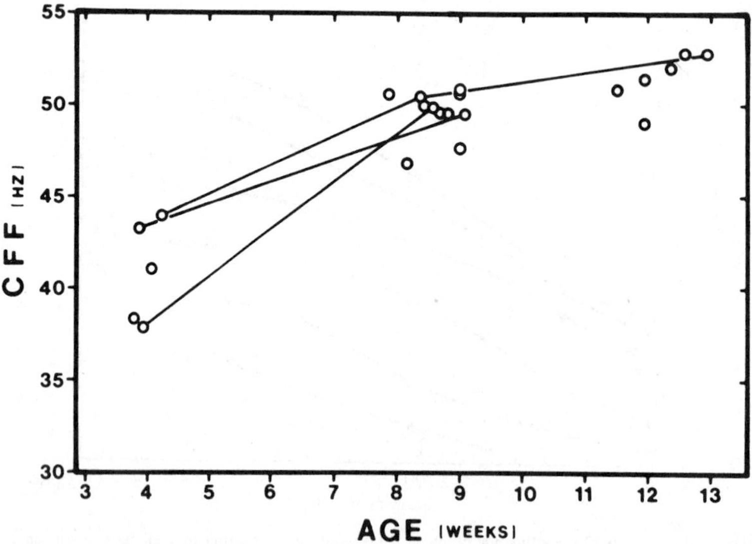

Figure 40. Critical flicker frequency (CFF) as a function of age as reported by Regal (1981). The highest flicker frequency to elicit 75% correct responding in a preferential looking paradigm is plotted. (From Regal, 1981.)

frequency. Under most conditions, the adult temporal contrast sensitivity function exhibits a bandpass characteristic; sensitivity is higher to intermediate frequencies around 15 Hz than to low or high frequencies (Kelly, 1961). Measurements of this function in infants would surely be useful because, in adults, it has revealed several important properties of the visual system and has been used to predict sensitivity to a wide variety of temporal stimuli (Kelly, 1972).

Motion

The temporal vision studies reviewed thus far have examined infant perception of very simple, unpatterned temporal stimuli. In the real world, however, most of the temporal variation in visual stimuli is associated with motion of one pattern(s) with respect to another.

Motion is a pervasive and extremely important aspect of the visual environment (Gibson, 1966). For example, movement of an observer or of an object under inspection causes motion in the retinal image of the object. If the object is rigid and fairly continuous in shape (e.g., a book), the motions of nearby portions of the object's image are similar. Hence, similarity of motion at two points is information that those two points belong to a single physical object. If, on the other hand, the motions of two points are quite dissimilar, this is information that an object boundary (or discontinuity in shape) exists between those points. This illustrates that perceptual analysis of the organization of motion in the retinal image can potentially be used to make inferences about the structure of the outside world. Several experimental demonstrations have shown that adults actually use motion information to make such inferences (e.g., Ullman, 1979; Wallach & O'Connell, 1953).

Recognizing the importance of motion, researchers have examined infants' processing of both simple spatial-temporal interactions and moving stimuli. Moskowitz and Sokol (1980), for example, measured VEPs from 2 to 6 months using counterphase flickering checkerboards. Check size and flicker rate were varied orthogonally to ascertain the character of spatial-temporal interactions. They found that the spatial response function depended on flicker rate; that is, at high flicker rates, VEP amplitude was greatest for large checks but, at low flicker rates, it was greatest for smaller checks. Moskowitz and Sokol also observed that this spatial-temporal interaction changed with age. Most notably, the largest VEP amplitude was observed for higher temporal and higher spatial frequencies with increasing age. The 3- and 4-month data are both similar and dissimilar from the adult data of this experiment. For large check sizes, the temporal frequency at which the maximum VEP response occurs is 3 to 5 Hz for both 3- to 4-month-olds and adults. For smaller check sizes, however, the peak response occurs at a flicker frequency of 5 to 6 Hz in 3- to 4-month-olds and 3 Hz in adults. Thus, the Moskowitz and Sokol results for large check sizes are congruent with the above-mentioned flicker studies using unpatterned stimuli. Smaller check sizes, on the other hand, reveal a dissimilarity between infant and adult temporal selectivity.

Caution is required before using such VEP data to infer what the development of spatial-temporal interactions may be for visual thresholds measured using other techniques. As Regan (1972) has argued, for adult VEPs, the observed spatial-temporal interactions may be caused by the peculiar temporal summating properties of the VEP itself. For this reason, Karmel, Lester, McCarvill, Brown, and Hofmann (1977) explored the relationship between visual preference and VEP for flickering patterns. In their preference experiment, they presented simultaneously two identical checkerboards flickering in an on and off fashion at different rates to 3-month-olds. They found the longest fixation durations for a flicker frequency of about 5 Hz. In the VEP experiment, only one checkerboard was present at a time. The largest VEP amplitude was for a 5-Hz flicker, suggesting a link between the VEP and visual preference. Unfortunately, check size in the VEP study was only about one-half the check size in the preference study, so the two experiments were not directly comparable.

Our knowledge of the development of motion perception per se is quite limited. In the remainder of this section, we review studies of basic capabilities. Some studies of the perception of rigidity are not reviewed here because they are considered in detail in Gibson and Spelke's chapter (see Vol. 3, Chap. 1).

Many researchers have reported that infants prefer to fixate moving as opposed to static patterns (e.g., Carpenter, 1974), but few have examined this in detail. Atkinson et al. (1977a) compared 1-, 2-, and 3-month-olds' contrast sensitivity and visual acuity for static and drifting sine wave gratings. The drifting gratings were moved in such a way as to produce a local flicker rate of 3 Hz, so velocity and spatial frequency were inversely proportional. Thresholds under the two temporal conditions were estimated using FPL for a low spatial frequency grating (0.2 c/deg), for a mid-frequency grating (0.4 c/deg for 1-month-olds and 0.9 c/deg for 2- and 3-month-olds), and for the highest detectable frequency (the visual acuity cutoff). The results revealed higher sensitivity, at all ages, to drifting than to static gratings for low and intermediate spatial frequencies. In contrast, the acuity cutoff was similar for drifting and static gratings. The adults yielded qualitatively similar results: drift enhanced sensitivity to 0.2 to 0.9 c/deg but did not to 4.8 c/deg, a spatial frequency similar to the acuity cutoffs of 2- and 3-month-olds. It is tempting to conclude that movement enhances the visibility of coarse but not fine patterns in infants. Unfortunately, these data may not be conclusive on this point. Since Atkinson et al. used a constant local flicker rate of 3 Hz to set the drift rate of their gratings, the *velocity* of drift was quite low for higher spatial frequencies like those at the acuity cutoff. Consequently, we do not know if higher velocities would have yielded higher sensitivities. Future research in this area might follow Kelly's (1979) observation that measurements of contrast sensitivity at a constant local flicker rate represent an unnatural situation because different spatial frequencies are tested at different velocities. In the real world, all of the spatial frequency components of a moving object move at the same velocity. Thus, we might learn more about basic elements of motion perception if velocity, rather than flicker rate, were held constant in such experiments.

Volkmann and Dobson (1976) have studied the visual preferences of 1-, 2-, and 3-month-olds for oscillating checkerboards. Check size was always 5½ deg. The checkerboards were moved left and right at rates from 0.06 to 2 Hz. They found at all ages that 1.5 Hz was most preferred.

Lasky and Gogel (1978) asked whether 5-month-olds perceive relative motion of simple displays in the same way adults do. The stimuli they used are illustrated and described in Figure 41. They found that 5-month-olds responded to changes in these stimuli as though the changes induced different directions of relative motion. Although alternative interpretations existed, this is an interesting approach that warrants further attention.

The investigation of the development of temporal vision has just begun, but already interesting observations have appeared. For example, temporal resolution, unlike spatial resolution, appears to be essentially mature by 2 or 3 months of life. Preliminary evidence, however, suggests that spatial-temporal interactions are not mature by this age. This latter finding is not surprising given the deficits 2- and 3-month-olds exhibit in pattern vision per se. The development of motion perception and the process by which infants use motion gradients to make inferences about the outside world are important topics that warrant more experimental attention.

DEPTH PERCEPTION

As we stated in the introduction, we believe the fundamental purpose of vision is to mediate the recognition of objects and the determination of their spatial layout in the environment. Knowing the layout of objects is essential to the guidance of motor activity. Depth perception—the process by which the distance of objects is gauged—is obviously crucial to determining spatial layout but, as we will see, it may also be important to the object recognition process.

The fundamental problem to be explained in the study of depth perception is how we come to see things three-dimensionally. The problem is set by

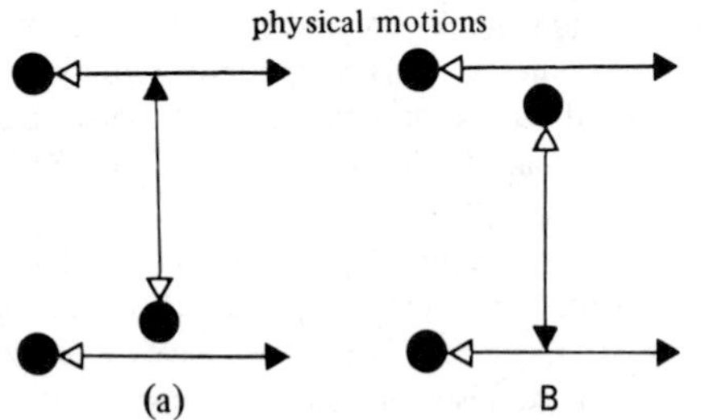

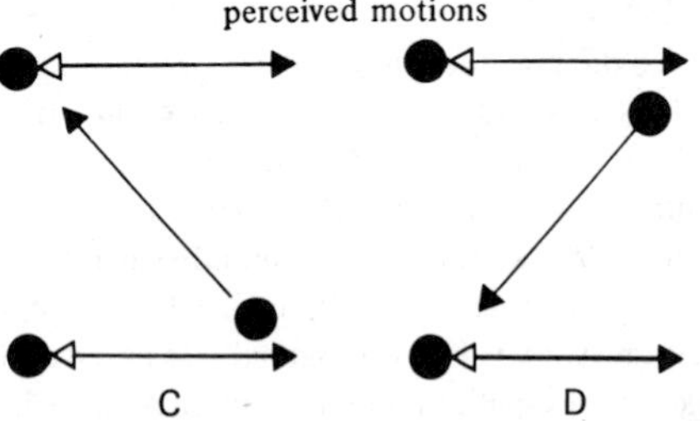

Figure 41. The experimental displays used by Lasky and Gogel. The left half of the figure shows the actual dot motions. Two dots in each display were moved left and right in parallel paths. A third dot was moved up and down between the paths of the first two. The movements were synchronized such that in one complete cycle all three dots returned to their initial positions simultaneously. The only difference between the motions in displays A and B is the motion of the third dot relative to the other two. In display A, the third dot moves up as the other two move from left to right. In display B, the third dot moves down as the other two move from left to right. The phase difference between displays A and B has a large perceptual effect. The right half of the figure shows the motions adults perceive. The perceived path of the third dot varies as shown in C and D for displays A and B, respectively. (From Lasky & Gogel, 1978.)

the structure of the eye. The retinal surface on which optical images are projected is two-dimensional, so it can only indicate the direction from which a beam of light comes and not, in any obvious way, the distance to the reflecting surface from which the beam came.

Since the problem of converting such a two-dimensional representation into a three-dimensional percept is both difficult and important, it is not surprising that the visual system uses a variety of information sources. These sources can be divided into three classes, each of which contains multiple cues to depth: binocular information, monocular static information, and kinetic information. The multiplicity of depth cues used by the visual system is essential because different cues provide reliable information in different situations. For example, binocular disparity (discussed in detail below) is a powerful depth cue but only for objects within a few meters of the observer. Aerial perspective (the shift of hue toward blue and the loss of contrast that accompanies distance), on the other hand, is only effective for objects that are miles away. The situational dependence and information value of some, but not all, depth cues have been examined. Gibson (1950, 1966) and others explored the information value of a number of cues and, recently, some formal models concerning texture gradients (Stevens, 1981), interposition (Huffman, 1971), optical flow (Longuet-Higgins & Prazdny, 1980; Prazdny, 1980), and binocular disparity (Marr, 1982) have appeared.

The multiplicity of cues whose effectiveness varies from situation to situation raises an intriguing problem: How does the visual system normally arrive at a cohesive interpretation of depth? Most researchers have argued that this is not a serious problem because, outside of the laboratory, information from various sources is generally in agreement (e.g., Hochberg, 1971b). This is often not true, however, as illustrated in the following example. Consider again the operation of two depth cues: binocular disparity and aerial perspective. If two objects—one composed of a high-contrast, green material and the other of a low-contrast, blue material—are both 1 meter from an observer, disparity cues would signal equidistance while aerial perspective cues would signal that the green object is closer. In this situation, adults rely on the disparity information and, therefore, judge that the objects are equidistant. If two large objects composed of the same materials as those above are both 1 mile from an observer, the disparity and aerial perspective cues would once again signal equidistance and nonequidistance, respectively. In this case, however, observers rely on the aerial perspective cue and judge the green object to be nearer. Thus, the problem of interpreting and integrating depth information from different sources is nontrivial in everyday as well as laboratory settings.

Before turning to work on the development of depth perception, we should mention a potential link between depth perception and object recognition. As mentioned earlier, Marr (1982) has hypothesized that the visual system converts visual inputs into object-centered representations. The recovery of information in the retinal image to implement this conversion in his model requires an analysis of depth relationships in the image of the object. Thus, from some theoretical perspectives, depth information may be an integral part of the object recognition process.

There is now a lengthy literature on the development of depth perception that has been reviewed by Pick and Pick (1970), Yonas and Pick (1975), Rosinski (1977), Aslin and Dumais (1980), and Yonas and Owsley (in press). The majority of infant studies have researched the global question: When does the perceptual appreciation of depth first develop? Until recently, most did not attempt to isolate individual depth cues to determine young infants' ability to utilize such cues. In general, we follow this chronology in our discussion, first considering the general issue of discriminating three-dimensional from two-dimensional objects and then moving to the individual depth cues that mediate such discriminations. As part of our discussion of individual cues, we also consider whether these cues mediate an appreciation of depth. Finally, we consider the mechanisms underlying the development of depth perception.

A number of researchers have shown that very young infants can discriminate three-dimensional from two-dimensional stimuli. Fantz (1961), for example, presented a disk and a sphere to infants as young as 1 month of age. The infants showed significant preference for the sphere over the disk, which indicated that they could discriminate the two. Campos, Langer, and Krowitz (1970) placed 2-month-olds face down on either the shallow or deep side of a visual cliff apparatus (Walk & Gibson, 1961). Greater heart rate deceleration occurred on the deep side, indicating the ability to differentiate the two sides. One might conclude from the Fantz and Campos et al. demonstrations that 1- and 2-month-olds perceived depth. But an alternative explanation exists; namely, the infants may not have perceived depth but rather responded to a specific stimulus variable such as contour density. The major problem in research on infant depth perception has been distinguishing these alternative accounts. Consequently, researchers have taken two approaches: (1) examining in some detail infants' sensitivity to individual depth cues with the hope of showing that discrimination occurs only with values that specify depth and (2) examining infants' appreciation of depth information by looking for depth-appropriate behaviors.

Two general classes of depth cues have been identified: monocular cues and binocular cues (Gibson, 1966; Kaufman, 1974). We consider binocular depth cues, and the development of binocular vision in general before turning to monocular depth cues.

Binocular Vision and Convergence

When one looks at an object, each eye receives a slightly different view of it. This slight discrepancy between the two retinal images is called binocular parallax. The mature visual system can use this information to determine the solidity or three-dimensionality of objects. A special case of binocular parallax can be generated with two-dimensional patterns presented separately to the two eyes. The difference between the two patterns is called *binocular disparity;* the resulting perception of depth is called *stereopsis.* In normal adults, stereopsis is exquisitely sensitive; the smallest amount of disparity necessary to perceive depth is only 5 to 15 sec of arc (Westheimer & McKee, 1980). For this and other reasons, stereopsis has often been regarded as the most refined of binocular visual capabilities. Worth (1915) believed that stereopsis was the highest level in a hierarchy of binocular functions. In particular, he stated that stereopsis required two other, lower order binocular functions: (1) bifoveal fixation, the ability to direct both eyes toward a common point in space, and (2) fusion, the combining of the two somewhat disparate retinal images into a single percept. It now appears that bifoveal fixation and fusion are not necessary for at least rudimentary stereopsis (e.g., Westheimer & Mitchell, 1958), but they are important for fine stereopsis. We use Worth's hierarchy as a framework for the discussion of the development of binocular vision (Aslin & Dumais, 1980, suggested this framework).

Bifoveal fixation allows the eyes to be directed toward the same part of an object. The object then stimulates corresponding points in the two retinas. When the eyes are not aligned (i.e., bifoveal fixation is not present), diplopia (perceived double images) or suppression of the input to one eye results. Diplopia and suppression are associated with markedly reduced stereopsis, so bifoveal fixation is necessary for fine stereopsis.

Several investigators have used corneal photography to examine the development of the vergence eye movements (convergence and divergence) that allow bifoveal fixation. Wickelgren (1967, 1969) and Maurer (1974) estimated the direction of gaze of the two eyes in newborn and older infants who were viewing a single visual target. Both investigators concluded that the pupil centers of young infants generally straddle the location of the target or, in other words, that the lines of sight are more divergent than they should be for bifoveal fixation. Maurer reported that the amount of divergence decreased during the first 2 or 3 months. These findings imply that bifoveal fixation is absent in neonates. This may be unwarranted, however.

Slater and Findlay (1972) argued that the apparent divergence is a measurement artifact resulting from difficulty in estimating the line of sight (visual axis) from photographs of the pupil and the corneal reflections of reference lights. The artifact is caused by the discrepancy between the eye's optic axis (which is what corneal photography assesses) and the visual axis. The optic axis of each eye projects temporally relative to the visual axis. This means the optic axes are always more divergent than the visual axes. The angle between the optic and visual axes—the angle alpha—is greater in newborns (8 to 10 deg) than in adults (4 to 5 deg; Bennett & Francis, 1969; Mann, 1964).

Because the angle alpha remains constant for all angles of convergence, Slater and Findlay (1975) and Aslin (1977) assessed bifoveal fixation by measuring changes in vergence for different target distances. Both studies employed corneal photography. Slater and Findlay presented stationary targets to newborns at 5, 10, and 20 inches. They observed appropriate changes in vergence between the 10- and 20-inch target distances but not between those distances and the 5-inch distance. Aslin measured changes in vergence to an alternately approaching and receding target. He found that 2- and 3-month-olds converged and diverged in the appropriate direction and often with the appropriate magnitude. One-month-olds also converged and diverged in the correct direction but with insufficient magnitude to maintain constant bifoveal fixation. Both experiments revealed considerable between- and within-subject variability, particularly among the younger infants. Thus, appropriate changes in binocular eye alignment occur in very young infants, but the accuracy of such changes is quite variable. Because of this variability, much of the neonate's visual experience must consist of misaligned images. The consistency of eye alignment appears to improve during the first few months of life, so the problem of misaligned images is transitory.

Fusion, the combining of the two retinal images into a single percept, has been the most difficult of the three levels of binocular vision to study in infants. It is not necessarily a prerequisite for stereopsis because adults can make stereoscopic discriminations with stimuli that cannot be fused (Westheimer & Mitchell, 1958). However, it is probably necessary for fine stereopsis. Only one infant study to date has attempted to examine the development of fusion. Aslin (1977) used prisms placed in front of one eye to introduce binocular disparity. Adult responses in this situation consist of a biphasic eye movement involving a saccadic and a vergence component. Aslin found that infants 3 and 4½ months old generally did not exhibit the saccadic refixation. Six-month-olds, on the other hand, usually did. Aslin concluded that either the younger infants did not realign their eyes (change vergence) after the introduction of the prism or that they did realign but only by using a vergence eye movement. Aslin and Dumais (1980) hypothesized that this experiment demonstrates fusion in 6-month-olds, but the experiment may simply demonstrate appropriate attempts to maintain bifoveal fixation and tell us nothing about fusion.

The most important question in the study of binocular development has been whether infants are capable of stereoscopic depth perception. Stereopsis is the appreciation of the relative distance of objects based on binocular disparity alone. Because the perception of depth is a subjective experience, it has been difficult to find an appropriate dependent measure of stereopsis in infants. Infant stereopsis research has taken two approaches: (1) studies of the development of disparity detection and (2) studies of the development of depth-appropriate responses to stereoscopic displays.

The detection of disparity is necessary for stereoscopic depth perception because disparity is the adequate stimulus for stereopsis. Disparity detection is not sufficient for stereopsis, however, because an observer may be able to detect disparity without appreciating the relative depth specified.

Several investigators have examined the development of disparity detection. Appel and Campos (1977) used a habituation-dishabituation paradigm in a study of 2-month-olds. The stimuli were stereoscopic photographs of a single object (line stereograms). They found that infants who were habituated to a photograph with no disparity would dishabituate when disparity was subsequently introduced. Unfortunately, significant dishabituation was not observed when the photograph with disparity served as the habituation stimulus and the one without disparity served as the test stimulus. The results, therefore, were not conclusive. Furthermore, the type of stereoscopic display used by Appel and Campos does not minimize potential monocular cues for discriminating the disparate and nondisparate stimuli.

Held, Birch, and Gwiazda (1980) also used line stereograms to study disparity detection developmentally. A number of infants were tested longitudinally. The amount of disparity presented was varied from 58 min to 1 min. The results showed that most infants reliably detected the larger disparities by 4 months. By 5 to 6 months, most demonstrated the detection of a 1-min disparity. Thus, the development of accurate disparity processing appeared to begin generally in the third month and to progress very rapidly thereafter. Held et al. presented a number of control conditions to determine if monocular cues or nonstereo binocular cues were contributing to their findings. Those conditions yielded generally negative results, so it appears that the infants' responses were based on stereopsis. They also noted that the development of crossed disparity processing (disparity specifying an object closer than the fixation point) seemed to precede that of uncrossed disparity processing (disparity specifying an object farther than the fixation point). Birch, Gwiazda, and Held (1982) confirmed this result.

The random-dot stereogram developed by Julesz (1960, 1971) presents binocular disparity while minimizing potential monocular cues. Atkinson and Braddick (1976) used random-dot stereograms to assess the ability of 2-month-olds to detect disparity. Preferential looking and habituation-dishabituation paradigms were used. Both yielded somewhat ambiguous results. In the preference experiment, two of the four infants tested exhibited significant preferences for stereograms with disparity over those without. The habituation study yielded similar results: Two of the four infants demonstrated the ability to discriminate stimuli with horizontal disparity (the direction of disparity which is the adequate stimulus for stereopsis) from stimuli with vertical disparity and from stimuli with no disparity. These results suggest that some 2-month-olds are able to detect disparity.

Fox, Aslin, Shea, and Dumais (1980) conducted a more extensive study with elegant stimulus control. The stimuli were dynamic, random-dot stereograms (Shetty, Brodersen, & Fox, 1979) that effectively eliminated any potential monocular cues. Fox et al. presented a small region of horizontal disparity embedded in a larger field of no disparity. Adults perceived the disparate region as standing out in depth from the rest of the display. In testing infants, Fox et al. moved the disparate region on each trial from the center to either the left or right of the display. An adult observer, who could not see the display, made a forced-choice judgment of the direction of motion. Forty infants between 2 and 5 months of age were tested. The results indicated that infants older than 3 months could reliably detect a large disparity. Younger infants did not demonstrate reliable detection. This demonstrates the ability to detect disparity by 3 months of age, but does not necessarily imply the presence of stereopsis. To look for evidence of stereopsis, the authors conducted another experiment in which the magnitude of disparity was varied. For adults, stereopsis is disrupted at very large disparities, although the perception of disparity per se is still possible. Fox et al. found that 3- to 5-month-olds reliably oriented toward the stereoscopic form at disparities for which adults experienced stereoscopic depth and did not orient at disparities for which adults did not experience depth. They concluded then that 3- to 5-month-olds possess stereopsis. This conclusion may, however, be unwarranted. At large disparities, their subjects in fact reliably oriented away from the stereoscopic form, which implies that they could detect the disparate region but found it aversive. So the infants, unlike adults, may have been responding to the same stimulus dimension in both the small and large disparity conditions.

Petrig, Julesz, Kropfl, Baumgartner, and Anliker (1981) also examined the development of disparity detection using dynamic, random-dot stereograms (and correlograms). Infants from 7 to 48 weeks of age were tested using VEPs. The correlograms alternated at 2.5 Hz from a display in which the pattern elements were perfectly correlated between the two eyes to a display in which the elements were perfectly negatively correlated. Adults with stereopsis perceive such a stimulus as alternating between a flat surface (correlated phase) and a "wooly" surface (negatively correlated phase). The stereograms also alternated at 2.5 Hz, but from a display with no disparity to one with checkerboard patches of disparity. Adults with stereopsis perceived this stimulus as oscillating between a flat surface and a checkerboard standing out in depth. Petrig et al. found significant VEPs to the alternating correlograms and stereograms in all infants 17 weeks of age or older. None of the infants less than 9 weeks of age exhibited significant VEPs to these stimuli. The 9- to 17-week period was transitional. Since the displays effectively eliminated monocular cues, the authors concluded that infants begin to detect disparity around 2 months but do not do so consistently until about 4 months.

The studies reviewed above on the detection of binocular disparity used a variety of different stimuli and response measures. For this reason, one might not expect the results to agree, but the agreement is actually quite good. Figure 42 illustrates this. It shows the percentage of infants in each study who demonstrated the ability to detect disparity as a function of age. The disparity magnitudes presented varied from study to study and are noted in the caption. The figure shows clearly that the ability to detect disparity is first evident between 2 and 3 months of age and is demonstrable in virtually all infants by 5 to 6 months.

These consistent data suggest the question: What mechanism(s) is(are) responsible for the development of disparity detection? We discuss three possibilities that have also been considered elsewhere (Aslin & Dumais, 1980; Held et al., 1980). First, perhaps the visual acuity (see *Visual Acuity* above) and contrast sensitivity (see *Contrast Sensitivity* above) of the young infant are too poor to allow disparity detection and stereopsis. This hypothesis has face validity since disparity detection and stereopsis require the comparison of two monocular

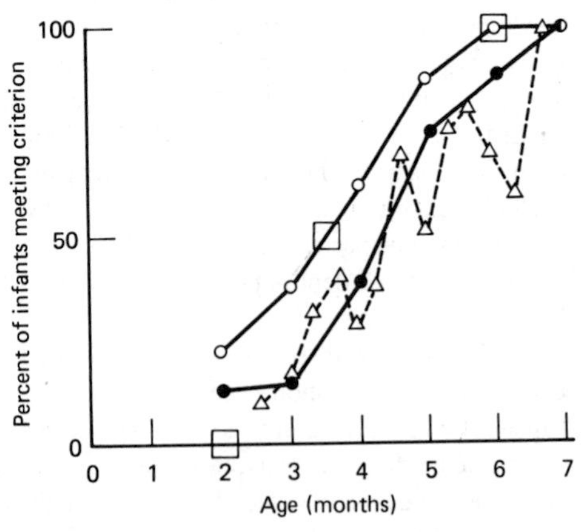

Figure 42. Detection of binocular disparity at different ages. Three different experiments are summarized. The percentage of infants meeting the criterion for detection in each experiment is plotted as a function of age. Open and filled circles: data from Birch et al. (1982) for disparities of 58 minutes of arc (open circles) and 1 minute of arc (filled circles). Large open squares: data from Petrig et al. (1981). Open triangles: data from Fox et al. (1979) and unpublished data from R. Aslin. (From Teller, 1982.)

images. If those images are poor in quality, any comparison of them should suffer correspondingly. Westheimer and McKee (1980) have studied this in adults by measuring the effect on stereoacuity of artificially reducing acuity and contrast sensitivity. They found that such reductions led to consistent decreases in stereoacuity. For example, stereoacuity fell by a factor of 6 (from 3–6 sec to 19–37 sec) when acuity was reduced to approximately that of a 2-month-old. This illustrates that a visual acuity deficit alone leads to lower stereoacuity but cannot account for the failure of most 2-month-olds to demonstrate the ability to detect even large disparities. Westheimer and McKee also observed that simulated reductions in contrast sensitivity caused reductions in stereoacuity, but again the reductions were too small to argue that infants' contrast sensitivity deficits alone (or the acuity and contrast sensitivity deficits combined) can account for their inability to detect even large disparities. Thus, the low acuity and contrast sensitivity of young infants may contribute to their stereoscopic deficits, but they cannot account for them by themselves.

A second possibility is that bifoveal fixation is too imprecise early in life to allow disparity detection. This hypothesis also has some face validity. When an observer is improperly converged on a target, the stereoscopic images may fall on parts of the retina that are too disparate for adequate binocular comparisons. This hypothesis alone is unlikely to account for the early deficits in disparity detection, however, because infants converge reasonably accurately before they consistently exhibit disparity detection (Aslin, 1977; Slater & Findlay, 1975).

The third possibility is that disparity-detecting mechanisms per se are the constraining factor early in life and, as they develop, the ability to detect disparity emerges and improves. Because it is impossible to study disparity-detecting mechanisms in humans directly, only indirect evidence can be garnered to evaluate this hypothesis. The development of disparity-detecting mechanisms—binocular visual cortical neurons—has been examined electrophysiologically in kittens (see our discussion above on *Visual Cortex*). Pettigrew (1974) found that most cortical neurons were binocular in newborn kittens but that they did not respond differentially to a fairly broad range of binocular disparities. With normal visual experience, the range of disparities to which individual neurons responded decreased. By 5 weeks of age, a population of neurons, each finely tuned to a narrow range of disparities, was present. Thus, in cats at least, disparity-detecting mechanisms are very coarsely tuned early in life and become more finely tuned during infancy with appropriate visual experience. One would expect that the ability to demonstrate disparity detection behaviorally would improve correspondingly. Timney (1981) has shown this to be the case. Using a behavioral technique, he showed that binocular disparity thresholds were very poor in newborn kittens yet improved to adultlike levels by 6 weeks of age. This is suggestive, but indirect, evidence that the development of disparity mechanisms is responsible for the emergence of stereopsis in humans.

Other indirect evidence comes from studies of visual experience. The role of visual experience in the development of binocular vision has been an important topic for both theoretical and clinical reasons. Most of this work has focused on the visual cortex (see our discussion on *Visual Cortex*), but confirmatory behavioral experiments have been conducted. The binocularity of cortical neurons in kittens and young monkeys is quite susceptible to disruption. Rearing under conditions of monocular deprivation or artificial strabismus causes a profound loss of binocularity and hence of disparity selectivity among such neurons (Hubel & Wiesel, 1965a; Wiesel & Hubel, 1965). If disparity-selective cortical neurons are essential to stereopsis, one would expect such animals to exhibit quite poor stereopsis, if any at all. Blake and Hirsch (1975) and Packwood and Gordon (1975) have confirmed this. They raised kittens under a condition of alternating monocular occlusion, a rearing condition known to disrupt cortical binocularity but not visual acuity. Their kittens performed quite poorly compared to normals in a behavioral test of disparity detection.

These animal results led two groups of investigators to search for analogous effects in humans (Banks et al., 1975; Hohmann & Creutzfeldt, 1975). Both studies used a psychophysical measure, interocular transfer of the tilt aftereffect (the apparent shift of a vertical target's orientation following exposure to a tilted target), to assess binocular function in children and adults who had received anomalous visual experience during some period of their lives. The anomalous experience resulted in each case from strabismus (misalignment of the two eyes). Although all subjects had correctly aligned eyes at the time of testing, only those who had strabismus during the first three years of life showed profound deficits. Figure 43 shows estimates of susceptibility to anomalous experience based on these experimental results. Apparently, a sensitive period exists in humans, just as it does in cats and monkeys.

In summary, the ability to detect binocular disparity, the adequate stimulus for stereopsis, seems to

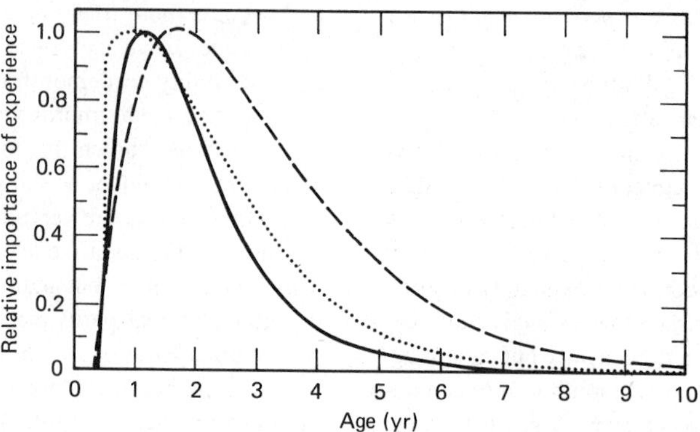

Figure 43. Estimates of how the importance of visual experience for the development of binocularity varies with age. The functions are those which yielded the highest correlations between measured and estimated binocularity for three groups of strabismics. The dashed line represents the best-fitting function for the congenital esotropes studied by Banks et al. (1975). The dotted line represents the best-fitting function for the late-onset esotropes studied by Banks et al. The solid line is the best-fitting function obtained for the late-onset esotropes studied by Hohmann and Creutzfeldt (1975). (From Aslin & Banks, 1978.)

emerge between 2 and 3 months of life and to improve rapidly thereafter. In large part, this emergence and rapid growth are probably the result of the development of binocular mechanisms per se.

The detection studies reviewed above show that infants can detect horizontal disparity, the adequate stimulus for stereopsis, by about 3 months of age. Unfortunately, they do not tell us with certainty whether infants at that age actually experience the depth relations specified by binocular disparity. Two possibilities exist: (1) The experience of depth specified by binocular disparity first appears at the time disparity detection emerges and (2) the experience of depth develops only after the ability to detect disparity. One can investigate this issue by determining when depth-appropriate responses such as reaching or avoidance can be elicited by stereoscopic displays.

Bower (1971, 1972) and Bower, Broughton, and Moore (1970) reported that infants as young as 7 days of age reach appropriately to the "location" of a stereoscopically presented object (virtual object) and become upset by the lack of tactual feedback from their reaches. Unfortunately, these results are probably not reliable. Dodwell, Muir, and DiFranco (1976) and Ruff and Halton (1977) failed to observe either directed reaching or emotional upset under conditions quite similar to Bower's. Consequently, there is no reliable evidence that neonates experience the depth relations specified in stereoscopic displays.

Reaching is better developed in older infants, so Gordon and Yonas (1976) examined reaches and other behaviors in 5- and 6-month-olds when presented a stereoscopic display. They found that reaches were directed to about the same location regardless of the "distance" of the virtual object. However, three other measures—position of the infant's head, number of reaches, and number of prehensile behaviors—varied appropriately with the virtual object's distance. Two other experiments, by Bechtoldt and Hutz (1979) and Field (1977), found that infants reached appropriately to stereoscopic displays by 5 to 7 months.

Another study by Yonas, Oberg, and Norcia (1978) used a stereoscopic display whose apparent distance changed rapidly over time, thereby simulating the approach of an object on a collision course with the infant's face. Five-month-olds, but not 3½-month-olds, exhibited more fixation, reaching, head withdrawal, and blinking on trials in which the virtual object loomed toward the infant than on trials in which distance was not specified.

The Gordon and Yonas (1976), Bechtoldt and Hutz (1979), and Yonas et al. (1978) results imply that the depth relations specified by binocular disparity are appreciated by 5 months of age. The failure to observe evidence of stereopsis at 3 to 3½ months could be the result of an inability to appreciate stereoscopic depth, but it could also be the result of an inability to respond in a depth-appropriate manner. The latter explanation cannot be rejected at this point because the responses used to date—reaching (Bechtoldt & Hutz, 1979; Field, 1977; Gordon & Yonas, 1976) and defensive reactions to impending collision (Yonas et al., 1978)—do not appear to be mature before 4 to 5 months (White, Castle, & Held, 1964; Yonas, Bechtold, Frankel,

Gordon, McRoberts, Norcia, & Sternfels, 1977). Consequently, we cannot yet distinguish the two possible relationships between the development of disparity detection and stereopsis discussed above.

Another ambiguity in the existing studies of depth-appropriate behaviors concerns the type of stereoscopic displays used. Aslin and Dumais (1980) and Yonas and Owsley (in press) pointed out that virtual object displays provide no contours (other than the edge of the field itself) to lock convergence onto the screen. Hence it is possible that infants converge to the disparate object instead. It is unclear, then, whether binocular disparity or convergence is the most salient depth cue in these displays. Von Hofsten's (1977) finding that 5- to 8-month-olds can use convergence angle to gauge visually guided reaching lends credence to this argument.

Monocular Depth Cues

Binocular information is, of course, not the only means to specify depth. In this section, we consider the other source of depth information: monocular depth cues. Some monocular depth cues require motion either by the observer or the object, and some do not. We will discuss the latter, static depth cues first and then turn to kinetic depth cues.

Static cues are often called *pictorial cues* because they are used by artists to create the impression of depth on a flat surface. Such cues include linear perspective, interposition, texture gradients, relative and familiar size, and aerial perspective (see Hochberg, 1971b, for descriptions). Gibson (1950) has noted that many of these cues are closely related. Another monocular, static cue—visual accommodation (see our discussion above on *Visual Accommodation*)—will not be considered here because it is at best a weak depth cue (Hochberg, 1971b).

The study of infant sensitivity to pictorial cues has been impeded by difficulties in developing appropriate stimuli. For example, most pictures with rich perspective cues specifying depth also provide conflicting monocular and binocular information that the picture is flat. Consequently, infants could fail to respond to the depth specified in such a stimulus for at least two reasons. First, they may not be sensitive to pictorial cues and hence do not appreciate the depth specified. Second, they may actually be sensitive to pictorial cues and appreciate the depth specified but rely more on the other information which specifies a flat display. Yonas and his colleagues have solved this problem to a considerable degree by independently manipulating the salience of pictorial and nonpictorial cues. In the next several paragraphs we review their elegant series of studies on the development of pictorial depth cues.

Yonas, Cleaves, and Pettersen (1978) investigated infants' sensitivity to linear perspective by examining their ability to utilize that depth cue to guide their reaching. The primary stimulus was a trapezoidal window (Ames, 1951) presented parallel to the frontoparallel plane. Adults viewing the stimulus monocularly thought, incorrectly, that the larger side of the window was nearer. Yonas et al. manipulated binocular cues by incorporating monocular and binocular conditions. They found that 7-month-olds under monocular conditions reached more frequently to the "near" than to the "far" side of the trapezoidal window even though the window was actually frontoparallel. A picture of a 7-month-old reaching in this manner is shown in Figure 44. This result suggests that 7-month-olds pick up and use linear perspective cues. To rule out the possibility that the infants were simply reaching to the larger of the two sides, Yonas et al. presented a size-control display in the frontoparallel plane; the size of the two sides differed, but no linear perspective cues were

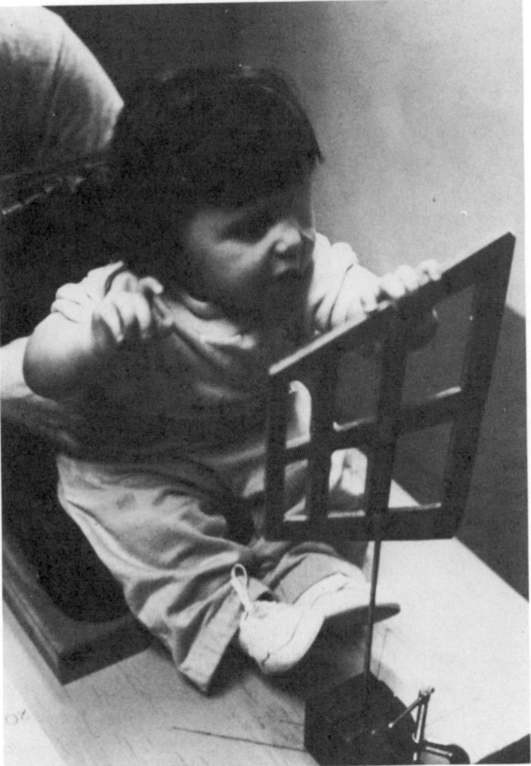

Figure 44. Seven-month-old infant grasping the frontal trapezoidal window while wearing an eye patch. (From Yonas & Granrud, 1983.)

provided. When presented this control stimulus, 7-month-olds reached equally often to the two sides. Further investigation revealed that binocular viewing eliminated the reaching bias toward the "near" side of the trapezoidal window. Thus, when conflicting binocular information was present, obedience to linear perspective cues disappeared in 7-month-olds.

Yonas et al. also explored younger ages. They found under monocular conditions that 5-month-olds, unlike 7-month-olds, reached about equally often to the "near" and "far" sides of the trapezoidal window. This result was not caused by a simple lack of specificity in the reaches of 5-month-olds because, when presented a slanted rectangular window (a nonillusory stimulus), they reached more frequently to the near side.

It is tempting to conclude that the utilization of linear perspective cues develops between 5 and 7 months of age. Yonas and his colleagues were concerned, however, that 5-month-olds in their experiment may have appreciated the depth specified by linear perspective but did not rely on it in the face of conflicting information (e.g., texture gradients, motion parallax) that the trapezoidal window was in the frontoparallel plane. They (Kaufmann, Maland, & Yonas, 1981) hoped to create a more sensitive test by comparing reaches to two different stimuli: a slanted trapezoidal window, in which the physically smaller side was closer to the infant than the larger side, and an equally slanted rectangular window. Viewing was monocular in all conditions. Five-month-olds were not influenced by the different perspective information in the two windows: They favored the physically closer side in both cases. Seven-month-olds, on the other hand, were again strongly affected by perspective information: They favored the closer side of the rectangular window but exhibited significantly less preference with the trapezoidal window.

The Yonas et al. (1978) and Kaufmann et al. (1981) reports indicate that the sensitivity to, and utilization of, one pictorial depth cue—linear perspective—emerges between 5 and 7 months of age. Critics might caution that an alternative explanation still remains: Infants 5 months of age or younger may actually appreciate the depth specified by linear perspective but ignore this information when other, conflicting cues, such as texture gradients, motion parallax, among others, are present. In other words, if a situation could be devised in which *only* linear perspective information was present, 5-month-olds might yet demonstrate their appreciation of it. We believe such a criticism is carrying the analytic approach a bit too far. First, it is not clear that such a display is physically realizable. Second, we believe the most important data for developmental theories will not be the age norms at which different depth cues, when presented in isolation, are first used. More important will be descriptive statements on how reliance on different cues varies as their salience is manipulated at different ages. So we believe it is reasonable to conclude that the utilization of linear perspective, in situations where its salience is enhanced above that of other depth cues, develops between 5 and 7 months of age.

Yonas and his colleagues have explored the development of other pictorial cues. Yonas, Pettersen, and Granrud (1982) found that familiar size is also an effective depth cue for 7-month-olds. They again used reaching as the index of depth perception. The familiar objects were two types of photographs of the faces of the infants' mothers. One type was smaller than life size while the other was larger. The unfamiliar objects were a small and large checkerboard. All were presented at the same distance. When viewing monocularly, 7-month-olds reached more often to the large face than to the small face. This appeared to reflect utilization of familiar size rather than relative size because no difference in reaching toward the two unfamiliar checkerboards was observed. The preference for the large face was eliminated with binocular viewing, so it was not caused by a simple preference to reach for large things. The 5-month-olds failed to provide evidence of sensitivity to familiar size; they reached as often to the large and small faces and the large and small checkerboards under monocular and binocular viewing conditions.

Granrud and Yonas (cited by Yonas and Granrud, in press) examined infants' sensitivity to the pictorial cue of interposition. The stimuli they used are depicted in Figure 45. Stimuli A and B had identical outer contours. They differed only in that interposition was specified in A and not B. Stimuli A and C had identical segments, but interposition was specified in A only. The 7-month-olds showed a significant preference, under monocular viewing conditions, to reach for the apparently nearer side of stimulus A but showed no preference with stimuli B and C. The 5-month-olds exhibited no reaching preference for any of the stimuli. Therefore, it appears that 7-month-olds utilize interposition information to gauge depth but that 5-month-olds do not.

In summary, Yonas and his colleagues have produced convincing evidence that sensitivity to pictorial (monocular, static) depth cues develops between 5 and 7 months of age, which is somewhat

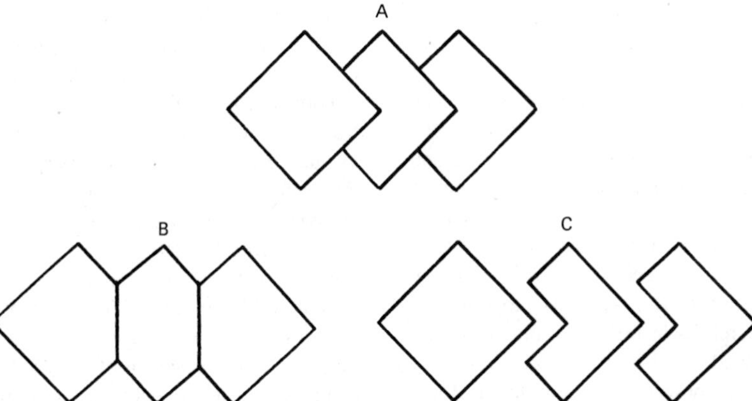

Figure 45. Schematic drawing of the interposition stimuli used by Granrud and Yonas. Stimuli A and B had identical outer contours, but interposition was specified in A and not B. Stimuli A and C had identical segments, but interposition was not specified in C. (Adapted from Yonas & Granrud, 1983.)

later than the emergence of sensitivity to binocular cues.

Kinetic information for depth is produced by changes over time in the retinal image. These changes can be created by movements of the observer's head or body (as is the case with motion parallax), or they can be created by movements of objects in the environment (as is the case in optical expansion and perspective transformation). Presumably, kinetic depth information is available throughout development since object and self-induced motion are common events independent of age. Moreover, the encoding of kinetic information could be simpler early in life than the encoding of other kinds of depth information. For example, the encoding of binocular information may be more difficult since it first requires proper alignment of the eyes. Consequently, it is somewhat surprising that kinetic information, unlike other sources of depth information, has not received much experimental attention. Only two aspects of kinetic information have been pursued developmentally in any detail: (1) the development of sensitivity to, and appreciation of, optical expansion cues for impending collision and (2) the development of visual proprioception for controlling posture. The latter aspect is discussed in our section above on *Postural Control*.

As an object approaches an observer (or an observer approaches an object), the retinal image of the object expands centrifugally. Indeed, centrifugal expansion alone can produce a powerful illusion of impending collision (Schiff, 1965). Similarly, centripedal or shrinking patterns are seen as receding. Bower, Broughton, and Moore (1971) investigated neonates' reactions to the approach of real objects. They reported, without providing much detail, that infants less than 3 weeks of age rotated their heads upward, raised their hands between the object and their faces, widened their eyes, and became quite upset emotionally. This constellation of behaviors seemed to reflect attempts to avoid the object. Bower et al. also studied the reaction to optical expansion alone. Using a shadow-casting device, like the one Schiff (1965) described, they projected the shadow of a solid object onto a screen. The shadow was made to expand or contract, which, to adults, specified the approach or withdrawal of an object, respectively. Avoidance behaviors were observed in the expansion trials, although not as consistently as in the real object condition. Ball and Tronick (1971) confirmed this result with a somewhat different display. They observed avoidance behaviors in 1-month-olds for symmetrical optical expansion (which specifies a direct collision or hit) but not for asymmetrical expansion (which specifies a miss). These two studies indicated that human neonates appreciate the impending collision specified by centrifugal optical expansion alone.

Yonas et al. (1977) conducted a well-controlled, thorough series of experiments that challenged the interpretations offered by Bower et al. and Ball and Tronick. They argued that the components of infants' reactions in those studies may have been the result of simply tracking a rising contour in the displays rather than avoiding a perceived impending collision. Three experiments were conducted, but the first was the most important. In this one, three conditions were presented to infants from 1 to 9 months of age: (1) symmetrical optical expansion of a solid form (specifying a direct collision), (2) asymmetrical expansion of the form (specifying a miss), and (3) a rising contour of a nonexpanding form (which did not specify collision). The infants' responses to each of these displays were scored using objective, quantitative criteria. The results revealed significant upward head rotation at all ages to both the symmetrical expansion and the rising contour. Indeed, no differences were observed between those two conditions on any of the response dimensions until 4 to 6 months. By then, reliable differences in the blinking frequency were seen. At 8 to 9 months, consistent differences in frequency of arm raising were also obtained. Significant head withdrawal and fussiness were not observed, contrary to the Bower et al. (1971) report.

In a second experiment, Yonas et al. looked at the reactions of 1- to 2-month-olds to stimuli whose expansion did not involve a rising contour. Infants responded similarly to trials in which a collision with the chest was specified and trials in which a miss was specified. Yonas et al. concluded that infants do not appreciate the impending collision specified by symmetrical optical expansion until 4 to 6 months of age. Of course, it remains possible that infants appreciate the significance of optical expansion earlier, but either do not rely on it in the face of conflicting binocular and monocular information that the surface is not approaching or do not yet have the response repertoire to react appropriately.

Yonas, Pettersen, Lockman, and Eisenberg (1980) studied the parameters of optical expansion that produce avoidance in more detail. Three types of stimuli were used in these experiments. One was a symmetrical expansion (or contraction) with the expansion rate (or contraction rate) increasing geometrically. This specified an object approaching (or withdrawing) at a constant rate. The second was a symmetrical expansion (or contraction) with a constant expansion (or contraction) rate. This specified an object slowing down as it approached (or speeding up as it withdrew). The third was a sudden darkening or lightening of the entire stimulus display. Yonas et al. looked for evidence of defensive reactions by comparing rates of blinking and head withdrawal in the two versions (expansion vs. contraction or darkening vs. lightening) of each stimulus type. Three- and 4-month-olds were much more likely to blink and withdraw from the geometrically expanding display than from the geometrically contracting display. None of the other conditions yielded a significant difference. Thus, their avoidance behavior was fairly specific; it was elicited only in the condition specifying a constant rate of approach. One-month-olds were only tested on the geometrically expanding/contracting displays and on the constant-rate expanding/contracting displays. In both conditions, they blinked and withdrew more frequently to the expanding version. Thus, their avoidance behavior was not specific. It would be interesting to know if the sudden darkening/lightening condition would yield differential responses at this age. Unfortunately, Yonas et al. (1980) did not use this condition with 1-month-olds.

Ball and Vurpillot (1976) noted that approaching surfaces are often specified by changes in texture rather than by expansion of a closed figure. They compared the effectiveness of texture flow, specifying either the approach or withdrawal of a surface, to the effectiveness of closed figure expansion or contraction. Their 2-month-old subjects exhibited avoidance behavior on the approaching texture trials only, which implies that texture flow is more salient than closed figure expansion early in life. Yonas and Owsley (in press) raised the possibility, however, that Ball and Vurpillot's findings reflect infants' tracking of rising texture elements in the upper visual field, so some further study is needed.

The role of texture was also examined by Carroll and Gibson (1981). They examined whether 3-month-olds could distinguish an approaching object from an approaching aperture. These two conditions were specified by differential texture flow. In the approaching object condition, expanding texture filled the central region of the stimulus. In the approaching aperture condition, expanding texture filled the peripheral regions in the stimulus. Carroll and Gibson observed considerably more avoidance to the approaching object than to the approaching aperture. This suggests that 3-month-olds can use different patterns of texture flow to distinguish between the consequences of the two events.

Thus, infants by 3 to 4 months of age demonstrate their sensitivity to, and appreciation of, kinetic depth cues that specify impending collision. Their perceptual knowledge is reasonably specific in this regard; 3- and 4-month-olds respond differentially to expansions specifying a hit rather than a miss, to expansions specifying a constant rather than a decreasing rate of approach, and to expansions specifying an approaching object rather than an approaching aperture. One should note, however, that it is premature to conclude that younger infants do not possess the same perceptual knowledge, because they actually may but simply do not exhibit it.

In summary, infants exhibit sensitivity to all three classes of depth information (kinetic, binocular, and monocular) by 7 months of age. Sensitivity to these three classes seems to develop in a sequence. Kinetic information appears first, then binocular, and finally monocular static information. The next step is to examine the mechanisms by which these sensitivities develop.

Mechanisms of Development

In our review of binocular vision, we discussed several experiments in animals and humans that have demonstrated the importance of early visual experience to the development of the ability to detect disparity. The role of experience in the development of the ability to appreciate depth information is also an important topic, but little experimental attention has been devoted to it. Recently, though, some work concerning the avoidance response on the visual cliff has appeared. Current opinion is that many infants will crawl across the deep side soon after they learn to crawl (Campos, Hiatt, Ramsay, Henderson, & Svejda, 1978; Scarr & Salapatek, 1970). The question then arises: What determines the avoidance response in individual infants? Rader, Bausano, and Richards (1980) and Richards and Rader (1981) examined this by evaluating which of the three subject variables—age at onset of crawling, age at testing, and number of weeks of crawling experience—was the best predictor of the avoidance response. Age at onset of crawling turned out to be the most reliable predictor in both experiments, an intriguing result that merits further consideration.

Summary

In summary, we have learned a great deal in the past decade about the development of depth perception. In rough outline, sensitivity to the three major classes of depth information appears to emerge in a sequence: kinetic information appears first, then binocular, and, finally, monocular static information. This summary statement may prove to be too simple because with further experimentation we may learn, for example, that some kinetic cues emerge later than some binocular cues. How the infant learns to interpret and integrate information from these different sources is an intriguing but unexplored question. It is presumably even more difficult for infants than for adults because the infant's "hardware" changes dramatically with age, causing continual changes in the meaning of particular values of binocular disparity and other important cues.

CONCLUSION

In this section we discuss two topics fairly briefly. First, we review the neurally based theories of infant visual perception described in our earlier section on this topic and summarize the evidence for and against each of them. Second, we outline in general terms the advances made in the field of infant visual perception in the last decade and describe some possible directions for research in the next.

Three models of early visual development—Bronson (1974), Maurer and Lewis (1979), and Haith (1980)—were described above in some detail. Each model was based on anatomical/physiological mechanisms. Bronson (1974) hypothesized that early visual development can be characterized by differential rates of development among two physically and functionally distinct subsystems: the primary (geniculocortical) and secondary (collicular) visual systems. The secondary system develops earlier, so a neonate's visual behavior should correspond roughly to a decorticate adult's visual behavior. The general notion that the visual cortex and superior colliculus subserve different functions is supported by a number of anatomical, physiological, and behavioral findings. However, some of Bronson's anatomical and physiological claims are probably false (see our discussion on *Neurally Based Theories of Infant Visual Perception* for details). In reality, the retinal periphery is not overrepresented in the secondary system. Furthermore, the primary and secondary systems are not actually parallel; instead, there are significant interactions between them. Finally, Bronson's view that the visual cortex is dysfunctional early in life is probably incorrect; VEP and anatomical observations suggest that the cortex is capable of some function at birth, though it is assuredly rather primitive. In spite of these criticisms, a wide range of infant data are consistent with Bronson's model. Many of the deficits observed before 2 months are consistent with the notion that the visual cortex is quite immature. Eye movement systems guided primarily by subcortical mechanisms are more refined early in life than systems guided by cortical mechanisms (see *Visuomotor Mechanisms* above). OKN is asymmetric in neonates just as it is in decorticate and deprived cats (see *Optokinetic Nystagmus* above). Moreover, neonates are subject to the "externality" effect and so are decorticate monkeys (see *Internal-External Effects* above). It would be quite interesting to look for form discrimination and generalization deficits, as Ganz and Haffner (1974) have in deprived cats, but this has not been done with neonates.

In conclusion, Bronson's view of two parallel systems, one of which is functional at birth and one of which is not, is probably too extreme. The general idea, however, that the unfolding of visual capabilities early in life is mediated primarily by cortical maturation is consistent with a variety of empirical observations.

Maurer and Lewis (1979) proposed a related version of the two visual systems model. Their model emphasized differences between X and Y cells (see *Developmental Anatomy and Physiology* above). Recall that X cells are supposedly designed for detailed pattern analysis and Y cells for the detection and localization of visual stimuli. Maurer and Lewis hypothesized that the X pathway to the cortex and the Y pathway to the colliculus are functional at birth. They also hypothesized that the Y pathway to the cortex becomes functional between 1 and 2 months, as does the Y pathway from the cortex to the colliculus. This model is consistent with a number of anatomical and physiological findings primarily in cats; however, we questioned it earlier on a number of grounds. We restate two of our criticisms here. First, it is unclear whether X and Y cells really form two functionally distinct categories of cells, particularly in primates and at higher levels in the visual pathway. Second, cells in the superficial layers of the monkey's superior colliculus do not seem to depend significantly on cortical development as they do in cats. Thus, Maurer and Lewis' argument that some collicular functions depend on the development of the visual cortex may not be valid for primates (consider, for example, binocularity).

Several behavioral findings are reasonably consistent with the Maurer and Lewis model. For example, OKN is asymmetric and some pattern discrimination capability exists in neonates, as predicted. Some other findings, however, are inconsistent. According to their model, X cells, which are responsible for fine pattern analysis, are mature at birth, whereas cortical Y cells, which are responsible for fine temporal resolution, are immature. One would expect then that visual acuity, an index of fine pattern vision, should be relatively good early in life and temporal resolution relatively poor. In fact, the data suggest just the opposite (see our sections above on *Visual Acuity* and *Flicker*).

Finally, Haith (1980) proposed a "cortical firing rate" model that posits that the visual cortex controls visuomotor behavior even in newborns. An infant's behavior changes with age as the receptive fields of cortical cells become more refined. Although it seems likely that the visual cortex is involved in visuomotor behavior from birth onward, the model has two shortcomings. First, it does not explain well the variety of visual capacities young infants do not possess (symmetric OKN, discrimination of internal elements in compound figures, etc.). Second, the model is nearly impossible to test because one cannot collect data on the characteristics of single cortical cells in human infants.

These three models all have some specific deficiencies. Nonetheless, they have been very useful in guiding empirical and theoretical work in the last decade. The three models concur that many of the changes in early visual development reflect growth of the visual cortex. This, of course, cannot be the whole story since profound changes occur at other loci in the visual pathway, but the general idea does seem to be useful. Future research, however, must strive to specify the relationship between perceptual and cortical development much more clearly. *What* properties of the developing cortex are most important, and *how* do these properties determine perceptual function? Reasonable answers to these questions are needed to test and elaborate the cortical growth hypothesis. Such answers will not come easily for, as Barlow (1979) has pointed out, the relationship between cortical and perceptual function has not been specified very clearly in adults, let alone in infants.

In 1970, a single chapter in Carmichael's *Manual* summarized work on infancy (Kessen, Haith, & Salapatek, 1970). Indeed, only 13 pages were devoted to infant visual perception. The ensuing years have yielded an exciting and significant expansion of our understanding of early visual perception. Consequently, a whole chapter is now devoted to the topic (and, even here, much work has been treated too cursorily or overlooked altogether).

Where has the work since 1970 brought us? Clearly, the description of several significant aspects of visual perception at different ages is well underway. A number of such advances have been reviewed above. However, many lines of research in this field have not been particularly illuminating. In most of these cases, the empirical and theoretical work has addressed paradigm-specific questions. In other words, the goal appears to have been the explanation of various observations within a particular experimental paradigm rather than the description and understanding of the development of visual capabilities that are fundamentally important to infants. A good example of such a case is the pattern preference literature. This literature has not provided much more than a list of stimulus dimensions that influence infants' fixation preferences among nonrepresentational patterns. The list allows some predictions of which patterns are preferred over others but, as we pointed out in the section on *Pattern Preferences,* it has not really illuminated infants' general pattern visual capabilities.

How might the likelihood of such unrewarding excursions be diminished? As we stated in the introduction, it is extremely useful to give serious thought to the everyday functions each visual capability is designed to serve for humans in general and infants in particular.[11] Accordingly, we attempted in each section above to sketch a plausible outline of the normal function of the visual capability in question. We hope these modest outlines can in some cases help guide experimental and theoretical work to more significant aspects of visual development.

In closing, we wish to describe two aspects of visual development that are extremely important, yet have not been considered in detail. First, we argued in the introduction that the mature visual system must extract "valid" clues to objects' identities and positions in the environment. What these clues are and how they might actually be extracted (even in adults) are, in general, poorly understood questions. Given the difficulty researchers have had in identifying the clues and the mechanisms for extracting them, one wonders how infants develop the requisite skills to identify and utilize "valid" sources of information. If the mechanisms for extracting such information are not predetermined, infants may have to discover those types of information through experience with the environment. The explanation of how this is accomplished appears to be an exceedingly difficult problem. Currently, most theories and models do not even consider this problem and those that do (e.g., Gibson, 1969) have not yet identified specific, testable mechanisms.

Second, once some capability develops and "valid" information can be used to infer the structure of the external world, infants must somehow maintain stability of the representation of this structure, despite dramatic changes in the "hardware" of their visual system. Consider, for example, the representation of the spatial layout of objects and the use of that representation to guide reaches. The distribution and connectivity of several levels in the visual pathway (e.g., retinal neurons) change significantly during the first year. Thus, the central representation of spatial layout must change, too. Consequently, the maintenance of accurate reaching demands constant recalibrations between central representations and motor commands. This also seems to be a fundamental aspect of perceptual development, yet few researchers have examined it.

Currently, our understanding of these two aspects of perceptual development is fragmentary at best. The explanation of them is an ample challenge for the next decade of research.

NOTES

1. Tests of linear spatial summation are conducted in the following manner. A sine wave grating is positioned over the cell's receptive field and exchanged periodically with a uniform field of the same average luminance. For cells with linear spatial summation, a position can be found at which the exchange evokes no response.

2. More recently, some controversy has arisen over these findings. Stryker and Sherk (1975) raised kittens in Blakemore and Cooper drums but were unable to replicate their physiological findings using a more rigorous, computer-controlled methodology. However, this failure to replicate was restricted to the Blakemore and Cooper experiment because they were able to replicate Hirsch and Spinelli's results when they used their goggle-rearing technique (Stryker, Sherk, Leventhal, & Hirsch, 1978).

3. In addition, two versions of each of these combinations were used: one with a regular arrangement of elements and one with a slightly irregular arrangement. This variable had a small, but significant, effect on preferences. We do not consider it here, however, because the main interest in the current discussion is the size and number manipulation.

4. Note that the horizontal axis plots the square root of contour density. Since there is no theoretical importance to the square root of contour density, it seems to us that it would, in general, be best to plot such functions in units of contour density. This allows one to avoid many of the machinations necessary to compare stimuli of different overall sizes (Greenberg & Blue, 1975; Greenberg & O'Donnell, 1972; Karmel, 1974).

5. To see how overall size is related to contour density, consider a 10 × 10 deg checkerboard with 1 deg checks and a 2 × 2 deg checkerboard with 1 deg checks. Both have a contour density when computed in degrees of visual angle (Karmel, 1974) of 2.0. In other words, increasing the size of a pattern by adding more pattern elements of the same size has no effect on contour density.

6. We have pointed out above that linear systems analysis provides a complete characterization of a system's input-output relationship so long as the system possesses certain strictly defined properties. We noted that the adult visual system, and presumably the infant system as well, does not exactly meet

these requirements but that, with certain restrictions on the stimuli used, the approach can be successfully applied. One of these properties is linearity, which we noted is probably not much of a problem when one studies patterns near their detection thresholds. In this section, however, we are considering infants' discrimination of, and preference for, supra-threshold patterns. Thus, the assumption of linearity may be violated. Banks and Salapatek (1981) and Banks and Ginsburg (in press) have used an empirical approach to this problem: If the linear systems' predictions are generally accurate, violations of the linearity assumption must not have been severe enough to invalidate the approach.

7. First, Hainline and Lemerise did not calibrate their measurements, a particular problem with the measurement system they used. When calibration was performed in another experiment, average corrections of ± 3 to 4 deg (6 to 8 deg total) were required (Hainline, 1981). For example, one subject required a 7 deg correction. Consequently, Hainline and Lemerise had difficulty evaluating what part(s) of the figures was (were) being fixated. This was particularly true for the small figure whose total width was less than the technique's measurement error. Second, the statistical tests they used were not suitable for assessing relative scanning breadth. Specifically, measures such as fixation variance, average number of subareas fixated in the whole visual display, and average length of eye movement are indices of absolute rather than relative scanning extensiveness. Finally, the most relevant test of age-related changes in scanning breadth (their Table 3) was performed in a manner that would mask various sorts of single-feature or narrow scanning. For each infant and stimulus, the proportion of fixations falling in each of the four quadrants of the screen was calculated. Then an analysis of variance was performed for each quadrant with age as a between-subjects factor. The statistical results are shown in column 8 of their Table 3. This analysis does not index scanning extensiveness well for two reasons: (1) The data were collapsed across stimuli so an infant who fixated a single quadrant for one stimulus and a different quadrant for another stimulus would be treated as an extensive rather than a narrow scanner; (2) separate analyses were conducted for each quadrant collapsed across subjects of a given age; so if infants in one age group were narrow scanners, but preferred different quadrants among themselves, the group as a whole would appear to be extensive scanners.

8. Segregation is often referred to as figure-ground segregation, that is, the organization of a unified figure standing in front of a diffuse background. We regard figure-ground segregation as a special case of the general segregation process, so we use the more general term throughout.

9. Powers et al. point out that the adults were only about 50 and 10 times more sensitive than 1-month-olds and 3-month-olds, respectively. This means that a signal initiated by the absorption of only a few hundred quanta of light passes all the way through the infant's visual system to evoke a reliable behavioral response. This is a remarkable level of sensitivity, particularly in light of the traditional view of poor vision early in life. This result also illustrates the sensitivity of the FPL technique.

10. This point is actually somewhat controversial. Sandell, Gross, and Bornstein (1979), for example, have argued the opposite:

> There is a close relationship between human wavelength discriminability and hue categorization (naming): Regions of relatively good wavelength discrimination correspond closely with hue boundaries, and regions of relatively poor wavelength discrimination correspond closely with hue categories. (p. 634)

A close look at the reports they cite to buttress their argument reveals that the relationship between discrimination and naming functions is not that close. Smith (1971), for example, attempted to predict the wavelength discrimination function from the hue-naming function. He showed that the general shape could be predicted, but not all the peaks and valleys and their locations, as was implied by Sandell et al.

11. We hope it is clear from previous sections that our view is not extreme on this point. For example, we certainly do not believe that only naturalistic settings should be used for perception experiments. On the contrary, well-controlled laboratory experiments are extremely useful, but only when the aspect of visual behavior under study has some important function in everyday environments.

REFERENCES

Abramov, I., Gordon, J., Hendrickson, A., Hainline, L., Dobson, V., & LaBossiere, E. The retina of the newborn human infant. *Science*, 1982, *217*, 265–267.

Albrecht, D. G., DeValois, R. L., & Thorell, L. G. Visual cortical neurons: Are bars or gratings the optimal stimuli? *Science*, 1980, *207*, 88–90.

Allen, J. *Visual acuity development in human infants up to 6 months of age*. Unpublished doctoral dissertation, University of Washington, 1978.

Alpern, M. Vergence and accommodation. I. Can change in size induce vergence movements? *American Medical Association Archives of Ophthalmology*, 1958, *60*, 355–357.

Alpern, M. Types of movement. In H. Davson (Ed.), *The eye. Muscular mechanisms* (Vol. 3). New York: Academic Press, 1969.

Alpern, M. Effector mechanisms in vision. In J. W. Kling & L. A. Riggs (Eds.), *Woodworth and Schlosberg's experimental psychology* (3rd ed.). New York: Holt, Rinehart and Winston, 1971.

Ames, A. Visual perception and the rotating trapezoidal window. *Psychological Monographs*, 1951, Series No. 324.

Ames, E. W., & Silfen, C. K. *Methodological issues in the study of age differences in infants' attention to stimuli varying in movement and complexity*. Paper presented at the meeting of the Society for Research in Child Development, Minneapolis, 1965.

Anderson, K. V., & Symmes, D. The superior colliculus and higher visual functions in the monkey. *Brain Research*, 1969, *13*, 37–52.

Andriessen, J. J., & Bouma, H. Eccentric vision: Adverse interactions between line segments. *Vision Research*, 1976, *16*, 71–78.

Appel, M. A., & Campos, J. J. Binocular disparity as a discriminable stimulus parameter for young infants. *Journal of Experimental Child Psychology*, 1977, *23*, 47–56.

Armington, J. C. *The electroretinogram*. New York: Academic Press, 1974.

Aslin, R. N. Development of binocular fixation in human infants. *Journal of Experimental Child Psychology*, 1977, *23*, 133–150.

Aslin, R. N. Development of smooth pursuit in human infants. In D. F. Fisher, R. A. Monty, & J. W. Senders (Eds.), *Eye movements: Cognition and visual perception*. Hillsdale, N.J.: Erlbaum, 1981.

Aslin, R. N., & Banks, M. S. Early visual experience in humans: Evidence for a critical period in the development of binocular vision. In H. L. Pick, Jr., H. W. Leibowitz, J. E. Singer, A. Steinschneider, & H. W. Stevenson (Eds.), *Psychology: From research to practice*. New York: Plenum Press, 1978.

Aslin, R. N., & Dumais, S. T. Binocular vision in infants: A review and a theoretical framework. In L. Lipsitt & H. Reese (Eds.), *Advances in child development and behavior*. New York: Academic Press, 1980.

Aslin, R. N., & Jackson, R. W. Accommodative-convergence in young infants: Development of a synergistic sensory-motor system. *Canadian Journal of Psychology*, 1979, *33*, 222–231.

Aslin, R. N., & Salapatek, P. Saccadic localization of peripheral targets by the very young human infant. *Perception and Psychophysics*, 1975, *17*, 293–302.

Atkinson, J., & Braddick, O. Stereoscopic discrimination in infants. *Perception*, 1976, *5*, 29–38.

Atkinson, J., & Braddick, O. Development of optokinetic nystagmus in infants: An indicator of cortical binocularity? In D. F. Fisher, R. A. Monty, & J. W. Senders (Eds.), *Eye movements: Cognition and visual perception*. Hillsdale, N.J.: Erlbaum, 1981.

Atkinson, J., Braddick, O., & French, J. Infant astigmatism: Its disappearance with age. *Vision Research*, 1980, *20*, 891–893.

Atkinson, J., Braddick, O., & Moar, K. Contrast sensitivity of the human infant for moving and static patterns. *Vision Research*, 1977, *17*, 1045–1047. (a)

Atkinson, J., Braddick, O., & Moar, K. Development of contrast sensitivity over the first 3 months of life in the human infant. *Vision Research*, 1977, *17*, 1037–1044. (b)

Atkinson, J., Braddick, O., & Moar, K. Infants' detection of image defocus. *Vision Research*, 1977, *17*, 1125–1126. (c)

Atkinson, J., & French, J. Astigmatism and orientation preference in human infants. *Vision Research*, 1979, *19*, 315–317.

Aulhorn, E., & Harms, H. Visual perimetry. In D. Jameson & L. M. Hurvich (Eds.), *Handbook of sensory physiology. Visual psychophysics* (Vol. VII/4). New York: Springer-Verlag, 1972.

Awaya, S., Miyake, Y., Amaizumi, Y., Shiose, Y., Kanda, T., & Komuro, K. Amblyopia in man suggestive of stimulus deprivation amblyopia. *Japanese Journal of Ophthalmology*, 1973, *17*, 69–82.

Bach, L., & Seefelder, R. *Atlas zur Entwicklungsgeschichte des Menschlichen Auges*. Berlin: Verlag von Wilhelm Engelmann, 1914.

Baker, F. H., Grigg, P., & von Noorden, G. K. Effects of visual deprivation and strabismus on the responses of neurons in the visual cortex of the monkey, including studies on the striate and prestriate cortex in the normal animal. *Brain Research*, 1974, *66*, 185–208.

Ball, W., & Tronick, E. Infant responses to impending collision: Optical and real. *Science*, 1971, *171*, 818–820.

Ball, W., & Vurpillot, E. Perception of movement in depth in infancy. *L'Annee Psychologique,* 1976, *76,* 383–399.

Banks, M. S. Infant refraction and accommodation. *International Ophthalmology Clinics,* 1980, *20,* 205–232. (a)

Banks, M. S. The development of visual accommodation during early infancy. *Child Development,* 1980, *51,* 646–666. (b)

Banks, M. S. The development of spatial and temporal contrast sensitivity. *Current Eye Research,* 1982, *2,* 191–198.

Banks, M. S. How should we characterize visual stimuli? In N. Krasnegor & G. Gottlieb (Eds.), *The measurement of vision and audition during the first year of life.* Norwood, N.J.: Ablex Press, in press.

Banks, M. S., Aslin, R. N., & Letson, R. D. Sensitive period for the development of human binocular vision. *Science,* 1975, *190,* 675–677.

Banks, M. S., & Ginsburg, A. P. Early visual preferences: A review and a new theoretical treatment. In H. W. Reese (Ed.), *Advances in child development and behavior.* New York: Academic Press, in press.

Banks, M. S., & Salapatek, P. Acuity and contrast sensitivity in 1-, 2-, and 3-month-old human infants. *Investigative Ophthalmology and Visual Science,* 1978, *17,* 361–365.

Banks, M. S., & Salapatek, P. Infant pattern vision: A new approach based on the contrast sensitivity function. *Journal of Experimental Child Psychology,* 1981, *31,* 1–45.

Banks, M. S., & Stephens, B. R. The contrast sensitivity of human infants to gratings differing in duty cycle. *Vision Research,* 1982, *22,* 739–744.

Barlow, H. B. Dark and light adaptation: Psychophysics. In D. Jameson & L. Hurvich (Eds.), *Handbook of sensory physiology. Visual psychophysics* (Vol. VII/4). New York: Springer-Verlag, 1972.

Barlow, H. B. Three theories of cortical function. In R. D. Freeman (Ed.), *Developmental neurobiology of vision.* New York: Plenum Press, 1979.

Barlow, H. B., Blakemore, C., & Pettigrew, J. D. The neural mechanism of binocular depth discrimination. *Journal of Physiology,* 1967, *193,* 327–342.

Barlow, H. B., Fitzhugh, R., & Kuffler, S. W. Dark adaptation, absolute threshold and Purkinje shift in single units of the cat's retina. *Journal of Physiology,* 1957, *137,* 327–337.

Barnet, A., Lodge, A., & Armington, J. Electroretinogram in human infants. *Science,* 1965, *148,* 651–654.

Barrera, M. E., & Maurer, D. Recognition of mother's photographed face by the three-month-old infant. *Child Development,* 1981, *52,* 714–716.

Barten, S., Birns, B., & Ronch, J. Individual differences in the visual pursuit behavior of neonates. *Child Development,* 1971, *42,* 313–319.

Beasley, W. C. Visual pursuit in 109 white and 142 Negro newborn infants. *Child Development,* 1933, *4,* 106–120.

Bechtold, A. G., Bushnell, E. W., & Salapatek, P. *Infants' visual localization of visual and auditory targets.* Paper presented at the meeting of the Society for Research in Child Development, San Francisco, 1979.

Bechtoldt, H. P., & Hutz, C. S. Stereopsis in young infants and stereopsis in an infant with congenital esotropia. *Journal of Pediatric Ophthalmology,* 1979, *16,* 49–54.

Bedrossian, R. H. The effect of atropine on myopia. *Annals of Ophthalmology,* 1971, *3,* 891–897.

Belkin, M., Yinon, U., Rose, L., & Reisert, I. Effect of visual environment on refractive error of cats. *Documenta Ophthalmologica,* 1977, *42,* 241–301.

Bennett, A. G., & Francis, J. L. Aberrations of optical images. In H. Davson (Ed.), *The eye. Visual optics and the optical space sense* (Vol. 4). New York: Academic Press, 1969.

Berlin, B., & Kay, P. *Basic color terms: Their universality and evolution.* Berkeley: University of California Press, 1969.

Berlyne, D. E. The influence of the albedo and complexity of stimuli on visual fixation in the human infant. *British Journal of Psychology,* 1958, *56,* 315–318.

Berman, N., Blakemore, C., & Cynader, M. Binocular interaction in the cat's superior colliculus. *Journal of Physiology,* 1975, *246,* 595–615.

Berry, R. N. Quantitative relations among vernier, real depth, and stereoscopic depth acuities. *Journal of Experimental Psychology,* 1948, *38,* 708–721.

Bertenthal, B. I., Campos, J. J., & Haith, M. M. Development of visual organization: The perception of subjective contours. *Child Development,* 1980, *51,* 1072–1080.

Birch, E. E., Gwiazda, J., & Held, R. Stereoacuity development for crossed and uncrossed disparities in human infants. *Vision Research,* 1982, *22,* 507–513.

Blake, R., & Hirsch, H. V. B. Deficits in binocular depth perception in cats after alternating monocular deprivation. *Science,* 1975, *190,* 1114–1116.

Blakemore, C. The conditions required for the maintenance of binocularity in the kitten's visual cortex. *Journal of Physiology,* 1976, *261,* 423–444.

Blakemore, C. The development of stereoscopic mechanisms in the visual cortex of the cat. *Proceedings of the Royal Society of London (Ser. B),* 1979, *204,* 477–484.

Blakemore, C., & Cooper, G. F. Development of the brain depends on the visual environment. *Nature,* 1970, *228,* 477–478.

Blakemore, C., & Donaghy, M. Co-ordination of head and eyes in the gaze changing behaviour of cats. *Journal of Physiology,* 1980, *300,* 317–335.

Blakemore, C., Garey, L. J., & Vital-Durand, F. The physiological effects of monocular deprivation and their reversal in the monkey's visual cortex. *Journal of Physiology,* 1978, *283,* 223–262.

Blakemore, C. B., & Sutton, P. Size adaptation: A new aftereffect. *Science,* 1969, *166,* 245–247.

Blakemore, C., & Van Sluyters, R. C. Reversal of the physiological effects of monocular deprivation in kittens: Further evidence for a sensitive period. *Journal of Physiology,* 1974, *237,* 195–216.

Blakemore, C., & Van Sluyters, R. C. Innate and environmental factors in the development of the kitten's visual cortex. *Journal of Physiology,* 1975, *248,* 663–716.

Blakemore, C., Van Sluyters, R. C., Peck, C. K., & Hein, A. Development of cat visual cortex following rotation of one eye. *Nature,* 1975, *257,* 584–586.

Blakemore, C., & Vital-Durand, F. Development of the neural basis of visual acuity in monkeys. Speculation on the origin of deprivation amblyopia. *Transactions of the Ophthalmological Societies of the United Kingdom,* 1980, *99,* 363–368.

Bodis-Wollner, I. Visual acuity and contrast sensitivity in patients with cerebral lesions. *Science,* 1972, *178,* 769–771.

Boettner, E. A., & Wolter, J. R. Transmission of the ocular media. *Investigative Ophthalmology,* 1962, *1,* 776–783.

Boltz, R. L., Manny, R. E., & Katz, B. J. The effects of induced optical blur on infant visual acuity. *American Journal of Optometry and Physiological Optics,* in press.

Bonds, A. B. Development of orientation tuning in the visual cortex of kittens. In R. D. Freeman (Ed.), *Developmental neurobiology of vision.* New York: Plenum Press, 1979.

Bonds, A. B., & Freeman, R. D. Development of optical quality in the kitten eye. *Vision Research,* 1978, *18,* 391–398.

Boothe, R. G. Development of spatial vision in infant macaque monkeys under conditions of normal and abnormal visual experience. In R. N. Aslin, J. R. Alberts, & M. R. Petersen (Eds.), *Development of perception: Psychobiological perspectives. The visual system* (Vol. 2). New York: Academic Press, 1981.

Boothe, R. G., Greenough, W. T., Lund, J. S., & Wrege, K. A quantitative investigation of spine and dendrite development of neurons in visual cortex (area 17) of *Macaca nemestrina* monkeys. *Journal of Comparative Neurology,* 1979, *186,* 473–490.

Boothe, R. G., Williams, R. A., Kiorpes, L., & Teller, D. Y. Development of contrast sensitivity in infant *Macaca nemestrina* monkeys. *Science,* 1980, *208,* 1290–1292.

Bornstein, M. H. Qualities of color vision in infancy. *Journal of Experimental Child Psychology,* 1975, *19,* 401–419.

Bornstein, M. H. Infants are trichromats. *Journal of Experimental Child Psychology,* 1976, *21,* 425–445.

Bornstein, M. H. Chromatic vision in infancy. In H. W. Reese & L. P. Lipsitt (Eds.), *Advances in child development and behavior* (Vol. 12). New York: Academic Press, 1978.

Bornstein, M. H. "Human infant color and color perception" reviewed and reassessed: A critique of Werner and Wooten (1979a). *Infant Behavior and Development,* 1981, *4,* 119–150.

Bornstein, M. H., Ferdinandsen, K., & Gross, C. G. Perception of symmetry in infancy. *Developmental Psychology,* 1981, *17,* 82–86.

Bornstein, M. H., Kessen, W., & Weiskopf, S. Color vision and hue categorization in young human infants. *Journal of Experimental Psychology, Human Perception and Performance,* 1976, *2,* 115–129.

Bower, T. G. R. Discrimination of depth in premotor infants. *Psychonomic Science,* 1964, *1,* 368.

Bower, T. G. R. The determinants of perceptual unity in infancy. *Psychonomic Science,* 1965, *3,* 323–324. (a)

Bower, T. G. R. Stimulus variables determining space perception in infants. *Science,* 1965, *149,* 88–89. (b)

Bower, T. G. R. Slant perception and shape constancy in infants. *Science,* 1966, *151,* 832–834.

Bower, T. G. R. Phenomenal identity and form perception in an infant. *Perception and Psychophysics,* 1967, *2,* 74–76.

Bower, T. G. R. The object in the world of the infant. *Scientific American,* 1971, *225,* 30–38.

Bower, T. G. R. Object perception in infants. *Perception,* 1972, *1,* 15–30.

Bower, T. G. R. *Development in infancy.* San Francisco: W. H. Freeman and Company, 1974.

Bower, T. G. R., Broughton, J. M., & Moore, M. K. Demonstration of intention in the reaching behavior of neonate humans. *Nature,* 1970, *228,* 679–681.

Bower, T. G. R., Broughton, J. M., & Moore, M. K. Infant responses to approaching objects: An indicator of response to distal variables. *Perception and Psychophysics,* 1971, *9,* 193–196.

Boycott, B. B., & Dowling, J. E. Organization of primate retina: Light microscopy. *Philosophical Transactions of the Royal Society of London (Ser. B),* 1969, *255,* 109–184.

Boynton, R. M. *Human color vision.* New York: Holt, Rinehart and Winston, 1979.

Braddick, O., Atkinson, J., French, J., & Howland, H. C. A photorefractive study of infant accommodation. *Vision Research,* 1979, *19,* 1319–1330.

Braddick, O., Campbell, F. W., & Atkinson, J. Channels in vision: Basic aspects. In R. Held, H. W. Leibowitz, & H. -L. Teuber (Eds.), *Handbook of sensory physiology. Perception* (Vol. VIII). New York: Springer-Verlag, 1978.

Brandt, T., Wenzel, & Dichgans, J. Die Entwicklung der visuellen Stabilisation des aufrechten Standes beim Kind: Ein Reifezeichen in der Kinderneurologie. *Arch. Psychiat. Nervenkr.,* 1976, *223,* 1–13.

Brennan, W. M., Ames, E. W., & Moore, R. W. Age differences in infants' attention to patterns of different complexity. *Science,* 1966, *151,* 354–356.

Bronson, G. W. The postnatal growth of visual capacity. *Child Development,* 1974, *45,* 873–890.

Bronson, G. W. *The scanning patterns of human infants: Implications for visual learning.* Norwood, N.J.: Ablex, 1982.

Brookman, K. E. *Ocular accommodation in human infants.* Doctoral dissertation, Indiana University, 1980.

Brunswik, E. *Perception and the representative design of psychological experiments* (2nd ed.). Berkeley: University of California Press, 1956.

Buisseret, P., & Imbert, M. Visual cortical cells: Their developmental properties in normal and dark reared kittens. *Journal of Physiology,* 1976, *255,* 511–525.

Bulpitt, C. J., & Baum, J. D. Retinal photography in the newborn. *Archives of Disease in Childhood,* 1969, *44,* 499–503.

Burnham, D. K., & Dickinson, R. G. The determinants of visual capture and visual pursuit in infancy. *Infant Behavior and Development,* 1981, *4,* 359–372.

Bushnell, I. W. R. Modification of the externality effect in young infants. *Journal of Experimental Child Psychology,* 1979, *28,* 211–229.

Butterworth, G., & Hicks, L. Visual proprioception and postural stability in infancy: A developmental study. *Perception,* 1977, *6,* 255–262.

Campbell, F. W., Carpenter, R. H. S., & Levinson, J. Z. Visibility of aperiodic patterns compared with that of sinusoidal gratings. *Journal of Physiology,* 1969, *204,* 283–298. (a)

Campbell, F. W., Cooper, G. F., & Enroth-Cugell, C. The spatial selectivity of the visual cells of the cat. *Journal of Physiology,* 1969, *203,* 223–235. (b)

Campbell, F. W., & Green, D. G. Optical and retinal factors affecting visual resolution. *Journal of Physiology,* 1965, *181,* 576–593.

Campbell, F. W., & Gubisch, R. W. Optical quality of the human eye. *Journal of Physiology,* 1966, *186,* 558–578.

Campbell, F. W., & Maffei, L. Electrophysiological evidence for the existence of orientation and size detectors in the human visual system. *Journal of Physiology,* 1970, *207,* 635–652.

Campos, J. J., Hiatt, S., Ramsay, D., Henderson, C., & Svejda, M. The emergence of fear on the visual cliff. In M. Lewis & L. Rosenblum (Eds.), *The origins of affect.* New York: Plenum Press, 1978.

Campos, J. J., Langer, A., & Krowitz, A. Cardiac responses on the visual cliff in prelocomotor human infants. *Science,* 1970, *170,* 196–197.

Cannon, M. W., Jr. Contrast sensitivity: Psychophysical and evoked potential methods compared. *Vision Research,* 1983, *23,* 87–95.

Caron, A. J., Caron, R. F., & Carlson, V. R. Infant perception of the invariant shape of objects varying in slant. *Child Development,* 1979, *50,* 716–721.

Caron, R. F., Caron, A. J., & Caldwell, R. C. Satiation of visual reinforcement in young infants. *Developmental Psychology,* 1971, *5,* 279–289.

Carpenter, G. C. Visual regard of moving and stationary faces in early infancy. *Merrill-Palmer Quarterly,* 1974, *20,* 181–184.

Carroll, J. J., & Gibson, E. J. *Infants' differentiation of an aperture and an obstacle.* Paper presented at the meeting of the Society for Research in Child Development, Boston, 1981.

Chow, K. L., & Spear, P. D. Morphological and functional effects of visual deprivation on the rabbit visual system. *Experimental Neurology,* 1974, *42,* 429–447.

Cohen, L. B. Observing responses, visual preferences, and habituation to visual stimuli in infants. *Journal of Experimental Child Psychology,* 1969, *7,* 419–433.

Cohen, L. B. Attention-getting and attention-holding processes in infant visual preferences. *Child Development,* 1972, *43,* 869–879.

Cohen, L. B., DeLoache, J. S., & Strauss, M. S. Infant visual perception. In J. D. Osofsky (Ed.), *Handbook of infant development.* New York: Wiley, 1979.

Conel, J. L. *The postnatal development of the human cerebral cortex* (Vols. 1–7). Cambridge, Mass.: Harvard University Press, 1939–1963.

Cook, R. C., & Glasscock, R. E. Refractive and ocular findings in the newborn. *American Journal of Ophthalmology,* 1951, *34,* 1407–1413.

Cornell, E. H. Infants' visual attention to pattern arrangement and orientation. *Child Development,* 1975, *46,* 229–232.

Cornsweet, T. N. *Visual perception.* New York: Academic Press, 1970.

Cowey, A., & Perry, V. H. The projection of the fovea to the superior colliculus in rhesus monkeys. *Neuroscience,* 1980, *5,* 53–61.

Cowey, A., & Rolls, E. T. Human cortical magnification factor and its relation to visual acuity. *Experimental Brain Research,* 1974, *21,* 447–454.

Cragg, B. G. The development of synapses in kitten visual cortex during visual deprivation. *Experimental Neurology,* 1975, *46,* 445–451. (a)

Cragg, B. G. The development of synapses in the visual system of the cat. *Journal of Comparative Neurology,* 1975, *160,* 147–166. (b)

Crawford, M. L. J., Blake, R., Cool, S. J., & von Noorden, G. K. Physiological consequences of unilateral and bilateral eye closure in macaque monkeys: Some further observations. *Brain Research,* 1975, *84,* 150–154.

Crick, F. H. C., Marr, D. C., & Poggio, T. An information-processing approach to understanding the visual cortex. In F. O. Schmitt, F. G. Worden, G. Adelman, & S. G. Dennis (Eds.), *The organization of the cerebral cortex.* Cambridge, Mass.: MIT Press, 1981.

Cruikshank, R. M. The development of visual size constancy in early infancy. *Journal of Genetic Psychology,* 1941, *58,* 327–351.

Cynader, M., & Berman, N. Receptive-field organization of monkey superior colliculus. *Journal of Neurophysiology,* 1972, *35,* 187–201.

Cynader, M., Berman, N., & Hein, A. Cats raised in a one-directional world: Effects on receptive fields in visual cortex and superior colliculus. *Experimental Brain Research,* 1975, *22,* 267–280.

Cynader, M., Berman, N., & Hein, A. Recovery of function in cat visual cortex following prolonged visual deprivation. *Experimental Brain Research,* 1976, *25,* 139–156.

Cynader, M., & Chernenko, G. Abolition of directional selectivity in the visual cortex of the cat. *Science,* 1976, *193,* 504–505.

Cynader, M., & Mitchell, D. E. Monocular astigmatism effects on kitten visual cortex development. *Nature,* 1977, *270,* 177–178.

Daniels, J. D., Pettigrew, J. D., & Norman, J. L. Development of single-neuron responses in kitten's lateral geniculate nucleus. *Journal of Neurophysiology,* 1978, *41,* 1373–1393.

Dannemiller, J. L., & Banks, M. S. The development of light adaptation in the human infant. *Vision Research,* in press.

Daw, N. W., Berman, N. E. J., & Ariel, M. Interaction of critical periods in the visual cortex of kittens. *Science,* 1978, *199,* 565–567.

Day, R. H. The physiological basis of form perception in the peripheral retina. *Psychological Review,* 1957, *64,* 38–48.

Day, R. H., & McKenzie, B. E. Perceptual shape constancy in early infancy. *Perception,* 1973, *2,* 315–320.

Day, R. H., & McKenzie, B. E. Constancies in the perceptual world of the infant. In W. Epstein (Ed.), *Stability and constancy in visual perception. Mechanisms and processes.* New York: Wiley, 1977.

Day, R. H., & McKenzie, B. E. Infant perception of the invariant size of approaching and receding objects. *Developmental Psychology,* 1981, *17,* 670–677.

Dayton, G. O., Jr., & Jones, M. H. Analysis of characteristics of fixation reflexes in infants by use of direct current electrooculography. *Neurology,* 1964, *14,* 1152–1156.

Dayton, G. O., Jr., Jones, M. H., Aiu, P., Rawson, R. A., Steele, B., & Rose, M. Developmental study of coordinated eye movements in the human infant. I. Visual acuity in the newborn human: A study based on induced optokinetic nystagmus recorded by electrooculography. *Archives of Ophthalmology*, 1964, *71*, 865–870. (a)

Dayton, G. O., Jr., Jones, M. H., Steele, B., & Rose, M. Developmental study of coordinated eye movements in the human infant. II. An electrooculographic study of the fixation reflex in the newborn. *Archives of Ophthalmology*, 1964, *71*, 871–875. (b)

Dember, W. N., & Earl, R. W. Analysis of exploratory, manipulatory, and curiosity behaviors. *Psychological Review*, 1957, *64*, 91–96.

de Monasterio, F. M. Properties of concentrically organized X and Y ganglion cells of macaque retina. *Journal of Neurophysiology*, 1978, *41*, 1394–1417.

Derrington, A. M., & Fuchs, A. F. Spatial and temporal properties of X and Y cells in the cat lateral geniculate nucleus. *Journal of Physiology*, 1979, *293*, 347–364.

Derrington, A. M., & Fuchs, A. F. The development of spatial-frequency selectivity in kitten striate cortex. *Journal of Physiology*, 1981, *316*, 1–10.

Derrington, A. M., & Hawken, M. J. Spatial and temporal properties of cat geniculate neurones after prolonged deprivation. *Journal of Physiology*, 1981, *314*, 107–120.

DeValois, R. L., Albrecht, D. G., & Thorell, L. G. Spatial frequency selectivity of cells in macaque visual cortex. *Vision Research*, 1982, *22*, 545–559.

DeValois, R. L., Morgan, H., & Snodderly, D. M. Psychophysical studies of monkey vision. III. Spatial luminance contrast tests of macaque and human observers. *Vision Research*, 1974, *14*, 75–81.

Dews, P. B., & Wiesel, T. N. Consequences of monocular deprivation on visual behavior in kittens. *Journal of Physiology*, 1970, *206*, 437–455.

Dichgans, J., & Brandt, T. Visual-vestibular interaction: Effects on self-motion perception and postural control. In R. Held, H. W. Leibowitz, & H. -L. Teuber (Eds.), *Handbook of sensory physiology. Perception* (Vol. VIII). New York: Springer-Verlag, 1978.

Dineen, J. T., & Meyer, W. J. Developmental changes in visual orienting behavior to featural versus structural information in the human infant. *Developmental Psychobiology*, 1980, *13*(2), 123–130.

Dobson, V. Spectral sensitivity of the two-month infant as measured by the visually evoked cortical potential. *Vision Research*, 1976, *16*, 367–374.

Dobson, V., Mayer, D. L., & Lee, C. P. Visual acuity screening of preterm infants. *Investigative Ophthalmology and Visual Science*, 1980, *19*, 1498–1505.

Dobson, V., & Teller, D. Y. Visual acuity in human infants: A review and comparison of behavioral and electrophysiological studies. *Vision Research*, 1978, *18*, 1469–1483.

Dobson, V., Teller, D. Y., & Belgum, J. Visual acuity in human infants assessed with stationary stripes and phase-alternated checkerboards. *Vision Research*, 1978, *18*, 1233–1238.

Dobson, V., Teller, D. Y., Lee, C. P., & Wade, B. A behavioral method for efficient screening of visual acuity in young infants. I. Preliminary laboratory development. *Investigative Ophthalmology and Visual Science*, 1978, *17*, 1142–1150.

Dodt, E., & Wadensten, L. The use of flicker electroretinography in the human eye. *Acta Ophthalmologica*, 1954, *54*, 163–180.

Dodwell, P. C. *Visual pattern recognition*. New York: Holt, Rinehart and Winston, 1970.

Dodwell, P. C., & Freedman, N. L. Visual form discrimination after removal of the visual cortex in cats. *Science*, 1968, *160*, 559–560.

Dodwell, P. C., Muir, D., & DiFranco, D. Responses of infants to visually presented objects. *Science*, 1976, *194*, 209–211.

Donovan, A. The postnatal development of the cat's retina. *Experimental Eye Research*, 1966, *5*, 249–254.

Dreher, B., Fukada, Y., & Rodieck, R. W. Identification, classification and anatomical segregation of cells with X-like and Y-like properties in the lateral geniculate nucleus of old-world primates. *Journal of Physiology*, 1976, *258*, 433–452.

Duke-Elder, S., & Cook, C. *System of ophthalmology* (Vol. III). St. Louis: Mosby, 1963.

Dunn, J. S. Development of the human neural retina. *Journal of Anatomy*, 1972, *111*, 510–512.

Edwards, S. B., Ginsburgh, C. L., Henkel, C. K., & Stein, B. E. Sources of subcortical projections to the superior colliculus in the cat. *Journal of Comparative Neurology*, 1979, *184*, 309–330.

Ellingson, R. J. Cortical electrical responses to visual stimulation in the human infant. *Electroencephalography and Clinical Neurophysiology*, 1960, *12*, 663–677.

Enoch, J. M., & Rabinowicz, I. M. Early surgery and visual correction of an infant born with unilateral eye lens opacity. *Documenta Oph-*

thalmologica, 1976, *41,* 371–382.

Enroth-Cugell, C., & Robson, J. G. The contrast sensitivity of retinal ganglion cells of the cat. *Journal of Physiology,* 1966, *187,* 517–552.

Estevez, O., & Cavonius, C. R. Low-frequency attenuation in the detection of gratings: Sorting out the artifacts. *Vision Research,* 1976, *16,* 497–500.

Fagan, J. F., III Infant recognition memory: Studies in forgetting. *Child Development,* 1977, *48,* 68–78.

Fantz, R. L. The origin of form perception. *Scientific American,* 1961, *204,* 66–72.

Fantz, R. L. Pattern vision in newborn infants. *Science,* 1963, *140,* 296–297.

Fantz, R. L. Visual perception from birth as shown by pattern selectivity. In H. E. Whipple (Ed.), New issues in infant development. *Annals of New York Academy of Science,* 1965, *118,* 793–814.

Fantz, R. L., & Fagan, J. F., III. Visual attention to size and number of pattern details by term and preterm infants during the first six months. *Child Development,* 1975, *16,* 3–18.

Fantz, R. L., Fagan, J. F., III, & Miranda, S. B. Early visual selectivity as a function of pattern variables, previous exposure, age from birth and conception, and expected cognitive deficit. In L. B. Cohen & P. Salapatek (Eds.), *Infant perception: From sensation to cognition. Basic visual processes* (Vol. 1). New York: Academic Press, 1975.

Fantz, R. L., & Miranda, S. B. Newborn infant attention to form of contour. *Child Development,* 1975, *46,* 224–228.

Fantz, R. L., & Nevis, S. Pattern preferences and perceptual-cognitive development in early infancy. *Merrill-Palmer Quarterly,* 1967, *13,* 77–108.

Fantz, R. L., Ordy, J. M., & Udelf, M. S. Maturation of pattern vision in infants during the first six months. *Journal of Comparative Physiological Psychology,* 1962, *55,* 907–917.

Field, J. Coordination of vision and prehension in young infants. *Child Development,* 1977, *48,* 97–103.

Fincham, E. F. The accommodation reflex and its stimulus. *British Journal of Ophthalmology,* 1951, *35,* 381–393.

Fincham, E. F., & Walton, J. The reciprocal actions of accommodation and convergence. *Journal of Physiology,* 1957, *137,* 488–508.

Fiorentini, A., & Maffei, L. Spatial contrast sensitivity of myopic subjects. *Vision Research,* 1976, *16,* 437–438.

Fisher, C. B., Ferdinandsen, K., & Bornstein, M. H. The role of symmetry in infant form discrimination. *Child Development,* 1981, *52,* 457–462.

Flandrin, J. M., & Jeannerod, M. Superior colliculus: Environmental influences on the development of directional responses in the kitten. *Brain Research,* 1975, *89,* 348–352.

Flandrin, J. M., Kennedy, H., & Amblard, B. Effects of stroboscopic rearing on the binocularity and directionality of cat superior colliculus neurons. *Brain Research,* 1976, *101,* 576–581.

Flom, M. C., Weymouth, F. W., & Kahneman, D. Visual resolution and contour interaction. *Journal of the Optical Society of America,* 1963, *53,* 1026–1032.

Fox, R., Aslin, R. N., Shea, S. L., & Dumais, S. T. Stereopsis in human infants. *Science,* 1980, *207,* 323–324.

Freeman, R. D., Mitchell, D. E., & Millodot, M. A. Neural effect of partial visual deprivation in humans. *Science,* 1972, *175,* 1384–1386.

Fregnac, Y., & Imbert, M. Early development of visual cortical cells in normal and dark-reared kittens: Relationship between orientation selectivity and ocular dominance. *Journal of Physiology,* 1978, *278,* 27–44.

Fulton, A. B., Dobson, V., Salem, D., Mar, C., Petersen, R. A., & Hansen, R. Cycloplegic refractions in infants and young children. *American Journal of Ophthalmology,* 1980, *90,* 239–247.

Ganon, E. C., & Swartz, K. B. Perception of internal elements of compound figures by one-month-old infants. *Journal of Experimental Child Psychology,* 1980, *30,* 159–170.

Ganz, L. Innate and environmental factors in the development of visual form perception. In R. Held, H. W. Leibowitz, & H. -L. Teuber (Eds.), *Handbook of sensory physiology. Perception* (Vol. VIII). New York: Springer-Verlag, 1978.

Ganz, L., & Haffner, M. E. Permanent perceptual and neurophysiological effects of visual deprivation in the cat. *Experimental Brain Research,* 1974, *20,* 67–87.

Ganz, L., & Wilson, P. D. Innate generalization of a form discrimination without contouring eye-movements. *Journal of Comparative and Physiological Psychology,* 1967, *63,* 258–269.

Gaskill, J. D. *Linear systems, Fourier transforms, and optics.* New York: Wiley, 1978.

Gayl, I. E., Roberts, J. O., & Werner, J. S. Linear systems analysis of infant visual pattern preferences. *Journal of Experimental Child Psychol-*

ogy, 1983, *35*, 30–45.

Geisler, W. S. Initial-image and afterimage discrimination in the rod and cone systems. *Journal of Physiology*, 1979, *294*, 165–179.

Geisler, W. S. Increment threshold and detection latency in the rod and cone system. *Vision Research*, 1980, *20*, 981–994.

Gibson, E. J. *Principles of perceptual learning and development*. New York: Appleton-Century-Crofts, 1969.

Gibson, J. J. *The perception of the visual world*. Boston: Houghton Mifflin, 1950.

Gibson, J. J. *The senses considered as perceptual systems*. Boston: Houghton-Mifflin, 1966.

Ginsburg, A. P. *Visual information processing based on spatial filters constrained by biological data*. Doctoral dissertation, University of Cambridge, 1978.

Girton, M. R. Infants' attention to intrastimulus motion. *Journal of Experimental Child Psychology*, 1979, *28*, 416–423.

Glickstein, M., & Millodot, M. Retinoscopy and eye size. *Science*, 1970, *168*, 605–606.

Goldberg, M. E., & Wurtz, R. H. Activity of superior colliculus in behaving monkey. III. Cells discharging before eye movements. *Journal of Neurophysiology*, 1972, *35*, 575–586. (a)

Goldberg, M. E., & Wurtz, R. H. Activity of superior colliculus in behaving monkey. IV. Effects of lesion on eye movements. *Journal of Neurophysiology*, 1972, *35*, 587–596. (b)

Goldman, P. S., & Nauta, W. J. H. Autoradiographic demonstration of a projection from prefrontal association cortex to the superior colliculus in the rhesus monkey. *Brain Research*, 1976, *116*, 145–149.

Goodkin, F. The development of mature patterns of head-eye coordination in the human infant. *Early Human Development*, 1980, *4*, 373–386.

Goodman, J. W. *Introduction to Fourier optics*. New York: McGraw-Hill, 1965.

Gordon, B. Receptive fields in deep layers of cat superior colliculus. *Journal of Neurophysiology*, 1973, *36*, 157–178.

Gordon, F. R., & Yonas, A. Sensitivity to binocular depth information in infants. *Journal of Experimental Child Psychology*, 1976, *22*, 413–422.

Gorman, J. J., Cogan, D. G., & Gellis, S. S. An apparatus for grading the visual acuity of infants on the basis of opticokinetic nystagmus. *Pediatrics*, 1957, *19*, 1088–1092.

Gorman, J. J., Cogan, D. G., & Gellis, S. S. A device for testing visual acuity in infants. *Sight-Saving Review*, 1959, *29*, 80–84.

Green, D. G. Regional variations in the visual acuity for interference fringes on the retina. *Journal of Physiology*, 1970, *207*, 351–356.

Green, D. G., & Campbell, F. W. Effect of focus on the visual response to a sinusoidally modulated spatial stimulus. *Journal of the Optical Society of America*, 1965, *55*, 1154–1157.

Green, D. G., Powers, M. K., & Banks, M. S. Depth of focus, eye size, and visual acuity. *Vision Research*, 1980, *20*, 827–835.

Greenberg, D. J., & Blue, S. Z. Visual complexity in infancy: Contour or numerosity? *Child Development*, 1975, *46*, 357–363.

Greenberg, D. J., & O'Donnell, W. J. Infancy and the optimal level of stimulation. *Child Development*, 1972, *43*, 639–645.

Gstalder, R. J., & Green, D. G. Laser interferometric acuity in amblyopia. *Journal of Pediatric Ophthalmology*, 1971, *8*, 251–256.

Guernsey, M. A quantitative study of the eye reflexes in infants. *Psychological Bulletin*, 1929, *26*, 160–161.

Guillery, R. W. Binocular competition in the control of geniculate cell growth. *Journal of Comparative Neurology*, 1972, *144*, 117–129.

Guillery, R. W. The effect of lid suture upon the growth of cells in the dorsal lateral geniculate nucleus of kittens. *Journal of Comparative Neurology*, 1973, *148*, 417–422.

Gwiazda, J., Brill, S., Mohindra, I., & Held, R. Infant visual acuity and its meridional variation. *Vision Research*, 1978, *18*, 1557–1564.

Hainline, L. Developmental changes in visual scanning of face and nonface patterns by infants. *Journal of Experimental Child Psychology*, 1978, *25*, 90–115.

Hainline, L. Eye movements and form perception in human infants. In J. W. Senders, R. A. Monty, & D. F. Fisher (Eds.), *Eye movements and the higher psychological processes*. Hillsdale, N.J.: Erlbaum, 1981.

Hainline, L., & Lemerise, E. Infants' scanning of geometric forms varying in size. *Journal of Experimental Child Psychology*, 1982, *33*, 235–256.

Haith, M. M. *Rules that babies look by*. Hillsdale, N.J.: Erlbaum, 1980.

Haith, M. M., Bergman, T., & Moore, M. J. Eye contact and face scanning in early infancy. *Science*, 1977, *198*, 853–855.

Haith, M. M., Goodman, G. S., Godwyn, M., & Montgomery, L. *A longitudinal study of infants' visual scanning and discrimination of form*. Paper presented at the International Conference on

Infant Studies, Austin, Texas, March 1982.

Haith, M. M., Kessen, W., & Collins, D. Response of the human infant to level of complexity of intermittent visual movement. *Journal of Experimental Child Psychology*, 1969, *7*, 52–69.

Hamasaki, D. I., & Flynn, J. T. Physiological properties of retinal ganglion cells of 3-week-old kittens. *Vision Research*, 1977, *17*, 275–284.

Hamasaki, D. I., & Sutija, V. G. Development of X- and Y-cells in kittens. *Experimental Brain Research*, 1979, *35*, 9–23.

Hamer, R. D., Alexander, K. R., & Teller, D. Y. Rayleigh discriminations in human infants. *Vision Research*, 1982, *22*, 575–588.

Hansen, R. M., & Fulton, A. B. Behavioral measurement of background adaptation in infants. *Investigative Ophthalmology and Visual Science*, 1981, *21*, 625–629.

Harris, L., Atkinson, J., & Braddick, O. Visual contrast sensitivity of a 6-month-old infant measured by the evoked potential. *Nature*, 1976, *264*, 570–571.

Harris, L. R. The superior colliculus and movements of the head and eyes in cats. *Journal of Physiology*, 1980, *300*, 367–391.

Harris, P., & MacFarlane, A. The growth of the effective visual field from birth to seven weeks. *Journal of Experimental Child Psychology*, 1974, *18*, 340–348.

Harter, M. R., Deaton, F. K., & Odom, J. V. Maturation of evoked potentials and visual preference in 6-45 day old infants: Effects of check size, visual acuity, and refractive error. *Electroencephalography and Clinical Neurophysiology*, 1977, *42*, 595–607. (a)

Harter, M. R., Deaton, F. K., & Odom, J. V. Pattern visual evoked potentials in infants. In J. E. Desmedt (Ed.), *Visual evoked potentials in man: New developments*. Oxford: Clarendon Press, 1977. (b)

Harter, M. R., & Suitt, C. D. Visually-evoked cortical responses and pattern vision in the infant: A longitudinal study. *Psychonomic Science*, 1970, *18*, 235–237.

Harting, J. K., Hall, W. C., Diamond, I. T., & Martin, G. F. Anterograde degeneration study of the superior colliculus in *Tupaia glis:* Evidence for a subdivision between superficial and deep layers. *Journal of Comparative Neurology*, 1973, *148*, 361–386.

Haynes, H., White, B. L., & Held, R. Visual accommodation in human infants. *Science*, 1965, *148*, 528–530.

Hebb, D. O. *The organization of behavior*. New York: Wiley, 1949.

Hecht, S., & Mintz, E. U. The visibility of single lines at various illuminations and the basis of visual resolution. *Journal of Genetic Physiology*, 1939, *22*, 593–612.

Heck, J. The flicker electroretinogram of the human eye. *Acta Physiologica Scandinavica*, 1957, *39*, 158–166.

Heck, J., & Zetterström, B. Analyse des photopischen Flimmerelektroretinogramms bei Neugeborenen. *Ophthalmologica*, 1958, *135*, 205–210.

Held, R. Dissociation of visual functions by deprivation and rearrangement. *Psychologische Forschung*, 1968, *31*, 338–348.

Held, R. Development of visual acuity in normal and astigmatic infants. In S. J. Cool & E. L. Smith, III (Eds.), *Frontiers in visual science*. New York: Springer-Verlag, 1978.

Held, R. Development of visual resolution. *Canadian Journal of Psychology*, 1979, *33*, 213–221.

Held, R., Birch, E., & Gwiazda, J. Stereoacuity of human infants. *Proceedings of the National Academy of Sciences, U.S.A.*, 1980, *77*, 5572–5574.

Hendrickson, A., & Kupfer, C. The histogenesis of the fovea in the macaque monkey. *Investigative Ophthalmology*, 1976, *15*, 746–756.

Hering, E. Über Individuelle Verschienheiten des Farbensinnes. *Lotos, Naturwissenschaftliche Zeitschrift* (n.F.), 1885, *6*, 142–198.

Hershenson, M. Visual discrimination in the human newborn. *Journal of Comparative Physiological Psychology*, 1964, *58*, 270–276.

Hershenson, M., Munsinger, H., & Kessen, W. Preferences for shapes of intermediate variability in the newborn human. *Science*, 1965, *147*, 630–631.

Hickey, T. L. Postnatal development of the human lateral geniculate nucleus: Relationship to a critical period for the visual system. *Science*, 1977, *198*, 836–838.

Hickey, T. L., & Guillery, R. W. Variability of laminar patterns in the human lateral geniculate nucleus. *Journal of Comparative Neurology*, 1979, *183*, 221–246.

Hirsch, H. V. B., & Spinelli, D. N. Visual experience modifies distribution of horizontally and vertically oriented receptive fields in cats. *Science*, 1970, *168*, 869–871.

Hirsch, H. V. B., & Spinelli, D. N. Modification of the distribution of receptive field orientation in cats by selective visual exposure during development. *Experimental Brain Research*, 1971, *13*,

509–527.

Hirsch, M. J. Changes in astigmatism during the first eight years of school—An interim report from the Ojai longitudinal study. *American Journal of Optometry*, 1963, *40*, 127–132.

Hitchcock, P. F., & Hickey, T. L. Prenatal development of the human lateral geniculate nucleus. *Journal of Comparative Neurology*, 1980, *194*, 395–411.

Hochberg, J. Attention, organization and consciousness. In D. Mostofsky (Ed.), *Attention: Contemporary theory and analysis*. New York: Appleton, 1970.

Hochberg, J. Perception. I. Color and shape. In J. W. Kling & L. A. Riggs (Eds.), *Woodworth and Schlosberg's experimental psychology* (3rd ed.). New York: Holt, Rinehart and Winston, 1971. (a)

Hochberg, J. Perception. II. Space and movement. In J. W. Kling & L. A. Riggs (Eds.), *Woodworth and Schlosberg's experimental psychology* (3rd ed.). New York: Holt, Rinehart and Winston, 1971. (b)

Hoffmann, K. -P., & Sherman, S. M. Effects of early binocular deprivation on visual input to cat superior colliculus. *Journal of Neurophysiology*, 1975, *38*, 1049–1059.

Hoffmann, K. -P., & Stone, J. Conduction velocity of afferents to cat visual cortex: A correlation with cortical receptive field properties. *Brain Research*, 1971, *32*, 460–466.

Hohmann, A., & Creutzfeldt, O. D. Squint and the development of binocularity in humans. *Nature*, 1975, *254*, 613–614.

Horsten, G. P. M., & Winkelman, J. E. Electrical activity of the retina in relation to histological differentiation in infants born prematurely and at full term. *Vision Research*, 1962, *2*, 269–276.

Horsten, G. P. M., & Winkelman, J. E. Electroretinographic critical fusion frequency of the retina in relation to the histological development in man and animals. *Ophthalmologica*, 1964, *18*, 515–521.

Howland, H. C. Infant eyes: Optics and accommodation. *Current Eye Research*, 1982, *2*, 217–224.

Howland, H. C., Atkinson, J., Braddick, O., & French, J. Infant astigmatism measured by photorefraction. *Science*, 1978, *202*, 331–333.

Howland, H. C., & Howland, B. Photorefraction: A technique for study of refractive state at a distance. *Journal of the Optical Society of America*, 1974, *64*, 240–249.

Hubel, D. H., & Wiesel, T. N. Receptive fields, binocular interaction and functional architecture in the cat's visual cortex. *Journal of Physiology (London)*, 1962, *160*, 106–154.

Hubel, D. H., & Wiesel, T. N. Receptive fields of cells in striate cortex of very young, visually inexperienced kittens. *Journal of Neurophysiology*, 1963, *26*, 994–1002.

Hubel, D. H., & Wiesel, T. N. Binocular interaction in striate cortex of kittens reared with artificial squint. *Journal of Neurophysiology*, 1965, *28*, 1041–1059. (a)

Hubel, D. H., & Wiesel, T. N. Receptive fields and functional architecture in two non-striate visual areas (18 and 19) of the cat. *Journal of Neurophysiology*, 1965, *28*, 229–289. (b)

Hubel, D. H., & Wiesel, T. N. Receptive fields and functional architecture of monkey striate cortex. *Journal of Physiology (London)*, 1968, *195*, 215–243.

Hubel, D. H., & Wiesel, T. N. Cells sensitive to binocular depth in area 18 of the macaque monkey cortex. *Nature (London)*, 1970, *225*, 41–42. (a)

Hubel, D. H., & Wiesel, T. N. The period of susceptibility to the physiological effects of unilateral eye closure in kittens. *Journal of Physiology*, 1970, *206*, 419–436. (b)

Hubel, D. H., & Wiesel, T. N. Laminar and columnar distribution of geniculocortical fibers in the macaque monkey. *Journal of Comparative Neurology*, 1972, *146*, 421–450.

Hubel, D. H., & Wiesel, T. N. Sequence regularity and geometry of orientation columns in the monkey striate cortex. *Journal of Comparative Neurology*, 1974, *158*, 267–293. (a)

Hubel, D. H., & Wiesel, T. N. Uniformity of monkey striate cortex: A parallel relationship between field size, scatter, and magnification factor. *Journal of Comparative Neurology*, 1974, *158*, 295–305. (b)

Hubel, D. H., & Wiesel, T. N. Functional architecture of macaque monkey visual cortex. *Proceedings of the Royal Society of London (Ser. B)*, 1977, *198*, 1–59.

Hubel, D. H., Wiesel, T. N., & LeVay, S. Plasticity of ocular dominance columns in monkey striate cortex. *Philosophical Transactions of the Royal Society*, 1977, *B 278*, 377–409.

Huffman, D. A. Impossible objects as nonsense sentences. *Machine Intelligence*, 1971, *6*, 295–323.

Humphrey, N. K. What the frog's eye tells the monkey's brain. *Brain, Behavior and Evolution*, 1970, *3*, 324–337.

Humphrey, N. K. Vision in a monkey without striate

cortex: A case study. *Perception,* 1974, *3,* 241–255.

Humphrey, N. K., & Weiskrantz, L. Vision in monkeys after removal of the striate cortex. *Nature,* 1967, *215,* 595–597.

Ingram, R. M., & Barr, A. Changes in refraction between the ages of 1 and 3½ years. *British Journal of Ophthalmology,* 1979, *63,* 339–342.

Ittelson, W. H., & Ames, A., Jr. Accommodation, convergence, and their relation to apparent distance. *Journal of Psychology (London),* 1950, *30,* 43–62.

Jacobson, M. *Developmental neurobiology.* New York: Plenum Press, 1978.

Jeffrey, W. The orienting reflex and attention in cognitive development. *Psychological Review,* 1968, *75,* 323–334.

Jones, M. C. The development of early behavior patterns in young children. *Pedagogic Seminary,* 1926, *33,* 537–585.

Julesz, B. Binocular depth perception of computer-generated patterns. *Bell System Technical Journal,* 1960, *39,* 1125–1162.

Julesz, B. *Foundations of cyclopean perception.* Chicago: University of Chicago Press, 1971.

Kahn, A. J. Ganglion cell formation in the chick neural retina. *Brain Research,* 1974, *63,* 285–290.

Kaplan, E., & Shapley, R. M. X and Y cells in the lateral geniculate nucleus of macaque monkeys. *Journal of Physiology,* 1982, *330,* 125–143.

Karmel, B. Z. The effect of age, complexity, and amount of contour density on pattern preferences in human infants. *Journal of Experimental Child Psychology,* 1969, *7,* 339–354.

Karmel, B. Z. Contour effects and pattern preferences in infants: A reply to Greenberg and O'Donnell (1972). *Child Development,* 1974, *45,* 196–199.

Karmel, B. Z., Lester, M. L., McCarvill, S. L., Brown, P., & Hofmann, M. J. Correlation of infants' brain and behavior response to temporal changes in visual stimulation. *Psychophysiology,* 1977, *14,* 134–142.

Karmel, B. Z., & Maisel, E. B. A neuronal activity model for infant visual attention. In L. B. Cohen & P. Salapatek (Eds.), *Infant perception: From sensation to cognition. Basic visual processes* (Vol. 1). New York: Academic Press, 1975.

Kaufman, L. *Sight and mind.* New York: Oxford University Press, 1974.

Kaufmann, R., Maland, J., & Yonas, A. Sensitivity of 5- and 7-month-old infants to pictorial depth information. *Journal of Experimental Child Psychology,* 1981, *32,* 162–168.

Kellman, P. J., & Spelke, E. S. *Infants' perception of partly occluded objects: Sensitivity to movement and configuration.* Paper presented at the meeting of the Society for Research in Child Development, Boston, 1981.

Kelly, D. H. Visual responses to time-dependent stimuli. I. Amplitude sensitivity measurements. *Journal of the Optical Society of America,* 1961, *51,* 422–429.

Kelly, D. H. Flicker. In D. Jameson & L. M. Hurvich (Eds.), *Handbook of sensory physiology. Visual psychophysics* (Vol. VII/4). New York: Springer-Verlag, 1972.

Kelly, D. H. Motion and vision. II. Stabilized spatiotemporal threshold surface. *Journal of the Optical Society of America,* 1979, *69,* 1340–1349.

Kessen, W., Haith, M. M., & Salapatek, P. H. Human infancy: A bibliography and guide. In P. H. Mussen (Ed.), *Carmichael's manual of child psychology* (Vol. 1, 3rd ed.). New York: Wiley, 1970.

Kessen, W., Salapatek, P., & Haith, M. The visual response of the human newborn to linear contour. *Journal of Experimental Child Psychology,* 1972, *13,* 9–20.

Kluver, H. Visual functions after removal of the occipital lobes. *Journal of Psychology (London),* 1941, *11,* 23–45.

Kluver, H. Functional significance of the geniculostriate. *Journal Bio. Symp.,* 1942, *7,* 253–299.

Koenderink, J. J., Bouman, M. A., Bueno de Mesquita, A. E., & Slappendel, S. Perimetry of contrast detection thresholds of moving spatial sine wave patterns. III. The target extent as a sensitivity controlling parameter. *Journal of the Optical Society of America,* 1978, *68,* 854–865.

Koffka, K. *Principles of gestalt psychology.* New York: Harcourt, Brace, 1935.

Köhler, W. *Gestalt psychology.* New York: Mentor, 1959.

Kratz, K. E., Mangel, S. C., Lehmkuhle, S., & Sherman, S. M. Retinal X- and Y-cells in monocularly lid-sutured cats: Normality of spatial and temporal properties. *Brain Research,* 1979, *172,* 545–551.

Kremenitzer, J. P., Vaughan, H. G., Jr., Kurtzberg, D., & Dowling, K. Smooth-pursuit eye movements in the newborn infant. *Child Development,* 1979, *50,* 442–448.

Kuffler, S. W. Discharge patterns and functional organization of mammalian retina. *Journal of Neurophysiology,* 1953, *16,* 57–68.

Kuffler, S. W., & Nicholls, J. G. *From neuron to brain: A cellular approach to the function of the nervous system.* Sunderland, Mass.: Sinauer Associates, 1976.

Larsen, J. S. The sagittal growth of the eye. IV. Ultrasonic measurement of the axial length of the eye from birth to puberty. *Acta Ophthalmologica,* 1971, *49,* 873–886.

Lasky, R. E., & Gogel, W. C. The perception of relative motion by young infants. *Perception,* 1978, *7,* 617–623.

Leahy, R. L. Development of preferences and processes of visual scanning in the human infant during the first 3 months of life. *Developmental Psychology,* 1976, *12*(3), 250–254.

Lee, D. N., & Aronson, E. Visual proprioceptive control of standing in human infants. *Perception and Psychophysics,* 1974, *15,* 529–532.

Leehey, S. C., Moskowitz-Cook, A., Brill, S., & Held, R. Orientational anisotropy in infant vision. *Science,* 1975, *190,* 900–902.

Lehmkuhle, S., Kratz, K. E., Mangel, S. C., & Sherman, S. M. Spatial and temporal sensitivity of X- and Y-cells in dorsal lateral geniculate nucleus of the cat. *Journal of Neurophysiology,* 1980, *43,* 520–541.

Leibowitz, H. W., & Owens, D. A. New evidence for the intermediate position of relaxed accommodation. *Documenta Ophthalmologica,* 1978, *46,* 133–147.

Leibowitz, H. W., & Post, R. B. The two modes of processing concept and some implications. In J. Beck (Ed.), *Organization and representation in perception.* Hillsdale, N.J.: Erlbaum, 1982.

Leibowitz, H. W., Shupert-Rodemer, C., & Dichgans, J. The independence of dynamic spatial orientation from luminance and refractive error. *Perception and Psychophysics,* 1979, *25,* 75–79.

Lennie, P. Parallel visual pathways. *Vision Research,* 1980, *20,* 561–594.

Lettvin, J. Y., Maturana, H. R., Pitts, W. H., & McCulloch, W. S. Two remarks on the visual system of the frog. In W. A. Rosenblith (Ed.), *Sensory communication.* Cambridge, Mass.: MIT Press, 1961.

LeVay, S., Stryker, M. P., & Shatz, C. J. Ocular dominance columns and their development in layer IV of the cat's visual cortex: A quantitative study. *Journal of Comparative Neurology,* 1978, *179,* 223–244.

LeVay, S., Wiesel, T. N., & Hubel, D. H. The development of ocular dominance columns in normal and visually deprived monkeys. *Journal of Comparative Neurology,* 1980, *191,* 1–51.

Leventhal, A. G., & Hirsch, H. V. B. Cortical effect of early selective exposure to diagonal lines. *Science,* 1975, *190,* 902–904.

Leventhal, A. G., & Hirsch, H. V. B. Effects of early experience upon the orientation sensitivity and the binocularity of neurons in the cat's visual cortex. *Proceedings of the National Academy of Sciences, USA,* 1977, *74,* 1272–1276.

Lewis, T. L., Maurer, D., & Kay, D. Newborns' central vision: Whole or hole? *Journal of Experimental Child Psychology,* 1978, *26,* 193–203.

Lippe, W., & Rubel, E. W. Development of the place principle: Tonotopic organization. *Science,* 1983, *219,* 514–516.

Lodge, A., Armington, J., Barnet, A., Shanks, B., & Newcomb, C. Newborn infants' electroretinograms and evoked electroencephalographic responses to orange and white light. *Child Development,* 1969, *40,* 267–293.

Longuet-Higgins, H. C., & Prazdny, K. The interpretation of moving retinal images. *Proceedings of the Royal Society of London,* 1980, *B 208,* 385–387.

Lund, J. S., Boothe, R. G., & Lund, R. D. Development of neurons in the visual cortex (area 17) of the monkey (Macaca nemestrina): A Golgi study from fetal day 127 to postnatal maturity. *Journal of Comparative Neurology,* 1977, *176,* 149–188.

Maffei, L., & Fiorentini, A. Spatial frequency rows in the striate visual cortex. *Vision Research,* 1977, *17,* 257–264.

Maisel, E. B., & Karmel, B. Z. Contour density and pattern configuration in visual preferences in infants. *Infant Behavior and Development,* 1978, *1,* 127–140.

Mandelbaum, J., & Sloan, L. L. Peripheral visual acuity: With special reference to scotopic illumination. *American Journal of Ophthalmology,* 1947, *30,* 581–588.

Mann, I. C. *The development of the human eye.* London: British Medical Association, 1964.

Marg, E., Freeman, D. N., Peltzman, P., & Goldstein, P. J. Visual acuity development in human infants: Evoked potential measurements. *Investigative Ophthalmology,* 1976, *15,* 150–153.

Marr, D. *Vision: A computational investigation into the human representation and processing of visual information.* San Francisco: W. H. Freeman and Company, 1982.

Maurer, D. *The development of binocular convergence in infants.* Doctoral dissertation, University of Minnesota, 1974.

Maurer, D. Infant visual perception: Methods of study. In L. B. Cohen & P. Salapatek (Eds.),

Infant perception: From sensation to cognition. Basic visual processes (Vol. 1). New York: Academic Press, 1975.

Maurer, D., & Lewis, T. L. Peripheral discrimination by 3-month-old infants. *Child Development,* 1979, *50,* 276–279.

Maurer, D., & Salapatek, P. Developmental changes in the scanning of faces by young infants. *Child Development,* 1976, *47,* 523–527.

Mayer, D. L., & Dobson, V. Visual acuity development in infants and young children, as assessed by operant preferential looking. *Vision Research,* 1982, *22,* 1141–1151.

McCall, R. B., & Kagan, J. Attention in the infant: Effects of complexity, contour, perimeter, and familiarity. *Child Development,* 1967, *38,* 939–952.

McCall, R. B., & Melson, W. H. Complexity, contour and area as determinants of attention in infants. *Developmental Psychology,* 1970, *3,* 343–349.

McGinnis, J. M. Eye movements and optic nystagmus in early infancy. *Genetic Psychology Monographs,* 1930, *8,* 321–430.

McGurk, H. The role of object orientation in infant perception. *Journal of Experimental Child Psychology,* 1970, *9,* 363–373.

McKee, S. P., & Nakayama, K. *The detection of motion in the peripheral visual field.* Paper presented at the meeting of the Association for Research in Vision and Ophthalmology, Sarasota, Florida, 1982.

McKenzie, B. E., & Day, R. H. Distance as a determinant of visual fixation in early infancy. *Science,* 1972, *178,* 1108–1110.

McKenzie, B. E., & Day, R. H. Infants' attention to stationary and moving objects at different distances. *Australian Journal of Psychology,* 1976, *28,* 45–51.

McKenzie, B. E., Tootell, H. E., & Day, R. H. Development of visual size constancy during the 1st year of human infancy. *Developmental Psychology,* 1980, *16,* 163–174.

Milewski, A. E. Infants' discrimination of internal and external pattern elements. *Journal of Experimental Child Psychology,* 1976, *22,* 229–246.

Milewski, A. E. Young infants' visual processing of internal and adjacent shapes. *Infant Behavior and Development,* 1978, *1,* 359–371.

Milewski, A. E. Visual discrimination and detection of configurational invariance in 3-month infants. *Developmental Psychology,* 1979, *15,* 357–363.

Miller, M., Pasik, P., & Pasik, T. Extrageniculostriate vision in the monkey. VII. Contrast sensitivity functions. *Journal of Neurophysiology,* 1980, *43,* 1510–1526.

Millodot, M. Retinoscopy and the refraction of infants. *Ophthalmic Optician,* 1972, *12,* 1130–1132.

Miranda, S. B. Visual abilities and pattern preferences of premature infants and full-term neonates. *Journal of Experimental Child Psychology,* 1970, *10,* 189–205.

Miranda, S. B., & Fantz, R. L. Distribution of visual attention by newborn infants among patterns varying in size and number of details. *Proceedings of the Annual Convention of the American Psychological Association,* 1971, *6,* 181–182.

Misumi, J. Experimental studies of the development of visual size constancy in early infancy. *Japanese Journal of Psychology,* 1951, *20,* 16–26.

Mitchell, D. E., Freeman, R. D., Millodot, M., & Haegerström, G. Meridional amblyopia: Evidence for modification of the human visual system by early visual experience. *Vision Research,* 1973, *13,* 535–558.

Mitchell, D. E., Giffin, F., Wilkinson, F., Anderson, P., & Smith, M. L. Visual resolution in young kittens. *Vision Research,* 1976, *16,* 363–366.

Moffett, A. Stimulus complexity as a determinant of visual attention in infants. *Journal of Experimental Child Psychology,* 1969, *8,* 173–179.

Mohindra, I., Held, R., Gwiazda, J., & Brill, S. Astigmatism in infants. *Science,* 1978, *202,* 329–331.

Mohler, C. W., & Wurtz, R. H. Organization of monkey superior colliculus: Intermediate layer cells discharging before eye movements. *Journal of Neurophysiology,* 1976, *39,* 722–744.

Morgan, J. B., & Morgan, S. S. Infant learning as a developmental index. *Journal of Genetic Psychology,* 1944, *65,* 281–289.

Moskowitz, A., & Sokol, S. Spatial and temporal interaction of pattern-evoked cortical potentials in human infants. *Vision Research,* 1980, *20,* 699–707.

Moskowitz-Cook, A. The development of photopic spectral sensitivity in human infants. *Vision Research,* 1979, *19,* 1133–1142.

Mower, G. D., & Christen, W. G. Effects of early monocular deprivation on the acuity of lateral geniculate neurons in the cat. *Brain Research,* 1982, *255,* 475–480.

Muir, D. W., & Mitchell, D. E. Visual resolution and experience: Acuity deficits in cats following early selective visual deprivation. *Science,* 1973, *180,* 420–422.

Munsinger, H., & Weir, M. W. Infants' and young children's preference for complexity. *Journal of*

Experimental Child Psychology, 1967, *5,* 69–73.

Myers, R. E. Visual deficits after lesions of brain stem tegmentum in cats. *Archives of Neurology,* 1964, *11,* 73–90.

Nodine, C. F., Carmody, D. P., & Kundel, H. L. Searching for Nina. In J. W. Senders, R. A. Monty, & D. F. Fisher (Eds.), *Eye movements and the higher psychological processes.* Hillsdale, N.J.: Erlbaum, 1978.

Norman, J. L., Pettigrew, J. D., & Daniels, J. D. Early development of X-cells in kitten lateral geniculate nucleus. *Science,* 1977, *198,* 202–204.

Norton, T. T. Receptive-field properties of superior colliculus cells and development of visual behavior in kittens. *Journal of Neurophysiology,* 1974, *37,* 674–690.

Norton, T. T., & Lindsley, D. B. Visual behavior after bilateral superior colliculus lesions in kittens and cats. *Federation Proceedings,* 1971, *30,* 615.

Noton, D., & Stark, L. Scanpaths in eye movements during pattern perception. *Science,* 1971, *171,* 308–311.

Nystrom, M., Hansson, M. B., & Marklund, K. Infant preference for intermittent light. *Psychological Research Bulletin, Lund U.,* 1975, *15,* 1–11.

Oesterberg, G. A. Topography of the layer of rods and cones in the human retina. *Acta Ophthalmologica,* 1935, Suppl. VI.

O'Leary, D. J., & Millodot, M. Eyelid closure causes myopia in humans. *Experientia,* 1979, *35,* 1478–1479.

Oster, H. *Color perception in ten-week-old infants.* Paper presented at the meeting of the Society for Research in Child Development, Denver, Colorado. April 1975.

Owens, D. A. A comparison of accommodative responsiveness and contrast sensitivity for sinusoidal gratings. *Vision Research,* 1980, *20,* 159–167.

Owens, D. A., & Held, R. The development of ocular accommodation. In R. Pigassou-Albouy (Ed.), Cahiers de l'orthoptie (Vol. 3). Toulouse, France: AFIM Documents, 1978.

Packwood, J., & Gordon, B. Stereopsis in normal domestic cat, Siamese cat, and cat raised with alternating monocular occlusion. *Journal of Neurophysiology,* 1975, *38,* 1485–1499.

Pasik, P., & Pasik, T. Oculomotor functions in monkeys with lesions of the cerebrum and the superior colliculi. In M. B. Bender (Ed.), *The oculomotor system.* New York: Harper and Row, 1964.

Pasik, P., Pasik, T., & Schilder, P. Extrageniculostriate vision in the monkey: Discrimination of luminous flux-equated figures. *Experimental Neurology,* 1969, *24,* 421–437.

Pass, A. F., & Levi, D. M. Spatial processing of complex stimuli in the amblyopic visual system. *Investigative Ophthalmology and Visual Science,* 1982, *23,* 780–786.

Pearson, R. M. The objective determination of vision and visual acuity. *British Journal of Physiological Optics,* 1966, *23,* 107–127.

Peeples, D. R., & Teller, D. Y. Color vision and brightness discrimination in two-month-old human infants. *Science,* 1975, *189,* 1102–1103.

Peeples, D. R., & Teller, D. Y. White-adapted photopic spectral sensitivity in human infants. *Vision Research,* 1978, *18,* 49–59.

Peiper, A. Über die Helligkeits- und Farbenempfindungen der Frühgeburten. *Archiv für Kinderheilkeit,* 1927, *80,* 1–20.

Peiper, A. *Cerebral function in infancy and childhood.* New York: Consultants Bureau, 1963.

Petrig, B., Julesz, B., Kropfl, W., Baumgartner, G., & Anliker, M. Development of stereopsis and cortical binocularity in human infants: Electrophysiological evidence. *Science,* 1981, *213,* 1402–1405.

Pettersen, L., Yonas, A., & Fisch, R. O. The development of blinking in response to impending collision in preterm, full term, and postterm infants. *Infant Behavior and Development,* 1980, *3,* 155–165.

Pettigrew, J. D. The effect of visual experience on the development of stimulus specificity by kitten cortical neurones. *Journal of Physiology,* 1974, *237,* 49–74.

Pettigrew, J. D. The paradox of the critical period in striate cortical development. In C. Cotman (Ed.), *Neuronal plasticity.* New York: Raven, 1978.

Pettigrew, J. D., & Freeman, R. D. Visual experience without lines: Effect on developing cortical neurons. *Science,* 1973, *182,* 599–601.

Pick, H. L., Jr., & Pick, A. D. Sensory and perceptual development. In P. H. Mussen (Ed.), *Carmichael's manual of child psychology* (Vol. 1, 3rd ed.). New York: Wiley, 1970.

Pinter, R. B., & Harris, L. R. Temporal and spatial response characteristics of the cat superior colliculus. *Brain Research,* 1981, *207,* 73–94.

Pipp, S. L. *A test of theories of infant visual behavior in the first two months of life.* Doctoral dissertation, University of Denver, 1978.

Pirchio, M., Spinelli, D., Fiorentini, A., & Maffei, L. Infant contrast sensitivity evaluated by evoked potentials. *Brain Research,* 1978, *141,* 179–184.

Pöppel, E. Comment on "Visual system's view of acoustic space." *Nature,* 1973, *243,* 231.

Powers, M. K., & Dobson, V. Effect of focus on visual acuity of human infants. *Vision Research,* 1982, *22,* 521–528.

Powers, M. K., Schneck, M., & Teller, D. Y. Spectral sensitivity of human infants at absolute visual threshold. *Vision Research,* 1981, *21,* 1005–1016.

Prazdny, K. Egomotion and relative depth from optical flow. *Biological Cybernetics,* 1980, *36,* 87–102.

Pulos, E., Teller, D. Y., & Buck, S. Infant color vision: A search for short wavelength-sensitive mechanisms by means of chromatic adaptation. *Vision Research,* 1980, *20,* 485–493.

Rabin, J., Van Sluyters, R. C., & Malach, R. Emmetropization: A vision-dependent phenomenon. *Investigative Ophthalmology and Visual Science,* 1981, *20,* 561–564.

Rader, N., Bausano, M., & Richards, J. E. On the nature of the visual-cliff avoidance response in human infants. *Child Development,* 1980, *51,* 61–68.

Rakic, P. Prenatal development of the visual system in the rhesus monkey. *Philosophical Transactions of the Royal Society,* 1977, *B 278,* 245–260.

Rakic, P. Developmental events leading to laminar and areal organization of the neocortex. In F. O. Schmitt, F. G. Worden, G. Adelman, & S. G. Dennis (Eds.), *The organization of the cerebral cortex.* Cambridge, Mass.: MIT Press, 1981.

Rakic, P., & Sidman, R. L. Supravital DNA synthesis in the developing human and mouse brain. *Journal of Neuropathology and Experimental Neurology,* 1968, *27,* 246–276.

Rashbass, C. The relationship between saccadic and smooth tracking eye movements. *Journal of Physiology (London),* 1961, *159,* 326–338.

Ratliff, F. *Mach bands: Quantitative studies on neural networks in the retina.* San Francisco: Holden-Day, 1965.

Rayner, K. Eye movements in reading and information processing. *Psychological Bulletin,* 1978, *85,* 618–660.

Regal, D. M. Development of critical flicker frequency in human infants. *Vision Research,* 1981, *21,* 549–555.

Regal, D. M., & Salapatek, P. *Eye and head coordination in human infants.* Paper presented at the meeting of the Association for Research in Vision and Ophthalmology, Sarasota, Florida, 1982.

Regan, D. *Evoked potentials in psychology, sensory physiology and clinical medicine.* London: Chapman and Hall, 1972.

Regan, D. Assessment of visual acuity by evoked potential recording: Ambiguity caused by temporal dependence of spatial frequency selectivity. *Vision Research,* 1978, *18,* 439–443.

Regan, D., & Richards, W. A. Independence of evoked potentials and apparent size. *Vision Research,* 1971, *11,* 679–684.

Reinecke, R., & Cogan, D. Standardization of objective visual acuity measurements. *Archives of Ophthalmology,* 1958, *60,* 418–421.

Richards, J. E., & Rader, N. Crawling-onset age predicts visual cliff avoidance in infants. *Journal of Experimental Psychology: Human Perception and Performance,* 1981, *7,* 382–387.

Riggs, L. A. Visual acuity. In C. H. Graham (Ed.), *Vision and visual perception.* New York: Wiley, 1965.

Ripps, H., & Weale, R. A. Visual adaptation. In H. Davson (Ed.), *The eye. Visual function in man* (Vol. 2A). New York: Academic Press, 1969.

Robinson, D. A. The oculomotor control system: A review. *Proceedings of the Institute of Electrical and Electronic Engineers,* 1968, *56,* 1032–1049.

Robinson, D. A. The physiology of pursuit eye movements. In R. A. Monty & J. W. Senders (Eds.), *Eye movements and psychological processes.* Hillsdale, N.J.: Erlbaum, 1976.

Robinson, D. L., & Jarvis, C. D. Superior colliculus neurons studied during head and eye movements of the behaving monkey. *Journal of Neurophysiology,* 1974, *37,* 533–540.

Robson, J. G. Spatial and temporal contrast-sensitivity functions of the visual system. *Journal of the Optical Society of America,* 1966, *56,* 1141–1142.

Rock, I. *An introduction to perception.* New York: Macmillan, 1975.

Rosenquist, A. C., & Palmer, L. A. Visual receptive field properties of cells in the superior colliculus after cortical lesions in the cat. *Experimental Neurology,* 1971, *33,* 629–652.

Rosinski, R. R. *The development of visual perception.* Santa Monica, Calif.: Goodyear Publishing Company, 1977.

Rosvold, H. E., Mishkin, M., & Szwarcbart, M. K.

Effects of subcortical lesions in monkeys on visual-discrimination and single-alternation performance. *Journal of Comparative and Physiological Psychology*, 1958, *51*, 437–444.

Rubel, E. W., & Ryals, B. M. Development of the place principle: Acoustic trauma. *Science*, 1983, *219*, 512–514.

Ruff, H. A. Infant recognition of the invariant form of objects. *Child Development*, 1978, *49*, 293–306.

Ruff, H. A., & Birch, H. G. Infant visual fixation: The effect of concentricity, curvilinearity, and the number of directions. *Journal of Experimental Psychology*, 1974, *17*, 460–473.

Ruff, H. A., & Halton, A. Is there directed reaching in the human neonate? *Developmental Psychology*, 1977, *14*, 425–426.

Rusoff, A. C., & Dubin, M. W. Development of receptive-field properties of retinal ganglion cells in kittens. *Journal of Neurophysiology*, 1977, *40*, 1188–1198.

Rusoff, A. C., & Dubin, M. W. Kitten ganglion cells: Dendritic field size at 3 weeks of age and correlation with receptive field size. *Investigative Ophthalmology and Visual Science*, 1978, *17*, 819–821.

Salapatek, P. *Visual scanning of geometric figures by the human newborn*. Paper presented at the meeting of the American Psychological Association, New York, 1966.

Salapatek, P. Visual scanning of geometric figures by the human newborn. *Journal of Comparative and Physiological Psychology*, 1968, *66*, 247–258.

Salapatek, P. Pattern perception in early infancy. In L. B. Cohen & P. Salapatek (Eds.), *Infant perception: From sensation to cognition. Basic visual processes* (Vol. 1). New York: Academic Press, 1975.

Salapatek, P., Aslin, R. N., Simonson, J., & Pulos, E. Infant saccadic eye movements to visible and previously visible targets. *Child Development*, 1980, *51*, 1090–1094.

Salapatek, P., & Banks, M. S. Infant sensory assessment: Vision. In F. D. Minifie & L. L. Lloyd (Eds.), *Communicative and cognitive abilities—Early behavioral assessment*. Baltimore: University Park Press, 1978.

Salapatek, P., Bechtold, A. G., & Bergman, J. *Pupillary response in 1- and 2-month-old infants*. Paper presented at the meeting of the Psychonomic Society, Washington, D.C. November 1977.

Salapatek, P., Bechtold, A. G., & Bushnell, E. W. Infant visual acuity as a function of viewing distance. *Child Development*, 1976, *47*, 860–863.

Salapatek, P., & Kessen, W. Visual scannings of triangles by the human newborn. *Journal of Experimental Child Psychology*, 1966, *3*, 155–167.

Salapatek, P., & Kessen, W. Prolonged investigation of triangles by the human newborn. *Journal of Experimental Child Psychology*, 1973, *15*, 22–29.

Samorajski, T., Keefe, J. R., & Ordy, J. M. Morphogenesis of photoreceptor and retinal ultrastructure in a sub-human primate. *Vision Research*, 1965, *5*, 639–648.

Sandell, J. H., Gross, C. G., & Bornstein, M. H. Color categories in macaques. *Journal of Comparative and Physiological Psychology*, 1979, *93*, 626–635.

Santonastaso, A. La refrazione oculare nei primi anni di vita. *Annali di Ottalmologia e Clinica Oculista*, 1930, *58*, 852–885.

Scarr, S., & Salapatek, P. Patterns of fear development during infancy. *Merrill-Palmer Quarterly*, 1970, *16*, 53–90.

Schaller, M. J. Chromatic vision in human infants: Conditioned operant fixation to "hues" of varying intensity. *Bulletin of the Psychonomic Society*, 1975, *6*, 39–42.

Schiff, W. The perception of impending collision: A study of visually directed avoidant behavior. *Psychological Monographs*, 1965, *79*, Whole No. 604.

Schiller, P. H., & Koerner, F. Discharge characteristics of single units in superior colliculus of the alert rhesus monkey. *Journal of Neurophysiology*, 1971, *34*, 920–936.

Schiller, P. H., & Stryker, M. Single-unit recording and stimulation in superior colliculus of the alert rhesus monkey. *Journal of Neurophysiology*, 1972, *35*, 915–924.

Schiller, P. H., Stryker, M., Cynader, M., & Berman, N. Response characteristics of single cells in the monkey superior colliculus following ablation or cooling of visual cortex. *Journal of Neurophysiology*, 1974, *37*, 181–194.

Schiller, P. H., True, S. D., & Conway, J. L. Deficits in eye movements following frontal eye-field and superior colliculus ablations. *Journal of Neurophysiology*, 1980, *44*, 1175–1189.

Schmitt, F. O., Worden, F. G., Adelman, G., & Dennis, S. G. (Eds.). *The organization of the cerebral cortex*. Cambridge, Mass.: MIT Press, 1981.

Schneider, G. Two visual systems. *Science*, 1969,

163, 895–902.

Schor, C., & Narayan, V. The influence of field size upon the spatial frequency response of optokinetic nystagmus. *Vision Research*, 1981, *21*, 985–994.

Schwartz, M., & Day, R. H. Visual shape perception in early infancy. *Monographs of the Society for Research in Child Development*, 1979, *44*, No. 7.

Sekuler, R. Visual motion perception. In E. C. Carterette & M. P. Friedman (Eds.), *Handbook of perception. Seeing* (Vol. 5). New York: Academic Press, 1975.

Shapley, R. M., & So, Y. -T. Is there an effect of monocular deprivation on the proportion of X and Y cells in the cat lateral geniculate nucleus? *Experimental Brain Research*, 1980, *39*, 41–48.

Shatz, C. J., & Stryker, M. P. Ocular dominance in Layer IV of the cat's visual cortex and the effects of monocular deprivation. *Journal of Physiology*, 1978, *281*, 267–283.

Sherman, S. M. The effect of superior colliculus lesions upon the visual fields of cats with cortical ablations. *Journal of Comparative Neurology*, 1977, *172*, 211–230.

Sherman, S. M., Hoffmann, K. -P., & Stone, J. Loss of a specific cell type from dorsal lateral geniculate nucleus in visually deprived cats. *Journal of Neurophysiology*, 1972, *35*, 532–541.

Sherman, S. M., & Stone, J. Physiological normality of the retina in visually deprived cats. *Brain Research*, 1973, *60*, 224–230.

Sherman, S. M., Wilson, J. R., Kaas, J. H., & Webb, S. V. X- and Y-cells in the dorsal lateral geniculate nucleus of the owl monkey (*Aotus trivirgatus*). *Science*, 1976, *192*, 475–477.

Shetty, S. S., Brodersen, A. J., & Fox, R. System for generating dynamic random-element stereograms. *Behavioral Research Methods and Instrumentation*, 1979, *11*, 485–490.

Shinkman, P. G., & Bruce, C. J. Binocular differences in cortical receptive fields of kittens after rotationally disparate binocular experience. *Science*, 1977, *197*, 285–287.

Shively, J. N. Fine structure of the postnatal development of the canine retina. *American Journal of Veterinary Research*, 1971, *32*, 383–392.

Shlaer, R. Shift in binocular disparity causes compensatory change in the cortical structure of kittens. *Science*, 1971, *173*, 638–641.

Shlaer, S. The relation between visual acuity and illumination. *Journal of General Physiology*, 1937, *21*, 165–188.

Slater, A. M., & Findlay, J. M. The measurement of fixation position in the newborn baby. *Journal of Experimental Child Psychology*, 1972, *14*, 349–364.

Slater, A. M., & Findlay, J. M. Binocular fixation in the newborn baby. *Journal of Experimental Child Psychology*, 1975, *20*, 248–273.

Slater, A. M., & Sykes, M. Newborn infants' visual responses to square wave gratings. *Child Development*, 1977, *48*, 545–554.

Smith, D. P. Derivation of wavelength discrimination from colour-naming data. *Vision Research*, 1971, *11*, 739–742.

Snyder, A. W. The physics of vision in compound eyes. In H. Autrum (Ed.), *Handbook of sensory physiology. Vision in invertebrates* (Vol. VII/6A). New York: Springer-Verlag, 1979.

Sokol, S. Measurement of infant visual acuity from pattern reversal evoked potentials. *Vision Research*, 1978, *18*, 33–40.

Sokol, S. Pattern elicited ERGs and VEPs in amblyopia and infant vision. In J. Armington, J. Krauskopf, & B. Wooten (Eds.), *Visual psychophysics: Its physiological basis*. New York: Academic Press, 1980.

Sokol, S. Infant visual development: Evoked potential estimates. In I. Bodis-Wollner (Ed.), *Annals of the New York Academy of Sciences*, in press.

Sokol, S., & Dobson, V. Pattern reversal visually evoked potentials in infants. *Investigative Ophthalmology*, 1976, *15*, 58–62.

Sokol, S., Moskowitz, A., & Paul, A. Visual evoked potential estimates of the amplitude of accommodation in human infants. *Vision Research*, in press.

Sokoloff, L., Reivich, M., Kennedy, C., Des Rosiers, M. H., Patlak, C. S., Pettigrew, K. D., Sakurada, O., & Shinohara, M. The (^{14}C) deoxyglucose method for the measurement of local cerebral glucose utilization: Theory, procedure, and normal values in the conscious and anesthetized albino rat. *Journal of Neurochemistry*, 1977, *28*, 897–916.

Sorsby, A., Benjamin, B., & Sheridan, M. Refraction and its components during the growth of the eye from the age of three. *Medical Council Special Report*, Series No. 301. London: Her Majesty's Stationery Office, 1961.

Sorsby, A., & Sheridan, M. Refraction and its components during the growth of the eye. *Special Report Series Medical Research Council*, 1961, Series No. 301.

Spear, P. D., & Braun, J. J. Pattern discrimination following removal of visual neocortex in cat. *Ex-*

perimental Neurology, 1969, *25*, 331–348.

Spears, W. C. Assessment of visual preference and discrimination in the four-month-old infant. *Journal of Comparative and Physiological Psychology*, 1964, *57*, 381–386.

Spears, W. C. Visual preference in the four-month-old infant. *Psychonomic Science*, 1966, *4*, 237–238.

Spira, A. W., & Hollenberg, M. J. Human retinal development: Ultrastructure of the inner retinal layers. *Developmental Biology*, 1973, *31*, 1–21.

Sprague, J. M., & Meikle, T. H., Jr. The role of the superior colliculus in visually guided behavior. *Experimental Neurology*, 1965, *11*, 115–146.

Stein, B. E. Development and organization of a multimodal representation in cat superior colliculus. *Federation Proceedings*, 1978, *37*, 2240–2245.

Stein, B. E., & Clamann, H. P. Control of pinna movements and sensorimotor register in cat superior colliculus. *Brain Behavior and Evolution*, 1981, *19*, 180–192.

Stein, B. E., Clamann, H. P., & Goldberg, S. J. Superior colliculus: Control of eye movements in neonatal kittens. *Science*, 1980, *210*, 78–80.

Stein, B. E., & Edwards, S. B. Corticotectal and other corticofugal projections in neonatal cat. *Brain Research*, 1979, *161*, 399–409.

Stein, B. E., & Gallagher, H. L. Maturation of cortical control over superior colliculus cells in cat. *Brain Research*, 1981, *223*, 429–435.

Stein, B. E., Lábos, E., & Kruger, L. Long-lasting discharge properties of neurons in the kitten midbrain. *Vision Research*, 1973, *13*, 2615–2619. (a)

Stein, B. E., Lábos, E., & Kruger. L. Sequence of changes in properties of neurons of superior colliculus of the kitten during maturation. *Journal of Neurophysiology*, 1973, *36*, 667–679. (b)

Stein, B. E., Magalhães-Castro, B., & Kruger, L. Relationship between visual and tactile representations in cat superior colliculus. *Journal of Neurophysiology*, 1976, *39*, 401–419.

Sterling, P. Quantitative mapping with the electron microscope: Retinal terminals in the superior colliculus. *Brain Research*, 1973, *54*, 347–354.

Sterling, P., & Wickelgren, B. G. Visual receptive fields in the superior colliculus of the cat. *Journal of Neurophysiology*, 1969, *32*, 1–15.

Stevens, K. A. The information content of texture gradients. *Biological Cybernetics*, 1981, *42*, 95–105.

Stone, J., & Dreher, B. Projection of X- and Y-cells of the cat's lateral geniculate nucleus to areas 17 and 18 of visual cortex. *Journal of Neurophysiology*, 1973, *36*, 551–567.

Stone, J., Dreher, B., & Leventhal, A. Hierarchical and parallel mechanisms in the organization of the visual cortex. *Brain Research*, 1979, *180*, 345–394.

Stone, J., & Freeman, R. B., Jr. Neurophysiological mechanisms in the visual discrimination of form. In R. Jung (Ed.), *Handbook of sensory physiology. Central processing of visual information. Part A.* (Vol. VII/3). New York: Springer-Verlag, 1973.

Stone, J., & Fukuda, Y. Properties of cat retinal ganglion cells: A comparison of W-cells with X- and Y-cells. *Journal of Neurophysiology*, 1974, *37*, 722–748.

Strauss, M. S., & Curtis, L. E. *Infant perception of patterns differing in goodness of form*. Paper presented at the meeting of the Society for Research in Child Development, Boston, 1981.

Stromberg, E. Über Refraktion und Achsenlange des Menschlichen Auges. *Acta Ophthalmologica*, 1936, *14*, 281–297.

Stryker, M. P., & Sherk, H. Modification of cortical orientation selectivity in the cat by restricted visual experience: A reexamination. *Science*, 1975, *190*, 904–906.

Stryker, M. P., Sherk, H., Leventhal, A. G., & Hirsch, H. V. B. Physiological consequences for the cat's visual cortex of effectively restricting early visual experience with oriented contours. *Journal of Neurophysiology*, 1978, *41*, 896–909.

Stuart, J. A., & Burian, H. M. A study of separation difficulties: Its relationship to visual acuity in normal and amblyopic eyes. *American Journal of Ophthalmology*, 1962, 53, 471–477.

Studdert-Kennedy, M., Liberman, A. M., Harris, K. S., & Cooper, F. S. Motor theory of speech perception: A reply to Lane's critical review. *Psychological Review*, 1970, *77*, 234–249.

Teller, D. Y. The forced-choice preferential looking procedure: A psychophysical technique for use with human infants. *Infant Behavior and Development*, 1979, *2*, 135–153.

Teller, D. Y. Scotopic vision, colorvision, and stereopsis in infants. *Current Eye Research*, 1982, *2*, 199–210.

Teller, D. Y., Allen, J. L., Regal, D. M., & Mayer, D. L. Astigmatism and acuity in two primate infants. *Investigative Ophthalmology and Visual Science*, 1978, *17*, 344–349.

Teller, D. Y., & Bornstein, M. H. Infant color vision. In P. Salapatek & L. B. Cohen (Eds.), *Handbook of infant perception*, in press.

Teller, D. Y., Morse, R., Borton, R., & Regal, D. Visual acuity for vertical and diagonal gratings in human infants. *Vision Research,* 1974, *14,* 1433–1439.

Teller, D. Y., Peeples, D. R., & Sekel, M. Discrimination of chromatic from white light by two-month-old human infants. *Vision Research,* 1978, *18,* 41–48.

Thomas, H. Visual fixation responses of infants to stimuli of varying complexity. *Child Development,* 1965, *36,* 629–638.

Thomas, H. Discrepancy hypotheses: Methodological and theoretical considerations. *Psychological Review,* 1971, *78,* 249–259.

Timney, B. Development of binocular depth perception in kittens. *Investigative Ophthalmology and Visual Science,* 1981, *21,* 493–496.

Tootell, R. B., Silverman, M. S., & DeValois, R. L. Spatial frequency columns in primary visual cortex. *Science,* 1981, *214,* 813–815.

Treiber, F., & Wilcox, S. Perception of a "subjective" contour by infants. *Child Development,* 1980, *51,* 915–917.

Trevarthen, C. Two mechanisms of vision in primates. *Psychologische Forschung,* 1968, *31,* 299–337.

Trincker, D., & Trincker, I. Die Ontogenetische Entwicklung des Helligkeits und Farbensehens beim Menschen. I. Die Entwicklung des Helligkeitssehens. (The ontogenetic development of brightness and color vision in man. I. The development of brightness.) *Graefes Archiv for Clinical and Experimental Ophthalmology,* 1955, *156,* 519–534. Translated and reprinted in Y. Brackbill & G. G. Thompson (Eds.), *Behavior in infancy and early childhood.* New York: The Free Press, 1967.

Tronick, E. Stimulus control and the growth of the infant's effective visual field. *Perception and Psychophysics,* 1972, *11,* 373–375.

Tronick, E., & Clanton, C. Infant looking patterns. *Vision Research,* 1971, *11,* 1479–1486.

Tucker, G. S., Hamasaki, D. I., Labbie, A., & Muroff, J. Anatomic and physiologic development of the photoreceptor of the kitten. *Experimental Brain Research,* 1979, *37,* 459–474.

Tversky, B. Eye fixations in prediction of recognition and recall. *Memory and Cognition,* 1974, *2,* 275–278.

Ullman, S. *The interpretation of visual motion.* Cambridge, Mass.: MIT Press, 1979.

Updyke, B. V. Characteristics of unit responses in superior colliculus of the Cebus monkey. *Journal of Neurophysiology,* 1974, *37,* 896–909.

van Alphen, G. W. H. M. On emmetropia and ametropia. *Ophthalmologica,* 1961, *142* (Suppl.), 1–92.

van Giffen, K., & Haith, M. M. Infant visual response to gestalt geometric forms. *Infant Behavior and Development,* submitted manuscript.

Van Hof-van Duin, J. Development of visuomotor behavior in normal and dark reared cats. *Brain Research,* 1976, *104,* 233–241. (a)

Van Hof-van Duin, J. Early and permanent effects of monocular deprivation on pattern discrimination and visuomotor behavior in cats. *Brain Research,* 1976, *111,* 261–276. (b)

Van Hof-van Duin, J. Direction preference of optokinetic responses in monocularly tested and normal kittens and light-deprived cats. *Archives of Italian Biology,* 1978, *116,* 471–477.

van Meeteren, A. *Spatial sinewave response of the visual system.* Institute for Perception TNO Report No. IZF-1966-7, 1967.

Van Nes, F. L., & Bouman, M. A. Spatial modulation transfer in the human eye. *Journal of the Optical Society of America,* 1967, *57,* 401–406.

Van Sluyters, R. C., & Blakemore, C. Experimental creation of unusual neuronal properties in visual cortex of kittens. *Nature,* 1973, *246,* 506–508.

Van Sluyters, R. C., & Levitt, F. B. Experimental strabismus in the kitten. *Journal of Neurophysiology,* 1980, *43,* 686–699.

Virsu, V., & Rovamo, J. Visual resolution, contrast sensitivity, and the cortical magnification factor. *Experimental Brain Research,* 1979, *37,* 475–494.

Virsu, V., Rovamo, J., Laurinen, P., & Näsänen, R. Temporal contrast sensitivity and cortical magnification. *Vision Research,* 1982, *22,* 1211–1217.

Vital-Durand, F., Garey, L. J., & Blakemore, C. Monocular and binocular deprivation in the monkey: Morphological effects and reversibility. *Brain Research,* 1978, *158,* 45–64.

Vitova, Z., & Hrbek, A. Developmental study on the responsiveness of the human brain to flicker stimulation. *Developmental Medicine and Child Neurology,* 1972, *14,* 476–486.

Volkmann, F. C., & Dobson, M. V. Infant responses of ocular fixation to moving visual stimuli. *Journal of Experimental Child Psychology,* 1976, *22,* 86–99.

Von Hofsten, C. Binocular convergence as a determinant of reaching behavior in infancy. *Perception,* 1977, *6,* 139–144.

von Noorden, G. K., & Crawford, M. L. J. Lid closure and refractive error in macaque monkeys. *Nature,* 1978, *272,* 53–54.

von Noorden, G. K., Dowling, J. E., & Ferguson, D. C. Experimental amblyopia in monkeys. I. Behavioral studies of stimulus deprivation amblyopia. *Archives of Ophthalmology,* 1970, *84,* 206–214.

Vos, J. J., Lazet, A., & Bouman, M. A. Visual contrast thresholds in practical problems. *Journal of the Optical Society of America,* 1956, *46,* 1065–1070.

Vurpillot, E., Ruel, J., & Castrec, A. L'organisation perceptive chez le nourrisson: Reponse au tout ou à ses éléments. *Bulletin de Psychologie,* 1977, *327,* 396–405.

Walk, R. D., & Gibson, E. J. A comparative and analytical study of visual depth perception. *Psychological Monographs,* 1961, *75*(Whole No. 519).

Wallach, H., & O'Connell, D. N. The kinetic depth effect. *Journal of Experimental Psychology,* 1953, *45,* 205–217.

Weidman, T. A., & Kuwabara, T. Development of the rat retina. *Investigative Ophthalmology,* 1969, *8,* 60–69.

Welch, M. J. Infants' visual attention to varying degrees of novelty. *Child Development,* 1974, *45*(2), 344–350.

Werner, J. S. *Developmental change in scotopic sensitivity and the absorption spectrum of the human ocular media.* Unpublished doctoral dissertation, Brown University, 1979.

Werner, J. S. Development of scotopic sensitivity and the absorption spectrum of the human ocular media. *Journal of the Optical Society of America,* 1982, *72,* 247–258.

Werner, J. S., & Wooten, B. R. Human infant color vision and color perception. *Infant Behavior and Development,* 1979, *2,* 241–274.

Wertheimer, M. Untersuchungen zur Lehre von der Gestalt. II. *Psychologische Forschung,* 1923, *4,* 301–350.

Westheimer, G. Eye movement responses to a horizontally moving visual stimulus. *American Medical Association Archives of Ophthalmology,* 1954, *52,* 932–943.

Westheimer, G. The spatial sense of the eye. *Investigative Ophthalmology and Visual Science,* 1979, *18,* 893–912.

Westheimer, G. The spatial grain of the perifoveal visual field. *Vision Research,* 1982, *22,* 157–162.

Westheimer, G., & McKee, S. P. Stereoscopic acuity with defocused and spatially filtered retinal images. *Journal of the Optical Society of America,* 1980, *70,* 772–778.

Westheimer, G., & Mitchell, A. M. Eye movement responses to convergence stimuli. *Archives of Ophthalmology,* 1958, *55,* 848–857.

Wheeless, L. L., Jr., Boynton, R. M., & Cohen, G. H. Eye movement responses to step and pulse-step stimuli. *Journal of the Optical Society of America,* 1966, *56,* 956–960.

White, B., Castle, R., & Held, R. Observations on the development of visually directed reaching. *Child Development,* 1964, *35,* 349–364.

Wickelgren, B. G. Superior colliculus: Some receptive field properties of bimodally responsive cells. *Science,* 1971, *173,* 69–72.

Wickelgren, L. W. Convergence in the human newborn. *Journal of Experimental Child Psychology,* 1967, *5,* 74–85.

Wickelgren, L. W. The ocular response of human newborns to intermittent visual movements. *Journal of Experimental Child Psychology,* 1969, *8,* 469–482.

Wiesel, T. N., & Hubel, D. H. Comparison of the effects of unilateral and bilateral eye closure on cortical unit responses in kittens. *Journal of Neurophysiology,* 1965, *28,* 1029–1040.

Wiesel, T. N., & Hubel, D. H. Ordered arrangement of orientation columns in monkeys lacking visual experience. *Journal of Comparative Neurology,* 1974, *158,* 307–318.

Wiesel, T. N., & Raviola, E. Increase in axial length of macaque monkey eye after corneal opacification. *Investigative Ophthalmology and Visual Science,* 1979, *18,* 1232–1236.

Williams, R. W., & Chalupa, L. M. Prenatal development of retinocollicular projections in the cat: An anterograde tracer transport study. *Journal of Neuroscience,* 1982, *2,* 604–622.

Wilmer, H., & Scammon, R. Growth of the components of the human eyeball. I. Diagrams, calculations, computation and reference tables. *Archives of Ophthalmology,* 1950, *43,* 599–619.

Wilson, M. E., & Toyne, M. J. Retino-tectal and cortico-tectal projections in *Macaca mulatta. Brain Research,* 1970, *24,* 395–406.

Wolff, P. H. Observations on newborn infants. *Psychosomatic Medicine,* 1959, *21,* 110–118.

Wolff, P. H., & White, B. L. Visual pursuit and attention in young infants. *Journal of the American Academy of Child Psychiatry,* 1965, *4,* 473–484.

Wood, C., Spear, P., & Braun, J. Direction-specific deficits in horizontal optokinetic nystagmus following removal of visual cortex in the cat. *Brain Research,* 1973, *60,* 231–237.

Wood, I. C. J., & Tomlinson, A. The accommodative response in amblyopia. *American Journal of Optometry and Physiological Optics,* 1975, *52,* 243–247.

Woodruff, M. E. Cross sectional studies of corneal and astigmatic characteristics of children between the twenty-fourth and seventy-second months of life. *American Journal of Optometry,* 1971, *48,* 650–659.

Wurtz, R. H., & Goldberg, M. E. Activity of superior colliculus in behaving monkey. III. Cells discharging before eye movements. *Journal of Neurophysiology,* 1972, *35,* 575–586.

Yakovlev, P. I., & LeCours, A. The myelogenetic cycles of regional maturation of the brain. In A. Minkowski (Ed.), *Regional development of the brain in early life.* Philadelphia: F. A. Davis Company, 1967.

Yarbus, A. L. *Eye movements and vision.* New York: Plenum Press, 1967.

Yonas, A., Bechtold, A. G., Frankel, D., Gordon, F. R., McRoberts, G., Norcia, A., & Sternfels, S. Development of sensitivity to information for impending collision. *Perception and Psychophysics,* 1977, *21*(2), 97–104.

Yonas, A., Cleaves, W., & Pettersen, L. Development of sensitivity to pictorial depth. *Science,* 1978, *200,* 77–79.

Yonas, A., & Granrud, C. Development of depth sensitivity in infants. In J. Mehler (Ed.), *Beyond the blooming, buzzing confusion: Neonate and infant cognition,* in press.

Yonas, A., Oberg, C., & Norcia, A. Development of sensitivity to binocular information for the approach of an object. *Developmental Psychology,* 1978, *14*(2), 147–152.

Yonas, A., & Owsley, C. Development of spatial vision in infants. In P. Salapatek & L. Cohen (Eds.), *Handbook of infant perception.* New York: Academic Press, in press.

Yonas, A., Pettersen, L., & Granrud, C. E. Infants' sensitivity to familiar size as information for distance. *Child Development,* 1982, *53,* 1285–1290.

Yonas, A., Pettersen, L., & Lockman, J. Young infants' sensitivity to optical information for collision. *Canadian Journal of Psychology,* 1979, *33,* 268–276.

Yonas, A., Pettersen, L., Lockman, J., & Eisenberg, P. *The perception of impending collision in 3-month-old infants.* Paper presented at the International Conference of Infant Studies, New Haven, Connecticut, 1980.

Yonas, A., & Pick, H. L. An approach to the study of infant space perception. In L. B. Cohen & P. Salapatek (Eds.), *Infant perception: From sensation to cognition. Perception of space, speech, and sound* (Vol. 2). New York: Academic Press, 1975.

Young, F. A. The effect of restricted visual space on the refractive error of the young monkey eye. *Investigative Ophthalmology,* 1963, *2,* 571–577.

Young, L. R. Pursuit eye tracking movements. In P. Bach-y-Rita & C. C. Collins (Eds.), *The control of eye movements.* New York: Academic Press, 1971.

Zaporozhets, A. V., & Zinchenko, V. P. Development of perceptual activity and formation of a sensory image in the child. In A. Leontyev, A. Luria, & A. Smirnov (Eds.), *Psychological research in the U.S.S.R.* (Vol. 1). Moscow: Progress Publishers, 1966.

Zetterström, B. Flicker electroretinography in newborn infants. *Acta Ophthalmologica,* 1955, *33,* 157–166.

Zuckerman, C. B., & Rock, I. An appraisal of the roles of past experience and innate organizing processes in visual perception. *Psychological Bulletin,* 1957, *54,* 269–296.

AUDITORY DEVELOPMENT AND SPEECH PERCEPTION IN INFANCY*

8

RICHARD N. ASLIN, *Indiana University*
DAVID B. PISONI, *Indiana University*
PETER W. JUSCZYK, *University of Oregon*

CHAPTER CONTENTS

*Preparation of this chapter was supported in part by a Research Career Development award (HD–00309) to Richard N. Aslin and by research grants to Richard N. Aslin (HD–11915), David B. Pisoni (MH–24027), and Peter W. Jusczyk (HD–15795). We thank Mary Buuck, Sandra Shea, and Marthalyn Wayne for bibliographic assistance and Nancy Layman for manuscript preparation. The helpful critical comments provided by Eileen C. Schwab, Joan M. Sinnott, and Amanda C. Walley are gratefully acknowledged.

INTRODUCTION

Auditory signals play a major role in communicative behaviors as well as providing important information concerning the location and acoustic characteristics of objects in space. Although a sophisticated understanding of auditory development has long been the goal of researchers in psychology, medicine, child development, and the speech sciences, many basic questions concerning the development of auditory function have remained unanswered. Prior to 1970, the study of auditory development in human infants generated very little highly quantified and reliable data, even though numerous clinical reports and qualitative observations were published. In the first four editions of this Handbook, Pratt (1931, 1933, 1946, 1954) devoted only five pages to his summary of auditory sensitivity in the neonate. Riesen (1960) covered the topic of auditory sensation and perception in human infants in two pages. And, as recently as the last edition of the Handbook, despite enormous growth in the study of the infant's visual system, Kessen, Haith, and Salapatek (1970) summarized the topic of human auditory development in less than three pages.

There are many reasons why the development of auditory function in human infants has eluded detailed study until the past decade. First, the auditory system is devoid of unique behavioral responses, such as the presence of eye movements and fixations in the visual modality, that are linked specifically to the processing of auditory inputs. There are, of course, several general response systems, such as startle reflexes, orienting responses, and psychophysiological measures (heart rate, galvanic skin response [GSR], respiration, evoked potentials), that could be employed as indices of auditory function. However, none of these responses is elicited solely by auditory stimuli. Thus, the choice of response measure has been guided largely by convenience or personal preference rather than by its validity as an index of auditory function.

Second, the characteristics of auditory stimuli in the majority of pre-1970 studies with infants lacked important controls. The first study to use an audiometer in assessing the infant's auditory function was reported by Haller (1932). However, in the ensuing 40 years, specification of the auditory stimulus has been qualitative at best, including such noise generators as clickers, crumpled paper, gongs, bells, rattles, whistles, and voices. As a result of this tendency to ignore the precise specification of auditory stimuli, the replicability of results with infants has been quite poor.

Third, the combination of loosely defined responses and poorly specified stimuli has had the effect of eliminating a rich and productive approach to the study of sensory and perceptual development, namely, the use of psychophysical methods. If one has available a reliably elicited and measurable behavioral or psychophysiological response as well as a quantifiable and manipulable stimulus, then one can systematically vary specific aspects of the stimulus and record variations in the quantitative aspects of the response. This psychophysical approach, despite a long tradition in the adult literature (Boring, 1942; Stevens, 1951), has only recently been applied to the study of visual development (see Teller, 1979, for a general review) and auditory development (e.g., see Hecox, 1975; Trehub, Schneider, & Endman, 1980). This recent trend toward the use of the psychophysical approach in studies of auditory and visual development in infants is due in part to the development of new methodological techniques. However, many of these techniques, even though available for at least 20 years, have not been employed in systematic psychophysical studies of basic visual and auditory functioning. We suspect that, as in many other areas of science, two literatures (adult and infant) have evolved relatively independently, with little overlap in methods or data bases. Particularly fruitful advances in the area of sensory and perceptual development appear to have been associated with collaborative efforts among researchers from the adult and infant areas or with a researcher trained in the more sophisticated adult area who became interested in developmental issues.

Fourth, the auditory system has traditionally been less well understood than the visual system—from the anatomy and sensory coding at the auditory periphery to the neurophysiology of the central auditory pathways. As a result, whether or not one actually believes that our knowledge of the visual system is correct, hypotheses about visual development have been more easily generated and questions have been addressed with the confidence that the endpoint of development is quantifiable. In addition, systematic manipulations of visual input to developing organisms have been made and dramatic deficits, which can be related to specific neural systems, have been discovered (see recent reviews in Aslin, Alberts, & Petersen, 1981; Freeman, 1979). Only recently have such studies of auditory deprivation been extended to neural mechanisms in the mammalian auditory system (see Clopton, 1981). Finally, without examples from the nonhuman literature, researchers studying human auditory development have not had the benefit of analogies derived from animal research, a strategy that has proven fruitful to the study of human visual development.

In contrast to these issues concerning the development of basic auditory abilities, the area of infant speech perception has undergone a remarkable metamorphosis in the past decade. In the previous edition of the Handbook (Mussen, 1970), no data were reported on infant speech perception. Ten years later, dozens of empirical studies have been published as well as several reviews of this burgeoning literature (Aslin & Pisoni, 1980b; Eilers, 1980; Eimas, 1975b, 1978; Eimas & Tartter, 1979; Jusczyk, 1981; Kuhl, 1976b, 1978, 1979a, 1980; Morse, 1978, 1979; Trehub, 1979; Walley, Pisoni, & Aslin, 1981). Interestingly, many of the problems that have impeded progress in studying basic auditory abilities in infants have been overcome in the study of infant speech perception. For example, new methods for assessing the infant's sensitivity to differences in speech signals have been developed, most notably the high amplitude sucking (HAS) procedure (Siqueland & DeLucia, 1969) and the operant head-turning procedure (Moore, Wilson, & Thompson, 1977). In addition, stimulus specification has been perhaps the key aspect of studies of speech perception and great care has been taken to control minute aspects of the speech signals presented to infants. Finally, the entire area of infant speech perception was motivated by empirical findings and theories with a long tradition in the adult speech perception literature. Thus, in contrast to the two relatively independent lines of research on basic auditory sensitivities in infants and adults, studies of infant and adult speech perception have in many respects operated as a unified area.

Despite the similarities between the infant and adult speech perception areas with regard to theories and stimulus control, two issues have constrained the manner in which the development of speech perception has been studied. First, the close association between the adult and infant speech perception literatures has often promoted the rapid adoption of theories from adult speech perception in explaining similar data gathered from infants. These theories and their implications regarding the mechanisms underlying infant speech perception, although seemingly straightforward, have subsequently been questioned by several researchers who view the infant speech perception data from a nonlinguistic (acoustic) perspective. Second, as in the case of studies of basic auditory abilities in infants, the use of psychophysical methods to study infant speech perception has been rare. This stems in part from a theoretical perspective in the adult speech perception literature that characterized speech signals as unique acoustic stimuli and, thus, not subject to the same methods of investigation used to study less complex sounds. Again, however, this view has recently been questioned by researchers who disagree with the hypothesis that speech signals are analyzed in a specialized manner by infants.

This chapter provides a comprehensive review of two related areas of perceptual development in infants—basic auditory abilities and speech processing abilities—that have followed quite different paths of investigation during the past decade. Because the area of basic auditory abilities in infants has not received extensive coverage in previous editions of the Handbook, we will devote a separate discussion to the anatomy and neurophysiology of the developing auditory system as well as a review of recent quantitative studies of auditory function in human infants. The major part of this chapter, however, will be devoted to the description of theoretical issues and empirical findings in the area of infant speech perception. This latter topic is unique in that it spans the areas of basic auditory development and linguistics and it may involve general cognitive mechanisms as well. Before proceeding to the empirical review of audition and speech perception, however, we will first provide an overview of those critical questions we believe researchers must consider in conducting and evaluating research in these areas. Our purpose in outlining these questions is to place the empirical findings reviewed in later discussions in this chapter into a coherent perspective. In addition, we will briefly review the methods that have been applied to the study of auditory function and speech perception in infancy. These methodological issues are particularly important because they influence the types of conclusions that may be drawn from empirical studies with infants.

Critical Issues in Auditory Development

The most elementary question one could raise concerning the development of auditory abilities is whether infants can hear at birth. This apparently simple question, however, has not received a definitive answer. As a result, if infants do not show evidence for a functioning auditory system at birth, then one can ask at what postnatal age does auditory function begin? Alternatively, perhaps the newborn has a functioning auditory system but lacks the behavioral or physiological systems required to indicate that such is the case. If newborns do show evidence of a functioning auditory system, then at what prenatal age did it become functional? Thus, the first question concerning the development of auditory abilities in infants is: At what age does the auditory system begin to function?

When it has been determined at what age (prenatal or postnatal) auditory function begins, it becomes imperative to determine the precise characteristics of this functioning. Is the infant as sensitive as the mature adult to variations in intensity and frequency? If not, then how does one characterize the newborn's abilities and what is the normative developmental sequence of emerging auditory sensitivities? Are there certain classes of sounds (e.g., speech) to which the infant, like the adult, is more attuned, or are all types of acoustic input processed by the infant auditory system in a similar (but perhaps inefficient) manner? Thus, the second question concerning the development of auditory abilities in infants is: How does the infant's sensitivity to various auditory inputs change during development?

If the development of auditory sensitivity can be precisely specified, then one can begin to examine the factors that are responsible for this normative course of development. Does the infant require general auditory stimulation during some early period of development for the normal changes in sensitivity to occur, or does auditory sensitivity undergo normal changes without any acoustic input? If some general auditory input is necessary for normative auditory development, then are there additional specific aspects of that auditory input that are necessary for the development of specific auditory sensitivities? Thus, the third question concerning the development of auditory abilities in infants is: What general or specific aspects of auditory experience (if any) are necessary for the normative development of auditory sensitivities?

Finally, when all three of the previous questions have been satisfactorily addressed (at least in a preliminary manner), one can begin to ask what types of mechanisms underlie the normative development of auditory function. For example, if auditory input is *not* necessary for normal auditory development, then any change in auditory function must be accompanied by some anatomical or physiological constraints that are overcome during ontogeny. If general or specific auditory experience *is* required for normative auditory development, then these experiences may act as additional modifiers of the anatomical and physiological changes that occur without auditory experience. In most instances, it will be impossible to answer this question without recourse to the study of nonhuman species. However, the judicious use of available human anatomical data, gross physiological recordings from humans, and detailed anatomical and neurophysiological measures from related species should lead to a reasonable set of theoretical principles of auditory development. Thus, the fourth question concerning the development of auditory abilities in infants is: What mechanisms (anatomical, physiological, motoric, etc.) underlie the normative development of auditory function in infants?

These four questions also serve as a useful guide to investigations of speech perception in human infants. Thus, one can ask whether infants, who have been shown to be sensitive to various auditory inputs, are also sensitive to various aspects of speech signals that are used contrastively in natural languages. In the case of speech sounds, then, the first question is concerned with discriminative abilities, that is: When do infants become capable of discriminating the various acoustic parameters that differentiate speech signals? Similarly, the second question becomes: How do the infant's sensitivities to various speech contrasts change during development? The third question is identical to that raised for basic auditory development: What general or specific aspects of auditory experience (if any) are necessary for the normative development of speech perception? And, the fourth question includes a small addendum: What mechanisms underlie the normative development of speech perception in infants and do these mechanisms differ from those that operate in the processing of nonspeech signals? Finally, an additional question can be raised that is unique to speech sounds. Because speech sounds are employed in communicative behaviors, there are often many acoustic differences in the speech signal that are ignored by mature perceivers. Thus, invariant meaning-conveying units of speech contain irrelevant (but potentially discriminable) acoustic information. The final question concerning the development of speech perception, therefore, is: Can infants ignore variations in acoustic information when such variations are irrelevant to the task of speech perception as a linguistic process?

The foregoing questions provide us with a framework within which studies of basic auditory abilities and speech perception in infants can be evaluated. Typically, several of these questions have been addressed in the same study of infant audition or speech perception. However, the entire set of questions offers a comprehensive goal for those who hope to obtain a complete description of the developing auditory system. As such, we have only begun to obtain answers to these questions. It has been difficult to assess the validity of many preliminary answers to these questions because of inadequate methods of assessment. It is to these methodological issues that we now turn so that the empirical findings reviewed in later discussions can be evaluated cautiously.

Methodological Techniques

During the past century, since the early reports by Preyer (1888, 1889), six general types of response measures have been used to assess auditory function in infants. These six methods are listed in Table 1, along with various subtypes that have been used to measure different aspects of auditory function. In this discussion, we briefly review each of these six methodologies. In later discussions, as we review specific studies of audition and speech perception, we will further examine these methods as they apply to specific interpretive issues in auditory and speech perception research.

Table 1. **Response Measures Used to Assess Auditory Function in Infants**

1. **Elicited Motor Responses**
    - (a) **Gross motor activity**
    - (b) **Respiration**
    - (c) **Auropalpebral response (blinking)**
    - (d) **Response inhibition (sucking, blinking)**
    - (e) **Head turning**
2. **Cardiac and Electrodermal Responses**
    - (a) **Heart rate change: fixed trials**
    - (b) **Heart rate change: no delay**
    - (c) **Skin potential**
3. **Electrophysiological Responses**
    - (a) **Auditory evoked response (AER)**
    - (b) **Auditory brainstem response (ABR)**
    - (c) **Electrocochleogram (ECoG)**
4. **Visual Fixation Responses**
    - (a) **Habituation-dishabituation**
    - (b) **Response to novelty**
    - (c) **Auditory-visual pairing**
5. **High Amplitude Sucking (HAS)**
    - (a) **Single stimulus contrast**
    - (b) **Alternating postshift contrast**
    - (c) **Multiple preshift tokens**
6. **Conditioning**
    - (a) **Classical**
    - (b) **Two-alternative button press**
    - (c) **Unidirectional head turn**
    - (d) **Two-alternative head turn**

Elicited Motor Responses

The first method that has been used to study auditory function in infants consists of observing gross motor activity during the presentation of various types of auditory stimuli. Preferably, the observer who is judging the responses of the infant is blind to the timing of stimulus presentations to guard against biased judgments. In addition, no-signal control trials should be presented, both as a check for observer bias and to assess the infant's level of spontaneous (i.e., false positive) responding. These two control procedures are particularly important in light of Moncur's (1968) demonstration that even trained observers show false positive judgments on 39% of no-signal control trials.

Recently, several semiautomated recording devices have been designed and implemented to measure the gross motor responses of infants to auditory stimuli (Altman, Shenhav, & Schaudinischky, 1975; Bennett, 1979; Simmons, McFarland, & Jones, 1979). These various electromechanical recording devices offer the advantage of a response measure that eliminates the need for a human observer. However, it should be noted that a human scorer must judge the output of the electromechanical device. Thus, like any other objectively recorded response, the determination of a response threshold is subject to scorer error. Nevertheless, these semiautomated recording devices, with the use of a predetermined scoring criterion, are a significant advance over the on-line or videotaped observation of gross motor responses.

A second type of motor response elicited by auditory stimuli is a change in respiration. Presumably, this respiratory change is a component of the orienting response to any novel, suprathreshold stimulus. Like gross motor responding, changes in respiration can be detected by human observers, but the reliability of such judgments is typically quite low. Several investigators have used various transducing devices, such as a mercury strain gauge, to record respiratory responses in infants (Bennett & Lawrence, 1980; Heron & Jacobs, 1969; Steinschneider, 1968). However, in general, these procedures have been somewhat unreliable, primarily because of the many spontaneous changes in respiratory rate and amplitude present in both alert and sleeping infants. Thus, although respiratory responses (with the advantage of objective recording) have the potential to be a reliable measure of auditory function, the sensitivity of the measure is as yet insufficient to detect small differences in auditory sensitivity.

A third type of motor response elicited by auditory stimuli is the auropalpebral or eyelid response. The sudden onset of a sound typically results in an orienting response. A widening or closing of the eyelids is one component of this response, depending on the intensity of the stimulus (Demetriades, 1923). Several investigators have employed this response as a measure of auditory sensitivity in newborns (Froding, 1960; Froeschels & Beebe, 1946; Wedenberg, 1956). However, none of these studies has shown a systematic relation between stimulus intensity or frequency and the presence of the auropalpebral response. For example, Kearsley (1973) found that newborns either open or close their eyes to the presentation of a pure tone or white noise, but there was little consistency in the relation between stimulus intensity, frequency, or rise time and the frequency of the eyelid responses. Thus, the auropalpebral response does not appear to be a sensitive or reliable indicator of auditory processing in the developing infant. However, newborns do show evidence of shifting their gaze toward a visual stimulus immediately following the onset of a sound. This ocular localization response occurs if the auditory signal is presented on the same side of midline as the visual stimulus (Mendelson & Haith, 1976). Bechtold, Bushnell, and Salapatek (1979) have also shown that 2-month-olds shift their gaze appropriately to the right or left of midline following the presentation of an auditory stimulus in total darkness. Thus, subtle aspects of oculomotor behavior appear to provide a reliable indicator of auditory function in young infants who lack a large repertoire of well-controlled behaviors.

Another component of the orienting response is the inhibition of an ongoing behavior. If infants show a cessation or attenuation of behavior as a result of an auditory signal, then auditory responsiveness must be present. Several studies have employed sucking suppression as a dependent measure of auditory responsiveness (Keen, 1964; Sameroff, 1967, 1970; Soderquist & Hoenigmann, 1973), but as in the case of respiration, the dynamic nature of spontaneous sucking has not as yet resulted in a detailed and reliable measure of auditory responsivity. Recently, several investigators have studied the inhibition of startle blink responses to auditory signals (Berg, 1980; Graham, Strock, & Ziegler, 1981). Although these inhibition measures appear promising as a technique for studying auditory responsiveness in very young infants, they have not as yet been studied extensively.

The final motor response that has received a significant amount of use in the study of auditory function in infants is head turning. In the present context, we will only consider unconditioned head turning because conditioned head turning involves a quite different set of procedures. The advantage of head turning as a dependent measure is its ease of scoring, which can be reliably accomplished on-line by an observer. The disadvantage of head turning is that very young infants have poor motor control over the neck muscles involved in head movements. In addition, the head-turning response itself is a component of the orienting response and, thus, demands a directional response to be interpretable by the scorer. If, however, an infant turns its head leftward to a sound source located left of midline and rightward to a source located on the right, then, at least, a binary decision has been made concerning the location of the sound source. The use of bilateral head-turning responses, therefore, in conjunction with a counterbalanced order of sound source locations, can be used to assess the infant's ability to detect the presence of an auditory input. Clearly, however, an infant's failure to turn in the direction of the stimulus could be the result of factors other than the inability to detect the presence of the sound (e.g., the inability to localize the sound). And, until recently (e.g., Muir & Field, 1979), localizing head turns in infants under 3 months of age had not been demonstrated. Finally, the use of unconditioned head turning as a measure of discrimination rather than detection has not been reported.

Cardiac and Electrodermal Responses

The second major method that has been applied to the assessment of infant auditory function is the use of heart rate and skin resistance (potential) responses. As a measure of detection, both cardiac and skin potential responding can be elicited as a component of the orienting response to any novel stimulus. Despite widespread use of the cardiac orienting response as a measure of auditory responsivity in infants, the majority of such studies have used auditory stimuli as a powerful elicitor of cardiac responding rather than as a well-controlled independent variable (see review by Graham, Anthony, & Zeigler, in press). The magnitude of the cardiac response (acceleratory or deceleratory) elicited by the presentation of a specific auditory stimulus can be used as a measure of auditory detection. However, to obtain a stable measure of cardiac responding, it is necessary to average the responses from several presentations. Moreover, because the cardiac response itself typically lasts from 10 to 30 sec., it is necessary to repeat the trials at fairly lengthy intervals. In addition, it is known that the magnitude of the cardiac response habituates over trials if the same stimulus is repeated (see Woodcock, 1971). Thus, these effects of recovery time and habituation must be taken into account in any study using a simple cardiac detection method.

Perhaps the most widespread use of the cardiac response has been as a measure of discrimination. Given the fact that the magnitude of the cardiac response habituates over repeated trials, it is possible to present a novel stimulus after a criterion of cardiac habituation has been reached, thereby eliciting a second orienting response. The magnitude of this reorienting or dishabituation response, compared to a no-change control group, can provide a measure of discrimination between the first and second auditory stimuli. The foregoing procedure has been used in several studies of auditory discrimination with infant subjects, including studies of intensity (Bartoshuk, 1964; Moffitt, 1973) and speech discrimination (Lasky, Syrdal-Lasky, & Klein, 1975; Moffitt, 1971).

Although cardiac dishabituation has been used as a reliable indicator of auditory discrimination, this procedure has several inherent problems. First, there are many different criteria one could use to assess the level of habituation to the first stimulus prior to introducing the second (novel) stimulus. Often, a fixed number of trials has been presented to all infants, with one group subsequently receiving the novel stimulus and the other group receiving no change in the stimulus (control). However, as Cohen and Gelber (1975) have pointed out in the case of such studies using visual fixation as a dependent measure, individual infants may not encode the stimulus at the same rate and, therefore, a uniform criterion of habituation will not have been met prior to the dishabituation trials. Thus, failures to show evidence of above-control dishabituation are difficult to interpret because discrimination of the two auditory stimuli requires encoding of the first stimulus, a fact that may have been precluded by the short familiarization period. Use of an individually determined criterion of habituation would seem to be an obvious solution to this problem (thus ensuring a uniform level of encoding), but the difficulty of on-line scoring of the magnitude of the cardiac response has (until recent computer technologies) effectively limited the use of such automated procedures.

A second problem associated with the cardiac dishabituation procedure is the fact that long interstimulus intervals operate against the rapid encoding of the initial auditory stimulus. Typical interstimulus intervals are in the 10- to 30- sec. range, a length of time that places quite a memory demand on the infant. Studies of speech perception that have used the cardiac dishabituation procedure have adopted two solutions to this problem. The first was to repeat the stimulus, say a 500-msec speech sound, several times (e.g., 10), followed by an intertrial interval of 10 to 30 sec. during which the cardiac response returns to baseline. Thus, each train of 10 stimuli acts as the equivalent of a single stimulus presentation, but the infant would have the advantage of hearing the stimulus 10 times more often than in the single presentation procedure. The second approach to overcoming lengthy interstimulus intervals was to eliminate them entirely. Leavitt, Brown, Morse, and Graham (1976) and Miller and Morse (1976) simply repeated the train of identical stimuli for 30 sec. followed immediately by a second train of novel stimuli for another 30 sec. Another group of infants received the same initial stimulus train followed by another identical stimulus train, thus acting as a no-change control group. This *no-delay* cardiac dishabituation procedure was found to be a more sensitive indicator of stimulus discrimination than the discrete trials procedure described above, presumably because it reduced the encoding demands required of the infant to compare the two stimuli. Moreover, the technique can be used to test a variety of stimulus contrasts in a short period of time as well as to obtain multiple dishabituation trials with the same contrast. Recall that the discrete trials procedure typically uses only a single dishabituation trial. Thus, groups of infants must be tested to assess the reliability of the dishabituation response. In the no-delay procedure, each infant could serve as its own control and many trials with the same contrast could be presented to the same infant, although such within-subject designs have been rare.

The third and final problem with the cardiac dishabituation procedure concerns the interpretation of dishabituation response magnitudes. Just as there are constraints on the magnitude of the cardiac response to the initial stimulus presentation, primarily due to the absolute level of the tonic heart rate, so too are there constraints on the magnitude of the cardiac response to the novel stimulus presentation. If two different contrasts are presented to two separate groups of infants and one contrast results in a significantly greater magnitude of cardiac dishabituation, then the novel stimulus associated with the greater dishabituation must in some sense be more discriminable in comparison to the initial stimulus. However, it is difficult to measure how much more discriminable the stimulus contrast is, given the unscaled nature of dishabituation magnitudes. A statistically reliable difference in dishabituation magnitudes may indicate a tenfold or a hundredfold difference in discriminability. Also, given the physiological limits placed on the magnitude of cardiac responses, it is very likely that a ceiling effect is present in cardiac dishabituation measures. Thus, there may be a bias against obtaining a statistically significant differential cardiac dishabituation. In summary, the use of cardiac measures of detection and discrimination are potentially powerful techniques for auditory assessment in infants. However, each specific procedure has its limitations, many of which are shared by the other measures reviewed below.

Although cardiac responses have been used extensively in assessing infant auditory function, a related psychophysiological response, skin potential, has only rarely been used with infants (Crowell, Davis, Chun, & Spellacy, 1965). As a component of the orienting response, transient changes in skin potential can be used as a measure of detection in a manner identical to the use of heart rate responses. Similarly, the habituation of the skin potential response can be used, with appropriate change and no-change groups, to assess response dishabituation to a novel auditory stimulus. Despite the possible utility of skin potential responses in assessing infant auditory function, few studies have employed the response as a dependent measure. This stems in part from the large change in basal skin resistance that occurs during early infancy. Just as cardiac responsivity changes during the first few postnatal months, so too does the ease of eliciting a skin potential response. In the case of heart rate, this maturational change in the response system itself has not posed as severe a problem as has the skin potential response because the latter system has in many cases been reported to be absent in the newborn. Nevertheless, all response systems undergo change during the early postnatal period, and researchers must grapple with this interpretive problem in evaluating the effectiveness and validity of developmental data on auditory sensitivity.

Electrophysiological Responses

The third major class of response measures used to assess infant auditory function—evoked neural responses—is similar in many respects to the motor-, cardiac-, and electrodermal-orienting responses discussed above. Presentation of a suprathreshold auditory stimulus elicits a synchronous pattern of electrical activity in various regions of the brain that can be amplified and displayed with the use of appropriate signal-averaging techniques. In adults, systematic and reliable relationships can be observed between aspects of the auditory signal and the magnitude and characteristic shape of several auditory evoked responses. Three general types of evoked responses have been used in the past, both with adult and infant subjects, as measures of auditory responsivity. The first two are recorded with gross electrodes attached to the scalp. The most common technique, the auditory evoked response (AER), is obtained by averaging the electrical responses of a time-locked stimulus that is repeatedly presented to the subject. The resultant average waveform is characterized by several negative and positive peaks, with amplitudes of 10 to 20 μV, that occur within 300 msec of stimulus onset. Recently, the early components of the AER waveform, which were previously undetected because of their low amplitude (less than 1 μV), have been found to be systematically related to auditory responsivity in adults (Jewett, Romano, & Williston, 1970). Seven distinct peaks in the first 10 msec of the AER waveform were noted, and these peaks have subsequently been correlated with specific neural loci along the auditory pathway. Animal research has identified the underlying neural locus of these peaks in the subcortical areas of the auditory system. Thus, the short latency waveform has been termed the auditory brainstem response (ABR).

Several systematic reviews of both the AER and ABR techniques have appeared in the literature (e.g., Picton, Hillyard, Krausz, & Galambos, 1974). Hecox (1975, in press), and Reneau and Hnatiow (1975) have reviewed the applicability of these techniques for the assessment of auditory function in infants. Perhaps the greatest difficulty with the AER technique is that variations in state of arousal greatly affect the amplitude and latency of the peaks in the waveform (Picton & Hillyard, 1974). Thus, most studies have been conducted on infants who are asleep because, in adults, the thresholds obtained during sleep are only slightly elevated compared to thresholds obtained during periods of alertness. The greatest difficulty with the ABR technique is that the very short latency of the waveform demands the use of very brief stimuli, typically clicks of less than 1 msec. As a result, the frequency characteristics of the stimulus are not easily varied. In fact, even filtered clicks contain a relatively broadband frequency spectrum. Thus, ABR responses have been used primarily as tests of the functional integrity of various peripheral neural structures, particularly those that are diagnosed by abnormally long latencies in the ABR waveform.

The third electrophysiological recording technique that has been used to assess auditory function in infants is the electrocochleogram (ECoG). This technique involves the placement of either a gross electrode in the external auditory canal or a needle electrode through the tympanic membrane into the middle ear near the cochlea (see Aran, 1978). Obviously, the latter procedure involves sedation of the subject and, thus, is not practical for large-scale assessment of auditory function in normal infants. Electrocochleogram recordings obtained with external electrodes can potentially provide measures of three gross electrical responses: the cochlear microphonic (CM), the summating potential (SP) and the action potential (AP) (see review by Eggermont, 1976). The AP response is of greatest importance to the assessment of auditory function because it is believed to be a reflection of the gross response of the auditory (eighth) nerve. In adults, the latency of the AP decreases and the amplitude increases as stimulus intensity is increased. Moreover, psychophysically determined thresholds are very closely related to the thresholds obtained with the AP response. However, the very short latency (approximately 2 msec) of the ECoG limits its use to click or short tone-burst stimuli. Because the amplitude of the response is much greater than the ABR, however, it is possible to present masking stimuli to assess AP amplitudes for relatively narrow frequency bands. As yet, such techniques have not been applied to infants.

Visual Fixation Responses

The fourth technique that has been applied to the assessment of auditory function in infants involves the use of visual fixation durations as a dependent measure of auditory discrimination. Many studies have shown that infants presented with successive views of a visual pattern (e.g., a checkerboard) show a decrement in the duration of their first fixation to that pattern. By repeatedly presenting the visual pattern until a criterion of habituation has been reached, it is possible to assess visual discrimination by changing the visual pattern for one group of subjects (experimental) and not changing the pattern for another group of subjects (control). If the experimental group shows a recovery (dishabituation) of fixation duration to the novel pattern that is greater than any recovery shown by the control group, then discrimination can be inferred.

Boyd (1975) found that a similar technique can be used to assess auditory discrimination. The visual pattern remains invariant during the entire procedure. Initially, the pattern is presented simultaneously with an auditory stimulus. When the infant looks away from the visual pattern, the duration of the first fixation is recorded, the visual and auditory stimuli are removed, and the next trial of auditory-visual pairing is initiated. Trials are repeated until a criterion of habituation of the visual fixation response is met. For subjects in the experimental group, the first posthabituation trial now consists of the same visual stimulus paired with a novel auditory stimulus, whereas control subjects receive no change in either the visual or the auditory stimulus. Auditory discrimination is indicated by a significant dishabituation of the visual fixation response for the experimental group compared to the no-change control group. Although this visual habituation technique appears to have promise as a useful measure of auditory function in infants, particularly because visual fixation responses can be observed over a very broad age range, the technique has not received extensive use (see, however, Bundy, 1980). Colombo and Bundy (1981) have also shown that 4-month-olds prefer to fixate one of two identical visual stimuli if fixation of one stimulus (e.g., the left) results in presentation of a sound. In addition, they found that if two different sounds (e.g., a voice vs. white noise) are made contingent upon fixation of the two stimuli, infants prefer to fixate the target that is paired with the voice stimulus. Without further stimulus pairings, however, it is unclear whether this technique will prove to be a sensitive indicator of auditory discrimination in infants.

High Amplitude Sucking (HAS)

Perhaps the most widely used technique for studying speech perception in infants is the HAS procedure originally developed by Siqueland and Delucia (1969). This technique employs a response that even newborns are capable of producing and capitalizes on the naturally attention-getting (reinforcing) properties of novel stimulation. Thus, the technique is classified as one of conjugate reinforcement because a spontaneous behavior (sucking) can be brought under stimulus control through the use of response-contingent stimulation without the need for an external reinforcing stimulus. The auditory stimulus is made contingent upon a criterion-level sucking response, and the auditory stimulus itself (along with control over its presentation) takes on reinforcing properties for the infant. However, because the reinforcing property of the auditory stimulus depends upon its novelty, the contingent sucking response typically declines (satiates) after an initial period of response acquisition. If the infant shows a criterion-level decline in response rate, then a change in the auditory stimulus should result in an increase in the reinforcing value of the stimulus. A no-shift control group provides a comparison to guard against spontaneous shifts in sucking rate that are not linked to the properties of the auditory stimuli. Thus, as shown in Figure 1, the HAS procedure consists of four parts: baseline, acquisition, satiation, and recovery. If a group of infants shows response recovery after the auditory stimulus has been changed, and a no-shift control group does not show response recovery, then it can be concluded that the shift group discriminated the two auditory stimuli.

An interesting modification of the HAS procedure has been devised by Spring and Dale (1977). During the postshift phase of their experiment, they presented subjects with an alternating series of stimuli consisting of a novel stimulus and the original

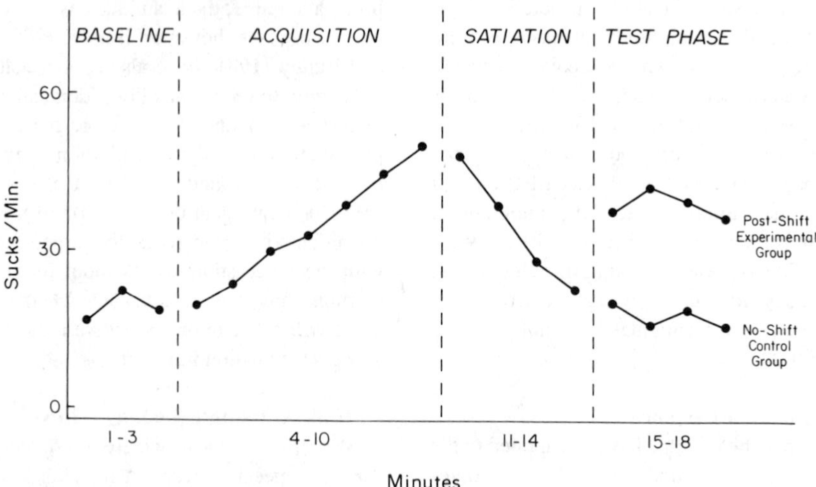

Figure 1. Schematic illustration of data from the HAS technique showing the four phases of the procedure and typical outcomes for the experimental and control groups.

preshift stimulus. Spring and Dale hypothesized that the alternating sequence would be more potent in promoting discrimination because it should reduce the memory load for the infant by allowing repeated comparisons of the novel and original stimuli. This procedure has also been used by Eilers (1977). A final modification of the HAS procedure consists of presenting multiple sound stimuli (in random order) during the preshift phase in an attempt to habituate the infant to some feature or attribute shared by the stimuli. If the infant has extracted the invariant feature, postshift responding should not increase to a new stimulus that also contains the shared feature. This modified HAS procedure has been used by Miller and Eimas (1979), Eimas and Miller (1980a, 1980b), and Jusczyk and Derrah (in preparation). Further details about the HAS procedure and its rationale can be found in Trehub and Chang (1977) and Williams and Golenski (1978).

The HAS technique has been particularly instrumental in recent advances in the area of infant speech perception. There are, however, several disadvantages associated with the HAS technique. First, the progression through a four-part experiment, typically lasting 8 to 15 min., is quite demanding on young infants. Thus, the subject attrition rate has often been in the 50% to 75% range. Second, it is crucial that the infant's baseline rate of criterion-level sucks be within the range of 20 to 40 sucks/min. If the baseline is set lower than 20 sucks/min., then acquisition is difficult for the infant and subsequent satiation may not occur because the criterion of response decrement (typically 2 successive min. with a 30% decrement) cannot be reached if the sucking rate cannot be increased during acquisition. If the baseline is set higher than 40 sucks/min., it is very likely that the criterion of response decrement will be met even though acquisition has not occurred. Moreover, the likelihood of subsequent postshift recovery is high because the response decrement may have been a transient decline unrelated to the reduction in the reinforcing properties of the auditory stimulus. Clearly, however, the no-shift control group would provide a check for this possibility. In short, the HAS technique requires a careful set of checks to ensure that the infant's range of sucking responses can both increase and decrease relative to the initial baseline rate.

The third and final difficulty with the HAS technique is the fact that only a single data point is obtained as a result of the entire four-part procedure (a limitation characteristic of most habituation-dishabituation procedures). In other words, the postshift sucking rate either recovers from habituation or it does not; there are no repeated assessments of dishabituation. In addition, because of the relatively high variance in sucking responses across sessions and between subjects, typically only group data have been used in making comparisons between shift and no-shift conditions (see Mehler & Bertoncini, 1981, for an exception). Thus, as with all the other techniques reviewed earlier, the performance of individual infants cannot be interpreted. Nevertheless, the HAS procedure has proven to be remarkably productive, primarily because it has shown infants to be much more sensitive to subtle kinds of auditory information than previously thought possible. Apparently, the repetitions of the initial stimulus in the phases prior to recovery, and the attention-getting aspect of the auditory stimulus which is under the control of the infant, provide for a very sensitive indicator of auditory discrimination. The HAS technique has not received much use in assessing basic auditory abilities in infants, nor has it proven useful with infants older than 4 or 5 months of age. However, it remains one of the primary assessment techniques in the area of infant speech perception.

Operant and Classical Conditioning

Both classical and operant conditioning have been used in conjunction with various response measures to assess auditory abilities in human infants. Classical conditioning involves the pairing of the auditory signal (the conditioned stimulus or CS) with an unconditioned stimulus (UCS) that elicits an unconditioned response (UCR). After several trials of this pairing of CS and UCS, the UCR becomes associated with the CS, even though the CS alone did not elicit the UCR prior to the CS-UCS pairing. Thus, the response becomes a conditioned response (CR). If the infant exhibits evidence of a CR in the presence of a CS-only stimulus, then the CS (in this case an auditory signal) must have been detected by the infant. In addition, if variations in the quality of the CS are made on trials subsequent to acquisition of the CR, it is possible to assess whether the infant can detect variations in the CS. Presumably, if the novel auditory signal is similar to the CS, then the CR will be present. If, however, the infant can discriminate the novel auditory signal from the CS, then the CR will decrease in magnitude or frequency of occurrence.

Classical conditioning procedures require a fairly extensive series of trials during which the CS and UCS are paired. Thus, the procedure demands a lengthy period of time during which the infant must be attentive to the stimuli and during which the UCR must not habituate. Moreover, in very young infants, there are few responses that are easily and reliably elicited by auditory signals. Nevertheless, Marquis (1931) and Kasatkin and Levikova (1935) have reported that young infants can be classically conditioned to an auditory signal. Although subsequent investigators have questioned the validity of these early studies (see Pratt, 1946), more recent evidence clearly shows that classical conditioning can be obtained in young infants using auditory signals as the CS (Lintz, Fitzgerald, & Brackbill, 1967; Sommer & Ling, 1970). However, widespread use of classical conditioning as a measure of auditory sensitivity or discrimination in infants is unlikely to occur unless procedures allowing for more rapid acquisition of the CR can be developed.

Two operant conditioning techniques have been used to assess auditory function in infants. The first involves a two-alternative manual response in which the infant is rewarded for pushing a button by being allowed to hear a brief auditory stimulus. Friedlander (1968, 1970) and Glenn, Cunningham, and Joyce (1981) have used this technique to assess the preferences of infants for various types of auditory stimuli. In general, the technique has only been successful with infants who can reach to press a button and who are motivated (during a very lengthy testing session) to respond differentially to one of two auditory signals. Clearly, if no preference is exhibited, one cannot conclude that the infant is incapable of discriminating between the two signals because the signals may not be preferred differentially. Moreover, because the only reward for responding is the opportunity to hear one of two signals (that do not change during the experiment), overall preferences are likely to underestimate the true discriminative capacities of the infant. Thus, although studies using this two-alternative button-pressing technique have addressed questions concerning the infant's auditory preferences, investigations of auditory sensitivity and the limits of auditory discrimination will probably require an external reinforcer in addition to the auditory signal itself.

The second operant conditioning technique that has proven particularly useful as a reliable measure of auditory function in infants is the head-turning response in conjunction with an external visual reinforcer. This technique was originally described by Suzuki and Ogiba (1961). In their study, the infant was presented with a laterally positioned sound. If the infant oriented to the location of the sound by a head-turning response toward the sound source, an animated toy located adjacent to the sound source was activated. Because infants often show habituation of the orienting response toward a sound, the external visual reward presumably motivates the infant to look away from the experimenter toward the location of the sound (and reinforcing toy). This technique has the advantage of rapid conditioning (because the response is often initially based on an unconditioned orienting response toward the sound), little response habituation over the course of 30 to 50 trials, and the potential for generating data from individual infants rather than being limited to group means as in other techniques. The requirements for obtaining reliable and valid individual subject data involve controlling for both response bias and experimenter bias (see Aslin & Pisoni, 1980a). In the initial applications of the head-turning technique, the observer of the infant's head-turning responses was aware of the timing and quality (above or below threshold) of the stimulus. Thus, the observer may have recorded a head-turning response when, in fact, no response occurred. In addition, response bias, or the presence of false positive responses, must be guarded against to ensure that the infant is not simply exhibiting a head-turning response at random toward the location of the auditory signal. Catch trials, which contain no signal, must be presented to assess the level of false alarms.

To date, four versions of the head-turning technique have been used to assess various aspects of the infant's auditory and speech perception abilities. The first version consists of a simple auditory threshold procedure in which the infant hears no sound until a signal, of varying intensity, is presented. The infant's task is to respond to any just-detectable sound. By varying the intensity of the signal, it is possible to generate a threshold for detectability that can be compared across different stimulus characteristics (e.g., frequency; see Berg & Smith, in press; Sinnott, Pisoni, & Aslin, in press).

The second version of the head-turning technique is identical to the first except that two sound locations are used. The infant is centered between two speakers and silence is interrupted by a signal presented from one of the two speakers. The first directional head-turning response is scored and correlated with the location (right or left) of the sound source. By using a random assignment of sound source locations, the infant's percent correct for directional head-turning responses toward the signal can be computed. In this case, because a two-alternative procedure is used, no catch trials are required (either random right-left responding or 100% directional bias would result in a 50% correct level of responding). Again, by appropriate manipulations of the characteristics of the auditory signal, it is possible to obtain reliable thresholds for infants (e.g., see Trehub, Schneider, & Endman, 1980).

The third version of the head-turning technique involves the addition of a repeating (or background) stimulus that is interrupted by the presentation of a different (or target) stimulus. In contrast to the first two cases in which there was no signal acting as a background, this third version is a discrimination procedure, allowing for assessment of the infant's ability to differentiate between two suprathreshold auditory stimuli. In this version, it is essential that catch trials are presented to the infant to assess the level of false positive responding. A catch trial consists of informing the observer that a scoring interval is occurring, but not changing the background stimulus to the target stimulus during this interval. Thus, experimenter bias is eliminated by ensuring that the observer is unaware of the type of trial being presented (stimulus change vs. no-change control), and the infant's response bias is assessed by comparing the response rate during change and no-change trials. In initial applications of this discriminative response technique, many of these controls were not employed to guard against experimenter bias and an inadequate number of test trials was used to assess the reliability of the infant's responding. However, recent studies have employed such safeguards, and the technique has proven to be highly reliable (see the controversy between Eilers, Gavin, & Wilson, 1979; Aslin & Pisoni, 1980a; and Eilers, Gavin, & Wilson, 1980).

The fourth and final version of the head-turning technique involves the addition of a trials-to-criterion measure to the basic discriminative response procedure described above. After the infant has shown evidence of discriminating two stimuli, additional stimuli are added to the background set to assess the ease of ignoring variations in these background stimuli. Additional targets are also presented to determine if the infant can attend to common aspects of the target set. By appropriately choosing stimuli for the background and target sets that contain easily discriminable variations in several acoustic parameters, it is possible to use this multiple background- and target-set procedure to assess the ease with which infants can form categories for acoustic signals. Kuhl (1980) has employed this procedure to assess which acoustic aspects of speech stimuli are most easily grouped into perceptual categories.

Although the head-turning technique, in all its variations, appears to offer several distinct advantages over other auditory assessment procedures, it too suffers from several disadvantages. First, reliable head-turning responses under the control of visual reinforcement do not appear to be present in infants under 5 or 6 months of age (Moore, Wilson, & Thompson, 1977). Thus, many questions concerning the early months of auditory development cannot be addressed with the same technique that is used with older infants. As a result, the only technique that at present can provide individual subject data cannot be used until the infant has already had 6 months of postnatal auditory experience. Second, although most infants quickly learn the "game" involved in turning toward the sound source to view the visual reinforcer when the auditory discrimination is easy, subtle differences between the background and target stimuli appear to demand high levels of attentiveness. Thus, attrition rates for easily discriminable vowel stimuli may only be 5% to 20% (Kuhl, 1979b), whereas attrition rates for more difficult consonant contrasts may be as high as 75% (Katz & Jusczyk, 1980). Third, the ability to collect highly reliable discrimination data from individual infants necessitates that the reinforcing value of the visual display remain fairly constant over trials or over testing sessions. Clearly, the effectiveness of an invariant visual reinforcer is unlikely to remain constant. Thus, in the future, more powerful and variable visual reinforcers will have to be developed to optimize the infant's performance and reduce habituation effects over lengthy periods of data collection.

Summary and Cautionary Note

All of the methodological techniques outlined in this discussion have certain advantages and disadvantages that must be carefully evaluated both in selecting a measure for a prospective experiment and in determining whether empirical results have been interpreted appropriately. In addition, *all* of the techniques described earlier suffer from the problem of uncertainty associated with measuring auditory function in a developing organism. Typically, developmentalists are interested in the change in auditory function across age and experiential history. Given an organism that is clearly undergoing rapid advances in motor, attentional, and motivational systems in parallel with presumed changes in sensory and perceptual sensitivity, it is crucial to be aware of the potential confounding of these various systems as one draws conclusions about the infant's perceptual development. When any improvement in performance on an auditory task is documented in the developing infant, it is absolutely essential to ask whether such an improvement could be due to nonperceptual factors, such as improvements in response systems, attentiveness, or familiarity with the testing situation. Unfortunately, we do not have any single technique, other than auditory evoked potentials, that can be used in precisely the same manner with both infants and adults. In addition, auditory evoked potentials cannot provide answers to all of the basic questions one could ask about the development of auditory function (e.g., discrimination of sounds).

ANATOMY AND NEUROPHYSIOLOGY OF THE AUDITORY SYSTEM

The auditory system consists of a series of components that transform airborne sound-pressure variations into neural signals that are analyzed and interpreted by several regions of the central nervous system. In this discussion, we briefly review this process of transformation from physical acoustics to auditory perception. Many of the functional properties of various structures in the adult auditory system are unknown at present. Moreover, even less is known about the developmental status of these auditory structures. Thus, in addition to providing a concise background on the structure and function of the mammalian auditory system, we will provide a description of the many differences between the infant and adult auditory system that could potentially affect the level of auditory function in the developing human infant. The interested reader should consult Rubel (1978) for an extensive review of the anatomy, neurophysiology, and behavioral responsiveness of the developing mammalian auditory system.

The Auditory Periphery

The essential structure of the peripheral auditory apparatus is shown in Figure 2. There are three divisions of the auditory periphery: the outer, middle, and inner structures of the ear. The outer ear consists of the pinna (external earflap) and the auditory canal that leads to the tympanic membrane (eardrum). The middle ear consists of the three auditory ossicles (bones), which transmit the vibrations of the tympanic membrane to the inner ear. The inner ear consists of the cochlea, which contains the auditory hair cells that act as the neural receptors for the transmission of oscillations of the fluid in the cochlea to the auditory branch of the eighth nerve. In the following discussions, we will review what is known about the manner in which these three portions of the auditory periphery influence auditory function as well as the possible influences on auditory function resulting from differences in the structure and size of the infant's peripheral auditory apparatus.

The Outer Ear

The primary function of the auditory canal is to capture and direct airborne sound pressure variations for transmission to the tympanic membrane. Because the canal is a tube, it has a natural resonance frequency; that is, sounds within a certain frequency range are enhanced as a result of reflections off the internal wall of the canal. In adults, the gain (amount of enhancement) in sound pressure level (SPL) resulting from the size and shape of the canal has been

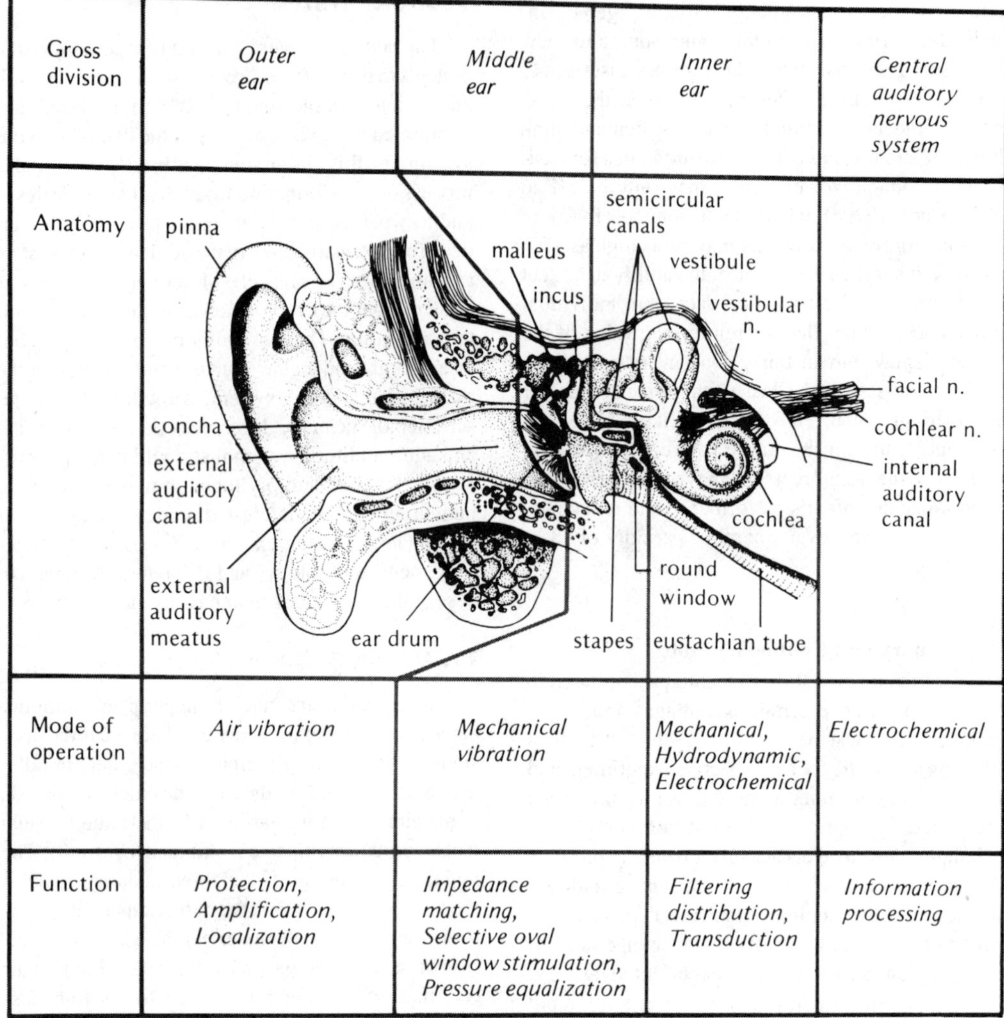

Figure 2. Cross-section of the human ear showing the three major divisions (outer, middle, and inner ear), their mode of operation, and their presumed function. (Reprinted from Yost & Nielsen, 1977)

shown to be up to 15 dB in the frequency range from 1.5 to 7 kHz, with a peak at approximately 3 kHz (Wiener & Ross, 1946).[1] Because the resonance characteristics of the canal are largely determined by its length, the infant's canal probably has a significantly higher resonance frequency (extrapolated by us to have a peak at 5 kHz) than the adult's. Although this developmental shift in the resonance frequency may appear to be small, it could, with the addition of other small differences in the same direction, account for some of the functional differences between basic auditory abilities in infants and adults.

Two other anatomical aspects of the outer ear may affect the infant's perception of sound locus and intensity: interaural separation and the shape of the pinna. Interaural separation (the distance between the two pinnae) provides three types of acoustic information that could be potentially useful in localizing a sound source: (1) relative intensity, (2) time-of-arrival, and (3) phase. For any sound source positioned off the midline, the intensity of the signal reaching the auditory canal will be greater for one ear than for the other. The relative loss in intensity is inversely proportional to the square of the additional distance traveled in reaching the "far" ear. This interaural intensity difference, however, is typically very small. A more important aspect of interaural separation is the shadowing effect that occurs for sounds located off the midline. The head acts as a baffle that creates a region of relatively low sound intensity at the "far" ear. Shadowing is greatest for high-frequency sounds because low-frequency sound waves are not greatly distorted by objects (e.g., the head) that are small relative to the sound's wavelength (low-frequency sounds have long wavelengths). In adults, a 5 kHz tone presented 90° laterally from the midline creates a sound shadow of up to 20 dB (Fedderson, Sandel, Teas, & Jeffress, 1957). For a newborn, with an interaural separation that is approximately 50% less than an adult's, the sound shadow would be expected to be shifted toward higher frequencies, although this prediction has not been verified empirically.

Interaural differences in the time-of-arrival of a sound are also dependent upon interaural separation. The onset of a sound (regardless of its frequency) will reach the "near" ear before the "far" ear, provided that the sound source is not positioned along the midline. For adults, this time-of-arrival difference is greatest (approximately 0.6 msec) when the sound source is positioned 90° laterally from the midline. For newborns, their smaller interaural separation would reduce the absolute magnitude of this time difference, presumably reducing its effectiveness as a cue to the locus of a sound source.

The relative phase of a pure tone can provide localization information because the peaks and troughs of the sinusoidal signal reach the two ears at different times. Variations in phase (measured independently of time-of-arrival differences) have been shown to be effective as a cue to sound localization for adults, but only for frequencies whose wavelength is greater than the interaural separation (approximately below 2,800 Hz in adults). Higher frequencies result in the matching of a peak (or trough) with a later occurring peak (or trough). In fact, phase differences are not an accurate source of information for frequencies above approximately 1,000 Hz (Yost, 1974). In newborns, the smaller interaural separation would indicate an even higher frequency range within which phase differences could act as an effective sound localization cue, provided of course that infants were capable of processing phase relationships.

Finally, the pinnae act as deflectors (transformers) of sounds entering the auditory canal. Sounds originating from behind are attenuated relative to sounds originating from in front of the listener. This differential attenuation is particularly relevant to the localization of sounds along the midline because the absence of the pinnae would result in time-of-arrival and phase information that was equivalent for sounds located in front of, or behind, the listener. Although head movements can effectively clarify this midline localization task, brief acoustic events (e.g., clicks) or poor head control could contribute to poor localization abilities in the infant if the pinnae were grossly different from the adult. No anatomical data on the morphological development of the pinnae are available to evaluate this potential effect, but no major influence appears to be evident.

In summary, both the higher resonance characteristics of the infant's auditory canal and the smaller interaural separation (primarily via differential shadowing effects) could alter the young infant's processing of sounds relative to the adult. Relative sensitivity might be expected to be shifted toward higher frequencies and sound localization might also be biased toward the use of higher frequencies. Time-of-arrival and phase information would appear to be less effective in sound localization because of the infant's smaller interaural separation. However, it should be emphasized that none of these factors has been investigated systematically and all of the predicted developmental differences are quite small compared to the empirically reported deficits in infant auditory function.

The Middle Ear

The primary function of the middle ear is to transmit the sound-induced vibrations of the tympanic membrane to the fluid-filled cochlea. This process may appear to be simple, but a series of complex adaptations have made a potentially ineffective transfer remarkably efficient. Because sounds are carried through the air, whereas the neural receptors in the cochlea are surrounded by fluid, there is a large impedance mismatch between the tympanic membrane and the cochlear fluid. In other words, the amount of energy required to induce an equivalent pressure variation in air versus fluid is quite different because of the difference in the densities of the two media. Two structural factors appear to have evolved to overcome this inherent impedance mismatch. First, the three ossicles—malleus, incus, and stapes—act as a lever in transmitting the vibrations from the tympanic membrane. In adults, this lever action enhances the transmitted force by a factor of 1.3. Second, and more important, the difference in size between the tympanic membrane and the stapes footplate (the surface that induces vibrations of the cochlear fluid) acts as an amplifier. In adults, this size ratio provides an additional enhancement of approximately 17 times. Thus, these two structural aspects of the middle ear account for a twenty-twofold increase in the efficiency with which sound pressure variations are transmitted from the air to the fluid of the cochlea. Without this structural enhancement, the impedance mismatch would result in a 27 dB loss between the auditory canal and the cochlea. (These values are based on Yost & Nielson's, 1977, summary.)

The effectiveness of the infant's middle ear in transmitting sounds to the cochlea has not been determined with the accuracy of similar measurements from adults. Anatomical data show that the sizes of the ossicles, including the size of the stapes footplate, reach adult levels in the eighth prenatal month (Bast & Anson, 1949). However, the tympanic membrane does not reach adult size until the second postnatal year (Ballenger, 1969). Yet, because of differences in the compliance of the tympanic membrane, it is possible that this difference in size has little functional significance. For example, it is known that the actual size of the adult tympanic membrane is 65 mm^2, but the size of the effective region of the tympanic membrane (the region that actually vibrates) is only 55 mm^2. Thus, although the infant's tympanic membrane is smaller than the adult's, its greater compliance may overcome this potential loss in amplification relative to the constant size of the stapes footplate. Although techniques exist (e.g., laser holography) to examine the effective region of the infant's tympanic membrane, such measurements have not as yet been reported.

Although the primary transduction process performed by the middle ear is from airborne sound to vibrations of the fluid in the cochlea, two other methods exist that could stimulate the cochlea via different mechanisms. One method is bone conduction in which airborne vibrations are carried directly by the skull to the cochlear fluid (see Tonndorf, 1976, for a comprehensive review). This method is very inefficient for airborne sounds, but a mechanical vibration applied directly to the skull can result in suprathreshold auditory stimulation, particularly for low frequencies. A second, and more efficient, method involves the transmission of sounds through a fluid-filled media. In utero, the auditory canal and the middle ear of the fetus are filled with fluid. Sounds traveling through the uterine wall are transmitted with relatively little attenuation, provided they are below 1,000 Hz (Armitage, Baldwin, & Vince, 1980). Thus, the potential exists for a significant prenatal auditory influence in humans if the auditory system is functional during the late prenatal period.

In the postnatal period, a method exists for determining the effectiveness with which airborne sounds are transmitted through the middle ear. A technique called impedance audiometry consists of varying the relative pressure between the auditory canal and the middle ear chamber and measuring the compliance of the tympanic membrane (see review by Cone & Gerber, 1977). If the infant's tympanic membrane is stiff, sounds will be reflected rather than transmitted to the ossicles and on to the cochlea. In contrast, a highly compliant tympanic membrane will absorb the sound pressure variations and set the ossicles in motion. However, even a compliant tympanic membrane can be rendered ineffective if the pressure of the middle ear chamber is less than the pressure in the auditory canal. This negative pressure forces the tympanic membrane into the middle ear chamber, thus reducing its effective range of motion. A common condition during infancy and early childhood is a partial or complete blockage of the eustachian tube that connects the middle ear chamber with the throat. This tube functions to maintain the pressure balance between the middle ear chamber and the auditory canal. An infection of the eustachian tube (otitis media) can severely retard the effectiveness with which sounds are transmitted by the middle ear. Moreover, with otitis media, fluid often collects in the middle ear chamber, further degrading the transduction of energy from the tympanic membrane to the cochlea.

Several types of impedance audiometry are used to assess the integrity of the middle ear. The most common type, called tympanometry, involves the measurement of sound energy that has been reflected from the tympanic membrane. As shown in Figure 3, a sealed tube is placed into the auditory canal and a microphone records the reflected energy of a constant sound source as variations in pressure are induced. A normal tympanogram should show a peak in reflected sound energy under balanced pressure conditions, that is, when no positive or negative pressure has been induced in the canal. A peak in the tympanogram at zero pressure indicates that the tympanic membrane is maximally compliant under normal conditions. A peak in the tympanogram at either a high- or low-pressure level indicates that compliance of the tympanic membrane under normal conditions is being attenuated by a negative or positive relative pressure in the middle ear chamber.

The use of impedance audiometry with infants as young as 2 hr. after birth has been reported by Keith

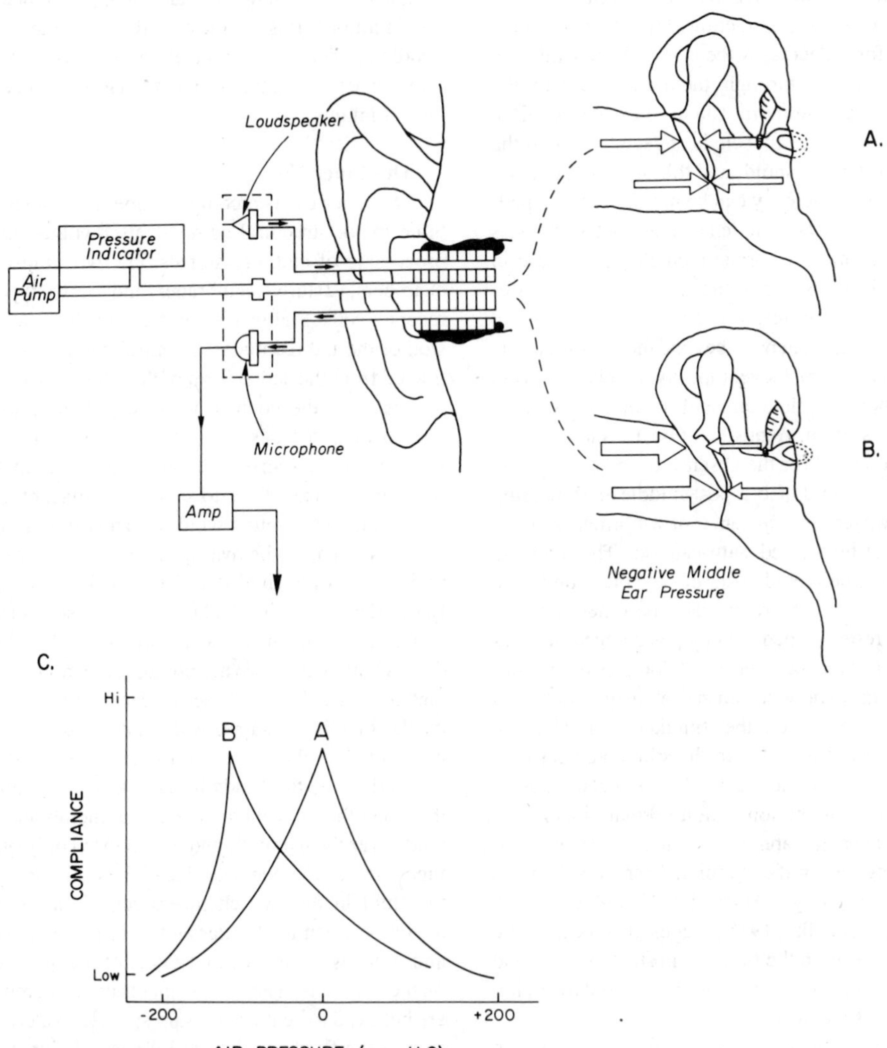

Figure 3. Illustration of the device used in tympanometry to measure middle ear pressure: (A) Balanced pressure between the outer and middle ear. (B) Negative middle ear pressure relative to the outer ear, indicating noncompliant (stiff) tympanic membrane. (C) Sample tympanograms based on (A) and (B). (Redrawn from Jerger, 1970; Copyright 1970, American Medical Association)

(1973, 1975). The majority of those infants tested had a tympanogram similar to records obtained with older children and adults. However, Paradise, Smith, and Bluestone (1976) have reported that in infants under 7 months of age with a middle ear infection verified by otoscopic examination, nearly half display a normal tympanogram. This high level of false negative diagnosis using tympanometry was not found in infants older than 7 months; it may result from the greater compliance of the walls of the auditory canal in younger infants. Thus, tympanometry is a useful but not completely error-free measure of middle ear function in infants.

A final issue related to impedance audiometry is the recording of the so-called acoustic reflex. The stapes is held in place in the oval window of the cochlea by the adjacent ossicle (the incus), by ligaments, and by the stapedius muscle. The stapedius muscle acts as a dampening device to prevent the stapes from "bouncing" between the incus and the oval window at high oscillation amplitudes (high sound intensities). Contraction of the stapedius muscle, therefore, decreases the effective transmission of sound energy through the middle ear to the cochlea. The minimum sound pressure level at which the stapedius muscle is engaged is called the acoustic reflex threshold, and this sudden reduction in middle ear efficiency can be measured by impedance audiometry as a sudden increase in the stiffness of the tympanic membrane (actually a decrease in the compliance of the entire ossicular chain). Because the acoustic reflex must be mediated by an analysis of sound intensity beyond the middle ear, its presence at a normal level (approximately 100 dB to 110 dB above absolute threshold) indicates an intact middle ear system. Acoustic reflex thresholds above this normal level (or the absence of the reflex) may indicate a central (i.e., post-middle ear) hearing loss. However, the presence of a normal acoustic reflex must be viewed with caution. The inducing sound can be delivered to one ear and the compliance response can be recorded from the other ear. Because the reflex is mediated by postcochlear mechanisms (e.g., the perception of loudness), the opposite ear may show the normal acoustic reflex via a bilateral response from the stimulated ear. Thus, an abnormal acoustic reflex in the stimulated ear may indicate either a middle ear defect or a central hearing loss. In conjunction with a normal bilateral reflex, however, the abnormal reflex indicates a central hearing loss in the stimulated ear. Results from several studies (e.g., Abahazi & Greenberg, 1977; Margolis & Popelka, 1975) suggest that the acoustic reflex is present in the first few postnatal weeks and that decreasing signal intensity is required to elicit it as the infant matures.

The developmental implication of middle ear function for hearing in infants centers on the efficiency with which sounds of various frequencies and intensities are accurately transmitted to the oval window of the cochlea. The overall structure of the ossicles appears to be nearly adultlike at the time of birth, and the functional size and compliance of the tympanic membrane appears to match closely that of the adult. However, the shorter length of the infant's auditory canal would appear to provide a shift in peak sensitivity toward higher frequencies. In addition, the smaller length and diameter of the eustachian tube in infants appear to increase the risk of infection and its resultant change in the compliance of the tympanic membrane. Nevertheless, many normal infants have little or no measurable loss in middle ear function relative to adult norms. Thus, although checks on middle ear function may be advisable in determining the cause of apparent hearing loss in infants, it is not the case that all infants have middle ear deficits. The inner ear appears to be the primary peripheral locus for explanations of hearing loss in infants.

The Inner Ear

The inner ear is a complex tube that consists of three major structural components involved in the processing of auditory signals: (1) two fluid-filled chambers, (2) three membranes, and (3) two types of receptor cells. Figure 4 illustrates a schematized version of these three major structural components extracted from the actual form of the cochlea shown in Figure 2. If the cochlea were uncoiled, it would consist of two tubes, one of which runs from the footplate of the stapes at the oval window to the end of the cochlea and back to a location adjacent to the stapes called the round window. Thus, vibration of the stapes against the oval window induces pressure variations in the fluid that fills this dual chamber. Located between this dual chamber is a second self-contained chamber called the cochlear duct. This duct is bounded by two membranes, the more important of which is called the basilar membrane. The basilar membrane supports the inner and outer hair cells that are the receptors for the sound-induced oscillations of the fluids in the cochlea. A smaller third membrane, called the tectorial membrane, extends over the hair cells and is supported only on the inner side of the cochlear duct. Thus, vibrations of the fluid in the two chambers sets up a shearing action between the basilar and tectorial membranes and induces complex movements of the stereocilia on the hair cells. These movements of the stereocilia are believed to be the necessary stimulus for conversion of the fluid oscillations into neural signals.

Although the foregoing account is greatly oversimplified, it should be clear that the action of the various fluids, membranes, and hair cells in the cochlea is extremely complex even for the simplest of auditory stimuli. There are, however, some relatively simple descriptions of these actions that have been discovered, largely through the efforts of von Bekesy (1960). Because the basilar membrane forms the base for the hair cells, it has received the most thorough investigation. As shown in Figure 5, the basilar membrane actually increases in width by a factor of 5 from the base (the end nearest the oval window) to the apex of the cochlea. This increase in width, although camouflaged by the decrease in overall width of the cochlea from base to apex, is accompanied by a hundredfold increase in elasticity. The result of these anatomical characteristics is a

A.

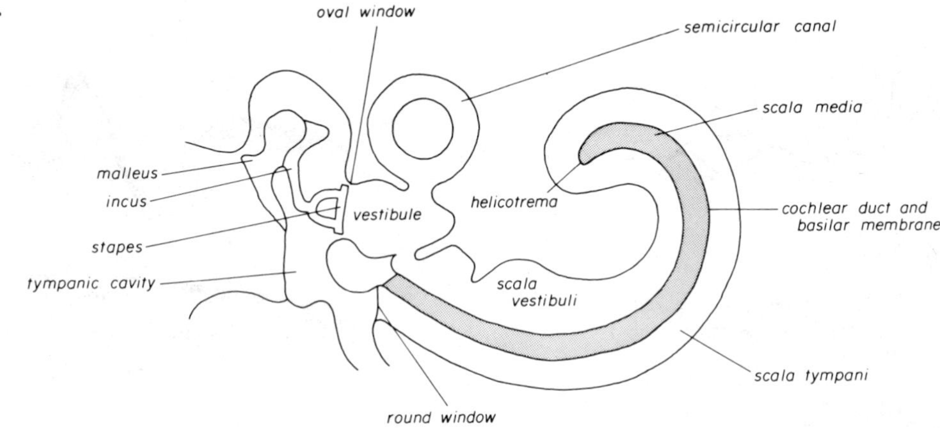

B.

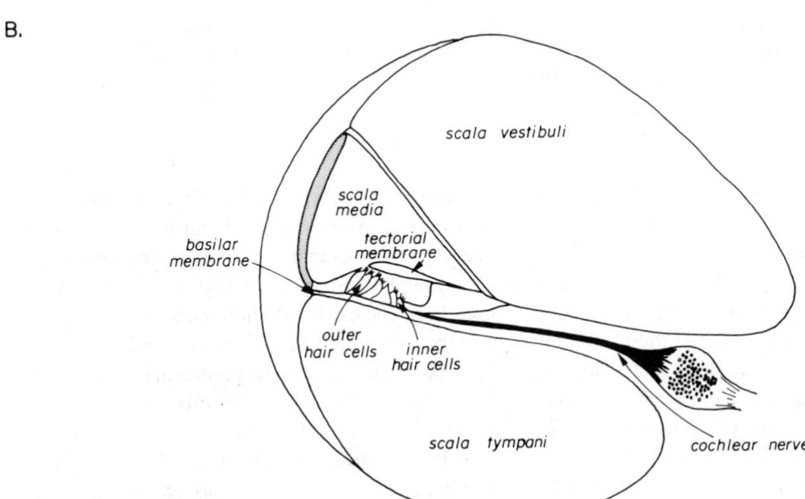

Figure 4. (A) Diagram of the inner ear showing the major features of the cochlea (uncoiled for simplicity). (Redrawn from Zemlin, 1981) (B) Cross-section of the cochlea illustrating the basilar and tectorial membranes and the inner and outer hair cells. (Redrawn from Langman, 1963)

basilar membrane that vibrates differentially as a function of the frequency and amplitude of sound transmitted via the stapes. The stiff basal end of the basilar membrane vibrates most readily to high frequencies, whereas the more elastic apical end vibrates most readily to low frequencies. Complex auditory signals composed of many different component frequencies will create a complex traveling wave along the basilar membrane so that each component frequency induces a displacement of the basilar membrane that corresponds to the relative amplitude of that component frequency within the complex signal. The amplitude envelope of this traveling wave along the basilar membrane illustrates how frequency information is coded. The point of maximum displacement of the basilar membrane is frequency specific, with high frequencies represented near the base and low frequencies represented near the apex. Note that both low and high frequencies induce displacement of the basilar membrane near the base, but only low frequencies displace the apical end.

Although the function of inner and outer hair cells is still controversial (see Dallos, 1981, for a

A.

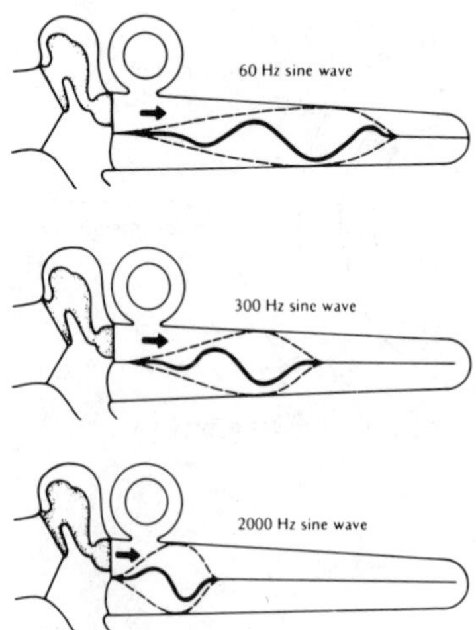

B.

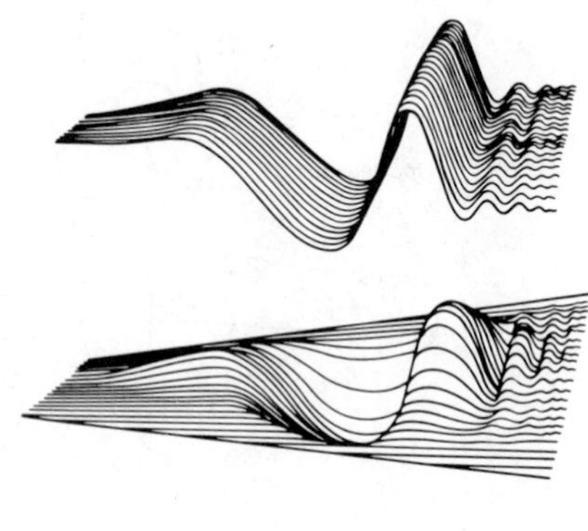

Figure 5. (A) Illustration of the vibration of the basilar membrane to three different sound frequencies. (Adapted from Zemlin, 1981; reprinted from Yost & Nielsen, 1977) (B) Illustration of a standing wave along the basilar membrane and its increasing width from base to apex. (Reprinted from Tonndorf, 1960)

recent review), it is known that 95% of the afferent nerve fibers from the cochlea to the central auditory areas originate from the inner hair cells (Spoendlin, 1978). The hair cells also have an efferent neural input from more central auditory areas and, in contrast to the afferent system, 80% of these efferent fibers terminate on the outer hair cells (Iurato, 1974). Electrophysiological and behavioral evidence have strongly implicated the outer hair cells in determining absolute intensity thresholds (Ryan & Dallos, 1975). However, for suprathreshold stimuli, Prosen, Moody, Stebbins, and Hawkins (1981) have shown in the guinea pig that loss of the outer hair cells does not significantly impair thresholds for intensity differences. Data on the contribution of inner and outer hair cells to frequency sensitivity and frequency discrimination are currently unclear.

The developmental implications of these findings on the structure and function of the inner ear in infants leave many unanswered questions. Although the size and gross structure of the cochlea are nearly adultlike at birth (Bast & Anson, 1949), it is unclear whether the microstructure of the basilar and tectorial membranes as well as the inner and outer hair cells are fully developed at birth. For example, the relative stiffness of the infant's basilar membrane at various locations from base to apex is unknown. The functional significance of current anatomical data is also unclear. For example, the course of anatomical development during embryogenesis proceeds from the base to the apex of the basilar membrane (Bredberg, 1967). Thus, on strictly anatomical grounds, one might predict that sensitivity to low frequencies would lag behind the development of sensitivity to high frequencies. In addition, anatomical data suggest that the inner hair cells mature before the outer hair cells. Thus, one might predict that the contribution of the efferent (outer hair cell) system would lag behind the afferent (inner hair cell) system. In addition, Pujol, Carlier, and Devigne (1978) have shown in kittens that efferent neurons are probably at a competitive disadvantage compared to afferent neurons because the afferents eventually dominate (95%) the overall number of connections made to inner hair cells. Therefore, the implications of these anatomical findings on the development of the inner ear for changes in auditory function are not clear; careful studies of the relation between anatomy and function will be needed in the future.

Neural Pathways and Response Characteristics

The neuroanatomy of the auditory system is extremely complex. The afferent pathways from cochlea to auditory cortex are shown in simplified form in Figure 6. The efferent pathways are less well understood and will be excluded from further discussion despite their potential importance as an inhibitory influence in auditory processing.

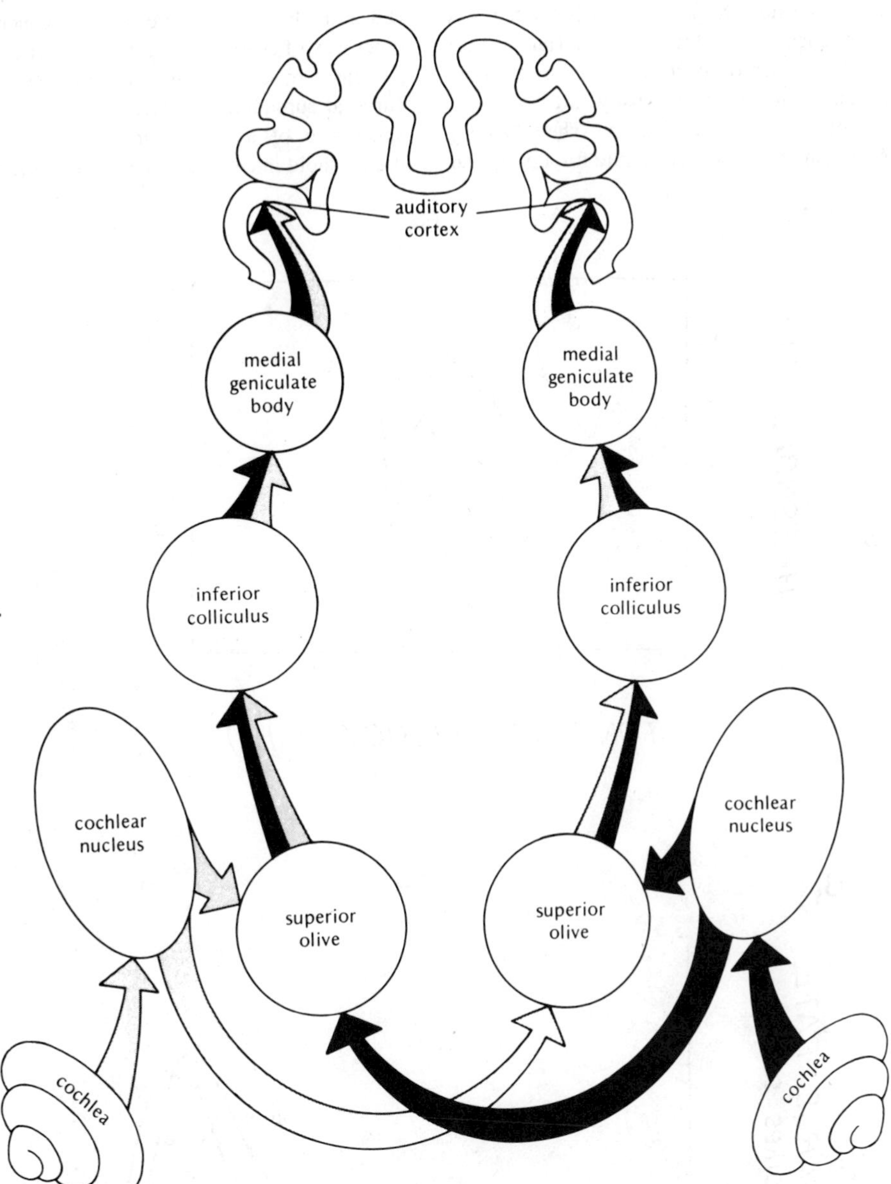

Figure 6. Major afferent pathways of the auditory system. (Reprinted from Yost & Nielsen, 1977)

Single Unit Responses

The sound-induced mechanical stimulation of the hair cells in the cochlea results in a graded electrical potential that triggers a neural impulse in the auditory nerve. Pujol and Hilding (1973) have shown that the kitten's peripheral auditory system is functional within 2 days of birth (based on recordings of the cochlear microphonic and the action potential of the auditory nerve). Recordings from single neurons in the auditory nerve in various species of mammals (see the classic report on the cat by Kiang, Watanabe, Thomas, & Clark, 1965) have revealed several characteristics of neural coding. First, each neuron in the auditory nerve shows an increase in the frequency of discharge (spike rate) dependent upon both the intensity and frequency of the sound impinging upon the animal. The threshold for each neuron corresponds to the intensity of sound required to raise the spike rate above the neuron's spontaneous level of responding. However, this threshold for neural responsiveness is limited to a restricted range of sound frequencies. Thus, the response of each neuron is characterized by a tuning curve that illustrates the intensity threshold as a function of frequency (see Fig. 7A). The frequency that results in the highest spike rate for a particular neuron is the characteristic or best frequency. Another way of characterizing the selectivity of neural responses in single units is to examine the tuning curve at suprathreshold levels (see Fig. 7B). The spike rate of a neuron at each of several suprathreshold intensities is recorded as a function of

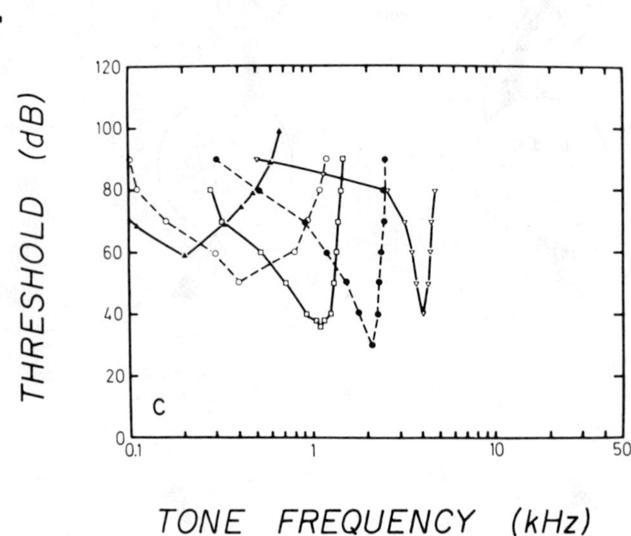

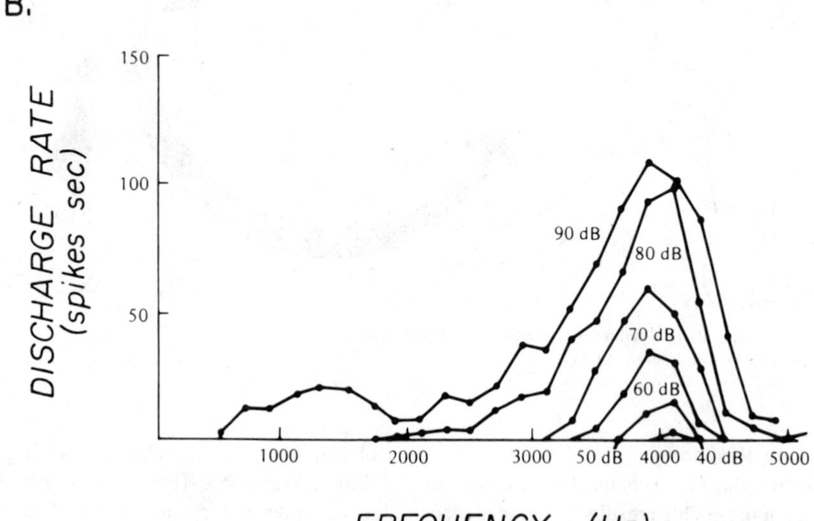

Figure 7. (A) Tuning curves from single neurons in the auditory nerve of the monkey showing the threshold level for exceeding a criterion spike rate as a function of tone frequency. (Reprinted from Evans, 1975) (B) Rate of response curves from single neurons in the cat showing the spike rate at several intensities as a function of frequency. (Reprinted from Rose, Hind, Anderson & Brugge, 1971)

frequency. The band width of each neuron's tuning curve varies as a function of intensity, but typically the characteristic frequency (highest relative spike rate) remains invariant. Romand (1979) has recently shown in kittens that the tuning curves of single neurons in the auditory nerve undergo rapid sharpening during the postnatal period from 20 to 30 days. Further studies will be required to determine whether this rapid development at a relatively peripheral level of the auditory system is dependent on specific auditory inputs during the postnatal period.

A second response property of single neurons in the auditory nerve is the phase locking of the spike rate to the periodicity of the sound input. For frequencies below 1 kHz, the output of the neuron may correspond to the oscillations of the pure-tone input (i.e., one spike per cycle of the sinusoidal stimulus). Although the refractory period of the neuron prevents perfect phase locking for higher frequencies, there may be a partial locking for frequencies up to 5 kHz if the neuron discharges to every second or third cycle of the sinusoid. Thus, for relatively low-frequency sounds, the discharge rate of the neuron could provide a code for the frequency of the sinusoid. However, for complex sounds composed of several sinusoids, the phase locking of the neuron is likely to be based on the periodicity of the sound rather than on the frequency of each component sinusoid. A possible mechanism for coding the individual sinusoidal components involves the place along the basilar membrane from which the neuron originates. Because high frequencies are best transmitted by vibrations of the base of the basilar membrane and low frequencies by vibrations near the apex, an analysis system that kept track of *which* neuron was firing and from *where* along the basilar membrane it originated could presumably provide accurate frequency coding. The fact that frequency sensitivity far exceeds the 5 kHz upper limit on phase locking also implies that some sort of place organization operates in the analysis of high frequencies. Finally, it should be noted that intensity is encoded by the discharge rate of an entire population of neurons because each neuron's response range is only a fraction of the dynamic range of the entire auditory nerve.

The termination area of neurons originating in the cochlea is a brainstem region called the cochlear nucleus (see Fig. 6). Second-order neurons in the cochlear nucleus maintain a tonotopic organization so that adjacent locations along the basilar membrane are similarly represented in the spatial arrangement of neurons that send their axons on to the superior olivary nuclei. This tonotopic organization provides additional support for the operation of a place-coding mechanism in the analysis of frequency information in the auditory system. The response characteristics of single neurons in the cochlear nucleus are somewhat more complex than those of the first-order neurons originating in the cochlea (Pfeiffer, 1966). Recently, several classification schemes have been devised to characterize these diverse response properties (e.g., Evans, 1975), not only because more variance is evident in the cochlear nucleus than in primary afferents but also because responses to complex auditory signals are not always predictable from an analysis of responses to single sinusoids. This fact emphasizes the nonlinearity associated with the integration of auditory information as it travels from peripheral to central areas of the auditory system.

The results of single unit recordings from the cochlear nucleus in infant cats and rats have recently been reported (Brugge, Javel, & Kitzes, 1978; Clopton, 1979). In both species, these second-order neurons have very broad tuning curves and very high thresholds. During the first 3 to 4 postnatal weeks for both species, the tuning curves take on the narrow shape typical of the adult animal. Brugge et al. (1978) have found differential rates of development in the cat for different response properties of these neurons. Tuning curve shapes change rapidly, followed by a reduction in response thresholds and response latencies and finally the phase locking to low-frequency tones. At present, the contribution of auditory experience to these developmental trends in the cat is unknown. However, in the rat, the neurons in the cochlear nucleus are susceptible to monaural deprivation. Coleman and O'Conner (1979) have shown that in rats receiving attenuated input to one ear from the 10th postnatal day there is a reduction in cell size in the ipsilateral cochlear nucleus but a very small reduction in the contralateral cochlear nucleus (as one would expect from the pathways shown in Fig. 6). Binaural deprivation resulted in no measurable decrease in cell size. Finally, monaural deprivation beginning on postnatal day 16 resulted in a less severe ipsilateral deficit, suggesting that auditory experience is heavily weighted during the first few days of auditory input (the auditory canal in the rat does not open fully until postnatal day 10).

The termination site of second-order neurons from the cochlear nucleus includes (among other areas) the superior olivary complex (see review by Brugge & Geisler, 1978). This brainstem region is the first known location at which axons from both cochleas converge, thus providing binaural neural input. The discharge characteristics of these third-order neurons are similar to those in the cochlear nucleus, but they are, in addition, selective for interaural intensity and time-of-arrival differences. Goldberg and Brown (1969) have shown that very small interaural intensity differences can modulate the response rate of neurons in the superior olive of the dog. They have also shown that neurons in the superior olive have a characteristic delay time so that interaural time-of-arrival differences influence the neuron's discharge rate. These findings, replicated by Moushegian, Rupert, and Gidda (1975) in the rat, illustrate an important type of information that is used by animals to localize sound sources. Recently, Feng and Rogowski (1980) have shown that in monaurally occluded rats during postnatal days 12 to 60, there is a laterally biased anatomical morphology among neurons in the superior olive. Binaurally occluded rats do not show this biased anatomy, suggesting that the balance of binaural inputs during an early sensitive period affects the growth of neural connections. Presumably, these neural changes are responsible for the subsequent behavioral deficits found in monaurally deprived animals.

One of the primary termination sites of axons from the superior olivary complex is the inferior colliculus. The binaural property of neurons from the superior olive is also a response characteristic of inferior colliculus neurons. Clopton and his colleagues (Clopton, 1979; Clopton & Silverman, 1977, 1978; Silverman & Clopton, 1977) have shown that for rats receiving monaural deprivation shortly after the time of ear opening, there are a number of deficits in the response characteristics of inferior colliculus neurons. When the deprived ear is stimulated, the latency of the neural response is increased, discharge threshold is increased, and frequency selectivity is degraded. Moreover, there is a dramatic loss in the inhibitory influence (normally exerted by the deprived ear) on the discharge characteristics of neurons in the ipsilateral colliculus. Thus, as shown in Figure 8, monaural deprivation beginning at postnatal day 10 eliminates the binaural (ipsilateral) suppression effect typical of normal adult collicular neurons. A normal period of binaural experience prior to deprivation attenuates this deficit. Thus, there appears to be a sensitive period for the maintenance of binaural connections in the midbrain of the developing rat. More detailed experien-

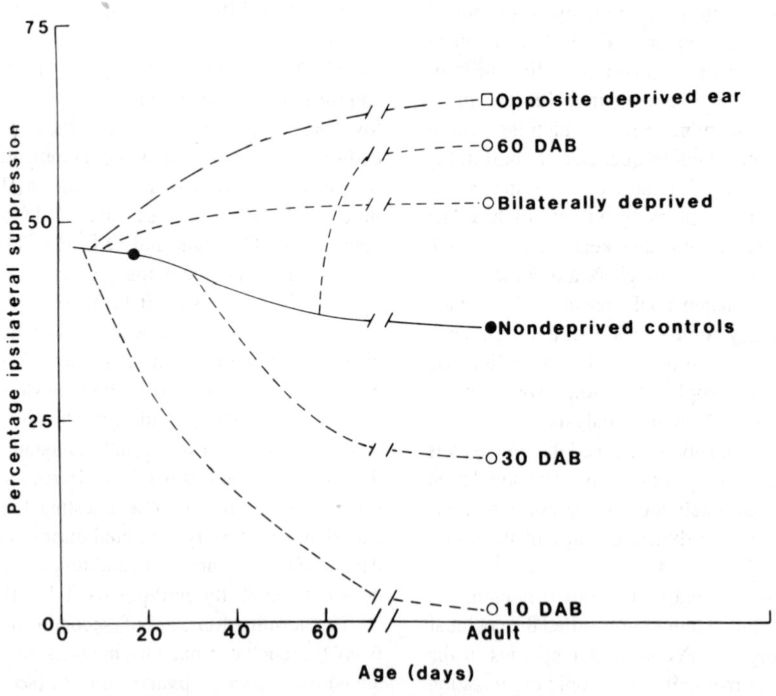

Figure 8. Ipsilateral suppression of single unit responding in the inferior colliculus as a function of age for five sound deprived groups of rats and a control group. DAB = days after birth that the auditory meatus (either one or both) was occluded. (Reprinted from Clopton, 1981)

tial manipulations are needed to define precisely the necessary conditions for this maintenance process, and other regions of the brain should be investigated to check for redundant neural mechanisms that could mediate recovery of function. Moreover, species differences may exist. For example, Moore and Irvine (1980) have recently reported that inferior colliculus neurons in normally reared kittens show little or no change in response characteristics during the first 3 postnatal weeks. However, they have yet to alter the kitten's auditory input during this early postnatal period to examine the system's plasticity.

This brief review illustrates the many complex aspects of neural responding that occur along the auditory pathway. Similar developmental findings have been reported for several other species (e.g., mice: Willott & Shnerson, 1978; bats: Brown, Grinnell, & Harrison, 1978). In general, the development of the auditory pathway proceeds from peripheral to central neural regions. For example, Pujol (1972) showed in kittens that single unit latencies reached adult levels by 18, 25, 37, and 40 days after birth for the cochlear nucleus, inferior colliculus, medial geniculate, and auditory cortex respectively. It should be clear that research on the neurophysiological development of the auditory system is just beginning to reveal some of the basic properties that underlie auditory function as well as the range of susceptibility to early auditory experience.

Gross Electrical Recordings

The data obtained from microelectrode recordings of single unit activity in the auditory system have provided new information about the onset of function and the stimulus specificity of neural responding. However, similar data cannot be gathered from human adults or infants. Thus, less invasive techniques have been devised to assess auditory function. The latency and amplitude characteristics of the averaged waveform recorded from adults with scalp electrodes have been summarized by Picton et al. (1974). As summarized earlier (see *Methodological Techniques*) and illustrated in Figure 9, there are three general latency components of the auditory evoked potential. Difficulties in eliminating arousal effects from the mid-latency and late-latency components (Picton & Hillyard, 1974) have led to the adoption of the early components, or auditory brainstem response (ABR), as a useful developmental tool in assessing auditory function.

The ABR in human adults was initially described

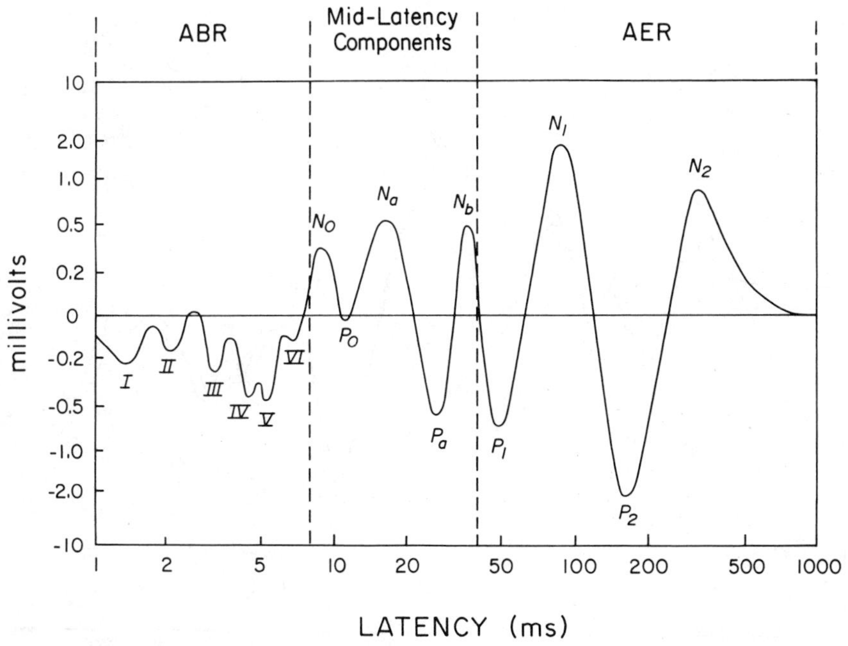

Figure 9. The gross electrical response recorded from the auditory system showing the amplitude and latency of the three major divisions of the auditory evoked waveform. (Redrawn from Picton, Hillyard, Krausz, & Galambos, 1974)

by Jewett et al. (1970) and Jewett and Williston (1971). As shown in Figure 10, the ABR consists of at least seven distinct peaks or troughs in the averaged waveform. Subsequent research (e.g., Don, Eggermont, & Brackmann, 1979) has shown that the latency and amplitude of several aspects of the ABR are highly correlated with the audiogram (detection thresholds at various frequencies) in adults. The ABR recordings from cats (Buchwald & Huang, 1975; Jewett, 1970) have identified the primary neural generators for each of the first five peaks: I—the auditory nerve, II—the cochlear nucleus, III—the superior olivary complex, IV—the lateral lemniscus, and V—the inferior colliculus. These general conclusions have been confirmed in human adults who have documented lesions of the auditory pathway (Starr & Hamilton, 1976).

In a study of developing cats and rats, Jewett and Romano (1972) recorded ABR amplitudes and latencies to click stimuli during the first 4 postnatal months. They found that the latencies of the major peaks of the ABR waveform did not reach adult levels until approximately the end of the third postnatal month. They also found that, as in adult animals, increases in click intensity resulted in an increase in the amplitude of the ABR waveform as well as a decrease in the latency of each peak. Finally, they found that developmental decreases in latency were greater for the later peaks of the ABR waveform. This last finding suggests that, although all neural components of the auditory pathway show postnatal development, the more central regions have a longer maturational period. These findings have been replicated and extended in several more recent studies of the kitten's auditory system (e.g., Shipley, Buchwald, Norman, & Guthrie, 1980).

In summary, the use of evoked potentials, particularly those generated from subcortical regions, has proven very useful in diagnosing the functional status of different levels of the developing auditory system. It appears from the findings on cats and rats that a very significant change in auditory function occurs during the early postnatal period. However, studies of auditory deprivation using evoked potential recordings have not been conducted. Thus, we do not as yet know whether these postnatal changes

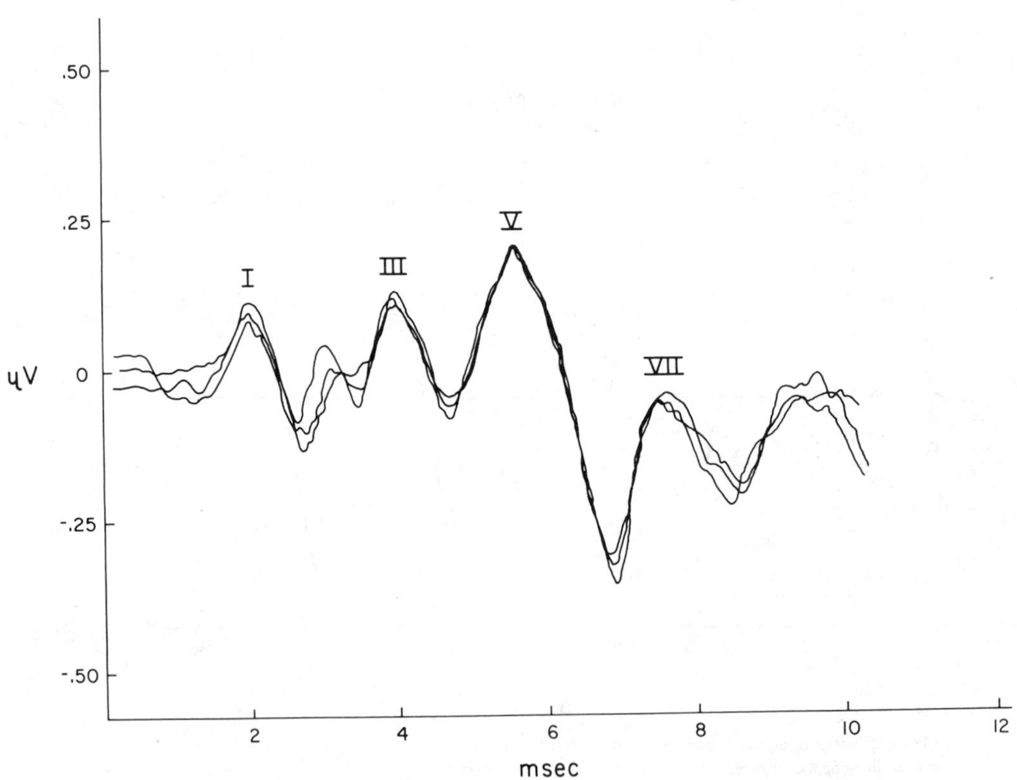

Figure 10. The seven major components of the ABR. (Redrawn from Hecox, 1975)

in auditory responsiveness are influenced by the quality of early experience. Finally, we do not know whether evoked potential measures, although highly correlated with single unit measures, accurately reflect perceptual function in developing organisms. It is possible that differences in either the AER or ABR obtained from the developing infant reflect an improved synchrony of neural events rather than an improvement in hearing. The relation between the neural and perceptual levels requires a behavioral assessment of hearing. This relation, which is critical to the interpretation of many phenomena in sensory and perceptual development, is addressed next.

AUDITORY DEVELOPMENT IN HUMAN INFANTS

In our discussion, *Critical Issues in Auditory Development,* we raised four questions that could serve as a guide to investigations of auditory development in human infants:

1. At what age does auditory function begin?
2. How does auditory sensitivity change during development?
3. Does auditory experience influence the course of auditory development?
4. What mechanisms underlie developmental changes in auditory sensitivity?

The questions of functional onset (1) and developmental change (2) have received the most attention in studies of human auditory development, largely because experiential manipulations (3) are difficult to conduct and underlying mechanisms (4) are difficult to document. Unfortunately, interpretations of empirical findings on both the onset of function and the course of development have been obscured by difficult methodological issues. For example, conclusions regarding the age at which the auditory system begins to function are often based on a response system (e.g., AER, HR, HAS, or head turn) that itself undergoes considerable development independently of any sensory input. Such response-system developments may result in overestimates of developmental changes in auditory sensitivity with increasing age or experience. The development of auditory sensitivity is also confounded by potential age differences in attentional state or response criteria. In other words, the endpoint of auditory development has been quantified in highly motivated and attentive adults whose willingness to respond under conditions of uncertainty can be assessed with a fair degree of accuracy. Attentional states in infants can only be inferred from a limited behavioral repertoire, and the response criteria used by the infant are typically unmeasurable, even with assessments of response bias using signal detection procedures. It is not surprising, therefore, that many contradictions regarding both the onset of auditory function and developmental changes in auditory sensitivity exist in the literature.

In this discussion we will review those empirical findings on auditory development in human infants that are relevant to the four questions raised earlier (*Critical Issues in Auditory Development*) and repeated above. Our goal here is to be comprehensive, not encyclopedic. As a prelude to this selective review, we will first consider a set of goals that may have guided past research in this area. We do not suggest that such an organized process was actually followed by any single researcher, but rather that such a set of rationales could account for the progress that has been made in the area of infant audition over the past century.

Historical Background

It seems reasonable to assume that most researchers of human infants have been concerned with whether or not *newborns* can hear. Presumably, few researchers seriously considered the possibility that auditory function could begin prenatally because (1) fetal research was too difficult to perform and newborns were not readily accessible as subjects, (2) the process of sound transmission and hearing *in utero* did not seem plausible and no simple intervention technique could effectively alleviate any prenatal auditory deficit, or (3) a reasonable first step was to document auditory function in newborns before tackling the more difficult question of prenatal antecedents. Given the choice of newborns as the primary subject population, it was necessary to choose an auditory stimulus for testing purposes. In the absence of data on newborn auditory thresholds, it made sense to select a stimulus that sounded quite loud to most adults. Often, the choice of a stimulus was clearly arbitrary. Yet, only intuition could serve as a guide to this selection process (even for the sophisticated adult psychoacoustician). One might wonder why systematic variations in stimulus intensity or quality were not commonplace, but the goal appeared to be the documentation of reliable responding by the newborn to *any* auditory stimulus. Finally, a response measure was needed to assess the newborn's detection of the auditory stimulus. Again, in the absence of easily controlled and quantifiable dependent measures, response selection (overt behaviors) was based largely on convenience or on assumptions that covert measures (HR, AER, etc.) were more sensitive indices of auditory responsiveness.

The result of these various research strategies was to present the newborn with an intense sound on one or more trials and to record the presence or absence of a criterion response. With the aid of hindsight, the outcome of these procedures was predictable. Some researchers chose stimuli that were above the newborn's threshold and others did not. Given inadequate control over key variables, such as the frequency content of the stimulus and the ambient noise level of the testing environment, as well as the likelihood of large fluctuations in the newborn's attentional state, the seemingly discrepant findings on newborn hearing were not surprising. Moreover, the skill of the experimenter in reliably recording and scoring different responses as well as the sensitivity of the response itself further obscured the issue of newborn hearing. These methodological difficulties, in the absence of an external referent for newborn hearing levels, led many researchers to hypothesize several reasons for the elusive nature of responses to sound by the newborn. For example, Pratt (1933) cites six possible causes for the absence (or reduced sensitivity) of hearing in the newborn:

1. Fluid in the middle ear.
2. Occlusion of the auditory canal.
3. Inefficient mobility of the tympanic membrane.
4. Immobile ossicles.
5. Labor and delivery complications.
6. Immaturity of the auditory nerve.

Far from being naive, these six explanations are nearly identical to those that might be raised today given the same inconsistencies in the literature. Nevertheless, the empirical evidence at that time for hearing in the newborn was inconclusive. Over a decade later, however, Pratt (1946) was willing to conclude that: "The newborn is not deaf, but there is little evidence that it makes pitch discriminations or differential responses correlated with the complexity characteristics of auditory stimuli" (p. 213).

Perhaps the greatest difficulty faced by researchers (past and present) of auditory development is what to conclude on the basis of negative evidence of auditory responsiveness. A failure by the newborn to provide a consistent response to an auditory stimulus could indicate several things, including (1) the absence of auditory function; (2) selection of a stimulus intensity below the newborn's threshold; (3) selection of a stimulus that was processed (i.e., "heard") but not responded to, either via active inhibition or general indifference; or (4) selection of an insensitive or immature response system. As a research strategy, therefore, the trial-and-error style of the past was frequently misleading and often counterproductive. It is essential to anchor the absence of responding to certain stimuli against the presence of responding to at least one stimulus type or level. If all other procedures are identical, failures to respond are more easily interpreted. As mentioned in the introduction to this chapter, this technique is the essence of the psychophysical method. Unfortunately, only in rare instances have investigators of infant audition adopted such a research strategy. Instead, the half century from Pratt (1933) to the present has seen the repetition of trial-and-error research with infants, albeit with new and more sensitive measures of auditory responsiveness. In the review to follow, we will focus on the more recent (post-1970) studies of infant audition that have begun to answer all four of the questions we raised above and, in particular, those studies that have employed psychophysical methods.

Thresholds and Masking

Before proceeding to a review of the data from infants on thresholds for auditory signals, it is important to clarify the manner in which auditory stimuli are quantified. In the 1930s, experiments conducted by several researchers established a sound pressure level of 0.0002 dynes/cm^2 as the threshold for young adults presented with pure tones between 1,000 Hz and 4,000 Hz. Thus, when a stimulus is defined relative to this adult standard, it has a decibel value referred to as sound pressure level (SPL). However, the threshold intensities of pure tones differ considerably as a function of frequency. In an attempt at standardization, the International Organization for Standardization (ISO) and the American National Standards Institute (ANSI) established psychophysical norms for each frequency. These norms are referred to as hearing level (HL), or hearing threshold level. Thus, a particular pure tone that is referenced to physical intensity has an SPL value as well as a psychophysically based HL value. Because infants may have a set of threshold values that is different from adults, the use of adult HL values could be misleading. In addition, there are interindividual differences in adults' absolute thresholds. Thus, in some experiments it is more appropriate to anchor each subject's threshold to a psychophysical judgment under a specific set of testing conditions rather than to an absolute physical intensity. The term sensation level (SL) is used to refer to the difference in intensity between the individual subject's threshold and a suprathreshold stimulus.

A second important aspect of auditory testing is the psychophysical criterion used in deciding what sound intensity is the subject's threshold. Typically, a series of intensities is presented to the subject according to one of three major procedures: (1) a random sequence of intensities (the method of constant stimuli), (2) an ascending and descending sequence of intensities (the method of limits), or (3) a sequence of intensities that are decreased until the subject fails to detect them and increased until detection is reinstated, thereby generating a series of above- and below-threshold judgments (an adaptive staircase procedure). The essence of each of these three procedures is to generate a set of judgments that fall just above and below the subject's threshold. In this way, one can be sure that sounds of some intensity were actually detected, whereas sounds of a lesser intensity were not detected.

Each of these three procedures has some advantages and disadvantages. For example, the method of constant stimuli requires either some knowledge of the general range of stimuli that are likely to be near threshold, or a subject who is capable of providing a very large number of judgments for all the possible intensities that could be presented. This procedure, therefore, is quite costly in time and effort. However, it has the advantage of generating a complete psychometric function. As shown in Figure 11, there are two general procedures for obtaining psychophysical data in a threshold task. In the first procedure (Fig. 11A), an interval is defined during which a signal may or may not be presented. The subject must indicate whether the signal was present or absent during this interval. If the signal is below threshold, the probability of a yes judgment will be 0 (or near 0, depending on the subject's likelihood of making a yes response by chance). As the signal intensity is increased, the probability of a yes response will increase, approaching 1.0 at very high intensity levels. In this yes/no procedure, the signal intensity corresponding to the 0.5 level of a yes response is typically defined as the threshold.

In the second psychophysical procedure (Fig. 11B), the subject must indicate whether the signal was detected by making one of two mutually exclusive responses (e.g., yes if the signal was detected, no if it was not detected). Because the subject is forced to make a response, the minimum level of correct responding is 0.5 rather than 0. Thus, the psychometric function extends from a probability of 0.5 correct at low signal intensities to 1.0 at high

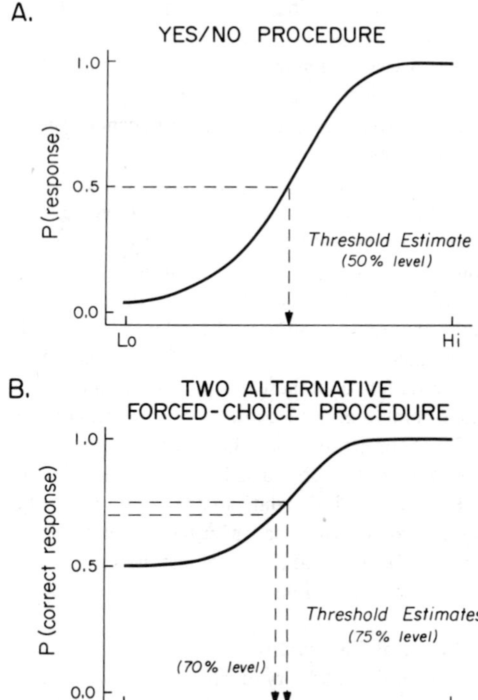

Figure 11. Schematic psychometric functions for: (A) The yes/no or single-interval procedure. (B) The two-alternative forced-choice procedure.

intensities. The task of the experimenter who has obtained the data shown in Figure 11B is to select a percent correct value that corresponds to the subject's threshold. Unfortunately, this threshold criterion is somewhat arbitrary. Typically, 75% correct is used as the threshold criterion because it is the point where the psychometric function has the steepest slope and, therefore, the least likely location for chance responding to contaminate the data. However, in many instances the subject does not reach 100% correct even for very intense sounds. Thus, the point halfway between chance responding and asymptotic performance (e.g., 80% correct) is chosen as the estimate of threshold (in this example such a criterion would be 65% correct) because this point corresponds to the steepest slope of the psychometric function. Finally, other investigators simply choose the point on the psychometric function that is just significantly above chance responding. This point is determined by the variance in the subject's judgments (and, of course, the number of judgments made at each intensity level). The point here is that threshold criteria are selected in a rather arbitrary manner. Thus, unless the experimental conditions are identical when comparing data collected in two different laboratories, the *absolute* threshold values may be misleading, even though relative values (e.g., at different frequencies) may be comparable.

In testing infants, it is often unrealistic to expect that reliable data can be gathered for a large number of stimulus intensities in a given testing session. Thus, the method of limits or a variety of staircase procedures have been used to reduce the number of trials required to estimate the infant's threshold. Rather than attempt to gather data for the entire psychometric function, these two procedures focus on a single point (e.g., 50% correct for yes/no procedures or 70% correct for two-alternative forced-choice procedures). The only disadvantage of these staircase procedures is that threshold responding must be stable, that is, many trials near the threshold intensity must be gathered to ensure that the subject was not responding randomly.

Prenatal Thresholds

The onset of auditory function is dependent upon both peripheral factors, such as the opening of the auditory canal, and central factors, such as the presence of neural processing mechanisms. The development of peripheral and central auditory mechanisms proceeds at different rates among members of different species, thereby altering the onset of auditory function with respect to an obvious developmental marker, such as hatching or birth. However, for some species whose sensory systems are precocial (such as ducklings), the onset of auditory function precedes the abrupt transition into the external auditory environment (e.g., posthatching). To document the onset age of human auditory function, several researchers over the past century have investigated the possibility that the human fetus has a functioning auditory system.

The first investigations of auditory function in the human fetus consisted of verbal reports by pregnant women (e.g., Forbes & Forbes, 1927). The women in these studies typically reported a sudden movement of the fetus several seconds after a loud noise was presented in the extrauterine environment. These anecdotal reports were documented by systematic studies of fetal movement. For example, Sontag and Wallace (1935) presented a 120-Hz vibration directly to the abdomen of women during the last trimester of pregnancy. Movements of the fetus were recorded by a set of pressure sensors attached to the abdominal wall. Reliable movement responses became evident during the 31st week of gestation, increasing in frequency of occurrence to 86% during the last prenatal month. Bernard and Sontag (1947) extended this study by recording fetal heart rate changes to the presentation of auditory stimuli. Although the prenatal age of onset of the heart rate acceleration response was not determined, a reliable heart rate response with a latency of 10 to 15 sec. was obtained. In addition, there was a slight tendency for higher frequencies (above 2,000 Hz) to elicit reduced heart rate acceleration.

These early studies of fetal responsiveness to sound are subject to a number of methodological concerns. First, the pregnant women were aware of the timing of stimulus presentations, either by hearing the sounds or feeling the vibrations delivered to their abdomens. Thus, it is unclear whether the response of the fetus was mediated by the sensory apparatus of the fetus or the mother. Although the relatively short response latencies (less than 20 sec.) in these studies precluded a fetal response mediated by maternal hormones, it is quite possible that the fetal response was triggered by a maternal muscular contraction to the startle effect from stimulus onset. Second, although the vibratory stimulus presented to the fetus was nominally an auditory signal, it was also capable of transmitting tactile vibrations to the fetus via the mother's abdominal wall, her uterus, and the amniotic fluid. Thus, it is unclear whether the movement response of the fetus (assuming no influence by the mother) resulted from stimulation of the fetus's skin or cochlea.

In the past 10 years, several studies of heart rate and brain evoked potential responses from fetuses have been conducted. Grimwade, Walker, Bartlett, Gordon, and Wood (1971) reported convincing evidence that fetal heart rate responses are not mediated by the mother. For example, they recorded both fetal and maternal heart rate changes and found that fetal responses had very short latencies (approximately 5 sec.), maternal responses were absent, and fetal responses were present even on those trials in which the mother did not hear the sound (via a speaker placed in the birth canal). It is interesting to note that Grimwade et al. used a 500- to 1,000-Hz stimulus because their measurements of sounds transmitted through the maternal abdominal wall suggested a significant attenuation of frequencies above 1,000 Hz (Walker, Grimwade, & Wood, 1971). Walker et al. also found that the ambient noise level in the intrauterine environment was approximately 85 dB SPL. Thus, significant masking of moderately intense sounds from the extrauterine environment may preclude effective stimulation of the fetal auditory system. Two recent reports using a more sophisticated hydrophone than the one employed by Walker et al. (1971) (Armitage et al., 1980; Querleu & Renard, 1981) have demonstrated that auditory signals below 1,000 Hz are transmitted from the external environment to the amniotic sac with little attenuation. Thus, external sounds below 1,000 Hz and above 85 dB SPL may provide sufficient stimulation to activate the peripheral auditory apparatus of the fetus. However, no study has recorded the response of the fetus to auditory signals differing in intensity or frequency. Without such psychophysical data it is unclear whether the auditory system alone is mediating the fetus's responsiveness to vibratory stimuli. Finally, auditory evoked potentials, recorded both through the maternal abdominal wall (Sakabe, Arayama, & Suzuki, 1969) and from the fetal scalp during labor (Scibetta, Rosen, Hochberg, & Chik, 1971), have confirmed the presence of at least rudimentary neural activity in the auditory system prior to birth.

In summary, it is likely, particularly in light of anatomical and electrophysiological data (see below), that the auditory system of the human fetus is functional in at least a rudimentary sense several weeks prior to birth. Premature infants, once they have passed through the first critical hours postpartum, show evidence of auditory responsivity on a variety of measures. However, no conclusive evidence has as yet been provided to document the onset of auditory function *in utero*. It is possible that auditory neural mechanisms are functional prior to birth but peripheral obstructions imposed by the uterine environment may impede or delay the onset of hearing until the birth process is complete.

Neonatal Thresholds

The study of auditory thresholds in infants has focused primarily on the newborn. In general (see Weir, 1979), there are two prevailing opinions supported by different sets of empirical research: (1) newborns show elevated thresholds (approximately 40 dB relative to adults) at all frequencies and (2) newborns show elevated thresholds compared to adults, with an additional sensitivity deficit at high frequencies. Evidence in support of these two viewpoints has been summarized by Eisenberg (1976) and Schneider, Trehub, and Bull (1979). Unfortunately, there is no simple explanation that can account for these differing viewpoints, such as the use of unusual stimuli or unique assessment procedures. In addition, the evidence supporting a high-frequency insensitivity among newborns has been criticized on procedural grounds. For example, Hutt, Hutt, Lenard, von Bernuth, and Muntjewerff (1968) recorded electromyographic (muscle activity) responses from newborns presented with sine- and square-wave stimuli at frequencies of 70, 125, 250, 500, 1,000, and 2,000 Hz. They also presented tape-recorded human voices matched in intensity (75 dB SPL) to the sine- and square-wave stimuli. Their results showed that the most potent stimuli were the square waves of low frequency, with human voices and low-frequency sine waves less potent and higher frequency square and sine waves ineffective in eliciting the muscle response. A follow-up study by Lenard, von Bernuth, and Hutt (1969) recorded the cortical AER to sine-wave, square-wave, and voice stimuli (80 dB SPL). They found that the low-frequency (125 Hz) square-wave stimulus and the human voice (uttering "baby") elicited a much larger AER amplitude than either the higher frequency square-wave stimulus (1,000 Hz) or the two sine-wave stimuli (125 and 1,000 Hz). They also found that the 125-Hz square-wave and a broadband (white noise) stimulus elicited a large amplitude AER. As Bench (1973) has correctly noted, a square-wave stimulus actually contains a broad spectrum of frequencies with decreasing amplitudes at harmonics above the fundamental frequency. The 125-Hz square-wave stimulus, therefore, differed considerably in band width from the 125-Hz sine-wave stimulus. Similarly, the voice, although containing low frequencies, was also a relatively broadband stimulus.

In contrast to Bench (1973), Lenard et al. (1969), and Hutt (1973) have argued that band width alone cannot account for the apparently greater responsiveness to low-frequency stimuli. Lenard et al. (1969) showed that the amplitude of the AER was greater for the 125-Hz square-wave stimulus than for the white-noise stimulus, even though their band widths were equated. In addition, hi-pass and low-pass filtered white-noise stimuli with band widths differing by a factor of 10 elicited identical AER amplitudes. Lenard et al. (1969) concluded, on the basis of these and similar results in the literature, that the newborn is differentially tuned to the frequencies that carry much of the distinctive information in spoken language (i.e., low frequencies).

Similar arguments regarding the greater responsiveness of newborns to low frequency and broadband stimuli have been made by Eisenberg (1970). In addition, the difficulty in obtaining reliable responses to pure-tone (sine-wave) stimuli has frequently been noted in the literature. For example, Turkewitz, Birch, and Cooper (1972) found that newborns showed no reliable heart rate, eye-movement, or finger-movement responses to sine-wave stimuli at 250, 500, 1,000, 2,000, 4,000, and 8,000 Hz. In contrast, these same newborns showed reliable responses to a white-noise stimulus equated in intensity to the pure tones (90 dB SPL). The heart rate response, despite evidence for its increasing magnitude with stimulus intensity (Bartoshuk, 1964), has not proven to be a reliable indicator of auditory thresholds for sine-wave stimuli. As a result, Schulman (1973) and Steinschneider, Lipton, and Richmond (1966) used warbled tones (frequency modulated over time) and white noise respectively to elicit reliable heart rate changes in newborns. In both cases, the threshold levels were in the 55 to 90 dB SPL range.

The only behavioral method that has provided reliable auditory thresholds in newborns is a sucking technique devised by Eisele, Berry, and Shriner (1975). The rate of sucking was linked to the intensity of a pure tone, thereby generating a series of bursts and pauses that corresponded to a staircase threshold method used in adults (the von Bekesy technique). Although these data from 100 neonates provided thresholds of 59, 62, and 68 dB at 1,000, 2,000, and 4,000 Hz respectively, it is not clear that this sucking technique provides a valid threshold assessment. For example, the rate of sucking in the HAS procedure increases for suprathreshold stimuli; cyclical baseline rates of sucking are present even in the absence of stimulation. Thus, the variance in intensity levels corresponding to the initiation and termination of the sucking response was very high in the Eisele et al. (1975) study. Nevertheless, this report is one of the few attempts to provide systematic behavioral data on auditory thresholds in newborns.

Other researchers have attempted to determine newborn thresholds for pure tones with the cortical AER. Taguchi, Picton, Orpin, & Goodman (1969) recorded the AER in over 200 neonates. Tone-burst stimuli (60 msec in duration) with frequencies of 500, 1,000, and 2,000 Hz were presented at a rate of 1 per 5 sec. A descending method of limits beginning at 70 dB HL (relative to adult norms) was used to estimate newborns' thresholds at each frequency based on the AER amplitude. During the first two postnatal days, the newborns showed thresholds in the 30 to 50 dB range, with a slight trend toward higher sensitivity to the lower frequencies and lower thresholds (up to 10 dB) in deep sleep than in light sleep. Engel and Young (1969) also recorded the AER from over 100 newborns using 500 msec sine-wave stimuli with frequencies of 250, 500, 1,000, 2,000, 4,000, and 8,000 Hz. A modified method of limits was also used to determine the amplitude threshold of the AER as stimulus intensity was varied between 70 dB and −20 dB HL (relative to adult norms). In contrast to Taguchi et al. (1969), the results of the Engel and Young (1969) study showed little difference between newborn and adult hearing levels. Thresholds at all frequencies tested were within 15 dB of adult norms with a slightly higher sensitivity to the two lowest frequencies. The reason for this discrepancy in estimated newborn thresholds between these two studies is not readily apparent. Both used slow stimulus repetition rates, a parameter known to affect the amplitude of the AER. One possibility, however, is the rise time of the pure tones. Taguchi et al. (1969) used a 30 msec rise time, whereas Engel and Young (1969) used a 10 msec rise time. More abrupt onsets have the effect of increasing the band width of the stimulus, and Lenard et al. (1969) have shown that larger band widths result in higher AER amplitudes. Nevertheless, these two studies indicate that the AER can be used as a reliable index of auditory function for pure-tone stimuli.

One unfortunate aspect of the AER is its dependence on the state of the infant. In contrast, the ABR does not change in latency or amplitude as the arousal level of the subject varies (Picton & Hillyard, 1974). Thus, newborns can be studied in a sleeping state to simplify the recording procedures. Initial work using the ABR in neonates (Leiberman, Sohmer, & Szabo, 1973) was followed by a series of studies from Galambos' laboratory (Hecox & Galambos, 1974a, 1974b; Hecox, Squires, & Galambos, 1974; see review by Hecox, 1975). As summarized in the discussion on *Gross Electrical Recordings,* the ABR response is elicited by click stimuli with durations typically less than 1 msec. Newborns show longer latencies to the major peaks of the ABR waveform than do adults, and Hecox (1975) has estimated the newborn's threshold to be 17 dB greater than the adult. Schulman-Galambos and Galambos (1979) have replicated this finding of less than a 20 dB difference in the ABR threshold for a sample of over 200 newborns compared to adult hearing levels.

Starr, Amlie, Martin, and Sanders (1977) have documented the presence of the ABR in premature infants beginning in the 28th week of gestation. In addition, they showed that the decrease in latency for each peak of the ABR waveform (also documented in detail by Hecox, 1975, for older infants) was closely correlated with conceptional age rather than postnatal age. Although the Starr et al. (1977) study was not specifically intended as an assessment of thresholds, they found that an AER could be elicited in a preterm infant during the 25th gestational week using the same stimulus intensity (65 dB) that failed to elicit a reliable ABR until the 28th gestational week. One possible explanation raised by Starr et al. to account for this discrepancy is that all electrophysiological responses require synchronous neural firing to provide an AER or ABR waveform. However, the ABR is best elicited by transient stimuli (clicks or fast rise times), whereas the AER response can be elicited by longer duration stimuli that may be facilitated by temporal summation. In fact, Stockard, Stockard, Westmoreland, and Corfits (1979) have shown that the initial direction of sound pressure variation (rarefaction vs. condensation) during a click can significantly influence the shape and amplitude of the newborn's ABR waveform. Thus, as Hecox (1975) has correctly noted, each location along the auditory pathway may have its own characteristic latency and age of onset dependent upon the maturation of underlying anatomical and physiological mechanisms.

In summary, little good behavioral data exist on newborn auditory thresholds for simple or complex stimuli. Psychophysical methods have rarely been used, except in several recent studies employing electrophysiological responses. These studies of brain activity in response to sine-wave and click stimuli support the view that auditory function begins prior to birth. Thresholds, however, are at least 10 to 20 dB higher than adults. Unfortunately, newborn thresholds as a function of stimulus frequency have not been determined, primarily because behavioral data are unreliable and electrophysiological procedures are limited to rapid stimulus onsets or clicks (see the later discussion on *Masking* for at least one exception). Thus, although ABR procedures now provide a reliable screening device for detecting gross hearing losses in newborns, the absolute level of newborns' thresholds at various frequencies remains unresolved.

Postnatal Threshold Changes

Perhaps the greatest problem associated with the assessment of changes in the infant's auditory threshold is the absence of a measurement technique that can be used with infants of widely varying ages. The recent advances in ABR techniques would seem to provide an obvious choice because of their minimal dependence on motor and attentional systems that change dramatically during the first postnatal year. Unfortunately, absolute ABR threshold estimates during an extensive postnatal period have not been reported in the literature. However, Hecox (1975) has reported that the latency of each peak in the ABR waveform decreases during the first 12 to 18 postnatal months. The latency to wave I declines to an adult level by 7 months postnatally, whereas latencies to waves III and V do not reach an adult level until at least 12 months postnatally. Because wave I reflects the action potential of the eighth nerve, these findings suggest that a large component of the latency decrease in waves III and V is the result of peripheral development in the auditory apparatus. However, development beyond the eighth nerve also appears to occur in the postnatal period. This dual contribution of peripheral and central areas of the auditory system to ABR development has been confirmed by other researchers for ABR latencies (Salamy & McKean, 1976; Salamy, McKean, & Buda, 1975) as well as ABR amplitudes (Salamy, Fenn, & Bronshvag, 1979). These developmental changes in ABR latencies and amplitudes, although suggestive of improvements in thresholds, may, in fact, indicate only that auditory signals are processed more rapidly as the infant's neural mechanisms mature. In the absence of ABR thresholds as a function of age, such a possibility (though implausible) cannot be dismissed.

In the past 5 years, several researchers have turned to behavioral measures in an attempt to assess developmental changes in infant auditory thresholds. These behavioral data have been collected not only to provide converging evidence for AER, ABR, and heart rate responses but also to examine the possibility that electrical responses may not indicate "hearing" by the infant. Although a behavioral response in a nonverbal subject is just as ambiguous as any other response, many researchers feel more comfortable if the criterion response can be directly related to an overt behavior (e.g., head turning) that is correlated with verbal reports of hearing in older subjects.

A precursor to the most recent studies of auditory thresholds was a report by Hoversten and Moncur (1969) in which psychophysical methods were used to assess thresholds in 3- and 8-month-old infants. Although these investigators used two uncontrolled stimuli (female voice, music), they also used white-noise and two sine-wave stimuli (500 and 4,000 Hz). A randomized sequence of stimuli at five intensities (15, 30, 45, 60, and 75 dB HL relative to adult norms) was presented to each infant, and two observers recorded gross motor responses during a 30-sec. poststimulus interval. No-stimulus control trials were interspersed throughout the testing session to assess false alarm rates, and the observers were unaware of the characteristics of the stimulus presented on each trial to guard against observer bias. The results of this study showed that the observers were reliable (false alarm rate < 20%) and that the psychometric functions were consistent (i.e., percent correct increased with increasing stimulus intensity). Threshold estimates (50% correct) were approximately 43, 42, and 72 dB HL for the white noise, 500 Hz, and 4,000 Hz stimuli respectively among the 3-month-olds. Corresponding thresholds for the 8-month-olds were 30, 34, and 57 dB. Thus, a significant improvement with age in overall threshold level was found as well as a relative insensitivity to high-frequency stimuli.

One problem associated with gross motor responses, even when they are used in the context of a reliable psychophysical experiment (e.g., Hoversten & Moncur, 1969), is that the infant is provided with little external motivation to respond to the auditory stimuli. Thus, unless the stimuli spontaneously engage the infant's attentional or motivational system, detection may occur without an overt response that can be reliably observed. If one is only interested in *relative* thresholds as a function of frequency, this limitation of spontaneous response measures may not pose a serious problem unless attentional systems are selectively attuned to certain frequency bands. However, if one can enhance the salience of the detection task, it is more likely that the infant will attend to all auditory signals. The foregoing rationale provided the basis for what has been called visual reinforcement audiometry (Liden & Kankkunen, 1969; Moore, Thompson, & Thompson, 1975). Detection of a sound is paired with a visual reinforcer to maintain a high rate of head turning over the course of 30 to 50 trials (see description of this procedure in the discussion on *Operant and Classical Conditioning*). Moore and Wilson (1978) used this head-turning procedure along with a staircase algorithm to estimate thresholds (50% correct) for 500, 1,000, and 4,000 Hz warbled tones. They reported thresholds in the 15 to 20 dB SPL range for all three stimuli among groups of 6- and 12-month-olds (thresholds using earphones were slightly higher, but this difference is not relevant to the comparisons discussed here). Thus, Moore and Wilson (1978) found that infants show thresholds in a visually reinforced procedure that are 25 to 35 dB lower than the thresholds reported by Hoversten and Moncur (1969) using a spontaneous (nonreinforced) procedure. In addition, the much higher thresholds for high-frequency stimuli reported by Hoversten and Moncur (1969), as well as by numerous other investigators, were not found by Moore and Wilson (1978).

The visually reinforced head-turning procedure was subsequently modified by Trehub et al. (1980) and Schneider, Trehub, and Bull (1980) to assess auditory thresholds for octave-band noise stimuli in 6- to 24-month-olds. In their procedure, the infant must make a directional head turn (right vs. left) toward a speaker from which the stimulus is presented. In contrast to the unidirectional head-turning response (with no-stimulus control trials) used by Moore and Wilson (1978), the procedure used by Trehub et al. (1980) and Schneider et al. (1980) is a two-alternative forced-choice task with an unlimited response period (instead of a discrete 5- or 6-sec. response window). Trehub et al. (1980) tested groups of 6-, 12-, and 18-month-olds using octave-band noises with center frequencies of 200, 400, 1,000, 2,000, 4,000, and 10,000 Hz. Each frequency was presented at four intensities to provide a threshold estimate (65% correct) based on psychometric functions averaged across infants within each age group. As shown in Figure 12, threshold estimates decreased with increasing stimulus frequency. Adults tested under the same conditions, but with a 75% correct threshold criterion, showed a relatively flat threshold function across the different stimulus frequencies. These findings led Trehub et al. (1980) to conclude that there is a developmental improvement in auditory sensitivity (reflected in the different slopes of the functions for infants and adults) and that this development is characterized by an improvement in low-frequency sensitivity. Schneider et al. (1980) subsequently found that 6- to 24-month-olds show a greater similarity to adults in their thresholds at 19,000 Hz than at 10,000 Hz (see Fig. 12). Thus, it appears from these data that infants are more adultlike in their thresholds for high-frequency sounds and that the development of auditory sensitivity is primarily marked by improvements in low-frequency sensitivity.

Although the approach used in the studies by Trehub et al. (1980) and Schneider et al. (1980) employed rigorous psychophysical methods, there are several questions that can be raised concerning their experimental procedures and conclusions. First, the two-alternative head-turning task clearly involves the localization of the sound source. In adults, sound localization is dependent, in part, upon the frequency of the stimulus (Jeffress, 1975; Searle, Braida, Davis, & Colburn, 1976). For example, as noted by Clifton, Morrongiello, Kulig, and Dowd (1981a), binaural time-of-arrival differences are an effective sound localization cue for frequencies below 1,500 Hz, whereas binaural intensity differences are primarily mediated by higher frequencies. If sensitivity to interaural intensity information

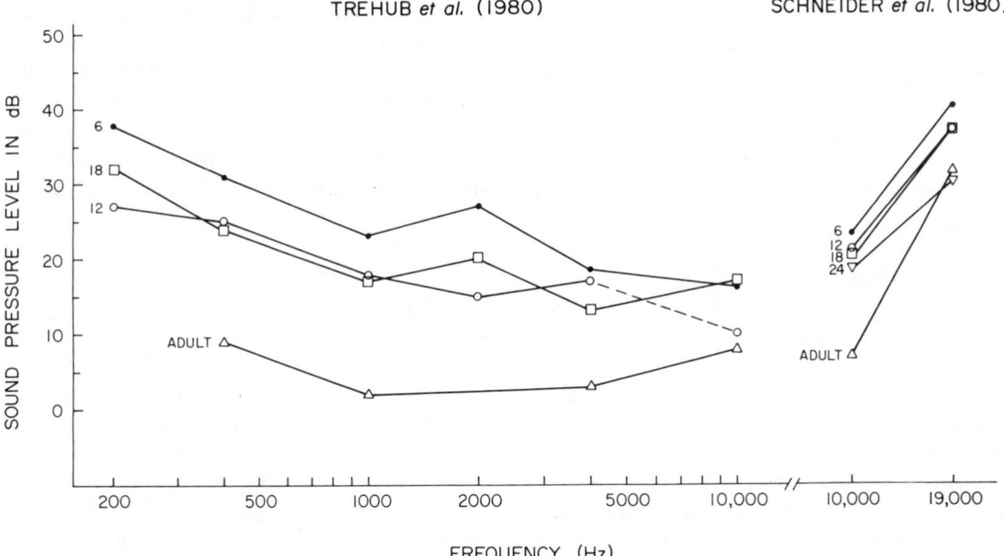

Figure 12. Threshold estimates from infants and adults using octave-band noises at several frequencies. The dashed line for 12-month-olds represents an extrapolated value because their performance was never below criterion at 10,000 Hz. (Redrawn from Trehub, Schneider, & Endman, 1980, and Schneider, Trehub, & Bull, 1980; copyright 1980 by the American Association for the Advancement of Science)

precedes (or is initially more robust than) the development of sensitivity to time-of-arrival differences, infants should show more accurate localization of high-frequency sounds. Thus, the developmental changes in the thresholds obtained by Trehub et al. (1980) and Schneider et al. (1980) may be confounded with the development of sound localization abilities. Trehub et al. (1980) were aware of this possible confound; in fact, they stated that octave-band stimuli were chosen because the infants had difficulty localizing pure tones (increasing band width improves sound localization in adults).

A second issue related to the Trehub et al. (1980) study is their use of different threshold criteria for infants (65% correct) and adults (75% correct). Their rationale was that the infants did not always show 100% correct responding at the highest intensity level. As seen from our introductory discussion about thresholds and masking, if asymptotic performance along the psychometric function does not reach 100% correct, the threshold criterion is sometimes set at the midpoint between peak performance and chance performance. Trehub et al. (1980) stated that the peak performance of the infants in their study (approximately 85% correct) was less than 100% correct because of attentional deficits and high task demands. Thus, they chose 65% correct as their threshold criterion for the infants because this level was significantly above chance. However, some of the infant psychometric functions in this study did approach 100% correct, and the functions for the youngest age group did not employ an intensity level high enough to determine if performance had reached an asymptote. Thus, the rationale for selecting different threshold criteria for the infants and adults is questionable.

The effect of employing two different threshold criteria in the Trehub et al. (1980) study was to bring the functions for the infant groups closer to the adult group. As a result, the infant thresholds at higher frequencies appeared to be nearly identical to the adult thresholds because of the difference in slope between the infant and adult functions. Clearly, there is no simple way to equate the overall level of performance between infants and adults. The task demands and attentional/motivational levels of the two age groups are vastly different in spite of the laudable attempt to equate the testing situations. The data do, however, show differences in the slope of the threshold-by-frequency functions. If these differences in slope are real (and not subject to the localization confounding mentioned above), then the results demonstrate a developmental change in threshold sensitivity. However, it remains unclear from these findings whether there is an improvement in low-frequency sensitivity or whether adults show a loss of high-frequency sensitivity after infancy (or both). As Nozza (1981) has pointed out, if one shifted the threshold functions of the infants relative to the adult function, the infants and adults would have nearly identical thresholds at the *lower* frequencies. Such a possibility (raised but rejected by Schneider et al. 1980) would imply that adults have suffered a high-frequency loss sometime after infancy. Data on hair cell loss in the basal cochlea during postnatal development (Bredberg, 1981) provide suggestive anatomical evidence in support of a high-frequency loss in adulthood. In addition, Saunders, Dolgin, and Lowry (1980) have shown in mice that improvements in midfrequency and high-frequency sensitivity between 12 and 24 days postnatally are followed by a significant high-frequency loss between 24 and 65 days postnatally. Although these data are from a different species and were obtained from recordings at the level of the cochlear nucleus, they raise the possibility that losses in high-frequency sensitivity are not without precedent in the mammalian auditory system. Thus, the interpretation offered by Trehub et al. (1980) and Schneider et al. (1980) regarding the development of frequency sensitivity should be evaluated with caution until further data have been collected to clarify the adults' performance at high frequencies.

Two more recent studies have provided additional data on auditory thresholds in 6- to 18-month-olds. Sinnott, Pisoni, and Aslin (in press) have reported thresholds for pure tones in 7- to 11-month-olds using the unidirectional head-turning procedure. An adaptive staircase algorithm was used to estimate thresholds (50% correct) at 250, 500, 1,000, 2,000, 4,000, and 8,000 Hz for both 0.5- and 1.0-sec. tones. Figure 13 illustrates the performance of an infant during the threshold procedure. As in the Trehub et al. (1980) study, Sinnott et al. (in press) found that adult thresholds, under testing conditions identical to those used with the infants, were flat

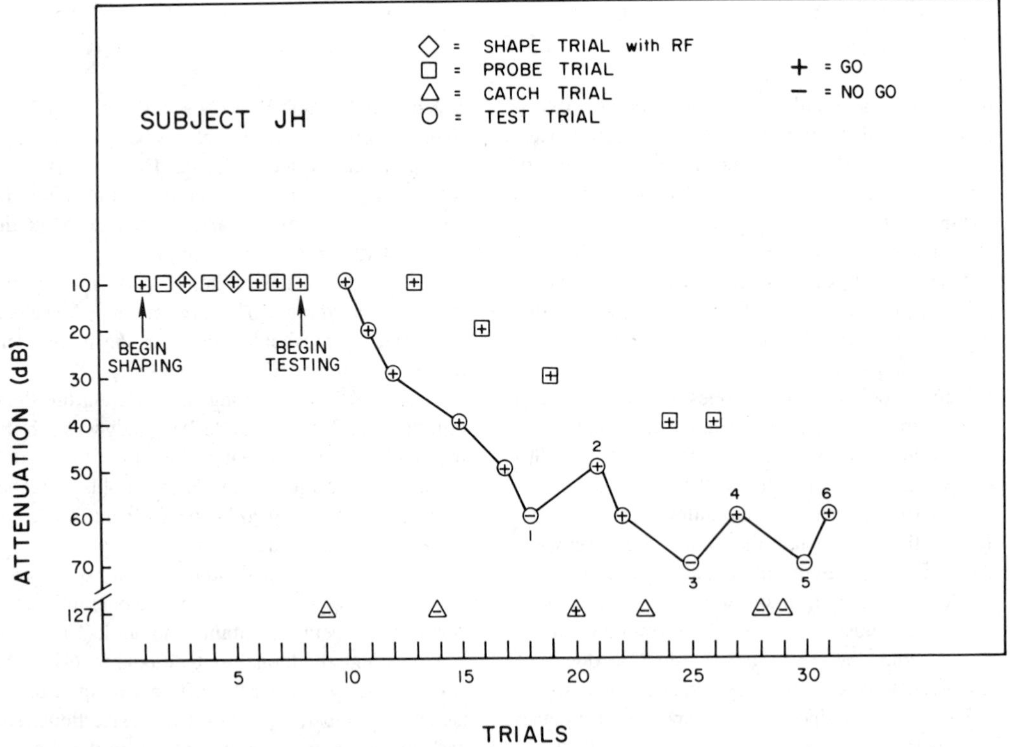

Figure 13. Trial-by-trial record of an experimental session from an infant tested with the unidirectional head-turning procedure using an adaptive staircase algorithm. (Reprinted from Sinnott, Pisoni, & Aslin, in press)

across the 0.5- to 8-kHz range of frequencies. Infant thresholds were between 17 and 27 dB higher than the adults' thresholds, and the lowest threshold (25 dB SPL) was at the highest frequency (8 kHz). Thus, there is some support for the Trehub et al. (1980) finding of a relatively greater sensitivity to high-frequency sounds among infants, despite the fact that Sinnott et al. (in press) used pure tones (rather than octave-band noises) and a unidirectional head-turning response (rather than a sound localization procedure).

In contrast to the Trehub et al. (1980) study, Sinnott et al. (in press) used the same threshold criterion (50% correct) for infants and adults. If Trehub et al. had used the same criterion for their infants and adults, their obtained infant thresholds would have been approximately 30 to 40 dB higher than adult thresholds. Thresholds obtained from the infants in the Sinnott et al. (in press) study were approximately 10 dB closer to the adult thresholds. This apparently greater sensitivity of the unidirectional (yes/no) head-turning procedure compared to the two-alternative (localization) head-turning procedure is particularly curious in light of a recent methodological study by Trehub, Schneider, and Bull (1981). They found that infants have *higher* thresholds if the window for making a response is decreased from an unlimited duration to 5 sec. This 5-sec. response window is approximately the duration used by Sinnott et al. (in press) and the unlimited response window was used in the Trehub et al. (1980) study. At the present time, the discrepancy in absolute threshold levels between these two studies remains unresolved.

Berg and Smith (in press) have also measured thresholds for pure tones (500, 2,000, and 8,000 Hz) in 6- to 18-month-olds. They used the unidirectional head-turning procedure and an adaptive staircase technique similar to the one used by Sinnott et al. (in press). Infants showed overall threshold estimates that were approximately 15 dB higher than adults tested under identical conditions. However, infants tested with headphones showed a relative insensitivity to the 8,000-Hz tone, whereas infants tested with loudspeakers (as in Sinnott et al., in press) showed equal threshold estimates at all three frequencies. Thus, in contrast to Trehub et al. (1980) and Schneider et al. (1980), Berg and Smith (in press) found no evidence for an increased sensitivity to high-frequency stimuli. It is unclear whether this difference is attributable to task differences (i.e., the use of a two-alternative forced-choice vs. a yes/no procedure) or some other variable.

In summary, evidence of developmental changes in auditory thresholds has been obtained largely by recent applications of visually reinforced head-turning techniques. These techniques have been restricted to infants older than the 5th postnatal month, thereby limiting conclusions about auditory development in the early postnatal period. Changes in thresholds appear to be evident between infancy and adulthood, but the absolute level of infants' sensitivity at various stimulus frequencies remains unclear. Studies that have shown infants to be relatively more sensitive than adults to high frequencies (above 4 kHz) may indicate that an improvement in low-frequency sensitivity occurs during early development or that a loss of high-frequency sensitivity occurs after infancy.

Masking

The presence of background noise during a threshold task can significantly reduce or mask the absolute level of auditory sensitivity. Masking studies with infants provide information not only about sound detection in noise but also about the frequency selectivity of the auditory system. If the signal is a pure tone presented in background noise, the frequency and band width of the noise will differentially affect detection of the signal. For example, a pure-tone signal will not be masked by noise unless the frequency of the pure tone overlaps the band width of the noise. In fact, two pure tones can mask each other if they are close in frequency (within the so-called critical band; see Scharf, 1970). If the critical band, which is approximately 1/3 octave in adults, were larger in infants, this would imply a deficit in detecting the individual frequency components of a complex (broadband) stimulus. Thus, masking studies with infants could provide important information concerning their ability to detect frequency-specific information (such as formants) within complex auditory signals (such as speech).

Hecox and Galambos (1974b) have examined the frequency selectivity of the ABR in newborns, older infants, and adults by presenting clicks embedded in broadband masking noise. Clicks have a very broad spectrum and, thus, impart motion along nearly the entire length of the basilar membrane. By altering the low-frequency cutoff of the masking noise, Hecox and Galambos were able to assess frequency-specific changes in ABR latency and amplitude to click stimuli. In newborns, there was little attenuation of ABR amplitude unless the broadband masker extended below 2,000 Hz. In 10-day-olds and 10-week-olds, this attenuation effect was present if the masker extended below 10,000 Hz. In addition, the attenuation effect in adults was present regardless of the low-frequency cutoff of the masker. These findings imply that the ABR is less dependent on high-frequency information during early postnatal development. Such a finding is consistent with Hecox's (1975) ABR threshold data in newborns that showed a very small latency shift with changes in click intensity. This latency-intensity relation is indicative of a high-frequency hearing loss in adults. However, it is also possible that the developmental changes in ABR frequency selectivity are unrelated to hearing thresholds but instead reflect a developmental change in the areas of the basilar membrane that contribute most strongly to the ABR response.

Although Hecox (1975) reported that newborns show little difference in the ABR to clicks presented at rates of 10/sec. versus 30/sec., Despland and Galambos (1980) have shown that the ABR is absent in premature infants if the click rate is higher than 40/sec. It is possible that each click in a series masks the preceding or following click. Recently, Lasky and Rupert (in press) have conducted a series of experiments on temporal masking of the ABR in newborns. To unconfound the influence of forward and backward masking in a train of clicks, they presented a broadband masker (up to 50 msec duration) either before or after a single click stimulus. The duration of the silent interval between the masker and the click was also varied. Little evidence of backward masking was obtained in either newborns or adults. However, a strong forward masking effect was present in both newborns and adults. Decreases in the masker-to-click interval increased the masking effect (longer ABR latencies). In addition, increases in masker duration affected ABR latencies to a greater extent in newborns than adults, whereas increases in masker intensity affected both newborn and adult ABR latencies equally. Thus, forward masking in newborns is qualitatively similar to masking in adults, but the temporal resolution of the ABR appears to improve markedly during the postnatal period. Finally, Lasky and Rupert (in press) found that newborns and adults show the same ABR latency decrease with increasing click intensity (40 μsec/dB). Thus, the greater forward masking effect found for newborns implies an approximately 10 dB greater attenuation of the click for newborns than adults when presented after an identical masking stimulus.

Bull, Schneider, and Trehub (1981) and Trehub, Bull, and Schneider (1981) have assessed masking of octave-band noise and speech stimuli respectively with the two-alternative head-turning procedure. In both studies, a continuous broadband masking stimulus was presented at one of two intensities (42 or 60 dB SPL) and the target signal was presented at one of five different intensities. Bull et al. (1981) used a 4,000 Hz target signal and Trehub, Bull, and Schneider (1981) used a tape-recorded speech segment containing the utterance "Hi there." Group psychometric functions for 6-, 12-, 18-, and 24-month-olds as well as adults were obtained and thresholds for both infants and adults were based on a 65% correct criterion. The 18 dB difference in the two masking levels resulted in a 18.6 dB increase in the infants' threshold for the 4,000-Hz octave-band noise and a 14 dB increase in the infants' threshold for the speech stimulus. Adults showed a 19 dB increase in threshold for the 4,000-Hz octave-band noise and a 17.25-dB threshold increase for a 4,000-Hz pure tone. These results were interpreted as evidence that infants may be more severely impaired than adults in detecting auditory signals in the natural environment where ambient noise levels are often greater than 60 dB SPL. However, in both of these studies the authors argued that absolute thresholds are unlikely to be similar in infants and adults. If for procedural or motivational reasons, thresholds were actually similar across this age range (6 months to adulthood), the effect of masking noise would be invariant. The primary contribution of these two studies was the documentation of a consistent relation in infants and adults between increases in masker intensity and increases in signal intensity at threshold. Any conclusions about the effects of environmental noise on infants' auditory processing must await further supporting evidence.

Further evidence for masking effects in infants and adults comes from a study by Nozza (1981). He used the unidirectional head-turning procedure with 6- and 12-month-olds and with adults. A broadband masking stimulus was presented continuously and target signals consisting of 1,000-Hz and 4,000-Hz pure tones were introduced through a single earphone. A staircase testing procedure was used to estimate thresholds (50% correct criterion). As in the Bull et al. (1981) and Trehub, Bull, and Schneider (1981) studies, the infants showed elevated thresholds compared to adults. However, the slope of the threshold functions for the two signal frequencies was constant for all three age groups. Thus, the relation between signal intensity and background noise appears to be constant during development despite developmental differences in the estimates of absolute threshold. Nozza (1981) also provided evidence for frequency selectivity by computing the critical ratios (signal intensity at masked threshold divided by spectrum level of the noise), an indirect estimate of the critical band. Although the infant's frequency selective mechanism varied in the same proportion as the adult's, the dependence of the critical ratio on absolute thresholds resulted in an estimated frequency selectivity that was much larger in infants than adults. Nozza argued that this developmental difference in critical ratios may be largely due to differences in nonsensory (task) variables. However, such a conclusion must await a more direct estimate of the critical band in infants and adults.

In summary, data from infants using both the ABR and head-turning procedures support the conclusion that a similar mechanism underlies masking in infants and adults. Thresholds are elevated in proportion to the increase in the intensity of the masking noise. Infants appear to require a greater absolute level of signal intensity compared to adults to detect a target embedded in a masking noise of constant intensity. However, the increase in signal intensity required by infants to detect the target is proportional to the estimates of infants' absolute thresholds. Thus, the mechanism underlying masking in infants and adults does not appear to vary developmentally. Estimates of frequency selectivity in infants indicate poorer resolution of individual frequency components within a complex auditory stimulus compared to adult frequency selectivity. However, these estimates are subject to alternative interpretations, including the greater dependence of infant threshold data on nonsensory factors (e.g., task difficulty and response criterion effects).

Intensity and Frequency Discrimination

Despite the importance of the ability to detect differences in the intensity and frequency of auditory signals, little psychophysical research on infants has actually been conducted. The absence of these developmental data is particularly surprising because discrimination of complex auditory signals, such as speech, may depend on the ability to resolve subtle differences in frequency and intensity. One of the few published studies of intensity discrimination is a report by Moffitt (1973) in which 6-month-olds were presented with a 500-Hz tone in a heart rate habituation-dishabituation paradigm. After six habituation trials during which the tone was presented at 75 dB SPL, a dishabituation trial was presented with the tone intensity increased to 85 dB SPL. A reliable increase in the magnitude of the heart rate response occurred on the dishabituation trial compared to a no-change control group. Thus, infants can discriminate a 10-dB increment in intensity, but their difference limen (DL) for intensity and any developmental changes in intensity resolution are unknown.

Currently, Sinnott, Aslin, and Pisoni (in preparation) are gathering intensity DLs from 7- to 12-month-olds using the unidirectional head-turning procedure. An adaptive staircase procedure is being used to estimate the smallest intensity increment (or decrement) required for reliable detection by the infants. Ten infants provided threshold estimates; DLs as low as 3 dB were obtained for a 1,000-Hz pure tone. Trehub and Schneider (in press) and Schneider and Trehub (in press) have also recently reported preliminary results on intensity increment thresholds using broadband noise signals. They have reported increment thresholds as low as 0.8 dB in 12-month-olds. Additional work in this area can be expected in the near future.

Data on frequency discrimination by infants are slightly more extensive than data on intensity discrimination. Early studies using gross motor and sucking responses provided conflicting evidence with respect to frequency discrimination. For example, Leventhal and Lipsitt (1964) recorded gross behavioral responses in newborns when a pure tone was changed from 200 to 500 Hz and from 200 to 1,000 Hz. No significant evidence of discrimination was obtained for either frequency difference. Wormith, Pankhurst, and Moffitt (1975) used the HAS procedure to assess discrimination of a 200- to 500-Hz frequency shift in 1-month-olds. In contrast to Leventhal and Lipsitt (1964), Wormith et al. (1975) found that this frequency difference was discriminated. Finally, Trehub (1973) used the HAS procedure to assess discrimination of a 100- to 200-Hz (square-wave) contrast, a 1,000- to 2,000-Hz (square-wave) contrast, and a 200- to 1,000-Hz (sine-wave) contrast. Contrary to the findings of Wormith et al. (1975), Trehub found no reliable evidence of frequency discrimination in her groups of 5- to 16-week-olds. Thus, data on frequency discrimination remain equivocal.

Olsho, Schoon, Sakai, Turpin, and Sperduto (1982) used the unidirectional head-turning procedure to assess frequency discrimination for pure tones in 5- to 8-month-olds. A repeating background tone of 1,000, 2,000, or 3,000 Hz was interrupted by the presentation of a target tone of a different frequency. The frequency difference between the target and background tones was initially set at 96 Hz and gradually decreased according to a staircase algorithm. Estimates of the minimum frequency difference between target and background required for discrimination (70% correct criterion) were quite variable, but in general infants reliably detected a 2% change in frequency. In contrast, adults detected frequency differences of 1% or less. Unfortunately, the DL data from individual infants at each of the three background frequencies were highly variable. Thus, the slope of the Weber function (Δ f/f) could not be compared between infants and adults. It remains unclear, therefore, whether infants show an overall improvement in frequency discrimination during development or whether nonsensory factors underlie the infant-adult differences.

In summary, data from infants on intensity and frequency discrimination are sparse. The few studies that have been published suggest that infants in the second 6 postnatal months are capable of making relatively good intensity (3 to 5 dB) and frequency (2%) discriminations. However, these two topics will require additional research to chart accurately the development of intensity and frequency discrimination abilities.

Sound Localization

Perception of the spatial position of sounds involves not only the detection of a sound's location with respect to an egocentric coordinate system (e.g., 10° to the right of midline) but also the resolution of small differences in spatial position. Only the most crude measurements of sound localization (right vs. left of midline) have been attempted with infants and no data have been gathered on the spatial resolution for sounds. The traditional view of sound localization (e.g., Chun, Pawsat, & Forster, 1960) has been that infants do not show body, head, or eye orientation to the locus of a sound source until the 4th or 5th postnatal month. However, Wertheimer (1961) reported that a newborn infant exhibited reliable ocular orientation to the right or left of midline when presented with a click stimulus. Two independent observers recorded these ocular movements to sound on 52 trials during the newborn's first 10 postnatal min. This brief report led many investigators to reevaluate the traditional view that young infants cannot localize sounds, particularly because Wertheimer's neonatal subject was born without obstetrical medication (a relatively uncommon occurrence prior to the 1970s).

Criticisms of the Wertheimer study centered on the fact that the observers of the newborn's ocular behavior were aware of the direction of the sound source. Subsequent replication attempts (Butterworth & Castillo, 1976; McGurk, Turnure, & Creighton, 1977) failed to find evidence of ocular orientation to an off-midline sound. However, other studies using different stimuli and response measures (e.g., Alegria & Noirot, 1978; Leventhal & Lipsitt, 1964; Turkewitz, Birch, Moreau, Levy, & Cornwell, 1966; Turner & MacFarlane, 1978) have reported reliable responses in newborns to right-left differences in sound location.

In the past few years, several reports have provided convincing evidence of sound localization in newborns (e.g., Clifton, Morrongiello, Kulig, & Dowd, 1981b; Field, Muir, Pilon, Sinclair, & Dodwell, 1980; Mendelson & Haith, 1976; Muir & Field, 1979; see reviews by Clifton et al., 1981a; Muir, Abraham, Forbes, & Harris, 1979). In the Muir and Field (1979) study, 2- to 4-day-olds were presented with a tape-recorded rattle sound from one of two loudspeakers located 90° on either side of the newborn's midline. Experimental trials consisted of a 20-sec. presentation of the stimulus from one of the two loudspeakers; control trials consisted of a 20-sec. silent interval. Videotapes of the behavioral responses of the newborns were later scored by two independent observers who were unaware of the type of trial (sound or silence) or the location of the sound source. The newborns reliably oriented toward the location of the sound by making a correct lateral head turn on 74% of the experimental trials (17% error rate, 9% no-response rate). In contrast, on control trials, the newborns showed a high no-response rate (40%) as well as a bias for rightward head turns (43% vs. 17% to the left). Response latencies were very long, averaging 2.5 sec., and the head-turn response was sluggish (latency to complete the head turn averaged nearly 6 sec.). In a study of prematurely born infants (32 to 37 weeks postconception), Muir, Campbell, Low, Killen, Galbraith, and Karchmar (1978) found that sound localization occurred at a rate of 87% correct, but response latencies were approximately 12 sec. Thus, past failures to observe reliable orientation toward sounds in newborns may have resulted from expectations of shorter response latencies as well as the failure to allow the infants to turn their heads easily (a problem overcome in more recent studies by having an experimenter support the head while holding the infant in a supine position). The results of these two studies, therefore, provide good evidence that newborns exhibit reliable orientation toward the location of a lateral sound source.

A follow-up study by Field et al. (1980) tested sound localization in newborns and 1-, 2-, and 3-month-olds using procedures similar to those used by Muir and Field (1979). Side-appropriate head turns were present on 80% of the trials for infants in all age groups except the 2-month-olds, whose performance was approximately 55% correct. This decline in performance at 2 months was puzzling in light of data from Field, DiFranco, and Dodwell (1979) who found that 2½-month-olds localized a voice stimulus on approximately 75% of the trials. To clarify this discrepancy, Muir et al. (1979) conducted a longitudinal assessment of sound localization with four infants who were tested repeatedly between birth and 4 months of age. The infants showed a consistent decline in performance from nearly 100% correct shortly after birth to 50% correct or less during the period from 40 to 100 days after birth. Between 100 and 120 days after birth, however, localization recovered to nearly 100% correct. Muir et al. (1979) also tested three of the infants in total darkness, using an infrared video camera, to determine if visual information may have distracted the infants during the postnatal period when sound localization performance declined. No differences in sound localization were found under these two conditions (lighted room vs. darkness). Thus, the temporary decrement in head orientation to sounds appears to be reliable and not based on a temporary period of visual distraction. The discrepancy between the Field et al. (1979) and Muir et al. (1979) studies results from 2½-month-olds appears to reside in the lateral extent of the loudspeaker locations from midline (45° vs. 90° respectively).

The findings of reliable head orientation to sound in newborns and a temporary decrement in these responses during the second and third postnatal months have been replicated by Clifton et al. (1981a, 1981b). In a procedure nearly identical to the one used by Muir and Field (1979), Clifton et al. (1981b) found that newborns reliably oriented toward the location of a tape-recorded rattle sound (58% response rate, 95% correct). Control trials on which the sound was presented simultaneously from both loudspeakers resulted in few head turns (16% response rate). In a study of 5- to 6-month-olds, Clifton et al. (1981a) found evidence of reliable sound localization to a stimulus consisting of clicks presented at a rate of 5/sec., whereas 6- to 9-week-olds did not show reliable evidence of sound localization.

In a follow-up study, Morrongiello, Clifton, and Kulig (1982) examined sound localization in newborns and 5-month-olds to determine whether the frequency characteristics of the stimulus influenced orienting performance. The original broadband rattle stimulus as well as filtered versions of this stimulus were presented to each infant. The filtered stimuli consisted of low frequencies (less than 1,600 Hz), midfrequencies (1,000 to 3,000 Hz), and high frequencies (above 1,800 Hz). Both newborns and 5-month-olds showed more frequent head turns toward the sound source if it contained high frequencies. Thus, for newborns, the percentage of correct head turns increased from the low-pass to the mid-range to the high-pass stimulus, and the original broadband rattle stimulus was equivalent in effectiveness to the high-pass stimulus. The 5-month-olds showed the same pattern of results, except that the low-pass and mid-range stimuli did not differ from each other in eliciting the head-turning response. These results imply that sounds containing frequencies above 1,800 Hz are more effective in eliciting a head-turning response. Morrongiello et al. also recorded heart rate changes to the presentation of the four stimuli during the localization task. Despite the differential head-turning performance as a function of stimulus frequency, however, reliable heart rate changes were shown for all stimuli and no differences were found as a function of frequency.

Clifton et al. (1981a, 1981b) have also investigated the ability of newborns and older infants to localize a sound based solely on interaural time-of-arrival differences. If identical sounds are presented from two laterally positioned loudspeakers but one sound precedes the other by several msec, adults report that the sound appears to have originated from the loudspeaker that presented the leading sound. This auditory illusion is called the precedence effect. If the delay between sound onsets is small, only a single centrally located sound will be perceived; if the delay is long (e.g., 50 msec or longer), two discrete sound onsets will be perceived. Clifton et al. (1981a) showed that 5- to 6-month-olds reliably localized a precedence-effect stimulus (7-msec delay) and that the performance on these trials was identical to performance on trials in which the sound was presented only from a single loudspeaker. However, in a study of newborns, Clifton et al. (1981b) found no evidence that precedence-effect stimuli were localized, despite strong evidence for localization of sounds presented from a single loudspeaker. In fact, the newborns responded to the precedence-effect stimulus in a manner nearly identical to that shown on control trials in which there was no delay in the onset of a sound presented from both loudspeakers. A study of 6- to 9-week-olds indicated that the temporal onset asynchrony was detected but no reliable head-turning responses were observed. Bundy (1980) has also reported that 16-week-olds, but not 8-week-olds, can detect interaural time-of-arrival differences. Based on these developmental differences, Clifton et al. (1981a, 1981b) suggested that binaural information in brief auditory stimuli (or stimuli with rapid onsets) may require processing by cortical areas of the auditory system, which may not be fully developed in newborns. This suggestion awaits further empirical evidence to eliminate simpler explanations based on developmental changes in temporal processing and auditory-motor coordination.

In summary, recent data on auditory localization in infants provide evidence for abilities previously believed to be present only in much older infants. Newborns are able to orient their heads reliably toward the location of a sound, at least in a simple two-choice (right-left) task. However, this spontaneous head-turning response declines in frequency of occurrence during the 2nd and 3rd postnatal months. In the 4th postnatal month, orientation to sounds reappears as a robust response, but it is more subject to habituation effects. Finally, in the presence of a visual reinforcer, the head-turning response toward a sound can be maintained for a large number of trials (Moore et al., 1975; Trehub, Schneider, & Bull, 1981).

These recent findings on auditory localization in infants have not addressed the precise mechanisms underlying this ability or their susceptibility to the effects of early experience. Studies of auditory localization in developing cats (Clements & Kelly, 1978b) and guinea pigs (Clements & Kelly, 1978a) have demonstrated that (1) orienting responses (locomotion) toward a sound emerge at different postnatal ages in different species, (2) the absence of binaural information impairs localization behavior, and (3) monaural blockage during the early postnatal period impairs subsequent localization behavior despite removal of the ear blockage. Thus, it is possible that effective sound localization is dependent upon the absence of early binaural imbalances. These findings are of great importance to an understanding of sound localization in human infants, particularly because selective deprivation experiments cannot be conducted on humans. Further use of animal models will undoubtedly assist in clarifying the developmental processes and mechanisms that underlie human auditory function.

DEVELOPMENT OF SPEECH PERCEPTION IN INFANCY

Background on Adult Speech Perception

The study of speech perception in infants has been motivated largely by empirical findings and theoretical issues from the area of adult speech perception. A number of advances in speech analysis and synthesis occurred shortly after World War II, primarily as a result of the development of the sound spectrograph and the pattern playback. Researchers at Haskins Laboratories took advantage of these technological developments and, in the 1950s and 1960s, conducted a wide variety of studies of adults' perception and production of speech. These studies led to a view of speech perception that formed the basis for the majority of adult and infant speech perception studies in the 1960s and 1970s. In the following discussion, we first review several of the major findings from these early studies of adult speech perception and production because they provide the background for subsequent research on infant speech perception. We will then review several recent findings that challenge traditional views of adult speech perception, particularly those that have important implications for speech perception studies on infants.

Linguistic Structure of Speech

Theorists have assumed that speech perception entails several stages of processing, including acoustic, phonetic, and phonological as well as syntactic, semantic, and pragmatic levels of analysis. In the normal course of linguistic communication, we are typically conscious only of the words and sentences spoken to us and not of the speech sounds themselves. Except under special circumstances, such as listening to a foreign accent, a speech synthesizer, or a child's first words, we do not separate the perception of speech as an acoustic event from its subsequent linguistic interpretation as a series of meaningful words and sentences. For the most part, the earliest stages of speech perception appear to be carried out almost automatically, that is, without the conscious awareness or control of the listener.

Because most of our awareness of spoken language is based primarily on meanings and not on sounds, it is important for researchers to consider some of the aspects of the sound structure of language—specifically, the functional categories (phonemes) that have been developed in linguistic science. Research on adult and infant speech perception has generally assumed that phonemes form the basic objects of perception and, as a consequence, most experimental work has been guided by this assumption.

Although the speech signal that impinges upon the ear of the listener varies more or less continuously as a function of time, the adult listener perceives an utterance as consisting of a sequence of discrete segments. The segments that the listener perceives are based on the functional sound categories of the language community—the phonemes. A phoneme is usually considered to be the smallest unit of speech that signals a difference in meaning between two linguistic forms. However, the phoneme is actually an abstract concept because it does not represent a unique instance of a sound (i.e., a phonetic segment or phone) but instead refers to a derived or abstract class of sounds that function in similar ways in a given language.

To illustrate how the phonemic principle works, consider the differences between the words *bin* and *pin*. At the lowest level of linguistic analysis, the phonetic level, the first segment of each word is different. The difference lies both in the articulation of the sound and in its acoustic properties. Because the phonetic difference between these sounds serves to distinguish different linguistic forms in English, these segments are considered to be members of different classes of phonemes, /b/ and /p/. Thus, the phonetic differences between [b] and [pʰ] are retained at a more abstract level, the phonological level, where linguistically significant information is represented.

The situation is, however, somewhat more complicated in the case of sound segments that are phonetically different but do not serve to contrast different linguistic forms in a specific language. For example, in English, the initial stop consonant in *pin* ([pʰ]) is phonetically aspirated (i.e., it is produced with a brief puff of air when the lips are released), whereas the stop consonant in *spin* ([p]) has no aspiration. At the phonetic level, the two *p*'s are represented as distinct phonetic segments ([pʰ] and [p]); they are produced differently and are, therefore, acoustically distinct. At the phonological level, however, the two sounds are considered to be allophones or variants of the same phoneme category /p/. This is true because the feature of aspiration that distinguishes these two sound segments does not serve to contrast linguistic forms in English. In some languages, such as Thai, the feature of aspiration does serve to contrast forms, and, in such cases, the two phonetic segments [pʰ] and [p] represent functionally different phonemes.

The symbol /p/ in the preceding example has no unique phonetic status itself; it simply stands for a class of sounds having related properties. Some members of the class are in complementary distribution, that is, phonetic segments occur in contexts in which other segments do not appear. For example, the [kʰ] in *keep* is produced further forward in the vocal cavity than the [kʰ] in *coop* and this difference is predictable in terms of the properties of the following vowel. Members of a particular class of phonemes also have similar articulatory and acoustic attributes. For example, the two *k* sounds referred to above are both voiceless velar stop consonants, even though they have slightly different places of articulation.

Thus, there are two distinct levels of linguistic representation, a phonetic level and a phonological level. The phonological representation is assumed to be more abstract than the phonetic representation. Segments that differ at the phonetic level may be treated as functionally the same at the phonological level, depending on whether the allophonic variations serve a distinctive function in the particular language. However, the distinction between phonetic and phonological levels has little importance for naive adult listeners who typically perceive speech in terms of the phonological categories (i.e., the phonemes) of their language. They often fail to perceive subtle differences at the phonetic level.

It should be noted that even the description of speech at a phonetic level is not regarded as a true representation of the physical events associated with speech. A phonetic transcription is neither a physical description of the speech signal produced by the vocal tract nor a detailed specification of the resultant acoustic signal. The speech signal transcribed by a phonetician has undergone a great deal of abstraction and categorization before being represented as a sequence of discrete phonetic segments and features.

Acoustic Structure of Speech Signals

Speech signals have numerous distinctive acoustic properties or attributes that are used in the earliest stages of perceptual analysis. In this section, we will briefly consider some aspects of the way speech is produced by the vocal apparatus because the articulatory system constrains the types of acoustic signals produced by the vocal tract. The basic principles of sound production and acoustic filtering that are carried out in the human vocal tract are now understood in considerable detail (Fant, 1960; Flanagan, 1972; Stevens & House, 1956). The human vocal tract may be thought of as an acoustic tube of varying cross-sectional area that extends from the glottis to the lips. The upper right-hand panel of Figure 14 shows a midsagittal outline of the vocal tract during the production of a neutral vowel. An additional tube, the nasal tract, can be connected to the system by lowering the soft palate (velum) as in the production of nasal and nasal-like sounds.

The overall shape of the vocal tract can be changed very rapidly by varying the position of the lips, jaw, tongue, and velum. The cross-sectional area of the vocal tract can be varied from complete closure, as in the production of a stop consonant (e.g., [p]), to about 20 cm^2, as in the production of an open vowel (e.g., [a]). When the velum is lowered, the nasal tract is also excited and this excitation produces changes in the spectral properties of the radiated sound output.

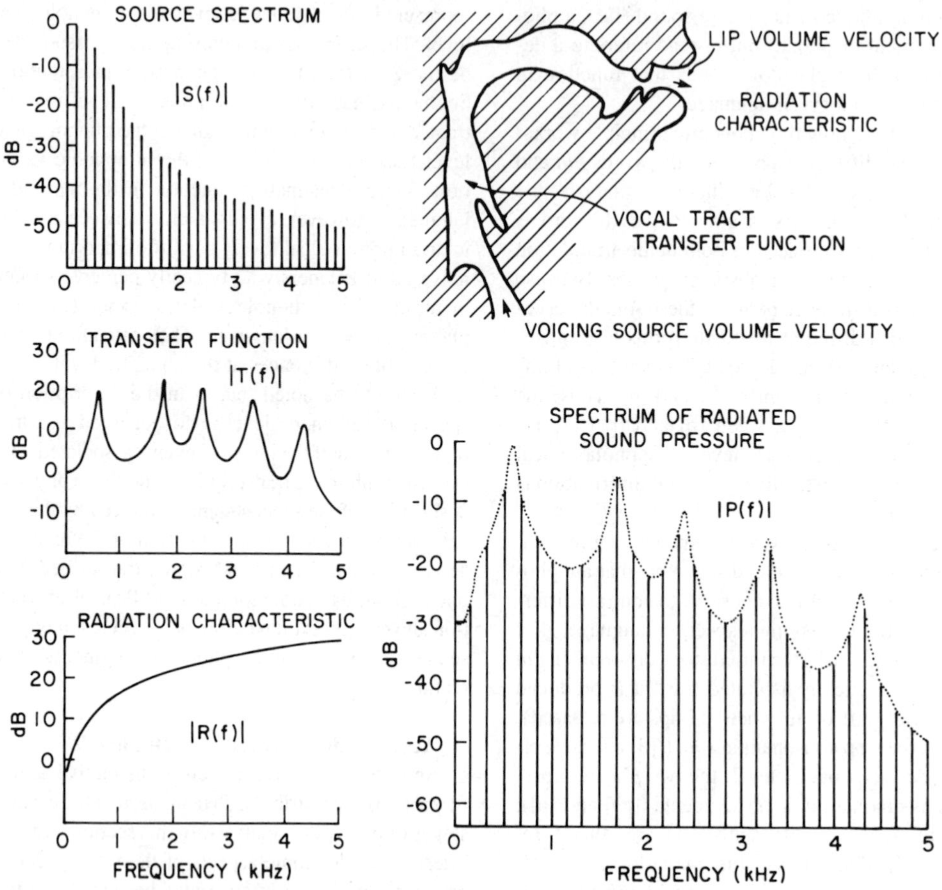

Figure 14. Contribution of source spectrum, vocal-tract transfer function, and radiation characteristic to the spectrum envelope of the radiated sound pressure. (Courtesy of Dr. Dennis Klatt; reprinted from Pisoni, 1978)

Sound is generated in the vocal tract by either forcing air through the glottis (i.e., the space between the vocal folds) to produce a quasiperiodic sound source (voicing) or by creating a noisy turbulence in the vicinity of a constriction in the vocal tract. Both sound sources can be used to excite the vocal tract above the larynx. For some sounds, like nonnasalized vowels, there is a direct acoustic transmission path between the glottis and the lips, whereas for other sounds, such as nasals, there are significant side branches in the transmission path that introduce changes in the distribution of spectral energy.

The vocal system acts as a time-varying filter with resonant properties that influence the sound waves generated in the vocal tract. The sound pressure radiated from the lips may be thought of simply as the product of the source spectrum S(f), the vocal tract transfer function T(f), and the radiation characteristic of the vocal tract R(f). The power spectrum of the radiated sound pressure P(f) is given by the following equation:

$$P(f) = S(f) \times T(f) \times R(f)$$

Each of these components is shown separately in the left-hand column of Figure 14. The spectrum envelope, P(f), of the radiated sound pressure, which displays the relative distribution of energy at different frequencies, is shown in the bottom right-hand corner of the figure. As shown here, the speech production mechanism consists of two relatively independent components: (1) mechanisms that contribute primarily to the generation of sound energy (i.e., the source) and (2) mechanisms that function to modify the sound energy (i.e., the filter).

For a periodic sound, such as a vowel, the sound source consists of a line spectrum with components at multiples of the fundamental frequency (|S(f)| in Fig. 14). The amplitude of these components is attenuated by about 12 dB per octave at high frequencies. When the vocal tract is excited by this voicing source, it acts as a filter to reinforce some frequencies and to attenuate others. The vocal tract transfer function shown in the middle panel on the left of Figure 14 can be characterized by a number of natural resonant frequencies or formants that change as the vocal tract changes from one articulatory position to another. As a consequence, the radiated sound output reflects the natural resonant frequencies that are favored by the system. These formant frequencies appear as peaks in the power spectrum. Finally, the radiation characteristic reflects the relation between acoustic volume velocity at the mouth opening and sound pressure at some distance from the lips. This effect occurs primarily at low frequencies: The slope of the spectrum envelope of the radiated sound pressure drops by about 6 dB/octave as shown in the lower right-hand panel of Figure 14. This reduces the intensity differences between low and high frequency harmonics originally displayed in |S(f)|.

In summary, the vocal tract acts as a linear, time-varying filter that imposes its transmission properties on the frequency spectra of the sound sources generated in the vocal tract. As the vocal tract changes its shape during the production of different sounds, the properties of the transfer function change, as does the spectrum of the sound output.

Some Attributes of Speech Sounds

One traditional approach to the description of speech sounds has been to classify them in terms of the degree of vocal tract constriction employed in their production. At one extreme are the vowels and vowel-like sounds that are produced with a relatively unconstricted vocal tract. Liquids, glides, and fricatives have intermediate constrictions, whereas stop consonants represent the other extreme with complete closure of the vocal tract at some point of articulation. Figure 15 shows midsagittal outlines of X-ray tracings of vocal tract shapes for the vowels [i], [a], and [u]. These tracings show the cross-sectional area of the vocal tract as a function of distance from the glottis (i.e., area functions) and their respective spectrum envelopes. When the tongue body is high and fronted as in [i], the oral cavity is relatively constricted, whereas when the tongue is low, as in [a] and [u], the oral cavity is relatively large. In contrast, the pharyngeal cavity is relatively large for [i] and [u] but more constricted for [a]. The cross-sectional area functions of the vocal tract, as shown in the middle panel of Figure 15, reflect these differences in position of the tongue body and degree of constriction in the vocal tract. The effect of these variations in vocal tract shape on the spectra of the sound output is shown by the differences in the corresponding spectrum envelopes on the far right of Figure 15.

The frequency of the first formant (F1) is low for [i] and [u], reflecting, in part, the relatively large pharyngeal cavity compared to [a], where F1 is high. On the other hand, the frequency of the second formant (F2) is high for [i] due to the narrow oral cavity and is low for [u] as a result of lip rounding, which increases the overall length of the oral cavity. Although a simple relation exists between formant frequency and cavity affiliation for the point vowels [i], [a], and [u], it is not possible to associate a particular formant frequency with a specific cavity resonance for all vowels (see Fant, 1960, for further discussion). Nevertheless, vowels are produced with a relatively unconstricted vocal tract that generates sounds with well-defined formant structures. From acoustic analysis and synthesis experiments, researchers have found that the relative positions of the lowest two or three formant frequencies are sufficient to distinguish different vowels in both production and perception (see Delattre, Liberman, Cooper, & Gerstman, 1952; Peterson & Barney, 1952; Stevens & House, 1956).

In contrast to vowels, the production of consonants is characterized by a highly constricted or even occluded vocal tract. Consider, for example, the production of a fricative sound (e.g., [f]) in which there is a turbulent noise source generated at the point of constriction. The spectrum of this noise source is continuous; that is, energy is distributed across all frequencies rather than being restricted to only harmonics of the fundamental, as is the case for a voiced sound, such as a vowel. The spectrum of the radiated sound output for a fricative sound is the product of the source function and the vocal tract transfer function as in the case of vowels. However, the sound source for fricatives is located above the glottis. Thus, the sound output is influenced not only by structures above the source, but also, to a lesser extent, by structures below the sound source as well as the specific properties of the constriction itself. Differences in the production of fricatives are reflected in the relative frequency of noise, its bandwidth, and its overall intensity. These attributes have been shown to be important perceptual cues for different fricative sounds (Delattre, Liberman, & Cooper, 1955; Harris, 1958; Heinz & Stevens, 1961; Stevens, 1960).

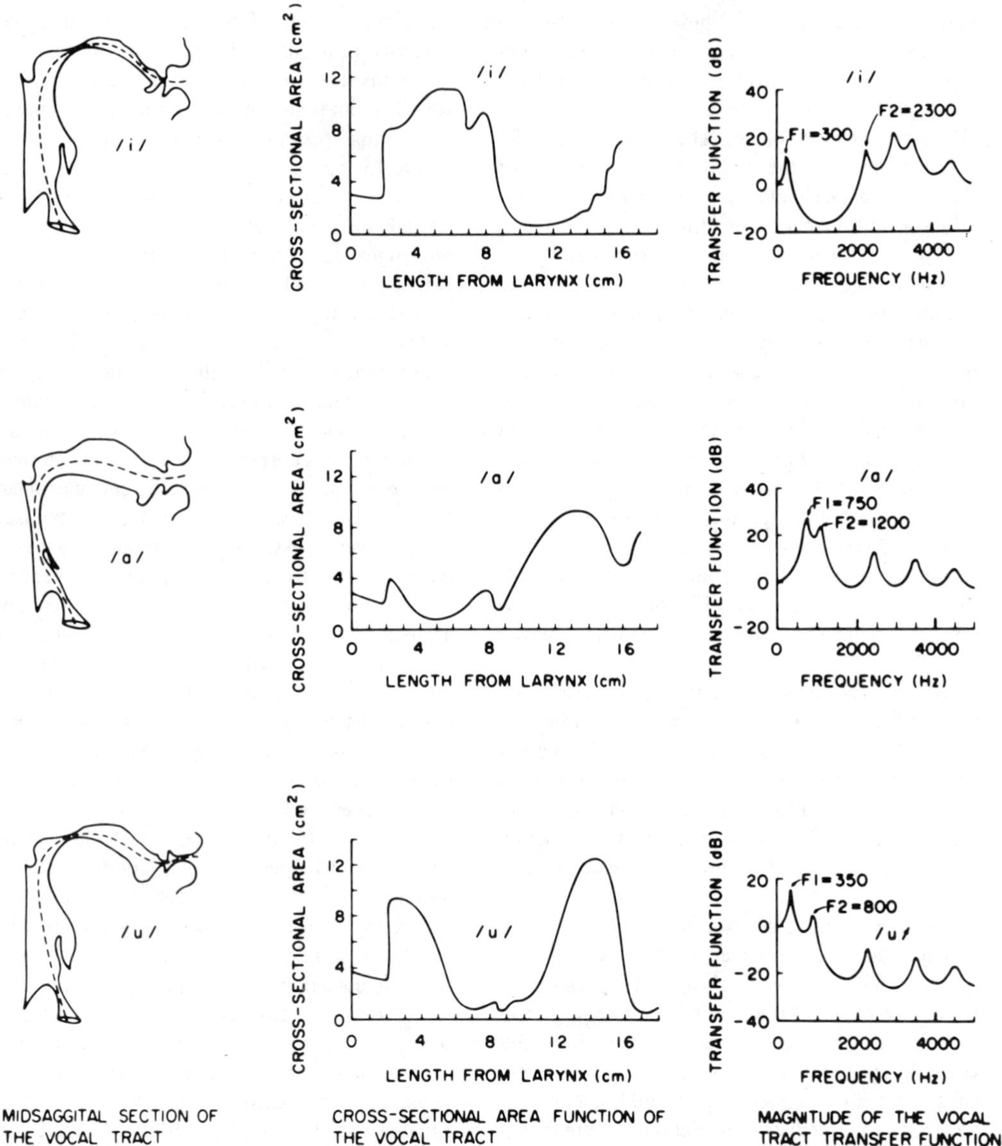

Figure 15. Illustrations of the outline shape of midsagittal sections of the vocal tract, cross-sectional area functions, and the corresponding vocal-tract transfer functions for the vowels [i], [a], and [u]. (From Lieberman, Crelin, & Klatt, 1972; reproduced by permission of the American Anthropological Association)

The production of stop consonants, liquids, and glides is characterized by total or virtual closure of the vocal tract, followed by a more abrupt opening (or release). During closure, no sound is produced and air pressure builds up behind the point of closure in the vocal tract. At the release of an initial stop, for example, there is an abrupt change in the shape of the vocal tract that results in a rapid spectral change over a very brief period of time as the articulators move toward the position appropriate for the next sound. These rapid formant transitions systematically affect the rate of frequency change and the position of the formant frequencies in terms of the place and type of closure (see Liberman, Delattre, Gerstman, & Cooper, 1956; Stevens & House, 1956). Differences in place of articulation among the stop and nasal consonants are cued primarily by the direction and extent of the second and third formant transitions. The liquids [r] and [l] are differentiated from stops primarily by relatively slow formant transitions into the following vowel. The segment [r] differs from [l] in terms of the direction of the third formant transition. The glides [w] and [j] are distinguished from stops in terms of both duration and rate of change of the transitions of the first two formants. These transitions are longer and usually slower for the glides than for the stops. Glides and stops are perceptually distinguished by the duration and extent of the formant transitions (Schwab, Sawusch, & Nusbaum, 1981).

Voicing distinctions among consonants have received a great deal of attention in the recent speech perception literature. For consonants in final position, voicing can be cued by the duration of the preceding vowel (Denes, 1955; Raphael, 1972). The duration of articulatory closure has been shown to cue voicing differences between stops in intervocalic (medial) position (Lisker, 1957). Voice onset time (VOT), a complex articulatory timing dimension, has been shown to characterize the voicing distinctions between stop consonants in syllable initial position (i.e., [b, d, g] vs. [p, t, k]; Lisker & Abramson, 1964). Acoustically, VOT involves simultaneous changes in the relative onset of voiced excitation, the amplitude of the F1 transition, and the presence of aspiration in the higher formants during this time period.

The acoustical structure of speech can be examined by considering a broadband sound spectrogram of an utterance, such as the one shown in Figure 16. Typically, time is represented on the abscissa and frequency on the ordinate. The relative concentration of energy at each frequency is shown by the degree of darkness on the trace. The horizontal bars represent concentrations of energy that occur at the natural resonant frequencies (formants) of the vocal tract. These dark bands can most easily be seen in the lower frequency regions of a spectrographic representation of vowel and vowel-like sounds. The closely spaced repetitive striations that occur during vowels and other voiced sounds reflect the presence of individual pulses of air passing through the glottis (i.e., glottal pulses), whereas the more randomly structured portions of the spectrogram reflect the presence of turbulence or noise.

An inspection of Figure 16 reveals the presence of numerous discrete acoustic segments in the sound spectrogram. However, these acoustic segments do not always correspond in any simple way to the phonetic segments that result from perceptual analysis, nor do they correspond to linguistic units, such as morphemes or words. Thus, from this analysis, it has become quite clear to many investigators that, at the acoustic level, speech sounds are not represented discretely in time like beads on a string or bricks in a wall. Instead, successive speech sounds appear to be merged together or encoded with each other in a complex way. The nature of this encoding for any particular speech segment is dependent upon the context in which the phoneme occurs. This context dependency in the perception of phonetic segments reflects the interaction between successive articulatory movements in speech production. The production of speech may be thought of as consisting of a sequence of maneuvers from one idealized articulatory position or target to another. During fluent, con-

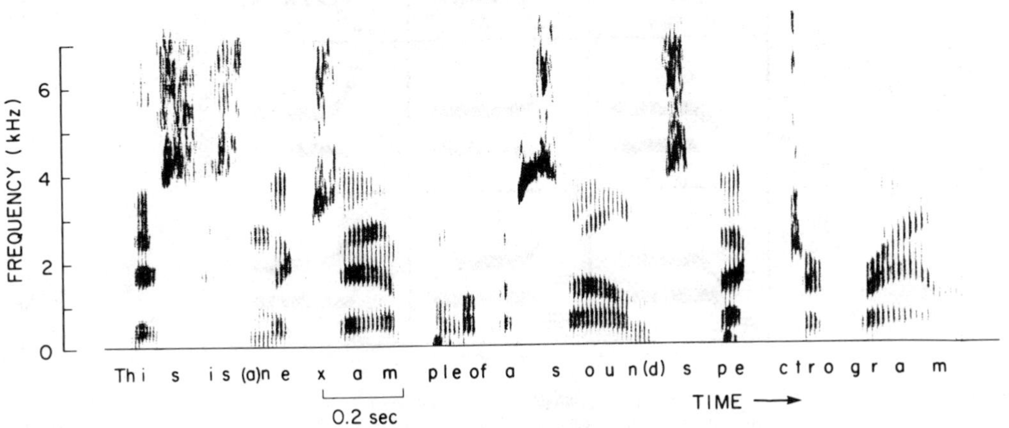

Figure 16. Broadband spectrogram of the utterance: "This is an example of a sound spectrogram."

nected speech, the articulatory apparatus frequently moves so rapidly from one position to another that the target positions are often not fully reached. Thus, there is undershooting of the ideal articulatory configurations. Moreover, the production of new target configurations is often initiated and executed before the previous target has actually been fully reached.

The complexity of coarticulation effects in speech production is mirrored in the relation between a phoneme and the physical signal. This relation is, however, becoming more clearly understood as additional studies of speech analysis and synthesis are conducted. For example, some idea of the relation between acoustic cues and phonemic structure can be seen in Figure 17, which shows stylized acoustic patterns for nine consonants followed by the vowel [a]. When converted to sound on the Pattern Playback synthesizer (Cooper, Liberman, & Borst, 1951), these patterns produce reasonably intelligible approximations of the intended syllables. As shown in Figure 17, the acoustic cues that distinguish place, manner, and voicing among these consonants show a systematic relation when the vowel is the same in each syllable. In these examples, place of articulation is cued primarily by differences in the direction and extent of the F2 transition. Stops are distinguished from nasals by the presence of a low-frequency nasal resonance. The voicing differences between [b, d, g] and [p, t, k] are distinguished by the relative onset of F1 to F2.

The situation is, however, substantially more complicated when the vowel context of the syllable changes. As shown in the middle panel of Figure 18, the acoustic cues for a particular consonant, for example, the [d] segments, vary and are coarticulated with the following vowel. As a consequence, it has been extremely difficult to find a simple invariant acoustic attribute that corresponds uniquely to the same stop consonant in all vowel environments (Cooper, Delattre, Liberman, Borst, & Gerstman, 1952). The results of early synthesis experiments with two-formant patterns failed to establish acoustic invariants for the various places of articulation in stop consonants (see Liberman, Cooper, Shankweiler, & Studdert-Kennedy, 1967, for a review and interpretation of these early studies).

One should not conclude from these results that there are no invariant acoustic attributes for stop consonants in natural speech. Instead, a more reasonable conclusion, given our current knowledge, is that the invariant attributes are unlikely to be found in terms of relatively simple acoustic properties as displayed in the sound spectrogram. Recent work employing more sophisticated methods of analysis has demonstrated that there are general properties of the acoustic signal that may uniquely specify a particular place of articulation in stop consonants independent of vowel context (Kewley-Port, 1980; Stevens & Blumstein, 1978). The extent to which invariant, context independent acoustic cues to

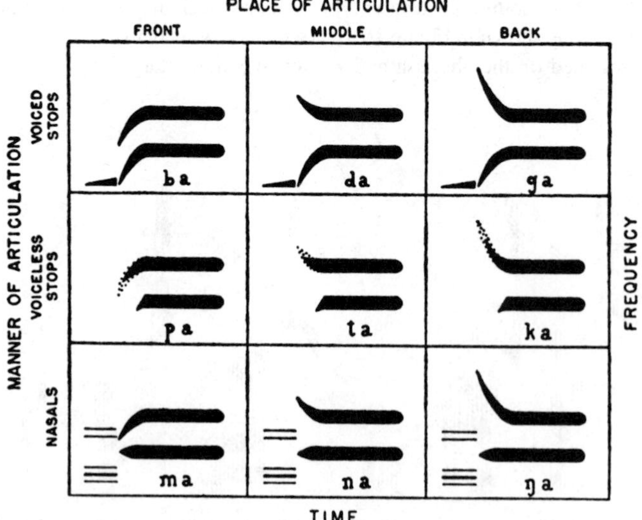

Figure 17. Schematized sound spectrograms for nine consonant-vowel syllables illustrating the acoustic cues for place, manner, and voicing. (Reprinted from Liberman, Ingeman, Lisker, Delattre, & Cooper, 1959)

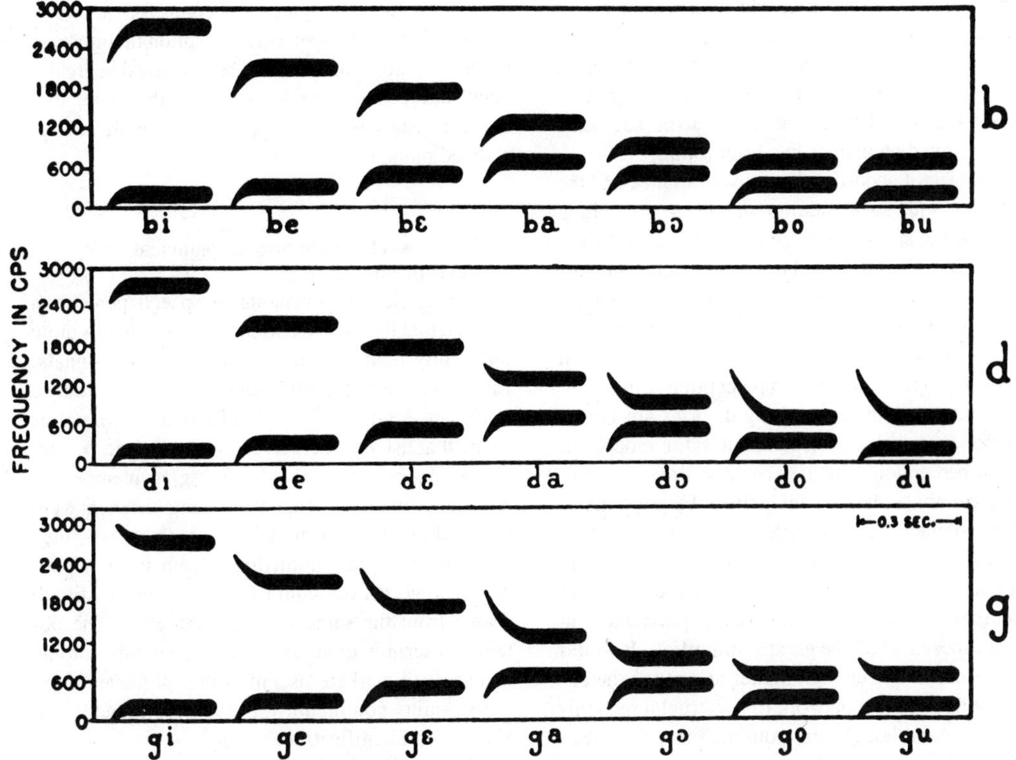

Figure 18. Schematized sound spectrograms showing the formant transitions that are appropriate for the voiced stop consonants [b], [d], and [g] before various vowels. (Reprinted from Delattre, Liberman, & Cooper, 1955)

phonemes can be identified in the speech signal has been a topic of some controversy in both the adult and infant speech perception literature (see Chapin, Tseng, & Lieberman, 1982). Because of the importance of this issue, we will consider it again in greater detail later (*Sensory and Interpretive Coding of Speech Signals*).

Linearity, Invariance, and Segmentation

One of the most important problems in the field of speech perception is that the speech signal fails to meet what Chomsky and Miller (1963) referred to as the conditions of linearity and invariance. The *linearity condition* states that for each phoneme there must be a particular stretch of sound in the utterance such that if phoneme *X* is to the left of phoneme *Y* in the phonemic representation, the stretch of sound associated with *X* must precede the stretch of sound associated with *Y*. The *invariance condition* states that for each phoneme *X* there must be a specific set of criterial acoustic attributes or features associated with it in all contexts. These features must be present whenever *X* or some variant of *X* occurs *and* they must be absent whenever some other phoneme occurs in the representation.

As noted earlier, it has been extremely difficult to identify acoustic segments or features that match the perceived phonemes independently of context. As a result of various coarticulation phenomena in speech production, there is a great deal of acoustic variability brought about by the surrounding phonetic environment and the overlapping articulatory gestures. Often a single acoustic segment contains information about several neighboring linguistic segments; thus, the signal fails to meet the linearity condition. Conversely, the same linguistic segment is often represented acoustically in quite different ways, depending on the phonetic context, rate of speaking, and individual talker and, thus, fails to meet the invariance condition.

Because of the failure to meet the linearity and invariance conditions, investigators have found it difficult to generate a set of rules for segmenting speech into acoustically defined units that are independent of adjacent segments. Although some segmentation is possible according to strictly acoustic criteria (see Fant, 1962), the number of acoustic segments is typically greater than the number of phonemes in the utterance. Moreover, no simple invariant mapping between these acoustic segments and perceived phonemes has been found.

The lack of acoustic-phonetic invariance and the problems with segmentation suggested something unique about speech as an acoustic stimulus (Liberman, 1957). Certainly, relations between segments of the acoustic signal and units of linguistic analysis are complex, and this, in turn, places certain constraints on the classes of perceptual theories that might be proposed for speech perception. For example, filter or template-matching theories are generally believed to be poor candidates for models of speech perception primarily because linguistic segments cannot be defined exclusively by physical attributes of the acoustic signal. As Chomsky and Miller (1963) remarked, if both the invariance and linearity conditions were met, the task of building machines capable of recognizing phonemes in human speech would be greatly simplified. It would surely be a simple enough matter to arrange the appropriate filters in a network to construct a recognition device. Although numerous attempts have been made along these lines in the past, the results have generally been unsuccessful because of the inherent variability of the physical signal. It is, therefore, not at all surprising that passive theories of speech recognition involving template matching and filtering are considered to be poor candidates for models of human speech perception, particularly models of fluent or continuous speech processing (Cole, 1980).

To deal with the contextual variability of phonemes and the complex relation between acoustic signal and phonetic segment, investigators have proposed perceptual models based on specialized feature detectors. It was originally assumed that these complex phonetic feature detectors processed quite diverse acoustic inputs equivalently. Thus, this approach provided one way to avoid the invariance and segmentation problems. However, as we discuss later, the results of selective adaptation studies indicate that, if there are feature detectors, they are quite sensitive to a number of contextual variables. Moreover, most of the evidence provided in support of specific phonetic feature detectors is weak and subject to alternative acoustically based interpretations (Pisoni & Tash, 1975; Sawusch & Jusczyk, 1981). Because it seems unlikely that young infants employ higher level linguistic information in speech processing, such feature detector approaches have become popular in trying to account for the major findings in the infant speech perception literature. A number of these findings will be discussed in greater detail later, after we review one of the major theoretical issues in adult speech perception: a specialized mode of perception.

The Speech Mode and Categorical Perception

The earliest experiments in speech perception showed that listeners respond to speech signals quite differently than they do to other auditory signals. Liberman and his colleagues (Liberman, Harris, Hoffman, & Griffith, 1957) at Haskins Laboratories found that listeners perceived synthetic speech stimuli varying between [b], [d], and [g] as members of discrete categories. When these same listeners were required to discriminate pairs of these sounds, they could discriminate stimuli drawn from different phonetic categories but could not discriminate stimuli drawn from the same phonetic category. The obtained discrimination functions were nonmonotonic and showed marked discontinuities at places along the stimulus continuum that were correlated with changes in identification.

The ideal case of this form of perception, what has become known in the literature as categorical perception, is illustrated in Figure 19. In an experiment such as the one described above, two or more stimuli from different phonemic categories are selected to represent endpoints and a continuum of synthetic stimuli is generated to span these categories. Subjects are required to carry out two tasks: identification and discrimination. In the identification task, stimuli are selected from the continuum and presented one at a time in random order for labeling into categories defined by the experimenter. In the discrimination task, pairs of stimuli are selected from the continuum and presented to listeners for some discriminative response.

The typical finding in a categorical perception experiment is that listeners can discriminate two speech sounds that are identified as belonging to different phonemic categories in their language much better than they can discriminate two stimuli that are identified as the same phoneme, even though the acoustic (i.e., physical) differences between the two stimulus pairs are equivalent. This kind of result was considered by Liberman et al. (1957) and others at the time to be quite unusual in light of the discrimination results obtained in most psychophysical experiments with nonspeech stimuli. In general, nonspeech stimuli that vary along a single physical

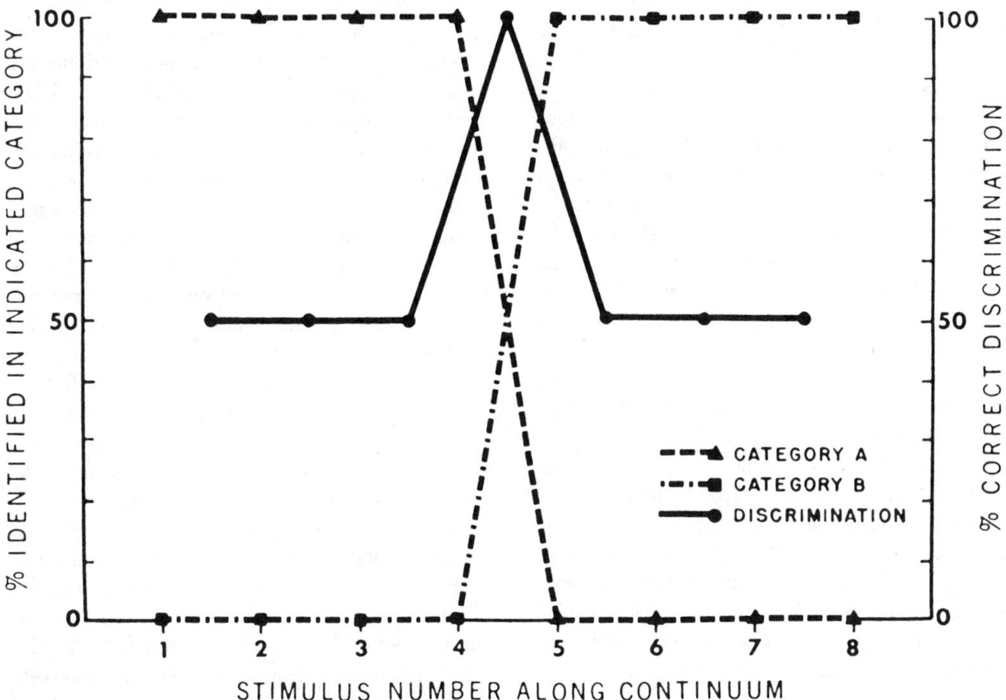

Figure 19. Idealized form of categorical perception showing the identification function (left ordinate) and the ABX discrimination function (right ordinate). (Reprinted from Studdert-Kennedy, Liberman, Harris, & Cooper, 1970; copyright 1970 by the American Psychological Association)

dimension are perceived continuously, that is, discrimination functions are typically monotonic with the physical scale. As is well known, there are capacity limitations on absolute identification by human adults (Miller, 1956). In experimental tests listeners can discriminate many more acoustic stimuli than they can identify in absolute terms (Pollack, 1952, 1953). However, in the case of categorical perception of speech, the situation is quite different—discrimination appears to be no better than absolute identification. In the extreme case of categorical perception, discrimination performance can be predicted from the identification function under the strong assumption that the listener can discriminate two stimuli only to the extent that these stimuli are identified as different on an absolute basis (Liberman et al., 1957).

These initial perceptual findings with stop consonants led to a similar experiment with synthetic vowels that varied in acoustically equal steps through the range [i], [I], and [ɛ]. Fry, Abramson, Eimas, and Liberman (1962) reported that, like nonspeech signals, these stimuli are perceived continuously. The discrimination functions did not show discontinuities that were related to category boundaries along the stimulus continuum, but instead showed that they were relatively flat (i.e., monotonic) across the entire continuum. Moreover, it was observed that the synthetic vowels used in this experiment were, in general, more discriminable than stop consonants, indicating that listeners could perceive many more intraphonemic differences.

The differences in perception between stop consonants and steady-state vowels have been assumed to reflect two different modes of perception, a categorical mode and a continuous mode. Categorical perception reflects a mode of perception in which each acoustic pattern is *always* and *only* perceived as a token of a particular phonetic type (Studdert-Kennedy, 1974). Listeners can discriminate between two different acoustic patterns if the stimuli have been categorized into different phonetic categories, but they cannot discriminate two different acoustic patterns that have been categorized into the same phonetic category. Information about the acoustic properties of these stimuli appears to be unavailable for purely auditory judgments as a consequence of phonetic classification. What remains available to the decision process is a more abstract and permanent code resulting from the listener's interpretation or coding of the stimulus event (see Pisoni, 1971, 1973; Pisoni & Tash, 1974).

In contrast to categorical perception, continuous perception may be thought of as reflecting an auditory mode of perception in which discrimination is independent of category assignment. Although listeners can assign acoustically different stimuli to the same category, they may still discriminate between tokens selected from the same category. Thus, an auditory, nonphonetic basis for discrimination is available to the listener.

For a number of years, the categorical perception results were assumed to be unique to speech perception and primarily a consequence of phonetic categorization. Indeed, the differences in perception between consonants and vowels led Liberman (1970a, 1970b) to argue strongly for a specialized mode of perception, a speech mode, to characterize the way in which these stimuli are perceived. Other findings suggested that a specialized perceptual mechanism, a special speech decoder, may exist for processing speech sounds (Studdert-Kennedy & Shankweiler, 1970).

In addition to the proposal that there are two modes of speech perception (categorical and continuous), the differences in perception between consonants and vowels were also interpreted as support for the motor theory of speech perception (Liberman, Cooper, Harris, & MacNeilage, 1963). According to the strong version of motor theory, articulatory processes are assumed to mediate recognition of the incoming acoustic signal. As discussed earlier, stop consonants are produced in a discontinuous way by a constriction at a particular place in the vocal tract, whereas vowels are produced by continuous changes in the overall shape of the vocal tract. The strong version of the motor theory assumed that although the appropriate acoustic cues for consonants could be described by an acoustic continuum, these stimuli are perceived discontinuously (i.e., categorically) because the articulations underlying the production of these sounds are essentially discontinuous. In contrast, vowels are perceived continuously because their production entails continuous changes in the articulators from one position to another. Although the original accounts of the motor theory (Liberman, 1957; Liberman et al., 1963) assumed that articulatory movements themselves and their sensory effects mediated perception, more recent versions of the theory (Liberman et al., 1967; Studdert-Kennedy, 1974) have placed the articulatory reference at the level of the neuromotor commands.

The major reason for proposing a motor theory of speech perception was to provide a solution to the absence of invariance between acoustic attribute and perceived phoneme. According to Liberman (1957), there is a simpler relation between articulation and perception than between acoustic information and perception. At the time, it was claimed that the articulatory movements and motor commands for a particular phoneme showed less contextual variability than the resultant acoustic manifestation of the phoneme. However, research on the electromyography of speech production has not borne out this assumption (MacNeilage, 1963).

The notion that categorical perception reflects a mode of perception that is unique to speech and the claims associated with the motor theory have come under strong criticism from a number of directions over the last few years. Several investigators have argued that the differences in perception between consonants and vowels reflect differences in the psychophysical properties of the acoustic information that distinguishes these two classes of speech sounds (Lane, 1965; Pisoni, 1971; Studdert-Kennedy, 1974). For the stop consonants, there is a relatively complex relation between a phoneme and its sound representation; the essential acoustic cues are contained in the rapidly changing spectrum at onset (i.e., the release burst and formant transitions), which is weak, relatively brief in duration (30 to 50 msec), and transient in nature. In contrast, the cues to the vowels involve changes in the steady-state frequencies of the first three formants, which have a relatively long duration and more uniform spectral properties as well as greater intensity in comparison to consonants. As support for this, Fujisaki and Kawashima (1969, 1970) and Pisoni (1971, 1975) have shown that the differences in perception between consonants and vowels are due, in part, to the duration of the acoustic cues. Vowels of very short duration (i.e., 40 to 50 msec) are perceived more categorically than identical signals having longer durations (Pisoni, 1975).

Other findings indicate that categorical perception is also due, in part, to limitations on the encoding processes in short-term memory that result from the particular type of discrimination task that is used (Pisoni, 1971, 1973, 1975). The ABX procedure was used in almost all of the early speech perception experiments that demonstrated categorical perception. In this task, the subject is presented with three sounds successively, ABA or ABB. A and B are always acoustically different and the subject has to indicate whether the third sound in the triad (X) is identical to the first or second sound. This is basically a recognition memory paradigm. To solve the discrimination task, the subject is forced to encode individual stimuli in temporal succession and then base the decision on the encoded representations in short-term memory. In a number of experiments, Pisoni (1971, 1973) has shown that differences between categorical and continuous modes of perception are strongly dependent on the short-term memory requirements of the particular discrimination procedure and the level of stimulus encoding required to perform the task.

Several recent experiments employing *non*-speech stimuli have also demonstrated that categorical perception may not be peculiar to speech sounds or to a specialized speech mode, but it may be a more general property of perceptual and cognitive processes that involve categorization and coding of complex stimulus inputs (see Bruner, 1957; see also *Perception of Nonspeech Signals by Adults and Infants*). These recent studies have shown that categorical perception of both speech and complex nonspeech signals can be accounted for, in part, by the presence of well-defined psychophysical boundaries that separate stimuli into distinctive perceptual categories and by the use of perceptual codes or labels that can be used to encode these stimulus attributes into short-term memory. This revised account of categorical perception, therefore, involves two distinct components, a sensory component and a labeling or interpretative component. Early explanations of categorical perception stressed only the labeling component (Liberman et al., 1967). If categorical perception were based only on verbal labels and encoding processes in short-term memory, as Fujisaki and Kawashima (1969, 1970) and Massaro (1976) have argued, we would expect to find comparable categorical-like discrimination functions for vowels and other steady-state signals that can be labeled easily and consistently. However, the available evidence indicates that although labeling and coding may account for some aspects of vowel discrimination, particularly the results obtained with very short vowels, they cannot account for all of the relevant findings. For example, comparable categorical-like ABX discrimination functions have been obtained for stop consonants and nonspeech signals in the absence of specific labeling instructions (Miller, Wier, Pastore, Kelly, & Dooling, 1976; Pisoni, 1977; Sachs & Grant, 1976). Although it is possible to argue that subjects did use correct verbal labels for the speech stimuli in this task, it seems unlikely that they could have used them with the nonspeech signals because marked discontinuities were also found in the shape of the discrimination functions. Thus, the discrimination findings with nonspeech signals provide support for a sensory component to categorical perception that consists of a psychophysically based notch or discontinuity in the stimulus continuum at the category boundary. Similar interpretations of the infant discrimination data for speech and nonspeech signals have been proposed recently, and these interpretations are discussed more fully later (see *Perception of Nonspeech Signals by Adults and Infants*).

Despite the evidence for a sensory component to categorical perception, it should be pointed out that the category boundaries for phonetic features are not inherently fixed perceptual thresholds because there are differences in the location of these boundaries that are also a function of the linguistic experience of the listener. Indeed, as Popper (1972) has suggested, "people who speak different languages may tune their auditory systems differently" (p. 218). Cross-language research with adults has shown, in fact, that the categorizations imposed on synthetic test stimuli are based on both the acoustic attributes of the stimuli and the linguistic experience of the listener. To take one example, Abramson and Lisker (1970) generated a continuum of synthetic stimuli varying in VOT between [da] and [t^ha] and presented them in a labeling task to listeners from three different language backgrounds. The labeling functions for English, Thai, and Spanish subjects are displayed in Figure 20. As shown, these listeners categorized the same synthetic stimuli in quite different ways depending on the phonological structure of their native language. The phoneme boundaries are not only located at different positions along the continuum in each case but the Thai subjects also show additional perceptual categories. This result was expected because in Thai a phonological distinction is made between the voiceless aspirated stop [t^h] and the voiceless unaspirated stop [t]. This phonetic difference is not realized phonologically in either English or Spanish and consequently fails to play a role in the listener's identification and discrimination. The phonological systems of different languages, therefore, make use of the acoustic distinctions that exist between different speech sounds in quite different ways. Cross-language studies of VOT have also been carried out with young prelinguistic infants in an attempt to determine the effects of linguistic experience on speech perception. These developmental studies, which were motivated by the earlier Lisker and Abramson results (1964, 1970), will be discussed in greater detail later (see *Cross-language Studies of Infant Speech Perception* and *Role of Experience in the Development of Speech Perception*).

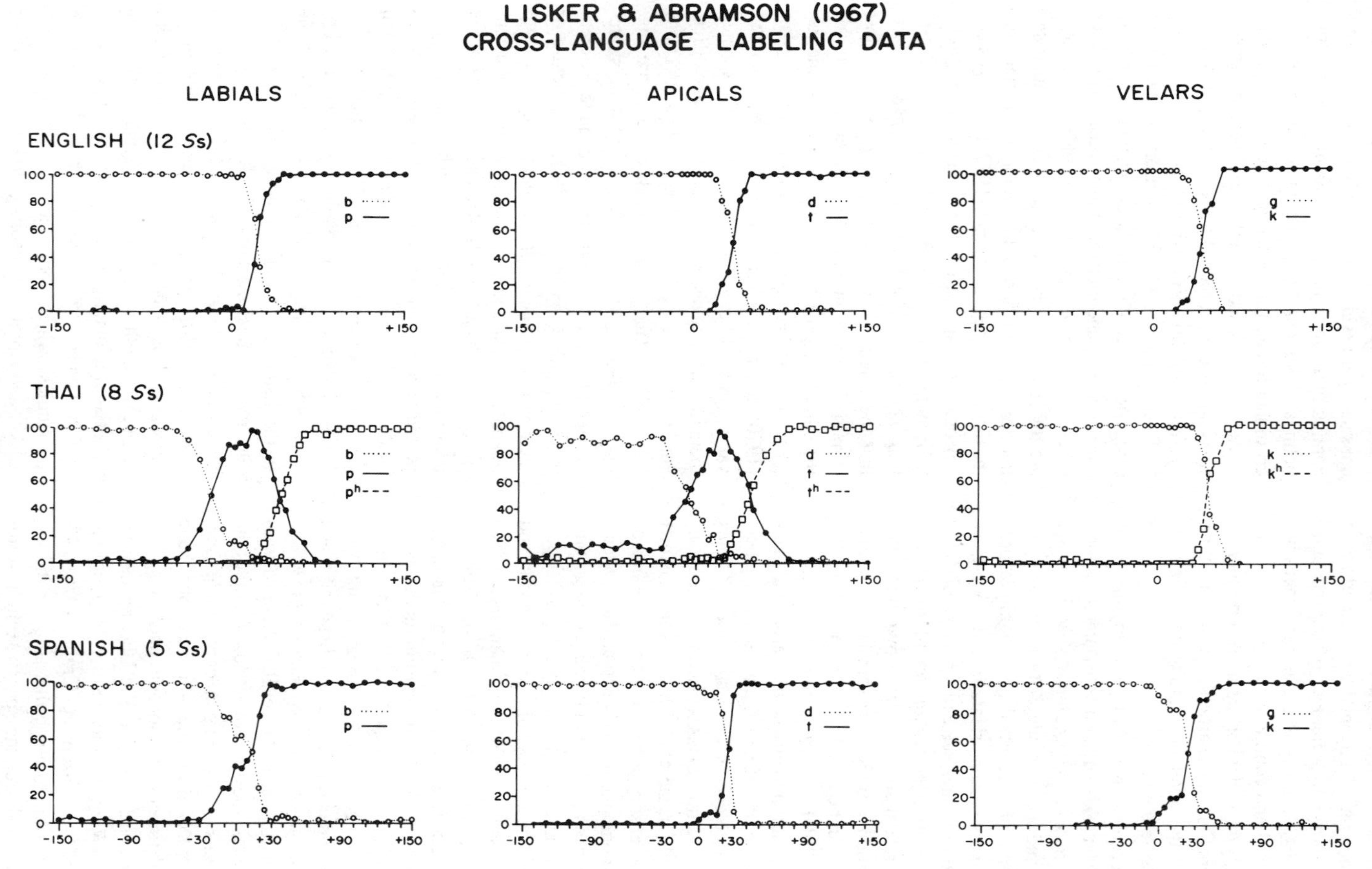

Figure 20. Adult cross-language labeling functions for synthetic labial, apical, and velar stop consonants varying in VOT obtained from native speakers of English, Thai, and Spanish. (Redrawn from Lisker & Abramson, 1970)

Feature Detectors in Speech Perception

To explain the results of the categorical-like discrimination performance shown by infants (see *Place of Articulation in Stop Consonants*), Eimas (1974) proposed that speech perception may be based on sets of feature detectors that are finely tuned to restricted ranges of acoustic information in the speech signal. This particular idea did not originate with Eimas. Several other investigators earlier suggested the possibility that some sort of feature-detecting mechanism might be involved in speech perception (e.g., see Abbs & Sussman, 1971; Liberman et al., 1967; Lieberman, 1970; Stevens, 1972; Whitfield, 1965). However, it was Eimas and Corbit (1973) who introduced an experimental paradigm, selective adaptation, that revealed the operation of these hypothesized detectors (see Cooper, 1979, for a recent review). In selective adaptation, the repeated presentation of a stimulus alters the perception of a set of test stimuli. For example, in their initial study, Eimas and Corbit (1973) investigated the voicing feature and showed that adaptation with the syllable [ba] caused the locus of the phonetic category boundary between [ba] and [pʰa] to shift toward the [ba] end of the continuum. Stimuli near the boundary, which were identified as [ba] when the listener was in an unadapted state, were subsequently labeled as [pʰa] after adaptation with [ba]. Similar findings were obtained when [pʰa] was used as the adaptor; that is, the locus of the phonetic boundary shifted toward the [pʰa] end of the stimulus continuum. Eimas and Corbit also showed that these results were not specific to the syllables or phonetic segments in the test series but were due instead to adaptation to a specific attribute or feature in the consonants. This conclusion was based on the results of cross-series tests in which adaptation to the voiceless bilabial stop [pʰa] produced approximately equivalent shifts in the identification functions for a series of alveolar stop consonants (i.e., [d] and [tʰ]) as it did for the bilabial stop series (i.e., [b] and [pʰ]). In both cases, the locus of the phonetic boundary shifted toward the voiceless end of the continuum. These results are shown in Figure 21 for one of the subjects in the Eimas and Corbit study.

In another experiment, Eimas and Corbit (1973) showed that the peak in the discrimination function also shifted after adaptation, suggesting that the shifts in the labeling function were not due simply to a response bias introduced by changing the stimulus probabilities. Furthermore, Eimas, Cooper, and Corbit (1973) showed that the adaptation effects were not mediated solely by the peripheral auditory system because presentation of the adaptor and test stimuli to different ears still produced large and reliable shifts in the locus of the phonetic boundary (see also Sawusch, 1977a, 1977b).

At the time, Eimas and Corbit (1973) and Eimas et al. (1973) argued that the selective adaptation results provided convincing support for the existence of detectors specialized for processing phonetic features rather than the acoustic attributes that form the basis for these phonetic distinctions. However, their original conclusions have been shown to be incorrect because more recent work has demonstrated that adaptation effects in speech perception are related more to the spectral similarity between test series and adaptor than to phonetic similarity (see Bailey, 1975; Cooper & Blumstein, 1974; Pisoni & Tash, 1975; Tartter & Eimas, 1975). One of the questions currently under investigation is whether the selective adaptation results are due to fatigue of mechanisms that process the acoustic attributes of speech stimuli, their more abstract phonetic features, or both (see Eimas & Miller, 1978; Sawusch & Jusczyk, 1981). The specific details of the arguments are intricate and need not concern us here. The importance of the adaptation work is that it demonstrates that the perceptual system responds to certain acoustic attributes of speech signals and that these attributes are precisely those that underlie distinctions between phonetic segments.

As we will see later, one of the intriguing questions that infant speech perception work has raised concerns the extent to which environmental input determines the development and sensitivity of these hypothesized feature detectors. There is an extensive literature on the role of early experience in the development of the visual system that indicates that early environmental experience can modify the selectivity of cortical cells in kittens (see recent reviews in Aslin, Alberts, and Petersen, 1981; Freeman, 1979; Movshon & Van Sluyters, 1981). The analogy between this developmental work and the data on infant speech perception has already been drawn by Eimas (1978) who argued that the lack of experience with specific phonetic contrasts in the local environment during language acquisition modifies the appropriate detectors by reducing their sensitivity. Some detectors originally sensitive to certain phonetic distinctions may be captured or subsumed by other detectors after exposure to specific acoustic stimuli from the linguistic environment. The nonspecific detectors might, therefore, assume the specificity for only those attributes present in the stimuli to which they are exposed. Although such an account appears intriguing at first glance, the available data suggest that the develop-

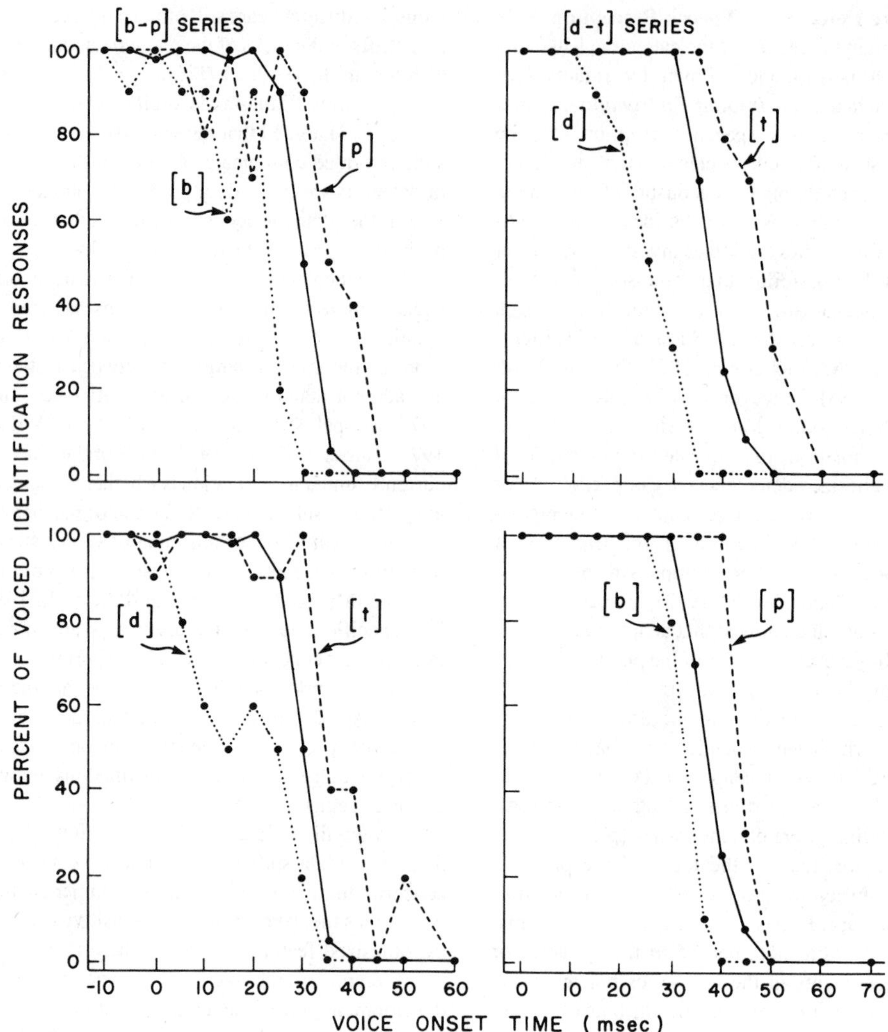

Figure 21. Identification functions obtained with and without adaptation for a single subject. The functions for the [b-p] series are shown on the left; the ones for the [d-t] series are on the right. The lower two functions in each panel show the results of cross-series adaptation when the adaptor was selected from a different test series. In each panel, the solid lines show the unadapted identification functions, the dotted and dashed lines show the functions obtained after adaptation. (Reprinted from Eimas & Corbit, 1973)

mental course of speech perception in infants is substantially more complicated than originally assumed by the early workers in this field (see Aslin & Pisoni, 1980b; Jusczyk, 1981, 1982; MacKain, 1982; Walley, Pisoni, & Aslin, 1981).

Discrimination of Speech Sounds by Infants

The primary question of interest to the early researchers of infant speech perception (see *Critical Issues in Auditory Development*) was whether young infants are capable of discriminating the various acoustic parameters that differentiate speech signals. When these studies were initiated in the late 1960s, there was still considerable doubt concerning precisely how the capacity for discriminating speech sounds arose. A view held by some researchers studying adults maintained that speech perception capacities developed out of experiences that infants had in listening to their own productions of speech sounds (Fry, 1966; Liberman, 1957). Although it is possible that babbling may play an important role in sharpening or tuning the infant's discriminative capacities, it is clear that young infants are capable of speech sound discrimination well before they begin producing any recognizable speech sounds on their own. This discussion provides an overview of research directed at defining the extent of infants' capacities for discriminating different kinds of phonetic contrasts. Three basic questions are discussed: (1) the age of onset for speech discrimination, (2) the change in sensitivity to speech contrasts with age and/or listening experience, and (3) the mechanisms underlying speech discrimination.

Voicing Distinctions Between Stop Consonants

The most extensively studied set of speech contrasts has been those involving differences in voicing. In particular, the bulk of the research has centered around the infant's ability to discriminate differences in VOT. Studies of the VOT cue have been popular with researchers of infants primarily because an extensive literature exists for adults' perception of this cue (e.g., Liberman, Harris, Kinney, & Lane, 1961; Lisker & Abramson, 1970). Moreover, because the research with adults indicated that VOT was perceived categorically, the question naturally arose as to whether young infants also perceive these stimuli in a categorical manner.

The pioneering study in this area by Eimas, Siqueland, Jusczyk, and Vigorito (1971) examined 1- and 4-month-olds' perception of VOT differences in synthetic speech tokens of the syllables /ba/ and /pa/. The objective of this study was twofold. First, Eimas et al. wished to find out if infants had any capacity at all for discriminating differences in VOT. Second, they sought to determine whether infants, like adults, showed any tendency toward categorical discrimination of VOT. To address these questions, Eimas et al. employed the HAS procedure and examined performance with several different VOT pairs. The two stimuli in each pair differed from each other by 20 msec of VOT. One pair contained stimuli selected from different VOT categories based on the judgments of English-speaking adults (i.e., +20 msec /ba/ vs. +40 msec /pa/) and the other pairs contained stimuli selected from within the same VOT category (i.e., −20 msec /ba/ vs. 0 msec /ba/ or +60 msec /pa/ vs. +80 msec /pa/). The results of the study by Eimas et al. showed that both 1- and 4-month-olds discriminated the between-categories pair (+20/+40) but that neither age group discriminated the within-categories pairs (−20/0 or +60/+80).

On the basis of these results, Eimas et al. (1971) drew the following conclusions: (1) the mechanisms underlying the infant's discrimination of VOT differences may well be part of the biological makeup of the organism (i.e., they are presumably innate), (2) the infants perceived the sounds in a manner approximating categorical perception by adults, and (3) the findings suggested perception in a linguistic mode. The third conclusion is the one that has proven the most controversial. It was based upon the finding that infants' discrimination of VOT differences was, like adults, categorical and upon the assumption that categorical perception is unique to speech sounds. Despite the fact that the latter assumption has been shown to be questionable, this study demonstrated a number of important phenomena and single-handedly established the field of infant speech perception. Eimas and his colleagues succeeded in demonstrating that infants as young as 1 month have the perceptual capacity to discriminate speech syllables differing solely in VOT and, more important, that this capacity is constrained so that not all VOT differences are equally discriminable. Instead, the VOT difference that the infants detected was precisely the one that crossed the phonemic category boundary for English-speaking adults.

The finding by Eimas et al. (1971) that infants are sensitive to a distinction between voiced and voiceless stop consonants has been replicated on a number of occasions. For example, Trehub and Rabinovitch (1972) found that infants discriminated a voiced/voiceless distinction between [d] and [t] as well as between [b] and [p]. However, because they used natural speech tokens, it is likely that other cues besides VOT helped to mark the voiced/voiceless distinction. In a subsequent study, Eimas (1975b) used synthetic speech syllables and found that infants discriminated a 50 msec VOT difference that crossed the phonemic boundary between /d/ and /t/. However, the infants did not show evidence of discriminating VOT differences of the same magnitude between syllables chosen from within the same phonemic category (e.g., /da$_1$/ vs. /da$_2$/). Thus, Eimas extended his earlier findings by demonstrating that VOT differences in the vicinity of the voiced/voiceless boundary are discriminated categorically for apical stops [d, t] as well as for labial stops [b, p].

In summary, several studies of the perception of VOT have demonstrated that shortly after birth infants are capable of discriminating certain speech contrasts. Furthermore, in at least one important respect (viz., categorical discrimination of VOT information in the region of the English voiced/voiceless boundary), infants' discrimination capacity appears to be comparable to that of adults. However, the mechanism underlying this VOT discrimination ability remains unclear. The two alternative explanations (phonetic and acoustic) are still competing for empirical confirmation (see *Mechanisms Underlying Infant Speech Perception*).

Place of Articulation in Stop Consonants

Another major focus of early research with infants has been on the perception of information relating to place of articulation in consonants. Evidence gained from research on the perception of place information by adult subjects has long played a critical role in shaping theories of speech perception. As we already noted, early investigations suggested that invariant acoustic cues do not exist for the perception of place of articulation in stop consonants (e.g., Liberman et al., 1967). More recent attempts to identify invariant features for the perception of stop consonants have reexamined various acoustic correlates that may underlie the perception of differences in place of articulation (cf. Kewley-Port, 1980; Searle, Jacobson, & Rayment, 1979; Stevens & Blumstein, 1978). Hence, information concerning the infant's ability to discriminate differences in place of articulation might be expected to play a critical role in any theory of the development of speech perception.

The first reported study of infants' discrimination of syllables differing in place of articulation was conducted by Moffitt (1971). He employed the heart rate dishabituation measure to assess the ability of 5-month-olds to discriminate differences between synthetic tokens of [ba] and [ga]. He found evidence of significant changes in heart rate following a change from one speech syllable to the other and concluded that the infants could discriminate the difference between [ba] and [ga]. Subsequently, these findings were replicated by Morse (1972) who employed the HAS procedure in a study of 2-month-olds. In addition, Morse found that the acoustic information underlying the [b-g] contrast was responded to differently when it occurred in a nonspeech context. This latter study raised the possibility that infants might engage some form of specialized processing of speech signals (for further details see *Perception of Nonspeech Signals by Adults and Infants*).

Neither Moffitt (1971) nor Morse (1972) tested whether infants display categorical discrimination of place information. Such an investigation was, however, conducted by Eimas (1974) who synthesized a continuum of stimuli between [dae] and [gae] by varying the onset frequency of F2 and F3 (see Pisoni, 1971). Using HAS, Eimas (1974) presented groups of 2-month-olds with either between-category or within-category contrasts of similar magnitudes and found that infants' discrimination of place information was categorical. In a follow-up study, Eimas (1974) employed a set of synthetic speech stimuli consisting of only two formants. In these stimuli, only the direction and extent of the second formant transition was varied. Adult listeners identified these synthetic stimuli as [bae] or [dae]. Once again, by presenting different groups of infants with contrasts chosen from either within or between the adult phonemic categories, Eimas was able to demonstrate that infants' discrimination of these sounds was also categorical. Moreover, Eimas found that this pattern of discrimination held only when the relevant acoustic differences (i.e., the formant transitions) occurred in the context of *speech* syllables, again suggesting the existence of specialized processing mechanisms for speech sounds. Till (1976) has reported similar findings in a study employing the heart rate dishabituation procedure (for further discussion see *Perception of Nonspeech Signals by Adults and Infants*).

To this point, our discussion of the perception of place contrasts by infants has been limited to studies in which place information was signaled by differences in the formant transitions. However, there are a number of other acoustic cues that can be used to support perception of place information (e.g., see the excellent discussion of this point by Dorman, Studdert-Kennedy, & Raphael, 1977). For instance, Miller, Morse, and Dorman (1977) examined the infant's sensitivity to one of these cues—the release burst. Using the heart rate paradigm, they presented infants with a contrast between the syllables [bu] and [gu]. The stimuli differed only in the nature of the initial burst cue. Both stimuli were derived from the same natural speech token of [bu]. However, for the [gu] stimulus the initial [b] burst was removed and replaced by a [g] burst. The results of Miller et al. (1977) indicated that this initial burst difference was sufficient for the infant's discrimination of the two syllables.

More recently, Walley (1979) investigated whether infants could discriminate synthetic [ba], [da], and [ga] stimuli. She used the operant head-turning procedure and presented 6- to 9-month-olds with either full-cue stimuli (five formants plus the burst) or partial-cue stimuli (two formants without the burst). Infants discriminated both the partial-cue stimuli from each other and the full-cue stimuli from each other. Thus, it appears that infants can utilize information from either bursts or formant transitions (or both) to discriminate differences in place of articulation in stop consonants.

Before concluding our discussion of the infant's

capacity for discriminating stop consonants differing in place of articulation, we should note that several other studies have demonstrated that infants are also sensitive to place contrasts that occur in either the medial or final positions of utterances (Jusczyk, 1977a; Jusczyk & Thompson, 1978; Williams, 1977a). These studies will be examined at length in the discussion on *Context Effects and Cue-Trading Relations*.

In summary, research on the infant's perception of place of articulation in stop consonants indicates that: (1) infants are sensitive to place differences; (2) they are capable of discriminating place differences on the basis of burst cues, formant transition cues, or some combination of the two; (3) the discrimination of at least one of these cues, formant transitions, is categorical; and (4) differences have been found in the infant's responsiveness to what appears to be the same acoustic information in speech and nonspeech contexts.

Contrasts Between Fricative Segments

As in the case of stop consonants, fricatives may differ from one another in terms of voicing and place of articulation. Both features have been explored in research with infants, although the data regarding voicing differences are limited to a single contrast ([s]-[z]). Eilers (1977) and Eilers, Wilson, and Moore (1977) have examined the discrimination of the voicing contrast between [s] and [z]. In a study with 3-month-olds using the HAS procedure, Eilers failed to find evidence of discrimination of [sa] from [za], although the same voicing contrast was discriminated in syllable-final position (i.e., [as]-[az]). This finding implied that not all phonetic contrasts are equally discriminable for infants and led Eilers to test older infants. She tested 6-month-olds using the head-turning paradigm and found that they were able to distinguish [sa] from [za] (Eilers et al., 1977). Consequently, Eilers et al. (1977) suggested that the discrimination of voicing differences in fricatives develops with increasing experience in the language-learning environment. However, Eilers' results have been challenged by a number of investigators who have raised serious questions about the experimental procedures and methods of analyses used in these studies. In particular, Eimas and Tartter (1979) and Jusczyk (1981) have argued that Eilers' method of testing for significant postshift recovery with the HAS procedure may have caused her to underestimate the probability that infants can distinguish the [sa]-[za] contrast. Hence, the issue of whether 3-month-olds are capable of distinguishing voicing contrasts in fricatives remains unresolved.

Considerably more research on the infant's capacity to distinguish place of articulation differences between fricative segments has been carried out. Eilers and Minifie (1975) used the HAS procedure in a study with 2- to 4-month-olds and found evidence for the discrimination of a [sa]-[Θa] pair. In a more extensive cross-sectional study, Eilers et al. (1977) employed the head-turning procedure to examine the discrimination of a variety of fricative contrasts by infants at different age levels. Eilers et al. found that both 6- and 12-month-olds discriminated [sa] from [Θa]. However, neither age group provided evidence of discriminating [fa] from [Θa] and only the 12-month-olds appeared to discriminate [fi] from [Θi]. Eilers et al. concluded that developmental changes occur in the infant's ability to detect some fricative contrasts during the first year of life. However, Jusczyk (1981) has pointed out that the natural speech tokens of [fa] and [Θa] used by Eilers et al. (1977) were only correctly identified by adult listeners 70% and 60% of the time respectively. Thus, the ambiguous nature of the test stimuli coupled with the small number of test trials (three change and three control trials) employed by Eilers et al. (1977) may have resulted in the underestimation of the infant's discriminative capacities for these contrasts.

Empirical support for this contention comes from recent studies reported by Holmberg, Morgan, and Kuhl (1977) and Jusczyk, Murray, Murphy, Levitt, and Carden (in preparation). Holmberg et al. (1977) tested 6-month-olds using the head-turning paradigm and reported evidence that infants could detect a [f]/[Θ] contrast in both the initial ([fa] vs. [Θa]) and final ([af] vs. [aΘ]) positions of syllables. Holmberg et al. employed a different criterion for discrimination than Eilers et al. (1977). The measure used by Holmberg et al. (1977) was similar to a training paradigm, in that infants were tested repeatedly until they attained a performance level of 8 correct responses out of 10 trials (5 change and 5 control trials). On the average, it took the subjects of Holmberg et al. 68 trials to achieve this criterion (this was about twice as long as it took them to master a [sa]/[Θa] contrast). Thus, although the [fa]/[Θa] contrast appears to be a more difficult one, Holmberg et al. have provided evidence that 6-month-olds can discriminate it if the appropriate test conditions are used. Similarly, Jusczyk et al. (in preparation) found evidence that 2-month-olds are capable of distinguishing synthetic speech tokens of [fa] from [Θa] and, moreover, that discrimination along this continuum appears to be categorical. Jusczyk et al. (in preparation) verified and extended these findings in a subsequent experiment with natural speech tokens by showing that 2-month-olds could discriminate contrasts between the voiced fricative pair [va] and [ða] as well as the voiceless pair [fa] and [Θa]. Therefore, it seems reasonable to conclude that infants as young as 2-months of age do, in fact, have the sensory-perceptual capacity to discriminate place of articulation differences between fricative segments.

Other Consonantal Contrasts

Investigators have also examined the infant's ability to discriminate a variety of other consonantal contrasts. Many of these studies have been directed toward contrasts based on differences in manner of articulation in consonants. For instance, Eimas and Miller (1980b) studied the infant's capacity to detect the oral/nasal contrast that distinguishes [ba] from [ma]. By varying two factors, the amount of nasal resonance and the starting frequency of the first formant, they constructed a synthetic speech continuum ranging from [ma] to [ba]. Eimas and Miller (1980b) tested 2- to 4-month-olds using the HAS procedure by presenting either within-category pairs (i.e., [ma_1] vs. [ma_2] or [ba_1] vs. [ba_2]) or between-category pairs (i.e., [ma] vs. [ba]). Interestingly, although the infants discriminated the between-category pairs, there was no evidence that discrimination of these pairs was reliably better than discrimination of the within-category pairs. In other words, the infants' discrimination of the oral/nasal distinction was noncategorical. In this respect, the infants differ from adult subjects who do show categorical perception for the same stimuli (Miller & Eimas, 1977). Eimas and Miller's (1980b) interpretation of this discrepancy between the infant and adult data is that infants are better able to make within-category distinctions along the oral/nasal continuum and that linguistic experience may function to reduce this capacity for making within-category discriminations along this continuum (see also Eimas, 1975a). However, such a conclusion is probably premature because, although in the right direction, the difference in postshift responding for the within-category group was not reliably greater than that of the control group. Hence, the most that can be said at this time is that there is little evidence showing that infants discriminate an oral/nasal contrast in a categorical manner.

Hillenbrand, Minifie, and Edwards (1979) also investigated the infant's ability to make distinctions on the basis of changes in manner of articulation. Their investigation focused on whether infants are sensitive to cues that distinguish stops, glides, and dipthongs. The parameter they varied was the tempo of spectral change, a complex cue consisting of both the duration of the formant transitions and the rate of frequency change. For stops, such as [bɛ], formant transition durations are very short (35 msec) and, therefore, the rate of frequency change is quite fast. For glides, such as [wɛ], formant transition durations are longer (120 msec) and the rate of frequency change is slower. And, for dipthongs, such as [uɛ], the formant transitions are still longer (250 msec) and the corresponding rate of frequency change is even slower. Hillenbrand et al. used the head-turning paradigm to test a group of 6- to 8-month-olds and found that infants could discriminate contrasts among [bɛ], [wɛ], and [uɛ] when the stimuli were computer-modified natural tokens. Results for synthetic speech tokens were similar except that most infants failed to discriminate the [wɛ]/[uɛ] contrast. However, because Hillenbrand et al. employed only a six-trial (three change and three control) criterion to assess discrimination performance, it is likely that with a more sensitive measure infants could discriminate the synthetic [wɛ]/[uɛ] pair. In any event, the Hillenbrand et al. study demonstrated that infants can discriminate manner distinctions based upon tempo of spectral change.

In addition to the studies directed at manner contrasts, several other kinds of consonantal contrasts have also been examined. Using the HAS procedure, Jusczyk, Copan, and Thompson (1978) found that infants could discriminate the glides [w] and [j] on the basis of formant transition differences. Similarly, Eimas and Miller (1981) reported that infants were capable of discriminating a [ma]/[na] contrast when it was cued by formant transition differences. In both of these studies, the findings were consistent with previous studies demonstrating that infants are sensitive to differences in place of articulation in stops and fricatives.

Finally, one other phonetic contrast ([r]-[l]) has been investigated in infants. Perception of this contrast may have important implications for the development of speech perception for a number of reasons. For example, in speech production it emerges relatively late in development (Strange & Broen, 1981; Templin, 1957). In addition, it is known that some foreign speakers, such as Japanese, have difficulty in mastering this English contrast (Miyawaki, Strange, Verbrugge, Liberman, Jenkins, & Fujimura, 1975). In fact, Miyawaki et al. found marked differences between Japanese and American adults in the way they perceived a synthetic speech continuum ranging from [ra] to [la]. Specifically, the American listener's perception of this continuum was categorical, whereas the Japanese listener's was continuous. When the critical information distinguishing these speech stimuli (i.e., the F3 transition) was presented in isolation (so that it no longer sounded like speech), both groups of listeners exhibited continuous perception. Since the [r]-[l] distinction is phonologically distinctive in English but not in Japanese, Miyawaki et al. concluded that the absence of categorical perception for this speech contrast in Japanese adults is the result of linguistic experience (see also Pisoni, Aslin, Perey, & Hennessy, 1982; Strange & Jenkins, 1978).

To determine whether English-speaking adults *acquire* the ability to discriminate the [ra]/[la] distinction or whether Japanese-speaking adults *lose* this ability, Eimas (1975a) tested 2- and 3-month-old infants from English-speaking families on this same [ra]/[la] contrast. He found that they responded in much the same way as English-speaking adults. That is, the infants displayed categorical discrimination of stimuli chosen from the [ra]/[la] continuum. In another condition, the infants exhibited continuous discrimination when the same F3 transition information was presented in isolation. On the basis of these results, Eimas argued that infants may be endowed with mechanisms specialized for speech processing. According to Eimas, the absence of experience with a particular phonetic contrast may eventually lead to a loss of sensitivity to that contrast. (For further discussion of these conclusions, see *Perception of Nonspeech Signals by Adults and Infants* and *Cross-language Studies of Infant Speech Perception*). To summarize, several investigations of infant speech perception have shown that infants are capable of distinguishing between a wide variety of consonantal contrasts. In addition, many of these contrasts are discriminated in a categorical-like manner.

Distinctions Between Vowels

In contrast to the perception of consonants, vowels appear to be perceived in a manner analogous to that of many simple nonspeech sounds. This is perhaps best demonstrated by the repeated finding that vowels tend to be perceived continuously by adults. That is, within-category discrimination tends to be considerably better than chance (e.g., Fry, Abramson, Eimas, & Liberman, 1962; Pisoni, 1973, 1975; Stevens, Liberman, Studdert-Kennedy, & Ohman, 1969). Although it has been demonstrated that the degree to which both consonants and vowels are perceived in a continuous manner is subject to experimental manipulation (e.g., see Carney, Widin, & Viemeister, 1977; Pisoni, 1973, 1975; Pisoni & Lazarus, 1974; Repp, Healy, & Crowder, 1979; Samuel, 1977), claims about differences in perception between vowels and consonants still appear to be well founded (Perey & Pisoni, 1977). For this reason, it would be of interest to determine whether there are any important differences in the infant's perception of vowels and consonants.

Trehub (1973) used the HAS paradigm to investigate the infant's perception of natural speech tokens involving two vowel contrasts: [a]/[i] and [i]/[u]. She also examined the consequences of presenting the [a]/[i] contrast in the context of an accompanying stop consonant ([pa]/[pi] or [ta]/[ti]). Her results indicated that infants were able to distinguish all of the contrasts. Moreover, there was no evidence of any difference between subjects who received the [a]/[i] contrast in isolation and those who received it in the context of an accompanying stop consonant.

Trehub's findings with respect to the [a]/[i] distinction were replicated by Kuhl and Miller (1975b) who showed (using HAS) that infants could discriminate this contrast, even in the presence of irrelevant pitch changes, such as those produced by varying intonation contours (see also Carrell, Smith, & Pisoni, 1981). Using the head-turning procedure with 6-month-olds, Kuhl (1980) extended these findings in a study that varied both intonation contour and speaker's voice. She found that the infants were able to detect an [a]/[i] contrast despite the presence of potentially distracting nonphonemic information. More recently, Kuhl & Miller (1982) obtained similar results with an [a]/[ɔ] contrast.

Although the studies reviewed thus far indicate that infants are capable of discriminating various vowels, they leave unanswered the question of whether vowel discrimination is continuous or categorical. This latter issue has been addressed in two studies by Swoboda and his colleagues. Swoboda, Morse, and Leavitt (1976) tested 2-month-olds with the HAS procedure on a series of contrasts from a continuum ranging from [i] to [I]. They found that infants discriminated not only the between-category items but also the within-category items. Moreover, there was no evidence that the infants' performance on the between-category items was any better than on within-category items. Thus, these results imply that infants' discrimination of contrasts on the [i]/[I] continuum was continuous rather than categorical. In this respect, the infant data parallel those observed in earlier studies with adults (e.g., Fry et al., 1962; Pisoni, 1973, 1975; Stevens et al., 1969).

In a second study, Swoboda, Kass, Morse, and Leavitt (1978) sought additional parallels between infants' and adults' perception of vowels. Studies with adults suggest that the use of long vowel durations increases the likelihood of observing continuous (i.e., good within-category) discrimination

(Pisoni, 1973, 1975; Repp et al., 1979). In contrast, when vowel durations are shorter, the discrimination data are more categorical. The most widely accepted explanation of these results is one that posits both acoustic and phonetic memory codes for speech signals (Fujisaki & Kawashima, 1969; Pisoni, 1973, 1975). Information in the acoustic code is assumed to decay more rapidly than information in the phonetic code. As a result, procedures that reduce the availability of acoustic information are more likely to result in categorical-like discrimination. To determine whether infants are similarly affected by such procedures, Swoboda et al. (1978) used the HAS technique to examine infants' perception of vowel stimuli with very short durations (60 msec) and vowels with longer durations (240 msec). Unfortunately, the results of this second study did not resolve the issue of how stimulus duration affects the infants' perception of vowels. Although only the subjects in the between-category conditions displayed a reliable increase in sucking during the postshift period, the difference in performance between subjects in this condition and those in the within-category condition was not significant. Nevertheless, Swoboda et al. (1978) took these results to be an indication that short duration vowels are discriminated in a more categorical-like manner than longer duration vowels. Given the ambiguous nature of the Swoboda et al. (1978) results, further experimentation is clearly necessary before it can be concluded that infants' discrimination of short-duration vowels is more categorical than it is for long-duration vowels.

In addition to the studies just reviewed, several investigators have examined the capacity of infants from English-speaking environments to discriminate vowel contrasts that are phonologically distinctive in another language. These studies will be discussed in more detail later (see *Cross-language Studies of Infant Speech Perception*). In summary, the research on infants' discrimination of vowels indicates that they are able to detect subtle contrasts between vowels. Moreover, it appears that, like adults, infants display continuous perception of phonetic contrasts along selected vowel continua.

Summary

The studies reviewed in the preceding discussion established that, from an early age, infants are capable of discriminating a wide variety of phonetic contrasts in spoken language. Moreover, it seems clear that the basic sensory mechanisms underlying categorical discrimination are present, if not immediately from birth, then within the first month of life. In addition, these studies of speech discrimination have implications for the nature of the mechanisms underlying speech perception and for the role of early experience in the development of speech perception. We now turn to a more detailed examination of these interpretive issues.

Mechanisms Underlying Infant Speech Perception

The initial studies of infant speech perception led to several conclusions regarding the nature of the perceptual mechanisms underlying discrimination of phonetic contrasts. First, because infants were found to discriminate speech contrasts in the first month of life without any explicit training, it was assumed that the basic perceptual mechanisms were innate. Second, evidence of categorical discrimination and of differences in processing speech and nonspeech sounds led some researchers to propose that the underlying mechanisms were specialized for speech processing. In this discussion we examine each of these issues in light of more recent evidence that challenges the view that infants perceive speech in a specialized linguistic or speech mode.

Perception of Nonspeech Signals by Adults and Infants

At the time of their original study, Eimas et al. (1971) argued that the mechanisms underlying the infant's discrimination of speech were not only innate but also unique to processing spoken language. This latter claim was based largely on the belief that categorical perception was unique to speech. The basis for this assumption was that when the critical cues for the perception of a particular phonetic contrast were removed from a speech context, perception of these same cues was no longer categorical but was continuous (e.g., Liberman et al., 1961; Mattingly, Liberman, Syrdal, & Halwes, 1971). Because infants in the Eimas et al. (1971) study displayed categorical discrimination of synthetic speech sounds differing in VOT, the authors based their claims for language-specific mechanisms on the further assumption that infants would exhibit continuous discrimination of the same acoustic information in a nonspeech context. The results of several subsequent studies on the discrimination of nonspeech contrasts appeared to justify the Eimas et al. (1971) assumption that infants respond differently to speech and nonspeech contrasts.

The first comparison of speech and nonspeech discrimination in infants was reported in a study conducted by Morse (1972). Drawing upon the logic of the earlier studies of speech and nonspeech processing in adults (e.g., Liberman et al., 1961; Mattingly et al., 1971), Morse presented infants with the same acoustic information in both speech and nonspeech contexts. He employed a consonant-vowel (CV) syllable pair ([ba]/[ga]) and a nonspeech chirp version of this pair. The syllable pair differed solely in terms of differences in the second and third formant transitions of each syllable. The nonspeech chirps were created by presenting only those portions of the speech patterns that distinguished the two syllables (i.e., the F2 and F3 transitions). Morse did not directly assess whether infants showed categorical discrimination of these nonspeech stimuli but simply looked for any differences in the infants' discrimination of the speech and nonspeech stimuli. The overall analysis of his results indicated no difference in the infants' responsiveness to the speech and nonspeech stimuli. However, discrimination performance for the nonspeech sounds was bimodally distributed; about half of the infants showed evidence of discrimination, whereas the other infants were at chance. Based on these findings, Morse argued that infants were responding differentially to speech and nonspeech sounds (for further discussion of this point see Jusczyk, 1981).

A more extensive study of infants' differential responsiveness to speech and nonspeech sounds was carried out by Eimas (1974). He tested directly for categorical discrimination of the same acoustic variations in both speech and nonspeech contexts. For this purpose, he selected CV syllables and chirps from the stimuli used by Mattingly et al. (1971) in their study with adults. Specifically, the speech stimuli were selected to provide both between-category comparisons (e.g., [bae] vs. [dae]) and within-category comparisons (e.g., [bae_1] vs. [bae_2]). Because these were synthetic stimuli composed of only two formants, the comparable nonspeech test pairs were created by utilizing only the second formant transitions of the syllables. Thus, for each pair of speech syllables, there was a comparable nonspeech chirp pair. Eimas' results indicated that the infants' discrimination of the speech contrasts was categorical: Pairs of syllables from opposite sides of the adult phonetic boundary were discriminated, whereas pairs of syllables from the same category were not. In comparison, although infants were able to discriminate the chirps, there was no indication that the chirps corresponding to between-category pairs were better discriminated than ones corresponding to within-category pairs. Hence, infants' discrimination of the nonspeech control stimuli appeared to be continuous.

Eimas' (1974) finding of a difference in the way certain acoustic cues were discriminated in speech and nonspeech contexts was replicated in a study by Till (1976). Till also investigated the discrimination of the acoustic cues for place of articulation (i.e., [ba] vs. [da]) in both speech and nonspeech contexts. However, unlike Eimas (1974), he employed a nonspeech control that involved inverting the F1 pattern. Hence, as opposed to the F2 formant chirps that Eimas had used, Till's (1976) patterns contained information in the general frequency region of F1 and were equivalent in duration to the speech stimuli. Although Till used different nonspeech control stimuli and a different measure of discrimination (heart rate dishabituation), his findings were essentially the same as those reported by Eimas (1974). Categorical discrimination was observed for the speech stimuli but not for the nonspeech control signals.

Eimas (1975a) extended these initial speech-nonspeech comparisons to an examination of infants' perception of the acoustic differences which signal the [ra]/[la] distinction. As described earlier, a study of adults by Miyawaki et al. (1975) had shown that changes in the initial steady-state frequency of F3 were sufficient to cue a distinction between [ra] and [la]. Moreover, for American adults, although not for Japanese adults, the F3 cue was perceived categorically in the speech context but continuously when the cue was presented in a nonspeech context. Eimas (1975a) found that infants responded similarly to American adults, that is, they displayed categorical discrimination for the speech but not for the nonspeech sounds. In Eimas' view, the performance of the infants reflected the "natural" state of the perception of speech and nonspeech stimuli. He, therefore, attributed the continuous perception of Japanese adults in the Miyawaki et al. (1975) study to a *loss* of sensitivity to the [r]-[l] distinction as a result of the absence of specific early exposure to this contrast (see Pisoni et al., 1982, for further discussion).

In summary, the early studies comparing perception of speech and nonspeech stimuli had an important impact on the way in which researchers viewed the perceptual mechanisms underlying infant speech perception. The repeated demonstrations that infants responded differentially to what was apparently the same acoustic information in speech and nonspeech contexts provided further support for the belief that different types of perceptual mechanisms underlie speech and nonspeech processing. It should be noted here that the claims for specialized speech-processing mechanisms rested not only on the assumption that categorical discrimination was limited to speech but also on the belief that infants were responding to the *same acoustic information* differentially in speech and nonspeech contexts. Hence, merely demonstrating that categorical discrimination exists for certain classes of nonspeech sounds was not sufficient to refute the claims for the operation of a specialized speech-processing mode. It would also be necessary to demonstrate that infants fail to respond differentially to the same acoustic information in speech and nonspeech contexts or that the particular nonspeech control stimuli used previously were inappropriate because they did not contain the same acoustic information as speech.

In several recent studies of nonspeech perception by adults, it has become clear that categorical perception is *not* unique to speech signals. For example, Cutting and Rosner (1974) demonstrated categorical perception for nonspeech musical sounds varying in rise time that could be labeled as plucks or bows. Miller et al. (1976) have shown comparable categorical perception effects for nonspeech stimuli varying in the onset of a noise preceding a buzz. And, in another study, Pisoni (1977) has reported categorical perception for stimuli differing in the relative onset time of two-component pure tones. In each case, these nonspeech experiments showed that discrimination was better for pairs of stimuli selected from different perceptual categories than for pairs of stimuli selected from the same category. Moreover, discrimination of stimuli from within a perceptual category was very close to chance as predicted by the categorical perception model.

These results obtained with nonspeech stimuli have provided some insight into the underlying basis of categorical perception for speech stimuli. These nonspeech experiments have succeeded in demonstrating categorical perception when previous attempts have failed, primarily for three reasons. First, recent investigations have employed relatively complex acoustic signals in which only a single component was varied relative to the remainder of the stimulus. In most of the earlier nonspeech experiments only very simple stimuli were used (see Eimas, 1963). Second, although these complex stimuli may be characterized as varying in linear steps along some physical continuum, the stimuli may have perceptual attributes or qualities that define quantal regions along the stimulus continuum separated by natural psychophysical boundaries. Within these regions sensitivity is low, but between these regions it is high (see Miller et al., 1976). Finally, because the stimulus continuum can be partitioned into several perceptually distinctive categories, subjects can easily employ a set of verbal labels or descriptive perceptual terms to encode these signals into short-term memory. These perceptual codes can then be used to categorize stimuli presented in a subsequent ABX discrimination task.

The recent findings that certain classes of nonspeech sounds are perceived categorically by adults has prompted a reexamination of previous interpretations of the infant's perception of nonspeech sounds. This reexamination has included (1) a determination of whether certain classes of nonspeech signals are discriminated categorically by infants and (2) a search for parallels in the infant's discrimination of speech and nonspeech contrasts that may reveal analogous underlying mechanisms.

Jusczyk, Rosner, Cutting, Foard, and Smith (1977) investigated whether or not infants show categorical discrimination for nonspeech contrasts differing in rise time. They employed the nonspeech stimuli that the adults in the Cutting and Rosner (1974) study had labeled as plucks and bows and tested 2-month-old infants using the HAS procedure. Pairs of stimuli differing in rise time were selected from either within the same adult category (e.g., 0 msec vs. 30 msec of rise time—both of which are perceived as plucks) or between the two adult categories (e.g., 30 msec vs. 60 msec of rise time—perceived as pluck and bow respectively). Jusczyk et al. (1977) found that only the between-category pairings were discriminated by the infants. Therefore, the infant's discrimination of the rise-time dimension for nonspeech sounds appeared to be categorical and was, therefore, similar to the findings with adults.[2]

The Jusczyk et al. (1977) results provided the first indication that categorical discrimination by infants is not limited solely to the perception of speech signals. Further support for this contention was provided in a second study by Jusczyk et al. (1980). These investigators examined the infant's ability to discriminate complex nonspeech sounds differing in their temporal onset characteristics. One objective of this study was to determine whether temporal-order information is discriminated categorically by infants. In addition, Jusczyk et al. (1980) wished to explore any possible links between the ability to respond to temporal-order differences in the relative onsets of nonspeech signals and the ability to discriminate differences in VOT.

As noted earlier, Pisoni (1977) found similarities to VOT perception in adults' identification and discrimination of two-component tone stimuli differing in relative onset time. The correspondence between tone onset time (TOT) and VOT perception suggested to Pisoni a common basis in the human auditory system for the perception of temporally ordered events (see also Hirsh, 1959; Miller et al., 1976).

Accordingly, Jusczyk et al. (1980) sought to determine whether there was a common psychophysical basis for the infants' responsiveness to TOT and VOT stimuli. They explored this possibility by presenting 2-month-olds with contrasts from various points along the TOT continuum. Three of the stimulus pairings consisted of items chosen from within the same adult perceptual category, whereas the two remaining contrasts consisted of stimuli from different adult categories. The infants displayed evidence of discriminating temporal-order information and, like adults, they appeared to divide the TOT continuum into three categories. However, for infants, the two regions of highest discriminability along the continuum were shifted toward slightly larger stimulus values than those observed for adults. In particular, the infants discriminated the −70/−40 msec and +40/+70 msec contrasts, both of which are, for adults, within-category contrasts. Jusczyk et al. (1980) predicted that the infants would discriminate only those pairs that crossed the adult category boundaries at −20 msec and +20 msec. Thus, in contrast to the adult studies that showed a close correspondence in the locations of the TOT and VOT boundaries, this study with infants indicates a slight discrepancy in the precise location of their estimated boundaries for the speech and nonspeech stimuli. Because the HAS technique only permits a rather crude estimate of the infant's category boundaries, some caution is necessary in interpreting the discrepancy between the infants' perception of the TOT and VOT series. Nevertheless, these findings demonstrate that infants are sensitive to the relative timing of events at stimulus onset.

Eilers, Morse, Gavin, and Oller (1981) have provided evidence that infants may not be capable of making fine temporal-order discriminations in speech stimuli that differ solely in VOT. They used the head-turning procedure to examine 6- to 8-month-olds' discrimination of [du] and [tu] stimuli (both natural and synthetic) that differed in VOT by 20 msec. The other cues associated with the voicing distinction between [d] and [t] (aspiration, F1 cutback, duration, and extent of the F1 transition) were held constant in these stimuli by selecting a vowel that had a minimal F1 transition. Although infants discriminated a full-cue d/t distinction (that adults judged to be good exemplars of [d] and [t]), they failed to discriminate the 20-msec VOT difference when it was the only cue to voicing.

These results on VOT discrimination may provide one explanation for the findings on TOT discrimination by Jusczyk et al. (1980). The larger values of TOT required for the infants to discriminate temporal order may be attributed to the fact that the TOT stimuli differed solely in temporal-order information, whereas the VOT stimuli used in past studies of infant discrimination contained numerous additional acoustic cues for the voicing distinction (see Stevens & Klatt, 1974). Nevertheless, the Jusczyk et al. (1980) study is suggestive of a possible link between the discrimination of temporal-order information and the discrimination of VOT contrasts. However, based on these findings and other more recent data with adults (see Summerfield, 1982), it seems unlikely that temporal-order information provides the sole basis for the adult's or infant's discrimination of VOT. Instead, temporal-order information appears to be one of several acoustic cues that might be used in combination to support the perception of VOT differences (Lisker, 1975, 1978).

The categorical discrimination of nonspeech sounds observed in recent investigations raises the question of why several earlier studies only found continuous discrimination for nonspeech contrasts. Given that infants have the capacity to discriminate nonspeech contrasts categorically, why should isolating a speech cue (i.e., presenting it in a nonspeech context) result in continuous discrimination? As some investigators (e.g., Eimas, 1974) have argued, one possibility is that the infant employs different perceptual mechanisms for processing speech and nonspeech signals. Such an account would have difficulty explaining recent evidence that nonspeech sounds are perceived categorically. A more attractive explanation is that the early studies employing nonspeech control signals really did not present infants with the *same acoustic information* in both speech and nonspeech contexts. Recall that these nonspeech contexts were created by systematically deleting F1 transition information on the grounds that such information was redundant across the stimulus pairs. However, Jusczyk, Smith, and Murphy (1981) have shown that the removal of F1 information may, in fact, have substantial effects on perception if the analysis of these signals is conducted not on individual formants but on the relationships between the formants (i.e., if the perception relies on overall spectral shape). Support for this contention comes from two studies with adult subjects. First, Pisoni (1976) found that the inclusion of the F1 transition in chirplike nonspeech stimuli produced sharp discontinuities in discrimination performance (characteristic of speech contrasts) rather than the flat discrimination functions observed for chirp patterns lacking F1 cues. Second, Jusczyk et al. (1981) reported marked differences in adult subjects' classification of chirp patterns with and without F1 information. Hence, infants' failure to show categorical discrimination for nonspeech chirps may be attributed to the omission of critical acoustic information in the stimulus pattern rather than to some inherent difference in the processing of speech and nonspeech signals.

Studies comparing the perception of speech and nonspeech signals have played an important role in past arguments concerning the existence and operation of a specialized speech processing mode, and will no doubt continue to do so in the future. However, the recent investigations of nonspeech processing in infants point more clearly toward similarities rather than differences in the way in which speech and nonspeech contrasts are perceived by adults and infants. These investigations have established that categorical discrimination occurs for nonspeech as well as for speech contrasts; additional attempts have been made to find nonspeech perceptual analogues for a number of speech dimensions. The results from the latter investigations have supported the existence of such parallels but no firm conclusions can be made at present. Undoubtedly, the most fruitful grounds for future research on the perception of speech and nonspeech signals will be directed at issues surrounding context effects and cue-trading relations (see *Context Effects and Cue-Trading Relations*) and to the continued search for nonspeech analogues to phonetic dimensions that will help to specify the psychophysical principles underlying speech perception.

Cross-language Studies of Infant Speech Perception

A natural extension of the early research on speech discrimination by infants was to examine the degree to which infants are sensitive to contrasts that do not occur in their native-language environment. Not only do cross-language studies extend our knowledge of the variety of contrasts that infants discriminate but, more important, they also bear closely on the role of early experience in the development of speech perception capacities. In particular, cross-language studies have been used to determine the degree to which the perceptual categories observed for a particular group of infants represent universal phonetic categories. As such, cross-language studies form an integral part of any attempt to map out the set of basic abilities humans have for speech perception.

Much of the work in this area has focused on the ability of infants from English-speaking environments to discriminate phonetic contrasts that do not occur in English. Recall that the Eimas et al. (1971) study demonstrated that infants have the capacity to distinguish between two modes of voicing along the VOT continuum, that is, between the voiced bilabial stop /ba/ and the voiceless /pa/. However, as discussed briefly earlier (see *The Speech Mode and Categorical Perception*), Lisker and Abramson (1964, 1970) found evidence for at least three modes of voicing in their cross-language experiments with adults. The third category, which corresponds to a prevoiced stop, is one not employed in English, but one that is used in a number of other languages including Thai. Given the results of Eimas et al. (1971), which strongly implied an innate basis for the perception of the voiced/voiceless distinction, it was only natural to expect that infants would also discriminate VOT contrasts between prevoiced and voiced stops.

Eimas (1975b) reported two attempts to determine whether infants were sensitive to prevoiced/voiced contrasts in stops differing in VOT. His results were equivocal for several reasons. First, the VOT differences that he used were much larger (80 msec) than those used for the comparable voiced/voiceless distinction (20 msec). Second, although he did find some weak evidence that one group of infants could discriminate a prevoiced/voiced contrast (−70 msec/+10 msec), the performance of this group was not reliably different from a group that received a contrast from within the prevoiced category (−150 msec/−70 msec). Thus, the results suggested that infants from an English-speaking environment were marginally sensitive to VOT differences in the prevoiced/voiced region, but there was no firm evidence that discrimination of these contrasts was categorical.

Eimas' (1975b) findings raised a number of questions about the development of infant speech perception capacities, particularly in view of his contention that performance on the voiced/voiceless contrast reflected the operation of innate perceptual mechanisms. One could ask why infants should display greater sensitivity to VOT differences in the voiced/voiceless region of the VOT continuum compared to the prevoiced/voiced region. Is it possible that only the voiced/voiceless boundary is innately determined or that even the limited experience with English that 2-month-olds have is sufficient to desensitize them to the prevoiced/voiced contrast? Or, is there some other explanation for this discrepancy? Although some investigators (e.g., Eilers, Gavin, & Wilson, 1979) have argued in favor of the first (experiential) possibility, the results of additional research in this area (e.g., Aslin, Pisoni, Hennessy, & Perey, 1981; Lasky et al., 1975; Streeter, 1976) strongly favor the view that experience is not the major determinant of VOT perception in early infancy and that acoustic rather than phonetic factors underlie the infant's discrimination of VOT differences.

Lasky et al. (1975) employed the heart rate procedure to investigate the discrimination of VOT contrasts by Guatemalan infants between 4 and 6½ months. Their study of infants from a Spanish-speaking environment has a direct bearing on the role of early linguistic experience in speech perception because the infants came from a language environment in which the major VOT boundary differs considerably from English (Lisker & Abramson, 1970; Williams, 1977b). That is, the VOT boundary in Spanish is centered around 0 msec rather than at +25 msec as in English. Thus, if anything, the early linguistic experience of the infants tested by Lasky et al. (1975) should have biased their discrimination performance away from the English boundary and toward the Spanish boundary. However, Lasky et al. found that their infant subjects exhibited two regions of high sensitivity to VOT differences, neither of which corresponded precisely to the Spanish boundary. Instead, one region (between +20 and +60 msec VOT) coincided with the voiced/voiceless boundary and the other (between −20 and −60 msec VOT) coincided with the prevoiced/voiced boundary. A third contrast between −20 and +20 msec VOT, which straddled the adult Spanish boundary, was not discriminated by the infants. Hence, it appears (at least from this study) that the linguistic environment had little effect on the infants' sensitivity to VOT differences during the first few months of life.

This conclusion is bolstered by findings from another study with infants from a non-English-speaking environment. Using the HAS procedure, Streeter (1976) found that Kikuyu infants also discriminated both prevoiced/voiced and voiced/voiceless contrasts. Again, what is interesting about these results is that one of these contrasts, the voiced/voiceless distinction, does not occur in the language-learning environment to which these infants were exposed.

Hence, there is strong evidence that infants from three diverse language backgrounds (English, Spanish, Kikuyu) are capable of discriminating VOT contrasts that cross a universal voiced/voiceless category boundary regardless of the phonological relevance of that phonetic category in their native-language environment. In contrast, the only strong evidence for the capacity to discriminate VOT contrasts between the prevoiced category and the voiced category comes from the two studies that tested infants whose native language employs the prevoiced/voiced distinction phonemically (Spanish and Kikuyu). These findings raised the possibility that all three modes of voicing described by Lisker and Abramson (1964) are not universal in the sense of being innate and that early experience in a language environment may enhance the infant's ability to discriminate phonetic contrasts in the prevoiced/voiced region of the VOT continuum.

Three studies investigated these two hypotheses. Eilers, Wilson, and Moore (1979) tested eight 6-month-old infants from an English-speaking environment on several VOT contrasts that spanned a 30-msec range along the VOT continuum (from −60 msec to +70 msec). Using the head-turning procedure, they found that the majority of the infants reliably discriminated the VOT contrast (+10 msec/+40 msec) that spanned the voiced/voiceless boundary of English-speaking adults. Eilers, Gavin, and Wilson (1979) extended these findings to test directly whether infants from different language environments would show VOT discrimination that matched the categories used by adult speakers of their native language. Groups of infants from Spanish-speaking and English-speaking communities were tested individually using the head-turning procedure. The infants from the English-speaking environment displayed reliable evidence of discriminating the VOT contrast (+10 msec/+40 msec) that crossed the adult English boundary. These infants did not discriminate the VOT contrast that crossed the adult Spanish boundary (−20 msec/+10 msec). However, the infants from the Spanish-speaking environment showed reliable evidence of discriminating the Spanish contrast *and* the English contrast. Eilers, Gavin, and Wilson (1979) concluded that the voiced/voiceless distinction is more salient acoustically, whereas the prevoiced/voiced distinction is not. Thus, they interpreted their results as evidence for an effect of early linguistic (listening) experience on the infants from the Spanish-speaking environment who apparently became more sensitive to the prevoiced/voiced distinction than infants from the English-speaking environment.

Although the Eilers, Wilson, and Moore (1979) and Eilers, Gavin, and Wilson (1979) studies provided an important advance by introducing the head-turning paradigm to the infant speech perception area, there were a number of serious methodological problems with both studies, including possible experimenter bias effects and the use of a limited number of trials (three test and three control). The Eilers, Gavin, and Wilson (1979) study was also of great interest because it was the first and only experiment that tested infants from two language communities in the same laboratory with the same VOT stimuli. Unfortunately, the methodological and interpretive difficulties associated with this latter study prevent any firm conclusions regarding the effects of early experience on VOT discrimination (see critique by Aslin & Pisoni, 1980a and the reply by Eilers, Gavin, & Wilson, 1980).

In an attempt to clarify the role of early experience in VOT discrimination, Aslin, Pisoni, Hennessy, and Perey (1981) conducted a study to assess the ability of infants from an English-speaking environment to discriminate several VOT contrasts along a −70 msec to +70 msec continuum. A head-turning procedure similar to that used by Eilers, Gavin, and Wilson (1979) was employed to measure discrimination. Potential experimenter and response bias effects were eliminated by using a computer-controlled, adaptive-staircase algorithm. This procedure enabled Aslin et al. (1981) to gather data from each infant on several VOT contrasts and to estimate the smallest VOT difference (Δ VOT) required for reliable discrimination from a set of standard background VOT values (−70, −50, −20, 0, +20, +50, +70 msec). The infants provided evidence of discriminating VOT contrasts that straddled *both* the voiced/voiceless and prevoiced/voiced boundaries. However, the threshold Δ VOT values were considerably larger in the minus region of the VOT continuum than in the plus region. Thus, infants are capable of discriminating the prevoiced/voiced contrast (all infants tested met the 80% correct criterion on the −70/0 msec contrast). But, as discussed earlier, the acoustic attributes associated with this nonphonemic contrast are less discriminable than those associated with the voiced/voiceless contrast that is phonemic in English.

Past failures to find strong evidence for infants' discrimination of the prevoiced/voiced distinction have undoubtedly been due, in part, to the selection of relatively small VOT contrasts (30 msec or less). The Aslin et al. (1981) study may have benefited from the fact that the staircase algorithm provides the infant with larger and presumably more easily discriminable VOT differences prior to the smaller VOT differences near the Δ VOT threshold. This, in turn, may have focused the infants' attention on the critical acoustic cues associated with differences in voicing. Nevertheless, it is clear that infants from an English-speaking environment, despite the absence of listening experience with the prevoiced/voiced distinction, possess the basic sensory capacity to make this discrimination. Whether early listening experience with the prevoiced/voiced distinction acts to enhance this basic sensory ability will remain unclear until infants from two different language environments are tested under the same conditions.

The foregoing results have implications for the level (or levels) of processing that underlies the ability of infants to discriminate VOT differences in the prevoiced/voiced region. Some investigators have interpreted the asymmetry in discriminability between the prevoiced/voiced and voiced/voiceless distinctions as evidence for a phonetic mode in the perception of the voiced/voiceless distinction. The basis of this interpretation is that the superior discriminability in the voiced/voiceless region of the VOT continuum must be the result of an additional level of processing associated with phonetic categorization. However, several lines of empirical evidence from cross-language and nonspeech studies favor a nonphonetic basis for the infant's discrimination of all VOT differences. First, a similar asymmetry in the discrimination of TOT differences in the lead and lag regions of this nonspeech continuum has also been found by Pisoni (1977). The poorer discrimination of both TOT and VOT differences in the lead (prevoiced) region of these continua is probably due, in part, to the poorer temporal resolving power of the auditory system for a high-frequency component preceded by a low-frequency component (Danaher, Osberger, & Pickett, 1973). Second, all studies of infants' VOT discrimination have found evidence of reliable discrimination of VOT contrasts in the voiced/voiceless region regardless of the phonological appropriateness of this voicing distinction in the infants' native language. Third, adults from various language communities are able to discriminate VOT contrasts that are not phonemic in their native language if a discrimination procedure (e.g., AX) is used to reduce the encoding requirements of the testing situation. For example, Streeter (1976) found that adult speakers of Kikuyu could reliably discriminate the nonphonemic voiced/voiceless bilabial stops and Williams (1977b) found that Spanish adults could discriminate the voiced/voiceless bilabial stops that cross the English-category boundary. In addition, Eilers, Wilson, and Moore (1979) and Aslin et al. (1981) found that English-speaking adults could discriminate nonphonemic VOT contrasts in the minus region of the VOT continuum. The foregoing evidence does not imply that adults fail to use a phonetic or phonemic level of analysis in the processing of running speech. However, a purely sensory basis for infants' discrimination of isolated VOT contrasts can account for all of the empirical findings that have been reported over the past decade. Thus, until convincing evidence is provided for the operation of a phonetic level of analysis in infants' perception of speech, a purely sensory or psychophysically based level of analysis can account for the current empirical findings.

Other research suggests that cross-language commonalities in perceptual boundaries for infants are not limited to the perception of VOT differences. Trehub (1976a) investigated the ability of infants from English-speaking homes to discriminate foreign-language contrasts between both consonants and vowels. In one experiment, she presented infants with a fricative contrast ([řa]/[za]) that occurs in Czech but not in English. Using natural speech tokens produced by Czech speakers, she employed the HAS procedure to test 1- to 4-month-olds on this contrast. Her results indicated that this contrast was readily discriminated by the infants. In a second experiment, Trehub (1976a) examined the discrimination of a foreign-language vowel contrast. She presented 1- to 4-month-olds from English-speaking homes with a distinction between the nasalized versus nonnasalized pair, [pã]/[pa]. This distinction is one that occurs in both Polish and French but not in English. Moreover, according to Jakobson (1968), it is one of the last phonemic distinctions that children learn to produce accurately. Once again, Trehub (1976a) found that the infants had no difficulty in discriminating this contrast. Hence, Trehub's findings provide another indication that little or no specific experience is required for infants to discriminate phonetic contrasts.

Trehub (1976a) obtained one other result that has influenced the way in which researchers view the role of early experience in the development of speech perception. She tested a group of English-speaking adults who had no knowledge of Czech on the same [řa]/[za] contrast used with the infants in her earlier study. In comparison to the infants, the adults appeared to display considerable difficulty in discriminating this contrast, especially when compared to their performance on an English contrast between [ri] and [li]. One way to interpret these findings is to assume that early experience with a particular language functions to reduce the listener's sensitivity to nonphonemic contrasts rather than to increase sensitivity to contrasts that are relevant to the phonology of the infant's native language (see Pisoni et al., 1982). However, there was some indication, even in Trehub's (1976a) data, that the apparent loss of discriminative capacity by adults was not permanent because performance on the foreign-language contrast was still reliably above chance. It should be noted that Trehub made no attempt to train her adult subjects on these foreign-speech contrasts. More recent data on adults' discrimination of non-English VOT contrasts will be discussed later (see *Role of Experience in the Development of Speech Perception*).

Two other studies have tested infants' discrimination of non-English phonetic contrasts. Eilers, Gavin, and Oller (1982) tested two groups of infants, one from a Spanish-speaking environment and one from an English-speaking environment. Three natural speech contrasts were used: (1) [aza] versus [asa], a voiced/voiceless fricative contrast that is phonemic in English, (2) [aɾa] versus [ara], a tapped versus trilled *r* contrast that is phonemic in Spanish, and (3) [za] versus [řa], a distinction that had been used by Trehub (1976a) and that is phonemic in Czech. Data from 40 trials on each contrast were gathered from each infant using the head-turning procedure. Their results indicated that the English fricative contrast and the Czech contrast were discriminated by the infants from a Spanish-speaking environment, despite the fact that neither contrast is phonemic in Spanish. The Spanish contrast, however, was only discriminated by the infants from the Spanish-speaking environment. For the two contrasts that were discriminated by both groups of infants, the performance of the Spanish infants exceeded that of the English infants. Eilers et al. (1982) interpreted these findings as evidence that Spanish infants may be more attuned to a broader range of phonetic contrasts regardless of the phonological relevance of the contrasts to their native language. Their heightened sensitivity may be the result of a more diverse set of listening experiences during early infancy. Nevertheless, any experiential effect is unlikely to be mediated by a phonetic level of analysis because the Spanish and English infants did not receive specific listening experience with the Czech contrast and the Spanish infants received only limited bilingual experience with the English contrast.

Werker, Gilbert, Humphrey, and Tees (1981) have obtained further evidence that infants can discriminate speech contrasts that are not phonemic in their native language. Werker et al. also used the head-turning procedure to test a group of infants from an English-speaking environment on two Hindi and one English natural-speech contrasts: (1) /Ta/ versus /ta/, a voiceless unaspirated versus dental stop; (2) /tʰ/ versus /dʰ/, a voiceless aspirated versus breathy dental stop; and (3) /ba/ versus /da/, voiced stops differing in place of articulation. The infants discriminated all three contrasts despite the nonphonemic status of the two Hindi pairs. Werker et al. also tested two groups of English-speaking adults on the two Hindi contrasts. One group was totally naive to the task and the other group was trained in a manner similar to the infants (i.e., with shaping and reinforcement). Both groups of adults showed some evidence of discriminating the /t^h/ versus /d^h/ contrast, but only the trained adults showed any evidence of discriminating the /Ta/ versus /ta/ contrast. Thus, infants appear to be more sensitive to some phonetic contrasts than adults. Whether the adults have, in fact, suffered a permanent loss of the sensory or perceptual capacity to discriminate nonphonemic contrasts will be a topic addressed later (see *Role of Experience in the Development of Speech Perception*).

Two conclusions can be drawn from this review of cross-language studies of infant speech perception. First, for at least some phonetic contrasts, specific listening experience is not required for discrimination to emerge. Infants from diverse language backgrounds show a close correspondence in the regions of highest discriminability along phonetic continua. Thus, the most important factor controlling the young infant's responsiveness to speech appears to be a basic set of innate perceptual mechanisms rather than exposure to specific types of early linguistic experience. This is not to say that experiential factors play no role in speech perception. Indeed, such experiences may exert an influence that might become apparent only at some later time in development. The point we wish to make here is simply that whatever the nature of infants' early experiences with language, the discrimination results to date suggest that they do not appear to manifest themselves during the first few months of life. Second, the exact nature of the innate mechanisms governing speech discrimination during infancy is presently unknown, despite its prominent status as a topic of current empirical research and theorizing. However, available empirical findings provide little support for the view that infants perceive speech sounds on a phonetic basis. If a phonetic mode of analysis is operative in infancy, however, then there must be universal phonetic categories built into the infant's auditory system and these categories must be capable of some postnatal shifts as a result of linguistic experience (see *Role of Experience in the Development of Speech Perception*). Moreover, if a phonetic mode underlies the perception of speech in infants, then one would predict that nonhuman species, who do not employ human speech distinctions in their communicative systems, should not exhibit humanlike discrimination and categorization of speech. This latter claim will be examined in the next discussion.

Species Specificity in Speech Perception

Perhaps the strongest evidence that infants process speech in a specialized manner would consist of demonstrations that other animal species, who are also limited to nonverbal response indices, perform differently on tasks that measure speech discrimination and categorization. Presumably, these nonhumans do not have access to the phonology of any human language and, therefore, would not be expected to process human speech with specialized mechanisms. Thus, it is important to know from the standpoint of understanding the *development* of speech processing whether the acoustic attributes of any signals that undergo specialized processing differ from species to species. We now examine this issue of species-specific processing of biologically relevant acoustic signals by considering several examples from the animal literature (see Bullock, 1977). Although the findings from nonhuman species are interesting in their own right, our intent here is to broaden the perspective from which researchers typically conceptualize the speech perception process in human infants, children, and adults. Two specific examples will suffice to highlight the major issues involved in an understanding of species-specific coding of biologically significant acoustic signals.

Evidence supporting species-specific processing of a limited set of communicative gestures must demonstrate (1) that only members of the target species process their communicative gestures efficiently and (2) that this bias in favor of the target species is *not* solely the result of a superior or specialized sensory apparatus. Precisely such evidence has been obtained by Zoloth, Petersen, Beecher, Green, Marler, Moody, and Stebbins (1979). The target species was the Japanese macaque, a species whose communicative calls have been extensively studied in the field (Green, 1975a, 1975b). Zoloth et al. (1979) chose to study two categories of calls, a smooth early coo and a smooth late coo, each of which is associated with quite different social contexts in the natural habitat of the Japanese macaque. The control species was the non-Japanese macaque, who possesses a sensory apparatus and a general intellectual level that is nearly identical to the Japanese macaque but whose communicative call system does not utilize the particular call categories chosen from the repertoire of the Japanese macaque. Thus, the calls under investigation were biologically significant only to the target species and not to the control species.

The basic design of the Zoloth et al. (1979) study (see review by Petersen, 1981) was to train macaques to exhibit a discriminative response when a change occurred from one exemplar of the smooth early type of coo to one exemplar of the smooth late type of coo. Once this initial two-choice discrimination was learned, other exemplars of the smooth early and smooth late types were added to the testing situation to determine how easily the animals could generalize these new calls to the classes of smooth early and smooth late. Presumably, if the two calls were relevant in a natural communicative context for the Japanese macaques, then the addition of slightly different examples of these calls would pose no great difficulty and generalization would be rapid. However, if the two calls were *not* communicatively relevant, as in the non-Japanese macaques, then generalization would not be rapid because each new exemplar would have to be added to a previously unknown class of sounds. Results from the Zoloth et al. study supported the above predictions. Japanese macaques generalized their discriminative responding to new examples of smooth early and smooth late calls at a much more rapid rate than the non-Japanese macaques.

These findings suggest that communicatively relevant acoustic signals are processed in a specialized manner by members of a particular target species. However, the results of the Zoloth et al. (1979) study could be explained on the basis of the Japanese macaques' greater familiarity with the nature of the stimuli used in the study. That is, the superior performance of the Japanese macaques may not have been the result of a species-specific mechanism but rather it may have resulted from having experienced the calls more often during the pretesting period. Zoloth et al. addressed this potential problem by testing both Japanese and non-Japanese macaques using a procedure identical to their first experiment but with two types of calls that were *not* communicatively relevant for the Japanese macaques. Exactly the same stimuli as in the first experiment were used, except that they were not grouped into smooth early and smooth late types. Instead, the stimuli were grouped into low-pitched and high-pitched types. Pitch is not in itself a communicatively relevant dimension for the Japanese macaque. Therefore, one would predict that as more and more examples of high- and low-pitched stimuli, some smooth early and some smooth late, were added to the discrimination task, Japanese macaques would have great difficulty generalizing the discriminative response. Non-Japanese macaques, however, would be expected to show no decrement in generalization performance for the two pitch types compared to the smooth early and smooth late types tested in the first experiment. Results from this second experiment again supported the general hypothesis of species-specific perception by the Japanese macaques. The communicatively irrelevant dimension of pitch was very difficult for the Japanese macaques to learn, whereas the non-Japanese macaques showed more rapid generalization to the two general pitch types. Presumably, either non-Japanese macaques use pitch in a communicative manner or they find pitch an easier acoustic attribute to attend to than the acoustic attributes present in the smooth early and smooth late calls used by Japanese macaques.

The results of the two experiments reported by Zoloth et al. provide strong evidence of a constraint on the processing of biologically significant acoustic signals. It remains unclear, however, whether this constraint is governed by genetic or experiential factors. Although one might be tempted to assume that Japanese macaques have evolved a species-specific communicative code that is completely specified by genetic factors, it is also quite possible that some, little, or none of the species-specific nature of Japanese macaque calls is determined by genetic factors. As discussed later (see *Role of Experience in the Development of Speech Perception*), during some early period of postnatal development, the auditory system of Japanese macaques may acquire a specialized call-processor for the types of signals present in their auditory environment. It remains to be seen whether the macaque call system is genetically specified, as in crickets (Hoy, Hahn, & Paul, 1977), or whether some aspect of auditory experience during a sensitive period in early development shapes the course of species-specific acoustic analysis.

Although the case of macaque call perception is potentially relevant to the issues surrounding infant speech perception, the study of developing macaques is just now beginning (Kuhl, 1982). A much more extensively studied communicative system is that of the songbirds, particularly the varieties of sparrows studied by Peter Marler and his associates. As reviewed by Marler (1970), a number of important conclusions have been reached concerning the development of sparrow song. First, isolation-reared sparrows fail to develop a normal species-specific song repertoire. Second, sparrows reared in an environment devoid of their own species' song but containing a song from another sparrow species also fail to develop a normal species-specific song repertoire. Third, if both species-relevant and species-irrelevant songs are present during early rearing (a situation similar to conditions in the natural habitat), then only the species-typical song becomes a part of the sparrow's vocal repertoire. Thus, there is a clear bias for sparrows to acquire a species-specific vocal repertoire, and this bias may be thought of as a clear example of a constraint on learning within the realm of communicative signals.

One final conclusion concerns the period of development during which song learning occurs in sparrows. Previous research had established that the presence of species-typical song was only necessary during a 10- to 50-day posthatching sensitive period. Song input delivered before or after this sensitive period resulted in a vocal repertoire similar to that of isolation-reared sparrows. Finally, sparrows who were experimentally deafened after the sensitive period but prior to the normal onset of adultlike song production developed an abnormal song. Sparrows deafened after adultlike song production had been attained did not lose their species-typical song-production behavior. Thus, it appears that sparrows must have auditory feedback from their own vocalizations in addition to species-specific early experience for the normal song repertoire to develop.

Marler and Peters (1977) extended this line of research by presenting sparrows with synthetic acoustic signals that contained features of two naturally occurring songs from two different sparrow species. The synthetic song tokens were presented to one of the sparrow species during the 20- to 50-day age period. Results showed that only the species-relevant song tokens were actually produced by the sparrows in adulthood. In an additional experiment, sparrows were reared by canaries and also given early natural song input (via tape recordings) from two sparrow species, one species-relevant and the other species-irrelevant. Only the species-relevant sparrow song was produced by the foster-reared sparrows in adulthood. One final interesting aspect of this study is the observation that sparrows do not produce their species-specific song until several weeks after the sensitive period. This finding implies that sparrows begin to produce their song on the basis of a memory trace of their species-specific song rather than from currently available perceptual models. Thus, the Marler and Peters study showed that (1) sparrows are constrained in the kind of songs they will produce, (2) early experience must match this constrained class of species-specific song, and (3) song production develops from a template of the song, a template presumably stored, refined, or consolidated during an early sensitive period.

The foregoing examples of specialized processing for species-relevant auditory signals have led several researchers to draw parallels between animal communication and infant speech perception (e.g., see Marler & Peters, 1981). The key questions in this area are whether human infants process speech sounds differently from nonspeech sounds and, if so, whether early auditory experience influences these specialized processing mechanisms. One avenue for investigating the first question is to choose a nonhuman species and ask whether it also shows evidence of specialized processing of human speech. If such cross-species evidence fails to support a species-specific model of speech perception, then either one would have to abandon the notion of specialized speech mechanisms in human infants or one would have to postulate that these specialized mechanisms are shared by other nonhuman species as well.

The first cross-species study of human speech perception was conducted by Kuhl and Miller (1975a). They trained chinchillas to escape from a compartment of their cage when one type of speech sound was presented and to inhibit the escape response when another type of speech sound was presented. Failure to escape resulted in shock and inhibition of escape resulted in a liquid reward. In two experiments, Kuhl and Miller found that the chinchilla could discriminate a natural speech [d]-[t] contrast produced by two male and two female talkers in three vowel contexts ([ti], [ta], [tu] vs. [di], [da], [du]). They also found that the chinchilla could discriminate a synthetic [da]-[ta] contrast. A discrimination phase in which the VOT values of the two stimuli were 0 and +80 msec respectively was followed by a generalization phase in which intermediate VOT values (10 to 70 msec) were presented. The results of this generalization procedure indicated that the chinchilla divides the VOT continuum into two relatively discrete categories, as evidenced by the steep slope of the generalization function (analogous to a labeling function in adults).

Kuhl and Miller (1978) extended these findings by presenting chinchillas with VOT continua for three places of articulation in syllable-initial stops ([b-p], [d-t], [g-k]). Generalization functions were gathered after discrimination of the 0-msec and +80-msec endpoints and discrete categories were observed. In addition, the category boundaries for the three continua showed a systematic shift toward more positive VOT values as place of articulation moved from labial to velar to alveolar. This interaction effect between place of articulation and voicing boundary is precisely the same as that found in human adults (see Miller, 1977; Sawusch & Pisoni, 1974).

Kuhl (1981) has also reported the chinchilla's thresholds for detecting differences in VOT. Each animal received a repeating (background) stimulus (e.g., +30 msec VOT) that was interrupted by several repetitions of a different (target) VOT value (e.g., +60 msec). A staircase procedure was used to increase and decrease the VOT difference between the target and background, thereby obtaining a threshold Δ VOT value for discrimination of VOT at several background VOT values. The results, based on 75% correct responding, indicated that the chinchilla is most sensitive to VOT differences (i.e., displays the smallest Δ VOT) at approximately +30 msec, a value that is very close to the peak in VOT sensitivity and the category boundary for voicing in adults (see Sachs & Grant, 1976).

In another study, Burdick and Miller (1975) showed that chinchillas generalize quite readily from a single [a]-[i] vowel contrast to a set of 24 [a]'s and 24 [i]'s recorded from four different speakers using three different pitch contours. Thus, in a manner similar to the Zoloth et al. (1979) study of transfer in the macaque's perception of species-specific calls, the chinchilla demonstrated rapid transfer of a speech category (vowel color) despite irrelevant variations in pitch contour and talker. Finally, Miller and Kuhl (1976) reported limited success in discrimination of place of articulation in natural-speech contrasts. They found that chinchillas could discriminate a [b]-[d] and a [d]-[g] contrast. However, the [b]-[g] contrast, which is cued solely by differences in the third formant, was not discriminated. This failure may be due to the poorer high-frequency sensitivity of the chinchilla compared to human adults.

The perceptual results from the chinchilla, because they conform quite closely with data from human adults and infants, provide convincing evidence that the categorical perception of speech signals by human infants does not necessarily imply a specialized speech perception mechanism. Further investigations of other nonhuman species, particularly the monkey, were undertaken, in part, to ensure that these results from chinchillas were not due to a species-specific effect or to the particular methods of testing employed.

Morse and Snowden (1975) studied the ability of rhesus macaques to discriminate place of articulation differences among [b], [d], and [g] by using the heart rate procedure. They presented both within-category and between-category contrasts as well as no-change control trials. The results indicated that monkeys could discriminate both between- and within-category distinctions in place of articulation. Thus, monkeys can discriminate speech contrasts, but their discrimination does not appear to be categorical as in human adults and infants.

Sinnott, Beecher, Moody, and Stebbins (1976) conducted two experiments with macaques. The monkeys were trained to release a contact key in response to changes in a repeating background sound. The monkeys discriminated a [ba]-[da] contrast and generalized rapidly both to natural speech tokens produced by eight male speakers and to synthetic speech tokens. The monkeys were also tested on a synthetic [ba]-[da] continuum, but they did not display any evidence of categorical discrimination. However, an AX procedure, such as the one used by Sinnott et al. (1976), requires little encoding and may have allowed the monkeys to make within-category discriminations.

Waters and Wilson (1976) tested rhesus macaques' discrimination of synthetic [b]-[p] and [d]-[t] contrasts. The monkeys were required to escape to avoid shock after a change in the speech signal. The original training stimuli had VOT values of −140 msec and +140 msec, −100 msec and +100 msec, or 0 msec and +140 msec. Subsequent test stimuli were presented with VOT values between the two training stimuli. Interpolated category boundaries for all the animals were in the plus VOT region (mean value = +22 msec). Thus, the monkeys could discriminate the synthetic VOT contrasts but, in the absence of finer test contrasts, the presence of categorical discrimination could not be determined.

The foregoing three studies of speech perception in monkeys provide somewhat more conflicting evidence compared to the humanlike performance of the chinchilla. It appears that categorical perception is present in chinchillas but not in monkeys. However, several of the monkey studies employed methods of assessment or stimulus sets that did not allow for a strong test of the presence of categorical perception. Recently, Kuhl and Padden (in press-a, in press-b) have conducted two studies of speech perception in macaques that provide stronger evidence for categorical perception.

The first study examined perception of the place of articulation distinction [b, d, g] using a same/different task in which the monkey was required to release a contact key whenever a stimulus change occurred. Discrimination data were collected for seven contrasts along the [b, d, g] continuum. The results indicated that peaks in discrimination were located at the two human adult category boundaries. Thus, macaques appear to show the same categorical discrimination of place of articulation differences that has been found for human infants (Eimas, 1974).

The second study by Kuhl and Padden (in press-b) examined VOT discrimination in macaques for three synthetic continua [b-p, d-t, and g-k]. As in their first experiment (in press-a), a same/different task was used to assess both within- and between-category discrimination of VOT contrasts. The results indicated that between-category contrasts were discriminated better than within-category contrasts. In addition, the between-category contrast straddled a different VOT value that corresponded to adults' category boundaries at the three different places of articulation. This shift in peak VOT discriminability as a function of place of articulation was also found in chinchillas (Kuhl & Miller, 1978) and mirrors the effect found in human adults.

These recent findings by Kuhl and Padden (in press-a, in press-b) provide stronger evidence that categorical discrimination of stop consonants is not unique to humans. The close parallels between certain aspects of human speech perception by animals and human infants have led to speculations about common underlying mechanisms in the mammalian auditory system among diverse species. Thus, as Kuhl (1978) has argued, the basis for speech perception in human infants may reside in general properties of the auditory system that are common to a wide variety of species. Presumably, the human speech processing system has capitalized on these general auditory mechanisms to reduce the complexity of segmenting speech sounds into discrete categories (see Stevens, 1975). The notion that the sound structure of language evolved to fit the perceptual characteristics of the auditory system is, of course, quite speculative. One could also argue that articulatory constraints placed pressure on languages to use certain auditory distinctions and the auditory system evolved to process these critical dimensions more easily (see Studdert-Kennedy, 1977). It is also possible that the animals tested in these recent studies of speech perception have been selectively influenced by the types of early auditory input presented to them in captivity. That is, chinchillas and monkeys reared in English-speaking environments may have different perceptual capabilities than similar members of their species reared in the wild or in non-English-speaking animal colonies. Until tests of animals reared in controlled auditory environments have been conducted, this latter possibility cannot be eliminated. Nevertheless, the claim that human infants process speech signals in a specialized manner has been severely weakened by these recent findings from nonhuman species.

Processing of Complex Speech Dimensions by Infants

Although studies of speech discrimination for simple phonetic contrasts have provided a wealth of information about the young infant's ability to perceive various distinctions used in natural language, speech perception entails more than simple discrimination. After a decade of research on infant speech perception, it is fair to say that every phonetic contrast presented to infants has been shown to be discriminated prior to 12 months of age. Thus, more complex aspects of speech perception, such as the categorization of speech sounds, would appear to be a logical next step in delineating the infant's speech-processing abilities.

Context Effects and Cue-Trading Relations

The first attempt to explore the effects of different contexts on the infant's discrimination of phonetic contrasts involved varying the position of the target contrast within an utterance. Jusczyk (1977a) used the HAS procedure to investigate the 2-month-old's capacity for discriminating the [d]-[g] contrast in syllable-final position. Previous work by Shvachkin (1973) suggested that 1-year-olds do not discriminate syllable-final contrasts until some time after they are able to discriminate syllable-initial contrasts. However, Shvachkin's task was one that involved *phonemic* perception. That is, the young child had to learn to associate correctly a set of nonsense syllables with a set of nonsense objects. Thus, the discrimination involved learning to associate meaning with the syllables, a more difficult task than simple segmental discrimination.

Jusczyk (1977a) tested infants on a variety of syllable-final contrasts (e.g., [ag]/[ad], [bag]/[bad], [bag]/[bam]) to determine if infants could discriminate these contrasts and if discrimination was affected by the number of common segments shared by the syllables (e.g., one common segment [ag]/[ad] or two common segments [bag]/[bad]). In addition, Jusczyk directly compared the discrimination performance of infants on the same phonetic contrast in syllable-initial positions (i.e., [dab]/[gab]) and syllable-final positions (i.e., [bad]/[bag]). The results indicated that infants were capable of discriminating syllable-final contrasts involving a single phonetic feature, such as place of articulation. Moreover, there was no evidence that discrimination performance was affected by the number of shared segments in the test pair. Finally, it appeared that the syllable-final contrasts posed no more difficulty for the infants than the syllable-initial ones. Thus, Jusczyk was able to demonstrate convincingly that 2-month-olds have the basic capacity to perceive phonetic contrasts beyond those contained in the initial segments of CV syllables.

Jusczyk's finding that syllable-initial contrasts are no more discriminable than syllable-final contrasts apparently contradicts Shvachkin's (1973) earlier report. Thus, it appears that discriminability per se was not the reason that Shvachkin's subjects had difficulty with contrasts differing in their final segments. However, an important stimulus variable may account for this apparent discrepancy. Jusczyk (1977a) employed stimuli in which the final stops were accompanied by release bursts. Often in natural speech and perhaps in Shvachkin's (1973) study as well release bursts are absent from final segments. As Malecot (1958) showed with adults, segments without bursts are less discriminable than those with bursts. Consequently, it is possible that if Jusczyk (1977a) had employed syllable-final contrasts *without* release bursts, he would have found that such contrasts were less discriminable for infants than syllable-initial contrasts. Some empirical support for this notion comes from an investigation by Williams (1977a). She also used the HAS procedure to test the 2-month-old's discrimination of syllable-initial ([da]/[ga]) and syllable-final ([ad]/[ag]) contrasts. In contrast to Jusczyk (1977a), however, she employed consonants *without* release bursts in the syllable-final pair. Her results indicated that although the syllable-initial contrast was discriminated, the syllable-final contrast was not. Thus, it appears that information contained in the release burst may be critical for the infant's discrimination of place of articulation in syllable-final contrasts. However, further investigations involving a direct comparison of the discriminability of a particular contrast with and without burst cues are required before drawing any firm conclusions on this matter (see Bush & Williams, 1977; Walley, 1979).

In summary, there is evidence from several sources that infants are capable of discriminating at least some kinds of phonetic contrasts in syllable-final as well as syllable-initial position. However, these results do not necessarily imply that the infant uses the same kind of information to discriminate a particular phonetic contrast in both syllable-initial and syllable-final positions. Indeed, to succeed on a discrimination task like the ones employed in the studies described earlier, the infants need not recognize any commonality between phonetic segments in syllable-initial and syllable-final positions. Instead, all that is required is that the infant discriminate *any* acoustic difference between the speech contrasts. This issue is discussed further when we examine cue-trading relations.

Another prominent aspect of the speech signal that provides phonetic information is pitch contour. Although by definition such prosodic information is carried across two or more syllables, there have been some attempts to investigate perception of suprasegmental information in units as small as single syllables. Kuhl and Miller (1975b) used the HAS procedure to examine the effects of varying the pitch contour of a syllable on vowel discrimination. For one group of infants, a contrast between [a] and [i] was accompanied by an irrelevant variation in pitch contour (monotone vs. a rise-fall contour). During the preshift phase, each subject heard one of the two vowels alternating between the different pitch contours. Kuhl and Miller found that infants were able to discriminate the vowel contrast despite irrelevant pitch variation. Thus, their study provided some indication that the infant's capacity for phonetic discrimination is not affected by variations in pitch contour (see also Carrell et al., 1981).

As noted earlier, suprasegmental information is typically examined in utterances that are longer than a single syllable. For example, words longer than a single syllable vary internally in terms of syllable-stress patterns. Indeed, in some cases distinctions between words are made largely on the basis of differences in stress patterns (e.g., recórd vs. récord, contráct vs. cóntract, condúct vs. cónduct), some of which are accompanied by a reduction of vowel duration in the unstressed syllable. Consequently, the most natural place to look for possible effects of suprasegmental cues on phonetic perception is in contrasts between multisyllabic utterances. Jusczyk and Thompson (1978) assessed the consequences of positioning a place of articulation contrast (i.e., [b]/[g]) in multisyllabic tokens. By utilizing multisyllabic stimuli, Jusczyk and Thompson were able to examine several factors simultaneously. First, they examined whether suprasegmental information interacts in any interesting way with phonetic information to affect the discriminability of the contrasts. For instance, does syllable stress serve to direct attention to a phonetic contrast that might otherwise be unnoticed (e.g., is a [dabá]/[dagá] contrast more discriminable than a [dába]/[dága] contrast)? Second, they examined the effects of locating a phonetic contrast in either the initial (e.g., [bada] vs. [gada]) or medial ([daba] vs. [daga]) position of a bisyllabic utterance. Using the HAS procedure, Jusczyk and Thompson found that 2-month-olds were able to discriminate the [b]/[g] contrast in either the initial or medial portion of the bisyllabic utterances regardless of whether or not the contrast occurred in a stressed or unstressed syllable. Furthermore, there was no indication that contrasts that appeared in stressed syllables were any more discriminable than those in unstressed syllables.

These findings are in agreement with those of Williams (1977a) who used a different place of articulation contrast. She examined the discrimination of a [d]/[g] contrast in the medial position of bisyllabic utterances for both stressed (e.g., [agá]/[adá]) and unstressed (e.g., [ága]/[áda]) syllables and found that infants were able to discriminate the contrast regardless of stress pattern. Moreover, there was no evidence that syllable stress had any effect on discriminability.

Although it might appear that syllable stress has little effect on the discrimination of phonetic distinctions, both studies involving multisyllables focused on contrasts between stop consonants. Stops contain several acoustic characteristics that mark their appearance in an utterance. One prominent feature is the presence of a silent interval (corresponding to vocal tract closure) followed by an abrupt onset of spectral energy. It is possible that these acoustic characteristics are sufficient to call attention to stops so that syllable stress would produce no appreciable gain in discriminability. It is also possible that the effects of syllable stress might show up only in contrasts between phonetic segments that lack silent closures and abrupt onsets. Jusczyk et al. (1978) used the HAS procedure to examine one such contrast involving the glide pair [w]/[j]. Their experimental design was basically the same as Jusczyk and Thompson's (1978), namely, discriminability of the contrast was tested in initial and medial positions in bisyllabic utterances and in both stressed and unstressed syllables. The results were consistent with their earlier findings for stops. Infants displayed reliable evidence of discriminating the [w]/[j] contrast in all situations. More important, there was no indication that syllable stress improved discrimination performance. On the basis of these results, Jusczyk et al. (1978) argued that syllabic stress may have little or no effect on the infant's ability to perceive phonetic contrasts in situations in which one meaningless utterance is pitted against another. It is still possible, of course, that syllable stress does affect discrimination in certain language-learning situations in which the child's attention must be devoted simultaneously to phonological, syntactic, semantic, and even pragmatic considerations. In this case, we might expect stress to play a more prominent role in marking the location of syllables or segments within syllables.

In addition to the research investigating the perception of place of articulation contrasts in different phonetic contexts, there has been some attempt to investigate the discrimination of voicing contrasts in multisyllabic utterances. Trehub (1976b) used the HAS procedure to test 1- to 4-month-olds on their ability to discriminate a voicing contrast embedded in bisyllabic and trisyllabic utterances. She found that infants were able to discriminate [b] from [p] in bisyllables (e.g., [aba]/[apa] and [kaba]/[kapa]) provided that the individual syllable durations were 500-msec long. For contrasts presented in bisyllabic and trisyllabic utterances with syllable durations of 300 msec, there was no evidence of discrimination, even when the contrast occurred in a stressed syllable. It is unclear why infants discriminated the voicing contrasts in the 500-msec syllables but not in the 300-msec syllables. Trehub's explanation was that temporal constraints on speech processing limit the infant's ability to discriminate speech presented at rapid rates. But this proposal seems unlikely in view of Jusczyk and Thompson's (1978) finding that infants can discriminate contrasts in syllables with a duration of only 208 msec. Another possibility is that the 500-msec and 300-msec syllables differed with regard to the presence of some critical acoustic feature. Whichever explanation is actually correct, it is interesting that Trehub (1976b) also found no indication that a stressed syllable improved the discriminability of the phonetic contrast for the infants. Thus, it appears that whether an infant will discriminate a particular phonetic contrast in multisyllabic utterances is not directly related to the occurrence of syllable stress.

Another major source of contextual variation in natural speech is produced by changes in speaking rate. At first glance, such changes in speaking rate might not appear to pose a problem for the listener; however, there are a number of phonetic contrasts that are cued by both absolute and relative temporal durations of acoustic events (see Port, 1981a, 1981b). For example, examination of the phonetic distinction between [ba] and [wa] indicates that the duration of the formant transitions is a sufficient cue for signaling this contrast (Miller & Liberman, 1979). However, Miller and Liberman also found in their study of adults that the critical formant transition duration that marks this distinction varies as a function of total syllable duration. For example, whereas the [ba]/[wa] boundary value is approximately 32 msec for syllables 80 msec in duration, it is 47 msec for syllables with durations of 296 msec. In other words, the adult listener appears to compensate for the overall duration of the utterance in the course of deciding what phonetic segment is uttered. However, the perceptual compensation is not based solely on duration; instead, the specific nature of the information that is contained in the longer duration utterance also plays an important role. Miller and Liberman (1979) found that increasing the duration of the steady-state portion of the vowel in a syllable, as might occur when speaking rate declines, had the effect of shifting the perceptual boundary toward longer transition duration values. In contrast, an equivalent increase in syllable duration produced by adding a final stop consonant to the steady-state vowel (thus *not* slowing the speaking rate) actually produced shifts in boundaries toward *shorter* duration values. Hence, it is not just syllable duration per se but also syllable structure that appears to determine the compensation made in perceiving the [ba]/[wa] contrast. For this reason, Miller and Liberman argued that the location of the phonetic boundary was governed by estimates of speaking rate (however, see Carrell, Pisoni, & Gans, 1980).

If Miller and Liberman's (1979) view is correct, the young child who is learning distinctions, such as the one between [ba] and [wa], must be able to compensate for differences in a talker's speaking rate. Eimas and Miller (1980a) sought to determine the extent to which infants might already possess such an ability. They found a close correspondence between the infants' discrimination of syllables varying in transition duration and the results obtained with adults by Miller and Liberman (1979). Using the HAS procedure, they showed that infants display categorical discrimination for formant transition differences and that the region of highest discriminability shifted as overall syllable duration was varied. For 80-msec syllables, infants discriminated a contrast between syllables with transition durations of 16 and 40 msec, but they did not discriminate between syllables with transition durations of 40 and 64 msec (both of the latter tokens are perceived as [wa] by adults). For syllables with overall durations of 296 msec, the results were just the opposite; the 40/64 pair was discriminated but the 16/40 pair was not (both of the latter tokens are perceived as [ba] by adults). Eimas and Miller (1980a) interpreted these findings as evidence that infants were responsive to differences in rate of speaking and, thus (by implication), were engaging in some form of specialized processing of speech sounds.

Although the Eimas and Miller (1980a) results indicate that infants' discriminative capacities are dependent on contexts, such as those introduced by changes in speaking rate, these results do not necessarily point to the existence of any specialized speech processing mechanisms. In their study with infants, Eimas and Miller did not test whether increasing overall syllable duration by adding formant transitions to the end of the syllables (i.e., adding a final stop consonant) resulted in a shift of highest discriminability toward pairs with shorter transition durations. A finding of this sort would provide some indication that the internal structure of the syllable also affects the discrimination of the initial formant transition durations. However, even then, the possibility would remain that general auditory processing mechanisms, as opposed to ones limited to speech, were responsible for the infants' discrimination performance.

This possibility of a nonphonetic basis for their findings receives strong support from the results of a study by Carrell et al. (1980). They showed that adults perceive nonspeech sine-wave analogs of [ba] and [wa] (containing rapid changes in the spectrum at stimulus onset) in precisely the same manner as the speech tokens used by Miller and Liberman (1979) and Eimas and Miller (1980a). That is, the labeling boundaries for these nonspeech tokens shifted with the overall duration of the stimulus. Moreover, the direction of the boundary shifts for these nonspeech signals was the same as the boundary shifts for the speech signals, that is, boundaries shifted toward longer transition durations when "vowel" duration was increased and toward shorter transition durations when a "consonant" was added to the end of the signal. In addition, Jusczyk, Pisoni, Fernald, Reed, and Myers (1983) have shown that 2-month-olds, tested with the same sine-wave stimuli used by Carrell et al. (1980), discriminated the same durational contrasts as the infants tested by Eimas and Miller (1980a) with speech sounds. That is, for 80-msec stimuli, the infants discriminated a 15/35-msec transition duration pair but not a 35/55-msec pair, whereas for 295-msec stimuli, the infants discriminated a 35/55-msec transition duration pair but not a 15/35-msec pair. Thus, discrimination of these nonspeech contrasts is categorical in the same way as Eimas and Miller's (1980a) results using [ba]-[wa] speech contrasts. In conclusion, the Eimas and Miller results demonstrate that certain contextual variables appear to influence the infant's discriminative capacities, but they do not establish a locus for these effects in specialized speech processing mechanisms.

The phenomenon studied by Eimas and Miller

(1980a) indicates one way in which different cues can interact during the course of speech perception. The two cues they studied (formant transition duration and overall syllable duration) played an important role in signaling different sorts of information in the speech signal (viz., phonetic identity and speaking rate respectively). However, equally common in speech perception are those occasions in which two or more cues interact to signal the presence of a particular phone (e.g., see Dorman et al., 1977). In these cases, it becomes possible to study the relative contribution of each cue to the perception of a particular phone across different contexts. In a number of studies with adults, researchers at Haskins Laboratories have demonstrated the existence of trading relations between various cues in speech perception (e.g., Dorman et al., 1977; Lisker, 1978; Mann & Repp, 1980, 1981; Repp, 1982).

The presence of trading relations in speech perception is taken to be a mark of the flexibility of the underlying perceptual apparatus. In effect, the listener has the freedom to accept a wider range of tokens as alternative members of a given phonetic type. Naturally, it is of interest to know the origins of the perceptual abilities that underlie these trading relations. Indeed, one possibility is that trading relations arise as a result of associating the acoustic correlates of different aspects of various articulatory gestures. Because the reference point here is articulation, these accounts assume that the listener has knowledge of the characteristics of the speech production system prior to the recognition of trading relations in speech perception. Such knowledge of the vocal tract characteristics could be either an intrinsic part of the specialized innate speech processing mechanisms or a consequence of learning to link one's own articulatory gestures with their acoustic correlates. An alternative explanation of trading relations in perception is that they have their origins in the way in which the auditory system is organized to deal with the simultaneous occurrence of different types of acoustic information. By this account, one would expect to see similar sorts of trading relations between acoustic cues in nonspeech contexts. Unfortunately, up to the present time there has been very little research directed at these issues, particularly with regard to comparisons with nonspeech signals (see, however, Carrell et al., 1980; Nusbaum, 1981).

Relatively little is currently known about the infant's perception of trading relations in speech. The most extensive study in this area was conducted by Jusczyk et al. (in preparation). In a series of experiments they tested infants' sensitivity to both formant transition and spectral noise cues for place of articulation in fricatives. Previous work with adult subjects suggested that an intricate relation between these two cues exists in the perception of fricatives. For example, Harris (1958) found that although both cues are important for the distinction between [fa] and [Θa], formant transition cues appear to predominate. More recently, Carden, Levitt, Jusczyk, and Walley (1981) attempted to assess whether the formant transition cues were sufficient to cue the distinction between [fa] and [Θa]. Using natural speech tokens of these syllables, they removed the frication portion from each stimulus, leaving only the formant transitions and the following vowel. To their surprise, Carden et al. found that the truncated versions of [fa] and [Θa] were labeled consistently by adults as [ba]. Further experimentation using synthetic speech indicated that this effect could not be ascribed to the absence of some critical difference in the absent frication portions of [fa] and [Θa]. Synthetic speech sounds constructed with the identical frication noise for both fricatives produced exactly the same effect, namely, its removal from the stimuli caused the resulting sounds to be perceived as [ba]. Carden et al. argued that the frication noise provided subjects with the necessary context to perceive the formant transition differences that also distinguish [fa] and [Θa].[3]

Jusczyk et al. (in preparation) drew upon these earlier findings with adults in examining the infant's ability to utilize formant transition and spectral noise cues in the perception of fricative contrasts. In their first experiment, they investigated whether formant transition differences provide a sufficient cue for the infant's discrimination of [fa] and [Θa]. Using the HAS procedure, one group of infants heard a contrast between natural speech tokens of [fa] and [Θa] and a second group heard a contrast between truncated versions of these syllables (i.e., the syllables minus the frication noises). In agreement with the results of Carden et al. (1981), Jusczyk et al. (in preparation) found that although the infants discriminated the [fa]/[Θa] contrast, they did not discriminate the truncated versions of these stimuli. Thus, without the different frication noises, the formant transition differences present in the truncated syllables were not sufficient to support discrimination by the infants. Jusczyk et al. conducted a second experiment to ascertain whether differences in the frication portions of the syllables enabled the infants to discriminate [fa] and [Θa]. One group of infants heard a contrast consisting of the spectral noise (frication) portions of [fa] and [Θa] directly appended to the vowel [a]. Thus, no formant transitions were present in these stimuli. The aim here was to determine if the spectral noise difference alone was sufficient to signal this contrast.

In another experiment, Jusczyk et al. (in preparation) tested an additional group of subjects to see whether the presence of a constant frication noise provides a context or reference that would allow infants to discriminate the formant transition differences as Carden et al. (1981) found for adults. The stimuli for this contrast were composed of a constant frication noise appended to truncated [fa] and [Θa] syllables (i.e., ones containing only formant transitions and vowels). Jusczyk et al. (in preparation) found that both sets of contrasts were discriminable for the infants. Therefore, there is sufficient information in the spectral noise differences between [fa] and [Θa] to cue this contrast. Yet, it is also the case that the presence of even a constant frication noise can serve as an appropriate context for the detection of formant transition differences present between [fa] and [Θa]. Thus, Jusczyk et al. demonstrated that, under the proper circumstances, infants are able to utilize either formant transition or spectral noise differences to signal the [fa]/[Θa] contrast. The factors that determine precisely which cue the infant will use are not known at present, but evidently the formant transition differences are only effective in the presence of an accompanying frication noise. The latter result directly parallels the findings observed by Carden et al. (1981) in their study with adults. Could it be that the frication noise is a useful context for the infants because it cues them about a difference in manner of articulation? Or is there a more general psychophysical explanation for this result? Only further experimentation can decide this issue. Regardless of how it is resolved, the results of Jusczyk et al. (in preparation) do indicate that infants' discriminative capacities are affected by at least some trading relations between different speech cues.

A second investigation of the infant's sensitivity to trading relations was reported by Morse, Eilers, and Gavin (1982). They employed the head-turning procedure to test whether 6- to 8-month-old infants could discriminate an invariant phonetic contrast that is signaled by different acoustic cues. A number of investigations with adults have shown that the addition of a brief silent interval spliced between the [s] and [lit] of [slit] results in the perception of [split] (e.g., Bastian, Eimas, & Liberman, 1961; Fitch, Halwes, Erickson, & Liberman, 1980; Marcus, 1978). In addition to the silent duration interval, the [p] in [split] in natural speech is also cued by the presence of formant transitions. Fitch et al. (1980) demonstrated the existence of a trading relation between the silent interval and formant transition cues in adults' perception of [slit] and [split]. In two experiments, Morse et al. (1982) sought to determine if infants were also sensitive to these trading relations. In the course of their two experiments, Morse et al. examined performance on three different contrasts. As a check on the infant's ability to discriminate [slit] from [split], one test condition employed a natural speech contrast (the [slit]/[split] condition). A second test condition was designed to investigate whether infants could discriminate natural speech tokens of [slit] from ones containing an interval of silence after the [s] (the [slit]/[slit]+s condition). The latter tokens were perceived by adults as [split]. Finally, the third pairing focused on the infant's ability to distinguish natural speech tokens of [split] from [slit] tokens with the silent interval included after the [s] (the [split]/[slit]+s condition). Because both of these stimuli were perceived by adults as [split], this test condition was designed to determine whether infants also recognize some sort of equivalence between silent intervals and formant transition cues for [p].

Morse et al. (1982) reported that infants can discriminate [slit] from [slit]+s and that they respond in a similar manner to the [slit]+s and the [split] stimuli. The latter claim was based chiefly on the observation that infants did not discriminate a contrast between [slit]+s and [split] because a direct test of responding to the [slit]/[split] contrast yielded no evidence of discrimination.[4] Although the basic idea behind the Morse et al. study is interesting and potentially important, especially in light of the recent adult literature on cue trading, the study itself has a number of methodological problems. For example, Morse et al. used natural speech stimuli and, as a result, they were unable to carefully control a number of important stimulus parameters. In addition, they developed a new statistical criterion based on the z-statistic to test the hypothesis that the infants as a group exceeded chance expectation levels of responding on the speech contrasts. This z-test ignores the between-subject variance that is crucial to a meaningful test of differences between group means. Given these problems, any conclusions regarding the results of the Morse et al. study must await further empirical research.

In summary, the effects of syllable context and cue-trading relations appear to operate in a similar manner in infants' and adults' perception of speech: (1) infants are capable of detecting phonetic contrasts across different positions in words, (2) infants' sensitivity to phonetic contrasts shows evidence of perceptual compensation to changes associated with different speaking rates, and (3) infants appear to display evidence of integrating multiple sources of information in the discrimination of several diverse phonetic contrasts.

Categorization and Perceptual Constancy

The mature perceiver of speech is not only adept at discriminating speech sounds but is also able to recognize the phonetic identity of physically different versions of the same sound. Researchers of infant speech perception have long been interested not only in the infant's ability to recognize differences between sounds but also in their ability to recognize similarities between sounds. Unfortunately, the latter interest has been a much more difficult one to pursue, chiefly because of the lack of adequate measures of categorization in infants. As a result, much of the available information regarding the infant's categorization of speech has been acquired through indirect measures involving discrimination. Despite the limitations of these measures, much useful information has been gained in the last few years.

The research questions in this area fall into two major domains: (1) perceptual constancy and (2) the nature of the categories that the infant employs in processing speech. The perceptual constancy issue has been investigated almost exclusively by Kuhl and her colleagues (Hillenbrand, 1980; Holmberg et al., 1977; Kuhl, 1979a, 1979b, 1980; Kuhl & Miller, 1975b, 1982). These studies have focused on the infant's ability to ignore irrelevant variations in either pitch or characteristics of the speaker's voice. The most common method has been to present infants with a fixed set of stimulus dimensions and to see whether discrimination performance is maintained when irrelevant variations in pitch contour and speaker's voice are introduced. Continued successful discrimination performance is taken as an indication that the infant recognizes the inherent phonetic identities of the test stimuli despite the irrelevant changes in speaker's voice and pitch contour.

The first evidence that infants display some degree of perceptual constancy for speech was reported in a study by Kuhl and Miller (1975b). They used the HAS procedure to test the ability of 1- to 4-month-olds to discriminate a phonetic contrast ([a]/[i]) in the face of irrelevant changes in pitch contour. During the preshift phase of the experiment, one of the vowels (e.g., [a]) was presented and varied randomly between two pitch contours (monotone and rise-fall). During the postshift phase, the other vowel (e.g., [i]) was introduced with the same pitch variations. The results indicated that infants could detect the shift from one vowel to the other despite the potential distraction caused by the pitch contour variations. Although these results do not provide direct support for the claim that infants actually perceive phonetic similarities between the different versions of each vowel, they do indicate that infants are at least able to tolerate some physical variation in the cues to these perceptual categories in making the critical distinction between vowels.

Another attempt to measure perceptual constancy was carried out by Kuhl (1979b) in an experiment with 6-month-olds using the head-turning procedure. Once again, Kuhl employed an [a]/[i] contrast, but varied the speaker's voice and pitch contour. Using a transfer of training paradigm, she first had each infant meet a discrimination criterion for the [a]/[i] contrast when speaker's voice and pitch contour were held constant. After mastering the initial discrimination, the infants completed a number of successive training stages in which irrelevant variations in speaker's voice and pitch contour were introduced into the stimulus items. The variations ultimately included tokens from three different talkers and two different pitch contours. Despite these variations, infants were able to maintain the discrimination between the [a] and [i] tokens. As a check on whether the training procedure she employed was responsible for the infant's success, Kuhl ran an additional experiment in which she eliminated the successive training phases so that the infants moved directly from initial training to the final test stage. Once again, infants proved capable of discriminating the [a]/[i] contrast. Hence, it appears that the infant does not require direct training to ignore variations introduced by changes in speaker's voice and pitch contour. Instead, the infant appears to be able to apply this ability to the test situation with very little training.[5]

How broad is the infant's capacity for perceptual constancy with speech sounds? In the study described earlier, Kuhl employed synthesized tokens generated by an adult male, an adult female, and a child talker. The absolute values of the formant frequencies of vowels undergo a considerable shift across this range of speakers, although the relative positions of the formants remain fairly constant and there is only a slight overlap for the third formant of the two vowels. Thus, it is possible that infants could have maintained the discrimination on the basis of

F1 or F2 differences between the stimuli. It would be interesting to know whether the infants could maintain such a high level of performance for stimuli in which there is a greater degree of overlap between formants. In fact, Kuhl and Miller (1982) reported the results of a study on the [a]/[ɹ] contrast that approximates that situation. Although infants required more initial training trials than for the [a]/[i] contrast, nevertheless, they were successful in discriminating the [a]/[ɔ] contrast. Once the initial training stage was passed, the infants had little difficulty coping with the variations in speaker's voice or pitch contour despite the fact that the [a] and [ɔ] tokens from different speakers had formant frequencies with similar absolute values. Thus, it appears that the infants were able to extract some measure of commonality across the variations of each vowel. Moreover, the infant's capacity for ignoring irrelevant differences among tokens of a given phonetic segment is not limited to vowels. In another study, Holmberg et al. (1977) found that infants were also able to respond consistently in discriminating the fricative contrasts [s]/[ʃ] and [f]/[Θ] despite variations in speaker's voice and pitch contour.

It should be noted that the procedure that Kuhl and her colleagues have employed is not a true generalization procedure and, thus, does not demonstrate that infants have innate categories for phonetic segments. Rather, the procedure involves a transfer of training or learning paradigm because all responses were reinforced. Kuhl and her associates have suggested in these experiments that it is possible to train infants to ignore changes in speaker's voices and pitch contours in responding to phonetic contrasts. Although it is extremely unlikely that infants would have been able to master such a task without recognizing some commonality between the different tokens of the same phonetic segment, it is important to test for such a possibility in future work. One could employ the same set of tokens used in previous experiments but require infants to learn an arbitrary grouping of these tokens (i.e., one in which tokens from the two phonetic categories are mixed and assigned to two new categories not based on a common set of phonetic dimensions; see also Kuhl, 1981). If infants failed to learn such an arbitrary grouping or learned it with considerably more difficulty than the phonetic groupings, one could be fairly confident in claiming that infants recognize a perceptual similarity among tokens from the same phonetic category. Ultimately, the strongest test for perceptual constancy would be one involving a direct measure of categorization. For example, one could train infants to identify each vowel with a particular response and then introduce new variants of the vowels and observe which response the infant made to each stimulus. This would be one way of establishing the limits of the infant's capacity for perceptual constancy. In the absence of these more precise measures, the data of Kuhl and her co-workers (see summary in Kuhl, 1980) suggest that infants have at least some degree of perceptual constancy for phonetic segments.

Another issue of fundamental importance in understanding infant speech perception concerns the nature of the perceptual categories that infants may use in dividing up the speech stream. Research in this area provides a characterization of the way in which speech sounds are represented internally by the infant. In recent years, there has been a great deal of speculation concerning the nature of the early categories used in speech perception. For the most part, proponents of the view that the infant possesses specialized speech perception mechanisms have argued for the existence of categories corresponding to linguistic units, such as phones and phonetic features (e.g., Eimas, 1982; Eimas, in press). Proponents of a more generalized auditory account of infant speech perception have favored a representation in terms of somewhat larger units, such as syllables (e.g., Bertoncini & Mehler, 1981; Jusczyk, 1982; Jusczyk, in press; Studdert-Kennedy, 1980). Although there have been a number of studies directed at this issue, the data are sparse and in many cases open to alternative explanations. The main problem is again the lack of an effective methodology to measure categorization. Still, the data derived from indirect measures of categorization represent the only information we have concerning the nature of the categories underlying infant speech perception.

A number of attempts have been made to determine whether infants represent speech in terms of traditional phonetic categories. One ambitious attempt was made by Fodor, Garrett, and Brill (1975) who employed a left/right head-turning procedure with 4-month-old infants. Fodor et al. reasoned that if phonetic categories are available to the infant, then it should be easier to learn a head-turning task in which the same response was required to items from the same phonetic category (e.g., [pi] and [pu]) as opposed to items from different phonetic categories (e.g., [pi] and [ka]). Fodor et al. selected their stimuli so that members of the nonphonetic grouping shared an important acoustic feature (frequency of the burst). Previous work by Liberman, Delattre, Cooper, and Gerstman (1954) with synthetic stimuli and by Schatz (1954) with natural speech had shown that if the burst cue from [pi] is removed and placed before the vowel [a], the resulting stimulus is actually perceived by adults as [ka]. Thus, in designing their study Fodor et al. (1975) were able to compare directly groupings based on phonetic identity against ones based on acoustic identity. Their results indicated that infants performed reliably better for the phonetic groupings than for the acoustic groupings; hence, Fodor et al. concluded that infants represent speech in terms of phonetic categories. However, the subjects of Fodor et al. never attained very high levels of proficiency, even with the phonetic groupings. In fact, they made correct anticipatory head turns on fewer than 50% of the test trials and their overall hit rates were scarcely better than their false-alarm rates. Several factors may have been responsible for the infants' low-performance level, including the fact that it is extremely difficult to use a head-turning procedure effectively in speech perception studies with infants younger than 5½ months of age (Moore et al., 1977). Because the overall performance levels were so low, the results of this study must be interpreted cautiously.

Holmberg et al. (1977) used a somewhat different approach in their study of phonetic categorization by 6-month-olds. Using a variant of the operant head-turning procedure (see Kuhl, 1979a, 1979b), Holmberg et al. (1977) tested the 6-month-old's capacity to discriminate [f]/[Θ] and [s]/[ʃ] contrasts when vowel context (e.g., [fa], [fi], [fu]) and utterance position (e.g., [fa], [af]) varied randomly. The infants were first trained to discriminate a contrast between two syllables (e.g., [fa] and [Θa]). Irrelevant changes in vowel context and utterance position were then introduced in subsequent phases of the experiment. Holmberg et al. found that infants were able to maintain the discrimination between the fricatives despite the changes in vowel context and utterance position. They concluded that the infants showed strong evidence of phonetic categorization for fricatives. However, Holmberg et al. did not test whether a grouping according to the phonetic categories ([f] and [Θ] or [s] and [ʃ]) was easier for their infants to learn than an arbitrary grouping of the same syllables. Thus, the evidence for phonetic categorization was indirect.

In their study, Holmberg et al. (1977) examined fricative contrasts because the acoustic cues for fricatives vary with vowel context. However, it is well known that fricatives exhibit much less contextual variation from surrounding vowels than do stop consonants or nasals. Hence, stronger support for the existence of phonetic categories in infant speech perception would come from a demonstration involving stop consonants. Katz and Jusczyk (1980) undertook such an investigation to determine whether infants display phonetic categorization of [b] and [d] across four different vowel contexts. They utilized the same head-turning procedure as Kuhl (1979a, 1979b), but in addition to training phases involving stimulus groupings according to phonetic categories, they employed training phases involving arbitrary groupings of the stimuli. Thus, training proceeded in the following manner. All subjects were initially trained to discriminate a contrast between [bi] and [di]. However, in the next stage of training, half of the subjects were transferred to a task in which they had to discriminate a pair of contrasts, such as [bi] and [bɛ] from [di] and [dɛ], whereas the other half of the subjects were trained on an arbitrary (nonphonetic) grouping of the same stimuli (e.g., [bi] and [dɛ] vs. [di] and [bɛ]). Because the latter grouping of the syllables has no common phonetic basis, subjects could only perform successfully on the discrimination task if they memorized the stimulus sets. Subjects who successfully completed the second stage of training advanced to the final stage, which involved four different vowel contexts. Subjects in the phonetic condition were tested for their discrimination of [bi], [bo], [be], and [bɚ] from [di], [do], [de], and [dɚ]. Subjects in the arbitrary condition were tested for their discrimination of [bi], [de], [bo], and [dɚ] from [di], [be], [do], and [bɚ]. Katz and Jusczyk (1980) argued that if the phonetic groupings were more easily learned than the arbitrary ones, the results would provide strong support for the view that infants are capable of some form of phonetic categorization. The results indicated that infants were only able to perform above chance on a transfer task involving a phonetic grouping of the syllables. No subject succeeded in the transfer task involving the arbitrary groupings.

Although these results provide support for phonetic categorization, this account must be tempered by Katz and Jusczyk's (1980) finding that no subject in the phonetic grouping ever successfully completed the final stage of training. There was no evidence for phonetic categorization of [b] and [d] when four different vowel contexts were presented. What evidence there was for phonetic categorization came only from those conditions in which two different vowel contexts were used. Such results are problematic for the view that infants categorize speech phonetically because true phonetic categorization should occur across *all* vowel contexts. The fact that infants displayed phonetic categorization only across two vowel contexts may be an indication that infants at this age are severely limited in their ability to represent speech in terms of phonetic categories. Alternatively, it is possible that infants do represent speech sounds phonetically, but the task demands of the head-turning procedure interact in some way to prevent them from displaying these abilities in this setting (for further discussion of this point see Jusczyk, 1982).

Jusczyk and Derrah (in preparation) also examined the phonetic categorization issue using a task that imposes less cognitive demands than the head-turning procedure. Borrowing their rationale from earlier studies of categorization employing visual habituation measures (e.g., Bornstein, Kessen, & Weiskopf, 1976; Cohen & Strauss, 1979), they modified the HAS procedure to study phonetic categorization. Jusczyk and Derrah (in preparation) hoped to show that repeated exposure to different instances of a particular phonetic category would result in less responding for a new instance of the same category than for a new instance of a different category. The suggestion that infants might display phonetic categorization in this setting rested on three assumptions: (1) that infants would perceive the similarity between category members, (2) that infants would become satiated to the category as a whole, and (3) that any effects of novelty for a new member of the familiar category would be offset by the satiation to the category as a whole. The test procedure involved presenting infants with a randomly ordered series of the syllables [bi], [ba], [bo], and [bɚ] during the preshift phase of the HAS procedure. During the postshift phase, some of the infants heard a stimulus set that consisted of the four preshift syllables plus [bu] (a new instance from the familiar category). For other infants, the postshift set included the four preshift stimuli plus [du] (a stimulus from a new phonetic category). Once again, the results failed to support predictions from the phonetic categorization hypothesis. The difference between responding to a new instance from a familiar category and responding to a new instance from a new category was in the predicted direction, but it was not statistically significant.

The absence of compelling evidence for perceptual categorization in terms of phonetic segments has not deterred some researchers from looking for the existence of categories at a lower level, namely, the level of phonetic features. Hillenbrand (1980) tested the ability of infants to respond to categories organized according to an oral/nasal feature distinction. He used the operant head-turning procedure (Kuhl, 1979a, 1979b) and presented infants with syllables containing the voiced stop consonants [b], [d], and [g] as background stimuli. The change stimuli were syllables containing the nasal consonants [m], [n], and [ŋ]. In addition, Hillenbrand presented another group of infants with an arbitrary grouping of the same syllables. Thus, he was able to assess whether infants found the discrimination based on the phonetic feature distinction inherently easier than the discrimination involving the arbitrary grouping. The results indicated that the infants displayed substantially higher rates of correct responding on change trials for the phonetic feature-based groupings than for the arbitrary groupings. Hillenbrand interpreted these findings as evidence that infants are able to perceptually organize speech sounds on the basis of phonetic feature similarity. Although his results are consistent with this conclusion, they are also open to another interpretation. For example, the oral/nasal distinction for consonants is marked very clearly in the acoustic signal by the presence of a nasal resonance preceding the nasal consonants. Therefore, it is possible that infants in the phonetic feature condition based their discrimination on the presence of a salient acoustic correlate (nasal resonance) rather than on some abstract phonetic feature representation derived from an analysis of the syllable structure.

A similar interpretation can be raised concerning the results of another recent study that reported that infants utilize a phonetic feature organization in categorizing speech sounds. Miller and Eimas (1979) attempted to determine whether infants are sensitive to the phonetic feature structure of a single consonant. Whereas the results from the early studies of speech perception demonstrated that infants can discriminate consonants differing in a single phonetic feature, such as voicing (see *Discrimination of Speech Sounds by Infants*), these findings did not establish that infants treat phones as combinations of phonetic features. Miller and Eimas proposed that infants may process available information about phonetic feature values independently rather than as integral parts of the same phonetic segment. They presented infants with some contrasts that were characterized by a change in a single phonetic feature across the stimulus set. Thus, a randomly ordered series of [ba] and [da] tokens during the HAS preshift period was followed by a randomly ordered series of [pa] and [ta] tokens in a test condition to examine the infants' abilities to extract a voicing contrast between the stimuli. An analogous condition pairing [ba] and [pa] against [da] and [ta] was arranged to examine the discrimination of place of articulation. However, the critical test condition for their hypothesis was one that paired [ba] and [ta] during the preshift period against [da] and [pa] during the postshift period. For this (recombined) condition, both values of the voicing feature (voiced and voiceless) and both values of the place feature (labial and alveolar) were included in both stimulus pairs; however, the specific combinations of the phonetic features differed for the preshift and postshift pairs. Miller and Eimas argued that discrimination of this contrast should only occur if infants are abstracting out the particular combination of features in the consonants. They also conducted a second experiment in which the stimulus pairs differed in place of articulation and manner of articulation (i.e., [ba], [da], [ma], [na]). The results of both studies indicated that infants discriminated the contrasts when a single feature was varied across the stimulus sets and when the features were recombined. Moreover, there were no reliable differences in performance between the condition in which a single feature was varied and the condition in which the features were recombined. On the basis of these findings, Miller and Eimas concluded that infants are sensitive to the combinations of features that define phonetic segments and, therefore, that infants analyze phonetic segments into features.

Another interpretation of the results obtained by Miller and Eimas (1979) is that their experimental conditions did not provide an adequate test of the hypothesis that infants perceive speech sounds according to a set of phonetic features. To succeed on these discrimination tasks, the infants need not have extracted any phonetic feature description of the stimuli. Instead, the infants only had to recognize that at least one of the postshift stimuli was different from the two preshift stimuli. Hence, subjects tested in the single feature condition did not need to recognize that the two preshift stimuli (e.g., [ba] and [da]) shared a common phonetic feature (voicing) that differed from one shared by the postshift stimuli (e.g., [pa] and [ta]). Nor did subjects in the recombined condition need to analyze the stimuli they heard into combinations of voicing and place features. Instead, all that was required of the infant was a response based on recognition that the syllables as wholes differed from one another in the preshift and postshift sets. Although Miller and Eimas considered this holistic explanation of their results, they rejected it on the grounds that there is "extensive behavioral as well as neurophysiological evidence for an analysis into components or features in human and non-human pattern perception" (1979, p. 355). However, the issue is precisely whether infants do, in fact, engage in phonetic feature processing. Unfortunately, Miller and Eimas' results are not sufficient to differentiate between holistic and phonetic feature processing in infant speech perception.

The lack of compelling evidence for perceptual categorization at either the phonetic segment or phonetic feature level has led some investigators to argue in favor of the syllable as the basic unit of infant speech perception (Bertoncini & Mehler, 1981; Jusczyk, 1982, in press). Although not entirely free from contextual influences by surrounding units, syllables appear to undergo considerably less context-conditioned variation than phonetic segments. For this reason, syllables or syllablelike structures have been proposed as the basic perceptual units in several models of adult processing (e.g., Klatt, 1979, 1980; Savin & Bever, 1970; Wickelgren, 1969a, 1969b). Moreover, as Jusczyk (1982, in press) has pointed out, during the earliest stages of language acquisition the child's primary task is to differentiate between the various words in the language. Hence, attending to similarities between individual phonetic segments of different words could prove to be a hindrance to successful language acquisition because of the arbitrary relationship that exists between sound and meaning in language. For example, although the words *cake* and *rake* sound more similar than *cake* and *pie*, the meanings of the latter pair are far more similar. This is not to say that the ability to recognize phonetic similarities between different words is without relevance to the child. Such an ability is crucial for learning to read and for discovering the phonological regularities that exist in spoken language. However, neither of these skills is likely to emerge until after the child has already acquired a working vocabulary of the language; the chief route toward the latter goal seems to be in learning to distinguish between different words.

Despite the arguments in favor of the syllable as the basic unit of infant speech perception, there is little direct evidence to support this notion. At present, there has been only one reported attempt to demonstrate that the syllable is the basic unit of analysis for infants. Bertoncini and Mehler (1981) attempted to show that infants are more sensitive to differences between true syllables than they are to nonsyllabic units composed of speech sounds. They employed a version of the HAS procedure and presented different groups of infants with consonant-vowel-consonant (CVC) contrasts ([pat] vs. [tap]) or consonant-consonant-consonant (CCC) contrasts ([pst] vs. [tsp]). In addition, they tested a group of infants on the same CCC contrast embedded in a vowel context. They argued that this vowel-consonant-consonant-consonant-vowel (VCCCV) contrast ([upstu] vs. [utspu]) might be easier than the original CCC contrast because it provided infants with a syllable structure that was unavailable in the

CCÇ contrast. Unfortunately, Bertoncini and Mehler's results are difficult to interpret. All three types of contrasts were discriminated by the infants based on an index of postshift dishabituation. This measure provided some indication of better discrimination performance by the CVC group but no firm evidence of better discrimination by the VCCCV group than by the CCC group. Because the former—but not the latter—results are in accordance with Bertoncini and Mehler's hypothesis, the study is inconclusive. Moreover, there is an alternative explanation for their results. The [s] may have masked information about the accompanying consonants to a greater degree than did the [a]. Therefore, Bertoncini and Mehler's experiment may not provide a suitable test for the syllable hypothesis.

In summary, the nature of the categories used by infants in perceiving speech is still an elusive problem. Research on these issues has been hampered by the absence of an adequate measure of perceptual categorization. However, based on the available data, it appears that infants may segment speech into units of syllable-size or larger. Whether infants represent syllables as configurations of smaller units, such as phonemes or features, is unclear at the present time.

Recognition of Speaker's Voice by Infants

One aspect of infant speech perception that has received little attention concerns the ability to recognize the voices of different speakers. As indicated above, the work of Kuhl (1980) and her colleagues has demonstrated that under some circumstances infants are able to ignore differences in the quality of speakers' voices. To what extent are infants also capable of detecting differences between voices, and what information might they use for this purpose?

The existing studies of voice recognition by infants have all focused on the ability to recognize a familiar voice (the mother's) in contrast to a stranger's voice. The earliest study in this area was conducted by Mills and Melhuish (1974). They tested 20- to 30-day-old infants using a modified version of the HAS procedure. After an initial 6-min. period in which a contingency between sucking and tape-recorded presentations of a stranger's voice was established, two 3-min. test periods followed in which sucking was reinforced by either live presentations of the mother's voice or tape-recorded presentations of a second stranger's voice. The results indicated that the infants' sucking rates were significantly higher to the mother's voice during the postshift period than to the second stranger's voice. Unfortunately, the live versus tape-recorded presentations were confounded with the mother's and stranger's voices. This confounding was avoided in a subsequent study by Mehler, Bertoncini, Barriere, and Jassik-Gerschenfeld (1978). These investigators also used the HAS procedure to present 4- to 6-week-olds with 20-sec. speech segments produced by the infant's mother or by the mother of another infant. In addition to the manipulation of familiarity of voice, Mehler et al. tested for the effects of prosodic information by varying the intonation of the adult utterances. Each mother produced a tape-recording that consisted of highly intonated speech directed to the infant as well as utterances spoken in a monotone. The results of this study indicated that infants preferred the mother's voice, but only when it was highly intonated. Mehler et al. interpreted these results as evidence that by at least 1 month of age infants have the capacity to recognize their mother's voice. In addition, prosodic information (in the form of intonation contours) may play a critical role in controlling the recognition process.

Additional evidence for voice recognition in even younger infants has been provided by DeCasper and Fifer (1980). They used a modified version of the sucking procedure to assess the preference of 3-day-old infants for their mother's voice compared to the voice of another infant's mother. The results indicated that the newborns preferred the mother's voice over the stranger's voice. An intriguing aspect of this study is the fact that, at most, the infants had only 12 hr. of postnatal contact with their mothers. Although it is possible that such a limited period of exposure to the mother's speech was sufficient to induce a voice preference, it is also possible that the critical information for maternal voice preference is provided during the intrauterine period. This latter possibility receives some support from the fact that speech sounds produced by the mother (or other speakers) can reach the fetus. Two recent studies, one with sheep (Armitage et al., 1980) and the other with humans (Querleu & Renard, 1981), used hydrophones placed in the amniotic sac to record the sounds transmitted through the mother's abdominal wall. Sounds with frequencies of 1,000 Hz or less were transmitted from the external environment to the hydrophone with little attenuation, whereas higher frequencies were greatly attenuated. Because much of the prosodic information contained in speech is carried in the frequency range of 100 to 1,000 Hz, it is likely that Mehler et al. (1978) were correct in assigning a critical status to prosodic cues for voice recognition in early infancy. It is important to note that vowel information (contained in at least the first two formants) would not appear to be a likely candidate for transmission to the fetus because, in a number of cases, the second formant is above 1,000 Hz. However, Spence and DeCasper (1982) have recently reported that newborns prefer to listen to a tape recording of their mother's voice reading a familiar prose passage. Prior to birth, each mother recited a particular prose passage a number of times over several weeks. Presumably, this prenatal experience was sufficient to induce a behavioral preference (assessed by a sucking technique) for the familiar passage over an unfamiliar passage also tape-recorded by the mother. The specific acoustic attributes of the passage that led to this preference have not been identified.

The full range of the infant's sensitivity to prosodic information, particularly with regard to its role in voice recognition, has only begun to be explored. As noted earlier, a number of studies have shown that very young infants are capable of distinguishing between utterances solely on the basis of prosodic cues (e.g., Jusczyk & Thompson, 1978; Kuhl & Miller, 1975b; Morse, 1972; Spring & Dale, 1977). Moreover, it has long been assumed that infants are especially sensitive to prosodic information (e.g., Kaplan & Kaplan, 1971; Weir, 1962). However, until recently little attention has been given to the kind of prosodic information available in speech sounds directed to the infant or to a description of the infant's sensitivity to this information. Studies of the prosodic features of mothers' speech to infants are beginning to reveal some potentially important patterns. For example, recent investigations using acoustical analysis procedures (e.g., Fernald & Simon, 1981; Stern, Spieker, & MacKain, 1982) have supported earlier anecdotal reports that high-pitch and exaggerated intonation contours are present in adults' speech to young children. These acoustic correlates appear to be present in such diverse languages as Luo (Blount, 1972), Arabic (Ferguson, 1964), Spanish (Blount & Padgug, 1977), Comanche (Ferguson, 1964), and American English (Garnica, 1977). In particular, Stern et al. (1982) observed changes in the prosodic features (intonation contour, timing, and rhythm) of speech directed to infants between birth and 6 months of age. Fernald and Simon (in press) found that German mothers markedly vary the tonal and temporal patterns of their speech when addressing newborns as opposed to adults. Over 77% of the utterances directed to infants fell into a limited set of prosodic patterns (e.g., expanded intonation contours and whispered speech) that were rarely found in adult speech.

The repeated finding of exaggerated intonation contours in speech directed to infants led Fernald (1981) and Fernald and Kuhl (1981) to undertake a systematic investigation of the infant's sensitivity to a number of the acoustic attributes of what has become known as motherese (Newport, 1977). First, Fernald (1981) developed a procedure to determine if 4-month-olds prefer to listen to motherese versus adult speech that is not directed to an infant. The infants were familiarized with both types of speech (tape recordings from four unfamiliar female voices) by presenting each type from one of two laterally positioned loudspeakers (counterbalanced positions between infants). Then, the presentation of each sound type was made contingent upon the head-turning responses of the infant (i.e., the sound acted as a reinforcer for directional head turns). The infants showed significantly more head turning (i.e., preference) toward the loudspeaker associated with the motherese sounds. Thus, some of the same acoustic attributes present in motherese appear to control the infant's listening preference.

Fernald and Kuhl (1981) extended this initial demonstration of the infant's preference for motherese by isolating one of its major acoustic attributes: expanded pitch contours. They analyzed the pitch contours in the motherese and nonmotherese tapes used by Fernald (1981). These pitch contours were then synthesized to produce two sets of sine-wave stimuli that contained none of the complex spectral information found in natural speech (see Remez, Rubin, Pisoni, & Carrell, 1981). Using the same preferential head-turning technique, they found that 4-month-olds made significantly more head turns to hear the motherese pitch contours than the nonmotherese pitch contours. Whether absolute pitch level or the amount of pitch excursion is more important in mediating this preference for motherese remains unclear. However, once the appropriate acoustic dimensions have been isolated, research can begin on which aspects of the speaker's voice serve to distinguish it as unique to the infant.

In summary, these pioneering studies in the area of voice recognition and speaker preference by young infants will not only lead to further research on the acoustic information that is most salient to the infant but also to a better understanding of the role that early auditory experience plays in the development of speech perception.

Role of Experience in the Development of Speech Perception

A number of findings reviewed in the preceding four discussions have led to claims for a significant influence of early linguistic experience in determining the ability of infants and adults to perceive various speech sounds. Some of these claims are based on logical arguments stemming from clear differences in speech perception among adults in diverse language communities. Other claims are based on empirical findings from infants, findings that may or may not receive confirmation as new and more sensitive assessment techniques are developed in the future. And, some of the claims are based on theoretical interpretations of data gathered from adults and infants, interpretations that have often been made without a consideration of viable alternatives. In this discussion, we offer a perspective from which the effects of early linguistic experience can be viewed. This perspective is intended to be general rather than directed toward a particular theory of speech perception. In developing this view, we will also consider the empirical evidence from adults and infants that bears on the issue of early experiential effects in speech perception. Finally, we will offer an account of the way experience influences the developing child's perception of speech.

Processes of Developmental Change

Despite the extensive body of empirical data on infant speech perception gathered over the past decade, there still exists a strong tendency toward theoretical simplification in describing the ontogeny of various infant speech processing capacities, that is, toward explaining them either in vague terms of learning or by recourse to strong nativist accounts. In contrast, several researchers working in the area of visual system development have begun to appreciate the many diverse and interactive roles that genetic and experiential factors can play in the development of sensory and perceptual systems. For example, some of the neural mechanisms underlying visual functioning are not present at birth, nor do they emerge during development as a simple consequence of a genetically controlled plan or maturational schedule. Instead, early visual experience appears to influence strongly the course of visual system development (see Aslin, Alberts, & Petersen, 1981). Experience does not, however, totally control the outcome of visual system development because some genetically specified limits are clearly placed on how much and at what point in development such early experience can influence visual system structure and function.

It has become clear from the study of visual system development that a simple dichotomy between nativist and empiricist accounts of the process of development is simply inadequate to capture the complex genetic and environmental interactions that underlie normal perceptual development (see Aslin, 1981). The following discussion is motivated primarily by our concern for providing a more explicit and coherent framework from which to view the course of perceptual development, particularly the development of speech perception. The need for such a theoretical framework in understanding the processes involved in the development of speech perception is particularly important in light of the many seemingly diverse and conflicting empirical findings that have appeared in the infant speech perception literature in recent years, many of which we have described earlier in this chapter.

Gottlieb (1976a, 1976b, 1981; see also *Models of Development, Vol. II, chap. 1*) has provided an account of some of the possible roles that early experience can play in behavioral development. His conceptualization of these experiential processes seems particularly relevant and amenable to the development of speech perception (see Aslin & Pisoni, 1980b). According to our application of Gottlieb's initial framework, there are four basic ways in which early experience could influence the development of speech processing abilities (see Fig. 22).

First, a perceptual ability may be fully developed at birth but requires certain specific types of early experience to maintain the integrity of that ability. The absence or degradation of the requisite early experience can result in either a partial or a complete loss of the perceptual ability, a loss that may be irreversible despite subsequent experience. For example, the work of Hubel and Wiesel (1965, 1970) on the visual system of the kitten showed, among other things, that the full complement of neural cells responsible for binocular vision was present at birth, although the neural cells lost their function if the kittens were deprived of binocular vision during a sensitive period. Early experience in this case served to maintain the functional integrity of the mechanisms underlying binocular vision (see also Blakemore, 1976).

Second, an ability may be only partially developed at birth, requiring specific types of early experience to facilitate or attune the further development of that perceptual ability. The lack of early experience with these stimuli that may serve a facilitating function could result either in the absence of any further development or a loss of that ability in comparison to its level at birth. As an example of a facilitating effect of experience, Gottlieb has shown that ducklings' subsequent preference and recognition of species-specific calls is modified by their own vocalizations prior to, and shortly after, hatching (see review in Gottlieb, 1981). If these self-

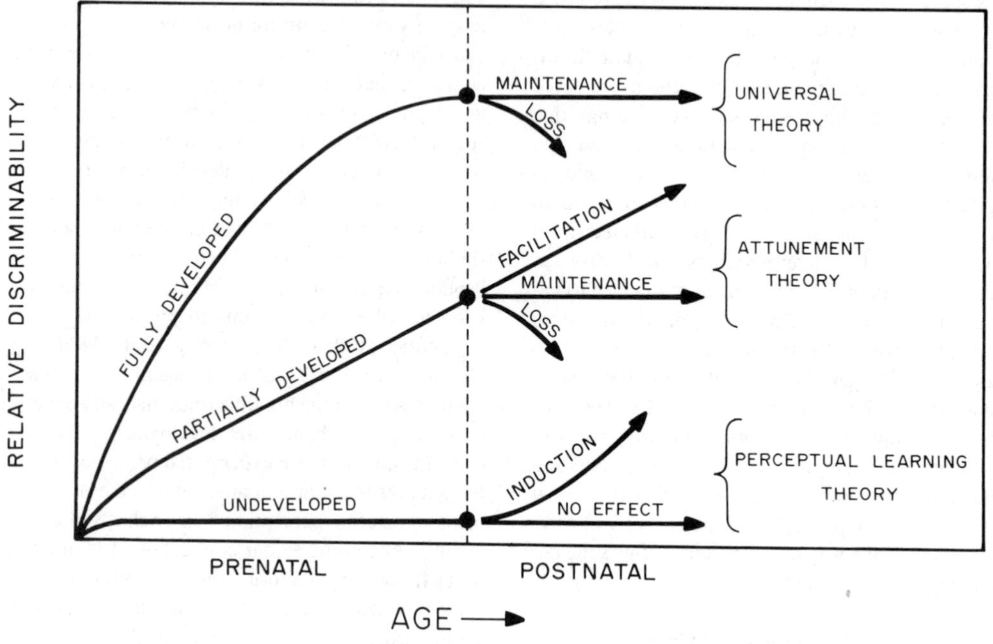

Figure 22. Illustration of the major roles that early auditory experience may play in modifying the relative discriminability of speech sounds. (Reprinted from Aslin & Pisoni, 1980b)

produced vocalizations are prevented from occurring (through devocalization techniques) in the early stages of development, the developmental rate of preference for species-specific calls declines and the ability to discriminate and recognize particular calls is substantially reduced.

Third, a perceptual ability may be absent at birth and its development may depend upon a process of induction based on early experience. The presence of a particular ability, then, would depend to a large extent on the presence of a particular type of early experience. For example, it is well known that specific early experiential inputs to young ducklings lead to imprinting to a particular stimulus object. This phenomenon can be taken as an instance of inducing a behavioral preference (Hess, 1972). Thus, in this case, a particular early experience is *necessary* for the subsequent development of a particular preference or tendency.

Finally, early experience may exert no role at all in the development of a particular perceptual ability; that is, the ability may be either present or absent at birth and it may remain, decline, or improve in the absence of any particular type of early experience. Absence of experiential effects is difficult to identify and often leads to unwarranted conclusions, especially those that assume that an induction process might be operative. For example, it is quite common for investigators to argue that if an ability is absent at birth but then observed to be present sometime after birth, the ability must have been learned (see Eilers, Gavin, & Wilson, 1979). In terms of the conceptual framework outlined above, this could be an instance of induction. Yet, it is quite possible that the ability simply unfolded developmentally according to a genetically specified maturational schedule—a schedule that required no particular type of early experience. Fantz, Fagen, and Miranda (1975) have provided an interesting example of this by demonstrating that preferences for patterned stimuli by full-term and premature infants is correlated with gestational rather than postnatal age. This unfolding of an ability may be thought of as adhering to the general class of maturational theories of development. As an example, although general motor activity is necessary to prevent the atrophy of various muscle systems, many of the classic studies by Gesell in the 1930s demonstrated that no specific training experience was necessary for infants to acquire the ability to walk (see review in Gesell & Ames, 1940). Thus, the complexity of these numerous alternatives—maintenance, facilitation, induction, and maturation—and their possible interactions should serve to caution researchers against drawing premature conclusions about the developmental course of specific perceptual abilities.

An elaboration of Gottlieb's (1981) scheme of the roles of early experience when applied to the development of speech perception generated four general classes of theories: universal theory, attunement theory, perceptual learning theory, and maturational theory. Universal theory assumes that, at birth, infants are capable of discriminating all the possible phonetic contrasts that may be used phonologically in any natural language. According to this view, early experience functions to maintain the ability to discriminate phonologically relevant distinctions—those actually presented to the infant in the language-learning environment. However, the absence of exposure to phonologically irrelevant contrasts results in a selective loss of the ability to discriminate those specific contrasts. The perceptual mechanisms responsible for this loss of sensitivity may be either neural or attentional (or both). These two alternatives also make several specific predictions concerning the possible reacquisition of the lost discriminative abilities in adults, an important topic in its own right (see *Sensory and Interpretive Coding of Speech Signals*).

Attunement theory assumes that, at birth, all infants are capable of discriminating at least some of the possible phonetic contrasts contained in the world's languages but that the infant's discriminative capacities are incompletely developed or possibly quite broadly tuned. Early experience, therefore, functions to align or to sharpen these partially developed discriminative abilities. By this account, phonologically irrelevant contrasts might be discriminable in early development but the absence of these contrasts in the language-learning environment would result in an attenuation of discriminability later in life (see Eimas, 1975a; Pisoni et al., 1982).

In contrast with the other two views, perceptual learning theory assumes that the ability to discriminate any particular phonetic contrast is dependent upon specific early experience with that contrast in the language-learning environment. The rate of development could be very fast or very slow, depending on the relative importance of the phonetic contrasts during early life, the relative psychophysical discriminability of the acoustic cues underlying the phonetic contrast compared with other phonetic contrasts, and the attentional state of the infant. According to this view, however, phonologically irrelevant contrasts would never be discriminated better than the phonologically relevant ones present in the language-learning environment.

Finally, maturational theory assumes that the ability to discriminate a particular phonetic contrast is independent of any specific early experience; it simply unfolds according to a predetermined developmental schedule. All possible phonetic contrasts would be discriminated equally well irrespective of the language environment, although the age at which specific phonetic contrasts could be discriminated would depend on the developmental level of the underlying sensory mechanisms. For example, if infants did not show sensitivity to high frequencies until later in development, one would not expect them to discriminate phonetic contrasts that are differentiated by high-frequency information (e.g., the higher formants).

These four classes of theories of perceptual development make rather specific predictions about the developmental course of speech perception in infants and young children. It is important to note that it is unlikely any single class of theory will uniquely account for all of the data on the development of speech perception. Instead, it seems reasonable to us that some hybrid of these theories will provide the best description of the development of specific speech-sound contrasts. In fact, this view of parallel developmental processes appears to be supported by current empirical findings (see *Relations Between Early Perceptual Abilities and Phonological Development*).

The perceptual findings reviewed earlier in this chapter indicate that early experience may modify the perceptual categories for speech that are assumed to be present and functional at birth. There are several ways in which early experience could selectively modify the perceptual mechanisms and, therefore, influence the overall discriminability of phonetic contrasts found in natural-language environments. Figure 23 outlines several forms that this selective modification might take with reference to the shape and level of typical adult ABX discrimination functions.

First, stimuli in the region of a boundary between two perceptual categories may become either more discriminable or less discriminable, processes we have called enhancement and attenuation. The process of enhancement may account for the heightened discriminability of stops in the prevoiced region of the VOT continuum by Thai speakers. In contrast, the process of attenuation may account for the poor discriminability of VOT differences in the prevoiced region by English speakers and the apparent de-

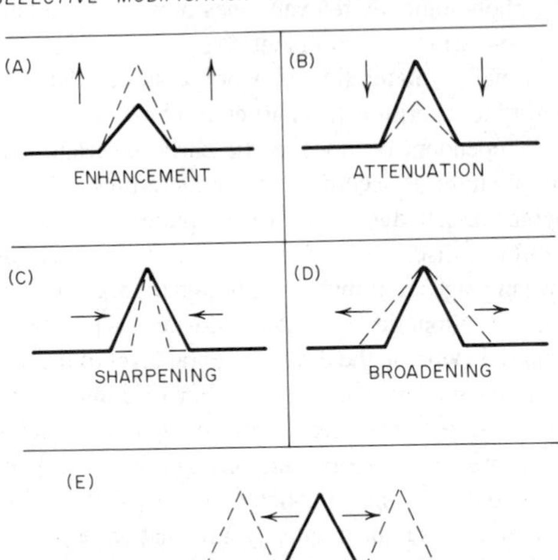

Figure 23. Five processes by which early experience in a particular language environment may selectively modify the relative discriminability of speech sounds based on schematized ABX functions. (Reprinted from Aslin & Pisoni, 1980b)

crease in discriminability of the English [r]-[l] contrast by Japanese speakers (see Pisoni et al., 1982, for further discussion of these issues).

Perception of speech stimuli in the region of a perceptual boundary may also become more finely tuned or more poorly tuned, processes we have called sharpening and broadening. On the one hand, the process of sharpening may account for the discrete and well-defined crossover points observed in adult labeling functions obtained for synthetic stop consonants. On the other hand, the process of broadening may account for the finding that vowels are more discriminable overall than consonants as well as for the wider region of heightened discriminability of VOT found in Spanish subjects who apparently rely on several other cues to voicing in addition to VOT (Abramson & Lisker, 1970, 1973; Williams, 1977b, 1977c).

Finally, the perceptual boundary may undergo a shift, a process we have called realignment. This effect of early experience may account for the differences in the voiced/voiceless boundary observed between English and Spanish stops as reported in studies by Lisker and Abramson (1970), Williams (1977b, 1977c), and Eilers, Gavin, and Wilson (1979).

From our earlier discussion of the perception of voicing and place of articulation by infants, it should be obvious that the major roles of early experience cannot be uniformly invoked to account for the development of the ability to discriminate *all* speech contrasts found in spoken language. Clearly, there are numerous variables and factors that will determine which particular ontogenetic function in Figure 22 best characterizes the developmental course of a particular phonetic contrast. For example, the auditory system of humans may well be specialized for processing certain very specific types of acoustic attributes at an early age, perhaps even at birth. If some phonetic contrasts in a language are based on these distinctive acoustic properties, the infant should be able to discriminate these contrasts with practically no experience in the language-learning environment short of auditory deprivation. However, if a certain amount of neural maturation or specific early experience is required for discrimination of these acoustic properties, we would anticipate a delay or developmental lag in discrimination of these phonetic contrasts.

The hybrid or parallel view of the role of early experience in the development of speech perception proposed here is not entirely without precedent or empirical support. Recent work on visual system development in animals has shown, for example, that most visual cortical neurons are characterized by their simultaneous responsiveness to several aspects of stimulus structure, such as direction of movement, orientation, and retinal disparity. Yet, the mechanisms underlying the development of each type of stimulus specificity is quite different. The property of directional selectivity is present at birth and undergoes little improvement or loss unless the animal is deprived of stimulus movement (see Olson & Pettigrew, 1974). The property of orientation selectivity is also present at birth, but the sharpness of each neuron's orientation specificity depends on the quality of early experience (Sherk & Stryker, 1976). And the property of disparity selectivity appears to be nearly absent at birth and the neurons acquire (within broad limits) the range of disparity values experienced during early life (Pettigrew, 1974). Thus, three of the theories we outlined in the speech perception domain—universal, attunement, and perceptual learning—could be thought of as analogous to three general mechanisms by which early experience influences visual system development. Moreover, the work on visual system development emphasizes the fact that parallel developmental mechanisms can, in fact, operate upon different aspects of the *same* sensory input and underlie what are apparently the same general perceptual abilities in the adult. With respect to speech perception, it should be obvious that only a very detailed description of the development of these discriminative abilities will enable us to distinguish between the various types of complex interactions among genetic and experiential factors.

Sensory and Interpretive Coding of Speech Signals

One of the central issues in discussions of infant speech perception is the level of processing presumed to underlie discrimination and categorization (see *Mechanisms Underlying Infant Speech Perception*). As discussed briefly earlier (*Background on Adult Speech Perception*), there are two general levels of speech processing that have been postulated: sensory (acoustic) and interpretive (phonetic). Support for a sensory level comes from several lines of evidence, most notably the correspondence between basic psychophysical aspects of auditory perception and the discrimination and categorization of speech sounds by human adults, infants, and nonhuman animals. Support for an interpretive level also comes from several lines of evidence, including evidence of perceptual constancy, that is, the presence of context-conditioned variability in the relation between acoustic attributes and phonetic identity. This context conditioning is most clearly illustrated in the acoustic correlates of place of articulation in CV syllables (see Fig. 18). The finding that potential cues for place of articulation, as seen in sound spectrograms, are context dependent has been an important justification for the claim that speech perception involves specialized processing mechanisms (e.g., Liberman & Studdert-Kennedy, 1978).

Recently, several theorists have attempted to circumvent many of the problems associated with an interpretive account of speech perception by proposing that the sound spectrogram is an impoverished representation of the speech signal. For example, rather than accepting the traditional view that there are no acoustic attributes (or set of attributes) that correspond uniquely to phonetic segments, Stevens and Blumstein (1978, 1981) have looked at alternative ways of representing the speech signal in an attempt to find invariant underlying acoustic-phonetic correspondences. Their analysis technique consists of integrating the acoustic waveform across a fixed time window and displaying the spectrum of the signal. For various reasons, they chose a window of 26 msec and initially limited their analyses to the onsets (the first 26 msec) of stop consonants in syllable-initial position. Figure 24 illustrates the relation between a traditional sound spectrogram and Stevens and Blumstein's spectral analysis.

Note that for the stop consonants differing in place of articulation (e.g., [b, d, g] vs. [p, t, k]), the onset spectra have characteristic shapes. Stevens and Blumstein (1978) have claimed that these general shapes remain invariant across different vowel contexts in CV syllables, thus providing a potentially invariant acoustic-phonetic correspondence. Such correspondences are clearly absent from analyses of formant transitions and bursts in a sound spectrogram (see Fig. 18), a fact that has been referred to as context dependency. To a first approximation, therefore, Stevens and Blumstein may have provided a new method for speech analysis that could uncover invariant acoustic-phonetic properties. If these properties are truly context *in*dependent, then a simple network of spectral templates could form the initial basis for speech perception.

There are a number of problems with the details of Stevens and Blumstein's (1978) approach to characterizing phonetic segments in terms of context-independent spectral templates. For example, the general characteristics of the spectral templates do not hold across syllable position (e.g., the spectra for [da] and [ad] are not equivalent). Thus, a second level of phonetic correspondence must be posited within Stevens and Blumstein's framework. In addition, Walley and Carrell (in press) have shown that when a CV syllable contains formant transition cues for one place of articulation but the overall spectral shape for a different place of articulation, adults more frequently label the syllable according to its formant transition cues. Thus, the secondary context-dependent cues (i.e., the formant transitions) appear to override the presumably primary context-independent cues (the properties of the onset spectrum). Recent analyses of the speech of young children (Chapin, Tseng, & Lieberman, 1982) provide converging evidence in support of Walley and Carrell's (in press) findings.

A possible solution to the problems with Stevens and Blumstein's (1978) account is to propose that listeners use the dynamic information contained in formant transitions, that is, *changes* in spectral energy over time as opposed to a static spectral sample at stimulus onset. This alternative has served as the basis for Kewley-Port's (1980) work on place of articulation in which a spectral analysis of 26-msec sections of the stop consonant waveform are performed every 5 msec. Figure 25 shows examples of these running spectral displays that have been successfully used by Kewley-Port to establish invariant context-independent characteristics of stop consonants in a variety of vowel contexts. These dynamic spectral characteristics are capable of accounting for several higher level, context-dependent effects in stops without recourse to a theory that postulates the interaction of multiple cues to phonetic segment identity. For example, several of the effects associ-

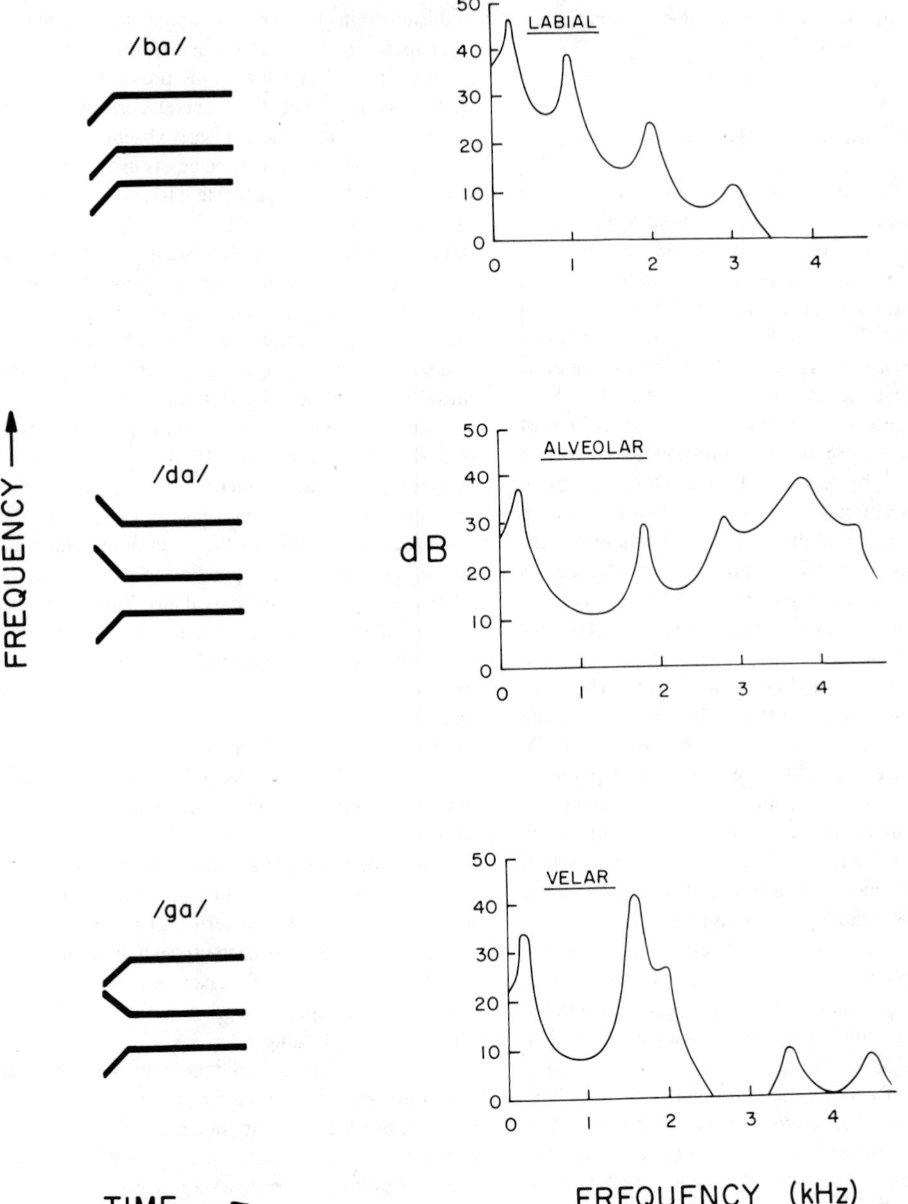

Figure 24. Schematic representation of the formant patterns associated with labial-, alveolar-, and velar-voiced stop consonants and the corresponding onset spectra.

ated with cue-trading relations may consist of invariant spectral properties that do not involve separate acoustic cues. Clearly, such a possibility demands careful investigation in the future.

Another means of investigating the issue of sensory versus interpretive coding of speech has been to gather cross-language perceptual data. Presumably, when we listen to a foreign language for the first time, we do not engage in an interpretive analysis of the phonetic segments. Rather, the speech stream is processed solely by sensory coding mechanisms. Although some investigators have hypothesized that the difference in speech perception abilities among members of different language communities is the

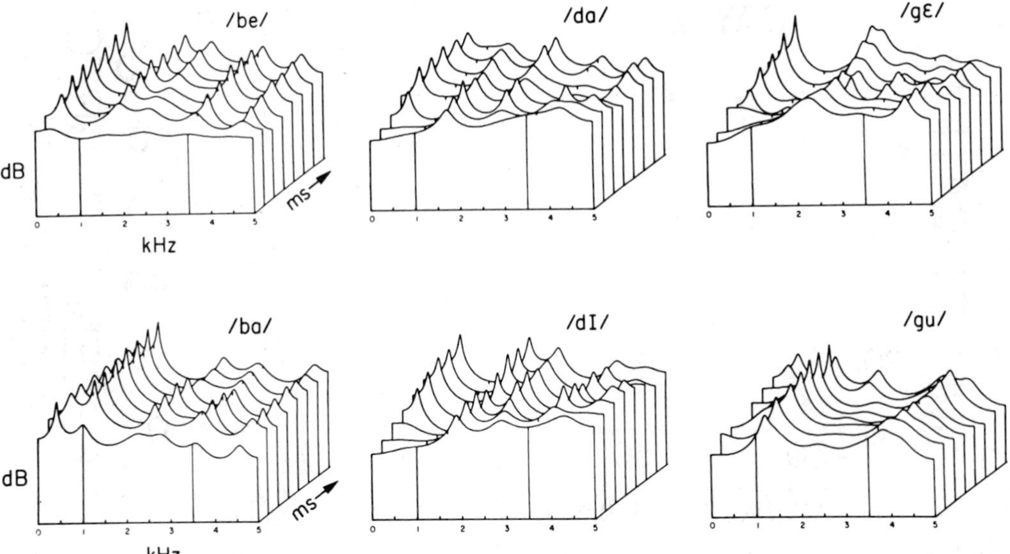

Figure 25. Running spectral displays for labial-, alveolar-, and velar-voiced stop consonants in two vowel contexts. (Reprinted from Kewley-Port, 1980)

result of the selective and permanent loss of underlying perceptual mechanisms (either phonetic or auditory), other investigators have hypothesized that such cross-language deficits are the result of undeveloped (or unused) attentional mechanisms that can be reacquired by appropriate training procedures. For example, Strange and Jenkins (1978) have reviewed the early research that attempted to train adults to discriminate speech contrasts that are not phonemic in their native language. They concluded that, in general, adults are incapable of reacquiring speech processing skills that they presumably possessed as infants. Although none of the studies cited in support of this claim attempted to match the consistency and duration of the young child's normal language experience, arguments regarding the permanence of these speech processing deficits have been made. Obviously, it is difficult to prove that adults (or infants) are incapable of acquiring an ability under some as yet untried training regimen. However, the claim for permanent perceptual deficits has been widely accepted in the absence of empirical evidence to support a training effect.

Recently, Pisoni et al. (1982) provided a demonstration of retraining that was so simple it was not even considered a training study per se. English-speaking adults were presented with bilabial stops, differing in VOT from −70 to +70 msec, in standard identification and ABX discrimination tasks. In contrast to the original Lisker and Abramson (1964, 1970) studies, however, the subjects were given a third response category in the identification task; that is, instead of asking the subjects to label the CV syllables according to the phonemic categories of their native language, they were given a three-alternative response with the categories /pa/, /ba/, and /mba/. The third response does not correspond to a phonemic category in English but it seemed obvious that Lisker and Abramson's (1970) identification data were confounded by the number of response categories provided to their subjects. The only training received by the subjects in the Pisoni et al. (1982) study was a sequence of 10 repetitions of each of the three stimuli in an order that guaranteed each subject understood how the three response categories were to be used.

The results of this study are shown in Figure 26. Note that on the identification task, despite the absence of feedback on each trial, the subjects were able to divide the VOT continuum into *three* perceptual categories, one of which did not correspond to a voicing category that is phonemic in English. The ABX discrimination data confirmed that two regions of heightened discriminability were located at the prevoiced/voiced and voiced/voiceless category boundaries. Although discrimination of tokens near the prevoiced/voiced boundary was not as good as discrimination near the voiced/voiceless boundary, a nearly identical asymmetry has been reported by Lisker and Abramson (1970) for Thai subjects de-

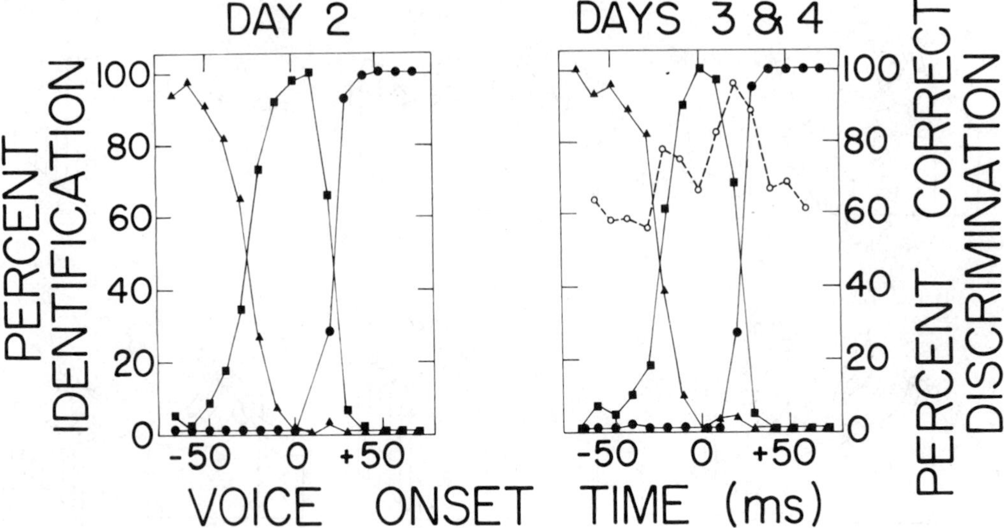

Figure 26. Average identification and ABX discrimination functions for native speakers of English presented with synthetic VOT series encompassing three different voicing categories. (Reprinted from Pisoni, Aslin, Perey, & Hennessy, 1982; copyright 1982 by the American Psychological Association)

spite the phonological relevance of the prevoiced/voiced distinction in their language.

The implication of these results is *not* that experience plays little or no role in speech perception. It is possible that Thai subjects tested under identical conditions would show superior performance compared to English subjects. Certainly one would expect to find cross-language differences in the perception of continuous speech where there are critical temporal constraints on understanding the linguistic message. However, it is clear from the results of Pisoni et al. (1982) that the underlying sensory mechanisms that enable infants and adults from a variety of language backgrounds to discriminate VOT contrasts are not permanently lost as a result of early linguistic experience. There may be transient effects of early experience, including some that influence the sensory coding of speech signals. However, the contribution of such effects does not appear to lead to an irreversible loss of the speech perception abilities that are needed to learn (or relearn) a new phonetic or phonological system (see also Carney et al., 1977).

To date, the weight of the empirical evidence from studies of human adults, infants, and nonhuman animals supports the view that *all* infant speech perception findings can be accounted for by a sensory-based processing mechanism. This does not mean that an interpretive mechanism could not also account for the data from infants. However, such a proposal is not parsimonious, particularly because there is no empirical evidence that provides convincing support for a phonetic mode of processing in infants or animals. Nevertheless, at some point in development, speech signals must undergo interpretive as well as sensory processing.

Relations Between Early Perceptual Abilities and Phonological Development

A conservative view of language development would posit that the kinds of speech perception capacities included in the infant's innate endowment would be language independent, that is, broad enough to permit the acquisition of the phonological structure of any human language. Given the fact that the phonological systems of various natural languages differ markedly, one would expect the speech signal to be analyzed initially by the infant's auditory system in a manner that constitutes only an approximation to the phonological categories used by adult members of the infant's native language community. The final step in the infant's adaptation to a particular phonological system would consist of a fine tuning of the relevant perceptual mechanisms to coincide precisely with the phonetic distinctions employed in the infant's native language.

Although at present we do not have precise information regarding the infant's categorization of speech sounds (native or nonnative), several lines of evidence from discrimination and perceptual constancy studies support the view that infants may initially partition the speech signal on the basis of well-defined psychophysical properties rather than on phonetic categories. Nevertheless, at some point in the course of language acquisition, infants from different language environments must begin to process the acoustic information contained in the speech signal differently from nonspeech and foreign speech contrasts because cross-language studies of adults have documented differential responsiveness to phonemic versus nonphonemic contrasts. Thus, the infant's categorization of speech sounds must eventually shift from a psychophysical to a phonological basis. At this later stage, the same acoustic information that was previously available to the infant is still present but the infant presumably processes that information beyond the sensory level.

An account of this shift from psychophysical to phonetic processing of speech has been delineated recently by Jusczyk (in press). This approach assumes that the impetus for the shift is the infant's desire to communicate, that is, the task of assigning meaning to a given utterance. This goal encourages the child to attend in a new way to the similarities and differences that exist in the acoustic attributes of the utterance. The child must be able to focus attention on precisely those acoustic variations that result in a change in the meaning of the utterance. Feedback (parental or contextual) about the meaning of the utterance enables the child to isolate those properties of the acoustic signal that play a critical role in the specific language being learned. In effect, the process of mapping sounds to meanings provides the child with an important check on the consequences that different acoustic attributes have for conveying a particular message.

Delineating just what acoustic properties are the most critical for the child is presumably closely tied to the phonological constraints operating in the particular language-learning environment. Thus, as the child begins to acquire the phonological structure of the language, various aspects of the available acoustic information are weighted according to their salience in marking distinctive phonetic contrasts in the language. Therefore, the shift from a psychophysical categorization of speech to a phonological one may involve the assignment of a new set of weightings to the various aspects of acoustic information in the speech signal. As a result, the child now begins to treat speech sounds differently than nonspeech sounds. In summary, the present model proposes that the child develops the appropriate working representation of the phonological structure of a particular language by developing an appropriate set of weightings for extracting specific acoustic attributes from the speech signal. A similar process probably occurs in the learning of a second language. Hence, the bilingual speaker would be expected to employ different weightings for each language. Some support for this latter notion comes from Williams (1977b, 1977c) and Diehl, Elman and McCusker (1978) who have found that fluent bilingual speakers show two sets of category boundaries along the voicing continuum that are dependent on the language context.

One consequence of this view is that the speech mode may be more appropriately regarded as the deployment of an interpretive or attentional weighting scheme rather than the activation of a specialized perceptual mechanism. Some otherwise puzzling findings are also accounted for by this approach. For example, studies of adults using the selective adaptation procedure indicate that shifts in category boundaries are tied to acoustic rather than phonetic properties of the stimuli (Diehl, 1981; Sawusch, 1977a, 1977b; Sawusch & Jusczyk, 1981; Studdert-Kennedy, 1980). In contrast, studies that have employed ambiguous sine-wave stimuli (e.g., Bailey, Summerfield, & Dorman, 1977; Best, Morrongiello, & Robson, 1981) have found different perceptual boundaries for the same stimuli under speech and nonspeech instruction sets. And, recent findings have shown that subjects' interpretation of one speech cue can be influenced by their expectations about another cue. For example, Carden et al. (1981) demonstrated that instructions regarding manner of articulation of a syllable (i.e., whether it contained a stop or a fricative) affected adult subjects' place of articulation judgments (i.e., whether a stimulus was considered to be labial or dental). All of these findings are consistent with the view that different schemes for weighting the acoustic information are employed in each situation.

Finally, the notion that the speech mode undergoes considerable development is consistent with findings on the effects of early linguistic experience. As noted earlier, several studies have demonstrated that young infants can discriminate foreign speech contrasts and that adult speakers may be less sensitive to certain foreign language contrasts than infants. One possible explanation for this presumed decline in perceptual ability is that certain underlying mechanisms atrophy as a result of nonuse in the native language environment. However, any notion that permanent damage to underlying mechanisms occurs as a result of nonuse is countered by the finding that relatively short periods of training can greatly improve the discrimination performance of nonnative listeners (Pisoni et al., 1982; Werker et al., 1981). In fact, the latter results suggest that poor performance on the part of nonnative listeners may be an attentional deficit brought about by many years of practice in learning to ignore or deemphasize those aspects of the acoustic signal that are not pertinent to the phonological constraints of the listener's native language. That the poor performance of a nonnative listener is rooted in an attentional deficit rather than a sensory one follows directly from a model that equates the speech mode with an interpretive weighting scheme.

The present account is only a preliminary step in the process of delineating what weightings the infant applies to the speech signal and how these weightings change during development. It is possible, as Bertoncini and Mehler (1981) have suggested, that infants initially attend most closely to the entire syllable rather than to specific components or features associated with a phonetic representation. For example, infants do not appear to recognize a commonality among syllables that share initial stop consonant segments (e.g., /bi/, /ba/, /bo/; Katz & Jusczyk, 1980). Studies of the older child's ability to report on the identity of a phonetic segment that appears in different words suggest that attention to the level of phonetic segments may not be complete until the child is ready to read (Jusczyk, 1977b; Liberman, Shankweiler, Carter, & Fischer, 1974; Walley, Smith, & Jusczyk, 1980). Although it is possible that the child engages in some form of analysis at the level of phonetic segments prior to the onset of reading skills, other investigators of phonological development (e.g., Menyuk & Menn, 1979) have suggested that the initial phonological distinctions made by the child involve syllable-sized units and only later does the child engage in an analysis of words into phonetic segments. This notion that the child may not begin to analyze speech into the smallest possible units is prevalent in other areas of language acquisition. For example, Rosch and Mervis (1981) have applied this whole-to-part notion in their discussions of prototypes as basic semantic categories, and Bowerman (1981) and Bever (1982) have applied it in descriptions of syntactic development.

It was argued earlier that the phonological structure of the native language influences the weighting of acoustic information in the speech signal. What, then, contributes to the assignment of the weighting factors? An illustrative example is the voicing dimension. Although voicing differences are used to describe a variety of phonetic contrasts in different languages, there is strong evidence that distinctly different cues may be involved in different phonological systems. For example, the use of the terms voiced and unvoiced in describing English stop consonants is somewhat inappropriate because, as Ladefoged (1971) has noted, the English voicing distinction is actually a contrast between aspirated and unaspirated stops. In contrast, Spanish employs a difference in voicing per se for this distinction. Thus, these two languages use different aspects of the acoustic signal to make a voicing distinction in labial stop consonants. As a result, the assignment of weighting factors to the same acoustic signal should be different in English and Spanish, and this is precisely the effect reported in studies of English-Spanish bilinguals (Diehl, Elman, & McCusker, 1978; Williams, 1977b, 1977c).

These cross-language findings on differential weightings applied to the same speech signal receive some support from studies of speech production. For example, Macken (1980) found that children learning English seemed to produce appropriate VOT distinctions at an earlier age than children learning Spanish. Macken noticed that the children learning Spanish were contrasting the segments on the basis of a stop-spirant feature rather than VOT. A subsequent analysis of adult speakers of Spanish revealed that the stop-spirant feature was substituted for VOT 30 to 40% of the time in initial position. Macken also found that the children learning Spanish acquired appropriate VOT productions earlier for initial stops in the labial place of articulation. Spanish uses many more voicing contrasts for labials than for other places of articulation, suggesting that the children were attending to the distributional aspects of the adults' productions. While these data are from production, rendering any direct inferences about perceptual analysis problematic, they are suggestive of a process by which the phonological structure of the child's native language could influence the development of a phonetic representation. It would be of great interest to determine what the perceptual categories of the children were during the early period of speech production.

A final question raised by this account of differential weightings of speech inputs concerns the dimensions of salience that determine the child's current weighting scheme or representation. A problem faced by all current theories of phonological development is that a characterization of the child's representation of sounds and meanings based on the child's productions may be confounded by developmental constraints on the articulatory system. One approach for circumventing this problem is to look for evidence of systematic patterns in the productions (and nonproductions, see Menn, 1980) made by the child. It is unlikely that we can assume that the underlying representation is equivalent to the set of phonetic contrasts that the infant is capable of discriminating. There is evidence from several studies (e.g., Garnica, 1973; Shvachkin, 1973) that the child may not employ the discriminative capacities that we know to be present in early infancy. Moreover, Locke (1979) has noted that the ability to discriminate a given phonetic contrast on a specific comparison test does not ensure that the contrast will be discriminated in all contexts, nor does it ensure that the dimension underlying discrimination of the contrast is a part of the child's phonological representation. The question of what the psychologically relevant dimensions are for the perceiver is, of course, a critical question for the entire field of speech perception. Often researchers assume that, just because a stimulus set can be described adequately in a certain way, this description must be the one used by the perceiver (see Schwab, Sawusch, & Nusbaum, 1981, for a recent counterexample).

In summary, the field of infant speech perception has been provided with a wealth of new information on the discriminative capabilities of young infants presented with a wide variety of phonetic contrasts. Future research efforts will likely focus on the *use* of these discriminative abilities in analyzing speech inputs and the organization of these inputs into a phonological representation for subsequent speech productions. The validity of the notion of a set of differential weightings of the speech signal will require more sensitive methods for studying speech perception, especially categorization, during the second year of life.

SUMMARY AND CONCLUSIONS

In this chapter, we have examined the explosive growth that has occurred during the past decade in the number of studies of basic auditory development and speech perception in human infants. In an attempt to briefly summarize these findings, we return to the set of questions that provided a framework for our review. First, in the area of basic auditory abilities, we described evidence from fetal and prematurely born infants that auditory function begins several weeks before the 40th postconceptional week. However, the quality of this early auditory function is unknown because of the restricted range of sounds that reach the fetus and the possibility that tactile rather than cochlear stimulation may mediate the fetal response to extrauterine sounds. Postnatal changes in auditory sensitivity are also not fully understood because of difficulties in applying an invariant method of measurement over a broad age range. Thus, despite clear changes during the postnatal period in such measures as the ABR, it remains unclear whether hearing improves or whether neural response systems become more synchronized. In fact, although nearly all studies of infant hearing have found at least a 15- to 20-dB threshold deficit relative to adults, it is possible that nonsensory factors (such as attention and criterion differences) may account for much of this discrepancy. Nevertheless, infants and adults do appear to show reliable differences in auditory sensitivity to sounds of varying frequency.

The precise role of early experience in human auditory development is also unclear and, unfortunately, largely untestable. Evidence from other species suggests that auditory deprivation in the form of monaural attenuation significantly impairs sound localization abilities. However, the applicability of these findings to human infants will remain unclear until more satisfactory animal models of human auditory development are discovered. Finally, the mechanisms underlying auditory development are largely unknown. It would appear from anatomical findings that the basic peripheral auditory apparatus is quite mature at birth. However, the development of cochlear functioning and the more central areas of the human auditory system has eluded systematic study, primarily because noninvasive techniques are required. Again, the development of an animal model of the human auditory system would greatly facilitate the study of the mechanisms underlying auditory development.

In the area of speech perception we have much more information concerning each of the five questions raised in the *Introduction*. First, there is evidence for discrimination of nearly all the phonetic contrasts that have been presented to infants. These findings do not imply that few developmental changes occur in the processing of speech sounds by infants. Instead, most of the phonetic distinctions employed in natural languages contain acoustic attributes that the auditory system is capable of discriminating at an early age. As in the case of basic auditory sensitivity, however, few studies have addressed developmental changes in speech perception, primarily because available methods of measurement do not provide a fine-grained analysis of speech discrimination in young infants. Nevertheless, infants are adept at discriminating a vast array of speech contrasts, and this fact provides strong support for the assumption that infants possess specialized speech processing skills. However, evidence from nonhuman species as well as similar discrimination performance by infants for nonspeech signals provides a forceful counterargument to the claim for a specialized speech mode. An alternative view is that general properties of the mammalian auditory system underlie much of the infant's speech discrimination performance.

Additional evidence from cross-language studies of infant speech perception also supports the view that a set of general auditory abilities underlies the infant's processing of speech sounds. Nearly all of the cross-language evidence suggests that infants from a wide variety of language-learning environments discriminate speech sounds in much the same manner. At present, evidence for the effect of early linguistic experience in infant speech perception is equivocal. Thus, until more detailed discrimination and categorization studies are conducted, the status of experiential influences will remain unclear. Finally, the evidence for perceptual categorization in infants supports the view that certain acoustic attributes are more salient than others and that the most salient attributes guide the process of category formation. Unfortunately, the limited data base on speech categorization precludes a complete account of the infant's skill at forming categories, particularly in light of the diverse set of acoustic attributes that are used in various languages.

In conclusion, the areas of infant speech perception and audition have shown remarkable growth in the past decade. The development of new methods of measurement coupled with a trend toward the use of sophisticated psychophysical techniques will undoubtedly lead to additional progress in describing the ontogeny of auditory function in the decade ahead.

NOTES

1. The dynamic range of the human auditory system is very large (approximately 10 to the 15th power). To provide a more manageable metric for this range, stimulus intensity is converted to a logarithmic scale. Thus, a decibel (dB) is defined as 10 log E1/E2, where E1 is the intensity of a sound and E2 is a referent intensity (typically the absolute threshold). Thus, if E1 is 20 dB more intense than E2, the actual difference in intensity is a factor of 1,000. Note, however, that the physical energy of the sound may not correspond to the perceived intensity (loudness) of the sound.

2. Recently, Rosen and Howell (1981) have provided evidence that nonspeech stimuli differing in rise time are not perceived categorically by adults. This finding contradicts the report by Cutting and Rosner (1974). It appears that errors were made in the synthesis of the original stimuli used by Cutting and Rosner to test adults and subsequently by Jusczyk et al. (1977) to test infants. The noncategorical nature of adults' perception of rise-time differences has also been reported by Kewley-Port and Pisoni (1982). Although these recent nonreplications of the Cutting and Rosner (1974) study render the Jusczyk et al. (1977) findings from infants equivocal, they do not detract from the other evidence of categorical discrimination of nonspeech signals differing in TOT reported by Jusczyk, Pisoni, Walley, and Murray (1980).

3. A possible explanation of these results might appear to lie in some sort of auditory masking effect. However, in a subsequent experiment using stimuli from synthetic speech continua, Carden et al. (1981) ruled out such an explanation by demonstrating that the same effect could be obtained in the absence of any physical cue for frication by manipulating subjects' expectations regarding the manner of articulation for the syllables. Thus, Carden et al. interpreted their results as indicating that the perception of place of articulation cues depends on the perception of manner of articulation.

4. Morse et al. (1982) reported that pooling the results from the [slit]/[slit]+s and the [slit]/[split] conditions did yield evidence of discrimination. However, the fact remains that they did not obtain any evidence for discrimination of the [slit]/[split] contrast, even with the unorthodox statistical measures that they used.

5. Bundy, Colombo, and Singer (1982) have recently reported that 4-month-olds do not exhibit pitch discrimination. The infants were habituated to a three-note melody whose spectral composition was either constant (containing the fundamental frequency) or randomly varying (with or without the fundamental frequency). Heart rate dishabituation was shown only to the melody whose spectral composition remained invariant during the habituation phase. Thus, infants may not be able to extract pitch from complex sounds until after 4 months of age. If this pitch-extraction process were difficult for the infants tested by Kuhl (1980), then the ease with which these infants "ignored" pitch variations may not indicate perceptual constancy per se but a tendency to ignore small stimulus differences.

REFERENCES

Abahazi, D. A., & Greenberg, H. J. Clinical acoustic reflex threshold measurements in infants.

Journal of Speech and Hearing Disorders, 1977, *42*, 514–519.

Abbs, J. H., & Sussman, H. M. Neurophysiological feature detectors and speech perception: A discussion of theoretical implications. *Journal of Speech and Hearing Research*, 1971, *14*, 23–36.

Abramson, A. S., & Lisker, L. Discriminability along the voice continuum: Cross-language tests. *Proceedings of the Sixth International Congress of Phonetic Sciences*, 1967. Prague: Academia, 1970.

Abramson, A. S., & Lisker, L. Voice-timing perception in Spanish word-initial stops. *Journal of Phonetics*, 1973, *1*, 1–8.

Alegria, J., & Noirot, E. Neonate orientation behavior towards human voice. *International Journal of Behavioral Development*, 1978, *1*, 291–312.

Altman, M. M., Shenhav, R., & Schaudinischky, L. Semi-objective method for auditory mass screening of neonates. *Acta Oto-Laryngologica*, 1975, *79*, 46–50.

Aran, J.-M. Contribution of electrocochleography to diagnosis in infancy: An eight-year survey. In S. E. Gerber & G. T. Mencher (Eds.), *Early diagnosis of hearing loss*. New York: Grune & Stratton, 1978.

Armitage, S. E., Baldwin, B. A., & Vince, M. A. The fetal sound environment of sheep. *Science*, 1980, *208*, 1173–1174.

Aslin, R. N. Experiential influences and sensitive periods in perceptual development: A unified model. In R. N. Aslin, J. R. Alberts, & M. R. Petersen (Eds.), *Development of perception: Psychobiological perspectives*, Vol. 2, *The visual system*. New York: Academic Press, 1981.

Aslin, R. N., Alberts, J. R., & Petersen, M. R. (Eds.), *Development of perception: Psychobiological perspectives*, Vol. 2, *The visual system*. New York: Academic Press, 1981.

Aslin, R. N., & Pisoni, D. B. Effects of early linguistic experience on speech discrimination by infants: A critique of Eilers, Gavin and Wilson (1979). *Child Development*, 1980, *51*, 107–112. (a)

Aslin, R. N., & Pisoni, D. B. Some developmental processes in speech perception. In G. H. Yeni-Komshian, J. F. Kavanagh, & C. A. Ferguson (Eds.), *Child phonology*, Vol. 2, *Perception*. New York: Academic Press, 1980. (b)

Aslin, R. N., Pisoni, D. B., Hennessy, B. L., & Perey, A. J. Discrimination of voice onset time by human infants: New findings and implications for the effects of early experience. *Child Development*, 1981, *52*, 1135–1145.

Bailey, P. J. *Perceptual adaptation in speech: Some properties of detectors for acoustical cues to phonetic distinctions*. Unpublished doctoral dissertation, Cambridge University, 1975.

Bailey, P. J., Summerfield, A. Q., & Dorman, M. F. On the identification of sine-wave analogs of certain speech sounds. *Status Report on Speech Research* (SR 51–52). New Haven, Conn.: Haskins Laboratories, 1977.

Ballenger, J. J. *Diseases of the nose, throat, and ear*. Philadelphia: Lea & Febiger, 1969.

Bartoshuk, A. K. Human neonatal cardiac responses to sound: A power function. *Psychonomic Science*, 1964, *1*, 151–152.

Bast, T. H., & Anson, B. J. *The temporal bone and the ear*. Springfield, Ill.: Charles C. Thomas, 1949.

Bastian, J., Eimas, P. D., & Liberman, A. M. Identification and discrimination of a phonemic contrast induced by silent interval. *Journal of the Acoustical Society of America*, 1961, *33*, 842.

Bechtold, A. G., Bushnell, E. W., & Salapatek, P. *Infants' visual localization of visual and auditory targets*. Paper presented at the meeting of the Society for Research in Child Development, San Francisco, March 1979.

Bench, J. "Square-wave stimuli" and neonatal auditory behavior: Some comments on Ashton (1971), Hutt et al. (1968) and Lenard et al. (1969). *Journal of Experimental Child Psychology*, 1973, *16*, 521–527.

Bennett, M. J. Trials with the auditory response cradle. *British Journal of Audiology*, 1979, *13*, 125–134.

Bennett, M. J., & Lawrence, R. J. Trials with the auditory response cradle. *British Journal of Audiology*, 1980, *14*, 1–6.

Berg, K. M., & Smith, M. C. Behavioral thresholds for tones during infancy. *Journal of Experimental Child Psychology*, in press.

Berg, W. K. *Auditory inhibition of infants' reflexblinks: Enhancement by near-threshold stimuli*. Paper presented at the meeting of the International Conference on Infant Studies, New Haven, Conn., April 1980.

Bernard, J., & Sontag, L. W. Fetal reactivity to tonal stimulation: A preliminary report. *Journal of Genetic Psychology*, 1947, *70*, 205–210.

Bertoncini, J., & Mehler, J. Syllables as units in infant speech perception. *Infant Behavior & Development*, 1981, *4*, 247–260.

Best, C. T., Morrongiello, B., & Robson, R. Perceptual equivalence of acoustic cues in speech and nonspeech perception. *Perception & Psy-*

chophysics, 1981, *29,* 191–211.

Bever, T. G. Regression in the service of development. In T. G. Bever (Ed.), *Regressions in development: Basic phenomena and theoretical alternatives.* Hillsdale, N.J.: Erlbaum, 1982.

Blakemore, C. The conditions required for the maintenance of binocularity in the kitten's visual cortex. *Journal of Physiology (London),* 1976, *261,* 423–444.

Blount, B. G. Aspects of socialization among the Luo of Kenya. *Language Sociology,* 1972, *1,* 235–248.

Blount, B. G., & Padgug, E. J. Prosodic, paralinguistic and interactional features in parent-child speech: English and Spanish. *Journal of Child Language,* 1977, *4,* 67–86.

Boring, E. G. *Sensation and perception in the history of experimental psychology.* New York: Appleton-Century, 1942.

Bornstein, M. H., Kessen, W., & Weiskopf, S. Color vision and hue categorization in young human infants. *Journal of Experimental Psychology: Human Perception and Performance,* 1976, *2,* 115–129.

Bowerman, M. Reorganizational processes in lexical and syntactic development. In L. Gleitman & E. Wanner (Eds.), *Language acquisition: State of the art.* Cambridge, Eng.: At the University Press, 1981.

Boyd, E. F. Visual fixation and voice discrimination in 2-month-old infants. In F. D. Horowitz (Ed.), Visual attention, auditory stimulation, and language discrimination in young infants. *Monographs of the Society for Research in Child Development,* 1975, *39,* (5–6, Serial No. 158).

Bredberg, G. The human cochlea during development and aging. *Journal of Laryngology and Otology,* 1967, *81,* 739–758.

Bredberg, G. *The anatomy of the developing ear.* Paper presented at the Erindale symposium: Auditory development in infancy, Toronto, June 1981.

Brown, P. E., Grinnell, A. D., & Harrison, J. B. The development of hearing in the pallid bat, *Antrozous pallidus. Journal of Comparative Physiology,* 1978, *126,* 169–182.

Brugge, J. F., & Geisler, C. D. Auditory mechanisms of the lower brainstem. In W. M. Cowan, Z. W. Hall, & E. R. Kandel (Eds.), *Annual review of neuroscience* (Vol. 1). Palo Alto, Calif.: Annual Reviews, 1978.

Brugge, J. F., Javel, E., & Kitzes, L. M. Signs of functional maturation of peripheral auditory system in discharge patterns of neurons in anteroventral cochlear nucleus of kitten. *Journal of Neurophysiology,* 1978, *41,* 1557–1579.

Bruner, J. S. Neural mechanisms in perception. *Psychological Review,* 1957, *64,* 340–358.

Buchwald, J. S., & Huang, C. M. Far-field acoustic response: Origins in the cat. *Science,* 1975, *189,* 382–384.

Bull, D., Schneider, B. A., & Trehub, S. E. The masking of octave-band noise by broad-spectrum noise: A comparison of infant and adult thresholds. *Perception & Psychophysics,* 1981, *30,* 101–106.

Bullock, T. H. (Ed.). *Recognition of complex acoustic signals.* Berlin: Dahlem Konferenzen, 1977.

Bundy, R. S. Discrimination of sound localization cues in young infants. *Child Development,* 1980, *51,* 292–294.

Bundy, R. S., Colombo, J., & Singer, J. Pitch perception in young infants. *Developmental Psychology,* 1982, *18,* 10–14.

Burdick, C. K., & Miller, J. D. Speech perception by the chinchilla: Discrimination of sustained /a/ and /i/. *Journal of the Acoustical Society of America,* 1975, *58,* 415–427.

Bush, M. A., & Williams, S. K. L. *Infant place discrimination of voiced stop consonants with and without release bursts.* Paper presented at the meeting of the Acoustical Society of America, University Park, Pa., June 1977.

Butterworth, G., & Castillo, M. Coordination of auditory and visual space in newborn human infants. *Perception,* 1976, *5,* 155–160.

Carden, G., Levitt, A., Jusczyk, P. W., & Walley, A. C. Evidence for phonetic processing of cues to place of articulation: Perceived manner affects perceived place. *Perception & Psychophysics,* 1981, *29,* 26–36.

Carney, A. E., Widin, G. P., & Viemeister, N. F. Noncategorical perception of stop consonants differing in VOT. *Journal of the Acoustical Society of America,* 1977, *62,* 961–970.

Carrell, T. D., Pisoni, D. B., & Gans, S. J. *Perception of the duration of rapid spectrum changes: Evidence for context effects with speech and nonspeech signals.* Paper presented at the meeting of the Acoustical Society of America, Los Angeles, November 1980.

Carrell, T. D., Smith, L. B., & Pisoni, D. B. Some perceptual dependencies in speeded classification of vowel color and pitch. *Perception & Psychophysics,* 1981, *29,* 1–10.

Chapin, C., Tseng, C., & Lieberman, P. Short-term release cues to stop-consonant place of articulation. *Journal of the Acoustical Society of America,* 1982, *71,* 179–186.

Chomsky, N., & Miller, G. A. Introduction to the formal analysis of natural languages. In R. D. Luce, R. Bush, & E. Galanter (Eds.), *Handbook of mathematical psychology* (Vol. 2). New York: Wiley, 1963.

Chun, R. W. M., Pawsat, R., & Forster, F. M. Sound localization in infancy. *Journal of Nervous and Mental Diseases,* 1960, *130,* 472–476.

Clements, M., & Kelly, J. B. Auditory spatial responses of young guinea pigs (*Cavia porcellus*) during and after ear blocking. *Journal of Comparative and Physiological Psychology,* 1978, *92,* 34–44. (a)

Clements, M., & Kelly, J. B. Directional responses by kittens to an auditory stimulus. *Developmental Psychobiology,* 1978, *11,* 505–511. (b)

Clifton, R. K., Morrongiello, B. A., Kulig, J. W., & Dowd, J. M. Developmental changes in auditory localization in infancy. In R. N. Aslin, J. R. Alberts and M. R. Petersen (Eds.), *Development of perception: Psychobiological perspectives,* Vol. 1, *Audition, somatic perception, and the chemical senses.* New York: Academic Press, 1981. (a)

Clifton, R. K., Morrongiello, B. A., Kulig, J. W., & Dowd, J. M. Newborns' orientation toward sound: Possible implications for cortical development. *Child Development,* 1981, *53,* 833–838. (b)

Clopton, B. M. The development of hearing. In T. Ruch & H. D. Patton (Eds.), *Physiology and biophysics.* Philadelphia: W. B. Saunders, 1979.

Clopton, B. M. Neurophysiological and anatomical aspects of auditory development. In R. N. Aslin, J. R. Alberts, & M. R. Petersen (Eds.), *Development of perception: Psychobiological perspectives,* Vol. 1, *Audition, somatic perception, and the chemical senses.* New York: Academic Press, 1981.

Clopton, B. M., & Silverman, M. S. Plasticity of binaural interaction. II. Critical period and changes in midline response. *Journal of Neurophysiology,* 1977, *40,* 1275–1280.

Clopton, B. M., & Silverman, M. S. Changes in latency and duration of neural responding following developmental auditory deprivation. *Experimental Brain Research,* 1978, *32,* 39–47.

Cohen, L. B., & Gelber, E. R. Infant visual memory. In L. B. Cohen & P. Salapatek (Eds.), *Infant perception: From sensation to cognition* (Vol. 1). New York: Academic Press, 1975.

Cohen, L. B., & Strauss, M. S. Concept acquisition in the human infant. *Child Development,* 1979, *50,* 419–424.

Cole, R. A. (Ed.). *Perception and production of fluent speech.* Hillsdale, N.J.: Erlbaum, 1980.

Coleman, J. R., & O'Connor, P. Effects of monaural and binaural sound deprivation on cell development in the anteroventral cochlear nucleus of rats. *Experimental Neurology,* 1979, *64,* 553–566.

Colombo, J., & Bundy, R. S. A method for the measurement of infant auditory selectivity. *Infant Behavior & Development,* 1981, *4,* 219–233.

Cone, B. K., & Gerber, S. E. Impedance measurements. In S. E. Gerber (Ed.), *Audiometry in infancy.* New York: Grune & Stratton, 1977.

Cooper, F. S., Delattre, P. C., Liberman, A. M., Borst, J. M., & Gerstman, L. J. Some experiments on the perception of synthetic speech sounds. *Journal of the Acoustical Society of America,* 1952, *24,* 597–606.

Cooper, F. S., Liberman, A. M., & Borst, J. M. The interconversion of audible and visible patterns as a basis for research in the perception of speech. *Proceedings of the National Academy of Sciences,* 1951, *37,* 318–325.

Cooper, W. E. *Speech perception and production: Studies in selective adaptation.* Norwood, N.J.: Ablex, 1979.

Cooper, W. E., & Blumstein, S. A "labial" feature analyzer in speech perception. *Perception & Psychophysics,* 1974, *15,* 591–600.

Crowell, D. H., Davis, C. M., Chun, B. J., & Spellacy, F. J. Galvanic skin reflex in newborn humans. *Science,* 1965, *148,* 1108–1111.

Cutting, J. E., & Rosner, B. S. Categories and boundaries in speech and music. *Perception & Psychophysics,* 1974, *16,* 564–570.

Dallos, P. Cochlear physiology. In M. R. Rosenzweig & L. W. Porter (Eds.), *Annual review of psychology* (Vol. 32). Palo Alto, Calif.: Annual Reviews, 1981.

Danaher, E. M., Osberger, M. J., & Pickett, J. M. Discrimination of formant frequency transitions in synthetic vowels. *Journal of Speech and Hearing Research,* 1973, *16,* 439–451.

DeCasper, A. J., & Fifer, W. P. Of human bonding: Newborns prefer their mothers' voices. *Science,* 1980, *208,* 1174–1176.

Delattre, P. C., Liberman, A. M., & Cooper, F. S. Acoustic loci and transitional cues for consonants. *Journal of the Acoustical Society of America,* 1955, *27,* 769–773.

Delattre, P. C., Liberman, A. M., Cooper, F. S., &

Gerstman, L. J. Observations on one- and two-formant vowels synthesized from spectrographic patterns. *Word,* 1952, *8,* 195–210.

Demetriades, T. The cochlea-palpebral reflex in infants. *Annals of Otology, Rhinology and Laryngology,* 1923, *32,* 894–903.

Denes, P. Effect of duration on perception of voicing. *Journal of the Acoustical Society of America,* 1955, *27,* 761–764.

Despland, P. A., & Galambos, R. The auditory brainstem response (ABR) is a useful diagnostic tool in the intensive care nursery. *Pediatric Research,* 1980, *14,* 154–158.

Diehl, R. L. Feature detectors for speech: A critical reappraisal. *Psychological Bulletin,* 1981, *82,* 1–18.

Diehl, R. L., Elman, J. L., & McCusker, S. B. Contrast effects on stop consonant identification. *Journal of Experimental Psychology: Human Perception and Performance,* 1978, *4,* 599–609.

Don, M., Eggermont, J. J., & Brackmann, D. E. Reconstruction of the audiogram using brain stem response and high-pass noise masking. *Annals of Otology, Rhinology and Laryngology,* 1979, *88*(suppl. 57), 1–20.

Dorman, M. F., Studdert-Kennedy, M. G., & Raphael, L. J. Stop consonant recognition: Release bursts and formant transitions as functionally equivalent, context-dependent cues. *Perception & Psychophysics,* 1977, *22,* 109–122.

Eggermont, J. J. Electrocochleography. In W. D. Keidel & W. D. Neff (Eds.), *Handbook of sensory physiology* (Vol. 5/3). Berlin: Springer-Verlag, 1976.

Eilers, R. E. Context sensitive perception of naturally produced stop and fricative consonants by infants. *Journal of the Acoustical Society of America,* 1977, *61,* 1321–1336.

Eilers, R. E. Infant speech perception: History and mystery. In G. H. Yeni-Komshian, J. F. Kavanagh, & C. A. Ferguson (Eds.), *Child phonology,* Vol. 2, *Perception.* New York: Academic Press, 1980.

Eilers, R. E., Gavin, W. J., & Oller, D. K. Cross-linguistic perception in infancy: Early effects of linguistic experience. *Journal of Child Language,* 1982, *9,* 289–302.

Eilers, R. E., Gavin, W. J., & Wilson, W. R. Linguistic experience and phonemic perception in infancy: A cross-linguistic study. *Child Development,* 1979, *50,* 14–18.

Eilers, R. E., Gavin, W. J., & Wilson, W. R. Effects of early linguistic experience on speech discrimination by infants: A reply. *Child Development,* 1980, *51,* 113–117.

Eilers, R. E., & Minifie, F. Fricative discrimination in early infancy. *Journal of Speech and Hearing Research,* 1975, *18,* 158–167.

Eilers, R. E., Morse, P. A., Gavin, W. J., & Oller, D. K. Discrimination of voice onset time in infancy. *Journal of the Acoustical Society of America,* 1981, *70,* 955–965.

Eilers, R. E., Wilson, W. R., & Moore, J. M. Developmental changes in speech discrimination in infants. *Journal of Speech and Hearing Research,* 1977, *20,* 766–780.

Eilers, R. E., Wilson, W. R., & Moore, J. M. Speech discrimination in the language-innocent and language-wise: A study in the perception of voice onset time. *Journal of Child Language,* 1979, *6,* 1–18.

Eimas, P. D. The relations between identification and discrimination along speech and nonspeech continua. *Language and Speech,* 1963, *6,* 206–217.

Eimas, P. D. Auditory and linguistic processing of cues for place of articulation by infants. *Perception & Psychophysics,* 1974, *16,* 513–521.

Eimas, P. D. Auditory and phonetic coding of the cues for speech: Discrimination of the [r-l] distinction by young infants. *Perception & Psychophysics,* 1975, *18,* 341–347. (a)

Eimas, P. D. Speech perception in early infancy. In L. B. Cohen & P. Salapatek (Eds.), *Infant perception: From sensation to cognition* (Vol. 2). New York: Academic Press, 1975. (b)

Eimas, P. D. Developmental aspects of speech perception. In R. Held, H. Leibowitz, & H. L. Teuber (Eds.), *Handbook of sensory physiology: Perception* (Vol. 8). Berlin: Springer-Verlag, 1978.

Eimas, P. D. Speech perception: A view of the initial state and perceptual mechanisms. In J. Mehler, M. Garrett, & E. Walker (Eds.), *Perspectives on mental representation: Experimental and theoretical studies of cognitive processes and capacities.* Hillsdale, N.J.: Erlbaum, 1982.

Eimas, P. D. Some constraints on a model of infant speech perception. In J. Mehler & R. Fox (Eds.) *Neonate cognition: Beyond the blooming, buzzing confusion.* Hillsdale, N.J.: Erlbaum, in press.

Eimas, P. D., Cooper, W. E., & Corbit, J. D. Some properties of linguistic feature detectors. *Perception & Psychophysics,* 1973, *13,* 247–252.

Eimas, P. D., & Corbit, J. D. Selective adaptation

of linguistic feature detectors. *Cognitive Psychology,* 1973, *4,* 99–109.

Eimas, P. D., & Miller, J. L. Effects of selective adaptation on the perception of speech and visual patterns: Evidence for feature detectors. In R. D. Walk & H. L. Pick (Eds.), *Perception and experience.* New York: Plenum, 1978.

Eimas, P. D., & Miller, J. L. Contextual effects in infant speech perception. *Science,* 1980, *209,* 1140–1141. (a)

Eimas, P. D., & Miller, J. L. Discrimination of the information for manner of articulation. *Infant Behavior & Development,* 1980, *3,* 367–375. (b)

Eimas, P. D., & Miller, J. L. Organization in the perception of segmental and suprasegmental information by infants. *Infant Behavior & Development,* 1981, *4,* 395–399.

Eimas, P. D., Siqueland, E. R., Jusczyk, P. W., & Vigorito, J. Speech perception in infants. *Science,* 1971, *171,* 303–306.

Eimas, P. D., & Tartter, V. C. On the development of speech perception: Mechanisms and analogies. In L. P. Lipsitt & H. W. Reese (Eds.), *Advances in child development and behavior* (Vol. 13). New York: Academic Press, 1979.

Eisele, W. A., Berry, R. C., & Shriner, T. A. Infant sucking response patterns as a conjugate function of change in the sound pressure level of auditory stimuli. *Journal of Speech and Hearing Research,* 1975, *18,* 296–307.

Eisenberg, R. B. The organization of auditory behavior. *Journal of Speech and Hearing Research,* 1970, *13,* 454–471.

Eisenberg, R. B. *Auditory competence in early life.* Baltimore: University Park Press, 1976.

Engel, R., & Young, N. B. Calibrated pure tone audiograms in normal neonates based on evoked electroencephalographic responses. *Neuropaediatrie,* 1969, *1,* 149–160.

Evans, E. F. Cochlear nerve and cochlear nucleus. In W. D. Keidel & W. D. Neff (Eds.), *Handbook of sensory physiology* (Vol. 5/2). Berlin: Springer-Verlag, 1975.

Fant, C. G. M. *Acoustic theory of speech production.* The Hague: Mouton, 1960.

Fant, C. G. M. Descriptive analysis of the acoustic aspects of speech. *Logos,* 1962, *5,* 3–17.

Fantz, R. L., Fagan, J. F., & Miranda, S. B. Early visual selectivity. In L. B. Cohen & P. Salapatek (Eds.), *Infant perception: From sensation to cognition* (Vol. 1). New York: Academic Press, 1975.

Feddersen, W. E., Sandel, T. T., Teas, D. C., & Jeffress, L. A. Localization of high frequency tones. *Journal of the Acoustical Society of America,* 1957, *29,* 988–991.

Feng, A. S., & Rogowski, B. A. Effects of monaural and binaural occlusion on the morphology of neurons in the medial superior olivary nucleus of the rat. *Brain Research,* 1980, *189,* 530–534.

Ferguson, C. A. Baby talk in six languages. *American Anthropology,* 1964, *66,* 103–114.

Fernald, A. *Four-month-olds prefer to listen to "motherese."* Paper presented at the meeting of the Society for Research in Child Development, Boston, April 1981.

Fernald, A., & Kuhl, P. K. *Fundamental frequency as an acoustic determinant of infant preference for motherese.* Paper presented at the meeting of the Society for Research in Child Development, Boston, April 1981.

Fernald, A., & Simon, T. Expanded intonation contours in mothers' speech to newborns. *Developmental Psychology,* in press.

Field, J., DiFranco, D., & Dodwell, P. Auditory-visual coordination in 2½-month-old infants. *Infant Behavior & Development,* 1979, *2,* 113–122.

Field, J., Muir, D., Pilon, R., Sinclair, M., & Dodwell, P. Infants' orientation to lateral sounds from birth to three months. *Child Development,* 1980, *50,* 295–298.

Fitch, H. L., Halwes, T., Erickson, D. M., & Liberman, A. M. Perceptual equivalence of two acoustic cues for stop-consonant manner. *Perception & Psychophysics,* 1980, *27,* 343–350.

Flanagan, J. L. *Speech analysis, synthesis, and perception* (2nd ed.). New York: Academic Press, 1972.

Fodor, J. A., Garrett, M. F., & Brill, S. L. Pi ka pu: The perception of speech sounds by prelinguistic infants. *Perception & Psychophysics,* 1975, *18,* 74–78.

Forbes, H. S., & Forbes, H. B. Fetal sense reaction: Hearing. *Journal of Comparative Psychology,* 1927, *7,* 353–355.

Freeman, R. D. *Developmental neurobiology of vision.* New York: Plenum, 1979.

Friedlander, B. Z. The effect of speaker identity, voice inflection, vocabulary, and message redundancy on infants' selection of vocal reinforcement. *Journal of Experimental Child Psychology,* 1968, *3,* 443–459.

Friedlander, B. Z. Receptive language development in infancy: Issues and problems. *Merrill-Palmer Quarterly,* 1970, *16,* 7–52.

Froding, C. A. Acoustic investigation of newborn infants. *Acta Oto-Laryngologica,* 1960, *52,*

31–40.

Froeschels, E., & Beebe, H. Testing the hearing of newborn infants. *Archives of Otolaryngology,* 1946, *44,* 710–714.

Fry, D. B. The development of the phonological system in the normal and deaf child. In F. Smith & G. A. Miller (Eds.), *The genesis of language.* Cambridge, Mass.: MIT Press, 1966.

Fry, D. B., Abramson, A. S., Eimas, P. D., & Liberman, A. M. The identification and discrimination of synthetic vowels. *Language and Speech,* 1962, *5,* 171–189.

Fujisaki, H., & Kawashima, T. On the modes and mechanisms of speech perception. *Annual Report of the Engineering Research Institute* (Vol. 28). Tokyo: University of Tokyo, Faculty of Engineering, 1969.

Fujisaki, H., & Kawashima, T. Some experiments on speech perception and a model for the perceptual mechanism. *Annual Report of the Engineering Research Institute* (Vol. 29). Tokyo: University of Tokyo, Faculty of Engineering, 1970.

Garnica, O. The development of phonemic speech perception. In T. E. Moore (Ed.), *Cognitive development and the acquisition of language.* New York: Academic Press, 1973.

Garnica, O. Some prosodic and paralinguistic features of speech to young children. In C. E. Snow & C. A. Ferguson (Eds.), *Talking to children: Language input and acquisition.* Cambridge, Eng.: At the University Press, 1977.

Gesell, A. L., & Ames, L. B. The ontogenetic organization of prone behavior in human infancy. *Journal of Genetic Psychology,* 1940, *56,* 247–263.

Glenn, S. M., Cunningham, C. C., & Joyce, P. F. A study of auditory preferences in nonhandicapped infants and infants with Down's syndrome. *Child Development,* 1981, *52,* 1303–1307.

Goldberg, J. M., & Brown, P. B. Response of binaural neurons of dog superior olivary complex to dichotic tonal stimuli: Some physiological mechanisms of sound localization. *Journal of Neurophysiology,* 1969, *32,* 613–636.

Gottlieb, G. Conceptions of prenatal development: Behavioral embryology. *Psychological Review,* 1976, *83,* 215–234. (a)

Gottlieb, G. The roles of experience in the development of behavior and the nervous system. In G. Gottlieb (Ed.), *Neural and behavioral specificity.* New York: Academic Press, 1976. (b)

Gottlieb, G. The roles of early experience in species-specific perceptual development. In R. N. Aslin, J. R. Alberts, & M. R. Petersen (Eds.), *Development of perception: Psychobiological perspectives,* Vol. 1, *Audition, somatic perception, and the chemical senses.* New York: Academic Press, 1981.

Graham, F. K., Anthony, B. J., & Zeigler, B. L. The orienting response and developmental processes. In D. Siddle (Ed.), *The orienting response.* Chichester, Eng.: Wiley, in press.

Graham, F. K., Strock, B. D., & Zeigler, B. L. Excitatory and inhibitory influences on reflex responsiveness. In W. A. Collins (Ed.), *Aspects of the development of competence.* Hillsdale, N.J.: Erlbaum, 1981.

Green, S. Dialects in Japanese monkeys: Vocal learning and cultural transmission of locale-specific behavior? *Zeitschrift für Tierpsychologie,* 1975, *38,* 304–314. (a)

Green, S. The variation of vocal pattern with social situation in the Japanese monkey (*Macaca fuscata*): A field study. In L. Rosenblum (Ed.), *Primate behavior* (Vol. 4). New York: Academic Press, 1975. (b)

Grimwade, J. C., Walker, D. W., Bartlett, M., Gordon, S., & Wood, C. Human fetal heart rate change and movement in response to sound and vibration. *American Journal of Obstetrics and Gynecology,* 1971, *109,* 86–90.

Haller, M. W. The reactions of infants to changes in the intensity and pitch of pure tone. *Journal of Genetic Psychology,* 1932, *40,* 162–180.

Harris, K. S. Cues for the discrimination of American English fricatives in spoken syllables. *Language and Speech,* 1958, *1,* 1–7.

Hecox, K. Electro-physiological correlates of human auditory development. In L. B. Cohen & P. Salapatek (Eds.), *Infant perception: From sensation to cognition* (Vol. 2). New York: Academic Press, 1975.

Hecox, K. Auditory psychophysics. In P. Salapatek & L. B. Cohen (Eds.), *Handbook of infant perception.* New York: Academic Press, in press.

Hecox, K., & Galambos, R. Brainstem auditory evoked responses in human infants and adults. *Archives of Otolaryngology,* 1974, *99,* 30–33. (a)

Hecox, K., & Galambos, R. Frequency specificity of the human brainstem evoked response. *Journal of the Acoustical Society of America,* 1974, *56,* S63. (b)

Hecox, K., Squires, N., & Galambos, R. Dependence of human brainstem evoked potentials on signal duration and rise-fall time. *Journal of the Acoustical Society of America,* 1974, *56,* Suppl. 1, S63.

Heinz, J. M., & Stevens, K. N. On the properties of voiceless fricative consonants. *Journal of the Acoustical Society of America,* 1961, *33,* 589–596.

Heron, T. G., & Jacobs, R. Respiratory curve responses of the neonate to auditory stimulation. *International Audiology,* 1969, *8,* 71–84.

Hess, E. H. "Imprinting" in a natural laboratory. *Scientific American,* 1972, *227,* 24–31.

Hillenbrand, J. M. *Perceptual organization of speech sounds by young infants.* Unpublished doctoral dissertation, University of Washington, 1980.

Hillenbrand, J. M., Minifie, F. D., & Edwards, T. J. Tempo of spectrum change as a cue in speech-sound discrimination by infants. *Journal of Speech and Hearing Research,* 1979, *22,* 147–165.

Hirsh, I. J. Auditory perception of temporal order. *Journal of the Acoustical Society of America,* 1959, *31,* 759–767.

Holmberg, T. L., Morgan, K. A., & Kuhl, P. K. *Speech perception in early infancy: Discrimination of fricative consonants.* Paper presented at the meeting of the Acoustical Society of America, Miami Beach, Florida, December 1977.

Hoversten, G. H., & Moncur, J. P. Stimuli and intensity factors in testing infants. *Journal of Speech and Hearing Research,* 1969, *12,* 687–702.

Hoy, R., Hahn, J., & Paul, R. C. Hybrid cricket auditory behavior: Evidence for genetic coupling in animal communication. *Science,* 1977, *195,* 82–83.

Hubel, D. H., & Wiesel, T. N. Binocular interaction in striate cortex of kittens reared with artificial squint. *Journal of Neurophysiology,* 1965, *28,* 1041–1059.

Hubel, D. H., & Wiesel, T. N. The period of susceptibility to the physiological effects of unilateral eye closure in kittens. *Journal of Physiology (London),* 1970, *206,* 419–436.

Hutt, S. J. Square-wave stimuli and neonatal auditory behavior: Reply to Bench. *Journal of Experimental Child Psychology,* 1973, *16,* 530–533.

Hutt, S. J., Hutt, C., Lenard, H. G., von Bernuth, H., & Muntjewerff, W. J. Auditory responsitivity in the human neonate. *Nature,* 1968, *218,* 888–890.

Iurato, S. Efferent innervation of the cochlea. In W. D. Keidel & W. D. Neff (Eds.), *Handbook of sensory physiology* (Vol. 5/1). Berlin: Springer-Verlag, 1974.

Jakobson, R. *Child language, aphasia and phonological universals.* The Hague: Mouton, 1968.

Jeffress, L. A. Localization of sound. In W. D. Keidel & W. D. Neff (Eds.), *Handbook of sensory physiology* (Vol. 5/2). Berlin: Springer-Verlag, 1975.

Jerger, J. Clinical experience with impedance audiometry. *Archives of Otolaryngology,* 1970, *92,* 311–324.

Jewett, D. L. Volume conducted potentials in response to auditory stimuli as detected by averaging in the cat. *Electroencephalography and Clinical Neurophysiology,* 1970, *28,* 609–618.

Jewett, D. L., & Romano, M. N. Neonatal development of auditory system potentials averaged from the scalp of rat and cat. *Brain Research,* 1972, *36,* 101–115.

Jewett, D. L., Romano, M. N., & Williston, J. S. Human auditory evoked potentials: Possible brainstem components detected on the scalp. *Science,* 1970, *167,* 1517–1518.

Jewett, D. L., & Williston, J. S. Auditory evoked far fields averaged from the scalp of humans. *Brain,* 1971, *94,* 681–696.

Jusczyk, P. W. Perception of syllable-final stop consonants by 2-month-old infants. *Perception & Psychophysics,* 1977, *21,* 450–454. (a).

Jusczyk, P. W. Rhymes and reasons: Some aspects of the child's appreciation of poetic form. *Developmental Psychology,* 1977, *13,* 599–617. (b)

Jusczyk, P. W. Infant speech perception: A critical appraisal. In P. D. Eimas & J. L. Miller (Eds.), *Perspectives on the study of speech.* Hillsdale, N.J.: Erlbaum, 1981.

Jusczyk, P. W. Auditory versus phonetic coding of speech signals during infancy. In J. Mehler, M. Garrett, & E. Walker (Eds.), *Perspectives on mental representation: Experimental and theoretical studies of cognitive processes and capacities.* Hillsdale, N.J.: Erlbaum, 1982.

Jusczyk, P. W. On characterizing the development of speech perception. In J. Mehler & R. Fox (Eds.), *Neonate cognition: Beyond the blooming, buzzing confusion.* Hillsdale, N.J.: Erlbaum, in press.

Jusczyk, P. W., Copan, H. C., & Thompson, E. J. Perception by two-month-olds of glide contrasts in multisyllabic utterances. *Perception & Psychophysics,* 1978, *24,* 515–520.

Jusczyk, P. W., & Derrah, C. A study of phonetic categorization in 2-month-olds. Manuscript in preparation.

Jusczyk, P. W., Murray, J., Murphy, C., Levitt, A., & Carden, G. Perception of place of articulation in fricatives and stops by infants. Manuscript in preparation.

Jusczyk, P. W., Pisoni, D. B., Fernald, A., Reed, M., & Myers, M. Durational context effects in the processing of nonspeech sounds by infants. Paper presented at the meeting of the Society for Research in Child Development, Detroit, April 1983.

Jusczyk, P. W., Pisoni, D. B., Walley, A. C., & Murray, J. Discrimination of relative onset time of two-component tones by infants. *Journal of the Acoustical Society of America,* 1980, *67,* 262–270.

Jusczyk, P. W., Rosner, B. S., Cutting, J. E., Foard, F., & Smith, L. B. Categorical perception of non-speech sounds by two-month-old infants. *Perception & Psychophysics,* 1977, *21,* 50–54.

Jusczyk, P. W., Smith, L. B., & Murphy, C. The perceptual classification of speech. *Perception & Psychophysics,* 1981, *30,* 10–23.

Jusczyk, P. W., & Thompson, E. J. Perception of a phonetic contrast in multisyllabic utterances by two-month-old infants. *Perception & Psychophysics,* 1978, *23,* 105–109.

Kaplan, E., & Kaplan, G. The prelinguistic child. In J. Elliot (Ed.), *Human development and cognitive processes.* New York: Holt, Rinehart & Winston, 1971.

Kasatkin, N. I., & Levikova, A. M. On the development of early conditioned reflexes and differentiations of auditory stimuli in infants. *Journal of Experimental Psychology,* 1935, *18,* 1–19.

Katz, J., & Jusczyk, P. W. *Do six-month-olds have perceptual constancy for phonetic segments?* Paper presented at the International Conference on Infant Studies, New Haven, Conn., April 1980.

Kearsley, R. B. The newborn's response to auditory stimulation: A demonstration of orienting and defensive behavior. *Child Development,* 1973, *44,* 582–590.

Keen, R. Effects of auditory stimuli on sucking behavior in the human neonate. *Journal of Experimental Child Psychology,* 1964, *1,* 348–354.

Keith, R. Impedance audiometry with neonates. *Archives of Otolaryngology,* 1973, *97,* 465–467.

Keith, R. Middle ear function in neonates. *Archives of Otolaryngology,* 1975, *101,* 376–379.

Kessen, W., Haith, M. M., & Salapatek, P. Human infancy: A bibliography and guide. In P. H. Mussen (Ed.), *Carmichael's manual of child psychology* (3rd ed.). New York: Wiley, 1970.

Kewley-Port, D. Representations of spectral change as cues to place of articulation in stop consonants. *Research on Speech Perception* (Technical Report No. 3). Bloomington: Indiana University, 1980.

Kewley-Port, D., & Pisoni, D. B. Discrimination of rise time in nonspeech signals: Is it categorical or noncategorical? *Journal of the Acoustical Society of America,* 1982, *71,* Suppl. 1, S36.

Kiang, N. Y.-S., Watanabe, T., Thomas, E. C., & Clark, L. F. *Discharge patterns of single fibers in the cat's auditory nerve.* Cambridge, Mass.: MIT Press, 1965.

Klatt, D. H. Speech perception: A model of acoustic-phonetic analysis and lexical access. *Journal of Phonetics,* 1979, *7,* 279–312.

Klatt, D. H. Speech perception: A model of acoustic-phonetic analysis and lexical access. In R. A. Cole (Ed.), *Perception and production of fluent speech.* Hillsdale, N.J.: Erlbaum, 1980.

Kuhl, P. K. Speech perception in early infancy: The acquisition of speech-sound categories. In S. K. Hirsh, D. H. Eldridge, I. J. Hirsh, & S. R. Silverman (Eds.), *Hearing and Davis: Essays honoring Hallowell Davis.* St. Louis: Washington University Press, 1976.

Kuhl, P. K. Predispositions for the perception of speech-sound categories: A species-specific phenomenon? In F. D. Minifie & L. L. Lloyd (Eds.), *Communicative and cognitive abilities: Early behavioral assessment.* Baltimore: University Park Press, 1978.

Kuhl, P. K. The perception of speech in early infancy. In N. J. Lass (Ed.), *Speech and language: Advances in basic research and practice* (Vol. 1). New York: Academic Press, 1979. (a)

Kuhl, P. K. Speech perception in early infancy: Perceptual constancy for spectrally dissimilar vowel categories. *Journal of the Acoustical Society of America,* 1979, *66,* 1668–1679. (b)

Kuhl, P. K. Perceptual constancy for speech-sound categories in early infancy. In G. H. Yeni-Komshian, J. F. Kavanagh, & C. A. Ferguson (Eds.), *Child phonology,* Vol. 2, *Perception.* New York: Academic Press, 1980.

Kuhl, P. K. Discrimination of speech by nonhuman animals: Basic auditory sensitivities conducive to the perception of speech-sound categories. *Journal of the Acoustical Society of America,* 1981, *70,* 340–349.

Kuhl, P. K. Personal communication, March 1982.

Kuhl, P. K., & Miller, J. D. Speech perception by the chinchilla: Voiced-voiceless distinction in alveolar plosive consonants. *Science,* 1975, *190,* 69–72. (a)

Kuhl, P. K., & Miller, J. D. Speech perception in early infancy: Discrimination of speech-sound categories. *Journal of the Acoustical Society of America,* 1975, *58,* Suppl. 1, S56. (b)

Kuhl, P. K., & Miller, J. D. Speech perception by the chinchilla: Identification functions for synthetic VOT stimuli. *Journal of the Acoustical Society of America,* 1978, *63,* 905–917.

Kuhl, P. K., & Miller, J. D. Discrimination of auditory target dimensions in the presence or absence of variation in a second dimension by infants. *Perception & Psychophysics,* 1982, *31,* 279–292.

Kuhl, P. K., & Padden, D. M. Enhanced discriminability at the phonetic boundary for the place feature in macaques. *Journal of the Acoustical Society of America,* in press. (a)

Kuhl, P. K., & Padden, D. M. Enhanced discriminability at the phonetic boundaries for the voicing feature in macaques. *Perception & Psychophysics,* in press. (b)

Ladefoged, P. *Preliminaries to linguistic phonetics.* Chicago: University of Chicago Press, 1971.

Lane, H. L. The motor theory of speech perception: A critical review. *Psychological Review,* 1965, *72,* 275–309.

Langman, J. *Medical embryology.* Baltimore, Maryland: Williams & Wilkins, 1963.

Lasky, R. E., & Rupert, A. L. Temporal masking of auditory evoked brainstem responses in human newborns and adults. *Hearing Research,* in press.

Lasky, R. E., Syrdal-Lasky, A., & Klein, R. E. VOT discrimination by four to six and a half month old infants from Spanish environments. *Journal of Experimental Child Psychology,* 1975, *20,* 215–225.

Leavitt, L. A., Brown, J. W., Morse, P. A., & Graham, F. K. Cardiac orienting and auditory discrimination in 6-week-old infants. *Developmental Psychology,* 1976, *12,* 514–523.

Leiberman, A., Sohmer, H., & Szabo, G. Cochlear audiometry (electro-cochleography) during the neonatal period. *Developmental Medicine and Child Neurology,* 1973, *15,* 8–13.

Lenard, H. G., von Bernuth, H., & Hutt, S. J. Acoustic evoked responses in newborn infants: The influence of pitch and complexity of the stimulus. *Electroencephalography and Clinical Neurophysiology,* 1969, *27,* 121–127.

Leventhal, A. S., & Lipsitt, L. P. Adaptation, pitch discrimination, and sound localization in the neonate. *Child Development,* 1964, *35,* 759–767.

Liberman, A. M. Some results of research on speech perception. *Journal of the Acoustical Society of America,* 1957, *29,* 117–123.

Liberman, A. M. The grammars of speech and language. *Cognitive Psychology,* 1970, *1,* 301–323. (a)

Liberman, A. M. Some characteristics of perception in the speech mode. In D. A. Hamburg (Ed.), *Perception and its disorders: Proceedings of the Association for Research in Nervous and Mental Diseases.* Baltimore: Williams & Wilkins, 1970. (b)

Liberman, A. M., Cooper, F. S., Harris, K. S., & MacNeilage, P. F. A motor theory of speech perception. In C. G. M. Fant (Ed.), *Proceedings of the speech communication seminar,* Stockholm, September 1962. Stockholm: Royal Institute of Technology, Speech Transmission Laboratory, 1963.

Liberman, A. M., Cooper, F. S., Shankweiler, D. P., & Studdert-Kennedy, M. G. Perception of the speech code. *Psychological Review,* 1967, *74,* 431–461.

Liberman, A. M., Delattre, P. C., Cooper, F. S., & Gerstman, L. J. The role of consonant-vowel transitions in the perception of the stop and nasal consonants. *Psychological Monographs,* 1954, *68* (8, Whole No. 379).

Liberman, A. M., Delattre, P. C., Gerstman, L. J., & Cooper, F. S. Tempo of frequency change as a cue for distinguishing classes of speech sounds. *Journal of Experimental Psychology,* 1956, *52,* 127–137.

Liberman, A. M., Harris, K. S., Hoffman, H. S., & Griffith, B. C. The discrimination of speech sounds within and across phoneme boundaries. *Journal of Experimental Psychology,* 1957, *54,* 358–368.

Liberman, A. M., Harris, K. S., Kinney, J. A., & Lane, H. L. The discrimination of relative-onset time of the components of certain speech and nonspeech patterns. *Journal of Experimental Psychology,* 1961, *61,* 379–388.

Liberman, A. M., Ingeman, F., Lisker, L., Delattre, P. C., & Cooper, F. S. Minimal rules for synthesizing speech. *Journal of the Acoustical Society of America,* 1959, *31,* 1490–1499.

Liberman, A. M., & Studdert-Kennedy, M. G. Phonetic perception. In R. Held, H. Leibowitz, & H. L. Teuber (Eds.), *Handbook of sensory physiology: Perception* (Vol. 8). Berlin: Springer-Verlag, 1978.

Liberman, I. Y., Shankweiler, D., Fisher, F. W., & Carter, B. Explicit syllable and phoneme segmentation in the young child. *Journal of Experimental Child Psychology,* 1974, *18,* 201–212.

Liden, G., & Kankkunen, A. Visual reinforcement audiometry. *Acta Oto-Laryngologica,* 1969, *67,* 281–292.

Lieberman, P. Towards a unified phonetic theory. *Linguistic Inquiry,* 1970, *1,* 307–322.

Lieberman, P., Crelin, E. S., & Klatt, D. H. Phonetic ability and related anatomy of the newborn and adult human, Neanderthal man, and the chimpanzee. *American Anthropologist,* 1972, *74,* 287–307.

Lintz, L. M., Fitzgerald, H. E., & Brackbill, Y. Conditioning the eyeblink response to sound in infants. *Psychonomic Science,* 1967, *7,* 405–406.

Lisker, L. Closure duration and the intervocalic voiced-voiceless distinction in English. *Language,* 1957, *33,* 42–49.

Lisker, L. Is it VOT or a first-formant transition detector? *Journal of the Acoustical Society of America,* 1975, *57,* 1547–1551.

Lisker, L. In qualified defense of VOT. *Language and Speech,* 1978, *21,* 375–383.

Lisker, L., & Abramson, A. S. A cross language study of voicing in initial stops: Acoustical measurements. *Word,* 1964, *20,* 384–422.

Lisker, L., & Abramson, A. S. The voicing dimension: Some experiments in comparative phonetics. *Proceedings of the Sixth International Congress of Phonetic Sciences,* 1967. Prague: Academia, 1970.

Locke, J. The child's processing of phonology. In W. A. Collins (Ed.), *The Minnesota symposium on child psychology* (Vol. 12). Hillsdale, N.J.: Erlbaum, 1979.

MacKain, K. S. Assessing the role of experience on infants' speech discrimination. *Journal of Child Language,* 1982, *9,* 527–542.

Macken, M. A. Aspects of the acquisition of stop systems: A cross linguistic perspective. In G. H. Yeni-Komshian, J. F. Kavanagh, & C. A. Ferguson (Eds.), *Child Phonology,* Vol. 1, *Production.* New York: Academic Press, 1980.

MacNeilage, P. F. Electromyographic and acoustic study of the production of certain final clusters. *Journal of the Acoustical Society of America,* 1963, *35,* 461–463.

Malecot, A. Acoustic cues for nasal consonants: An experimental study involving a tape-splicing technique. *Language,* 1958, *32,* 274–284.

Mann, V. A., & Repp, B. H. Influence of vocalic context on perception of the [ʃ]-[s] distinction. *Perception & Psychophysics,* 1980, *28,* 213–228.

Mann, V. A., & Repp, B. H. Influence of preceding fricative on stop consonant perception. *Journal of the Acoustical Society of America,* 1981, *69,* 548–558.

Marcus, S. M. Distinguishing "slit" and "split"—An invariant timing cue in speech perception. *Perception & Psychophysics,* 1978, *23,* 58–60.

Margolis, R. H., & Popelka, G. R. Static and dynamic acoustic impedance measurements in infant ears. *Journal of Speech and Hearing Research,* 1975, *18,* 435–443.

Marler, P. A comparative approach to vocal learning: Song development in white-crowned sparrows. *Journal of Comparative and Physiological Psychology,* 1970, *71,* 1–25.

Marler, P., & Peters, S. Selective vocal learning in a sparrow. *Science,* 1977, *198,* 519–521.

Marler, P., & Peters, S. Birdsong and speech: Evidence for special processing. In P. D. Eimas & J. L. Miller (Eds.), *Perspectives on the study of speech.* Hillsdale, N.J.: Erlbaum, 1981.

Marquis, D. Can conditioned responses be established in the newborn infant? *Journal of Genetic Psychology,* 1931, *39,* 479–492.

Massaro, D. W. Auditory information processing and short-term memory. In W. K. Estes (Ed.), *Handbook of learning and cognitive processes.* Hillsdale, N.J.: Erlbaum, 1976.

Mattingly, I. G., Liberman, A. M., Syrdal, A. K., & Halwes, T. Discrimination in speech and nonspeech modes. *Cognitive Psychology,* 1971, *2,* 131–157.

McGurk, H., Turnure, C., & Creighton, S. J. Auditory-visual coordination in neonates. *Child Development,* 1977, *48,* 138–143.

Mehler, J., Bertoncini, J., Barriere, M., & Jassik-Gerschenfeld, D. Infant recognition of mother's voice. *Perception,* 1978, *7,* 491–497.

Mendelson, M. J., & Haith, M. M. The relation between audition and vision in the human newborn. *Monographs of the Society for Research in Child Development,* 1976, *41,* (4, Serial No. 167).

Menn, L. Phonological theory and child phonology. In G. H. Yeni-Komshian, J. F. Kavanagh, & C. A. Ferguson (Eds.), *Child phonology,* Vol. 1, *Production.* New York: Academic Press, 1980.

Menyuk, P., & Menn, L. Early strategies for the perception and production of words and sounds. In P. Fletcher & M. Garman (Eds.), *Studies in language acquisition.* Cambridge, Eng.: At the University Press, 1979.

Miller, C. L., & Morse, P. A. The "heart" of categorical speech discrimination in young infants. *Journal of Speech and Hearing Research,* 1976,

19, 578–589.

Miller, C. L., Morse, P. A., & Dorman, M. F. Cardiac indices of infant speech perception: Orienting and burst discrimination. *Quarterly Journal of Experimental Psychology,* 1977, *29,* 533–545.

Miller, G. A. The perception of speech. In M. Halle (Ed.), *For Roman Jakobson.* The Hague: Mouton, 1956.

Miller, J. D. Perception of speech sounds in animals: Evidence for speech processing by mammalian auditory mechanisms. In T. H. Bullock (Ed.), *Recognition of complex acoustic signals.* Berlin: Dahlem Konferenzen, 1977.

Miller, J. D., & Kuhl, P. K. *Discrimination of speech-sound categories by the chinchilla: A progress report on syllable-initial voiced-plosive consonants.* Paper presented at the meeting of the Acoustical Society of America, Washington, D.C., April 1976.

Miller, J. D., Wier, C. C., Pastore, R., Kelly, W. J., & Dooling, R. J. Discrimination and labeling of noise-buzz sequences with varying noise-lead times: An example of categorical perception. *Journal of the Acoustical Society of America,* 1976, *60,* 410–417.

Miller, J. L., & Eimas, P. D. Studies on the perception of place and manner of articulation: A comparison of the labial-alveolar and nasal-stop distinctions. *Journal of the Acoustical Society of America,* 1977, *61,* 835–845.

Miller, J. L., & Eimas, P. D. Organization in infant speech perception. *Canadian Journal of Psychology,* 1979, *33,* 353–367.

Miller, J. L., & Liberman, A. M. Some effects of later-occurring information on the perception of stop consonant and semivowel. *Perception & Psychophysics,* 1979, *25,* 457–465.

Mills, M., & Melhuish, E. Recognition of mother's voice in early infancy. *Nature,* 1974, *252,* 123–124.

Miyawaki, K., Strange, W., Verbrugge, R., Liberman, A. M., Jenkins, J. J., & Fujimura, O. An effect of linguistic experience: The discrimination of [r] and [l] by native speakers of Japanese and English. *Perception & Psychophysics,* 1975, *18,* 331–340.

Moffitt, A. R. Consonant cue perception by twenty- to twenty-four-week-old infants. *Child Development,* 1971, *42,* 717–731.

Moffitt, A. R. Intensity discrimination and cardiac reaction in young infants. *Developmental Psychology,* 1973, *8,* 357–359.

Moncur, J. P. Judge reliability in infant testing. *Journal of Speech and Hearing Research,* 1968, *11,* 348–357.

Moore, D. R., & Irvine, D. R. F. Development of binaural input, response patterns, and discharge rate in single units of the cat inferior colliculus. *Experimental Brain Research,* 1980, *38,* 103–108.

Moore, J. M., Thompson, G., & Thompson, M. Auditory localization of infants as a function of reinforcement conditions. *Journal of Speech and Hearing Disorders,* 1975, *40,* 29–34.

Moore, J. M., & Wilson, W. R. Visual reinforcement audiometry (VRA) with infants. In S. E. Gerber & G. T. Mencher (Eds.), *Early diagnosis of hearing loss.* New York: Grune & Stratton, 1978.

Moore, J. M., Wilson, W. R., & Thompson, G. Visual reinforcement of head-turn responses in infants under 12 months of age. *Journal of Speech and Hearing Disorders,* 1977, *42,* 328–334.

Morrongiello, B. A., Clifton, R. K., & Kulig, J. W. Newborn cardiac and behavioral orienting responses to sound under varying precedence-effect conditions. *Infant Behavior & Development,* 1982, *5,* 249–260.

Morse, P. A. The discrimination of speech and nonspeech stimuli in early infancy. *Journal of Experimental Child Psychology,* 1972, *14,* 477–492.

Morse, P. A. Infant speech perception: Origins, processes and *alpha centauri.* In F. D. Minifie & L. L. Lloyd (Eds.), *Communicative and cognitive abilities: Early behavioral assessment.* Baltimore: University Park Press, 1978.

Morse, P. A. The infancy of infant speech perception: The first decade of research. *Brain, Behavior & Evolution,* 1979, *16,* 351–373.

Morse, P. A., Eilers, R. E., & Gavin, W. J. The perception of the sound of silence in early infancy. *Child Development,* 1982, *53,* 189–195.

Morse, P. A., & Snowdon, C. T. An investigation of categorical speech discrimination by rhesus monkeys. *Perception & Psychophysics,* 1975, *17,* 9–16.

Moushegian, G., Rupert, A. L., & Gidda, J. S. Functional characteristics of superior olivary neurons to binaural stimuli. *Journal of Neurophysiology,* 1975, *38,* 1037–1048.

Movshon, J. A., & Van Sluyters, R. C. Visual neural development. In M. R. Rosenzweig & L. W. Porter (Eds.), *Annual review of psychology* (Vol. 32). Palo Alto, Calif.: Annual Reviews, 1981.

Muir, D., Abraham, W., Forbes, B., & Harris, L.

The ontogenesis of an auditory localization response from birth to four months of age. *Canadian Journal of Psychology*, 1979, *33*, 320–333.

Muir, D., Campbell, D., Low, J. A., Killen, H., Galbraith, R., & Karchmar, J. *Neonatal assessments of intrauterine growth in retarded, premature, and asphyxiated infants: Group differences and predictive value*. Paper presented at the meeting of the Canadian Psychological Association, Ottowa, June 1978.

Muir, D., & Field, J. Newborn infants orient to sounds. *Child Development*, 1979, *50*, 431–436.

Mussen, P. H. *Carmichael's manual of child psychology* (3rd ed.). New York: Wiley, 1970.

Newport, E. L. Motherese: Speech of mothers to young children. In N. J. Castellan, D. B. Pisoni, & G. R. Potts (Eds.), *Cognitive theory*, Vol. 2. Hillsdale, N.J.: Erlbaum, 1977.

Nozza, R. J. *Detection of pure tones in quiet and in noise by infants and adults*. Unpublished doctoral dissertation, University of Washington, 1981.

Nusbaum, H. C. *Capacity limitations in phoneme perception*. Unpublished doctoral dissertation, State University of New York at Buffalo, 1981.

Olsho, L. W., Schoon, C., Sakai, R., Turpin, R., & Sperduto, V. Preliminary data on frequency discrimination in infancy. *Journal of the Acoustical Society of America*, 1982, *71*, 509–511.

Olson, C. R., & Pettigrew, J. D. Single units in visual cortex of kittens reared in stroboscopic illumination. *Brain Research*, 1974, *70*, 189–204.

Paradise, J. L., Smith, C., & Bluestone, C. D. Tympanometric detection of middle ear effusion in infants and young children. *Pediatrics*, 1976, *58*, 198–206.

Perey, A. J., & Pisoni, D. B. Dual processing versus response-limitation accounts of categorical perception: A reply to Macmillan, Kaplan, and Creelman. *Journal of the Acoustical Society of America*, 1977, *62*, Suppl. 1, S60–61.

Petersen, M. R. Perception of acoustic communication signals by animals: Developmental perspectives and implications. In R. N. Aslin, J. R. Alberts, & M. R. Petersen (Eds.), *Development of perception: Psychobiological perspectives*, Vol. 1, *Audition, somatic perception, and the chemical senses*. New York: Academic Press, 1981.

Peterson, G. E., & Barney, H. L. Control methods used in a study of the vowels. *Journal of the Acoustical Society of America*, 1952, *24*, 175–184.

Pettigrew, J. D. The effect on the development of stimulus specificity by kitten cortical neurones. *Journal of Physiology (London)*, 1974, *237*, 49–74.

Pfeiffer, R. R. Classification of response patterns of spike discharges for units in the cochlear nucleus: Tone-burst stimulation. *Experimental Brain Research*, 1966, *1*, 220–235.

Picton, T. W., & Hillyard, S. A. Human auditory evoked potentials. II: Effects of attention. *Electroencephalography and Clinical Neurophysiology*, 1974, *36*, 191–199.

Picton, T. W., Hillyard, S. A., Krausz, H. I., & Galambos, R. Human auditory evoked potentials. I: Evaluation of components. *Electroencephalography and Clinical Neurophysiology*, 1974, *36*, 179–190.

Pisoni, D. B. On the nature of categorical perception of speech sounds. *Supplement to Status Report on Speech Research* (SR–27). New Haven, Conn.: Haskins Laboratories, 1971.

Pisoni, D. B. Auditory and phonetic memory codes in the discrimination of consonants and vowels. *Perception & Psychophysics*, 1973, *13*, 253–260.

Pisoni, D. B. Auditory short-term memory vowel perception. *Memory & Cognition*, 1975, *3*, 7–18.

Pisoni, D. B. Some effects of discrimination training on the identification and discrimination of rapid spectral changes. *Research on Speech Perception* (Progress Report No. 3). Bloomington: Indiana University, 1976.

Pisoni, D. B. Identification and discrimination of the relative onset of two component tones: Implications for voicing perception in stops. *Journal of the Acoustical Society of America*, 1977, *61*, 1352–1361.

Pisoni, D. B. Speech perception. In W. K. Estes (Ed.), *Handbook of learning and cognitive processes*, Vol. 6. Hillsdale, N.J.: Erlbaum, 1978.

Pisoni, D. B., Aslin, R. N., Perey, A. J., & Hennessy, B. L. Some effects of laboratory training on identification and discrimination of voicing contrasts in stop consonants. *Journal of Experimental Psychology: Human Perception and Performance*, 1982, *8*, 297–314.

Pisoni, D. B., & Lazarus, J. H. Categorical and noncategorical modes of speech perception along the voicing continuum. *Journal of the Acoustical Society of America*, 1974, *55*, 328–333.

Pisoni, D. B., & Tash, J. B. Reaction times to comparisons within and across phonetic categories. *Perception & Psychophysics*, 1974, *15*, 285–290.

Pisoni, D. B., & Tash, J. B. Auditory property detectors and processing place features in stop consonants. *Perception & Psychophysics,* 1975, *18,* 401–408.

Pollack, I. The information in elementary auditory displays. *Journal of the Acoustical Society of America,* 1952, *24,* 745–749.

Pollack, I. The information in elementary auditory displays II. *Journal of the Acoustical Society of America,* 1953, *25,* 765–769.

Popper, R. D. Pair discrimination for a continuum of synthetic voiced stops with and without first and third formants. *Journal of Psycholinguistic Research,* 1972, *1,* 205–219.

Port, R. F. Linguistic timing factors in combination. *Journal of the Acoustical Society of America,* 1981, *69,* 262–274. (a)

Port, R. F. On the structure of the phonetic space with special reference to speech timing. *Lingua,* 1981, *55,* 181–219. (b)

Pratt, K. C. The neonate. In C. Murchison (Ed.), *A handbook of child psychology.* Worcester, Mass.: Clark University Press, 1931.

Pratt, K. C. The neonate. In C. Murchison (Ed.), *A handbook of child psychology* (2nd ed.). Worcester, Mass.: Clark University Press, 1933.

Pratt, K. C. The neonate. In L. Carmichael (Ed.), *Manual of child psychology.* New York: Wiley, 1946.

Pratt, K. C. The neonate. In L. Carmichael (Ed.), *Manual of child psychology* (2nd ed.). New York: Wiley, 1954.

Preyer, W. *The mind of the child. Part I. The senses and the will.* New York: Appleton, 1888.

Preyer, W. *The mind of the child. Part II. The development of the intellect.* New York: Appleton, 1889.

Prosen, C. A., Moody, D. B., Stebbins, W. C., & Hawkins, J. E. Auditory intensity discrimination after selective loss of cochlear outer hair cells. *Science,* 1981, *212,* 1286–1288.

Pujol, R. Development of tone-burst responses along the auditory pathway in the cat. *Acta Oto-Laryngologica,* 1972, *74,* 383–391.

Pujol, R., Carlier, E., & Devigne, C. Different patterns of cochlear innervation during the development of the kitten. *Journal of Comparative Neurology,* 1978, *177,* 529–536.

Pujol, R., & Hilding, D. Anatomy and physiology of the onset of auditory function. *Acta Oto-Laryngologica,* 1973, *76,* 1–10.

Querleu, D., & Renard, K. Les perceptions auditives du foetus humain. *Médicine et Hygiène,* 1981, *39,* 2102–2110.

Raphael, L. J. Preceding vowel duration as a cue to the perception of the voicing characteristic of word-final consonants in American English. *Journal of the Acoustical Society of America,* 1972, *51,* 1296–1303.

Remez, R. E., Rubin, P. E., Pisoni, D. B., & Carrell, T. D. Speech perception without traditional speech cues. *Science,* 1981, *212,* 947–950.

Reneau, J., & Hnatiow, G. Z. *Evoked response audiometry: A topical and historical review.* Baltimore: University Park Press, 1975.

Repp, B. H. Phonetic trading relations and context effects: New experimental evidence for a speech mode of perception. *Psychological Bulletin,* 1982, *92,* 81–110.

Repp, B. H., Healy, A. F., & Crowder, R. G. Categories and context in the perception of isolated steady-state vowels. *Journal of Experimental Psychology: Human Perception and Performance,* 1979, *5,* 129–145.

Riesen, A. H. Receptor functions. In P. H. Mussen (Ed.), *Handbook of research methods in child development.* New York: Wiley, 1960.

Romand, R. Development of auditory nerve activity in kittens. *Brain Research,* 1979, *173,* 554–556.

Rosch, E., & Mervis, C. B. Categorization of natural objects. In M. R. Rosenzweig & L. W. Porter (Eds.), *Annual review of psychology.* Palo Alto, Calif.: Annual Reviews, 1981.

Rose, J. E., Hind, J. E., Anderson, D. J., & Brugge, J. F. Some effects of stimulus intensity on response of auditory nerve fibers in the squirrel monkey. *Journal of Neurophysiology,* 1971, *34,* 685–699.

Rosen, S. M., & Howell, P. Plucks and bows are not categorically perceived. *Perception & Psychophysics,* 1981, *30,* 156–168.

Rubel, E. W. Ontogeny of structure and function in the vertebrate auditory system. In M. Jacobson (Ed.), *Handbook of sensory physiology: Development of sensory systems* (Vol. 9). Berlin: Springer-Verlag, 1978.

Ryan, A., & Dallos, P. Absence of cochlear outer hair cells: Effect on behavioral auditory threshold. *Nature,* 1975, *253,* 44–46.

Sachs, R. M., & Grant, K. W. *Stimulus correlates in the perception of voice onset time (VOT): II. Discrimination of speech with high and low stimulus uncertainty.* Paper presented at the Meeting of the Acoustical Society of America, San Diego, Calif., November 1976.

Sakabe, N., Arayama, T., & Suzuki, T. Human fetal evoked response to acoustic stimulation. *Acta Oto-Laryngologica,* 1969, *252,* 29–36. (Suppl.)

Salamy, A., Fenn, C. B., & Bronshvag, M. Ontogenesis of human brainstem evoked potential amplitude. *Developmental Psychobiology,* 1979, *12,* 519–526.

Salamy, A., & McKean, C. M. Postnatal development of human brainstem potentials during the first year of life. *Electroencephalography and Clinical Neurophysiology,* 1976, *40,* 418–426.

Salamy, A., McKean, C. M., & Buda, F. B. Maturational changes in auditory transmission as reflected in human brain stem potentials. *Brain Research,* 1975, *96,* 361–366.

Sameroff, A. Non-nutritive sucking in newborns under visual and auditory stimulation. *Child Development,* 1967, *38,* 443–452.

Sameroff, A. Changes in the non-nutritive sucking response to stimulation during infancy. *Journal of Experimental Child Psychology,* 1970, *10,* 112–119.

Samuel, A. G. The effect of discrimination training on speech perception: Noncategorical perception. *Perception & Psychophysics,* 1977, *22,* 321–330.

Saunders, J. C., Dolgin, K. G., & Lowry, L. D. The maturation of frequency selectivity in C57BL/6J mice studied with auditory evoked response tuning curves. *Brain Research,* 1980, *187,* 69–79.

Savin, H. B., & Bever, T. G. The nonperceptual reality of the phoneme. *Journal of Verbal Learning and Verbal Behavior,* 1970, *9,* 295–302.

Sawusch, J. R. Peripheral and central processes in selective adaptation of place of articulation in stop consonants. *Journal of the Acoustical Society of America,* 1977, *62,* 738–750. (a)

Sawusch, J. R. Processing of place information in stop consonants. *Perception & Psychophysics,* 1977, *22,* 417–426. (b)

Sawusch, J. R., & Jusczyk, P. W. Adaptation and contrast in the perception of voicing. *Journal of Experimental Psychology: Human Perception and Performance,* 1981, *7,* 408–421.

Sawusch, J. R., & Pisoni, D. B. On the identification of place and voicing features in synthetic stop consonants. *Journal of Phonetics,* 1974, *2,* 181–194.

Scharf, B. Critical bands. In J. V. Tobias (Ed.), *Foundations of modern auditory theory* (Vol. 1). New York: Academic Press, 1970.

Schatz, C. The role of context in the perception of stops. *Language,* 1954, *30,* 47–56.

Schneider, B. A., & Trehub, S. E. Behavioral assessment of basic capabilities. In S. E. Trehub & B. A. Schneider (Eds.), *Auditory development in infancy.* New York: Plenum, in press.

Schneider, B. A., Trehub, S. E., & Bull, D. The development of basic auditory processes in infants. *Canadian Journal of Psychology,* 1979, *33,* 306–319.

Schneider, B. A., Trehub, S. E., & Bull, D. High-frequency sensitivity in infants. *Science,* 1980, *207,* 1003–1004.

Schulman, C. A. Heart rate audiometry. Part I. An evaluation of heart rate response to auditory stimuli in newborn hearing screening. *Neuropaediatrie,* 1973, *4,* 362–374.

Schulman-Galambos, C., & Galambos, R. Brain stem evoked response audiometry in newborn hearing screening. *Archives of Otolaryngology,* 1979, *105,* 86–90.

Schwab, E. C., Sawusch, J. R., & Nusbaum, H. C. The role of second formant transitions in the stop-semivowel distinction. *Perception & Psychophysics,* 1981, *29,* 121–128.

Scibetta, J. J., Rosen, M. G., Hochberg, C. J., & Chik, L. Human fetal brain responses to sound during labor. *American Journal of Obstetrics and Gynecology,* 1971, *109,* 82–85.

Searle, C. L., Braida, L. D., Davis, M. F., & Colburn, H. S. Model for auditory localization. *Journal of the Acoustical Society of America,* 1976, *60,* 1164–1175.

Searle, C. L., Jacobson, J. Z., & Rayment, S. G. Stop consonant discrimination based on human audition. *Journal of the Acoustical Society of America,* 1979, *65,* 799–809.

Sherk, H., & Stryker, M. P. Quantitative study of cortical orientation selectivity in visually inexperienced kittens. *Journal of Neurophysiology,* 1976, *39,* 63–70.

Shipley, C., Buchwald, J. S., Norman, R., & Guthrie, D. Brain stem auditory evoked response development in the kitten. *Brain Research,* 1980, *182,* 313–326.

Shvachkin, N. Kh. The development of phonemic speech perception in early childhood. In C. A. Ferguson & D. I. Slobin (Eds.), *Studies of child language development.* New York: Holt, Rinehart & Winston, 1973.

Silverman, M. S., & Clopton, B. M. Plasticity of binaural interactions. I. Effect of early auditory deprivation. *Journal of Neurophysiology,* 1977, *40,* 1266–1274.

Simmons, F. B., McFarland, W. H., & Jones, F. R. Automated hearing screening techniques for newborns. *Acta Oto-Laryngologica,* 1979, *87,* 1–8.

Sinnott, J. M., Aslin, R. N., & Pisoni, D. B. Discrimination of intensity differences in pure tones and vowels by infants. Manuscript in preparation.

Sinnott, J. M., Beecher, M. D., Moody, D. B., & Stebbins, W. C. Speech sound discrimination by monkeys and humans. *Journal of the Acoustical Society of America,* 1976, *60,* 687–695.

Sinnott, J. M., Pisoni, D. B., & Aslin, R. N. A comparison of pure tone auditory thresholds in human infants and adults. *Infant Behavior & Development,* in press.

Siqueland, E. R., & DeLucia, C. A. Visual reinforcement of non-nutritive sucking in human infants. *Science,* 1969, *165,* 1144–1146.

Soderquist, D. R., & Hoenigmann, N. Infant responsivity to pure tone stimulation. *Journal of Auditory Research,* 1973, *13,* 321–327.

Sommer, F. G., & Ling, D. Auditory testing of newborns using eyeblink conditioning. *Journal of Auditory Research,* 1970, *10,* 292–295.

Sontag, L. W., & Wallace, R. F. The movement response of the human fetus to sound stimuli. *Child Development,* 1935, *6,* 253–258.

Spence, M. J., & DeCasper, A. J. *Human fetuses perceive maternal speech.* Paper presented at the meeting of the International Conference on Infant Studies, Austin, Tex., March 1982.

Spoendlin, H. The afferent innervation of the cochlea. In R. F. Naunton & C. Fernandez (Eds.), *Evoked electrical activity in the auditory nervous system.* New York: Academic Press, 1978.

Spring, D. R., & Dale, P. S. Discrimination of linguistic stress in early infancy. *Journal of Speech and Hearing Research,* 1977, *20,* 224–232.

Starr, A., Amlie, R. N., Martin, W. H., & Sanders, S. Development of auditory function in newborn infants revealed by auditory brainstem potentials. *Pediatrics,* 1977, *60,* 831–839.

Starr, A., & Hamilton, A. E. The correlation between confirmed sites of neurological lesions and abnormalities of far-field auditory brainstem lesions. *Electroencephalography and Clinical Neurophysiology,* 1976, *41,* 595–608.

Steinschneider, A. Sound intensity and respiratory responses in the neonate. *Psychosomatic Medicine,* 1968, *30,* 534–541.

Steinschneider, A., Lipton, E., & Richmond, J. Auditory sensitivity in the infant: Effect of intensity on cardiac and motor responsivity. *Child Development,* 1966, *37,* 233–252.

Stern, D. N., Spieker, S., & MacKain, C. Intonation contours as signals in maternal speech to prelinguistic infants. *Developmental Psychology,* 1982, *18,* 727–735.

Stevens, K. N. Toward a model for speech recognition. *Journal of the Acoustical Society of America,* 1960, *32,* 47–55.

Stevens, K. N. The quantal nature of speech. In E. E. David, Jr., & P. B. Denes (Eds.), *Human communication: A unified view.* New York: McGraw-Hill, 1972.

Stevens, K. N. The potential role of property detectors in the perception of consonants. In C. G. M. Fant & M. A. A. Tatham (Eds.), *Auditory analysis and perception of speech.* New York: Academic Press, 1975.

Stevens, K. N., & Blumstein, S. E. Invariant cues for place of articulation in stop consonants. *Journal of the Acoustical Society of America,* 1978, *64,* 1358–1368.

Stevens, K. N., & Blumstein, S. E. The search for invariant acoustic correlates of phonetic features. In P. D. Eimas & J. L. Miller (Eds.), *Perspectives on the study of speech.* Hillsdale, N.J.: Erlbaum, 1981.

Stevens, K. N., & House, A. S. Studies of formant transitions using a vocal tract analog. *Journal of the Acoustical Society of America,* 1956, *28,* 578–585.

Stevens, K. N., & Klatt, D. H. Role of formant transitions in the voiced-voiceless distinction for stops. *Journal of the Acoustical Society of America,* 1974, *55,* 653–659.

Stevens, K. N., Liberman, A. M., Studdert-Kennedy, M. G., & Ohman, S. E. G. Cross-language study of vowel perception. *Language and Speech,* 1969, *12,* 1–23.

Stevens, S. S. *Handbook of experimental psychology.* New York: Wiley, 1951.

Stockard, J. E., Stockard, J. J., Westmoreland, B. F., & Corfits, J. L. Brainstem auditory-evoked responses. *Archives of Neurology,* 1979, *36,* 823–831.

Strange, W., & Broen, P. A. The relationship between perception and production of /w/, /r/, and /l/ by three-year-old children. *Journal of Experimental Child Psychology,* 1981, *31,* 81–102.

Strange, W., & Jenkins, J. J. Linguistic experience and speech perception. In R. D. Walk & H. L. Pick (Eds.), *Perception and experience.* New York: Plenum, 1978.

Streeter, L. A. Language perception of 2-month-old infants shows effects of both innate mechanisms and experience. *Nature,* 1976, *259,* 39–41.

Studdert-Kennedy, M. G. The perception of speech. In T. A. Sebeok (Ed.), *Current trends in linguistics* (Vol. 12). The Hague: Mouton, 1974.

Studdert-Kennedy, M. G. Universals in phonetic structure and their role in linguistic communication. In T. H. Bullock (Ed.), *Recognition of com-*

plex acoustic signals. Berlin: Dahlem Konferenzen, 1977.

Studdert-Kennedy, M. G. The beginnings of speech. In G. B. Barlow, K. Immelman, M. Main, & L. Petrinovich (Eds.), *Behavioral development: The Bielefeld interdisciplinary project*. New York: Cambridge University Press, 1980.

Studdert-Kennedy, M. G., Liberman, A. M., Harris, K. S., & Cooper, F. S. Motor theory of speech perception: A reply to Lane's critical review. *Psychological Review*, 1970, *77*, 234–249.

Studdert-Kennedy, M. G., & Shankweiler, D. Hemispheric specialization for speech perception. *Journal of the Acoustical Society of America*, 1970, *48*, 579–594.

Summerfield, Q. Differences between spectral dependencies in auditory and phonetic temporal processing: Relevance to the perception of voicing in initial stops. *Journal of the Acoustical Society of America*, 1982, *72*, 51–61.

Suzuki, T., & Ogiba, Y. Conditioned orientation reflex audiometry. *Archives of Otolaryngology*, 1961, *74*, 192–198.

Swoboda, P., Kass, J., Morse, P. A., & Leavitt, L. A. Memory factors in infant vowel discrimination of normal and at-risk infants. *Child Development*, 1978, *49*, 332–339.

Swoboda, P., Morse, P. A., & Leavitt, L. A. Continuous vowel discrimination in normal and at-risk infants. *Child Development*, 1976, *47*, 459–465.

Taguchi, K., Picton, T. W., Orpin, J. A., & Goodman, W. S. Evoked response audiometry in newborn infants. *Acta Oto-Laryngologica* (Suppl.), 1969, *252*, 5–17.

Tartter, V. C., & Eimas, P. D. The role of auditory and phonetic feature detectors in the perception of speech. *Perception & Psychophysics*, 1975, *18*, 293–298.

Teller, D. Y. The forced-choice preferential looking procedure: A psychophysical technique for use with human infants. *Infant Behavior & Development*, 1979, *2*, 135–153.

Templin, M. Certain language skills in children. *Institute of Child Welfare Monographs* (No. 26). Minneapolis: University of Minnesota Press, 1957.

Till, J. A. *Infants' discrimination of speech and nonspeech stimuli*. Paper presented at the meeting of the American Speech and Hearing Association, Houston, Tex., November 1976.

Tonndorf, J. Shearing motion in scala media of cochlear models. *Journal of the Acoustical Society of America*, 1960, *32*, 238–244.

Tonndorf, J. Bone conduction. In W. D. Keidel & W. D. Neff (Eds.), *Handbook of sensory physiology* (Vol. 5/3). Berlin: Springer-Verlag, 1976.

Trehub, S. E. Infants' sensitivity to vowel and tonal contrasts. *Developmental Psychology*, 1973, *9*, 91–96.

Trehub, S. E. The discrimination of foreign speech contrasts by infants and adults. *Child Development*, 1976, *47*, 466–472. (a)

Trehub, S. E. *Infants' discrimination of multisyllabic stimuli: The role of temporal factors*. Paper presented at the meeting of the American Speech and Hearing Association, Houston, Texas, November 1976. (b)

Trehub, S. E. Reflections on the development of speech perception. *Canadian Journal of Psychology*, 1979, *33*, 368–381.

Trehub, S. E., Bull, D., & Schneider, B. A. Infants' detection of speech in noise. *Journal of Speech and Hearing Research*, 1981, *24*, 202–206.

Trehub, S. E., & Chang, H. Speech as reinforcing stimulation for infants. *Developmental Psychology*, 1977, *13*, 170–171.

Trehub, S. E., & Rabinovitch, M. S. Auditory-linguistic sensitivity in early infancy. *Developmental Psychology*, 1972, *6*, 74–77.

Trehub, S. E., & Schneider, B. A. Recent advances in the behavioral study of infant audition. In S. E. Gerber (Ed.), *Development of auditory behavior*. New York: Grune & Stratton, in press.

Trehub, S. E., Schneider, B. A., & Bull, D. Effect of reinforcement on infants' performance in an auditory detection task. *Developmental Psychology*, 1981, *17*, 872–877.

Trehub, S. E., Schneider, B. A., & Endman, M. Developmental changes in infants' sensitivity to octave-band noises. *Journal of Experimental Child Psychology*, 1980, *29*, 282–293.

Turkewitz, G., Birch, H. G., & Cooper, K. Responsiveness to simple and complex auditory stimuli in the human newborn. *Developmental Psychobiology*, 1972, *5*, 7–19.

Turkewitz, G., Birch, H. G., Moreau, T., Levy, L., & Cornwell, A. C. Effect of intensity of auditory stimulation on directional eye movements in the human neonate. *Animal Behavior*, 1966, *14*, 93–101.

Turner, S., & MacFarlane, A. Localization of human speech by the newborn baby and the effects of pethidine (''meperidine''). *Developmental Medicine and Child Neurology*, 1978, *20*, 727–734.

von Bekesy, G. *Experiments in hearing*. New York:

McGraw-Hill, 1960.

Walker, D. W., Grimwade, J. C., & Wood, C. Intrauterine noise: A component of the fetal environment. *American Journal of Obstetrics and Gynecology,* 1971, *109,* 91–95.

Walley, A. C. Infants' discrimination of full and partial cues to place of articulation in stop consonants. *Research on Speech Perception* (Progress Report No. 5). Bloomington: Indiana University, 1979.

Walley, A. C., Smith, L. B., & Jusczyk, P. W. Classification of CV syllables by readers and prereaders. *Research on Speech Perception* (Progress Report No. 6). Bloomington: Indiana University, 1980.

Walley, A. C., & Carrell, T. D. The role of the CV syllable onset spectrum and formant transitions in the adult's and child's perception of place of articulation. *Journal of the Acoustical Society of America,* in press.

Walley, A. C., Pisoni, D. B., & Aslin, R. N. The role of early experience in the development of speech perception. In R. N. Aslin, J. R. Alberts, & M. R. Petersen (Eds.), *Development of perception: Psychobiological perspectives,* Vol. 1, *Audition, somatic perception, and the chemical senses.* New York: Academic Press, 1981.

Waters, R. S., & Wilson, W. A. Speech perception by rhesus monkeys: The voicing distinction in synthesized labial and velar stop consonants. *Perception & Psychophysics,* 1976, *19,* 285–289.

Wedenberg, E. Auditory tests on newborn infants. *Acta Oto-Laryngologica,* 1956, *46,* 446–461.

Weir, C. Auditory frequency sensitivity of human newborns: Some data with improved acoustic and behavioral controls. *Perception & Psychophysics,* 1979, *26,* 287–294.

Weir, R. H. *Language in the crib.* The Hague: Mouton, 1962.

Werker, J. F., Gilbert, J. H. V., Humphrey, K., & Tees, R. C. Developmental aspects of cross-language speech perception. *Child Development,* 1981, *52,* 349–355.

Wertheimer, M. Psychomotor coordination of auditory and visual space at birth. *Science,* 1961, *134,* 1692.

Whitfield, I. C. "Edges" in auditory information processing. *Proceedings of the XXIII International Congress of Physiological Sciences.* New York: Excerpta Medica Foundation, 1965.

Wickelgren, W. A. Auditory or articulatory coding in verbal short-term memory. *Psychological Review,* 1969, *76,* 232–235. (a)

Wickelgren, W. A. Context-sensitive coding in speech recognition, articulation, and development. In K. N. Leibovic (Ed.), *Information processing in the nervous system.* Berlin: Springer-Verlag, 1969. (b)

Wiener, F. M., & Ross, D. A. The pressure distribution in the auditory canal in a progressive sound field. *Journal of the Acoustical Society of America,* 1946, *18,* 401–408.

Williams, L. *The effects of phonetic environment and stress placement on infant discrimination of place of stop consonant articulation.* Paper presented at the Second Boston University Conference on Language Development, Boston, October 1977. (a)

Williams, L. The perception of stop consonant voicing by Spanish-English bilinguals. *Perception & Psychophysics,* 1977, *21,* 289–297. (b)

Williams, L. The voicing contrast in Spanish. *Journal of Phonetics,* 1977, *5,* 169–184. (c).

Williams, L., & Golenski, J. Infant speech sound discrimination: The effects of contingent versus noncontingent stimulus presentation. *Child Development,* 1978, *49,* 213–217.

Willott, J. F., & Shnerson, A. Rapid development of tuning characteristics of inferior colliculus neurons of mouse pups. *Brain Research,* 1978, *148,* 230–233.

Woodcock, J. M. Terminology and methodology related to the use of heart rate responsivity in infancy research. *Journal of Experimental Child Psychology,* 1971, *11,* 76–92.

Wormith, S. J., Pankhurst, D., & Moffitt, A. R. Frequency discrimination by young infants. *Child Development,* 1975, *46,* 272–275.

Yost, W. A. Discrimination of interaural phase differences. *Journal of the Acoustical Society of America,* 1974, *55,* 1299–1303.

Yost, W. A., & Nielsen, D. W. *Fundamentals of hearing.* New York: Holt, Rinehart & Winston, 1977.

Zemlin, W. R. *Speech and hearing science.* Englewood Cliffs, N.J.: Prentice-Hall, 1981.

Zoloth, S., Petersen, M. R., Beecher, M., Green, S., Marler, P., Moody, D., & Stebbins, W. Species-specific perceptual processing of vocal sounds by Old World monkeys. *Science,* 1979, *204,* 870–873.

INFANT COGNITION 9

P. L. HARRIS, *Oxford University*

CHAPTER CONTENTS

INTRODUCTION

This chapter is divided into six main parts. In the introduction, the theoretical framework for research on infant cognition is examined. The next three sections focus on research findings in particular content areas: space, identity, and action. The fifth section turns to the issues of measurement and prediction. The sixth and final section examines the hypothesis that the infant's cognitive achievements toward the end of the sensorimotor period constitute prerequisites for the emergence of language.

The major goal of this first section is to indicate some of the key theoretical issues in infant cognition. An examination of the philosophical background to modern infant research will be followed by an examination of four contemporary theorists. Whether we look at philosophical writing before this century or at modern psychological theories, three issues recur.

Theoretical Issues

The Role of Interpretation

The first issue concerns the extent to which perceptual experience requires interpretation for it to be meaningful. This question is especially likely to arise when the objectivity of the infant's view of the world is considered. On the one hand, it is possible to argue that the infant, particularly the newborn infant, lives in a subjective world of sensations, which require reinterpretation before they can provide objective information about the world. On the other hand, it can be argued that perception supplies the neonate with valid information about the world more or less immediately, however limited that supply of information might be initially. The opposition between these two points of view will be especially clear when we compare the theories of Piaget and Gibson.

The Role of Experience

The second issue concerns the role of experience. First, we may ask whether there is any major role for experience. The answer to this question obviously depends in part on the answer given to the earlier question regarding the extent to which perceptual sensations require interpretation. If they do not, then experience will merely supplement an initial kernel of already objective information, or perhaps allow the infant to detect that information more efficiently, but it will not have a major role in establishing the infant's basic view of the world. If, on the other hand, we do allow a relatively important role for experience we are then forced to ask the second question: What types of experience are critical in producing cognitive change? Some theorists stress the importance of active motor exploration by the infant whereas others stress the role of visual observation per se.

The Role of Representation

The third issue to be examined concerns the extent to which the infant's behavior should be seen as a response to the immediate perceptual world, as opposed to a mental world based on remembered information, imagery, or some other type of representational system. Some theorists have implied that the neonate's reactions, in particular, are influenced by the immediate perceptual field, whereas others have implied that the neonate's mental life, far from being restricted to the here and now, is rich enough to represent intended or desired states of affairs as well as past events. This question is also linked to the preceding one. If a minor role is attributed to experience, then it will appear necessary to supply the infant's mind with certain ideas on an innate basis. Equally if experience is accorded a relatively important role in permitting the development of a representational code, that code might be based on active motor experience, or visual observation.

Philosophical Background

Questions about the origins of human cognition have a history that reaches back beyond the beginning of modern experimental research on infants and indeed well beyond the beginnings of psychology itself. The framework for some of the questions we will consider in this chapter was built in the seventeenth and eighteenth centuries by philosophers concerned with the origins and validity of human knowledge. In particular, we may examine the debate between the empiricists and the rationalists.

The Debate Between Empiricism and Rationalism

The British empiricists Locke, Berkeley, and Hume argued that our fundamental ideas of color, of space, and so forth, are provided by perceptual experience. Hume put the argument as follows:

> But though our thought seems to possess this unbounded liberty, we shall find upon a nearer examination that it is really confined within very narrow limits, and that all this creative power of the mind amounts to no more than the faculty of compounding, transposing, augmenting or diminishing the materials afforded us by the senses and experience. When we think of a golden mountain, we can only join two consistent ideas, gold and mountain with which we were formerly acquainted. (Hume, 1904, Section II, paragraph 5)

In contrast, the rationalist position, particularly that developed by Kant, held that although experience furnishes the mind with data about the real world, the interpretation of that data is supplied by certain built-in categories of the mind, such as the concepts of space or causality.

If we examine some of the current research questions concerning cognition in infancy, we shall see that this opposition between empiricism and rationalism still lies behind a good deal of research. Consider, for example, the perception of depth, a topic that will be taken up in more detail later. The most detailed empiricist account of depth perception was provided by Berkeley in his famous *Essay Towards a New Theory of Vision* (Berkeley, 1910). He argued that we must learn to perceive the third dimension of space because the retinal image is only two-dimensional. By touching objects and by moving toward them, we come to make associations between particular visual cues and tactual or motor experiences. For example, in order to view an object at a certain distance, the eyes converge for that distance. We can directly sense the angle at which the eyes are converged, and this visual cue, though not giving rise to an impression of depth in and of itself, can in combination with the tactual and motor experiences that come to be associated with it serve as a sign or index of a particular distance. Berkeley admitted, then, that certain sensory inputs such as visual cues cannot themselves give rise to the idea of distance. However, by making use of the concept of association between various types of sensory experience, such as tactual and visual experience, Berkeley was able to trace back the idea of distance to a sensory experience.

Berkeley's empiricism provides an answer to the three issues outlined earlier: the need for reinterpretation, the role of experience, and the origins of ideas or representations. First, he denies that the infant's initial visual experience of the world provides the infant with valid information. Berkeley argues that visual sensations are necessarily two-dimensional, whereas the world and the infant's movements within that world are arranged in three dimensions. Thus these flat visual sensations require reinterpretation. Second, Berkeley specifies how experience can supply that reinterpretation. By associating visual sensations with tactual and motor sensations, the infant will learn eventually to use visual sensations as cues for the idea of depth. Finally, Berkeley answers the question of how the mind comes to represent aspects of the world that are not directly perceived: The idea of depth is ultimately derived from tactual and motor experience, and eventually comes to be aroused in the absence of that experience by associated cues, namely visual sensations.

The contrast between Kant and Berkeley emerges clearly if we examine how Kant faced the same three issues. Kant insisted that the mind imposes spatiality on sensations. Thus whereas Berkeley claimed that visual but not tactual sensation needed reinterpretation, Kant argued that all sensations are interpreted in the light of intellectual categories. Second, although Berkeley gave an important role to tactual experience in educating the subject about the meaning of visual sensations, Kant did not regard sensory experience, be it visual or tactual, as having any formative role. Finally, unlike Berkeley who argued that the idea of depth was derived ultimately from experience, Kant argued that it is part of the innate equipment of the mind to furnish an idea of depth.

Piaget

Among contemporary theorists, Piaget's ideas have dominated the study of infant cognition to a remarkable degree. In other chapters of these volumes, the broader outline of Piaget's theory is described. Later in this chapter I shall explore in detail recent efforts to check and reinterpret Piagetian claims regarding the development of object permanence. In this section, I wish to indicate the general framework that Piaget has offered for the study of infant cognition.

Piaget's work on infancy is presented in three volumes: *The Origins of Intelligence in Children* (1952), *The Construction of Reality in the Child* (1954), and *Play, Dreams and Imitation in Childhood* (1951). For the most part, these investigations were based on close observation of the development of his own three children in the first 2 years of life.

Six Content Areas Divided into Six Stages

Piaget traces the course of development within six content areas: so-called circular reactions; imitation, and the understanding of time, space, causality, and the permanent object. Across all of these content areas, Piaget divides the course of development into six sequential stages and claims that within certain limits the infant's development proceeds in parallel across the various content areas. The evidence for this claim will be examined when we turn to psychometric investigations of infant cognition. The claim amounts to the prediction that an infant who is at, say, Stage 3 for the development of object permanence will also be at Stage 3, approximately, for the development of imitation and all the other content areas.

Perhaps the best place to begin with a description of the various sequences is with the development of circular reactions. These circular reactions or sensorimotor schemes are of fundamental importance in Piagetian theory because they constitute the ultimate building blocks for cognitive development. As we shall discuss in more detail later, Piaget argues that infants acquire knowledge of the world by acting on it, and their initial modes of activity are organized in terms of the basic circular reactions such as sucking, looking, and grasping. A circular reaction is an organized act that tends to produce stimuli that lead to its subsequent re-elicitation. For example, as infants suck, they produce tactile pressure on the mouth, which tends to elicit further sucking. In the course of development, such building blocks undergo differentiation and refinement in that they are adjusted to suit a wider and wider range of objects. In the case of grasping, for example, infants gradually adjust their grasp to a variety of differently shaped objects. The circular reactions or schemes also become integrated, one with another; for example, the act of grasping eventually becomes coordinated with the act of looking so that infants come to reach out and grasp objects smoothly and effectively. By the final two stages of the six-stage development of circular reactions, two important changes have occurred. First, in the fifth stage the differentiation of schemata becomes deliberate rather than random: More specifically, infants deliberately vary their reactions to an object in order to deal with its novel aspects. For example, Piaget describes Jacqueline at 14 months, who finds that certain movements of her fingers cause a box to tilt; she goes on to vary the conditions of this movement until she succeeds in tilting the box back up. A second important achievement, which emerges in the sixth stage of sensorimotor intelligence, is the capacity for internal representation. Piaget argues that this capacity permits the infant to experiment not simply with overt actions as described above for the fifth stage, but also to try out various possibilities in a purely mental fashion. Jacqueline again provides an illustration of such mental representation. She arrives at a closed door, which is difficult to open because she is carrying a blade of grass in each hand.

> When she wants to leave the room, things become complicated. She puts the grass on the floor and grasps the doorknob. But then she perceives that in pulling the door toward her she will simultaneously chase away the grass which she placed between the door and the threshold. She therefore picks it up in order to put it outside the door's zone of movement. (Piaget, 1952, p. 339)

Here, the possible mishap and its prevention are apparently envisaged ahead of Jacqueline's overt action of placing the grass outside of the door's zone of movement.

If we turn now to the development of imitation we see that it develops along similar lines according to Piaget (1951). In the initial stages, imitation consists simply in the repetition of the type of circular reactions that Piaget described in *The Origins of Intelligence in Children*. Such imitative acts occur because infants in the early stages fail to make any sharp distinction between the acts of the person being imitated and their own imitative acts. Thus infants incorporate the sensory input they are provided with by an adult act, such as hand clapping, into their own circular reactions. As we saw above, such circular reactions tend to be repeated when the appropriate feedback is available. So, given that infants confuse another's acts with their own, it makes little difference that the source of this sensory feedback is actually another person.

By the age of 18 months, imitation has, in common with infants' other practical activities, become freed from the need for support from immediate input. In the final stage of imitation, infants are able to engage in delayed imitation: Having seen a model produce a given act, hours or even days before, they remain capable of imitating what they have seen. Second, infants are capable of imitating certain new behaviors even if they have never before performed them. Both of these abilities imply the capacity for some type of internal representation of another's acts, even acts that are not within the infant's repertoire. The parallels with the development of the circular reactions are relatively clear.

If we turn to the four remaining content areas, we can see how the developing capacity for mental representation, which allows infants to organize their actions in advance, also enables them to grasp the organization of the spatiotemporal world and to shape their actions accordingly. For example, with respect to the concept of the permanent object, neonates, according to Piaget, have no conception of an object that is not present within the immediate perceptual field. Their conception of the object is restricted to the set of actions that can be directed at the immediately visible object. Once the object disappears, so that it no longer engages any sensorimotor scheme, infants assume it has ceased to exist. Thus a change of position is confused with a change of state. By the end of the sensorimotor period, on the other hand, infants can imagine the movements of an object that is hidden in a container and subjected to various displacements within that container, as well as the actions needed to restore the object to view again after its disappearance. This development in the capacity to represent the invisible object also reflects, according to Piaget, infants' increasing objectivity: No longer perceiving the object and their actions on it as indissociable, so that the object is assumed to cease to exist once they cease to act on it, infants at the end of the sensorimotor period acknowledge that the object's existence and its displacements in space can occur quite independently of their actions or perceptions regarding the object.

A similar picture emerges with regard to the developing concept of space. Initially, infants can only specify an object's position with regard to their own bodily actions on it. So, for example, they can turn toward an object in the corner of their eye. However, such objects are not perceived as existing within an independent amodal space. When infants hear an object to one side of them, they do not, according to Piaget, turn to look at it, because this would presuppose an intercoordination between the various local spaces within which they execute the various circular reactions such as looking and listening. Only gradually are such local spaces linked together in a common space so that auditory information can guide visual orientation and so forth. In the final stage of sensorimotor intelligence, infants' spatial understanding permits them to imagine the displacements of an object, be they visible or invisible as noted above. This capacity for mental representation also eventually includes the infant's own body and its displacements. That is to say, infants can imagine their own change of position relative to other objects without actually moving. Such an accomplishment is obviously invaluable for solving various types of spatial problems. One of Piaget's observations is as follows:

> Laurent clings to his father with his left hand and with his right tries to pull an iron gate toward him. . . . He succeeds to a slight degree but does not succeed in opening it wide. He stops, then

> suddenly leads me to the other side of the wall; there without any hesitation or false move, he pushes the gate with both hands and thus succeeds in opening it. Hence he has gone around the object, representing to himself, ahead of time the path to follow since the gate is not transparent. (Piaget, 1954, p. 232)

Analogous developments are described by Piaget regarding the concepts of time and causality. At first, the infant's notion of time is restricted to a specification of the order in which certain behaviors can be executed, whereas at the end of the sensorimotor period, time is regarded as an independent dimension, within which the infant's activities and also events in which he or she did not participate directly may be arranged. Likewise, causality is initially understood exclusively in terms of the infant's own activities and desires, but by the end of the sensorimotor period, the infant can conceive of a causal relation existing between other people and objects, to which the infant is a mere bystander.

Having given an account of Piaget's description of the course of development across the six content areas, we may specify Piaget's position in relation to the three key issues raised earlier: the roles played by interpretation, experience, and representation.

Objectivity and the Need to Reinterpret Perceptual Experience

Brainerd (1978a) points out that the objectivity of the infant's view of the world is a major theme of Piaget's writing on infancy. Piaget is strongly of the opinion that the sensorimotor schemes of the neonate do not provide valid information about the outside world. At first, the neonate only conceives of a permanent object—of space, time, and causality—in terms of practical activities toward objects. Gradually, as infants understand more and more about the way in which the spatiotemporal world is organized, they subordinate their actions to that organization in order to achieve their own practical ends. Thus, perceptual encounters are slowly reinterpreted as infants gain a more objective understanding of the world. To take but one example, neonates only acknowledge the existence of an object to the extent that it actually engages their sensorimotor schemes, be it looking at, touching, or sucking the object. Once these schemes are not engaged—for example when the object disappears out of the perceptual field—neonates react as if the object no longer existed. They make no effort to recover it. This fallacious assumption that the object has ceased to exist is abandoned as they come to reinterpret the disappearance of the object in the light of their understanding that objects continue to exist—or remain permanent as Piaget puts it—even when they do not engage any sensorimotor schemes.

The Role of Experience

Piaget attributes a major role to experience in cognitive development, but it is important to stress that he dissents not only from the traditional rationalist postulate of innate ideas, but also from the empiricist postulate that knowledge derives from perceptual experience.

Piaget is sympathetic to the empiricist position in so far as it recognizes the implausibility of assuming that innate ideas would be adequate to supply an objective understanding of the world. Such a preestablished harmony between our conceptual categories and the nature of the world seems unlikely. Thus Piaget praises the empiricists for acknowledging that there is a role for experience in the acquisition of knowledge. However, he criticizes them for assuming that the mind is a tabula rasa whose knowledge is restricted to the impress of experience. Even in the neonate we see that experience is assimilated to certain simple structures, namely the sensorimotor schemes.

To the extent that rationalism stresses the contribution made by the knowing subject, Piaget is sympathetic. However, for Piaget, such a contribution is in a constant state of revision and improvement. The rationalist position, in contrast, emphasizes the importance of innate conceptual categories and therefore allows little room for the gradual elaboration of conceptual structures in the course of development. Thus Piaget agrees with Kant when he argues that the subject imposes concepts such as causality and time on his or her perceptual experience, but he disagrees with Kant in so far as he argues that such concepts are only gradually constructed in the course of development and should not be regarded as innate.

How then does experience help the infant to construct new conceptual categories? Piaget stresses the active role of the infant in the acquisition of knowledge rather than the passive absorption of perceptual experience. The infant's activity is important in two ways. In the first place, the infant actually produces transformations in the course of exercising the sensorimotor schemes. So, for example, the infant does not simply passively observe the reappearance of an object that has vanished. At first by chance, and later more deliberately, eye movements or groping movements in the direction of disappearance serve to bring about the reappearance of the object. Second, the infant's hypotheses about the world are not a simple copy of what is perceived but are based on the actions or schemes that transform reality from one state to another. This can also be explained with reference to the example of the permanent object. Because an invisible object offers no perceptual information, almost by definition, it is easy to see that the infant's understanding that it continues to exist is not simply some mental copy of a perceptual experience; instead, the idea of permanence is ultimately based on the infant's grasp of how action can transform invisibility into visibility, always provided it is adjusted to the precise trajectory and displacements of the invisible object. We can summarize the role of experience by saying that infants act on the world, and observing the resulting transformations, their perception of the here-and-now world is gradually impregnated with knowledge of the acts that led up to it, and that could transform it yet again.

Piaget's avoidance of both rationalism and empiricism is also linked to another hallmark of Piagetian theory: the emphasis on invariant ordinal sequences of development. In later sections, the examples of object permanence and imitation will be described in more detail. For the moment we may note that such ordinal sequences grow out of the interplay between experience and the preexisting sensorimotor schemes. An analogy with the growth of science is useful: A hypothesis is used to guide experimental observations; such observations throw up unexpected new data that lead to a revision of the hypothesis, and a new direction for experimental observation. Similarly, as infants act on the world they encounter new relationships between acts and outcomes. These relationships are incorporated into the schemes, making them more elaborate. When these new schemes are deployed, new relationships are discovered and the cycle begins again. Thus if we observe infants longitudinally, we will observe a sequence of more and more elaborated and coordinated sensorimotor schemes.

The Role of Representation

Finally, we may survey Piagetian theory in the light of the third issue raised earlier: To what extent does Piaget regard the infant's reactions during the first weeks as being restricted to the immediate here-and-now world? It should be clear by now that Piaget does indeed see the neonate as starting off at a stage of more or less immediate reactivity to externally available stimulation, so long as that stimulation fits in with some preexisting scheme. Gradually, infants exhibit an increasingly planful organization of their sensorimotor activities which, while directed at the achievement of some practical goal in the outside world, are nevertheless based on the mental representation of anticipated outcomes. A full capacity for representation emerges in the sixth and final stage of sensorimotor intelligence, representation being the internalized execution of a sensorimotor scheme rather than its overt execution.

It is important to note that although two of Piaget's developmental themes, namely the increasingly objective view of the world taken by the infant and the increasing use of inner mental representation, appear to be conceptually inseparable, this is not necessarily the case. Traditional psychoanalytic theory—criticized at length by Piaget in *Play, Dreams and Imitation in Childhood* (Piaget, 1951)—shows how these two themes can, at least in principle, be severed. Psychoanalytic theorists typically acknowledge that infants cannot distinguish between the external world and their own actions on it, but such theorists also claim that infants have a rich representational capacity, in so far as they can imagine various types of wish fulfillment. As a result, neonates of the psychoanalytic school are likely not only to confuse their own actions with the external world, but also to confuse the products of their own imagination with the states of affairs that actually do obtain. The less imaginative Piagetian neonate is saved, at least, from this latter confusion.

Gibson

J. J. Gibson is not usually thought of as a developmental psychologist and has certainly written very little on the topic of infant cognition as such. Nevertheless, like Piaget, Gibson is strongly theoretical in his writing, and like Piaget has attempted to address some of the epistemological implications of his theorizing. Gibson is particularly interesting in so far as he offers a sharp contrast to Piagetian writings, and in my view students of perceptual and cognitive development during infancy will increasingly see Gibson as a radical alternative. Indeed, E. J. Gibson and her students have begun to explore the implications of this alternative view for the study of perceptual development in infancy (E. J. Gibson, 1969, 1977; Gibson & Spelke, *vol. III, chap. 1*).

Richness of Available Stimulation

J. J. Gibson (1950) points out that the study of psychophysics has proceeded in a secure fashion by seeking an empirical correspondence between the stimulus and its conscious result. For example, perceived color is related to variations in the wavelength of light; and perceived musical tone is related to variations in the frequency of air vibration. Such psychophysical correspondences, as they may be termed, can be studied without recourse to the intervening physiological processes provided lawful relationships can be found.

If we now try to extend this program to space perception, it appears at first sight to be impossible. As Berkeley pointed out, the retinal image is two-dimensional. How then could it register three dimensions of a physical layout so as to yield our conscious impression of depth? Gibson argued that the search for psychophysical correspondence can be pursued

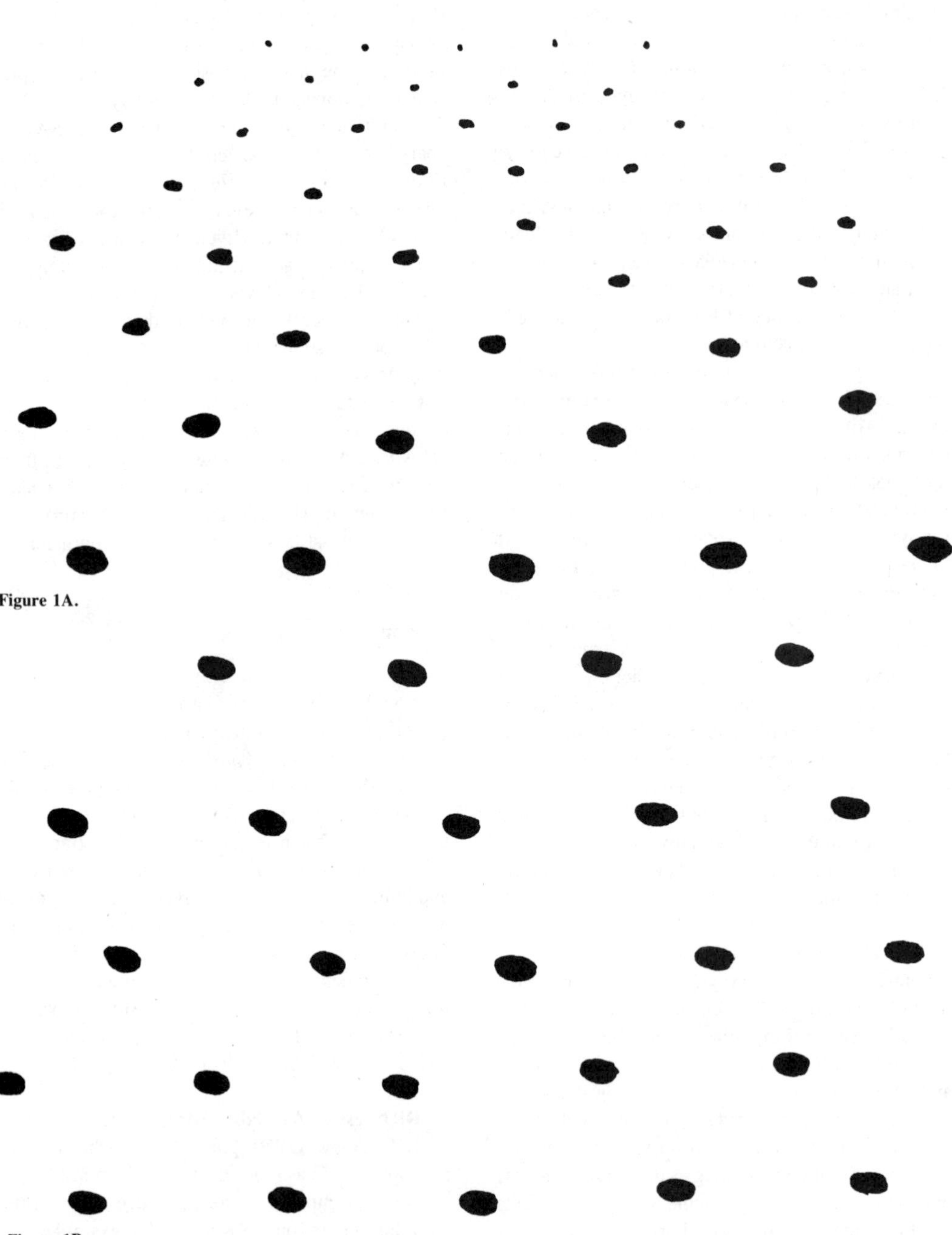

Figure 1A.

Figure 1B.

into the realm of space. However, instead of focusing on a single spot of light of a given wavelength and intensity, we must turn our attention to variation in the relations among different spots of the image. These relations are organized in ways that can inform the perceiver about the objective spatial properties of the environment. Consider Figure 1A and B, for example. A glance indicates that the texture in Figure 1A but not in Figure 1B forms a gradient. In fact, in Figure 1A, the texture gradient resembles that which we can observe as we look out across a landscape. Gibson points out that such texture gradients, which are a natural part of most landscapes, provide us directly with information about relative distance. If the perceptual system can register information about texture gradients, then it can by implication register information about depth.

Gibson has argued further that it is not only the static layout of the environment, which offers us directly perceptible information. The transformations of and within that environment also provide information. For example, certain types of information specify a movement of an object, whereas others specify movement of an observer. Figure 2 illustrates an object located on a texture gradient. Figure 3A illustrates the approach of the object toward th observer, and Figure 3B illustrates the approach of the observer toward the object. Note that in Figure 3B, the entire optic array undergoes an expansion. This transformation constitutes what might be called visual proprioception. Although we tend to think of information about our locomotion as coming from inside the body, Gibson's analysis of the available stimulation indicates that there is visual information available as well.

In drawing our attention to the fact that the environment is rich in information and in stressing that psychologists should identify carefully the nature of the available information, Gibson spells out the implications of his position for various theoretical controversies in psychology (J. J. Gibson, 1979). I shall focus on the three issues raised earlier: the role of interpretation in perception, the role of experience, and the extent to which the infant is disposed to use a system of representation.

Direct Visual Perception

If the environment is rich in organized information, it becomes feasible to think of the infant as being equipped with a perceptual system that can detect that information from birth. Indeed it is feasible to think of the neonate not simply as detecting cues for depth or motion but as perceiving depth and motion directly. This is in fact the position adopted by J. J. Gibson (1979), and it is useful to emphasize the difference between a "cue" theory of perception and a theory of "direct" perception.

Berkeley, it will be remembered, argued that visual sensations such as the felt angle of convergence of the eyes could serve as cues for depth by dint of their eventual association with other sensations such as tactual contact with the object or motor movement toward it. In Berkeley's account, then, tactual sensations inform the infant or adult about depth directly whereas visual sensations serve only as cues or indices of the more directly informative sensations, namely tactual sensations. Gibson, in contrast, argues that there is nothing special about tactual information. Although such information can provide us with direct information about depth, so also can visual cues such as binocular convergence and texture gradients.

Gibson's approach contrasts not only with traditional empiricist approaches to perception, but also with Piaget's emphasis on the need to reinterpret perceptual information in terms of constructed concepts. To bring out this contrast more clearly, we may focus again on the development of object permanence. According to Piaget, the neonate has no conception of the continued existence of a hidden object. Gradually, having discovered that certain simple actions such as manual groping or visual search can restore perceptual contact with an object that has disappeared, the infant adopts the hypothesis that although objects cease to exist when they disappear, they can be brought back into existence by such actions. The restricted and ultimately fallacious nature of this hypothesis is revealed by the fact that having successfully found an object in one place, the infant returns to that place, even after seeing the object disappear at a quite different place. Eventually this hypothesis is abandoned as the infant comes to appreciate that an object is typically to be found at the place or container where it was last seen to disappear. Because almost by definition there do not appear to be any perceptual cues to indicate the continued existence of a *hidden* object, and because the infant only gradually comes to exhibit accurate search, making a considerable number and variety of search errors along the way, it is hard not to sympathize with Piaget's hypothesis that the infant constructs the idea of a permanent object.

Nevertheless, J. J. Gibson (1966) points out that when something disappears from sight by being screened or covered, there is a progressive "wiping out" of a greater and greater surface area of the object as the cover is drawn over the object. Such perceptual information differs from that which is

Figure 2.

Figure 3A.

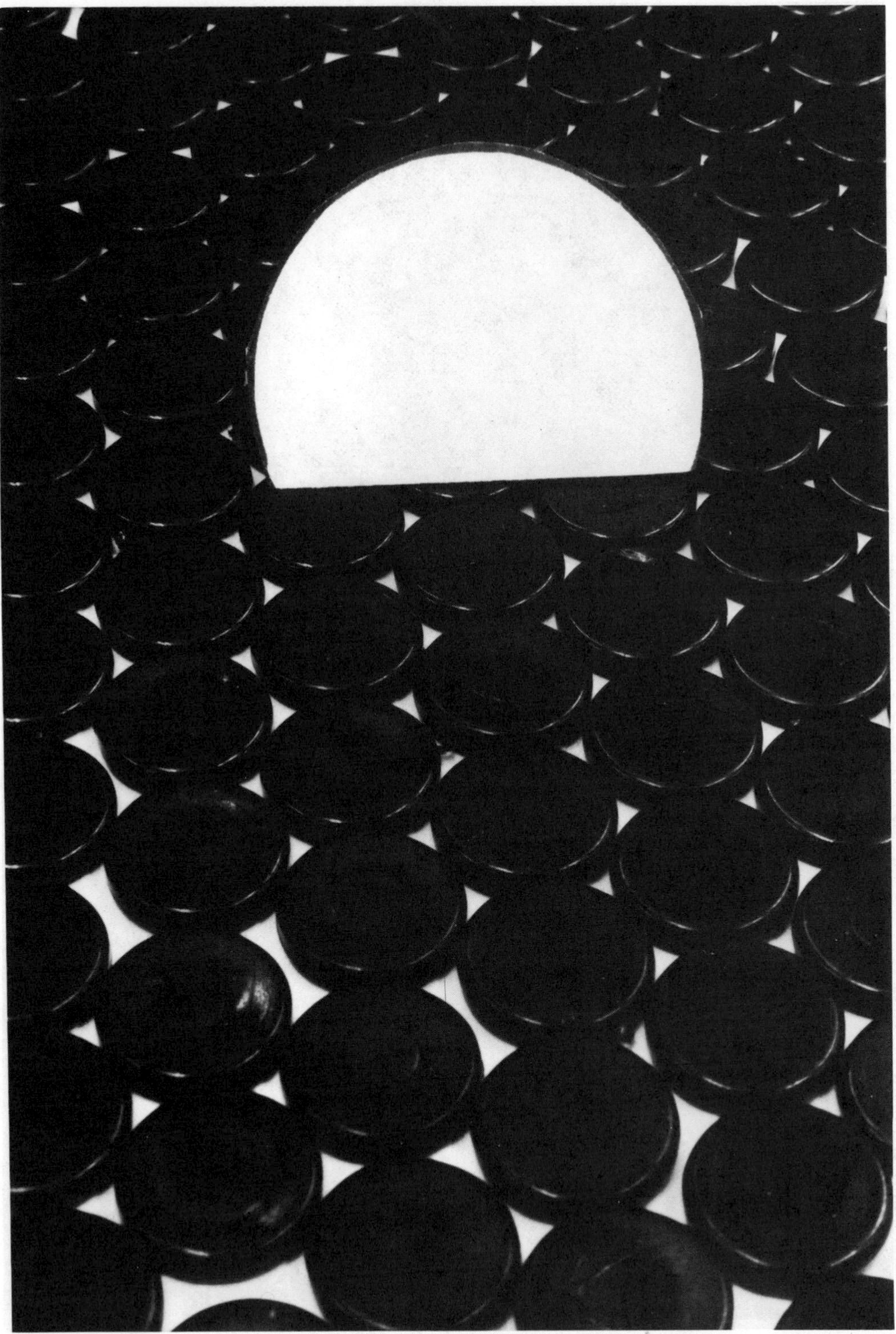

Figure 3B.

available if the object undergoes a different type of disappearance. For example, if the object gradually fades into the background or implodes, the visual information specifying these two events is quite different from that specifying gradual occlusion. Thus Gibson (1966) writes: "The child must distinguish, or learn to distinguish, between these two kinds of optical transformation in order to perceive when a thing merely goes out of sight and when it vanishes, but he does not have to 'construct' reality out of impermanent sensations (Piaget, 1954)" (p. 285). Thus Gibson's account draws attention to the fact that, although there are no perceptual cues to indicate the location of an object during the time that it is hidden, such cues are available at the moment of disappearance to indicate either the continued existence of the object, as in the case of gradual occlusion, or its disintegration, as in the case of implosion. Indeed, as we have noted, Gibson would not even refer to such visual sensations as cues at all, because this immediately assumes that they are mere substitutes for or indices of some firmer or more palpable information regarding the object's continued existence.

In summary, Gibson disagrees with empiricists on the one hand and Piaget on the other. The empiricists emphasize that certain types of perceptual sensations, especially tactual sensations, supply an interpretation of otherwise uninformative visual stimuli. Piaget emphasizes that action-derived intellectual constructs such as the notion of object permanence permit a reinterpretation of initially misleading visual stimuli. In contrast to both, Gibson argues that the perceptual world, including the visual world, affords valid information, which requires no interpretation or supplementation.

The Role of Experience

What approach does Gibson take to the role of experience? Because Gibson argues that the infant can pick up perceptual information from birth, and because he is reluctant to admit that such information requires any kind of interpretation in order to provide valid evidence about the state of the world and the perceiver's relation to it, it might be thought that Gibson's theory leaves precious little room for learning through experience. In a sense this is true; the older child is unlikely, within Gibson's framework, to arrive at radically new conclusions about the world, whereas both Piaget and the traditional empiricist position do postulate such new insights. Nevertheless, Gibson does admit an important role for learning. He suggests that the perceptual system becomes more finely tuned or resonates more clearly to the information that is available in the environment. This process of fine tuning operates in two ways. First, with repeated exposure to a set of objects falling into the same class, the observer becomes better able to detect those features that distinguish that class of objects from other objects, and eventually the features that distinguish between various members of the same class (Gibson & Gibson, 1955). Eleanor Gibson (1969) has described what this process of differentiation might involve for the perception of faces by the infant. At first, the infant might have differentiated features that distinguish faces from nonfaces: eyes, mouth, an oval head shape, and so forth. At this point, however, the infant would still fail to differentiate between individual faces. Gradually, however, the infant would learn to attend to the appropriate distinctive features while ignoring those that stay constant across faces. To take a simple example, faces differ from one another only marginally in the horizontal alignment of the eyes within the head. On the other hand, they do differ from one another considerably in the length of the nose or chin. Thus attention to the latter features would help an infant to differentiate one face from another whereas attention to the former feature would not.

E. Gibson (1969) also indicates the link between perceptual schemata and feature differentiation. According to Kagan (1965), whose ideas will be discussed in more detail in the next section, a mental schema provides a basis for distinguishing between faces. In contrast, E. Gibson (1969) argues that until the features that are invariant across faces, but that distinguish faces from other objects, have been isolated, it is not clear what should be entered into a schema. Accordingly, she argues that the schema for "faces in general" emerges as a result of the differentiation process, not before.

A second learning process concerns the detection of invariants, which can be of two broad types. First, an individual object will have certain invariant properties despite transformation of other properties. For example, a face can be transformed in its orientation from full-face to profile, but its shape will remain invariant. Second, a given class of objects will have certain invariant features across individual members, despite variation in other features. Again, using the example of faces, as we noted above, the horizontal alignment of the eyes will be invariant across different faces, whereas the length of the nose will not.

In emphasizing the importance of invariants, the Gibsons highlight an important difference between their account of development and that of Piaget.

Piaget argues that the infant constructs the idea of invariance by acting on objects so as to transform them and then annulling such transformations by returning to the starting point. Thus the existence of an object remains invariant, despite its disappearance. In contrast, the Gibsons insist that such invariants are not intellectual constructs derived from acting on the environment; they can be detected in the environment. The infant can observe that certain types of displacement do leave an object's shape, or its existence, unaltered. Thus to return to an earlier analogy, Piaget implies that the infant and young child is in a certain way like an experimental physicist who interprets and reinterprets data in the light of observations that are guided by particular hypotheses. The Gibsons, on the other hand, imply that the developing child is like an increasingly skilled observer such as an astronomer: Over time, the astronomer becomes better able to notice the features that distinguish one galaxy from another and yet also better able to detect the wavelike configurations that recur across galaxies in different regions of the sky.

A Minor Role for Representation

Finally, we may turn to the issue of representation. Do the Gibsons believe that the infant gradually becomes less reactive to the immediate perceptual world and gradually comes to represent a remembered or anticipated world instead? They dissent from such a view in so far as it implies a gradual subordination of the perceived to the conceived. Eleanor Gibson (1969) has been quite explicit on this point:

> What is wrong with saying that the young child is stimulus bound, and that cognitive development is a liberation from these bonds by the operations of intelligence? This is Piaget's opinion. One must admit its popularity and pervasiveness, for a neonate's attention does seem to be captured by a few kinds of events in its environment. But the developmental change is not one of doing without stimulus information; it is one of seeking stimulus information in a directed, systematic fashion. (p. 448)

Such a conclusion is, of course, perfectly reasonable, once one accepts along with Gibson that the environment affords information to an observer in a direct fashion. Thus for both J. J. Gibson and E. J. Gibson, the only difference between the neonate and the infant at the end of the sensorimotor period would consist in their ability to pick up information from the environment. Indeed, in certain ways the older infant will be more rather than less reactive to the information available. This is not to deny, of course, that there are processes such as imagery or expectation. Indeed it may be that the neonate and the 18-month infant differ in such representational capacities. The Gibsons only wish to insist that the infant need not have recourse to such mental processes in order to gather valid information about the world.

Kagan

Control of Attention by Developing Schemata

In various theoretical statements, Kagan (1970, 1976, 1979) has tried to integrate the considerable amount of research on infant attention. To immediately highlight the difference between Kagan and Gibson, we may note that the Gibsons are for the most part concerned with the ways in which a stimulus provides information once it is attended to. In contrast, Kagan has addressed the question of what factors govern the distribution of attention in the first place. For this reason, Kagan is more inclined than the Gibsons to invest the infant with mental structures and schemata, so as to account for the infant's tendency to select from the available information.

In the first months of life, Kagan suggests that attention is controlled by the physical aspects of the stimulus itself, rather than by any stored experience with that stimulus. In particular, infants are attentive to stimuli that are marked by change, such as movement or the transitions from light to dark that can be seen in a contoured stimulus. In the course of development, however, the infant begins to develop schemata that Kagan (1979, p. 164) defines as "an abstract representation of an event that retains the relations among the physical dimensions of the original experience—be it object, sound, smell, or dynamic sequence." Such internal representations of previous perceptual encounters alter the infant's distribution of attention. Specifically,

> the child's attention tends to be prolonged to those events that are a little different—but not extremely different—from the one that created the original schema. Thus a 4-month old infant with a schema for its parents' faces will look a long time at a picture or a sculpture of a face in which the eyes are arranged vertically rather than horizontally. But infants will not look very long at a face that does not contain eyes. (Mussen, Conger, & Kagan, 1979, p. 135)

This hypothesis is generally known as the discrepancy hypothesis.

Kagan (1979) argues that a further change in the functioning of schemata occurs at about 8 months. First, if infants are tested across a large age range ($3\frac{1}{2}$–29 months) for their attentiveness to a repeated event, a drop in attention is found at about 7 to 8 months, both for American and for Guatemalan infants. Kagan's interpretation of this age change is that from 3 to 7 months, attention wanes because the infant is developing mental schemata, which permit a more and more rapid assimilation of a repeated event. Attention begins to increase after 8 months because of the emergence of a new tendency: to compare current inputs in an active fashion to a stored representation so as to understand the way in which the current input is a transformation of the stored representation.

As further evidence for this claim, Kagan (1979) also reports work on the development of search for a hidden object indicating that at around 8 months, infants engage in more active search despite increasingly long delays, the absence of the sought-for object, and the substitution of a new one.

The Role of Interpretation

In the opening section, attention was drawn to the disagreement among theorists regarding the role of interpretation. So far we have seen that Piaget agrees with the empiricists in stressing that the infant needs to reinterpret initially uninformative or misleading perceptual information so as to reach sound conclusions about the world. In contrast, the Gibsons deny that interpretation of perceptual input is needed. Provided the infant attends to the appropriate relations and transformations within the optic array, valid information is there to be found. Kagan adopts yet a third position with regard to the role of interpretation. He stresses the fact that all perceptual input is assimilated to perceptual schemata from a very early age. Changes in the course of development are attributed to the increasing availability of schemata and the more active processes of comparison. However, such interpretative processes serve a distinct role in Kagan's theory. Unlike the theorists discussed hitherto, he does not introduce such interpretive processes in order to explain the infant's ability to come to valid conclusions about the world. Instead, he introduces such processes so as to explain the infant's distribution of attention. So far as Kagan is concerned, the infant simply assimilates perceptual input to schemata of varying degrees of complexity and the validity or objectivity of such schemata is not discussed.

In making a comparison between his own ideas and those of Piaget, Kagan has been inclined to stress the fact that his own notion of a schema is less tied to active manipulation than is the case within Piagetian theorizing. Thus Kagan suggests that the infant can form a schema for an object on the basis of mere visual inspection. "Available evidence is consonant with the view that infants can acquire knowledge of an event by looking, listening or smelling; it is not always necessary that they manipulate it" (Kagan, 1979, p. 165). This comparison, however, appears to miss a more essential difference between the two theorists. Piaget is concerned with the infant's understanding of how particular states of the world can be transformed into other states. Kagan, in contrast, is primarily concerned with the child's representation of a given state of the world; to the extent that the infant might represent a transformation, Kagan only implies that the infant can store some kind of abstract copy of that transformation. Yet, as Piaget would be quick to point out, the ability to store a copy is not adequate to ensure understanding of a transformation and it is with the acquisition of such understanding that Piaget is concerned. For example, the fact that the infant can store a mental representation or schema for the optical information that is available when an object moves behind a screen is in no sense a guarantee that the infant can understand how that transformation has been brought about and how it can be undone by the infant's own intervention. Moreover—and this brings us to the reason why Piaget stresses active manipulation—it may be that infants come to understand those transformations of the world more rapidly if they bring them about themselves rather than observing others producing them. Thus Piaget's focus on the importance of manipulation needs to be seen within the context of his account of how the infant moves from a subjective to an objective view of the world.

In summary, Kagan stresses the importance of interpretation but in order to explain the distribution of the infant's attention, not the validity of the infant's knowledge. Moreover, because Kagan is not concerned with the development of objectivity, he discusses knowledge in terms of the storage of a schema for an object or event; such schemata may be based on visual inspection rather than active experimentation.

The Role of Experience

What view does Kagan take regarding the role of experience in cognitive development? Compared to other theorists, Kagan is unusual in being fairly explicit about the existence of innate processes, which guide the course of development, but which will not necessarily be detectable at birth. Thus Kagan interprets the changing role of the schema in the light of a maturationally controlled growth function, which contrrols the infant's memorial ability. Support for such a maturational timetable is provided by cross-cultural work in which the timetable for such changes in memory processes appears to be universal.

Nevertheless, as should be apparent from the above discussion, the elaboration of particular schemata (as opposed to the role of the schemata in general) will depend on specific encounters with the world. In particular, encounters that are somewhat but not maximally different from existing schemata will elicit the most attention and therefore have the most formative role in revision of those existing schemata. Unfortunately, Kagan has not been very precise about how exactly such revisions occur. For example, does the infant create a new schema, which in some way averages across the old schema and the newly encountered stimulus? Alternatively, does the new encounter merely strengthen those aspects of the schema with which it does overlap while attenuating those aspects from which it deviates? Kagan does not specify, but as we shall see in discussing the question of object identity, experimental work is gradually being guided by those more precise questions.

Development of Representation

Finally, Kagan's approach can be related to the issue of whether the infant gradually becomes less and less responsive to immediate stimulus input. It should be apparent from the above description of Kagan's theory and empirical findings that such a shift away from reactions to the immediate physical input is indeed central to Kagan's theory. Nevertheless, although Piaget and Kagan concur in this respect, this should not obscure the fact that the end point of development during the period of infancy is somewhat different for the two theorists. As noted earlier, Piaget invokes the concept of internal representation in order to explain how the infant is able to envisage certain outcomes and to act accordingly. Moreover, as discussed earlier, Piaget attributes representational capacities to the infant only at the end of the sensorimotor period at approximately 18 months of age. Even when the infant searches for a fully hidden object at around 8 to 9 months, Piaget insists that such behaviors do not involve any true representation of the hidden object, because the infant will search at a previously correct hiding place even though the object has been seen to disappear at a new hiding place.

Kagan differs from Piaget with respect to both the role of representational processes and the timetable for their emergence. For Kagan, as we have seen, representational capacities are recruited in order to explain the infant's distribution of attention to a visible event, so that the objectivity or validity of such processes is not at issue. Kagan is therefore inclined to attribute a representational capacity even at 3 to 4 months. Admittedly the function of those processes will change in the course of development but the ability to represent previous objects and events, independent of the current availability of those particular objects and events, is an early attainment.

Bruner

Growth of Skill, Intention, Reordering, and Modularization

Bruner (1973) has argued that much of development in infancy can be seen as the growth of skill. Behind this apparently innocent-sounding word, there is a good deal of psychological meaning. Bruner views skilled activity as goal-oriented activity, which is composed of a set of sequentially organized constituent parts. Skilled motor activity is like language in certain ways. First, it is possible to reorder some components and still achieve the same goal; second, components can be transposed from one context to another. Thus creative recombination is a hallmark of both language and skill.

Bruner argues that even from the outset the infant's motor activities are under the control of an intention, despite the fact that the skill may still be in a crude and rudimentary form. For example, when one observes infants at around 4 months of age—at the onset of visually guided reaching—various components of the act of reaching are triggered and appear to signal ahead of time their intention to take the object even though the capacity to realize that intention is very limited. Infants stare at the object to be taken, pump their arms up and down, open and close their hands as if the hands were about to capture the object, and even open and close their mouths as if in anticipation of eventually bringing the object to the mouth.

These observations illustrate two claims that Bruner regards as central to the ontogeny of skill. First, the actions of the neonate do not randomly achieve a particular goal: The means to achieve the goal and the appropriate consummatory activity are typically preadapted rather than learned constituents of the motor act. Second, these constituents are often executed in the wrong order. Thus, strictly speaking, until the infant has reached out for the object, it is premature to clench the hand. Similarly, until the object has been clasped and brought to the mouth, there is no point in opening the mouth. As Bruner (1973, p. 2) puts it, "Initial arousal is often followed by a loosely ordered sequence of constituent acts that will later occur in an appropriate serial order to achieve the end state toward which the intention appears to be steering."

Bruner stresses two sources for the constituent parts of skilled action. First, there is an innate repertoire of action patterns that are evoked by an encounter with an appropriate object or event in the environment. Second, there is the use of so-called mastery play, in which the infant seeks to fit an object into a variety of activities and to extend each activity to all those objects that afford an opportunity. So, the infant who has learned to hold onto an object, holds it to look at it, to shake it, to bang it, and so forth. Similarly, when the infant has acquired the bimanual skill of holding an object in one hand while fingering it with the other, this skill is applied to a whole range of objects.

Such component parts are eventually modularized in the course of repeated use. By modularization, Bruner refers to several processes: An act is "made more automatic, less variable, and achieves a predictable spatio-temporal patterning" (Bruner, 1970, pp. 70–71). Thus in the course of repeated use an act is more smoothly executed and typically executed in a shorter time. An important consequence of such modularization is that the infant's attention is less dominated by the execution of the act. This frees attention, such that the act can be inserted into some other goal, or a particular subcomponent can be elaborated.

Finally, Bruner (1973) emphasizes the fact that whereas the environment might afford feedback regarding the appropriateness of a given act, environmental feedback or reinforcement is scarcely responsible for the initial selection of that act as potentially appropriate. Thus Bruner takes issue with studies of operant learning in which there is a relatively arbitrary link between a given act and a particular outcome arranged by the ingenuity of the experimenter, rather than any natural fit between a given act and an environmental consequence. Bruner concludes:

> There are, as ethologists have insisted, natural "chunks" of behaviour, natural orderings of constituents, etc. The ordinary operant conditioning paradigm—choose any operant and bring it under the control of a stimulus and a reinforcer—is no more revealing of the growth of skill than the rate of learning of paired associates is relevant to the learning of language. (Bruner, 1973, p. 10)

Emphasis on Motor Acts Rather Than Perception

This review of Bruner's account of skill acquisition indicates that his focus of attention is somewhat different from that of the other three theorists. Simply stated, Bruner is less interested in the infant's perception of the world than in the infant's overt and observable actions. As a result, the question of whether or not Bruner believes that the infant's initial perception requires interpretation in order to provide valid information about the world can scarcely be considered. Nevertheless, Bruner does in fact provide an implicit answer to this question. He argues that the infant's motor acts exhibit a high degree of preadaptation. Such preadaptation necessarily depends on the extraction of valid information about the objects to be acted on. To give one example, Bruner and Koslowski (1972) have reported that well before the infant can execute a smoothly executed reach for an object, the components of the reach are adapted to the size of the object: A small object elicits bimanual fingering at the midline, whereas a larger object elicits manual activity in which the hands are not united at the midline. Thus to the extent that Bruner deals with the infant's perception of the world, he is much closer to the Gibsons' notion of direct perception than to Piaget's insistence on the need to interpret initial perceptions in the light of constructed cognitive categories. Of course, Piaget does admit that even the neonate exhibits well-adapted sensorimotor schemes such as sucking and looking, but he never admits that these are anything other than highly local and specific adaptations, in need of considerable extension and intercoordination throughout the sensorimotor period.

The Role of Experience

Bruner is, as noted above, explict about the relative contribution of innate factors and experience in the acquisition of skill. The basic components of a particular skill are preadapted to the achievement of a particular goal. Experience teaches the infant how to order those components, how to integrate them into a smoothly executed motor act, and how to free attention so that the act can be elaborated or inserted as a subcomponent into a more complex act. Again,

Bruner's account differs quite sharply from that of Piaget. Whereas Bruner argues that the means to achieve a goal and the consummatory act that is its terminus are preadapted, Piaget argues that deliberate means selection can only emerge toward the end of the sensorimotor period, following an earlier stage in which schemes are linked together on an unsystematic basis.

The Nature of Representation in Infancy

Before undertaking research on infants, Bruner and his colleagues (Bruner, Olver, Greenfield, et al., 1966) had suggested that the mental code by which the growing child represents the world gains new media in the course of development. The very young infant is restricted to an action-based code, which is later supplemented by the use of imagery and language. However, this tripartite distinction between different types of representation was not taken up in Bruner's subsequent empirical work with infants. Instead, he concentrated on skilled action in infancy, ignoring the question of when and how the infant becomes capable of using imagery and language.

Nevertheless, we may ask whether Bruner invests the infant with a complex action-based representational system. In particular, does Bruner assume that the neonate is capable of planned representation of future actions, or is the neonate restricted to a more or less involuntary and stimulus-bound reactivity? Again, it is clear that Bruner's emphasis is surprisingly nativistic, especially when contrasted with that of Piaget. Bruner insists that skilled activity is, from the outset, under the control of a mentally represented intention, which steers the infant toward its realization. Such a system of mental representation is no doubt relatively circumscribed, especially when compared to the representational capacities with which Piaget endows the infant at the end of the sensorimotor period. However, Bruner sees such an ability to represent intention as the foundation of skilled sensorimotor activity rather than its crowning achievement.

Current Status of the Four Theories

Without doubt, Piaget's ideas continue to dominate research on infant cognition. Nevertheless, as I shall attempt to show in the discussion of particular content areas, his ideas are being challenged in several ways. First, with regard to the role of interpretation, it seems likely that Piaget has underestimated the ability of the infant to extract valid information about the world. Gibson's emphasis on direct visual perception therefore becomes much more appropriate. We shall note the way in which the Gibsonian challenge has been launched with respect to space perception and crossmodal integration. With regard to the role of experience, it is clear that the infant's knowledge does not always develop in a stagelike fashion. In certain domains experience appears simply to extend but not alter the infant's initial mode of perception. Again, these findings accord with the Gibsonian emphasis on the fine tuning of a rich capacity for information extraction rather than the radical revision of false theories of the world. Finally, with regard to the capacity for representation, there is evidence suggesting that it comes to guide attention and imitation from an early age, in line with Kagan's theorizing.

All this evidence suggests that cognitive development is neither so uniform nor so integrated as Piaget would have us believe. The organization of subaspects of the world—for example, the domain of space and the domain of action—cannot be described by a small set of principles, and the infant tries to understand different domains in different ways. Indeed, as we shall see in the section on psychometrics, which follows our examination of specific content areas, even if we stick to the domains that Piaget investigated, the idea of uniformly paced development across a wide set of cognitive domains is an illusion. Cognitive development, even when it involves the type of constructive sequences that best suit the Piagetian model, is more piecemeal and local than he suggested (Harris & Heelas, 1979). Accordingly, we can proceed to look at particular domains, making the relatively safe assumption that the infant too is incapable of finding a small set of principles that unites them all.

Three different domains will be examined: space, identity, and action. Within each of these domains, I shall again try to show the relevance of the three issues that have been introduced: the roles of interpretation, experience, and representation. Having introduced the major ideas of Bruner, Kagan, Gibson, and Piaget, I shall not review their position with respect to each of the domains to be discussed. Rather, I shall draw in particular theorists to the extent that their ideas have guided experimental investigations. Nevertheless, the ensuing sections will not consist solely of a historical record. Where a particular theoretical stance seems especially relevant but has been neglected, I shall attempt to indicate this.

SPACE

In the introduction a contrast was drawn between Gibson's emphasis on direct visual perception and

Piaget's assertion that the infant's concept of space is only gradually constructed. In this section, three aspects of spatial development will be considered where this disagreement provides an ever-present backdrop: the development of depth perception, of crossmodal coding, and of object permanence.

The link between these three topics is clear in both theoretical positions. Piaget argues that the neonate is equipped only with a set of separate sensorimotor schemes: For example, looking and grasping are not integrated. Crossmodal coding is necessarily impossible until these schemes are integrated. Moreover, because, according to Piaget, the construction of depth depends on an appreciation of what particular visual cues mean in terms of action, the neonate necessarily has no appreciation of depth. Only gradually as a result of the integration of vision first with reaching, and then with locomotion, is an idea first of near space and then of far space constructed. Finally, the integration of schemes is a precondition for the construction of the permanent object. At first the infant merely perceives insubstantial images that come into and go out of existence. Gradually permanence is attributed to them, as such images are linked with certain tactual consequences, and as procedures are discovered for recovering them after visual loss.

Similarly, Gibson's theory of direct visual perception leads him to adopt a consistent approach to each of the three topics. He asserts that information, such as positional information, is common to different modalities. Thus initially separate modalities do not require integration. They are necessarily united by virtue of their ability to pick up multimodal information. Second, the infant does not construct an idea of space. There is information in the optic array sufficient to specify depth directly. Finally, the various types of disappearance directly specify the difference between temporary occlusion and permanent annihilation.

Below, we turn to a more detailed scrutiny of each of the three topics, taking up the issue of crossmodal integration first.

Crossmodal Integration in Space

Objects offer information to more than one perceptual modality. For example, the human face can be seen, touched, and heard. Moreover, the information offered to the various modalities can be related across those modalities. A face is in the same position whether it is seen or heard; its shape is the same whether it is seen or touched; the movements of the lips are correlated with the sounds made by the voice. According to traditional empiricist theories of perception, such correlations are perceived because experience in the two modalities is linked by associative experience. For example, when an object is simultaneously touched and seen, the infant comes to associate a set of visual experiences with a set of tactual experiences, so that eventually one set of experiences can conjure up a memory of the other. The implication of such an account is that the links between the modalities are arbitrary rather than necessary; an object seen to be round could presumably come to be associated with an object felt to be square, provided the two sets of experiences were systematically paired.

Piaget (1952) comes very close to an empiricist account of crossmodal perception, the only major difference being that whereas traditional empiricist accounts stressed the temporal association of sensations across modalities, Piaget stresses the reciprocal coordination of sensorimotor schemes such as looking and touching rather than the sensations that they might produce. Thus as a result of the simultaneous activation of schemes associated with different modalities, the infant comes to achieve some measure of crossmodal unity. Because according to Piaget such reciprocal coordination of schemes does not occur at birth, there is no crossmodal unity at birth.

In contrast to this account, J. J. Gibson (1966) and E. J. Gibson (1969) have argued that there is information about objects that is amodal in that it can be picked up from more than one modality. For example, if an object's position is referred to the self, then the infant can discover by vision, touch, or hearing that it is either straight ahead or 45° in the right periphery. Similarly, if the tempo of the father's voice and the tempo of his lip movements are both perceived by the infant and referred to a common temporal dimension, then the infant can discover by listening or by looking what that tempo is. Thus the Gibsons claim, in line with their emphasis on direct perception, that links between the modalities do not need to be manufactured on the basis of experience by association, nor by any type of intellectual construction. They are specified by the information available in the environment.

Three Levels of Crossmodal Integration

To what extent does the infant appreciate the multimodal nature of objects? In order to answer this question, we shall have to be a good deal more precise. I have argued that we can conceive of crossmodal integration as taking place at three levels (Harris, 1979). At the first elementary level, information in one modality might provide directional information for the receptors in one or more of the other modalities. For example, the sound of an object might alert the infant both to look out and to reach in a given direction. It would not be surprising if such orientation mechanisms were innate because objects that make a sound do generally offer the possibility of visual and tactual information from the same spatial location. An innate system to capitalize on such overlap therefore becomes plausible. Of course there are artificial separations that occur. At the cinema, the moving lips that we see on the screen are not typically the spatial source for the sound track. Yet even when confronted with such artificial separations we tend to perceive the voice as coming from the moving lips, just as it does in the real world, an illusion that ventriloquists are happy to hide behind.

At the second level, there might be a more complex form of crossmodal integration where infants not only orient their receptors on the basis of information in one modality, but predict that information is available in a second modality, once an appropriate adjustment of the receptors has been made. For example, infants might hear a sound to their left and turn their eyes in that direction. So far, this adjustment of the receptors constitutes evidence for integration at level one only. If, however, the infants indicate that they expect to see something, this would indicate crossmodal integration at the second level. Hence this second level of crossmodal integration goes beyond the first level: Information in one modality is not simply used to guide the receptors in another modality, but is used to make a prediction that feedback will be available in that second modality, provided the receptors are directed toward the appropriate position in space.

At the third level of integration, the infant might be able to anticipate the specific type of feedback that will be available in one modality on the basis of information in another modality. Thus the infant might anticipate that an object that looks round will also feel round. Similarly, lips moving at a particular tempo ought to be accompanied by a voice speaking at a similar tempo. It is important to note that this third level of integration, although apparently more complex than the second, does not necessarily presuppose that second level. Thus it might be possible to detect correlations between the tempo of a voice and the movement of the lips without knowing that such correlations typically emanate from the same spatial source.

Below, I shall examine evidence for crossmodal integration at the first two levels. The third level concerns object identity rather than object location and accordingly it will be taken up when the more general issues of object identity and object classification are discussed.

Vision and Hearing

With regard to vision and hearing, there is some controversial evidence that the neonate can use auditory information to guide the direction of gaze. Wertheimer (1961) tested infants only a few minutes old and found that they turned their eyes toward the sound of a click either to their left or their right. This finding has been replicated by Mendelson and Haith (1976) using a somewhat different experimental arrangement. They tested infants who were 2 or 3 days old rather than a few minutes old and they used a human voice as a sound source. However, other experimenters have found either that there is little systematic relationship between sound direction and eye movements (McGurk, Turnure, & Creighton, 1977), or observed eye movements contralateral to the direction of sound (Butterworth & Castillo, 1976). Crassini and Broerse (1980) have carried out what appears to be the most systematic study to date. They found that lateral eye movements occurred more often than chance to a human voice but that failure to make a response was also quite frequent. Moreover, they found no clear relationship between the probability of responding and the degree of lateral displacement.

Other evidence indicates that this relatively fragile capacity for directing the eyes toward a sound source should be treated only as evidence for integration at the first level. That is to say, the evidence does not show that neonates expect to find some visual stimulation located at the sound source. Thus Mendelson and Haith (1976) report that such eye movements occurred even when infants were lying in darkness, and Turkewitz, Birch, Moreau, Levy, and Cornwell (1966) observed such eye movements (with the help of electrodes) even when infants had their eyes closed. Neither of these results suggests that the infant is turning to seek out visible stimulation. Indeed, given the imprecision in the infant's eye movements toward a sound source, such expectations would be quite inappropriate, because the infant would encounter frequent violations.

Nevertheless, the minimal coordination between the schemes of listening and looking, present at birth, does not fit in with Piaget's claim that the schemes are only coordinated in the course of development. Such minimal coordination is, on the other hand, perfectly compatible with the Gibsonian claim that information about position, particularly position relative to the self, is not tied to any particular modality.

Given that the neonate does look toward a sound source, at what point in development does he or she come to expect to see something there? Aronson and Rosenbloom (1971) investigated this question by presenting 4- to 8-week infants with a sight—their mother—separated from a sound source, her voice, which emanated from a loudspeaker at some distance. They claimed that the infants were upset by this separation of sight and sound, suggesting that infants of 6 weeks do expect to find a visible stimulus (and indeed a very specific visible stimulus, given that the voice and a loudspeaker were always colocated) when they turn toward a sound source. However, these findings have not been replicated by other investigators (Condry, Haltom, & Neisser, 1977; McGurk & Lewis, 1974). Indeed, my expectation would be that the separation of sights and sounds is not particularly disturbing even for older children and adults, because as mentioned earlier in connection with ventriloquism, a visual capture appears to occur such that a sound is displaced toward an appropriate visual source.

Vision and Touch

We may approach the relationship between vision and touch in terms of the same two levels of integration: When do infants reach toward a visible object and when do they expect to find something tangible there?

In order to find out whether a visible stimulus would elicit appropriate spatial orientation of the hands, Bower, Broughton, and Moore (1970b) placed objects at various locations around infants of 2 weeks. The infants were reported to reach in the appropriate direction for the object, although their ballistic arm movements did not always result in contact with the object. These findings suggest that infants can orient their hands and arms in the appropriate lateral direction toward a visible stimulus much as they are able to orient their eyes in the appropriate lateral direction to an auditory stimulus.

However, such precocity has proved difficult to replicate. Recent studies by Dodwell, Muir, and Di Franco (1976) and by Ruff and Halton (1978) have reported a much slower timetable for the development of accurate reaching, in conformity with earlier reports (Gesell & Thompson, 1934; Piaget, 1952; White, Castle, & Held, 1964). Ruff and Halton (1978) carried out a close replication of the study by Bower et al. (1970b). They presented nine infants ranging from 7 to 15 days of age with a small sphere, placed at three different positions around the infant: midline, 45° right, and 45° left. A base line was used in which no object was present and the number of extensions with and without the object could then be compared. Extensions proved to be as frequent with no target as with a target. Moreover, contacts with the object occurred on only about a third of arm extensions and, given the frequent number of extensions when no target was present, were probably fortuitous rather than intentional. Thus it seems safer to accept that visually directed reaching emerges at around 4 to 5 months, as suggested by the earlier studies.

Nevertheless, there are various indications that Piaget's description of the gradual coordination of looking and reaching, and more specifically, his claim that such coordination depends on visual monitoring of the moving hand, appear to be in error. Instead, the evidence suggests that various properties of the object provide directional information for the arm and hand even when reaching consists of a ballistic swipe such that visual guidance during the actual reach seems unlikely. First, Lasky (1977) found that reaching for a visible object was disrupted at 5½ months if infants could not see their hands, but such disruption did not occur in younger infants. Second, infants are quicker to reach out for a target (Rezba, 1977) and reach out for it more frequently (Field, 1976) if it is within reach rather than beyond reach, although the reaches themselves are inaccurate swipes rather than object-directed reaches.

In summary, there appears to be some innate coordination between looking and reaching, contrary to Piaget's claims that the two schemes are initially separate. This is not to deny of course that visual monitoring of reaching may occur in older infants. Indeed, given the fact that infants can adjust to prismatic displacement (McDonnel, 1975), it seems virtually certain that such on-line visual guidance does occur. However, such visual guidance is an elaboration of rather than a precondition for visually triggered reaching.

Moving up to level two of crossmodal integration, we may ask whether the infants expect to be able to touch the visible object that they reach out for. There are now several experiments that have attempted to answer this question, but they do not provide a wholly consistent picture. Bower et al. (1970a) presented a virtual object (similar to that to be described in connection with depth perception), which looked solid and tangible but which was actually an optical illusion, so that the infant's hand would pass straight through with no tactual feedback being provided. The authors reasoned that infants who expected to be able to touch a visible object, which looked hard and solid, should exhibit surprise and distress when their hands passed straight through it. In line with these expectations, the authors claimed that infants from 2 weeks to 6 months old showed emotional upset when they reached out to touch the object and found nothing there. Indeed the older infants appeared to try to resolve the mystery. They stared at their hands, rubbed their hands together, and banged them on the table, as if checking that their hands could still produce tactual feedback under familiar circumstances.

In contrast to these findings, Field (1977) and Gordon and Yonas (1976) failed to find any evidence of emotional upset among 5-month infants when they reached out for a visible object. In both studies, fingering movements at or near the location of the object were observed. Such behavior might suggest that infants expect to obtain tactual feedback from the object, but it could be that the sight of the object simply elicits fingering movements without the infant having any clear expectation of what they should produce, much as the neonate might look toward a sound source with no specific expectation.

Gordon, Lamson, and Yonas (1978) report some later research on the virtual object situation in which infants of 5½, 7½, and 9½ months were tested. Do older infants exhibit surprise even if 5½-month infants do not? In fact, Gordon et al. (1978) found little change across the three age groups. The most frequent response was a continuation of the reach or the instigation of another reach but without any emotional reaction or attempts to check the sensitivity of the hand to tactual feedback.

Conclusions

In summary, the evidence indicates that infants are equipped from birth to use auditory information to orient their eyes, albeit inaccurately, toward a sound source. Similarly, an object within reach triggers swiping movements of the hand and arm, even though such movements may often not result in tactual contact with the object. Although not explicitly predicted by Gibsonian theory, such mechanisms provide a rudimentary basis for detecting information that is correlated across the two modalities. Moreover, such coordinations indicate that Piaget has exaggerated the extent to which the various schemes for listening, looking, and touching are separate from one another in the earliest months. Nevertheless, although infants appear to have a rudimentary ability to pick up correlated information, there is no clear evidence in the preceding review that shows that they expect such correlated information to emanate from a single location. Thus although newborns can turn their eyes toward a sound, there is no indication that they expect something to be visible in the direction that they turn. Similarly, when infants of 4 to 5 months direct their hands toward a visible object, there is no evidence that they expect to find something tangible when their hands reach the visible object. When we turn to a discussion of the infant's search for a hidden object, we shall continue to find evidence that is consistent with the claim that, at least until 9 months, the infant does not realize that the visual and tactual aspects of an object are colocated.

Depth

Is depth perceived directly or constructed? J. J. Gibson (1979, p. 286) writes: "No one ever saw the world as a flat patchwork of colours—even Bishop Berkeley or Baron von Helmholtz, who believed firmly that the cues for depth were learned." In this quote, Gibson clearly reveals his belief that the infant does not have to learn to see the third dimension. In contrast, Piaget argued that the child's understanding of space is only gradually constructed. Piaget adopts a metaphor that is strikingly similar to the "flat patchwork" that Gibson rejects. "The sky seems to us a big spherical or elliptical cover on whose surface move images without depth which alternately interpenetrate and detach themselves: sun and moon, clouds, the stars as well as the blue, black or grey spots which fill the interstices" (Piaget, 1954, p. 162). This cover or patchwork on whose surface objects are not arranged one overlapping the other or one behind the other, but merely touch or intermingle, is, according to Piaget, the way in which the infant in the first two stages of sensorimotor intelligence (i.e., approximately 0–5 months) perceives the whole of space. During the third stage, the coordination of vision and reaching enables the infant to construct a zone of near space in which relations in depth are understood distinct from the zone of distant space that lies quite literally beyond the infant's grasp. "Distant space remains analogous to the sky in immediate perception, whereas near space is comparable to our perception of the terrestrial environment in which planes of depth are regulated by action" (Piaget, 1954, p. 163).

Sight and prehension permit the construction of depth within near space because children can discover the concept of "in front of" and "behind" by noticing how their hands either disappear behind an object to be grasped, or occlude it as they pass in front. Eventually children will discover that objects are also arranged in depth, one behind the other, beyond the zone of prehension or grasping. To do this, they must presumably be able to displace themselves by bending or crawling.

We see clearly then that Piaget and Gibson differ in the role that they assign to action. Gibson would expect depth perception to precede appropriately adjusted spatial behavior, whereas Piaget would expect depth perception to follow from the adjustments and accommodations that the reaching or crawling infant must make. More specifically, Gibson and Piaget differ with respect to the roles of interpretation and experience. Gibson denies that interpretation of visual information is necessary and does not ascribe any important role to experience, be it visual, prehensile, or locomotor in the perception of depth. Piaget, on the other hand, insists that visual information must be interpreted, and such interpretation results from motor experience.

In the review of experimental evidence that follows it will be useful to draw a distinction between two types of research: studies of the infant faced with an object just within or beyond reach, and studies of the infant faced with a cliff. By eventually putting the results of these two sets of studies together, we can obtain a reasonable longitudinal picture.

Binocular Cues and the Study of Reaching

For infants to adjust their reach to the distance of an object, they must be able to use either convergence or binocular disparity. Recent evidence shows that although binocular convergence increases in probability and latency during the first 6 months of life (Aslin, 1977), a limited ability to adjust the angle of convergence in accordance with the distance of the object appears to be available from birth (Slater & Findlay, 1975a, 1975b).

Fusion of the images available from each eye (that is, stereopsis) depends on extremely precise convergence. Haith and Campos (1977) point out that even a minute amount of deconvergence—an amount too small to be detected by our current measurement techniques—will prevent stereopsis. However, we do know that the 2-month infant can detect the shift from nondisparity to disparity (Appel & Campos, 1977; Atkinson & Braddick, 1976), and this detection is usually taken to depend on the ability to achieve stereopsis at least some of the time.

Thus current evidence is consistent with two possibilities: On the one hand, there may be an ability to achieve both convergence and stereopsis from birth; alternatively, convergence may be transitory and imprecise during the first weeks of life, so that convergence plus stereopsis emerges from only 2 months onward. In either case, however, it looks as if the neonate has the capacity to pick up cues for distance well before accurate reaching for objects emerges. However, such experiments indicate only that the infant can detect the binocular depth cues of convergence and disparity. It is perfectly possible for the infant to detect such cues without knowing that they indicate anything about depth. This takes us back to the point made by Berkeley himself. There are depth cues available, but it is by no means certain that such cues are automatically taken to signify depth or distance.

Piaget follows Berkeley quite explicitly in this respect: "As Berkeley said, it is necessary to distinguish vision as a sensory factor from the judgments we bring to bear upon it" (Piaget, 1954, p. 135). He also argues, like Berkeley, that it is only the child's activities that lead to the construction of the third dimension. If this position is correct, we would expect an initial period in which the infant reaches for an object both within reach and out of reach if only binocular cues are available to indicate its distance.

Information for depth can be restricted to binocular cues in two ways. First, the infant can be fitted with a pair of prisms that alter the apparent distance of an actual object. Van Hofsten (1977) carried out this experiment and found that infants of 5 to 8 months adjusted their reach to the apparent distance of the object, although as Yonas (1979) points out, the basis for judging the accuracy of reaching was not specified in any detail. In a second type of experiment, a stereoscopic shadow caster can be used to produce a so-called virtual object, which looks perfectly tangible but is nothing more than an optical illusion (Bower, 1974). Using such an apparatus, Gordon and Yonas (1976) presented 5½-month infants with a virtual object at three distances: 15, 20, and 30 cm. The first two locations were judged to be within the infants' reach but the last was judged to be just beyond. Gordon and Yonas found little indication that the end points of the reaches varied reliably with the location of the virtual object. On the other hand, various other measures did indicate a sensitivity to distance. When the object was within reach, the infants did not lean so far forward, they reached out more frequently, and they made more grasping movements. In a follow-up study with infants of 5½, 7½, and 9½ months (Gordon et al., 1978), all three age groups reached out more frequently and did not lean so far forward when the virtual object was within reach. However, the accuracy of the reach increased reliably with age. Whereas the 5½-month infants placed their hands at a more or less constant distance from their bodies irrespective of the distance of the object from them, the two older groups adjusted their reach to the distance of the object. Yonas (1979) concludes: "Apparently, at 5½ months it is the trunk rather than the arms that responds with more precision to binocular depth information" (p. 92). This conclusion is interesting because it suggests that Berkeley and Piaget are probably wrong, although the argument is rather indirect. If the infant had to discover that binocular cues specify the distance of an object, we would surely expect such cues to be effective to the extent that they helped the infant produce actual tactual feedback by touching the object. Thus binocular cues ought to have their most direct effect on the response immediately preceding tactual feedback, such as the extension of the hand, rather than on responses that serve as a motor "framework," such as the angle of the trunk. Certainly such an analysis would follow from a simple learning theory approach in which reinforcement (i.e., tactual feedback in this case) has the strongest impact on the immediately prior response rather than temporally more distant responses. However, the findings of Gordon and Yonas (1976) and Gordon et al. (1978) indicate that if reinforcement is having any effect at all, it affects temporally distant responses such as the adjustment of the torso as well as temporally proximate responses such as frequency of reaching; and in the case of one temporally proximate response, namely the extension of the hand and arm, it has no detectable effect. Indeed, because of the inaccuracy of the infant's reach, it is conceivable that torso adjustment has no appreciable effect on the likelihood of making tactual contact with the object, so that we can scarcely speak of such adjustments being rewarded by tactual contact. All of these points suggest that the infant does not start off perceiving a flat world and gradually discover that there are cues to depth. Binocular cues such as convergence and stereopsis may specify depth as directly as a transition from light to dark specifies an edge. This conclusion is, of course, precisely the type of conclusion that is favored by J. J. Gibson (1979). Nevertheless, it must be admitted that the empirical support for Gibson's conclusion is somewhat indirect.

The evidence also provides rather firm support for Bruner's emphasis on the preadapted nature of the reaching skill, an emphasis, which, as was mentioned earlier, fits in comfortably with Gibson's stress on direct perception. Adjustment of the torso prefigures successful reaching just as the infant's mouthing prefigures grasping the object and carrying it to the mouth. Such constituents of the skill are exhibited before they are incorporated into successful reaching. Moreover, as Bruner (1973) implies, such constituents are adjusted to the nature of the target, but not apparently on the basis of reinforcement.

Studies of Prereaching Infants

Given that certain constituents of the reach are adjusted to the distance of the object, as soon as reaching emerges, can even prereaching infants perceive depth on the basis of binocular information alone? If the emergence of reaching is not necessary in order to teach the infant how to interpret cues for depth, then we should expect to find such evidence. Yonas, Oberg, and Norcia (1978) used a stereoscopic shadow caster to create a moving virtual object, apparently on a collision path with the viewer's nose. The behavior of the 20-week infants clearly suggested that they were trying to avoid a collision with the approaching virtual object. In contrast, the behavior of the 14-week infants gave little indication that they perceived the object to be on a collision path. However, an experiment by Rezba (1977) showed that infants of 15 weeks were quicker to reach out for a virtual object within reach than a virtual object out of reach, although the reaches themselves, as in the experiments of Gordon and Yonas (1976) with older infants, were inaccurate swipes rather than accurate object-directed reaches. Such behavior again supports the conclusion reached above, that the infant's reaching shows adjustment to the distance of the object before such adjustment is likely to have any systematic consequences in terms of tactual contact with the object.

Studies on the Visual Cliff

The evidence presented above is consistent with the claim that the infant perceives depth before the experience of reaching. Can we extend this claim to distances beyond the infant's reach? Are these too arranged in depth by the infant before locomotor experience? Campos, Hiatt, Ramsay, Henderson, and Svejda (1978) have reviewed recent evidence pertaining to the infant's reaction to the visual cliff. Contrary to the widely accepted conclusion that infants show fear of the deep side of a visual cliff as soon as they can locomote, Campos et al. (1978) report that such fear only emerges some days or weeks after the onset of crawling. One possible interpretation of these results is that infants might not perceive depth at all. This seems unlikely given the evidence on reaching reviewed earlier. Moreover, Campos et al. (1978) were able to provide additional counterevidence by showing that virtually all infants make a visual placing response when lowered toward the shallow side of the visual cliff but not toward the deep side, the placing response being defined as extension of the arms plus fanning of the fingers before tactual contact with the glass surface.

A second and initially more attractive explanation of the results is that although infants can perceive depth, they only gradually learn to be afraid of it, perhaps as a result of falling. In support of this explanation, Campos et al. (1978) report a monotonic relationship between crawling experience and hesitation when infants were confronted with the deep rather than the shallow side: Experienced infants hesitated longer. On the other hand, Rader, Bausano, and Richards (1980) could find no support for the role of crawling experience in producing fear of the cliff. One group of infants who began crawling quite late (after 6½ months), and who had only about 4 weeks crawling experience, avoided the visual cliff; a second group who began crawling earlier (before 6½ months), and had about 11 weeks crawling experience, did not avoid the visual cliff. Thus, in this experiment, infants with more crawling experience were less likely to avoid the deep side. Rader et al. (1980) concluded that avoidance is probably controlled by a maturational timetable rather than amount of crawling experience: Specifically, infants who start crawling early are more likely to cross the deep side than those who start crawling late. This conclusion was confirmed in a follow-up study by Richards and Rader (1981), which showed that age of onset of crawling, but neither age of testing nor amount of crawling experience, predicted avoidance. Rader et al. (1980) spell out their argument by claiming that when crawling emerges late, it is elicited only by visual information specifying a support. Thus these authors see the avoidance response not as a reaction to fear, but simply as the nonelicitation of a motor program that occurs only in the presence of a particular stimulus input. In support of this interpretation, Rader et al. (1980) also found that few infants avoided the cliff when they were given the opportunity of locomoting in a walker rather than crawling. If avoidance of the cliff reflected fear rather than the suppression of a particular motor program, one would expect it to extend to a different motor program such as locomotion in a walker.

To what extent do these data provide support for the claims of either Piaget or Gibson? Gibson's stress on direct visual perception allows us to explain the various spatially adjusted behaviors of the infant: the placing response and the avoidance of the cliff. The only difficulty for Gibson's approach is that some early crawling infants do not avoid the cliff. Is Piaget's account of the gradual construction of space able to explain this latter finding more successfully? As noted earlier, Piaget distinguishes between the infant's perception of near space and of far space. We could conclude that the placing response of the infant reflects an understanding of near space, because it is elicited when the shallow side of the cliff approaches the zone of prehension. The deep side, on the other hand, lies beyond that zone and might be perceived as a surface at some indeterminate distance just beyond reach, but precisely because of its indeterminate location might fail to elicit an appropriate avoidance response from the infant. There are, however, severe difficulties for the Piagetian approach. First, Rader et al. (1980) and Richards and Rader (1981) could find no evidence that crawling experience led to avoidance, contrary to Piaget's constructivist position. Second, some early findings run precisely contrary to the Piagetian notion of an ever-expanding sphere. Walk (1979) sums up these problematic findings as follows:

> The same percentage of 7–9 and 10–13 month-old infants crawled to the mother at the deep side with 40 inches of visual depth, and only a few more of the younger group crawled to her with 20 inches; but with 10 inches of visual depth, 68% of the 7–9 month-old children crossed the deep side to the mother as compared to 23% of the 10–13 month-olds. (pp. 82–83)

Here we find that there is an increasing differentiation with age of depth within near space rather than far space, quite contrary to what Piaget would expect.

Overview of the Experimental Evidence

The evidence presented above suggests that the infant exhibits a variety of spatially adjusted behaviors before the opportunity to practice those behaviors or to encounter their consequences. Such a conclusion argues against Piaget's conclusion that an idea of space must be constructed but is compatible with Gibson's emphasis on the fact that the visual world offers information for depth, which is as rich and as valid as that obtained as a result of touch or locomotion.

Having reached this conclusion, several important caveats must be made. First, it is most unlikely that infants learn nothing from active reaching or locomotion. As Bower (1974) has pointed out, given that the distance between the eyes alters during growth, and also the length and power of the limbs, some ability to recalibrate motor commands may be vital. Yet even allowing for the possibility of recalibration through experience, the timetable for the onset of reaching and crawling in the human infant is sufficiently inflexible that some genetically programmed initial calibration of the system would be quite reasonable. So, for example, infants might reach out for objects that fall within a given angle of convergence. Also, there may be compensatory growth patterns, which limit the need for recalibration. For example, although the increase in interocular distance with growth means that objects are fixated with a wider angle of convergence, which might elicit underreaching, the length of the arm is increasing, thereby compensating for underreaching. Nevertheless, it seems unlikely that there is perfect compensation occurring throughout the visuomotor system, so that some recalibration may well be needed. The classic experiments on prism adaptation and the work of Held and Hein (1963) indicate that active movement may be an important factor in such recalibration.

A second qualification is that even spatially adjusted behavior that is exhibited without learning does not conclusively show that the infant perceives depth. Thus having rejected Piaget's account, and having noted that current evidence is largely compatible with Gibson's emphasis on direct perception, we should not automatically conclude that Gibson's theory is indeed correct. Recent evidence shows that adults with specific types of brain damage can exhibit reaching movements and eye movements in the appropriate direction toward stimuli that they claim to be unable to see (Pöppel, Held, & Frost, 1973; Weiskrantz, 1977). Clearly, if spatially adjusted behavior is present without any perceptual experience at all, it is plausible to suppose that reaching in the young infant is adjusted for distance without any concomitant perceptual experience of depth being available (see Figure 4A).

A related objection to that made above is to argue, not that infants have no perceptual experience at all of spatial cues, but simply that such cues are linked to a given motor response without there being

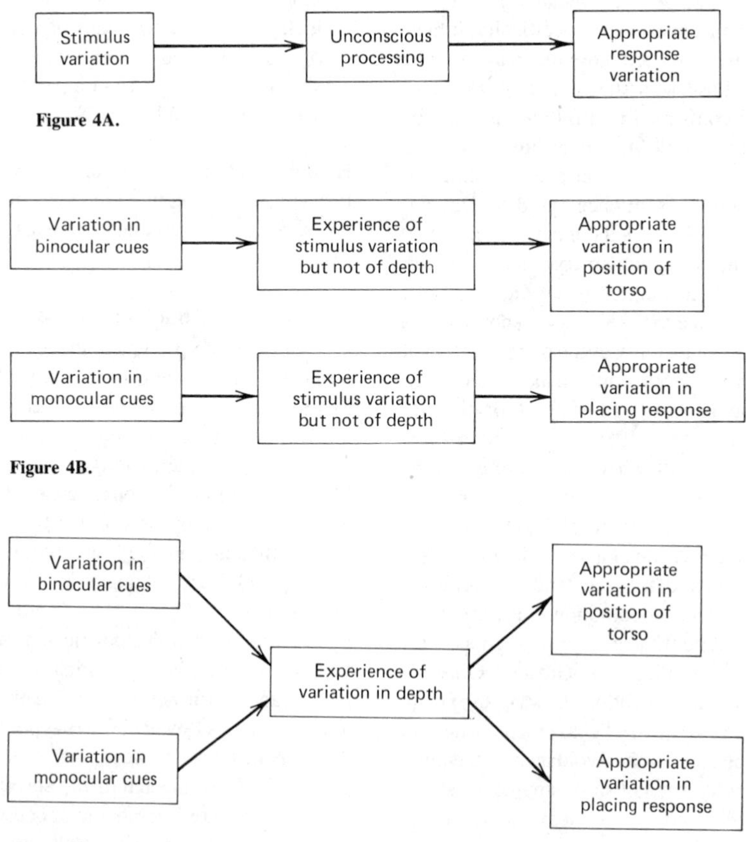

Figure 4A.

Figure 4B.

Figure 4C.

any accompanying experience of depth. Thus infants might adjust their torsos to variation in binocular cues without experiencing such binocular cues as specifying an object at a particular distance. Equally, infants might adjust their arms and fingers by means of the placing response to the variation in monocular cues that arises as they are lowered toward a surface (see Figure 4B). Evidence suggesting that infants exhibit appropriate motor programs in only a very localized fashion was found, it will be recalled, by Rader et al. (1980). Infants who would not crawl over the visual cliff would venture to cross it in a walker.

The strongest evidence against the above objections and in favor of the claim that the infant does perceive depth would be to show transfer of response, or better still, of a set of responses from one type of depth information to another. Figure 4C illustrates a system in which such transfer would be possible. The need for such transfer experiments has been discussed by Bower (1972) and by Yonas and Pick (1975), although, regrettably, no such experiments have been published as yet.

Object Permanence

On the basis of various errors manifested by young infants in their search for hidden objects, Piaget (1954) reached some startlingly radical conclusions concerning the spatial naivete of the young infant. As a result of Piaget's theorizing, the development of search behavior has become one of the most thoroughly investigated areas of cognitive development in infancy (Harris, 1975). I shall first give an outline of Piaget's theory and then review some of the many recent studies that have attempted to replicate the developmental sequence observed by Piaget and to check his interpretation of that sequence.

Piaget claimed to observe six stages in the development of search. In the first two stages, the infant virtually ignores the object unless it is clearly within the perceptual field. In the final stage, the infant can find the object even if it has been moved around while invisible—for example, by being moved in a container or in the experimenter's hand. The following description indicates what happens at each stage in more detail.

Sequence of Stages

Stage 1 and 2: 0 to 4 months. No active search is exhibited. Infants simply continue to look in the same direction as they did before the object began to move or disappear.

Stage 3: 4 to 8 months. Infants now begin to exhibit a set of minimal adjustments to the disappearance or movement of the object. For example, if the object is moving, infants show some anticipation of its future position by looking in its direction of travel. If the object is tugged out of their hands, they grope after it in the direction of its movement. If the object is partially hidden by a cloth, they will pull it from under the cloth, but not when the object is fully hidden.

Stage 4: 8 to 12 months. Infants are now able to search for an object that is completely hidden as opposed to half-hidden by a cloth. However, there is an important restriction on this new ability: If the object is moved to a new hiding place in full view, and made to disappear at this new hiding place, infants return to the old place and mistakenly search there as if expecting to find the object there again.

Stage 5: 12 to 18 months. Infants now avoid the type of perseverative errors described for Stage 4, but still encounter difficulty if the object is not fully visible as it is moved to its hiding place. For example, if the experimenter hides the object in one hand and then moves it to a hiding place, infants will tend to search in the experimenter's hand.

Stage 6: Approximately 18 months onward. The invisible movements that disrupted search at the previous stage can now be taken into account.

Before asking how Piaget interprets this developmental sequence, we may first look briefly at studies that have attempted to replicate Piaget's original findings without focusing directly on the adequacy of his interpretation. These replication studies are virtually unanimous in their confirmation of Piaget's findings. Thus whether the tasks are presented to the infant in their supposed order of difficulty (Corman & Escalona, 1969; Uzgiris & Hunt, 1975), or in a random order (Kramer, Hill, & Cohen, 1975), the same order of difficulty as that observed by Piaget is found. Only one possible exception to this virtual unanimity may be noted. Miller, Cohen, and Hill (1970) were unable to arrange their items in the sequence of difficulty predicted by Piaget (1954). However, even this exception does not appear to be a robust finding, because a later study conducted in the same laboratory (Kramer et al., 1975) did agree with Piaget's original findings.

In short, whether we examine Piaget's original data or subsequent replication studies, there is little doubt that the infant's ability to search for a hidden object becomes progressively more sophisticated. Moreover, this progressive sophistication can be tapped by a fairly simple set of tasks that can be arranged in a stable order of difficulty for virtually all the infants who have been tested so far. However, the fact that observers have been able to replicate Piaget's original findings should not, in itself, convince us that Piaget's interpretation of those findings is correct. It is to that somewhat radical interpretation that we can now return.

Piaget concluded that in the first two stages of search the infant's view of the universe is quite different from that of an adult. Adults believe that a hidden object, whether it be in their pockets or on the other side of the world, continues to exist despite the fact that they are unable to see it. Infants, according to Piaget, do not share this belief at all. They stick, in an empirical fashion, to the evidence provided by their senses. Because an invisible object, by definition, offers no information to the perceptual system, they treat it as if it did not exist. What happens then, when the object comes back into view? For an adult this is merely a change in the perceptual status of the object; what was invisible has been brought back into view. For the infant, however, the object's reappearance is tantamount to its re-creation and therefore constitutes a change in its existential status. Thus the infant lives in an ever-changing world where objects are continually made and unmade. Given this ''skeptical'' attitude on the part of the young infant, the failure to search for a hidden object becomes perfectly reasonable. Because the infant does not believe that the hidden object continues to exist, there is little reason to search for it.

The skepticism regarding permanence is slowly undermined as infants act on the world. They discover that various actions on their part are sufficient to bring the object back into contact with their perceptual systems, be it the hand or the eye. Some of these simple discoveries are described above in connection with Stage 3 search behaviors. However, such discoveries take us to a second fundamental misconception that young infants have. Instead of regarding the reappearance of the object as being attributable to their having searched correctly for an object that exists quite independently of that search, they attribute the object's reappearance to the fact that their search activities have brought the object back into existence again. This problem or misconception reflects the so-called egocentricity of infants: their tendency to see objects and events as being at the disposal of their own actions rather than understanding that their actions must be subordinate to the independent spatiotemporal regularities of the world.

The gradual emergence of a belief in permanence and the gradual waning of egocentricity provide a fairly satisfactory account of the six-stage sequence. In Stages 1 and 2 infants have no belief in permanence, and have not yet discovered the potential effectiveness of their own actions in bringing the object back into view. By Stage 3 some of those discoveries have been made in a restricted fashion. By Stage 4 the belief in the efficacy of action has progressed to the point where infants believe that their search activity is capable of bringing an object back into view even if they have seen it disappear at a quite different location. During Stages 5 and 6, infants come to understand the independent existence not simply of an object that has disappeared from sight but also one that is displaced even after its disappearance. According to Piaget, this latter type of search depends on the emergence of an ability to imagine the invisible trajectory of the hidden object. The ability to have an image of the hidden object is something that Piaget is reluctant to attribute to the infant in earlier stages of search and is a hypothesis with which students of language development have been very intrigued, because the capacity to represent an absent object seems to be an important precondition for conventional language use.

Is there a major theoretical alternative to Piaget which can account for the findings? Currently, it is fair to say that no one has offered a systematic alternative to Piaget's account, particularly because, as we saw earlier, the large-scale replication studies provide considerable support for the sequence predicted by Piaget. Nevertheless, it is worth considering what such an alternative account might be like even if it has not been fully worked out. As for the development of crossmodal coding and depth perception, we may look initially to Gibson for the most radical alternative to Piaget. Piaget claims that permanence is an intellectual construction by which initially misleading data such as the covering of the object are reinterpreted to indicate the temporary occlusion of the object rather than its annihilation. In contrast, Gibson asserts that annihilation and temporary disappearance look quite different. An object being occluded by a cloth or screen is gradually wiped out as more and more of its surface is obscured by the leading edge of the occluding surface. On the other hand, an object that has been annihilated either goes out of sight instantly—in the way that a bubble suddenly bursts—or its entire boundary is suddenly altered as it implodes or explodes. An infant who sees the difference between these visual events is potentially able to predict the reappearance of the occluded object but the continued loss of the annihilated object. Accordingly, the first goal of a Gibsonian experimenter would be to show that such differences are perceived even by young infants, and appropriate predictions made. In a subsequent section, I shall discuss the research of Bower (1967) and Spelke (1979c), which has been directed at these issues.

Nevertheless we may ask, even at this juncture, what would be the next step if such research successfully demonstrated an early concept of permanence. A major question would still be unresolved. What is the significance of the ordinal sequence of search behaviors, especially because such sequences are, as indicated in the introduction, a hallmark of Piagetian theory? A possible answer to this question is to dismiss the psychological importance of such sequences. Brainerd (1978b) has recently attempted to do this and his argument has been spelled out in relation to object permanence by Cornell (1979b). Cornell points out that an infant who can search correctly for an object hidden under one of two screens (Stage 5) must necessarily be able to search for an object hidden by a single screen (Stage 4). Thus the fact that infants invariably attain Stage 4 before Stage 5 can be attributed to the fact that the two stages constitute part of what Brainerd (1978b) has called a measurement sequence that "occurs when each item in the sequence consists of the immediately preceding item plus some new things" (p. 176). Such items are ordered in terms of logic rather than psychology, because there is no empirical possibility for attaining a more complex item prior to a simpler one. Even so, we cannot dismiss the object permanence sequence as having no psychological importance. We may take resolution of the A$\bar{B}$ error as a case in point. At Stage 4, according to Piaget, the infant can search correctly at an initial location A, but perseverates to A if the object is hidden at a new location B. At Stage 5, the infant can search correctly at A or B. Clearly, both Brainerd (1978b) and Cornell (1979b) are right to point out that the Stage 5 task presupposes solution of the Stage 4 task and therefore involves a measurement sequence. However, Piaget describes something more than a measurement sequence. He argues that the infant returns to A when the object disappears at B, but there are other logical possibilities such as searching randomly or not searching at all. Moreover, even if Piaget were wrong about the exact form of the error, the measurement sequence itself still deserves psychological analysis: It might be harder to search at a new place as compared to an initial hiding place, because a change of motor response is required, or a change of place, or both.

Thus wherever measurement sequences occur, Brainerd (1978b) is right to point out that we need not waste research effort by demonstrating their universality. Such universality is necessarily the case. However, we can ask questions about what precisely infants have learned to do when they are able to solve "the immediately preceding item plus some new things" (Brainerd, 1978b, p. 176). Without further experimental analysis, we cannot know which component(s) of those "new things" is preventing infants from performing as adequately as they did on the preceding item. Accordingly, the exact nature of the object permanence sequence is of psychological importance, and as yet few investigators other than Piaget have offered any explanation for that sequence. This applies particularly to Piaget's most radical critic, Gibson, whose remarks on object permanence pertain chiefly to the infant's perception of disappearance rather than the elaboration of the infant's ability to find an object once it has disappeared. The following review will therefore address two issues: the status of the infant's early perceptual knowledge, and Piaget's explanation for the object permanence sequence.

Stages 1 and 2

During Stages 1 and 2 Piaget claimed that the infant's ignorance of the permanence of hidden objects is reflected in the absence of any kind of search behavior other than the tendency to stare at the place where the object was last seen. One might argue, however, that the infant either lacks the motor ability to search or simply does not know where to search, but does have a belief in permanence. To substantiate this latter claim, Bower (1967a) investigated the reactions of 2-month infants to various types of disappearance, distinguished by J. J. Gibson (1966) and earlier by Michotte (1955). Infants were trained to suck for an auditory reward, a sphere being visible throughout the training period. Bower examined the effect of disappearance of the sphere on the rate of sucking. The sphere was made to disappear in one of four ways: (1) gradual occlusion by a screen, (2) gradual fading, (3) an instantaneous occlusion by a screen, and (4) an instantaneous implosion. Sucking was least disrupted by (1), which, according to Michotte (1955), specifies the continued existence of the invisible object unlike the other three types of disappearance.

In three follow-up studies the effect of the various types of disappearance on spontaneous sucking was examined. The results showed that slow gradual occlusion led to the most suppression, but that sucking quickly recovered when the object reappeared, especially after a short interval. Bower interpreted these results as showing that infants suppress sucking while they wait for a gradually occluded object to reappear. If the rate of occlusion is too fast, or the time of reappearance too delayed, such expectations are abandoned.

These experiments provide good evidence that the event of gradual occlusion is seen as different from other types of disappearance by young infants. However, it is not clear how infants interpret gradual occlusion. Bower argues that infants interpret gradual occlusion as indicating the continued existence of the object. However, there are at least two problems with this argument. First, no statistical techniques were used to compare responses to the different conditions, despite the use of a small number of subjects (four to six) per condition. Second, Bower interprets sucking suppression in Experiments 2 to 4 as indicating that infants are waiting for the return of the occluded object. In Experiment 1, however, infants maintained rather than suppressed sucking when the bull's-eye disappeared. Given these interpretive problems and the fact that no replication studies have been reported, the safest conclusion at present is that young infants can distinguish different types of disappearance at a perceptual level, but we do not know what predictions they make on the basis of these different types of disappearance.

In any case, Bower (1967a) reports a final study whose results were especially clear and indicate that the development of object permanence is likely to involve more than the gradual refinement of perceptual distinctions available in the earliest weeks. The duration of active manual search was studied in this final experiment, a measure that does not have the interpretive problems associated with sucking. Infants of 5 to 12 months were presented with object disappearances at various rates of occlusion. Infants of 12 months were equally persistent for slow, fast, and even instantaneous rates of occlusion, whereas the persistence of younger infants declined as the rate of occlusion increased. This result is very important for the disagreement between Gibson and Piaget. It suggests that older infants have acquired some type of conceptual overrule, which deletes the information provided by purely perceptual data. An instantaneous occlusion induces a similar overrule in adults, according to Michotte (1962). They make statements such as, "It looks as if it vanished into thin air, but I know it must be somewhere."

Research on Stages 1 and 2 can be summarized then in the following way. First, no investigator has successfully challenged Piaget's claim (1954) that very young infants exhibit virtually no active search for a vanished object. There is, however, some evidence to indicate that infants can see the difference between various types of disappearance. In particular, young infants respond differentially to gradual occlusion. However, it would be premature to interpret such differential responding as a belief in permanence. At best, it might index an expectation that the object might reappear, but even if this were the correct interpretation of the infant's differential response, a belief in reappearance is not tantamount to a belief in permanence, because an object may reappear by dint of its re-creation rather than its continued existence. In any case, whatever the reactions of young infants to gradual occlusion, older infants do not guide their search solely in terms of reliable perceptual data. They search even for objects that have been instantaneously occluded, a disappearance that adults find quite mysterious.

Piaget diagnosed Stage 3 in terms of several behaviors: reactions to a partially occluded object, visual tracking, and the emergence of manual search. Research on each of these behaviors is examined below.

Stage 3: Reactions to a Partially Occluded Object

Piaget argues that infants in Stage 3 realize that a partially occluded object extends behind an occluding screen. Accordingly, on the basis of Piagetian theory, it would not be expected that infants younger than 5 months will show any understanding of partial occlusion. Bower (1967b) investigated the reaction of 5-week-old infants to partial occlusion by means of a learning experiment. Infants were rewarded for sucking in the presence of a partially screened wire triangle (see top of Figure 5). Subsequently, infants were given transfer tests to four nonoccluded stimuli (see bottom of Figure 5). Infants exhibited most generalization to the complete triangle, leading Bower to conclude that infants realized that the boundaries of the partially occluded triangle had extended behind the screen.

Kellman and Spelke (1979) examined the reactions of 4-month-old infants to partially occluded stimuli, using a habituation procedure. Infants were first presented with a rod that was partially screened by a block, and then tested for transfer of habituation to either the complete rod or a rod divided into two sections, corresponding to the parts of the rod originally visible in the occluded display. Contrary to what might be expected on the basis of Bower's (1967b) results, there was no indication that infants recognized the complete stimulus as equivalent to the partially occluded stimulus. However, in a follow-up study in which the rod was moved from side to side behind the block, recognition did occur in the

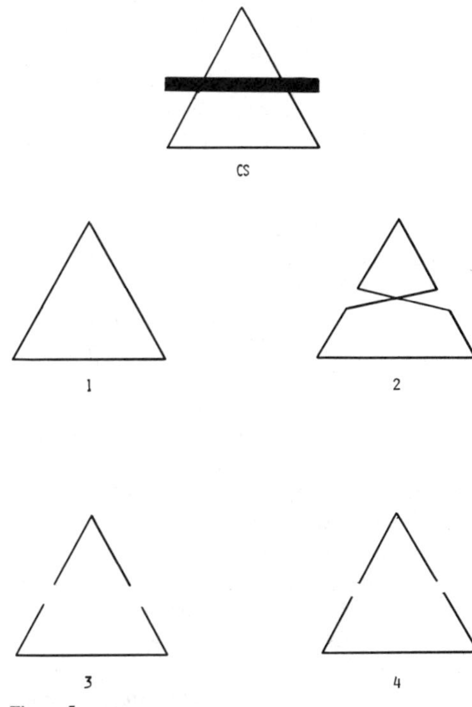

Figure 5.

form of boredom with the apparently familiar complete rod and interest in the incomplete rod. As Spelke (1979c) points out, the two parts of the rod were united in the moving display by the law of common fate.

Taken togeher these results suggest that Piaget may have exaggerated the extent of the young infant's naivete. Infants at 4 months or younger appear to be able to recognize a completely visible object as equivalent to a partially occluded object, particularly if they have seen the partially occluded object in motion. These data then provide some support for the Gibsonian claim that Piaget has neglected the richness of the stimulation available to the infant. Nevertheless, whatever perceptual capacities we invest in the young infant, the fact remains that search skill does increase in accuracy and sophistication. If we attribute a full-fledged object permanence to the young infant, and currently available evidence does not yet entitle us to do that, we are still left with the problem of offering a different account from Piaget's of the development in search skill.

Stage 3: Visual Tracking

Piaget (1954) argued that although the infant at Stage 3 shows a rudimentary appreciation of the future positions of a moving object, such an appreciation is based on local contingencies rather than any insight into the fact that an object remains in existence even as it moves invisibly behind a screen.

Nelson (1971) carried out one of the most thorough studies on the development of visual tracking, and his results provide a good starting point. He presented a group of younger infants (3 to 6 months) and a group of older infants (6 to 9 months) with a train that travelled around a rectangular track, one side of which was covered by a tunnel. Infants in both age groups successfully tracked the train for most of its visible journey around the train, once they had spotted it. When the train entered the tunnel for the first time, infants in both age groups looked at the point of entry. They rarely looked at the point of exit, so that there was a brief 1- to 2-sec. delay before they spotted the train after its re-emergence. By the final trial, subjects looked further toward the exit point but still anticipated the train's re-emergence on only the minority of trials. These results suggest that even by 9 months infants keep track of a moving invisible object on a purely empirical basis. Infants did not spontaneously look over at the exit point on the initial trial, and even on the last trial, infants typically shifted their gaze toward the exit point, without actually looking at the exit point ahead of the train's re-emergence. In a more recent study Meicler and Gratch (1980) tested infants of 5 and 9 months with a somewhat shorter screen, but reached similar conclusions. Anticipation of the train's re-emergence at the exit point never occurred among 5-month-olds and occurred only occasionally among 9-month-olds.

The infant's expectations about a moving object can also be diagnosed by presenting a repeated movement pattern and then introducing some transformation of that pattern. Experimenters have introduced transformations that fall into three categories, which are examined in turn below: changes of direction, changes in the temporal aspect of the trajectory, and changes in the identity of the moving object.

Nelson (1971) observed infants' reactions to a change of direction in which entry and exit points of the tunnel were reversed as compared to the initial trials. The behavior of the infants indicated that they had acquired only a very local rule on the initial trials. Faced with a change of direction, infants again reverted to looking at the entry point rather than shifting their gaze along the trajectory.

Reactions to an alteration in the temporal aspects of the trajectory have been examined by several investigators. In their study of 5- and 9-month-old infants, Meicler and Gratch (1980) included two unexpected-stop trials, in which the object remained out of view behind the screen for 10 sec. The two age groups behaved roughly as they had on standard trials in which occlusion time was much shorter (1.8 sec.): Five-month infants tended to look away or stare only briefly at the screen; but tended not to show any definite expectancy about which edge would be the point of exit.

Other investigators have introduced a sudden stop ahead of the screen rather than behind it, with contradictory results. Muller and Aslin (1978) found that infants of 2, 4, and 6 months simply stopped tracking. Bower, Broughton, and Moore (1971), and Bower and Paterson (1973), on the other hand, observed what they called "false anticipations." Infants between 3 and 5 months were likely to turn away from the arrested object to a point further along its usual trajectory, as if expecting to rediscover the object there. Simonoux and Decarie (1979) also observed such false anticipations, but unlike Bower and his colleagues found that such errors increased rather than decreased with age. However, in those studies in which false anticipations have been found, the infant's line of gaze was observed for several seconds after the arrest of the object. The shift of gaze might reflect boredom or simple eye-head realignment rather than visual search. Indeed, given the infrequency of genuine anticipatory visual search in 9-month-olds, and given that Muller and Aslin (1978) did not find such false anticipations, it seems unlikely that 3-month infants possess definite expectations, either valid or false, about the possible whereabouts of a mobile but temporarily stationary object.

Turning finally to the transformation of identity, the results of three experiments indicate that this change produces little alteration in infants' tracking. Muller and Aslin (1978) observed the reactions of 2-, 4-, and 6-month infants to the emergence of an object different in identity from that which had disappeared behind the screen. Whether the object's shape or color was altered, infants usually tracked it continuously when it emerged, just as they did when it emerged unaltered on standard trials. Meicler and Gratch (1980) obtained similar results with 5- and 9-month-old infants: Infants mostly began to track the object once it emerged, and rarely looked back at the screen as if in search of the original object. Infants did exhibit somewhat more puzzled frowning when a new object emerged. However, it is not clear whether this reaction was to the relative unfamiliarity of the emerging object or its lack of correspondence with the object that disappeared. Thus Goldberg (1976) carried out a study of 5-month-olds, which was similar to that of Meicler and Gratch (1980), but she ensured that the new object that re-emerged was sometimes more familiar than the original object that had disappeared. She found that there was no variation in visual fixation or affectivity (as measured by heart rate) that was systematically associated with a change of identity during the occlusion period.

Thus in three experiments infants ranging from 2 to 9 months show no systematic variation in their tracking and at best an ambiguous frown when one object disappears behind a screen and another emerges. These conclusions contrast quite sharply with those reached by Moore, Borton, and Darby (1978). They found that infants of 5 and 9 months produced more looking back or looking away when identity was altered during occlusion. One possible explanation for these discrepant results is that the object in the study by Moore et al. (1978) emerged from behind the screen, travelled to one side of the horizontal track, and stopped before a new trial was begun; whereas in the experiments by Muller and Aslin (1978), Meicler and Gratch (1980), and Goldberg (1976), object movement was continuous across trials. A continuously moving object might capture attention, suppressing search for the original object, whereas an object at rest might release attention. However, this explanation does not indicate why a change of identity had no effect on heart rate (Goldberg, 1976).

In summary, infants can learn to turn toward the place where a moving object will reappear, but such behavior appears to be little more than a learned extension of tracking. Even at 9 months, infants do not spontaneously turn to where an object is likely to re-emerge, such as the far side of a screen or tunnel; nor do they ever consistently turn to a place of re-emergence before that re-emergence. The local and empirical nature of the infant's acquired expectancies is reflected in several other ways. When the object's direction of disappearance is reversed, infants revert to staring at the place of disappearance, and no longer extend their gaze along the object's trajectory. When the object remains hidden behind a screen for an extended period, infants fixate the screen in general rather than the previous exit point. Finally, if a new object emerges, most but not all investigators have been unable to detect any alteration in the infant's tracking. Virtually all of these findings can be accommodated quite easily by Piagetian theory.

Stage 3: Emergence of Manual Search

Recent evidence on the emergence of manual search also lends broad support to Piaget's claim that the young infant does not believe in the permanence of a hidden object. First, it is now clear that the infant's failure to search under a cloth at around 6 months cannot be attributed to a lack of manual skill. When a transparent cloth rather than an opaque cloth is used, the infant is more likely to retrieve the object (Bower & Wishart, 1972; Gratch, 1972), although both types of cloth would seem to require approximately the same motor skills. Moreover, just as Piaget might expect, manual search exhibits a series of gradual improvements in sophistication, which have more to do with the increasing ability to dispense with perceptual information about the object than any improvement in motor skill. At around 6½ to 7½ months the infant will withdraw a clasped object from underneath a cloth, but only at 8 months will the infant retrieve an object that has been touched before but not throughout its disappearance (Harris, 1971). Finally, at around 12 months, the infant will search for an object that has not been touched before its disappearance (Harris, 1971).

Diamond (1981) has examined the development of the infant's ability to retrieve an object without using line-of-sight information. The object was visible inside a transparent box with an opening. Infants of 6 to 7 months reach more or less exclusively along the line of sight, so that they are unable to retrieve the object through the opening if in order to reach into the box they must make a manual detour off the line of sight. By 8 to 11 months, such a detour is made, provided the infant has first looked at the toy through the opening by looking around or over the protruding edge of the box. By 12 months, successful retrieval can occur whether the infant has looked through the opening or not. Diamond's findings with respect to the use of line-of-sight information suggest a three-step sequence similar to that described above for tactual information. In both cases, the young infant requires the continuous availability of perceptual information, be it tactual feedback of line-of-sight information, in order to retrieve the object successfully. Subsequently, the infant can retrieve the object if such information has been available but is not available at the moment of retrieval. Finally, retrieval can occur whether or not such information has been available. Thus the development of manual search does, as Piaget insisted, appear to reflect the infant's growing ability to dispense with perceptual input; it does not simply reflect an improvement in motor skill.

One puzzling piece of evidence from a Piagetian point of view comes from Bower and Wishart (1972), who found that infants of 5 months, presented with a free-standing object, which is suddenly made invisible by switching out the room lights, will search in the dark for the object and make manual contact with it. At present it is not clear whether such manual contact can be attributed to random flailing in the dark or alternatively to a reach that is initiated prior to the switching out of the lights. Were either of these hypotheses tenable, and replication studies are required to test them, the apparent threat to Piaget's argument would be easily eliminated.

On the other hand, one further piece of evidence is more troublesome. Several investigators, including Piaget himself, have reported that at the age of 4 to 5 months, infants will carry an object held in their hands into the visual field (Bower et al., 1970a; Piaget, 1952; White, Castle, & Held, 1964). Why should such an ability emerge so early, particularly when the infant of up to 6½ months will not withdraw a clasped object from underneath an opaque cloth? Unless we are prepared to argue that withdrawal of the hand from under a cloth requires more motor skill than the simple transport of a held object into the visual field, we are again led back to the possibility that the way in which an object disappears may be an important factor, even when the actions that bring about its appearance are roughly equivalent: The object held in the hand outside of the visual field is never seen to disappear, unlike the object clasped at the midline that is covered by a cloth. Piaget offers little insight into such phenomena because he talks globally about the infant's difficulty with disappearance rather than particular kinds of disappearance.

Stage 4: The A$\bar{B}$ Error

The Stage 4 infant's return to a previous hiding place has been a popular research problem, because it appears to illustrate so neatly Piaget's claim that the infant is egocentric. Piaget argued that the infant, having successfully found the object at A, believes the existence of the object to be contingent on search at A. Hence even when the object is seen to have disappeared at B, search is directed at A. There is now a good deal of evidence to suggest that Piaget's original characterization of the Stage 4 error is not quite right. First, return to the previous location is certainly not as systematic as Piaget claimed: It does not occur on 100% of all test trials but on approximately 50%, sometimes more and sometimes less depending on the exact experimental setup (Butterworth, 1974, 1975, 1977). Second, the perseverative error sometimes occurs even if the object remains fully visible at a new location rather than being hidden at a new location (Butterworth, 1975; Harris, 1974). Third, the error disappears altogether if the infant is allowed to search as soon as the object disappears at the new hiding place rather than being forced to wait for a second or more (Gratch, Appel, Evans, LeCompte, & Wright, 1974; Harris, 1973). These three pieces of evidence indicate that perseverative error is in certain ways a more transient phenomenon than Piaget suggested, being less frequent and even altogether avoidable under certain conditions; they also indicate that the error is more pervasive than Piaget indicated, because it persists even in the face of a visible object.

Recent research also shows that the association between the hiding place and the object hidden is a more potent determinant of perseveration than the frequency with which a given motor action has caused the object to reappear. In order to vary the latter factor, investigators have varied the number of times that the infant makes a response to the initial hiding place, while holding constant the number of times that the object reappears from under that cover, for example, by having the experimenter rather than the infant make the object reappear on several trials. Such studies have not provided any consistent evidence that the frequency of prior approach to the initial hiding place influences the likelihood of perseverative error (Evans, 1973; Landers, 1971; Sophian & Wellman, 1982).

On the other hand, it is now clear that the association between the object and its place of disappearance can help or hinder the infant. If there is no cover or landmark with which the object can be readily associated at its initial hiding place, then the infant is less likely to return there when the object is moved to a new hiding place (Butterworth, 1974; Lucas & Uzgiris, 1977). Conversely, when the object can be linked with an easily identifiable object at its new hiding place—for example, a cup in its normal orientation rather than upside down (Freeman, Lloyd, & Sinha, 1980)—the infant is less likely to return to the old hiding place.

Finally, we may consider an important methodological issue raised by Cummings and Bjork (1977) and Sophian and Wellman (1982). These authors note that an error rate of 50% does not clearly show that infants are perseverating. Random responding on the part of the entire sample of infants would also produce such a result. To control for this possibility Sophian and Wellman (1982) tested infants of 9 and 16 months with three hiding places: A, B, and C. The object was hidden for several trials at A and then hidden at B. They found that 9-month infants who erred on B trials were equally likely to search at A and C, suggesting that they were indeed responding randomly. The 16-month infants, on the other hand, tended to return to A if they erred. Although this result does appear to call into question the claim that 9-month infants exhibit perseveration, there are two important caveats. First, the introduction of three hiding places may have confused infants so that they were reduced to more or less random responding on B trials. Second—and more important for the conclusions reached above—the fact that the infant returns to either hiding place A or C (which were identical in appearance) can be interpreted as showing that the infant has come to associate the object with a particular type of landmark, irrespective of the motor response required to recover it from that landmark. Completely random responding, in which the infant searches in any direction whatever irrespective of the presence of covers or hiding places, has not been observed. These conclusions, of course, are quite compatible with those reached above.

Spatial Coding and the A$\bar{B}$ Error

In line with the above emphasis on the fact that infants guide their search, whether it be accurate or perseverative, in terms of identifiable, external landmarks such as covers and cloths, there is now considerable evidence that infants' spatial coding does undergo a shift toward the use of external landmarks in the second 6 months of life. Such evidence comes not only from studies within the conventional object permanence literature but also from studies directed at spatial learning. Because these two sets of studies tell a rather similar story, they will be considered together.

In an initial study, Bremner and Bryant (1977) obtained results suggesting that infants were returning to search at a particular place relative to their own body. However, a later experiment led Bremner (1978b) to moderate this emphasis on self-related or egocentric coding. Provided the two hiding places were distinct from one another and provided the infants were moved relative to these distinctive covers (rather than the covers being moved relative to the infants), they tended to go back to the initial hiding place even when this involved the adoption of a new motor response, and hence a change in egocentric direction. A similar use of framework cues rather than egocentric cues emerged in a subsequent experiment (Bremner, 1978a), in which the displacement of the infant or the covers was carried out within a trial, immediately after the object had been hidden but before the infant could reach out to find it.

A recent study by Acredolo (1979) produced similar results. The majority of a group of 8- to 9-month infants were able to find an object that they saw hidden under a cloth even though they were rotated to the far side of the cloth after the object had been made to disappear, thereby requiring a change in their motor response. This accuracy was only found, however, when infants were tested in their homes, presumably because a number of familiar landmarks were available. When tested in an unfamiliar but landmark-filled office or a relatively plain laboratory, most infants revealed the use of an egocentric code because they reached in the direction that would have been correct had they not been rotated to the far side of the cloth.

Finally, Benson and Uzgiris (1981) have carried out a study similar to that of Acredolo in that infants watched the object being hidden from one point in the room but were required to search from a different point in the room. Accordingly, correct search could not be based on the position of the object relative to the self at the time of hiding. Benson and Uzgiris (1981) found that correct search from the new room position was more likely if infants had actively moved there rather than being passively carried. Such a result is not surprising when it is borne in mind that active locomotion might well instruct infants that a self-related code remains valid only so long as they remain stationary.

Perhaps the clearest evidence for the increasing use of landmarks by older children, when such landmarks are available, comes from research on spatial learning in which the infant is trained to orient visually toward a particular part of the room in order to see a visual novelty, then moved relative to that visual target and tested on a set of transfer trials. On such trials, Cornell and Heth (1979) found that their youngest group—infants of 4 months—tended to perseverate by making the same response even though they had been rotated 180°; the two older groups of 8 and 12 months were more likely to look toward the target despite their change of position.

Acredolo (1978) carried out a similar study but systematically varied the presence or absence of a useful landmark. After a 180° rotation, the youngest group of 6 months tended to perseverate irrespective of the presence or absence of a landmark. The 11-month infants were more accurate if a landmark was present, whereas the 16-month infants were accurate whether or not a landmark was present. Finally, although Acredolo and Evans (1979) and Rieser (1979) have found evidence of nonegocentric responding in 6-month infants when a salient landmark is used, such responding is fragile and inconsistent compared to that obtained in older infants.

In summary, these various experiments show that infants increasingly make use of landmarks to guide their spatial behavior, be it visual orientation or reaching. At around 6 months, the use of a landmark is fragile and is typically dominated by egocentric responding. By approximately 9 to 11 months, landmarks are used more consistently if available, but infants fall back on egocentric responding if no landmark is available. Finally, at around 16 months, it appears that infants can take into account the fact that they have altered their position (passively) even if no landmark is available.

The A$\bar{B}$ Error: Conclusions

The above findings suggest that by 9 months at any rate, the infant's search for a hidden object may not be as egocentric as Piaget implies. The evidence suggests that the infant links an object with a given position rather than the activities that brought about its reappearance. Moreover, position is increasingly specified during the second 6 months of life in relation to external landmarks, rather than previous self-related positions. If this is the case, there is little point in claiming that the infant believes the existence of the object to be solely dependent on previous actions toward it; the infant may be simply confused about the whereabouts of the object. I shall return to this point later in considering theoretical alternatives to Piaget's position.

Stages 5 and 6: Search Despite Invisible Displacement

The Piagetian tasks at Stages 5 and 6 involve a rather complicated sequence of events: First the object is hidden inside a container and moved in that container; then it is invisibly transposed from that container to a new hiding place. Some recent studies have dispensed with the transposition from one container to another and simply looked at the effect of invisible movement. Despite this simplification, performance is not usually error-free until 18 months or older (Wishart & Bower, 1982). However, above chance performance has been observed even at 9 months under certain conditions. Provided the object is hidden in one of two distinctive rather than identical containers, search is fairly accurate despite the transposition of the containers after the object has been hidden (Bremner, 1978a; Cornell, 1979a; Goldfield & Dickerson, 1981). These results are, of course, compatible with the claim made earlier that infants increasingly guide their search in terms of distinctive landmarks.

Finally, we may ask if there is any evidence regarding Piaget's claim that Stage 6 marks the point at which the infant can fully represent the absent object for the first time. Supportive evidence for this claim has been provided by Ramsay and Campos (1978). Infants who had reached Stage 6 were more likely to smile if they found a toy that they had seen hidden, but to persist in searching if they found a different toy. Similarly, infants in Stage 6 who were told to look for a named object (which they had not actually seen disappear) were likely to smile if they found that object, but likely to persist in searching if they found a different object. Ramsay and Campos (1978) argue that although infants can recognize a toy switch prior to Stage 6, it is only at Stage 6 that the infant can recall the identity of the object to be found, so that its recovery elicits a smile and its absence elicits further search. The findings of Le Compte and Gratch (1972), who looked at infants' reactions to a toy switch, are compatible with this conclusion. They had infants of 9, 12, and 18 months find a toy three times in succession at one place. On the fourth trial, infants saw the same toy hidden, but the experimenter substituted another toy after its disappearance so that infants found a grossly different object. The 18-month-old infants were likely to look puzzled and also to search for the missing toy. The 9-month-old infants tended to examine the new toy with hesitation, suggesting that they had detected the toy switch. The 12-month group fell in between these two types of reactions. If we assume that only the eldest group had reached Stage 6, these results are broadly in line with what Ramsay and Campos (1978) would expect: A toy switch can be detected before Stage 6, but not until then is the missing toy sought.

We should, however, be cautious in our interpretation. It is conceivable that even before Stage 6 the infant can recall the identity of the missing object, but faced with its absence from the expected hiding place does not know where else to search. This possibility highlights an important problem in using search tasks, such as the missing toy or toy switch paradigms, to diagnose the infant's representational capacities. Search for the missing toy presupposes two potentially distinct types of representation: first, the ability to represent the identity of the hidden object despite its invisibility; and second, the ability to represent where it should or might be. Piaget's account of the development of representation tends to collapse together these two potentially distinct abilities. However, it is conceivable that the first ability is present without the second. Thus an infant might be able to recall the identity of the absent object yet fail to exhibit any persistent search for it when it is missing from the place where it disappeared. This point will be important when we come to consider the infant's ability to represent the identity of an object irrespective of its hidden location. It will also be important when we discuss the infant's ability to talk about or understand references to absent objects. Although several investigators have supposed that such an ability depends on the attainment of Stage 6, this conclusion may be incorrect because Stage 6 assumes the representation of the actual or possible location of the hidden object as well as its identity.

Summary of Experimental Studies

The above review, whether it be that of the large-scale replication studies or of the more detailed experimental studies, indicates that Piaget's theory of object permanence has survived very well indeed considering the fairly massive research activity that has been directed toward it. In the first place, it is clear that Piaget is quite right in his claim that the infant's early search is very limited indeed and that in the course of development more and more sophisticated search patterns are acquired. The development of such abilities cannot be simply explained in terms of the gradual surmounting of mnemonic or motor difficulties. This conclusion is especially clear when we examine perseverative errors at Stage 4. Search at a new hiding place involves the same motor skills as search at an old hiding place. Moreover, in terms of the length of time in which the infant must remember the presence of the invisible object, the two tasks are also equivalent. Nevertheless, search at a new hiding place is error prone whereas search at an old hiding place is not. We are forced then to agree with Piaget that the infant's difficulties are probably conceptual in nature. Should we then go the whole way with Piaget and conclude that the two central difficulties are those that were identified earlier, namely the absence of a belief in the permanence of the invisible object and the infant's vulnerability to egocentricity? I am not sure that we should. First, the infant is sometimes puzzled about the location of a visible object as well as an invisible object. It is not clear how the infant's lack of a belief in object permanence can account for such errors. Of course, it might be argued that such errors constitute dramatic evidence in favor of Piaget's second postulated difficulty: the infant's egocentricity. However, this defense of Piaget is blocked because there is now considerable evidence that the errors to which Piaget himself attached so much importance, namely perseverative $A\bar{B}$ errors, cannot be interpreted as the repetition of a previously successful response. Particularly when the previous hiding place has been associated with a distinctive landmark, the infant appears to be returning to that landmark rather than repeating a previous motor response. Moreover, errors in manual search are only apparent when the infant searches after a short delay. If immediate search is permitted, perseverative errors in manual search are eliminated. These findings cannot be readily explained in terms of infantile egocentricity. Instead, we can simply conclude that the infant is easily muddled about where an object is to be found without reaching the more radical conclusion that the infant believes the object's existence and location is dependent on previous actions. Once this is admitted, we may ask whether we need to assume that the infant has no belief in the permanence of objects, or to put the same point somewhat differently, we may argue that the infant simply differs from the adult in having a more limited set of routines for recovering a hidden object. The infant is much more rapidly faced with the impasse that we feel as adults when we are confronted by a clever conjuror: The conjuror's assistant has been made to vanish and we simply do not know where to begin looking for her once the conjuror has demonstrated that our most obvious hunches (behind the curtain, underneath the cupboard, etc.) are clearly false. At this point, we as adults obviously do not conclude that the assistant has ceased to exist, yet our puzzlement is presumably no less than that of an infant who searches in the wrong place. Indeed it might be claimed that adults never truly attain object permanence. What they do attain is an increasingly rich repertoire for finding objects. If this is the case, it may be psychologically inappropriate to ask when an infant has acquired the concept of object permanence.

Alternative Theories

Several investigators have proposed alternatives to Piaget's original theory. In this section I review these alternatives and propose briefly the interpretation that I favor myself. For a more exhaustive scrutiny of these various alternatives the reader is referred to Harris (in press).

Bower (1974, 1977, 1979) offers a radical alternative to Piaget's theory. He attempts to shift attention away from the problem of permanence to the problem of object position. In this respect his proposals are in line with the comments made above. However, Bower's proposals are radical in that he claims that the infant has more or less solved the problem of permanence by the age of 2 to 3 months. Two pieces of evidence are proposed to support this claim, which have both been mentioned briefly in previous sections. First, Bower used surprise indices to argue that the 2- to 3-month infant expects an occluded object to reappear (Bower, 1967a). Second, Bower and Wishart (1972) have reported that an infant of 5 months will reach out in the dark to make manual contact with an object visible a few seconds before. Of these two pieces of evidence, the second is stronger and deserves replication.

Moore and Meltzoff (1978) share some of Bower's dissatisfaction with Piagetian theory but they have been less radical in their proposals. Instead of maintaining, like Bower, that the young infant already possesses a concept of permanence, they agree with Piaget in admitting that this concept emerges only gradually in the course of infancy. However, Moore and Meltzoff (1978) agree with Bower (1974, 1977, 1979) in claiming that the infant has difficulty in uniting the various loci of a given object. Such loci are first united for a visible object and then for an invisible object. The problem for the infant in both cases is to reidentify an object as the same object across intervals of time during which it may have moved or disappeared. For example, the infant might find an object under a cloth after it has been hidden there by the experimenter, but for the infant to see this reappearance as related to the earlier disappearance, the infant must acknowledge that the same object is involved, both at the time of disappearance and reappearance. In order to understand that it is the same object, the infant needs to acquire what Moore and Meltzoff (1978) describe as rules for identity. They conceive of these at three levels: first, rules for understanding the continued identity of an object that either moves or alternatively remains stationary; second, rules for unifying a stationary with a moving object; and third, rules for maintaining the identity of an object across disappearance and reappearance.

These proposals dispose of the notion of egocentricity and they also assimilate the infant's difficulties in dealing with an invisible object to a much wider issue than that of permanence, namely, how an object is to be relocated and reidentified across visible as well as invisible displacements. However, there are several difficulties. First, false anticipations in tracking have not been found by all investigators, yet such errors are important for the claims of Bower and Moore and Meltzoff concerning the infant's difficulties in uniting the loci of a visible object. Second, Moore and Meltzoff (1978) do not appear to be able to explain the fact that difficulties in the manual retrieval of visible objects persist well after 9 months, because they imply that by that age the infant faces difficulties only in dealing with invisible objects. Third, Moore and Meltzoff (1978) ignore the fact that perseverative errors in manual search disappear if the infant is permitted to search immediately at a new hiding place.

Butterworth (1975, 1978), like Moore and his colleagues (Moore, 1975; Moore & Meltzoff, 1978), stresses the problem of object identity, but offers a different account of how the infant comes to solve this problem. Butterworth argues that the infant can unite the various successive positions of an object by linking them together through a third term. For example, the infant might notice an object's position relative to the self at a given moment (e.g., "to my left, within reaching distance"). If a similar-looking object occupies the same position at a later moment in time, the infant might conclude that the object's position has not altered. Indeed Butterworth (1978) goes on to suggest that the identity of the object can be deduced from the fact that it has occupied a stable position over time. In this fashion, the self can be used as a third term to unite the various positions of an object and to reidentify it as the same object. Logically speaking, however, there appears to be a flaw in this argument. Clearly the infant might actually be looking at the object that was seen a moment ago. Alternatively, the infant might be looking at a similar-looking object, which has replaced the first. An analogous problem arises with a second hypothesis of Butterworth, namely that the infant can use a stable framework as a way of linking up the various positions of a moving as opposed to a stationary object. The same objection applies because two successive sightings of an object having a constant location, despite its movement in relation to a stable framework (e.g., "within this room"), do not guarantee that the same object is involved in both sightings.

These logical difficulties, however, do not detract from an important contribution that Butterworth has made in emphasizing the various ways in which an object's position may be encoded. Even if we admit that such encodings do not solve the problem of identity for the infant, we are still encouraged to be more precise about the way in which the infant might conceive of the position of an object, be it visible or hidden.

Bremner (1980) has taken up the distinction made by Butterworth between a self-related code and a framework code in offering an intriguing analysis of perseverative errors in manual search. Bremner notes that infants, especially under about 8 or 9 months, are unable to crawl and hence unable to alter their position relative to an object in front of them. As a result, young infants might notice the position of an object relative to their own body and come to regard this as an overly reliable specification of an object's position. Once infants begin to crawl and hence to alter the position of objects relative to their own body, they are forced to abandon their belief in the stability of object positions and instead to use a framework code in which the object's position is specified relative to distinctive landmarks, for example, "above the cot" or "under the cloth," and so forth.

Bremner's account has the attractive feature of offering a functional context for the infant's errors. However, as even the above brief description indicates, it is far from being a full-scale account of the development of search. Indeed, if we look back at all the alternatives discussed above, it is clear that none of them has the full sweep of Piaget's original proposals. Investigators have tended to concentrate on a fairly narrow range of findings, typically those uncovered in their own laboratory. Nevertheless, these alternative proposals have introduced some novel and potentially fruitful concepts into theorizing about the development of search. First, the ideas of Bower (1974, 1977, 1979), of Moore and Meltzoff (1978), and of Butterworth (1978) locate the problem of object disappearance in terms of the more pervasive issue of how an infant comes to see the various successive positions of an object, be it visible or invisible, as united with one another. Second, Butterworth (1978) and Bremner (1980) have made an important distinction between two types of spatial codes: the self-related code and the framework code. I believe these two contributions can be integrated into a more adequate interpretation of search development and I shall attempt this below.

Object Categories and the Location of Individual Objects

Two hypotheses will be advanced: one concerned with the successive positions of a single object, and the other with the coding of spatial position. The first hypothesis can best be explained by contrasting single objects with multiple instances of a class of objects. The successive appearances of a single object are contingent on one another in an entirely lawful fashion. Indeed they are mutually exclusive: A single object cannot appear in more than one place at any given moment. This rule obviously does not hold for two instances of a given class of objects. Not only does their spatial relationship to one another follow, at best, local and relatively arbitrary rules, but their distinct positions may be simultaneously as opposed to successively occupied. Moreover, the displacements of a single object provide information both about where it will be and where it will no longer be. In contrast, the displacement of one member of a pair or class of objects has no consequences for the future locations of other instances, except under the special condition that the two instances are spatially conjoined in some way so that the movement of one impels the movement of the other.

An examination of the errors that the infant makes during search development suggests that the infant has not grasped that the relationships that hold between successive positions of a single object are lawful. For example, the infant does not regard the movement of an object to a new hiding place, or even its visibility at a new hiding place (Butterworth, 1977; Harris, 1974), as evidence that is incompatible with the presence of the object at the previous location. Thus it looks as if the infant starts with the assumption that the various appearances of a single object are linked in no more than an empirical fashion, just as the appearances of separate instances of the same class of objects are linked in no more than an empirical fashion. The development of search then is the gradual discovery that the displacements of a single object conform to a lawful pattern that enables predictions to be made from present location or trajectory to future location or trajectory.

Since the relationships that exist between the earlier and later positions of a single object are lawful and regular, why should infants be so slow to discover them? There appear to be at least two possible reasons. First, infants are often confronted with apparent violations. As noted above, the spatial relations between members of a class of objects are arbitrary: Two members of a class of objects can appear simultaneously in different positions and the movement of one member has no bearing on the location of the other. Infants who are confronted by an environment that presents such irregularity may find it difficult to discover the more specific regularity that pertains to a single member of the class. A second possibility is that infants are confused not by the complexity of the environment, but by limitations on their own information-processing capacity. The successive positions of a single object will only appear to be lawfully related if infants can retain information about temporal order. If they cannot retain such information, or can only retain it briefly, they will confuse earlier and later positions. As a result, infants will neither be able to predict an object's future position from its current position, nor eliminate earlier positions as possible locations for the object. All past and current positions will be equally valid candidates for making predictions and deletions.

The second hypothesis is that infants come to remember an object's position in terms of two spatial codes. A self-referent code that guides eye- and hand-movements to objects located around the infant's body is probably available from an early age. However, ample evidence has also been presented to show that infants remember an object's location in terms of distinctive landmarks in the environment. This landmark or framework code has the advantage that it does not require updating when the infant moves. An object remains under a cloth even if the infant crawls to the other side of the cloth. Accordingly, infants are likely to adopt such a code as an alternative or addition to the self-referent code, when they become more mobile.

We may now combine these two hypotheses into an overall explanation of search development. The young infant will initially be confused about the displacements of a single object whose position is encoded in terms of the self-referent code. Similar problems will recur with the emergence of the framework code. Below, these hypotheses are related in more detail to the development of search. This interpretation differs from that of Piaget in arguing that displacements of all kinds, both visible and invisible, will be a source of potential difficulty for the infant. In stressing the problems that infants have in integrating the successive positions of a single object, the present account obviously comes close to the suggestions made by Bower (1979), by Moore and Meltzoff (1978), and by Butterworth (1978), but it attempts to explain a wider range of findings.

Visual Tracking Revisited

From previous discussion, it was apparent that infants could learn the local relationships that might hold between the successive appearances of an object as it moves back and forth. For example, infants can learn to turn toward the reappearance of a train at the far end of a tunnel once it has entered that tunnel. To our adult eyes there is only one train involved throughout. However, the infant may well be responding simply to an empirical link between two similar-looking objects: one that enters the tunnel on one side and another that emerges a couple of seconds later from the other side. Accordingly, if the train's direction of travel is reversed, we would not expect the infant to spontaneously turn to the new exit point. Rather, the infant would have to rediscover in an empirical fashion the link between disappearance and reappearance. These are exactly the results that Nelson (1971) obtained for infants of 5 and 9 months.

Once an empirical link between two successive locations of an object was learned by an infant, false anticipations might occur in which although the object is visibly stationary at some distance from its place of reappearance, the infant nevertheless turns to that place of reappearance. Such false anticipations would constitute excellent evidence for the assertion that successive locations are not mutually exclusive for the infant. Bower et al. (1971) and Bower and Paterson (1973) have, in fact, claimed to observe that 2- to 3-month infants do inspect a stationary object and then turn to the far end of the tunnel expecting its reappearance as on previous trials. However, attempts to replicate these findings have failed, so that they should not be seen as firm support for the present interpretation.

The Emergence of Manual Search Revisited

The infant's difficulty in removing a grasped object, or one that has just been touched, from under a cloth, may also be interpreted in the light of the above hypothesis. Just as the infant may have difficulty in seeing the successive within-modality appearances of a given object as being lawfully related appearances of the same object, so the infant may fail to regard the crossmodal appearances—for example, the tactile and the visual appearance of the same object—as lawfully related appearances of a single object. It is not enough for the infant to realize that the tactile appearance of, say, a sphere has an equivalence to the visual appearance of a sphere in so far as both indicate a common round shape. This, as we shall see in a later section, is something that an infant of 6 months can indeed appreciate. What the infant must also realize is that these two sources of information are colocated. Hence a movement of the clasped object into the visual field will necessarily produce a displacement of the visible object into the visual field. That infants do not appear to realize this is indicated by the fact that infants younger than 6½ months will not withdraw an object that they are grasping from underneath a cloth, even though they have the motor skills to withdraw an object that is visible underneath a transparent rather than an opaque cloth. Further support for the claim that infants do not expect visual and tactual information to be colocated was presented in the earlier discussion on crossmodal integration. Even at 9 months infants show no obvious surprise when they reach out to a visible object and discover it to be intangible (Yonas, 1979).

The above findings indicate how important it is to distinguish between crossmodal integration of position and crossmodal integration of shape. Admittedly, these two aspects of crossmodal integration are often united: Visual and tactual information that emanates from the same place often emanates from a single object, and therefore information for shape is equivalent across the two modalities. Yet the environment also affords the infant opportunities to touch an object in one place while looking at an identically shaped object in another. Hence it would not be surprising if an infant of 6 months could detect the equivalence of shape across modalities, without assuming that inputs from one modality will be correlated with inputs from a second modality whenever they belong to a single object in one location.

The A$\bar{B}$ Error Revisited

Elsewhere (Harris, 1977) I have discussed the problems that arise in keeping the specification of an object's position up to date. An object's position can be encoded in relation to the body as being "straight ahead," "to my left," and so forth. Provided the object remains in the visual field, infants ought to be able to keep their encoding of its position up to date, whether they move or the object moves. For both types of movement, the changing relationship between object and observer is continuously specified by the visible object. As I turn my head and eyes to the right, an object that was straight ahead continuously traverses my visual field and ends up in my left peripheral field. The same thing happens if the object moves to the left; it will end up in the same place within my visual field, although in this case its motion will be accompanied by continuous occlusion of the background, and we know that infants will be tempted to track it under such circumstances (Harris, Cassell, & Bamborough, 1974).

The situation is obviously much more complicated for a hidden object. Whether the object or the observer moves, there is no visible feedback from the object to indicate that a previous specification of the object's position should be deleted and replaced with a more up-to-date specification. One solution to this problem is to use an allocentric or framework code rather than an egocentric code. Whereas the position of an object relative to the self is altered whenever the self moves, the position of an object relative to some landmark or framework feature remains invariant despite movements of the self. Thus an object remains under or adjacent to a particular cover whatever the movements of the infant relative to both object and cloth. It seems likely, then, and this postulate is borne out by other investigators, that there is an increasing tendency during the second 6 months of life to encode the position of an object relative to a framework feature (Acredolo, 1978; Cornell & Heth, 1979).

The development of such a framework code may

well be related to the emergence of locomotion in the infant, because as noted by Bremner and Bryant (1977), locomotion would instruct the infant that objects do not remain fixed relative to the self. Certainly, infants appear to search more accurately after a self-initiated change of position than a passive change of position (Benson & Uzgiris, 1981). However, a study comparing crawling and precrawling infants of the same age has yet to be carried out.

Whatever the origin of the use of a framework code, it leads infants into difficulties: They tend to return to a previously valid framework location even if they have seen an object move to a new position. If we consider once more the potential obstacles to understanding discussed earlier, such an error can be explained. First, the infant may be muddled by the complexity of the environment. Frequently, the infant will have seen one instance of a class of objects being displaced, while a second member of that class remains at a particular framework location. Indeed, containers for a particular category of objects, such as biscuit tins, bead boxes, cereal bowls, and so forth, will frequently confirm for the infant that the displacement of one object of a given description from that container need in no way entail that the container will cease to supply further objects of the same description. Second, the discovery that the successive positions of a single object are mutually exclusive depends on a retention of temporal order information. Without such information, infants would be forced to search indiscriminately at the past or current hiding place. Thus, whether we focus on the complexity of the environment or possible limits on the infant's information-processing capacity, we may say that the infant will not treat the relationship between a previously encoded framework location for the object and a movement of that same object away from the framework location as a mutually exclusive relationship.

This analysis can be applied to perseverative errors in manual search in the following way. Having encoded the object's position as being related to a given cloth, the infant fails to regard the movement of the object to a new hiding place as information that precludes the presence of the object at the original framework location. Precisely why the absence of delay helps the infant to avoid making perseverative errors is not clear at present, but the above analysis suggests the beginnings of an answer. The object that is moved by the experimenter to hiding place B provides continuous visible feedback that will ensure a correct specification of its new position at the moment it disappears. Hence, provided the infant relies on some immediate memory for its last visible position in the visual field, search will be accurately directed toward A. However, as soon as the infant shifts his or her postural orientation toward B, or turns away from B completely, no visible feedback is available to indicate the object's new position within the visual field. If the infant does not regard a previously encoded framework location and a movement of the object away from that location as mutually exclusive, position A will continue to be a potential hiding place for the object in the infant's eyes, and search at A will be likely.

Is there any strong evidence against the above account? One recent study does raise certain doubts. Corter, Zucker, and Galligan (1980) have carried out a test of Stage 4 responding using the mother as the hidden object rather than an inanimate object. The mother disappeared through one doorway for one or two trials, and then disappeared through a second. Faced with a change of hiding place, infants tended to crawl to the previous hiding place; visual search was directed unsystematically to both doors. In addition, before reaching the room to which their search was directed, infants showed more stress when faced with the change of hiding place. Thus such distress seemed to reflect the infant's conflict over the correct place to search and was not simply a negative reaction to not having yet found the mother.

Most important, from the point of view of the theory being advanced here, is the finding that perseverative errors in search are not confined to classes of inanimate objects of which the infant might have seen several members, but are also extended to an object that is clearly unique in the world of the infant and that the infant can certainly distinguish by the age of 8 or 9 months from other persons. Does such a finding call into question the idea that the infant cannot unite the successive appearances of the mother into a single unique person? Certainly Corter et al. (1980) have argued that infants' perseverative errors in searching for their mothers cast doubt on the claim of Moore (1975) and Moore and Meltzoff (1978) that the infant does not reidentify the same object in different places as the same object. However, Corter et al. (1980) seem to be adopting an adult point of view with respect to the uniqueness of the mother. Unless the infant were equipped with the rules for understanding the displacements of a single unique object, there is no reason to credit the infant with a belief in only one mother. The infant sees the mother disappear in a given place and reappear in a mysterious fashion either at the same place or at another place. Such evidence is perfectly compatible with the possibility of having more than one mother.

Admittedly, infants have never seen more than

one mother simultaneously, whereas they will certainly have seen more than one cup or orange simultaneously. Accordingly, one might be tempted to say that infants will assume uniqueness in the absence of simultaneous instances of a given object. However, such an assumption by the infant is more complicated than it looks. Because both the mother and the head and eyes of the infant are mobile, the mother will at successive moments occupy different loci in the infant's visual field. Thus infants must distinguish between simultaneously different and successively different positions if they are to conclude that their mothers are unique. At present, we know so little about the infant's notions of time that the above argument is hard to evaluate. Suffice it to point out that Corter et al. (1980) are implicitly crediting infants with sophisticated temporal concepts, while at the same time providing excellent evidence for their spatial naivete. Such a combination is highly counterintuitive.

Object Permanence: Conclusions

In the introduction, it was pointed out that Piaget and Gibson have sharply disagreed about the origin and nature of object permanence, Piaget stressing the constructive intellectual activity of the infant, and Gibson stressing the information available in the environment for extraction by the infant. Where do we stand in relation to these two theories after the above review of recent evidence? First, even if we accept with Gibson that information for permanence is directly available and also that the infant can detect that information, there are several findings that are difficult to reconcile with Gibson's approach. First, even if the very young infant can perceive the information for permanence, search in the first 5 months is nonexistent or consists of highly local groping and tracking routines. Second, when search does emerge in a more systematic fashion, it is frequently error prone, even in the face of a visible object (Butterworth, 1977; Harris, 1974). Such errors are very hard to reconcile with the Gibsonian claim that the infant's behavior is best understood in the light of an analysis of the information available in the environment as opposed to speculations about the infant's set of inferences or hypotheses about that environment. At the very least, we must admit that infants' hypotheses lead them astray at certain points in development.

Should we then adopt the standard constructivist position advocated by Piaget, which views the child as a naive scientist constructing false but temporary theories about the nature of objects? The ordinal stages of search replicated by so many investigators do suggest that the infant is revising provisional hypotheses in the light of fresh data. However, I would argue, in line with the alternative account developed above, that Piaget has misstated the question that the infant comes to answer. He proposes that the infant comes to resolve the question of whether objects continue to exist when they are hidden. I would argue instead that the infant comes to resolve the question of where to search for an object; any belief in object permanence is no more than an epiphenomenon of the fact that the infant's search strategies will eventually be sufficiently accurate to ensure success on most occasions, so that failure will elicit surprise and a fresh application of the search repertoire. Although the difference between these two approaches may sound subtle, there is a critical difference. It concerns the nature of the perceptual feedback available to the infant in the two cases. Piaget characterizes the infant as seeking to resolve a philosophical question rather than an empirical one: There is no perceptual information to the infant to indicate whether an object actually does remain in existence when it is hidden. (Even the different types of disappearance events distinguished by Gibson only permit predictions, ultimately, about whether or not an object can be found again.) In contrast, the question of whether and where an object may be found following its disappearance is an empirical question. Given that the infant's search will either be successful or unsuccessful, the environment will provide information about whether an accurate prediction has been made or not.

Thus the alternative account outlined above borrows from both Piagetian and Gibsonian theory. In line with Piaget and in contrast to Gibson, it endows the infant with false theories. On the other hand, by investing the infant with the empirical question "Where is an object to be found?", it stresses the informative role of the environment in providing a direct answer much as Gibson might envisage. Piaget readily admits that in terms of his own framework, feedback from the environment is not enough.

> This discovery [of object permanence] simultaneously presupposes two things: 1) experience, since only the failure of his initial search teaches the child that the object is no longer where it was found the first time but rather where it was last hidden, and 2) deduction, since without reciprocal assimilation of schemata the child would not succeed in postulating . . . their permanence

once and for all, particularly when he has not found them where he first looked for them. (Piaget, 1954, p. 107)

By denying that the infant ever does postulate permanence, we avoid the need to attribute deductive capacities to the infant.

IDENTITY

Detection of Invariance

In the previous section, I discussed how the infant comes to identify repeated appearances of the same object as actually belonging to a single unique object. Identity over time was established in terms of the continuity of the object as specified by its visible location or inferred from various indices such as landmarks or containers. I concluded that the infant's capacity to understand the displacements of an object, visible or invisible, was crucial for the realization that he or she was dealing with a single object.

In this section, we turn to another aspect of identity, or rather to two aspects of identity, which have been approached in a similar fashion experimentally. First we will consider the extent to which the infant can overlook certain variations in an object's appearance as it is subjected to various types of displacement, such as rotation or being moved toward and away from the observer. Such movements alter certain aspects of an object's appearance but leave other aspects unaltered. The experimental question to be answered is whether the infant can detect such invariance despite the accompanying variation.

The second and related aspect of identity concerns the issue of category membership. Objects that belong to the same category—for example, the category of male faces—share certain features with one another, and also differ in certain features. In order to perceive that an object belongs to a particular category, the infant needs to be able to detect the invariance despite the accompanying variation. Thus it is apparent that the question of category membership and the detection of shape constancy across various types of displacement are similar problems, in that they require that the infant see invariance in the presence of variation. As indicated in the introduction, the detection of invariance is a key process in the Gibsons' approach to perceptual learning (E. J. Gibson, 1969; J. J. Gibson, 1979). In accord with their direct theory of perception, they argue that there are invariants of stimulation, which the infant becomes better able to detect; such an improvement does not require that the infant enrich the information given by attaching similar or higher order responses to initially disparate stimuli. I shall argue, however, that the direct theory is inadequate in its explanation of the detection of invariance across examples of a category. An alternative approach is to assume that category members are coded in terms of their similarity to a mental prototype or schema as advocated by Kagan (1971). In the introduction, it was pointed out that Kagan has argued that infants from a relatively early age can build up a mental schema that may not correspond to any object that the infant has actually seen, but rather constitutes an idealized version of a set of objects. Although Kagan has been quite vague about how such schemata are formed, we shall see that recent research by Cohen (1979) and Strauss (1979) among others provides strong support for the claim that such prototypical representations do exist in the mind of the infant.

Eventually, when some of the evidence has been presented for the infant's ability to detect invariance of shape across displacement and invariance of shape across members of a category, I shall ask whether or not there are important differences between the detection of invariance in the two contexts. Thereafter, the infant's grasp of identity across modalities rather than within modalities will be examined. Finally, research on self-identity will complete the section.

Invariance and Changes of Orientation

Various studies have examined the extent to which the infant can detect similarities across different orientations of the same stimulus. Such studies have typically used the habituation paradigm. The infant is first familiarized with one or more stimuli and then tested for the extent to which that familiarity is transferred to other stimuli that vary in their similarity to the stimuli presented during the familiarization phase. The general assumption is that infants will devote more attention in the test phase to stimuli that appear novel rather than familiar.

Fagan (1976) used the habituation technique to show, first of all, that 6-month infants could distinguish between two orientations of the same face. Thus they would pay more attention to a novel orientation than to a familiar, previously shown orientation. Subsequently, he was able to show that 6-month infants could also treat these discriminable orientations of the same form as having something in common. Infants transferred their habituation from a specific face in one orientation to the same face in a different orientation. Transfer of habituation was indexed by the fact that infants spent less time looking at a face that was novel in identity but familiar in orientation as compared to a face novel in both identity and orientation. Thus this pair of experiments indicates that although infants can perceive the difference between two orientations of the same face, they can also see that those two orientations have something in common with one another.

Cohen and Strauss (1979) compared three age groups in an experiment somewhat similar to that of Fagan (1976). In one condition, infants of 18 to 30 weeks were habituated to a picture of a female face shown repeatedly in the same pose. When a novel picture was introduced, either the same female in a new pose or a different female, attention recovered, indicating discrimination of both orientation and identity. In a second condition, infants were habituated to the same female face, but this time shown in a variety of poses. Cohen and Strauss (1979) reasoned that such variegated experience might instruct the infants to treat the various poses as instances of a single concept. The eldest group, aged 30 weeks, appeared to construct such a concept, because when they were shown another instance of the same concept, a picture of the same woman in a completely novel pose, they showed no recovery of attention; only when they were shown a picture falling outside of the putative concept—a picture of a different female altogether—did they dishabituate. In contrast, the younger infants, those under 30 weeks, dishabituated whether they were shown the same woman in a novel pose or a totally novel face, suggesting that they had not constructed a concept to include the various possible orientations of the familiar face but had simply registered which specific orientations of the face they had previously seen.

The ability to detect invariance of shape across changes in orientation appears to emerge at less than 30 weeks of age provided simple geometric stimuli are used. Thus Caron, Caron, and Carlson (1979) found that 12-week infants, habituated to a square tilted backward at 60°, recovered when the same stimulus was placed upright. Nevertheless, infants of the same age exposed to a variety of slants of the same stimulus spent less time looking at an upright square than an upright trapezoid. Thus taken together, these results show that 12-week infants can perceive a change in the orientation of a simple geometric shape, but once they have been exposed to several orientations of that shape, regard any new orientation as relatively familiar compared to a new shape in a new orientation.

These experiments concur, then, in showing that the infant is capable of detecting that different orientations of the same shape have something in common. Moreover, it is important to underline that the infant is not simply insensitive to the difference between the various orientations of the object. Differences between orientations can be detected but they do not lead the infant to treat the various orientations as totally dissimilar because habituation is transferred from one orientation to another.

Invariance Across Exemplars of a Category

Are infants also capable of treating different instances, not of the same object, but of the same class of objects as similar to one another? The question of category membership has been tackled by Cohen and Strauss (1979). Infants of 30 weeks were shown a variety of female faces in a variety of poses in order to establish a category of "female faces in general." Afterwards, infants showed transfer of habituation both to a female face that they had previously seen and also to a completely novel female face. Presumably, both faces were assimilated to the category of female faces in general. However, this conclusion ought to be accepted tentatively because no male face was included to show that dishabituation would occur for a stimulus falling outside the putative category of female faces in general.

Fagan (1979) reports experiments where such a precaution was taken. Provided infants of 7 months had seen more than one male face, they appeared to construct a category of "male faces in general" such that they transferred habituation to a novel male face that fell within the putative category but not to a novel female face that fell outside it. When the same experiment was repeated, but infants were presented with only one male face during the familiarization phase, they paid an equal amount of attention to a novel male face and to a novel female face. Accordingly, these results suggest that infants must be exposed to several instances from a putative category if that category is to be constructed.

The habituation technique has also been used to study categorization of a much more disparate set of objects. Ross (1980) presented infants of 12, 18, and 24 months with a variety of exemplars from a given toy category. Some categories were chosen for the relatively marked perceptual similarity of individual exemplars: for example, the category of O-shaped red wooden blocks ranging in diameter from 5 to 10 cm. In contrast, other categories were chosen for the heterogeneity of their exemplars: for example, furniture exemplars varying in height, shape, material, and color. After several members of a given category had been presented in a familiarization phase, a comparison pair was presented that consisted of a new member of the category previously presented (e.g., another type of furniture) and a member of a novel category (e.g., a type of food). Attention waned for successive presentations of exemplars from the homogeneous categories but not for exemplars from the heterogeneous categories. Nonetheless, in the comparison test, transfer of habituation was found irrespective of the type of category. Thus infants turned away from an exemplar drawn from a previously presented category and spent more time looking at the exemplar from the novel category. These results are striking in that selective attention was observed in the comparison test even when highly disparate exemplars had been presented during the habituation period.

Conditions for Detecting Invariance

The evidence presented so far shows that at least by the age of 6 to 7 months, and sometimes earlier, the infant is able to perceive that different orientations of the same object have something in common and also that different members of the same category have something in common. In both cases, moreover, similarity is detected despite the ability to distinguish between the various orientations or category instances. What are the optimal conditions for the detection of invariance? There is now considerable evidence that concept attainment is promoted by variegated experience. As mentioned earlier, Fagan (1979) contrasted two types of familiarization experiences. In one, infants only viewed a single instance from the category of male faces; in a second, they viewed more than one instance. Only the latter group showed the categorical transfer pattern of habituation to a novel male face and dishabituation to a novel female face. The former group treated the two faces as equally unfamiliar.

The experiment by Cohen and Strauss (1979) also indicates that variegated experience promotes concept attainment, or rather, to put the point somewhat more accurately, the breadth of an infant's familiarization experience is related to the breadth of the concept that is constructed. Thus infants who were exposed repeatedly to the same face in the same orientation treated a novel orientation of that face, or a completely novel face, as equally unfamiliar. Such infants appeared to have constructed a fairly narrow category, namely "a particular female in a particular orientation." In contrast, infants who were familiarized to a variety of poses of the same female, rather than a single pose, did not dishabituate to a novel pose of the same female. Instead, they only dishabituated when they were presented with a face that was different in both identity and orientation, that is to say a completely unfamiliar female in a new pose. These latter infants appeared to have constructed a broader concept, not "a particular female in a particular orientation," but "a particular female, irrespective of orientation." Apparently, the variegated experience with different orientations of the same face led infants to delete or attenuate orientation as a salient feature for identifying concept members.

The Coding of Invariance Across Category Members

Earlier, two approaches to the detection of invariance were mentioned: the Gibsons' emphasis on the extraction of invariants that are actually present in the pattern of stimulation; and schema theories, as proposed by Kagan and others, stressing that similar stimuli are referred to some common prototype, which may in some way go beyond or abstract from the actual pattern of stimulation. In his most recent book, J. J. Gibson (1979) was especially concerned with the detection of invariance over time in a single persisting object. Kagan, on the other hand, has been more concerned with the ability to refer several similar objects to a common class. Gibson (1979) himself notes that different processes may operate in these two cases: "In the case of the persisting thing, I suggest, the perceptual system simply extracts the invariants from the flowing array; it *resonates* to the invariant structure or is *attuned* to it. In the case of substantially distinct things, I venture, the perceptual system must *abstract* the invariants" (p. 249). Nevertheless, Gibson is loath to admit that the process of abstraction in any sense goes beyond the information in the optic array: "The latter process has been interpreted to imply an intellectual act of lifting out something that is mental from a collection of objects that are physical, of forming an abstract concept from concrete percepts but that is very dubious" (p. 249). In this section, however, I shall try to show that some form of intellectual abstraction must be postulated to account for infant categorization.

In order to envisage what is involved in the process of abstraction, we may use a simplified analogy. Consider two faces, each drawn on some material such as tracing paper. If these pictures are now superimposed one on top of the other, there will be some features for which there is a more or less perfect superimposition and some features, which are sited differently or shaped differently throughout the set of faces (see Figure 6A). We might argue that habituation is built up to the extent that there is per-

Figure 6A.

fect superimposition for some of the lines (see Figure 6B). Attention will be given to a stimulus to the extent that it did not have features overlapping with such invariant features.

We could, on the other hand, base habituation on a different principle. As we look at the set of faces one on top of the other, the contours of each face will be distributed or scattered across a given area. By drawing a line at the central tendency or midpoint of this distribution, we could obtain an "average face," which in principle need not correspond with any particular face or any particular feature from the set of faces, just as a true average for a set of numerical scores need not correspond to any particular score. Habituation would then be extended to a stimulus to the extent that it was similar to this prototype.

To carry this analogy a little further, we need to represent the fact that the average face that the infant derives from a variegated set is different from the average that is derived from a narrower set, as the experiments of Fagan (1979) and Cohen and Strauss (1979) have indicated. To achieve this, we may represent a widely scattered set of features by a faint average line and a narrowly scattered set of features by a bold average line. If we assume that the infant now compares novel stimuli to this prototype, and in particular to the more boldly represented features in the prototype, we can capture the fact that variegated experience with respect to, say, orientation would lead the infant to pay less attention to a change of orientation, whereas narrow experience with respect to orientation would lead the infant to dishabituate to a change of orientation.

Which of these two types of habituation do infants display? The most suggestive evidence comes from a recent experiment by Strauss (1979). He presented 10-month infants with a set of faces that differed along various dimensions such as the length of the nose and the distance between the eyes. The results showed that a face containing the average of these various values was perceived as familiar and elicited no dishabituation response; in fact, this face was seen as more familiar than a face containing values that had actually been presented more frequently than the average value. Strauss concluded that infants perform in the same way as adults do for certain stimulus sets: They average across the presented values. The implication is that they eventually abstract a prototype, which need not correspond to any actually presented stimulus, so that a stimulus corresponding to that prototype appears to be more familiar than previously encountered stimuli.

As Strauss (1979) points out, such an averaging ability implies that infants are not simply detecting which values are always present across a set of category exemplars, nor even which values are most frequently present. Instead they actively determine an average value that need not correspond to any previously experienced stimulus. Such an averaging process would seem to involve precisely the type of intellectual abstraction or of "lifting out something that is mental" that Gibson (1979) was loath to admit.

Does such an averaging model account for all categorization processes? Strauss (1979) notes that this is unlikely, because certain discontinuous features (e.g., red/green, wood/plastic) cannot be averaged. Moreover, research with adults (Goldman & Homa, 1977; Neumann, 1977) indicates that instead of averaging, subjects sometimes count features and construct a prototype out of the most frequently occurring features even for continuously distributed feature values. Counting rather than averaging is especially likely when the varying feature values are

Figure 6B.

easily discriminated from one another. Of course, to the extent that the discriminative capacity of the infant is less than that of the child or adult, one would expect infants to adopt an averaging model more frequently than a counting model. Nevertheless, Sherman (1981) has successfully shown that infants of 10 months do sometimes adopt a counting model, and indeed she has found that the modal prototype was regarded as more familiar than the mean prototype for the stimuli that she employed. Similarly, in the case of furniture exemplars used by Ross (1980), which varied in form, color, material, and height, it seems likely that infants adopted a counting strategy, at least for the dimensions of material and color.

To summarize the discussion so far, then, we may propose three principles of category formation. First, where feature values are discontinuous it seems likely that infants will incorporate the most frequently occurring feature into a prototype. Second, where feature values are drawn from a narrow range along a continuum, they will be averaged. Third, it seems likely that a prototype for a category will reflect the heterogeneity of that category. This will necessarily be the case if features are counted, but even if they are averaged, it could still be achieved by incorporating some index of the scatter or standard deviation of a set of exemplars into the prototype. Below we consider two further issues that arise in relation to the detection of invariants or similarities across a range of stimuli.

The Detection of Invariants and the Detection of Differences

The Gibsons (E. J. Gibson, 1969; J. J. Gibson, 1979) have argued that perceptual learning consists of two related processes: the extraction of invariants and the differentiation of distinctive features. As we have seen, the results obtained by Strauss (1979) show that the infant does not simply extract invariant features, but, at least under some conditions, averages over a set of feature values. As a result, the infant comes to perceive a novel stimulus as quite familiar. It is hard to see how the Gibsons' emphasis on the extraction of invariance from the stimulus array can explain such a finding.

A second problem arises for the Gibsons' theory if we attempt to specify the relationship between the detection of invariance and the differentiation of distinctive features. The detection of invariance involves the search for similarities across a class of stimuli. The differentiation process, on the other hand, is facilitated to the extent that the perceiver concentrates on those features that vary within the class. This point was raised in the introduction when it was pointed out that it would be unhelpful to focus attention on the horizontal alignment of the eyes in trying to distinguish one face from another, because virtually all faces have horizontally aligned eyes. On the other hand, the shape of the nose varies markedly across faces and this would be a useful feature to concentrate on. In short, the differentiation process requires adoption of the following rule: Attend to dimensions of variation, and ignore dimensions that exhibit little variation.

Now consider once again the detection of invariance or the search for similarities. First, the infant appears to treat the average as the most representative value for a range of values. Second, the infant appears to create a prototype, which emphasizes relatively invariant or narrowly scattered dimensions of variation. For example, in the experiment of Cohen and Strauss (1979) described earlier, infants who repeatedly saw the same female in the same pose showed a recovery of attention if they were presented with the same female in a new pose. Presumably, the constancy of orientation during the habituation period led infants to construct a category in which orientation was encoded. Support for this conclusion comes from the fact that infants exposed during the habituation period to a variety of poses of the same woman showed no recovery of attention when she was presented in yet another novel pose. Thus the search for invariance or relative invariance requires adoption of the following rule: Attend to dimensions that exhibit little variation in constructing a prototype, and ignore dimensions of variation.

The problem for the Gibsons' theory should now be clear. The concentration on relative invariance leads the infant to do precisely the opposite of what is called for by the process of differentiation. The former leads to the storage of features that do not vary, whereas the latter calls for selective attention to those that do. Because the Gibsons do not offer any clear account of when one process operates and not the other, they can only account for any given result by calling on either process in an ad hoc fashion.

Is it possible to specify in more detail how both processes might coexist? We might envisage a storage system along the following lines. Upon encountering any specific stimulus, the infant retrieves that prototype to which it bears the most resemblance. A comparison process ensures in which features of the specific stimulus are encoded in terms of their degree of correspondence with the prototype. A record of these degrees of correspondence is then stored. In the short term, discrimination between any two stimuli can be facilitated by ignoring features showing a marked correspondence with the prototype and paying particular attention to all other features. These noncorresponding features will consist of two types: First, major departures from the prototype, and second, features that are highly variable across members of the category, so that they are not emphasized in the prototype. Since both of these types of features will tend to distinguish between instances of a category, whereas prototypical features will not, such selective attention will clearly help the discrimination process.

We may now consider how such a stored representation might be modified in the course of time. During subsequent encounters with other stimuli, the infant will typically encode and store minor departures rather than major departures. This follows from the fact that if a prototype reflects either mean or modal values of past encounters, then future encounters will tend to show minor departures from the prototype rather than major departures. If we assume, in addition, that repetition of given values leads to a reactivation or strengthening of those values, then it also follows that the infant will continue to be able to access minor departures, whereas major departures will undergo forgetting due to a lack of reactivation. This latter assumption is well justified on the basis of recent research by Rovee-Collier, Sullivan, Enright, Lucas, and Fagen (1980). Three-month-old infants learned to move a crib mobile, which was attached to their ankle by a ribbon. Forgetting is typically complete after 8 days, in the sense that the infant's response rate has returned to the level exhibited before any training. However, a brief exposure to the mobile (with no ribbon present) 24 hours before retention testing was sufficient to eliminate forgetting almost entirely, so that infants responded as much as they had done immediately after the original training. Even more surprising is the finding that such reactivation is effective even if it occurs 24 hours before a retention test given 2 or 4 weeks after the original learning, that is, when complete forgetting would normally have occurred. Rovee-Collier et al. (1980) conclude therefore that stimulus repetition even with fairly extended intervals is sufficient to ensure retrieval of information that would otherwise be inaccessible. Moreover, Enright (1981) has shown that reactivation only occurs if the reactivation cue is highly similar to the original stimulus. Accordingly, it is reasonable to assume that if particular stimulus values are repeated, reactivation will occur, but a stimulus showing a major departure from the prototype will not tend to reactivate a stimulus showing a minor departure, and vice versa.

From the above assumptions, it follows that a memory for a given encounter will, in the course of time, tend to reflect those aspects of the stimulus that it shares with other stimuli; aspects of the stimulus that are not shared with other stimuli will not be re-encountered with any great frequency and, in the absence of reactivation, forgetting will occur. Putting the same point somewhat differently, any given memory will eventually assume a prototypical character in the long term. Short-term storage, on the other hand, is both prototypical and idiosyncratic according to the above assumptions: A particular stimulus is referred to and compared with a prototype that it resembles, so that the degree to which each feature does or does not correspond with the prototype can be encoded.

The above model offers a solution to the problem of how the infant can attend to dimensions of variation while also concentrating on invariance. In the short term, any given stimulus is encoded in terms of its degree of correspondence with the prototype. Thus the availability of a prototype ensures that the infant can discriminate between members of a category by paying special attention to features showing little or no correspondence with the prototype. In the long term, however, the representation of a given stimulus reflects a concentration on relative invariance, like the prototype itself; the absence of reactivation deletes relatively variable features from memory.

This model allows us to explain two intriguing results. Rovee-Collier and Sullivan (1980) trained infants of 3 months to move a mobile by kicking a leg. Infants were tested again 1, 2, 3, or 4 days later, either with the same mobile or a new one. Use of a new mobile at the shorter retest intervals reduced responding, presumably because infants did not identify it as the mobile they had seen during acquisition. Retesting after 4 days, on the other hand, produced a high level of responding whether the original or a new mobile was used. The implication is that after 4 days, infants had forgotten the details of the original mobile, and therefore "recognized" the new as well as the original mobile as a cue for foot kicking. This result readily follows from the assumptions made above: Although delay will ensure the maintenance by repetition of those features of the mobile that it tends to share with other mobiles, it will not ensure retention of its idiosyncratic features. Hence a new mobile will be indistinguishable from the original mobile at longer delay intervals.

Fagan and Singer (1979) gave infants a short-term recognition test in which infants of 5 months were shown a previously encountered picture of a face now paired either with a face of the same sex and age, but which according to adult judgment was quite distinct in overall appearance (e.g., a roundfaced man paired with a gaunt-looking man), or alternatively with a face similar in overall appearance but drawn from a different age or sex category (e.g., a roundfaced man paired with a roundfaced baby). The results indicated that infants spent more time looking at the unfamiliar face if it differed from the familiar face in terms of age and sex rather than overall physical appearance. Thus, pursuing the examples given above, having previously seen a roundfaced man, infants were more likely to treat a roundfaced baby as novel than a gaunt-looking man. These findings fit into the above model in the following way. The process of prototype construction will be accelerated to the extent that a narrow range of variation is found in a set of stimuli, again by dint of repetition, because a narrow range of variation will ensure repetition or at least virtual repetition. For example, faces of babies show a narrow range of variation with respect to certain features such as the shape of the nose, the vertical location of the eyes within the head, and so forth. Accordingly, a prototypical baby face should emerge, reflecting those features that infants have in common, or with respect to which they show only minor variation. Similarly, a prototypical male face should emerge. Particular faces will be treated as more or less equivalent on a recognition test depending on two factors: first, whether they are referred to the same prototype or not; and second, whether they depart from that prototype in similar ways. A roundfaced adult male and the face of a baby will be referred to different prototypes and also depart from those prototypes in distinct ways. Conversely, two males will be referred to the same prototype even though one might be roundfaced and the other gaunt. Thus the above model offers an explanation of why two physically similar faces will appear relatively distinct provided they are drawn from different age and sex categories.

One final point needs to be made with regard to the ability to construct prototypes. It seems likely that such an ability is very important when the child comes to acquire language. If the child always recognizes a particular dog in relation to some stored prototype, and if he regards object names as labels to be applied to any object that approximates a stored prototype, then we would expect children to extend the names that they learn for a specific object, such as the family dog encountered in a particular location, to other dogs encountered in other locations. This generalizing ability is of course exactly what we do observe in young children as they learn to talk. The work on perceptual classification suggests that the foundations for such naming abilities are being laid well before the infant either comprehends or produces any speech.

Nevertheless, as we shall see later, the ability to generalize creates as well as solves several problems for the infant. Nothing in a particular label indicates to the infant how general a category is being indicated. Can "Mommy" be applied to one particular woman, to care-takers, or to all women? As we shall see, in the early stages of language acquisition, the child is not sure of the answer to these questions.

Variation Produced by Rigid and Nonrigid Motion, and Variation Between Category Members

We may now turn to two further questions. We can couch the first in terms of the perception of faces, although it applies in principle to all objects. As infants look at the various faces in their environment, they will be confronted by three distinct types of variation: First, they will see the same face from different orientations, for example, a full face versus a profile; second, they will see a given face vary in shape as its expression changes; third, they will see variation between faces belonging to different individuals. We have already seen that the infant can detect similarities despite the existence of such variation. Thus a given face looks familiar despite a change of orientation, and two faces look similar, particularly if they are of the same sex or age. It also seems likely, although we have reviewed no relevant evidence, that infants can detect similarities in a given face across changes of facial expression. Granted that the infant does perceive similarities across all three types of variation, we may move on to a higher order issue. Does the infant perceive similarities, not just across a particular variation, such as a rotation, but across a set of related variations, such as the set of rigid rotations? Moreover, if the infant can perceive similarities across the various rigid rotations of an object, can these be distinguished from a different type of movement such as takes place during a smile or frown? Recent evidence strongly suggests that young infants do possess such higher order abilities. Gibson, Owsley, and Johnston (1978) presented 5-month infants with an object undergoing various types of rigid movement: rotation around the frontal, horizontal, or vertical axes; or a movement toward and away from the subject. Having viewed any three of these four types of rigid motion, infants were offered a choice: They could either watch another rigid motion (the fourth type that they had not previously seen) or a different type of nonrigid motion, a deformation brought about by squeezing of the object. Infants appeared to recognize the new rigid motion as similar to those that they had previously seen, because they preferred to look at the novel squeezing movement. Similar results were obtained by Gibson, Owsley, Walker, and Megaw-Nyce (1979), who tested still younger infants of 3 months.

In a further experiment, Walker, Owsley, Megaw-Nyce, Gibson, and Bahrick (1980) posed the complementary question: Can infants see similarities across different types of nonrigid motion and distinguish such movements from a rigid movement? Infants were exposed to two of the following types of squeezing motion: a rippling motion; a folding around the vertical axis produced by pressing both sides of the back of the object; a similar type of folding, but around the horizontal axis. Subsequently, three different types of posthabituation trial were presented: the unseen squeezing motion; the squeezing motions presented in the habituation phase; and a novel type of motion, that is, a rigid rotation. Only subjects exposed to the latter stimulus showed dishabituation.

In summary, these experiments show that infants of 3 months can, in some sense, group together different types of transformations: Those movements that do not deform the object, but simply alter its orientation or position, are treated as similar to one another. In addition, those movements that do deform an object—the various types of squeezing transformation such as occur when a face changes its expression—are also treated as similar. Given the young infant's ability to group transformations in this fashion, it would not be very surprising if the infant were able to go one step further and to distinguish the transformations that can occur within an object, namely rotation and squeezing, from those variations that are not underpinned by any type of conventional transformation at all: specifically, the variation that can be observed when one looks at two different instances of a category of objects, such as the category of male faces.

It is important for the infant to be able to sort out this problem for several reasons. First, consider the infant who is learning the meaning of *Daddy* and the meaning of *man*. The word *Daddy* can be applied to only one person, but it can be applied irrespective of his orientation and indeed irrespective of his facial expression. In contrast, the word *man* can be applied to various instances of a much wider category. An infant who cannot sort out the variations that can occur within an object from those that can occur across different instances of a given category would never acquire the meaning of *Daddy* as distinct from the meaning of *man*. The two types of variation would be equivalent and as a result the words would be hopelessly confused.

The second problem that the infant must be able to solve in understanding within-object variation as opposed to within-category variation, is how to annul a within-object transformation. Let us make this abstruse-sounding issue a bit more concrete. Piaget makes several observations on the reactions of Laurent to various orientations of his feeding bottle. At the age of 7 months, Laurent can manage to rotate the feeding bottle if it is presented to him the wrong way around. However, he only does this if the nipple is visible. If the bottle is oriented in such a way that the nipple is completely invisible, Piaget reports the following reaction: "He looks at it for one or two seconds and begins to howl without making any attempt at reversal. Fifth attempt (same position); Laurent looks, begins to suck the glass (the bottom), and howls again" (Piaget, 1954, Observation 78, p. 142). Thus Laurent shows no appreciation of the fact that he is being confronted with the same bottle in a different orientation, and reacts instead as if it were a bottle (because he sucks its bottom), but one that is inexplicably different from the bottle he normally encounters.

Regrettably, very little research has been carried out since Piaget's observations on this topic. As we have seen, even infants of 12 weeks are capable of recognizing a simple shape such as a square when it is rotated from a tilted to an upright position, but such a recognitive ability is not equivalent to an appreciation of how actually to bring about such a change of orientation. Gibson has emphasized the extent to which invariants are available in the stimulus array, which might help the infant to achieve shape constancy. Piaget, on the other hand, has emphasized the extent to which the infant may not understand the reversibility of certain transformations. At present, we have no insight into the developmental relationship between these two abilities. It is conceivable but unlikely that the mere detection of invariants in the stimulus array is sufficient to teach the infant how to rotate an object to the upright position. It seems more likely that only through active experimentation does the infant learn how to rotate an object to a desired orientation. These two possibilities are of course similar to those we have examined in relation to object permanence. Although Gibson has stressed the fact that there is information available during the disappearance of an object to specify its continued existence, Piaget has preferred to concentrate on the extent to which the infant knows how to undo the transformation in question, that is to bring the object back into view again. Finally, it is interesting to note that the Gibsonian approach, or variants of it, has dominated research on so-called shape constancy, whereas the Piagetian approach has dominated research on object permanence. Ideally, both approaches should be compared in tackling each of the two issues.

Summary and Conclusions

In this section, an apparently disparate set of issues has been raised. It may be useful to try to recapitulate some of the main points. First, we have seen that although infants can detect differences between two orientations of the same object, they can detect similarities despite those differences. The same applies to exemplars of the same category. Although infants can see the difference between two female faces, or two items of furniture, they are still able to see certain similarities among female faces, and among items of furniture. The basis for such a generalizing ability is not fully worked out, but research on category formation indicates that it is not simply a question of extracting invariants from the stimulus array. Instead the infant constructs a schema or prototype such that novel items that are similar to that prototype may be perceived as more familiar than previously encountered items.

Three additional problems face the infant: how to perceive similarities among stimuli without ignoring the idiosyncrasies of a particular stimulus; how to distinguish within-object variation, such as rotation of a feeding bottle, from between-object variation, such as exists among various types of bottles; and finally, how to effect or annul within-object variation such as a change of orientation. A solution to the first problem was proposed in terms of a short- and long-term storage system: Short-term representation of a particular stimulus reflects both its idiosyncrasies and its similarities relative to other members of its category, whereas long-term storage increasingly reflects only those properties of the stimulus that it shares with other members—that is, it will assume an increasingly prototypical character.

With regard to the second problem, it was argued that current evidence indicates that infants can distinguish between different types of within-object change: rigid motion versus nonrigid motion. Accordingly, it seems likely that they can distinguish the changes in appearance brought about by these latter two types of transformations from those variations that distinguish one member of a category from another. Finally, with regard to the third problem, it was pointed out that even if infants can see that different orientations of an object have something in common, they may still be unable to bring about a change of orientation. Thus infants may reveal their perception that the top and bottom of their feeding bottle have something in common by sucking on the bottom end of the bottle but they may not know how to turn the bottle around.

Crossmodal Integration: Identity

Previously I asked whether the infant lives in a world that has a spatial unity across the various perceptual modalities. In this section, we turn to crossmodal integration at the level of identity. This question was originally posed to John Locke by Molyneux. He asked whether a blind man whose sight was restored by some miracle would instantly recognize a cube as distinct from a sphere. If discriminations that can be made on a tactile basis—and we may presume that a blind person could distinguish between a cube and a sphere on a tactile basis—are automatically converted into the visual modality, then the blind man could presumably recognize a cube as soon as his sight was restored. On the other hand, if the conversion of information from the tactile modality to the visual modality depends on the simultaneous experience of having touched and looked at the same object, then the blind man, deprived of such bimodal experience, would have no basis for converting his rich tactile experience into a visual capacity for discrimination.

Gibson and Piaget would give different answers to Molyneux. Gibson argues that certain types of information are not exclusively visual or tactual, or for that matter, auditory. For example, information about shape is available to both vision and touch. Information about rhythm can be seen, felt, and heard. To the extent that a blind person had learned the features that distinguish between a cube and a sphere, and to the extent that those same distinctive features were present in the visual modality, Gibson would predict that the blind man whose sight was restored would see the differences between the two shapes. With respect to the period of infancy itself, Gibson would expect crossmodal integration to be present provided infants could make the relevant within-modal discriminations. During infancy, there might be an improvement in the ability to pick up distinctive features within the various modalities, but Gibson would not anticipate any improvement in the ability to translate information across the modalities independent of improvement in within-modality discriminative ability.

Piaget comes very close to adopting a straightforward empiricist account of crossmodal integration, so he would not expect a blind man to distinguish shapes once his sight was restored. For Piaget, as for the empiricists, crossmodal integration depends on the simultaneous experience of having touched and looked at the same object. He differs from the empiricists only in stressing a different aspect of that experience (Spelke, in press). Whereas the empiricists stress the fact that visual and tactual sensations that occur together or follow each other closely in time will come to be associated, Piaget emphasizes the coordination of the schemes that yield those sensations. So, to the extent that an object can be simultaneously assimilated to visual and tactual schemes, a basis for crossmodal integration is provided.

Below we look in more detail at the results that have been obtained with infants. As for spatial integration, we shall consider first the relationship between vision and hearing, and then the relationship between vision and touch.

Vision and Hearing: Nonarbitrary Correlations

The physical world does not always offer a systematic correlation between auditory and visual input. Although there is a very close relationship between visual and tactual information because it is difficult to alter the touchable surface of an object without simultaneously altering its visible appearance, it is clear that there are no necessary correlations between, for example, the voice and the external shape of a person. Moreover, some sounds such as the rushing wind have no visible accompaniment; or, as in the case of many mechanical objects, whatever visible accompaniment there might be to their operation is hidden from view. Nevertheless, there are certain correlations that exist between sights and sounds. Consider, for example, the temporal correlation between the movements of a speaker's lips and the sound produced. As adults, we have a great sensitivity to this correlation, a sensitivity which can be irritating if we are watching a film that is badly dubbed or in which the film and the sound track are badly synchronized. Our appreciation of dance and ballet also depends in part on our ability to detect an abstract temporal synchrony between the rhythm of the music and the rhythm of the performers.

Spelke (1979a) reports a series of experiments concerned with the infant's ability to detect such correlations. In an initial study (Spelke, 1976), 4-month infants watched two events, one a film of a woman playing "peekaboo," the other a film of some percussion instruments being played. Infants viewed these films side by side. A speaker located between the two films played the sound track first appropriate to one film and then the other. The experimental question was whether the infants would notice the correlation between the sound and one of the films and look at the appropriate film. To check that such a preference was not attributable to the type of film, irrespective of the sound track, a control group of infants viewed the films with no accompanying sound track. The results indicated that when a sound track was available, infants tended to watch the film appropriate to it; this was especially clear for the film of the percussion instruments. Similar results were obtained by Bahrick, Walker, and Neisser (1978).

In a subsequent study, Spelke (1979b) asked whether the results of the initial studies were based on learned associations or on the ability to detect relatively novel correlations between sounds and sights. Infants of 4 months were presented with two films, each showing a toy animal being lifted and dropped to the ground (by invisible strings). A percussion sound, either a thump or a gong, accompanied each landing, but because the animals were lifted and dropped at different rates the accompanying sound tracks were made up of a percussion sound that occurred at different rates. The experimental question was whether an infant hearing one of these sound tracks would turn to watch the film that went with it. Because the sounds were counterbalanced relative to the two animals, it was possible to determine whether the infant was responding to the temporal correlation rather than to some familiar association between sights and sounds. The results indicated a slight preference for the film matching the sound track. However, a set of so-called search trials produced firmer results. On these trials, one of the two sound tracks was played briefly and the infant's choice of film directly after its cessation was observed. For the most part, infants turned to the film that fitted the sound track they had just heard. Moreover, they did this even if they had had no prior simultaneous exposure to the film and its accompanying sound track. This latter result suggests that subjects could remember what the temporal pattern of the sound track had been and subsequently match that to a particular film. Thus the data suggest that infants can detect correlations between remembered events and currently perceived events, and not simply between two currently perceived events.

In the preceding study, infants might have been detecting two types of correlation: the temporal *simultaneity* of a given sound and the sight of the animal falling to the ground, or alternatively, the similarity in the *tempo* of the sound track and the movements of the animal, whether or not those two tempos were in strict synchrony. Studies in which the infants listened to a sound track and could then search for a film showing either a movement at the same tempo as the sound track (but not in synchrony) or, alternatively, simultaneous events (of a different tempo) indicated that infants would seek out either of these correlations (Spelke, 1979b).

Taken together these various results fit quite comfortably into Gibsonian theory. The infant does not appear to depend on learned associations between sights and sounds, but can detect similarities in the temporal patterning of sights and sounds, whether they typically co-occur in the natural world or not. As Spelke (in press) has pointed out, it is more difficult to see how the traditional empiricist or the Piagetian approach could handle the results. First, the finding that infants can detect commonalities of tempo across sights and sound, irrespective of synchrony, is hard to explain for any theory that stresses co-occurrence of either sensations or schemes. Second, with regard to Piaget's emphasis on the coordination of schemes rather than sensations, it is not obvious how the detection of a particular tempo can be construed, within either the visual or auditory modality, in terms of the mere activation of schemes, because there is no obvious pattern of activity that might serve as an encoding device.

Vision and Hearing: Arbitrary Links

As noted earlier, sights and sounds may go together in a relatively arbitrary fashion. For example, we may have learned to associate the face and voice of a given person, but there is nothing about the structure of the physical world that dictates that such a face should be linked to such a voice. Conceivably, Piagetian theory might be more appropriate for explaining the detection and retention of such essentially arbitrary links. Lyons-Ruth (1977) familiarized 4-month infants with a particular toy and the sound that it produced. Subsequently, the infants tended to look more at the familiar toy when the sound was played than to a novel toy that had no learned association with the sound. In a similar experiment, Spelke and Owsley (1979) took advantage of a previously established link: that between the audible and visible characteristics of the parents. Infants listened to a recording of the voice of one of their parents, which emanated from a source located between the infant's mother and father. Infants from 3½ to 7½ months tended to spend more time looking at the parent whose voice they could hear. Because both parents were in fact sitting motionless without moving their lips, this behavior must have reflected the infant's learned association of a particular voice with a particular face. A similar experiment using toy animals and a brief familiarization period demonstrated an ability to learn such links quite rapidly.

Nevertheless, it would not be surprising if there were constraints on such learning. If, for example, simultaneity were the only constraint, a sound might be wrongly associated with any object infants were looking at when they heard it. At present, it is not clear how such constraints operate. Thus Lawson (1980) found that a sound and a moving object were associated provided they were spatially contiguous; temporal synchrony of the movement and the sound without contiguity did not lead to a learned association. On the other hand, recent results have shown that spatial contiguity is not a necessary condition for forming an association. Spelke (1981) found that associations were formed on the basis of temporal synchrony despite a spatial separation between moving object and sound source. Similarly, Bahrick, Walker, and Neisser (1981) found that even when two films were superimposed on the same screen, 4-month infants attended preferentially to the film that was synchronized with the sound source, as revealed in a subsequent habituation test, even though both films had been colocated and equidistant from the sound source. One possible explanation of these conflicting results is that an association can be formed on the basis of synchrony provided the spatial separation is relatively small as in the case of Spelke's experiments (1981), and those of Bahrick et al. (1981). Certainly, as adults we are rarely troubled by the spatial separation of lips and voice at the movies.

Vision and Touch

Bower, Broughton, and Moore (1970b) claimed that neonates exhibit hand shaping as they reach toward an object, suggesting that the visual appearance of the object was guiding their tactual expectations and hence the shaping of their hands. However, Gordon and Yonas (1976) failed to observe such precise motor coordination in older infants of 5½ months. Their report runs as follows: "The infant often closed his hand in front or to the side of the object, undershot or overshot the object or hit the object with the back of the hand" (p. 419). Such imprecision scarcely includes the possibility of accurate handshaping.

There is nevertheless good evidence that infants in the first year of life can translate tactual information into visual information. Bryant, Jones, Claxton, and Perkins (1972) made use of the interest that infants of 8 months show in noisy objects to examine their crossmodal abilities. An object was placed in their hands without its being visible and the object was made to produce an attractive noise. Subsequently the infants were offered the choice between two objects: the potentially noisy object that they had felt in their hands and a differently shaped object. Most infants reached out for the object that they had felt, presumably in order to get it to make a noise. Because their reach was based on the visible appearance of the object and because their only other experience with the object had been when they felt it in their hands, the experiment clearly indicates an ability to store some description of the object based on tactual experience and to match this up with some aspect of the object's visible appearance.

Rose, Gottfried, and Bridger (1981) have also shown that infants can store a description of an object based on visual experience and match this up with some aspect of the object's tactual appearance. Year-old infants were presented with an object either for visual inspection, or in darkness, so that only tactual inspection was possible. Subsequently, when offered a choice between the familiar object and a novel object, both types of objects being presented in darkness, infants preferred to touch the novel object, suggesting that they recognized the familiar object whether they had only touched it before or only looked at it.

At what age do such crossmodal abilities emerge? Recent evidence has tended to place it at an increasingly young age. Gottfried, Rose, and Bridger (1977) found evidence of crossmodal abilities at 8 months, and Ruff and Kohler (1978) at 6 months. What is still unclear from these reports is exactly how the crossmodal translation process is acquired. By the age of 6 months, the infant may have spent a good deal of time engaged in simultaneous visual and tactual inspection of objects (Harris, 1972). Such inspection might facilitate the simultaneous activation of visual and tactual schemes, which Piaget regards as necessary for the development of a crossmodal "dictionary."

The strongest evidence against the Piagetian account has been reported by Meltzoff and Borton (1979). They presented infants of approximately 4 weeks with a pacifier to suck, which had either a stippled or a plain surface. After 90 sec. of such tactual exploration infants were presented with the two similarly shaped objects for visual inspection alone. Two experiments indicated that subjects preferred to look at the shape that they had sucked. As Meltzoff and Borton (1979) point out, these results indicate that the neonate is able to store some representation of the tactually perceived shape and match it with the subsequently presented visible shape. Such results cast strong doubts on an empiricist or associative account because it is obviously very difficult to suck and look at an object simultaneously. At best such associations would depend on links made between past tactual experience and present visual experience. However, it is not at all clear how the infant would know which visible object to link up with past tactual experience. These results also suggest, contrary to Piaget's assertion, that even the neonate is capable of storing and retrieving an image or representation of an object, although admittedly the results of Meltzoff and Borton (1979) imply only that a visually perceived object can be *recognized* in relation to a prior tactual experience; there is no evidence from these experiments that the neonate is capable of *recalling* a representation of the tactually perceived object in the absence of any current perceptual input regarding the object.

Finally, we may return to an apparent conflict between two sets of findings. On the one hand, the evidence reviewed in this section shows that infants even as young as 1 month and certainly by 6 to 8 months are able to remember something about an object's tactually perceived shape, and to match that memory to a visually perceived shape. On the other hand, in discussing crossmodal spatial integration, results were reviewed that showed that infants exhibit little surprise when they reach out for an object that looks hard and find that their hand passes straight through it (Gordon & Yonas, 1976). Similarly, Bushnell (1980, reported in Spelke, in press) found that 8-month infants who reached for a visible object and encountered an object that felt different in size, shape, or texture from its visible appearance, showed no surprise. Only at 9½ months was some degree of surprise displayed. How should this discrepancy be interpreted? One possibility is that the infant is better at translating from touch to vision, than from vision to touch. The experiments where successful crossmodal translation has been shown in infants under 1 year of age have all tested the use of a tactual memory to guide visual inspection. The experiments in which no surprise has been manifested assess the infant's tendency to be surprised when current tactual experience violates expectations based on earlier visual inspection. However, this explanation of the discrepancy seems dubious. After all, once the infant has failed to touch a virtual object or touched a solid object, these tactual experiences may be used to generate expectations that can be compared to the infant's visual experience and found not to match. Thus the experiments by Gordon and Yonas (1976) and Bushnell (1980, reported in Spelke, in press) involve a violation of expectations derived from tactual as well as visual input.

Another explanation of the discrepancy between the two sets of results is that infants can generate expectations or predictions from one modality to another, but do not react to or become aware of a violation of those expectations (Spelke, in press). In the same way, in reviewing depth perception it was noted that young infants may perceive depth but show no affective reaction to it. One problem with this interpretation is that although in the case of depth perception we can easily imagine the type of experiences that would elicit an affective reaction, it is hard to imagine what these would be in the case of crossmodal integration.

In line with the separation of different levels of crossmodal integration discussed earlier, I favor a third interpretation of the discrepancy. Where infants are given a tactual experience, and this tactual experience influences their subsequent visual inspection, we need only postulate an ability to detect tactual and visual correspondence at the level of identity. The conflict experiments, on the other hand, require that infants not only realize that a particular visual shape matches a particular tactual shape, but also that the two encounters should be colocated. If infants do not realize this there is no reason for them to be puzzled by the conflict situations, because they will certainly have touched a surface different from the one they are looking at on many occasions in the past, provided they are looking in one direction and reaching in another.

In summary, the available evidence suggests that young infants have two initially separate systems for dealing with visual/tactual relationships. First, they are equipped with the ability to reach in the appropriate direction for a visible object. Second, the infant can detect correspondences between visually and tactually perceived shapes. During the first 9 months of life there is no consistent evidence that these two systems are coordinated, such that infants who reach out for a visible object expect to obtain tactual feedback of a specific kind when their hands reach the location of the visible object.

Crossmodal Integration and Identity: Conclusions

In the introduction to this section, the different theoretical approaches of Gibson and Piaget to crossmodal integration were discussed. The results from both the study of visual/auditory correlations and visual/tactual correlations are consistent with Gibson's claim that infants are sensitive to amodal information that can be specified by more than one modality. The findings that infants can detect quite unfamiliar correlations (Spelke, 1979a), and can do so under circumstances in which associative experience is unlikely to have an effect (Meltzoff & Borton, 1979), cast doubt on the Piagetian account of crossmodal perception at the level of identity.

Nevertheless, when the findings on crossmodal integration with regard to both position and identity are considered together, the evidence suggests that these two types of crossmodal integration are not coordinated one with another. More specifically, there is evidence that the neonate or young infant can use information in one modality to guide the receptors in another modality. Sounds guide looking, and sights guide reaching. In addition, auditory/visual and visual/tactual correspondences in rhythm and shape, respectively, can be detected. However, there is no consistent evidence that young infants are distressed when the receptors for two modalities are directed toward the same location in space and encounter noncorrelated information at that place. Whereas some early investigations suggested that infants reacted with distress to such mismatches, more recent studies have consistently reported no distress. This conclusion is certainly compatible with Piaget's theorizing because it suggests that the infant does not realize that the different modalities of information for a given object operate within a common space. Indeed, Piaget may be right to assert that such a common space is only gradually constructed. What he appears to have underestimated is the fact that the infant appears to possess two important sets of tools for engaging in such a constructive process: the ability to guide receptors in one modality by means of another, and the ability to detect amodal correlations.

Self-identity

Direct Perception Versus Construction of the Self

Virtually every writer on the topic of the discovery of the self in infancy has started from the assumption that the neonate has no conception of the self. Thus Piaget argues that the neonate begins life in a state of adualism, in which the distinction between self and outer world is absent. All that the infant has are certain sensations and experiences, but no appreciation of whether they emanate from an external world as in the case of perceptions, or from the self as in the case of memories, pains, and desires. Moreover, infants only gradually come to distinguish outcomes for which they are entirely responsible from those that are independent of the self. For example, we saw that at the fourth stage of object permanence, infants do attribute some minimal independent existence to the hidden object because they search for it even though it is completely hidden; but according to Piaget infants think that they bring about the re-creation of the object. A similar egocentricity obtains with respect to causality. Infants credit other people with the power to achieve some outcome: They grasp an adult's hand and press it against the cord of their baby swing in order to get the adult to make it move. Yet, according to Piaget, infants still believe that their own intervention, such as grasping or poking the adult's hand, is necessary to set this latter agent in motion. Only at the end of the sensorimotor period can infants conceive of and search for objects and agents quite independent of the self.

J. J. Gibson (1979), on the other hand, has argued that so far as the bodily self is concerned, information is available in early infancy to distinguish it from the external world. On first reflection, it seems unlikely that infants could have any perception of their own heads or faces. Only with the aid of a mirror might they gradually discover that they possess eyes, ears, a nose, and so on, just like the faces they see around them. According to this approach, then, the major source of information about the self would be supplied by two sources: the infant's perception of his or her own body, particularly the more mobile parts of that body, such as the hands; and the kinesthetic feedback supplied whenever the infant moves any part of the body. Thus Lewis and Brooks (1975) write: "The kinaesthetic feedback produced by our own actions is continuous and such action-outcome contingencies must theoretically form the basis for self-recognition" (p. 121). Such accounts, however, ignore the actual nature of the visual field, which has been analyzed most thoroughly by J. J. Gibson (1979). Our field of view has boundaries, which, although vague and indistinct, are nevertheless boundaries. These consist of the head and the nose. That the nose forms a constant part at least of the adult field of view, is easily checked by closing one eye. Thus the self is a constant feature of the visual field because it visibly occludes part of the visual world. Such occlusions have regularities that are similar to the occlusions produced by a conventional moving object in that they consist of "an accretion of optical structure at the leading edge with deletion of structure at the trailing edge" (J. J. Gibson, 1979, p. 112).

Moreover, as Gibson points out, the other features of the body, the trunk and the limbs, also occlude part of the visual world; but they differ from the head and nose with respect to their distance from the point of observation. The nose and orbit sweep across the surface behind them at the greatest rate whenever one moves one's head. Thus Gibson suggests that the experience of the self as being in the head, or at least as most centrally located within the head rather than the body, has its basis in optical information rather than any unanalyzable intuition.

In addition, an analysis of the optical information available to the infant suggests that there is at least one route—whether or not the neonate takes up that route is another question—by which the neonate can escape the adualism that is assumed by virtually every other developmental theorist regarding the period immediately after birth. The nose, head, limbs, and extremities occupy relatively fixed positions with respect to the point of observation. All other objects in the infant's environment, on the other hand, will be seen to undergo reduction in the retinal size as the infant is transported from place to place or as objects and people spontaneously move away.

Finally, as Bower (1974) has suggested, the fact that one can see oneself within the visual field permits clear distinctions to be made between movements that are initiated by the observer and movements that belong to objects in the outside world. Upon moving the head, the position of all objects within the observer's visual field is altered, but the projection of the head and nose onto the visual field remains constant. On the other hand, whenever an object moves in the world, the projection of all other objects in the external world and the projection of the self remains constant. Only the moving object alters its position relative to both of these. Finally, upon moving one's eyes, the projection of the self will take up a different position within the field of view of the observer, but will remain in a constant position relative to all the other objects in the world. Thus the infant is in a position to distinguish between (1) a change in the field of view brought about by a movement of the head, (2) the movement of an object relative to the self, and (3) a change in the field of view brought about by an eye movement rather than a movement of the head.

At the present time it is fair to say that Gibson's analysis of the optical information available to specify the self, and Bower's supplementary remarks on the perception of movement, constitute an analysis of the information that the infant might use. We have no clear evidence that the neonate does in fact discriminate between these various optical events. Nevertheless, such analyses do, in my view, provide a healthy antidote to the assumption that the self is necessarily mysterious and beyond the grasp of the human neonate. We should not take that assumption for granted simply because there is virtually no psychologist except Gibson who has ever questioned it.

Experimental Studies Falling Within Gibson's Framework

Although evidence with regard to the neonate is lacking, evidence with regard to the older infant is beginning to accumulate. The evidence indicates that the infant can discriminate between different types of movement and responds in an appropriate fashion to such movements. For example, Harris, Cassell, and Bamborough (1974) showed that infants of 2 months and older were more likely to track an object moving against a stationary background than an object that moved together with a moving background moving at the same rate. The accretion and deletion of optical structure that is specified by the moving object as it successively occludes the background constitutes the information par excellence for object movement, and infants appear to respond to it with the appropriate response, namely tracking, from an early age. The motion of the object unaccompanied by such occlusion information reduces tracking considerably.

How then does the infant respond to movement of the whole field? As was suggested above, this is the usual optical accompaniment to movement of the observer. Unless we are in an artificial environment, we are virtually never exposed to an actual movement of the whole visual framework. Hence adults may conclude, upon observing such an event, that they are moving rather than the outside world. Do infants draw the same conclusions from movements of the visual framework? Lee and Aronson (1974) placed infants of 12 months and up on a stable floor inside a moveable room; infants faced the interior end wall of the room, and when the whole room was moved, the end wall appeared to approach toward or recede from them. Such an expanding or contracting flow of optical information typically specifies forward or backward motion of the observer. Thus infants detecting such an event might tend to attribute it to their own motions rather than the movement of the room, and as a result initiate some countermovement to compensate for the momentary (nonexistent) loss of balance. The infants tested did in fact sway, stagger, and fall in ways that were appropriate to the feedback provided by the moving room. If the end wall moved toward them, thereby providing the optical information normally associated with forward motion, they compensated by falling backward.

The infants tested were capable of standing, so that one might assume that such a reaction to the visual frame depends on the experience of standing or at least crawling. However, a report by Butterworth and Hicks (1977) indicates that such experience is not necessary. They tested infants who could sit but not stand, as well as infants who could both sit and stand unsupported. The younger infants, who were unable to crawl, showed much the same reactions as the older infants to the experience of the moving room. Indeed, if anything, older infants exhibited an increasingly mild reaction depending on the amount of experience that they had had with the posture under investigation. Presumably this result indicates that the visual framework is used from the start to maintain a given posture, and only gradually can the infant recognize cases where such movements of the visual framework, being unaccompanied by any postural alteration, do not require any type of compensation.

Butterworth (1980) has suggested that this delayed appearance of the ability to distinguish a true change of posture (i.e., one that does require compensation) from an apparent change, as specified by the visual framework, must mean that the infant has an implicit but not an objective self-knowledge. I am not convinced that such a distinction can be maintained. Even adults remain susceptible to information from the visual framework such that they will draw conclusions, which in objective terms are false. For example, a fast car chase filmed from the driver's position, with rapid changes of altitude as the car climbs and drops, can induce a feeling of nausea in the comfortably seated and totally immobile moviegoer. Yet we need not conclude that such nauseous feelings indicate any lack of objective self-awareness. Similarly, even if infants feel themselves to be toppling over when the moveable room is displaced, we may not conclude from such a localized lack of objectivity that they do not have objective self-awareness. Indeed there is a sense in which, once Gibson's analysis is taken seriously, it becomes misleading to talk in terms of objective versus subjective knowledge. Because the information is picked up directly, we cannot speak of its being objective or subjective without introducing some additional yardstick, which has no place in Gibsonian theory. The infant who compensates for the displacement of the room can only be regarded as lacking in objectivity if we insist that infants are correcting for a (nonexistent) loss of balance. But this is precisely what infants are not apparently compensating for. Instead they are reversing the perceived displacement of the room relative to their own point of observation, a relative displacement that objectively took place. Older infants, who take into account both the visual framework and their own postures are in Gibsonian terms simply picking up more information, rather than attaining objectivity.

In summary, we have seen that Gibson has offered an interesting account of the ways in which the visual field specifies the existence, location, and displacements of the observer. We have reviewed preliminary evidence indicating that in the early months of the first year of life the infant is sensitive to such information. Finally, we have noted that the distinction between objective and subjective knowledge cannot be maintained within Gibson's framework; the infant develops not from subjective to objective knowledge, but from the detection of less information to the detection of more information.

Self and Mirror

Infants might realize that they have a face and body without recognizing their own particular face or body when seen in a mirror. When does this type of self-recognition emerge? Gallup (1970) devised a neat test of whether primates recognized their own face in a mirror as belonging to them rather than some other animal. Red dye was painted on the ears of chimpanzees and rhesus monkeys while they were anesthetized. When they awoke and were permitted to examine their reflection in a mirror, Gallup observed whether they explored the reflection of their dyed ears in the mirror or fingered their own ears under guidance from the mirror. Only in the latter case could one conclude that the primates were capable of recognizing that the reflection in the mirror was that of their own face. The results indicated that the chimpanzees did reach for their own ears, whereas the monkeys directed their exploration at the mirror.

Lewis and Brooks (1975) made use of a similar technique to study the development of self-recognition in human infants. Rouge was applied to the infants' faces by their mothers under the guise of wiping their faces. When they were subsequently confronted with a floor-length mirror, none of the 9- and 12-month-old infants, 25% of the 15- and 18-month infants, and 75% of the 21- and 24-month infants touched their noses.

Bertenthal and Fischer (1978) have attempted to look at self-recognition across a wider range of tasks, which they argue form an invariant developmental sequence. In Task 1, infants are simply tested for the ability to look at some part of their mirror images. In Tasks 2 and 3, infants are expected to locate an object immediately above their bodies by means of its reflection in a mirror. Thus infants might look at their reflections in the mirror and, seeing a hatlike object above their heads in the mirror, look up in order to find it. In Task 4, infants are tested for their ability to touch their noses after seeing their rouged noses in the mirror. Thus this task is modeled after those of Gallup (1970) and Lewis and Brooks (1975). Finally, in Task 5, infants are tested for their ability to give their names, when asked: "Who's that?," of their own mirrored reflections. The results indicated that the five tasks did form an invariant sequence between the ages of 6 and 24 months.

From the point of view of the results reported earlier, Tasks 2 and 3 are particularly interesting. When infants are not expected to locate a particular spot on their bodies as required by the rouge test, but simply to direct their visual regard to a particular region adjacent to the body, the task can be solved at an earlier age.

Self as Similar to Others

Hitherto, we have discussed the infant's self-perception without reference to other people. However, one aspect of self-recognition is the ability to regard oneself as similar to particular classes of other people, be it people of the same age or the same sex. This aspect of self-recognition has recently been investigated in an interesting series of studies by Lewis and Brooks (1975).

In an initial study, they observed infants ranging from 7 months to 19 months confronted by various other people including an unfamiliar child. The results indicated that infants were more disturbed by an unfamiliar adult than by an unfamiliar child. It does not seem feasible to construct an argument showing that children are more familiar to infants than are adults. Accordingly, Lewis and Brooks hypothesized that the infants were in part using their own self as a reference point, in which case an older child would seem less unfamiliar and less frightening than an unfamiliar adult; support for this interpretation was provided by additional studies in which fixation to pictures of various persons was studied. The results indicated that infants tended to look longer at a picture of a baby of the same sex as themselves as compared to a picture of a baby of the opposite sex. Such a result is extremely hard to understand unless we accept first that the infant has some knowledge of his or her own sex, and second, that the infant is capable of recognizing other infants as belonging to the same category.

Conclusions

Sketchy as the above findings are, they suggest at the very least that infants' discovery of their bodily self is not a single unified process. Nor is there any particular magic moment when self-awareness suddenly emerges. In line with Gibson's theory of direct perception, infants of 6 months can distinguish those optical changes that normally accompany the movement of the external object from those that accompany their own changes of position. In reaction to both of these optical changes, infants behave in appropriate ways by tracking in the first case and by seeking to readjust their posture in the second. On the other hand, there are indications that infants gradually construct a more and more elaborate notion of their bodily self throughout the sensorimotor period. The results of Bertenthal and Fischer (1978) are especially interesting in this respect. Henceforward, investigators need to be explicit about which aspects of the infant's self-percept or self-concept are being studied.

One additional point worth mentioning is that the studies cited above refer almost exclusively to visual indices of the self: The constraints on the visual field offered by the observer's body, observations of the limbs, recognition of the reflection of the self, and recognition of similar others. We know virtually nothing about what might be called biographical self-awareness. Such self-awareness depends on an appreciation of the fact that certain experiences are not simply ongoing or past events but belong to one's own particular biography. Current research is completely silent on the point at which infants or children become aware of themselves having a coherent biography in which they themselves have been experiencers or agents of particular events distinct from those events that are simply reported to them, or that they have imagined. Such memories clearly depend on a concept of oneself as a psychological subject having a continuity across successive spatial and temporal loci. Without such a concept, one's own biography is indistinguishable from general historical knowledge on the one hand, and dreams and fantasies on the other.

ACTION AND IMITATION

Introduction

In this section we examine one important index of the infant's ability to represent action: the ability to imitate the actions of someone else. Imitation rests on several abilities. In the first place, the infant must be able to encode another's movement as a visual event, or to encode another's vocalization as an auditory event. Second, the infant must be able to translate such visual or auditory events into a set of matched motor commands. Finally, the infant must be able to execute those commands in the appropriate serial order. In addition to these basic requirements, it is also possible to introduce a mnemonic factor: a delay between the model's actions and the time at which the infant produces a copy. Such a delay must be mediated by storage of the representation of the visual event, or storage of its translation into a set of motor commands.

Piaget (1951) has offered a theoretical account of imitation in which he argues for the relatively slow development of two of the components described above: the ability to translate another's actions into a set of motor commands and the ability to store a representation of an act to be imitated. The slow development of the translation component is attributable to two factors: From a relatively early age infants can imitate actions provided they are familiar and provided they produce some type of feedback that can be readily matched to the actions of the model. Actions that are unfamiliar and actions that infants cannot see or hear themselves perform are only imitated toward the middle and end of the sensorimotor period. The slow development of the memory component is illustrated by the fact that initially infants can imitate acts that they have just seen performed but do not reproduce acts witnessed hours or days before until the end of the sensorimotor period.

Replication studies of Piagetian findings on imitation fall into two broad types, similar to those described for the development of object permanence. First, there are the relatively broad-scale studies of the sequence of development postulated by Piaget, studies that examine imitation across a relatively large age range and a wide range of tasks. Second, there are more focused studies of a particular age group, especially the neonate, in which Piagetian claims may be challenged rather than replicated. I shall first review the broad-scale studies before turning to the more restricted challenges to Piagetian theory.

Broad-Scale Replications

Uzgiris (1972) reports a longitudinal study of 12 infants between the ages of 1 month and 2 years, and Uzgiris and Hunt (1975) report the results of several cross-sectional studies. Overall, the findings suggest a four-step course to the development of imitation. In the first step, infants only reproduce acts that are already within their repertoire and that produce feedback that is similar to that produced by the acts of the model. For example, infants can imitate cooing sounds such as "uuh" or "aah." Such sounds are already within their repertoire because they are produced spontaneously, and whether the infant or the model produces the sounds, the auditory feedback is similar. In the second step, infants alternate in a turn-taking fashion with the experimenter and are not simply triggered by the experimenter as is often the case in the fist step; moreover, they attempt to reproduce unfamiliar acts or complex acts composed of unfamiliar schemes, but fail to reproduce the whole act. For example, they reproduce the wrong sound in response to an unfamiliar vocalization from the experimenter, or, rather than banging two blocks together, they bang one on the table. In the third step, infants attempt to approximate the adult model in a more active fashion, correcting errors in the process; for example, they might open and close their mouths in response to the experimenter's blinking, then shut their eyes tight, and then eventually blink. Finally, in the fourth stage, infants produce unfamiliar sounds and actions in a fairly direct fashion, even when these include gestures that they cannot see themselves perform.

The Translation Component

The sequence suggested by Uzgiris (1972) and Uzgiris and Hunt (1975) corresponds fairly well to the sequence proposed by Piaget, but there is little systematic evaluation of Piaget's claim that the ability to translate the model's acts into a set of motor commands undergoes development. Indeed, Piaget asserts that the translation component changes in a qualitative fashion in the course of development. Very young infants are able to imitate actions that they can see themselves perform because they fail to distinguish a model's behavior and its accompanying visual and auditory feedback from their own. Because in any case an action by the infant tends to have a circular excitatory effect, as described in the introduction to Piagetian theory, the sight or sound of an adult model has a similar effect.

Only later are infants able to imitate actions that they cannot see themselves perform. To explain this development Piaget invokes the possibility of tactual mediation. An infant equipped with rules for translating visual input into tactual input, or for discovering such rules of translation would be able to note a correspondence between, for example, the sight of the mother's nose and the feel of his or her own nose. Because the establishment of such visual/tactual correspondences is relatively slow according to Piaget, he argues that the imitation of invisible gestures does not emerge until Stage 4, or approximately 8 to 12 months of age.

There are various reasons for subjecting Piaget's claim to critical scrutiny. First, it seems difficult to imagine how infants could establish a very exact correspondence between the component parts of an adult's face and their own rather differently shaped face. Even admitting that infants can ride roughshod over these dissimilarities, it is not at all clear how, once such visual/tactual correspondences have been established, they will help infants to reproduce the actual motor gesture. After all, it is one thing to be able to grasp one's tongue and to know that it has roughly the same shape as an adult's tongue; it is quite another thing to know that the act of tongue protrusion can be reproduced by executing a particular set of motor commands. Tactual information does not appear to be linked in any obvious way with such motor commands or with any accompanying kinesthetic feedback.

Nevertheless, it might be thought that the infant's ability to imitate an increasingly complex and unfamiliar series of actions proves that the translation component must be undergoing development. There is an alternative interpretation, however. Piaget (1952) argues that the infant's ability to engage in a complex series of actions to reach a particular goal develops during the sensorimotor period even in situations where there is no question of imitation. For example, the ability to negotiate a detour or remove an obstacle so as to recover an attractive toy improves independent of any prior modeling by the adult. Much the same type of development is described by Bruner (1970), although Bruner speaks of the modularization of skills rather than the coordination of schemes. Accordingly, the fact that the infant can imitate an increasingly complex set of actions, including unfamiliar actions, may simply reflect the infant's general improvement in skilled action, rather than any improvement in the ability to translate the model's acts into motor commands. A concrete analogy might make the ambiguity of Piaget's claim more obvious. A novice typist might at first be incapable of listening to the teacher dictate a given sentence and then typing it out. Any subsequent improvement in the ability to perform this task is almost certainly a result of an improvement in typing skill considered purely as a motor skill, and not to any improvement in the ability to translate spoken utterances into a string of letters and words. Accordingly, the novice typist will exhibit no deficit in such "translation" skills if a different output medium is chosen such as writing; nor is there likely to be any improvement in writing as a result of learning to type. Similarly, the development of imitation can be seen as the application of an invariant "translation" ability to an increasingly sophisticated capacity for generating and executing a set of motor commands. In the next section, we examine evidence favoring the view that the translation component does remain invariant.

Imitation of Invisible Gestures by the Neonate?

Zazzo (1957) was one of the earliest investigators to report, in a case study, imitation of facial gestures in the first 2 or 3 weeks of life. Since that time, other investigators have published similar findings (Gardner & Gardner, 1970; Maratos, 1973; Meltzoff & Moore, 1977). The study by Meltzoff and Moore is the most systematic and deserves a relatively detailed description. Infants between 12 and 21 days were presented with four different gestures to imitate: three facial gestures (tongue protrusion, lip protrusion, and mouth opening) and one manual gesture (sequential finger movements). Their efforts to reproduce these gestures were videotaped, and subsequently coders were invited to view a randomly ordered set of the infants' imitative efforts and to decide in each case which of the four gestures had just been modeled. Raters were able to identify above chance level which of the four gestures had just been modeled. As Moore and Meltzoff (1977) point out, it seems unlikely that infants of such a tender age would be able to make use of the tactual mediation proposed by Piaget, even if this mechanism did not suffer from the inherent implausibilities mentioned above.

Meltzoff and Moore (1977) also consider the possibility that such early imitation might be based on an innate releasing mechanism such as that described by Tinbergen (1951). According to this view, the various gestures are fixed action patterns that are released by the corresponding adult gestures, which serve as sign stimuli. Meltzoff and Moore (1977) reject this view on two counts. First, they argue that the lack of stereotypy in the infant's response argues against such an interpretation; and second, they note that it is somewhat cumbersome to postulate a set of four fixed action patterns.

Nevertheless, a recent report by Jacobson (1979) does lend some support to the notion that certain sign stimuli may serve as releasers of particular actions in the neonate. Jacobson observed infants at 6, 10, and 14 weeks in a longitudinal study; on each test occasion, infants were presented with five different stimuli. Two of these corresponded to those modeled in the study carried out by Meltzoff and Moore (1977), namely tongue protrusion and hand movements. The remaining stimuli had only an abstract correspondence to these gestures. For example, Jacobson presented a ball and a pen being moved toward the infant's mouth on the ground that such approach movements might be equally likely to provoke tongue protrusion. Similarly, the lowering and raising of a ring was thought to be likely to provoke hand movements. The results supported these expectations: At 6 weeks, not only tongue protrusion itself, but also the approach of the ball and pen were likely to elicit tongue protrusion to a greater extent than either the movement of the hand or the ring. Thus tongue protrusion was not elicited exclusively by the adult's modeling of tongue protrusion but also by two other approach movements bearing only an abstract similarity to tongue protrusion itself. By 14 weeks, imitation was more selective because tongue protrusion was primarily elicited by the demonstration of tongue protrusion itself, but this effect was limited to infants whose mothers had demonstrated tongue protrusion in the interim on a more or less daily basis. Imitative movements of the hand increased rather than declined during the initial months of life. As for tongue protrusion, however, support was obtained for the claim that imitation is a reaction to specific releasing stimuli, because the movement of the ring was as effective in eliciting hand movements as the modeling of hand movements themselves.

To what extent do the findings of Jacobson provide a genuine rebuttal of the claim advanced by Meltzoff and Moore (1977) that the neonate is capable of selective imitation? Close inspection of Jacobson's data reveals that the majority of infants tested at 6 weeks exhibited more tongue protrusion to the modeling of tongue protrusion itself than to the other two so-called sign stimuli. Moreover, tongue protrusion was more frequent after the modeling of tongue protrusion than after any other gesture. Burd and Milewski (1981) also report that infants of 2, 6, and 10 weeks exhibited more tongue protrusion to the tongue model than to any other stimulus including pen movements. The evidence is consistent with the claim that infants encode human movement into fairly abstract motion configurations, which inanimate objects may approximate. Thus the weight of the evidence is still, in my view, in favor of the hypothesis that the neonate can engage in selective imitation, with some generalization to similar-looking stimuli. Further research may indicate with more precision exactly how the infant codes motion such that inanimate objects can appear to mimic human motion.

Two Alternatives to Piagetian Theory

If we accept that Meltzoff and Moore have demonstrated selective imitation in that an abstract code is available for translating perceived movements into a set of motor commands, it is clear that Piagetian theory will need considerable revision. Two major alternatives suggest themselves. One possibility is that neonates set out with an abstract system for representing both perceived movement and their own movement in some type of common code. Far from being the final achievement of the sensorimotor period, such a code would be a basis for development. Once this is accepted, it becomes questionable whether there is any major change in the translation component, contrary to Piaget's claim. The increasing sophistication of the infant's imitative repertoire can be attributed to the fact that the infant's repertoire for skilled movement in general, spontaneous as well as imitative, is undergoing considerable development throughout infancy.

A second possibility is that the precocious behavior of the neonate observed by Meltzoff and Moore (1977) is replaced by a more mature form of imitation in the course of development. A report by Maratos (1973) lends some support to this possibility. Twelve female infants were studied on a longitudinal basis over the first 6 months of life. Maratos found that tongue protrusion is present at 1 month and then decreases until it becomes only sporadic from 2½ months onward. A similar developmental pattern was also found for mouth movements and side-to-side movements of the head, but the evidence is harder to interpret because mouth movements were frequent even in the absence of a model, and side-to-side movements of the head might be a tracking response rather than true imitation. The imitation of finger movements and sounds exhibited a different developmental pattern, being rare or nonexistent in the first 2 months of life but increasing thereafter.

Taking the results of Maratos (1973) as a whole, there appear to be two developmental patterns: In the first pattern there is a drop in imitation from the neonatal period onward; whereas for the second pattern there is a virtual absence of imitation during the neonatal period and a steady rise during the succeeding 6 months. Responses of the head and mouth tend to fall in the first pattern, whereas responses of the limbs, particularly the fingers, and also the vocal tract fall into the second pattern. Why should there be such strikingly different developmental patterns for these different response systems? One possible critical difference between the response patterns is that movements of the head and mouth are not accompanied by any feedback except kinesthetic feedback. In contrast, movements of the fingers and vocal tract produce visible and audible feedback in addition to the feedback produced by the motor movement itself. Hence it is possible that imitation can be triggered in two ways: either by a direct translation of the model's movements into motor commands, or by an indirect translation in which the model's movements are linked with the feedback associated with such movements, much as Piaget envisaged. The development of imitation in the latter mode would necessarily be slower because it would depend on the extent to which infants produce such movements themselves, and it would also, as Piaget argues, be more difficult to achieve the less a given movement produces perceptual feedback that is similar across model and imitator.

In order to explain the decline of tongue protrusions and the like, it can be argued that the first direct mode of translation—from perceived gesture to motor command—might be gradually replaced by an indirect mode. To the extent that infants produce movements that they cannot see in response to demonstrations by a model, the kinesthetic feedback consequent on such movements will eventually come to be associated with the model's demonstrations. Eventually, the model's gestures might arouse both memories of kinesthetic feedback, and also, the motor commands that lead to such feedback. Thus, all gestures might come to be imitated on the basis of an indirect translation process, those with auditory or visible feedback starting off in the indirect mode and those with kinesthetic feedback only shifting over to the indirect mode after an initial learning experience based on a short-lived period of direct translation.

This latter account has the advantage over Piaget's in admitting the existence both of precocious imitation in the neonate and of a more or less extended period of improvement during the infancy period. However, the postulated switch from direct to indirect translation does not accord very precisely with the developmental facts. Maratos (1973) observed that imitative tongue protrusion declined during the first weeks of life to become only sporadic from 2½ months onward. Piaget (1951), on the other hand, argues that the imitation of invisible gestures such as tongue protrusion emerges at around 8 to 12 months. Although the developmental decline and the subsequent re-emergence of imitative tongue protrusion might be regarded as evidence consistent with the shift in translation mode postulated above, it is not at all clear why according to this model there should be such a lengthy quiescent period from 2 to 8 months.

In summary, the choice between these two alternative accounts boils down to a choice between developmental change in either of two components in the mechanism for imitation: change in motor skill with zero or minimal change in the translation component, or change in the translation component over and above any changes in motor skill.

PSYCHOMETRIC ISSUES

In this section I raise three questions. First, can an infant's intellectual status predict later intelligence? Second, what contribution does heredity make to individual differences during infancy? Third, do psychometric data lend support to the claim that sensorimotor intelligence is organized into a set of sequential stages?

The Prediction of Later Intelligence

Evidence for Poor Predictive Validity

There is currently a firm consensus that infant intelligence tests have poor long-term predictive validity. As Brooks and Weinraub (1976) have indicated, severe doubts were cast on their predictive validity from the 1930s onward. As a reaction to such poor predictive power, a second wave of tests were devised in the 1940s, including the Cattell, Northwestern, and Griffiths tests; but these tests did not succeed in undermining the basic conclusion that infant tests of intelligence are poor predictors of preschool or school-age intelligence. Only at the lower end of the intelligence scale is reasonable predictive validity obtained. Thus Knobloch and Pasamanick (1960, 1967) found a substantial correlation between 1st- and 3rd-year scores ($r = .48$), and between 1st and 8- to 10-year scores ($r = .70$). In these studies, the Gesell Developmental Schedule was used to carry out the infant testing and the Stanford-Binet was used at later ages.

McCall (1979) has surveyed the evidence on the stability of intelligence from a variety of sources and reaches two conclusions. First, the correlation between performance on an infant test and subsequent IQ increases linearly with the age at which the infant is tested. Childhood IQ (i.e., averaged over the years from 3 to 18) correlates very poorly with performance during the first 6 months, approximately .12, and rises gradually to .26, .39, and .49 at 7 to 12, 13 to 18, and 19 to 30 months, respectively. Second, the prediction from infant test to later IQ tends to be stronger the younger the child. Thus scores during the infancy period correlate .40, .25, and .28 with IQ at 3 to 4, 5 to 7, and 8 to 18 years, respectively.

Even when predictive validity within the time period of infancy is examined, correlations are still relatively small across age. Thus when scores from 1 to 3 months are used to predict scores from 4 to 6 months, a time span of approximately 3 months, the correlation in test scores is .52 when averaged across several studies, but the correlation drops sharply as the time span is increased and is virtually nonexistent when performance beyond the first year is predicted. In contrast, McCall (1979) points out that the median year-to-year correlation for childhood IQ is dramatically higher, at .90.

Explanations of Poor Predictive Validity

Why should the predictive validity of infant intelligence tests, both within the period of infancy and from infancy to childhood, be so weak? One possible interpretation of the results is that scores at any given age are inherently unreliable, so that long-term predictive validity cannot be expected. However, when test-retest intervals are abbreviated to less than 30 days, then the correlation between tests is substantial (i.e., .80 and higher), a reliability that approximates that which can be obtained with IQ tests during childhood. Admittedly, investigators have not uniformly obtained such high reliabilities. Thus Horner (1980) found test-retest correlations ranging from .42 to .96 for the Bayley test depending on the age and sex of the subgroup under investigation. However, given the small size of the subgroups ($n = 12$), an occasional low correlation is unremarkable.

An alternative explanation for poor predictive validity is that the very nature of infant intelligence and childhood intelligence is different, at least with respect to the sources of variation between individuals. For example, it might be claimed that during the first 2 years of life, the infant is engaged in the acquisition of fundamental and routine sensorimotor skills; individual variation in such skills will show little relationship to the individual variation that is to be found in the more symbolic verbal and spatial skills that characterize later intelligence. This hypothesis is not unreasonable, but it does require some qualification. As stated earlier, the intelligence of retarded children is well predicted by their performance on infant tests of intelligence. Hence for a subsection of the population, there is a fairly strong stability between early performance and later intelligence. One possible explanation of this link is that the retarded child's performance is weighted toward performance items rather than symbolic items, and such items will be more similar to those found in tests of infant intelligence.

A third possible interpretation of the weak link between infant and childhood intelligence is that because infant tests have been devised for ease and reliability of administration, there has been a concentration on overt, easily codable motor or vocal behaviors. Thus it is conceivable that tests that introduced items that depend on more subtle observations of attention, habituation, concept formation, and so forth, rather than the more obviously codable motor skills, might show a stronger link with later intelligence. However, recent efforts in this direction (Kagan, 1971; Kagan, Kearsley, & Zelazo, 1978) have not uncovered much greater stability than that found in conventional tests of intelligence. Nevertheless, it is possible that tests that focus on the emergence of verbal comprehension skills will exhibit stronger correlations with later IQ. This expectation is consistent with the finding that predictions to later IQ become stronger as standard infant tests become more verbal in character (McCall, Eichorn, & Hogarty, 1977; McCall, Hogarty, & Hurlburt, 1972).

Heritability and Performance on Infant Tests

Genetic factors might influence infant intelligence in two important ways. First, they might influence individual differences in performance. Second, they might underpin a species-typical pattern of development in which very little individual variation is observed. I shall concentrate here on the first type of influence.

McCall (1979) examines three sources of evidence regarding individual differences in intelligence during infancy: parent/child concordance, sibling concordance, and twin concordance. Evidence from the Berkeley Growth Study and the Fels Longitudinal Study shows that the correlation between the level of infant intelligence during the first 2 years and the intelligence of the infant's parent is virtually nonexistent. This conclusion is valid whether the parent's adult intelligence or the parent's intelligence as an infant is entered into the correlation (Eichorn, 1969). Because parents and children share, on average, half their genes, these data provide no support for the claim that variation between infants in test performance is partially under genetic control. A similar conclusion emerges from data on siblings, who also, on average, share half their genes. Same-age sibling correlations are approximately .20 for any given assessment within the first 2 years, although this figure rises to .40 if four different assessments for each sibling are averaged (McCall, 1972). Both of these figures fall short of the correlations that can be obtained between siblings for childhood or adult IQ.

The third source of data on the heritability of individual differences comes from a comparison of MZ and DZ twins. If there is a strong genetic component to individual variation in intelligence during infancy, then MZ twins, who have identical genes, ought to show much greater concordance than DZ twins, who like sibling and parent/child pairs, share only half their genes, on average.

In a series of papers, Wilson and his colleagues (Wilson, 1973; Wilson & Harping, 1972) have argued that there is a significantly greater concordance for MZ twins than for DZ twins (.81 vs. .68, averaged over the entire infancy period). These data are problematic for two reasons. First, the DZ correlation is surprisingly high, especially when it is compared to the correlations discussed earlier for siblings and parent/child pairs. From a strictly genetic point of view, these three different types of pairs should exhibit a similar level of concordance. The obvious conclusion therefore is that environmental conditions, either pre- or postnatal or both, operate to increase the similarity of DZ twins. Such factors would presumably operate to increase the concordance of MZ twins, also, to either the same or, more likely, to a greater extent. Thus it is not clear either that the high absolute levels of concordance for MZ pairs, or their greater concordance than DZ pairs, necessarily reflects a strong genetic component to variation in infant intelligence.

The second problem with the data presented by Wilson and his colleagues has been pointed out by Nichols and Broman (1974). They noted that MZ twins show a higher incidence of severe retardation than DZ twins. Accordingly, the high overall concordance for MZ twins might be due primarily to the high concordance for low-scoring twins. To check this possibility, they eliminated twin pairs in which one twin scored less than 50 (on the Bayley scale) and found that the difference between MZ and DZ twins was eliminated. Nevertheless, when Wilson and Matheney (1976) eliminated low-scoring pairs from their original sample, they continued to find that MZ pairs had a higher concordance than DZ pairs (.81 vs. .62).

In summary, data from three different sources provide some measure of support for the hypothesis that a genetic blueprint exerts a strong influence on individual patterns of infant mental development, but the bulk of the evidence is inconsistent with such a hypothesis.

Stages in Infant Intelligence?

Stages Derived from Piaget's Theory

In a previous section, it was established that infant tests of intelligence have poor predictive validity across time in that the rank order of individuals is preserved in only a modest fashion. Here we consider a question about the organization of an individual's performance at a given point in development. To what extent is an infant's performance on any one item at a particular age related to performance on other items at the same age? Even though long-term predictive validity might be low, it could be argued that such lack of predictive validity reflects the fact that infant intelligence has a different organization at different points in development, but that at any given age, when a particular type of organization predominates, similar performance across disparate items is to be expected.

This question has not been systematically pursued by the creators of infant intelligence tests, but it is a question that arises from the sensorimotor scales that have been based on Piagetian theorizing. Uzgiris (1976) has noted that Piaget's account of cognitive development across the six content areas described in the introduction suggests that an infant's level of development is fairly uniform across the various content areas. However, there are certain difficulties associated with testing this prediction. Available evidence suggests that the transition from one stage to another within any particular content area is gradual rather than abrupt. Corman and Escalona (1969) have reported that infants rarely pass all the items associated with Stage *n*, for a particular content area, before passing any items associated with $n + 1$. This finding emerged for both their object permanence scale and their space scale. For infants who show behaviors straddling two stages, some decision must be made in order to assign them to a specific stage. However, Piagetian theory gives no clear guidelines as to how this should be done. Piaget commented on the infant's tendency to straddle two stages, as follows:

> It is perfectly normal that these behaviour patterns of the fourth stage are constituted sporadically from the middle of the third stage. . . . Inversely, it is evident that the behaviour patterns belonging to a given stage do not disappear during the following stages but conserve a role whose importance only diminishes very gradually (and relatively). (Piaget, 1952, p. 214)

Such a conclusion is compatible with the finding that although a group of infants typically pass through a sequence of items in a fixed order, the repeated testing of individual infants will sometimes reveal backsliding from one test occasion to another. Such regressions in the course of repeated testing have been noted by Kopp, Sigman, and Parmelee (1974) and by Uzgiris (1973). Inevitably such fluctuations in performance will tend to reduce the ease with which a consistent level of performance across different content areas can be observed.

Evidence from Retarded Children

From a variety of studies, it is clear that infants do not always exhibit congruent performance across content areas. One of the earliest investigations was carried out by Woodward (1959), who tested 147 mentally retarded children on three scales modeled on Piaget's observations: circular reactions, problem solving (the use of a string, support, rake, etc., to retrieve a desired object), and object permanence.

For the first two scales, 45% of the subjects were classified as concordant—that is to say they were classified as being at the same stage for both scales. For the relation between object permanence and a scale combining items from both of the first two scales, concordance was higher at 87%. Woodward suggested that the emotional instability of many subjects may have led to frequent false negatives and a consequent reduction in concordance. As we shall see, however, Woodward's finding that concordance is by no means universal has proved to be quite unexceptional.

Rogers (1977) tested 40 profoundly retarded children aged 8 to 14 years on four areas of functioning: object permanence, space, causality, and imitation. The tasks were in part based on existing instruments (Corman & Escalona, 1969; Miller et al., 1970), and in part developed from Piaget's observations. Although correlations between these four areas proved moderately high (.48–.67), the range of concordance (10–58%) was even lower than that observed by Woodward (1959). Finally, Dunst and Rheingrover (1981) found concordance levels from 28% to 39% depending on the mental age of the group in question. Nevertheless, using a variety of statistical techniques (hierarchical cluster analysis, factor analysis, and multidimensional scaling), Dunst and Rheingrover concluded that performance on two scales—object permanence and means-end analysis—did show some covariation. The possibility of finding more local types of congruence will be taken up again when we turn to normal subjects.

Evidence from Normal Infants

Turning to observations of normal subjects within the period of infancy, Kopp, Sigman, and Parmelee (1974) tested 24 infants on a longitudinal basis between 7 and 18 months. They made use of seven subtests, initially devised by Casati and Lezine (1968) and based on Piaget's observations. The seven subtests were drawn from four content areas: object permanence, the use of intermediaries, object exploration, and object combination. Only .9% of the infants exhibited a concordant performance across all seven subtests, and when all of the subtests were intercorrelated with one another for each age of observation, only a very small fraction of these intercorrelations proved significant, and none of these exceeded .60. The authors conclude: "It is clear from these data that sensorimotor development is characterised by unevenness and the capabilities exhibited in one area of performance have little relationship to abilities measured in another aspect of performance at a given age" (p. 692).

A similar conclusion was reached by King and Seegmiller (1973), who tested a variable number (51–27) of infants at 14, 18, and 22 months with the Bayley tests and seven Piagetian scales based on Uzgiris and Hunt (1966); see also Uzgiris & Hunt, 1975. The intercorrelations for the seven Piagetian scales at each of the three ages yielded mostly insignificant results. Uzgiris (1973) reported a similar longitudinal study based on 12 infants assessed between 1 month and 2 years on four Piagetian scales (see Uzgiris & Hunt, 1975). The vast majority of intercorrelations between these scales at each month of testing were insignificant, although for short periods of time (4–6 months; 5–8 months; 14–19 months) significant correlations between a particular pair of scales, but by no means all scales, were observed. Finally, Bates et al. (1979) looked at the intercorrelations in performance among four scales similar to those developed by Uzgiris and Hunt (1975). A group of 25 infants were studied between the ages of 8 and 13 months. All four measures correlated with one another at close to chance levels. Assessments of play behavior did manifest low correlations with the four scales. For example, symbolic play correlated with imitation and means-end relationships, whereas manipulative play correlated with object permanence. However, these correlations may simply reflect the fact that assessment of play and the Uzgiris and Hunt (1975) scales tapped similar behaviors. For example, symbolic play included pretending to use a telephone, which is an obvious case of imitation. Manipulative play included the emptying and filling of containers, which is similar to the skill of hiding and uncovering an object.

In short, these studies indicate that correlated performance between scales, where these scales clearly tap different behaviors, is the exception rather than the rule.

Supportive Evidence?

There are a small number of studies that, at first glance, appear to be exceptions to the negative picture presented above. Paraskevopoulos and Hunt (1971) carried out a cross-sectional study of children exposed to different rearing conditions. The authors administered tests of object permanence, vocal imitation, and gestural imitation to three groups: a home-reared group, a group being raised in an orphanage with a good staff/child ratio (1 : 3), and a group being raised in an orphanage with a poor staff/child ratio (1 : 10). Within each rearing condition, high intercorrelations between the three scales were found ranging from .78 to .93. Why should Paraskevopoulos and Hunt (1971) have obtained results that run contrary to those of virtually every other investigator? One likely explanation is that they used an unusual cross-sectional method in which children of various ages were assessed. It is quite conceivable that the rank order of subjects on each scale was strongly correlated with age, in which case the rank orders for a given pair of tests would intercorrelate with one another. Moreover, it is important to note that a correlation would be obtained even if subjects were advanced by a stage or several stages on one scale relative to another, because a rank order correlation is sensitive only to an individual child's ordinal position relative to other children for a given scale and not to the absolute level of performance. This interpretation gains weight from two additional points. First, the other investigators grouped subjects by age whereas Paraskevopoulos and Hunt looked at a wide age within each rearing condition. It is highly likely that the variance in individual performance across tests that is associated with differences in *age* is both greater and more stable than the variance that is associated with individual differences in *precocity* at any given age level. In the second place, Paraskevopoulos and Hunt (1971) themselves provide additional evidence showing that the level of performance in two different task domains is relatively independent: Whereas for the object permanence scale, development within the orphanage with a poor staff/child ratio was retarded relative to the other two groups, for the vocal imitation scale the home-reared group was relatively advanced and the two orphanage-reared groups equally delayed.

Fischer and his colleagues (Bertenthal & Fischer, 1978; Watson & Fischer, 1977) have also reported evidence that appears to support the notion of yoked development across task domains, but which on closer scrutiny, and in line with Fischer's own developmental theory (Fischer, 1980), supports the claim that task domains are relatively independent. Bertenthal and Fischer (1978) examined the relationship between object permanence, using the Uzgiris and Hunt (1975) scale, and a sequence of self-recognition tasks (discussed earlier in connection with the self-concept). Six age groups were tested between the ages of 6 and 24 months. Correlation between the two scales was quite high (.82), contrary to the authors' expectation of a low correlation. In addition, Watson and Fischer (1977) examined the relationship between the development of pretend play and object permanence in infants of 14, 19, and 24 months, and found a moderate correlation of .62. However, as noted in the discussion of the results obtained by Paraskevopoulos and Hunt (1971), to the extent that progress along any two developmental sequences increases with age, rank order correlations will prove significant provided a wide enough age range is used, because variation in infants' ages will lead to a fairly stable rank order across both sequences or scales. In line with this cautious attitude toward interdependence is the further result noted by Watson and Fischer: When stages were defined for both object permanence and pretend play in terms of Fischer's neo-Piagetian theory (Fischer, 1980), concordance of stage was observed for approximately half of the subjects only.

One final study by Fischer and his colleagues requires discussion. Jackson, Campos, and Fischer (1978) examined the development of object permanence while varying three factors: spatial factors regarding the type of displacement and hiding (e.g., big screens vs. small cloths), the nature of the object hidden (e.g., mother vs. inanimate object), and the degree of practice with the task. Infants were tested within a very narrow age band (6–8¼ months), so that concordant performance across these various manipulations is not likely to be attributable to an overall correlation of performance with age. The results indicated that the practice and task factors both produced marked variation in level of performance. On the other hand, the nature of the object hidden produced only slight variability in performance. This latter finding is important because it indicates that concordant performance can be obtained across some types of task variation even if a lack of concordance is the more common result.

Conclusions Regarding Piagetian Stages

The above review has indicated three conclusions. First, whenever a group of infants of a given age is examined for correlations or concordance across different developmental sequences or scales, low correlations and frequent lack of concordance are obtained. This conclusion holds for normal infants as well as retarded children. Second, if a wide age range is assessed on two developmental sequences or scales, moderate to strong correlations in performance across the scales may be found. However, such results provide no support for the claim that development within the two domains is interdependent rather than independent. If development on both scales is age linked, then the rank order for individuals will tend to coincide across the two scales producing a significant rank order correlation. Indeed, even if there were not a single example of stage concordance throughout the entire subject pool, a strong correlation might still be obtained. Thus reports of correlated performance on two scales, particularly where a large age range is used, indicate little more than the fact that performance tends to improve with age on several fronts. Third, and finally, there is some preliminary evidence that certain task manipulations do not alter the level of performance within a given developmental sequence.

Returning to the broader question of stages of development within the infancy period, we may say that there is ample evidence that infants' performance on a given scale improves with age such that tasks may be placed in a more or less invariant developmental sequence. Earlier in this chapter, the evidence pertaining to object permanence was discussed in this light, but the evidence is by no means restricted to object permanence (Uzgiris & Hunt, 1975) or to sequences based on Piaget's observations (Bertenthal & Fischer, 1978; Watson & Fischer, 1977). In this narrow sense, the concept of a stage of development remains useful for the infancy period. Much less useful is the notion that an infant's stage of development within one task sequence can be used to predict the infant's stage of development within other task sequences. In this respect, the pattern of development for the infant appears to be similar to that for the older child (Fischer, 1980) and for the adult (Harris & Heelas, 1979). Thus we should think of the infant's development as proceeding simultaneously, but not synchronously, along several relatively independent task sequences. In the future, it is to be hoped that investigators will attempt to demarcate the extent to which performance *within* any particular task sequence remains stable despite variability in task parameters (see Jackson et al., 1978), even though the level of performance *across* different scales—for example, object permanence and imitation—may be quite variable.

Stages Derived from Psychometric Data

The above conclusions apply most directly to task sequences that have been devised within a Piagetian or neo-Piagetian framework. Recently, an alternative approach to the question of stages has been explored by McCall and his colleagues (McCall, 1979; McCall et al., 1977) using longitudinal psychometric data on infant performance on California Pre-School tests (forerunners of the Bayley). McCall makes use of two types of data. First, he has examined longitudinal records in order to find out what the principal components of the test are at particular ages. Thus to give a simplified illustration, at 3 to 4 months a test might principally carry items concerned with the active production of perceptual consequences (head turning, banging, etc.). At 21 months, items might be principally concerned with budding linguistic abilities: comprehension, imitation, and vocalization. By examining the principal components at various ages, it is possible to discover periods in which the character of the components is altering slightly if at all, and periods in which the components alter markedly. By analogy with Piagetian stages, the former pattern would correspond to a within-stage period and the latter to a between-stage period.

The second source of data concerns the stability of individual differences both within and across such putative stages. Conceivably, despite the changing nature of the items that make up the infant intelligence tests at various ages, such items might all be manifestations of some single underlying intellectual ability, variably distributed across individuals. In this case, an infant who was precocious at head turning and banging would also be expected to be precocious at verbal tasks. More generally, the rank ordering of a group of infants should be preserved across several test occasions. As we have already seen, the data on the predictive validity of infant tests, even within the infancy period, render the hypothesis of a single intellectual ability untenable. McCall's stage-based framework permits a different question to be asked about predictive validity. We may inquire whether the rank order of individuals remains more stable within a putative stage than from one stage to another, especially where it is possible to equate the two time intervals. If stability is greater within stage boundaries than across stage boundaries, it becomes feasible to assume that infancy is a period in which a sequence of relatively distinct mental abilities wax and wane, each of them having an independent pattern of individual variation.

McCall et al. (1977) made use of data from the Berkeley Growth Study in order to check whether there were dips in the size of the cross-age correlations. These occurred at 8, 13, and 21 months. Moreover, analysis of the principal components indicated that the item composition of the first principal component tended to alter at these same ages, while remaining relatively invariant between these ages. Thus, taken together, the analysis of principal components and the longitudinal analysis of variation between individuals suggest that mental development in infancy is composed of a set of distinct stages or abilities, each having a particular content and a distinctive pattern of individual variation.

From an examination of the items characterizing the principal component within each stage, McCall

(1979) offered a description of five successive stages, which bear some resemblance to those described by Piaget and by Uzgiris (1976). In Stage 1 (0–2 months) most behaviors are under tight endogenous, particularly state-based, control. Test behaviors include reflexive looking, alerting, and visual tracking. Stage 2 (2–7 months) is characterized by acts that produce perceptual consequences. In Stage 3 (7–13 months), goal-oriented behavior emerges, in which means and ends are separated. In Stage 4 (13–21 months) infants can link one entity to another, including a name with its referent. Finally, in Stage 5 (21 months onward) relationships between entities can be symbolically coded (e.g., size relationships, locative relations, etc.).

Although McCall has adopted an original approach to existing longitudinal data, certain weaknesses are apparent. In the first place, McCall (1979) distinguishes sharply between what he refers to as developmental function and the study of individual differences. A developmental function is a species-typical developmental curve. Piagetian theory, for example, emphasizes the developmental function for various achievements and errors that are to be found across all infants during the sensorimotor period. In contrast, the study of individual differences emphasizes the rank order, and also the stability of a rank order across time, that can be observed when individuals are examined at various points along one or more developmental functions. McCall readily admits that the study of a developmental function and the study of individual differences in the growth of that function are independent fields of study. Nevertheless, he restricts himself to an examination of the developmental function by means of the study of individual differences. He does this in two ways. First, stages are in part identified by means of dips in the pattern of cross-age correlation. Second, stages are identified in terms of the principal components at various ages, but such an identification rests on an analysis of items showing variation between individuals. Items that show minimal or zero variation between individuals are not included in infant tests of intelligence for obvious reasons. Accordingly, species-typical achievements, particularly those that emerge at approximately the same time for all individuals, will not be included in a test of mental development. Thus despite his admonition to developmental psychologists that they have neglected the importance of developmental functions in their search for stable individual differences, McCall's methods are equally biased by a focus on individual differences.

A second problem with McCall's approach is that the diversity of test behaviors at a given stage renders a coherent account of the nature of that stage very difficult indeed. At present, McCall's characterization of a given stage—for example, the grasp of entity/entity relations—is too vague to permit sharp predictions about what behaviors should and should not be observed during that stage.

Third, and finally, McCall and his colleagues provide little direct evidence that items that fall within a given stage produce a concordant performance across a given sample of infants, such that performance on one item can be used to predict performance on other items at the same stage. Admittedly, the initial mode of construction of the infant tests will tend to guarantee that particular items are of an approximately equal level of difficulty at any given age. Moreover, from the fact that McCall (1979) has reported that rank order does remain relatively stable across certain ages but not others, it is tempting to conclude that some concordance across items will be found for those periods. However, such a conclusion is invalid. Suppose, for example, that for a given period of infancy, say 7 to 13 months, cross-age correlations are relatively stable. Such a result does not depend in any way on yoked performance across items during that period. Provided individual infants perform consistently, whether it be a good performance or a bad performance, on the same items, they could retain their rank order relative to other individuals. Such stability of rank order would obtain, even if the constellation of passed and failed items varies on a random basis from individual to individual, so that, for example, infant n consistently passes Items 1 to 5 but not Items 6 to 10, whereas infant $n + 1$ passes Items 2, 4, 6, and 8 but none of the remaining items. Nevertheless, given that infant tests make use of a wide range of items, and have been administered to large samples of infants on a longitudinal basis, they may yet provide us with important information about those items that do elicit concordant performance, but this is an empirical question for the future.

Psychometric Data: Overall Conclusions

We have reached three main conclusions in this review of psychometric data. First, an infant's performance on a test of intelligence predicts very little about later preschool or school-age intelligence. The most plausible explanation of such poor predictive validity is not that infant tests are inherently unreliable, but that variation in the symbolic capacities that determine performance on intelligence tests for children and adults has no measureable manifestation in infancy. It is important to note that this conclusion tells us nothing about whether or not infants are capable of symbolic or representational thought. They may be capable of such thought but exhibit little or no stable individual variation in that capacity during the period of infancy.

The second conclusion we have reached is that there is only limited evidence for the hypothesis that genetic factors play an important part in determining individual differences in performance on infant intelligence tests. Data based on parent/child and sibling concordance provide no support for the hypothesis, but there is some evidence, albeit disputed, based on the study of MZ and DZ twins. Again, it should be noted that this conclusion pertains only to individual differences. There may well be a genetically controlled species-typical pattern for which little variation between individuals is observed.

Third, and finally, not only is it difficult to predict how infants will perform in the future from how they perform now, it is also difficult to predict how infants will perform in one sensorimotor domain from their performance in another domain. It is conceivable that analysis of Piagetian tasks and also of infant intelligence tests will indicate that performance is congruent across a narrower range of task variation, but at present this is a research issue for the future rather than a well-established conclusion.

LANGUAGE AND COGNITIVE DEVELOPMENT

There are many aspects to language development: perception of speech sounds, articulation of those sounds, ability to take turns with an interlocutor, and acquisition of semantics and of syntax. I shall be concerned here with only one question: To what extent does the infant either comprehend or produce language by recruiting the conceptual knowledge that has been built up before the development of language?

Cognitive Prerequisites for Language Production

One of the earliest contributions to the debate regarding the relevance of early cognitive development for language was made by Sinclair (1971). Using Piagetian theory, she argued that the capacity for representation characteristic of Stage 6 was a crucial precondition for the emergence of productive naming and two-word utterances. This claim has been advanced in slightly different ways by a host of recent investigators into early language. Before looking at the evidence, it is worth dwelling on exactly what is being assumed in such a hypothesis and what sort of evidence ought to be collected to substantiate it. In fact, I shall argue that the plethora of findings in the area is marred by the absence of any serious consideration of these questions.

The Assumptions Behind the Hypothesis

Piaget, who uses a fairly stringent criterion for representation, argues that it emerges in Stage 6 of the sensorimotor period, when the capacity to search for an object despite invisible displacements of that object and also the capacity for delayed imitation and "insightful" problem solving emerges. From these various performances we can infer that the ability to represent in some way a hidden object or to represent a set of acts has emerged. However, it is important to notice that we cannot assume that these abilities have *only* emerged at Stage 6; indeed some investigators (Moore & Meltzoff, 1978) have argued that such capacities have emerged much earlier. At best, then, we can say that the capacity for some kind of representation has emerged by Stage 6, *if not earlier*.

If we turn to the production of language we can again assert that the production of words that make reference to absent objects or actions presupposes some kind of representation capacity. Where objects or actions are present in the immediate environment we can at best assume that words might be linked with some recognitive schema, which is triggered by a direct perceptual encounter.

What Sinclair and others have suggested is that the ability to represent objects and actions in search, delayed imitation, and insightful problem solving are preconditions for the ability to make verbal references to absent objects or actions. This claim contains at least two highly questionable assumptions. First, there is no a priori reason to think that the representational code that is used in the two cases is the same one. The way in which I represent the meaning of a word such as *dog*, linked as it probably is to a variety of dogs in a variety of settings, may have little to do with the way in which I represent the identity and location of a particular object in a particular location. As has been indicated in various sections throughout this review, the notion of a unique displaceable object is distinct from the notion of a particular class of objects, and there is little reason to suppose that their mental representations are inextricably linked.

Second, even if it is true that the mental code deployed in search tasks, for example, is the same mental code as that deployed in referring to an absent object, it does not follow that the ability to solve a particular search task is a prerequisite for the ability to refer to an absent object. This becomes obvious once it is admitted that both abilities depend on the coordination of a capacity for mental representation with additional skills: the ability to track an object or container and to engage in a sustained series of search actions at various containers in the case of advanced tasks of the object permanence sequence, and the ability to associate and produce a set of sounds in the case of speech production. To the extent that the timetable for the emergence of these additional skills is slower for search than for speech production, then advanced search skills may well emerge after rather than before various types of speech production, despite their deployment of a common mental code.

Accordingly, the cognitive prerequisites hypothesis, when examined closely, is actually much closer to what Bates and her colleagues (Bates, Benigni, Bretherton, Camaioni, & Volterra, 1977, 1979) have referred to as the ''shared-base'' model. This model assumes that certain cognitive and verbal abilities share a common component without assuming that the former are prerequisites for the latter. It is perhaps with this point in mind that most investigations of the early relationship between thought and language have looked for a temporal correlation between the two domains only; they have not sought to establish that the solution of certain cognitive tasks invariably precedes the attainment of certain language skills.

The Validity of Correlational Evidence

Let us suppose that a relatively high correlation emerges between, for example, the solution of Stage 6 object permanence tasks and some aspect of language development, even after the effect of age has been partialed out. What can be concluded from such a correlation? In the first place, it is obvious that the correlation might be attributable to the fact that language development is a precondition for object permanence. Second, and more plausibly, the correlation may be a result of some third variable that operates on both cognitive and verbal development, despite the absence of any causal link between the two. For example, if positive environmental influences exist both for early cognitive development and the development of language, such influences may well be correlated with one another. A home that stimulates cognitive development by the provision of toys and opportunities for exploration may also be a home where the infant will be frequently spoken to. Similarly, if cognitive and verbal development are at least partially under the control of maturational factors, correlated mechanisms may control maturation in the two domains. Under certain circumstances it may be possible to partial out the influence of such third variables. However, a final difficulty will still remain: A correlation between the development of language and thought may result from the existence of certain shared skills—a shared base, to use the terminology of Bates et al. (1977, 1979)—but skills other than those being targeted by the investigator. Thus most cognitive and linguistic tasks depend to some extent on the recruitment of attention and motor skills. Variation in these skills among infants may yield a correlated performance on a cognitive and a verbal task, whether or not the two tasks depend on some common representational code as hypothesized by the investigator.

Can experimental methods rather than psychometric methods provide less ambiguous data? The strongest form of support for a causal link between cognitive and verbal development might be a training study in which training is given in one domain, and generalization to the other domain is subsequently assessed. The cognitive prerequisites hypothesis predicts that generalization should be unidirectional: from cognitive development to language development. On the other hand, as Bates et al. (1977, 1979) point out, the shared-base model is compatible with bidirectional training effects. Such a study, if it were successful in showing either uni- or bidirectional effects, would provide strong evidence for there being a causal link between the two domains. Again, however, that causal link would be hard to interpret unless the investigator were sure that the effect of the training program was restricted to the particular prerequisite or shared component under scrutiny. Moreover, negative results would also be hard to interpret. Because of the potential importance of additional skills peculiar to either the cognitive or verbal domain, a training study might produce negative results despite there being a causal link between the two domains. For example, a search task and a naming task might share a common mental code for representing an invisible object. Hence it might be expected that any training on the search task that produced an acceleration in the ability to represent an invisible object would improve naming. This assumption ignores the possibility that additional skills required by the naming task, such as name retrieval or articulation skills, may put a ceiling on performance in that task, so that generalization of training from the cognitive to the verbal domain would not occur.

Before turning to look at the available evidence in more detail, it will be useful to recapitulate the points that have been made so far. Most investigators have adopted a correlational approach in looking at the early link between language and thought. A positive correlation between development in the two domains is hard to interpret. It may reflect the fact that certain cognitive skills are prerequisites for certain verbal achievements. It may also reflect the existence of some hypothetical shared base, such as a common mental code for representing absent objects. However, positive correlations are also compatible with a variety of other possibilities. First, there may be verbal prerequisites to certain cognitive achievements. Second, variables such as a stimulating environment or maturational status may operate on both cognitive and verbal development, irrespective of the presence or absence of a causal link between these two spheres of development. Third, even if such variables can be shown to have no effect, the component that is shared by cognitive and verbal development alike may not correspond to the component hypothesized by the investigator: It may involve attentional or motor skills, for example, rather than the use of a common representational code. Finally, even training studies would be difficult to interpret, because training might improve a component not included in the hypothesis, or fail to train additional skills necessary for generalization of training from one domain to another. With these problems of interpretation in mind, we may turn to an examination of the available evidence, which is predominantly correlational in nature.

Evidence Linking Early Cognitive and Verbal Development

Diary-Based Evidence

Ingram (1978) examined various diaries of language development, including that of Piaget (1951). His goal was to "attempt to determine the extent to which sensori-motor stages represent cognitive precursors to language development" (Ingram, 1978, p. 262). He does not specify which of the various content areas he sees as a primary prerequisite. Instead, he agrees with Piaget in assuming that sensorimotor development proceeds at approximately the same pace across the various content domains. Ingram comes to the conclusion that in Stage 5, the first words appear. These do not usually number more than 10; they are usually uttered only in the presence of a particular object or in connection with certain routine actions, but are not narrowly tied to any specific context.

In Stage 6, Ingram claims that there are several changes: First there is a spurt in vocabulary, and with the attainment of representation toward the end of Stage 6, reference to past rather than present events is made, multiword utterances emerge, and the question "What is it?" is used to ask the name of things.

Ingram's review suffers from several of the weaknesses outlined in the methodological critique put forward earlier. The evidence is based simply on the fact that the two lines of development appear to be roughly synchronous for several children. Such a correlation might be due to the fact that both developments are linked to age, much as locomotion and language comprehension emerge in a roughly synchronous fashion. However, Ingram's diary review offers no possibility of partialing out the contribution of age to the putative correlation. Even if this were possible, some other third variable such as environmental stimulation might still produce such a correlation. Finally, even if no such third variable could be found, language and cognition might both depend on skills other than the emergence of a capacity for representation.

Bloom (1975) summarizes her view of the relation between cognition and early language as follows:

> The different words that Allison used, and the way in which she used them, appeared to be functions of her underlying cognitive development (p. 267).
>
> The use of relational terms such as "more" and "there" predominate in the first half of the second year and noun forms, or references to classes of objects, do not come to predominate in child lexicons until the achievement of object constancy in the second half of the second year. (p. 268)

However, a cursory examination of Bloom's data reveals that these claims are based on very flimsy evidence indeed. First, Bloom observed only one subject. Second, she fails to provide any detailed evidence about Allison's stage of intellectual development, except as it is manifested in her utterances. Third, diary-based observations of apparent co-occurrence are vulnerable to all the objections mentioned above in relation to Ingram (1978).

Correlational Evidence: Normal Subjects

Zachry (1978) carried out a cross-sectional investigation of 24 infants between 12 and 24 months of age. Infants were assessed on both sensorimotor cognitive development and language in an effort to "test Piaget's general contention that representational thought develops before 'true language' . . . and . . . to indicate the specific sensorimotor precursors of the first sentences'' (p. 681). Cognitive development was assessed by means of the Uzgiris and Hunt scales (Uzgiris & Hunt, 1975) in all six of the Piagetian content areas. Only items relating to Stages 4, 5, and 6 were used because it was assumed that infants fell within or beyond this range. Spontaneous verbalizations were recorded during a free-play session with the parent or caretaker. Subjects were assigned to a stage for the various content areas on the basis of the highest item passed within each content area.

In order to relate progress in cognitive development to progress in language, Zachry (1978) rated infants in terms of the number of content areas in which they attained Stage 6 performance, and plotted this in relation to the number of different language categories employed by each infant. The results indicated that these two developmental functions increased in parallel. However, there was no obvious relationship between the attainment in specific content areas and the emergence of particular language categories. Perhaps even more disturbing for proponents of the cognitive prerequisites hypothesis is Zachry's observation that there was a rank order correlation of .75 between cognitive development as indexed by the number of areas in which Stage 6 had been attained and chronological age. Because it is a safe assumption that language development also correlates with age, the fact that number of Stage 6 attainments and language development correlates cannot be taken as evidence that the former is a prerequisite for the latter.

Corrigan (1978) offers one of the most cautious evaluations of the cognitive prerequisites hypothesis to date. In a longitudinal study of three children from the age of approximately 10 to 29 months, Corrigan examined the relationship between the development of object permanence and the development of language. Thus Corrigan's study differs from Ingram's and from Zachry's in that she focuses on a specific content area rather than the whole range of sensorimotor contents, and (in line with much of the psychometric evidence discussed earlier) she does not assume that the infant's progress in the various content areas is interrelated in any stagelike fashion. Language development was also assessed differently. Because the three infants were producing only single words for many observational sessions, the conventional mean-length-of-utterance index remained invariant. Accordingly, progress was assessed in terms of the gradual transition from nonlexical vocalizations to items that could be glossed as adult lexical items. Nonlexical items were assigned a score of .5 and lexical items a score of 1. Because there was an increasing tendency to use only lexical items, progress was reflected in terms of a transition from a mean language score of .5 to 1 and beyond. The object permanence scale was a more refined version of that developed by Uzgiris and Hunt (1975). Finally, unlike other investigators, Corrigan predicted only a moderate correlation between object permanence and language development because both develop with age.

The results indicated that development on the language scale and the object permanence scale were both correlated with age and with each other (from .68 to .97). However, once age was partialed out, the intercorrelation of the language scale and the object permanence scale dropped considerably for each child (to .18, .46, and 0).

Further analysis hinted that there might be some more subtle relationship between development on the two scales, but the evidence was slender: Near the time that object permanence was achieved, in the sense that the infant searched systematically back through a set of three screens to find the object that has been deposited invisibly at the first of the three, a slight spurt in vocabulary was observed. Moreover, for all three children the word *allgone* tended to emerge at around the same time.

Corrigan's evaluation of Bloom's proposals (Bloom, 1973) produced a negative picture. First, there was no evidence that function forms such as *more* were more frequently produced than substantives before the attainment of object permanence (as defined above), nor did they have any greater endurance because they did not appear in any more sessions than the substantives.

Overall, Corrigan's study provides no strong evidence for a clear and systematic relationship—even of a correlational nature—between object permanence development and language development. Moreover, Corrigan makes the important point that a particular Piagetian stage can be quite a lengthy business. The three children studied—John, Mindy, and Ashley—remained at Stage 6, which encompassed six different tasks, for 5, 6, and 7 months, respectively. Because a good deal of progress in language occurred during this period, investigators will have to be quite specific about which particular aspects of a given stage they believe to be prerequisites for a given development.

Correlational Evidence: Retarded Subjects

Moore and Meltzoff (1978) have taken a different tack from most other writers in speculating about the cognitive bases for language. Rather than concentrate exclusively on the way in which the infant's understanding of the world might be a possible basis for talking about that same world, Moore and Meltzoff point out that the infant also has to discover something about the nature of language before it can be used properly. Thus, for Moore and Meltzoff, the infant must understand language as a symbolic medium as well as a carrier of a particular message.

They suggest that there are four stages in the child's growing understanding of the medium. First, the infant fails to grasp that there is any link between an adult's utterance and some ongoing stage of affairs. Next, the infant begins to note that transformations of the world (e.g., objects disappearing or coming into view) are frequently accompanied by an adult vocalization. At this point however, the infant perceives no systematicity in the specific utterances that go with specific events. In the third stage, the infant notes that adults repeat specific vocalizations in a consistent fashion to accompany specific events but does not detect which particular vocalization goes with which particular event. Accordingly, the infant employs certain consistent but essentially idiosyncratic vocalizations to go with particular objects on the one hand, and particular transformations (actions, displacements, etc.) on the other.

Moore and Meltzoff also discuss the way in which the cognitive system will determine whether or not the infant can detect invariance in the physical world itself: invariance in the identity of particular objects despite their disappearance, rotation, and so forth; and invariance in the identity of particular transformations such as actions and displacements despite their being applied to a wide variety of objects. Such invariant objects and transformations must be detected if the infant is to perceive eventually that there are also certain invariant relationships between particular adult vocalizations and particular objects or events, as discussed above.

In order to provide support for these ideas, Moore and his colleagues (Moore, Clark, Mael, Myers, Rajotte, & Stoel-Gammon, 1977) observed a group that deviated from the normal pattern of cognitive development, namely a group of mentally retarded children, and checked whether or not there was a concomitant deviation in language development. An object permanence scale, initially devised by Moore (1973, 1975), was used to assess the cognitive development of a group of 11 Down's syndrome children ranging from 3 years 8 months to 5 years 3 months. In addition, they checked the mean length of the five longest utterances. Correlational analyses indicated that there was a strong relationship between the cognitive measure and both language measures, even when age was partialed out. Moreover, Moore et al. (1977) went on to partial out mental age on the grounds that variations in object permanence ability as well as language might be two independent symptoms of a third variable, namely intellectual status. However, when mental age (as assessed by the Bayley) was removed, there was still a strong correlation (.80) between object permanence and language ability.

This study provides one of the firmest pieces of evidence in favor of there being some relationship between cognitive status and language acquisition. However, even this study suffers from three important weaknesses. First, the study does not prove that object permanence abilities have any causal link with language development. As discussed earlier, such abilities might covary with language development because both cognitive and linguistic abilities are correlated with some third variable. The authors have provided some of the first evidence that obvious candidates for such a third variable, namely age and mental status, cannot account for the results. Nevertheless it is still possible, albeit unlikely, that environmental stimulation has produced the correlation. A second problem is that even when obvious third variables have been ruled out, a correlation between language and thought need not result from their deployment of an ability to detect invariance. As noted earlier, language production and search require several additional skills, including memory, attention, and motor skills. The status of Down's syndrome children on such skills could conceivably produce a common rank order for both language production and search. Third, and finally, Moore and Meltzoff (1978) do not clearly indicate why the length of utterance should be so firmly linked to object permanence. Although their theory does appear to make predictions about the ages at which consistent common and proper nouns might be acquired as a function of the development of object permanence, predictions that were not tested, it makes no specific link between object permanence and length of utterance. Indeed, most of their discussion regarding the detection of invariance in the physical world and concomitant invariance in the language medium itself pertains more directly to comprehension than to production. In short, what appears to be the strongest piece of evidence for a link between object permanence and language development is not informed by any theoretical analysis, except that which is tangential to the evidence available.

Conclusions

The evidence for a link between cognitive and verbal development has been reviewed and found to be weak. Two studies based on diary records of individual subjects offered no independent assessment of cognitive development, or, having done so, failed to show that the temporal link between cognitive development and language was anything more than two relatively independent developments, each associated with age. This skepticism is strengthened by correlational evidence derived from normal subjects: Where age was partialed out, the correlation between cognitive and linguistic status was trivial. Only one study based on Down's syndrome children (Moore et al., 1977, discussed in Moore & Meltzoff, 1978) provided correlational evidence that held firm when age and indeed mental status was partialed out of the correlation. However, such evidence provides only ambiguous evidence for a causal link between cognitive and verbal development: Both domains may be influenced by some hitherto unexamined third variable, such as environmental stimulation; or, more likely, the two domains may share a common skill that is ignored by the hypothesis under scrutiny.

Alternative Formulations

Bates and her colleagues (Bates et al., 1977, 1979) have provided an interesting discussion of the many potential relations between language and thought, of which three are especially relevant to the present discussion. First, certain cognitive attainments might serve as prerequisites to language development. Second, certain mental operations might be preconditions for carrying out specific cognitive tasks, such as object permanence, and certain linguistic tasks, such as word combination. This shared-base hypothesis differs from the cognitive prerequisites hypothesis in predicting that the emergence of successful performance in the cognitive and linguistic tasks will tend to be temporally correlated, but that performance in the cognitive task need not necessarily antedate performance on the linguistic task. Correlational evidence pertinent to these two models has been reviewed above, with the exception of the data collected by Bates and her colleagues; this will be examined below.

The third possible relation between language and thought is one of analogy. Consider, for example, the fact that there are certain parallels between the emergence of sentence embedding in language development and the use of embedded structures in the building of a hierarchically arranged mobile (Greenfield, 1978). Success on the former task is achieved by 5 years of age, but in the construction task only by 9 to 11 years. Here we have an analogous sequence of development within two separate domains. The temporal gap between development in the two domains strongly suggests that the two developments are not psychologically related at all, but that something about the two types of problems dictates a similar solution, or sequence of solutions in both cases. Bates et al. (1977, 1979) discuss an interesting example of a related issue in ethology. Different animals may exhibit similar solutions to a given survival problem because they are descendants from some common stock (similarity by homology), or alternatively because the range of solution is so restricted that similar solutions are found by different species (similarity by analogy). For example, duck feet and fish fins have a similar webbing structure. Homology would be established if it could be shown that the similarity was a result of some common inheritance. Analogy would be established, if in the absence of any common inheritance, the two species had independently evolved a similar solution to the problem of locomotion through water. Translating this back into the question of the relation between language and thought, we may note that parallel development in these two domains might be an example of homologous developments attributable to the fact that language and cognition have some common basis such as the capacity for representation, or an example of analogous developments because the two domains invite similar solutions or analogous sequences of solutions.

How can these three types of relationships between language and thought be distinguished from one another empirically? Bates et al. (1977, 1979) discuss several possibilities. First, the prerequisites model predicts that certain cognitive achievements will precede language development, whereas the other two models make no claims about sequence. As we have seen, most investigators have not examined the sequence issue, despite its importance for distinguishing the two alternatives discussed by Bates et al. (1977, 1979). The models also differ with regard to the effects of training. The prerequisites model predicts that where such effects occur, they should be unidirectional from thought to language; the shared-base model, on the other hand, can handle bidirectional training effects; the analogy model predicts no training effects at all. Training studies would be complicated by the potential need for additional skills for an effect of training to be shown; this point was raised earlier. However, because no investigator has attempted a training study, it need not be elaborated further.

Bates et al. (1977, 1979) also discuss the relevance of correlational data. They suggest that the prerequisites model and the shared-base model predict correlations between the domains of language and thought, whereas the analogy model does not. Strictly speaking, this is correct. However, as Bates et al. (1979) admit, the existence of a correlation does not eliminate the possibility of a mere analogy. For example, intuitive consideration of the evidence provided by Moore and his colleagues is quite compatible with the notion of analogous development. Object permanence scales typically contain items that vary in terms of the number of elements required for their solution. Thus simpler tasks involve a single visible hiding, more complex tasks involve several hidings, and very complex tasks involve invisible displacements between those several hidings. Clearly, in some loose sense the infant is being required to integrate more and more elements for task solution. In a similar fashion, longer utterances require the integration of more elements than do short ones. Hence it would not be so surprising if development in these two spheres ran in parallel. Second, to the extent that the environmental conditions that foster the development of search skills are also correlated with the environmental conditions that foster language development—or alternatively, development in both spheres depends on additional skills such as attentional or motor skills—one would expect progress in the two domains to be correlated even where age and mental age have been partialed out. Thus although the analogy model does not actually predict the existence of correlations, like the cognitive prerequisite and shared-base models, it is compatible with the existence of correlations between language and cognition.

There is one further point. The correlational approach probes development by looking at individual differences in rates of development, or more precisely by looking at the extent to which the rank order of individuals in one domain is similar to the rank order for individuals in another domain. Whenever there is little or no variation between individuals on their attainment within a given domain, correlations will not be found. The absence of a correlation is therefore compatible with similarity by analogy, with the existence of a shared base, and also with the cognitive prerequisites model.

In summary, both the presence and the absence of correlations between domains are compatible with all three models described by Bates et al. (1977, 1979). Given these weaknesses of the correlational approach, weaknesses that Bates et al. (1979) admit for the most part, it is disappointing that these same authors offer an avalanche of correlational data in an effort to provide support for the shared-base model. The main findings and their ambiguities will be reviewed briefly. The subjects were 25 infants, studied between the ages of 9½ and 12½ months. During four home visits at the ages of approximately 9½, 10½, 11½, and 12½ months, infants were assessed on four somewhat modified Piagetian scales: object permanence, spatial relations, means-end relations, and imitation. Various aspects of the infants' communicative and play behavior were also assessed, by means of a maternal interview as well as experimental observation.

The authors proceeded to correlate scores across sessions and across domains. So, for example, object permanence at the first observational session would be correlated with object permanence at the second, third, and fourth sessions as well as with language comprehension, gestural communication, and so on, at each of the four sessions. I shall concentrate here on only the links between communication and the neo-Piagetian measures of object permanence, spatial relations, imitation, and means-end relations. Although there were some relationships between play and communication, these varied in incomprehensible ways depending on whether play was assessed by means of a maternal interview or experimenter observation, and also depending on the language measure in question.

Performances on the object permanence and spatial relations scales were poor predictors of communicative development. These negative findings, especially those for object permanence, endorse the general conclusion reached earlier, with the exception of the findings reported by Moore et al. (1977). On the other hand, the two other cognitive scales—imitation and means-end relations—did produce modest correlations, both with gesture and with language development. Examination of the various aspects of language development showed that these correlations were more frequent for production than for comprehension. Why should this be the case? A partial answer is that language production, unlike comprehension, involves some of the same behaviors. Thus the Uzgiris and Hunt scale for imitation (1975) involves both vocal and gestural imitation, as does the use of gesture and the development of language production. Because the same behaviors are involved, the correlations are scarcely surprising. Such an explanation is less appropriate for the means-end scale. This scale taps the infant's skill in using an intermediary, such as a support or rake, to reach a goal object. Similarly, gestures and early productive speech are often used to get a human intermediary to reach a goal object for the infant. However, the correlation is of some interest because the same behaviors are not involved. On the other hand, it is not at all obvious how the correlations should be interpreted. First, Bates et al. (1979) treat them as evidence for their shared-base model, but we have seen that the other two models—the prerequisites model and the analogy model—are not incompatible with the existence of correlations between language and thought. Second, even if we accept the notion of a shared base, it does not tell us very much about what psychological operations are actually shared. On the one hand, it might be that infants who understand the use of inanimate tools are quick to understand how language and gesture can recruit animate intermediaries. On the other hand, we need not necessarily invoke a cognitive shared base. Active children who manipulate their environment may simply have more occasion to resort to gestural and linguistic performatives when they encounter an obstacle. Alternatively, parents who provide a physical environment where means-end relations can be discovered may be the most responsive to such performatives. Until we know which aspects of the means-end scale are predictive of language development, a question Bates and her colleagues are currently trying to answer (Bates et al., 1979), the findings cannot be interpreted with any certainty. At best, then, we may conclude that Bates et al. 1979) have reported some suggestive but many ambiguous findings.

The Development of Comprehension

Language and Thought Reconsidered: A Problem of Translation?

In the previous section, we saw that there was little consistent evidence that the course of cognitive development, at least when that course is defined in terms of Piagetian stages, is correlated with the timetable for language production. Further evidence that throws doubt on the usefulness of the cognitive prerequisites hypothesis or its variants comes from an examination of the course of development for comprehension. Although investigators have rarely acknowledged the fact, certain hypotheses about the link between language production and cognitive development have been framed in such a way that they ought to apply equally to language comprehension. Below, I shall examine evidence indicating that comprehension develops well ahead of production. We may draw two possible conclusions from this finding. First, we might conclude that the cognitive achievements deemed to be necessary for production have actually emerged considerably earlier, given that comprehension is so advanced. Alternatively, we may conclude that comprehension abilities have developed in the absence of such cognitive achievements. If we accept this second argument, it is also tempting to claim that the occasional synchrony between the emergence of particular cognitive abilities and particular aspects of language production is merely fortuitous. Whichever of these two conclusions is adopted, there will be little likelihood of predicting the rate of development of language production from knowledge of the infant's status on nonverbal cognitive tasks.

An alternative hypothesis is that the timetable for language development with respect to both comprehension and production depends on the ease with which a translation between available concepts and language can be made by the child (Harris, 1982). This hypothesis appears to have several advantages over the cognitive prerequisites hypothesis or its variants such as the shared-base model. First, it accepts the reasonable assumption that there is a language of thought (Fodor, 1976), which is nonverbal and must be translated into conventional language. It denies, however, that there is any simple link between developments in the language of thought and the acquisition of language. Thus the child's nonverbal cognitive achievements are poor predictors of language development, consistent with the evidence reviewed above. Second, it claims that the timetable of language development is governed, not by the availability of cognitive concepts as such, but by the ease with which they can be translated into conventional language. Such a translation process will be governed in part by the ease with which the infant can discern an adult's intended meaning. Thus concepts that are equally available to an infant may differ in the precocity with which they are translated by the infant into conventional language, and concepts that the infant has fully available may be mistranslated into conventional language. Third, in so far as the translation process from language to thought may not be equivalent to the translation process from thought to language, the above hypothesis is not embarrassed by the fact that comprehension typically precedes production.

Below, evidence is reviewed that illustrates these last two points: the lag between comprehension and production and the mistranslations that can occur as the infant struggles to map available concepts onto conventional language. The evidence to be reviewed relies on various methods: naturalistic observation by the experimenter, mothers' diary records, and experimental procedures. At least for older infants, it seems likely that these disparate methods yield concordant results. Thus, by the age of 13 months,

Thomas, Campos, Shucard, Ramsay, and Shucard (1981) found that experimental procedures using signal-detection analysis of infant looking confirmed mothers' reports of what nouns their infants did and did not understand.

The Rate of Growth of Comprehension

Benedict (1979) traced the development of comprehension in eight infants between the ages of 9 and 20 months. The results indicated that comprehension development began at around 9 months, whereas production typically began at about 12 months; similarly, the 50-word level was reached at about 13 months in comprehension but not until 18 months in production. As these two time spans imply, the rate of acquisition measured in terms of the mean number of new words acquired per month was different for comprehension and production. These results indicate that the spurt in vocabulary, which Bloom (1973) links to the acquisition of object permanence, has taken place approximately 3 to 5 months earlier for comprehension. Indeed, on the average, children understood 50 words before they were able to produce 10 words. For individual children, the number of words that were understood at the point that 10 words were produced ranged from 30 to 182, with a mean of 60 words. Thus not only does comprehension precede production for all children, but additionally the degree of that precedence is subject to considerable variation when individual children are examined.

An examination of the types of words that were understood and produced indicated several important similarities, and no substantial differences. For both comprehension and production, nominals (i.e., words for people, animals, and objects) composed more than half the vocabulary. Action words that either accompanied or elicited actions of the children or games in which they participated, formed the next largest category for both comprehension and production. Finally, words referring to attributes, and words expressive of various affective states and social relationships (e.g., want, hi, etc.), formed two relatively small categories for both comprehension and production. The only slight difference between the two vocabularies lay in the relatively greater proportion of action words in comprehension.

Understanding Word Combinations

Huttenlocher (1974) reported some provocative findings regarding the ability of a 14-month infant to understand contrastive items such as "Where is your shoe (nose)?" and "Where is Mommy's shoe (nose)?". A second, somewhat older child of 17 months was able to understand sentences in which three rather than two of the items were used contrastively, for example: "Give (show) Mommy (me) the baby's (your) bottle."

Sachs and Truswell (1978) assessed 12 children aged 16 to 24 months, none of whom had produced two-word combinations, for their ability to understand sentences containing two contrasting items, for example: "Kiss (bang) duck (car)." The results showed that children were able to respond correctly to each of the four instructions forming at least one complete set of contrasting two-word sentences. As the preceding examples suggest, children were not only able to comprehend sentences referring to relatively well-practiced and familiar activities (e.g., "Kiss Mummy"), they were also able to understand sentences referring to novel acts or at least novel combinations of acts with particular objects. They responded to sentences such as "Pat candle," "Tickle book," and "Kiss plane." Such evidence indicates that the child's understanding was not based on a separately acquired understanding of each of the four sentences composing a set of contrasts, but was based on some kind of creative comprehension process set in operation by hearing a particular sentence for the first time.

These data, particularly the findings with respect to the accurate comprehension of novel combinations, suggest that neo-Piagetians such as Bloom (1973), Ingram (1978), and Moore and Meltzoff (1978) have underestimated the abilities of the child by concentrating on production only. Whereas the emergence of two-word utterances does occur typically at around 18 months and might be related to completion of Stage 6 of object permanence or of Stage 6 in general, given its dependence on mental combination, the above data indicate that the understanding of novel combinations can occur before the production of a single two-word utterance, and by implication before the completion of Stage 6, although it must be admitted that Sachs and Truswell (1978) did not make any independent assessment of cognitive development in their subjects.

In the next section, we shall turn to the final area of comparison between production and comprehension: the consistent usage of certain substantives. In particular, we shall focus on the phenomenon of overextension, which appears to differ sharply in frequency for comprehension and production.

Overextensions in Comprehension and Production

Two recent studies by Gruendel (1977) and Rescorla (1980) provide us with a natural history of overextensions in the first months of language acquisition. Gruendel (1977) studied two children, one from 12 to 24 months, and the other from 13 to 25 months. During this period each child's productive vocabulary grew from 10 words to more than 130 words, and approximately 10% of these words were produced in an overextended fashion. Rescorla (1980) collected data on six children from the age of 12 months for a period of 6 to 8 months up to the point where each child had a productive vocabulary of approximately 75 words. Rescorla found that 33% of the total number of words produced by the six children were overextended one or more times. Overextensions were probably more frequent in Rescorla's study because she used more liberal criteria for overextension, and also because she focused on the first 75 words rather than the first 130. In any case, we can conclude that overextension is a significant aspect of acquisition, especially for words acquired early. Rescorla's description of one child's use of the word *clock* provides a simple illustration of the phenomenon. The child first used the word correctly for an unfamiliar picture of a cuckoo clock, and immediately afterward for his parents' alarm clock. He then extended the word to many other clocks, but also to other objects including watches, dials, bracelets, and a buzzing radio and telephone.

An early attempt to account for such overextensions was made by Clark (1973), who argued that word meaning can be composed of semantic features such as +male and +human and +married. The words *man* and *husband* share certain features (i.e., +human; +male), but husband has an additional feature (i.e., +married). Similarly, *father* might be composed of the features: +human; +male; +caretaker (roughly speaking, anyway). Clark (1973) pointed out that children who acquired the word *Dada* but attached to it only two features, +human and +male, would extend the word not only to their own fathers but potentially to any Tom, Dick, or Harry that they set eyes on.

However, there are problems for the feature hypothesis. In the first place, it is difficult to find a single feature that is common to the whole set of objects across which an infant might extend a particular word. Consider, for example, the following report by de Villiers and de Villiers (1978). Their son, Nicholas, learned to call the family dog by his name, Nunu, and then extended the word Nunu to other animals and birds as well as to furry objects such as slippers and coats. He also said it while cuddling a warm blanket. Already one can see that it is difficult to find a common feature across these various referents, unless it is something vague such as texture. Even if this is accepted, however, the most exotic extension reported by de Villiers and de Villiers is very hard to explain. Nicholas pointed to some black pitted olives on top of a salad and said "Nunu." His parents were puzzled until they realized that the black olives, which were wet and shiny, looked a bit like Nunu's nose. Although an imaginative feature theorist might be able to find a common feature linking dogs and blankets on the one hand and dogs and olives on the other, blankets and olives would appear to have no features in common. Rescorla (1980) confirms that such overextensions where no single feature characterizes all exemplars formed a substantial proportion (39%) of the overextended words in her study.

The second difficulty for the feature hypothesis concerns the failure to find overextensions in comprehension. If the young child thinks that the word *dog* means something like *animal,* in so far as it can be extended to sheep and horses as well as dogs, then if asked to pick out a picture of a dog, the child should as readily choose a picture of a sheep or horse as a dog. Similarly, Nicholas when asked to find Nunu ought to be as likely to come back with an olive or blanket as Nunu herself. However, in the two longitudinal studies reported above, a marked discrepancy was found between comprehension and production. Gruendel (1977) looked for overextensions in comprehension but found none. Rescorla (1980) also reports that there were numerous cases of a lack of symmetry between comprehension and production, although occasional overextensions in comprehension were noted.

Thompson and Chapman (1977) carried out an experimental study of the asymmetry. They tested five children between the ages of 20 and 27 months. In the initial sessions, the children's tendency to make overextensions was established by presenting them with various pictures to be named. For example, a child who overextended the word *doggie* would be presented with various appropriate referents (i.e., pictures of dogs), various referents likely to elicit an overextension (i.e., pictures of other animals), and various inappropriate referents (pictures of vehicles, household items, etc.). This procedure served to establish that the infants would produce the word for appropriate referents, would also produce it for overextended referents, but would not produce it for objects falling outside of the (overextended) category. All the words eventually selected referred to people, animals, or objects (e.g., *daddy, doggie, apple, ball*).

In examining the children's overextensions, it was apparent that a common feature governing their usage was often hard to discover. For example, one child used the word *apple* for pictures of apples, bananas, pears, and a teapot. Neither edibility nor a round shape characterizes all of these objects. These data fit in with the observations of de Villiers and de Villiers (1978) and of Rescorla (1980), cited earlier.

In the final two or three sessions with the children, their comprehension was tested by presenting pictures of an appropriate referent together with an overextended exemplar (e.g., pursuing the above example of *doggie,* a dog and a sheep); or alternatively by pairing an overextended exemplar with an inappropriate referent (e.g., a sheep and a train); or finally by pairing two inappropriate exemplars (e.g., a bicycle and a train). For each pair of pictures, the experimenter cited one of the child's overextended words and asked the child to indicate which picture depicted the named item. Subjects chose the correct referent rather than the overextended exemplar for 12 of the 20 words. Correct choice was especially apparent for the 7 words referring to people. When the overextended exemplar was paired with an inappropriate exemplar, the majority of choices were directed toward the overextended exemplar. When there were two inappropriate exemplars presented together, children typically refused to make a choice.

These results argue against the missing feature hypothesis, which predicts that comprehension data should mirror production data. One way to account for the discrepancy between comprehension and production is to adopt a "limited vocabulary" hypothesis—that is, to argue that the child knows the full meaning of the word, as revealed by the comprehension data, but produces overextensions so as to make up for a limited vocabulary. Thus, not knowing the word for horse, the child produces instead a word for an admittedly different, but nonetheless similar animal whose name is known, such as a dog. However, this account fails to acknowledge that overextensions were sometimes observed even in comprehension, although in the minority of cases and never in connection with people. Admitting this problem for the limited vocabulary hypothesis, Thompson and Chapman (1977) develop two alternative accounts, but a subsequent report by Fremgen and Fay (1980) indicates that the limited vocabulary hypothesis may still be the best explanation of the data. They tested a large number of children in much the same way as Thompson and Chapman (1977), with one important modification: Apprehensive that with repeated testing subjects might select an overextended exemplar because their initially accurate choice of a correct exemplar was succeeded by another trial in Thompson and Chapman's study, (1977) Fremgen and Fay (1980) tested each child only once on a word. Their results were clear-cut. With 16 children tested on a total of 27 words, they found no instance in the comprehension test of overextension. These results appear to provide strong support for the limited vocabulary hypothesis: Asked to select a dog from several animals, children can do so; but not knowing the name of certain animals, such as horses and sheep, they overextend the word *dog*.

However, the limited vocabulary hypothesis does oversimplify the situation somewhat. Fremgen and Fay (1980) provide evidence showing that it is not the case that children who overextend the word *dog* to a sheep know nothing about the word *sheep*. When the overextended exemplar (e.g., a sheep) was named by the experimenter appropriately and subjects were asked to select it from a group of four pictures, they did one of two things. They either refused to make a choice, suggesting in accord with the limited vocabulary hypothesis, that they did not know the name at all. Alternatively, they correctly chose the sheep, indicating that they understood the correct name although they themselves had been unable to produce it. Thus, Fremgen and Fay (1980) refine the limited vocabulary hypothesis as follows: Children may suffer from a problem of limited vocabulary either because they do not know the word and would not recognize it, or because they cannot retrieve the word themselves but would recognize it. In either case, however, the result is the same: the production of an overextended substitute.

I am not convinced that Fremgen and Fay (1980) are correct. The following hypothesis illustrates the possibility that it may not be easy for a child to map concepts onto language, and such mapping problems may be especially acute for production. We may assume that children bring to the language acquisition task concepts organized around a prototype, as discussed in the section on identity. Such concepts may be fairly detailed, reflecting a narrow concept such as the category of dogs, or less detailed, reflecting a wider concept such as the category of animals. On hearing a dog called "dog," the child has no way of knowing the level of generality the term implies. For all the child knows, *dog* may actually mean *animal*. Thus the child will tend to associate the word both with the category of dogs, and the category of animals, and will use the word *dog* for instances of either category. These assumptions explain overextensions. Why, according to this hypothesis, are overextensions so infrequent in comprehension? We may use the prototype notion again, by assuming that the child selects from the available items the exemplar most similar to those prototypes that have been associated with the word *dog*. A dog will be similar both to the child's dog and to animal prototypes; an overextended exemplar such as a cat or sheep will be similar to the latter only. Thus, given a choice between an appropriate and an overextended exemplar, the child will select the appropriate exemplar, despite not knowing the proper range of extension of the term being used.

What will the child do, however, if no correct exemplar is available? Recall that Thompson and Chapman (1977) paired overextended exemplars with completely inappropriate exemplars. No correct exemplar was available. Under these circumstances, children should tend to choose the overextended exemplar, and this is what Thompson and Chapman (1977) found. Moreover, it is likely that a similar situation will sometimes arise during naturalistic observation: The child will be unable to find a correct exemplar and will choose an overextended exemplar. Consistent with this expectation, Rescorla (1980) reports occasional overextensions in comprehension.

How can we distinguish the limited vocabulary hypothesis of Fremgen and Fay (1980) from the alternative outlined above? The two hypotheses differ on one crucial point. The limited vocabulary hypothesis assumes that the child really knows the meaning of *dog,* but not knowing the correct word for sheep, overextends *dog*. The alternative hypothesis that I have proposed claims that the child does not know whether dog means *dog* or *animal*. The two hypotheses make different predictions about what should occur when the child begins to acquire words for other animals. Fremgen and Fay (1980) should predict that once the child has overcome vocabulary limitations, overextensions should stop. However, the child who is not sure whether *dog* covers all animals, or just dogs, may continue to use the word *dog* for cats or sheep even after acquiring the words *cat* or *sheep,* just as adults use both the word *animal* and the word *dog* to make reference to dogs.

Rescorla (1981) reports that overextensions do not immediately disappear when a more appropriate term has been acquired. For example, all of Rescorla's six subjects overextended the word *car*. Although all subjects did eventually narrow their usage of this term, three subjects were observed to overextend the word even when they had acquired other vehicle terms such as *bike, truck,* and *bus*. Thus the acquisition of adjacent terms may help to limit overextensions but there is no indication that they do so immediately. To the extent that the child should, in the long run, come to acquire a variety of words associated with a given abstract prototype (e.g., *dog, cat, sheep,* associated with the abstract prototype for animals, and *car, bus, truck,* associated with the abstract prototype for vehicles), the tendency to use any single term in an overextended fashion should eventually be weakened.

Language and Cognitive Development: Conclusions

The cognitive prerequisites hypothesis and its variants are not unreasonable, at first glance. Starting from the assumption that speech involves the translation of ideas into language, it predicts that the infant must be able to solve particular nonverbal cognitive tasks (C) that tap those ideas, before productive language (L) will be found. This prediction about the temporal sequence of development has for the most part been tackled in a somewhat indirect fashion by looking at the extent to which infants advanced in cognitive development are also advanced in language production.

Closer inspection of the hypothesis and the evidence for it reveals a thicket of problems. Where negative evidence is obtained—and for the most part this has been the outcome of most recent research—it is still possible to hang on to the cognitive prerequisites hypothesis: First, low variation between individuals in the rates of development of either C or L may reduce or eliminate correlations between the two domains despite the fact that C is a prerequisite for L; second, tasks that test C or L may require the recruitment of additional skills (e.g., manual skills for C, articulation skills for L), and such additional skills may also serve to eliminate any temporal link between the manifestations of C and L.

On the other hand, where positive correlations are obtained the picture is equally unclear. The existence of shared skills (e.g., memory and attention skills) across C and L may have produced the correlation, rather than the capacities targeted by the experimenter. Equally, environments that stimulate C may stimulate L whether or not they share any skills or capacities.

An examination of the development of comprehension offered a less ambiguous way of evaluating the cognitive prerequisites model. Although investigators have rarely been explicit about the matter, it seems unlikely that comprehension would rest on a different set of cognitive achievements from production. Accordingly, one might expect speech production and comprehension alike to develop in approximate temporal synchrony, and to both depend for their emergence on a common set of cognitive achievements. The available evidence shows, however, that in several aspects of language that have been targeted by advocates of the cognitive prerequisites hypothesis—namely the rate of vocabulary growth, the ability to handle word combinations, and the consistent use of substantive forms—production lags behind comprehension. The existence of this lag indicates that it is most unlikely that the timetable for production is governed simply by the emergence of certain cognitive prerequisites.

One possible explanation of the lag, consistent with current versions of the cognitive prerequisites model, is that comprehension and production recruit different cognitive categories. This seems highly unlikely, however, given the marked overlap in content for the two domains.

To explain the existence of the lag despite similarity of content, an alternative to the cognitive prerequisites hypothesis was proposed: It was argued that the timetable for both comprehension and production may depend, not on the emergence of ideas as such, but on the ease with which a translation can be effected between thought and language. Because this translation moves in one direction for comprehension and the reverse direction for production, it is conceivable that the two translation processes are of unequal difficulty, such that production lags behind comprehension.

Finally, one asymmetry between comprehension and production was examined in more detail: Overextensions are rare in comprehension but characteristic of production, an asymmetry that is inconsistent with feature-based models of semantic development. A more promising explanation of this asymmetry focuses on the translation processes involved and is therefore consistent with the above hypothesis.

FINAL CONCLUSIONS

Three questions were raised in the introduction regarding the roles of interpretation, of experience, and of representation. We may now return to these issues in the light of the evidence reviewed.

The Role of Interpretation

The conflict over the role of interpretation was most clearly seen when the theories of Piaget and Gibson were compared. With regard to crossmodal integration, depth, object permanence, and the self, Gibson has emphasized the richness of information that is directly available to the infant. Piaget, in contrast, has argued that in the same four areas the infant must gradually come to reinterpret impoverished or misleading sensations in terms of constructed intellectual categories. The evidence presented suggests that Piaget has underestimated the information available to young infants, and in several cases has also ignored infants' capacity to detect that information. On the other hand, there is ample evidence that infants do modify their interpretation of that information as Piaget has argued. To take three examples, young infants can detect depth information but show no fear of depth; they can detect a new place of hiding but return to an old one; and they can detect matched inputs in the same place while showing no surprise at conflicting inputs. In all of these areas, it looks as if infants only gradually come to learn that their actions will be associated with particular consequences: Venturing over the cliff may lead to a fall; search at an old hiding place rather than the most recent one can lead to a failure to find the desired object; orienting to one place with eyes and hands or eyes and ears typically reveals matched inputs across modalities.

Should we then agree with Piaget's conclusion that infants construct cognitive categories with which to reinterpret ambiguous or misleading stimuli? I prefer an alternative conclusion: Infants are not imposing an intellectual category on inherently ambiguous data, but coming to detect the correlations in the data that their actions reveal. Thus infants come to impregnate initially neutral stimuli with knowledge of the perceptual consequences they signal. Such a conclusion allows us to see cognitive development as a matter of more skilled detection and anticipation rather than intellectual construction. The clearest example of the difference between these two approaches was discussed earlier in connection with object permanence. Provided we view the infant as attempting to locate an object rather than speculating about its permanence, we can see how the infant will gradually discover that certain types of disappearance must be followed by search in a particular direction if the object is to be found again.

Such an approach is, in fact, not far from that adopted by J. J. Gibson (1979) in his theory of affordances. He too argues that perceptual data can come to specify certain consequences for action, and these can be picked up in the course of interacting with the world. Nevertheless, there are two reasons, in my view, for not agreeing completely with Gibson. First, as we have discussed in connection with category formation, even basic perceptual processes are not a simple matter of detection. Infants are capable of averaging across category instances so that a previously unseen stimulus that corresponds to that average is seen as highly familiar. Paradoxically, then, although "intellectual" categories such as object permanence can be redefined so that they involve no more than the capacity for detecting and anticipating the location of an object, the process of perception itself cannot be defined so readily in terms of detection; the infant extrapolates beyond the perceptual information that is actually given.

The second problem with Gibson's approach is that it tends to see development as an increasingly sophisticated pickup of information. This sanguine view does not leave much room for the way in which infants are led astray by their own expectations. For example, the infant will turn away from an object visible at a new location and search at an old one. In short, the ability to detect structure leads to the expectation of structure, and such expectations may be false.

The Role of Experience

The role of experience is intimately connected to the role of interpretation. In the introduction, two possible roles for experience were described: Experience might extend an initial kernel of already objective information processing, so that the infant comes to see differences more acutely and similarities more widely. Alternatively, experience might permit the infant to revise false ideas about the world. In deciding between these two approaches, we may note first of all that the capacity of the young infant for detecting information is much greater than was envisaged by Piaget. First, the neonate is equipped with a variety of behaviors that are adjusted to a three-dimensional space. Second, within the first months of life, the infant can use information in one modality to guide the receptors for a second modality and is attentive to correlations across modalities when they are available. Third, the neonate can discriminate between different types of object disappearance and can imitate invisible gestures. On the other hand, an important role does remain for experience. Even if the infant exhibits appropriate actions in a variety of situations, these are frequently unaccompanied by the appropriate expectations. Thus, although infants of 4 to 9 months will reach out for a visible object, the majority of recent reports indicate that they are not surprised at finding an impalpable object there. In the course of a few trials, infants of the same age can learn to turn toward the place where an object will reappear, but they are not obviously surprised if it fails to reappear, nor do they adjust their visual search if the object disappears in a different direction. It appears then that experience plays a role not so much in leading to the integration of initially separate schemes, as Piaget argued, but in teaching the infant the perceptual consequences of schemes that are already activated by the appropriate sensory circumstances.

Nevertheless, it is important to note that we have very little experimental information on the exact way in which the infant extracts information from experience. We have Piaget's own suggestive observations and we have a handful of learning experiments. Ideally, we need to know what changes can be brought about in the infants' expectations by means of laboratory training studies, and we need to check the ecological validity of such training studies by watching the infants' spontaneous exploration outside of the laboratory. Such a two-pronged approach is necessary because the fact that changes can be brought about in one way within the laboratory is no guarantee that such a training study replicates the natural learning conditions for the infant outside the laboratory.

Perhaps the most suggestive results reported in this chapter regarding the role of experience come from studies of perceptual categorization: Several experiments have indicated that the breadth of a constructed category is determined by the heterogeneity of the infant's prior experience. Dimensions of experience will come to be ignored even when a new value along that dimension is presented. Such findings ought to be replicated outside the laboratory by showing that infants exposed to a variety of instances of a particular category of objects will have formed a broader category than infants exposed to one or two instances only.

The Role of Representation

Two conclusions have been reached with respect to representation. First, if we examine the developmental evidence, we should be cautious in accepting Piaget's claim that the capacity to represent an invisible state of affairs is absent until the end of the sensorimotor period. The most interesting evidence has been provided by Meltzoff and Moore (1977), who found that neonates could imitate previously exhibited motor gestures. Additional evidence is furnished at a later stage of development by studies of perceptual categorization. The infant of 10 months exhibits habituation to a stimulus that has not been seen before but that corresponds to a mental prototype. An ability to use such a prototype appears to demand an ability more akin to recall than to recognition. The apparently familiar stimulus has not actually been seen before and is not therefore in any true sense being recognized. Conversely, a previously seen stimulus that could be truly recognized is seen as less familiar so long as it does not correspond to the stored prototype. Thus the distribution of attention is governed less by recognition than by the recall of previously encountered stimuli, or rather by the recall of some schema abstracted from those stimuli.

The second conclusion is that it may be illegitimate to think of the capacity for representation as emerging in a unified fashion at any single point in development. We have just seen that the capacity to recall previously seen motor gestures is present in the neonate, and that the recall of a category prototype is available before the end of the first year. The ability to represent an invisible trajectory, on the other hand, may, as Piaget argues, be attained only at the end of the sensorimotor period. These diverse developmental functions all point to the conclusion—commonplace among students of adult memory—that the process of recall is not a single process but varies with the nature of the materials.

Finally, we may turn to two general issues that have emerged repeatedly in the course of this chapter and that are in certain respects mirror images of one another. First, to what extent is the infant's progress in one domain independent of progress in another? Second, where developmental progress necessarily rests on an integration of domains, how can such progress be best understood?

The Independence of Task Domains

The psychometric data on infant intelligence suggests that it is probably time to abandon the notion of developmental synchrony across a wide variety of task domains. Much more important is a deeper consideration of why some tasks within a domain are more difficult than others. Thus the Piagetian approach to infant intelligence needs bisection. His emphasis on the importance of ordinal sequences remains an enduring contribution, but the implication that infants' progress in any one domain is synchronous with their progress in another has not been upheld by the psychometric data.

With regard to the ordinal sequence of object permanence, a considerable effort has been expended in attempting to establish whether or not Piaget's interpretation of the sequence is correct. An explanation that is at once more inclusive than Piaget's in stressing infants' difficulties with changes of position as well as disappearance, and yet more restricted than Piaget's in not being linked to any across-the-board emergence of representational skills, can best handle the data currently available.

Such analytical work indicates that even where an ordinal sequence may, in part, constitute what Brainerd (1978) has called a measurement sequence, experimental analysis is still required to establish what particular skills are improving within a sequence. Moreover, the existence of a measurement sequence does not indicate how far the infant can transfer the skills that are assumed to develop within any such sequence. Thus Jackson, Campos, and Fischer (1978) have demonstrated that certain aspects of the object permanence task may be altered without leading to fluctuations in levels of performance (e.g., the nature of the object hidden), whereas other changes (e.g., the type of screen) do produce fluctuations. These data indicate that although stages may not exist across a wide task spectrum, we should not abandon the search for stability in the level of performance within a narrower task spectrum.

The same theme of asynchronous development also emerged from a review of so-called cognitive prerequisites to language. The evidence suggests that the timetable for language development is not dictated by nonlinguistic cognitive achievements, and indeed even when the occasional correlation between the domains of language and thought is obtained, its interpretation is fraught with difficulty.

Translation Between Domains

In the course of reading through the various content areas—crossmodal integration, imitation, and language development—the reader may have noticed a recurrent question and a recurrent set of methodological issues. It is worthwhile focusing on this commonality in a more explicit fashion. In these various areas, the question arises as to whether events, ideas, or patterns of stimulation in one domain can be translated into a corresponding set of expectations or actions in another domain. Various illustrations of such translation processes are illustrated in Figure 7. The figure makes clear that any failure to observe the activities associated with execution (the boxes furthest to the right) can be attributed to a breakdown in at least three locations: the detection phase, the translation phase, and the execution phase. Investigators have tended to focus on one of these phases with respect to any particular translation problem while neglecting the others as possible loci for failure. Thus proponents of the cognitive prerequisites hypothesis with regard to speech production have concentrated on the perception or recall phase, that is, the extent to which the infant can come up with the ideas that can be translated into

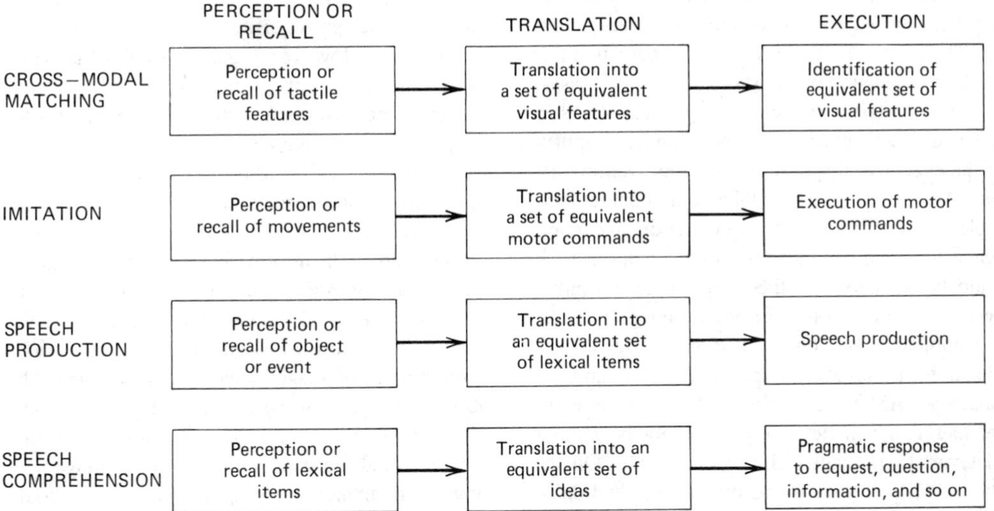

Figure 7.

speech. Conversely, investigations of the development of imitation have focused on the development of the translation component, and in connection with delayed imitation on the recall component. However, as the review of the relevant evidence has shown, it is equally plausible to suppose that the age changes are actually located in components different from those targeted by the majority of investigators. To review briefly: With regard to crossmodal integration, the early emergence of the ability to detect crossmodal correlations suggests that development may take place exclusively in the capacity to detect and recall an object in one modality, or to select an object in a second modality. The translation component may remain invariant with age. Certainly where the relevant controls have been included (Bryant, 1968, 1974), age changes may be attributed exclusively to within-modal discriminative capacity and not to the translation component.

With regard to language production, investigators have focused almost exclusively on the detection-and-recall component, but this seems unlikely to be the brake on language production because comprehension presupposes the same component but exhibits a developmental function that starts earlier and grows faster. Consideration of the other two components suggests two possibilities. First, the executive processes associated with comprehension—obeying instructions, answering questions nonverbally by looking or pointing—may be simpler to carry out than the production of speech sounds. This seems unlikely, however, given that meaningless vocalizations can be made both before and during the emergence of meaningful vocalizations. Accordingly, the most plausible candidate for a brake on the rate of growth of productive speech would appear to be the translation component. This hypothesis implies, as discussed in an earlier section, that the translation component is asymmetric in that moving from ideas to lexical items is harder than the reverse process, although no detailed explanation for this asymmetry has been advanced.

Turning finally to imitation, it was argued that the capacity to imitate single isolated gestures, together with the fact that the neonate is unable to generate complex sequences of movements, raises the possibility that the brake on development with regard to imitation is located in the execution component, and not, as is usually supposed to be the case, in either the recall or translation of perceived gestures.

The above review, then, indicates that questions of translation or mapping can be misleading. Problems can arise in any of the three components, and if the above analysis is only partially correct, investigators have mistakenly focused on one component to the exclusion of the other two. Having indicated the dimensions of the problem and its implication for three different areas, we may turn to two related issues: one methodological, the other theoretical. First, we may ask what strategies can be adopted to locate what have been referred to in passing as developmental brakes. The second issue concerns the nature of such constraints, once they have been diagnosed.

Taking up the methodological issue, it is immediately apparent that successful execution implies the successful function of the perception-and-recall phase on the one hand and the translation phase on the other. Unsuccessful execution is more ambiguous. The problem may be located in perception or recall, in translation or in execution. In such cases, the methodological challenge is to devise tasks in which successful execution is possible by simplifying the executive response or by circumventing the translation component. To take some concrete examples, if the lag between production and comprehension involves the translation component, it would be unlikely that the adoption of a simpler executive process would eliminate the lag. Thus the developmental function ought to be similar for vocalization, nonverbal gestures, and American Sign Language (ASL), in so far as the translation of meaning into vehicle will presumably be similar whatever the particular choice of vehicle. On the other hand, if it were found that the production of ASL among children of deaf parents was noticeably in advance of the production of speech among children of hearing parents, this would be reasonable grounds for the conclusion that the developmental brake on productive speech was located in the executive component. Evidence on this issue is mixed: Bonvillian, Orlansky, and Novack (1981) report that the onset of language production was earlier for signing children, but combinations were produced much closer to the norms for spoken language. Clearly such research will be important in the future as a means of evaluating the cognitive prerequisites hypothesis as well as the translation hypothesis advanced above.

An example of circumvention of the translation component can be given from the study of crossmodal integration. Bryant, Jones, Clayton, and Perkins (1972) found that infants of 8 months could solve a crossmodal tactual/visual problem with one shape but not another. Were the infant to be tested on visual/visual and tactual/tactual matching tasks as well as a crossmodal task with the same shape, it would be possible to establish whether the difficulty lay in the reception of the tactual information, its translation into a visual equivalent, or the selection of the visual match (Bryant, 1968).

Turning finally to the theoretical issue, the evidence indicates that a developmental brake may be variously located in the perception/recall component, the translation component, or the execution component. If the perception/recall component is assumed to be a prerequisite, but the developmental brake is located further along the system in either of the other two components, it is a waste of time to look for correlations between the development of the perception/recall component and the execution component. This seems to be why so little evidence for the cognitive prerequisites hypothesis has been forthcoming. However, Figure 7 also illustrates that even in the absence of correlational evidence a hypothetical prerequisite may actually be a prerequisite. To put the point another way, the development of any system of skills will be dictated by the pace of development of the most retarded component.

Accordingly, just as we have ultimately become skeptical about the information that correlational evidence can provide regarding the relationship between language and thought, we should extend the same point to the asynchronies found for the various content areas of Piaget's sensorimotor stages. The absence of a synchrony between Stage 6 of object permanence and Stage 6 of imitation—or, for that matter, the absence of a synchrony for Stage 4 of object permanence and Stage 6 of imitation—should not blind us to the possibility that one may be a prerequisite for the other, or that the two tasks may share a common component of some kind. Equally, however, because the evaluation of such claims is so tricky, it may be more fruitful to try to find out what constitutes the developmental brake for any given cognitive system rather than the list of prerequisites for that system. Paradoxically, a developmental brake is by its nature at the cutting edge of developmental change.

REFERENCES

Acredolo, L. Development of spatial orientation in infancy. *Developmental Psychology,* 1978, *14,* 224–234.

Acredolo, L. P. Laboratory versus home: The effect of environment on the 9-month-old infant's choice of spatial reference system. *Developmental Psychology,* 1979, *15,* 585–593.

Acredolo, L. P., & Evans, D. Developmental changes in the effects of landmarks on spatial behavior. Paper presented at the meeting of the Society for Research in Child Development, San Francisco, March 1979.

Appel, M., & Campos, J. J. Binocular disparity as a discriminable stimulus parameter in early infancy. *Journal of Experimental Child Psychology,* 1977, *23,* 47–56.

Aronson, E., & Rosenbloom, S. Space perception in early infancy: Perception within a common auditory visual space. *Science,* 1971, *172,* 1161–1163.

Aslin, R. N. Development of binocular fixation in human infants. *Journal of Experimental Child Psychology,* 1977, *23,* 133–150.

Atkinson, J., & Braddick, O. Stereoscopic discrimination in infants. *Perception,* 1976, *5,* 29–38.

Bahrick, L., Walker, A., & Neisser, U. *Infants' perception of multimodal information in novel events.* Paper presented at the meeting of the Eastern Psychological Association, Washington, D.C., March 1978.

Bahrick, L., Walker, A., & Neisser, U. Selective looking by infants. *Cognitive Psychology,* 1981, *13,* 377–390.

Bates, E., Benigni, L., Bretherton, I., Camaioni, L., & Volterra, V. From gesture to the first word: On cognitive and social prerequisites. In M. Lewis & A. Rosenblum (Eds.), *Interaction, conversation and the development of language.* New York: Wiley, 1977.

Bates, E., Benigni, L., Bretherton, I., Camaioni, L., & Volterra, V. *The emergence of symbols.* New York: Academic Press, 1979.

Benedict, H. Early lexical development: Comprehension and production. *Journal of Child Language,* 1979, *6,* 183–200.

Benson, J. B., & Uzgiris, I. C. *The role of self-produced movement in spatial understanding.* Paper presented at the meeting of the Society for Research in Child Development, Boston, April 1981.

Berkeley, G. *An essay towards a new theory of vision.* New York: E. P. Dutton, 1910. (Originally published, 1709.)

Bertenthal, B. I., & Fischer, K. W. Development of self-recognition in the infant. *Developmental Psychology,* 1978, *14,* 44–50.

Bloom, L. *One word at a time: The use of single word utterances before syntax.* The Hague: Mouton, 1973.

Bloom, L. Language development. In F. D. Horowitz (Ed.), *Review of child development research* (Vol. 4). Chicago: University of Chicago Press, 1975.

Bonvillian, J. D., Orlansky, M. D., & Novack, L. L. *Early sign language acquisition and its relation to cognitive and motor development.* Paper presented at the meeting of the Society for Research in Child Development, Boston, April 1981.

Bower, T. G. R. The development of object-permanence: Some studies of existence constancy. *Perception and Psychophysics,* 1967, *2,* 411–418. (a)

Bower, T. G. R. Phenomenal identity and form perception in an infant. *Perception and Psychophysics,* 1967, *2,* 74–76. (b)

Bower, T. G. R. Object perception in infants. *Perception,* 1972, *1,* 15–31.

Bower, T. G. R. *Development in infancy.* San Francisco: Freeman, 1974.

Bower, T. G. R. *A primer of infant development.* San Francisco: Freeman, 1977.

Bower, T. G. R. *Human Development.* San Francisco: Freeman, 1979.

Bower, T. G. R., Broughton, J. M., & Moore, M. K. The coordination of visual and tactual input in infants. *Perception and Psychophysics,* 1970, *8,* 51–53. (a)

Bower, T. G. R., Broughton, J., & Moore, M. K. Demonstration of intention in the reaching behavior of neonate humans. *Nature,* 1970, *228,* 5172. (b)

Bower, T. G. R., Broughton, J. M., & Moore, M. K. Development of the object concept as manifested in the tracking behavior of infants between 7 and 20 weeks of age. *Journal of Experimental Child Psychology,* 1971, *11,* 182–193.

Bower, T. G. R., & Paterson, J. G. The separation of place, movement and object in the world of the infant. *Journal of Experimental Child Psychology,* 1973, *15,* 161–168.

Bower, T. G. R., & Wishart, J. G. The effects of motor skill on object permanence. *Cognition,* 1972, *1,* 165–171.

Brainerd, C. J. *Piaget's theory of intelligence.* Englewood Cliffs, N.J.: Prentice-Hall, 1978. (a)

Brainerd, C. J. The stage question in cognitive-developmental theory. *The Behavioural and Brain Sciences,* 1978, *2,* 173–213. (b)

Bremner, J. G. Egocentric versus allocentric spatial coding in nine-month-old infants: Factors influencing the choice of code. *Developmental Psychology,* 1978, *14,* 346–366. (a)

Bremner, J. G. Spatial errors made by infants: Inadequate spatial cues or evidence of egocentrism? *British Journal of Psychology,* 1978, *69,* 77–84. (b)

Bremner, J. G. The infant's understanding of space. In M. V. Cox (Ed.), *Are young children egocentric?* London: Concord, 1980.

Bremner, J. G., & Bryant, P. E. Place versus response as the basis of spatial errors made by young infants. *Journal of Experimental Child Psychology,* 1977, *23,* 162–171.

Brooks, J., & Weinraub, M. A history of infant intelligence testing. In M. Lewis (Ed.), *Origins of intelligence.* New York: Plenum, 1976.

Bruner, J. S. The growth and structure of skill. In K. Connolly (Ed.), *Mechanisms of motor skill development.* New York: Academic Press, 1970.

Bruner, J. S. Organization of early skilled action.

Child Development, 1973, *44,* 1–11.

Bruner, J. S., & Koslowski, B. Visually preadapted constituents of manipulatory action. *Perception,* 1972, *1,* 3–14.

Bruner, J. S., Olver, R. R., Greenfield, P. M. et al. *Studies in cognitive growth.* New York: Wiley, 1966.

Bryant, P. E. Comments on the design of cross-modal matching and cross-modal transfer experiments. *Cortex,* 1968, *4,* 127–137.

Bryant, P. E. *Perception and understanding in young children.* London: Methuen, 1974.

Bryant, P. E., Jones, P., Claxton, V., & Perkins, J. Recognition of shapes across modalities by infants. *Nature,* 1972, *240,* 303–304.

Burd, A. P., & Milewski, A. E. *Matching of facial gestures by young infants: Imitation or releasers?* Paper presented at the meeting of the Society for Research in Child Development, Boston, April 1981.

Butterworth, G. *The development of the object concept in human infants.* Unpublished doctoral dissertation, University of Oxford, 1974.

Butterworth, G. Object identity in infancy: The interaction of spatial location codes in determining search errors. *Child Development,* 1975, *46,* 866–870.

Butterworth, G. Object disappearance and error in Piaget's stage IV task. *Journal of Experimental Child Psychology,* 1977, *23,* 391–401.

Butterworth, G. Thought and things: Piaget's theory. In A. Burton & J. Radford (Eds.), *Perspectives on thinking.* London: Methuen, 1978.

Butterworth, G. The origins of auditory-visual perception and visual proprioception in human development. In H. A. Pick & R. Walk (Eds.), *Perception and experience* (Vol. 2). New York: Plenum, 1980.

Butterworth, G., & Castillo, M. Coordination of auditory and visual proprioception in newborn human infants. *Perception,* 1976, *5,* 155–160.

Butterworth, G., & Hicks, L. Visual proprioception and postural stability in infancy: A developmental study. *Perception,* 1977, *6,* 255–262.

Campos, J. J., Hiatt, S., Ramsay, D., Henderson, C., & Svejda, M. The emergence of fear on the visual cliff. In M. Lewis & L. A. Rosenblum (Eds.), *The development of affect.* New York: Plenum, 1978.

Caron, A. J., Caron, R. F., & Carlson, V. R. Infant perception of the invariant shape of objects varying in slant. *Child Development,* 1979, *50,* 716–721.

Casati, I., & Lezine, I. *Les étapes de l'intelligence sensori-motrice.* Paris: Editions du Centre de Psychologie Appliquée, 1968.

Clark, E. What's in a word? On the child's acquisition of semantics in his first language. In T. E. Moore (Ed.), *Cognitive development and the acquisition of language.* New York: Academic Press, 1973.

Cohen, L. B. Our developing knowledge of infant perception and cognition. *American Psychologist,* 1979, *34,* 894–899.

Cohen, L. B., & Strauss, M. S. Concept acquisition in the human infant. *Child Development,* 1979, *50,* 419–424.

Condry, S. M., Haltom, M., Jr., & Neisser, U. Infant sensitivity to audio-visual discrepancy. *Bulletin of the Psychonomic Society,* 1977, *9,* 431–432.

Corman, H. H., & Escalona, S. K. Stages of sensorimotor development: A replication study. *Merrill-Palmer Quarterly,* 1969, *15,* 351–361.

Cornell, E. H. The effects of cue reliability on infants' manual search. *Journal of Experimental Child Psychology,* 1979, *28,* 81–91. (a)

Cornell, E. H. The stage heuristic in the study of sensorimotor intelligence. *The Behavioural and Brain Sciences,* 1979, *1,* 140. (b)

Cornell, E. H., & Heth, C. D. Response versus place learning by human infants. *Journal of Experimental Psychology: Human Learning and Memory,* 1979, *5,* 188–196.

Corrigan, R. Language development as related to stage 6 object permanence development. *Journal of Child Language,* 1978, *5,* 173–189.

Corter, C. M., Zucker, K. J., & Galligan, R. F. Patterns in the infant's search for mother during brief separation. *Developmental Psychology,* 1980, *16,* 62–69.

Crassini, B., & Broerse, J. Auditory visual integration in neonates: A signal detection analysis. *Journal of Experimental Child Psychology,* 1980, *29,* 144–155.

Cummings, E. M., & Bjork, E. L. *Piaget's stage IV object concept error: Evidence of perceptual confusion, state change, or failure to assimilate?* Paper presented at the meeting of the Western Psychological Association, Seattle, April 1977.

de Villiers, P. A., & de Villiers, J. G. *Language acquisition.* Cambridge, Mass.: Harvard University Press, 1978.

Diamond, A. *Retrieval of an object from an open box: The development of visual-tactile control of reaching in the first year of life.* Paper presented at the meeting of the Society for Research in Child Development, Boston, April 1981.

Dodwell, P. C., Muir, D., & Di Franco, D. Responses of infants to visually presented objects. *Science,* 1976, *194,* 209–211.

Dunst, C. J., & Rheingrover, R. M. *The stage concept revisited: Methodological considerations and strategies.* Paper presented at the meeting of the Society for Research in Child Development, Boston, April 1981.

Eichorn, D. H. *Developmental parallels in the growth of parents and their children.* Presidential address, Division 7, APA, September 1969.

Enright, M. L. *The role of context similarity in memory reactivation and generalisation in three-month-old infants.* Paper presented at the meeting of the Society for Research in Child Development, Boston, April 1981.

Evans, W. F. *The Stage IV error in Piaget's theory of object concept development: An investigation of the role of activity.* Unpublished dissertation proposal, University of Houston, 1973.

Fagan, J. F., III. Infants' recognition of invariant features of faces. *Child Development,* 1976, *47,* 627–638.

Fagan, J. F., III. The origins of facial pattern recognition. In M. H. Bornstein & W. Kessen (Eds.), *Psychological development from infancy: Image to intention.* Hillsdale, N.J.: Lawrence Erlbaum, 1979.

Fagan, J. F., III, & Singer, L. T. The role of simple feature differences in infant recognition of faces. *Infant Behaviour and Development,* 1979, *2,* 39–46.

Field, J. Relation of young infants' reaching behaviour to stimulus distance and solidity. *Developmental Psychology,* 1976, *12,* 444–448.

Field, J. Co-ordination of vision and prehension in young infants. *Child Development,* 1977, *48,* 97–103.

Fischer, K. W. A theory of cognitive development: The control and construction of hierarchies of skills. *Psychological Review,* 1980, *87,* 477–531.

Fodor, J. A. *The language of thought.* Sussex: Harvester, 1976.

Freeman, N., Lloyd, S., & Sinha, C. G. Infant search tasks reveal early concepts of containment and canonical usage of objects. *Cognition,* 1980, *8,* 243–262.

Fremgen, A., & Fay, D. Overextensions in production and comprehension: A methodological clarification. *Journal of Child Language,* 1980, *7,* 205–211.

Gallup, G. G. Chimpanzees: Self-recognition. *Science,* 1970, *167,* 86–87.

Gardner, J., & Gardner, H. A note on selective imitation by a 6-week-old infant. *Child Development,* 1970, *41,* 1209–1213.

Gesell, A., & Thompson, H. *Infant behaviour.* New York: McGraw-Hill, 1934.

Gibson, E. J. *Principles of perceptual learning and development.* New York: Appleton-Century-Crofts, 1969.

Gibson, E. J. *The ecological optics of infancy: The differentiation of invariants given by optical motion.* Presidential address, DRV 3, APA, 1977.

Gibson, E. J., Owsley, C. J., & Johnston, J. Perception of invariants by five-month-old infants: Differentiation of types of motion. *Developmental Psychology,* 1978, *14,* 407–415.

Gibson, E. J., Owsley, C. J., Walker, A., & Megaw-Nyce, J. Development of the perception of invariants: Substance and shape. *Perception,* 1979, *8,* 609–619.

Gibson, E. J., & Spelke, E. The development of perception. In P. Mussen (Ed.), *Handbook of child psychology.* Vol. III. New York: Wiley, 1983.

Gibson, J. J. *The perception of the visual world.* Boston: Houghton-Mifflin, 1950.

Gibson, J. J. *The senses considered as perceptual systems.* Boston: Houghton-Mifflin, 1966.

Gibson, J. J. *The ecological approach to visual perception.* Boston: Houghton-Mifflin, 1979.

Gibson, J. J., & Gibson, E. J. Perceptual learning: Differentiation or enrichment? *Psychological Review,* 1955, *62,* 32–41.

Goldberg, S. Visual tracking and existence constancy in 5-month old infants. *Journal of Experimental Child Psychology,* 1976, *22,* 478–491.

Goldman, D., & Homa, D. Integrative and metric properties of abstracted information as a function of category discriminability, instance variability, and experience. *Journal of Experimental Psychology: Human Learning and Memory,* 1977, *3,* 375–385.

Gordon, F. R., Lamson, G., & Yonas, A. *Reaching to a virtual object.* Unpublished manuscript, University of Minnesota, 1978.

Gordon, F. R., & Yonas, A. Sensitivity to binocular depth information. *Journal of Experimental Child Psychology,* 1976, *22,* 413–422.

Gottfried, A. W., Rose, S. A., & Bridger, W. H. Cross modal transfer in human infants. *Child Development,* 1977, *48,* 118–123.

Gratch, G. A study of the relative dominance of vision and touch in six-month-old infants. *Child Development,* 1972, *43,* 615–623.

Gratch, G., Appel, K. J., Evans, W. F., LeCompte,

G. K., & Wright, N. A. Piaget's Stage IV object concept error: Evidence of forgetting or object conception? *Child Development*, 1974, *45*, 71–77.

Greenfield, P. M. Structural parallels between language and action in development. In A. Lock (Ed.), *Action, gesture and symbol*. New York: Academic Press, 1978.

Gruendel, J. M. Referential extension in early language development. *Child Development*, 1977, *48*, 1567–1576.

Haith, M. M., & Campos, J. J. Human infancy. *Annual Review of Psychology*, 1977, *28*, 251–293.

Harris, P. L. Examination and search in infants. *British Journal of Psychology*, 1971, *62*, 469–473.

Harris, P. L. Infants' visual and tactual inspection of objects. *Perception*, 1972, *1*, 141–146.

Harris, P. L. Perseverative errors in search by young infants. *Child Development*, 1973, *44*, 28–33.

Harris, P. L. Perseverative search at a visibly empty place by young infants. *Journal of Experimental Child Psychology*, 1974, *18*, 535–542.

Harris, P. L. Development of search and object permanence during infancy. *Psychological Bulletin*, 1975, *82*, 332–344.

Harris, P. L. The child's representation of space. In G. Butterworth (Ed.), *The child's representation of the world*. New York: Plenum, 1977.

Harris, P. L. Perception and cognition in infancy. In K. Connolly (Ed.), *Psychology Survey No. 2*, London: George Allen & Unwin, 1979.

Harris, P. L. Cognitive prerequisites to language? *British Journal of Psychology*, 1982, *73*, 187–195.

Harris, P. L. The development of search. In P. Salapatek & L. B. Cohen (Eds.), *Handbook of infant perception*. New York: Academic Press, in press.

Harris, P. L., Cassell, T., & Bamborough, P. Tracking by young infants. *British Journal of Psychology*, 1974, *65*, 345–349.

Harris, P. L., & Heelas, P. Cognitive processes and collective representations. *European Journal of Sociology*, 1979, *20*, 211–241.

Held, R., & Hein, A. Movement produced stimulation in the development of visually-guided behaviour. *Journal of Comparative and Physiological Psychology*, 1963, *56*, 872–876.

van Hofsten, C. Binocular convergence as a determinant of reaching behavior in infancy. *Perception*, 1977, *6*, 139–144.

Horner, T. M. Test-retest and home-clinic characteristics of the Bayley scales of infant development. *Child Development*, 1980, *51*, 751–758.

Hume, D. *An enquiry concerning human understanding*. Chicago: Open Court, 1904.

Huttenlocher, J. The origins of language comprehension. In R. Solso (Ed.), *Theories in cognitive psychology*. Hillsdale, N.J.: Lawrence Erlbaum, 1974.

Ingram, D. Sensori-motor intelligence and language development. In A. Lock (Ed.), *Action, gesture and symbol*. New York: Academic Press, 1978.

Jackson, E., Campos, J. J., & Fischer, K. W. The question of decalage between object permanence and person permanence. *Developmental Psychology*, 1978, *14*, 1–10.

Jacobson, S. W. Matching behavior in the young infant. *Child Development*, 1979, *50*, 425–430.

Kagan, J. *The growth of the "face" schema: Theoretical significance and methodological issues*. Paper presented at the meeting of the American Psychological Association, Chicago, September 1965.

Kagan, J. The determinants of attention in the infant. *American Scientist*, 1970, *58*, 298–306.

Kagan, J. *Change and continuity in infancy*. New York: Wiley, 1971.

Kagan, J. Emergent themes in human development. *American Scientist*, 1976, *64*, 186–196.

Kagan, J. Structure and process in the human infant: The ontogeny of mental representation. In M. H. Bornstein & W. Kessen (Eds.), *Psychological development from infancy: Image to intention*. Hillsdale, N.J.: Lawrence Erlbaum, 1979.

Kagan, J., Kearsley, R. B., & Zelazo, P. R. *Infancy: Its place in human development*. Cambridge, Mass.: Harvard University Press, 1978.

Kellman, P., & Spelke, E. *Perception of partly occluded objects in infancy*. Paper presented at the meeting of the Society for Research in Child Development, San Francisco, March 1979.

King, W. L., & Seegmiller, B. Performance of 14- to 22-month-old black, firstborn male infants on two tests of cognitive development. *Developmental Psychology*, 1973, *8*, 317–326.

Knobloch, H., & Pasamanick, B. An evaluation of the consistency and predictive value of the forty week Gesell development schedule. In G. Shagass & B. Pasamanick (Eds.), *Child development and child psychiatry*. Psychiatric Research Reports of the American Psychiatric Association, 1960, *13*, 10–13.

Knobloch, H., & Pasamanick, B. Prediction from assessment of neuromotor and intellectual status in infancy. In J. Zubin & G. A. Jervis (Eds.),

Psychopathology of mental development. New York: Grune & Stratton, 1967.

Kopp, C. B., Sigman, M., & Parmelee, A. H. A longitudinal study of sensori-motor development. *Developmental Psychology,* 1974, *10,* 687–695.

Kramer, J., Hill, K., & Cohen, L. Infant's development of object permanence: A refined methodology and new evidence of Piaget's hypothesized ordinality. *Child Development,* 1975, *46,* 149–155.

Landers, W. F. The effect of differential experience on infants' performance in a Piagetian Stage IV object-concept task. *Developmental Psychology,* 1971, *5,* 48–54.

Lasky, R. E. The effect of visual feedback of the hand on the reaching and retrieval behaviour of young infants. *Child Development,* 1977, *48,* 112–117.

Lawson, K. R. Spatial and temporal congruity and auditory-visual integration in infants. *Developmental Psychology,* 1980, *16,* 185–192.

LeCompte, G. K., & Gratch, G. Violation of a rule as a method of diagnosing infants' levels of object concept. *Child Development,* 1972, *43,* 385–396.

Lee, D., & Aronson, E. Visual proprioceptive control of standing in human infants. *Perception and Psychophysics,* 1974, *15,* 529–532.

Lewis, M., & Brooks, J. Infants' social perception: A constructionist view. In L. B. Cohen & P. Salapatek (Eds.), *Infant perception: From sensation to cognition* (Vol. 1). New York: Academic Press, 1975.

Lucas, T. C., & Uzgiris, I. C. Spatial factors in the development of the object concept. *Developmental Psychology,* 1977, *13,* 492–500.

Lyons-Ruth, K. Bimodal perception in infancy: Response to auditory visual incongruity. *Child Development,* 1977, *48,* 820–827.

Maratos, O. *The origin and development of imitation in the first six months of life*. Paper presented at the annual meeting of the British Psychological Society, Liverpool, April 1973.

McCall, R. B. Similarity in I.Q. profile among related pairs: Infancy and childhood. *Proceedings of the 80th Annual Convention of the American Psychological Association,* 1972, *7,* 79–80.

McCall, R. B. The development of intellectual functioning in infancy and the prediction of later IQ. in J. D. Osofsky (Ed.), *The handbook of infant development*. New York: Wiley, 1979.

McCall, R. B., Eichorn, D. H., & Hogarty, P. S. Transitions in early mental development. *Monographs of the Society for Research in Child Development,* 1977, *42* (3, Serial No. 171).

McCall, R. B., Hogarty, P. S., & Hurlburt, N. Transitions in infant sensorimotor development and the prediction of childhood IQ. *American Psychologist,* 1972, *27,* 728–748.

McDonnel, P. M. The development of visually-guided reaching. *Perception and Psychophysics,* 1975, *18,* 181–185.

McGurk, H., & Lewis, M. Space perception in early infancy: Perception within a common auditory-visual space? *Science,* 1974, *186,* 649–650.

McGurk, H., Turnure, C., & Creighton, S. J. Auditory-visual coordination of neonates. *Child Development,* 1977, *48,* 138–143.

Meicler, M., & Gratch, G. Do 5-month olds show object conception in Piaget's sense? *Infant Behaviour,* 1980, *3,* 265–282.

Meltzoff, A., & Borton, R. W. Intermodal matching by human neonates. *Nature,* 1979, *282,* 403–404.

Meltzoff, A., & Moore, M. K. Imitation of facial and manual gestures by human neonates. *Science,* 1977, *198,* 75–78.

Mendelson, M., & Haith, M. M. The relation between audition and vision in the human newborn. *Monographs of the Society for Research in Child Development,* 1976, *41,* 1–61.

Michotte, A. Perception and cognition. *Acta Psychologica, 1955, 11,* 69–91.

Michotte, A. *Causalité, permanence et réalité phénomenales*. Louvain: Publications Universitaires Belgium, 1962.

Miller, D., Cohen, L., & Hill, K. A methodological investigation of Piaget's theory of object concept development in the sensory-motor period. *Journal of Experimental Child Psychology,* 1970, *9,* 59–85.

Moore, M. K. *The genesis of object permanence*. Paper presented at the meeting of the Society for Research in Child Development, Philadelphia, April 1973.

Moore, M. K. *Object permanence and object identity: A stage-developmental model*. Paper presented at the meeting of the Society for Research in Child Development, Denver, April 1975.

Moore, M. K., Borton, R., & Darby, B. L. Visual tracking in young infants: Evidence for object identity or object permanence? *Journal of Experimental Child Psychology,* 1978, *25,* 183–198.

Moore, M. K., Clark, D., Mael, M., Myers, G., Rajotte, P., & Stoel-Gammon, C. *The relationship between language and object permanence development: A study of Down's infants and children*. Paper presented at the meeting of the Society for Research in Child Development, New Orleans, March 1977.

Moore, M. K., & Meltzoff, A. N. Imitation, object permanence and language development in infancy: Toward a neo-Piagetian perspective on communicative and cognitive development. In F. D. Minifie & L. L. Lloyd (Eds.), *Communicative and cognitive abilities—Early behavioral assessment*. Baltimore: University Park Press, 1978.

Muller, A. A., & Aslin, R. N. Visual tracking as an index of the object concept. *Infant Behavior and Development*, 1978, *1*, 309–319.

Mussen, P. H., Conger, J. J., and Kagan, J. *Child development and personality*. New York: Harper & Row, 1979.

Nelson, K. E. Accommodation of visual-tracking patterns in human infants to object movement patterns. *Journal of Experimental Child Psychology*, 1971, *12*, 182–196.

Neumann, P. G. Visual prototype formation with discontinuous representation of dimensions of variability. *Memory and Cognition*, 1977, *5*, 187–197.

Nichols, P. L., & Broman, S. H. Familial resemblances in infant mental development. *Developmental Psychology*, 1974, *10*, 442–446.

Paraskevopoulos, J., & Hunt, J. McV. Object construction and imitation under differing conditions of rearing. *Journal of Genetic Psychology*, 1971, *119*, 301.

Piaget, J. *Play, dreams and imitation in childhood*. New York: Norton, 1951.

Piaget, J. *The origins of intelligence in children*. New York: International University Press, 1952.

Piaget, J. *The construction of reality in the child*. New York: Basic Books, 1954.

Pöppel, E., Held, R., & Frost, D. Residual visual function after brain wounds involving the central visual pathways in man. *Nature*, 1973, *243*, 295–296.

Rader, N., Bausano, M., & Richards, J. E. On the nature of the visual-cliff avoidance response in human infants. *Child Development*, 1980, *51*, 61–68.

Ramsay, D. S., & Campos, J. J. The onset of representation and entry into Stage 6 of object permanence development. *Developmental Psychology*, 1978, *14*, 79–86.

Rescorla, L. A. Overextension in early language development. *Journal of Child Language*, 1980, *7*, 321–335.

Rescorla, L. A. Category development in early language. *Journal of Child Language*, 1981, *8*, 225–238.

Rezba, C. *A study of infant binocular depth perception*. Unpublished undergraduate honors thesis, University of Minnesota, 1977.

Richards, J. E., & Rader, N. Crawling-onset age predicts visual cliff avoidance in infants. *Journal of Experimental Psychology: Human Perception and Performance*, 1981, *7*, 382–387.

Rieser, J. Spatial orientation of six-month-old infants. *Child Development*, 1979, *50*, 1078–1087.

Rogers, S. J. Characteristics of the cognitive development of profoundly retarded children. *Child Development*, 1977, *48*, 837–843.

Rose, S. A., Gottfried, A. W., & Bridger, W. H. Cross-modal transfer and information-processing by the sense of touch in infancy. *Developmental Psychology*, 1981, *17*, 90–98.

Ross, G. S. Categorization in one- to two-year-olds. *Developmental Psychology*, 1980, *16*, 391–396.

Rovee-Collier, C. K., & Sullivan, M. W. Organisation of infant memory. *Journal of Experimental Psychology: Human Learning and Memory*, 1980, *6*, 798–807.

Rovee-Collier, C. K., Sullivan, M. W., Enright, M. L., Lucas, D., & Fagen, J. W. Reactivation of infant memory. *Science*, 1980, *208*, 1159–1161.

Ruff, H. A., & Halton, A. Is there directed reaching in the human neonate? *Developmental Psychology*, 1978, *14*, 425–426.

Ruff, H. A., & Kohler, C. J. Tactual-visual transfer in six month old infants. *Infant Behavior and Development*, 1978, *1*, 259–264.

Sachs, J., & Truswell, L. Comprehension of two-word instructions by children in the one-word stage. *Journal of Child Language*, 1978, *5*, 17–24.

Sherman, T. *Categorization skills in infants*. Paper presented at the meeting of the Society for Research in Child Development, Boston, April 1981.

Simonoux, K., & Decarie, T. G. Cognition and perception in the object concept. *Canadian Journal of Psychology*, 1979, *33*, 396–407.

Sinclair, H. Sensorimotor action patterns as a condition for the acquisition of syntax. In E. Ingram & R. Huxley (Eds.), *Language acquisition: Models and methods*. New York: Academic Press, 1971.

Slater, A. M., & Findlay, J. M. Binocular fixation in the newborn baby. *Journal of Experimental Child Psychology*, 1975, *20*, 248–273. (a)

Slater, A., & Findlay, J. M. The corneal reflection technique and the visual preference method:

Sources of error. *Journal of Experimental Child Psychology,* 1975, *20,* 240–247. (b)

Sophian, C., & Wellman, H. M. *Selective information use and perseveration in the search behaviour of infants and young children.* Unpublished manuscript Department of Psychology, Carnegie-Mellon University, 1982.

Spelke, E. Infants' intermodal perception of events. *Cognitive Psychology,* 1976, *8,* 553–560.

Spelke, E. S. Exploring audible and visible events in infancy. In A. D. Pick (Ed.), *Perception and its development: A tribute to Eleanor J. Gibson,* Hillsdale, N.J.: Lawrence Erlbaum, 1979. (a)

Spelke, E. S. Perceiving bimodally specified events in infancy. *Developmental Psychology,* 1979, *15,* 626–636. (b)

Spelke, E. *Perception in infancy.* Paper presented at a symposium on human development, La Jolla Conference on Cognitive Science, August 1979. (c)

Spelke, E. The infant's acquisition of knowledge of bimodally specified events. *Journal of Experimental Child Psychology,* 1981, *31,* 279–299.

Spelke, E. The development of intermodal perception. In L. Cohen & P. Salapatek (Eds.), *Handbook of infant perception.* New York: Academic Press, in press.

Spelke, E. S., & Owsley, C. Intermodal exploration and knowledge in infancy. *Infant Behavior and Development,* 1979, *2,* 13–27.

Strauss, M. S. Abstraction of prototypical information by adults and 10-month-old infants. *Journal of Experimental Psychology: Human Learning and Memory,* 1979, *5,* 618–632.

Thomas, D. G., Campos, J. J., Shucard, D. W., Ramsay, D. S., & Shucard, J. Semantic comprehension in infancy: A signal detection analysis. *Child Development,* 1981, *52,* 798–803.

Thompson, J. R., & Chapman, R. S. Who is "Daddy" revisited: The status of two-year-olds' overextended words in use and comprehension. *Journal of Child Language,* 1977, *4,* 359–375.

Tinbergen, N. *A study of instinct.* New York: Oxford University Press, 1951.

Turkewitz, G., Birch, H. G., Moreau, T., Levy, L., & Cornwell, A. C. Effect of intensity of auditory stimulation on directional eye movements in the human neonate. *Animal Behaviour,* 1966, *14,* 93–101.

Uzgiris, I. C. Patterns of vocal and gestural imitation in infants. In F. Monks, W. Hartup, & J. de Wit (Eds.), *Determinants of behavioural development.* New York: Academic Press, 1972.

Uzgiris, I. C. Patterns of cognitive development in infancy. *Merrill-Palmer Quarterly,* 1973, *19,* 181–204.

Uzgiris, I. C. Organization of sensorimotor intelligence. In M. Lewis (Ed.), *Origins of intelligence.* New York: Plenum, 1976.

Uzgiris, I. C., & Hunt, J. McV. *An instrument for assessing infant psychological development.* Mimeographed paper, Psychological Development Laboratories, University of Illinois, 1966.

Uzgiris, I. C., & Hunt, J. *Assessment in infancy: Ordinal scales of psychological development.* Champaign: University of Illinois Press, 1975.

Walk, R. D. Depth perception and a laughing heaven. In A. D. Pick (Ed.), *Perception and its development: A tribute to Eleanor J. Gibson.* Hillsdale, N.J.: Lawrence Erlbaum, 1979.

Walker, A. S., Owsley, C. J., Megaw-Nyce, J., Gibson, E. J., & Bahrick, L. E. Detection of elasticity as an invariant property of objects by young infants. *Perception,* 1980, *9,* 713–718.

Watson, M. W., & Fischer, K. W. A developmental sequence of agent use in late infancy. *Child Development,* 1977, *48,* 828–836.

Weiskrantz, L. Trying to bridge some neuropsychological gaps between monkey and man. *British Journal of Psychology,* 1977, *68,* 431–445.

Wertheimer, M. Psycho-motor coordination of auditory-visual space at birth. *Science,* 1961, *134,* 1692–1696.

White, B., Castle, P., & Held, R. Observations on the development of visually-directed reaching. *Child Development,* 1964, *35,* 349–364.

Wilson, R. S. Testing infant intelligence. *Science,* 1973, *182,* 734–737.

Wilson, R. S., & Harpring, E. B. Mental and motor development in infant twins. *Developmental Psychology,* 1972, *7,* 277–287.

Wilson, R. S., & Matheny, A. P., Jr. Retardation and twin concordance in infant mental development: A reassessment. *Behavior Genetics,* 1976, *6,* 353–358.

Wishart, J. G., & Bower, T. G. R. The development of spatial understanding in infancy. *Journal of Experimental Child Psychology,* 1982, *33,* 363–385.

Woodward, M. The behaviour of idiots interpreted by Piaget's theory of sensori-motor development. *British Journal of Educational Psychology,* 1959, *29,* 60–71.

Yonas, A. Studies of spatial perception in infancy. In A. D. Pick (Ed.), *Perception and its development: A tribute to Eleanor J. Gibson.* Hillsdale, N.J.: Lawrence Erlbaum, 1979.

Yonas, A., Oberg, C., & Norcia, A. Development of sensitivity to binocular information for the approach of an object. *Developmental Psychology,* 1978, *14,* 147–152.

Yonas, A., & Pick, H. L., Jr. An approach to the study of infant space perception. In L. Cohen & P. Salapatek (Eds.), *Infant perception: From sensation to cognition* (Vol 2). New York: Academic Press, 1975.

Zachry, W. Ordinality and interdependence of representation and language development in infancy. *Child Development,* 1978, *49,* 681–687.

Zazzo, P. La problème de l'imitation chez le nouveau-né. *Enfance,* 1957, *2,* 135–142.

SOCIOEMOTIONAL DEVELOPMENT* | 10

JOSEPH J. CAMPOS, *University of Denver*
KAREN CAPLOVITZ BARRETT, *University of Denver*
MICHAEL E. LAMB, *University of Utah*
H. HILL GOLDSMITH, *University of Texas at Austin*
CRAIG STENBERG, *Texas Christian University*

CHAPTER CONTENTS

*All authors contributed to all sections of this chapter; however, the section on emotional development was principally the responsibility of Campos and Barrett; the section on temperament—Goldsmith, Campos, and Barrett; and the section on social development—Lamb, Barrett, and Campos. The authors were supported by grants and fellowships from the Spencer foundation, The American Association of University Women, the National Institute of Mental Health (MH-23556, MH-22803-11, & MH-08239), and the National Science Foundation (BNS-8021615).

We are especially grateful to Dr. Marilyn Svejda and Mrs. Charlotte Henderson, who aided immensely in the preparation of this chapter.

In recent years, it has become increasingly apparent that emotional development and social development are intimately interrelated, especially during the period of infancy. In particular, the *expressions* of emotion are proving to be central regulators of interpersonal interactions. Moreover, social relationships, such as affectional *attachments,* are, in turn, prototypical influences on emotionality. Finally, it has become clear that certain of these social/emotional phenomena, namely temperamental dispositions, appear to have traitlike qualities that not only differ across individuals but also account for important differences in how members of dyads relate to one another, and how individuals engage in cognitive and perceptual tasks. It is these three closely related aspects of infantile development that we will discuss in the present chapter. Focusing primarily on the period of infancy, we will first discuss emotions and their development. Next, we will discuss temperament, followed by a treatment of attachment and affiliative relations during infancy.

In our treatment of the topic of emotion, we will attempt to provide the background for the remarkable surge of interest in this field. Although we will not be encyclopedic in our treatment, we will describe some of the methodological and theoretical developments that have revolutionized our understanding of emotion within the past 10 years; we will attempt to bridge two hitherto separate literatures—that on adult emotional expression and that on infant emotional development; and we will draw implications for the study of emotional development that stem from the new perspective on emotions.

EMOTIONS AND THEIR DEVELOPMENT

Prologue

All basic psychological processes have proved remarkably difficult to define, but perhaps none has been as resistant as the concept of emotion. It has at times been considered synonymous with certain classes of stimulation, with patterns of facial expression, with autonomic reactivity, with the disruption of behavior, with perception of peripheral autonomic and muscular feedback, with rather special states of consciousness, and with thalamic, hypothalamic, or limbic activity. None of these definitions has proved adequate, and the time has come to attempt a different approach to characterizing the inclusion and exclusion criteria of emotion.

In this chapter, we do not presume to solve the recurrent problem of definition. However, we will propose a new working definition of emotion. It differs from others in rejecting the possibility of an ostensive definition of emotion. That is, no emotional state is ever specified by a single, unambiguous behavioral measure or even by a pattern or set of behaviors. Emotions can sometimes be inferred from facial or vocal expressions, sometimes from observing the person's train of thought, at times by noting what the person chooses to do, and on occasion, even from what the person does *not* do: to attempt to determine the *pattern* of behavior that specifies an emotional state seems doomed to imprecision because at any given time, totally dissimilar behaviors can be produced by the same emotional process. Emotions are such protean and abstruse phenomena that we feel the first step in describing the nature of emotions involves specifying what emotions do rather than cataloguing their physical attributes. What permits classification of these diverse manifestations into a single unitary category is, thus, the common function served by the diverse expressions and instrumental activities.

Looked at in this functionalist way, emotions can be defined in terms of the *conjunction* of four criteria. One criterion is that, like cognitions and drives, *emotions regulate internal psychological processes*—influencing the selection of information from the perceptual world, the flow and processing of information once it has been detected, and the selection of response outputs of the organism. Emotions both energize and steer behavior, help tune the organism to the environmental information that is most relevant to the organism at the time, and facilitate or occasionally impede working memory, inferential capacities, and problem solving.

A second criterion is that, in a manner rather similar to language, *emotions crucially regulate social and interpersonal behaviors.* Emotions do this primarily (although not exclusively) through their multiple expressive channels (typically, the face, voice, gesture, certain physiological reactions, and other means discussed by researchers in the area of nonverbal communication). Emotional expressions of one person can elicit contagious or resonant emotional states in another; they can produce empathic responses; they can disambiguate uncertain circumstances; and they can specify action consequences of the expressor to the perceiver of the expression. When conceptualized this way, emotions become a fourth fundamental category of perception along with depth, form, and motion—all of which are critical for adaptation to the social and physical world. Accordingly, there is a need to describe the multiple sources of emotional information in the environment that have in common specification of emotional state (in other words, the analogues for emotion to retinal disparity, motion parallax, interposition, acoustic localization, convergence, kinesthetic depth, etc.). We also need to describe the susceptibilities or attunements of the organism that facilitate or impede the detection of emotional information.

The third criterion is that *emotions can be differentiated from drives, in that emotions are specified by unique patterns of facial, vocal, or gestural expressions*. This is not say that hunger or other drives cannot be identified by instrumental actions, like foraging, or by conditions that terminate behaviors, like food for a hungry animal. However, emotions can be identified by expressive criteria in addition to those voluntary behavioral reactions that identify drives.

Finally, unlike language or cognition, *the basic emotions*—which we believe include joy, anger, disgust, surprise, fear, sadness, sexual ardor, affection, and possibly others—*utilize a noncodified, prewired communication process,* a process now known to require no social learning either for the *reception* of at least some facial and gestural signals (Kenney, Mason, & Hill, 1979; Mendelson, Haith, & Goldman-Rakic, 1982; Sackett, 1966) or for the *production* of such (Boucher & Carlson, 1980; Ekman & Friesen, 1972; Ekman, Sorenson, & Friesen, 1969; Steiner, 1973).

We emphasize that these criteria taken singly do not discriminate emotions from other fundamental psychological processes. However, just as primates cannot be differentiated from other species on the basis of any single trait or criterion but rather by the joint presence of several factors, so the scope of emotion is potentially definable by the joint operation of the four criteria we have just described.

Moreover, given the central role of presocialized expressive channels in this conceptualization of emotion, the study of emotion in human infancy becomes central to the understanding of the role of emotion in human behavior in general. In the discussions that follow, we will review the dramatic changes in the treatment of emotion by psychology, describe some of the reasons for the present interest in human emotions, and further explicate our conceptualization of the nature of emotion as well as the implications of this conceptualization for understanding emotional development, temperament, and social development.

Introduction

One of the most striking developments in contemporary psychological theory is the resurgence of interest in the field of human emotions. Until recently, emotions suffered from a not-very-benign neglect by psychologists, except from a few isolated theorists and researchers (e.g., Plutchik, 1962; Tomkins, 1962, 1963). The neglect seemed well justified: Emotions appeared not to be amenable to measurement with any degree of specificity; they seemed to play no causal role in behavioral explanations; they appeared to be irrelevant to the basic constructs and the most central conceptualizations of human behavior, especially those originating within experimental psychology; and they were much too closely linked to a naive, romanticized, and unscientific language. What progress had been made in understanding emotion had not been made by psychologists but rather by neurophysiologists working with brain structures or with neural transmitters (Grossman, 1967; Snyder, 1978).

This neglect did not always exist. At one time, the conscious aspect of emotion, called affect or hedonic tone by theorists like Wundt (1904), Titchener (1905), Allport (1924), or Beebe-Center (1932), constituted one of the three central topics in psychological theory, along with sensation and association. Moreover, in Breuer and Freud's (1895) early theory of psychopathology, affect also played a central explanatory role. Strangulated affect, for instance, was believed to account for the formation of neurotic symptoms in hysteric patients. So long as introspection and verbal reports were the preferred methods in psychological research, affect was revealed directly and unequivocally. Although controversy surrounded the nature of affect, it did not revolve around its reality or its importance but rather the number of dimensions of which it was constituted. Early behaviorist theories (J. B. Watson, 1930) also gave emotional reactions a central role in explaining behavior. J. B. Watson proposed three innate emotions, in part because he claimed to have observed them in neonates but also, in part, because he recognized their biological adaptive significance.

By the late 1920s, however, the theoretical importance of the conscious feeling state of affect as well as the behavioral patterns constituting emotion began to be questioned. By that time, the method of introspection had been discredited and affect thus lost both its theoretical appeal and its method of verification. Freud abandoned his notions linking repressed affect to symptom formation and proposed his well-known instinct or drive theories, which made affect the *result* of increases or decreases in drive rather than the *cause* of symptom formation. Furthermore, not long after J. B. Watson proposed his theory of three innate emotions, research by Sherman (1927a, 1927b) and later Dennis (1940) led to dissatisfaction with the behavioral and expressive criteria for emotion. Whereas J. B. Watson (1930) had proposed that the researcher could identify the type of elicitor by viewing the type of expressive response, Sherman (1927a, 1927b) argued that emotions can be identified by observers only if one already knows the stimulus circumstances. Sherman's data and arguments implied that emotions were a mere rubric for categorizing stimulus inputs: using emotions as unifying constructs seemed unnecessary at best, erroneous at worst (Bentley, 1928; Skinner, 1953).

By 1933, some psychologists were predicting that the term emotion would eventually disappear from psychology (Duffy, 1934; Meyer, 1933), a prediction which almost came true in the 1970s. Consider that in 1954 Woodworth and Schlosberg's *Experimental Psychology,* one of the standard reference sources of the time, included 3 chapters, out of a total of 24, devoted to emotions. These primarily concerned difficulties in measuring emotions, and contained a proposed dimensional approach to conceptualizing both physiological reactions and the recognition of emotional expressions in others. By 1971, when Kling and Riggs edited the third edition of the same reference work, there were *no* chapters devoted to emotion out of a total of 21 in the book. Moreover, there was not even an entry under emotion in the index and only scattered references to related phenomena, such as conditioned emotional response and emotionality. Consider also the previous edition of this *Handbook* (Mussen, 1970). It reflected the same trend: although each edition prior to 1970 had included a chapter on emotion, neither volume of the 1970 version did, and the handbook's indices were equally skimpy on the topic, being limited to 23 entries. As seemed appropriate in discussing phenomena of secondary importance, whatever there was of significance in the field of emotion was subsumed under other rubrics then considered to be more central (e.g., aggression, attachment, cognition, early experience).

Of course, there seemed to be noteworthy exceptions to the neglect of emotion, but these exceptions prove to be more apparent than real. Two dramatic and influential ones deserve specific mention. One is Schachter and Singer's (Schachter, 1970; Schacter & Singer 1962; Schachter & Wheeler, 1962) theory of physiological arousal, cognition, and emotion. In their model, emotion was conceptualized as a composite of autonomic arousal plus cognition (i.e., the labeling by the subject of the reason for the arousal). By explicitly proposing that physiological arousal probably was the same for all emotions but that the cognitive labeling was not, Schachter and Singer implied that to understand emotion one must really understand cognition. Accordingly, Schachter and Singer's work fostered rather than challenged the beliefs that emotions had no biological specificity and were processes of secondary significance. Although they considered how the manipulations of cognitions or physiological arousal influenced behavior, they treated emotions much like a psychophysicist treats color vision, stopping at the level of self-report. For Schachter, then, as for many others, emotions were essentially epiphenomenal.

The second apparent exception took place within developmental psychology. In the 1940s, 1950s, and 1960s, there was an abundance of research on social smiling, anaclitic depression, separation and stranger anxiety, and fear of heights or looming stimuli. However, except for the conceptualizations of theorists like Bowlby (1951) and Spitz (1950, 1965), the motivation for conducting such studies was to use emotions to index something else—usually a perceptual or cognitive process.

Consider the work with the visual cliff (Walk & Gibson, 1961) or with looming stimuli (Ball & Tronick, 1971; Bower, Broughton, & Moore, 1970). Almost all of the research on these two paradigms was centered on what infants' reactions revealed about depth perception or sensitivity to optical expansion patterns (T. G. R. Bower, 1974). It is only recently that a few researchers have begun to relate these paradigms to the development of emotions (Campos, Hiatt, Ramsay, Henderson, & Svejda, 1978; Cicchetti & Sroufe, 1978; Scarr & Salapatek, 1970).

A similar example may be found in the research on the development of smiling: Kagan's (1971) interest in the emergence of smiling at 6 to 10 weeks of age was based on his theory that smiling results when sensory input is assimilated effortfully to emergent schemas (i.e., representations of prior inputs). Because his interests were in memory more than in emotion, he preferred not to focus his important early research on the study of how joy may motivate rehearsal of a new skill, how it may help consolidate information into memory, how it may mediate generalization of the skill to a new task, or how the smile is involved in affective sharing of a new accomplishment with the caretaker. His interests, instead, led him to study how memory changes with age and how it seems to have a maturational substrate (Kagan, 1976). The smile was, for Kagan and others (e.g., McCall, 1972; J. S. Watson, 1972), a convenient and sensitive dependent variable, but any other dependent variable might as easily have served the same purposes.

Stranger and separation distress were also of interest at the time primarily because of their apparent dependence on cognitive development (Décarie, 1974; Schaffer, 1974). For instance, separation and stranger distress were believed to measure discrepancies from schemas (G. W. Bronson, 1968), the establishment of a permanent image of the mother (Brossard, 1974), or the formation of unconfirmed hypotheses (Kagan, Kearsley, & Zelazo, 1978). Those investigating separation or stranger anxiety, like those studying the smile, only rarely (e.g., Clarke-Stewart, 1978a; Dixon, Yogman, Tronick, Adamson, Als, & Brazelton, 1981) speculated about the possible consequences or functions that these processes played in the social or intellectual life of the infant. As in Schachter and Singer's (1962) work, the emphasis was on cold cognition rather than emotion. Thus, although the developmental work was titularly on emotion, its conceptual focus was often more relevant to the study of perception, memory, or sensorimotor intelligence.

The Shift in the Zeitgeist: Methodological Advances

The neglect of emotion has begun to be replaced in recent years with a dramatic reevaluation of the importance of emotion, its consequences, and its development from infancy to old age (Malatesta, 1981a). One reason for this dramatic shift has been a proliferation of methodologically sound technologies for emotion measurement. Most noteworthy among these technologies are those for scoring facial expression.

The recent research on facial expression has been extremely influential in fostering the sudden emergence of interest in emotions and their development. It was research on the facial expression of emotion that clearly demonstrated that emotions have measurement specificity and that at least some emotions appear to have a biological basis. Research on facial expressions also has made possible the construction of very precise methods of scoring emotional reactions and has uncovered the close link between emotions and social regulation. Moreover, some theories (e.g., Izard, 1971; Tomkins, 1962, 1963) allude to a close link between feedback from the facial musculature and the *conscious experience* of affect, thus suggesting that one road to the study of feeling state is through the study of facial expressions. Furthermore, unresolved issues about the nature of facial expression of emotions have led to an integration of two formerly disparate disciplines—the study of emotions in adults and the study of emotional development in infancy. One of the central issues in present-day theories of adult emotion concerns the extent to which facial expression patterns are innate. If so, some or most basic emotions may be observable in the presocialized infant.

For these reasons, more work has been done on facial expressions than on any other expressive channel. We will review this important work now. In particular, we will (1) review the empirical research that led to a dramatic change in attitude about the relevance of facial expressions for research on emotion, (2) describe some methodological developments in facial expression scoring that promise to provide a new level of precision in emotion measurement, (3) allude to some of the problems that are encountered by researchers studying emotional expressions in infancy, and (4) summarize some of the major research findings to date on facial expressions of emotion in infancy. We will end this discussion with a brief critique of the conceptual and empirical work on facial expressions.

The Facial Expression of Emotion in Infancy

The Rediscovery of the Specificity of Facial Expressions of Emotion. Recent research has sharply challenged the heretofore widespread conviction that facial expressions provide no reliable information about discrete emotions. In particular, the work of Ekman (1972), Izard (1971, 1972, 1979), and Tomkins (1962, 1963) has demonstrated that some emotions can be recognized from changes in facial patterning, even in the absence of contextual information—contrary to the opinions of Landis (1929) and Sherman (1927a). The most compelling evidence for this proposition has been provided by cross-cultural experiments conducted independently by Ekman and Izard (Ekman & Friesen, 1972; Ekman, Sorenson, & Friesen, 1969; Izard, 1971). The inspiration for the research of each of these investigators was the theory of Silvan Tomkins. Using Tomkins's description of specific facial patterns associated with particular emotions, each researcher constructed a set of still photographs of persons whose faces were configured in the theoretically predicted fashions. These photographs were then shown to persons from five literate cultures in Ekman's study (Ekman et al., 1969) and nine literate cultures in Izard's study (Izard, 1971). These observers were asked to choose from a list of emotion labels the term that most accurately matched the picture. There was considerable intraculture and interculture agreement in both studies for distinctive facial patterning of happiness, sadness (sometimes termed distress), surprise, fear, anger, and disgust. Izard also found evidence for interjudge agreement on shame and interest across cultures, but Ekman and Oster (1979) criticized these findings—because head position and not facial expression may have provided the basis for these judgments—and the findings have not been corroborated.

Studies of literate cultures, however, cannot demonstrate biologically based universality: These cultures can and do communicate with one another; thus, culturally learned symbols of emotion might become widely accepted. With this in mind, Ekman and his colleagues (Ekman et al., 1969; Ekman & Friesen, 1972) studied facial expressions in two preliterate cultures. Subjects were asked to pose expressions they might observe following specific, culture-appropriate events (e.g., the death of a child) and to choose the correct expression from among pictures of peak expressions. This study confirmed that preliterate adults not only configured their faces in the same manner as persons from a literate culture but also discriminated posed pictures representing happiness, sadness, disgust, and anger in the same manner as did literate adults. However, although the preliterate group discriminated fear and surprise from other expressions, they did not distinguish them from each other. Thus, Ekman reported strong evidence for the cross-cultural recognizability of four emotions (happiness, sadness, disgust, and anger) as well as suggestive evidence for three additional emotions (surprise, fear, and interest). The cross-cultural work has had major implications for the study of emotions in human infancy because if some facial emotional patterns appear to be universal and under biological control, some of these emotional patterns may be observable in infancy as well (Izard, 1978).

The Biological Adaptive Value of Facial Expressions. A second consideration suggesting the unlearned nature of some facial expressions of emotion—and, hence, the possibility of their being observed in early development in humans—comes from theories speculating about the adaptive value of facial expressions. A number of theorists (Andrew, 1963; Darwin, 1872/1975; Tinbergen, 1951; van Hoof, 1962) have argued that these facial patterns evolved from biologically adaptive behaviors connected with such activities as grooming, vision, respiration, and fighting: Through the process of natural selection, facial movements that initially functioned as such serviceable associated habits may have come to serve as social cues about internal states and environmental events.

For example, two facial patterns are reliably recognized cross-culturally as anger. The facial movement patterns are the same in two of three facial regions—the upper portion containing the eyebrows and forehead as well as the middle portion with the eyes, lids, nose, and cheeks. However, in one configuration, the mouth is open and squarish; in the other, the lips are pressed tightly together. Theorists (Darwin, 1872/1975; Ekman, 1972; Izard, 1979; Spencer, 1890) have proposed that these features may have originally served several adaptive functions.

The lowering of the eyebrows may have served to enhance visual acuity by shielding the eyes from direct sunlight. The tensing and narrowing of the eyelids may have accompanied visual concentration and further served to shield the eyes from the sun and protect them somewhat from other environmental intrusions (e.g., wind, dust, moderately sized objects). Taken as a gestalt, these movements in the upper portion of the face convey the impression of a determined, foreboding, penetrating countenance, both signaling and enhancing readiness for combat. The flaring of the nostrils may have facilitated the rapid, intense intake of oxygen and provided a measure of protection against external blocking of the air passage. The open mouth display may have originally functioned to bare the teeth for biting attack. As Darwin 1872/1975 hypothesized: "We may suspect . . . that our semi-human progenitors uncovered their canine teeth when preparing for battle as we still do when feeling ferocious or when merely sneering at or defying someone without any intention of making a real attack with our teeth" (pp. 251–242).

The closed-mouth display on the other hand may be a socially acquired expression that emerges as the angry animal or person learns to conceal or disguise the bare-toothed expression. Such concealment may serve either of two goals: to control the outward manifestations of anger altogether or to gain advantage over an adversary through the element of surprise. Another speculation regarding the closed-mouth face is that it results from arousal of less intense anger. Similar speculations have been made regarding other basic emotional expressions.

The fact that some facial patterns have proved cross-culturally recognizable has had important consequences for infancy and emotion reseachers. Facial scoring techniques have been created and refined to identify these emotional expressions and permit discrimination among them. As a result, the study of the facial expressions of infants has become an important means of investigating discrete emotional expressions as well as of validating the various scoring schemes.

Facial Expression Measurement. The existing facial measurement systems may be grouped into three categories: template-based, anatomically comprehensive, and inductively derived systems (Ekman & Oster, 1979). Template-based systems (e.g., Ekman & Friesen's, 1975, Facial Affect Scoring Technique [FAST] or Izard's, 1980, Maximally Discriminative Facial Movement [MAX]) identify full-faced patterns of facial muscle movements empirically or theoretically linked to discrete emotions. For example, the sadness template will include several facial movements: raising the inner corners of the brows to form inverted v's, pulling down the corners of the mouth, and often pushing up the chin.

Anatomically comprehensive systems (e.g., Ekman & Friensen's, 1978, Facial Action Coding System [FACS]) include not only such emotionally significant movement patterns but also all other movement possibilities as well.

Inductively derived systems have generally been developed using ethological observational methods to derive ethograms of apparently meaningful regularities of facial behavior. Although such systems have been developed for infants (Nystrom, 1974; Young & Decarie, 1977), children (Brannigan & Humphries, 1972; Grant, 1969; McGrew, 1972), and adults (Grant, 1969), methodological difficulties have limited their usefulness. They often confound behavioral description and inferential labeling (e.g., specifying a facial movement as an angry frown). Moreover, the codes frequently are imprecisely described, leaving considerable interpretive latitude to scorers. The facial patterns are not anatomically precise and are sometimes inaccurate (Ekman, 1982). Finally, the movements are not linked, theoretically or empirically, to facial information cross-culturally recognized as emotionally discrete.

By contrast, both the anatomically comprehensive and theory-based comprehensive systems provide a means for determining whether any given facial expression contains any or all of the essential features of universally recognized emotions. These scoring systems are all based on descriptive, noninferential categories specifying a number of distinct facial muscle configurations in each of the three regions described earlier (eyebrows/forehead; eye/lids/nose/cheeks; and mouth). Moreover, there is general agreement among the systems regarding the emotionally meaningful configurations within each facial region as well as which, of the plethora of possible combinations of these movements, unambiguously identify particular emotions. Because each of the fundamental emotions is defined as a specific and exclusive set of movements, expressions of one emotion can be differentiated from the others as well as from patterns that do not specify any single emotion (e.g., blends of components indicative of more than one emotion, or configurations not expressing any universally recognizable emotion).

When observers score facial activity using these systems, they judge the presence or absence of each of the movement categories within each facial region. They do not base their categorization of a movement on their perceptions of the emotional content of the expression. The researcher later determines that an emotion is present when the categorizations of the observed movements meet a preselected or predicted criterion (which may be unknown to the scorers) or when statistical comparison indicates that the relative proportions of facial movement components expected to be present in response to elicitors of one emotion are high relative to those expected to be associated with a different emotion (Hiatt, Campos, & Emde, 1979).

Currently, the most widely used anatomically comprehensive approach is FACS (Ekman & Friesen, 1976, 1978). Ermiane and Gergerian (cited in Ekman & Friesen, 1976) have published a similar system but, as Ekman (1982) notes, reliability data have not been presented nor is there information about how the system is to be taught. FACS, which is designed to record all visible changes of the facial musculature, distinguishes 24 discrete action units, 20 miscellaneous actions more grossly defined in terms of their anatomical basis (e.g., cheek puff), and 14 action units designating head and eye positions (Ekman & Friesen, 1978).

The comprehensive of FACS offers a number of advantages. FACS can be used to detect previously undocumented regularities in facial action and, in turn, to determine whether these regularities signal

Table 1. **Facial Expression Criteria and Illustrations**

Maximally Discriminative Facial Movements (MAX) Codes

Brows (*B*); (Forehead [*F*]; Nasal root [*N*]	Eyes/Nose/Cheeks	Mouth/Lips
20. *B*: Raised in arched or normal shape. (F: Long transverse furrows or thickening; *N*: Narrowed.)	30. Enlarged, roundish appearance of eye region owing to tissue between upper lid and brow being stretched (upper eye furrow may be visible); upper eyelids not raised.	50. Opened, roundish or oval.
21. *B*: One brow raised higher than other (other one may be slightly lowered).	31. Eye fissure widened, upper lid raised (white shows more than normal).	51. Opened, relaxed.
22. *B*: Raised; drawn together, straight or normal shape. (*F*: Short transverse furrows or thickening in mid-region; *N*: Narrowed.)	*33*. Narrowed or squinted (by action of eye sphincters or brow depressors).	52. Corners pulled back and slightly up (open or closed).
23. *B*: Inner corners raised; shape under inner corner. (*F*: Bulge or furrows in center above brow corners; *N*: Narrowed.)	36. Gaze downward, askance.	53. Opened, tense, corners retracted straight back.
24. *B*: Drawn together, but neither raised nor lowered. (Vertical furrows or bulge between brows.)	37. Eye fissure scrouged, tightly closed.	*54*. Angular, squarish (open).
25. *B*: Lowered and drawn together. (*F*: Vertical furrows or bulge between brows; *N*: Broadened, bulged.)	*38*. Cheeks raised.	56. Corners drawn downward—outward (open or closed); chin may push up center of lower lip.
	39. Gaze cast downward, head tilted back.	59A(= 51/66). Opened, relaxed; tongue forward (beyond gum line), may be moving.
	42. Nasal bridge furrowed (or shows lumpy ridge running diagonally upward from nasolabial fold.) (42 need not be coded separately; it can be used as an additional cue in coding *54* and 59B.)	59B(= 54/66). Opened, angular, upper lip pulled up; tongue forward (beyond gum line), may be moving.
		61. Upper lip raised on one side.
		63. Lower lip lowered (may be slightly forward).
		64. Lower lip (or both lips) rolled inward (not illustrated and not observed in our video records of infants).
		65. Lips pursed.
		66. Tongue forward (beyond gum line), may be moving.

(*continued*)

specific emotions. It can be used to study culture-specific as well as cross-culturally universal expressions. It can assist in determining whether specific actions, sequences of actions, variations in intensity, timing of actions, or some combination best specify particular emotions. Moreover, it facilitates the study of a wide range of facial behaviors that may be self-regulatory or socially communicative but not necessarily emotional, such as lip biting or winking.

Moreover, this system has been adapted for application to infants' expressions, Although an infant's facial musculature is the same as that of an adult, there are some marked differences in appearance that result from the infant's substantial deposits of subcutaneous fat, differences in proportions and dimensions of skeletal parts (Oster, 1982), the buccal fat pad, the sucking lip, and so on. Oster (1982) has adapted FACS to take account of these differences.

The major disadvantage of FACS is that its comprehensiveness makes it quite time consuming to use. Substantial time must be invested in learning the codes reliably, maintaining scorer accuracy, and scoring videotapes. The system is not well suited to live coding and, even with videotape, requires numerous tape passes and slow-motion viewing to be satisfactorily applied.

However, as alluded to earlier, the system has clear advantages as well. Because FACS make no a priori assumptions about which facial configurations have significance, but codes all visible patterning, it can be used to construct special purpose scoring systems that include and exclude various action units on the basis of some set of criteria. Ekman is currently

Table 1. *(Continued)*

Partial List of Formulas Used to Identify Discrete Emotions and the Infant Pain Expression

Interest:* *IE
Any one or more of the following movement units (A)

		A	
20	30	51	65
24	33	59A	66
25	38		

if the following movements (B) are *not* presented simultaneously:

		B	
21	31	50	61
22	37	52	63
23		53	64
		54	
		56	
		59B	

IE blends: Movements that can participate in IE blends
24 33,38 51,59A 65,66
33, 38 must not be concomitant with 25 or 37

Enjoyment-Joy:* *EJ
38 + 52

Surprise-Astonishment:* *SA
20 + 30 + 50

Sadness-Dejection:* *SD
23 + 33,38 + 56

Anger:* *AR
25 + (33, 38) + 54

Disgust:* *DR
25 + 33, 38 + 59B + 63

Contempt:* *CS
21 + 61 + 39

Fear:* *FT
22 + 31 + 53

Shame:* *SH
36 + 64 + 75 (head lowered)

Discomfort-Pain:* *DP
25 + 37 + 54

constructing such a shorthand instrument—tentatively called EMFACS—(Emotion Facial Action Coding System—for use by researchers who only wish to answer questions about whether a certain universally recognizable emotion or blend of emotions was present in a given behavioral sample.

Izard's (1980) MAX is currently a widely used template-based coding system designed specifically for use with infants. The MAX system identifies 27 distinct components, 26 of which are patterns of facial muscle movements derived from theory and empirical data regarding those facial configurations that universally specify each of 10 discrete emotions. The other movement involves an eye glance or head tilt.

These 27 components may be organized to form patterns that specify random facial posturing, blends of emotions, or discrete emotions, including interest-excitement (IE), enjoyment-joy (EJ), surprise-astonishment (SA), sadness-dejection (SD), anger-rage (AR), disgust (DR)-contempt (CS), fear-terror (FT), shame-shyness (SH), discomfort-pain (DP), or distress-anguish. The codes for these discrete emotions and the configurations are listed in Table 1 and illustrated in Figure 1. These codes appear to be especially useful when researchers are interested in the presence of cross-culturally recognized emotions or blends. MAX is decidedly easier to use than FACS. Its use, however, is limited to determining whether samples of behavior match the predicted template. It does not assess emotion intensity; nor does it capture movement regularities not already anticipated by the theoretical underpinnings of the system. Finally, no data yet clearly establish the validity of some of MAX's configurational judgments. For example, the design of MAX presumes that when an infant closes his eyes tightly while his brows are lowered and his mouth is square, then the infant is experiencing pain-discomfort. By contrast, if the eyes are open, then the infant is regarded as angry. This distinction may make some theoretical sense, in that pain is an inward experience not re-

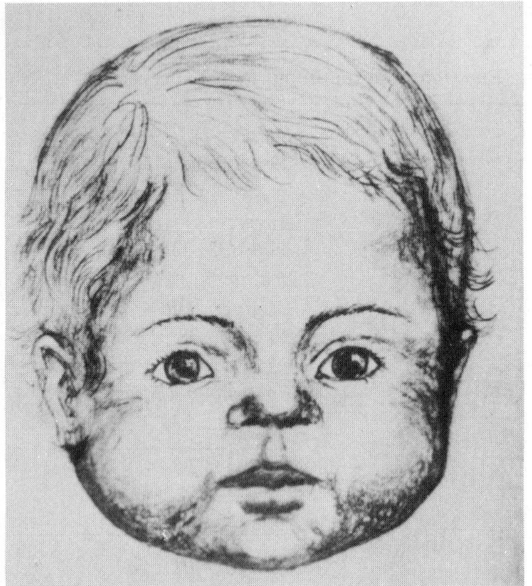

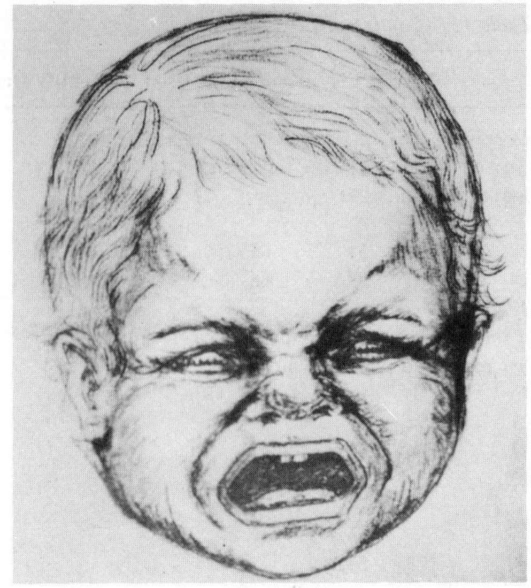

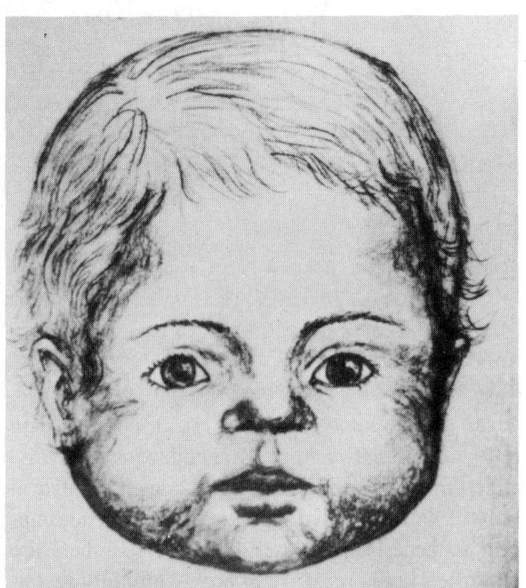

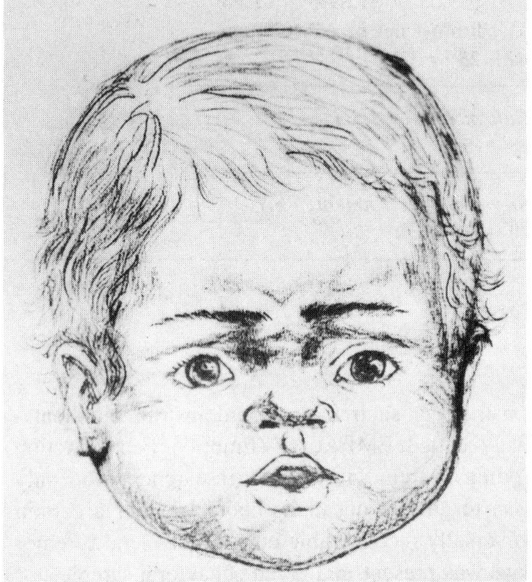

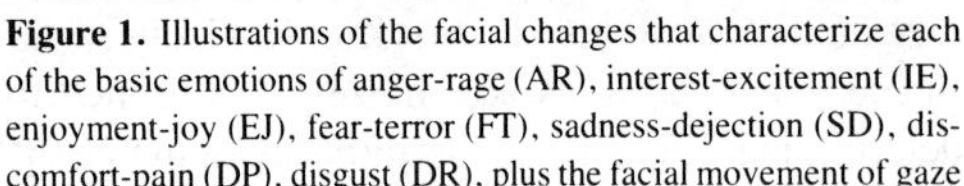

Figure 1. Illustrations of the facial changes that characterize each of the basic emotions of anger-rage (AR), interest-excitement (IE), enjoyment-joy (EJ), fear-terror (FT), sadness-dejection (SD), discomfort-pain (DP), disgust (DR), plus the facial movement of gaze aversion. These illustrations are taken from Izard's Maximally Discriminative Facial Movement Scoring System (1979). The numbers to the left of the figures refer to the facial movement code numbers presented in Table 1.

quiring vision for adaptation, whereas anger usually presumes an external target and a threatened attack for which visual acuity may be crucial. However, the significance of eyes open versus eyes shut has not been empirically established.

Izard has introduced another scoring system, (AFFEX), which identifies the same emotions as MAX at a more global level (Izard & Dougherty, 1980, 1982). AFFEX requires judges to be trained first in MAX and in its templates, then to make judgments about the presence of emotions from the pattern of the entire face scored at once rather than three facial regions scored separately (Izard, 1979). Although the system offers great advantages in terms of efficiency of scoring time, it shares the same difficulties as the MAX system (because it uses

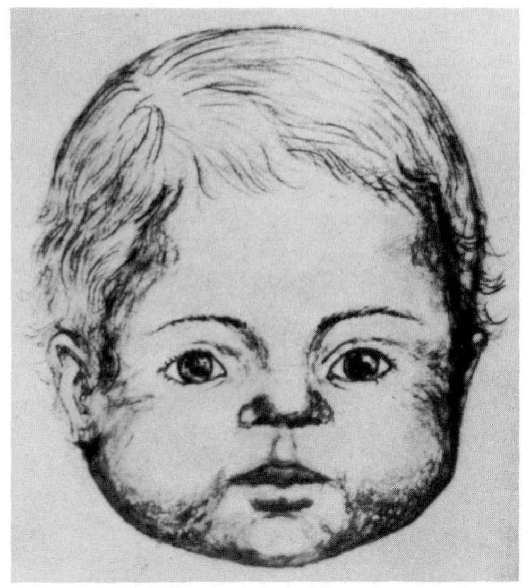

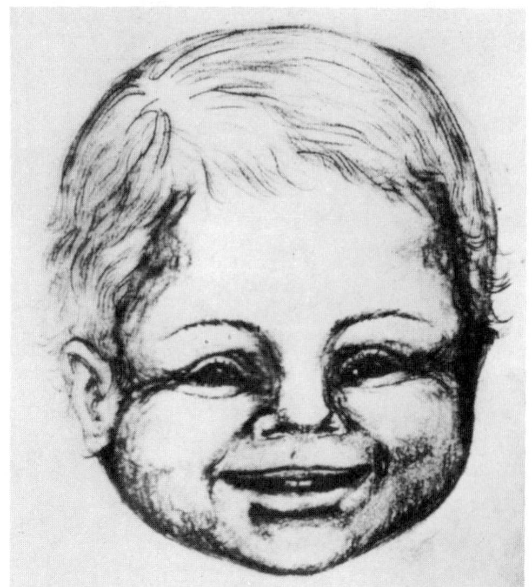

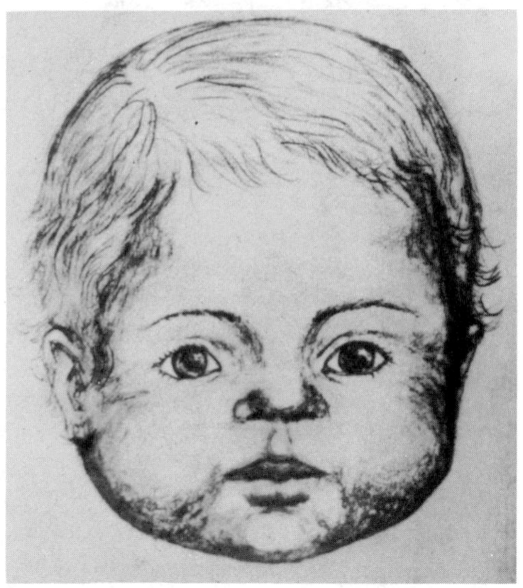

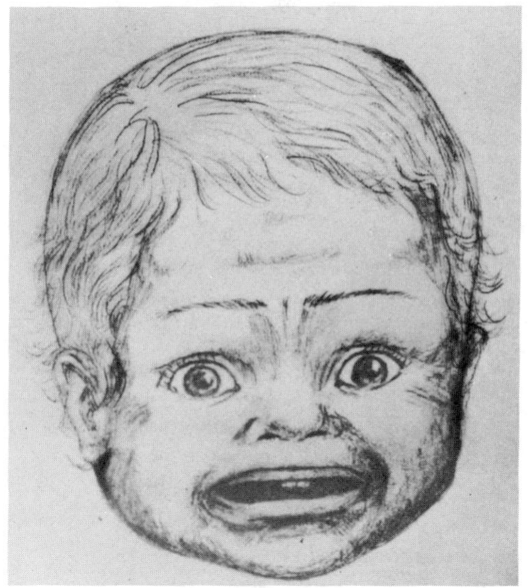

Figure 1 —***Continued***

the same templates). In addition, AFFEX may fail to detect subtle blends of emotions (1) by not detecting micromomentary changes of the facial musculature (as may occur in masking) or (2) by registering a discrete emotion as occurring when not all predicted movements are present.

Recent Studies of Facial Expression of Emotion in Infancy. Researchers studying emotional expressions in adults have noted that the universal expression forms are not invariably observed in response to an emotion-arousing event. Individuals vary greatly both in the ways they respond to specific situations (e.g., smiling or crying at a wedding) and in the intensity of their reactions (consult *Infant Temperament*). Also, considerable cultural variability exists with respect to norms (what Ekman,

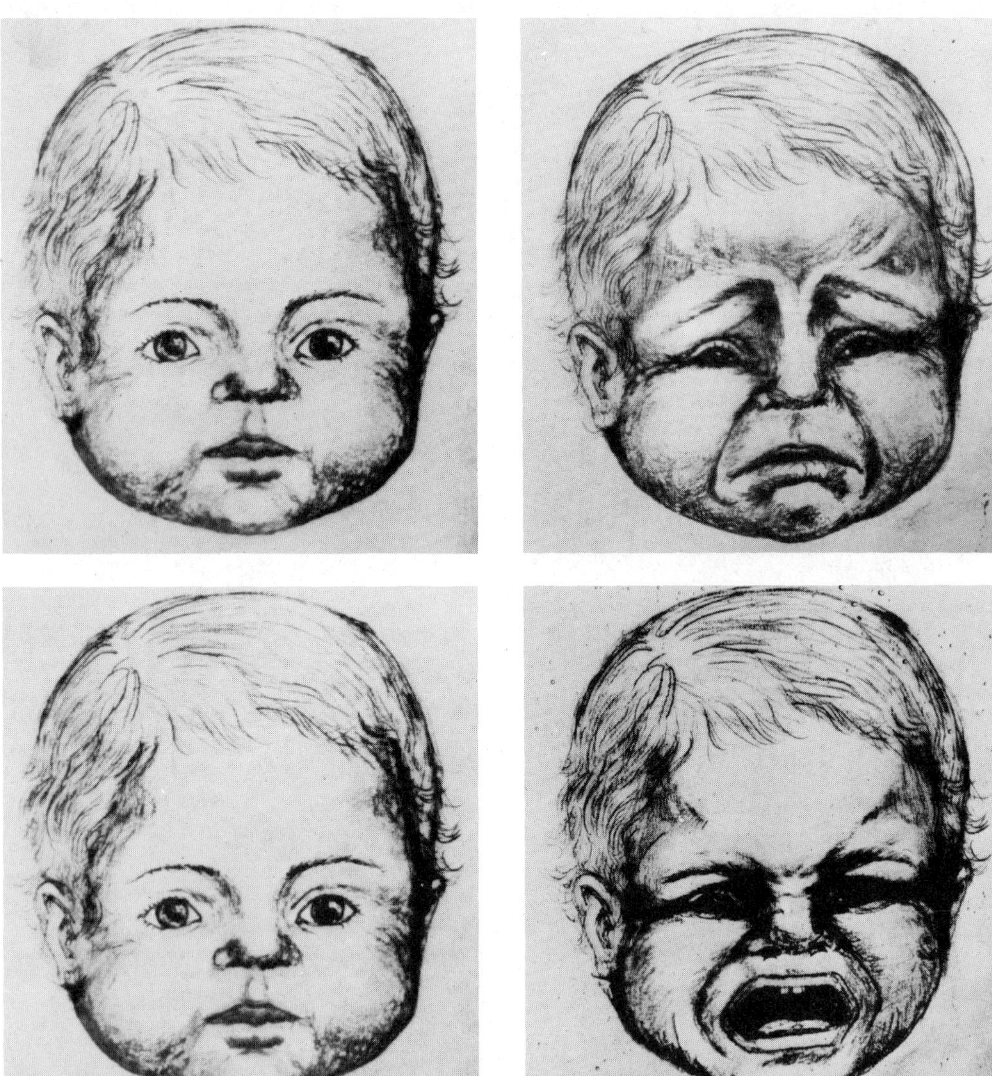

Figure 1. —*Continued*

1980, calls cultural display rules) governing the content and intensity of emotional expressions (see also Birdwhistell, 1970; M. Mead, 1975). For example, Ekman and Friesen (1972) find that when Japanese and American subjects watch stress-inducing or neutral films by themselves, the facial responses of the two nationalities are very similar. However, when their reactions to the films are observed by another person, the Japanese subjects evidence more smiling and constriction of facial responsivity than do Americans. There is even some indication that cultural variables may result in modifications of universal expression patterns. For instance, Heider (1974) reported that members of the Dani preliterate culture in New Guinea do not show clear anger but a blend of emotions, including disgust components. Furthermore, the study of naturally occurring emotions is compromised by the capacity of persons to abort facial expressions, to express them in the absence of an accompanying feeling state (simulation), or to alter them (masking), for example, by substituting other movements (Ekman, 1980; Izard, 1977).

These human capabilities have lent great significance to the study of emotional expression in infan-

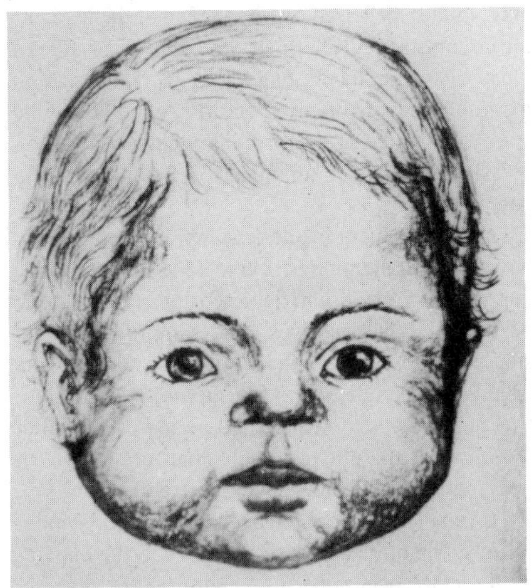

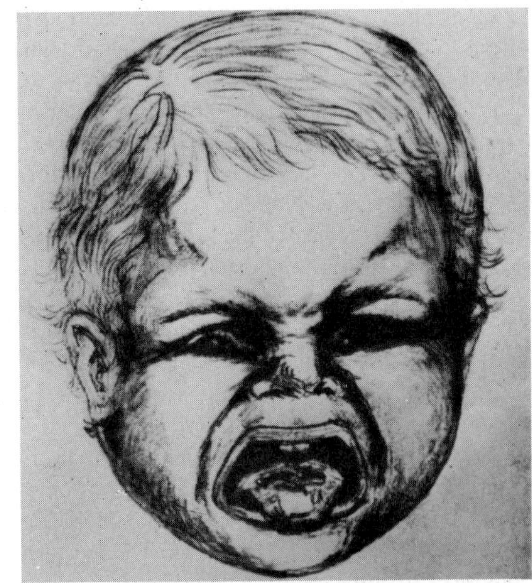

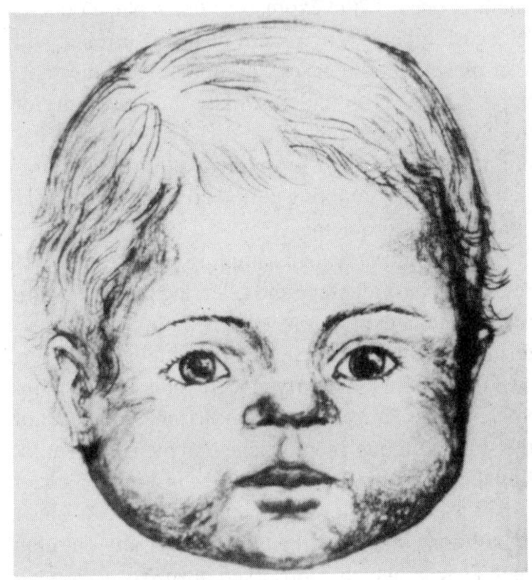

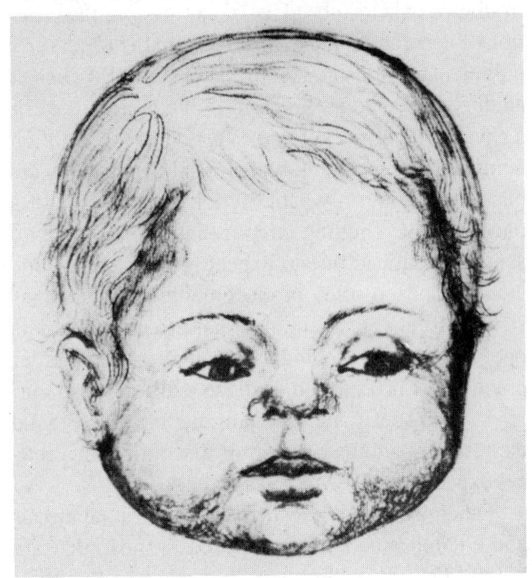

Figure 1. —*Continued*

cy. Although infants also display considerable individual differences in the content and intensity of their reactions to environmental events, the complexity of their reactions is limited by the level of their perceptual and cognitive skills. For example, the emotional significance of an event, such as rolling a ball to an infant and then retrieving it, may become more difficult to predict once the child has acquired an understanding of the game of catch. Prior to the child's understanding the game she might typically show positive or negative reactions as the ball approaches and is taken away. Once the child knows how to play the game, however, her reactions may be influenced not only by the event per se but also by her disposition toward playing that game at that time.

Further, unlike older individuals, infants are less likely to display complex combinations of emotional expressions or to hide their emotions. First, they have not yet become strongly influenced by social display rules governing affective expressions. Also, young infants probably do not possess the requisite cognitive abilities to mask their facial responses intentionally. Finally, infants are incapable of appreciating as many aspects of a situation as are older persons and are less sophisticated in coping with emotion-eliciting events. Thus, they are unlikely to react to eliciting situations with as complex an array of responses as older children or adults. The deliberate disguise of an emotion, for instance, may require a capacity as advanced as that of deferred imitation, which may not appear until the second year of life (Piaget, 1951, 1954). Emotional reactions in infancy, then, remain less confounded by the factors found in adults' expressions. Thus, the issue of universals of expression of discrete emotions may be more validly investigated with infants.

Methodological Problems in Facial Expression Research with Infants. Although theoretically significant, research on facial expressions of emotion in human infancy encounters formidable methodological and conceptual problems. The most serious of these obstacles is the problem of accuracy. In studies of actor-posed facial expression, the criterion of accuracy is the match between the observer's judgment and the intent of the actor. Or, in studies of adults' spontaneous expressions of emotion, the criterion is often the expressor's report of the emotion being experienced. But when facial expressions are elicited by stimuli, what criterion of accuracy does one use? The eliciting circumstances that common sense would lead one to expect to bring about one emotion all too often produce another emotion instead. Moreover, a stimulus that effectively elicits one emotion in one individual may elicit another emotion, or no emotion at all, in a different person. How, then, does one ascertain that observed facial expression patterns confirm or disconfirm theoretical expectations?

Other problems concern the study of spontaneous and elicited emotions as opposed to those that are posed. One such problem is created by emotion blends. When an actor poses a facial expression pattern, he can control facial movements so that only components of one particular emotion are expressed. However, in real life, a single eliciting event is likely to produce several emotions, not just one. Moreover, the blending can take place simultaneously (e.g., when a facial expression of anger is accompanied by components of disgust) or sequentially (e.g., when surprise gives way quickly to joy or to fear).

Another problem, not so difficult in principle to control as the first two, is the influence of the background context on coders' emotion judgments. As we noted earlier, many critics of facial expression research have pointed out that emotion judgments that *seem* to be determined by a facial expression may, in fact, be based on knowledge of the instigating circumstances (Sherman, 1927a, 1927b). Judges must, therefore, be presented with facial expression recordings devoid of any suggestion of context if the study is directed at determining whether facial expressions reliably communicate emotional states to perceivers.

A final problem is one of sampling from the behavior record the time period to be judged for facial expressions of emotion. Two scoring schemes have been used. One involves time sampling. For instance, the researcher can record all facial behaviors or judges can code their perception of a given emotion or emotions for a specified period of time after the onset of the elicitor (e.g., Hiatt et al., 1979). This method encounters a major difficulty however. If a given facial expression occurs very briefly and is followed by other expressions, the record will overrepresent the occurrence of blends—in this case, sequential ones. If the expression takes place outside the scoring period, no record of its occurrence will take place. In both cases, the outcome of the sampling scheme is to underestimate the specificity of the facial expressions elicited. Because facial expressions can change so rapidly, altering the duration of the time-sampling period does not necessarily eliminate the problem.

The second prevalent sampling scheme involves reviewing the videotape and selecting the best examples of facial expressions that meet any a priori determined templates (e.g., Izard, Huebner, Risser, McGinnes, & Doughterty, 1980). This approach involves the use of coders naive as to the hypotheses of the study, although sophisticated in measuring emotional expressions in the face. For instance, a coder can be asked to review segments of a tape to discover expressions that meet the template for any emotion such as fear, which is observed during or following an eliciting event. When such expressions are selected, they can be shown to naive judges to determine the probability of their judging the expression to be a fearful one or the expression can be subjected to detailed facial movement analysis to confirm that the pattern of facial movement indeed exists as predicted. This approach can avoid the problem of inadvertent scoring of sequential emotional blends. However, its difficulty is that it can capitalize on chance or coincidental facial movements that happen momentarily to meet the a priori criteria. This approach, then, can result in overrepresentation of the likelihood of finding discrete facial patterns. To date, no widely agreed on method of facial expression sampling has been developed.

Studies of Facial Expressions of Emotion in

Infancy. One of the most comprehensive studies of facial expression patterning to date is that of Hiatt and her collaborators (1979). They employed six situations—two presumed to elicit each of three emotions—joy, fear, and surprise. Determination was made of whether the two situations presumed to elicit the same emotional state produced similar facial expression patterns to one another but different patterns than did the situations designed to elicit different emotional states. The investigators took care to confirm, using nonfacial criteria, that the eliciting circumstances produced the desired emotion (i.e., by verifying whether the elicitors produced expected behavioral reactions, such as the visual cliff eliciting failure to cross to the mother or a suddenly vanishing toy producing prolonged looking at the point of disappearance).

A time-sampling scheme was used to score facial movements, and Ekman and Friesen's (1975) FAST—as modified by the investigators—was used to code all facial movements observed within the designated time window. These facial movements were then tabulated as the proportion of facial movements that had been predicted to occur for the given emotion elicitor and the proportion of movements that had not been predicted to occur. These two figures permitted assessment of whether the elicitors (e.g., the two happy conditions) produced the predicted facial movements (e.g., the four components of a happy face in the modified FAST scheme) significantly more than they produced facial movements not predicted for those elicitors (e.g., disgust, fear, anger components, etc.). Such patterning was observed for both joy as well as both surprise elicitors, but not for either fear elicitor (one was the direct placement atop the deep side of the visual cliff and the other was the approach of a stranger). The authors concluded that strong evidence was found for some types of facial patterning in 10- to 12-month-old infants.

This study was followed up by one on the facial expression of anger in 7-month-old infants by Stenberg, Campos, and Emde (1983). The emotion elicitor used was the removal of a teething biscuit just prior to the baby's placing it in her mouth and a similar time-sampling and modified FAST scoring method used to determine facial expression movement patterning. Strong evidence of the patterning of anger was found: prior to the first biscuit-removal trial, only 3% of anger-related facial movements were observed; after removal, the anger facial movements increased to 29%. On the other hand, nonanger components did not change as a function of the frustration, the observed nonanger components being 6% prior to, and 9% after, removal. Findings became even stronger on subsequent trials: By the last trial scored, a sharp increase in anger components again was evident, although now the prestimulus period also contained a large proportion of anger components (prestimulus = 32%; poststimulus = 66%). Nonanger components again remained constant (prestimulus = 6%; poststimulus = 9%).

Stenberg (1982) replicated these findings, using a different elicitor (arm restraint), a different component scoring technique (MAX), and a different sampling method (selection of the first negative facial expression for scoring regardless of which type of negative affect). In this study, 1-, 4-, and 7-month-olds were tested: the findings are presented in Figure 2. As can be seen in this figure, anger facial movement components are rarely observed before restraint. After restraint, the proportion of anger components rises sharply at each age. Moreover, at 4 and 7 months of age, the proportion of nonanger components elicited by the restraint task was small. (Children 1 month old, but not older infants, tended to close their eyes and protrude their tongues, neither movement being expected for anger expressions.) Further analyses by Stenberg revealed that 5 of the 16 four-month-olds tested and 6 of the 16 seven-month-olds met the extremely stringent criterion of facial patterning of showing *all four* MAX components pertaining to the template of anger and *no other* MAX components indicative of other negative emotions.

Izard and his collaborators (e.g., Izard, Hembree, Dougherty, & Coss, in press) have studied the facial expression reactions of infants at various ages to the stress of receiving innoculations. Using the MAX templates and a 10-second time sampling procedure, Izard et al. reported a sharp increase in the duration of time that anger is expressed between the ages of 8 and 19 months. Before 19 months of age, the predominant expression is one of distress, which includes eyes screwed tightly as well as an open, square mouth, and eyebrows drawn together.

Izard's approach to facial expression studies has sometimes differed from the previous ones, in that it focuses on whether college students, nurses, or mothers agree with one another on what emotional expression is present in a photograph of a baby's reaction to the innoculation (Izard et al., 1980). In general, the judgment data he reports demonstrate that the facial expressions matching his templates for certain discrete emotions, like surprise, sadness, joy, and anger, are judged at well above chance

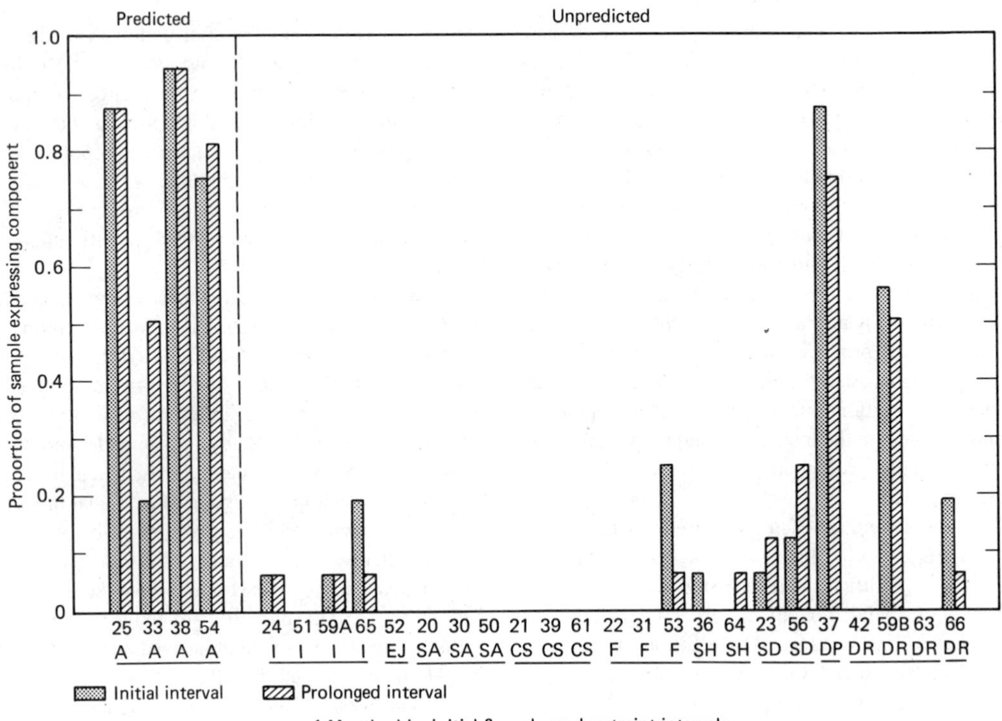

Figure 2. The MAX facial movement patterns in response to restraint reported by Stenberg (1972) for 1-, 4-, and 7-month-old infants. The solid bars represent data from 3 sec. intervals encompassing the first intense negative facial expression observed in the videotape (which negative expression did not need to be anger). The crosshatched bars represent data from the 3-sec, interval just prior to the termination of restraint. The numbers under the bars represent the MAX facial code numbers presented in Table 1: *A* stands for anger, *I* for interest, *EJ* for enjoyment-joy, *SA* for surprise-astonishment, *CS* for contempt, *F* for fear, *SH* for shame, *SD* for sadness-dejection, *DP* for discomfort-pain, and *DR* for disgust.

levels. Moreover, Izard reports that the accuracy of judgments does not differ significantly between still photos and videotape segments of the facial expressions, a finding also reported by Emde, Kligman, Reich, and Wade (1978).

The third major line of research on infant facial expression has concerned neonates' responses to various taste stimuli Rosenstein and Oster (1981), for instance, tested 2-hour-old infants' responses to various taste substances, which to adults taste sour, sweet, salty, and bitter. Selecting the peak expression of the infant in response to the stimuli, they coded the infants' responses using FACS. They reported strong evidence of differentiation of facial response patterns to positive versus negative solutions but little evidence for differentiation within negative elicitors. A follow-up judgment study revealed that judges were able to identify infants' facial expressions to the sweet versus the bitter substance but were inaccurate in recognizing reactions to sour and salty stimuli.

Steiner (1973) reported that infants' facial expression reactions to similar taste stimuli became much more differentiated during the period beginning immediately after birth and ending 3 days later. The weak evidence for differentiation of facial patterns on other than a hedonic-tone dimension by Rosenstein and Oster (1981) could, thus, result from the less-than-optimal state of the infant after the stress of birth.

In summary, much progress has been made in our understanding of facial expressions in general and infant facial expressions in particular. Strong evidence of the universality of certain expressions had been generated. The data on anger is particularly impressive, given the consistent reports of anger facial patterns to different elicitors using different coding systems and sampling approaches.

Moreover, facial action coding techniques based on these universal facial configurations have potentiated the study of emotion, especially in preverbal infants. The study of infants' facial expressions, al-

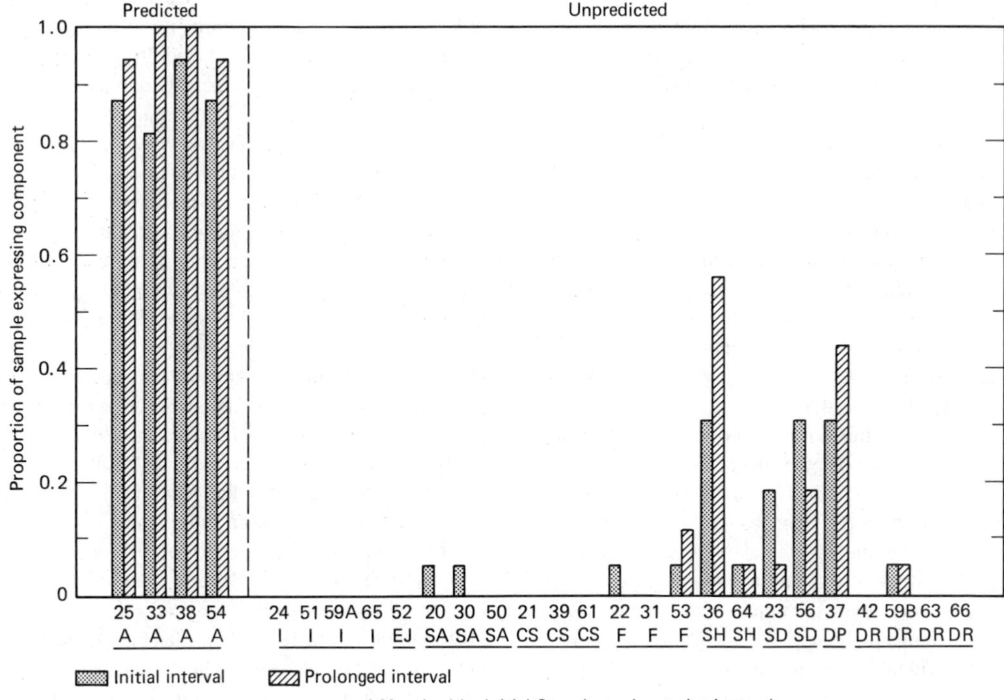

4 Month olds, initial & prolonged restraint intervals

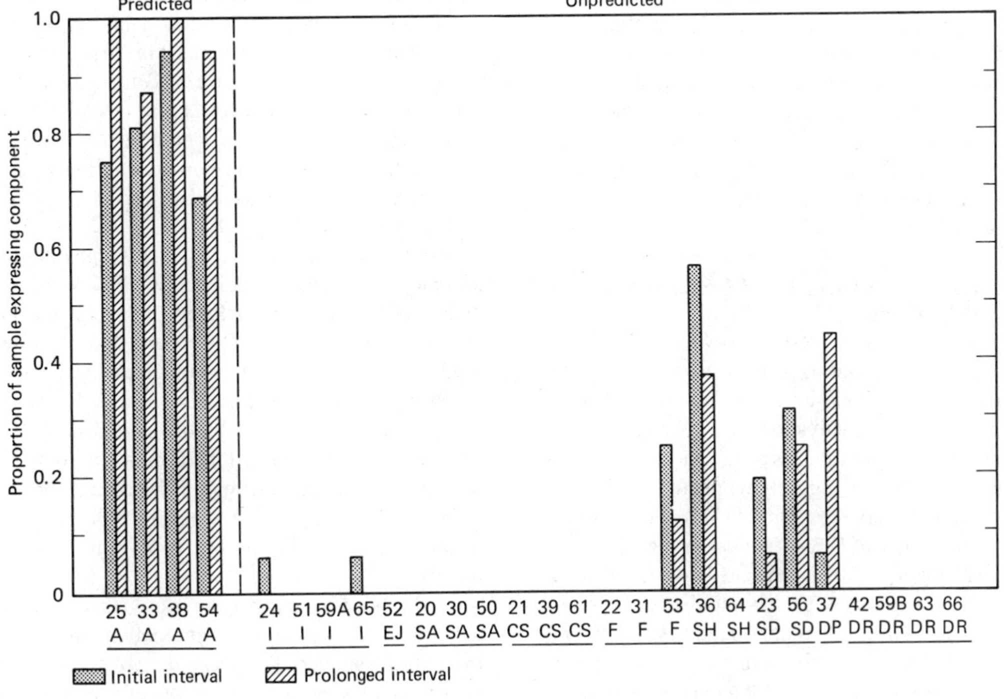

7 Month olds, initial & prolonged restraint intervals

Figure 2. ***—Continued***

though fraught with its own set of methodological difficulties, may be especially enlightening, in that it may uncover the relative roles of biology and socialization in the ontogenesis of emotional expressions, especially when such studies are combined with research on blind or deaf infants or with studies on different races and cultures.

As we mentioned earlier, the study of facial expressions has been so prevalent that, at times, facial expressions have seemed isomorphic with emotion. This dominance of the field by facial expressions is unfortunate for two reasons. In the first place, the impression is created that we have much more evidence for discrete measurement of emotion by means of the face than is yet the case. Although findings are promising, we need to pursue the study of discrete emotions other than those yet investigated (e.g., sadness, which to date has been studied sensitively only by Gaensbauer, 1980). We also need to understand why facial expression patterns of fear have been so difficult to identify cross-culturally and to document in human infants. Is the theory-derived template in error? Does fear show more interindividual variation than does anger? Or do our laboratory and observational measures of fear not adequately elicit the emotion in as clear and intense a fashion as is necessary?

The second unfortunate outcome of the emphasis on facial expression measurement has been the relative neglect of the study of the other expressive channels in infancy. As we will see, the state of knowledge concerning vocal and gestural expressions of emotion is immature compared to what we know regarding facial emotion. Nevertheless, there is increasing evidence to indicate that emotion specificity is not the exclusive province of facial expressions. We now turn to the study of the expression of emotion through the voice.

The Vocal Expression of Emotion in Adults and Infants

Background. There is now clear and consistent evidence that vocal expressions convey information about dimensional properties, like hedonic tone and level of activation, and discrete emotions, like anger, fear, joy, surprise, and sadness. The available evidence suggests judgment accuracy rates of approximately 60% for vocal samples compared to a chance rate of 12%—figures that are all the more remarkable considering the methodological inadequacy of some of the studies and the rather esoteric affect states that judges are sometimes given to rate (e.g., indifference, boredom, jealousy) (for a review, see Scherer, 1981). Moreover, every emotion identified in the cross-cultural studies of facial expression recognition has been shown in one or another study of Western cultures to be identified in vocal expressions as well. In addition, there has been considerable progress in analyzing the acoustical properties of the voice that specify emotional information to the perceiver. Innovative approaches are now verifying that these properties can be synthesized to generate artificial affect-specifying vocal patterns (Scherer, 1979a), and great strides are being made in identifying the neurophysiological basis of affect vocalizations (Jürgens, 1979). Given these promising developments, it is surprising that so little research on the vocal expression of emotion has been carried out with infants. Our review, accordingly, will emphasize the findings from research with adults or children (see also Malatesta, 1981b).

A number of rather different research methods have been used to study the relationship between vocal patterns and emotion judgments. The objective of each method has been to control for nonemotional sources of variance and to manipulate those features of the voice believed to carry the emotional information. For instance, Sherman (1927b) manipulated singing to determine whether emotions could be identified in the voice when eliciting context, facial expression, body movement, semantic information, and even certain types of acoustic information, such as pitch, intensity, and duration were controlled. Subjects sang five notes in E major and then in A major, having been instructed to convey one of four emotions: surprise, fear-pain, sorrow, or anger-hate. The notes were limited in duration to 1- to 2-seconds. Despite the limited acoustic information available to the perceivers and despite Sherman's expectations that there would be no specificity of emotion judgment, all emotions were identified accurately—sorrow and anger-hate especially were readily identifiable.

Another popular method that yields high rates of accuracy of judgment—despite lacking ecological validity—involves reading letters of the alphabet in various tones of voice. Dusenbury and Knower (1939) reported accuracy rates ranging from 75% to 91% for judgments of pain, determination, fear, and joy. Davitz and Davitz (1959) reported accuracy rates well above chance for 10 emotions (anger, fear, happiness, jealous, love, nervousness, pride, sadness, satisfaction, and sympathy). Anger was identified most readily in this study, fear the least readily.

A number of researchers have used the *standard text passage* to test accuracy of emotion judgments from vocal samples. This method involves an actor or actress reading an identical set of sentences in different tones of voice. Fairbanks and Pronovost

(1938) reported accuracy rates of 66% for fear, 78% for anger and grief, 84% for contempt, and 88% for indifference—results that far exceed chance expectations. Dimitrovsky (1964) used this approach with children ranging in age from 5 to 12 years and found that children at all ages accurately identified sadness, happiness, anger, and loving expressions. She also reported that the accuracy of identification increased monotonically with age, confirming a conclusion from a sketchy early study by Gates (1925).

Voice sounds from *filtered speech* have also communicated specific emotions to listeners, but this method appears to produce much lower accuracy rates than other methods. The purpose of filtering is to eliminate the high-frequency sounds that carry the semantic information while preserving the lower frequency sounds, which are presumed to carry the emotional information. Using this method applied to sounds obtained from real-life situations, Soskin and Kauffman (1961) obtained significant agreement on 10 of their 15 voice samples. McCluskey, Albas, Niemi, Cuevas, and Ferrer (1975) used this method in a cross-cultural and developmental study of emotion recognition in which they found that Mexican children were more sensitive to vocal expressions of emotion than Canadian children were.

The consistency of these findings regarding emotion judgments has led researchers to analyze some of the acoustic features that may account for the emotion judgments (Williams & Stevens, 1981). To date, the important acoustic features have not been specified as successfully as have the components of facial expression. Nevertheless, a number of regularities have emerged that center on prosodic parameters, such as pitch level, pitch range, pitch variability, loudness, and tempo. The relationship between these parameters and various discrete emotions and the emotional dimensions of evaluation, activation, and potency are listed in Table 2.

Pitch level was analyzed as long ago as 1935 by Skinner, who found it to reliably differentiate the expression of happiness and sadness. Happiness was reported to have a much higher pitch than sadness, which, in turn, had nearly the same pitch as that in the normal voice. Fairbanks and Pronovost (1938) reported similar findings for grief and also demonstrated that grief had a low pitch range, the lowest mean inflectional range of the emotions they studied, and the lowest rate of pitch change. On the other hand, anger was characterized by a relatively high median pitch level, wide pitch range within short time intervals, and widest mean inflectional range, whereas fear had the highest median pitch level, widest pitch range, rapid pitch changes, and wide mean inflectional range.

Using more advanced techniques, Williams and Stevens (1972) obtained similar results to those of Skinner (1935) and Fairbanks and Pronovost (1938) for the emotions of sadness, anger, and fear. Profes-

Table 2. **Summary of Results on Vocal Indicators of Emotional States**

Emotion	Pitch level	Pitch range	Pitch variability	Loudness	Tempo
Happiness-joy	High	?	Large	Loud	Fast
Confidence	High	?	?	Loud	Fast
Anger	High	Wide	Large	Loud	Fast
Fear	High	Wide	Large	?	Fast
Indifference	Low	Narrow	Small	?	Fast
Contempt	Low	Wide	?	Loud	Slow
Boredom	Low	Narrow	?	Soft	Slow
Grief-sadness	Low	Narrow	Small	Soft	Slow
Evaluation	?	?	?	Loud	?
Activation	High	Wide	?	Loud	Fast
Potency	?	?	?	Loud	?

(Revised from Scherer, 1979b, p. 513. Reprinted with permission of Plenum Press.)

sional actors uttered standard phrases and sentences while portraying different emotional situations that were part of a dramatic play. The utterances were then subjected to spectrographic analyses. Measures of median fundamental frequency and fundamental frequency range differentiated sorrow (reduced fundamental frequency and narrow range), anger (high fundamental frequency and narrow range), and fear (low fundamental frequency and occasional contour peaks). In addition, duration of the utterance and rate of articulation were found to differentiate the various expressions. Sorrow was characterized by an increase in the duration of an utterance and a decrease in the rate of articulation when compared to the normal voice. Angry utterances tended to be longer, with vowels and consonants more precisely articulated than in normal voice utterances. The same precision of articulation was found in fear as in anger, but the duration of an utterance was much greater than that for anger and neutral utterances.

Some early research suggested that the sequential pattern of the utterance may be an important component in the communication of emotion. Sequential pattern includes such features as stress, intonation contour, and pauses. Dusenbury and Knower (1939) found that when judges heard only the first or the last 6 letters of an 11-alphabet-letter utterance expressed emotionally, the accuracy of their judgments was decreased. The percentage of correct judgments for anger-hate-rage went from 78% to about 60%, glee-merriment went from 81% to about 35%, and fear-terror-horror went from 82% to about 50%. Yet, even with these changes, the percentages of accuracy were beyond chance expectation.

To explore more completely the importance of the sequential pattern of speech on emotional expression recognition, Knower (1941) compared the accuracy of emotional expression identification in recordings of voices played in normal sequence (forward) with those same recordings of voices played in reverse. As in the Dusenbury and Knower (1939) study, emotions were expressed by reciting letters of the alphabet. Knower (1941) found that the accuracy rate of the judgments in the reverse condition was much lower (43%) compared to the rate obtained in the normal voice-forward condition (89%). (Recognition rates for specific emotions were not provided). However, even the lower accuracy rate was nearly five times over chance expectation. According to Knower, the sequential pattern of speech is an important part of emotional expression communication, but other physical attributes (e.g., intensity) also play a significant role.

The investigations of Scherer and associates (Scherer, 1979a, 1979b, 1982; Scherer & Ekman, 1982; Scherer, Koivumaki, & Rosenthal, 1972) comprise some of the most extensive efforts to identify patterns of vocal cues that may characterize discrete emotions in the voice. To identify the minimum set of vocal cues that would be sufficient to communicate several basic emotions, listeners in one study (Scherer et al., 1972) rated content-masked voice samples on 20 semantic differential scales. Pitch level, pitch variation, amplitude level and variation, and rate of articulation were found to constitute a minimum set of vocal cues that may communicate affect.

To specify further the precise nature of vocal cues or cue combinations that allow for recognition of emotion in the voice, Scherer and Oshinsky (1977) used the Moog synthesizer to manipulate independently five acoustic cues that previous research had demonstrated to communicate emotional meaning in the voice. In this way, 64 cue combinations were generated and presented to raters who were to indicate whether the samples expressed happiness, interest, anger, fear, boredom, sadness, disgust, contempt, or elation. Cue combinations were also rated on 10-point scales for pleasantness, activity, evaluation, and potency. Results indicated that raters achieved a significant level of agreement in judgments of the various emotions. Emotion judgments were particularly influenced by pitch variation and tempo. Extreme pitch variation produced ratings of highly pleasant, active emotions, such as happiness and surprise. Fast tempo led to attributions of high activity and potency, as in the emotions of fear, happiness, anger, and interest. The results of this study were replicated, using a larger number of judges (Scherer, 1979a). In addition, highly significant effects on emotional expression recognition were found for two new parameters: duration and filtration (lack of overtones).

Of these 64 acoustical cue combinations, 16 were then selected to represent happiness, sadness, anger, and fear, and raters were required to choose from a pair of alternative labels the one best describing each stimulus. As in the previous study, judges' accuracy was well beyond chance expectation. The results of the several studies using the Moog synthesizer, then, are in accordance with those of studies using human voice samples, attesting to the synthesizer's usefulness in research on the acoustics of vocal affect.

Studies of Vocalic Expression of Emotion in Human Infants. There is virtually no work on the specificity of vocalic expressions of emotion in human infancy. What research exists bears on three issues: Whether the infant's cry conveys discrete messages about the infant's state of hunger, pain, or anger (Wolff, 1969); whether the cry can specify brain damage or risk factors in development (Fisichelli & Karelitz, 1962; Murry & Murry, 1980); and the effect of crying either on other infants (Martin & Clarke, 1982; Sagi & Hoffman, 1976; Simner, 1971) or on the caretaker (e.g., Bell & Ainsworth, 1972; Gewitz & Boyd, 1977; Goldberg, 1977). We review the issue of the effects of the infant's cry on the caretaker (see *Social Development in Infancy*) and will cover the effect of the cry on other neonates when we discuss emotions as organizers of interpersonal and intrapsychic processes.

In terms of the distinction between various types of infant vocalizations, Wolff's (1969) description of patterns and causes of crying, based on extensive home observations of 18 infants, has yet to be surpassed for breadth and depth of observation. Wolff categorized cries into three basic types: the anger cry, characterized by loud and prolonged vocalization; the hunger cry (also called the basic cry), characterized by a rhythmic and repetitive vocalization; and the pain cry, characterized by a sudden onset, an initial long cry, and extended breath holding. Although Wolff did not experimentally investigate the signal function of the cry, he did observe how mothers responded to tape recordings of pain cries played in the infant's room. In the home setting, the pain cry was a peremptory signal that induced alarm and apprehension in the mothers as well as an immediate response. The anger cry was also reported to be more effective in inducing the mother to approach the infant than the basic cry. However, because Wolff's study did not control for acoustic intensity, several critics have called into question Wolff's claim of message specificity in the voice (e.g., Murray, 1979). Also, Richards and Bernal (1972) have reported that mothers judge the infant's state not from the cry, but from context: mothers look at the clock and estimate whether the baby is likely to be hungry or not. If the time is too short for hunger to be a likely determinant of crying, the mother then posits an alternative interpretation of the cause of the baby's crying.

The other signal features of the cry that have been studied extensively are those that might specify clinical abnormality in the newborn. The hope that analysis of cries can provide a rapid method of diagnosing neurological abnormalities (Bax, 1975; Zeskind, 1981) has yet to be realized however. Most recently, researchers have been investigating whether cry types can be related to the child's prognosis when at risk for illness or developmental deviation. Zeskind (1981), for instance, reported that malnourished infants have more variability in fundamental frequency and more harmonic distortion than do normal controls. Asphyxiated infants have significantly shorter cries, higher fundamental frequencies, and less stable cry signals than do controls (Michelsson, Sirvio, & Wasz-Hockert, 1977). The interested reader is referred to a thorough review of this literature by Hollien (1980).

In summary, the promising studies of identification of emotion in the voice performed to date with adults have not been extended to the study of vocalic expression of emotion in infancy (see Malatesta, 1981b). It is particularly ironic (and a testimonial to the domination of recent psychology by cognitive and psycholinguistic concerns) that although dozens of studies of speech perception and production have been carried out in infancy, there is only a modest literature on emotion vocalics. This is likely to change in the next few years. Because we now have ascertained some of the facial expression patterns expectable in response to certain situations, we can use this information to help anchor inferences regarding the emotion specified by vocal expressions under the same eliciting conditions.

The Shift in the Zeitgeist: Theoretical Advances

The changes taking place in methodology have not been the only advancements promoting and being promoted by the change in zeitgeist. Theory and research in virtually all areas of psychology have reflected the change in attitude toward emotion. Researchers in the field of information processing—long noted for ignoring emotion—now consider the role of emotion in such processing to be one of the most critical issues of the day (Norman, 1980). A symposium on cognition-emotion interrelationships has recently been held in the very center of artificial intelligence and computer modeling of cognition—Carnegie-Mellon University (Fiske & Clarke, 1982). Attempts are now being made to effect computer simulations of affective processes and to conceptualize the influence of real-world factors, which invariably seem to involve emotion, on cognitive processes (Neisser, 1976). Important applications of memory and cognitive research, such as studies of memory in eyewitnesses, are now attempting to determine how emotions affect the registration, storage, and retrieval of information from memory (Goodman & Haith, in preparation).

In social development, increasing numbers of researchers are realizing that the study of interaction is predicated on the study of emotions as both goal and monitor of dyadic relationships (Brazelton, 1983; Cohn & Tronick, 1982; Sroufe, 1979a, 1979b; Stern, 1977). Theories that once specified generalized arousal or activation as the goals of interaction are now being replaced with others that propose instead hedonic processes to explain dyadic interaction (Brazelton, 1983; Stoller & Field, 1982). Such conceptualizations, in turn, have generated interest in identifying characteristic individual differences both in the ability of each member of a dyad to read emotional signals and to transmit such signals (DePaulo & Rosenthal, 1982; Emde, Gaensbauer, & Harmon, 1982; Field, 1982).

In the field of language, there is increasing interest in tracing the roots of symbolic communication to its possible nonverbal origins in human emotional interchanges (Bruner, 1977; Bullowa, 1979; Ziajka, 1981). There is a rediscovery of emotion as a rudimentary and biologically prewired process of communication that may underlie subsequent gestural and symbolic communication. Fernald (in press), for instance, describes how maternal affective-intonation patterns (an aspect of motherese) facilitates the segmentation of the auditory stream of speech for the infant, thereby advancing both auditory-pattern recognition and eventual semantic comprehension.

In perception, there is growing realization that emotional expressions constitute prototypic affordances—that is, perceptual invariants that derive meaning from the action consequences that they provide to the perceiver (Gibson, 1979; McArthur & Baron, in press). McArthur and Baron (in press) capture the new importance of emotional expressions for an ecological theory of social perception when they state, "A stress on the adaptive significance of emotional expressions shifts the emphasis in the study of emotion perception from *emotion as phenomenal experience to emotion as a guide to action*" (emphasis added). The perception of emotion in others is also posing fascinating questions about whether an emotion detected in another generates an emphatic, resonant reaction in oneself (Neisser, 1976).

Psychiatrists and clinical psychologists, who always ascribed some significance to emotions, are increasingly conceptualizing phenomena like empathy and moral development in affective rather than purely cognitive terms (e.g., Feschbach, 1982; Hoffman, 1982; Radke-Yarrow & Zahn-Waxler, 1982). Furthermore, new and excitingly detailed proposals for reviving the importance of affect in psychoanalytic theory are now being articulated (Emde, 1980a, 1980b).

Emotion as an Organizational Construct

It is customary to believe that important changes in a zeitgeist, such as those currently taking place, represent merely the swing of the pendulum backward—namely, to an unimaginative rediscovery of the problems and issues of an earlier day. However, this is not entirely the case with the changes taking place today. There is literally a new perspective on emotions—what has been called the organizational approach (Emde, 1980a, 1980b; Sroufe, 1979a, 1979b)—an approach, based on systems theory (Bertalanffy, 1968; Buckley, 1968), that emphasizes the role of emotions as determinants and regulators of both intrapersonal and interpersonal behaviors and that stresses the adaptive role of emotions. This approach also shares many features in common with Izard's differential emotions theory (Izard, 1977, 1978).

Such approaches view emotion as organizational in at least three different senses: (1) emotion terms help conceptually structure events and behaviors, providing coherent summaries for multiple functional relationships; (2) emotional processes regulate both intrapsychic and interpersonal interactions; and (3) emotion elicitation reflects an organism's coordination of events with his own active strivings. We will elaborate on each of these uses of the term organizational.

1. *Emotion words as hypothetical constructs.* One of the perplexing features of psychological phenomena is that the very same input to the organism can result in multiple outputs and very different inputs can result in the same output. Strictly operational attempts to describe complex event-outcome relationships invariably involve so many specific relationships that they become incomprehensible or are so specialized that they are observable only under highly constraining, ecologically invalid laboratory conditions.

As an alternative to such approaches, one may hypothesize that some construct underlies many observables. A construct is a hypothesized variable that helps simplify and explain the multiple functional relationships possible among variables. Such constructs are particularly useful in cases, like emotion, in which (1) dependent variables are not highly correlated with one another, yet show some empirically derived or theoretically postulated coherence and (2) each of several independent variables are thought, again on either a priori or a posteriori grounds, to elicit a similar process in the organism. N. E. Miller (1959) used such an approach to link multiple experimental means of increasing drives in laboratory rats with multiple means of measurement of drive increase.

Emotions are particularly prone to be manifested in multiple and somewhat independent ways, and they can be elicited by multiple situational and imaginal events. For instance, a single event can elicit at least five different general manifestations of an emotion such as anger: a particular facial configuration, a characteristic tone of voice, an abrupt gesture, a hostile reaction, or an autonomic pattern consisting of flushing of the face, dilation of certain arteries, and increases in diastolic blood pressure (Schwartz, Weinberger, & Singer, 1981). There are at least three reasons why it is rare, however, that a given episode of anger results in changes across all these modes of expression.

First, reliable individual differences influence the patterning of responses to stressors. The work of Buck (1975, 1977), Eysenck (1967), and Jones (1930, 1950) has demonstrated that subjects who are facially quite expressive are often autonomically hyporesponsive, and that subjects who are facially bland are autonomically quite reactive. Thus, across sets of response variables, consistent event-reaction relationships can be found, but within a single response category, whether facial or autonomic, there is considerable variance.

Second, some testing contexts differentially influence the probability of elicitation of different channels of emotional expression. This takes place, for instance, when a subject is tested alone versus in the company of another. We have already described Ekman's (1972) finding that Japanese subjects were much more facially expressive when tested alone than when tested in the presence of another member of their culture. Ekman had predicted this effect on the basis of what is known about the tendency in Japanese culture to mask negative expressions. However, other expressions of emotions, not quite so subject to socialization, would not be expected to demonstrate as strong an effect of testing context. Similarly, Campos, Emde, Gaensbauer, and Henderson (1975) reported that, under some circumstances, heart rate was more sensitive than behavior and that, under other circumstances, the reverse was the case. It is, therefore, critical to consider the multiple ways that emotions can be expressed as well as their contextual dependencies to avoid inferential error.

The third reason why one does not expect emotion to be manifested across all possible response modes is that the manner of expression of an emotional construct changes dramatically in the course of development. For instance, early in life, the emerging attachment of the infant toward its mother may be expressed primarily by the differential reinforcing potential of the mother (e.g., DeCasper & Fifer, 1980; Mills & Melhuish, 1974); later, it is manifested also by differential smiling (Ambrose, 1961; Spitz & Wolf, 1946); still later, by differential cardiac reactions to stressors in the presence of the mother (Campos, 1976); at later ages, by contact maintenance and proximity seeking (Waters, 1978); and during toddlerhood, by language and gestural communication. It is only by considering the various alternative means by which attachment can be expressed that any sense has been made of individual differences in the attachment of an infant to the mother. As Sroufe and Waters (1977a) put it when they described their early findings on the remarkable stability of attachment:

> Infants who did not initiate contact and turned away when being held by mother on reunion, for example, may or may not have exhibited this *behavior* on reunion at 18 months. But they were likely to show some kind of avoidance (turning away, ignoring, gaze aversion, etc.). *It is the organization of behavior, the adaptational patterns, the quality of the affective bond that has been shown to be stable, not particular discrete behaviors* maintained by contingent maternal responses. (p. 1193, emphasis added)

Not only can emotions be expressed in a multiplicity of ways but they can also be produced by a plethora of events. For instance, anger can be elicited by prohibitions, insults, physical restraint, removal of desired objects, and so on. Thus, if one has n possible elicitors of an emotional reaction and n possible means of expressing the hypothetical state, there are numerous possible functional relationships, a state of affairs graphically portrayed in Figure 2. It is here that the use of emotion terms as organizational constructs is useful. As can be seen in Figure 3, the intervening construct of anger neatly summarizes the multiple functional relationships possible between eliciting events and response outputs. In that figure, nine functional relationships are reduced to three between input and construct and to three between construct and output. As Hinde (1972) points out, the greater the number of eliciting circumstances and the greater the number of response modes, the greater the economy of description provided by the emotion term. Moreover, given the typically low intercorrelations among alternative emotional reactions, there is a potentially great increase in explanatory value gained through the use of the intervening construct.

2. *Emotions as organizers of interpersonal and intrapsychic processes.* One of the reasons why so much interest has been generated recently on human emotions is that, contrary to once-widespread opin-

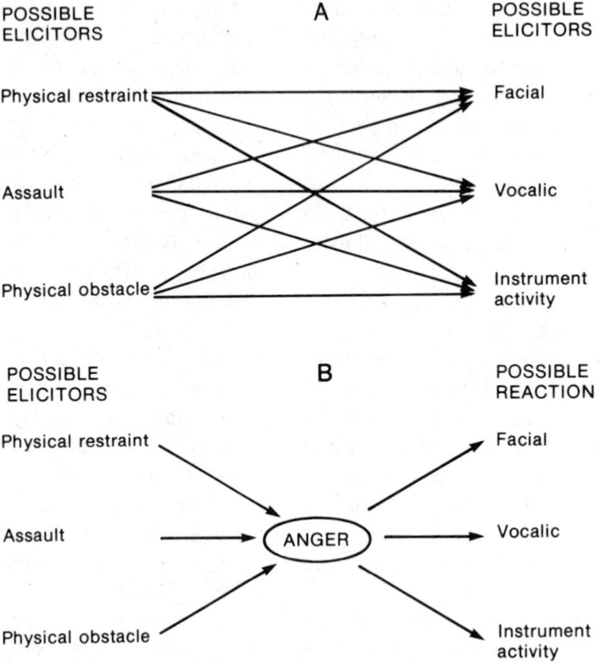

Figure 3. Relationships between three independent and three dependent variables (panel A) and between three independent variables, one emotional construct, and three dependent variables. This figure is adapted from one in Hinde (1972), which, in turn, was based on one presented in N. E. Miller (1959).

ion, emotions clearly influence psychological functions. As we mentioned earlier, there has been a long tradition of treating affect and emotion as epiphenomenal (Kagan, 1978; Ryle, 1950; Skinner, 1953). Emotions have been conceptualized, at best, either as end states in causal chains or as nuisance variables to be controlled to eliminate measurement noise. When not considered epiphenomenal, emotions were considered to be disorganizing, that is, as disruptions to the smooth execution of cognitive or motoric plans. However, the new systems view of human emotions emphasizes that every part plays a role in the total adaptation of the organism. Consequently, researchers now try to specify how emotions regulate behavior and not just how they disrupt it. Emotions are viewed as regulators, in contradistinction to causes, because the role they serve in the total system is highly context dependent. Thus, under some conditions (which we have just begun to conceptualize), emotions will play a crucial and adaptive role in human behavior. Under other circumstances, their contemporaneous role will be minimal (as in automatisms). Under still others, emotions will be disruptive and upsetting.

Emotional Expressions as Organizers of Behavior in Social Settings. The most noteworthy contemporary research is taking a contextually dependent view of the way emotions influence social, perceptual, or cognitive processes (Emde, 1980a, 1980b; Klinnert, 1981; Sroufe, 1977; Sroufe, Waters, & Matas, 1974; Stern, 1977; Tronick, Ricks, & Cohn, 1982). Consider the recent research on affective communication in infancy, including that on the social referencing phenomenon (Campos & Stenberg, 1981; Feinman, 1982; Feinman & Lewis, in press; Klinnert, Campos, Sorce, Emde, & Svejda, 1983; Lewis & Feiring, 1981). When a person faces an uncertain event, the person tends to seek out and use the facial, vocal, and gestural emotional expressions of others to help disambiguate the uncertainty (Campos & Stenberg, 1981).

A particularly dramatic study with 1-year-olds, using a modified visual cliff, exemplifies the power of affective communication as well as the contextual dependence of the regulatory consequences of emotional communication (Sorce, Emde, Campos, & Klinnert, 1981). When 1-year-old infants attempting to cross to the mother on a visual cliff were faced with an apparent 4-ft. dropoff, they avoided crossing to the mother. When there was no apparent dropoff on a modified deep side, the infants did not even seek affective information or, on those rare cases when they did, such information did not influence the tendency to cross to the mother. However, when the dropoff on the deep side was set at an intermediate level—somewhat intrinsically fear provoking but not so much that crossing was impeded entirely—infants characteristically (1) looked to the mother and (2) used the specific facial affective information the mother provided to determine whether to cross to her or not. In this study, if the mother posed a fear face, no infant out of 17 tested was observed to cross the deep side. On the other hand, if the mother posed a happy face, 15 of 19 infants crossed. Similar findings were obtained when mothers posed anger or interest faces: only 11% of the infants tested crossed when the mother posed anger, whereas 75% crossed when she posed interest. Finally, when a separate group of infants was exposed to the mother's pose of sadness (an emotion contextually inappropriate to crossing or not crossing the deep side of the visual cliff), an intermediate number of infants crossed (33%), but the infants showed evidence of extensive vacillation over whether to cross or not.

Subsequent research has demonstrated that the emotional expression of another adult, not just the mother, can regulate the infant's behavior (Klinnert, Emde, Butterfield, & Campos, 1983). Thus, when an ambiguous toy moves into a room where baby, mother, and familiarized woman are located, the familiarized adult's facial expressions strongly influence the baby's behavior. If the adult poses a joy face, the infant tends to approach and touch the toy significantly more than when the adult poses a fear face. Because the mother's expressions are held constant in this study, the findings demonstrate that 1-year-olds seek out, and are responsive to, the facial expressions of persons other than the attachment figure.

Other studies have demonstrated that vocal expressions of emotion (specifically fear, anger, and joy) significantly influence the behavior of infants as young as 8.5 months when the vocal expressions are uttered as infants tentatively approached an unfamiliar toy (Svejda & Campos, 1982). Infants approached a toy more closely and resumed activity more quickly on a subsequent trial following a happy vocalization from the mother than following either an angry or fearful vocalization.

Even the infant's reactions to strangers, long considered to be a biologically prewired phenomenon (Freedman, 1974), can be influenced by the emotional communication between the mother and her infant in the first year of life (Boccia & Campos, 1983; Feinman & Lewis, in press; Lewis & Feiring, 1981). It is now known that the entry and approach of a stranger is an uncertain event for the infant. At one time, the checking back-and-forth between mother and stranger that the baby engages in on the approach of a stranger was thought to be a facial comparison process resulting in a discrepancy reaction (Campos & Stenberg, 1981; Feinman, 1982). However, now it seems more likely to reflect a deliberate search for emotional information from the mother (Feinman, 1982; Sorce, Emde, & Frank, 1982).

To test the possibility that emotional communication from the mother to the baby can influence the baby's reaction to the stranger, Boccia and Campos (1983) instructed the mother (1) to utter a single abrupt and unfriendly hello and to pose a slight frown on her face or (2) to utter a cheery hello and to smile at both baby and stranger. They reported that in the mother-wary condition, 8.5-month-old infants showed marked cardiac accelerations to the stranger, less smiling, and more distress than when the mother posed the cheery hello and the smile. In the latter condition, infants show heart rate deceleration. The results of a study by Feinman and Lewis (in press), who used a somewhat comparable test situation, were similar but not so clear, possibly because they contrasted only joy and neutral conditions.

Perhaps the most remarkable testimony to the importance of emotions as social regulators is the early age when the effects of nonverbal communication or its perturbation can be noted. For instance, a sighted infant born to blind parents shows marked deviations in its usual pattern of eye-to-eye contact. Whereas it will establish eye-to-eye contact with a sighted adult, it does not do so with its parents, even in the first 3 months of life. The parents have to substitute other means of interaction, such as bathtub play or play with objects, to prevent developmental deviation (Adamson, Als, Tronick, & Brazelton, 1977).

It has been reported that 3-month-olds are seriously upset when they encounter their mother in a still-faced and unreactive pose. The infants appear to initiate interaction by smiling and looking toward their mothers but, when the expected social response is replaced by the inert pose, the infants stop interacting and withdraw (Tronick, Als, Adamson, Wise, & Brazelton, 1978). Most recently, Cohn and Tronick (1982) explicitly manipulated the mother's affective behavior and similarly found powerful effects of this manipulation on the behavior of 3-month-olds. The mothers were instructed to pose a depressed feeling state, expressed by a slow and monotonous tone of voice, minimal movement of the arms and body, and absence of touching the baby. When encountering such a posture, the infants showed much more gaze aversion, protest behavior, and crying than when the mother behaved normally. Moreover, Cohn and Tronick reported that the sequential relationships among behaviors of the infants exposed to depressed versus normal mothers differed: Under normal conditions the infants usually shifted from play to looking at the mother and then to smiling; by contrast, in the mother-depressed condition, the infants' behavior shifted from one negative state to another. These findings suggest that young infants are sensitive to some aspects of the mother's emotional state, although it will remain for future work to determine what affective communicative channels mediate these consequences.

A related finding comes from the work of Mehler and his associates (Mehler, Bertoncini, Barriére, & Jassik-Gerschenfeld, 1978). They showed that 6-week-old infants could discriminate the mother's voice from that of a stranger, although only when the mother's voice was spoken in a normal tone of voice, which presumably carried some affective information. When the mother spoke in a monotone, the infants failed to discriminate mother from stranger. This study raises the possibility that early discrimination of mother from stranger is facilitated by emotional information associated with her. Fernald (in press) has also made a similar point.

One of the most important ways in which emotions regulate social behavior is by making possible the process of empathy. Hoffman (1976, 1978, in press), for instance, believes that empathy has dissociable cognitive and affective roots. The latter, he believes, originates in the neonate. He and Sagi (Sagi & Hoffman, 1976), replicated Simner's (1971) finding that newborn infants cry in response to the cry sounds of another newborn, a finding subsequently replicated by Martin and Clarke (1982). These results suggest that even the newborn can respond in kind to the distress of another human, a rudimentary kind of empathic response. Hoffman (1978, in press) postulates increasingly complex levels of sensitivity to the distress of another throughout development, beginning with simple classical conditioning whereby such empathic affective arousal enables the child to associate the cues of another's distress with her own distress feelings. A more complex type of associational process constitutes Hoffman's third level: When a person observes another experiencing an emotion, the combination of the other's expressive reactions and the situation the child is in may remind the person of analogous situations in which she experienced emotion. Thus, vicarious emotion may be felt. Hoffman (1978, in press) also describes a theory proposed by Lipps (1906), who held that humans experience an innate, isomorphic response to another person's expression of emotions. In support of Hoffman's position, Klinnert, Campos, Sorce, Emde, and Svejda 1983) have also speculated on the possibility that an emotional resonance exists that permits the perceiver to feel directly (and not merely mimic or mirror) the emotion expressed by another in certain contexts. Because, Hoffman (1978, in press) notes, all of these levels of appreciation of another's affective experience can take place during infancy, the roots of empathy may be found in the affective interchanges between an infant and others.

Finally, Zahn-Waxler, Radke-Yarrow, and King (1979) have shown that 1½- to 2½-year olds not only are aware of the meaning of others' distress reactions but also often attempt to make reparation for distress they have caused or to help a distressed person even when they did not cause the distress. Hoffman's (1978, in press) theory and the data of Zahn-Waxler et al. (1979), thus, demonstrate the crucial significance that the perception of emotional expressions in another has for determining prosocial behavior.

Thus, another's emotional communication can regulate one's reaction to that person, to other persons, or to ambiguous events. Moreover, the power of emotional expressive communication is not limited to infancy (Feinman, 1982). On the contrary, it is part of the everyday aura of interpersonal interaction, influencing everything from friendship to the doctor-patient relationship, as several (e.g., Hill, Siegelman, Gronsky, Sturniolo, & Fretz, 1981; Milmoe, Novery, Kagan, & Rosenthal, 1974) have argued. Yet to be investigated in early infancy is what happens when there is incongruence of emotional communication among channels. Such an issue is significant not only for identifying which channels of emotional communication are peremptory but also for determining whether personality development in infants and young children is influenced by a different kind of double bind—one that involves contradiction between two nonverbal channels, such as the face and voice, rather than between a verbal and a nonverbal message. The studies to date also emphasize the importance of context for understanding emotional communication and call for extensive elaboration of what could be called a theory of the context dependence of behavior regulation through emotional expression. Sroufe et al. (1974) were among the first to emphasize the importance of such a theory for the ultimate understanding of the quality and intensity of emotional reactions.

Emotions as Organizers of Cognitive Processes. Emotional communication through face, voice, and gesture is not only a powerful influence on others' behavior but also a profound influence on one's own cognitive processes. For instance, emotional communication can mediate learning processes that are crucial for survival. Infants and toddlers do not have to learn to avoid dangerous plants, electric outlets, and similar hazards by directly experiencing the harmful effects. Nor do they have to await the maturation of verbal communication skills to do so. It seems likely that infants acquire such adaptive habits (and sometimes some maladaptive ones) by associating specific hazards with the caregiver's emotional communications. Such a learning process may help account for the development of fear of heights in human infants: a wealth of data now demonstrates that infants become wary of heights only *after* the acquisition of crawling (despite beliefs that fear of heights is innate) (Bertenthal, Campos, & Barrett, in press; Campos, et al., 1978). But precisely how does crawling determine wariness of heights? The increased probability of falling accidents is not a likely explanation for the majority of infants. Neither the research by Campos et al. (1978) nor that by Walk (1966) supports such an explanation for the developmental changes shown by most subjects. It seems more likely that the infant acquires fear by associating heights with the mother's emotional reactions to near falls and to precarious situations. Bowlby (1973) has discussed how emotional expressions can mediate fear contagion, as has Bandura (1977). Like Bowlby and Bandura, we propose that emotional communication subserves biologically adaptive learning. If that is so, then it is particularly surprising that no studies on such expression-mediated learning have been attempted with either human infants or toddlers and that only a few studies with monkeys have been attempted (R. Miller, 1967).

There have been many other recent attempts to relate emotions to the registration, storage, and retrieval of information from memory. These studies differ from the earlier ones by manipulating feeling states or central affective processes rather than expressive ones. This new line of research revives, although in methodologically much more sophisticated ways, one which has a long but frequently interrupted history. For instance, Bain (1859) and Spencer (1890) had proposed in the nineteenth century that humans tend to remember pleasant experiences and to forget unpleasant ones; Freud proposed in numerous instances that one is prone to deny unpleasant perceptions and to repress undesired memories. Rapaport (1961) summarized many of these classic views and presented the findings of several experiments related to the issue of whether the quality or the intensity of an emotional reaction influences memory. He concluded that affective intensity had its major effect on memory, not on specific emotional quality. However, recent findings are leading to a reconsideration of Rapaport's conclusions.

The most relevant of the recent studies involves the well-designed investigations by G. Bower and his associates (1981) at Stanford. One of G. Bower's experiments captures particularly well the importance of emotions as organizational constructs. In that study, subjects were presented with lists of material to be learned while they were in each of four hypnotically induced states: joy, sadness, anger, or fear. The subjects were then brought back to the laboratory for a recall test, which was conducted while the subjects were in either the same or a different emotional state as that during their initial learning of the memory list. G. Bower's preliminary findings were dramatic: retention was highest when recall of a list took place in the same emotional state as in acquisition—regardless of what that state was; it was poorest when recall occurred in the emotional state opposite to that in acquisition (e.g., sadness-joy, anger-fear); and it was intermediate when recall took place in the other two emotional states. G. Bower concluded that hypnotically induced feeling states created nodes around which registration of information into memory was organized, which nodes were reinstated when the subject was in the same affective state later, thus permitting easier access to the information when the same state was later induced.

G. Bower (1981) also described how emotions influence the cognitive processes of free association, semantic elaboration, interpretation of imaginative stories, selective learning, and certain perceptual effects. The influence of emotion on cognition, thus, was shown to be powerful and widespread.

Zajonc (1980) has also been influential in restoring interest in how emotions influence both cognitions and perceptions. He sharply challenged the belief that affect necessarily follows cognition, and he has presented evidence in support of the notion that affect and cognition show different functional relationships with environmental stimulation presented at the threshold of identification. Beginning with the assumption (based on some of his earlier work) that familiarity with a stimulus leads to preference for it, Zajonc familiarized subjects with certain nonsense figures. Then, he presented both familiar and unfamiliar figures at the perceptual threshold to these subjects, asking them to (1) indicate whether or not they had seen each figure before and (2) the degree of their preference for each figure (whether they reported seeing it or not). His results indicate that subjects preferred familiar stimuli, even when they could not identify them as familiar (Kunst-Wilson & Zajonc, 1980). From this and other lines of evidence, Zajonc (1980) concluded that affect can precede cognition and often can determine the nature of the cognitions that follow it.

Emotions have always been known to influence performance on various tasks, with the intensity of emotional arousal influencing performance in an inverted U-shaped fashion (the Yerkes-Dodson law). As usually conceptualized, however, the quality of the discrete emotional state has not been treated as a parameter of the relationship between intensity of arousal and performance. It is conceivable, however, that positive emotions, like joy, may show inverted U-shaped functions that peak at very high levels of arousal, with performance suffering only when joy approaches mania. On the other hand, anger might show inverted U performance that peaks at fairly low levels of intensity. This possibility has been recently investigated by Meng, Henderson, Campos, and Emde (1983) with 16-month-old infants. The infants were divided into two groups: one underwent the stress of two maternal separations, the other played joyfully with a series of puppets. After a brief interval, the subjects were given a problem to solve adapted from one designed by Bruner and Koslowski (1972): Infants had to rotate a bar away from them to bring toward them a toy on the other side of the bar. The results obtained were quite promising: The greater the intensity of happiness in the puppet task, the better the performance up to a certain point, then performance decreased. On the other hand, the greater the intensity of distress elicited by the separation, the poorer the subsequent performance. In short, different functions—one curvilinear and one linear—related emotion intensity and performance for the two hedonically different background conditions.

We know from classic studies, such as those of Easterbrook (1959) that emotional stress influences perception by constricting the visual field toward the center of vision; we also know that the social class (and, hence, the probable value to a child of money) influences the child's report of the apparent size of a coin (Bruner & Postman, 1947). However, most of the classic research has not related perception to discrete emotions. Yet, if discrete emotions are adaptive, one would expect certain perceptual processes to be influenced quite specifically by the nature of the emotion. Does anger, for instance, raise pain thresholds as an adaptive preparation for the likelihood of injury following attack? Does fear lower thresholds of sensitivity to sudden stimuli and to certain environmental events that can specify danger? Does the emotion of disgust influence taste and smell thresholds? Questions such as these deserve careful investigation (Erdelyi, 1974).

3. *Emotions as related to the strivings of the individual.* In a field that abounds with puzzles and paradoxes, perhaps the most vexing problem has been to explain on a priori grounds exactly what produces emotions. Most theorists have ignored the problem altogether or postulated mechanistic approaches that simply do not do justice to the variety of emotions that a single event can elicit. By a mechanistic approach, we mean one that stresses the capacity of a stimulus to elicit a response without consideration of the particular context (including the social context in the environment and the motivational state of the organism) that both the stimulus and the emoting person are in.

These mechanistic approaches frequently postulate classical conditioning or unlearned responses to simple physical stressors as models of emotion elicitation and are particularly prevalent in certain fields. For instance, physiological psychologists employ such models almost exclusively in much of their work on emotions. Even Sylvan Tomkins (1982), who more than any other single person is responsible for the revival of interest in human emotions, has taken a mechanistic approach to the problem of emotion elicitation. According to Tomkins, emotions are elicited by neural activation, and the specific quality of the emotion is determined by the direction and gradient of such activation. Fear, for instance, results when the gradient of neural activation is steep and positive; interest, when the gradient is positive but more gradual; joy, when the gradient is negative; and laughter, when the gradient is both negative and steep. Tomkins's approach, however, seems both implausible and reductionistic. First, no operationalization of neural activation is proposed, and one can, thus, think of apparent exceptions to his theoretical principles. For instance, excited joy can follow unexpected good news (which conceivably involves an increase rather than a decrease in the gradient of neural activation). Moreover, the theory does not specify how real-life events are mapped onto gradients of neural firing. As a result, the applicability of Tomkins's theory to predict the emotional states and reactions of humans in real-life situations seems questionable.

The basic issue is to account for why the same stimulus can account for different emotional reactions in the same person at different times and in different people at the same time. A related problem involves explaining why sometimes the absence of stimulation produces emotional reactions (e.g., as happens when a passive aggressive inaction produces intense anger in another). We propose that any approach that attempts to explain emotion elicitation purely on the basis of environmental stimulation is fundamentally flawed. We will also take issue with memory-based attempts to explain the same phenomena. Our approach denies that there are any purely reflexive elicitors of emotional responses: Even such powerful elicitors of emotional reaction, such as swaddling for soothing, prove to be influenced powerfully by the state of the organism. Giacoman (1971), for instance, reported that swaddling is maximally effective as a soother when the infant is in a hunger state, and is minimally so when the infant is alert and satiated. Similarly, dropping an infant from a height can be the source of intense distress or it can elicit peals of laughter; a mask worn by the mother can produce smiling, whereas when worn by a stranger, it elicits fear (Sroufe & Waters, 1976; Sroufe & Wunsch, 1972).

The role of context in emotion elicitation has rarely been considered by researchers (with the exception of Sroufe's group at Minnesota). As a result, there is little empirical documentation of the significance of context for a theory of emotion elicitation at this time. Instead of context, most researchers in infancy to date have emphasized the importance of memory and sensorimotor cognitive capacities for the elicitation of different emotional reactions to the same stimulus. Hebb's (1946) theory of emotion and contemporary revisions of it (e.g., G. W. Bronson, 1968; Kagan, 1971; McCall & McGhee, 1977; Rothbart, 1973; Schaffer, 1971, 1974) have been particularly influential in this regard.

Initially, Hebb's theory attempted to explain only fear of unusual or novel events without reference to classical conditioning or innateness. It was an attractively simple theory, going beyond mechanistic stimulus-response (S-R) theories of emotion in only one major way—emphasizing the importance of degree of discrepancy from past experience as the factor that accounts for the elicitation of diverse emotional reactions to the same stimulus. Hebb proposed that when stimulation is processed in the central nervous system, it produces neurophysiological circuits called phase sequences. These phase sequences, once well established, are activated whenever a subject encounters a similar stimulus in the future. If, however, the new stimulus is not sufficiently similar to maintain the smooth activation of the phase sequence, the disruption of neural timing and patterning in the brain is reflected in the periphery by fear.

This simple theory was subsequently extended to explain a broad array of emotional reactions, including surprise, boredom, interest, laughter, degree and intensity of hedonic tone, and joy (see McCall & McGhee, 1977, for an excellent elaboration of some of these points). Without past experiences with familiar stimuli, a new stimulus cannot produce disruption. The stimulus is either ignored or attended to only slightly. If the stimulus is quite familiar, it matches the central store too well and it is not attended to either—habituation or boredom results (Berlyne, 1960; Sokolov, 1963). If the stimulus begins to be assimilated with some difficulty to the central memory store, smiling occurs (Kagan, 1971). If the discrepancy between input and memory is moderate, regardless of the direction of the discrepancy, positive emotions occur; if the discrepancy is too great, negative ones are elicited (Haber, 1958). Although the theory was never extended to account for sadness, affection, sexual ardor, or anger (despite some confusing remarks on the latter by Hebb, 1946), it clearly addressed the issue of how the same stimulus can result in so many different emotional reactions.

Unfortunately, the theory did not succeed in explaining why the same or similar stimuli could so often elicit such diverse emotional reactions (Cohn & Tronick, 1982; Sroufe et al., 1974; Sroufe & Waters, 1976). A wealth of subsequent research has shown that discrepancy per se proves insufficient to account for the quality of an emotional state (e.g., G. W. Bronson, 1972; Brooks & Lewis, 1976; Clarke-Stewart, 1978b; Haith & Campos, 1977). This point was surprisingly made by Hebb himself (1949), a mere three years after he published his original paper. Two problems in particular beset Hebb's original hypothesis: (1) contrary to what his theory seemed to predict, human infants showed evidence of well-established memories of their mothers long before they experienced fear of unfamiliar persons (G. W. Bronson, 1972; Schaffer, 1966b); and (2) as Hebb (1949) pointed out, the same discrepant event could elicit dramatically different emotional reactions in the same animal or in animals with presumably the same memory stores. Hebb reported that he presented chimpanzees with an anesthetized chimpanzee, a cast of a chimpanzee's face, or a cured chimpanzee hide, and he said that "such stimulation may be primarily a source of profound *excitation,* rather than specifically fear-producing; the excitation was usually followed by avoidance, but sometimes by aggression, and sometimes it produced a marked autonomic reaction combined with apparent friendliness" (p. 243). Some other explanatory principle, thus, needed to be proposed to account for the conversion of a discrepant event into an emotional reaction.

In an attempt to preserve the attractive simplicity of Hebb's discrepancy hypotheses of emotion elicitation, yet to permit explanation of why emotions seemed to differ so dramatically in quality to the same discrepant event, many theorists proposed cognitive corollaries to Hebb's notions of discrepancy. Almost without exception, these theorists addressed the first of the two problems in Hebb's theory (i.e., why fear of strangers emerged so much later than the formation of memory schemas of the mother), and they ignored the second problem (why the same discrepant event elicits so many diverse emotional qualities). Fear, for instance, was considered to emerge when discrepancy was supplemented by object permanence (Schaffer, 1966b), person permanence (Brossard, 1974), the infant's understanding of causality (Goulet, 1974), the child's recall-memory capacities (Schaffer, 1974), the capacity to evoke hypotheses that are subsequently disconfirmed (Kagan et al., 1978), or the understanding of means-ends relationships (Scarr & Salapatek, 1970), and so on.

However, none of these corollaries has proved any more successful in accounting for the emergence of fear than discrepancy was (Clarke-Stewart, 1978b; Haith & Campos, 1977). No theory to date has clearly articulated precisely why object permanence or these other capacities should be related to the expression or experience of any emotional state. The postulation of these cognitive capacities has rested on an apparent coincidence in time of onset of the cognitive capacity and the emotional reaction to a specific circumstance. However, in studies in which age is held constant and the presence and absence of the cognitive capacity in question is permitted to vary, the presence of the emotional reaction (typically fear, but sometimes anger) is found not to relate to the predicted sensorimotor underpinning (Campos et al., 1978; Scarr & Salapatek, 1970; Stenberg et al., 1983). Moreover, Brooks and Lewis (1976) tested infants between 6 and 18 months of age (i.e., infants who presumably possess the requisite Piagetian sensorimotor capacities postulated as corollaries by neo-Hebbian theorists). These infants showed wariness to unfamiliar full-sized adults, friendliness to unfamiliar children, and uncertain reactions to unfamiliar midgets. Clearly, sensorimotor capacities per se are also unrelated to the apparent emergence of different emotional states.

These problems with purely cognitive interpretations of emotion elicitation lead us to propose an alternative conceptualization of this little-understood, yet critically important, process. Our alternative conceptualization has two major principles. First we propose that only when cognition is in the service of the goals and strivings of the organism will it be involved in the elicitation of emotion. This interweaving of event and goal provides an explanation as to why the same unexpected snowfall will elicit joy in someone who wants to go skiing, fear in someone who needs to travel to another city unprepared, anger in an individual who has to shovel a driveway rather than rest, pride in someone who predicted the snowfall with a new theory, and even guilt in the person who interprets it as retribution for a transgression. Second, it is the significance of the goal (however that significance is produced) and not mere discrepancy of an event from a memory store that accounts for the intensity of the emotion elicited. We are only now beginning to understand what produces significance for an individual (see Mandler, 1982). We will elaborate later some of the aspects likely to enter into individual differences in the value of an event for an individual.

Emotion Elicitation as Related to Goals and Their Value. There is little doubt that the long history within psychology of avoiding teleological explanations has influenced the field's reluctance to relate emotions to goals. But the traditional objections to purposivistic explanations of behavior need not apply to the study of emotions. For instance, the concept of goal need not imply consciousness of purpose. Many goals are promoted by socialization; thus, many emotional reactions are intimately related to conscious social goals. But not all goals are socially constructed. Some concern the very survival of the organism and are probably prewired influences on even neonatal emotionality (a point implied by Emde, 1982, in discussing the pre-representational self").

Nor is goal synonymous with drive (although drives may generate goals). Systems engineers talk about end states and system objectives, such as the task of getting traffic from the suburbs to downtown and back. Piagetian theory also specifies end states without which cognitive development cannot be understood (Piaget, 1950), and Bowlby (1969) familiarized psychologists with the usefulness of the concept of set point. These types of goals not only need not be conscious but need not be impelled by tissue deficits or strong stimuli.

Recently, a few theorists have attempted to specify the types of goals involved in eliciting various emotions. Roseman (1979), for instance, described six factors that enter into the elicitation of most discrete emotions. The two major ones involve goals: One is a dimension of motivational state—defined simply as what the organism wants or does not want. The second is the person's situational state—the extent to which the goal appears achievable. To understand the simplest emotions, according to Roseman, one must understand the comparison between these two states. Joy, for instance, results from having what one wants; sadness from not having what one wants.

According to Roseman, the experience of more complex emotions involves the interplay of other factors related to the comparison between state and goal. For instance, a third factor, probability, by which Roseman means the subject's estimate of the likelihood that something desirable or undesirable will happen, influences the elicitation of hope and fear. Hope results when a person feels she may get what she wants. Fear, on the other hand, occurs when a person anticipates that she may get what she does not want. When a fourth factor, agency (attribution of causality for the situational state), is added, pride, dislike, and a shamelike state called regret can be predicted. A fifth factor, called legitimacy, involves the perception of the fairness of others' actions toward oneself. It plays a role in the elicitation of anger and guilt, Finally, the unexpectedness of an event influences emotion primarily by increasing the intensity of the emotional expression and experience.

Roseman's approach has many difficulties with it. A major one is its failure to consider the developmental roots of some of the emotions he attempts to explain. As we have seen, there is now little doubt that anger expressions are clearly observable by 4 months of age. But are we to say the 4-month-olds have a sense of legitimacy? Three-month-olds express fearlike withdrawal to looming stimuli (Yonas, 1981). Are we to say that the infant has a sense of probability at such an age? Moreover, the theory ignores important complexities in the development of certain emotions. Guilt, for instance, may require prior experience of perceiving others' emotional reactions (Hoffman, 1982, in press), as well as complex capacities to internalize social rules. Roseman's (1979) approach does not do full justice to these complexities.

Another related difficulty with Roseman's approach is that the cognitions relating goals to events appear cold, calculating, and conscious. Roseman appears to suggest that prior to experiencing an emotion a person combines bits of information in a controlled, highly structured fashion, and ipso facto feels an emotion. However, we agree with Zajonc (1980) that this does not seem to be the process through which emotion is elicited. Information leading to emotion elicitation does not appear to be categorized in an objective, logical fashion but rather in a personalized and evaluative fashion. Most important, the goals on which emotion focuses must be significant ones—ones that have value to that individual.

We are only now beginning to analyze exactly what is meant by these concepts of value and significance as related to emotions (Mandler, 1982). For now, we must be content to specify some processes that we believe lead persons to characterize some goals as more significant than others. Clearly, some goals are significant because biological endowment has deemed them so. All animals have built-in significant goals of breathing, obtaining food, and so on—that is, maintaining the physical integrity of the organism or the self. This is not to suggest that the significance of such goals for an individual can not be altered. It most definitely can. However, these goals as well as behaviors serving these goals are endowed with initial significance by the genetic makeup of the organism. Significance, thus, need not be calculated nor even thought out.

Most goals, however, do not have built-in significance, but rather obtain significance through socialization and other forms of acquisition of experience as such processes transact with the constitutional makeup of the individual. Goals may acquire significance through direct instruction by family members, by hero figures, by members of a subculture, or by society in general. Goals may obtain significance through a person's observation of the effects of social and nonsocial events on others (e.g., in a social-referencing situation, as described earlier). They may become important because of idiosyncratic experiences of an individual. In fact, if such experiences are too idiosyncratic, these may lead to neurotic emotional reactions, such as phobias. Finally, significance can be acquired through cognitive estimation, as Lazarus (1968) and Roseman (1979) emphasize. The list of experiences that endow goals with significance is endless. However, significance must be endowed on a goal before such a goal is implicated in emotion elicitation.

Moreover, although significance of goals is by no means easy to assess, experimentalists need not despair that it can never be operationalized (Sroufe & Waters, 1977a). The significance of a goal to an individual may be operationally determined by using converging measures, by judging the extent to which behavior is organized around that goal. These behaviors do not only include emotional expressions, instrumental actions, and verbalizations. They also include the selection of perceptions, the choice of cognitions, and the interpretations given to ambiguous events. Indeed, these are the criteria used by sensitive clinicians to infer conflict states in the person. We merely add that the same methods can be used to make sense of what is eliciting a person's emotions, not merely to infer the presence of conflicts.

With this concept in mind, let us outline our conceptual framework for the elicitation of emotion—a framework that we feel is applicable to even the youngest human infant. Table 3 presents the scheme for elicitation of what seem to be five of the most significant basic or fundamental emotions. We define basic emotions in terms of five criteria. One is that, to be classified as basic, the expressive reaction belonging to that state must have been shown to be recognizable cross-culturally, as Izard (1971) and Ekman (1972) have argued, although we add sexual ardor and affection as candidates for such universal recognition despite the minimal research on these two emotions even within a culture. Second, the emotional state must have clear evolutionary antecedents in nonhuman primates, as do fear, anger,

Table 3. **Generalized Schema for Predicting Elicitation of Some Basic Emotions**

Emotion	Goal	Appreciation	Action tendency	Adaptive function
Joy	Any significant objective	Goal is perceived or predicted to be attained	Approach Energizing	Reinforcement of successful strategy Facilitation of rehearsal of new skill Encourages response to new challenges Social message to initiate or continue interaction
Anger	Any significant objective	Perception of or anticipation of an obstacle to attainment of goal; perception of obstacle as not easily removable	Elimination (not just removal) of properties of an object that make it an obstacle	Restoration of progress toward a goal Effecting a change in behavior of a social other In later development: revenge, retaliation
Sadness	Securing or maintaining an engagement with either an animate or inanimate object	Perception of the goal as unattainable	Disengagement	Conservation of energy Eventual redirection of resources to other pursuits perceived to be more attainable Encourages nurturance from others
Fear	Maintenance of integrity of the self, including self-survival, and later, self-esteem	Perception that the goal is not likely to be attained, unless protective action is taken	Flight, withdrawal	Survival Avoidance of pain Maintenance of self-esteem Alert others to avoid the situation or help
Interest	Engagement or involvement in a task or event	Perception that information is potentially relevant to any goal	Receptor orientation; processing of information	Extraction of information from environment Socially, to reflect willingness to enter into a relationship, consider future action

surprise, disgust, sexual ardor, interest, sadness, affection and perhaps other states (Chevalier-Skolnikoff, 1973; Izard, 1977). Third, the emotion must be able to be expressed in more than one modality (i.e., they can be specified separately by facial expressions, vocal expressions, and gestures, as discussed earlier. Fourth, these emotions must be recognizable and must regulate social interaction, even in the absence of social experience (the evidence here is less strong than for cross-cultural identification, but see Kenney et al., 1979; Mendelson et al., 1982; and Sackett, 1966—all of whom have shown that infant primates are influenced profoundly by unlearned social signals from conspecifics). Finally, some researchers (e.g., Izard, 1978) expect most, if not all, of the basic emotions to be potentially observable in infancy.

In Table 3, we have employed the term appreciation to underscore our conviction that higher order cognitions are neither necessary nor even sufficient for the elicitation of emotion. For instance, it is well known in clinical circles that merely cognizing a problem does not necessarily result in emotional changes. Moreover, in everyday life, we can fully know that an event is not dangerous, yet our fear can persist in full intensity. As long ago as the Middle Ages, Aquinas discussed *vis estimativa* (roughly translated as power of estimation) as a fundamental, even presensory, power of the mind to appreciate the significance of events without conscious reflection (Arnold, 1960). Aquinas's concept was discarded along with the myriad other scholastic distinctions that proliferated at the time. However, as Arnold (1960) has pointed out, the concept of *vis estimativa* perhaps should have survived. Like *vis estimativa,* our concept of appreciation may operate at the level of sensation, perception, or cognition. Moreover, the concept of appreciation connotes that value has been added to information as it is being processed. In our view, the value results from the interaction between events, the relationship of events to one's goals, and the significance of the related goals.

Any significant objective may be implicated in eliciting joy or anger; however, joy is elicited when the goal is appreciated as likely to be obtained, whereas anger occurs when an obstacle makes the goal difficult to obtain. Sadness and interest also involve similar goals to one another—each involves engagement with an animate or inanimate object. In sadness, such an engagement is deemed unattainable; whereas in interest, the engagement has been attained; moreover, maintenance of the engagement is relevant to a higher order goal (e.g., learning something new, developing a love relationship). Fear is related to a specific and basic goal—maintenance of the integrity of the self. We must emphasize again that this self may be as rudimentary as the physical self (i.e., the body) or as advanced as the psychological self (i.e., the self-concept or its components). We will elaborate on this idea shortly.

Note also that in this conceptualization, because goals may be prewired and appreciations may be extremely rudimentary, the emotional life of the young infant may be much more differentiated than was once believed. We will discuss later (in *Emotional Development in Infancy*), the empirical evidence supporting our proposition that there may be a core of differentiated affective continuity throughout the life span.

In summary, our purpose in proposing this new conceptualization of the elicitation of emotions is to account for the diversity of emotions that the same stimulus can elicit and the singularity of emotion that diverse events can bring about. We reject the notion that general cognitive developments, such as object permanence or person permanence, can account for this diversity. Although recognizing the significance of information processing in the elicitation of affect, we believe that it is a special kind of information processing—that which relates events to goals, and that which gives significance to goals—that brings about different emotional reactions to the same event or the same reaction to different events. With few exceptions (e.g., Arnold, 1960; Lazarus, 1968; Mandler, 1982; Roseman, 1979; Zajonc, 1980), theorists have ignored the distinction between general cognitive ability and what we are calling the capacity to appreciate relevance.

Emotional Development in Infancy

What is Emotional Development the Development of?

Our conceptualizations of emotional development have changed dramatically in recent years. At issue in these changing conceptualizations have been (1) whether emotions emerge in the course of development and, if so, what mechanisms account for their emergence; (2) whether and how cognitive, perceptual, and motoric developments relate to emotional developments; (3) under what conditions both the feeling states and the expressive reactions of the individual become socialized with age; (4) how reactions to others' emotional expressions change with age; and (5) what accounts for the developmental changes evident in the baby's reception of emotional signals.

The Development of Emotional Reactivity in In-

fancy. At one time, considerable attention was devoted to studying the emergence of emotions during infancy. Many of these studies, implicitly or explicitly, were influenced by Bridges's (1930, 1932) theory of emotional differentiation with age. She proposed that at birth, neonates demonstrate only undifferentiated emotion—general excitement. In succeeding weeks and months, Bridges proposed, the combined influence of learning, maturation, cognitive development, and new motoric abilities leads to the differentiation of negative and positive emotions. For instance, distress differentiates out of excitement at 3 weeks of age, anger differentiates out of distress at 4 months, disgust from anger at 5 months, and fear from disgust at 6 or 7 months. The positive emotions show a developmental sequence whereby first delight emerges (at 3 months), then elation, and, finally, affection—the latter two emerging in the seond half-year of life.

In recent years, Bridges's theory has increasingly been called into question as researchers have observed what appear to be more specific emotional expressions in the neonate. Izard's (Buechler & Izard, 1983; Izard, 1978; Izard & Buechler, 1978, 1981, in press) and Sroufe's (1979b) theories of emotional development illustrate this evolution of thought rather clearly: Izard (1978) specifies that some, but not all, discrete emotions emerge in the course of development, and Sroufe (1979) argues that precursors of the major emotions are already observable in the neonate. We, in turn, will argue that emotional states, not just precursors, can be observed in the newborn and young infant, although obviously expressions such as laughter are not.

Izard's Theory of Emotional Development. Izard's approach has three fundamental postulates: (1) that the newborn possesses several quite discrete emotions evidenced by specific facial expressions (for Izard, patterned facial expressions are closely linked to corresponding emotional experiences), (2) that emotions emerge when they first become adaptive in the life of the organism, and (3) that emotions show their developmental onset in close simultaneity with, but not as a result of, changes in the perceptual, cognitive, and motoric capacities of the organism. In connection with the last postulate, Izard argues that emotional development is frequently more significant for perceptual and cognitive development than the reverse. For instance, the disequilibrium that Piaget (1950, 1981) and Cicchetti & Pogge-Hesse (1981) propose as a motivator of cognitive advancement seems to be an emotional state. Emotions may highlight perceptual arrays and draw attention to the physical and psychological boundaries of the self. They motivate the expansion of the child's cognitive and physical world by eliciting and reinforcing exploration. Moreover, they help bond humans together into social groups, ranging from the mother-infant dyad to the peer-interactional group.

The newborn, according to Izard, shows the emotions of interest, disgust, distress, as well as a startlelike precursor of surprise. These emotions are critical for the newborn's adaptation to his extrauterine existence. Without interest, for example, cognitive development would not be possible: the newborn would not note nor appreciate information from the environment, because he would lack the attention and allocation of mental resources that permit both perceptual and stimulus-response learning. Without disgust, noxious substances might be ingested and threaten the infant's survival. Without distress, the infant would not be able to communicate to the mother or anyone else that some caretaking action is needed to change his state of discomfort. Finally, without startle, neonates would have few or no defensive capabilities.

In the course of the following four months, according to Izard, the emotions of anger, surprise, and joy emerge. Joy, for instance, emerges at 1 to 3 months of age, in rough synchrony with the capacity to discriminate social from nonsocial objects in the environment and, thus, in time to begin to function as an important social regulator. Anger becomes possible (and adaptive) at the point in development when the emergence of new voluntary behaviors, particularly means-end activities, permit the child to act on the source of his frustrations.

The emotions of fear and shyness emerge in the second half-year, during which time they are central influences on the infant's reactions to strangers. Fear does not emerge before this period because, as an extremely noxious emotion, it would be maladaptive, according to Izard, unless the infant possessed means to cope with it. The new motoric skills possible during the second half-year, such as locomotion, intentional communication, and voluntary use of emotional expressivity, provide the child with many new coping strategies not possible before. Fear's emergence in synchrony with these other capacities (especially crawling and creeping and other forms of voluntary proximity-seeking behaviors) adaptively facilitates the development of the attachment system by giving the child greater motivation to use the mother as a haven of safety (Bowlby, 1969). Shyness emerges at a time when the infant's sense of self is beginning to blossom, and it profoundly influences the child's self-concept, not only by emphasizing the child's ineptitudes but also by motivating the development of compensatory competencies.

In Izard's theory, then, some basic emotions systems emerge at particular points in development. Moreover, such emergence is synchronous with, but not caused by, developments in motor, perceptual, and cognitive capacities. As we will see, recent data suggest that the basic emotion systems may not emerge but may rather be observable in some form in early infancy. Moreover, perceptual, cognitive, and motoric factors may influence the development of particular emotional reactions to specific elicitors. For example, it is now quite clear that self-produced locomotion is a determinant of wariness of heights. Bertenthal et al. (1983) reported that the development of wariness of heights, both as assessed on the visual cliff and as reported by mothers, is a function of the first four to six weeks of locomotor experience, not age per se. In support of their conclusion, they cited experimental evidence that prelocomotor infants provided with artificial self-produced locomotor experience (walkers) show cardiac accelerations on being lowered to the deep side of the cliff, whereas prelocomotor infants without walker experience show decelerations. Moreover, in a case study described in their report, an intellectually normal infant who received locomotion-impeding casting to correct an orthopedic anomaly did not show cardiac acceleration on descent to the cliff until 10 months of age—approximately one month after the cast had been removed and locomotion had first become possible. These studies, taken together with the animal work on the kitten carousel by Held and Hein (1963), point to the importance of cognitive and motoric developments as determinants of, not mere accompaniments of, the onset of emotional reactions to this situation.

In Izard's theory of emotion, facial expressions are deemed crucial for the experience of emotional states, and the development of the expressive capacity is a major criterion for concluding that the emotion has developed. In places, Izard (1971) has argued that the feedback from the facial musculature accounts for the unique feeling state specific to each affect. Although he has softened this position somewhat (Izard, 1977; Izard et al., in press), he has been criticized for drawing an isomorphism between facial expressions and corresponding emotional states (Sroufe, 1979b). For this reason, those who are less convinced of the primacy of facial expressions as measures of emotional state have rejected his approach to emotional development. Sroufe (1979b) is one who takes sharp issue with Izard on the nature of emotional development.

Sroufe's Theory of Emotional Development. Sroufe (1979b), in contrast to both Izard (1978) and Bridges (1932), proposes that the neonate manifests precursors of at least three emotions: wariness-fear, rage-anger, and pleasure-joy. What changes with development, according to Sroufe, are the cognitive level of the baby, the systems available to express emotions. (e.g., laughter), and coping capacities (e.g., locomotion). These three developments ensure that with increasing age, the infant will experience more complex emotions. Indeed, Sroufe (like Lewis & Brooks-Gunn, 1978, 1979) argues that true emotions are not possible until the child has a differentiated sense of self, a development that Sroufe places around the third quarter-year of life.

We will only describe one example of the developments that Sroufe posits for an emotional system. The precursor of wariness-fear, for Sroufe, is observable in the neonatal period when certain compelling environmental stimuli produce obligatory attention. However, once the child is capable of forming representations of prior experience and of detecting discrepancies, wariness becomes possible (at around 4 months of age). With greater experience, the child not only reacts warily to discrepancies but also assimilates events to negative schemas (roughly speaking, learned expectations that something undesirable will happen). At this time true fear becomes possible because the child has differentiated her self from the outside world, as evidenced by the child's level of object permanence. Anxiety emerges at 12 months of age, and shame (an emotion that Sroufe (1979b) links to the fear system, in contrast to Izard, 1978) is experienced by 18 months.

There are several serious difficulties with Sroufe's (1979b) theory of emotional development, most of which concern how cognitive development is related to emotional development. Sroufe's scheme does not specify how or why higher levels of cognition should lead to more complex emotional experiences. His theory seems to us to encounter all the problems of approaches that fail to take into account the organism's strivings, as we elaborated earlier. Accordingly, the postulation of cognitive prerequisites (e.g., object permanence) for the experience of fear seems gratuitous. A second problem with the theory is that subsequent research has shown that some of the mechanisms Sroufe poses for emotional development do not apply. For instance, the argument that fear at 8 months of age is based on learning that something harmful will come about because of generalizations from past experiences is based on rather flimsy evidence of a change in the factor structure of infant's reactions to strangers before and after 6 months of age (see G. W. Bronson, 1978). Recent reviews of the literature on fear of strangers at 8 months of age downplay the importance of learned expectations (see Clarke-Stewart,

1978a; Horner, 1980; Smith, 1979). Moreover, as we mentioned earlier, the emergence of fear of heights and looming stimuli have not yet been shown to result from negative encounters, such as falls or other painful experiences (Bertenthal et al., 1983; Walk, 1966; Yonas, 1981). As we alluded to earlier, we believe that one cannot determine whether or not a cognition will lead to an emotion without considering the goals of the organism. Sroufe's (1979b) theory lacks this emphasis.

A New Approach to Understanding Emotional Development. Like Sroufe, we believe that discrete emotion systems may be observable in the neonate. Moreover, we also agree that critical developments in cognitive capacities influence emotions, in that cognition is part (but only part) of what affects the child's appreciation of the significance of an event for his own biologically determined or voluntarily determined objectives. However, we stress that emotional development should not be viewed as a mere exemplar of cognitive development: instead, we feel that just as significant as changes in the development of general cognitive and perceptual capacities are changes in the goals of the organism with development. Moreover, if, as we believe, the elicitation of an emotion is determined by a particular relationship between a type of goal and a type of appreciation of how events relate to the goal, then it is possible for this relationship to be invariant across development while both goals and cognitions change. For example, anger may be elicited in persons of any age: the neonate may show anger following the appreciation that a preadapted end state is blocked (e.g., impeding the baby's movement when it is exercising reflexive movements—cf. Stenberg, (1982); an 8-month-old may show anger when she anticipates that an event will impede progress toward a visible goal; a 2-year-old may be angered by the content of a verbal remark that may thwart progress toward a symbolic goal, like play; a 10-year-old may be angered by an insult; and so forth. Similar considerations apply to other fundamental emotions.

We propose seven postulates to describe the most important features of emotional development:

1. There is a set of differentiated core emotion states that are present throughout the lifespan.
2. As cognitive development proceeds and as new goals appear in the life of the child, complex intercoordinated emotions become evident.
3. The effectiveness of specific eliciting circumstances changes as the organism develops.
4. The relationship between emotional expression and emotional experience changes as the organism develops.
5. Coping responses to emotions change as the organism develops.
6. Emotions become socialized as the organism develops.
7. Receptivity to others' emotional expressions changes as the organism develops.

We will now examine each of these postulates in turn.

1. *There is a set of differentiated core emotion states that are present throughout the lifespan.* We postulate that many fundamental emotions (not just their precursors) should be observable much earlier than the theories discussed so far would admit. The empirical evidence to date seems to support this theoretically derived expectation. For instance, two separate carefully executed interview studies of mothers' reports of their infants' emotional expressions in the first three months of life have revealed that mothers report far higher incidences of discrete emotional expressions in their babies than had ever been thought possible before. Johnson, Emde, Pannabecker, Stenberg, and Davis (1982) found that even at 1 month of age, 84% of the mothers interviewed stated that their babies expressed anger, 58% reported fear, 74% surprise, 95% joy, 34% sadness, and 99% interest. This study, like all others depending on maternal report, is subject to numerous biases, but several factors lead us to propose that the mothers' reports are valid—that is, the data may be more an indication of responses by the baby than attributions by the mothers. For instance, when carefully interviewed about the bases for their judgments, mothers typically alluded to either discrete facial or vocal criteria (e.g., eye widening for surprise, distinctive vocal and facial qualities for anger, and a contented look, albeit one without a smile for joy). They also mentioned distinctive instrumental reactions, like defensive movements for fear or slashing about for anger (Klinnert, Sorce, Emde, Stenberg, & Gaensbauer, in press).

But evidence for the early manifestation of discrete emotions is not limited to studies using maternal reports. Newborns in alert waking states show facial patterns akin to hedonic tone in response to sweet versus sour and bitter substances (Steiner, 1973) and to facial imitation tasks (Field, Woodson, Greenberg, & Cohen, 1982). When the mother's voice is made contingent on sucking, both increases and decreases in sucking rate of 3-day-old infants can be operantly conditioned to the mother's (but not a stranger's) voice as reinforcer (DeCasper & Fifer, 1980), suggesting that the mother's voice quickly acquires positive reinforcing and perhaps hedonically pleasant qualities as well for the newborn infant. When the neonate is shifted from a contingent schedule of reinforcement to a noncontingent one, the infant's reaction becomes hedonically negative (DeCasper & Carstens, 1981). Field (1982) has reported that facial expressions of surprise are elicited in neonates by administering certain Brazelton Neonatal Behavioral Assessment Scale (NBAS) items that involve a change in instigating circumstances.

As discussed earlier, in Stenberg's (1982) study of anger, some (although not all) anger facial expression components were expressed by 1-month-olds. Moreover, Stenberg suggested that vocal expressions of emotion recorded in this situation seemed to be communicative of anger even at 1 month of age. Furthermore, despite criticisms described earlier, the conclusions of Wolff's (1969) study of anger vocalizations still remain viable and deserve more careful study.

Facial and postural expressions of sadness, an emotion long thought to emerge only after the child has a sufficiently elaborated cognitive representation of the mother (i.e., at about 6 months of age) (Bowlby, 1951), have been observed in a 3.5-month-old girl subject to intense abuse and neglect (Gaensbauer, 1980; Gaensbauer & Hiatt, in press). Because the facial expression recordings were taken for the first time at that age, it is conceivable that the child showed facial expressions of sadness at an even younger age.

Fear has not been studied in very young infants except indirectly when investigators have looked at reactions to looming stimuli. In these studies, the withdrawal component of fear is clearly present at 3 months of age, possibly earlier (Bower, Broughton, & Moore, 1970; Yonas, 1981). Unfortunately, because the studies with looming stimuli addressed issues relevant to perception rather than to emotion, the requisite converging operations relevant to confirming or disconfirming the presence of fear were never taken. Moreover, it is conceivable that sudden loss of support might elicit facial or other indications of fear even in the neonate. Irwin's (1932) study on the phenomenon restricted itself to gross limb movements and the presence of crying.

In short, the possibility cannot be ruled out that the emotional life of the newborn and very young infant might include members of all basic emotion families: joy, surprise, anger, fear, disgust, interest, sadness, and possibly sexual ardor (cf. J. B. Watson, 1930, concerning neonatal sexuality) and affection. To the extent that each family may involve only rudimentary biological goals and quite elementary sensory appreciations, it should be possible for these emotions to be elicited in this period.

We portray each basic emotion as a family to highlight our belief that, although all members of the family share crucial features of feeling tone, expressive patterning, action tendency, and (most important) particular relationships between the organism's goals and events (i.e., the affective core of emotion), each particular instance of the emotion is likely to differ somewhat from each other. This is especially true when one examines emotion across the lifespan. For example, the fear that a 3-month-old seems to express in response to a looming stimulus (Yonas, 1981) is likely to be different from that of an adult on hearing that all of his financial assets are in jeopardy owing to a projected change in the stock market. In these two examples, the level of goal differs: the threat to the baby is loss of the physical integrity of the bodily self, whereas that to the adult is loss of the integrity of his self-esteem. Moreover, the level of the appreciation differs: The baby faces the quick approach of a concrete object, whereas the adult thinks of an impending event's effect on a symbolic, socialized goal. Obviously, maintenance of respect for oneself as a provider for one's family would not be a goal for the child. What is invariant is the type of goal (maintenance of integrity of the self) and the appreciation (that there is a low probability of achieving a goal unless remedial action is taken).

Cognitive development, socialization, or the specific features of the situation may slightly alter any or all aspects of the emotion, so that one particular family member differs from another. Still, the crucial aspects of these emotions (again—the type of goal, the type of appreciation, the type of action tendency) are the same, identifying both as members of the same family (see Table 3).

2. *As cognitive development proceeds and as new goals appear in the life of the child, complex intercoordinated emotions become evident.* In Table 4, we present a schema for the more developmentally advanced emotions of shame, guilt, envy, and depression. We propose that these emotions are analogous to complex intercoordinations of sensorimotor schemes, the intercoordination often assuming properties not present in the constitutent emotional states. During late infancy, childhood, and adult-

hood, intercoordinated emotions, such as shame, guilt, jealousy, embarrassment, and many others, make their appearance. These emotions have many attributes in common with basic emotions, including their capacity to regulate the perceptual, cognitive, and social experiences of the individual. However, they are also quite distinguishable from the basic emotions. First of all, the goals around which these emotions are centered are exclusively socialized goals. By contrast, the primary emotions initially are evoked in relationship to biological goals, although they eventually are evoked in relationship to socialized goals as well. Second, although these later appearing emotions often have expressive accompaniments in face, voice, or gesture, no one has successfully demonstrated patterning in all three channels, and what patterning is obtained seems to consist of complex blending of the primary emotional expressions and feelings (Izard, 1972). A related point is that, with the possible exception of shame (Izard, 1971), the evidence for cross-culturally universal recognition of the later appearing emotions is poor (Ekman, Friesen, & Ellsworth, 1972). Finally, such emotions as guilt, envy and jealousy do not seem to have been observable in nonhumans, although it would not surprise us to find evidence for some of these emotions in the higher primates.

Given that this chapter concerns emotion in infancy, it is beyond its scope to present a long list of such emotions or to detail their many important and distinguishing features. However, in Table 4, we outline some important features of four of these emotions, which, lacking a better label, we will call the complex emotions.

Notice in Table 4 that these emotions seem to involve different goals from one another. For example, shame is differentiated from guilt in that shame has explicit or implicit reference to others' judgments of important attributes of oneself and the resulting sadness at losing the esteem or love of others. The drooping posture, tucked head, and occasional tears arising from shame may reflect this sadness.

An important attribute of guilt that is not high-

Table 4. **Generalized Schema for Predicting Elicitation of More Complex Emotions**

Emotion	Goal	Appreciation	Action tendency[a]	Adaptive function[b]
Shame	Maintenance of others' respect and affection, preservation of self-esteem	Perception of loss of another's respect or affection; perception that others have observed one doing something bad	Like those of sadness, anger (at self), and fear	Maintenance of social standards
Guilt	Meeting one's own internalized standards	Anticipation of punishment because one has not lived up to an internalized standard	Like those of fear and anger	Encouragement of moral behavior
Envy	Obtaining a desired object	Perception that an object cannot be had because another has it; one's deficits prevent oneself from attaining the object	Like those of sadness and anger	Motivates achievement so as to obtain similar goods
Depression	Having the respect and affection of both others and one's self	Perception of lack of love or respect from both others and oneself; perception of lack of possibility of attaining any significant goal	Like sadness and anger (at self)	Elicits affection and nurturance from others; conservation of energy

Note:
[a]Action tendencies for complex emotions are specific forms of action tendencies of component emotions.
[b]Any of these emotions can become maladaptive if severe or prolonged.

lighted in Table 4 is guilt's associated action tendency of expiation. As Berscheid and Walster (1967), Carlsmith and Gross (1969), Regan, Williams, and Sparling (1972), and others have demonstrated, inculcation of guilt in a subject increases the likelihood that the subject will engage in altruism. Interestingly, given that guilt seems to include a strong fear component, such a subject may be most altruistic to persons other than the one injured by the guilt-producing transgression. Perhaps subjects are attempting to alleviate their anger at themselves by allowing themselves to behave morally, yet avoid the reminder that they behaved immorally and should be punished.

Another important feature distinguishing among these emotions is the degree to which the self is injured. Shame results from injury to any important aspect of one's self-concept (a self-concept that may be quite unsophisticated because even toddlers seem to experience shame). Guilt, on the other hand, results from injury to one specific aspect of the self—one's moral standards. Envy, not surprisingly often viewed as petty, involves primarily attributes regarding one's ability to secure desired goods. Finally, depression, which may be the most devastating of all of these emotions, involves injury to the entire self-system, including the person's beliefs regarding the way others view the person's self.

3. *The effectiveness of specific eliciting circumstances change as the organism develops.* This principle has been implicitly recognized by most researchers, but we believe widely misinterpreted, in that specific situations deemed prototypic elicitors of specific emotional states are studied and results interpreted as reflecting a general emergence of that emotion across situations. Such was the case in the study of negative reactions to strangers, the study of which was frequently equated with the development of fear in general. However, this assumption of prototypicality of discrete situations is discordant with the data observed. For instance, Scarr and Salapatek (1970) reported that the development of fear of strangers correlated only with the development of the perceptually similar fear of masks. These authors were able to find no general pattern of correlations indicating that any of their test situations (the visual cliff, loud noises, mechanical toys) correlated with all other situations. What positive correlations they obtained were interpretable as testing order artifacts.

The appearance of smiling to social stimuli has frequently been taken as the hallmark of the emergence of joy. However, Emde and Harmon (1972) reported that infants smiled at numerous other stimuli, including bull's-eyes, bells, and other nonsocial stimuli before the social smile was well established. Emde and Harmon's study, thus, provides further support to the lack of correlation expectable between reactions to a presumably prototypic stimulus and to other elicitors of the same emotional state. It appears that in the field of emotional development, as in the study of cognitive development (Fischer, 1980), task specificity between environmental stimulation and the organism's response is the rule rather than the exception.

4. *The relationship between emotional expressions and emotional experience changes as the organism develops.* We believe that during a brief period after birth, the emotional expressions manifested by the infant (e.g., the smile or a fully patterned angry facial expression) may be poorly coordinated with the underlying emotional state, probably because of neurological immaturity. Stenberg and Campos (in press), for example, found that in response to restraint, neonates manifest some nonanger facial components (eye closing and tongue protrusion) along with anger components. It seems probable that the inappropriate components constitute overflow or noise in the expression. That is, owing to neurological immaturity, contextually inappropriate components (e.g., those related to disgust or pain states) are expressed along with the appropriate ones. Another example is the rapid-eye-movement-sleep-state smile of the neonate. Although it is now clear that this smile is not associated with either environmental stimuli or with endogenous digestive states, as had once been believed (e.g., Emde & Harmon, 1972), it is not clear what does trigger it. It seems quite possible and even likely that this smile is *not* a reflection of joy, as later smiles will be.

After this early period, expressions are likely to become more closely coordinated with the corresponding emotional state. However, as early as 3 months of age, infants may begin to be exposed to socialization aimed at dissociating expression of emotion from the emotional state (Malatesta & Haviland, 1982). By late childhood and early adulthood, few emotions are expressed completely freely—all may be subject to control in accordance with cultural display rules, personal display rules, and so on (cf. Ekman, 1980). It is likely that control of expression, in turn, influences the emotional state of the expressor (e.g., Izard, 1971; Laird, 1974). Moreover, it is also possible that minute, covert facial muscle movements corresponding to the "true" emotion continue to promote some experience of that emotion (Schwartz, Fair, Salt, Mandel, Klerman, 1976). Still, there is no doubt that overt expression may not resemble underlying emotion.

5. *Coping responses to emotion change as the*

organism develops. Our fifth postulate concerns an obvious yet neglected feature of emotional development. As a person becomes more competent motorically and cognitively, there arise new capacities for coping with emotion or even short-circuiting elicitation of a particular emotion. Such coping capacities dramatically influence the impact of emotion by (1) changing the phenomenological experience of emotion and (2) changing the regulatory impact of emotion. For example, when the infant acquires the ability to crawl, she can better control an interaction with the stranger (G. W. Bronson, 1972). As such, she may ensure that the stranger's behavior does not impinge on her sensorimotor goals. Accordingly, an infant who would otherwise be distressed at interacting with the stranger may not only avoid becoming distressed but may also show pleasure at interacting with the unfamiliar person. Alternatively, if the stranger's actions begin to arouse wariness in the infant, the infant may withdraw, preventing the negative emotion from becoming intense. In fact, as Gunnar (Gunnar, 1980; Gunnar-vonGnechten, 1978) has demonstrated, coping skills may transform negative emotions to pleasurable feelings of efficacy, feelings that should motivate further exploration of novel events.

The last two aspects of emotional development (i.e., 6. *Emotions become socialized as the child grows older* and 7. *Receptivity to others' emotional expressions changes as the organism develops*) have received special and increasing attention in recent years and, therefore, will be discussed in greater detail here.

Socialization of Emotion

Introduction. During the late 1950s and the 1960s when behaviorism was prevalent, many sought to demonstrate that emotions were acquired through conditioning. Brackbill (1958), for example, demonstrated that smiling in 4-month-old infants could be both operantly conditioned and extinguished and Brossard and Decarie (1968) explicated particular forms of conditioning that were most successful in affecting the smiling response. The studies by Sherman (1927a, 1927b) and others (described earlier) seemed consistent with this learning theory approach: there were no universal emotions; emotions were learned like any other behaviors. Yet, as we have already noted, research of Ekman, Izard, and others provided compelling evidence that certain basic emotions are universal across cultures. Ekman and his associates were quick to point out that both positions were correct: at least certain aspects of emotionality—in particular, the expressive aspects—are dramatically affected by enculturation. Acquisition of display rules comprises an important form of socialization of emotional expressions. In this discussion, we will examine some forms of display rules and some effects that such rules may have on expressive behavior. Moreover, as Hochschild (1975) and Lewis and Michalson (1982b) have noted, socialization does not merely affect expression of emotion, it affects the very nature of the emotional experience. Culture may dictate the circumstances under which emotions are experienced, the targets toward whom emotions can or should be felt and expressed, the value of feeling and expressing emotions, the labels given to emotional states, and how emotions are managed. Moreover, society's demands create the need for certain role-taking emotions, such as shame, envy, or embarrassment. Finally, socialization influences a person's responses to others' emotions. We will briefly describe these facets of emotion socialization, ending with a brief discussion of the sparse evidence regarding the beginnings of such processes in infancy.

Display Rules. As indicated earlier, display rules indicate when individuals, cultural groups, or subgroups should and should not express particular emotions. For example, in middle-class American culture, it is expected that close female relatives of a person who dies will express sadness at that relative's funeral. In other cultures, it may be expected that such female relatives exaggerate their sadness, whereas in still other cultures, they may be expected to smile and mask their grief. Note that both the intensity and the quality of the emotional expression are prescribed for a particular subgroup (in this case, women) of a particular culture under particular conditions. Display rules may lead one to exaggerate, dampen, or neutralize a particular emotion, or even to simulate another emotion under particular circumstances (Ekman, 1980; Lewis & Michalson, 1982b). A culture may even specify that only a particular subgroup may ever openly express particular emotions. Moreover, as we will see later, socialization begins quite early; it may be observed in infancy. Such early indoctrination regarding display rules may lead to the developmental progression (mentioned earlier), in which emotional expressions are at first, during the neonatal period, slightly uncoordinated in relationship to the underlying emotional state (owing perhaps to the immaturity of the nervous system). Then, during the first months, prior to the impact of much socialization, the expressions are closely connected to the infant's state, and gradually through infancy and childhood expressions become divorced to some extent from the state.

Feeling Rules. Within psychology, less has

been articulated about feeling rules—rules dictating what a person, subgroup, or cultural group should feel under particular conditions. Hochschild (1975) described three types of appropriateness of feelings: (1) clinical appropriateness (whether in a particular culture a particular feeling is considered healthy or sick), (2) a moral appropriateness (whether an emotion is considered legitimate for a particular group to express toward another group), and (3) social-situational appropriateness (whether it is considered reasonable to experience a particular emotion under particular circumstances).

An interesting variant of clinical inappropriateness may be inferred from Levy's (1973) description of Tahitian emotionality. In Tahiti, it appears that grief is so completely disallowed that no label exists for such an affect. Yet, under appropriate circumstances, such as the loss of a mate, a feeling state, which we would call grief, is experienced. Having no category for such a state, Tahitians seem to have no recourse other than to consider the strange feeling an indicator of illness.

An example in which only a particular elicitor of an emotion is proscribed as sick may be found in middle-class American society. Some persons derive extreme pleasure from being, or watching others be, mutiliated or injured. These elicitors of pleasure are sufficiently common that we have labels for persons who are influenced by them (masochism and sadism), yet most members of our society would view such pleasure as sick.

Note that in each of these examples certain members of the society experience the feelings in question. Still, there is such a strong prohibition against the feelings that those experiencing them are considered sick.

Members of cultures also are strongly socialized regarding moral appropriateness of different feelings. For example, in our culture, it is considered morally inappropriate to feel strong anger toward someone who inadvertently causes damage. As is well known, children must develop an understanding of this notion of intentional versus unintentional wrongdoing (Piaget, 1932). Perhaps the most extreme and harmful example of moral inappropriateness occurs when an infant's prolonged or high-pitched crying elicits anger and abuse from a parent. Although it is clear that the strongest sanctions are exacted against those who act on such angry feelings, those persons who feel anger under those conditions may consider themselves to be reacting immorally.

Social-situational inappropriateness usually is less stringently prohibited. An example of this type of inappropriateness would be if a woman felt a strange sense of relief when her husband, with whom she was happily married, was sent across the country on a long business trip. However, if social-situational inappropriateness becomes too extreme, it may become clinical inappropriateness.

Labeling of Emotions. One clear way in which emotions are socialized is by the labeling of them. A particular culture's set of emotion labels is often a vivid reflection of the society's structure. For example, Lutz (1982) notes that many of the emotion terms of the Ifaluk reflect the relative ranks of the emoting person and the target of the emotion. For example, *fago* refers to an emotion similar to love, which is felt by a fortunate person toward a less fortunate person. Although social rank certainly plays a role in defining some emotion words in English (e.g., one would rarely feel contempt for someone whom one greatly respected), rank does not seem as crucial in defining our emotions as it does in defining those of the Ifaluk.

It seems likely that labeling of emotions influences one's responses to those states. We already noted Tahitians' beliefs that they were ill when they felt grief. Furthermore, labeling need not be verbal. Recently, theorists have suggested that caregivers' actions toward their infants may lead to the children's developing incorrect labels for their psychological states. For example, a caretaker may implicitly label a cry of distress or loneliness as hunger by giving the child a bottle. Bruch (1961) believes that a long-term pattern of this practice may lead to the child's maladaptive overeating when he is depressed or lonely in later life.

Role-taking Emotions. One class of emotions, which Shott (1979) calls role-taking emotions, is of central importance in maintaining social order and, as such, seems especially subject to socialization. These emotions, such as jealousy, envy, embarrassment, pride, shame, and guilt, are explicitly social, requiring a comparison to, or evaluation by, another person (or by a cognitive generalized other) (G. Mead, 1934). In light of the profound influence of emotions on memory, the importance of role-taking emotions becomes apparent. These emotions serve to highlight in memory the important features of a person's culture. Through guilt, shame, and pride, moral principles are driven into memory. Through envy, social dominance hierarchies are underscored. Thus, socialization is bidirectionally related to role-taking emotions: The particular elicitors of such emotions must be culturally transmitted, and, in turn, such emotions inculcate in individuals a deeper understanding of the beliefs, structures, and mores of their culture.

Responses to Others' Emotions. Hoffman (in

press) gives an excellent account of the development of empathy. Briefly, it appears that certain forms of reflexive emotional resonance, such as empathic crying (Martin & Clarke, 1982; Sagi & Hoffman, 1976; Simner, 1971) may be evident as early as the neonatal period. Still, empathic responses are clearly influenced by socialization practices. We can witness such socialization within middle-class American culture by noting the effect of changes in childcare practices on empathic responses. Parents following the dictates that one should ignore crying outbursts (to avoid spoiling the child) would soon extinguish their own empathic responses to crying, whereas followers of Ainsworth (1979) might learn to respond empathically to the first precry whimpers. Children soon learn not to laugh when another child falls or is injured but rather to comfort and help them in some fashion (Radke-Yarrow & Zahn-Waxler, 1982).

Less obvious but quite intriguing is the concept that certain empathic responses—responses indicating elicitation of another's emotion in an observer of that emotion—may exacerbate the original person's distress. For example, anger in response to another person's anger might cause escalation of angry responses. Thus, for some emotions or situations, socialization may induce diminished empathy. This notion becomes especially intriguing when viewed in the context of Malatesta and Haviland's (1982) study described later.

Research on Socialization of Emotion in Infancy. Despite the abundance of interesting questions to study regarding early socialization of emotion, there is a dearth of research regarding the *process* of socialization of emotion during infancy. Most research (e.g., Greif, Alvarez, & Ulman, 1981; Saarni, 1979, 1980; Shenum & Bugental, 1982) has concerned socialization of emotions in older, verbal children. Stenberg and Campos (1983) did address the socialization of the target of a specific emotional expression. They reported that by 4 months of age, infants specifically orient their anger expressions toward the immediate source of what is frustrating them (the experimenter's hands); by 7 months of age, they direct their anger toward the social source of the frustration (the experimenter or the mother who is permitting the impediment to movement). They also reported that at 7 months the anger display is still the primitive bared-teeth expression, leaving open the question of when infants begin to cover their teeth by pressing their lips tightly together—the pattern more commonly reported in older persons.

The two major programs of research on socialization of emotion in infancy are those of Malatesta and Haviland (Haviland, 1977; Malatesta & Haviland, 1982), and by Lewis and his collaborators (e.g., Lewis & Michalson, 1982a). Haviland (1977) reported that the same videotape of an infant expressing emotions was viewed as more negative when it was labeled boy than when it was labeled girl. Malatesta and Haviland (1982) followed up this study with one of mothers' reactions to their 3- and 6-month-old infants' expressions. They found that mothers quite frequently responded to their infants' expressions with expression changes of their own. In most cases, mothers matched their babies' expressions, with a few exceptions. Infants' pain expressions were never observed to be precisely matched. Moreover, mothers responded differently to boys' versus girls' pain expressions: boys were ignored 95% of the time (100% for 6-month-olds), whereas girls were responded to with knitted brow quite frequently, as if mothers were empathizing with girls' pain. Boys' anger, on the other hand, was responded to with knitted brow, whereas girls' anger was more frequently responded to with an angry expression. These findings are particularly intriguing when one notes middle-class society's greater prohibition of female than male anger. If, as some research suggests (e.g., Sorce et al., 1982; Svejda & Campos, 1982), an adult's anger expression leads to avoidance of the activity or object being engaged in, female infants may show dampened anger as a result of mother's matching expression. On the other hand, the knitted brow may imply sympathy for male's anger.

Reactions to Others' Facial Expressions During Infancy and Beyond

These patterns of socialization highlight the interactive nature of emotion. Because emotions are intimately connected with the process of social communication, the study of emotional development is incomplete without an analysis of how receptivity to emotional signals changes with age. The study of the receptive aspects of emotion, however, may be the most neglected topic in the entire field. To date, the most thorough developmental analysis is that of Charlotte Buhler (e.g., Buhler, 1930; Buhler & Hetzer, cited in Kreutzer & Charlesworth, 1973). She studied infants' responses to a positive face, a negative face, to positive and negative voices, and to threatening and affectionate arm gestures. She reported that by 5 months of age, some infants were capable of responding appropriately to angry facial expressions. By 7 months, the reaction to such expressions was evident in her entire sample.

Buhler (1930) subsequently constructed a developmental scale, the norms of which demonstrated that at 5 months, infants responded with the appropriate emotional or behavioral expression to combinations of vocal and facial information; at 6 months, they responded to vocal emotional information without accompanying facial information; and at 7 months, they responded to facial emotional information without vocal accompaniment. At 9 months, her infants responded differently to threatening versus friendly gestural information.

These important findings have been followed up by remarkably few studies, and these have been unpublished (e.g., Charlesworth & Kreutzer, 1973; Klinnert, Sorce, & Emde, 1982; Kreutzer & Charlesworth, 1973). In a recent discussion, Klinnert, Campos, Sorce, Ende, & Svejda (1983) attempted to integrate what was known about the development of a child's use of facial expression information and proposed that such usage proceeded through several levels. (Too little is known about infants' and children's sensitivity to vocal or gestural information to permit the construction of a developmental model of receptivity to vocal affect.)

The first level, predicted to last from birth to about 6 weeks of age, is characterized by minimal attention to internal details of visual gestalts, such as the face (Hainline, 1978; Haith, Bergman, & Moore, 1977; Maurer & Salapatek, 1976). This characteristic impedes visual access to the areas of the face that specify emotional information; hence, the neonate is not expected to discriminate consistently among facial expressions of emotion, let alone utilize the information for behavior regulation.

The second level, predicted to last from the time that infants reliably begin scanning interior details of the face until about 4 or 5 months of age, is characterized by the ability to discriminate facial expressions that specify emotional state without necessarily appreciating the emotional meaning of such expressions. Numerous studies (e.g., Barrera & Maurer, 1981; LaBarbera, Izard, Vietze, & Parisi, 1976; Young-Browne, Rosenfeld, & Horowitz, 1977) have shown that 3- and 4- month-olds dishabituate to changes in facial expression in pictorial displays. However, as has been pointed out repeatedly in the literature on infant perception (e.g., Appel & Campos, 1977; Lamb & Campos, 1982), dishabituation to changes in complex visual displays (e.g., a happy from an angry face) in no way implies that one emotion is being discriminated from another. The discrimination can be mediated by a featural rather than configurational discrimination. For instance, Oster and Ewy (cited in Oster, 1981) demonstrated discrimination of smiling from nonsmiling faces only when teeth were visible in the smile, thus raising the possibility that contour density may have mediated the apparent discrimination of happiness from other emotions. Other studies, which at first seem interpretable as evidence for the detection of emotional information in the face, can also be explained more parsimoniously. The studies by Tronick (e.g., Cohn & Tronick, 1982; Tronick et al., 1978) have shown that when mothers remain still-faced or depress their level of interaction, 1- to 3-month-olds withdraw and become fussy. These findings, however, are interpretable in terms of the importance of contingency in social interaction at 1 to 3 months. They lack the experimental operations necessary to infer that infants appreciate the emotional state of the mother's facial expressions.

The third level involves what we have called emotional resonance: the infant reacts with a positive or negative expression, depending on the affective quality specified by the facial configuration. It is during this age period, which Klinnert, Campos, Sorce, Ende, & Svejda (1983) predicted to last from 4 or 5 months to 9 months of age, that infants in both Buhler's (1930) and Kreutzer and Charlesworth's (1973) studies began responding emotionally to other's facial and vocal displays of emotion—a capacity that we feel may be made possible by changes in the baby's ability to appreciate the entire facial *gestalt* (Bushnell, 1982).

Whereas in the third level, discrete emotional communication can first take place between the infant and another person, the fourth level, which begins at 8 to 9 months of age, is characterized by the communication between infant and another becoming extended to include a third event in the environment. During this period, the infant can appreciate what in the environment is the target of the other person's emotional reaction, much as the infant at this age begins to understand the referent of the mother's pointing or gaze behavior (e.g., Leung & Rheingold, 1981; Scaife & Bruner, 1975). Accordingly, during this period, social referencing begins. Social referencing is the deliberate search for emotional information in another person's face, voice, and gesture to help disambiguate uncertainties in the environment, and it is an instance of a two-person communication about a third event (Klinnert, Campos, Sorce, Ende, & Svejda, 1983).

Further changes in the understanding of emotions take place in subsequent years, and have been well described by Harter (1979); at first, children do not seem to understand that an individual can feel two emotions at the same time; later, they understand that a person can feel two emotions, but sequentially; ultimately, at 9 or 10 years of age, children understand that a person can feel two quite opposite emotions simultaneously.

The lack of replicated work in this area makes any proposal regarding emotional development quite tentative, and several issues raised by recent studies need to be addressed. For instance, Field et al. (1982) and Field and Walden (1982) have reported that infants at 3 days of age imitate components of facial expressions of sadness, joy, and surprise. These remarkable findings raise fundamental questions about whether the receptive capacities of neonates are as well developed as their expressive capacities seem to be. However, previous work on neonatal imitation (Meltzoff & Moore, 1977) has failed to replicate (Hayes & Watson, 1981). Will this more recent neonatal imitation be replicated? Is it possible that, as with certain neonatal reflexes (e.g., Zelazo, 1976), a capacity that is present at a reflexive level in the neonate submerges only to reappear at a higher level of organization later (T. Bower, 1976)? Moreover, it is now clear that when provided with moving displays, infants show better capacity to appreciate the affective information conveyed in expressions (Walker, 1982); the ages provided in the model of Klinnert, Campos, Sorce, Ende, & Svejda (1983) are then only approximations. On the whole, then, one of the most fundamental issues in the study of emotion is that of the development of emotional communication.

Conclusion

In the first section of this chapter, we have presented an emerging conceptualization of the nature of human emotions and their development. Our aim has not been to offer an encyclopedic review of the literature on the various emotional domains that have been so widely studied. We refer the reader to recent reviews that are much more comprehensive than we can be in the present volume. The literature on fear of strangers, for instance, has been well covered by Clarke-Stewart (1978b), Horner (1980), Smith (1979), and Sroufe (1977); that on reactions to looming stimuli by Yonas (1981); and that on heights by Bertenthal et al. (1983). Those interested in the literature on the development of anger should consult Stenberg (1982). The development of smiling and laughter has been dealt with by Sroufe and Waters (1976), and curiously, little has been added since to their conceptualizations. We will discuss separation distress in *Social Development in Infancy* as well as the development of attachment—a major component of which is the discrete emotion of affection.

We have stressed a new orientation to the study of emotions and their development in an attempt to elucidate just what we do not know and, hence, to help direct future research in this field. Despite major advances in both methodology and theory in the last decade, we have only begun to explore the new conceptualization of emotions. This conceptualization involves the following major propositions:

1. That emotions should be studied because of what they do and because of the adaptive functions that they play for both internal and social regulation rather than because of what they index or reflect.
2. That emotions are intimately linked to, yet dissociable from, expressive reactions in face, voice, and gesture.
3. That emotions can serve as both end states (e.g., pleasant hedonic tone) and mediators of the changes in behavior required to ensure progress toward an end state (e.g., anger, fear).
4. That certain aspects of emotions (e.g., paralinguistic reactions, expressions like laughter) undergo developmental reorganization but other aspects of emotion probably do not.
5. That certain emotions require minimal social experience for their expression and recognition, other emotions are heavily dependent on socialization for their construction and elicitation, but all have biological roots in common.
6. That we must understand more about the goals and strivings of the person before we can understand either the elicitation of emotion in ourselves or another or before we can place into context the emotional expressions of others as they impact ourselves—a point made by Trevarthen (1979, 1982).

Emotions have always been conceptualized as closely related to the development of an individual's personality. The conceptualization of emotion that we presented in this section has implications for understanding the construct of infant temperament as well as the burgeoning field of social development. We will address each of these areas in turn.

INFANT TEMPERAMENT

Introduction

One of the most significant recent developments in the field of human infancy has been the dramatic rise of interest in the causes, consequences, and measurement of stable individual differences in human infancy, especially those individual differences that are believed to be at the root of adult personality. Loosely unified under the rubric of temperament, the study of individual differences in infancy has attracted attention from a remarkably diverse number of sources, starting with personality theory and extending to psychophysiology, education and learning theory, and social development. Given such a diversity of conceptual roots, there is little wonder that the concept of temperament has proved so difficult to pinpoint (Plomin, 1982).

One difficulty comes about because the different approaches to the study of temperament have often had different purposes for their interest in individual differences. Some approaches (e.g., learning theory) have stressed the internal organizing features of temperament, such as its role in the ease of establishment and extinction of conditioned responses (Eysenck, 1967; Gray, 1964; Pavlov, 1927; Rothbart & Derryberry, 1983). Other approaches have emphasized the role of temperament as a major influence on interpersonal interactions (e.g., R. Q. Bell, 1968) and neglected the internal organizing functions. A few investigators, such as Brazelton (1973), have stressed both the internal and the interpersonally organizing functions. Still others (e.g., Kagan, Reznick, Clarke, Snidman, & Garcia-Coll, in press) have proposed that some types of temperament may show far more stability and continuity between infancy and later life than the more widely studied processes of cognition and attachment.

A second difficulty arises because each theoretical approach has brought to the study of infant temperament a preferred method of investigation (e.g., questionnaire assessment vs. laboratory testing), different explanatory goals (long-term clinical predictions vs. explanation of the contemporaneous influences on mother-infant relationships), and different criteria of scientific proof (e.g., clinical case histories vs. correlational longitudinal approaches with large groups). To clarify the concerns of the various constituencies responsible for current interest in temperament, we will review each briefly.

Personality Theory

Many theorists view temperament as an important subdomain in the broader field of personality psychology. That is, according to one's theoretical predilections, temperament may be considered as the heritable, the early appearing, or the stable aspects of personality. The tradition of personality research has given rise to the widespread interest in change and consistency in individual differences in various temperament traits. Much of the research done in this tradition has been unabashedly empirical. Any phenomenon that proved to be stable was, prima facie, important. Moreover, it did not matter whether the behavior predicted at later ages was morphologically similar to the predictor. What mattered was the degree of the relationship (Bell, Weller, & Waldorp, 1971). Theory generally followed research rather than the reverse. Kagan and Moss's (1962) attempt to trace the origins and development of personality was one of the first systematic studies of the continuities and discontinuities in personality development from early infancy on. Such an endeavor had undoubtedly received encouragement from the report by Neilson (1948) describing a surprising degree of stability in the personality of Shirley's babies studied as adolescents 15 years later. Moreover, the Fels Longitudinal Study (which formed the data base for the Kagan and Moss, 1962, book) had been antedated by numerous demonstrations of stable individual differences in early infancy (e.g., Bayley, 1956). The influence of this approach is still evident in attempts to generate empirical scales that predict later behavior from early infancy (Lerner, Palermo, Spiro, & Nesselroade, 1982; Waldrop, Bell, McLaughlan, & Halverson, 1978).

Psychophysiology and Psychosomatic Medicine

The interest in studying individual differences in infancy that originated in the study of autonomic response functions was also largely atheoretical, although the work of both John Lacey (e.g., 1959, 1967) and Frances Graham (e.g., Graham & Clifton, 1966) had important implications for understanding the functions that individual differences in autonomic patterns can serve for perception and cognition and even, to some extent, for interpersonal behavior (Lacey, Kagan, Lacey, & Moss, 1963).

In the 1950s, a number of researchers had demonstrated that individuals manifest stable patterns of physiological reactions termed individual response stereotypy (Lacey, 1959). This term refers to the observation that each individual has a characteristic pattern of autonomic reaction that is observable in response to many widely different stressors and that differs from the pattern observable in other individuals. For instance, one individual might react with the same pattern of extreme electrodermal responses, moderate changes in blood pressure, and minimal changes in heart rate in response to five different stressors. Another individual might show a different, but equally reliable, profile of autonomic response to the same stressors. These profiles proved to be stable in childhood, showing impressive test-retest stability across 4 years (Lacey & Lacey, 1962). Autonomic response stereotypy was believed to reflect a constitutional or hereditary predisposition because at the time autonomic patterns were not believed to be amenable to environmental modification. In addition to the basic research on autonomic patterning, other studies documented that stress-symptom relationships are mediated by specific organ sensitivities. For instance, Mirsky, Weiner, Thales, and Reiser (1957) documented that only those persons with a predisposition to react to stress with particularly high degrees of gastric secretions were at risk for ulcer formation. This led to a number of empirical studies to determine whether there was an innate basis for these autonomic predispositions and whether autonomic patterns were stable in the neonatal period (e.g., Birns, Blank, & Bridger, 1966; Bridger & Reiser, 1959; Grossman & Greenberg, 1957; Lipton, Steinschneider, & Richmond, 1965).

Moreover, as early as 1958, the Laceys (Lacey & Lacey, 1958a, 1958b) had speculated that individual differences in heart rate and blood pressure changes might serve important perceptual-cognitive and socially regulatory functions in the individual and might account in part for the trait of impulsivity. On the basis of extensive neurophysiological data, Lacey (Lacey, 1967; Lacey & Lacey, 1970) proposed that increases in heart rate and blood pressure tend to reduce cortical activity by indirectly blocking reticular activation through a complex circuit activated by peripheral autonomic feedback from the cardiovascular system. Increases in heart rate and blood pressure, thus, were predicted to result in reduced perceptual sensitivity, slowed motor function, and less impulsivity, whereas heart rate and blood pressure decreases were predicted to bring about the reverse pattern of behavior. Accordingly, individual differences in variability and direction of heart rate change were predicted to bring about important differences in both intrapersonal and interpersonal functions—the latter mediated through the link between cardiovascular function and impulsivity. These predictions received a measure of empirical support in studies by Lacey et al. (1963) and by Lacey and Lacey (1970). The hypothesis of Lacey and his colleagues, as translated by Graham and Clifton's (1966) theory of the relationship between the direction of heart rate change and orienting and defensive responding, led to a number of studies on the stability of individual differences in cardiac response to stimulation (e.g., Clifton & Graham, 1968; Lipton, Steinschneider, & Richmond, 1966). Most recently, Kagan and his collaborators (e.g., Garcia-Coll, 1981; Kagan, 1982a; Reznick, 1982) have linked heart rate to individual differences in temperament in infancy. Consistent with Lacey's theory, Kagan has reported that high and stable heart rates during conditions of information processing reflect inhibition and wariness on the part of the child (a condition Kagan calls vigilance), whereas low and variable rates reflect ease of engagement in the cognitive task and a calm behavioral disposition. Racial/ethnic group differences have also been found in both heart rate patterns and proneness to vigilance by Kagan's group (Kagan et al., 1978). For example, Chinese-American infants show more stable heart rate and greater vigilance than do Caucasian infants matched for sex and socioeconomic and rearing status. The relationship between individual differences in biological function and individual differences in wariness is presumed by Kagan to reflect maturational control, although environmental factors can often mask the child's behavioral inhibition.

A recent contribution of psychophysiology to the study of temperament involves the revival of interest in a phenomenon reported long ago by Jones (1930). He claimed that there was a surprising *negative* correlation between children's overt behavioral expressions of emotion (such as facial expressions) and their covert autonomic responses (e.g., electrodermal reactions). These findings, which have subsequently been confirmed by Buck (1975, 1977), were unexpected because it is usually assumed that there is a positive correlation between different indices of emotional reactivity (Duffy, 1962). Because many researchers assume that high autonomic activation expressed over a prolonged period of time results in tissue pathology, Field (1982) has proposed that the measurement of individual differences in behavioral-autonomic expressivity may allow identification in the infancy period of children at risk for subsequent stress-related disease. Field has also pointed out that the belief shared by Jones (1930), Buck, (1975, 1977), and others that these individual differences are due to differences in acculturation cannot entirely apply. She reports that even neonates show a similar negative correlation between autonomic and overt emotional expressions (Field, 1982). Nevertheless, the possibility remains that some children are encouraged to inhibit overt emotional expressions, whereas others are not, and that such inhibition amplifies autonomic emotional responding (Buck, 1975; Jones, 1950). The reverse relationship is also possible—that high autonomic reactivity facilitates the socialization of overt emotional expression (Eysenck, 1967).

Clinical Psychiatry

As in so many areas of research in human infancy, interest in temperament also came from clinicians who were impressed with the inability of the mother-infant experiential relationship, by itself, to account for subsequent clinical outcomes. As Escalona (1963) put it, there are numerous instances in which diametrically opposite maternal behavior leads to the precisely identical outcome, whereas there are instances in which extremely similar behavior on the part of mothers leads to very different infant outcomes. The influential New York Longitudinal Study (NYLS) initiated in the mid-1950s by Alexander Thomas, Stella Chess, Herbert Birch, and colleagues (Thomas & Chess, 1977, 1980; Thomas, Chess, & Birch, 1968; Thomas, Chess, Birch, Hertzig, & Korn, 1963)—which we will discuss in greater depth later (see *Thomas and Chess's Theory*)—was motivated by clinical experience suggesting that environmental factors alone cannot explain the nature and variability of behavioral problems. Thomas and Chess postulated that there may be constitutional susceptibilities to stress and stress reduction that, in the proper environment, may determine clinical outcomes. They were impressed by their observation that the infant, far from being a pliable organism subject only to the influence of the mother, frequently was a major source of influence on the mother's behavior. The same theme of the infant as an influence on the mother's behavior became the topic of influential papers by R. Q. Bell (1968)—and by others before him (Gewirtz, 1961; Korner, 1965)—in which a reinterpretation of the contribution of the child to parent-child relationships was proposed.

More recently, the theme of constitutional susceptibilities to psychopathology remains significant in theories, for example, that of Margaret Mahler (Mahler, Pine, & Bergman, 1975) and William B. Carey (1981), as well as in contemporary approaches to other early childhood disorders, for example, autism (Wing, 1976). This theme has been supplemented with a concern for the *invulnerability* of a large number of infants and children to even the most traumatic and repeated stressors (Rutter, 1979). A number of familial, economic, social, and experiential factors have been proposed as determinants of such invulnerability, but the infant's constitutional makeup is one of the most likely factors. For instance, Rutter (1979) reports that "even when there was marked disharmony in the home, the temperamentally easy child tended to escape much of the flak" (p. 296). The precise mechanism by which temperament buffers the child from stress is currently of great interest.

Behavior Genetics

With the upsurge of speculation about biological influences on human behavior, there came an attempt to demonstrate that variability in certain infant traits is associated with genetic differences. Following up early work by Jost and Sontag (1944) on the heritability of autonomic reactivity in young children as well as research on temperament in dogs (Freedman, 1958), Freedman and Keller (1963) reported significant heritabilities on the Bayley Infant Behavior Profile—a temperamentlike rating scale adjunct to the Bayley scales of intellectual and motor development. Freedman (1974) also demonstrated that the age of onset of emotional phenomena, like the social smile and stranger distress, was more similar in identical than in fraternal twins. Subsequent to this work and that of Gottesman (1963) on adolescent personality, there was a steady increase in what had previously been a dormant interest in behavior-genetic studies of temperament. Two decades later, a fairly extensive literature has been generated, indicating that a number of personality dimensions, especially extraversion-introversion, have significant genetic loadings (Goldsmith, 1983; see also *Scarr & Kidd, vol. II, chap. 6*). These findings have led some behavior geneticists, such as Goldsmith (Goldsmith & Campos, 1982b), Matheny (1980), and Plomin (1982), to explore which individual differences in infancy show genetic loading, and which do not.

Education

Educators were also interested in the concept of temperament. In the 1960s, considerable discussion had been generated regarding phenomena like hyperkinesis and disturbances in concentration as factors impairing children's functioning in schools. When individual differences in temperament began to be documented, their role in school adjustment attracted considerable interest (Carey, Fox, & McDevitt, 1977; Chess, Thomas, & Cameron, 1976; Garside, Birch, Scott, Chambers, Kolvin, Tweddle, & Barber, 1975; Gordon & Thomas, 1967; Sobesky, List, Holden, & Braucht, 1981). After reviewing the relevant literature, sketchy though it is, Keogh and Pullis (1980) concluded that available evidence suggests "that individual variations in temperament are important influences on a given child's success or failure in a social situation, be it family or preschool" (p. 270). This interest in the educational implications of temperament differences is consistent with theories that treat temperament as a mediator of learning. These include the classic Pavlovian concept of strength of the nervous system (Pavlov, 1927) as well as Eysenck's (1967) view that characteristic differences in ease of acquisition and extinction of responses distinguish introverts and extraverts. The evidence for individual differences in conditionability early in infancy (Fitzgerald & Brackbill, 1976) suggests the possibility of tracing putative temperamental modulators of learning to earlier developmental periods.

Developmental Psychology

A final source of our present conceptualization of temperament lies within the traditional domain of developmental psychology. Following an era of baby biographies, Gesell and Ames (1937) and Shirley (1933) demonstrated significant—although far from complete—stability of various temperament traits during infancy. Their methods involved gathering extensive objective data on small samples, forming ratings from clinical impressions extracted from these data, and attempting to match ratings across time periods. Neilson (1948) was able to obtain significant degrees of matching between Shirley's (1933) personality sketches of her infants and similar sketches made during adolescence. There followed larger scale, multipurpose longitudinal studies that included assessment of the stability of temperament dimensions (Kagan & Moss, 1962; Schaefer & Bayley, 1963).

Definition of Temperament

Given the diverse sources of interest in temperament, it is not surprising that vagueness plagues current definitions and theories of temperament. Temperament often seems to refer to *any* differences among individual infants, a tendency exacerbated by the frequent tendency to define temperament operationally (i.e., as the temperament scales measure it). Recent reviews, however, have decried the lack of conceptual focus of temperament research and called for agreement on which individual differences to call temperament related and which to call something else (Hubert, Wachs, Peters-Martin, & Gandour, 1982; Plomin, 1982). In our discussion, *Theories of Temperament,* we attempt a conceptual approach that links temperament closely to individual differences in emotionality, and we try to show how such an approach integrates many of the major alternative positions in the field to date.

Most attempts to conceptualize temperament have begun with G. W. Allport's (1937) definition: "Temperament refers to the characteristic phenomena of an individual's emotional nature, including his susceptibility to emotional stimulation, his customary strength and speed of response, the quality of his prevailing mood, and all peculiarities of fluctuation and intensity of mood; these phenomena being regarded as dependent on constitutional make-up, and therefore largely hereditary in origin" (p. 54).

This definition captures the important notions that temperament, mood, and emotion are closely related, that temperament is stable rather than fluctuating, that it concerns dispositions rather than discrete behaviors, that it is closely linked to biological factors, and that it involves parameters of emotional responsiveness, such as latency, amplitude, and duration of behavior.

The definition, however, lacks any stress on the functions that temperament plays in the life of the infant or, for that matter, the adult, because nothing in this definition of temperament limits its applicability to infancy (see Lerner & Lerner, in press). Like emotion, temperament is of contemporary interest because it has both intrapersonal and interpersonal organizational functions. Intrapersonally, the temperament concept helps to account for individual differences in degree of engagement by problem-solving tasks, in attention to significant environmental stimuli, and in the probability that certain responses (e.g., distress, smiling) will be elicited and others not. It is probably of even more interest because it reflects individual differences in behaviors that influence others in the environment. Indeed, one of the original sources of interest in the investigation of temperament was the realization that the same parent frequently behaved differently to different children (Thomas & Chess, 1977) and that these differences were a function of how the children behaved toward the parent. That realization led researchers to supplement the then-prevalent conception of direction of effects as being almost exclusively mother-to-infant with one that emphasized bidirectional influences (Tronick, Als, & Brazelton, 1980). Because most approaches to temperament also consider temperamental dispositions to be biological in origin and heritable (Buss & Plomin, 1975), temperament meets the same three criteria that help to differentiate the domain of emotions from that of other fields: (1) it organizes internal psychological processes, (2) it directly influences interpersonal interactions and (3) it has phylogenetic, species-specific, or heritable roots.

However, the term temperament is not synonymous with emotion. Temperament refers to stable individual differences in parameters of hedonic tone, arousal, and discrete emotions like anger or fear, whereas emotion concerns the normative affective and expressive processes themselves. Thus, all human beings will manifest fear, joy, anger, interest, increased or diminished activity, and so forth.

These are the normative aspects of emotion. However, some show a very low threshold for fearfulness and others a high one. Some will show anger long after the provocation has passed, others will calm quickly. Some will be very active in most situations, whereas others are quiescent. These are the individual differences that we feel are temperament related—again we emphasize, they are not restricted to infancy. An adult who is characteristically prone to smile and gesture in a friendly fashion to others is demonstrating individual differences in temperament, as is an infant who behaves similarly.

Not all individual differences in the behavior of human infants are temperamental in nature, either on the basis of the common usage of the term temperament or on the basis of the conceptual framework we propose. There are categories of individual differences that are studied primarily because they are indices of something else that is more fundamental. As usually conceptualized, individual differences in these indicator variables do not serve an organizing function. Consider the difference between individuality in handedness (by consensus, a nontemperament trait) and in crying (a protypical expression of temperament). Handedness is studied because it is presumed to reflect important aspects of underlying brain function, like the organization of hemispheric specialization for speech (see *Kinsbourne & Hiscock, vol. II, chap. 4*), because it predicts future language performance (Ramsay, 1980) or because it may be related to deficits or unusual performance in reading and writing, like mirror imaging (Hardyck & Petrinovich, 1977; Naylor, 1980). No one proposes that handedness organizes brain function, determines the growth of vocabulary, or leads the child to reverse the perception or production of letters. Moreover, although handedness under certain circumstances strongly influences interpersonal functions—for example, when certain cultures proscribe the adoption of sinistrality—such interpersonal influence is conditioned by society. There are doubtless many cultural groups who pay no attention to a child's emerging handedness.

By way of contrast, temperamental differences have clear intrapersonal and interpersonal ramifications. For example, individual variations in crying produce important differences among infants in their intrapersonal psychological processes. A crying infant shuts out the world perceptually, frequently directs little or no attention to even the most significant environmental stimulation, disengages from whatever task in which he is involved, and emits behaviors, like tensing or striking out, at the expense of other, more desirable, behaviors. The more a baby cries, the more learning, habituation, and problem solving are impeded or prevented altogether (Hutt, Lenard, & Prechtl, 1969). In short, crying powerfully influences what we have been classifying as internal psychological processes.

Although differences in crying may at times reflect hunger or illness, temperamental influences likely exert more profound and pervasive effects upon individual differences in crying. The cry also has immediate effects on those within earshot of the child, creating a sense of discomfort, which, in turn, motivates them to take steps to terminate the cry. If caregivers fail in these attempts to stop the crying, they become frustrated and their distress is augmented. If they succeed, they generally feel confident and satisfied. Moreover, we would predict that cross-cultural data would show a far more prevalent and universal pattern of response to individual differences in the infant's cry than to individual differences in handedness, which would suggest that there is fundamental link between the infant's signal transmission and the listener's signal reception.[3] Moreover, individual differences in crying behaviors show fairly strong evidence of heritability. In a recent twin study of infant temperament, Goldsmith and Campos (1982a) calculated heritabilities in the .50 range for 9-month-olds in response to certain distress-provoking stimuli, such as the deep side of the visual cliff or the approach by strangers. Goldsmith & Campos (1982a) also found similar heritability for the fear and anger scales, as reported by mothers in Rothbart's Infant Behavior Questionnaire (Rothbart, 1981a), scales that are heavily loaded with questions regarding the infant's frequency of crying.

Other examples of individual differences that are not temperament related include individual differences in the detection of spatial frequencies, which are used to identify ophthalmological difficulties in the baby (e.g., Salapatek & Banks, 1977); differences in recognition memory in infancy, which predict later IQ (e.g., Fagan & McGrath, 1981); changes in reflex functions, which are used to determine levels of brain maturation (Peiper, 1963); or measures of brainstem-evoked potentials, which indicate risk for later developmental disorders (Shucard, Shucard, & Thomas 1982). On the other hand, the individual differences that are probably temperament related include such traits as timidity, distractability, irritability, soothability, activity level, and possibly many more. As is the case with the fundamental emotions, there is no consensus regarding an exhaustive list of prototypic temperament domains.

A second defining feature of temperament is stability: individual differences in temperamental dispositions are expected to be maintained across time as well as to be consistent across situations. A child with a low threshold for crying, for example, would be likely to cry with little provocation under circumstances ranging from moderately loud sounds to minor intrusiveness of a strange person. Such a child would be expected to cry more frequently than a child with a higher threshold for crying on several testing occasions, even weeks apart. Moreover, the source of such ability should be the infant's predisposition rather than the stability of the environment.

The expectation of temperament stability needs to be qualified in two ways, however, to make it applicable to the infancy period. First, it is unnecessary to require that the various aspects of temperament be stable from the neonatal period onward. The stability may be confined to the intervals between periods of behavioral reorganization, such as those suggested by Piaget (1951, 1954); Kagan, (1971); Emde, Gaensbauer, and Harmon (1976); and McCall (1979). The second qualification is that the same underlying temperament dimension may be elicited by different events and indexed by different manifest behaviors during successive developmental periods. For instance, low threshold to fear may be manifested as crying inconsolably when placed on the deep side of the visual cliff at 8 months, clinging to the mother at 18 months when a jack-in-the-box pops up (but not crying on the visual cliff at this age), and screaming on a roller coaster at 8 years (but not clinging to mother when viewing jack-in-the-boxes nor crying on the visual cliff at this age). Both the events that elicit fearfulness and the behaviors expressing fearfulness change at different points in development; however, the child still is high in fearfulness relative to others of the same age. A particularly dramatic illustration of this point has come from the work of Bell et al. (1971). They reported that babies whose reactions to interruption of sucking were characterized by quick reaction and hard crying were not only more incoordinated and arrhythmic as preschoolers but also were more passive and lethargic. Similarly, Yang and Halverson (1976) reported that crying in response to aversive stimuli in the neonatal period predicts the rather different discrete behaviors of disruptive and socially unacceptable behavior.

A third distinction between temperament and emotion relates to the difference between the parameters of a phenomenon and the phenomenon itself. We are proposing that the content domains of the individual differences in temperament are emotional in nature and that the appropriate measures of temperament consist of differences in the temporal or intensive characteristics of the discrete emotions or of the more general dimensions of hedonic tone and arousal level. For example, two infants may both smile at a stimulus but differ characteristically in certain temporal parameters of smiling, such as the latency to smile, the rise time of the smile, the tempo of accompanying expressions (Kagan, 1971), and the smile's duration and recovery time. Infants may also differ in the amplitude of the smile, its threshold of elicitation, and the vigor and patterning of fine and gross motor activities, such as the bouncing and bicycling that accompanies enthusiastic smiling (Emde & Harmon, 1972). Accordingly, our definition of temperament is quite straightforward. *Temperament refers to individual differences in the intensive and temporal parameters of behavioral expressions of emotionality and arousal, especially as these differences influence the organization of intrapersonal and interpersonal processes.* This definition subsumes many of the phenomena that other investigators have identified as temperament related, but it highlights gaps in the approaches taken by some who are interested in the study of temperament. A brief review of some influential approaches to temperament helps clarify similarities and differences among theories.

Theories of Temperament

Thomas and Chess's Theory

Thomas and Chess's (1977) approach to temperament, which was derived from the NYLS, is certainly the most widely cited by developmental and clinical researchers. Thomas and Chess define temperament as behavioral style—the how, not the why of behavior. We believe that the intensive and temporal parameters of behavioral expression described are precisely what constitute such style of behavior. However, Chess and Thomas rule out the *content* of behavior from their definition of temperament as style, whereas we believe that temperament is intimately related to content (e.g., the discrete emotions) and also that stylistic differences in response parameters are not necessarily correlated from one dimension of emotionality to the next. That is, Thomas and Chess believe that a child with a low threshold for crying will also likely have a low threshold for smiling, anger, and distraction. We, however, do not hold such a belief, primarily because it seems unduly restraining for theory and because we and others have found a lack of empirical support for the notion (Goldsmith & Campos, 1982b; Rothbart, 1981a, 1981b).

Thomas and Chess (1977) emphasize the importance of interactive processes—both between infant temperament and parental caregiving style and between temperament, motives, and abilities within the individual—for later development and mental health. They endorsed the notion of goodness-of-fit between an individual's temperamental characteristics and the environment (primarily the rearing environment) as a central feature of their interactive viewpoint. This interactive orientation, although open to challenge as being so general that it offers few guidelines for contemporary research (Lamb, 1980), does redress the imbalance of earlier theories of temperament that were heavily imbued with biological determinism.

Thomas and Chess's (1977) framework has special relevance to the ongoing controversy regarding continuity/discontinuity of temperament. Most recent researchers conclude that, in the face of apparent discontinuity of temperamental traits, underlying continuity can be uncovered if the correct conceptual framework and research strategy are taken. One point relevant to this conclusion is the fact that the same trait may be manifested through different behaviors during different developmental periods—as we discussed earlier. The other points are closely related to the aforementioned goodness-of-fit notion. Early temperament is thought to predict subsequent behavior only when considered in the context of the parents' and other socializers' reactions and expectations (Thomas & Chess, 1977, 1980). Goodness-of-fit between infant and caregiver greatly influences the socialization process.

If an infant's traits are offensive to the caregiver, the caregiver is likely to modify the environment so that the infant becomes unlikely to manifest the temperamental trait or to condition the child to avoid expressing the trait. In either case, the child will express the trait more at time 1 than at time 2. Therefore, for a researcher to witness continuity across time she must place the child in a situation that powerfully elicits the trait in question and do so under conditions that minimize socialized control of the trait's expression.

Lerner and Lerner (in press) have extended the goodness-of-fit conceptualization by proposing that temperament research should entail simultaneous study of temperament and its context of expression. Indeed, the Lerners propose that researchers "move to a second level of abstraction, measuring both the person's temperament and the contextual demands." Multivariate relational scores expressing the good-of-fit between temperament dimensions and contextual demands are expected to predict psychosocial adaptation. In the absence of such goodness-of-fit measures, the Lerners expect little construct validity for temperamental attributes alone. Their work clearly demonstrates the important impact that Thomas and Chess's approach has had on developmental psychology.

Thomas and Chess (1977) propose nine dimensions of temperament: activity level, rhythmicity, approach-withdrawal, adaptability, intensity of reaction, threshold of responsiveness, quality of mood, distractibility, and attention span/persistence. (These dimensions will be described more fully later.) From these dimenisons, they derive three temperamentally based typological characterizations of infants: the *easy* child (seen in 40% of their sample and characterized by high rhythmicity, positive mood, high approach, high adaptability, and low intensity); the *difficult* child (seen in 10% of their sample and characterized by the opposite pattern); and the *slow-to-warm-up* child (seen in 15% of the sample and characterized by high activity, withdrawal, low adaptability, negative mood, and low intensity).

Although this typological approach has been widely used, it has serious problems. First, note that easy and difficult are not so much types as they are the opposite poles of a complex dimension. This necessarily oversimplifies the true state of individual differences in any study of temperament because the distribution of cases is likely to be small at the extremes of any dimension. (There are few highly difficult or extremely easy children). Moreover, although an easy-difficult dimension has emerged in other studies using maternal report (e.g., Stevenson-Hinde & Simpson, in press), the dimension in other samples is not constituted by the five predicted dimensions (Plomin, 1982). In fact, it is not clear that the dimensions that purportedly comprise the typologies are themselves reliable clusters of characteristics; the nine NYLS dimensions frequently do not emerge in factor-analytic studies despite the use of scales designed specifically to tap the nine dimensions. Add to these difficulties the other problems that are characteristic of the use of typologies, such as the implicit value judgments being made regarding the individual types, the difficulties arising in statistical analyses of nominal data, and the lack of differentiation of potentially important differences within a type. It seems reasonable to conclude that a dimensional approach is preferable, especially for nonclinical research. Thus, for the remainder of this discussion, we will focus on dimensional approaches to temperament.

Buss and Plomin's Theory

Another theoretical approach to dimensions of temperament is that of Buss and Plomin (1975), which was supplemented by Plomin and Rowe (1979). These authors endorse G. W. Allport's (1937) definition cited earlier, but the key feature of their temperament theory is the postulation of five inclusion criteria that are biological or developmental in nature. These criteria require that valid dimensions of temperament be (1) heritable, (2) stable, (3) predictive of adult personality, (4) adaptive (in the evolutionary sense), and (5) perhaps present in other animals. (This last criterion has been emphasized by Diamond, 1957). Consideration of the evidence relevant to these criteria led Buss and Plomin (1975) to postulate four broad dimensions of temperament: emotionality, activity, sociability, and impulsivity (EASI).

Buss and Plomin's theory is interactive in three ways: (1) the child elicits certain types of parental behaviors as a function of her temperament (differences in emotionality and impulsivity being especially likely to elicit differences in the amount of parental controlling behavior), (2) the impact of such parental behaviors varies as a function of children's temperament, and (3) the efficacy of modeling of parental behavior is a function of temperamental similarity between parent and child. This approach seems quite promising; however, as we noted earlier, it may be unduly restricting because it requires that a child who is emotional under fear-eliciting conditions, for example, be similarly emotional under joy-eliciting conditions. We believe it is more useful to propose separate temperament dimensions pertaining to particular emotions.

Rothbart and Derryberry's Theory

An approach that does incorporate emotion-specific content in its temperament dimensions is that of Rothbart and Derryberry (1982). Rothbart and Derryberry recently proposed a multilevel theory of temperament that seeks to integrate the views of adult temperament represented by Eysenck (1967), Gray (1973), and Zuckerman (1979) and related Eastern European concepts of the reactivity of the nervous system (e.g., Pavlov, 1927; Strelau, 1975; Teplov, 1964) with research on social and emotional development during infancy. The key concepts in Rothbart and Derryberry's (1982) theory are reactivity of the nervous system and self-regulation of reactivity:

> In this chapter, we will define temperament as constitutional differences in reactivity and self-regulation, with "constitutional" seen as the relatively enduring biological makeup of the organism influenced over time by heredity, maturation, and experience. By "reactivity" we refer to the characteristics of the individual's reaction to changes in the environment, as reflected in somatic, endocrine, and autonomic nervous systems. By "self-regulation" we mean the processes functioning to modulate this reactivity, e.g., attentional and behavioral patterns of approach and avoidance.

Examples of self-regulation include approach and avoidance behavior and channeling of attention. In discussing reactivity and self-regulation, these authors emphasize that the two constructs can be utilized to describe temperament at the neural level (the level of interacting physiological systems) and at the behavioral level. Rothbart and Derryberry (1982) specify the somatic, endocrine, and autonomic response systems (including motor activity, facial expressions, vocal activity, and emotional reactions) through which reactivity and self-regulation are expressed. They also discuss the intensive and temporal response characteristics of these response systems: intensity (the peak level of excitement), threshold (sensitivity to low-intensity stimulation), latency of response, rise time of response (the interval from onset to peak intensity), and recovery time. Individual differences in these five elements of the phasic nature are *not* necessarily expected to be consistent across the various response systems.

In agreement with our view, Rothbart and Derryberry (1982) clearly reject the notion of temperament as merely style and place, affective-motivational systems at the center of the developing personality. These authors also postulate a connection between temperament and affect, in that the emotion systems constitute one of the response systems for reactivity. Thus, one aspect of temperament would be threshold of reactivity in the fear response system. However, in contrast to our position, variability in the perceptual and cognitive system (e.g., the alerting, orienting, and detecting components of attention) are postulated to be components of temperament. Indeed, the explication of the theory is so wide ranging that it is difficult to determine just which individual differences in the infant's behavioral repertoire are *not* temperament related. The theory describes phenomena related to perception, cognition, motivation, and emotion at neural, physiological, behavioral, and dyadic levels of analysis.

In concordance with our approach, however, Rothbart has recently begun to explore the social regulatory functions of temperament (Rothbart, 1981b), citing the work of Fraiberg (1977) and Moss and Robson (1970) on the importance of parent sensitivity to individual differences in expressive patterns of infants. She also speculates about the need for the mother to engage in more active regulation of her baby's behavior when the infant is either extremely irritable or the victim of genetic or congenital disorders.

It is possible to conceptualize most of the temperament dimensions suggested by these three theories by combining a dimension of affect and its expression with one or more parameters of temperament. The temperament dimensions listed in Table 5 are those suggested by Rothbart (1981b), Buss and Plomin (1975), and Thomas and Chess (1977); the discrete affects used are those described by Ekman (1972) and Izard (1977) plus a category of general arousal (Duffy, 1962; Lindsley, 1951); and the parameters of temperament are those used by Rothbart and Derryberry (1982).

The three groups of temperament dimensions in Table 5 differ in level of the specificity of their relationship to discrete affects: Rothbart's (1981b) dimensions are quite congruent with a discrete affect approach; Buss and Plomin's (1975) dimensions are affect related, but much broader than those of Rothbart; and Thomas and Chess's (1977) categories are more difficult to classify, although they are, as a

Table 5. **Mapping of Selected Dimensions of Temperament onto Affects**

Temperament dimension	Affects
Activity level[a]	General arousal expressed via the motoric system
Smiling and laughter	Happiness or pleasure
Fear	Fear
Distress to limitations	Anger
Soothability	Recovery time of negative affect, given appropriate stimulation by caretaker
Undisturbed persistence	Duration of interest
Emotionality[b]	Fear, anger, and distress
Activity	General arousal expressed via the motor system
Sociability	Interest and positive affects expressed toward people
Impulsivity	Latency of expression of affect or activity
Activity level[c]	General arousal expressed via the motor system
Approach/withdrawal	The initial balance of positive and negative affect (plus associated motor activity) given a novel stimulus
Rhythmicity	No clear relationship
Adaptability	Higher order construct involving, in part, the degree to which initial affective reactions to novel stimuli can be modified
Threshold	A parameter of affect (as well as of other phenomena)
Intensity	A parameter of affect
Mood	Characteristic balance of positive and negative affect
Distractability	Latency of response to a new stimulus, given ongoing activity
Attention span/persistence	Duration of interest/duration of interest given a new stimulus

Notes:
[a]Rothbart, 1981b.
[b]Buss and Plomin, 1975.
Adapted from Goldsmith and Campos (1982b).
[c]Thomas and Chess, 1977.

group, more related to the parameters of temperament than to the dimensions of affect.

Research Issues in the Study of Temperament

From the theoretical perspectives discussed, we can identify three major substantive issues for temperament research: (1) biological contributions, (2) continuity over time, and (3) influence on interpersonal relationships. In addition to these concerns, measurement of temperament has proved a vexing issue, and we will discuss this problem as well. Although clinical and educational implications of temperament are of great importance, these are beyond the scope of this chapter. Plomin (1982) provides an excellent discussion of these issues. Our review is somewhat selective, focusing only on those studies that are most relevant to our discussion.

Measurement of Temperament

Issues in the Measurement of Temperament. Infant temperament has been measured by means of parental report (interviews, questionnaires), observer ratings, or direct behavioral recording. Primarily as a result of the historical influence of the NYLS and subsequent questionnaires based on that study, it is common to find the construct of temperament uncritically equated with parental report as assessed by scales of one sort or another. There has frequently been a failure to appreciate the distinctions between parental report and direct observational measures of temperament. Attention to measurement issues should aid in avoiding these pitfalls.

The conceptualization presented in our earlier discussion, *Theories of Temperament* has a number of important implications for the measurement of temperament, both by questionnaire and in the laboratory. First, because temperament refers to a disposition and not to any specific occurrence of a behavior, single-instance assessment of temperament is not advisable; neither single behavioral items on a questionnaire nor single occurrences of behavior in the laboratory are likely to capture significant individual differences in temperament. Instead, temperament is to be discovered in the commonality among items or occurrences of behavior.

Furthermore, a critical implication of most definitions of temperament is that *there are no behaviors that are unique to a given dimension of temperament.* For example, the frequency of crying may be indicative of the degree to which an infant is prone to distress (a temperament characteristic); however, at times, crying may be indicative of hunger (which, not being affect related by our definition of emotion, is not a temperamental characteristic).

This fact underscores the necessity of attending to situational context. In questionnaires or in the laboratory, the aim of temperament assessment should be to focus both the stimulus situation and the coding of responses to lessen the probability of the coded behaviors being nontemperament related. For example, if the researcher wishes to use crying as a measure of temperamental fearfulness, he should ensure that the infant is not in a tired state, which could produce fussiness. A slightly more complex precaution related to situational context involves discrimination among various dimensions of temperament. For example, in attempting to assess anger during a frustrating situation, it is important to avoid novel elements in the situation, which might elicit fear.

Third, there are problems associated with attempting to assess temperament across too broad an age range with a single instrument, whether the instrument is a questionnaire or a battery of laboratory tests. These problems arise from the changes in expression of temperament that are due to such factors as cognitive and motoric development (e.g., Lerner et al., 1982, attempted to deal with many of these problems in constructing their Dimension of Temperament Survey [DOTS]). The desirability of incorporating measures of stability into the assessment process should be apparent, as should the advantages of using measures with built-in stability, that is, measures averaged across more than one occasion.

A final issue involves the difficulty in successfully disentangling temperament measures of the infant from measures of caretaker interaction. When using parental-report measures, one must accept the fact that the parent's *perception* of temperament is what is being assessed. Then, one can evaluate the degree of distortion introduced by this perception in relationship to the purpose of one's assessment (e.g., Bates, Freeland, & Lounsbury, 1979; Goldsmith & East, 1981). For the purposes of some studies, the caregiver's perception of the infant's temperament (which we might label tempercept) may be precisely the construct of importance (W. B. Carey, 1982). For example, if one is interested in goodness-of-fit between infant and caregiver, that caregiver's perception, not the infant's endogenous characteristic, is the variable of interest. However, if one is interested in determining the influence of the infant's disposition on the infant's reactions to a new event (e.g., one's experimental manipulation), one must isolate the dispositional characteristic from rater biases. Toward this end, one might include validity scales on a questionnaire, use other converging measures of temperament (which would be contaminated by fewer, less powerful, or different sources of bias), or make direct attempts to measure parental biasing factors (e.g., assess parental personality). In the laboratory, one can, of course, minimize the parent's role in temperament assessment, but this factor must be balanced against concerns about ecological validity.

The Questionnaire Approach. The questionnaire approach to temperament assessment was dominant in the 1970s, but there are serious questions concerning the quality of the research instruments that were available. Two generic psychometric concerns should be raised regarding temperament questionnaires. First, selection of the initial item pool, always a rational decision, determines to an important degree the characteristics of scales derived from the pool. Obviously, if one includes no activity items in the initial pool, no scale construction technique will yield an activity-level scale. Second, various scale-construction approaches, such as factor analysis, maximization of internal consistency, and inductive item assignment, entail different assumptions about the independence of temperament dimensions in the nature and the breadth of temperament dispositions.

Because the NYLS temperament categories are directly targeted as the temperament traits in most measures (13 of the 22 temperament questionnaires, rating scales, checklists, and interview schedules are reviewed by Hubert et al., 1982), it is important to note the derivation process for the 9 NYLS dimensions. According to Thomas and Chess (1977), "Nine categories of temperament were established by an inductive content analysis of the parent interview protocols for the infancy periods of the first 22 children studied" (p. 20). This procedure has resulted in several problems:

1. There are no guidelines for replication in other research projects.
2. Whether the same categories would be uncovered at later ages is not known.
3. The 9 categories refer to seemingly disparate levels of analysis, as indicated in Table 5.
4. There is a lack of discriminant validity among the proposed categories, both in the NYLS interview measures and in W. B. Carey (1970, 1972), McDevitt and Carey (1978), and Thomas and Chess's (1977) questionnaire measures (Martin & Pfeffer, 1980; Rowe & Plomin, 1977; Vaughn, Taraldson, Chrichton, & Egeland, 1980).
5. Independent attempts to operationalize some of the 9 dimensions using caretaker-report questionnaires have not been successful (e.g., Pedersen, Anderson, & Cain, 1977; Rothbart, 1981b).

For these reasons and others, investigators recently have derived, usually through factor analysis, smaller sets of scales from NYLS-derived items (e.g., see Rowe & Plomin, 1977; Scholom, Zucker, & Stollack, 1979; Sobesky et al., 1981). Such efforts are likely to be psychometrically more satisfactory than the 9 original scales; however, the rationale for selection of the initial item pool places important constraints on the dimensions that can be rederived.

The NYLS spawned the construction of a number of pencil-and-paper temperament scales, the most widely used of which has been W. B. Carey's (1970, 1972) Infant Temperament Questionnaire (ITQ). The early research with this instrument has been reviewed thoroughly by Sostek and Anders (1977), Campbell (1979), Scholom and Schiff (1980), as well as others cited in Thomas and Chess (1977). The ITQ was initially devised as a pediatric screening device and has had unwarranted application in developmental research, given its unsatisfactory psychometric characteristics of low internal consistency and lack of discriminant validity. Unfortunately, the unwarranted application of this scale has run the risk of generating unfairly negative connotations regarding the validity of the measurement of infant temperament, when it is the specific operationalization of the construct that can be questioned. To help circumvent some of these problems, Carey and McDevitt (1978) have made important changes and constructed a Revised Infant Temperament Questionnaire (RITQ), the early research on which demonstrates much more adequate psychometric properties. Because of these problems with the initial ITQ, we will not review empirical research based on it.

Table 6 and its associated notes present standardization, reliability, and validity data for the five most widely used parental-report questionnaires. Each may be an appropriate choice for certain applications; however, given the paucity of data regarding these scales' validity, one should exercise caution in interpreting them.

None of the questionnaires shows impressive interrater agreement, a finding that implies either that rater perception of temperament independent of actual behavior is salient or that actual infant temperament is conditioned differently by interaction with various caregivers. In comparing the scales, one might note the following: (1) the revised Carey scales show weaker internal consistency and (probably) less discriminant validity than the others presented in Table 6, (2) the Infant Characteristics Questionnaire (ICQ) makes no claim of being a comprehensive assessment of temperament, and (3) the modest correlations between questionnaire scales

Table 6. Correlational Reliability and Validity Evidence for Temperament Questionnaire Commonly Used for Infants and Toddlers

Questionnaire and scales[a]	Internal consistency	Short-term stability	Rater agreement: Mother-father	Rater agreement: Mother-other	Longer-term stability	Evidence for discriminant validity	Evidence for Convergence with observational measures[y]
Revised Infant Temperament Questionnaire (RITQ)[b]							
Activity	.64	.78[k]	.58[p]	.23[p]	range = .24–.58, median = .38[u]	Not available for standardization sample	Approach r = .40 with fear of strangers in lab.[z] 4/8 significant rs with home observations.[aa] Studies using previous form of ITQ show that difficult designation predicts crying.[bb]
Rhythmicity	.65	.75	.59	.31			
Approach	.71	.77	.55	.27			
Adaptability	.57	.74	.35	.11			
Intensity	.56	.66	.12	.06			
Mood	.53	.81	.30	.33			
Persistence	.62	.74	.00	.04			
Distractability	.49	.75	.45	.24			
Threshold	.57	.74	.28	.25			
Toddler Temperament Scale (TTS)[c]							
Activity	range = .53–.86, median = .70 for 1–2 yr-olds and .72 for 2-3 yr.-olds[h]	range = .69–.89, median = .81[l]	.28[q]	.35[q]	NA	7/36 interscale r's > .50; appears to have 3-factor structure at 12 mo.[x]	Approach, r = .50 with inhibition measures.[cc] Activity, approach, mood, persistence, and distractability show r's of −.06, .47, .34, .34, and .30 with conceptually similar ratings made from videotaped lab episodes.[x]
Rhythmicity			.48	.43			
Approach			.59	.56			
Adaptability			.61	.44			
Intensity			.33	.26			
Mood			.58	.20			
Persistence			.56	.42			
Distractability			.45	.21			
Threshold			.25	.30			
Infant Characteristics Questionnaire (ICQ)[d]							
Fussy-difficult factor[e]	.79[i]	.70[m]	.61[r]	.34[m]	.57 (.71)[y]	Factor analytic derivation	r's = .22 with fussiness and −.18 with unsoothability (home ratings).[d] Cries of infants high on factor are rated more irritating and spoiled and show different acoustic properties.[dd]

(continued)

Notes:

[a]Only English-language instruments are tabulated. Substantial research on Swedish questionnaires is available (see Bohlin, Hagekull, & Lindhagen, 1981; McNeil & Persson-Blennow, 1982).

[b]Primary reference, Carey and McDevitt (1978). $N = 203$; Age: 4 to 8 months. Data from other sources as cited.

[c]Primary reference, Fullard, McDevitt, and Carey (1978). Data from other sources as cited.

[d]Primary reference, Bates, Freeland, and Lounsbury (1979). N varies for different analyses as noted. Data from other sources as cited.

[e]Factors accounting for less variance in the ICQ are not considered.

[f]Primary reference, Rothbart (1981a). $N = 94$ 3-month-olds, 115 6-month-olds, and 106 12-month-olds in three longitudinally studied cohorts. 463 questionnaires analyzed. Data from other sources as cited.

[g]Primary reference, Rowe and Plomin (1977). $N = 182$ twins; Age: 5 months to 6 years. Similar data are available for the EASI questionnaire (Emotionality, Activity, Sociability, Impulsivity) (Buss & Plomin, 1975), which has highly overlapping item content for the first three scales. Data from other sources as cited.

[h]McDevitt and Carey (1979). $N = 304$; Age: 1 to 3 years. Lower estimates are reported by Hermanns (cited in Hubert, Wachs, Peters-Martin, & Gandour, 1982).

[i]Bates, Freeland, and Lounsbury (1979). $N = 196$. Similar findings reported by Goldsmith, Reeser-Danner, and Pomerantz (1983).

[j]Values shown are means of the 3-, 6-, 9-, and 12-month estimates. Similar data are presented for another sample by Rothbart (1980, 1981b) and in another study by Goldsmith and Campos (1982a). In the latter study, $N = 249$; Age = 9 months.

[k]Mean interval 25.1 days; $N = 41$.

[l]McDevitt and Carey (1979). $N = 47$; Interval: 1 month as cited in Hubert, Wachs, Peters-Martin, and Gandour (1982).

[m]$N = 98$. Mother × observer in home.

[n]Values shown are means of three cohorts for the 9 to 12 months interval. Additional stability data provided by Rothbart (1981b).

[o]$N = 31$, Average test-retest interval: 1 week.

[p]Field and Greenberg (1982). $N = 16$.

[q]Field and Greenberg (1982). $N = 33$.

[r]$N = 89$.

[s]$N = 22$. Mother × father or babysitter. Questionnaires completed at approximately the same time. Considerably lower values were reported by Goldsmith and Campos (1982a) with fathers unselected as to caregiving responsibilities and with questionnaires completed in successive weeks.

[t]Lyon and Plomin (1981). EASI questionnaire value in parenthesis is for impulsivity scale.

[u]McDevitt and Carey (1981). $N = 115$; RITQ at mean age 5.6 months, TTQ at 23.4 months.

[v]Bates (personal communication cited in Hubert, Wachs, Peters-Martin, & Gandour, 1982). $N = 127$; ICQ at 6 months, CCQ at 24 months. Value in parentheses is from Bates (personal communication cited in Hubert, Wachs, Peters-Martin, & Gandour, 1982). $N = 122$; ICQ at 13 months, CCQ at 24 months.

[w]Rothbart (1981a). $N = 36$ (cohort 1); IBQ at ages 3 and 12 months. See Rothbart (1981b) and Rothbart (1981a) for other, similar stability data. Values in parentheses are from Thompson and Lamb (1982, 1983). IBQ at ages 12½ and 19½ months.

[x]Wilson and Matheny (in press). $N = 48$; Age: 12 months.

[y]Evidence is presented only from studies relating questionnaire scales with relatively objective nonquestionnaire measures of the same or conceptually similar measures. See Hubert, Wachs, Peters-Martin, and Gandour (1982) for other evidence of construct validity.

[z]K. Berberian, as cited in S. Carey (1981). $N = 60$.

[aa]Searls, Fullard, and McDevitt (in press). $N = 20$.

[bb]See S. Carey (1981).

[cc]Garcia-Coll (1982).

[dd]Lounsbury and Bates (1982).

(continued)

Table 6. *(Continued)*

Questionnaire and scales[a]	Internal consistency	Short-term stability	Rater agreement: Mother-father	Rater agreement: Mother-other	Longer-term stability	Evidence for discriminant validity	Evidence for Convergence with observational measures[y]
Infant Behavior Questionnaire (IBQ)[f]							
Smiling and laughter	.79[j]	.72[n]	.45[s]		.57 (.76)[w]	No interscale r's, .36, most substantially lower	Fear predicts concurrent stranger sociability at 12½ and 19½ mos. (r's = .38, −.47); Activity level, distress to limitations, and smiling and laughter predict stranger sociability at 19½ mo. (r's = −.45, −.34, and .36) (Thompson & Lamb in press, 1982, 1983). IBQ × HO r's = .35, .50, .38, and .09 for activity, smiling, fear, and distress to limitations, respectively.[ee]
Duration of orienting	.72	.64	.46		.11 (.67)		
Soothability	.79	.29	.54		.41 (.46)		
Fear	.82	.61	.66		.06 (.65)		
Distress to limitations	.79	.65	.60		.25 (.61)		
Activity level	.79	.68	.69		.48 (.53)		
Colorado Childhood Temperament Inventory (CCTI)[g]							
Sociability	.88	.58[o]	.42[t]		NA	Factor analytic derivation; r = −.42, soothability × emotionality; other interscale r's < .25	Activity, r = .75 with very reliable actometer measures.[ff]
Emotionality	.80	.72	.27				
Activity	.82	.80	.44				
Attention span-persistence	.79	.77					
Reactions to food	.77	.74					
Soothability	.73	.43					

[ee]Rothbart, (1980). N = 46; Data for 9-month-olds; 3- and 6-month data also available.
[ff]Eaton (in press). N = 27; Mean age: 50.4 months.

and home observations or global ratings may be attenuated by low reliability of the latter.

There is an interesting contrast between the Infant Behavior Questionnaire (IBQ) and the EASI approaches in dealing with the issue of situational context in temperament assessment by questionnaire. The IBQ specifies the situational context for every item on a scale, whereas the EASI implicitly asks the respondent to generalize across all relevant situations. For example, an IBQ activity-level item is: "When placed in an infant seat or car seat, how often did the baby squirm and turn body?" An EASI activity-item is: "Child is always on the go." An assumption of the IBQ approach is that the test designer has sampled adequately the situations relevant to the expression of the targeted temperament dimensions; an assumption of the EASI apporach is that the respondent attends to the relevant situations and weighs each appropriately in formulating his answers. Judging which approach is superior must await additional evidence.

Although sacrificing the depth of knowledge about the child that the parental report provides, structured observations made by trained examiners also provide measures of temperament. The most prominent of such instruments are Bayley's (1969) Infant Behavioral Record (IBR), Brazelton's (1973) NBAS, and various clinical rating scales, such as the Nurses' Scale for Rating Neonates (Haar, Welkowitz, Blau, & Cohen, 1964).

It is important to note that neither the IBR nor the NBAS were designed primarily as temperament-assessment instruments, and both have weaknesses when used for this purpose. Because these instruments are well known, we will not review them here. Applications of the IBR (and its previous versions) may be found in Schaefer and Bayley (1963), Matheny (1980), and Goldsmith and Gottesman (1981). Sameroff (1978) and Goldsmith and Campos (1982b) discuss limitations of using the NBAS to assess temperament.

The Observational and Laboratory Approaches. Recently, laboratory and home observation measures of temperament have begun to supplement assessments (cf. Goldsmith, Duncan, & Henderson, 1981; Kagan, 1971; Kagan et al., 1978; Lytton, 1980; Lytton, Martin, & Eaves, 1977; Plomin & Foch, 1980; Plomin & Rowe, 1979; Rothbart, 1981a, 1981b; Rothbart, in press; Wilson & Matheny, in press). This paradigmatic trend promises to bring temperament research closer to the mainstream of developmental psychology.

The laboratory approach has its own set of unique problems. First, laboratory assessments, just like questionnaires, need to meet various psychometric criteria. Furthermore, to assess temperament sensitively, laboratory paradigms need to be modified to maximize individual differences. This can be accomplished by devising graded measuring scales that show high variance for behavioral measures and by adjusting the difficulty levels of dichotomous variables. In addition, both internal consistency reliability and stability need to be computed for laboratory measures, just as one would do for questionnaire scales. To achieve satisfactory internal consistency *and* an adequate sampling for situations, fairly extensive series of laboratory paradigms are necessary.

How do these new laboratory assessments compare to the more traditional home observation and questionnaire measures? Evidence is only beginning to accumulate, but early indications are that the two types of temperament assessment correlate between .30 and .40 (sometimes lower). Rothbart (1981a, 1981b) reported correlations in the .30s between IBQ scales and corresponding home observations. Bates et al. (1979) found low but significant correlations between the ICQ fussy-difficult factor and home observation factors of fussiness ($r = .22$) and unsoothability ($r = .18$). Because the home observation factors showed only modest stability over a few days (r's = .46 and .20 respectively), however, the import of the minimal evidence for convergent validity is unclear. Goldsmith and Campos (1982a) reported r's varying from .20 to .50 between the IBQ activity level, smiling and laughter, and fear scales on the one hand and the corresponding laboratory composites on the other hand. Wilson and Matheny (in press), using a multivariate approach to relate laboratory ratings to Toddler Temperament Scale (TTS) data, found a significant (uncorrected) canonical R of .60; however, there were only modest relationships at the level of specific laboratory ratings versus TTS scores. Lemly and Schwarz (1979) reported that 2-year-olds' responses to a stranger in the laboratory were predicted by EASI emotionality and sociability scores derived from combined maternal and paternal ratings.

Perhaps the most encouraging evidence comes from Eaton's (in press) demonstration of strong convergence (r's of about .70) among parental questionnaire reports of activity level, staff ranking in a nursery school setting, and actometer measures. Eaton's key insight was that actometer measures needed to be recorded on multiple occasions (he used 13) if reliable laboratory measures are desired.

Summary of Measurement Considerations. In their review of a number of paper-and-pencil temperament-assessment instruments for infants as well as older children, Hubert et al. (1982) report that half the available scales have no documented validity data. Further, these reviewers suggest that methodological problems of inadequate reliability of instruments, small sample sizes, and the presence of statistically significant but low-validity coefficients confound interpretations in this area. The key practical implication we draw from the information reviewed is that the temperament construct should not be method bound. Uncritical equation of temperament with the questionnaire approach is to be avoided. On the other hand, objectivity does not ensure reliability of measurement. Cross-method convergence is to be desired highly (Plomin, 1982).

Origins of Temperament: Biological Influences

Substantial evidence for the influence of genotype on behavior has been accumulating. Such evidence is crucially important, given that most theories of temperament postulate some innate component. The majority of research on the genetics of temperament has involved adolescents and adults (see *Scarr & Kidd, vol. II, chap. 6*) in whom most personality characteristics show moderate heritability; the strongest evidence emerging for the temperamentlike dimension of introversion-extraversion has been shown to have a moderate genetic loading. In addition, Buss and Plomin's (1975) review of research with adults and children uncovered evidence for the heritability of behaviors in three broad domains: emotionality, activity, sociability. A fourth dimension, impulsiveness, showed less impressive evidence of heritability.

Recently, there has been a flurry of research on the genetics of infant temperament. Most studies have tested twins and used either paper-and-pencil questionnaires or parental interviews. Although there are some exceptions across studies to the generally reported findings, there is fairly consistent evidence for heritability of activity level and sociability and some evidence for heritability of attention span, emotionality, and discrete emotional predispositions. For instance, Goldsmith and Gottesman (1981) employed a version of Bayley's (1969) IBR and reported significant (h^2 = .44) levels of genetic variance for an activity-level factor at 8 months of age. Cohen, Dibble, and Grawe (1977) reported strong evidence for genetic variance in activity level (which they called behavior modulation) in a large cross-sectional twin study that used maternal and paternal ratings. (The twins in this study, however, ranged in age from 1 to 6 years of age). Using the Colorado Childhood Temperament Inventory, (CCTI), Plomin and Rowe (1977) reported significantly greater identical than fraternal co-twin similarity for the activity-level factor. Harris and Rose (1977) reported similar findings using the EASI temperament questionnaire developed by Buss and Plomin (1975). Using Rothbart's (1981a) IBQ with 9-month-old twins, Goldsmith and Campos (1982a) found moderate evidence for heritability for activity level (h^2 = .36). On the other hand, Matheny (1980) analyzed the Bayley IBR at 3, 6, 9, 12, 18, and 24 months and uncovered little evidence for the heritability of an activity-level factor before 18 months. At 18 and 24 months, however, monozygotic (MZ) correlations were significantly greater than dizygotic correlations (DZ) for the activity-level factor.

Sociability is another trait fairly consistently found to have a significant genetic loading. In Matheny's (1980) study, for instance, a test affect/extraversion factor showed significant genetic variance, although not at every testing age. Harris and Rose (1977), Plomin and Rowe (1977), and Torgensen and Kringlen (1978) similarly reported evidence for the heritability of sociability. One exception to this trend is the study by Goldsmith and Gottesman (1981), which did not find significant genetic variance in an interest-in-persons factor at 8 months of age. These authors expressed reservations, however, regarding the generalizability of their interest-in-persons factor to the broader domain of infant sociability.

Task orientation and attention span have also been reported to show heritability (Cohen et al., 1977; Matheny, 1980; Plomin & Rowe, 1977), as have maternal ratings of fear and distress to limitations taken from the Rothbart IBQ (Goldsmith & Campos, 1982a). Finally, Plomin and Rowe (1977) and Harris and Rose (1977) reported that their emotionality subscales showed significantly greater identical than fraternal co-twin similarity.

An intriguing and unexpected finding reported in two very different twin studies is that the consistency of an infant's behavior across situations may itself be a trait under genetic control. In one study (Goldsmith, 1978), the finding was obtained with a parental-report instrument, the Rothbart IBQ—a scale that explicitly varies situational context across items. In the second study (Matheny & Dolan, 1975), comparisons were made of infants' adaptability across both playroom and Bayley test settings. Not only were identical co-twins more similar to one another than fraternals in a given setting but also the profile of adaptability across the two test situations showed more similarity for identical twins.

These studies, thus, support the expectation that at least some temperament characteristics have a biological basis. It is especially encouraging that the dimensions showing possible heritability in infancy in parental-report measures are similar to those found with adults. These findings are particularly impressive when one considers the limitations of parental-report instruments described earlier (Bates, 1980; Hubert et al., 1982). Nevertheless, a serious problem has occasionally been reported by investigators using twins—a problem that calls into question some of the assumptions of the twin method to assess heritability. For instance, Plomin and Rowe (Plomin, 1982; Plomin & Rowe, 1977) reported that the fraternal co-twin similarity obtained in their study was lower on many scales than genetic theory would predict. That is, because fraternal twins share roughly one-half of their segregating genes, whereas identicals share all, the fraternal twin correlation on a given trait that shows significant heritability should be approximately 50% that of the identicals. However, Plomin (1981) reported identical twin correlations of around .50, whereas fraternal twin correlations hovered around 0. Harris and Rose (1977) ran into a similar problem, as did Torgensen and Kringlen (1978). On the other hand, Goldsmith and Gottesman (1981), Goldsmith and Campos (1982a) and Matheny (1980) did not encounter this problem.

It is not entirely clear either why the fraternal co-twin correlations have been so low nor why there have been inconsistencies in encountering this difficulty. However, the prevalance of the problem has led behavior geneticists (e.g., Goldsmith, 1983; Plomin, 1982) to propose that twin studies be supplemented, whenever possible, by other types of behavior-genetic approaches, such as adoption studies and family studies, before firm conclusions are drawn regarding genetic influences on early temperament. Unfortunately, there is a dearth of evidence from such other behavior-genetic approaches. Available adoption data related to temperament is either retrospective (e.g., Caderot, Cunningham, Loftus, & Edwards, 1975) or focuses on childhood personality rather than infant temperament (see also Loehlin, Horn & Willerman, 1981; *Scarr & Kidd, vol. II, chap. 6*). The completion of the Colorado Adoption Project (Plomin, in press) should help to shed light on this issue however.

Only recently have behavior-genetic studies of infant temperament begun to use home observations or laboratory assessments. Too few home observation or laboratory-based genetic studies have been reported to permit definite conclusions, but several studies have found significant evidence for genetic influence on characteristics measured by way of laboratory observations. The Matheny and Dolan (1975) study of adaptability measured across different situations was one study providing positive findings. In addition, other studies have uncovered genetic influence on dimensions related to negative reactivity to strangers. For instance, Plomin and Rowe (1979) studied home behavior in a sample of 22-month-old twins and reported significant heritable variation in social behaviors directed toward a stranger, but not toward the mother. The pioneering study by Freedman and Keller (1963) reported a fascinating but somewhat anecdotal result from a small twin sample observed at home: They observed striking concordance in the time of emergence of the affect-related phenomena of social smiling and stranger distress. This interesting finding deserves a more rigorous replication. Early results from an extensive laboratory-based infant twin study have been reported by Goldsmith and Campos (1982a). They found that roughly 30% of the variance in composite, objective laboratory-based measures of overt distress in a stranger-approach paradigm and overt distress while avoiding the deep side of a visual cliff could be attributed to genetic influences in 9-month-olds. More subtle indications of fear and avoidance, such as latency to cross the visual cliff or backing away from the cliff edge, did not show heritable patterns. Similarly, measures of intense positive emotionality (laughing and motoric activation) demonstrated significant heritablilty (h^2 = .47 and .44 respectively), whereas smiling measures showed no significant genetic effects in the same joy-eliciting situations.

In contrast to activity-level reports provided by parents, activity level of infants when assessed in the laboratory has not yet been shown to be heritable. Goldsmith and Campos (1982a) reported that identical co-twins were only slightly more similar than fraternal on measures of locomotive activity taken during free play at 9 months of age, and Lytton (1980) reported little evidence for genotypic effects for measures of aspects of activity and negatively toned actions. We suspect that some laboratory-testing contexts may seriously constrain activity level in infancy, thereby reducing observed variance in infant movement patterns.

In summary, then, parental-report data on temperament reveal moderate levels of genetic influence for many of the dimensions studied. In addition, as Loehlin and Nichols (1976) and Rowe and Plomin

(1981) report, the salient environmental influences on temperament, as well as later personality, that emerge from the behavior-genetic analyses appear to be those that make members of a family *different* from one another rather than, as is usually expected, more similar to one another. The accumulated empirical behavior-genetic data on laboratory studies and home observations do not allow so clear a conclusion, but the results to date are encouraging.

Tantalizing findings have emerged from nongenetic studies that examine those psychophysiological or biochemical factors that may provide clues to the endophenotypic (Gottesman, 1974) substrates of temperament. As we mentioned earlier, Kagan (Kagan, 1982a; Kagan et al., in press) reported that inhibited (timid, fearful) infants show less heart rate variability during a cognitively engaging task than less inhibited children, a tendency that proved stable on retesting several months later. In Kagan's laboratory, Garcia-Coll (1981) reported a moderate correlation between laboratory measures of inhibition and parental perception of similar behavior; higher scores on this dimension were again related to lower heart rate variability, although the relationship held strongly only for boys. Kagan et al. (1978) also demonstrated that this psychophysiological dimension differentiated Caucasian and Oriental infants.

Rappaport, Pandorini, Renfield, Lake, and Ziegler (1977) found that another physiological variable in newborns, elevated levels of the enzyme dopamine hydroxylase, predicted (to a low but significant degree) parental report of infants' fussiness and negative emotional reactions at 5 months of age. Some of these relationships were replicated at 1 year of age.

The extensive research on biological correlates of adult sensation seeking (Zuckerman, 1979), a dimension widely regarded as temperament related, is also quite intriguing. High scores on questionnaire measures of sensation seeking (or its subscales) correlated positively with several physiological measures, for example, the higher the sensation seeking reported, the greater the magnitude of various indices of physiological reactivity, including the electrodermal orienting response; and the higher the cortical average-evoked response, the greater the levels of gonadal hormones and the lower the levels of platelet moneine oxidase (an enzyme which, in the form present in the brain, regulates norepinephrine levels). Furthermore, twin studies demonstrate a strong genetic influence on scores on this questionnaire (Fulker, Eysenck, & Zuckerman, 1980) as well as on some of the questionnaire's above-mentioned biological correlates. Although no *common* genetic basis for the biological and behavioral correlates of the sensation-seeking construct has been demonstrated, the accumulated biologically oriented research perhaps brings us closer to the point of synthesis of genetics-physiology-temperament relationships than does the work on any other temperament dimension, with the possible exception of Eysenck's (1967; 1981) extraversion dimension.

Continuity of Temperament

A defining characteristic of temperament, explicitly made by Buss and Plomin (1975) and implicitly by most other theorists, is that it should be stable. Our selective empirical review must be limited to stability within the infancy period; the broader issue of long-term stability is treated by Lewis and Starr (1979) and Beckwith (1979). The reader is also referred to a review of continuities in the areas of patterns of attention, activity, and intensity of response by Dunn (1980). The stability data summarized here were chosen because of their relevance to other issues treated in this discussion. We will first discuss data derived from more traditional questionnaire and interview measures of temperament. Then we will highlight results from home observation and laboratory studies. These latter results have not all been conceptualized as being temperament related.

Using parental-report methodology, Carey and McDevitt (1978) obtained correlations ranging from .24 to .58 for the nine NYLS dimensions when their original ITQ was given at a median age of 5.6 months and the TTS (Fullard, McDevitt, & Carey, 1978) was completed about 18 months later. As indicated in Table 6, Rothbart (1981a) assessed parental perception of temperament at 3, 6, 9, and 12 months and found a pattern indicating increasing stability of her scales during the infant's first year. For example, the fear scale longitudinal r's were .23 (3 to 6 months), .59 (6 to 9 months), and .69 (9 to 12 months). However, activity-level and smiling-and-laughing scales did remain quite stable throughout infancy (r's for six-month intervals in the .60s).

Employing NYLS-style interviews, Torgensen and Kringlen (1978) obtained 2- to 9-month stabilities ranging from .03 to .48 (median r, .21). This compares to Thomas and Chess's (1977) own reports from the NYLS of Year 1 to Year 2 stabilities (where each year is a composite of several ratings) of −.05 to .47 (median r, .38).

Peters-Martin and Wachs (1981), in a study of both stability and predictive validity, administered Brazelton's (1973) NBAS examination at 1 month; Carey and McDevitt's (1978) RITQ at 6 months; and

Fullard and his co-workers' (1978) TTS along with Caldwell's (1978) HOME inventory (a measure of certain features of the home environment that are believed to affect development) and Uzgiris & Hunt's (1975) Infant Psychological Development Scale, (a measure of cognitive development) at 12 months. Again, modest stability of the temperament measures was uncovered. There were numerous substantial correlations among the 12-month TTS dimensions, cognitive measures, and HOME measures.

In a longitudinal study using maternal interviews to assess temperament in 137 pairs of twins, Matheny, Wilson, Dolan, and Krantz (1981) employed intrapair comparisons of temperament to address issues of stability and genetics. Over a broad span of the infancy period (6 to 24 months), significant stability was demonstrated for four associated activity and negative-emotion-related variables and for three associated sociability variables (cuddling, accepting people, smiling). Additional support for stability of observer ratings of irritability and closely related variables comes from studies of Bayley (1956), Moss (1967), and Shirley (1933); these studies yielded *r*'s of roughly .4 to .6 for intervals of approximately 3 months. Schaefer and Bayley (1963) report a strikingly high *r* of .82 from 11 to 14 months for irritability; lower *r*'s were reported for other temperament-related dimensions.

All of these studies employed questionnaire and interview approaches however; thus, stability of actual infant behavior is confounded with stability of parental attribution of infant behavior. Some limited but promising evidence of temperamental stability, however, has also emerged from home observation studies. For example, Clarke-Stewart, Umeh, Snow, and Pederson (1980) derived a composite measure of sociability from home observations at 12, 18, 24, and 30 months of age. Individual differences in sociability directed toward mother and stranger showed low and insignificant *r*'s until the age of 24 months, when modest stability emerged. Rothbart (1981a) reported three-month stabilities, over two intervals, of home observation measures of activity, smiling and laughing, fear, and anger, which averaged respectively .31, .39, .24, and .25. From these and other home observation studies (e.g., Bell & Ainsworth, 1972; Fish & Crockenberg, 1981; Lytton, 1980; Moss, 1967), we can draw the tentative conclusion that stability of individual differences is usually apparent, but not high, in home observation studies. However, such studies depend on recording of discrete behaviors, and extensive observation time is required for reliable results (see Waters, 1978, for details). Thus, the lower stability shown with home observation techniques as opposed to parental reports may be due to attenuation of home observation correlations because of unreliability and does not necessarily imply a bias in the other more reliable measures.

Observations and experimental measures recorded in more controlled settings also yield some support for stability of infant temperament, particularly in the realms of activity level and irritability. For example, Korner, Hutchinson, Koperski, Kraemer, and Schneider (1981) assessed individual differences in newborn activity and crying with several objective measures and, in general, found high day-to-day stability. Such differences, moreover, appeared to be unaffected by birth circumstances. When we consider other studies demonstrating stability of early activity level (e.g., Campbell, Kuyek, Lang, & Partington, 1971) and the predictive value of higher activity level for such personality characteristics as control, compliance, lower levels of inhibition, and greater competitive, outgoing, and manipulative behavior in older children (Buss, Block, & Block, 1980), support appears to be growing for the importance of activity level, the theoretical significance of which was first described by Escalona (1968) and Schaffer (1966a). The temperamental characteristic of vigilance or wariness is also proving to be remarkably stable. Moreover, the stability is reflected in both cardiovascular and behavioral assessments of the characteristic (Kagan et al., in press). For instance, Chinese-American infants have been reported to show stability coefficients approximating .60 across a period of 12 months. In addition, infants found by Garcia-Coll (1981) to be extremely inhibited or vigilant continue to be assessed as such when retested in both laboratory and home 1 year later (Kagan et al., in press).

An issue that has several parallels with the continuity issue is the question of the cross-situational generality of a temperamental characteristic assessed at the same point in time. There is little a priori reason to expect a uniform answer to the question of how broad temperament dimensions might be. Cross-situational consistency is an issue to be investigated separately for each dimension. Although this has been the object of much controversy and study by researchers in personality and social psychology, the issue is not generally focused on in the same manner by infancy researchers.

One lesson to be learned from recent research in social psychology is that one cannot expect to demonstrate cross-situational consistency unless the situations involved are assimilated similarly by the individuals being tested. This means that we must understand the coherence of situations from the individual's point of view. From either Kagan's (1971) or Piaget's (1950) theoretical perspectives, the infant's cognitive development can be expected to modulate his understanding of the relationship between situations, and this must somehow be taken into account when investigating cross-situational consistency.

To establish cross-situational consistency using the questionnaire approach, one needs to show strong intercorrelations among items that inquire about the same or related behavioral responses in different situations. To date, Rothbart's IBQ is the only instrument that explicitly varies situational context across items. The relatively high internal consistency of the IBQ scales reported by Rothbart (1981b) implies that cross-situational consistency does exist, at least according to the report of the mother or rater.

Using the laboratory approach, one must demonstrate that individual differences in the same or similar behaviors are correlated in different situations designed to elicit such behavior. This strategy, however, has been used in only a handful of studies. Matheny and Dolan (1975), in a study cited earlier in a different context, used this strategy successfully, as have Goldsmith and Campos (1982a), who reported modest intersituational consistency in 9-month-olds.

If we take seriously the conceptual issues raised in this and the preceding discussion on stability, a major measurement problem in studying temperament from a developmental perspective is apparent: There may be differences *between* individuals that are due to particular infants being developmentally advanced or slow relative to others rather than to such infants' temperamental predispositions. For example, one child may show no fear on the visual cliff, whereas another shows great fear. This may simply be because the former child had not as yet developed an appreciation of the significance of the dropoff. On the other hand, there may be differences *within* individuals' reactions to different situations, despite the existence of a stable temperamental predisposition, because of differences in the assimilability of the various situations.

Temperament and Cognition

Earlier, we argued that emotions serve to organize various aspects of behavior and that temperament consists largely of individual differences in emotionality. Accordingly, individual differences in temperament should predict individual differences in those aspects of behavior that emotions are thought to organize.

Although this line of reasoning has guided much less research than have the issues of biological influence and psychometric assessment, there is now good evidence that a concurrent relationship exists between temperament and cognition, that temperamental dispositions predict subsequent cognitive performance. There is also a small but growing body of theory specifying processes by which temperament may influence cognitive growth (e.g., Escalona, 1963; Kagan et al., in press; Keogh, 1982).

There is plentiful evidence that temperamental traits related to the emotion of interest—namely, persistence or its variants, such as attention span, goal orientation, and distractability—predict individual differences in cognitive functioning. For instance, persistence was found to correlate with Bayley mental scale scores both concurrently (Matheny, Dolan, & Wilson, 1974; Seegmiller & King, 1975) and predictively over a 3-year span (Goldsmith & Gottesman, 1981). Concurrent relationships have also been reported for 12-month-olds between persistence and distractability subscales of the TTQ on the one hand and sensorimotor development, as measured by most of the Uzgiris and Hunt (1975) scales, on the other hand (Peters-Martin & Wachs, 1981). Several of these correlations were sizable, reaching $r = .60$. In addition, McCall, Eichorn, and Hogarty (1977) and Yarrow, Rubenstein, and Pedersen (1975) have found correlations between cognitive competence and the infant's alertness, attentiveness to objects, persistence on tasks, and goal-directed behaviors. Moreover, the evidence indicates that temperamental persistence affects cognitive growth over and above performance on specific tasks. For instance, Keogh and her colleagues (Keogh, 1982) reported that persistence not only predicted IQ and grades in school but also correlated with teachers' estimates of ability when IQ was held constant. Thus, temperamental persistence seems to be related to cognitive growth.

Another dimension of temperament that may organize cognition is activity level. Perhaps the most persuasive arguments on this issue have been made by Escalona (1968), who described how active versus inactive infants encounter different patterns of experience that, in turn, lead to differences in ego development. Differences in activity level at 8 months of age predict differences in Stanford-Binet IQ taken at 4 years of age (Goldsmith, 1978); moreover, substantial concurrent correlations between activity level and various Piagetian tasks have been reported (Peters-Martin & Wachs, 1981). However, to date, insufficient attention has been given to differences in quality of activity level: activity that has an undercontrolled and impulsive quality seems likely to show predictions in the opposite direction from well-modulated, task-oriented activity.

A third dimension of temperament thought to be relevant to individual differences in cognitive activity is positive affect, which we will consider jointly with positive affect directed toward other persons (a component of sociability). For example, amount of pleasure shown by 18- and 24-month-old infants during administration of the Cattell and Piaget object-permanence scales predicted 3-year-old-performance on the Stanford-Binet (Birns & Golden, 1972). In addition, Beckwith, Cohen, Kopp, Parmalee, and Marcey (1976) reported that infants who smiled more and vocalized more to an unfamiliar observer at 8 months of age also had higher sensorimotor scores and Gesell development quotient (DQ) scores. The importance of this result is heightened by the fact that the measure of sociability was taken outside the test situation and nevertheless predicted mental status. Infant sociability and cognitive test performance have been reported to be correlated in a number of other studies (Bayley & Schaefer, 1964; Crano, 1977; Stevenson & Lamb, 1981). Significantly, cognitive performance and sociability remain correlated even when performance on the most socially laden cognitive test items are excluded from the cognitive scores (Lamb, Garn, & Keating, 1981). The influence of temperament on cognition may thus be much more profound than the mere facilitation of the testing process.

Susceptibility to distress, not surprisingly, hinders cognitive development. Fear of unusual stimuli, frustration with difficult tasks, and problems with emotional communication with caregivers and teachers can result in behavioral disorganization. Such disorganization can prevent learning in the immediate situation and, through a series of influences on both the child and others, can limit future opportunities for cognitive growth. It can also account for the suggestion in reports by Thomas and Chess (1977), Sostek and Anders (1977), as well as others (Field, Hallock, Ting, Dempsey, Dabiri, & Shuman, 1978) that difficult infants show slower cognitive development.

However, just as emotions can be organizing as well as disorganizing, depending on context, so can otherwise undesirable temperamental traits be organizing: Reznick (1982), for instance, reported that infants who on both behavioral and cardiovascular criteria are classified as vigilant and wary tend to be much more sensitive to subtle differences in environmental stimulation.

In summary, the findings to date provide converging evidence that the development of cognitive competence is influenced by temperamental dimensions. Infants who tend to explore the environment, orient to interesting features of it, and respond in a well-modulated fashion to stimulation are likely to develop superior cognitive skills. Current research is beginning to explore the mechanisms and processes involved in these relationships.

Temperament and Social Interaction

Temperament is not simply an interactional phenomenon, in that it does exist apart from the interactional process. However, as we noted earlier, caretaker-infant interaction influences the expression of temperament. Also, most dimensions of temperament are typically observed in the context of social interaction; thus, assessments of temperament may be confounded with interactional processes. Finally, as we stressed earlier, an important feature of temperament is its role in regulating social interaction. For these reasons, we believe the relationship between temperament and social interaction deserves special attention.

Temperament should be especially influential on parent-infant attachment for several reasons. We have argued that temperament is closely related to emotion, and investigators agree that attachment refers to the presence of an affective bond between parent and infant. Few would doubt that social interaction involves affective communication, and one of the primary tenets of attachment theory (Ainsworth, Blehar, Waters, & Wall, 1978) is that the quality of mother-infant social interaction greatly influences the attachment process. This nexus of relationships suggests that individual differences in temperament could conceivably affect attachment in any of several ways. For instance, individual differences in temperament at birth and afterward might influence the mother's social responsiveness to her infant with consequences for the type of relationship that the child develops with the mother (see *The Role of Temperament in Strange-Situation Classification*). Alternatively, individual differences in maternal social responsiveness to the infant may affect both the quality of attachment and some of the parameters of expression of temperament. As an example, an infant might learn from observing her mother that there are a number of features of the environment of which to be fearful and, if the learning is of sufficient breadth, the child may show cross-situationally stable low thresholds for fearfulness (Campos & Stenberg, 1981). Still another way in which temperament may be related to attachment is as one of the factors that determine the classification of infants' individual differences in "security of attachment." That is, temperament may affect the assessment of attachment. We will discuss these issues further and bring evidence to bear on them in a later section.

Conclusions

In the preceding discussion, we have suggested that there are broad ties between the concept of temperament and the primary topic of this chapter, socioemotional development. Our emphasis in discussing the emotions was on their role as organizers of behavior. If temperament is accurately defined as individual differences in the expression of emotionality, then temperamental differences should predict stable individual variations in the organization of some aspects of cognition and social interaction. As the core of personality, temperament dimensions should also organize the development of later appearing, more complex personality traits.

A handful of studies point to the plausibility of considering temperament as one of the influences on differences in the organization of other behaviors. Schaffer and Emerson's (1964) research on cuddliness and Wolff's (1969) on irritability suggest that early temperament differences affect the pattern of infant-caregiver social interaction, as does the work on temperament and attachment to be reviewed later.

There is also evidence of an influence of temperament on cognitive development. Several studies have shown that the temperament dimension of persistence is predictive of IQ, although some results may be task specific (e.g., Goldsmith & Gottesman, 1981; Matheny, Dolan, & Wilson, 1976). Clarke-Stewart et al. (1980) suggest possible relationships between sociability and measures of IQ and language development. Peters-Martin and Wachs (1981) reported a number of correlations among parental perception measures of temperament and Piagetian tests of cognitive functioning. Given the extensive goodness-of-fit research on the relationship between temperament and educational adjustment at later ages (e.g., Keogh, 1982; Lerner et al., 1982; List, 1981), the study of temperament-cognition interaction is potentially fruitful. Advances await guidance from as yet undeveloped theory.

A particularly useful study for demonstrating the regulatory functions of temperament is Olweus's (1980) path-analytic investigation of the determinants of aggressive behavior in adolescent boys. Retrospective maternal and paternal ratings of active, hot-headed versus calm temperament in early childhood directly predicted later aggression. Of prime interest here, however, is Olweus's replicated finding that early activity and emotionality indirectly predicted aggression through its tendency to cause the mother to become more permissive of aggressive behavior. Thus, individual differences in temperament lead to differences in parental behavior, which, in turn, regulate later development. We predict that a similar state of affairs exists for other dimensions of temperament and other interactive social behaviors and would encourage investigations along this line. However, a final caveat regarding such studies is that temperament is only one of several possible regulators leading to developmental differences. Future research programs must recognize such higher order contexts.

SOCIAL DEVELOPMENT IN INFANCY

Introduction

Ever since the early work on the devastating effects of maternal deprivation, the study of social interaction has been central in developmental theory. Indeed, social development has probably been the single most popular topic of research and theorizing in infancy. Popular issues include: assessments of the infant's social repertoire, the caretaker's pattern of behavior toward the infant, and, occasionally, dyadic assessments of infant-caretaker interaction (Lamb, Suomi, & Stephenson, 1979). Most recently, the study of social interaction has expanded to include even more complex social relationships, such as peer and sibling relationships (Dunn & Kendrick, 1981; Lamb & Sutton-Smith, 1982; Lewis & Rosenblum, 1978), the mother-father-infant triad (Belsky, 1981; Lamb, 1979; Parke, Power, & Gottman, 1979; Pedersen, 1980) and the entire family system.

Much of the research to date has involved assessing what infants and adults bring to the interaction and the relationships. For infants, this includes the species-typical human behaviors that help integrate children into the social world. This involves studying sucking, states of sleep and wakefulness, sensitivity to visual- and auditory-stimulus patterns, social communicative behaviors (e.g., gazing and eye contact), play, and, of course, emotional patterns.

When focused on adults, the research has frequently addressed the adult's contributions to interaction, such as their repertoire of soothing techniques, their caretaking style, the frequency with which they play with or intrude on what the baby is doing, their sensitivity to the baby's social signals, their skill in pacing activities according to the baby's intellectual development, and their attitudes about parenting and childcare.

Over the years, the theoretical assumptions that have guided the research have changed, although the ultimate research objectives have remained the same. The primary objective has always been to assess the influence of caretaking on the child's intellectual and personality development. Since the 1930's, however, at least four different theoretical approaches have guided research (Schaffer, 1977). The first of these stressed the importance of infant care. Early psychoanalytic reconstructions had highlighted the importance of breast versus bottle feeding, demand versus schedule feeding, gradual versus abrupt weaning, and easy versus difficult bowel and bladder training as determinants of early fixations in ego development. These fixations were believed to produce personality traits, such as the oral personality (marked by dependency or verbal aggressiveness) and the anal personality (marked by stinginess, compulsiveness, or sloppiness). A great deal of cross-cultural research resulted from this line of thinking—both in its initial psychoanalytic form and in the social learning version created by a group of social scientists at Yale (e.g., Whiting & Child, 1953). This line of research came to an abrupt end with the publication of a very thorough review showing that there was no apparent relationship between physical care and later personality (Caldwell, 1964).

A second and somewhat different perspective on the importance of early social interaction came from the studies done primarily in the 1940s on the consequences of maternal deprivation. These studies were summarized very effectively by Bowlby, who proposed that mother love in infancy is as essential for mental health as vitamins and proteins are for physical health (Bowlby, 1951). The study of maternal deprivation, like that on physical care, arose from psychoanalytic theory but from a different branch of it. Following publication of *The Ego and the Id,* (Freud, 1927), some psychoanalysts became intrigued with how the ego emerged and drew its energies from the id—which, according to Freud, was the primordial source of all mental energies. In *The Ego and the Id*, Freud proposed that by both frustrating and satisfying the baby in just the right proportion, the mother (or primary caretaker) helped the reality principle to emerge from the pleasure principle. This notion, in turn, led to interest in the study of the absence of the mother in early and later infancy as a means of elucidating the rule of mother-infant interaction in ego development. Maternal deprivation was expected to produce deficiencies in all aspects of human psychological function controlled by the ego, including delay of gratification, language development, intelligence, emotional development, defense mechanisms, and control over body functions. The early work of Goldfarb (1943), Spitz (1946), and Bowlby (1951) seemed to support these predictions, and the stage was set for a large volume of research designed to determine which factors accounted for the destructive effects observed. However, later reviews by Pinneau (1955), Casler (1961), and Yarrow (1961) called into question the psychoanalytic interpretations of these findings, suggesting instead that the amount and quality of stimulation normally provided by the mother were crucial mediators of the effects of maternal deprivation. These reviews, together with the intriguing theories of Harlow (Harlow & Zimmermann, 1959), Hebb (1949), Levine (1961), Melzack, (1954), as well as many others using animal models (e.g., Newton & Levine, 1968) stimulated research on the effects of early experience on neurophysiological and psychological functioning (Thompson & Grusec, 1970).

This third approach to the study of mother-infant interaction stressed the significance of the mother as a source of physical stimulation. This was a very exciting approach because it promised to explain cognitive, emotional, and personality development without appeal to such principles as need reduction, mothering, associationistic or conditioning processes, and heredity or maturation (except insofar as sensitive periods of susceptibility to stimulation were invoked). Casler (1961), for example, stated that "the physical, intellectual, and emotional deficits often observed in individuals deprived of 'mothering' during early infancy can best be explained in terms of perceptual deprivation" (p. 42). An early study by Harlow and Zimmermann (1959) apparently demonstrated that contact comfort played a central role in determining infant monkeys' attachment to surrogates. This study, along with those revealing dramatic and long-lasting effects of handling in early infancy on both emotionality and maze performance in rodents (Denenberg, 1964), seemed at first to support Casler's (1961) view, as did studies of the cognitive and personality consequences of sensory deprivation in adults (Heron, 1957). During the 1960s and early 1970s, therefore, the mother's importance seemed to derive from her role as a provider of stimulation. A study by Korner and Grobstein (1966) was frequently cited to illustrate the role of the mother as provider and mediator of stimulation. These investigators showed that when a neonate was held to an adult's shoulders, the child's attentiveness increased, and it was, thus, able to extract more stimulation from its environment. This clearly exemplified the indirect effect of caretaking on intellectual growth. Another widely cited example of the importance of stimulation came from Brackbill's work on soothing (Brackbill, 1971; Brackbill, Adams, Crowell, & Gray, 1966). She stressed that the soothing effects of stimuli, such as heartbeat sounds (Salk, 1960, 1962, 1973), came not from a history of association between such sounds and a pleasant state in the uterus but from the heartbeat's continuous, repetitive qualities. The more continuous the stimulation and the more modalities continuously stimulated, the greater the effectiveness of a given intervention for soothing. Brackbill (1971) also noted that such interventions helped the child to attend to his environment or to rest and restore his physical energies. Other investigators argued that mobiles and other sources of pleasing stimulation should induce motoric and intellectual growth (White, Held, & Castle, 1967).

The contingency between the child's behavior and resulting stimulation was also of great interest during this period. For instance, Watson and Ramey (1972) speculated that the infant's attachment to the parent resulted not from the parent's role in need reduction but from the contingent manner in which the parent stimulated the infant in response to infant behaviors, such as cooing or crying. There was nothing uniquely human about this process of contingency-based attachment: Watson reported that infants became emotionally responsive to their contingently controlled mobiles to the extent that mothers used them as surrogate baby-sitters and that some infants were distressed when the mobiles were removed.

However, the emphasis on mother as stimulation proved to be short lived. Studies by Casler (1965) failed to show that stimulation of institutionalized human infants produced much cognitive growth. Nor did physical stimulation necessarily have beneficial nor large-magnitude effects on the psychological development of preterm infants reared in stimulus-barren isolettes (Fagan & Singer, 1981; Katz, 1971; Kramer, Chamorro, Green, & Knudtson, 1975: Porter, 1972; Ramey, Zeskind, & Hunter, 1981). Moreover, sharp theoretical criticisms by Bronfenbrenner (1968) and Bowlby (1969) led researchers to seek new ways of explaining how mother-child interactions influenced the child's cognitive and personality development.

This led to the fourth and currently most popular perspective for researchers of mother-infant interaction—a viewpoint based on ethology. One of the guiding premises of the ethological approach is that social behavior is adaptive not because it promotes interaction but because it increases the evolutionary fitness of the individuals. Accordingly, ethologists emphasize species-specific behaviors that have evolved to serve social-communicative or social-regulatory functions. This emphasis has resulted in numerous studies concerned with the social functions of specific behaviors. For example, smiling apparently serves to initiate and maintain social interaction (Brazelton, Tronick, Adamson, Als, & Wise, 1975); head orientation and gaze aversion can attenuate or even terminate interaction (Stern, 1974); the infant's state of sleep-wakefulness communicates readiness or reluctance to engage in social activity (Sander, 1975, 1977); and crying, according to some (e.g., Wolff, 1969), specifies the infant's state of anger, hunger, or pain. Furthermore, the perception of faces has been a major topic of investigation (e.g., S. Carey, 1981; Vine, 1973) because of its great importance for both social identification and the communication of action tendencies.

Contemporaneous with this perspective is the psychoanalytic theory of Margaret Mahler, which has had a great influence on clinical psychology. Mahler's theory has generated much less empirical data and will, therefore, be discussed more briefly than will ethological theory. Still, because of its impact on clinical practitioners, we believe it should be described. Our discussion of infantile social development is exhaustive, instead it is selectively representative. We discuss the Mahlerian and ethological approaches and then describe some important contemporary research on related issues.

Mahler's Theory of Separation-Individuation

One of the central tenets of psychoanalytic theory since Freud has been the conviction that a stable relationship with the mother is crucial not only for the infant's survival but also for the development of ego functions (Blanck & Blanck, 1974). According to many psychoanalytic theorists, two circumstances produce an absolute dependence on the mother. One of these is the immaturity of the infant's sensory and motor apparatus, resulting from the baby's birth at an earlier and less mature stage of physical development than any other higher primate. The second is the dependency of the infant's ego development upon identification with emotionally invested social objects, the most important of which is the mother (Brenner, 1955). By ministering to the infant's physical needs, and, importantly, by creating a stable emotional climate, the mother becomes an organizer of the child's perceptual, cognitive, social, and emotional development. By corollary, any deficiencies she has as a caretaker and as a partner in affective interactions (and any constitutional inability on the part of the infant to utilize her as such) contribute to the development of psychopathology.

One of the most influential recent expositions of the psychoanalytic tradition has been provided by Margaret Mahler (Mahler et al., 1975; McDevitt, 1975). Her work comprises a further elaboration of psychoanalytic perspectives—such as those of Freud (1927) and Spitz (1946) (alluded to above as the second perspective)—that played a seminal role in the conceptualization of social development during earlier decades. Mahler posits that during the first four years of life, the normal infant proceeds through three distinct phases of development, which she calls the autistic, the symbiotic, and the separation-individuation phases. Each of these phases has specific developmental tasks associated with it. The failure to accomplish a task effectively leads either to a psychopathological reaction specific to that period or regression to a developmentally lower level of organization. In the autistic period, the risk is early childhood autism (Mahler, 1958); in the symbiotic period, it is symbiotic psychosis (Mahler, 1968); and in the separation-individuation phase, it is the borderline personality disorder (Mahler et al., 1975). Each of these disorders and their relationship to developmental deviations will now be described.

The Autistic Phase (0 to 2 Months of Age)

Like many psychoanalysts, Mahler (1958, 1968) believes that the infant enters the world with little or no capacity to understand the environment. Thus, the infant's consciousness is dominated by internal bodily sensations, while a stimulus barrier (an innate unresponsiveness to outside stimuli) protects the infant against extremes of stimulation, producing an environment approximating the prenatal state. The neonate's primary goal is internal homeostasis. Homeostasis is closely linked to tension reduction, some of which is under endogenous control (e.g., urination, sneezing) and some of which is under the mother's control (e.g., feeding, holding, diapering, soothing). At the beginning of this stage, the infant can only distinguish between tension and relief, pain and pleasure, and good versus bad feelings. As the mother ministers consistently to the infant's needs, however, the repetitive association of tension reduction with maternal features (e.g., the tone of voice, the pressure from the mother holding the infant, oral sensations from sucking the breast, etc.) leads the infant to take notice of her. If the infant does not acquire even a rudimentary capacity to distinguish the ministrations of the mother from self-generated tension reductions, then she will be at risk for early infantile autism, which Mahler views as an absence of boundaries between self and world. Mahler holds that self-mutilation, such as repetitive head banging and self biting by autistic children, is symptomatic of this difficulty, because it represents an attempt to sharpen awareness of self-other boundaries.

The Symbiotic Phase (2 to 5 Months of Age)

The infant enters the symbiotic phase when he acquires a dim awareness of the relationship between the mother's presence (or, at least, the presence of parts of her body, such as the breast) and the reduction of tension. At this point, the stimulus barrier is replaced by a new protective shield—a belief that baby and mother form a single, omnipotent unit separate from the rest of the world. The symbiotic phase is marked by an intrapsychic process, but it has externally observable characteristics. From the intrapsychic perspective, the baby cannot yet perceive mother as a separate person, and so he cannot dissociate his own wishes and mother's satisfaction of these wishes into separate events with separate determinants. From the perspective of an external observer, the symbiotic phase is characterized by a mutual cuing between mother and infant. The infant's cues are primitive affective sensorimotor reactions, such as cries, coos, and social smiles. These elicit caretaking and other ministrations from sensitive mothers and, thus, produce in the infant a state of pleasantness owing to tension reduction and a sense of the mother's emotional tone (e.g., loving care), which depends on both the appropriateness of the ministrations relative to the infant's needs and the specific qualities of the mother's touch, facial expressions, and vocalizations. Mother and infant, thus, convey their wishes and reactions to each other by means of rudimentary affective exchanges. Mahler's (1958, 1968) notion of mutual cuing is echoed in Bowlby's (1969) theory as well as the widely cited works of Brazelton et al. (1975), Sander (e.g., 1975, 1977), Stern (1977), and others (e.g., Tronick et al., 1980).

For Mahler (1958, 1968), the resultant intrapsychic state is absolutely critical for normal development, especially social development. Indeed, Mahler believes that all subsequent social relationships—not just the mother-infant relationship—originate in the symbiotic phase. Symbiosis also affects the organization of the baby's memory. It facilitates the formation of a primitive memory trace of the mother and helps to invest that trace with positive affective significance. This investment, in turn, helps the child to differentiate between the mother and other external objects and between the self and other objects. It also lays the foundation for differentiation of two images, those of the good mother and the bad mother.

Most infants resourcefully adjust their cues to their mother's characteristics, and most mothers sensitively and promptly meet their infant's needs. For such infants, ego development proceeds normally. However, if interactional deficits or constitutional problems cause the infant to maintain or revert to this symbiotic mode of thought, the infant will manifest a profoundly distorted view of reality, which Mahler (1958, 1968) labels symbiotic psychosis. Mahler proposes that psychotics have no sense of self, only a sense of fusion with everything in the world along with either a feeling of contentment or a sense of total diffusion and resulting panic or rage. In the face of this panic, individuals frantically attempt to establish parasitic relationships with anyone who will gratify their needs.

Separation-Individuation Phase (5 Months to 25 to 36 Months of Age)

Those developing normally next enter a phase poetically described by Mahler (1968) as a second birth experience, a phase during which the child gradually constructs the mental concepts of self and other. As with the term symbiosis, separation and individuation refer to intrapsychic constructs. Separation describes the capacity to recognize that other human beings are not a part of the self. This discrimination serves as the foundation for learning about and caring about other persons. Individuation, by contrast, describes the developing sense of identity as an autonomous human being. This self-concept integrates perception, memory, cognition, emotion, and other ego functions into a single unitary personality. Mahler (1958, 1968) describes four subphases of the separation-individuation period: differentiation, practicing, rapprochement, and the beginnings of emotional object constancy. Each new stage is marked by a new sense of self and object as well as more complex levels of memory organization, anticipation, intentionality, frustration tolerance, identification, defensive structure, and reality testing.

The differentiation subphase lasts from approximately 5 to 10 months of age and begins what Mahler (1968) colorfully calls the hatching out of the symbiotic phase. This subphase is marked by the emergent discrimination of mother from other people and is followed by the development of a preference for her. This preference is initially revealed by differential smiling to the mother, by looking more in her direction, and by quieting more quickly in her presence. It is later confirmed first by the 7- to 8-month-old's tendency to look back and forth from the mother as if comparing her features with those of others and later by the emergence of separation distress. Another crucial source of evidence that the infant has established a positive, trusting, relationship is the *absence* of intense stranger distress. Indeed, one of the unusual features of Mahler's theory is her proposal that there is an inverse relationship between the intensity of stranger distress and the intensity of the child's trust in the mother.

With the advent of skillful locomotor capacities, the practicing subphase begins—a subphase that lasts from 10 to 12 until 16 to 18 months of age. During this phase, infants rapidly become aware that their bodies are distinct from those of their mothers, and numerous autonomous ego functions emerge and undergo further development. Mahler believes that efficient self-produced locomotion is a particularly important influence during this subphase because no other experience so clearly demonstrates to the child her physical separateness or so readily facilitates exploration of the physical world. During this time, perhaps owing to parallel developments in cognition but more probably because of an increase in the strength of the affective bond between the child and her mother, the child's internal image of the mother becomes stronger and more differentiated. She begins to use the word mama, anticipates mother's departures, becomes consciously aware of the relationship between mother's absence and the child's own distress, and starts to use evocative memory to remember her mother when she is gone. The more positive the relationship, the more comforting the memory image is. Although the infant displays less need for physical closeness to the mother than previously, the mother's presence or absence does have a distinct impact on the infant's affective state. While the mother is in the room, the infant often ventures away from her and appears to be exhilarated and enthralled by these exploratory ventures. Occasionally, she returns to the mother for brief periods of physical contact. Mahler (1968) describes this as emotional refueling. In the mother's absence, the infant's state appears more low keyed than when the mother is present and the infant seems less inclined to engage the physical world. These concepts resemble Bowlby's (1969) and

Ainsworth's (1973) notion that attachment figures provide secure bases for exploration (discussed later).

As toddlers acquire a still more elaborate conception of their autonomy and separateness through the exercise of locomotor skills and their burgeoning representational intelligence, they enter the rapprochement subphase. This period, which extends from approximately 15 to 22 months, is marked by a shift in toddlers' feelings about their mothers. Toddlers become less tolerant of their mothers' absences. The low-keyed demeanor of the previous phase gives way initially to increased activity and restlessness. Shortly thereafter, dramatic increases in the incidence of separation distress and stranger anxiety are often observed, although once again Mahler (1968) cautions that intense separation and stranger reactions signal that problems may exist in the mother-infant relationship. Furthermore, where babies once showed only exhilaration in the mother's presence, as toddlers they show a wider and more complex array of emotions. Mahler infers from these reactions that the mother has become a more important figure for the toddler. During this stage, she notes, the toddler's attention shifts dramatically back toward the mother even while the toddler continues to maintain some degree of physical separation. Some toddlers may watch their mothers carefully as if following their every move, while occasionally darting away from them. According to Mahler, this pattern reveals a fundamental ambivalence wherein the child wishes to be reunited with mother, yet, at the same time, desires independence. At this point, the mother's consistent emotional availability to the child is very important: "Predictable emotional involvement on the part of the mother seems to facilitate the rich unfolding of the toddler's thought processes, reality testing, and coping behavior by the end of the second or the beginning of the third year" (Mahler et al., 1975, p. 79).

At the same time, Mahler notes that the toddler benefits from a mother who is ready to encourage the child's independence. At this point, the toddler begins to make a critical shift from earlier mental organizations that maintain grand delusions (e.g., wishes for symbiotic union or intense fears that mother will cease to exist physically when she departs) to more elaborate mental constructions in which toddlers wish for their mothers' love and fear its loss. For the first time, toddlers begin to understand that conflicts may exist between their interests or desires and those of their mothers. Moreover, the desire to be loved by mother plays an important role in the internalization of rules (i.e., in superego formation).

From 24 to 36 months and sometimes beyond, the older toddler shifts from using the mother as a secure base for exploration to internalizing a stable mental representation of her as a person for whom the child cares deeply. Mahler (1968) (like other psychoanalytic theorists) labels this achievement the establishment of libidinal object constancy. By this term, she means that the child has acquired a concept of the mother that: (1) can be recalled in her absence, (2) is invested with strong feelings, and (3) represents her as a separate person with both positive and negative attributes. Mahler suggests that the child has arrived at this cognitive-emotional level when he can tolerate separation from the mother for long periods of time, yet still greet her positively when she returns. With development toward this level comes an increase in the child's feelings of trust, security, affection, and confidence as well as a tendency to engage in cooperative play, sharing, empathic behavior, and an ability to cope with frustration.

Developmental problems that arise after entry into the separation-individuation phase, but prior to the next phase of development, are labeled borderline personality disorders. Depending on when they occur in the separation-individuation process, borderline disorders themselves may be differentiated along a continuum ranging from near-psychotic symbiotic difficulties to neuroticlike problems. If problems arise in the earliest subphase, according to Mahler, the person later struggles with desires for, and fears of, annihilation or fusion. At a slightly higher level, the person fears the loss of the loved object: separation from that object is affectively comparable to the death or disappearance of that object. At a still higher level, the person fears the loss of love. Real or fantasized changes in the attitudes of caring persons toward the individual produce deep and intense emotional reactions—reactions that are defended against by the use of primitive coping strategies. One of these, called splitting, entails characterizing persons or events as all good or all bad and responding to them accordingly. Extended use of such a mechanism distorts the person's view of reality.

Mahler (1968) argues that inappropriate maternal behavior plays a major role in the formation of borderline problems. At one extreme, the mother may cling to the child, fostering a return to symbioticlike interactions. At the other, she may not provide enough support and nurturance for the child to overcome the fearful prospect of becoming separate and individuated.

Critique of Mahler's Theory

Among the most influential aspects of the theory

have been: (1) its conviction that the quality of mother-infant interaction has a profound effect on normal development and pathology; (2) its insistence that affective cues are the fundamental building blocks of the mother-infant relationship and, thus, have profound influences on both the development of self and of all social relationships; (3) its suggestion that the infant acquires a sense of separation and individuation as a result of prolonged sequential developmental processes; and (4) its postulation that certain specific pathologies result from the inadequate resolution of particular developmental tasks (often owing to, or exacerbated by, faulty maternal care). Mahler's suggestion that self-produced locomotion may be associated with the emergence of a number of perceptual, affective, and emotional competencies has received a measure of empirical support: Mobile infants show sharp increases in emotional communication with the mother, use their mother's emotional signals more effectively than prelocomotor infants, and also show different types of emotional reactions in standard eliciting situations (Bertenthal et al., 1983).

The theory, however, has a number of critical weaknesses. Despite rich anecdotal descriptions, there is little empirical support for a number of Mahler's hypotheses. The developmental sequence Mahler proposes has not been corroborated empirically; therefore, many crucial features of the theory remain speculative. For example, there is no evidence that phase-specific developmental deviations produce late-emerging discrete psychopathology (a deficiency that applies also to other ego analytic conceptualizations, such as those of Kernberg, 1967, and Kohut, 1972). This aspect of Mahler's theory appears contrary to transactional models of development (e.g., Sameroff & Chandler, 1975) and is postulated on the basis only of retrospective reconstructions and clinical case studies.

In addition, some findings directly contradict several of Mahler's positions. First, a primary cause of psychotic disturbances appears to be biogenic dysfunction, not developmental fixation (Snyder, 1978). Second, the notion of a stimulus barrier has been called into question by research demonstrating that the neonate is able to process complex environmental stimuli (e.g., Cohen & Salapatek, 1975; Field, 1982; Mendelson & Haith, 1977). Moreover, although Mahler hypothesizes that the absence of stimulation facilitates physiological growth, most researchers believe that stimulation facilitates maturation of the central nervous system (*Gottlieb, vol. II, chap. 1*). Also, Mahler's (Mahler et al., 1975) claim that stranger anxiety is mild at about 8 months and becomes more intense after 15 months has not been confirmed empirically (e.g., Lester, Kotelchuck, Spelke, Sellers, & Klein, 1974). Finally, while Mahler's formulations occasionally make reference to constitutional factors that may influence normal and pathological development, her theory does not take into account contemporary temperament research nor the mounting evidence supporting genetic predispositions to psychosis. These omissions have limited the acceptance of her ideas by many psychologists.

Another problem concerns Mahler's misleading and confusing terminology. Constructs like symbiosis or practicing are particularly troublesome because they appear to describe observable interactions or behavior, whereas they actually refer to intrapsychic states. Although Mahler's poetic style is often enticing, it frequently lacks scientific precision.

Mahler's focus on intrapsychic processes leads to several related difficulties. Often, she fails to specify operationally which features of mother-infant interaction produce an intrapsychic acquisition or reorganization. Furthermore, Mahler may place too much significance on the intrapsychic process of internalizing the mental image of the mother. For instance, Mahler and others have argued that because the acquisition of libidinal object constancy is of such central importance to the infant, person permanence should precede object permanence (e.g., S. M. Bell, 1970). However, the evidence cited in support of this hypothesized decalage is seriously flawed methodologically (see Jackson, Campos, & Fischer, 1978) and was not replicated (Levitt, 1982).

Ethological Attachment Theory

Background

Research on infant socioemotional development in the last two decades has been more dramatically and directly influenced by the ethological-evolutionary perspective offered by Bowlby (1958, 1969) and Ainsworth (Ainsworth, 1969, 1973, 1979; Ainsworth et al., 1978) than by that of Mahler. Bowlby was initially trained as a psychoanalyst, and one of his goals in developing the ethological-attachment theory was to replace with an evolutionary biological model the outmoded and indefensible notion that infants become attached to their caretakers because of the caretakers' association with satisfaction of hunger. Bowlby's basic assumption is that, as a result of selection pressures over the course of human evolution, infants are born with a repertoire of behavioral tendencies that would be of survival value in the environment of evolutionary adaptedness. Because human infants are incapable of caring for themselves, it is highly adaptive for them to seek proximity to, or physical contact with, the adults who can protect them against predators while providing the food and care that they need to survive.

Whereas some species produce precocious young who are able to attain and maintain proximity using their own locomotor capacities (e.g., ungulates), the young of most primates—especially humans—are not able to do this. Instead, they can attain proximity/contact during early infancy only by signaling others to initiate proximity to them, for example, by crying or smiling. Among humans, therefore, infant-adult proximity depends not only on the ability of infants to emit proximity-promoting signals but also on the complementary tendency of adults to respond to these signals. (See Frodi & Lamb, 1978; Frodi, Lamb, Leavitt, & Donovan, 1978; and Frodi, Lamb, Leavitt, Donovan, Neff, & Sherry, 1978, for empirical documentation of these tendencies using psychophysiological techniques.) According to the ethological-attachment theorists, both tendencies reflect evolved adaptations. These theorists argue that, by virtue of these adaptations, infants form attachments to those people who have consistently and repeatedly responded in appropriate fashion to the infants' proximity-promoting signals—that is, people on whom infants can count to provide protection and care when they need it. The basis of the specific affectional bond between infant and adult is, thus, a feeling of basic trust, confidence, or security on the part of the infant (cf. Bischof, 1975; Bowlby, 1973; Lamb, 1981a, 1981c; Sroufe, 1977). Variations in the adult's tendencies to respond promptly and appropriately, according to this theory, influence individual differences in infant-parent attachment (as elaborated in the discussion of *Ainsworth's Strange Situation and the Security of Attachment*).

In addition to being influenced by evolutionary biology, Bowlby was influenced by control systems theory. According to the control systems approach, various behaviors that can each serve the same function or goal are grouped together as a set or control system. For example, seemingly disparate behaviors, such as smiling, crying, or locomoting, can all serve the goal of maintaining proximity to the caretaker. As the term control implies, the behaviors within the system are governed to attain the end goal served by the system.

A control system is activated when changing circumstances lead the organism to adjust its set goal to a status different from the current state. The control system ceases to activate behavior when the new set goal has been achieved. Like a thermostat, individuals are constantly appraising their current status relative to their set goals.

In the case of attachment, the infant's desire for proximity or contact with the attachment figure is not constant; instead, it varies depending on a variety of endogenous and exogenous factors. Bowlby (1969) suggests that infants appraise or evaluate these conditions to determine how much proximity or contact they need to feel secure. They then compare this need—the set goal—with their current proximity status. If they need more proximity than they currently have, proximity-promoting behaviors will be activated. If not, infants will be able to explore the environment or interact with others. Wariness of novel people or environments as well as fatigue, sickness, and so on, increases the felt need for proximity and, thus, activates proximity-promoting (or attachment) behaviors. As novelty decreases, wariness declines, and the child may shift from avoiding the novel adult and seeking the proximity of an attachment figure to interacting with the novel adult and moving away from the attachment figure.

Because these behavioral changes depend on the individual's appraisal of the current circumstances, the appraisal process is also affected by past experiences that have shaped her perception of how much proximity is needed in particular circumstances. An individual whose attachment figure has been unreliable or inaccessible in the past may require greater proximity to the adult at all times than one who can count on the adult's prompt availability for example. These predictions affected development of Ainsworth and Wittig's (1969) Strange Situation, a paradigm designed to measure individual differences in the security of attachment (see *Ainsworth's Strange Situation and the Security of Attachment*).

Bowlby (1969) highlights four major functions of behavior in the infancy period—each coordinated by a different behavioral system: proximity seeking in the service of protection or care, coordinated by the *attachment* system; avoidance of events or people that are potentially dangerous, coordinated by the *fear/wariness* system; playful social interaction (other than that to obtain protection or care), controlled by the *affiliation* system; and investigation of the nonsocial environment, controlled by the *exploration* system. Activation of any of these behavioral systems affects the operation of the others. For example, wariness leads to an inhibition of affiliation and exploration owing to the activation of attachment behavior, whereas the absence of wariness produces a reduced need for proximity, which, in turn, potentiates exploration and affiliation.

Bowlby's use of behavioral biology and control systems theory not only provided a novel conceptualization of attachment and a testable set of predictions (Bischof, 1975; Rajecki, Lamb, & Obmascher, 1978; Sroufe & Waters, 1977a) but also suggested a new way of viewing the organization of infant behavior. Instead of classifying behaviors on the basis of their morphological similarities and dissimilarities, for example, Bowlby (1969) proposed that we classify them on the basis of their functional similarities or dissimilarities. (Indeed, Bowlby's view influenced the conception of emotion proposed earlier in this chapter). Thus, separation protest (crying), locomotor approach, and clinging to an adult can be classified as attachment behaviors because all serve to bring about or maintain proximity/contact. Control systems coordinate behaviors that are functionally similar, activating any of a number of behaviors, depending on the circumstances. Moreover, any of these behaviors may serve a given function on one occasion and another function on a different occasion. Thus, to understand an infant's behavior, one should not thoughtlessly tabulate occurrences of discrete behaviors; instead, one should focus on the organization or integration of behaviors according to their function.

Development of Attachment

Similarly to Mahler and Freud, Bowlby (1969) describes an ontogenetic sequence in the development of infant-adult attachments. During the first one to two months, infants emit proximity-promoting signals indiscriminately; provided that someone responds to their signals, infants are content. However, as they develop the capacities to distinguish among adults and to remember the frequency and hedonic quality of past interactions with them, infants start to exhibit preferences. They may be soothed more readily by some adults than by others, and they may respond more positively to playful social bids from such preferred adults. Until about 6 to 8 months of age, however, infants seem willing to accept the ministration and attention of less preferred individuals, whereas after about 6 to 8 months, infants may protest when separated from their preferred adults. This transition coincides with the emergence of the infant's capacity to locomote independently; then, infants can achieve proximity/contact of their own accord and are not always dependent on the adults' willingness to respond to their signals.

A final transition occurs sometime during the third year of life, when children acquire the capacity to recognize that others (e.g., their attachment figures) have desires and needs of their own that have to be taken into account when interacting with them (Marvin, 1977). This transition marks the onset of what Bowlby (1969) calls the phase of goal-corrected partnerships, wherein both partners consider the interests of themselves, the other, and the dyad.

Bowlby's Attachment Theory: Implications for Personality Development

Bowlby's theory has implications that far transcend infancy and the preschool years. One of the most important and most controversial aspects of Bowlby's (1969) theory of attachment is his claim that early attachment relationships play a critical role in the formation of an individual's later personality. Much of the controversy concerning this position has arisen from other researchers' misinterpretation of Bowlby's views. It is, therefore, important to clarify Bowlby's position.

Working Models. Bowlby proposes that, during infancy, childhood, and adolescence, individuals gradually build working models of the world and of themselves by the aid of which they perceive events, forecast the future, and construct plans.

> In [the person's] . . . model of the world . . . a key feature is his notion of who his attachment figures are, where they may be found, and how they may be expected to respond. Similarly, in the working model of the self that anyone builds a key feature is his notion of how acceptable or unacceptable he himself is in the eyes of his attachment figures." (Bowlby, 1973, p. 203)

Bowlby argues that these working models of self and world are based on the individual's actual experiences with attachment figures: each set of experiences gives rise to complementary models of (1) the attachment figure as either an accessible, responsive, loving individual or as an inaccessible, unresponsive, unloving individual and (2) the self as either an endearing, worthy, lovable person or as a loathesome, unworthy, unlovable person. These working models then organize the individual's reaction to the environment. In particular, a working model based on the caretaker's prompt and appropriate response to a child when the child is wary or distressed inculcates a sense of security—a belief that the child can explore the world and interact with others safely. The caretaker's failure to respond promptly and appropriately on the other hand predisposes a child to develop a chronically anxious or inhibited style of approaching the environment.

Personality may, thus, develop in a variety of

ways, depending on a child's experiences. Bowlby acknowledges that a child's constitution influences his personality, but he considers interactions with attachment figures to play a central role in shaping personality development. Bowlby's view, thus, constrasts sharply with a purely maturational point of view wherein, given a minimally normal environment, a biologically based temperament determines the individual's reactions toward the world (e.g., Kagan, 1974). Bowlby's view also contrasts with Mahler's theory, in that, according to Bowlby, (1973) atypical development can be produced by traumatic disruptions in social attachment at points beyond the discrete stages identified by psychoanalytic theorists. Accordingly, the development of atypical or pathological models of self and world is not stagebound. Similarly, normal development is not due to successful passage through the developmental stages but to the formation and maintenance of positive working models, which the individual continues to define and modify throughout infancy, childhood, and adolescence. However, as the child grows older and the models become better defined and elaborated, radical changes in personality become less likely.

Monotropy. As already described, personality development is greatly influenced by experiences with attachment figures. All attachment figures, however, are not equally important in shaping personality: according to Bowlby (1969), one individual is particularly important. Bowlby proposed the term monotropy to capture the apparent predisposition of individuals to form one primary attachment relationship. Bowlby proposed that the relationship to this person—usually the primary caretaker—developed before any other attachments and remained more important than them. This notion that infants form a hierarchy of attachment figures has, as we will see, received some empirical support. Inappropriate interpretation of monotropy, however, has led to confusion. Many investigators believe that Bowlby predicted drastic, irreversible consequences when infants are reared by persons other than their natural mothers—something that clearly does not happen. In part, this confusion stems from Bowlby's unfortunate use of the term mother. When Bowlby coined the term monotropy, he exemplified the concept by stating, "Good mothering from any kind woman ceases to satisfy him . . . only his own mother will do" (Bowlby, 1958, p. 370). However, within that very article, and even more clearly in later articles and books, Bowlby applied the term mother to any primary attachment figure—a particular caring, responsive individual. For the typical, home-reared Western infant, the primary attachment figure is the natural mother, but may be the father, a grandparent, a nursemaid, and so on. Bowlby did not mean to imply that having a caretaker other than the natural mother inevitably or even typically led to abnormal personality development. Instead, he suggested that the unavailability of any particular caring and responsive individual might predispose the child toward undesirable personality development.

Childhood Experiences That Promote Atypical Rather Than Typical Development. What are the experiences that predispose individuals to abnormal or normal personality development? The most clear-cut and extreme disturbance of the attachment relationship is created when, from a very early age, the child is institutionalized under conditions that preclude development of a secure relationship with one particular individual. Several investigators have studied the development of such children, in one case (B. Tizard, cited in Rutter, 1982) following their progress until adulthood. The results of these studies suggest that institutionalization under these conditions, especially when combined with other undesirable circumstances may—but does not always—affect personality development adversely.

A recent longitudinal investigation of institutionalized children has revealed, in keeping with Bowlby's (1973) theory, that children's social relationships in general and attachment relationships in particular are adversely affected by early institutionalization (Tizard & Hodges, 1978; Tizard & Rees, 1975; Tizard and Tizard, 1971). The children studied were primarily born to young, unwed women from working-class backgrounds and were institutionalized from before 4 months of age until they were adopted, placed in foster homes, or returned to their natural mothers. The institutions were of high quality in most respects; however, the caretaking strategy was designed to prevent children from forming strong attachments to particular nurses. Moreover, staff turnover was astoundingly rapid in these institutions: about 50 different nurses had cared for the average child by the time she was 4½ years old.

When children were 4½ and 8 years old, Tizard (Tizard & Hodges, 1978; Tizard & Rees, 1975; Tizard & Tizard, 1971) contrasted the behavior of children in four groups: (1) children who had remained institutionalized, (2) children from the institutions who had been adopted, (3) children from the institutions who were returned to their mothers, and (4) a comparison group of children from intact, working-class families in London. Whereas natural parents and those in the control group were very young and from the working class, adoptive parents were older and from the middle class.

At 4½ years of age, both institutionalized and ex-institutionalized children manifested atypical social behavior, including indiscriminate and excessive friendliness to strangers (ex-institutionalized children only), marked attention seeking, poor peer interactions, and clinginess (continuously institutionalized children only). Despite their clinginess, however, continuously institutionalized children had only shallow attachments to their caretakers; 2 showed no preferences among nurses, and many of those who showed preferences were not disturbed when "their" nurse was off duty or even when she left the institution. Of 26 children, 18 were said not to care deeply about anyone. Thus, at age 4½, institutionalized children seemed unattached, at least by caretaker report.

By age 8, however, the ex-institutionalized children who had been restored to their own mothers seemed to have especially severe difficulties. Almost two thirds of the restored children, compared with less than one third of the institutionalized and control group children and less than one tenth of the adopted children, had received professional help for behavior problems. Moreover, significantly more institutionalized and restored children than adopted or working-class children were not closely attached to their caretakers. Further, this apathy was apparently reciprocated: most mothers of restored children said that they did not feel deeply for those children, and only about half the caretakers of restored and institutionalized children played with their children during the week, compared to 90% of the adoptive parents and 72% of the working-class parents.

According to ratings by the children's teachers, however, even adopted children had significantly more behavior problems in school than did control children and other classmates (although these were not as severe as those of restored children). It is difficult to account for these discrepant reports. Perhaps the adoptive parents' attitudes and behavior altered their perceptions of the children's behavior and/or affected the children's actual behavior in relation to them. Alternatively, it is possible that teachers somehow knew of their students' histories and this jaundiced *their* perceptions. The accuracy of caretaker and teacher reports cannot be ascertained from these data.

Bohman and Sigvardson (1980) followed a similar group of institution-reared children until age 15, at which time they compared: Group 1—children reared from about 5 months of age by adoptive parents, Group 2—children raised by their biological mothers (who were usually unmarried) from about 7 months age, and Group 3—children placed in foster homes after about 9 to 11 months in the institution. At age 15, significantly more Group 2 and Group 3 children manifested maladjustment (tension, withdrawal, aggression, inability to concentrate, poor peer relationships, etc.) than did their classmates.

All of these findings suggest that early institutionalization may have lasting effects on personality development, predisposing children to become anxiously or shallowly attached to their caregivers and to have difficulty interacting with peers and teachers and controlling their own behavior. These findings are consistent with Bowlby's (1973) predictions. However, contrary to Bowlby's predictions, institutionalized and ex-institutionalized children were not particularly fearful or phobic, except to the extent that fearfulness possibly produced clinginess.

One problem with all these studies, moreover, is that they relied on others' reports, which (as we have discussed earlier) are colored by the reporter's attributions as well as by the child's behavior. However, P. Dixon (cited in Rutter, 1979) reportedly confirmed many of Tizard's (Tizard & Hodges, 1978; Tizard & Reese, 1975) findings with in-school behavioral observations. Another problem with these studies is that they tell us nothing about the quality of care received by children after removal from the institution. Good relationships with both substitute or adoptive caretakers should minimize symptoms, whereas later relationships with overtly rejecting caretakers should increase their intensity.

Noninstutionalized Children. Bowlby (1973) predicts abnormal development not only for children who experience long periods of institutionalization but also for those experiencing less extreme circumstances. In particular, he predicts atypical development when attachment figures punish children by threatening to abandon them, commit suicide, or stop loving them, or have anxious attachment relationships with their own parents or spouses. Tizard (Tizard & Hodges, 1978; Tizard & Reese, 1975) provides data that indirectly support Bowlby's (1973) predictions. When she studied the 4½-year-olds, she found that 8 of the 15 mothers of restored children, compared with only 2 of the 24 adoptive mothers, threatened to reinstitutionalize their children. This behavior may have contributed to the anxiety shown by these children at age 8.

Bowlby (1973) also discusses several studies and case histories suggesting a connection between threats of separation or loss of love on the one hand and fearfulness, school-phobia, and disordered mourning on the other hand. These studies require careful replication and extension, using better methods and larger samples.

Even more disconcerting are studies supporting the link Bowlby hypothesizes between the anxious attachments of parents and their children's atypical development. Bowlby (1973) submits that each individual's working models of attachment figures and self affect the organization of attachment behavior toward their spouses and the organization of caretaking behavior toward their children, either because the parents redirect anger from their own parents to their spouses or children, misattribute the parent's rejection, or model their own parents' angry, rejecting behavior. Many abusive parents, in fact, claim to have been abused themselves (Bowlby, 1980; Rutter, 1979). More recently, B. Tizard (cited in Rutter, 1982) found that women raised in institutions were more likely than home-reared working-class parents to have illegitimate children, to marry disturbed men, and to be bad parents themselves. Frommer and O'Shea (1973a, 1973b), similarly, found that mothers who experienced disrupted homes during their childhood had undesirable parenting styles. However, institution-reared women who married stable partners and had satisfactory marriages were also likely to be better parents according to Tizard (Rutter, 1982). This suggests that there may not be a direct relationship between the parents' childhood experiences and their own parenting style.

Several other studies suggest intergenerational continuity of anxious attachments and unsatisfactory development: children of couples experiencing marital discord, separation, or divorce are more likely to have interpersonal difficulties during adulthood (Cass & Thomas, 1979) and unsatisfactory marriages (Jonsson, 1967; Rutter & Madge, 1976). It appears, then, that anxious attachment may affect not only each individual's development, but the development of his children as well.

Moreover, several studies (Rutter, 1979; Rutter, Yule, Quinton, Rowlands, Yule, & Berger, 1975; Vaillant, 1977) indicate that a combination of factors, such as the parents' marital conflict, parent-child separations, and parental rejection, is much more pathogenic than any single event. Such findings support Bowlby's (1973, 1980) belief that each person's working models are continuously modified by important events in their lives. Vaillant (1977), for example, found that adjustment at age 30 was unrelated to whether or not the men in his study had a cold rejecting mother. However, a composite score was strongly related to adult adjustment. The composite score included: assessments of (1) the overall home environment in childhood, (2) the security of the home atmosphere in childhood, (3) the security of the mother-child relationship, (4) the security of the father-child relationship, (5) the adequacy of sibling relationships, (6) psychological problems in childhood, (7) physical health in childhood, and (8) high school accomplishments (academic, social, and athletic). Those with a low composite score (the loveless) were viewed as unable to play: they did not participate in sports, take vacations, or play games with friends. In addition, the loveless were unable to trust others, were emotionally disturbed, and were more physically ill relative to the lucky (those with the highest scores).

In conclusion, there is much evidence that is consistent with Bowlby's (1973, 1980) theoretical predictions. However, no study clearly demonstrates that defective attachment relationships per se lead to abnormal personality development or to deficits in social and parenting skills. Ainsworth and her colleagues (1978) have attempted to investigate Bowlby's notions more directly (see *Ainsworth's Strange Situation and the Security of Attachment*).

Possible Mechanisms for Abnormal Personality Development. The studies reviewed earlier indicate that abnormal development is by no means inevitable, even under the most adverse conditions. What might be the mechanisms by which abnormal attachment experiences lead to atypical development? Bowlby (1973) suggests that atypical working models are developed, but how do these abnormal working models influence behavior? According to Bowlby, they influence behavior by a process called defensive exclusion. Defensive exclusion involves actively preventing incoming information from being processed consciously. As a result of this exclusion, the behavioral systems that incoming information would normally activate become either partially or totally deactivated. Bowlby contends that if a child's attachment behaviors elicit rejection from the attachment figure, that person may later exclude information pertaining to the rejection and deactivate the behaviors leading to this rejection. Moreover, Bowlby, in agreement with such theorists as Bateson, Jackson, Haley, and Weakland (1956), suggests that parents may promote defensive exclusion by behaving in a rejecting fashion while saying that they love their children. According to Bowlby, all defense mechanisms may be viewed as particular forms of defensive exclusion.

Bowlby's hypothesis has been both supported and modified by findings from a careful study by Vaillant (1977). He studied the relationship between the background and personality characteristics of male Ivy League students and their success as adults.

He found that adjustment in adulthood (overall adjustment, rewarding career, marital adjustment, friendship patterns, psychological adjustment, medical history, etc.) was highly correlated with the types of defense mechanisms used. Those who mainly employed mechanisms such as turning against the self and projection (both of which Bowlby, 1973, considers to be common among anxiously attached persons), were more poorly adjusted than were those whose predominant mechanisms were those like sublimation, altruism, and humor, which have beneficial effects for others. Perhaps the style of defensive exclusion determines, at least in part, whether adverse childhood experiences will or will not be pathogenic.

Conclusions. Although much more research is needed regarding Bowlby's theory of personality development, there is a growing body of evidence available that is consistent with his point of view. Abnormal attachment experiences have been linked to such diverse adult conditions as depression and loneliness (Shaver & Rubenstein, 1980), character disorders (Cass & Thomas, 1979), and phobias (Bowlby, 1973). Moreover, there is some evidence that secure attachments throughout childhood and adolescence may partially offset the effects of adverse early experiences. In recent years, extensive attempts have been made to assess the quality of attachment relationships in hopes of predicting later development. We now turn to this burgeoning literature.

Ainsworth's Strange Situation and the "Security of Attachment"

Background

In his writings, Bowlby emphasized that attachment figures served two interrelated functions for young infants. One was to provide children with secure bases for exploration of the environment, thereby facilitating cognitive growth. The second was to afford children a haven of safety when they encountered threats, thus permitting children to regulate their level of stress.

These notions of the caretaker as a secure base and as a haven of safety helped stimulate the development of a paradigm that has become the most popular procedure for assessing infant-adult attachments. The paradigm is the Strange Situation, devised by Ainsworth and her colleagues (Ainsworth et al., 1978; Ainsworth & Wittig, 1969). Prior to development of this paradigm, attachment was usually operationalized in terms of unitary behavioral dimensions, such as separation protest, the amount of time spent in proximity to mothers, and the relative degree of positive expressions directed to the mother rather than to a stranger. Before Ainsworth, separation protest was the most popular index of attachment, in part because of Spitz's report (e.g., Spitz, 1946; Spitz, 1965) that the more favorable the relationship between mother and child before prolonged separation, the more intense the child's separation distress and the more likely the anaclitic depression during such separations. Fleener and Cairns (1970), Schaffer and Emerson (1964), and Tennes and Lampl (1964) were among those using separation protest as an index of attachment.

The use of proximity seeking as an index was prompted by its use in the studies of mother love in monkeys by Harlow and Zimmermann (1959). When applied to humans, proximity seeking involved determining how long an infant spent within a zone of physical proximity to the adult (e.g., Cohen & Campos, 1974; Kotelchuck, Zelazo, Kagan, & Spelke, 1975). The assumption was that such scores reflected the strength or intensity of the attachment relationship and that investigators could, thus, compare the degree of attachment to mother, father, substitute caretaker, or unfamiliarized adult (L. Cohen, 1974; Masters & Wellman, 1974). Other researchers used the relative frequency or duration of smiling to mothers and strangers to index the growth of the child's attachment to the mother (e.g., Ambrose, 1961; Spitz & Wolf, 1946). The more positive the reaction to the mother, the more intense the attachment was assumed to be.

Ainsworth (Ainsworth, 1973; Ainsworth & Wittig, 1969) did not reject the validity of these approaches to the study of normative questions about age differences in specific attachment behaviors or relative preferences for mothers or fathers. However, she felt that these measures did not adequately capture individual differences in the quality of attachment, that is, in whether a child appeared to be secure or insecure in the presence of her caretaker. Nor did these measures seem related to individual differences in the childcare practices of the mothers she studied in the longitudinal study (Ainsworth et al., 1978) described later in our discussion. Her approach also revealed the enduring aspects of attachment relationships: later work using her paradigm revealed remarkable individual consistency over a 6-month-period (Waters, 1978) and even longer (Sroufe, in press), whereas previous approaches had not (Masters & Wellman, 1974).

The eight episodes of the Strange Situation are described in Table 7. These episodes are designed to assess a number of ways in which an attachment relationship can be manifested. During Episode 1, the infant is introduced to the setting, devised in accordance with Bowlby's (1969) view that the attachment system is best observed when fear and distress are activated. Hence, the Strange Situation involves the use of an unfamiliar room to elicit fear of novelty. In Episode 2, parent and child are alone in the room so that observers can assess the extent to which the parent is used as a secure base for exploration. In Episode 3, the focus is on reactions to an unfamiliar adult and the use of the parent as a haven of safety when somewhat upset by the intrusive actions of the stranger. Separation distress is assessed when the parent leaves the child alone with the stranger in Episode 4, whereas in Episode 6, researchers assess separation distress in a more stressful context—being left alone. Episodes 5 and 8 reveal the quality of the child's reaction on being reunited with the parent. The child's ability to be soothed by the stranger is assessed in Episode 7, and is compared with the child's reaction when soothed by the parent in Episode 8. Because the Strange Situation was designed for the assessment of individual differences, sequence effects are of little consequence.

Bowlby's theorizing has had obvious effects on the interpretation of individual differences in the Strange Situation. First, separation protest is viewed not merely as an index of individual differences in attachment but as a precondition for the elicitation of behavior patterns reflecting the security of attachment (i.e., use of the caretaker as a secure base and as a haven of safety as well as reactions to reunion with the caretaker). In addition, a systems approach to measurement is used. For instance, proximity seeking is not defined in physical terms, such as by the distance between adult and baby at any given time. Proximity can be sought by crying and emitting a pickup bid or by active locomotion. The systems approach to measurement is also evident in the emphasis on the patterns of response in the situation

Table 7. **Summary of Episodes of the Strange Situation**

Number of episode	Persons present	Duration	Brief Description of Action
1	Mother, baby, and observer	30 sec.	Observer introduces mother and baby to experimental room, then leaves.
2	Mother and baby	3 min.	Mother is nonparticipant while baby explores; if necessary, play is stimulated after 2 min.
3	Stranger, mother, and baby	3 min.	Stranger enters. Min. 1: stranger silent. Min. 2: stranger converses with mother. Min. 3: stranger approaches baby. After 3 min. mother leaves unobtrusively.
4	Stranger and baby	3 min.[a] or less	First separation episode. Stranger's behavior is geared to that of baby.
5	Mother and baby	3 min.[b] or more	First reunion episode. Mother greets and comforts baby, then tries to settle him again in play. Mother then leaves, saying bye-bye.
6	Baby alone	3 min.[a] or less	Second separation episode.
7	Stranger and baby	3 min.[a] or less	Continuation of second separation. Stranger enters and gears her behavior to that of baby.
8	Mother and baby	3 min.	Second reunion episode. Mother enters, greets baby, then picks him up. Meanwhile stranger leaves unobtrusively.

Notes:

[a]Episode is curtailed if the baby is unduly distressed.

[b]Episode is prolonged if more time is required for the baby to become reinvolved in play.

(Schwartz, 1982). As we will see, no single discrete response, like smiling, nor any unitary dimension, like avoidance, distinguishes all the theoretically significant individual differences observed in the Strange Situation. Also consistent with Bowlby's theorizing is the heavy emphasis on social signaling, as evident in the type of greeting the baby gives the attachment figure on that person's return to the room.

The first step in scoring the infant's Strange Situation performance is to score the child's behavior on five 7-point scales called interactive categories: Proximity seeking, contact maintaining, proximity and interaction avoidance, contact and interaction resistance, and distance interaction. The definitions of these scales are provided in Table 8. These variables are used to create a typology of individual differences presumed to reflect security of attachment.

The use of patterns of variables to understand individual differences is most clearly exemplified by the classification of infants' reactions in the Strange Situation into three general types, A, B, and C.

Group A infants (whom Ainsworth et al., 1978, term "anxiously attached—avoidant") conspicuously avoid their caretaker during the reunion episodes, fail to cling when held, and tend to treat the stranger the same way as, or sometimes more positively than, their caretaker. There are two subgroups: A1 infants, who show clear-cut avoidance and A2 infants, who mingle avoidance with proximity seeking to, and contact maintaining with, their

Table 8. **Definitions of Ainsworth Interactive Scales**

Interactional variable	Definition
1. Proximity and contact seeking	The intensity and persistence of the baby's efforts to gain (or regain) physical contact (or more weakly, proximity) with an adult.
2. Contact maintaining	The degree of activity and persistence in the baby's efforts to maintain physical contact with an adult once she has gained it (especially such active resistance to being released as clinging or protesting); also, behaviors, such as sinking in while held, which tends to delay the adult's attempts to release the baby (i.e., to prolong contact by not signaling readiness for release).
3. Proximity and interaction avoidance	The intensity, persistence, duration, and promptness of any active avoidance of proximity or interaction, even across a distance, especially in reunion episodes. Included here are aborted approaches on reunion, turning the face away when greeted, prolonged pout, and refusal to make eye contact or to interact, and mild signs of wariness of the stranger accompanied by retreat to the mother. This scale does not include behavior that denotes only active interest in toys by an infant who is not distressed by separation or by the presence of a stranger.
4. Contact resistance	The intensity and frequency or duration of negative behavior evoked by a person who comes into contact or proximity with the baby, especially behavior accompanied by signs of anger. Relevant behaviors include pushing away, dropping or hitting toys offered, body movements in resistance to being held. More diffuse indications include tantrums and especially a prolonged pout or cranky fussing or other signs of inability to be comforted by contact with the adult. The behavior may alternate with active efforts to achieve or maintain contact, and both can be scored high in the same episode.
5. Distance interaction	Spontaneous indications of positive interest in an adult in the absence of proximity. Includes smiling, vocalizing, gestures, and play carried out with some attempts to elicit the adult's interest or interaction.

attachment figures. Approximately 20% to 25% of middle-class samples in the United States display the A1 or A2 patterns.

Group B infants (termed "securely attached") tend to seek proximity to, and contact with, attachment figures, particularly during reunion episodes. Moreover, such infants manifest clear preferences for their caretakers over the stranger. This group, into which approximately 65% of middle-class American infants are classified, is composed of four subgroups: B1 infants, who rely mainly on distal modes of interaction with their caretakers and may show some avoidance; B2 infants, who may show some avoidance during the first reunion but who eventually seek proximity; B3 infants, who conspicuously seek proximity and contact with their attachment figures during reunions and show virtually no avoidance or resistance; and B4 infants, who rather ineffectually but persistently seek contact with their caretakers and who constantly monitor attachment figures, becoming distressed during separation and showing some resistance upon reunion.

Group C infants (termed "ambivalently attached" or "resistant") tend to resist interaction and contact with their caretaker, yet they also manifest contact- and proximity-seeking behavior. Group C infants seek proximity and contact before separation, moreover, which may inhibit their exploration of the novel environment. There are two subgroups: C1 infants combine marked proximity and contact seeking with conspicuously angry, resistant behavior (e.g., hitting or pushing attachment figures away), whereas C2 infants show both passive proximity/contact seeking (by crying rather than reaching or approaching) and some resistance.

The relationship between the interactive category scores and the classification of infants into the A, B, and C groups is shown in Table 9. Clearly no single variable distinguishes the three types of attachment from one another. Proximity seeking, for instance, differentiates A infants from both B and C infants, as do avoidance and contact maintaining. Resistance differentiates C from both B and A infants, but not the latter two groups from one another. Similarly, C infants are distinguished from both A and B infants by the amount of crying.

So widely used is Ainsworth's system that the term "quality of attachment" has become synonymous with "Strange Situation classification." It is often assumed that these classifications fully capture individual differences in the security of caretaker-infant relationships and reflect differences in relationships built on the history of interactions with sensitive or insentitive caretakers rather than constitutional differences among infants.

Based on these assumptions, researchers often relate Strange Situation classification to various measures of child or caretaker behavior and conclude that "security of attachment" is (or is not) related to the other constructs. To evaluate such

Table 9. **Summary of Strange-Situation Classifications**

		Classification Criteria (Reunion Episodes 5 and 8)[a]				
Classification	**Descriptor**	**Proximity seeking**	**Contact maintaining**	**Proximity avoiding**	**Contact resisting**	**Crying**
A (2 subgroups)	Avoidant	Low	Low	High	Low	Low (preseparation), high or low (separation), low (reunion)
B (4 subgroups)	Secure	High	High (if distressed)	Low	Low	Low (preseparation), high or low (separation), low (reunion)
C (2 subgroups)	Ambivalent	High	High (often preseparation)	Low	High	Occasionally (preseparation), high (separation), moderate to high (reunion)

Notes:
[a]Typical of the group as a whole; subgroups differ in nonreunion episodes and to some extent in reunion behavior. See Ainsworth, Blehar, Waters, & Wall (1978) for detailed classification instructions.
(From Waters, 1978.)

studies, however, it is crucial to know:

1. Do Strange Situation classifications reflect important individual differences in patterns of parent-infant interaction in the home?
2. Do infants really fall into three fairly global types, as has been claimed?
3. Is there stability over time in Strange Situation behavior, and what factors account for instability when it is observed?
4. Does the A, B, C classification system make possible the prediction of later social and personality development as well as cognitive engagement, as attachment theory predicts?

The evidence bearing on these questions was recently reviewed by Lamb, Thompson, Gardner, Charnov, and Estes (in press-a, in press-b), to whom readers are referred for further details. Their conclusions are briefly summarized and occasionally supplemented here.

Antecedents of Strange Situation Classification

Maternal Sensitivity. One of the initial predictions of Ainsworth et al. (1978) is that the "quality" of each infant's attachment to his caretaker depends on the sensitivity of the caretaker to the infant's social signals. Although Ainsworth (1979) and Bowlby (1973) acknowledge that infant characteristics affect parent-infant interaction and the adult's sensitivity, they consistently emphasize the adult's influence on the infant. Ainsworth (1979) and Main and Weston (1982) have proposed that the mothers of future A babies express controlled anger toward, and rejection of, the infants, whereas the mothers of C babies are insensitive and inept but not rejecting. As a result of interacting repeatedly with such a caretaker, "The C baby fears that he will not get enough of what he wants; the A baby fears what he wants" (Ainsworth et al., 1978, p. 130). Mothers of B babies on the other hand are more affectionate, engage in more physical contact, are more effective in soothing their infants, greet their infants more positively, engage in more face-to-face interaction, and are in general less intrusive and better able to assess the infant's needs (Ainsworth et al., 1978).

The evidence for these claims has come primarily from a longitudinal study conducted in Baltimore by Ainsworth and her students (Ainsworth, Bell, & Stayton, 1971, 1972, 1974). This study involved visiting homes for about 4 hours approximately every 3 weeks throughout the first year. A Strange Situation assessment in the laboratory occurred when the infants were 1 year old. Three more recent longitudinal studies have since obtained data bearing on the relationship between maternal sensitivity and Strange Situation classifications. As we will see, these later studies, like the original Baltimore study, provide only weak support for the hypothesis that differences in Strange Situation behavior are determined by differences in caretaker sensitivity.

The Baltimore study involved 26 infants and their mothers, of whom 3 were later excluded because valid data could not be obtained in the Strange Situation. Although this study has generated an impressive number of publications (Ainsworth, 1979; Ainsworth & Bell, 1969; Ainsworth et al., 1971, 1972, 1974; Bell & Ainsworth, 1972; Blehar, Lieberman, & Ainsworth, 1977; Stayton & Ainsworth, 1973; Stayton, Ainsworth, & Main, 1973; Tracy & Ainsworth, 1981; Tracy, Lamb, & Ainsworth, 1976) and although this study is an excellent source of interesting hypotheses, its design and execution preclude any definitive conclusions (Lamb, Thompson, Gardner, Charnov, & Estes in press-a, in press-b) pointed to four major methodological weaknesses.

First, all of the home measures were developed post hoc, often by individuals who were aware of the infants' Strange Situation classifications and of the general hypotheses. The opportunity for contamination was thus high, especially because many of the variables, such as maternal sensitivity and cooperativeness, are somewhat subjective. The multiple measures were derived from the same narratives dictated by the same individuals—a situation ensuring nonindependence and allowing leeway for the observers' biases to exert a profound impact. Unfortunately, although the investigators were careful to provide coefficients of intercoder agreement, interobserver agreement in the home was never assessed quantitatively. Moreover, these narratives were used to compute duration scores, even though time was coded crudely at best.

Second, the sample size was too small to draw any meaningful conclusions. Of the 23 infants, 13 were in the B, 6 in the A and only 4 in the C group. As a result, it was difficult to obtain any statistically significant differences between the mothers of B- and A-group infants or between mothers of B- and C-group infants. Instead, we have only descriptive data of uncertain reliability because of the potentially large sampling error.

Third, although the theory predicts that mothers of A and C babies should differ from one another, the differences observed between mothers of A and C babies appear to be very modest in contrast to the differences between mothers of B babies on the one hand, and mothers of A or C babies on the other hand (see Table 10). Reports in secondary sources of substantial differences between mothers of A and C babies are simply unsupported empirically.

Fourth, Ainsworth did not adequately consider the possibility that some of the reported differences in maternal behavior were accounted for by infant characteristics. Ainsworth and her colleagues tend to assume that the direction of influence proceeds from mother to baby rather than bidirectionally.

Despite these weaknesses, the study is of great heuristic value, although cross-validation is badly needed. In one attempted replication, the Grossmanns (Grossmann & Grossmann, 1982; Grossmann, Grossmann, Huber, & Wartner, 1981) studied 49 West German infants and mothers from birth. Mother-infant interaction was observed in the home at 2, 6, and 10 months of age. From narrative accounts of the home observations, scorers rated maternal sensitivity, using the rating scales and coding conventions of Ainsworth et al. (1978). The Grossmanns reported a number of differences between their findings and Ainsworth's. Specifically, they found that 49% of their infants fell into the A classification, compared with 25% in the United States. B babies constituted only 40% of their sample compared with 65% in most U.S. studies. Because the study was carried out in a different country and because it is not clear yet what the causes of the cross-national differences may be, these findings require strict caution in interpretation.

However, contrary to expectations from Ainsworth's theory, the Grossmanns did not find any clear relationship between Strange-Situation behavior and ratings of maternal sensitivity. For instance, they reported that at 2 months, the mothers of B infants were significantly more sensitive than those of C babies, but not more sensitive than mothers of A babies. At 6 months, mothers of B babies were more sensitive than mothers of either A or C infants, but by 10 months of age, all the mothers were equally sensitive! Furthermore, even when they were significant, the differences between the means of the mothers on the sensitivity scale were much less pronounced in Germany than they were in the Baltimore study. Grossmann and Grossmann (1982) also reported that at 10 months the mothers of

Table 10. **Behavior Displayed at Home by the Mothers of Infants in the Three Strange Situation Groups (Mean Scores for the Fourth Quarter)**

Maternal Behavior	Group A $N = 6$	Group B $N = 13$	Group C $N = 4$
Responsiveness to Infant Crying			
Ignoring of crying (episodes per hour)	2.06	1.50	2.35
Unresponsiveness to crying (minutes per hour)	3.26[d]	1.27	4.44[c]
Behavior Relevant to Separation/Reunion			
Acknowledging baby when entering room	17.83[b]	34.46	23.00[a]
Behavior Relevant to Close Bodily Contact			
% of pick-ups in which M behaves affectionately	8.83[b]	24.00	4.00[d]
% of pick-ups that are abrupt or interfering	20.33[c]	9.08	14.25
% of holding time in which M is tender, careful	8.67	21.62	3.00[a]
% of holding time in which M is inept	9.83[a]	3.85	15.00[b]
% of holding time occupied with routines	21.33	17.38	46.25
Behavior Relevant to Infant Obedience			
Frequency of verbal commands	2.37	2.57	2.03
Frequency of physical interventions	1.32[a]	.58	1.33
General Characteristics (Ratings)			
Sensitivity-insensitivity to signals	2.42[d]	6.48	2.38[d]
Acceptance-rejection	3.75[d]	7.62	5.38[c]
Cooperation-interference	3.58[d]	7.30	4.25[d]
Accessibility-ignoring	3.83[c]	6.62	3.50[c]

Notes: Significance of *t* test comparing Group B with Group A or Group C

[a]p < .10.

[b]p < .05.

[c]p < .01.

[d]p < .001.

the B3 infants were almost as insensitive as the A infants' mothers, contrary to the findings of Ainsworth et al. (1978).

Another recent longitudinal study (Egeland & Farber, in preparation) is distinguished by its use of: an extremely large lower class sample (267 primiparae and their infants); prenatal and postnatal assessments of maternal attitudes and characteristics using standardized instruments; Brazelton neonatal assessments in the first 10 days of life; maternal reports of infant temperament at 6 months; observational assessments of mother-infant interaction during feeding at both 3 and 6 months; a play session at 6 months; and Strange Situation assessments at 12 months and 18 months.

Because these poor and primarily (62%) single mothers were more likely to be in states of economic and social stress than were Ainsworth's or Grossmann's middle-class subjects, this study does not really constitute a replication of Ainsworth et al. (1978). Nevertheless, like the study by the Grossmanns (1982), Egeland and Farber's (in preparation) findings cast doubt on the generalizability of the claims of Ainsworth et al. (1978) concerning the relationship between maternal sensitivity and Strange Situation classifications. For instance, although they reported some significant correlations between ratings of maternal sensitivity using Ainsworth's scales and Strange Situation classification at 12 and 18 months, in no case were the same measures significantly related to classification at both ages. In all, no consistent relationships were found between maternal characteristics and Strange Situation classifications.

A subsample of Egeland and Farber's (in preparation) subjects were studied by Vaughn, Gove, and Egeland (1980), who compared the attachment status at 12 and 18 months of age of infants whose mothers had returned to work by 12 months (Early Work, $N = 34$), between 12 and 18 months (Late Work, $N = 18$), or not at all (No Work, $N = 52$). Vaughn et al. (1980) reported a greater proportion of A ("avoidant") infants in the Early Work group than in the Late Work and No Work groups; however, the proportion of A and C infants combined did not differ across the three groups. Without knowledge of the alternative care arrangements received by the infants whose mothers returned to work, however, interpretation of these findings is difficult.

Less uncertain are the effects of extremely poor maternal care—including abuse or neglect. Examining a subsample of Egeland's sample, Egeland and Sroufe (1981) found that when maternal care was extremely poor, infants were more likely to be classified as A or C. The pattern of effects was different for 12- and 18-month Strange Situation assessments, however. Abusive/neglectful caretaking was associated with C group classification at 12 months and with A group classification at 18 months. In another sample, Lamb, Gaensbauer, Malkin, and Shultz (in preparation) reported that most abused or neglected infants showed avoidance of their abusive parents on reunion when assessed at an average age of 19 months.

Finally, Crockenberg (1981) reported a study relating infant irritability in the neonatal period; maternal responsiveness to distress at 3 months; maternal reports of social support, also at 3 months; and Strange Situation classification at 12 months in 48 mother-infant pairs. She reported that maternal responsiveness predicted B classification at 12 months only in mothers with low reported social support.

In summary, then, the empirical evidence in support of the claim of a relationship between maternal behaviors considered to indicate sensitivity and Strange Situation classification seems to be weaker than many reports have claimed. Most studies report some positive findings, but when more than one assessment of maternal sensitivity is performed, the multiple assessments rarely provide consistent relationships with single Strange Situation classifications. And when multiple Strange Situation classifications are performed, the maternal sensitivity variables that correlate with one Strange Situation do not relate to the second, and those that correlate with the second do not relate with the first.

The Role of Temperament in Strange Situation Classification. In addition to maternal sensitivity, individual differences in Strange Situation classification can reflect the role of individual differences in temperament. With some exceptions, Ainsworth and her colleagues (1978) have consistently deemphasized the role of endogenous infant characteristics in shaping Strange Situation behavior. However, temperament can influence Strange Situation classifications in at least three ways. The first interpretation, which involves only a minor change in emphasis from Ainsworth's position, is that the infant's own characteristics influence the mother's interaction, which then determines the infant's "security of attachment" (Waters & Deane, 1982). Thus, the more sensitive a caretaker is, the more secure the child; however, in some cases, even an exquisitely sensitive mother will have difficulty coping with an extremely irritable infant, producing an interactional failure reflected in the infant avoiding or resisting the mother.

A second interpretation follows Thomas and

Chess (1977) in suggesting that an important predictor of quality of attachment is the goodness-of-fit between infants and their caretakers. Instead of proposing that caretakers vary on a unidimensional scale of sensitivity, proponents of this view argue that it is critical to consider various caretaker characteristics in relation to various infant characteristics. For example, an emotionally expressive, active caretaker might create distress in a child who has a low threshold of negative reactivity to stimulation, whereas she might interact quite smoothly with an alert infant who has a high threshold for distress. Because few caretakers would fit well with highly irritable or passive infants, such babies would be more likely to form insecure attachment relationships. Like the first position, the goodness-of-fit interpretation of mother-infant interaction still implies that the quality of the parent-child interaction is the mediator of the relationship between early individual differences and the Strange Situation classifications.

The third interpretation directly challenges the basic assumption of Ainsworth et al. (1978) that the Strange Situation assesses the "quality" of the mother-infant interaction. Instead, the observed differences are assumed to be a direct reflection of the child's characteristic pattern of reaction to stress (i.e., the child's endogenous temperament, regardless of history of interaction with the parent). This position has been most clearly articulated by Kagan (1982b). He argues that behavior in the Strange Situation is directly and profoundly influenced by the child's threshold for distress. Babies classified as A are believed to be temperamentally calm babies, cry little upon separation, and, hence, show little need to seek proximity to the mother on reunion; C babies on the other hand are extremely easy to stress and become prone to anger toward the caregiver for leaving them and for failing to soothe them. B babies are intermediate in proneness to distress, and, hence, appear to show a more normal pattern. Because the proneness to distress and wariness may be endogenous and evident even in the neonatal period (Miyake 1983), the individual differences in Strange Situation classification imply little or nothing about mother-infant interactional differences. In line with Kagan's (1982b) position, Gaensbauer, Shultz, and Connell (in press), using a modified Strange-Situation procedure, reported that the infant's contact maintenance and degree of avoidance of the mother on reunion was predictable from the degree of negative emotion expressed by the infant during the separation: If the infants were quite upset by the separation, they showed marked contact-maintaining behaviors as well as little avoidance. If the infants were not upset by the separation, avoidance was maximal. Gaensbauer et al. (in press) thus suggested that "avoidant" babies may appear so on reunion with the mother simply because they are not distressed by separation.

Ainsworth downplayed the importance of temperamental characteristics in accounting for individual differences in maternal sensitivity and, eventually, in Strange Situation classification—in part, because of a widely cited study she and Sylvia Bell did that suggested the direction of effects proceeded from mother to infant rather than the reverse (Bell & Ainsworth, 1972). They reported that maternal unresponsiveness to infant crying predicted later irritability more strongly than the infant's early irritability predicted maternal unresponsiveness to crying. The logic of their study was that infants did not show stable individual differences in crying patterns until the last quarter of the first year, suggesting that differences in the infant's threshold to distress emerged and were not present from the start. On the other hand, the mother's unresponsiveness to crying *was* significantly stable from one quarter to the next throughout the first year. Furthermore, the mother's unresponsiveness to crying in one quarter was in most cases significantly correlated with the infant's irritability in the next quarter, whereas infant irritability did not predict subsequent maternal responsiveness until the second half-year of life. According to Bell and Ainsworth, this set of findings suggested that the degree of infant distress resulted from maternal unresponsiveness, rather than that the infant's irritability shaped maternal behavior.

Unfortunately, serious methodological and statistical problems compromise the conclusions of this study. First, both the amount of distress and the degree of responsiveness depended on imprecise estimates of duration, with substantial opportunity for observer bias to affect the results. Second, the quarter-to-quarter stability coefficients for the mother's unresponsiveness were not statistically compared with the corresponding stability coefficients for the infant's crying. In fact, the stability coefficients for infant crying are reported only for the last quarter, creating the impression that prior stability coefficients were 0, when they may have been nearly as large as the maternal coefficients, but fallen just short of statistical significance.

Similarly, the failure to contrast statistically the correlations between maternal unresponsiveness and the infant's subsequent crying on the one hand with the correlations between infant crying and subsequent maternal unresponsiveness on the other hand makes the conclusions about the direction of effects untenable. In fact, the key correlations do not seem to have been significantly different from one another. Accordingly, Bell and Ainsworth's study does not demonstrate that infant irritability is determined by mother-infant interaction rather than by infant temperament. Gewirtz and Boyd (1977) describe still other serious methodological problems in Bell and Ainsworth's (1972) study.

Some evidence has been reported that infant characteristics in the neonatal period predict future A, B, and C classification. For instance, Connell (1976) found that future C babies had lower Apgar scores and weighed less at birth than did future A and B babies. Waters, Vaughn, and Egeland (1980) reported a similar relationship between later C group classifications and 5-minute Apgars as well as an even more interesting difference at 7 days of age between future C babies and other babies. That is, on the Brazelton NBAS, future C babies were rated as having significantly more nonoptimal behaviors than did future B or A babies. The C babies as neonates oriented less to both animate and inanimate stimuli, had weak muscle tone, less head and upper body control, and displayed more spontaneous startle reactions. In general, they also seemed less alert than did other babies. All of these characteristics might make it difficult to stimulate such babies without causing distress. There were also interesting differences reported between the two future C subgroups: C1 babies, who would later show active resistance and ambivalence, were as neonates irritable, more quickly excitable, and adjusted their bodies less when held. C2 babies on the other hand, who in the Strange Situation manifest markedly passive behavior, as neonates showed poor muscle tone, such as when pulled to a sitting position.

There seems to be little doubt that some of the variance of Strange Situation behavior is related to temperamental traits, such as irritability, although the precise mechanism by which irritability produces Strange Situation behavior remains uncertain. Sagi, Lamb, Lewkowicz, Shoham, Dvir, and Estes (in press) reported that even though the Strange Situation classifications of infants tested with their mothers were independent of those obtained when the infants were tested with their fathers, there was a subgroup of infants who tended to respond with extreme distress each time they were seen in the Strange Situation. Most of these infants were classified into the C group with both parents. Moreover, Ainsworth et al. (1978) reported, but did not emphasize, that C babies are cry-babies at home during the first year of life and appear to differ from A and B babies in *every single Strange Situation episode* on the basis of crying.

However, it would be an error to conclude at this time that temperament is the only, or even the major, determinant of Strange Situation classification. Unfortunately, some of the findings relating neonatal behavior of the Strange Situation must be viewed cautiously. First of all, Waters et al. (1980) reported no consistent association between 10-day Brazelton scale scores and later Strange Situation classification. If there were clear relationships between endogenous characteristics and later behavior in the Strange Situation, they should have been evident in *both* the 7- and the 10-day assessments, but the associations were significant only for the former. Second, the data of Waters et al. (1980) were derived from a subsample of Egeland's subjects. However, when Egeland and Farber (in preparation) sought to confirm the initial findings of Waters et al. (1980) no consistent relationships between neonatal assessments and later Strange Situation behavior were found.

The findings of Connell (1976) are also difficult to evaluate: he used a very unconventional way of classifying his infants (a discriminant function analysis), and his significant neonatal to one-year relationships represented a small proportion of the many relationships tested.

There are also findings indicating that individual differences in patterns of Strange Situation behavior are not simply manifestations of infant temperament. Thompson and Lamb (1982; in preparation), for example, showed that the individual differences in emotional expressiveness were significantly and independently related to both parental reports of infant temperament and to attachment classification. In addition, several researchers (Grossmann, Grossmann, Huber, & Wartner, 1981; Lamb, Hwang, Frodi, & Frodi, 1982; Lamb, 1978c; Main & Weston, 1981; Sagi, Lamb, Estes, Shoham, Lewkowicz, & Dvir, 1982) have shown that the Strange Situation classification given an infant tested with the mother is independent of the classification given the same infant with the father. One would expect that, if Strange Situation classification simply reflected aspects of infant temperament, infants would behave similarly when seen in the situation with either of their two parents.

In summary, there seems to be some evidence that C babies may be difficult babies from earliest infancy and that certain aspects of their Strange Situation performance (e.g., their threshold to cry and their passivity) may be evident long before the attachment relationship is built. However, the precise contribution of other temperamental factors to Strange Situation performance and the specific mechanism by which temperament influences classification status awaits careful investigation.

Do the Ainsworth Groups and Subgroups Provide the Best Way of Summarizing Individual Differences?

So widely accepted is the system of Ainsworth et al. (1978) for classifying individual differences in the Strange Situation that few have stopped to ask whether the A, B, C trichotomy constitutes a valid way of clustering individual differences (exceptions are Connell & Goldsmith, 1982; Gardner, Lamb, & Thompson, in preparation; Lamb, Thompson, Gardner, Charnov, & Estes, in press-a, in press-b). The question is an important one, given that Ainsworth and her colleagues arrived at the A, B, C clustering on an a posteriori basis. They first derived their subgroups by seeking similarities among two or more infants. Subsequently, they searched for similarities among subgroups and, in this fashion, derived the major groups. Ainsworth et al. (1978) later subjected to multiple discriminative function analysis a number of the variables that discriminated between the groups that she considered "securely" attached (i.e., B infants) as compared to those considered "insecurely" attached (i.e., A and C). In this procedure, sets of data on individuals who have been classified into separate groups are used to create weighted equations of variables that best predict the group membership of the individuals. These predictor equations can then be applied to the original data or cross-validated in other samples (see Connell, 1976). The percentage of individuals correctly reclassified into their original groups by means of the discriminant functions quantifies the extent to which group assignment effectively summarizes individual differences. Two comments are in order here. First, the results of this analysis must be interpreted cautiously because it capitalizes on chance differences between groups. Accordingly, the reclassification by Ainsworth et al. (1978) using this method does not demonstrate the validity of the A, B, C typology, especially as the variables included in the analysis were selected not on theoretical grounds but on the basis of their ability to distinguish the groups in the first place. The validity of Ainworth's system was also not adequately tested by Connell (1976), who used weights derived from the sample of Ainsworth et al. (1978) to classify subjects in a different sample. Connell (1976) reported a 97% rate of successful reclassification using the discriminant function, but his success rate was exaggerated by eliminating his B1 and B4 infants, who appeared to resemble A and C infants (respectively) more than they resembled other Bs. In addition, he used both statistical and intuitive procedures when developing his discriminant functions. (See Lamb, Thompson, Gardner, Charnov, & Estes, in press-a, for a more extended discussion of this issue.)

The second problem with discriminant-function analyses is that they answer the question: Can one optimally weight a set of variables to discriminate among the three groups? However, the more important question is: Given the behaviors said to describe important individual differences (e.g., the interactive categories described in Table 8), do infants fall into three clear and distinct groups defined by these variables, and do these three groups coincide with the A, B, and C classifications? For the latter question, discriminant analysis is inappropriate, and cluster analysis is more appropriate (Lamb, Thompson, Gardner, Charnov, & Estes, in press-a; Gardner et al., in preparation).

Lamb and his colleagues employed cluster analyses on five samples of infants tested in the Strange Situation: (1) the 43 infants seen at 12½ months in the Thompson, Lamb, and Estes (1982) study; (2) the same infants seen at 19½ months; (3) Swedish infants seen at 11 or 13 months (Lamb, Hwang, Frodi, & Frodi, 1982); (4) 68 infants seen between 11 and 14 months of age in Israeli kibbutzim (Sagi et al., in press; and American infants seen at 12 or 13 months by Belsky, Rovine, and Taylor (in press)). Infants were classified using global judgments into the A, B, or C groups and were subjected to cluster analysis using the five interactive scores.

Some of the results are presented in Tables 11a and 11b. They show that there is some truth to the claim that the A, B, and C groupings summarize individual differences. They also suggest, however, that the categories of Ainsworth et al. (1978) do not constitute an optimal system for summarizing individual differences in Strange Situation behavior. The borders dividing the A, B, and C groups did not fall where the Ainsworth system says they should, and differences within the B group were greater than were differences between the A and B groups. Moreover, the degree of fit between the statistical clusters and the Ainsworth classifications declined with departures—with respect to age or culture—from the sample of middle-class 12-month-old Americans used by Ainsworth to devise her typology. Lamb, Thompson, Gardner, Charnov, and Estes, (in press-b) concluded that there seems to be an underlying continuum (or several continua) that has (have) been artificially trichotomized. This implies that re-

Table 11a. **Composition of Empirically Derived Clusters Using Data for the Michigan Infants at 12½ Months**

	Cluster 1	Cluster 2	Cluster 3	Not clustered
A1	3	0	0	0
A2	4	0	0	0
B1	1	0	0	0
B2	10	3	0	0
B3	0	11	0	0
B4	0	5	0	0
C1	0	0	4	0
C2	1	0	0	1

[a]From Gardner, Lamb, & Thompson, in preparation.

Table 11b. **Composition of Empirically Derived Clusters Using Data for the Michigan Infants at 19½ Months**

	Cluster 1	Cluster 2	Cluster 3
A1	3	0	0
A2	2	1	0
B1	8	0	0
B2	1	5	0
B3	0	9	0
B4	0	6	0
C1	0	3	4
C2	0	1	0

[a]From Gardner, Lamb, & Thompson, in preparation.

searchers should keep open the possibility of developing new ways of grouping subjects. Proponents of the traditional approach to the A, B, C classification could rightly point out, however, that the cluster analytic approach does not differentially weight the interactive categories in ways theory might suggest. In addition, the cluster analyses do not take into account the sequencing of behaviors, except to the extent that sequencing is reflected in the interactive categories themselves. Therefore, the "best" way of classifying infants' Strange Situation behavior remains at issue.

Is There Stability Over Time in Strange Situation Classifications?

One reason for the current popularity of research on attachment is that, in keeping with Bowlby's (1969) predictions, "security of attachment" promises to be a source of continuity in development (Sroufe, 1978, 1979a). A construct, like "security of attachment," must, however, be at least somewhat stable itself if it is to organize an individual's socioemotional and cognitive development. Thus, the temporal stability of A, B, C classifications has been the subject of many investigations. In 1978, Waters published a rather remarkable article revealing near-perfect consistency between 12 and 18 months of age in infants' Strange Situation classifications. However, similar studies by others have since produced a more complex picture. Table 12 summarizes the results of eight studies in which the standard Strange Situation procedure has been employed to assess the security of infant-mother attachments on two temporally separated occasions. Three of the studies show stability coefficients that are little better at all than chance, two show near-perfect stability, and the other three report coefficients between these two extremes. What might be the sources of these differences and similarities?

The investigators who find low temporal stability typically attribute this to the intervention of changing family circumstances or to high degrees of stress that precipitate renegotiation of the attachment relationships. Waters's (1978) middle-class sample was selected to minimize the likelihood of such changes and stresses between the two assessments to maximize the likelihood of finding stable individual differences in the security of attachment. However, the studies reporting low stability utilized samples undergoing greater stress or changing family circumstances.

Ainsworth et al. (1978), for example, attributed the low (57%) stability in their 2-week longitudinal study to increased distress in the second assessment (carryover effects), which led to an overall increase in the activation of attachment behavior. This interpretation was supported by the shift of all initial A babies into the B group on retest and of one-sixth of the B babies into the C group on retest. (Incidentally, these findings also suggest that individual differences in Strange-Situation behavior might best be viewed in the context of one or more continua rather than discrete categories.)

Similarly, Vaughn et al. (1979), with a sample of 100 infants and their socioeconomically disadvantaged mothers, found that only 62% received the same classification at both 12 and 18 months of age. However, Vaughn and his colleagues found that the mothers of infants who changed from "secure" (B) to "insecure" (A or C) reported a greater number of

Table 12. **Stability of A, B, C Classification**

Study	*N* of subjects (Age at time 1, Age at Time 2)	Classification at Time 2	Classification at Time 1: A	B	C	% agreement expected by chance	Overall observed % agreement	B % agreement observed	Not B % agreement observed
Ainsworth (sample 3 in Ainsworth, Blehar, Waters, & Wall, 1978)	23 (50 wk., 52 wk.)	A	0	0	0	54%	57%	86%	11%
		B	7	12	1				
		C	0	2	1				
Connell (1976)	46 (12 mo., 18 mo.)	A	11	2	0	52%	81%	90%	71%
		B	4	26	1				
		C	0	1	1				
Waters (1978)	50 (12 mo., 18 mo.)	A	9	0	0	46%	96%	100%	90%
		B	1	30	1				
		C	0	0	9				
Vaughn, Egeland, Sroufe, & Waters (1979)[a]	100 (12 mo., 18 mo.)	A	11	7	5	44%	62%	82%	38%
		B	10	45	11				
		C	2	2	6				
Main & Weston (1981)[b]	30 (12 mo., 20 mo.)		not provided			36%	80%	not provided	
Thompson, Lamb, & Estes (1982)	43 (12½ mo., 19½ mo.)	A	1	5	0	52%	53%	67%	23%
		B	5	20	4				
		C	1	5	2				
Egeland & Sroufe (1981), inadequate care[a]	25 (12 mo., 18 mo.)	A	4	2	3	33%	48%	78%	31%
		B	2	7	5				
		C	1	0	1				
Egeland & Sroufe (1981), excellent care[a]	32 (12 mo., 18 mo.)	A	3	2	1	60%	81%	92%	50%
		B	1	22	1				
		C	1	0	1				

Note:
[a]These samples are drawn from the same population and may include some of the same subjects. Therefore, caution is required in interpretation.
[b]Also included a new category, unclassified.

stressful family events between the two assessments than did the mothers of infants who were secure in both assessments. Contrary to theoretical expectations, however, change from what Vaughn et al. (1979) considered "insecure" to "secure" classifications was *not* associated with appreciably fewer stressful events between the time infants were 12 and 18 months of age.

In a more recent study of an unselected middle-class sample, Thompson et al. (1982) found that only 23 of 43 infants (53%) were assigned the same overall attachment classification at both ages. The temporal consistency of classification subgroups, moreover, was only 26%. Like Vaughn et al. (1979), Thompson et al. (1982) found that the occurrence of one or more important changes in family circumstances during the first year was associated with change in the baby's attachment status between the two assessments and that the relationship between changing family circumstances and attachment stability was even stronger when family events occuring at any time before the second assessment were considered. However, in the study of Thompson et al. (1982), changes in classification were bidirectional; there was no tendency for family stresses to make attachments more "insecure," as they had in the sample of Vaughn et al. In other words, some infants changed from "insecure" to "secure" in the face of changing family circumstances, whereas others changed from "secure" to "insecure". Egeland and Sroufe (1981), finally, found that temporal stability was lower in a sample of infants whose parents abused or neglected them than among infants who received excellent care. Again, the changes were bidirectional, with more infants becoming "secure" than becoming "insecure" over time.

Closer examination of Table 12 reveals a potential source of instability that was confounded with stress. Note that there was always higher stability in B-group classifications than A- and C-group classifications and that there is a tendency for "insecure" babies to become "secure". One explanation of these findings suggested by Thompson et al. (1982) is that they reflect real differences in the stability of different types of relationships: Due to a self-righting tendency (Sameroff & Chandler, 1975), infants become secure in their relationships to insensitive caretakers by adjusting their own behavior. Perhaps the increased competence of older children facilitates such adjustment.

However, these findings may be explained by methodological as well as substantive factors. Two examples of such methodological factors involve biases in the criteria used to assign infants to A, B, or C groups. First, there may be a bias, using these criteria, to classify children as B babies. Thus, any particular infant would be more likely to be spuriously classified as B on either occasion, leading to greater spurious stability of B infants than to A or C infants *and* to a tendency for infants classified as A or C to be spuriously classified as B when seen again. Waters's (1978) random data analyses provide some support for the existence of such a bias.

Another possibility is that the rating criteria, which were derived on a 12-month-old population may lead to increased incidence of B-group classification when applied to 18-month-olds. For instance, it is possible that the Strange-Situation procedure is somewhat less stressful for older than younger infants and less overt insecurity is manifested; thus, using the same criteria for "insecurity," one might find fewer signs of such "insecurity" at follow-up.

Finally, all thinking about the stability of the A, B, and C classification will benefit from the realization that there is an unknown error rate in the classification at both initial testing and follow-up in these studies. We refer this time not to error in scoring procedure but rather to the failure of the classification to reflect "true" quality of attachment on certain occasions.

Summary

The evidence reviewed in this discussion suggests that it may not be justifiable to equate "security of attachment" with "Strange-Situation classification": B classifications may or may not reflect "secure attachment," whereas A and C classifications may or may not reflect "insecure attachment."

Investigations conducted in other countries provide further support for this possibility. As discussed earlier, the Grossmanns (1982) found a much higher proportion of A babies in West Germany than is typically found in middle-class American samples. The Grossmanns also reported that German parents encourage their infants to be independent. Perhaps the greater proportion of A infants in that study reflected not "insecurity of attachment" or maladaptive parent-infant relationships but the desired outcome of conscious parental strategies. Similarly, Miyake (1983) reported an unusually high proportion (37%) of C babies in Japan, whereas Sagi et al (1982, in press) found an unusually high proportion of C babies among infants on Israeli kibbutzim. Does this indicate that Japanese and Israeli 12-month-olds are more ambivalently attached than American 1-year-olds? It seems presumptious to assume this in the absence of further converging evidence regarding the validity of the procedure. Rearing condition in these cultural contexts may ensure that many Japanese and Israeli infants are far more intensely stressed by the Strange Situation than American infants are. Given the weak relationships between maternal variables and Strange Situation classifications, the less-than-optimal success of the A, B, C clustering for capturing individual differences, the lack of stability in A and C classifications, and these cross-cultural findings, there is a clear need for researchers to differentiate the construct (security of attachment) from index (Strange Situation classification). Evidence besides A, B, or C classification is necessary to make any inferences about "security of attachment."

Do Strange Situation Classifications Make Meaningful Predictions About Later Behavior?

In view of the above conclusion, one cannot assume that associations between Strange Situation classifications and later development necessarily imply a relationship between "security of attachment" and later development. In recent years, however, considerable excitement has been generated by claims concerning the predictive validity of Strange Situation classifications. These claims have been exciting because so few measures of individual differences in infancy are related to assessments made in either the preschool or school years. Moreover, the findings concerned seem to demonstrate that the Strange Situation, indeed, measures the "security of attachment." A more detailed review of these findings is provided by Lamb et al. (Lamb, Thompson, Gardner, Charnov, & Estes, in press-a, in press-b).

Studies on the predictive validity of Strange Situation classifications are of two general types—those dealing with cognitive performance and engagement and those dealing with aspects of social and personality development. Few researchers have examined differences in cognitive performance as a function of Strange Situation classification because attachment theorists would not predict differences in cognitive abilities between members of the three Strange Situation groups: As Sroufe (in press) puts it, "well functioning children may be relatively high or low in intelligence and many severely limited children have adequate intelligence." However, attachment theorists do predict important differences in task engagement, in the patterning of specific abilities, and in the style (i.e., the emotional accompaniments) of cognitive performance (Sroufe & Waters, 1977a). The studies on social and personality development have addressed the hypothesis that B babies should later show more "adaptive" functioning. However, "adaptive functioning" has not been well defined operationally.

S. M. Bell (1970) was the first to relate attachment classification to the development of person and object permanence. Her study exemplifies those concerned not so much with overall cognitive performance as with the patterning of specific cognitive abilities. Many theorists have observed that mother is an object whom the child invests with great affect. Accordingly, Piaget (1954) predicted that infants would typically perform better on cognitive tasks requiring that they search for their mother (person permanence) than on tasks requiring them to search for inanimate toys (object permanence). S. M. Bell (1970) reported that person permanence scores were indeed higher than object permanence scores in 23 of her 33 subjects. All 23 subjects were B babies, leading S. M. Bell to claim that the more secure the attachment relationship, the more articulate the baby's ability to understand the mother's permanence. Security of attachment, thus, seemed related to at least one important aspect of cognitive development.

Main (1973) later related the security of attachment at 12 months of age to (among other variables) performance on a Bayley assessment at 20.5 months. She reported that B babies scored higher than A and C-group babies. Matas, Arend, and Sroufe (1978) could not replicate this finding, although Strange Situation behavior at 18 months of age was related to measures of problem solving and play at 24 months of age. B-group infants engaged in more symbolic play, were more enthusiastic and compliant in problem-solving tasks, exhibited fewer frustration-related and distress-related behaviors and more positive affect, and showed less negative affect than did A- and C-group infants. Two studies reported that B-group infants displayed more sophistication in both social (Bretherton, Bates, Benigni, Camaioni, & Volterra, 1979) and nonsocial (Bretherton et al., 1979; Matas et al., 1978) tool-use tasks than A and C infants did. Overall, then, the evidence concerning the relationship between Strange Situation behavior and measures of cognitive performance or engagement appears strong.

Similarly, several studies report significant associations between Strange Situation behavior and later assessments of social and personality functioning. Main (Londerville & Main, 1981; Main 1973) found B-group infants to be more compliant, cooperative, and less disobedient and to show more of a gamelike spirit and more positive affect than A- and

C-group infants. Erickson and Crichton (1981), Maslin and Bates (1982), Matas et al. (1978), and Sroufe and Rosenberg (1982) also reported that B-group babies were the most compliant babies in their samples. Pastor (1981), reported that B-group babies were later more sociable with peers, whereas Easterbrooks and Lamb (1979), who only studied infants from the four B subcategories, reported that the B1 and B2 infants were more sociable than B3 and B4 infants. Main and Weston (1981) reported that B-group infants were most sociable with adults; whereas Thompson and Lamb (1983), reported that B1 and B2 infants were most sociable to strangers, while B3, B4, and C2 infants were the least sociable. Similar results concerning Strange Situation classification of infants tested with their fathers were reported by Lamb, Hwang, Frodi, and Frodi (1982).

Three other studies are cited particularly often because they appear to show a relationship between early Strange Situation classifications (usually at 18 months of age) and later assessments of the children's personalities. Sroufe (in press) recently reported a study of 39 children about 4 years of age who were invited to participate in a special nursery school program. Most of the children in this sample had obtained the same Strange Situation classification at 12 and 18 months of age. Teachers observed the children's behavior and subsequently described their characteristics on a variety of questionnaires. The children were also observed by research assistants. Sroufe reported that B infants showed more ego resiliency, more self-esteem, higher "agency," (as rated by the teachers), more positive affect, less dependency, higher social competence, greater popularity, and more empathy than the A- and C-group children. The A-group children were said to be more hostile, isolated, and disconnected, whereas the C-group children were impulsive and helpless.

Arend, Gove, and Sroufe (1979) relocated 12 B and 14 non-B children from the sample of Matas et al. (1978) when the children were between the ages of 54 and 79 months. Q-sorts and laboratory assessments revealed that the B babies were more ego resilient and more curious than the non-B babies. Using a modification of the Strange Situation procedure, Waters, Wippman, and Sroufe (1979) related "security of attachment" at 15 months of age to preschool behavior. They reported that B-group babies demonstrated greater peer competence and greater ego strength than did non-B children.

As Lamb, Thompson, Gardner, Charnov, and Estes (in press-a, in press-b) point out, these studies appear to provide strong evidence for the predictive validity of the Strange Situation classifications. However, these data are not as strong as they seem. Several of the studies in this area are methodologically flawed. In some studies, the researchers assessing the later characteristics could have known, or been able to make informed guesses, of the Strange Situation behavior of the children they were assessing. As was mentioned earlier, S. M. Bell (1970) and Chazan (1981) not only used a faulty method for assessing person permanence but also reported results that have not been replicated (Jackson et. al., 1978; Levitt, 1982). Similarly, the DQ differences between B- and non-B-group infants reported by Main (1973) have not been replicated by Pastor (1981), Matas et al. (1978), nor Egeland and Farber (in preparation). Main (1973) failed to control for preexisting differences in DQ before comparing B- and non-B groups on other measures.

Nevertheless, there is sufficient evidence that early Strange Situation behavior predicts later behavior in some contexts. How are we to interpret these data? There are at least two possible ways of explaining the relationship between Strange Situation classifications and later measures. First, it may be that the relationship between the child and the attachment figure remains stable, thus mediating the continued differences in performance across a period of time. Second, a pattern of adaptive cognitive and social functioning may be established in infancy and remain stable despite the intervention of later experiences or of minor changes in social relationships. The latter seems to be the interpretation offered by Sroufe (in press), although he did not attempt to assess parent-child relationships in the 4-year-olds to rule out the other possible explanation. The first interpretation is supported by the fact that relationships between early assessments of "attachment security" and later child measures are significant if and only if there is stability in parent-child relationships or factors likely to potentiate such stability (see Lamb, Thompson, Gardner, Charnov, & Estes, in press-a, in press-b for a more extended discussion). However, the second interpretation remains viable because even relatively stable characteristics are by no means impervious to major environmental influences.

Mothers' Attachment to Their Infants: Bonding

Not only the Strange Situation and infants' attachment to their mothers have been the object of intense study by researchers; mothers' attachment to their infants bonding has received great attention as well. In fact, in the last decade, one of the most influential and controversial areas of research has concerned such mother-to-infant bonding (Klaus & Kennell, 1976). Although the definition of this term has shifted over the years to include all processes by which a mother becomes attached to her infant (see Klaus & Kennell, 1982), its common usage refers to a much more specific phenomenon: The establishment of a long-lasting, affectionate attachment of a mother toward her infant as the result of the mother's skin-to-skin contact with her newborn during a hormonally determined sensitive period lasting for a few hours after birth.

The concept of bonding has revolutionized obstetric practices in the United States. Before the 1970s, birth was often treated as a surgical experience rather than an emotional one. The mother and baby were rarely given more than a brief glimpse of one another and were, thus, prevented from sharing the period of marked alertness that often characterizes the first few hours of a newborn's postnatal existence. Moreover, when mothers did receive their infants, it was after silver nitrate had been placed in the babies' eyes, markedly impeding eye-to-eye contact (Butterfield, Emde, Svejda, & Neiman, 1982). In the rare cases when mothers were allowed to hold or contact their infants, it was often done during painful episiotomy repairs, which prevented the mothers from attending fully to their offspring, and worse yet, associated the infants with pain rather than joy.

The bonding concept suggested that the treatment of birth as a surgical procedure had at least one major psychological cost: preventing the optimal attachment of mothers to their newborn babies. In the process, proponents of bonding sensitized medical personnel to the social effects of medical interventions in the perinatal period. Klaus, Kennell, and their collaborators' (Klaus & Kennell, 1976) at Case Western Reserve University argued, on the basis of both animal studies and clinical observations with humans, that the prevention of early contact between mothers and newborns had major negative consequences for both mothers and infants. The animal work most relevant to their position involved ungulates, like sheep and goats, although studies of maternal behavior in both rats and monkeys were also pertinent. The studies of maternal separation in sheep and goats best documented a sensitive period for the establishment of a bond between mother and infant. For instance, when ewes are separated from their lambs immediately after delivery and reunited some 2 to 3 hours later, the mothers reject the young by butting and shoving them aside (Collias, 1956; Hersher, Moore, & Richmond, 1958; Hudson & Mullord, 1977; Klopfer, 1971). However, as little as 5 minutes of postpartum contact with the offspring results in dramatically different behavior: The mothers accept their offspring even after 2-hour separations.

Other studies showed that the hormonal condition of female rats crucially affected the initiation of maternal behavior (Lamb, 1975; Rosenblatt, 1970). Ordinarily, 5 to 10 days of exposure to pups is necessary to elicit maternal behavior from nonpregnant animals. However, the amount of exposure needed drops as pregnant rats approach parturition, and it can also be reduced in virgin or hysterectomized female rats by employing hormonal treatments designed to mimic the final stages of pregnancy (Bridges, Rosenblatt, & Feder, 1978; Bridges, Zarrow, & Denenberg, 1973; Krehbiel & LeRoy, 1979; Rosenblatt & Siegel, 1975; Siegel & Rosenblatt, 1978; Zarrow, Gandelman, & Denenberg, 1971). In nonhuman primates, Cross and Harlow (1963) demonstrated that after giving birth, female rhesus monkeys looked at infant monkeys more, suggesting a hormonal priming to become attentive to immature members of the species. Furthermore, Meier (1965) reported that laboratory-reared rhesus monkeys who delivered vaginally accepted their young, whereas those who delivered by cesarean section did not.

Work with humans suggested that mothers who were separated from their newborns for medical reasons (typically, prematurity) often seemed to be less attached to their infants when ultimately reunited. Many of these mothers reportly rejected and some even abused their offspring later (Leifer et al., 1972). This made pediatricians wonder whether the medical intervention necessary to save the life of the premature incurred the cost of creating deviant maternal attachment. The work on rats, sheep, and monkeys, however, raised the possibility that by simply ensuring contact between mothers and neonates in the immediate postpartum period, pediatricians might prevent or attenuate the ill effects of subsequent separations.

The early work on bonding in humans was impressive; it appeared to demonstrate that a few hours of additional contact between mothers and newborns had beneficial effects long after birth. Klaus, Jerauld, Kreger, McAlpine, Steffa, and Kennell (1972) studied 14 low income, predominantly black, unmarried primiparae who were given 1 hour of nude skin-to-skin contact with their newborns during the first 3 hours after delivery, plus an additional 5 hours of contact on each of the next 3 days. In a contrast group, 14 mothers were given only a brief glimpse of the baby after birth, brief contact at 6 to 8 hours for purposes of identification, and then 20 to

30 minutes of contact every 4 hours until discharge. One month after birth, the mothers in the extended contact condition reported being more reluctant to leave their infants with babysitters, paid more attention to their infants during pediatric examinations, soothed the baby more, and engaged in more behaviors like fondling and en face positioning. When their infants were 1 year old, the early contact mothers reportly missed their babies more when they returned to work, stayed closer to their babies during an examination, and soothed and kissed them more often (Kennell, Jerauld, Wolfe, Chesler, Kreger, McAlpine, Steffa, & Klaus, 1974). When the infants were 2 years old, the extended contact group used more questions and adjectives and gave fewer commands (Ringler, Kennell, Jarvella, Navojosky, & Klaus, 1975).

These remarkable findings were reinforced by the results of a study in Guatemala (Hales, Lozoff, Sosa, & Kennell, 1977). Three groups of 20 mothers were studied. Mothers in one group were given 45 minutes of nude skin-to-skin contact after birth and rooming-in started 12 hours postpartum. Mothers in a second group were given 45 minutes of nude skin-to-skin contact, but not until 12 hours after birth, at which time rooming-in began. Mothers in a third group were given no skin-to-skin contact, but, as in the other groups, rooming-in began at 12 hours postpartum. The study showed that 36 hours after delivery, the mothers who experienced early contact were more affectionate than those in the no contact group.

A substantial number of studies have since explored the role of early contact in mother-infant bonding. These studies have been the focus of recent reviews by Goldberg (in press), Harmon (1981), Lamb (1982), Lamb and Hwang (1982), and Svejda, Pannabecker, and Emde (1982), which should be consulted by those seeking greater detail. These reviewers called into question the robustness of the bonding phenomenon and documented serious ethical questions raised by overinsistence on the need for mothers to experience nude skin-to-skin contact at birth. Moreover, the research to date has been plagued by basic methodological problems. In some studies, for instance, research subjects in the experimental condition may very well have realized that they were receiving special treatment from highly regarded medical personnel. Only a few researchers (e.g., Svejda, Campos, & Emde, 1980) have controlled for such Hawthorne effects and have determined that nursing personnel treated experimental and control group mothers similarly. Another problem is that of experimentwise error. In a study with 20 dependent variables, one significant result is likely to occur by chance. In many studies on bonding, however, one significant result in the context of numerous nonsignificant findings has been regarded as confirmation of the bonding hypothesis. A third problem concerns the precise meaning of a replication. Frequently, investigators fail to replicate a previous finding at the level of a discrete variable (e.g., en face behavior) but do find a significant difference on another discrete variable (e.g., smiling) that indexes the same global construct, maternal attachment. Still other difficulties involve the selection of measures of maternal attachment that are of questionable validity, and the use of observers who are not blind with regard to the hypotheses of the study or to the group assignment of the subjects. Finally, there are problems with respect to preexisting group differences. Few studies avoid all of these pitfalls, and because of the flawed data base, conclusions about the bonding phenomenon are necessarily equivocal. Nevertheless, there seems to be an emerging consensus that the effects of early mother-infant contact are weak, short lived, apply only to some mothers, and do not involve biological factors.

In a methodologically careful study done in Germany, Grossmann, Thane, and Grossmann (1981) reported weak positive effects of contact, which attenuated over time. Grossmann and her colleagues divided primiparous mothers randomly into four groups: (1) an early contact group, which involved at least 30 minutes of contact with the newborns within the first postpartum hour; (2) an extended contact group, which involved 5 hours of rooming-in per day; (3) an early and extended contact group, which combined both treatments 1 and 2; and (4) a control group, which involved the standard hospital routine: a brief glimpse after delivery, medical care, and then placement of the clothed baby in a bassinet near the mother's bed. Feedings were filmed on days 2 to 3, 4 to 5, and 7 to 9 (mothers in Germany usually have a 10-day lying-in period). Mothers in the early contact group showed more tender touching and cuddling during the first two observations than did mothers in the extended contact and control groups, but these differences disappeared by the third observation. In addition, these differences were evident only among mothers who had planned the pregnancy in the first place. Extended contact seemed to have no effect. Other careful studies using short-term outcome measures have reported either equivocal effects (Hopkins & Vietze, 1977) or no effects (Svejda et al., 1980) of early contact.

De Chateau and Wiberg (1977a, 1977b) in Sweden have studied both the short-term and long-term consequences of additional skin-to-skin contact. They compared: (1) 22 middle-class Swedish primiparae who were given 15 minutes of extra contact with their neonates beginning 10 minutes after delivery, (2) 20 primiparae receiving standard hospital treatment who served as controls, and (3) 20 multiparae receiving the standard hospital treatment. Unlike Hales et al. (1977), de Chateau and Wiberg (1977a) did not find that early contact mothers were more affectionate 36 hours after delivery than control group mothers. The differences they did find (e.g., mother sitting up, mother leaning on elbow, and mother holding infant) do not indicate greater maternal affection or competence. A follow-up of these subjects when the infants were 3 months of age (de Chateau & Wiberg, 1977b) revealed that early contact mothers kissed and held their infants more in the "en face" position and cleaned them less than did control mothers. The early contact infants also cried less and smiled and laughed more than did infants in the control group. At 1 year of age, the early contact mothers held their infants more closely, engaged in more nonfunctional touching, and talked more warmly than did the control group mothers (de Chateau & Wiberg, in press), although no statistical comparisons were presented to support any inferences.

This study has been sharply criticized by Lamb and Hwang (1982) for the way in which conclusions about early contact have been drawn, even though the number of significant differences is about at the chance level. Lamb and Hwang also questioned the comparability of groups at the outset of the study. The early contact mothers had more frequently attended antenatal parenting classes, and it is not clear that mothers were randomly assigned to groups. At best, the study produced weak support for the bonding hypothesis; at worst, even those supportive findings are subject to several alternative interpretations.

The long-term effects of both early and extended contact were also studied by Siegel and his collaborators (Siegel, Bauman, Schaefer, Saunders, & Ingram, 1980). They studied 202 women, mostly black and unmarried, using both interviews and observations to derive factors dealing with maternal acceptance of the infant, maternal stimulation, and maternal consoling. Follow-up observations took place at both 4 and 12 months. The findings of Siegel et al. (1980) showed again that the effects of early and extended contact are weak: at 4 months of age, contact accounted for only 2.8% of the variance in maternal acceptance and 3.3% in maternal consoling, whereas at 12 months, contact accounted for only 3.2% of the variance in infant positive/negative behavior.

The conclusions of Siegel et al. (1980) summarize well the current status of research on bonding: "Even though we found some enhancement of maternal attachment during the first year of life by early and extended contact, it appears that programs other than early and extended contact . . . must be developed to produce substantial influences on attachment . . . among mothers comparable to those in our study" (p. 189).

Father-Infant Interaction

Although mother-infant relationships have long been considered important phenomena to investigate, the importance of father-infant relationships has been directly studied only recently. In earlier studies, the importance of the father's role was typically assessed by measuring the impact of his absence (or, occasionally, his unavailability) on children's development. These studies suggested that fathers did have an important influence on child development. Father absence, when it began prior to the child's fifth birthday, adversely affected both socioemotional and cognitive development. Boys without fathers were reportedly less aggressive, more dependent, less masculine in their choice of games, and less masculine in their responses to projective tests (e.g., Hetherington & Deur 1971; Sears, 1951). Moreover, the impulse control and moral development of both boys and girls seemed impaired (e.g., Hoffman, 1970; Mischel, 1961; Wallerstein & Kelly, 1976). Other studies suggested that early father absence was associated with deficits in IQ and a feminized cognitive style in boys—deficits that could still be detected when children were entering college (e.g., Blanchard & Biller, 1971; Carlsmith, 1964; Radin, 1981).

In each case, these studies suggested that paternal influences began quite early in child development. The findings regarding sex-role development apparently held true only for children whose fathers left or died prior to their fifth birthday. The cognitive deficits, too, were inversely related to the age at which children lost their fathers. Carlsmith (1964), in fact, observed the most severe cognitive deficits among children who had lost their father prior to 6 months of age.

These early studies, however, have been roundly criticized for failing to control other influences, such as socioeconomic status and amount of life stress (Herzog & Sudia, 1973). Nevertheless, the results at least suggested that fathers influence their children's development, and the criticisms merely highlighted the need to study paternal influences in a more direct fashion—by examining father-child interactions. Here we are concerned only with studies of father-infant interaction and focus on six related issues:

1. How much time do fathers spend with their infants?
2. Are fathers attentive to their infants' signals?
3. What is the nature of father-infant interaction?
4. How does father-infant interaction differ from mother-infant interaction?
5. Do infants form attachments to their fathers?
6. Most important, is there evidence that specific qualities of father-infant interaction influence infants' social and cognitive development?

The Extent of Father-Infant Interaction. Several researchers have attempted to determine how much time average fathers spend with their infants. As one might expect, the estimates vary widely, even when one considers only traditional families. One early study (Pedersen & Robson, 1969) found that, according to maternal report, fathers of 8 to 9½-month-old infants were home between 5 and 47 hours per week at times when the infants were awake (M = 26 hours). The fathers reportedly spent between 45 minutes and 26 hours each week actually interacting with their babies. From interviews with the parents of 6- to 21-month-olds, Kotelchuck (1975) later reported that fathers spent an average of 3.2 hours per day with their children, as compared with 9 hours spent by mothers. Similarly, the parents interviewed by Golinkoff and Ames (1979) reported figures of 3.16 and 8.33 hours per day respectively. By contrast, fathers interviewed by Lewis and Weinraub (1974) reported much less interaction than this: the average was 15 to 20 minutes per day. Perhaps the variability among these estimates is attributable to socioeconomic or subcultural differences among the populations studied.

Paternal Sensitivity. Determining how much time the average father spends with his baby, however, may be much less important than determining how effectively he interacts with the baby. Here the major variable studied has been parental sensitivity to infants' signals. As described earlier, parental sensitivity is believed to affect the security of infant-parent attachment, and is, thus, an important dimension to study.

In an early interview study, Greenberg and Morris (1974) found that most fathers reported elation at the birth of their infants—a reaction that Greenberg and Morris termed engrossment. Parke and his colleagues (Parke & O'Leary, 1976; Parke, O'Leary, & West, 1972) observed mothers and fathers in a maternity ward and found that, contrary to popular belief, the fathers were neither inept nor uninterested in interacting with their newborns. Indeed, all but a few measures showed that the fathers and mothers were equivalently involved in interaction. When observed feeding their 3-month-old infants, both fathers and mothers responsed to infant cues either with social bids or by adjusting the pace of the feeding (Parke & Sawin, 1977, 1980). Although the fathers were capable of behaving sensitively, however, they tended to yield responsibility for caretaking to their wives when not asked to demonstrate their competence for the investigators.

In some studies, moreover, differences have been observed between males and females in responsiveness toward infants or toward infant signals, such as smiles and cries. There is at present a controversy as to whether these differences are due primarily to biological or social factors. Feldman and Nash (Feldman & Nash, 1977, 1978; Feldman, Nash, & Cutrona, 1977; Nash & Feldman, 1982) argued for a social interpretation of the sex differences. They offered this interpretation on the basis of studies in which they observed male and female children, adolescents, unmarried college students, childless couples, and parents individually while they sat in a waiting room with an unfamiliar infant and his mother. They found that females were more behaviorally responsive to babies than were males only during early adolescence and early parenthood; there were no sex differences in responsiveness in the remaining groups. Feldman and Nash inferred from these data that sex differences in responsiveness to infants are evident only during stages of life when individuals are under social pressure to respond in a conventionally sex-typed fashion.

Frodi and Lamb (Frodi, Lamb, Leavitt, & Donovan, 1978; Frodi, Lamb, Leavitt, Donovan, Neff, & Sherry, 1978) observed similar behavioral but no physiological differences between males and females in responsiveness to babies and also concluded that social rather than biological factors were responsible. For instance, Frodi and Lamb (1978) found that, although there were no sex differences in 8- and 14-year-olds' physiological (blood pressure and skin conductance) responses to crying or smiling infants, 14-year-old females were more behaviorally responsive to infants in a waiting room situation like that of Feldman and Nash.

On the other hand, there is evidence that biological factors play a role in sex differences in responsiveness to infants. Chandler (1977) reported that even when age was held constant, girls differed from boys in nurturance to infants and small animals only when they had reached puberty—as assessed by biological indices, like menarche and the appearance of pubic hair.

Regardless of the sources for the differences observed in responsiveness, the data suggest that men—even traditionally uninvolved fathers—*can* be as responsive to their babies as women are. However, it is not clear that fathers typically *are* as responsive as mothers.

Characteristics of Mother- and Father-Infant Interaction. Responsiveness aside, several studies have been designed to determine whether mothers and fathers provide different types of experiences for their infants, and the data consistently suggest that they do. When videotaped in face-to-face interaction with their 2- to 25-week-old infants in a recent study, fathers tended to provide staccato bursts of both physical and social stimulation, whereas mothers tended to be more rhythmic and containing (Yogman, Dixon, Tronick, Als, Adamson, Lester, & Brazelton, 1977). During visits to hospitalized premature infants, mothers were responsive to social cues, fathers to gross motor cues (Marton & Minde, 1980). Lamb (1976a, 1977c) found that fathers tended to engage in more physically stimulating and unpredictable or idiosyncratic play with their 7- to 13-month-old infants than did mothers. Because these types of play elicited more positive responses from the infants, the average response to play bids by fathers was more positive than was the average response to maternal bids. Clarke-Stewart (1978), and Power and Parke (1979) later confirmed that mothers and fathers engaged in different types of play, although Belsky (1979) did not find differences of this kind. Lamb (1976a, 1977c) also found that mothers were more likely to hold infants in the course of caretaking, whereas fathers were more likely to hold them either to play with them or in response to their requests to be held. The first of these findings was replicated by Belsky (1979). Not surprisingly, infants responded more positively to being held by their fathers than by their mothers (Lamb, 1976a, 1977c).

Data gathered by interview confirm that, in traditional families, fathers are identified with playful interaction, whereas mothers are associated with caretaking (Clarke-Stewart, 1978a; Kotelchuck, 1975; Rendina & Dickerscheid, 1976; Richards, Dunn, & Antonis, 1975). However, Pedersen, Cain, and Zaslow (1982) found that these patterns of involvement may change when both parents are employed. Employed mothers stimulated their infants more than the unemployed mothers did; moreover, employed mothers were far more actively involved in interaction than their husbands were. Although maternal responsibility for childcare did not differ depending on maternal employment status, fathers with unemployed wives played with their infants more than their wives did, whereas the pattern was reversed in families with employed mothers.

Differences in Mothers' and Fathers' Perceptions of and Interactions with Sons and Daughters. Parental behavior is influenced not only by the parents' gender but by infants' gender as well. Even during the newborn period, fathers and mothers perceive their sons to have masculine characteristics and their daughters to have feminine ones; these differences in perception are most extreme among fathers who have seen but not held their babies (Rubin, Provenzano, & Luria, 1974). Moreover, fathers and mothers differ not merely in their perceptions, but in their treatment of newborn boys and girls as well. Fathers of boys respond to their sons' vocalizations more often than do the fathers of girls. Moreover, fathers vocalize to and touch their firstborn sons more than other infants (Parke & O'Leary, 1976; Parke & Sawin, 1975).

The differential treatment of sons and daughters is not confined to the newborn period. Fathers of 3-week-old and 3-month-old boys visually and tactually stimulate their infants more than do fathers of like-aged girls (Parke & Sawin, 1975, 1980). Mothers show the opposite pattern of behavior—stimulating 3-week-old and 3-month-old girls more than they do boys. Similarly, fathers of 15- to 24-month-old boys were observed to vocalize to their babies more than mothers did (Lamb, 1977a, 1977b). However, similar differences were not observed in these studies for parents' interactions with 12- to 13-month-old sons. Nevertheless, in general, it seems that fathers and mothers tend to stimulate same-sex infants more than opposite-sex infants. Perhaps these differences affect the establishment of gender role and gender identity.

The Formation of Infant-Father Attachment. Father-infant interaction is likely to have its most immediate impact on the formation of attachment and affiliative (playmate) relationships. The studies reviewed later indicate that infants do form attachments to their fathers. They also reveal a somewhat less clear picture of the features of father-infant interaction that might influence the development of attachments; in general, the relationships between these features and the strength of attachment vary depending on which index of attachment is employed.

Schaffer and Emerson (1964) used separation distress as their index of attachment and found that, according to maternal report, many infants began to protest separation from their fathers at about the same age (7 to 9 months) as they began protesting separations from their mothers. Moreover, by 18 months of age, 71% of the infants reportedly protested separation from both parents. Schaffer and Emerson concluded that babies became attached to those with whom they interacted regularly, regardless of involvement in caretaking.

Pedersen and Robson (1969) used infants' responses to reunion following day-long separations as their index of attachment, and they reported, like Schaffer and Emerson (1964), that infants become attached to both parents. However, they found different relationships between strength of attachment and father-infant interaction than had Schaffer and Emerson. For male infants, the intensity of greeting behavior was correlated with the frequency of paternal caretaking, paternal patience with infant fussing, and the intensity of father-infant play. For female infants, however, intensity of greeting behavior was only correlated with the fathers' reported apprehension over well-being.

Another series of studies, using several indices of attachment, yielded even more complex results (Kotelchuck, 1972, 1975, 1976). Although these studies showed that infants became attached to both parents (infants protested when left alone by either parent, explored little while the parents were absent, and greeted them both positively when they returned), there was an inverse relationship between the amount of protest following separation from fathers and the degree of paternal involvement in caretaking. Heightened paternal involvement also seemed to delay the onset of separation protest (Kotelchuck, 1972; Lester et al., 1974). On the other hand, other dependent measures (proximity seeking toward, and amount of, interaction with fathers) suggested that increased paternal involvement in caretaking was associated with increased infant-father attachment.

These contradictory findings and the counterintuitive relationships between separation protest and the extent of paternal childcare (but see Mahler's predictions, discussed earlier, that such protests should be inversely related to strength of attachment) suggest that the intensity of separation protest may not measure intensity of attachment. This conclusion is strengthened by the evidence that separation protest often fails to reveal differences that are evident on other measures (e.g., Cohen & Campos, 1974; Stayton, Ainsworth, & Main, 1973).

A more recent investigation, employing a composite proximity-seeking and contact-maintaining score as the index of attachment, revealed that fathers' sensitivity, playfulness, and the time spent face to face with their 2-month-old infants predicted the intensity of infant-father attachment at 7½ months of age (Chibucos & Kail, 1981). Thus, the preponderance of the evidence suggests a positive relationship between paternal interaction and the intensity of attachment.

A Hierarchy of Attachment Figures? As mentioned earlier, Bowlby's concept of monotropy implies that infants' prefer one attachment figure over all others. Bowlby (1969) proposes that, although infants may have many playmates and subsidiary attachment figures, they selectively direct attachment behaviors toward their preferred figure, especially when they are distressed. This prediction brings clarity to what would otherwise be a series of apparently contradictory findings. Although most studies in which infants were not exposed to stress reported no consistent preferences, studies in which infants were stressed and were allowed to choose between their parents have more consistently shown that most infants chose their mothers.

Neither Feldman and Ingham (1975), who did not allow infants to choose between parents, nor Willemsen, Flaherty, Heaton, and Ritchey (1974), who neither exposed infants to stress nor allowed a choice, found differences between infants' behavior toward mothers versus fathers. In the nonstressful home environment, 7 to 13-month old infants showed no preferences for either parent on attachment behavior measures (Lamb, 1976a, 1977c). Between 15 and 24 months of age, the infants, especially the boys, showed preferences for their fathers on these measures, perhaps because fathers interacted more with them (Lamb, 1977a). Lewis and his colleagues, however, found that although unstressed 2-year-olds showed no preference for mothers or fathers, 1-year-olds touched, stayed near, and vocalized to their mothers more than their fathers (Ban & Lewis, 1974; Lewis, Weinraub, & Ban, 1972).

The same infants who were observed under low stress conditions in Lamb's (1976a, 1977a, 1977c) longitudinal study were also observed in more stressful laboratory contexts at 12 and 18 months (Lamb, 1976a). When 12- and 18-month-old infants became distressed and only one parent was present, the display of attachment behaviors increased and the infants organized their behavior similarly regardless of which parent was present. When both parents were present, however, distressed infants turned to their mothers preferentially.

Similarly, Cohen and Campos (1974) observed

infants' propensity to seek comfort from their mothers, fathers, or a stranger following separation from a parent. On such measures as frequency of approach, speed of approach, time in proximity, and use of the parent as a "secure base" from which to interact with a stranger, 10-, 13-, and 16-month-old infants showed preferences for their mothers over their fathers as well as clear preferences for fathers over strangers. However, contrary to these findings, 8- and 24-month-old infants in other studies did not show any preferences (Lamb, 1976b, 1976c). Perhaps the hierarchy among attachment figures is marked only during a relatively brief period or perhaps the 8- and 24-month samples were unusual. Further research is needed to explicate the relationships among interaction history, stress, and infants' preference for particular attachment figures.

Father-Infant Interaction and Cognitive Development. Although there is a wealth of research and theory linking mother-infant interaction and cognitive development (Bullowa, 1979; Clarke-Stewart, 1973; Shinn, 1978; Stevenson & Lamb, 1981), much less has been written about the relationship between father-infant interaction and cognitive development. Those studies that have been carried out indicate that fathers do influence their infants' cognitive development, although this effect may be mediated by maternal behavior (Clarke-Stewart, 1978b). Pedersen, Rubenstein, and Yarrow (1980) found a positive relationship between the amount of contact infants had with their fathers and infants' DQs. Clarke-Stewart (1978) found that although Bayley DQs were related to the amount of verbal and material stimulation provided by mothers, they were less consistently related to the amount of verbal and material stimulation by fathers. However, these infants' DQs were systematically related to the amount of play provided by fathers, the positiveness of the fathers' ratings of their infants, and the amount of infant-father interaction during a home observation. Cross-lagged analyses suggested that the direction of effects went as follows: Mother influences child, child influences father, and father influences mother, but the small sample size in Clarke-Stewart's study precludes strong conclusions.

Preterm Infants

In the previous discussions, we have noted that the characteristics of both parents and infants seem to influence parent-infant interaction as well as the infants' subsequent development. Moreover, as a result of interaction, both parents and infants appear to change one another.

This transactional approach has been particularly helpful in understanding the development of atypical infants. Recent studies of preterm infants (defined as infants born after less than 35 weeks of gestation and who weigh less than 2,500 grams at birth) reveal that parents of preterm infants and parents of full-term infants do interact differently with their infants. Moreover, these differences seem to have long-term consequences when (but only when) they are compounded by continued ill health or impoverished family environments.

Early researchers seeking direct linear relationships between infants' preterm status and their intellectual development were puzzled to find that although, on the average, preterms scored lower than did normal infants (Caputo & Mandell, 1970; Davies & Stewart, 1975; Sameroff & Chandler, 1975), the vast majority of preterm infants developed normally.

In an important review of this early literature, Sameroff and Chandler (1975) noted that socioeconomic status influenced the long-term impact of preterm delivery and of perinatal anoxia. The studies they reviewed repeatedly showed, except when the medical risk was extreme, that preterm delivery and birth complications had measurable effects only on infants in lower socioeconomic groups (Drillien, 1964; Francis-Williams & Davies, 1974; Illsley, 1966; McDonald, 1964). Enduring characteristics of the environment were more influential than such single critical incidents as preterm delivery (Drage, Barondes, & Fisher, 1969; Smith, Flick, Ferriss, & Sellman, 1972), suggesting that the effects of preterm delivery on later development were not due to delivery status per se but to a complex interaction among medical risk factors and postnatal experiential factors. Sameroff and Chandler (1975) and later Olson and Lamb (1982) proposed that the development of preterm infants was determined by the interaction among three types of variables: infant characteristics (including neurological damage or maturity, temperament, behavior, attractiveness), parental characteristics (including attitudes and behavioral styles related to social class, preparation for, and skills in, parenting, etc.), and the physical environment (including richness and patterning of stimulation).

Many recent studies have found that the mothers of preterm and full-term infants interact differently with their children. Prior to discharge, the mothers of preterms express less confidence in their parenting abilities than do mothers of full-terms, particularly if they have been denied contact with their babies (Seashore, Leifer, Barnett, & Leiderman, 1973). Moreover, their parental behavior is different: Prior to discharge, mothers of preterms less often touch their infants affectionately, hold them closely, or smile at them than do the mothers of full-term infants, regardless of the amount of prior contact (DiVitto & Goldberg, 1979; Leifer, Leiderman, Barnett, & Williams, 1972).

Mothers of preterm and full-term infants continue to interact differently during the months that follow. In particular, mothers of preterms seem more active or intrusive in interacting with their infants. When their babies are 1 to 4 months old, the mothers of preterms more actively initiate and maintain interactions than do mothers of full-terms (Brown & Bakeman, 1977, 1979), stimulating their infants during feeding, even while the infants are sucking (Field, 1980). By the time their infants are 2 years old, the mothers of preterms use fewer statements and more imperatives than do mothers of full-term 2-year olds.

These differences in maternal behavior may arise, at least in part, from differences in the infants' behavior. Newborn preterms score less optimally on the Brazelton neonatal assessment scales (Field, 1980) and are less alert and responsive (DiVitto & Goldberg, 1979) than are full-terms. Compared with full-term infants, 4-month-old preterms score lower on the Denver Developmental Screening Test, vocalize less (Field, 1980), are fussier and avert gaze from their mothers more frequently (Field, 1977, 1979a), and still are somewhat less responsive (Goldberg, Brachfeld, & DiVitto, 1980). At 8 months, preterms play less and fuss more than do full-terms (Brachfeld, Goldberg, & Sloman, 1980); at 2 years, they have shorter mean lengths of utterance, smaller vocabularies, and talk less than do full-terms. It is likely that maternal and infant behavior influence one another throughout infancy.

Differences in the quality of interaction may have long-term effects. There is some evidence that language development at 2 years of age is correlated with aspects of the mother-infant interaction at 4 months. Furthermore, the readiness of caretakers and preterm infants to engage in positive social interaction with each other during the first eight months of life appears modestly related to infant cognitive performance at 9 months of age (Beckwith et al., 1976). These relationships, which are similar to those reported in samples of full-term infants (Clarke-Stewart, 1973; Yarrow et al., 1975), underscore the potential formative importance of parent-infant interaction. In fact, a large comprehensive study of preterm infants showed that patterns of infant-parent interaction distinguished infants who remained at risk for developmental failure from those developing normally (Sigman & Parmelee, 1979).

Societal Influences on Attachment and Development

Nonmaternal Care

Sameroff (1982) has recently expanded his transactional model to include a higher order influence on persons and their immediate environment—societal changes. Nowhere has the impact of societal change been observed more keenly than in relation to the care of infants. Whether because of current societal emphasis on self-realization for women through the pursuit of rewarding careers or because of economic hardship forcing women to work, recent statistics show that 36% of the mothers of infants and toddlers are employed outside the home, either full- or part-time (Glick & Norton, 1979). Most of these infants receive supplementary care outside the family, but some are cared for by their fathers. In this discussion, we will review evidence concerning the effects of nonmaternal care on infant development. We will discuss research concerning daycare, maternal employment, and increased paternal care separately, even though these often co-occur in reality, because research on these three topics has proceeded independently.

Daycare. At one time, it was feared that children in daycare settings might suffer consequences qualitatively similar to those that follow prolonged separation or institutionalization—specifically, intellectual and language deficits, superficial friendliness, strong defenses against deep emotional involvement in others, and extreme ambivalence toward their mothers (Bowlby, 1951).

An early study by Blehar (1974) seemed to validate this concern. Using the Strange Situation to test children 5 months after enrollment, she reported that children entering daycare at 2 years of age seemed to be avoidant of their mothers on reunion, whereas those who entered daycare at 3 years of age seemed to behave angrily. Several other studies reviewed by Clarke-Stewart and Fein (*vol. II, chap. 11*) reported that, when tested in the Strange Situation, infants in daycare were more likely to be judged avoidantly attached than were home-reared infants. Further, Moore (1975) followed a group of English children for many years and reported that unstable supplementary care in the preschool years predicted maladjustment in adolescence.

By contrast, however, most studies show daycare has no adverse effects on child-mother attachment (Barahal, 1977; Brookhart & Hock, 1976; Cochran, 1977; Doyle, 1975; Doyle & Somers, 1975; Lieberman, 1977; Portnoy & Simmons, 1978; Ragozin, 1980; Roopnarine & Lamb, 1978, 1980).

Daycare children not only develop preferences for their mothers (Farran & Ramey, 1977; Kagan et al., 1978; Maccoby & Feldman, 1972), they also form attachments to consistent supplementary caretakers (Fox, 1977; Sagi et al., in press; Willis & Ricciuti, 1974). Several researchers using similar procedures and measures have failed to replicate Blehar's (1974) findings (Blanchard & Main, 1979; Moskowitz, Schwarz, & Corsini, 1977; Ragozin, 1980; Roopnarine & Lamb, 1978), leading Blanchard and Main (1979) to suggest that Blehar (1974) may have observed temporary adjustment difficulties shortly after enrollment in daycare rather than enduring consequences. Moore's (1975) study is hard to evaluate because alternative care experience was confounded with family instability. Moreover, even if daycare did produce more A-group attachments, this may in some cases reflect the greater independence of daycare children rather than insecurity of attachments.

If daycare has no adverse effects on infant-mother relationships, does it affect children's interactions with unfamiliar adults? To date, no consistent differences have been found. Schwarz, Strickland, and Krolick (1974) reported that daycare children were more physically and verbally aggressive toward, and less cooperative with, adults than were home-reared children, but these findings have not replicated in three other studies (Clarke-Stewart, 1980; Lay & Meyer, 1972; Macrae & Herbert-Jackson, 1976). Similarly, McCutcheon and Calhoun (1976) reported that because of their greater involvement with peers, daycare children interacted less with adults. However, just the opposite was found in two other studies (Cochran, 1977; Finkelstein & Wilson, 1977). These discrepancies are hard to explain because researchers have not used standardized measures.

Does daycare adversely affect children's peer relationships—for example, by increasing their aggressiveness? Here again the findings seem to be inconsistent. Schwarz et al. (1974) reported that center-reared children were more aggressive than were home-reared children of the same age. However, similar effects were not observed in China (Kessen, 1975) nor in the Soviet Union (Bronfenbrenner, 1970) by informal observers. Moreover, Becker (1977) reported that, for home-reared children, regular contact with peers (like that daycare children experience) increased peer competence.

Although the evidence thus suggests that daycare has no necessary or consistent ill effects on young children, it would be premature to conclude that none occur. First, most of the research has been concerned with center-based care, even though only 10% of the children receiving supplementary care are enrolled in such centers (Belsky & Steinberg, 1978). Second, many of the studies have involved outcome measures (e.g., amount of distress on separation) that are of questionable validity. Third, few studies involve preenrollment assessments to determine whether the daycare and home-care groups are initially comparable: those that have done so (Roopnarine & Lamb, 1978, 1980) suggest that preenrollment differences may be greater than later ones! Fourth, researchers have implicitly assumed that the daycare experience is similar for all young children. They have, thus, failed to take into account such factors as quality of care, caretaker-child ratio, number and age of other children, and childcare philosophy, all of which are likely to have a significant effect on the child's development. Thus, little is known about the manner in which different aspects of extrafamilial care affect early child development (Belsky & Steinberg, 1978; Belsky, Steinberg, & Walker, 1982).

Maternal Employment. By contrast, studies of maternal employment have revealed consistent relationships between employment and both maternal attitudes and caretaking behavior. Moreover, these attitudes and behaviors seem to influence the infants' attachment behaviors toward their mothers.

For instance, mothers who resumed paid work early in the infants' lives reported being less anxious about separation from their infants and more trusting of supplementary caretakers than were unemployed mothers (Hock, 1978). Employed mothers were found, not surprisingly, to have a higher career orientation than unemployed mothers. More surprising, perhaps, was the negative correlation between career orientation and reported infant-attachment behavior: The greater the mothers' career orientation, the less the reported separation distress in their infants. In addition, Hock reported that the greater their career orientation, the less mothers reported anxiety about separation and apprehension about alternate caretakers. On the other hand, all of these negative correlations among employed mothers' attitudes toward separation and alternative caretakers and perceptions of infant distress were positive for unemployed mothers (Hock, 1978, 1980; Hock, Christman, & Hock, 1980). It thus seemed that mothers who were confident in their career commitment and in alternative childcare arrangements were rewarded with less anxious children. At least, that is what these mothers reported!

Another group of researchers likewise concluded that maternal employment did not influence infant-attachment behavior, although the mothers' attitudes toward employment did (Owen, Chase-Lansdale, & Lamb, in preparation). Employed mothers valued work more and parenthood less than did the unemployed mothers. In addition, employed mothers reported receiving less support from families and friends for their childcare plans and only marginally more help from their husbands (who on the other hand reported that they provided substantially more help!) than did the nonemployed mothers. Satisfaction with parenthood was positively correlated with the value of parenthood and was negatively correlated with both the perceived value of work and resentment of the infant. These attitudes were related to individual differences in the infants' Strange Situation behavior at 12 months of age. Non-B babies tended to have mothers who valued work highly, and valued parenthood less. Although employed mothers were somewhat more likely to have A- or C-group infants than were nonworking mothers, this finding was mediated by the attitudinal differences reported earlier. Employed mothers who valued both parenthood and work tended to have B-group babies, indicating that maternal employment per se does not necessarily result in "insecure" mother-infant attachments.

One other recent study also showed that infants were more likely to have non-B-group attachments to their mothers if their mothers were employed outside the home (Vaughn, Gove, & Egeland, 1980). Thompson et al. (1982), however, reported that the infants of employed mothers were not more likely to be rated as "insecure." Indeed, some infants shifted into the B classification between 12 and 19 months of age when mothers worked outside the home. Furthermore, when infants of employed mothers are cared for by a consistent caretaker in a home setting, with no more than one other child present, few differences in Strange Situation behavior are observed. In one study (Burke & Weir, 1976), for instance, the infants of nonworking mothers were the ones who showed negative behavior—displaying more resistant (angry) behavior toward the stranger in the Strange Situation.

S. Cohen (1978) explored the effects of maternal employment on mother-infant interaction and infant cognitive performance in a sample of preterm infants. Maternal employment had no apparent effect in the first year of life, but by the second year, differences were evident: the nonworking mothers had more positive interactions with their infants, who vocalized more and had higher developmental quotients. Unfortunately, the findings of this study are hard to interpret because there were differences between the two groups at the outset: Women who later sought employment had smaller and lighter infants and were more likely to be single parents. Consequently, it is not clear that the group differences should be attributed to maternal employment status.

In all, these studies suggest that although maternal employment may have adverse effects on infant development, it need not. Moreover, the effects that have been found may be due to differences in maternal attitudes and behavior and the quality of alternative childcare rather than to maternal employment per se.

Paternal Care. In a few families today, fathers assume primary responsibility for childcare. There has been little research on the parental behavior of such fathers, and the available results are inconsistent. Field (1978) observed primary caretaking fathers, secondary caretaking fathers, and primary caretaking mothers engaging in face-to-face interaction with their 4-month-old infants. She found that the primary caretaking fathers and mothers smiled more and emitted more imitative grimaces and high-pitched imitative vocalizations than did secondary caretaking fathers, whereas the primary and secondary caretaking fathers engaged in more poking and game playing and less holding of the infant's limbs than did primary caretaking mothers. Unfortunately, only 3 minutes of interaction were recorded per dyad and no secondary caretaking mothers were studied, making it impossible to assess the effects of gender and parental role in a factorial design.

In a longitudinal study of highly involved Swedish fathers, their wives, and their infants, Lamb and his colleagues (Lamb, Frodi, Frodi, & Hwang, 1982; Lamb, Frodi, Hwang, Frodi & Steinberg, 1982a, 1982b) found that parental gender had a greater effect on parental behavior than did caretaking role. Home observations at 3, 8, and 16 months of age revealed that the Swedish mothers resembled American mothers in their tendency to hold, tend to, display affection toward, smile at, and vocalize to their infants more than fathers, and this was true regardless of relative parental involvement in caretaking. Unfortunately, none of the fathers in these studies were primary caretakers from birth on. Moreover, the average highly involved father only assumed primary responsibility for about 3 months, beginning when the infants were weaned at 5 to 6 months of age. Regardless of degree of paternal involvement, the 8- and 16-month-old infants showed preferences for their mothers on attachment behavior measures (Lamb, Frodi, Hwang, & Frodi, 1983). Moreover, although the "security" of infant-father attachment in the Strange Situation was correlated with infant sociability toward unfamiliar adults, degree of paternal involvement did not affect either sociability or the relative predictive validity of the two infant-parent attachments (Lamb, Hwang, Frodi, & Frodi, 1982).

Peer Interactions

The return of mothers to work while their children are infants has not only determined who cares for those infants; for those infants placed in daycare, it has also provided increased opportunity for interacting with peers. Moreover, contrary to widespread belief, even young infants do seem to interact with those peers. Most research on infant-infant interaction has focused on the structure of such interactions, indicating that from earliest infancy children react to one another and that their interactions with peers become more complex and sophisticated as infants become more cognitively, vocally, physically, and socially competent.

During the first 2 months of life, extensive visual regard is the usual mode of interaction between familiar infants (Bridges, 1933; Lichtenberger, 1965; Vincze, 1971), while during the next 2 months, touching becomes increasingly prominent (Lichtenberger, 1965; Shirley, 1933; Vincze, 1971). During the third-quarter year of life, interactions become colored with positive affect: Peer-directed smiling and approaching/following become important features of infant-infant interactions. From this point on, the complexity of peer interaction increases logarithmically: in the last quarter of the first year of life, giving and accepting toys first occurs, as does engagement in conventional games, such as peek-a-boo, ball, and chase (Bridges, 1933; Durfee & Lee, 1973; Lichtenberger, 1965; Maudry & Nekula, 1939; Vincze, 1971). Vocal exchanges involving turn-taking as well as social imitation have been observed among peers from the fifth-quarter year of life (Bridges, 1933; Eckerman, Whatley, & Kutz, 1975; Lichtenberger, 1965). Moreover, the frequency and complexity of such exchanges and of negative incidents, such as fighting over toys, increase over the course of the second year (Becker, 1977; Eckerman et al., 1975; Field, 1979a; Maudry & Nekula, 1939; Mueller & Brenner, 1977; Mueller & Rich, 1976).

Researchers have disagreed regarding the onset of true peer interaction, depending on their implicit definitions of this term (Field & Roopnarine, 1982). Although some reciprocal exchanges occur during the first year, they become much more common during the second year of life; by contrast, social behaviors that do not elicit responses are much more common in the first year than they are later (Durfee & Lee, 1973; Mueller & Lucas, 1975; Ross & Goldman, 1977). Regardless of one's definition of true interaction, however, it is clear that peers affect one another from earliest infancy. (We have already documented the contagious effects of peer crying in the neonatal period: Martin & Clarke, 1982; Sagi & Hoffman, 1976; Simner, 1971).

Influences on Peer Interactions. A number of factors affect the amount and complexity of peer interaction. Familiarity if one important variable. Researchers find that infants interact more, initiate a larger number of more complex interactions, and display more positive affect when interacting with familiar rather than with unfamiliar peers (Becker, 1977; Bridges, 1933; W. Bronson, 1975; Field & Ignatoff, 1980; Fischoff, 1974; Lewis, Young, Brooks, & Michalson, 1975; Young & Lewis, 1979). W. Bronson (1975) has suggested that this is because familiar peers are simply more predictable; however, prior experience with peers also facilitates interaction with new (i.e., unfamiliar) peers.

Another factor that influences peer interaction is the number of infants in the group. In fact, the developmental changes in complexity of interaction described occur only in dyadic rather than small-group contexts (W. Bronson, 1974, 1975; Vandell, 1976). Moreover, Dragsten and Lee (1973) found that the effects of group size on peer interaction were greater than the effects of familiarity.

The presence of adults also affects peer interactions. Peers interact with each other less when their mothers are present than when they are absent (Field, 1979a; Rubenstein & Howes, 1976). Nevertheless, in many contexts, infants still interact more with peers than with their mothers.

The physical context is also important: Infants and toddlers pay more attention to peers in their own homes than in unfamiliar settings (Becker, 1977; Fischoff, 1974; Rubenstein & Howes, 1976). Siblings, too, appear to interact with each other much less when observed in an unfamiliar laboratory (Lamb, 1978a, 1978b) than when observed in their own homes (Abramovitch, Pepler, & Corter, 1982). The presence of toys affects peer interaction as well, although this effect seems quite complex. Mueller and Lucas (1975) noted that toys often enhanced the positiveness of peer interaction—especially in the fourth- and fifth-quarter years—because they gave infants a common focus (exploration of the toys) and thus facilitated their discovery of each other. However, toys may have less effect on pairs or groups of unfamiliar infants and toddlers than on familiar dyads (Lewis et al., 1975). Moreover, although the number of toys is directly related to the positiveness of interactions (Buhler, 1933; Maudry & Nekula, 1939), the presence of toys diminishes the amount of attention actually directed toward peers (Eckerman & Whatley, 1977; Ramey & Finkelstein, 1978; Vandell, Wilson, & Buchanan, 1980).

Individual Differences. Peer interactions are also influenced by individual differences in sociability that are stable from the first year of life onward. There are stable individual differences in the frequency of initiations, the probability of successful initiations, the probability of accepting others' initiatives, and the frequency of directed social behaviors (W. Bronson, 1975; Lamb, 1978a; Lee, 1973; Vandell, 1976). Two potential determinants of these individual differences—sibling status and Strange Situation classification—have been explored empirically. Although contrary findings were reported by Shirley (1933), researchers have recently reported that latter-born infants are less sociable than are firstborns (Lewis et al., 1975; Vandell, Wilson, & Whalen, 1981). Furthermore, infants who are frequently exposed to older children other than siblings have fewer and briefer interactions with peers (Vandell et al., 1981), even though, as noted earlier, experience with peers is associated with increased sociability. Perhaps the negative effects of encounters with older children are due to the fact that interactions with older children involve more passive watching and submission than do interations with peers (Abramovitch, Corter, & Lando, 1979; Lamb, 1978a, 1978b).

Furthermore, as mentioned earlier, B-group infants—especially B1 and B2 infants—appear more socially competent with peers than those in the A and C groups (Easterbrooks & Lamb, 1979; Pastor, 1981; Sroufe, in press; Waters, Wippman, & Sroufe, 1979).

Summary

In the preceding section, we provided a somewhat selective discussion of the literature on infantile social development, focusing on those issues around which we feel the most influential current research has centered. We first described two important theories of social development—Mahler's (Mahler et al., 1975) theory of separation-individuation, which primarily has influenced clinicians, and the Bowlby-Ainsworth approach, which has had a profound effect on developmental researchers.

Next, we reviewed work on Strange Situation assessments of infants' attachment to their mothers, followed by research on mothers' bonding to their infants. In each of these cases, we described intense controversies regarding interpretation of findings.

Then, we discussed father-infant interaction and the development of father-infant attachment, providing evidence that, although fathers seem capable of caring for their infants just as sensitively as mothers, most fathers today may not act on such skills. Moreover, under conditions of stress, infants raised in most contemporary American families still seem to turn preferentially to their mother rather than their father, at least during certain periods of development.

Finally, we described data bearing on current issues of social significance: parent-child interaction with preterm infants, nonmaternal care of infants, and infant-infant interaction. As the length and diverse contents of this section indicate, social development during infancy has been a popular focus for researchers and theorists in the last decade. Still, as the raging controversies described in several sections suggest, many questions remain unanswered—much research remains to be done.

EPILOGUE

In each of the three major sections of this chapter, we have attempted to document the role that emotion, temperament, and social interaction play as important regulators of human behavior. We would now like to briefly trace some of the general implications for future research.

First, we predict a decline in the number of descriptive studies of socioemotional development and an increase in those dealing with the determinants and consequences of socioemotional phenomena. This trend is already clear in the field of attachment, and is now beginning to be evident in research on emotion and temperament as well.

Second, the concern with determinants and consequences in socioemotional development will lead researchers to search for naturalistic and ecologically valid approaches to test the effects that temperament, emotion, and social interaction have on other phenomena. Accordingly, we expect a resurgence of interest in cross-cultural research, in research with special populations such as the deaf and the blind, and in research with groups varying in child-rearing practices within our own culture. Such research is uniquely suited to investigate current issues such as those on the universality or cultural specificity of socioemotional processes, or the way in which particular experiences direct the course of socioemotional development.

Third, we predict increasing methodological sophistication in studies of social interaction; in particular the new technologies for assessing facial and vocal expressions are likely to be applied soon to assess individual differences in the quality of caretaker-infant interaction. Moreover, we can expect great advancements in measuring specific emotional states, both in laboratory and naturalistic settings.

Fourth, we predict a dramatic increase in research on socioemotional processes during the child's second and third years of life. At these ages, important complex emotions like shame, guilt, and envy begin to appear. Emotional experience and expression begin to be socialized extensively, and the appearance of language and symbolic capacities provide the child powerful new means of regulating and understanding emotions and social interaction.

Other predictions could be made, but those listed already make it clear that the excitement that exists today concerning research on socioemotional development will continue for many years. It seems to us that we are on the threshold of a period of major discovery and growth of knowledge about emotional and social development, a period that may rival that of the cognitive revolution of the 1950s and the psycholinguistic revolution of the 1960s.

NOTES

[1]This is not to suggest that there should be no cultural differences in reactions to individual differences in parameters of emotionality. It is conceivable that some cultures might welcome high activity levels and, thus, encourage active children. Other cultures however might restrict activity levels forcefully (Thomas & Chess, 1981). What we are proposing here is rather a dimension of the impact that individual differences in emotionality have—a dimension that ranges from social codified interpretations of individual differences in behavior to genetically conditioned reactivity to individual differences. Reactions to what we are proposing as temperamental traits are closer to the genetically conditioned end of the dimension.

REFERENCES

Abramovitch, R., Corter, C., & Lando, B. Sibling interaction in the home. *Child Development,* 1979, *50,* 997–1003.

Abramovitch, R., Pepler, D., & Corter, C. Patterns of sibling interaction among preschool-age children. In M. E. Lamb & B. Sutton-Smith (Eds.), *Sibling relationships: Their nature and importance across the life span.* Hillsdale, N.J.: Erlbaum, 1982.

Adamson, L., Als, H., Tronick, E., & Brazelton, T. B. The development of social reciprocity between a sighted infant and her blind parents. *Journal of the American Academy of Child Psychiatry,* 1977, *16,* 194–207.

Ainsworth, M. D. S. Object relations, dependency and attachment: A theoretical review of the infant-mother relationship. *Child Development,* 1969, *40,* 969–1025.

Ainsworth, M. D. S. The development of infant-mother attachment. In B. M. Caldwell & H. N. Ricciuti (Eds.), *Review of child development research* (Vol. 3). Chicago: University of Chicago Press, 1973.

Ainsworth, M. D. S. Attachment as related to mother-infant interaction. In J. S. Rosenblatt, R. A. Hinde, C. Beer, & M. Busnel (Eds.), *Advances in the study of behavior* (Vol. 9). New York: Academic Press, 1979.

Ainsworth, M. D. S., & Bell, S. M. Some contemporary patterns of mother-infant interaction in the feeding situation. In A. Ambrose (Ed.), *Stimulation in early infancy.* New York: Academic Press, 1969.

Ainsworth, M. D. S., Bell, S. M., & Stayton, D. J. Individual differences in strange-situation behavior of one-year-olds. In H. R. Schaffer (Ed.), *The origins of human social relations.* New York: Academic Press, 1971.

Ainsworth, M. D. S., Bell, S. M., & Stayton, D. J. Individual differences in the development of some attachment behaviors. *Merrill-Palmer Quarterly,* 1972, *18,* 123–143.

Ainsworth, M. D. S., Bell, S. M., & Stayton, D. J. Infant mother attachment and social development: "Socialization" as a product of reciprocal responsiveness to signals. In M. P. M. Richards (Ed.) *The integration of a child into a social world.* Cambridge: Cambridge University Press, 1974.

Ainsworth, M. D. S., & Blehar, M., Waters, E., & Wall, S. *Patterns of attachment.* Hillsdale, N.J.: Erlbaum, 1978.

Ainsworth, M. D. S., & Wittig, B. Attachment and exploratory behavior of one-year-olds in a strange situation. In B. Foss (Ed.), *Determinants of infant behavior* (Vol. 4). New York: Wiley, 1969.

Allport, F. *Social psychology.* Boston: Houghton Mifflin, 1924.

Allport, G. W. *Personality: A psychosocial interpretation.* New York: Holt, 1937.

Ambrose, J. The development of the smiling response in early infancy. In B. Foss (Ed.), *Determinants of infant behavior* (Vol. 1). New York: Wiley, 1961.

Andrew, R. Evolution of facial expression. *Science,* 1963, *142,* 1034–1041.

Appel, M., & Campos, J. J. Binocular disparity as a discriminable stimulus parameter for young infants. *Journal of Experimental Child Psychology,* 1977, *23,* 47–56.

Arend, R., Gove, F., & Sroufe, L. A. Continuity of individual adaptation from infancy to kindergarten: A predictive study of ego-resiliency and curiosity in preschoolers. *Child Development,* 1979, *50,* 950–959.

Arnold, M. *Emotion and personality.* New York: Columbia University Press, 1960.

Ball, W., & Tronick, E. Infant response to impending collision: Optical and real. *Science,* 1971, *171,* 818–820.

Bain, A. *The emotions and the will.* London: J. W. Parker and Son, 1859.

Ban, P., & Lewis, M. Mothers and fathers, girls and boys: Attachment behavior in the one-year-old. *Merrill-Palmer Quarterly,* 1974, *20,* 195–204.

Bandura, A. *Social learning theory.* Englewood Cliffs, N.J.: Prentice-Hall, 1977.

Barahal, R. *A comparison of parent-infant attachment and interaction patterns in day care and non-day care family groups.* Unpublished doctoral dissertation, Cornell University, 1977.

Barrera, M., & Maurer D. The perception of facial expressions by the three-month-old. *Child Development,* 1981, *52,* 203–206.

Bates, J. E. The concept of difficult temperament. *Merrill-Palmer Quarterly,* 1980, *26,* 299–320.

Bates, J. E., Freeland, C., & Lounsbury, M. Measurement of infant difficultness. *Child Development,* 1979, *50,* 794–803.

Bateson, G., Jackson, D., Haley, J., & Weakland, J. Toward a theory of schizophrenia. *Behavioral Science,* 1956, *4,* 251–264.

Bax, M. Clinical analysis of the cry. *Developmental Medicine and Child Neurology,* 1975, *17,* 799–801.

Bayley, N. Individual patterns of development. *Child Development,* 1956, *27,* 45–74.

Bayley, N. *Bayley scales of infant development.* New York: Psychological Corporation, 1969.

Bayley, N., & Schaefer, E. Correlations of maternal and child behaviors with the development of mental abilities: Data from the Berkeley growth study. *Monographs of the Society for Research in Child Development,* 1964, *29*(6, Whole No. 97).

Becker, J. A learning analysis of the development of peer oriented behaviors in nine-month-old infants. *Developmental Psychology,* 1977, *13,* 481–491.

Beckwith, L. Prediction of emotional and social behavior. In J. Osofsky (Ed.), *Handbook of infant development.* New York: Wiley, 1979.

Beckwith, L., Cohen, S., Kopp, C., Parmalee, A., & Marcy, T. Caregiver-infant interaction and early cognitive development in preterm infants. *Child Development,* 1976, *47,* 579–587.

Beebe-Center, J. *The psychology of pleasantness and unpleasantness.* New York: Van Nostrand, 1932.

Bell, R. Q. A reinterpretation of the direction of effects in studies of socialization. *Psychological Review,* 1968, *75,* 63–72.

Bell, R. Q., Weller, G., & Waldrop, M. F. Newborn and preschooler: Organization of behavior and relations between periods. *Monographs of the Society for Research in Child Development,* 1971, *36*(1 and 2, Serial No. 142).

Bell, S. M. The development of the concept of the object and its relationship to infant-mother attachment. *Child Development,* 1970, *41,* 291–312.

Bell, S. M., & Ainsworth, M. Infant crying and maternal responsiveness. *Child Development,* 1972, *43,* 1171–1190.

Belsky, J. Mother-father-infant interaction: A naturalistic observational study. *Developmental Psychology,* 1979, *15,* 601–607.

Belsky, J. Early human experience: A family perspective. *Developmental Psychology,* 1981, *17,* 3–23.

Belsky, J., Rovine, M., & Taylor, D. The origins of individual differences in infant-mother attachment: Maternal and infant contributions. *Child Development,* in press.

Belsky, J., & Steinberg, L. D. The effects of daycare: A critical review. *Child Development,* 1978, *49,* 929–949.

Belsky, J., Steinberg, L. D., & Walker, A. The ecology of child care. In M. E. Lamb (Ed.), *Nontraditional families: Parenting and child development.* Hillsdale, N.J.: Erlbaum, 1982.

Bentley, M. Is "emotion" more than a chapter heading? In C. Murchison (Ed.), *Feelings and emotions—The Wittenberg Symposium.* Worcester, Mass.: Clark University Press, 1928.

Berlyne, D. *Conflict, arousal, and curiosity.* New York: McGraw-Hill, 1960.

Berscheid, E., & Walster, E. When does a harm-doer compensate a victim? *Journal of Personality and Social Psychology,* 1967, *6,* 435–441.

Bertalanffy, L. von. *General systems theory: Foundations, development, applications.* New York: George Braziller, 1968.

Bertenthal, B., Campos, J., & Barrett, K. Self-produced locomotion: An organizer of emotional, cognitive, and social development in infancy. In R. N. Emde & R. J. Harmon (Eds.), *Continuities and discontinuities in development.* New York: Plenum, 1983.

Birdwhistell, R. *Kinesics and context.* Philadelphia: University of Pennsylvania Press, 1970.

Birns, B., Blank, M., & Bridger, W. The effectiveness of various soothing techniques on human neonates. *Psychosomatic Medicine,* 1966, *28,* 316–322.

Birns, B., & Golden, M. Prediction of intellectual performance at 3 years from infant tests and personality measures. *Merrill-Palmer Quarterly,* 1972, *18,* 53–58.

Bischof, N. A systems approach toward the functional connections of attachment and fear. *Child Development,* 1975, *46,* 801–817.

Blanchard, M., & Main, M. Avoidance of the attachment figure and social-emotional adjustment in daycare infants. *Developmental Psychology,* 1979, *15,* 445–446.

Blanchard, R., & Biller, H. Father availability and academic performance among third-grade boys. *Developmental Psychology,* 1971, *4,* 301–305.

Blanck, G. & Blanck, R. *Ego psychology: Theory and practice.* New York: Columbia University Press, 1974.

Blehar, M. Anxious attachment and defensive reactions associated with daycare. *Child Development,* 1974, *45,* 683–692.

Blehar, M., Lieberman, A. F., & Ainsworth, M. Early face-to-face interaction and its relation to later infant-mother attachment. *Child Development,* 1977, *48,* 182–194.

Boccia, M., & Campos, J. *Maternal emotional signalling: Its effect on infants' reaction to strangers.* Paper presented at the meeting of the Society for Research in Child Development, Detroit, April 1983.

Bohlin, G., Hagekull, B., & Lindhagen, K. Dimensions of infant behavior. *Infant Behavior and Development,* 1981, *4,* 83–96.

Bohman, M., & Sigvardson, S. Long-term effects of early institutional care: A prospective longitudinal study. In S. Chess & A. Thomas (Eds.), *Annual progress in child psychiatry and child development.* New York: Brunner/Mazel, 1980.

Boucher, J., & Carlson, G. Recognition of facial expressions in three cultures. *Journal of Cross-Cultural Psychology,* 1980, *11,* 263–280.

Bower, G. Mood and memory. *American Psychologist,* 1981, *36,* 128–148.

Bower, T. G. R. *Development in infancy.* San Francisco: W. H. Freeman, 1974.

Bower, T. G. R. Repetitive processes in child development. *Scientific American,* 1976, *235,* 38–47.

Bower, T. G. R., Broughton, J., & Moore, M. Infant responses to approaching objects: An indicator of response to distal variables. *Perception & Psychophysics,* 1970, *9,* 193–196.

Bowlby, J. *Maternal care and mental health.* Geneva: World Health Organization, 1951.

Bowlby, J. The nature of the child's tie to his mother. *International Journal of Psychoanalysis,* 1958, *39,* 350–373.

Bowlby, J. *Attachment and loss,* vol. 1, *Attachment.* New York: Basic Books, 1969.

Bowlby, J. *Attachment and loss,* vol. 2, *Separation.* New York: Basic Books, 1973.

Bowlby, J. *Attachment and loss,* vol. 3, *Loss.* New York: Basic Books, 1980.

Brachfeld, S., Goldberg, S., & Sloman, J. *Parent-infant interaction in free play at 8 and 12 months: Effects of prematurity and immaturity.* Manuscript submitted for publication, 1980.

Brackbill, Y. Extinction of the smiling response in infants as a function of reinforcement. *Child Development,* 1958, *29,* 115–124.

Brackbill, Y. Cumulative effects of continuous stimulation on arousal level in infants. *Child Development,* 1971, *42,* 17–26.

Brackbill, Y., Adams, G., Crowell, D., & Gray, M. Arousal level in neonates and preschool children under continuous auditory stimulation. *Journal of Experimental Child Psychology,* 1966, *4,* 178–188.

Brannigan, C., & Humphries, D. Human non-verbal behavior, a means of communication. In N. Blurton-Jones (Ed.), *Ethological studies of child behaviour.* Cambridge: At the University Press, 1972.

Brazelton, T. B. *Neonatal behavioral assessment scale.* Philadelphia: J. B. Lippincott, 1973.

Brazelton, T. B. Precursors for the development of emotions in early infancy. In R. Plutchik & H. Kellerman (Eds.), *Emotions in early development,* vol. 2, *The emotions.* New York: Academic Press, 1983.

Brazelton, T. B., Tronick, E., Adamson, L., Als, H., & Wise, S. Early mother-infant reciprocity.

In M. Hofer (Ed.), *Parent-infant interaction.* Amsterdam: Excerpta Medica, 1975.

Brenner, C. *An elementary textbook of psychoanalysis.* New York: Doubleday, 1955.

Bretherton, I., Bates, E., Benigni, L., Camaioni, L., & Volterra, V. Relationships between cognition, communication, and quality of attachment. In E. Bates, L. Benigni, I. Bretherton, L. Camaioni, & V. Volterra (Eds.), *The emergence of symbols: Cognition and communication in infancy.* New York: Academic Press, 1979.

Breuer, J., & Freud, S. Studies in hysteria. *Nervous and Mental Disease Monographs,* 1895, No. 61.

Bridger, W., & Reiser, M. Psychophysiological studies of the neonate: An approach toward the methodological and theoretical problems involved. *Psychosomatic Medicine,* 1959, *21,* 265–276.

Bridges, K. M. A genetic theory of the emotions. *Journal of Genetic Psychology,* 1930, *37,* 514–527.

Bridges, K. M. Emotional development in early infancy. *Child Development,* 1932, *3,* 324–341.

Bridges, K. M. A study of social development in early infancy. *Child Development,* 1933, *4,* 36–49.

Bridges, R., Rosenblatt, J. S., & Feder, H. Serum progesterone concentrations and maternal behavior in rats after pregnancy termination: Behavioral stimulation after progesterone withdrawal and inhibition by progesterone maintenance. *Endocrinology,* 1978, *102,* 258–267.

Bridges, R., Zarrow, M. X., & Denenberg, V. H. The role of neonatal androgen in the expression of hormonally induced maternal responsiveness in the adult rat. *Hormones and Behavior,* 1973, *4,* 315–322.

Bronfenbrenner, U. Early deprivation: A cross-species analysis. In G. Newton & S. Levine (Eds.), *Early experience and behavior.* Springfield, Ill.: Charles C. Thomas, 1968.

Bronfenbrenner, U. *Two worlds of childhood.* New York: Simon & Schuster, 1970.

Bronson, G. W. The fear of novelty. *Psychological Bulletin,* 1968, *69,* 350–358.

Bronson, G. W. Infants' reactions to unfamiliar persons and novel objects. *Monographs of the Society for Research in Child Development,* 1972, *37*(Serial No. 148).

Bronson, G. W. Aversive reactions to strangers: A dual process interpretation. *Child Development,* 1978, *49,* 495–499.

Bronson, W. Mother-toddler interaction: A perspective on studying the development of competence. *Merrill-Palmer Quarterly,* 1974, *20,* 275–301.

Bronson, W. Peer-peer interactions in the second year of life. In M. Lewis & L. A. Rosenblum (Eds.), *Friendship and peer relations.* New York: Wiley, 1975.

Brookhart, J., & Hock, E. The effects of experimental context and experiential background on infants' behavior toward their mothers and a stranger. *Child Development,* 1976, *47,* 330–340.

Brooks, J., & Lewis, M. Infants' responses to strangers: Midget, adult, and child. *Child Development,* 1976, *47,* 323–332.

Brossard, L., & Décarie, T. Comparative reinforcing effects of eight stimulations on the smiling responses of infants. *Journal of Child Psychology and Psychiatry,* 1968, *9,* 51–60.

Brossard, M. The infant's conception of object permanence and his reactions to strangers. In T. Décarie (Ed.), *The infant's reaction to strangers.* New York: International Universities Press, 1974.

Brown, J. V., & Bakeman, R. *Behavioral dialogues between mothers and infants: The effects of prematurity.* Paper presented at the meeting of the American Pediatric Society, San Francisco, April 1977.

Brown, J. V., & Bakeman, R. Relationships of human mothers with their infants during the first year of life. In R. W. Bell & W. P. Smotherman (Eds.), *Maternal influences and early behavior.* New York: Prentice-Hall, 1979. (Spectrum Books).

Bruch, H. Transformation of oral impulses in eating disorders. *Psychiatry Quarterly,* 1961, *35,* 458.

Bruner, J. Early social interaction and language acquisition. In H. R. Schaffer (Ed.), *Studies in mother-infant interaction.* New York: Academic Press, 1977.

Bruner, J., & Koslowski, B. Learning to use a lever. *Child Development,* 1972, *43,* 790–799.

Bruner, J., & Postman, L. Emotional selectivity in perception and reaction. *Journal of Personality,* 1947, *16,* 69–77.

Buck, R. Nonverbal communication of affect in children. *Journal of Personality and Social Psychology,* 1975, *31,* 644–653.

Buck, R. Nonverbal communication of affect in preschool children: Relationships with personality and skin conductance. *Journal of Personality and Social Psychology,* 1977, *35,* 225–236.

Buckley, W. (Ed.), *Modern systems research for the behavioral scientist.* Chicago: Aldine, 1968.

Buechler, S., & Izard, C. E. On the emergence,

functions, and regulation of some emotion expressions in infancy. In R. Plutchik & H. Kellerman (Eds.), *Emotions in early development,* vol. 2, *The Emotions.* New York: Academic Press, 1983.

Buhler, C. *The first year of life.* New York: John Day, 1930.

Buhler, C. The social behavior of children. In C. Murchison (Ed.), *Handbook of child psychology.* Worcester, Mass.: Clark University Press, 1933.

Bullowa, M. *Before speech: The beginning of interpersonal communication.* New York: Cambridge University Press, 1979.

Burke, R., & Weir, T. Relationship of wives' employment status to husband, wife, and pair satisfaction and performance. *Journal of Marriage and the Family,* 1976, *38,* 279–287.

Bushnell, J. Discrimination of faces by young infants. *Journal of Experimental Child Psychology,* 1982, *33,* 298–308.

Buss, A. H., & Plomin, R. *A temperament theory of personality development.* New York: Wiley, 1975.

Buss, D. M., Block, J. H., & Block, J. Preschool activity level: Personality correlates and development implications. *Child Development,* 1980, *51,* 401–408.

Butterfield, P., Emde, R. N., Svejda, M., & Neiman, S. Silver nitrate and the eyes of the newborn: Effects on parental responsiveness during initial social interaction. In R. N. Emde & R. J. Harmon (Eds.), *The development of attachment and affiliative systems: Psychobiological aspects.* New York: Plenum, 1982.

Cadoret, R., Cunningham, L., Loftus, R., & Edwards, J. Studies of adoptees from psychiatrically disturbed biological parents. II. Temperamental, hyperactive, anti-social and developmental variables. *Journal of Pediatrics,* 1975, *87,* 301–306.

Cairns, R. Attachment and dependency: A psychobiological and social-learning synthesis. In J. A. Gewirtz (Ed.), *Attachment and dependency.* New York: Wiley, 1972.

Caldwell, B. The effects of infant care. In M. Hoffman & L. Hoffman (Eds.), *Review of child development research* (Vol. 1). New York: Russell Sage Foundation, 1964.

Caldwell, B. *Manual of the HOME scale for measuring the environment.* Unpublished manuscript, 1978.

Campbell, D., Kuyek, J., Lang, E., & Partington, M. Motor activity in early life. Daily motor activity output in neonatal period. *Biology of the Neonate,* 1971, *181,* 108–120.

Campbell, S. Mother-infant interactions as a function of maternal ratings of temperament. *Child Psychiatry and Human Development,* 1979, *10,* 67–76.

Campos, J. J. Heart rate: A sensitive tool for the study of emotional development. In L. P. Lipsitt (Ed.), *Developmental psychobiology: The significance of infancy.* Hillsdale, N.J.: Erlbaum, 1976.

Campos, J. J., Emde, R. N., Gaensbauer, T. J., & Henderson, C. Cardiac and behavioral interrelationships in the reactions of infants to strangers. *Developmental Psychology,* 1975, *11,* 589–601.

Campos, J. J., Hiatt, S., Ramsay, D., Henderson, C., & Svejda, M. The emergence of fear of heights. In M. Lewis & L. Rosenblum (Eds.), *The development of affect.* New York: Plenum, 1978.

Campos, J. J., & Stenberg, C. Perception, appraisal, and emotion: The onset of social referencing. In M. E. Lamb & L. R. Sherrod (Eds.), *Infant social cognition: Empirical and theoretical considerations.* Hillsdale, N.J.: Erlbaum, 1981.

Caputo, D. V., & Mandell, W. Consequences of low birth weight. *Developmental Psychology,* 1970, *3,* 363–383.

Carey, S. The development of face perception. In G. Daview, H. Ellis, & J. Shepherd (Eds.), *Perceiving and remembering faces.* New York: Academic Press, 1981.

Carey, W. B. A simplified method of measuring infant temperament. *Journal of Pediatrics,* 1970, *77,* 188–194.

Carey, W. B. Measuring infant temperament. *Journal of Pediatrics,* 1972, *81,* 414.

Carey, W. B. Clinical appraisal of temperament. In M. Lewis & A. Taft (Eds.), *Developmental disability in preschool children.* New York: Prentice-Hall 1981. (Spectrum Books)

Carey, W. B. Validity of parental assessment of development and behavior. *American Journal of Diseases of Children,* 1982, *136,* 97–99.

Carey, W. B., Fox, M., & McDevitt, S. Temperament as a factor in early school adjustment. *Pediatrics,* 1977, *60,* 621–624.

Carey, W. B., & McDevitt, S. Revision of the infant temperament questionnaire. *Pediatrics,* 1978, *61,* 735–739.

Carlsmith, L. Effect of early father absence on scholastic aptitude. *Harvard Educational Review,*

1964, *34,* 3–21.

Carlsmith, L., & Gross, A. Some effects of guilt on compliance. *Journal of Personality and Social Psychology,* 1969, *11,* 232–239.

Casler, L. Maternal deprivation: A critical review of the literature. *Monographs of the Society for Research in Child Development,* 1961, *26*(2, Serial No. 80).

Casler, L. Effects of extra tactile stimulation on a group of institutionalized infants. *Genetic Psychology Monographs,* 1965, *71,* 137–175.

Cass, L., & Thomas, C. *Childhood pathology and later adjustment.* New York: Wiley, 1979.

Chandler, J. V. *Sex differences in the nurturant responses of adolescent children.* Unpublished doctoral dissertation, University of Denver, 1977.

Charlesworth, W., & Kreutzer, M. Facial expressions of infants and children. In P. Ekman (Ed.), *Darwin and facial expression.* New York: Academic Press, 1973.

Chazan, S. Development of object permanence as a correlate of dimensions of maternal care. *Developmental Psychology,* 1981, *17,* 79–81.

Chess, S., Thomas, A., & Cameron, M. Temperament: Its significance for school adjustment and academic achievement. *New York Educational Review,* 1976, *7,* 24–29.

Chevalier-Skolnikoff, S. Facial expression of emotion in nonhuman primates. In P. Ekman (Ed.), *Darwin and facial expression.* New York: Academic Press, 1973.

Chibucos, T., & Kail, P. Longitudinal examination of father-infant interaction and infant-father interaction. *Merrill-Palmer Quarterly,* 1981, *27,* 81–96.

Cicchetti, D., & Sroufe, L. A. An organizational view of affect: Illustration from the study of Down's syndrome infants. In M. Lewis & L. Rosenblum (Eds.), *The development of affect.* New York: Plenum, 1978.

Cicchetti, D., & Pogge-Hesse, P. The relation between emotion and cognition in infant development. In M. E. Lamb & L. R. Sherrod (Eds.), *Infant social cognition: Empirical and theoretical considerations.* Hillsdale, N.J.: Erlbaum, 1981.

Clarke-Stewart, K. A. Interactions between mothers and their young children: Characteristics and consequences. *Monographs of the Society for Research in Child Development,* 1973, *38*(6–7, Serial No. 153).

Clarke-Stewart, K. A. And daddy makes three: The father's impact on mother and young child. *Child Development,* 1978, *49,* 466–479. (a)

Clarke-Stewart, K. A. Recasting the Lone Stranger. In J. Glick & K. A. Clarke-Stewart (Eds.), *Studies in social and cognitive development* (Vol. 1). New York: Gardner Press, 1978. (b)

Clarke-Stewart, K. A. The father's contribution to children's cognitive and social development in early childhood. In F. A. Pedersen (Ed.), *The father-infant relationship: Observational studies in a family context.* New York: Praeger, 1980.

Clarke-Stewart, K. A., Umeh, B. J., Snow, M. E., & Pederson, J. A. Development and prediction of children's sociability from 1 to 2-1/2 years. *Developmental Psychology,* 1980, *16,* 290–302.

Clifton, R. K., & Graham, F. K. Stability of individual differences in heart rate activity during the newborn period. *Psychophysiology,* 1968, *5,* 37–50.

Cochran, M. M. A comparison of group day and family child rearing patterns in Sweden. *Child Development,* 1977, *48,* 702–707.

Cohen, D. J., Dibble, E., & Grawe, J. M. Fathers' and mothers' perceptions of children's personality. *Archives of General Psychiatry,* 1977, *34,* 480–487.

Cohen, L. The operational definition of human attachment. *Psychological Bulletin,* 1974, *81,* 207–217.

Cohen, L., & Campos, J. Father, mother and stranger as elicitors of attachment behaviors in infancy. *Developmental Psychology,* 1974, *10,* 146–154.

Cohen, L., & Salapatek, P. (Eds.) *Infant perception: From sensation to cognition.* New York: Academic Press, 1975.

Cohen, S. Maternal employment and mother-child interaction. *Merrill-Palmer Quarterly,* 1978, *24,* 189–197.

Cohn, J. F., & Tronick, E. Z. Communicative rules and the sequential structure of infant behavior during normal and depressed interaction. In E. Z. Tronick (Ed.), *The development of human communication and the joint regulation of behavior.* Baltimore: University Park Press, 1982,

Collias, N. E. The analysis of socialization in sheep and goats. *Ecology,* 1956, *37,* 228–239.

Connell, D. B. *Individual differences in attachment: An investigation into stability, implications, and relationships to structure of early language development.* Unpublished doctoral dissertation, Syracuse University, 1976.

Connell, J. P., & Goldsmith, H. H. A structural modeling approach to the study of attachment and strange situation behaviors. In R. N. Emde & R. J. Harmon (Eds.), *The development of attachment and affiliative systems.* New York: Plenum, 1982.

Crano, W. What do infant mental states test? A cross-lagged panel analysis of selected data from the Berkeley growth study. *Child Development*, 1977, *48*, 144–151.

Crockenberg, S. B. Infant irritability, mother responsiveness, and social support influences on the security of infant-mother attachment. *Child Development*, 1981, *52*, 857–865.

Cross, H. A., & Harlow, H. F. Observation of infant monkeys by female monkeys. *Perceptual and Motor Skills*, 1963, *16*, 11–15.

Darwin, C. *The expression of the emotions in man and animals*. Chicago: University of Chicago Press, 1975. (Originally published, 1872).

Davies, P. A., & Stewart, A. L. Low-birth weight infants: Neurological sequelae. *British Medical Bulletin*, 1975, *3*, 85–89.

Davitz, J., & Davitz, L. The communication of feelings by content-free speech. *Journal of Communication*, 1959, *9*, 6–13.

Décarie, T. (Ed.) *The infant's reaction to strangers*. New York: International Universities Press, 1974.

DeCasper, A. J., & Carstens, A. A. Contingencies of stimulation: Effects on learning and emotion in neonates. *Infant Behavior & Development*, 1981, *4*, 19–36.

DeCasper, A. J., & Fifer, W. Of human bonding: Newborns prefer their mothers' voices. *Science*, 1980, *208*, 1174–1176.

de Chateau, P., & Wiberg, B. Long-term effect on mother-infant behaviour of extra contact during the first hour post partum: I. First observations at 36 hours. *Acta Paediatrica Scandinavica*, 1977, *66*, 137–143. (a)

de Chateau, P., & Wiberg, B. Long-term effect on mother-infant behaviour of extra contact during the first hour post partum. II. Follow-up at three months. *Acta Paediatrica Scandinavica*, 1977, *66*, 145–151. (b)

de Chateau, P., & Wiberg, B. Long-term effects on mother-infant behaviour of extra contact during the first hour post-partum. *Developmental Medicine and Child Neurology*, in press.

Denenberg, V. H. Critical periods, stimulus input, and emotional reactivity. *Psychological Review*, 1964, *71*, 335–351.

Dennis, W. Infant reactions to restraint. *Transactions of the New York Academy of Science*, 1940, *2*, 202–217.

DePaulo, B., & Rosenthal, R. Measuring the development of sensitivity to nonverbal communication. In C. E. Izard (Ed.), *Measuring emotions in infants and children*. New York: Cambridge University Press, 1982.

Diamond, S. *Personality and temperament*. New York: Harper, 1957.

Dimitrovsky, L. The ability to identify the emotional meaning of vocal expressions at successive age levels. In J. Davitz, (Ed.), *The communication of emotional meaning*. New York: McGraw-Hill, 1964.

DiVitto, B., & Goldberg, S. The development of early parent-infant interaction as a function of newborn medical status. In T. M. Field, A. Sostek, S. Goldberg, & H. H. Shuman (Eds.), *Infants born at risk*. New York: Prentice-Hall, 1979. (Spectrum Books)

Dixon, S., Yogman, M. W., Tronick, E., Adamson, L., Als, H., & Brazelton, T. B. Early infant social interaction with parents and strangers. *Journal of the American Academy of Child Psychiatry*, 1981, *20*, 32–52.

Doyle, A. B. Infant development and day care. *Developmental Psychology*, 1975, *11*, 655–656.

Doyle, A. B., & Somers, K. *The effect of group and individual day care on infant development*. Paper presented at the meeting of the Canadian Psychological Association, Quebec, June 1975.

Drage, J. S., Barondes, H. W., & Fisher, P. D. The Apgar score and four-year psychological examination. In *Perinatal factors affecting human development* (Publication No. 185). Geneva: World Health Organization, 1969.

Dragsten, S. S., & Lee, L. C. *Infants' social behavior in a naturalistic vs experimental setting*. Paper presented at the meeting of the American Psychological Association, Montreal, August 1973.

Drillien, C. M. *The growth and development of the prematurely born infant*. London: E. & S. Livingston, 1964.

Duffy, E. Emotion: An example of the need for reorientation in psychology. *Psychological Review*, 1934, *41*, 184–198.

Duffy, E. *Activation and behavior*. New York: Wiley, 1962.

Dunn, J. F. Individual differences in temperament. In M. Rutter (Ed.), *The scientific foundations of developmental psychiatry*. London: Heinemann, 1980.

Dunn, J. F., & Kendrick, C. Interaction between young siblings: Associations with the interactions between mother and first-born. *Developmental Psychology*, 1981, *17*, 336–343.

Durfee, J. T., & Lee, L. C. *Infant-infant interaction in a day care setting*. Paper presented at the meeting of the American Psychological Association, Montreal, August 1973.

Dusenbury, D., & Knower, F. Experimental studies

of the the symbolism of action and voice. II. A study of the specificity of meaning in abstract tonal symbols. *Quarterly Journal of Speech,* 1939, *25,* 6–75.

Easterbrook, J. The effect of emotion on cue utilization and the organization of behavior. *Psychological Review,* 1959, *66,* 183–201.

Easterbrooks, M. A., & Lamb, M. E. The relationship between quality of infant-mother attachment and infant competence in initial encounters with peers. *Child Development,* 1979, *50,* 380–387.

Eaton, W. Measuring activity level with actometers: Reliability, validity, and arm length. *Child Development,* in press.

Eckerman, C., & Whatley, J. Toys and social interaction between infant peers. *Child Development,* 1977, *48,* 1645–1656.

Eckerman, C., Whatley, J., & Kutz, S. Growth of social play with peers during the second year of life. *Developmental Psychology,* 1975, *11,* 42–49.

Egeland, B., & Farber, E. A. Antecedents of infant-mother attachment relationships in economically disadvantaged families. (Article in preparation).

Egeland, B., & Sroufe, L. A. Attachment and early maltreatment. *Child Development,* 1981, *52,* 44–52.

Ekman, P. Universals and cultural differences in facial expressions of emotion. In J. Cole (Ed.), *Nebraska Symposium on Motivation.* Lincoln: University of Nebraska Press, 1972.

Ekman, P. Biological and cultural contributions to body and facial movement in the expression of emotions. In A. Rorty (Ed.), *Explaining emotions.* Berkeley: University of California Press, 1980.

Ekman, P. Methods for measuring facial action. In K. Scherer & P. Ekman (Eds.), *Handbook on methods in research on nonverbal communication.* New York: Cambridge University Press, 1982.

Ekman, P., & Friesen, W. Constants across cultures in the face and emotion. *Journal of Personality and Social Psychology,* 1972, *17,* 124–129.

Ekman, P., & Friesen, W. *Unmasking the face: A guide to recognizing emotions from facial clues.* Englewood Cliffs, N.J.: Prentice-Hall, 1975.

Ekman, P., & Friesen, W. Measuring facial movement. *Environmental Psychology and Verbal Behavior,* 1976, *1,* 56–75.

Ekman, P., & Friesen, W. *Facial action coding system.* Palo Alto, Calif.: Consulting Psychologists Press, 1978.

Ekman, P., Friesen, W., & Ellsworth, P. *Emotion in the human face: Guidelines for research and an integration of findings.* New York: Pergamon, 1972.

Ekman, P., & Oster, H. Facial expressions of emotion. *Annual Review of Psychology,* 1979, *30,* 527–554.

Ekman, P., Sorenson, E., & Friesen, W. Pan-cultural elements in the facial expression of emotion. *Science,* 1969, *164,* 86–88.

Emde, R. N. Toward a psychoanalytic theory of affect. I. The organizational model and its propositions. In S. Greenspan & G. Pollock (Eds.), *The course of life: Psychoanalytic contributions toward understanding personality development.* Washington, D.C.: U.S. Government Printing Office, 1980. (a)

Emde, R. N. Toward a psychoanalytic theory of affect. II. Emerging models of emotional development in infancy. In S. Greenspan & G. Pollock (Eds.), *The course of life: Psychoanalytic contributions toward understanding personality development.* Washington, D.C.: U.S. Government Printing Office, 1980. (b)

Emde, R. N. *The pre-representational self and its affective core.* Paper presented at the meeting of the Los Angeles Psychoanalytic Society, February 1982.

Emde, R. N., Gaensbauer, T. J., & Harmon, R. J. Emotional expression in infancy: A biobehavioral study. *Psychological Issues* (Vol. 10, No. 37). New York: International Universities Press, 1976.

Emde, R. N., Gaensbauer, T. J., & Harmon, R. J. Using our emotions: Principles for appraising emotional development and intervention. In M. Lewis & L. Taft (Eds.), *Developmental disabilities: Theory, assessment, and intervention.* New York: SP Medical & Scientific Books, 1982.

Emde, R. N., & Harmon, R. J. Endogenous and exogenous smiling systems in early infancy. *Journal of the American Academy of Child Psychiatry,* 1972, *11,* 77–100.

Emde, R. N., Kligman, D., Reich, J., & Wade, T. Emotional expression in infancy: I. Initial studies of social signaling and an emergent model. In M. Lewis & L. Rosenblum (Eds.), *The development of affect.* New York, Plenum, 1978.

Erdelyi, M. A new look at the new look: Perceptual defense and vigilance. *Psychological Review,* 1974, *81,* 1–25.

Erickson, M., & Crichton, L. *Antecedents of compliance in 2-year-olds from a high-risk sample.* Paper presented at the meeting of the Society for Research in Child Development, Boston, April 1981.

Escalona, S. K. Patterns of infantile experience and the developmental process. *Psychoanalytic Study of the Child,* 1963, *18,* 197–244.

Escalona, S. K. *The roots of individuality: Normal patterns of development in infancy*. Chicago: Aldine, 1968.

Exline, R. Gaze behavior in infants and children: A tool for the study of emotions? In C. E. Izard (Ed.), *Measuring emotions in infants and children*. New York: Cambridge University Press, 1982.

Eysenck, H. J. *The biological basis of personality*. Springfield, Ill.: Charles C. Thomas, 1967.

Eysenck, H. J. *A model for personality*. Berlin: Springer-Verlag, 1981.

Fagan, J. F., & McGrath, S. K. Infant recognition memory and later intelligence. *Intelligence,* 1981, *5,* 121–130.

Fagan, J. F., & Singer, L. Intervention during infancy: General considerations. In S. Friedman & M. Sigman (Eds.), *Preterm birth and psychological development*. New York: Academic Press, 1981.

Fairbanks, G., & Pronovost, W. Vocal pitch during simulated emotion. *Science,* 1938, *88,* 383–386.

Farran, D. C., & Ramey, C. T. Infant day care and attachment behaviors toward mothers and teachers. *Child Development,* 1977, *48,* 1112–1116.

Feinman, S. Social referencing in infancy. *Merrill-Palmer Quarterly,* 1982, *28,* 445–470.

Feinman, S., & Lewis, M. Social referencing and second order effects in ten-month-old infants. *Developmental Psychology,* in press.

Feldman, S. S., & Ingham, M. Attachment behavior: A validation study in two age groups. *Child Development,* 1975, *46,* 319–330.

Feldman, S. S., & Nash, S. C. The effect of family formation on sex stereotypic behavior: A study of responsiveness to babies. In W. Miller & L. Newman (Eds.), *The first child and family formation*. Chapel Hill: University of North Carolina Press, 1977.

Feldman, S. S., & Nash, S. C. Interest in babies during young adulthood. *Child Development,* 1978, *49,* 617–622.

Feldman, S. S., Nash, S. C., & Cutrona, C. The influence of age and sex on responsiveness to babies. *Developmental Psychology,* 1977, *13,* 675–676.

Fernald, A. The perceptual and affective salience of mothers' speech to infants. In L. Feagans, C. Garvey, & R. Galinkoff (Eds.), *The origins of growth of communication*. Norwood, N.J.: Ablex, in press.

Feshbach, N. Sex differences in empathy and social behavior in children. In N. Eisenberg-Berg (Ed.), *The development of prosocial behavior*. New York: Academic Press, 1982.

Field, T. M. Effects of early separation, interactive deficits, and experimental manipulations on infant-mother face-to-face interaction. *Child Development,* 1977, *48,* 763–771.

Field, T. M. The three Rs of infant-adult interactions: Rhythms, repertoires, and responsivity. *Journal of Pediatric Psychology,* 1978, *3,* 131–136.

Field, T. M. Interaction patterns of high-risk and normal infants. In T. M. Field, A. Sostek, S. Goldberg, & H. H. Shuman (Eds.), *Infants born at risk*. New York: Prentice-Hall, 1979. (Spectrum Books) (a)

Field, T. M. Visual and cardiac responses to animate and inanimate faces by young term and preterm infants. *Child Development,* 1979, *50,* 188–194. (b)

Field, T. M. Interactions of preterm and term infants with their lower- and middle-class teenage and adult mothers. In T. M. Field, S. Goldberg, D. Stern, & A. Sostek (Eds.), *High-risk infants and children*. New York: Academic Press, 1980.

Field, T. M. Individual differences in the expressivity of neonates and young infants. In R. Feldman (Ed.), *Development of nonverbal behavior in children*. New York: Springer-Verlag, 1982.

Field, T. M., & Greenberg, R. Temperament ratings by parents and teachers of infants, toddlers, and preschool children. *Child Development,* 1982, *53,* 160–163.

Field, T. M., Hallock, N., Ting, G., Dempsey, J., Dabiri, C., & Shuman, H. H. A first-year follow-up of high-risk infants: Formulating a cumulative risk index. *Child Development,* 1978, *49,* 119–131.

Field, T. M., & Ignatoff, E. *Interaction of twins and their mothers*. Unpublished manuscript, University of Miami, 1980.

Field, T. M., & Roopnarine, J. L. Infant peer interactions. In T. M. Field, A. Huston, H. Quay, L. Troll, & G. Finley (Eds.), *Review of human development*. New York: Wiley, 1982.

Field, T. M., & Walden, T. Perception and production of facial expressions in infancy and early childhood. In H. W. Reese & L. P. Lipsitt (Eds.), *Advances in child development and behavior* (Vol. 16). New York: Academic Press, 1982.

Field, T. M., Woodson, R., Greenberg, R., & Cohen, D. Discrimination and imitation of facial expressions by neonates. *Science,* 1982, *218,* 179–181.

Finkelstein, N. W., & Wilson, K. *The influence of daycare on social behaviors towards peers and adults*. Paper presented at the meeting of the Society for Research in Child Development, New Orleans, March 1977.

Fischer, K. W. A theory of cognitive development: The control and construction of hierarchies of skills. *Psychological Review,* 1980, *87,* 477–531.

Fischoff, A. *A comparison between peer-oriented social behavior of kibbutz and city infants in different settings.* Unpublished master's thesis, Hebrew University of Jerusalem, 1974.

Fish, M., & Crockenberg, S. B. Correlates and antecedents of nine-month infant behavior and mother-infant interaction. *Infant Behavior & Development,* 1981, *4,* 69–82.

Fiske, M., & Clarke, S. *Cognition and emotion: The Carnegie-Mellon Symposium.* Hillsdale, N.J.: Erlbaum, 1982.

Fitzgerald, H., & Brackbill, Y. Classical conditioning in infancy: Development and constraints. *Psychological Bulletin,* 1976, *83,* 353–376.

Fleener, D., & Cairns, R. Attachment behaviors in human infants: Discriminative vocalization on maternal separation. *Developmental Psychology,* 1970, *2,* 215–223.

Fox, N. Attachment of kibbutz infants to mother and metapelet. *Child Development,* 1977, *48,* 1228–1239.

Fraiberg, S. *Insights from the blind.* New York: Basic Books, 1977.

Francis-Williams, J., & Davies, P. A. Very low birth weight and later intelligence. *Developmental Medicine and Child Neurology,* 1974, *16,* 709–728.

Freedman, D. Constitutional and environmental interactions in rearing of four breeds of dogs. *Science,* 1958, *127,* 585–586.

Freedman, D. *Human infancy: An evolutionary perspective.* Hillsdale, N.J.: Erlbaum, 1974.

Freedman, D., & Keller, B. Inheritance of behavior in infants. *Science,* 1963, *140,* 196–198.

Freud, S. *The ego and the id.* London: Hogarth Press, 1927.

Frodi, A. M., & Lamb, M. E. Sex differences in responsiveness to infants: A developmental study of psychophysiological and behavioral responses. *Child Development,* 1978, *49,* 1182–1188.

Frodi, A. M., Lamb, M. E., Leavitt, L. A., & Donovan, W. L. Fathers' and mothers' responses to infant smiles and cries. *Infant Behavior & Development,* 1978, *1,* 187–198.

Frodi, A. M., Lamb, M. E., Leavitt, L. A., Donovan, W. L., Neff, C., & Sherry, D. Fathers' and mothers' responses to the faces and cries of normal and premature infants. *Developmental Psychology,* 1978, *14,* 490–498.

Frommer, E., & O'Shea, G. Antenatal identification of women liable to have problems in managing their infants. *British Journal of Psychiatry,* 1973, *123,* 149–156. (a)

Frommer, E., & O'Shea, G. The importance of childhood experience in relation to problems of marriage and family-building. *British Journal of Psychiatry,* 1973, *123,* 157–160. (b)

Frye, D. *The problem of infant day care.* Unpublished manuscript, Yale University, 1979.

Fulker, D., Eysenck, S. B. G., & Zuckerman, M. A genetic and environmental analysis of sensation seeking. *Journal of Research in Personality,* 1980, *14,* 261–281.

Fullard, W., McDevitt, S., & Carey, W. B. *Toddler temperament scale.* Unpublished manuscript, Temple University, 1978.

Gaensbauer, T. J. Anaclitic depression in a three-and-a-half-month-old child. *American Journal of Psychiatry,* 1980, *137,* 841–842.

Gaensbauer, T. J., & Hiatt, S. Facial communication of emotion in early infancy. *Journal of the American Academy of Child Psychiatry,* in press.

Gaensbauer, T. J., Shultz, L., & Connell, J. P. Emotion and attachment: Interrelationships in a modified "strange situation" paradigm. *Developmental Psychology,* in press.

Garcia-Coll, C. *Psychophysiological correlates of a tendency toward inhibition in infants.* Unpublished doctoral dissertation, Harvard University, 1981.

Gardner, W. P., Lamb, M. E., & Thompson, R. A. *How consistently are the Strange Situation classifications applied?: An exploration using cluster analysis.* Article in preparation.

Garside, R. F., Birch, H., Scott, D., Chambers, S., Kolvin, I., Tweddle, E. G., & Barber, L. M. Dimensions of temperament in infant school children. *Journal of Child Psychology and Psychiatry and Allied Disciplines,* 1975, *16,* 219–231.

Gates, G. A test for ability to interpret facial expressions. *Psychological Bulletin,* 1925, *22,* 120.

Gesell, A., & Ames, L. Early evidence of individuality in the human infant. *Scientific Monthly,* 1937, *45,* 217–225.

Gewirtz, J. A. A learning analysis of the effects of normal stimulation, privation, and deprivation on the acquisition of social motivation and attachment. In B. Foss (Ed.) *Determinants of infant behavior* (Vol. 1). New York: Wiley, 1961.

Gewirtz, J. A., & Boyd, E. F. Does maternal responding imply reduced infant crying? A critique of the 1972 Bell and Ainsworth report. *Child Development,* 1977, *48,* 1200–1207.

Giacoman, S. Hunger and motor restraint on arousal and visual attention in the infant. *Child Development,* 1971, *42,* 605–614.

Gibson, J. J. *The ecological approach to visual perception.* Boston: Houghton Mifflin, 1979.

Glick, P. C., & Norton, A. J. Marrying, divorcing, and living together in the U.S. today. *Population Bulletin,* 1979, *32*(Whole No. 5).

Goldberg, S. Parent-to-infant bonding: Another look. *Child Development,* in press.

Goldberg, S., Brachfeld, S., & DiVitto, B. Feeding, fussing and play: Parent-infant interaction in the first year as a function of prematurity and prenatal medical problems. In T. M. Field, S. Goldberg, D. Stern, & A. Sostek, (Eds.), *High-risk infants and children.* New York: Academic Press, 1980.

Goldfarb, W. Infant rearing and problem behavior. *American Journal of Orthopsychiatry,* 1943, *13,* 249–265.

Goldsmith, H. H. *Behavior-genetic analyses of early personality (temperament): Development perspectives from the longitudinal study of twins during infancy and early childhood.* Unpublished doctoral dissertation, University of Minnesota, 1978.

Goldsmith, H. H. Behavior-genetic studies of personality. *Child Development,* 1983, *54,* 331–355.

Goldsmith, H. H., & Campos, J. J. *Infant temperament: Genetics and generalizability.* Paper presented at the meeting of the American Psychological Association, Washington, D.C., August 1982 (a)

Goldsmith, H. H., & Campos, J. J. Toward a theory of infant temperament. In R. N. Emde & R. J. Harmon (Eds.), *The development of attachment and affiliative systems: Psychobiological aspects.* New York: Plenum, 1982. (b)

Goldsmith, H. H., Duncan, K. S., & Henderson, C. *A laboratory based twin study of infant emotional development.* Paper presented at the meeting of the Society for Research in Child Development, Boston, April 1981.

Goldsmith, H. H., & East, P. L. *Parental perception of infant temperament: Validity and genetics.* Paper presented at the meeting of the Society for Research in Child Development, Boston, April 1981.

Goldsmith, H. H., & Gottesman, I. I. Origins of variation in behavioral style: A longitudinal study of temperament in young twins. *Child Development,* 1981, *52,* 91–103.

Goldsmith, H. H., Reiser-Danner, L., & Pomerantz, S. *Maternalattitudinal structure as a contributor to infant temperament.* Paper presented at the meeting of the Southwestern Psychological Association, San Antonio, Tex., April 1983.

Golinkoff, R. M., & Ames, G. J. A comparison of fathers' and mothers' speech with their young children. *Child Development,* 1979, *50,* 28–32.

Goodman, G., & Haith, M. *Eyewitness testimony in children.* Manuscript in preparation, University of Denver, 1982.

Gordon, E., & Thomas, A. Children's behavioral style and the teacher's appraisal of their intelligence. *Journal of School Psychology,* 1967, *5,* 292–300.

Gottesman, I. I. Heritability of personality: A demonstration. *Psychological Monographs,* 1963, *77,* 1–21.

Gottesman, I. I. Developmental genetics and ontogenetic psychology: Overdue detente and propositions from a matchmaker. In A. Pick (Ed.), Minnesota Symposia on Child Psychology (Vol. 8). Minneapolis: University of Minnesota Press, 1974.

Goulet, J. The infant's conception of causality and his reactions to strangers. In T. Décarie (Ed.), *The infant's reaction to strangers.* New York: International Universities Press, 1974.

Graham, F. K., & Clifton, R. K. Heartrate change as a component of the orienting response. *Psychological Bulletin,* 1966, *65,* 305–320.

Grant, E. Human facial expression. *Man,* 1969, *4,* 525–536.

Gray, J. A. (Ed.) *Pavlov's typology.* New York: Macmillan, 1964.

Gray, J. A. Causal theories of personality and how to test them. In J. Royce (Ed.), *Multivariate analysis and psychological theory.* New York: Academic Press, 1973.

Greenberg, M., & Morris, N. Engrossment: The newborn's impact upon the father. *American Journal of Orthopsychiatry,* 1974, *44,* 520–531.

Greif, E., Alvarez, M., & Ulman, K. *Recognizing emotions in other people: Sex differences in socialization.* Paper presented at the meeting of the Society for Research in Child Development, Boston, April 1981.

Grossman, H., & Greenberg, N. Psychosomatic differentiation in infancy: I. Autonomic activity in the newborn. *Psychosomatic Medicine,* 1957, *19,* 293–306.

Grossman, S. *A textbook of physiological psychology.* New York: Wiley, 1967.

Grossmann, K., Thane, K., & Grossmann, K. E. Maternal tactual contact of the newborn after various postpartum conditions of mother-infant contact. *Developmental Psychology,* 1981, *17,* 159–169.

Grossmann, K. E., & Grossmann, K. *Maternal sensitivity to infants' signals during the first year as related to the year-old's behavior in Ainsworth's strange situation in a sample of Northern German families.* Paper presented at the meeting of the International Conference on Infant Studies, Austin, Tex., March 1982.

Grossmann, K. E., Grossmann, K., Huber, F., & Wartner, U. German children's behavior towards their mothers at 12 months and their fathers at 18 months in Ainsworth's strange situation. *International Journal of Behavioral Development,* 1981, *4,* 157–181.

Gunnar, M. Control, warning signals, and distress in infancy. *Developmental Psychology,* 1980, *16,* 281–289.

Gunnar-vonGnechten, M. Changing a frightening toy into a pleasant toy by allowing the infant to control its actions. *Developmental Psychology,* 1978, *14,* 157–162.

Haar, E., Welkowitz, J., Blau, A., & Cohen, J. Personality differentiation of neonates. *Journal of the American Academy of Child Psychiatry,* 1964, *3,* 330–342.

Haber, R. Discrepancy from adaptation level as a source of affect. *Journal of Experimental Psychology,* 1958, *56,* 370–375.

Hainline, L. Developmental changes in visual scanning of face and nonface patterns by infants. *Journal of Experimental Child Psychology,* 1978, *25,* 90–115.

Haith, M. M., Bergman, T., & Moore, M. Eye contact and face scanning in early infancy. *Science,* 1977, *198,* 853–855.

Haith, M. M., & Campos, J. J. Human infancy. *Annual Review of Psychology,* 1977, *28,* 251–294.

Hales, D., Lozoff, B., Sosa, R., & Kennell, J. Defining the limits of the maternal sensitive period. *Developmental Medicine and Child Neurology,* 1977, *19,* 454–461.

Hardyck, C., & Petrinovich, L. Left-handedness. *Psychological Bulletin,* 1977, *84,* 385–404.

Harlow, H. F., & Zimmermann, R. Affectional responses in the infant monkey. *Science,* 1959, *130,* 421–432.

Harmon, R. J. The perinatal period: Infant and parents. In J. Spittell (Ed.), *Clinical medicine,* vol. 12, *Psychiatry,* Hagerstown, Md.: Harper & Row, 1981.

Harris, E. L., & Rose, R. J. *Personality resemblance in twin children: Comparison of self-descriptions with mothers' ratings.* Paper presented at the meeting of the 2nd International Congress on Twin Studies, Washington, D.C., 1977.

Harter, S. *Children's understanding of multiple emotions: A cognitive-developmental approach.* Address presented at the Symposium of the Jean Piaget Society, Philadelphia, June 1979.

Haviland, J. Sex-related pragmatics in infants. *Journal of Communication,* 1977, *27,* 80–84.

Hayes, L., & Watson, J. B. Neonatal imitation: Fact or artifact? *Developmental Psychology,* 1981, *17,* 655–660.

Hebb, D. On the nature of fear. *Psychological Review,* 1946, *53,* 259–276.

Hebb, D. *The organization of behavior.* New York: Wiley, 1949.

Heider, K. *Affect display rules in the Dani.* Paper presented at the meeting of the American Anthropological Association, New Orleans, 1974.

Held, R., & Hein, A. Movement-produced stimulation in the development of visually-guided behavior. *Journal of Comparative and Physiological Psychology,* 1963, *56,* 872–876.

Heron, W. The pathology of boredom. *Scientific American,* 1957, *196,* 52–56.

Hersher, L., Moore, A., & Richmond, J. Effect of post-partum separation of mother and kid on maternal care in the domestic goat. *Science,* 1958, *128,* 1342–1343.

Herzog, E., & Sudia, C. F. Children in fatherless families. In B. M. Caldwell & H. N. Ricciuti (Eds.), *Review of child development research* (Vol. 3). Chicago: University of Chicago Press, 1973.

Hetherington, E. M., & Deur, J. L. Effects of father absence on child development. *Young Children,* 1971, *26,* 233–242.

Hiatt, S., Campos, J., & Emde, R. N. Facial patterning and infant emotional expression: Happiness, surprise, and fear. *Child Development,* 1979, *50,* 1020–1035.

Hill, C. E., Siegelman, L., Gronsky, B. R., Sturniolo, F., & Fretz, B. R. Nonverbal communication and counseling outcome. *Journal of Counseling Psychology,* 1981, *28,* 203–212.

Hinde, R. A. Concepts of emotion. In *Physiology, emotion, and psychosomatic illness* (Ciba Foundation Symposium No. 8). Amsterdam: Elsevier, 1972.

Hochschild, A. The sociology of feeling and emotion: Selected possibilities. In M. Millman & P. Kanter (Eds.), *Another voice*. Garden City, N.Y.: Doubleday, 1975. (Anchor Books).

Hock, E. Working and nonworking mothers with infants: Perceptions of their careers, their infants' needs, and satisfaction with mothering. *Developmental Psychology*, 1978, *14*, 37–43.

Hock, E. Working and nonworking mothers and their infants: A comparative study of maternal caregiving characteristics and infant social behavior. *Merrill-Palmer Quarterly*, 1980, *26*, 79–102.

Hock, E., Christman, K., & Hock, M. Factors associated with decisions about return to work in mothers of infants. *Developmental Psychology*, 1980, *16*, 535–536.

Hoffman, M. Moral development. In P. Mussen (Ed.), *Carmichael's manual of child psychology* (Vol. 2, 3rd ed.). New York: Wiley, 1970.

Hoffman, M. Empathy, role-taking, guilt and the development of altruistic motives. In T. Likona (Ed.), *Moral development: Current theory and research*. New York: Holt, 1976.

Hoffman, M. Toward a theory of empathic arousal and development. In M. Lewis & L. Rosenblum (Eds.), *The development of affect*. New York: Plenum, 1978.

Hoffman, M. The measurement of empathy. In C. E. Izard (Ed.), *Measuring emotions in infants and children*. New York: Cambridge University Press, 1982.

Hoffman, M. Interaction of affect and cognition in empathy. In C. E. Izard, J. Kagan, & R. Zajonc (Eds.), *Emotion, cognition, and behavior*. New York: Cambridge University Press, in press.

Hollien, H. Developmental aspects of neonatal vocalizations. In T. Murry & J. Murry (Eds.), *Infant communication: Cry to early speech*. Houston: College Hill Press, 1980.

Hopkins, J., & Vietze, P. *Postpartum early and extended contact: Quality, quantity, or both?* Paper presented at the meeting of the Society for Research in Child Development, New Orleans, March 1977.

Horner, T. Two methods of studying stranger reactivity in infants: A review. *Journal of Child Psychology and Psychiatry*, 1980, *21*, 203–219.

Hubert, N., Wachs, T. D., Peters-Martin, P., & Gandour, M. The study of early temperament: Measurement and conceptual issues. *Child Development*, 1982, *53*, 571–600.

Hudson, S. J., & Mullord, M. M. Investigations of maternal bonding in dairy cattle. *Applied Animal Ethology*, 1977, *3*, 271–276.

Hutt, S., Lenard, H., & Prechtl, H. Psychophysiological studies in newborn infants. In L. P. Lipsitt & H. W. Reese (Eds.), *Advances in child development and behavior* (Vol. 4). New York: Academic Press, 1969.

Illsley, R. Early prediction of prenatal risk. *Proceedings of the Royal Society of Medicine*, 1966, *59*, 181–184.

Irwin, O. Infant responses to vertical movement. *Child Development*, 1932, *3*, 167–169.

Izard, C. E. *The face of emotion*. New York: Appleton-Century-Crofts, 1971.

Izard, C. E. *Patterns of emotions*. New York: Academic Press, 1972,

Izard, C. E. *Human emotions*. New York: Plenum, 1977.

Izard, C. E. On the ontogenesis of emotions and emotion-cognition relationships in infancy. In M. Lewis & L. Rosenblum (Eds.), *The development of affect*. New York: Plenum, 1978.

Izard, C. E. *The maximally discriminative facial movement scoring system*. Unpublished manuscript, University of Delaware, 1979.

Izard, C. E., & Buechler, S. Aspects of consciousness and personality in terms of differential emotions theory. In R. Plutchik & H. Kellerman (Eds.), *Emotion: Theory, research, and experience*, Vol. 1, *Theories of emotion*. New York: Academic Press, 1981.

Izard, C. E., & Buechler, S. Theoretical perspectives on emotions in developmentalal disabilities. In M. Lewis & L. Taft (Eds.), *Development disabilities: Theory, assessment, and intervention*. New York: Medical and Scientific Books, in press.

Izard, C. E., & Dougherty, L. *A system for identifying affect expressions by holistic judgments (Affex)*. Unpublished manuscript, University of Delaware, 1980.

Izard, C. E., & Dougherty, L. Two complementary systems for measuring facial expressions in infants and children. In. C. E. Izard (Ed.), *Measuring emotions in infants and children*. New York: Cambridge University Press, 1982.

Izard, C. E., Hembree, E., Dougherty, L., & Coss, C. Changes in two- to nineteen-month-old infants' facial expressions following acute pain. *Development Psychology*, in press.

Izard, C. E., Huebner, R., Risser, D., McGinness,

G., & Dougherty, L. The young infant's ability to produce discrete emotion expressions. *Developmental Psychology,* 1980, *16,* 132–140.

Jackson, E., Campos, J., & Fischer, K. The question of decalage between object permanence and person permanence. *Developmental Psychology,* 1978, *14,* 1–10.

Johnson, W., Emde, R. N., Pannabecker, B., Stenberg, C., & Davis, M. Maternal perception of infant emotion from birth through 18 months. *Infant Behavior & Development,* 1982, *5,* 313–322.

Jones, H. The galvanic skin reflex as related to overt emotional expression. *Child Development,* 1930, *1,* 106–110.

Jones, H. The study of patterns of emotional expression. In M. Reymert (Ed.), *Feelings and emotions.* New York: McGraw-Hill, 1950.

Jonsson, G. Delinquent boys, their parents and grandparents. *Acta Psychiatrica Scandinavica,* 1967, *43,* suppl. 195.

Jost, H., & Sontag, L. W. The genetic factor in autonomic nervous system function. *Psychosomatic Medicine,* 1944, *6,* 308–310.

Jürgens, U. Vocalization as an emotional indicator: A neuroethological study in the squirrel monkey. *Behavior,* 1979, *69,* 88–118.

Kagan, J. *Change and continuity in infancy.* New York: Wiley, 1971.

Kagan, J. Discrepancy, temperament and infant distress. In M. Lewis & L. A. Rosenblum (Eds.), *The origins of fear.* New York: Wiley, 1974.

Kagan, J. Emergent themes in human development. *American Scientist,* 1976, *64,* 186–196.

Kagan, J. On emotion and its development: A working paper. In M. Lewis & L. Rosenblum (Eds.), *The development of affect.* New York: Plenum, 1978.

Kagan, J. Heart rate and heart rate variability as signs of a temperamental dimension in infants. In C. E. Izard (Ed.), *Measuring emotions in infants and children.* New York: Cambridge University Press, 1982. (a)

Kagan, J. *Psychological research on the human infant: An evaluative summary.* New York: W. T. Grant Foundation, 1982. (b)

Kagan, J., Kearsley, R., & Zelazo, P. R. *Infancy: Its place in human development.* Cambridge: Harvard University Press, 1978.

Kagan, J., & Moss, H. *Birth to maturity.* New York: Wiley, 1962.

Kagan, J., Reznick, S., Clarke, C., Snidman, N., & Garcia-Coll, C. Cardiac correlates of behavioral inhibition in the young child. In M. Coles, J. Jennings, & J. Stern (Eds.), *Festschrift for John Lacey.* Stroudsburg, Pa.: Hutchinson Ross, in press.

Katz, V. Auditory stimulation and developmental behavioı of the premature infant. *Nursing Research,* 1971, *20,* 196–201.

Kennell, J., Jerauld, R., Wolfe, H., Chesler, D., Kreger, N., McAlpine, W., Steffa, M., & Klaus, M. Maternal behavior one year after early and extended postpartum contact. *Developmental Medicine and Child Neurology,* 1974, *16,* 172–179.

Kenney, M., Mason, W., & Hill, S. Effects of age, objects, and visual experience on affective responses of rhesus monkeys to strangers. *Developmental Psychology,* 1979, *15,* 176–184.

Keogh, B. Children's temperament and teachers' decisions. In R. Porter & G. Collins (Eds.), *Temperamental differences in infants and young children.* London: Pitman, 1982.

Keogh, B., & Pullis, M. Temperament influences on the development of exceptional children. In B. Keogh (Ed.), *Advances in special education* (Vol. 1). Greenwich, Conn.: JAI Press, 1980.

Kernberg, O. Borderline personality organization. *Journal of the American Psychoanalytic Association,* 1967, *15,* 641–685.

Kessen, W. *American delegation on early childhood development in the People's Republic of China.* New Haven, Conn.: Yale University Press, 1975.

Klaus, M., Jerauld, R., Kreger, N., McAlpine, W., Steffa, M., & Kennell, J. Maternal attachment: Importance of the first postpartum days. *New England Journal of Medicine,* 1972, *286,* 460–463.

Klaus, M., & Kennell, J. *Maternal-infant bonding.* St. Louis: C. V Mosby, 1976.

Klaus, M., & Kennell, J. *Parent-infant bonding.* St. Louis: C. V. Mosby, 1982.

Kling, L., & Riggs, E. (Eds.), *Woodworth and Schlosberg's experimental psychology* (3rd ed.). New York: Holt, Rinehart & Winston, 1971.

Klinnert, M. *The regulation of infant behavior by maternal facial expression.* Unpublished doctoral dissertation, University of Denver, 1981.

Klinnert, M., Campos, J. J., Sorce, J., Emde, R. N., & Svejda, M. Emotions as behavior regulators: Social referencing in infancy. In R. Plutchik & H. Kellerman (Eds.), *Emotions in early development,* vol. 2, *The emotions.* New York: Academic Press, 1983.

Klinnert, M., Emde, R. N., Butterfield, P., & Campos, J. J. *Emotional communication from familiarized adults influences infants' behavior.* Paper presented at the meeting of the Society for Research in Child Development, Detroit, April 1983.

Klinnert, M., Sorce, J., & Emde, R. N. *Differential reactions of one-year-olds to discrete emotional expressions.* Paper presented at the meeting of the International Conference on Infant Studies, Austin, Tex., March 1982.

Klinnert, M., Sorce, J., Emde, R. N., Stenberg, C., & Gaensbauer, T. J. Continuities and change in early affective life: Maternal perceptions of surprise, fear, and anger. In R. N. Emde & R. J. Harmon (Eds.), *Continuities and discontinuities in development.* New York: Plenum, in press.

Klopfer, P. Mother love: What turns it on? *American Scientist,* 1971, *49,* 404–407.

Knower, F. Analysis of some experimental variations of simulated vocal expressions of the emotions. *Journal of Social Psychology,* 1941, *14,* 369–372.

Kohut, H. Thoughts on narcissism and narcissistic rage. *Psychoanalytic Study of the Child,* 1972, *27,* 360–401.

Korner, A. F. Mother-child interaction: One-way or two-way street? *Social Work,* 1965, *10,* 47–51.

Korner, A. F., & Grobstein, R. Visual alertness as related to soothing in neonates: Implications for maternal stimulation and early deprivation. *Child Development,* 1966, *37,* 867–876.

Korner, A. F., Hutchinson, C. A., Koperski, J. A., Kraemer, H. C., & Schneider, P. A. Stability of individual differences of neonatal motor and crying pattern. *Child Development,* 1981, *52,* 83–90.

Kotsch, W., Gerbing, D., & Schwartz, L. The construct validity of the differential emotions scale as adapted for children and adolescents. In C. E. Izard (Ed.), *Measuring emotions in infants and children.* New York: Cambridge University Press, 1982.

Kotelchuck, M. *The nature of the child's tie to his father.* Unpublished doctoral dissertation, Harvard University, 1972.

Kotelchuck, M. *Father caretaking characteristics and their influence on infant father interaction.* Paper presented at the meeting of the American Psychological Association, Chicago, September 1975.

Kotelchuck, M. The infant's relationship to the father: Experimental evidence. In M. E. Lamb (Ed.), *The role of the father in child development.* New York: Wiley, 1976.

Kotelchuck, M., Zelazo, P. R., Kagan, J., & Spelke, E. Infant reactions to parental separations when left with familar and unfamiliar adults. *Journal of Genetic Psychology,* 1975, *126,* 255–262.

Kramer, M., Chamorro, I., Green, D., & Knudtson, F. Extra tactile stimulation of the premature infant. *Nursing Research,* 1975, *24,* 324–334.

Krehbiel, D. A., & Leroy, L. M. The quality of hormonally stimulated maternal behavior in ovariectomized rats. *Hormones and Behavior,* 1979, *12,* 243–252.

Kreutzer, M., & Charlesworth, W. *Infants' reactions to different expressions of emotions.* Paper presented at the meeting of the Society for Research in Child Development, Philadelphia, Pa.: March 1973.

Kunst-Wilson, W., & Zajonc, R. Affective discrimination of stimuli that cannot be recognized. *Science,* 1980, *207,* 557–558.

LaBarbera, J., Izard, C. E., Vietze, P., & Parisi, S. Four- and six-month-old infants' visual responses to joy, anger, and neutral expressions. *Child Development,* 1976, *47,* 535–538.

Lacey, J. Psychophysiological approaches to the evaluation of psychotherapeutic process and outcome. In E. Rubenstein & M. Parloff (Eds.), *Research in psychotherapy.* Washington, D.C.: American Psychological Association, 1959.

Lacey, J. Somatic response patterning and stress: Some revisions of activation theory. In M. Appley & R. Trumbull (Eds.), *Psychological stress: Issues in research.* New York: Appleton-Century-Crofts, 1967.

Lacey, J., Kagan, J., Lacey, B., & Moss, H. The visceral level: Situational determinants and behavioral correlates of autonomic response patterns. In P. H. Knapp (Ed.), *Expression of the emotions in man.* New York: International Universities Press, 1963.

Lacey, J., & Lacey, B. The relationship of resting autonomic activity to motor impulsivity. *Research in Nervous and Mental Disease,* 1958, *36,* 144–209. (a)

Lacey, J., & Lacey, B. Verification and extension of the principle of autonomic response specificity. *American Journal of Psychology,* 1958, *71,* 50–73. (b)

Lacey, J., & Lacey, B. The law of initial value in the longitudinal study of autonomic constitution: Reproducibility of autonomic responses and response patterns over a four-year interval. *Annals of the New York Academy of Sciences,* 1962, *98,* 1257–1290.

Lacey, J., & Lacey, B. Some autonomic-central

nervous system interrelationships. In P. Black (Ed.), *Physiological correlates of emotion.* New York: Academic Press, 1970.

Laird, J. Self-attribution of emotion: The effects of expressive behavior on the quality of emotional experience. *Journal of Personality and Social Psychology,* 1974, *29,* 475–486.

Lamb, M. E. Physiological mechanisms in the control of maternal behavior in rats: A review. *Psychological Bulletin,* 1975, *82,* 104–119.

Lamb, M. E. Interaction between eight-month-old children and their fathers and mothers. In M. E. Lamb (Ed.), *The role of the father in child development.* New York: Wiley, 1976. (a)

Lamb, M. E. Interactions between two-year-olds and their mothers and fathers. *Psychological Reports,* 1976, *38,* 447–450. (b)

Lamb, M. E. Parent-infant interaction in eight-month-olds. *Child Psychiatry and Human Development,* 1976, *7,* 56–63. (c)

Lamb, M. E. Twelve-month-olds and their parents: Interaction in a laboratory playroom. *Developmental Psychology,* 1976, *12,* 237–244. (d)

Lamb, M. E. The development of mother-infant and father-infant attachments in the second year of life. *Developmental Psychology,* 1977, *13,* 637–648. (a).

Lamb, M. E. The development of parental preferences in the first two years of life. *Sex Roles,* 1977, *3,* 495–497. (b)

Lamb, M. E. Father-infant and mother-infant interaction in the first year of life. *Child Development,* 1977, *48,* 167–181. (c)

Lamb, M. E. The development of sibling relationships in infancy: A short-term longitudinal study. *Child Development,* 1978, *49,* 1189–1196. (a)

Lamb, M. E. Interactions between 18-month-olds and their preschool-aged siblings. *Child Development,* 1978, *49,* 51–59. (b)

Lamb, M. E. Qualitative aspects of mother- and father-infant attachments. *Infant Behavior & Development,* 1978, *1,* 265–275. (c)

Lamb, M. E. The effects of the social context on dyadic social interaction. In M. E. Lamb, S. J. Suomi, & G. R. Stephenson (Eds.), *Social interaction analysis.* Madison: University of Wisconsin Press, 1979.

Lamb, M. E. Unfulfilled promises. (Review of *The dynamics of psychological development* by Alexander Thomas & Stella Chess). *Contemporary Psychology,* 1980, *25,* 906–907.

Lamb, M. E. Developing trust and perceived effectance in infancy. In L. P. Lipsitt (Ed.), *Advances in infancy research* (Vol. 1). Norwood, N.J.: Ablex, 1981. (a)

Lamb, M. E. The development of father-infant relationships. In M. E. Lamb (Ed.), *The role of the father in child development.* (Rev. ed.). New York: Wiley, 1981. (b)

Lamb, M. E. The developmental of social expectations in the first year of life. In M. E. Lamb & L. R. Sherrod (Eds.), *Infant social cognition: Empirical and theoretical considerations.* Hillsdale, N.J.: Erlbaum, 1981. (c)

Lamb, M. E. Early contact and mother-infant bonding: One decade later. *Pediatrics,* 1982, *70,* 763–768.

Lamb, M. E., & Campos, J. J. *Development in infancy: An introduction.* New York: Random House, 1982.

Lamb, M. E., Frodi, A. M., Frodi, M., & Hwang, C. P. Characteristics of maternal and paternal behavior in traditional and nontraditional Swedish families. *International Journal of Behavioral Development,* 1982, *5,* 131–141.

Lamb, M. E., Frodi, A. M., Hwang, C. P., Frodi, M., & Steinberg, J. The effects of gender and caretaking role on parent-infant interaction. In R. N. Emde & R. J. Harmon (Eds.), *The development of attachment and affiliative systems,* New York: Plenum, 1982. (a)

Lamb, M. E., Frodi, A. M., Hwang, C. P., Frodi, M., & Steinberg, J. Mother- and father-infant interaction involving play and holding in traditional and nontraditional Swedish families. *Developmental Psychology,* 1982, *18,* 215–221. (b)

Lamb, M. E., Frodi, M., Hwang, C. P., & Frodi, A. M. Effects of paternal involvement on infant preferences for mothers and fathers. *Child Development,* 1983, *54,* 450–458.

Lamb, M. E., Gaensbauer, T. J., Malkin, C. M. & Shultz, L. *The effects of abuse and neglect on security of infant-adult attachment.* Article in preparation, 1982.

Lamb, M. E., Garn, S., & Keating, M. Correlations between sociability and cognitive performance among eight-month-olds. *Child Development,* 1981, *52,* 711–713.

Lamb, M. E., & Hwang, C. P. Maternal attachment and mother-neonate bonding: A critical review. In M. E. Lamb & A. L. Brown (Eds.), *Advances in developmental psychology* (Vol. 2). Hillsdale, N.J.: Erlbaum, 1982.

Lamb, M. E., Hwang, C. P., Frodi, A. M., & Frodi, M. Security of mother- and father-infant attachment and its relation to sociability with strangers in traditional and nontraditional Swedish families. *Infant Behavior & Development,* 1982, *5,* 355–367.

Lamb, M. E., Suomi, S. J., & Stephenson, G. R. (Eds.) *Social interaction analysis*. Madison: University of Wisconsin Press, 1979.

Lamb, M. E., Sutton-Smith, B. (Eds.) *Sibling relationships: Their nature and significance across the life span*. Hillsdale, N.J.: Erlbaum, 1982.

Lamb, M. E., Thompson, R. A., Gardner, W. P., Charnov, E., & Estes, D. *Patterns of attachment reassessed*. Hillsdale, N.J.: Erlbaum, in press. (a)

Lamb, M. E., Thompson, R. A., Gardner, W. P., Charnov, E. L., & Estes, D. Security of infantile attachment as assessed in the strange situation: Its study and biological interpretation. *Behavioral and Brain Sciences*, in press. (b)

Landis, C. The interpretation of facial expression of emotion. *Journal of General Psychology*, 1929, *2*, 59–72.

Lay, M., & Meyer, W. *Effects of early daycare experience on subsequent observed program behaviors* (Final report to the Office of Education [Subcontract 70–007]). Syracuse, N.Y.: Children's Center, 1972.

Lazarus, R. Emotions and adaptation: Conceptual and empirical relations. In W. Arnold (Ed.), *Nebraska Symposium on Motivation*. Lincoln: University of Nebraska Press, 1968.

Lee, L. C. *Social encounters of infants: The beginnings of popularity*. Paper presented at the meeting of the International Society for the Study of Behavioral Development, Ann Arbor, Mich., August 1973.

Leifer, A., Leiderman, P., Barnett, C., & Williams, J. Effects of mother-infant separation on maternal attachment behavior. *Child Development*, 1972, *43*, 1203–1218.

Lemly, E., & Schwarz, J. *Temperament and child rearing antecedents of two-year-olds' reactions to male and female strangers*. Paper presented at the meeting of the Society for Research in Child Development, San Francisco, March 1979.

Lerner, J. V., & Lerner, R. M. Temperament and adaptation across life: Theoretical and empirical issues. In P. B. Baltes & O. G. Brim (Eds.), *Life-span development and behavior* (Vol. 5). New York: Academic Press, in press.

Lerner, R. M., Palermo, M., Spiro, A., & Nesselroade, J. Assessing the dimensions of temperamental individuality across the life-span: The dimension of temperament survey (DOTS). *Child Development*, 1982, *53*, 149–160.

Lester, B., Kotelchuk, M., Spelke, E., Sellers, M., & Klein, R. Separation protest in Guatemalan infants: Cross-cultural and cognitive findings. *Developmental Psychology*, 1974, *10*, 79–85.

Leung, E., & Rheingold, H. Development of pointing as a social gesture. *Developmental Psychology*, 1981, *17*, 215–220.

Levine, S. Psychophysiological effects of early stimulation. In E. Bliss (Ed.), *Roots of behavior*. New York: Hoeber, 1961.

Levitt, M. *Object permanence and attachment: Another look*. Unpublished manuscript, Florida International University, 1982.

Levy, R. *Tahitians*. Chicago: University of Chicago Press, 1973.

Lewis, M., & Brooks-Gunn, J. Self-knowledge and emotional development. In M. Lewis & L. Rosenblum (Eds.), *The development of affect*. New York: Plenum, 1978.

Lewis, M., & Brooks-Gunn, J. *Social cognition and the acquisition of self*. New York: Plenum, 1979.

Lewis, M., & Feiring, C. Direct and indirect interactions in social relationships. In L. P. Lipsitt (Ed.), *Advances in infancy research* (Vol. 1). Norwood, N.J.: Ablex, 1981.

Lewis, M., & Michalson, L. The measurement of emotional state. In C. E. Izard (Ed.), *Measuring emotions in infants and children*. New York: Cambridge University Press, 1982. (a)

Lewis, M., & Michalson, L. The socialization of emotions. In T. M. Field & A. Fogel (Eds.) *Emotion and interaction: Normal and high risk infants*. Hillsdale, N.J.: Erlbaum, 1982. (b)

Lewis, M., & Rosenblum, L. A. *The development of affect*. New York: Plenum, 1978.

Lewis, M., & Starr, M. Developmental continuity. In J. Osofsky (Ed.), *Handbook of infant development*. New York: Wiley, 1979.

Lewis, M., & Weinraub, M. Sex of parent versus sex of child: Socio-emotional development. In R. Riehart, R. Friedman, & R. Vande Wiele (Eds.), *Sex differences in behavior*. New York: Wiley, 1974.

Lewis, M., Weinraub, M., & Ban, P. *Mothers and fathers, girls and boys: Attachment behavior in the first two years of life*. Educational Testing Service Research Bulletin, Princeton, N.J., 1972.

Lewis, M., Young, B., Brooks, J., & Michalson, L. The beginning of friendship. In M. Lewis & L. A. Rosenblum (Eds.), *Friendship and peer relations*. New York: Wiley, 1975.

Lichtenberger, W. *Mitmenschliches Verhalten eines Zwillingspaares in seinen ersten Lebensjahren*. Munich: Ernst Reinhardt, 1965.

Lieberman, A. F. Preschoolers' competence with a peer: Relations with attachment and peer experience. *Child Development*, 1977, *48*, 1277–1287.

Lindsley, D. B. Emotion. In S. S. Stevens (Ed.), *Handbook of experimental psychology*. New York: Wiley, 1951.

Lipps, T. Das Wissen von Fremden Ichten. *Psychologische Untersuchungen*, 1906, *1*, 694–722.

Lipton, E. L., Steinschneider, A., & Richmond, J. B. The autonomic nervous system in early life. *New England Journal of Medicine*, 1965, *273*, 147–153.

Lipton, E. L., Steinschneider, A., & Richmond, J. B. Autonomic function in the neonate. VII. Maturational changes in cardiac control. *Child Development*, 1966, *37*, 1–16.

List, K. *Temperament and behavior problems in preschool*. Unpublished doctoral dissertation, University of Denver, 1981.

Loehlin, J. C., Horn, J. M., & Willerman, L. Personality resemblance in adoptive families. *Behavior Genetics*, 1981, *11*, 309–330.

Loehlin, J. C., & Nichols, R. *Heredity, environment, and personality: A study of 850 twins*. Austin: University of Texas Press, 1976.

Londerville, S., & Main, M. Security of attachment, compliance and maternal training methods in the second year of life. *Developmental Psychology*, 1981, *17*, 289–299.

Lounsbury, M., & Bates, J. The cries of infants of differing levels of perceived temperamental difficultness: Acoustic properties and effects on likeness. *Child Development*, 1982, *53*, 677–686.

Lutz, C. The domain of emotion words on Ifaluk. *American Ethologist*, 1982, *9*, 113–128.

Lyon, M., & Plomin, R. The measurement of temperament using parental ratings. *Journal of Child Psychology and Psychiatry*, 1981, *22*, 47–53.

Lytton, H. *Parent-child interaction: Socialization process observed in twin and singleton families*. New York: Plenum, 1980.

Lytton, H., Martin, N., & Eaves, L. Environmental and genetical causes of variation in ethological aspects of behavior in two-year-old boys. *Social Biology*, 1977, *24*, 200–211.

Maccoby, E., & Feldman, S. S. Mother-attachment and stranger reactions in the third year of life. *Monographs of the Society for Research in Child Development*, 1972, *37*(1, Serial No. 146).

Mahler, M. Autism and symbiosis: Two extreme disturbances of identity. *International Journal of Psychoanalysis*, 1958, *39*, 77–83.

Mahler, M. *On human symbiosis and the vicissitudes of individuation*. New York: International Universities Press, 1968.

Mahler, M., Pine, F., & Bergman, A. *The psychological birth of the human infant*. New York: Basic Books, 1975.

Main, M. *Exploration, play, and cognitive functioning as related to mother-child attachment*. Unpublished doctoral dissertation, Johns Hopkins University, 1973.

Main, M., & Weston, D. The quality of the toddler's relationship to mother and father: Related to conflict behavior and the readiness to establish new relationships. *Child Development*, 1981, *52*, 932–940.

Main, M., & Weston, D. Avoidance of the attachment figure in infancy: Descriptions and interpretations. In J. Stevenson-Hinde & C. Murray Parkes (Eds.), *The place of attachment in human infancy*. New York: Basic Books, 1982.

Malatesta, C. Affective development over the lifespan: Involution or growth? *Merrill-Palmer Quarterly*, 1981, *27*, 145–173. (a)

Malatesta, C. Infant emotion and the vocal affect lexicon. *Motivation and Emotion*, 1981, *5*, 1–23. (b)

Malatesta, C., & Haviland, J. Learning display rules: The socialization of emotion expression in infancy. *Child Development*, 1982, *53*, 991–1003.

Mandler, G. The structure of value: Accounting for taste. In M. Fiske & S. Clarke (Eds.), *Cognition and emotion: The Carnegie-Mellon Symposium*. Hillsdale, N.J.: Erlbaum, 1982.

Martin, G., & Clarke, R. Distress crying in neonates: Species and peer specificity. *Developmental Psychology*, 1982, *18*, 3–10.

Martin, R., & Pfeffer, J. *A report on an item analysis, reliability, and validity study of the Thomas, Chess, and Korn temperament questionnaire—Parent form—for children age 3 to 7* (Report No. 2). Unpublished manuscript, University of Georgia, 1980.

Marton, P. L., & Minde, K. *Paternal and maternal behavior with premature infants*. Paper presented at the meeting of the American Orthopsychiatric Association, Toronto, April 1980.

Marvin, R. S. An ethological-cognitive model for the attenuation of mother-child attachment behavior. In T. M. Alloway, L. Krames, & P. Pliner (Eds.), *Advances in the study of communication and affect*, vol. 3, *The development of social attachment*. New York: Plenum, 1977.

Maslin, C. A., & Bates, J. E. *Anxious attachment as a predictor of disharmony in the mother-toddler relationship*. Paper presented at the meeting of the International Conference on Infant Studies, Austin, Tex., March 1982.

Masters, J., & Wellman, H. The study of human infant attachment: A procedural critique. *Psychological Bulletin,* 1974, *81,* 218–237.

Matas, L., Arend, R., & Sroufe, L. A. Continuity of adaptation in the second year: The relationship between quality of attachment and later competence. *Child Development,* 1978, *49,* 547–556.

Matheny, A. P. Bayley's infant behavior record: Behavioral components and twin analyses. *Child Development,* 1980, *51,* 1157–1161.

Matheny, A. P., & Dolan, A. Persons, situations, and time: A genetic view of behavioral change in children. *Journal of Personality and Social Psychology,* 1975, *32,* 1106–1110.

Matheny, A. P., Dolan, A., & Wilson, R. S. Bayley's infant behavior record: Relations between behaviors and mental test scores. *Developmental Psychology,* 1974, *10,* 696–702.

Matheny, A. P., Dolan, A., & Wilson, R. S. Twins: Within-pair similarity on Bayley's infant behavior record. *Journal of Genetic Psychology,* 1976, *128,* 263–270.

Matheny, A. P., Wilson, R. S., Dolan, A., & Krantz, J. Behavioral contrasts in twinships: Stability and patterns of differences in childhood. *Child Development,* 1981, *52,* 579–588.

Maudry, M., & Nekula, M. Social relations between children of the same age during the first two years of life. *Journal of Genetic Psychology,* 1939, *54,* 193–215.

Maurer, D., & Salapatek, P. Developmental changes in the scanning of faces by young infants. *Child Development,* 1976, *47,* 523–527.

McArthur, L. Z., & Baron, R. Toward an ecological theory of social perception. *Psychological Review,* in press.

McCall, R. Smiling and vocalization in infants as indices of perceptual-cognitive processes. *Merrill-Palmer Quarterly,* 1972, *18,* 341–347.

McCall, R. Qualitative transitions in behavioral development in the first two years of life. In M. Bornstein & W. Kessen (Eds.), *Psychological development from infancy: Image to intention.* Hillsdale, N.J.: Erlbaum, 1979.

McCall, R., Eichorn, D., & Hogarty, P. Transitions in early mental development. *Monographs of the Society for Research in Child Development,* 1977, *42*(3, Serial No. 171).

McCall, R., & McGhee, P. The discrepancy hypothesis of attention and affect in infants. In I. Uzgiris & F. Weizman (Eds.), *The structuring of experience.* New York: Plenum, 1977.

McCluskey, K. W., Albas, D. C., Niemi, R. R., Cuevas, C., & Ferrer, C. A. Cross-cultural differences in the perception of the emotional content of speech: A study of the development of sensitivity in Canadian and Mexican children. *Developmental Psychology,* 1975, *11,* 551–555.

McCutcheon, B., & Calhoun, K. Social and emotional adjustment of infants and toddlers to a day care setting. *American Journal of Orthopsychiatry,* 1976, *46,* 104–108.

McDevitt, J. Separation, individuation, and object constancy. *Journal of the American Psychoanalytic Association,* 1975, *23,* 713–742.

McDevitt, S., & Carey, W. B. The measurement of temperament in 3–7 year old children. *Journal of Child Psychology and Psychiatry and Allied Disciplines,* 1978, *19,* 245–253.

McDevitt, S., & Carey, W. B. *Stability of ratings versus perceptions of temperament from early infancy to 1 to 3 years.* Paper presented at the meeting of the Society for Research in Child Development, San Francisco, March 1979.

McDevitt, S., & Carey, W. B. Stability of ratings versus perceptions of temperament from early infancy to 1–3 years. *American Journal of Orthopsychiatry,* 1981, *11,* 342–345.

McDonald, A. D. Intelligence in children of very low birth weight. *British Journal of Preventive and Social Medicine,* 1964, *18,* 59–74.

McGrew, W. *An ethological study of children's behavior.* New York: Academic Press, 1972.

McNeill, T., & Persson-Blennow, I. Temperament questionnaires and clinical research. In R. Porter & G. Collins (Eds.), *Temperamental differences in infants and young children.* London: Pitman, 1982.

Macrae, J., & Herbert-Jackson, E. Are behavioral effects of infant daycare program specific? *Developmental Psychology,* 1976, *12,* 269–270.

Mead, G. *Mind, self, and society: From the standpoint of a social behaviorist.* Chicago: University of Chicago Press, 1934.

Mead, M. Review of *Darwin and facial expression,* P. Ekman (Ed.). *Journal of Communication,* 1975, *25,* 209–213.

Mehler, J., Bertoncini, J. Barriére, M., & Jassik-Gerschenfeld, D. Infant recognition of mother's voice. *Perception,* 1978, *7,* 491–497.

Meier, G. W. Maternal behavior of feral- and laboratory-reared monkeys following the surgical delivery of their infants. *Nature,* 1965, *206,* 492–493.

Meltzoff, A. N., & Moore, M. K. Imitation of facial and manual gestures by human neonates. *Science,* 1977, *198,* 75–78.

Melzack, R. The genesis of emotional behavior: An

experimental study of the dog. *Journal of Comparative and Physiological Psychology,* 1954, *47,* 166–168.

Mendelson, M., & Haith, M. The relation between audition and vision in the human newborn. *Monographs of the Society for Research in Child Development,* 1977, *41*(Serial No. 167).

Mendelson, M., Haith, M., & Goldman-Rakic, P. Face scanning and responsiveness to social cues in infant rhesus monkeys. *Developmental Psychology,* 1982, *18,* 222–228.

Meng, Z., Henderson, C., Campos, J., & Emde, R. N. *The effects of background emotional elicitation on subsequent problem solving in the toddler.* Unpublished manuscript, University of Denver, 1983.

Meyer, M. That whale among the fishes—the theory of emotions. *Psychological Review,* 1933, *40,* 292–300.

Michelsson, K., Sirvio, P., & Wasz-Hockert, D. Pain cry in fullterm asphyxiated newborn infants correlated with late findings. *Acta Paediatrica Scandinavica,* 1977, *66,* 611–616.

Mills, M., & Melhuish, E. Recognition of mother's voice in early infancy. *Nature,* 1974, *252,* 123–124.

Miller, N. E. Liberalization of basic S-R concepts. In S. Koch (Ed.), *Psychology: The study of a science.* New York: McGraw-Hill, 1959, 196–292.

Miller, R. Experimental approaches to the physiological and behavioral concomitants of affective communication in rhesus monkeys. In S. Altman (Ed.), *Social communication among primates.* Chicago: University of Chicago Press, 1967.

Milmoe, S., Novery, M., Kagan, J., & Rosenthal, R. The mother's voice: Postdictor of aspects of her baby's behavior. In S. Weitz (Ed.), *Nonverbal communication: Readings with commentary.* New York: Oxford University Press, 1974.

Mirsky, A., Weiner, H., Thales, M., & Reiser, M. Etiology of duodenal ulcer. I. Relation of specific psychological characteristics to rate of gastric secretion (serum pepsinogen). *Psychosomatic Medicine,* 1957, *19,* 1–10.

Mischel, W. Father-absence and delay of gratification. *Journal of Abnormal and Social Psychology,* 1961, *62,* 116–124.

Miyake, K., & *Relation of temperamental disposition to attachment classification.* Paper presented at the meeting of the Society for Research in Child Development, Detroit, April 1983.

Moore, T. Exclusive early mothering and its alternatives: The outcomes to adolescence. *Scandinavian Journal of Psychology,* 1975, *16,* 255–272.

Moskowitz, D., Schwartz, J. D., & Corsini, D. Initiating day care at three years of age: Effects on attachment. *Child Development,* 1977, *48,* 1271–1276.

Moss, H. Sex, age, and state as determinants of mother-infant interaction. *Merrill-Palmer Quarterly,* 1967, *13,* 19–36.

Moss, H., & Robson, K. The relation between the amount of time infants spent at various states and the development of visual behavior. *Child Development,* 1970, *41,* 509–517.

Mueller, E., & Brenner, J. The growth of social interaction in a toddler playgroup: The role of peer experience. *Child Development,* 1977, *48,* 854–861.

Mueller, E., & Lucas, T. A developmental analysis of peer interaction among toddlers. In M. Lewis & L. A. Rosenblum (Eds.), *Friendship and peer relations.* New York: Wiley, 1975.

Mueller, E., & Rich, A. Clustering and socially-directed behaviors in a playgroup of 1-year-old boys. *Journal of Child Psychology and Psychiatry,* 1976, *17,* 315–322.

Murray, A. Infant crying as an elicitor of parental behavior: An examination of two models. *Psychological Bulletin,* 1979, *86,* 191–215.

Mussen, P. *Carmichael's manual of child psychology* (3rd ed). New York: Wiley, 1970.

Nash, S. C., & Feldman, S. S. Sex role and sex-related attributions: Constancy or change across the family life cycle? In M. E. Lamb & A. L. Brown (Eds.), *Advances in developmental psychology* (Vol. 1). Hillsdale, N.J.: Erlbaum, 1982.

Naylor, H. Reading disability and lateral asymmetry: An information-processing analysis. *Psychological Bulletin,* 1980, *87,* 531–545.

Neilson, P. Shirley's babies after fifteen years: A personality study. *Journal of Genetic Psychology,* 1948, *73,* 175–186.

Neisser, U. *Cognition and reality.* San Francisco: W. H. Freeman, 1976.

Newton, G., & Levine, S. *Early experience and behavior.* Springfield, Ill.: Charles C. Thomas, 1968.

Norman, D. Twelve issues for cognitive science. *Cognitive Science,* 1980, *4,* 1–32.

Nystrom, M. Neonatal facial-postural patterning during sleep: I. Description and reliability of observation. *Psychological Research Bulletin,* 1974, *14,* 1–16.

Olson, G. M., & Lamb, M. E. Premature infants:

Cognitive and social development in the first year of life. In J. Stark (Ed.), *The special child.* New York: Human Sciences Press, 1982.

Olweus, D. Familial and temperamental determinants of aggressive behavior in adolescent boys: A causal analysis. *Development Psychology,* 1980, *16,* 644–660.

Oster, H. "Recognition" of emotional expression in infancy? In M. E. Lamb & L. R. Sherrod (Ed.), *Infant social cognition: Empirical and theoretical considerations.* Hillsdale, N.J.: Erlbaum, 1981.

Oster, H. Measuring facial movement in infants. In P. Ekman & W. Friesen (Eds.), *Analyzing facial action.* New York: Plenum, 1982.

Owen, M. T., Chase-Lansdale, L., & Lamb, M. E. *The relationship between mother-infant and father-infant attachments.* Article in preparation, 1982.

Parke, R. D., & O'Leary, S. Father-mother-infant interaction in the newborn period: Some findings, some observations and some unresolved issues. In K. Riegel & J. Meacham (Eds.), *The developing individual in a changing world,* vol. 2, *Social and environmental issues.* The Hague: Mouton, 1976.

Parke, R. D., O'Leary, S., & West, S. Mother-father-newborn interaction: Effect of maternal medication, labor and sex of infant. *Proceedings of the 80th Annual Convention of the American Psychological Association,* 1972, *7,* 85–86.

Parke, R. D., & Sawin, D. B. *Infant characteristics and behavior as elicitors of maternal and paternal responsibility in the newborn period.* Paper presented at the meeting of the Society for Research in Child Development, Denver, April 1975.

Parke, R. D., & Sawin, D. B. *The family in early infancy: Social interactional and attitudinal analyses.* Paper presented at the meeting of the Society for Research in Child Development, New Orleans, March 1977.

Parke, R. D., & Sawin D. B. The family in early infancy: Social interactional and attitudinal analyses. In F. A. Pedersen (Ed.), *The father-infant relationship: Observational studies in a family context.* New York: Praeger, 1980.

Pastor, D. L. The quality of mother-infant attachment and its relationship to toddlers' initial sociability with peers. *Developmental Psychology,* 1981, *17,* 326–335.

Pavlov, I. *Conditioned reflexes.* London: Oxford University Press, 1927.

Pedersen, F. A. (Ed.), *The father-infant relationship: Observational studies in the family context.* New York: Praeger, 1980.

Pedersen, F. A., Anderson, B., & Cain, R. *An approach to understanding linkages between the parent-infant and spouse relationships.* Paper presented at the meeting of the Society for Research in Child Development, New Orleans, March 1977.

Pedersen, F. A., Cain, R. & Zaslow, M. Variation in infant experience associated with alternative family roles. In L. Laosa & I. Sigel (Eds.), *The family as a learning environment.* New York: Plenum, 1982.

Pedersen, F. A., & Robson, K. Father participation in infancy. *American Journal of Orthopsychiatry,* 1969, *39,* 466–472.

Pedersen, F. A., Rubenstein, J. L., & Yarrow, L. J. Infant development in father-absent families. *Journal of Genetic Psychology,* 1980, *135,* 51–61.

Peiper, A. *Cerebral function in infancy and childhood.* New York: Consultants Bureau, 1963.

Peters-Martin, P., & Wachs, T. D. *A longitudinal study of temperament and its correlates in the first year of life.* Paper presented at the meeting of the Society for Research in Child Development, Boston, April 1981.

Piaget, J. *The moral judgment of the child.* London: Routledge & Kegan Paul, 1932.

Piaget, J. *The psychology of intelligence.* Paterson, N.J.: Littlefield, Adams, 1950.

Piaget, J. *The origins of intelligence.* New York: Basic Books, 1951.

Piaget, J. *The construction of reality in the child.* New York: Basic Books, 1954.

Piaget, J. *Intelligence and affectivity.* Palo Alto: Annual Reviews, 1981.

Pinneau, S. The infantile disorders of hospitalism and anaclitic depression. *Psychological Bulletin,* 1955, *52,* 429–451.

Plomin, R. Heredity and temperament: A comparison of twin data for self-report questionnaires, parental ratings, and objectively assessed behavior. *Proceedings of the Third International Congress on Twin Studies.* New York: Alan R. Liss, 1981.

Plomin, R. Childhood temperament. In B. Lahey & A. Kazdin (Eds.), *Advances in clinical child psychology* (Vol. 6). New York: Academic Press, 1982.

Plomin, R. The Colorado adoption project. *Child Development,* in press.

Plomin, R., & Foch, T. A twin study of objectively assessed personality in childhood. *Journal of*

Personality and Social Psychology, 1980, *39,* 680–688.

Plomin, R., & Rowe, D. A twin study of temperament in young children. *Journal of Psychology,* 1977, *97,* 107–113.

Plomin, R., & Rowe, D. Genetic and environmental etiology of social behavior in infancy. *Developmental Psychology,* 1979, *15,* 62–72.

Plutchik, R. *The emotions: Facts, theories, and a new model.* New York: Random House, 1962.

Porter, L. The impact of physical-physiological activity on infants' growth and development. *Nursing Research,* 1972, *21,* 210–219.

Portnoy, F., & Simmons, C. Daycare and attachment. *Child Development,* 1978, *49,* 239–242.

Power, T. G., & Parke, R. D. *Toward a taxonomy of father-infant and mother-infant play patterns.* Paper presented at the meeting of the Society for Research in Child Development, San Francisco, March 1979.

Radin, N. The role of the father in cognitive, academic, and intellectual development. In M. E. Lamb (Ed.), *The role of the father in child development* (Rev. ed.). New York: Wiley, 1981.

Radke-Yarrow, M., & Zahn-Waxler, C. Roots, motives, and patterns in children's prosocial behavior. In J. Reykowski, J. Karylowski, D. Bartal, & E. Staub (Eds.), *Origins and maintenance of prosocial behavior.* New York: Plenum, 1982.

Ragozin, A. Attachment behavior of daycare children: Naturalistic and laboratory observations. *Child Development,* 1980, *51,* 409–415.

Rajecki, D. W., Lamb, M. E., & Obmascher, P. Toward a general theory of infantile attachment: A comparative review of aspects of the social bond. *Behavioral and Brain Sciences,* 1978, *1,* 417–463.

Ramey, C. T., & Finkelstein, N. W. Contingent stimulation and infant competence. *Journal of Pediatric Psychology,* 1978, *3,* 89–96.

Ramey, C. T., Zeskind, P., & Hunter, R. Biomedical and psychosocial intervention for preterm infants. In S. Friedman & M. Sigman (Eds.), *Preterm birth and psychological development.* New York: Academic Press, 1981.

Ramsay, D. Onset of unimanual handedness in infants. *Infant Behavior & Development,* 1980, *3,* 377–385.

Rapaport, D. *Emotions and memory.* New York: Science Editions, 1961.

Rappaport, J., Pandorini, C., Renfield, M., Lake, C., & Ziegler, M. Newborn beta-hydroxylase, minor physical anomalies, and infant temperament. *American Journal of Psychiatry,* 1977, *134,* 676–679.

Regan, D., Williams, M., & Sparling, S. Voluntary expiation of guilt. *Journal of Personality and Social Psychology,* 1972, *24,* 42–45.

Rendina, I., & Dickerscheid, J. D. Father involvement with first-born infants. *Family Coordinator,* 1976, *25,* 373–379.

Reznick, S. *The development of perceptual and lexical categories in the human infant.* Unpublished doctoral dissertation, University of Colorado, 1982.

Richards, M. P. M., & Bernal, J. An observational study of mother-infant interaction. In N. Blurton-Jones (Ed.), *Ethological studies of child behaviour.* New York: Cambridge University Press, 1972.

Richards, M. P. M., Dunn, J. F., & Antonis, B. *Caretaking in the first year of life: The role of fathers' and mothers' social isolation.* Unpublished manuscript, Cambridge University, 1975.

Ringler, N., Kennell, J., Jarvella, R., Navojosky, B., & Klaus, M. Mother-to-child speech at 2 years—effects of early postnatal contact. *Behavioral Pediatrics,* 1975, *86,* 141–144.

Roopnarine, J. L., & Lamb, M. E. The effects of day care on attachment and exploratory behavior in a strange situation. *Merrill-Palmer Quarterly,* 1978, *24,* 85–95.

Roopnarine, J. L., & Lamb, M. E. Peer and parent child interaction before and after enrollment in nursery school. *Journal of Applied Developmental Psychology,* 1980, *1,* 77–81.

Roseman, I. *Cognitive aspects of emotion and emotional behavior.* Paper presented at the meeting of the American Psychological Association, New York, September 1979.

Rosenblatt, J. S. Views on the onset and maintenance of maternal behavior in the rat. In L. Aronson, E. Toback, J. S. Rosenblatt, & D. Lehrman (Eds.), *Development and evolution of behavior* (Vol. 1). San Francisco: W. H. Freeman, 1970.

Rosenblatt, J. S., & Siegel, H. Hysterectomy-induced maternal behavior during pregnancy in the rat. *Journal of Comparative and Physiological Psychology,* 1975, *89,* 685-700.

Rosenstein, D., & Oster, H. *Facial expression as a method for exploring infants' taste responses.* Paper presented at the meeting of the Society for Research in Child Development, Boston, April 1981.

Ross, H. S., & Goldman, B. M. Establishing new social relations in infancy. In T. M. Alloway, L. Krames, & P. Pliner (Eds.), *Advances in commu-*

nication and affect (Vol. 3). New York: Plenum Press, 1977.

Rothbart, M. K. Laughter in young children. *Psychological Bulletin,* 1973, *80,* 247–255.

Rothbart, M. K. *Longitudinal home observation of infant temperament.* Paper presented at the meeting of the International Conference on Infant Studies. New Haven, Conn., April 1980.

Rothbart, M. K. *Infant temperament and early social interaction.* Paper presented at the meeting of the Society for Research in Child Development, Boston, April 1981. (a)

Rothbart, M. K. Measurement of temperament in infancy. *Child Development,* 1981, *52,* 569–578. (b)

Rothbart, M. K. The concept of difficult temperament: A critical analysis. *Merrill-Palmer Quarterly,* in press.

Rothbart, M. K., & Derryberry, D. Development of individual differences in temperament. In M. E. Lamb & A. L. Brown (Eds.), *Advances in developmental psychology* (Vol. 1). Hillsdale, N.J.: Erlbaum, 1982.

Rothbart, M. K., & Derryberry, D. Emotion, attention, and temperament. In C. E. Izard, J. Kagan, & R. Zajonc (Eds.), *Emotion, cognition, and behavior.* New York: Cambridge University Press, in press.

Rowe, D., & Plomin, R. Temperament in early childhood. *Journal of Personality Assessment,* 1977, *41,* 150–156.

Rowe, D., & Plomin, R. The importance of non-shared (E1) environmental influences in behavioral development. *Developmental Psychology,* 1981, *17,* 517–531.

Rubenstein, J. L., & Howes, C. The effects of peers or toddler interaction with mother and toys. *Child Development,* 1976, *47,* 597–605.

Rubin, J., Provenzano, F., & Luria, Z. The eye of the beholder: Parents' views of sex of newborns. *American Journal of Orthopsychiatry,* 1974, *43,* 720–731.

Rutter, M. Maternal deprivation, 1972–1978: New findings, new concepts, new approaches. *Child Development,* 1979, *50,* 283–305.

Rutter, M. *Developmental continuities and discontinuities: Empirical and conceptual perspectives.* Paper presented at the meeting of the Developmental Psychobiology Research Group, Estes Park, Colo., June 1982.

Rutter, M., & Madge, N. *Cycles of disadvantage: A review of the research.* London: Heinemann, 1976.

Rutter, M., Yule, B., Quinton, D., Rowlands, O., Yule, W., & Berger, M. Attainment and adjustment in two geographical areas. III. Some factors accounting for area differences. *British Journal of Psychiatry,* 1975, *126,* 520–533.

Ryle, G. *The concept of mind.* New York: Barnes & Noble, 1950.

Saarni, C. Children's understanding of display rules for expressive behavior. *Developmental Psychology,* 1979, *15,* 424–429.

Saarni, C. *Observing children's use of display rules: Age and sex differences.* Paper presented at the meeting of the American Psychological Association, Montreal, September 1980.

Sackett, G. P. Monkeys reared in isolation with pictures as visual input: Evidence for an innate releasing mechanism. *Science,* 1966, *154,* 1468–1472.

Sagi, A., & Hoffman, M. Empathic distress in the newborn. *Development Psychology,* 1976, *12,* 175–176.

Sagi, A., Lamb, M. E., Estes, D., Shoham, R., Lewkowicz, K. S., & Dvir, R. *Security of infant-adult attachment among kibbutz-reared infants.* Paper presented at the meeting of the International Conference on Infant Studies, Austin, Tex., 1982.

Sagi, A., Lamb, M. E., Lewkowicz, K. S., Shoham, R., Dvir, R., & Estes, D. Security of infant-mother, -father, and -metapelet attachments among kibbutz-reared Israeli children. In I. Bretherton (Ed.), The strange situation: New direction for research. *Monographs of the Society for Research in Child Development,* in press.

Salapatek, P., & Banks, M. Infant sensory assessment: Vision. In F. Minifie & L. Lloyd (Eds.), *Communicative and cognitive abilities: Early behavioral assessment.* Baltimore: University Park Press, 1977.

Salk, L. The effects of the normal heartbeat sound on the behavior of the newborn infant: Implications for mental health. *World Mental Health,* 1960, *12,* 168–175.

Salk, L. Mother's heartbeat as an imprinting stimulus. *Transactions of the New York Academy of Science,* 1962, *24,* 753–763.

Salk, L. The role of the heartbeat in the relations between mother and infant. *Scientific American,* 1973, *228,* 24–29.

Sameroff, A. Organization and stability of newborn behavior: A commentary on the Brazelton neonatal behavior assessment scale. *Monographs of the Society for Research in Child Development,* 1978, *43*(5–6, Serial No. 177).

Sameroff, A. The environmental context of developmental disabilities. In D. D. Bricker (Ed.), *Intervention with at-risk and handicapped infants: From research to application*. Baltimore: University Park Press, 1982.

Sameroff, A., & Chandler, M. Reproductive risk and the continuum of caretaking casualty. In F. Horowitz, E. M. Hetherington, S. Scarr-Salapatek, & G. Siegel (Eds.), *Review of child development research* (Vol. 4). Chicago: University of Chicago Press, 1975.

Sander, L. W. Infant and caretaking environment: Investigation and conceptualization of adaptive behavior in systems of increasing complexity. In E. J. Anthony (Ed.), *Explorations in child psychiatry*. New York: Plenum, 1975.

Sander, L. W. The regulation of exchange in infant-caregiver systems and some aspects of the context-contrast relationship. In M. Lewis & L. A. Rosenblum (Eds.), *Interaction conversation and the development of language*. New York: Wiley, 1977.

Scaife, M., & Bruner, J. The capacity for joint visual attention in the infant. *Nature*, 1975, *253*, 265–266.

Scarr, S., & Salapatek, P. Patterns of fear development during infancy. *Merrill-Palmer Quarterly*, 1970, *16*, 53–90.

Schachter, S. *Emotion, obesity, and crime*. New York: Academic Press, 1970.

Schachter, S., & Singer, J. Cognitive, social, and physiological determinants of emotional state. *Psychological Review*, 1962, *69*, 379–399.

Schachter, S., & Wheeler, L. Epinephrine, chlorpromazine, and amusement. *Journal of Abnormal and Social Psychology*, 1962, *65*, 121–128.

Schaefer, E., & Bayley, N. Maternal behavior, child behavior and their intercorrelations from infancy through adolescence. *Monographs of the Society for Research in Child Development*, 1963, *28*(3, Whole No. 87).

Schaffer, H. R. Activity level as a constitutional determinant of infantile reaction to deprivation. *Child Development*, 1966, *37*, 595–602 (a)

Schaffer, H. R. The onset of fear of strangers and the incongruity hypothesis. *Journal of Child Psychology and Psychiatry*, 1966, *7*, 95–106. (b)

Schaffer, H. R. Cognitive structure and early social behavior. In H. R. Schaffer (Ed.), *The origins of human social relations*. New York: Academic Press, 1971.

Schaffer, H. R. Cognitive components of the infant's response to strangeness. In M. Lewis & L. A. Rosenblum (Eds.), *The origins of fear*. New York: Wiley, 1974.

Schaffer, H. R. *Studies in mother-infant interaction*. New York: Academic Press, 1977.

Schaffer, H. R., & Emerson, P. The development of social attachments in infancy. *Monographs of the Society for Research in Child Development*, 1964, *29*(3, Serial No. 94).

Scherer, K. Acoustic concomitants of emotional dimensions: Judging affect from synthesized tone sequences. In S. Weitz (Ed.), *Nonverbal communication*. New York: Oxford University Press, 1979. (a)

Scherer, K. Nonlinguistic vocal indicators of emotion and psychopathology. In C. E. Izard (Ed.), *Emotions in personality and psychopathology*. New York: Plenum, 1979. (b)

Scherer, K. Speech and emotional states. In J. Darby (Ed.), *Speech evaluation in psychiatry*. New York: Grune & Stratton, 1981.

Scherer, K. The assessment of vocal expression in infants and children. In C. E. Izard (Ed.), *Measuring emotions in infants and children*. New York: Cambridge University Press, 1982.

Scherer, K., & Ekman, P. *Handbook of methods in nonverbal research*. New York: Cambridge University Press, 1982.

Scherer, K., Koivumaki, J., & Rosenthal, R. Minimal cues in the vocal communication of affect: Judging emotions from content-masked speech. *Journal of Psycholinguistic Research*, 1972, *1*, 269–285.

Scherer, K., & Oshinsky, J. Cue utilization in emotion attribution from auditory stimuli. *Motivation and Emotion*, 1977, *1*, 331–346.

Scholom, A., & Schiff, G. Relating infant temperament to learning disabilities. *Journal of Abnormal Child Psychology*, 1980, *8*, 127–132.

Scholom, A., Zucker, R. A., & Stollak, G. E. Relating early child adjustment of infant and parent temperament. *Journal of Abnormal Child Psychology*, 1979, *7*, 297–308.

Schwartz, G. Psychophysiological patterning and emotion revisited. In C. E. Izard (Ed.), *Measuring emotions in infants and children*. New York: Cambridge University Press, 1982.

Schwartz, G., Fair, P., Salt, P., Mandel, M., & Klerman, G. Facial muscle patterning to affective imagery in depressed and non-depressed subjects. *Science*, 1976, *192*, 489–491.

Schwartz, G., Weinberger, D., & Singer, J. Cardiovascular differentiation of happiness, sadness, anger and fear following imagery and exercise. *Psychosomatic Medicine*, 1981, *43*, 343–364.

Schwarz, J. D., Strickland, R. G., & Krolick, G.

Infant day care: Behavioral effects at preschool age. *Developmental Psychology,* 1974, *10,* 502–506.

Searls, E., Fullard, W., & McDevitt, S. Relationships between infant temperament questionnaire ratings and observations during a short home visit. *Infant Behavior & Development,* in press.

Sears, P. Doll-play aggression in normal young children: Influence of sex, age, sibling status, and father's absence. *Psychological Monographs,* 1951, *66,* 295–324.

Seashore, M., Leifer, A., Barnett, C., & Leiderman, P. The effects of denial of early mother-infant interaction on maternal self-confidence. *Journal of Personality and Social Psychology,* 1973, *26,* 369–378.

Seegmiller, B., & King, W. Relations between behavioral characteristics of infants, their mothers' behaviors, and performance on the Bayley mental and motor scales. *Journal of Psychology,* 1975, *90,* 99–111.

Shaver, P., & Rubenstein, C. Childhood attachment experience and adult loneliness. In L. Wheeler (Ed.) *Review of personality and social psychology* (Vol. 1). Beverly Hills, Calif.: Sage Publications, 1980.

Shenum, W., & Bugental, D. The development of control over affective expression in nonverbal behavior. In R. Feldman (Ed.), *Development of nonverbal behavior in children.* New York: Springer-Verlag, 1982.

Sherman, M. The differentiation of emotional responses in infants: I. Judgments of emotional responses from motion picture views and from actual observations. *Journal of Comparative Psychology,* 1927, *7,* 265–284. (a)

Sherman, M. The differentiation of emotional responses in infants: II. The ability of observers to judge the emotional characteristics of the crying of infants and of the voice of an adult. *Journal of Comparative Psychology,* 1927, *7,* 335–351. (b)

Shinn, M. Father absence and children's cognitive development. *Psychological Bulletin,* 1978, *85,* 295–324.

Shirley, M. *The first two years: A study of twenty-five babies.* Minneapolis: University of Minnesota Press, 1933.

Shott, S. Emotion and social life; A symbolic interactionist analysis. *American Journal of Sociology,* 1979, *84,* 1317–1334.

Shucard, J., Shucard, D. W., & Thomas, D. G. *Relationships between hand preference and evoked potential asymmetries in 6-month-old infants.* Paper presented at the meeting of the Society for Psychophysiological Research, Minneapolis, October 1982.

Siegel, E., Bauman, K., Schaefer, E., Saunders, M., & Ingram, D. Hospital and home support during infancy: Impact on maternal attachment, child abuse and neglect, and health care utilization. *Pediatrics,* 1980, *66,* 183–190.

Siegel, H., & Rosenblatt, J. S. Duration of estrogen stimulation and progesterone inhibition of maternal behavior in pregnancy-terminated rats. *Hormones and Behavior,* 1978, *11,* 12–19.

Sigman, M., & Parmelee, A. H. Longitudinal evaluation of the high risk infant. In T. M. Field, A. Sostek, S. Goldberg, & H. H. Shuman (Eds.), *Infants born at risk.* New York: Prentice-Hall, 1979. (Spectrum Books)

Simner, M. Newborn's response to the cry of another infant. *Developmental Psychology,* 1971, *5,* 136–150.

Skinner, B. *Science and human behavior.* Glencoe, Ill.: Free Press, 1953.

Skinner, R. E. A calibrated recording and analysis of the pitch, force, and quality of vocal tones expressing happiness and sadness and a determination of the pitch and force of the subjective concepts of ordinary soft and loud tones. *Speech Monographs,* 1935, *2,* 81–137.

Smith, A. C., Flick, G. L., Ferriss, G. S., & Sellman, A. H. Prediction of developmental outcome at seven years from prenatal, perinatal and postnatal events. *Child Development,* 1972, *43,* 495–507.

Smith, P. K. The ontogeny of fear in children. In W. Sluckin (Ed.), *Fear in animals and man.* New York: Van Nostrand Reinhold, 1979.

Snyder, S. Dopamine and schizophrenia. In L. Wynne, R. Cromwell, & S. Matthysse (Eds.), *The nature of schizophrenia: New approaches to research and treatment.* New York: Wiley, 1978.

Sobesky, W., List, K., Holden, D., & Braucht, N. *Dimensions of child temperament in school settings.* Paper presented at the meeting of the Society for Research in Child Development, Boston, April 1981.

Sokolov, Y. *Perception and the conditioned reflex.* New York: Pergamon, 1963.

Sorce, J., Emde, R. N., Campos, J. J., & Klinnert, M. *Maternal emotional signaling: Its effect on the visual cliff behavior of one-year-olds.* Paper presented at the meeting of the Society for Research in Child Development, Boston, April 1981.

Sorce, J., Emde, R. N., & Frank, M. Maternal referencing in normal and Down's Syndrome infants: A longitudinal study. In R. N. Emde & R. J. Harmon (Eds.), *The development of attachment and affiliative systems: Psychobiological aspects*. New York: Plenum, 1982.

Soskin, W., & Kauffman, P. Judgment of emotion in word-free samples. *Journal of Communication*, 1961, *11*, 73–80.

Sostek, A., & Anders, T. Relationships among the Brazelton neonatal scale, Bayley infant scales, and early temperament. *Child Development*, 1977, *48*, 320–323.

Spencer, H. *Principles of psychology*. New York: Appleton, 1890.

Spitz, R. Anaclitic depression. *Psychoanalytic Study of the Child*, 1946, *2*, 313–342.

Spitz, R. Anxiety in infancy: A study of its manifestations in the first year of life. *International Journal of Psychoanalysis*, 1950, *31*, 138–143.

Spitz, R. *The first year of life*. New York: International Universities Press, 1965.

Spitz, R., & Wolf, K. The smiling response: A contribution to the ontogenesis of social relations. *Genetic Psychology Monographs*, 1946, *34*, 57–125.

Sroufe, L. A. Wariness of strangers and the study of infant development. *Child Development*, 1977, *48*, 731–746.

Sroufe, L. A. Attachment and the roots of competence. *Human Nature*, 1978, *1*, 50–57.

Sroufe, L. A. The coherence of individual development: Early care, attachment, and subsequent developmental issues. *American Psychologist*, 1979, *34*, 834–842. (a)

Sroufe, L. A. Socioemotional development. In J. Osofsky (Ed.), *Handbook of infant development*. New York: Wiley, 1979. (b)

Sroufe, L. A. Individual patterns of adaptation from infancy to preschool. In M. Perlmutter (Ed.), *Minnesota Symposia on Child Psychology* (Vol. 16). Hillsdale, N.J.: Erlbaum, in press.

Sroufe, L. A., & Rosenberg, D. *Coherence of individual adaptation in lower class infants and toddlers*. Paper presented at the meeting of the International Conference on Infant Studies, Austin, Tex., March 1982.

Sroufe, L. A., & Waters, E. The ontogenesis of smiling and laughter: A perspective on the organization of development in infancy. *Psychological Review*, 1976, *83*, 173–189.

Sroufe, L. A., & Waters, E. Attachment as an organizational construct. *Child Development*, 1977, *48*, 1184–1199. (a)

Sroufe, L. A., & Waters, E. Heart rate as a convergent measure in clinical and developmental research. *Merrill-Palmer Quarterly*, 1977, *23*, 3–27. (b)

Sroufe, L. A., Waters, E., & Matas, L. Contextual determinants of infant affective response. In M. Lewis & L. A. Rosenblum (Eds.), *The origins of fear*. New York: Wiley, 1974.

Sroufe, L. A., & Wunsch, J. The development of laughter in the first year of life. *Child Development*, 1972, *43*, 1326–1344.

Stayton, D. J., & Ainsworth, M. Individual differences in infant responses to brief, everyday separations as related to other infant and maternal behaviors. *Developmental Psychology*, 1973, *9*, 226–235.

Stayton, D. J., Ainsworth, M., & Main, M. Development of separation protest in the first year of life. *Developmental Psychology*, 1973, *9*, 213–225.

Steiner, J. E. The gustofacial response: Observation on normal and anencephalic newborn infants. In J. F. Bosma (Ed.), *Fourth symposium on oral sensation and perception*. Bethesda, Md.: U.S. Department of Health, Education, and Welfare, 1973. (DHEW Publication No. NIH 73–546.)

Stenberg, C. *The development of anger facial expressions in infancy*. Unpublished doctoral dissertation, University of Denver, 1982.

Stenberg, C., & Campos, J. The development of the expression of anger in human infants. In M. Lewis & C. Saarni (Eds.), *The socialization of affect*. New York: Plenum, 1983.

Stenberg, C., Campos, J., & Emde, R. The facial expression of anger in seven month old infants. *Child Development*, 1983, *54*, 178–184.

Stern, D. Mother and infant at play: The dyadic interaction involving facial, vocal, and gaze behaviors. In M. Lewis & L. A. Rosenblum (Eds.), *The effect of the infant upon the caregiver*. New York: Wiley, 1974.

Stern, D. *The first relationship: Infant and mother*. Cambridge: Harvard University Press, 1977.

Stevenson, M. B., & Lamb, M. E. The effects of social experience and social style on cognitive competence and performance. In M. E. Lamb & L. R. Sherrod (Eds.), *Infant social cognition: Empirical and theoretical considerations*. Hillsdale, N.J.: Erlbaum, 1981.

Stevenson-Hinde, J., & Simpson, A. Temperament and relationships. In R. Porter & G. Lawrenson (Eds.), *Temperamental differences in infants and young children*. London: CIBA Publications, in press.

Stoller, S., & Field, T. M. Alteration of mother and

infant behavior and heart rate during still-face perturbation of face-to-face interaction. In T. M. Field & A. Fogel (Eds.), *Emotion and early interaction*. Hillsdale, N.J.: Erlbaum, 1982.

Strelau, J. Reactivity and activity style in selected occupations. *Polish Psychological Bulletin*, 1975, *6*, 199–206.

Svejda, M., & Campos, J. *The mother's voice as a regulator of the infant's behavior*. Paper presented at the meeting of the International Conference on Infant Studies, Austin, Tex., March 1982.

Svejda, M., Campos, J., & Emde, R. N. Mother-infant "bonding": Failure to generalize. *Child Development*, 1980, *51*, 775–779.

Svejda, M., Pannabecker, B., & Emde, R. N. Parent-to-infant attachment: A critique of the early "bonding" model. In R. N. Emde & R. J. Harmon (Eds.), *The development of attachment and affiliative systems: Psychological aspects*. New York: Plenum, 1982.

Tennes, K., & Lampl, E. Stranger and separation anxiety in infancy. *Journal of Nervous and Mental Diseases*, 1964, *139*, 247–254.

Teplov, B. M. Problems in the study of general types of higher nervous activity in man and animals. In J. A. Gray (Ed.), *Pavlov's typology*. New York: Macmillan, 1964.

Thomas, A., & Chess, S. *Temperament and development*. New York: Brunner/ Mazel, 1977.

Thomas, A., & Chess, S. *The dynamics of psychological development*. New York: Brunner/Mazel, 1980.

Thomas, A., & Chess, S. Individuals as producers of their development. In R. N. Lerner & N. A. Busch-Rossnagel (Eds.), *Individuals as producers of their development*. New York: Academic Press, 1981.

Thomas, A., Chess, S., & Birch, H. *Temperament and behavior disorders in children*. New York: New York University Press, 1968.

Thomas, A., Chess, S., Birch, H., Hertzig, M., & Korn, S. *Behavioral individuality in early childhood*. New York: New York University Press, 1963.

Thompson, R. A., & Lamb, M. E. Stranger sociability and its relationship to temperament and social experiences during the second year. *Infant Behavior and Development*, 1982, *5*, 277–288.

Thompson, R. A., & Lamb, M. E. Security of attachment and stranger sociability in infancy. *Developmental Psychology*, 1983, *19*, 184–191.

Thompson, R. A., & Lamb, M. E. *Assessing qualitative dimensions of emotional responsiveness in infants*. Article in preparation.

Thompson, R. A., Lamb, M. E., & Estes, D. Stability of infant-mother attachment and its relationship to changing life circumstances in an unselected middle class sample. *Child Development*, 1982, *53*, 144–148.

Thompson, W., & Grusec, J. Studies of early experience. In P. Mussen (Ed.), *Carmichael's manual of child psychology* (Vol. 2, 3rd ed.). New York: Wiley, 1970.

Tinbergen, N. *The study of instinct*. Oxford: Oxford University Press, 1951.

Titchener, E. G. *Experimental psychology: A manual of laboratory experiments*. New York: Macmillan, 1905.

Tizard, B., & Hodges, J. The effect of early institutional rearing on the development of eight-year-old children. *Journal of Child Psychology and Psychiatry*, 1978, *19*, 99–118.

Tizard, B., & Rees, J. The effect of early institutional rearing on the behaviour problems and affectional relationships of four-year-old children. *Journal of Child Psychology and Psychiatry*, 1975, *16*, 61–74.

Tizard, J., & Tizard, B. The social development of two year old children in residential nurseries. In H. R. Schaffer (Ed.), *The origins of human social relations*. New York: Academic Press, 1971.

Tolman, E. C. *Purposive behavior in animals and men*. New York: Century, 1932.

Tomkins, S. *Affect, imagery, consciousness*, vol. 1, *The positive affects*. New York: Springer-Verlag, 1962.

Tomkins, S. *Affect, imagery, consciousness*, vol. 2, *The negative affects*. New York: Springer-Verlag 1963.

Tomkins, S. Affect theory. In P. Ekman (Ed.), *Emotion in the human face*. New York: Cambridge University Press, 1982.

Torgensen, A. M., & Kringlen, E. Genetic aspects of temperamental differences in infants: A study of same-sexed twins. *Journal of the American Academy of Child Psychiatry*, 1978, *17*, 433–444.

Tracy, R. L., & Ainsworth, M. D. S. Maternal affectionate behavior and infant-mother attachment patterns. *Child Developmental*, 1981, *52*, 1341–1343.

Tracy, R. L., Lamb, M. E., & Ainsworth, M. D. S. Infant approach behavior as related to attachment. *Child Development*, 1976, *47*, 571–578.

Trevarthen, C. Communication and cooperation in early infancy: A description of primary intersubjectivity. In M. Bullowa (Ed.), *Before speech:*

The beginning of interpersonal communication. New York: Cambridge University Press, 1979.

Tronick, E. Z., Als, H., Adamson, L., Wise, S., & Brazelton, T. B. The infant's response to entrapment between contradictory messages in face-to-face interaction. *Journal of the American Academy of Child Psychiatry,* 1978, *17,* 1–13.

Tronick, E. Z., Als, H., & Brazelton, T. B. Monadic phases: A structural descriptive analysis of infant-mother face to face interaction. *Merrill Palmer Quarterly,* 1980, *26,* 3–24.

Tronick, E. Z., Ricks, M., & Cohn, J. F. Maternal and infant affective exchange: Patterns of adaptation. In T. M. Field (Ed.), *Emotion and early interaction.* Hillsdale, N.J.: Erlbaum, 1982.

Uzgiris, I., & Hunt, J. *Assessment in infancy: Ordinal scales of psychological development.* Urbana: University of Illinois Press, 1975.

Vaillant, G. E. *Adaptation to life.* Boston: Little, Brown, 1977.

Vandell, D. L. *Toddler sons' social interaction with mothers, fathers, and peers.* Unpublished doctoral dissertation, Boston University, 1976.

Vandell, D. L., Wilson, K. S., & Buchanan, N. R. Peer interaction in the first year of life: An examination of its structure, content, and sensitivity to toys. *Child Development,* 1980, *51,* 481–488.

Vandell, D. L., Wilson, K. S., & Whalen, W. T. Birth-order and social-experience differences in infant-peer interaction. *Developmental Psychology,* 1981, *17,* 438–445.

van Hoof, J. Facial expressions in higher primates. *Symposium of the Zoological Society of London,* 1962, *8,* 97–125.

Vaughn, B., Deinard, A. & Egeland, B. Measuring temperament in pediatric practice. *Journal of Pediatrics,* 1980, *96,* 510–514.

Vaughn, B., Egeland, B., Sroufe, L. A., & Waters, E. Individual differences in infant-mother attachment at twelve and eighteen months: Stability and change in families under stress. *Child Development,* 1979, *50,* 971–975.

Vaughn, B., Gove, F., & Egeland, B. The relationship between out-of-home care and the quality of infant-mother attachment in an economically disadvantaged sample. *Child Development,* 1980, *51,* 1203–1214.

Vaughn, B., Taraldson, B., Crichton, L., & Egeland, B. Relationships between neonatal behavioral organization and infant behavior during the first year of life. *Infant Behavior & Development,* 1980, *3,* 47–66.

Vaughn, B., Taradlson, B., Chrichton, L., & Egeland, B. The assessment of infant temperament: A critique of the Carey infant temperament questionnaire. *Infant Behavior & Development,* 1981, *4,* 1–18.

Vincze, M. The social contacts of infants and young children reared together. *Early Child Development and Care,* 1971, *1,* 99–109.

Vine, I. The role of facial-visual signaling in early social development. In M. Von Cranach & I. Vine (Eds.), *Studies of interaction and expression in man and chimpanzee.* New York: Academic Press, 1973.

Waldrop, M. F., Bell, R. Q., McLaughlan, B., & Halverson, C. F. Newborn minor physical anomalies predict short attention span, peer aggression, and impulsivity at age 3. *Science,* 1978, *199,* 563–565.

Walk, R. The development of depth perception in animals and human infants. *Monographs of the Society for Research in Child Development,* 1966, *31*(Whole No. 5).

Walk, R., & Gibson, E. A comparative and analytical study of visual depth perception. *Psychological Monographs,* 1961, *75*(15, Whole No. 5).

Walker, A. Intermodal perception of expressive behaviors by human infants. *Journal of Experimental Child Psychology,* 1982, *33,* 514–535.

Wallerstein, J. S., & Kelly, J. B. The effects of parental divorce: Experiences of the child in later latency. *American Journal of Orthopsychiatry,* 1976, *46,* 256–269.

Waters, E. The reliability and stability of individual differences in infant-mother attachment. *Child Development,* 1978, *49,* 483–494.

Waters, E., & Deane, D. Infant-mother attachment: Theories, models, recent data, and some tasks for comparative developmental analysis. In L. W. Hoffman, R. A. Gandelman, & H. R. Schiffman, (Eds.), *Parenting: Its causes and consequences.* Hillsdale, N.J.: Erlbaum, 1982.

Waters, E., Vaughn, B., & Egeland, B. Individual differences in infant-mother attachment relationships at age one: Antecedents in neonatal behavior in an urban, economically disadvantaged sample. *Child Development,* 1980, *51,* 208–216.

Waters, E., Wippman, J., & Sroufe, L. A. Attachment, positive affect, and competence in the peer group: Two studies in construct validation. *Child Development,* 1979, *50,* 821–829.

Watson, J. B. *Behaviorism.* Chicago: University of Chicago Press, 1930.

Watson, J. S. Smiling, cooing, and "the game." *Merrill-Palmer Quarterly,* 1972, *18,* 341–347.

Watson, J. S., & Ramey, C. T. Reactions to response-contingent stimulation in early infancy. *Merrill-Palmer Quarterly,* 1972, *18,* 219–228.

White, B., Held, R., & Castle, P. Experience in early human development. Part 1: Observations on the development of visually-directed reaching. In J. Hellmuth (Ed.), *Exceptional infant: The normal infant.* Seattle: Special Child Publications, 1967.

Whiting, J., & Child, I. *Child training and personality. A cross cultural study.* New Haven, Conn.: Yale University Press, 1953.

Wiesenfeld, A., Malatesta, C., & DeLoach, L. Differential parental response to familiar and unfamiliar distress signals. *Infant Behavior & Development,* 1981, *4,* 281–295.

Willemsen, E., Flaherty, D., Heaton, C., & Ritchey, G. Attachment behavior of one-year-olds as a function of mother vs. father, sex of child, session, and toys. *Genetic Psychology Monographs,* 1974, *90,* 305–324.

Williams, C., & Stevens, K. Emotions and speech: Some acoustical correlates. *Journal of the Acoustical Society of America,* 1972, *52,* 1238–1250.

Williams, C., & Stevens, K. Vocal correlates of emotional states. In J. Darby (Ed.), *Speech evaluation in psychiatry.* New York: Grune & Stratton, 1981.

Willis, A., & Ricciuti, H. *A good beginning for babies.* Ithaca, N.Y.: College of Human Ecology, Cornell University, 1974.

Wilson, R. S., & Matheny, A. P. Assessment of temperament in infant twins. *Development Psychology,* in press.

Wing, L. *Early childhood autism.* Oxford: Pergamon, 1976.

Wolff, P. H. The natural history of crying and other vocalizations in early infancy. In B. Foss (Ed.), *Determinants of infant behavior* (Vol. 4). New York: Wiley, 1969.

Woodworth, R. S., & Schlosberg, H. S. *Experimental psychology.* New York: Holt, 1954.

Wundt, W. *Principles of physiological psychology,* New York: Macmillan, 1904.

Yang, R., & Halverson, C. A study of the "inversion of intensity" between newborn and preschool-age behavior. *Child Development,* 1976, *47,* 350–359.

Yarrow, L. J. Maternal deprivation: Toward an empirical and conceptual reevaluation. *Psychological Bulletin,* 1961, *58,* 459–490.

Yarrow, L. J., Rubenstein, J. L., & Pederson, F. A. *Infant and environment: Early cognitive and motivational development.* New York: Wiley, 1975.

Yogman, M. W., Dixon, S., Tronick, E., Als, H., Adamson, L., Lester, B., & Brazelton, T. B. *The goals and structure of face-to-face interaction between infants and fathers.* Paper presented at the meeting of the Society for Research in Child Development, New Orleans, March 1977.

Yonas, A. Infants' responses to optical information for collision. In R. Aslin & Petersen (Eds.), *Development of perception: Psychobiological perspectives.* (Vol 2). New York: Academic Press, 1981.

Young, G., & Décarie, T. An ethology-based catalogue of facial/vocal behaviour in infancy. *Animal Behaviour,* 1977, *25,* 95–107.

Young, G., & Lewis, M. Effects of familiarity and maternal attention on infant peer relations. *Merrill-Palmer Quarterly,* 1979, *25,* 105–119.

Young-Browne, G., Rosenfeld, H., & Horowitz, F. Infant discrimination of facial expressions. *Child Development,* 1977, *48,* 555–562.

Zahn-Waxler, C., Radke-Yarrow, M., & King, R. A. Child rearing and children's prosocial initiations toward victims of distress. *Child Development,* 1979, *50,* 319–330.

Zajonc, R. Feeling and thinking: Preferences need no inferences. *American Psychologist,* 1980, *35,* 151–175.

Zarrow, M. X., Gandelman, R., & Denenberg, V. H. Prolactin: Is it an essential hormone for maternal behavior in the mammal? *Hormones and Behavior,* 1971, *2,* 343–354.

Zelazo, P. R. From reflexive to instrumental behavior. In L. P. Lipsitt (Ed.), *Developmental psychobiology: The significance of infancy.* Hillsdale, N.J.: Erlbaum, 1976.

Zeskind, P. Behavioral dimensions and cry sounds of infants of differential fetal growth. *Infant Behavior & Development,* 1981, *4,* 297–306.

Ziajka, A. *Prelinguistic communication in infancy.* New York: Praeger, 1981.

Zuckerman, M. *Sensation seeking: Beyond the optimal level of arousal.* Hillsdale, N.J.: Erlbaum, 1979.

EARLY CHILDHOOD PROGRAMS 11

K. ALISON CLARKE-STEWART, *University of Chicago*
GRETA G. FEIN, *University of Maryland*

CHAPTER CONTENTS

INTRODUCTION

As stated in the Preface to the third edition, the purpose of the *Manual of Child Psychology* is to provide a "comprehensive and accurate picture of the current state of knowledge . . . in the most important research areas of the psychology of human development" (Mussen, 1970, p. vii). In keeping with this purpose, the third edition contained a chapter entitled ''Studies of Early Experience,'' in which Thompson and Grusec critically reviewed experiments that ''leave no doubt that early experience is extremely important'' (p. 565). Wisely, these authors set wide boundaries around key terms: ''Early'' covered all age levels from conception to maturity; ''experience'' could include prenatal exposure to drugs or maternal disease, as well as behavioral events; and ''important'' meant dimensions such as the extent or generality of change, the likelihood of spontaneous recovery (or regression), and the ease with which the change might be reversed. Considering these wide boundaries, it is interesting that human studies comprised only 22 of the chapter's 69 pages, the remainder being devoted to animal research. In the section on human subjects there was only one page devoted to the impact of nursery school attendance, another for studies of disadvantaged children, and about six pages on the formation and disruption of social attachments.

Not surprisingly, for an article prepared well before its 1970 publication date, there were few warnings that a field of inquiry dominated by animal models, in which extensions to human beings meant the sacrifice of scientific rigor, was already becoming caught in a tidal wave of antipoverty programs, infant, preschool, and parent interventions, and debates about community change, working mothers, school reform, economic justice, and civil rights. Most important from the perspective of this chapter, in now a fourth edition of the *Manual*, there was no warning that a scant decade later the field would be drowning in a deluge of reports, studies, analyses, reanalyses, aggregations, and disaggregations concerned with what happened when a limited set of psychological ideas were used to serve the purposes of national reform.

Ideally, authors updating a chapter in a previous edition of the *Manual* would look at earlier themes and provide a thorough account of how a given area arrived at its current state, along with a description of that state. In collecting material for the present chapter, however, it soon became clear that the issue of ''early experience'' had changed in so many important ways that the area was no longer what it had been, or perhaps what it might have become, if child psychologists had not in the 1960s left their laboratories and joined other social scientists in a richly supported and unprecedented opportunity to conduct what Bronfenbrenner (1979) calls the ''ecological experiment''—an experiment conducted for ''heuristic purposes'' to analyze the complex relations between a child and the environment in the hope that by trying ''to budge the one'' one might ''see what happens to the other.''

Early Childhood Programs

The 1960s and 1970s produced a flood of ecological experiments attempting to alter the early experiences of young children, especially those whose environments were considered disadvantageous for development. Programs to compensate for presumed deficits in these environments appeared suddenly and proliferated rapidly. Experimental preschool programs were created in the laboratories of child development researchers and tested in communities across the country; Head Start was conceived and soon expanded to a national scale, reaching hundreds of thousands of preschool children; traditional nursery schools were revitalized by input from developmental research and grew in popularity; day care became an increasing necessity for working parents and an arena for educational programming; parent training programs based on theories of child development were designed and disseminated; and popular books, articles, and TV shows uncovered a large audience hungry for knowledge and advice about child development. Developmental psychologists were ready to change the world; their proposals to structure children's experiences in ways different from those traditionally accomplished by untutored parents at home were made with enthusiasm and optimism.

This early childhood ''movement,'' and the programs it spawned, was so swift, salient, and significant that it soon dominated the study of children's early experience. Laboratory and animal research on the effects of early experience continued, but was overshadowed by the bulk of these programmatic interventions. It was for this reason that the present chapter became a treatment of early childhood programs instead of an update of Thompson and Grusec's chapter on early experience. In compiling a literature for this chapter, we made no attempt to match Thompson and Grusec's comprehensive coverage of research on early experience. We omitted laboratory manipulations, physiological interventions, studies of parental care, and research using animal subjects, and chose to focus solely on field studies of recent programs affecting the real-life experiences of young children.

We deemed these programs worthy of attention for several reasons. One reason was that early childhood programs are relatively new and we know very little about them. A second reason was that, since programs are involving increasing numbers of children, it seemed important to find out about their effects. A third reason to focus on these programs was that by examining the programs and their effects we thought we might learn something about educational practice and how to improve it. And the fourth reason, of particular relevance to an audience of researchers in child development, was our belief that these programs can serve as the basis for a new research paradigm, a research paradigm that can provide important information about processes of child development and educational change.

A New Paradigm

The research paradigm which characterizes studies of early childhood programs is "new" in its clear departure from traditional basic research in child development and different for its move into new areas of applied research which until now have been left unexamined. Research on field programs represents a dramatic shift from the carefully controlled experimental model, in which one variable is manipulated and one outcome is measured at a time, to a much looser kind of research, in which manipulations are complex and effects multiple and murky. The canons of traditional experimental methodology are stretched to the breaking point when applied to these programs and, as a consequence, when programmers and policymakers demand meaningful answers to seemingly straightforward questions about the programs, they are often disappointed. But this kind of research, though difficult, is potentially very valuable. Studies of early childhood programs require a difficult to achieve balance between theory and practice—a balance that has not yet occurred in developmental psychology. The programs offer a unique opportunity to map the theoretical domain of child development by studying systematic variation in programs and effects, in input and output, while providing the option of strengthening educational practice by extending ideas drawn from developmental theory. Focusing on the studies of these programs can help conceptualize and clarify this research paradigm in which psychologists and educators, scientists and practitioners, work reciprocally.

There is a myth about how scientific knowledge accumulates, to which many, including scientists, subscribe. The myth is that detached scientists acquire general knowledge that, when disseminated to the public, is discovered by technicians, who recognize its practical value. The myth rests on the belief that general knowledge follows only from "basic" research, which is experimental, analytic, conducted in a laboratory vacuum, and uncontaminated by the complexities of real life. Actually, even in other areas of psychology, striking theoretical advances have grown out of research that was deliberately wholistic and conducted in field settings, utilizing observational procedures and addressing the specific problems of "practitioners" (e.g., Garner, 1972; see also Reese & Overton, 1980). Elegant theory may develop in tandem with sophisticated practical problem solving, and general knowledge may be the end product of an ongoing exchange between general and specific knowledge, between scientist and technician. Paradoxically, the psychological laboratory, with its meticulous controls, often yields only highly specific knowledge; it takes a "real-life" investigation to test the generality of findings.

In developmental psychology, the opportunity for such investigation is provided by early childhood programs. In fact, these programs may tell us more about developmental processes than we learn in laboratory experiments. The study of such programs may not yield unqualified facts or unconditional answers; however, it can add to our understanding and to our general knowledge about child development. Finding that some children improve in a program and others do not raises questions about individual differences in development. Finding that some programs "work" and others do not suggests hypotheses about environmental contributions to development. The analysis of systematic variation between programs or program components can illuminate relative influences on development. The application of theoretical constructs to program practices can advance the refinement and elaboration of theoretical formulations within general theories of child development. Most child development theories tend to focus on particular, even narrow, aspects of development rather than on the "whole" child. But practice has difficulty preserving these boundaries because the real child laughs, cries, speaks, moves, and looks in rapid sequence or simultaneously in ways that reflect thoughts, emotions, intentions, hopes, and expectations. To put a theory into practice, thus, may entail stretching its boundaries to encompass problems initially peripheral to the theory itself. For example, Piaget's theory of cognitive development is not really about education, but it has been stretched to apply to preschool programs. Piaget's research methods, his notions of developmental stages, and his view of the child as active constructor, all have been applied somewhat differently in early childhood programs designed by Lavatelli (1970); Weikart, Rogers, Adcock, and McClelland (1971); and Kamii and DeVries (1977). Thus, though it has not provided explicit curriculum guidelines, Piaget's theory has offered ways of conceptualizing an educational program. On the other hand, if these programmatic applications of the theory can serve to identify environments that enrich or accelerate children's development, this could contribute to a more detailed, more differentiated, and more finely tuned general theory of cognitive development.

The reciprocal relationship between theory and practice offered by early childhood program research can be illustrated by describing one particular study we know well, a study we did with William Kessen in New Haven (Kessen, Fein, Clarke-Stewart, & Starr, 1975). This study was designed to examine the effects of variation in two components of an early childhood program: the curriculum (emphasizing language, play, or social activities) and the target participants (mothers, children, or both). An attempt was made to control all other variables. Participants were all of the same age (12 months) and socioeconomic (working class) status, were in the program the same length of time (18 months) and for the same number of sessions (42), and had the same "teachers" (female research assistants), who used the same instructional strategies (demonstration and discussion). Assessment of the performance of mothers and children on a wide range of measures taken before the program began and at 6-month intervals thereafter did not confirm the clear picture that had been suggested initially by child development theory: a matching of curricular input with measures of performance for that aspect of development (e.g., language improving most for participants in the language curriculum group) and a clear causal path of influence from teacher to mother to child. Results were complicated by unexpected factors among the individual children (such as the child's sex), their mothers (e.g., their initial directiveness), and the real-life context in which they lived (e.g., the family support network). The study thus showed our working hypotheses to be simplistic and suggested the need for futher refinement and elaboration of our child development theory before further effort was spent fine-tuning program curricula.

Point of View

In this chapter we try to wring general information about child development and educational practice from the world of early childhood programs. We attempt to illustrate the interrelationship between theory and practice by discussing the results of program evaluations in terms of possible explanations for observed effects. We use the literature on these programs not as the basis for facts or specific knowledge but as a source that expands our understanding of developmental and educational processes by raising questions as often as answering them.

It is our conviction that this is the most productive utilization of currently available information, and it has guided our organization of this chapter. Here you will find no comprehensive catalog of early childhood programs and their outcomes. (For child-focused experimental programs, more comprehensive reviews of these programs can be found in Fein & Clarke-Stewart, 1973; Horowitz & Paden, 1973; Mann, Harrell, & Hurt, 1978; for parent-focused interventions in Chilman, 1973; Clarke-Stewart & Apfel, 1979; Croate & Glover, 1977; Goodson & Hess, 1976; and Gray & Wandersman, 1980; for infant-focused programs in Beller, 1979; for day care programs in Belsky & Steinberg, 1978; Belsky, Steinberg, & Walker, 1982; Bronfenbrenner, Belsky, & Steinberg, 1976; Kilmer, 1979; Ricciuti, 1976; Rutter, 1982; Silverstein, 1977; for nursery school programs in Stukat, 1969; Swift, 1964.) In this chapter you will find instead a selective review of this literature, intended to raise and illuminate questions about processes of program-induced changes in children's psychological development. Our selectivity has led us to give particular coverage to research in which attempts have been made to describe what happens to children when they attend early childhood programs, in which observational methods have been used and social and emotional as well as cognitive outcomes have been assessed. It is our hope that this kind of systematic study and the kind of analyses illustrated in this chapter will permit richer inferences about environment-child interactions and strengthen the methodology of applied developmental psychology.

Limitations

Some limitations in the chapter's content are a result of our deciding to deal with general process issues rather than specific studies. Other limitations are the results of the work done in the field and the current state of the art, not of our selectivity, and we have tried to compensate for these limitations. The research on early childhood programs that formed the corpus for our review has been limited by a lack of systematic organization and analysis. Programs are diverse and scattered. To compensate for this we have provided a taxonomy of program dimensions and components. The research has also been limited by unacknowledged values, assumptions, and social pressures. To bring some of these underlying factors into the open, we have included a section on the historical and social context of early childhood programs. Research on programs for young children has been further limited by methodological problems and, therefore, we have offered a discussion of some of the important issues in program evaluation. Finally, the literature on early childhood programs has been limited in one more way, which we could not compensate for: the biases of selective reporting and publication. A federally funded survey of research on Head Start programs conducted by Mann et al. (1978) clearly illustrates these biases. These investigators located 59 studies considering the impact of Head Start programs, 27 of which were unpublished doctoral dissertations. The unpublished dissertations were likely to find "no impact" (about 50%), whereas published national evaluation studies invariably found a "positive impact." Of the 762 references listed, less than a third were published articles, and relatively few of these were in peer reviewed journals. Much of the research on child development programs has never been published in any form, although some reports have been deposited in public archives, such as the ERIC Clearinghouse. The observations in this chapter must be viewed, therefore, as representing only a sampling of the empirical research conducted during the 1960s and 1970s in the area of early childhood, based, as they are, on available reports, most of them published. The sampling probably reflects both the most adequate research and the most positive.[1] This bias we can only acknowledge and warn the reader of.

Organization

The organization of the chapter is as follows: First, an overview of the domain to be reviewed, outlining the dimensions of early childhood programs, is offered. Second, there is a discussion of the historical and social context in which these programs are embedded. Third, salient methodological issues in the evaluation of these programs are discussed. Fourth, the results of such evaluations are presented to illustrate program effects and the processes underlying them. Finally, some conclusions following from this analysis and review are made about how research on early childhood programs can in the future illuminate more clearly theories and descriptions of child development and educational practice.

DEFINITIONS AND DIMENSIONS

Early childhood programs include nursery schools and day care centers, Head Start programs and day care homes, community preschools and experimental early education programs, parent training and parent education. They are not necessarily formal or explicitly educational, but all have in common the provision of some form of regular and systematic experience beyond what young children ordinarily receive from their parents at home. They are characterized by extreme diversity on a wide variety of dimensions. As a first step in our review of these programs, therefore, we look at a number of these dimensions. It is by comparing the effects of programs as they differ along these dimensions that we may ultimately gain a deeper understanding of child development and educational practice.

Organization of Programs

Table 1 summarizes a number of dimensions that affect the organization of early childhood programs, and it begins to illustrate at a broad level the complexity and diversity of the programs. An early childhood program may originate in any one of a variety of ways (see Figure 1). A program may be

Table 1. **Organizational Dimensions**

Sponsor	*Funding Source*
Legislature	**Government**
Entrepreneur	**Private enterprise**
Parents	**Nonprofit organization**
Community group	
Social service agency	
Researcher	
Company	
Scale	*Accountability*
National	**Individual parents**
Multiple	**Licensers**
Single	**Sponsors**
	Researchers
Director	*Staff Roles*
Clinician	**Teacher**
Administrator	**Social worker**
Educator	**Researcher**
Social worker	**Caregiver**
Researcher	**Therapist**
Caregiver	**Nutritionist**
	Nurse
	Aide
	Custodian
Participants	*Services*
"Targets"	**Health**
"Clients"	**Nutrition**
"Patients"	**Social work**
"Consumers"	**Education**
"Students"	**Training**
"Constituents"	**Diagnosis**
	Transportation

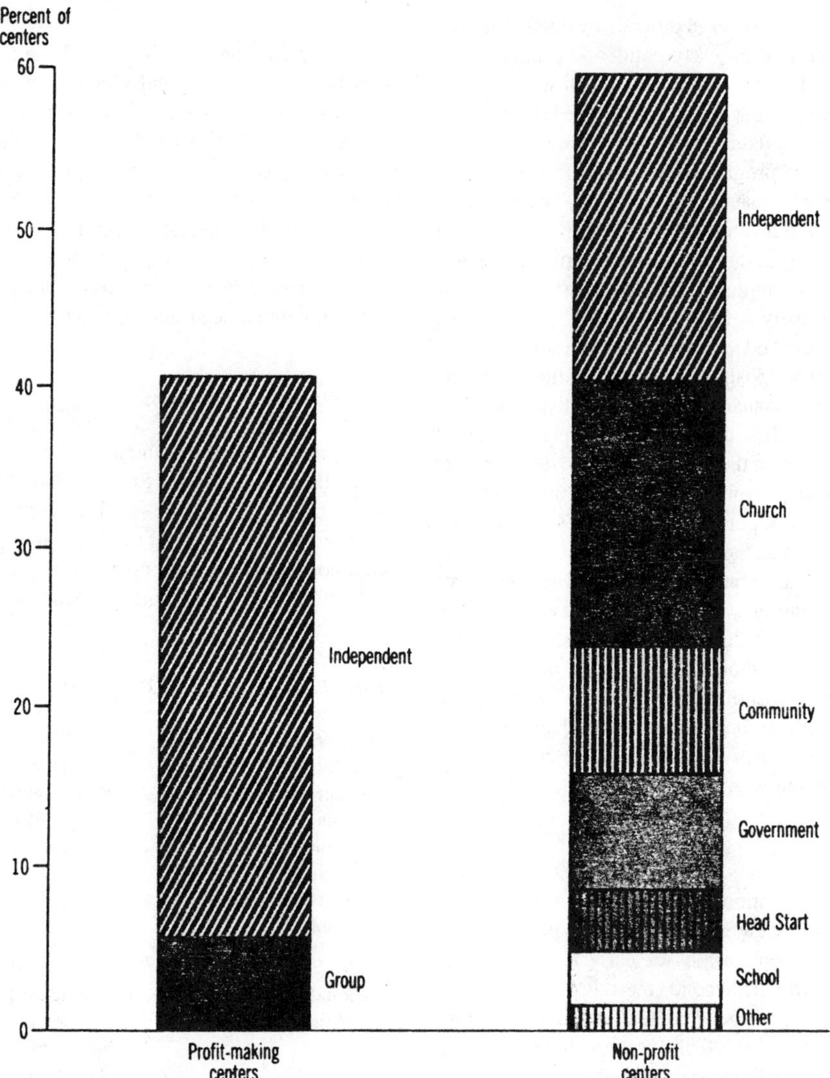

Figure 1. Legal status and sponsorship of day care centers. (From Nancy B. Dearman and Valena White Plisko. *The Condition of Education.* Washington, D.C.: National Center for Educational Statistics, 1980.)

established or funded by a government office. Head Start programs, a national network of part-time preschool programs for disadvantaged children, which originated in the federal Office of Child Development, are perhaps the best known exemplars of such programs. Government-funded programs are usually for "special" children (poor, handicapped, of minority status), stress education or treatment, and meet approved standards of quality. They may be operational, service-oriented programs (like Head Start) or research and demonstration programs (like the Parent Child Development Centers, more of which will be said later). However, a relatively small proportion of available programs is of this type. Only 9% of current day care center programs, for example, get direct government funding (Coelen, Glantz, & Calore, 1978; Frost & Schneider, 1971).

On the other hand, a program may be set up and sponsored by a community group or a social service organization (a church, a service club, Easter Seals, or Red Feather) and supported by charitable donations, perhaps supplemented with parental fees.

These programs are also usually for poor children, but they are more likely to emphasize physical caretaking and personal attention rather than education or treatment. Third, parents themselves may start and staff a program cooperatively; this kind of program is usually used by middle or upper income families in which parents have time available for working in the program. In planning the program the organizers are likely to stress shared values and ideology over education and physical caretaking (Frost & Schneider, 1971). Fourth, a program may be created for the purpose of research, funded with support from government, private foundations, and sometimes parental or university contributions. The aim of these experimental programs is usually intervention and improvement, "to serve the needs and interests and enhance the personal welfare of the target individuals" (Bermont, Kelman, & Warwick, 1978, p. 29), or the testing of some theoretical question (e.g., comparing "structured" and "open" teaching methods). Industrial day care, a fifth type of early childhood program, is receiving more attention lately. These programs originate as a fringe benefit in large companies, unions, or institutions, such as hospitals, and are established to keep employees at work and happy. They often offer a full range of services, and company policy may carry over into the program (e.g., hygienic emphasis in a hospital program; Garland & White, 1980).

Finally and most commonly, a program may originate with an individual entrepreneur: a babysitter or day care home provider, a neighborhood nursery school owner, a "Ma and Pa" in a proprietary day care center, or an operator of a facility in a commercial chain of franchised early childhood centers (KinderCare, Mary Moppet, Children's World). The "programs" falling into this category range from a private residence with only one or two children (a day care home or the child's own home) to large commercial centers with 300 or more children. About half the existing center day care programs are in this category (Coelen et al., 1978; Dearman & Plisko, 1980). These programs are supported entirely by parent fees and operated for profit. They are less likely than publicly funded programs to have eligibility criteria, highly trained personnel, an educational curriculum, or social services. Commercial day care centers are likely to stress the physical facility; private individuals are likely to stress supervision and physical care; and private nursery schools are likely to stress creative expression and social adjustment (Frost & Schneider, 1971).

Linked to these general dimensions of the source and sponsorship of a program are other aspects of organizational structure, such as who directs the program and the respective roles of staff and participants (researcher and subjects, social worker and cases, administrator and clients, therapist and patients, provider and consumers, teacher and students). Another organizational aspect is who supervises the program. Most often it is the responsibility of the parents and staff to monitor the program, but in experimental programs there is supervision by the research investigator; in programs that are part of a training and support network of day care homes or centers there is supervision by the training institution; and in licensed programs there is some supervision by the state. Yet another organizational factor is the scale of the program. Programs can range in size, from a single, independent setting to multiple associated settings [e.g., a chain of commercial day care centers like KinderCare or a widely replicated experimental program like the Mother Child Home Program (Levenstein, 1977)], or they can be as large as a national program like Head Start. A final organizational dimension is the range of services offered by a program: health, nutrition, education, transportation, and so on.

These organizational features of early childhood programs undoubtedly affect the content of the program, though the links have not yet been studied as systematically as one might wish (Belsky et al., 1982). The effect of source and sponsor, for example, is suggested by the distinction between private and public day care centers: Publicly funded centers have been observed to have, on the average, better adult-child ratios (1:6 vs. 1:8), more teachers with training in child development (66% vs. 44%), teachers who have been in the center longer (3 vs. 2 years), more parent involvement, higher quality overall, and more comprehensive services (Coelen et al., 1978; Keyserling, 1972). Similarly, licensed day care home providers are more likely than unlicensed individuals to talk, help, teach, and play with the children, to provide a stimulating physical environment, including music, dancing, books, and educational TV, and to serve nutritious food (Fosburg, Hawkins, Singer, Goodson, Smith, & Brush, 1980; Stallings, 1980). These organizational features thus can be seen as overarching and indirect influences on the context and nature of early childhood programs.

Assumptions and Values

At the other extreme, also wielding an indirect influence on program content, are the assumptions and values that underlie these programs. These di-

Table 2. **Assumptions and Values**

Nature of the "Problem"	***Nature of the "Solution"***
Poor physical environment	**Prevention**
Parent not available	**Amelioration**
Parent not competent	**Rehabilitation**
Lack of school preparation	**Acceleration**
Lack of social training	**Service**
Nature of Intervention	***Source of Program Objectives***
Coercive	**Generalized virtues**
Manipulative	**Normative standards**
Persuasive	**Developmental potential**
Facilitative	**Emancipation ethic**
	Health
Nature of Development	***Theory of Development***
Nature/nurture	**Psychoanalytic**
Critical periods	**Learning**
	Cognitive
Nature of the Child	***Role of the Parent***
Exploratory	**Uninvolved**
Expressive	**Mediator**
Learning	**Teacher**
Sociable	**Therapist**
Constructive	

mensions of early childhood programs are outlined in Table 2.

One critical assumption has to do with the purpose of the program or the "problem" it addresses. Day care, for example, is a response to the inability of parents to care for their children during the day. Parent training is a response to the perception that parents are unable to provide the best or proper care for their children. Early childhood education programs identify as the "problem" particular shortcomings in children's home environments; for instance, inadequate preparation for school is identified as the problem in the Distar program (Bereiter & Engelmann, 1966); lack of social interaction with peers in traditional nursery schools; less than adequate training in social skills in Bank Street sponsored programs (Biber, 1977); dearth of stimulating physical materials and knowledge about how to use them in toy-lending programs (Nimnicht, Arango, & Adcock, 1977).

Related to these assumptions about the nature of the problem are assumptions about appropriate solutions. A program may be aimed simply at providing a service or resource for working parents, or it may attempt to influence children's development. If the second case, a program may aim at prevention, amelioration, or rehabilitation of delayed or inadequate development; or it may be an attempt to speed up the child's development beyond the normal rate; or it may offer enriching experiences intended to enhance development. Even within a Piagetian framework, there are some programs based on the assumption that the appropriate solution is acceleration, getting children to the next developmental stage faster, and so they offer structured learning opportunities calculated to move the child ahead: hiding games to develop object permanence, weight and volume experiments to encourage conservation, ordering problems to foster seriation, labeling exercises to speed up classification skills (e.g., Gordon, Guinagh, & Jester, 1977; Lavatelli, 1970; Weikart et al., 1971). Other programs also inspired by the spirit of Piagetian theory strive for enrichment, offering a variety of materials and social games with the purpose of encouraging children to come up with interesting ideas, problems, situations, and questions (Kamii & DeVries, 1977; Kohlberg & DeVries, 1983).

Assumptions about the problem and the solution are, in turn, related to assumptions about effective and appropriate implementation strategies—strategies that range from the most intrusive coercion to the most indirect facilitation—and to the particular objectives or desired outcomes of the program. These objectives might be drawn from a set of generalized virtues or idealized traits (children should be good, independent, sociable, and bright), from a vision of good physical and mental health (children should be happy, healthy, and rosy-cheeked), from normative standards for development (children should have school-readiness skills by the time they are 5 years old), from the notion that one should fulfill his or her individual potential (children should be working at the top of their capacity), or from an "emancipation ethic" (program objectives should be left up to the individual parent to decide).

Underlying early childhood programs are also some basic assumptions about the nature of development and the abilities of children. One critical assumption about development concerns how much impact the environment has: Is development propelled primarily by nature or by nurture? The content and style of programs vary dramatically, depending on the programmers' position on this issue; at one extreme, a rich environment may be provided for children to explore with minimal instruction or interference, and, at the other extreme, a prescribed, didactic regimen of academic drills may be the basis of a program. A second important assumption about development concerns the existence of critical periods in development. This assumption is likely to dictate the target age of children in the program and to determine how closely activities are linked with age. And a third assumption about development, with implications for curriculum programming, has to do with how children progress and thus what kind of behavior is encouraged (e.g., exploring materials, creating art, acting roles, learning lessons, interacting socially, constructing experiments). Programs may also reflect curricular biases rooted in a particular theory of development, for example, psychoanalytic, cognitive (Piaget or Montessori), or learning theory.

Finally, there are assumptions about the appropriate role of parents in the program (Fein, 1980). Parents may be viewed as irrelevant or even possibly as a negative influence and thus may be ignored—for example, parents are noble creatures, but "I just happen not to have complete faith in them as teachers during the period I happen to think is the most important in the child's entire life" (Caldwell, 1968, p. 75). Or parents may be viewed as important mediators of their children's experiences and as sources of continuity in their children's lives, sheltering them, transmitting societal expectations to them, and negotiating with other systems to secure the resources their children require; thus their involvement in the program may be encouraged (e.g., Berger & Neuhaus, 1977; Powell, 1979). Or, finally, parents may be seen not merely as mediators, but as teachers or therapists for their children and in the program may be trained to carry out these tasks more effectively (e.g., Andrews, Blumenthal, Bache, & Weiner, 1975; Gordon et al., 1977; Kessen et al., 1975; Levenstein, 1977; Lombard, 1982).

These underlying dimensions of early childhood programs, though not exhaustively described, serve to illustrate assumptions implicit in current programs—assumptions that wind their way through the history of early childhood education, as we will discover in the next section. But before we begin that discussion, there are two final sets of dimensions that are particularly relevant.

Program Variables

The first set of dimensions consists of variables that are most directly related to children's experiences in the program, and thus most likely to explain observed program effects. These program variables are presented in Table 3.

We can divide program variables into two types.

Table 3. **Program Variables**

Goals	*Size*	*Target*
Educational	One child	Child
Custodial	Small group	Parent
Therapeutic	Large class	Parent-child dyad
Developmental		Family
Managerial		
Intensity	*Methods*	*Location*
Length of program	Direct instruction	Own home
Length of session	Modeling	Other home
Number of sessions	Interaction	Center
Schedule of sessions	Discovery	Laboratory
	Discussion	Hospital
		School
		Mobile unit
Curriculum Emphasis	*Staff*	
Discipline	Sex	
Social relations	Age	
Emotional health	Education	
Cognitive development	Training	
Language abilities	Experience	
Academic skills	Relation to child	
"Whole child"	Number	
	Behavior	
	Attitudes	

The first type includes general setting variables, such as the location, size, targets, and intensity of the program. A program may be located in the child's own home (with a tutor, social worker, home visitor, or babysitter), in someone else's home (a day care home or a neighborhood playgroup), or in some institutional setting (a school, day care center, laboratory, or hospital). It may involve one child, a few children, or many. In home settings the number of children seldom exceeds 6; usually it is fewer than 3 (Fosberg et al., 1980). In centers, programs with as many as 300 children are possible, but about 50 is typical. The children in these center programs are then divided into classes or groups, the maximum size of which, in licensed programs, is determined by age; the average class size is 10 for toddlers and 18 for preschoolers (Coelen et al., 1978). The program may focus on children, parents, or both. It may be scheduled (or the child may attend) for a month or a year; it may be a daily or a weekly program, lasting a half hour, a half day, or a full day.

The second type of program variable involves the staff. Early childhood programs vary in the number of adults present, the ratio of adults to children, the background characteristics of staff members (training, education, experience, age), their attitudes toward children and education, and of course, most relevant, the kinds of interactions they have with the child. Related to this last factor are the kinds of activities the program provides for its participants. These activities may be custodial (feeding, dressing, supervising play) or educational (lessons, guided interactions, structured tasks). If educational, the activities may be slanted toward social competence (e.g., games), emotional expression (e.g., drama or therapy), cognitive abilities (e.g., puzzles), language (e.g., stories), academic skills (e.g., drills), or all of the above. Just how implicitly or overtly educational the activities are depends on the instructional techniques employed. These can include direct instruction in lectures and tutorials, indirect instruction in discussions, interaction, and modeling sessions, or unstructured "discovery" methods.

Table 4. **Participant Characteristics**

Child	*Parent*
Age	Socioeconomic status
Temperament	Behavior
Prior history	Attitudes
Developmental level	
Special needs	

Participant Characteristics

Finally, programs vary not just in these "input" variables but in the characteristics of their participants (Table 4). Since these characteristics are related to the type of program the children are in (e.g., poor children receive academic instruction, while middle-class children are offered social enrichment), they also may contribute to the effects of the program input. Among the myriad possible characteristics of children that could be discussed, some of those that would appear to be relevant as potential mediators of program experience are age, sex, temperament, prior history (e.g., less than adequate parental care, a poor physical environment, or social isolation), and special needs (e.g., physical or mental handicaps). Among the possible characteristics of parents, those of interest might include socioeconomic status, ethnicity, work status, intelligence, disciplinary attitude and practices, caretaking, and verbal stimulation of the child.

These four sets of dimensions—organizational factors, assumptions and values, program variables, and participant characteristics—illustrate the range, diversity, and complexity of early childhood programs. It is not possible in this chapter to discuss in detail the effects or implications of each of these dimensions or to systematically compare programs on all dimensions—neither space nor data is available for that task. Nor will we be trying in our review to identify what is the ideal or optimal position on each dimension. In subsequent sections of the chapter we discuss only some of the most influential and well-researched dimensions. Our purpose in naming these dimensions here is to provide a rough taxonomy of early childhood programs, to illustrate their enormous complexity and to serve as an overview and organizer for the field.

HISTORICAL AND SOCIAL CONTEXTS

It has become axiomatic in psychology to assume that notions drawn from culture invade the core metaphors, definitions, concerns, and assumptions of psychological theory (e.g., Kessen, 1979). The point of view that espouses cultural relativity stresses the instability of our vision of the child and shifting enthusiasms that seem to have less relation to empirical evidence or sustained scientific inquiry than to broad social and economic forces (Lasch, 1977, 1979) or ethnocentric biases (Cole & Bruner, 1971). In the midst of the potentially endless discontinuities this viewpoint allows, however, fluctuations in developmental psychology can be seen as swings between opposite poles of two major continua. In matters of theory, there are swings resulting from the unresolved epistemological tension between nature and nurture; and, in matters of practice, there are shifts resulting from the ideological tension between parent or society as the ultimate authority in the rearing of children. Each of these continua has marked conceptions of development in early childhood for at least 400 years of thought, and each can provide a focus for summarizing salient aspects of the historical and social context for current early childhood programs and research. To focus on these dimensions necessarily limits us to an overly simple account of social history, but it is hoped that narrative cohesion will compensate for oversimplification. For more elaborate presentations of the complex historical forces impinging on child development research and social programs for children, the interested reader is referred to Eller (1956), Fein (1980), Glaser (1982), Kessen (1979), Ross (1979), Sunley (1955), and Wishy (1972).

The Beginnings

Ideas about the education and rearing of young children emerged with clarity and force in Europe during the Protestant Reformation of the sixteenth century. It was during this period that the family began to acquire many of its contemporary characteristics, and it was also in this period that the idea of childhood as a special time of life became a matter of serious discussion (see Aries, 1962; Lasch, 1977). These ideas were compelling extensions of revolutionary religious, political, and moral visions accompanying pervasive social and economic changes. Ideas about the family and the child were elaborated and strengthened by a broader intellectual framework into which they fit quite comfortably. Descartes' "I think, therefore I am" paved the way for new concepts of self, personal consciousness, and individual autonomy, and new definitions of the child and the adult as persons. Shortly thereafter, the empiricists argued that the child comes into the world as a "tabula rasa" and is shaped by experience into an adult human being. These were awesome and thoroughly optimistic visions, replacing the authority of kingdom and church with the authority of the individual person, and replacing the immutability present at birth with the malleability offered by education.

These two optimistic ideas—of a self-conscious and responsible individual and an uplifting education—merged in two contrary ways. On the one hand, religious leaders argued that careful and vigilant nurture could contain and inhibit an individual's inborn proclivity to evil. To be effective, training had to begin at an early age; the infant's willfulness and passion had to be curbed and never indulged. The educational attitude emerging from this perspective was repressive, intolerant of individual diversity, and aimed ultimately at producing compliant and conforming adults.

On the other hand, a more benign concept of nurture and education appeared during this period in the writings of John Amos Comenius (Eller, 1956). Firmly rejecting the Calvinist doctrine of infant depravity, Comenius claimed that children came into the world innocent and unable to discern between good and evil. He proclaimed love as the child's right, "descended from heaven," arguing that "no man" can "dispossess them of this inheritance" for children "come from our own substance" and "deserve to be loved by us, certainly not less than we love ourselves" (Eller, 1956, p. 61).

Comenius offered a radical vision of education. Without benefit of a scientific theory of human development, he designed a pedagogy based on assumptions regarding children's changing capacities from birth to adolescence. Taking into account institutional matters, he proposed a sequence of four schools. The first, the "School of the Mother," covered the first 6 years of a child's life. The others were roughly equivalent to the contemporary sequence of elementary, secondary, and higher education. In the first handbook written for the education and rearing of infants, Comenius held that most children should remain in the School of the Mother until 6 years of age, because until then they require more personal and individual care than the teacher of a group of children could give, and because until the brain is "rightly consolidated" it is enough that the child learn "spontaneously . . . in play whatever may be learned at home" (Eller, 1956, p. 116). In addition, Comenius offered a set of child-rearing principles to guide the parent in promoting the child's spiritual, physical, and mental health. The infant's education must begin at birth, for "a young sapling, planned for a tree, must be planted, watered, hedged around for protection and propped up" (p. 67). However, "parents are often incompetent to instruct their children, or unable because of duties or family affairs, or deem instruction of trifling importance" (p. 67), in which case young children might be handed over for instruction to "righteous, wise, and good persons." With considerable clarity, Comenius outlined the format that guided subsequent reformers: (1) Parents are to be in charge of rearing children during the period of infancy, (2) parents can benefit from guidance in that task, and (3) under circumstances of parental incompetence or unwillingness, the task might be taken over by others. But the persons (parents or others) and the places (home or school) represented separate and autonomous institutions connected only by the child who might travel unaided from one to another.

Early Childhood Education in U.S. History

The ideas of Comenius and his religious counterparts have emerged with considerable regularity in the discussion of early child development and education since his time, and they were a part of the intellectual tradition of those who settled in America. Whether depraved or innocent, children were certainly malleable, and the well-being of society hinged on the outcome of education. In cyclical fashion, reformers suggested two solutions to provide such education. Some reformers, thinking that parents were unable to rear children unaided, took upon themselves the task of providing such aid. Others, more pessimistic about alleviating parental incompetence, set out to save children by separating them from deviant parents (Ross, 1979).

It was at the beginning of the nineteenth century that ideas about child rearing first came into wide circulation. It was also about that time that reformers in a thriving and liberated nation turned their attention to the children of the poor. Abandoned or neglected by dissolute or incompetent parents, these children desperately needed enlightened training. Sunday schools were expanded to week days in order to provide such training. In the words of one enthusiastic Boston supporter writing in 1828, citizens were urged to have "compassion for the . . . poor little ones who have no nursery and no mother deserving the name, and not to rest until every section of the city has its infant school" (Kuhn, 1947, p. 27).

But then, the country discovered public corruption, greed, and immorality in high places. The spoils system and the misdeeds of the Jacksonian presidency were viewed as evidence that the nation had lost the virtues of an earlier time. In the self-scrutiny that followed, there were many who suggested that America's fall from grace had occurred because children were no longer being reared as they ought to be (Wishy, 1972). Pamphlets, tracts, magazines, and sermons on child rearing inundated the public and were purchased by anxious middle-class parents. "Mothers' Associations," study groups of mothers interested in child rearing, expanded rapidly, and the first magazine for mothers appeared in 1832.

What counsel were the experts giving in this flood of material? Not surprisingly, it was contradictory. Some writers advised repression and the rod. Others, who soon became the dominant force, recommended firmness, affection, and respect for the child's individual interests. In a perceptive analysis, Wishy (1972) suggested that there was a more basic and, perhaps, unresolvable conflict. Although vastly transformed from its original philosophical form, Americans had come to believe deeply in the ultimate authority of the individual, in the legitimacy of self-interest, and in the idea that social benefits will be gained when self-interest is exercised. Social reciprocity (one good turn deserves another) was a practical ethic that fit individualism better than the ethic of social responsibility. Thus child-rearing advice focused on social reciprocity, with platitudes to accommodate social responsiblity. Interest in the informed parent soon waned, however, and, by 1850, *Mothers' Magazine* had stopped publishing, Mothers' Associations lost membership, and the first parenting crusade came to an end.

According to some analysts, the parenting movement had its base in small rural communities (Kuhn, 1947) and its demise may, in part, have reflected the rise of cities and the rapid growth of industries. By mid-century, jobs were in abundance and people came from the American countryside and northern Europe to take them. The participation of women in the work force rose to about 20%, and a significant number were mothers. They were also predominantly foreign born and poor and they worked in the sweat shops and factories for long hours and low pay. Who took care of their children? Some children, of course, worked alongside their parents; others stayed at home to mind the even younger ones. But these adjustments conflicted with the goals of a new crusade—the Americanization of the foreign born. In the great debate over public education, the major argument for the common school stressed acculturation and the inadequacies of the foreign-born parent. And so again, interest shifted to child rearing by persons other than parents, and infant schools became a popular reform (Addams, 1910; Fein & Clarke-Stewart, 1973). These establishments were called "day nurseries" rather than "infant schools," a name change reflecting the young ages of the children, the concern with health and physical care, and the emerging professional identity of child-care workers as "nurses."

If Calvinist child rearing had lost out as the preferred way of rearing children at home, it was revived in the new institution. Children were to be clean, orderly, and compliant. In the institutional child-care literature of the period, little attention was paid to the young child's need to explore, discover nature, or play.

These two contrasting emphases—parent and home versus professional teacher and institution—continued to occupy the attention of reformers in alternating fashion until recent times. Perhaps too much ought not to be made of what may be superficial economic and political correlates of these shifts. Generally, however, institutionalized child care has been recommended for the children of the poor in times of affluence and industrial expansion, while upsurges in parent education have occurred in times of economic hardship.

The second great upsurge of popular parent education appeared in the 1880s, when the nation was reeling from economic recession and the scandals of the Grant administration. For the first time, parent education acquired an organizational structure, a recognized national leadership, and, with the active participation of G. Stanley Hall, expert authority derived from the new empirical study of children. The Society for the Study of Child Nature (later to become the Child Study Association of America) was formed in 1888, followed in 1897 by the prestigious and influential National Congress of Mothers (later to become the National Congress of Parents and Teachers, still later, the Parent-Teacher Association). This was a grass-roots, voluntary, and essentially middle-class movement. It appealed to mothers preoccupied with rearing children in what were becoming increasingly isolated, nuclear, urban households. The organization provided research reports and study guides, whereas the mothers themselves provided a spirit of sharing and mutual support. Although the dominant theme was self-improvement, the movement's missionary zeal carried over to societal improvement and, in local communities, the mothers organized political campaigns on behalf of child labor laws, prohibition, pure food and drug acts, housing codes, and so forth (Schlossman, 1976; Sunley, 1955; Wishy, 1972).

In the new wave of immigration preceding World War I, interest once again shifted to the institutional care of poor children. Settlement houses and the new social worker profession championed the needs of abandoned, neglected, and abused children, achieving national attention in the first White House Conference on Children (1909). The profession also gained a national, organizational structure with the creation of the Children's Bureau under the leadership of Grace Abbot.

By the second decade of the twentieth century, the rift seemed complete—exponents of parent education on one side of the argument and professionals in favor of institutional care on the other. Those experts in favor of parent education played an inspirational, advisory role, providing parents with supposedly scientific information about the development of children and the implications of child-rearing practices. Parents were the program implementers. On the other hand, "experts" in favor of institutional care became both conceptualizers and implementers, identifying issues, designing programs, and providing the institutional framework to address these issues. If parent education was a populist women's movement, group care became a professional women's movement that increasingly stressed direct services by trained persons to a relatively passive clientele.

Some signs of compromise between these two opposing views began to appear in the 1930s as middle-class mothers discovered the nursery school. For the first time, in substantial numbers, the young children of middle-class families entered secular, institutional environments. Some were dominated by professionals (teachers rather than nurses); some were dominated by parents; and some combined parent education and professional child care (Fein & Clarke-Stewart, 1973; Swift, 1964). In an extension of the voluntaristic, participatory spirit of the mothers' movement, there appeared a new form of child care—the parent cooperative nursery school.

The severity of the Great Depression, the pressure on middle-class women to find employment, and the formation of WPA day nurseries contributed further to the participation of middle-class families in institutional forms once assigned exclusively to the poor. The industrial mobilization of World War II operated in a similar fashion. However, the participation of parents in these arrangements was not encouraged; the children were there, but parents were not.

Serious attention to the relationship between parent and institution did not emerge until the 1960s. Poverty programs of this period attempted to implement a sweeping and, of course, controversial reconceptualization of the role of parent and nonprofessionals in early childhood programs. At the core was the idea that the domains of parent and professional were overlapping and that authority was reciprocal. If the trend in the past was toward a growing separation between home and institution, notions about parent participation and parent control in the 1960s set in motion a movement for reunion.

Poverty Programs of the 1960s

The spirit of the 1960s was brewed in the Great Depression and World War II (Sarason, 1978). The former established social welfare as entitlement, whereas the latter placed science and technology in the service of a moral crusade against evil, as dusty notions of justice, freedom, and dignity acquired new urgency from horrifying evidence that these notions might be successfully challenged.

On the scientific-technological side, the postwar period began with the publication of *Cybernetics* (Wiener, 1948), and heady notions of control systems and information processing complemented the birth and rapid development of high-speed computers. The new technology made possible a stunning achievement. In 1957, the Soviet Union launched the first earth satellite. Human ingenuity had overcome a powerful natural force. But the ingenuity was Russian, not American. An alarmed Congress and a supportive military blamed the failure not on parents, but on America's outdated and decrepit educational system. Within a year, Congress provided the initiative for a sweeping modernization of American schooling. The National Defense Act of 1958 offered scholarships, loans, and grants to improve teaching in science and mathematics and to provide counseling and testing services to identify quickly and accurately talented young people. By 1961, President Kennedy promised that within the decade America would land a man on the moon, and, in keeping with that promise, the federal government supported a vast array of space-related training, research, and development efforts (Kiesler, 1979).

Suddenly, there was a massive federal investment in what had traditionally been a decentralized and provincial educational enterprise (Levitan & Taggart, 1976). Curriculum development, once the province of educators and publishers, became the province of mathematicians and scientists. The new math and the new science that emerged offered a sweeping revision of the traditional curriculum. But the revisionist spirit did not stop with the content of teaching. Teaching methods were also affected. The notion of programmed instruction, introduced by Skinner (1958), was well suited to the promise of computers, and predictions were made that these amazing devices would soon be commonplace appliances in schools and homes. In early childhood education, these ideas had their most vivid practical expression in the talking typewriter (Moore & Anderson, 1968, 1969). It is only now, however, with the advent of the low cost microcomputer, that educators have begun to explore the bolder idea that young children can be taught to program computers and thereby come in contact with powerful ideas in mathematics and science (Papert, 1980).

The curriculum movement of the early 1960s expressed the belief that all things could be taught to all—its spirit nicely captured by Bruner's radical and euphoric hypothesis that any subject matter could be taught effectively in an intellectually honest form to any child at any age—and in that sense carried with it the optimism of the first reformation. But missing was Comenius's insight that education must concern itself with soul as well as mind (Eller, 1956). Matters of conscience and morality did not emerge with force until the mid-1960s, with the emerging Civil Rights Movement.

The moral issues of World War II simmered during the postwar period. In 1954, the Supreme Court ruled unanimously that racial segregation in public schools was inherently a denial of equality of educational opportunity. In the historic decision, *Brown* v. *Board of Education,* the court referenced seven works by social scientists demonstrating that segregation had a damaging effect on the psychological development of black children (Loftus & Monahan, 1980). In the 1954 decision, the court called for "all deliberate speed," but the attempt by blacks to implement the decision produced a violent reaction from whites. In response, President Eisenhower directed federal troops to protect the rights of black children to attend a white high school in Little Rock, Arkansas. As Sarason (1978) notes, the ugliness of Little Rock was viewed in the living rooms of millions of Americans. In a sense, the postwar technology of television meant that 40 million Americans could watch Little Rock as it happened; cruelty and hatred within America was communicated with an energizing immediacy and vividness beyond the reach of sermons or scholarly analyses. The national response, supportive and compassionate, brought with it sympathy for the emerging civil rights movement and a growing challenge to segregation, discrimination, and inequity. A Catholic became president, and that president was assassinated. In 1963, 250,000 people marched to Washington and in 1964, Congress responded with the Civil Rights Act and the Economic Opportunity Act. The first added economic penalties to civil rights violations, whereas the second provided the economic resources that could be withheld. The Economic Opportunity Act mandated the "maximum feasible participation" of the poor, a mandate with as many interpretations as there were interpreters. Within a mere decade, the nation had reached for the not so proverbial moon, convinced that people of all races and creeds would soon homestead the heavens.

Social scientists, also, spoke to the facts of poverty (Harrington, 1962), its forms (Lewis, 1966; Moynihan, 1964) and its solutions (Cloward & Ohlin, 1960), giving scholarly expression to social and political ideas that were already in motion. Their constituents held two shared beliefs—that poverty was the problem and that change was possible. But they disagreed about whether individual change, through education, or institutional change, through politics, provided the best means for achieving a brighter, better world.

The case for individual change grew out of a problem that would be pressing for some time in the future. The massive testing of men eligible for induction in the armed forces in the early 1960s had revealed that one-third were mentally unqualified for military service (Moynihan, 1964). They lacked the basic skills needed to participate in the work force and in defense of the nation. The explanation provided by social scientists was that the poverty of the parents was being passed on to these men through a disordered and chaotic home life that failed to encourage the acquisition of attitudes needed to succeed in school, where basic skills were acquired (Moynihan, 1964; President's Panel on Mental Retardation, 1963). In keeping with this point of view, analysts recommended programs of "compensatory education" for children in poor families. Presumably, these programs would provide what the low-income home lacked, namely an opportunity for children to acquire the attitudes and information conducive to school learning.

A major program that eventually implemented these recommendations was Head Start, an educational, social, and health program of national scope aimed at individual change for disadvantaged preschool youngsters. The program was established in 1965, following the recommendations of a panel of distinguished experts (Cooke, 1965), and it has survived to this day. Initially suggested as an experimental program for 2,500 children, the numbers expanded to 50,000 and then to 100,000 by the time serious planning began. But the idea was an instant political success, and federal support expanded to meet popular demand. In its first summer, Head Start served 561,000 children in about 2,400 communities at a cost of $95 million. Beginning in the fall of 1965, the first full year program served 20,000 children; in 1979 Head Start served over 349,000 children with an annual budget of over $500 million. According to its founders, the intention of the Head Start program was to ameliorate the effects of poverty on the physical and psychological well-being of children (Cooke, 1965; Zigler & Valentine, 1979) but, according to others, its intention was to promote institutional change through political action, creating jobs and changing attitudes in the community (Payne & Mercer, 1973; Valentine & Stark, 1979). Unfortunately for researchers, in defining Head Start as both a community action program and an educational program, themes that were seemingly divergent in theory—that is, institutional change and individual change—converged in practice. This complicated the already difficult tasks of conceptualizing, implementing, and evaluating a major and unwieldy new program for children. As a result, research on evaluations of the effects of Head Start have been controversial, inconsistent, and far from conclusive.

Experimental Programs and Developmental Psychology

Although Head Start became the best known symbol of the War on Poverty, it was not the only program that sprang up during the 1960s era of educational optimism, aimed at ameliorating the effects of poverty on young children. A variety of experimental early childhood programs were designed by child psychologists in sites across the country. They ranged from daily tutoring of children in homes (e.g., Schaefer & Aaronson, 1972) to full-time comprehensive care in a center (e.g., Ramey & Mills, 1977). They focused on parents (Gordon et al., 1977), or children (e.g., Bereiter & Engelmann, 1966), or both (e.g., Klaus & Gray, 1968). These experimental programs more clearly than Head Start reflected and influenced theorizing and research in developmental psychology.

As conceptualized in the 1960s, early education reflected a theoretical shift within psychology and a new interest in the developing child. Psychology was rediscovering cognition in the form of sophisticated theories of information processing and control systems (Garner, 1972), and the infant's ability to perceive patterns and complexity and to acquire language was emerging as amenable to systematic study (Berlyne, 1958; Brown, 1958; Fantz, 1958).

These shifts were cogently synthesized by Hunt (1961). In the influential book *Intelligence and Experience,* Hunt challenged the notion of fixed intelligence in a manner that ensured child development research a privileged position in the social programs of the decade. Briefly, Hunt marshaled evidence from studies of animals and children to support the view that intelligence was not fixed and that the young in particular were both vulnerable and malleable. Vulnerability was illustrated by the disastrous effects of institutionalization on young children (e.g., Dennis & Dennis, 1941; Dennis & Najarian, 1957; Spitz, 1946), generally interpreted as the consequence of environmental deprivation whether maternal or physical (Bowlby, 1951; Casler, 1961). The malleability of children was illustrated by the amazing recovery of such children when deleterious environments were altered (e.g., Dennis & Sayegh, 1965; Skeels & Dye, 1939; Spitz, 1946). The special sensitivity of the early years, conceived either as a critical period or more mildly as an optimal period, gained support not only from Hunt's empirical synthesis, but from the theories of Hebb (1949) and Erikson (1950), from the dramatic phenomenon of imprinting (Lorenz, 1952), and from a consequential analysis of longitudinal variations in the stability of IQ scores (Bloom, 1964).

However, as presented in the literature of the 1960s (see Hess & Bear, 1968, for illustrations of these conceptualizations), the position on early experience lacked the interpretive statements necessary for conceptual or empirical testing. First, there was ambiguity in the conceptualization of "early." Was "early" to be interpreted according to age or developmental status? Was the early-late contrast relative, or was it in reference to some absolute system of age or stage markings? Was "early" a dimension of experience orthogonal to duration, priorness, or recency—and if so, how was the natural confounding of such things to be conceptualized? Second, there was even greater ambiguity in the conceptualization of "experience." Fundamental issues of experience as available, effective, perceived, or conceived were never debated, although positions with respect to such issues are embedded in serious psychological theories.

The child development literature of the 1960s also contained evidence that low-income children performed poorly in school and on tests of IQ and achievement (see Hess, 1970), and the cause of this retardation was presumed to be environmental deficiencies in the low-income home. However, whether rich or poor, the home environments of young children had not been systematically observed. In child psychology, interest in the observation of children's behavior in natural environments had atrophied since the 1930s, and most studies of parent behavior used the self-reports of middle-class parents. In the absence of systematic evidence, the homes of poor children were variously characterized as understimulating, overstimulating, or inappropriately stimulating (cf. Clarke-Stewart, 1977; Fein & Clarke-Stewart, 1973). Analysts eventually settled on the concept of "cultural deprivation" to describe the disadvantage inherent in the lower class home, which restated the observation that poor children did not do well in school.

Into the melee, Hunt (1964) also contributed the theoretical notion that successful development required exposure to experiences matched in quantity or complexity to the level of development already achieved by the child. The suggestion was in keeping with other attempts to revise learning theory in the light of evidence from the new cognitive psychology, attempts which redefined stimulation to take into account the stimulated individual (e.g., Berlyne, 1960). But as a method of facilitating development, the notion of "the match" posed an interesting problem for future research rather than a basis for practical programs. What exactly constitutes a match, and how might a proper match be promoted? The remarkable answer—preschool education—had little to do with psychological theory and its unsolved problems.

After proposing preschool education as an antidote for deleterious home environments, many psychologists were content to pass the task of specifying and generating corrective environments to preschool educators. In practice, thus, the "match" was interpreted to mean whatever a good nursery school offered. Matters that might have been settled in theory but were not, were, in fact, settled in practice. The irony in these programs was that an environment with dubious benefits, designed to promote social skills in middle-class children, was adopted as the model environment for improving the school success of poor children.

The irony was soon apparent, however, and with support from federal and private agencies psychologists in the late 1960s and 1970s developed a wide variety of preschool models as small-scale experimental efforts more directly linked to psychological theories, which attempted to elaborate the notions of "early," "experience," and "the match." Many of these programs preserved the traditional boundaries of nursery schools (child-centered programs attended by children between the ages of 3 and 5 for a few hours a day, 2 to 5 days a week), changing only the content of the preschool experience (see Day & Parker, 1977; Fein & Clarke-Stewart, 1973; Horowitz & Paden, 1973). As an alternative to exploration and free play, the content of a program might offer a highly organized academic curriculum (e.g., Bereiter & Engelmann, 1966) or focus on traditional psychoanalytic concepts of security and trust (Beller, 1974); it might use concepts derived from operant learning theory (Reynolds & Risley, 1968) or attempt a marriage between psychoanalytic and cognitive theory (Biber, 1977). Other programs did not follow even the form of traditional nursery schools. Some extended the hours to full-time day care, while others extended the age downward to infancy or upward to school age. In one of the more intensive group efforts, full-time care began when the children were infants and continued until the children entered first grade (Heber, 1978). In one of the less intensive efforts, 1 hour of individualized sessions began when the children were 2 or 3 years of age and continued for 8 months (Palmer & Siegel, 1977). These experimental preschool programs clearly went beyond the traditional preschool, stressing a variety of theoretical perspectives, materials, and techniques.

Programs and Research in the 1980s

By the mid-1970s, the War on Poverty was reduced to defensive skirmishes as the confident affluence of the preceding decade was replaced by the uncertainties of inflation and unemployment. Corruption in government supported movements for decentralization and deregulation. These events were accompanied by a growing emphasis on parent education, individual empowerment, and the family as a mediating structure (e.g., Berger & Neuhaus, 1977; Gaylin, Glasser, Marcus, & Rothman, 1978). Federal support for early childhood programs receded and relatively few new efforts appeared. In the 1980s, the programs that are most likely to affect young children will be those that are responses to the economic realities of working mothers rather than those intended to reform the disadvantaged. The limited funding that is available for research on programs will most likely go toward the study of monitoring, licensing, and evaluating existing programs rather than for setting up new model programs. Emphasis will be on cost effectiveness, delivery systems, and the role of parents as facilitators of their children's educational experiences in a voluntary rather than manipulated way (*Federal Register,* November 16, 1981). This shifts the emphasis from ameliorative experimental preschool programs to day care and other nongovernmental human services.

The most recent estimate (*Federal Register,* November 16, 1981) is that, in the United States, 9 out of 10 households with children under the age of 4 (42 million children) will use some form of day care in the 1980s. This state of affairs is dramatically different from the situation even a decade ago. With the 1980s, day care has become an important facet of the ecology of childhood. This increase in the use of day care is the direct result of the rapid rise in the numbers of mothers of young children who are employed in full-time or part-time jobs outside the home. The percentage of mothers of preschool children in this country who work has more than doubled since the mid-1960s: 20% in 1965, 29% in 1975, 42% in 1980, 48% in 1982—and it is expected to continue its climb for the next decade (Hofferth, 1979). Paralleling this increase in the number of working mothers has been an increase in the number of preschool children living with single parents: Divorces in families with preschool children rose from 7% in 1948 to 18% in 1978; the number of unmarried women having and deciding to keep their babies rose from 5% in 1950 to 11% in 1970. It is estimated that out of every 10 children born in the 1970s, 4 will spend time in a one-parent home. The rise in single-parent families has also increased the need and use of day care. Single mothers are likely to work (56% of the single vs. 33% of the married mothers of preschool children work) and are unlikely to live with another adult who could provide child care. Even though remarriage has kept pace with divorce (9 out of 10 divorced women remarry), during the interim period of single parenthood there is need for day care.

These are the clearest demographic statistics showing a basis for the increased use of day care, but we might also note that other social trends point in the same direction: Feminism has freed women from the notion that child care is their exclusive duty; the human potential "movement" with its focus on self-fulfillment has done the same for parents (and grandparents) of both sexes; the decrease in family size has made in-house babysitting less available; the increase in geographic mobility of the nuclear family household has further separated young parents from the possibility of supplementary child care by relatives; and the stress placed by psychologists and educators on the importance of educational programs in early childhood has increased the desirability and availability of preschool facilities. In spite of these trends, the majority (55%) of preschool children whose mothers work outside the home are cared for by a relative (father, grandmother, sibling, sister), most often in the child's own home, while the mother works. If a relative is not available, the most popular alternative is to have the child cared for by a (nonrelated) caregiver (32%), most often in the caregiver's home (a day care home). The least common arrangement (13%) is the one that has received the most attention: the day care center or nursery school (Coelen et al., 1978; Department of Labor, 1977; Frost & Schneider, 1971).

In the 1970s, day care was enthusiastically advocated or adamantly opposed largely on ideological and political grounds in the absence of empirical evidence. Extrapolations were made from limited or inappropriate data. For example, children's progress in high-quality centers was used as the basis for promoting day care (Caldwell, 1970); their retardation in residential institutions as a way to denounce day care (Fraiberg, 1977). Unfortunately, the first research to study day care effects was designed in ways that supported investigators' ideological or theoretical biases (cf. Lieberman, 1978). Researchers whose theory suggested that day care could be harmful to children's emotional development—apparently agreeing with the statement "If Bowlby['s theory of the development of attachment] is to be taken seriously, then human decency requires that children younger than 3 years of age be forbidden to attend nursery schools or day care centers" (Hogan, 1975)—studied children in mediocre day care settings (Blehar, 1974; Vaughn, Gove, & Egeland, 1980). On the other hand, researchers convinced day care was beneficial for children's cognitive development set up and evaluated model programs (Garber & Heber, 1980; Ramey & Mills, 1977).

Reflected in the day care studies of the 1970s was the familiar theme of different factions supporting the authority of either professionals (pro-day care) or parents (anti-day care), a theme further reflected in practical decisions about the degree of parent involvement, control, communication, and choice in day care. Research on day care in the 1980s shows promise of a more balanced stance, not biased for or against day care, but taking day care as a given and collecting descriptive evidence about children's experiences in a variety of day care programs (e.g., Belsky et al., 1982). This kind of research is more likely to yield useful information about educational practice and developmental theory than the simple "day care is good or bad" research that preceded it. We may look forward to continued, if slow, progress in the accumulation of knowledge about child development as research on early childhood programs moves through the next decade of history and toward the next edition of the *Manual of Child Psychology*.

EVALUATION ISSUES

Today, however, in reviewing the recent literature on early childhood programs, one is struck most forcibly by how much we still do not know. Although a great many program evaluations have been carried out, involving hundreds of measures, subjects, and dollars, we are still not completely clear about the effects of early childhood programs. The reason for the discrepancy between the weight of data collected and the clarity of information produced lies partially in the methodological problems that confront the researcher in this area. Since these problems plague all investigations of early childhood programs, rather than criticizing individual studies we have provided here a general discussion of problematic issues in evaluation. We discuss these issues at some length because of our conviction that, if these methodological problems are solved, research on early childhood programs can make a significant contribution to both child development theory and early childhood education. The methodological problems that we discuss fall into four general categories. One concerns the nature of the program "treatment"—what it was supposed to be and what it actually was. A second concerns the research design required to establish effectiveness and the factors in the field that compromise even well-designed studies. A third concerns how effectiveness is to be measured. And the fourth concerns the interpretations of the results obtained.

Treatment

In the traditional experimental study, conditions of training are embedded in a broader paradigm of established scientific practice that includes theory, definitions, procedures, and instrumentation learned by the experimenter through intensive and rigorous professional preparation (e.g., Kuhn, 1962; Reese & Overton, 1980). Under these circumstances, treatments can be parsimoniously and precisely described, and those trained in the profession can understand and, if they wish, replicate the treatment. The technical description is accepted as what happened, unless the results are anomalous or replication fails. But when a new paradigm emerges, as was the case with research on early childhood programs, practice becomes fluid and descriptions of "treatment" uncertain. This uncertainty is magnified several times over when the new paradigm involves field study—because when researchers move from laboratory to field, they must give up elegance for the pursuit of relevance, forfeiting a large degree of both simplicity and control.

What Is the Treatment in Early Childhood Programs?

In field studies of early childhood programs, in particular, the treatment is enormously complex. "Day care," for example, is neither simple nor even a single treatment (although it is often discussed as if it were). The term "day care" subsumes a wide range of child-care arrangements, including care by a babysitter, in a day care home, or in a center, and within each arrangement there is variation in the setting, program, staff, and clientele (as shown in Tables 3 and 4). Even within a single setting, the treatment is multidimensional, involving space, materials, curriculum, and the adult-child ratio. Moreover, for any individual child, the day care "treatment" often includes more than one such setting: A child may be in a center in the morning, with a babysitter in the afternoon, and participate in a play group on the weekend. All of these experiences would be part of the child's day care "treatment." Even when the "treatment" in question is an experimental one deliberately instituted by the investigator, rather than being "found" in the real world, the treatment is complex. As we illustrated in our earlier section, *Definitions and Dimensions,* treatment involves a configuration of factors on multiple dimensions, including personal qualities of the educator, content of the curriculum, its theoretical underpinnings, instructional methods, location, and intensity. Whether experimental or "real world," the complexity of the treatment in these programs exacerbates the loss of control that results simply from locating them in the field.

In the laboratory, the experimenter's intervention is rarely exposed to systematic observation (even though such observation might clarify considerably the relationship between experimenter and child on which inferences depend). In the field, documentation of this kind might well be essential. Although control and simplicity may have to be sacrificed in the field, specificity does not. Several studies (e.g., Miller & Dyer, 1975; Stallings, 1975) have demonstrated the feasibility of specifying program practices by careful description and documentation of day-to-day activities in early childhood programs.

Observing Program Practices

Some of the problems associated with treatment specification emerged in the Head Start Planned Variation (HSPV) study (see Bissell, 1973; Datta, 1975; Lukas, 1975). The purpose of the study was to determine which of several curriculum models had the greatest impact on children from low-income families. The study was precipitated by the basically negative results of overall Head Start evaluations (e.g., Cicirelli, 1969), which did not fit with evidence from experimental studies suggesting that preschool programs, if properly conceptualized and implemented, might have a substantial impact. The assumptions of the study were that effective curriculum was the key to effective programs and that models developed in laboratory-like university settings could be easily transported to new locations. In keeping with these assumptions, several early childhood curriculum models were installed in numerous sites throughout the country, and an effort was made to assess the extent to which curriculum models were implemented in these sites as well as to evaluate their effects. Although several previous studies had compared the effectiveness of different curriculum models (e.g., Karnes, Teska, & Hodgins, 1970; Weikart & Weigerink, 1968), there were few previous attempts to compare curriculum practices in action. In the HSPV study, classroom practices were globally rated by sponsors and observed according to behavioral criteria by outside observers.

The efforts to assess the implementation of varied models under field conditions uncovered substantial problems in program evaluation. One problem was the possibility that, to do justice to its theoretical basis, each program model might require its own distinctive observational system. If so, the implications of comparing different models across markedly different theoretical systems need to be considered. Presumably, for example, the social experiences required to promote trust (Beller, 1974) will differ from the object contacts required to enhance sensorimotor intelligence (Gordon et al., 1977). Behavioral specification of these two types of programs may require different observational units and behavioral definitions.

Another problem was that, when judged subjectively by model sponsors, some of the models evaluated in the HSPV study were not fully implemented and the level of implementation varied substantially among sites implementing the same model (Lukas, 1975). Some models are apparently easier to implement than others and, when this is so, model type and quality of implementation are confounded in outcome assessments. Also, the implementation criteria are easier to specify for some models than others. For example, it is easier to specify prescribed teacher-led activities and their frequency than the duration of children's spontaneous intellectual experiences or the teacher behaviors likely to facilitate such experiences. These problems call for a sustained research effort that has not as yet appeared.

The best designed study hinges on the assumption that a treatment occurred for one or more groups and not for others. But the actual experiences of program (or control) children are rarely studied (Cronbach, 1975; Willis, 1978). Poorly implemented efforts do not constitute a replicable treatment. Since programs are ongoing entities, program "drift" further complicates program specification. Small experimental efforts are most likely to represent fully implemented and, therefore, specifiable treatments, but even these have not been specified sufficiently to permit the type of analyses required for the development of a serious program technology.

The problems in monitoring program practices in small-scale experimental programs are magnified many times in studies of ongoing community-based programs. For the former programs, curriculum, philosophy, staffing, and setting may be explicit and therefore specifiable, but in most community programs, practices are likely to be specified only to the extent of adult-child ratio, at best. Since the community programs may not be meaningfully described in terms of their *theoretical* distinctions, it is important for investigators to make on-site observations in order to specify program practices in them.

Participant Perspectives

An intervention program or "treatment" might be delivered but whether it is "consumed" is another matter. The problem is nicely illustrated by a particular program that provided nutritional supplements for malnourished pregnant women (Herrera, Mora, Christianson, Ortiz, Clement, Vuozi, Waber, Deparades, & Wagner, 1980). In the program, food supplements began to be offered during the first or second trimester of pregnancy. Consumption was carefully monitored. Of the 850 supplementary calories of food provided to the mothers, it was found that, on the average, only 490 were ingested. Moreover, 360 of these calories replaced the calories that the women would otherwise have obtained in their normal diets. In effect, either the mothers did not consume the food supplements or they substituted the supplements for food already in their diets. Nor surprisingly, the birth weight difference for supplemented versus unsupplemented mothers was modest, significant for male infants but not for females.

These findings illustrate some of the problems endemic in intervention research. The monitoring of consumption is much more difficult in educational interventions, but the need to assess the intervention from the perspective of the participants is nonetheless present (Zimiles, 1977). An intervention might fail because it is poorly delivered; but it might also fail because it is poorly received. There is a clear need to evaluate a program at the level of the experiences of individual participants. It is not sufficient to specify program practices at the level of the curricular orientation or the adult-child ratio. To know how the program is consumed, the relevant observation may be how much a child interacts in a particular way with an adult, or what the child does with particular types of materials. It is not enough to know that a program recommends that mothers play with their children; the appropriate assessment is whether the mother, in fact, did play with her child more or differently as a result of the recommendation.

Research Design

Randomization and Control

Random assignment of participants to treatment and control groups is generally viewed as the cornerstone of sound experimentation (e.g., Frye, 1982). However, in the research on early childhood programs, randomization has been the exception rather than the rule (see Andrews et al., 1975; Gordon et al., 1977; Klaus & Gray, 1968; Palmer & Siegel, 1977; Ramey & Mills, 1977; Weikart et al., 1978, for important exceptions). The climate of the 1960s and 1970s favored the provision of services on a first-come-first-served basis, and more important, perhaps, the resolution of policy or program conflicts by political rather than scientific methods. In spite of intellectual arguments favoring systematic social experimentation, the arbitrariness of random assignment and the top-down administration required by studies of this type conflict with the voluntarist tradition of the country and the general belief that any service no matter how untested is better than no service at all (Cohen, 1975). In the 1980s, if one can project from current political views and fiscal policies of nonsupport for social science, randomization is not likely to become more common. Moreover, in research on existing programs rather than on experimental interventions, randomization is unlikely *ever* to be a feasible strategy for assigning children to groups.

Even if randomization is possible, it is not without its own problems (Seitz, 1982). There are different ways in which random assignment can be implemented. For example, participants can be randomly assigned before or after being solicited for the study. However, some investigators have argued that attrition and participant satisfaction might be influenced by pre- or post-solicitation randomization procedures (Andrews et al., 1975). One virtue of randomization is its ability to eliminate selection bias. But, if the program is demanding, randomly assigned participants might selectively drop out or for other reasons be unable to continue in the program (Schweinhart & Weikart, 1980). What is more, those who seek out or volunteer for experimental efforts may differ from those who do not; if so, the results will apply only to participation-prone people rather than to the general population of individuals for whom the program is presumably designed.

For various reasons, therefore, nonrandomization procedures have been used to define or select comparison groups rather than the conventional randomly assigned control groups. These procedures may involve the selection of a comparison group from a presumably equivalent school or community (e.g., Abelson, Zigler, & DeBlasi, 1974; Herzog, Newcomb, & Cisin, 1974), or from children in the same public school classrooms as those who received intervention (e.g., Beller, 1974), or from families matched on such characteristics as SES and ethnicity (e.g., Kagan, Kearsley, & Zelazo, 1978). In some studies, the comparison group is based on a sample of children who enter the same program at a later age or at a later time (e.g., Cochran, 1977; Roopnarine & Lamb, 1978, 1980; Smith, 1975). Problems associated with these procedures have been discussed by Campbell and Stanley (1967), Campbell and Erlbacher (1970), Smith (1975a), and Cronbach and Furby (1970). Some of the most relevant of these problems for early childhood program research include the following: Subjects in different comparison conditions may not be equally accessible to the investigator (e.g., children in day care centers are more accessible than those in day care homes). Different recruitment strategies may be used for different groups (e.g., recruiting day care children through the program and home care children through the parents). Finding matched groups when treatments covary with the criteria for matching is extremely difficult (e.g., use of day care covaries with maternal work and marital status and parents' selection of the type of day care arrangement covaries with their SES). "Nontreated" comparison subjects are often the recipients of some "hidden treatment" (e.g., children not in an early childhood program may watch "Sesame Street"; children not in day care may experience frequent babysitting or participate in a play group). The ideal design in which subjects are randomly chosen from randomly chosen classrooms in randomly chosen communities is likely to be impractical.

The unsettled question is what compromises in subject selection entail the least inferential costs. Rather than forcing a match by including atypical subjects, investigators may broaden the definition of a treatment (so that "day care" becomes "day care *plus* maternal employment and attitudes" or "day care *in the context of* free parental choice"). They may study the "program" of nontreated subjects and take this into account. They may use more than one comparison group so that they can examine systematic variation along significant dimensions across treated and nontreated groups. Or they may use statistical procedures through which confounding factors might be controlled and true scores estimated. Even these statistical procedures are not without problems (see Cohen, 1975; Datta, 1979), but their use would be a step beyond the current level of statistical analysis in most studies.

Attrition

Attrition was once something people talked about but rarely translated into systematic analyses. In studies of school curriculum reform, the problem was minor because the children were a captive audience and attrition was likely to be uncorrelated with treatments. However, in studies of early childhood programs, attrition is a major problem. In studies of model programs, attrition has run as high as 50% from the time participants were recruited to the time the program terminated (Andrews et al., 1975). In day care studies, not only do parents drop out of the study or, for that matter, out of day care, day caregivers "drop out" of providing care, and children are switched from one day care program or arrangement to another with great frequency (Ambron, 1980; Clarke-Stewart, in preparation).

Lazar and Darlington (1982) offer an unusually careful analysis of attrition issues. According to these investigators, there are at least five specific questions an attrition analyst might address: (1) rate of attrition (i.e., the percent of the initial sample remaining at the completion of the study), (2) differential rate of attrition (i.e., different attrition rates for treatment and control groups), (3) main attrition effects (i.e., whether the sample differed from the dropouts on some important pretest characteristic), (4) differential attrition effect (i.e., whether different kinds of children were selectively retained in treatment and control groups), and (5) equivalence of final groups (i.e., whether final treatment and control groups differed on some important pretest characteristic). The appropriate analyses depend on adequate pretest information, complete and consistent data collection over time, decisions concerning missing data, and the definition of dropout status. The value of these analyses is manifold. They permit some assessment of whether the treatment introduced selection factors, whether differential attrition produced nonequivalent groups, and whether findings for the final sample can be generalized to the population from which the initial sample was drawn.

Generalizability

Another source of problems in research on early childhood programs has been the need or tendency of investigators to overgeneralize: to extrapolate from one kind of institution (e.g., an orphanage or a kibbutz) to another (e.g., day care centers), to generalize from one type of program (e.g., a model program) to another (e.g., a community program), from one particular program (e.g., Levenstein's Mother Child Home Program) to others (e.g., all maternal training programs), or from one group of subjects (e.g., middle-class white subjects) to another (e.g., poor black subjects). To overcome this problem, representative sampling is needed: sampling across settings and subjects and replication of programs or program comparisons. A word must be said about representative replication. Unlike the replication (actually duplication) of a laboratory treatment, for which specification of treatment can be made to the level of lumens and decibels, investigators of early childhood programs might more productively aim for replication in which programs as well as subjects systematically differ in known and relevant ways. The replication strategy proposed for evaluating the Parent Child Development Centers—three different models, each first to be replicated by different staffs on three similar populations and then to be replicated on three different populations—might serve as a model. To make generalizations about the effects or effectiveness of early childhood programs, the phenomena of interest in this kind of field research should be sturdy enough to appear in approximations of the same program (besides which, exact duplication of a complex program may be impossible).

Studies Within Studies

Although early childhood program studies are conducted in the field, it is possible for investigators to incorporate more controlled experimentation *within* the overall program treatment. Researchers may manipulate the adult-child ratio (Ruopp, Travers, Glantz, & Coelen, 1979), class size and materials (Smith & Connolly, 1981), or storage facilities (shelves or boxes; Montes & Risley, 1975) in day care centers, for example, or they may institute systematic variation of curricula or participants in a training program (Kessen et al., 1975). This research strategy of combining experimental and quasi- or non-experimental designs offers the possibility of combining the best of both worlds—relevance and elegance—and may help identify the processes of change or components of effectiveness in any program.

Longitudinal Design

Given the nature of the research questions involved in evaluations of early childhood programs, the advantages of a longitudinal design for evaluating effects would seem to be obvious. Only through comparison of children's developmental progress over time can researchers establish the existence or duration of "transition" effects, differentiate acceleration (rate) of development from enhancement (level) of abilities, distinguish gains in children's performance from nondeclines in performance, separate effects of age and program duration, plot the trajectory of program-induced change for individuals or groups, and determine the minimum length of the program to have a measurable effect. Unfortunately, longitudinal designs have been rare in this area of research. Longitudinal follow-up in field studies of early childhood programs is extraordinarily difficult not only for the same reasons that apply to all longitudinal research (e.g., measurement problems and changes in federal funding priorities), but because of the high probability of subject disappearance and treatment instability. Nevertheless, there must be more efforts to do longitudinal work.

Data Analyses

The development of high-speed computers supported the technology of space flight, but it did little to support sophisticated research on early childhood programs. Large quantities of data could be efficiently processed, but the analyses that most researchers performed consisted of simple univariate analyses of variance or calculation of correlations. Univariate thinking exaggerated the importance of single-score test instruments. Innovative efforts to assess social, emotional, or selected aspects of cognitive functioning were disparaged because often the multiple measures of these functions were analyzed singly as if they were separate, unrelated variables, thus exceeding statistically permissible variable-to-subject ratios. Moreover, when such multiple univariate analyses were performed, there were problems in interpreting the results (e.g., Beller, 1974; Gordon et al., 1977). Suppose 15 variables were analyzed, and 4 showed significant differences and the remainder were in the same direction? How were these findings to be interpreted? Multivariate analyses could help. Their usefulness lies in their ability to eliminate significant findings that have been inflated by chance or to reveal underlying dimensions of behavior or ability. In some studies, multivariate analyses might be difficult because of missing data, a problem made more troublesome when the study is longitudinal and the subjects with missing data change from one test point to another. But they can then provide the "backbone" of analysis while univariate tests with more complete data fill in details.

The computer also offers other advantages to the investigator of complex programs, advantages that are not presented by a statistical analysis of variance. In particular, more sophisticated analytic techniques (like regression analysis, path analysis, covariance, or causal model analysis) can elucidate the processes of change in such programs. This can be done in a number of ways. One is by relating program treatment (or, more specifically, the individual child's experience in the program) to that child's performance outcomes. A second way is by placing the treatment/outcome relationship in the context of other individual characteristics or experiences of the child. These individual characteristics or experiences would include family differences (size, SES), parental differences (attitudes, expectations, behavior), and child differences (age, temperament, prior history). They could be related to treatment and outcome either by examining trait-by-treatment interactions, or by partialing out nonprogram differences. And the third way statistical analyses can elucidate the processes of change is by examining all these relationships as they change longitudinally, through some kind of sequential or causal analysis (see Price, 1976; Rogosa, 1978). By using these kinds of analyses, investigators could go beyond the overall, average effects of their programs and begin to understand if a program affects children's development, how it does so, and for whom, when, and under what circumstances. Ultimately, this will be more informative and useful than any simple success-or-failure verdict that relies simply on a test of mean differences between groups. Because even randomized designs are likely to become compromised by selective attrition, the assumption that treatment groups differ only on program variables is suspect. Even groups matched on macrovariables such as social class or neighborhood may differ on other variables associated with child development outcomes. The assumption that the haphazardness of day care services produces a sort of "natural" randomization of children in different settings has been challenged (Powell, 1980). It is more reasonable to assume that a variety of family and parental factors, some of which may be associated with child development outcomes, govern parental decisions to use day care, the parents' search for suitable arrangements, and, therefore, children's participation in different programs. If so, investigators need to incorporate an approach used by epidemiological researchers, in which a large number of potentially confounding variables are tested in preliminary analyses and those associated with the risk or benefit factor of interest are used as covariates in control analyses.

The assumption has usually been made that observed differences between program and comparison group children are a direct result of the program; that is, the program changed the child or, in the case of a parent-training program, the program changed the parent and the parent changed the child. This assumption is not proven, or even tested, by simple ANOVA statistics. By using more sophisticated statistical analyses, the investigator can examine possible indirect effects—mediated, for example, through the child's influence on the parent or through parental expectations and attitudes—rather than, or in addition to, direct program effects.

Outcome Assessment

The social programs of the 1960s and 1970s were accompanied by an intense scrutiny of psychological tests and their use in the assessment of disadvantaged children. Substantive issues concerned the tests' narrowness of scope, lack of diagnostic sensitivity, focus on achievement rather than process, and their susceptibility to situational and motivational factors (Cole & Bruner, 1971; Mercer, 1974; Zigler, Abelson, & Seitz, 1973). In somewhat altered form, these issues apply to the use of psychological tests in the evaluation of early childhood programs (Zigler & Trickett, 1978).

As we indicated earlier, early childhood programs vary considerably in their governing philosophies. Some programs stress the "whole" child, others stress particular aspects of development (e.g., language, cognition, or social relations), and still others stress academic skills. Individual investigators have sometimes developed or adopted instruments to assess these particular program outcomes: for example, autonomy and aggression (Beller, 1974), self-concept (Beller, 1974; Gordon et al., 1977), attachment (Caldwell, Wright, Honig, & Tannenbaum, 1970), curiosity (Arkes & Boykin, 1971; Miller & Dyer, 1975), teacher behavior (Lally & Honig, 1977b), and maternal behavior (Andrews et al., 1975); Schaefer & Aaronson, 1977). However, most studies have tended to rely almost exclusively on standardized tests of IQ or achievement, and reviewers have often singled out results from standardized tests to the exclusion of others because they offered a common basis for comparison.

The emphasis on IQ and achievement tests has been attributed to several factors. First, the concepts of IQ and school achievement have a long history; they have been comparatively well measured, and over the years a substantial research effort has identified a large collection of correlates between IQ and other aspects of functioning (see Anderson & Messick, 1974). Second, equally valid and reliable instruments for measuring other abilities or personal characteristics were not available. Finally, the national mission which brought these early childhood programs into being was concerned primarily with intellectual functioning related to the acquisition of high-level technical skills. President Johnson had promised that early intervention would put low-income children "on an equal footing with their classmates as they enter school" (Zigler & Valentine, 1979, p. 69), and policymakers wanted to know whether this promise was kept.

Negative findings from early studies of Head Start (Cicirelli, 1969) and equally discouraging findings from the study of Head Start Planned Variation (Rivlin & Timpane, 1975; Smith, 1975a) created something of a crisis. Statistical witchcraft could demonstrate gains in children that attended regular Head Start classrooms, but it could not convincingly demonstrate additional gains from specially conceived programs that were supposed to overcome the admitted inadequacies of Head Start (see Cohen, 1975; Datta, 1975; Harmon & Hanley, 1979; Trickett, 1979, for somewhat different views of these inadequacies). Those who were sponsors of planned variation programs protested that the standard assessment instruments of intelligence and achievement did not reflect the specific purposes of their programs. Smith (1975b) offered a compromise for the future in which measures of interest to policymakers would be used as well as those that reflect program goals. However, these noncognitive measures were to meet psychometric standards of reliability and validity.

Social Competence

These and other pressures energized the search for a concept that would represent something more than intelligence or school achievement. *Social competence* became that concept, and numerous efforts to define it were undertaken (Zigler & Trickett, 1978). One such effort involved the convening of a panel of experts, an effort which produced a list of 29 virtues reflecting the diverse theoretical and philosophical orientations of the participants (Anderson & Messick, 1974). Yet efforts to develop test batteries to measure these characteristics were often unsuccessful (Raizin & Bobrow, 1974). Another approach began with Head Start performance standards (e.g., health and nutrition, cognitive and language skills, self-concept, etc.) and devised adequate instruments to assess these aspects of program goals (Taub & Wilkerson, 1977). Attempts to reduce the complexity of these dimensions or reorganize them according to simplifying conceptual schemes often yielded a mixed list of variables, including physical growth, IQ, and achievement tests, and a variety of noncognitive measures often reflecting the preferences of a particular investigator.

The dilemma posed by Kohlberg and Mayer (1972) in their discussion of different assessment models (i.e., bag-of-virtues, prediction-of-success, normative-expectation, and theory-guided) has not been resolved, nor have issues concerning the situational appropriateness of behavior, typical versus maximal performance, performance versus ability, or achievement versus process (Anderson & Messick, 1974; Fein, 1981; Glick, 1968). At present, the concept of social competence may be more a vision of a mature child psychology or an umbrella covering diverse and nonstandardized observational measures of children's social behavior, than a practical guide for immediate test construction.

Psychometrics or Edumetrics?

The appropriateness of using classical psychometric criteria in the evaluation of educational programs has been seriously challenged (e.g., Bersoff, 1973; Carver, 1974; Levine, 1979; Tyler, 1967; Tyler & Wolf, 1974). For example, IQ and achievement tests have been specifically designed to measure stable differences among individuals and to screen out environmental variations attributable to teachers, schools, local communities, or other variable life experiences. A psychometrically good test is one in which some children are consistently winners and others losers. Moreover, on standardized achievement tests, the scores of disadvantaged children are usually on the low end of the performance range, with fewer than 10% of the test items being at a level of difficulty that most of them can pass. These tests, standardized on a diverse population of children, will be insensitive to individual differences among disadvantaged children; for these children, the tests are not reliable measures of individual variation. One might add that the emotional impact of taking a test in which most items are difficult also has a negative effect on performance (e.g., see Zigler & Butterfield, 1968). Norm-referenced tests pose other problems, as well, namely that they may bear little relevance to the particular goals of particular educational programs. According to some investigators, programs can only be held accountable for the particular content they set out to transmit.

By contrast, criterion-referenced tests are keyed to curriculum content areas, the idea being that all children can begin as losers and end up winners (e.g., Carver, 1974; Tyler & Wolf, 1974). Several early childhood programs have developed criterion-referenced tests for assessing language (Palmer & Siegel, 1977), mathematical concepts (Wang, 1973), and social judgments (Spivak & Shure, 1974). The organization of criterion-referenced tests reflect notions of either developmental progression or logical relations among concepts. However, by their very nature, these tests cannot be used in the longitudinal assessment of program outcomes.

Social Indicators

A new kind of measure of long-term benefits has begun to appear in the program evaluation literature (e.g., Abelson, 1974; Gordon et al., 1977; Lazar & Darlington, 1982; Schweinhart & Weikart, 1980). This kind of measure is similar to actuarial or epidemiological indicators insofar as it depends on matters of public record (e.g., school attendance, retention in grade, assignment to special education). As a measure of long-term outcomes, these indicators have numerous advantages. For one, they represent widely shared values and, in this sense, they can be viewed as a special type of criterion-referenced standard (i.e., all children should be at grade level, no child should require special education, etc.). For another, since disadvantaged children are overrepresented on many of these indicators, differences can be detected with a reasonable sample size of children. However, positive findings do not lend themselves to easy interpretation. If program children do not differ from nonprogram children on measures of school achievement, do positive findings on measures of grade retention or assignment to special education mean that children are held back or assigned to special education classes because of reasons other than academic criteria? If so, what are these criteria and why do children who have been exposed to a brief period of intervention during the preschool years manage to meet them? And finally, these indicators reflect minimal rather than optimal levels. Positive findings may reassure policymakers that the investment in early childhood programs is cost-effective, but they are unlikely to reassure those concerned with broader social values.

Observations as Outcomes

Another alternative to a standardized, psychometric testing of outcomes is to use observations of children's behavior in either natural or semistructured situations. This strategy has been used most often in the socioemotional domain, while cognitive outcomes have typically been assessed with tests. For example, in the National Day Care Study (Stallings & Wilcox, 1976), children's cooperation, compliance, helping, dependency, and aggression were observed in the day care setting, whereas language, memory skills, and task persistence were tested. However, it may be possible to assess intellectual development through unstructured observations as well (Carew, 1980). Observation of children's behavior in the natural setting of a home or program offers a degree of "ecological validity" not obtained in unfamiliar test situations. The familiar setting is more likely to elicit a normal range of responses and may reveal strong feelings, functional intelligence, and creative expression not observable in tests.

But, of course, there are problems in using observations as measures of "outcome." They are not a substitute for, but a supplement to, tests. One important problem is noncomparability across settings (from center to center, home to home, or center to home), and inconsistency across situations (from free play to lesson to lunch; Stallings & Wilcox, 1976). A second problem is the confounding in some observations of "treatment" with "outcome" (e.g., observing day care children in their day care centers and home parent care children at home). A third problem is the lower reliability and agreement between observers in natural observations in comparison to test results. A solution to the problems of comparability, consistency, and confoundability is the observation of behavior in a standard, semistructured situation (such as the ubiquitous laboratory playroom). This strategy substitutes the problem of generalizability for those of comparability, consistency, and confoundability. But this problem can at least be attacked by demonstrating that the data yield valid measures of the construct being assessed, or by broadening the scope of the semistructured situation to include a variety of tasks and examiners in repeated or lengthy observations. The semistructured assessment situation does not have to remain limited to the "strange situation with strange adults for the briefest possible period of time," a setting criticized by Bronfenbrenner (1979). Work needs to be done to explore the assessment possibilities offered by semistructured situations.

Work also needs to be done on developing coding systems for observations made in either unstructured or semistructured situations. Typically, behavior is coded into frequencies and analyzed linearly. This follows the simple assumption that more is better and ignores the possibility that meaningful differences in children's behavior are qualitative and that significant relations are "U" or "S" shaped. It also ignores the possibility of devising scales that measure a developmental progression of different types of behavioral competence. Measures involving style, duration, level, and intensity of children's behavior and superordinate categories of behavior should also be explored. Other issues still remaining for methodological investigation include establishing the lengths of observations necessary to get reliable, valid, and sufficient data in different situations.

Procedural Details

Whatever method of assessment is used, it is essential that its procedures be practical, reliable, relevant, and appropriate for the age of the child. Field research has not been held to the procedural refinements expected of laboratory studies. Investigators rarely report whether examiners were aware of treatment conditions or whether program and control participants were equally familiar with the place of testing or the examiner. Information concerning the number, training, conspicuousness, and reliability of the examiners is often omitted. Control or discussion of some of these refinements is feasible in field studies and would enhance the efficiency and the validity of field research and the interpretation of outcomes. Seldom has there been systematic field testing of assessment instruments prior to data collection, but this is a valuable if not necessary step, particularly with less tried and tested assessment methods.

Exemplary Studies

Before leaving the discussion of evaluation issues and problems, it seems reasonable to highlight a few of the studies that have attempted to solve some of these problems. At the Frank Porter Graham Center (Ramey & Mills, 1977) and in the Milwaukee Project (Garber & Heber, 1980), disadvantaged subjects were randomly assigned to treatment conditions (model day care programs or traditional home care). They were assessed repeatedly with a battery of diverse tests and observations as investigators followed a transactional model of development, assessing multiple determinants of change and looking for "ripple effects" at the levels of family, neighborhood, and community.

Investigators in two national studies of day care, the National Day Care Study (Ruopp et al., 1979) and the National Day Care Home Study (Fosberg et al., 1980), first field tested and subsequently used a large number of instruments, not just IQ tests, to assess the performance of children in day care. They then used multivariate statistics to analyze the wealth of data obtained from these assessments, statistics they were able to use because of their large samples (64 centers in the National Day Care Study and 793 day care homes in the National Day Care Home Study). Special efforts were also made in these studies to ensure that subjects and the programs they attended were representative of day care users and programs in the United States. Detailed data for the National Day Care Study were collected in Atlanta, Detroit, and Seattle; for the National Day Care Home Study, in Los Angeles, San Antonio, and Philadelphia; and broader survey data were collected nationwide. In addition, the National Day Care Study attempted an experimental manipulation of adult-child ratios and teacher education within the framework of nonexperimental, observational data collection, and followed the children in the experiment longitudinally to evaluate the effects of the manipulation.

Cochran and his collaborators in Sweden (Cochran, 1977; Gunnarsson, 1977, 1978) and Golden and his associates in New York City (Golden, Rosenbluth, Grossi, Policare, Freeman, & Brownlee, 1978) studied a range of existing day care programs. They included in their studies both day care centers and day care homes and compared children's activities and behavior in the two types of day care. As in the National Day Care Study, they sampled widely from existing day care programs, collected both cross-sectional and longitudinal data, assessed a variety of developmental outcomes, and analyzed how children's experiences in day care were related to these outcomes. Unlike the National Day Care Study, these studies included children who were not (yet) in day care.

The Chicago Study of Child Care and Development (Clarke-Stewart, in preparation) was another investigation that related children's experiences in existing day care arrangements to a range of developmental outcomes. This study broadened "day care" beyond day care centers and day care homes to include babysitters, nursery schools, and combinations of these. The performance of children in each of these different kinds of day care was then compared with that of children who were in the exclusive care of their parents. All children were observed intensively at home as well as in their day care settings, in standard, semistructured situations as well as in their spontaneous activities, and in unfamiliar laboratory settings as well as in familiar home conditions. To provide a context for an interpretation of observed differences in children's performance, researchers interviewed parents and day care providers about their values, attitudes, backgrounds, experience, and education. The sample was relatively large (150 children) and included a range of ages (from 2 to 4 years) and day care settings (over 80).

All subjects were recruited in the same way (through parents, not day care facilities), and they were followed longitudinally over a year and a half to investigate changes in their day care experiences and their development over time.

Finally, the Parent Child Development Centers (PCDCs) followed a unique research model. Three experimental intervention programs in New Orleans (Andrews et al., 1975), Houston (Leler, Johnson, Kahn, Hines, & Torres, 1975), and Birmingham (Lasater, Malone, & Ferguson, 1975) each focused on training low-income parents in a context of comprehensive health, educational, and social services. Families were randomly assigned to treatment conditions, and extensive efforts were made to evaluate the progress of mothers and children through the course of the program, which lasted 2 to 4 years. The three programs exemplified three very different approaches to early childhood education: In Houston, hispanic families with 1-year-old infants were visited by a paraprofessional trainer at home every week and participated in workshops and English classes for 1 year. In the second year children attended nursery school at the center four mornings a week, while their mothers learned about home management, driving, and child development. In Birmingham, black and white low-income mothers of 3-month-old infants were trained in child development by means of a hierarchical network of more advanced mothers (who had been in the program longer) teaching less advanced mothers, using techniques like demonstration, reinforced practice, written instruction, and discussion. In New Orleans a center program for poor black mothers of 2-month-old infants consisting of discussion groups, supervised practice, home resource workshops, and general educational classes was compared with a weekly home visiting program.

The central idea behind the PCDC project was that early childhood programs must be developed and studied as a top-down configuration of related factors rather than as a bottom-up addition of presumably independent factors. The premise was that different program models could be equally effective, but that it was necessary first to create, describe, and test these models, and then to examine attributes of these configurations for hypotheses about the properties of successful programs. The PCDCs were also conceived as a multistage experimental effort predicated on the notion that useful technical innovation required a step-by-step research, development, and utilization effort (Dokecki, Hargrove, & Sandler, 1980; Kiesler, 1979; Rivlin & Timpane, 1975; Robinson, 1972, 1975). The purpose of the first stage was to develop, document, and test theory-based models under well-controlled conditions with random assignment and systematic assessment. In the next stage, these models were to be systematically replicated in new settings. Replication studies would identify essential model characteristics and create a mechanism for maintaining the effectiveness and integrity of the original models under less stringently controlled field conditions. This stage would permit further testing and revision on a small scale, but the major focus would be the analysis and solution of field implementation problems, especially those concerned with the specification of standards and criteria for determining when a model is fully implemented (cf. Cronbach, 1975). In the third stage, a large-scale field study would be undertaken to find out how the models worked under a variety of conditions and with a variety of populations. Finally, the results of the field testing and the program technology would be made available to those who wished to adopt one or another of the PCDC models. Had the experiment been completed, information would have been gathered on the side effects of economic support policies and on the benefits for parents and children of educational support systems focused specifically on parent training. However, since the replication study has been terminated for lack of funds, information will be limited to the small samples in the initial programs.

These studies provide exemplary research designs for evaluating early childhood programs, but none has solved *all* the problems presented by this area of research. There is much work ahead.

Interpretation

There are problems in the evaluation of early childhood programs, not only at the levels of treatment, design, and assessment, but at the level of interpretation of results. Problems exist for both the individual investigator and the reviewer. For the individual investigator, interpretive problems include the meaning of "no difference" between program and comparison groups—Is it that the program had no effect or that the assessment instrument was not sufficiently sensitive?—and problems resulting from naive, and unwarranted, assumptions about causal processes and direction. For the reviewer, problems of interpretation involve the difficulty of comparing or aggregating results from different studies (see Block, 1976; Hedges, 1982; Light & Smith, 1971).

Aggregation

Aggregation is especially difficult when different measures are used in the different studies, but it also applies when apparently the same measure is used (e.g., ratings made by different observers in different studies), or when different coding systems are applied and are not comparable, or even when an identical standardized measure is used. (What does it mean if six studies show significant gains and six do not?) The problem of outcome measurement differences between studies is also often exacerbated by unmeasured treatment differences.

One strategy reviewers have followed is to identify a large number of programs, classify these according to the variables of interest (e.g., curriculum structure, participant characteristics, location, or duration), and then tally how many programs within each category report positive, negative, or null outcomes on different measures (e.g., Bronfenbrenner, 1974; Goodson & Hess, 1976; Mann et al., 1978). The problem in simply combining groups of programs is that programs are likely to differ on variables other than the one of interest, and program variables are likely to be intercorrelated (White, Day, Freeman, Hantman, & Messenger, 1973). Those programs designed to yield comparative data present a better base for discussion because the reviewer is able to state the conditions under which a particular effect is found, but relatively few programs have been designed to examine internal variations. Reviewers also differ in the criteria they use to select programs. Some seem to require only that outcome data are reported (e.g., Datta, 1979; Goodson & Hess, 1976); others apply some standards of scientific quality (e.g., Bronfenbrenner, 1974); and still others separate experimental and quasi-experimental designs, excluding those that fail to meet minimal design criteria (e.g., Lazar & Darlington, 1982). If the criteria are too stringent, the number of programs available for analysis will be drastically reduced. But if the criteria are too liberal, the analyses may be misleading.

Procedures for determining overall trends in the findings range from simple counting (e.g., Goodson & Hess, 1976) to more sophisticated statistical procedures for aggregating data, either using raw data from individual studies or combining the results of analyses from individual studies (e.g., Hedges, 1982; Lazar & Darlington, 1982; Walberg, 1981). Unfortunately, the statistical procedure, the preferable strategy, has not often been used in reviewing the effects of early childhood programs.

In this area of research, as we have mentioned, the reviewer's problem is further complicated because only a small proportion of early childhood program evaluations are published, and those that are published tend to reflect more positive results and to receive special attention. Since there is currently no national registry, abstract system, or comprehensive data bank, the completeness or representativeness of a review cannot be determined by either the reviewer or the reader. When reviewers attempt to make fine programmatic distinctions, completeness and representativeness become important issues. The quality of research also becomes important. Unfortunately for the reviewer, however, many early childhood programs were initially intended as demonstrations or service programs, and evaluation was not a central mission. Therefore, even if evaluations were done, they were not usually of the highest scientific quality.

Application

Finally, there have been problems in the application of results to practice or policy. Policy recommendations have often been based on overgeneralization, extrapolating from experimental model programs to "real world" community programs, as was the case with the results of the Consortium for Longitudinal Studies (Lazar, Hubbell, Murray, Rosche, & Royce, 1977) and their applications to Head Start. Policy recommendations have been subject to oversimplification, without attention to subtle differences between programs or individual differences in program effects. And they have not escaped misrepresentation by ignoring unfounded and untested assumptions—for instance, the assumption that if a given program "succeeded" and children's behavior changed, then *each* of that program's components is necessarily effective and systematic manipulation of these components independently is not required.

In this section, we have presented the major methodological issues and problems in current research on early childhood programs. The problems are many and complex, but potentially solvable. Unfortunately, resources were not available to us in preparing this chapter to solve all these problems, or even to aggregate the results of the available, if flawed, evaluations of early childhood programs statistically. Like most reviewers before us, we have resorted to the conventional and less adequate strategies of qualitative weighing and quantitative tallying of results from individual studies, always with the aim of producing an integrated, conceptually consistent, and convincing account of early childhood programs and their effects. This account is presented in the next section. We have taken the liberty of using the term "effects," even though, strictly speaking, the self-selection of subjects into program or nonprogram samples in many of the available studies makes it impossible to establish causation unambiguously. The reader should keep in mind, therefore, that the title of the next section refers to hypothetical effects not necessarily "true" effects.

PROGRAM EFFECTS AND EXPLANATIONS

Our procedure in reviewing empirical results consisted of examining observed differences between program and nonprogram children in the context of variation in assessment methods (situation, measures), child characteristics (age, sex, temperament), family factors (socioeconomic level, parental attitudes and behavior), and program conditions (type, quality, amount), and to relate the results of this examination to generalizations from research on the "normal" course of development in "untreated" children. Hypotheses were made about the possible processes by which programs may affect children's development, including direct effects on the child of the experience in the program or of separation from parents which the program required, indirect effects on the child through the impact of the program on the parents or on family circumstances, and interactive effects resulting from the combination of child, family, and program factors. These hypotheses were then "tested" against the relevant available data. The hypotheses may be not be exhaustive, but they are, at least, relatively wide ranging and illustrate the kind of analysis we believe to be important in this area.

Day Care and the Child's Attachment to the Mother

Since the question of possible detrimental effects of early childhood programs on children's emotional development—particularly on the relationships children have with their mothers—has been of such central theoretical and practical concern, we begin our review of research in this area with findings on the effects of day care on attachment. Attachment is a key concept in current theories about early social and emotional development. It is drawn originally from Bowlby's work (Bowlby, 1969), which was refined by Ainsworth (1973) and more recently by Sroufe and Waters (1977). According to these theorists the infant's tendency to seek and maintain physical proximity to its mother is adaptive from an evolutionary perspective. The infant maintains proximity by signaling and later by locomotion, and this proximity serves as a facilitator, mediator, and behavioral indicator of an underlying bond, an enduring and focused relationship between the child and mother. Theory and empirical work suggest that before the end of the first year every normally developing child forms an attachment to a primary caregiver, as evidenced by selective proximity-seeking behavior. There are, however, differences in the quality of these relationships of attachment. The optimal attachment pattern of "secure" attachment is characterized by a balanced integration of proximity seeking and independent exploration, and by trust and enjoyment in the interaction (Ainsworth, Blehar, Waters, & Wall, 1978).

Studies of children in day care that have focused on this concept of attachment suggest quite unequivocally that these children are attached to their mothers, and that this attachment is not replaced by their relationship with another caregiver. Although infants in day care form an affectionate relationship with an involved and stable caregiver—a relationship which parallels and functions similarly to the attachment to mother, in that it offers comfort and security (Anderson, Nagle, Roberts, & Smith, 1981; Cummings, 1980; Ricciuti, 1974)—they still overwhelmingly prefer their mothers to this other caregiver. They go to mother for help (Farran & Ramey, 1977), stay closer to her (Cummings, 1980; Farran & Ramey, 1977; Finkelstein & Wilson, 1977; Kagan et al., 1978; Ragozin, 1975), approach her more often (Bryant, Harris, & Newton, 1980; Mayall & Petrie, 1977), go to her when distressed or bored, or claim they would (Kagan et al., 1978; Lippman & Grote, 1974), and interact with her more (Finkelstein & Wilson, 1977; Ricciuti, 1974) in assessment situations. In the day care center, they do not greet the teacher in the morning with the same joy as they greet their mother at night; they do not behave as if the caregiver is a substitute mother (Kagan et al., 1978).

For some, this evidence that young children in day care, like those in the traditional arrangement of care by parents, become attached to their mothers has been sufficient evidence to conclude that day care is not detrimental to early emotional development. Nevertheless, there is still the question of whether there are differences in the *quality* of the mother-child attachment relationship between children in day care and those that are not. The first study to address this question (Caldwell et al., 1970) brought in an encouraging verdict: Whether they were attending a day care center or not, no differences were observed in children's nurturance, affiliation, hostility, dependence, or happiness with mother. But was this because the measures used in this study were too global? Because the observers knew which children were in day care and wanted them to look normal? Because these children were fortunate enough to be in a model day care center? Because they were old enough to have formed an attachment to mother before they started day care? Other studies subsequently have used other methods and samples to study further the effects of day care on attachment. Overall, these results too have been positive. That is, on most measures of attachment, in most studies, no unfavorable differences have been found between children in day care and those not in day care. Reviewers, for the most part, have been content to conclude that day care has no consistent, discernible, disruptive, or harmful effects on attachment (Belsky & Steinberg, 1978; Belsky, Steinberg, & Walker, 1982; Bronfenbrenner, Belsky, & Steinberg, 1976; Kilmer, in press; Ricciuti, 1976; Rutter, 1982; Silverstein, 1977)—though all point out that evidence is still limited (e.g., to day care in high-quality centers), and Rutter and Silverstein caution that more *subtle* ill effects may yet be discovered in some very young children.

Because attachment is difficult to assess, and because some studies *do* document differences in attachment on some measures, it seems important that we probe as deeply as possible before dismissing the possibility that day care, while it may not have grossly damaging effects on attachment, may have some impact. We should probe not only by collecting more data with more sensitive instruments in future research, but by analyzing consistencies in the available data.

Altogether 28 studies comparing children in day care with those not in day care on the dimension of attachment were located for this review: Blehar, 1974; Brookhart and Hock, 1976; Caldwell et al., 1970; Carr, 1973; Clarke-Stewart, in preparation; Cochran, 1977; Cornelius and Denney, 1975; Cummings, 1980; Doyle, 1975; Doyle & Somers, 1978; Everson, Ambron, Kermoian, & Romo, 1981; Hock, 1976, 1980; Hock and Clinger, 1980; Kagan et al., 1978; Lippman & Grote, 1974; Moskowitz, Schwarz, & Corsini, 1977; Portnoy & Simmons, 1978; Ragozin, 1975, 1977; Ricciuti, 1974; Romaine & Teets, 1972; Roopnarine & Lamb, 1978; Rubenstein, Howes, & Boyle, 1981; Schwartz, 1983; Vaughn et al., 1980; Wille & Jacobson, 1982; and Wynn, 1979. Although the differences in attachment revealed by these studies are not enormous or uniform across all measures or samples, they do show some consistency in their direction.

Nature of the Difference in Attachment

Within the general domain of attachment, there are three dimensions that have been suggested as possible indicators of attachment: reaction to separation, physical proximity and contact, and response at reunion. We discuss each of these in turn.

Separation Distress. Of the studies assessing children's reaction to separation from mother in a laboratory situation, seven found no difference in whether children cried or searched for the absent mother [Hock, 1976, 1980; Portnoy & Simmons, 1978; Ragozin, 1977; Ricciuti, 1974; Roopnarine & Lamb (on search for mother), 1978; Wynn, 1979]; two found more distress in home care children (Moskowitz et al., 1977; Roopnarine & Lamb, 1978); two found more distress in day care children (Blehar, 1974; Clarke-Stewart, in preparation); one found a higher mean level of distress in home care children, but in this study more day care mothers were not even able to leave the room for the brief separation (Doyle & Somers, 1978); and one found more separation distress in children from day care *homes* but less in children from day care *centers* (Everson et al., 1981). One reason for these inconsistent findings is suggested in a recent report by Wille and Jacobson (1982). These investigators compared three groups of 18-month-olds: a home care group, a group that spent a few hours a week in a nursery program, and a group that spent extensive time in a program. The relationship between program attendance and separation distress was curvilinear: The most distressed children were those who spent either all their time with mother or considerable time in day care. Since day care attendance is not an all-or-none condition, different criteria for assigning children to comparison groups are likely to yield inconsistent and contradictory findings.

Physical Proximity. Table 5 lists the studies that have assessed the second dimension of attachment: physical closeness and contact with mother in a standard laboratory situation that included the presence of a stranger and several brief separations from mother. Of the seventeen studies listed, ten studies (8 to 17) found no difference between day care and home care children; three studies [5, 6 (boys), 7] found that day care children sought proximity to mother less; and four studies, although they found no significant difference in overall proximity to mother, found some indications of greater distance, in that day care children spent more time away and assumed a greater maximum distance from mother (1), initiated proximity less (2), spent less time in physical contact (3), and were more distant when a stranger was present or after a separation (4). No study reported a difference in the direction of greater proximity to mother for day care children. So although the difference in mean level was not always statistically significant, when a difference did ap-

Table 5. **Laboratory Studies Comparing Day Care and Home Care Children on Measures of Proximity Seeking**

	Age at Assessment (months)	Age Began Day Care (months)	Length in Day Care (mean, range)	Type of Day Care
Finding day care children more distant on some measure:				
1. Wynn, 1979	18–30	<30	10 (4–24)	Center
2. Ragozin, 1977	17–38	12–24	16 (≥4)	Center
3. Roopnarine & Lamb, 1978	40	37	3	Center
4. Clarke-Stewart, in preparation	30–60	21–53	12 (3–13)	Center
5. Ricciuti, 1974	16	<6	12 (11–14)	Center
6. Moskowitz et al., 1977	42	36	6	Center
7. Schwartz, 1983	18	<6	16 (12–18)	Home
Finding no difference in proximity seeking on some measure:				
1. Wynn, 1979	18–30	<30	10 (4–24)	Center
2. Ragozin, 1977	17–38	12–24	16 (≥4)	Center
3. Roopnarine & Lamb, 1978	40	37	3	Center
4. Clarke-Stewart, in preparation	30–60	21–53	12 (3–18)	Home
8. Doyle, 1975	5–30	<24	7	Center
9. Doyle & Somers, 1978	10–42	<12	14 (12,15)	Center and Home
10. Portnoy & Simmons, 1978	41–45	12,24	20 (9,32)	Center and Center plus home
11. Cornelius & Denney, 1975	48–72	>30	15 (6–28)	Center
12. Cummings, 1980	12–28	<24	10 (5–15)	Center
13. Romaine & Teets, 1972	12–24	<12	8 (>3)	Center
14. Hock 1973b, 1980	10–12	<6	7 (2–12)	Center and Home
15. Carr, 1973	21–36	<36	?	Center
16. Blehar, 1974	30,40	25,35	5	Center
17. Everson et al., 1981	18–30	12–24	6	Center and Home

pear it was always in the same direction, with day care children seeking and maintaining less physical proximity with their mothers than home care children.

Response to Reunion. The third dimension that has been used to assess attachment is the child's response to reunion with mother after a brief separation. On this dimension, three general patterns of reaction to reunion have been observed in home-reared children: secure, angry-ambivalent, and avoidant. With respect to the first of these classifications, studies comparing home-reared and day care children's reactions to reunion after a laboratory separation have consistently found no difference in the percentage of children classified as secure (Clarke-Stewart, in preparation; Doyle, 1975; Doyle & Somers, 1978; Portnoy & Simmons, 1978; Ricciuti, 1974; Roopnarine & Lamb, 1978; Vaughn et al., 1980). Similarly, studies have found no difference in the percentage of children classified as angry-ambivalent or in the intensity of children's resistance to mother (Everson et al., 1981; Hock, 1976, 1980; Moskowitz et al., 1977; Portnoy & Simmons, 1978; Ricciuti, 1974; Schwartz, 1983; Vaughn et al., 1980). Only one investigator found part of her sample (the 3-year-olds) more angry and resistant in day care than in home care (Blehar, 1974). But in several other studies the (nonsignificant) trend was for day care children to be *less* angry-ambivalent than home care children (Clarke-Stewart, in preparation; Schwartz, 1983; Vaughn et al., 1980). It seems unlikely, therefore, that day care increases anxious anger or ambivalence.

Perhaps this is not surprising, since this category of attachment has been found to be more frequent in children who exhibited disturbances as neonates (Waters, Vaughn, & Egeland, 1980), suggesting there may be some innate or congenital factor in this pattern of maladjusted attachment, which would make it less susceptible to environmental influence. What Blehar's results reflect may not be pathologically anxious anger and resistance, but simply noncompliance to mother's wishes when after a brief separation the mother attempts to pick up her 3-year-old child. Picking the child up, as suggested by the standard "strange situation" procedure, may be less common or appropriate at this age than earlier (when the difference was not observed even in Blehar's study), and the child's reaction may reflect resistance to this perceived restriction or intrusion rather than to mother per se. Greater noncompliance to mother's requests has been reported for day care children in other studies and situations (Clarke-Stewart, in preparation; Rubenstein, Howes, & Boyle, 1981; Vroegh, 1976).

Unlike the first two categories of response to reunion, relatively consistent differences have been observed across studies for the third category, avoidance (see Table 6). Three studies (7, 8, 9) did not find enough avoidance (or avoidant subjects) to analyze for day care effects; six [5, 6, 10, 11, 12, 2 (late day care group)] did not find a significant difference between day care and home care children; but four [1, 2 (early day care group), 3, 4 (boys)] found day care children significantly more likely to show avoidance or to be classified as "avoidant." In no study was a difference in avoidance in the opposite direction found.

To summarize, children in day care are more likely than children at home to position themselves farther away from mother, to spend less time close to or in physical contact with mother, and to ignore or avoid mother after a brief separation. The difference is not observed in every child or every study, but the consistent direction of the differences observed suggests that a meta-analysis might reveal a significant difference overall. Day care children are *not* more likely than home care children to be anxious or angry, or to protest or ignore the mother's leaving.

Meaning of the Difference in Attachment

In the literature on attachment, it has been suggested that children who avoid their mothers during the reunion episode of the laboratory sequence are "disturbed." Although they may appear precociously independent, since they spend their time in the strange situation actively and happily involved with toys or strangers, the fact that these children do not greet or initiate contact or interaction with mother after a separation indicates, according to some, that they are maladjusted. Avoidance does not simply reflect lack of interest (Matas, Arend, & Sroufe, 1978; Sroufe & Waters, 1977). It represents a cutoff of arousal in an approach-avoidance conflict, which protects the child from a rebuff that he or she has come to expect when seeking close physical contact with mother. The avoidant child is suppressing the proximity-seeking attachment that would ordinarily be expressed (Main, 1977).

But does the lower level of proximity seeking observed among day care children reflect this same conflict? The inference has been drawn that day care children who display avoidance and are more distant are also more disturbed (Blehar, 1974; Vaughn et

Table 6. **Laboratory Studies Comparing Day Care and Home Care Children on Measures of Proximity Avoidance**

	Age at Assessment (months)	Age Began Day Care (months)	Length in Day Care (mean, range)	Type of Day Care
	Finding day care children showing more avoidance behavior			
1. Schwartz, 1983	18	<6	16 (12–18)	Home
2. Vaughn et al., 1980	12,18	<12	6 (1–12)	Home
3. Blehar, 1974	30,40	25,35	5	Center
4. Hock, 1976, 1980	10–12	<6	7 (2–12)	Center
	Finding no difference in proximity avoidance			
2. Vaughn et al., 1980	12,18	12–18	3 (1–6)	Home
5. Portnoy & Simmons, 1978	41–45	12,24	20 (9,32)	Center plus home
6. Moskowitz et al., 1977	42	36	6	Center
7. Roopnarine & Lamb, 1978	40	37	3	Center
8. Doyle, 1975	5–30	24	7	Center
9. Doyle & Somers, 1978	10–42	12	14 (12,15)	Center and Home
10. Clarke-Stewart, in preparation	30–60	21–53	12 (3–18)	Center and Home
11. Wynn, 1979	18–30	30	10 (4–24)	Center
12. Everson et al., 1981	18–30	12–24	6	Center and Home

al., 1980). While this may, of course, be the case, it is possible that what is coded as avoidance among day care children is not identical to, does not have the same history as, and will not predict the same outcomes as what is coded as avoidance among home care children (cf. Main, 1977). The "avoidance" category is very responsive to contextual variation. It can disappear when the same infants are retested in the strange situation two weeks later, and the proportion of children classified as "avoidant" varies substantially from sample to sample (e.g., being twice as high in a West German sample as in American samples; Grossmann, Grossmann, Huber, & Wartner, 1981). In children receiving care exclusively from mother avoidance may be a pathological response reflecting an interactive history with a rejecting mother, while for children in day care greater distance from, or ignoring of, mother at reunion may be an adaptive response reflecting a habitual reaction to repeated daily separations and reunions. In these latter children, greater physical distance from mother and apparent avoidance may, in fact, signal a precocious independence. There is clear evidence that normal development proceeds toward greater mother-child distance from 1 to 4 years of age (Anderson, 1972; Clarke-Stewart & Hevey, 1981; Marvin, 1977; Rheingold & Eckerman, 1970). Among day care children, those who maintained more distance from mother (if not those who were classified as more "avoidant"; see Blanchard & Main, 1979; Lieberman, 1977) have been observed to be more, not less, socially competent (Clarke-Stewart, in preparation). Moreover, although day care children have been observed to be more distant or avoidant than home care children, they have not been found to be less sociable or cooperative with their mothers—quite the reverse (Carr, 1973; Clarke-Stewart, in preparation; Farran & Ramey, 1977; Garber & Heber, 1980; Ragozin, 1977). And in the Vaughn et al. (1980) sample, the early day care children, who were more avoidant than home care children at 12 and 18 months, were not socially or intellectually different from them at 24 months (Farber & Egeland, 1982).

It seems likely that the "avoidant" classification is more frequent for day care than home care samples, because it is singling out two kinds of children. The first kind is the insecure children who exhibit avoidance rather than anger-ambivalence as their anxious pattern because their mothers are not as often around to direct anger toward. The second kind is the secure children who interact with toys and people independently of mother, who maintain greater physical distance from her when she is there, and who ignore her return after she has been absent, because they are used to interacting with other people without mother or because they are accustomed to the mother's coming and going. There is no way to determine at this point if the apparent avoidance of mother observed in day care children in *some* studies is a disturbed or an adaptive pattern. We can, however, look into some possible explanations of how this attachment pattern in day care children may come about.

Causes of Distance and Avoidance in Day Care Children

Greater distance and avoidance in day care children can be explained in several ways, some more plausible than others. In the following discussion we propose and "test," using available data and hypotheses, issues that might be pursued in future studies.

Transitory Reaction. It has been suggested that the reason Blehar (1974) found day care children to be more avoidant than home care children, while Portnoy and Simmons (1978) did not, was that Blehar's subjects had been in day care a briefer time (5 months) than Portnoy and Simmons's (9 months) (Belsky & Steinberg, 1978; Portnoy & Simmons, 1978; Rutter, 1982). Tables 5 and 6 present the duration of day care experience for children in the studies reviewed. To all appearances, length of time in day care is not related to proximity seeking or avoidance. Mean length of time in day care is 10 months for studies showing an effect on proximity and also for those showing no differences; it is 8½ months for those finding a difference in avoidance and also for those finding no difference. Studies where children had been in day care less than 6 months [Blehar, 1974; Roopnarine & Lamb, 1978; Vaughn et al., 1980 (late day care group)] were not more likely to find avoidance than studies of children who had been in day care longer. Schwartz (1983) found no relation between avoidance and length of day care experience, ranging from 12 to 18 months.[2] There *may* be a transition effect, but, if so, it must occur within the first 2 months of day care attendance. This period has also been suggested as sufficient for adjustment to nursery school; that is, by then newcomers' behavior is indistinguishable from that of other children who have been in nursery school longer (Feldbaum, Christenson, & O'Neal, 1980; McGrew, 1972; Smith, 1974). In fact, since Roopnarine and Lamb (1978) found more differences between day care and home care children the week *before* day care began than 3 months after, the transition most likely starts before the day care begins, when mothers are likely to be using makeshift and unstable arrangements for care or preparing themselves and their children for the impending change. What is more, the effect of the transition is likely to be in the direction of more, not less, proximity seeking. Roopnarine and Lamb found more proximity-seeking contact, search, and crying in the pre-day-care children than in the children remaining at home. The observed difference of greater distance or avoidance in day care children thus does not seem to be a result of initial adjustment to day care.

Bond Formation or Disruption. There are two possibilities related to the *timing* of the day care experience. One is that day care children are more distant because the attachment they formed to mother was never as intense. This might be the case if day care began in the critical first year (cf. Ainsworth et al., 1978; Bowlby, 1969). The second possibility is that day care children are more distant because disruption after the bond is formed has led to protest and then detachment (Robertson & Robertson, 1971). This might be the case if the child was put in day care after the first year. It is difficult to separate these two possibilities on the basis of available data, since most studies of day care have included a range of ages and have not analyzed their results for age effects (see Tables 5 and 6). There is, however, some suggestion that the probability of avoidance is greater if day care begins in the first year. In studies in which all subjects started day care in the first year of life, and avoidance was measured (four studies), three found significantly higher levels of avoidance in day care children (Hock, 1976, 1980; Schwartz, 1983; Vaughn et al., 1980); in the fourth study (Doyle & Somers, 1978) avoidance was observed too infrequently in either group to analyze. On the other hand, in studies in which all subjects began day care after the first year and avoidance was measured (seven studies), only one found more avoidance in day care children (Blehar, 1974, for 2½-years-olds more than 3½-year olds), while six did not (Clarke-Stewart, in preparation; Everson et al., 1981; Moskowitz et al., 1977; Portnoy & Simmons, 1978; Roopnarine & Lamb, 1978; Vaughn et al., 1980). In the Vaughn study, moreover, more avoidance was found for day care children only when day care began in the first year and not when it began in the second year. Although half of the latter group of infants changed attachment category after they began day care, only 11% of them became more avoidant; 28% of them changed to "secure."

For measures of proximity seeking or distance, as opposed to avoidance, age of beginning day care does not seem to be so clearly related to outcome. Of studies where all subjects began day care in the first year, two found day care children more distant (Ricciuti, 1974; Schwartz, 1983), and four did not (Doyle & Somers, 1978; Hock, 1976, 1980; Romaine & Teets, 1972); of studies of children beginning day care later, four found *some* evidence of greater distance (Clarke-Stewart, in preparation; Moskowitz et al., 1977; Ragozin, 1977; Roopnarine & Lamb, 1978); four did not (Blehar, 1974; Cornelius & Denney, 1975; Everson et al., 1981; Portnoy & Simmons, 1978). The suggestion that day care children are different from parent care children because they do not form as intense attachment bonds to their mothers, thus, is supported by the observed differences in avoidance but not by the differences in physical distance.

One specific hypothesis, within the general hypothesis that avoidance or distance in day care children is the result of disruption of an already formed bond, is that avoidance results when day care begins in the second year, since attachment is expressed most intensely during this period, and since only after the child is 2 or 3 years she or he can understand or tolerate separation (Mahler, Pine, & Bergman, 1975; Marvin, 1977; Weinraub & Lewis, 1977). Studies in which children began day care between 1 and 3 years (Carr, 1973; Cummings, 1980; Doyle, 1975; Everson et al., 1981; Portnoy & Simmons, 1978; Ragozin, 1977; Vaughn et al., 1980; Wynn, 1979) did not, however, seem to be represented disproportionately among the studies finding differences in avoidance or distance: None (of four) found that day care children were more avoidant; only two (of eight) found them more distant. Thus this hypothesis found no support.

Unfortunately, in most of these studies of day care and attachment the age of beginning day care has been confounded with the age at which attachment was assessed and consequently with the appropriateness of the assessment method. The "strange situation" was designed for and has been validated with 12- to 18-month-olds, not 2- to 5-year-olds. Ainsworth et al. (1978) noted that, as an assessment of attachment, the strange situation loses predictive power after 2 years. Perhaps the reason that studies of older children are not as likely to show an effect of day care on attachment, therefore, is that the strange situation simply does not reveal such differences. Only Vaughn et al. (1980) and Everson et al. (1981) assessed all children at less than 2 years and looked for age effects. Vaughn et al. separated those beginning day care into first- or second-year starters and did find an age effect: Avoidance was more likely for those who started day care in the first year than the second. Everson et al. separated day care children into 12- to 18-month versus 19- to 24-month starters and did not find an age effect in this older age range. Thus, these two studies, using the strange situation at appropriate ages, do support the hypothesis that greater distance and avoidance in day care children is most likely if day care begins in the first year of life.[3] Further support comes from a study using an entirely different assessment method. Lippman and Grote (1974) asked 4-year-old children whom they would like to be with if they were happy, sad, scared, or sick. Of the children who had begun day care in the first year of life, only one-fifth gave a parent as their choice of companion in these situations; half of the children beginning day care after 2 years of age chose a parent.

To summarize, although the data available can only be considered as very tentative, there is some suggestion that avoidance is most likely to distinguish day care and home care children if day care begins in the first year. Thus, the observed difference in attachment may reflect the formation of a less intense bond with mother for day care children. There is no evidence that greater distance or avoidance reflects the disruption of a bond already formed.

Separation from Mother. According to Bowlby (1973), separation from the attachment figure is the key to detachment; it is dangerous and whenever possible should be avoided. It is this view, in fact, that first alerted parents and psychologists to the possible dangers of day care, since day care involves the daily separation of mother and child. Bowlby's claim was based on his reading of the literature on long-term separation (e.g., in institutions or hospitals), and it is a grave error to extrapolate from those settings to day care. The acute distress and subsequent detachment of children separated from their parents as noted by Bowlby was no doubt because separation for these children was continuous and prolonged, beyond control or comprehension. This is not the case for children in day care. Nevertheless, since, at least superficially, distance and avoidance resemble a mild form of detachment, it is important to examine the available evidence to see whether the observed day care differences may be the result of separation per se. In fact, Vaughn has suggested that day care children are avoidant because they interpret their mothers' absence as rejection. This kind of interpretation by 1-year-old children would seem to strain the cognitive capacities of naive creatures who scarcely have attained an *incomplete* notion of person permanence.

There are also two empirical suggestions that separation is not the culprit. First, children have been observed in the day care setting when the mother leaves. When the child is left for the first time, crying is common for children under 2½ years, but rare for older children (Blurton Jones & Leach, 1972). It is less common, even for young children, if a sibling accompanies them (Blurton Jones & Leach, 1972). Over the next few months of attending day care or preschool, this protest reaction decreases, and overt distress is no longer observed (Cummings, 1980; Kagan et al., 1978; Ragozin, 1975; Smith & Connolly, 1972). So the separation itself becomes an accepted part of the daily routine, not a traumatic event. Second, variations in the degree of avoidance or distance are related to the type of day care the child is in. Although greater distance and avoidance have been observed, across studies, for children in either day care centers or day care homes (see Tables 5 and 6), two studies comparing these two types of day care found center children to be more distant or avoidant than those in day care homes or with babysitters (Clarke-Stewart, in preparation; Hock, 1976). This, too, suggests that the observed difference in distance and avoidance is the result of more than separation from mother per se, since separation occurs with equal frequency and regularity in both these day care arrangements. It is interesting to note that Rutter (1979), more recently reviewing the literature on long-term separations which Bowlby relied on (e.g., Heinicke & Westheimer, 1965; Hinde & Spencer-Booth, 1970, 1971; Moore, 1969; Robertson & Robertson, 1971), concluded that, even in these cases, separation by *itself* did not cause detachment or affectionless psychopathy, since these outcomes were affected by the kind of substitute care given during the separation and by the mother's response at and after reunion.

Substitute Attachment. We know that some children in day care do form close relationships with their day caregivers (Anderson et al., 1981; Cummings, 1980; Ricciuti, 1974). Even though mother is still preferred to this caregiver, could the child's attachment to her be diluted (or replaced) by such a "competing" attachment? Unfortunately, no studies have assessed and "weighed" the individual child's attachment to both mother and another caregiver. As we did previously, therefore, we must try to answer this obvious and simple question from a combination of indirect sources of evidence.

We know that the child is more likely to develop an attachment to a caregiver who interacts with him more (Anderson et al., 1981; Cummings, 1980). We also know that the kind of caregiver who interacts with the child more is likely to be a babysitter or day care home provider rather than a day care center teacher (Cochran, 1977; Prescott, 1978). If the avoidance of day care children were caused by a competing attachment with their caregiver, we would predict that the most distant and avoidant children would be those cared for by a babysitter; next would be those in a day care home; and least would be those in a center. Tallying across studies in Tables 5 and 6 we find, contrary to prediction, that avoidance and distance are more likely in day care centers (8 of 15 studies) than in day care homes (2 of 7 studies) or with babysitters (1 of 3 studies). In looking at the results of studies that have compared different types of day care in the same study, again there is no support for the hypothesis that children with babysitters or in day care homes are more distant or avoidant than those in day care centers (Clarke-Stewart, in preparation; Doyle & Somers, 1978; Everson et al., 1981; Hock, 1976; Portnoy & Simmons, 1978), nor that children with babysitters are more avoidant than those in day care homes (Clarke-Stewart, in preparation; Hock, 1976). Steinberg and Green (1977) report that more mothers are likely to *perceive* a weakened attachment bond when their child is with a babysitter in their home (40%) than when their child is in a day care home or center (10%). Yet these mothers may have perceived a weaker attachment to themselves when care was provided by a babysitter because they were more likely to see more of the child's interactions with the babysitter and, competitively, compare them with their own.

We might also expect avoidance of the mother would increase as the child stayed in the day care program longer, or would be greater if the child were in day care full-time rather than part-time, since these children would have had the opportunity to form a closer relationship with the caregiver (Cummings, 1980; Leiderman & Leiderman, 1974; Smith, Eaton, & Hindmarsh, in press). But, as we have discussed, there is no evidence that greater distance or avoidance is related to length of time in day care, and although there is a trend for children in full-time day care to be more avoidant than those in part-time day care (Blanchard & Main, 1979; Clarke-Stewart, in preparation; Everson et al., 1981; Schwartz, 1983), the difference was significant in only one study (Schwartz, 1983).

More important than these comparisons of different kinds or durations of day care, however, is the fact that there is no evidence that having an attachment to more than one person in *any* environment, not just day care, dilutes the child's "primary" attachment (cf. Smith, 1980). Children form attachments to fathers, siblings, grandmothers—even blankets (Clarke-Stewart, 1978; Lamb, 1977; Main & Weston, 1981; Passman & Weisberg, 1975)—and this does not interfere with their attachment to mother. Attachment is not stronger or more secure in single-parent families, or where the child is not attached to the father. In single-parent families, children are less likely to be securely attached to mother than in two-parent families (Vaughn et al., 1980); while in two-parent families, children securely attached to one parent tend also to be securely attached to the other and are better off emotionally when this is the case (Main & Weston, 1981). To summarize, it seems unlikely that the greater avoidance or distance from mother noted for day care children results from replacing attachment to mother with another attachment relationship.

Too Many Caregivers. The suggestion that day care children are more avoidant because they have too many caregivers and so cannot form attachments to any, like the preceding hypothesis, derives from Bowlby's (1969) notion of monotropy—that attachment is formed to a single person only. Bowlby based this notion on studies showing that children in institutions with many and changing caregivers had impaired social-emotional relationships. Since, as we have mentioned, there are obvious dangers in extrapolating from the effects of residential institutions to the effects of day care, we need to look closely at the evidence regarding the number and stability of caregivers for day care children.

Throughout the world it is the rule, not the exception, for children to be cared for by more than one caregiver and to form more than one attachment (see Smith, 1980). In 186 nonindustrial societies Weisner and Gallimore (1977) found only five where the mother was the child's "almost exclusive" caregiver. And in industrialized nations, too, it has been found that children spend more time in the care of mother plus someone else than in care of mother alone (e.g., Lawson & Ingleby, 1974). Thus, while it may be true that having "too many" caregivers is bad, "too many" does not mean more than one. Since four is the average number in cultures as diverse as the Hausau (Marvin, 1977) and the British (Tizard & Tizard, 1971), "too many" may mean more than four. According to maternal reports, home-reared children can apparently form secure and intense attachments to as many as four people (Marvin, 1977; Schaffer & Emerson, 1964); more than that does seem to affect intensity (Schaffer & Emerson, 1964). If the number of caregivers were responsible for the greater distance and avoidance from mother observed in day care children, we would expect to see more distance in center day care children (with more than one caregiver) than in home day care children (with a single caregiver). There is some evidence supporting this prediction, both across studies (as we described in the discussion of the preceding hypothesis) and within studies (Clarke-Stewart, in preparation; Hock, 1976). However, we would also expect that the intensity of the child's attachment to mother would be related to the number of caregivers, with whom he or she interacted. In the Chicago Study of Child Care and Development (Clarke-Stewart, in preparation), the group of day care children exhibiting the lowest mean level of proximity with mother, on the average, interacted with four different adults during a 2-hour observation, while the group with the highest mean level of proximity interacted with two. But the correlation between proximity and the number of interacting adults was not statistically significant. In another study, attachment to mother was unaffected by the number of caregivers (one vs. five) who were assigned to look after the child in a day care center (Wilcox, Staff, & Romaine, 1980). Unfortunately for our purposes here, in the latter study children were not given exclusive care by their assigned caregivers. Even the children assigned to a single caregiver interacted with the other four caregivers to some extent. Thus, this study did not really provide an adequate test of the multiple-attachment hypothesis. Neither study, however, provides evidence that the lower level of proximity seeking observed in day care children is the result of their interacting with more caregivers.

Regarding the stability of caregivers, the prediction could be made that children who have changed caregivers more frequently would be less attached to mother. But the two studies to examine this question have not found support for this prediction. Schwartz (1983) found avoidance of mother unrelated to number of changes of caregiver, and Moore (1969) found that children who had been in unstable care arrangements were more clinging and dependent on mother, not more distant. Given that even day care children, like home care children (and unlike children in most residential institutions), do have one stable attachment figure—the mother—these results are not too surprising.

To summarize, then, while there is no strong evidence supporting the hypothesis that the difference in distance or avoidance between day care and home care children results from the fact that day care children have "too many" caregivers, the possibility cannot be ruled out that interacting regularly with a large number of people may encourage or support greater distance or independence in the mother-child relationship (and possibly in the other relationships as well).

Poor Quality Day Care. It has also been suggested that the reason some day care children are more distant or avoidant from mother is that they are in less than adequate day care (Anderson et al., 1981; Belsky & Steinberg, 1978; Farber & Egeland, 1982; Rutter, 1982). Here, the argument is that the child is less attached to mother because of a rejecting or insensitive caregiver to whom the child cannot form an attachment and from whom the child generalizes to mother. This argument does not receive empirical support. Avoidance and distance were observed for children in both optimal day care settings (Hock, 1976; Ricciuti, 1974; Wynn, 1979) and ordinary day care settings (Blehar, 1974; Clarke-Stewart, in preparation; Schwartz, 1983; Vaughn et al., 1980); and in two studies to analyze the relation between attachment to mother and quality of day care (Clarke-Stewart, in preparation; Schwartz, 1983), no relation was found. This argument is not a very compelling one anyway since, if there is any connection *between* the child's various attachment relationships, it seems more plausible that one good relationship would provide a buffer for a poor one than that one poor relationship would destroy a good one (cf. Rutter, 1979a).

Maternal Availability. The mother's availability would seem to be the most obvious and reasonable hypothesis to account for observed day care effects: Day care children are more distant or avoidant of mother simply because they have spent less time with her. Three kinds of research are pertinent to this hypothesis: (1) descriptions of how much time day care children compared with home care children spend with their mothers or spend interacting with their mothers; (2) comparisons of the effects of full-time versus part-time day care; (3) analyses of the relation between attachment and the amount of time or interaction with mother. None provides strong evidence supporting this hypothesis.

First, it is hard to judge how much time working mothers actually spend with their children compared to the "exclusive caregiver" or "traditional mothers", who are busy with housework and personal activities. Studies that have addressed this question of the effect of maternal employment on child care (Clarke-Stewart, in preparation; Curtis, 1976; Howell, 1973a; Robinson, Yerby, Fieweger, & Somerick, 1977; Thomopoulos & Huyck, 1976; Walker & Woods, 1972; Young, 1975) paint a consistent picture of the working mother juggling the time demands of home and work, and coping with this overload largely by giving up her own free time and the pursuit of personal interests. Working mothers may complete household tasks in less time (Hoffman & Nye, 1974; Robinson et al., 1977) or have more help with these tasks (e.g., from husbands), but the time they claim to spend in child care—bathing, feeding, dressing, chauffeuring, playing, teaching—is the same whether the mother is employed or not (Walker & Woods, 1972). A working mother's activities with her child just have to be more carefully planned and scheduled than if she were not working.

Second, in the studies comparing attachment of children in part-time or full-time care (or analyzing its relationship to the number of hours per week in day care), as we mentioned earlier, although the trend is for full-time day care children to be more distant, only one study found this difference significant.

And third, for the traditionally parent-reared children, attachment quality has not been found to be related to the amount of time a child spends with mother (Clarke-Stewart, 1973; Rutter, 1974; Schaffer & Emerson, 1964). Some minimum amount of time and interaction, certainly, is necessary for the formation of an attachment (Ainsworth, 1973), but what that amount is has not yet been established. It seems quite likely that children in day care see their mothers a sufficient amount to form an attachment. Even children in day care 40 hours a week spend three times this amount of time at home.

Given the evidence from these three kinds of research, then, it seems unlikely that maternal availability alone accounts for the observed home care/day care difference in distance and avoidance.

Maternal Accessibility. This hypothesis speaks to the possibility that working mothers, even though they may spend enough time with their children to ensure the formation of an attachment, may not be as emotionally or psychologically accessible. The double burden of family and job is reflected in the mother's psychological state. Working mothers feel overworked and tired. They feel that life is hard (Wright, 1978). Many feel lonely. There are compensations, of course—they enjoy their jobs and meeting people, they may have a better self-image, and they claim to be in better health (Curtis, 1976; Gold & Andres, 1978; Hoffman & Nye, 1974; Thomopoulos & Huyck, 1976; Welch & Booth, 1977); however, they feel rushed, harried, and guilty about the job they are doing as mothers (Burke & Weir, 1976; Hoffman & Nye, 1974; Thomopoulos & Huyck, 1976; Vaughn et al., 1980; Welch & Booth, 1977), and they often experience more marital conflict (Burke & Weir, 1976; Hoffman & Nye, 1974; Howell, 1973a). Could such stress be reflected in the mother-child relationship?

The investigators who have looked at this question most directly say "yes." Vaughn and his associates assessed overall family stress (ill health, money problems, work pressures) in poor families with young children. Children whose families experienced more stress were more likely to shift from secure to anxious attachment (70% of them to the avoidant attachment category; Vaughn, Egeland, & Sroufe, 1979). The combined stress of single parenthood plus full-time employment was especially likely to be reflected in avoidance: 48% of the children of single working mothers versus 23% of those of single nonworking mothers, 31% of married working mothers, and 4% of married nonworking mothers were classified as avoidant (Vaughn et al., 1980). Bryant et al. (1980), too, noted that children who were withdrawn and detached had experienced a combination of day care and problems at home that were likely to make mother less accessible (divorce, illness, etc.), and Crockenberg (1981) found avoidant attachment more likely in children whose mothers had no social support. Finally, among home-reared children, twins—a family condition that may also lead to reduced maternal accessibility—have been observed to be more avoidant than only children (Hock, Coady, & Cordero, 1973). Maternal accessibility does seem to matter then—probably more than availability per se—but what about specific maternal behaviors?

Maternal Insensitivity. In studies of the normal course of development in home-reared children, the best predictor of the quality of the child's attachment is not maternal availability or accessibility but, specifically, maternal sensitivity. Intense, affectionate, sensitive, and responsive mothering is related to the development of a secure attachment (Ainsworth, 1973; Ainsworth et al., 1978; Rutter, 1979), while maternal rejection and submerged anger communicated through aberrant reactions to close bodily contact, a lack of facial expression, and a lack of reciprocity are related to the development of avoidant attachment (Ainsworth, 1973; Ainsworth et al., 1978; Main, 1977; Rosenberg, 1975). It is possible, therefore, that the difference observed in attachment quality between day care and home care children derives from differences in maternal behavior. Ideally, the behavior of the mothers of avoidant day care children would be examined to test this hypothesis. Only one study (Farber & Egeland, 1982) has included an analysis that speaks to this issue. Correlations were calculated between children's attachment classification (secure or avoidant) and maternal behavior variables, observed at 6 months, in a group of mothers who put their children in day care in their first year (the Vaughn et al., 1980, early day care sample). No significant relationship was found between attachment and maternal sensitivity.

Lending indirect support to this finding are the results of numerous studies comparing the behavior of working and nonworking mothers, which also have not found significant differences in affectionate and sensitive behavior or attitudes in standard situations (Clarke-Stewart, in preparation; Cohen, 1978; Hock, 1980; Ragozin, 1977; Rubenstein et al., 1981; Schubert, Bradley-Johnson, & Nuttal, 1980), in natural interactions (Clarke-Stewart, in preparation; Farber & Egeland, 1982; Hock, 1980; Schwartz, 1983; Vaughn et al., 1980), on questionnaires (Blehar, 1974; Gold & Andres, 1978; Hock, 1980), or according to psychologists' ratings (Moore, 1969), either before or after they began work. In general, working mothers do not appear to differ in ways that would be expected to generate greater avoidance in their children and, in fact, have been observed to play and show affection to the child more frequently than nonworking mothers in play times with their child at the end of the day (Pedersen, Cain, Zaslow, & Anderson, 1980; Schwartz, 1983).

There are but a few hints of a difference in the direction of greater insensitivity for mothers of children in day care: Cohen (1978) found working mothers to provide their children with less positive attention and reciprocal interaction, but only in a sample that confounded work status with marital status (more employed mothers were single parents). Hock (1980) and Moore (1969) found working mothers to be less invested in the maternal role and in their children but, again, there were confounded factors. More predictive of maternal differences than work status alone seemed to be the combination (and compatibility) of work status and attitudes toward working. In Hock's research (1976, 1978, 1980; Hock, Christman, & Hock, 1980), children of working mothers were more distant or resistant if the mother thought she should be the child's exclusive caregiver but was not. This parallels other studies showing that, if a working mother is dissatisfied with her role, her behavior is less playful, involved, warm, and effective (Harrell & Ridley, 1975; Hoffman, 1961), and it suggests that, while working mothers as a whole may not be insensitive or rejecting, there may be some among them for whom the combination of work status and dissatisfaction is related to less involved interaction with their children. One special group of mothers in Hock's study intended, when the baby was born, to stay home, but by 12 months had gone to work. Relative to those who said they would stay home and did, mothers who returned to work were less positive about their maternal role, more career oriented, took their baby's fussiness as a personal affront, and thought the baby was less positively and strongly attached at 3 months. Since babies are not, in observable ways, attached at 3 months, this difference was largely in the eye of the beholder, suggesting that differences in maternal attitude predating work or placement of the child in day care are in the direction of greater distance for some day care mothers. Finally, in the Farber and Egeland (1982) study, although the avoidance of the early day care children was not related to the mother's observed sensitivity, it was related to her lower desire for motherhood assessed prenatally.

In general, it seems unlikely that day care mothers as a group are more rejecting; but there may be *some* who are less invested in the maternal role or are less satisfied with it, who may be themselves more distant and less encouraging of physical contact, and this may be reflected in a higher percentage of avoidant children who later end up in day care.

Selective Placement. This finding about the qualities of mothers who choose to go to work and put their children in day care brings up another hypothesis regarding self-selection; namely, that parents selectively place children who are more avoidant or distant in early childhood programs. This possibility was explored in a prospective study by Blurton Jones, Ferreira, Brown, and MacDonald (1980) with the outcome of interest being the age at which mothers put their children into play groups or preschool programs. These investigators did find that children who maintained greater physical distance from their mothers in playroom assessments of free play during the second year of life were, subsequently, placed in preschool programs at younger ages. They suggest that mothers take children's readiness into account in making a decision about putting them in a play group or nursery school. We do not know, however, how hard the mothers were pushing the children's independence to attain this "readiness." Studies of natural mother-child interaction at home (e.g., Clarke-Stewart & Hevey, 1981) demonstrate that mothers do encourage children's autonomy at this age, and, in the Blurton Jones study, mothers who put their children in preschool earlier were also less likely to pick them up if they cried after a brief, standard separation—possibly in order to foster independence. Unfortunately, we cannot determine whether self-selection was based on characteristics of the child or the mother. Mothers may have been responding to their children's "spontaneous" independence by placing them in preschool earlier, or they may have been encouraging their children's independence all along, and early placement in a preschool was just one more way of doing so. Either way, whether independence was child-initiated or mother-induced, the generalizability to day care from the Blurton Jones study of play group and preschool placement is limited, since placement in day care is likely to be more contingent on the mother's plans, needs, and desire to work than simply on what is best, appropriate, or desired for the child. More important, the difference in distance observed by Blurton Jones before English children were placed in play groups has not been found in several American studies in which children's behavior was observed before they started nursery school or day care (Everson et al., 1981; Roopnarine & Lamb, 1978, 1980).

It is possible, of course, that there is selective placement of children in day care programs on the basis of some characteristic other than the quality of the attachment (like sex or birth order)—and this might account for observed differences. Not only mothers but day caregivers may be making selections on the basis of children's individual characteristics. It is a fact, for instance, that many day care centers admit only children who are toilet trained, and this criterion of physical maturity may well bias the day care center population toward more mature and, hence, more independent or distant children, at least in the age range when toilet training is a differentiating issue. In the preschool day care group children are more likely to be firstborn (Powell, 1980), a condition associated with greater sociability and assertiveness with peers and adults (Rosenberg & Sutton-Smith, 1973; Snow, Jacklin, & Maccoby, 1981). Unfortunately, the only studies that randomly assigned children to day care or home care did not include assessments of the quality of the children's attachment (Farran & Ramey, 1977; Garber & Heber, 1980), so this possibility cannot be ruled out. However, it seems likely that self-selection is at best a partial explanation for observed differences.

Interaction with Child Characteristics. The only individual characteristic that has been systematically examined for interactions with day care effects has been the child's sex. Studies consistently reveal more numerous and significant differences between home care and day care children for boys than for girls (Clarke-Stewart, in preparation; Cornelius & Denney, 1975; Hock, 1976; Moore, 1969; Moskowitz et al., 1977)—reflecting, perhaps, the greater susceptibility of boys to all kinds of environmental conditions (cf. Rutter, 1982). Moreover, it has been the day care boys who are more distant than home care boys in most studies (Carr, 1973; Clarke-Stewart, in preparation; Hock, 1976; Moskowitz et al., 1977). Unfortunately for those who would like to make this a simple generalization, one study found the opposite—that day care boys stayed closer to their mothers than did home care boys (Cornelius & Denney, 1975)—a discrepancy for which there is no clear explanation. At this time we must conclude that, while children's sex may contribute to the observed findings, and while this sex effect may be tied to differences in the treatment of male and female children, a satisfying explanation for these findings has not appeared.

Method of Assessment. The hypothesis that the observed difference between day care and home care children is a methodological artifact rather than a genuine difference in the mother-child relationship should also be explored. Perhaps day care children have simply had more experience in the type of situation used to assess attachment, so they find it less stressful and therefore exhibit less overt and intense attachment behavior (i.e., proximity). To examine this possibility, we might ask whether the same effects (or direction of effects) are observed across different assessment situations. Unfortunately for testing this hypothesis, one assessment situation has been used almost exclusively in these studies: Ainsworth's "strange situation," an assessment that combines an unfamiliar setting, an unfamiliar adult, and repeated separations from mother. All of these features are likely to be more common for day care children. How is the behavior of day care children affected by an unfamiliar setting, an unfamiliar person, or a separation, taken separately?

First, the setting: Day care children have been observed to be more comfortable than home care children in an unfamiliar setting (laboratory or new day care centers; Kagan et al., 1978; Moskowitz et al., 1977; Ramey, MacPhee, & Yeates, 1982; Schwarz, Strickland, & Krolick, 1973). So this factor likely contributes to the observed difference in proximity.

Second, the unfamiliar adults: When no stranger is present, day care children have not been found to be more distant from their mothers than home care children (Carr, 1973; Clarke-Stewart, in preparation). This suggests that the observation of distance and avoidance may be a result of the inclusion of a stranger in the attachment assessment. But although this facet of the strange situation may contribute to the observed difference in proximity, it is unlikely to be solely responsible for that difference. Day care children have only been observed to be more comfortable with a stranger in their mother's absence; overall they are not more friendly or less fearful (see the following discussion under *Less Wariness of Unfamiliar Adults*).

And finally, the separation: Differences in proximity have not been as marked before separation or without separation (Blehar, 1974; Caldwell et al., 1970; Carr, 1973; Clarke-Stewart, in preparation; Cornelius & Denney, 1975; Cummings, 1980), although they do still show up (Ricciuti, 1974; Schwartz, 1983). This factor, too, then, seems likely to contribute to the observed difference in proximity between day care and home care children, but cannot alone account for it.

Attachment theorists (Ainsworth, 1973; Bowlby, 1969) argue that some degree of stress is necessary in order to evoke observable attachment behavior. It is unfortunate for generalizations about the true effects of day care on attachment that the three factors inducing stress in the strange situation, which each apparently affects children's exhibition of attachment, are all more common for day care children. To eliminate possible confounding effects of these particular features, assessments should be made using other known stressors like fatigue or retesting, as well. At present, we cannot rule out the possibility that differences in distance or avoidance between day care and home care children are contributed to by the particular method of assessment that has been used. It is also troublesome that the strange situation has only been validated as an assessment of attachment up to 18 or 24 months of age, and we do not know what it indicates past that age.

In conclusion, it seems that there are several plausible hypotheses concerning the effects of day care on children's attachment to their mothers. Any simple statement regarding the meaning or etiology of these effects would be misleading. The best generalization we can make on the basis of our analysis of available—and limited—data is that when children are placed in day care, although they become or continue to be attached to their mothers, there may be differences in the quality of that relationship. These differences are in the direction of greater distance, avoidance, or independence from mother, and they show up in mildly stressful situations with unfamiliar people in unfamiliar places. They are most likely to be extreme if day care is begun in the first year, before a secure and stable attachment to mother has formed, and they are likely to be the result not only of the time the children spend away from mother and the amount of interaction they have with other caregivers, but perhaps also the differences in maternal attitudes and emotional accessibility that accompany the task of combining job and family. For most children this pattern of greater distance from mother probably reflects an adaptive reaction to a realistic appraisal of the situation rather than a pathological disturbance.

But the nature of the child's attachment relationship with mother is only one of several areas of concern in research on early childhood programs. Another important area is the child's social relationships with peers and unrelated adults. We turn to this area next.

Social Development in Early Childhood Programs

A substantial number of researchers have been interested in the social development of children attending day care, early education, and nursery school programs, particularly in these children's interactions with peers and nonparental adults (Allen & Masling, 1957; Blanchard & Main, 1979; Blehar, 1974; Braun & Caldwell, 1973; Brookhart & Hock, 1976; Bryant et al., 1980; Clarke-Stewart, in preparation; Cochran, 1977; Cornelius & Denney, 1975; Doyle, 1975; Fein & Moorin, 1980; Fein, Moorin, & Enslein, 1982; Finkelstein & Wilson, 1977; Fowler, 1978; Fowler & Khan, 1974; Gehler, 1972; Golden et al., 1978; Gunnarsson, 1977, 1978; Harrold & Temple, 1960; Hock, 1976, 1980; Hock & Clinger, 1980; Kagan et al., 1978; Keister, 1970; Lally & Honig, 1977b; Lay & Meyer, 1972; Lieberman, 1977; Lippman & Grote, 1974; Moore, 1969, 1975; Moskowitz et al., 1977; Peaslee, 1976; Ragozin, 1975, 1977; Ramey & Mills, 1977; Ramey et al., 1982; Ramey, Dorval, & Baker-Ward, in press; Raph, Thomas, Chess, & Korn, 1968; Ricciuti, 1974; Rubenstein & Howes, 1979; Rubenstein et al., 1981; Saunders & Keister, 1972, 1979; Schwarz et al., 1973; Schwarz, Strickland, & Krolick, 1974; Vroegh, 1976). Reviewers of these studies (or at least of those done before 1979) generally have concluded that children attending these programs interact more with peers—both positively and, often, negatively—and that they are less cooperative and responsive with adults than home care children. They also agree that evidence even for these general statements is as yet limited (Belsky & Steinberg, 1978; Belsky, Steinberg, & Walker, 1982; Bronfenbrenner, Belsky, & Steinberg, 1976; Ricciuti, 1976; Silverstein, 1977; Sjolund, 1971).

In our reading of this literature the most consistent finding seemed to be that children who are attending or have attended early childhood programs are more socially competent or mature. We base this conclusion on the following evidence: Children attending early childhood programs are more self-confident, more self-assured, more outgoing, and are less timid and fearful (Moore, 1969, 1975; Ramey et al., 1982; see Sjolund, 1971); they are more assertive—for example, tell the examiner "I don't know," or ask another child to share (Lally & Honig, 1977b; Lippman & Grote, 1974; Rubenstein et al., 1981; see Sjolund, 1971), more self-sufficient and independent of parent or teacher (Fowler, 1978; Harrold & Temple, 1960; Moore, 1969, 1975; see Sjolund, 1971), and yet more helpful and cooperative with peers, mothers, or examiners when the situation requires it (Clarke-Stewart, in preparation; see Sjolund, 1971). They are more verbally expressive (Fowler & Khan, 1974; Stukat, 1973) and are more knowledgeable about the social world—for example, about sex roles, emotional labels, social problem solving, and perspective taking (Clarke-Stewart, in preparation), about their names, addresses, and birthdays (Cochran, 1977). They are more comfortable in a new or stressful situation (Kagan et al., 1978; Moskowitz et al., 1977; Schwarz et al., 1973), more realistic about their achievements (Lippman & Grote, 1974), and more competent to manage on their own (Cochran, 1977; Stukat, 1973). They are less stereotyped in their play (Clarke-Stewart, in preparation), more curious and more persistent on a task (Miller & Dyer, 1975); and more mature in their figure drawing (Lippman & Grote, 1974) and in their pretend play (Fein, Moorin, & Enslein, 1982). When they get to school, they are better adjusted, more task oriented and goal directed, and show more leadership and persistence (Fowler & Khan, 1974; Harrold & Temple, 1960; Lally & Honig, 1977b; Ramey et al., 1982; see Sjolund, 1971). They score higher on a rating of social competence tapping the following qualities: cooperation in shared activities, awareness of social norms and conventions, appropriate independence, friendliness, responsiveness and social confidence in interactions (Clarke-Stewart, in preparation).

The exhibition of greater social competence or maturity by these children is not always "positive," however. Children in early childhood programs are not only more independent, they have also been observed to be less polite, less agreeable, less respectful of others' rights, and less compliant with maternal directives or teacher demands (Clarke-Stewart, in preparation; Fowler, 1978; Moore, 1969, 1975; Rubenstein et al., 1981; Sjolund, 1971; Vroegh, 1976). They have been found to be not only more assertive, but also louder, more aggressive, rebellious, bossy, belligerent, irritable, and hostile (Fowler & Khan, 1974; Harrold & Temple, 1960; Lally & Honig, 1977b; Moore, 1969, 1975; Ramey et al., 1982; Rubenstein et al., 1981; Schwarz et al., 1974)[4]—especially if the family or school context allows or supports this (Fowler & Khan, 1974; Lally & Honig, 1977b). Nevertheless, while these latter behaviors may not be positive, even these differences are in a direction that, in general, reflects greater maturity, since these kinds of behavior have been found to increase with increasing age of the child through this preschool period (e.g., Clarke-Stewart, in preparation; Greif, 1977; Hartup, 1974; Parten, 1932).

A few studies or measures do not exhibit significant differences on dimensions of social competence (Braun & Caldwell, 1973; Fowler, 1978, for children over 3 years; Golden et al., 1978; Lippman & Grote, 1974; Saunders & Keister, 1979; Winnett, Fuchs, Moffatt, & Nerviano, 1977), but generally the consistency of the findings is impressive. They are replicated across studies; for example, in Sjolund's 1971 survey of 56 studies of children in nursery school only three found no difference. Findings are always in the same direction; in only one study (Peaslee, 1976) of a very poor day care program was there a significant difference in the opposite direction. Significant findings occur in different assessment situations (in tests and observations; in the program setting and outside; with peers and adults; with strangers and acquaintances) and with different kinds of subjects (boys and girls, at different SES levels). And, finally, they appear as the outcome of different kinds of programs; for example, kibbutzim (Nahir & Yussen, 1977; Shapira & Madsen, 1974); part-time as well as full-time day care center programs (e.g., Clarke-Stewart, in preparation); model as well as mediocre programs (e.g., Clarke-Stewart, in preparation; and Ramey et al., in press).

In this section, we look at evidence regarding the effects of early childhood programs on social development and, as we did for the effects on attachment, we look not just at the consistent outcomes, but discuss the meaning and possible processes underlying the apparent effects.

Interpreting the Difference in Social Competence

Rejection of Adult Standards. Is it the case that the apparent "competence" of children in early childhood programs really just reflects a lack of conformity to, or a rejection of, adult standards as was suggested by Bronfenbrenner, Belsky, and Steinberg (1976)? This would seem to be too general a statement. These children conform less to some demands by adults, while still conforming to other adult standards. Program children have been observed to be not so likely to comply with maternal demands, for example, but they have at the same time been observed to be more spontaneously helpful and comforting to mother and to cooperate more with her in games—showing a sensitivity to adult expectations for these kinds of behavior (Clarke-Stewart, in preparation). What is more, their mothers have been observed to issue fewer demands to them than mothers of children not in early childhood programs (Clarke-Stewart, in preparation), perhaps making it appear that program children are less dominated by adults or adult standards. This hypothesis of differential conformity to adult standards has not really been tested, but it seems more likely that program children are socialized to a different set of standards, which may be more peer oriented than traditional parental socialization standards, than that they simply have not achieved or are rejecting adult standards.

Less Wariness of Unfamiliar Adults. Another possibility is that the apparent social competence of program children is a reflection of the fact that these children, having had more experience with nonparental adults, are friendlier or less afraid with unfamiliar adult "examiners" and, therefore, are able to cooperate more in assessments, thus appearing more competent. However, this explanation also seems inadequate. In an unfamiliar situation with a noninteractive stranger, many studies find no difference between program and nonprogram children in social interaction, proximity, or fear (Brookhart & Hock, 1976; Clarke-Stewart, in preparation; Cornelius & Denney, 1975; Hock & Clinger, 1980; Kagan et al., 1978; Ragozin, 1977; Saunders & Keister, 1979). And when there is a difference, it is more likely the nonprogram children who appear interested, friendly, and positive with the stranger (Blehar, 1974; Clarke-Stewart, Umeh, Snow, & Pederson, 1980; Doyle, 1975; Moskowitz et al., 1977; Ragozin, 1977; Ricciuti, 1974). Only when mother is not present are program children less likely to resist the stranger (Hock & Clinger, 1980). Only when the stranger is interactive and initiates a task or test are they more friendly and cooperative (Clarke-Stewart, in preparation; Ramey et al., in press). Thus it seems that observed differences in social competence do not simply reflect differences in sociability with unfamiliar adults (friendliness or fear), but a difference in sensitivity to social situations.

Sociability Versus Social Maturity. Is the greater social competence observed in children attending early childhood programs a result of these children's having had more experience with other children, and this experience making them friendlier or more oriented toward peers and, therefore, more cooperative or competent? In the peer group, children who have been in an early childhood program or have been in a program longer have been observed to be more popular (Allen & Masling, 1957), to form relationships more easily and more often (Gehler, 1972), and to interact with other children more often and more positively or agreeably (Lay & Meyer, 1972; Macrae & Herbert-Jackson, 1976; Schwarz et al., 1974). Results of these studies are influenced by the fact that the children in the early childhood programs knew their particular classmates better, however, confounding friendship with friendliness. Since no difference has been observed in the level of play and positive effect shown with a peer when children in a day-care program are compared with parental care children at home with a familiar playmate (Rubenstein & Howes, 1979), it might be better to compare sociability of both program and nonprogram children with equally unfamiliar or familiar children. In studies using this approach, the majority find no difference between program and nonprogram children in initiating social interaction with the peer (Clarke-Stewart, in preparation; Fein & Moorin, 1980; Fein, Moorin, & Enslein, 1982; Finkelstein & Wilson, 1977; Kagan et al., 1978; Lieberman, 1977; Raph et al., 1968). Some find small differences in the direction of greater sociability for program children: less apprehension, but only at 20 months (Kagan et al., 1978); more social initiation, but only for boys (Wynn, 1979); more approach to other children, but only at the beginning of the play group (Ricciuti, 1974). So it appears that, if there is a difference in sociability with unfamiliar children favoring those in early childhood programs, it is not large, long-lasting, or consistent. In fact, one study found that in pairs of home care and day care toddlers it was the home care children who initiated more interaction with their partners (Doyle, 1975). It does not appear that the observed difference in social competence is attributable to differential sociability with peers.

On the contrary, a number of studies have documented the tendency of children in early childhood programs to be more antisocial toward their peers. Although this tendency is *not* inevitably observed (e.g., Clarke- Stewart, in preparation, with friend or in second year of day care; Macrae & Herbert-Jackson, 1976; Ramey et al., in press, in the day care center), it occurs with enough regularity and consistency to disconfirm the hypothesis that the observed difference in social competence indicates only a difference in positive sociability (e.g., Clarke-Stewart, in preparation, with unfamiliar peer in the first year of day care; Doyle, 1975; Harrold & Temple, 1960; Lally & Honig, 1977b;

Ramey et al., in press, in kindergarten; Schwarz et al., 1974). The combination of more positive *and* more negative social behavior with peers suggests something more complex than just simple friendliness. Since, as we have mentioned, in the course of "normal development" from 2 to 4 years, the age range of most of these studies, there is an increase in the frequency of aggression, as well as of cooperation, role play, and social interaction, it may signal greater social maturity.

Cognitive Development. Perhaps, given this suggestion of differential maturity favoring children attending early childhood programs, the reason that these children appear more socially competent is that they are more advanced cognitively and this advance shows itself in social skills as well as intellectual abilities. This may indeed be part of the explanation. It is most likely to account for the differences observed in children's social knowledge, for instance. But not all the social differences observed (e.g., friendliness, helpfulness, nonconformity) are likely to reflect only cognitive ability. How large a part cognitive ability is of the explanation we do not know. This is a question that needs further research and statistical analysis, which can control or partial out cognitive factors.

Independence from Mother. Another possible interpretation of the observed differences in social competence between early childhood program and nonprogram children is that the difference is the result of, or is the same as, the greater physical independence of mother that has been noted for day care children. Program children may appear to be more mature and self-sufficient because they are more distant from their mothers and therefore can interact sociably with a variety of other partners. It is true that a secure or distant relationship with mother may support or even allow the development of autonomous social competence with mother, strangers, and peers. Correlations between social competence and attachment to mother have been noted by Clarke-Stewart (in preparation), Londerville and Main (1981), and Matas et al. (1978). But they are clearly not the same thing. What is more, evidence of competence is not restricted to interaction with mother; it shows up as readily with other partners.

Endurance of the Effect. Finally, there is the question of whether the observed difference in social competence reflects a permanent enhancement by the program of children's social skills or simply an acceleration of social maturity. This may be the most interesting and important question—but its answer is not yet clear. The difference in social competence is apparently not related to the age at which the child begins the program. Whether a child enters the program before 2, at 2, at 3, or at 4 years of age does not seem to matter—he or she will still exhibit this increased competence relative to a child who stays at home, according to the range of ages in studies cited and findings that specifically compared children of different ages (Clarke-Stewart, in preparation; Ferri, 1980; Golden et al., 1978; Hock, 1976).[5] And the difference increases or is maintained over a period of up to 2 years (Blanchard & Main, 1979; Clarke-Stewart, in preparation; Fowler, 1978; Raph et al., 1968; Schwarz et al., 1974; Vroegh, 1976).

But is the effect permanent? It does seem to carry over into the first few school grades (Lally & Honig, 1977b; Ramey et al., in press; Sjolund, 1971), and in one longitudinal study, using tests taken from 6½ to 15 years of age, Moore (1975) found a consistent pattern of nonconformity, outgoingness, fearlessness, and aggressiveness in children who had experienced a program of nonparental care in their first 5 years. But in most longitudinal studies of children in early childhood programs, the differences tend to decrease with time (Harrold & Temple, 1960; Lally & Honig, 1977b; Ramey et al., in press; and see Sjolund, 1971). (The Moore study may have confounded program experience with family factors that continued through the school years.) The answer to the question of enhancement versus acceleration is still not settled. On the basis of available data, we suspect that at least part, but probably not all, of the effect for children who subsequently receive "typical" kindergarten and elementary school experience is merely acceleration rather than permanent enhancement of social competence.

Having described the pattern of differences in social development, and having explored possible interpretations of this observed pattern, we now turn to an examination of the possible processes by which such a pattern might occur. Unfortunately, we know less about the "normal" course of development for social competence than we do for other aspects of development, such as attachment or intellectual development. Nevertheless, we can look for logical "causes" in the early childhood program, in the family, and in the child.

Causal Factors in the Program

Experience with Peers. Perhaps the most obvious hypothesis would be that it is simply the fact that children in early childhood programs have more experience with peers, and this experience leads to their increased social competence. Peers offer models for imitation (Abramovitch & Grusec, 1978; Lougee, 1978; Pfeifer, 1971), tutors (Allen & Feldman, 1976), reinforcers (Lamb & Roopnarine, 1979), competitive partners (Moely, Skarin, & Weil, 1979), and congenial and cooperative playmates (Rubenstein & Howes, 1976). Only peers do certain things together, like using the teeter-totter, playing with a jack-in-the-box, jumping off a platform 20 times, or playing peek-a-boo under a blanket. The kinds of social behavior that have been observed more frequently among children who are in early childhood programs occur because peers are salient, their behavior is interesting, and it is not customary for an adult to perform these kinds of acts. Program children thus could benefit from (1) opportunities for *any* interaction with other children, (2) more of such interaction, (3) interaction with more children, or (4) interaction with a greater variety of children. We consider each of these possibilities.

Opportunity for any Peer Interaction. We do know that with a *familiar* playmate, the level of social play (including cooperation, reciprocity, and refusing to follow) is higher than with an unfamiliar peer (Doyle, Connolly, & Rivest, 1980; Gottman & Parkhurst, 1980; Lewis, Young, Brooks, & Michalson, 1975; Rubenstein & Howes, 1979). This suggests that experience with a peer acquaintance might benefit the child by giving him or her the opportunity to practice the more advanced social skills that occur only with such a friend. A study by Becker (1977) with 9-month-olds tested the generalizability of social behavior from a peer acquaintance to a peer stranger. Pairs of firstborn infants were brought together for 10 one-hour play sessions in one or the other's home. With increased familiarization, infants increased in the amount, complexity, and responsiveness of social engagement. On the eleventh session, an unfamiliar peer, who had not been in the experiment, came to visit, and the social behavior observed with the peer friend was found to generalize to the new playmate. This provides some support for the potential value of building social skills through interaction with a peer. Lieberman's (1977) finding that having a regular peer playmate before nursery school was related to interactive chains with an unfamiliar peer in the laboratory, chains which were longer and more responsive, gives further support. And there is additional support: Mueller and Brenner's (1977) finding that participation by 12- to 16-month-olds in a weekly play group was associated with increased social interaction and skill, and Vandell, Wilson, and Whalen's (1981) finding that 6- to 9-month-olds who had experience with an agemate were most successful at initiating interaction with a peer.

The question, then, is: Can experience with a peer be the reason children in early childhood programs are more socially competent? If it were, one would expect that children in day care homes (with other children) would be as socially competent as children in day care centers, for example. But they are not. The studies cited as finding differences in social competence are all of children in center programs, and the consistent finding when the two kinds of settings are compared is that children in centers are more socially competent in the ways we have described than those receiving supplementary care in homes (Bruner, 1980; Clarke-Stewart, in preparation; Saunders & Keister, 1979; Steinberg & Green, 1979; Vroegh, 1976). One would also expect that children in day care homes would be more socially competent than children with babysitters. Again, this is not so (Clarke-Stewart, in preparation). So it seems it is not just *any* experience with a peer. Even if peer experience is *part* of the reason for greater social competence in program children, it is not the whole explanation.

More Interaction with Peers. Perhaps it is not that children in early childhood programs have just *any* interaction with another child or children, but that they have *more* of it. Is this the reason day care center children are more socially competent than children in day care homes? We can ask the question: Is the amount of peer interaction different in day care homes and day care centers? It is not, according to Howes and Rubenstein (1981) and Clarke-Stewart (in preparation): Children in day care homes, day care centers, and nursery schools all averaged the same number of verbal exchanges with peers in a 2-hour observation in the day care setting. Perhaps the more important question, though, is whether the amount of peer interaction a child has is related to social competence. In the Chicago Study of Child Care and Development (Clarke-Stewart, in preparation), the amount of interaction a child was observed to have with peers was not related to the level of social competence evident in standard assessments. Again, therefore, although evidence relating to the hypothesis is as yet limited, what little there is does not support the hypothesis that social competence in children attending early childhood programs arises simply from their having more interaction with peers (cf. Hartup, 1976; West, 1974).

Interaction with More Peers. The number of peers encountered clearly differentiates children in day care centers from those in day care homes. For example, in the Chicago Study of Child Care and Development (Clarke-Stewart, in preparation) an estimate of the number of different children interacted with was 2 in home care with parents or a babysitter, 3 in a day care home, and 10 in a nursery school or day care center. Moreover, this estimate of the number of different children an individual interacted with *was* found to predict the child's social competence. This factor may, then, help explain observed differences in social competence between program and nonprogram children. It should not, however, be concluded that because children in centers interact with more other children and this is related to greater social competence, that, having more children to interact with is necessarily better. In fact, having more than 20 different children in a class has a *negative* effect on the quality of social interaction (Ruopp et al., 1979; Smith & Connolly, 1981; Sylva, Roy, & Painter, 1980).

Interaction with More Diverse Peers. It may be advantageous for the development of social competence for children to interact not only with *more* children, but with different *kinds* of children, although the evidence is scattered. In mixed-sex nursery school groups, for example, girls were observed to be more independent and boys to be more socially responsive than they were in same-sex groups (Greenberg & Peck, 1974)—both differences might be considered to reflect greater social competence. In mixed-age groups, children, especially the younger ones, have been found to experience more frequent and complex peer interactions than in single-age groups (Beller, Litwok, & Sullivan, undated; Body, 1955; Fosburg et al., 1980; Furman, Rahe, & Hartup, 1979; Goldman, 1981; Jersild & Markey, 1935; Markey, 1935; Murphy, 1937), and in a standard situation children from mixed-age classes are more socially competent (cooperative, persistent, flexible, etc.; Beller et al., undated). These advantages of heterogeneity have been observed in day care centers, day care homes, and nursery schools. Unfortunately for our purposes here, however, the studies have not controlled the qualities of teacher behavior, such as nurturance, responsiveness, and sensitivity, that accompany heterogeneity. Therefore, the observed advantages of mixed groupings may be the result of teacher differences rather than differences in peer interactions per se. What is more, since the age range of children in day care homes is, on the average, *wider* than in day care centers (Fosburg et al., 1980, versus Ruopp et al., 1979), and since day care homes and day care centers are equally likely to include both boys and girls, heterogeneity of age and sex cannot explain the observed difference in social competence that distinguishes children in center and home programs. The advantage of more diversity may be superseded by the disadvantage of children's relative competence in this case. The wider age range in day care homes merely gives children the opportunity to interact with socially less competent infants. This would not be expected to enhance their social skills.

To summarize, the evidence on experience with peers suggests that the advantage of early childhood programs for the development of children's social competence is not likely to be the result of these children's simply having an opportunity to interact with one other child, nor of their having more frequent opportunities to interact with this other child or with more than one child. The variety of different children they interact with may contribute to social competence, especially if these children are more socially competent than themselves, but this factor has not been separated from associated differences in teachers' behavior. Experience with peers appears to be, at best, a partial explanation for differences in social competence.

Activities with Materials. Perhaps the reason for the greater social competence of children in early childhood programs lies not in the number of peers or peer interactions they experience, but in the kinds of things the children do together in the two kinds of settings. Activities that lead to peer conflict and cooperation or to more complex peer skills may be more common in early childhood programs than in homes. Some researchers have looked at children's behavior in various activity areas in preschool settings. Advanced social behaviors such as cooperation, conversation, and complex interaction with peers are more common with the following kinds of materials: dolls, dressups, dramatic props, blocks, outdoor or large equipment like slides or stairs, and social toys (like checkers, pickup sticks, or Playdoh); they are less common with small toys, puzzles, art supplies, intellectual exercises, and books (Connolly & Smith, 1978; Eckerman & Whatley, 1977; Fiene, 1973; Green, 1933; Howes & Rubenstein, 1981; Mueller, 1979; Quilitch & Risley, 1973; Rohe & Patterson, 1974; Shure, 1963; Smith & Connolly, 1981; Sylva et al., 1980; Tizard, Philips, & Plewis, 1976a; Van Alstyn, 1932). Are the former kinds of materials found more frequently in programs than in homes? Materials in programs and homes have not been comprehensively inventoried, but counter to the hypothesis, dolls, dressups, and dramatic props have been found to be more common in homes than centers (Fiene, 1973; Rubenstein & Howes, 1979), while large equipment is found in both (in different forms, such as slides in centers, stairs in homes). It seems unlikely, therefore, that physical materials and equipment are responsible for observed differences in children's social competence.

Experience with Nonparental Adults. A substantial amount of the child's social experience in early childhood programs involves not other children, but a nonparental adult caregiver or teacher. Younger children in a program, in fact, spend more of their time interacting with the adult caregiver than they do with other children (42% vs. 6% at 1 year and 28% vs. 11% at 2 years; Finkelstein, Dent, Gallagher, & Ramey, 1978). Not until 4 years is peer interaction more frequent than adult-child interaction (Tizard, Philips, & Plewis, 1976b). Consequently, we might expect that social interaction with the adult caregiver would be one aspect of the day care experience that would foster children's social competence. In general, the presence of an adult has been observed to modulate and facilitate peer interaction (Sylva et al., 1980) and, on the individual level, the amount of interaction the child has with the teacher has been found to predict her or his later social competence (Golden et al., 1978). It seems very likely that the caregiver plays a central role in developing children's social competence. As yet, however, the data are not available to elucidate the process by which that influence occurs.

Children in *all* kinds of early childhood programs interact with nonparental adults substantially more than do children being raised exclusively by parents, but they interact significantly more with a caregiver when they are in a day care home or with a babysitter than when they are in a center program (Clarke-Stewart, in preparation; Cochran, 1977; Golden et al., 1978; Prescott, 1973; Sale & Torres, 1971; Tyler & Dittman, 1980). Since it is the children in center programs who are more advanced in social skills, it is unlikely that simply having more experience with nonparental adults increases social competence. Most likely, nonparental caregivers are valuable in their influence on children's social competence because of the particular ways they behave with the children. Here, we investigate two kinds of behavior that may be related to the development of social competence: discipline and teaching.

Studies of both mother-child and caregiver-child relationships have consistently demonstrated associations between discipline and development. In early childhood programs, indicators of social competence for individual children or groups of children have been found to be positively related to teachers' encouragement, nurturance, responsiveness, suggestions, and positive control and negatively related to their directiveness, restrictiveness, and negative control (Espinosa, 1980; Golden et al., 1978; Hamilton & Gordon, 1978; Prescott, Jones, & Kritchevsky, 1967; Rubenstein & Howes, 1979; Stallings, 1975).[6] Similarly, in studies of mother-child relationships, indicators of social competence have been found to be related to discipline that is affectionate, positive, and encouraging of autonomy, and negatively related to discipline that is negative and authoritarian (see Clarke-Stewart & Apfel, 1979).[7]

Perhaps children in early childhood programs are more socially competent because the caregivers in these settings are less authoritarian than mothers or other home caregivers. What is the evidence regarding differences in the methods of discipline used by teachers and mothers? Hess, Price, Dickson, and Conroy (1981) interviewed and observed 67 mothers and 34 day care center teachers.[8] Teachers were more flexible, indirect, and moderate in their requests and more likely to encourage the child's self-direction and independence; mothers were more directive, task oriented, likely to appeal to their own authority, and concerned about the child's development of social skills like politeness. These findings—in the predicted direction—are generally supported by results of other studies, which have found teachers to be less restrictive, demanding, and authoritarian than mothers (Ambron, 1979; Gunnarsson, 1977, 1978; Rubenstein & Howes, 1979). The differences are not simply a function of different levels of education—though teachers also generally have higher levels of education than the mothers of the children in their programs, and this makes the differences more marked (Hess et al., 1981; Winetsky, 1978). Day care home providers and babysitters, like mothers, have been observed to be more controlling than teachers (in fact, they are even more controlling than mothers; Bryant et al., 1980; Cochran, 1977; Howes & Rubenstein, 1981; Prescott, 1973; Sale & Torres, 1971; Tyler & Dittman, 1980). Thus the limited data we have on caregiver discipline do support the hypothesis that the development of social competence of children in early childhood programs may be facilitated by the supportive, nonauthoritarian discipline of the teacher.

Teachers and trained caregivers have also been observed to differ from mothers and untrained caregivers in a second way: in the amount of direct teaching they do with the children in their care (Clarke-Stewart, in preparation; Espinosa, 1980; Fosburg et al., 1980; Lazar & Darlington, 1982; Prescott et al., 1967; Ruopp et al., 1979; Tyler & Dittman, 1980). Teaching, too, has been found to predict differences in children's social competence (Clarke-Stewart, in preparation). This may be another way of accounting for differences observed between children in center programs and those in homes, since children in day care homes, with babysitters, or with their own mothers, on the average, have been found to be exposed to less adult caregiver teaching than those in day care centers, nursery schools, or model preschool programs (Clarke-Stewart, in preparation).

We do not know whether this kind of teaching was specifically directed toward social skills like cooperation and perspective taking, but indirect evidence from a variety of training studies suggests that it might have been. Children's social competence (as exhibited by sharing, independence, and perspective taking) has been significantly improved by direct training, demonstration, and deliberate encouragement of social skills like cooperation, helping, role taking, and interpersonal problem solving, and by guided activities that offer opportunities to use these skills (Iannotti, 1978; Orlick, 1981; Reuter & Yunik, 1973; Saltz, Dixon, & Johnson, 1977; Serbin, Connor, & Citron, 1978; Silvern, Waterman, Sobesky, & Ryan, 1979; Spivak & Shure, 1974; Van Lieshout, Leckie, & Smits-Van Sonsbeek, 1973; Yarrow, Scott, & Waxler, 1973). In the Silvern et al. study, for instance, direct training in interpersonal problem solving increased children's perspective-taking ability, whereas unguided activities with other children (like no intervention of any kind) did not. Cross-program comparisons among a variety of preschool programs also have shown that those focused most directly on sociability ("traditional" nursery schools or Bank Street programs) have the most socially skilled (cooperative, participative—and aggressive) children (Miller & Dyer, 1975; Stallings, 1975). So it seems quite plausible that the systematic teaching of social skills *could* be an important contributor to the development of social competence among children in early childhood programs, but further examination through detailed observations made on site in these programs is necessary to confirm this likely hypothesis.

Factors in the Family

We now turn to the possibility that the difference in social competence observed for children attending early childhood programs comes not from their direct experience in the program but from concomitant differences in their families.

It could, perhaps, be that mothers of children in early childhood programs differ from those who are exclusive or primary caregivers for their children in ways that we know, on the basis of correlational study, are likely to foster social competence: for example, being less authoritarian and more didactic. Do mothers of program children exhibit more of these qualities? The data are very sketchy, but the studies that have compared mothers whose children are or are not in such programs have either found no difference in discipline or teaching (Clarke-Stewart, in preparation, for teaching; Hock, 1980; Ramey et al., 1982; Rubenstein et al., 1981) or differences in the predicted direction (Clarke-Stewart, in preparation, for directiveness; Fowler, 1978; Moore, 1969).[9] Consequently, we cannot rule out the possibility that maternal differences contribute to the development of social competence in program children.

It could also be that the father's participation in child care in these families contributes to the higher level of social competence observed in the children. Having a more involved father does predict greater competence for children in traditional, alternative, and divorced families (Bloom-Feshbach, 1979; Clarke-Stewart, 1980; Hetherington, Cox, & Cox, 1978; Radin, 1976, 1981). And one might expect that fathers whose children are in early childhood programs would be more involved in child care, since, in these studies, their wives are more likely to be employed. The evidence for father participation as a factor is extremely limited, however. Although a few studies have suggested that husbands of working women are more intensely involved in child care than those whose wives are not employed (Draeger, 1977; Hoffman & Nye, 1974; Pedersen et al., 1980; Young, 1975), others find that there is no difference in the fathers' time commitment to child care or household work that is dependent on their wives' employment (Meissner, Humphreys, Meis, & Schea, 1975; Robinson et al., 1977; Walker & Woods, 1972). To arrive at some conclusion, studies of father-child correlations in program as well as nonprogram families and in families using center day care versus home care are needed.[10]

Factors in the Child

Finally, there is the possibility that it is something in the children themselves that accounts for the differences observed in their social competence. Perhaps they are selected for an early childhood program (by staff or parents) because they are already more socially competent. This possibility cannot be ruled out. As we have mentioned, many day care centers take toddlers only after they are toilet trained, and perhaps for very young children they use other selection criteria based on maturity as well, forcing mothers who must work to utilize day care homes or babysitters. Moreover, children have been found to be placed by their mothers in preschool earlier if they are more socially competent (both more sociable and more aggressive with a peer at 15 to 21 months of age; Blurton Jones et al., 1980), and there may be a tendency for firstborns, who have these characteristics (Rosenberg & Sutton-Smith, 1973; Snow et al., 1981), to be overrepresented in preschool populations. Nevertheless, it seems unlikely that this kind of selectivity would be the sole contributor to differences between children in center programs and in home care, since for children over 2 or 3 years of age centers would be unlikely to be able to select on the basis of maturity without more screening than is commonly done, and since a parent's decision to use a day care center program rather than a home day care arrangement is likely to involve more non-child-related factors than their decision to participate in a play group or nursery school. Moreover, the one study to assign subjects randomly to a day care program and measure their social competence (Ramey et al., 1982) also found differences in social competence favoring the program children. However, because it is so difficult in studies of early childhood programs, particularly in studies of day care programs, to eliminate self-selection factors by exact matching or random assignment, to disconfirm the self-selection hypothesis more effort needs to be put into assessing preprogram differences between the self-selected groups; then, if necessary, the differences can be controlled statistically. One study to assess prenursery school differences in children's social interactions with peers found no measurable differences between future nursery and nonnursery school attendees 2 months before the program began (Roopnarine & Lamb, 1980). But more efforts of this kind are necessary before self-selection factors can be eliminated as an explanation.

To conclude, advanced social competence that has been observed in children attending early childhood programs most likely arises from a combination of variables. It is unlikely that a single factor alone accounts for the differences reported. It may be that children in these programs develop social competence because (or when) they are given direct, though not necessarily formal, "instruction" in social skills, in a context where peers and nonparental adults offer the opportunity to practice social skills, where independence and self-direction are allowed and encouraged, and where independence is reinforced by similar values and parental behaviors at home. Nor is the process likely to be in one direction only: The social skills that the program initiates in the child may then affect the child's interactions with his or her parents (Rubenstein & Howes, in press; Vandell, 1979). The process of developing social competence is most likely multidirectional as well as multidimensional.

Intellectual Development, School Success, and Early Education

Of all the studies of children in day care that have included some measure of children's intelligence or intellectual development, only one (Peaslee, 1976) reported significantly higher IQ, language, and perceptual scores for children reared at home in comparison to those of similar family background in day care. The 2-year-olds in this study had been in day care since early infancy, and the day care centers they attended met only minimal licensing standards. Adult-child ratios in these centers ranged from 1:16 to 1:24, and care was custodial at best. All the other studies available for this review showed that children in day care centers do as well as those at home (Adamson, 1971; Doyle, 1975; Doyle & Somers, 1978; Farber & Egeland, 1982; Gunnarsson, 1977; Hock, 1976; Keister, 1970; Larson, 1973; Rubenstein & Howes, 1979; Taylor, 1976), or that they do better, at least for a time or on some measures (Caldwell, 1970; Clarke-Stewart, in preparation; Cochran, 1977; Fowler, 1978; Fowler & Khan, 1974; Garber & Heber, 1980; Golden et al., 1978; Kagan et al., 1978; Lally & Honig, 1977b; Macrae & Herbert-Jackson, 1976; Provost, 1980; Ramey et al., 1982; Robinson & Robinson, 1971; Rubenstein et al., 1981; Saunders & Keister, 1972, 1979; Winnett et al., 1977). The findings of these studies, showing an overall probability of higher performance on tests of intellectual development for children in day care, parallel earlier studies that demonstrated higher IQ and achievement scores for children attending or having attended nursery school (e.g., Allen & Masling, 1957; Harrold & Temple, 1960; Stukat, 1969; and see Sjolund, 1971; Swift, 1964). In Sjolund's review of this literature examining 36 studies, 21 showed that nursery school children were advanced in intellectual development; the other 15 showed no significant difference. This finding also parallels findings of significant, if temporary, gains in IQ resulting from participation in experimental preschool education programs (e.g., Bereiter & Engelmann, 1966; Gray & Klaus, 1970; Horowitz & Paden, 1973; Karnes, Hodgins, & Teska, 1969; Lazar & Darlington, 1982; Nimnicht, 1967; Van de Riet & Van de Riet, 1969; Weikart, Bond, & McNeil, 1978). These programs, uniformly, evidenced higher IQ scores in their participants when compared to control group children at the end of the program. Evaluations of community preschool programs, such as Head Start (see Mann et al., 1978) or public school programs (e.g., DiLorenzo, Salter, & Brady, 1969), too, have documented significant IQ advantages for children attending the programs.

Reviews of the literature on early childhood programs (e.g., Beller, 1979; Belsky & Steinberg, 1978; Bronfenbrenner et al., 1976; Horowitz & Paden, 1973; Kilmer, in press; Ricciuti, 1976; Silverstein, 1977) generally agree that such programs present no negative effects on intellectual development (often with the caveat that only "high-quality" programs have been studied). They are more cautious in concluding that programs have a facilitative effect, saying either that they have no facilitative effect or that they have only a short-term or modest facilitative effect, that they are facilitative only for poor children or only for children over 18 months of age, or that they are facilitative only if the program is a "model" one. However, since research has been skewed toward sampling only these subjects and programs, these cautions should be viewed as the result of gaps in our knowledge rather than of proof that early childhood programs do *not* generally have facilitative effects.

With or without these cautions and qualifications, these conclusions present a number of questions concerning the meaning of any observed differences in intellectual development and the processes by which differences might have occurred. These questions will be addressed next.

Nature of Differences in Intellectual Development

Aspects of Intellectual Development Affected. The most common assessment of intellectual development in studies of early childhood programs has been the standardized IQ test. Differences favoring program children have been consistently revealed in these assessments. Of studies reporting a significant difference in IQ scores, the size of the difference ranged from 6 points (Golden et al., 1978) to 34 points (Robinson & Robinson, 1971, for low SES black children). Although several experimental programs had maximum differences in mean scores exceeding 15 points (Caldwell, 1970; Garber & Heber, 1980; Robinson & Robinson, 1971), most were less than this. Thus, since the magnitude of the difference did not generally exceed one standard deviation, a difference that can be produced simply by more "sensitive" testing (Zigler & Butterfield, 1968), it is conceivable that the observed difference was produced by the greater cooperativeness of program children with the experimenter (discussed in the previous section). However, parallel differences favoring program children have also been observed in assessments of intellectual development based on maternal reports (e.g., Steinberg & Green, 1977) and teacher ratings (e.g., Stukat, 1969), so it seems unlikely that test cooperativeness alone accounts for the observed differences in IQ scores.

Assessments of particular *kinds* of intellectual abilities have also been made. In these assessments, differences favoring program children have been found in eye-hand coordination (Cochran, 1977; Kagan et al., 1978), in creative, exploratory, and ingenious use of materials (Clarke-Stewart, in preparation; Harrold & Temple, 1960; Provost, 1980), in memory span (Clarke-Stewart, in preparation; Ramey et al., 1982), in knowledge about the physical world and social roles (Clarke-Stewart, in preparation; Stukat, 1969), in perceptual, spatial, and conceptual perspective taking (Clarke-Stewart, in preparation), and in arithmetic (Ramey et al., 1982). There is also the suggestion that program children excel in problem solving or reasoning (Clarke-Stewart, in preparation; Fowler, 1978; Garber & Heber, 1980; Macrae & Herbert-Jackson, 1976); only one study (Schwarz et al., 1973) did not find a difference on this dimension. Moreover, there are consistent indications of advanced language development in program children: comprehension, fluency, naming objects, concepts, vocabulary, verbal expressiveness, and mean length of utterance (Andrews et al., 1975; Clarke-Stewart, in preparation; Fowler, 1978; Fowler & Khan, 1974; Garber & Heber, 1980; Lally & Honig, 1977b; Lasater et al., 1975; Ramey et al., 1978; Rubenstein et al., 1981; Stukat, 1969). The only language assessments that did not favor program children was an assessment of everyday use of language (Golden et al., 1978) and a subset of verbal items from the Bayley test (Kagan et al., 1978; a subset on which, in this particular study, working-class children scored higher than middle-class children). The results of all these studies assessing children's intellectual abilities directly are corroborated by interviews with mothers (Steinberg & Green, 1977). Mothers using day care center programs claimed that their children learned more about concepts, arithmetic, and practical knowledge than they would have at home. They reported only one negative effect of program attendance: Children learned more "bad language." In brief, then, differences favoring children in early childhood programs appear across a range of intellectual abilities, including both verbal and nonverbal skills, things that are likely to be directly taught (e.g., drawing figures) and those not taught (e.g., perspective taking or digit span), and things that could be learned from materials (e.g., eye-hand coordination) as well as from other people (e.g., language).

Reliability of Observed Differences. Only a handful of the studies of early childhood programs that assessed intellectual development with a standardized measure during the time the children were in attendance or had just completed the program found no difference favoring program participants. Peaslee's study we have mentioned. One other study was Taylor's (1976), in which program and nonprogram children were *matched* on IQ at the beginning of the study and tested only 6 months later. And in several other studies differences, though nonsignificant, were in the direction favoring children in the program (Doyle & Somers, 1978; Lambie, Bond, & Weikart, 1974; Palmer & Siegel, 1977). Thus, the difference in intellectual performance favoring children in early childhood programs, although its size does depend to some extent on age and other factors, appears to be quite reliable overall.

Significance of the Difference

What is the significance of the observed difference between program and nonprogram children in intellectual performance? Do early childhood programs actually increase the rate or level of intellectual development for children in attendance, or do they merely prevent the decline that would otherwise occur in their underprivileged participants? Is the effect permanent or temporary?

Improvement Versus Prevention. Reviewers of the research on day care programs (e.g., Belsky & Steinberg, 1978; Ricciuti, 1976) have generally favored an interpretation of observed effects that suggests that program attendance prevents or retards the decline in children's intellectual performance which would otherwise be observed. But the interpretation that some programs actually increase children's development is also plausible. In the eight studies of children in day care reporting longitudinal data on IQ, six show an absolute gain in IQ scores for day care children while in the program, not just maintenance of IQ level (Caldwell, 1970; Fowler, 1978, from 6 to 30 months; Fowler & Khan, 1974; Garber & Heber, 1980; Robinson & Robinson, 1971; Saunders & Keister, 1972, 1979); while in two studies (of lower class children), the day care children merely maintained or declined slightly in their initial IQ level, and home care children declined significantly more (Golden et al., 1978; Ramey et al., in press). Experimental preschool programs have also generally found absolute gains (as well as relative gains) in their participants by the end of the program (e.g., Bereiter & Engelmann, 1966; Lasater et al., 1975; Leler et al., 1975; Levenstein, 1977; Miller & Dyer, 1975; Van De Riet & Van De Riet, 1969; Weikart et al., 1978). It seems reasonable, therefore, to conclude that the "effect" is sometimes an improvement, not merely a prevention of decline.

Permanent or Temporary? A related issue concerning the significance of the intellectual gains in program children is whether the differences observed are permanent or temporary. To answer this question, we need longitudinal studies following children after the programs have ended. From the longitudinal follow-up studies available, the answer seems quite clear—program effects on IQ are not permanent. Day care has been found to accelerate early intellectual development while children are in attendance, but by 5 years of age home care children "catch up" and the difference diminishes or disappears (Fowler, 1978; Fowler & Khan, 1974; Lally & Honig, 1977; Ramey et al., 1982). This is likely because home care children by this age are having comparable experiences in kindergarten or have had such experiences in nursery school. Only in one study (Garber & Heber, 1980) were significant differences in IQ between day care and home care children maintained past first grade. Perhaps this was because when these very poor home care children did get to school their experiences there were still not sufficiently supportive of intellectual development to allow them to catch up.

Similarly, studies of Head Start and experimental preschool programs find that differences between program and control children appear by the end of the program but diminish over time (Bronfenbrenner, 1974; Datta, 1975; Lazar & Darlington, 1982; Mann et al., 1978; Schaefer & Aaronson, 1977). As with the studies of day care, studies of model programs show an increase in the IQ scores of control children when they enter regular school and, then, for these disadvantaged children, a progressive decline in *both* program and control groups thereafter. By third grade, IQ differences have, for the most part, disappeared.

The only study to find long-term effects up to 12 years later was the multiprogram secondary analysis of 14 experimental programs conducted by the Consortium on Longitudinal Studies (Darlington, Royce, Snipper, Murray, & Lazar, 1980; Lazar & Darlington, 1982). This analysis demonstrated that, when confounding variables were controlled, preschool programs, regardless of curriculum design or participant focus, had a strikingly long-term effect on children's development—though not on IQ. The most informative part of the analysis was based on 8 projects initiated in the 1960s. Some of the initial investigators had conducted follow-up testing after the program terminated and during the school years. When the children were tested in 1976 as part of the organized follow-up effort, they ranged in age from 10 to 17 years and were 7 to 12 years removed from the programs in which they had participated. The analyses of these data showed not only that IQ effects lasted for only about 2 years after intervention and then began to fade but that, in spite of the diversity in school policies, children who participated in these early childhood programs were less likely to have repeated a grade or to have been placed in special education classes than those who did not. Program children were also less likely to engage in delinquent behavior in adolescence (Schweinhart & Weikart, 1980).

The implications of these positive outcomes are considerable, and several interpretations of the reported effects are possible. Some interpreters note that most programs involved parents to some degree, and others propose a chain of effects in which a preschool experience might facilitate a successful first-grade experience, which then becomes the basis of success in second grade, and so forth (Lazar & Darlington, 1982; Schweinhart & Weikart, 1980; Zigler & Trickett, 1978). Subsequent studies might attempt to sort out these possibilities, but longitudinal studies of this type are difficult to sustain at a level required to test specific hypotheses.

Variation in Effects

Although gains in intellectual development have been observed consistently across different studies of different programs using different measures, there may still be systematic variation in the size or probability of these effects. Here we examine several of the dimensions that might produce such variation.

Duration of Participation. Results pertaining to the effect of the length of children's participation in a program are not clear. For one thing, length of participation has not been systematically separated from the age at which children have begun the program (cf. Beller, 1979; Clarke-Stewart & Apfel, 1979; Fein & Clarke-Stewart, 1973). But even if we settle for a relationship between intellectual gains and length-plus-age, results are not consistent. Fowler and Khan (1974), Clarke-Stewart (in preparation), and Winnett et al. (1977) found that children who started a program earlier and stayed longer made more gains, but Golden et al. (1978), Larson (1973), Tizard, Philips, and Plewis (1976c), and Blurton Jones et al. (1980) found that intellectual level was not related to length or age. Lay and Meyer (1972) observed that children who had started earlier and been in day care longer were *less* likely to spend their time in day care in the areas where intellectual activities would be more frequent. And Lally and Honig (1977b) found that participation in a program for longer than 3 years was related to *decreased* scores. In experimental programs, no difference in effects related to length of participation was found by Andrews et al. (1975), Lombard (1973), Love, Nauta, Coelen, Hewett, and Ruopp (1976), Klaus and Gray (1968), and Lazar and Darlington (1982). The best we can say at this point is that it seems unlikely that there is a simple, monotonic relationship between length of attendance in a program and intellectual gains, but as yet definitive studies of this dimension are not available.

Age Effects. Results of different studies using subjects of different ages are quite consistent on the relationship between age and program effects. Differences seem to be smaller or less likely in the first 18 months of life (Cochran, 1977; Fowler, 1978; Garber & Heber, 1980; Gordon et al., 1977; Lambie et al., 1974; Lally & Honig, 1977b; Ramey et al., 1982; Robinson & Robinson, 1971); after that age, differences are consistently observed up to 4 years (Clarke-Stewart, in preparation; Cochran, 1977; Fowler & Khan, 1974; Garber & Heber, 1980; Golden et al., 1978; Kagan et al., 1978; Lally & Honig, 1977b; Lazar et al., 1977; Ramey et al., 1982; Robinson & Robinson, 1971; Rubenstein et al., 1981; Weikart et al., 1978) and do not seem to be related to age within that period (Andrews et al., 1975; Caldwell, 1970; Clarke-Stewart, in preparation; Golden et al., 1978; Hock, 1976; Karnes et al., 1969; Lazar et al., 1977; Levenstein, 1977; Morris, London, & Glick, 1976; Robinson & Robinson, 1971; Ruopp et al., 1979).

Perhaps differences do not appear in the first 18 months of life because available tests are not sufficiently subtle to reveal them. It may be that the particular skills that early childhood programs enhance (like drawing, creative use of materials, or verbal fluency) come into play only after the age of 18 months. It may be that the infant is biologically "buffered" in infancy so that any average environment providing good physical care is sufficient for normal intellectual development. Or, it may be that experience in a program is cumulative and takes 18 months to have a measurable effect. Only the last possibility can be definitely ruled out since, at later ages, program effects of day care have been observed in a shorter period than 18 months (e.g., Clarke-Stewart, in preparation; Palmer & Siegel, 1977), and, as we have mentioned, there is no evidence of a monotonic relationship between length of program experience and intellectual development. Otherwise, it could be the tests, the skills, or the nature of early intellectual development that accounts for the observed age-related effects on intellectual abilities. Problems of predictability of later IQ scores from infant tests or from early experience have been discussed at length (e.g., Carew, 1980; Kagan et al., 1978; McCall, 1979). For now, the question of program effects in the first 18 months of life will have to remain open, pending further research more directly focused on this issue.

Individual Children. Differential effects of early childhood programs on boys and girls have been noted in some studies (Cochran, 1977; Fowler & Khan, 1974; Gordon et al., 1977; Kessen et al., 1975; Lally & Honig, 1977b; Miller & Dyer, 1975); but they are not consistent enough to formulate any sex-related generalizations. Greater gains in programs have also been observed for Chinese and black children (if lower or working class; Kagan et al., 1978; Robinson & Robinson, 1971) compared to white children, but there have been too few studies on which to base any hypotheses about race.

Only one study that we were able to find looked at the relationship between intellectual gains and children's temperament. This study (Ramey et al., 1982) showed that infants with an "easy" temperament gained more in a model day care program than in home care, while difficult babies gained more at home; but, later on, both easy and difficult children did better in the day care program, making it appear likely that the impact of temperament is related to the age of the child.

Socioeconomic status is the one characteristic that has been reported often enough in early childhood research to examine systematically. This is particularly true in research on day care programs, since experimental compensatory education programs have focused exclusively on the disadvantaged lower SES children. Reviewers of the research on day care (e.g., Belsky & Steinberg, 1978) have concluded that the facilitative effect of day care programs is to be found only for lower class children. On the basis of data now available, however, this conclusion does not seem warranted. Of the studies documenting day care gains, half sampled lower class children (Caldwell, 1970; Garber & Heber, 1980; Golden et al., 1978; Lally & Honig, 1977b; Ramey et al., 1982; Robinson & Robinson, 1971), and half looked at mixed, working, or middle class samples (Clarke-Stewart, in preparation; Cochran, 1977; Fowler, 1978; Fowler & Khan, 1974; Kagan et al., 1978; Rubenstein et al., 1981). Moreover, in studies that compared effects for different SES levels, although one (Robinson & Robinson, 1971) found the difference accentuated for lower class subjects (the difference between home care and day care groups was 29 IQ points for lower class and 13 for middle-class children), in others (Fowler & Khan, 1974; Kagan et al., 1978) comparable differences were reported for lower class and middle-class subjects (19 and 16 IQ points, respectively, in Fowler & Khan; 6 and 5 in Kagan et al.). What is more, in the Fowler and Khan study middle-class children continued to gain as long as the program continued, while lower class children began to drop. In Garber and Heber's (1980) intervention with low-income, high-risk children, children from less risky (relatively higher low SES) families gained more than those with the highest risk.

In brief, then, we have at present no evidence to suggest that program effects on intellectual development are limited to any single group based on race, sex, SES, or temperament.

Factors Producing Intellectual Gains in Program Children

The next set of issues we look at concerns the possible processes by which the intellectual gains of children in early childhood programs may have occurred. Although predictors of intellectual development in these programs have not received the attention of researchers until very recently, there have been numerous studies identifying associations between children's IQ and features of their home environments or their lives in residential institutions. These studies (reviewed in Clarke-Stewart & Apfel, 1979) document the fact that young children growing up in severely depriving institutions, where there are few playthings, limited opportunities for motor activity, and infrequent contact with adult caregivers, have retarded intellectual development (by as much as 50 IQ points by 1 or 2 years of age), while in institutions that offer books and movies, trips and outings, and an adequate number of caregivers who are interested in promoting children's development, intellectual development is significantly less retarded. Similarly, studies of children being raised at home demonstrate that intellectual development is related to aspects of the environment. One significant aspect is stimulation by the mother—at first manifested by rocking, talking, and playing with the infant using toys; later by providing the toddler with appropriate play materials and intellectual experiences, by sharing, expanding, and elaborating on the child's activities, and by entertaining and talking to the child; and still later by teaching and encouraging the child's achievement. Another aspect of the home environment that has been related to children's intellectual development is the mother's positive and contingent responsiveness—at first the mother responds to the infant's distress and communicative signals; later to the child's questions and interests. A third aspect of the home environment is the parent's positive control—manifested at first by allowing the infant freedom to explore, and later by providing the child with a moderate number of limits that are enforced firmly and consistently in a context of positive affect. Finally, there is the impact of the family constellation; firstborn children are intellectually advanced over children born later, presumably because they receive more intense stimulation from attentive parents (Zajonc & Markus, 1975).

The question for us here is: If early childhood programs accelerate children's intellectual development, why might that be? In this section we explore several possibilities.

Quantitative Differences Between Programs and Homes. Perhaps the reason early childhood programs have an effect on intellectual development is that they are like very good homes and children in them simply get *more* of the kinds of stimulating interaction we have just described as predicting IQ in children raised at home. This possibility has several testable implications. First, if this were the case, the intellectual gains related to participation in a program should occur (only or most clearly) for children from unstimulating homes who are placed in stimulating programs. Although this premise is testable, the data to test it are not readily available. The best we can do at this point is to let high and low SES stand as a crude index of more or less stimulating homes and let model versus community programs represent more or less stimulating programs. When model and community programs are compared, IQ effects for children from poor homes attending model programs do, on the average, tend to be greater than effects for children from poor or not-so-poor homes attending community programs. In the first group of model programs are studies by Beller (IQ difference = 10), Deutsch (IQ difference = 7), Gordon (IQ difference = 3), Gray (infant program; IQ difference = 7), Gray (combined program; IQ difference = 10), Karnes (IQ difference = 9), Levenstein (IQ difference = 8), Miller (IQ difference = 7), Miller (combined; IQ difference = 6), Palmer (IQ difference = 4), Weikart (infant program; IQ difference = 3), Weikart (preschool program; IQ difference = 11), all reported in Lazar and Darlington, 1982; and Fowler and Khan, 1974 (IQ difference = 16), Garber and Heber, 1980 (IQ difference = 26), Ramey et al., in press (IQ difference = 14), Robinson and Robinson, 1971 (IQ difference = 29). The mean IQ difference in the first group = 10.6. In the second group of community programs are studies of poor children by Golden et al., 1978 (IQ difference = 6), and studies of middle-class children by Doyle and Somers, 1978 (IQ difference = 8), Rubenstein et al., 1981 (IQ difference = 13), Taylor, 1976 (IQ difference = 1), Winnett et al., 1977 (IQ difference = 1). The mean IQ difference in the second group = 5.7. But we do not really have a numerous enough representation of community programs to provide a fair comparison. Moreover, there is some indication that middle- and working-class children in model programs do just as well as poor children in these programs (Fowler, 1978, IQ difference = 14; Fowler & Khan, 1974, IQ difference = 19; Robinson & Robinson, 1971, IQ difference = 13; mean IQ difference = 15). We need more studies of differential effects analyzed according to the mesh of home and program experiences, before we can begin to establish whether IQ effects are the result of quantitative differences between homes and early childhood programs.

A second kind of evidence that might argue for this hypothesis—that good preschool programs are like good homes in the stimulation they provide—would be if attendance in a full-time program had a greater effect than attendance in a part-time program, since it would then provide even more stimulation to the child. Again, unfortunately, this question cannot be definitively answered from available data, but the data that are available do not offer support for this hypothesis. Program comparisons suggest that part-time programs have as large an effect as full-time programs (Adamson, 1971; Biemiller, 1978, 1981; Clarke-Stewart, in preparation; Lazar & Darlington, 1982; Taylor, 1976; Winnett et al., 1977).[11]

More convincing than this kind of evidence would be evidence that early childhood programs offer children more space, toys, or equipment, and that this is what predicts their intellectual development. Here again, however, what evidence there is argues against, not for, the hypothesis. Although, all other things being equal, extreme differences in the space per child have indeed been related to children's behavior and development (Connolly & Smith, 1978; Espinosa, 1980; Prescott et al., 1967; Rohe & Patterson, 1974; Ruopp et al., 1979; Smith & Connolly, 1981; Wachs, 1978), this relationship cannot explain the observed advantages of center programs over home care, since the classrooms or centers in which preschool programs are typically located offer less space than children have at home.

Compared to the home environment, there may or may not be more toys or varied objects to play with, look at, and explore in early childhood programs—it depends on the particular program and the particular home. Golden et al. (1978) found there were more toys in centers; Prescott et al. (1967) and Rubenstein and Howes (1979) found there were not. But probably this factor also is not critical. As at home, where it is whether the parent plays with the child using the toys rather than just their availability that predicts development (e.g., Belsky, 1980; Clarke-Stewart, 1973), studies of the effects of number of toys in early childhood programs suggest that they are not a simple enhancer of development. Although the type and number of toys available affect the activities children do with them (Rohe & Patterson, 1974; Smith & Connolly, 1981), there is no relation between the number of toys accessible or even played with and children's performance on tests of intellectual development (e.g., Belsky, 1980; Golden et al., 1978; Levenstein, 1970; Rubenstein & Howes, 1979; Tamminen, 1967).

Another kind of evidence that could support the hypothesis that the difference between program and home experiences is quantitative would be the finding that teachers or caregivers in early childhood programs give children more stimulating attention and interaction than they would receive at home. The intellectual development of individual children or classes in these programs has been found to be related to the amount of teacher or caregiver stimulation and interaction they receive (e.g., Carew, 1980; Clarke-Stewart, in preparation; Espinosa, 1980; Golden et al., 1978; Rosenshine, 1971; Ruopp et al., 1979; Soar & Soar, 1976; Stallings, 1975). But do children in early childhood programs receive more stimulation from teachers than home care children do from their mothers? Given the adult-child ratios in most programs, there is a limit on the amount of interaction that takes place between the teacher and each child. In fact, of the studies comparing the amount of verbal interaction with mother (for home care children) and teacher (for program children), one found there was no difference (Rubenstein & Howes, 1979); while two others (Clarke-Stewart, 1981; Tizard, Carmichael, Hughes, & Pinkerton, 1980) found that children at home heard more utterances from mother than children in programs did from a teacher or caregiver. Once again, then, data do not support the hypothesis.

Furthermore, final disconfirmation comes from comparisons of home- and center-based day care programs, which consistently suggest that children in day care homes have more verbal exchanges with their caregivers than children in day care centers have with their teachers (Cochran, 1977; Golden et al., 1978; Prescott, 1973; Sale & Torres, 1971; Tyler & Dittman, 1980)—yet their intellectual development is usually not enhanced (Adamson, 1971; Clarke-Stewart, in preparation; Cochran, 1977; Golden et al., 1978; Saunders & Keister, 1972; Vroegh, 1976; Winnett et al., 1977).

To summarize, there is simply no direct evidence that children in early childhood programs benefit intellectually because of quantitative differences between home and program experiences. Yet, although children in center programs, whose intellectual development is advanced over that of children at home, hear less adult speech directed at them, a significantly greater proportion of that speech may be *teaching*. In the Chicago Study of Child Care and Development (Clarke-Stewart, in preparation)[12] 27% of the speech addressed to children by center teachers was classified as teaching and only 10% of the speech of mothers to their children was so coded, while for children in home day care programs, whose intellectual development is *not* so advanced over children at home with mother, the proportion of teaching by the caregiver was comparable to that by the mother (11%). In this sense, then, it seems likely that the gains in intellectual development observed in early childhood programs are the result of qualitative, not quantitative, differences in home and program environments, and it is to that possibility we turn next.

Qualitative Differences Between Programs and Homes. Some of the most suggestive evidence in support of the hypothesis that program effects are the result of qualitatively different experiences for children are the findings that the observed differences in intellectual development have occurred exclusively in center day care programs not in home day care programs and that, in studies comparing children's development in different kinds of day care, children in center programs have consistently scored higher than children in home day care programs (Adamson, 1971; Clarke-Stewart, in preparation; Golden et al., 1978; Saunders & Keister, 1972; Vroegh, 1976; Winnett et al., 1977).[13] In the New York Infant Day Care Study (Golden et al., 1978), for example, children in day care homes and centers stayed at the same level of intellectual performance until 18 months of age, but then those in day care homes dropped (to the same level as children in home care), while center children maintained their level. Occasionally, children in home day care have been observed to do even worse on IQ tests than children in home care with parents (Schachter, 1981). In a study by Saunders and Keister (1972), 2-year-old children in a model day care center gained, while those in day care homes lost IQ points. And, in the Chicago Study of Child Care and Development (Clarke-Stewart, in preparation), on all measures of cognitive development, there was a clear and significant division between children in homes (with parents, day care providers, or babysitters) and in centers (nursery schools, day care centers, or nursery school plus babysitters), favoring centers. Moreover, in the Chicago study, when children changed from home care to a center program over the course of the year-long investigation, this was reflected in a significantly higher *gain* in scores on the measure of cognitive development assessed at two separate times. Interviews with mothers conducted by Steinberg and Green (1977) support these observed differences in cognitive development; 66% of the mothers of children in day care center programs (vs. 46% of those with children in day care homes or 22% of those with babysitters) thought their children's intellectual development had been enhanced by day care attendance.[14]

However, centers differ from homes in a number of qualitative ways. Can we be more specific about what aspects of a center program might be responsible for the cognitive advances observed? Here we explore the possibilities that the effect is the result of the other children, the physical setting, the educational curriculum, the teacher, or the institutional regulations.

Peers. Although playing with a peer raises the complexity and creativity of children's activities with materials over what they are when children are alone (Cohen & Tomlinson-Keasey, 1980, for boys; Rabinowitz, Moely, Finkel, & McClinton, 1975; Rubenstein & Howes, 1976; Sylva et al., 1980), studies of different kinds of programs suggest that intellectual gains are not the result of children's opportunities for peer interaction. First, if peers were the critical factor, then *all* group programs, not just center programs, should show the effect. But, as we have just indicated, day care home programs do not show the effect, despite the fact that in day care homes children interact with peers as much as children do in day care centers (Clarke-Stewart, in preparation; Howes & Rubenstein, 1981). Second, in programs where children have more peer interaction, cognitive gains are not higher (Lazar & Darlington, 1982; Miller & Dyer, 1975; Weikart et al., 1978). And, third, in programs with more children in the class, effects on intellectual development are detrimental, not helpful, to play activities (Smith & Connolly, 1981; Sylva et al., 1980) and intellectual development (Ruopp et al., 1979), findings consistent with sibling differences associated with birth order (Zajonc & Markus, 1975). Altogether, then, there seems little evidence to support the proposition that the experiences that foster intellectual development are provided simply by the presence or activities of other children.

Physical Materials. What about the possibility that different physical equipment and materials are provided in early childhood programs and homes? Within the program setting, children's play activities are, quite naturally, related to the specific equipment and materials with which they are engaged. "High-level" cognitively challenging and constructive activity with materials is more likely to occur with building materials, puzzles, books, academic materials, or in teacher-directed art or music (Shure, 1963; Sylva et al., 1980). These kinds of opportunities are likely to be more frequent in center programs than in children's homes. In homes, the opportunities are greater for tactile exploration with sand, soft objects, water, and dough, and for cooking, "messing around," and unstructured play (Cochran, 1977; Prescott, 1973; Rubenstein & Howes, 1979), but there are fewer academic or construction materials. The physical materials and equipment in centers, then, may allow more frequent intellectual activities. However, physical materials *alone* are unlikely to account for cognitive gains on standard tests, since just adding novel materials to preschool classrooms or having more varied materials accessible has not been found to lead to cognitive gains (Busse, Ree, Gatride, & Alexander, 1972; Mann & Taylor, 1973; Ruopp et al., 1979). It was in combination with teacher behavior that materials in these last studies were related to children's intellectual development.

Curriculum. This brings us to the next possibility—that it is the educational curriculum that accounts for observed differences in intellectual level. One obvious way in which center programs differ from home care or home day care is in the likelihood of an educational curriculum and formal instruction (Lippman & Grote, 1974). Although many centers are simply custodial and many homes do stress educational activities, these are generally *not* the kinds of settings that have been studied in the research on early childhood programs and that have had the accelerating effects on intellectual development that we are trying to explain. There are several hints that the educational curriculum may be a critical as well as distinguishing feature of the child's experience in the early childhood program. First, if we may assume that an educational developmental curriculum is more likely or at least more *explicit* in a model or experimental program than in a community program, then the indication that the former programs have more significant effects on intellectual development (documented under *Quantitative Dif-*

ferences Between Programs and Homes) would support this hypothesis. If we can assume that nursery school is more likely than a day care center to be educationally oriented (a reasonable assumption, given their respective histories), then evidence that nursery school children on the average have higher scores than day care center children (Adamson, 1971; Clarke-Stewart, in preparation; Winnett et al., 1977) would also support the hypothesis. (Since differences here were small or confounded with SES, however, this must be regarded strictly as a hint.) More direct evidence comes from a study by Ferri (1980) where the cognitive performance of children in a combined day nursery/nursery school (i.e., a day care center with educational activities) was higher than that of children in an unmodified day nursery. Tizard et al. (1976a) reported that middle-class children attending a noneducational day nursery did more poorly than expected on a cognitive test, while working-class children in an educational nursery school did better. But the issue of self-selection clouds these results.

Direct curriculum comparisons across programs or within programs provide better evidence that an educational curriculum affects intellectual outcomes, since in some of these comparisons it has been possible to use random assignment of children or classes to curricular groups. These comparisons show consistently that children in programs with more prescribed educational activities—such as lessons, "guided play" sessions, teaching of specific content, and more direct teacher instruction—spend more time in constructive and complex play and less time in social interactions with peers or doing nothing during class, and do better on IQ and achievement tests (Connolly & Smith, 1978; DiLorenzo et al., 1969; Fowler, 1978; Huston-Stein, Friedrich-Cofer & Susman, 1977; Johnson & Ershler, 1981; Johnson, Ershler, & Bell, 1980; Karnes, Hodgins, & Teska, 1968; Kirschner, 1970; Lazar & Darlington, 1982; Miller & Dyer, 1975; Rusk, 1968; Soar & Soar, 1976; Stallings, 1975; Sylva et al., 1980; Weikart, 1981). The more direct stimulation and teaching offered by the caregiver or teacher, the greater the children's cognitive competence and achievement (Clarke-Stewart, in preparation; Espinosa, 1980; Golden et al., 1978; Rosenshine, 1971; Soar & Soar, 1976; Stallings, 1975). There may even be a match between specific content taught and outcomes tested. For example, Fowler's (1978) program stressed problem solving in visual-spatial skills, and this was the area in which program children showed superior performance on the Griffith's IQ test. An educational curriculum seems to be a likely candidate for explaining the intellectual advances of children in early childhood programs on standardized tests. Even in community day care center programs, children are likely to be the recipients of more teaching than if they were in day care homes, with babysitters, or with their mothers (Biemiller, Avis, & Lindsay, 1979; Clarke-Stewart, in preparation; Lippman & Grote, 1974). In day care homes, "teaching" is likely to be casual and informal. Children have more free time and time alone; and they learn from messing around, exploring, and helping the caregiver, from real-life tasks and role models, not from educational curricula or lessons. They have to meet fewer expectations, answer fewer questions, and follow fewer rules than children in centers (Cochran, 1977; Espinosa, 1980; Prescott, 1973; Sale & Torres, 1971; Tyler & Dittman, 1980). Unless the day care home provider is part of a training and support network and has a professional self-concept, she is unlikely to have child development or education as a goal for the child (Belsky et al., 1982; Espinosa, 1980). Most day care homes are informal and unlicensed—and even if licensed, this just means they are likely to be more stable, safe, with better food, and the caregiver more helpful but not more educational.[15] Generally, the caregiver does housework and the children are on their own about half the time. Active involvement in teaching, playing, directing, and helping the children takes up only a small part of the caregiver's time (12% in unlicensed, 13% in licensed, and 17% in sponsored day care homes; Stallings, 1980).

Rules and Schedules. But there are qualitative aspects other than the educational curriculum that distinguish center programs from home care. One, related to curriculum, is the type of institutional rules and schedules that prevails in centers. In center programs, regulations are more likely to be fixed and based on the needs of the group rather than the individual. Thus, children in centers must learn to recognize and adapt to abstract, arbitrary, general rules; while at home children operate in a concrete, "hands on" context, where rules and schedules, as such, are limited. It has been suggested (e.g., Bruner, Olver, & Greenfield, 1966; Cole, Gay, Glick, & Sharp, 1971) that schooling in this institutionalized sense facilitates the development of test-taking skills, knowledge, and disciplined behavior in instructional situations in which children in preschool programs are advanced. One might also expect that the effects of adapting to this aspect of institutional life would appear within a relatively brief period (as they do) and would be as likely to appear in part-time programs as in full-time (as they do). This aspect of early childhood programs is one that deserves further exploration.

Teacher Style. We now come to the last of the ways we will consider in which centers and homes differ—the way in which the caregiver's attitudes and behavior influence children's intellectual gains. Mothers and teachers differ in their relationship to the child, the context in which they interact with the child (public vs. private), and their training in child development. In addition, there may be other distinguishing characteristics like age and SES: Teachers tend to be older and more middle class than the majority of mothers using their services, while day care home providers are also older, but usually of lower SES. All of these differences have implications for the kinds of behavior characteristic of teachers and of mothers.

The effect of the caregiver's training in child development has been established within the population of day care teachers and providers: Caregivers with more training (beyond a minimal, "token" level) are more interactive, didactic, helpful, and verbal (Espinosa, 1980; Fosburg et al., 1980; Lazar & Darlington, 1982; Prescott et al., 1967; Ruopp et al., 1979; Stallings, 1980; Tyler & Dittman, 1980)—and the children in their care make more cognitive gains (Ruopp et al., 1979). But whether it is the direct result of training or of other distinguishing characteristics, teachers, providers, and mothers exhibit distinctly different styles—of interacting with materials, of managing and disciplining the children, of simply conversing with them—any one of which might enhance or inhibit children's intellectual development.

As we have already mentioned, in independent studies, the same patterns have emerged: To facilitate the child's use of materials or performance of tasks, mothers are more likely to demand, direct, restrict, and interrupt; teachers are less directive and more likely to offer explanations and help, make the task a game, and respond to the child's initiation of play (Hess et al., 1981; Rubenstein & Howes, 1979). The teacher's style may be so indirect, in fact, that many mothers do not even see the "hidden" educational agenda in nursery school activities. In one study (Tizard, 1977), mothers thought the sand in the nursery classroom was to remind children of the seashore and the water was to get children interested in washing up, not, as the teachers intended, to encourage children's imaginations or to teach concepts like weight, volume, and flotation.

Disciplinary differences between mothers and teachers parallel these differences in interactive style; teachers have been observed to be less authoritarian than mothers (Cochran, 1977; Hess et al., 1981; Rubenstein & Howes, 1979). Day care home providers, on the other hand, are more like mothers in control (more prohibitive than teachers and less likely to train independence; Cochran, 1977; Prescott, 1973; Sale & Torres, 1971; Tyler & Dittman, 1980). Since authoritarian discipline and restrictive interaction have been found to predict children's intellectual development in school settings as well as at home (Hamilton & Gordon, 1978; Prescott et al., 1967; Rubenstein & Howes, 1979; Swift, 1964), it seems reasonable that this qualitative difference between home and center care is part of the explanation for the observed differences in children's intellectual performance.

The quality of adult-child conversations at home or at school may also help account for these differences. At home with mother or a day care provider, conversations are longer (Tizard et al., 1980), include more complex and meaningful utterances (Fiene, 1973), and offer children more opportunities to ask questions and express opinions (Cochran, 1977; Prescott, 1978; Tyler & Dittman, 1980); in day care centers or nursery schools, conversations are more likely to take the form of teacher questions and child answers (Cochran, 1977; Fiene, 1973; Prescott, 1973; Tyler & Dittman, 1980). In homes, conversations are more "inductive" (Prescott, 1978; Tizard et al., 1980): "What would you like for lunch?" might lead to a long discussion about people's food preferences, the time it takes to prepare food, which foods are more nutritious, and so forth. In center programs, conversations are more likely to be deductive. The parallel question would be "What are we having for lunch?" and might lead to a discussion of peas as an example of vegetables, what other vegetables the child can name, of what color, size, and so on.[16] We don't know the ramifications of these different conversational styles for the child's cognitive development, but it seems not unlikely that the kinds of verbal exchange occurring in early childhood programs, while they may be less inductive and meaningful, are precisely the kind that would prepare a child to do well on standardized tests of intelligence. They may not be designed to enhance practical problem solving or sensitivity to human needs—nor may programs foster these kinds of behavior. For example, in the Chicago Study of Child Care and Development, children in day care centers or nursery schools did not respond more "empathically" when the experimenter hurt herself or needed help. These kinds of skills may be "taught" at home to all children, whether they attend an early childhood program or not.

To summarize, it does appear plausible that

qualitative differences between experiences offered at home and in early childhood programs contribute substantially to the difference observed in children's intellectual development. These qualitative differences most likely center on the different interactive styles of mothers and teachers, styles bolstered by the availability of different kinds of equipment, activities, and rules in centers and homes. All these qualitative differences point in the direction of a more systematically educational environment in the preschool program, which is likely to facilitate children's intellectual development.

An alternative or additional explanation would be that there are differences in the experiences program and nonprogram children have at *home* that affect intellectual development. We turn to this possibility next.

Parental Effects. It is possible that the parents of children in early childhood programs provide experiences that other parents do not. This might happen for any of several reasons. In nonexperimental programs, it could happen through self-selection: Parents who are particularly stimulating with their children might also be more likely to place their children in day care center programs or nursery schools. In experimental programs or in comprehensive programs, it could happen through parent education or support: Being involved in an early childhood program might offer the mother more training in child development, or more opportunity to meet with other parents, and this could make her behavior with her child more intellectually stimulating. Or, finally, parents of program children might be more stimulating because of their children's influence on them: Children in early childhood programs might elicit more stimulating interaction from their parents because they themselves are more advanced, more interested, or more interesting. It is hard to separate these alternatives on the basis of the available data, but we can start by asking how the parents whose children are in early childhood programs are different from those whose children are not.

Of course, in well-controlled studies where every attempt has been made to match or randomly assign program and nonprogram families, there are large areas of overlap where no differences are observed (e.g., on the HOME scale: Blehar, 1974; Fowler & Khan, 1974; Ramey et al., in press; on family functioning: Golden et al., 1978; on the quality of mother-child interaction: Clarke-Stewart, in preparation; Rubenstein et al., 1981; Winnett et al., 1977). But when differences have been observed, even in these studies, they are in the predicted direction of greater verbal stimulation and playfulness in program mothers (Carr, 1973; Garber & Heber, 1980; Ramey et al., in press; Rubenstein et al., 1981) and higher educational aspirations for their children (Lippman & Grote, 1974).

As to whether these differences are the result of self-selection, parent education, or the child's influence, there are some suggestive data. Regarding self-selection, there is evidence that one reason parents send children to nursery school or day care centers rather than using home day care is in order to offer the child educational experiences—and they tend to be most satisfied with their day care arrangement, especially when they think the child is getting an education (Bone, 1977; Frost & Schneider, 1971; Handler & Fredlund, 1971; Hess et al., 1981). Moreover, when parents think the purpose of the program is educational rather than social, their children spend relatively more time in the program engaged in educational activities, while if the parents' attitude is that the purpose of nursery school is social, children spend more time in peer interaction (Meadows, Philips, Weaver, & Mably, 1977). So self-selection may contribute to the differences in parent behavior that have been observed in nonexperimental programs (e.g., Lippman & Grote, 1974; Rubenstein et al., 1981). However, it is difficult to see how self-selection could account for the parallel differences observed in experimental programs (e.g., Garber & Heber, 1980; Ramey et al., 1982).

Whether the differences in parental behavior are the result of parent education or children's influence is even harder to say. In nonexperimental programs, even those with no explicit parent education component, parents *claim* they learn more about child care as a result of their children's being in the program (Steinberg & Green, 1977). But little communication between parent and teacher has been observed to occur naturally (Powell, 1978), and when it *does* occur, it does not lead to more agreement between parent and teacher. So it is hard to see how parental behavior would change as a result of mere exposure to a day care program. In early childhood programs that make a deliberate effort through parent education or training to modify parents' behavior, positive changes have been found by the end of the program in how much mothers talk, teach, respond, discipline, and interact with their children (Andrews et al., 1975; Benson, Berger, & Mease, 1975; Gutelius, 1977; Lasater et al., 1975; Leler et al., 1975; Levenstein, 1977; Love et al., 1976; Wandersman & Wandersman, 1976). Yet changes in maternal behavior are not inevitably observed, even when these parent education efforts are made (Epstein & Evans, 1977; Fowler, 1978; Lally & Honig, 1977b; Slaughter, 1977). Nor are the changes in maternal behavior always in the desired direction of greater involvement or tolerance (Badger, Hodgins, & Burns, 1977; Kessen et al., 1975). More important, even if changes in maternal behavior have been observed to accompany advances in children's performance, it may not be that the changes in maternal behavior have caused or are responsible for the observed changes in the children's performance. What is needed to test this hypothesis is an analysis of the relationship between changes in maternal behavior and child behavior over time.

Only a handful of studies offers evidence of this kind. Kogan and Gordon (1975) observed that mothers' behavior changed during training sessions and children's behavior changed in the posttraining period, but they found no correlation between maternal change and child change for individual mother-child pairs. Andrews et al. (1975) found that mothers' behavior changed prior to the time treatment effects were observed in children's IQ, but the time differential by which maternal change preceded changes in children's motor and cognitive performance was slight and could be at least partially attributed to asynchrony in scheduling assessments. They did not analyze correlations between maternal change and child change. Kessen et al. (1975), examining both changes in group means and correlational patterns, found no evidence that changes in maternal behavior either preceded or caused increments in children's performance and, indeed, found that children's changes preceded maternal changes on several factors. Forrester, Boismier, and Gray (1977) found that the correlation between children's IQ at the beginning of the program and maternal stimulation at the end was stronger than that between maternal stimulation at the beginning and children's IQ at the end. Since the opposite direction of influence has been observed for comparable variables and for same-age children in families *not* participating in a parent training program (Clarke-Stewart, 1973), this correlational pattern may reflect a treatment effect. To clarify the causal pattern, we need a further breakdown into treatment periods during the program.

The results of these investigations of changes in mothers' and children's behavior do not support the hypothesis that children's advanced development is the direct result of parental intervention. The case for parental influence as a causal explanation is further undermined by the following findings: (1) children in early childhood programs modify their mothers' behavior by asking them to watch, read, play, and answer questions, and, as a result, mothers give more information and are more stimulating and responsive (Falender & Heber, 1975; Garber & Heber, 1980; Gray & Klaus, 1970; Ramey et al., in press); (2) measures involving the child are more susceptible to program-induced change than are measures of maternal behavior or attitudes (Kogan & Gordon, 1975; Lally & Honig, 1977b; Leler et al., 1975; Sonquist, 1975); and (3) child-focused early childhood programs are at least as effective as mother-focused or mother-child-focused ones in producing gains in children's intellectual performance (cf. Clarke-Stewart & Apfel, 1979, pp. 87ff). In brief, we have no support for the hypothesis that improvements in children's performance in early childhood programs are the result of parents' influence.

Thus, while advances in children's intellectual development may be the result of both indirect (parent-mediated) and direct (program-induced) influences working in concert, it seems unlikely that in most early childhood programs indirect effects would be of primary importance. As further support for this conclusion, it should be noted that, for children who are in full-time day care center programs, the correlation between children's IQ and maternal stimulation that has been consistently observed in studies of nonprogram children gradually declines (see Clarke-Stewart & Apfel, 1979; Fowler, 1978; and Ramey et al., in press).

The final hypothesis we consider regarding the etiology of gains in intellectual development for children in programs is another kind of self-selection—self-selection according to the child's characteristics.

Selective Placement. It may be that children in early childhood programs are already more advanced intellectually and have been selectively placed in programs for that reason. Although this kind of selection may augment program effects in real-world programs (as we suggested in the discussion on social competence), selective placement cannot alone account for all observed differences, because gains were also observed in those studies in which children were initially matched on IQ (Fowler, 1978), or, more importantly, when children were randomly assigned to the program (Garber & Heber, 1980; Lazar & Darlington, 1982; Ramey et al., in press). However, the tendency for IQ gains to diminish after the program ends even in these well-controlled studies prevents us from dismissing self-selection as a factor in accounting for the gains observed in early childhood programs.

To summarize very briefly the results of this analysis of early childhood programs and intellectual development, it appears that the acceleration of intellectual development observed in many children attending preschool programs is attributable primarily to the structured educational activities and teaching encountered in the supportive, child-oriented atmosphere of the program, augmented by further stimulating interactions with their parents—some of which the children themselves initiate.

Physical Health and Development

For the sake of completeness, brief mention should be made of the effects of day care on children's physical health and development. Several studies have included examinations by pediatricians, ratings by teachers, questionnaires from mothers, or standardized tests concerning children's physical health and motor development. Their findings are quite consistent. When infants or children are from poor families, being in day care advances motor development and activity, increases height and weight, and decreases the likelihood of pediatric problems (Golden et al., 1978; Ramey et al., in press; Robinson & Robinson, 1971; Schwarz et al., 1974). For physical development (height, weight, pediatric examination), day care in either a center or a home appeared to be advantageous (Golden et al., 1978), but for motor development the advantage has been found only in centers (Vroegh, 1976). These advantages for physical and motor development occurred in both community (Golden et al., 1978; Vroegh, 1976) and model day care programs (Ramey et al., in press; Robinson & Robinson, 1971).

What is the reason for these observed differences? First, day care centers are likely to provide more opportunities for locomotor activity than poor homes—there are play yards, indoor spaces where motor activity is encouraged, and other children to romp with. These factors have been suggested as the reason motor development is more advanced in some residential institutions than others (Dennis, 1960). It seems likely it would be reflected in the effect of day care as well. Day care centers also provide better physical care than poor homes (supervised medical screening, immunization, nutrition, safety; Golden et al., 1978), which could be associated with the advantage in physical development. However, there does not seem be a simple link between differences in height or weight and in nutrition, since nutrition was better in day care centers than in day care homes, yet day care center children were not taller or heavier (Golden et al., 1978).

When middle-class children make up a substantial percentage of the sample, these differences between day care and home care children in height, motor development, and motor activity are not observed (Douglas & Blomfield, 1958; Fowler & Khan, 1974; Keister, 1970; Macrae & Herbert-Jackson, 1976). This is probably because middle-class homes provide nutrition and opportunities for locomotor activity that are equally good to those found in day care centers.

The health of children in day care is another story. Regardless of their family's socioeconomic status, children in day care centers have been observed to have more frequent (though not more severe) infectious diseases (flu, colds, runny noses, respiratory ailments, rashes) than children in homes (Berfenstam & William-Olsson, 1973; Douglas & Blomfield, 1958; Doyle, 1975; Keister, 1970; Steinberg & Green, 1977). This difference, too, occurred in model as well as community centers. To account for this day care effect, we need nothing more complicated than a modern explanation of germ theory and contagion.

Summary of Program Effects

When children are placed in day care or an early childhood education program, there are likely to be some differences in their relationship with mother, their interactions with peers, and their performance on intellectual tasks. In this review we attempted to describe and explain these differences. Unfortunately, in no instance was it possible to offer a completely satisfactory explanation of the differences, although some explanations did seem more plausible than others.

The evidence indicates that day care children become or continue to be attached to their mothers, but that there may be differences in the direction of greater avoidance, independence, or distance from mother. In explaining these differences, it was not possible to dismiss with confidence the competing interpretations holding that these effects reveal (1) a disturbance in the child's relationship with mother, (2) adaptive and psychologically healthy independence of mother, or (3) inadequate control over confounding factors or assessment artifacts. Similar interpretive difficulties appear in the research on peer interaction. Although one can look at the evidence and say that children in early childhood programs are more socially mature than those who are not in programs, this interpretation presupposes a developmental model of peer behavior in which, depending on the age of the child, more mature children may display more negative as well as more positive social behavior, along with qualitatively more sophisticated social behavior. The case for greater intellectual gains in program children is somewhat more straightforward. Yet we know little about the particular intellectual processes affected, how much the apparent gains are by-products of the greater social competence of day care children, or how the preschool gains become translated into less school failure.

CONCLUSIONS

The naturalist John Muir once observed that, in nature, everything is hooked to everything else. In the case of the young child, these links are mediated by social institutions—psychological as well as physical contexts—which themselves are hooked to the broader society. In this chapter, we have viewed the early childhood program as a major institutional context for the care and rearing of the young, a context likely to become more pervasive and salient in the years ahead.

Our review of these programs was guided by an emerging and promising paradigm in which human behavior is studied in the contexts in which it is enmeshed. At its center, the paradigm is aimed at comprehending the mundane events of a young child's life. This aim, however, is embedded in an effort to untangle the awesomely intricate web of contingencies that shape and order equally intricate processes of development. In part, this review was a paradigmatic exercise: When programs—themselves multilayered configurations—are treated as psychologically meaningful units of analysis, what, if anything, can be said about processes of development? This exercise required the assumption that in these early childhood programs we would find events of sufficient scope and diversity to be treated as experiential or environmental variables likely to influence developmental outcomes. As it turned out, this assumption was a safe one. Almost every variable of traditional interest in child development can be found when particular forms of these programs are studied—temporal variables (age of entry and of testing, time away from mother, duration of attendance), social-interactive variables (caregiver, peer, and parental behavior), physical environment variables (materials and playthings), and other variables derived from these. However, in preschool programs, these variables are confounded. Even though more refined categories and measurements will sharpen future analyses, we do not envision nor do we recommend thinking of these variations as a master factorial design in which each program dimension is crossed with every other. The way things are "hooked up"—historical events to ideologies, ideologies to curricula, curricula to settings, settings to family circumstances, and so on—needs to be studied more carefully before attempts are made to examine program effects.

In treating the research on early childhood programs as we have—as a new paradigm, with attention to historical and societal forces, field methods, ecological validity, and configural arrangements—several important issues in the field of child development were brought to our attention. These issues appear at a number of levels, including definitional, methodological, theoretical, metatheoretical, and practical.

Definitional Problems

Early childhood programs do not exist "out there," neatly ordered and precisely marked. The attempt to study these programs requires a preliminary intellectual effort in which settings are classified according to explicit criteria, often those developed by licensing or other governmental agencies. These classifications, embedded in a historical and social context, have social meanings—not one but several—that compete for attention in the research. Numerous classification schemes are possible but, whichever schemes are used, none will be free of surplus social meanings and none will be culturally neutral or detached from the researcher's personal perspective.

This recognition of the bias inherent in program research is not intended as a criticism or apology. Quite the contrary. The problem of cultural bias infuses all of developmental research; it is only more obvious, and more easily identified, in the study of early childhood programs. Our response to the problem in this review was to adopt a classification scheme that seemed to be useful to us, in 1982, and therefore there was much discussion of similarities and differences among "centers," "family day care homes," "babysitters," and "home-reared" children. We gave less stress to other ways of classifying children's experience (e.g., intervention vs. nonintervention programs, profit vs. nonprofit programs), although a convincing case might have been made for these classifications. Our choice of categories was governed by several considerations. First, similar categories are used in the national census and by public agencies and, therefore, the information derived from child development studies that is organized according to these categories can be used to interpret secular changes in child care arrangements or to inform public policy debates. Second, these classifications do, in fact, represent qualitatively different child care settings. Since some of these types of care can be subdivided further, where appropriate we described variations among center programs or family day care programs, among experimental programs using different curricula or child development approaches. Our organization, suited to our own purposes and reflecting the current early childhood scene, is obviously not the only one. Defining early childhood programs will continue to be a problem each researcher or reviewer must solve anew.

Methodological Complexities

Field research presents substantial methodological difficulties. But if we seemed to imply that field research was qualitatively more difficult than research in the laboratory, the implication was unintended. Research paradigms fall along a continuum from in vitro to in situ studies, from strenuous attempts to hold living systems still to equally strenuous attempts to glimpse these systems in full motion. Difficulties confront researchers at all points on the continuum.

For those who work in field settings, the major difficulty is control. Even when randomized designs are used, attrition rapidly produces a quasicorrelational design. In the new paradigm, randomization is used whenever possible—but the investigator must assume that the design is really correlational. Potentially confounding covariates therefore must become important objects of study in their own right—not just the standard covariates (e.g., SES, sex, and parity), but covariates that tap the motivation, understanding, and personal dispositions of the participants.

Theoretical Models

Much of the research reviewed in this chapter was based on a linear model of environmental and developmental processes. And yet, in some instances, the data make sense only when a curvilinear model is considered. On the input side, a linear model says that the more the better (or the more the worse). In this model, for example, more time away from mother, more frequent separations, more substitute caregivers should predict greater disturbances in the mother-child relationship. But the data indicate that some time away from mother, some separation, and some care from persons other than the mother might be better than none at all or too much. How then will a midway optimum be conceptualized? One solution is to enter curvilinear terms into our predictive models. Another is to reconceptualize the underlying dimensions.

On the output side there may also be curvilinear functions. For example, the evidence indicates that children who attend early childhood programs are socially more outgoing and skilled—but also more likely to have conflicts with peers. How should these findings be interpreted? We suggested that between the ages of 2 and 5 children become more socially active, but that this increased activity yields some social conflicts that later decrease as children become better able to negotiate disagreements. If so, the interpretation of day care effects will depend on the age of the child—at an early age, more conflict behavior represents greater maturity; at a later age, less maturity. Missing, but needed, is a theoretical model of social development appropriate for this age range, one in which the social desirability of a particular behavior is distinguished from its developmental significance.

Metatheoretical Dilemmas

From "Cause" to "Contribution"

In an early draft of this chapter, we often used the term "cause" in discussing program factors responsible for child development outcomes. Gradually, however, we began to realize that the word "cause" was inappropriate to the paradigm we were using. Conceptually, it is possible to think "cause" while using a paradigm that cannot establish "cause" in the manner achieved by a true experiment. But in thinking this way, we are in danger of ignoring conceptions that might be more useful and appropriate for a research paradigm in which a configuration of factors "contribute" to outcomes rather than "cause" easily separated effects.

A similar problem is faced by epidemiologists studying factors that contribute to human disease or its alleviation. For this reason, epidemiologists refer to "risks" or "benefits," and their analytical models are designed to specify those risk or benefit factors that contribute to a particular outcome (Cowan & Leviton, 1980). Were we to adopt this strategy in the study of early childhood programs, we would examine a multivariate model in which each of several risk factors might contribute to developmental effects and together account for a substantial amount of outcome variation. Each contributing factor might itself be further refined and reentered into the model. When interventions are attempted, models can be compared (pretreated vs. posttreated or treated vs. untreated) for changes in the configuration of contributing factors. If, for example, prefamiliarization procedures reduced the distance-avoidance effect, some factors such as maternal stress might continue to account for attachment differences while other factors such as sex of child might no longer be related to these effects.

The Concept of Application

There are also metatheoretical problems associated with the distinction between a theory of development and a theory of practice (Fein & Schwartz, 1982). How do notions of development "apply" to notions of practice—and how do notions of practice "apply" to a theory of development? Suppose we gain from a theory of development some understanding of how children's attachment to mother is likely to be modified as a result of a day care experience; suppose this understanding involves dimensions such as time away from mother and caregiver behavior with the child. One tendency of child development theorists is to convert this understanding into recommendations such as "part-time care is desirable" and "caregivers ought to be responsive."

Now, look at the way day care settings typically handle the separation situation and respond to the mother and to the child. Or consider the stresses placed on the full-time working mother. Conceivably, improved practices might change the current research findings; however, the possibility can only be examined in conjunction with a theory of practice in which procedures for change have been developed. Findings from child development research can provide an impetus for change—and the tools of child development research can provide a way of assessing whether change has occurred—but a parallel, quasi-independent body of knowledge, a coherent technology of practice, is needed to create real-life dimensions of variation that may not currently exist. This technology will offer effective and reproducible procedures for generating these dimensions. These procedures can then be incorporated into the research methodology, contributing to the technical operations used to define new developmental constructs. This relationship between theory and practice (or more accurately between theories aimed at explanation and theories aimed at doing) is discussed in detail elsewhere (Fein & Schwartz, 1982). An illustration might clarify what we mean. Suppose that day care attendance encourages greater avoidance of mother. Is this an inevitable consequence of day care attendance, or does the effect reflect only current day care practices? If the latter is true, what might these practices be? Perhaps infants are placed in out-of-home day care arrangements before their attachment to mother has formed. Perhaps the separation and reunion of mother and child are managed abruptly, without providing children and their mothers support to ease the transition from home to program and from program to home. What kinds of arrangements or procedures would provide these supports, and how can their effectiveness be verified? The task of the practitioner would be to propose, justify, implement, and monitor day care arrangements and procedures. The procedures themselves might be designed to extend or test hypotheses derived from developmental theory. For example, based on the theoretical notion that young children are anxious or wary with strangers, a day care procedure might include visits from the caregiver at home before an out-of-home placement begins, with each visit planned to include playful interactions with the child. These visits might continue until some criterion is met—for example, the child cheerfully stays alone with the caregiver. Other hypotheses might relate to children's reactions to unfamiliar peers or to the physical features of the day care setting. The developmentalist's job would be to determine whether these procedures changed the effects of day care on children's attachment.

Practical Concerns

Finally, there is the practical issue of what to say to parents who must make decisions about putting their young children in day care or early childhood programs. The message suggested by the available data is basically reassuring. If children are placed in a decent program after 2 years of age, effects, if any, are likely to be positive. Children's development of social and intellectual skills is likely to be advanced, and there are no apparent detrimental effects on their emotions. Developmental acceleration is especially likely in programs that offer systematic educational activities and opportunites for social interaction and exploration of materials. For children less than 1 year of age, there may be some effect on the mother-child relationship, an effect which *may* be negative, especially if the mother's work responsibilities absorb much of her emotional energy and if the family situation does not alleviate these pressures.

Before translating this message into practical decisions about real children, however, parents (and their advisors) need to be reminded of several things. First, they need to remember that there are severe limitations in the research from which these suggestions were drawn. Studies were inevitably of volunteer subjects attending relatively good programs, which, for the most part, they had selected themselves. "Effects" were assessed with fairly gross measures, during the program or shortly thereafter, by white middle-class researchers with their own values, standards, and biases. The research evaluating preschool programs, thus, offers no guarantees to a parent about an individual child, a particular setting, or the long-term effects on the child, the family, or society.

Second, in addition to appreciating the limitations of the research, parents need to realize that real decisions must ultimately rest not on research findings but on their own personal needs and values. It is they who must weigh the advanced social and intellectual skills which an early childhood program might foster in their child against the possibility of more intense noncompliance and aggressiveness concomitantly. It is they who must decide whether they want to stress socialization for school success (by enrolling the child in a center program) or socialization for family harmony (by keeping the child at home).

Finally, although the prevalent fears of parents in the 1970s—that day care would lead to intellectual retardation, emotional disturbance, or excessive dependence on peers—may now be laid to rest, there is a new fear that has been expressed (Suransky, 1982). This is the concern that speeding up children's development or thrusting them into an adultlike world of rules and schedules too early is, itself, negative or will have negative effects. It is feared that an early childhood program will deprive children of the idyllic and innocent childhood we have so carefully and enlightenedly constructed for them (Aries, 1962). Can these programs have short-term negative ramifications as preschool programmed children find further schooling beneath their advanced abilities? Or will there be long-term negative effects as these children reach adolescence and adulthood, procreation and parenthood, without the inner core of primitive and prolonged playfulness a "traditional" childhood provides? We have no answer to this concern, nor is an empirical answer likely to be forthcoming. These concerns, too, must be confronted by each individual parent and judged according to personal values, economic needs, and financial circumstances.

Hope for the Future

If you will permit us a flight of fancy, the state of the art in early childhood education is reminiscent of that in aviation circa 1900, when the Wright brothers set out to build a flying machine. The contribution of child development theory to this art is not unlike the contribution of classic aerodynamic theory to early aviation; it was trial-and-error glider experiments rather than elegant mathematical equations that produced the wing configurations first needed to stay aloft. Only later were mathematical equations integrated with a practical knowledge of flying.

Those who initiated early childhood programs in the 1960s remind us of the Wrights' tinkering in their backyard; and the research material covered in this *Handbook* holds the promise of inspiring theories yet to come. We are not yet flying a Concorde, nor have we figured out how to rear a child on the moon, but our current designs are better than hot-air balloons and we have begun to appreciate the intricacies of child rearing on earth. With a more symbiotic interplay of developmental theory, educational practice, and parental concerns, in a favorable sociopolitical climate, the next half-century could see the field of child development, too, inspire new visions and ventures.

NOTES

1. We have taken the results of these studies more or less at face value, but the reader should be aware that the veracity of some of the most favorable results (e.g., Garber & Heber, 1980) has been challenged by critics (see Page, 1975).

2. Only Blanchard and Main (1979) found a decrease in attachment the longer children were in day care, from 12 to 25 months, but after 12 months in day care this could hardly be a "transition" effect.

3. Unfortunately, even these two studies are not strictly comparable, since the age range of day care commencement in the one group that showed greater avoidance (the early starters in Vaughn et al., 1980) was longer (1 year) than in the other three groups (6 months).

4. It is not simply that for day care children "familiarity breeds contempt" either; the greater aggressiveness of day care children was observed with unfamiliar as well as familiar peers.

5. Although two studies point to age 2 as being a particularly beneficial time to start day care for children's social competence (Bryant et al., 1980; Largman, 1976), stronger evidence (cited) suggests the effect occurs regardless of age.

6. Independence, cooperation, initiative, play level, task persistence, and involvement were the indicators of social competence.

7. Friendliness, maturity, cooperation, independence, and social responsibility were the indicators of social competence.

8. Unfortunately for our purposes in this comparison, these were mothers of children attending day care, not home care mothers.

9. Since Ramey and Farran randomly assigned subjects to program or nonprogram groups, it is not surprising they found no difference.

10. Belsky (1980) suggests that the best combination for fostering the child's exploratory competence is for both parents to be affectionate and playful, but for fathers to be more stimulating than mothers (which would be the situation when the mother works). Unfortunately, however, his conclusion was based on possibly biased observations at the *end* of the day (when father has just gotten home). In Clarke-Stewart's (1980) study, in observations made at other times of the day, relatively higher stimulation from mothers than fathers predicted children's social competence.

11. Unfortunately, studies comparing full-time day care with part-time nursery school tend to have samples confounded by SES (e.g., Winnett et al., 1977), but even when this variable is controlled (in Biemiller, 1978; Clarke-Stewart, in preparation), the finding is the same.

12. Rubenstein and Howes (1979) did not find that day caregivers did more teaching than mothers; perhaps this was a function of the young ages of their subjects (under 2 years).

13. Only three studies have not shown an advantage for day care centers over day care homes: Cochran (1977) in Sweden, Doyle and Somers (1978) in Canada, and Scarr (1981) in Bermuda.

14. This discussion is not meant to imply that center programs are inevitably superior to or more effective than home-based programs. Home-based parent training programs have been observed to have positive effects (see Clarke-Stewart & Apfel, 1979). This is merely a way of trying to understand what *kinds* of experiences in programs might be responsible for the observed gains in intellectual development.

15. There may be a problem of sampling bias here: It is easier to locate day care centers than day care homes. But even when an effort is made to find excellent day care homes (Golden et al., 1978) or to make subject recruitment for home and center groups equivalent (Clarke-Stewart, in preparation), these differences have been observed.

16. The homes where these inductive conversations were observed (Cochran, 1977; Prescott, 1973; Tizard et al., 1980) were middle or working class.

REFERENCES

Abelson, W. D. Head Start graduates in school. In S. Ryan (Ed.), *A report on longitudinal evaluations of preschool programs.* Washington, D.C.: DHEW Publication No. (OHD) 74-24, 1974.

Abelson, W. D., Zigler, E., & DeBlasi, C. Effects of a four year Follow Through program on economically disadvantaged children. *Journal of Educational Psychology,* 1974, *66,* 756–761.

Abramovitch, R., & Grusec, J. E. Peer imitation in a natural setting. *Child Development,* 1978, *49,* 60–65.

Adamson, G. What kind of pre-school care? *New Society,* 1971, July 29, 199.

Addams, J. *Twenty years at Hull House.* New York: New American Library, 1910.

Ainsworth, M. D. The development of infant-mother attachment. In B. M. Caldwell & H. N. Ricciuti (Eds.), *Review of child development research* (Vol. 3). Chicago: University of Chicago Press, 1973.

Ainsworth, M. D., Blehar, M., Waters, E., & Wall, S. *Patterns of attachment: Observations in the strange situation and at home.* Hillsdale, N.J.: Lawrence Erlbaum Associates, 1978.

Allen, G. B., & Masling, J. M. An evaluation of the effects of nursery school training on children in the kindergarten, first, and second grades. *Journal of Educational Research,* 1957, *51,* 285–296.

Allen, V. L., & Feldman, R. S. Studies on the role of the tutor. In V. L. Allen (Ed.), *Children as tutors.* New York: Academic Press, 1976.

Ambron, S. *Causal models in early education research.* Unpublished report, Boys Town Center for the Study of Youth Development, Stanford University, 1979.

Ambron, S. *Day care and early social development.* Unpublished report, Boys Town Center for the Study of Youth Development, Stanford University, 1980.

Anderson, C. W., Nagle, R. J., Roberts, W. A., & Smith, J. W. Attachment to substitute caregivers as a function of center quality and caregiver involvement. *Child Development,* 1981, *52,* 53–61.

Anderson, J. W. Attachment behavior out of doors. In N. Blurton Jones (Ed.), *Ethological studies of child behaviour.* Cambridge, Eng.: Cambridge University Press, 1972.

Anderson, S., & Messick, S. Social competency in young children. *Developmental Psychology,* 1974, *10,* 282–293.

Andrews, S. R., Blumenthal, J. B., Bache, W. L., & Wiener, G. *New Orleans Parent-Child Development Center* (Fourth Year Report OCD 90-C-381). New Orleans: University of New Orleans, March 1975.

Arend, R., Gove, F. L., & Sroufe, L. A. Continuity of individual adaptation from infancy to kindergarten: A predictive study of ego-resiliency and curiosity in preschoolers. *Child Development,* 1979, *50,* 950–959.

Aries, P. *Centuries of childhood: A social history of family life* (R. Baldick, trans.). New York: Random House, 1962.

Arkes, H. R., & Boykin, A. W. Analysis of complexity preference in Head Start and nursery school children. *Perceptual and Motor Skills,* 1971, *33,* 1131–1137.

Badger, E., Hodgins, A., & Burns, D. *Altering the behavior of adolescent mothers: A follow-up evaluation of the Infant Stimulation/Mother Training Program.* Paper presented at the Nassau County Coalition for Family Planning Conference, Westbury, N.Y., November 1977.

Baumrind, D. Childcare practices anteceding three patterns of preschool behavior. *Genetic Psychology Monographs,* 1967, *75,* 43–88.

Becker, J. M. A learning analysis of the development of peer-oriented behavior in nine-month-old infants. *Developmental Psychology,* 1977, *13,* 481–491.

Beller, E. K. The impact of early education on disadvantaged children. In S. Ryan (Ed.), *A report on longitudinal evaluations of preschool programs.* Washington, D.C.: DHEW Publication No. (OHD) 74-24, 1974.

Beller, E. K. Early intervention programs. In J. Osofsky (Ed.), *Handbook of infant development.* New York: Wiley, 1979.

Beller, E. K., Litwok, E., & Sullivan, K. *An observational study of interaction in daycare.* Unpublished manuscript, Temple University, undated.

Belsky, J. A family analysis of parental influence on infant exploratory competence. In F. A. Pedersen (Ed.), *The father-infant relationship: Observational studies in the family setting.* New York: Praeger, 1980.

Belsky, J., & Steinberg, L. D. The effects of daycare: A critical review. *Child Development,* 1978, *49,* 929–949.

Belsky, J., Steinberg, L. D., & Walker, A. The ecology of daycare. In M. Lamb (Ed.), *Childrearing in nontraditional families.* Hillsdale, N.J.: Lawrence Erlbaum Associates, 1982.

Benson, L., Berger, M., & Mease, W. Family communication systems. *Small Group Behavior,* 1975, *6,* 91–104.

Bereiter, C., & Engelmann, S. *Teaching disadvantaged children in the preschool.* Englewood Cliffs, N.J.: Prentice-Hall, 1966.

Berfenstam, R., & William-Olsson, I. *Early child care in Sweden.* London: Gordon & Breach, 1973.

Berger, P. L., & Neuhaus, R. J. *To empower people: The role of mediating structures in public policy.* Washington, D.C.: American Enterprise Institute for Public Policy Research, 1977.

Berlyne, D. E. The influence of the albedo and complexity of stimuli on visual fixation in the human infant. *British Journal of Psychology,* 1958, *49,* 315–318.

Berlyne, D. E. *Conflict, arousal, and curiosity.* New York: McGraw-Hill, 1960.

Bermont, G., Kelman, H. C., & Warwick, D. P. (Eds.). *The ethics of social intervention.* Washington, D.C.: Hemisphere, 1978.

Bersoff, D. N. Silk purses in sows' ears: The decline of psychological testing and a suggestion for its redemption. *American Psychologist,* 1973, *28,* 892–899.

Biber, B. A developmental-interaction approach: Bank Street College of Education. In M. C. Day & R. K. Parker (Eds.), *The preschool in action* (2nd ed.). Boston: Allyn & Bacon, 1977.

Biemiller, A. *Kindergarten programmes: The effects of regular half day, alternate full day, and daily free day programmes.* Final report of research funded by the Ministry of Education, Ontario, ONO1480, December 1978.

Biemiller, A. *The effects of kindergarten programs and teachers' perceptions of "thriving," "average," & "non-thriving" status on children's functioning in kindergarten and grades one and two.* Final report of research funded by the Ministry of Education, Ontario, June 1981.

Biemiller, A., Avis, C., & Lindsay, A. Application of Watt's Human Interactional Scale to the study of competence-supporting aspects of day care environments. *Canadian Journal of Behavioral Science,* 1979, *11,* 356–360.

Bissell, J. S. Planned variation in Head Start and Follow Through. In J. C. Stanley (Ed.), *Compensatory education for children ages two to eight: Recent studies of educational intervention.* Baltimore: The Johns Hopkins University Press, 1973.

Blanchard, M., & Main, M. Avoidance of the attachment figure and social-emotional adjustment in day-care infants. *Developmental Psychology,* 1979, *15,* 445–446.

Blehar, M. C. Anxious attachment and defensive reactions associated with day care. *Child Development,* 1974, *45,* 683–692.

Block, J. H. Issues, problems, and pitfalls in assessing sex differences: A critical review of *The psychology of sex differences. Merrill-Palmer Quarterly,* 1976, *22,* 283–308.

Bloom, B. S. *Stability and change in human characteristics.* New York: Wiley, 1964.

Bloom-Feshbach, S. *Separation reactions and nursery school adjustment.* Unpublished doctoral dissertation, Yale University, 1979.

Blurton Jones, N. G., Ferreira, M. C., Brown, M. F., & MacDonald, L. *Behaviour of one-year-old children that predicted the age at which they started preschool: An illustration of the perils of self-selected samples.* Unpublished manuscript, University of London Institute of Child Health, 1980.

Blurton Jones, N. G., & Leach, G. Behavior of children and their mothers at separation and greeting. In N. G. Blurton Jones (Ed.), *Ethological studies of child behavior.* Cambridge, Eng.: Cambridge University Press, 1972.

Body, M. K. Patterns of aggression in the nursery school. *Child Development,* 1955, *26,* 3–11.

Bone, M. *Preschool children and the need for day care.* London: Her Majesty's Stationery Office (Office of Population Censuses & Surveys, Social Survey Division), 1977.

Bowlby, J. *Maternal care and mental health.* World Health Organization Monograph No. 2. Geneva: World Health Organization, 1951.

Bowlby, J. *Attachment and loss,* Vol. 1, *Attachment.* London: Hogarth (New York: Basic Books), 1969.

Bowlby, J. *Attachment and loss,* Vol. 2, *Separation.* New York: Basic Books, 1973.

Braun, S. J., & Caldwell, B. M. Emotional adjustment of children in day care who enrolled prior to or after age of three. *Early Child Development and Care,* 1973, *2,* 13–21.

Bronfenbrenner, U. *Is early intervention effective? A report on longitudinal evaluations of preschool programs* (Vol. 2). Washington, D.C.: Department of Health, Education, and Welfare, 1974.

Bronfenbrenner, U. *The ecology of human development.* Cambridge, Mass.: Harvard University Press, 1979.

Bronfenbrenner, U., Belsky, J., & Steinberg, L. *Day care in context: An ecological perspective on research and public policy* (a review prepared for the Office of the Assistant Secretary for Planning & Evaluation, Department of Health, Education, and Welfare. Cornell University, December, 1976.

Brookhart, J., & Hock, E. The effects of experiential background on infants' behavior toward their mothers and a stranger. *Child Development,* 1976, *47,* 333–340.

Brown, R. How shall a thing be called? *Psychological Review,* 1958, *65,* 14–21.

Bruner, J. *Under five in Britain.* London: Grant McIntyre, 1980.

Bruner, J. S., Olver, R., & Greenfield, P. *Studies in cognitive growth.* New York: Wiley, 1966.

Bryant, B., Harris, M., & Newton, D. *Children and minders.* London: Grant McIntyre, 1980.

Burke, R., & Weir, T. Relationship of wives' employment status to husband, wife and pair satisfaction and performance. *Journal of Marriage and the Family,* 1976, *38,* 279–287.

Busse, T. V., Ree, M., Gatride, M., & Alexander, T. Environmentally enriched classrooms and the cognitive and perceptual development of Negro preschool children. *Journal of Educational Psychology,* 1972, *63,* 15–21.

Caldwell, B. The fourth dimension in early childhood education. In R. Hess & R. Bear (Eds.), *Early education.* Chicago: Aldine-Atherton, 1968.

Caldwell, B. M. The rationale for early intervention. *Exceptional Children,* 1970, *36,* 717–726.

Caldwell, B., Wright, B., Honig, A., & Tannenbaum, G. Infant day care and attachment. *American Journal of Orthopsychiatry,* 1970, *40,* 397–412.

Callahan, S. C. *The working mothers.* New York: Macmillan, 1971.

Campbell, D. T., & Erlebacher, A. How regression artifacts in quasi-experimental evaluations can mistakenly make compensatory education look harmful. In J. Hellmuth (Ed.), *Disadvantaged child,* Vol. 3, *Compensatory Education: A National Debate.* New York: Brunner/Mazel, 1970.

Campbell, D. T., & Stanley, J. C. *Experimental and quasi-experimental designs for research.* Chicago: Rand McNally, 1967.

Carew, J. Experience and the development of intelligence in young children. *Monographs of the Society for Research in Child Development,* 1980, *45*(1–2, Serial No. 183).

Carr, S. J. *Sex, daycare, and mother-child attachment.* Unpublished doctoral dissertation, Georgia State University, 1973.

Carver, R. B. Two dimensions of tests: Psychometric and edumetric. *American Psychologist*, 1974, *29*, 512–518.

Casler, L. Maternal deprivation: A critical review of the literature. *Monographs of the Society for Research in Child Development*, 1961, *26* (2, Serial No. 80).

Chilman, C. S. Programs for disadvantaged parents: Some major trends and research. In B. M. Caldwell & H. N. Ricciuti (Eds.), *Review of child development research*, Vol. 3. Chicago: University of Chicago Press, 1973.

Cicirelli, V. G. *The impact of Head Start: An evaluation of the effects of Head Start on children's cognitive and affective development* (Vols. 1 and 2). Washington, D.C.: National Bureau of Standards, Institute for Applied Technology, 1969.

Clarke-Stewart, K. A. Interactions between mothers and their young children: Characteristics and consequences. *Monographs of the Society for Research in Child Development*, 1973, *38*(6–7, Serial No. 153).

Clarke-Stewart, K. A. *Child care in the family: A review of research and some propositions for policy*. New York: Academic Press, 1977.

Clarke-Stewart, K. A. And daddy makes three: The father's impact on mother and young child. *Child Development*, 1978, *49*, 466–478.

Clarke-Stewart, K. A. The father's contribution to child development. In F. A. Pedersen (Ed.), *The father-infant relationship: Observational studies in a family context*. New York: Praeger Special Studies, 1980.

Clarke-Stewart, K. A. Observation and experiment: Complementary strategies for studying day care and social development. In S. Kilmer (Ed.), *Advances in early education and day care*, Vol. 2. Greenwich, Conn.: JAI Press, 1981.

Clarke-Stewart, K. A. *The Chicago Study of Child Care and Development*. Report in preparation, 1982. (Available from author, Department of Education, the University of Chicago.)

Clarke-Stewart, K. A., & Apfel, N. Evaluating parental effects on child development. In L. S. Shulman (Ed.), *Review of research in education*, Vol. 6. Itasca, Ill.: Peacock, 1979.

Clarke-Stewart, K. A., & Hevey, C. A. Longitudinal relations in repeated observations of mother-child interaction from 1 to 2½ years. *Developmental Psychology*, 1981, *17*, 127–145.

Clarke-Stewart, K. A., Umeh, B. J., Snow, M. E., & Pederson, J. A. Development and prediction of children's sociability from 1 to 2½ years. *Developmental Psychology*, 1980, *16*, 290–302.

Cloward, R. A., & Ohlin, L. E. *Delinquency and opportunity: A theory of delinquent gangs*. New York: Free Press, 1960.

Cochran, M. M. A comparison of group day and family child-rearing patterns in Sweden. *Child Development*, 1977, *48*, 702–707.

Coelen, C., Glantz, F., & Calore, D. *Day care centers in the U.S., 1976–1977* (Final report of the National Day Care Study, Vol. 3). Cambridge, Mass.: Abt Associates, 1978.

Cohen, D. K. The value of social experiments. In A. M. Rivlin & P. M. Timpane (Eds.), *Planned variation in education: Should we give up or try harder?* Washington, D.C.: Brookings, 1975.

Cohen, N. L., & Tomlinson-Keasey, C. The effects of peers and mothers on toddlers' play. *Child Development*, 1980, *51*, 921–924.

Cohen, S. E. Maternal employment and mother-child interaction. *Merrill-Palmer Quarterly*, 1978, *24*, 189–197.

Cole, M., & Bruner, J. S. Cultural differences and inferences about psychological processes. *American Psychologist*, 1971, *26*, 867–876.

Cole, M., Gay, J., Glick, J. A., & Sharp, D. W. *The cultural context of learning and thinking: An exploration in experimental anthropology*. New York: Basic Books, 1971.

Connolly, K. J., & Smith, P. K. Experimental studies of the preschool environment. *International Journal of Early Childhood*, 1978, *10*, 86–95.

Cooke, R. *Recommendations for a Head Start program by a panel of experts*. Baltimore: Johns Hopkins University, 1965.

Cornelius, S. W., & Denney, N. W. Dependency in day care and home care children. *Developmental Psychology*, 1975, *11*, 575–582.

Cowan, L. D., & Leviton, A. Epidemiologic considerations in the study of the sequelae of low level exposure. In H. L. Needleman (Ed.), *Low level lead exposure: The clinical implications of current research*. New York: Raven Press, 1980.

Croate, J., & Glover, K. A history and evaluation of parent education. *The Family Coordinator*, 1977, *26*, 151–158.

Crockenberg, S. B. Infant irritability, mother responsiveness, and social support influences on the security of infant-mother attachment. *Child Development*, 1981, *52*, 857–865.

Cronbach, L. J. Beyond the two disciplines of scientific psychology. *American Psychologist*, 1975, *30*, 116–127.

Cronbach, L. J., & Furby, L. How should we measure change—Or should we? *Psychological Bulletin*, 1970, *74*, 68–80.

Cummings, E. M. Caregiver stability and day care.

Developmental Psychology, 1980, *16,* 31–37.

Curtis, J. *Working mothers.* New York: Doubleday, 1976.

Darlington, R. B., Royce, J. M., Snipper, A. S., Murray, H. W., & Lazar, I. Preschool programs and the later school competence of children from low-income families. *Science,* 1980, *208,* 202–204.

Datta, L. E. Design of the Head Start Planned Variation experiment. In A. M. Rivlin & P. M. Timpane (Eds.), *Planned variation in education: Should we give up or try harder?* Washington, D.C.: Brookings, 1975.

Datta, L. Another spring and other hopes: Some findings from national evaluations of Project Head Start. In E. Zigler & J. Valentine (Eds.), *Project Head Start: A legacy of war on poverty.* New York: Free Press, 1979.

Day, M. C., & Parker, R. K. *The preschool in action* (2nd ed.). Boston: Allyn & Bacon, 1977.

Dearman, N. B., & Plisko, V. W. *The condition of education.* Washington, D.C.: National Center for Educational Statistics, 1980.

Demos, J. *A little commonwealth.* New York: Oxford University Press, 1970.

Dennis, W. Causes of retardation in institutional children: Iran. *Journal of Genetic Psychology,* 1960, *96,* 47–59.

Dennis, W., & Dennis, M. G. Infant development under conditions of restricted practice and minimum social stimulation. *Genetic Psychology Monographs,* 1941, *23,* 149–155.

Dennis, W., & Najarian, P. Infant development under environmental handicap. *Psychological Monographs,* 1957, *71*(7, Whole No. 436).

Dennis, W., & Sayegh, Y. The effect of supplementary experience upon the behavioral development of infants in institutions. *Child Development,* 1965, *36,* 81–90.

Department of Labor, Bureau of Labor Statistics. *U.S. working women: A data book.* Washington, D.C.: U.S. Government Printing Office, 1977.

DiLorenzo, L. T., Salter, R., & Brady, J. J. *Prekindergarten programs for educationally disadvantaged children* (Final report, Project No. 3040, New York State Education Department, Office of Research and Evaluation, Contract No. OE 6-10-040). Washington, D.C.: United States Department of Health, Education, and Welfare, Office of Education, Bureau of Research, December 1969.

Dokecki, P. R., Hargrove, E.C., & Sandler, H. M. *An overview of the Parent Child Development Centers social experiment.* Paper presented at the Parent Education and Public Policy Conference, University of North Carolina, Chapel Hill, March 1980.

Douglas, J. W., & Blomfield, J. W. *Children under five.* London: Allen & Unwin, 1958.

Doyle, A. Infant development in day care. *Developmental Psychology,* 1975, *11,* 655–656.

Doyle, A., Connolly, J., & Rivest, L. The effect of playmate familiarity on the social interactions of young children. *Child Development,* 1980, 51, 217–223.

Doyle, A., & Somers, K. The effects of group and family day care on infant attachment behaviours. *Canadian Journal of Behavioural Science,* 1978, *10,* 38–45.

Draeger, C. B. *Parental investment and the use of alternative child care arrangements.* Unpublished master's thesis, University of Chicago, June 1977.

Eckerman, C. O., & Whatley, J. Toys and social interaction between infant peers. *Child Development,* 1977, *48,* 1645–1656.

Eller, E. M. (Ed.). *The school of infancy by John Amos Comenius.* Chapel Hill: University of North Carolina Press, 1956.

Epstein, A. S., & Evans, J. L. *Parenting: Processes and programs.* Unpublished manuscript, High Scope, November 1977.

Erikson, E. H. *Childhood and society.* New York: Norton, 1950.

Espinosa, L. *An ecological study of family day care.* Unpublished doctoral dissertation, University of Chicago, 1980.

Everson, M. D., Ambron, S. R., Kermoian, R., & Romo, V. *The impact of day care on attachment behavior among 12 to 24 month-olds.* Unpublished manuscript, Stanford University, 1981.

Falender, C. A., & Heber, R. Mother-child interaction and participation in a longitudinal intervention program. *Developmental Psychology,* 1975, *11,* 830–836.

Fantz, R. L. Pattern vision in young infants. *Psychological Record,* 1958, *8,* 43–47.

Farber, E. A., & Egeland, B. Developmental consequences of out-of-home care for infants in a low-income population. In E. F. Zigler & E. W. Gordon (Eds.), *Day care: Scientific and social policy issues.* Boston: Auburn House, 1982.

Farran, D. C., & Ramey, C. T. Infant day care and attachment behaviors toward mothers and teachers. *Child Development,* 1977, *48,* 1112–1116.

Fein, G. G. The informed parent. In S. Kilmer (Ed.), *Advances in early child care and develop-*

ment. Greenwich, Conn.: JAI Press, 1980.

Fein, G. G. The physical environment: Stimulation or evaluation? In R. Lerner & H. Busch (Eds.), *Individuals as producers of their own development: A life span perspective*. New York: Academic Press, 1981.

Fein, G., & Clarke-Stewart, A. *Day care in context*. New York: Wiley, 1973.

Fein, G. G., & Moorin, E. R. Group care can have good effects. *Day Care and Early Education*, 1980, *7*, 14–17.

Fein, G. G., Moorin, E. R., & Enslein, J. Pretense and peer behavior: An intersectoral analysis. *Human Development*, 1982, *25*, 392–406.

Fein, G. G., & Schwartz, P. Developmental theories and early education. In B. Spodek (Ed.), *Handbook of early childhood education*. New York: Free Press, 1982.

Feldbaum, C. L., Christenson, T. E., & O'Neal, E. C. An observation study of the assimilation of the newcomer to the preschool. *Child Development*, 1980, *51*, 497–507.

Ferri, E. Combined nursery centres. *Concern* (National Children's Bureau), No. 37, Autumn 1980.

Field, T. Interaction behaviors of primary versus secondary caretaker fathers. *Developmental Psychology*, 1978, *14*, 183–184.

Fiene, R. J. *The differential structural characteristics of sentences formed by preschool children in family and group day care centers*. Stony Brook, N.Y.: State University of New York, Department of Psychology, 1973. (ERIC Document Reproduction Service No. ED 094 849)

Finkelstein, N. W., Dent, C., Gallagher, K., & Ramey, C. T. Social behavior of infants and toddlers in a day care environment. *Developmental Psychology*, 1978, *14*, 257–262.

Finkelstein, N. W., & Wilson, K. *The influence of day care on social behaviors towards peers and adults*. Paper presented at the meeting of the Society for Research on Child Development, New Orleans, March 1977.

Forrester, B. J., Boismier, N. O., & Gray, S. W. *A home-based intervention program with mothers and infants*. Unpublished manuscript, George Peabody College for Teachers, Nashville, 1977.

Fosburg, S., Hawkins, P. D., Singer, J. D., Goodson, B. D., Smith, J. M., & Brush, L. R. *National Day Care Home Study* (Contract No. HEW 105-77-1051). Cambridge, Mass.: Abt Associates, 1980.

Fowler, W. *Day care and its effects on early development: A study of group and home care in multi-ethnic, working-class families*. Toronto: The Ontario Institute for Studies in Education, 1978.

Fowler, W., & Khan, N. *The later effects of infant group care: A follow-up study*. Toronto: Ontario Institute for Studies in Education, 1974.

Fraiberg, S. *Every child's birthright. In defense of mothering*. New York: Basic Books, 1977.

Frost, J., & Schneider, H. *Types of day care and parents' preferences* (Final Report: Part VII). 1971. (ERIC Document Reproduction Service No. ED 068 195)

Frye, D. The problem of infant day care. In E. F. Zigler & E. W. Gordon (Eds.), *Day care: Scientific and social policy issues*. Boston: Auburn House, 1982.

Furman, W., Rahe, D. F., & Hartup, W. W. Rehabilitation of socially withdrawn preschool children through mixed-age and same-age socialization. *Child Development*, 1979, *50*, 915–922.

Garber, H., & Heber, R. *Modification of predicted cognitive development in high-risk children through early intervention*. Paper presented at the meeting of the American Educational Research Association, Boston, April 1980.

Garland, C., & White, S. *Children and day nurseries*. London: Grant McIntyre, 1980.

Garner, W. R. The acquisition and application of knowledge. *American Psychologist*, 1972, *27*, 941–946.

Gaylin, W., Glasser, I., Marcus, S., & Rothman, D. *Doing good: The limits of benevolence*. New York: Pantheon, 1978.

Gehler, W. The development of social behavior in preschool and elementary children. *Early Child Development and Care*, 1972, *1*, 227–235.

Glaser, R. Instructional psychology: Past, present and future. *American Psychologist*, 1982, *37*, 292–305.

Glick, J. Some problems in the evaluation of preschool intervention programs. In R. D. Hess & R. M. Baer (Eds.), *Early education*. Chicago: Aldine, 1968.

Gold, D., & Andres, D. Relations between maternal employment and development of nursery school children. *Canadian Journal of Behavioural Science*, 1978, *10*, 116–129.

Golden, M., Rosenbluth, L., Grossi, M. T., Policare, H. J., Freeman, H., Jr., & Brownlee, E. M. *The New York City Infant Day Care Study*. New York: Medical and Health Research Association of New York City, 1978.

Goldman, J. A. Social participation of preschool children in same- versus mixed-age groups. *Child Development*, 1981, *52*, 644–650.

Goodson, B. D., & Hess, R. D. *The effects of parent training programs on child performance and parent behavior*. Unpublished manuscript, Stanford University, 1976.

Gordon, E. W., & Shipman, S. Human diversity, pedagogy, and educational equity. *American Psychologist,* 1979, *34,* 1030–1036.

Gordon, I. J., Guinagh, B., & Jester, R. E. The Florida Parent Education Infant and Toddler Programs. In M. C. Day & R. K. Parker (Eds.), *The preschool in action* (2nd ed.). Boston: Allyn & Bacon, 1977.

Gottman, J. M., & Parkhurst, J. T. A developmental theory of friendship and acquaintanceship processes. In W. A. Collins (Ed.), *Minnesota symposium on child psychology,* Vol. 13. Hillsdale, N.J.: Lawrence Erlbaum, Associates, 1980.

Gray, S. W., & Klaus, R. A. The Early Training Project: A seventh year report. *Child Development,* 1970, *41,* 908–924.

Gray, S. W., & Wandersman, L. P. The methodology of home-based intervention studies: Problems and promising strategies. *Child Development,* 1980, *51,* 993–1009.

Green, E. H. Group play and quarrelling among preschool children. *Child Development,* 1933, *4,* 302–307.

Greenberg, S. B., & Peck, L. F. *A study of preschoolers' spontaneous social interaction patterns in three settings: All female, all male, and coed.* Paper presented at the meeting of the American Educational Research Association, Chicago, March 1974.

Greif, E. B. Peer interactions in preschool children. In R. A. Webb (Ed.), *Social development in childhood: Day care programs and research.* Baltimore: Johns Hopkins University Press, 1977.

Grossmann, K. E., Grossmann, K., Huber, F., & Wartner, U. German children's behaviors toward their mothers at 12 months and their fathers at 18 months in Ainsworth's strange situation. *International Journal of Behavioral Development,* 1981, *4,* 157–181.

Gunnarsson, L. *The Swedish Childrearing Study: A longitudinal study of children in different childrearing environments—First follow up.* Paper prepared for the Conference on Research Perspectives in the Ecology of Human Development, Cornell University, August 1977.

Gunnarsson, L. O. *Children in day care and family care in Sweden: A follow up.* Unpublished doctoral dissertation, University of Michigan, 1978.

Gutelius, M. F. *Mobile unit for child health supervision* (Interim Report, No. RO1-MH-9215). Ely, Vt., 1977.

Hamilton, V. J., & Gordon, D. A. Teacher-child interactions in preschool task persistence. *American Educational Research Journal,* 1978, *15,* 459–466.

Handler, E., & Frelund, J. *Differences between highly satisfied and not highly satisfied clients of day care centers,* 1971. (ERIC Document Reproduction Service No. ED 068 165)

Harmon, C., & Hanley, E. J. Administrative aspects of the Head Start program. In E. Zigler & J. Valentine (Eds.), *Project Head Start.* New York: Free Press, 1979.

Harrell, J. E., & Ridley, C. A. Substitute child care, maternal employment and the quality of mother-child interaction. *Journal of Marriage and the Family,* 1975, *37,* 556–564.

Harrington, M. *The other America: Poverty in the United States.* New York: Macmillan, 1962.

Harrold, M. V., & Temple, M. H. *A study of children in the admission classes of four infant schools.* Unpublished thesis, Child Development Centre, Institute of Education, University of London, 1960. Cited in W. VanderEyken, *The preschool years* (4th ed.). Harmondsworth, Middlesex, England: Penguin Books, 1977.

Hartup, W. W. Aggression in childhood: Developmental perspectives. *American Psychologist,* 1974, *29,* 336–341.

Hartup, W. W. Peer interaction and the behavioral development of the individual child. In E. Schoplel & R. J. Reichler (Eds.), *Psychopathology and child development.* New York: Plenum, 1976.

Hebb, D. O. *Organization of behavior.* New York: Wiley, 1949.

Heber, F. R. Sociocultural mental retardation—A longitudinal study. In D. Forgay (Ed.), *Primary prevention of psychopathology.* Vol. 2, *Environmental influences.* Hanover, N.H.: University Press of New England, 1978.

Hedges, L. V. Estimating effect size from a series of experiments. *Psychological Bulletin,* 1982, *92,* 490–499.

Heinicke, C. M., & Westheimer, I. *Brief separations.* New York: International Universities Press, 1965.

Herrera, M. G., Mora, J. O., Christianson, N., Ortiz, N., Clement, J., Vuozi, L., Waber, D., Deparades, B., & Wagner, M. Effects of nutritional supplementation and early education on physical and cognitive development. In R. R. Turner & H. W. Reese (Eds.), *Life-span developmental psychology: Intervention.* New York: Academic Press, 1980.

Herzog, E., Newcomb, C. H., & Cisin, I. H. Double deprivation: The less they have, the less they learn. In S. Ryan (Ed.), *A report on longitudinal evaluations of preschool programs.* Washington, D.C.: DHEW Publication No. (OHD) 74-24, 1974.

Hess, R. D. Social class and ethnic influences upon socialization. In P. H. Mussen (Ed.), *Carmichael's manual of child psychology* (Vol. 2, 3rd ed.). New York: Wiley, 1970.

Hess, R. D., & Bear, R. M. (Eds.). *Early education.* Chicago: Aldine, 1968.

Hess, R. D., Price, G. G., Dickson, W. P., & Conroy, M. Different roles for mothers and teachers: Contrasting styles of child care. In S. Kilmer (Ed.), *Advances in early education and day care.* Greenwich, Conn.: JAI Press, 1981.

Hetherington, E. M., Cox, M., & Cox, R. *Family interaction and the social, emotional, and cognitive development of children following divorce.* Paper presented at the Symposium on the Family: Setting Priorities. Sponsored by the Institute for Pediatric Service of the Johnson & Johnson Baby Company, Washington, D.C., May 17–20, 1978.

Hinde, R. A., & Spencer-Booth, Y. Individual differences in the responses of Rhesus monkeys to a period of separation from their mothers. *Journal of Child Psychology and Psychiatry,* 1970, *11,* 159–176.

Hinde, R. A., & Spencer-Booth, Y. Effects of brief separation from mother on Rhesus monkeys. *Science,* 1971, *173,* 111–118.

Hock, E. *Alternative approaches to childrearing and their effects on mother-infant relationship* (Final report, OCD-CB-490), 1976.

Hock, E. Working and nonworking mothers with infants: Perceptions of their careers, their infants' needs, and satisfaction with mothering. *Developmental Psychology,* 1978, *14,* 37–43.

Hock, E. Working and nonworking mothers and their infants: A comparative study of maternal caregiving characteristics and infant social behavior. *Merrill-Palmer Quarterly,* 1980, *26,* 79–102.

Hock, E., Christman, K., & Hock, M. Factors associated with decisions about return to work in mothers of infants. *Developmental Psychology,* 1980, *16,* 535–536.

Hock, E., & Clinger, J. B. Behavior toward mother and stranger of infants who have experienced group day care, individual care, or exclusive maternal care. *The Journal of Genetic Psychology,* 1980, *137,* 49–61.

Hock, E., Coady, S., & Cordero, L. *Patterns of attachment to mother of one-year-old infants.* Paper presented at the meeting of the Society for Research in Child Development, Philadelphia, March 1973.

Hofferth, S. L. Day care in the next decade: 1980–1990. *Journal of Marriage and the Family,* 1979, *41,* 649–658.

Hoffman, L. W. Effect of maternal employment on the child. *Child Development,* 1961, *32,* 187–197.

Hoffman, L. W., & Nye, F. I. *Working mothers: An evaluative review of the consequences for wife, husband, and child.* San Francisco: Jossey-Bass, 1974.

Hogan, R. The terror of solitude. *Merrill-Palmer Quarterly,* 1975, *21,* 67–74.

Honig, A. S., Lally, J. R., Webb, L., Armstrong, F., & Wright, N. S. *Effects of testing style on language scores of four-year-old low-income ''control'' children in intervention projects.* Paper presented at the meeting of the Society for Research in Child Development, Denver, April 1975.

Horowitz, F. D., & Paden, L. Y. The effectiveness of environmental intervention programs. In B. M. Caldwell & H. N. Ricciuti (Eds.), *Review of child development research,* Vol. 3. Chicago: University of Chicago Press, 1973.

Howell, M. C. Employed mothers and their families (I). *Pediatrics,* 1973, *52,* 252–263. (a)

Howell, M. C. Effects of maternal employment on the child (II). *Pediatrics,* 1973, *52,* 327–343. (b)

Howes, C., & Rubenstein, J. L. Toddler peer behavior in two types of day care. *Infant Behavior and Development,* 1981, *4,* 387–394.

Hunt, J. *Intelligence and experience.* New York: Ronald, 1961.

Hunt, J. M. The psychological basis for using preschool enrichment as an antidote for cultural deprivation. *Merrill-Palmer Quarterly,* 1964, *10,* 209–248.

Huston-Stein, A., Friedrich-Cofer, L., & Susman, E. J. The relation of classroom structure to social behavior, imaginative play, and self-regulation of economically disadvantaged children. *Child Development,* 1977, *48,* 908–916.

Iannotti, R. J. Effect of role-taking experiences on role taking, empathy, altruism, and aggression. *Developmental Psychology,* 1978, *14,* 119–124.

Jersild, A. T., & Markey, F. V. Conflicts between preschool children. *Child Development Mono-*

graphs, 1935, No. 21.

Johnson, J. E., & Ershler, J. Developmental trends in preschool play as a function of classroom program and child gender. *Child Development,* 1981, *52,* 995–1004.

Johnson, J. E., Ershler, J., & Bell, C. Play behavior in a discovery-based and a formal-education program. *Child Development,* 1980, *51,* 271–274.

Kagan, J., Kearsley, R. B., & Zelazo, P. R. *Infancy: Its place in human development.* Cambridge, Mass.: Harvard University Press, 1978.

Kamii, C., & DeVries, R. Piaget for early education. In M. C. Day & R. K. Parker (Eds.), *The preschool in action* (2nd ed.). Boston: Allyn & Bacon, 1977.

Karnes, M. B., Hodgins, A., & Teska, J. A. An evaluation of two preschool programs for disadvantaged children: A traditional and highly structured experimental preschool. *Exceptional Children,* 1968, *34,* 667–676.

Karnes, M. B., Hodgins, A. S., & Teska, J. The effects of short term instruction at home by mothers of children not enrolled in a preschool. In *Research and development program on preschool disadvantaged children* (Final report to the U.S. Office of Education). Washington, D.C., 1969.

Karnes, M. B., Teska, J. A., & Hodgins, A. S. The effects of four programs of classroom intervention on the intellectual and language development of 4-year-old disadvantaged children. *American Journal of Orthopsychiatry,* 1970, *40,* 58–76.

Keister, M. E. *"The good life" for infants and toddlers.* Washington, D.C.: National Association for the Education of Young Children, 1970.

Kessen, W. The American child and other cultural inventions. *American Psychologist,* 1979, *34,* 815–820.

Kessen, W., Fein, G., Clarke-Stewart, A., & Starr, S. *Variations in home-based infant education: Language, play, and social development* (Final report to the Office of Child Development, Grant No. 1 OCD-CB-98). Department of Health Education and Welfare, August 1975.

Keyserling, M. D. *Windows on day care. A report on the findings of members of the National Council of Jewish Women on day care needs and services in their communities.* ERIC Document Reproduction Service No. ED 063 027 1972.

Kiesler, S. Federal policies for research on children. *American Psychologist,* 1979, *34,* 1009–1016.

Kilmer, S. Infant-toddler group day care: A review of research. In L. Katz (Ed.), *Current topics in early childhood education,* Vol. 3. Norwood, N.J.: Ablex, 1979.

Kirschner Associates. *A national survey of the Parent-Child Center Program* (report prepared for the Office of Child Development, Department of Health, Education, and Welfare, Contract No. B89-4557).

Klaus, R. A., & Gray, S. W. The Early Training Project for Disadvantaged Children: A report after five years. *Monographs of the Society for Research in Child Development,* 1968, *33*(4, Serial No. 120).

Kogan, K. L., & Gordon, B. N. A mother-instruction program: Documenting change in mother-child interactions. *Child Psychiatry and Human Development,* 1975, *5,* 190–200.

Kohlberg, L., & DeVries, R. *Developmental psychology in early education.* New York: Longman, 1983.

Kohlberg, L., & Mayer, R. Development as the aim of education. *Harvard Educational Review,* 1972, *42,* 449–496.

Kuhn, A. L. *The mother's role in childhood education. New England concepts, 1830–1860.* New Haven, Conn.: Yale University Press, 1947.

Kuhn, T. S. *The structure of scientific revolutions.* Chicago: University of Chicago Press, 1962.

Lally, J. R., & Honig, A. S. The Family Development Research Program. In M. C. Day & R. K. Parker (Eds.), *The preschool in action* (2nd ed.). Boston: Allyn & Bacon, 1977. (a)

Lally, J. R., & Honig, A. S. *The Family Development Research Program* (Final report, No. OCD-CB-100). Syracuse, N.Y.: University of Syracuse, 1977. (b)

Lamb, M. E. The development of mother-infant and father-infant attachments in the second year of life. *Developmental Psychology,* 1977, *13,* 637–648.

Lamb, M. E., & Roopnarine, J. L. Peer influences on sex-role development in preschoolers. *Child Development,* 1979, *50,* 1219–1222.

Lambie, D. Z., Bond, J. T., & Weikart, D. P. Home teaching of mothers and infants. Ypsilanti, Mich.: *High Scope,* 1974.

Largman, R. R. *The social-emotional effects of age of entry into full-time group care.* Unpublished doctoral dissertation, University of California, Berkeley, 1976.

Larson, J. C. *Extended day-care attendance and first grade school performance.* ERIC Document Reproduction Service No. ED 078 947, 1973.

Lasater, T. M., Malone, P., & Ferguson, C. *Birmingham Parent-Child Development Center*

(Progress report to Office of Child Development). Birmingham, Ala.: University of Alabama, 1975.

Lasch, C. *Haven in a heartless world.* New York: Basic Books, 1977.

Lasch, C. *The culture of narcissism.* New York: Norton, 1979.

Lavatelli, C. S. *Piaget's theory applied to an early childhood curriculum.* Boston: Center for Media Development, 1970.

Lawson, A., & Ingleby, J. D. Daily routines of preschool children: Effects of age, birth order, sex, and social class, and developmental correlates. *Psychological Medicine,* 1974, *4,* 399–415.

Lay, M. Z., & Meyer, W. J. *Effects of early day care experience on subsequent observed program behaviors* (Final report to the Office of Education, Subcontract 70-007). Syracuse, N.Y.: Children's Center, Syracuse University, 1972. (ERIC Document Reproduction Service No. ED 068 149, 1970)

Lazar, I., & Darlington, R. B. Lasting effects of an early education. *Monographs of the Society for Research in Child Development,* 1982, *47*(2–3, Serial No. 195).

Lazar, I., Hubbell, R., Murray, H., Rosche, M., & Royce, J. *The persistence of preschool effects: A long-term follow-up of fourteen infant and preschool experiments* (Final report to Office of Human Development Services, Grant No. 18-76-07843). Ithaca, N.Y.: Community Services Laboratory, Cornell University, 1977.

Leiderman, P. H., & Leiderman, G. F. Affective and cognitive consequences of polymatric infant care in the East Africa Highlands. In A. D. Pick (Ed.), *Minnesota Symposium on Child Psychology* (Vol. 8). Minneapolis: University of Minnesota Press, 1974.

Leler, H., Johnson, D. L., Kahn, A. J., Hines, R. P., & Torres, M. *Houston Parent-Child Development Center* (Progress report to Office of Child Development, Grant No. CG60925). Houston, Tex.: University of Houston, 1975.

Levenstein, P. Cognitive growth in preschoolers through verbal interaction with mothers. *American Journal of Orthopsychiatry,* 1970, *40,* 426–432.

Levenstein, P. The Mother-Child Home Program. In M. C. Day & R. K. Parker (Eds.), *The preschool in action* (2nd ed.). Boston: Allyn & Bacon, 1977.

Levine, M. The academic achievement test: Its historical context and social functions. *American Psychologist,* 1979, *31,* 228–238.

Levitan, S. A., & Taggart, R. *The promise of greatness.* Cambridge, Mass.: Harvard University Press, 1976.

Lewis, M., Young, G., Brooks, J., & Michalson, L. The beginning of friendship. In M. Lewis & L. Rosenblum (Eds.), *Friendship and peer relations.* N.Y.: Wiley-Interscience, 1975.

Lewis, O. The culture of poverty. *Scientific American,* 1966, *215,* 19–25.

Lieberman, A. F. Preschoolers' competence with a peer: Relations with attachment and peer experience. *Child Development,* 1977, *48,* 1277–1287.

Lieberman, A. F. Psychology and day care. *Social Research,* 1978, *45,* 416–451.

Light, R. J., & Smith, P. V. Accumulating evidence: Procedures for resolving contradictions among different research studies. *Harvard Educational Review,* 1971, *41,* 429–471.

Lippman, M. Z., & Grote, B. H. *Social emotional effects of day care* (Final report, Office of Child Development, DHEW. June 1974. (ERIC Document Reproduction Service No. ED 110 164)

Loftus, E. G., & Monahan, J. Trial by data: Psychological research as legal evidence. *American Psychologist,* 1980, *35,* 270–283.

Lombard, A. D. *Home Instruction Program for Preschool Youngsters* (HIPPY). Unpublished manuscript, The National Council of Jewish Women, Center for Research in Education of the Disadvantaged, School of Education, The Hebrew University of Jerusalem, September 1973.

Lombard, A. D. *Success begins at home: Educational foundations for preschoolers.* New York: Heath, 1982.

Londerville, S., & Main, M. Security of attachment, compliance, and maternal training methods in the second year of life. *Developmental Psychology,* 1981, *17,* 189–199.

Lorenz, K. Z. *King Solomon's ring.* New York: Crowell, 1952.

Lougee, M. D. *Children's imitation of younger and older peers.* Unpublished doctoral dissertation, University of Minnesota, 1978.

Love, J. M., Nauta, M. J., Coelen, C. G., Hewett, K., & Ruopp, R. R. *National Home Start Evaluation* (Final report to Office of Child Development, HEW-105-72-1100). Department of Health, Education, and Welfare. Cambridge, Mass.: Abt Associates, 1976.

Lukas, C. V. Problems in implementing Head Start Planned Variation models. In A. M. Rivlin & P. M. Timpane (Eds.), *Planned variation in education: Should we give up or try harder?* Washington, D.C.: Brookings, 1975.

Macrae, J. W., & Herbert-Jackson, E. Are behavioral effects of infant day care programs specific? *Developmental Psychology*, 1976, *12*, 269–270.

Mahler, M. S., Pine, F., & Bergman, A. *The psychological birth of the human infant*. New York: Basic Books, 1975.

Main, M. B. Analysis of a peculiar form of reunion behavior seen in some day care children: Its history and sequelae in children who are home-reared. In R. A. Webb (Ed.), *Social development in childhood: Day care programs and research*. Baltimore: Johns Hopkins University Press, 1977.

Main, M., & Weston, D. R. The quality of the toddler's relationship to mother and father: Related to conflict behavior and the readiness to establish new relationships. *Child Development*, 1981, *52*, 932–940.

Mann, A. J., Harrell, A., & Hurt, M. *A review of Head Start research since 1969 and an annotated bibliography*. Washington, D.C.: U.S. Government Printing Office, No. 017-092-00037-5, 1978.

Mann, M., & Taylor, A. The effects of multisensory learning systems on the concept formation of young children. *Journal of Research and Development in Education*, 1973, *6*, 35–43.

Markey, F. V. Imaginative behavior of preschool children. *Child Development Monographs*, 1935, Serial No. 18.

Marvin, R. S. An ethological-cognitive model for the attenuation of mother-child attachment behavior. In T. Alloway, P. Pliner, & L. Krames (Eds.), *Attachment behavior*. New York: Plenum, 1977.

Marvin, R. S., VanDevander, T. L., Iwanaga, M. I., & Levine, R. A. Infant-caregiver attachment among the Hausa of Nigeria. In H. McGurk (Ed.), *Ethological factors in human development*. Amsterdam: North Holland, 1977.

Matas, L., Arend, R. A., & Sroufe, L. A. Continuity of adaptation in the second year: The relationship between quality of attachment and later competence. *Child Development*, 1978, *49*, 547–556.

Mayall, B., & Petrie, P. *Minder, mother, and child*. London: University of London, Institute of Education (Studies in Education, 5), 1977.

McCall, R. B. The development of intellectual functioning in infancy and the prediction of later IQ. In J. Osofsky (Ed.), *Handbook of infant development*. New York: Wiley, 1979.

McGrew, W. C. Aspects of social development in nursery school children with emphasis on introduction to the group. In N. Blurton Jones (Ed.), *Ethological studies of child behavior*. London: Cambridge University Press, 1972.

Meadows, S., Philips, J., Weaver, J., & Mably, S. *Adults' and children's views on education, and their behavior at home and in nursery school: A report on two pilot studies*. Paper given at the BPS London Conference, December 19, 1977.

Meissner, M., Humphreys, E., Meis, C., & Schea, J. No exit for wives: Sexual division of labour and the cumulation of household demands. *Canadian Review of Sociology and Anthropology*, 1975, *12*, 424–439.

Mercer, J. R. A policy statement on assessment procedures and the rights of children. *Harvard Educational Review*, 1974, *44*, 125–141.

Miller, L. B., & Dyer, J. L. Four preschool programs: Their dimensions and effects. *Monographs of the Society for Research in Child Development*, 1975, *40*(5–6, Serial No. 162).

Moely, B. E., Skarin, K., & Weil, S. Sex differences in competition-cooperation behavior of children at two age levels. *Sex Roles*, 1979, *5*, 329–342.

Montes, F., & Risley, T. R. Evaluating traditional day care practices: An empirical approach. *Child Care Quarterly*, 1975, *4*, 208–215.

Moore, O. K., & Anderson, A. R. The responsive environment project. In H. R. Hess & R. Bear (Eds.), *Early education*. Chicago: Aldine-Atherton, 1968.

Moore, O. K., & Anderson, A. R. Some principles for the design of clarifying education environments. In D. A. Goslin (Ed.), *Handbook of socialization theory and research*. Chicago: Rand-McNally, 1969.

Moore, T. W. Effects on the children. In S. Yudkin & A. Holme (Eds.), *Working mothers and their children*. London: Sphere Books, 1969.

Moore, T. Exclusive early mothering and its alternatives: The outcomes to adolescence. *Scandanavian Journal of Psychology*, 1975, *16*, 255–272.

Morris, A. G., London, R., & Glick, J. Educational intervention for preschool children in a pediatric clinic. *Pediatrics*, 1976, *57*, 765–768.

Moskowitz, D. S., Schwarz, J. C., & Corsini, D. A. Initiating day care at three years of age: Effects on attachment. *Child Development*, 1977, *48*, 1271–1276.

Moynihan, D. P. The president's task force on manpower conservation. In D. P. Moynihan (Ed.), *One-third of a nation: A report on young men found unqualified for military service*. Washington, D.C.: U.S. Government Printing Office, 1964.

Mueller, E. (Toddlers + toys) = (An autonomous social system). In M. Lewis & L. A. Rosenblum (Eds.), *The child in its family*. New York: Plenum, 1979.

Mueller, E., & Brenner, J. The origins of social skills and interaction among playgroup toddlers. *Child Development*, 1977, *48*, 854–861.

Murphy, L. B. *Social behavior and child personality*. New York: Columbia University Press, 1937.

Mussen, P. H. (Ed.). *Carmichael's manual of child psychology* (3rd ed.). New York: Wiley, 1970.

Nahir, H. T., & Yussen, S. R. The performance of kibbutz- and city-reared Israeli children on two role-taking tasks. *Developmental Psychology*, 1977, *13*, 450–455.

Nimnicht, G. *Research on the New Nursery, Part 1. A summary of the evaluation of the experimental program for deprived children at the New Nursery School using some experimental measures*. Unpublished manuscript, Colorado State College, 1967.

Nimnicht, G., Arango, M., & Adcock, D. The Parent/Child Toy Library Program. In M. C. Day & R. K. Parker (Eds.), *The preschool in action* (2nd ed.). Boston: Allyn & Bacon, 1977.

O'Connor, M. The nursery school environment. *Developmental Psychology*, 1975, *11*, 556–561.

Orlick, T. D. Positive socialization via cooperative games. *Developmental Psychology*, 1981, *17*, 426–429.

Page, E. B. Miracle in Milwaukee: Raising the IQ. In B. Z. Friedlander, G. M. Sterret, & G. E. Kirk (Eds.), *Exceptional infant*. New York: Brunner/Mazel, 1975.

Palmer, F. H., & Siegel, R. J. Minimal intervention at ages two and three and subsequent intellective changes. In M. C. Day & R. K. Parker (Eds.), *The preschool in action* (2nd ed.). Boston: Allyn & Bacon, 1977.

Papert, S. *Mindstorms: Children, computers, and powerful ideas*. New York: Basic Books, 1980.

Parten, M. B. Social participation among preschool children. *Journal of Abnormal Social Psychology*, 1932, *27*, 243–269.

Passman, R. H., & Weisberg, P. Mothers and blankets as agents for promoting play and exploration by young children in a novel environment: The effects of social and nonsocial attachment objects. *Developmental Psychology*, 1975, *11*, 170–177.

Payne, J. S., & Mercer, C. D. *Head Start—Tragicomedy with epilogue*. New York: Behavioral Publications, 1973.

Peaslee, M. V. *The development of competency in 2-year-old infants in day care and home reared environments*. Unpublished doctoral dissertation, Florida State University, 1976.

Pedersen, F., Cain, R., Zaslow, M., & Anderson, B. *Variation in infant experience associated with alternative family role organization*. Paper presented at the International Conference on Infancy Studies, New Haven, April 1980.

Pfeifer, M. R. *The effects of varying age-grade status of models on the imitative behavior of six-year-old boys*. Unpublished doctoral dissertation, University of Delaware, 1971.

Portnoy, F. C., & Simmons, C. H. Day care and attachment. *Child Development*, 1978, *49*, 239–242.

Powell, D. R. The interpersonal relationship between parents and caregivers in day care settings. *American Journal of Orthopsychiatry*, 1978, *48*, 680–689.

Powell, D. R. Family-environment relations and early child-rearing: The role of social networks and neighborhood. *Journal of Research and Development in Education*, 1979, *13*, 1–11.

Powell, D. R. *Finding child care: A study of parents' search processes*. Unpublished manuscript, Merrill-Palmer Institute, 1980.

Prescott, E. *A comparison of three types of day care and nursery school-home care*. Pasadena, Calif.: Pacific Oaks College, 1973. (ERIC Document Reproduction Service No. ED 078 910)

Prescott, E. Is day care as good as a home? *Young Children*, 1978, *33*, 13–19.

Prescott, E., & Jones, E., with Kritchevsky, S. *Group day care as a child-rearing environment. An observational study of day care programs*. Pasadena, Calif.: Pacific Oaks College, 1967.

President's Panel on Mental Retardation. Report of the task force on prevention, clinical services, and residential care. Washington, D.C.: Public Health Service, 1963. (University Microfilms No. 77-7, 149)

Price, G. G. How cognitive abilities of preschool children are influenced by maternal teaching behavior: A causal model analysis. Unpublished doctoral dissertation, Stanford University, 1976.

Provost, M. A. The effects of day care in child development. *Canada's Mental Health*, 1980, *28*, 17–20.

Quilitch, H., & Risley, T. The effects of play materials on social play. *Journal of Applied Behavior Analysis*, 1973, *6*, 573–578.

Rabinowitz, F., Moely, B. E., Finkel, N., & McClinton, S. The effects of toy novelty and social interaction on the exploratory behavior of preschool children. *Child Development,* 1975, *46,* 286–289.

Radin, N. The role of father in cognitive, academic, and intellectual development. In M. E. Lamb (Ed.), *The role of the father in child development.* New York: Wiley, 1976.

Radin, N. Childrearing fathers in intact families. I. Some antecedents and consequences. *Merrill-Palmer Quarterly,* 1981, *27,* 489–514.

Ragozin, A. *Attachment and day care children; field and laboratory findings.* Paper presented at the meeting of the Society for Research in Child Development, Denver, April 1975.

Ragozin, A. S. *Attachment behavior of day care and home-reared children in a laboratory setting.* Paper presented at the meeting of the Society for Research in Child Development, New Orleans, March 1977.

Raizen, S., & Bobrow, S. B. *Design for a national evaluation of social competence in Head Start children* (Prepared for the Office of Child Development, Department of Health, Education, and Welfare, R-1557-HEW). Santa Monica, Calif.: Rand, 1974.

Ramey, C. T., Dorval, B., & Baker-Ward, L. Group day care and socially disadvantaged families: Effects on the child and the family. In S. Kilmer (Ed.), *Advances in early education and day care,* (Vol. 3). Greenwich, Conn.: JAI Press, in press.

Ramey, C. T., MacPhee, D., & Yeates, K. O. Preventing developmental retardation: A general systems model. In L. Bond & J. Joffe (Eds.), *Facilitating infant and early childhood development.* Hanover, N.H.: University Press of New England, 1982.

Ramey, C. T., & Mills, P. J. Social and intellectual consequences of day care for high-risk infants. In R. A. Webb (Ed.), *Social development in childhood: Day care programs and research.* Baltimore: Johns Hopkins University Press, 1977.

Raph, J. B., Thomas, A., Chess, S., & Korn, S. Influence of nursery school on social interactions. *American Journal of Orthopsychiatry,* 1968, *38,* 144–152.

Reese, H. W., & Overton, W. F. Models, methods, and ethics of intervention. In R. R. Turner & H. W. Reese (Eds.), *Life-span developmental psychology.* New York: Academic Press, 1980.

Reuter, J., & Yunik, G. Social interaction in nursery schools. *Developmental Psychology,* 1973, *9,* 319–325.

Reynolds, N. J., & Risley, T. R. The role of social and material reinforcers in increasing talking of a disadvantaged preschool child. *Journal of Applied Behavior Analysis,* 1968, *1,* 253–262.

Rheingold, H. L., & Eckerman, C. O. The infant separates himself from his mother. *Science,* 1970, *168,* 78–83.

Ricciuti, H. N. Fear and the development of social attachments in the first year of life. In M. Lewis & L. A. Rosenblum (Eds.), *The origins of fear.* New York: Wiley, 1974.

Ricciuti, H. N. *Effects of infant day care experience on behavior and development: Research and implications for social policy.* (Review prepared for the Office of the Assistant Secretary for Planning and Evaluation, Department of Health, Education, and Welfare). Cornell University, 1976.

Rivlin, A. M., & Timpane, M. P. Planned variations in education: An assessment. In A. M. Rivlin & P. M. Timpane (Eds.), *Planned variation in education: Should we give up or try harder?* Washington, D.C.: Brookings, 1975.

Robertson, J., & Robertson, J. Young children in brief separation: A fresh look. *Psychoanalytic Study of the Child,* 1971, *26,* 264–315.

Robinson, H. B., & Robinson, N. M. Longitudinal development of very young children in a comprehensive day care program: The first two years. *Child Development,* 1971, *42,* 1673–1683.

Robinson, J. P., Yerby, J., Fieweger, M., & Somerick, N. Sex-role differences in time use. *Sex Roles,* 1977, *3,* 443–458.

Robinson, M. *Parent-Child Development Centers: An experiment in infant-parent interventions and systematic testing of social innovations* (R & D Planning memorandum, Office of Research Plans and Evaluation). Washington, D.C.: Office of Economic Opportunity, 1972.

Robinson, M. *Introduction to the Parent-Child Development Centers.* Paper presented at the meeting of the Society for Research in Child Development, Denver, April 1975.

Rogosa, D. Causal models in longitudinal research: Rationale, formulation, and interpretation. In J. R. Nesselroade & P. B. Baltes (Eds.), *Longitudinal research in human development: Design and analysis.* New York: Academic Press, 1978.

Rohe, W., & Patterson, A. H. The effects of varied levels of resources and density on behavior in a day care center. In D. H. Carson (Ed.), *Man-Environment Interactions.* EDRA, 1974.

Romaine, M. F., & Teets, S. *A comparison of attachment behavior observed in day care and home-reared infants* (The University of Tennessee). Paper presented at the Southeastern Conference on Research in Child Development, Williamsburg, Va., April 1972.

Roopnarine, J. L., & Lamb, M. E. The effects of day care on attachment and exploratory behavior in a strange situation. *Merrill-Palmer Quarterly*, 1978, *24*, 85–95.

Roopnarine, J. L., & Lamb, M. E. Peer and parent-child interaction before and after enrollment in nursery school. *Journal of Applied Developmental Psychology*, 1980, *1*, 77–81.

Rosenberg, B. G., & Sutton-Smith, B. Family structure and sex-role variations. In J. K. Cole & R. Dienstbier (Eds.), *Nebraska Symposium on Motivation*, (Vol. 21). Lincoln: University of Nebraska Press, 1973.

Rosenberg, S. E. *Individual differences in infant attachment: Relationships to mother, infant, and interaction system variables*. Unpublished doctoral dissertation, Bowling Green State University, 1975. (Dissertation Abstracts International, 1975, *36*, 1930B; University Microfilms No. 75-22, 954)

Rosenshine, B. *Teaching behaviors and student achievement*. Windsor, England: National Foundation for Educational Research in England and Wales, 1971.

Ross, C. J. Early skirmishes with poverty: The historical roots of Head Start. In E. Zigler & J. Valentine (Eds.), *Project Head Start: A legacy of the War on Poverty*. New York: Free Press, 1979.

Rubenstein, J., & Howes, C. The effects of peers on toddler interaction with mother and toys. *Child Development*, 1976, *47*, 597–605.

Rubenstein, J. L., & Howes, C. Caregiving and infant behavior in day care and in homes. *Developmental Psychology*, 1979, *15*, 1–24.

Rubenstein, J. L., & Howes, C. Adaptation to day care. In S. Kilmer (Ed.), *Advances in early education and day care*, (Vol. 4). Greenwich, Conn.: JAI Press, in press.

Rubenstein, J. L., Howes, C., & Boyle, P. A two year follow-up of infants in community based infant day care. *Journal of Child Psychology and Psychiatry*, 1981, *22*, 209–218.

Rubenstein, J. L., Pedersen, F. A., & Yarrow, L. J. What happens when mother is away: A comparison of mothers and substitute caregivers. *Developmental Psychology*, 1977, *13*, 529–530.

Ruopp, R., Travers, J., Glantz, F., & Coelen, C. *Children at the center*. Cambridge, Mass.: Abt Associates, 1979.

Rusk, B. A. *An evaluation of a six-week Head Start program using an academically oriented curriculum: Canton, 1967*. Unpublished manuscript, University of Illinois, 1968.

Rutter, M. *The qualities of mothering: Maternal deprivation reassessed*. New York: Jason Aronson, 1974.

Rutter, M. Maternal deprivation, 1972–1978: New findings, new concepts, new approaches. *Child Development*, 1979, *50*, 283–305. (a)

Rutter, M. Separation experiences: A new look at an old topic. *Journal of Pediatrics*, 1979, *95*, 147–154. (b)

Rutter, M. Social-emotional consequences of day care for preschool children. In E. F. Zigler & E. W. Gordon (Eds.), *Day care: Scientific and social policy issues*. Boston: Auburn House, 1982.

Sale, J. S., & Torres, Y. L. *I'm not just a babysitter*. A descriptive report of the community family day care project. Pasadena, Calif.: Pacific Oaks College, 1971. (ERIC Document Reproduction Service No. ED 056758)

Saltz, E., Dixon, D., & Johnson, J. Training disadvantaged preschoolers on various fantasy activities: Effects on cognitive functioning and impulse control. *Child Development*, 1977, *48*, 367–380.

Sarason, S. B. An unsuccessful war on poverty? *American Psychologist*, 1978, *33*, 831–839.

Saunders, M., & Keister, M. *Family day care: Some observations*. ERIC, 1972.

Saunders, M. M., & Keister, M. E. *Follow-up studies of children enrolled in a group day care program in infancy*. Unpublished manuscript, Department of Child Development and Family Relations, University of North Carolina at Greensboro, 1979.

Scarr, S. *On the development of competence and the indeterminate boundaries between cognition and motivation: A genotype-environment correlation theory*. Paper prepared for the Conference on Home Influences on School Achievement, Wisconsin Research and Development Center, Madison, Wis., October 1981.

Schachter, F. F. Toddlers with employed mothers. *Child Development*, 1981, *52*, 958–964.

Schaefer, E. S., & Aaronson, M. Infant Education Project: Implementation and implications of the home-tutoring program. In R. K. Parker (Ed.), *The preschool in action*. Boston: Allyn & Bacon,

1972 (2nd ed. 1977).

Schaffer, H. R., & Emerson, P. E. The development of social attachments in infancy. *Monographs of the Society for Research in Child Development,* 1964, *29*(3, Serial No. 94).

Schlossman, S. Before Home Start: Notes toward a history of parent education in America, 1897–1929. *Harvard Educational Review,* 1976, *46,* 436–467.

Schubert, J. B., Bradley-Johnson, S., & Nuttal, J. Mother-infant communication and maternal employment. *Child Development,* 1980, *51,* 246–249.

Schwartz, P. M. Length of daily separations due to child care and attachment behaviors of 18 month-old infants. Child Development, 1983, in press.

Schwarz, J. C., Krolick, G., & Strickland, R. G. Effects of early day care experience on adjustment to a new environment. *American Journal of Orthopsychiatry,* 1973, *43,* 340–346.

Schwarz, J. C., Strickland, R. G., & Krolick, G. Infant day care: Behavioral effects at preschool age. *Developmental Psychology,* 1974, *10,* 502–506.

Schweinhart, L. J., & Weikart, D. P. Young children grow up: The effects of the Perry Preschool Program on youths through age 15. *Monographs of the High Scope Educational Research Foundation,* 1980, No. 3.

Seitz, V. A methodological comment on "The problem of infant day care." In E. F. Zigler & E. W. Gordon (Eds.), *Day care: Scientific and social policy issues.* Boston: Auburn House, 1982.

Serbin, L. A., Connor, J. M., & Citron, C. C. Environmental control of independent and dependent behaviors in preschool girls and boys: A model for early independence training. *Sex Roles,* 1978, *4,* 867–875.

Shapira, A., & Madsen, M. Between- and within-group cooperation and competition among kibbutz and nonkibbutz children. *Developmental Psychology,* 1974, *10,* 140–145.

Shure, M. E. Psychological ecology of a nursery school. *Child Development,* 1963, *34,* 979–999.

Silvern, L. E., Waterman, J. M., Sobesky, W., & Ryan, V. L. Effects of a developmental model of perspective taking training. *Child Development,* 1979, *50,* 243–246.

Silverstein, L. *A critical review of current research on infant day care.* Paper prepared for the six-country study "Alternative Policies for Caring for Children Under the Age of Three," November 1977.

Sjolund, A. *The effect of day care institutions on children's development: An analysis of international research.* Copenhagen: The Danish National Institute of Social Research, February 1971.

Skeels, H. M., & Dye, H. B. A study of the effects of differential stimulation on mentally retarded children. *Proceedings of the American Association of Mental Deficiency,* 1939, *44,* 114.

Skinner, B. F. Teaching machines. *Science,* 1958, *128,* 969–977.

Slaughter, D. T. *Parent education for low-income black families.* Paper presented at General Mills American Family Forum, Washington, D.C., October 1977.

Smith, M. S. Design strategies for experimental studies. In A. M. Rivlin & P. M. Timpane (Eds.), *Planned variation in education: Should we give up or try harder?* Washington, D.C.: Brookings, 1975. (a)

Smith, M. S. Evaluation findings in Head Start planned variations. In A. M. Rivlin & P. M. Timpane (Eds.), *Planned variation in education: Should we give up or try harder?* Washington, D.C.: Brookings, 1975. (b)

Smith, P. K. Social and situational determinants of fear in the playgroup. In M. Lewis & L. A. Rosenblum (Eds.), *The origins of fear.* New York: Wiley, 1974.

Smith, P. K. Shared care of young children: Alternative models to monotropism. *Merrill-Palmer Quarterly,* 1980, *26,* 371–390.

Smith, P. K., & Connolly, K. Patterns of play and social interaction in preschool children. In N. Blurton Jones (Ed.), *Ecological studies of child behavior.* Cambridge, Eng.: Cambridge University Press, 1972.

Smith, P. K., & Connolly, K. J. *The behavioral ecology of the preschool.* Cambridge, England: Cambridge University Press, 1981.

Smith, P. K., Eaton, L., & Hindmarsh, A. How one-year-olds respond to strangers: A two person situation. *Journal of Genetic Psychology,* in press.

Snow, M. E., Jacklin, C. N., & Maccoby, E. E. Birth-order differences in peer sociability at thirty-three months. *Child Development,* 1981, *52,* 589–595.

Soar, R. S., & Soar, R. M. *An attempt to identify measures of teacher effectiveness from four studies.* Paper presented at the American Educational Research Association Meeting, San Francisco, April 1976.

Sonquist, H., *A model for low-income and chicano parent education.* Final report, Santa Barbara

Family Care Center, California, 1975. (ERIC Document Reproduction Service No. ED 113 063)

Spitz, R. A. Hospitalism. *Psychoanalytic Study of the Child,* 1946, *2,* 113–117.

Spivak, G., & Shure, M. B. *Social adjustment of young children.* San Francisco: Jossey-Bass, 1974.

Sroufe, L. A., & Waters, E. Attachment as an organizational construct. *Child Development,* 1977, *48,* 1184–1199.

Stallings, J. A. Implementation and child effects of teaching practice in Follow-Through classrooms. *Monographs for the Society for Research in Child Development,* 1975, *40*(3, Serial No. 163).

Stallings, J. A. An observational study of family day care. In J. C. Colbert (Ed.), *Home day care: A perspective.* Chicago: Roosevelt University, 1980.

Stallings, J. A., & Wilcox, M. A. *Collecting data for a day care study at the national level.* Paper presented at the meeting of the American Educational Research Association, San Francisco, April 1976.

Steinberg, L. D., & Green, C. *Three types of day care: Choices, concerns, and consequences.* Unpublished manuscript, University of California, Irvine, 1977.

Steinberg, L. D., & Green, C. *How parents may mediate the effect of day care.* Paper presented at the meeting of the Society for Research in Child Development, San Francisco, March 1979.

Stukat, K. G. *Lekkskolans inverkan pa barns utveckling* (The influence of preschool on the child's development), 1969. Cited in R. Berfenstam, & I. William-Olsson, *Early child care in Sweden.* London: Gordon & Breach, 1973.

Sunley, R. Early nineteenth century American literature on childrearing. In M. Mead & M. Wolfenstein (Eds.), *Childhood in contemporary cultures.* Chicago: University of Chicago Press, 1955.

Suransky, V. *The erosion of childhood.* Chicago: University of Chicago Press, 1982.

Swift, J. W. Effects of early group experience: The nursery school and day nursery. In M. L. Hoffman & L. W. Hoffman (Eds.), *Review of child development research.* New York: Russell Sage Foundation, 1964.

Sylva, K., Roy, C., & Painter, M. *Child watching at play group and nursery school.* London: Grant McIntyre, 1980.

Tamminen, A. W. *An evaluation of a preschool training program for culturally deprived children.* Unpublished manuscript, University of Minnesota, 1967. (ERIC Document Reproduction Service No. ED 019 135)

Taub, H., & Wilkerson, D. *A proposal for the development of measures of social competence.* Proposal submitted by Mediax Associates to the Office of Child Development, Department of Health, Education, and Welfare, March 25, 1977.

Taylor, L. J. Outcome and process evaluation of a day care centre. *Canadian Journal of Behavioural Science,* 1976, *8,* 410–413.

Thomopoulos, E., & Huyck, M. H. *Love and labor: Happy wives, worried mothers.* Paper presented at the convention of the American Psychological Association, Washington, D.C., 1976.

Thompson, W. R., & Grusec, J. Studies of early experience. In P. H. Mussen (Ed.), *Carmichael's manual of child psychology.* New York: Wiley, 1970.

Tizard, B. No common ground? *Times (London) Educational Supplement,* May 27, 1977, No. 15.

Tizard, B., Carmichael, H., Hughes, M., & Pinkerton, G. Four-year-olds talking to mothers and teachers. In L. A. Hersoveval (Ed.), *Language and language disorders in childhood (Supplement No. 2, Journal of Child Psychology and Psychiatry).* London: Pergamon Press, 1980.

Tizard, B., Philips, J., & Plewis, I. Play in preschool centres. II. Effects on play of the child's social class and of the educational orientation of the centre. *Journal of Child Psychology and Psychiatry,* 1976, *17,* 265–274. (a)

Tizard, B., Philips, J., & Plewis, I. Play in preschool centres. I. Play and measures and their relation to age, sex, and I.Q. *Journal of Child Psychology and Psychiatry,* 1976, *17,* 251–264. (b)

Tizard, B., Philips, J., & Plewis, I. Staff behaviour in preschool centres. *Journal of Child Psychology and Psychiatry,* 1976, *17,* 21–33. (c)

Tizard, J., & Tizard, B. The social development of two-year-old children in residential nurseries. In H. R. Schaffer (Ed.), *The origins of human social relations.* New York: Academic Press, 1971.

Trickett, P. Career development in Head Start. In E. Zigler & J. Valentine (Eds.), *Project Head Start: A legacy of the War on Poverty.* New York: Free Press, 1979.

Tyler, B., & Dittman, L. Meeting the toddler more than halfway: The behavior of toddlers and their caregivers. *Young Children,* 1980, *35,* 39–46.

Tyler, R. W. Changing concepts of educational evaluation. *Perspectives of curriculum evaluation. AREA monograph series on curriculum evaluation.* Chicago: Rand-McNally, 1967.

Tyler, R. W., & Wolf, R. M. *Crucial issues in testing.* Berkeley, Calif.: McCutcheon, 1974.

Valentine, J., & Stark, E. The social context of parent involvement in Head Start. In E. Zigler & J. Valentine (Eds.), *Project Head Start: A legacy of the War on Poverty.* New York: Free Press, 1979.

Van Alstyn, D. *Play behavior and choice of play materials of preschool children.* Chicago: University of Chicago Press, 1932.

Vandell, D. L. Effects of a playgroup experience on mother-son and father-son interaction. *Developmental Psychology,* 1979, *15,* 379–385.

Vandell, D. L., Wilson, K. S., & Whalen, W. T. Birth-order and social-experience differences in infant-peer interaction. *Developmental Psychology,* 1981, *17,* 438–445.

Van de Riet, V., & Van de Riet, H. *A follow-up evaluation of the effects of a unique sequential learning program, a traditional preschool program, and a no-treatment program on culturally deprived children* (University of Florida, Contract No. B89-4425). Department of Health, Education, and Welfare, December 1969.

Van Lieshout, C. F., Leckie, G., & Smits-Van Sonsbeek, B. *The effect of a social perspective-taking training on empathy and role-taking ability of preschool children.* Paper presented at the International Society for the Study of Behavioral Development, Ann Arbor, Mich., August 1973.

Vaughn, B., Egeland, B., & Sroufe, L. A. Individual differences in infant-mother attachment at twelve and eighteen months: Stability and change in families under stress. *Child Development,* 1979, *50,* 971–975.

Vaughn, B. E., Gove, F. L., & Egeland, B. The relationship between out-of-home care and the quality of infant-mother attachment in an economically disadvantaged population. *Child Development,* 1980, *51,* 1203–1214.

Vroegh, K. *Infant day care: Some research findings.* Unpublished manuscript, Institute for Juvenile Research, Chicago, 1976. (ERIC Document Reproduction Service No. ED 145 968)

Wachs, T. D. The relationship of infants' physical environment to their Binet performance at 2½ years. *International Journal of Behavioral Development,* 1978, *1,* 51–65.

Walberg, H. *Home environment and school learning: Some quantitative models and research synthesis.* Paper presented at conference: Home influences on school achievement, Wisconsin Research and Development Center, University of Wisconsin, Madison, October 1981.

Walker, K. E., & Woods, M. E. *Time care of family members.* Use-of-Time Research Project, Human Ecology, Cornell University (Working Paper No. 1), September 1972.

Wandersman, L. P., & Wandersman, A. *Facilitating growth for all the family in adjustment to a newborn.* Paper presented at the National Conference on Family Relations, New York, October 1976.

Wang, M. C. Psychometric studies in the validation of an early learning curriculum. *Child Development,* 1973, *44,* 54–60.

Waters, E., Vaughn, B. E., & Egeland, B. R. Individual differences in infant-mother attachment relationships at age one: Antecedents in neonatal behavior in an urban, economically disadvantaged sample. *Child Development,* 1980, *51,* 208–216.

Weikart, D. P. Effects of different curricula in early childhood intervention. *Educational Evaluation and Policy Analysis,* 1981, *3,* 25–35.

Weikart, D. P., Bond, J. T., & McNeil, J. T. The Ypsilanti Preschool Project: Preschool years and longitudinal results. *Monographs of the High Scope Educational Research Foundation,* 1978, No. 3.

Weikart, D. P., Rogers, L., Adcock, C., & McClelland, D. *The cognitively oriented curriculum: A framework for preschool teachers.* Urbana: University of Illinois—NAEYC, 1971.

Weikart, D. P., & Wiegerink, R. Initial results of a comparative preschool curriculum project. *Proceedings of the 76th Annual Convention of the American Psychological Association,* 1968, *3,* 597–598.

Weinraub, M., & Lewis, M. The determinants of children's responses to separation. *Monographs of the Society for Research in Child Development,* 1977, *42*(4, Serial No. 172).

Weisner, T. S., & Gallimore, R. My brother's keeper: Child and sibling caretaking. *Current Anthropology,* 1977, *18,* 169–190.

Welch, S., & Booth, A. Employment and health among married women with children. *Sex Roles,* 1977, *3,* 385–397.

West, H. Early peer-group interaction and role-taking skills: An investigation of Israeli children. *Child Development,* 1974, *45,* 1118–1121.

White, S. H., Day, M. C., Freeman, P. K., Hantman, S. A., & Messenger, K. P. *Federal pro-*

grams for young children: Review and recommendations. Washington, D.C.: Government Printing Office, 1973.

Wiener, N. *Cybernetics*. New York: Wiley, 1948.

Wilcox, B. M., Staff, P., & Romaine, M. F. A comparison of individual with multiple assignment of caregivers to infants in day care. *Merrill-Palmer Quarterly,* 1980, *26,* 53–62.

Wille, D., & Jacobson, J. *Development of capacity to cope with brief parental separations at 18 months*. Paper presented at the International Conference on Infant Studies, Austin, Texas, March 1982.

Willis, G. *Qualitative evaluation: Concepts and cases in curriculum criticism*. Berkeley, Calif.: McCutcheon, 1978.

Winetsky, C. S. Comparison of the expectations of parents and teachers of preschool children. *Child Development,* 1978, *49,* 1146–1154.

Winnett, R. A., Fuchs, W. L., Moffatt, S., & Nerviano, V. J. A cross-sectional study of children and their families in different child care environments. *Journal of Community Psychology,* 1977, *5,* 149–159.

Wishy, B. *The child and the republic*. Philadelphia: University of Pennsylvania Press, 1972.

Wright, J. D. Are working women *really* more satisfied? Evidence from several national surveys. *Journal of Marriage and the Family,* 1978, *40,* 301–313.

Wynn, R. L. *The effect of a playmate on day care and home-reared toddlers in a strange situation*. Paper presented at the meeting of the Society for Research in Child Development, San Francisco, March 1979.

Yarrow, M. R., Scott, P. M., & Waxler, C. Z. Learning concern for others. *Developmental Psychology,* 1973, *8,* 240–260.

Young, S. F. *Paternal involvement as related to maternal employment and attachment behavior directed to the father by the one-year-old infant*. Unpublished doctoral dissertation, Ohio State University, 1975.

Zajonc, R. B., & Markus, G. B. Birth order and intellectual development. *Psychological Review,* 1975, *82,* 74–88.

Zigler, E., Abelson, W., & Seitz, V. Motivational factors in the performance of economically disadvantaged children on the Peabody Picture Vocabulary Test. *Child Development,* 1973, *44,* 294–303.

Zigler, E., & Butterfield, E. C. Motivational aspects of changes in IQ test performances of culturally deprived nursery school children. *Child Development,* 1968, *39,* 1–14.

Zigler, E., & Trickett, P. K. IQ, social competence, and evaluation of early childhood intervention programs. *American Psychologist,* 1978, *33,* 789–799.

Zigler, E., & Valentine, J. *Project Head Start: A legacy of the War on Poverty*. New York: Free Press, 1979.

Zimiles, H. A radical and regressive solution to the problem of evaluation. In L. G. Katz (Ed.), *Current topics in early childhood education,* (Vol. 1). Norwood, N.J.: Ablex, 1977.

ATTENTION, LEARNING, AND MEMORY IN INFANTS* | 12

GARY M. OLSON, *University of Michigan*
TRACY SHERMAN, *University of California at Los Angeles*

CHAPTER CONTENTS

*Preparation of this chapter was supported by a Research Career Development Award (HD 00169) and a research grant (HD 10486) from the National Institute of Child Health and Human Development to the first author and by a postdoctoral fellowship from the National Institute of Mental Health (MH 16381) and UCLA to the second author. The authors are grateful for the comments of Joseph Campos, Marshall Haith, Joan Olson, Judith Reitman, Mark Strauss, and Barbara Zimmerman at various stages in the writing of this chapter. Bonnie Holcomb used her expertise in word processing to transform successive drafts from chaos to order and Mary Jo Blahna provided editorial assistance.

INTRODUCTION

Birth marks the transition from life in an environment with information of limited richness to what James (1890) suggested is the "blooming, buzzing confusion" of the external world. As we all know, it is a world filled with events and objects presenting information to all of the senses. Some of the senses, particularly vision and audition, have especially rich information available to them. The infant comes equipped with many skills for coping with this world. Other chapters in this volume document the sensory and perceptual capacities of the infant that govern the range and character of the information from the world that is available to the infant. In this chapter we will focus on how the infant attends to the information that is presented by the senses, and how information comes to have an enduring effect on the infant through learning and memory.

All too often psychologists have reduced the study of specific phenomena to issues surrounding particular tasks or paradigms. This has certainly been true in the history of the study of learning and memory and has also characterized the study of these phenomena in infancy. In our view, this approach limits our understanding, because one of the most essential qualities of a useful explanation of a set of phenomena is transferability or generalizability. A conceptualization of learning and memory that is confined to traditional tasks is weak at best. Learning and memory are central to intelligent behavior and thus form an important component of almost any psychologically important domain. If our knowledge of learning and memory is not developed to be general, our understanding of virtually any psychological phenomenon we might examine will be seriously incomplete. Developing a useful conceptualization of learning and memory in the sense we have just been discussing is of course extremely challenging. In this chapter we will offer a theoretical framework for interpreting the specific tasks and phenomena that have resulted from a period of intense experimental study of learning and memory in infants.

Science is rooted in its methods, and thus the chapter begins with a review of the experimental methods that have been used to study attention, learning, and memory in infants. The focus of this section will be the methodological issues involved in the use of various tasks and measures. Although we will focus on the most commonly used tasks and methods, we will also briefly examine a wider range of behaviors that can be studied. Next, we will review the research literature in order to draw conclusions about the infant's developing skills, focusing on research carried out in the last decade or so. Given that infancy is a period of great change, we will give special attention to the nature of the infant's skills at different periods of development. A final section will present a characterization of the information processing skills implicated in the various behaviors exhibited by the infant. The methods used to study infants will be analyzed in terms of this general conceptual framework, and some generalizations about the nature of acquisition and retention in infancy will be proposed. We will also speculate about the mechanisms of development.

Our primary focus is on how the infant acquires and retains information. To put it differently, we are mainly interested in how the infant comes to know rather than in what the infant knows. However, these two issues are inextricably linked: what is attended to, learned, and remembered is related to what is known. The topics of sensation, perception, and cognition, which are covered in other chapters in this volume, are directly related to attention, learning, and memory. Thus, we will necessarily cover some material that appears in other chapters. However, our focus on acquisition and retention will give our discussion of these topics a different character.

METHODS FOR STUDYING ATTENTION, LEARNING, AND MEMORY

Almost all that the infant does has the potential for revealing information about learning and memory abilities. However, in this chapter we will confine ourselves to those behaviors that have actually been used by investigators to study these abilities. In this section we will describe the methods that have been used and will discuss the advantages, disadvantages, and special methodological issues associated with their use. The goal of the study of infant information processing is to learn about the mental processes and structures that represent the source of the ability to learn and remember. Specific laboratory tasks have complex, indirect relationships to these mental phenomena, but they are our primary path to inferences about them. Ultimately, however, it is the mental phenomena, not the tasks, that are the object of our inquiry. In the section titled *Conceptual Framework* we will discuss how performance in some of these tasks is related to one conception of the internal processes and structures.

Measures of Attention

Because learning and memory depend on attentional processes, we will begin our survey by examining methods that have been used to study attention. There are at least two distinct senses of attention that must be kept separate. The first is the overall level of activation or *arousal*. A person can be alert, drowsy, drugged, or asleep, and these differences affect the acquisition and retention of environmental information. The second sense of attention is that of *selection*. There is far more information in the environment than the limited-capacity human information processing system can handle at once, so a person must selectively attend to what is presented to the senses, either as an outcome of certain involuntary reflexes or as part of controlled, voluntary examination of the perceptual field. Recent research has shown that selection in adults is not merely a matter of receptor orientation but involves purely central, cognitively controlled components (Neisser, 1967; Posner, 1978).

There is a possible third sense of attention that is related to both of these first two. Kahneman (1973) described this as the intensive aspect of attention, or *effort*. We are all familiar with the idea of "paying attention." As an aspect of selectively attending to a certain feature of the environment we can devote more effort to its processing. Kahneman argued that this aspect of attention should be considered distinct from arousal, and other theoreticians have supported this view (e.g., Norman & Bobrow, 1975). Conceptually, this means that even within a given state of general arousal there is a pool of attentional resources that can be allocated or used differentially. We are not sure how clearly this third sense of attention can be differentiated within the phenomena available for study in infancy, so we will not consider effort separately from arousal. However, distinguishing between arousal and effort will ultimately be important for a developmental theory of attention.

We will divide our review of methods of studying attention into two broad sections, the first on arousal and the second on selection. Our goal in each section is to discuss briefly the nature of the methods and their role in the studying of the infant's information processing abilities. In many cases very detailed reviews are available elsewhere, so we will not duplicate these discussions here.

Measures of Arousal and Attentiveness

The overall level of arousal or attentiveness is an important feature of the infant's behavior. The most general index of this is the infant's *state*, but other measures of arousal—more typically psychophysiological measures—are used too. These other measures can be used to index the level of arousal associated with specific stimuli, and in so doing they provide an important link to the study of selection.

State. The concept of state refers to the overall level of alertness or arousal in the infant. It is usually measured by means of a series of behaviorally determined categories that have been described by various investigators (e.g., Ashton, 1973; Korner, 1972; Parmelee & Stern, 1972; Prechtl & Beintema, 1964; Wolff, 1966), though state clearly has psychophysiological correlates in such measures as the electroencephalogram (EEG) or even heart rate (e.g., Campos & Brackbill, 1973). A typical set of state categories are regular sleep, irregular sleep, drowsiness, alert inactivity, waking activity, and crying (Korner, 1972; Wolff, 1966). These categorizations can be made very reliably, and a large body of research now exists on both the nature of these categories and their correlates. A more complete discussion of state is available in the chapter by Parmelee and Sigman in this volume.

State is an important variable in studies of learning and memory in infants. Infants, especially in the earliest months, can cycle through various states quite rapidly. For instance, Clifton and Nelson (1976) reported that the average duration of an awake, alert state in a newborn is about 10 minutes. Many experimental sessions with infants last long enough for state changes to occur. It is crucial to distinguish state changes from the types of behavioral changes used to infer retention. Infant experiments often involve having the infant do something repetitive, and such activities, or even the passage of time, can lead to state changes that can confound our observations. Since state cycling is more erratic and state duration is shorter during the earliest months of infancy (Parmelee, 1974), these problems can be especially acute when working with newborns and infants during the first couple of months (e.g., Clifton & Nelson, 1976).

State is also an important theoretical variable. Campos and Brackbill (1973) found that infants who were in different states or who underwent different state histories during an habituation experiment had different patterns of heart rate behavior across the session. Interestingly, habituation to auditory or olfactory stimuli can occur when the infant is asleep throughout the session (Campos & Brackbill, 1973; Engen & Lipsitt, 1965; Engen, Lipsitt, & Kaye, 1963). These studies point to the theoretical importance and practical usefulness of exploring acquisition and retention as a function of state variables. For obvious reasons, most investigators confine their study to alert, awake infants, and presumably this is the state in which learning from the outside world is most effective. However, a complete picture of the infant's abilities requires that a broader range of states be considered.

Heart Rate. The autonomic nervous system responds to novel, intense, or particularly significant environmental events through a number of general body reactions such as changes in blood vessel diameters, heart rate, sweat gland activity, stomach contractions and secretions, pupil dilation, respiration rate, and EEG activity. Many of these changes can be measured, and they provide useful indicators of a person's responsiveness to environmental events. Pavlov (1927) noted that many of these autonomic indicators participated in what he called the *orienting reflex,* a complex of responses elicited by novel stimuli. The fact that the orienting reflex habituates as a novel stimulus is presented repeatedly further contributed to the interest in it, since it could serve as an index of both attentiveness and adaptation to recurring events. Discussions of orienting by Berlyne (1960) and Sokolov (1963) had a major influence on developmental psychologists. Because the infant has a limited number of behaviors that can be easily measured and has no linguistic skills with which to report internal states, the autonomic correlates of the orienting reflex have been extremely important to the study of infant attention. Heart rate has been the most common psychophysiological measure of orienting used with infants, but in the next two sections we will briefly describe some other measures that have been used.

It has long been known that the rate at which the heart beats is sensitive to environmental events. This fact, along with theoretical interest in the nature of psychophysiological responsivity to the environment and the development of effective means of measuring heart rate, has made this a popular measure of infant attention. A number of reviews of the measure, including discussions of its collection, meaning, and limitations, have appeared, and we urge the interested reader to examine these papers for details (e.g., Campos, 1976; Clifton, 1974; Graham & Jackson, 1970; Porges, 1974). We will not discuss how heart rate is actually measured. There are many important technical issues concerning this, and we refer the reader to such sources as Graham and Jackson (1970) and Richards (1980). Instead, our discussion will focus on some general methodological issues that have arisen in studies of infant attention.

One classic problem with the measurement of any psychophysiological response is the accurate measurement of a baseline. Generally, long intertrial intervals must be used to allow the heart rate to return to a baseline following stimulus presentation. It is important to measure the baseline throughout an experimental session since it can change value as time passes. For instance, heart rate changes as state changes (Campos & Brackbill, 1973). Therefore there are some constraints on the types of experiments for which heart rate is an appropriate measure.

Related problems are the control of the heart rate response to background events that might affect the baseline. For instance, Gregg, Clifton, and Haith (1976) and M. N. Nelson, Clifton, Dowd, and Field (1978) describe an interaction between heart rate and sucking behavior that led M. N. Nelson et al. (1978) to recommend that studies that measure heart rate should not use pacifiers. Sucking on the pacifiers produced clear effects on heart rate, making it impossible to measure the effect of primary variables without major complications. It is essential that great care be used to control for these kinds of background influences, because serious problems of interpretation arise if one's primary dependent variable is being affected by factors that are inadvertently left uncontrolled.

Heart rate can either accelerate or decelerate from the baseline, and Graham and Clifton (1966), in an influential paper, attributed different significance to these two kinds of changes. In their view, heart rate *deceleration* is a component of orienting or attention, whereas heart rate *acceleration* is a component of the defensive or fear reaction. There is a large empirical literature on this, and some have questioned the support for Graham and Clifton's (1966) directional thesis (e.g., Barry & Maltzman, 1982). In some situations it may be theoretically important to distinguish these two types of reactions (e.g., Campos, 1976), but in many of the applications we will consider in this chapter the crucial fact is that the heart rate *changes* from baseline in response to an event and with repetition of the event there comes a point where such change is no longer observed. Porges (1974; Porges, Arnold, & Forbes, 1973; Porges, Stamps, & Walter, 1974) proposed that heart rate *variability* might be a more useful indicator of infant attention than changes in the mean rate, an emphasis that would also avoid the issue of directionality.

Heart rate is an extremely important measure in infancy. With modern technology it can be easily and reliably measured at most ages, and its sensitivity to environmental events makes it a useful indicator of attentional processes. It can be used with stimuli in any modality or infants in almost any state. Enough is now known about the behavior of this measure in infancy so that the thoughtful and knowledgeable investigator can use it for a very wide range of situations.

Pupil Dilation. The pupils dilate and constrict in response to environmental events other than changes in illumination, and with appropriate photographic techniques these changes can be precisely measured. Brackbill and Fitzgerald have used it in several studies of classical conditioning (Brackbill, Fitzgerald, & Lintz, 1967; Brackbill, Lintz, & Fitzgerald, 1968; Fitzgerald, Lintz, Brackbill, & Adams, 1967) and in a study of attention to social and nonsocial stimuli (Fitzgerald, 1968). Unlike heart rate, it fits a more limited range of situations and is more difficult to measure and analyze. Nonetheless, in the Brackbill and Fitzgerald work it clearly seems to have been an effective and revealing measure. Fitzgerald (1968) found greater pupillary dilation to photographs of faces than to nonsocial stimuli for infants from 1 to 4 months of age, and at 4 months he found greater pupillary dilation to the face of a stranger than to that of the mother.

Electroencephalogram (EEG). The electrical activity of the brain that can be measured by recording from the scalp of humans is known as the EEG and serves as a useful indicator of attentional states. The EEG can manifest electrical activity that is specific to the presentation of environmental stimuli. This stimulus-specific activity is known as an *evoked potential.* Although sometimes the evoked potential can be seen against the background of EEG activity from a single stimulus presentation, it is more commonly measured by averaging the EEG in response to a series of stimulus presentations. Such average evoked potentials have been successfully used with infants (Ellingson, 1967; Karmel & Maisel, 1975). Most of the early work measured infant responses to unpatterned flashes of light, but Karmel and his associates have successfully measured infant *visual evoked potentials* (VEP) to patterned stimuli, finding that the VEP varied in systematic ways to different patterns.

Hofmann, Salapatek, and Kuskowski (1981) reported an application of the evoked potential method relevant to memory. Several investigators have found that adults shown an enhancement or elevation of the component of the VEP that occurs 300 msec after stimulus onset when in tasks that involve selective attention, novelty, detection, and matching (Courchesne, Hillyard, & Galambos, 1975; Sutton, Braren, Zubin, & John, 1965; Thatcher, 1977). This is called the *late positive component* or LPC. Hofmann et al. presented 3-month-old infants with a familiarization period in which one of two square wave gratings was presented at least 40 times. During a subsequent test phase the other grating was presented 20% of the time. They found an LPC for the trials on which the novel grating was presented but not on the trials when the familiar one was presented. This suggests that VEP is a useful method for studying memory phenomena as well as attentional phenomena.

Sucking Suppression. We have just examined a set of three psychophysiological measures of arousal or activation. There are some behavioral measures as well. The human information processing system has limited capacity to carry out simultaneous activities. If attention or processing resources are devoted to one activity, performance on other activities must suffer (Broadbent, 1958, 1971; Kahneman, 1973; Norman & Bobrow, 1975). A nice example is the suppression of sucking activity due to attention to novel stimuli. Several observers (Bronshtein, Antonova, Kamenetskaya, Luppova, & Sytova, 1958; Fleischl, 1957; Piaget, 1952) reported that young infants would inhibit their sucking when presented with novel visual or auditory stimuli. However, as was noted by Kessen, Haith, and Salapatek (1970), this sucking suppression effect has had a mixed history in subsequent literature. Some investigators were able to reproduce the effect, but many were not (see Kessen et al., 1970, for details). The method has not been used extensively, though Girton (1979) recently used it successfully to study attention in 1-month-old infants.

Measures of Selective Attention

Through the use of careful experimental designs the psychophysiological and behavioral measures we have just reviewed can be used to study aspects of selective attention. Studies of stimulus discrimination using these measures as indicators of processing can suggest what aspects of stimuli infants are attending. However, more direct techniques are available, at least for visual processing, and in this section we will review two of them.

The study of selective attention is the measurement of what the infant is attending to. In adults, this can be examined for any sensory modality through the use of special experimental paradigms. However, most of these paradigms use the subject's verbal sophistication for comprehending and following instructions and the subject's fine motor control for responding. Neither of these skill systems is available with infants. Thus, the study of selective attention in infants has largely been confined to visual processing. We will describe two methods which are identical in their logic: both monitor where the infant

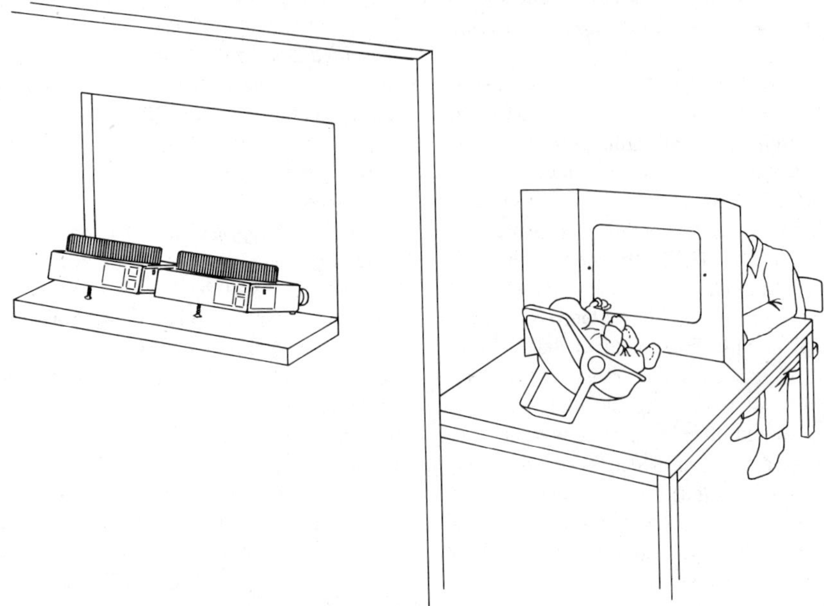

Figure 1. Typical apparatus for observing corneal reflections of stimuli in infants. Stimuli are projected onto the screen in front of the infant in a darkened room. The observer watches the infant's eyes through a small peephole in the screen. There are two peepholes so interobserver reliability can be monitored.

is looking. They differ only in their precision, but this difference is crucial, since wholly different instrumentation and analysis are required.

Visual Preferences. Following the lead of Fantz (1958, 1961), investigators of infant attention realized that one of the simplest ways to study the selection of visual stimuli by infants is to monitor where their eyes are directed. Even the newborn infant can selectively fixate elements of its visual world, and this behavior has turned out to be a powerful tool for investigators of infant attention and cognition.

The monitoring of infant eye movements can proceed at several levels of detail. As it is used by Fantz (1958, 1961) and by hosts of subsequent investigators, general fixations on one or more stimuli can be recorded. For example, one can present a single stimulus to an infant and measure how long the infant looks at it during a fixed exposure period or how long the infant's first look to it is. Alternatively, one can present two or more stimuli to the infant and record the fixation times to each during a test interval. The goal is to measure whether any portion of the stimulus is fixated. No consideration is given in this technique to which part of the stimulus is fixated.

The technique is very simple and highly reliable. The stimuli are shown to the infant and an observer views the reflection of the stimuli from the infant's cornea (corneal reflection technique). (See Figures 1 and 2.) Superimposition of a stimulus on the infant's pupil is taken as an indication of attention. This is easily observed, and the reliability of this measure among trained observers is very high (see, e.g., Fagan, 1972). In such studies, the stimuli typically subtend several degrees of visual angle, and when there are several of them, the stimuli are also separated by several degrees, making the observer's

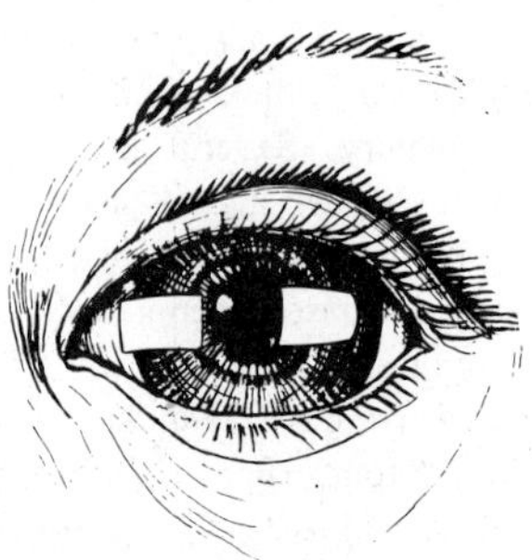

Figure 2. Observer's view of the reflection of stimuli off the infant's cornea.

judgments quite simple. It is clearly impractical for observers to judge the finer details of the eye fixations they are observing. Rather, they can make gross judgments about fixation on a target or not, or judge fixations between two stimuli. Given the high reliability and simplicity of this measure, it is not surprising that most studies of infant attention and cognition have used some variant of it.

Stimulated by Fantz's (1958, 1961, 1963, 1965, 1966) pioneering investigations, many investigators have collected information about the patterns of infant attention to many types of stimuli. Excellent reviews of this work are available (e.g., Appleton, Clifton, & Goldberg, 1975; Bond, 1972; Cohen, DeLoache, & Strauss, 1979; Fantz, Fagan, & Miranda, 1975; Hershenson, 1967; Karmel & Maisel, 1975; Kessen, Salapatek, & Haith, 1972; Stone, Smith, & Murphy, 1973), including discussions of many issues and concepts that have arisen in the study of infant visual preferences. We will discuss many of these matters in a later section.

One major issue that has not received sufficient discussion is the scaling and measurement of such preferences. The study of preferences is for all practical purposes the study of *relative* preferences: the level of attention to any particular stimulus is easiest to interpret if it is compared to that of other stimuli. But how exactly should these comparisons be made? A number of nontrivial questions arise. First, what is the measure that ought to be used? This is complicated because with infants we start with a measure of looking time, which is at best an indirect measure of preference. Adults in a preference or choice experiment understand that they are to provide relative judgments among stimuli. Infants, however, are merely visually exploring a perceptual array presented to them. Looking times probably are not an interval or ratio scale of the underlying psychological dimensions, meaning that at most we can infer ordinal relationships among stimuli on the basis of them.

Another problem is the interpretation of even those ordinal relationships in relation to stimulus domains. Investigators are often interested in psychological properties of stimuli, such as faceness or complexity. For the most part, the selection of stimuli for infant visual preference studies has proceeded informally and intuitively. Checkerboards of varying size, faces with normal and scrambled components, and various types of geometrical figures are typical stimuli in such studies. Stimuli selected in this way are then used to make inferences about the development of visual preferences or other psychologically important domains. However, the psychological dimensions of the stimuli are almost always based on the investigator's intuitions about the stimulus domain. It need not be this way. In an important methodological and theoretical article, H. Thomas (1973) showed how it is possible to approach these issues in a more sophisticated way. When it is claimed that infants are sensitive to various dimensions of stimuli, such as complexity, is their behavior really compatible with a formal concept of dimension? It is in principle possible to answer such questions by applying appropriate scaling and measurement techniques to the analysis of infant preference data. Thomas did just this, applying Coombs' (1964) unfolding theory to several sets of infant data. He showed how one can rigorously verify that there are unitary dimensions underlying a set of stimulus preferences and describe in a theoretically more appropriate fashion the nature of infant preferences. Other reports that use Coombs' technique include Jones-Molfese (1972, 1975) and H. Thomas and Jones-Molfese (1977).

These important measurement issues have often been neglected in the infant preference literature. The cost of such neglect can be very high: the interpretation of stimulus preferences without proper sensitivity to scaling and measurement issues can lead to faulty conclusions about infant attention and cognition. These issues also arise when we use the infant's preference score as if it were a ratio or even an ordinal scale value, averaging, for example, over preference problems or correlating preference scores with other dependent variables (e.g., Fagan & McGrath, 1981). In each case, the investigator must consider the implications of his or her performing statistical operations on values that do not meet the properties required to use the statistic in the conventional manner. In a later section, we will consider in more detail a specific domain: the assessment of the discrepancy hypothesis of infant attention.

Eye Fixations. In the previous section we talked about global eye fixations. It is also possible to measure detailed eye fixations. These techniques have been used most extensively with infants in the first few months of life, since they require that the infant lie quite still, something very hard to achieve with the active infant of 3 months or older. An excellent description of the general methodology used in these studies can be found in Haith (1980). A popular technique, first described by Salapatek and Kessen (1966) and by Haith (1969), uses infrared photography of the infant's eye. Figure 3 shows the apparatus used by Haith. The infant is placed on its back and is presented stimuli on a screen directly above it. Embedded in the screen is a camera and a series of small infrared light sources used as refer-

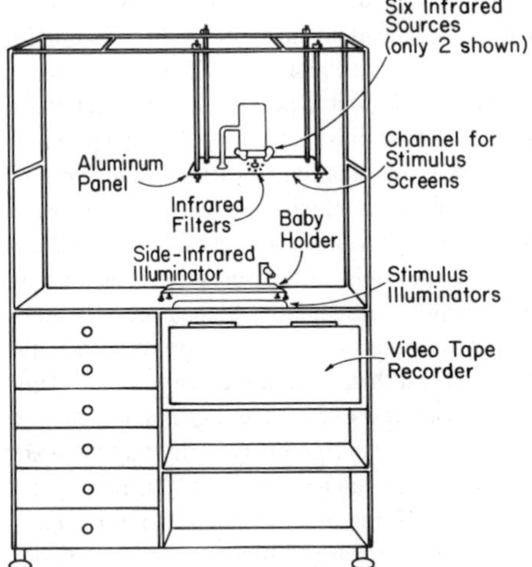

Figure 3. Illustration of the apparatus used to record eye movements in newborn infants in Haith (1980). The infant lies on the baby holder and views the overhead stimulus screens while the infrared TV camera records the infant's eyes on videotape. The infrared light sources provide both invisible illumination for recording and reflections on the infant's eyes. These reflections are used to determine the location of the infant's fixations. See Haith (1980) for further details.

ence points. These markers are invisible to the infant but appear in the film or videotape as small points reflected off the infant's eyes. The infant's attention to various stimuli is recorded on film or videotape, and scorers later reconstruct the infant's point of fixation on each frame or during each time period with the aid of the infrared reference points. A variety of assumptions must be made for this reconstructive technique to work. There has been some controversy about the need to introduce corrections in the data analysis to take into account the relationship between surface of the eye and the point of the retina being stimulated at any given instant by stimuli that are also reflected from the retina (Haith, 1980; Salapatek, Haith, Maurer, & Kessen, 1972; Slater & Findlay, 1972). These details are important for anyone who is contemplating using this technique, and we refer such persons to these references.

What emerges from these observations is a moment-by-moment record of which part of the stimulus the infant has fixated on. The technique allows one to locate the infant's fixation within 3 to 5 degrees of visual angle, meaning that in general fairly large stimuli must be presented to the infant if one is interested in selective fixation of various parts of it. Figure 4 shows some typical data using these procedures. This figure shows a newborn infant's scanning of a triangle. The lines indicate the path followed by the eye as it surveys the stimulus. Since the record obtained is a dynamic one, it is possible to obtain not just the path of the eye movement but the amount of time devoted to fixation of various features of the stimulus.

As was mentioned, these techniques have been used mainly with very young infants. Haith (1980) noted that one's first impression of such data is that the infant is a "'dynamic' information *seeker*" rather than a "'static' stimulus *selector*" (p. 14), a point of view reflected in the conception of infant information processing being developed in this chapter. Given how useful the study of eye movements has been in the study of adult cognition (e.g., Monty & Senders, 1976), it would be highly desirable to record the eye movements of older infants in order to get detailed information about the early development of attention and encoding strategies. Recent work by Haith and his colleagues (Haith, Goodman, Goodwyn, & Montgomery, 1982) and by Bronson (1982) has begun to do just this.

Shifts in Attention that Imply Learning and Memory

We have already noted that the infant's attention to stimuli is affected by stimulus familiarity. Other things being equal, novel stimuli elicit more attention than familiar ones. In general, attention to stimuli *habituates* as the stimuli are presented repeatedly. No phenomenon in infant behavior has been as extensively and as effectively used as this. The explosion of research on infant perception, learning, memory, and cognition in the past 15 years has been due in large part to the use of the habituation paradigm. Habituation is a simple and reliable phenomenon, easy to measure and evident in many domains. As we will see throughout this chapter, the habituation paradigm has been used in an incredible variety of innovative studies of infant abilities. Because it is such an important method, we will give it more detailed consideration than the other methods we are reviewing.

There are many specific ways in which habitua-

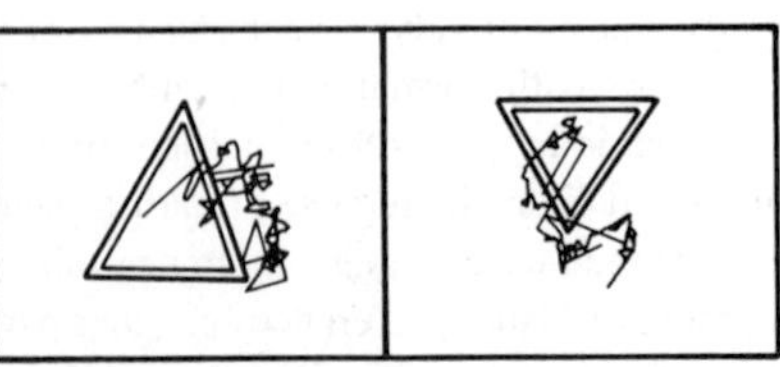

Figure 4. The scan paths of a newborn infant examining a triangle. (From Salapatek & Kessen, 1973.)

tion phenomena can be used in the laboratory. However, in actual practice, two broad classes of methods have been used, the basic habituation task and the paired-comparison task. We will describe each of these in turn. The reader should keep in mind that, given the basic logic of the phenomena, any number of hybrids of these two classes of paradigms are possible if they should better suit the purposes of an experimental design.

The Habituation Task

The logic of the habituation method is simple. A stimulus is presented and some measure of orientation or attention to it is monitored. Initially, the infant will attend quite readily to this stimulus because it is a novel event. If the stimulus is presented a number of times in succession, or if it is made available for an extended period of time, the infant's attention wanes. The link to memory is the assumption that the different pattern of attention to the stimulus early and late in the series of presentations occurs because the infant remembers the stimulus. In line with the assumption first clearly specified by Sokolov (1963), the level of attention to the stimulus is interpreted to be due to the extent to which the current perceptual trace of it matches traces that are available in memory.

Of course, there are many factors other than familiarity that affect the level of attention to stimuli. Methodological advances in the study of habituation have led to greater sophistication about how to distinguish among these various factors. Early attempts to measure infant habituation were often plagued by incomplete controls. In a major analysis of habituation, Jeffrey and Cohen (1971) described the issues of control and method that are pertinent to using this task with infants. Although we will discuss these issues in some detail below, we will not duplicate their historical review of habituation with infants, and we strongly recommend this major paper for this perspective.

An habituation task is defined by several basic components. The most basic one is the trial, the series of discrete presentations of the stimuli. Trials in turn are comprised of two broad classes: familiarization trials and posthabituation trials. The familiarization trials are those in which the stimulus or stimuli whose habituation is being measured are presented. Habituation is the decline in attentiveness over these familiarization trials. On the posthabituation trials a further series of presentations of familiar and novel stimuli is used to ensure that the lower level of attentiveness found on later familiarization trials is specific to the familiar stimuli. This is revealed by significantly greater attentiveness to novel stimuli than to the familiar ones on the posthabituation trials.

The role of the posthabituation trials is crucial. A decline in attentiveness across a series of familiarization trials can arise for a number of reasons. For instance, the infant may change state—become drowsy or irritable. Some general type of receptor or effector fatigue can occur. These general changes in the infant's responsiveness have a different conceptual status than a specific loss of attentiveness due to the formation of a memory trace because the infant has learned about the habituation stimulus. If the decline in attentiveness is due to general factors, the novel and familiar stimuli ought to be attended to at roughly equal levels, whereas if a memory trace has been established and the infant is still capable of being attentive, the novel stimulus ought to elicit significantly greater attention than the familiar one.

Even this is not sufficient. Stimuli are not equal in their power to elicit attention because of factors other than their relative novelty. To take an extreme example, a gray patch and a moving, talking face are going to elicit extremely different amounts of visual attention from an infant who has seen neither before. If we presented the gray patch during the familiarization trials and then found greater looking toward the face when we presented it as a novel stimulus, we would not have a very convincing argument against nonspecific changes in attention. Thus, greater looking toward the novel stimulus on a posthabituation trial does not guarantee that the decline in looking during familiarization is an indication of memory for the habituated stimulus. Two classes of remedies are available for this problem. One is to measure the preferences for the stimuli independent of the habituation experiment. This could be done by presenting the stimuli to subjects who had seen neither before, in order to measure their relative strengths of eliciting attention. The other remedy is to counterbalance stimuli in the design of the habituation experiment so that any particular stimulus serves equally often as an old and a novel stimulus in the overall design. This would then mean that the *net* effects averaged over subjects in any condition could not be due to *a priori* stimulus preferences.

The traditional way of running an habituation task with infants is to use what is called a *fixed-trials procedure*. Each trial consists of the presentation of the to-be-habituated stimulus for a prespecified interval of time. The level of attention during this interval is the basic dependent variable. A fixed number of such trials are presented during the familiarization phase, and the decline in attentiveness is measured by an analysis of variance with trials as a factor. The ideal posthabituation sequence would have at least one novel stimulus followed by at least one further presentation of the familiar stimulus.

During the 1970s a new variant of the habituation task became popular, the so-called *infant control procedure* (Cohen & Gelber, 1975; Horowitz, Paden, Bhana, & Self, 1972). Several important changes were made. First, the nature of individual trials was altered to consist of one unlimited look by the infant. Second, the familiarization portion was run to a criterion of habituation rather than for a fixed number of trials. Third, because of the use of a criterion, some new issues pertaining to the posthabituation trials arose. The infant control task has become popular because of a number of conceptual, analytic, and procedural advantages this paradigm has over the standard fixed-trial procedure. However, there are also potential pitfalls. Since it is so important, we will discuss this version of the habituation task in some detail. For purposes of illustration, we will confine our discussion to an experiment using visual stimuli.

The Nature of the Trial. The traditional infant habituation experiment had a fixed-trial structure. The stimulus was presented to the infant for a fixed period of time, and the measure of attention—most often looking time or heart rate—was collected during this interval. Often, though not always, investigators timed the trial from the infant's first look at the stimulus, but the end of a trial *always* depended on the expiration of a fixed interval. In the infant control procedure, the trial begins when the infant looks at the stimulus and lasts until the infant looks away. Often an intertrial event such as an off-screen blinking light is used to control the infant's attention between trials. Usually, the stimulus is taken away as soon as the infant looks away.

Many investigators using this type of trial have noted that the infants are less fussy and more cooperative than in the fixed-trial task (e.g., Cohen & Gelber, 1975; Olson & Sherman, 1978). Having the stimuli come and go according to the infant's behavior gives the experiment a natural interactive flow that is less disruptive to the infants. Furthermore, a single fixation appears to have theoretical elegance. It is logical for theories of infant visual attention to focus on what it is that holds or releases the infant's looking. Interestingly, this kind of trial makes more obvious the fact that infants—especially those beyond 3 months—seem to be trying to figure out the event structure of the experiment. Some infants in the infant control procedure will "play games" with the experiment, seemingly using their fixations to try to figure out what happens with the stimuli. This aspect of the infant's behavior is seldom analyzed, although it is of course a possible feature of *any* experimental situation.

The infant control trial is not without its problems. Ames, Hunter, Black, Lithgow, and Newman (1978) argued that the judgment of the end of a fixation is subject to serious problems of observer reliability. What counts as the end of a look and hence the end of a trial? The problem is discriminating between a clear look away from the stimulus and a momentary flit of attention off the target. The former is clearly the end of a fixation, whereas the latter could be viewed as insufficient for terminating a trial. Some investigators have dealt with this problem by requiring that looks away must be of some minimum duration, such as a half second or even longer, before they count it as an off-target look. Computer programs or electronic circuitry linked to the observer can make such judgments. Ames et al. (1978) argue that the best solution is to use two observers and have the trial end only when both observers agree that the infant is no longer looking at the stimulus (a suggestion originally made by Horowitz et al., 1972). This method generally produces a high level of agreement.[1]

Number of Trials: The Criterion. A second issue is how many familiarization trials should be presented prior to the posthabituation sequence. Traditionally, a fixed number of trials was presented, and habituation was tested by doing an analysis of variance of trials across the whole group of subjects. However, any student of learning knows that there are always individual differences in the rate of learning. Why not tailor the number of trials to the learner's speed? In typical learning tasks, a criterion of mastery is defined and a subject continues until this criterion is met. For instance, in paired-associate learning, two adjacent perfect runs through the list of pairs is a typical criterion. Theoretically, there are a wide range of reasons why it is nice to be able to equate subjects on their degree of learning. For example, in studies of transfer or forgetting, inferences about the size of effects are facilitated by equating subjects' initial level of learning. Of course, no matter what domain one is looking at, it is often difficult to operationalize equivalence of learning. The domain of infant habituation is no exception.

The heart of the criterion problem is what behavior should count as the state of habituation. Many psychophysiological measures have natural baselines, and a nonarbitrary criterion for any of these would be some number of trials in a row with no departure from baseline. However, *looking* does not have a naturally defined baseline, and so a more arbitrary convention must be used to signal achievement of habituation.

Cohen and Gelber (1975) discussed in detail the general issue of how to define a criterion for looking time. There are two broad strategies: the criterion can be defined in relation to the infant's initial level of looking in the task, or it can be defined in some *a priori* manner. A definition based on the infant's initial level of performance assumes that habituation is a decline in looking relative to where the infant starts out. Hence, this class of criteria are called *relative* criteria. Cohen and Gelber (1975) argued that the most reasonable relative criterion is one based on a proportional change in the infant's looking, say 50% of where they started. An alternative relative criterion would be to require an infant's looking to decline by some fixed amount relative to where it started. So, for example, the criterion might be met if the looks on three trials in a row were at least 5 seconds below the average of the first three looks. (Because of the typical trial-by-trial variability in the length of infant looks, it is important to average several trials together for specifying either the initial levels or the achievement of criterion.)

Another class of possibilities is to define a criterion that is independent of where an infant starts out. For instance, if we knew that most infants fixate objects for approximately 2 to 4 seconds when scanning a series of familiar ones, it might make sense to define looks of 3 seconds or less as a criterion for achieving habituation. This would be an *absolute* criterion. In this scheme, each infant is assumed to have the same baseline of looking when a stimulus is regarded as familiar, even though they each show differential reactions (in terms of length of fixation) when stimuli are new. Hence, each infant is required to achieve the same level of performance before he or she is considered to have habituated to the target stimulus.

Both kinds of criteria present problems. The relative criterion seems inappropriate for a subject who starts out with some very long looks. Let's consider an example. Suppose the infant looked at the stimulus for 100 seconds on the first few trials, so that a look of 50 seconds would be adequate for achieving a 50% proportional relative criterion. For the moment we are ignoring the problem of trial-by-trial variability. It is difficult to believe that an infant who is looking 50 seconds at a stimulus before looking away has lost interest in it. Yet such extreme looks do occur, so this is not an abstract problem. Intuitively, it seems more satisfying to count as habituated an infant who is looking quite briefly at the stimulus. However, even with this intuition, it may be reasonable to assume that brief looks are different for different infants, allowing for some degree of relativity in their final level of looking. Nevertheless, looks as long as 10 seconds or more just do not seem to be good indicators of loss of interest.[2]

Although there are problems using the relative criterion with the infant who starts out looking very long, *both* criteria have difficulty with the infant who starts out looking very briefly. An absolute decline from the initial level of looking will be impossible to achieve for an infant whose initial looks are shorter than the criterion change required. A proportional decline from an already low level of looking may be difficult or impossible to achieve in a practical number of trials. However, with an absolute criterion, the initial looks of a short looker may already be below the criterion. This leads to the paradox that the infant is classified as having habituated when it begins. This does not seem reasonable. The problems of the short looker are severe, so much so that some investigators of habituation (e.g., McCall) have often excluded them from their analyses.

Both criteria present difficulties in developmental comparisons or stimulus comparisons. Younger infants tend to look at a particular stimulus longer than older ones. With a relative criterion, the younger infants will have a much easier criterion to meet. On the other hand, should infants of different ages, who clearly have different tempos of visual exploration and response to novelty, be required to reach the same absolute criterion? If not, what absolute criterion for 4-month-olds matches what absolute criterion for 8-month-olds? For the same reasons, these criteria present problems in stimulus comparisons or other experimental manipulations of the habituation trials. Stimuli differ in their capacity to elicit attention. What criterion would ensure equivalent degrees of learning if comparisons were to be made in, say, the long-term retention of different stimuli?

As was mentioned at the beginning of this section, criteria were introduced into learning studies to enable the experimenter to equate subjects for degree of learning. In the field of infant habituation it is not clear which type of criterion and which specific criteria within a type will allow the experimenter to infer that equivalent degrees of learning have been achieved. Although many investigators of infant habituation have adopted the infant control procedure, there is very little evidence in the published literature of any concern with these issues. A solution will depend as much on greater theoretical understanding as it will on greater methodological sophistication.

Until the criterion can be defined in a nonarbitrary way, it is not clear that the use of a criterion in the infant control paradigm is superior to a fixed number of trials used in the classic fixed-trial paradigm.

Posthabituation Sequence. While a pattern of waning attentiveness to a repeating stimulus is the hallmark of habituation, the behavior on posthabituation tests is essential to distinguish between losses of attention due to true habituation and losses due to other factors, such as receptor or effector fatigue and changes of state. The importance of these controls cannot be underestimated. Studies that fail to use posthabituation trials or that fail to control for possible stimulus differences by counterbalancing or pre- and posttesting are inconclusive.

The use of a criterion of habituation introduces new problems in the design and interpretation of the posthabituation sequence. We have commented several times on the enormous trial-by-trial variability in infant looking times. Let us suppose we were running an infant control task with a criterion of three looks in a row that are less than 3 seconds. If we were to use a Monte Carlo procedure to generate a series of random looks with a constant mean and with variability that mimicked that of infants, we would find that with enough trials *any* sequence of such simulated looking data would achieve the criterion. This is so because eventually, by chance, three looks in a row that fell below the criterion would occur merely as a product of the variability of the looking times. With real infants there is some unknown probability that a criterion will be achieved by the chance occurrence of several short looks in a row rather than as the result of habituation. Such chance satisfactions of the criterion have an important implication for the postcriterion trials. By definition, under circumstances where criterion is met by chance the true mean value of the look lengths at that point is higher than the criterion level. Thus, on trials following criterion achievement, subjects who have achieved it by chance will have longer looks on the average because of regression to the mean. If the presentations are of a novel stimulus, there will be artificially high looking to this stimulus because of these regression phenomena. In other words, what would appear to the investigator as habituation followed by recovery to the novel stimulus would be due, in part, to an artifact of the use of a criterion of habituation in combination with normal trial-by-trial variability.

If all subjects achieved criterion by chance, then all of the subsequent elevation in looking would be due to regression effects. In actuality, however, only some proportion of subjects in an experiment would have achieved criterion by chance. The effect would still be to produce an artificially higher level of response on postcriterion trials. How can one cope with this situation? There are various possibilities. One is to keep running trials with the old stimulus *after* the criterion is met and then to compare the response to the novel stimulus with these unconstrained postcriterion trials. Data from an experiment in our laboratory illustrate this procedure. One hundred twenty 4-month-old infants were run to an absolute criterion of three looks in a row less than 3.15 seconds. Once criterion was reached, a postcriterion sequence of six trials was presented: two further presentations of the old stimulus, one presentation each of two novel stimuli, and finally two more presentations of the old stimulus. Three different stimuli were used in the overall design, and one-third of the subjects saw each of them as the old stimulus. For each old stimulus; the other two appeared as the novel stimuli, half in each order. The performance of the infants on the posthabituation trials is shown in Table 1. Notice that the level of responding to the old stimuli on the first two trials is above the criterion level of 3.15 sec., indicating a modest degree of regression. However, the level of performance on these two trials did not differ significantly from that on the last criterion trial. The looking to the novel stimuli is significantly longer than this level, and the looking to the old stimuli on the final two posthabituation trials is again significantly lower than to the novel stimuli. This pattern of low looking to further old stimuli, high looking to the novel stimuli, and low looking again to the old stimuli *after* the novel stimuli is the ideal pattern and is one way to control for regression effects due to chance attainment of the criterion. Further, the extent of regression effects on the immediate postcriterion trials can be tested with appropriate statistics.

Bertenthal, Haith, and Campos (in press) have proposed another way of handling these problems: a *partial-lag design.* Half the subjects continue past the criterion with at least one further presentation of the old stimulus, while the other half is shifted immediately to a novel stimulus. The former group is shifted to the novel stimulus too, but at a lag following criterion achievement. Two analyses can be done. In the first the two groups of subjects are compared on their first postcriterion trial, which is old for one group and novel for the other. In the second analysis various analyses can be done to estimate the size of the regression effect and thus allow for assessment of the extent of the novelty preference with the regression effect partialed out. This feature is

Table 1. **Postcriterion Performance in an Infant Control Habituation Task**

	Trial					
Stimulus	**Old**	**Old**	**New_1**	**New_2**	**Old**	**Old**
Checkerboard						
Mean	2.76	2.39	12.41	9.00	4.62	2.93
SD	1.59	1.54	12.90	9.01	5.14	1.73
Fabric swatch						
Mean	2.68	2.89	8.50	7.78	4.17	3.49
SD	1.76	1.95	6.71	5.73	3.08	2.83
Hearts pattern						
Mean	2.58	3.18	8.64	7.84	3.13	2.45
SD	1.45	2.29	5.71	6.46	1.59	1.62

Note: N = 40 for each stimulus.

especially important if one is using the size of the novelty preference to assess hypotheses about the discriminability of different stimuli, a common use of the habituation technique. The Bertenthal et al. (in press) paper should be consulted for a more complete discussion of these issues.

Design features in the posthabituation trials that address these regression phenomena are extremely important if one is using the infant control procedure and a criterion of habituation. In general investigators using the infant control habituation task have not considered these effects. Thus, a reader of the recent habituation literature should evaluate claims made about posthabituation performance with care.

For similar reasons, the use of a criterion can introduce precriterion artifacts as well. Cohen and Gelber (1975) and Cohen (1976) speculated on the possible theoretical importance of a ''peak'' in looking times they observed just prior to the achievement of criterion. Using backward habituation curves, in which the precriterion data are averaged backwards across trials from the point of criterion achievement, they observed that looking was fairly level across the precriterion trials but increased sharply just prior to criterion achievement. However, several investigators have noted (Cohen, 1976; Cohen & Menton, 1979; Olson & Sherman, 1978; Sherman & Olson, 1978) that this precriterion peak is an artifact of the use of a criterion. Since the criterion is achieved by means of short looks, the trials just before criterion by definition cannot have any of these short looks in them, since they would have been included in the criterion sequence. In other words, the trials just prior to criterion achievement do not represent a full sample of precriterion looks, because they cannot have any short looks. Hence, the mean of these trials will have to be longer than that of other precriterion trials. Melton (1936) discussed these phenomena especially clearly, and his paper is worthy of reading by anyone contemplating using a criterion of habituation.

These examples of criterion artifacts underscore the need to be thoughtful and cautious in analyzing data from the infant control paradigm. The data we see are a joint product of the infant's behavior and the window through which we have decided to look at this behavior. It is often a subtle task trying to figure out what is a property of the behavior and what is a property of the window.

The Paired-Comparison Task

Fantz (1964) and Fagan (1970) developed a special adaptation of the habituation procedure which has proven to be quite useful in the study of infant visual memory. The infant is exposed to a visual stimulus and then is tested for retention by being presented two stimuli simultaneously, the old one and a new one. Relatively greater looking toward the new stimulus implies retention. Reliably, more looking toward the old stimulus could also be used to infer retention in a properly counterbalanced design, but in practice infants of all ages usually look longer at the novel stimulus.

Though it is tempting to view this procedure as an analogue of the forced-choice recognition test used in memory research, this is inappropriate, since there is no notion of ''correct choice'' for the infant that guides its selection of stimuli. Rather, the paired-comparison task is more analogous to a choice or preference task. In principle, formal techniques used to analyze choice or preference data could be applied to paired-comparison data, though this has rarely been done (but see Thomas, 1973).

As with the habituation task, behavior in the paired-comparison task has multiple determinants. Figure 5 summarizes the kinds of factors that might govern an infant's choice between two stimuli, *A* and *B*. The relative novelty–familiarity of the stimuli is of primary importance in the memory experiment. In order to measure memory effects independent of the other determinants of choice, investigators typically do two things: (1) they choose stimuli that infants look at about equally often prior to familiarization with one of them, and (2) they counterbalance stimulus assignments over subjects, so that equal numbers see *A* and *B* as old stimuli in each condition of an experiment. As in the habituation paradigm, the counterbalancing ensures that experimental effects averaged over stimulus assignments are memory effects, and by choosing stimuli that elicit comparable levels of looking prior to familiarization, the experimenter attempts to control the variance that is due to stimulus assignments interacting with nonmemory factors.

There are situations where it may be undesirable or impractical to counterbalance in the way just described. Any scheme that partitions subjects on the basis of a characteristic of performance (e.g., aspects of familiarization looking) might not preserve the counterbalancing and thus would make it difficult to infer the memory consequences of these performance characteristics. Therefore, an alternative procedure is to determine the *a priori* choice levels empirically, either by testing subjects both before and after familiarization in a memory experiment or by collecting choice data from a comparable group of subjects. The first of these is better, since it takes into account individual variation in *a priori* choice

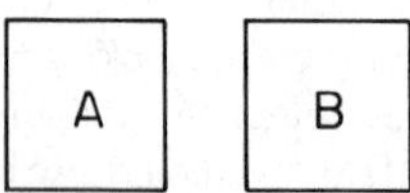

Figure 5. Determinants of looking on paired-comparison tests.

Table 2. **Sample Stimulus Counterbalancing for a Paired-Comparison Memory Experiment**

Familiarization Stimulus	Test Stimuli		
	Immediate	24-hour	1-week
1	4–1	1–2	1–3
	1–4	2–1	3–1
1	1–3	4–1	1–2
	3–1	1–4	2–1
1	1–2	1–3	4–1
	2–1	3–1	1–4
2	1–2	2–4	2–3
	2–1	4–2	3–2
2	2–3	1–2	2–4
	3–2	2–1	4–2
2	2–4	2–3	1–2
	4–2	3–2	2–1
3	1–3	3–4	2–3
	3–1	4–3	3–2
3	2–3	1–3	3–4
	3–2	3–1	4–3
3	3–4	2–3	1–3
	4–3	3–2	3–1
4	4–1	2–4	3–4
	1–4	4–2	4–3
4	2–4	3–4	4–1
	4–2	4–3	1–4
4	3–4	4–1	2–4
	4–3	1–4	4–2

Note: **Numbers refer to specific stimuli. For the test pairs, the *x–y* entries refer to the stimuli presented on the left and right of each portion of a paired-comparison test.**

factors. However, in cases where retention is being studied in relation to relatively brief experience with stimuli, pretests of choice might interfere with the experimental manipulations. In this case, group choice data might be the only recourse. In both instances, it is important to have control subjects who are familiarized to an irrelevant stimulus under comparable conditions so that general shifts in attention or regression to the mean artifacts can be evaluated. Still, though, even with assessing *a priori* differences, some preference effects may interact with memory effects such that memory effects may be swamped if a strongly nonpreferred item is serving as the novel test item or overly enhanced if a strongly preferred item serves as novel (as in the moving face example in the prior section). Problems of floor and ceiling effects may also arise if *a priori* preferences deviate greatly from 50%.

To provide a concrete illustration of the design and results of a simple paired-comparison experiment, we present part of a study run in our laboratory. In one part of this experiment, 34 8-month-old infants were tested for their ability to recognize colored photographs of faces. Three faces were used in a counterbalanced design, with both immediate and delayed tests. Table 2 shows how the counterbalancing worked. During familiarization, the to-be-remembered stimulus was presented to the infant until 60 seconds of total looking had been accumulated. A minicomputer connected to the observer stations kept track of how much looking the infant had done. Thus, each infant received the same total amount of exposure to the to-be-remembered stimulus. An alternative procedure is to present the to-be-remembered stimulus for a fixed interval, timed from the onset of the infant's first look to guarantee that *some* looking occurs. Under such conditions, one typically gets a wide range of individual differences in the total amount of looking to the old stimulus. At the end of this period, two 10-second paired-comparison trials were presented. The 10-second interval was timed from the onset of the infant's first look toward either picture, and its duration was independent of the actual amount of looking displayed by the infant. The second paired-comparison trial was identical to the first, except that the right-left position of the two pictures was reversed to control for any positional preferences infants might have.[3] The paired-comparison test was repeated 24 hours and 1 week later to provide measures of delayed recognition. It is important that the paired-comparison trials be brief so that significant amounts of learning about the new stimulus cannot occur during the test trial, obscuring memory performance. The most typical durations of such trials are 5 to 10 seconds.

There are several ways to measure performance in this task. The two most common are to compare the absolute amounts of looking with the old and new stimuli, or to calculate a percent-looking-to-novel score and compare it with 50%. The data from the experiment just described are shown in Table 3 analyzed both ways.[4] Generally, one summarizes the memory data across the two parts of the paired-comparison trial. The percent-looking-to-novel scores are calculated by summing up for each infant the total time spent looking at both the old and new stimuli and then calculating the following score:

$$\text{Percent-to-novel} = \frac{\text{Total to new}}{(\text{Total to new} + \text{Total to old})} \times 100$$

If subjects were to look equally often to the two stimuli, this score would be 50%. Significant departures from 50% indicate recognition of the old stimulus. Note that in this experiment infants looked significantly longer at the novel stimulus in two of the three delay conditions, indicating both immediate and 24-hour recognition. Further, the percent novelty measure yields results concordant with the total looking measure. This is typical.

One advantage of the paired-comparison technique is that it can be used to test memory under conditions of very limited familiarization. Both Fagan (1974) and Olson (1979) have found significant novelty preferences in a paired-comparison task with as little as a few seconds of familiarization. This is briefer than most single trials in an habituation task.

The multiple determinants of paired-comparison looking summarized in Figure 5 have an important effect on paired-comparison memory data. The ob-

Table 3. **Looking Data from a Typical Paired-Comparison Experiment**

Measure	Test Delay: Immediate	24-hour	1-week
Looking to novel stimulus			
Mean	9.69[a]	10.10[a]	8.70
SD	3.11	2.70	2.54
Looking to familiar stimulus			
Mean	7.17	6.89	8.29
SD	2.53	2.49	2.45
Percent looking to novel			
Mean	57.2[a]	60.0[a]	51.0
SD	13.1	12.2	11.3

[a] $p < .01$, two tailed.
Note: For each test delay, mean looking to novel stimulus was compared to mean looking to familiar stimulus, while percent looking to novel was compared to 50%. $N = 30$ for each cell.

served percent-to-novel scores rarely exceed 60% to 70%; novelty preferences as high as 80% to 90% are very rarely observed. This should be kept in mind when one is interpreting data from such experiments or when planning studies. Because of the limited range of such scores, the measure has a limited amount of sensitivity. It is difficult to find differences in percent novelty measures for two different conditions each of which is significantly greater than 50% unless a very large number of subjects are run (e.g., Welch, 1974). It is also difficult to find indications of memory when initial preferences are strong.

Savings and Reinstatement in Habituation

If something has been partially or completely learned, a later learning experience with it ought to lead to *savings* in relearning. In the logic of the habituation paradigm, where learning is measured by its effects on visual attention, savings phenomena ought to be shown by appropriate shifts in attention following a retention interval.

The most direct way of showing this would be to find that on a subsequent habituation experience, following either an earlier one or some other kind of familiarization, there was less looking at the outset or a criterion of habituation was achieved in a smaller number of trials relative to an appropriate control. A study from our laboratory shows how this might work (Olson, Zimmerman, & Sherman, in preparation). A group of premature infants was given an infant control visual habituation task on two occasions separated by 24 hours. The same old stimulus and the same novel stimuli were used on each day. Further, the entire habituation sequence was preceded by single presentations of four different warm-up stimuli, and the same warm-up stimuli were used on both days. A variety of measures of habituation showed savings: the length of the first fixation to the habituation stimulus was 3.6 seconds shorter on the second day, criterion was achieved in 3.9 fewer trials, and the total time needed to reach criterion was 52.3 seconds less. All of these effects were significant. However, neither the total looking to the prehabituation warm-up trials nor the total looking to the recovery trials during the posthabituation sequence showed any significant change across days, indicating that the savings effect was specific to the repeating stimulus and was not due to general shifts in attention across the two days.

A closely related phenomenon is the *reinstatement* effect. Several investigators have found that a brief reshowing of the to-be-remembered stimulus prior to a delayed paired-comparison test can facilitate recognition memory (Cornell, 1979; Fagan, 1978). Cornell's study illustrates the logic. He found that 5- to 6-month-old infants could recognize certain visual patterns in a paired-comparison experiment after only 10 or 20 seconds of familiarization when the test was immediate, but following a retention interval they showed no significant novelty preferences. However, if infants were shown the to-be-remembered stimuli for 5 seconds prior to the delayed recognition test—an exposure insufficient on its own to produce reliable recognition effects—they *did* show significant novelty preferences even after a delay. Such reinstatement effects are another manifestation of the savings phenomenon.

Savings or reinstatement effects are especially useful when one is studying retention over long intervals or after brief familiarization experiences. Investigators of learning and memory have long viewed savings in relearning as an especially sensitive measure of memory effects (e.g., T. O. Nelson, 1971). Although the techniques have not been widely used yet with habituation, there are sufficient numbers of positive examples to suggest it is an informative method for evaluating the limiting conditions of infant recognition memory.

Summary

The habituation phenomena open the door to the study of a number of important cognitive and perceptual processes. The earliest uses of the paradigm were designed to ask basic questions about learning and memory abilities in infants (see, e.g., Cohen & Gelber, 1975; Kessen et al., 1970; Olson, 1976). The amount, type, and spacing of the familiarization experiences and the delay between familiarization and novelty testing have obvious translations into basic questions about memory. By clever design of the familiarization sequences and novelty tests, one can ask a broad range of questions about perceptual discrimination, encoding processes, abstraction and classification, and indeed any psychological process that can be operationalized in terms of differential patterns of discrimination and generalization. In later sections we will see many examples of the innovative use of habituation phenomena in just these ways.

All of these manipulations are available with other paradigms, such as the conditioning methods to be described in the next section. However, these other methods have not been as widely or as successfully used with infants as the habituation method. Why? One reason is that the habituation method exploits basic attentional phenomena that are a natural part of the infant's everyday behavior. Even the most casual observer of infants notices the extent to which they attend to stimuli in the environment.

Thus, the behaviors that are central to the method are not contrived to fit the logic of a paradigm but are just the kinds of activities the infant does spontaneously on exposure to stimuli. Successful uses of conditioning paradigms are probably due in part to successful exploitation of natural infant behaviors. In general, however, teaching the infant to respond to stimuli in an experimenter-designated way is much more difficult to achieve than presenting stimuli and monitoring how the infant attends.

Conditioning Paradigms

The psychology of learning during the 1930s, 1940s, and 1950s was dominated by the study of conditioning, predominantly with animal subjects. During this period there were a few studies of conditioning in infants (e.g., Marquis, 1931; Wenger, 1936; Wickens & Wickens, 1940), though, as we will discuss below, they had serious methodological flaws. There is also a more recent literature on conditioning in infants, and although conditioning techniques have not been as widely used as habituation, they are common enough for us to devote some attention to their unique methodological issues. We will use the conventional divisions of classical and operant conditioning in our review.

Classical Conditioning

Although there are many variations to the basic procedure, classical conditioning consists in essence of the transfer of stimulus control from a stimulus that reliably elicits a reflex to one that was previously neutral. Thus, in Pavlov's famous experiment, the taste of food powder reliably elicited salivation but a neutral stimulus, a bell, initially did not. By repeatedly pairing the neutral bell with the taste of food powder, Pavlov's dogs came to salivate to the sound of the bell alone.

There are several key components to the classical conditioning paradigm. First, there must be an initial pattern of stimulus control in which one stimulus, called the unconditioned stimulus (UCS), reliably elicits an identifiable unconditioned response (UCR), while a second, called the conditioned stimulus (CS), does not elicit the response. Typically, simple reflexes like salivation to food, eye-blink to an air puff, or heart rate responses to loud tones or bright lights are studied. The UCS and CS are presented in a close temporal sequence during the *acquisition* phase of the experiment, optimally, with the CS preceding the UCS. After acquisition, an *extinction* phase is presented, in which the CS is presented by itself. The occurrence of responses to the CS during this extinction phase is the main indicator of conditioning. If the extinction phase continues without further presentations of the UCS, the response will eventually cease to occur.

Classical conditioning is one of the basic forms of learning, and ever since Pavlov's initial investigations it has been studied extensively. Most theorists recognize it as only one of a variety of forms of learning, but it is of special interest because of its phylogenetic generality. Further, classical conditioning is largely confined to the study of reflex activity, and it provides a means of studying learning and memory in organisms that have limited response repertoires. It is tempting to say it is also a simple form of learning, but anyone familiar with the full range of classical conditioning phenomena and the modern expectancy theories of these phenomena (e.g., Rescorla & Wagner, 1972; Wagner & Rescorla, 1972) would find this attribution misleading. However, it is fair to say that it is a *basic* form of learning, predominantly confined to psychophysiological reflexes, and of considerable usefulness in studying the nonverbal and motorically immature infant.

As with any of the experimental learning paradigms, it is important to differentiate various forms of pseudolearning from true learning. Each learning paradigm develops a repertoire of important controls that must be followed to do this, and classical conditioning is no exception. Repeatedly presenting a stimulus can make a response more likely to occur because of sensitization of the response rather than because of transfer of stimulus control. In order to rule this out, a control group is presented the UCS the same number of times as the experimental group but either without any presentation of the to-be-conditioned stimulus or with the CS and UCS presented in a random, unpaired fashion. Wickens and Wickens (1940) found that a group of infants who were presented with the UCS alone exhibited as many conditioned responses on a test trial as did those who had been given paired presentations of the CS and UCS. This implies that the responses occurring on the test trials were due to sensitization rather than to a transfer of stimulus control to the CS.

Rescorla (1967, 1972) argued, on the basis of a new conceptualization of the conditioning paradigm, that the UCS presented alone was not a good control for sensitization effects. He observed that in a classical conditioning paradigm the CS acquires informational value during the course of acquisition. That is, it comes to predict the occurrence of the UCS. Given this analysis, the important characteristic of the relationship between the CS and UCS is their correlation. In the typical paradigm these have a perfect positive correlation during acquisition.

Each time the CS occurs, the UCS occurs. However, presenting the UCS without the CS has a perfect negative correlation, which is also informationally relevant to the organism. A better control is to present the CS and UCS throughout the acquisition phase but with no correlation in their occurrence in time. In this way, both the experimental and the control groups would have the same number of presentations of the CS and the UCS. For experimental subjects the CS would always predict the occurrence of the UCS, whereas for control subjects the CS would have no information value.

An example of a classical conditioning study with infants is one of the experiments reported by Brackbill, Fitzgerald, and Lintz (1967). They examined the conditioning of both pupil dilation and pupil constriction to two CSs: a fixed time interval and a tone. In a third condition, these two CSs were combined. The UCS for pupil dilation was a change in illumination from the light to dark, and for constriction it was a change from dark to light. For the temporal CS for conditioning of dilation, the light remained on for 20 seconds and then went off for 4 seconds in a continuous cycle. The complementary arrangement—light off for 20 seconds and on for 4 seconds—was used for constriction. A test trial consisted of withholding the UCS, or in these cases either leaving the light on or off at the end of 20 seconds. The occurrence of the appropriate pupillary response on such test trials was an indication of successful conditioning. For conditioning with the tone plus interval, a brief complex sound was presented 1.5 seconds prior to the switch in illumination during the conditioning trials. During test trials the tone appeared in the same position relative to the interval but there was no change in illumination. Finally, in the tone alone condition, the tone again appeared 1.5 seconds prior to a change in illumination during conditioning, but now the intervals varied from 10 to 30 seconds, with an average of 20 seconds. Test trials again consisted of the tone alone.

Two control groups were used. In one, the light onset or offset occurred at random intervals ranging from 10 to 30 seconds, with an average of 20 seconds. This is a pseudoconditioning control for the time CS. A second control group was presented the sound CS concurrently with the UCS (light on or light off). In general, presenting the CS and the UCS concurrently, as opposed to having the CS precede the UCS, is ineffective in producing conditioning. This is clearly not quite the zero correlation control recommended by Rescorla, but it does provide a check on the tendency of the CS to potentiate the CR.

This study was run with infants whose ages averaged 53.3 days, and the results were quite clear. Four subjects were run in each of the three CS conditions for both dilation and constriction. All subjects in the time and the time-plus-sound groups showed conditioning: significant dilation for the dilation groups, significant constriction for the constriction groups. No subjects in the sound-alone group showed conditioning, nor did any subjects in the control groups. Interestingly, the time-plus-sound group conditioned to dilate their pupils showed significantly greater dilation than the time-only group, whereas the time-plus-sound group conditioned to constrict showed significantly less constriction than the time-only constriction group.

These data show that a simple psychophysiological response—pupil dilation—can be classically conditioned to a temporal stimuli. The design of the experiment is especially elegant in that the pupillary response can go in either direction, and conditions were arranged to condition the response in each direction. It is also significant that the sound-only group showed no evidence of conditioning. This pattern of findings is typical of the infant classical conditioning literature: some CS-UCS combinations have produced successful conditioning whereas others have proven resistant to conditioning. Fitzgerald and Brackbill (1976) and Sameroff and Cavanagh (1979), in reviewing the data, have concluded that infant classical conditioning supports the idea of there being constraints on learning, an idea that has received extensive discussion in the general literature on conditioning (e.g., Hinde & Stevenson-Hinde, 1973; Seligman, 1970).

Operant Conditioning

In operant conditioning, behavior is controlled by the presentation of reinforcement when specific stimulus-response pairs occur. A spontaneously emitted behavior is followed by a negative or a positive outcome. The negative tends to decrease the probability of occurrence of the response, the positive to increase it. Typically, the reinforcement is given in association with a discriminative stimulus of some sort, so that the measurement of response probability can occur in an identifiable experimental environment.

There is a very large literature on operant conditioning in infants, along with a large number of review articles (e.g., Kessen et al., 1970; Rovee-Collier & Gekoski, 1979; Rovee-Collier & Lipsitt, 1980; Sameroff & Cavanagh, 1979). There are many conceptual and methodological issues pertinent to this paradigm, many of which have been discussed extensively before. Our goal in this section will be to introduce the operant conditioning paradigm as it is typically used with infants and to highlight briefly some of the major methodological issues.

A number of stimuli and behaviors have been examined. For instance, early studies by Papousek (1959, 1961, 1967) examined infant head turns in response to auditory and visual stimuli, with food often used as the reinforcer. Several investigators have used head turns with complex visual or visual/auditory events as reinforcers (e.g., Fagen, 1977). Both nutritive (e.g., Sameroff, 1968, 1972) and nonnutritive (e.g., Siqueland & DeLucia, 1969) sucking have been studied, with many different types of stimuli. More recently, Rovee-Collier and her colleagues have conducted a wide range of studies examining reinforcement of infant foot kicks (e.g., Fagen & Rovee, 1976; Rovee & Fagen, 1976; Rovee & Rovee, 1969; Rovee-Collier, Sullivan, Enright, Lucas, & Fagen, 1980; Sullivan, Rovee-Collier, & Tynes, 1979). Finally, starting with a classic study by Rheingold, Gewirtz, and Ross (1959), there has been interest in the operant conditioning of infant vocalizations with social reinforcement.

To make the discussion concrete, we will consider a representative infant study, that by Rovee and Rovee (1969). This study used the conjugate reinforcement technique, in which the reinforcement is continuously available and its intensity depends directly upon the rate of response. This variant of the operant conditioning paradigm has been extremely popular in recent infant research. In the Rovee and Rovee study 10-week-old infants were tested in their cribs at home. A mobile that the infants had seen on their cribs for at least 6 weeks was at the foot end of the crib. For the experimental group of six infants, a soft silk cord linked the infant's left ankle to the mobile. Thus, infant foot or leg movements would cause the mobile to move. The experimental group received 27 minutes of testing. During the first 3 minutes the cord was attached to the foot but not to the mobile, and the baseline rate of foot kicking was assessed. Then there was a 15-minute acquisition period with the cord attached to both the infant's foot and the mobile. Finally, there was a 5-minute extinction period during which the cord was once again unattached to the mobile. Two minutes intervened between each part of the experiment to allow preparation for the next phase. Two control groups were used. In one, six infants received the same 27 minutes except that the cord was never attached to the foot. However, during the acquisition phase the mobile was moved by the experimenter to mimic what happened during the experimental group's acquisition phase. This provided noncontingent visual stimulation.[5] A second control group received the same series of presentations as the first one, but had the cord attached to their ankle so they could feel as well as see the experimenter's movements of the mobile.

Figure 6 shows the results. The dependent vari-

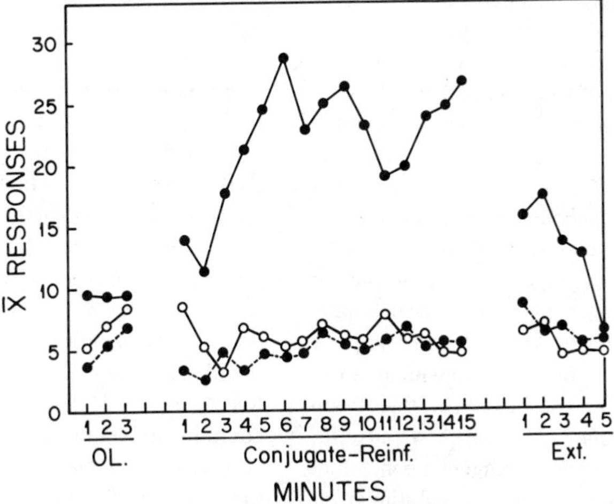

Figure 6. Rate of foot kicking as a function of reinforcement condition in the Rovee and Rovee (1969) study. Each point represents a minute of observation. Approximately 2 minutes separated conditions. The solid line is the experimental group and the dotted lines are two different control groups (filled circles = visual-somesthetic controls; open circles = visual only). See Rovee and Rovee (1969) for details.

able is the average number of foot kicks by the infants during each minute of the experiment. Note that a moderate rate of foot kicking occurred for all three groups during the baseline period. However, during acquisition, only the group whose foot kicks controlled the mobile increased their rate of responding. During the extinction phase, when foot kicks for the experimental group no longer controlled the mobile, the rate of responding fell off, coming to be indistinguishable from either of the control groups. On the other hand, neither control group showed any change in the rate of foot kicks across the session. The noncontingent stimulation provided during the acquisition phase had no effect on the response rate.

This is the classic pattern of behavior for an operant conditioning experiment. The conclusion one wants to draw is that the reinforcement provided during the acquisition phase influenced the rate of responding, specifically because there was a contingent relation between the infant's behavior and the occurrence of the reinforcing event.

As with any paradigm, there are always complicating issues that affect the interpretation of what is actually happening. An illustration of this is useful to examine. Bloom (1974, 1975, 1977a, 1977b, 1979; Bloom & Esposito, 1975) has published a series of reports on the social conditioning of infant vocalizations in 3-month-olds that present some important qualifications on what counts as evidence of infant learning skills. On the basis of two important earlier studies by Rheingold, Gewirtz, and Ross (1959) and Weisberg (1963), it had been assumed that the vocalizations of young infants could be operantly conditioned by adult's providing social reinforcement contingent upon such vocalizations. This particular process was of widespread theoretical interest because of the likely role that such social reinforcement could play in ordinary learning in the infant's everyday life. The conclusion of Bloom's series of studies and methodological discussions is that the research done so far probably does not demonstrate operant learning. Several facts contribute to this conclusion. In essence, the issue is one of appropriate controls. The standard procedure in the prior literature was to have a control group with an unresponsive adult. Rate of vocalization in this group was contrasted with another in which social reinforcements were provided contingent upon infant vocalizations. Bloom has found that the unresponsive adult has an inhibitory effect on infant vocalizations, undoubtedly because an unresponsive adult is an extremely strange stimulus in relation to the infant's experience (Bloom, 1977a). Moreover, a social adult appears to *elicit* vocalization, independent of whatever contingency exists between the adult's social behavior and the infant's vocalizations (Bloom, 1975; Bloom & Esposito, 1975). Although there are some differences in the pattern of infant responses under contingent versus noncontingent adult behavior (Bloom, 1977b; Bloom & Esposito, 1975), the general conclusion about this line of work is that *conditioning* of infant vocalizations has not been demonstrated (Bloom, 1979; see also Millar's, 1976, discussion of operant conditioning of social behaviors).

The careful analysis of the social conditioning paradigm by Bloom is yet another example of the importance of examining infant behavior in learning tasks in relation to (1) a careful analysis of the proper control procedures and (2) knowledge about the natural ecology of infant behaviors as they occur outside the laboratory. The 3-month-old infant is already a social creature, and its experiences in the laboratory cannot help being colored by the contrast between this particular little microworld and the world of its broader experiences. The 3-month-old infant has already learned much about people and their characteristics, and the social stimuli or social conditions presented by the experimenter to the infant will activate knowledge the infant brings to the situation. Events in the laboratory will be encoded and interpreted in light of this growing knowledge base stored in long-term memory. All too often laboratory studies ignore the meaningfulness of the situation presented to the infant. Bloom's work shows that by 3 months—and perhaps even earlier—failure to consider this aspect can possibly lead to spurious conclusions about the infant's capacities.

Savings and Reinstatement in Conditioning

The logic of savings and reinstatement phenomena that we briefly described for habituation holds as well for conditioning studies. The best example of such effects in this domain are the reinstatement effects in long-term memory for conditioned foot kicks demonstrated by Rovee-Collier, Sullivan, Enright, Lucas, & Fagen (1981). Using the conditioned foot kick procedure we described earlier, they found that if they gave a brief exposure to the reinforcing mobile 24 hours prior to a retention test, they could obtain significant retention over intervals as long as 4 weeks for infants who were 3 months old at the time of original training. Such long-term retention could not be demonstrated without the reinstatement procedure, nor was the reinstatement experience all by itself sufficient to produce learning. Just as with habituation, reinstatement and savings phenomena offer the investigator of infant conditioning an opportunity to look at performance under more extreme conditions of delay or original learning. Such investigations are important for exploring the full range of the infant's abilities.

A Hybrid Task: Habituation of Visual or Auditory Reinforcement

A task first used by Siqueland and DeLucia (1969) has come to be quite popular in studies of infant perceptual capacities, especially in the area of speech perception. We will describe the method through its most well-known instantiation, the Eimas, Siqueland, Jusczyk, and Vigorito (1971) study of infant perception of stop consonants. High-amplitude, nonnutritive sucking was the behavior that was measured. The infant was seated with a nipple to suck. The nipple was connected with equipment that monitored the rate of high-amplitude sucking (HAS). The baseline rate of sucking was established at the beginning of the session. Then the reinforcement phase began. A reinforcing event was made contingent on the infant's rate of sucking: the greater the rate of sucking, the more intense the reinforcement (up to a reasonable ceiling of intensity). In the original Siqueland and DeLucia (1969) study visual reinforcement was used, whereas in the Eimas et al. (1971) study the reinforcers were synthetic speech stimuli that were played over and over. When reinforcement begins the infants typically increase their rate of sucking. However, if the reinforcing stimulus remains the same, the infants eventually habituate to it and their rate of sucking declines. At some point (Eimas et al. used a relative criterion) the stimulus is changed for some of the infants. If the change is noticed, the rate of sucking recovers, but if the new stimulus is presented repetitively, it too will produce habituation of the sucking.

In the Eimas et al. (1971) study there were three groups of infants at each of two ages. The groups differed in what happened at the point of stimulus change following attainment of the habituation criterion. Group O, the control group, continued with the same reinforcer. That is, there was no change. Group D was changed to a new speech stimulus, which was hypothesized to be perceptually discriminable from the training stimulus. Group S was changed to a new stimulus which, while equally physically different as the Group D stimulus, was hypothesized to be indiscriminable from the original reinforcer (see Eimas et al., 1971, and Eimas, 1975, for a discussion of the rationale and significance of the study for speech perception). Figure 7 shows the data. Note that prior to the point of criterion attainment (the dashed line), all groups showed the pattern we described above: an initial increase from baseline with the onset of reinforcement followed by a decline in responding. Following criterion attainment the no-change control group (O) continued to decline. Group D showed significant recovery at both ages, while Group S did not differ significantly from the control group.

This paradigm has been the main task used for the study of infant speech perception (see reviews by Eimas, 1974, 1975; Morse, 1974, 1978), though other tasks have been used too. Butterfield and Cairns (1974) criticized the paradigm on several grounds, and Morse (1978) discussed these criticisms and replied to most of them. The investigator interested in the HAS technique should examine both of these papers. All in all, the task provides an attractive blend of two methodologies and should appeal particularly to the investigator interested in early discriminative capacities.

Summary

Though conditioning tasks were the earliest experimental methods used to study infant learning, they have not been as popular as habituation methods during the 1970s and 1980s. Classical conditioning work has all but disappeared from the literature, probably because it is so difficult to demonstrate and because the paradigm is not as popular in the general learning literature. However, operant conditioning is still a useful and moderately popular paradigm and is an extremely attractive task for studies of learning, memory, and discrimination where distinctive stimulus-response contingencies have an important methodological or conceptual role. For both classical and operant conditioning, substantial advances have been made in clarifying appropriate controls and procedures.

Imitation

Imitation refers to the ability of an organism to reproduce a behavior it has observed in another. In order for a behavior to be imitated, it must be represented by the organism in some way. For a behavior that the organism can observe itself performing, such as a hand gesture, the representation need not be an internal one. Imitation could occur by the organism's watching both the model's behavior and its own, and on the basis of these *external* representations attempt to bring the two into concordance through modifications of its own. For a behavior like a facial expression, where one cannot observe oneself, a more complex process involving *internal* representations of the original and copied behaviors

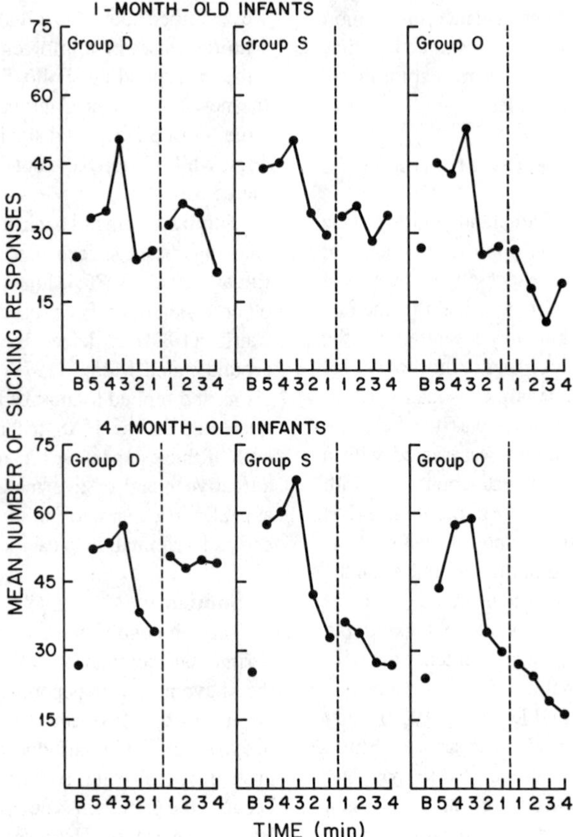

Figure 7. Data from the Eimas, Siqueland, Jusczyk, and Vigorito (1971) study.

must occur. Piaget (1962) argued that this latter kind of imitation should occur later than the former kind. Finally, if there is a delay between when the behavior is modeled and when it is imitated (so-called *deferred imitation*), memory for the behavior is required. Thus, depending on the exact conditions under which it is observed and the type of behavior imitated, the study of imitation can involve many issues that are relevant to the study of memory in infants.

There are further reasons why imitation is relevant to the concerns of this chapter. All theories of learning have recognized that imitation is a fundamental form of learning. Imitation provides a means through which significant forms of long-term learning can occur. The organism can gain a substantial amount of information about how to behave by attempting to reproduce behaviors it observes. The feedback obtained from its own behavior and from the environment on such occasions is extremely important for the development of many skills.

Many investigators agree that imitation undergoes considerable development during infancy (e.g., Kagan, Kearsley, & Zelazo, 1978; McCall, Parke, & Kavanaugh, 1977; Piaget, 1962; Uzgiris, 1972; Uzgiris & Hunt, 1975). Because it is an important form of learning, and because in its deferred form it is a central memory phenomenon, we treat it here as one of the core methods for studying learning and memory in infants. However, there is nowhere near as extensive a literature on infant imitation as one can find for *any* of the methods we have already reviewed. This neglect of imitation phenomena is unfortunate, for they offer a rich circumstance to learn about many features of the infant's information processing skills. In this section we will analyze some of the methodological issues involved in studying imitation, and in the section titled *Conceptual Framework* we will address the conceptual importance of imitation for the study of infant learning and memory.

The definition of imitation is simple, but in practice the study of imitation is complex because of the many phenomena that seem very much like imitation but are not. Piaget (1962), in his classic treatment of imitation, was very careful to distinguish true imitation from various forms of pseudoimitation. Recently a spirited controversy over whether or not newborn infants can imitate facial expressions (Meltzoff & Moore, 1977; Moore & Meltzoff, 1978) has raised many of the issues pertaining to the analysis of imitation. Since we want to draw proper inferences from behavior about the nature of learning and memory, it is important to examine these matters carefully. We will use an analysis of the Meltzoff and Moore (1977) studies as a concrete illustration of the methodological issues.

The definition of imitation is the starting point for our analysis. Imitation is the ability to reproduce a behavior that has been observed in another. Operationally, this is shown by a change in the likelihood of a target behavior following the observation by the imitator of the behavior in a model. However, most to-be-imitated behaviors have some nonzero base rate of occurrence. Further, the rate of occurrence can be influenced by other factors present in the imitation situation. For instance, the base rate of the behavior might shift spontaneously as time passes in the experiment. Controls with no modeling or with the modeling of behaviors different from the target behavior could handle this problem. The behavior of the model might have indirect or general effects on the imitator, such as generally potentiating or activating the behavior. That is, the model might have a nonspecific effect on the behavior in question. For instance, infants tend to stick out their tongues spontaneously, often in response to excitement. A model sticking its tongue out might get the infant very excited getting the infant to stick its tongue out because it is excited, not because it is imitating the model. Careful analysis of the mapping of modeled onto imitated behavior is needed to control for this. For example, if smiling also increased the rate of tongue protrusions, we would be safer concluding that it was general arousal that was responsible for the increase in tongue protrusions to the model's tongue protrusions. To eliminate the hypothesis of general arousal, the to-be-imitated behavior must be specific to the modeling of *that* behavior and no other. Finally, another problem is shaping effects by the model. In a typical imitation situation the model and the imitator are involved in a social interaction with continuous effects on each other. If what the model is doing is a reinforcing event for the infant, the effect of the model's behavior might be to affect the rate of the to-be-imitated behavior through operant conditioning (see discussions by Gewirtz & Boyd, 1976; Millar, 1976). Though this is an interesting form of learning, its mechanics are different than those involved in imitation, and the theoretical inferences one would draw would be different. Careful attention to the temporal contingencies of the model's and the imitator's behaviors are needed to differentiate conditioning or shaping from imitation.

When analyzed as we just have done, these imitation lookalikes seem quite different from imitation. Further, how to control for them seems straightforward. At a practical level, however, it is much more difficult. An ideal situation for observing imitation is in spontaneous interactive behaviors, say between an infant and a mother. Rich information can be obtained from such observations (e.g., Pawlby, 1977). However, in these circumstances the investigator has little control over factors that differentiate imitation from near misses. A more carefully controlled experimental situation is the obvious answer, but as a practical matter these conditions probably inhibit the occurrence of imitation in the infant. Further, because an imitation situation *necessarily* involves interaction between a model and an imitator, there is all kinds of room for covert, unintended contaminations to creep into the experiment.

Meltzoff and Moore (1977) claimed to demonstrate that infants less than a week old can imitate the facial expressions of an adult. The studies reported in the paper were remarkable for the care that went into their design. Meltzoff and Moore were well aware of the many phenomena that could appear to be imitation but are not, and thus they included many controls so they could distinguish imitation from its pretenders. However, because their conclusions were so controversial, a number of investigators examined the issue in great detail, and a series of reports appeared that raised a number of further methodological claims about the Meltzoff and Moore studies. In this exchange of views we see the subtlety involved in differentiating imitation from pseudoimitation.

Meltzoff and Moore reported two studies. In the first, four different gestures were modeled for the infant: tongue protrusion, mouth opening, lip protrusion, and a sequential finger movement (opening and closing in sequence the four fingers against the thumb). Each gesture was modeled for each infant in a different order. The session began with a 90-second baseline period in which the experimenter faced the infant with a neutral, unresponsive face. Each gesture was modeled four times in a 15-second modeling period, immediately followed by a 20-second response period in which the experimenter again resumed the neutral face. At the experimenter's discretion, up to three pairs of modeling and response intervals could be presented for each gesture in order to ensure that the infant had seen the modeled behavior. Half the time only one interval was required. The neutral face was presented for a 70-second interval between each gesture.

The infants were videotaped, and scorers who did not know what gesture had been modeled in any particular interval judged whether the gestures had occurred during the interval. Figure 8 shows the results. The cross-hatched bars represent the gesture that was modeled in that interval, and as can be seen, for each type of gesture the modeled gesture occurred more frequently than the others.

The design of this first experiment addressed several issues that could affect the inference that imitation had occurred. By having the same model demonstrate the different gestures, it was hoped that the role of the arousing properties of the particular face would be minimized. If general arousal in response to this particular face tended to produce tongue protrusions, and there was no specific imitation, then tongue protrusions ought to be observed just as frequently in response to all of the different modeled behaviors. To control for the experimenter's shaping the infant's behavior, the experimenter displayed an unresponsive, neutral face during the response period that followed the modeling of each behavior. Possible problems in subjective influences in scoring the data were controlled by having naive judges score the presence of the behaviors on videotaped records of the response intervals. These judges did not know which behavior had been modeled in a particular interval.

Seldom is any experimental design ironclad against possible objections, and knowing this to be the case, Meltzoff and Moore conducted a second experiment with further controls. In this study only two gestures were used: tongue protrusion and mouth opening. During the modeling period the infant had a pacifier in his or her mouth to prevent any direct shaping of the infant's behavior by the experimenter. The experimenter continued to demonstrate the gesture until satisfied that the infant had seen it for 15 seconds. The passive, neutral face was resumed before the pacifier was removed from the infant's mouth and a 150-second response period began. Throughout the response period the experimenter remained passive. As a check on this, the experimenter's face was also videotaped and later analyzed for any evidence of subtle forms of feedback to the infant (none was found). The results are shown in Figure 9. Again, there was significantly more of the modeled behavior than the unmodeled behavior in the response interval, once again showing selective imitation of a facial expression.

The results of these studies were startling. Prior to this report it was generally believed that the imitation of facial gestures is an important landmark of infant development, occurring late in the first year of life. According to Piaget (1962), a number of substantial cognitive skills are required in order to do this, and these skills do not appear until late in the

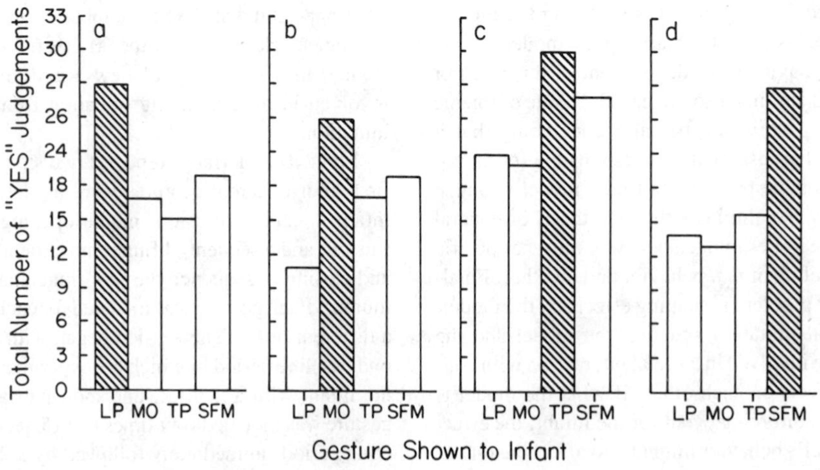

Figure 8. Data from Experiment 1 in Meltzoff and Moore (1977). The distribution of "yes" judgments as a function of the gesture shown to the infant is plotted. The maximum number of judgments was 36. Shaded bars indicate the behavior that modeled: LP = lip protrusion, MO = mouth opening, TP = tongue protrusion, and SFM = sequential finger movement. Copyright © 1977 by the American Association for the Advancement of Science.

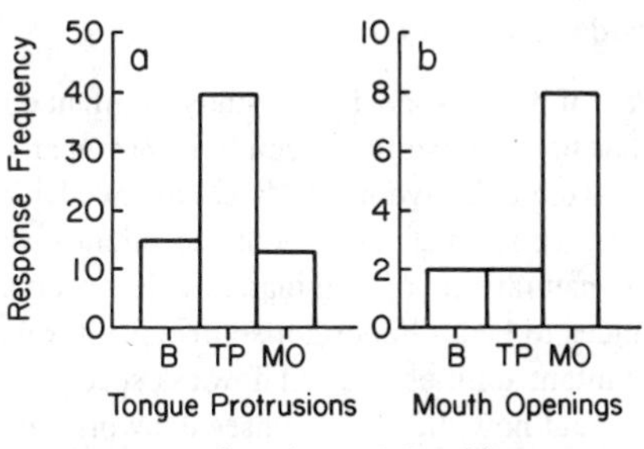

Figure 9. Data from Experiment 2 in Meltzoff and Moore (1977). In panel (a), tongue protrusion (TP) was modeled, and in panel (b) it was mouth opening (MO). B is the baseline period. Copyright © 1977 by the American Association for the Advancement of Science.

first year. The Meltzoff and Moore report suggested this was not true, that facial gestures could be imitated in the first week of life. As so often happens when a controversial finding is reported, a number of investigators attempted to replicate this work. At the 1979 meeting of the Society for Research in Child Development a number of reports of failure to replicate were presented (e.g., Hamm, Russell, & Koepke, 1979; Hayes & Watson, 1981; McKenzie & Over, in press; Waite, 1979). Several of these reports focused on methodological details of the tasks used by Meltzoff and Moore in an effort to understand why there was so much difficulty reproducing these startling findings.

In a nutshell, the problems exposed by these attempted replications had to do mainly with uncontrolled experimenter effects. Hamm et al. focused on the possibility of experimenter bias in the first study, where the number of repetitions of the modeling sequence was under the experimenter's control. Hamm et al. found that they obtained no evidence of imitation when the experimenter was forced to decide whether to repeat a modeling sequence prior to the response period, so the infant's behavior during this period could not influence the decision. Of course, part of the rationale for Meltzoff and Moore's second study was to minimize this objection. Hayes and Watson focused on the second study and found that the decision to remove the pacifier and begin a response period was subject to bias, since the experimenter could sense the mouth and tongue movements being made by the infant just before pacifier removal. Furthermore, in the Meltzoff and Moore study some of the time the experimenter used his or her finger as the pacifier, a procedure that would make the experimenter even more sensitive to the infant's behavior at this crucial transition point. Finally, Waite found that she could reproduce the Meltzoff and Moore findings only when the experimenter believed that neonatal imitation was possible, suggesting that the experimenters were introducing subtle influences on the infants' behavior. When the experimenter was naive or did not believe so, the findings could not be replicated.[6]

Imitation is, by definition, an interactive phenomenon. As can be seen in this series of studies and critiques, the control of extraneous factors in the interaction is an exceedingly subtle matter. In order to draw proper inferences about the infant's information processing capacities from imitation studies, it is essential to analyze the interactions between the model and the infant. Piaget (1962) himself was careful to point this out, and we must continue to use the same care that he used in his pioneering analyses of these phenomena. Imitation is an extremely important phenomenon and is in need of much more extensive investigation during the infant period.

Other Behaviors

Habituation, conditioning, and imitation are the most direct methods for studying learning and memory in infancy, but they are not the only behaviors that can provide information about basic information processing skills. In this section we will briefly review several other behaviors that have been systematically studied. These behaviors are especially useful for studying the infant's learning and memory skills in the second year, the period we know the least about. We will not present a detailed methodological discussion of these behaviors here but will merely call attention to a useful set of behaviors that should be given more attention by those interested in learning and memory.

Search and Object Permanence

Piaget (1954) used search behavior to study the development of the object concept. However, as Piaget himself as well as many other investigators (see Gratch, 1975) have noted, the infant's act of searching for something that is hidden involves a number of memory factors. Some sort of representation of the missing object must be held in memory to mediate the search. Further, such factors as the delay between hiding and searching have been shown to have major effects on search behavior (see Gratch, 1975). However, as in the case of imitation, the analysis of search behavior as memory phenomena is subtle and complex.

Sophian (1980) recently presented an elegant and informative review of the usefulness of the object search task for learning about infant memory skills. Rather than reproduce her discussion here, we refer the reader to her paper for details. Let us briefly summarize the main points, however. These tasks involve many kinds of specific memories: memories for objects that are currently hidden from view, memories for locations of objects or actions (e.g., hidings, findings), and memories of one's own actions. While object permanence tasks clearly involve recognition memory in various ways, they are especially intriguing because they most likely also involve other kinds of memory such as recall. Most theorists have argued that searching for a hidden object implies that the infant has an active representation of that object in mind. This representation, in conjunction with the goal of locating the object, leads to search. If this is the right analysis, then object search tasks may be one of the purest forms of recall in the infant: the activation of a memory trace via associated cues (e.g., the context of the task) in a way that does not produce an automatic response (as in classical conditioning). For this reason, we will review aspects of the object search literature in the next section.

Play

Developmental psychologists have long recognized that play is an extremely rich situation in which to examine cognitive development. Piaget (1962) was one of the first to highlight how the child's changing interactions with objects are indicative of cognitive maturity. Information processing skills are clearly involved in play, although because play—even when studied in the laboratory—occurs in rich, spontaneous contexts, it is often difficult to analyze the contributions of the various components of information processing skills. Nonetheless, we will later briefly review some of the research on play in discussing the skills of older infants.

Social Behavior

Like play, the infant's developing social behavior involves many components of the information processing system. The development of knowledge about persons is a paradigm case of the development of the knowledge base, the store of what is known that is contained in long-term memory (see Olson, 1981). Such well-known social behaviors as stranger fear and specific attachments are direct products of learning and memory. Seldom are social behaviors studied with questions of information processing skills paramount. Thus, as with play, there is little direct evidence from social behavior about the precise components of information processing skills. However, because it is such an important area of development, we will also give some attention to this research in our later review.

Methods: Summary

Part of the reason why the study of infant cognition has been so exciting recently is that an array of reliable and effective methods is now available for asking precise questions about the infant's skills. While naturalistic or seminaturalistic observation continues to be an important source of information about infant abilities, we can now ask specific questions about how the infant senses the world, how it attends, how it learns and remembers, and what it knows. Our review of research in the next section will focus on studies that have used laboratory tasks to study attention, learning, and memory. Most of this work has been done with infants in the first year. However, because we want to take a brief look at the infant during the second year, we will also look at some research on imitation, play, and social interactions, which provide what little evidence we have about the infant's information processing skills after twelve months.

ATTENTION, LEARNING, AND MEMORY IN INFANCY

In the following sections we will review the empirical work on infant attention, learning, and memory. The goal of this review is to portray accurately what is known about the infant's developing skills. The findings were generated using the methods just described in one-time brief encounters with different infants, but it is now possible to piece together a more or less coherent view about the functioning and development of the infant's attention, learning, and memory abilities. Our aim is to present a chronologically organized portrait of the infant's capacities during infancy, focusing on the first twelve months. In the section titled *Conceptual Framework* we will present a conceptual point of view in an effort to summarize the significance of what has been learned so far in this area.

A major goal of the review is to give direct attention to both the ways in which the infant's skills seem to change during this period and the mechanisms that might be responsible for such change. Though we will organize our review by age, within each age we will pick up a major theme or two that seem to us to be especially salient during that period and will give it a more extended discussion. We will first present what is known about the capacities of the newborn. With what capacities does the child enter the world? Then, in our discussion of the early months we will focus on the role that changes in sensory, perceptual, and attentional skills play on the ability to pick up information from the environment. These skills appear to undergo rapid maturational change during the early months. By the middle of the first year the infant's expanding knowledge base (the store of all that is known that is contained in long-term memory) begins to play a major role in the acquisition and retention of information. This role becomes increasingly dramatic as the infant's physiological hardware achieves a large proportion of its maturity and such major skills as easy locomotion, language, and play begin to appear late in the first year and into the second. Throughout this whole period there are marked developments in the infant's response capacities, with enormous consequences for the cognitive skills we are examining. Further, there are major shifts in motivations and goals, which have large effects on observed behavior.

In the classic psychology of learning and memory, the focus has always been on the learning and retention of information in laboratory settings. The amount of information learned is modest, and memory is examined over brief periods of time. Virtually all of the methodologies and the studies of infants that use them have a similar focus. However, contemporary cognitive psychologists have become increasingly interested in the major, long-term learning that occurs in environments such as school or in the learning of major skills or expertises. Schemes, scripts, frames, and other theoretical constructs have been described, and research on learning and memory has shifted focus to such long-term learning. The recent experimental work on learning and memory has given very little attention to long-term learning. Even the most casual observer would agree that an enormous amount of long-term learning occurs during infancy. Of course much of Piaget's theory of infancy is concerned with long-term learning. We will describe long-term learning in our review and will discuss possible mechanisms and research directions for the study of such learning.

Each chronologically organized section will in turn be organized into several major categories. After the general themes for that period are discussed, the existing research will be reviewed under the following headings: attention, acquisition, retention, knowledge base, and performance. Not every heading is used in each age period, since there are not always sufficient numbers of studies that fall into each category.

The Newborn

General Themes

The nature of the skills and knowledge possessed by the newborn infant is one of the classic questions in developmental psychology. As was indicated in the introduction, William James reflected a view widespread throughout much of this century of the newborn's world as a "blooming, buzzing confusion." Stone, Smith, and Murphy (1973), in their introduction to an edited collection of research on infancy, review a history of opinions about infant capacities that show that even until relatively recently it was thought that the newborn was capable of very little. One of the most dramatic shifts of opinions in recent developmental psychology has been the revision of the view of the newborn's capacities. As is evident in many of the chapters in this volume, careful and imaginative research has revealed a wide range of neonatal capacities. Consistent with these findings, one of our themes will be that the newborn *does* possess significant learning and memory skills. However, as often happens when the view of a field shifts dramatically, the emphasis given to the competence of the newborn has sometimes overshadowed the fact that the newborn has limited skills. The newborn is physiologically immature and inexperienced. These limits are a significant feature of the attention, learning, and memory skills evident during this period.

Attention: Attentiveness

As described in a previous section, the study of *state* is the study of the infant's overall state of alertness or attentiveness. Newborns and very young infants spend much of their time sleeping. When they are awake, the period of alertness is typically quite short. For example, on the basis of a broad survey of state data, Clifton and Nelson (1976) observed that except for feeding situations, over 90% of the alert periods in newborns last less than 10 minutes. This means that outside of the feeding situation (where alert periods may last as long as an hour), the newborn's exposure to the world while in what has to be considered the optimal state for learning is broken up into very small chunks, allowing little opportunity for sustained information pickup. This changes rapidly over the early months. Whereas the newborn has very limited periods of alertness, by 3 months the infant's average nonfeeding alert periods are 90 minutes, in comparison to an average of about 5 minutes in the newborn (see Clifton & Nelson, 1976).

These properties of the newborn present a major limitation on its ability to learn and remember. Effective learning takes sustained and organized attention over a sufficiently long period of time to allow for the construction of internal mental representations of experience that can be easily retrieved on appropriate occasions in the future. Except for the feeding situation, the newborn has few opportunities when such effective learning can occur. When this fact is combined with the sensory and perceptual limitations of the newborn and their limited response capacities, it is not surprising that we focus on the limitations faced by the newborn in contrast to the later periods of infancy.

The state variables that limit the infant's abilities to learn also limit the psychologist's ability to study learning and memory. Classical conditioning, operant conditioning, and habituation all make use of repeated presentations of stimuli. Given the limited periods of alertness in the newborn, the investigator must take great care not to confuse changes in the infant's behavior that are caused by state changes with changes that are caused by learning. This distinction is especially important when one is implementing the habituation paradigm, where one primary dependent variable is the change in responsivity due to repeated presentation of a stimulus. Clifton and Nelson (1976) reviewed a large number of studies of neonatal responsiveness and habituation and found that few investigators had given proper consideration to the potential confounding role of state changes in their assessment of neonatal behavior. They found that the experimental sessions in many studies were considerably longer than the 10-minute upper limit of 90% of newborn alert periods. Thus, the probability was very high that infants in these studies underwent a state change. Yet frequently these investigators either did not measure state variables or measured them inadequately.

Attention: Selection

Fantz (1958, 1961, 1963, 1965, 1966) conducted extensive investigations of newborn visual preferences which revealed that from birth the infant selectively fixates the visual world. Newborns look longer to patterned over unpatterned stimuli, as long as the patterns are large enough to compensate for the infant's limited acuity. Following Fantz's lead, many investigators have examined the visual preferences of newborns, attempting to uncover those dimensions of stimulus variation that either attracted or held the newborn's attention. One general conclusion is that newborns tend to look longer at stimuli that have moderate numbers of elements, such as the number of checks in a checkerboard, the number of turns in a random shape, the number of elements in a multielement display (see reviews by Bond, 1972; Fantz, Fagan, & Miranda, 1975; Hershenson, 1967). Older infants, in contrast, look longer at stimuli with a greater number of elements. The most plausible explanation for these developmental differences is that sensory limitations on the newborn's ability to see complex patterns account for their looking preferences (Banks & Salapatek, 1981). The patterns with simpler, bolder elements are easier for the newborn to see. We discuss this work in more detail later in the section on the first three months.

Another domain that has attracted much research is newborn attention to face patterns. Fantz (1963) and others (e.g., Stechler, 1964) found that newborns looked longer at schematic black and white faces than at other stimuli. However, newborns seem to look just as long at scrambled faces as at ones that have regularly arranged features (Fantz, 1966; Fantz & Nevis, 1967; Hershenson, 1964), suggesting that the "faceness" per se of such stimuli is *not* what the newborns are attending to. In fact, the most probable interpretation of newborn's attention to face stimuli is that faces happen to have many properties that attract and hold the newborn's attention, such as contour, multiple elements, and movement, but that faces per se have no particular innate significance for newborns (Olson, 1981; Sherrod, 1981).

The Fantz procedure monitors the infant's attention to global properties of stimulation. More detailed observations of infant attention have come from studies of eye fixations. As was described in the earlier section, these observations are based on photographic or videotaped records of the eye fixations that allow the investigator to determine within 3 to 5 degrees of visual angle where the infant is looking.

Haith (1980) has recently published an excellent summary of both methodology and research in this area. He proposed several broad conclusions about the newborn's scanning of the visual world. First, the newborn scans the world in an organized fashion. Even when there is no patterned stimulation, either in darkness or in lighted but patternless visual fields, the newborn scans the visual world in a controlled and systematic fashion. Second, when presented with a simple high contrast edge in the visual field, the newborn selectively fixates it for prolonged periods of inspection. Visual attention is clearly captured by such simple visual features. However, both Haith (1980) and Kessen et al. (1972) noted that more complex qualities of visual displays such as configurations of contours making up patterns do not seem to be very salient to newborns. Their general tendency, in marked contrast to infants even a month or two older, is to fixate an edge or contour and to direct their gaze back and forth across this specific feature. They tend not to engage in broad visual exploration of complex patterns.

Haith (1980) described the tendencies in newborn visual scanning in terms of a set of rules that nicely summarize much of the research:

Rule 1: If awake and alert and if light is not too bright, open eyes.

Rule 2: If in darkness, maintain a controlled, detailed search.

Rule 3: If in light with no form, search for edges by relatively broad, jerky sweeps of the field.

Rule 4: If an edge is found, terminate the broad scan and stay in the general vicinity of that edge. Attempt to implement eye movements that cross the edge. If such eye movements are not possible in the region of the edge (as is the case for edges too distant from the center of the field), scan for other edges.

Rule 5: While in the proximity of edges, reduce the dispersion of fixations perpendicular to the edges as local and resolvable contour-density increases.

Haith (1980) argued that a simple biological principle can account for these rules: "The newborn's visual-scanning activity is adapted to keep the firing rate of visual cortical neurons at a high level" (p. 107). He cites a wide range of data, both physiological and behavioral, to support both the rule system and his biological account of the adaptive significance of these rules. Further, he claims that these rules and the neural-firing account of them are specifically applicable to the early weeks of life. A variety of other factors come to control visual scanning as the infant matures.

Mendelson and Haith (1976) added further perspective to these conclusions by examining the role of auditory stimulation on newborn eye movements. They recorded newborn eye movements to darkness, to patternless light, and to patterned fields, and they found that in all situations newborn eye movements were affected by concurrent auditory stimulation. Furthermore, the spatial location of the sound source also affected eye movements. They conclude that the newborn is biologically predisposed to acquire information from the world in a fashion that uses concurrent visual and auditory information to control exploration.

On a somewhat different matter of considerable theoretical as well as practical importance, there is some evidence suggesting that very young infants show a preference for familiarity rather than a preference for novelty. Greenberg, Uzgiris, and Hunt (1970), Weizmann, Cohen, and Pratt (1971), and Wetherford and Cohen (1973) all reported some tendency for infants younger than 2 months to prefer familiar over novel stimuli, whereas older infants showed the more standard pattern of novel over familiar. However, the Friedman work to be described below showed a clear preference for novelty by newborns in a variety of experiments. These inconsistent findings have yet to receive a clear explanation.

Acquisition

Can the newborn infant learn and remember aspects of his or her experience? This classic question has received much attention, and the research on the issue is not without controversy. The newborn's limited perceptual and response capacities and the problems associated with the newborn's state organization produce many difficulties for the investigator of learning and memory. However, despite all the difficulty and controversy, the answer seems to be affirmative.

There is a moderately large literature on conditioning in newborns (see reviews by Lipsitt, 1963; Sameroff, 1971, 1972; Sameroff & Cavanagh, 1979). All of these reviews reach a similar conclusion: conditioning in the newborn is very hard to demonstrate. There are many reasons why this is the case. Conditioning studies with neonates are difficult to do, and seldom are studies run with adequate numbers of subjects or with proper controls. The issues of state that complicate studies of newborns are seldom adequately taken into account. There are few attempts to replicate studies, a fact that further weakens the empirical foundations for claims of successful conditioning.

In an effort to account for this pattern of weak and negative findings, Sameroff and Cavanagh (1979) applied the concept of preparedness or of constraints on learning to the case of newborn learning. The traditional view of conditioning has been that with proper parameters in a conditioning experiment essentially any response can be associated with any stimulus. Thus, in selecting stimuli and responses for conditioning experiments, investigators typically chose on the basis of convenience or some intuitions about simplicity. However, more recently a number of investigators have noted that there are important species-specific constraints on what can be learned (see discussions in Hinde & Stevenson-Hinde, 1973; Seligman, 1970). The organism's biology predisposes it to notice certain contingencies in its environment and not others. Typically, these contingencies are of adaptive significance. A classic example of this is the work of Garcia and his associates (e.g., Garcia & Koelling, 1966; see also Revusky & Garcia, 1970). Rats were given strong x-rays while drinking flavored water from an apparatus that also presented flashing lights and loud noises in response to the drinking. The x-rays made the rats sick, but not until an hour later. The rats associated the sickness with the taste of the water, but not with the lights and noise. However, other rats who were shocked while drinking from the same apparatus associated the shock with the lights and noise, not with the taste of the water. These patterns of association suggest that the rats were predisposed to link sickness with a consummatory activity like drinking but the shock with an intense environmental stimulus like the light or the noise. In general, results of this type suggest that organisms do not arbitrarily link stimuli and outcomes in their environment but rather are "prepared" to notice certain linkages and not others (Seligman, 1970).

Sameroff and Cavanagh (1979) argued that the human infant is also prepared to notice certain environmental contingencies and not others. They noted that the few examples of conditioning that seem to stand up to methodological scrutiny tend to involve biologically adaptive responses, such as sucking or head turning. Significantly, Fitzgerald and Brackbill (1976), in a review of research on infant classical conditioning, reached a very similar conclusion. They found that the pattern of successful and unsuccessful attempts at classical conditioning could best be accounted for by the concept of preparedness or of constraints on learning. For example, they noted that autonomic responses (e.g., pupil dilation) tend to be more readily conditioned to temporal CSs than to auditory, visual, or tactile CSs, while for somatic responses (e.g., eye blink) just the opposite is the case. Thus, one general conclusion we can reach about newborn learning capacities is that the newborn appears to be biologically predisposed to notice certain kinds of contingencies in its environment and not others, and that its ability to learn during the earliest weeks of life will be highly constrained by these predispositions.

A somewhat different kind of evidence regarding the learning abilities of newborns comes from research using variants of the habituation paradigm. The largest body of such work is a series of studies conducted by Friedman and his collaborators (Friedman, 1972a, 1972b, 1975; Friedman, Bruno, & Vietze, 1974; Friedman & Carpenter, 1971; Friedman, Carpenter, & Nagy, 1970; Friedman, Nagy, & Carpenter, 1970). The Friedman (1972a) study is a good example of this work. Forty infants ranging in age from 28 to 88 hours were presented with successive 60-second trials of either a 2 by 2 or a 12 by 12 black and white checkerboard that was attached to the side of their crib. Trials continued until there were two trials in a row that had an average of 8 seconds less looking than the average of the first two trials. This criterion was determined empirically in pilot work. When the criterion was reached, half the infants saw one more trial of the stimulus they had been seeing all along, and then they were shifted to the other pattern; the other half were shifted to the second pattern immediately after reaching criterion. The clear result was that those infants presented with the same pattern continued to look at the same level as they had been looking at the end of the habituation sequence, whereas those shifted to the other stimulus looked much longer. The results are shown in Figure 10. Notice that the experimental group, shifted after reaching the criterion, showed a significant rise in their level of attention, while the control group, who got another presentation of the old stimulus before being shifted, showed no recovery until the shift trial.

This pattern of results fits the classic criteria for the habituation paradigm, although it would have been useful if a final presentation of the old stimulus had been given *after* the recovery trial to ensure that there was retention of the familiar pattern. These results suggest that newborns can learn and remember. However, a criticism that has been leveled against Friedman's work, and that has been acknowledged by Friedman himself (e.g., Friedman, 1972a, 1975), is that only a small number of newborn subjects who attempt such studies actually show the pattern of behavior indicative of habituation and recovery. For example, in the Friedman

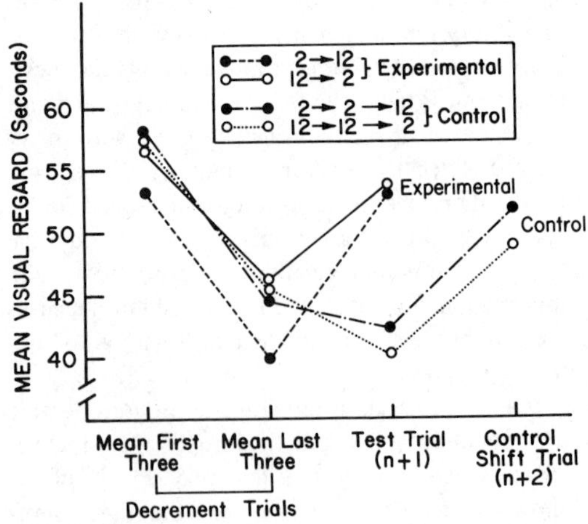

Figure 10. Total looking per trial in the Friedman (1972a) experiment.

(1972a) study described above, only 40 of the 90 infants who attempted the experiment completed it, and of these 40 only 29 individually showed recovery with presentation of the novel pattern. Using this strict criterion of success, only 32% of the infants he tested showed the behavior. The most conservative conclusion to draw from this is that *some* proportion of newborns can show recognition memory in an habituation experiment. However, we must in turn be cautious about being so cautious. First, it is risky to require that a specific individual show the novelty effect in an habituation experiment. The relative novelty of a stimulus is only one of several factors that control looking time, and on an individual trial one cannot be certain which of these several factors will win out. To put it differently, the relative novelty of a stimulus influences the mean of a hypothetical distribution of looking times that hold for that trial, but there is also considerable variability, and a certain proportion of trials in which the mean of the looking time has been shifted because of successful recognition memory and detection of stimulus novelty will nonetheless yield short looks. Of course, some short looks are undoubtedly also produced by nonrecognition, but we cannot tell which infants are which. Of course, by a similar argument, infants who did not recognize the new stimulus could have *long* looks by chance. As we saw in an earlier section, this is especially likely when a criterion of habituation is used. Therefore, to say that only 29 out of 40 infants in the Friedman study showed memory makes overly simplistic assumptions about the underlying processes. A second reason for not being overly cautious is that we do not know much about the 50 infants who failed to complete the experiment. Given all the problems with state in newborn research, one has to assume that the vast majority of these infants were lost because of an unacceptable state change that occurred during the experiment. Thirty-two of the 50 subjects in the Friedman study showed overt signs of such state changes, either crying or drowsiness and sleep. Another 13 did not meet the criterion of habituation, but it seems likely that at least some of these failures were also caused by state changes. Three more did not orient to the stimulus, but again state changes are likely to be implicated. So far as we know, no one has asked the obvious empirical question of whether on a different day those infants who cried, fell asleep, or failed to orient would successfully complete the habituation experiment. In short, it does not seem proper to conclude that complications of state in running an habituation experiment should lead to the overly cautious inference that only some newborns have recognition memory skills. This conclusion takes the data far too seriously, especially since no attempt was made to habituate the failed infants on another occasion.

A recent report by Slater, Morison, and Rose (in press) describes newborn habituation and recovery using visual stimuli with an infant control paradigm. Two large, vertically oriented stimuli were used, and half the infants were presented with each one as the familiarization stimulus. Habituation was to a criterion of three trials that were less than 50% of the first three trials. In their first study, twelve infants habituated to this criterion and then were immediately shown the other stimulus on a recovery trial. Significant recovery was found. Unfortunately, this design does not control for the regression effects that are present in the use of a criterion that we discussed in detail in the section on methodology. However, their second experiment did. In that study, eleven infants were given a series of paired-comparison test trials upon achieving the habituation criterion, and a significant preference for novelty was found. Thus, although the sample size is modest, the researchers have clear evidence of visual recognition memory in newborns. Further, their studies did not have the severe subject attrition problems of Friedman's: eight subjects did not complete the first experiment, and only two the second.

Given the importance of the issues, it is surprising to find such a modest and inconclusive literature on newborn habituation. The conclusion that newborns show visual recognition memory in habituation tasks is certainly in need of further empirical support.

Habituation phenomena should not be subject to the kinds of preparedness or constraints on learning considerations noticed in conditioning research. What is constrained in the conditioning situation is the ability to notice a *contingency* between environmental stimuli with particular outcomes. However, in the habituation experiment, we are measuring the tendency to orient toward events as a function of their relative novelty or familiarity. We would assume that the innate predisposition being revealed in this instance is an innate tendency to orient toward novel events. Of course, there will be innate components of attention that will play a role, such as preferences for pattern or contour, for motion, perhaps for color, and other stimulus characteristics. However, we would expect that habituation and recovery could be demonstrated for almost any stimuli that are perceptible to the neonate. At present the empirical base on newborn habituation is far too limited to do more than speculate about this possibility.

Retention

Virtually no studies exist that address the question of the newborn's ability to remember information over an interval. Most studies examine retention within the same session, usually immediately after the acquisition phase. Papousek (1959, 1961, 1967) used milk to reinforce infants' head turns in response to a discriminative sound, with a buzzer signaling a turn in one direction and a bell the other. Ten trials were given each day over a prolonged period of time and continued until there were five correct responses in a row within a given day's session. Infants who started his conditioning procedure during the neonatal period did not typically reach his criterion of learning until nearly 1 month of age. Thus, the learning he was observing was gradual, and what was learned was being retained from session to session and hence over long periods of time. However, there is no way of telling what kind of retention existed during the neonatal period.

The First 3 Months

General Themes

Although the neonate can attend to the world in an organized way and can learn and remember information from it, one is struck by the limits that exist on these skills. These limits continue to dominate the infant's information processing skills during the first three months of life. However, this is a period when the rapid maturation of the nervous system plays a major role in lessening the impact of these limits. At 3 months of age the infant's states have become much more organized, and there are longer periods of alertness. Perceptual sensitivities have improved, with obvious consequences for attention and acquisition. Basic skills of learning and memory emerge very clearly, though still with important limits that we will characterize in this section.

Attention: Attentiveness

One of the most remarkable developments during the first three months is the regularization of state cycles (Parmelee, 1974; Parmelee & Stern, 1972). The newborn infant's states are labile and erratic. The mean duration of alert states is short, and the pattern of state transitions is often irregular. By 3 months, longer periods of alertness are evident. Sleep–wake cycles are more regular. As a result, many more opportunities for extended learning are present, with the consequence that much more learning is evident. It is also not surprising that the amount of research conducted with 3-month-olds is substantially greater than with infants between the newborn stage and 3 months. The greater state regularity—combined with better perceptual sensitivity, better motor control, and other maturational factors—make the 3-month-old a far superior research subject.

Attention: Selection

A number of studies using the preferential looking technique have attempted to characterize those aspects of stimuli that account for the infant's preferences. Among the many aspects that have been noted are: (1) a preference for greater complexity as measured by number of checks in a checkerboard or similar metric (e.g., Brennan, Ames, & Moore, 1966; Greenberg, 1971; Greenberg & O'Donnell, 1972; Hershenson, 1964; Hershenson, Munsinger, & Kessen, 1965; Ruff & Birch, 1974); (2) a preference for curved lines over straight ones (e.g., Fantz, 1965; Fantz, Fagan, & Miranda, 1975; Fantz & Nevis, 1967; Ruff & Birch, 1974); (3) a preference for irregular patterns over regular ones (e.g., Fantz, 1965; Fantz et al., 1975); (4) a preference for patterns with high contour density over those with low (Karmel, 1969a, 1969b; Karmel & Maisel, 1975); (5) a preference for concentric over nonconcentric stimuli (Ruff & Birch, 1974); and (6) a preference for symmetrical over asymmetrical stimuli (Fantz et al., 1975). There are clearly a wide range of characteristics of stimuli that are relevant to selective attention in infants.

Although the list of such characteristics is quite lengthy, for it to be useful one would like to translate such an empirical base into some generalizations about infant attention that are more informative about the underlying dimensions of selective attention. There have been various attempts to do this. We will not review all such suggestions here, although we will allude to several. One view is that there are innate preferences for certain stimuli of functional importance to the infant, such as faces (e.g., Fantz, 1961; Gibson, 1969). This view, although it has aroused considerable interest and speculation among those interested in social development (e.g., Klaus & Kennell, 1976), seems to have little empirical support (Olson, 1981; Sherrod, 1981). Another view that has received much attention in the infant literature is the discrepancy hypothesis. We will discuss this more fully in the section on 3- to-6-month-olds, because the bulk of the research pertaining to this hypothesis has been conducted with infants in this age range. The view posits that infants prefer to attend to stimulation that is moderately discrepant from internal cognitive standards and that these internal cognitive standards change with development in orderly ways.

Two views that we will discuss in more detail in this section are the contour density theory of Karmel and his associates (Karmel, 1969a, 1969b; Karmel & Maisel, 1975) and the theory of pattern vision based on the contrast sensitivity function recently proposed by Banks and Salapatek (1981). The main reason for discussing these theories in this section is that their primary data base has been with infants in the first three months and their underlying mechanisms are closely tied to the physiological bases that we feel provide the major source of limitations on infant attention during this early period.

Karmel's theory is similar to Haith's (1980) theory of neonatal eye movements that we discussed earlier, in that it is based on the assumption that infant attention to patterns is controlled by the presence of contours in the visual field. Both theories are rooted in the physiological fact that the visual system is known to have primitive units that are sensitive to contour (e.g., Hubel & Wiesel, 1959, 1962). Karmel extends the idea by positing attention to be a function of the average density of contour in complex visual patterns. Karmel's hypothesis is straightforward. He argues that contour density is a major determinant of visual preferences and that these preferences at any particular age are an inverted U-shaped function of density. That is, there is a particular contour density that is most preferred at a given age. With development, the maxima of these inverted *U*s shift toward greater densities: older infants prefer patterns with more contour in them than do younger infants. A neurological account is provided for these phenomena. It is postulated that there are particular contour densities that elicit maximal neural firings from visual receptive fields and that the preferences are directly related to these neural outputs. With neural maturation, receptive fields sensitive to patterns with denser contours come to give maximal firings, leading to the observed shifts in pattern preferences. In Karmel and Maisel (1975) both behavioral and evoked potential data are presented that are consistent with this account.

This extension beyond the simple rules that Haith (1980) developed to account for neonatal eye movements is useful and seems to account for certain aspects of pattern preferences in very young infants. It should be noted that Rule 5 of Haith (1980) provides a mechanism for the contour density effect, in that in the presence of contour the infant scans more narrowly, with the result that patterns with much perceptible contour are fixated longer than patterns with less contour. However, the construct of average contour density is also limited. The visual world contains information about qualities other than contour: texture, color, motion, and so on. Further, contour density cannot be the only relevant quality of contour; contour configuration is also an important characteristic for differentiating among meaningful patterns.

Banks and Salapatek (1981) have recently presented a new analysis of early visual development in infants that has relevance for the kind of preference data we have been describing. The heart of the theory is a linear systems analysis of the properties of the visual system. In acoustics, the complex waveform of a particular sound can be decomposed by Fourier analysis into a series of sine waves with particular weights or coefficients indicating the relative strength of that particular sine wave in the original waveform. A two-dimensional variant of the same kind of analysis can be done on a visual pattern, resulting in the decomposition of a two-dimensional pattern into weighted sine wave components that characterize the pattern. A variety of psychophysical and physiological data suggest that this process might provide a reasonable approximation to how the visual system analyzes two-dimensional patterns (see Banks & Salapatek, 1981, and this volume, for details).

One way to characterize the sensitivity of the visual system to fine pattern is to measure its contrast sensitivity function. This is an empirically determined function which relates sensitivity to sine wave components. Figure 11 shows contrast sensitivity functions for 1-, 2-, and 3-month-old infants. Several properties are relevant. First, the visual system shows greater sensitivity to moderate wavelengths than to very short or very long ones. Second, sensitivity changes across the first three months, with the older infants showing more net contrast sensitivity than the younger ones. Third, the change is not monotonic. The older infants show greater sensitivity at moderate and short wavelengths (high spatial frequency) than the younger ones, but not at long wavelengths. The low-frequency falloff characteristic of the 3-month-olds is typical of the adult contrast sensitivity function. Intuitively, what these data show are that the infant's sensitivity to fine pattern detail increases over the first few months. This is similar to earlier claims that showed that the infant's acuity improved over the first few months, but the characterization of the change in terms of the contrast sensitivity function is more exact because it shows the changes in sensitivity to a whole spectrum

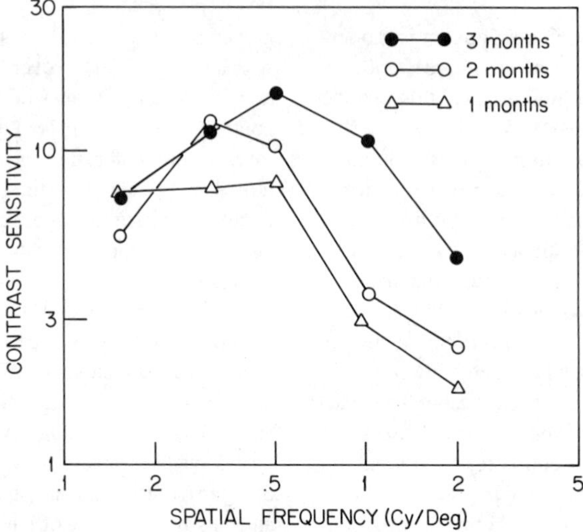

Figure 11. Average contrast sensitivity functions for 1-, 2-, and 3-month-old infants. (From Banks & Salapatek, 1981.)

of spatial frequencies. Acuity is a measure of maximal sensitivity only.

Banks and Salapatek (1981) suggested that these facts about the early development of the infant's contrast sensitivity function could account for developmental data on visual preferences during this period. Of greatest interest to us is their analysis of the checkerboard preference data that we described earlier in this section. Figure 12 shows their analysis. The black dots are a summary of empirical data on infant preferences for checkerboards during the first few months of life (based on a comparable plot in Karmel & Maisel, 1975). Banks and Salapatek attempted to predict these preferences by performing the following analysis. Checkerboards of varying check size were Fourier analyzed to obtain their spectral composition (see Kelly, 1976). Each checkerboard's Fourier analysis yielded a component with a highest amplitude, and the assumption was made that infants' preference behavior was governed by this highest amplitude component. In particular, for a particular age the maximally preferred checkerboard would be the one whose highest frequency component matched the peak of the contrast sensitivity function for that age. These were estimated from the data, and the predicted most-preferred checkerboards are shown in Figure 12 as small white squares. As is evident, these predictions are quite accurate. These predictions are not based in any way on the infants' behavior in the preference tasks, but rather are based on assessments of the infant's acuity for sine waves of various spatial frequencies. Thus, through their theory Banks and Salapatek have integrated data from two distinct domains: visual preferences for checkerboards and a description of the visual system in terms of its contrast sensitivity.

In the same spirit as the theories of Haith (1980) and Karmel (Karmel & Maisel, 1975) that we have already examined, Banks and Salapatek (1981) relate empirical data about developmental changes in behavioral preferences during early infancy to basic facts about the development of the visual system. We have claimed that a dominant property of these early months is the constraining influence of the infant's maturing nervous system, and implicit in all of these theories is the principle that basic facts about this early maturation, combined with simple assumptions about how behavior depends upon these basic facts (e.g., Haith's rule system), can account for behavioral preferences of very young infants.

In addition to research that has provided data on infants' global preferences in looking, there is some research that provides detailed information on the nature of infant eye movement patterns when inspecting a specific visual stimulus. Salapatek (1975) described an important shift in infant visual attention that occurred across the first three months. Studies of the eye movements of newborns revealed a clear pattern of visual fixations on simple figures: fixation on outer contours, with maximal attention elicited by such prominent contour features as the corners of squares or the points of triangles. Salapatek (1975) reported two striking developmental trends in how young infants scan simple geometric figures. First,

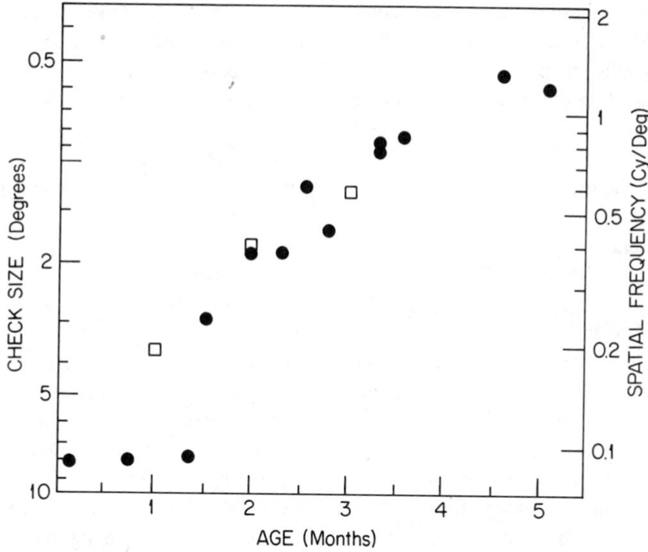

Figure 12. Comparison of observed and predicted checkerboard preferences from Banks and Salapatek (1981). The filled symbols represent the most preferred check size for a particular age based on preference studies, while the open symbols represent predictions from the Banks and Salapatek (1981) theory. Their article should be consulted for details.

the newborn or 1-month-old tends to focus on a single peripheral feature and devotes extensive attention to it. Occasionally more global scanning will be observed, but it has a very disorganized appearance to it. By 2 months the infants give evidence of more organized, global scanning. Second, when compound figures were used, that is, figures that had both an external and an internal component, the younger infants seldom looked at the internal elements. Their visual attention tended to be captured by the external contour, and their scanning almost never included the internal details. By 2 months this pattern had changed. The 2-month-olds regularly inspected the internal components.

Maurer and Salapatek (1976) and Haith, Bergman, and Moore (1977) looked at infant eye movements when viewing faces, and several important findings emerged. Consistent with the data of Salapatek (1975), there was extensive scanning of the perimeter of the faces, with little attention paid to the central features by the youngest infants (Maurer and Salapatek studied 1- and 2-month-olds, Haith et al. 1- to 3-month-olds). Both studies found little difference in the scanning of mother's versus stranger's face, though Maurer and Salapatek found evidence of *less* scanning of the mother at 1 month only. The youngest infants spent much time looking at portions of the visual field off the faces. In the Maurer and Salapatek study, 57% of the fixations at 1 month were off the face entirely. The fact that the young infants spent so little time fixating the face at all, and that even then most of the fixations were on the perimeter of the face, suggests that the infants were taking in little information that would allow them to discriminate the faces from each other or from other visual patterns.

Milewski (1976) showed that this developmental shift in the infants' pattern of attention has important consequences for the encoding and retention of simple figures. He presented infants with compound visual stimuli consisting of an external and an internal geometric shape. In order to assess what the infants had learned, he then presented paired-comparison test trials in which the novel stimuli differed from the familiar in either their external shape, their internal shape, or both. Four-month-old infants could make all of the discriminations: external only, internal only, or both. However, 1-month-olds could make discriminations *only* when the familiar and novel stimuli differed in their external contour. They showed no discrimination when the two stimuli differed only in their internal shapes. Several control experiments showed that the problem with the 1-month-olds could be attributed to the organization of their attention and encoding. They *could* discriminate the internal figures when the external ones were absent. Further, they could discriminate compound stimulus changes when the changes were made in one of two adjacent figures rather than in one that was embedded in the other. In short, the younger infants appeared to be unable to shift their attention from the external figure to the internal one and thus did not encode the internal component of the embedded compound figure.

Several more recent studies have added important qualifications to Milewski's findings. Both Bushnell (1979) and Girton (1979) found that 1-month-olds *did* encode the central elements of a stimulus when these elements moved relative to the outer contour during presentation. Also important are Bushnell's (1979) finding that the encoding of the inner elements under such conditions was *not* at the expense of encoding the outer contour; the infants dishabituated to outer contour changes even under the condition where the inner elements were moving during presentation. Ganon and Swartz (1980) found that 1-month-olds encoded inner elements when they consisted of patterns that were highly preferred by infants of that age. Once again, they found that this encoding was not at the expense of the encoding of the outer contour.

Nonetheless, very young infants appear to have some limits on their ability to encode complex patterns. Unlike older infants, they are less likely to encode internal elements of such stimuli unless they are moving or are especially salient. Milewski (1978) found a general bias in 1-month-olds to encode the larger member of a stimulus whether the smaller one was contained in the larger one or was presented alongside it. However, the development of attentional skills that allow more general encoding of stimuli occurs rapidly. All of these studies agree that by 2 or 3 months of age infants show successful encoding of outer and inner or large and small elements of more complex stimuli, at least under typical habituation conditions where there is extended familiarization. When familiarization time is limited, one plausible hypothesis is that the ontogenetic order would reappear, determining what gets encoded earliest. However, there are no studies of this.

The picture of selective attention during these early months is one of gradual growth from highly constrained scanning of the world, with severe implications for what can be noticed and encoded, to more global scanning and hence more general encoding of information. The development during this period is dramatic. The newborn's visual attention is dominated by simple principles, focusing on the crossing of local contours, possibly to maximize cortical neural firing in its immature visual system. By 3 months there has been sufficient maturation of the visual system to produce both higher-quality visual information (Salapatek & Banks, 1978) and more elaborate exploration of visual stimuli (Salapatek, 1975). The result is greater opportunity for learning and more effective encoding of stimuli. The implications for retention are clear.

Acquisition

Studies of learning and memory during this period show an uneven though perhaps explicable distribution by age. There is a large bulge of studies examining the learning of 3-month-olds, but relatively few for the period between the neonate and the 3-month-old. We have just examined in the previous section a series of studies of the "externality effect," all of which show successful learning by 1- and 2-month-olds using the standard habituation paradigm. Other studies showing clear evidence of learning prior to 3 months using standard habituation or paired-comparison procedures include Lewkowicz and Turkewitz (1980), Maurer and Barrera (1981), and Treiber and Wilcox (1980). A variety of studies, many of them designed to investigate early speech perception, have shown learning during this period using the hybrid high amplitude sucking paradigm of Siqueland and DeLucia (1969) described in an earlier section. We reviewed in that section the study of Eimas et al. (1971), who found that 1-month-olds habituated to synthetic speech stimuli and showed recovery and rehabituation to certain kinds of stimulus changes. There are many other studies like this. Included among them are Milewski and Siqueland (1975), Morse (1972), Swoboda, Kass, Morse, and Leavitt (1978), Swoboda, Morse, and Leavitt (1976), Trehub (1973, 1976), Trehub and Rabinovitch (1972), and Wormith, Pankhurst, and Moffitt (1975). Aslin, Pisoni, and Jusczyk (this volume) provide an in-depth review of this research. These studies show clearly that the infant prior to 3 months of age can learn in a variety of situations.

A much larger and more systematic literature appears for 3-month-olds. By this age a broad and diverse range of learning skills are apparent. There is a modest literature employing habituation-based techniques, and it consistently shows facile learning on the part of three-month-olds (e.g., Barrera & Maurer, 1981a, 1981b, 1981c; A. J. Caron, Caron, & Carlson, 1978, 1979; R. F. Caron, Caron, Carlson, & Cobb, 1979; Cook, Field, & Griffiths, 1978; Glanville, Best, & Levenson, 1977; Milewski, 1979; Young-Browne, Rosenveld, & Horowitz, 1977). An impressive diversity of stimuli and specific learning conditions appear in these studies, suggesting the robustness of habituation-like phenomena by this age. For example, Barrera and Maurer (1981a, 1981b, 1981c) and Young-Browne et al. (1977) examined 3-month-olds' recognition memory for social stimuli, including facial expressions, the mother's face, and discrimination of stranger's faces. Cook et al. (1978) examined memory for solid form, and the studies by the Carons and their colleagues and by Milewski (1979) studied recognition of shapes. In short, by 3 months the infant readily shows recognition memory for social and nonsocial stimuli following moderate amounts (i.e., a few minutes at most) of familiarization.

There is a substantial literature on the operant conditioning of 3-month-olds that provides further insight into the nature of learning skills at this age. We have already examined some of this literature in our earlier discussion of the operant conditioning method. In this section we will briefly summarize the scope of some of this research to provide a further indication of the nature of the infant's learning and memory skills at 3 months.

The vast bulk of the research conducted by Rovee and her associates using the operant foot-kick paradigm originally developed by Rovee and Rovee (1969) has used 3-month-old subjects (Fagen & Rovee, 1976; Fagen, Rovee, & Kaplan, 1976; Mast, Fagen, Rovee-Collier, & Sullivan, 1980; McKirdy & Rovee, 1978; Rovee-Collier & Capatides, 1979; Rovee-Collier, Morrongiello, Aron, & Kupersmidt, 1978; Rovee-Collier, Sullivan, Enright, Lucas, & Fagen, 1981; Rovee & Fagen, 1976; Sullivan, Rovee-Collier, & Tynes, 1979). Most of these studies use similar acquisition conditions, namely, the foot-kick conditioning procedure and its controls as described in the section on methodology. The major variation among these studies is in the test trials following acquisition, either in their retention delay or in the relationship between the test and acquisition stimuli. Some of the studies have included variation in the number of elements present in the mobiles used for acquisition (Fagen & Rovee, 1976; Mast et al., 1980; McKirdy & Rovee, 1978), and these show that learning can occur in a number of different contexts. Overall, the body of work conducted by Rovee and her colleagues shows that the 3-month-old can be readily conditioned.

In the section on operant conditioning methodology we reviewed an extensive series of studies on the social conditioning of infant vocalizations in 3-month-olds that were conducted by Bloom (1974, 1975, 1977a, 1977b, 1979; Bloom & Esposito, 1975). As we summarized there, Bloom found that this paradigm had several methodological problems that cast doubt on the conclusion that 3-month-old vocalizations had been *conditioned* in such experiments. The negative conclusions of Bloom about the social conditioning research do not lead to the broader conclusion that 3-month-olds cannot learn. There is far too much evidence that shows that by 3 months the infant is an active and competent learner. However, learning skills must be analyzed in relation to other developments occurring in the infant, such as the changing goals and motives that govern the infant's behavior in particular situations or the ever-increasing knowledge base that can contain behavioral routines for dealing with familiar and meaningful situations. As we noted before, Bloom's work highlights the need to examine the infant's behavior in the context of the broader meaning or significance of the stimuli encountered in typical laboratory tasks.

Retention

There are a handful of studies of infants in this age range that show that these infants have a growing retentive capacity. The studies of Papousek described earlier, which involved long-term learning, showed that within the first month the infant possesses the capacity to remember a learned response from day to day. Weizmann, Cohen, and Pratt (1971) also studied long-term familiarization at one and two months, providing further evidence of retention across daily sessions. The most impressive data on retention come from Rovee's operant foot-kick research. A number of the studies at 3 months were done with conditioning sessions spread out over a number of days. These studies thus provide evidence of long-term retention. In addition, in several studies Rovee and her colleagues have studied long-term retention directly.

Sullivan et al. (1979) found evidence of positive responding and of savings in relearning over intervals as long as 192 hours in 3-month-olds. They reported two studies. In both of them, there were two acquisition sessions that were held 24 hours apart. In one of the two studies a third session was held 96, 144, 192, or 336 hours after the second one. The data are shown in Figure 13. The first two panels show the acquisition data over the two training sessions. The 336-hour group did not show significant retention or savings when compared with the first session whereas all of the other groups did. Further, the 336-hour group showed significant forgetting when compared with day 2. Although the groups on day 3 did not differ significantly from each other, there is certainly a trend for lower performance on

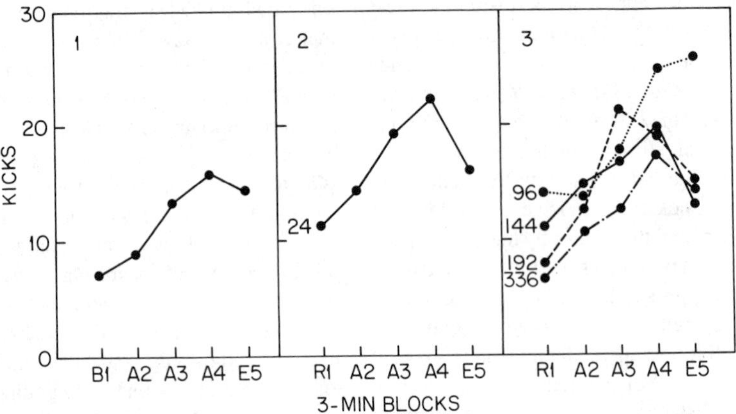

Figure 13. Data from Sullivan, Rovee-Collier, and Tynes (1979), showing mean footkicks per minute over successive blocks of trials. Sessions 1 and 2 were separated by 24 hours for all subjects, and session 3 followed session 2 by the number of hours shown for the different curves in panel 3.

the retention test with increasing delays.

Mast et al. (1980) reported transfer of training from a mobile with six or ten elements to one with two elements over a 24-hour interval. Groups that had been trained on either a six- or ten-element mobile showed savings 24 hours later when compared with a group that had no prior experience with either mobile.

In a study we reviewed earlier, Rovee-Collier et al. (1981) provided infants with a brief exposure of the reinforcer 24 hours prior to retention testing. This produced evidence of memory as long as four weeks after original training. As we noted earlier, the reactivation treatment, as they described the brief exposure procedure, was of insufficient duration to produce new learning; its effect had to be to "remind" the infant of the earlier learning experience.

All of these studies show that by 3 months the infant can remember a learned contingency over very long intervals. Similar data do not yet exist for recognition as measured in the habituation task, nor do we know much about the *development* of long-term memory over these early months. However, by 3 months the infant appears to have considerable capacity for long-term retention.

3 to 6 Months

General Themes

The second three months of life are characterized by elaboration of the infant's basic information processing skills. The degree of physiological maturation that so limited the infant during the early months now provides the infant with the foundational skills to become an increasingly active information processor. The infant is curious about the world, is learning and remembering much about it, and is highly motivated to explore and learn. Attention is both controlled and actively exploratory. Acquisition is facile, and information can be retained over very long intervals. The knowledge base has become substantial enough for there to be marked effects of knowledge on the encoding and representation of new information. Motor skills have matured enough for the infant to be a much more active participant in the exploration of the world. Smiling and other facial expressions have emerged to make the infant an active social partner, a step of major significance for learning and memory. By the end of this period the infant has in place the skills for a series of major achievements in cognitive and social development that will begin in the second half of the first year.

Attention: Attentiveness

The infant of 3 to 6 months is an ideal research subject. There are long periods of alert attentiveness, which, when coupled with the infant's still limited mobility, make for a cooperative subject for studying perceptual and cognitive development. The ease of working with these infants certainly accounts in large part for the huge number of studies that have been conducted using infants at these ages. Physiological limits on attentiveness are less salient at these ages than during the first few months. While issues of state and its control during studies still remain, these problems provide much less of a constraint on infant research than they did with younger subjects.

Attention: Selection

The infant of 3 to 6 months has become an extremely active information processor. Basic perceptual sensitivities have matured to the point where in most sensory domains the level of functioning is approaching adult levels (see Aslin et al., *vol. II, chap. 8* and Banks & Salapatek, *vol. II, chap. 7*). Thus, good quality information from the environment is available to the infant. Locomotor skills are still limited, but infants have better control over their head so even if they are limited to a single location in space they can scan the world about them much more easily. Reaching and grasping improve dramatically over this period (e.g., Field, 1976a, 1976b; Lasky, 1977; Provine & Westerman, 1979; von Hofsten, 1980; von Hofsten & Lindhagen, 1979; Willatts, 1979), substantially expanding the infant's capacity to acquire information. Visual attention continues to develop in the ways begun during earlier months: increasingly active exploration of the visual world characterized by shorter average looking times and preference for ever more complex or meaningful patterns. Objects that can be looked at and manipulated hold especially great attentional value. Finally, with substantial amounts of long-term learning adding large amounts of new information to the knowledge base, attention comes increasingly to be controlled by what the infant knows about the objects and events of its world. This is especially true in the social domain (e.g., Olson, 1981).

We will now look at some of these developments in a little more detail. Cohen (1972) introduced a useful distinction between the attention-getting and attention-holding properties of stimuli, and the empirical work he has done to explore these phenomena was done with infants in this age range. The Cohen (1972) study found that 4-month-old infants' latency of turning toward a checkerboard stimulus was more determined by the size of the checks, whereas the duration of their fixation once they had looked was more determined by the number of checks. Although these findings have unfortunately not been followed up by subsequent investigations, they suggest a hypothesis about attention that should be investigated. In particular, they suggest that the *attraction* of attention might be due mainly to gross physical characteristics of stimuli. That is, attention-getting is seen to be under the control of innate mechanisms that orient the infant to such salient properties of the environment as bold patterns, large objects, motion, sudden changes of illumination, and loud sounds. The hypothesis, then, is that attention-getting may not change much with development. However, what *holds* attention ought to undergo substantial developmental change, since variables such as the fine detail of patterns or their meaningfulness will determine how long patterns are fixated. Cohen, DeLoache, and Rissman (1975) explicitly compared attention-holding and attention-getting in an infant control visual habituation experiment with 4-month-olds. They found that attention-holding habituated but not attention-getting. For the males, the length of looks decreased over trials. However, the latency to turn toward the stimulus remained constant for both males and females. In a later study DeLoache, Rissman, and Cohen (1978) found changes in attention-getting over trials, with infants generally turning faster to the stimuli as the experiment progressed. However, neither of these studies included any developmental data: both of them tested 4-month-old infants. Most studies of infant attention have measured only attention-holding, so there is little direct evidence that can be examined to assess the hypothesis just sketched. These two facets of selective attention deserve more systematic developmental investigation.

The major developments in attention-holding during this period continue along the lines described for the period prior to 3 months. Over the early months infants look less and less at simple two-dimensional patterns, preferring to look at patterns with greater numbers of elements, more angles, and in general larger amounts of that elusive quality, visual "complexity" (Fantz & Fagan, 1975; Fantz, Fagan, & Miranda, 1975). Figure 14 shows repre-

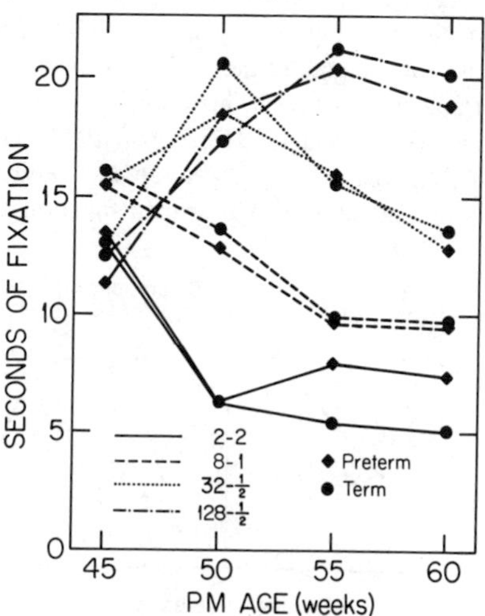

Figure 14. Visual preferences for patterns varying in number of elements. (From Fantz & Fagan, 1975.)

sentative data. This figure plots seconds of cumulative fixation out of 36 seconds of total exposure time for a series of patterns containing different numbers and sizes of elements. The ages are weeks of postmenstrual (PM) time. All patterns receive roughly the same amount of looking at 1 month (45 weeks PM), but by 4½ months (60 weeks PM) the patterns with smaller numbers of large elements (2-2) receive much less attention than those with large numbers of small elements (128¼). These data are typical of what many investigators have found: with increasing age infants will fixate longer patterns that have more elements or details.

What controls infant attention? If we focus on looking times as a measure of attention, the question becomes: What controls how long an infant looks at a visual pattern? Part of the answer has to do with how well the infant sees the pattern (e.g., Banks & Salapatek, 1981). As we saw in the section on the first three months, it is possible to predict the visual preferences of very young infants on the basis of some simple assumptions about the effect of contrast sensitivity on looking. Undoubtedly, over the first three to four months how well the infant sees the pattern is a major determinant of changes in preferences. However, there are other factors as well. One important determinant is what alternatives are available, although surprisingly, this area has not been systematically investigated. Another important determinant of attention that has produced much discussion is the relationship between the infant's representation of the currently available stimulus and the information or knowledge available in long-term memory that is potentially related to this representation. There are two views of this relationship, shown schematically in Figure 15. One view, shown on the left, is that the greater the difference between the input and information in memory, the greater the attention (e.g., Cohen, 1973; Fagan, 1977a; Olson, 1976). Alternatively, the *discrepancy hypothesis* posits that attention is a U-shaped function of the

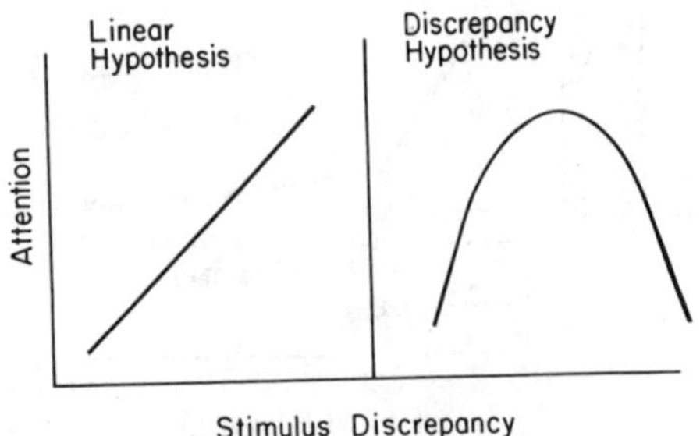

Figure 15. Hypothesized relationships between attention and stimulus discrepancy.

difference between a present input and a representation in the knowledge base, with attention maximal at intermediate levels of discrepancy.

The discrepancy hypothesis is an important theory with substantial historical roots (see, e.g., Dember & Earl, 1957; Hebb, 1949; Kagan, 1971; McCall & McGhee, 1977; McClelland & Clark, 1953; Thomas, 1971). The core idea, as applied to infant attention, is that attention should be maximal when the stimulus differs from a stored comparison by some optimal, intermediate amount. This relationship can be explained on a variety of cognitive or motivational grounds (see Thomas, 1971). In essence, stimuli that are too discrepant from a standard are posited to be less pleasant and less useful for learning than those that are moderately discrepant (which is presumably at least part of the reason for attending longer). The cognitive account would emphasize that it is sensible to attend to experiences somewhat different but not too different from what one knows since they ought to produce maximal new learning. An experience too different from what one knows will be uninterpretable and therefore very difficult to learn from. An experience that is too similar to what is already known can by definition provide very little in the way of new learning.

The major empirical claim derived from the discrepancy hypothesis is that measures of attention will show an inverted U-shaped function of stimuli arranged according to their degree of discrepancy from a standard. Consider an example. Figure 16 shows the stimuli used in the study by McCall, Kennedy, and Appelbaum (1977). For an infant who was familiarized with stimulus A, the stimuli B, C, and D would represent successively greater degrees of discrepancy from the standard. A favorable empirical outcome for the discrepancy hypothesis would be that infants gave maximal attention to C, with lower levels given to both B and to D, following familiarization with A. The data are shown in Figure 17. These data are based on difference scores between experimental and control conditions in a complex experimental design, and the original paper should be consulted for details. The results clearly look like those predicted by the discrepancy hypothesis. Other discussions of infant attention data bearing on this theory include those of Cohen and Gelber (1975), Kagan (1971), Kagan, Kearsley, and Zelazo (1978), McCall and Kagan (1967), and McCall and McGhee (1977).

There are two types of problems with empirical evaluations of the discrepancy hypothesis. The first problem is to verify that the stimuli selected by the experimenter in fact form an ordered, unidimen-

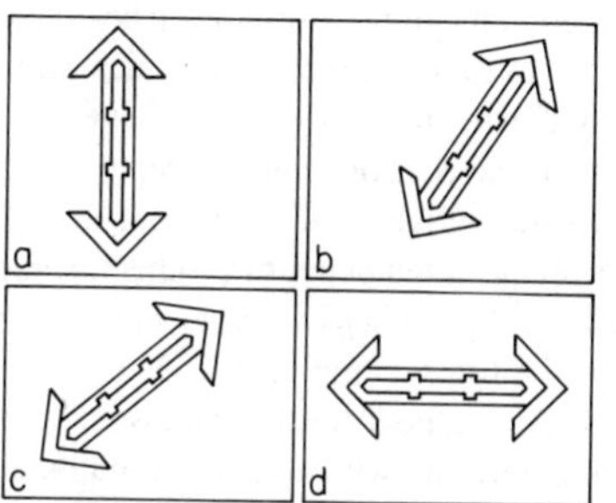

Figure 16. Stimuli used by McCall, Kennedy, and Appelbaum (1977).

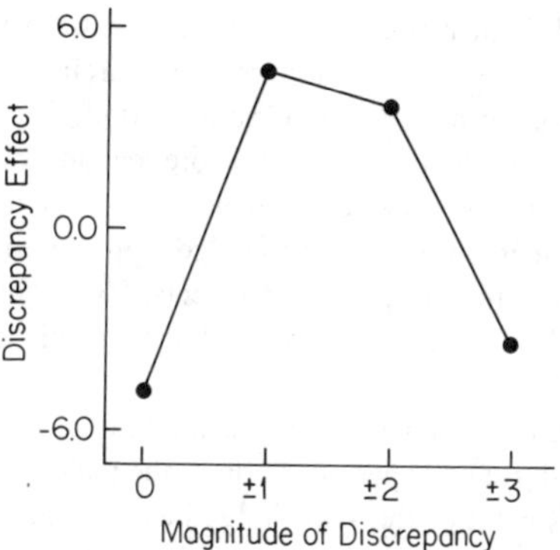

Figure 17. Data from McCall, Kennedy, and Appelbaum (1977).

sional scale for the subject. Thomas (1971) emphasized that unless the investigator can document that the stimuli do in fact form a unidimensional scale for the subject, the data are uninterpretable. If the psychologist orders the stimuli in a manner that differs from the infant's internal scale, or if the putative unidimensional scale is in fact a multidimensional one, the data plotted along the psychologist's *a priori* unidimensional scale are meaningless. In actual fact, almost no studies of the discrepancy hypothesis with infants have assessed the structure of the stimulus scale. Most are constructed on intuitive grounds, using the adult experimenter's casual judgments. Stimuli are typically not even scaled using adult subjects.

The second problem is that while an inverted U-shaped function supports the theory, assuming that the stimuli have been scaled, it is not clear what evidence would ever disconfirm it. Finding that infant attention is a monotonic function of discrepancy, either ascending or descending, is not in itself sufficient to disconfirm the theory unless independent evidence can be presented about the representativeness of the range of stimuli used in the experiment. It could always be argued that such monotonic functions were just one tail of the expected nonmonotonic function. Thus, in order for the theory to be tested in an unambiguous way, the relevant range of stimulus variation needs to be specified independently of the test of the theory. Few investigators have done this in studies of infant attention.

McCall, Kennedy, and Appelbaum (1977) argued that since neither objection can be adequately met in any particular experiment, the strategy for testing the theory is to examine data from a wide range of situations and use the method of "converging operations" (Garner, Hake, & Eriksen, 1956). Consistent findings across a range of conditions that differ in what the theory says ought to be irrelevant ways should lend support to the theory. Indeed, in answer to the second objection, they point out that there are certain outcomes that *are* inconsistent with the discrepancy hypothesis (e.g., noninverted U-shape, S-shape). Further, they argue that clear evidence of inverted U-shaped functions *do* disconfirm a theory that predicts linear functions. They list a number of studies that report findings favoring the discrepancy hypothesis. They conclude that "25 demonstrations of the inverted-U function represent a converging trend . . . which renders the discrepancy hypothesis a plausible concept" (p. 784). Cohen and Gelber (1975) noted that the pattern of support and nonsupport for the discrepancy hypothesis had some consistency to it. Studies that report linear functions tend to produce discrepancy by varying the number of elements that are changed in the stimuli or by varying the number of dimensions changed. On the other hand, studies reporting inverted-U functions tend to produce discrepancy by means of small, continuous changes in the stimuli, such as varying its orientation (e.g., Figure 16) or elongation.

The advocate of the linear hypothesis would not be fully assuaged by these counterarguments. The empirical claim about the number of studies supporting the theory must be tempered by consideration of the wide range of studies that have been done and the relative proportion of them that have yielded clear inverted U-shaped functions. Often there seems to be a haphazard pattern of outcomes, with linear or inverted-U functions arising in an unsystematic way over variations in stimuli, experimental conditions, or even dependent variables (e.g., heart rate versus looking). Further, given the nature of the theory, it is not clear why inverted-Us ought to be found for some kinds of stimulus manipulations and not others. Nothing in the theory as presently developed has explained the pattern of results noted by Cohen and Gelber (1975). In sum, while the discrepancy hypothesis is an intriguing theoretical possibility which has generated a large amount of research on infant attention during the 3- to 6-month period, its present status is still tentative. New theoretical analyses are needed that present a detailed account of the mechanisms of attention and knowledge representation responsible for the predicted effects. This would in turn allow for clearer empirical tests of this important issue.

There are other important attentional developments during this period. Perhaps the major one, the development of the knowledge base and its effects on attention and encoding, will be treated more fully in the next section. Before concluding this section we want to examine briefly one other phenomenon, the development of coordination between looking and reaching.

Schaffer (1971, 1975) suggested that looking and manipulating are not in concordance until the infant is 8 or 9 months of age. He based his conclusion on a series of studies in which 9-month-old infants showed concordance between looking and manipulating in responding to novel and familiar stimuli, but 6-month-olds did not (Schaffer, Greenwood, & Parry, 1972; Schaffer & Parry, 1969, 1970). Rubenstein (1974) reported that 6-month-olds *did* show concordance of looking and manipulating in responses to novel and familiar stimuli. Schaffer (1975) criticized Rubenstein's study on methodological grounds, pointing out that the same object had been used as the familiar object for all subjects and that since common toys were used as stimuli, there had been no control for extra-experimental familiarity. However, Ruff (1976) and Rubenstein (1976) both reported concordance of looking and manipulating in 6-month-old infants in studies where these factors *were* controlled. Given the contrasting results between the earlier studies and the more recent ones by Rubenstein and Ruff, it seems as though differential manipulation of novel and familiar objects is a less robust behavior than is looking. However, the 6-month-old infant is capable of displaying coordinated attention in two extremely important ways: visual exploration and manual exploration. The coordination of these two activities provides the infant with a type of control over the proximal environment that significantly enhances the opportunities for learning.

Acquisition

The major developments affecting learning during this period are changes in the infant's ability to encode experience. By encoding we mean the process through which environmental information is represented in the mind. Stimuli can be given physical descriptions, but the way in which stimuli are represented in the mind is subject to several levels of transformation. Sensory and perceptual processes determine the initial transformation; some stimulus qualities are detected better than others, some not at all, and all are given a *psychological* representation based on the transducing properties of the sensory channels. At the next level, processes of selective attention determine which of the stimulus qualities that can be sensed are actually noticed. Through the process of perceptual learning it is possible to alter which features of the world are even noticed (E. Gibson, 1969). Finally, cognitive processes affect how environmental information is interpreted. For example, as adults we encode our experiences in terms of meaningful objects and events; we see chairs, tables, people, and organized patterns of actions such as greetings, not mere patterns of light.

Encoding affects learning because it determines both what is learned and how quickly learning occurs. Thus major developmental changes in encoding skills have a major impact on the development of learning. What factors might play a role in producing developmental changes in the ability to encode a stimulus? There are several possibilities: (1) increased sensory and perceptual sensitivity, (2) changes in the speed and reliability of internal operations, (3) changes in attentional strategies, and (4) growth in the knowledge base. Each of these is a significant source of change during this period. Possibilities (1) and (2) most likely result from postnatal maturation of the central nervous system, especially the visual system (Bronson, 1974; Salapatek, 1975). As the visual system matures, the data that reach the infant's active memory are of increasingly good quality, and this development is important because the quality of sensory information places an upper bound on the encoding process (what is encoded can be no better than the quality of the raw input). Similarly, general maturational factors probably increase the speed and reliability of mental operations. These changes can also be selectively facilitated by experience. For example, various skills probably become more automatic, less effortful, as they become more and more highly practiced (LaBerge & Samuels, 1974; Posner, 1978; Schneider & Shiffrin, 1977; Shiffrin & Schneider, 1977).

There also may be a maturational component to the development of attentional strategies (Bronson, 1974; Salapatek, 1975). Research on infant eye movements has shown that there are major shifts in the nature of the infant's scanning of visual patterns over the first few months. The newborn's limited scanning of the visual world is in marked contrast to the active, exploratory scanning of the 2- or 3-month-old. Thus, not only does the older infant have better quality input because of sensory maturation, it is also gathered in a more systematic, organized fashion. There is also evidence that infants of 4 to 6 months can make use of comparative information in the environment in encoding a pattern. Fagan (1978), Ruff (1978), and Olson (1979) all found that visual patterns presented in spatial or temporal contiguity to a to-be-remembered pattern affected the encoding of the latter. So far there have been no developmental studies of the influence of contextual stimuli on encoding, but presumably the younger infant is not as likely to use such information as effectively as the older one. Such contextual influences are similar to the attentional effects that are at the heart of E. Gibson's (1969) account of perceptual learning. Comparative information of this type is also central to the development of classes or concepts, a topic that will be discussed in the next age period.

Finally, a rich knowledge base should have important effects on encoding. It is well known from studies of adult cognition that knowledge has important effects on the perception and retention of experience. Some of the best demonstrations of this fact have come from studies of perception and memory in games like chess or Go. Highly skilled players retain more information from a meaningful board pattern than do less skilled ones, whereas level of skill does not affect memory performance for meaningless board configurations (Chase & Simon, 1973; Reitman, 1976). The superior knowledge of the expert leads to quicker and more effective encoding of meaningful patterns. Since the infant is learning an enormous amount about the world, it seems quite likely that the older infants would have an advantage relative to the younger infant similar to that enjoyed by the expert in these adult studies. Fagan's (1972) studies of infant face recognition suggest that this is true. He presented 6-month-old infants with a right-side-up face and found that they could discriminate this familiar face from a novel right-side-up face. However, when he presented the same face upside down for the same familiarization period, infants of the same age could not discriminate this from a novel upside-down face. Presumably the infant's knowledge of faces makes the encoding of the right-side-up stimulus easier than encoding the same stimulus when it is presented upside down. These effects have not been investigated developmentally, but since it is already clear that there are developmental shifts in infants' knowledge of faces (Olson, 1976, 1981), this seems like a rich domain in which to examine the effects of knowledge on recognition memory.

As a result of the developments that contribute to greater coding skills, infants of this age have the capacity to remember visual patterns on the basis of only a few seconds of experience. Fagan (1974) found that 21- to 25-week-old infants could successfully recognize simple patterns on the basis of an average of 3.4 seconds of looking when these patterns were tested against novel distractors that differed from the target in a number of ways. When the tests required more subtle discriminations, such as between a target and a novel item that varied only in the arrangement of small elements or between a target and a novel item that were both photos of human faces, longer cumulative study times were needed before successful paired-comparison recognition was demonstrated. Unfortunately, type of stimulus and degree of difference between old and new patterns on the test were confounded in this experiment, so we cannot clearly differentiate the encoding of the to-be-remembered stimulus from similarity effects at the time of the test. Nonetheless, the study does show that by 5 to 6 months infants can encode a pattern well enough to show a novelty preference on the basis of very little experience.

Three other reports supplement these findings. Fagan (1977b) found that infants who averaged 22.6 weeks of age were able to discriminate a photograph of a face from a line drawing of the same face on the basis of an average of 4.6 seconds of looking. The minimum time needed to discriminate a photo of a face from an inverted photo of the same face was an average of 14.5 seconds. Olson (1979) found that 16- to 21-week-old infants were able to recognize stimuli that differed from their test distractor in both color and internal detail on the basis of 8 to 13 seconds of looking during familiarization. Finally, Cornell (1979) reported that 5- to 6-month-old infants could discriminate various old and new stimuli on the basis of 10 to 20 seconds of cumulative looking. Interestingly, he also tested delayed recognition for items that had been exposed for these brief durations and found that these same infants did not look differentially to old and new stimuli after retention intervals ranging from 40 seconds to 48 hours, unless they were presented with a brief "reminder" prior to test (see next section on *Retention*).

The implications of these studies is that during this period the infant's encoding skills have developed to the point where information can be extracted from the world and stored in memory relatively quickly. Lasky and Spiro (1980) reported a study that provides some important perspectives on this issue: though the infant of 3 to 6 months has come a long way from the neonatal period, there is still considerable development to come in information processing skills. They presented visual patterns from the Fagan (1974) study to 5-month-old infants in 100-msec flashes. Each presentation was followed by a masking stimulus at a delay of either 0, 250, 500, or 2,000 msec. Forty-five such presentations were given to the infants during the familiarization period. Only in the condition with the 2,000-msec delay between the stimulus and the masker did a significant novelty preference occur. Unfortunately, Lasky and Spiro did not run an important control, namely, groups who were presented the familiarization stimulus without the mask but with the same interstimulus intervals. The group with the 0-msec delay had a total familiarization period that was roughly 90 seconds shorter than the 2000-msec delay condition, and without the no-mask control we don't know if the recognition effect was due to the presence of the mask or the spacing of familiarization stimuli. However, there certainly is the suggestion that infants require a longer period of time following stimulus presentation to encode what they have just seen than do older children and adults. The intriguing methodology of Lasky and Spiro suggests a number of important studies that could be done during the infant period that would provide substantial insights into critical components of the information processing system.

These studies show that during the 3- to 6-month period infants acquire the ability to extract information quickly and effectively from the world around them and, at least under conditions in which several different aspects of the stimuli differ between test item and distractor, these infants can show reliable recognition memory on the basis of a relatively few seconds of experience. The infant is not yet an adult, however: this process of developmental increase in processing speed continues for a long period (e.g., Wickens, 1974).

Retention

During this period excellent long-term retention emerges. There are several lines of work showing that retention over periods of days and weeks can be demonstrated in infants between 3 and 6 months of age. In the previous section we described the work of Rovee-Collier and her associates which showed that 3-month-olds remembered the contingency between kicking their foot and moving a crib mobile over intervals as long as 2 to 4 weeks under conditions where they were presented a reminder, or upon reactivation of the conditioned response. In this section we will examine evidence from habituation-based paradigms on retention over long intervals.

The best evidence of long-term recognition memory is the set of studies reported by Fagan (1973). He presented a variety of stimuli to infants who were 21 to 25 weeks old and tested for recognition at intervals ranging up to 14 days. His data are shown in Figure 18. For most of the stimuli recognition was excellent over all of the intervals tested. Only the three-dimensional face masks tested at a delay yielded percent-to-novel scores that were not different from chance.

Unfortunately, there are no other published reports of recognition data where the testing occurred over intervals as long as this. However, there are other data which tested recognition at shorter intervals and which yield a picture of the 3- to 6-month-old's retentive capacities that are consistent. Martin (1975) found 24-hour recognition memory in 5-month-olds using a habituation savings technique. Cornell (1979) found significant long-term recognition for 5- to 6-month-olds for intervals ranging up to 48 hours, using the savings technique we described in the section on methodology. Finally, there is a series of studies that have found little evidence of forgetting in recognition memory across delays of a few minutes up to several hours (Bornstein, 1976; Cohen, DeLoache, & Pearl, 1977; Fagan, 1971, 1977b; McCall, Kennedy, & Dodds, 1977; Olson, 1976) and which support a consistent picture of robust recognition memory capabilities in the 3- to 6-month-old infant, at least when the initial exposure to the old stimulus is longer than a few seconds.

There has been considerable interest in whether or not visual recognition memory in infants is subject to interference. Fagan (1970, 1973) reported some interference effects, and a trio of papers by Fagan (1977b), Cohen, DeLoache, and Pearl (1977), and McCall, Kennedy, and Dodds (1977) examined this issue in more detail, using several methodologies. The most surprising finding from all of these studies is the apparent resistance of infant visual memories to interference from intervening experience. While there were conditions in these experiments that produced some interference, these interference effects were not terribly robust. For instance, Fagan (1977b) found that brief reminders that were themselves too short to produce learning undid the interference effects he had found. McCall et al. (1977) reported that the extent of interference was related to the degree to which infants habituated to the intervening stimuli, suggesting that well-encoded intervening experiences are more likely to

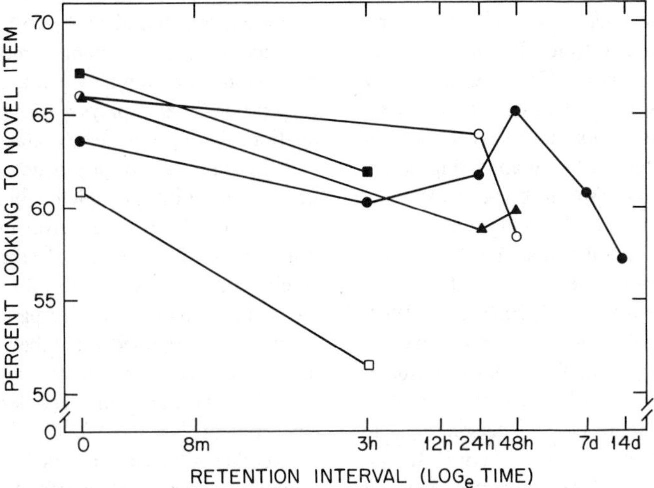

Figure 18. Recognition memory performance in the Fagan (1973) study. The time scale is in log (minutes), but for ease of reading is shown in minutes (m), hours (h), and days (d). The different lines are for different stimuli: PF = photographs of faces, MD = black and white stimuli varying multidimensionally, PA = small elements varying in pattern or arrangement, and FM = three-dimensional face masks.

lead to interference than poorly encoded ones. In total, however, these studies suggest that once an infant has encoded a visual experience, it is not highly probable that subsequent experiences are going to interfere with it. This finding is consistent with the earlier retention data, which showed that visual recognition memory persisted over long retention intervals for infants in the 3- to 6-month period.

Knowledge Base

We have mentioned several times the importance of the infant's developing knowledge base. The presence of greater and better organized knowledge about the world has enormous consequences for information processing. As we already mentioned, it affects perception, attention, acquisition, and undoubtedly also retention. In this section we will briefly review some of the major developments during this period in one of the most significant areas of knowledge acquisition for the very young infant: knowledge of persons.

There are many types of knowledge of persons that develop during this period. First, there is knowledge of specific persons, particularly the mother or the primary care-giver. Second, there is knowledge of the concept of persons in general. Both kinds of knowledge have several aspects to them. There is knowledge of the perceptual characteristics of either specific persons or of persons in general. However, there is also knowledge of what Olson (1981) has called the *dispositional characteristics* of persons. This is knowledge about the types of behaviors typical of either specific persons or persons in general. For instance, one type of dispositional knowledge is knowledge about how a person will react if I do something, such as smile. Clearly such knowledge is an integral part of a mature concept of person.

Olson (1981) has reviewed evidence pertaining to the development of all these types of knowledge, so here we will only briefly summarize the main conclusions. First, regarding knowledge of specific persons, it is for the period after 3 months of age that the evidence is clear that infants can discriminate their mother from an unfamiliar woman. It may be that such discrimination occurs earlier, but the studies of very young infants have many serious flaws, and the only unambiguous data on such discrimination exist for infants older than 3 months. This ability has enormous implications for learning in general and social development in particular.

There is little evidence of a concept of a person prior to 2 or 3 months. Faces and voices are potent elicitors of attention during these early months, but there is no evidence that this attention is due to the faceness of such stimuli as opposed to a variety of perceptual qualities (e.g., contour, movement) that are intrinsically attractive to the infant (Cohen, DeLoache, & Strauss, 1979). There is little evidence that young infants respond to faces as configurations. They tend to attend to local features such as the hairline or eyes (Caron, Caron, Caldwell, & Weiss, 1973; E. Gibson, 1969; Maurer & Salapatek, 1976). However, behaviors suggestive of a rudimentary concept of person begin appearing during the 3- to 6-month period. Smiling comes to be selectively elicited by human voices during the first month and by faces by 3 months, showing a great increase to social stimuli in general around 4 months (Ambrose, 1961; Gewirtz, 1965; Rheingold, 1961; Wolff, 1963). During this period social stimuli come to control the elicitation of babbling and the termination of crying (e.g., Bowlby, 1969), and by 3 months a stationary, nonresponsive person seems to have a suppressive effect on infant behavior (Bloom, 1977a, 1979). The infant's perceptual knowledge of persons is also developing. Sherrod (1981) reviewed the research on faces as physical stimuli, summarizing the evidence on the infant's emerging appreciation of the distinctive qualities of faces as physical events. Again, the evidence suggests that substantial development occurs during the 3- to 6-month period. Caron et al. (1973) found that by 5 months infants appreciated the configural properties of faces. Similarly, Fagan (1972) found that 5-month-olds could remember right-side-up faces after a brief familiarization but not upside-down ones.

In sum, the infant's knowledge of persons undergoes major development during the first six months. Persons have many properties that attract the infant's attention, and interactions with persons constitute a significant portion of the infant's experience. Most of the evidence suggests that the greater attention paid to persons during the first few months does not imply the existence of a person concept. However, during the second quarter of the first year the infant's behavior increasingly suggests that a rudimentary concept is present and developing (see Olson, 1981, and Sherrod, 1981, for more detailed discussions).

Performance

Major advances in motor skills occur during this period, and they have substantial implications for learning and memory. Motorically, newborns are helpless, limited information extractors, but during the 3- to 6-month period many information-seeking and exploratory behaviors emerge, giving the infants greater control of the stimulation they received from objects and events in its world. The infant's manual skills begin to show significant precision. Reaching and grasping improve and are accompanied by an informationally relevant activity that has not been given sufficient attention: mouthing. Being able to manipulate objects is a major cognitive advance, for it gives infants some degree of control over the information they extract. Mouthing of objects probably also plays a role in information extraction. During this period infants also learn to sit without support and gain better control over their heads. This ability, coupled with improved sensory and perceptual capacities, gives infants greater control over the kinds of distal stimulation they will receive. Lacking locomotor skills, infants cannot yet move themselves to another part of their world in order to explore objects, but they can at least orient themselves so as to gain better views or to hear more clearly what is going on in another part of their local environment.

Another relevant behavior is social smiling and socially directed vocalizations, which appear during this period. People are one of the richest sources of information in the infant's world. The infant's ability to influence the behavior of persons through his or her own behavior is of major cognitive significance. This allows the infant to shape or control some of the information that is made available and provides an essential source of interactions for learning about the *contingencies* that are an important part of social knowledge (cf. Olson, 1981). Such contingent interactions are a significant part of cognitive development (e.g., Clarke-Stewart, 1973). In sum, during this period infants acquire the ability to control information in their world, both through general motor development and through aspects of social development.

6 to 12 Months

General Themes

The second half of the first year is dominated by different general themes than the first half. As we have just reviewed, the first six months produce an enormous change in basic information processing skills. Sensory and perceptual skills become much more refined. The disorganization of the newborn's states disappears. The 6-month-old has substantial periods of alertness. Exploration of the world and active acquisition of knowledge characterize the 6-month-old. Acquisition skills are excellent: Information can be extracted and stored on the basis of limited experience. Retention is also good: Information can readily be retained over periods of days and weeks, even on the basis of modest amounts of experience.

During the second half of the first year these basic skills are put to use in several major developments. First, there is extensive growth of the knowledge base. The infant learns a large amount about its world and organizes this knowlege in systematic, even if still infantile, ways. The infant's current knowledge about the world will dominate new learning. Second, skills of abstraction and classification develop. The infant develops the ability to group and classify entities of its experience in useful ways. Classification skills play a major role in the emergence of the cognitive skill that will eventually signal the transition out of infancy: language. The first rudiments of language begin to appear at the end of the first year. Third, the beginnings of language represent a major cognitive step in that abstract symbols will enter the world of thought. Few maintain that these skills are present in the second half of the first year, but their foundations begin to appear in functional and symbolic play, imitation, and social interaction.

Attention

Unlike for the early months of infancy, there are no detailed studies of the attentional skills of infants during the second half year of life. However, we can make some inferences about the infant's attentional capacities during this period on the basis of indirect evidence. We start with the issue of states of alertness and general arousal. There is steady development of sleep and wake patterns during the first year. During the first four months the total time spent sleeping per day changes very little, but at 4 months most sleep is at night and there are prolonged periods of wakefulness (Berg & Berg, 1979; Parmelee, 1974). The emergence of regular sleep patterns over the early months of infancy is interpreted by many investigators as a sign of the physiological maturation of the brain (Berg & Berg, 1979; Emde & Robinson, 1979; Parmelee, 1974). These changes could also signal a shift in the ability of the brain to process incoming information, affecting the infant's capacity to learn and remember. At the very least, the emergence of night sleep and prolonged periods of wakefulness gives the infant more sustained, intensive periods for learning, and all the indications suggest that during the latter two-thirds of the first year the infant is an eager and active learner. These longer periods of wakefulness in turn allow for more prolonged periods of investigation, play, and social interaction. The infant during this period is often alert and very engaging. To be sure, there are still regular and lengthy daytime sleep sessions, and these will persist for several years in most children, but the infant has come a long way from the early months of sporadic alertness and frequent sleep cycles.

For the young infant our consideration of selective attention was narrowly focused on visual processing, including visual preferences and eye movements. During the second half of the first year selective attention must be considered more broadly. The infant's developing motor abilities have a substantial impact on the ability to attend selectively during this period. The ability to sit up, crawl, stand with support, and walk with support appears during this time. Indeed, a significant number of infants can stand and walk alone by 12 months (Shirley, 1931). Similarly, during this period the infant comes to have considerable ability to grasp and manipulate objects. Thus, selective attention during this period refers not merely to the selective visual fixation of patterns of objects, but also to selective reaching, grasping, mouthing, manipulating, and locomoting toward. This richer array of behaviors permits a wide range of important questions about attention to be addressed, though until now few have been explored in this age range.

The predominant changes in selective attention during this period are due to changes in the knowledge base. We boldly make this assertion on the basis of limited data, since there is little direct work on selective attention during this period. However, several major developments support the idea that what the infant knows comes to determine increasingly what the infant pays attention to. One source of evidence is the infant's social and emotional development. Although faces and persons have had significant stimulus value for the infant earlier, during the second half of the first year there is clearly enough knowledge about persons in the infant's memory to allow a host of important social behaviors to appear that are based on such knowledge. The appearance of selective social smiling to familiar rather than unfamiliar adults, of stranger anxiety, and of the behavioral indicants of specific attachments are all attentional phenomena with knowledge as a central component. In all of these domains, there is substantial development during the second half of the first year (an excellent summary of social and emotional development appears in Lamb & Campos, 1982). Social interactions in general, and imitation and play in particular, reflect the influence of social cognition on patterns of selective attention. The infant is eager to engage in interactions with adults but attends to features of these interactions on the basis of knowledge. Thus, the mother or other primary care-giver receives increasing amounts of attention from the infant, presumably because the infant has learned that a variety of important needs can be satisfied by this specific social agent. However, selective attention to the mother is not invariant. For instance, in the presence of the mother as a secure base, the infant will attend to and explore novelty in the environment, including strangers (see Lamb & Campos, 1982, for details). Thus, across the whole spectrum of social behaviors, one sees complex, contingent patterns of selective attention that depend upon the status of the events or persons as social entities and upon the context in which the infant finds itself.

Another domain with substantial development during this period is the object concept. Piaget's (1954) pioneering description of the development of the object concept pointed out a number of ways in which the infant's attention to objects changes during this period. It is during this period that the infant will search for an object that has been totally hidden from view. Furthermore, an exceedingly interesting error appears during this period: the so-called Stage IV error. When an object is hidden in a new location after a series of hidings in which an infant has successfully retrieved it, the infant searches for it at the old location. This error has been given a number of interpretations, and numerous factors have been implicated in its appearance, including perceptual, attentional, and memory ones (see reviews by Gratch, 1975, 1979; Harris, *vol. II, chap. 9*). What seems quite clear, however, is that during this period the infant's selective attention to objects in its world is being increasingly affected by what it knows about objects in general, as well as what it knows about particular objects. The infant has expectations about what objects ought to be like, where they ought to be, and what they ought to do, and its attention is guided by these expectations.

Acquisition and Retention

There is a considerable body of research on learning and memory in 6- to 12-month-old infants, although much of it is carried out with questions other than the retentive capacities of the infant as their focus. As we noted in the previous section, by 6 months the infant is a competent learner, as manifested in habituation and conditioning tasks. During this period there is continued evidence of the infant's ability to recognize previously experienced stimuli on the basis of modest amounts of familiarization and over long retention intervals. This ability is based on conditioning (e.g., Casey, 1979; Fagen, 1977; Finkelstein & Ramey, 1977; Millar & Schaffer, 1972; Millar & Watson, 1979; Silverstein, 1972; Silverstein & Lipsitt, 1974) and habituation or paired-comparison studies (e.g., Fagan, 1978; Gottfried & Rose, 1980; Gottfried, Rose, & Bridger, 1978; Kagan et al., 1978; Lester, 1975; McCall, 1979; Parry, 1972; Rose, 1981; Schaffer, Greenwood, & Parry, 1972; Schaffer & Parry, 1970; Soroka, Corter, & Abramovitch, 1979), the latter group using both visual and manipulatory measures.

In the previous section on attention we indicated that much evidence for the development of selective attention comes from studies of social development and of the emergence of the object concept. Not surprisingly, there is considerable research on learning and memory in these same contexts. There are a variety of studies that examine these skills with respect to social stimuli and social interactions (e.g., Eckerman & Whatley, 1975; Jacobson, 1980; Kaltenbach, Weinraub, & Fullard, 1980; Levitt, 1980; Ross, 1975; Ross, Rheingold, & Eckerman, 1972). Many of these studies focus on the emergence of wariness toward strangers, a significant indicator of long-term learning as well as emotional development. Similarly, a number of studies examine memory factors in the object search task (e.g., Cummings & Bjork, 1981a, 1981b; Gratch, Appel, Evans, LeCompte, & Wright, 1974; Ramsay & Campos, 1975; Schubert & Gratch, 1981). Piaget (1954) himself pointed out that the traditional object search task has significant memory components, and these studies indicate more formally that such factors as retention delay between the hiding and the opportunity for search or the number of alternative locations to search can substantially influence the infant's performance. This finding suggests that although the infant's information processing skills have progressed remarkably from the neonatal period, as with an older child or an adult, limitations of memory are going to constrain performance in many domains. In order for proper inferences about cognitive and social development to be drawn, it is important that memory factors involved in tests of these more general abilities be thoroughly understood.

One significant ability clearly emerges during this period: the ability to imitate. Although the empirical literature is modest, those studies that do exist show that by 12 months the infant has a limited ability to imitate actions and facial expressions modeled by an adult experimenter (Abravenel, Levan-Goldschmidt, & Stevenson, 1976; Kaye & Marcus, 1978; McCall, Parke, & Kavanaugh, 1977). Although imitation *appears* during this period, there is substantial subsequent development of this important ability (McCall et al., 1977). For example, McCall et al. (1977) found no evidence of delayed imitation prior to 18 months, consistent with Piaget's (1962) claim that delayed imitation is closely linked to the emergence of symbolic representations. The emergence of imitation has two implications. On the one hand, it represents a substantial set of skills, as many analyses of imitation have shown (Guillaume, 1971; Parton, 1976; Piaget, 1962). This is why the issue of whether or not the neonate imitates, which we discussed in an earlier section, is so significant. On the other hand, it offers the infant a new means through which to acquire knowledge from the world. Although the role of imitation in the development of such substantial skills as language is complex (see, e.g., de Villiers & de Villiers, 1978), there is little doubt that it plays a significant role in the learning of many cognitive skills. It certainly is the source of interactions with adults that form a rich forum for learning (e.g., Pawlby, 1977).

Knowledge Base

Since the major developments pertaining to the growth of attention, learning, and memory skills during this period are due to changes in the knowledge base, we now turn to a specific consideration of the nature of these changes. The primary domain we will examine is the general development of classes or categories as constituents of the infant's knowledge base. Although there may be earlier manifestations of this, there is a growing body of recent literature that documents the infant's ability to group its experience into classes and categories in the second half of the first year.

The classic studies of learning and memory using shifts of attention focused on memory for specific items. Thus, in a classic infant habituation experiment a single stimulus is presented repeatedly and recovery of habituation is examined by the presenting of another specific stimulus. A classic paired-comparison experiment is similar in this regard. Although successful habituation-dishabituation or paired-comparison behavior meant that the infant had recognized some commonality across a series of separate trials and thus had abstracted information from the temporally and contextually varying particulars of individual trials, the core experience—the to-be-remembered stimulus—was at least nominally the same. Therefore, presumably these studies were focusing on *recognition of recurrence,* that is, recognition that this specific pattern is one that was experienced before. During the 1970s a new type of study has emerged, one that focuses on *recognition of class or category membership.* In these studies infants are presented with a variety of stimuli, typically drawn from some class or category that is specified by the experimenter. The recognition test is a test for generalization; test trials consist of presenting novel instances from the class or category that was used during familiarization along with novel instances from a different category. Assuming appropriate controls have been used, the inference one would draw from discriminative behavior on such test trials is that the infants noticed the abstract property shared by the category members during familiarization and, upon noticing this same property in the novel within-category item on the test, the infant regarded the "novel" item as less novel than the outside-category test item. Thus there would be preferential looking toward the outside-category stimulus.

There are many important conceptual and methodological issues that pertain to experiments of this type. To facilitate our discussion, we will present an example of such a study so we can tie our points into a concrete case. The study by Strauss and Curtis (1981) on the infant's concept of number will serve as our example. The question they addressed was whether or not 10- to 12-month-old infants are able to discriminate stimuli that differ only in their numerosity. To study this, they presented infants with a series of familiarization trials in which each trial contained the same number of items. In one condition the infants saw different items (e.g., dogs, houses) in different sizes and positions on each trial (Heterogeneous Condition). In another (Homogeneous Condition), the same item type (e.g., dogs) was presented on each trial, with the size and position varied. However, in both conditions the *number* of items presented on each trial was constant. Different infants were familiarized with 2, 3, 4, or 5 items per trial. An infant control procedure with a relative criterion was employed. Following habituation, four test trials were presented, two with the same numerosity as familiarization and two with either $N + 1$ or $N - 1$ items. Different groups were tested on the 2 versus 3, 3 versus 4, and 4 versus 5 discriminations. For the 2 versus 3 discrimination, all infants were able to make the discrimination regardless of the familiarization condition (Homogeneous versus Heterogeneous). In the 4 versus 5 discrimination no infants showed differential attention on the test trials. An interaction of familiarization and sex occurred for the 3 versus 4 contrast. Females in the Homogeneous and males in the Heterogeneous conditions discriminated 3 from 4. Strauss and Curtis (1981) concluded that these data showed that preverbal infants possess the ability to apprehend the numerosity of perceptual displays, at least for small numbers. A study by Starkey and Cooper (1981) reported similar results for younger infants (4 to 6 months).

What are studies of this type about? The first

issue is the definition of a class or category. We will propose a definition that fits the spirit of the studies that have been done with infants. A class or category is a mental representation of the common elements of a set of distinct experiences *that are known to be distinct by the infant*. Distinct events whose differences are not noticed because of sensory or perceptual limitations or incomplete encoding do not produce category knowledge. The differences among the items in a class or category must be *noticed but ignored* by the infant.

Second, does the typical categorization experiment teach the infant the category or does it provide an opportunity for the infant to manifest category knowledge the infant already brings to the experiment? It seems improbable that Strauss and Curtis (1981) and Starkey and Cooper (1981) taught the infants in their studies the concept of numerosity. More likely, the infants came to the experiments with it and exhibited it under the conditions of the tasks. Category learning of this type is probably an extended process, based on long-term learning. A small number of trials in the laboratory cannot teach an infant the concept of numerosity. However, nothing in these experiments or any others that have been done contain evidence to support this supposition. The distinction between category learning and category recognition is an important one, and it would be useful to see proposals for how to differentiate the two.

Third, the perceptual knowledge displayed in a typical categorization experiment should not be thought of as concept knowledge. Concepts embody many types of knowledge, of which perceptual knowledge is only one. For instance, the concept of a face, of person, or of number is not exhausted by the perceptual knowledge that underlies the abilities infants have to notice categorizations built into experimental designs in recent studies. The perceptual knowledge is an important constituent of *some* concepts. These studies should properly be thought of as studies on the use of knowledge about perceptual categories. Otherwise misleading claims about infant abilities can result when terms like "concept" are thrown around too loosely.

What are the implications of these issues for categorization experiments? There are several. First, the precise nature of the category being investigated must be explicated so the types of controls to be run are clear. In particular, the relevant and irrelevant perceptual features for any particular category must be explicitly defined. In the Strauss and Curtis (1981) and Starkey and Cooper (1981) studies the investigators wanted to examine the infants' conception of numerosity. They wanted to have the numerosity of their displays constant across familiarization trials, but irrelevant features that might also attract the infants' attention had to be controlled. Item identity, item size, item orientation, and the configuration of items in the display are all irrelevant features. Therefore, these irrelevant features were varied from trial to trial so that the infants' test behavior could not be based on these features. These issues are very tricky, and presumably there will be continuing debate among investigators interested in perceptual categorization as to whether irrelevant and relevant features have been properly defined and controlled in particular experiments.

Second, there must be evidence that the infants can tell the different exemplars of the category apart. Few existing studies have coped with this issue in a satisfactory way. Some of the earliest studies that suggested infants were capable of displaying categorical knowledge in attentional experiments (e.g., Cornell, 1974; McGurk, 1972) did not address this issue at all. Some more recent studies (e.g., Cohen & Strauss, 1979; Fagan, 1976) showed that infants at the age tested could discriminate the stimuli used in the categorization experiment, but the studies did not assess whether the infants in fact could do so *under the conditions of presentation used in the categorization experiment itself*. A recent study by Sherman (1980) directly addressed this issue. She used a subset of the face stimuli that Strauss (1979) had used but employed a familiarization procedure which required that the infant demonstrate discrimination between category exemplars as they were presented for familiarization. Thus, her procedure guaranteed that the infants could discriminate all the category exemplars under the conditions used in the category study. She still found evidence of categorization at 10 months, although the pattern of results regarding the infant's representation of the central tendency of the category was different than that reported by Strauss (1979). Although there were some other differences in the details of these two studies, it at least raises the possibility that the kinds of categorization behavior one finds in infants may be strongly influenced by the extent to which one has guaranteed that the infants have discriminated the category exemplars *in the category experiment itself*. The criterion used in the Sherman (1980) study is quite stringent. In adult experiments it is often the case that the subjects know that the stimuli are different from trial to trial but they cannot discriminate those they have seen from novel members of the same category (e.g., Posner & Keele, 1968, 1970). Knowing that the items are different is a more appropriate prerequisite for categorization in the sense we mean than remembering the specific instances. Yet testing for memory of specific instances is the most direct way of testing with infants that they can tell the items apart. However, requiring memory for specific instances may affect the way in which categorization occurs.

Let us now briefly examine the categorization literature for the 6- to 12-month period, where most of the recent research has been done. The infant's ability to recognize categories of perceptual stimuli has been investigated in a number of particular domains: shape independent of specific orientation (McGurk, 1972), gender of pictures of faces (Cohen & Strauss, 1979; Cornell, 1974; Fagan, 1976), same face independent of pose (Cohen & Strauss, 1979; Fagan, 1976), the form of objects independent of size, color, and orientation (Ruff, 1978), faces generated from a common pool of features versus faces having totally novel features (Sherman, 1980; Strauss, 1979), types of motion (E. Gibson, Owsley, & Johnston, 1978), toys representing letters, men, animals, foods, and furniture (Ross, 1980), and numerosity (Starkey & Cooper, 1981; Strauss & Curtis, 1981). Strauss (1979) investigated not just whether categorization occurs but also the nature of the representation of categories, focusing on the question of prototypes or the representation of the central tendency of a category, an important conceptual advance that is at the heart of general issues of the nature of categorization (cf. Smith & Medin, 1981). All of these studies used the habituation logic.

The safest conclusion at present is that perceptual categorization emerges during the 6- to 12-month period. There are many results that support this conclusion, including the most stringent tests (e.g., Sherman, 1981). So far the question of whether categorization occurs earlier than 6 months is indeterminate. Studies conducted with younger infants have not examined whether the familiarization stimuli could be discriminated (e.g., Cornell, 1974; E. Gibson et al., 1978). It seems *probable* that some form of categorization skill is present prior to 6 months, but so far it has not been identified in appropriately controlled experiments.

What kinds of categories are recognized during this period? As was indicated above, most studies have examined categories from the real world, such as faces and various two- and three-dimensional objects. The evidence that real-world categories like furniture, animals, and foods emerge toward the end of this period (Ross, 1980) is important. These are the kinds of categories that will be labeled by the words the child acquires in his or her native language. Indeed, there have been several interesting recent experiments that have studied this link. Oviatt (1980) and D. G. Thomas, Campos, Shucard, Ramsey, and Shucard (1981) studied the tendency of infants to turn toward pictures of objects that were named. As we will see in the next section, infants just beyond this period begin to display the ability to look longer at pictures or objects that are named (Oviatt, 1980; D. G. Thomas et al., 1981), providing evidence of the emerging link between perceptual categories and the early stages of language acquisition. Although the methods for studying categorization are still relatively new, they promise to provide significant information about the development of categorization skills during the prelinguistic period.

The ability to classify or categorize experiences is basic to intelligence. The fact that we have examined the recent literature on categorization skills in infants in a section on the second six months of life is probably a temporary symptom of present research methods. Categorization skills may be very basic and thus may be part of the infant's cognitive repertoire long before 6 months. What's clear during the 6- to 12-month period is that these skills are well-developed. Now that researchers have begun to ask questions about the nature of these skills and the knowledge they in turn construct in memory, we would expect rapid progress in our understanding of the ontogeny of the process of categorization.

The Second Year: 12 to 24 Months

There is distressingly little research available on the development of learning and memory skills during the second year of life. This makes it difficult to present a precise picture of the infant's abilities during this period. By knowing where the 12-month-old is coming from and where the 24-month-old is going, it is possible to speculate about information processing capacities that develop during the second year, but few of these speculations can be tied to observations. Because of the limited data, our review of this period will be both briefer than for other periods and more general. Our goal is to highlight the kinds of phenomena that *have* been studied that hint at the infant's information processing skills.

There is almost no work during this period using habituation and paired-comparison tasks. Since these tasks primarily tap recognition memory, we know little about how recognition memory develops during the second year. However, it seems likely that the most profound changes in this ability occur quite early, say in the first six months, and that although adult levels of recognition performance have not been achieved during the second year, the rate of change in these abilities is much less substantial than during the earliest months of infancy. As the knowledge base is enriched and elaborated, encoding and attentional processes are affected. Also there may be further improvements in the speed and efficiency of the processes underlying recognition, due to further neural maturation and practice. All in all, however, recognition memory is a skill that is present early.

Nevertheless, there are major developments during the second year. We will describe three: the emergence of symbolic representations, the development of recall abilities, and the development of imitation abilities. All of these are significantly related to the major overriding development that is occurring during the second year, the emergence of language. There is probably no cognitive change more profound than the acquisition of language. In the verbally sophisticated child or adult the presence of linguistic skills has a major impact on most cognitive functioning. Language is a major factor in learning and memory. What makes the early months of infancy so interesting is that this important influence is missing. Language starts to appear late in the first year and continues throughout the second year, signaling the end of infancy and marking a deep change in the nature of cognition.

Piaget's characterization of sensorimotor intelligence is a description of mental life without language or symbolic thought. Perceptions and actions are the dominant forms of internal processes, and Piaget made the strong claim that in the absence of symbolic representations objects and events cannot be thought about or recalled in their absence. The transition from sensorimotor intelligence to preoperational thought at around 2 years is signaled by several significant achievements. One is clearly the appearance of language. In addition, symbolic play, deferred or delayed imitation, and a fully elaborated object concept also mark the transition. The key feature among these latter phenomena is the ability to represent an absent object or event, which according to Piaget requires symbolic thought. Thus, at a theoretical level the key feature is the acquisition of symbolic representations. Mandler (in press, a) has provided an excellent discussion of the emergence of symbolic thought, and we do not want to duplicate her review here. As she summarizes, there is a growing body of research that indicates that symbolic thought develops earlier than Piaget had thought. He had put this achievement in the 18- to 24-month period, whereas the work Mandler reviews suggests symbolic thought may be present at around 12 months. Regardless of the exact age, the appearance of symbolic thought is the dominant cognitive achievement of the second year.

In our review of infant memory abilities we have not yet discussed the development of recall. Recognition and recall are two basic forms of memory performance. In recognition, the to-be-remembered item is actually presented to the person, and the response we look for is an indication of familiarity. Has the item been experienced before? In recall, however, the to-be-remembered item is to be produced by the person. We as the experimenters present a cue, and what we want from the person is a specific target behavior. Unfortunately, these operational descriptions of recall and recognition are too narrow. By the characterization we have given of recall, such tasks as classical and operant conditioning would seem to qualify as instances of recall. However, these tasks seem to require different cognitive skills than the act of recalling a word list by a verbal adult or the act of recalling a prior experience. It's difficult to pin down what the difference is. Voluntariness is one possible difference. A classically conditioned response occurs automatically, and the traditional view of operant conditioning is that it occurs without conscious awareness (Dulany, 1968). These begin to be theoretical distinctions, however, and exactly how they are to be operationalized is difficult to specify (Dulany, 1968).

What might count as evidence of recall in the infant? We maintain that neither classical nor operant conditioning represent recall in the sense intended by Piaget or, more recently, by Mandler (in press, a). There are other behaviors that seem more probable. Ashmead and Perlmutter (1980) had parents of infants keep diaries of events they observed that indicated memory for past events on the part of their children. There were ample indications of recall-like activities in the infants, all of whom were less than a year old. Most of the parents reported incidents in which their infant searched for a hidden object at a known location. This included looking for objects in a location where they had seen it only once. Huttenlocher (1974) describes children of roughly 1 year of age locating named objects even when they are not in sight. Indeed, searching for hidden objects, especially in the typical Piagetian object search task, is a particularly good indicator of recall-like abilities. Sophian (1980) has reviewed a number of such studies from this perspective.

Another achievement that requires recall-like processes is imitation. It is scarcely surprising that Piaget linked the development of recall and of symbolic thought more generally with the appearance of deferred or delayed imitation, which is the ability to reproduce a modeled behavior after an interval of time has passed. Piaget claimed his studies of his own children showed that this ability did not appear until Stage VI, at roughly 18 to 24 months. Unfortunately, there is almost no research on deferred imitation. McCall, Parke, and Kavanaugh (1977) studied the development of imitation in infants ranging from 12 to 36 months. A model performed actions with various objects, and the infant was given an opportunity to imitate the action. The youngest infants in their study showed little evidence of imitation when the test occurred 24 hours after the original modeling, but by 24 months deferred imitation was readily observed, consistent with Piaget. Interestingly, in one study the 24-month-olds showed just as much deferred imitation when their *first* opportunity to imitate occurred 24 hours after the modeling as when they had had an immediate opportunity to model in addition to the 24-hour test. Thus, to the extent that deferred imitation counts as recall, this ability is readily evident by the end of the second year.

But what about earlier? In the McCall, Parke, and Kavanaugh (1977) study the 1-year-olds showed little evidence of deferred imitation. However, since the researchers were interested in how the properties of the to-be-imitated behaviors affected the rate of imitation, they presented each infant with fourteen different object-action pairs. This is a large memory load, and it is conceivable that they simply overloaded the younger infants, who would be expected to have more difficulty encoding these pairs because of a more limited knowledge base. Indeed, in one of their studies they did find that with 2-year-olds they obtained a higher rate of deferred imitation when they presented a smaller number of more highly salient object-action pairs. Research needs to be done with younger infants using smaller sets of to-be-remembered actions before we can conclude that deferred imitation does not occur until the end of the second year.

In sum, although there is little research available to trace the details, there are substantial developments during the second year of life in information processing capacities, all linked to the development of language and symbolic thought. We hope that there will be increasing interest among investigators in tracing out the details of these developments.

CONCEPTUAL FRAMEWORK

The past quarter of a century has produced major advances in our understanding of the human information processing system. These advances, in the areas of perception, attention, learning, memory, and cognition, provide the basis for the general sketch of human information processing to be presented in this section. This conceptualization will serve as a framework for examining the methods and findings we have reviewed in this chapter. Our goal is to highlight in a theoretical sense what is known and to provide a guide for future research on infant attention, learning, and memory.

The general sketch we will provide is essentially a sketch of the organization of memory and of its interface with input and output processes. The information processing system is rooted in memory. The capacity to store and access information in an effective way is at the heart of intelligent behavior. Adaptation depends upon retaining a record of interactions with the environment and ultimately of constructing generalizations based on these interactions. Perceptual and attentional processes can be modified on the basis of experience if a capacity for keeping mental records is available. Complex cognitive processes like language require enormous amounts of computational and archival memory. Even simple forms of adaptation such as habituation or conditioning require memory traces of various types. In short, memory is at the heart of all human behavior.

Most of what has been learned about the general organization of information processing has come from research on adults and older children, but we are making the strong assumption that there is continuity from the infant to older children and adults. The conceptual scheme we will review here has not come from infant research. However, we feel it is a conceptual scheme that is productive for examining the broad range of infant information processing skills. Since we do not have space to develop this view in detail, our strategy is to describe conceptual distinctions at a general level and then illustrate how they apply to some representative infant phenomena. The analysis is developed in greater detail in Olson and Sherman (in press).

We will first present an overview of the organization of the conceptual scheme. Then we will examine in more detail each of the central components of the scheme. Throughout, our goal will be to provide concepts that are useful in examining what is known about infant memory. In the last part of this section we will discuss some specific topics in infant learning and memory using the concepts we have developed.

Overall Organization

A schematic representation of the major components of the information processing system appears

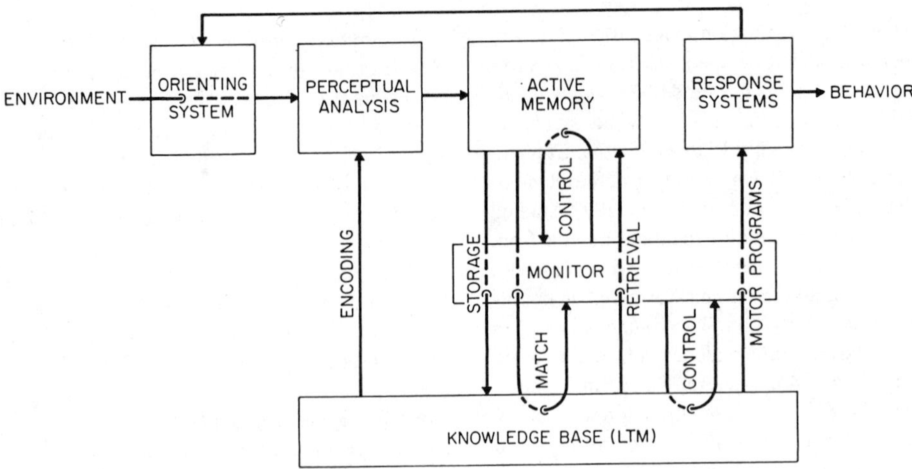

Figure 19. Major components of the human information processing system.

in Figure 19. The major components of the system are: (1) the *perceptual system,* which encodes stimuli received from the external world; (2) the *active memory,* the currently active set of information, both from perception and from the knowledge base; (3) the *response system,* which initiates and controls actions, including the *orienting system,* a special aspect of the response system which controls the orientation of the perceptual analyzers; (4) the *knowledge base,* the store of everything that is known, both in the sense of facts and of skills or procedures, and including affective as well as cognitive components of knowledge; and (5) the system *monitor,* the special set of routines responsible for the control of information processing and the regulation of system goals. We cannot stress too much the fact that these are not necessarily descriptions of different places in the nervous system. Of course, perceptual processes depend in their initial stages on the various specific sensory systems and specific pathways to specialized portions of the brain for vision, hearing, and so forth. Similarly, actions are performed by particular effectors that have specific loci of control in the brain and specific pathways of activation. However, with regard to the interactions of information in the center of the system and the distinctions between active memory, the knowledge base, and the system monitor, we wish to claim only that the distinctions we make are functional ones, not neurological ones. There is adequate evidence to support the usefulness of making these functional distinctions (see, e.g., Anderson, 1976; Newell & Simon, 1972).

Given that our focus in this chapter is infant attention, learning, and memory, we will examine how these skills are embodied in the scheme shown in Figure 19. We need to know how information from the environment is noticed and encoded. This involves examining perception and attention. However, the noticing and encoding of information also depends on system goals and motives, which we describe as monitor functions. Further, the knowledge base plays a major role in the pickup of information from the environment. Once noticed and encoded, information may have a range of effects of varying permanence on the system. New entries may be made in the knowledge base. Information may be activated with consequences for active processing. Goals or motives may be modified. In adults internal processing can occur independently of the immediate external input. Information is retrieved from the knowledge base for various purposes, and a wide range of internal computations may occur. An interesting though difficult-to-investigate question is the extent of such purely internal processing in infants. Finally, whether as a result of environmental inputs or purely internal processing, the activities of the cognitive system *may* ultimately lead to overt actions. As empirical psychologists, we are confined to studying those processes that have external outputs. This study is especially restrictive with infant subjects since they have a more limited range of behaviors than the motorically skilled and verbal child or adult. While we are not concerned with the nature of motor behavior in infants per se, we cannot ignore this domain because of the major developments that occur during infancy. Not only are we confined to examining internal processes that have external outputs, we also have to examine those behaviors that arise in response to identifiable inputs, either from the external environment or from observable aspects of the organism's internal environment. Our goal is to infer the internal mental processes that mediate learning and memory, an effort that must be anchored in specifiable inputs at one end and observable behavior at the other.

Sensation and Perception

Learning is constrained by what can be sensed, what can be perceived. The infant's sensory and perceptual systems differ in a variety of ways from the adult's. There are several issues to consider: (1) the nature of the infant's environment as a possible source of information; (2) the structural or functional characteristics of the infant's sensory equipment and associated orientation systems that might constrain information pickup, and the way these develop during the infant period; and (3) the nature of perceptual learning and its relation to other forms of learning.

The Infant's World as an Information Source

Probably no perceptual psychologist has done more to force us to think about the nature of the world as a source of information than J. J. Gibson (1950, 1966, 1979). There has been a long-standing tradition in perceptual psychology to think of the world as presented to the perceptual systems as "punctate and momentary" (Turvey, 1975, p. 137). This view assumes that the perceptual systems operate on narrow time slices consisting of an array of discrete elements. Wholistic elements of perception such as the orderly flow of events or the stability of objects must be constructed from the impoverished data of experience.

Gibson's challenge to this view was to argue that the information in the environment is quite rich. The primary data of perception are invariants extracted from the normally dynamic objects and events as viewed by a multimodal perceptual system, rather than the moment-by-moment snapshots of the traditional view. The wholes of experience, such as objectness or constancies, are themselves primitives rather than constructions from elementaristic data. Gibson's theory has been vague about just what it is in the environment that the organism senses. What are the invariants of perceptual experience? Although the absence of clear specifications of perceptual invariants has limited the appeal of his theory, he nonetheless has forced perceptual psychologists to think more carefully about what it is in the environment that the perceptual systems pick up.

The psychologist who has most developed Gibson's case in the infancy area is T. G. R. Bower (1974, 1977a, 1977b, 1979). Although his work has been extremely controversial, it has forced investigators to think very carefully about what the infant's experience might be like. What is a simple stimulus for an infant, and what is a complex one? One can get very different answers to this question as a function of what one believes about Gibson's analysis. Take one example: the human face. Most studies present the infant with drawings or photographs of two-dimensional faces, at least partly because such stimuli seem "simple." This assumption would fit with the snapshot view of perception. However, if the infant attends to the invariants of moving, three-dimensional, multimodal stimuli such as those normally encountered in the real world, then a two-dimensional, static, unimodal view of a face could be psychologically "complex" compared with real faces (see a more complete discussion of this example in Olson, 1981). This fact in turn might imply that it would be easier for the infant to show recognition memory for moving, full-color, three-dimensional faces than for black-and-white photographs of faces. No data yet exist for this very straightforward comparison.

A second issue about the nature of the infant's world is the types of experiences infants have. What is an infant's day-to-day world like? Most studies of this experience have focused on social interactions, especially with the primary care-taker (e.g., Ainsworth & Bell, 1974; Clarke-Stewart, 1973; Elardo, Bradley, & Caldwell, 1977; Yarrow, Rubenstein, & Pederson, 1975), on physical properties of the home environment (e.g., Elardo et al., 1977; Wachs, 1978, 1979; Wachs, Francis, & McQuiston, 1979; Yarrow et al., 1975), on differences between cultures (e.g., Leiderman, Tulkin, & Rosenfeld, 1977), or on some special domains, such as the intensive care units in which premature infants often spend many of their early days (e.g., Cornell & Gottfried, 1976; Lawson, Daum, & Turkewitz, 1977). What type of stimulation is a typical normal infant exposed to? Certainly the dominant forms are associated with social interactions with primary care-givers. However, other persons are experienced to varying degrees, and there are many nonsocial situations, such as lying alone in one's crib. Further, the world of the infant changes drastically following the onset of locomotor skills. For the preperambulatory infant, the effectively available world is controlled by others. Once the infant can crawl, sit, stand up, and walk, the range of experiences and the dependence on the infant's own actions change in profound ways. Thus, during the infant period there is great change in the world that is presented to the senses.

Constraints Imposed by the Sensory and Perceptual Systems

The sensory systems are sensitive to only a limited range of environmental information. For example, only a small portion of the electromagnetic or acoustic spectra is detectable. Further, physical constraints impose limits. We can see only within a rough hemisphere surrounding what our eyes are focused on. These constraints define the range of opportunities for information pickup.

We are interested mainly in the *differences* in constraints between infants and adults. How similar are the basic perceptual sensitivities? If there are differences, what is the pattern of development? Does the immaturity of motor systems limit the pick-up of information (e.g., through eye movements)? All of the evidence indicates that there are large changes in basic sensory and perceptual sensitivites during the first year of life (see, e.g., Aslin et al., *vol. II, chap. 8;* Banks & Salapatek, *vol. II, chap. 7;* Cohen, DeLoache, & Strauss, 1979; Cohen & Salapatek, 1975; Salapatek & Banks, 1978). No matter what sensory or perceptual skill is examined, the newborn has limited abilities. However, development of the sensory systems due to maturation is rapid during the first six months. Thus, not only will the infant's basic perceptual sensitivity be a limiting factor on its ability to learn and remember, its rapid development will contribute to change in these abilities.

Perceptual Learning

J. J. Gibson (1966) and E. Gibson (1969) have argued that perceptual learning is the process of coming to attend to relevant features of the perceptual world. We learn to notice those distinctive features that differentiate among objects of events that matter to us, and we learn to ignore those differences among experiences that are irrelevant to our purposes. Thus, the sonar operator learns which noises are relevant to the task of detecting objects underwater and which are irrelevant. Nothing new is *sensed.* Rather, the features of experience come to be attended to differentially.

The possibilities for such perceptual learning are enormous during infancy. One domain that has attracted analytic attention is faces (E. Gibson, 1969; Sherrod, 1981). E. Gibson (1969), for example, has described how the infant learns to attend to the various features of the human face. Exactly how such development proceeds is difficult to untangle because of the concurrent changes in basic sensitivity. However, it is highly likely that substantial amounts of perceptual learning in the sense we are describing occur. The net effect of such development is an infant who attends to the world in a more effective manner, devoting perceptual processing to those characteristics of the world that are related to the types of objects and events important to the infant's activities.

Sensation and Perception: Summary

Because of these three sources of concurrent change during infancy—the nature of the world as an information source, the structural limits of the sensory and perceptual systems, and perceptual learning—there is substantial change in the nature of the information presented to the infant's cognitive system. Thus, during the early months of life there are changes in the *opportunity* to learn that are as profound as any possible changes in the *ability* to learn. Sorting out an overall account of the infant's abilities and the ways they change requires careful analysis of the *source* of performance characteristics. Certainly during the early months of infancy sensory, perceptual, and motor factors are likely to play a large role.

Active Processing

The human information processing system has basic, central limitations on the amount of information that can be activated or processed at any moment in time. This limitation has been variously characterized as a limited-capacity memory store (Newell & Simon, 1972; Simon, 1974), as a limited pool of processing resources (Kahneman, 1973; Norman & Bobrow, 1975), and as a limitation on the number of active nodes in a memory network (Anderson, 1976). The common theme among all of these is that there is an upper bound on the amount of information that can be currently active and available for immediate processing and that this limitation is a major determiner of the form of information processing in humans.

There are two basic ways of conceptualizing this limitation. First, there is a limit on immediate memory. Typically, it is thought that only five to seven "units" of information can be active at any given moment. This figure arises from work on immediate memory span (Miller, 1956; Simon, 1974) and from attempts to do computer simulations of human performance with realistic structural constraints (e.g., Newell & Simon, 1972). The exact quantitative characteristics of the limitation are not as important for our purposes as the fact of the limitation. Immediate memory can hold roughly a half dozen units, not a hundred or an unlimited number. The ambiguity about "units" is intentional. One of the basic characteristics of immediate memory is that its "units" are based on what is known. Information that has been grouped or "chunked" (Miller, 1956) in the knowledge base is more readily held in an active state in immediate memory than the same information in an unchunked format. Thus, knowing more about a domain makes it easier to remember items in immediate memory (Chase & Simon, 1973; Reitman, 1976).

Second, there are limits on attention. The extreme description of this limit is that attention can be allocated to only one thing at a time. Norman and Bobrow (1975) proposed a more general form of this limit on attention. They suggested there is a limited pool of processing energy. Several tasks can tap this limited pool, but at some point performance on the multiple tasks breaks down because the limited resources have been exceeded. The single-task position claims that attention can be switched among tasks, yielding functional time-sharing, but that such switching is itself limited and costly, yielding once again a breakdown in performance as the number of tasks or their specific demands become too great.

The idea of limited attention has an important corollary. Tasks will be performed in parallel successfully to the extent that they do not take attention. This fact in turn implies that tasks that can be performed automatically can be performed in parallel with tasks that demand attention. Many examples of this are readily available with adults—driving a car, singing a song, and thinking about one's research can proceed in parallel until one of the automatic activities (presumably one of the first two, as when there is a sudden emergency on the road) demands attention and displaces the others. Thus, the automatization of various functions is an advantage (see LaBerge & Samuels, 1974; Schneider & Shiffrin, 1977; Shiffrin & Schneider, 1977). Automatization of skills enables the individual to perform multiple tasks concurrently. For skills that are hierarchically organized (such as reading), automatization of lower level skills (such as letter recognition) will allow attention to be allocated to high-level processes (such as comprehension).

There are many possibilities for how these limits might be manifested in infancy. The basic capacities of immediate memory and attention might be more limited in infants. At a minimum, because of the less-developed knowledge base of the infant, there will be less chunking and less automatic processing. Further, infants might have more limited schemes for switching or sharing attention, degrading performance in situations where there are competing demands. Finally, infants clearly have fewer skills automated. Thus, all of these factors put the infant at a relative disadvantage for effective and efficient information processing. Further, developments in any and each of these domains (knowledge base, attentional resources, automatization, etc.) can account for many of the developmental changes seen throughout the infant period.

So far we have discussed two broad kinds of limits—those on immediate memory and those on attention—as characteristics of active processing. These limits are the most fundamental central constraints on human information processing. They determine the ways in which a human's processing resources are constrained in real time. Another characteristic of active processing, which will be described in more detail in the next section but which needs to be mentioned here, is the goal structure (or motivational structure) active at the time information processing is taking place. Processing does not occur in a vacuum but typically occurs in the service of various goals. The moment-by-moment allocation of the limited resources of memory and attention must be considered with respect to current goals. For some kinds of goals, focusing the resources on one task may be optimal, whereas for other goals the spreading of resources across a wide range of tasks may be optimal. Developmental changes in goals or motives probably interact strongly with the development of ways to cope with the limitations of active processing.

Response Processes

The only mental processes we can examine are those that have observable correlates. Thus, the study of attention, learning, and memory, like any other psychological investigation, must of necessity consider the nature of *behavior:* the actions and responses that are measured as part of our inquiry. In adults, the exact nature of action—while in itself an incredibly important and interesting domain of investigation (e.g., Gallistel, 1980; Turvey, 1975)—seldom intrudes into our studies of the properties of learning and memory. This is in large part because the exact nature of the actions performed are irrelevant to what is measured. In a normal, verbal adult, the use of instructions and the exploitation of a wide range of well-articulated behaviors make the exact behavior to be measured in any experiment almost arbitrary. If we want verbal recall, we can have the subject write down the responses, type them into a computer terminal, or say them out loud, and usually the details of these responses are not important. Furthermore, if we are studying long-term memory or long-term learning, there is little likelihood that there will be any substantial change in the repertoire of response processes available to use on various test occasions.

However, with the infant things are quite different. The newborn and very young infant is motorically immature. Both the peripheral and the central components of action and its control are immature. Further, there is enormous change during infancy. Just contrast the newborn with the walking, talking 2-year-old. From the most basic reflexes and psychophysiological reactions to motor behaviors such as reaching, grasping, and locomoting, there is change. Thus, the choice of a behavior to measure and its interpretation across different ages must be sensitive to the incredible development in response capacity that is occurring during infancy.

As we indicated in our prior discussion of representation, action may have another important role. Several theorists (e.g., Piaget, Bruner, Mandler) have suggested that *action* may be the infant's predominant form of encoding experiences. If this is correct, then not only is change in action an important methodological consideration, it may also affect in a substantial way what is being encoded and remembered. Thus, the analysis of action may be a central problem for the study of information processing in infancy.

Although such theorists as Piaget and Bruner have made action a central component of their theories of infant information processing, in general their proposals have been made at a very general level and have not been exploited in any systematic fashion by those who have examined attention, learning, and memory. As the study of action develops in general (e.g., Gallistel, 1980), we can hope that the analysis of infant information processing will incorporate a more thorough treatment of this domain.

Knowledge Base

Long-term memory is at the heart of intelligence. Even the simplest kind of adaptation to the environment requires that an organism modify some internal structures in an appropriate manner and retain these modifications for later use. More complex forms of adaptation require advanced sensory, locomotive, and manipulative skills, but in order for these skills to be effective it is necessary to have an ample and organized knowledge base. Higher levels of intelligence do not result from the proliferation of elementary sensorimotor adaptations but are based on complex systems of organization, synthesis, control, and abstraction that are all part of a sophisticated knowledge base. Higher intelligence is both a quantitative and a qualitative change in the nature of the knowledge base. Abstractions from the environment, theories and causal accounts of these abstractions, symbolic systems, belief systems, reasoning systems, and more come to dominate the knowledge base.

The systematic study of knowledge is of recent origin within the mainstream of cognitive psychology. It took the popularization of Piaget, theoretical pressure from Chomsky, and the objectification of issues of knowledge by artificial intelligence to make knowing a central issue in cognitive psychology. As a result, questions of how knowledge is acquired, represented, stored, organized, and retrieved have become central puzzles. The study of semantic memory, central to both cognitive psychology and artificial intelligence in the past decade, is basically the study of the knowledge base. The content of the knowledge base is diverse. It includes both the particulars of individual experiences and generalizations or abstractions due to recurring experiences or to instruction. It includes declarative and procedural knowledge, knowing *that* and *knowing how to* (Winograd, 1975). Knowledge may be perceptual-like or symbolic (Kosslyn, 1980). In short, the knowledge base is the store of all that is known.

There are vast differences between the infant's knowledge base and that of an older child or adult. Further, there are enormous changes in the knowledge base during the infant period. As a result of the baby's interactions with people and objects, the infant learns an enormous amount about the social and physical world. This developing knowledge base is a product of the infant's developing learning and memory skills and in turn plays a substantial role in shaping or influencing the infant's developing ability to learn and remember. Thus, a systematic treatment of the nature of the knowledge base and its development is of central importance for understanding the infant's information processing skills. Here we can only provide a brief overview of the issues. More detailed discussions appear in Olson and Sherman (in press) and Olson and Strauss (in press). The discussion of the knowledge base will focus on four major topics: (1) *representation:* the character of the knowledge in the data base in terms of its format and organization; (2) *entry:* the entry of new information into the knowledge base; (3) *access:* the locating or activating of knowledge in the data base; and (4) *fate:* the status of knowledge with the passage of time (either clock time or event time).

Representation

We mean by representation what Mandler (in press, a) describes as "knowledge and the way in which it is organized," that is, "both what is known and how that knowledge is structured." She distinguishes this from "representation as the use of symbols," a more traditional sense of the term. In this sense, representational thought refers specifically to thought based on language or symbols, with abstract entities "representing" aspects of reality. However, as used in contemporary discussions in cognitive psychology or artificial intelligence, representation refers more broadly to *any* system of internal representation, including sensory- and motor-based systems as well as abstract, symbolic ones.

Issues of representation are not new to the infancy area. Piaget's theory directly pertains to what is known and how what is known is structured. His characterization of how object knowledge develops is an excellent example of a theory of knowledge representation (Piaget, 1954). More generally, his whole characterization of sensorimotor intelligence and its contrast with later forms of intelligence is a proposal for how knowledge is represented in the infant. Similarly, Bruner's (1966) proposal that during infancy there is a progression from enactive encoding, rooted primarily in action, to ikonic encoding, rooted in perception, is a theory of the development of the representation of knowledge. A thorough discussion of issues of representation, including their application to infancy, is found in Mandler (in press, a).

Issues of knowledge representation are extremely important. How an information processing system chooses to represent something will determine its availability on future occasions, its effect on future learning, its relation to other knowledge, and even what gets stored, since different modes of representation will weight features of an experience in different ways. The issues are especially interesting in infancy because of the absence of language. Language is an extremely important representational system in older children and adults, and all theories of cognitive development have correctly stressed the importance of the acquisition of language for thought. Infancy is interesting in two ways. In early infancy there is no linguistic or languagelike representational system available. As we mentioned above, most theorists have supposed that information is represented in memory in codes with strong connections to the motor and sensory systems. However, during infancy the foundations are established for the acquisition of the verbal system. Thus, infancy will be a period where the representational formats available are quite different than they are later, and where there is much change over the course of later infancy.

Entry

Entry and access are the touchstones linking active processing to the knowledge base. As information is generated from perceptual inputs or through thought, it may be entered in a relatively permanent form into the knowledge base. What will be entered is governed by attention and goals or motivations. How it will be entered is determined by the repertoire of representations available and by the manner and intensity of active processing devoted to it. Principles of information entry are known as learning, memory storage, assimilation, or even understanding. These are the principles by which the information processing system alters its knowledge base as a result of experience with both the world of perception and the world of inner thought. These modifications include changes in both procedural and declarative knowledge as well as changes at all levels of abstraction and generality. Included also are changes with systemwide effects, such as changes in the way in which the system copes with information processing (what Klahr and Wallace, 1976, have called principles of self-modification). However, human information processing is not modifiable without bound. There are broad functional constraints, probably of biological origin, that limit the way the system operates. The limits of immediate memory and attention constrain learning. Further, there may be constraints on the kinds of environmental contingencies that can be noticed or encoded (Fitzgerald & Brackbill, 1976; Hinde & Stevenson-Hinde, 1973), as we mentioned earlier in our discussions of classical conditioning.

Entry of knowledge is typically context dependent. Interpretations of experience are provided by routines which use the information in the current knowledge base. In part, such context-dependent processing assists in the organization of new inputs for future retrieval. The new is related to the old and is stored in this relative fashion. Presumably, then, an account of the principles of information entry must reflect this dependence upon context and the current knowledge base.

Although there is a rich traditional literature on the psychology of learning (e.g., G. H. Bower & Hilgard, 1981), it is only fairly recently that learning has again been systematically studied by those interested in both human and artificial information processing systems (e.g., Anderson, 1981, 1982; Holland, 1975; Michalski, Carbonell, & Mitchell, 1983). The few preliminary models of infant learning that exist (e.g., Cohen & Gelber, 1975; Fagan, 1977a; Olson, 1976) have not yet tapped the rich literature on learning that is beginning to appear.

Access

Entry of information in terms of what is already known suggests that access will often depend upon possession of relevant retrieval information. In adults, this is clearly the case for recall, and it is probably true of recognition as well (Tulving & Thomson, 1973). Information in long-term memory is stored in relation to other things: the knowledge it was assimilated to, the spatiotemporal context in which it was experienced, and the thoughts and goals present when it was experienced. Successful access often depends on activating this contextual information. The principles of activation, memory search, and retrieval are of great interest to investigators of natural and artificial intelligence. Much activation of information may be highly automatic, for example as spreading activation through an organized memory network (Anderson, 1976; Posner, 1978). Other ways of access are more strategic and planful, involving careful encoding of the inputs and intelligent search through the knowledge base.

The automatic activation of information is a very basic property of memory and is probably central to all of the tasks used to study memory in infancy. For instance, in adults a well-learned item like a letter or a word, when presented visually, usually automatically activates its name, categorical information, and semantic associates (Posner, 1978). These may have important consequences for information processing despite the fact that their activation may not have been the goal of the perceptual or cognitive routine that generated the stimulus input. This class of processes, whereby memory nodes and pathways are automatically activated via the presence of a representation, is basic to all cognitive operations. It is exactly these more automatic operations that are at the heart of learned adaptations, and their influences upon action provide the key for the study of the knowledge base in organisms of a wide range of complexity.

There are other varieties of access to the knowledge base that are characteristic of human cognition, although they may not be characteristic of the very young infant. These are operations whose primary goal is to activate some set of memory nodes specifically via associated pathways. *Redintegrative memory* seeks to activate an entire complex via a part, and *recall* tries to activate a memory structure (simple or complex) through the medium (cues) of pathways and structures that are not a part of the target structure. Redintegrative and recall memory often involve elaborate search, with many similarities to problem solving. The contrast between automatic activation of memory information and effortful search and retrieval is important, for it is one component of the differences between such basic forms of learning as conditioning and habituation and more cognitive forms of learning that will appear later in the developing child.

Fate

Fate is the issue of how information might be lost. There are three types of accounts: (1) Information is lost track of, much as a book might be misplaced in a library or, perhaps more accurately, a small part of the card catalog is rearranged or lost. In this account, the information is still there but for the time being there is no access to it because appropriate or effective retrieval cues are unavailable. (2) Information is destroyed by other information. The purest form of this account is the metaphor of the computer memory. The information in a memory register is destroyed when a new item is entered. It is now permanently gone. The unlearning mechanism of classical interference theory is an example of such a mechanism (Barnes & Underwood, 1959; Melton & Irwin, 1940). (3) Information spontaneously decays with the passage of time. This has been another popular account, although it has proven to be very difficult to test (see Klatzky, 1980, for an instructive review of some of the literature). In this account a memory trace is assumed to have some inherent instability, probably associated with the biological mechanisms responsible for memory traces, perhaps a shift over time in the signal/noise ratio of some kind of statistical process that differentiates meaningful information (memory traces) from background activity (John, 1967). In a system like the human brain with many complicated microprocesses and significant levels of spontaneous activity, shifts in the resolution of encoded information over time do not appear to be at all implausible.

There is currently no final answer as to how many of these mechanisms of memory trace loss are functional in human cognition. There is a widespread belief, on the basis of pretty good evidence, that (1) holds. Decay theories are popular and plausible but exceedingly difficult to test (e.g., Reitman, 1971, 1974; Shiffrin, 1973; Shiffrin & Cook, 1978). Overwriting or unlearning accounts are popular for immediate memory but much less so for long-term memory (e.g., Reitman, 1970). There is a sense in which the difference between (1) on the one hand and (2) and (3) on the other is untestable. In the face of the nonretrievability of a particular piece of information, the trace availability hypothesis can retreat into the claim that the right set of retrieval cues have not yet been located. Indefinite regress of this form makes it impossible to distinguish availability hypotheses from those that posit trace loss. However, the availability hypothesis acts as a useful heuristic for thinking about the mechanics of memory access.

The availability hypothesis can explain a number of phenomena in infant memory. For illustration, we will examine some recognition memory phenomena. The typical recognition study consists of a familiarization and a test phase. During familiarization, the pattern that is to be remembered is made available to the infant according to some experimental scheme. The infant attends to the pattern, and an encoding of it is available in active memory. Exactly what gets coded depends on the infant's attentional strategies and upon information present in the knowledge base. The presence of a representation in active memory provides an opportunity for storing of information in long-term memory about the stimulus and its context. The test phase consists of a subsequent presentation of the familiarized pattern, with either a successive (in habituation studies) or simultaneous (in paired-comparison studies) contrast with a novel pattern. Once again, the patterns are encoded, and then the activated encoding is matched against information stored in long-term memory. The degree of match between the presently activated encoding and those stored in memory leads to the shifts in attention that are characteristic of test-phase behavior in habituation or paired-comparison experiments.

If the to-be-remembered pattern is encoded differently at test than at initial familiarization, it will not be recognized. Thus, factors contributing to variability in encoding will tend to produce poorer recognition (see G. H. Bower, 1972; E. Martin, 1968). Generally, immediate recognition ought to be better than delayed recognition, since the encoding of the target pattern most likely includes information about the general context (both internal and external) and there is likely to be more similarity of context over short delays than over long ones. Immediate recognition may also be aided by the presence of a trace in active memory. All of the factors we have discussed that differentiate the younger from the older infant will tend to produce more variable encoding. Familiarization intervals that are short relative to the infant's attentional skills, to processing speed, or to facilitatory effects of the knowledge base will tend to produce incomplete encodings. If sufficiently incomplete, they may not even mediate immediate recognition, but they will certainly have major effects on delayed recognition. However, even with ample familiarization time, the factors that characterize the younger infant such as incomplete perceptual development, a limited knowledge base, and less efficient processing would tend to produce variability in encoding a pattern on different occasions and produce poorer recognition, particularly at delays.

This discussion of recognition can be summarized in terms of two major classes of predictions. In what follows, the locution "knowledgeable infant" refers to knowledge relative to the stimulus domain under investigation. Thus, for faces, the knowledgeable infant is one who has information stored in his or her knowledge base about human faces as a general class. The first prediction is that younger infants or less knowledgeable ones should take longer to achieve a given level of encoding. More concretely, such infants should tend to habituate more slowly or should require more familiarization to achieve a novelty preference for a given paired-comparison test. However, a concrete example suggests why one must be careful in separating memory effects from other factors. Consider Fagan's (1972) finding that infants recognized right-side-up but not upside-down faces. This might lead one to predict that infants would habituate more slowly to upside-down faces. However, this might not be the case. In addition to familiarity effects that result from the match process, infants also acquire various approach or avoidance tendencies based on the types of outcomes associated with particular type of stimuli (Zeaman, 1976). Faces as a class might have many bases for approach tendencies, leading an infant to look longer at meaningful faces and, as a result, habituate more slowly. On the other hand, if one has a novelty preference between two similarly oriented faces as the performance criterion, the encoding prediction would be on safer ground. Specifically, a positive novelty preference might be achieved for right-side-up faces on the basis of less total looking than for upside-down ones.

The second prediction is that the younger or less knowledgeable infant will show poorer delayed recognition. Since several factors can contribute to good immediate recognition, the encoding variability argument most clearly bears on delayed recognition. Of course, as is well known, predictions regarding retention must take into account degree of initial learning. One might suspect that habituating infants to a common criterion would accomplish this, but we discussed the problems associated with the use of a criterion of habituation in an earlier section. Thus, a more adequate control would be to equate the degree of learning by presenting familiarization stimuli as long as is necessary to achieve a novelty preference criterion on a series of paired-comparison tests. Under these conditions, younger or less knowledgeable infants should show poorer delayed recognition because of greater encoding variability.

These are illustrations of how these concepts could be applied to studies of retention in infants. There is another phenomenon that is often linked to these concepts, namely, *infantile amnesia*. This is the inability of older children or adults to recollect anything from infancy. The usual account of this phenomenon (Neisser, 1962, 1967; Schachtel, 1947, 1959) is that the mental context of infancy and early childhood is so different from later childhood and adulthood that whatever information remains from that period cannot be accessed. Schachtel's (1959) detailed discussion of this account is as good a statement of the position as exists.

Monitor

Any complex information processing system must have a system of control whereby activities are monitored and competition among competing processes is mediated. Furthermore, since activities occur in the context of goals or motives, the status of goals and changes in goal structure must be coordinated. It is these broad functions of the control of mental activity and of the coordination of goal or motivational structure that we subsume under the heading of *monitor*. We do not imply that these functions are carried out in any specifiable *place* in the information processing system. Instead, in discussing these matters under a single heading, we mean only to highlight their importance.

Control

Control is central to an adaptive, purposive system. As was stated above, behavior is typically in the service of one or more goals, as well as being constantly responsive to the vagaries of the external world. Such flexible purposiveness requires the capacity to monitor the functioning of many systems and to coordinate the internal mental processes that underlie behavior.

One of the important lessons from the study of information processing systems is that a system of overall organization, control, and communication is essential for effective computation of complex functions. The significant characteristics of a complex information processing system, as described by Simon (1969), are: (1) hierarchical organization of components, (2) decomposition of the total system into subsystems, and (3) repetitive use of similar components. In their own way, each of these characteristics underscores the importance of central control. The marshaling of the system resources and skills in the service of ever-changing goals requires a control structure that is capable of tests, place-keeping, and other coordination and control functions.

What is the infant's system of control like? How do these control functions develop? What system of control is present at birth? These are important questions that are difficult to address on the basis of available data. An example of a hypothesis that pertains to this domain is Bronson's (1974) proposal that during the early months of infancy there is a shift in the control of visual processing from the phylogenetically older second visual system to the primary visual system. He traces the implications of this view for such phenomena as visual attention, including visual preferences and eye movements. More recently, Posner and Rothbart (1981) have offered a similar proposal for the early development of the control of attention. They argue, on the basis of adult data, that there are two separable systems for visual attention: one that controls eye movements and one that controls the movement of attention. Their hypothesis is that initially infant eye movements are under exogenous control, with little voluntary control over the direction of gaze. They speculate that the infant may be learning to coordinate these two systems. Regardless of the adequacy of either Bronson's or Posner and Rothbart's hypotheses, they are both examples of proposals for how internal control might develop in early infancy.

Control processes are relatively easy to study in the case of vision, where visual preferences and eye movements are available as a rich source of data to guide hypothesis formation. Control issues are also important in other domains, including such purely central activities as planning, the monitoring of memory processes, and the regulation of goals. Most of the work on control has been done in artificial intelligence (see, e.g., Nilsson, 1982; Winston, 1977), and a number of concepts are emerging that could be useful for psychologists interested in the development of information processing.

The assumption that the central control processes in humans are sequential is a dominant theoretical bias in contemporary cognitive psychology. The bias has its roots in the computer metaphor and in the introspective impression of a single-channel flow of active processing. Most, though not all, conceptions of attention have adhered to some variant of the one-thing-at-a-time principle of focal attention. Explicit models of complex information processing (e.g., Anderson, 1976; Newell & Simon, 1972) have assumed that at any given instant in time active processing is occurring in the service of one particular goal or subgoal. This is not to deny that a large amount of parallel computation occurs. Rather, it is simply that the control or monitor functions, which we are roughly equating with focal attention, operate in an inherently sequential fashion. Presumably significant aspects of perceptual or memory processing operate in an inherently parallel fashion (Anderson, 1976; McClelland, 1979; Rumelhart, 1977). An important developmental issue is the extent to which sequential processing emerges during development as opposed to occurring from the beginning. In many ways even the newborn seems to manifest sequential processing. Haith (1980), for example, describes the organized and sequential fashion in which infants scan their visual world. From his descriptions it is easy to speculate that the infant is born as an inherently serial processor of the type described by Newell and Simon (1972). Whether the infant can handle perceptual or memory tasks in parallel, though, is an open question. As was mentioned earlier, component processes that are automated in the older child or adult may still require focal attention in the infant. Thus, the infant may be even more of a serial processor than the child or adult, with concomitant limitations in the information processing capabilities. However, further theoretical and empirical analysis is needed.

Motives

Motivation is an important and complex subject, one that has been ignored until recently in cognitive psychology but that is extremely important in early cognitive development. So often the goal structure of an organism is assumed to be determined by the task set up by the experimenter. This assumption is risky enough with an adult subject, but it is totally unacceptable with infants. Without language for instructions, and without any sense on the infant's part that an experimental task is a situation in which cooperation is desired, the infant's goals are minimally controlled by the experimenter. Failure to take into account what the infant is doing in a laboratory task can seriously distort the inferences one draws from laboratory performance. The earlier discussion of Bloom's studies on social conditioning of vocalizations provides a good example of this.

It is useful to draw a distinction between *biological* and *cognitive* motivation. Flavell (1977) distinguished between those goals whose aims are *extrinsic* to the cognitive system and those that are *intrinsic*. Examples of extrinsic goals would be food, water, sex, or social approval. They are extrinsic in the sense that their primary end is not the modification of cognitive structures but rather the satisfaction of basic needs. Most of these needs are biological in origin and correspond to the basic forms of reinforcement studied by traditional learning theorists. On the other hand, intrinsic motivation has as its primary aim the modification of cognitive structures. When Butler (1953, 1954) discovered that a monkey could perform a variety of tasks in order to get a brief look through a window at such things as another monkey, an electric train, or even an empty box, he had discovered something about cognitive motivation. It is now well known that many human (and nonhuman) activities must be explained on the basis of cognitive motives—curiosity, dissonance reduction, confirmation seeking, and the like. As Flavell (1977) describes it, the human—in particular, the child—is "an organism that idly learns when there is no practical need to do so, that tries to learn what it most needs to learn, and that finds it rewarding both to learn these things initially and also to solidify and perfect its learning through subsequent practice" (p. 24).

Motivational constructs have been an important part of theories of infant cognition (e.g., Bowlby, 1969; Piaget, 1952, 1954, 1962). Nonetheless, work on infant attention, learning, and memory has given scant attention to motivation, with the exception of the discrepancy hypothesis we discussed earlier. It is essential that future work on these topics take account of what are undoubtedly profound changes in motivation during the infant period.

Motivation and emotion are closely related, and the study of emotional development in infants is a major topic (e.g., Lamb & Campos, 1982; Lewis & Rosenblum, 1974, 1978; Sroufe, 1979). However, there is almost no work linking emotional development with learning and memory in infants. Recently, cognitive psychologists in general have given emotion and affect more attention (e.g., Clark & Fiske, 1982). The relation between the two areas of emotion and learning would seem to be a topic to which those who study infants could make a major contribution.

Conceptual Analysis of the Habituation and Paired-Comparison Tasks

In order to bring together the various conceptual strands we have been discussing, we will now analyze the habituation task in relation to the schema that was described in Figure 19. To simplify our discussion, we will confine our analysis to tasks with visual stimuli. However, the entire analysis could be transformed *ceteris paribus* to tasks using nonvisual stimuli.

Consider a single trial in the infant-controlled visual habituation task. Our goal is to describe the mechanisms that determine how long the infant looks at the stimulus on each trial. What controls the infant's initial fixation of the stimulus? In the typical habituation experiment the infant is seated or held in a relatively impoverished environment so as to make the stimulus more salient. For instance, the room may be darkened and slides projected onto a screen. Or the apparatus may contain a large, relatively featureless screen that partially encloses the area in which the infant is located. When the stimulus is presented, there are not many alternatives for the infant to look at, and so basic attention-getting routines will have a strong tendency to divert the infant's attention to the stimulus.

Once the stimulus is fixated, it undergoes perceptual encoding. This consists of the transformation of the stimulus energy arriving at the senses into an internal code. Consistent with recent analyses of the representation of visual information in cognitive models, the internal code can be thought of as a structural description of what is perceived (Anderson, 1980; Palmer, 1977, 1978; Winston, 1975). A variety of factors influence the structural description given to a stimulus, and all of them are highly relevant to what happens in an habituation experiment. First, the vocabulary of nodes and relations available for composing structural descriptions will define the set of descriptions that are possible. Presumably a number of these elements are innate. The visual system is primed to notice certain features of the world, and even the infant is especially attentive to contours and configurations of contours like corners (Haith, 1980). Similarly, relations like adjacency and part-whole might be primitive elements in such descriptions. However, as a result of perceptual learning, other elements will enter the vocabulary used for composing structural descriptions. Further, as a result of experience, particular patterns that are meaningful will become grouped or organized and may themselves become elementary units from which structural descriptions can be comprised. Modifications in the vocabulary available for composing structural descriptions will be a major source of developmental change.

Second, and closely related to the first, the structural description will be influenced by the way in which the stimulus is attended to. Indeed, some theorists (e.g., Noton & Stark, 1971) have proposed that the pattern of scans used in examining a stimulus is part of the representation of the stimulus. The evidence for this point of view is not clear, but, to consider it at a more basic level, in order for an element of a stimulus to be coded it probably has to be looked at (assuming it cannot be inferred on the basis of information in the knowledge base). Thus, the newborn, with its extremely limited scans of figures, is likely to encode a stimulus quite differently than an older infant who scans a figure much more completely. How stimuli are scanned is in turn related to general attentional strategies and to the development of knowledge.

The role of these first two factors has been vividly demonstrated in studies of board games like chess or Go. As we noted earlier, highly skilled players retain more information from meaningful board configurations than do less skilled ones, whereas level of skill does not affect performance with meaningless board configurations (Chase & Simon, 1973; Reitman, 1976). The superior knowledge of the expert leads to quicker and more effective encoding of the meaningful patterns because of a richer vocabulary of possible codes and because of knowledge-based scanning of the array. We would expect the acquisition of knowledge during infancy to have substantial effects on coding, analogous to those displayed by skilled adults when compared with unskilled ones.

A third factor that influences encoding is the representation of the context. Both the external environment and the infant's internal environment provide a context in which an object or event is experienced, and this context is given an explicit representation. The representation of the context is important, because it is well known from studies of adult memory that contextual influences on encoding play a major role in recognition (see G. H. Bower, 1972; E. Martin, 1968). If two different occurrences of a stimulus are encoded with markedly different contexts, the extent to which they are perceived as a match will be severely affected. Similarly, if two different stimuli are encoded in essentially the same context, their similarity will be enhanced.

A final factor that influences encoding is the speed with which it occurs. Knowledge affects encoding speed: the more one knows, the faster a given display can be encoded (Chase & Simon, 1973; Reitman, 1976). In the case of infants, their relative degree of neurological maturity will also affect encoding speed. It seems highly probable, although it is difficult to cite definitive evidence, that there is marked development during infancy in both the speed and the variability of neural activity, with the net effect that internal events occur more quickly in the older infant than in the younger one. This has important effects on encoding. Given that there is a background of ongoing activity that will affect how long an infant will persist in attending to something, if encoding is slow there will be a tendency to form incomplete encodings of objects or events before attention shifts to other stimuli.

The process of encoding leads to an active memory trace of the thing being attended. Several important processes occur when the information is in this state. First, traces in the knowledge base or long-term memory are activated. To put it differently, a matching process occurs, which provides information that can be the basis of recognition. The output of this activation or match process is information about the relative familiarity of the stimulus that will affect, in infants, the sense of novelty or familiarity that is one major determinant of the length of attention. Second, information associated with the long-term trace of the stimulus—if there is one—will be activated. Human memory is fundamentally associative, so that activation of particular memory traces tends to produce activation of closely associated traces. These associated traces can, in the case of an infant in an habituation experiment, affect the length of a fixation. For instance, even though the mother is very familiar to the infant, she would undoubtedly elicit prolonged fixation because of knowledge associated with her perceptual representation in the knowledge base that leads to expectations of, for example, social interactions (see fuller discussion in Olson, 1981). Third, new information about the activated representation will be stored in the knowledge base. Many kinds of information can be stored: characteristics of the object itself (its structural description), characteristics of the context, associated events (e.g., what occurs before or after it, what is done with it, how it behaves), and relations between the presently activated representation and representations retrieved from memory. These are all aspects of learning.

The duration of the infant's look on such a trial is influenced by the nature of the encoding, by the nature of the information activated or retrieved from the knowledge base, and by the nature of the external and internal context. The routines that control attention use the information so obtained in conjunction with other information about general or specific goals, information from the internal environment (e.g., hunger, toilet needs), and other ongoing mental activity to shift the gaze from the stimulus at some point. This process of shifting the gaze is not determined solely by the memory processes surrounding the active representation of the stimulus. There is a whole background of activity relevant to this. However, on balance, a stimulus that activates little information in memory will be fixated longer, whereas one that is very familiar will be fixated less unless there is knowledge associated with it that suggests otherwise (e.g., the mother example).

Across a series of trials in an habituation experiment information about the stimulus will be stored, so that on later trials increasingly more information will be available in the knowledge base and, again on balance, attention to the stimulus will wane. The average early trial will be longer than the average late trial, but given the multitude of influences on this process, one would expect the trial-by-trial variability found in habituation experiments. In other words, both long and short looks can occur anywhere in the sequence.

The extension of this analysis to other types of habituation experiments or to the paired-comparison task is straightforward. In the traditional habituation task the stimulus is presented on each trial for a predetermined period. The process we described simply recurs within a trial; the attention-getting and attention-holding processes occur cyclically during the course of a trial, with the same net effect on total fixation time per trial over the course of the experiment. In the paired-comparison task the only major difference is that more than one stimulus is available, so that when fixation of one ends there is another salient stimulus that can be fixated. A particularly important implication of this is that the comparison of stimulus representations is facilitated by having the recently activated trace of one pattern available while the other pattern is being fixated. This situation could aid the recognition process and the learning process in a variety of obvious ways (Fagan, 1976, 1978; Olson, 1979; Ruff, 1978).

The purpose of this example is to show for a representative task how the distinctions we have been discussing in this section maps onto the behavior actually observed. Olson and Sherman (in press) present a more detailed analysis of this and other tasks. The study of infant learning and memory has up to now been quite descriptive and atheoretical and has often been narrowly focused on the tasks used to study the infant. The data base is now sufficiently large so that serious theoretical work can begin. It is through careful and comprehensive theoretical analysis that the study of infant attention, learning, and memory will ultimately yield rich fruits for both the study of infancy and the study of cognitive development.

SUMMARY AND CONCLUSIONS

Despite the great length of this chapter, we have discussed only a subset of the important topics in the areas of attention, learning, and memory in infants. Our review of published literature has been quite selective. We have focused on the discussion of methodology and the examination of the research literature for developmental progressions. We have also presented a conceptual scheme that attempts to connect the infant literature with the broader literature on cognition and information processing. Fortunately, there are other reviews that offer different perspectives and give prominence to other research (e.g., Cohen, 1976; Cohen & Gelber, 1975; Fagan, 1975, in press; Fitzgerald & Brackbill, 1976; Kessen et al., 1970; Mandler, in press; Olson, 1976; Olson & Strauss, in press; Rovee-Collier & Gekoski, 1979; Rovee-Collier & Lipsitt, 1980; Ruff, in press; Sameroff, 1972; Sameroff & Cavanagh, 1979; Watson, 1980; Werner & Perlmutter, 1979).

There are two important topics we considered including in this chapter but excluded for reasons of space. One is research on individual differences. We have discussed the information processing skills of the modal infant, ignoring the large and conceptually interesting variations among infants in performance on the tasks we have reviewed. One of the classic questions in all of developmental psychology is whether individual differences in childhood or beyond can be predicted from infant behavior. This issue is made all the more interesting because of recent reports by Fagan (in press; Fagan & McGrath, 1981; Fagan & Singer, in press) and others (e.g., Lewis & Brooks-Gunn, 1981) that infant memory performance is correlated with later measures of intelligence. Such findings hold much potential interest for developmental psychologists, but there is still extensive conceptual and empirical work to be done before their status is clear. In fact, there is surprisingly little work on the extent and stability of cross-sectional individual variation in performance on the basic tasks we reviewed in the section titled *Methods for Studying Attention, Learning, and Memory.*

A second important topic is the nature of attention, learning, and development in special populations of infants. Because of the enormous practical importance of early risks and hazards in infancy, there is a large and growing body of research on the developing abilities of infants who are born with birth defects or undergo early risks such as prematurity, anoxia, obstetrical medication, and other neonatal hazards. As methods for assessing attention, learning, and memory have become more sophisticated and reliable, these tasks have been used extensively in studies of special populations. Up to now, the published literature reporting such studies has not been systematically reviewed or integrated with the broader range of work on infant information processing. In principle, however, such data could be quite important in distinguishing among alternative theoretical accounts of infant information processing phenomena.

As the research reviewed in this chapter has revealed, there are several broad conclusions one can reach at this time. First, there has been substantial advancement in methods. The investigator of infant information processing has available a broad range of demonstrably reliable tasks. We have learned how to use these tasks to ask basic questions about infant abilities and to move beyond the narrow confines of parametric task manipulations or task-specific conclusions.

Second, an articulated portrait of the early development of infant information processing skills is beginning to emerge. We reviewed some of the details in the section titled *Attention, Learning, and Memory in Infancy.* During the earliest months of infancy the infant's skills are shaped by neurological and psychomotor immaturity. The infant's information processing is limited by constraints on sensory, perceptual, and attentional processes and by more central constraints on efficient, complex processing. However, over these early months of infancy there is rapid development in all of these skills. By 5 or 6 months of age recognition memory skills are excellent. During the latter portions of the first year the basic skills of acquisition and retention are applied to establishing a rich knowledge base, to classifying and categorizing the elements of experience into perceptual categories. This knowledge base plays an increasing role in information processing, affecting mental skills at all levels. As the infant develops new ways to represent information, skills such as imitation and recall appear. These in turn enlarge the infant's ability to acquire and use information from the world. During the second year these developments converge to yield language development, perhaps the single most profound change that occurs in the child's cognitive development.

Although there is now a substantial data base on the development of attention, learning, and memory, there are still serious gaps in our knowledge. Most research has been done during the first six months, so we know much less about the 6- to 24-month period. There are very few developmental or longitudinal studies, so most of what we know about change comes from piecing together results from a wide range of data collected under different circumstances. Finally, although there have been a few attempts made to provide broader conceptual frameworks, the study of infant memory has been predominantly empirical and has had few connections with the general study of either infants or memory. We know a lot more about what infants can do than we did when the last Carmichael revision appeared, but we still have a long way to go before we fully understand how these basic skills develop during infancy.

NOTES

1. In our laboratory, the two observers agree within 0.5 sec. on over 90% of the trials, and disagreements have no relationship to the role of the trial (e.g., warm-up, familiarization, posthabituation) in the experiment.

2. Of course, long looks per se do not necessarily indicate active processing. The phenomenon of the vacant stare is familiar to anyone who works with younger infants.

3. Many observers have noted that infants tend to look more toward the right side of such two-stimulus displays.

4. Although 34 infants were run in this experiment, attrition from missed appointments, equipment failure, and other miscellaneous sources meant that for each cell in Table 3 the data for only 30 infants were available. Even though exact counterbalancing of the three stimuli was not preserved for these 30 observations, the means for these 30 did not differ in any instance from a subset of the infants for whom exact counterbalancing was preserved.

5. This is not an ideal control for visual feedback because of the very real possibility of experimenter bias affecting the nature and timing of the mobile movements.

6. As this chapter was going to press, a report appeared by Field, Woodson, Greenberg, and Cohen (1982) that described imitation of facial expressions by neonates whose average age was 36 hours. Although the procedure differed somewhat from that used by Meltzoff and Moore (1977), the Field et al. report does not address the full range of criticisms raised in response to the Meltzoff and Moore work. Clearly, the question of whether neonates can imitate is still an open one.

REFERENCES

Abravanel, E., Levan-Goldschmidt, E., & Stevenson, M. B. Action imitation: The early phase of infancy. *Child Development,* 1976, *47,* 1032–1044.

Ainsworth, M. D. S., & Bell, S. M. Mother-infant interaction and the development of competence. In K. J. Connolly & J. Bruner (Eds.), *The growth of competence.* New York: Academic Press, 1974.

Ambrose, J. A. The development of the smiling response in early infancy. In B. M. Foss (Ed.), *Determinants of infant behavior* (Vol. 1). London: Methuen, 1961.

Ames, E. W., Hunter, M. A., Black, A., Lithgow, P. A., & Newman, F. M. Problems of observer agreement in the infant control procedure. *Developmental Psychology,* 1978, *14,* 507–511.

Anderson, J. R. *Language, memory, and thought.* Hillsdale, N.J.: Erlbaum, 1976.

Anderson, J. R. *Cognitive psychology and its implications.* San Francisco: W. H. Freeman, 1980.

Anderson, J. R. (Ed.). *Cognitive skills and their acquisition.* Hillsdale, N.J.: Erlbaum, 1981.

Anderson, J. R. Acquisition of cognitive skill. *Psychological Review,* 1982, *89,* 369–406.

Appleton, T., Clifton, R., & Goldberg, S. The development of behavioral competence in infancy. In F. D. Horowitz (Ed.), *Review of child development research* (Vol. 4). Chicago: University of Chicago Press, 1975.

Ashmead, D. H., & Perlmutter, J. Infant memory in everyday life. In M. Perlmutter (Ed.), *New directions for child development: Children's memory* (Vol. 10). San Francisco: Jossey-Bass, 1980.

Ashton, R. The state variable in neonatal research: A review. *Merrill-Palmer Quarterly,* 1973, *19,* 3–20.

Banks, M. S., & Salapatek, P. Infant pattern vision: A new approach based on the contrast sensitivity function. *Journal of Experimental Child Psychology,* 1981, *31,* 1–45.

Barnes, J. M., & Underwood, B. J. Fate of first-list associations in transfer theory. *Journal of Experimental Psychology,* 1959, *58,* 97–105.

Barrera, M. E., & Maurer, D. Discrimination of strangers by the three-month-old. *Child Development,* 1981, *52,* 558–563. (a)

Barrera, M. E., & Maurer, D. The perception of facial expressions by the three-month-old. *Child Development,* 1981, *52,* 203–206. (b)

Barrera, M. E., & Maurer, D. Recognition of mother's photographed face by the three-month-old infant. *Child Development,* 1981, *52,* 714–716. (c)

Barry, R. J., & Maltzman, I. Heart rate deceleration is not an orienting reflex; heart rate acceleration is not a defensive reflex. Manuscript submitted for publication, 1982.

Berg, W. K., & Berg, K. M. Psychophysiological development in infancy: State, sensory function, and attention. In J. D. Osofsky (Ed.), *Handbook of infant development.* New York: Wiley, 1979.

Berlyne, D. E. *Conflict, arousal, and curiosity.* New York: McGraw-Hill, 1960.

Bertenthal, B. I., Haith, M. M., & Campos, J. J. The partial-lag design: A method for controlling spontaneous regression in the infant-control habituation paradigm. *Infant Behavior and Development,* in press.

Bloom, K. Eye contact as a setting event for infant learning. *Journal of Experimental Child Psychology,* 1974, *17,* 250–263.

Bloom, K. Social elicitation of infant vocal behavior. *Journal of Experimental Child Psychology,* 1975, *20,* 51–58.

Bloom, K. Operant baseline procedures suppress infant social behavior. *Journal of Experimental Child Psychology,* 1977, *23,* 128–132. (a)

Bloom, K. Patterning of infant vocal behavior. *Journal of Experimental Child Psychology,* 1977, *23,* 367–377. (b)

Bloom, K. Evaluation of infant vocal conditioning. *Journal of Experimental Child Psychology,* 1979, *27,* 60–70.

Bloom, K., & Esposito, A. Social conditioning and its proper control procedures. *Journal of Experimental Child Psychology,* 1975, *19,* 209–222.

Bond, E. K. Perception of form by the human infant. *Psychological Bulletin,* 1972, *77,* 225–245.

Bornstein, M. H. Infants' recognition memory for hue. *Developmental Psychology,* 1976, *12,* 185–191.

Bower, G. H. Stimulus-sampling theory of encoding variability. In A. W. Melton & E. Martin (Eds.), *Coding processes in human memory.* Washington, D.C.: Winston, 1972.

Bower, G. H., & Hilgard, E. R. *Theories of learning* (5th ed.). Englewood Cliffs, N.J.: Prentice-Hall, 1981.

Bower, T. G. R. *Development in infancy.* San Francisco: W. H. Freeman, 1974.

Bower, T. G. R. *The perceptual world of the child.* Cambridge, Mass.: Harvard University Press, 1977. (a)

Bower, T. G. R. *A primer of infant development.* San Francisco: W. H. Freeman, 1977. (b)

Bower, T. G. R. *Human development.* San Francisco: W. H. Freeman, 1979.

Bowlby, J. *Attachment.* New York: Basic Books, 1969.

Brackbill, Y., Fitzgerald, H. E., & Lintz, L. M. A developmental study of classical conditioning. *Monographs of the Society for Child Development,* 1967, *32* (Whole No. 116).

Brackbill, Y., Lintz, L. M., & Fitzgerald, H. E. Differences in the autonomic and somatic conditioning of infants. *Psychosomatic Medicine,* 1968, *30,* 193–201.

Brennan, W. N., Ames, E. W., & Moore, R. W. Age differences in infants' attention to patterns of different complexities. *Science,* 1966, *151,* 354–356.

Broadbent, D. E. *Perception and communication.* New York: Pergamon Press, 1958.

Broadbent, D. E. *Decision and stress.* New York: Academic Press, 1971.

Bronshtein, A. I., Antonova, T. G., Kamenetskaya, A. G., Luppova, N. N., & Sytova, V. A. On the development of the functions of analyzers in infants and some animals at the early stage of ontogenesis. In *Problems of evolution of physiological functions.* Moscow Academy of Science, 1958. Israel Program for Scientific Translations, 1960. Pp. 106–116. (U.S. Department of Commerce OTS 60-51066.)

Bronson, G. The postnatal growth of visual capacity. *Child Development,* 1974, *45,* 873–890.

Bronson, G. *The scanning patterns of human infants: Implications for visual learning.* Norwood, N.J.: Ablex, 1982.

Bruner, J. S. On cognitive growth. In J. S. Bruner, R. R. Olver, & P. M. Greenfield (Eds.), *Studies in cognitive growth.* New York: Wiley, 1966.

Bushnell, I. W. R. Modification of the externality effect in young infants. *Journal of Experimental Child Psychology,* 1979, *28,* 211–229.

Butler, R. A. Discrimination learning by rhesus monkeys to visual exploration motivation. *Journal of Comparative and Physiological Psychol-*

ogy, 1953, 46, 95–98.

Butler, R. A. Incentive conditions which influence visual exploration. *Journal of Experimental Psychology,* 1954, *48,* 19–23.

Butterfield, E. C., & Cairns, G. F. Discussion summary—infant reception research. In R. L. Schiefelbusch & L. L. Lloyd (Eds.), *Language perspectives—acquisition, retardation, and intervention.* Baltimore: University Park Press, 1974.

Campos, J. J. Heart rate: A sensitive tool for the study of emotional development in infancy. In L. P. Lipsitt (Ed.), *Developmental psychobiology: The significance of infancy.* Hillsdale, N.J.: Erlbaum, 1976.

Campos, J. J., & Brackbill, Y. Infant state: Relationship to heart rate, behavioral response and response decrement. *Developmental Psychobiology,* 1973, *6,* 9–19.

Caron, A. J., Caron, R. F., Caldwell, R. C., & Weiss, S. J. Infant perception of the structural properties of the face. *Developmental Psychology,* 1973, *9,* 385–399.

Caron, A. J., Caron, R. F., & Carlson, V. R. Do infants see objects or retinal images? Shape constancy revisited. *Infant Behavior and Development,* 1978, *1,* 229–243.

Caron, A. J., Caron, R. F., & Carlson, V. R. Infant perception of the invariant shape of objects varying in slant. *Child Development,* 1979, *50,* 716–721.

Caron, R. F., Caron, A. J., Carlson, V. R., & Cobb, L. S. Perception of shape-at-a-slant in the young infant. *Bulletin of the Psychonomic Society,* 1979, *13,* 105–107.

Casey, M. B. Color versus form discrimination learning in 1-year-old infants. *Developmental Psychology,* 1979, *15,* 341–343.

Chase, W. G., & Simon, H. A. Perception in chess. *Cognitive Psychology,* 1973, *4,* 55–81.

Clark, M. S., & Fiske, S. T. *Affect and cognition: The 17th Carnegie Symposium on Cognition.* Hillsdale, N.J.: Erlbaum, 1982.

Clarke-Stewart, K. A. Interactions between mothers and their young children: Characteristics and consequences. *Monographs of the Society for Research in Child Development,* 1973, *38* (Whole No. 153).

Clifton, R. K. Heart rate conditioning in the newborn infant. *Journal of Experimental Child Psychology,* 1974, *18,* 9–21.

Clifton, R. K., & Nelson, M. N. Developmental study of habituation in infants: The importance of paradigm, response system, and state. In T. J. Tighe & R. N. Leaton (Eds.), *Habituation: Perspectives from child development, animal behavior, and neurophysiology.* Hillsdale, N.J.: Erlbaum, 1976.

Cohen, L. B. Attention-getting and attention-holding processes of infant visual preferences. *Child Development,* 1972, *43,* 869–879.

Cohen, L. B. A two process model of infant visual attention. *Merrill-Palmer Quarterly,* 1973, *19,* 157–180.

Cohen, L. B. Habituation of infant visual attention. In T. J. Tighe & R. N. Leaton (Eds.), *Habituation: Perspectives from child development, animal behavior, and neurophysiology.* Hillsdale, N.J.: Erlbaum, 1976.

Cohen, L. B., DeLoache, J. S., & Pearl, R. A. An examination of interference effects in infants' memory for faces. *Child Development,* 1977, *48,* 88–96.

Cohen, L. B., DeLoache, J. S., & Rissman, M. W. The effect of stimulus complexity on infant visual attention. *Child Development,* 1975, *46,* 611–617.

Cohen, L. B., DeLoache, J. S., & Strauss, M. S. Infant visual perception. In J. D. Osofsky (Ed.), *Handbook of infant development.* New York: Wiley, 1979.

Cohen, L. B., & Gelber, E. R. Infant visual memory. In L. B. Cohen & P. Salapatek (Eds.), *Infant perception: From sensation to cognition* (Vol. 1). New York: Academic Press, 1975.

Cohen, L. B., & Menten, T. G. The rise and fall of infant habituation. Paper presented at the Biennial Meeting of the Society for Research in Child Development, San Francisco, March 1979.

Cohen, L. B., & Salapatek, P. (Eds.). *Infant perception: From sensation to cognition* (2 vols.). New York: Academic Press, 1975.

Cohen, L. B., & Strauss, M. S. Concept acquisition in the human infant. *Child Development,* 1979, *50,* 419–424.

Cook, M., Field, J., & Griffiths, K. The perception of solid form in early infancy. *Child Development,* 1978, *49,* 866–869.

Coombs, C. H. *Theory of data.* New York: Wiley, 1964.

Cornell, E. H. Infants' discrimination of photographs of faces following redundant presentations. *Journal of Experimental Child Psychology,* 1974, *18,* 98–106.

Cornell, E. H. Infants' recognition memory, forgetting, and savings. *Journal of Experimental Child Psychology,* 1979, *28,* 359–374.

Cornell, E. H., & Gottfried, A. W. Intervention

with premature human infants. *Child Development,* 1976, *47,* 32–39.

Courchesne, E., Hillyard, S. A., & Galambos, R. Stimulus novelty, task relevance and the visual evoked potential in man. *Electroencephalography and Clinical Neurophysiology,* 1975, *39,* 131–143.

Cummings, E. M., & Bjork, E. L. The search behavior of 12 to 14 month-old infants on a five-choice invisible displacement hiding task. *Infant Behavior and Development,* 1981, *4,* 47–60. (a)

Cummings, E. M., & Bjork, E. L. Search on a five-choice invisible displacement hiding task: A rejoinder to Schubert and Gratch. *Infant Behavior and Development,* 1981, *4,* 65–67. (b)

DeLoache, J. S., Rissman, M. W., & Cohen, L. B. An investigation of the attention-getting process in infants. *Infant Behavior and Development,* 1978, *1,* 11–25.

Dember, W. N., & Earl, R. W. Analysis of exploratory, manipulatory, and curiosity behaviors. *Psychological Review,* 1957, *64,* 91–96.

de Villiers, J. G., & de Villiers, P. A. *Language acquisition.* Cambridge, Mass.: Harvard University Press, 1978.

Dulany, D. E. Awareness, rules, and propositional control: A confrontation with S-R behavior theory. In T. R. Dixon & D. L. Horton (Eds.), *Verbal behavior and general behavior theory.* Englewood Cliffs, N.J.: Prentice-Hall, 1968.

Eckerman, C. O., & Whatley, J. L. Infants' reactions to unfamiliar adults varying in novelty. *Developmental Psychology,* 1975, *11,* 562–566.

Eimas, P. D. Linguistic processing of speech by young infants. In R. Schiefelbusch & L. Lloyd (Eds.), *Language perspectives—acquisition, retardation, and intervention.* Baltimore: University Park Press, 1974.

Eimas, P. D. Speech perception in infancy. In L. B. Cohen & P. Salapatek (Eds.), *Infant perception: From sensation to cognition* (Vol. 2). New York: Academic Press, 1975.

Eimas, P. D., Siqueland, E. R., Jusczyk, P., & Vigorito, J. Speech perception in infants. *Science,* 1971, *171,* 303–306.

Elardo, R., Bradley, R., & Caldwell, B. M. A longitudinal study of the relation of infants' home environments to language development at age three. *Child Development,* 1977, *48,* 595–603.

Ellingson, R. J. The study of brain electrical activity in infants. In L. P. Lipsitt & C. C. Spiker (Eds.), *Advances in child development and behavior* (Vol. 3). New York: Academic Press, 1967.

Emde, R. N., & Robinson, J. The first two months: Recent research in developmental psychobiology and the changing view of the newborn. In J. Noshpitz & J. Call (Ed.), *Basic handbook of child psychiatry.* New York: Basic Books, 1979.

Engen, T., & Lipsitt, L. P. Decrement and recovery of responses to olfactory stimuli in the human neonate. *Journal of Comparative and Physiological Psychology,* 1965, *59,* 312–316.

Engen, T., Lipsitt, L. P., & Kaye, H. Olfactory responses and adaptation in the human neonate. *Journal of Comparative and Physiological Psychology,* 1963, *56,* 73–77.

Fagan, J. F., III. Memory in the infant. *Journal of Experimental Child Psychology,* 1970, *9,* 217–226.

Fagan, J. F., III. Infants' recognition memory for a series of visual stimuli. *Journal of Experimental Child Psychology,* 1971, *11,* 244–250.

Fagan, J. F., III. Infants' recognition memory for faces. *Journal of Experimental Child Psychology,* 1972, *14,* 453–476.

Fagan, J. F., III. Infants' delayed recognition memory and forgetting. *Journal of Experimental Child Psychology,* 1973, *16,* 424–450.

Fagan, J. F., III. Infant recognition memory: The effects of length of familiarization and type of discrimination task. *Child Development,* 1974, *45,* 351–356.

Fagan, J. F., III. Infant recognition memory as a present and future index of cognitive abilities. In N. R. Ellis (Ed.), *Aberrant development in infancy: Human and animal studies.* Hillsdale, N.J.: Erlbaum, 1975.

Fagan, J. F., III. Infants' recognition of invariant features of faces. *Child Development,* 1976, *47,* 627–638.

Fagan, J. F., III. An attention model of infant recognition. *Child Development,* 1977, *48,* 345–359. (a)

Fagan, J. F., III. Infant recognition memory: Studies in forgetting. *Child Development,* 1977, *48,* 68–78. (b)

Fagan, J. F., III. Facilitation of infants' recognition memory. *Child Development,* 1978, *49,* 1066–1075.

Fagan, J. F., III. Infant memory: History, current trends, relations to cognitive psychology. In M. Moscovitch (Ed.), *Infant memory.* New York: Plenum, in press.

Fagan, J. F., III, & McGrath, S. K. Infant recognition memory and later intelligence. *Intelligence,* 1981, *5,* 121–130.

Fagan, J. F., III, & Singer, L. T. Infant recognition memory as a measure of intelligence. In L. P.

Lipsitt (Ed.), *Advances in infancy research* (Vol. 2). Norwood, N.J.: Ablex, in press.

Fagen, J. W. Interproblem learning in ten-month-old infants. *Child Development,* 1977, *48,* 786–796.

Fagen, J. W., & Rovee, C. K. Effects of quantitative shifts in a visual reinforcer on the instrumental response of infants. *Journal of Experimental Child Psychology,* 1976, *21,* 349–360.

Fagen, J. W., Rovee, C. K., & Kaplan, M. G. Psychophysical scaling of stimulus similarity in 3-month-old infants and adults. *Journal of Experimental Child Psychology,* 1976, *22,* 272–281.

Fantz, R. L. Pattern vision in young infants. *Psychological Review,* 1958, *8,* 43–47.

Fantz, R. L. The origin of form perception. *Scientific American,* 1961, *204,* 66–72.

Fantz, R. L. Pattern vision in newborn infants. *Science,* 1963, *140,* 296–297.

Fantz, R. L. Visual experience in infants: Decreased attention to familiar patterns relative to novel ones. *Science,* 1964, *146,* 668–670.

Fantz, R. L. Visual perception from birth as shown by pattern selectivity. *Annals of the New York Academy of Science,* 1965, *118,* 793–814.

Fantz, R. L. Pattern discrimination and selective attention as determinants of perceptual development from birth. In A. H. Kidd & J. L. Rivoire (Eds.), *Perceptual development in children.* New York: International University Press, 1966.

Fantz, R. L., & Fagan, J. F., III. Visual attention to size and number of pattern details by term and preterm infants during the first six months. *Child Development,* 1975, *46,* 3–18.

Fantz, R. L., Fagan, J. F., III, & Miranda, S. B. Early visual selectivity as a function of pattern variables, previous exposure, age from birth and conception, and expected cognitive deficit. In L. B. Cohen & P. Salapatek (Eds.), *Infant perception: From sensation to cognition* (Vol. 1). New York: Academic Press, 1975.

Fantz, R. L., & Nevis, S. Pattern preferences and perceptual-cognitive development in early infancy. *Merrill-Palmer Quarterly,* 1967, *13,* 77–108.

Field, J. The adjustment of reaching behavior to object distance in early infancy. *Child Development,* 1976, *47,* 304–308. (a)

Field, J. Relation of young infants' reaching behavior to stimulus distance and solidity. *Developmental Psychology,* 1976, *12,* 444–448. (b)

Field, T. M., Woodson, R., Greenberg, R., & Cohen, D. Discrimination and imitation of facial expressions by neonates. *Science,* 1982, *218,* 179–181.

Finkelstein, N. W., & Ramey, C. T. Learning to control the environment in infancy. *Child Development,* 1977, *48,* 806–819.

Fitzgerald, H. E. Autonomic pupillary reflex activity during early infancy and its relation to social and nonsocial visual stimuli. *Journal of Experimental Child Psychology,* 1968, *6,* 470–482.

Fitzgerald, H. E., & Brackbill, Y. Classical conditioning in infancy: Development and constraints. *Psychological Bulletin,* 1976, *83,* 353–376.

Fitzgerald, H. E., Lintz, L. M., Brackbill, Y. B., & Adams, G. Time perception and conditioning an autonomic response in human infants. *Perceptual and Motor Skills,* 1967, *24,* 479–486.

Flavell, J. H. *Cognitive development.* Englewood Cliffs, N.J.: Prentice-Hall, 1977.

Fleischl, M. F. The problem of sucking. *American Journal of Psychotherapy,* 1957, *11,* 86–97.

Friedman, S. Habituation and recovery of visual response in the alert human newborn. *Journal of Experimental Child Psychology,* 1972, *13,* 339–349. (a)

Friedman, S. Newborn visual attention to repeated exposure of redundant versus "novel" targets. *Perception and Psychophysics,* 1972, *12,* 291–294. (b)

Friedman, S. Infant habituation: Process, problems and possibilities. In N. Ellis (Ed.), *Aberrant development in infancy.* Hillsdale, N.J.: Erlbaum, 1975.

Friedman, S., Bruno, L. A., & Vietze, P. Newborn habituation to visual stimuli: A sex difference in novelty detection. *Journal of Experimental Child Psychology,* 1974, *18,* 242–251.

Friedman, S., & Carpenter, G. C. Visual response decrement as a function of age of human newborn. *Child Development,* 1971, *42,* 1967–1973.

Friedman, S., Carpenter, G. C., & Nagy, A. N. Decrement and recovery of response to visual stimuli in the newborn infant. *Proceedings of the 78th Convention of the American Psychological Association,* 1970, *5,* 273–274.

Friedman, S., Nagy, A. N., & Carpenter, G. C. Newborn attention: Differential response decrement to visual stimuli. *Journal of Experimental Child Psychology,* 1970, *10,* 44–51.

Gallistel, C. R. *The organization of action: A new synthesis.* Hillsdale, N.J.: Erlbaum, 1980.

Ganon, E. C., & Swartz, K. B. Perception of internal elements of compound figures by one-month-old infants. *Journal of Experimental Child Psy-*

chology, 1980, *30,* 159–170.

Garcia, J., & Koelling, R. Relation of cue to consequence in avoidance learning. *Psychonomic Science,* 1966, *4,* 123–124.

Garner, W. R., Hake, H. W., & Eriksen, C. W. Operationism and the concept of perception. *Psychological Review,* 1956, *63,* 149–159.

Gewirtz, J. L. The course of infant smiling in four childrearing environments in Israel. In B. M. Foss (Ed.), *Determinants of infant behavior* (Vol. 3). London: Methuen, 1965.

Gewirtz, J. L., & Boyd, E. F. Mother-infant interaction and its study. In H. W. Reese (Ed.), *Advances in child development and behavior* (Vol. 11). New York: Academic Press, 1976.

Gibson, E. *Principles of perceptual learning and development.* New York: Appleton-Century-Crofts, 1969.

Gibson, E., Owsley, C., & Johnston, J. Perception of invariants by five-month-old infants: Differentiation of two types of motion. *Developmental Psychology,* 1978, *14,* 407–415.

Gibson, J. J. *The perception of the visual world.* Boston: Houghton Mifflin, 1950.

Gibson, J. J. *The senses considered as perceptual systems.* Boston: Houghton Mifflin, 1966.

Gibson, J. J. *The ecological approach to visual perception.* Boston: Houghton Mifflin, 1979.

Girton, M. R. Infants' attention to intrastimulus motion. *Journal of Experimental Child Psychology,* 1979, *28,* 416–423.

Glanville, B. B., Best, C. T., & Levenson, R. A cardiac measure of cerebral asymmetries in infant auditory perception. *Developmental Psychology,* 1977, *13,* 54–59.

Gottfried, A. W., & Rose, S. A. Tactile recognition memory in infants. *Child Development,* 1980, *51,* 69–74.

Gottfried, A. W., Rose, S. A., & Bridger, W. H. Effects of visual, haptic, and manipulatory experiences on infants' visual recognition memory for objects. *Developmental Psychology,* 1978, *14,* 305–312.

Graham, F. K., & Clifton, R. K. Heart-rate change as a component of the orienting response. *Psychological Bulletin,* 1966, *65,* 305–320.

Graham, F. K., & Jackson, J. C. Arousal systems and infant heart rate responses. In H. W. Reese & L. P. Lipsitt (Eds.), *Advances in child development and behavior* (Vol. 5). New York: Academic Press, 1970.

Gratch, G. Recent studies based on Piaget's view of object concept development. In L. B. Cohen & P. Salapatek (Eds.), *Infant perception: From sensation to cognition* (Vol. 2). New York: Academic Press, 1975.

Gratch, G. The development of thought and language in infancy. In J. Osofsky (Ed.), *Handbook of infant development.* New York: Wiley, 1979.

Gratch, G., Appel, K. J., Evans, W. F., LeCompte, G. K., & Wright, N. A. Piaget's stage IV object concept error: Evidence of forgetting or object conception? *Child Development,* 1974, *45,* 71–77.

Greenberg, D. J. Accelerating visual complexity levels in the human infant. *Child Development,* 1971, *42,* 905–918.

Greenberg, D. J., & O'Donnell, W. J. Infancy and the optimal level of stimulation. *Child Development,* 1972, *43,* 639–645.

Greenberg, D. J., Uzgiris, I. C., & Hunt, J. M. Attentional preference and experience. III: Visual familiarity and looking time. *Journal of Genetic Psychology,* 1970, *117,* 123–135.

Gregg, C., Clifton, R. K., & Haith, M. A possible explanation for the frequent failure to find cardiac orienting in the newborn infant. *Developmental Psychology,* 1976, *12,* 75–76.

Guillaume, P. *Imitation in children.* Chicago: University of Chicago Press, 1971.

Haith, M. M. Infrared television recording and measurement of ocular behavior in the human infant. *American Psychologist,* 1969, *24,* 279–283.

Haith, M. M. *Rules that babies look by: The organization of newborn visual activity.* Hillsdale, N.J.: Erlbaum, 1980.

Haith, M. M., Bergman, T., & Moore, M. J. Eye contact and face scanning in early infancy. *Science,* 1977, *198,* 853–855.

Haith, M. M., Goodman, G. S., Goodwyn, M. A., & Montgomery, L. A longitudinal study of infant's visual scanning and discrimination of form. Paper presented at the International Conference on Infant Studies, Austin, Texas, March 1982.

Hamm, M., Russell, M., & Koepke, J. Neonatal imitation? Paper presented at the Biennial Meeting of the Society for Research in Child Development, San Francisco, March 1979.

Hayes, L. A., & Watson, J. S. Neonatal imitation: Fact or artifact? *Developmental Psychology,* 1981, *17,* 655–660.

Hebb, D. O. *The organization of behavior.* New York: Wiley, 1949.

Hershenson, M. Visual discrimination in the human newborn. *Journal of Comparative and Physiological Psychology,* 1964, *58,* 270–276.

Hershenson, M. Development of the perception of

form. *Psychological Bulletin,* 1967, *67,* 326–336.

Hershenson, M., Munsinger, H., & Kessen, W. Preference for shapes of intermediate variability in the newborn human. *Science,* 1965, *147,* 630–631.

Hinde, R. A., & Stevenson-Hinde, J. (Eds.). *Constraints on learning.* New York: Academic Press, 1973.

Hofmann, M. J., Salapatek, P., & Kuskowski, M. Evidence for visual memory in the averaged and single evoked potentials of human infants. *Infant Behavior and Development,* 1981, *4,* 185–205.

Holland, J. H. *Adaptation in natural and artificial systems.* Ann Arbor: University of Michigan Press, 1975.

Horowitz, F., Paden, L., Bhana, K., & Self, P. An infant-control procedure for studying infant visual fixations. *Developmental Psychology,* 1972, *7,* 90.

Hubel, D. H., & Wiesel, T. N. Receptive fields of single neurones in the cat's striate cortex. *Journal of Physiology,* 1959, *148,* 574–591.

Hubel, D. H., & Wiesel, T. N. Receptive fields, binocular interaction and functional architecture in the cat's visual cortex. *Journal of Physiology,* 1962, *160,* 106–154.

Huttenlocher, J. The origins of language comprehension. In R. L. Solso (Ed.), *Theories in cognitive psychology: The Loyola symposium.* Hillsdale, N.J.: Erlbaum, 1974.

Jacobson, J. L. Cognitive determinants of wariness toward unfamiliar peers. *Developmental Psychology,* 1980, *16,* 347–354.

James, W. *The principles of psychology.* New York: Holt, 1890.

Jeffrey, W. E., & Cohen, L. B. Habituation in the human infant. In H. W. Reese (Ed.), *Advances in child development and behavior* (Vol. 6). New York: Academic Press, 1971.

John, E. R. *Mechanisms of memory.* New York: Academic Press, 1967.

Jones-Molfese, V. J. Individual differences in neonatal preferences for planometric and stereometric visual patterns. *Child Development,* 1972, *43,* 1289–1296.

Jones-Molfese, V. J. Preferences of infants for regular and distorted facial stimuli. *Child Development,* 1975, *46,* 1005–1009.

Kagan, J. *Change and continuity in infancy.* New York: Wiley, 1971.

Kagan, J., Kearsley, R. B., & Zelazo, P. R. *Infancy: Its place in human development.* Cambridge, Mass.: Harvard University Press, 1978.

Kahneman, D. *Attention and effort.* Englewood Cliffs, N.J.: Prentice-Hall, 1973.

Kaltenbach, K., Weinraub, M., & Fullard, W. Infant wariness toward strangers reconsidered: Infants' and mothers' reactions to unfamiliar persons. *Child Development,* 1980, *51,* 1197–1202.

Karmel, B. Z. The effects of age, complexity, and amount of contour on pattern preferences in human infants. *Journal of Experimental Child Psychology,* 1969, *7,* 339–354. (a)

Karmel, B. Z. Complexity, amounts of contour, and visually dependent behavior in hooded rats, domestic chicks, and human infants. *Journal of Comparative and Physiological Psychology,* 1969, *69,* 649–657. (b)

Karmel, B. Z., & Maisel, E. B. A neuronal activity model for infant visual attention. In L. B. Cohen & P. Salapatek (Eds.), *Infant perception: From sensation to cognition* (Vol. 1). New York: Academic Press, 1975.

Kaye, K., & Marcus, J. Imitation over a series of trials without feedback: Age six months. *Infant Behavior and Development,* 1978, *1,* 141–155.

Kelly, D. H. Pattern detection and the two-dimensional Fourier transform: Flickering, checkerboards and chromatic mechanisms. *Vision Research,* 1976, *16,* 277–287.

Kessen, W., Haith, M. M., & Salapatek, P. Human infancy: A bibliography and guide. In P. Mussen (Ed.), *Carmichael's manual of child psychology.* New York: Wiley, 1970.

Kessen, W., Salapatek, P., & Haith, M. M. The visual response of the newborn to linear contour. *Journal of Experimental Child Psychology,* 1972, *13,* 9–20.

Klahr, D., & Wallace, J. G. *Cognitive development: An information-processing view.* Hillsdale, N.J.: Erlbaum, 1976.

Klatzky, R. L. *Human memory: Structures and processes* (2nd ed.). San Francisco: W. H. Freeman, 1980.

Klaus, M. H., & Kennell, J. H. *Maternal-infant bonding.* St. Louis: C. V. Mosby, 1976.

Korner, A. F. State as variable, as obstacle, and as mediator of stimulation in infant research. *Merrill-Palmer Quarterly,* 1972, *18,* 77–94.

Kosslyn, S. M. *Image and mind.* Cambridge, Mass.: Harvard University Press, 1980.

LaBerge, D., & Samuels, S. J. Toward a theory of automatic information processing in reading. *Cognitive Psychology,* 1974, *6,* 293–323.

Lamb, M. E., & Campos, J. J. *Development in infancy.* New York: Random House, 1982.

Lasky, R. E. The effect of visual feedback of the hand on the reaching and retrieval behavior of young infants. *Child Development,* 1977, *48,* 112–117.

Lasky, R. E., & Spiro, D. The processing of tachistoscopically presented visual stimuli by five-month-old infants. *Child Development,* 1980, *51,* 1292–1294.

Lawson, K., Daum, C., & Turkewitz, G. Environmental characteristics of a neonatal intensive-care unit. *Child Development,* 1977, *48,* 1633–1639.

Leiderman, P. H., Tulkin, S. R., & Rosenfeld, A. *Culture and infancy: Variations in the human experience.* New York: Academic Press, 1977.

Lester, B. M. Cardiac habituation of the orienting response to an auditory signal in infants of varying nutritional status. *Developmental Psychology,* 1975, *11,* 432–442.

Levitt, M. J. Contingent feedback, familiarization, and infant affect: How a stranger becomes a friend. *Developmental Psychology,* 1980, *16,* 425–432.

Lewis, M., & Brooks-Gunn, J. Visual attention at three months as a predictor of cognitive functioning at two years of age. *Intelligence,* 1981, *5,* 131–140.

Lewis, M., & Rosenblum, L. (Eds.). *The origins of fear.* New York: Wiley, 1974.

Lewis, M., & Rosenblum, L. (Eds.). *The development of affect.* New York: Plenum, 1978.

Lewkowicz, D. J., & Turkewitz, G. Cross-modal equivalence in early infancy: Auditory-visual intensity matching. *Developmental Psychology,* 1980, *16,* 597–607.

Lipsitt, L. P. Learning in the first year of life. In L. P. Lipsitt & C. C. Spiker (Eds.), *Advances in child development and behavior* (Vol. 1). New York: Academic Press, 1963.

Mandler, J. M. Representation. In J. H. Flavell & E. M. Markman (Eds.), *Manual of child psychology (Vol. 2): Cognitive development.* New York: Wiley, in press. (a)

Mandler, J. M. Representation and retrieval in infancy. In M. Moscovitch (Ed.), *Infant memory.* New York: Plenum, in press. (b)

Marquis, D. P. Can conditioned responses be established in the newborn infant? *Journal of Genetic Psychology,* 1931, *39,* 479–492.

Martin, E. Stimulus meaningfulness and paired-associate transfer: An encoding variability hypothesis. *Psychological Review,* 1968, *75,* 421–441.

Martin, R. M. Effects of familiar and complex stimuli on infant attention. *Developmental Psychology,* 1975, *11,* 178–185.

Mast, V. K., Fagen, J. W., Rovee-Collier, C. K., & Sullivan, M. W. Immediate and long-term memory for reinforcement context: The development of learned expectancies in early infancy. *Child Development,* 1980, *51,* 700–707.

Maurer, D., & Barrera, M. Infants' perception of natural and distorted arrangements of a schematic face. *Child Development,* 1981, *52,* 196–202.

Maurer, D., & Salapatek, P. Developmental changes in the scanning of faces by infants. *Child Development,* 1976, *47,* 523–527.

McCall, R. B. Individual differences in the pattern of habituation at 5 and 10 months of age. *Developmental Psychology,* 1979, *15,* 559–569.

McCall, R. B., & Kagan, J. Stimulus-schema discrepancy and attention in the infant. *Journal of Experimental Child Psychology,* 1967, *5,* 381–390.

McCall, R. B., Kennedy, C. B., & Appelbaum, M. I. Magnitude of discrepancy and the distribution of attention in infants. *Child Development,* 1977, *48,* 772–785.

McCall, R. B., Kennedy, C. B., & Dodds, C. The interfering effect of distracting stimuli on the infant's memory. *Child Development,* 1977, *48,* 79–87.

McCall, R. B., & McGhee, P. E. The discrepancy hypothesis of attention and affect in human infants. In I. C. Uzgiris & F. Weizmann (Eds.), *The structuring of experience.* New York: Plenum, 1977.

McCall, R. B., Parke, R. D., & Kavanaugh, R. D. Imitation of live and televised models by children one to three years of age. *Monographs of the Society for Child Development,* 1977, *42*(Whole No. 173).

McClelland, D. C., & Clark, R. A. Antecedent conditions for affective arousal. In D. C. McClelland, J. W. Atkinson, R. A. Clark, & E. L. Lowell (Eds.), *The achievement motive.* New York: Appleton-Century-Crofts, 1953.

McClelland, J. L. On the time relations of mental processes: An examination of systems of processes in cascade. *Psychological Review,* 1979, *86,* 287–330.

McGurk, H. Infant discrimination of orientation. *Journal of Experimental Child Psychology,* 1972, *14,* 151–164.

McKenzie, B., & Over, R. Young infants fail to imitate facial and manual gestures. *Infant Behavior and Development,* in press.

McKirdy, L. S., & Rovee, C. K. The efficacy of auditory and visual conjugate reinforcers in infant conditioning. *Journal of Experimental Child Psychology,* 1978, *25,* 80–89.

Melton, A. W. The end-spurt in memorization curves as an artifact of the averaging of individual curves. *Psychological Monographs,* 1936, *47,* 119–134.

Melton, A. W., & Irwin, J. M. The influence of degree of interpolated learning on retroactive inhibition and the overt transfer of specific responses. *American Journal of Psychology,* 1940, *53,* 173–203.

Meltzoff, A. N., & Moore, M. K. Imitation of facial and manual gestures by human neonates. *Science,* 1977, *198,* 75–78.

Mendelson, M. J., & Haith, M. M. The relation between audition and vision in the human newborn. *Monographs of the Society for Child Development,* 1976, *41*(Whole No. 167).

Michalski, R. S., Carbonell, J. G., & Mitchell, T. M. *Machine learning: An artificial intelligence approach.* Los Altos, Calif.: William Kaufmann, 1983.

Milewski, A. E. Infants' discrimination of internal and external pattern elements. *Journal of Experimental Child Psychology,* 1976, *22,* 229–246.

Milewski, A. E. Young infants' visual processing of internal and adjacent shapes. *Infant Behavior and Development,* 1978, *1,* 359–371.

Milewski, A. E. Visual discrimination and detection of configurational invariance in 3-month infants. *Developmental Psychology,* 1979, *15,* 357–363.

Milewski, A. E., & Siqueland, E. R. Discrimination of color and pattern novelty in one-month human infants. *Journal of Experimental Child Psychology,* 1975, *19,* 122–136.

Millar, W. S. Operant acquisition of social behaviors in infancy: Basic problems and constraints. In H. W. Reese (Ed.), *Advances in child development and behavior* (Vol. 11). New York: Academic Press, 1976.

Millar, W. S., & Schaffer, H. R. The influence of spatially displaced feedback on infant operant conditioning. *Journal of Experimental Child Psychology,* 1972, *14,* 442–453.

Millar, W. S., & Watson, J. S. The effect of delayed feedback on infant learning reexamined. *Child Development,* 1979, *50,* 747–751.

Miller, G. A. The magical number seven, plus or minus two: Some limits on our capacity for processing information. *Psychological Review,* 1956, *63,* 81–97.

Monty, R. A., & Senders, J. W. (Eds.). *Eye movements and psychological processes.* Hillsdale, N.J.: Erlbaum, 1976.

Moore, M. K., & Meltzoff, A. N. Object permanence, imitation, and L development: Toward a neo-Piagetian perspective on cognitive and communicative development. In F. Minifie & L. Lloyd (Eds.), *Communicative and cognitive abilities—early behavioral assessment.* Baltimore: University Park Press, 1978.

Morse, P. A. The discrimination of speech and nonspeech stimuli in early infancy. *Journal of Experimental Child Psychology,* 1972, *14,* 477–492.

Morse, P. A. Infant speech perception: A preliminary model and review of the literature. In R. Schiefelbusch & L. Lloyd (Eds.), *Language perspectives—acquisition, retardation, and intervention.* Baltimore: University Park Press, 1974.

Morse, P. A. Infant speech perception: Origins, processes, and *Alpha Centauri.* In F. D. Minifie & L. L. Lloyd (Eds.), *Communicative and cognitive abilities—early behavioral assessment.* Baltimore: University Park Press, 1978.

Neisser, U. Cultural and cognitive discontinuity. In T. E. Gladwin & W. Sturtevant (Eds.), *Anthropology and human behavior.* Washington, D.C.: Anthropological Society of Washington, 1962.

Neisser, U. *Cognitive psychology.* New York: Appleton-Century-Crofts, 1967.

Nelson, M. N., Clifton, R. K., Dowd, J. M., & Field, T. M. Cardiac responding to auditory stimuli in newborn infants: Why pacifiers should not be used when heart rate is the major dependent variable. *Infant Behavior and Development,* 1978, *1,* 277–290.

Nelson, T. O. Savings and forgetting from long-term memory. *Journal of Verbal Learning and Verbal Behavior,* 1971, *10,* 568–576.

Newell, A., & Simon, H. A. *Human problem solving.* Englewood Cliffs, N.J.: Prentice-Hall, 1972.

Nilsson, N. J. *Principles of artificial intelligence.* Los Altos, Calif.: William Kaufmann, 1982.

Norman, D. A., & Bobrow, D. G. On data-limited and resource-limited processes. *Cognitive Psychology,* 1975, *7,* 44–64.

Noton, D., & Stark, L. Scanpaths in eye movements during pattern perception. *Science,* 1971, *171,* 308–311.

Olson, G. M. An information processing analysis of visual memory and habituation in infants. In T. J. Tighe & R. N. Leaton (Eds.), *Habituation: Perspectives from child development, animal behavior, and neurophysiology.* Hillsdale, N.J.: Erlbaum, 1976.

Olson, G. M. Infant recognition memory for briefly presented visual stimuli. *Infant Behavior and Development,* 1979, *2,* 123–134.

Olson, G. M. The recognition of specific persons. In M. E. Lamb & L. R. Sherrod (Eds.), *Infant social cognition: Empirical and theoretical considerations.* Hillsdale, N.J.: Erlbaum, 1981.

Olson, G. M., & Sherman, T. Varying the criterion in the infant controlled visual habituation task: Methodological and theoretical implications. Report No. 108, Developmental Program, Department of Psychology, University of Michigan, August 1978.

Olson, G. M., & Sherman, T. A conceptual framework for the study of infant mental processes. In L. P. Lipsitt (Ed.), *Advances in infancy research* (Vol. 3). Norwood, N.J.: Ablex, in press.

Olson, G. M., & Strauss, M. S. A theory of infant memory. In M. Moscovitch (Ed.), *Infant memory.* New York: Plenum, in press.

Olson, G. M., Zimmerman, B. L., & Sherman, T. Visual attention and risk status in premature infants. Manuscript in preparation.

Oviatt, S. L. The emerging ability to comprehend language: An experimental approach. *Child Development,* 1980, *51,* 97–106.

Paivio, A. *Imagery and verbal processes.* New York: Holt, Rinehart and Winston, 1971.

Palmer, S. E. Hierarchical structure in perceptual representation. *Cognitive Psychology,* 1977, *9,* 441–474.

Palmer, S. E. Fundamental aspects of cognitive representation. In E. Rosch & B. Lloyd (Eds.), *Cognition and categorization.* Hillsdale, N.J.: Erlbaum, 1978.

Papousek, H. A method of studying conditioned food reflexes in young children up to the age of 6 months. *Pavlov Journal of Higher Nervous Activities,* 1959, *9,* 136–140.

Papousek, H. Conditioned head rotation reflexes in infants in the first months of life. *Acta Pediatrica,* 1961, *50,* 565–576.

Papousek, H. Experimental studies of appetitional behavior in human newborns and infants. In H. W. Stevenson, E. H. Hess, & H. L. Rheingold (Eds.), *Early behavior.* New York: Wiley, 1967.

Parmelee, A. H., Jr. Ontogeny of sleep patterns and associated periodicities in infants. In F. Falkner, N. Kretchmer, & E. Rossi (Eds.), *Modern problems in paediatrics* (Vol. 13). Basel: S. Karger, 1974.

Parmelee, A. H., Jr., & Stern, E. Development of states in infants. In C. D. Clemente, D. P. Purpura, & F. E. Mayer (Eds.), *Sleep and the maturing nervous system.* New York: Academic Press, 1972.

Parry, M. H. Infants' responses to novelty in familiar and unfamiliar settings. *Child Development,* 1972, *43,* 233–237.

Parton, D. A. Learning to imitate in infancy. *Child Development,* 1976, *47,* 14–31.

Pavlov, I. P. *Conditioned reflexes.* New York: Oxford, 1927.

Pawlby, S. J. Imitative interaction. In H. R. Schaffer (Ed.), *Studies in mother-infant interaction.* New York: Academic Press, 1977.

Piaget, J. *The origins of intelligence in children.* New York: W. W. Norton, 1952.

Piaget, J. *The construction of reality in the child.* New York: Basic Books, 1954.

Piaget, J. *Play, dreams, and imitation in childhood.* New York: W. W. Norton, 1962.

Piaget, J., & Inhelder, B. *Memory and intelligence.* New York: Basic Books, 1973.

Porges, S. W. Heart rate indices of newborn attentional responsivity. *Merrill-Palmer Quarterly,* 1974, *20,* 231–254.

Porges, S. W., Arnold, W. R., & Forbes, E. J. Heart rate variability: An index of attentional responsivity in human newborns. *Developmental Psychology,* 1973, *8,* 85–92.

Porges, S. W., Stamps, L. E., & Walter, G. F. Heart rate variability and newborn heart rate responses to illumination changes. *Developmental Psychology,* 1974, *10,* 507–513.

Posner, M. I. *Chronometric explorations of mind.* Hillsdale, N.J.: Erlbaum, 1978.

Posner, M. I., & Keele, S. W. On the genesis of abstract ideas. *Journal of Experimental Psychology,* 1968, *77,* 353–363.

Posner, M. I., & Keele, S. W. Retention of abstract ideas. *Journal of Experimental Psychology,* 1970, *83,* 304–308.

Posner, M. I., & Rothbart, M. K. The development of attentional mechanisms. In J. H. Flowers (Ed.), *Nebraska symposium on motivation, 1980: Cognitive processes.* Lincoln: University of Nebraska Press, 1981.

Prechtl, H. F. R. Brain and behavioural mechanisms in the human newborn infant. In R. J. Robinson (Ed.), *Brain and early behavior.* New York: Academic Press, 1969.

Prechtl, H. F. R. The behavioral states of the newborn infant (a review). *Brain Research,* 1974, *76,* 185–212.

Prechtl, H., & Beintema, D. The neurological examination of the full-term newborn infant. *Little Cub Clinics in Developmental Medicine,* 1964, *12,* 1–74.

Provine, R. R., & Westerman, J. A. Crossing the

midline: Limits of early eye-hand behavior. *Child Development,* 1979, *50,* 437–441.

Ramsay, D. S., & Campos, J. J. Memory by the infant in an object notion task. *Developmental Psychology,* 1975, *11,* 411–412.

Reitman, J. S. Computer simulation of an information-processing model of short-term memory. In D. A. Norman (Ed.), *Models of human memory.* New York: Academic Press, 1970.

Reitman, J. S. Mechanisms of forgetting in short-term memory. *Cognitive Psychology,* 1971, *2,* 185–195.

Reitman, J. S. Without surreptitious rehearsal, information in short-term memory decays. *Journal of Verbal Learning and Verbal Behavior,* 1974, *13,* 365–377.

Reitman, J. S. Skilled perception in Go: Deducing memory structures from inter-response times. *Cognitive Psychology,* 1976, *8,* 336–356.

Rescorla, R. A. Pavlovian conditioning and its proper control procedures. *Psychological Review,* 1967, *74,* 71–80.

Rescorla, R. A. Informational variables in Pavlovian conditioning. In G. H. Bower (Ed.), *The psychology of learning and motivation* (Vol. 6). New York: Academic Press, 1972.

Rescorla, R. A., & Wagner, A. R. A theory of Pavlovian conditioning: Variations in the effectiveness of reinforcement and nonreinforcement. In A. H. Black & W. F. Prokasy (Eds.), *Classical conditioning II.* New York: Appleton-Century-Crofts, 1972.

Revusky, S., & Garcia, J. Learned associations over long delays. In G. H. Bower (Ed.), *The psychology of learning and motivation* (Vol. 4). New York: Academic Press, 1970.

Rheingold, H. L. The effect of environmental stimulation upon social and exploratory behavior in the human infant. In B. M. Foss (Ed.), *Determinants of infant behavior* (Vol. 1). London: Methuen, 1961.

Rheingold, H. L., Gewirtz, J. L., & Ross, H. W. Social conditioning of vocalization in the infant. *Journal of Comparative and Physiological Psychology,* 1959, *52,* 68–73.

Richards, J. E. The statistical analysis of heart rate: A review emphasizing infancy data. *Psychophysiology,* 1980, *17,* 153–166.

Rose, S. A. Developmental changes in infants' retention of visual stimuli. *Child Development,* 1981, *52,* 227–233.

Ross, G. S. Categorization in 1- to 2-year-olds. *Developmental Psychology,* 1980, *16,* 391–396.

Ross, H. S. The effects of increasing familiarity on infants' reactions to adult strangers. *Journal of Experimental Child Psychology,* 1975, *20,* 226–239.

Ross, H. S., Rheingold, H. L., & Eckerman, C. O. Approach and exploration of a novel alternative by 12-month-old infants. *Journal of Experimental Child Psychology,* 1972, *13,* 85–93.

Rovee, C. K., & Fagen, J. W. Extended conditioning and 24-hour retention in infants. *Journal of Experimental Child Psychology,* 1976, *21,* 1–11.

Rovee, C. K., & Rovee, D. T. Conjugate reinforcement of infant exploratory behavior. *Journal of Experimental Child Psychology,* 1969, *8,* 33–39.

Rovee-Collier, C. K., & Capatides, J. B. Positive behavioral contrast in 3-month-old infants on multiple conjugate reinforcement schedules. *Journal of the Experimental Analysis of Behavior,* 1979, *32,* 15–27.

Rovee-Collier, C. K., & Gekoski, M. J. The economics of infancy: A review of conjugate reinforcement. In H. W. Reese & L. P. Lipsitt (Eds.), *Advances in child development and behavior* (Vol. 13). New York: Academic Press, 1979.

Rovee-Collier, C. K., & Lipsitt, L. P. Learning, adaptation, and memory. In P. M. Stratton (Ed.), *Psychobiology of the human newborn.* London: Wiley, 1980.

Rovee-Collier, C. K., Morrongiello, B. A., Aron, M., & Kupersmidt, J. Topographical response differentiation and reversal in 3-month-old infants. *Infant Behavior and Development,* 1978, *1,* 323–333.

Rovee-Collier, C. K., Sullivan, M. W., Enright, M., Lucas, D., & Fagen, J. W. Reactivation of infant memory. *Science,* 1980, 208, 1159–1161.

Rubenstein, J. A concordance of visual and manipulative responsiveness to novel and familiar stimuli in six-month-old infants. *Child Development,* 1974, *45,* 194–195.

Rubenstein, J. Concordance of visual and manipulative responsiveness to novel and familiar stimuli: A function of test procedures or prior experience? *Child Development,* 1976, *47,* 1197–1199.

Ruff, H. A. The function of shifting fixations in the visual perception of infants. *Child Development,* 1975, *46,* 857–865.

Ruff, H. A. The coordination of manipulation and visual fixation: A response to Schaffer (1975). *Child Development,* 1976, *47,* 868–871.

Ruff, H. A. Infant recognition of the invariant form of objects. *Child Development,* 1978, *49,* 293–306.

Ruff, H. A. Infant memory from a Gibsonian point of view. In M. Moscovitch (Ed.), *Infant memory*. New York: Plenum, in press.

Ruff, H. A., & Birch, H. G. Infant visual fixation: The effect of concentricity, curvilinearity, and number of directions. *Journal of Experimental Child Psychology*, 1974, *17*, 460–473.

Rumelhart, D. E. Toward an interactive model of reading. In S. Dornic (Ed.), *Attention and Performance VI*. Hillsdale, N.J.: Erlbaum, 1977.

Salapatek, P. Visual scanning of geometric figures by the human newborn. *Journal of Comparative and Physiological Psychology*, 1968, *66*, 247–258.

Salapatek, P. Pattern perception in early infancy. In L. B. Cohen & P. Salapatek (Eds.), *Infant perception: From sensation to cognition* (Vol. 1). New York: Academic Press, 1975.

Salapatek, P., & Banks, M. Sensory assessment: Vision. In F. Minifie & L. Lloyd (Eds.), *Communicative and cognitive abilities: Early behavioral assessment*. Baltimore: University Park Press, 1978.

Salapatek, P., Haith, M. M., Maurer, D., & Kessen, W. Error in the corneal-reflection technique: A note on Slater and Findlay. *Journal of Experimental Child Psychology*, 1972, *14*, 493–497.

Salapatek, P., & Kessen, W. Visual scanning of triangles by the human newborn. *Journal of Experimental Child Psychology*, 1966, *3*, 155–167.

Salapatek, P., & Kessen, W. Prolonged investigation of a plane geometric triangle by the human newborn. *Journal of Experimental Child Psychology*, 1973, *15*, 22–29.

Sameroff, A. J. The components of sucking in the human newborn. *Journal of Experimental Child Psychology*, 1968, *6*, 607–623.

Sameroff, A. J. Can conditioned responses be established in the newborn infant? *Developmental Psychology*, 1971, *5*, 1–12.

Sameroff, A. J. Learning and adaptation in infancy: A comparison of models. In H. W. Reese (Ed.), *Advances in child development and behavior* (Vol. 7). New York: Academic Press, 1972.

Sameroff, A. J., & Cavanagh, P. J. Learning in infancy: A developmental perspective. In J. D. Osofsky (Ed.), *Handbook of infant development*. New York: Wiley, 1979.

Schachtel, E. G. On memory and childhood amnesia. *Psychiatry*, 1947, *10*, 1–26.

Schachtel, E. G. *Metamorphosis: On the development of affect, perception, attention, and memory*. New York: Basic Books, 1959.

Schaffer, H. R. Cognitive structure and early social behavior. In H. R. Schaffer (Ed.), *The origins of human social relations*. New York: Academic Press, 1971.

Schaffer, H. R. Concordance of visual and manipulative responses to novel and familiar stimuli: A reply to Rubenstein (1974). *Child Development*, 1975, *46*, 290–291.

Schaffer, H. R., Greenwood, A., & Parry, M. H. The onset of wariness. *Child Development*, 1972, *43*, 165–176.

Schaffer, H. R., & Parry, M. H. Perceptual-motor behavior in infancy as a function of age and stimulus familiarity. *British Journal of Psychology*, 1969, *60*, 1–9.

Schaffer, H. R., & Parry, M. H. The effects of short-term familiarization on infants' perceptual-motor coordination in a simultaneous discrimination situation. *British Journal of Psychology*, 1970, *61*, 559–569.

Schneider, W., & Shiffrin, R. M. Controlled and automatic human information processing: I. Detection, search, and attention. *Psychological Review*, 1977, *84*, 1–66.

Schubert, R. E., & Gratch, G. Search on five-choice invisible displacement task: A reply to Cummings and Bjork. *Infant Behavior and Development*, 1981, *4*, 61–64.

Seligman, M. E. P. On the generality of the laws of learning. *Psychological Review*, 1970, *77*, 406–418.

Sherman, T. L. *Categorization skills in infants*. Unpublished doctoral dissertation, University of Michigan, 1980.

Sherman, T., & Olson, G. M. Pre-criterion behavior in infant visual habituation. Paper presented at the International Conference on Infant Studies, Providence, R.I., March 1978.

Sherrod, L. R. Issues of cognitive-perceptual development: The special case of social stimuli. In M. E. Lamb & L. R. Sherrod (Eds.), *Infant social cognition: Empirical and theoretical considerations*. Hillsdale, N.J.: Erlbaum, 1981.

Shiffrin, R. M. Information persistence in short-term memory. *Journal of Experimental Psychology*, 1973, *100*, 39–49.

Shiffrin, R. M., & Cook, J. R. Short-term forgetting of item and order information. *Journal of Verbal Learning and Verbal Behavior*, 1978, *17*, 189–218.

Shiffrin, R. M., & Schneider, W. Controlled and automatic human information processing: II. Perceptual learning, automatic attending, and a general theory. *Psychological Review*, 1977, *84*, 127–190.

Shirley, M. M. *The first two years: A study of twen-*

ty-five babies (Vol. 1). Minneapolis: University of Minnesota Press, 1931.

Silverstein, A. Secondary reinforcement in infants. *Journal of Experimental Child Psychology,* 1972, *13,* 138–144.

Silverstein, A., & Lipsitt, L. P. The role of instrumental responding and contiguity of stimuli in the development of infant secondary reinforcement. *Journal of Experimental Child Psychology,* 1974, *17,* 322–331.

Simon, H. A. *The sciences of the artificial.* Cambridge, Mass.: M.I.T. Press, 1969.

Simon, H. A. How big is a chunk? *Science,* 1974, *183,* 482–488.

Siqueland, E. R., & DeLucia, C. A. Visual reinforcement of nonnutritive sucking in human infants. *Science,* 1969, *165,* 1144–1146.

Slater, A. M., & Findlay, J. M. The measurement of fixation position in the newborn baby. *Journal of Experimental Child Psychology,* 1972, *14,* 349–364.

Slater, A. M., Morison, V., & Rose, D. Visual memory at birth. *British Journal of Psychology,* in press.

Smith, E. E., & Medin, D. L. *Categories and concepts.* Cambridge, Mass.: Harvard University Press, 1981.

Sokolov, E. N. *Perception and the conditioned reflex.* New York: Macmillan, 1963.

Sophian, C. Habituation is not enough: Novelty preferences, search, and memory in infancy. *Merrill-Palmer Quarterly,* 1980, *26,* 239–257.

Soroka, S. M., Corter, C. M., & Abramovitch, R. Infants' tactual discrimination of novel and familiar tactual stimuli. *Child Development,* 1979, *50,* 1251–1253.

Sroufe, L. A. Socioemotional development. In J. D. Osofsky (Ed.), *Handbook of infant development.* New York: Wiley, 1979.

Starkey, P., & Cooper, R. G. Perception of number by human infants. *Science,* 1980, *210,* 1033–1035.

Stechler, G. Newborn attention as affected by medication during labor. *Science,* 1964, *144,* 315–317.

Stone, L. J., Smith, H. T., & Murphy, L. B. (Eds.) *The competent infant: Research and commentary.* New York: Basic Books, 1973.

Strauss, M. S. Abstraction of prototypical information by adults and 10-month-old infants. *Journal of Experimental Psychology: Human Learning and Memory,* 1979, *5,* 618–632.

Strauss, M. S., & Curtis, L. E. Infant perception of numerosity. *Child Development,* 1981, *52,* 1146–1152.

Sullivan, M. W., Rovee-Collier, C. K., & Tynes, D. M. A conditioning analysis of infant long-term memory. *Child Development,* 1979, *50,* 152–162.

Sutton, S., Braren, M., Zubin, J., & John, E. R. Evoked potential correlates of stimulus uncertainty. *Science,* 1965, *150,* 1187–1188.

Swoboda, P. J., Kass, J., Morse, P. A., & Leavitt, L. A. Memory factors in vowel discrimination of normal and at-risk infants. *Child Development,* 1978, *49,* 332–339.

Swoboda, P. J., Morse, P. A., & Leavitt, L. A. Continuous vowel discrimination in normal and at risk infants. *Child Development,* 1976, *47,* 459–465.

Thatcher, R. W. Evoked potential correlates of delayed letter-matching. *Behavioral Biology,* 1977, *19,* 1–23.

Thomas, D. G., Campos, J. J., Shucard, D. W., Ramsay, D. S., & Shucard, J. Semantic comprehension in infancy: A signal detection analysis. *Child Development,* 1981, *52,* 798–803.

Thomas, H. Discrepancy hypothesis: Methodological and theoretical considerations. *Psychological Review,* 1971, *78,* 249–259.

Thomas, H. Unfolding the baby's mind: The infant's selection of visual stimuli. *Psychological Review,* 1973, *80,* 468–488.

Thomas, H., & Jones-Molfese, V. Infants and I scales: Inferring change from the ordinal stimulus selections of infants for configural stimuli. *Journal of Experimental Child Psychology,* 1977, *23,* 329–339.

Trehub, S. E. Infants' sensitivity to vowel and tonal contrasts. *Developmental Psychology,* 1973, *9,* 91–96.

Trehub, S. E. The discrimination of foreign speech contrasts by infants and adults. *Child Development,* 1976, *47,* 466–472.

Trehub, S. E., & Rabinovitch, M. S. Auditory-linguistic sensitivity in early infancy. *Developmental Psychology,* 1972, *6,* 74–77.

Treiber, F., & Wilcox, S. Perception of a "subjective" contour by infants. *Child Development,* 1980, *51,* 915–917.

Tulving, E., & Thomson, D. M. Encoding specificity and retrieval processes in episodic memory. *Psychological Review,* 1973, *80,* 352–373.

Turvey, M. T. Perspectives in vision: Conception or perception? In D. Duane & M. Rawson (Eds.), *Reading, perception and language.* Baltimore, Md.: York, 1975.

Uzgiris, I. C. Patterns of vocal and gestural imitation. In F. Monks (Ed.), *Determinants of behavioral development.* New York: Academic Press,

1972.

Uzgiris, I. C., & Hunt, J. M. *Assessment in infancy*. Chicago: University of Illinois Press, 1975.

von Hofsten, C. Predictive reaching for moving objects by human infants. *Journal of Experimental Child Psychology*, 1980, *30*, 369–382.

von Hofsten, C., & Lindhagen, K. Observations on the development of reaching for moving objects. *Journal of Experimental Child Psychology*, 1979, *28*, 158–173.

Wachs, T. D. The relationship of infant's physical environment to their Binet performance at 2-½ years. *International Journal of Behavioral Development*, 1978, *1*, 51–65.

Wachs, T. D. Proximal experience and early cognitive-intellectual development: The physical environment. *Merrill-Palmer Quarterly*, 1979, *25*, 3–41.

Wachs, T. D., Francis, J., & McQuiston, S. Psychological dimensions of the infant's physical environment. *Infant Behavior and Development*, 1979. *2*, 155–161.

Wagner, A. R., & Rescorla, R. A. Inhibition in Pavlovian conditioning: Application of a theory. In R. A. Boakes & M. S. Halliday (Eds.), *Inhibition and learning*. New York: Academic Press, 1972.

Waite, L. H. Early imitation with several models: An example of socio-cognitive and socio-affective development. Paper presented at the Biennial Meeting of the Society for Research in Child Development, San Francisco, March 1979.

Watson, J. S. Memory in infancy. In J. Piaget, J. P. Bronkart, & P. Mounoud (Eds.), *Encyclopédie de la pleiade: La psychologie*. Paris: Gallimard, 1980.

Weisberg, P. Social and nonsocial conditioning of infant vocalizations. *Child Development*, 1963, *34*, 377–388.

Weizmann, F., Cohen, L. B., & Pratt, J. Novelty, familiarity, and the development of infant attention. *Developmental Psychology*, 1971, *4*, 149–154.

Welch, M. J. Infants' visual attention to varying degrees of novelty. *Child Development*, 1974, *45*, 344–350.

Wenger, M. A. An investigation of conditioned responses in human infants. *University of Iowa Studies in Child Welfare*, 1936, *12*(No. 1), 7–90.

Werner, J. S., & Perlmutter, M. Development of visual memory in infants. In H. W. Reese & L. P. Lipsitt (Eds.), *Advances in child development and behavior* (Vol. 14). New York: Academic Press, 1979.

Wetherford, M. J., & Cohen, L. B. Developmental changes in infant visual preferences for novelty and familiarity. *Child Development*, 1973, *44*, 416–424.

Wickens, D. D. Temporal limits of human information processing: A developmental study. *Psychological Bulletin*, 1974, *81*, 739–755.

Wickens, D. D., & Wickens, D. A study of conditioning in the neonate. *Journal of Experimental Psychology*, 1940, *26*, 94–102.

Willatts, P. Adjustment of reaching to change in object position by young infants. *Child Development*, 1979, *50*, 911–913.

Winograd, T. Frame representations and the declarative/procedural controversy. In D. G. Bobrow & A. Collins (Eds.), *Representation and understanding*. New York: Academic Press, 1975.

Winston, P. H. Learning structural descriptions from examples. In P. H. Winston (Ed.), *The psychology of computer vision*. New York: McGraw-Hill, 1975.

Winston, P. H. *Artificial intelligence*. Reading, Mass.: Addison-Wesley, 1977.

Wolff, P. Observations on the early development of smiling. In B. M. Foss (Ed.), *Determinants of infant behavior* (Vol. 2). London: Methuen, 1963.

Wolff, P. H. The causes, controls, and organization of behavior in the neonate. *Psychological Issues*, 1966, *5*, Monograph No. 17.

Wolff, P. H. Organization of behavior in the first three months of life. In J. I. Nurnberger (Ed.), *Biological and environmental determinants of early development*. Baltimore: Williams & Wilkins, 1973.

Wormith, S. J., Pankhurst, D., & Moffitt, A. R. Frequency discrimination by young infants. *Child Development*, 1975, *46*, 272–275.

Yarrow, L. J., Rubenstein, J. L., & Pederson, F. A. *Infant and environment: Early cognitive and motivational development*. Washington, D.C.: Hemisphere, 1975.

Young-Browne, G., Rosenfeld, H. M., & Horowitz, F. D. Infant discrimination of facial expressions. *Child Development*, 1977, *48*, 555–562.

Zeaman, D. The ubiquity of novelty-familiarity (habituation?) effects. In T. J. Tighe & R. N. Leaton (Eds.), *Habituation: Perspectives from child development, animal behavior, and neurophysiology*. Hillsdale, N.J.: Erlbaum, 1976.

RISK FACTORS IN DEVELOPMENT* 13

CLAIRE B. KOPP, *University of California, Los Angeles*

CHAPTER CONTENTS

Developmental risk factors refer to a wide range of biological and environmental conditions that are associated with increased probability for cognitive, social, affective, and physical problems. In some instances, the probabilities are very high, for example, with anomalies of autosome chromosomes, whereas lower probabilities are associated with other conditions, such as preterm birth without complications or adverse social conditions. Because almost every individual in the former instance is similarly and seriously affected, a major health goal is to work toward prevention of the condition or, if it does occur, to provide amelioration to the extent that it is possible to modify sequelae. With conditions associated with lower incidence rates, goals not only include prevention but also proper identification and interventions for those children who show signs of problems.

Prevention, identification, and intervention represent substantive challenges and demand the integration of social, political, and professional resources. Developmentalists are increasingly called upon to contribute their expertise to the multiple dimensions of risk conditions. Actually, our discipline has long been involved in identification of, and interventions for, children with problems. More recently, however, we have attempted to explicate the processes within, and external to, the child that exacerbate or attenuate the influence of risk factors. A discussion of these efforts directed toward children stressed by risk factors that are biologic in origin is the focus of this chapter. Risk factors represent diverse entities and have markedly variable outcomes; therefore, the first part of this chapter describes what they are and traces their influence from an historical perspective.

HISTORICAL FACTORS

In industrialized nations, the major contributions to risk have changed over time. To understand the nature and complexities that characterize the study of these influences, these introductory comments review the sources of problems and their epidemiology from a recent historical perspective. The summary is necessarily brief and highlights general trends.

*Preparation of this chapter was supported in part by Contract 300–77–0306, Office of Special Education, and by Grant 40–820–B–59527 from the Spencer Foundation. This support is gratefully acknowledged. Appreciation is extended to Nancy Baker, Stefan Hastrup, and Peggy Stuppy for their diligent library research, to Massie Oshita for assistance with references, and to Gretchen Geiser for invaluable help in both areas. To Richard Q. Bell, Pamela A. Davies, David Gibson, Antoinette Krupski, Lewis P. Lipsitt, and the editors of this volume, I extend my thanks for thoughtful and helpful comments.

A scant 100 years ago, childhood morbidity and mortality were very high. Urbanization and industrialization brought health problems to the forefront because of close living quarters, lack of sanitation, and squalor. Children were among the most vulnerable members of society. In 1869, the prominent physician, J. L. Smith, estimated that 53% of all deaths in New York City occurred to children under 5 years and 26% to children under 1 year of age. Further, he believed that one fourth to one third of all children born in the city died by age 5 (J. L. Smith, 1869).

J. L. Smith attributed the causes of mortality to:

1. Congenital factors (e.g., cyanosis, syphilitic infections, ''perturbating influences upon the mother,'' and many unknown conditions) that were mostly unpreventable and virtually untreatable.
2. ''Natural feebleness'' of the infant and young child's system that was exacerbated by the pregnant mother having tuberculosis, syphilis, or rachitis (rickets); these diseases further weakened the infant constitution.
3. The postnatal infectious diseases of childhood, including scarlet fever, smallpox, measles, bronchitis, and croup.
4. Antihygienic living conditions owing to poverty or gross parental negligence, which led to Asiatic cholera, cholera infantum, diphtheria, and typhus fever.
5. Careless management of young children with regard to dress and subsequent exposure to cold, with the consequent occurrence of respiratory infections, ''a very cold week always increases the mortality of the very young and very aged'' (J. L. Smith, 1869, p. 26).
6. Use of artificial feeding techniques for infants and provision of indigestable food for children that led to diarrhea, emaciation, and death.

J. L. Smith noted that morbidity and mortality problems were most acute in city living but were present in rural settings as well. In New York City, for example, he found that the mortality of foundlings who were artificially fed reached almost 100%. In contrast, J. L. Smith felt the effects would not be so devastating in the country. There, sunlight helped to develop a robust constitution and cow's milk, being clean and fresh, would not necessarily harm the infant.

Of the six broad categories described by J. L. Smith (1869), four can be considered postnatal causes and two prenatal, one of which was likely influenced by postnatal rearing conditions. Not surprisingly, most medical treatment of the time focused on attempts to alleviate postnatal conditions, although attention was also directed toward the need to improve health of pregnant women, particularly the poor (Combe, 1845). As will be seen shortly, postnatal risk conditions currently account for only a small proportion of serious developmental problems.

Risks for young children seemed little changed in the latter part of the nineteenth century. In his personal memoirs, Abt (1944) recounted the high infant and child mortality and morbidity rates that existed at the turn of the century. (Mortality has been estimated at 10% for newborns [Shapiro, Schlesinger, & Nesbitt, 1968].) In addition to the causes noted by J. L. Smith, Abt mentioned tuberculous, meningitis, traumatic accidents, and scurvy, which resulted from depletion of vitamins in milk that had been boiled for too long a time.

During Abt's 50-year career as a pediatrician, he witnessed the advent of antitoxin for diphtheria, serum to attenuate the effects of measles, widespread vaccination for smallpox, a vaccine for whooping cough, supervised milk supply, improved home and community sanitation, introduction of incubators for preterm infants, and so forth. In the *Abt-Garrison History of Pediatrics,* Abt (1965) also discussed specific events and years that had important ramifications for child health. In the 1920s, for example, a simple resuscitation device was introduced to prevent asphyxiation; in the 1930s sulfa and antibiotic drugs appeared; in the 1940s penicillin was introduced. Also in the 1930s and 1940s, research pointed to viral causes of influenza, mumps, rubella, and some forms of encephalitis.

These treatments and procedures alongside better overall maternal and child care, improvement in medical facilities, and changing economic and environmental conditions had a pronounced effect. By the mid-1940s, a rapid decline in postnatal causes of infant mortality rates was noted (Monroe & Anderson, 1963; Shapiro et al., 1968). Table 1 provides information on causes of mortality, changes in these causes, and incidence rates from the early part of the century to the present time. For the most part, changes in mortality rates were accompanied by a decline in postnatal causes of serious kinds of morbidity (e.g., central nervous system impairment, sensory disorders, paralysis, and mental retardation).

In this country, the 1920s also heralded interest in perinatal factors (Monroe & Anderson, 1963). Medical research started to unravel the dynamics of pregnancy and its complications, and obstetric surgery improved. Moreover, graduate training in obstetrics was fostered, and a liaison between obstetricians and pediatricians showed tentative beginnings.

The major shift in attention to perinatal problems stemmed from a confluence of events that occurred between the 1930s and the 1950s. For instance, the specialty of pediatrics began to establish formalized criteria for training and board certification (Hughes, 1980). Thus, a trained cadre would be available to assume major responsibility for the care of children. From another quarter there was a call for revised standards for registering the length of pregnancy and birthweight on birth certificates. These were required by the late 1940s and called attention to mortality rates among small infants (Silverman, 1980). Yet another push came from post-World War II goals to build specialized infant care centers with government funding (Gordon, 1975; Silverman, 1980). Naturally, infants with perinatal problems were referred to these facilities. Technology, too, was changing. Thus, transparent incubators began to be used in infant nurseries, making the previously swaddled small infant who had labored breathing immediately visible, and pediatricians increasingly gained control (from obstetricians) of the care of these children (Hughes, 1980; Silverman, 1980). Whereas almost a century had to elapse before postnatal mortality and morbidity was appreciably reduced, between 1942 and the early 1950s, perinatal mortality declined considerably (Shapiro et al., 1968). Unfortunately, it leveled off in the late 1950s and 1960s, but it is once again showing a decline (Chase, 1977; Shapiro et al., 1968).

But the history of changing practices in perinatal medicine are more complex than the preceding suggests. There were failures in treatments as well as successes. Excellent summaries of past and current practices employed with very low birthweight in-

Table 1. **Examples of Incidence Rates and Causes of Mortality Among Children 1 to 4 Years: United States 1920–1975[a,b]**

Cause of Death	1920	1940	1960	1970	1975
All causes per 100,000	987.2	289.6	108.8	84.5	70.8
Accidents: nonmotor vehicles	71.1	36.3	21.5	20.0	17.9
Accidents: motor vehicles		12.4	10.0	11.5	10.3
Congenital anomalies		10.3	12.8	9.7	8.9
Influenza & pneumonia	283.7	62.5	16.2	7.6	4.1
Malignancies			10.8	7.5	5.6
Symptoms & ill-defined conditions			2.8	2.1	2.7
Meningitis			2.8	1.9	1.7
Acute respiratory infections	12.3	8.9		1.7	
Enteritis, other diarrheal diseases	141.3	30.2	3.2	1.4	0.7
Meningococcal infections			1.4	1.0	0.6
Gasteritis, etc.			0.1		
Bronchitis			1.1		
Measles	56.4				
Tuberculosis	45.4	12.3			
Whooping cough	57.7	9.7			
Diphtheria	90.5	9.0			
Streptococcal sore throat, scarlet fever	23.2				
Dysentery	12.8				
Other	192.8	91.2	25.3	20.1	33.0

Notes: [a]Caution in interpreting data over time is necessary; criteria for diagnoses change and diagnostic classifications undergo modifications. Detailed documentation of changes in categories is found in publications of the National Center for Health Statistics.

[b]Blanks in columns indicate item was not measured or that incidence rates were quite low.

Source: Adapted from Vaughan & McKay, 1975, and U.S. Public Health Services Statistics, 1975.

fants are found in Davies (1976) and Silverman (1980). Both authors addressed issues related to mortality and morbidity and noted instances where outcome was affected by iatrogenic causes (e.g., pediatricians not sufficiently trained to resuscitate tiny infants, use of questionable and unproved treatments, insufficient use of clinical trials, failure to maintain infant body temperature, etc.).

Table 2 depicts examples of current mortality rates for infants under 1 year of age. Overall, successes outweigh setbacks as the data show sharp decreases for asphyxia, immaturity, and birth injuries. These encouraging signs are tempered by other findings that reveal substantial differences in mortality between white and nonwhite samples (Placek, 1977).

The last 30 years have also witnessed overall decreases in infant morbidity so that severe sequelae as a result of perinatal factors are substantially reduced in advantaged communities (Hagberg, 1975, 1978; Reed & Stanley, 1977; Usher, 1977). A case in point is the occurrence of spastic diplegia that shows major reductions in low birthweight infants who are more than 1,500 g (Davies & Tizard, 1975; Hagberg, 1975, 1979; Hagberg, Hagberg, & Olow, 1975; Jones, Cummins, & Davies, 1979). Although progress will continue to be made, the percentage of future improvements will be relatively small compared to what has gone before (Hagberg, 1975).

In spite of these positive trends, additional efforts must be directed to high-risk perinatal events that still occur. Half of high-risk pregnancies, for example, are associated with adverse perinatal sequelae (Vaughan & McKay, 1975). Although reproductive problems are still not fully understood, it is clear that outcome, in part, depends on the quality of care provided during pregnancy. Outcome also depends on the quality of care at birth and later (Hobel, 1978; Stanley & Alberman, 1978). Quality often suffers under poverty circumstances, underscoring the fact that a marked relationship exists between untoward socioeconomic conditions and perinatal complications (Birch & Gussow, 1970).

Also at this time, uneasiness and concern are increasingly focused upon risk factors that arise in the prenatal period. Their influence on serious kinds of morbidity is very high, representing 85% to 90% of all cases of severe handicapping conditions. Table 3 shows the percentage of severe mental retardation from prenatal and untraceable causes. Note that the Swedish studies, which are the most recent, coincide with Hagberg's (1975) estimate. Using another statistic, we find the incidence rate of severe mental retardation to be about 3 to 5 per 1,000 (Abramowicz & Richardson, 1975).

Unfortunately, many prenatal influences are far less amenable to early identification and prevention than perinatal or postnatal conditions. As a result, numerous prenatal risk influences are discovered in retrospect long after they have occurred and often

Table 2. **Examples of Incidence Rates and Causes of Infant Mortality: Birth to 1 Year: United States 1965, 1970, 1975, 1980**[a,b]

Cause of Death	1965	1970	1975	(Jan. to June) 1980[c]
All causes per 100,000 live births	2,469.6	2,001.1	1,606.9	1,320.0
Asphyxia of newborn, unspecified	410.3	262.9	128.8	40.0
Immaturity, unqualified	383.8	234.6	139.9	120.0
Respiratory distress syndrome[d]		119.5	123.3	150.0
Congenital anomalies	357.5	310.7	272.9	260.0
Influenza and pneumonia	287.4	168.9	70.0	30.0
Birth injuries	205.2	64.2	52.5	30.0
Sudden infant death syndrome[e]				170.0

Notes: [a]Public Health Service Statistics supply information about other causes of death; the ones provided here are among the most common.

[b]Caution in interpreting data over time is necessary; criteria for diagnoses change and diagnostic classifications undergo modifications. Detailed documentation of changes in categories is found in publications of the National Center for Health Statistics.

[c]This is an extrapolation based upon estimated infant mortality rates for 1,000 live births.

[d]Respiratory distress syndrome was introduced as a category in 1968.

[e]Sudden infant death syndrome was introduced as a category in 1973.

Source: Adapted from Vaughan & McKay, 1975, and U.S. Public Health Service Statistics, 1975, 1980.

Table 3. **Origin of Severe Mental Retardation According to Four Epidemiological Studies with Somewhat Different Criteria for Their Groupings**

	Drillien (1966) (Edinburgh) n = 218; IQ ≤ 54 Born 1950–56 %	McDonald (1973) (Quebec) n = 507; IQ ≤ 50 Born 1958 %	Gustavson et al. (1977a,b) (Uppsala) n = 122; IQ ≤ 50 Born 1959–70 %	Gustavson et al. (1977c) (Västerbotten) n = 161; IQ ≤ 50 Born 1959–70 %
Prenatal	56	44	73	68
(genetic)	(36)	(44)	(43)	(52)
(other)	(20)		(30)	(16)
Untraceable	20	30–37	12	22
Perinatal	13	7–11	10	8
Postnatal	9	9–12	3	1
Infantile psychosis + mental retardation	2	2	2	1

Source: Hagberg, 1978, in Ciba Foundation Symposium No. 59 [new series], *Major mental handicap: Methods and costs of prevention.* Amsterdam, Elsevier, 1978. Reprinted by permission.

long past the birth of the child. In addition, the links between prenatal influences and outcomes are sometimes tenuous or obscure and may involve a host of interacting variables (e.g., maternal age, metabolic and endocrine disturbances, placental atypicalities, exposure to certain toxic substances, etc.).

Other ambiguities and complexities are inherent in the study of prenatal influences. For example, individuals and groups differ in their vulnerability to deleterious factors, sometimes as a function of genetic factors, at other times environmental factors—and often both. Moreover, effects on the developing organism are a function of the character of the disruptive agent and developmental status at the time of disruption. The impact of interfering agents occurring during early prenatal life may result in gross structural defects, whereas a later influence may result in growth retardation and functional disturbances. The outcomes for adverse prenatal influences may range from death, malformation, growth retardation, major developmental problems, subtle functional deficits, or no detectable sequelae (Kopp & Parmelee, 1979; Wilson, 1973).

The fact that there are many unknowns associated with the study of prenatal risk factors is not surprising, given the brief time span of formal research. In terms of diagnosis, it was as recent as 1941 that Gregg (1941) described a relationship between rubella in pregnant women and cataracts in their children and that Warkany and Nelson (1941) reported upon the effects of adverse environmental factors upon the growth of mammalian fetuses. Similarly, it was only two decades ago that Lejeune (Lejeune, Gautier, & Turpin, 1959) and his associates pinpointed an additional chromosome as the cause of Down syndrome (DS) and as recent as 1961 that a drug (thalidomide) was identified as the cause of limb abnormalities (McBride, 1961). Even though significant advances in knowledge have been made about the genetic and environmental conditions that cause developmental problems, there are still a number of children with major sequelae where the etiology is unknown (between 20% to 60% are estimated to have undefined or unknown etiologies [Hagberg, 1978; Wilson, 1977a]).

Turning from issues of identification and epidemiology to a concern about developmental effects of risk influences, it is evident that the developmentalists' contribution is a recent one. Follow-up studies of preterms, physically handicapped, and mentally retarded go back to the 1920s (see, e.g., Barker, Wright, Meyerson, & Gonick, 1953; Benton, 1940), but they were often implemented by physicians, psychiatrists, or educators. When psychologists were involved with risk or nonnormal groups (e.g., Barker, Goldstein, etc.), they tended to study the functioning of older children or adults. The systematic examination of the psychological development of infants and children exposed to risk factors is a recent phenomenon. Many of the pioneers in the field—Graham, Honzik, Lipsitt, Werner—to name but a few, began their research as recently as 20 to 25 years ago. Although different motives propelled these individuals to the study of risk, all tried to understand the relationship between untoward biological risk events and developmental outcome. All became involved in pioneering longitudinal studies and produced data that formed the core of our current knowledge. Since this initial period of study, many more developmentalists have been involved in research on risk. In addition to contributing to longitudinal research, numerous kinds of cross-sectional studies have been initiated to examine processes that mediate problem development (Kopp & Parmelee, 1979).

Because research on risk factors and development has grown almost exponentially in the last decade, it is appropriate to provide an examination of the state of the art, highlighting what is known, illuminating questions and issues, and offering suggestions for additional research strategies. These are the aims of this chapter.

CHAPTER ORGANIZATION

The chapter is organized as follows: First, definitions and current epidemiologic perspectives are introduced. Examples are provided of the diverse kinds of prenatal, perinatal, and postnatal events that alone or in combination impair development. Influences on development are also described.

A second section is concerned with identification. This topic centers on the techniques and measures used by developmentalists to assess delay or retardation and to pinpoint areas of a child's strengths and weaknesses. Issues associated with identification techniques are highlighted.

The third section is devoted to an examination of research conducted by developmentalists on different risk conditions. Discussion opens with examination of strategies employed in longitudinal, cross-sectional, and mixed paradigms. Following this, research directed to two specific domains, DS (representing a prenatal influence) and preterm birth (perinatal influence) is discussed. A common format is employed in which studies are grouped either by longitudinal follow-up approaches or cross-sectional strategies. Findings from each are examined and integrated as far as possible. This section is not meant to be a compendium of all risk research that has a developmental orientation but rather provides exemplars of approaches that are currently being utilized.

In the final section, three issues related to research are singled out for additional comments. It is argued that attending to these problems can lead to more systematic research and interpretable findings. The problems noted include the need to use theory/models as conceptual frameworks, to extend the focus of study to family and community influences that interact with biological risk factors, and to characterize samples with adequate specificity.

RISK FACTORS: DEFINITIONS AND TIMING

One of the ways to consider the potential influence of risk factors is to make a categorical distinction between events that arise during prenatal life in contrast to those that occur during the perinatal and postnatal periods. Prenatal life consists of two major stages, embryonic and fetal. The former covers the first 12 weeks and is the time when structures are formed. The latter encompasses the remainder of pregnancy and is the period of cell growth and differentiation. However, cell growth does not cease at birth, it continues for 1½ years of postnatal life (Dobbing, 1976).

In some instances, events that arise in the prenatal period are not independent of insults that occur perinatally. Forceful statements of this nature were made by Knobloch and Pasamanick (1966) who spoke of the continuum of reproductive casualty, implicating early stress to later vulnerability. In like manner, Sameroff and Chandler (1975) described the continuum of caregiving casualty, implicating prenatal and perinatal factors with postnatal environmental conditions. These principles are useful underpinnings for the following discussion of prenatal risk influences.

Prenatal

The prenatal period encompasses the time from conception to the 7th prenatal month for epidemiological considerations, and in other contexts, through the entire pre-birth period. Subsumed under prenatal risks are defects of genetic origin, including those related to mutant dominant or recessive genes and those related to chromosomal abnormalities. In these instances, the developmental die is cast (so to speak), in that the organism is affected at the time of conception. Unless there is some kind of ameliorating treatment (e.g., special diet for phenylketonuria [PKU]), the individual irrevocably will have some kind of syndrome or disease associated with minor or major problems. During prenatal life, environmental factors (e.g., drugs, viruses) also have powerful in utero effects with the severity of outcome resulting, in part, on the timing of the insult. Table 4 includes examples of prenatal risk factors, organized by genetic and environmental categories, that have developmental implications. Additional comments about some of them are given below.

Genetic Factors

Mendelian Inheritance. Mutant genes may be on an autosomal or sex-linked chromosome (location) and have a single (heterozygous) or double (homozygous) dosage (McKusick, 1969); therefore, the developmental consequences will vary widely. Individuals with a recognized autosomal dominant syndrome have inherited mutant genes from only *one* affected parent, therefore, the dosage they receive is single. In general, these individuals are less severely affected than those with diagnosed autosomal recessive conditions. In the latter conditions, mutant genes are inherited from *both* parents, thus, the dosage is double.

Autosomal dominant gene mutations often do not involve developmental delay and mental retardation because those mutations that are very serious are also life threatening. Because reproduction in these circumstances is often impossible, the mutant gene tends to disappear from the pool (McKusick, 1969). In contrast, mental retardation and severe developmental problems are manifest in a number of autosomal recessive conditions. These mutant genes frequently affect biochemical reactions that impinge on functions of the brain involving amino acid patterns, enzyme production, metabolic pathways, accumulation of substrate material, and the amount of metabolites present. Although the brain may be affected, the individual's life is not necessarily threatened. Whereas not all autosomal recessive conditions result in mental retardation, at least one third to one half are associated with mental retardation and contribute 3% to 6% of the severely retarded (Moser, 1975; Nora & Fraser, 1974).

Homozygous mutant genes are a cause of inborn errors of metabolism, more than 100 of which have been identified, with about half of these associated with mental retardation (Moser, 1975). These disorders are associated with aberrant activities of a particular enzyme; some are not produced at all, others are produced in an abnormal form, still others operate in atypical ways (Nora & Fraser, 1974). Among the inborn errors of metabolism are disorders of mucopolysaccharide metabolism, which consist of heterogeneous conditions that involve accumulation of the acid in body tissues. Although the behavioral and developmental aspects of these disorders seem similar, they are in fact biochemically different (Horwitz, 1979). Another group of inborn errors of metabolism includes the protein metabolism disorders, such as PKU and maple syrup urine disease. The most widely known of these disorders, PKU results from insufficient activity of the enzyme responsible for converting phenylalanine to tyrosine. Consequently, biochemical dysfunction occurs that leads to an excessive buildup of amino acid phenylalanine, an essential dietary amino acid related to the formation of body protein. This results in further biochemical, physiologic, and pathologic effects that contribute to irreversible changes in the central nervous system leading to mental retardation.

Other diagnostic conditions associated with mutant genes are listed in Table 4 along with their related outcomes. It can be seen that in most cases the effects on development are severe. Fortunately, however, treatments that ameliorate or bypass the problems have been identified for several disorders, the most notable one being PKU (see Moser, 1975, for examples of dietary treatments). In this instance, dietary restrictions lead to essentially normal development (Dobson, Kushida, Williamson, & Friedman, 1976).

Polygenic and Multifactorial Influences. Genetic factors combined with environmental agents contribute to a varied group of developmental problems. The term multifactorial has been used to describe situations where simple Mendelian models do not explain familial distributions of deleterious outcomes (Fraser, 1976; Thompson & Thompson, 1980). The multifactorial concept encompasses polygenic inheritance where a number of genes may exert an influence over a characteristic, individual thresholds of liability and relative risk for acquiring a malformation, and environmental influences. Stated another way, there are interactions of genetic transmission, individual predisposition to a condition, and environmental factors.

Thompson and Thompson (1980) outlined some of the characteristics of multifactorial inheritance including (1) the correlation between relatives is proportional to their genes in common (i.e., parent-child, ½; grandparent-child, ¼); (2) the mean of a trait for offspring is between parental value and population mean; (3) if a threshold trait is more frequent in one sex, the recurrence risk is higher for relatives of individuals of the less susceptible sex; (4) the lower the population risk, the greater the relative increase for siblings; (5) the recurrence risk is higher when more than one family member is affected; and (6) the more severe the malformation, the higher the recurrence risk.

One of the major challenges found in multifactorial inheritance is determining how much individual contributors influence outcome. For example, the development of complex characteristics

Table 4. Examples of Risk Factors in Development[a]

	Incidence[b]	Physical Signs	Early Developmental Course	Trends in Developmental Outcomes
PRENATAL—Genetic Factors:				
A. Mendelian inheritance				
1. Recessive genes				
Inborn errors of metabolism (Milunsky, 1979)				
Cerebral lipidoses				
Tay Sachs disease	1:3,600 among Ashkenazy Jews		Apparently normal until 5 to 8 months, then rapid deterioration and developmental delay	Death in early childhood
Mucopolysaccharidoses (Leroy, 1979; Lorincz, 1978; Thompson & Thompson, 1980)				
Hunter syndrome (x-linked)	.66:100,000	Growth retardation, skeletal deformities, visceral enlargements	Problems noted in infancy (hypotonia, joint restriction, noisy breathing, etc.)	Moderate to severe mental retardation
Scheie syndrome	1:500,000	Skeletal deformities, visual symptoms		Normal intelligence
Hurler syndrome	1:100,000	Visual symptoms, skeletal deformities, visceral enlargements	Diagnosed about 1 to 3 years (delayed speech and general development, noisy behavior, etc.)	Severe mental retardation, neurological and behavior problems; death in mid-adult life.

Note: Blanks indicate specific information could not be located or that the heading was not applicable.

[a]Many articles have been written about each of the risk conditions listed above, however, only a few of the most general references are provided for the reader. My thanks to S. Cedarbaum, M.D., of the University of California, Los Angeles, for reviewing the entries in this table. The ultimate responsibility for its content, of course, is mine.

[b]Incidence figures often vary among investigators. Where the variation is appreciable, ranges are listed. In a few cases, incidence figures could not be located.

[c]DQ refers to developmental quotient.

Table 4. *(Continued)*

	Incidence[b]	Physical Signs	Early Developmental Course	Trends in Developmental Outcomes
Carbohydrate (Moser, 1975)				
Galactosemia (Fishler, Donnell, Bergren, & Koch, 1972)	1:50–120,000	Enlarged liver, jaundice	More than 50% die in early infancy	*Untreated:* mental retardation *Treated early:* intelligence is in normal range; some difficulties with visual perceptual tasks
Protein				
Phenylketonuria (PKU)	1:10–20,000	Fair skin, light hair color, spasticity	Developmental delay if not treated by dietary restrictions	*Untreated:* severe mental retardation for most, behavior problems, irritability, seizures *Treated:* function within normal range
2. Dominant genes				
Tuberculous sclerosis	1:500,000	Facial lesions, cutaneous plaques	Seizures, developmental delay	*Variable:* about 50% mental retardation; internal organ involvement
B. Polygenic inheritance: Multifactorial				
Neural tube defects (Leck, 1977)				
Anencephaly	<.5 to 4.5:1,000, depends on geographic locale	Absence of most of cortex	Death occurs within first weeks/months of life	
Spina bifida	<.5 to 4:1,000, also depends on geographic locale	Lesion or separation of vertebrae elements: exposure or herniation of neural, spinal, or brain tissues	Range of neurologic impairment, developmental delays; higher lesions associated with greater incidence of mortality or severe problems; may develop hydrocephalus	*Variable:* from severe impairment to no intellectual problems; range of physical, genitourinary problems; range of emotional, language, and behavior problems

(continued)

Table 4. *(Continued)*

	Incidence[b]	Physical Signs	Early Developmental Course	Trends in Developmental Outcomes
C. Chromosomal disorders (Gorlin, 1977; Hsu & Hirschhorn, 1977; Robinson, Lubs, Bergsma, 1979)				
Autosomes				
Trisomies				
Trisomy 13 (Patau syndrome)	1:6,000	Sloping forehead, wide sagittal suture, arhinencephaly, holoprosencephaly, ocular disorder	46% mortality in 1 month, 70% in 6 months; less than 5% survive after 12 months—seizures, deafness	Severe mental retardation
Trisomy 18 (Edward syndrome)	1:3,000–7,000 births, 4 to 1 female–male ratio	Microcephaly, flexion deformities of fingers, short sternum, heart disease, foot deformities, craniofacial anomalies	30% mortality in 1 month, 50% in 2 months; less than 10% live past 12 months—developmental retardation, feeding difficulties	Severe mental retardation
Trisomy 21 (DS)—translocation: 3.5% of cases; mosaicism, 2% to 3% of cases	1:500–1,000 births—mother 21 years, 1 per 2,500 births; mother, 40 years, 1 in 50 births	Oblique palpebral fissures, absence of sinuses, flattened profile, ear anomalies, cardiac problems, hands short; simian crease, skeletal anomalies	Early development is not greatly delayed but rate of change slows during 1st year and into 2nd and 3rd years; decline in DQ[c] and IQ to 3rd and 4th years, then some stabilization; effects of intervention are ambiguous	IQ scores from 40 to 70, occasionally up to 90; home reared are higher functioning than institution reared; abstract reasoning and language are major problem areas
Deletions				
4p- (Wolf-Hirschhorn syndrome)	45 cases reported as of 1976	Ocular problems, facial anomalies, microcephaly, growth retardation	Psychomotor retardation seizures	Mental retardation
5p- (cri du chat)	1:50,000	Microcephaly, neuromuscular anomalies, short stature	Psychomotor retardation seizures	Mental retardation
18p-	85 cases reported to 1976; 2:1 female predilection	Variable phenotype, somatic growth retardation	Developmental delay	Mental retardation

Table 4 (*Continued*)

	Incidence[b]	Physical Signs	Early Developmental Course	Trends in Developmental Outcomes
D. Sex chromosome disorders				
Klinefelter syndrome (47, XXY); variants include 47, XXYY, XXXY, XXXXY	2–13:1,000 live male births	Clinical features become most apparent at puberty, long lower extremities, testes fail to enlarge, facial hair sparse	Motorically slow, some incoordination	75% have normal intelligence; some language delays noted
47, XYY, XYYY, XYYYY	1:700 births	Children are tall, mild facial and body alterations	Possibility of lower intelligence, poorer social adaptation than found in 46, XY controls	
47, XXX	1–11:1,000 live female births		Delay in early motor and speech development, incoordination	Some mild depression of IQ scores, a few with mild mental retardation, some problems in verbal abilities
Turner syndrome (45, X)	1:2,500–10,000	Short stature, amenorrhea and sterility, broad chest and infantile external genitalia	Early diabetes, hypertension	Some individuals have mild mental retardation, some spatial problems
PRENATAL—Environmental Factors:				
E. Infections (Alford, Reynolds, & Stagno, 1975; MacDonald & Tobin, 1978; Remington & Desmonts, 1976; Stagno, Dworsky, Torres, Mesa, Hirsh, 1982; Whitley, Nahmias, Visintine, Fleming, Alford, 1980)				
Toxoplasmosis	1:5–6.4:1,000 in mother; .75–1.3:1,000 in fetus		Range is from asymptomatic to severe problems to death; seizures, microcephaly, hydrocephaly	*Variable:* severe to no mental retardation, seizures, visual defects, neurological problems

(*continued*)

Table 4 (*Continued*)

	Incidence[b]	Physical Signs	Early Developmental Course	Trends in Developmental Outcomes
Rubella	Epidemic: 20–40:1,000 in mother; 4–30:1,000 in fetus	Auditory, visual impairment, small stature, cerebral palsy	Asymptomatic to severe problems	*Variable:* severe mental retardation to no problems; mental retardation rates range from 7% to 37%; autism, reactive behavior disorders
Cytomegalovirus (CMV)	.2 to 2.2% of all live births	Auditory, visual impairments	Range is from asymptomatic to severe problems to death	*Variable:* of infected fetuses, estimate 50+% without problems, 25% with mild handicaps, 15% with severe handicaps, 5% death
Herpes simplex virus (HSV)	10–15:1,000 in mother; .03–.33:1,000 in newborn	Congenital malformations, visual, auditory impairment, cerebral palsy	Range is from asymptomatic to severe problems to death	*Variable.*
F. Drugs and chemicals				
Alcohol (fetal alcohol syndrome) (DHEW, 1978; D. W. Smith, 1979)	1:750–1,000	Cardiac defects, joint anomalies, short stature, low birthweight, microcephaly, facial abnormalities	Neonatal sleep and behavioral irregularities	*Variable:* severe to mild retardation or no discernible problems; possible hyperactivity
Thalidomide (Leck, 1977)		Amelias and phocomelias, more of upper than lower limbs; cardiac defects, sensory problems	May be delayed due to motoric limitations	*Variable:* small proportion with mental retardation, majority with normal or above intelligence; some behavior disorders noted
Mercury (Harada, 1978)	To 1976: 40 cases in Minemata area, 8 others to 1978	6 months of age or after: neck weakness, disturbance of body growth	Delay	Seizures, mental retardation, neurological and sensory problems, motor impairment
G. Maternal (Ounsted & Ounsted, 1973)				
Endogenous				
Size, general health, placental integrity		Born small for gestational age or reduced birthweight		*Variable:* appears to be highly related to a host of postnatal rearing conditions

Table 4 (*Continued*)

	Incidence[b]	Physical Signs	Early Developmental Course	Trends in Developmental Outcomes
Exogenous				
Diet, geography, economic circumstances				
PERINATAL:				
A. Asphyxia (Gluck, 1977; Novy, 1973)	20% of newborns experience a degree of oxygen deprivation that may have an effect on outcome		Variable	*Variable:* large majority show no serious sequelae
B. Low birthweight, preterm (≤ 2,500 g) ≤ 37 weeks	7.4% of live births	May be small for gestational age or of appropriate weight	Variable	*Variable:* dependent on age and size at birth, complications, and type of care given during illness and later
C. Neonatal intracranial hemorrhage (Donat, Okazaki, & Kleinberg, 1979; Larroche, 1977)	Approximately 1% of all live births; of infant deaths, hemorrhage found in 25% preterm and 10% neonates	If untreated, increase in head size	Variable	*Variable:* but seems to be associated with high incidence of neurological problems
POSTNATAL:				
A. Nutritional deficiencies (Beaton & Bengoa, 1976; Brozek, 1979)				
Protein-calorie malnutrition (PCM)	Severe PCM: 0.5% to 20% depending on locale, greatest incidence in economically poor areas	Marasmus: extreme wasting, growth failure; kwashiorkor: endematous, reduction of muscle tissue	Apathy, hyperirritability, physical inactivity	*Variable:* depends on child health prior to malnutrition onset, duration of malnourishment, rearing conditions, economic and social factors

(*continued*)

Table 4 (Continued)

	Incidence[b]	Physical Signs	Early Developmental Course	Trends in Developmental Outcomes
Anemias (iron, folate, B_{12})	Anemia tropical areas, 40% in first year of life; native American children, 20+%	None to dysfunction in major systems	Variable	Decreased energy, inattention, sleeplessness, etc.
B. Accidents (Bond, 1978)	28 million children harmed in 1975; age and sex related (e.g., poisonings highest in preschool years, automobile, bicycle, etc., in school years; male accident victims outnumber females)	Depends on site and extensiveness of injury	Variable	Estimates range from 5,000 to 50,000 with neurological sequelae; intellectual deficit, impaired attention and memory, increase in physical activity, disturbance of sleep and eating
C. Infections (Bear, 1978; Gotoff & Gotoff, 1978)				
Meningitis (Sell, Merrill, Doyne, & Zimsky, 1972; Tejani, Dobias, & Sambursky, 1982)	Neonatal: 26:100,000; childhood: 48:100,000 for hospitalization rate	Visual and auditory impairment	Variable	*Variable:* no effects to mental retardation, brain damage, and auditory impairment, in approximately 10% of cases
D. Toxic substances				
Lead (Chisolm & Barltrop, 1979; Rutter, 1980; Sahu, 1977)	40–65:1,000	Neurological manifestations		Estimates range for sequelae of intoxication from 25% to 90%; blood lead concentration—J 5.8μg mol/1; mental retardation, seizures, cerebral palsy, behavior and learning disorders

depends on any number of genes, and the exact contributions of each is unknown. Moreover, numerous environmental factors are also involved, but how they interface positively or negatively with genetic factors is not understood. It is not surprising, therefore, to note that the term multifactorial has been criticized for being oversimplified and nonheuristic. However, Fraser (1976) suggests that with care, underlying principles of multifactorial inheritance can be used to gain a better understanding of the distributions and thresholds underlying major problems and their genetic and environmental contributors.

The most notable examples of multifactorial patterns of influence are found with congenital malformations (e.g., clubfoot, spina bifida, cleft palate, pyloric stenosis, etc.), albeit malformations also stem from aberrant genetic and chromosomal conditions. A congenital malformation has its origins during the early weeks of embryonic life when organs are being formed (Wilson, 1973). Among the most serious are those that involve the central nervous system. Commonly called neural tube defects, one group includes spina bifida (spina bifida aperta or spina bifida cystica refers to exposure of neural tissue and open spinal canal, meningomyelocele defines herniation of malformed spinal tissue and meninges, and meningocele refers to herniation of a portion of brain through a defect in the skull), another group includes anencephaly (Leck, 1977). A range of developmental outcomes from mild problems to death is associated with spina bifida malformations; in contrast, sustained life is incompatible with anencephaly.

Neural tube defects show variation across locales, with the highest incidence found in Ireland and Wales (Leck, 1977). In addition, within these populations, incidence varies with social class. Nonetheless, a genetic bias is implicated in these malformations because they show clear sex and ethnic differences that persist even after migration to other geographic locales (Carter, 1971, 1974; Leck, 1977). Moreover, the rate of malformations among siblings is far higher than would be expected by chance.

Disorders of Autosomes. One of the principal causes of developmental problems arises with chromosomal anomalies. Estimates suggest that one third or more of prenatal causes of mental retardation stem from aberrant chromosomes. Since chromosomal studies began, more than 50 disorders of this nature have been identified (de Grouchy & Turleau, 1977). A few of the syndromes are very rare, for example, only 45 cases of Wolf-Hirschhorn's syndrome (4p-) were identified to 1976 (Gorlin, 1977). Others, such as DS (trisomy 21), are relatively common, occurring about 1 in 500 to 1000 live births (Hirschhorn, 1973; Thompson & Thompson, 1973, 1980).

In general, incidence figures related to chromosomal abnormalities are couched in approximations; however, chromosomal aberrations, even allowing for imprecision, are not unusual. Some findings suggest that between 3% and 6% of known conceptions show evidence of an embryo with abnormal chromosomes; of these, 90% will be aborted subsequently (Ford, 1973; Jacobs, 1972, 1979). Alternatively, Thompson and Thompson (1980) cite figures suggesting that incidence of chromosome abnormalities in early abortion is more than 60%, and in later ones about 5%. Overall, these authors indicate that 1 in 13 conceptuses has a chromosomal abnormality. About half of chromosomally atypical abortuses have an additional autosome, whereas many of the remaining are sex-chromosome related (Jacobs, 1972, 1979). Many chromosomal variants are so lethal that they are rarely seen in surviving newborns; nonetheless, approximately 1% of live neonates show chromosomal aberration of one or another kind (Ford, 1973; McKusick, 1969). There are, however, some chromosomal errors that are not associated with obvious syndromes (DeMyer, 1975).

One of the reasons chromosomal anomalies may lead to mental retardation is due to imbalance of genetic material created by either excessive or depleted amounts of chromosome (Ford, 1973; Hirschhorn, 1973). Clinical conditions associated with excess chromosomal material are commonly found in the autosomal trisomies, that is, the individual has 3 chromosomes where there should be a pair, which results in 47 chromosomes rather than 46. Trisomy 21 (DS), trisomy 13 (Patau syndrome), and trisomy 18 (Edward syndrome) are representative of this diagnostic condition. The most common of these is DS; the others, fortunately rare, are associated with very severe malformations, severe intellectual deficit, and relatively early mortality (see Table 4).

The majority of trisomies seem to derive from imperfect meiosis. In this process of cell division, there is duplication and then division of chromosomes. It is during meiosis that a chromosome may break off or an error can occur in division so that two chromosomes do not separate from each other.

Hirschhorn (1973) estimates that imperfect meiosis may account for 70% of individuals affected by the three trisomies, 21, 13, and 18 because cells in meiosis seem to be particularly sensitive to viral influences, X rays, and chemicals (Hirschhorn, 1973). Recent studies strongly suggest that many cases of nondisjunction occur in meiosis (Magenis, Overton, Chamberlin, Brady, & Lovrien, 1977; Tsuji & Nakano, 1978).

More intensively studied than any other chromosomal anomaly, DS shows a dramatic increase in incidence with the age of the mother. Thus, the rate for a woman under 30 is 1 in 1,500 and for a woman past 45 years, 20 or greater per 1,000 (J. D. Erickson, 1979; Smith & Wilson, 1973; Zarfas & Wolf, 1979).[1] Neither sex (Thompson & Thompson, 1973) nor ethnic differences (Kashgarian & Rendtorff, 1969) affect incidence, although underascertainment may affect rates given for the latter (J. D. Erickson, 1979).

A number of speculations have been advanced about the association between DS and maternal age, including the effect of delayed fertilization, physiological changes in the reproductive system, seasonality, accelerated aging in young mothers, maternal thyroid antibodies, radiation, and viruses (see Magenis et al., 1977, for references). Magenis et al. (1977) suggest that delayed fertilization and fallopian tube malfunction can be ruled out as factors because most dysfunction of maternal origin occurs in the first stage of meiosis.

In addition to maternal age, paternal age has also been implicated in DS (Magenis et al., 1977; Matsunaga, Tonomura, Oishi, & Kikuchi, 1978; Stene, Fischer, Stene, Mikkelson, & Peterson, 1977; Stene & Stene, 1977). However, it is thought that the data on paternal effects are still inconclusive or if effects exist that they are quite small compared to maternal age effects (J. D. Erickson, 1979). However, it is now clear that extra paternal chromosomes contribute to DS in perhaps as many as one third of cases (J. D. Erickson, 1979; Mikkelsen, Hallberg, & Poulsen, 1976).

Although the underlying central nervous system mechanism that mediates developmental retardation in DS remains elusive, anatomic and neurophysiologic studies provide leads, including incomplete myelination, cellular agenesis, diminution of cortical cells and dendritic spines, and early cortical atrophy (Benda, 1969; Ellis, McCulloch, & Corley, 1974; Marin-Padilla, 1972). Moreover, an abnormal aging pattern likened to early senile degeneration with concomitant histologic abnormalities has also been identified (Burger & Vogel, 1973; Ellis et al., 1974; Jervis, 1970; Ohara, 1972).

In addition, various EEG and average evoked response abnormalities have been found, particularly with regard to larger evoked response amplitudes and long latencies in visual, auditory, and somatosensory systems (Barnet & Lodge, 1967; Barnet, Ohlrich, & Shanks, 1971; Callner, Dustman, Madsen, Schenkenberg, & Beck, 1978; Ellingson, Menoloscino, & Eisen, 1970; Gliddon, Busk, & Galbraith, 1975; Straumanis, Shagass, & Overton, 1973). There is also indication that developmental changes in auditory evoked responses observed in the first year of life with normal children is not mirrored in DS, at least up to 12 months of age, possibly affecting regulation of sensory input (Barnet & Lodge, 1967; Barnet et al., 1971). In any event, differences in cerebral inhibition of auditory stimuli are noted in early infancy. Whether these differences diminish over time or represent a real variation in functioning remains an unanswered question.

Disorders of Sex Chromosomes. In addition to developmental problems that arise from too many or too few autosomes, problems can stem from aberrant numbers of sex chromosomes. This condition is relatively common among risk disorders (approximately .25% of newborns), but fortunately the developmental sequelae tend to be mild. In recent years, a considerable amount of attention has been focused on syndromes that have multiple Xs or Ys (Robinson, Lubs, & Bergsma, 1979; Robinson, Lubs, Nielsen, & Sørensen, 1979; Robinson, Puck, Pennington, Borelli, & Hudson, 1979). For the most part, studies mentioned in Robinson, Lubs, and Bergsma as well as other research suggests that mental development tends to be in the normal range, although problems have been noted in language and spatial abilities (Leonard & Schowalter, 1979). (See also *Scarr & Kidd, vol. II, chap. 6,* for additional discussion on genetics.)

Environmental Factors

Infections. Infectious agents, particularly viruses, can have a profound effect on the developing fetus. If the infection occurs early in intrauterine life, malformations may occur that resemble classic defects of embryogenesis (Kurent & Sever, 1977); if the infection occurs later, growth retardation and functional problems may arise (Wilson, 1973; 1977c). Infectious agents attack the placenta, for example, cytomegalovirus (CMV) and rubella cause lesions in villous tissue with later tissue destruction (Benirschke, 1977). This has the effect of reducing nutrient intake to the embryo or fetus.

Toxoplasmosis, rubella, CMV, and herpes are infections that have thus far been identified with developmental problems. Of these, the latter three are viruses. Because viral infections are often undetected during pregnancy, establishing links between an infection and developmental outcomes may be difficult; however, the effects of rubella and CMV are well documented. The rubella virus affects the placenta in all cases; however, placental infection does not necessarily mean fetal infection. If the fetus is affected, the infection can be widespread or be limited to a few organs (Kurent & Sever, 1977).

Rubella is one of the few infections where congenital malformations can be linked directly to gestational age at the time of infection. Maternal infection in the 1st month of pregnancy is associated with abnormality in 50% of the infants, the 2nd month with 22%, and the 3rd to 5th months with 6% to 8%. Cataracts and heart defects had the highest occurrence (each 10%) when infections occurred at 4 weeks prenatal life, whereas microcephaly and mental retardation showed a peak occurrence (each 10%) when infections occurred at 7 weeks (Dekaban, O'Rourke, & Corman, 1958).

The CMV is part of the herpes group. Approximately 3% of pregnant women are infected (Kurent & Sever, 1977). Because women can be host to the infection and yet show no clinical signs, it is not known when in intrauterine life the fetus is most susceptible to infection. The problems presented by CMV can be substantial. First, developmental outcomes include microcephaly, hydrocephaly, encephalitis, blindness, seizures, and microthalmia; second, the number of children with problems may also be sizable. Kurent and Sever (1977) estimate that 1 in 1,000 infants is damaged by CMV.

Drugs. Ever since the devasting effects of thalidomide were identified, awareness of drugs as potential teratogens has been heightened; however, a vast array of drugs are still available by prescription and over-the-counter sales. Arena (1979) reports that a recent study indicated that the average pregnant woman took six prescribed and four over-the-counter drugs. Other studies (cited in Hill & Stern, 1979) show that a sizable number of pregnant women consume large amounts of caffeine in their diets.

Several major problems arise in studying drugs or any other potentially teratogenic agent for their developmental effects. Animal models, for example, are useful to the extent that they can mirror the human system, but the thalidomide experience has shown that they may not do so (Arena, 1979; Fraser, 1977a; Hill & Stern, 1979). Unfortunately, the actual test of a teratogenic agent for humans is the human organism; therefore, most of the time knowledge of effects is gained retrospectively (Fraser, 1977a). After-the-fact reports are often subject to varied interpretations. Other problems associated with determining drug effects pertains to the state of the art in methodology. Tests are relatively crude even with animals that mimic humans. Moreover, epidemiologic surveys often have sampling and reporting problems. Complications also arise when trying to evaluate particular types of drug susceptibilities or the effects of drug interactions. The following discussion about drug effects is drawn primarily from Wilson (1973, 1977a) because his conceptual scheme is particularly clear.

Drug effects on the fetus are not confined to the action of a single agent but are presumed to stem from interactions of two or more drugs (Wilson, 1977a). Interactive effects have already been clearly identified in mature humans and in laboratory animals (Wilson, 1977b). Although Wilson (1977a) estimates that known drugs and chemicals account for 4% to 5% of developmental defects, he believes the figure would be higher if more were known about drug interactions.

Although the most obvious drug effects—malformations, such as phocomelias (limb abnormalities), that were associated with thalidomide—draw public attention, Wilson (1973, 1977a) suggests the range of potential outcomes include prenatal or perinatal death, malformation, prenatal or postnatal growth retardation, and postnatal functional aberrations. The period of greatest vulnerability for the organism occurs during the first 2 to 3 months after conception, although there is continued risk during the rest of prenatal life. Therefore, Wilson (1977b) uses the term developmental toxicity instead of teratogenicity to reflect ongoing risk.

When considering deleterious effects of drugs, Wilson (1977a) separates drugs that are known to be deleterious agents from those that are suspect or those that thus far have no known association with harmful effects. The drug categories thus far defined are (1) established as being embryotoxic, (2) suspected, (3) possibly embryotoxic under certain conditions of dosage or combination, and (4) not embryotoxic (for other classifications see Arena, 1979, and Hill & Stern, 1979).

Under the established embryotoxic category are thalidomide, androgenic hormones, and folic agent antagonists. The effects of thalidomide are well documented (see Decarie, 1969; McBride, 1961). Androgenic hormones lead to masculinization of female fetuses, and use of folic acid antagonists in the early months of pregnancy leads to death or malformation.

Several drugs are suspected of causing developmental problems, although alternative causes may be implicated. Among these drugs are alcohol, anticonvulsants, alkylating agents, and oral hypoglycemic agents (Wilson, 1977a). Those that are possible embryotoxic agents include female sex hormones, tranquilizers, salicylates, antibiotics, antituberculous drugs, quinine, anesthetics, insulin, and lithium carbonate (used for manic-depressive disorders). Wilson (1977a) notes this latter group includes drugs widely used and only occasionally implicated in developmental problems or for which the evidence for toxic effects is sparse.

Finally, some drugs have been intensively investigated because of some adverse reports about developmental effects (Wilson, 1977a). Although contradictory findings occasionally appear, overall the drugs (under likely usage) that thus far do not show embryotoxicity include imprimine (used for treatment of depression), LSD, marijuana, sulfanomides, antihistamines, adrenocortical steroids, narcotics, barbiturates, and some sedatives (Wilson, 1977a). It should be noted that some disagreement exists about drug effects. Whereas Wilson (1977a), for example, indicates quinine as a possible embryotoxic agent, Vaughan and McKay (1975) suggest it is a conclusive cause of abortion.

Behavioral teratogenesis, a domain of inquiry established in the past decade, is the study of behavioral change that results from administration of drugs during the prenatal period (Golub & Golub, 1981). In their comprehensive review of research, Golub and Golub evaluated evidence for a wide range of substances, commented on the search for animal models, and discussed critical periods for teratogenic effects. They noted that because the field is new, definitions of behavioral toxicity are often unclear and confounding effects such as social class are often not measured. Findings, therefore, should be interpreted with considerable caution.

Other Agents. Numerous other agents, including forms of radiation, chemicals, gases, and extremes of temperature, have been implicated in developmental defects (Brent, 1977; Edwards & Wanner, 1977; Wilson, 1977b, 1977c). In some cases, the effect is presumed because of tests made with animal models (e.g., temperature), in other instances, the link between agent and outcome for humans is uncontestable (e.g., the link between mercury and cerebral palsy).

As with other noxious agents, the outcomes identified for humans range from death, malformations, to growth retardation (Brent, 1977). Although not always clearly known (Wilson, 1977b, 1977c), much appears to depend on period of gestation, dosage level, the number of agents involved and their possible interactive effects, rate of absorption, physical form of the agent, entry path (through the maternal tissues for radiation or from the mother to the placenta to the fetus in the case of drugs), characteristics of the placenta, individual susceptibility, health and diet of the mother, and the nature of the environment (Brent, 1977; Fraser, 1977b; Wilson, 1977c).

One final word about the environment is relevant. With the increasing entry of women into the workplace, the potential for occupationally related reproductive hazards has increased considerably (Sever, 1981). Exposure to substances in the workplace has varied effects on the potential health and well-being of the fetus and child, including spontaneous abortions, late fetal deaths, chromosome malformations, intrauterine growth retardation, developmental disabilities, chronic diseases, and behavioral disorders (Sever, 1981). In addition, female fertility and altered sex ratios of offspring may occur. Although problems inherent in determining exposure and relating it to outcome are particularly difficult, no less a challenge is found in the sociopolitical and legal issues that arise in documenting and regulating worker exposure to hazards (Sever, 1981). Invasion of privacy and its ramifications are major concerns.

Maternal Factors. In addition to toxic substances directly ingested or absorbed into the maternal body, there are internal maternal conditions that are considered to be sources of risk. Included are maternal cyanotic heart disease, toxemia, renal disease, physical or structural features of the uterus that restrict transport functions, and aberrant placental conditions relating to size, structural features, cysts, infections, edema, or thrombosis (DeMyer, 1975; Gruenwald, 1975; Ounsted & Ounsted, 1973; Vorherr, 1975). Abnormal placental attachments also may lead to poor fetal nourishment. Other maternal factors that affect fetal development include maternal ethnicity, size, general health, nutrition, weight gain during pregnancy, geographic locale of residence, and social class (Ounsted & Ounsted, 1973). Some of these influences are nonpathological in nature; nonetheless, it is highly probable that many maternal factors are complexly interrelated so that an unfortunate combination of them leads to fetal deprivation. In sum, any maternal condition that impairs fetal oxygen and nutrient transport or exchange of metabolic waste products (Vorherr, 1975) has the potential to affect deleteriously ongoing development of the fetus.

Summary. The précis given above and in

Table 4 attest to the exceedingly diverse and complex kinds of risk factors that may arise during prenatal life. In spite of this diversity, many of these risk factors lead to similar adverse outcomes, including developmental delay, mental retardation with and without structural abnormalities, emotional disturbances, and physical, neurological, and sensory disorders. The fact that these profound consequences are so pervasive raises questions about the strategies that must be mounted to reduce prenatal risks. Although this issue is beyond the scope of this chapter, it has implications for social and medical policies, and developmentally oriented research.[2]

Perinatal

The perinatal period roughly extends from the 7th month of pregnancy to the 28th day of infant life. (Some consider the period lasts only until the 7th day of life.) Natal and perinatal causes of mortality and morbidity include disorders of delivery, neonatal infections, asphyxia, hypoglycemia, prematurity, cardiac and respiratory difficulties, and a host of other conditions. Some perinatal events have their origins in prenatal factors. Thus, infants born prior to term and who are underweight for gestational age were actually subjected to prenatal risk conditions that affected their intrauterine nutrition. In other instances, a full-term infant could show signs of distress during the birth process, having experienced an antepartum hemorrhage. The infant's ability to withstand stresses that arise in the perinatal period depends on the integrity of the central nervous system, which in some cases has been compromised by earlier events. In the long term, however, many perinatal complications have less effect on intellectual outcome than social-class variables (Broman, Nichols, & Kennedy, 1975).

Asphyxia. Asphyxia accounts for a high proportion of problems that arise in the late perinatal period and is a major hazard of early birth (Pape & Fitzhardinge, 1981; Usher, 1975). It is found in 1 in 200 infants weighing 2,500 g or more, but in 1 in 2 infants who weigh less than 1,000 g. Asphyxia in the newborn period refers to difficulty in initiating or sustaining respiration that leads to oxygen deprivation and carbon dioxide accumulation.

The site and distribution of cerebral damage is a function of the neurodevelopmental maturity of the infant and severity and duration of the insult (Pape & Fitzhardinge, 1981). In preterm infants, periventricular hemorrhage and infarction are major problems whereas in full-term infants, cerebral edema, boundary zone infarction, and necrosis of thalamic and brainstem nuclei may occur (Pape & Fitzhardinge, 1981).

Anoxia, often the precursor of asphyxia, refers to reduction of oxygen in body tissues. According to Adamsons (1975), about 20% of newborns experience some degree of anoxia that is sufficiently severe to impinge on future development. Equally important, anoxia (or asphyxia) is the leading cause of death in the fetal and neonatal periods (Adamsons, 1975; Volpe, 1977).

Although textbooks provide definitions of anoxia and asphyxia, it is often difficult to obtain precise clinical descriptions of asphyxia in very sick, vulnerable infants whose symptoms often show considerable variability (Adamsons, 1975). This impacts on the ability to make meaningful evaluations about outcome; however, available evidence suggests that many infants who have experienced asphyxia do not show long-term sequelae. Of those who do, the consequences can be very serious and include cerebral palsy and mental retardation. As noted earlier, outcome in part depends on the integrity of the central nervous system prior to the stress of asphyxia.

Immaturity. Immaturity is also a mixed diagnostic entity and includes infants born early and of weight appropriate-for-gestational-age (AGA) as well as those who are undersized for age. With specific reference to preterm birth, this category includes infants born at or before 37 weeks of gestation and who weigh 2,500 g or less.

Because confusion still exists about terminology, it is useful to summarize past and current practices. In the early days of clinical and follow-up studies, considerable doubt existed about accurate labeling of samples. Therefore, in 1948, the World Health Organization (WHO) suggested that the label premature be used for infants born weighing less than 2,500 g. This led to confusion because clinicians found it difficult to measure gestational age with some degree of certainty. By 1961 (WHO, 1961), the term low birthweight superceded the label of premature. And, as reliable neurological and physical signs were identified for gestational age (Dubowitz, Dubowitz, & Goldberg, 1970; Saint-Anne Dargassies, 1966), percentile charts developed (Lubchenco, 1970; Lubchenco, Hansman, & Backström, 1967), and ponderal indices formulated (Miller & Hassanein, 1971), it began to be possible to evaluate infants by both gestational age and weight criteria. Samples could be subdivided by infants born small-for-gestational-age (SGA) or AGA.

More recently, the label preterm has been used to signify infants born before their expected date of delivery.

Given the striking diversity of preterm samples, it is not surprising to find numerous causal factors implicated for early births, although the exact causes of preterm birth are in many cases unclear. Among the conditions that have an association are maternal health and nutritional status prior to pregnancy; maternal age, height, and weight; weight gain; smoking; use of drugs during pregnancy; uterine problems; lack of prenatal care; social class; ethnic group membership; geography (Bergner & Susser, 1970; Hardy & Mellits, 1977; Lubchenco, 1976; Meyer, 1977; Miller, Hassanein, Chin, & Hensleigh, 1976; Morton, 1977; Naylor & Myrianthopoulos, 1967; Niswander, 1977; Ounsted & Ounsted, 1973).

Obstetric factors associated with prematurity are varied; Niswander (1977) categorized them as poor obstetric history, malformations of the genital tract, medical disease prior to pregnancy (e.g., pneumonia, asthma, diabetes, etc.), diseases peculiar to pregnancy (e.g., placenta previa, abruptio placentae, hypertensive disease of pregnancy, etc.), iatrogenic and miscellaneous causes (e.g., elective induction of labor, etc.). Socioeconomic and ethnic factors are clearly associated with prematurity, with the poor and nonwhite populations showing relatively high incidence rates (Garn, Shaw, & McCabe, 1977). Nonetheless, economic status does not fully account for the data, thus, genetic factors may be influential (Garn et al., 1977). Consumption of alcohol, smoking, nutrition, and a host of other variables are also implicated (van den Berg, 1977).

Early birth and immaturity have shown a decline in mortality and morbidity in the last 20 years (Chase, 1977). Among infants born 2,500 g or less, 1960 neonatal deaths were approximately 18 per 1,000 live births, whereas in 1975 it was 11.6 per 1,000 live births (Lee, Paneth, Gartner, Pearlman, & Gruss, 1980). Much of this improvement has been attributed to improved perinatal care. (See Table 2 for more recent trends in mortality in unqualified immaturity.) It is unfortunate, however, that infant mortality rates in the United States are still high when compared to other industrialized countries. Data from 1973 showed that even the mortality rate among U.S. Caucasians was 14.8 per 1,000, which is higher than Sweden's 9.6 per 1,000 (Chase, 1977).

Because multiple etiological factors operate in prematurity, interventions directed at just one condition will not have a major impact (Emanuel, 1977). Emanuel suggests that prematurity will be reduced appreciably when certain social, cultural, and economic changes are made alongside contributions from medicine and behavioral science.

Declines in morbidity parallel mortality data. Drillien, over 20 years ago (1961), noted that 40% of her total sample showed intellectual and neurologic sequelae. Today, morbidity is quite low among the heavier and healthier preterm infants and generally ranges from 10% to 30% for the very low birthweight and sick infant (see Table 8 for details; also see Ciba Foundation, 1978, for overviews; Davies, 1976, Lubchenco, 1976).

In sum, perinatal risk factors may arise from untoward maternal conditions, infant prenatal stresses, or events that emerge only in the last weeks of pregnancy or at birth. Outcome ranges from death to normal functioning; however, many perinatal stresses are temporary, thus, most infants eventually show normal functioning. The percentage of children with severe residuals is considerably less than that found with prenatal conditions. Perinatal mortality and morbidity are also influenced by adverse environmental circumstances.

Postnatal

Postnatal refers to the period that begins after 28 days of life and later. For ease of interpretation, many child statistics, particularly mortality, refer to events that occur to children who are less than 1 year of age, between 1 and 5 years of age, and between 5 and 14 years of age.

In industrialized nations, the contribution of postnatal illness, disease, and accidents to severe developmental sequelae is relatively small. In contrast to the relatively optimistic picture found in affluent nations, the rates of mortality and morbidity observed in poorer, developing nations, particularly for infants under 1 year of age, are high. Disease, infections, malnutrition, and poverty are common. Often, however, it is difficult to distinguish the unitary contributions made by adverse postnatal factors to impairment because deleterious conditions are also influenced by the health and nutrition of the child's parents, pregnancy events, and the circumstances at birth. The cumulative effect of stresses leads to a vulnerable child.

In this country (as noted in Table 1), childhood accidents account for a significant amount of mortality in early life; morbidity rates are generally unknown. Motor vehicle accidents are the leading cause of accidental deaths (Scherz, 1981; Williams,

1981). Even in noncrashes, children are at risk in automobiles because of sudden stops and turns, particularly when unrestrained with seatbelts (Agran, 1981).

In our country, in addition to accidents, concern is increasingly directed toward the nutritional status of children. Severe malnutrition is rarely found in the United States, albeit chronic undernutrition is relatively widespread. Undernutrition may have serious, long-lasting consequences. Concentration, reading ability, motivation, and activity often show impairment, even if overall cognitive skills do not show major retardation (Read, 1975, 1977).

Common forms of nutritional deficit occur as a result of inadequate intake of specific vitamins, calcium, and iron (Greene, 1977). Often observed among the poor minorities and native Americans, chronic undernutrition is associated with the factors that coexist with poverty. These are inadequate housing, health care, and education; nonaccess to inexpensive nutritious food; and child neglect and abuse. Of native American Indian children, 10% to 20% are estimated to have nutritional deficiencies (Moore, Silverberg, & Reed, 1972).

Among the most frequently found nutritional problems is nutritional anemia, which is a condition resulting from inability to maintain a normal hemoglobin concentration because of inadequate supply of essential nutrients containing iron, folic acid, and B_{12} (Layrisse, Roche, & Baker, 1976). Infections (e.g., hookworms), may exacerbate an already inadequate situation. Other nutritional problems include iron deficiencies, which are the most prevalent of all nutritional lacks (Layrisse et al., 1976) and are particularly common among the poor (Woodruff, 1977). Rapid growth of tissue mass and blood volume in young children demands adequate sources of iron (Layrisse et al., 1976), and it now seems that 6- to 18-month-olds are particularly vulnerable to iron deficiencies. Iron, however, is important during all of childhood because basal requirements increase even though growth requirements lessen. Folate, also necessary for metabolic functions, can be deficient because of preterm birth, artificial feeding of infants, poverty, and food faddism (Layrisse et al., 1976; Neumann, 1979). Vitamin B_{12}, associated with maintenance of the integrity of the nervous system, is primarily obtained from animal sources (Layrisse et al., 1976). Marked inadequacies can lead to neurological and mental disorder.

In sum, accidents, illnesses, and nutritional factors are among important postnatal risk factors. Severe sequelae account for a small proportion of outcome; nonetheless, it is likely that postnatal risk events contribute a sizable number of children who show school and learning problems.

Summary

This overview opened with a brief historical recounting of the changing influence of risk factors. A century ago, postnatal causes of mortality and morbidity were high. These gave way in the face of improved health and economic conditions alongside advances in treatment and care. Before and after World War II, attention was directed to perinatal factors. Within a relatively short space of time, improvements were noted; unfortunately, a disproportionate number of high-risk pregnancies and adverse socioeconomic conditions continue to contribute to perinatal risk. Finally, it was noted that the most common causes of severe developmental problems currently stem from prenatal influences. Regretfully, they are not easy to prevent or to detect.

The second part of the overview provided a summary of various kinds of prenatal, perinatal, and postnatal risks. Distinguishing characteristics were mentioned, and outcomes were described.

IDENTIFYING THE CHILD WHO HAS A DEVELOPMENTAL PROBLEM

In the previous section, discussion called attention to risk factors that influence infants and young children. Because many risk factors are associated with higher probabilities of developmental problems, the challenge is to identify correctly the specific infant or child whose development is suspect or frankly abnormal. This is a far more complex task than was once thought and one that has led to polarized stands. This section focuses on the philosophical basis of identification, the techniques used within the identification process, and the issues that have arisen in practice. Discussion opens with comments on definitions and a highlight of issues, then it turns to examination of specific assessment and diagnostic techniques.

Identification is a complex, ongoing process by which an infant/child is evaluated with a set of techniques along with clinical judgment and is labeled as normal, suspect, or abnormal/delayed/retarded. Many times, this process is directed toward groups exposed to a risk event (e.g., preterms), with the hope that the child with a problem will be identified early. At other times, the identification process begins either (1) after a screening examination has suggested a child's development is suspect or abnormal or (2) because parents, relatives, or teachers suspect that the child's development is not proceeding well. Whatever its origins, the process of identification must be appropriate to children of diverse ages, characteristics, and backgrounds.

Depending on the age of the child, identification requires use of developmental or intelligence tests, neurological and other clinical examinations, educational assessments, sound clinical judgment, and knowledge of actuarial statistics vis-à-vis risk and handicapping conditions. There is also growing realization that no single measure is sufficiently adequate for identification; therefore, use of several assessment techniques and repeated measurements are necessary. Specific approaches that are used must vary with the age of the child, initial diagnosis, and the most obvious presenting symptomatology.

One of the most enduring and controversial issues about early identification involves infant assessment and prediction to later development. Since the early part of the twentieth century, there have been professionals who firmly believed that assessment measures would be able to define accurately normal and abnormal/delayed infants and children, gauge the prognosis of the delayed, and provide specificity about strengths and weaknesses. Whether or not these expectations have been met is still a moot point. There are those who have forcefully argued in the affirmative for measures currently available (e.g., Illingworth & Birch, 1959; Knobloch & Pasamanick, 1963) as well as others who suggest that the prediction issue is a relative one and hinges on the age of the child (e.g., early vs. late infancy) and the nature of the risk or handicapping condition (e.g., mild vs. severe impairment) (see Kopp & McCall, 1982); still others indicate that the right instrument is still to be developed but that once it is, high predictive levels will occur.

As will be seen later, at this point there is no single assessment technique that meets all needs and all demands. Further, although it is possible to identify the young infant with a contemporaneous problem, it is often impossible to predict correctly all of those who will continue to have problems. There are no existing techniques that take into account and insert into a formula the nature of individual development (including learning and adaptation patterns), both the kind of caregiving that is provided and other experiential factors, and, of course, the type of risk event the child was exposed to as well as its interactions and influences on all of the above.

Although high levels of individual predictive accuracy from very early infancy may never be achieved (and probably should not be achieved if flexibility and qualitative and quantitative growth are cornerstones of the developmental model), assessment techniques provide valuable information for the identification process. In particular, they provide quantified findings about groups of infants, some of whom will require careful monitoring with respect to ongoing developmental status. Monitoring is extremely valuable because it primes sensitivity to child skill and behavior, and it often signals the time for introduction of specific intervention services.

Another highly charged issue in identification concerns the use of standardized intelligence tests to define low levels of intellectual functioning. Many initial challenges to this use stemmed from situations where the test was deemed inappropriate for minority groups (Mercer, 1973); however, more recently some of these same issues have surfaced with respect to identification of intellectual performance of biologically at-risk groups. Additional related problems have been outlined by Maloney and Ward (1976) who noted that psychological tests take on a status and implication of their own. As such, they are often viewed as end points rather than as one step in a data-collection process. When the tests are considered as the sum total of the identification or diagnostic process, they unfairly weight that aspect of performance and thereby penalize the child. Other important competencies are overlooked.

Maloney and Ward (1976) also called attention to differences between psychometric testing and psychological testing. The former, they suggested, is strictly oriented to measurement and is focused on describing and studying groups. In contrast, the latter is primarily problem and process oriented and should be devoted to an analysis of the overall functioning of an individual child. All too often, the psychometric rather than the psychological approach underlies the identification process for the at-risk preschool or school-aged child.

In the following discussion, an overview is provided about assessment measures that have been used as part of the identification process for children who may have problems. These measures include neonatal measures, psychometrically derived infant measures, Piagetian-based infant measures, unitary indices (e.g., visual attention, habituation, cry, parent-infant interaction patterns) of infant performance, and preschool and school-age psychometric intelligence tests. Some of the infant techniques have been highly developed and utilize formalized procedures; others, however, do not do so because they are still in their earliest stages of development. Almost all have shown at least modest correlations for groups of children tested during infancy and a later period.

Neonatal Tests

In a sense, the forerunner of neonatal tests can be traced back to Gesell's (1945) *The Embryology of Behavior: The Beginnings of the Human Mind* in which he carefully documented the visual and motoric responses of preterm and full-term infants. Subsequently, André-Thomas and Saint-Anne Dargassies (1960) and other European clinicians developed neonatal examinations (for a discussion, see Parmelee, 1962). In the United States, Graham, Matarazzo, and Caldwell (1956) designed the first formal assessment measure designed to detect signs of newborn abnormality. The five scales (visual, auditory, maturational, tonicity, and irritability) were standardized on a large number of infants and included information on test-retest, split-half, and interobserver reliabilities. Concurrent reliability and predictive relationships were also studied (Corah et al., 1965; Graham et al., 1956; Graham, Pennoyer, Caldwell, Greenman, & Hartmann, 1957). Longitudinal analyses on the original Graham test and its successor, the Graham-Rosenblith (Rosenblith, 1961; Rosenblith & Lipsitt, 1959), produced very modest coefficients between the newborn period and childhood performance.

In the same or intervening periods, additional newborn measures were developed, some designed exclusively to detect the newborn in need of immediate medical attention (Apgar, 1953), others focused on determining gestational age (Dubowitz et al., 1970; Farr, 1968). Several measures have been developed as tests of newborn neurology and behavior (see Amiel-Tison, 1968; also see Self & Horowitz, 1979, for an overview). The following discussion centers on the Prechtl and Beintema (1964) examination, Parmelee's Newborn Neurological Examination (Parmelee, 1974), and the Brazelton Neonatal Behavioral Assessment Scale (BNBAS) (Brazelton, 1973) because they are the most widely used measures.

The Prechtl scale (Prechtl, 1977; Prechtl & Beintema, 1964) contains neurological and reflex oriented items with a goal of testing the structural and functional integrity of the nervous system (Prechtl, 1973). Acknowledging that different philosophical perspectives can be brought to the task, Prechtl (1975) viewed the nervous system as an information processing apparatus that manifests known and testable neural functions at different developmental stages. He also believes that certain patterns of abnormalities have significance for later functioning (Prechtl & Beintema, 1964); more recently, however, Prechtl (1977) has argued against using abnormal neonatal performance to predict later neurological functioning. He does call for monitoring of infants who show atypical signs.

The strength of the Prechtl measure lies in its careful conception, delineation of standardization procedures (environmental conditions, infant posture and state, etc.), and well-defined scoring system. The full test, however, is lengthy and requires an extensive period of time for administration. This point is particularly troublesome when an infant is very small or very ill. Recently Prechtl (1977) published a 10-min. screening examination designed to detect signs of paresis (weakness), hemisyndrome (problems on one side of the body), and nervous excitability. Using this measure, findings from the Groningen Perinatal Project reveal that the rate of false negatives among 80 neurologically abnormal neonates was low, but the rate of false positives was high, underscoring the presence of transient neonatal problems (Bierman-van Eendenburg, Jurgens–van der Zee, Olinga, Huisjes, & Touwen, 1981).

The relationship of neurological status to other events has been examined with the Prechtl-Beintema examination, as has the predictive validity of the assessment. Findings revealed that neonatal neurological status and nonoptimal conditions during pregnancy were associated (Prechtl, 1968). Long-term prediction with the measure yielded low to moderate correlation coefficients and depended on the particular sample that Prechtl (1968, 1975) employed. Prechtl (1975) also noted that individual differences in early days of life "may reflect mainly the differences in physiological adaptation, and may contain relatively little information of prognostic value for the later life of the infant" (p. 76).

The Parmelee Newborn Neurological examination (Parmelee, 1974) contains a number of reflex and state items found in the Prechtl examination. Parmelee's primary goal, however, was to provide clinicians with a standardized technique that could be administered relatively easily and quickly to assess the status of sick or at-risk infants.

The first section of the examination contains reflex and behavioral pattern items (e.g., head turning, hand to mouth, leg withdrawal) scored on a scale that includes a range from normal tone to absent responses. The second section includes evaluation of eye movement, tremor, cry, and body movements. In addition, scores for changes in states of arousal can be given throughout the examination. This provides clinicians with a strategy to evaluate infant response to arousing and soothing stimuli. The strength of the Parmelee examination lies in its comprehensiveness and its brevity; it takes only a short time to administer.

Although the Parmelee examination was not designed primarily for predictive purposes, it has been used in longitudinal studies. In the Infant Studies Project, for example, data collected on a preterm sample reveal a small correlation with 4-month performance, but the coefficients decreased markedly for 2-year performance (Parmelee, 1976).

The Brazelton Neonatal Behavioral Assessment Scale (BNBAS) (Brazelton, 1973, 1978) examines reflex responsiveness, behavioral organization, modulation of state, and interactional responses to people and stimuli. Using these indices, an indication of neurophysiological regulation and processes of adaptation can be obtained. These are defined as the capacity to achieve smooth state transitions, be attentive to differences in social stimuli, show cyclical social interactions, and demonstrate coordinated motor responses.

The BNBAS was originally designed as a tool to understand the organization of newborn behavior, the range of individual differences that are manifested, and the ways that newborns shape their caregivers' behaviors (Brazelton, 1978). Moving beyond this, attempts were made to use the examination with a wide range of infants reared under vastly different circumstances (see review in Sameroff, 1978). More recently, it has been used with infants at risk to identify their threshold levels, ability to attend, and organization of states (Als, 1978; Als, Tronick, Lester, & Brazelton, 1979; Sostek, Quinn, & Davitt, 1979). Attempts are also being made to interpret the responses infants give on the examination to parents to facilitate their understanding of infant clues and signals (Als et al., 1979).

One of the strengths of the BNBAS is its inclusiveness. It is, in fact, one of the most extensive neonatal assessment techniques in existence. Because of this, at first it was presumed that the examination would be a good predictor of later developmental functioning. Indeed, with some high-risk or unusual groups (e.g., infants with birthweight markedly below expectation for gestation), the predictive usefulness of the instrument may be greater than for other measures (Tronick & Brazelton, 1975). However, it is now realized that the BNBAS, although a very valuable technique for contemporaneous neonatal assessment, does not provide a crystal-clear view of the future (Horowitz, Sullivan, & Linn, 1978; Sameroff, 1978).

In sum, under most circumstances, the neonatal assessment techniques have limited usefulness in identifying infants who may continue to have problems. Even after major stresses in early life, many infants recover and go on to develop normally (for a recent example see Bierman-van Eendenburg, Jurgens-van der Zee, Olinga, Huisjes, & Touwen, 1981). The tests are, nonetheless, sensitive measures for evaluation of contemporaneous newborn status and thereby alert clinicians to the need to continue monitoring infants.

Developmental Measures

A number of recent reviews and articles have analyzed the content of the traditional assessment measures (e.g., Bayley, Cattell, Gesell, Griffiths, etc.), discussed their strengths and weaknesses, and analyzed their predictive value for normally developing samples (Brooks & Weinraub, 1976; Honzik, 1976; McCall, 1979; McCall, Hogarty, & Hurlburt, 1972; Stott & Ball, 1965; Thomas, 1970). As the findings are well known, it is not necessary to restate this material; therefore, the discussion that follows focuses primarily on use of developmental tests with infants stressed by biological conditions.

By far, the assessment measure that is most commonly used to analyze the developmental level of infants is Bayley's (1969) Scales of Infant Development. The scales provide valuable information about the development of children who do not have major neurological/sensory sequelae and who are not markedly delayed (less than 50 developmental quotient [DQ]). However, three issues have surfaced with use of Bayley scales (or indeed with any other developmental measure); one concerns age corrections made for preterm infants, another relates to suitability for certain kinds of handicapped children, and the third concerns predictions to later development.

One of the most highly charged controversies in assessment of preterm infants focuses on contrasting views of the effect of neurological maturation upon developmental performance. Those in favor of age correction argue that maturational phenomena influence the timing of emergence of key infant behavior and, therefore, infant performance should be gauged from time of conception rather than from time of birth (see Parmelee & Schulte, 1970). Thus, postmenstrual (or conceptional) age or an adjusted postnatal age correction is made. Others, however, state that experience rather than maturation is the crucial factor and use unadjusted postnatal age indices (Goldstein, Caputo, & Taub, 1976).

At this time, empirical evidence supports use of age corrections. In the newborn period, for example, Schulte, Linke, Michaelis, and Nolte (1969) showed that nerve conduction velocity was dependent on conceptional age and Dreyfus-Brisac (1964) demonstrated age-dependent development of the EEG. Moreover, Hunt and Rhodes (1977) sequentially tested a group of preterms and found that unadjusted age scores led to a large number of delayed infants who, in fact, did not seem to be impaired. By 2 years of age, many of these children showed catch-up phenomena. In other words, the amount of prematurity became less important and had markedly attenuated effects the older the age of the infant.

Another issue found with traditional developmental measures concerns the problems that are encountered when the tests are used with children who are blind, motorically impaired, or very low functioning. The authors of the tests did not specifically design them for use with these groups, did not include these children in their standardization samples, and offered no suggestions for adapting the tests for special needs (e.g., visual, motor impairment). As a result, assessments made with these groups can be problematic.

To counteract these difficulties, numerous individuals have undertaken to develop new assessment instruments (for a listing, see Johnson & Kopp, 1980). The rationale underlying development of new measures varies widely and includes the need for a shorter test, a test that can be used by nonpsychologists, a parent-report test, a more extensive test, and so forth. Unfortunately, many of the newer measures do not have adequate sample sizes; do not provide standardization data, reliability, and validity findings; or give clearly defined administration or scoring procedures (Johnson & Kopp, 1980). Moreover, there is a concern about the conceptual rationale underlying choice of test items for inclusion. Few of the new measures provide theoretically or empirically derived rationales for item selection. Instead, factors, such as ease of testing, entered into the decision-making process. This practice has probably led to inclusion of items that have questionable bearing on the child's general competence. At this time and with the need as great as it is, it would be helpful if developmentalists met this problem directly.

Finally, it has been suggested that beyond the value of helping to identify children with delays, developmental tests could be good prognosticators of outcome for at-risk and handicapped samples (Drillien, 1961; Illingworth & Birch, 1959; Knobloch & Pasamanick, 1960, 1963; Knobloch, Rider, Harper, & Pasamanick, 1956). Indeed, the literature is replete with statements to the effect that the tests predict for individual infants. However, a close examination of data suggests that a more cautious interpretation of prediction is warranted.

Table 5 and Table 6 provide data about coefficients obtained with at-risk and handicapped groups from infancy onward. In general, the pattern that appears indicates that low coefficients can be expected when the initial test is given in early infancy and the subsequent test is given in early childhood or later. By later infancy, the coefficients rise dramat-

Table 5. **Correlations Between Infant Test Scores and Childhood IQ for At-Risk Samples**

Childhood Age of Test (Years)	Age of Infant Test (Months)			
	1–6	7–12	13–18	19–36
8–18				.71[f], .46[f]*, .52[f]*
5–7	.54[a]	.57[a]		
3–4		.37[b]*, −.11[b]; .48[c]		.86[b]
2	.29[e], .42[d]	.44[b]*, .30[b]; .07[d], .39[d]; .48[e]	.63[d]	

Notes: *Sample restricted to subjects scoring below a cut-off at both ages.
[a]Drillien, 1961.
[b]Hunt, 1979.
[c]Knobloch & Pasamanick, 1960;
[d]Siegal, Saigal, Rosenbaum, Young, Berenbaum, & Stoskop, undated.
[e]Sigman, 1980.
[f]Werner, Honzik, & Smith, 1968.
Adapted from Kopp & McCall, 1982.

Table 6. **Correlations Between Infant Test Scores and Childhood IQ for Clinic and Handicapped Samples**

Childhood Age of Test (Years)	Age of Infant Test (Months) 1–6	7–12	13–18	19–36
8–18				
5–7	.26[e]	.51[e]; .11, .73, .50[d]		.81[e]; .59, .76, .64[d]
3–4	.20[a]	.64[a]	.72[a], .63[c]	.83[a]
± 2	.63[e], .36[b]	.76[f], .72[c]; .39[g]	.77[f]	

Notes: [a]Carr, 1975: DS.
[b]Dicks-Mireaux, 1966: DS (author's calculation).
[c]M. T. Erickson, 1968: "young M.R."
[d]Fishler, Graliker, & Koch, 1965: cerebral palsy, congenital anomalies, DS.
[e]Fishman & Palkes, 1974: spina bifida.
[f]Goodman & Cameron, 1978: clinic population.
[g]Share, Webb, & Koch, 1961: DS.
Adapted from Kopp & McCall, 1982.

ically for handicapped groups and somewhat less so for at-risk groups. However, coefficients obtained from diagnostic groups vary considerably. Those that probably contain a substantial number of misclassified infants because of motor impairments (cerebral palsy) are lower than those obtained from groups who have a more generalized form of retardation (DS).

Kopp and McCall (1982) have speculated about reasons underlying earlier and increased levels of prediction for samples of handicapped. They suggest that the nature of a handicap may impose constraints or limitations upon qualitative changes in development that occur at about 2 to 3 months, 8 to 9 months, 12 months, and 18 months. Thus, at each period there can be an incomplete stage transition with a concomitant high retention of immature patterns of functioning. Kopp and McCall (1982) further hypothesize that the tendency toward immature patterns persists and, thus, the infant loses ground at each period of qualitative shift. As a consequence, with repeated testing, the infant will tend to occupy the same relative position leading to stability.

It is probable that failure to negotiate a stage, in part, depends on the type of risk event to which the child was exposed. With DS, for example, Gibson (1978) noted that children have difficulty in making transitions from sensorimotor to symbolic thought. Many show overall cognitive levels no higher than that of 2 to 3 years of age, albeit rote-memory skills and social training are more advanced. Gibson's comments are corroborated by the stability coefficients reported in Table 6, which show high coefficients for DS samples by the 2nd and 3rd years.

In addition to instances of early stability, there continues to be a subset of children who defy their early classifications. That is, they show intellectual gains or, unfortunately, losses over the course of testing periods. In a recently reported longitudinal study, the children that showed the most upward shift in functioning were young, perinatally stressed boys who had initial test scores higher than 50 (Goodman & Cameron, 1978).

Altogether, review of the literature suggests that five patterns of development have been identified for children exposed to biological risks:

1. Normal development during infancy and thereafter.
2. Delayed or suspect development during infancy and mental retardation during childhood and later.
3. Normal development during infancy and mental retardation during school years (Chess, 1974).
4. Delayed development during infancy and normal intellectual status during childhood (Chess, 1974; Hohman & Freedheim, 1959; Saint-Anne Dargassies, 1979).
5. Oscillating developmental status during infancy and childhood (e.g., normal, abnormal, normal; abnormal, normal, abnormal; etc.) (Hunt, 1979; Saint-Anne Dargassies, 1979).

Several explanations have been advanced to account for shifting developmental patterns. One, for example, relates to the fact that a stress (e.g., anoxia, toxemia, etc.) may shock the system to such an extent that it takes an appreciable amount of time to attain (or regain) integrated functioning. In other instances, an infant may be considered delayed during early life because of motoric limitations but, with the advent of language, can develop a new and effective way of dealing with the environment. This situation is often true of children with cerebral palsy.

Alternatively, some groups of children appear to be developmentally normal during infancy but show major problems later on. In part, this may reflect inadequacies in the child-rearing environment (Sameroff & Chandler, 1975). It may also result from sleeper effects imposed by the early risk event. That is, the stresses do not influence the generalized sensorimotor repertoire, but they impose constraints on the growth of specific abilities that are needed to meet challenges set forth by social and educational systems.

Finally, it is noted that attempts have been made to improve predictions by including sex, socioeconomic status (SES), and clinical judgments or by using multiple-regression techniques (Escalona, 1950; Escalona & Moriarty, 1961; Knobloch & Pasamanick, 1966; McCall, 1979; Werner, Honzik, & Smith, 1968; Willerman, Broman, & Fiedler, 1970). Although these have added more precision, prognostic assessments for the individual child still remain a challenge. Also suggested, but not verified as yet, is that formal inclusion of processing skills, such as indices of attention, play, and social interactions, might improve short-term predictions (Kopp, 1979; Zelazo, 1979).

Because of the problems outlined above, still other methods of assessing infants and children have been introduced. Some of these are considered next.

Piagetian-Based Measures

During the last decade, investigators turned to Piagetian measures, particularly sensorimotor series, in an attempt to gain more comprehensive assessments and to determine if they offered better prediction than the standardized psychometric measures. The three commonly used sensorimotor measures, Uzgiris and Hunt (1975), Einstein series (Corman & Escalona, 1969), and the Casati and Lézine (Casati & Lézine, 1968; Kopp & Sigman, 1968/1972) share many content features. They provide item and stage analyses of object permanence, means-end exploration, and various forms of problem solving. Imitation scales are also included in the Uzgiris and Hunt series.

From a practical standpoint, the questions that have to be asked about the Piagetian measures relate to their concurrent and predictive validity. With respect to the former, there are no empirical data about the value or accuracy of Piagetian measures when compared to traditional developmental assessments in the identification of a child with developmental problems. Instead, findings tell us that sensorimotor series have been extensively used for assessment or training with moderately and severely impared children whose mobility is markedly restricted or whose intellectual skills are very limited (e.g., see Brassell & Dunst, 1976; Kahn, 1976, 1978; Kopp & Shaperman, 1973; Robinson, 1974; Woodward, 1959). The scales have also been used to explore the relationship between level of sensorimotor development and development of expressive language (Kahn, 1975).

With respect to predictive utility, data are scant. Findings obtained from the Infant Studies Project (Parmelee, 1976; Parmelee, Kopp, & Sigman, 1976) indicated that the relationship between 9-month sensorimotor performance and 25-month Bayley Mental Development Index (MDI) scores was .30 in a heterogeneous sample of 87 preterm infants. In general, it is fair to state that the long-term value of Piagetian measures for special groups of infants has not been demonstrated.

Measurement of Specific Types of Behavior

The last few years have also witnessed other efforts to identify from among at-risk groups, children who will show later-development problems. These new efforts have focused on evaluations of specific kinds of behavior and then related behavioral responses obtained in early life to intellectual performance during childhood. Historical precedence for this strategy derives from studies in which language development of females (Cameron, Livson, & Bayley, 1967), awareness of perceptual contingencies (McCall et al., 1972), and response decrement (Lewis, Goldberg, & Campbell, 1969) showed modest predictive coefficients from early life.

Examples of these approaches are as follows. Miranda and Hack (1979) have explored the predictive utility of a neonatal visual-perception measure and reported that their unqualified ratings of normal and abnormal were highly predictive. Approximately 80% of normal children were correctly classified, whereas only 1 of 14 abnormal children was incorrectly labeled. Their initial procedure involved presentation of stimulus pairs. Elementary responses included fixating the target, whereas a higher level involved discriminating a pattern from a plain stimulus or between two patterns that differ in brightness contrast. Finally, the highest level demanded a discrimination between two patterns on the basis of size or number, with the other controlled. Other observations, such as blank stare or inadequate turning of eyes to stimuli, were also recorded. A rating of normal indicated the infant fixated actively and quickly, whereas a rating of abnormality denoted failure to fixate the stimuli, turning of the eyes, or discriminations at chance levels. Outcome measures included testing with the Bayley scales or the Stanford-Binet at age 2 or 3 years.

A problem with this and similar procedures lies in sample delineation. Some samples contain markedly heterogeneous groups of infants, a few with conditions associated with known retardation, and others who are at risk only briefly. Use of heterogeneous samples often increases predictive coefficients for a designated group but does not specify outcome for individual children.

A visual attention strategy is also being employed by Fagan (Fagan & McGrath, 1981; Fagan & Singer, in press). Initially, Fagan suggested that because visual selectivity in infancy varied as a function of rearing conditions and as a diagnostic problem, it should be possible to relate these differences to later cognitive functioning (Fagan, 1975). In a more recent work, Fagan and Singer (in press) argue that "the infant's ability to recognize a previously seen stimulus may involve processes similar to those tapped on later intelligence tests and, thus, may validly reflect early intelligence." Further, they stated that to predict later intelligence, one has to sample infant behaviors that are similar in kind or tap processes that relate to later functioning. Thus, they implied infant discrimination, retention, and identification correspond to intelligence test items, such as discrimination of stimuli, retention of new information, identification of similarities, and definition of words.

In the initial report on predictive validity, Fagan (Fagan & McGrath, 1981) retested normally developing 4- to 6-year-old children who during infancy had been given multiple-paired presentations of stimuli either for novelty preferences or recognition with facial or abstract stimuli. A recognition score was based on the mean percent of total fixations paid to novel targets. The follow-up score was derived from performance on a vocabulary test. The obtained coefficients for these measures were .37 ($n = 54$) at 4 years and .66 ($n = 20$) at 6 years for normally developing, moderate to high SES groups. These findings, the authors (Fagan & McGrath, 1981) suggested, indicate that variation in infant recognition-memory reflects and predicts variation in general intellectual functioning. Thus, they noted further, the measure has usefulness as a screening device. These findings, although interesting, were on small samples and data collection was made on samples that were not originally recruited for longitudinal predictive studies. Whether or not this reflects unknown biases can not be determined.

More recently, Fagan (Fagan & Singer, in press) attempts to show that the measure has concurrent validity, in that it distinguishes performance between various risk groups and a normally developing sample. No predictive data are available for these children.

Still other approaches are being tried. For example, Lipsitt (1979a, 1979b) and colleagues are attempting to determine whether sucking, heart rate, and habituation are indices that will forecast developmental problems. On another front, Zelazo and Kearsley (Kearsley & Zelazo, 1975; Zelazo, 1979) are exploring the older infant's reaction to perceptual-cognitive events as a tool for more accurate assessment of infants with motor problems. These techniques are still in their early stages of development and their ultimate value remains to be evaluated.

Because many believe that traditional assessments only convey a partial amount of information about infant functioning, attempts have been made to utilize analyses of mother-infant interactions as indices of current and future performance. These involve documenting the nature, frequency, and duration of various kinds of behaviors in which each member of the dyad engages (Bakeman & Brown, 1977; Beckwith, Cohen, Kopp, Parmelee, & Marcy, 1976; DiVitto & Goldberg, 1979; Field, 1979a). In general, the predictive utility is modest with coefficients highest at younger ages (Bakeman & Brown, 1977, 1980; Beckwith et al., 1976). In some instances, virtually no relationship is obtained between early interaction and later performance (Bakeman & Brown, 1980). In a recent paper, Uzgiris (1980) questioned the merits of these types of predictive analyses and noted that interactional measures are usually employed in a single context and only at one time period. Although they have the virtue of enlarging the repertoire of behaviors that are assessed, in actuality, the ongoing process is not examined.

Perhaps, however, the crucial issue does not relate to methodology but rather to the nature of the young human. Infants may be buffered against minor variations in caregiving (Dunn, 1975) because of strong evolutionary adaptations (Scarr-Salapatek, 1976). Such adaptations permit them to acquire fundamental sensorimotor behaviors within the range of most caregiving situations. Given this species similarity, it may be very difficult to detect subtleties in early social interactions that accurately foretell poor outcome for one child and good outcome for another. In instances where interactions are grossly deviant for prolonged periods, one does not need a formal measurement tool to surmise problematic outcome.

In sum, renewed efforts are being made to predict developmental outcome for infants. Although it is too soon to evaluate the results, it is probable that the findings will prove to be no better or no worse than those reported previously. However, it is unlikely that single units of behavior will reflect infant potential any more effectively than the group of indices found in the standard development tests.

Preschool and School-Age Measures

The issue of accurate and appropriate identification continues into the preschool and school-age periods. For some at-risk children, problems begin to surface when they are placed in cognitively challenging situations (Chess, 1974), for others it is a matter of resolving what looked like earlier patterns of suspect development.

For preschool-age children, the McCarthy scales (1972) or the Wechsler Preschool and Primary Scale of Intelligence (WPPSI) (Wechsler, 1967) tend to be used for identification. However, a major problem concerning their use pertains to the fact that their basal ages do not actually overlap the ceiling age of the Bayley scales (Bayley, 1969). The McCarthy scales, for example, were designed to be used with 30-month-olds and up. In practice, a number of delayed or handicapped children who reach ceiling levels on the Bayley pass very few basal levels on the McCarthy (Bernheimer, 1980).

By the later preschool period, the Stanford-Binet (1973) or the revised Wechsler Intelligence Scale for Children (WISC-R) (Wechsler, 1974) are employed for assessment. Although not fully documented, there is a preference (e.g., in preterm research) for the WISC-R because verbal and performance scores can be separated. This is helpful in identifying strengths and problems because it is not uncommon for some children to show higher levels of ability on verbal than on performance tests (Francis-Williams & Davies, 1974). In addition to the standardized developmental intelligence tests, language scales and social maturity tests are often included in a test battery.

Two central issues arise in the identification process used with older children who either appear to have a problem or are diagnosed as intellectually retarded. The first concerns the controversial and highly charged issue of intelligence testing with special groups (Maloney & Ward, 1976; Mercer, 1973). Of concern are questions related to the content of intelligence tests, the meaning of diagnosis and clinical judgments, definitions of mental retardation (classification has been revised three times since 1961 [the most recent version is in Grossman, 1977]), and cultural values and priorities that look favorably on certain kinds of child behaviors.

The second issue, that of predictive validity, surfaces less often with this age group than with younger children because intellectual functioning shows more intrachild stability after the age of 5 (Honzik, MacFarlane, & Allen, 1948; Kopp & McCall, 1982; McCall, 1979). However, a number of investigators have suggested that stability coefficients in mental test performance among retarded children are markedly higher than those obtained with nonretarded children. In actuality, coefficients are fairly high for both groups. Cross-age correlations from Honzik et al. (1948) show a coefficient of .79 for children between 9 and 13 years of age; findings from the Fels and Berkeley studies show a slightly higher coefficient for children of the same age (cited in McCall, 1979).

Scores taken from an institutionalized sample of retarded individuals showed a coefficient of .761 for those who had tests 5 years apart (Sloan & Harmon, 1947). Not surprisingly, when coefficients were computed with short test-retest intervals, the coefficients were quite high. Throne, Schulman, & Kasper (1962) reported a correlation of .95 between tests taken over a 3- to 4-month period of 39 retarded children from 11 to 14 years old. Similarly, Collman and Newlyn (1958) obtained a correlation of .93 for retarded children (6 to 14.11 years old) retested anywhere from after 4 weeks to 1 year.

There is always the sobering realization that even when a child's developmental picture looks grim, change can occur. Chess and her associates (Chess, 1977; Korn, Chess, & Fernandez, 1978) noted that 37% of their rubella sample was retarded at preschool but that only 25% were retarded at school age. It does appear, however, that fewer numbers of retarded children than nonretarded show major shifts in intellectual ability. Among normal children, Honzik et al. (1948) noted that a third of their sample showed sizable shifts between childhood and adolescence, and 1 in 7 children in the Fels study shifted 40 or more points (McCall, Appelbaum, & Hogarty,

1973). In contrast, with retarded samples, Kopp and McCall (1982) found a range of change from 10 to 30 points, and a smaller proportion of sample change which depended on the nature of the nonnormal sample that was employed.

Summary

The purpose of this section was to recount information about the kinds of measures used to assess individual infants and children who have problems in developmental or intellectual functioning. The strengths and weaknesses of individual measures were enumerated and issues central to each were discussed. The implications of this material go beyond this chapter because professionals need to approach the whole area of identification with considerable wariness. There are no miraculous techniques that provide easy and highly accurate screening or assessment.

RESEARCH ABOUT RISK INFLUENCES: EFFECTS ON DEVELOPMENT

From preceding discussions, it is apparent that the number of prenatal, perinatal, and postnatal conditions that influence development is extensive and that the extent and range of effects is wide. Because each of the conditions requires knowledge about effects for purposes of prevention, treatment, and provision of services, the study of risk has grown almost exponentially. The developmentalist's role has included the introduction of, first, a developmental orientation and concern for qualitative and quantitative change and, second, fostering a research climate that focuses on processes rather than end points or products.

Mixed blessings have come from the expansion of research levels and goals; the benefits are unmistaken, but problems have arisen owing to growth of an unsystematic and uncohesive research literature that has rarely been synthesized and critically reviewed. Two recent notable exceptions are Gibson's (1978) examination of the DS research literature and Sameroff and Chandler's (1975) analysis of findings about reproductive and caregiving risks.

No single review can hope to integrate and evaluate the vast amount of existing research literature. Rather, the goal of this section is twofold: (1) to discuss a few research strategies that have been employed and in so doing to integrate findings into a more cohesive picture and (2) to describe and organize research collected with specific diagnostic groups. It is hoped that this dual approach will highlight the strengths and weaknesses of past research efforts and focus directions for future studies. This section leads to the final part of the chapter, which is concerned with directions for future research.

Methodological Paradigms

Longitudinal Follow-up Research

The most commonly adopted strategy in risk research is the longitudinal follow-up study. The pitfalls inherent in longitudinal research have been documented extensively (Schaie, 1965; Wohlwill, 1973) and are also addressed in Volume I of the Handbook. Not surprisingly, many longitudinal follow-up studies focused on early developmental risk contain problems. Among them are failure to take into account cohort trends; use of comparison groups that are not representative or equivalent to the index group; exclusion of, or confounding of, important environmental variables; and a restricted range of analytic techniques. In the following discussion, some general comments about the goals, strategies, advantages, and shortcomings of longitudinal risk research are highlighted. Here, the focus is on issues that are particularly pertinent to risk conditions rather than on methodological or statistical shortcomings that cut across all longitudinal research.

Longitudinal research that is concerned with developmental follow-up or outcome of children exposed to a risk condition has as its fundamental operative mode the grouping of children by common symptoms, physical and neurological signs, or by a diagnostic label. After the initial examination period, development is monitored at prescribed intervals for a set length of time. The overriding goal of most longitudinal research is to determine the effects of condition *X* on developmental outcome up to $time_1$, $time_2$, and so on. A partial list of longitudinal studies completed in the last two decades includes research on children who experienced anoxia in the neonatal period (Corah, Anthony, Painter, Stern, & Thurston, 1965; Graham, Ernhart, Thurston, & Craft, 1962; Graham et al., 1957); those born preterm (see Table 8); infants who showed neurologic signs in the newborn period (Parmelee, Minkowski, Saint-Anne Dargassies, Dreyfus-Brisac, Lézine, Berges, Cervin, & Stern, 1970; Prechtl, 1968); infants whose mothers had rubella in pregnancy (Chess, 1974); children born with congenital malformations owing to teratogenic effects of thalidomide (Decarie, 1969; Decarie & O'Neill, 1974); infants born with defects of the spinal cord (Diller, Gordon, Swinyard, & Kastner, 1969; Hunt & Holmes, 1975; Laurence, 1966; Laurence & Tew,

1967; Tew & Laurence, 1972); children with DS (Carr, 1975; Dicks-Mireaux, 1972; Share, Koch, Webb, & Graliker, 1964); and infants with diagnosed PKU (Baumeister, 1967; Berman, Waisman, & Graham, 1966; Lonsdale & Foust, 1970; Steinhausen, 1974).

Another category of longitudinal research involves evaluation of specific interventions administered to prenatally or perinatally stressed infants (e.g., through neonatal intensive care units, phototherapy, surgical interventions, changes in dietary intake for preterms, introduction of parents into intensive care nurseries, provision of sensory stimulation to preterms, etc.). Dependent variables include the incidence of mortality or neurologic sequelae, sensory disorders, cerebral palsy, and developmental status. Exemplars of research monitoring medical-based interventions include studies by Alden, Mandelkorn, Woodrum, Wennberg, Parks, and Hodson (1972); Carrier, Doray, Stern, and Usher (1972); Mawdsley, Rickham, and Roberts (1967); Davies and Tizard (1975); and Hagberg, Olow, and Hagberg (1973). Examples of research on social and other nonmedical types of interventions include studies by Leiderman, Leifer, Seashore, Barnett, and Grobstein (1973), and Barnard (1973).

Classifications of Outcome. By far, the most commonly used index of outcome is performance measured by developmental or intelligence tests. Typically, findings are reported in terms of the risk groups's means and ranges of performance. If a comparison group has been employed, the risk and comparison scores are subjected to tests of statistical significance. Other comparisons may be utilized, including performance by SES categories, sex, or ethnicity.

The continuing influence of a risk event can be discounted when the risk group's performance on an intelligence test closely approximates that of a comparison group. In contrast, the risk event can be considered to have a major and continuing influence when a group's performance is clearly in the deviant or retarded level (e.g., three or more standard deviations below the mean). However, problems of interpretation surface about the effect of a risk influence when outcome scores fall in borderline ranges. Is, for example, an IQ of 85 the result of a primary influence of the biological risk condition, the environment, family-genetic influence, or all three?

In the last few years, there are indications that efforts are being made to collect background information about a child's family, social class, ethnic-group membership, and parents' education levels. In a few instances, interactional data have been obtained. However, only large studies have enough subjects to analyze outcome by levels of social class (e.g., see Francis-Williams & Davies, 1974). Consequently, most researchers use broad descriptors (e.g., samples are primarily middle class or primarily Caucasian to delineate simple background). Rarely, however, are inferential statistics used to analyze for main or interactive effects of background influences. The problems related to interpretation of findings that this practice causes are by no means trivial.

Other difficulties arise in interpreting the magnitude of effects when definitions of borderline versus retarded functioning vary from one researcher to the next. In some studies, retardation is defined as an IQ score below 85, in others it is below 70. Not only do these definitions vary within professional disciplines, they also vary across disciplines (medicine, psychology, education).

In addition to psychometrically defined outcomes, other indices are employed, including the number of children with sensory impairment, neurologic disorders, and behavioral or psychiatric symptoms. Further, some studies include information about specific language delays or educational problems as manifested by reading problems, special school placements, or perceptual disorders. Interpretative problems arise if these scores are reported only in terms of mean performance and compared with those of a nonrisk group. In these cases, it becomes impossible to determine if the score reflects extreme performance of a few members of the group or a wide distribution of scores as a whole.

In instances where outcomes are variable, ranging from severe impairment to normal functioning, researchers have attempted to define levels of sequelae (e.g., Brimblecombe, Edelsten, & Rubissow, 1978; Kitchen, Ryan, Richards, McDougall, Billson, Keir, & Naylor, 1980). Mild impairment, for example, may consist of an IQ between 70 and 85 and a minor sensory or neurological problem. In contrast, severe impairment can represent IQs below 50, major motor impairments, or a combination of these. As yet, these indices of severity are individualized and only rarely are they commonly applied to children enrolled in different longitudinal studies.

Being able to determine outcome is obviously a primary concern for longitudinal researchers. An intensive debate recently appeared in the *Lancet* (1980) around interpretation of outcome data for low birthweight infants. This was followed by recommendations for design, analysis, and reporting

(Kiely & Paneth, 1981). Because problems in interpretation of data are commonplace in longitudinal risk research, the topic is discussed again later (*Research Issues*).

Conceptual Underpinnings of Longitudinal Research. In their classic discussion, Sameroff and Chandler (1975) described the linear, unidimensional model that so often characterizes the study of risk conditions. Essentially, proponents of the model argue that risk effects are noninteractive and permanent. Unfortunately, in some conditions this is the case, although Sameroff and Chandler found numerous examples of perinatal risk where it was not. Their argument about the importance of models is a compelling one and has been discussed often; it does not need review here.

However, longitudinal developmental risk research is decidedly atheoretical. This characteristic is so pervasive, in fact, that it is possible to enumerate the few exceptions. Decarie (1969) explicitly linked research questions that were derived from theory to her longitudinal follow-up of thalidomide children. Specifically, she asked how the object concept and child-parent attachment could develop, given that many of the sample children lacked prehension, could never integrate that scheme with others, nor could they cling or follow. By using nontraditional measurement techniques, Decarie (1969) showed that most thalidomide children attained these competencies by using vision, oral exploration, and whatever segments of limbs they possessed. In addition, the sample children were routinely tested with standardized measures so that their ongoing development could be evaluated.

Decarie's precision in laying out a theoretically derived study was paralleled in Fraiberg's (Fraiberg, 1968, 1971; Fraiberg & Freedman, 1965) studies of blind infants. Here, psychoanalysis and Piagetian principles were used to formulate questions about ongoing ego and cognitive development. Fraiberg, too, used specific concepts to ask her questions. Taking one very brief example from her rich theoretical discussions, she described Spitz's comments about infants' hands being able to achieve "a progressive independence from the oral zone . . ." leading to greater coordination with the visual system. Using this as a point of departure, Fraiberg carefully observed the mouth and hand explorations demonstrated by blind and sighted infants. She then described adaptive and nonadaptive hand use of blind children and concomitant effects on their ego growth. Much of this theoretically derived follow-up material is presented in clinical-type reports, but standardized indices were also employed (as appropriate) in her studies.

To some extent, theory was employed in the Infant Studies Project (a longitudinal study of preterm infants), setting the stage for adoption of a few of the measurement techniques that were employed (Parmelee, Kopp, & Sigman, 1976). Specifically, Kopp (Kopp, 1974, 1976) used Piagetian theory to undergird questions about the types and level of action schemes employed (Uzgiris, 1967) and the course of sensorimotor development demonstrated by preterm infants.

The use of theory (discussed again, see *The Role of Theory*) not only guides questions that are asked (thus, focusing research) but also has the potential of fostering use of comparable longitudinal strategies across several risk groups. Thus, an array of findings can be systematically generated about a specific aspect of functioning of children exposed to risk. For example, for theoretical and practical reasons, it would be helpful to know if and how attachment processes, which are considered to be species typical (Bowlby, 1969; see also *Campos, Goldsmith, & Svejda, vol. II, chap. 10*), are affected by different risk conditions.

The conceptual framework of longitudinal studies also benefits by building in approaches that combine use of qualitative and quantitative measurement strategies (noted earlier in relation to Fraiberg, 1968, 1971). The only large-scale longitudinal risk study that systematically used both is Chess's (Chess, 1974, 1977) follow-up of rubella children. Her contribution is unique because she postulated different forms that development could take between children and, in the course of development, for a single child.

The developmental patterns are worth repeating because of their potential value in laying out a series of questions that can be addressed only in a longitudinal study. Chess's (1974) developmental patterns are presented first, followed by examples provided by this author.

1. A crossover effect of a handicapping condition can occur when a problem in one area causes problems in other areas of functioning. For example, being retarded may affect social interactions, not because of limited intellect per se but because a child does not recognize the necessity of taking turns or sharing with peers. (For a discussion of social intelligence in retarded children, see Greenspan, 1979.)

2. A defect in a function may be present but not identified until it fails to emerge and undergo

changes in a hierarchical fashion. Memory is one example where the developmental function changes, thus, organic impairment could affect memory, but the defect could be very subtle in early life and go unnoticed until a later age when the child is unable to produce more complex memory strategies. (See Brown, 1974.)

3. A weakness may not change but its handicapping influence can increase as age-related cognitive demands become more complex. Hearing impairment is a relevant example here. Most infants even with profound hearing loss function quite well during the sensorimotor period because of the here-and-now concrete nature of caregiver demands. Problems surface when the child is exposed to, or is expected to produce, higher order concepts that require the juxtaposition of complex ideas in the abstract. Deaf children are often at a disadvantage in these situations. (For discussions, see Liben, 1978; Meadow, 1980.)

4. The effect of a problem may be more pronounced at an earlier age but increasing cognitive skills and motivation may attenuate some of the effects of the handicap. Infants with motor impairments are severely hampered in object explorations or interpersonal expressions of affiliation, but with the emergence of language, an alternative path to knowledge and communication is available to them.

5. Individual differences in mastery of handicaps may occur owing to individual differences in child temperament and interactions with parents or teachers. Thomas, Chess, & Birch's, 1968, study of temperament suggests that a mismatch in child and parent temperament leads to stress in the relationship and parent avoidance or denial of child needs. Although the normal child can seek relief from other quarters, the handicapped child is more restricted. The consequences for a moody and withdrawn child who is considered by caregivers to be difficult and who has a handicap can be cognitive, motivational, or social failure.

Another aspect of Chess's research strategy that has significance for conceptual underpinnings is her concern for developmental change. Her diligence in following the rubella sample to the school years (Chess, 1977; Korn et al., 1978) is not unique, but her interest in documenting signs of individual growth (or deterioration) is rare and required adequate planning in the early stages of research.

Specification of Independent or Contributing Variables. The question of timing of a risk event and its effects is an issue that cuts across all of the follow-up studies mentioned in this review. As noted earlier, the sequelae of an early prenatal stress is fairly obvious (e.g., structural impairment); the actual timing of a postnatal risk event can be documented fairly easily. However, determining the actual timing of late prenatal or perinatal cases (e.g., preterm birth, anoxia, etc.) is more difficult. In the last two decades, additional specificity about timing and its effects has been introduced by subcategorizing preterms into subgroups based on small-for-dates (inadequate intrauterine nutrition) and appropriate-for-dates assessments. Although outcome data for the two groups are currently inconclusive (Francis-Williams & Davies, 1974; Kitchen et al., 1980; Neligan, Kolvin, Scott, & Garside, 1976; Parkinson, Wallis, & Harvey, 1981), analyses utilizing these subgroups at least affords the opportunity to explore further the separate and combined consequences of prenatal and perinatal stress.

More recently, other strategies have been adopted in an attempt to be more specific about stress events and the timing of stress for infants. Drillien (Drillien, 1972; Drillien, Thomson, & Burgoyne, 1980), for example, categorized low birthweight infants on the basis of:

1. No evidence of adverse factors in early pregnancy or the third trimester.
2. Evidence of adverse factors operating in early pregnancy (e.g., major or several minor congenital anomalies).
3. Adverse factors operating in late pregnancy (e.g., maternal pre-eclampsia).
4. Indeterminate causes.

Preliminary support for use of the early pregnancy subgrouping was demonstrated by the finding of Drillien et al. (1980) that in longitudinal studies, this category of children showed an increased degree of impairment and an increased percentage of exclusions from normal school.

Using another approach, Sostek et al. (1979) grouped infants on the basis of type of birth, and illness with and without evidence of central nervous system impairment. Preliminary data analyses indicate that the impaired infants are doing less well than nonimpaired infants. However, the authors' data are confounded by lack of age correction or information about gestational ages represented in the sample subsets.

Cohort Effects and Secular Changes. Generally, only large, well-funded projects are able to collect a broad array of information; thus, having an extensive outcome data base tends to be the exception rather than the rule in longitudinal risk studies. As a result, findings of large studies are cited many years after the data were first published and sometimes bear little relationship to prevailing health, medical practices, and social conditions. An example can be found in the perinatal risk literature, where outcomes of cohorts born in the 1950s and early 1960s were repeatedly used to characterize the developmental potential of perinatal risk groups born in the 1970s. The cohorts were not equivalent because of changes in neonatal intensive care; thus, the earlier data were, at best, only partially relevant to the more recent scene.

Secular effects can also arise in the course of a single study where intake may extend to several years. Major changes in the nature of direct treatment are usually documented (see Table 8), however, more subtle or indirect changes are not. Thus, changes in economic conditions, enrollments in training programs designed for support professionals, or day-to-day working conditions may have significant, but unrecorded, implications for the development of the early and later born children in a cohort.

Finally, influences akin to cohort effects can emerge when a condition is relatively rare so that only a few subjects are entered into a study in the space of a year. A researcher might have to wait 5 years to recruit an adequate follow-up sample. A case in point is the current effort to determine the developmental course of children diagnosed as having fetal alcohol syndrome (FAS) (Streissguth, Landesman-Dwyer, Martin, & Smith, 1980). Relatively few children are known to have this disorder. All manner of experiential, social, medical, and intervention events can occur over the years that adequate-sized samples of FAS are to be generated.

Cross-sectional, Convergence, Mixed Paradigms

Cross-sectional Paradigms. Another major category of research involves comparisons made between groups of children who were stressed by risk factors and those who were not. Studies in this genre focus upon differences in characteristics, performance, or the nature of social interactions of the two groups. In some instances, the comparison involves subjects categorized solely by class membership (e.g., preterm) and not necessarily because the subjects show deviant functioning.

Most often, the emphasis in cross-sectional studies is on group performance. Rarely do researchers discuss individual variability within each group and the extent to which scores of children in the risk sample overlap those in the comparison sample. Inclusion of this unit of measurement would indicate the proportion of children in risk groups who clearly fall outside the range of variation of majority performance.

Cross-sectional designs have several merits that probably account for their increased use in studying the effects of risk. They "represent an economy in time and effort and allow total samples to be studied" (Clarke, 1978). Moreover, they allow more rapid testing of theoretical propositions than do longitudinal paradigms (Bell, 1953).

Problems are found as well. Most of the time, results obtained do not correspond with those obtained from longitudinal studies. This may occur for a variety of factors: sample attrition or constant retesting in the longitudinal study or secular changes (Clarke, 1978). Lack of correspondence may also be due to inadequate sample selection of either the cross-sectional or longitudinal studies.

Moreover, the data base in cross-sectional studies is less rich than that obtained in longitudinal research, thus, the number of testable ideas that emerge will be fewer. Finally, major problems arise in cross-sectional studies when samples are not drawn from the same cohorts, are nonrepresentative, or the tasks given to different aged samples are not comparable in meaning (Garmezy & Levine, 1977; Wohlwill, 1973). When these conditions arise, Garmezy and Levine (1977) noted, "deforming conclusions can be drawn about the developmental emergence of specific processes" (p. 211).

At this point in time, the two most obvious problems in cross-sectional studies of risk effects pertain to sample representativeness and to limitations in the number of ages studied to define the growth of developmental functions. With respect to the former, it is clear that adequate sample representation is only possible when one has the potential to draw from the pool of all members of a risk group. Because that is not feasible, researchers draw from the pool of subjects available in their own geographic locales (this, of course, applies to subjects selected for longitudinal research as well). But one pool may be very different from another selected elsewhere. Consider, as an example, the preterm subjects studied by Rose, Gottfried, and Bridger (1979) on visual-memory tasks. The children were drawn largely from a low socioeconomic group of predominantly Hispanic and black heritage living in the Bronx, New York, which is a community with major social and economic problems. However, another study of preterms' visual responses utilized only Caucasian infants reared by parents living in a less stressed urban community (Fantz & Fagan, 1975). Which sample is representative of preterms in general? If findings differ regarding the implications of early birth (as, for example, they do in these two studies), which set actually reflects the primary contribution made by preterm birth?

Sample representativeness issues also surface with regard to groups selected as comparisons to the risk sample. Because samples may differ from the population as a whole on variables other than the stress of a risk event, investigators turn to matching techniques and match comparison subjects on selected variables (e.g., age, sex, SES factors, etc.). However, matching has well-documented problems (Kerlinger, 1964). To circumvent these limitations, researchers, particularly in the area of childhood psychopathology, have been drawing two comparison samples, one is matched and the other is randomly selected from the population as a whole. This approach has the merit of allowing comparisons to be made across the combination of samples and, thus, to test the pattern of results. To my knowledge, this strategy has not been employed in studies of risk effects.

Turning to the issue of developmental functions, it is evident that one of the most common uses of the cross-sectional paradigm in developmental research with nonrisk samples involves determining the form (direction, shape, and parameters) of a developmental function (Wohlwill, 1973). To this end, many age groups are employed and, although it may be difficult to determine exactly the contributors of changes that occur over time, at the very least the direction of changes can be ascertained.

The situation that prevails in cross-sectional research with risk samples is markedly different. Studies have been directed to very few age periods and involve analysis of a limited number of developmental functions. In the literature on preterm infant development, for example, by far the largest number of studies exist on newborn characteristics and the least on older infants. Using preterms again as an example, a review of the literature reveals less than a dozen studies of any kind of cognitive processing skill and most do not overlap on task, age, or other background characteristics. Moreover, most involved one-time comparisons, which makes it impossible to plot the course of a developmental function, much less to attempt to unravel contributors to change. Unfortunately, this lack of an adequate data base has not deterred some investigators from drawing some far-reaching conclusions about the problems of children stressed by a risk event.

Convergence Approach. The convergence, or sequential, approach was designed as an antidote to cohort problems generated by cross-sectional and longitudinal designs (Bell, 1953, 1954; Schaie, 1965; Wohlwill, 1973). Using this strategy, different cross-sectional samples are followed with partially overlapping periods. To my knowledge, there is no study of risk factors that has employed this design.

Mixed Paradigms. The programmatic research initiated at Case Western Reserve by Fantz, Fagan, and Miranda (1975) has effectively combined use of short-term longitudinal and cross-sectional studies. Their research focused on the development of visual-processing skills utilized by samples of normally developing, DS, and preterm infants. In some instances, a cross-sectional study was first carried out and followed by a longitudinal study so that a trend found in one could be checked out in another. Often, the age groups employed in both paradigms overlapped. Moreover, the same kind of visual-processing skills were analyzed for the different risk groups.

The mixed paradigm can also be particularly advantageous for studying individual differences in risk groups. For example, within-group variability can be identified by using a cross-sectional approach, and the implications of that variability can be evaluated by turning to a short-term longitudinal approach.

Research on Specific Diagnostic Conditions

Down Syndrome (DS)

The very first descriptions of the developmental course of DS (mongolism, as it was referred to in past years) occurred in the nineteenth century and took the form of clinical reports (Gibson, 1978). These were "anecdotal, subjective and unreliable but rich in clinical observation . . ." (p. 35) and later were superceded by use of Binet tests (Gibson, 1978). Although narrower in scope than clinical reports, psychometric testing had the advantage of permitting large-scale assessment of many individuals, evaluation of their progress over time, and assessment of the effects of diverse kinds of rearing conditions.

At present, a rich and extensive literature exists that documents the intellectual, behavioral, neurological, and psychophysiological functioning of DS individuals across the life span. Much of this material has been admirably synthesized and critiqued in the last few years by Belmont (1971) and Gibson (1978). Rather than attempt to repeat what has already been skillfully stated, this review will focus on an analysis of research devoted to infancy. The early life of young DS children is a topic that has benefited from considerable interest and research in the last few years and has not been extensively examined in previous reviews.

In the first part of this review, attention is directed to longitudinal follow-up studies that document the course of development in the first few months and years of life. Topics specifically addressed center on the issue of developmental declines and when they first begin to appear as well as the nature of test-retest predictive coefficients found in early life. An analysis of cross-sectional and other kinds of studies comprises the second part of this review. Here, findings are examined to determine how observations of behavioral attributes of DS infants aids the interpretation of longitudinal findings.

Longitudinal Follow-up Research on Early Development. To set the stage for discussion, it will be helpful to review briefly the long-term course of mental development in DS. Developmentally, the DS infant seems very similar to normal infants; however, this changes over a few years. By school age, DS children are substantially behind their peers in level of abilities and attainment of skills as reflected by IQ differences. Not infrequently, there can be 50 or more points between the two groups. Typically, IQs range from 20 to 70 (Koch & de la Cruz, 1975; Smith & Wilson, 1973), although occasionally they may be in the 80s in cases of partial translocation (Rosecrans, 1971). The skills most impaired involve abstract reasoning and language, whereas abilities related to accomplishment of simple tasks, rote skills, and noncomplex language are less involved (Cornwell, 1974; Lenneberg, Nichols, & Rosenberger, 1962). During the childhood period, mental-growth changes become appreciably slow for most DS individuals (Melyn & White, 1973; Morgan, 1979; Ross, 1962; Silverstein, 1966; Zeaman & House, 1962).

The issue of decelerating rates of intellectual growth in DS has provoked much controversy. Earlier reports suggested a progressive retardation occurred (Masland, Sarason, & Gladwin, 1958), others believed deterioration in abilities set in at age 4 (Gesell & Amatruda, 1941), still others argued that a slow but steady progress could be documented. In summarizing the earlier literature, Kopp and Parmelee (1979) noted that if declines were reported, they were attributed to inability of DS children to keep pace with rapid conceptual growth of middle childhood, to reflect poor environmental conditions, to be a manifestation of dissimilarity of skills measured during infancy and childhood (e.g., sensorimotor vs. language-oriented tasks), to be a function of test artifact, or to signify biologically based deterioration.

Some of the longitudinal studies initiated in the 1950s with DS infants helped to clarify the nature of early development. Actually, one of the major studies was started because of concern about validity of predictions of early developmental test scores (Fishler et al., 1965; Koch, Share, Webb, & Graliker, 1963; Share, Webb, & Koch, 1961). This concern was then extended to an interest in the rates of developmental changes manifested by DS children. The findings of Koch and his colleagues are of interest on two counts. First, with regard to predictive validity, these investigators noted that stability for test-retest performance appeared at about 18 months. Thus, it could be surmised that something was happening to intellectual growth around that age.

In examining their articles, there is no doubt that Koch and his colleagues accurately pinpointed an important age period. The correlation coefficients are very high for test-retest after about 18 months or so. In some instances, they are high for earlier ages, but the data are not consistent. Specifically, in reviewing three publications, it is apparent that one or more factors (e.g., possibly marked variability in the sample) dramatically influenced the nature of predictive coefficients obtained with the younger aged sample when its size increased from an n of 16 to an n of 31. However, these very same changes had little effect on predictive coefficients made on test scores obtained at 1½ years and later, and the coefficients were uniformly high irrespective of sample size (they ranged from .85 with an $n = 16$ to .97 with $n = 31$).

The second important set of findings that emerged from these studies was the further delineation of developmental changes manifested by DS children. The children did, in fact, develop additional intellectual skills, albeit their rate of change showed a progressive decrement. During the first year, growth averaged 6 months; the second year, 5 months; and the third year, 4 months. Thus, taken as a group, the children progressed but compared to their peers they retrogressed and showed declines in development.

As noted above, deceleration in developmental growth had been reported by Gesell and Amatruda (1941) as occurring around 3 to 4 years of age, but the Koch group documented its emergence as early as the 2nd year. These findings took on added significance because they were obtained with children who were home reared and presumably ruled out effects owing to poor or neglectful caregiving situations. Moreover, the fact that declines were noted to occur during the time that language often emerged suggested that other factors could account for a slowdown in mental growth. Fortunately, two additional longitudinal studies helped clarify the developmental picture. Both included samples of infants who were tested often during the early years and both included comparison groups of normally developing infants (Carr, 1975; Dicks-Mireaux, 1972).

Carr's (1975) sample included 54 DS children (home and institution reared) matched for sex, age, and social class with normal controls. After testing at 1.5, 6, 10, 15, 24, 36, and 48 months, Carr found a deceleration in development that began to emerge at 6 months, was readily apparent at 10 months (the mean scores dropped by 30 points between 6 weeks and 10 months), and then leveled out by ages 2 to 3. Predictive test-retest coefficients conformed to the developmental regression data in that low coefficients were obtained between 6 and 36 months (.29) but rose markedly between 15 and 48 months (.72), indicating increasing stability of performance.

In addition, Carr noted environmental effects on performance with home-reared children scoring higher than institution-reared children. Moreover, she was able to demonstrate that language ability per se was not the crucial factor in developmental retrogression because the declines she observed actually began long before functional language emerged in the infant's repertoire.

The issue of declines was also addressed by Dicks-Mireaux (1972) who pursued a slightly different statistical course than Carr (1975). A group of DS infants was followed from approximately 10 weeks to 78 weeks of age and compared to normal infants tested cross-sectionally. Five age periods, 16, 28, 40, 52, and 78 weeks, were chosen for test administration of Gesell schedules. Examination of developmental quotients showed each group exhibiting a downward trend in scores; among the normal group it was slight (although marked with some irregularity), but for the DS sample there was less irregularity but a much steeper decline, reaching its maximum at 52 weeks of age.

To examine trends in the data, Dicks-Mireaux (1972) used covariance and regression equations of mental age over chronological age. Statistical support was found for a strong linear relationship for development of the normal group of infants, whereas a curvilinear relationship was observed for data derived from the DS group. My interpretation of the trends depicted graphically by Dicks-Mireaux indicate that the slope for the DS infants started to move away from a linear trend about 40 weeks of age, thus supporting Carr's (1975) findings. Dicks-Mireaux (1973) reached three conclusions: DS infants show a steady rate of development but it is slower than normal, and there is "progressive deterioration" in the rate of longitudinal development.

In sum, taken together, the findings reveal a slowing down of developmental growth in the 1st year of life for many DS infants, although individual differences are noted. Because variability is reported in both rates of growth and deceleration, prediction from early to later mental abilities is problematic in the 1st year, but rises appreciably in the 2nd (see also Kopp & McCall, 1982).

Two hypotheses have been advanced to account for longitudinal findings about mental development. Gibson (1978), for example, suggested that the level of development reached by many DS individuals is actually no more than 2 to 3 years of mental age. He hypothesized that the manipulation of symbols and images provided "something of a developmental wall for the syndrome," although he notes the first five sensorimotor stages unfold reliably. Parenthetically, Gibson (1978) suggests that many older DS individuals transcend these intellectual limitations by developing good rote-memory abilities, social habits, and language skills.

Kopp and Parmelee (1979), interested in the issue of declines in early life, adopted both a Piagetian and an information processing perspective to explain developmental patterns. They suggested that the developmental shift presumed to occur in the latter part of the 1st year (Piaget, 1952, 1954) might not be fully negotiated by DS infants. Kopp and Parmelee (1979) reasoned that, because DS infants did not respond to complex visual stimuli like normally developing infants (see Fantz, Fagan, & Miranda, 1975), at some level the DS infants had difficulty processing stimuli. They further speculated that the problem in cognitive processing affected, in some unspecified way, the transition to a higher level of functioning. Thus, Kopp and Parmelee (1979) continued, scores between the two groups should begin to diverge at this point. Examination of data in the next discussion allows a preliminary evaluation of the information processing skills of DS infants and possible implications for stage transformations.

One of the issues yet to be resolved is whether the observed pattern of declines is reversible. Several reports indicate that DS infants and young children provided with early and sensitive interventions show a more optimal developmental course than samples receiving no intervention (Bidder, Bryant, & Gray, 1975; Connolly & Russell, 1976; Hayden & Haring,

1976; Rynders & Horrobin, 1975); in contrast, a recent study of a short-term intervention showed no significant differences between the experimental and control groups (Piper & Pless, 1980). But sample sizes are small, statistical evaluations limited, and the follow-up period generally short. Not surprisingly, the merits of intervention programs continue to be debated (for recent examples, see Bricker, Carlson, & Schwarz, 1981; Browder, 1981; Denhoff, 1981; Ferry, 1981). As Gibson (1978) noted, some programs show promising effects in social, emotional, and motoric domains and may in fact attenuate arousal/attention problems commonly observed in DS. Whether the effects are long lasting remain to be determined.

Cross-sectional and Other Research on DS Infants. It is fortunate that renewed interest in DS in general and an awakening concern for handicapped infants in particular has led to increasing research directed at the very young DS child. Because this research has not been systematically reviewed, the focus of this discussion is to provide a summary of the topics that have been addressed and the nature of findings. The studies will be organized around several themes or headings to determine what inferences can be made about the development of DS infants.

First, because the content of the studies is exceedingly diverse, the research is categorized by domains of functioning—social-emotional, perceptual, language, and so forth. This strategy, although somewhat artificial, forces a closer analysis of specific attributes than might otherwise be possible. A second column provides information about subject characteristics. This detail is necessary because the samples differ so markedly from one another. A third theme concerns developmental delays and notes whether lags were found in a particular domain of functioning. Although the prevailing belief is that DS infants are delayed in all domains, there is evidence from studies of older DS children that indicates some areas of functioning (e.g., learning simple rote-memory tasks) are not that discrepant from those manifested by peers of similar chronological age.

Fourth, three separate headings are used to note whether researchers reported differences or similarities in developmental sequences, structure (or organization of behavior), and processes. The rationale underlying selection of these categories stems from research in mental retardation. For example, Weisz and Zigler (1979, in press) reviewed an extensive number of Piagetian-based studies that employed mentally retarded (MR) children as subjects. Review of findings indicated that both the organization and sequence of developmental structures (i.e., the organization of thought) as described by Piaget (1952, 1954, 1970) were found in the familial retarded *if* they were examined at the same developmental/mental age that Piaget proposed for normal children. The findings, although remarkably similar, were not as clearcut when studies included subjects with genetic or physiological defects (e.g., some minor variations in sequence were noted).

In other instances, researchers in the field of mental retardation have attempted to determine if structural or process differences are at the basis of variations in functioning or mentally retarded and normal individuals (see Campione & Brown, 1977; Karrer, Nelson, & Galbraith, 1979; Spitz, 1963, 1979). Here, structure refers to invariant components of a system much like the hardware of a computer (Campione & Brown, 1977; Newell & Simon, 1972), and, of course, the analogy stems from the information processing orientation to cognition. Also, in this view, processes, specifically control processes, are considered to be strategies that individuals bring to bear on tasks. Control processes can involve organization of material, rehearsal, and production of strategies used in memory, problem solving, and so forth (see Flavell & Wellman, 1976, for memory).

Current research findings suggest that as far as memory and problem solving skills are concerned, process limitations rather than structural impairments separate the thinking of MR individuals from that of their age peers (see Borkowski & Wanschura, 1974; Brown, 1974; Butterfield & Belmont, 1977; Spitz, 1979). However, the argument is far from settled.

Although there are a number of limitations in using the structure-process distinction with younger organisms—not the least of which is the evolving acquisition of structures during infancy and the immaturity of existing infant thought processes—the distinction does serve a useful purpose. It allows one to go beyond discussions of developmental problems that are addressed primarily in terms of delay and examine other ways that DS infants differ from their normally developing counterparts. Examination of an infant's information processing ability or use of control processes has credibility because incipient forms of some control processes have been inferred to occur by the end of the 1st year (e.g., conscious awareness, Collins & Hagen, 1979; planfulness, Piaget, 1952, 1954; hypothesis testing, Kagan, 1971; use of agents, Watson & Fischer, 1977). This is not to suggest, however, that infants are able to think consciously about the content of their thoughts.

The studies, their findings, and the inferences made about the findings are depicted in Table 7. Note that S and D are used to signify evidence (or inference) of similarities or differences between DS and normally developing infants.

Turning first to the issue of delay, analysis of the Delays Noted column shows that those investigators who utilized DS and normal infants matched by chronological age often reported delays in one or more facets of behavior. This is true, for example, of smiling, perceptual responsiveness, and the onset of social speech. However, delay was not characteristic of all behaviors, notable exceptions pertain to early visual perceptual abilities and reduplicated babbling. Both of these may be so basic to human existence and so tied to biological underpinnings and maturational factors that DS conditions are not severe enough to disrupt the timing of their emergence.

What meaning does this checkered pattern of delay convey? The picture is clouded because large numbers of stressed infants (*not* DS, and not with other chromosomal problems) who show developmental delays during infancy become essentially normal later on, but DS infants do not. It may turn out that certain patterns of delay are more sensitive indicators of future developmental status than others.[3] Perhaps too, developmental outcome hinges on a relationship between the domain of functioning that is delayed *and* a level of delay that is consistently demonstrated. In any event, the fact that behavioral delays exist does not explain why DS development proceeds the way it does.

Examination of the two columns Structure or Organization and Developmental Sequence of behaviors indicate that no investigator reported variations in either. The inference is that these sensorimotor behaviors have a firm biological basis that reflects strong evolutionary pressures and are distorted only in the wake of profound organismic damage (Piaget, 1970; Scarr-Salapatek, 1976).

In contrast to these similarities, interesting group differences emerge in the information processing column and pertain to behaviors demonstrated by DS compared to normally developing children. In some instances, the DS response is weak and used far less regularly than observed with younger aged normal infants. This characteristic has been observed with smiling, laughter, and fear responses, leading Cicchetti and Sroufe (1976) to hypothesize that the underlying problem was a deficiency in processing of information. Coupled with marked hypotonia, some DS infants could not build up sufficient tension to generate a strong affective response.

Differences are also apparent when performance is analyzed on perceptual-cognitive tasks. DS infants tend to overlook parts of stimulus configurations presented in studies of visually mediated perception, attention, and recognition memory (Cohen, 1981; Fantz et al., 1975; Miranda & Fantz, 1973, 1974). This difficulty, not a function of impaired sensory acuities, was reported, for example, in recognition-memory studies (Fantz et al., 1975). Here, the DS sample appeared to have difficulty "interpreting" or discriminating stimuli that had relatively complex elemental arrangements. The researchers interpreted the findings as signifying cognitive limitations of DS infants. Would, in fact, these differences be attenuated if the groups had been equated for developmental age? It does not seem likely because inspection of graphs provided in Fantz et al. (1975) suggest that even the oldest DS infants (30 to 40 weeks) did not show the level of response that younger normal infants (8 to 16 weeks, 17 to 29 weeks) were capable of.

The problems noted in DS responses to two-dimensional complex stimuli were not unique to the tasks that were employed or the age that was studied. Both Jones (1980), in an analysis of nonverbal communication, and Krakow and Kopp (1982), in examination of patterns of attention, reported that visual regard was deployed differently by DS infants. Of importance, in each study the DS children were matched by developmental age to normally developing infants.

In the Jones (1980) study, DS children used far less referential eye contact (a two-party communication about a third event) than did normal children. This is a complex behavioral act where the infant has to pause in an activity, direct eye contact to mother to elicit a response, and on receiving same, return to the activity. This chain of events requires the infant to attach some meaning to the act of engaging another person in an activity and then interpreting explicit or subtle facial expressions, gestures, or verbal replies.

Krakow and Kopp (1982) also found that DS infants in a laboratory situation did less visual monitoring of their environs (e.g., mother, examiner, room) and showed more repetitive object play. Although the infants were capable of demonstrating more complex forms of visual interchange of object-mother-object, they rarely used these higher levels of behavior.

What emerges from some of the findings reported in Table 7 is that DS infants have difficulty in

Table 7. Developmental Studies of Down Syndrome (DS) Infants: Similarities and Differences in Behavior

Behavior Studied	Sample: n, Age Type, Developmental Performance, etc.	Characteristics of Behavior				
		Delays Noted	Structure or Organization[a]	Developmental Sequence	Information Processing[b]	Author Comments
Sensorimotor landmarks as described in developmental tests (e.g., head control, transfer of objects, sits unsupported, walks alone, etc.) (Carr, 1975; Coraza, Dameron, 1963; Dicks-Mireaux, 1966; Gesell & Amatruda, 1941; Share et al., 1964)	DS infants of varied ages; tested by CA[d] and compared to normative standards	Considerable variability across test items and among children; fine motor items often less delayed than locomotion or first word (may be delayed 1 or more years)	S[c]	Similar in most cases but nonlinear growth patterns noted for DS	S	
Emotional/affective development						
Social smiling (Emde & Brown, 1978)	n = 6, birth to 6 months	Social smiling delayed	S	S	Dampened response, used inconsistently, irregular eye contact	
Laughter (Cicchetti & Sroufe, 1976)	n = 14 (16M, 8F); CA = 4–24 months; 11 trisomy, 2 mosaics, 1 translocation; home reared (data on normal samples collected earlier)	Laughter: delayed from 6 to 15 months, md 10 months	S	S	Rarely laughed	Tie between affect and cognition more apparent with DS than ND[e]

Behavior Studied	Sample: n, Age Type, Developmental Performance, etc.	Characteristics of Behavior				
		Delays Noted	Structure or Organization[a]	Developmental Sequence	Information Processing[b]	Author Comments
Distress or crying to visual loom and visual cliff (Cicchetti & Sroufe, 1978)	n = 120 DS, 90 ND; 4 to 16 months; 114 trisomy; 3 each mosaics, translocations; home reared		S	S	DS show less crying at 8–12 months to loom than ND; DS show paucity of distress at deep side of visual cliff	DS infant's slowness becomes apparent when meaning of event needs to be abstracted; may also have physiological deficit, suggested by low level of distress shown
Self-recognition (Mans, Cicchetti, & Sroufe, 1978)	n = 55 DS, CA age range 15 to 48 months; 51 trisomy 21, 3 mosaic, 1 translocation; home reared	22% showed recognition at 15–22 months, 89% 34–48 months; recognition related to developmental test scores	S	S	S	
Social						
Strange situation (Berry, Gunn, & Andrews, 1980)	n = 18 (12M, 6F) $\bar{x}$ CA = 24 months (SD 6 months), $\bar{x}$ DA[f] = 14 months, 25 days (SD 4 months); 17 trisomy, 1 translocation; home reared		S		Children were sensitive to strange situation, separation from mother, and to presence of a strange person; almost all cried when mother left room	

Notes: [a]Structure refers either to the organization of behavior in the Piagetian sense or to the basic elements of the human repertoire.
[b]Information processing refers to ways of handling information or strategies used in situations.
[c]S = similarities found; D = differences found.
[d]CA = chronological age.
[e]ND = normally developing infant/child.
[f]DA = developmental age.
[g]DQ = developmental quotient.
[h]Refers to Piaget's sensorimotor stages.

Table 7. (*Continued*)

Behavior Studied	Sample: n, Age Type, Developmental Performance, etc.	Characteristics of Behavior: Delays Noted	Structure or Organization[a]	Developmental Sequence	Information Processing[b]	Author Comments
Attachment						
Strange situation (Serafica & Cicchetti, 1976)	n = 12 DS, 12 ND; CA = median age 33.5, 32.8 months; DS $\bar{x}$ DQ = 56.45[g]; home reared		S	S	Both groups used smiling as a response, both used locomotion to gain proximity to mother; crying and vocalization used less by DS	DS may interpret strange situation differently from ND, possibly less sensitive to cues denoting novelty
Use of signals: looking, smiling, vocalization (Markowitz, 1980)	n = 3 DS, 3 ND; CA = 5 to 7 months; 1 trisomy, 1 mosaic, 1 translocation; developmental age match at 5 months; home reared	Onset of social smile	S	S	Both groups used *en face* vocalizations; DA match showed no differences; younger DA infants less *en face;* DS overall did more looking at mother's body than ND	
Prelinguistic communications (Jones, 1980)	n = 6 DS, 6 ND; CA = 8 to 24 months, 3 to 13 months; infants matched on DA, sex, SES, ordinality; matched DA ranged from 8 to 19 months		S	S	Overall many similarities; differences: DS showed more ritual-nonverbal interchanges, less referential looking, less consideration of role in vocal dialogue	Mothers of DS had more failed bids to child, tended to be more directive; in using less referential eye contact, DS infants "depriving themselves of a very rich source of relevant information"

(*continued*)

Behavior Studied	Sample: n, Age Type, Developmental Performance, etc.	Characteristics of Behavior: Delays Noted	Structure or Organization[a]	Developmental Sequence	Information Processing[b]	Author Comments
Play						
Pretend play (Hill & McCune-Nicolich, 1981)	n = 30 DS (16 males); CA = 20–53 months; DA = 12–26 months; home reared		S	Similar for levels of play		
Vocalization						
Premeaningful vocalizations: emission and length of utterances; types of vowels and consonants (Dodd, 1972)	10 DS, 10 ND; CA = 9–13 months; MDI = 56.8 (9.7), 112.5 (11.3); all trisomy 21; English-speaking families		Number, range, length of utterances similar; emotional tone, tension, activity, manipulation, body motion less for DS	S	S	Babbling is a nonlearned behavior and not closely linked with level of intelligence or later articulatory proficiency
Premeaningful vocalizations: reduplicated babbling; place of consonant articulation; vocalic productions (Smith & Oller, in press)	10 DS, 9 ND; first 15 months of life; all Ss had normal hearing	Both groups produced canonical, reduplicated babbling at 8–8½ months; similar shift in production frequency for alveolars and velars at 6 months	Consonant and vocal development similar	S		

(continued)

Table 7. (*Continued*)

Behavior Studied	Sample: n, Age Type, Developmental Performance, etc.	Characteristics of Behavior: Delays Noted	Structure or Organization[a]	Developmental Sequence	Information Processing[b]	Author Comments
Communicative and sensorimotor development (Greenwald & Leonard, 1979)	n = 15 DS below 30 months; 6 = Stage 4[h]; 9 = Stage 5 performance; IQs = 37 to 79 ($\bar{x}$ 62); n = 20 nonretarded children, 10 = Stage 4, 10 = Stage 5; IQs ≥ 90; all home reared, no hearing loss		Both groups showed more advanced types of behavior with increasing developmental age	S	DS relied more on gestures	
Contingent and noncontingent stimulation of vocalization and looking behavior (Gunn, Berry, & Andrews, 1979)	n = 10 DS (8M, 2F); CA = 4–19 months; MDI = <50–107				Neither condition increased infant vocalization; decrease in looking at mother during base-line stage following maternal vocalization	"Looking behavior may be an important indication of competence"
Language and sensorimotor development (Mahoney, Glover, & Finger, 1981)	n = 18 DS, 18 ND; CA = 24–38 months, $\bar{x}$ 29.1; 12–19 months, $\bar{x}$ 16.3; DA = 13–23 months, $\bar{x}$ 16.8; 12–23 months, $\bar{x}$ 17.1; home reared, English speaking; matched on DA and sex	DS delayed in expressive receptive language			DS used vocal imitation less than ND; no difference for gestural imitation	

(*continued*)

Behavior Studied	Sample: n, Age Type, Developmental Performance, etc.	Characteristics of Behavior: Delays Noted	Structure or Organization[a]	Developmental Sequence	Information Processing[b]	Author Comments
Auditory functions						
Visual reinforcement audiometry (VRA)—head turn to a complex noise signal reinforced by a complex visual stimulus (Greenberg, Wilson, Moore, & Thompson, 1978)	20 DS; CA = 6–36 months (from larger sample of 41 Ss with ages to 6 years); MDI measurements taken; most trisomy; health screened	When CA used, less than 50% of 13 to 24-month-olds showed localization to sound; by 6 years all localized; when DA used, high rate of success noted at 10 months in contrast to normal infants who show consistent VRA at 5–6 months	S	S	S	Speculate if differences are a function of inappropriate scaling of abilities of DS on developmental test or reflects inability to deal effectively with auditory cues in modality-specific manner
Visual processing/ attention						
Visual preferences (Miranda & Fantz, 1973)	n = 40, 20 DS (11M, 9F), 20 ND; $\bar{x}$ CA = 34.4 weeks, 31.6 weeks; $\bar{x}$ MDI = 48.2, 101.7; all home reared; no oculomotor defects or severe organic disease		S		Both show preferences for novel over familiar; DS longer attention to stimulus pattern; ND more differential fixation and greater responsiveness to stimuli of behavioral significance	

(*continued*)

Table 7. *(Continued)*

Behavior Studied	Sample: *n*, Age Type, Developmental Performance, etc.	Characteristics of Behavior: Delays Noted	Structure or Organization[a]	Developmental Sequence	Information Processing[b]	Author Comments
(Fantz et al., 1975)	n = 31 DS, 28 ND (variable numbers of Ss in each test session), followed from 5–33 weeks of age; matched on gestation, race, siblings, parent education; no visual deficits or other illnesses; all home reared; tested biweekly, at home	Most stimuli configurations (e.g., bull's eye vs. stripes, resolution of pairs of stripes, schematic faces) showed delays for DS, ranged from 2 weeks to 4 months; group differences greatest in later months	S	Changing preferences for one vs. another stimuli was noted once for ND but not for DS	Both look selectively at patterns with more elements, angles, and contours	Delays in development of selective attention may be indicative of retarded perceptual-cognitive development; some results suggested deficient utilization of experience
Recognition memory (Miranda & Fantz, 1974)	n = 28 DS (11F, 17M), 46 ND (18F, 28M); 3 CA age levels: 8–16 weeks (median 13), 17–29 weeks (median 24), 30–40 weeks (median 35 ND, median 37 DS); no oculomotor disorder or severe organic disease; Ss matched for sex, gestational age, age, parent education, siblings	Overall, delayed onset for novelty responses	S	S	At two older age groups, novelty preference shown by both groups; photographs looked at by oldest DS and two older ND groups; no DS group responded to element arrangement but two oldest ND groups did	DS have capacity to acquire, store, retrieve information at an early age; possible specific delay in form perception; differences not believed to be due to sensory or motor factors

(continued)

Table 7. (*Continued*)

Behavior Studied	Sample: n, Age Type, Developmental Performance, etc.	Characteristics of Behavior				
		Delays Noted	Structure or Organization[a]	Developmental Sequence	Information Processing[b]	Author Comments
Habituation (Cohen, 1981)	n = 8 DS, 8 ND; CA = 19, 23, 28 weeks; all Ss matched for age, sex, SES, and number of times tested	Habituation and dishabituation seen in DS at 28 weeks, whereas present at all three ages for ND	S	S	Number of habituation trials similar, but DS longer fixation times than ND	
Patterns of attention (Krakow & Kopp, 1982)	n = 16 DS, 40 ND (63% m)/(50% m); CA = $\bar{x}$ 29.2 months, 15.4 months; DA = $\bar{x}$ 59.4, 113.2; developmental age match = 17¾ months; all Ss home reared; vision normal or corrected	(Matched for DA)	S	S	No group differences in overall duration of engagement with toys; differences: DS show less socially oriented time, fewer monitoring glances to environment, more total time unoccupied, more stereotypic play	DS pattern reflects limited repertoire; data run counter to belief that DS are highly social, whether this reflects limitations in processing nuances of situation or effects of intervention or both is not clear

attending to, discriminating, and encoding subtle or complex signals. Because nuances are often lost to them, their own behavior reflects less richness than that of peers of the same developmental age. The data, albeit limited, also show that problems in handling complex stimuli increasingly appear during the last part of the 1st year. These problems continue into the 2nd and 3rd years of life as social and task demands begin to be placed on the child. Thus, congruent with longitudinal data (Carr, 1975; Dicks-Mireaux, 1972), during the first year the DS child begins to fall increasingly behind more normally developing peers and this is reflected in developmental performance patterns.

The interpretation that very young DS children have difficulty acquiring and communicating some types of information parallels findings derived from studies of older MR children. For example, Zeaman and House's (1963) classic studies of visual discrimination showed that MR individuals often had difficulty responding to relevant stimulus dimensions. Fagan's (1968) research on memory indicated that MR children had difficulty encoding material. Similarly, control strategies used by these children in memory tasks are deficient, but they are not absent (Campione & Brown, 1977; Spitz, 1979). Compared to normally developing children, MR children do less spontaneous rehearsal, organization of material, and elaboration; in addition, they do less monitoring of their own activities.

Although the data base is small, these parallels in restricted use of monitoring activities and simple strategies employed as learning supports (e.g., using parents as a source of approval or going to them for help) warrant additional study. They may further our understanding of the ways information is acquired and transmitted, and why developmental growth or delays occur. They may also foster our understanding of deceleration patterns that were described earlier. Being less responsive to the environment than their peers, DS infants may not have the same propulsion for accommodative change (Piaget, 1952, 1954) or incentives for psychological change (Kagan, Kearsley, & Zelazo, 1978). Accordingly, the dissolution of old forms of functioning (Vygotsky, translated by Zender & Zender, 1974) and the emergence of new forms (Kagan et al., 1978; Piaget, 1952, 1954) may take on an entirely different cast in DS. Thus, as Kopp and Parmelee (1979) speculated earlier, developmental transitions might not be as sharply defined for DS as for normally developing children.

The preceding discussion focused exclusively on behavioral attributes of DS infants; however, this review would be incomplete if reference was not made to interactional and communicative studies of DS infants and their parents.

In general, the first studies of handicapped and delayed infants and children suggested that parents of retarded and handicapped children were more directive and controlling and less contingent than parents of normally developing children (Jones, 1977; Kogan, 1980; Kogan & Gordon, 1975; Kogan & Tyler, 1973; Vietze, Abernathy, Ashe, & Faulstich, 1978). Subsequently, this research emphasis was modified as researchers asked if delays in language development of DS children reflected interactional deficiencies between the children and their parents or fundamental cognitive problems (Buium, Rynders, & Turnure, 1974). Parental limitations were implicated because the DS sample was exposed to increased parent utterances and imperatives and less grammatically complete sentences.

More recently, investigators, using a developmental approach that takes into account the level of the child's functioning, report different findings. Parents clearly adjust their interactions to the nature of the child's responsivity, irrespective of chronological age. When a DS child's developmental level of language-production is equated to that of a normally developing child, findings reveal that parents talk more and use more complex phrasing to developmentally older children than younger ones (Buckhalt, Rutherford, & Goldberg, 1978; Gunn, Clark, & Berry, 1980; Rondal, 1977). Finally, it is interesting to note that parents are able to produce spontaneously effective teaching strategies to help their DS children become more verbal, given information about stages of language development (Cheseldine & McConkey, 1979).

Despite this intuitively sensitive approach to parenting, interactions between DS children and their caregivers pose numerous problems that can be categorized around the issue of abnormality. As noted above and in Table 7, DS children do not give clearly interpretable signals, are often inattentive, show reduced levels of visual contact, exhibit "no space"[4] communication, and verbalize little (Emde & Brown, 1978; Jones, 1977; Krakow & Kopp, 1982; Markowitz, 1980; Stone & Chesney, 1978). Aside from the frustration this brings to parenting, it also fosters more talking and doing than might be manifested by parents of normal children. This probably does not reflect conscious desires to be controlling but rather attempts to propel the child to become more involved. This adaptive behavior has parallels to behaviors observed by Kaye (1979) in studies of normally developing infants and their mothers. He noted that mothers assume a major, often unilateral, role in controlling the state and behavior of their very young children. Kaye interpreted the behavior as reflecting maternal agendas that are geared toward promoting certain kinds of responses.

In sum, the findings reported for the development of DS suggests that in early life sequences and organization of behaviors that mirror structural aspects of the repertoire are by and large comparable for DS and normal children. Differences in handling information have been noted and linked to longitudinal findings. Support for this inference awaits empiric study.

Finally, it is clear that many of the cross-sectional studies that have been reported represent the training interests and biases of individual researchers. This is hardly surprising. However, the resultant research lacks cohesiveness and systematic frameworks. The fact is that a more unified approach toward studying DS infants could lead to fundamental research about the early development of children who *will be* retarded. It is highly likely that some of the findings will pertain *only* to DS. On the other hand, it is probably the case that elucidation of developmental processes will have relevance for other groups. The example set by Decarie (1969) is relevant to this purpose. The physical impairments of thalidomide children set them apart from motorically intact infants, yet the questions asked and the answers obtained furthered our overall understanding of sensorimotor development.

Preterm Birth

The risk condition of preterm birth (before 37 completed weeks of gestation)[5] offers compelling reasons why caution should underlie generalizations made about outcome. Preterm birth does not represent a homogeneous condition and long-term effects depend on any number of variables, including when and where the infant was born, its condition and size at birth, the nature of treatment that was provided, the quality and training of professional staff giving the treatment, economic resources of the family and local community, and the personal resources of the child's family.

Turning first to historical trends, mortality and morbidity data for preterms have shown marked variation in the last 60 to 70 years. From about 1920 or so onward, mortality trends show a linear decrease, whereas the course of morbidity findings show a curvilinear trend with initially low rates, then higher ones, and more recently, lower rates. Overall morbidity trends have to be inferred because most countries did not systematically record data of this kind. With this caveat in mind, reviews written about studies executed in the 1920s and 1940s reported that most surviving preterms did not show major sequelae and their intelligence was not inferior to full-terms. Albeit some behavioral and educational problems were noted (Benton, 1940; Beskow, 1949). During this same period, however, mortality was high for the sickest and tiniest infants, and there was minimal use of aggressive treatment techniques.

By the 1950s and into the 1960s, the picture had changed markedly. Longitudinal findings began to reveal disconcertingly high rates of cerebral palsy, major mental handicaps, or lesser intellectual deficits among surviving preterms (Drillien, 1964; Lubchenco, Horner, Reed, Hix, Metcalf, Cohig, Elliott, & Bourg, 1963; Wiener, 1962; Wright, Blough, Chamberlin, Ernest, Halstead, Meirer, Moore, Naughton, & Newell, 1972). Earlier findings regarding low morbidity were ignored because they were felt to be inaccurate or they were criticized because of sample shortcomings (Drillien, 1964). In retrospect, it is likely that the initial reviews accurately portrayed morbidity until the late 1940s. What occurred during the 1950s and early 1960s was the initiation of aggressive and often untested treatment regimes that were not always effective (Reynolds, 1978; Silverman, 1980), albeit an increase occurred in the number of very tiny infants who survived.

The changing modes of treatment have to be placed in context to understand why preterm birth began to be perceived as a very harmful stress to the infant. The treatment picture is complicated and somewhat obscure because a full historical account has yet to be written. Apparently, however, in the early part of the twentieth century, it was obstetricians who cared for newborns and obstetricians who controlled newborn nurseries (Parmelee, 1980). Pediatricians began to be consulted in the 1920s and 1930s and were routinely found in U.S. nurseries in the late 1940s (although not yet in British ones) (Douglas & Gear, 1976; Parmelee, 1980). But systematized training programs for pediatricians were just starting in the 1930s and were far from being well established even 10 to 15 years later (Hughes, 1980). Added to this factor was the dramatic growth in hospital units directed toward the care of the newborn and the introduction of technology into nurseries (Silverman, 1980). Transparent incubators, oxygen piped from a central source directly to incubators, airlocks for resuscitation were just some of the innovations (Silverman, 1980). So, at the time that many obstetricians moved away from the care of newborns, there were insufficient numbers of highly trained specialist pediatricians to take their place. The demand grew as hospitals were built. Most pediatricians did not have expertise in treating very sick tiny infants who teetered on the edge of survival and who had fragile central nervous systems and sensory organs. In discussing the role of English pediatricians with low birthweight infants, Davies (1976) noted, "theirs was not an instant success story. . . . Faced suddenly with the resuscitation at birth of very small infants, often done efficiently previously by anaesthetists or obstetricians, they did not cut dashing figures" (p. 91). The pediatricians, Davies (1976) continued, used intubation as a last resort and substituted modes of treatment that lacked physiological basis and actually harmed the infant. To compound matters, preterm infants were routinely kept at lower temperatures than they should have been, and they were frequently given too liberal dosages of drugs. The importance of preventing biochemical disturbances was not appreciated (Reynolds, 1978). Many preterm infants were seriously damaged by these practices or lack of them. Blindness, cerebral palsy, and mental retardation were found in thousands of children.

Silverman (1980) is just as critical of his American colleagues. In his book, *Retrolental Fibroplasia. A Modern Parable,* he deplored the rush to technology, lack of clinical trials, pressures to use new treatments touted by experts, exploitation of a confused situation by the media, and the attitudes that suggested accidents were the price of progress. Silverman's (1980) point of view may not be universally accepted, but his indictment of the forces that pushed pediatricians toward use of certain deleterious practices has implications for any professional group that provides treatment or care for children.

Several changes occurred that led to more adept care and lower morbidity. For example, a subspeciality arose in pediatrics in which a core of clinicians received specialized training in newborn care. This group, neonatologists, is now routinely found in newborn intensive care units. Many communities in this country and elsewhere introduced a hierarchical system of care in which routine births were treated in local facilities (primary care centers), whereas sick and high-risk infants and mothers were transported to regionalized care centers that had specialists and a high level of technology (tertiary care centers). Successful and unsuccessful modes of treatment began to be documented and evaluated and led to changes in care as appropriate (see Davies, 1976; Reynolds, 1978, Silverman, 1980). Research into physiology and biochemistry increased (Silverman, 1980).

From approximately midpoint in the 1960s, as new treatment modes were introduced, morbidity rates began to improve overall for preterm infants and the level of severe handicapping conditions dropped. (Lest the erroneous impression be given that all major problems have been solved, it is noted that striking a balance in treatment is still a concern, for example, too little oxygen and cerebral palsy occurs, too much oxygen and retrolental fibroplasia occurs. In the data to be reported in the next discussion, it may appear that this positive trend is leveling off for the very tiny infant (i.e., less than 1,500 g). An increasing number of these infants are being saved, often with forms of mechanical assistance; however, the morbidity rates for some samples are high (Britton, Fitzhardinge, Ashby, 1981; Ciba Foundation, 1978; Marriage & Davies, 1977; Pape & Fitzhardinge, 1981). Hagberg, Hagberg, and Olow (1982) have even noted a slight increase in cerebral palsy during the early part of the 1970s. Some problems arise in attempting to draw conclusions about general trends because many more studies of very tiny (often ventilated) infants currently exist than are available for larger preterm infants. Those few studies that are available show positive trends for the latter.[6]

During the time that iatrogenic causes of handicap were so prominent, there was little differentiation about individual factors that affected outcome. To be sure, the worst outcomes were found among the poorest (Drillien, 1964), but these were group trends that were reported. Slowly, additional perspectives began to appear indicating a far more complicated picture than the recent literature portrayed. Parmelee (Parmelee & Haber, 1973), for example, argued forcefully that preterms were not a homogeneous group and that conditions related to recurring and serious stresses would have a far greater impact upon development than just the fact of early birth. Thus, noting variation in health status was important.

Still others began to realize that outcome findings sometimes reflected the fact that investigators included in their samples infants who had major problems (e.g., chromosome anomaly) *not* attributed to preterm birth. This led to a more discriminating approach with respect to the kinds of infants included in follow-up studies. Infants with chromosomal or genetic conditions began to be excluded. Moreover, concerned attempts were made to classify infants by weight for gestational age (Neligan et al., 1976). Finally, of course, came the compelling argument that a biological risk could not be considered apart from the child's environment (Sameroff & Chandler, 1975). Given a poor environment, the chances for poor outcome were high; therefore, adequate documentation of sample background characteristics was essential.

The following review begins with an overview of longitudinal follow-up data reported on cohorts studied from 1965 onward and attempts to synthesize an exceedingly diverse set of follow-up studies. This is followed by presentation of cross-sectional and other types of behavioral studies, all of which pertain to the infancy period. This age group is examined because almost all older children have been studied in a longitudinal fashion with the traditional psychometric examinations or by school performance.

Longitudinal Follow-up Research. The last decade has been witness to an unprecedented number of longitudinal studies of preterms. Most are of relatively short duration and last into the child's early years, albeit one or two have followed the children into late childhood. The studies reviewed in Table 8 share in common the use of preterm subjects and the fact that they began in 1965 and after. Other than these similarities, the studies differ in enrollment of sick and well infants, types of treatment provided, range of included birthweights and gestational ages, size of samples, use of control or comparison groups, outcome measures employed, duration of follow-up period, explicit information about family background conditions. Some sample diversity is inevitable because a subtantial number of small infants had hyaline membrane disease or required mechanical ventilation. (Reynolds, 1978, reported approximately 50% for each condition.) In any event, a cautious approach to interpretation of outcome findings is essential.

Several trends are apparent and can be highlighted. First, as has been noted earlier and elsewhere (Davies, 1976; Davies & Stewart, 1975; Drillien, 1975), remarkable advances in intensive care technology, including careful monitoring of infant condition and improved means of temperature control and respiration therapy, have led to a reduction in severe sequelae. In some instances, the changes that were instituted were exceedingly well documented. For example, Prod'hom and Calâme (1978) noted that between 1961 and 1965 changes were introduced in feeding techniques and intravenous fluid therapy. During 1966 to 1968, better control of hypoxemia occurred, and in 1971 artificial ventilation began to be employed. In the last reported period of 1974–1975, the authors noted that "medical and nursing managements have not changed, but the techniques used were less aggressive to the infant" (p. 265).

Second, there is considerable variation in outcome as a function of type of infant treated (Hein & Brown, 1981; Pape & Fitzhardinge, 1981). Handicaps will be greatest among groups who are growth retarded, neurologically abnormal, or extremely immature (Pape & Fitzhardinge, 1981). As one example, some tertiary care centers that serve very sick and very tiny infants from a wide geographic locale show particularly grim statistics. Fitzhardinge, Kalman, Ashby, and Pape (1978) documented the course of 250 infants of less than 1,500-g birthweight who were referred to an intensive care unit in a tertiary care hospital (designated center for high-risk newborns). The center served 65 other community hospitals with transport time varying from 20 min. to 4 hr. Of entering newborns, 66% survived. Of these, 149 were followed to 2 years of age, with 30% showing signs of major handicapping conditions. Infants at the very highest risk for outcome were those who had intracranial hemorrhage, a finding reported by others, including an investigator from the 1940s (Beskow, 1949). Somewhat lower risk was found for those who were small for their gestational age and a still slightly lower risk for those born weighing less than 1,000 g.

Because a few other tertiary care centers report outcome data with relatively high percentages of adverse sequelae (Hunt, 1979; Kitchen et al., 1979, 1980)—although not as high as Fitzhardinge et al. (1978)—there is a concern about exercising heroic efforts to save damaged infants (Ciba Foundation, 1978). There is, in fact, some feeling that some very sick, tiny newborns actually represent damaged fetuses that under ordinary care would not have survived. There is agreement, however, that some improvement in the number of cases with severe retardation may come about by avoiding genetically high-risk pregnancies, improved antenatal surveillance, monitoring of labor, and excellent neonatal care (Alberman, 1978; Hagberg, 1978); a decline in the incidence of cerebral palsy should occur with the introduction and use of advanced perinatal techniques (Ciba Foundation, 1978).

Not all tertiary care or specialized centers show such adverse outcomes. As shown in Table 8, findings suggest that severe handicapping conditions have occurred in 10% to 15% of samples, a finding reported in other reviews. Specifically, longitudinal studies of preterms born in the mid-1960s indicate severe neurological or intellectual sequelae for about 15% of their total samples and in the 1970s about 10% (see reviews of Davies & Stewart, 1975; Kopp & Parmelee, 1979; Stewart, Turcan, Rowlings, Hart, & Gregory, 1979). For the most part, these samples included infants at 37 weeks or less and a range of birthweights from 2,500 g downward.

Table 8. Annotations of Preterm Follow-up Studies with Part or All of Cohorts Born 1965 or Later

Authors	Follow-up Sample[a]	Length of Follow-up	Outcome Findings[b]	Comments
I. Samples: ≤ 2,500 g, ≤ 37 weeks				
Bakeman & Brown, 1980; Brown & Bakeman, 1980	Cohort born 1975: n = 26 PT, BW x̄ 1627 g (205), GA x 32.4 weeks (4.4); n = 23 FT. All infants healthy, without neurological or physical abnormalities. All infants black; maternal age, education, income comparable	3 years	1. IQ: PT = 81.5 (12.4), FT = 94.5 (14.2) 2. No group differences found for social competence or social participation	No indication of AGA[c] or SGA
Caputo, Goldstein, & Taub, 1979; Taub, Goldstein, & Caputo, 1977	Cohort born 1965 and later: n = 137 premature, singleton and twin births, BW 1,400–2,500 g; n = 96 nonpremature. Multiethnic, SES primarily middle class, mixed parity. Follow-up study begun in early 1970s: n = 38, premature; n = 26, nonprematures	7–9½ years	1. IQ: PT, full scale, M (Male) = x̄ 100.6, F (Female) = x̄ 100.2; verbal, M = x̄ 101.6, F = x̄ 103.2; performance, M = x̄ 99.7, F = x̄ 96. FT, full scale, M = x̄ 110, F = x̄ 106.8; verbal, M = x̄ 106.1, F = x̄ 106.1; performance M = x̄ 112.4, F = x̄ 105.2 2. 3 of 7 WISC-R subscales show significant differences between PT and FT. Overall performance scale significantly differed 3. Significant differences in Visual Motor Gestalt Test	No indication of AGA or SGA. Social class factor significantly related to IQ; BW significantly related to performance IQ

Notes: [a]Samples varied considerably; details are provided as possible.
[b]Outcomes do not necessarily reflect the same indices, particularly for handicaps, mental retardation, and so on. Where possible, details are provided.
[c]AGA = appropriate-for-gestational-age; SGA = small-for-gestational-age.
[d]PT = preterm; BW = birthweight; GA = gestational age; FT = full-term.

Table 8. (*Continued*)

Authors	Follow-up Sample[a]	Length of Follow-up	Outcome Findings[b]	Comments
			4. No group differences in personal-social behavior, social history, school functioning	
Drillien et al., 1980	Cohort born 1966–1970: *n* = 261. 31% ≤ 1,500 g, 69% 1,501–2,000 g. *n* = 111 control children selected from local schools	Birth to 7 years	1. IQ: PT = 101, FT = 106; variation in scores by social class, range of 19 points for PT, 26 points for FT 2. Handicapping conditions: ≤ 1,500 g = 14%, 1,501–2,000 g = 12%; M, 14%, F, 10%. Greater % in SGA than AGA 3. Additive impairment score: poorest scores for lowest BW children with abnormal neurologic status or adverse factors in early pregnancy	
Escalona, 1980, 1982	Cohort born 1975–1976: *n* = 114; BW < 2250 g, GA 4 weeks premature; 70 AGA, 27 SGA (at 7 months); 50% black, 25% Hispanic, 25% Caucasian; 20% below poverty income, 33% on welfare (at any one time), 25% middle class	Birth to 3½ years	1. $\bar{x}$ IQ at 40 months (*n* = 97), 89.3 (17.2), range 66 to 114 2. 26% of low SES quartile scored less than 70 IQ at 40 months 3. No differences found in 40-month test between AGA and SGA 4. Psychological maladjustment noted in 27 children at 40 months. Their IQ scores were 81 in contrast to 92.5 for adjusted group	Findings reported exclude severely delayed children (< 75 at 7 months of age). Maladjustment defined as prolonged behavior problems reported by family and judged significant by psychiatric criteria

(*continued*)

Table 8. (*Continued*)

Authors	Follow-up Sample[a]	Length of Follow-up	Outcome Findings[b]	Comments
Nelson, 1979	Cohort period unstated: $n = 45$ premature, BW ≤ 2,500 g. Singletons. SGA excluded. Multiethnic, primarily low SES, 10% teenage mothers	18 months for some of the sample	1. Developmental: MDI[e] = 99.9 (9.1), PDI[f] = 97.3 (11.4) 2. Subgroups: ≤ 1,500 g ($n = 28$); MDI = 93.9 (20.1), PDI = 92.4 (19.6); BW = 1,500–2,500 g ($n = 17$); MDI = 83.9 (25.0), PDI = 81.6 (24.4)	Author speculates that necessity for respiratory ventilation may have to do with 1,500–2,500 g group scores
Sabel, Olegård, & Victorin, 1976	3-year follow-up of 6,700 nonselected infants born in Swedish hospital, 1969–1970. At 3 years of age, 6,596 children were alive	3 years	1. BW ≤ 1,500 g ($n = 17$), no severe motor or mental handicaps 2. BW 1,501–2,000 g —13% rate of severe sequelae (2, slight hemiparesis; 2, severe diplegia; 1, severe diplegia & mental retardation; 1, sensorineural deafness with hearing aid	
Sigman & Parmelee, 1979	Cohort born 1971–1972: $n = 126$ (99) preterm ≤ 37 weeks, BW ≤ 2,500 g. Multiethnic, mixed SES, mixed parity. $n = 29$, FT	2 years	1. Developmental: MDI = 97.5 (20.4), range 50–159, 15% < 80 2. Subset: high risk vs. low risk; MDI high = ($n = 61$), 93.59 (19.30); low = ($n = 65$), 101.15 (20.96) 3. Highest MDI scores obtained by high SES, English-speaking firstborn, lowest by low SES, Spanish-speaking later-born; range 29 points	Sample excluded children with major anomalies; AGA and SGA analyzed together. Predictive analyses showed prediction better for F than M, English-speaking than Spanish-speaking subjects

[e]MDI = Bayley scales: mental development index.
[f]PDI = Bayley scales: psychomotor development index.
[g]HMD = hyaline membrane disease.
[h]DQ = developmental quotient.

Table 8. (Continued)

Authors	Follow-up Sample[a]	Length of Follow-up	Outcome Findings[b]	Comments
Sostek et al., 1979	Cohort born 1976, 1977: n = 118 high-risk prematures and FTs. Infants with chromosomal anomalies excluded, infants with congenital malformations included. Infants separated into groups by type of birth, health status, central nervous system involvement, also subdivided by ventilation treatment. Multiethnic, SES	9 months; range from x̄ 4.2 months to x̄ 9.4 months	1. FT ill infants scored highest on developmental test (MDI) and PT ill with central nervous system signs scored lowest; range 35 points	No indication of GA variation by group, or comparability of central nervous system involvement for samples
Stewart, Turcan, Rawlings, Hart, & Gregory, 1978	Cohort born 1966–1976: BW ≤ 1,500 g; n = 259 (follow-up), x̄ BW 1,236 g, x̄ GA 30 weeks; BW 1,501–2,500 g; n = 124; BW 1,000 g with HMD[g], n = 123	18 months to 8 years	1. BW ≤ 1,500 g: (a) 8.5% (n = 22) significantly handicapped (1.5% cerebral palsy, 1.5% < 70 DQ[h], 4% multiple handicaps). No significant differences in incidence of handicap between inborn and transfer infants, AGA and SGA, or 500–1,000 g and 1,001–1,500 g. Significant differences between children who required ventilation and those who did not. Handicaps in ventilated group were associated with respiratory failure in conjunction with abnormal central nervous system signs, perinatal	40% of ≤ 1,500 g infants died in first 28 days of life, 6% more died by 2 years. Illness associated with convulsions made biggest perinatal contribution to DQ in multiple regression analysis. No information about social class or ethnic factors

(continued)

Table 8. (*Continued*)

Authors	Follow-up Sample[a]	Length of Follow-up	Outcome Findings[b]	Comments
			asphyxia, or apnoeic spells. (b) IQ: 12% of children over 3 years in 1966–1971 group had scores below 84. At 8 years, 18% had minor problems in handicaps requiring additional help in school, 6% attended special schools 2. 1973 cohort of 1,501–2,500 g at 18 months showed no major handicaps 3. 1970–1976 cohort of mechanically ventilated infants at 18 months showed 6% with major handicaps	
II. Samples: ≤ 1,500 g				
Alden et al., 1972	Cohort 1965–1970: $n = 20$ surviving infants, BW < 1,000 g	Birth to 6 years	1. During infancy, 12 infants had normal DQs, 6 had "high abnormal abnormal to borderline" (70–89), and 2 with congenital defects were severely retarded 2. 5 infants have retrolental fibroplasia, 3 minimal spasticity, 2 have congenital	88% mortality in original sample of 161
Bethenod, Bourgeois, Sann, Cottancin, Riegal, Fau, Vachet, & Saumir, 1979	Cohort 1967–1976: $n = 40$ surviving preterms, < 1,001 g	1 to 10 years	1. Overall 85.7% showed no neurologic sequelae and 70% (of 31 tested) showed IQ > 80	Overall mortality rate was 71.2%

Table 8. *(Continued)*

Authors	Follow-up Sample[a]	Length of Follow-up	Outcome Findings[b]	Comments
			2. IQ scores for oldest children are lower than scores for younger children. Of *tested* children, x̄ scores are: 1967 (n = 4) IQ = 83; 1968 (n = 5) IQ = 95; 1969 (n = 4) IQ = 105; 1970 (n = 6) IQ = 85; 1972 (n = 1) IQ = 107; 1973 (n = 4) IQ = 109; 1974 (n = 2) IQ = 72, 100; 1976 (n = 4) IQ = 92. 3. Many psychoaffective problems were noted	
Britton et al., 1982	Cohort 1974–1977 n = 38 surviving infants, BW < 801 g	2 years	1. 22% had severe handicap (DQ < 70, neurological problems, etc.); 27% had moderate handicap (DQ 70–84, mild cerebral palsy, seizures) 2. Delayed speech common 3. Health problems continued into 2nd year 4. No differences found for AGA and SGA groups 5. Poor outcome for infants with asphxyia, apnea, < 700 g	n = 158 transferred infants from a wide geographic area, 91% admitted within 12 hours of birth; 119 died in NICU
Davies, 1975; Davies & Tizard, 1975	Cohort 1961–1970: BW ≤ 1,500 g (Hammersmith subset)	Middle childhood (varying ages)	1. (a) 1961–1964 cohort: 7 children with cerebral palsy; 3.4% each visual, hearing, and minor neurological problems (b) 32% of AGA had IQ over 100	Infants born at hospital or admitted soon after birth. Sample included in later group had increased food intake in first week and better maintenance of body temperature. No correction for PT birth

(continued)

Table 8. (*Continued*)

Authors	Follow-up Sample[a]	Length of Follow-up	Outcome Findings[b]	Comments
			2. (a) 1965–1968: no cerebral palsy; 1.9% with visual, 2.8% with hearing, 4.8% with minor neurological problems (b) 62% of AGA had IQ over 100	
Francis-Williams, & Davies, 1974	Cohort born 1961–1968: n = 120. BW ≤ 1,500 g (Hammersmith subset)	4–12 years	1. *Full-scale IQ:* (a) AFD (n = 72) = 99.2, SFD (n = 33) = 99.2.[i] (b) No relationship between IQ and BW or GA, or IQ and neonatal illness. (c) Differences in the mean IQ and social class are highly significant. (d) IQ and sex was significant with Ms averaging higher scores than Fs. (e) 7 children had IQs below 70, 5 were SFD 2. *Verbal vs. performance IQs:* As many as ⅕ of the children had a performance IQ 15 points or more below verbal 3. *Reading tests:* The group of children born 1965–1968 were superior over the group born 1961–1964	No correction for PT births. Infants born at hospital or admitted shortly after birth

[i]AFD = appropriate-for-dates; SFD = small-for-dates.

Table 8. (*Continued*)

Authors	Follow-up Sample[a]	Length of Follow-up	Outcome Findings[b]	Comments
Hunt, 1979, 1981	Cohort period 1965–1978: (follow-up ongoing) 173 infants < 1,500 g	8 years (103 tested at 2,3 years; 72 at 4–6 years, 30 at 8 years)	1. Most data reported are for 4–6-year-olds. IQ ranged from 52 to 140; 14% had scores below 68. 14% of children with IQ scores 68–83 "had definite disabilities," 18% with IQs in normal range "had definite disabilities" 2. 4 children with scores below 60 were born before 1969 3. Of 29 children with HMD, 65.5% had handicaps; of those without, 32.6% had handicaps 4. Precise prediction from infancy to childhood for individual cases was problematic even for extreme cases	Information about GA, social class, and ethnicity not provided
Kitchen et al., 1979, 1980	Cohort 1966–1970: n = 158 very low BW infants 1,000–1,500 g (74 received routine care, 84 received intensive care). n = 43 normal BW children entered in latter phases of study. Children were primarily low SES	8 years	1. No statistically significant differences between intensive and routine care for handicaps and disabilities 2. Significantly more profound or severe handicaps in intensive care group (17 vs. 6)	This study was in part a controlled clinical trial of neonatal intensive care in Melbourne, Australia. Authors note their test data "compares unfavourably" with other recent findings, suggest may be due to very low BW and poor social conditions. Correction made for PT birth

(*continued*)

Table 8. (*Continued*)

Authors	Follow-up Sample[a]	Length of Follow-up	Outcome Findings[b]	Comments
			3. Full scale IQ = 89, range < 50 to > 110. Less than 10% of routine care, and approximately 15% of intensive care had IQs < 70; IQ by BW: < 1,000 g (n = 10)-full-scale 79.4 (15.7), verbal 76.4 (17.6), performance 85.1 (16.7); 1,000–1,500 g (n = 143)-full-scale 89.4 (15.7), verbal 90.1 (17.8), performance 90.3 (15.1); normal BW (n = 43)-full-scale 98.8 (15.7), verbal 96.2 (15.9), performance 102.7 (16.7) 4. 10.1% had serious residual disabilities (e.g., IQ < 69, or deafness); 37.3% had significant but lesser degrees of abnormality (e.g., IQ < 84, reading delay, visual problems, etc.); 41.8% had a reasonably satisfactory outcome but, of this group, ⅓ are at risk for future educational difficulties 5. Reading ability: 39.7% not retarded, 44.4% retarded 1–17 months, 12.6% retarded > 17 months, 3.3%	

Table 8. (*Continued*)

Authors	Follow-up Sample[a]	Length of Follow-up	Outcome Findings[b]	Comments
			testing precluded by handicap; no significant differences with comparison group 6. 4.7% of children handicapped or disadvantaged by unfavorable family circumstances could not attend normal school	
Koops & Harmon, 1980	Cohorts born 1975 and later: ≤ 1,500 g, n = 160, all referrals to neonatal center; n = 166 referrals to perinatal center (in utero transport). Follow-up samples, n = 95, n = 60 respectively	8–23 months	1. Moderate/severe psychomotor retardation in 29% of infants in both groups 2. Moderate to severe neuromotor handicap in about ⅓ of each group	Survival rate was 75% for neonatal center, 68% for perinatal center
Pape, Buncie, Ashley, & Fitzhardinge, 1978	Cohort born 1974: BW ≤ 1,000 g, GA 24–32 weeks (27.7); n = 46 (17M, 29F) (Toronto subset)	2 years	1. Major neurologic defects, 9%; minor neurologic defects, 37% 2. Retrolental fibroplasia (16%) 3. Developmental status: $\bar{x}$ MDI—80.2 (24.8), $\bar{x}$ PDI—80.9 (21.7)	53% mortality. Neonatal diagnosis of intracranial hemorrhage or seizures was strongly correlated with severe abnormalities. No relationship could be demonstrated between DQ and SES. Complications of pregnancy or delivery, asphyxia, RDS[j], apnea or prolonged ventilation not specifically linked with later defects. The BWs of the handicapped infants were significantly lower than the rest of the sample

(*continued*)

Table 8. (*Continued*)

Authors	Follow-up Sample[a]	Length of Follow-up	Outcome Findings[b]	Comments
Prod'hom & Calâme, 1978	3 cohort periods: 1966–1968; 1971–1973; 1974–1975. n = 57, 41, 56. BW ≤ 1,500 g (1966 cohort retrospective, 1971 & 1974 prospective)	2 years	1. Sequelae for 1966 cohort showed 1.7% with cerebral palsy, 3.5% blind, 24.6% with DQ/IQ less than 80; 1971 cohort figures are 4.9, 2.4, and 4.9 respectively	Neonatal center in Lausanne admits all high-risk newborns and receives about 7% of the 5,000–7,000 deliveries per year. 40% of infants are born in the university hospital; others come from locals of varying proximities. No SES data provided. Authors emphasize only major sequelae are reported
Ruiz et al., 1981	Cohort 1976–1978: n = 38 infants, BW < 1,001 g (range 680 to 990 g)	1 year	1. 53% of sample developing normally; 21% had minor problems 2. Ventilated infants (n = 20) had significantly poorer outcome than nonventilated infants 3. n = 4 with severe RLF 4. n = 10 with severe handicaps, n = 7 with multiple handicaps, n = 3 with severe neurologic impairment or marked delay	35% of 134 infants survived neonatal period. Inborn and transfer infants in sample

Table 8. (*Continued*)

Authors	Follow-up Sample[a]	Length of Follow-up	Outcome Findings[b]	Comments
Siegel et al., undated	Cohort period: 1975–1976: n = 80, < 1,500 g. AGA and SGA separated. n = 68 FTs matched for sex, parity, SES, and maternal age	2 years	1. Overall sequelae: 12.5% PT were blind, had cerebral palsy, or severe developmental delay. 2. Percent of specific language delays: AGA singleton: 29%; SGA singleton: 14%	Data reported with and without age corrections
Teberg et al., 1982	Cohort period 1973–1975: n = 178, ≤ 1,500 g seen for follow-up (represents almost 75% of sample). n = 23, ≤ 1,000 g, n = 155, 1,001–1,500 g; 26% SGA. Mexican-Americans, 61%, blacks, 25%, Caucasians, 12%	1–3 years	1. No differences in neurological outcomes for smaller vs. larger infants. Higher incidence of problems for infants who required ventilation 2. Developmental: normal (MDI > 85) 66%, suspect (MDI 75–84) 18%, abnormal (MDI < 75) 16%. A greater number of ventilated infants had abnormal DQs than nonventilated. No differences in scores for AGA and SGA 3. Visual impairment in 8% (severe in 2+%); middle ear obstruction in 24%	Hospital serves low-income area in Los Angeles and averages very high number of births per year (in 1980, approximately 12,000). Outcome data not reported by social-class levels

(*continued*)

Table 8. (*Continued*)

Authors	Follow-up Sample[a]	Length of Follow-up	Outcome Findings[b]	Comments
III. Samples: Respiratory problems, ventilated, resuscitated, etc.; birthweights vary				
Field, Dempsey, & Shuman, 1979	Study 1: Cohort born 1972–1973: n = 21 RDS, GA x̄ 32 weeks, BW x̄ 1,700 g, x̄ 2.6 days negative pressure respiration, x̄ 37 days hospitalization; n = 21 matched controls, GA 39 weeks, BW x̄ 3,300 g. Mixed sex, parity, primarily middle class	4 years	1. Stanford-Binet, Vineland showed no significant group differences 2. Significant group differences on behavior problem checklist and number of signs of minimal brain dysfunction 3. 24% hearing deficits and language-production delays	Subjects were matched by postconceptional age
	Study 2: Cohort born 1975: n = 21 RDS, GA x̄ 32 weeks, BW x̄ 1,000 g, 2.9 days positive pressure ventilation; 44 days hospitalization; n = 21, matched controls, GA 40 weeks, BW x̄ 3,300 g	2 years	1. Bayley MDI and PDI scores: PT-RDS 95.38 (17.45), 89.90 (16.77); controls 105.72 (14.28), 104.21 (17.23) 2. Significant mean group differences in social maturity, behavior problems, and minimal brain dysfunction favoring controls	Subjects were matched by postconceptional age

[j]RDS = respiratory distress syndrome.

Table 8. (*Continued*)

Authors	Follow-up Sample[a]	Length of Follow-up	Outcome Findings[b]	Comments
Fisch, Bilek, Miller, & Engel, 1975	Cohort born 1959–1966: Singleton births only. Of 280 infants born with respiratory distress syndrome, *n* = 58 survivors evaluated at 4 years. From pool of 35,198 normal control infants, each RDS infant was matched with 5 controls on hospital of birth, BW, SES, gestation, race, *n* = 290. Three subgroups: < 1,501 g, 1,501–2,500 g, > 2,500 g	4 years	1. Neurological evaluation: At 1 year RDS group had significantly more neurological abnormalities than unmatched controls in the two upper BW groups; by 4 years, convergence in the incidence of abnormal neuromotor performances of RDS group and unmatched controls for lower two BWs. 2. Psychologic evaluation at 4 years: Majority of RDS group were capable of normal psychomotor performance. IQ: < 1,501 g, RDS 83.4, control 83.4; 1,501–2,500 g, RDS 92.5, control 93; > 2,500 g, RDS 93; control 100.9. Weight group of > 2,500 g had significantly more psychomotor abnormalities than either controls 3. SES: Difference in median IQ score for children from the highest and lowest SES group is 30 points for matched controls and 43 points for RDS group	Majority did not receive ventilatory assistance. 81 infants of original 280 survived first year.

(*continued*)

Table 8. (*Continued*)

Authors	Follow-up Sample[a]	Length of Follow-up	Outcome Findings[b]	Comments
Fitzhardinge, Papel, Arstikoitis, Boyle, Ashby, Rowley, & Netley, 1976	Cohort born 1970–1973: *n* = 75, 36M, 39F. BW < 1,501 g. 3M, 7F were SGA; 3M, 10F < 1,000 g All had mechanical ventilation. Social class varied (Toronto subset)	2 years	1. Central nervous system sequelae at 2 years: (a) 14 Ms, 7 Fs had major neurologic defects; (b) 17 children had minor deviations in muscle tone, tendon reflexes hyperactivity, and short attention span; (c) 3 children had seizures 2. 1 year Bayley x̄ MDI = 93.5; 29 scored less than 80; no significant differences by sex, AGA or SGA, pulmonary vs. respiratory illness. Significant difference in MDIs between high-risk pregnancy and normal pregnancy outcomes (90.7 vs. 106); and between children with and without major neurologic defect (73.6 vs. 101.7)	Tertiary care center. All patients were referred initially because of neonatal illness or size. Immediate postnatal care varied considerably, as did transport time to hospital. Age corrections made for prematurity. "Sample . . . by no means represents a normal group of low-birth-weight infants"
Harrod, L'Heureux, Wangensteen, Hunt, & Long, 1974	Cohort born 1970–1971: *n* = 22 surviving infants with RDS. Infants treated with intermittent positive pressure. BW: x̄ 2.07 kg (1.07 to 3.44), GA: 30 to 41 weeks	Variable to 5 years	1. Developmental assessment: 15 normal, 7 had developmental difficulties (e.g., failure of gross motor on screening examination, immature attention span, language retardation); of these 1 had significant problems	

Table 8. (Continued)

Authors	Follow-up Sample[a]	Length of Follow-up	Outcome Findings[b]	Comments
Hommers & Kendall, 1976	Cohort born 1973–1974 < 1,500 g; resuscitation, intubation, massage, sodium bicarbonate, etc. n = 59, 1973; n = 44, 1974; 21% SGA, n = 42 follow-up	9–31 months	1. DQ = x̄ 102, range 77 to 120 2. No major handicaps, one mild hemiplegia 3. Presence of adverse social factors, x̄ DQ = 99, no adverse social factors, x̄ DQ = 104	Mortality: no survivors < 500 g, 21% 501–1,000 g, 65% 1,001–1,500 g
Johnson, Malachowski, Grobstein, Welsh, Daily & Sunshine, 1974	Cohort born September 1962–July 1969: 196 infants ventilated; 66 survived, n = 55, long-term survivors. BW 870–4,337, x̄ 2,319; GA 26–40, x̄ 34.6. (Mechanical ventilation used)	2.8–9.7 years, x̄ 5.7 years	1. Sequelae: 10% had abnormalities of general neurologic function; 11% spasticity; minor problems 8% 2. Sensory problems: hearing loss 10%; visual: blind, 2%; strabismus and refraction error 26% 3. Severe disorders, 4%; EEG abnormalities, 32% 4. Severe handicaps: 50% of 1,500 g, 14% of 1,501–2,000 g, 18% of 2,001–2,500 g, 6% of 2,500 g	Highest mortality among < 1,500 g
Marriage & Davies, 1977	Cohort born 1966–1973: n = 77 surviving infants who received mechanical ventilation. BW: 840–5,340 g. GA 27–40 weeks (Hammersmith subset)	2–9 years	1. Neurological abnormality: of 73 children tested, 11 had neurological problems: 3 with BW ≤ 1,500 g, 6 1,501–2,500 g, 2 > 2,500 g 2. Significant association of seizures in the early neonatal period with other abnormal neurological signs	77% transferred to Hammersmith hospital

(*continued*)

Table 8. (*Continued*)

Authors	Follow-up Sample[a]	Length of Follow-up	Outcome Findings[b]	Comments
			3. Overall neurological sequelae is 15%, compared to eight other studies of mechanically ventilated infants where sequelae ranged from 4% to 30% (median 16–17%)	
Minkowski, Amiel-Tison, Cukier, Dreyfus-Brisac, Reber, & Bethman, 1977	Two cohort periods, 1967–1970, 1973–1974: All with HMB. (1) 1967–1970: n = 79 infants survived without ventilation. n = 99 with ventilation (n = 80 long-term survivors). BW: ≤ 1,500 g, 33%; GA: < 37 weeks, 93%. (2) 1973–1974: n = 84 survived with ventilation (follow-up, n = 50). BW: < 1,500 g, 18%; GA < 37 weeks, 81%. About ⅔ of survivors were M; ¼ were multiple births	Cohort (1) 4–6 years Cohort (2) 1–2 years	1. Tone and motor abnormalities; 1967–1970: normal 41.5%; transitory abnormalities to 18 months 35%; post 18 months persistent abnormalities 24% of which 15% were major. Figures for 1973–1974 are 60%, 23.6%, 16.3%, 5.5% respectively 2. Major defects (hydrocephalus, seizures, DQ < 70, etc.) 1967–1970: 36.7%; 1973–1974: 20.2% 3. Minor defect (strabismus, mild to moderate motor abnormalities, DQ 70 to 90, etc.). 1967–1970: 58.2%, 1973–1974: 45.6% 4. DQ: 1967–70, > 90: 63.5%, 70 to 90 = 30%, < 70 = 8.75%; 1973–1974, > 90 = 76%, 70 to 90 = 20%, < 70 = 4%	In first cohort, 44.5% died, in second, 42% died. HMD was graded as to severity. Age correction employed. No family or demographic information provided

Table 8. ***(Continued)***

Authors	Follow-up Sample[a]	Length of Follow-up	Outcome Findings[b]	Comments
Outerbridge & Stern, 1972	n = 84. BW = 1,050–4,360 g. GA: 27–42 weeks. All had respiratory failure in the newborn period requiring support with negative pressure; 74 had RDS	1–6 years	1. Sequelae: 16% show abnormal neurological functioning; 1 child has retrolental fibroplasia 2. Developmental: 45 children > 24 months of age evaluated: 20 were slow, 17 of these only in speech development 3. 4 of 5 five-year-old children previously considered to be slow later showed normal speech and IQs: 11/12 children > 5 years have IQs in normal range	Age correction used. Authors believe data to be encouraging and children will ultimately have the potential to lead useful and rewarding lives in society
Stahlman, Hedvall, Dolanski, Faxelius, Burko, & Kirk, 1973	Cohort born 1961–1966: n = 85 infants who had clinical HMB. 21 required ventilation during acute phase. Control: 29 siblings, over 2 years and 2,500 g BW	6 years	1. Developmental and emotional status: mean DQs of infants with BW < 2,000 is lower than DQs of infants > 2,000; DQs differed according to educational level and occupation	No correction for prematurity. Most infants of less than 1,500 g BW who required assisted ventilation died during these years. Size was, thus, a large determinant of survival in all respirator infants

However, the fact that outcomes are most severe for very sick, very low birthweight infants who require assistance support Parmelee's (Parmelee & Haber, 1973) contention that within-group health differences have developmental implications. However, as Parmelee and his associates' data revealed (Littman, 1979; Sigman & Parmelee, 1979), many serious perinatal events and medical risks were not associated with deleterious outcomes. Indeed, social-class factors were more important for child outcome to age 2 years than were perinatal factors.

Third, the environmental correlates of social class continue to have an impact on the development of preterms; unfortunately, however, many samples are still poorly delineated with respect to background and environmental variables. This is an especially pressing omission because preterm birth and deleterious outcome have long been linked to variations in family conditions (Benton, 1940; Birch & Gussow, 1970; Drillien, 1964; Sameroff & Chandler, 1975). In the current studies, as much as 30 points separates the intellectual performance of advantaged and disadvantaged children and often outweighs effects owing to preterm birth.

Fourth, there is still a tendency to report data primarily focused on group performance with little attention paid to within-group variability. It is virtually impossible to identify important mediating outcome influences for children who have specific kinds of characteristics, who have received specialized kinds of treatments, and who are reared in certain conditions. Some attempts have been made by examining the relationship of birthweight, gestational age, and neonatal illness to DQ or IQ, and also by reporting outcome by sex and social class (Fisch, Bilck, Miller, & Engel, 1975; Francis-Williams & Davies, 1974; Pape, Buncie, Ashby, & Fitzhardinge, 1978; Sigman & Parmelee, 1979). None of the neonatal relationships proved to be significant. Francis-Williams and Davies (1974) also provided data for small-for-dates and appropriate-for-dates groups that turned out to be an important distinction in their sample. The Infant Studies Project findings (Sigman & Parmelee, 1979) also furnished evidence of within-group differences as a function of SES, language spoken in the home, and ordinality of the child. Later born children who were from low SES, Spanish-speaking families scored 29 points lower on the MDI than firstborn, high-SES children from English-speaking families.

Review of the literature suggests that additional specificity about factors that carry weight for individual outcome should occur when the following characteristics and conditions are systematically examined: type and quality of care provided in hospital settings (Prod'hom & Calâme, 1978; Stanley & Alberman, 1978), the size and health status of infants in the sample (Ambrus, Weintraub, Niswander, Fischer, Fleishman, Bross, & Ambrus, 1970; Fisch et al., 1975; Fitzhardinge et al., 1978; Grigoroiv-Serbanescu, 1981; Hunt, 1979; Johnson et al., 1974; Kitchen et al., 1979, 1980; Minkowski et al., 1977; Ounsted, Moar, & Scott, 1982; Sostek et al., 1979), inborn versus transfer status (Britton, Fitzhardinge, & Ashby, 1981; Davies, 1976), delineation of sample characteristics by whether weight was appropriate for gestational age (Francis-Williams & Davies, 1974; Neligan et al., 1976; Pape et al., 1978), early versus late period of prenatal stress (Drillien, Thomson, & Burgoyne, 1980; Parkinson, Wallis, & Harvey, 1981), and measures of family background (Fisch et al., 1975; Francis-Williams & Davies, 1974; Kitchen et al., 1980; Sigman & Parmelee, 1979).

Each of the above has been implicated in outcome, but no researcher has included all of these variables in analyses. It may be that the only way to achieve this kind of integrated approach is for several researchers to combine their subject pool to create one very large sample. Use of sophisticated analytic techniques could be employed to reduce irrelevant variance.

Finally, analysis of the findings in Table 8 yields insufficient evidence to support or refute earlier findings about untoward numbers of educational difficulties experienced by children, particularly males, who were born preterm (Caputo & Mandell, 1970; Davies & Stewart, 1975; Parkinson et al., 1981; Rubin, Rosenblatt, & Balow, 1973). Differences in functioning on performance versus verbal portions of intelligence tests were reported by both Francis-Williams and Davies (1974) and Caputo and his co-workers (Caputo, Goldstein, & Taub, 1979, 1981). The former reported 20% of the sample had this discrepancy, whereas no indication about proportions was given by the latter. Whether or not this factor actually exists currently and is independent of specific adverse family characteristics is as yet unknown. Moreover, the overall relationships postulated between perinatal complications and school problems are not strong and are unclear (Rubin & Balow, 1977). The fact that this inconclusive situation exists has ramifications for cross-sectional research. As will be seen in the following discussion, several recent studies are predicated on the fact that preterms as a group have difficulty with information processing skills. But the proposed relation is by no means well documented.

Summarizing the above and the data in Table 8, it appears that:

1. As a group, with all weights averaged together, preterm infants of this generation show less serious sequelae and higher intelligence test scores than cohorts of a generation ago.
2. Healthy, heavier infants show less untoward sequelae when contrasted to lighter and sicker infants.
3. Group trends are reported with little emphasis on individual variability.
4. School problems continue to be found in a percentage of children, but the contributors of these have not been teased out.
5. Studies have differed markedly in outcome measures, definition of normality and abnormality, descriptions of subjects, and provision of background information. There seems to have been little attempt to utilize more uniform measures.
6. Environmental contributors to risk have rarely been spelled out but, where they are given, a substantial difference in performance is found between advantaged and disadvantaged children.

Cross-sectional and Short-term Longitudinal Studies. Given that the risk for mortality and morbidity increase with lower birthweights and younger gestational ages, researchers have grappled with attempts to define more precisely the characteristics of infants born early. One of the first questions asked centered on performance as a consequence of having additional extrauterine experience rather than intrauterine experience. Gesell and Amatruda (1941) and later Saint-Anne Dargassies (1966) asked this question about visual responsiveness. Both investigators reported heightened attentiveness by preterms tested at their term dates, but this response pattern was short-lived and, in a matter of weeks, terms and preterms were similar.

The issue of group differences has been addressed more vigorously in recent years. This interest was spurred by the findings of the 1950s and 1960s that showed that some preterms had later intellectual problems. Therefore, it was assumed that performance in early life would reflect some of these difficulties. Three themes of contemporary research can be identified. The first started about 15 to 20 years ago and focused upon neurophysiological and behavioral differences primarily found in the newborn period. Some of this emphasis extends to current studies. The second focus started with the seminal studies of Leifer, Leiderman, Barnett, and Williams (1972) who reported that mothers of preterm infants who were separated from them in the newborn nursery had more family problems later on than mothers who had newborn contacts. Subsequent studies explored variations of this, looking for evidence of enduring effects in the caregiver-infant relationship. Most recently, research has focused on elucidating transactional effects (Sameroff & Chandler, 1975). The third theme, which began a few years ago and continues to receive considerable emphasis, is concerned with identifying deficits in information processing that appear in preterm samples. It is presumed that these relate to difficulties later encountered in school settings.

Although these emphases overlap in time and the thematic categories are somewhat artificial, they serve as an organizational strategy for this review. The overall goal is to examine what these data add to our knowledge about preterms' long-range development.

The largest group of research data exists for infants labeled preterm or low birthweight, irrespective of the relationship of gestational age and weight. The studies cited below will rely on this general classification, separating as possible those findings reported for samples characterized by different weight/gestational-age relationships.

Turning to the first wave of research and to newborn data, there is no doubt that being born early changes, at least for a time, the organization of early behavior. It is not at all clear why this phenomenon occurs, but it is most apparent in the newborn period. Preterm infants tested at their term dates (often not classified within the studies by AGA, SGA, neurological stress, or health status) show instances of both mature and immature development when contrasted with full-terms. This is apparent in arousal; sleep states; neuromuscular functioning; visual, auditory, and tactile responsiveness; sucking behavior; EEG patterns; visually evoked responses; and sound detection (Bench & Parker, 1971; Chappell, Boismier, & Meier, 1973; Dreyfus-Brisac, 1966, 1970; R. Engel, 1965; Gesell & Amatruda, 1941; Hack, Mostow, & Miranda, 1976; Howard, Parmelee, Kopp, & Littman, 1976; Kopp, Sigman, Parmelee, & Jeffrey, 1975; Michaelis, Parmelee, Stern, & Haber, 1973; Parmelee, Schulte, Akiyama, Wenner, Schultz, & Stern, 1968; Rose, Schmidt, & Bridger, 1976; Sainte-Anne Dargassies, 1966; Stern, Parmelee, Akiyama, Schulz, & Wenner, 1969). Many of these differences have been documented in earlier reviews (Kopp & Parmelee, 1979; Parmelee, 1975) and require only summary comment here.

At 40 weeks of conceptual age (gestational age + duration of postnatal life), preterms show the same kinds of behaviors that full-term newborns demonstrate (e.g., visual scanning and responsivity, auditory detection, tactile sensitivity, activation of arousal and soothing mechanisms, and facilitation and inhibition of neuromuscular responses). Nonetheless, there are unmistakable indicators of differences, in some cases differences manifested by a majority of one group, in other cases, only by some. Consider for example, neurological organization. A third or more preterm infants tested at their term dates are more hypotonic than full-term infants (Dreyfus-Brisac, 1966, 1970; Howard et al., 1976). Howard et al. (1976) noted a pattern of response that reflected uneven neurologic maturation and organization of the nervous system. Preterm infants had more weak responses than term infants, although they also had arousal levels that were at least equal to, or greater than, the terms. As a group, they were more difficult to soothe. Descriptions of individual infants corroborate this uneven level of responses (Als et al., 1979).

Most studies indicate overlapping distributions of responses rather than two distinct independent patterns of response. For example, distribution of terms and preterms' fixation responses revealed that both groups were represented at each of five levels of first fixation (Kopp et al., 1975). Overall, however, group means showed consistently greater fixation for preterm samples than for terms (Kopp et al., 1975; Sigman, Kopp, Littman, & Parmelee, 1977). Similarly, Friedman, Jacobs, and Wirthmann (1980) examined sensory processing in full-term and preterm healthy black infants who were equated for environmental factors. Considerable overlap of responses was noted but significant differences were found in the speed of response to visual stimuli favoring full-terms, responsiveness to initial auditory stimulation (with full-term females most responsive and preterm females least responsive), and response decrement criterion again favoring full-terms. In all, 12 comparisons were made (3 sensory modalities and 4 response measures), of these, 3 showed significant group differences.

Differences in mean scores, although readily apparent, do not spell deviancy. The fact that these differences occur represents an unexplained developmental phenomenon but one that does not necessarily have long-term implications. Indeed, no significant relationships were found in one study that systematically explored variation in preterm versus full-term neonatal behavioral and neurophysiological organization to performance at age 2 years (Parmèlee, 1976; Sigman & Parmelee, 1979). Although newborn studies of preterms are inherently interesting, it is unlikely that differences that are found in comparison with full-term infants will shed much light on the reasons underlying the appearance of later problems.

Turning to the second research focus, it is likely that a combination of factors (medical, social, research zeitgeist) led to concern about interactions between preterms and their caregivers. During the 1960s, a period when outcome for these infants seemed particularly bleak, descriptions of parent responses to the early birth of a child focused on grief, loss of self-esteem, and crises (Caplan, Mason, & Kaplan, 1965). In contrast, anecdotal reports supplied by parents and relatives of tiny infants born a generation or two earlier suggested fewer psychic aftereffects subsequent to preterm birth. This was probably due to the need for families to mobilize their own resources to keep the infant warm and alive (e.g., cotton batting wrapped around an infant who was then placed in a shoe box on a table near a woodburning stove and watched vigilantly) (Hastrup, 1980).

More recent reports of parent responses to preterm births suggest that early grief and anxiety may not last as long as that reported by Caplan et al. (1965), although the shock of seeing a scrawny, weak infant attached to a myriad of life-support measures must leave an indelible impression. In any event, a recent study showed that mothers observed in a preterm nursery markedly increased their smiling and touching of infants by the second week of life (Minde, Trehub, Corter, Boukydis, Celhoffer, & Marton, 1978). Whether family distortion patterns (e.g., separation, divorce) reported in earlier samples continues, is unknown, for now (Leifer et al. 1972).

During the 1960s, parents were excluded from intensive care nurseries; thus, attempts to bring them into contact with their infants (Barnett, Leiderman, Grobstein, & Klaus, 1970) were met with optimism. However, the fact that many parents approached their infants tentatively and behaved differently to them (Leifer et al., 1972) reinforced the idea that patterns of interactions were bound to be distorted. Reports about the incidence of child abuse directed toward preterms gave additional credence to this perspective (Elmer & Gregg, 1967; Klein & Stern, 1971).

Subsequently, it was suggested that there was a sensitive period for maternal attachment (Fanaroff, Kennell, & Klaus, 1972; Klaus & Kennell, 1976; Klaus, Kennell, Plumb, & Zuelke, 1980). These authors argued that both the conditions of birth of a premature infant and isolette care interfered with the initial development of the mother and child relationship. Observing groups of separated and contact mother-infant dyads, they cited findings showing more enface holding and fondling for early-contact mothers. From these complex beginnings, a body of research began to grow that was centered around infant-mother interactions (see Goldberg, 1978, for a recent review; see also *Emotional and Social Development, vol. II, chap. 10*).

The role of separation was explored further. More recent findings suggest that differences found between groups of full-term and preterm dyads were not adequately accounted for by just the variable of separation. Specifically, mothers of preterm infants (whether they had experienced separation or not) exhibited less ventral contact and less smiling with their infants than mothers of full-term infants (Leiderman et al., 1973; Leiderman & Seashore, 1975). However, these findings were somewhat ambiguous because the infants were observed at ages calculated by date of discharge from the hospital rather than corrections for preterm birth. Nonetheless, by the 2nd year, most reported differences had disappeared.

Separation could, however, exaggerate differences that actually had their origins in other characteristics. In another study of separation and contact, no differences were found in maternal interactive behaviors related to separation per se of mother and infant (Field, 1977). However, differences were found in maternal behaviors related to the risk level of the infant. Mothers of high-risk infants were found to be more active in face-to-face interaction with their infants than were mothers of non-high-risk infants. Field (1977) obtained a powerful sex interaction that she attributed to the weaker signals given by high-risk males to their caregivers.

Other investigators have also reported more intense, active, or different behaviors demonstrated by mothers of older preterm infants compared to full-terms (DiVitto & Goldberg, 1979; Field, 1977, 1979a). Goldberg and her colleagues (DiVitto & Goldberg, 1979; Goldberg, 1978; Goldberg, Brachfeld, & DiVitto, 1980) suggested that these patterns of activity required a great deal of adaptation, thus, the stress for parents could be substantial and might have long-term implications.

The nature of these implications began to be addressed in a series of studies emanating from Georgia with black infants (Bakeman & Brown, 1977, 1980), from California with a mixed ethnic and social-class sample (Beckwith et al., 1976; Beckwith & Cohen, 1980; Cohen & Beckwith, 1977, 1979; Parmelee et al., 1976), and from the northeast (two separate series) with many preterms who had been ill and who were primarily Caucasian (DiVitto & Goldberg, 1979; Field, 1979a).

Bakeman and Brown (1977, 1980) found that none of the early maternal interactive behaviors that they had examined had any relationship to child intelligence test performance measured at 3 years. Bakeman and Brown's observations had been taken on three occasions during the first part of the 1st year of life in feeding situations. In these first observations, they did find marked differences between preterm and full-terms, with the former being difficult to feed and less responsive to interactions (Brown & Bakeman, 1980).

The UCLA group (Infant Studies Project) found a relationship between maternal interactions and infant competence at age 9 months and at 2 years (Beckwith et al., 1976; Beckwith & Cohen, 1980; Cohen & Beckwith, 1979; Parmelee, Beckwith, Cohen, & Sigman, 1980). Many of the relationships that are reported accounted for a relatively small amount of later performance (Beckwith & Cohen, 1980).

Differences were also noted between the Caucasian subsample when compared with the entire sample; furthermore, predictive relations varied as a function of social class (which was confounded with ethnicity) and sex. Middle-class girls were the most competent group at age 2 years, and earlier caregiver behaviors showed higher coefficients for them than for males. (Parenthetically, Kopp & Vaughn [1982] found that a greater number of infant measures showed moderate or better predictive coefficients for females than for males.) Ordinal position has also been implicated as an influential variable (Cohen & Beckwith, 1977; Sigman, Cohen, Beckwith, & Parmelee, 1981). Taken together, the findings suggest that a firstborn female preterm reared in an English-speaking home by educated and sensitive parents will show better development at age 2 years than other groups. But how these variables interrelate and how much they account for is difficult to determine from the data as reported.

Several important differences may account for the small, albeit discrepant, findings between the UCLA and Georgia studies. The UCLA study involved over 100 infants of diverse ethnic and SES backgrounds who also had varied risk histories. The data were collected when infants were 1 and 8 months in several situations, including feeding. In contrast, Bakeman and Brown (1977, 1980) studied a small, homogeneous sample of very poor black mothers and their healthy preterm infants. The variability between the samples could account for the differences in level of predictive coefficients that were found.

On the basis of these and other findings, it seems reasonable to state that it is unlikely that very specific caregiver acts will be found that show high and enduring relationships to child functioning from early infancy to childhood. Instead, intuitively it seems that we should expect multifaceted caregiver attributes, such as sensitivity or extreme insensitivity coupled with changing developmental attributes, or qualities of infants to have long-term effects.

A number of years ago, Escalona (1963, 1968) called attention to behavioral characteristics of healthy, full term infants. Some were very quiet, whereas others were highly active and consistently explored their milieu. The quietest infants showed better performance when guided by maternal directions. In contrast, some of the active infants did best when caregivers receded to the background. The fact that parents were able to adjust to these attributes is not surprising; similarly, the fact that parents are able to adjust to the differences in behaviors manifested by their preterm infants is not surprising either.

However, the reality of the situation is that preterm infants can be especially vulnerable because a greater number of parental adjustments have to be made to uneven developmental patterns or variations in sleep and feeding cycles. Forces that potentially interfere with caregiver coping include disturbed parents (Klein & Stern, 1971); young, single, uneducated parents (Fanaroff et al., 1972; Field, Widmayer, Stunger, & Ignatoff, 1980); lack of support systems (Hunter, Kilstrom, Draybill, & Loda, 1978); and family neglect (Hunter et al., 1978). In the face of these adverse circumstances, poor outcome for preterms can result.

Finally, it is noted that numerous interventions have been directed toward preterm infants and their parents. The findings, summarized thoroughly by Cornell and Gottfried (1976), indicate there is mixed evidence for short-term gains in functioning as a result of interventions provided early in life. Similar effects continue to be reported (Field et al., 1980; Leib, Benfield, & Guidubaldi, 1980). It is unlikely, however, that early gains will be maintained unless programs continue into the child's preschool years, or beyond.

Turning to the final focus of study—in the last decade, the study of information processing abilities of preterms was initiated. Research centered primarily upon visual attention, recognition memory, exploratory and play behavior. A few studies were implemented because of interest in pursuing the issue of conceptual-age matches and involved postnatal and postmenstrual behavior comparisons (see Fantz & Fagan, 1975). Others, however, were predicated on the assumption that later educational problems shown by school-aged preterms should have counterparts in early functioning (e.g., see Fagan & Singer, in press; Rose, Gottfried, & Bridger, 1978).

The validity of that supposition is not known. One factor that causes interpretative problems is that older preterm infants (just like their younger counterparts) often show subtle differences in behavior when they are compared with full-term infants of similar conceptual ages. Why this occurs is not well understood. However, some of these differences are probably shortlived and have little bearing on development; on the other hand, others may have significance for long-term competencies. The challenge for developmentalists is to determine which differences reflect noise and which are truly important. As will be seen in the forthcoming paragraphs, this level of sophistication has not been reached as yet.

Table 9 lists recent studies that have been devoted to examination of information processing abilities. Looking first at the tasks that have been presented and the ages that were represented, it is evident that the most commonly employed paradigm involved measurement of a variant of visual responsivity in the first 4 months of life. Somewhat less emphasis has been placed on measuring visual and manipulative acts demonstrated by infants during the latter part of the 1st year. In any event, none of the studies utilized identical procedures.

Examination of subject characteristics reveals considerable sample heterogeneity with respect to social class, ethnic affiliation, and presence of birth complications. How influential these factors are is yet to be determined. However, Kagan (1971), and more recently Cohen (1981) and Rose et al. (1978) reported variations in full-term performance on visual perceptual tasks as a function of social-class and ethnic factors. These variables may be operating upon preterm performance as well. However, it is difficult to sort out the influence of these factors because comparison samples are either nonequivalent in this respect or the variables were unmeasured.

Table 9 also reveals that contemporary health status, ordinality, and current level of developmental performance were rarely documented in studies. The latter omission is particularly important because heterogeneity in this variable may signal nonequivalence in developmental abilities between comparison samples. Utilization of developmental-age matches is just beginning to surface in the developmental literature (see Kopp & Krakow, 1982), although the issue of mental-age matches as had a long and controversial history in mental retardation (see Ellis, 1963; Zigler, 1968). Although arguments are still encountered, concerted efforts have been made to report both chronological and mental age in studies of retarded children. This strategy is justified by the need to be able to make some inferences about the basic intellectual capabilities of children who are being compared with one another. The approach used in mental retardation research has clear implication for research utilizing any type of risk, handicapped, or developmentally delayed group of infants.

It is also important to document the developmental functioning of preterm and term samples even when handicapped and severely delayed infants are excluded from a study. The reason is that children who have been exposed to a biological risk often show a slightly slower rate of development (albeit in the normal range) and their health course may be a bit more unstable than full-term normal infants. The latter, in fact, are often slightly precocious. However, these kinds of variations in functioning (e.g., 6 weeks difference in developmental level) may not be detected if the groups are only selected by chronological age. The ability that is being evaluated and the task that is utilized may be more appropriate for the developmentally older infants. Thus, differences emerge, not necessarily because of deficits but because the two groups are not age equivalent.

Returning again to Table 9, the findings reported about the information processing deficits of preterm infants appear to be fragile, and the generalizations made about impaired functioning are unwarranted at this time. Overall, the magnitude of differences that are reported is slight. In the few instances where major differences were found, they could easily be accounted for by social class, ethnic factors, health status, or any number of variables other than preterm birth.

It should also be noted that even when group differences seem profound, they do not necessarily have implications for later performance. The studies executed by Kopp (1976), Sigman and Parmelee (1974), and Sigman (1976) all reported some differences in term and preterm performance, albeit some more than others. Many of these studies were part of the Infant Studies Project battery of measures (Parmelee, Kopp, & Sigman, 1976), and many of the sample children were part of the longitudinal cohort. In each case, analysis of performance on the measures showed only modest correlations to developmental level at 2 years (Parmelee, 1976). Whether a larger relationship would have been found to a direct analysis of childhood informational processing skills is not known.

Finally, in addition to the problems noted above, it seems that the overall research strategy being employed in these and similar studies has some fundamental flaws. There is, first of all, no unifying conceptual or theoretical model (or set of models) that has guided the research. Instead, studies have been loosely tied to very general constructs that have not been explicitly defined. Second, there has been no concerted effort to explore the growth of developmental functions of preterms as has been done for normally developing term infants. A case in point are the elegant studies of visual attention that mapped out the perceptual abilities of very young infants or the development of play in older infants. We do not know if and how developmental functions of preterms and fullterms parallel or diverge. Additional systematic study is needed.

In sum, the preceding paragraphs have presented an overview of preterm infancy research. It was noted that differences between terms and preterms emerged but that many of the differences were of low magnitude and some could have been accounted for by other variables. At this point, the cross-sectional literature seems to have very limited application to longitudinal outcome findings. They do not explain the why and how of either major or minor sequelae.

RESEARCH ISSUES

The following points have been made in the preceding discussions:

1. A variety of biological risk conditions can assault the organism at the time of conception or during prenatal, perinatal, and postnatal life.
2. Outcome varies and depends upon the particular type and timing of influence. In general, the earlier the insult, the greater the effects. The range of outcome for all perinatal and postnatal insults is from severe impairment to normal development, but the processes accounting for variability are not fully documented or understood.
3. Factors within the environment act upon biological risk by heightening or attenuating effects; in some instances (e.g., perinatal stress), environmental influences may supercede the effect of biological risk. Biological risk and adverse rearing conditions combined appear to have greater negative effects than either alone, but the exact nature of the contributors has rarely been identified.
4. Research on outcome often takes the form of longitudinal follow-up studies where incidence and level of mental retardation, presence of neurological disorders, and educational problems are documented for each type of diagnosis. Outcome-oriented approaches have not elucidated processes of development.
5. Attempts to unravel process and understand other aspects of developmental functioning of children stressed by risk is a recent phenomenon. Topics addressed, primarily by cross-sectional studies, include parent-child interactions, perceptual processes, and so forth. Studies conducted along these lines are exceedingly diverse and fragmented. At best, conclusions from these studies are limited.
6. Studies of individual variability are rare.
7. Innovative approaches to the study of risk effects are available and have generated rich data bases and hypotheses.

This summary brings into focus one of the most pressing challenges confronting the student of risk. How can a more cohesive definitive body of information about the effects of risk be systematically acquired? I suggest we need first to lay out carefully the kinds of knowledge that are necessary; second,

Table 9. **Performance of Preterm (and Term) Infants on Perceptual-Cognitive Tasks**

		Sample Characteristics of Preterms									
Behavior	Test Age	GA[a]	BW[b]	Complications[c]	Current Health Status	Current Devel. Status	Ordinal[d]	SES[e]	Ethnic[f]	Sex	Findings
Visual attention to size/pattern (Fantz & Fagan, 1975)	PN[g]: 5 to 25 weeks, PM: 45 to 60 weeks (1–5 months)	$\bar{x}$ 35 weeks	$\bar{x}$ 1,992 g	minor	H[h]				C[i]		1. No differences when PM age used for both groups; differences found if PN used
Visual discrimination: relational information (Caron & Caron, 1981)	52 to 64 weeks conceptional age (12–24 weeks)	median 33 weeks (27–36)	median 1,620 g (910–2,580)	varying, all in ICU[j]				M+[k]	C+	even	1. No overall differences in habituation 2. Differences found in configuration scores: PT[l] failed to exceed chance on 4 problems, whereas T[l] did; PT scores lower than T

Notes: [a]Gestational age.
[b]Birthweight.
[c]Birth complications.
[d]Ordinal position in family.
[e]Socioeconomic status.
[f]Ethnic membership.
[g]PN = postnatal age; PM = postmenstrual age.
[h]H = healthy.
[i]C = Caucasian.
[j]ICU = intensive care nursery.
[k]M = middle class; H.S. = high school education.
[l]PT = preterm; T = term.

(continued)

Table 9. (*Continued*)

Behavior	Test Age	GA[a]	BW[b]	Complications[c]	Current Health Status	Current Devel. Status	Ordinal[d]	SES[e]	Ethnic[f]	Sex	Findings
Visual/cardiac responses: inanimate/animate faces (Field, 1979b)	3 months, corrected	x̄ 32 weeks					later+	M	C	even	1. No group differences in inanimate preferences, animate faces, overall gaze alternation, baseline heart rate, heart rate during stimulus presentation, etc. 2. Differences: PT less visual responsiveness to spontaneous mother face, higher cardiac rate to same
Visual preferences (Sigman & Parmelee, 1974)	58 weeks conceptional age (4 months)	x̄ 33.6 weeks (27–36)	4 lb. 4 oz. (2/10–5/7)					H.S.		even	1. No group differences in degree of preference or overall attention; both look longer at complex than simple

(*continued*)

Table 9. (*Continued*)

Behavior	Test Age	GA[a]	BW[b]	Complications[c]	Current Health Status	Current Devel. Status	Ordinal[d]	SES[e]	Ethnic[f]	Sex	Findings
											2. T more attentive to face pattern; T show greater differentiation of novel over familiar
Auditory discrimination (O'Connor, 1980)	57 weeks conceptional age (4 months)	$\bar{x}$ 31.97 weeks (3.19)	$\bar{x}$ 1,748 g (510.27)	All in ICU	No central nervous system damage			mixed	mixed	even	1. No differences in rate of response decrement and in response to novel stimulus
Haptic exploration/visual recognition (Rose et al., 1979)	$\bar{x}$ 28.6; $\bar{x}$ 53.4 weeks (7 & 12 months)	$\bar{x}$ 33.4, 33.7 weeks	$\bar{x}$ 1,610 g; 1,738 g					80% L		50+ F	1. No differences in age progression to handle stimuli 2. Differences in evidence of memory at 6 months, and at 12 months PT performance similar to 6 months FT performance

(*continued*)

Table 9. (*Continued*)

Behavior	Test Age	GA[a]	BW[b]	Complications[c]	Current Health Status	Current Devel. Status	Ordinal[d]	SES[e]	Ethnic[f]	Sex	Findings
Crossmodal transfer (Rose et al., 1978)	$\bar{x}$ 54.4 weeks (2.83)	$\bar{x}$ 32.6 weeks (2.5)	$\bar{x}$ 1,651 g (303) (30% < 1,500 g)	All in ICU				$\bar{x}$ 12.5 years education and income lower for PT than middle class FT	mixed (% not equiv. to FT-MSES)	even	1. No group differences in visual recognition memory; in magnitude of novelty percentages; fixation times to familiar stimuli 2. Differences in crossmodal novelty tasks and looking at novel stimulus both favoring FT middle class over FT lower class and PT
Action-schemes (Kopp, 1976)	8 months, corrected	(< 37 weeks)	(≤ 2,500 g)		H	N[m]					1. No differences in type of action scheme used or proportion of time in object involvement

[m]N = normal.

(*continued*)

Table 9. *(Continued)*

Behavior	Test Age	GA[a]	BW[b]	Complications[c]	Current Health Status	Current Devel. Status	Ordinal[d]	SES[e]	Ethnic[f]	Sex	Findings
											2. Differences in duration of two (of 7) individual modes of object exploration
Exploratory behaviors (Sigman, 1976)	8 months, corrected (34.6 weeks)	x̄ 33.5 weeks (2.4)	x̄ 1,992.26 g (380.66)			some high risk		50% M, L (by education)		even	1. Familiar: no group difference over all 10 trials; first 2 trials PT explore familiar stimulus longer 2. Novel: no group effect 3. By risk: no differences in familiar; significant difference in novel favoring low risk
Sensorimotor performance (Kopp et al., 1975)	9 months (39.4 weeks) corrected age	(≤ 37 weeks)	(≤ 2,500 g)			DQ ≥ 90		H, L (by education)	85% C		1. No differences found

(continued)

Table 9. (*Continued*)

Behavior	Test Age	GA[a]	BW[b]	Complications[c]	Current Health Status	Current Devel. Status	Ordinal[d]	SES[e]	Ethnic[f]	Sex	Findings
Spontaneous play (Ungerer & Sigman, 1980)	13½ months, 22 months, corrected ages	< 37 weeks	< 2,500 g		H	N	½ first born	H.S.+	mixed	both	1. No differences in four categories of play when age correction used; differences emerge when age correction not employed

to organize strategies to gather this information; and third, to move to multivariate analytic techniques to determine the multiple contributions of multiple kinds of effects. This last point is beyond the scope of the chapter.

What is it that we need to know? Table 10 provides examples of the kinds of information professionals might do well to think about as studies are contemplated, and then collect such data, when possible, as studies are implemented. The categories listed are oversimplified and very general versions of specific research domains.

First, as a general organizational strategy, each diagnostic entity should be considered as a separate unit of study. This stance is warranted because as yet there is no compelling evidence that shows that deleterious outcomes observed as a result of condition *a* (e.g., DS) are identical to deleterious outcomes that stem from condition *b* (e.g., birth injury). Instead, at present, we know that mental retardation, as measured by performance on a psychometric test is found in both conditions. Although this information is not to be scoffed at, it is nonspecific and does not indicate the why and how of impaired mental functioning within and across diagnostic groups. Until it has been demonstrated that diagnostic labels do not serve a useful categorizational purpose, I suggest the labels be maintained.

The second and third columns refer to basic epidemiologic information that ought to be available for each diagnosis. Often these data are collected by public health, educational, and medical agencies, and are useful for planning and implementing developmental research. Mortality data for most conditions are collected with a fair degree of accuracy (David, 1980). Morbidity data, however, are recorded less systematically and depend on the vagaries of operation of individual local agencies.

Columns 4 and 5 pertain directly to the developmental research plan, and call attention to the processes or systems that may be influenced by a risk condition. Column 4 calls for specifying which domain of functioning—cognitive processes, linguistic abilities, social skills—is affected. Here, the researcher lays out the what and how of study and fills in relevant details once data have been analyzed. Column 5 asks the investigator to specify how a domain of functioning is affected. This may be documented by examining the nature of performance, developmental change, level of competencies attained, or sequential patterns of change. Other areas of inquiry might include analysis of an individual's repertoire (Corman & Escalona, 1969; Kopp & Parmelee, 1979; H. Werner, 1948) or the adaptability of responsiveness (Block & Block, 1979; Lewin, 1935). These have been implicated as important sources of individual differences among normally developing individuals and could prove to be interesting kinds of individual differences found with less serious forms of risk sequelae.

Column 6 focuses attention upon the need to study specific child or setting variables that exacerbate or attenuate the effects of biological risk. As an example of child variables, findings show that lan-

***Table 10.* Information Needed About Effects and Mediators of Risk**

			Developmental Research Questions			
Diagnostic Condition	**Incidence**	**Percent Affected**	**Developmental Systems/Processes Involved**	**Types of Involvement**	**Mediators of Risk Influences**	**Individual Variability**
D_1	1:	Mortality: by age; Morbidity: any level of sequelae on standardized tests, neurological examinations, etc.	Perceptual/cognitive (attention, memory, etc.) Language Affective Social Neurological Motor, etc.	Rate of development Level of development obtained Sequence Breadth of repertoire Flexibility of behavior, patterns of functioning, etc.	Within child conditions: language, social skills, etc. External child conditions: caregiving, social supports, educational programs, etc.	Organization of behavior Coping skills Growth spurts, etc.
D_2	Etc.					

guage skills offer the motorically impaired child a vehicle for social interactions (Kopp & Shaperman, 1973), or an easy-going temperament of a rubella child can foster parent-child relationships (Korn et al., 1978). Setting variables include poverty or affluence, presence or lack of support systems, inadequate versus adequate education. All have been implicated in outcome, particularly for perinatal stress (Werner, Bierman, & French, 1971; Werner & Smith, 1977).

In practice, only a limited number of these child and setting sources of variation have been studied. A rare exception are the Kauai studies, where a confluence of biological, social, and developmental characteristics were identified as important predictors to 18-year-old behavioral functioning. These include moderate-severe perinatal stress, congenital defects, low SES at birth and at 2 and 10 years, level of maternal education below 8 years, low family stability between 2 and 8 years, very high or very low infant responsiveness at age 1 year and low social responsiveness, a Cattell score below 80 at age 2 years, and the need for long-term mental health services or placement in a learning disability class at age 10 years. The presence of four or more of these variables set the stage for serious coping problems by the second decade of life (E. E. Werner, 1979).

The final column calls attention to the need to examine individual children in a case study mode to understand patterns of developmental functioning within a risk condition. Recognition of unique attributes draws upon perspectives advanced by Escalona (1963, 1968) and Murphy (Murphy, 1956; Murphy & Moriarity, 1976) who described patterns of behavior that suggested resiliency, adaptability, and coping, or vice versa. Werner and Smith (1982) have been analyzing individual patterns for children stressed by perinatal risk and found that many childhood problems improved during adolescence. When problems persisted, they were associated with higher rates of moderate to severe perinatal stress, congenital defects, handicapping conditions, chronic poverty, or parent psychopathology. Alternatively, attributes and features associated with child resiliency included a strong bond between infant and caregiver, high activity levels during infancy, social responsivity, presence of support systems for family, presence of models for the children and, overall, strong social bonds. The results of these studies provide numerous leads that could be explored in future research.

It is evident that the list of research needs found in Table 10 presents an extremely complex goal that can be met only with sophisticated research designs and statistical tools. Some of these are yet to be determined. Nonetheless, it is possible at present to work toward filling in the details of this (or any other) model. Tactics that can be adopted to aid research efforts are now discussed.

The Role of Theory

Theories and models are especially useful in laying out questions about developmental phenomena that potentially are influenced by risk influences. Cognition, language, social skills, interaction patterns are but a few of the domains that lend themselves to questions dictated by theory. As an example, Bowlby (1969) and Ainsworth (1973) have suggested that immature organisms are socially primed and have social signals especially designed for early interactions. Observations made of blind and DS infants indicate some distortion in social signals (Emde & Brown, 1978; Jones, 1980; Markowitz, 1980). How common are these distortions to other risk conditions? Do distortions impair the development of attachment? What kind of caregiver adaptation patterns attenuate the potential effects of distortion? That this very fundamental level of asking questions provides information about the organization of behavior in the face of risk is attested to by studies of DS infants using attachment theory (Serafica & Cicchetti, 1976; Markowitz, 1980), the utilization of Piagetian theory by Decarie (1969) in the study of thalidomide children, or by Kopp and Shaperman (1973) who examined the development of a child with major birth defects.

One of the best early examples of the role of theory evolved from Piaget and Inhelder's (1947) premise that theory could be used to study and to understand mental operations in the retarded. They insisted that dependence on traditional intelligence tests could not define how contemporary or past accomplishments, or lack of them, were obtained. Nor, they further stated, did a derived mental age "correspond to any natural phase of mental development" (p. 401). Inhelder's (1968) study of retarded children and adults using Piagetian theory as foundation is clearly the classic research of the genre, and her findings were seminal. She reported that many retarded seemed fixated at early levels of reasoning development and some even oscillated between levels. These latter individuals, she decided, had fragile thought mechanisms that were also easily perturbed by environmental situations. Subsequent studies extended Inhelder's theory-based paradigm by examining mentally retarded children with respect to age of stage acquisition and effects of training on performance as well as evidence of sequence, structure, and decalages. As a result, a meaningful corpus of knowledge has been accumulated about mentally retarded children (see examples of sensorimotor functioning in Brassell & Dunst, 1976; Kahn, 1976; Robinson, 1974; Woodward, 1979).

Research exploring the effects of risk factors is not necessarily limited to the use of the grand developmental theories. Others have amply demonstrated the value of mini theories or approaches using information processing models. The study of memory functioning among mentally retarded children is one example (see Campione & Brown, 1977; Hagen & Stanovich, 1977). Although these approaches generally have not been developmentally oriented, adoption of information processing approaches that utilize a developmental stance is becoming more commonplace among normal children (see Siegler, 1978). Thus, translation to risk groups should not prove to be difficult.

Questions that lend themselves to an information processing approach include: What kinds of strategies do children (who have been stressed by an identifiable risk event) generate to control their attention, or memory? How do these change over time? Are risk events equivalent in influence upon the production of strategies at any given age? How much individual variability in production of strategies can be noted within a risk condition?

In addition to the above, questions can be posed around patterns of ability rather than a single index of performance. Das (1972), for example, specifically examined reasoning and memory in retarded children in terms of Zigler's (1968) developmental theory of mental retardation, and less directly to a defect position (Luria, 1963). Accordingly, children were matched for mental age and their modes of problem solving were explored. Despite mental-age matches, nonretarded children were superior to retarded on certain tasks, a finding that Das (1972) interpreted as reflecting differential modes of processing. A variant of this strategy has been adopted for studies of patterns of attention among handicapped infant samples who have known and unknown etiologies (see Krakow & Kopp, 1982). In this instance, developmental age matches were employed, then similarities and differences between diagnostic groups and normally developing children were examined.

Mediators of Risk: Setting Variables

Virtually everyone now agrees that conditions surrounding the child influence developmental outcome subsequent to biological stress. This point has been made by Barker et al. (1953), Lewin (1935), Roskies (1972) and a host of others in the past 40 years. But problems have arisen either because single units of setting characteristics have been employed (e.g., social class) or, if multiple indices have been utilized, they have not been integrated into a systematic framework. As a result, a loosely connected set of findings exist about environmental influences. These are overinterpreted and overgeneralized to children stressed by biological risk events.

Utilization of coherent frameworks may move us to more systematic accumulation and integration of data centered around setting variables. I suggest that as a first step we examine child and environment with comprehensive ecological perspectives. Fortunately, several system-oriented models have been generated over the last decade that lend themselves to this orientation (e.g., see Sameroff, 1975; Sameroff & Chandler, 1975). These models share a concern for the changing interplay of individual and settings. And, of equal importance, attempts are being made to apply data analytic techniques to the system's conceptualization.

One of the most comprehensive perspectives is found in Bronfenbrenner's (1977, 1979) ecological orientation to development that focuses upon accommodations that occur between the changing human being and the changing properties in the setting in which the person lives. The ecological environment has been described in terms of *microsystem* (patterns of activities experienced by a person in a given setting), *mesosystem* (interrelations between two or more settings in which the person participates), *exosystem* (one or more settings that indirectly affect the individual), and *macrosystem* (belief systems that influence the other systems).

Bronfenbrenner's model has the potential virtue of drawing attention to very specific child characteristics that may be found subsequent to biological stress and the variety of setting variables that may influence outcome. In this system, a changing child with evolving needs and abilities is at the core of the eco setting. The child will impact family members, peers, and teachers in different ways during the course of development, calling forth differential responses. The presence of this dynamic interplay makes a compelling argument for developmentally oriented analyses of child and the interactions.

The potential richness of the ecological model is found in Bronfenbrenner's conceptualization of the exo, meso, and macro systems. Using this as a guide, it should be possible, for example, to identify, document, and measure the influence upon child and family of specific exosystem supports (e.g., health and educational agencies, access to media, recreational facilities, etc.). Attempts along this vein have been made in the area of child abuse (Garbarino, 1976).

Similarly, systematic delineation and subsequent analysis of social forces and their indirect effects upon child and family should prove to be very illuminating. What happens, for example, to parental attitudes and behaviors directed to their biologically stressed children when professionals debate the merits of pregnancy screening for the presence of biological risk (see Kolata, 1980, on screening for spina bifida) or when once socially condoned practices are frowned upon because of currently perceived risks (use of drugs or alcohol, dietary restrictions, pollutant disposal practices, etc.)? These are just a few of the ways that the ecological perspective can be exploited in the study of risk effects.

In addition to the Bronfenbrenner (1977, 1979) perspective, other system-oriented approaches have been developed. G. L. Engel (1977, 1980), for example, introduced a biopsychosocial model to be used in the study of effects that arise subsequent to an illness. G. L. Engel's model spells out a range of interacting systems (from molecular to macro) that change when an illness occurs. One of G. L. Engel's major points is that physicians should no longer approach the study of illness solely with a medical model that fosters attention to just the disease process.

In a similar fashion, Greene (1977), an anthropologist, developed a model of interrelating environmental, biological, and sociocultural systems that he used to study the interactive effects of longstanding nutritional deficiencies. Greene's research focused on endemic goiter commonly found in an Ecuadorian community where iodine malnutrition was severe. He explored the nature of effects that occurred, the impact of widespread retardation (as a result of the deficiency) on the community, and, in turn, the meaning of reduced community resources for the individuals living in that setting.

These system approaches are interesting, have merit, and offer useful ways to confront the issue of studying setting variables. Obviously, they do not offer instant panaceas for solving the problems of teasing out processes and interactions. However, their strength lies in the fact that they force investigators to go beyond a single event (risk) in exploring the multiple factors that mediate outcome. And, the models forcefully demonstrate how mediators can be placed into cohesive perspective.

Subject Variables

The preceding paragraphs dealt with broad research issues related to risk events. These final paragraphs focus on a more narrow issue but one that is extremely important at this stage of research. That is the problem of employing well-defined samples so that interpretation of findings is not hampered by lack of clarity about subject characteristics.

Research on developmental risk is a relatively recent phenomenon and as such we have borrowed from other research and clinical fields. For example, it is likely that the practice of using risk categories stemmed from clinical settings in which physicians wanted to alert colleagues about infants and mothers who required close observation to prevent illness or death. In time, the term was taken from the clinical setting and directly translated into subject categories for research purposes. In like manner, the term educable mentally retarded (EMR) has been used in educational settings to label children who are in need of specialized teaching programs. The label was subsequently extended to research with EMR serving as the classification of children being studied (MacMillan, Meyers, & Morrison, 1980). However, the term is so broad that it reveals little about the characteristics of the samples (MacMillan et al., 1980). This criticism applies equally as well to the term risk; it has little value for the researcher who is trying to unravel the specific main and interactive effects of specific risk events.[7]

The developmentally oriented researcher studying risk factors has generally used some of the strategies employed in the study of normally developing children. Thus, age, sex, and broad descriptive variables of social class (and sometimes ethnicity) have often been given for sample descriptors. More recently, investigators began to suggest that these terms were insufficient to describe risk samples. Therefore, some studying preterm infants added information about gestational age, birthweight, and corrected age. Sometime later, a few began to report if samples were small-for-dates or appropriate-for-dates. Similarly, increased concern for sample specificity slowly entered the research literature on DS triggered by reports that suggested the level of mental retardation for trisomy 21 was lower than that found among mosaics. As a result, type of DS began to be reported.

By and large, these concerns about sample definition are not universal. However, investigators must exert additional effort to characterize their samples of risk, delayed, and handicapped children more fully to elucidate specific characteristics that contribute to reported differences (Kopp & Krakow, 1982). Utilization of this strategy would have the effect of making comparisons across studies easier and, in the long run, findings more interpretable than they are now.

It seems essential to define samples in terms of very specific child characteristics, such as chronological and developmental age, presence of central nervous system impairments, and visual and auditory functioning. However valuable this information is, it is not obtained without effort and expense. Table 11 lays out some of the advantages and disadvantages of collecting and reports these subject characteristics. Overall, the merits of describing these facets outweigh negative aspects. Finally, Table 12 lists background and demographic variables that ought to be considered in describing samples.

In sum, this last section has been devoted to highlighting problems in research. As such, it has reflected the negative rather than the positive aspects of our accomplishments. However, in the short space of time that the developmental aspects of risk effects have been systematically studied, great strides have been made in our understanding, albeit much remains to be accomplished. It is hoped that this review of risk factors in development will serve as a catalyst for some of these future endeavors.

NOTES

1. Precise incidence rates are difficult to ascertain because of current changes in the ages that women choose to become pregnant and because of elective abortion practices.

2. Discussions of ethical and social issues related to prenatal risk, prevention, and genetic counseling can be found in Fletcher, 1979; Hamerton, 1979; Milunsky, 1976; Motulsky, 1974; Nadler, 1976;

Table 11. **Advantages and Disadvantages of Approaches Used to Describe Samples**

Approach	Advantages	Disadvantages
Diagnosis (medical) (e.g., rubella, autism, DS)	Determine if nature of disorder is associated with specific characteristics Useful for studying chromosomal anomalies, single gene disorders, etc. Determine range of individual variation in relatively well-defined group	May result in a wide range of CA or DA levels represented
Known evidence of central nervous system impairment	Notes presence of organicity and resulting long-term prognosis	Difficult to ascertain central nervous system involvement among infants with exception of severely impaired
Chronological age (CA)	Notes length of experience, useful for investigation of similarities as a function of experience	May result in a wide range of developmental levels and, therefore, procedures used may be appropriate for only part of sample. May also confound DA with CA differences
Developmental age (DA); Mean length of utterance or other developmental variable	Exploration of range of individual variability in performance of infants of similar developmental level. Useful for study of behavioral characteristics, styles, information processing variables, parental practices	May have extensive ranges of CA, DQ[a], or experience in sample: problems of history, maturation effects may arise
Postmenstrual or conceptional age	Useful for exploring developmental phenomena and parental caregiving variables irrespective of infant extrauterine experience Affords investigation of effects of prematurity per se	Confounds effects of extrauterine experience: history, maturation problems may arise

Note: [a]DQ = developmental quotient.

Table 12. **Background and Demographic Variables to Consider in Sample Description**

Sex
SES (maternal education, paternal education, income level)
Ethnic/language background
Parental ages
Birth order/parity
Family constellation
Rearing conditions, including intervention status, alternate care, and out-of-home placement
Prenatal and perinatal history
Length of hospitalization
Past and current health status (cardiac, respiratory, etc.)
Sensory abilities (visual, auditory acuity)

Reilly & Milunsky, 1979; Sorenson, Swazey, & Scotch, 1981; and Thompson, 1979.

3. Gibson (1981) suggests that delay in the "rate of decay of primitive reflexes" may markedly constrain the development of body positioning, locomotion, exploration, fixation, and attention. Accordingly, accessibility to the environment would be limited because of "aberrant reflex dynamics in DS" (see details in Cowie, 1970). It would be feasible and interesting to compare the development of DS and non-DS infants who have comparable delays in reflex maturation and similar kinds of low muscle tone.

4. "No space" refers to communications where the child utters a vocalization and *does not wait* for a response from the partner. In the case of DS infants, Jones (1977) reported numerous instances of less than ½ sec. between vocalizations (i.e., "no space"), thus mother and child verbalize simultaneously.

5. Low birthweight refers to infants born at 2,500 g or less.

6. P. A. Davies (1980) has two comments that are pertinent to this discussion. First, she suggests that morbidity trends may show an artifact because of decreasing mortality, "for every hundred low birth weight . . . children born, there may be as many handicapped survivors now when mortality is low as when mortality was very high. When expressing handicap as a percentage of *survivors* a very low mortality rate must make handicap appear in a favourable light."

Second, Davies emphasizes that many studies emanate from centers that deal with very selected populations and small numbers, "and that the truth probably does *not* lie with them, but with the *true* population surveys which are in such regrettably short supply."

7. Recognizing that risk labels are convenient descriptors for certain children and that different risk factors can lead to similar types of risk status, it is suggested that risk terminology be confined to non-research settings. It is also suggested that it may be useful to introduce additional specificity so that professionals share a common frame of reference. Thus, the membership of at-risk groups can be defined at the outset.

One approach is to use categories: (1) Groups where there is clear evidence of distortion in brain structure or some type of chronic malfunction in the central nervous system so that virtually all individuals within a given diagnostic category show some level of developmental delay during infancy and invariably become intellectually retarded during childhood and later years. This group is not really at risk; instead, they have a known and essentially irreversible handicapping condition (congenital malformations, mental retardation, neurological sequelae, etc.). Tjossem (1976) labeled this group with the term *established risk.* In the interest of clarity, it might be useful to use either established risk or handicapped to designate these children and to reserve the term risk for those children who *may* or *may not* develop problems. (2) Children who were exposed to one or more kinds of organismic stresses during the prenatal, perinatal, or postnatal periods and where documentation shows long-term outcome is variable. Some children will demonstrate serious sequelae (e.g., mental retardation, neurological signs) but numerous others will show no untoward signs. Although the incidence of developmental problems is higher for these children than for the population as a whole, it is still far less than for the irreversible handicapping conditions discussed above. In many instances, deleterious rearing conditions have a far more pervasive effect on outcome than the biological stresses (Broman et al., 1975; Davies & Stewart, 1975; Sameroff & Chandler, 1975; Werner et al., 1971); however, the biological stress may make the children less resistant to environmental deprivations. (3) Children who have a physical or sensory impairment that either occurred secondary to a prenatal condition (e.g., cataracts after a rubella infection) or is a primary condition that occurred during postnatal life (e.g., amputation as a result of an accident). Here, sensory or motor impairment is a key component of risk status. (4) Children with subtle problems or suspect kinds of early development. Here risk status is a function of questionable development. Some children may be mildly delayed, others moderately so, a few may show delay in only one or two areas of functioning. These children may also have two or more minor anomalies and unusual facial characteristics or they may demonstrate transient incoordination. Although these point to stress in the prenatal period, it is often difficult to isolate the untoward event in early life that is linked to their developmental problems. Many are particularly difficult to diagnose in the early months of life because the signs are subtle. Once identified, however, some move into the mentally retarded category in time, whereas others progress and eventually appear normal. (5) Children reared in economically deprived families and communities that are associated with undernutrition and inadequate health care, housing, and educational facilities. These are children at biosocial risk. However, the biologic risk these children are exposed to differs a magnitude from those described earlier, and in some instances effects are subtle. Many exist with marginal health status experiencing frequent colds, chronic low-grade infections, undernutrition, and physical abuse.

REFERENCES

Abramowicz, H. Z., & Richardson, S. A. Epidemiology of severe mental retardation in children: Community studies. *American Journal of Mental Deficiency,* 1975, *80,* 18–39.

Abt, I. A. *Baby doctor.* New York: McGraw-Hill, 1944.

Abt, I. A. (Ed.) *Abt-Garrison history of pediatrics.* Philadelphia: W. B. Saunders, 1965.

Adamsons, K. Obstetric considerations in the prevention of perinatal asphyxia. In K. Adamsons & H. Fox (Eds.), *Progress in clinical and biological research* (Vol. 2). New York: Alan R. Liss, 1975.

Agran, P. F. Motor vehicle occupant injuries in noncrash events. *Pediatrics,* 1981, *67,* 838–840.

Ainsworth, M. D. S. In B. M. Caldwell & H. N. Ricciuti (Eds.), *The development of infant-mother attachment.* Chicago: University of Chicago Press, 1973.

Alberman, E. D. Main causes of major mental handicap: Prevalence and epidemiology. In (Ciba Foundation Symposium No. 59 [new series] *Major mental handicap: Methods and costs of prevention*). Amsterdam: Elsevier, 1978.

Alden, E. R., Mandelkorn, T., Woodrum, D. E., Wennberg, R. P., Parks, C. R., & Hodson, W. A. Morbidity and mortality of infants weighing less than 1,000 grams in an intensive care nursery. *Pediatrics,* 1972, *50,* 40–49.

Alford, C. A., Reynolds, D. W., & Stagno, S. Current concepts of chronic perinatal infections. In L. Gluck (Ed.), *Modern perinatal medicine.* Chicago: Year Book Medical Publishers, 1975.

Alford, C. A., Stagno, S., Reynolds, D. W., Dahle, A., Amos, C., Saxon, S. Long term mental and perceptual defects associated with silent intrauterine infections. In L. Gluck (Ed.), *Intrauterine asphyxia and the developing fetal brain.* Chicago: Year Book Medical Publishers, 1977.

Als, H. Assessing an assessment: Conceptual considerations, methodological issues, and a perspective on the future of the neonatal behavioral assessment scale. In A. J. Sameroff (Ed.), *Organization and stability of newborn behavior: A commentary on the Brazelton neonatal behavior assessment scale. Monographs of the Society for Research in Child Development,* 1978, *43*(5–6, Serial No. 177).

Als, H., Tronick, E., Lester, B., & Brazelton, T. B. Specific neonatal measures: The Brazelton neonatal behavioral assessment scale. In J. D. Osofsky (Ed.), *Handbook of infant development.* New York: Wiley, 1979.

Ambrus, C., Weintraub, D., Niswander, K., Fisher, L., Fleishman, J., Bross, I. D. J., & Ambrus, J. L. Evaluation of survivors of respiratory distress syndrome at 4 years of age. *American Journal of Diseases of Children,* 1970, *120,* 296–302.

Amiel-Tison, C. Neurological evaluation of the maturity of newborn infants. *Archives of Disease in Childhood,* 1968, *43,* 89–93.

André-Thomas, C. Y., & Saint-Anne Dargassies, S. *The neurological examination of the infant.* London: Medical Advisory Committee of the National Spastics Society, 1960.

Apgar, V. Proposal for a new method of evaluation of newborn infants. *Current Researches in Anesthesia and Analgesia,* 1953, *32,* 260–267.

Arena, J. M. Drug and chemical effects on mother and child. *Pediatric Annals,* 1979, *8,* 690–697.

Bakeman, R., & Brown, J. V. Behavioral dialogues: An approach to the assessment of mother-infant interaction. *Child Development,* 1977, *48,* 195–203.

Bakeman, R., & Brown, J. V. Early interactions: Consequences for social and mental development at three years. *Child Development,* 1980, *51,* 437–447.

Barker, R. G., Wright, B. A., Meyerson, L., & Gonick, M. R. *Adjustment to physical handicap and illness: A survey of the social psychology of physique and disability.* New York: Social Science Research Council, 1953.

Barnard, K. E. A program of stimulation for infants born prematurely. Paper presented at the meeting of the Society for Research in Child Development, Philadelphia, March 1973.

Barnet, A. B., & Lodge, A. Click evoked EEG responses in normal and developmentally retarded infants. *Nature,* 1967, *214,* 252–255.

Barnet, A. B., Ohlrich, E. S., & Shanks, B. L. EEG evoked responses to repetitive auditory stimulation in normal and Down's syndrome infants. *Developmental Medicine and Child Neurology,* 1971, *13,* 321–329.

Barnett, C. R., Leiderman, P. H., Grobstein, R., & Klaus, M. Neonatal separation: The maternal side of interactional deprivation. *Pediatrics,* 1970, *54,* 197–205.

Baumeister, A. A. The effects of dietary control on intelligence in phenylketonuria. *American Journal of Mental Deficiency,* 1967, *71,* 840–847.

Bayley, N. *Manual for the Bayley scales of infant development.* New York: Psychological Corporation, 1969.

Bear, M. R. Meningitis in pediatric patients. *PAS Reporter,* 1978, *16,* 21–31.

Beaton, G. H., & Bengoa, J. M. *Nutrition in preventive medicine. The major deficiency syndromes, epidemiology, and approaches to control.* Geneva: World Health Organization, 1976.

Beckwith, L., & Cohen, S. E. Interactions of preterm infants with their caregivers and test performance at age two. In T. M. Field, S. Goldberg, D. Stern, & A. M. Sostek (Eds.), *High-risk infants and children: Adult and peer interactions.* New York: Academic Press, 1980.

Beckwith, L., Cohen, S. E., Kopp, C. B., Parmelee, A. H., & Marcy, T. Caregiver-infant interaction and early cognitive development in preterm infants. *Child Development,* 1976, *47,* 579–587.

Bell, R. Q. Convergence: An accelerated longitudinal approach. *Child Development,* 1953, *24,* 145–152.

Bell, R. Q. An experimental test of the accelerated longitudinal approach. *Child Development,* 1954, *25,* 281–286.

Belmont, J. M. Medical-behavioral research in retardation. In N. R. Ellis (Ed.), *International review of research in mental retardation* (Vol. 5). New York: Academic Press, 1971.

Bench, J., & Parker, A. Hyper-responsivity to sounds in the short-gestation baby. *Developmental Medicine and Child Neurology,* 1971, *13,* 15–19.

Benda, C. E. *Down's syndrome.* New York: Grune & Stratton, 1969.

Benirschke, K. Effects of placenta pathology on the embryo and fetus. In G. Wilson & F. C. Fraser (Eds.), *Handbook of teratology,* vol. 3, Comparative, maternal, and epidemiological aspects. New York: Plenum, 1977.

Benton, A. L. Mental development of prematurely born children. *American Journal of Orthopsychiatry,* 1940, *10,* 719–746.

Bergner, I., & Susser, M. W. Low birthweight and prenatal nutrition: An interpretative review. *Pediatrics,* 1970, *46,* 946–966.

Berman, P. W., Waisman, H. A., & Graham, F. K. Intelligence in treated phenylketonuric children—A developmental study. *Child Development,* 1966, *37,* 731–747.

Bernheimer, L. Personal communication, 1980.

Berry, P., Gunn, P., & Andrews, R. Behavior of Down syndrome infants in a strange situation. *American Journal of Mental Deficiency,* 1980, *85,* 213–218.

Beskow, B. Mental disturbances in premature children at school age. *Acta Paediatrica,* 1949, *37,* 125–149.

Bethenod, M., Bourgeois, J., Sann, L., Cottancin, G., Rigal, D., Fau, M., Vachet, M. F., & Saunier, B. Evolution des infants né avec un très petit poids de naissance 139 cas de poids inférieur à 1001g né entre 1967 et 1976. *Pediatrie,* 1979, *34,* 573–593.

Bidder, R. T., Bryant, G., & Gray, O. P. Benefits of Down's syndrome children through training their mothers. *Archives of Disease in Childhood,* 1975, *50,* 383–386.

Bierman-van Eendenburg, M. E. C., Jurgens-van der Zee, A. D., Olinga, A. A., Huisjes, H. H., & Touwen, B. C. L. Predictive value of neonatal neurological examination: A follow-up study at 18 months. *Developmental Medicine and Child Neurology,* 1981, *23,* 296–305.

Birch, H. G., & Gussow, J. D. *Disadvantaged children: Health, nutrition and social failure.* New York: Harcourt, Brace & World, 1970.

Block, J. H., & Block, J. The role of ego-control and ego-resiliency in the organization of behavior. In W. A. Collins (Ed.), *Theoretical perspectives in development.* Minnesota Symposia on Child Psychology (Vol. 13). Hillsdale, N.J.: Erlbaum, 1979.

Bond, M. R. Mental impairment following head injury. In C. H. Carter (Ed.), *Medical aspects of mental retardation* (2nd ed.). Springfield, Ill.: Charles C. Thomas, 1978.

Borkowski, J. G., & Wanschura, P. B. Mediational responses in the retarded. In N. R. Ellis (Ed.), *International review of research in mental retardation* (Vol. 7). New York: Academic Press, 1974.

Bowlby, J. *Attachment and loss,* vol. 1, *Attachment.* London: Hogarth, 1969.

Brassell, W. R., & Dunst, C. J. Comparison of two procedures for fostering the development of the object construct. *American Journal of Mental Deficiency,* 1976, *80,* 523–528.

Brazelton, T. B. Neonatal behavioral assessment scale. *Clinics in Developmental Medicine* (No. 50). Philadelphia: J. B. Lippincott, 1973.

Brazelton, T. B. Introduction. In A. J. Sameroff (Ed.), *Organization and stability: A commentary on the Brazelton Neonatal Behavior Assessment Scale.* Monographs of the Society for Research in Child Development, 1978, *43*(5–6, Serial No. 177).

Brent, R. L. Radiations and other physical agents. In J. G. Wilson & F. C. Fraser (Eds.), *Handbook of teratology,* vol. 1, *General principles and etiology.* New York: Plenum, 1977.

Bricker, D., Carlson, L., & Schwarz, R. A discussion of early intervention for infants with Down's syndrome. *Pediatrics,* 1981, *67,* 45–46.

Brimblecombe, F. S. W., Edelsten, A. D., & Rubissow, J. The use of special care unit, neonatal mortality and subsequent handicap. In F. S. W. Brimblecombe (Ed.), *Early separation and special care nurseries* Clinics in Developmental Medicine. No. 68 London: Heinemann, 1978.

Britton, S. B., Fitzhardinge, P. M., & Ashby, S. Is intensive care justified for infants weighing less than 801 gm at birth? *Journal of Pediatrics,* 1981, *99,* 937–944.

Broman, S. H., Nichols, P. L., & Kennedy, W. A. *Preschool IQ: Prenatal and early developmental correlates.* Hillsdale, N.J.: Erlbaum, 1975.

Bronfenbrenner, U. Toward an experimental ecology of human development. *American Psychologist,* 1977, *32,* 513–531.

Bronfenbrenner, U. *The ecology of human development. Experiments by nature and design.* Cambridge: Harvard University Press, 1979.

Brooks, J., & Weinraub, M. A history of infant intelligence testing. In M. Lewis (Ed.), *Origins of intelligence.* New York: Plenum, 1976.

Browder, J. A. The pediatrician's orientation to infant stimulation programs. *Pediatrics,* 1981, *67,* 42–44.

Brown, A. L. The role of strategic behavior in retardate memory. In N. R. Ellis (Ed.), *International review of research in mental retardation* (Vol. 7). New York: Academic Press, 1974.

Brown, J. V., & Bakeman, R. Relationships of human mothers with their infants during the first year of life: Effects of prematurity. In R. W. Bell & W. P. Smotherman (Eds.), *Maternal influence and early behavior.* Jamaica, N.Y.: Spectrum, 1980.

Brozek, J. *Behavioral effects of energy and protein deficits* (NIH Publication No. 79–1906). Washington, D.C.: U.S. Department of Health, Education, and Welfare, 1979.

Buckhalt, J. A., Rutherford, R. B., & Goldberg, K. E. Verbal and nonverbal interaction of mothers with their Down's syndrome and nonretarded infants. *American Journal of Mental Deficiency,* 1978, *82,* 337–343.

Buium, N., Rynders, J., & Turnure, J. Early maternal linguistic environment of normal and Down's syndrome language-learning children. *American Journal of Mental Deficiency,* 1974, *79,* 52–58.

Burger, P. C., & Vogel, F. S. The development of the pathologic changes of Alzheimer's disease and senile dementia in patients with Down's syndrome. *American Journal of Pathology,* 1973, *73,* 457–467.

Butterfield, E. C., & Belmont, J. M. Assessing and improving the executive cognitive functions of mentally retarded people. In I. Bialer & M. Sternlicht (Eds.), *Psychological issues in mental retardation.* New York: Psychological Dimensions, 1977.

Callner, D. A., Dustman, R. E., Madsen, J. A., Schenkenberg, T., & Beck, E. C. Life span changes in the average evoked responses of Down's syndrome and nonretarded persons. *American Journal of Mental Deficiency,* 1978, *82,* 398–405.

Campione, J. C., & Brown, A. L. Memory and metamemory in educable retarded children. In R. V. Kail, Jr., & J. W. Hagen (Eds.), *Perspectives on the development of memory and cognition.* Hillsdale, N.J.: Erlbaum, 1977.

Cameron, J., Livson, N., Bayley, N. Infant vocalizations and their role to mature intelligence. *Science,* 1967, *157,* 331–333.

Caplan, G., Mason, E., & Kaplan, D. M. Four studies of crisis in parents of prematures. *Community Mental Health Journal,* 1965, *1,* 149–161.

Caputo, D. V., Goldstein, K. M., & Taub, H. B. The development of prematurely born children through middle childhood. In T. M. Field, A. M. Sostek, S. Goldberg, & H. H. Shuman (Eds.), *Infants born at risk: Behavior and development.*

Jamaica, N.Y.: Spectrum, 1979.

Caputo, D. V., Goldstein, K. M., & Taub, H. B. Neonatal compromise and later psychological development: A ten-year longitudinal study. In S. L. Friedman & M. Sigman (Eds.), *Preterm birth and psychological development.* New York: Academic Press, 1981.

Caputo, D. V., & Mandell, W. Consequences of low birth weight. *Developmental Psychology,* 1970, *3,* 363–383.

Caron, A. J., & Caron, R. F. Processing of relational information as an index of infant risk. In S. L. Friedman & M. Sigman (Eds.), *Preterm birth and psychological development.* New York: Academic Press, 1981.

Carr, J. *Young children with Down's Syndrome.* London: Butterworth, 1975.

Carrier, C., Doray, B., Stern, L., & Usher, R. H. Effects of neonatal intensive care on mortality rates in the Province of Quebec. *Pediatric Research,* 1972, *6,* 408. (Abstract).

Carter, C. O. Incidence and aetiology. In A. P. Norman (Ed.), *Congenital abnormalities in infancy.* Oxford: Basil Blackwell, 1971.

Carter, C. O. Clues to the aetiology of neural tube malformations: Studies in hydrocephalus and spina bifida. *Developmental Medicine and Child Neurology,* 1974, *16,* 3–15.

Casati, I., & Lézine, I. *Les étapes de l'intelligence sensori-motrice.* Paris: Les Éditions du Centre de Psychologie Appliquée, 1968.

Chappell, P. J., Boismier, J. P., & Meier, G. The infant's entering repertoire. Paper presented at the meeting of the Society for Research in Child Development. Philadelphia, March 1973.

Chase, H. C. Time trends in low birth weight in the United States, 1950–1974. In D. M. Reed & F. J. Stanley (Eds.), *The epidemiology of prematurity.* Baltimore and Munich: Urban & Schwarzenberg, 1977.

Cheseldine, S., & McConkey, R. Parental speech to young Down's syndrome children: An intervention study. *American Journal of Mental Deficiency,* 1979, *83,* 612–620.

Chess, S. The influence of defect on development in children with congenital rubella. *Merrill-Palmer Quarterly,* 1974, *20,* 255–274.

Chess, S. Follow-up report on autism in congenital rubella. *Journal of Autism and Childhood Schizophrenia,* 1977, *7,* 69–81.

Chisolm, J., & Barltrop, D. Recognition and management of children with increased lead absorption. *Archives of Disease in Childhood,* 1979, *54,* 249–262.

Ciba Foundation. *Major mental handicap: Methods and costs of prevention* (Ciba Foundation Symposium No. 59 [new series]). Amsterdam: Elsevier, 1978.

Cicchetti, D., & Sroufe, L. A. The relationship between affective and cognitive development in Down's syndrome infants. *Child Development,* 1976, *47,* 920–929.

Cicchetti, D., & Sroufe, L. A. An organizational view of affect: Illustration from the study of Down's syndrome infants. In M. Lewis & L. A. Rosenblum (Eds.), *The development of affect.* New York: Plenum, 1978.

Clarke, A. D. B. Predicting human development: Problems, evidence, implications. *Bulletin of the British Psychological Society,* 1978, *31,* 249–258.

Cohen, L. B. Examination of habituation as a measure of aberrant infant development. In S. L. Friedman & M. Sigman (Eds.), *Pre-term birth and psychological development.* New York: Academic Press, 1981.

Cohen, S. E., & Beckwith, L. Caregiving behaviors and early cognitive development as related to ordinal position in preterm infants. *Child Development,* 1977, *48,* 152–157.

Cohen, S. E., & Beckwith, L. Preterm infant interaction with the caregiver in the first year of life and competence at age two. *Child Development,* 1979, *50,* 767–777.

Collins, J. T., & Hagen, J. W. A constructivist account of the development of perception, attention, and memory. In G. A. Hale & M. Lewis (Eds.), *Attention and cognitive development.* New York: Plenum, 1979.

Collman, R. D., & Newlyn, D. Changes in Terman-Merrill IQ's of mentally retarded children. *American Journal of Mental Deficiency,* 1958, *63,* 307–311.

Combe, A. *A treatise on the physiological and moral management of infants for the use of parents.* 4th Edinburgh Edition. New York: William H. Colyer, 1845.

Connolly, B., & Russell, F. Interdisciplinary early intervention program. *Physical Therapy,* 1976, *56,* 155–158.

Corah, N. L., Anthony, E. J., Painter, P., Stern, J. A., & Thurston, P. L. Effects of perinatal anoxia after seven years. *Psychological Monographs,* 1965, *79*(3, Whole No. 596).

Coraza, M. C. Motor development of DS toddlers measured by the Hahnemann pre-school scales for exceptional children. *Dissertation Abstracts International,* 1977, *38,* 2039A–2040A.

Corman, H. H., & Escalona, S. K. Stages of sensorimotor development; A replication study. *Merrill-Palmer Quarterly*, 1969, *15*, 351–361.

Cornell, E. H., & Gottfried, A. W. Intervention with premature human infants. *Child Development*, 1976, *47*, 32–39.

Cornwell, A. C. Development of language abstraction and numerical concept formation in Down's syndrome children. *American Journal of Mental Deficiency*, 1974, *79*, 179–180.

Cowie, V. *A study of the early development of mongols*. Oxford: Pergamon, 1970.

Dameron, L. E. Development of intelligence of infants with mongolism. *Child Development*, 1963, *34*, 733–738.

Das, J. P. Patterns of cognitive ability in nonretarded and retarded children. *American Journal of Mental Deficiency*, 1972, *77*, 6–12.

David, R. J. The quality and completeness of birthweight and gestational age data in computerized birth files. *American Journal of Public Health*, 1980, *70*, 964–973.

Davies, P. A. Infants of very low birthweight: An appraisal of some aspects of their present neonatal care and of their later prognosis. In D. Hull (Ed.), *Recent advances in pediatrics*. Edinburgh: Churchill Livingstone, 1976.

Davies, P. A. Personal communication, 1980.

Davies, P. A., & Stewart, A. L. Low-birth-weight infants: Neurological sequelae and later intelligence. *British Medical Bulletin*, 1975, *31*, 85–91.

Davies, P. A., & Tizard, J. P. M. Very low birthweight and subsequent neurological defect. *Developmental Medicine and Child Neurology*, 1975, *17*, 3–17.

Decarie, T. G. A study of the mental and emotional development of the thalidomide child. In B. M. Foss (Ed.), *Determinants of infant behaviour* (Vol. 4). London: Methuen, 1969.

Decarie, T. G., & O'Neill, M. Quelques aspects du développement cognitit d'enfants souffrant de malformation du à la thalidomide. *Bulletin de Psychologie*, 1974, *27*, 5–9.

de Grouchy, J., & Turleau, C. *Clinical atlas of human chromosomes*. New York: Wiley, 1977.

Dekaban, A., O'Rourke, J., & Corman, T. Abnormalities in offspring related to maternal rubella during pregnancy. *Neurology*, 1958, *8*, 387–392.

DeMyer, W. Congenital anomalies of the central nervous system. In D. B. Tower (Ed.), *The nervous system*, vol. 2, *The clinical neurosciences*. New York: Raven Press, 1975.

Denhoff, E. Current status of infant stimulation or enrichment programs for children with developmental disabilities. *Pediatrics*, 1981, *67*, 22–37.

Department of Health, Education, and Welfare (DHEW). *Vital statistics of the United States*, vol. 2, *Mortality* (*Part A*). Washington, D.C.: U.S. Government Printing Office, 1975.

Department of Health, Education, and Welfare (DHEW). Third special report to the U.S. Congress on alcohol and health. Washington, D.C.: U.S. Government Printing Office, June 1978. (Pat. No. (ADM) 78–568).

Dicks-Mireaux, M. J. Development of intelligence of children with Down's syndrome. *Journal of Mental Deficiency Research*, 1966, *10*, 89–100.

Dicks-Mireaux, M. J. Mental development of infants with Down's syndrome. *American Journal of Mental Deficiency*, 1972, *77*, 26–32.

Diller, L., Gordon, W. A., Swinyard, C. A., & Kastner, S. Psychological and educational studies with spina bifida children. Washington, D.C.: U.S. Department of Health, Education, and Welfare/U.S. Office of Education, 1969.

DiVitto, B., & Goldberg, S. The effect of newborn medical status on early parent-infant interaction. In T. Field, A. Sostek, S. Goldberg, & H. H. Shuman (Eds.), *Infants born at risk: Behavior and development*. Jamaica, N.Y.: Spectrum, 1979.

Dobbing, J. Vulnerable periods in brain growth and somatic growth. In D. F. Roberts & A. M. Thomson (Eds.), *The Biology of human fetal growth*. New York: Halsted Press, 1976.

Dobson, J. C., Kushida, E., Williamson, M., & Friedman, E. G. Intellectual performance of 36 phenylketonuria patients and their nonaffected siblings. *Pediatrics*, 1976, *58*, 53–58.

Dodd, B. J. Comparison of babbling patterns in normal and Down-syndrome infants. *Journal of Mental Deficiency Research*, 1972, *16*, 35–40.

Donat, J. F., Okazaki, H., & Kleinberg, F. Cerebellar haemorrhages in newborn infants. *American Journal of Diseases of Children*, 1979, *133*, 441.

Douglas, J. W. B., & Gear, R. Children of low birthweight in the 1946 national cohort. Behaviour and educational achievement in adolescence. *Archives of Disease in Childhood*, 1976, *51*, 820–827.

Dreyfus-Brisac, C. The electroencephalogram of the premature infant and full-term newborn. In P. Kellaway & I. Petersén (Eds.), *Neurological and electroencephalographic correlative studies in infancy*. New York: Grune & Stratton, 1964.

Dreyfus-Brisac, C. The bioelectric development of

the central nervous system during early life. In F. Falkner (Ed.), *Human development.* Philadelphia: W. B. Saunders, 1966.

Dreyfus-Brisac, C. Sleep ontogenesis in human prematures after 32 weeks of conceptional age. *Developmental Psychobiology,* 1970, *3,* 91–121.

Drillien, C. M. Longitudinal study of growth and development of prematurely and maturely born children: VII. Mental development, 2–5 years. *Archives of Disease in Childhood,* 1961, *36,* 233–240.

Drillien, C. M. *The growth and development of the prematurely born infant.* Edinburgh: Livingstone, 1964.

Drillien, C. M. Aetiology and outcome in low-birthweight infants. *Developmental Medicine and Child Neurology,* 1972, *14,* 563–574.

Drillien, C. M. Prevention of handicap in infants of very low birthweight. In D. A. A. Primrose (Ed.), *Proceedings of the Third Congress of the International Association for the Scientific Study of Mental Deficiency* (Vol. 1). Warsaw: Polish Medical Publishers, 1975.

Drillien, C. M., Jameson, S., & Wilkinson, E. M. I: Prevalence and distribution by clinical type and severity of defect. *Archives of Disease in Childhood,* 1966, *41,* 528–538.

Drillien, C. M., Thomson, A. J. M., & Burgoyne, K. Low-birthweight children at early school-age: A longitudinal study. *Developmental Medicine and Child Neurology,* 1980, *22,* 26–47.

Dubowitz, L. M. S., Dubowitz, V., & Goldberg, C. Clinical assessment of gestational age in the newborn infant. *Journal of Pediatrics,* 1970, *77,* 1–10.

Edwards, M. J., & Wanner, R. A. Extremes of temperature. In J. G. Wilson & F. C. Fraser (Eds.), *Handbook of teratology,* vol. 1, *General principles and etiology.* New York: Plenum, 1977.

Ellingson, R. J., Menoloscino, R. J., & Eisen, J. D. Clinical EEG relationships in mongoloids confirmed by karyotype. *American Journal of Mental Deficiency,* 1970, *74,* 645–650.

Ellis, N. R. The stimulus trace and behavioral inadequacy. In N. R. Ellis (Ed.), *Handbook of mental deficiency* (1st ed.). New York: McGraw-Hill, 1963.

Ellis, W. G., McCulloch, J. R., & Corley, C. L. Presenile dementia in Down's syndrome. *Neurology,* 1974, *25,* 101–106.

Elmer, E., & Gregg, G. Developmental characteristics of abused children. *Pediatrics,* 1967, *40,* 596–602.

Emanuel, I. Need for future epidemiologic research: Studies for prevention and intervention. In D. M. Reed & F. J. Stanley (Eds.), *The epidemiology of prematurity.* Munich and Baltimore: Urban & Schwarzenberg, 1977.

Emde, R. N., & Brown, C. Adaptation after the birth of a Down's syndrome infant: A study of six cases, illustrating differences in development and the counter-movement between grieving and maternal attachment. *Journal of the American Academy of Child Psychiatry,* 1978, *17,* 299–323.

Engel, G. L. The need for a new medical model: A challenge for biomedicine. *Science,* 1977, *196,* 129–136.

Engel, G. L. The clinical application of the biopsychosocial model. *The American Journal of Psychiatry,* 1980, *137,* 535–544.

Engel, R. Maturation changes and abnormalities in the newborn electroencephalogram. *Developmental Medicine and Child Neurology,* 1965, *7,* 498–506.

Erickson, J. D. Paternal age and Down's syndrome. *American Journal of Human Genetics,* 1979, *31,* 489–497.

Erickson, M. T. The predictive validity of the Cattell infant intelligence scale for young mentally retarded children. *American Journal of Mental Deficiency,* 1968, *72,* 728–733.

Escalona, S. K. The use of infant tests for predictive purposes. *Bulletin of the Menninger Clinic,* 1950, *14,* 117–128.

Escalona, S. K. Patterns of infantile experience and the developmental process. *Psychoanalytic Study of the Child,* 1963, *18,* 197–244.

Escalona, S. K. *The roots of individuality. Normal patterns of development in infancy.* Chicago: Aldine, 1968.

Escalona, S. K. Paper presented at the meeting of Child Development Section, American Academy of Pediatrics, Detroit, 1980.

Escalona, S. K. Babies at double hazard: Early development of infants at biologic and social risk. *Pediatrics,* 1982, *70,* 670–675.

Escalona, S. K., & Moriarty, A. Prediction of school-age intelligence from infant tests. *Child Development,* 1961, *32,* 597–605.

Fagan, J. F. Short-term memory processes in normal and retarded children. *Journal of Experimental Child Psychology,* 1968, *6,* 279–296.

Fagan, J. F. Infant recognition memory as a present and future index of cognitive abilities. In N. R. Ellis (Ed.), *Aberrant development in infancy.* Hillsdale, N.J.: Erlbaum, 1975.

Fagan, J. F., & McGrath, S. K. Infant recognition

memory and later intelligence. *Intelligence,* 1981, *5,* 121–130.

Fagan, J. F., & Singer, L. T. Infant recognition memory as a measure of intelligence. In L. P. Lipsitt (Ed.), *Advances in infancy research* (Vol. 2). Norwood, N.J.: Ablex, in press.

Fanaroff, A. A., Kennell, J. H., & Klaus, M. H. Follow-up of low birthweight infants—the predictive value of maternal visiting patterns. *Pediatrics,* 1972, *49,* 287–290.

Fantz, R. L., & Fagan, J. F. Visual attention to size and number of pattern details by term and preterm infants during the first six months. *Child Development,* 1975, *46,* 224–228.

Fantz, R. L., Fagan, J. F., & Miranda, S. B. Early visual selectivity. In L. B. Cohen & P. Salapatek (Eds.), *Infant perception: From sensation to cognition,* vol. 1, *Basic visual processes.* New York: Academic Press, 1975.

Farr, V. Estimation of gestational age by neurological assessment in the first week of life. *Archives of Disease in Childhood,* 1968, *43,* 353–357.

Ferry, P. C. On growing new neurons: Are early intervention programs effective? *Pediatrics,* 1981, *67,* 38–41.

Field, T. M. Effects of early separation, interactive deficits, and experimental manipulations on infant-mother face-to-face interaction. *Child Development,* 1977, *48,* 763–771.

Field, T. M. Interaction patterns of high-risk and normal infants. In T. Field, A. M. Sostek, S. Goldberg, & H. H. Shuman (Eds.), *Infants born at risk:* Jamaica, N.Y.: Spectrum, 1979. (a)

Field, T. M. Visual and cardiac responses to animate and inanimate faces by young term and preterm infants. *Child Development,* 1979, *50,* 188–194. (b)

Field, T. M., Dempsey, J. R., & Shuman, H. H. Developmental assessments of infants surviving the respiratory distress syndrome. In T. M. Field, A. M. Sostek, S. Goldberg, & H. H. Shuman (Eds.), *Infants born at risk. Behavior and development.* Jamaica, N.Y.: Spectrum, 1979.

Field, T. M., Sostek, A. M., Goldberg, S., & Shuman, H. H. (Eds.). *Infants born at risk: Behavior and development.* Jamaica, N.Y.: Spectrum, 1979.

Field, T. M., Widmayer, S. M., Stunger, S., & Ignatoff, E. Teenage, lower class, Black mothers and their preterm infants: An intervention and developmental follow-up. *Child Development,* 1980, *51,* 426–436.

Fisch, D., Bilek, M. K., Miller, L. D., & Engel, R. R. Physical and mental status at 4 years of age of survivors of the respiratory distress syndrome. *Journal of Pediatrics,* 1975, *86,* 497–503.

Fishler, K., Donnell, G. N., Bergren, W. R., & Koch, R. Intellectual and personality development in children with galactosemia. *Pediatrics,* 1972, *50,* 412–419.

Fishler, K., Graliker, B. V., & Koch, R. The predictability of intelligence with Gesell developmental scales in mentally retarded infants and young children. *American Journal of Mental Deficiency,* 1965, *69,* 515–525.

Fishman, M., & Palkes, H. The validity of psychometric testing in children with congenital malformations of the central nervous system. *Developmental Medicine and Child Neurology,* 1974, *16,* 180–185.

Fitzhardinge, P. M., Kalman, E., Ashby, S., & Pape, K. E. Present status of the infant of very low birthweight treated in a referral neonatal intensive care unit in 1974. In *Major mental handicap: Methods and costs of prevention* (Ciba Foundation Symposium No. 59 [new series]). Amsterdam: Elsevier, 1978.

Fitzhardinge, P. M., Pape, K. E., Arstikoitis, M., Boyle, M., Ashby, S., Rowley, A., & Netley, C. Mechanical ventilation of infants of less than 1,501 grams birth weight: Health, growth and neurologic sequelae. *Journal of Pediatrics,* 1976, *88,* 531–541.

Flavell, J. H., & Wellman, H. M. Metamemory. In R. V. Kail, Jr., & J. W. Hagen (Eds.), *Memory in cognitive development.* Hillsdale, N.J.: Erlbaum, 1976.

Fletcher, J. C. The morality and ethics of prenatal diagnosis. In A. Milunsky (Ed.), *Genetic disorders and the fetus: Diagnosis, prevention and treatment.* New York: Plenum, 1979.

Ford, E. H. R. *Human chromosomes.* New York: Academic Press, 1973.

Fraiberg, S. Parallel and divergent patterns in blind and sighted infants. *Psychoanalytic Study of the Child,* 1968, *23,* 264–300.

Fraiberg, S. Intervention in infancy: A program for blind infants. *Journal of the American Academy of Child Psychiatry,* 1971, *10,* 381–405.

Fraiberg, S., & Freedman, D. A. Studies in the ego development of the congenitally blind child. *Psychoanalytic Study of the Child,* 1965, *19,* 113–169.

Francis-Williams, J., & Davies, P. A. Very low birthweight and later intelligence. *Developmental Medicine and Child Neurology,* 1974, *16,*

709–728.

Fraser, F. C. The multifactorial/threshold concept—Uses and misuses. *Teratology*, 1976, *14*, 267–280.

Fraser, F. C. Relation of animal studies to man. In J. G. Wilson & F. C. Fraser (Eds.), *Handbook of teratology*, vol. 1, *General principles and etiology*. New York: Plenum, 1977. (a)

Fraser, F. C. Interactions and multiple causes. In J. C. Wilson & F. C. Fraser (Eds.), *Handbook of teratology*, vol. 1, *General principles and etiology*. New York: Plenum, 1977. (b)

Friedman, S. L., Jacobs, B. S., & Werthmann, M. W. *Visual behaviors of low medical risk preterms at expected date of birth*. Unpublished manuscript, 1980.

Garbarino, J. A preliminary study of some ecological correlates of child abuse: The impact of socioeconomic stress on mothers. *Child Development*, 1976, *47*, 178–185.

Garmezy, W., & Levine, V. T. Longitudinal vs. cross-sectional research in the study of children at risk for psychopathology. In J. S. Strauss, H. M. Babigian, & M. Roff (Eds.), *The origins and course of psychopathology*. New York: Plenum, 1977.

Garn, S. M., Shaw, H. A., & McCabe, K. D. Effects of socioeconomic status and race on weight-defined and gestational prematurity in the United States. In D. W. Reed & F. J. Stanley (Eds.), *The epidemiology of prematurity*. Baltimore and Munich: Urban & Schwarzenberg, 1977.

Gesell, A. L. *The embryology of behavior: The beginnings of the human mind*. New York: Harper, 1945.

Gesell, A. L., & Amatruda, C. S. *Developmental diagnosis*. New York: Hoeber, 1941.

Gibson, D. *Down's syndrome: The psychology of mongolism*. Cambridge, Mass.: Cambridge University Press, 1978.

Gibson, D. Personal communication, 1981.

Gliddon, J. B., Busk, J., & Galbraith, G. C. Visual evoked responses as a function of light intensity in Down's syndrome v. nonretarded subjects. *Psychophysiology*, 1975, *12*, 416–422.

Gluck, L. *Intrauterine asphyxia*. Chicago: Year Book Medical Publishers, 1977.

Goldberg, S. Prematurity: Effects on parent-infant interaction. *Journal of Pediatric Psychology*, 1978, *3*, 137–144.

Goldberg, S., Brachfeld, S., & DiVitto, B. Feeding, fussing, and play: Parent-infant interaction in the first year as a function of prematurity and perinatal medical problems. In T. M. Field, S. Goldberg, D. Stern, & A. M. Sostek (Eds.), *High-risk infants and children: Adult and peer interactions*. New York: Academic Press, 1980.

Goldstein, K. M., Caputo, D. V., & Taub, H. B. The effects of prenatal and perinatal complications on development at one year of age. *Child Development*, 1976, *47*, 613–621.

Golub, M. S., & Golub, A. M. Behavioral teratogenesis. In A. Milunsky, E. A. Friedman, & L. Gluck (Eds.). *Advances in perinatal medicine*, Vol 1. New York: Plenum, 1981.

Goodman, J. F., & Cameron, J. The meaning of IQ constancy in young retarded children. *Journal of Genetic Psychology*, 1978, *132*, 109–119.

Gordon, H. H. Perspectives of neonatology—1975. In G. B. Avery (Ed.), *Neonatology* (6th ed.). Philadelphia: J. B. Lippincott, 1975.

Gorlin, R. J. Classical chromosome disorders. In J. J. Yunis (Ed.), *New chromosomal syndromes*. New York: Academic Press, 1977.

Gotoff, S. P., & Gotoff, M. L. Infectious diseases. In C. H. Carter (Ed.), *Medical aspects of mental retardation* (2nd ed.). Springfield, Ill.: Charles C. Thomas, 1978.

Graham, F. K., Matarazzo, R. G., & Caldwell, B. M. Behavioral differences between normal and traumatized newborns: II. Standardization, reliability and validity. *Psychological Monographs*, 1956, *70*(21, Whole No. 428).

Graham, F. K., Pennoyer, M. M., Caldwell, B. M., Greenman, M., & Hartmann, A. T. Relationship between clinical status and behavior test performance in a newborn group with histories suggesting anoxia. *Journal of Pediatrics*, 1957, *50*, 177–189.

Graham, F. K., Ernhart, C. B., Thurston, D. L., & Craft, M. Development three years after perinatal anoxia and other potentially damaging new born experiences. *Psychological Monographs*, 1962, *76* (3, Whole No. 522).

Greenberg, D. B., Wilson, W. R., Moore, J. M., & Thompson, G. Visual reinforcement audiometry (VRA) with young Down's syndrome children. *Journal of Speech and Hearing Disorders*, 1978, *43*, 448–458.

Greene, L. S. Hyperendemic goiter, cretinism, and social organization in highland Ecuador. In L. S. Greene (Ed.), *Malnutrition, behavior, and social organization*. New York: Academic Press, 1977.

Greenspan, S. Social intelligence in the retarded. In N. R. Ellis (Ed.), *Handbook of mental deficiency: Psychological theory and research* (2nd ed.). Hillsdale, N.J.: Erlbaum, 1979.

Greenwald, C. A., & Leonard, L. B. Communicative and sensorimotor development of Down's syndrome children. *American Journal of Mental Deficiency,* 1979, *84,* 296–303.

Gregg, N. McA. Congenital cataract following German measles in the mother. *Transactions of the Ophthalmological Society of Austria,* 1941, *3,* 35–46.

Grigoroiv-Serbanescu, M. Intellectual and emotional development in premature children from 1 to 5 years. *International Journal of Behavioral Development,* 1981, *4,* 183–199.

Grossman, H. J. *Manual on terminology and classification in mental retardation.* Washington, D.C.: American Association on Mental Deficiency, 1977.

Gruenwald, P. *The placenta.* Baltimore: University Park Press, 1975.

Gunn, P., Berry, P., & Andrews, R. Vocalization and looking behaviour of Down's syndrome infants. *British Journal of Psychology,* 1979, *70,* 259–263.

Gunn, P., Clark, D., & Berry, P. Maternal speech during play with a Down's syndrome infant. *Mental Retardation,* 1980, *18,* 15–18.

Gustavson, K.-H., Hagberg, B., Hagberg, G., & Sars, K. Severe mental retardation in a Swedish county. I. Epidemiology, gestational age, birth weight and associated CNS handicaps in children born 1959–1970. *Acta Pediatrica Scandinavica,* 1977, *66,* 373–379. (a)

Gustavson, K.-H., Hagberg, B., Hagberg, G., & Sars, K. Severe mental retardation in a Swedish county. II: Etiologic and pathogenic aspects of children born 1959–1970. *Neuropaediatrie,* 1977, *8,* 293–304. (b)

Gustavson, K.-H., Holmgren, G., Jonsell, R., & Blomquist, H. Severe mental retardation in children in a northern Swedish county. *Journal of Mental Deficiency Research,* 1977, *21,* 161–177. (c)

Hack, M., Mostow, A., & Miranda, S. B. Development of attention in preterm infants. *Pediatrics,* 1976, *58,* 669–674.

Hagberg, B. Pre-, peri- and postnatal prevention of major neuropediatric handicaps. *Neuropaediatrie,* 1975, *6,* 331–338.

Hagberg, B. Severe mental retardation in Swedish children born 1959–1970: Epidemiological panorama and causative factors. In *Major mental handicap: Methods and costs of prevention* (Ciba Foundation Symposium No. 59) [new series]. Amsterdam: Elsevier, 1978.

Hagberg, B. Epidemiological and preventive aspects of cerebral palsy and severe mental retardation in Sweden. *European Journal of Pediatrics,* 1979, *130,* 71–78.

Hagberg, B., Hagberg, G., & Olow, I. The changing panorama of cerebral palsy in Sweden 1954–1970. I: Analysis of the general changes. *Acta Paediatrica Scandinavica,* 1975, *62,* 199–200.

Hagberg, B., Hagberg, G., & Olow, I. Gains and hazards of intensive neonatal care: An analysis from Swedish cerebral palsy epidemiology. *Developmental Medicine and Child Neurology,* 1982, *24,* 13–19.

Hagberg, B., Olow, I., & Hagberg, G. Decreasing incidence of low-birthweight diplegia—An achievement of modern neonatal care? *Acta Paediatrica Scandinavica,* 1973, *62,* 199–200.

Hagen, J. W., & Stanovich, K. G. Memory: Strategies of acquisition. In R. V. Kail, Jr., & J. W. Hagen (Eds.), *Perspectives on the development of memory and cognition.* Hillsdale, N.J.: Erlbaum, 1977.

Hamerton, J. L. Ethical considerations in newborn chromosome screening programs. In A. Robinson, H. A. Lubs, & D. Bergsma (Eds.), *Sex chromosome aneuploidy: Prospective studies on children.* (The National Foundation, March of Dimes Birth Defects: Original Article Series, Vol. 15, No. 1.) New York: Alan R. Liss, 1979.

Harada, M. Congenital Minamata disease: Intrauterine methylmercury poisoning. *Teratology,* 1978, *18,* 285–288.

Hardy, J. B., & Mellits, E. P. Relationship of low birth weight to maternal characteristics of age, parity, education and body size. In D. M. Reed & F. J. Stanley (Eds.), *The epidemiology of prematurity.* Baltimore and Munich: Urban & Schwarzenberg, 1977.

Harrod, J. R., L'Heureux, P., Wangensteen, O. D., & Hunt, C. E. Long term follow-up of severe respiratory distress syndrome treated with IPPB. *Journal of Pediatrics,* 1974, *84,* 277–286.

Hastrup, R. Personal communication, 1980.

Hayden, A. H., & Haring, N. G. *The acceleration and maintenance of developmental gains in Down's syndrome school-aged children.* Paper presented at the Fourth International Congress of the International Association for the Scientific Study of Mental Deficiency, 1976.

Hein, H. A., & Brown, C. J. Neonatal mortality review: A basis for improving care. *Pediatrics,*

1981, *68*, 504–509.

Hill, P. M., & McCune-Nicolich, L. Pretend play and patterns of cognition in Down's Syndrome children. *Child Development,* 1981, *52,* 611–617.

Hill, R. M., & Stern, L. Drugs in pregnancy: Effects on the fetus and newborn. *Drugs,* 1979, *17,* 182–197.

Hirschhorn, K. Chromosomal abnormalities I: Autosomal defects. In V. A. McKusick & R. Claiborne (Eds.), *Medical genetics.* New York: H. P. Publishing Co., 1973.

Hobel, C. J. ABCs of perinatal medicine. In (Ciba Foundation Symposium No. 59). [new series] *Major mental handicap: Methods and costs of prevention.* Amsterdam: Elsevier, 1978.

Hohman, L. B., & Freedheim, D. K. A study of IQ retest evaluation on 370 cases of cerebral palsy. *American Journal of Physical Medicine,* 1959, *38,* 180–187.

Hommers, M., & Kendall, A. C. The prognosis of the very low-birthweight infant. *Developmental Medicine and Child Neurology,* 1976, *18,* 745–752.

Honzik, M. P. Value and limitations of infant tests: An overview. In M. Lewis (Ed.), *Origins of intelligence.* New York: Plenum, 1976.

Honzik, M. P., MacFarlane, J. W., & Allen, L. The stability of mental test performance between two and eighteen years. *Journal of Experimental Education,* 1948, *17,* 309–324.

Horowitz, F. D., Sullivan, J. W., & Linn, P. L. Stability and instability of newborn behavior: The quest for elusive threads. In A. J. Sameroff (Ed.), *Organization and stability of newborn behavior: A commentary on the Brazelton neonatal behavior assessment scale. Monographs of the Society for Research in Child Development* 1978, *43*(5–6, Serial No. 177).

Horwitz, A. L. The mucopolysaccharidoses: Clinical and biochemical correlations. *American Journal of Mental Deficiency,* 1979, *84,* 113–123.

Howard, J., Parmelee, A. H., Kopp, C. B., & Littman, B. A neurological comparison of preterm and full-term infants at term gestational age. *Journal of Pediatrics,* 1976, *88,* 995–1002.

Hsu, L. Y. F., & Hirschhorn, K. Numerical and structural chromosome abnormalities. In J. C. Wilson & F. C. Fraser (Eds.), Mechanisms and Pathogenesis. *Handbook of Teratology,* vol. 2. New York: Plenum, 1977.

Hughes, J. G. *American Academy of Pediatrics: The first fifty years.* Evanston, Ill.: American Academy of Pediatrics, 1980.

Hunt, G. H., & Holmes, A. E. Studies in hydrocephalus and spina bifida. *Developmental Medicine and Child Neurology,* 1975, *17,* 65–70.

Hunt, J. V. Longitudinal research: A method for studying the intellectual development of high-risk preterm infants. In T. M. Field, A. Sostek, S. Goldberg, & H. H. Shuman (Eds.), *Infants born at risk: Behavior and development.* Jamaica, N.Y.: Spectrum, 1979.

Hunt, J. V. Predicting intellectual disorders in childhood for high-risk preterm infants. In S. L. Friedman & M. Sigman (Eds.), *Preterm and post-term births: Relevance to optimal psychological development.* New York: Academic Press, 1981.

Hunt, J. V., & Rhodes, L. Mental development of preterm infants during the first year. *Child Development,* 1977, *48,* 204–210.

Hunter, R. S., Kilstrom, N., Draybill, E. N., & Loda, F. Antecedents of child abuse and neglect in premature infants: A prospective study in a newborn intensive care unit. *Pediatrics,* 1978, *61,* 629–635.

Illingworth, R. S., & Birch, L. B. The diagnosis of mental retardation in infancy: A follow-up study. *Archives of Disease in Childhood,* 1959, *34,* 269–273.

Inhelder, B. *The diagnosis of reasoning in the mentally retarded* (2nd ed.). New York: John Day, 1968.

Jacobs, P. A. Human population cytogenetics. In J. de Grouchy, F. J. G. Ebling, & I. W. Henderson (Eds.), *Human genetics.* Amsterdam: Excerpta Medica, 1972.

Jacobs, P. A. The incidence and etiology of sex chromosome abnormalities in man. *Birth Defects,* 1979, *15,* 3–14.

Jervis, G. A. Premature senility in Down's syndrome. *Annals of the New York Academy of Science,* 1970, *171,* 559–561.

Johnson, J. D., Malachowski, N. C., Grobstein, R., Welsh, D., Daily, W. J. R., & Sunshine, P. Prognosis of children surviving with the aid of mechanical ventilation in the newborn period. *Journal of Pediatrics,* 1974, *84,* 272–276.

Johnson, K. L., & Kopp, C. B. *A bibliography of screening and assessment measures for infants.* Unpublished manuscript, University of California, Los Angeles, 1980.

Jones, O. H. M. Mother-child communication with prelinguistic Down's syndrome and normal infants. In R. Schaffer (Ed.), *Studies in mother-*

infant interaction. New York: Academic Press, 1977.

Jones, O. H. M. Prelinguistic communication skills in Down's syndrome and normal infants. In T. M. Field, S. Goldberg, D. Stern, & A. M. Sostek (Eds.), *High-risk infants and children: Adult and peer interactions.* New York: Academic Press, 1980.

Jones, R., Cummins, M., & Davies, P. A. Infants of very low birthweight: A 15-year analysis. *Lancet,* 1979, *1,* 1332–1335.

Kagan, J. *Change and continuity in infancy.* New York: Wiley, 1971.

Kagan, J., Kearsley, R. B., & Zelazo, P. R. *Infancy: Its place in human development.* Cambridge: Harvard University Press, 1978.

Kahn, J. V. Relationship of Piaget's sensorimotor period to language acquisition of profoundly retarded children. *American Journal of Mental Deficiency,* 1975, *79,* 640–643.

Kahn, J. V. The utility of the Uzgiris and Hunt scales of sensorimotor development with severely and profoundly retarded children. *American Journal of Mental Deficiency,* 1976, *80,* 663–665.

Kahn, J. V. Acceleration of object permanence with severely and profoundly retarded children. *AAESPH Review,* 1978, *3,* 15–22.

Karrer, R., Nelson, M. N., & Galbraith, G. Psychophysiological research with the mentally retarded. In N. R. Ellis (Ed.), *Handbook of mental deficiency: Psychological theory and research* (2nd ed.). Hillsdale, N.J.: Erlbaum, 1979.

Kashgarian, M., & Rendtorff, R. C. Incidence of Down's syndrome in American Negroes. *Journal of Pediatrics,* 1969, *74,* 468–471.

Kaye, K. Thickening thin data: The maternal role in developing communication and language. In M. Bullowa (Ed.), *Before speech. The beginning of interpersonal communication.* Cambridge, Eng.: At the University Press, 1979.

Kearsley, R. B., & Zelazo, P. R. *Intellectual assessment during infancy and early childhood.* Paper presented at the meeting of the New England Pediatric Society, Boston, 1975.

Kerlinger, F. N. *Foundations of behavioral research.* New York: Holt, Rinehart & Winston, 1964.

Kiely, J. L., & Paneth, W. Follow-up studies of low birthweight infants: Suggestions for design, analysis and reporting. *Developmental Medicine and Child Neurology,* 1981, *23,* 96–100.

Kitchen, W. H., Richards, A., Ryan, M. M., McDougall, A. B., Billson, F. A., Keir, E. H., & Naylor, F. D. A longitudinal study of very low-birthweight infants. II: Results of controlled trial of intensive care and incidence of handicaps. *Developmental Medicine and Child Neurology,* 1979, *21,* 582–589.

Kitchen, W. H., Ryan, M. M., Richards, A., McDougall, A. B., Billson, F. A., Keir, E. H., & Naylor, F. D. A longitudinal study of very low-birthweigh infants. IV: An overview of performance at eight years of age. *Developmental Medicine and Child Neurology,* 1980, *22,* 172–188.

Klaus, M. H., & Kennell, J. H. (Eds.) *Maternal-infant bonding.* St. Louis: C. V. Mosby, 1976.

Klaus, M. H., Kennell, J. H., Plumb, N., & Zuelke, S. Human maternal behavior at first contact with her young. *Pediatrics,* 1970, *46,* 187–192.

Klein, M., & Stern, L. Low birth weight and the battered child syndrome. *American Journal of Diseases of Children,* 1971, *122,* 15–18.

Knobloch, H., & Pasamanick, B. An evaluation of the consistency and predictive value of the 40 week Gesell development schedule. In C. Shagass & B. Pasamanick (Eds.), *Child development and child psychiatry.* Washington, D.C.: American Psychiatric Association, 1960.

Knobloch, H., & Pasamanick, B. Predicting intellectual potential in infancy. *American Journal of Diseases of Children,* 1963, *106,* 43–51.

Knobloch, H., & Pasamanick, B. Prospective studies on the epidemiology of reproductive casualty: Methods, findings and some implications. *Merrill-Palmer Quarterly,* 1966, *12,* 27–43.

Knobloch, H., Rider, R., Harper, P., & Pasamanick, B. Neuropsychiatric sequelae of prematurity: A longitudinal study. *Journal of the American Medical Association,* 1956, *161,* 581–585.

Koch, R., & de la Cruz, F. F. *Down's syndrome (mongolism): Research, prevention and management.* New York: Brunner/Mazel, 1975.

Koch, R., Share, J., Webb, A., & Graliker, B. V. The predictability of Gesell developmental scales in mongolism. *Journal of Pediatrics,* 1963, *62,* 93–97.

Kogan, K. L. Interaction systems between preschool handicapped or developmentally delayed children and their parents. In T. M. Field, S. Goldberg, D. Stern, & A. M. Sostek (Eds.), *High-risk infants and children: Adult and peer interactions.* New York: Academic Press, 1980.

Kogan, K. L., & Gordon, B. N. A mother-instruction program: Documenting change in mother-child interactions. *Child Psychiatry and Human Development*, 1975, *5*, 189–200.

Kogan, K. L., & Tyler, N. Mother-child interaction in young physically handicapped children. *American Journal of Mental Deficiency*, 1973, *77*, 492–497.

Kolata, G. B. Prenatal diagnosis of neural tube defects. *Science*, 1980, *209*, 1216–1218.

Koops, B. L., & Harmon, R. J. Studies on long-term outcome in newborns with birth weights under 1500 grams. In B. W. Camp (Ed.), *Advances in behavioral pediatrics. A research annual* (Vol. 1). Greenwich, Conn.: JAI Press, 1980.

Kopp, C. B. Fine motor behaviours of infants. *Developmental Medicine and Child Neurology*, 1974, *16*, 629–636.

Kopp, C. B. Action-schemes of 8-month-old infants. *Developmental Psychology*, 1976, *12*, 361–362.

Kopp, C. B. Mildly to moderately handicapped infants: What should influence your approach to measurement? In T. Black (Ed.), *Perspectives on measurement—A collection of readings for educators of young handicapped children.* Chapel Hill: University of North Carolina (TADS), 1979.

Kopp, C. B., & Krakow, J. B. *At-risk and handicapped infants: The issue of subject characteristics. Journal of Pediatric Psychology*, 1982, *7*, 361–374.

Kopp, C. B., & McCall, R. B. Predicting later mental performance for normal, at-risk, and handicapped infants. In P. B. Baltes & O. G. Brim (Eds.), *Life-span development and behavior* (Vol. 4). New York: Academic Press, 1982.

Kopp, C. B., O'Connor, M. J., Sigman, M., Parmelee, A. H., & Marcy, T. G. *Early cognitive development of pre-term and fullterm infants: Component structure of sensorimotor and developmental examination.* Paper presented at the Society for Research in Child Development, Denver, March 1975.

Kopp, C. B., & Parmelee, A. H. Prenatal and perinatal influences on behavior. In J. D. Osofsky (Ed.), *Handbook of infant development.* New York: Wiley, 1979.

Kopp, C. B., & Shaperman, J. Cognitive development in the absence of object manipulation during infancy. *Developmental Psychology*, 1973, *9*, 430.

Kopp, C. B., & Sigman, M. (with assistance of T. Marcy & M. J. O'Connor). *The stages of sensori-motor intelligence in the child from birth to two years*, by I. Casati & I. Lézine, unpublished.

Kopp, C. B., Sigman, M., Parmelee, A. H., & Jeffrey, W. E. Neurological organization and visual fixation in infants at 40 weeks conceptional age. *Developmental Psychobiology*, 1975, *8*, 165–171.

Kopp, C. B., & Vaughn, B. C. Sustained attention during exploratory manipulation as a predictor of cognitive competence in pre-term males. *Child Development*, 1982, *53*, 174–182.

Korn, S. J., Chess, S., & Fernandez, P. The impact of children's physical handicaps on marital quality and family integration. In R. M. Lerner & G. B. Spanier (Eds.), *Child influence on marital and family interaction: A life-span perspective.* New York: Academic Press, 1978.

Krakow, J. B., & Kopp, C. B. Sustained attention in young Down syndrome children. *Topics in early childhood special education*, 1982, *2*, 32–42.

Kurent, J. E., & Sever, J. L. Infectious diseases. In J. G. Wilson & F. C. Fraser (Eds.), *Handbook of teratology*, vol. 1, *General principles and ediology*. New York: Plenum, 1977.

Lancet. The fate of the baby under 1501g at birth (Editorial). *Lancet*, 1980, *1*, 461–463.

Larroche, J.-C. *Developmental pathology of the neonate*. Amsterdam: Excerpta Medica, 1977.

Laurence, K. M. The survival of untreated spina bifida cystica. *Developmental Medicine and Child Neurology*, 1966, *8*, 10–20. (Supplement 11)

Laurence, K. M., & Tew, B. J. Follow-up of 65 survivors from the 425 cases of spina bifida born in South Wales between 1956 and 1962. *Developmental Medicine and Child Neurology*, 1967, *9*, 1–3. (Supplement 13)

Layrisse, M., Roche, M., & Baker, S. J. Nutritional anemias. In G. H. Beaton & J. M. Bengoa (Eds.), *Nutrition in preventive medicine: The major deficiency syndromes, epidemiology, and approaches to control.* Geneva: World Health Organization, 1976.

Leck, I. Correlations of malformation frequency with environmental and genetic attributes in man. In J. G. Wilson & F. C. Fraser (Eds.), *Handbook of teratology*, vol. 3, Comparative, maternal, and epidemiologic aspects. New York: Plenum, 1977.

Lee, K.-S., Paneth, N., Gartner, L. M., Pearlman, M. A., & Gruss, L. Neonatal mortality: An analysis of the recent improvements in the United States. *American Journal of Public Health,* 1980, *70,* 15–21.

Leib, S. A., Benfield, D. G., & Guidubaldi, J. Effects of early intervention and stimulation on the preterm infant. *Pediatrics,* 1980, *66,* 83–90.

Leiderman, P. H., Leifer, A. D., Seashore, M. J., Barnett, C. R., & Grobstein, R. Mother-infant interaction: Effects of early deprivation, prior experience and sex of infant. *Early Development,* 1973, *51,* 154–175.

Leiderman, P. H., & Seashore, M. J. Mother-infant separation: Some delayed consequences. In *(Ciba Foundation Symposium No. 33) [new series] Parent-infant interaction.* Amsterdam: Elsevier, 1975.

Leifer, A. D., Leiderman, P. H., Barnett, C. R., & Williams, J. A. Effects of mother-infant separation on maternal attachment behavior. *Child Development,* 1972, *43,* 1203–1218.

Lejeune, J., Gautier, M., & Turpin, M. R. Etudes des chromosomes somatiques de neuf enfants mongoliens. *CR Academic Science,* 1959, *248,* 1721.

Lenneberg, E. H., Nichols, I. A., & Rosenberger, E. F. Primitive stages of language development in mongolism. *Disorders of Communication,* 1962, *1,* 119–137.

Leonard, M. F., & Schowalter, J. E. *Sex chromosome anomalies: A prospective look at development.* Paper presented at the meeting of the American Academy of Pediatrics, San Francisco, 1979.

Leroy, J. G. Management of the micropolysaccharidoses and allied disorders. In C. J. Papadatos & C. S. Bartsocas (Eds.), *The management of genetic disorders.* New York: Alan R. Liss, 1979.

Lewin, K. *A dynamic theory of personality.* New York: McGraw-Hill, 1935.

Lewis, M., Goldberg, S., & Campbell, H. A developmental study of information processing within the first three years of life: Response decrement to a redundant signal. *Monographs of the Society for Research in Child Development,* 1969, *34*(9, Serial No. 133).

Liben, L. S. (Ed.) *Deaf children: Developmental perspectives.* New York: Academic Press, 1978.

Lipsitt, L. P. Learning assessments and interventions for the infant born at risk. In T. Field, A. Sostek, S. Goldberg, & H. H. Shuman (Eds.), *Infants born at risk: Behavior and development.* Jamaica, N.Y.: Spectrum, 1979. (a)

Lipsitt, L. P. The newborn as informant. In R. B. Kearsley & I. E. Sigel (Eds.), *Infants at risk: Assessment of cognitive functioning.* Hillsdale, N.J.: Erlbaum, 1979. (b)

Littman, B. The relationship of medical events to infant development. In T. M. Field, A. M. Sostek, S. Goldberg & H. H. Shuman, (Eds.), *Infants born at risk: Behavior and development.* Jamaica, N.Y.: Spectrum, 1979.

Lonsdale, D. M. B., & Foust, M. Normal mental development in treated phenylketonuria—Report of 10 cases. *American Journal of Diseases of Children,* 1970, *119,* 440–446.

Lorincz, A. E. Mucopolysaccharidoses. In C. H. Carter (Ed.), *Medical aspects of mental retardation* (2nd ed.). Springfield, Ill.: Charles C. Thomas, 1978.

Lubchenco, L. O. Assessment of gestational age and development at birth. *Pediatric Clinics of North America,* 1970, *17,* 125–145.

Lubchenco, L. O. *The high risk infant.* Philadelphia: W. B. Saunders, 1976.

Lubchenco, L. O., Hansman, C., & Backström, L. Factors affecting fetal growth. In J. H. P. Jonxis, H. K. A. Visser, & J. A. Troelstra (Eds.), *Nutricia symposium: Aspects of prematurity and dysmaturity.* Leiden, the Netherlands: Stenfert Kroese, 1968.

Lubchenco, L. O., Horner, F. A., Reed, L. H., Hix, I. E., Jr., Metcalf, D. R., Cohig, R., Elliott, H. C., & Bourg, M. Sequelae of premature birth: Evaluation of premature infants of low birth weights at 10 years of age. *American Journal of Diseases of Children,* 1963, *106,* 101–115.

Luria, A. R. Psychological studies of mental deficiency in the Soviet Union. In N. R. Ellis (Ed.), *Handbook of mental deficiency: Psychological theory and research.* New York: McGraw-Hill, 1963.

MacDonald, H., & Tobin, J. O'H. Congenital cytomegalovirus infection: A collaborative study on epidemiological, clinical and laboratory findings. *Developmental Medicine and Child Neurology,* 1978, *20,* 471–482.

MacMillan, D., Meyers, C. E., & Morrison, G. M. System identification of mildly mentally retarded children: Implications for interpreting and conducting research. *American Journal of Mental Deficiency,* 1980, *85,* 108–115.

Magenis, R. E., Overton, K. M., Chamberlin, J., Brady, T., & Lovrien, E. Parental origin of the extra chromosome in Down's syndrome. *Human Genetics,* 1977, *37,* 7–16.

Mahoney, G., Glover, A., & Finger, I. The relationship between language and sensorimotor development among Down syndrome and developmentally normal children. *American Journal of Mental Deficiency,* 1981, *86,* 21–27.

Maloney, M. P., & Ward, M. P. *Psychological assessment: A conceptual approach.* New York: Oxford University Press, 1976.

Mans, L., Cicchetti, D., & Sroufe, L. A. Mirror reactions of Down's syndrome infants and toddlers: Cognitive underpinnings of self-recognition. *Child Development,* 1978, *49,* 1247–1250.

Marin-Padilla, M. Structural abnormalities of the cerebral cortex in human chromosomal aberrations: A Golgi study. *Brain Research,* 1972, *44,* 625–629.

Markowitz, S. Mother-infant interaction with Down syndrome and normal infants. Unpublished doctoral dissertation, University of California, Los Angeles, 1980.

Marriage, K. J., & Davies, P. A. Neurological sequelae in children surviving mechanical ventilation in the neonatal period. *Archives of Disease in Childhood,* 1977, *52,* 176–182.

Masland, R. L., Sarason, S. B., & Gladwin, T. *Mental subnormality: Biological, psychological, and cultural factors.* New York: Basic Books, 1958.

Matsunaga, E., Tonomura, A., Oishi, H., & Kikuchi, Y. Reexamination of paternal age effect in Down's syndrome. *Human Genetics,* 1978, *40,* 259–268.

Mawdsley, T., Rickham, P. O., & Roberts, J. R. Long term results of early operation of open myelomeningoceles and encephaloceles. *British Medical Journal,* 1967, *1,* 663–666.

McBride, W. G. Thalidomide and congenital abnormalities. *Lancet,* 1961, *2,* 1358.

McCall, R. B. Qualitative transitions in behavioral development in the first three years of life. In M. H. Bornstein & W. Kessen (Eds.), *Psychological development from infancy.* New York: Erlbaum, 1979.

McCall, R. B., Appelbaum, M. I., & Hogarty, P. S. Developmental changes in mental performance. *Monographs of the Society for Research in Child Development,* 1973, *38*(3, Serial No. 150).

McCall, R. B., Hogarty, P. S., & Hurlburt, N. Transitions in infant sensorimotor development: The prediction of childhood I.Q. *American Psychologist,* 1972, *27,* 728–748.

McCarthy, D. *Manual for the McCarthy scales of children's abilities.* New York: Psychological Association, 1970, 1972.

McDonald, A. D. Severely retarded children in Quebec: Prevalence, causes, and care. *American Journal of Mental Deficiency,* 1973, *78,* 205–215.

McKusick, V.A. *Human genetics* (2nd ed.). Englewood Cliffs, N.J.: Prentice-Hall, 1969.

Meadow, K. P. *Deafness and child development.* Berkeley: University of California Press, 1980.

Melyn, M., & White, D. Mental and developmental milestones of noninstitutional Down's syndrome children. *Pediatrics,* 1973, 52, 542–545.

Mercer, J. *Labeling the mentally retarded: Clinical and social system perspectives on mental retardation.* Berkeley, Calif.: University of California Press, 1973.

Meyer, M. B. Effects of maternal smoking and altitude on birth weight and gestation. In D. W. Reed & F. J. Stanley (Eds.), *The epidemiology of prematurity.* Baltimore and Munich: Urban & Schwarzenberg, 1977.

Mikkelsen, M., Hallberg, A., & Poulsen, H. Maternal and paternal origin of extra chromosome in trisomy 21. *Human Genetics,* 1976, *32,* 17–21.

Miller, H. C., & Hassanein, K. Diagnosis of impaired fetal growth in newborn infants. *Pediatrics,* 1971, *48,* 511–522.

Miller, H. C., Hassanein, K., Chin, T. D. Y., & Hensleigh, P. Socioeconomic factors in relation to fetal growth in white infants. *Journal of Pediatrics,* 1976, *89,* 638–643.

Milunsky, A. Current concepts in genetics. Prenatal diagnosis of genetic disorders. *New England Journal of Medicine,* 1976, *295,* 377–380.

Milunsky, A. (Ed.) *Genetic disorders and the fetus. Diagnosis, prevention, and treatment.* New York: Plenum, 1979.

Minde, K., Trehub, S., Corter, C., Boukydis, C., Celhoffer, L., & Marton, P. Mother-child relationships in the premature nursery: An observational study. *Pediatrics,* 1978, *61,* 373–379.

Minkowski, A., Amiel-Tison, C., Cukier, F., Dreyfus-Brisac, C., Reber, J. P., & Bethman, O. de. Long-term follow-up and sequelae of asphyxiated infants. In L. Gluck (Ed.), *Intrauterine asphyxia and the developing fetal brain.* Chicago: Year Book Medical Publishers, 1977.

Miranda, S. B., & Fantz, R. L. Visual preferences of Down's syndrome and normal infants. *Child Development,* 1973, *44,* 555–561.

Miranda, S. B., & Fantz, R. L. Recognition memory in Down's syndrome and normal infants. *Child Development,* 1974, *45,* 651–660.

Miranda, S. B., & Hack, M. The predictive value of

neonatal visual-perceptual behaviors. In T. M. Field, A. Sostek, S. Goldberg, & H. H. Shuman (Eds.), *Infants born at risk: Behavior and development*. Jamaica, N.Y.: Spectrum, 1979.

Monroe, L., & Anderson, O. W. *Health progress in the United States, 1900–1960*. Chicago: University of Chicago Press, 1963.

Moore, W. M., Silverberg, M. M., & Read, M. S. *Nutrition, growth and development of North American Indian children* (DHEW Publication No. [NIH] 72–26). Washington, D.C.: U.S. Government Printing Office, 1972.

Morgan, S. B. Development and distribution of intellectual and adaptive skills in Down syndrome children: Implications of early intervention. *Mental Retardation*, 1979, *17*, 247–249.

Morton, N. E. Genetic aspects of prematurity. In D. M. Reed & F. J. Stanley (Eds.), *The epidemiology of prematurity*. Baltimore and Munich: Urban & Schwarzenberg, 1977.

Moser, H. W. Biochemical aspects of mental retardation. In D. B. Tower (Ed.), *The nervous system*, vol. 2, *The clinical neurosciences*. New York: Raven Press, 1975.

Motulsky, A. G. Brave new world? *Science*, 1974, *185*, 653–663.

Murphy, L. B. *Personality in young children* (Vols. 1, 2). New York: Basic Books, 1956.

Murphy, L. B., & Moriarity, A. *Vulnerability, coping and growth from infancy to adolescence*. New Haven, Conn.: Yale University Press, 1976.

Nadler, H. L. Prenatal detection of genetic defects. *Advances in Pediatrics*, 1976, *22*, 1–81.

Naylor, A. F., & Myrianthopoulos, N. C. The relation of ethnic and selected socio-economic factors to human birth-weight. *Annals of Human Genetics*, 1967, *31*, 71–83.

Neligan, G. A., Kolvin, I., Scott, D. M., & Garside, R. F. Born too soon or born too small (Clinics in Developmental Medicine, No. 61). London: Heinemann, 1976.

Nelson, M. N. Bayley developmental assessments of low birthweight infants. In T. M. FIeld, A. M. Sostek, S. Goldberg, & H. H. Shuman (Eds.), *Infants born at risk: Behavior and development*. Jamaica, N.Y.: Spectrum, 1979.

Neumann, C. Nutrition and women: Facts and faddism. In C. B. Kopp (Ed.), *Becoming female*. New York: Plenum, 1979.

Newell, A., & Simon, H. A. *Human problem solving*. Englewood Cliffs, N.J.: Prentice-Hall, 1972.

Niswander, K. R. Obstetric factors related to prematurity. In D. M. Reed & F. J. Stanley (Eds.), *The epidemiology of prematurity*. Baltimore and Munich: Urban & Schwarzenberg, 1977.

Nora, J. J., & Fraser, F. C. *Medical genetics: Principles and practices*. Philadelphia: Lea & Febiger, 1974.

Novy, M. J. Evaluation and treatment of the fetus at risk. In R. E. Behrman (Ed.), *Neonatology: Diseases of the fetus and infant*. St. Louis: C. V. Mosby, 1973.

O'Connor, M. J. A comparison of preterm and full-term infants on auditory discrimination at four months and on Bayley scales of infant development at eighteen months. *Child Development*, 1980, *51*, 81–88.

Ohara, P. R. Electron microscopical study of the brain in Down's syndrome. *Brain*, 1972, *95*, 681–684.

Ounsted, M., Moar, V., & Scott, A. Growth in the first year of life: Effects of sex and weight for gestational age at birth. *Developmental Medicine and Child Neurology*, 1982, *24*, 356–365.

Ounsted, M., & Ounsted, C. On fetal growth rate. *Clinics in Developmental Medicine* No. 61. London: Heinemann, 1973.

Outerbridge, E. W., & Stern, L. Developmental follow-up of artificially ventilated infants with neonatal respiratory failure. *Pediatric Research*, 1972, *6*, 412.

Pape, K. E., Buncie, R. J., Ashby, S., & Fitzhardinge, P. M. The status at 2 years of low birth weight infants born in 1974 with birth weights of less than 1,000 gm. *Journal of Pediatrics*, 1978, *92*, 253–260.

Pape, K. E., & Fitzhardinge, P. M. Perinatal damage to the developing brain. In A. Milunsky, E. A. Friedman, & L. Gluck (Eds.) *Advances in perinatal medicine*, Vol. 1. New York: Plenum, 1981.

Parkinson, C. E., Wallis, S., & Harvey, D. School achievement and behaviour of children who were small-for-dates at birth. *Developmental Medicine and Child Neurology*, 1981, *23*, 41–50.

Parmelee, A. H. European neurological studies of the newborn. *Child Development*, 1962, *33*, 169–180.

Parmelee, A. H. *Newborn neurological examination*. Unpublished manuscript, 1974.

Parmelee, A. H. Neurophysiological and behavioral organization of premature infants in the first months of life. *Biological Psychiatry*, 1975, *10*, 501–512.

Parmelee, A. H. *Diagnostic and intervention studies of high-risk infants* (USPHS Contract No.

1–HD–32776). 1976. (Report)

Parmelee, A. H. Personal communication, 1980.

Parmelee, A. H., Beckwith, L., Cohen, S. E., & Sigman, M. *Social influences on infants at medical risk for behavioral difficulties.* Paper presented at the First World Congress on Infant Psychiatry, Estoril, Portugal, April 1980.

Parmelee, A. H., & Haber, A. Who is the risk infant? *Clinical Obstetrics and Gynaecology,* 1973, *16,* 376–387.

Parmelee, A. H., Kopp, C. B., & Sigman, M. Selection of developmental assessment techniques for infants at risk. *Merrill-Palmer Quarterly,* 1976, *22,* 177–199.

Parmelee, A. H., Minkowski, A., Saint-Anne Dargassies, S., Dreyfus-Brisac, C., Lézine, I., Berges, J., Chervin, G., & Stern, E. Neurological evaluation of the premature infant. *Biology Neonate,* 1970, *15,* 65–78.

Parmelee, A. H., & Schulte, F. S. Developmental testing of pre-term and small-for-dates infants. *Pediatrics,* 1970, *45,* 21–28.

Parmelee, A. H., Schulte, F. S., Akiyama, Y., Wenner, W., Schultz, M., & Stern, E. Maturation of EEG activity during sleep in premature infants. *Electroencephalography and Clinical Neurophysiology,* 1968, *24,* 319–329.

Piaget, J. *The origins of intelligence in children.* New York: International Universities Press, 1952.

Piaget, J. *The construction of reality in the child.* New York: Basic Books, 1954.

Piaget, J. Piaget's theory. In P. H. Mussen (Ed.), *Carmichael's manual of child psychiatry* (3rd ed.), vol. 1. New York: Wiley, 1970.

Piaget, J., & Inhelder, B. Diagnosis of mental operations and theory of the intelligence. *American Journal of Mental Deficiency,* 1947, *51,* 401–406.

Piper, M. C., & Pless, I. B. Early intervention for infants with Down syndrome: A controlled trial. *Pediatrics,* 1980, *65,* 463–468.

Placek, P. J. Maternal and infant health factors associated with low infant birthweight: Findings from the 1972 national natality survey. In D. M. Reed & F. J. Stanley (Eds.), *The epidemiology of prematurity.* Baltimore and Munich: Urban & Schwarzenberg, 1977.

Prechtl, H. F. R. Neurological findings in newborn infants after pre- and perinatal complications. In J. H. P. Jonxis, H. K. A. Visser, & J. A. Troelstra (Eds.), *Nutricia symposium: Aspects of prematurity and dysmaturity.* Leiden: Stenfert Kroese, 1968.

Prechtl, H. F. R. Problems and strategies in neurological assessment in infancy. In D. A. A. Primrose (Ed.), *Proceedings of the Third Congress of the International Association for the Scientific Study of Mental Deficiency* (Vol. 1). Warsaw: Polish Medical Publishers, 1975.

Prechtl, H. F. R. The neurological examination of the full-term newborn infant (2nd ed.) (Clinics in Developmental Medicine, No. 63). London: Heinemann, 1977.

Prechtl, H. F. R., & Beintema, D. J. The neurological examination of the full-term newborn infant. (Clinics in Developmental Medicine, No. 12). London: Heinemann, 1964.

Prod'hom, L. S., & Calâme, A. Follow-up studies of low birth weight infants. In J. H. P. Jonxis (Ed.), *Growth and development of full-term and preterm infants.* New York: Excerpta Medica, 1978.

Read, M. S. Anemia and behavior. *Modern Problems in Paediatrics,* 1975, *14,* 189–202.

Read, M. S. Malnutrition and human performance. In L. S. Greene (Ed.), *Malnutrition, behavior, and social organization.* New York: Academic Press, 1977.

Reed, D. M., & Stanley, F. J. *The epidemiology of prematurity.* Baltimore and Munich: Urban & Schwarzenberg, 1977.

Reilly, P. R., & Milunsky, A. Medicolegal aspects of prenatal diagnosis. In A. Milunsky (Ed.), *Genetic disorders and the fetus: Diagnosis, prevention, and treatment.* New York: Plenum, 1979.

Remington, J. S., & Desmonts, G. Toxoplasmosis. In J. S. Remington & J. O. Klein (Eds.), *Infectious diseases of the fetus and newborn infant.* Philadelphia: W. B. Saunders, 1976.

Reynolds, E. O. R. Neonatal intensive care and the prevention of major handicap. In *Major mental handicap: Methods and costs of prevention* (Ciba Foundation Symposium No. 59 [new series]). Amsterdam: Elsevier, 1978.

Robinson, A., Lubs, H. A., & Bergsma, D. (Eds.) *Sex chromosome aneuploidy: Prospective studies on children.* (The National Foundation, March of Dimes Birth Defects: Original Article Series, Vol. 15, No. 1.) New York: Alan R. Liss, 1979.

Robinson, A., Lubs, H. A., Nielsen, J., & Sørensen, K. Summary of clinical findings: Profiles of children with 47, XXY, 47, XXX, 47, XYY karyotypes. *Birth Defects,* 1979, *15,* 261–266.

Robinson, A., Puck, M., Pennington, B., Borelli, J., & Hudson, M. Abnormalities of the sex chromosomes: A prospective study on randomly identified newborns. *Birth Defects*, 1979, *15*, 203–241.

Robinson, C. Error patterns in level 4 and level 5 object permanence training. *American Journal of Mental Deficiency*, 1974, *78*, 389–396.

Rondal, J. A. Maternal speech in normal and Down's syndrome children. In P. Mittler (Ed.), *Research to practice in mental retardation*, vol. 2, *Education and training*. Baltimore: University Park Press, 1977.

Rose, S. A., Gottfried, A. W., & Bridger, W. H. Cross-modal transfer in infants: Relationship to prematurity and socioeconomic background. *Developmental Psychology*, 1978, *14*, 643–652.

Rose, S. A., Gottfried, A. W., & Bridger, W. H. Effects of haptic cues on visual recognition memory in fullterm and preterm infants. *Infant Behavior & Development*, 1979, *2*, 55–67.

Rose, S. A., Schmidt, K., & Bridger, W. Cardiac and behavioral responsivity to tactile stimulation in premature and full-term infants. *Developmental Psychology*, 1976, *12*, 311–320.

Rosecrans, C. J. A longitudinal study of exceptional cognitive development in a partial translocation Down's syndrome child. *American Journal of Mental Deficiency*, 1971, *76*, 291–294.

Rosenblith, J. F. *Manual for behavioral examination of the neonate as modified by Rosenblith from Graham*. Unpublished manuscript, 1961.

Rosenblith, J. F., & Lipsitt, L. P. Interscore agreement for the Graham behavior test for neonates. *Journal of Pediatrics*, 1959, *54*, 200–205.

Roskies, I. *Abnormality and normality: The mothering of thalidomide children*. Ithaca, N.Y.: Cornell University Press, 1972.

Ross, R. T. The mental growth of mongoloid defectives. *American Journal of Mental Deficiency*, 1962, *66*, 736–738.

Rubin, R. A., & Balow, B. Perinatal influences on the behavior and learning problems of children. In B. B. Lahey & A. E. Kazdin (Eds.), *Advances in child clinical psychology*. New York: Plenum, 1977.

Rubin, R. A., Rosenblatt, C., & Balow, B. Psychological and educational sequelae of prematurity. *Pediatrics*, 1973, *52*, 352–363.

Ruiz, M.P.D., LeFever, J. A., Hakanson, D. O., Clark, D. A., & Williams, M. L. Early development of infants of birth weight less than 1,000 grams with reference to mechanical ventilation in newborn period. *Pediatrics*, 1981, *68*, 330–335.

Rutter, M. Raised lead levels and impaired cognitive/behavioral functioning: A reveiw of the evidence. *Developmental Medicine and Child Neurology*, 1980, *22* (Supplement No. 42).

Rynders, J., & Horrobin, J. M. Project EDGE: The University of Minnesota's communication stimulation program for Down's syndrome infants. In B. L. Friedlander, G. M. Sterritt, & G. E. Kirk (Eds.), *Exceptional infant*, vol. 3, *Assessment and intervention*. New York: Brunner/Mazel, 1975.

Sabel, K.-G., Olegård, R., & Victorin, L. Remaining sequelae with modern perinatal care. *Pediatrics*, 1976, *57*, 652–658.

Sahu, S. Lead poisoning in children. *Paediatrician*, 1977, *6*, 262–270.

Saint-Anne Dargassies, S. Neurological maturation of the premature infant of 28 to 41 weeks gestational age. In F. Falkner (Ed.), *Human Development*. Philadelphia: W. B. Saunders, 1966.

Saint-Anne Dargassies, S. Normality and normalization as seen in a long-term neurological follow-up of 286 truly premature infants. *Neuropaediatrie*, 1979, *10*, 226–244.

Sameroff, A. J. Early influences on development: Fact or fancy? *Merrill-Palmer Quarterly*, 1975, *21*, 267–294.

Sameroff, A. J. (Ed.) Organization and stability: A commentary on the Brazelton neonatal behavior assessment scale. *Monographs of the Society for Research in Child Development*, 1978, *43*(5–6, Serial No. 177).

Sameroff, A. J., & Chandler, M. J. Reproductive risk and the continuum of caretaking casualty. In F. D. Horowitz, M. Hetherington, S. Scarr-Salapatek, & G. Siegel (Eds.), *Review of child development research* (Vol. 4). Chicago: University of Chicago Press, 1975.

Scarr-Salapatek, S. An evolutionary perspective on infant intelligence: Species patterns and individual variations. In M. Lewis (Ed.), *Origins of intelligence*. New York: Plenum, 1976.

Schaie, K. W. A general model for the study of developmental problems. *Psychological Bulletin*, 1965, *64*, 92–107.

Scherz, R. G. Fatal motor vehicle accidents of child passengers from birth through 4 years of age in Washington State. *Pediatrics*, 1981, *68*, 572–575.

Schulte, F. S., Linke, I., Michaelis, R., & Nolte, R. Excitation, inhibition, and impulse conduction in spinal motoneurones of preterm, term and small-for-dates newborn infants. In R. J. Robinson (Ed.), *Brain and early behavior*. London: Academic Press, 1969.

Self, P. A., Horowitz, F. D. The behavioral assessment of the neonate: An overview. In J. Osofsky (Ed.), *Handbook of infant development.* New York: Wiley, 1979.

Sell, S. H. W., Merrill, R. E., Doyne, E. O., & Zimsky, E. P. Long-term sequelae of *Hemophilus influenzae* meningitis. *Pediatrics,* 1972, *49,* 206–211.

Serafica, F. C., & Cicchetti, D. Down's syndrome children in a strange situation: Attachment and exploration behaviors. *Merrill-Palmer Quarterly,* 1976, *22,* 137–150.

Sever, L. E. Reproductive hazards of the workplace. *Journal of Occupational Medicine,* 1981, *23,* 685–691.

Shapiro, S., Schlesinger, E. R., & Nesbitt, R. E. L. *Infant, perinatal, maternal and childhood mortality in the United States.* Cambridge: Harvard University Press, 1968.

Share, J., Koch, R., Webb, A., & Graliker, B. V. The longitudinal development of infants and young children with Down's Syndrome (mongolism). *American Journal of Mental Deficiency,* 1964, *68,* 685–692.

Share, J., Webb, A., & Koch, R. A preliminary investigation of the early developmental status of mongoloid infants. *American Journal of Mental Deficiency,* 1961, *66,* 238–241.

Siegel, L. S., Saigal, S., Rosenbaum, P., Young, A., Berenbaum, S., & Stoskopf, B. *Correlates and predictors of cognitive and language development of very low birthweight infants.* Departments of Psychiatry and Pediatrics, McMaster University Medical Center, Hamilton, Ontario, Canada, undated.

Siegler, R. S. The origins of scientific reasoning. In R. S. Siegler (Ed.), *Children's thinking: What develops?* Hillsdale, N.J.: Erlbaum, 1978.

Sigman, M. Early development of preterm and full-term infants: Exploratory behavior in eight month olds. *Child Development,* 1976, *47,* 606–612.

Sigman, M. Personal communication, 1980.

Sigman, M., Cohen, S. E., Beckwith, L., & Parmelee, A. H. Social and familial influences on the development of pre-term infants. *Journal of Pediatric Psychology,* 1981, *6,* 1–12.

Sigman, M., Kopp, C. B., Littman, B., & Parmelee, A. H. Infant visual attentiveness as a function of birth condition. *Developmental Psychology,* 1977, 431–437.

Sigman, M., & Parmelee, A. H. Visual preferences of four-month-old premature and full-term infants. *Child Development,* 1974, *45,* 959–965.

Sigman, M., & Parmelee, A. H. Longitudinal evaluation of the preterm infant. In T. M. Field, A. M. Sostek, S. Goldberg, & H. H. Shuman (Eds.), *Infants born at risk: Behavior and development.* Jamaica, N.Y.: Spectrum, 1979.

Silverman, W. A. *Retrolental fibroplasia: A modern parable.* New York: Grune & Stratton, 1980.

Silverstein, A. B. Mental growth in mongolism. *Child Development,* 1966, *33,* 132–142.

Sloan, W., & Harmon, H. H. Constancy in IQ of mental defectives. *Journal of Genetic Psychology,* 1947, *71,* 177–185.

Smith, B. L., & Oller, D. K. A comparative study of pre-meaningful vocalizations produced by normal and Down's syndrome infants. *Journal of Speech and Hearing Disorders,* in press.

Smith, D. W. The fetal alcohol syndrome. *Hospital Practice,* 1979, *14,* 121–128.

Smith, D. W., & Wilson, A. H. *The child with Down's syndrome (mongolism).* Philadelphia: W. B. Saunders, 1973.

Smith, J. L. *A treatise on the diseases of infancy and childhood.* Philadelphia: Lea, 1869.

Sorenson, J. R., Swazey, J. P., & Scotch, N. A. Reproductive past. Reproductive future. Genetic counseling and its effectiveness. *Birth Defects: Original Article Series,* Vol. 17, *4,* 1981.

Sostek, A. M., Quinn, P. O., & Davitt, M. K. Behavior, development and neurologic status of premature and full-term infants with varying medical complications. In T. M. Field, A. M. Sostek, S. Goldberg, & H. H. Shuman (Eds.), *Infants born at risk: Behavior and development.* Jamaica, N.Y.: Spectrum, 1979.

Spitz, H. H. Field theory in mental deficiency. In N. R. Ellis (Ed.), *Handbook of mental deficiency: Psychological theory and research.* New York: McGraw-Hill, 1963.

Spitz, H. H. Beyond field theory in the study of mental deficiency. In N. R. Ellis (Ed.), *Handbook of mental deficiency: Psychological theory and research* (2nd ed.). Hillsdale, N.J.: Erlbaum Associates, 1979.

Stahlman, M., Hedvall, G., Dolanski, E., Faxelius, G., Burko, H., & Kirk, V. A six year follow-up of clinical hyaline membrane disease. *Pediatric Clinics of North America,* 1973, *20,* 433–446.

Stanford-Binet intelligence scale. Boston: Houghton Mifflin, 1973.

Stagnos, S., Dworsky, M. E., Torres, J., Mesa, T., Hirsh, T. Prevalence and importance of congenital cytomegalovirus infection in three different populations. *The Journal of Pediatrics,* 1982, *101,* 897–900.

Stanley, F. J., & Alberman, E. D. Infants of very

low birthweight. I: Perinatal factors affecting survival. *Developmental Medicine and Child Neurology,* 1978, *20,* 300–312.

Steinhausen, H. Psychological evaluation of treatment in phenylketonuria: Intellectual, motor and social development. *Neuropaediatrie,* 1974, *5,* 146–156.

Stene, J., Fischer, G., Stene, E., Mikkelson, M., & Peterson, E. Paternal age effect in Down's syndrome. *Annals of Human Genetics,* 1977, *46,* 299–306.

Stene, J., & Stene, E. Statistical methods for detecting a moderate paternal age effect on incidence of disorder when a maternal one is present. *Annals of Human Genetics,* 1977, *40,* 343–353.

Stern, E., Parmelee, A. H., Akiyama, Y., Schultz, M., & Wenner, W. Sleep cycle characteristics in infants. *Pediatrics,* 1969, *43,* 65–70.

Stewart, A. L., Turcan, D., Rawlings, G., Hart, S., & Gregory, S. Outcome for infants at high risk of major handicap. In (Ciba Foundation Symposium No. 59). [new series]. *Major mental handicap: Method and costs of prevention.* Amsterdam: Elsevier, 1978.

Stone, N., & Chesney, B. Attachment behaviors in handicapped infants. *Mental Retardation,* 1978, *16,* 8–12.

Stott, L. H., & Ball, R. S. Evaluation of infant and preschool mental tests. *Monographs of the Society for Research in Child Development,* 1965, *30*(3, Serial No. 101).

Straumanis, J. J., Shagass, C., & Overton, D. A. Somatosensory evoked responses in Down's syndrome. *Archives of General Psychiatry,* 1973, *29,* 544–549.

Streissguth, A. P., Landesman-Dwyer, S. L., Martin, J. C., & Smith, D. W. Teratogenic effects of alcohol in humans and laboratory animals. *Science,* 1980, *209,* 353–361.

Taub, H. B., Goldstein, K. M., & Caputo, D. V. Indices of prematurity as discriminators of development in middle childhood. *Child Development,* 1977, *48,* 797–805.

Teberg, A. J., Wu, P. Y. K., Hodgman, J., Mich, C., Garfinkle, J., Azen, S., & Wingert, W. Infants with birth weight under 1500 grams: Physical, neurological and developmental outcomes. *Critical Care Medicine,* 1982, *10,* 10–14.

Tejani, A., Dobias, B., & Sambursky, J. Long-term prognosis after H. *influenzae* Meningitis: Prospective evaluation. *Developmental Medicine and Child Neurology,* 1982, *24,* 338–343.

Tew, B. J., & Laurence, K. M. The ability and attainments of spina bifida patients born in South Wales between 1956–1962. *Developmental Medicine and Child Neurology,* 1972, Supplement 27, 124–131.

Thomas, A., Chess, S., & Birch, H. G. *Temperament and behavioral disorders.* New York: New York University Press, 1968.

Thomas, H. Psychological assessment instruments for use with human infants. *Merrill-Palmer Quarterly,* 1970, *16,* 179–223.

Thompson, J. S., & Thompson, M. W. *Genetics in medicine.* Philadelphia: W. B. Saunders, 1973.

Thompson, J. S., & Thompson, M. W. *Genetics in medicine,* 3rd Ed. Philadelphia: W. B. Saunders, 1980.

Thompson, M. K. Prenatal diagnosis and public policy. In A. Milunsky (Ed.), *Genetic disorders and the fetus: Diagnosis, prevention, and treatment.* New York: Plenum, 1979.

Throne, F. M., Schulman, J. L., & Kasper, J. C. Reliability and stability of the Wechsler intelligence scale for children for a group of mentally retarded boys. *American Journal of Mental Deficiency,* 1962, *67,* 455–457.

Tjossem, T. *Intervention strategies for high risk infants and children.* Baltimore: University Park Press, 1976.

Tronick, E., & Brazelton, T. B. Clinical uses of the Brazelton neonatal behavioral assessment. In B. L. Friedlander, G. M. Sterritt, & G. E. Kirk (Eds.), *Exceptional infant,* vol. 3, *Assessment and intervention.* New York: Brunner/Mazel, 1975.

Tsuji, K., & Nakano, R. Chromosome studies of embryos from induced abortions in pregnant women age 35 and over. *Obstetrics and Gynecology,* 1978, *52,* 542–544.

Ungerer, J. A., & Sigman, M. *An evaluation of spontaneous play as a clinical assessment procedure.* Paper presented at the Third International Conference on Early Identification of Children Who Are Developmentally at Risk. Jackson Hole, Wyoming, September 1980.

Usher, R. H. The special problems of the premature infant. In G. B. Avery (Ed.), *Neonatology* (6th ed.). Philadelphia: J. B. Lippincott, 1975.

Usher, R. H. Changing mortality rates with perinatal intensive care and regionalization. *Seminars in Perinatology,* 1977, *1,* 309–319.

Uzgiris, I. Ordinality in the development of schemas for relating to objects. In J. Hellmuth (Ed.), *Exceptional infant* (Vol. 1). Seattle: Special Child Publications, 1967.

Uzgiris, I. *Changing patterns of infant-environment interaction at various stages of development.* Paper presented at the Symposium on Biosocial Factors and the Infant Who Is at High Risk for Developmental Disabilities, University of Massachusetts Medical School, Worcester, May 1980.

Uzgiris, I. C., & Hunt, J. McV. *Assessment in infancy: Ordinal scale of psychological development*. Urbana: University of Illinois Press, 1975.

van den Berg, B. J. Epidemiologic observations of prematurity: Effects of tobacco, coffee and alcohol. In D. W. Reed & F. J. Stanley (Eds.), *The epidemiology of prematurity*. Baltimore and Munich: Urban & Schwarzenberg, 1977.

Vaughan, V. C., III, & McKay, R.J. The field of pediatrics. In V. C. Vaughan, III & R. J. McKay (Eds.), *Nelson textbook of pediatrics*. Philadelphia: W. B. Saunders, 1975.

Vietze, P., Abernathy, S., Ashe, M., & Faulstich, G. Contingency interaction between mothers and their developmentally delayed infants. In G. Sackett (Ed.), *Observing behavior*, vol. 1, *Theory and applications in mental retardation*. Baltimore: University Park Press, 1978.

Volpe, J. Observing the infant in the early hours after asphyxia. *Intrauterine asphyxia*. Chicago: Year Book Medical Publishers, 1977.

Vorherr, H. Placental insufficiency in relation to postterm pregnancy and fetal postmaturity. *American Journal of Obstetrics and Gynecology*, 1975, *123*, 67–103.

Warkany, J., & Nelson, R. C. Skeletal abnormalities in offspring of rats reared on deficient diets. *Anatomical Record*, 1941, *79*, 83–100.

Watson, M. W., & Fischer, K. W. A developmental sequence of agent use in late infancy. *Child Development*, 1977, *48*, 828–835.

Wechsler, D. *Pre-school and primary scale of intelligence*. New York: Psychological Corporation, 1967.

Wechsler, D. *Wechsler intelligence scale for children, revised (WISC-R)*. New York: Psychological Corporation, 1974.

Weisz, J. R., & Zigler, E. Cognitive development in retarded and non-retarded persons: Piagetian tests of the similar sequence hypothesis. *Psychological Bulletin*, 1979, *86*, 831–851.

Weisz, J. R., & Zigler, E. Cognitive development in retarded and nonretarded persons: A critical review of the Piagetian evidence. In E. Balla & E. Zigler (Eds.), *Developmental and difference theories of mental retardation*. Hillsdale, N.J.: Erlbaum, in press.

Werner, E. E. *The transactional model: Application to the longitudinal study of the high risk child on the island of Kauai, Hawaii*. Paper presented at the meeting of the Society for Research in Child Development, San Francisco, March 1979.

Werner, E. E., Bierman, J. M., & French, F. E. *The children of Kauai: A longitudinal study from the prenatal period to age ten*. Honolulu: University Press of Hawaii, 1971.

Werner, E. E., Honzik, M. P., & Smith, R. S. Prediction of intelligence and achievement at 10 years from 20 months pediatric and psychologic examination. *Child Development*, 1968, *39*, 1063–1075.

Werner, E. E., & Smith, R. S. *Kauai's children come of age*. Honolulu: University Press of Hawaii, 1977.

Werner, E. E., & Smith, R. S. *Vulnerable but invincible: A longitudinal study of resilient children and youth*. New York: McGraw-Hill, 1982.

Werner, H. *Comparative psychology of mental development* (Rev. ed.). Chicago: Follett, 1948.

Whitley, R. J., Nahmias, A. J., Visintine, A. M., Fleming, C. L., Alford, C. A. The natural history of herpes simplex virus infection of mother and newborn. *Pediatrics*, 1980, *66*, 489–494.

Wiener, C. Psychologic correlates of premature birth: A review. *Journal of Nervous and Mental Disease*, 1962, *134*, 129–144.

Willerman, L., Broman, S. H., & Fiedler, M. Infant development, preschool IQ, and social class. *Child Development*, 1970, *41*, 69–77.

Williams, A. F. Children killed in falls from motor vehicles. *Pediatrics*, 1981, *68*, 576–578.

Wilson, J. G. *Environment and birth defects*. New York: Academic Press, 1973.

Wilson, J. G. Current status of teratology. General principles and mechanisms derived from animal studies. In J. G. Wilson & F. C. Fraser (Eds.), *Handbook of teratology*, vol. 1, *General principles and etiology*. New York: Plenum, 1977. (a)

Wilson, J. G. Embryotoxicity of drugs in man. In J. G. Wilson & F. C. Fraser (Eds.), *Handbook of teratology*, vol. 1, *General Principles and etiology*. New York: Plenum, 1977. (b)

Wilson, J. G. Environmental chemicals. In J. G. Wilson & F. C. Fraser (Eds.), *Handbook of teratology*, vol. 1, *General principles and etiology*. New York: Plenum, 1977. (c)

Wohlwill, J. T. *The study of behavioral development*. New York: Academic Press, 1973.

Woodruff, C. W. Iron deficiency in infancy and childhood. *Pediatric Clinics of North America*, 1977, *24*, 85–94.

Woodward, W. M. The behavior of idiots interpreted by Piaget's theory of sensorimotor development. *British Journal of Educational Psychology,* 1959, *29,* 60–71.

Woodward, W. M. Piaget's theory and the study of mental retardation. In N. R. Ellis (Ed.), *Handbook of mental deficiency: Psychological theory and research* (2nd ed.). Hillsdale, N.J.: Erlbaum, 1979.

World Health Organization (WHO). *Public health and low birthweight: Report of Expert Committee on Maternal and Child Health* (Technical Report Series No. 217). Geneva: World Health Organization, 1961.

Wright, F. H., Blough, R. R., Chamberlin, A., Ernest, T., Halstead, W. C., Meirer, P., Moore, R. Y., Naughton, R. F., & Newell, F. W. A controlled follow-up study of small prematures born from 1952 through 1956. *American Journal of Diseases of Childhood,* 1972, *124,* 507–521.

Zarfas, D. E., & Wolf, L. C. Maternal age patterns and the incidence of Down's syndrome. *American Journal of Mental Deficiency,* 1979, *83,* 353–359.

Zeaman, D., & House, B. J. Mongoloid MA is proportional to log CA. *Child Development,* 1962, *33,* 481–488.

Zeaman, D., & House, B. J. The role of attention in retardates' discrimination learning. In N. R. Ellis (Ed.), *Handbook of mental deficiency: Psychological theory and research.* New York: McGraw-Hill, 1963.

Zelazo, P. R. Reactivity to perceptual-cognitive events: Application for infant assessment. In R. B. Kearsley & I. E. Sigel (Eds.), *Infants at risk: Assessment of cognitive functioning.* Hillsdale, N.J.: Erlbaum, 1979.

Zender, M. A., & Zender, B. F. Vygotsky's view about the age periodization of child development. *Human Development,* 1974, *17,* 24–40.

Zigler, E. Developmental versus difference theories of mental retardation and the problem of motivation. *American Journal of Mental Deficiency,* 1968, *73,* 536–556.

AUTHOR INDEX

SUBJECT INDEX